AGE, WEIGHT & DISTANCE TABLE
For use with Chase and Hurdle races

Distance	Age	Jan	Feb	Mar	Apr	May	June
2m	5	12—7	12—7	12—7	12—7	12—7	12—7
	4	11–13	12—0	12—1	12—2	12—3	12—4
2¼m	5	12—7	12—7	12—7	12—7	12—7	12—7
	4	11–12	11–13	12—0	12—1	12—2	12—3
2½m	5	12—7	12—7	12—7	12—7	12—7	12—7
	4	11–11	11–12	11–13	12—0	12—1	12—2
2¾m	5	12—6	12—7	12—7	12—7	12—7	12—7
	4	11–10	11–11	11–12	11–13	12—0	12—1
3m	5	12—6	12—6	12—7	12—7	12—7	12—7
	4	11—8	11–10	11–11	11–12	11–13	12—0

Distance	Age	July	Aug	Sep	Oct	Nov	Dec
2m	5	12—7	12—7	12—7	12—7	12—7	12—7
	4	12—4	12—5	12—5	12—6	12—6	12—7
	3	11—5	11—6	11—8	11—9	11–11	11–12
2¼m	5	12—7	12—7	12—7	12—7	12—7	12—7
	4	12—3	12—4	12—5	12—5	12—6	12—6
	3	11—4	11—5	11—7	11—8	11—9	11–10
2½m	5	12—7	12—7	12—7	12—7	12—7	12—7
	4	12—2	12—3	12—4	12—5	12—6	12—6
	3		11—4	11—6	11—7	11—8	11—9
2¾m	5	12—7	12—7	12—7	12—7	12—7	12—7
	4	12—2	12—3	12—4	12—5	12—5	12—6
	3					11—7	11—8
3m	5	12—7	12—7	12—7	12—7	12—7	12—7
	4	12—1	12—2	12—3	12—4	12—5	12—5
	3					11—6	11—7

For 6-y-o's and older, use 12-7 in all cases

Note Race distances in the above tables are shown only at ¼-mile intervals. For races of 2m1f use the 2¼-mile table weights; for races of 2m3f use 2½ miles; and so forth. For races over odd distances, the nearest distance shown in the table should be used. Races over distances longer than 3 miles should be treated as 3-mile races.

National Hunt Flat races A separate age, weight & distance table is used for NH Flat races but there is no weight-for-age allowance for 5-y-o's; over 2 miles from January to November the allowance for 4-y-o's is 1 lb less than it is over jumps.

CHASERS & HURDLERS 2002/03

Price £66.00

A TIMEFORM PUBLICATION

A Timeform Publication

Compiled and produced by

G. Greetham (Director), D. P. Cleary (Editor), M. J. Taylor (Handicapper), R. J. C. Austen, J. Early, J. Ingles, M. S. Rigg and E. K. Wilkinson (essays), P. E. Turner (additional research), S. Hindle (short commentaries), P. A. Muncaster (short commentaries and proof checking), G. Crowther (proof checking), M. Hall, D. Holdsworth, W. Muncaster, A-M. Stevens and R. Todd (production).

CONTENTS

5   Introduction

16   Timeform Champion Jumpers 2002/03

18   The Timeform 'Top 100'

20   2002/03 Statistics

23   Explanatory Notes

26   The Form Summaries and Rating Symbols

27   Chasers & Hurdlers 2002/03

997   Promising Horses

999   Selected Big Races 2002/03

1049   Index to Photographs

1055   Champions from the 'Chasers & Hurdlers' series

The age, weight and distance table, for use in applying the ratings in races involving horses of different ages, appears on the end paper at the front of the book

Chasers & Hurdlers 2002/03

Introduction

'Crisis? What crisis?' The *Sun*'s January 1979 headline over James Callaghan's response to questions about 'mounting chaos' in the so-called 'winter of discontent' has passed into folklore. The headline was merely an interpretation of the prime minister's reply at an airport press conference on his return from a summit in sun-drenched Guadeloupe, but it is widely credited with contributing to Labour's General Election defeat four months later (the editor of the *Sun* received a knighthood from incoming prime minister Margaret Thatcher). Headlines on the racing pages in the latest jumps season—'National Hunt under threat', 'Fears grow for Kempton'—reflected worries among followers of jumping about the future proliferation of all-weather Flat racing in the winter calendar. The number of tracks in Britain with artificial surfaces is likely to grow close to double figures, with a new course at Great Leighs in Essex due to open in autumn 2004 and Newbury, Newmarket, Sedgefield and Kempton in the process of, or talking about, applying for the necessary planning permission. All-weather racing, introduced in 1989 principally as a stand-by when jumping on turf was frozen off or courses waterlogged, now seems set for radical expansion, to the detriment of National Hunt racing. The British Horseracing Board's response seemed to some jumps fans at least to be very much of the 'crisis? what crisis?' variety.

The BHB's Racing Review committee on the future shape of the sport, set up against the backdrop of a forthcoming Office of Fair Trading report which is virtually certain to recommend deregulation, concentrated on Flat racing and sees the answer to the twin threats of the OFT report and a continuing decline in horseracing's share of an increasingly diverse but flourishing betting market as the expansion of all-weather and low-grade Flat racing, which will provide courses with more fixtures and also serve the betting shops. 'The shops are now open seven days a week, even when British racing is not taking place . . . we have no choice but to fight for our market share which has been dropping rapidly since betting tax was removed. As for quality, you only improve quality by improving your finances,' said BHB chairman Peter Savill in a full page interview in the *Daily Mail* in July in which jumping didn't get a single mention. Among the achievements Mr Savill said he was most proud of, incidentally, were: the creation of Shergar Cup day, an international jockeys' competition which has undergone several changes since its inauguration and has included the use of It's A Knockout-style jokers to gain double points; and the newly-introduced Summer Triple Crown and Grand Slam, which, along with the funding put in to guarantee the big bonuses, evaporated into thin air as early as the second leg in 2003. More about the possible effects on jumping—and the successful lifting of the threat to National Hunt racing at Kempton—can be found in the essay on Christmas Hurdle winner **Intersky Falcon**.

Victory number 1,700 on Mighty Montefalco at Uttoxeter in August saw Tony McCoy go to the top of the all-time jump jockeys' list in Britain

Jumping may have its problems—name a sport which hasn't—but at the top level it is as vibrant as at any time in its history. Sell-out crowds of over 50,000 on each of the three days of the Cheltenham Festival—total attendance 155,976—were complemented by a modern-day record of 68,389 for Grand National day. Attendances at the three days of Aintree reached 142,467, another modern-day record, and included 50,474 on the Friday. The Cheltenham Festival is set to become a victim of its own success when it is expanded to four days from 2005, a debatable decision which is discussed in the essay on **Native Upmanship**. There's also an interesting aside in the comment on **Sudden Shock** on a recent change made to the Festival programme. Both Cheltenham and Aintree benefited from good weather as the country basked in an unseasonably early spring, with the brightest and driest March for more than twenty years. Watering took place at both Cheltenham and Aintree because of the lack of rain, Aintree's policy being one of the issues, along with the size of the TV audience, covered in the essay on the very easy Grand National winner **Monty's Pass**. The essay also touches on the very successful challenge mounted by Irish-trained horses at the two big meetings. The six Irish-trained winners at Aintree, who included Monty's Pass—the third National winner in five years for Ireland—and Native Upmanship, were all for different trainers. **Moscow Flyer**, who won the Queen Mother Champion Chase from Native Upmanship, was the biggest Irish winner at Cheltenham where **Back In Front** and **Hardy Eustace** gave the visitors a double in the Grade 1 novice hurdles, the Supreme Novices' and the Royal & SunAlliance. Six Irish-trained winners at Cheltenham was the most since the seven in 1995/6 (eight, in 1957/8, is the record). Grand National-winning jockey Barry Geraghty rode five winners at the Cheltenham Festival to equal the record held jointly by Fred Winter, Jamie Osborne and Tony McCoy. Geraghty partnered Moscow Flyer and completed a Cheltenham double for trainer Jessica Harrington on the remarkable mare **Spirit Leader** in the County Hurdle.

Spirit Leader's County Hurdle victory was her third of the season in a major handicap. The start of the Tote Gold Trophy, another of the races she won, provided a high-profile example of the problems sometimes created with big fields by the Jockey Club's current starting procedure. The attempts of

After another sold-out Cheltenham Festival, the stands were packed for the Grand National meeting, the big day itself attracting a modern-day record crowd of 68,389

The County Hurdle—the mare Spirit Leader wins her third major handicap of the season, crowning a splendid Cheltenham Festival for her jockey Barry Geraghty

senior starter Simon Morant to despatch the twenty-seven runners at Newbury made for most uncomfortable watching, with the jockeys, many of them guilty of over-keenness, virtually ignoring the starter's pleadings to 'pull them back off the gate', 'take a turn back . . . that's all of you', culminating with shouts of 'GET OFF THE TAPE!' Similar antics led to a shambolic start to the Champion Hurdle, after the tape snapped, with the previous year's winner Hors La Loi III refusing to race when the field eventually got away after a long delay. The starter reported all the Champion Hurdle riders, except Hors La Loi's, for lining up before they were instructed to, all of them being cautioned by the stewards as to their future conduct at the start. Some of the other Cheltenham starts also left something to be desired and it wasn't the first time in recent years that starting at the Festival has given cause for concern. The Jockey Club insists that jump races should be started with the runners at a virtual standstill and their noses almost on the tape. Unfortunately, this leads to over-fussy starters taking things to ridiculous extremes to achieve a perfect line, with embarrassing consequences sometimes. As we have said before, starters should have the flexibility to make runners line up away from the tape before allowing them to walk in as the tape is released.

After the palaver at the start, the Champion Hurdle produced a most worthy winner in nine-year-old **Rooster Booster**, who had won the County Hurdle twelve months earlier. Rooster Booster's eleven-length winning margin over 33/1-shot **Westender**, who had been reluctant to race after the chaotic start, has been exceeded only twice in Champion Hurdle history, by twelve-length winners Istabraq in 1998 and Insurance back in 1932. Rooster Booster had won all four of his races in the current season in the build-up to Cheltenham, and four other Champion Hurdle runners had also been unbeaten during the season, including stable-companions Intersky Falcon and **Rhinestone Cowboy**, a novice whose progress really caught the eye and led to his starting favourite. The die was cast for Rhinestone Cowboy with a mistake at the second flight but he stayed on for third. Rooster Booster provided jockey Richard Johnson with his biggest success of the season. Johnson has been sidelined with a

*Champion Hurdle winner Rooster Booster with his trainer Philip Hobbs (left);
Richard Johnson, who lost his whip after the last, shows his feelings after Rooster Booster
is narrowly beaten by Sacundai in the Martell Aintree Hurdle (right)*

broken leg for part of each of the last two seasons, most recently after a fall at Newton Abbot in August which ended any hope he had of challenging Tony McCoy for the jockeys' title. Johnson is the nearest thing there is to a serious challenger to McCoy's crown and still ended the latest season as runner-up (for the sixth consecutive time), in the process becoming only the eighth jockey to ride a thousand winners over jumps in Britain, following Stan Mellor, John Francome, Peter Scudamore, Richard Dunwoody, Tony McCoy, Peter Niven and Adrian Maguire. Johnson passed the hundred-winner mark for the seventh consecutive season.

While Richard Johnson enjoyed other Cheltenham Festival victories on **One Knight** (Royal & SunAlliance Chase), **Young Spartacus** and the estimable mare **La Landiere**, McCoy managed only one win at the meeting, a hard-fought one aboard the well-backed **Liberman** in the Champion Bumper. McCoy's Festival experiences are recorded in the essay on **Golden Alpha**, on whom he broke his collar-bone in the Grand Annual. The same horse provided McCoy with a victory on his return at Aintree, one of two hundred and fifty-seven in all during the season, one hundred and ten ahead of Johnson. McCoy's much publicised pursuit of three hundred winners—more than a possibility when he reached the two-hundred mark in record time on **Lord Sam** at Kempton on Boxing Day—continued to raise his profile following his epic 2001/2 season when he surpassed Flat champion Sir Gordon Richards' enduring British record of two hundred and sixty-nine winners in a season, setting a new mark of two hundred and eighty-nine. McCoy's phenomenal achievements earned him an exalted third in the poll for BBC Sports Personality of The Year. Frankie Dettori was previously the best-placed jockey in the poll when filling third spot in 1996 following his 'Magnificent Seven' at Ascot; even Lester Piggott never finished higher than fourth. The day after Johnson was sidelined, McCoy reached another milestone in his brilliant career, surpassing Richard Dunwoody's record tally for a jump jockey when Mighty Montefalco provided the second leg of a double at Uttoxeter and took him on to 1,700. McCoy's latest jockeys' title puts him level on eight championships with Peter Scudamore.

The best race at the Cheltenham Festival, indeed probably the finest in terms of quality seen all season, was the Stayers' Hurdle featuring French-trained **Baracouda**, the exceptional novice **Iris's Gift** and Ireland's most popular jumper **Limestone Lad**, whose five victories in the latest season took his tally under National Hunt rules to thirty-five, a phenomenal total for any horse, Flat or jumps. Limestone Lad had to settle for third at Cheltenham as Baracouda held the game Iris's Gift by three quarters of a length to record his second successive victory in the event. If there is an argument for a fourth day at the Festival, it was provided by the Stayers' Hurdle which fully deserved to be the centrepiece of its own day. It was a pity the latest running took place in the shadow of the Cheltenham Gold Cup which was won imperiously by **Best Mate** who became the first to win the race in successive years since L'Escargot (whose career is touched on in Best Mate's essay) in 1970 and 1971. Best Mate confirmed himself a class apart from his contemporaries among the staying chasers—he also won the King George VI Chase at Kempton—but some of the extravagant comparisons with Arkle were completely unjustified on any rational appreciation of his actual performances. For those whose memories don't go back far enough to recall Arkle's career, some of the highlights are touched on in Best Mate's essay. Still only eight, Best Mate's rating of 182 places him behind only Arkle (212), Flyingbolt (210), Mill House (191), Desert Orchid (187), Dunkirk (186), Burrough Hill Lad (184) and Master Oats (183) among the top jumpers in Timeform's experience.

The third-fence exit in the Gold Cup of the season's top novice, Irish-trained **Beef Or Salmon**, whose successful season helped to get jockey Timmy Murphy back in the news for the right reasons, robbed the race of some interest. Racegoers will probably have to wait until the next Gold Cup to see whether Beef Or Salmon, whose four victories in Ireland (none of them, incidentally,

The race of the season—Baracouda, the novice Iris's Gift and Limestone Lad provide a memorable finish to the Bonusprint Stayers' Hurdle

Best Mate takes the final fence in the Tote Cheltenham Gold Cup

in races restricted to novices) included the Ericsson Chase and the Hennessy Cognac Gold Cup, really is a serious challenger to Best Mate. The Ericsson was among five new Grade 1 events sanctioned by the Irish Turf Club in the latest season, a topic discussed in the essay on Beef Or Salmon. Best Mate was one of ten winning favourites—a record—at the Festival meeting where, however, Gold Cup sponsors the Tote suffered some embarrassing system failures, including a crash lasting ten minutes just before their high profile sponsorship. The Queen presented the Gold Cup trophies on her first visit to Cheltenham racecourse in more than fifty years and also unveiled a sculpture of the Queen Mother, whose long association with jumping did so much to popularise the sport in the second half of the twentieth century. The Queen Mother's last winner First Love was successful at Folkestone for the Queen in the latest season, believed to be the first jumping winner to carry the royal 'purple, gold braid, scarlet sleeves' for over a century, more precisely since Ambush won the 1900 Grand National for the then Prince of Wales.

The Cheltenham Festival, incidentally, was excellent live viewing on Channel 4, though it was disappointing for those unable to watch in the afternoon that the highlights programme went out at the kind of hour when even witches have decided to call it a night. Channel 4 was also involved in setting up the new racing channel, attheraces, whose acquisition of media rights ultimately spelt the end for the Racing Channel which closed in January soon after failing to agree a contract to continue showing Irish racing. This left racing at a small number of British courses not contracted to attheraces available only on SIS, the betting shop service. Some reduction in terrestrial racing coverage was announced by Channel 4 whose short-lived lunchtime racing slot, which could have been a useful promotional vehicle for the sport, featured mostly modest racing and was dropped because of poor viewing figures.

The big spring Festivals at Cheltenham and Aintree were not conspicuously successful for either the season's champion trainer Martin Pipe or the season's leading owner David Johnson, but both were clear-cut winners in their category. The trainers' championship was traditionally decided on win-money until the BHB set up an 'official' championship in the 1993/4 season based on win-and-place earnings. David Nicholson became the first champion trainer under the new criteria that season, though Pipe overtook him in the last few weeks of the season in first-prize money. Leaving that season aside, Pipe has now been champion trainer thirteen times, surpassing the twentieth-century record tally of 'the Wizard of Manton' Alec Taylor who was champion on the Flat on twelve occasions between 1907 and 1925. Pipe's first-three earnings in the latest season of £2,491,352 were only a little short of the record he had set the previous season, though he finished ten short of the now-customary two-hundred winner mark (something he has achieved eight times and no other trainer, Flat or jumps, has ever managed). Pipe's principal patron David Johnson was champion owner for the third time, beating his own record for first-three prize money set the previous season. Johnson's horses won £863,902, prominent among them Cleeve Hurdle winner **Classified**, Thomas Pink Gold Cup winner **Cyfor Malta** (one of seven successes for the Pipe stable at Cheltenham's Open meeting), the very tough **Stormez**, whose long campaign began just a month after the close of the old season and ended with seconds in the Scottish National and the attheraces Gold Cup, and the top-class mare **Lady Cricket**, a previous winner of the Thomas Pink. Lady Cricket's retirement coincides, ironically, with the increasing of the mares' allowance from 5 lb to 7 lb in pattern races over jumps (there is more about efforts to encourage mares in the essay on **Ar Muin Na Muice**). Runner-up to Martin Pipe for the fifth successive year in the trainers' championship was Paul Nicholls whose stable also passed the two-million mark in first-three prize-money. Nicholls ended the season with one hundred and fifty-two winners at a ratio of winners to runners of just over one in four, the best among the top stables. The stable housed a particularly strong collection of two-mile chasers including Arkle winner **Azertyuiop**, a magnificent prospect, and established performers Tingle Creek winner **Cenkos** and Game Spirit winner **Kadarann**, as well as another leading novice **Le Roi Miguel**, in the same ownership as Cenkos. **Valley Henry**, who ran particularly well in the Gold Cup, was the stable's top staying chaser, though veteran **See More Business** continued to do sterling service.

'The Taunton ten'—champion trainer Martin Pipe with his jockeys (Tony McCoy, right) before saddling ten of the sixteen runners (the stable had 1st, 2nd, 4th, 5th & 6th) in a handicap hurdle at Taunton in January, equalling the number of runners he saddled in the 2001 Grand National

The stable's leading juveniles also contributed with big-race wins through **Le Duc** at Aintree and **Sporazene** at Punchestown (shortly after the end of the British season).

Three other stables—those of Jonjo O'Neill, Philip Hobbs and Nicky Henderson—also won over £1m in Britain in first-three prize money, the first time five jumps trainers have topped that mark in a season. It was a rare occurrence for Henderson to leave the Cheltenham Festival without at least one winner (details in **Fondmort**) but he ended a long drought at the Grand National meeting when **Irish Hussar** won the Mildmay Novices' Chase. The stable lost its dual King George third **Bacchanal** in a fall at Cheltenham in January. The O'Neill stable also had to come to terms with the death of one of its outstanding prospects **Coolnagorna** who broke a leg at Aintree. O'Neill had three winners at the Cheltenham Festival (including **Spectroscope** in the Triumph) and four at Aintree's Grand National meeting but he also faced a Jockey Club disciplinary hearing after the stable was found in breach of the so-called 'non-triers' rules for a third time during the season at Exeter in January. O'Neill was successful in his appeal to the Jockey Club over the Exeter case, which, along with the two others at Fakenham and Haydock, is covered in detail in the essay on the stable's Welsh National winner **Mini Sensation**. Another Cheltenham-Festival winning trainer (successful with **Xenophon**) in hot water was Tony Martin whose Grand National hope Davids Lad was banned for forty-two days by the Irish Turf Club after finishing last at Naas in February; the story is recounted in the introduction to the Nicholls-trained **Shotgun Willy** whose Grand National preparation contrasted sharply.

Nicholls, O'Neill, Hobbs and Henderson all added to their tally at the Punchestown Festival which took place after the end of the British season. **Flagship Uberalles** may have lost his two-mile crown to Moscow Flyer but his fortunes revived when he won the BMW Chase for the Hobbs yard, while **Quazar** landed the Emo Oil Champion Hurdle for O'Neill and **Royal Rosa** (sold at the end of the season for a record 340,000 guineas) won the Champion Bumper for Henderson. The Nicholls stable landed a Grade 1 double with Sporazene and Le Roi Miguel. The essay on another Punchestown winner **Rule Supreme** looks at the changes made to the programme at the meeting which also featured a French-trained Grade 1 winner in **First Gold** who followed up in the Punchestown Gold Cup after returning to form with a bang in the Martell Cup at Aintree. Readers should note that the form figures relate only to the defined British season, which ended on April 26th. Performances after that date at Punchestown and in significant French races are, however, detailed where relevant and covered fully in the essays. Other notable performers whose most important wins were recorded after the end of the British season include the Irish-trained mare **Nobody Told Me** who went on to spring a big surprise in France's top hurdle race the Grande Course de Haies d'Auteuil after taking the Menolly Homes Champion Novices' Hurdle at the Punchestown Festival. Leading French jumpers **Line Marine**, **Karly Flight** and the top four-year-old in Europe **Nickname** have also been given essays.

Away from the racecourse action, the sport continued to rake over the embers of the doping and race-fixing furore which had come into the open in June 2002 after reporting restrictions were lifted on a series of trials held after a long-running Customs & Excise investigation. The BBC's *Panorama* programme screened a documentary in October drawing, among other things, on allegations made in court about the racing activities of Brian Wright, the suspected mastermind of a global drug trafficking and money laundering operation. Eight individuals, including Wright who remains a fugitive from justice, were eventually 'warned off' by the Jockey Club at the end of 2002, including one of *Panorama*'s key witnesses ex-jockey and trainer Dermot Browne who received another twenty years, on top of an existing ban, after admitting doping. A report published in July 2003 by the Jockey Club's security review team, headed by a former chief constable Ben Gunn, concluded that there was no hard evidence to support the central allegations of widespread corruption made by *Panorama* and by another BBC programme *Kenyon Confronts*. The *Panorama* programme included an unsubstantiated assertion by the Jockey Club's former head of security Roger Buffham that 'a whole generation of National Hunt jockeys had close links to organised crime'.

Another of the eight 'warned off' by the Jockey Club was jump jockey turned bloodstock agent Graham Bradley who had fallen foul of the Jockey Club before and had admitted in court, whilst appearing as a witness, to passing 'privileged and sensitive' information to Brian Wright. Bradley was banned

Graham Bradley—fighting against a five-year ban from racing

for eight years for a series of offences, including passing on information for money, receiving presents from persons other than the owner of the horse he had ridden in a race, providing false information over his association with Brian Wright and entering the weighing room at two racecourses without permission. A punishment to fit the crimes? Hardly. Bradley wasn't found guilty of race-fixing or doping, for example, and the penalty seemed most severe compared to those imposed in some previous cases for similar breaches of the rules, for which suspensions have been weeks or months, not years. Bradley's sentence was reduced to five years on appeal in April but he has taken the case to the High Court, arguing that the punishment is disproportionate and that the ban interferes with his right to trade as a bloodstock agent. He obtained an injunction preventing the ban from taking effect until after the High Court hearing.

Another long-running saga, over the future of foxhunting, rumbled on, as did the attendant arguments about the wisdom or otherwise of racing's rulers in aligning the sport behind the Countryside Alliance's campaign to defend the blood sport. The Government published its Hunting Bill, which enshrined a number of stringent tests that fox hunts would have to pass if they were not to be disbanded. The plans to regulate hunting, rather than ban it, apparently had the agreement of the RSPCA and a number of animal welfare groups, but when the Bill came to the Commons in the summer of 2003 the Government staged a strategic retreat. After an impassioned five-and-a-half-hour debate on the second reading, the Hunting Bill was amended after an alternative proposal to ban hunting outright was carried by 362 votes to 154, a majority of 208. The Commons has now voted three times, by overwhelming majorities, for a ban on hunting with dogs—pledged in Labour's 1997 election manifesto—but still the future looks unclear. MPs supporting the measure confidently forecast that foxhunting will be banned outright by 2005, but this seems to depend on the Parliament Act's being used to overcome House of Lords opposition to an outright ban. But will the Government allow exceptional parliamentary procedure to put a bill on the statute book that has been fashioned by those who wrecked the Government's own bill? Meanwhile, the country should prepare for the largest protest yet by the Countryside Alliance, which has already staged two large-scale marches on London, the latest in September 2002 attended by an estimated 400,000, a figure agreed by both police and organisers.

There were a number of notable retirements from the ranks of the jockeys and trainers in the latest season. Nine-times Irish champion jump jockey Charlie Swan, who won more races over jumps in Ireland (1,188) than any other jockey and rode seventeen Cheltenham Festival winners, announced his retirement from the saddle at Aintree. He is to concentrate full time on training. Highlights of his career appear in the essay on AIG Europe Champion Hurdle winner **Like-A-Butterfly**, Swan's last ride when third in the Aintree Hurdle. He was successful at the Grand National meeting on Patriot Games, a horse he also trained. Another jockey with over 1,000 winners to his name, Adrian Maguire, announced his retirement in October on medical grounds, following the effects of a broken neck sustained in a fall at Warwick the previous season. Maguire won the Gold Cup on Cool Ground, the Queen Mother Champion Chase on Viking Flagship and the King George VI Chase on Barton Bank and Florida Pearl and was twice runner-up in the jockeys' championship, riding one hundred and ninety-four winners in 1993/4 when he lost out only by three to Richard Dunwoody. A veteran of the northern weighing room, the cheerfully enthusiastic Brian Storey, also called it a day and is to keep his links with racing by becoming a part-time starter. Storey has always been involved on the family farm and he even managed to milk the dairy herd at six in the morning on the day he gained his only Cheltenham Festival victory, on Sparky Gayle in the 1997 Cathcart. Jimmy FitzGerald and Josh Gifford, both handing over to sons, relinquished their training licences. Forgive'N Forget's 1985 Gold Cup victory was the greatest highlight in FitzGerald's fine career which also included a

In the winner's enclosure for the final time as a jockey—
Charlie Swan with Patriot Games at Aintree (owner J. P. McManus, right)

Four notable retirements: Josh Gifford (top left) and Jimmy FitzGerald (top right) both handed over their licences to sons; Adrian Maguire (bottom left) was forced to retire from the saddle through injury and northern stalwart Brian Storey took up a post as a starter's assistant

number of big-race winners on the Flat. Recent seasons, however, saw a decline in his fortunes and he retired at the end of February. Gifford, who went out on an appropriate note when Skycab won on the final day of the season, made a successful transition to training after a distinguished career in the saddle. Though champion jockey four times, he never won a trainers' championship but did saddle Grand National winner Aldaniti and a host of other major winners including **Deep Sensation**, who won the Queen Mother Champion Chase, Katabatic, Bradbury Star and Kybo.

As usual, the horses picked out in bold in this introduction are among the hundred or so with essays or extended entries. Along with the comprehensive photographic content, the essays are designed to help provide an accurate and permanent record of the jumping year, one of the main aims of *Chasers & Hurdlers*. The wealth of facts, analysis and opinion contained in the thousand or so pages is also designed to be of practical value to the punter, who will also find Timeform ratings and commentaries on those Irish-trained horses not seen out in Britain who showed fairly useful form or better in the latest season.

September 2003

Best Mate with husband and wife team Terry Biddlecombe and Henrietta Knight

CHAMPION JUMPER & BEST STAYING CHASER – RATED AT 182

BEST MATE

8 b.g. Un Desperado – Katday (Miller's Mate)
Owner Mr Jim Lewis   Trainer Miss H. C. Knight

BEST TWO-MILE CHASER – RATED AT 170p
MOSCOW FLYER
9 b.g. Moscow Society – Meelick Lady (Duky)
Owner Mr Brian Kearney   Trainer Mrs J. Harrington

BEST NOVICE CHASER — RATED AT 165p
BEEF OR SALMON
7 ch.g. Cajetano – Farinella (Salmon Leap)
Owner Mr B. J. Craig   Trainer Michael Hourigan

BEST PERFORMANCE IN A HUNTER CHASE – RATED AT 137P
KINGSCLIFF
6 b.g. Toulon – Pixies Glen (Furry Glen)
Owner Mr A. J. Sendell   Trainer Mrs S. Alner

BEST TWO-MILE HURDLER — RATED AT 170
ROOSTER BOOSTER
9 gr.g. Riverwise – Came Cottage (Nearly A Hand)
Owner Mr Terry Warner   Trainer P. J. Hobbs

BEST STAYING HURDLER — RATED 175
BARACOUDA
8 b.g. Alesso – Peche Aubar (Zino)
Owner J. P. McManus   Trainer F. Doumen

BEST NOVICE HURDLER – RATED AT 172
IRIS'S GIFT
6 gr.g. Gunner B – Shirley's Gift (Scallywag)
Owner Mr Robert Lester   Trainer Jonjo O'Neill

BEST JUVENILE HURDLER – RATED AT 142
NICKNAME
4 b.c. Lost World – Newness (Simply Great)
Owner Mrs Daniel Wildenstein   Trainer J-P. Gallorini

BEST BUMPER PERFORMER – RATED AT 123
RHINESTONE COWBOY
7 b.g. Be My Native – Monumental Gesture (Head For Heights)
Owner Mrs John Magnier   Trainer Jonjo O'Neill

THE TIMEFORM 'TOP 100' CHASERS AND HURDLERS

Hurdlers

175	Baracouda
172	Iris's Gift
172	Limestone Lad
170	Rooster Booster
167d	Deano's Beeno
164	Bannow Bay
161	Intersky Falcon
161	Laveron
159	Sacundai
159	Westender
158	Liss A Paoraigh
157	Bacchanal
157	Classified
156p	Rhinestone Cowboy
156d	Galant Moss
156	It Takes Time
156	Landing Light
156	Vic Toto
155	Santenay
155	Self Defense
154§	Brother Joe
154	Flame Creek
153	Karly Flight
152	El Fuego
152	Like-A-Butterfly
152	Quazar
152	Royal Emperor
151p	Back In Front
151	Coolnagorna
151	Great Love
151	Kimbi
150	Ballyhampshire Boy
150	Boss Doyle
150	Just Our Job
149	Davenport Milenium
149	Escort Boy
149	Hardy Eustace
149	In Contrast
148p	Lord Transcend
148	Dukeen
148	Tiger Groom
147	Geos
147	Native Emperor
147	Pizarro
147	Rougenoir
146p	Solerina
146§	Katiki
146	Douze Douze
146	Never
145p	Xenophon
145	Ilnamar
145	Inching Closer
145	Marble Arch
145	Saint des Saints
145	Scottish Memories
145	Spendid

145	Thisthatandtother
144+	Copeland
144+	Holy Orders
144	Lord Sam
144	Mr Cool
144	Stage Affair
143	Foreman
143	In The Forge
143	Spectrometer
143	Spirit Leader
143	Supreme Prince
142+	Desir d'Un Soir
142	Puntal
141p	Kicking King
141+	Tees Components
141	Cerilly
141	Polar Red
141	Rostropovich
141	Sh Boom
140p	Nobody Told Me
140p	Our Vic
140+	Ad Hoc
140	Emotional Moment
140	Eternal Spring
139p	Line Marine
139§	El Paso III
139	Chauvinist
139	Nil Desperandum
139	Samon
139	Stromness
139	Telimar Prince
139	The French Furze
138	Over The Bar
137+	Chopneyev
137	Comex Flyer
137	Kopeck
137	Korelo
137	October Mist
137	Oway
137	Patriot Games
137	Timber King
137	Tucacas
136§	Hors La Loi III
136	Frosty Canyon
136	Non So
136	See You Sometime

Chasers

182	Best Mate
172	Valley Henry
171	First Gold
171	Native Upmanship
170p	Moscow Flyer
169	Marlborough
168	Behrajan
167	Edredon Bleu
167	Hussard Collonges

167	Seebald
166	Bacchanal
166	Chives
166	Cyfor Malta
166	Truckers Tavern
165p	Beef Or Salmon
165	Lady Cricket
165	Rince Ri
164	Flagship Uberalles
164	Harbour Pilot
164	Tiutchev
163	Cenkos
163	Commanche Court
163	Kingsmark
162	Latalomne
162	See More Business
160	Foxchapel King
159p	Azertyuiop
159+	Line Marine
159§	El Paso III
159	Kadarann
159	Shotgun Willy
158	Double Car
158	Foly Pleasant
157	Gingembre
156p	Le Roi Miguel
156+	Ad Hoc
156	Colonel Braxton
156	Florida Pearl
156	La Landiere
155	Monty's Pass
155	Rougenoir
154	Douze Douze
154	Fondmort
154	Young Devereaux
154	Young Spartacus
152p	Irish Hussar
152	Batman Senora
152	Geos
152	Impek
152	Iris Bleu
152	Urga
151p	Keen Leader
151	Dark'n Sharp
151d	Fadalko
151	Poliantas
151	Royal Auclair
151	Stormez
151	Vol Solitaire
151	Youlneverwalkalone
150p	Jair du Cochet
150p	One Knight
150+	Escort Boy
150?	Sunny Flight
150x	Tresor de Mai
150§	Upgrade
150	Golden Alpha

18

150	Lord Noelie	146x	Iznogoud	144	Europa
150	Tarxien	146	Idole des Fontaines	144	More Than A Stroll
149	Jerico Vallis	146	Ilare	144	Red Striker
149	Mini Sensation	146	Isio	144	Royal Predica
149	Shooting Light	146	Joss Naylor	144	Turgeonev
148§	Carbury Cross	146	Ryalux	143+	It Takes Time
148	Ballinclay King	145	Eskleybrook	143	Alcapone
148	Davids Lad	145	Il'Athou	143	Bounce Back
148	Davoski	145	Le Sauvignon	143	Farmer Jack
148	Knife Edge	145	Rathgar Beau	143	Grey Abbey
148	Sackville	144x	You're Agoodun	143	Logician
147	Goguenard	144	Armaturk	143	Macs Gildoran
147	Wahiba Sands	144	Be My Royal	143	Shamawan

THE TIMEFORM TOP JUVENILES, NOVICES, HUNTER CHASERS AND NH FLAT HORSES

Juvenile Hurdlers
142 Nickname
138p Sporazene
137 Spectroscope
134 Malcom
134 Well Chief
133§ Le Duc
133 Royaleety
132 Bulougun
131 Don Fernando
130p Golden Cross
130 Do L'Enfant d'Eau
130 Kapgarde
129+ Starzaan
129 Far Pavilions
128 Bal de Nuit
128 Lilium de Cotte
128 Mutineer
127 Dashing Home
127 Ladykish
127 Mistanoora
127 Old California

Novice Hurdlers
172 Iris's Gift
156p Rhinestone Cowboy
155 Self Defense
152 Royal Emperor
151p Back In Front
151 Coolnagorna
149 Hardy Eustace
147 Pizarro
146p Solerina
145 Thisthatandtother
144 Lord Sam
143 Foreman
143 Supreme Prince
142+ Desir d'Un Soir
142 Puntal
141p Kicking King
141+ Tees Components
141 Sh Boom
140p Nobody Told Me

140p Our Vic

Novice Chasers
165p Beef Or Salmon
159p Azertyuiop
156p Le Roi Miguel
156 La Landiere
152p Irish Hussar
152 Impek
151p Keen Leader
151 Stormez
151 Vol Solitaire
150p Jair du Cochet
150p One Knight
150 Golden Alpha
150 Tarxien
146 Isio
146 Joss Naylor
145 Le Sauvignon
145 Rathgar Beau
144 Be My Royal
143+ It Takes Time
143 Farmer Jack

Hunter Chasers
138 Horus
137P Kingscliff
136 Earthmover
136 Sheltering
130 Barryscourt Lad
130 Macgeorge
130 Sulphur Springs
129 County Derry
128 Dorans Pride
127+ Thoseweredays
126p Lord Atterbury
126 Bright Approach
126 Last Option
124x Joint Account
124 Joe Blake
122 Divet Hill
119x Family Business
119 Mulkev Prince

118 Torduff Express
117 Quetal

National Hunt Flat Horses
123 Rhinestone Cowboy
119 Liberman
118 Control Man
118 Cornish Rebel
118 Royal Rosa
118 Trabolgan
117 Bold Bishop
117 Brave Inca
117 Royal Alphabet
117 Widemouth Bay
116+ Rakaposhi Lass
116 Classic Native
116 He's The Boss
116 Masteroffoxhounds
116 Rockstown Boy
115 Cloudy Grey
114 Armaguedon
114 Be Fair
114 Flexible Action
114 Mister Month
114 Sixo

2002/03 STATISTICS

The following tables show the leading owners, trainers, jockeys, sires of winners and horses over jumps in Britain during 2002/03. The prize-money statistics, compiled by *Timeform*, relate to win-money and to first-three prize money. Win money has traditionally been used to decide the trainers' championship, though since 1994 the BHB and the National Trainers' Federation have recognised championships decided by total prize money as determined by the *Racing Post*. The jockeys' championship has traditionally been decided by the number of winners. *NOTE: These statistics do not take account of the pending disqualification of a number of horses tested positive for morphine (see essay on Be My Royal).*

OWNERS (1,2,3 earnings)	Horses	Indiv'l Wnrs	Races Won	Runs	%	Stakes £
1 Mr D. A. Johnson	37	21	46	168	27.3	863,902
2 Mr J. P. McManus	64	26	33	185	17.8	730,291
3 Mr Jim Lewis	7	4	11	27	40.7	484,570
4 Mr Terry Warner	8	4	14	38	36.8	380,617
5 Sir Robert Ogden	33	17	23	117	19.6	374,972
6 Dee Racing Syndicate	1	1	1	1	100.0	348,000
7 Mr Trevor Hemmings	47	12	23	164	14.0	303,731
8 Mrs J. Stewart	7	4	4	25	16.0	272,796
9 Mrs John Magnier	3	2	6	10	60.0	247,227
10 Mrs G. Smith	8	6	14	33	42.4	201,423

OWNERS (by win-money)	Horses	Indiv'l Wnrs	Races Won	Runs	%	Stakes £
1 Mr D. A. Johnson	37	21	46	168	27.3	577,885
2 Mr J. P. McManus	64	26	33	185	17.8	568,936
3 Mr Jim Lewis	7	4	11	27	40.7	412,921
4 Dee Racing Syndicate	1	1	1	1	100.0	348,000
5 Mr Terry Warner	8	4	14	38	36.8	334,685
6 Sir Robert Ogden	33	17	23	117	19.6	270,700
7 Mrs J. Stewart	7	4	4	25	16.0	194,260
8 Mrs R. J. Skan	3	2	11	24	45.8	170,307
9 Mrs G. Smith	8	6	14	33	42.4	168,852
10 Ashleybank Investments Limited	28	17	37	98	37.7	165,776

TRAINERS (1,2,3 earnings)	Horses	Indiv'l Wnrs	Races Won	Runs	%	Stakes £
1 M. C. Pipe	220	94	190	950	20.0	2,491,352
2 P. F. Nicholls	142	84	152	583	26.0	2,077,046
3 Jonjo O'Neill	157	63	114	546	20.8	1,491,939
4 P. J. Hobbs	146	77	134	618	21.6	1,416,759
5 N. J. Henderson	116	46	69	394	17.5	1,008,080
6 Miss H. C. Knight	81	28	43	276	15.5	858,600
7 Miss Venetia Williams	113	46	78	476	16.3	664,880
8 Mrs S. J. Smith	76	33	74	352	21.0	611,998
9 Mrs M. Reveley	103	40	58	452	12.8	484,458
10 Ferdy Murphy	115	35	43	416	10.3	452,253
11 H. D. Daly	57	19	28	203	13.7	402,243
12 A. King	71	29	40	275	14.5	388,360

TRAINERS (by win-money)	Horses	Indiv'l Wnrs	Races Won	Runs	%	Stakes £
1 M. C. Pipe	220	94	190	950	20.0	1,639,264
2 P. F. Nicholls	142	84	152	583	26.0	1,550,056
3 Jonjo O'Neill	157	63	114	546	20.8	1,198,152
4 P. J. Hobbs	146	77	134	618	21.6	1,074,304
5 N. J. Henderson	116	46	69	394	17.5	611,830
6 Miss H. C. Knight	81	28	43	276	15.5	605,886
7 Miss Venetia Williams	113	46	78	476	16.3	449,958
8 Mrs S. J. Smith	76	33	74	352	21.0	444,966
9 Mrs J. Harrington, Ireland	6	3	5	10	50.0	350,900
10 James Joseph Mangan, Ireland	1	1	1	1	100.0	348,000
11 Mrs M. Reveley	103	40	58	452	12.8	324,076
12 H. D. Daly	57	19	28	203	13.7	306,639

TRAINERS (with 100+ winners)	Horses	Indiv'l Wnrs	Races Won	2nd	3rd	Runs	%
M. C. Pipe	220	94	190	116	110	950	20.0
P. F. Nicholls	142	84	152	106	70	583	26.0
P. J. Hobbs	146	77	134	99	85	618	21.6
Jonjo O'Neill	157	63	114	77	50	546	20.8

JOCKEYS (by winners)	1st	2nd	3rd	Unpl	Total Mts	%
1 A. P. McCoy	257	132	118	333	840	30.5
2 R. Johnson	147	116	111	351	725	20.2
3 A. Dobbin	109	65	43	261	478	22.8
4 M. A. Fitzgerald	77	71	45	255	448	17.1
5 R. Walsh	77	49	32	137	295	26.1
6 G. Lee	66	60	66	356	548	12.0
7 A. Thornton	62	95	65	299	521	11.9
8 W. Marston	61	39	55	290	445	13.7
9 B. Fenton	60	46	36	217	359	16.7
10 L. Aspell	59	59	64	311	493	11.9
11 J. Culloty	56	46	41	245	388	14.4
12 R. Thornton	50	69	59	309	487	10.2

JOCKEYS (1,2,3 earnings of £500,000+)	Races Won	Rides	%	Stakes £
1 A. P. McCoy	257	840	30.5	2,534,141
2 R. Johnson	147	725	20.2	1,658,220
3 R. Walsh	77	295	26.1	1,469,251
4 B. J. Geraghty	26	104	25.0	1,191,962
5 M. A. Fitzgerald	77	448	17.1	914,869
6 J. Culloty	56	388	14.4	878,159
7 A. Dobbin	109	478	22.8	815,566
8 A. Thornton	62	521	11.9	628,501
9 L. Aspell	59	493	11.9	589,706
10 T. J. Murphy	42	409	10.2	555,272
11 G. Lee	66	548	12.0	533,965
12 R. Thornton	50	487	10.2	515,803
13 W. Marston	61	445	13.7	515,316
14 N. Williamson	20	101	19.8	505,215

JOCKEYS (by win-money, £500,000+)	Races Won	Rides	%	Stakes £
1 A. P. McCoy	257	840	30.5	1,908,306
2 R. Johnson	147	725	20.2	1,219,962
3 R. Walsh	77	295	26.1	1,136,208
4 B. J. Geraghty	26	104	25.0	1,050,043

		1st	2nd	3rd	Unpl	Total Mts	%
5	A. Dobbin	109	478	22.8			650,513
6	J. Culloty	56	388	14.4			606,554
7	M. A. Fitzgerald	77	448	17.1			592,174

CONDITIONAL JOCKEYS

		1st	2nd	3rd	Unpl	Total Mts	%
1	M. Foley	41	36	26	195	298	13.7
2	K. Renwick	33	36	38	223	330	10.0
3	W. Hutchinson	31	20	29	131	211	14.6

AMATEUR RIDERS

		1st	2nd	3rd	Unpl	Total Mts	%
1	Mr Christian Williams	23	16	9	64	112	20.5
2	Mr G. Carenza	18	16	13	77	124	14.5
3	Mr J. E. Moore	16	13	9	95	133	12.0

SIRES OF WINNERS
(1,2,3 earnings of £225,000+)

		Races Won	Runs	%	Stakes £
1	Be My Native (by Our Native)	81	535	15.1	1,130,765
2	Roselier (by Misti IV)	84	544	15.4	902,677
3	Supreme Leader (by Bustino)	68	413	16.4	839,131
4	Montelimar (by Alleged)	30	219	13.6	698,211
5	Un Desperado (by Top Ville)	32	143	22.3	540,130
6	Strong Gale (by Lord Gayle)	39	340	11.4	477,282
7	Phardante (by Pharly)	48	469	10.2	472,501
8	Gunner B (by Royal Gunner)	30	169	17.7	419,417
9	Lord Americo (by Lord Gayle)	36	346	10.4	358,926
10	Glacial Storm (by Arctic Tern)	40	290	13.7	346,490
11	Riverwise (by Riverman)	7	39	17.9	311,214
12	Good Thyne (by Herbager)	32	254	12.5	247,596
13	Bob Back (by Roberto)	16	125	12.8	242,862
14	Sadler's Wells (by Northern Dancer)	25	203	12.3	239,963
15	Alflora (by Niniski)	30	250	12.0	239,744

SIRES OF WINNERS (by win-money)

		Indiv'l Horses	Wnrs	Races Won	Stakes £
1	Be My Native (by Our Native)	172	50	81	821,576
2	Roselier (by Misti IV)	151	48	84	689,892
3	Supreme Leader (by Bustino)	120	40	68	555,211
4	Montelimar (by Alleged)	65	21	30	543,019
5	Un Desperado (by Top Ville)	44	20	32	494,476
6	Strong Gale (by Lord Gayle)	86	27	39	327,524
7	Gunner B (by Royal Gunner)	48	14	30	301,677
8	Phardante (by Pharly)	128	34	48	281,465
9	Riverwise (by Riverman)	9	3	7	272,281
10	Lord Americo (by Lord Gayle)	80	21	36	245,074

LEADING HORSES (1,2,3 earnings)

		Races Won	Runs	Stakes £
1	Monty's Pass 10 b.g. Montelimar–Friars Pass	1	1	348,000
2	Best Mate 8 b.g. Un Desperado–Katday	3	3	322,725
3	Rooster Booster 9 gr.g. Riverwise–Came Cottage	5	6	299,831
4	Stormez 6 b.g. Ezzoud–Stormy Scene	7	12	173,621
5	La Landiere 8 b.m. Synefos–As You Are	7	8	151,056
6	Spirit Leader 7 b.m. Supreme Leader–That's The Spirit	3	3	147,900
7	Moscow Flyer 9 b.g. Moscow Society–Meelick Lady	1	2	145,000
8	Native Upmanship 10 ch.g. Be My Native–Hi'upham	1	1	142,000
9	Iris's Gift 6 gr.g. Gunner B–Shirley's Gift	6	7	141,398
10	Supreme Glory 10 b.g. Supreme Leader–Pentlows	0	5	132,000

EXPLANATORY NOTES

'Chasers & Hurdlers 2002/03' deals individually, in alphabetical sequence, with every horse that ran over the sticks or in National Hunt Flat races in Britain during the 2002/3 season, plus a number of foreign-trained horses that did not race here. For each of these horses is given (1) its age, colour and sex, (2) its breeding and, where this information has not been given in a previous Chasers & Hurdlers or Racehorses Annual, a family outline (3) a form summary giving its Timeform rating—or ratings—at the end of the previous season, followed by the details of all its performances during the past season, (4) a Timeform rating—or ratings—of its merit (which appears in the margin), (5) a Timeform commentary on its racing or general characteristics as a racehorse, with some suggestions, perhaps, regarding its prospects for 2003/4 and (6) the name of the trainer in whose charge it was on the last occasion it ran.

The book is published with a twofold purpose. Firstly, it is intended to have permanent value as a review of the exploits and achievements of the more notable of our chasers and hurdlers in the 2002/3 season. Thus, while the commentaries upon the vast majority of the horses are, of necessity, in note form, the best horses are more critically examined. The text is illustrated by half-tone portraits of the most notable horses (where these are available) and photographs of the major races. Secondly, the book is designed to help the punter to analyse races, and the notes which follow contain instructions for using the data.

TIMEFORM RATINGS

The Timeform Rating of a horse is simply the merit of the horse expressed in pounds and is arrived at by careful examination of its running against other horses using a scale of weight for distance beaten. Timeform maintains a 'running' handicap of all horses in training throughout the season.

THE LEVEL OF THE RATINGS

At the close of each season the ratings of all the horses that have raced are re-examined, and, if necessary, the general level of the handicap is adjusted so that all the ratings are kept at the same standard level from year to year. Some of the ratings may, therefore, be different from those in the final issue of the 2002/3 Timeform Chasing Black Book series.

RATINGS AND WEIGHT-FOR-AGE

The reader has, in the ratings in this book, a universal handicap embracing all the horses in training it is possible to weigh up, ranging from tip-top performers, with ratings from 170 upwards, down to the meanest platers, rated around the 60 mark. All the ratings are at weight-for-age, so that equal ratings mean horses of equal merit. In using Timeform to assess the prospects of various runners, allowance should be made for any difference specified by the Age, Weight and Distance Table at the front.

Steeplechase ratings, preceded by c, should not be confused with hurdle ratings, preceded by h. Where a horse has raced over fences and also over hurdles its ratings as a chaser and hurdler are printed one above the other, the steeplechase rating (c) being placed above the hurdle rating (h).

Thus with REGALITY c157
h143

the top figure, 157, is the rating to be used in steeplechases, and the one below, 143, is for use only in hurdle races. Where a horse has a rating based on its performance in a National Hunt Flat race (usually referred to in the text as a bumper) it is preceded by 'F'. The procedure for making age and weight adjustments to the ratings (i.e. for the calculation of Race Ratings) is as follows:

A. Horses of the Same Age

If the horses all carry the same weight there are no adjustments to be made, and the horses with the highest ratings have the best chances. If the horses carry different weights, jot down their ratings, and to the rating of each horse add one point for every pound the horse is set to carry less than 12st 7lb, or subtract one point for every pound it has to carry more than 12st 7lb. When the ratings have been adjusted in this way the highest resultant figure indicates the horse with the best chance at the weights.

Example (any distance: any month of the season)

Teucer	5 yrs (11-0) ..	Rating 140 ..	add 21	....	161
Kiowa	5 yrs (10-7) ..	Rating 125 ..	add 28	....	153
Golden Age	5 yrs (10-4) ..	Rating 120 ..	add 31	....	151

Teucer has the best chance, and Golden Age the worst

B. Horses of Different Ages

In this case, reference must be made to the Age, Weight and Distance Table at the front. Use the Table for steeplechasers and hurdlers alike. Treat each horse separately, and compare the weight it has to carry with the weight prescribed for it in the table, according to the age of the horse, the distance of the race and the month of the year. Then, add one point to the rating for each pound the horse has to carry less than the weight given in the table: or, subtract one point from the rating for every pound it has to carry more than the weight prescribed by the table. The highest resultant figure indicates the horse most favoured by the weights.

Example (2¾m steeplechase in January)

(Table Weights: 8-y-o 12-7; 7-y-o 12-7; 5-y-o 12-6)

Black Book	8 yrs (12-8) ..	Rating 140 ..	subtract 1 ..		139
Pressman	7 yrs (12-3) ..	Rating 132 ..	add 4	....	136
Copyright	5 yrs (12-7) ..	Rating 150 ..	subtract 1 ..		149

Copyright has the best chance, and Pressman the worst

Example (3m hurdle race in March)

(Table Weights: 9-y-o 12-7; 5-y-o 12-7; 4-y-o 11-11)

Oxer	9 yrs (10-12) ..	Rating 110 ..	add 23	..	133
Clairval	5 yrs (10-7) ..	Rating 119 ..	add 28	....	147
Gallette	4 yrs (10-7) ..	Rating 128 ..	add 18	..	146

Clairval has the best chance, and Oxer the worst

C. Horses in National Hunt Flat races

The procedure for calculating Race Ratings in National Hunt Flat races is precisely the same as in (A) or (B).

Example (2m N.H. Flat in February)

(Table Weights: 6-y-o 12-7; 5-y-o 12-7; 4-y-o 12-1)

Squall	6 yrs (10-12) ..	Rating 88 ..	add 23	....	111
Lupin	5 yrs (11-3) ..	Rating 97 ..	add 18	....	115
Chariot	4 yrs (10-9) ..	Rating 84 ..	add 20	....	104

Lupin has the best chance, and Chariot the worst

The National Hunt Flat ratings are on a scale comparable with that used for hurdlers and chasers. The ratings can therefore be used not only within the context of National Hunt Flat races themselves, but also as an indication of the potential form of such horses in their first few starts over jumps.

JOCKEYSHIP AND RIDERS' ALLOWANCES

For the purposes of rating calculations it should, in general, be assumed that the allowance the rider is able to claim (3 lb, 5 lb, or 7 lb) is nullified by his or her inexperience. Therefore, the *weight adjustments to the ratings should be calculated on the weight allotted by the handicapper, or determined by the conditions of the race,* and no extra addition should be made to a rating because the horse's rider claims an allowance. This is the general routine procedure; but, of course, after the usual adjustments have been made the quality of jockeyship is still an important factor to be considered when deciding between horses with similar chances.

WEIGHING UP A RACE

The ratings tell which horses in a particular race are most favoured by the weights; but complete analysis demands that the racing character of each horse is also studied carefully to see if there is any reason why the horse might be expected not to run up to its rating. It counts for little that a horse is thrown in at the weights if it has no pretensions whatever to staying the distance, or is unable to act on the prevailing going. Suitability of distance and going are no doubt the most important points to be considered, but there are others. For example, the ability of a horse to accommodate itself to the conformation of the track. There is also the matter of a horse's ability and dependability as a jumper and of its temperament: nobody would be in a hurry to take a short price about a horse with whom it is always an even chance whether it will get round or not, or whether it will consent to race.

A few minutes spent checking up on these matters in the commentaries upon the horses concerned will sometimes put a very different complexion on a race from that which is put upon it by the ratings alone. We repeat, therefore, that the correct way to use Timeform, or this annual volume, in the analysis of individual races is, first to use the ratings to discover which horses are most favoured by the weights, and second, to check through the comments on the horse to see what factors other than weight might also affect the outcome of the race.

THE FORM SUMMARIES

The form summaries enclosed in the brackets list each horse's performances in the last season in sequence, showing, for each race, its distance in furlongs, the state of the going and the horse's placing at the finish. Steeplechase form figures are prefixed by the letter 'c' and N.H. Flat race (bumper) form figures by the letter 'F', the others relating to form over hurdles.

The going is symbolised as follows: f–firm, m–good to firm, g–good, d–good to soft/dead, s–soft, v–heavy.

Placings are indicated up to sixth place, by superior figures, an asterisk denoting a win; and superior letters are used to convey what happened to the horse during the race: F–fell (F^3 denotes remounted and finished third); pu–pulled up; ur–unseated rider; bd–brought down; R–refused; rtr–refused to race; su–slipped up; ro–ran out; co–carried out; wd–withdrawn; dis–disqualified.

Thus, [2002/3 h82, F80: 16g 16s* c18g^{pu} 16f^2 c20v^F Apr 10] states that the horse was rated 82 over hurdles and 80 in bumpers at the end of the previous season. In the 2002/3 jumping season the horse ran five times; unplaced in a 2m hurdle race on good going, winning a 2m hurdle race on soft going, being pulled up in a 2¼m steeplechase on good going, running second in a 2m hurdle race on firm going and falling in a 2½m steeplechase on heavy going. Its last race was on April 10th.

Where sale prices are given they are in guineas unless otherwise stated. The prefix IR denotes Irish guineas, IR £ denotes Irish punts, $ refers to American dollars, francs refers to French francs and € indicates the euro. Any other currencies are converted into pounds sterling at the prevailing exchange rate.

THE RATING SYMBOLS

The following symbols, attached to the ratings, are to be interpreted as stated:-

p   likely to improve.

P   capable of *much* better form.

+   the horse may be better than we have rated it.

d   the horse appears to have deteriorated, and might no longer be capable of running to the rating given.

§   unreliable (for temperamental or other reasons).

§§   so temperamentally unsatisfactory as to be not worth a rating.

x   poor jumper.

xx   a very bad jumper, so bad as to be not worth a rating.

?   the horse's rating is suspect or, used without a rating, the horse can't be assessed with confidence or, if used in the in-season Timeform publications, that the horse is out of form.

CHASERS & HURDLERS 2002/03

AAVASAKSA (FR)   10 b.g. Dancing Spree (USA) – Afkaza (FR) (Labus (FR)) **c§§**
[2002/3 16d^{rtr} 16g^{rtr} Mar 23] workmanlike gelding: winning hurdler/chaser: usually **h§§**
blinkered/visored: thoroughly temperamental nowadays, and best left severely alone.
M. F. Harris

ABABOU (FR)   7 ch.g. Synefos (USA) – Racine Carree (FR) (Dom Racine (FR)) **c73**
[2002/3 c25g^6 Apr 14] ex-French gelding: fourth foal: dam lightly raced on Flat: maiden **h–**
hurdler/chaser in France for G. Cherel: unbeaten in 4 points in 2003: never dangerous in
maiden hunter at Hexham: tried blinkered. *Mrs Lucy Latchford*

ABAJANY   9 b.g. Akarad (FR) – Miss Ivory Coast (USA) (Sir Ivor) [2002/3 h85: 17g **h72**
16g^6 17g Jun 10] leggy gelding: fair on Flat: poor maiden hurdler: best around 2m with
emphasis on speed: acts on good to firm going: tried visored. *R. J. Baker*

ABALVINO (FR)   9 ch.g. Sillery (USA) – Abalvina (FR) (Abdos) [2002/3 c124, h–: **c127**
c16s^F c16v^3 c16v^3 c16d^2 c16d^2 c17d* c16g Apr 3] quite good-topped gelding: fairly **h–**
useful handicap chaser: generally ran well in 2002/3, making all in 5-runner event at
Newbury in February to win by 5 lengths from Ivanoph: bad mistake first final outing:
best around 2m: acts on heavy going: tongue tied: enthusiastic front runner: genuine.
P. R. Webber

ABANDON HOPE   7 ch.m. Jupiter Island – Band of Hope (USA) (Dixieland Band **F–**
(USA)) [2002/3 F–: F16s F17g Jun 12] well held in 3 bumpers. *W. Clay*

ABBEY DAYS (IRE)   6 ch.g. Be My Native (USA) – Abbey Emerald (Baptism) **h64**
[2002/3 F16v^4 F16g 19d^F 19g^5 Apr 19] lengthy gelding: first foal: dam winning 19f **F80**
hurdler: better effort in bumpers where fourth to Sh Boom at Wetherby: raced freely both
starts over hurdles, poor form on completed one. *Mrs H. Dalton*

ABBEYKNOCK BOY (IRE)   6 b. or br.g. Alphabatim (USA) – Haha Dash (IRE) **c73**
(Lord Ha Ha) [2002/3 h67, F–: 22d 23d 24d^3 22m^4 24d^{pu} 24v c20g c20d^3 c16g c24g^3 Mar **h67**
23] poor maiden hurdler/chaser: left I. Williams after sixth outing: stays 3m: acts on good
to soft going: visored once: has looked none too keen. *M. F. Harris*

ABBEY LAD   13 b.g. State Diplomacy (USA) – Another Pin (Pinza) [2002/3 c20d **c–**
c26m^R Jul 19] winning pointer: runner-up in hunter in 1998: left E. Fenwick, held when
refusing 3 out in maiden chase at Southwell (blinkered). *Mrs M. Reveley*

ABBEY'S GIRL (IRE)   7 b.m. Elbio – Abbey Trinity (IRE) (Tender King) [2002/3 **h–**
c22d^F Feb 8] first foal: dam ran once: of no account. *K. J. Burke, Ireland*

ABBOTS COURT (IRE)   8 b.g. Hallowed Turf (USA) – Coronea Sea Queen (IRE) **c61**
(Bassompierre) [2002/3 c–: c26m^4 May 3] big gelding: winning pointer: poor form
completed outing in novice chases. *R. H. Alner*

ABERFOYLE PARK (IRE)   9 b.g. Riverhead (USA) – Go For Doe (Whistling Deer) **c118**
[2002/3 c20d^3 c24g^4 c21d^F c19d^{pu} Feb 23] lengthy gelding: third foal: dam unraced: one-
time useful pointer: better completed effort in novice chases where fourth of 5 finishers to
Bold Investor at Kempton (possibly flattered): reportedly distressed final outing: will
prove best at 3m+. *R. H. Alner*

ABERNANT LADY   6 gr.m. Absalom – Hosting (Thatching) [2002/3 19f^4 Oct 9] **h–**
showed little in 3 maidens on Flat at 3 yrs for G. Ham: well held in novice on hurdling
debut. *A. G. Newcombe*

ABERTHATCH (FR)   4 b.f. Thatching – Academy Angel (FR) (Royal Academy **h97**
(USA)) [2002/3 16s^3 16d^2 Nov 30] lengthy filly: modest maiden on Flat (stays 1¼m):
similar form when placed both starts over hurdles. *M. J. Ryan*

ABINITIO LADY (IRE)   8 br.m. Be My Native (USA) – Chake-Chake (Goldhill) **h85**
[2002/3 h95: 16g^6 20d^4 16v^3 16g* Jun 15] modest hurdler: won mares novice at Hexham
in June: should stay 2½m: raced mainly on good going or softer. *Mrs M. Reveley*

A BIT OF FLUFF   11 b.m. Green Adventure (USA) – Cantabile (Bustino) [2002/3 **c–**
c24g^{pu} May 3] angular mare: winning pointer: no form over hurdles/in novice hunter **h–**
chase. *Lady Susan Brooke*

ABLE NATIVE (IRE)   6 b.m. Thatching – Native Joy (IRE) (Be My Native (USA))   **c89**
[2002/3 h106: c17d² c20g⁴ c16g⁵ 17d⁶ 20m 20g⁶ c24g* 19d⁶ 16d² 16v² 20m³ Apr 12]   **h96**
medium-sized mare: modest handicap hurdler: best effort over fences when winning
weak handicap at Fakenham in October: effective around 2m to easy 3m: unraced on firm
going, acts on any other: tried blinkered/in cheekpieces: tongue tied. *R. C. Guest*

ABLINGTON DOWN (IRE)   8 ch.m. Camden Town – Quarry Run (Parva Stella)   **h–**
[2002/3 22m Jun 14] winning pointer (rarely completes): visored, well beaten in maiden
on hurdling debut. *J. W. Mullins*

ABOVE THE CLOUDS   12 gr.g. Neltino – Goodnight Master (Gay Fandango   **c–**
(USA)) [2002/3 c21mᵖᵘ May 22] sturdy gelding: of little account. *Mrs M. Rigg*   **h–**

ABOVE THE CUT (USA)   11 ch.g. Topsider (USA) – Placer Queen (Habitat)   **c–**
[2002/3 c–, h91: 24g 19m⁶ 24m* 22g² 20m³ 26g 22d³ 24d⁶ 26g³ Mar 17] small gelding: **h87**
maiden chaser: modest handicap hurdler: won seller at Market Rasen in July: stays 3¼m:
acts on firm and good to soft going: held up. *C. P. Morlock*

ABSINTHER   6 b.g. Presidium – Heavenly Queen (Scottish Reel) [2002/3 16g 16g   **h–**
Mar 12] leggy gelding: half-brother to winning 17f hurdler Hadeqa (by Hadeer): fair on
Flat (effective up to 1½m): little show in 2 maiden hurdles. *M. R. Bosley*

ABSOLUTELY HOPEFUL   10 ch.g. Nearly A Hand – Owena Deep (Deep Run)   **c– x**
[2002/3 c–x, h79: 24gᶠ 22gᵖᵘ Jun 10] angular gelding: poor handicap hurdler: stays 3¼m: **h–**
raced mainly on good going or softer (acts on heavy): blinkered/tongue tied nowadays:
tends to make mistakes over fences: lazy. *C. P. Morlock*

ABSOLUTE MAJORITY   8 ch.g. Absalom – Shall We Run (Hotfoot) [2002/3   **h69**
17m⁴ 17mᵖᵘ Aug 5] poor maiden hurdler: should stay 2½m: acts on firm and good to soft
going: usually tongue tied. *H. S. Howe*

ABZUSON   6 b.g. Abzu – Mellouise (Handsome Sailor) [2002/3 F88: F16g⁶ F16s⁶   **h102**
19dᶠ 20vᵘʳ 19g² Feb 28] big gelding: fairly useful form in bumpers, won at Hexham very   **F96**
early in season: first completion in novice hurdles when ¾-length second to Handy
Money at Doncaster: stays 2½m: acts on heavy going. *J. R. Norton*

ACCADEMIC (IRE)   6 ch.g. Accordion – Giolla's Bone (Pitpan) [2002/3 F16d 19d⁵   **h90**
24vᵖᵘ Feb 15] IR £21,000 4-y-o: angular gelding: eleventh foal: half-brother to 5 winners,   **F80**
including Mutual Trust (by Pollerton) and Mutual Agreement (by Quayside), both fair
chasers up to 3¼m: dam behind in bumpers and maiden hurdle in Ireland: seventh in
maiden bumper on debut: shaped as if in need of experience when fifth in novice at Exeter
on hurdling bow, ran no sort of race next time: should stay beyond 19f. *S. E. H. Sherwood*

ACCEPTING   6 b.g. Mtoto – D'Azy (Persian Bold) [2002/3 22s 20d³ 20v⁵ 19s Dec   **h89**
14] compact gelding: half-brother to fair 2m hurdler Announcing (by Old Vic): one-time
fairly useful on Flat (stays 2m), well held since 2001: modest form over hurdles: stays
2½m. *J. Mackie*

ACCESS OVERSEAS   6 b.m. Access Ski – Access Advantage (Infantry) [2002/3   **h72**
h78: 22d³ 17f³ 16m⁴ 17s Nov 14] rather sparely-made mare: poor hurdler: effective
around 2m to 2¾m: acts on firm and good to soft going. *J. D. Frost*

ACCIPITER   4 b.g. Polar Falcon (USA) – Accuracy (Gunner B) [2002/3 F16d⁵ F17d³   **F90**
Feb 23] lengthy gelding: sixth foal: closely related to fairly useful 1½m winner Little
Pippin (by Rudimentary) and half-brother to several winners, including 1m to 13f winner
Star Precision (by Shavian) and useful staying hurdler Brave Tornado (by Dominion):
dam fairly useful though temperamental staying hurdler: fair form in 2 bumpers, though
outpaced 3f out when third to Heron's Ghyll in maiden at Hereford: will be suited by
further than 2m. *G. B. Balding*

ACCORDION GIRL (IRE)   5 b.m. Accordion – Triple d'Or (Golden Love) [2002/3   **F75**
F18f³ Apr 24] €21,000 4-y-o: fourth foal: dam, placed in bumpers, half-sister to useful
juvenile hurdler Dr Livingstone: poor form when third in bumper at Fontwell on debut.
J. W. Mullins

ACCYSTAN   8 ch.g. Efisio – Amia (CAN) (Nijinsky (CAN)) [2002/3 h73d: 16g³ 17s⁵   **h66**
19g Jun 12] quite good-topped gelding: poor handicap hurdler: best efforts around 2m on
good/good to firm going: tried blinkered. *A. Crook*

ACERTACK (IRE)   6 b.g. Supreme Leader – Ask The Madam (Strong Gale) [2002/3   **h66 p**
19d 16g 18s Feb 3] IR £21,000 4-y-o: lengthy gelding: fourth foal: half-brother to modest
staying chaser Calleva Star (by Over The River): dam winning pointer: poor form over
hurdles, not given at all a hard time in novice at Fontwell final start: likely to be suited by
2½m+: type to do better in handicaps. *R. Rowe*

ACHILLES WINGS (USA) 7 b.g. Irish River (FR) – Shirley Valentine (Shirley **h109**
Heights) [2002/3 h117: 16v³ 16d 20dᵖ Apr 4] leggy gelding: fair handicap hurdler:
reportedly suffered overreach second outing: stays 19f: acts on soft going, probably on
heavy. *Miss K. M. George*

ACKZO 10 b.g. Ardross – Trimar Gold (Goldhill) [2002/3 c132, h–: c28s⁴ c29vᵖ c30dᶠ **c124 §**
c25sᵖ Feb 23] sturdy gelding: fairly useful handicap chaser: left F. Murphy, respectable **h–**
effort at Haydock on reappearance, only completion in 2002/3: thorough stayer: acts on
good to firm and heavy going: blinkered nowadays: unreliable: joined R. Phillips.
D. McCain

ACOUSTIC (IRE) 9 br.g. Orchestra – Rambling Ivy (Mandalus) [2002/3 c92, h71: **c90**
c22d⁴ c25vᵖ c24d⁴ c23g⁴ c25g⁶ Apr 14] big, rangy gelding: novice hurdler: modest **h–**
maiden chaser: stays 3m: acts on soft ground. *O. Brennan*

ACQUITAINE (USA) 4 b.f. Colonial Affair (USA) – Arctic Eclipse (USA) (Northern **h–**
Dancer) [2002/3 16mᵖ 17f Oct 17] half-sister to winning 17f hurdlers Arctiid and Hard
Lines (both by Silver Hawk), latter also successful over fences: modest form in maidens
on Flat: no show in 2 juvenile hurdles, pulling hard on debut: sold 3,000 gns Newmarket
December Sales. *A. G. Newcombe*

ACT IN TIME (IRE) 11 b.g. Actinium (FR) – Anvil Chorus (Levanter) [2002/3 **c99**
c109, h–: c24dᵖ c26s⁴ Nov 6] good-topped gelding: fair handicap chaser: stays 29f: acts **h–**
on heavy and good to firm going: visored once: races prominently. *T. R. George*

ACTIVE ACCOUNT (USA) 6 b. or br.g. Unaccounted For (USA) – Ameritop **h–**
(USA) (Topsider (USA)) [2002/3 h–: 16g Mar 12] has reportedly had wind operation:
fairly useful on Flat (barely stays 11f): little show in 2 maiden hurdles. *Mrs H. Dalton*

ACTIVIST 5 ch.g. Diesis – Shicklah (USA) (The Minstrel (CAN)) [2002/3 h98: 20g³ **h95**
20g* 20g² Oct 12] sturdy, workmanlike gelding: fairly useful stayer on Flat: modest
hurdler: none too fluent but made all in maiden at Perth in September: stays 2½m: best
effort on good ground. *G. M. Moore*

ADALIE 9 b.m. Absalom – Allied Newcastle (Crooner) [2002/3 h86: 16g 20d⁵ 16s **c84**
16v³ c16s² 18v* c16g³ Mar 14] sturdy mare: poor hurdler: trained by J. Joseph first **h78**
3 starts: won amateur handicap at Fontwell in March, hanging left: similar form in 2
handicap chases (jumped poorly on debut): stays 19f: acts on heavy going. *P. J. Hobbs*

ADALPOUR (IRE) 5 b.g. Kahyasi – Adalya (IRE) (Darshaan) [2002/3 16g 16s² Dec **h77**
27] modest on Flat (stays 2m), successful twice early in 2003: settled much better than on
hurdling debut when second in seller at Leicester. *Miss J. Feilden*

ADAMANT APPROACH (IRE) 9 b.g. Mandalus – Crash Approach (Crash **c138 p**
Course) [2002/3 h145: c16s⁴ c16v* c16gᶠ c20g* c20mᶠ Apr 22] **h–**
 Adamant Approach and Cheltenham have not so far proved a winning
combination. Adamant Approach was ante-post favourite for the 2000 Champion
Bumper when a muscle problem developed the weekend before the Festival forcing
him to miss the race; he fell at the last when poised to win the 2002 Supreme
Novices' Hurdle; and then departed at the second when a 7/1-chance, disputing
third favouritism behind Azertyuiop and Impek, for the latest running of the Arkle
Chase. There's nothing in his record to suggest Adamant Approach would have
made much of an impression with the Arkle winner but he needed only to improve
a little to trouble the placed horses. The Arkle was Adamant Approach's third start
over fences, after finishing fourth to Native Scout in a hot maiden at Wexford on his
debut and spreadeagling his field in showing useful form to land a similar event at
Punchestown. Adamant Approach jumped well that day, as he also did when
beating Knock Knock with plenty in hand in a novice at Cork a couple of weeks
after Cheltenham, but mistakes cost him his chance in another Grade 1 novice on
his final start. This came in the Powers Gold Cup at Fairyhouse, a race which had
been set to feature another early Cheltenham casualty Beef Or Salmon until the
ground dried out. In the end only Thari and a stable companion One Night Out lined
up against Adamant Approach who started at 100/30-on, odds he was well on his
way to justifying when he failed to lift his back legs and took a crunching fall two
out. There is improvement in Adamant Approach, though he's getting on a bit to be
making a big impact at the highest level over fences (he was conceding at least two
years to his principal opponents at Cheltenham). Before his last two runs Adamant
Approach had looked best at around two miles, but he is clearly effective at two and

Greenstar Syndicate's "Adamant Approach"

a half when conditions aren't testing. He showed at Punchestown that he is effective on heavy ground, as well as under less testing conditions. Adamant Approach's pedigree has been fully detailed in previous Annuals, though he wasn't the only member of his family to have problems with fences in the latest season. His year-younger half-brother Approaching Land (by Dry Dock) managed to win a members point but only after reportedly making mistakes at seventeen of the eighteen fences. *W. P. Mullins, Ireland*

ADAMATIC (IRE) 12 b.g. Henbit (USA) – Arpal Magic (Master Owen) [2002/3 c105d, h–: c16d^{pu} May 13] tall gelding: fair handicap chaser at best: no form in points/ hunters: raced mainly around 2m on good going or firmer (though probably acts on any): visored once: held up. *Neil King* **c–** **h–**

ADDED DIMENSION (IRE) 12 b.g. Top Ville – Lassalia (Sallust) [2002/3 h84: 20g^F 22s 28g Mar 16] close-coupled gelding: poor handicap hurdler: no form in 2002/3: stays 21f: acts on any going: effective tongue tied or not. *N. A. Dunger* **h–**

ADECCO (IRE) 4 b.g. Eagle Eyed (USA) – Kharaliya (FR) (Doyoun) [2002/3 16f* 16d^6 16s^{pu} 16g^3 Dec 28] useful-looking gelding: first foal: dam 1¼m winner: won 1m maiden at Bad Harzburg in July (runner-up over 11f): fair juvenile hurdler: won at Ludlow in October: left C. Von Der Recke and failed to progress, though creditable effort in blinkers final outing: flashes tail under pressure, and temperament under suspicion: joined R. C. Guest. *Miss Venetia Williams* **h96**

ADELPHI BOY (IRE) 7 ch.g. Ballad Rock – Toda (Absalom) [2002/3 17g^2 Jun 12] modest and none too consistent on Flat (seems to stay easy 2m) nowadays: encouraging **h95**

second in novice at Market Rasen on hurdling debut in June: seemed likely to improve, but not seen out again: joined M. Todhunter. *M. C. Chapman*

ADELPHI THEATRE (USA)   6 b.g. Sadler's Wells (USA) – Truly Bound (USA)   **h103**
(In Reality) [2002/3 h114: 19dF 18d6 21m 20g Mar 25] useful-looking gelding: fair up to 2m on Flat: fair hurdler: every chance when falling heavily 2 out on reappearance: below form after: may prove best up to 2½m: acts on good to soft going. *R. Rowe*

ADEPT   4 b.f. Efisio – Prancing (Prince Sabo) [2002/3 16g5 16g Sep 26] fair maiden at   **h63**
best at 2 yrs for Sir Mark Prescott: poor form on first of 2 starts in juvenile hurdles, making mistakes. *C. W. Fairhurst*

AD HOC (IRE)   9 b.g. Strong Gale – Knockarctic (Quayside) [2002/3 c149+:   **c156 +**
25d5 24v* 24d2 24s3 c24g3 c36dur c29m* Apr 26]   **h140 +**

    As 'consolation' prizes go, they don't come much bigger than the attheraces Gold Cup at Sandown. The first prize of £87,000 must have all but made up for the disappointment connections felt after Ad Hoc's second successive departure when still moving well in the Grand National. Ad Hoc's victory in the 2001 Whitbread Gold Cup (now the attheraces) snatched a third owners' title on the final day of that season for Sir Robert Ogden. Ad Hoc's second victory in the race—his first over fences since—helped to salvage an otherwise relatively low-key season for the sizeable string of his owner, who went from seventh to fifth on the last day to finish with final 1,2,3 earnings of £374,972, nearly £500,000 less than the season's leading owner David Johnson.

    Ad Hoc seems to come to his best in the spring and his target all season was the National in which he had seemed sure to be concerned in the finish when brought down four out in 2002. There was no 'consolation' in the attheraces Gold Cup that season, Ad Hoc managing only a respectable fourth at Sandown, making little impression after coming under the whip four out. His running at least ensured that he would start the latest season on or around the handicap mark off which he had raced at Aintree. Connections set out to protect that mark—at least until the National weights were published—by campaigning Ad Hoc over hurdles in the first half of the season. Bought as a store as a three-year-old for IR 47,000 guineas, Ad Hoc had never previously run over hurdles, graduating straight from points into novice chases as a five-year-old. He made his belated hurdling debut in the Grade 2 John Smith's West Yorkshire Hurdle at Wetherby in early-November, finishing a patiently-ridden and one-paced fifth behind another smart stayer in the Ogden colours, the Hobbs-trained Brother Joe (the mauve and pink checks were also

attheraces Gold Cup Chase (Handicap), Sandown—
Ad Hoc follows up his 2001 Whitbread Gold Cup success; runner-up Stormez is not yet in picture

Sir Robert Ogden's "Ad Hoc"

carried successfully on the same card by the Henderson-trained Marlborough in the Charlie Hall Chase). Ad Hoc's form at Wetherby was more than good enough to win virtually any novice hurdle and he landed the odds with ease in a three-mile event at Ascot later in November, before being beaten a neck by Iris's Gift in a driving finish to the Grade 2 Bristol Novices' Hurdle at Cheltenham in December. That was useful form—the performance looked even better by the end of the season—and Ad Hoc's hurdling merit is better judged on that effort than on his odds-on defeat in a muddling Spa Hurdle at Cheltenham at the end of December when he was also probably unsuited by making the running.

Ad Hoc wasn't seen out in January or February but he showed he was bang on course for Aintree when third, replicating his placing of the previous year, in the William Hill National Hunt Handicap Chase when next seen out at the Cheltenham Festival. Ad Hoc started 9/1 fourth favourite for the Grand National, though he wasn't the shortest-priced of his stable's five runners who also included the favourite Shotgun Willy, the preferred mount of Ruby Walsh. The 33/1-shot Montifault was the only member of the Nicholls-trained quintet to complete the Grand National course, finishing a very tired fifth after being up there most of the way. Surprisingly, for a trainer noted for his chasers, Nicholls' Grand National record is very surprising—just three finishers from twenty-two runners, with Montifault faring by far the best. That Ad Hoc failed to get round was his own fault on this occasion. Held up as usual, he was travelling well enough and yet to be asked a question—though still with plenty of ground to make up—when he blundered and unseated Paul Carberry ('He was going well and we were unlucky to come down') at the nineteenth, much too far out this time to say whether he would have featured in the finish. One thing that can be said, however, is that if Ad Hoc had completed

32

and run to the form he showed when winning the attheraces Gold Cup next time, he'd have been first or second in the National. Ad Hoc produced a decisive turn of foot to quicken clear at Sandown after half a dozen had still looked in with a chance at the third last. With the race won before the final fence, Ad Hoc was kept up to his work by Walsh to win by nine lengths from the durable Scottish National runner-up Stormez, with the consistent pair Gunther McBride and Frosty Canyon third and fourth in a field which was, if anything, short of up-and-coming chasers, the runner-up and Keltic Heritage, who was running from 25 lb out of the handicap, being the only novices in the sixteen-runner line-up. Ad Hoc became the fourth dual winner of the race, following Larbawn, Diamond Edge and Topsham Bay. There was talk of Ad Hoc's being sent for the Grand Steeple-Chase de Paris at Auteuil in May but, in the end, he wasn't seen out again. He will presumably be brought along patiently with the Grand National as his principal target once more in the next season, though a rise of 9 lb in his BHB handicap mark after a career-best effort at Sandown means he is unlikely to look well treated at Aintree. Let's hope, however, that he puts in a clear round and gets the chance to show what he can achieve in the race. Normally a sound jumper nowadays, Ad Hoc has finished second in the Scottish National, as well as winning two 'Whitbreads', and is sure to get the trip; so far as his going requirements are concerned, he acts on ground ranging from good to firm to heavy.

			Lord Gayle (b 1965)	Sir Gaylord
	Strong Gale (br 1975)			Sticky Case
Ad Hoc (IRE) (b.g. 1994)			Sterntau (br 1969)	Tamerlane
				Sterna
	Knockarctic (ch 1983)		Quayside (ch 1967)	London Gazette
				Wong
			Knock Off (b 1972)	Arctic Slave
				Nidee

The lengthy Ad Hoc, from the last crop of Strong Gale, the predominant jumps sire of the 'nineties, has had his pedigree examined in previous Annuals. His dam, the winning Irish two-mile hurdler Knockarctic, is from a successful family. Ad Hoc's grandam Knock Off—a sister to the dam of Champion Chase winner Buck House—bred eight winners. Knockarctic herself has some way to go to match that figure, Ad Hoc being her third winner, following the winning hurdler/fair chaser Excuse Me Sir (by Glacial Storm) and Ad Hoc's sister Vallingale, a winning chaser. *P. F. Nicholls*

ADIOS AMIGO   4 ch.g. Efisio – Los Alamos (Keen) [2002/3 16d Nov 30] workman-like gelding: poor maiden on Flat, sold out of C. Thornton's stable 1,500 gns Doncaster October Sales: tailed off in juvenile on hurdling debut. *A. C. Whillans*   h–

ADJAWAR (IRE)   5 b.g. Ashkalani (IRE) – Adjriyna (Top Ville) [2002/3 16v^{pu} Dec 20] fairly useful on Flat (stays 1½m): reportedly had breathing problem when pulled up in Grade 2 novice at Ascot on hurdling debut. *H. Morrison*   h–

ADJIRAM (IRE)   7 b.g. Be My Guest (USA) – Adjriyna (Top Ville) [2002/3 h–§: 20g^6 18f^4 16g Nov 20] sturdy gelding: little form over hurdles: has looked ungenuine. *D. C. O'Brien*   h65 §

ADMIRAL NELSON (IRE)   8 b. or br.g. Phardante (FR) – Mulberry (FR) (Denel (FR)) [2002/3 22g^2 20m^{pu} 20m 24f^{pu} 24g^6 22d* 20s* 22s^{su} 20s 20s c20s c24v c22s c22s^6 24s Mar 16] lengthy gelding: has only one eye: modest hurdler: won handicaps at Thurles in October and Cork in November: soundly beaten over fences: probably stays 3m: acts on soft going: blinkered fourth outing (looked none too keen). *E. McNamara, Ireland*   c–
h90

ADMIRAL PEARY (IRE)   7 b. or br.g. Lord Americo – Arctic Brief (Buckskin (FR)) [2002/3 F96: F16m* F17m^3 24d^{pu} 22f^{ur} 16g^3 17g^2 16f^4 21f^6 22v* 25v* 19s^5 21s 26g^2 27f^F Apr 24] smallish, close-coupled gelding: fair form in bumpers, didn't need to be at best to win at Stratford in July: fair hurdler: won novice handicaps at Newton Abbot in November and Plumpton in December: best effort when second to Emphatic (ladies) in handicap at Huntingdon penultimate start: probably best at 2¾m+: acts on heavy and good to firm going: sketchy jumper (went markedly right at Plumpton): free-going sort. *C. R. Egerton*   h100
F93

ADMIRAL ROSE   9 b.g. Handsome Sailor – Rose Ravine (Deep Run) [2002/3 c24s^{ur} c19g^{pu} Apr 2] angular gelding: fair hurdler for N. Henderson: won point in January: c83
h–

33

would have shown fair form both starts in hunters had he completed: likely to have stayed 3m: acted on heavy going (won bumper on good to firm): dead. *Mrs Nicholas Jones*

ADRADEE (IRE) 9 b.m. Ajraas (USA) – Miss Tan A Dee (Tanfirion) [2002/3 19s 17s[6] 22d 19f[4] Mar 24] sparely-made mare: fair handicap hurdler at best: off over 2 years and poor in 2002/3: stays 19f: acts on soft and good to firm going, probably on firm: often tongue tied. *M. J. Weeden* — c–, h72

ADRIANS PRIDE 4 ch.f. Keen – Pride's Desire (Grey Desire) [2002/3 16m[pu] Oct 16] lengthy, angular filly: tailed off in 2 maidens on Flat: no show in juvenile on hurdling debut. *N. Wilson* — h–

ADRONIKUS (IRE) 6 ch.g. Monsun (GER) – Arionette (Lombard (GER)) [2002/3 h–: 20g 16m6 17m* 16g* 16g3 24m Apr 16] angular gelding: modest hurdler: won handicaps at Market Rasen (novice) in July and Fakenham (idled) in October: may prove best around 2m: acts on good to firm going: blinkered last 4 starts: tongue tied after reappearance. *D. J. Wintle* — h93

ADVANCE EAST 11 b.g. Polish Precedent (USA) – Startino (Bustino) [2002/3 c88, h–: c20d[pu] c19d[4] c20v[3] c16v[2] c16s[4] Mar 7] workmanlike gelding: has been hobdayed: handicap chaser, only poor form in 2002/3: stays 21f: acts on firm and soft going: tried blinkered, not since 1997/8: held up, and has found little. *M. J. M. Evans* — c78, h–

ADVICE TAKEN (IRE) 6 ch.g. Rashar (USA) – Cyrenaics (IRE) (Cyrano de Bergerac) [2002/3 F16v 21d[pu] 22m[pu] Apr 8] first foal: dam unraced: third in bumper on debut but no other form (ran out once), trained by Mrs P. Gavin prior to hurdling debut: sold 1,400 gns Doncaster May Sales. *R. H. Alner* — h–, F–

ADVOCATUS (GER) 5 b.g. Law Society (USA) – Aguilas (Konigsstuhl (GER)) [2002/3 20g5 20s4 Mar 15] good-topped ex-German gelding: successful over 11f at Krefeld in 2001, in frame 3 times on Flat since for C. Von Der Recke: poor form both starts in novice hurdles. *A. G. Hobbs* — h77

AEGEAN 9 b.g. Rock Hopper – Sayulita (Habitat) [2002/3 c100, h–: c25d[pu] c24m2 c24d* Aug 4] tall gelding: fair handicap chaser: improved last 2 starts, won quite valuable event at Perth in August: stays 25f: acts on good to firm and good to soft going: usually sound jumper. *Mrs S. J. Smith* — c114, h–

AEGEAN PIRATE (IRE) 6 b.g. Polykratis – Rusheen Na Corra (IRE) (Burslem) [2002/3 F16g[pu] Mar 14] first foal: dam ran once: pulled up in bumper on debut. *C. J. Hemsley* — F–

AELRED 10 b.g. Ovac (ITY) – Sponsorship (Sparkler) [2002/3 c102, h–: 18g4 e17d2 c16g6 c17s3 c16d2 c16s3 c16s* c20d c17d4 c16g2 c16g6 c20g Apr 23] sturdy gelding: lightly raced over hurdles: fair handicap chaser: won at Newcastle (has won/been placed in 10 of 11 races over fences there) in December: in-and-out form after: stays 2½m: acts on heavy and good to firm going: tongue tied first 3 starts: races prominently. *R. Johnson* — c106, h82

AFADAN (IRE) 5 br.g. Royal Academy (USA) – Afasara (IRE) (Shardari) [2002/3 h106: 16s 16d2 16d 16g Mar 14] sturdy gelding: fairly useful on Flat (probably stays 1¾m): fair handicap hurdler: raced mainly around 2m on good going or softer: tried tongue tied: unreliable. *J. R. Jenkins* — h106 §

A FEW BOB BACK (IRE) 7 b.g. Bob Back (USA) – Kottna (USA) (Lyphard (USA)) [2002/3 h106, F75: 22s* 20d* 21s3 24m3 20v 24s6 22m Apr 11] fair handicap hurdler: fractured cannon bone final 2001/2 start: improved on return, winning at Kelso and Ayr in November: below form last 3 outings: stays 25f: acts on soft and good to firm going: has won in blinkers/cheekpieces. *D. Eddy* — h112

AFICIONADO (IRE) 9 b.g. Marju (IRE) – Haneena (Habitat) [2002/3 h–: 17m6 Jul 28] of little account nowadays: tried blinkered. *R. Williams* — h–

AFISTFULLOFDOLLARS (IRE) 5 b.g. Be My Native (USA) – Myra Gaye (Corvaro (USA))] [2002/3 NR] ninth foal: brother to winning hurdler/fairly useful chaser Keiran, stays 25f, and half-brother to winning 17f hurdler Buckland Knight (by Commanche Run): dam unraced, from family of top-class 2m to 3m hurdler Gaye Brief and very smart staying jumper Gaye Chance: promising close third to Kim Fontaine in bumper at Punchestown on debut in early-May: should progress. *N. Meade, Ireland* — F100 p

AFRICA (IRE) 6 b.m. Namaqualand (USA) – Tannerrun (IRE) (Runnett) [2002/3 h71: 20d[pu] 16s[pu] Jun 13] 1¾m winner on Flat: little form over hurdles. *A. Streeter* — h–

AFRICAN DAWN 5 b.g. Spectrum (IRE) – Lamu Lady (IRE) (Lomond (USA)) [2002/3 17m[pu] 16m6 16d[pu] Nov 12] angular gelding: fair on Flat (stays 1¾m), claimed to — h–

join N. Littmoden £6,000 in April: not fluent and no form in 3 starts over hurdles, visored final one. *P. R. Webber*

AFRICAN WATERS (IRE)   6 ch.m. Be My Native (USA) – Queens Romance **c95 d**
(Imperial Fling (USA)) [2002/3 20s⁴ 20d² 20g⁴ 20m* 18d c20f* c22d² c24vᵘʳ c20v c21d⁵ **h100 d**
c20s⁴ c20sᵘʳ 20v c22s⁶ Mar 16] 25,000 3-y-o: lengthy mare: sixth foal: sister to bumper winner Native Affair and fairly useful hurdler/chaser Native Fling, stays 2½m: dam maiden hurdler: fair hurdler, won maiden at Wexford in July: often let down by jumping over fences, though won mares maiden at Clonmel in September: stays 2¾m: acts on firm and soft going: no form in blinkers: has had tongue tied. *C. F. Swan, Ireland*

AFRO MAN   5 b.g. Commanche Run – Lady Elle (IRE) (Persian Mews) [2002/3 F18d **h95**
17s 16g⁶ 18g⁴ Mar 17] 3,000 3-y-o: first foal: dam unraced sister to fair chaser Hunters **F—**
Creek, stays 2¾m: won second of 2 starts in maiden Irish points in 2002: bought 22,000 gns Doncaster May Sales: well held in bumper: best effort over hurdles fourth in novice at Fontwell, off bridle some way out: will be suited by 2½m+. *C. J. Mann*

AFTER ME BOYS   9 b.g. Arzanni – Realm Wood (Precipice Wood) [2002/3 h108: **h119**
20d² 24d* Mar 15] angular gelding: fairly useful handicap hurdler: off 16 months, better than ever in 2 starts in 2002/3, won at Newcastle in March: effective at 2½m to 3m: acts on any going: reliable. *Mrs S. J. Smith*

AFTER THE BLUE (IRE)   6 b.g. Last Tycoon – Sudden Interest (FR) (Highest **h89**
Honor (FR)) [2002/3 h89: 20mᶠ 20m* Jun 3] modest hurdler: won maiden at Huntingdon in June: stays 21f: acts on firm going: tongue tied: sold to join K. Wingrove 1,200 gns Doncaster March Sales. *C. J. Mann*

AFZARK   6 b.h. Afzal – Dark Deb (Black Minstrel) [2002/3 F17s F18d Feb 17] first **F—**
foal: dam, of little account, half-sister to useful staying chaser Cerimau: well held in 2 bumpers. *R. H. Alner*

AGAIN AN AGAIN (IRE)   7 b.g. Montelimar (USA) – Running Board (IRE) (Deep **h100**
Run) [2002/3 16m² F18d² 16d 20d 22g 18g* 16f* 16m 17d³ Oct 26] leggy gelding: fourth **F86**
foal: dam unraced sister to Champion Hurdle winners Morley Street and Granville Again: fair form in bumpers: fair hurdler: won handicaps at Downpatrick (novice) and Down Royal (improved effort when making nearly all) in September: best form around 2m: acts on firm and good to soft going: blinkered: has had tongue tied. *S. Donohoe, Ireland*

AGENT PROVOCATEUR (NZ)   7 b.g. Racing Is Fun (USA) – Silver Crest (NZ) **h—**
(Silver Dream) [2002/3 h–, F–: 20d Apr 29] lengthy gelding: no worthwhile form over hurdles: poor point winner in 2003. *S. B. Clark*

AGINCOURT (IRE)   7 b.g. Alphabatim (USA) – Miss Brantridge (Riboboy (USA)) **c85**
[2002/3 h66: 21d⁴ c25v³ c25s² c24d* c24d⁴ c25d⁴ Mar 6] workmanlike gelding: poor **h66**
handicap hurdler: better over fences, travelled more sweetly than usual when winning novice handicap at Ludlow in January: stays 25f: raced on good going or softer (acts on heavy): blinkered once: tends to get behind. *John R. Upson*

AGITANDO (IRE)   7 b.g. Tenby – Crown Rose (Dara Monarch) [2002/3 h114: 16g³ **h112 x**
16d 16s³ 16m 16d⁶ 16m³ 16m³ 16mᶠ Apr 22] sturdy gelding: fair hurdler: should stay 2½m: acts on soft and good to firm going: wore cheekpieces last 2 outings: has found little. *B. De Haan*

AHOOPOE   5 ch.g. Sir Harry Lewis (USA) – Aspark (Sparkler) [2002/3 F16g⁴ Mar 2] **F87**
workmanlike gelding: half-brother to 6f to 8.2f winner Amidst (by Midyan) and unreliable 6f performer Arturian (by Vaigly Great), both fairly useful: dam little worthwhile form: 66/1 and bit backward, 6 lengths fourth of 19 to Flower of Pitcur in bumper at Huntingdon on debut. *Mrs P. Robeson*

AIFUNG (IRE)   5 ch.m. Bigstone (IRE) – Palmyra (GER) (Arratos (FR)) [2002/3 F17g² **F89**
F16d⁶ F16m* F17g* Apr 21] 500 3-y-o: seventh foal: half-sister to German 6.5f to 7.5f winner Super Shirley (by High Estate): dam, German 2-y-o 6f winner, from good family: fair in bumpers, won at Huntingdon in October and Newton Abbot (made all in weak mares race) in April. *R. H. Buckler*

AIMEES MARK (IRE)   7 b. or br.g. Jolly Jake (NZ) – Wee Mite (Menelek) [2002/3 **h120**
20s* 22d 20s* 20s* 20v* 20s⁴ 24s 21g Mar 12] good-topped gelding: brother to winning hurdler/fairly useful chaser up to 25f Royal Jake: dam, fair hurdler/winning chaser, half-sister to smart chasers short of 3m Donohill and Winter Rain: bumper winner: fairly useful handicap hurdler: much improved in 2002/3, won at Cork in June, Naas in October and Punchestown (twice) in December: creditable ninth of 27 in Coral Cup at Cheltenham final start: stays 3m: raced on good going or softer (acts on heavy): races prominently. *F. Flood, Ireland*

AINE DUBH (IRE)   6 b.m. Bob Back (USA) – Deep Thyne (IRE) (Good Thyne   **h101**
(USA)) [2002/3 16s³ 16v 20s* 20g³ 20g⁶ Apr 20] leggy, plain mare: first foal: dam,
Irish bumper winner, sister to top-class hurdler Mighty Mogul: maiden on Flat: bumper
winner: fair hurdler: won mares maiden at Tramore in March: further improvement when
24 lengths third of 15 to Leinster in Grade 2 novice at Aintree despite being hampered 3
out and 2 out, but well held after in other graded events at Fairyhouse and Punchestown:
likely to stay beyond 2½m: acts on soft ground. *Kevin F. O'Donnell, Ireland*

AIN TECBALET (FR)   5 b.g. Riverquest (FR) – La Chance Au Roy (FR) (Rex   **c?**
Magna (FR)) [2002/3 17g⁴ c19g³ c17g* c17d³ 21s 18v⁵ 20v 24m Apr 16] medium-sized   **h87**
ex-French gelding: third foal: dam 11f winner in France: won 4-y-o chase at Meslay-
du-Maine in July (left G. Macaire after next start): maiden hurdler, modest form at best in
Britain: best form around 2m: tried blinkered. *N. J. Henderson*

AIR ATTACHE (USA)   8 b.g. Sky Classic (CAN) – Diplomatic Cover (USA) (Ro-   **c113**
berto (USA)) [2002/3 c16g* c17m² c21m³ c19m* Apr 21] fairly useful hurdler in 2000/1:   **h–**
off 22 months prior to winning novice chase at Hereford in June: sold out of C. Mann's
stable only 1,600 gns Doncaster September Sales after third start: easily won 17-runner
hunter at Hereford on return in spring: stays 21f: acts on firm going (not discredited on
good to soft): tongue tied. *K. R. Pearce*

AIRCON (IRE)   8 ch.g. Moscow Society (USA) – Corrielek (Menelek) [2002/3 c83,   **c82 x**
h–: c16mˢᵘ c19g² c19s⁵ c28sᵖᵘ c24gᵖᵘ Apr 19] good-topped gelding: maiden hurdler: **h–**
poor handicap chaser: seems best around 2½m: acts on firm and soft going: usually
visored, wore cheekpieces final outing: sketchy jumper: none too consistent. *R. Dickin*

AIR CONTROL (IRE)   8 b.g. Executive Perk – Sandy Jayne (IRE) (Royal Fountain)   **h–**
[2002/3 h–: 16d Feb 23] quite good-topped gelding: lightly raced and well held over
hurdles. *L. Lungo*

AIR OF CONFUSION   5 b.g. Mr Confusion (IRE) – First Born (Be My Native   **F74**
(USA)) [2002/3 F17d Nov 24] fourth foal: brother to fair 2¼m bumper winner Max Time:
dam modest maiden, suited by 1½m: 50/1, eighth of 20 in bumper at Aintree on debut.
Mrs K. Walton

AJAR (IRE)   13 b.g. Avocat – Door Belle (Fidel) [2002/3 c106, h–: c19d⁶ c24sʳᵗʳ   **c– §**
c20gᵖᵘ Mar 17] sturdy gelding: won 3 hunter chases in 2002: most reluctant year on,   **h–**
refused to race second outing and virtually did so final one (visored): stays 21f: acts on
good to firm and heavy going: has broken blood vessel: sketchy jumper: best avoided.
J. W. Mullins

AKARUS (FR)   8 b.g. Labus (FR) – Meris (FR) (Amarko (FR)) [2002/3 c21s 19s   **c128**
c21s² c22s 18s c21s³ c23s* 20v⁶ c20gᵖᵘ c21s c34s² Mar 15] ex-French gelding: eighth   **h113**
foal: half-brother to 9f winner Thaleia (by Iron Duke): dam 12.5f winner: fair maiden
hurdler: won very valuable Prix Montgomery (handicap) at Auteuil in November by ¾
length from Jerko Vallis: left C. Aubert after next start, upped in trip and easily best effort
in Britain when 1½ lengths second of 6 finishers to Intelligent in valuable handicap at
Uttoxeter: stays 4¼m: acts on soft going: effective with/without blinkers. *M. C. Pipe*

AKINA (NZ)   12 b.g. Ivory Hunter (USA) – Wairoa Belle (NZ) (Bold Venture (NZ))   **c– x**
[2002/3 c70x, h–: 20gᶠ 27mᵖᵘ May 7] lengthy gelding: won over hurdles in New Zealand,   **h– x**
little form in Britain: poor novice chaser: stays 3¼m: acts on heavy going: poor jumper:
won point in April. *J. Neville*

ALAGAZAM   5 ch.g. Alhijaz – Maziere (Mazilier (USA)) [2002/3 h–: 19g Apr 19]   **h–**
compact gelding: poor maiden on Flat: no form in 2 starts over hurdles a year apart
(pulled hard second time). *B. I. Case*

ALAKDAR (CAN)   9 ch.g. Green Dancer (USA) – Population (General Assembly   **c–**
(USA)) [2002/3 c82d, h–: 26s 24m⁶ 19m² Apr 15] good-topped gelding: poor chaser/   **h69**
novice hurdler: stays 3m: acts on firm and soft going. *C. J. Down*

ALAM (USA)   4 b.g. Silver Hawk (USA) – Ghashtah (USA) (Nijinsky (CAN))   **h104**
[2002/3 16d² 16d² 16v* 16d* Mar 1] sturdy gelding: half-brother to winning 2m hurdler
Mutazz (by Woodman): fair maiden on Flat (will probably stay 1½m): fair juvenile
hurdler: won at Ayr in January and Kelso in March: will stay beyond 2m: acts on heavy
going. *P. Monteith*

ALBAMART WOOD   7 gr.g. Gran Alba (USA) – Marty's Round (Martinmas)   **c–**
[2002/3 c21dᶠ c21d³ c16s⁶ c19d⁶ Feb 10] lengthy gelding: third foal: dam unraced: no
worthwhile form over fences, tongue tied last 2 starts. *R. J. Hodges*

ALBAMORES MADAM 8 gr.m. Gran Alba (USA) – Lady Gwenmore (Town And **h86** Country) [2002/3 21d 22d 22m⁴ 25m³ 26m⁵ Apr 21] angular mare: modest maiden hurdler, off nearly 3 years before reappearance: stays 25f: acts on good to firm going. *Dr J. R. J. Naylor*

ALBATROS (FR) 6 b. or br.g. Shining Steel – Abalvina (FR) (Abdos) [2002/3 h126: **c125** c20s² c16m* c17d² c16f* c17g^F c16v² c16v⁴ c17d⁶ c20m^F 18g⁴ Apr 21] angular gelding: **h114** fairly useful hurdler, well held in minor event at Fairyhouse and handicap at Punchestown in April: fairly useful novice chaser: won at Wexford in July and Listowel in September: better form after when in frame at Wexford (Grade 3) and Naas: best around 2m: acts on any going: effective tongue tied or not. *E. J. O'Grady, Ireland*

ALBERMARLE (IRE) 12 ch.g. Phardante (FR) – Clarahill (Menelek) [2002/3 c–x, **c– x** h81: c21d^pu c20v^pu 21m⁶ Apr 21] strong gelding: winning hurdler/chaser: no form in **h–** 2002/3: stays 2½m: acts on any going: tried blinkered: usually let down by jumping. *M. J. Gingell*

ALBERT HOUSE (IRE) 5 ch.g. Carroll House – Action Plan (Creative Plan (USA)) **F78** [2002/3 F17d F16m Mar 22] workmanlike gelding: fourth foal: half-brother to winning hurdler/fair chaser Fasgo, stays 25f, and fair staying winner Monte Grande (both by Montelimar): dam winning chaser around 2m: signs of ability in bumpers at Aintree and Newbury. *R. H. Alner*

ALBERTINO LAD 6 ch.g. Mystiko (USA) – Siokra (Kris) [2002/3 F77p: F16d⁴ Feb **F91** 23] workmanlike gelding: better effort in bumpers at Ayr (10 months apart) when 6¾ lengths fourth of 18 to Monet's Garden. *L. Lungo*

ALBERT SQUARE (IRE) 6 b.g. Alflora (IRE) – Place Stephanie (IRE) (Hatim **F79** (USA)) [2002/3 F16s⁶ F18d Feb 17] sturdy gelding: second foal: dam, modest novice hurdler who stayed well, out of half-sister to Irish 2000 Guineas winner Northern Treasure: shaped like a stayer when sixth of 20 in bumper at Kempton on debut: well held in similar event 3 weeks later. *R. Rowe*

ALBRIGHTON 8 b.g. Terimon – Bright One (Electric) [2002/3 c17s^F 20s 16s 16s **c– p** 22g² Apr 21] angular gelding: fair on Flat, won twice at 1¾m in August: fell only start **h111** over fences: fair handicap hurdler: effective at 2m to 2¾m: acts on good to firm going, probably on soft. *N. Meade, Ireland*

ALBUNDY (IRE) 4 b.g. Alzao (USA) – Grove Daffodil (IRE) (Salt Dome (USA)) **h80** [2002/3 16v^F 16g⁶ 17d⁴ 20d Apr 25] modest maiden on Flat (stays 2m, hinted at temperament) for M. Tompkins: best effort over hurdles when sixth in maiden juvenile at Wetherby: should stay beyond 2m. *B. Mactaggart*

ALBUQUERQUE (IRE) 6 b.h. Barathea (IRE) – Height of Passion (Shirley **h111** Heights) [2002/3 16s* 16d* 16v³ 16v² 16s 16d 16m⁶ Apr 22] useful at best on Flat (stays 1½m): fair hurdler: won novices at Wexford and Limerick in May: raced around 2m: acts on heavy and good to firm going: has had tongue tied. *T. J. O'Mara, Ireland*

ALCAPONE (IRE) 9 b.g. Roselier (FR) – Ann's Cap (IRE) (Cardinal Flower) **c143** [2002/3 c143, h–: 17d c20g³ c16s* c20v^ur c20s⁵ c17v^pu c16d^F c20d⁵ c25d⁶ c17g² c16m⁴ **h–** Apr 26] workmanlike gelding: has reportedly had back problem: winning hurdler: useful chaser: back to best when making virtually all in Grade 3 at Navan in November: creditable efforts last 2 starts, head second to Killultagh Storm in handicap at Fairyhouse and fourth of 5 to Seebald in very valuable minor event at Sandown: best form around 2m: acts on good to firm and heavy going: has worn near-side pricker: reportedly gurgled sixth outing before undergoing wind operation: usually races up with pace. *M. F. Morris, Ireland*

ALCATRAS (IRE) 6 b. or br.g. Corrouge (USA) – Kisco (IRE) (Henbit (USA)) **h78 §** [2002/3 19d 16d^rtr 19d Jan 27] IR £9,000 4-y-o: workmanlike gelding: first foal: dam unraced: won 4-runner maiden Irish point on debut in 2002: showed more temperament than ability over hurdles: refused to race second start. *B. J. M. Ryall*

ALCAYDE 8 ch.g. Alhijaz – Lucky Flinders (Free State) [2002/3 h88: 20g² Oct 6] **h87** compact gelding: modest maiden hurdler: stays 2¾m: raced on good going or softer (acts on soft). *J. Akehurst*

ALDERBELLE 5 b.m. Alderbrook – Lightning Belle (Belfort (FR)) [2002/3 F17m⁶ **h–** 17g⁶ 22d^pu 17m Oct 1] third foal: dam 2-y-o 5f winner: little sign of ability. *G. M. Moore* **F–**

ALDERFLY 5 b.g. Regal Embers (IRE) – Nyika (Town And Country) [2002/3 F17d **F–** F17m Oct 3] third foal: half-brother to bumper winner Peeyoutwo (by Golden Heights): dam well beaten over hurdles: well held in 2 bumpers. *J. L. Spearing*

ALDERLEY EDGE 9 gr.g. Scallywag – Le Madame (Le Bavard (FR)) [2002/3 24d[4] **h–**
20g[F] 26d[ur] 20m 22s 23v 24d[4] 27v[4] 24v[6] 27g[4] 23m[pu] Apr 21] lengthy gelding: has severe
stringhalt: third in bumper on debut: off 2 years and little show over hurdles. *K. S. Thomas*

ALDWYCH ARROW (IRE) 8 ch.g. Rainbows For Life (CAN) – Shygate (Shy **h90**
Groom (USA)) [2002/3 h–: 21g[3] 17m* 20m[2] 16m[6] Oct 24] neat gelding: poor on Flat
(stays 2m): modest novice hurdler: won at Sedgefield in October: will stay beyond 2½m:
raced only on good/good to firm going since debut: not a fluent jumper. *M. A. Buckley*

ALEEMDAR (IRE) 6 b.g. Doyoun – Aleema (Red God) [2002/3 16s[2] 18m[2] 16d* **h108 d**
17g* 16d 16g[4] 19d 17s 18g[4] 19m[5] 20g[5] Apr 21] half-brother to winning 2m hurdler
Aliwaiyn (by Shernazar): 9f winner in France at 3 yrs: fair hurdler: won novices at Naas
and Killarney in July: sold out of M. O'Brien's stable 17,000 gns Doncaster August Sales:
well below best subsequently: will prove best at sharp 2m: acts on soft and good to firm
going: tried blinkered. *Miss K. Marks*

ALEXANDER BOYZONE (IRE) 9 gr.g. Mandalus – Fane Bridge (Random Shot) **h–**
[2002/3 h–: 19g Oct 6] lengthy gelding: placed in bumpers: no form over hurdles, off at
least a year before each of last 2 appearances. *Miss M. E. Rowland*

ALEXANDER MILENIUM (IRE) 7 b.g. Be My Native (USA) – Kissowen (Pit- **c– p**
pan) [2002/3 F117: c17s[F] c21v[6] 16g[5] Apr 20] rangy, good sort: smart bumper winner: **h90 p**
second in Grade 1 at Punchestown in 2002: tailed off in 2003 renewal in late-April: **F–**
running quite encouraging first race over fences when falling 2 out in Grade 1 novice at
Leopardstown on reappearance: shaped as if having a problem subsequently, including
on hurdling debut: should stay at least 2½m. *W. P. Mullins, Ireland*

ALEXANDER PARK (IRE) 6 b.g. Yashgan – Lady Laramie (IRE) (Le Bavard **h–**
(FR)) [2002/3 27v[pu] 20s 26d 26g Mar 2] sturdy gelding: first foal: dam unraced half-sister
to dam of useful 2m to 2½m hurdler Notcomplainingbut and useful hurdler/chaser up to
25f Force Seven: no form over hurdles. *John R. Upson*

ALFA SUNRISE 6 b.g. Alflora (IRE) – Gipsy Dawn (Lighter) [2002/3 F82: F16d[2] **F104**
F18s* F17d Feb 23] angular gelding: best effort in bumpers (fairly useful form) when
winning at Fontwell in December by 17 lengths: will stay at least 2½m. *R. H. Buckler*

ALF LAUREN 5 b.g. Alflora (IRE) – Gokatiego (Huntercombe) [2002/3 F17g* Mar **F87**
22] eleventh foal: half-brother to fair 2m hurdler/chaser Strong Views (by Remainder
Man) and winning hurdler/chaser Come On Penny (by Rakaposhi King), stayed 2½m:
dam unraced: 7/2, won 8-runner bumper at Bangor on debut by 1¼ lengths from Imperial
Dream. *A. King*

ALFORENKA 6 ch.g. Alflora (IRE) – Tochenka (Fine Blue) [2002/3 F16v F16d[6] Mar **F–**
1] big, strong gelding: first foal: dam fairly useful staying chaser: green, well held in 2
bumpers. *H. D. Daly*

ALFRED THE GREY 6 gr.g. Environment Friend – Ranyah (USA) (Our Native **c93**
(USA)) [2002/3 c–, h–: c24m 24d c26m* Jul 19] leggy gelding: little form over hurdles: **h–**
left R. Hollinshead, much improved when winning maiden chase at Southwell in July:
not seen out again: stays 3¼m: acts on good to firm going: tried blinkered. *R. Wilman*

ALFY RICH 7 b.g. Alflora (IRE) – Weareagrandmother (Prince Tenderfoot (USA)) **h77**
[2002/3 h–, F–: 24s[pu] 17v[2] 21g* Mar 12] tall gelding: poor hurdler: won selling handicap
at Huntingdon in March: stays 21f: acts on heavy going. *P. M. Rich*

ALGARVE 6 b.g. Alflora (IRE) – Garvenish (Balinger) [2002/3 F17s[6] 19d 20m Apr **h–**
12] IR £45,000 4-y-o: useful-looking gelding: fourth foal: dam, novice hurdler/chaser, **F72**
half-sister to useful 2½m chaser Wayward King: sixth in bumper on debut: showed little
in 2 novice hurdles. *H. D. Daly*

ALHAURIN 4 ch.g. Classic Cliche (IRE) – Fairey Firefly (Hallgate) [2002/3 F16d **F–**
F16d Feb 25] quite good-topped gelding: second foal: dam, 6f winner, half-sister to very
smart staying hurdler/chaser Avro Anson: well held in 2 bumpers. *Miss J. A. Camacho*

ALHERI 12 gr.g. Puget (USA) – Miss Haddon (Free Boy) [2002/3 c–, h58: 20g[2] c25d[pu] **c64**
21g c24m[3] 20m[5] 26m[3] c25f[2] Oct 10] workmanlike gelding: poor maiden hurdler/chaser: **h76**
stays 3¼m: raced mainly on good going or firmer (acts on firm). *J. A. T. de Giles*

ALICE 6 b.m. Rambo Dancer (CAN) – Cold Line (Exdirectory) [2002/3 h–, F73: 21d[pu] **h59**
21g[3] Aug 1] smallish, sturdy mare: poor in bumpers, little form over hurdles: tried tongue
tied. *J. Hetherton*

ALICE REIGNS 6 b.m. Sir Harry Lewis (USA) – Richards Kate (Fidel) [2002/3 F88: 17d⁴ Nov 5] won only start in bumpers: favourite, found little for pressure when around 20 lengths fourth in mares novice at Folkestone on hurdling debut. *Mrs A. J. Perrett* **h–**

ALITTLEMOREACTION 5 b.g. Alflora (IRE) – Ilderton Road (Noalto) [2002/3 F16g F17g F18f Apr 24] unfurnished gelding: fourth foal: dam, poor 2m novice hurdler, half-sister to dam of smart hurdler/chaser up to 3m Slaney Native: tailed off in bumpers, sweated profusely on debut. *M. J. Roberts* **F–**

ALKA INTERNATIONAL 11 b.g. Northern State (USA) – Cachucha (Gay Fandango (USA)) [2002/3 h110: c17d⁵ c16s³ c17v⁵ 20d Feb 17] lengthy gelding: seemingly modest form in small fields first 2 starts in novice chases: fair hurdler: set pace and probably flattered when last of 7 in Grade 2 at Fontwell final outing: stays 21f, at least when conditions aren't testing: acts on heavy going: effective blinkered or not. *Mrs P. Townsley* **c95 h?**

ALLANTON BRIG 7 b.g. Milieu – Lurdenlaw Rose (New Brig) [2002/3 F–: 24sᵖᵘ Feb 24] lengthy gelding: no show in bumper and maiden hurdle. *R. Shiels* **h–**

ALL BART NATIVE (IRE) 8 br.g. Be My Native (USA) – Bissie's Jayla (Zambrano) [2002/3 c22d⁴ Nov 11] IR 18,500 3-y-o: third foal: dam unraced half-sister to top-class staying chaser Docklands Express: 20/1, some promise but reportedly finished lame when fourth of 5 finishers in easy winner Ask The Natives in novice chase at Fontwell on belated debut: clearly difficult to train. *L. Wells* **c94**

ALL BLEEVABLE 6 b.g. Presidium – Eve's Treasure (Bustino) [2002/3 h66: 16g² 16g³ 16m⁴ Apr 21] close-coupled gelding: poor novice hurdler: form only around 2m: acts on heavy going. *Mrs S. Lamyman* **h72**

ALLEGED AFFAIR (IRE) 6 gr.g. Safety Catch (USA) – Wren's Princess (Wrens Hill) [2002/3 F16g Dec 13] tall gelding: ninth foal: half-brother to fairly useful chaser King's Banker (by King's Ride), stays 25f, and winning pointer by Sharp Charter: dam, lightly-raced maiden, out of half-sister to very smart 2m to 2½m hurdler Fane Ranger: never-dangerous ninth of 18 in bumper at Doncaster on debut: will be suited by greater test of stamina. *O. Brennan* **F80**

ALLEGEDLY RED 4 ch.f. Sabrehill (USA) – Tendency (Ballad Rock) [2002/3 16g6 16g6 16v6 16d⁴ Feb 8] no form on Flat: signs of ability in claimer/sellers over hurdles: will prove best at 2m. *Mrs A. Duffield* **h64**

ALLEGED SLAVE (IRE) 8 ch.g. Husyan (USA) – Lek Dawn (Menelek) [2002/3 24v² 24v⁶ 20s⁵ Mar 15] workmanlike gelding: won maiden Irish point/runner-up in bumper in 2000: off nearly 3 years, 5 lengths second to Master McGrath in maiden at Chepstow, easily best effort over hurdles on return. *A. King* **h98**

ALLEGIANCE 8 b.g. Rock Hopper – So Precise (FR) (Balidar) [2002/3 h–: 16d Mar 8] leggy gelding: handicap hurdler, well held both starts since 2000/1: raced around 2m: acts on good to firm and heavy going: formerly blinkered/visored. *P. Wegmann* **h–**

ALLER MOOR (IRE) 12 b.g. Dry Dock – Boggy Peak (Shirley Heights) [2002/3 c25s⁸ c25g* c26mᵖᵘ Apr 17] rather leggy, workmanlike gelding: fairly useful hunter chaser nowadays: won at Hereford and Exeter in March: should stay beyond 25f: acts on soft going, seemingly unsuited by firmer than good: normally sound jumper who races with plenty of zest. *C. J. Gray* **c105**

ALL EYEZ ON ME (IRE) 6 b.g. Torus – Ella Rosa (Le Bavard (FR)) [2002/3 c20vᶠ c23vᵖᵘ c20dur c19dur 24sᵖᵘ 17g 21mᵖᵘ c19m⁶ Apr 5] IR £11,500 4-y-o: fourth foal: dam, winning hurdler who stayed 2½m, half-sister to useful 2m chaser Buckfast Abbey: no form over hurdles or fences (makes mistakes): wore cheekpieces last 2 starts. *Dr P. Pritchard* **c– x h–**

ALLEZ TOUJOURS (IRE) 8 b.g. Castle Keep – Adapan (Pitpan) [2002/3 17s⁴ 16s³ 19s c16dᵖᵘ c19dbd c16gᵖᵘ 24g³ Apr 21] lengthy ex-Irish gelding: fourth foal: half-brother to 2 winning pointers: dam unraced: poor maiden hurdler on balance: failed to complete all 3 starts over fences: should stay beyond 2m: acts on soft going. *M. Sheppard* **c– h71**

ALL GUNS BLAZING (IRE) 7 b.g. Un Desperado (FR) – Malone Ranger (Noble Philip (USA)) [2002/3 h96, F–: 20d⁶ c24dᶠ Nov 6] good-topped gelding: novice hurdler, modest form at best: fell second on chasing debut: likely to prove best at 3m+: acts on going softer than good. *John R. Upson* **c– h–**

ALL HONEY (IRE) 6 ch.m. Fourstars Allstar (USA) – A Bit of Honey (The Parson) [2002/3 h78, F87: 20s² 22v³ 16s⁴ 24d⁵ 20v⁴ 24s c20gᵖᵘ c25sᵖᵘ 20g Apr 21] leggy mare: bumper winner: poor maiden hurdler: failed to complete both starts over fences: stays 2¾m: raced on good going or softer (acts on heavy): tried blinkered. *Miss K. Marks* **c– h83 d**

ALLIGATOR ALLEY (IRE) 7 ch.g. Roselier (FR) – Ballyhoura Lady (Green Shoon) [2002/3 F16v F16v 24vᵖᵘ Jan 17] IR 32,000 4-y-o: smallish, sturdy gelding: ninth foal: half-brother to several winners, including fairly useful hurdler/chaser Duhallow Lodge (by Deep Run), stayed 3m: dam won up to 3m in Ireland: no sign of ability: visored on hurdling debut. *P. R. Webber* **h–** **F–**

ALLIMAC (IRE) 6 b.g. Alphabatim (USA) – Firewood (IRE) (Brush Aside (USA)) [2002/3 h96: c19g* c17g² c20f* c16g³ c19gᵖᵘ c20g* Apr 26] lengthy gelding: modest novice hurdler: better over fences, won novices at Hereford in May, Ludlow in October and Market Rasen (simple task) in April: acts on firm going (runner-up in bumper on good to soft): front runner: jumps soundly in main: reportedly broke blood vessel fourth and fifth starts. *Miss H. C. Knight* **c111** **h–**

ALL IN THE STARS (IRE) 5 ch.g. Fourstars Allstar (USA) – Luton Flyer (Condorcet (FR)) [2002/3 21gʳᵒ Mar 3] €7,500 4-y-o: fifth foal: half-brother to modest 2m hurdlers Executive Flyer (by Executive Perk) and Morning Mist (by Supreme Leader): dam, winning 2½m hurdler, half-sister to useful staying hurdler Petty Bridge: won maiden point in February (subsequently tested positive for morphine): keeping on in share of second when driving left and crashing through wing of final flight in 16-runner conditional jockeys novice at Market Rasen on hurdling debut. *D. P. Keane* **h75**

ALLOTROPE (IRE) 8 b.g. Nashwan (USA) – Graphite (USA) (Mr Prospector (USA)) [2002/3 h75: 24m 17d⁵ 24mᵖᵘ Apr 12] leggy gelding: poor handicap hurdler, sold out of Mrs M. Reveley's stable 900 gns Doncaster October Sales after second outing: no form after in points/hunter chase: stays 2¾m: acts on good to firm and heavy going: blinkered last 2 starts. *Lady Susan Brooke* **c–** **h–**

ALL OVER NOW (IRE) 6 b.m. Broken Hearted – Betty's Girl (Menelek) [2002/3 F17s 25dᴿ F16v⁴ F19v 20v² 20s⁵ Mar 15] medium-sized mare: third foal: dam winning staying chaser: won mares maiden point in Ireland in 2002: poor form in bumpers/over hurdles, left Miss V. Williams after second start. *Michael Cullen, Ireland* **h79** **F70**

ALL POINTS NORTH (IRE) 4 b.g. Distinctly North (USA) – Winscarlet North (Garland Knight) [2002/3 17g Aug 9] brother to modest hurdler up to 2¾m Gypsy and half-brother to winning Irish 3m chaser Lotto Lolly (by Un Desperado): modest maiden at 2 yrs, well held on Flat in 2002: well held in juvenile on hurdling debut. *M. W. Easterby* **h–**

ALL RIGHT CLARK (IRE) 10 ch.g. Tale Quale – Cappahard (Record Run) [2002/3 c16s* c17s⁶ c22d c16g* c19f⁴ Sep 28] half-brother to winning chasers Synieyourmissed (by King's Ride), stayed 2½m, and Crossofspancilhill (by Duky), stayed well: dam, poor Irish maiden, half-sister to dam of useful staying chaser Whaat Fettle: winning pointer: best efforts in steeplechases when winning handicaps at Tralee in June and Uttoxeter (conditional jockeys) in September: reportedly badly lame final start: bred to stay beyond 2m: acts on soft going. *N. F. Glynn, Ireland* **c82**

ALL SONSILVER (FR) 6 b.g. Son of Silver – All Licette (FR) (Native Guile (USA)) [2002/3 h97ᵖ: 16g* c16mᵖᵘ c20s² c24d³ c16d⁵ c21s* Feb 23] useful-looking gelding: successful twice from 3 starts over hurdles, including handicap at Hexham in April: off 6 months, modest form in novice chases on return, winning handicap at Ayr: stays 21f (not 3m): acts on soft going. *M. Todhunter* **c96** **h94**

ALLSTAR LEADER (IRE) 6 b.g. Fourstars Allstar (USA) – Rugged Leader (Supreme Leader) [2002/3 F16g 17dᶠ F16g 16d F20s 16d 20s 24s F16m⁶ Apr 22] leggy gelding: once-raced on Flat: fair form in bumpers but little show over hurdles. *S. O'Farrell, Ireland* **h–** **F88**

ALL THE COLOURS (IRE) 10 br.h. Classic Secret (USA) – Rainbow Vision (Prince Tenderfoot (USA)) [2002/3 c22d⁴ c24sᵖᵘ c24vᶠ Nov 22] stocky horse: fair on Flat (stayed 2m): fair maiden hurdler at best, generally well below form in 2001/2 for J. Mulhern: no form in 3 starts over fences, let down by jumping: should have stayed beyond 17f: acted on any going: dead. *Jonjo O'Neill* **c–** **h–**

ALLTIME DANCER (IRE) 11 b.g. Waajib – Dance On Lady (Grundy) [2002/3 c86, h–: c33g c24s⁵ Mar 7] compact gelding: one-time fairly useful hurdler: winning pointer: largely disappointing in steeplechases, leaving Mrs C. Lambert after reappearance in May: stays 3¼m: acts on firm and good to soft going: has won in blinkers. *Miss Kate Smyth* **c–** **h–**

ALLUDE (IRE) 4 b.g. Darshaan – Ahliyat (USA) (Irish River (FR)) [2002/3 16d³ 16v⁶ 17d⁵ 17g² 16g Apr 3] strong, lengthy gelding: fairly useful on Flat (stays 1½m), sold out of M. Grassick's stable 7,000 gns Newmarket Autumn Sales: fairly useful juvenile **h113**

hurdler: easily best efforts when third to Bal de Nuit at Kempton and eighth of 19 to Le Duc in Grade 2 at Aintree. *C. J. Mann*

AL MABROOK (IRE)   8 b.g. Rainbows For Life (CAN) – Sky Lover (Ela-Mana-Mou) [2002/3 h79: 17v⁶ 16g 21vᵖᵘ Jan 21] close-coupled gelding: maiden hurdler, no form in 2002/3: stays 21f: acts on firm and soft going: has worn cheekpieces/visor: races prominently: joined N. Richards. *K. A. Ryan*   **h–**

ALMANOSO   7 b.m. Teenoso (USA) – Almanot (Remainder Man) [2002/3 h68: 22vᵖᵘ 25v⁵ Dec 4] bad maiden staying hurdler. *R. Curtis*   **h–**

ALMAPA   11 ch.g. Absalom – More Fun (Malicious) [2002/3 c–, h79: 16m 16g⁴ 17m² 16m⁴ 17g⁶ 16g⁴ 18m* 17f⁴ c16f² Oct 24] leggy gelding: poor handicap hurdler: won seller at Fontwell in September: lightly-raced maiden chaser: raced mainly around 2m: acts on firm and good to soft going, not on soft/heavy: well below form in blinkers fifth start: consistent. *R. J. Baker*   **c77** **h76**

ALMARAVIDE (GER)   7 ch.g. Orfano (GER) – Allerleirauh (GER) (Espresso) [2002/3 17s Jan 25] smallish gelding: fairly useful hurdler in 2000/1: in need of run in handicap at Cheltenham on return: should stay beyond 19f: acts on heavy going. *M. Bradstock*   **h–**

ALMASHROUK (IRE)   6 b.g. Common Grounds – Red Note (Rusticaro (FR)) [2002/3 17d³ 16d 16s 16g 17g⁵ 17g Mar 20] smallish, sturdy gelding: maiden on Flat (probably stays 7f), no form in 2002, sold out of M. Channon's stable 800 gns Newmarket July Sales: signs of only a little ability over hurdles: has worn cheekpieces. *M. E. Sowersby*   **h–**

ALMAZARD   6 b.g. Mazaad – Almanot (Remainder Man) [2002/3 F18s F16s 22d 27vᵖᵘ Mar 3] stocky gelding: second foal: dam placed in bumper: no show in bumpers/ novice hurdles (blinkered): has jumped poorly/looked none too keen. *L. Wells*   **h–** **F–**

ALMIRE DU LIA (FR)   5 ch.g. Beyssac (FR) – Lita (FR) (Big John (FR)) [2002/3 22d² 22v⁶ 24v⁵ 20d* 22f² Mar 29] third foal: dam 15f hurdles winner: modest novice hurdler: won handicap at Newcastle in March: stays 2¾m: acts on firm and good to soft going: usually wears cheekpieces. *Mrs S. C. Bradburne*   **h91**

ALMNADIA (IRE)   4 b.f. Alhaarth (IRE) – Mnaafa (IRE) (Darshaan) [2002/3 17s² 16g⁶ 17g⁴ 17m³ 16m* 16m² 16d⁶ 16d⁴ 16d* 16s⁶ 16vᵖᵘ 19d 16g³ 16g⁵ Mar 25] smallish filly: modest on Flat (stays 1½m), sold out of G. Butler's stable 8,000 gns Newmarket July Sales: fair juvenile hurdler, claimed from D. Williams £5,200 fourth start: made all at Cheltenham in October and Fakenham in December: likely to prove best around 2m: acts on soft and good to firm going: front runner: tough. *S. Gollings*   **h99**

ALMONTASIR (IRE)   5 b.g. Distinctly North (USA) – My Blue (Scenic) [2002/3 F16gᵖᵘ F18sᵖᵘ Dec 26] first foal: dam, winning 3m hurdler, from family of high-class 1½m winner Pelerin: pulled up in 2 bumpers. *T. P. McGovern*   **F–**

ALMOST BROKE   6 ch.g. Nearly A Hand – Teletex (Pollerton) [2002/3 F98: 22d⁶ 20sᶠ 20m³ Apr 11] tall gelding: chasing type: modest form in novice hurdles: likely to prove suited by further than 2½m. *P. F. Nicholls*   **h97**

ALMOST FREE   6 b.g. Darshaan – Light Fresh Air (USA) (Rahy (USA)) [2002/3 17vᵖᵘ 16g² Jan 28] won around 1½m on Flat at 3 yrs for M. Johnston: much better effort in novice hurdles (reportedly had mucus on lungs on debut) when 5 lengths second to easy winner Brooklyn Breeze at Musselburgh. *B. S. Rothwell*   **h84**

ALMUTAN STAR   8 b.m. Almutanabbi – Salt of The Earth (Sterling Bay (SWE)) [2002/3 16mᵖᵘ May 6] no sign of ability on Flat or in conditional jockeys seller on hurdling debut. *J. Neville*   **h–**

ALPHABETIC   6 ch.g. Alflora (IRE) – Incamelia (St Columbus) [2002/3 F17f³ F16s F16g³ Apr 2] well-made gelding: third living foal: dam modest staying chaser: fair form when third in bumpers (reportedly had breathing problem in between): carries head high. *N. J. Henderson*   **F93**

ALPHA BLUES   8 ch.g. Acatenango (GER) – Alpha Belle (GER) (Runnett) [2002/3 c20v⁴ c17s⁴ c25s⁴ 20v⁴ 23s 16g 18g³ Apr 21] strong gelding: useful hurdler at best: generally out of sorts in 2002/3, and just fair form in maiden chases: should stay beyond 2½m: raced on good going or softer (poor efforts on heavy): blinkered fifth and final starts: front runner. *J. T. R. Dreaper, Ireland*   **c114** **h121 ?**

ALPHA CENTAURI (IRE)   9 ch.g. Alphabatim (USA) – Barna Glen (Furry Glen) [2002/3 21dᵖᵘ 17s⁵ c20vᵖᵘ c16sᵖᵘ Jan 14] strong, good-topped gelding: bumper winner in   **c–** **h93**

Ireland in 2000/1: missed 2001/2, other form only when fifth in novice hurdle at Bangor in December: may prove best around 2m: has looked headstrong. *Miss Venetia Williams*

ALPHA LEATHER   12 gr.g. Zambrano – Harvey's Choice (Whistlefield) [2002/3 c–, h–: c24m^pu c21g^4 c24m^5 c24s^4 Aug 1] tall gelding: no longer of any account: tried visored. *L. P. Grassick*   c–, h–

ALPHAMERICREDONION (IRE)   7 ch.g. Naheez (USA) – Radical Sovereign (Radical) [2002/3 F16f^4 F16m^6 F17d^6 F16d 20m^6 Dec 17] 9,000 5-y-o: second foal: dam in frame in bumper/2m maiden hurdle: modest in bumpers: sixth in maiden at Musselburgh on hurdling debut. *Mrs A. Duffield*   h80 F83

ALPHA NOBLE (GER)   6 b.g. Lando (GER) – Alpha (GER) (Frontal) [2002/3 16v^4 Dec 21] useful-looking gelding: useful on Flat (stays 1½m), won 3 times in Germany, including twice in 2002, sold out of P. Rau's stable 34,000 gns Newmarket Autumn Sales: shaped as if in need of experience when fourth to Mythical King in novice at Uttoxeter on hurdling debut, not fluent: should do better. *Miss Venetia Williams*   h90 p

ALPHA ROMANA (IRE)   9 b.g. Alphabatim (USA) – Stella Romana (Roman Warrior) [2002/3 c91+, h–: c16g* c21m^pu c24s^pu c16d c20m^F c16m^2 Apr 5] strong, lengthy gelding: fairly useful hunter chaser: won at Cheltenham in May: stays 21f: acts on good to firm going. *Mrs Susan E. Busby*   c100 h–

ALPHASUPREME (IRE)   6 ch.m. Alphabatim (USA) – Railway Rabbit (IRE) (Supreme Leader) [2002/3 F17m^4 F17m^5 Aug 26] first foal: dam, unplaced in bumpers, sister to fair staying hurdler Garryduff Supreme: better effort in bumpers at Newton Abbot when fourth to Sammy Samba in maiden on debut: will stay beyond 17f: joined C. Down. *Mrs P. N. Dutfield*   F74

ALPINE HIDEAWAY (IRE)   10 b.g. Tirol – Arbour (USA) (Graustark) [2002/3 c–, h62: 17g^5 17d^4 17d^6 Oct 31] angular gelding: poor hurdler: raced mainly around 2m: acts on firm going, probably on good to soft: tried in blinkers/visor/cheekpieces. *J. S. Wainwright*   c– h72

ALPINE MESSAGE   6 b.m. Tirol – Jupiter's Message (Jupiter Island) [2002/3 h72, F70: 16m 20s F16v F16v Dec 31] rather leggy mare: poor form in bumpers and over hurdles: well held in 2002/3: sold out of S. Keightley's stable 11,000 gns Newmarket July Sales after reappearance. *John Joseph Murphy, Ireland*   h– F–

ALPINE PANTHER (IRE)   10 b.g. Tirol – Kentucky Wildcat (Be My Guest (USA)) [2002/3 c25g^pu c22d^pu c24s^F c20d^5 c22m Mar 21] lengthy, angular gelding: one-time useful hurdler/fair maiden chaser: modest pointer nowadays: no form in hunters: stays 3m: acts on good to firm and good to soft going, probably on soft: tried blinkered/tongue tied. *C. R. Cox*   c– h–

ALPINE PRINCE   5 b.g. Rock Hopper – Sweet Lore (Law Society (USA)) [2002/3 F14d F16s 19d^pu 17m Apr 5] workmanlike gelding: third living foal: dam unraced, out of smart 1977 2-y-o Sweet And Lovely: no sign of ability, looking temperamental both starts in bumpers: tried blinkered/visored. *R. Dickin*   h– F–

ALPINE RACER (IRE)   4 b.g. Lake Coniston (IRE) – Cut No Ice (Great Nephew) [2002/3 16d 16g 16d^4 19d 21d^pu Apr 8] half-brother to one-time fairly useful hurdler Pietro Bembo (by Midyan), stays 19f: modest maiden on Flat (stays 1¼m): no worthwhile form over hurdles. *R. E. Barr*   h–

ALPINE SLAVE   6 ch.g. Alflora (IRE) – Celtic Slave (Celtic Cone) [2002/3 16d^6 21s^F 18s* 20g^3 Apr 2] 21,000 3-y-o: sturdy gelding: half-brother to smart hurdler/chaser Young Spartacus (by Teenoso), stays 3m, and modest hurdler/chaser Celtino (by Relkino), stayed 21f: dam, fair hurdler/fairly useful chaser, stayed well: fair novice hurdler: didn't need to be at best to win at Fontwell in March: should stay beyond 2½m. *J. T. Gifford*   h110

ALQABAS (IRE)   5 b.g. Nashwan (USA) – Harayir (USA) (Gulch (USA)) [2002/3 20g^ur 21v^pu 22s^pu 20m^5 Mar 19] temperamental maiden on Flat: has also looked less than keen when showing little over hurdles. *M. R. Hoad*   h– §

ALRAFID (IRE)   4 ch.c. Halling (USA) – Ginger Tree (USA) (Dayjur (USA)) [2002/3 16d^6 Feb 7] medium-sized colt: fairly useful on Flat, won at 1m only start at 3 yrs (reportedly finished lame), sold out of A. Stewart's stable 17,000 gns Newmarket Autumn Sales: shaped like non-stayer in juvenile on hurdling debut. *G. L. Moore*   h–

ALSCOT FOXY LADY (IRE)   6 b.m. Foxhound (USA) – Arena (Sallust) [2002/3 h–, F–: 16g 16s 16s^pu Dec 27] close-coupled mare: no sign of ability. *R. Dickin*   h–

ALSINA   12 b.g. Alias Smith (USA) – Tersina (Lighter) [2002/3 c–: c25d² c25d^pu   **c92**
c26d^pu c25g Apr 7] fair pointer: easily best effort in hunter chases when second in maiden
at Hexham: let down by jumping final start: stays 25f. *Peter Innes*

ALSKA (FR)   10 b. or br.m. Leading Counsel (USA) – Kolkwitzia (FR) (The Wonder   **c84**
(FR)) [2002/3 c83, h–: c21f⁴ c31m⁴ c24m⁴ c24s Feb 13] angular mare: winning hurdler: **h–**
poor maiden chaser: appears to stay 31f: acts on any going: tried blinkered/visored: sometimes let down by jumping. *P. L. Southcombe*

AL SKYWALKER (USA)   10 b.g. Skywalker (USA) – Bint Alnasr (USA) (Al Nasr   **h?**
(FR)) [2002/3 18s* 19s^pu 17s* 17d^pu 18f* 19f* 20f⁵ Apr 25] medium-sized gelding: one
of the leading hurdlers in USA, successful 11 times, 4 times in 2002/3, notably Grade 1
Carolina Cup at Camden in March by 6¾ lengths, conceding 8 lb, from Tres Touche:
earlier won Grade 3 events at Radnor (National Hunt Cup) in May and Far Hills
(Appleton Stakes) in October and valuable contest at Little Everglades in March: failed
to settle and soon weakened once tempo increased in Grade 2 at Cheltenham (sweating)
in December, pulled up after being hampered 2 out: stays 2½m: acts on soft and firm
going. *Jennifer Majette, USA*

ALTAREEK (USA)   6 b.g. Alleged (USA) – Black Tulip (FR) (Fabulous Dancer   **h75**
(USA)) [2002/3 F94: 19s³ 17s^pu 16d Feb 26] useful-looking gelding: bumper winner:
only poor form in novice hurdles. *J. M. Jefferson*

ALTAR SOCIETY   9 b.m. Roscoe Blake – Small Money (Altosa Palace) [2002/3   **h–**
20g⁵ 20m⁴ 16s 25d^pu 26m 22s^pu Aug 1] plain mare: no form over hurdles: has looked
temperamental in points: tried visored. *M. J. Gingell*

ALTAY   6 b.g. Erins Isle – Aliuska (IRE) (Fijar Tango (FR)) [2002/3 16m* 19d² 16g*   **h122 +**
16g² Apr 5] big, leggy gelding: fairly useful on Flat (stays 13f): quickly progressed
into fairly useful hurdler: won novice at Musselburgh in December and handicap at
Wetherby in March: excellent second to Risky Reef in valuable handicap at Aintree final
start: probably ideally suited by sharp 2m: acts on good to firm and good to soft going.
R. A. Fahey

ALTHREY RULER (IRE)   10 b.g. Phardante (FR) – Keego's Aunt (Tyrant (USA))   **h78**
[2002/3 h72: 17g 16m 20d³ 20g⁵ 24g^pu 21f² 24f⁵ Oct 24] angular gelding: poor hurdler:
left W. Clay after reappearance: stays easy 21f: acts on any going: tried blinkered.
F. Lloyd

ALTHREY TORCH (IRE)   11 b.g. Torus – Keep The Cut (Tarqogan) [2002/3 h83:   **h81**
24g⁵ May 3] useful-looking gelding: poor maiden hurdler: probably best up to 21f: acts
on soft and good to firm going: races prominently: rejoined F. Lloyd. *W. Clay*

ALTREGAN BOY (IRE)   11 b.g. Lancastrian – Please Oblige (Le Levanstell)   **c78**
[2002/3 c–, h–: c25d⁵ c25g^ur c23d^ur c26d⁵ c28s* c25v³ c23v⁴ Jan 1] workmanlike   **h–**
gelding: one-time fairly useful hurdler: 22 lb out of handicap, best effort over fences
when winning at Market Rasen in December: thorough stayer: acts on heavy going: has
been blinkered and tongue tied. *C. N. Kellett*

ALVARO (IRE)   6 ch.g. Priolo (USA) – Gezalle (Shareef Dancer (USA)) [2002/3 h67:   **c–**
16g 17d³ 17m^pu 16d³ 22d³ 22d* 19m³ 24g⁶ 24g 24g 26m² 23m 23d 24d 16d c25d³ c20s^pu   **h85**
24f 26m⁴ Apr 21] workmanlike gelding: well beaten completed start over fences (left
M. Chapman after next outing): modest hurdler: won novice at Cartmel in August: stays
3¼m when conditions aren't testing: acts on good to soft and good to firm going:
blinkered once: has looked far from keen. *D. J. Wintle*

ALVINO   6 b.g. Alflora (IRE) – Rose Ravine (Deep Run) [2002/3 F115: 19d³ 16m* Apr   **h112 p**
2] has plenty of scope: smart bumper winner: reportedly hobdayed prior to reappearance:
better effort over hurdles (reportedly finished distressed on debut) when winning novice
at Ludlow by 5 lengths from Forest Tune: bred to be suited by further than 2m: capable of
better. *Miss H. C. Knight*

ALWAYS A GAMBLE   6 br.m. Lord Americo – Gamblingway (Gambling Debt)   **F–**
[2002/3 F17f May 15] fourth foal: half-sister to winning pointer by Arctic Lord: dam
winning pointer: well behind in maiden bumper on debut. *Mrs H. Pudd*

ALWAYS RAINBOWS (IRE)   5 b. or br.g. Rainbows For Life (CAN) – Maura's   **h117**
Guest (IRE) (Be My Guest (USA)) [2002/3 16s* 16d^F 16v* 16d² 18d 16g Mar 17] useful-
looking ex-Irish gelding: fairly useful on Flat (stays 1½m), sold out of K. Prendergast's
stable 14,000 gns Newmarket Autumn Sales: fairly useful novice hurdler: won at
Wetherby in November and December, and would have won at Haydock in between but
for falling last: good second to impressive Rhinestone Cowboy in Grade 2 novice at

Wetherby, but long way below form both subsequent outings: likely to stay 2½m: acts on heavy ground: visored after second appearance. *B. S. Rothwell*

ALY DALEY (IRE) 15 ch.g. Roselier (FR) – Roses In June (Timobriol) [2002/3 c26d Jun 5] rangy gelding: fair chaser at best: well beaten in hunter at Cartmel in June: won points in March and April: stays 27f: acts on soft and good to firm going (ran poorly on firm): blinkered once. *D. T. Greenwood* c– h–

AMACITA 5 b.m. Shareef Dancer (USA) – Kina (USA) (Bering) [2002/3 17m⁴ 17sᵖᵘ 19d 26sᵖᵘ 20g Apr 21] poor maiden on Flat (probably best around 1½m) for Miss E. Lavelle: fourth in seller on hurdling debut: sold out of J. O'Shea's stable 500 gns Doncaster October Sales, no show after: tried in cheekpieces/tongue strap. *K. G. Wingrove* h78 d

AMANDA KASAKOVA 7 ch.m. Kasakov – Manna Green (Bustino) [2002/3 19d 17d Mar 2] little sign of ability. *J. R. Norton* h–

AMANDARI (FR) 7 ch.g. Petit Loup (USA) – Baby Sitting (FR) (Son of Silver) [2002/3 25g 20vᵒ 24s⁶ 24gᵖᵘ Apr 23] rather leggy ex-French gelding: half-brother to fairly useful hurdler Herakles (by Hero's Honor), stays 2½m: 1½m winner at 3 yrs in France, showed little on Flat in Britain in 2001: completed twice from 6 starts over hurdles up to 19f in French Provinces in 1999/00 for B. O'Sullivan: bought 8,200 gns Doncaster August Sales: no worthwhile form on return: has worn cheekpieces. *Mrs K. Walton* h–

AMARETTOFORANNA (IRE) 10 b.g. Satco (FR) – Candy Slam (Candy Cane) [2002/3 c96§, h–: c16d⁵ c21d* c16vᵖᵘ c19m⁵ c21s⁴ Mar 11] lengthy, sparely-made gelding: modest handicap chaser: made all in weak amateur event at Fakenham in December: below form otherwise in 2002/3: stays 25f: acts on soft and good to firm going: sometimes jumps left: unreliable: sold 3,000 gns Doncaster May Sales. *Ferdy Murphy* c90 § h–

AMARI (IRE) 8 ch.g. Grand Plaisir (IRE) – Teazle (Quayside) [2002/3 c85, h–: 16d 20d 26sᵖᵘ c25g Mar 17] angular gelding: winning pointer: maiden hurdler/chaser, no form in 2002/3. *A. G. Hobbs* c– h–

AMARONE 5 b.g. Young Ern – Tendresse (IRE) (Tender King) [2002/3 h83: 16g⁵ 17dᵖᵘ 16d* 16g 20d⁴ 19s⁵ Dec 5] compact gelding: poor hurdler: easily best effort in 2002/3 when winning conditional jockeys seller at Fakenham in October: best efforts at 2m: acts on soft going: blinkered/visored: moody. *M. J. Ryan* h80 §

AMATEUR DRAMATICS 7 b.g. Theatrical Charmer – Chaconia Girl (Bay Express) [2002/3 h–: 18d⁶ Dec 10] angular gelding: little sign of ability. *Mrs P. A. Tetley* h–

AMATHUS (IRE) 6 br.g. New Express – Mistress Sarah (Ashford (USA)) [2002/3 F17mᵘʳ F17d³ Sep 4] third foal: half-brother to 2¾m hurdle winner Days Destiny and fairly useful chaser Fleeting Mandate (both by Mandalus), stays 2½m: dam lightly-raced half-sister to fairly useful hurdler Fort Noel: better effort in bumpers (held when unseating after jumping a path on debut) when third of 7 to Be Fair at Newton Abbot, still green. *A. King* F72

AMBER DIVER (IRE) 9 ch.g. Seclude (USA) – Sugar Beet (Frigid Aire) [2002/3 c24d⁵ c16m c16g⁴ F16s c26d⁵ 20f⁵ 20f Sep 21] leggy gelding: fifth foal: dam unraced: placed in maiden points, no form otherwise: usually blinkered and tongue tied. *J. J. Lambe, Ireland* c– h– F–

AMBER GO GO 6 ch.m. Rudimentary (USA) – Plaything (High Top) [2002/3 h–: 20g 18g 20dᵖᵘ 20g 17mᵖᵘ 17m⁴ Apr 26] lengthy mare: form over hurdles only when winning bad maiden at Cartmel in June. *K. W. Hogg, Isle of Man* h61

AMBER GOLD 5 b.m. Tragic Role (USA) – Dark Amber (Formidable (USA)) [2002/3 F17d Jan 16] eighth foal: half-brother to fairly useful Italian middle-distance stayer Di Giacomo (by Bustino): dam, 1m winner at 4 yrs, half-sister to smart middle-distance stayer Rakaposhi King: last of 10 in bumper on debut. *Mrs S. M. Johnson* F–

AMBERLEIGH HOUSE (IRE) 11 br.g. Buckskin (FR) – Chancy Gal (Al Sirat (USA)) [2002/3 c130, h–: c24d³ 23m⁶ c24d³ c27d² 17s⁴ c28d c20g³ c36d³ Apr 5] lengthy gelding: winning hurdler: useful handicap chaser: has good record over National fences at Aintree, and easily best effort in 2002/3 when third of 14 finishers to Monty's Pass in Grand National final start: stays 4½m, effective at much shorter: acts on good to firm and heavy going: sound jumper. *D. McCain* c135 h104

AMBER LILY 11 ch.m. Librate – Just Bluffing (Green Shoon) [2002/3 h–: 17gᵖᵘ 22gᵖᵘ 19mᵖᵘ 16s³ 16mᶠ 16m⁶ Jun 29] sturdy mare: winning hurdler: showed little in 2002/3: tried blinkered. *Mrs S. M. Johnson* h–

AMBER MOSS 8 ch.g. Phardante (FR) – Queen's Darling (Le Moss) [2002/3 c90§, **c76 §** h–: c25g^{ur} c22m^6 c22v^4 c21d^6 c16m^4 c24g^4 c24g c20s^3 c20d^3 c20g^6 Apr 25] workmanlike **h–** gelding: winning hurdler: poor maiden chaser: generally out of sorts in 2002/3 (trained until after second start by Mrs S. Bradburne): stays 25f: acts on good to firm and heavy going: tried in cheekpieces: ungenuine. *Mrs C. J. Kerr*

AMBER PRINCE 5 b.g. Prince Des Coeurs (USA) – Run Amber Run (Run The **F–** Gantlet (USA)) [2002/3 F16g Mar 16] 4,200 (privately) 4-y-o: half-brother to several winners, including useful 5f (at 2 yrs) and 7f winner Moon Over Miami and fair hurdler Dare (both by Beveled) and smart middle-distance stayer Quick Ransom (by Hostage): dam, won up to 9f in USA, half-sister to smart 1m to 1½m colt Mr John: well beaten in bumper on debut. *P. D. Evans*

AMBERSONG 5 ch.g. Hernando (FR) – Stygian (USA) (Irish River (FR)) [2002/3 **h–** 16g 16m Sep 28] modest maiden on Flat (stays 1½m): well held both outings over hurdles. *Ian Williams*

AMBIDEXTROUS (IRE) 11 b.g. Shareef Dancer (USA) – Amber Fizz (USA) **c– §** (Effervescing (USA)) [2002/3 17m^{pu} 20s^{pu} 16m 20m 22m c19m^{pu} c22d^3 Oct 19] leggy **h– §** gelding: winning hurdler: no worthwhile form since 1999/00 and no aptitude for chasing: tried visored: ungenuine. *G. J. Smith*

AMBIENCE 6 ch.g. Wolfhound (USA) – Amber Fizz (USA) (Effervescing (USA)) **F82** [2002/3 F–: F14g^5 F16g Apr 1] best effort in bumpers when fifth at Hereford on reappearance: takes good hold: sold 2,800 gns Doncaster May Sales. *G. A. Swinbank*

AMBIENCE LADY 7 b.m. Batshoof – Upper Caen (High Top) [2002/3 F18s^4 16g^{ur} **h76** 20g 19m^3 17g^{pu} Apr 19] leggy mare: fair bumper winner in 1999/00: poor form on return, **F65** mostly over hurdles: amiss final start. *J. W. Mullins*

AMBLESIDE (IRE) 12 b.g. Kambalda – Noellespir (Bargello) [2002/3 c122, h–: **c115** c26v^4 c24s^3 c24s^5 c24v^5 c26g^{pu} Apr 19] rangy, useful-looking gelding: impresses in **h–** appearance: fairly useful handicap chaser: disappointed after second start: stays 3¼m, not testing 4¼m: acts on heavy going: mistakes when tried in blinkers: reportedly broke blood vessel third outing: usually races prominently/jumps soundly. *Mrs S. D. Williams*

AMBRY 6 b.g. Machiavellian (USA) – Alkaffeyeh (IRE) (Sadler's Wells (USA)) **h114 §** [2002/3 h106: 18m* 16g* 16d^6 20v^{ur} 17s 21m Feb 22] compact gelding: fair handicap hurdler: ridden by A. McCoy when winning at Fontwell (fortunate) and Towcester in May: amateur ridden, poor efforts last 2 starts: effective at 2m, should stay beyond 2½m: acts on heavy and good to firm going: blinkered/visored: needs plenty of driving/often looks unenthusiastic: best treated with caution: joined Mrs S. J. Smith. *G. L. Moore*

AMBUSHED (IRE) 7 b.g. Indian Ridge – Surprise Move (IRE) (Simply Great (FR)) **h95** [2002/3 h90: 16d^F 16g^3 16g^2 16s* 16v^4 16g Jan 17] modest hurdler: won maiden at Ayr in November: will prove best around 2m: acts on soft and good to firm going: consistent. *P. Monteith*

AMERICANCONNECTION (IRE) 7 b.g. Lord Americo – Ballyea Jacki (Straight **c–** Lad) [2002/3 20s c20s 20v Feb 11] tall ex-Irish gelding: half-brother to several winners, **h87** including modest staying hurdler Master William (by Pollerton) and fair 2½m hurdler Genetic George (by King's Ride): dam, winning Irish pointer, half-sister to dam of Sun Alliance Chase winner Brief Gale: eighth in bumper at Fairyhouse in April 2001: runner-up in maiden point on return in November: well held in maiden hurdles/chase: left W. Mullins before final start. *M. C. Pipe*

AMERICAN PRESIDENT (IRE) 7 br.g. Lord Americo – Deceptive Response **h106** (Furry Glen) [2002/3 F82?: 16m^6 16v^2 19d^3 Jan 24] sturdy gelding: fair form in novice hurdles, placed at Wetherby and Doncaster: will stay at least 2½m: free-going sort. *O. Brennan*

AMICA BELLA 6 b.m. Environment Friend – Pontevecchio Bella (Main Reef) **h–** [2002/3 h–: 20g^{pu} Feb 22] no sign of ability: tried in cheekpieces. *Mrs L. C. Jewell*

AMIR ZAMAN 5 ch.g. Salse (USA) – Colorvista (Shirley Heights) [2002/3 16m^5 **h104 p** 16d^2 Mar 6] sturdy gelding: fair up to 2m on Flat, sold out of J. W. Payne's stable 26,000 gns Newmarket Autumn Sales, successful in January: stiff task on hurdling debut, much better effort when 11 lengths second to Limerick Boy in maiden at Wincanton: will stay 2½m: likely to do better again. *J. R. Jenkins*

AMITGE (FR) 9 ch.m. Vaguely Pleasant (FR) – Ribbon In Her Hair (USA) (Sauce **c–** Boat (USA)) [2002/3 c–, h–: c20m^{ur} May 6] tall, angular mare: fairly useful chaser/ **h–**

hurdler at best: little encouragement in 2 chases since 2000/1: stays 2½m: probably acts on any going: tried blinkered/visored: not a fluent jumper: sold €36,000 Fairyhouse January Sales. *Miss Venetia Williams*

AMJAD 6 ch.g. Cadeaux Genereux – Babita (Habitat) [2002/3 h87: 16m⁴ 16m⁴ 16d⁴ 19m⁶ 17g* 16d⁶ 16d⁶ 16d Jan 24] leggy gelding: modest handicap hurdler: won conditional jockeys event at Carlisle in October: poor efforts last 3 starts: will prove best around 2m: acts on good to firm and good to soft going: pulls hard. *Miss Kate Milligan* **h87**

AMORELLO 5 b.m. Be My Native (USA) – Soundsgoodtome (Supreme Leader) [2002/3 F17d* F17m* Apr 17] unfurnished mare: traces of stringhalt: first foal: dam lightly-raced half-sister to dam of high-class hurdler up to 3m Marello, from family of high-class 2m chaser Bobsline: justified favouritism in mares bumpers at Taunton in January and Cheltenham (valuable listed event, niggled halfway but ran on well to beat Flame of Zara 2 lengths) in April: will stay at least 2½m: useful prospect. *N. J. Henderson* **F104**

AMPLIFI (IRE) 6 b.g. Phardante (FR) – Season's Delight (Idiot's Delight) [2002/3 16d² 16d Jan 18] 15,000 4-y-o: medium-sized gelding: third foal: dam, winning hurdler who stayed 2½m, half-sister to smart staying hurdler Celtic Isle: shaped encouragingly both starts over hurdles, seventh of 18 in novice at Wincanton: likely to be suited by 2½m: should progress. *P. J. Hobbs* **h100 p**

AMSARA (IRE) 7 b.m. Taufan (USA) – Legend of Spain (USA) (Alleged (USA)) [2002/3 17d 19mᵖᵘ 17m 17g 17d⁵ 17gᶠ 22g 20vᵖᵘ 16g 27sᵖᵘ Mar 11] angular mare: bad on Flat (stays 2m): no worthwhile form over hurdles. *A. C. Wilson* **h–**

AMUSEMENT 7 ch.g. Mystiko (USA) – Jolies Eaux (Shirley Heights) [2002/3 h–, F88: 17s⁶ 16d 19s⁴ 20gᵖᵘ Apr 21] leggy gelding: poor maiden hurdler: best efforts around 2m. *D. G. Bridgwater* **h71**

Mr Erik Thorbek's "Amorello"

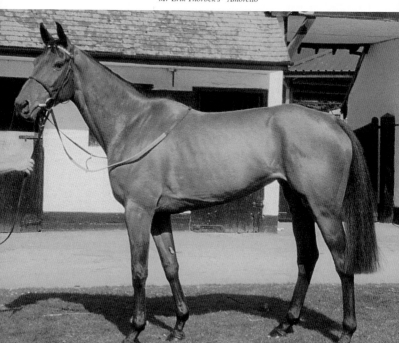

AMWELL STAR (USA) 5 gr.m. Silver Buck (USA) – Markham Fair (CAN) **h78**
(Woodman (USA)) [2002/3 h69: 17m³ 16g² 16m⁵ 20s³ 16d⁵ 21d 16d³ 17g^F 20m Mar 23]
workmanlike mare: poor maiden hurdler: probably stays 2½m: acts on soft and good to
firm going: wore cheekpieces last 3 starts. *J. R. Jenkins*

AMY'S GIFT 7 b.m. Lahib (USA) – Miss Amy Lou (IRE) (Gallic League) [2002/3 **c–**
c16m^ur Apr 5] first foal: dam, modest 2-y-o 5f winner, half-sister to useful performer up
to 7f Nashcash: no show in points/hunter chase (blinkered). *Miss A. J. Trim*

ANATAR (IRE) 5 b.g. Caerleon (USA) – Anaza (Darshaan) [2002/3 h–: 17g 17d* **h128**
16g* 16v² 16s* 16v* 16d 21g 20g* Mar 25] leggy gelding: progressive handicap hurdler,
won at Newton Abbot in September, Plumpton (novice) in October, Sandown (novice)
and Uttoxeter in December, and Ascot (beat No Collusion gamely by a head) in March:
will prove best up to 2½m: raced mainly on good going or softer (acts on heavy).
M. C. Pipe

ANBROOKA 8 ch.m. Meadowbrook – Angerton Annie (Waterfall) [2002/3 c23d^pu **c–**
c22m^F 20s⁶ 20d⁶ 26g⁵ 20f^pu Sep 15] workmanlike mare: fourth known foal: half-sister to **h–**
winning pointer by Zambrano: dam, bad maiden hurdler, half-sister to useful 2m to 3m
chaser Hindhope: winning pointer, no form otherwise. *Mrs H. O. Graham*

ANDALEER (IRE) 8 b.m. Phardante (FR) – Dunleer Duchess (Our Mirage) [2002/3 **c82**
h85, F85: 20d³ c19d² 20m^pu Jun 29] poor form when second in maiden at Hereford on **h79**
chasing debut: poor maiden hurdler: dropped away tamely in handicap at Worcester in
June, not seen out again: raced around 2½m, likely to prove effective over shorter: acts on
firm and good to soft going: takes good hold. *Mrs H. Dalton*

ANDREW DOBLE 4 ch.g. Sabrehill (USA) – Verchinina (Star Appeal) [2002/3 16g⁶ **h93**
17g 16d 17s^ur 16s³ 16v* 17d Feb 10] sturdy gelding: brother to fairly useful 2m
hurdler Inducement and half-brother to 2 winning hurdlers: fairly useful on Flat (stays
1¼m), sold out of M. Jarvis' stable 16,000 gns Newmarket July Sales: modest hurdler:
won handicap at Fakenham in January: likely to prove best around 2m: acts on heavy
going: headstrong. *Miss Venetia Williams*

ANDROMACHE 4 ch.f. Hector Protector (USA) – South Sea Bubble (IRE) (Bustino) **h–**
[2002/3 18s³ Mar 2] fair maiden on Flat (stays 1¼m), sold out of L. Cumani's stable 6,000
gns Newmarket December Sales: well-held third in juvenile at Fontwell on hurdling
debut, jumping with little fluency. *G. B. Balding*

ANDROMEDA (IRE) 4 b.f. Barathea (IRE) – Royal York (Bustino) [2002/3 16g **h–**
Sep 26] fair form on first of 2 starts on Flat for J. Noseda: well held in juvenile on hurdling
debut. *M. Todhunter*

ANDSUEPHI (IRE) 11 b.g. Montelimar (USA) – Butler's Daughter (Rhett Butler) **c–**
[2002/3 c–, h–: c23d^pu Mar 4] lengthy gelding: one-time useful handicap chaser: won **h–**
point in January, but ran poorly in hunter at Leicester next time: stays 3m, at least when
conditions aren't testing: acts on good to firm and heavy going: usually a sound jumper.
Mrs S. A. Hodge

ANDY GIN (FR) 4 b.g. Ski Chief (USA) – Love Love Kate (FR) (Saint Andrews **h120**
(FR)) [2002/3 17d* 17g Mar 13] leggy ex-French gelding: second foal: dam lightly-raced
on Flat: fairly useful on Flat (stays 15f), left R. Chotard after third in claimer in July: won
juvenile at Exeter on hurdling debut in January by 3½ lengths from Visibility: soundly
beaten in Triumph Hurdle at Cheltenham 6 weeks later: will stay beyond 17f. *P. J. Hobbs*

ANDY'S BIRTHDAY (IRE) 12 ch.g. King Luthier – Clonroche Abendego (Pauper) **c–**
[2002/3 c91, h80?: c24s⁴ c26v^pu c24d^pu Feb 7] angular gelding: modest handicap chaser: **h–**
out of sorts in 2002/3: stays 3¼m: best efforts on going softer than good (acts on heavy):
tried visored/in cheekpieces: tongue tied: usually forces pace: inconsistent. *Miss
S. J. Wilton*

ANGEL DELIGHT 7 gr.m. Seymour Hicks (FR) – Bird's Custard (Birdbrook) **h95**
[2002/3 h–, F77: 20g⁵ 21d⁵ 21d* 21s 21m⁵ 24m³ 24g² Apr 23] plain, angular mare:
modest hurdler: won mares novice handicap at Kempton in February: will prove best up
to 3m: acts on good to firm and good to soft going. *Miss Venetia Williams*

ANGEL DUST (FR) 7 b.m. Cadoudal (FR) – Silicity (FR) (Son of Silver) [2002/3 **c–**
c79, h–: c19s^pu c16s^ur c16s Feb 27] leggy mare: winning hurdler: poor maiden chaser: **h–**
bought out of C. Grant's stable 4,600 gns Doncaster August Sales: no show in 2002/3.
L. J. Williams

ANGELENA BALLERINA 5 b.m. Roselier (FR) – True Clown (True Song) [2002/3 F17f 20s^{ur} 17g^6 21d^{pu} Nov 26] leggy mare: fourth foal: half-sister to fair 2m chaser Percy Parkeeper and modest hurdler/chaser up to 25f Brambly Hedge (both by Teenoso): dam, winning chaser, stayed 3¼m: signs of ability in bumper, little show over hurdles. *N. A. Twiston-Davies* **h– F75**

ANGEL IN DISGUISE 11 b.m. Kind of Hush – Kasu (Try My Best (USA)) [2002/3 c–, h–: c20d^5 Apr 29] little sign of ability: tried visored. *N. B. Mason* **c– h–**

ANGEL'S FOLLY 4 b.f. Wesaam (USA) – Arum Lily (Bustino) [2002/3 16s 16v^3 16s* 16s^3 16s^6 Feb 22] smallish, close-coupled filly: dam winning staying hurdler: fair on Flat (best effort at 1¼m): fairly useful juvenile hurdler: won maiden at Gowran in January: likely to stay beyond 2m: raced mainly on soft/heavy going (well held under less testing conditions at Punchestown in early-May, blinkered there and previous start). *Miss F. M. Crowley, Ireland* **h111**

ANGIE GOLD 6 b.m. Mesleh – Gold Duchess (Sonnen Gold) [2002/3 F–: F16s F17v F16m^6 16g 20g^4 Apr 21] lengthy mare: no form in bumpers or novice hurdles. *Mrs S. J. Smith* **h– F–**

ANGIOLINI (USA) 6 ch.g. Woodman (USA) – Danse Royale (IRE) (Caerleon (USA)) [2002/3 16v 20g^4 16g 16f 16f^5 Sep 29] poor maiden on Flat (stays 13f): poor maiden hurdler: raced mainly at 2m: acts on firm going: tried blinkered: has had tongue tied. *N. F. Glynn, Ireland* **h69**

ANGLANIT (CZE) 4 b.c. Lanitos – Anglointernational (Millfontaine) [2002/3 16m^{pu} Nov 4] successful once (at 2 yrs) from 5 starts up to 7.5f in Czech Republic for J. Votavova: behind when pulled up lame in juvenile at Warwick on hurdling debut. *M. Pitman* **h–**

ANGUILLA 8 b.g. Rudimentary (USA) – More Wise (Ballymore) [2002/3 F–: 16g 25g^{pu} 20d 20g^2 Sep 14] poor novice hurdler: should be suited by further than 2½m. *P. T. Dalton* **h66**

ANIMAL CRACKER 5 gr.m. Primo Dominie – Child Star (FR) (Bellypha) [2002/3 17d^{pu} 17s Dec 12] modest on Flat (best efforts at 5f/6f): no show in 2 novice hurdles: joined J. Balding. *R. Curtis* **h–**

ANKLES BACK (IRE) 6 b.g. Seclude (USA) – Pedalo (Legal Tender) [2002/3 c20v^5 Jan 1] ninth foal: half-brother to modest hurdler Outfield (by Monksfield), stayed 3m, and modest staying chaser The Gallopin'major (by Orchestra): dam unraced half-sister to fair chaser Dream Isle, dam of Auntie Dot: runner-up in maiden Irish point in 2002: last of 5 finishers in maiden at Leicester on steeplechasing debut. *Mrs H. Dalton* **c–**

ANNA ALMOST 5 b.m. Tragic Role (USA) – Princess Hotpot (IRE) (King's Ride) [2002/3 F67: 16m^4 17s^{pu} 17g^3 16m^{ur} Mar 31] poor novice hurdler: raced around 2m: visored last 2 starts. *T. Wall* **h61**

ANNADAWI 8 b.g. Sadler's Wells (USA) – Prayers'n Promises (USA) (Foolish Pleasure (USA)) [2002/3 h71: 16g^{pu} May 29] workmanlike gelding: fair on Flat (stayed 1½m): poor maiden hurdler: raced at 2m on good going or softer: dead. *M. E. Sowersby* **h–**

ANNAGHMORE GALE (IRE) 9 br.g. Strong Gale – Kept In The Dark (Kemal (FR)) [2002/3 c16d^6 c24s^F c20g^2 c16m^3 c20m^2 c22d^F c20m* c21m^{pu} c16f^2 c20m^{rtr} c19m^{ur} Apr 21] rangy gelding: maiden hurdler: fair chaser: won handicap at Ballinrobe in August: sold out of D. Hughes' stable 15,000 gns Doncaster October Sales: temperamental efforts last 2 starts: stays 2½m: acts on firm and soft going: blinkered once: has had tongue tied: one to treat with caution. *Miss Sarah George* **c106 § h–**

ANNE-LISE 5 ch.m. Inchinor – Red Gloves (Red God) [2002/3 16s^4 16v Dec 21] small mare: modest on Flat (probably stays 1¼m): better effort in novice hurdles when fourth in mares event at Southwell for P. Mooney. *P. D. Evans* **h82**

ANNE NUTTER 4 ch.f. Kasakov – Bairn Glen (Bairn (USA)) [2002/3 16d^{pu} Nov 24] well held on Flat (has given trouble at start): pulled up early on hurdling debut. *I. W. McInnes* **h–**

ANNIE BYERS 7 ch.m. Sula Bula – Tuneful Flutter (Orchestra) [2002/3 F16s^2 F16s 21s 22v^4 19d^5 19m^3 22g^5 Mar 29] rather leggy, useful-looking mare: fourth known foal: half-sister to poor hurdler Spirit Level (by Sunley Builds), stayed 27f: dam rare twice: runner-up in maiden point in 2002: bought 6,200 gns Doncaster August Sales: runner-up on first of 2 starts in bumpers: poor novice hurdler: probably stays 2¾m: acts on good to firm and heavy going. *J. G. Portman* **h76 F91**

48

ANNIE FLEETWOOD 5 ch.m. Anshan – Gold Luck (USA) (Slew O' Gold (USA)) **h72**
[2002/3 F16g 20g⁶ 22m⁴ Apr 8] second foal: half-sister to 1m winner Top Hand (by First **F–**
Trump): dam unraced, out of smart winner up to 1¼m Rambushka: well beaten in bumper
on debut: signs of ability in 2 runs over hurdles. *C. P. Morlock*

ANNIEJO 4 br.f. Presenting – Lorna's Choice (Oats) [2002/3 F16v F16d F17g Mar 28] **F–**
third foal: half-sister to winning pointer by Milieu: dam poor maiden pointer/hurdler:
well held in 3 bumpers, looked awkward ride final outing. *W. McKeown*

ANNIES GOLD (IRE) 7 b.m. Spanish Place (USA) – Leventos (Le Moss) [2002/3 **h–**
19mᵖᵘ Apr 5] IR 3,000 4-y-o: fifth foal: dam placed in point: soon tailed off in maiden
hurdle on debut. *Mrs S. M. Johnson*

ANNODYCE 5 b.m. Faustus (USA) – Coleford (USA) (Secreto (USA)) [2002/3 h73: **h–**
16mᵖᵘ 16dᵖᵘ 16v⁵ 16s 16m⁵ 16m⁴ Apr 21] medium-sized mare: no worthwhile form over
hurdles. *Miss Z. C. Davison*

ANNO JUBILO (GER) 6 b. or br.g. Lando (GER) – Anna Maria (GER) (Night **h116**
Shift) [2002/3 16v² 16g* 16d⁴ 16d* 16g² Sep 1] won up to 11f on Flat in Germany: fairly
useful novice hurdler: won at Ballinrobe (maiden) in July and Roscommon in August:
raced at 2m. *C. F. Swan, Ireland*

ANNS GIRL 10 br.m. Newski (USA) – Nearly Married (Nearly A Hand) [2002/3 c–, **c–**
h96: 16mᵖᵘ 16g⁵ 16m 16m 16s 22d⁵ 19d⁵ 16v 17v⁵ 17g Mar 18] sturdy mare: **h86**
maiden chaser: modest handicap hurdler: best form up to 19f: acts on any going: tried
visored, usually blinkered: has broken blood vessel. *J. C. Fox*

ANOTHER ACE (IRE) 6 b.g. Synefos (USA) – Another Space (Brave Invader **c– p**
(USA)) [2002/3 c25dᵘʳ Mar 1] well-made gelding: half-brother to fair pointer Stoney
River (by Riverhead): dam lightly raced and no worthwhile form over hurdles: won
maiden Irish point on debut in 2002: unseated tenth on hunter chase debut. *P. D. Niven*

ANOTHER ARTHUR 7 b.g. Puissance – Traumatic Laura (Pragmatic) [2002/3 **h–**
18sᵖᵘ 16g Apr 1] poor maiden hurdler: showed nothing in 2002/3. *W. McKeown*

ANOTHER ASPECT (IRE) 4 b.g. Inzar (USA) – The Aspecto Girl (IRE) (Alzao **h–**
(USA)) [2002/3 16g 16s Mar 10] modest on Flat (should stay beyond 1m), below form in
early-2002: little encouragement in juvenile hurdles. *J. Cullinan*

ANOTHER BEEPER (IRE) 6 b.m. Accordion – Raymylettes Niece (IRE) (Dock **h–**
Leaf) [2002/3 F16d F16m 16s 18s 18s 24s 22dᵖᵘ 24g Feb 12] IR 3,000 3-y-o, IR £2,000 **F–**
4-y-o: second foal: dam unraced, from family of high-class chaser Another Coral: little
sign of ability: tried blinkered. *T. G. McCourt, Ireland*

ANOTHER BIT 6 ch.g. Henbit (USA) – Perrinpit Annapolis VII (Damsire Un- **h–**
registered) [2002/3 F16sᵘʳ F16s F17d 16g 17fᵘʳ 16f⁴ Apr 21] first foal: dam unraced: no **F–**
worthwhile form in bumpers or over hurdles: trained first 2 starts by Dr P. Pritchard.
J. C. Tuck

ANOTHER COPPER 7 ch.g. Bandmaster (USA) – Letitica (Deep Run) [2002/3 **c66**
c74, h77: c23f⁵ c26gᶠ c26gᵖᵘ 24v² 26mᶠ 24m⁵ Apr 10] compact gelding: winning chaser, **h89 ?**
trained first 3 starts by Mrs S. Williams: apparently suited best current form over hurdles, probably
flattered: should stay beyond 3m: acts on any going. *C. J. Down*

ANOTHER DIAMOND (IRE) 5 b.m. First Trump – Rockin' Rosie (Song) [2002/3 **h95**
16g⁵ 19v² 22m³ 19mᵖᵘ 22m* Apr 8] modest on Flat (seems to stay 1¾m) for
L. G. Cottrell: modest novice hurdler: blinkered, improved effort when winning maiden
at Exeter: stays 2¾m: acts on good to firm and heavy going. *C. J. Down*

ANOTHER DOTTIE (IRE) 10 b.g. Sharifabad (IRE) – Dottie's Wasp (Tarqogan) **c–**
[2002/3 20gᵖᵘ 21sᵖᵘ Nov 24] workmanlike ex-Irish gelding: fifth foal: half-brother to 2 **h–**
winning pointers: dam, placed in Irish bumpers, half-sister to very smart staying chaser
Arctic Call: runner-up on last of 3 starts in maiden Irish points in 2002, no form
otherwise: tried blinkered. *P. Butler*

ANOTHER DUDE (IRE) 6 br.g. Shardari – Gemma's Fridge (Frigid Aire) [2002/3 **h111**
h85: 17g² 16g* 19d² 16g² 19d* 18gᵖᵘ Mar 21] improved into fair novice hurdler in
2002/3, won at Catterick in November (handicap) and February: should stay 2½m: raced
on good going or softer (acts on heavy). *J. Howard Johnson*

ANOTHER FLY 9 b.m. Buckley – March Fly (Sousa) [2002/3 c–: c25mᵖᵘ 24dᵖᵘ **c–**
c25vᶠ Nov 8] runner-up in point, no form otherwise. *A. H. Mactaggart* **h–**

ANOTHER GENERAL (IRE) 8 ch.g. Glacial Storm (USA) – Whats In A Name **c120**
(IRE) (Le Moss) [2002/3 h122: c24s² c24d* c25s* Mar 8] angular gelding: fairly useful **h–**

hurdler: similar form in novice chases, won at Doncaster in January and Ayr (made hard work of landing odds) in March: will stay beyond 25f: raced on going softer than good (acts on heavy). *R. T. Phillips*

ANOTHER GRADUATE (IRE)   5 ch.g. Naheez (USA) – Another Daisy (Major F—
Point) [2002/3 F16m Feb 22] €4,800 4-y-o: smallish gelding: fifth foal: half-brother to winning hurdler/chaser Corbleu (by Corvaro), stays 25f: dam unraced: tailed off in bumper on debut. *John R. Upson*

ANOTHER HELPING (FR)   5 gr.g. Turgeon (USA) – Tabelbala (FR) (Nashamaa) F— §
[2002/3 F—: F17m F16dpu Mar 6] leggy gelding: no form in bumpers, looking temperamental. *J. R. Best*

ANOTHER JOKER   8 b.g. Commanche Run – Just For A Laugh (Idiot's Delight) c—
[2002/3 h100, F78: 16d 19d 17d⁵ c16g⁴ Mar 16] lengthy, workmanlike gelding: maiden h—
hurdler, modest at best: no danger after blunder second on chasing debut: stays 19f: acts on good to soft going: often takes good hold. *J. L. Needham*

ANOTHER KING   8 ch.g. Primitive Rising (USA) – Knocksharry (Palm Track) h—
[2002/3 h—: 22dpu Aug 26] strong, plain gelding: little sign of ability. *K. W. Hogg, Isle of Man*

ANOTHER MOOSE (IRE)   8 b.g. Mister Lord (USA) – Moose (IRE) (Royal Foun- c113
tain) [2002/3 c19d c26s² Mar 10] useful-looking gelding: fairly useful form in novice h—
hurdles in 2000/1: off 22 months, reportedly bled from nose both starts in novice chases (also withdrawn lame in between), though fair form and again jumped soundly when second in 3-finisher event at Plumpton: stays 3¼m: raced on going softer than good (acts on heavy): clearly not easy to train. *Miss E. C. Lavelle*

ANOTHER RALEAGH (IRE)   9 b.g. Be My Native (USA) – Caffra Mills (Pitpan) c136
[2002/3 c115, h100: c16m³ c20d² c20s² c20g* c20d² Feb 7] tall gelding: winning hurdler: h—
useful novice chaser: won handicap at Kempton in January: good neck second to Avalanche in similar event there final start, though edged left and caught close home: stays 2½m: acts on heavy going: consistent. *A. Ennis*

ANOTHER SPARKLE   6 gr.m. Bustino – Sparkling Time (USA) (Olden Times) F64
[2002/3 F16d F16g⁵ Dec 12] half-sister to several winners, including useful hurdler Coworth Park (by Wolver Hollow), stayed 3m, and useful chaser up to 25f Sparkling Cone (by Celtic Cone): dam ran twice at 2 yrs: showed bit more than on debut when fifth in mares bumper at Ludlow. *Miss Venetia Williams*

ANSAR (IRE)   7 b.g. Kahyasi – Anaza (Darshaan) [2002/3 h149: c17d* c20m* c17g² c129
c17d Mar 22] leggy gelding: smart hurdler: made good start to chasing career, easily h—
winning novices at Galway in August and Tralee in September: off over 5 months, not fluent when well held in similar event at Navan final start: stays 2½m: acts on soft and good to firm going. *D. K. Weld, Ireland*

ANTENNE (IRE)   6 b.m. Roakarad – Secrete Envie (USA) (Secreto (USA)) [2002/3 c— §
c?, h—: 24dpu c22dpu c20v⁴ 20spu Nov 27] lengthy mare: novice hurdler/chaser: no form in h— §
Britain, looking less than keen: left A. Crook after reappearance: tried blinkered/visored. *M. D. Hammond*

ANTHEMION (IRE)   6 ch.g. Night Shift (USA) – New Sensitive (Wattlefield) h— x
[2002/3 h—: 16gpu 17g⁴ 16s⁵ 16vpu 16g 17gpu 16gpu Apr 24] sparely-made gelding: not fluent and no worthwhile form over hurdles. *Mrs J. C. McGregor*

ANTONIO MARIANO (SWE)   12 b.g. Mango Express – Mango Sampaquita c96
(SWE) (Colombian Friend (USA)) [2002/3 c106, h–: c16gur c19g⁵ Jun 12] good-bodied h—
gelding: fair handicap chaser, below best completed start in 2002/3: raced mainly around 2m: acts on soft and good to firm going: tends to sweat. *Mrs L. C. Taylor*

ANTONY EBENEEZER   4 ch.c. Hurricane Sky (AUS) – Captivating (IRE) (Wolf- h83
hound (USA)) [2002/3 16mF 16m⁵ 16d Nov 12] leggy colt: modest on Flat (effective at 11f to 2m), successful in January: form in juvenile hurdles only when fifth of 21 to Fortunate Dave at Warwick: free-going sort. *C. R. Dore*

ANVIL LORD (IRE)   8 b.g. Lord Americo – Advance Notice (Le Bavard (FR)) h110
[2002/3 h105p: 24d³ 24s* 24spu Nov 17] compact gelding: pulled up in point in 1999: fair hurdler, lightly raced: won handicap at Navan in November: better at 3m than shorter: acts on soft going. *C. A. Murphy, Ireland*

ANXIOUS MOMENTS (IRE)　8 b.g. Supreme Leader – Ms Brooks (IRE) (Lord **h–**
Ha Ha) [2002/3 h124, F–: 16d 16v 16s Jan 12] tall gelding: fairly useful hurdler in
2001/2: little impact in valuable handicaps in 2002/3: will stay 2½m: raced on good going
or softer (acts on soft). *C. F. Swan, Ireland*

ANZAL (IRE)　5 b.g. Kahyasi – Anazara (USA) (Trempolino (USA)) [2002/3 F–: **h76**
20s^pu 16g^pu 22d^pu 17d^F 20d^4 16v 19m* 22g^6 Apr 19] small, leggy gelding: has reportedly
had breathing operation: poor hurdler: easily won novice handicap at Exeter in April:
should stay beyond 2½m: acts on good to soft and good to firm going: blinkered/tongue
tied third start. *D. R. Gandolfo*

APACHE IRELAND (IRE)　6 b.m. Mandalus – Brisbee (Prince Bee) [2002/3 16g^pu **h–**
22g^pu Mar 21] IR £4,000 4-y-o: fifth foal: half-sister to winning pointer by Satco: dam,
lightly-raced maiden, out of sister to smart 2½m chaser The Dealer: no sign of ability in
novice hurdles/points. *Mrs C. J. Kerr*

APADI (USA)　7 ch.g. Diesis – Ixtapa (USA) (Chief's Crown (USA)) [2002/3 h99: **h89**
16m^2 16g^3 19m^2 19g^4 17m^5 16m^ur 19d^2 21m^4 17d^3 16m^F 16g^3 19g^6 16g^F 16d^5 16d^4 16g^2
16m^5 17m^5 Apr 21] sturdy gelding: modest handicap hurdler: barely stays 19f: acts on
any going: headstrong, and usually held up. *M. C. Chapman*

APHELION　5 b.h. Superlative – Starchy Cove (Starch Reduced) [2002/3 16m^pu Jun **h–**
19] well held on Flat: showed nothing on hurdling debut: sold 800 gns Ascot July Sales.
N. M. Babbage

A PIECE OF CAKE (IRE)　10 gr.g. Roselier (FR) – Boreen Bro (Boreen (FR)) **c139**
[2002/3 c122, h–: c20v^ur c20v^2 c20v* c20d^ur c20v* c32g* Mar 21] good-topped gelding: **h–**
useful handicap chaser: in form of life in 2002/3, won 4-finisher events at Ayr in January
and February and valuable Ashleybank Investments Scottish Borders National at Kelso
in March: travelled well and always prominent when beating Interdit 5 lengths at latter:
effective at 2½m to 4m: has won on good to firm going, raced mainly on good or softer
(acts on heavy). *Mrs M. Reveley*

APOLLO THEATRE　5 b.g. Sadler's Wells (USA) – Threatening (Warning) [2002/3 **F98**
F18s^5 F17s^3 F17g^3 Mar 16] third foal: brother to smart 2001 2-y-o 1m winner Mutiny-
onthebounty: dam, 6f/7f winner, half-sister to St Leger/Gold Cup winner Classic Cliche:
third in bumpers at Folkestone, fairly useful form when beaten 1½ lengths by Samby in
maiden on second occasion. *R. Rowe*

APPLE JOE　7 b.g. Sula Bula – Hazelwain (Hard Fact) [2002/3 c–, h–: c23g^5 c24m^3 **c73**
22v^6 c25s^3 c22s^4 c26v^4 Feb 10] no form over hurdles: poor novice chaser: probably stays **h–**
25f: raced mainly on good going or softer. *Dr P. Pritchard*

Ashleybank Investments Scottish Borders National (Handicap Chase), Kelso—
top weight A Piece of Cake (nearest camera) challenges Interdit at the last

APPLE JOHN 14 b.g. Sula Bula – Hazelwain (Hard Fact) [2002/3 c88: c24m⁵ c23g **c85** c25s* c26vᵖᵘ 26s c20v⁴ Jan 1] tall, sparely-made gelding: modest handicap chaser: won **h–** amateur event at Hereford in November: well beaten only outing over hurdles: stays 25f: raced mainly on good going or softer (acts on heavy): blinkered once: often forces pace. *Dr P. Pritchard*

APPLEMIR GEORGE 8 b.g. Almushmmir – Lady Sweetapples (Super Song) **h–** [2002/3 h–, F–: 22fᵖᵘ May 10] rather sparely-made gelding: no form over hurdles: visored last 3 starts. *Jane Southcombe*

APPLEPIE LADY (IRE) 6 b.m. Lord Americo – Lady Bow (Deep Run) [2002/3 **h83** F83: F17m² F16m³ 21d⁵ 21d⁴ 19m⁵ Apr 8] good-topped mare: placed 3 of 4 starts in **F83** bumpers: poor form over hurdles: will probably stay beyond 21f. *A. J. Lidderdale*

APPROACHING LAND (IRE) 8 ch.g. Dry Dock – Crash Approach (Crash **h–** Course) [2002/3 20mᵖᵘ May 8] fifth foal: half-brother to smart 2m hurdler/winning chaser Adamant Approach (by Mandalus): dam unraced half-sister to Hennessy winner Approaching: successful on 2 of 3 completed starts in points, including in February: pulled up in novice hurdle at Wetherby. *M. W. Easterby*

APRIL ACE 7 ch.g. First Trump – Champ d'Avril (Northfields (USA)) [2002/3 h–: **h–** 16m 16s 16g Sep 14] won around 1m at 3 yrs on Flat: no form over hurdles. *R. J. Baker*

APRIL ALLEGRO (FR) 7 br.g. Doyoun – April Lee (Lyphard (USA)) [2002/3 c–, **c78** h130: c22d⁵ c24dᵖᵘ 24m 22g* Apr 21] compact gelding: very disappointing over **h123** fences: fairly useful handicap hurdler: won at Fairyhouse in April by 3½ lengths from Albrighton: stays 3m: acts on heavy and good to firm going: tried blinkered: has had tongue tied. *Michael Hourigan, Ireland*

APRIL CALL 7 b.m. Gildoran – Cloud Cuckoo (Idiot's Delight) [2002/3 h–, F–: **h–** 16mᵖᵘ 16mᵖᵘ Sep 7] of no account: sold £600 Ascot October Sales. *S. J. Gilmore*

APRIL LOUISE 7 b.m. Meqdaam (USA) – California Dreamin (Slip Anchor) **h94** [2002/3 h92+: 16g⁴ 17d³ 16f³ 20d 16mᵖᵘ Mar 19] plain, sparely-made mare: modest handicap hurdler: should stay 2½m: yet to race on heavy going, acts on any other. *T. Wall*

APRIL SPIRIT 8 b.m. Nomination – Seraphim (FR) (Lashkari) [2002/3 c81, h71: **c89** c23m c23g* c23m c21m³ c26m² c26m² c27d c20d³ c24s⁵ Dec 6] leggy, sparely-made **h–** mare: poor hurdler: modest handicap chaser: won at Worcester in July: stays 3¼m: acts on any going. *Mrs S. J. Smith*

APRIL TREASURE 8 b.m. Stani (USA) – Eleri (Rolfe (USA)) [2002/3 h58: 16d⁴ **c58** 16m² 19sᵖᵘ 16s⁴ 17m⁶ 17m 16g c16gᵖᵘ 19m⁴ c20fF Oct 10] leggy mare: bad maiden **h–** hurdler: held in second when falling 2 out in weak novice chase at Ludlow: probably stays 2½m: acts on soft and good to firm going, probably on firm. *Mrs P. Ford*

AQRIBAA (IRE) 5 b. or br.g. Pennekamp (USA) – Karayb (IRE) (Last Tycoon) **h62** [2002/3 h67: 17m⁵ 16f⁶ 17g Oct 15] poor maiden hurdler: raced around 2m on good going or firmer: takes good hold. *A. J. Lockwood*

AQUA PURA (GER) 4 b.c. Acatenango (GER) – Actraphane (Shareef Dancer **h–** (USA)) [2002/3 16d Dec 14] fair on Flat (stays 1½m) in Germany for A. Trybuhl, well held in Britain in October: 12/1 from 4/1, jumped badly when tailed off in juvenile at Fakenham on hurdling debut. *B. J. Curley*

AQUARIUS (IRE) 5 b.g. Royal Academy (USA) – Rafha (Kris) [2002/3 17f* 17v² **h107 d** 16v 24d 24s⁵ 22f⁵ 17m³ 16m³ Apr 21] angular gelding: half-brother to useful hurdler/ fairly useful chaser Fnan (by Generous), stays 3m: smart stayer on Flat for J. Dunlop, sold 12,500 gns Newmarket July Sales, little show in 4 starts for D. Nicholls: won novice at Taunton on hurdling debut in October: disappointing after, more than once staying as if amiss: should stay beyond 17f: tongue tied last 2 starts, visored final one. *M. C. Pipe*

AQUILA OCULUS (IRE) 5 b.m. Eagle Eyed (USA) – Out In The Sun (USA) (It's **h118** Freezing (USA)) [2002/3 17g⁴ 16g* 16f³ 16v⁶ 16s* Jan 4] third foal: half-sister to fair 2m hurdler Summer Break (by Foxhound): dam 2m hurdler: useful on Flat (stays 2m): fairly useful hurdler: progressive in 2002/3, winning handicaps at Tralee (4-y-o event) in August and Cork (mares) in January: raced around 2m: acts on any going. *Anthony Mullins, Ireland*

AQUILINE 5 ch.g. Sanglamore (USA) – Fantasy Flyer (USA) (Lear Fan (USA)) **h87** [2002/3 h94?: 16s² 17s 19d Mar 1] good-bodied gelding: modest form when runner-up twice over hurdles, well held otherwise: should stay beyond 2m: acts on soft going. *John A. Harris*

ARABIAN GOGGLES   4 ch.f. Cosmonaut – Jarrettelle (All Systems Go) [2002/3   **h–**
17f⁴ Oct 1] no form on Flat or in juvenile hurdle: sold £450 Ascot December Sales.
H. S. Howe

ARABIAN MOON (IRE)   7 ch.h. Barathea (IRE) – Excellent Alibi (USA) (Exceller   **h126**
(USA)) [2002/3 h113: 18g* 21m* 21g 21mᵖᵘ Apr 16] compact horse: fairly useful
hurdler: improved form when winning handicaps at Fontwell and Cheltenham in
October: off over 4 months, well below best last 2 starts: effective around 2m and stays
3m, at least when conditions aren't testing: acts on firm and good to soft going: has found
little. *S. Dow*

ARAF   4 b.g. Millkom – Euphyllia (Superpower) [2002/3 16m 16gᶠ 16d⁵ 16v⁵ Dec 20]   **h82**
medium-sized gelding: modest on Flat (stays 1½m), sold out of A. Newcombe's stable
6,400 gns Doncaster September Sales: best effort in juvenile hurdles when fifth to Red
Flyer at Newcastle third start: likely to prove best at 2m when conditions aren't testing.
N. Wilson

ARAGLIN   4 b.g. Sadler's Wells (USA) – River Cara (USA) (Irish River (FR)) [2002/3   **h–**
16m 17sᶠ 16d⁶ 19d 17g Mar 15] fair at best at 2 yrs (stays 9.4f): well held over hurdles:
blinkered last 3 starts. *Miss S. J. Wilton*

ARAMINTA   9 ch.m. Carlingford Castle – Abinovian (Ra Nova) [2002/3 c–, h74:   **c102 ?**
c26g Mar 13] sparely-made mare: winning hurdler: fairly useful pointer, successful in   **h–**
February (twice) and April: first completion in steeplechases (probably flattered) when
never-nearer seventh of 24 in Foxhunter at Cheltenham: stays 3¼m: acts on heavy
ground. *Mrs L. Pomfret*

ARAWAK PRINCE (IRE)   7 ch.g. College Chapel – Alpine Symphony (Northern   **c87**
Dancer) [2002/3 h87d: 17m* c16g² c20m⁴ 17mᵖᵘ Apr 21] leggy gelding: poor hurdler: **h87**
won seller at Southwell in August: beaten 2 lengths in 2-finisher novice at Worcester on
chasing debut: mistakes and less than keen next time: best around 2m: acts on good to
firm going, seemingly not on soft/heavy: often visored: races freely: has found little.
G. Prodromou

ARC EN CIEL   5 b.g. Rainbow Quest (USA) – Nadia Nerina (CAN) (Northern   **h–**
Dancer) [2002/3 19m Jul 4] fairly useful at 3 yrs on Flat (stays 1½m), no form in 2 starts
in 2002: well held in novice on hurdling debut. *Mrs L. Richards*

ARCHBISHOP   6 ch.g. Minster Son – Elitist (Keren) [2002/3 h–, F–: c16f⁵ c22g²   **c–**
c21g Oct 15] tall, quite good-topped gelding: no worthwhile form: sold 6,500 gns   **h–**
Doncaster November Sales. *T. D. Walford*

ARCHER FOR FOUR (USA)   4 b. or br.g. Royal Academy (USA) – Depelchin   **h–**
(USA) (Star de Naskra (USA)) [2002/3 16m 16d 16g Nov 23] workmanlike gelding: well
held on Flat and in juvenile hurdles: blinkered final start: pulls hard. *Ferdy Murphy*

ARCHIE BABE (IRE)   7 ch.g. Archway (IRE) – Frensham Manor (Le Johnstan)   **h93**
[2002/3 16sᶠ 16d⁴ 16d⁴ Feb 26] angular, workmanlike gelding: fair on Flat (stays 1½m),
successful in March: modest form in novice hurdles, fourth in large fields at Doncaster
and Wetherby: will probably stay beyond 2m. *J. J. Quinn*

ARCHON (IRE)   6 ch.g. Archway (IRE) – Lindas Delight (Batshoof) [2002/3 F91:   **h89**
17m⁴ Jul 15] runner-up in bumper on debut: modest on Flat (stays 1½m, has looked less
than keen): beaten about 10 lengths in novice at Newton Abbot on hurdling debut: will
prove best at 2m. *Mrs P. N. Dutfield*

ARCH STANTON (IRE)   5 b.g. Lahib (USA) – Sweet Repose (High Top) [2002/3   **h124**
16s⁵ 16s³ 16v² 16d² 16gˢᵘ Mar 11] fair on Flat (stays 1½m): easily best efforts over
hurdles when second in maidens at Leopardstown: fell on final start after third in Grade 1
novice at Cheltenham: likely to stay beyond 2m. *W. P. Mullins, Ireland*

ARCTIC CHALLENGE (IRE)   9 b.g. Glacial Storm (USA) – Ruckinge Girl (Ebor-   **c119**
neezer) [2002/3 c117§, h–: c20g* c20g⁴ c20m³ c19g⁴ c20g² c24mᵖᵘ Apr 21] rather leggy   **h–**
gelding: fairly useful handicap chaser: won at Worcester in May: better form in frame
after break next 4 starts: stays 21f: acts on good to firm and heavy going: usually races
prominently. *K. R. Burke*

ARCTIC COPPER (IRE)   9 b.g. Montelimar (USA) – Miss Penguin (General   **c142**
Assembly) [2002/3 c135, h–: c24g² c16s² c24s² c17v⁵ c24s⁵ c20s² c20d² c16d*   **h–**
c20g c17g³ Apr 20] good-topped gelding: useful chaser: won Grade 2 Paddy & Helen
Cox Memorial Newlands Chase at Naas in February: ran well when placed twice in April,
in handicap at Fairyhouse and Grade 1 event at Punchestown (tried in cheekpieces, beaten

Paddy & Helen Cox Memorial Newlands Chase, Naas—(left to right) Go Roger Go, Fadoudal du Cochet, Rathbawn Prince and the winner Arctic Copper all have a chance over the final fence

6 lengths by Flagship Uberalles): effective at 2m to 29f: raced on good going or softer (acts on heavy): usually blinkered, effective when not: has had tongue tied: jumped left throughout sixth start: not straightforward ride. *N. Meade, Ireland*

ARCTIC CORNER 9 b.m. Arctic Lord – Chatty Corner (Le Bavard (FR)) [2002/3 21gpu 17dF Jun 5] of little account. *N. Wilson* **h–**

ARCTIC DOUBLE (IRE) 6 b.g. Insan (USA) – Icy Queen (IRE) (Callernish) [2002/3 F91: 16m⁵ 21d⁵ Nov 25] rangy gelding: has scope: fair form in bumpers: never dangerous but not knocked about in novice hurdles at Wincanton and Ludlow: will stay 3m. *Miss H. C. Knight* **h73**

ARCTIC FANCY (USA) 10 ch.g. Arctic Tern (USA) – Fit And Fancy (USA) (Vaguely Noble) [2002/3 c116, h–: c19d* c20g Mar 12] good-topped gelding: fairly useful handicap chaser: off nearly 10 months, won at Doncaster in January by 1½ lengths from Super Nomad: stiff task at Cheltenham 7 weeks later: barely stays 3m: below form on firm going, acts on any other: usually races prominently: has hung left. *Miss H. C. Knight* **c125 h–**

ARCTIC FORCE (IRE) 6 b.g. Arctic Lord – Mogen (Adonijah) [2002/3 20m F16m³ F16f² F16f* F16f* Sep 26] strong gelding: half-brother to winning pointer by Brush Aside: dam unraced half-sister to smart chaser up to 3m Oregon Trail and smart hurdler up to 2½m Tiananmen Square: well held on hurdling debut (should be capable of better): useful form in bumpers: won at Clonmel and Listowel in September: changed hands €80,000 Goffs October Sale: far from discredited when eighth to Royal Rosa in Grade 1 at Punchestown in April: tongue tied on debut. *Paul A. Roche, Ireland* **h– p F105**

ARCTIC GAMBLE 11 b.g. Arctic Lord – Honey Gamble (Gambling Debt) [2002/3 c93: c23g² c24s⁶ c25d⁴ c24f² c25f* Apr 21] workmanlike gelding: modest chaser: won novice handicap at Taunton in March and 3-runner novice at Wincanton in April: stays 25f: best efforts on good going or firmer. *L. G. Cottrell* **c97**

ARCTIC GOLD (IRE) 6 b.g. Arctic Lord – Flashy Gold (Le Bavard (FR)) [2002/3 20gpu 17s³ 17s 16f 16g* 20g² c20f⁶ Apr 13] IR 5,000 3-y-o: half-brother to several winners, including fairly useful chaser Third Quarter (by Boreen), best up to 2½m: dam unraced from good jumping family: bumper winner: modest hurdler: made all in novice **c– h92**

at Kelso in October: soundly beaten in maiden at Listowel on chasing debut: stays 2½m: acts on good to firm going: should do better over fences. *C. F. Swan, Ireland*

ARCTIC GREY (IRE) 13 gr.g. Roselier (FR) – Our Hollow (Wolver Hollow) [2002/3 c25g^{pu} May 1] ex-Irish gelding: fair pointer: pulled up both starts in hunter chases. *Miss A. Nolan*

c–
h–

ARCTIC KING 10 b.g. Arctic Lord – Dunsilly Bell (London Bells (CAN)) [2002/3 c–, h–: c25s^F Mar 7] rangy gelding: poor chaser: won maiden point in February: stays 21f: acts on soft going: tried blinkered. *A. M. Lloyd*

c–
h–

ARCTIC LAGOON (IRE) 4 ch.g. Bering – Lake Pleasant (IRE) (Elegant Air) [2002/3 16g 16g^4 16g 16g^{pu} Apr 7] signs of ability in maidens on Flat, sold out of J. Fanshawe's stable £4,000 Ascot October Sales: poor form in juvenile hurdles, ran no sort of race on handicap debut: tongue tied on debut. *Mrs S. C. Bradburne*

h78

ARCTIC PLAYBOY 7 b.g. Petoski – Arctic Oats (Oats) [2002/3 F79: F16s^3 17s^4 20s Mar 6] angular gelding: easily best effort in bumpers when third at Newcastle on reappearance: well held in 2 novice hurdles. *G. A. Swinbank*

h–
F93

ARCTIC SANDY (IRE) 13 ch.g. Sandalay – Reach Here (Hereford) [2002/3 c–, h76: c16g^4 c20d^2 c21m^6 c21m^4 Aug 12] sparely-made gelding: novice hurdler: poor handicap chaser: barely stays 2½m: acts on any going: tried blinkered/visored. *A. Parker*

c76
h–

ARCTIC SKY (IRE) 6 b.g. Arctic Lord – Lake Garden Park (Comedy Star (USA)) [2002/3 F83: F17f^6 F17g* 20d^2 21s^2 21s 21g 21m* Apr 21] unfurnished gelding: best effort in bumpers when winning at Hereford in June: improved form over hurdles when winning handicap at Huntingdon in April: will stay beyond 21f: acts on soft and good to firm going: has jumped none too fluently. *N. J. Henderson*

h107
F94

ARCTIC SPIRIT 8 b.g. Arctic Lord – Dickies Girl (Saxon Farm) [2002/3 c91, h–: c19g^2 c20m^{pu} c16g c16g^3 c16s* c16s^6 c18m^3 c16f^6 Mar 29] close-coupled gelding: maiden hurdler: modest handicap chaser: won at Southwell in January: barely stays 19f: acts on heavy going, probably not on firmer than good: visored sixth and seventh outings: usually races prominently: sometimes makes mistakes. *R. Dickin*

c93
h–

ARCTIC SPLASH 8 ch.m. St Ninian – Arctic Oats (Oats) [2002/3 h63: 16d^2 20m^6 Jun 21] poor maiden hurdler: stays 21f: acts on firm and soft going. *G. A. Swinbank*

h62

ARCTIC STAR 8 b.g. Polar Falcon (USA) – Three Stars (Star Appeal) [2002/3 c25d^{pu} May 4] sparely-made gelding: poor maiden hurdler: successful all 3 completed starts in points: no show in hunter chase. *V. Thompson*

c–
h–

ARCTICTALDI (IRE) 13 br.g. Cataldi – Arctic Sue (Arctic Slave) [2002/3 c94, h79: c17d c16m^5 17d c16v^4 Jan 1] compact gelding: maiden hurdler: fair handicap chaser at best: bought out of B. Ellison's stable £1,700 Ascot June Sales: little show in 2002/3: barely stays 21f: acts on good to firm and heavy going: tried blinkered. *M. J. M. Evans*

c–
h–

ARCTIC TIMES (IRE) 7 ch.g. Montelimar (USA) – Miss Penguin (General Assembly (USA)) [2002/3 h88: c24v^2 c24d* c25g^2 Apr 5] novice hurdler: successful in 3 points in 2003 and hunter chase at Limerick in March: distant second to impressive Lord Atterbury in quite valuable novice hunter at Aintree following month: stays 25f: acts on heavy going. *Eugene M. O'Sullivan, Ireland*

c98
h–

ARDAN GLAS (IRE) 6 ch.g. Safety Catch (USA) – Jude's Hollow (IRE) (Hollow Hand) [2002/3 F16d^5 F16d Nov 17] tall gelding: third foal: dam unraced, from family of one-time useful hurdler up to 3m Valley Erne: fairly useful form when third in bumper at Cork in late-2000/1 on debut, but nowhere near that in 3 subsequent starts. *P. M. J. Doyle, Ireland*

F79

ARDASHIR (FR) 4 b.g. Simon du Desert (FR) – Antea (FR) (Esprit du Nord (USA)) [2002/3 16g 16d^{pu} Mar 10] leggy gelding: half-brother to fairly useful hurdler/fair chaser around 2m Delayed (by Fijar Tango): dam won over hurdles/on Flat in France: fairly useful on Flat (stays 13.5f), successful in June for R. Collet: little show in juvenile hurdles at Newbury and Stratford almost 3 months apart. *N. A. Twiston-Davies*

h–

ARDBEI (IRE) 14 ch.g. Le Bavard (FR) – Blackrath Girl (Bargello) [2002/3 c25g c25d^4 May 14] winning pointer: well beaten in 2 hunter chases: sold £1,500 Ascot June Sales. *G. W. Thomas*

c–

ARDEN HILLS (IRE) 9 b.g. Supreme Leader – Pisa (IRE) (Carlingford Castle) [2002/3 21s c20s^R 19d^6 16v* 22g^4 Apr 21] ex-Irish gelding: half-brother to fairly useful bumper winner Brutus McGregor (by Be My Native): won maiden Irish point in 2002:

c–
h75

yet to complete in steeplechases: poor hurdler: won conditional jockeys selling handicap at Chepstow in February: probably stays 2¾m: acts on heavy going. *J. D. Frost*

ARDENT SCOUT 11 b.g. Ardross – Vidette (Billion (USA)) [2002/3 c115§, h–: c24d* c25d³ c32m³ c22s² c27d* c28v² c28d Mar 1] rangy gelding: useful handicap chaser: won at Uttoxeter in May and Aintree (Tote Becher Chase, maintained good record over National fences by beating Amberleigh House 24 lengths) in November: good second of 7 to Mini Sensation in valuable event at Uttoxeter sixth outing: ran poorly at Haydock final one and missed Grand National through injury: stays 4m: has form on good to firm going, goes well on softer than good (acts on heavy): sound jumper: often races lazily, but much more consistent nowadays. *Mrs S. J. Smith*   **c130 h–**

ARDFINNAN (IRE) 10 b.g. Torus – O Tuk Deep (Deep Run) [2002/3 c74§, h87§: 21f³ May 11] angular gelding: winning hurdler/maiden chaser, fair at best: last of 3 in handicap hurdle only start in 2002/3: stays 2¾m: acts on soft and good to firm going: has jumped poorly all 4 starts in blinkers/visor: not one to trust. *Ian Williams*   **c– § h86 §**

ARDMAYLE (IRE) 9 b.g. Be My Native (USA) – Serena Bay (Furry Glen) [2002/3 c–: c27s⁴ Mar 11] successful in points in March and April: well held on completed start in hunters. *Mrs Richard Arthur*   **c–**

ARD NA CARRIG (IRE) 10 ch.g. Mister Lord (USA) – Coxtown Lass (IRE) (Selko) [2002/3 c–, h–: c20f³ Oct 10] no form outside points (won in March). *M. Sheppard*   **c– h–**

ARDOUR GLOWING 9 b.m. Ardross – Albaciyna (Hotfoot) [2002/3 24dᶠ 26sᵖᵘ Nov 23] medium-sized mare: fairly useful hurdler in 2000/1 for M. Pipe: failed to complete in handicaps both starts on belated return: stays 27f: acts on firm going (bumper form on soft). *D. A. Rees*   **h–**

ARDWELSHIN (FR) 5 b.g. Ajdayt (USA) – Reem Dubai (IRE) (Nashwan (USA)) [2002/3 16g 16mᵖᵘ Mar 22] workmanlike ex-Irish gelding: modest on Flat (barely stays 1½m), successful twice in 2002 for K. Prendergast: no show in 2 starts over hurdles. *B. G. Powell*   **h–**

Tote Becher Chase (Handicap), Aintree—
a clear-cut success for Ardent Scout and promising conditional Dominic Elsworth

ARGEEGEE 5 b.g. Terimon – Lunar Missile (Cruise Missile) [2002/3 F16m⁵ F17d **h–** 21g Mar 3] good-topped gelding: second foal: dam ran once: apparently easily better **F88 ?** effort in bumpers when fifth of 9 in falsely-run event at Huntingdon: showed nothing on hurdling debut. *S. Gollings*

ARGENTO 6 b.g. Weldnaas (USA) – Four M'S (Majestic Maharaj) [2002/3 F75: 16g³ **h113** 16d² 17d³ 16m* 17g* 17d² 16d² 16v² 16d⁶ 19d⁶ 16g² Apr 14] leggy gelding: fair novice hurdler: won at Hexham and Sedgefield in October: good second to Noshinannikin in handicap at former course final start: raced mainly around 2m: acts on good to firm and heavy going: reliable. *G. M. Moore*

ARGY BARGY (IRE) 6 b.g. Lord Americo – Bargy Fancy (Crash Course) [2002/3 **F–** F17g Oct 15] third foal: brother to winning pointer: dam unraced: no show in bumper on debut. *J. Wade*

A RIGHT SET TWO 11 ch.g. Island Set (USA) – Super Sol (Rolfe (USA)) [2002/3 **c–** c92, h–: c20sᵖᵘ 20gᵖᵘ Mar 2] workmanlike gelding: winning chaser, lightly raced nowa- **h–** days: no show in 2 novice hurdles. *R. M. Carson*

ARIJAZ 6 b.g. Teenoso (USA) – Zajira (IRE) (Ela-Mana-Mou) [2002/3 F–: F18m⁴ **F77** Mar 31] modest form on second of 2 starts in bumpers 22 months apart. *P. R. Webber*

ARIZONA (IRE) 5 b.g. Sadler's Wells (USA) – Marie de Beaujeu (FR) (Kenmare **h–** (FR)) [2002/3 16d Mar 5] no form on Flat at 3 yrs for S. Gollings: ninth of 21 in novice at Catterick on hurdling debut. *B. S. Rothwell*

ARJAYPEAR (IRE) 4 b.g. Petardia – Lila Pedigo (IRE) (Classic Secret (USA)) **h–** [2002/3 17sᵖᵘ 16s⁵ 17m Aug 17] poor maiden on Flat: little show in 3 juvenile hurdles, blinkered last 2: joined A. King. *John R. Upson*

ARLEQUIN DE SOU (FR) 9 b.g. Sir Brink (FR) – Colombine (USA) (Empery **c123** (USA)) [2002/3 c120, h–: c22m* c21dF c21v² c21s c26m⁶ Apr 16] lengthy, useful- **h–** looking gelding: winning hurdler: fairly useful handicap chaser: won at Haydock in October: weakened quickly at Cheltenham last 2 starts: stays 3m: acts on good to firm and heavy going: blinkered: races prominently: not an easy ride (has hung markedly left). *P. J. Hobbs*

ARMADA'S SECRET (IRE) 5 b.g. Un Desperado (FR) – Brigette's Secret (Good **F89** Thyne (USA)) [2002/3 F16s⁵ F16gᵖᵘ Mar 12] 29,000 3-y-o: third foal: half-brother to fairly useful hunter chaser Secret Streams (by Over The River): dam ran once: shaped quite well when fifth of 18 in bumper at Ludlow on debut: pulled up amiss next time. *K. C. Bailey*

ARMAGEDDON 6 b.g. Deploy – Arusha (IRE) (Dance of Life (USA)) [2002/3 h–: **h85** 19g⁵ 24d 21gᵖᵘ Mar 16] tall gelding: bumper winner: disappointing over hurdles. *O. Sherwood*

ARMAGUEDON (FR) 5 b.g. Garde Royale – Miss Dundee (FR) (Esprit du Nord **F114** (USA)) [2002/3 F105p: F14d* F14d* F16v³ F17g Apr 5] good-topped gelding: useful form in bumpers, made all to land odds easily at Newcastle in November and Ayr in December: found stamina stretched in Grade 2 events at Chepstow and Aintree last 2 starts: type to do well in 2m novice hurdles in 2003/4. *L. Lungo*

ARM AND A LEG (IRE) 8 ch.g. Petardia – Ikala (Lashkari) [2002/3 c16gᵖᵘ 16m **c–** 20dF 16s* 17m³ 16m⁴ 19d Oct 22] leggy gelding: winning bumper: pulled up on hunter **h83** chase debut, final outing for H. Davies: poor hurdler: made all in selling handicap at Worcester in August: likely to prove best up to 2½m: acts on soft and good to firm going: takes good hold. *Mrs D. A. Hamer*

ARMATURK (FR) 6 ch.g. Baby Turk – Armalita (FR) (Goodland (FR)) [2002/3 **c144** c144, h136: c17g³ c16d⁴ c16v² c21d* c20g c21g Apr 19] tall, angular gelding: useful **h–** hurdler: useful chaser: didn't need to be at best to win 4-runner minor event at Wincanton in February, going better than Upgrade when left clear 2 out: beaten 8 lengths by Geos in another small field for Grade 2 contest at Wetherby time before: well held in extremely valuable event in Japan final start: best form around 2m: acts on good to firm and heavy going: front runner who usually races with plenty of zest. *P. F. Nicholls*

ARMS ACROSSTHESEA 4 b.g. Namaqualand (USA) – Zolica (Beveled (USA)) **h80** [2002/3 16gF 16m⁵ 16f⁴ 16dᵖᵘ 16g⁴ 16d⁵ Dec 4] angular gelding: fair 1m winner on Flat: poor form in juvenile hurdles: likely to prove best at 2m: blinkered last 3 starts. *F. P. Murtagh*

*European Breeders Fund Crandon Park Stud Mares 'National Hunt' Novices' Hurdle Final
(Limited Handicap), Newbury—Ar Muin Na Muice lands some big bets;
Glenmoss Tara (left) gets the better of Blue Ride for second*

AR MUIN NA MUICE (IRE) 7 ch.m. Executive Perk – Raashideah (Dancer's **h134 +**
Image (USA)) [2002/3 F110: 20s* 24dᶠ 24v² 20d* 21m* Mar 22]

In the twenty years since Sea Spice won the inaugural running of the final
of the mares novice hurdle series at Newbury, many efforts have been made to
encourage the racing of mares over jumps. The following season a 5-lb allowance
for fillies and mares was introduced, and the number of races restricted to mares
continues to increase. From January 2004, owners' premiums are being introduced
to supplement prize-money won by most British-bred horses; the premium will be
50% for fillies and mares in races over jumps, with the aim of boosting demand for
British-bred fillies and mares for racing. There is now a similar mares series over
fences with a final at Uttoxeter in March, a listed bumper and a valuable limited
handicap hurdle run at the April meeting at Cheltenham, and there is talk of adding
a mares race to the programme for the Cheltenham Festival soon after the expansion to four days in 2005. Rewards for fillies and mares lurched towards the absurd
in 2003 with the first running of the Bewleys Hotels & EBF National Hunt Fillies
Championship Bumper at the Punchestown Festival shortly after the end of the
British season, the most valuable bumper of the season, but open only to fillies and
mares catalogued at the main NH sales the previous year at Goffs or Tattersalls
(Ireland). The event attracted a predictably large but ordinary field for the money
and—following an eleven-horse pile-up with a circuit to go—it took no more than
a fair performance to win it. Encouraging mares into jump racing and providing
opportunities for them, has obviously meant more mares winning races. Yet races
confined to them are seldom of much interest and mares continue to make only a
limited impact in open company. As for the idea that racing more mares will lead to
an improvement in the breed, the notion is surely fallacious. In *Chasers & Hurdlers
1983/84* five mares merited an essay: the smart hurdlers Buckbe and Stans Pride,
the useful staying hurdler Mayotte, the mares final winner Rose Ravine and Dawn
Run, the winner of the Champion Hurdle, Aintree Hurdle and Grande Course de
Haies d'Auteuil. In the latest edition seven British- and Irish-trained mares have a
full essay, and details of their breeding are an indictment of the efforts to improve
the breed by racing mares. Like-A-Butterfly and Solerina are out of maiden
hurdlers, the dams of Spirit Leader and Nobody Told Me were unraced and Ar Muin
Na Muice's dam won over six furlongs, while the two chasers among the septet,
Lady Cricket and La Landiere, are both French breds.

Few winners of the Newbury mares final between Rose Ravine and Ar
Muin Na Muice have merited more than a short comment in this Annual, and few

have gone on to notable success. The Champion Hurdle winner Flakey Dove is the glowing exception. Snitton Lane and Conquering Leader were useful winners of the race but the rest were nothing out of the ordinary. Rose Ravine won the following season's Stayers' Hurdle and has done well at stud, with the smart staying hurdler Cardinal Red and the smart staying jumper Frosty Canyon among her progeny. Ar Muin Na Muice showed useful form in winning at Newbury and is open to further improvement, though whether she'll be up to figuring in the top races against the current strong crop of staying hurdlers must be doubted. Sixteen went to post for the EBF and Crandon Park Stud-sponsored event in March but nine of them were out of the handicap and the market and the race were dominated by just three horses, Blue Ride and Glenmoss Tara, who were building winning sequences over hurdles, and Ar Muin Na Muice, a useful bumper performer for Caroline Hutchinson in Ireland before winning twice from four starts over hurdles for her current stable. Ar Muin Na Muice landed the odds with little fuss at Bangor in October and Wetherby in February and was also odds on when falling two out at Carlisle in November. She was held at the time but, as the winner Royal Emperor went on to show himself a smart hurdler, that was clearly a stiffer task than it looked. A defeat by the promising Supreme Toss at Uttoxeter on her other start also resulted from a jumping error, as Ar Muin Na Muice was going well when hitting three out. With form that clearly gave her a leading chance at Newbury, Ar Muin Na Muice was available at 7/2 in the morning but, in one of the major gambles of the season, after opening at 2/1 on the track, she was heavily backed down to 11/8 with one recorded bet of £400,000 to £200,000 on the books. In a race which suited her strong-galloping style down to the ground, Ar Muin Na Muice made most and, after seeing off the threat of Blue Ride before the last, she stayed on too well for Glenmoss Tara who came late for second. Ar Muin Na Muice won by two and a half lengths with four further back to Blue Ride, the trio well clear of the remainder.

The good-topped Ar Muin Na Muice isn't that fluent a jumper of hurdles but has the physique to make a chaser. As mares chases tend to be even weaker than

Mrs G. Smith's "Ar Muin Na Muice"

	Executive Perk (b 1985)	Lord Gayle (b 1965)	Sir Gaylord Sticky Case
Ar Muin Na Muice (IRE) (ch.m. 1996)		Areola (ch 1968)	Kythnos Alive Alivo
	Raashideah (b 1980)	Dancer's Image (gr 1965)	Native Dancer Noors Image
		Monaco Melody (b 1972)	Tudor Melody Albercaro

mares hurdles, she should be placed to win races if making the switch. Until Ar Muin Na Muice, her family was noted almost entirely for its Flat performers, most of them sprinters. All three dams in the bottom line of the pedigree won as two-year-olds. The dam Raashideah and third dam Albercaro were fairly useful, while Monaco Melody was a useful six-furlong winner. Both Albercaro, out of a half-sister to the good milers Faberge II and Turbo Jet, and Monaco Melody produced useful Flat performers, the former responsible for the sprinter Bold Tack and the middle-distance stayer Sleipnir, the latter for the two-year-old five-furlong winner Jeema (herself dam of two useful performers at short of a mile). When Ar Muin Na Muice was sold unbroken at the Goffs August Sale in 1999 for a mere IR 800 guineas, the only winning jumper to feature in her catalogue entry was Northern Ace, a winning hurdler/chaser in Ireland. Since then, a couple of Raashideah's off-spring have won under NH rules, Good Time Melody (by Good Thyne) developing into a fairly useful staying chaser while Aungier Gale (by Yashgan) has won a two-and-a-half-mile bumper. Raashideah's only other winner in a long career at stud is the Flat winner Brassy Nell (by Dunbeath). Ar Muin Na Muice—the name apparently means on the pig's back in Gaelic—has already shown she stays much further than might be expected from her pedigree and she will probably be effective beyond three miles, should she be given the chance. She acts on good to firm and heavy going. *Jonjo O'Neill*

A ROMP TOO FAR (IRE)   7 b.g. Eurobus – Saxa Princess (IRE) (Lancastrian) [2002/3 h76, F88: 21s^pu 25d 20d^pu 21g^pu Mar 12] medium-sized gelding: maiden hurdler, no form in 2002/3: wore cheekpieces last 2 starts. *K. C. Bailey*   **h–**

AROSEFORCLARE   7 b.m. Royal Vulcan – Lovelyroseofclare (Torus) [2002/3 h–, F–: 21d^pu 20v^pu 17m^ur Apr 26] no form over hurdles. *Miss K. M. George*   **h–**

ARRIBILO (GER)   9 b.g. Top Ville – Arborea (GER) (Priamos (GER)) [2002/3 h81: 16m² 16d⁶ 16v⁵ 16s^pu c16g^F 16s 17m³ 16m* Apr 21] good-topped gelding: modest hurdler, left P. Johnson after fourth start: won selling handicap at Huntingdon in April: very stiff task and held when falling 2 out on chasing debut: needs sharp 2m: acts on soft and good to firm going: tried visored/blinkered: has broken blood vessel: pulls hard, and has carried head high: unreliable. *B. P. J. Baugh*   **c–**
h91 §

ARROWS GOLD   5 b.g. Sure Blade (USA) – Gamefull Gold (Mummy's Game) [2002/3 17s 17v^F 20v⁶ 17g Mar 16] first foal: dam, modest hurdler, stayed 2¾m: well held over hurdles. *D. M. Grissell*   **h–**

ARTEMESIA   8 b.m. Teenoso (USA) – Annicomba Run (Deep Run) [2002/3 h74: 20g² 23d* 24d² 22g 21d 19s 20m* Apr 21] smallish mare: modest handicap hurdler: won at Fakenham in May (novice) and April, off 4 months before second occasion: stays 3m: acts on good to firm and good to soft going (bumper form on soft): none too consistent. *Ferdy Murphy*   **h85**

ARTEMISE (FR)   5 b.m. Cyborg (FR) – Articule (FR) (Art Francais (USA)) [2002/3 F16s F16s 17s^pu 16g² 17g^pu Apr 19] leggy mare: first foal: dam maiden half-sister to smart chaser around 2¾m Indian River: form only when second in weak mares maiden hurdle at Warwick. *A. King*   **h71 ?**
F–

ART EXPERT (FR)   5 b.g. Pursuit of Love – Celtic Wing (Midyan (USA)) [2002/3 17m^pu 16m Mar 23] modest maiden stayer on Flat: second start over hurdles, ninth of 17 in maiden at Huntingdon: likely to benefit from more of a test of stamina. *Mrs N. Macauley*   **h77**

ARTHUR PORTER   10 ch.g. Crawter – Chetsford Water (Sir Lark) [2002/3 c–: c17s^pu May 18] strong, workmanlike gelding: no show in 3 starts over fences. *P. R. Hedger*   **c–**

ARTHURS KINGDOM (IRE)   7 b.g. Roi Danzig (USA) – Merrie Moment (IRE) (Taufan (USA)) [2002/3 h70: 24g^pu 27g² 22d 24g⁵ 27d³ 27v³ 27s* 24m Mar 18] lengthy gelding: poor handicap hurdler: won at Sedgefield in March: stays 27f: acts on good to   **h70 §**

firm and heavy going: tried visored, wore cheekpieces last 3 starts: unreliable. *Miss Kate Milligan*

ART NOUVEAU 5 b.m. Cyrano de Bergerac – Norska (Northfields (USA)) [2002/3 F–: F17m Jun 1] well held in maiden bumpers. *J. A. Moore*   **F–**

ARUBA DAM (IRE) 5 br.m. Be My Native (USA) – Arumah (Arapaho) [2002/3 F16d Mar 6] eighth foal: half-sister to one-time fairly useful chaser up to 3m Shining Light (by Crash Course) and useful bumper winner Brave King (by King's Ride): dam unraced half-sister to useful staying chaser Castle Warden: well held in bumper at Wincanton on debut. *P. F. Nicholls*   **F–**

ARVI'S WAY 6 b.g. Alflora (IRE) – Gentle Madam (Camden Town) [2002/3 F84: F17d Nov 24] lengthy gelding: modest form on first of 2 starts in bumpers: will be suited by 2½m+. *Mrs S. J. Smith*   **F–**

ASADOR (FR) 7 ch.g. Kadounor (FR) – Apos (FR) (Baillamont (USA)) [2002/3 c122, h–: c19v* c19vF c16vF 20s Feb 8] tall, angular gelding: useful chaser: won handicap at Chepstow (comfortably by 4 lengths from Wain Mountain) in November: fell in similar events next 2 starts (about to be headed at last second occasion), not for first time went as if something amiss when returned to hurdles: stays 19f: acts on heavy and good to firm going: front runner. *P. F. Nicholls*   **c131 h–**

ASAS 9 b.g. Nashwan (USA) – Oumaldaaya (USA) (Nureyev (USA)) [2002/3 c21d5 16f Sep 23] angular gelding: fair hurdler/poor chaser at best, well held both starts in 2002/3: stays 21f: acts on firm ground: often blinkered/visored: has had tongue tied. *D. G. McArdle, Ireland*   **c– h–**

ASCOT TOUCH (IRE) 7 b. or br.g. Architect (USA) – Ascot Touchseal (NZ) (Mayo Mellay (NZ)) [2002/3 F17d 27v5 26d c24m6 c25g c27m5 Apr 26] no form outside points since debut in bumper in 2000/1, when trained by J. O'Neill: tried visored/in cheekpieces. *J. A. Moore*   **c– h– F–**

ASH BRANCH (IRE) 9 ch.g. Shardari – Etnas Princess (The Parson) [2002/3 h73: 20m* Aug 17] rangy gelding: improved effort over hurdles when winning maiden at Bangor in August: not seen out again: better around 2½m than 2m: acts on good to firm going. *Sir John Barlow Bt*   **h85**

ASHBURY STAR (NZ) 8 ch.g. Sumayr – Piaf's Star (NZ) (Famous Star) [2002/3 c92, h95: c18m2 c17d c17s5 c16dpu c17v4 c18fF4 Apr 24] big, strong gelding: modest hurdler/novice chaser, no form after reappearance: probably best around 2m: acts on good to firm and heavy going: tried blinkered/in cheekpieces: usually front runner: has looked less than keen. *Mrs N. Smith*   **c92 d h–**

ASHFIELD JAKE (IRE) 11 br.g. Jolly Jake (NZ) – Ashfield Rose (Mon Capitaine) [2002/3 c–, h–: 20spu 25gpu Jul 15] lengthy gelding: of little account. *S. T. Lewis*   **c– h–**

ASHGAN (IRE) 10 br.g. Yashgan – Nicky's Dilemma (Kambalda) [2002/3 c103, h–: c20m* c24mpu 20m* c21g2 c20m2 c21d4 c23g5 c24d 16d Dec 5] lengthy gelding: fair handicap chaser: won at Worcester in June: fairly useful hurdler, won handicap at same course in July: soundly beaten last 3 starts: best form at 2½m to 2¾m on good going or firmer: tried blinkered, raced freely in visor final outing. *Mrs H. Dalton*   **c103 h118**

ASHGAR (USA) 7 ch.g. Bien Bien (USA) – Ardisia (USA) (Affirmed (USA)) [2002/3 h109§: c23f3 c26g* c32m4 c26mF c26m2 c22mpu c21m2 c20g2 20d6 23v* 24dpu 20g5 20gpu Apr 24] quite good-topped gelding: fair hurdler/chaser at best, trained first 6 starts by P. Hobbs: successful over fences at Uttoxeter in May and hurdles at Wetherby (very simple task in seller) in November: reportedly bled/had breathing problem eleventh and final outings: stays 3¼m (found stamina stretched over 4m): acts on any going: usually blinkered: ungenuine. *M. D. Hammond*   **c105 § h98 §**

ASHLEYBANK HOUSE (IRE) 6 b.g. Lord Americo – Deep Perk (IRE) (Deep Run) [2002/3 F16s F16v4 20g5 Mar 17] IR 19,000 3-y-o, IR £36,000 4-y-o: well-made gelding: second foal: dam ran once: better effort in bumpers staying-on fourth to Carlton Climber at Newcastle: fifth of 13 to Gastornis in 2½m maiden at Wetherby on hurdling debut, not fluent at times and outpaced after 4 out in slowly-run race: will be suited by stiffer test of stamina: will improve for experience. *L. Lungo*   **h85 p F89**

ASHLEY BROOK (IRE) 5 ch.g. Magical Wonder (USA) – Seamill (IRE) (Lafontaine (USA)) [2002/3 F17g2 F14d3 F13s4 F16s* F17g Apr 5] strong gelding: second foal: dam ran twice over hurdles: best effort in bumpers granted stiffer test of stamina when dead-heating with Widemouth Bay at Ludlow in January, helping force good pace (soon clear) and rallying well once challenged: chased leader long way when seventh of 21 to   **F110**

Classic Native in strongly-run Grade 2 at Aintree 3 months later: interesting hurdling prospect. *K. Bishop*

ASHLEY MUCK 10 b.g. Gunner B – Miss Muck (Balinger) [2002/3 c126, h117: c20d^F c20v^4 c20d^4 c23f^3 Mar 27] compact gelding: fairly useful handicap hurdler/chaser: stays at least 21f: acts on any going: tried visored/blinkered: ungenuine. *M. C. Pipe* **c120 §**
h–

ASHMAN (IRE) 10 b.g. Ashmolean (USA) – Rhein Maiden (Rheingold) [2002/3 c–, h–: 17s^{pu} 16m^6 16s^3 c16g^5 c17g^F 16f 17d^{pu} Oct 19] lengthy gelding: winning 2m hurdler/novice chaser, capable of only poor form nowadays: acts on soft and good to firm going: tongue tied: very headstrong: sketchy jumper of fences. *R. N. Bevis* **c78 x**
h–

ASHNAYA (FR) 5 b.m. Ashkalani (IRE) – Upend (Main Reef) [2002/3 h–: 16g^5 16d^F 17g^2 17s* 20d^{pu} 21v^{pu} 16d Nov 25] poor hurdler: won novice handicap at Cartmel in August: should prove better at 2½m than 2m: raced on good going or softer (acts on soft): has worn blinkers/cheekpieces: no easy ride. *W. Storey* **h81**

ASHTON VALE 4 ch.g. Ashkalani (IRE) – My Valentina (Royal Academy (USA)) [2002/3 17d* 17m^2 16m^3 16f* 16f^5 16f^3 17m^3 Apr 26] sturdy gelding: fair maiden on Flat (stays 1¼m) for R. Hannon: fair juvenile hurdler: won at Newton Abbot in September and Wincanton (simple task) in October: likely to prove best at 2m: acts on firm and good to soft going: tongue tied last 5 starts. *P. F. Nicholls* **h97**

ASHTORETH (IRE) 4 ch.f. Ashkalani (IRE) – Sally Chase (Sallust) [2002/3 17m^3 17g^{pu} 17g 16v^2 16v^{pu} 17s^{pu} 17m^5 Apr 21] sturdy filly: half-sister to modest hurdler Bentley Manor (by M Double M), stays 2¾m: modest maiden on Flat (stays 1m), sold out of G. Butler's stable 1,100 gns Doncaster August Sales: poor juvenile hurdler: will prove best around 2m: acts on good to firm and heavy going: has pulled hard. *D. McCain* **h66**

ASHWELL BOY (IRE) 12 b.g. Strong Gale – Billys Pet (Le Moss) [2002/3 c129, h–: c16g^{pu} c19f^{pu} Mar 27] lengthy, angular gelding: useful handicap chaser at best: left M. Pipe after reappearance: pulled up in point/hunter subsequently: stays 25f: acts on any going: usually visored/blinkered since 2000/1: sometimes a weak finisher: prone to odd mistake. *B. R. Summers* **c–**
h–

ASIAN PERSUASION (IRE) 4 gr.g. Danehill Dancer (IRE) – Kaitlin (IRE) (Salmon Leap (USA)) [2002/3 16g^3 17g 16f^2 17f^5 16s^4 16d^{pu} 17d 16g Mar 14] close-coupled gelding: modest maiden on Flat (seems to stay easy 1¼m): poor juvenile hurdler: sold out of E. James's stable 5,500 gns Newmarket Autumn Sales after fourth outing: no form after, in cheekpieces last 2 starts: front runner: not a fluent jumper. *B. A. Pearce* **h77 d**

ASK FOR LUCK (IRE) 6 b.g. Camden Town – French Thistle (Kemal (FR)) [2002/3 F16s 20v 16g^{bd} 24d^3 Mar 1] IR £9,000 4-y-o: workmanlike gelding: fourth foal: dam unraced: last in Irish point in 2002: ninth of 22 only run in bumper: first form in novice hurdles when third to Fern Lord at Newbury: will stay beyond 3m. *J. G. Portman* **h89**
F83

ASK HENRY (IRE) 7 b. or br.g. Jolly Jake (NZ) – Pineway VII (Damsire Unregistered) [2002/3 c22d^2 c21d^2 c26v* c24g^2 c32g c25m^{pu} Apr 17] tall gelding: fifth known foal: half-brother to winning hurdler/top class chaser Valley Henry (by Step Together), stays 3¼m, and winning hurdler/fair chaser Templevalley (by King's Ride), stays 2½m: dam winning Irish pointer: winning pointer: useful novice chaser: won at Chepstow in January: better form when runner-up 3 times, to eased Stormez at Newbury next start: lame final outing: stays 3¼m (probably not 4m): best form on good/good to soft ground. *P. F. Nicholls* **c129**

ASKING 11 b.g. Skyliner – Ma Famille (Welsh Saint) [2002/3 c–, h81: 20g 17g 22d^2 19s^4 24v^2 22v 22d Mar 6] leggy gelding: let down by jumping both starts over fences: poor handicap hurdler: stays 3m: acts on good to firm and heavy going: effective visored or not. *M. Bradstock* **c–**
h81

ASK MARY 6 b.m. Endoli (USA) – Gold Nite (Nesselrode (USA)) [2002/3 F16s F16g F16m^4 16m Apr 22] first reported foal: dam unraced: no form in bumpers or maiden hurdle. *O. O'Neill* **h–**
F–

ASK ME WHAT (IRE) 6 b.m. Shernazar – Laffan's Bridge (IRE) (Mandalus) [2002/3 F17s* F17d^4 20v^3 17s* 21s^2 21m Mar 22] IR 4,400 3-y-o: unfurnished mare: second foal: dam, lightly-raced maiden, sister to useful staying hurdler Mandavi: fair form in bumpers (trained by W. Burke on debut in early-2001/2), winning at Folkestone in December: modest form in mares novice hurdles, won easily at Bangor in March: stays 21f: acts on good to firm and heavy going. *Miss Venetia Williams* **h89 +**
F89

ASKTHEJUDGE (IRE) 4 b.g. Revoque (IRE) – Law Student (Precocious) [2002/3 16d^{ro} 16g^2 Aug 28] fairly useful up to 9f on Flat, successful twice in 2002: length second **h111 p**

to Lost In The Rain in juvenile at Tralee on completed start over hurdles: should improve. *Francis Ennis, Ireland*

ASK THE NATIVES (IRE) 9 br.g. Be My Native (USA) – Ask The Lady (Over **c127** The River (FR)) [2002/3 c–, h–: c22d* c20g³ c24s² c21s⁵ Jan 25] useful-looking gelding: **h–** winning hurdler: fairly useful chaser: won novice at Fontwell in November: good placed efforts next 2 starts: stays 3m: acts on heavy going. *P. F. Nicholls*

ASPARAGUS (IRE) 9 b.g. Roselier (FR) – Arctic Bead (IRE) (Le Moss) [2002/3 **c120** c109, h109: c16s² c17g³ c16v² c19s³ c17d³ c21s* Mar 15] smallish gelding: fair hurdler: **h–** fairly useful handicap chaser: placed all starts in 2002/3, won at Uttoxeter: stays 21f: raced on good going or softer (acts on heavy): tongue tied: usually races prominently: genuine. *M. Sheppard*

ASSURED MOVEMENTS (USA) 7 b.g. Northern Flagship (USA) – Love At **h90** Dawn (USA) (Grey Dawn II) [2002/3 h89: 16d² 22f⁴ May 15] lengthy gelding: modest handicap hurdler: creditable efforts in frame in early-2002/3: effective at 2m to 2¾m: acts on soft and firm going: blinkered once: tongue tied: has looked none too keen. *Mrs D. A. Hamer*

ASSURED PHYSIQUE 6 b.g. Salse (USA) – Metaphysique (FR) (Law Society **h63** (USA)) [2002/3 h76: 16m⁶ 17s⁵ 20m 16m 17m⁶ Apr 15] poor maiden hurdler: likely to prove best around 2m: wears blinkers/cheekpieces: temperament under suspicion. *R. J. Baker*

ASTAFORT (FR) 4 ch.g. Kendor (FR) – Tres Chic (USA) (Northern Fashion (USA)) **h79** [2002/3 16d 16d⁴ 16v³ 16s 20v² 17d⁵ 16ur Mar 8] good-topped gelding: no form on Flat: modest juvenile hurdler: stays 2½m: acts on going softer than good (acts on heavy): whipped round start fifth outing. *A. C. Whillans*

ASTA LA VISTA (GER) 5 b.h. Nebos (GER) – Aminata (GER) (Local Suitor (USA)) **h76** [2002/3 16s⁵ Jan 13] brother to winning 17f chaser Alackaday: won once around 1¼m on Flat at 3 yrs, unplaced both starts in 2002: fifth of 10 to impressive Dancing Bay in novice at Plumpton on hurdling debut. *C. Von Der Recke, Germany*

ASTON MARA 6 b.g. Bering – Coigach (Niniski (USA)) [2002/3 h90: 20d⁵ 20d **h86** 20m⁴ 24g 23v³ 20s⁶ Nov 27] neat gelding: modest hurdler: stays 3m: acts on firm and soft going. *M. A. Buckley*

ASTONVILLE (FR) 9 b.g. Top Ville – Astonishing (BRZ) (Vacilante (ARG)) **c141** [2002/3 18s c19s⁴ c25s* 19v² c21v³ c22s Apr 13] very smart hurdler in 2000/1, just fairly **h128** useful form in 2002/3: demoted to second after beating Caballo Raptor a neck in minor event at Auteuil in December: useful chaser: won Group 2 Grand Steeple-Chase d'Enghien in November confidently ridden by length from Ty Benjam: good third to Line Marine in Group 3 at Auteuil in March: stays 25f: raced mainly on soft/heavy going. *M. Rolland, France*

ASTORMYDAYISCOMING 5 b.g. Alhaatmi – Valentine Song (Pas de Seul) **h79** [2002/3 16m² 20d⁴ 22d⁴ 16d² Nov 14] leggy gelding: poor maiden on Flat: similar form in frame all 4 starts over hurdles: effective at 2m, likely to stay 3m: has worn cheekpieces: joined G. Bridgwater. *W. M. Brisbourne*

ASTRAL PRINCE 5 ch.g. Efisio – Val d'Erica (Ashmore (FR)) [2002/3 h–: 16d 17s⁴ **h57** 17g⁶ 17d Oct 19] lengthy gelding: modest and unreliable on Flat (stays 1¼m): bad form over hurdles: raced around 2m: has worn cheekpieces/had tongue tied. *A. Crook*

ASTRO LINES (IRE) 9 ch.g. Classic Secret (USA) – Fado's Delight (Orchestra) **c88** [2002/3 c88, h–: c22g³ 25g⁴ Jul 15] sturdy gelding: modest chaser nowadays: pulled up **h–** in 2 points in February: stays 2¾m (beaten long way out in 25f claiming hurdle): acts on soft and good to firm going: reportedly lame on reappearance. *Ferdy Murphy*

ATALANTA SURPRISE (IRE) 6 ch.g. Phardante (FR) – Curragh Breeze (Furry **h76** Glen) [2002/3 F18m F16s F18v³ 18v⁶ 21s⁴ 20v 26spu 24mpu Mar 21] rather unfurnished **F76** gelding: eighth foal: brother to smart staying chaser Niki Dee and half-brother to fairly useful hurdler Dancing Dove (by Denel), stayed 2¾m: dam, Irish middle-distance winner/successful only start over hurdles, sister to useful staying hurdler Petty Bridge: modest form in bumpers: poor form over hurdles. *R. H. Buckler*

ATALYA 6 ch.g. Afzal – Sandy Looks (Music Boy) [2002/3 h91: 16d⁴ 17d c17vpu **c76** c16g³ c19m³ Apr 5] workmanlike gelding: modest handicap hurdler: poor novice chaser: **h96** left S. Sherwood after third start: raced around 2m: acts on any going: takes good hold. *S. T. Lewis*

ATAVISTIC (IRE)   11 b.g. Architect (USA) – Saceili (Saher) [2002/3 c130, h–: c28d* **c126**
c29s[6] c27d[pu] Jan 16] neat gelding: fairly useful handicap chaser: goes well fresh, and won **h–**
at Stratford in October: poor efforts both subsequent starts: stays 29f: acts on heavy
going: visored once: has good record on sharp tracks (successful 4 times at Taunton):
races prominently. *P. J. Hobbs*

ATHENIAN LAW   6 br.g. Darshaan – Titania's Way (Fairy King (USA)) [2002/3 **h102 +**
h97p, F92: 16g[3] Apr 23] won bumper and novice hurdle in 2001/2: third of 7 in handicap
hurdle at Perth only outing in 2002/3: raced around 2m: may still do better. *P. J. Hobbs*

ATHIRTY (IRE)   6 ch.g. Denel (FR) – Terrific Temp (Kemal (FR)) [2002/3 F–: F16g **F–**
Nov 9] well held in 2 bumpers, pulling hard only outing in 2002/3. *C. Tizzard*

ATHLEAGUE GUEST (IRE)   10 b.g. Be My Guest (USA) – Santella Bell (Ballad **c82**
Rock) [2002/3 c74+, h97d: c24d[pu] c20m c20s[3] c25d[pu] c19s[4] c20d[F] c20d[5] c24d[5] Mar 19] **h–**
lengthy gelding: winning hurdler: poor maiden chaser: stays 21f: acts on heavy going:
tried blinkered: reportedly lame final outing. *A. Sadik*

ATHNOWEN (IRE)   11 b.g. Lord Americo – Lady Bluebird (Arapaho) [2002/3 c71x, **c99 §**
h–: c19g[2] c25f[F] c24v[6] c20s[3] c16d[2] c16s[2] c19g[rtr] c21g[2] Apr 21] rangy gelding: modest **h– §**
handicap chaser: best effort when second from well out of weights at Newton Abbot:
refused to race previous start: stays 3m, effective at much shorter: acts on soft and good
to firm going: tried visored: sometimes let down by jumping. *J. R. Payne*

A THOUSAND DREAMS (IRE)   13 b.g. Aristocracy – Ardellis Lady (Pollerton) **c61**
[2002/3 c–, h–: c19g c18f* c16m[5] c16g[pu] c16m[pu] c16m[6] 18m[4] 16g[pu] Sep 14] lengthy **h–**
gelding: winning chaser: poor maiden hurdler: won selling handicap at Fontwell in June: stays
easy 21f: acts on firm going, probably unsuited by soft: lame final outing. *L. Waring*

A-TIME OF PEACE (IRE)   10 b.m. Royal Fountain – Sparkle For Me (Baragoi) **c–**
[2002/3 c–, h–: c20m[pu] May 6] leggy mare: little sign of ability: reportedly bled from **h–**
nose only outing in 2002/3. *R. Lee*

ATLANTIC CROSSING (IRE)   6 b.g. Roselier (FR) – Ocean Mist (IRE) (Crash **h99**
Course) [2002/3 F83: 20s[ur] 20s* 20d* 19d Jan 24] leggy, quite good-topped gelding: won
novice hurdles at Carlisle (made all) in November and Haydock in December: unsuited
by steady pace when only seventh of 20 in similar event at Doncaster in January: stiff task
when pulled up in Grade 1 novice at Punchestown in early-May: will be suited by 3m+:
type to do better over fences. *P. Beaumont*

ATLANTIC DRIFT (IRE)   9 b.g. Commanche Run – Cantafleur (Cantab) [2002/3 **c–**
c–, h–: 24g May 11] deep-girthed gelding: refused on chasing debut: poor maiden **h–**
hurdler: runner-up in point in February. *J. A. Moore*

ATLANTIC HAWK   5 b.g. Daar Alzamaan (IRE) – Pyewacket (Belfort (FR)) **F86**
[2002/3 F16v F16g[4] F16m[5] Apr 12] well-made gelding: second foal: dam tailed off in
bumpers: seemingly best effort in bumpers when fifth of 7 at Ayr, tending to hang under
pressure: pulled hard second start. *Ferdy Murphy*

ATLANTIC LADY (GER)   5 br.m. Dashing Blade – Atlantic City (GER) (Medicus **h84**
(GER)) [2002/3 17s[4] 16g[F] 16v[2] 20s 16v[6] 19s[pu] 17g Apr 19] leggy ex-German mare:
fairly useful on Flat at 3 yrs, successful over 7f and 1¼m: maiden hurdler, trained until
after fifth start by C. Von Der Recke: raced too freely both subsequent outings. *Mrs
N. S. Sharpe*

ATLANTIC POWER   10 gr.g. Golden Lahab (USA) – She Say She Will (Roselier **c71 §**
(FR)) [2002/3 h–: 24d[pu] c20d[2] c21d[pu] c21d[6] c25v[6] c24d[3] c25v[pu] 24v[pu] Jan 29] lengthy **h– §**
gelding: winning hurdler: poor maiden chaser: stays 3m: acts on good to firm and heavy
going: has worn cheekpieces: unreliable. *W. Storey*

ATLANTIC PRINCE (IRE)   7 b.g. Fairy King (USA) – Idle Chat (USA) (Assert) **h–**
[2002/3 h–: 18g May 29] of no account: usually tongue tied. *Mrs K. M. Lamb*

ATLANTIC RHAPSODY (FR)   6 b.g. Machiavellian (USA) – First Waltz (FR) **h121**
(Green Dancer (USA)) [2002/3 h127: 18s[5] 16s 16g 16v[5] 16m[4] Apr 22] leggy gelding:
useful on Flat up to 1½m: fairly useful hurdler, generally bit below best in 2002/3: may
prove best around 2m: acts on heavy going, probably on good to firm: successful only
start in tongue tie: patiently ridden. *T. M. Walsh, Ireland*

ATLANTICUS (IRE)   7 b.g. Kings Lake (USA) – Amazonia (GER) (Alpenkonig **c88**
(GER)) [2002/3 20g* c19g[4] Jan 18] lengthy, angular gelding: successful 4 times around **h73 +**
9f on Flat in Germany at 3/4 yrs for P. Lautner: fair form at best over hurdles in 2001/2 for
T. Cooper in Ireland: didn't need to run anywhere near that form when winning seller at
Fakenham in October: sold out of B. Curley's stable 5,800 gns Doncaster November

Sales: modest form when last of 4 finishers in novice at Catterick on chasing debut: stays 2½m: raced on good going or softer (acts on soft): has had tongue tied. *C. Grant*

ATLASTABOY (IRE) 7 b.g. Phardante (FR) – Corcaigh (Town And Country) [2002/3 **h105** F16s³ 20s³ 22s⁵ 24s⁶ 26g* Feb 22] well-made gelding: chasing type: fourth foal: dam **F94** winning hurdler/chaser up to 2½m: runner-up on second of 2 starts in Irish points: close third in bumper: best effort over hurdles when winning handicap at Huntingdon: stays 3¼m. *T. R. George*

ATOMIC BREEZE (IRE) 9 b. or br.g. Strong Gale – Atomic Lady (Over The River **c71 §** (FR)) [2002/3 c–, h–: c24dᵖᵘ c20mᶠ c22m⁴ c16m⁵ c20dᵖᵘ c26mᵘʳ c27g⁴ c28g² c27d³ **h–** c26dᵖᵘ c20g⁵ c26g* Apr 21] plain gelding: poor chaser: finally off mark in weak handicap at Carlisle: seems to stay 3½m: acts on good to firm and good to soft going: not a fluent jumper: inconsistent. *D. M. Forster*

ATTACK 7 gr.g. Sabrehill (USA) – Butsova (Formidable (USA)) [2002/3 F16m 16d **h87** 16m* 16d Nov 16] angular gelding: fair maiden on Flat (stays 13f): well held in bumper: **F–** enterprisingly ridden when making all in novice at Limerick in October, easily best effort over hurdles: tongue tied last 3 starts: sold 8,500 gns Doncaster November Sales. *Mrs J. Harrington, Ireland*

AT THE DOUBLE 7 b.g. Sure Blade (USA) – Moheli (Ardross) [2002/3 h70: 21d⁶ **h–** Nov 4] poor maiden hurdler: should stay beyond 3m: raced on good going or softer: tried visored. *P. Winkworth*

ATTICUS FINCH (IRE) 6 b.g. Witness Box (USA) – Dramatic Loop (IRE) (Balin- **c84** ger) [2002/3 c20g³ 16m⁵ 20s⁴ c16g⁴ 25dᵖᵘ c20v³ c16g* c17gᵘʳ c17gᶠ Apr 26] workman- **h84** like gelding: first foal: dam never ran: won maiden point in 2002: poor novice hurdler/ chaser: won handicap over fences at Wetherby in March: let down by jumping both subsequent starts: may prove best around 2m: free-going sort. *Mrs M. Stirk*

ATUM RE (IRE) 6 br.g. Be My Native (USA) – Collopy's Cross (Pragmatic) [2002/3 **h106** F91: 16vᵖᵘ 16d* 18d⁶ 17g⁵ Mar 29] tall, good-topped gelding: fair novice hurdler: won at Wincanton in February: raced around 2m on good going or softer: raced freely and found little final outing. *P. R. Webber*

AUBURN SPIRIT 8 ch.g. Teamster – Spirit of Youth (Kind of Hush) [2002/3 c83, **c86** h–: c24sᶠ c26sᵖᵘ c26s² c26s⁶ c24v² c26m* Apr 21] tall gelding: modest handicap chaser: **h–** fortunate to win at Plumpton in April: stays 3¼m: acts on good to firm and heavy going. *M. D. I. Usher*

AUCHONVILLERS 6 b.g. Deploy – Forbearance (Bairn (USA)) [2002/3 16m⁴ 20g⁵ **h71** Sep 14] half-brother to 2½m chase winner in Italy by Damister: fairly useful form around 1m on Flat (bred to be suited by 1¼m+) at 3 yrs for B. McMahon: fourth in novice at Worcester, better effort over hurdles: dead. *Mrs H. Dalton*

AUDACTER (IRE) 10 b.g. Strong Gale – Sue's A Lady (Le Moss) [2002/3 c106, **c117** h–: c25d³ c22m* c22g* c24f² c24d⁶ c20dᵖᵘ c21dᶠ Dec 17] sturdy gelding: fairly useful **h–** handicap chaser: won at Fontwell in August and October: stayed 3m well: acted on soft and firm going: dead. *L. Wells*

AUDIOSTREETDOTCOM 6 ch.g. Risk Me (FR) – Ballagarrow Girl (North **h91 §** Stoke) [2002/3 h84§: 20d⁴ 22v⁶ 21d 22d³ 20v 19s* 21s⁵ 21v³ 20v 21v⁶ 22s³ 21d² 24m⁶ Apr 12] lengthy gelding: modest handicap hurdler: won conditional jockeys event at Newbury in December: stays 2¾m: acts on heavy going, below form on good to firm: wears hood and cheekpieces: ungenuine. *G. B. Balding*

AUDITTY (IRE) 10 b.g. Montelimar (USA) – Tax Code (Workboy) [2002/3 c115, **c115 d** h–: c16g² c20m⁴ c16g³ c17m³ c16s⁴ c20d⁵ c20d c16f⁴ Mar 29] lengthy gelding: fairly **h–** useful handicap chaser: sold out of A. Moore's stable 15,000 gns Doncaster October Sales after fifth start, below form subsequently: stays 2½m: very best efforts on good going or firmer (acts on firm). *W. Jenks*

AUGATHELLA 6 b.g. Out of Hand – Choral Work (Song) [2002/3 F17d⁴ F16d Oct **F68** 23] stocky gelding: second foal: dam temperamental maiden: signs of a little ability when fourth of 7 in bumper at Newton Abbot on debut, well held in stronger contest at Chepstow following month. *W. S. Kittow*

AUGUSTUS MACRAE 6 b.g. Theatrical Charmer – More Wise (Ballymore) **F69** [2002/3 F16g May 8] fifth foal: dam, third in bumper, half-sister to useful 2m hurdler Skelum: eighth of 16 in bumper at Chepstow on debut. *Mrs L. Richards*

AUK 8 ch.g. Absalom – Lady Stock (Crofter (USA)) [2002/3 c–, h61: 16s⁶ 17s 16s⁵ **c–** 17s⁴ 16vᵖᵘ 16s⁴ 21g Mar 12] sturdy gelding: bad hurdler: raced mainly around 2m on **h55** going softer than good (acts on heavy). *Mrs P. Robeson*

AULD NICK (IRE) 5 b.g. Old Vic – Grey Tor (Ahonoora) [2002/3 F16s Dec 7] third **F74** known foal: half-brother to winning hurdlers up to 3m Tarrs Bridge and Holborn Hill (both by Riberetto), former useful: dam placed on only start over hurdles: eleventh of 22 in bumper at Warwick on debut. *M. C. Pipe*

AULD THYNES SAKE (IRE) 6 b.g. Good Thyne (USA) – La Fairy (IRE) (Lafon- **F96** taine (USA)) [2002/3 F17f⁴ F16m³ F16m Mar 22] 35,000 4-y-o: rather unfurnished gelding: second foal: dam unraced: in frame first 2 starts in bumpers, well held on final one: will stay at least 2½m: sold 63,000 gns Doncaster May Sales. *Mrs Merrita Jones*

AUNT ELSIE (IRE) 6 b.m. Norwich – Shayista (Tap On Wood) [2002/3 18m³ 16d³ **h89** 16dᵖᵘ 16m⁵ 16vᵖᵘ Dec 2] ex-Irish mare: second foal: half-sister to poor chaser Flying High (by Fayruz), stays 2½m: dam winning hurdler, stayed 2¾m: bumper winner: modest maiden hurdler: left V. Bowens after fourth start: reportedly lost action final outing: raced around 2m: acts on good to firm and good to soft ground (won bumper on soft): tried blinkered/tongue tied. *E. Sheehy, Ireland*

AUNT HILDA 4 b.f. Distant Relative – Aloha Jane (USA) (Hawaii) [2002/3 17d⁵ **h67** 17m 17g³ 17f³ 16d³ 16d 17sᵖᵘ 16vᵖᵘ Jan 22] fair maiden on Flat (probably stays 11.5f), sold out of J. Dunlop's stable 6,000 gns Doncaster August Sales: poor juvenile hurdler: raced around 2m: acts on firm and good to soft going: blinkered/visored after second start. *M. F. Harris*

AUNTIE BOB 5 b.m. Overbury (IRE) – Kadari (Commanche Run) [2002/3 F–: F16d **F–** F17g Jun 12] no form in 3 bumpers. *W. Clay*

AUSSI DON (IRE) 7 ch.g. Accordion – Maryland Flagship (Persian Bold) [2002/3 **h–** F16s 17dᵇᵈ Jan 16] thrice-raced in bumpers, failing to impress with attitude twice, trained **F–** on reappearance by V. Bowens: brought down on hurdling debut: dead. *P. F. Nicholls*

AUTCAESAR AUTNIHIL (IRE) 8 b.g. Supreme Leader – Monagey (Pimpernels **c–** Tune) [2002/3 h83?: c23g⁶ c24dᵖᵘ c23s⁴ c24gᶠ Mar 22] big, angular gelding: signs of **h–** only a little ability, left N. Chance after reappearance. *A. G. Juckes*

AUTUMN FANTASY (USA) 4 b. or br.c. Lear Fan (USA) – Autumn Glory (USA) **h84** (Graustark) [2002/3 16d⁶ 16s 16d 20g³ Mar 29] quite good-topped colt: fairly useful on Flat (stays 2m), sold out of J. Gosden's stable 35,000 gns Newmarket Autumn Sales: modest juvenile hurdler: should stay 2½m. *B. Ellison*

AUTUMN RAIN (USA) 6 br.g. Dynaformer (USA) – Edda (USA) (Ogygian (USA)) **h91 +** [2002/3 22dᵖᵘ 16d 21s⁶ 25d³ Dec 21] fairly useful on Flat (stays 1¼m), successful 3 times in 2002, sold out of N. Callaghan's stable 37,000 gns Newmarket July Sales: best effort over hurdles (caught eye on previous start) when third to Coolsan in novice at Warwick, weakening in straight: may be capable of better again returned to shorter. *D. L. Williams*

AUTUMN STROLL (IRE) 5 ch.g. Toulon – Bermuda Castle (Carlingford Castle) **F88** [2002/3 F16d F16m* F16g Jan 17] strong gelding: sixth foal: half-brother to fairly useful hurdler Patsy Veale (by Accordion), stays 21f: dam unraced: best effort in bumpers when landing odds at Musselburgh in December despite hanging right: pulled too hard final outing. *C. F. Swan, Ireland*

AVADI (IRE) 5 b.g. Un Desperado (FR) – Flamewood (Touching Wood (USA)) [2002/3 **F66** F17g Apr 19] 35,000 4-y-o: first foal: dam winning 2½m hurdler: eighth of 14 in maiden bumper at Newton Abbot on debut. *Mrs H. Dalton*

AVALANCHE (FR) 6 gr.g. Highest Honor (FR) – Fairy Gold (Golden Fleece (USA)) **c123** [2002/3 h93: c20v* c21dᶠ c20d* c20m² 22v c20gᵘʳ c20m⁴ Apr 26] big, workmanlike **h99** gelding: modest maiden chaser: fairly useful novice chaser: won at Leicester (maiden) in January and Kempton (handicap, beat Another Raleagh a neck) in February: should stay beyond 2½m: acts on good to firm and heavy going: pulls hard: usually sound jumper. *J. R. Best*

AVALON BUCK (IRE) 10 b.g. Buckskin (FR) – Lilly's Way (Golden Love) [2002/3 **c– x** c112d, h–: c25gᶠ c24s Mar 7] rather sparely-made gelding: fair hurdler: no form over **h–** fences since winning novice in 2001/2, generally failing to impress with jumping: stays 3m: raced mainly on going softer than good (acts on heavy): usually races prominently. *Miss Venetia Williams*

AVANTI EXPRESS (IRE) 13 b.g. Supreme Leader – Muckride Lady (Deep Run) **c117** [2002/3 c100, h–: c17g* c17d* c17gᵖᵘ Nov 30] strong, good sort: fairly useful handicap **h–**

chaser: successful twice at Stratford in October: effective around 2m and stays 25f: acts on good to firm and heavy going: effective with or without blinkers. *Miss E. C. Lavelle*

AVEBURY   7 b.g. Fairy King (USA) – Circle of Chalk (FR) (Kris) [2002/3 16m³ 16d³ 17m* 17g* 16g Aug 26] modest hurdler: tongue tied, won 2 novices at Sedgefield in summer: will prove best around 2m: yet to race on extremes of going. *G. M. Moore*   **h89**

AVEC PLAISIR (IRE)   8 ch.g. Grand Plaisir (IRE) – Ballinellard Lady (Fine Blade (USA)) [2002/3 c22dᵖᵘ c24dᵖᵘ c25sᵖᵘ Dec 31] good-topped gelding: modest form on second of 2 starts in novice hurdles in 2000/1: showed little over fences on return: stays 3m. *T. R. George*   **c–**
h–

A VENDRE (FR)   4 b.g. Kendor (FR) – Waaria (Shareef Dancer (USA)) [2002/3 17s⁴ 16vᵖᵘ 16v⁶ 16v Feb 4] fair maiden on Flat (barely stays 1¼m): visored, found little when fourth in juvenile seller at Taunton on debut, only form over hurdles. *M. C. Pipe*   **h72**

A VERSE TO ORDER   12 b.g. Rymer – Born Bossy (Eborneezer) [2002/3 c–, h–: 20gᵖᵘ Jul 10] strong gelding: of little account: tongue tied. *Mrs P. Ford*   **c–**
h–

AVITTA (IRE)   4 b.f. Pennekamp (USA) – Alinova (USA) (Alleged (USA)) [2002/3 16v* 16v² Feb 10] won once over 1½m from 4 starts on Flat in France in 2002, sold out of H-A. Pantall's stable 16,000 gns Newmarket July Sales: easily won juvenile at Fakenham on hurdling debut: odds on, found little when second in mares novice at Plumpton following month. *Miss Venetia Williams*   **h99**

AWAY HOME (IRE)   5 ch.g. Carroll House – Mugs Away (Mugatpura) [2002/3 F16v* F16d⁴ Mar 22] workmanlike gelding: half-brother to several winners, including Irish Grand National winner Glebe Lad (by Le Bavard) and fairly useful hurdler up to 2½m Stashedaway (by Treasure Hunter): dam lightly raced: improved efforts in bumpers in 2002/3 (tongue tied), winning maiden at Down Royal in February: will stay beyond 2m. *M. J. P. O'Brien, Ireland*   **F103**

AWESOME WELLS (IRE)   9 b.g. Sadler's Wells (USA) – Shadywood (Habitat) [2002/3 h–: 19g 17s⁴ 20s⁴ 17dᵖᵘ 16d* Mar 8] strong gelding: poor hurdler: won weak conditional jockeys handicap at Warwick: stays 2½m: raced on good going or softer (acts on soft): tongue tied last 3 outings. *D. J. Wintle*   **h74**

AY CARUMBA   6 b.g. Seymour Hicks (FR) – Aldington Peach (Creetown) [2002/3 F16sᵘʳ F18v F16s F16g Mar 12] unfurnished gelding: third foal: dam winning 2m selling hurdler: no show in bumpers. *J. F. Panvert*   **F–**

AYE AYE POPEYE (IRE)   5 ch.g. Imperial Frontier (USA) – Boskovice (IRE) (Flash of Steel) [2002/3 16d* 16d⁴ 16s 16g⁶ 16g 20sꟳ 20s 22s⁶ Dec 21] compact gelding: fourth foal: half-brother to 2 winners, including 2½m hurdler Allfourwhite (by Montelimar): dam unraced: fair at 1½m on Flat: fair hurdler: won novices at Clonmel in May and Punchestown (best effort, beat Mullacash a length) in April: best at 2m: acts on heavy going. *Mrs J. Harrington, Ireland*   **h112**

AYE SURELY (IRE)   9 b.g. Legal Circles (USA) – Uno Navarro (Raga Navarro (ITY)) [2002/3 c16d c20s* c22dꟳ c22v c19fᵇᵈ c17vꟳ c21sꟳ 20v⁴ 16s c16v⁵ c17s⁴ c20m⁴ 27g² Apr 19] leggy gelding: fourth known foal: half-brother to winning chaser Not My Line (by Entre Nous), stays 21f: dam unraced: fair hurdler/chaser on his day: won handicap chase at Limerick in July: sold out of M. Hourigan's stable 1,500 gns Doncaster March Sales after eleventh start: stays 27f: acts on heavy going: usually blinkered, not fluent and hung left when not final outing. *Mrs A. M. Thorpe*   **c101 d**
h89

AZERTYUIOP (FR)   6 b.g. Baby Turk – Temara (FR) (Rex Magna (FR)) [2002/3 h149: c17d* c16d* c16d* c16g* Mar 11]   **c159 p**
h–
Any winner of the Arkle Trophy has a hard act to follow given the achievements of those who have landed the race in the last fifteen years—between them, Waterloo Boy, Remittance Man, Klairon Davis, Flagship Uberalles, Tiutchev and Moscow Flyer have picked up seventeen Grade 1 races, including four Champion Chases. The latest winner Azertyuiop is a magnificent prospect and there is every reason to expect him to add his name to that list and, quite possibly, become another Champion Chase winner. Exuding a style and confidence reminiscent of Remittance Man in particular, he put up a performance at the Festival that was the equal of any at the meeting for sheer exhilaration, and very similar in merit to Moscow Flyer's in the race the previous year. Azertyuiop's style of racing, jumping with elan and lying close up or making the running, is in the best tradition of two-mile chasing, but an ability to quicken provides another valuable weapon in his armoury.

Granted normal improvement Azertyuiop will ensure that Moscow Flyer does not have things all his own way in championship races. Any clashes between them should be worth going a long way to see, especially as the Irish horse has a contrasting style, doing best when held up.

Azertyuiop was not far behind the best hurdlers switched to fences in the latest season but good as he was in that sphere, with a record including victories in the Kingwell Hurdle and Elite Hurdle, he had always been viewed by his connections as a chaser in the making. Paul Nicholls, who can usually sum up his horses' capabilities with great accuracy, acknowledged the fact after Azertyuiop's chasing debut in mid-October when saying: 'He was rated 150 over hurdles but he was never going to be a Champion Hurdle horse and I didn't train him too hard last season, because we were basically marking time before he went chasing.' The race concerned was a six-runner event at Market Rasen, in which Azertyuiop took a good hold—something he tends to do—and made most of the running to win by a distance, jumping well though tending to go slightly right at some fences. The contest lost any hint of competitiveness when Fait Le Jojo unseated at the ninth but Azertyuiop had that rival well beaten in fourth on his next appearance, in the Grade 2 Independent Newspaper November Novices' Chase at Cheltenham. Although opposed by four-time winner Golden Alpha and promising Stars Out Tonight, Azertyuiop started 5/4 favourite and justified the confidence in style, chasing Golden Alpha jumping well, challenging strongly at the third last, out jumping the leader and taking it up at the next before running on with gusto to win by sixteen lengths. This was just about the best performance by a novice to that point and Azertyuiop was promoted to ante-post favouritism for the Irish Independent Arkle Trophy at the Festival.

After bypassing the Henry VIII Novices' Chase at Sandown and the Denny Gold Medal at Leopardstown, and missing a run at Cheltenham over the New Year because of a muscle tear in his hind quarters, Azertyuiop had just one more run before the Festival, in a five-runner race at Wincanton in mid-February. None of his rivals could live with him and, with public confidence in him high, he started 5/4

Independent Newspaper November Novices' Chase, Cheltenham—
Azertyuiop is poised to challenge Golden Alpha three out

Irish Independent Arkle Challenge Trophy Chase, Cheltenham—Azertyuiop shows a decisive turn of foot two out as Impek (left) and Farmer Jack make mistakes, the third Isio is largely hidden by the winner

for the Arkle, the joint-shortest-priced favourite at the meeting with Cathcart winner La Landiere. Azertyuiop's eight opponents were by no means substandard and five had winning form, Impek (unbeaten in three runs, including the Henry VIII Chase), Isio (also with a record of three out of three), Farmer Jack (three wins), Hand Inn Hand (four wins) and the main Irish hope Adamant Approach, who had won one of his two starts. Azertyuiop's stable-companion Le Roi Miguel went off hell for leather but fell at the third—Adamant Approach had gone at the second—and the favourite then took it up. He produced a near-foot-perfect round of jumping and had the race in safe keeping once shaken up after two out, where he made the only semblance of a mistake. Impek, who had travelled through smoothly to stake his claim, was left for dead as Azertyuiop stretched clear, winning by eleven lengths with Isio third and Farmer Jack fourth. It was a breathtaking display by a horse who also looked the part beforehand, the tall, good-topped Azertyuiop impressing in appearance, continually taking the eye. The victory, the first for Nicholls at the Festival since See More Business in the 1999 Gold Cup, contributed £81,200 to the trainer's tally in a season which saw his team set personal records for wins, with one hundred and fifty-two races, and earnings, with £2,077,046 in 1,2,3 prize-money, which still left him £400,000 behind the champion Martin Pipe. Nicholls believes he has little chance of ever beating Pipe, given his stable's smaller size and usual lack of runners in summer jumps events, but he has every reason to anticipate the coming season with relish. He undoubtedly has something approaching an embarrassment of riches with his two-milers since, in addition to Azertyuiop and Le Roi Miguel, whose form late in the season lifted him right up the order, the stable also has established performers Cenkos and Kadarann. Given the lack of top-class opportunities for horses of this type it will be difficult to avoid clashes between them, and that will be greatly to the benefit of the racing public and the sport. The prospect of Azertyuiop and Le Roi Miguel taking on Moscow Flyer in the Tingle Creek Chase at Sandown, a course which should suit both the Nicholls horses ideally, is one to whet any appetite.

Mr J. Hales's "Azertyuiop"

		Northern Baby	Northern Dancer
	Baby Turk	(b 1976)	Two Rings
	(b 1982)	Vieille Villa	Kashmir II
Azertyuiop (FR)		(b 1974)	Vieille Demeure
(b.g. 1997)		Rex Magna	Right Royal V
	Temara (FR)	(br 1974)	Chambre d'Amour
	(b 1985)	Charabia	Bazin
		(b 1976)	Kachabia

Azertyuiop's sire Baby Turk is also responsible for his stable-mate Arma-turk, a front runner who is best at around two miles, a trip that also suits Azertyuiop though he probably stays two and a half. Not that Azertyuiop is likely to be raced beyond the minimum distance, judged on his trainer's comments. There is, how-ever, a reasonable amount of stamina in the dam's pedigree. Temara, an anglo-arab on her distaff side and by a stayer in Rex Magna, won four times at around a mile and a quarter. She has produced four other winners, all on the Flat as well as over jumps, notably Bipbap (by Dom Pasquini), successful in ten races and the best four-year-old chaser of his year in 1998 when landing the Prix Maurice Gillois. Bipbap finished third in the Prix La Haye Jousselin over nearly three and a half miles in 2001, beaten less than three lengths, and clearly stayed well. Azertyuiop's grandam Charabia won on the Flat and over jumps and foaled eight winners altogether, including three over jumps. Azertyuiop, a model of consistency, acts on soft and good to firm going and was not discredited on his only outing on heavy.
P. F. Nicholls

AZTEC RULE (IRE)   10 b.g. Strong Gale – Monksville (Monksfield) [2002/3 c–, **c–** h80: 22d^{pu} Aug 10] fell fourth on chasing debut: poor maiden hurdler: will stay 3m: raced **h–** mainly on good going or firmer (acts on firm): sold £2,500 Ascot November Sales, won maiden point in March. *R. Curtis*

AZUR TONIC (FR)   6 b.g. Muroto – Gym Tonic (FR) (Laostic (FR)) [2002/3 F18d^6 **h113** F16d^5 24m^6 24v* 22s* 24s^4 22v^3 Feb 6] fifth foal: half-brother to 15f hurdle winner **F81** Bleue Tonic (by Agent Bleue) and middle-distance winner Pre d'Azur (by Pietru): dam fair hurdler/1m to 1¼m winner on Flat: fair hurdler at best in bumpers: fair hurdler: won maiden at Clonmel in November and minor event at Thurles in December: stays 3m: acts on heavy going, well beaten only outing on good to firm. *Anthony Mullins, Ireland*

B

BABA AU RHUM (IRE)   11 b.g. Baba Karam – Spring About (Hard Fought) [2002/3 **c–** c106, h–: 17m 17m^5 Jul 19] lengthy gelding: fair chaser: fairly useful handicap hurdler at **h–** best, well held both starts in 2002/3: raced around 2m: acts on firm and good to soft going: makes mistakes over fences. *Ian Williams*

BABARULLAH   5 ch.g. Lucky Wednesday – Hantergantic (Van Der Linden (FR)) **F–** [2002/3 F16m Apr 10] second known foal: dam unraced: no show in bumper on debut. *B. R. Foster*

BABY GEE   9 ch.m. King Among Kings – Market Blues (Porto Bello) [2002/3 h75: **h86** 16v^4 17v* 16g^2 Feb 28] small mare: modest handicap hurdler: improved form when winning at Sedgefield in February: raced mainly around 2m on good going or softer (acts on heavy): game and consistent. *D. W. Whillans*

BABY JOHN (IRE)   10 b.g. Celio Rufo – Kings Princess (King's Ride) [2002/3 c–, **c–** h93d: c20g^5 c25g^F c27d^{pu} Oct 31] workmanlike gelding: winning chaser/maiden hurdler: **h–** no show in handicap chases in 2002/3, and soundly beaten in points subsequently: stays 2¾m: acts on good to firm and good to soft going. *Mrs Sarah Horner-Harker*

BACARDI BOY (IRE)   7 b.g. Lord Americo – Little Welly (Little Buskins) [2002/3 **h99** h111, F111: 24v* 24s^3 22s Mar 15] sturdy gelding: failed to complete in 2 Irish points: modest hurdler: below best in 2002/3, though won maiden at Chepstow in January: thorough stayer: raced on going softer than good (acts on heavy). *T. R. George*

BACCARAT (IRE)   9 b.g. Bob Back (USA) – Sarahlee (Sayyaf) [2002/3 c101, h–: **c88 x** c16d^{pu} c23d^{pu} c20g^3 c20g^{pu} Apr 25] strong, robust gelding: fair maiden chaser at best, **h–** modest form only completion in 2002/3: stays 21f: acts on heavy going: has reportedly had breathing problems (tongue tied final outing): often let down by jumping. *T. J. Fitzgerald*

BACCHANAL (IRE)   9 ch.g. Bob Back (USA) – Justitia (Dunbeath (USA)) **c166** [2002/3 c166, h–: 24g* c24s^3 c25s^F Jan 25] **h157**
The green screens going up in full public view around a stricken horse are an all-too-regular sight at jumping meetings, and adjusting to the loss of some of the leading lights each season is an unfortunate part of being a follower of the sport. Thankfully for racing's public relations, the vast majority of fractures sustained by racehorses happen during training, and, equally thankfully, only a relatively small proportion of those have a fatal outcome. The death and injury rate on course is highest in steeplechases which studies show account for around a third of all racing fatalities in Britain, despite steeplechases accounting for only about one seventh of all races. The majority of fatalities are associated with falls, including the one which led to the demise of the high-class Bacchanal, winner of the 2000 Stayers' Hurdle and twice third in the King George VI Chase. Bacchanal broke a hind leg at the eighth fence when favourite for the Pillar Property Chase at Cheltenham towards the end of January. Among others whose deaths on British racecourses made a significant impression in the latest season were: Its Time For A Win, killed in a fall in the Thomas Pink Gold Cup; Get Real, who shattered a hock in a fall at the second last when bidding for a fifth win at Ascot; former Stayers' Hurdle winner and dual Gold Cup third Dorans Pride, a fatality in the Foxhunter at the Cheltenham Festival; and Goguenard, killed in the Grand National. Readers will be

able to recall others for themselves. To illustrate that hurdling also carries risks, the leading novice Coolnagorna suffered fatal injuries in a fall at Aintree, and the promising juvenile Old California fell fatally in the Triumph Hurdle at the Festival. Others whom British jumping could ill afford to lose included the dual winner of the Grande Course de Haies d'Auteuil, Le Sauvignon, who collapsed and died after finishing second in the Feltham Novices' Chase at Kempton, and that other smart novice chaser Vol Solitaire, who received fatal injuries whilst out at grass in May, while in Ireland the top-class staying hurdler Bannow Bay died while undergoing surgery and Ballyhampshire Boy was put down as a result of injuries suffered in the Morgiana Hurdle.

Bacchanal was saddled for the Pillar Property Chase, in which he was tried in blinkers for the first time, with a view to helping connections decide whether the Gold Cup or a second Stayers' Hurdle would be his Cheltenham Festival target. Bacchanal's long-standing tendency to jump right had cost him ground in the previous year's Gold Cup, in which he dropped away to finish well beaten after starting second favourite. His flawed jumping technique was regarded as less of a hindrance on right-handed tracks and, in finishing a good third for the second year running in the King George VI Chase at Kempton in December, he showed that he was worth a place on merit in the Gold Cup field. But, immediately after that run—beaten a length and a half and four lengths by Best Mate and Marlborough—it seemed more likely that he would go for the Stayers' Hurdle. He had shown very smart form on his seasonal reappearance when winning the Cantor Sport Long Distance Hurdle at Newbury, which he contested in preference to tackling the same day's Hennessy Gold Cup under top weight. Bacchanal made all, drawing clear

Cantor Sport Long Distance Hurdle, Newbury—a final success for Bacchanal

some way from home with previous dual winner of the race Deano's Beeno, before asserting himself from two out and winning by five lengths and three from Native Emperor and Deano's Beeno. The Long Distance Hurdle turned out to be Bacchanal's last victory and, incidentally, his fourth in as many starts at left-handed Newbury, where he made a successful debut over fences and also won the AON Chase. Bacchanal won ten of his twenty races, his other major victories including the Feltham Novices' Chase at Kempton and the Reynoldstown Chase at Ascot. Despite being anything but a natural or fluent jumper of either hurdles or fences, Bacchanal only once failed to complete the course before the Pillar Property Chase, when falling at the first in the Mildmay Novices' Chase at Aintree.

			Roberto	Hail To Reason
		Bob Back (USA)	(b 1969)	Bramalea
		(br 1981)	Toter Back	Carry Back
Bacchanal (IRE)			(ch 1967)	Romantic Miss
(ch.g. 1994)			Dunbeath	Grey Dawn II
		Justitia	(b 1980)	Priceless Fame
		(ch 1987)	Royal Yacht	Riverman
			(b 1981)	Regal Style

The stocky Bacchanal, who stayed three miles and acted on good to firm and heavy going, was bred on Flat-racing lines. His sire Bob Back, winner of the Prince of Wales's Stakes at Royal Ascot, was being used as a dual-purpose stallion when Bacchanal's dam Justitia, a winner six times in Belgium, was mated with him. Justitia has bred a hurdle winner in Italy but her others have been Flat winners, the most notable of them the fairly useful sprinter Shatin Venture (by Lake Coniston). *N. J. Henderson*

BACHELORS PAD   9 b.g. Pursuit of Love – Note Book (Mummy's Pet) [2002/3   **h67** h78: 21d 16v² 17s⁶ 16g 17g⁴ 16m Apr 21] lengthy, angular gelding: poor handicap hurdler: raced mainly around 2m, should stay 2½m: acts on heavy going: usually wears cheekpieces: lazy. *Miss S. J. Wilton*

BACHIANA (FR)   6 ch.m. Exit To Nowhere (USA) – Etoile d'Ocean (USA) (Northern   **h–** Dancer) [2002/3 h81: 16mᵖᵘ 24d³ Aug 2] well-made mare: poor maiden hurdler: will prove best around 2m (didn't stay 3m): tried visored: has had tongue tied. *M. C. Pipe*

BACKBEAT (IRE)   6 ch.g. Bob Back (USA) – Pinata (Deep Run) [2002/3 h84+,   **h99** F106: 16d⁴ 19d* 20gᵖᵘ Apr 2] sturdy gelding: best effort in novice hurdles when making all at Newbury in February: ran no sort of race final outing: better around 2½m than shorter, and should stay further: raced only on good/good to soft going: usually sweats. *D. R. C. Elsworth*

BACKCRAFT (IRE)   5 b.g. Bob Back (USA) – Bawnanell (Viking (USA)) [2002/3   **h115** h109+: 16m* 19m⁴ 16vᵖᵘ 16v⁶ 22dᵖᵘ 18g 22gᵖᵘ Apr 7] lengthy gelding: fairly useful handicap hurdler: won at Wetherby in May: no form last 5 starts: best form at 2m: has won on heavy going, best form on good to firm. *L. Lungo*

BACKED TO EXACT (IRE)   9 b.g. War Hero – Panning (Pitpan) [2002/3 20g³   **h–** 20mᵖᵘ Jun 3] won maiden Irish point in 2000: has shown little in Britain, including over hurdles. *J. R. Cornwall*

BACK IN FRONT (IRE)   6 br.g. Bob Back (USA) – Storm Front (IRE) (Strong   **h151 p** Gale) [2002/3 F119: 16v² 16d* 20s* 16g* Mar 11]
   Twenty-five years on from his first winner of the Supreme Novices' Hurdle, Edward O'Grady trained a second when Back In Front came home ten lengths clear of Kicking King. The first O'Grady-trained winner was Golden Cygnet, the highest-rated novice hurdler since *Chasers & Hurdlers* began and described in the 1977/78 edition as the 'most exciting recruit for years'. As this was the era of Night Nurse, Sea Pigeon and Monksfield it's clear what a tremendous prospect Golden Cygnet was and what a cruel blow it was that he was fatally injured in a last-flight fall when poised to win the Scottish Champion Hurdle from Night Nurse and Sea Pigeon a month later. Back In Front is no Golden Cygnet at this stage but the way he won at Cheltenham marks him down as a leading Champion Hurdle contender for 2004. Waited with in a well-run race, he was travelling ominously well at the

top of the hill and quickened away impressively after two out, running on really strongly after the last. Back In Front jumped quickly and accurately, which along with his telling turn of foot, gives him two of the attributes required of Champion Hurdle winners. It wasn't a particularly strong renewal of the championship event for two-mile novice hurdlers, Rhinestone Cowboy and Self Defense, who would have been significant contenders, running in the Champion Hurdle instead, and only two of the other eighteen to line up—the Tolworth Hurdle winner Thisthatand-tother and the Ladbroke Handicap winner Chauvinist—within a stone of him on form beforehand. Back In Front's performance was well up to recent standards for the race, the ten-length gap to the runner-up being five less than Golden Cygnet had managed and surprisingly only the joint-third biggest winning margin in the last dozen years: Hors La Loi III (the only Supreme winner to go on to Champion Hurdle success since the race took its present form in 1972) won by seventeen in 1999 and the fragile Montelado won by twelve in 1993, Flown (1992) and Shadow Leader (1997) also winning by ten. There were also two equally notable winning margins recorded in the 'eighties—fifteen lengths by River Ceiriog in 1986 and ten by Browne's Gazette in 1984. Back In Front gave the Irish their fourth win in the last five runnings of the Supreme and, after a barren spell in the mid- and late-'eighties, there is something of the dominance previously enjoyed in this event—Golden Cygnet was the second of seven successive Irish-trained winners between 1977 and 1983.

Back In Front started 3/1 favourite at Cheltenham after finishing third in the 2002 Champion Bumper (behind Pizarro and Rhinestone Cowboy, who both also started favourite for their respective Festival events a year on) and winning two of his three previous outings over hurdles. The best of those runs in form terms actually came when he was beaten on his hurdling debut. Thrown in at the deep end, Back In Front acquitted himself really well when running Hardy Eustace to a length and a half at level weights in the Grade 1 Royal Bond Novices' Hurdle at Fairyhouse in early-December. Odds on for his next two appearances, Back In Front beat Arch Stanton by three quarters of a length in a maiden at Leopardstown at the end of January and Hidden Genius by fourteen in a two-and-a-half-mile

Gerrard Wealth Management Supreme Novices' Hurdle, Cheltenham—
Back In Front is well clear at the last

*Evening Herald Champion Novices' Hurdle, Punchestown—
another decisive success; third-placed Fota Island is also in shot*

novice at Limerick nearly a month later. Back In Front was already ante-post favourite for Cheltenham before he won the latter.

After Cheltenham, Back In Front was targeted at a Grade 1 double at the Punchestown Festival, shortly after the end of the British season. In doing so, he was seeking to emulate Davenport Milenium who in 2002 won a Grade 1 novice at the meeting as well as the Emo Oil Champion Hurdle. Back In Front started odds on for both events, the odds rather more justified on form in the Evening Herald Champion Novices' Hurdle than in the open event. Back In Front had little trouble beating the Supreme sixth Limerick Boy by two and a half lengths in an uncompetitive renewal of the novice event but had much more on his plate when taking on the tough and genuine Quazar in the Champion itself. In going down by a length, trying to concede 1 lb, Back In Front ran to his Cheltenham form. If it was a little disappointing that he couldn't find the turn of foot required at the end of a truly-run race, it may have been that two races in four days was a little too much for him at this stage of his career. He remains one of the main pretenders to Rooster Booster's crown in the next season.

		Roberto	Hail To Reason
	Bob Back (USA)	(b 1969)	Bramalea
	(br 1981)	Toter Back	Carry Back
Back In Front (IRE)		(ch 1967)	Romantic Miss
(br.g. 1997)		Strong Gale	Lord Gayle
	Storm Front (IRE)	(br 1975)	Sterntau
	(br 1988)	Tuneful	Reliance II
		(b 1971)	Song of The Coral

Back In Front, a workmanlike sort in appearance, isn't a particularly impressive individual and hasn't a lot to recommend him by way of pedigree either. Easily the most notable name in recent generations of his family is his dam Storm Front who was a useful hurdler and fairly useful chaser at around two and a half miles. Back In Front has form over that trip and acts on heavy going but is likely to

Mr D. Cox's "Back In Front"

prove ideally suited by around two miles and less testing ground. *E. J. O'Grady, Ireland*

BACK ON TOP (IRE)   9 b.g. Bob Back (USA) – Top Girl (IRE) (High Top) [2002/3 c107+, h–: c28s⁴ 24s 20d* 20s² Feb 22] good-topped gelding: fairly useful handicap hurdler: won at Gowran in February: much improved over fences when winning Castlemartin Stud Pat Taaffe Handicap at Punchestown in early-May by 20 lengths from Wotsitooya: should stay beyond 25f: acts on soft going. *J. L. Hassett, Ireland*   **c131**
h122

BACKSCRATCHER   9 b.g. Backchat (USA) – Tiernee Quintana (Artaius (USA)) [2002/3 16m 16d⁴ 17s 20s⁶ 21g 20m 22g³ Apr 26] rather leggy gelding: poor maiden hurdler: stays 2¾m: acts on good to soft going: blinkered fifth start (pulled hard): has looked none too easy ride. *John R. Upson*   **h76**

BACKSHEESH (IRE)   8 b.g. Bob Back (USA) – Kottna (USA) (Lyphard (USA)) [2002/3 c100, h–: c26gᵖᵘ Mar 13] tall gelding: fair chaser: won point in March: loose before start, pulled up in Foxhunter at Cheltenham later in month: stays 25f: acts on soft and good to firm going: tongue tied. *G. Tuer*   **c–**
h–

BACK TO BEN ALDER (IRE)   6 b. or br.g. Bob Back (USA) – Winter Fox (Martinmas) [2002/3 F16s* F16g Mar 12] IR 88,000 3-y-o: good sort: half-brother to several winners, including fairly useful 2m chaser Belstone Fox (by Buckskin): dam unraced half-sister to smart chaser Wild Fox and County Hurdle winner Java Fox: favourite, impressive when winning 20-runner bumper at Kempton on debut in January, beating Forever Dream 13 lengths: beaten long way out in Grade 1 at Cheltenham (reportedly returned with injuries to hind legs). *N. J. Henderson*   **F105**

BACKVIEW 11 ch.g. Backchat (USA) – Book Review (Balidar) [2002/3 h74: 24v³ **h87**
21s² 22v^{pu} Feb 11] compact gelding: modest hurdler: seemingly improved effort when
second in minor event at Warwick, then left M. Salaman: reportedly lame final outing:
stays 3m: acts on heavy going: tongue tied: front runner. *I. A. Wood*

BACLAMA (FR) 7 b.m. Siam (USA) – Santa Ana Wind (USA) (Empery (USA)) **c– §**
[2002/3 c94§, h97§: 16m 20d⁴ 16d⁵ 16s 17m⁶ 18m³ Sep 24] smallish mare: winning **h84 §**
hurdler/chaser, poor nowadays: best up to 2½m: acts on any going: visored last 2 starts:
weak finisher. *M. C. Pipe*

BADDA BING (IRE) 6 b.g. Marju (IRE) – Entracte (Henbit (USA)) [2002/3 16d 16v **h–**
16v^{pu} Jan 1] leggy gelding: seventh foal: half-brother to winning hurdler/fair chaser
up to 3m Maeterlinck (by Bluebird) and several winners on Flat: dam, useful French
2-y-o 7f winner, from outstanding Flat family: little worthwhile form over hurdles: tried
blinkered: dead. *Miss G. Lee, Ireland*

BADEN VUGIE (IRE) 6 bl.g. Hamas (IRE) – Bag Lady (Be My Guest (USA)) **c–**
[2002/3 h–: c16d c20s c20v⁴ c24g⁵ Mar 23] sturdy, lengthy gelding: little sign of ability: **h–**
sold out of H. Daly's stable 2,600 gns Doncaster January Sales after second start.
S. T. Lewis

BADGER BEER 11 b.g. Town And Country – Panda Pops (Cornuto) [2002/3 c100: **c79**
c21f³ c21m^{pu} May 22] workmanlike gelding: fair hunter chaser, well below form early in
season: won 2 points in April: stays 25f: acts on firm and good to soft going: tongue tied.
J. W. Dufosee

BADGERS GLORY 7 b. or gr.g. Neltino – Shedid (St Columbus) [2002/3 c–, h–, F–: **c–**
c26g^{pu} c20f⁴ c26m^{pu} Jul 19] little sign of ability: tried blinkered. *G. P. Enright* **h–**

BADWORTH GALE (IRE) 9 br.g. Strong Gale – Badsworth Madam (Over The **c–**
River (FR)) [2002/3 c22g c21m^{pu} Aug 12] won once from 6 outings in Irish points in
2000: no worthwhile form in steeplechases. *K. C. Bailey*

BAHAMIAN HEIR (IRE) 4 b.c. Lake Coniston (IRE) – Bally Souza (IRE) (Alzao **h–**
(USA)) [2002/3 16d 17g Mar 15] lengthy colt: modest maiden on Flat (stays 11f) when
trained by D. Nicholls: showed little in 2 juvenile hurdles. *N. Wilson*

BAHAMIAN SUN 4 b.g. Bahamian Bounty – Dear Person (Rainbow Quest (USA)) **h–**
[2002/3 17s⁶ Nov 29] half-brother to winning 21f chaser Figawin (by Rudimentary):
modest maiden on Flat (probably stayed 1½m): well held in juvenile on hurdling debut:
dead. *F. Jordan*

BAIE D'ALONG (FR) 4 b.f. Tel Quel (FR) – County Kerry (FR) (Comrade In Arms) **F–**
[2002/3 F17g⁵ Apr 21] fifth foal: half-sister to smart 2m chaser Turgeonev (by Turgeon)
and winner on Flat in Sweden by Subotica: dam won around 1m in France: tailed-off last
of 5 in mares bumper on debut. *N. J. Hawke*

BAILEY'S BRO (IRE) 6 br.g. Castle Keep – Boreen Bro (Boreen (FR)) [2002/3 **h–**
F16s 26g^{pu} Mar 2] IR £19,000 4-y-o: close-coupled gelding: fourth foal: brother to fair **F–**
hurdler/fairly useful chaser Kings Valley, stays 29f, and half-brother to 2 winners by
Roselier, smart staying hurdler Royal Emperor and useful chaser up to 4m A Piece of
Cake: dam, once-raced, from family of top-class chaser Kinloch Brae: no show in
bumper/maiden hurdle. *M. Bradstock*

BAILEY'S OF CASHEL (IRE) 8 ch.g. Husyan (USA) – Ballyharron (Deep Run) **h–**
[2002/3 24d^{pu} Aug 4] IR 3,200 2-y-o, IR 6,200 4-y-o: lengthy, workmanlike ex-Irish
gelding: second foal: half-brother to winning pointer by Good Thyne: dam, out of
half-sister to Grand National winner Grittar, showed little in bumpers: fair form on first
of 2 starts in bumpers in May 2000: runner-up in Irish point in 2001: bought 8,000 gns
Doncaster May (2001) Sales: showed little on hurdling debut. *L. Wells*

BAILEYS PRIZE (USA) 6 ch.g. Mister Baileys – Mar Mar (USA) (Forever Casting **h91 §**
(USA)) [2002/3 17d⁶ 17v⁴ 17s³ 19d⁴ 19d 19d² 18s Feb 3] medium-sized gelding: fair on
Flat (stays 1½m), sold out of M. Johnston's stable 12,000 gns Newmarket Autumn (2001)
Sales: modest novice hurdler: stays 19f: acts on soft going: less than keen. *C. J. Gray*

BAIRON (FR) 5 b.g. Subotica (FR) – Advantage (FR) (Antheus (USA)) [2002/3 **h113**
17m* 17m* Jul 15] ex-French gelding: second foal: half-brother to middle-distance
winner on Flat by Pistolet Bleu: dam, winning hurdler over 2m, half-sister to useful
chaser up to 2¾m Applescott: fair middle-distance stayer on Flat for B. Barbier: successful at Newton Abbot both starts in novice hurdles: will probably prove best around 2m:
looked type to continue improving but not seen out again. *P. F. Nicholls*

BAKIRI (IRE) 5 b.g. Doyoun – Bakiya (USA) (Trempolino (USA)) [2002/3 16d 16s 19d Jan 13] fairly useful on Flat (stays 1¼m) at 3 yrs for Sir Michael Stoute, no form in 2002: well held all 3 starts over hurdles. *R. T. Phillips*   **h–**

BAK ON BOARD 7 b.g. Sula Bula – Kirstins Pride (Silly Prices) [2002/3 h76: 22f^pu May 15] workmanlike gelding: poor maiden hurdler: won 2 points in February: probably stays 2¾m: acts on firm and good to soft going. *Mrs S. Gardner*   **c–** **h–**

BAK TO BILL 8 b.g. Nicholas Bill – Kirstins Pride (Silly Prices) [2002/3 h97: 22v² 22v³ 22s² 20v* 21m² 22s³ 22f⁴ Mar 29] lengthy gelding: fair handicap hurdler: won at Leicester in January by length from Formal Bid: ran well when in frame all other starts: stays 2¾m: acts on any going: often amateur ridden: consistent. *Mrs S. Gardner*   **h114**

BALAKAR (IRE) 7 b.g. Doyoun – Balaniya (USA) (Diesis) [2002/3 16v^pu 16s³ 21d 16g* 19m 16m* Apr 19] leggy ex-Irish gelding: modest hurdler: won handicap at Warwick in March and minor event at Plumpton in April: raced mainly around 2m: acts on soft and good to firm going: tried tongue tied, including at Plumpton. *M. F. Harris*   **h92**

BALANAK (USA) 12 b.g. Shahrastani (USA) – Banque Privee (USA) (Private Account (USA)) [2002/3 h90d: 22g 20v³ Jun 6] smallish, angular gelding: veteran hurdler, retains little ability and less enthusiasm: tried blinkered/visored: usually held up. *D. R. Gandolfo*   **h– §**

BALAPOUR (IRE) 5 b.g. Kahyasi – Balaniya (USA) (Diesis) [2002/3 h134: 16d 20s^ur 20v⁵ 20s³ 16v⁴ 16s^ur 20v^F 17g² 20g 16m^F Apr 22] smallish gelding: fairly useful hurdler: strong-finishing neck second to Spirit Leader in County Hurdle at Cheltenham in March: otherwise out of sorts: should stay at least 2½m: acts on firm and soft going (possibly not heavy): usually tongue tied: held up: inconsistent. *Patrick O. Brady, Ireland*   **h127 §**

BAL DE NUIT (FR) 4 gr.g. Balleroy (USA) – Eoline (FR) (In Fijar (USA)) [2002/3 15v^F c15s c17s³ c17v² 16d* 16d^F 17m* Apr 16] tall gelding: has plenty of scope: fourth foal: brother to Ephese, fair up to 1½m: dam 9f winner, fell only start over hurdles: maiden on Flat: fairly useful form when placed twice in 3-y-o chases at Enghien in November for J. Bertran de Balanda: useful form when winning both completed starts over hurdles, juveniles at Kempton in January and Cheltenham (beat Mistanoora a neck) in April: acts on good to firm and heavy going: type to make an impact in novice chases in 2003/4. *P. F. Nicholls*   **c117 +** **h128**

Concord Juvenile Filing Products Juvenile Novices' Hurdle, Cheltenham—
the grey Bal de Nuit gets the better of front-running Mistanoora

BALI BREEZE (IRE)   4 gr.f. Common Grounds – Bahia Laura (FR) (Bellypha)   h–
[2002/3 16v^{ur} 16s^{pu} 16g Feb 12] ex-Irish filly: fairly useful on Flat (stays 1¼m), sold out
of K. Prendergast's stable €15,000 Goffs November Sale: no form in 3 juvenile hurdles,
saddle slipped second start. *T. G. McCourt, Ireland*

BALINAHINCH CASTLE (IRE)   6 b.g. Good Thyne (USA) – Emerald Flair   h108
(Flair Path) [2002/3 22d* 25m* 24d^{pu} 24g^5 Apr 24]   IR 15,000 3-y-o: useful-looking
ex-Irish gelding: chasing type: fifth foal: half-brother to 3 winners, including useful
hurdler/winning chaser Count Campioni (by Brush Aside), stays 25f, and fairly useful
chaser Emerald Storm (by Strong Gale), stayed 3¼m: dam Irish 11f winner, half-sister to
smart chaser Southern Minstrel, effective at 2m to 3½m: runner-up in maiden point on
debut in 2002: fair form when winning novice hurdles at Exeter (amateurs) in October
and Warwick in November: no show either start after leaving J. O'Neill: will be suited by
thorough test of stamina. *Mrs L. B. Normile*

BALISTEROS (FR)   14 b.g. Bad Conduct (USA) – Oldbury (FR) (Fin Bon) [2002/3   c100
c114, h–: c27d^3 Apr 8] workmanlike gelding: prolific winning pointer, not so good   h–
nowadays, though won in January and March: without a win in hunters since 2000,
laboured effort at Sedgefield (bled from nose): stays 3½m: acts on heavy and good to
firm going: ran badly only start in visor: sometimes none too fluent: a difficult ride.
Mrs B. K. Thomson

BALI STRONG (IRE)   9 b.g. Strong Gale – Greavesfind (The Parson) [2002/3 h94:   h92
24m^4 27g^6 21m^2 26m^5 Oct 11] sturdy gelding: modest handicap hurdler: lame final
outing: stays 25f: acts on firm and good to soft going: tongue tied. *Ferdy Murphy*

BALKIRK   6 ch.g. Selkirk (USA) – Balenare (Pharly (FR)) [2002/3 h–, F–: 16m^4 16g^4 h79
16s^3 16s^{pu} 16v^{pu} Feb 10] angular gelding: poor novice hurdler: sold out of Mrs
M. Hambro's stable £3,600 Ascot August Sales before reappearance: raced mainly at 2m:
acts on soft and good to firm going: joined Mrs H. Bridges. *G. L. Moore*

BALLA D'AIRE (IRE)   8 b. or br.g. Balla Cove – Silius (Junius (USA)) [2002/3   c–
c–, h–: c17m^{pu} Jul 7] leggy gelding: winning pointer: poor maiden hurdler/chaser: tried   h–
blinkered. *K. F. Clutterbuck*

BALLADEER (IRE)   5 b.g. King's Theatre (IRE) – Carousel Music (On Your Mark)   h114
[2002/3 17s^F 16d^3 21s^2 19d^2 24d^6 Apr 4] leggy gelding: fairly useful on Flat (stays 2m)
for J. Hills: fair form in novice hurdles, best effort when 1½ lengths second of 21 to Fork
Lightning at Kempton third start: likely to stay 3m: acts on soft going. *Miss H. C. Knight*

BALLAD MINSTREL (IRE)   11 gr.g. Ballad Rock – Sashi Woo (Rusticaro (FR))   c–
[2002/3 c20d Feb 26] tall, good-topped gelding: fairly useful handicap chaser in 2000/1,   h–
well held only outing since: stays 2½m: acts on soft and good to firm going (ran poorly
on heavy): successful with/without blinkers: usually races prominently. *J. G. FitzGerald*

BALLARD CONNECTION   4 ch.f. Danzig Connection (USA) – Ballard Lady   h–
(IRE) (Ballad Rock) [2002/3 16v^{pu} 17d^{pu} Mar 2] no form on Flat or in 2 juvenile hurdles.
J. S. Wainwright

BALLARDS BOY (FR)   4 b.g. Sleeping Car (FR) – Anita (FR) (Olmeto) [2002/3   F–
F16m Mar 18] first foal: dam winning hurdler/chaser, stayed 2½m: well beaten in maiden
bumper on debut. *N. J. Pomfret*

BALLET RED   6 b.m. Sea Raven (IRE) – Cailin Rua (IRE) (Montelimar (USA))   h–
[2002/3 h–: 16g^{pu} May 17] angular mare: no worthwhile form. *R. D. Wylie*

BALL GAMES   5 b.g. Mind Games – Deb's Ball (Glenstal (USA)) [2002/3 h–: 16m^5 h74
17s^5 17d^3 Aug 26] close-coupled gelding: modest maiden on Flat (seems to stay 9f): poor
form over hurdles: raced around 2m: tried visored. *D. Moffatt*

BALLINA   11 b.g. Ayyabaan – Nicolene (Nice Music) [2002/3 20m^{pu} Jul 24]   c–
winning pointer/maiden hurdler/chaser, little sign of retaining ability: tried visored.   h–
J. G. M. O'Shea

BALLINCARA (IRE)   10 b.g. Broadsword (USA) – Four Sport (Swing Easy (USA))   c86 d
[2002/3 c20d* c18s^5 c20g c17g c20m^4 c19d^{pu} Mar 27] ex-Irish gelding: once-raced over   h–
hurdles: winning pointer: modest handicap chaser: won at Clonmel in May: sold out of
E. O'Grady's stable 5,000 gns Doncaster August Sales, resold £2,500 Ascot February
Sales: little show in points/hunter chase in Britain: stays 2½m: acts on good to soft
ground: tried blinkered. *Miss L. Blackford*

BALLINCLAY KING (IRE)   9 b.g. Asir – Clonroche Artic (Pauper) [2002/3 c128,   c148
h–: 20s^{pu} c25s^3 c25d^3 c21v* c21s^4 c36d^{pu} Apr 5] tall, rather leggy gelding: winning   h–
hurdler: smart handicap chaser: in good form in 2002/3, winning Unicoin New Homes

Unicoin New Homes Chase (Handicap), Cheltenham—Ballinclay King challenges between Grey Abbey and Saragann two out; runner-up Katarino is still to get in the picture

Chase at Cheltenham in January by 6 lengths from Katarino: good fourth to Lady Cricket in another valuable event there later in month: barely stays 25f: acts on heavy going: wore cheekpieces in 2001/2: has broken blood vessels, including when pulled up before halfway in Grand National at Aintree. *Ferdy Murphy*

BALLINURE BOY (IRE)   10 b.g. Meneval (USA) – Sweet Cahore (General Ironside) [2002/3 c21m* May 22] fairly useful pointer, successful in March and April: favourite, easily won maiden at Folkestone in May on hunter chase debut: will stay beyond 21f. *Mrs S. J. Hickman*   **c101**

BALL O MALT (IRE)   7 b.g. Star Quest – Vera Dodd (IRE) (Riot Helmet) [2002/3 F20f F18d⁴ F20s² F17s* F20s 18d⁵ 24v⁴ Mar 9] angular gelding: second foal: dam unraced: best effort in bumpers when making all at Bangor in December: better effort in maiden hurdles when fourth at Naas: stays 3m. *Ronald O'Leary, Ireland*   **h103 F98**

BALLYAMBER (IRE)   8 b.g. Glacial Storm (USA) – El Scarsdale (Furry Glen) [2002/3 c116, h134: c17v² c24v² c21v⁵ c21s³ Feb 9] tall, good sort: useful hurdler: fairly useful maiden chaser: creditable efforts first 3 starts: stays 3m well: best efforts on soft/heavy going. *W. P. Mullins, Ireland*   **c123 h–**

BALLYBAY DEMENSE (IRE)   7 b. or br.g. Bob Back (USA) – Coach Road (Brave Invader (USA)) [2002/3 c26sᵘʳ c24sᵘʳ c21s⁵ c24g³ Feb 22] IR 4,950 3-y-o: big gelding: half-brother to 4 winners, including winning staying chaser Biancone (by I'm A Star) and fair hurdler Laurens Fancy (by Sexton Blake), stays 3m: dam never ran: won maiden Irish point on debut in 2002: modest form in steeplechases: will probably stay beyond 3m. *L. A. Dace*   **c86**

BALLYBOUGH RASHER (IRE)   8 b.g. Broken Hearted – Chat Her Up (Proverb) [2002/3 c112, h93: c20m³ c22sᵘʳ c20d* c26sᵘʳ c24dᵖᵘ c32g⁴ c25dᵖᵘ Apr 4] sturdy gelding: useful handicap chaser: won at Aintree in November by 15 lengths from Maxie McDonald, dropped out in strongly-run race: usually let down by jumping otherwise in 2002/3: effective at 2½m to 4m: acts on soft and good to firm ground. *J. Howard Johnson*   **c131 x h–**

BALLYBROPHY (IRE)   8 gr.g. Roselier (FR) – Bavardmore (Le Bavard (FR)) [2002/3 c26s² c24s* c29d* Mar 8] workmanlike gelding: winning hurdler: progressive form in handicap chases on return from 2-year absence, winning at Ascot in February and Warwick in March: looks a thorough stayer: sound jumper: open to further improvement over fences. *S. E. H. Sherwood*   **c111 p h–**

BALLYCASSIDY (IRE)   7 br.g. Insan (USA) – Bitofabreeze (IRE) (Callernish) [2002/3 h129: c20d² c24d² c24s² 24m Apr 17] rather leggy gelding: won Irish point in 2000: fairly useful hurdler: runner-up in novice chases first 3 starts in 2002/3, fairly useful form on first occasion: ran moody race back over hurdles final outing: best at 3m+:   **c120 h–**

acts on good to firm and heavy going: blinkered third appearance: needs plenty of driving: sold to join P. Bowen 24,000 gns Doncaster May Sales. *A. King*

BALLYDAVID (IRE)   11 b.g. Lord Americo – Arctic Bavard (Le Bavard (FR)) [2002/3 c–, h–: 20g⁴ Apr 21] poor maiden hurdler/chaser, lightly raced: stays 21f: acts on good to firm going: has had tongue tied. *G. B. Balding*   c–
h60

BALLYGARVAN (IRE)   8 gr.g. King Luthier – Lackengarra Wood (Prince Regent (FR)) [2002/3 c115, h86: c25gᶠ Nov 9] workmanlike gelding: modest maiden hurdler: won on debut over fences in 2001/2: fell fatally on reappearance: would have stayed beyond 25f: raced on good going or softer (acted on heavy). *T. R. George*   c–
h–

BALLYGOBACKWARDS (IRE)   11 b.g. Lord Americo – Bargy Fancy (Crash Course) [2002/3 c–, h68: 16m⁶ 16gᶠ May 11] sturdy gelding: poor maiden hurdler/chaser: stays 21f: acts on good to firm and heavy going: tried blinkered. *C. T. Pogson*   c–
h61

BALLYHAMPSHIRE BOY (IRE)   7 b.g. Husyan (USA) – Dante's Ville (IRE) (Phardante (FR)) [2002/3 h147, F117: 16mˢᵘ 16dᶠ 16sᶠ Nov 17] smart hurdler: in contention when slipping up on reappearance, in front when falling 3 out in minor event at Cork next time: in process of showing improved form when falling last in Grade 2 at Navan (upsides winner Limestone Lad) final outing: should have stayed 2½m: raced mainly on going softer than good (showed promise on good to firm): raced prominently: dead. *Sean Aherne, Ireland*   h150

BALLYHARRY (IRE)   13 b.g. Phardante (FR) – Oakville Lady (Menelek) [2002/3 c–, h–: c25vᵖᵘ Nov 8] tall gelding: of little account nowadays: tried blinkered/visored. *P. Grindey*   c–
h–

BALLYKETTRAIL (IRE)   7 b.g. Catrail (USA) – Ballykett Lady (USA) (Sir Ivor) [2002/3 h124, F102: 16d³ 20g⁵ 16s 16s 16s 16s⁶ 16s 16s 16g² Apr 19] well-made ex-Irish gelding: will make a chaser: fairly useful hurdler: left C. Roche before final outing: has won at 2½m, best form at 2m: raced on good going or softer: has had tongue tied. *Jonjo O'Neill*   h118

BALLYKISSANN   8 ch.g. Ballacashtal (CAN) – Mybella Ann (Anfield) [2002/3 h52: 16m⁴ 22gᵖᵘ 22dᵖᵘ 16f⁵ 19f⁵ 19m 17sᵖᵘ Nov 21] tall, sparely-made gelding: bad maiden hurdler: tried blinkered: has had tongue tied. *J. C. Tuck*   h–

BALLYKNOCK ROSE (IRE)   8 ch.m. Cardinal Flower – Annamkerrig (Stetchworth (USA)) [2002/3 c16vᵖᵘ 19dᵖᵘ 20gᵖᵘ Apr 21] good-topped mare: fourth foal: dam unraced: in frame in maiden Irish points: no form in maiden chase (mistakes) or 2 starts over hurdles: left T. George prior to final outing. *L. P. Grassick*   c–
h–

BALLYKNOKAN LAD (IRE)   9 ch.g. Yashgan – Peace River (Over The River (FR)) [2002/3 c22d c17s⁵ c26m³ Aug 5] winning chaser: poor maiden chaser: stays 3¼m: acts on soft and good to firm ground: usually tongue tied. *D. P. Murphy, Ireland*   c69

BALLYLESSON (IRE)   8 b.g. Erdelistan (FR) – Three Dieu (Three Dons) [2002/3 18g³ 20m 21mˢᵘ c24gᶠ 20vᵖᵘ Feb 8] 5,000 4-y-o: half-brother to 3 winners, including fairly useful hurdler/chaser Hand Over (by Quayside), stayed 2½m: dam unraced half-sister to very smart hurdler Dondieu and smart staying chaser Anthony Watt: won maiden point in 2002: form over hurdles only when third in novice at Kelso in May: fell first on steeplechasing debut: should stay at least 2½m. *S. H. Shirley-Beavan*   c–
h84 d

BALLYLINE (IRE)   12 b.g. Electric – Miss Dikler (Tepukei) [2002/3 c96: c24m⁵ c25dᵖᵘ May 30] workmanlike gelding: handicap chaser: little form in early-2002/3: stays 25f: acts on soft and good to firm going: races prominently: none too consistent. *B. G. Powell*   c–

BALLY LIRA   11 b.m. Lir – Ballyorney Girl (New Member) [2002/3 c87§, h–§: c26v⁵ c32d c26s⁵ c26v* s30s³ c29g⁵ Mar 14] lengthy, sparely-made mare: chaser: travelled with much more fluency than usual and much improved when making all at Chepstow (first start since leaving P. Rodford) in February: well below that form otherwise in 2002/3: needs thorough test of stamina: acts on heavy going: visored once: has been ridden in spurs: unreliable. *S. C. Burrough*   c120 §
h– §

BALLYLUSKY (IRE)   6 b.g. Lord Americo – Blackbushe Place (IRE) (Buckskin (FR)) [2002/3 24d⁵ c22d² 20m³ 20d* 21s* 20d² 21s³ 22v⁴ 25g Mar 11] IR 17,000 3-y-o: medium-sized, well-made gelding: first foal: dam unraced: modest maiden chaser, placed all 3 completed starts: sold out of D. Wachman's stable 23,000 gns Doncaster May Sales after second outing: fairly useful handicap hurdler: much improved form subsequently, making all at Wetherby and Market Rasen in November: best effort when fourth to   c96 p
h119

Tote Scoop6 Handicap Hurdle, Wetherby—Ballylusky gains an all-the-way success in impressive fashion

Chopneyev in valuable race at Sandown: effective at 2½m to 3m: acts on good to firm and heavy ground: front runner: consistent: type to do better over fences in 2003/4. *Jonjo O'Neill*

BALLYMORE ROVER (IRE)   9 b.g. Euphemism – Tots Paradise (Roi Guillaume (FR)) [2002/3 h–: 22g⁵ 24m 24dᵖᵘ c23mᵖᵘ Jun 19] leggy gelding: no form over jumps. *Mrs A. C. Tate*   **c–**   **h–**

BALLYNATTIN BLUE (IRE)   10 ch.g. Good Thyne (USA) – Ballynattin Moss (Le Moss) [2002/3 h110: 24s³ 22v⁶ 24s Dec 18] tall gelding: fair handicap hurdler: appeared to run creditably on reappearance, but well below best both subsequent outings (reportedly lame on final one): best at 3m+: acts on heavy going. *J. N. R. Billinge*   **h102**

BALLYROBERT (IRE)   6 b. or br.g. Bob's Return (IRE) – Line Abreast (High Line) [2002/3 21v⁴ 16d c16v⁴ c20s⁶ c20d Mar 8] good-bodied gelding: fourth foal: half-brother to modest hurdler Killimor Castle (by Carlingford Castle), stays 3m: dam, 15f winner, sister to high-class 2m hurdler/smart Flat stayer Heighlin: ran 4 times in maiden Irish points in 2002, winning only completed start: poor form in novice hurdles and chases. *N. A. Gaselee*   **c80**   **h82**

BALLY'S BAK   5 ch.m. Bob Back (USA) – Whatagale (Strong Gale) [2002/3 F16s F16v³ F16d⁵ F16g 17g Apr 21] sturdy mare: third foal: dam, fair chaser, stayed 25f: easily best effort in bumpers when third at Newcastle: well beaten in novice on hurdling debut. *Mrs S. J. Smith*   **h–**   **F81**

BALLYSICYOS (FR)   8 b.g. Nikos – Bally Duke (FR) (Iron Duke (FR)) [2002/3 c111x, h131: 24d 24s³ 25g 24g 24m⁶ Apr 17] tall, angular gelding: fair chaser: fairly useful handicap hurdler: will stay beyond 25f: acts on soft and firm going: blinkered once: usually makes mistakes over fences. *M. C. Pipe*   **c– x**   **h125**

BALLYSTONE (IRE)   10 ch.g. Roselier (FR) – Gusseran Princess (Paddy's Stream) [2002/3 c120, h–: c25dᵖᵘ 24d² c31dᵘʳ 22v² c24m* c24gᵘʳ 24s* c24m² Apr 19] well-made gelding: fairly useful hurdler/handicap chaser: won over fences at Musselburgh in December and novice over hurdles at Carlisle in March: best at 3m+: acts on heavy and good to firm going: visored once, has worn cheekpieces (including at Musselburgh). *L. Lungo*   **c120**   **h115**

BALLYVADDY (IRE) 7 gr.g. Roselier (FR) – Bodalmore Kit (Bargello) [2002/3 c–, **c–** h91: 21d* 25v² 21d 22s⁴ 20g³ 21m* Apr 10] sturdy gelding: well held only completed **h110** start in novice chases: fair handicap hurdler: in good form in 2002/3, winning at Kempton in October and Ludlow in April: stays 25f: acts on good to firm and heavy going: tried in cheekpieces, has won in visor. *G. B. Balding*

BALLYWALTER (IRE) 7 ch.g. Commanche Run – Call Me Honey (Le Bavard **h71** (FR)) [2002/3 22mᶠ F18d⁵ 21s⁵ 21s 21s⁵ 25m⁵ Mar 31] lengthy ex-Irish gelding: chasing **F72** type: fourth foal: half-brother to bumper winner The Uilleann Piper (by Lord Americo): dam unraced half-sister to useful staying hurdler Jakarrdi: winning pointer in 2001: poor form in a bumper (final start for I. Ferguson) and over hurdles: stays 25f. *N. A. Gaselee*

BALNAGREINE (IRE) 10 b.g. Strong Gale – Regent Miss (Prince Regent (FR)) **c83** [2002/3 c70, h–: c24m² c24dᵖᵘ c22g Jun 12] winning pointer: maiden hurdler/chaser: best **h–** effort when second in handicap chase at Southwell in May: stays 3m: acts on firm going, possibly not on softer than good: blinkered once. *J. Mackie*

BALOO 7 b.g. Morpeth – Moorland Nell (Neltino) [2002/3 h82: 27g* 24g³ 22v⁴ 24v **h92** Nov 27] small gelding: modest handicap hurdler: won at Newton Abbot in July: stays 27f: probably acts on any going: effective tongue tied or not. *J. D. Frost*

BALSOX 7 b.g. Alzao (USA) – Bobbysoxer (Valiyar) [2002/3 16dᵖᵘ c19dᵖᵘ 20gᵖᵘ May **c–** 22] good-topped gelding: maiden hurdler/chaser: showed little in early-2002/3 (subse- **h–** quently placed in points): raced mainly around 2m, only on good/good to soft going: tried blinkered. *B. G. Powell*

BALTIC MAGIC (IRE) 9 b.g. Yashgan – Woolly (Giolla Mear) [2002/3 c–, h92: **c–** 19d May 14] modest hurdler/chaser: stays 3m: raced only on going softer than good (acts **h–** on heavy): usually blinkered/visored: sold 3,500 gns Doncaster August Sales, runner-up in points in February/March. *J. L. Spearing*

BALUCHI WAY 7 b.m. Nomadic Way (USA) – Kakapo (Oats) [2002/3 F17s F17m **F–** Jun 1] leggy mare: sixth foal: half-sister to winning 3m hurdler Maori Wisdom (by Be My Native): dam unraced half-sister to fairly useful staying hurdler Mynah Key: well held in 2 bumpers. *P. Beaumont*

BANASAN (IRE) 5 b.g. Marju (IRE) – Banaja (IRE) (Sadler's Wells (USA)) [2002/3 **h117** 16m 17g³ 16f* 16g⁴ 16s³ 20g³ Apr 20] leggy gelding: useful on Flat (will stay beyond 1½m), sold out of Sir Michael Stoute's stable €43,000 Goffs February (2002) Sale: fairly useful novice hurdler: didn't need to be at best to win maiden at Listowel in September: stays 2½m: acts on firm and soft going. *M. J. P. O'Brien, Ireland*

BANJO HILL 9 b.g. Arctic Lord – Just Hannah (Macmillion) [2002/3 h–: 18f² 20m³ **c110** 18m⁵ 22m³ 22g³ c20d² c20d⁵ c20g⁵ c20m* c21m* Apr 17] lengthy, good-bodied gelding: **h92** modest handicap hurdler: fair chaser: left C. Weedon prior to winning novice handicaps at Huntingdon in March and Cheltenham in April: should stay beyond 2¾m: acts on firm and good to soft going: has had tongue tied. *Miss E. C. Lavelle*

BANJO ISLAND (IRE) 5 b.m. Warcraft (USA) – Mandalaw (IRE) (Mandalus) **h–** [2002/3 F16g F17s⁵ 18s Dec 26] IR £4,000 3-y-o: third foal: sister to smart hurdler **F68** Coolnagorna, stayed 21f: dam unraced, from family of high-class staying chaser Bobby Grant: poor form in 2 bumpers: showed nothing on hurdling debut. *G. L. Moore*

BANKERSDRAFT 8 ch.g. Mazaad – Overdraft (Bustino) [2002/3 c–, h–: c16d⁶ **c64** c24gᶠ c20m³ Mar 23] compact gelding: first sign of ability when third in novice handicap **h–** chase at Huntingdon: has worn cheekpieces/had tongue tied. *R. C. Guest*

BANK ON LADY 5 ch.m. Dromod Hill – Sail On Lady (New Member) [2002/3 F16d **F–** F16m F16m Apr 10] third foal: half-sister to fair pointer Jimmy Jumbo (by Dragon Palace): dam of no account: well held in 3 bumpers. *R. J. Smith*

BANNERET (USA) 10 b.g. Imperial Falcon (CAN) – Dashing Partner (Formidable **c§§** (USA)) [2002/3 c§§, h§§: 21dᶠ 20g 16m⁶ c19fᴿ Mar 27] smallish gelding: maiden **h§§** hurdler, trained first 3 starts by T. Wall: has failed to complete in points/hunter chases: often blinkered/visored: thoroughly ungenuine. *F. L. Matthews*

BANNER GALE (IRE) 14 b.g. Strong Gale – Tipperary Special (Wrekin Rambler) **c–** [2002/3 c20dᶠ c21v⁴ c21sᵖᵘ c24v⁵ c25d⁵ c20gᵖᵘ Mar 23] workmanlike gelding: winning **h–** hurdler/maiden chaser, retains no ability: blinkered once. *Dr P. Pritchard*

BANNOW BAY (IRE) 8 b.g. Good Thyne (USA) – Derry Girl (Rarity) [2002/3 **h164** h168: 24s³ 24s³ Dec 28] well-made gelding: top-class hurdler: neck second, clear of remainder, to Baracouda in Stayers' Hurdle at Cheltenham final start in 2001/2: not quite at best in 2002/3, better effort when third of 5 to The Bunny Boiler in steadily-run handicap at Navan on reappearance: ideally suited by 3m+: won on good to firm going, best efforts on softer than good (acted on heavy): successful only run tongue tied: tough and consistent: dead. *C. Roche, Ireland*

BANSHA HOUSE   11 ch.g. Ardross – Proverbial Rose (Proverb) [2002/3 c25s^{pu} c–
c24m^{pu} Apr 2] lightly-raced winning hurdler: showed nothing in 2 hunter chases: should   h–
stay 3m. *Mrs Caroline Chadney*

BARABASCHI   7 b.g. Elmaamul (USA) – Hills' Presidium (Presidium) [2002/3 16m   h–
Oct 19] fairly useful at one time on Flat (stays 1m), only poor in 2002 (for D. Nicholls): well held in maiden on hurdling debut. *R. N. Bevis*

BARACOUDA (FR)   8 b.g. Alesso (USA) – Peche Aubar (FR) (Zino) [2002/3   **h175**
h169+: 20v* 25v^2 24g* Mar 13]

'The French are wiser than they seem,' wrote Francis Bacon. 'And the Spaniards seem wiser than they are.' Some four hundred years later, and leaving the Spanish question for another day, weighing up the French is as hot an issue as ever and the Bacon view isn't one that everyone goes along with. On the world political stage, the spring of 2003 saw the United States and British governments fall out with the French, and more specifically President Jacques Chirac, over policy towards Iraq. One of Britain's newspapers took to portraying Chirac as a worm and, across the Atlantic, assorted expressions of disgust included a restaurateur pouring a thousand dollars worth of French wine down his toilet, french fries renamed as freedom fries and a fourteen-ton armoured vehicle in Las Vegas grinding its way over a pile of 'French goods' including their flag, Chirac's portrait, a Paris travel guide, Perrier water, yoghurt and a French loaf. Hollywood personalities threatened to boycott the Cannes Film Festival. It was all pretty much unprecedented. In racing, of course, the French issue is something that seems never to go away. World leaders have merely begun to sound like the British media or punter when they get their knives out for a French jockey.

There was, to our knowledge, no mashing of their portraits by armoured vehicles, but Thierry Doumen and Jacques Ricou certainly got plenty of stick in Britain during the latest season. They must be used to it. Doumen in particular seems to have criticism follow him around on this side of the Channel and during 2001/2 the signs were that he would never win the doubters round as criticism centred on his riding of Baracouda, on whom he was in the process of compiling the sport's most impressive current winning sequence. In all, when the latest season commenced, Baracouda had eleven wins from fifteen starts and was on a winning run of nine in a row. He was still a novice when he won the Long Walk Hurdle in December 2000 by fourteen lengths. The form he showed that day put him among the very best novice hurdlers in the history of *Chasers & Hurdlers*. Among other exploits the following season, he took the Long Walk again, this time by twenty-four lengths, and a high-quality renewal of the Stayers' Hurdle at Cheltenham, confirming himself the season's best hurdler and earning the Timeform accolade of Champion Jumper. The only disappointment was that he had not crossed swords with the outstanding Irish hurdler Limestone Lad, who was forced to miss the Festival because of injury. The pair had never met.

Baracouda's bid to make it ten wins in a row came in the Pricewaterhouse-coopers Ascot Hurdle in November, immediately setting the tone for a season of burlesque achievement. He started 5/2-on against three opponents and what an extraordinary race it turned out to be. Two of the runners, Landing Light and Carlo-vent, ran nowhere near their best but 11/1-shot Mr Cool posed more than enough problems for Baracouda. A horse as good as Baracouda should not, all other things

Pricewaterhousecoopers Ascot Hurdle—not every picture tells a story;
Baracouda (left), nearly twenty lengths down two out, eventually beats Mr Cool a neck

being equal, have any trouble beating Mr Cool—39 lb separated them in the 2001/2 Timeform ratings—but all other things weren't equal at Ascot as, in addition to giving Mr Cool 8 lb, Baracouda also conceded him a lead of forty lengths. This was not entirely an act of generosity on the part of Thierry Doumen, nor one of opportunism on the part of Mr Cool's jockey Tony McCoy, but after the field of four took some thirteen seconds to respond to the tapes having risen, Mr Cool found himself in a lead of fifteen lengths not long after he was the first to put himself forward. This advantage was soon extended into a massive lead which still comprised some forty lengths when the field took the seventh of the eleven hurdles. Second favourite Landing Light made no contribution to the pursuit, while Carlovent simply isn't good enough to overturn a deficit of such proportions against his stablemate. However, Baracouda and Carlovent had reduced the margin to twenty lengths rounding the final turn, and, leaving Carlovent behind, Baracouda was only eleven lengths down at the last. Only eleven lengths! Getting the distance down to those proportions was an achievement in itself but when, in the heavy ground, the leader negotiated that flight like a tired horse, honourable defeat for Baracouda was surprisingly no longer the only possibility. Baracouda didn't take the last a great deal better than the leader but he was staying on strongly and came with a wet sail to head Mr Cool just before the post. Never a moment's doubt. 'He's perfectly amazing,' reported Doumen. 'I was just waiting for Baracouda to tell me when to attack.' Five days earlier, at Navan for his second race of the season, Limestone Lad had his own big scare in justifying odds of 11/8-on in a four-runner race, just getting the upper hand with Ballyhampshire Boy when that rival fell at the last. Over distances short of their best though, the top hurdlers in France and Ireland had both again emerged victorious.

Baracouda won by a neck at Ascot—with thirty lengths back to Carlovent —but from much of the comment and media reports afterwards, you would have thought he had lost. The real thing was just around the corner. Once again, the betting indicated a cakewalk for Baracouda when he attempted a third successive victory in the Long Walk at Ascot just before Christmas. At 11/4-on, Baracouda again encountered heavy going, this time over an extended three miles and a furlong. With outsider Young American, in the same ownership, seemingly there only to ensure that something made the running at a true pace, there were only three serious rivals and they did not look nearly serious enough. Deano's Beeno, sent off at 14/1 behind Native Emperor and Brother Joe, had not shown anything like his best for well over a year. At his best, however, Deano's Beeno was some 30 lb better than Mr Cool and a worthy opponent for Baracouda at level weights. The point was well made when Baracouda set about trying to catch him in the latest Long Walk. With no messing about this time up front, but a pretty good idea surely of how Baracouda might be beaten, McCoy on Deano's Beeno managed to stretch his advantage to at least ten lengths on the run down to Swinley Bottom; crucially, third-placed Baracouda was not on the second horse's quarters or anything near it, but another ten lengths back. A twenty-length disadvantage, even to Deano's Beeno, was something that Baracouda managed to eliminate, but on the run-in, having drawn upsides but never actually got his head in front, Baracouda's finishing effort expired and he went down by a length. It was widely believed that Deano's Beeno had been given too much rope. 'Doumen Gloom' proved highly popular among headline writers on both the tabloids and the broadsheets. For our part, Baracouda lost little in defeat against a rival who ran right up to his best under ideal conditions.

Winning on the best horse can lead to more praise than is deserved, losing on the best horse can gain more than its fair share of criticism, and few had any doubt that Baracouda was the best horse in the Long Walk. The best horse, but with flaws. If he had to be ridden like this, Baracouda was flawed indeed. 'Everything went all right,' reflected trainer Francois Doumen stoically. 'The only thing Thierry blamed himself for was that he actually came a bit too early. He should have left Deano's Beeno alone in front at the last and come to beat him after the last. There has been a bit of pressure on him not to leave it too late, and the criticisms that he is doing the wrong things maybe influenced Thierry to come a bit earlier than usual.' After Baracouda's previous race, in victory, the trainer commented 'Thierry has cold blood. If he had ridden the horse in a different way, he probably wouldn't have

Bonusprint Stayers' Hurdle, Cheltenham—three outstanding hurdlers in the race of the season; Iris's Gift (centre) and Limestone Lad finish second and third to Baracouda

won. This horse needs to be relaxed and then he can use that lethal turn of foot.' Circumstances in these two Ascot races made these tactics hard to execute. Some observers also questioned Baracouda's stomach for the fight. In the Ascot Hurdle, there were several strides approaching the second last when he carried his head awkwardly. Baracouda's tendency to idle in front—strange as it may seem for a horse that won by twenty-four lengths only twelve months earlier—was long-standing and well known but was there also now a certain idleness well before the finish as well? Baracouda's demeanour when asked to go about his business in the Long Walk was hard to gauge. The course was shrouded in fog. But all would surely be laid bare when he was also required to go in pursuit of Limestone Lad in the Bonusprint Stayers' Hurdle at Cheltenham.

Catching Limestone Lad is a stern test of any horse's stamina and resolution but the Stayers' seemed likely to suit Baracouda a lot better than the two races at Ascot. Most importantly, Baracouda would not have to lead the chase himself, he could follow others as they did their share of the donkey work for a change. Whether Limestone Lad could indeed be passed though, however favourable the circumstances, remained to be seen. Ireland's most popular horse had been in excellent form, taking his tally to five for the season when easily seeing off Boss Doyle and Bannow Bay at the Leopardstown Christmas meeting, though he too went to Cheltenham after a defeat, a narrow one at the hands of Like-A-Butterfly back over two miles in the AIG Europe Champion Hurdle. There was no remaining talk, incidentally, that it might be a realistic proposition for Baracouda similarly to drop back in distance to replace the same owner's Istabraq in the Champion Hurdle. A good job too, because, even in the absence of the 2002 runner-up Bannow Bay, who had suffered a life-ending injury, the Stayers' once again promised to be a better quality race than the Champion and it would have been a great loss to the racing public if the first clash between the French and Irish champions, something which had been in the offing for at least two years, had again failed to materialise. With Limestone Lad at the age of eleven, there would not have been many future opportunities. As it was, Limestone Lad's participation was threatened at one stage by a bout of coughing, but he recovered in time to take his chance. There were nine runners apart from the 'big two' and they had mopped up a total of nine pattern races between them earlier in the season. The aforementioned Deano's Beeno was one, sent off at 25/1, reflecting his lack of form over the course at Cheltenham, and there were three younger horses of considerable potential in unbeaten novice Iris's Gift, the Pipe-trained Classified, who looked set to improve for the step up in distance, and the reappearing Royal & SunAlliance Novices' Hurdle winner Galileo. Baracouda and Limestone Lad dominated both the build-up and the betting and were eventually sent off 9/4 co-favourites.

Baracouda and Limestone Lad were the very best that hurdling had to offer, both famous for taking their directly contrasting styles of running to the limits, the sport's most formidable front runner pitted against its most dramatic procrastinator. If horses can have charisma, this pair had it in abundance. It was easy to predict how the race might unfold and all the more thrilling to see as it came perfectly to fruition. Limestone Lad duly set a strong pace that gradually stretched the field and had nearly all of his rivals off the bridle more than a mile from home, with Baracouda all the while creeping closer. Seventh commencing the final circuit, Baracouda was fourth (with only four still in contention) at the third last, around seven lengths off the lead, and he had moved into third at the second last, on the heels of the leaders. The prize was still up for grabs entering the straight, but with the major, unexpected addition that Iris's Gift was there as well—three outstanding stayers instead of two. At the final flight, all three were in the air together, with Baracouda holding a slight lead from Iris's Gift, and Limestone Lad three quarters of a length behind them. Baracouda had played his hand a bit earlier than expected but, having wrested the advantage, he never looked like relinquishing it and passed the post to the good by three quarters of a length. Limestone Lad was five lengths back in third, with Classified thirteen lengths behind him in fourth.

If there is one good argument for a four-day Cheltenham meeting, apart from the fact that the racecourse and some owners, trainers and jockeys will make a lot more money, it was provided by the Stayers' Hurdle which fully deserved to be the centrepiece of its own day at the Festival. As it was, it was somewhat over-shadowed by the next event on the card, the Gold Cup, even though, for our money, the Stayers' was, as in 2002, the race of the meeting. The dead-heat between Night Nurse and Monksfield at Aintree in 1977 was the race before Red Rum's third Grand National win, and also didn't receive the coverage it deserved. As in 2002, Baracouda's Cheltenham performance was the best by any hurdler during the season and the latest renewal of the Stayers' represented better form than his first. Only two horses had previously won the Stayers' more than once, Crimson Embers in 1982 and 1986 (and most unlucky not to get it in the stewards' room in 1985) and Galmoy in 1987 and 1988. If he were to be returned for the race in 2004, still aged only nine, Baracouda would have a fine chance of becoming the first horse to win it three times. Three days after his latest win, however, Francois Doumen announced the intention to put him over fences. 'We have never schooled him but he is a very straightforward jumper and has great class,' he said. 'If he is to be a chaser, he must jump fences this year.' Interestingly, the trainer also admitted that he had spotted cause for concern with Baracouda earlier in the season, stating: 'He was having trouble with his neck and shoulder, but we managed to sort that out. You could see he wanted to get out on the track and race—not like before—and I was impressed the way he really put his neck out and stretched all the way to the line.'

A tall, leggy gelding, whose French pedigree has been detailed in past Annuals, Baracouda is effective at around two and a half miles given a test of stamina, but is best at three miles or further and, for one who stays so well, has an exceptional turn of foot. Baracouda built his reputation with victories in the mud, but the ground was only good to soft and then good for his two Stayers' Hurdle triumphs in which that turn of foot was seen to such good effect. With or without the problem with his neck and shoulder, it is clear now that Baracouda is not at all a straightforward ride. Thierry Doumen's post-race comments after the latest Stayers' were enlightening: 'After niggling away at Baracouda for much of the way in order to stay in touch with the leaders, I put my hands down at the top of the hill, stopped kicking, and told him "Come on friend, give me some help here". When I dropped my hands he simply picked up and took control. As a result, he was travelling much better in the second half of the race than the first. It's important to know him and to give him confidence.' A desire to 'stay in touch with the leaders' had not, of course, been noted in Baracouda's first two races of the season. When criticising the jockey, though, bear in mind, that Jim Culloty and Tony McCoy have both been beaten on Best Mate, a horse that in comparison to Baracouda could hardly be more straightforward. Above all, remember that since they arrived on the British racing scene, Doumen has been beaten only once on Baracouda. The same point naturally applies also to criticism of the horse. At what point are flaws really just idiosyncracies? Perhaps when the horse in question has

Mr J. P. McManus' "Baracouda"

Baracouda (FR) (b.g. 1995)	Alesso (USA) (b 1983)	Alleged (b 1974)	Hoist The Flag Princess Pout
		Leandra (b 1978)	Luthier Ady Endre
	Peche Aubar (FR) (b 1984)	Zino (b 1979)	Welsh Pageant Cyriana
		Salto Mortale (ch 1971)	Hul A Hul Dover Lassie

won eleven of his last twelve starts, including both the championship events he has contested. Baracouda and Doumen, Doumen and Baracouda, the two of them are a team, the jockey contributing to the huge excitement this horse creates every time he sets foot on a racecourse. Together they have proved almost, but not quite, unbeatable. For entertainment value, they have become irresistible. *F. Doumen, France*

BARAN ITSU   9 br.g. Itsu (USA) – Adelbaran (FR) (No Pass No Sale) [2002/3 c21m⁶ c16mᶠ c24s⁵ c17mᵖᵘ Aug 12] quite good-topped gelding: winning pointer: no form otherwise. *B. J. Llewellyn*   **c–**
h–

BARANNDEE (IRE)   8 b.m. Jurado (USA) – Last Princess (Le Prince) [2002/3 22m* 24d² c17s c18s c18s c20s⁶ c24s c20s⁶ Feb 8] half-sister to several winners, including smart staying chaser Strath Royal (by Furry Glen) and smart hunter chaser Wilbar (by Orchestra): dam, 2½m chase winner, half-sister to high-class 2m to 2½m chaser Artifice: first form over hurdles when winning maiden at Down Royal in May: found stamina stretched when second in weak 3m conditional jockeys handicap at Perth month later: well held over fences: has had tongue tied. *A. J. Martin, Ireland*   **c–**
h86

BARBIZON (NZ)   9 b.g. Oregon (USA) – Fleece Tum (NZ) (Umteen (NZ)) [2002/3 c–, h77; c20d* Nov 25] workmanlike gelding: winning hurdler: second run over fences   **c85**
h–

when winning novice handicap at Ludlow, despite jumping right: stays 21f: acts on soft going: tongue tied. *B. De Haan*

BARBURY HILL (IRE) 7 b.g. Rashar (USA) – Supreme Rehearsal (IRE) (Supreme **h67** Leader) [2002/3 h–, F79: 19g 16m6 19m Apr 5] medium-sized gelding: poor maiden hurdler. *A. King*

BARCELONA 6 b.g. Barathea (IRE) – Pipitina (Bustino) [2002/3 h102: 22m5 21d2 **h117** 16s4 20s6 21s4 21d 20g3 20g Apr 2] compact gelding: fair handicap hurdler on balance: stays 2½m: acts on firm and soft going: tried blinkered/in cheekpieces: tongue tied until after reappearance: none too consistent. *G. L. Moore*

BARCHAM AGAIN (IRE) 6 b.g. Aristocracy – Dante's Thatch (IRE) (Phardante **h91** (FR)) [2002/3 F16g 21d2 22dpu Feb 17] IR £13,000 4-y-o: first foal: dam placed in **F—** bumper/over hurdles in Ireland: showed little in bumper: much more promise when second in novice at Ludlow on hurdling debut: reportedly lost action final outing: should stay 3m. *K. C. Bailey*

BARDEN LADY 6 b.m. Presidium – Pugilistic (Hard Fought) [2002/3 h–: 21dpu 19mpu **h—** Jun 4] little sign of ability over hurdles. *H. D. Daly*

BARD OF DRUMCOO (IRE) 8 ch.g. Orange Reef – Sporting Houdini (Mon- **c72** seigneur (USA)) [2002/3 c21gF c24m6 Apr 21] ex-Irish gelding: no show in 3 runs for M. McElhone: bought 6,800 gns Doncaster May Sales: fair pointer, won in March and April: below that form on completed start in hunters. *M. A. Kemp*

BARDON BOY 9 ch.g. Rakaposhi King – Paper Dice (Le Dauphin) [2002/3 c25dpu **c—** May 14] workmanlike gelding: poor maiden steeplechaser: fair pointer, successful in **h—** February and March: stays 3m: acts on any going: tried blinkered: sometimes let down by jumping. *Mrs Monica Tory*

BAREME (FR) 4 b.g. Homme de Loi (IRE) – Roxa (FR) (Kenmare (FR)) [2002/3 16d6 **h119 p** 16d* Feb 7] rangy, useful-looking gelding: half-brother to 4 winners on Flat in France: dam won over 1¼m: won 1½m event from 4 starts on Flat in France at 3 yrs, sold out of H-A. Pantall's stable €38,000 Goffs November Sale: better effort in juvenile hurdles at Kempton when winning by 2½ lengths from Fantastic Champion: open to further improvement. *N. J. Henderson*

BARITO (GER) 6 b.g. Winged Love (IRE) – Blumme (CHI) (Jadar (CHI)) [2002/3 **c113** h113: 18d4 c17s2 c20s* c20s6 Mar 10] leggy gelding: fair hurdler: best effort over fences **h—** (reportedly lost shoe on debut) when winning novice at Plumpton in January: has won at 2½m, will probably prove better over shorter: acts on soft going: has pulled hard. *C. Von Der Recke, Germany*

BARKINGATTHEMOON 9 b.g. Seymour Hicks (FR) – China's Way (USA) **h—** (Native Uproar (USA)) [2002/3 h72: 20spu Jan 30] leggy gelding: poor maiden hurdler: showed little on reappearance (only second run in 3½ years): stays 19f: acts on good to firm going: often tongue tied. *J. Mackie*

BARLEY MEADOW (IRE) 11 ch.g. Phardante (FR) – Foredefine (Bonne Noel) **c—** [2002/3 c–, h82d: 20g3 16mur 21g c16d3 19g Jun 12] small, angular gelding: well held **h62 d** both starts over fences: poor handicap hurdler, on the downgrade: stays 21f, at least when conditions aren't ideal: acts on any going: tried blinkered, often visored: tongue tied: has looked none too keen. *R. Ford*

BARNARDS GREEN (IRE) 5 ch.g. Florida Son – Pearly Castle (IRE) (Carlingford **F75** Castle) [2002/3 F16m Feb 22] €9,400 4-y-o: lengthy gelding: third foal: dam lightly raced over hurdles: sixteenth of 19 in bumper at Kempton on debut, travelling well but very green when shaken up. *R. H. Alner*

BARNBURGH BOY 9 ch.g. Shalford (IRE) – Tuxford Hideaway (Cawston's **c110** Clown) [2002/3 c121, h–: c20spu c17mF c20m 17m3 c17s* 18s c20m4 Aug 17] smallish, **h115** close-coupled gelding: fairly useful hurdler/fair handicap chaser: won weak race over fences at Market Rasen in July: best around 2m: acts on good to firm and heavy going: sketchy jumper. *Miss Venetia Williams*

BARN DANCER (IRE) 8 b.m. Cataldi – Dancing Gale (Strong Gale) [2002/3 h–, **h—** F–: 16dpu 17dpu Oct 31] no sign of ability. *G. P. Kelly*

BARNEYSIAN 7 b.g. Petoski – Rosemoss (Le Moss) [2002/3 h70: 21s 17s 16d Mar **h—** 1] workmanlike gelding: signs of only a little ability over hurdles. *R. Dickin*

BARON ALLFOURS 11 gr.g. Baron Blakeney – Georgian Quickstep (Dubassoff **c—** (USA)) [2002/3 c67, h–: c26mpu Apr 21] poor maiden chaser: stays 3¼m: acts on firm **h—** and good to soft going. *Miss Z. C. Davison*

BARON CROCODILE 5 b.g. Puissance – Glow Again (The Brianstan) [2002/3 **h–**
17m 17g[pu] Aug 1] fair sprinter at best on Flat, below form in 2002 (left Mrs D. Sayer in
mid-June): tongue tied, no show in 2 novice hurdles: sold to join M. Todhunter 500 gns
Doncaster November Sales. *Mrs E. Slack*

BARON MONTY (IRE) 5 b.g. Supreme Leader – Lady Shoco (Montekin) [2002/3 **F106**
F16s[5] F16v* F16v* F17s[2] F17g Apr 5] lengthy gelding: seventh foal: half-brother to
useful hurdler/chaser Tonoco (by Teenoso), stays 25f: dam maiden half-sister to useful
hurdler/chaser Nodform, stayed 25f: useful form in bumpers: won at Ayr in January and
February: probably unsuited by less testing conditions when soundly beaten in Grade 2
at Aintree: will be suited by further than 17f: troublesome in preliminaries on debut.
C. Grant

BARONTINA 7 br.m. Baron Blakeney – Berina (Goldhills Pride) [2002/3 F16m[pu] **F–**
Jul 24] second foal: dam poor novice hurdler: showed nothing in bumper on debut.
H. H. G. Owen

BARON WINDRUSH 5 b.g. Alderbrook – Dame Scarlet (Blakeney) [2002/3 F14d **F–**
Nov 26] tall gelding: ninth foal: half-brother to fair chaser/modest hurdler Balleswhidden
(by Robellino), stayed 2½m, and one-time fairly useful 2m hurdler/useful hunter chaser
Good Glow (by Jalmood): dam unraced sister to Sun Alliance Hurdle winner Fealty: very
green when well held in bumper on debut. *N. A. Twiston-Davies*

BARRACAT (IRE) 6 b.g. Good Thyne (USA) – Helens Fashion (IRE) (Over The **F96**
River (FR)) [2002/3 F17d* May 14] 6,800 4-y-o: first foal: dam unraced won bumper at
Hereford on debut by 3½ lengths from Lady Terimond: seemed likely to progress but not
seen out again. *B. W. Hills*

BARRELBIO (IRE) 8 b.g. Elbio – Esther (Persian Bold) [2002/3 c86, h112: 22d[6] **c–**
20m 21g[6] 24g[pu] Sep 26] good-topped gelding: fair handicap hurdler: mostly well below **h–**
form for present stable, lame second start: barely stays 3m: acts on any going: blinkered
once: best held up. *F. P. Murtagh*

BARREN LANDS 8 b.g. Green Desert (USA) – Current Raiser (Filiberto (USA)) **c116**
[2002/3 h111: 16g* c17m[5] c21m[6] c19s[5] c16d[5] Dec 14] compact gelding: fairly useful **h116**
handicap hurdler, better than ever when winning at Aintree in May: easily best effort over
fences when winning handicap at Hereford in November, though possibly flattered in
strongly-run race: stays 19f: acts on soft and good to firm going. *K. Bishop*

BARRESBO 9 br.g. Barrys Gamble – Bo' Babbity (Strong Gale) [2002/3 h107: 22d* **h115**
20s[2] Feb 8] fairly useful handicap hurdler: won at Kelso in May: off 9 months, excellent
second to Inching Closer at Haydock: stays 3m: acts on heavy going. *A. C. Whillans*

BARROSA 4 b.f. Sabrehill (USA) – Shehana (USA) (The Minstrel (CAN)) [2002/3 **h–**
17m* Aug 17] half-sister to modest 2m hurdlers Blue Desert (by Elmaamul) and Legion
of Honour (by Ahonoora): poor maiden on Flat (best efforts at 6f): remote sixth in
juvenile at Bangor on hurdling debut. *Miss K. M. George*

BARROW DRIVE 7 b.g. Gunner B – Fille de Soleil (Sunyboy) [2002/3 h127, **c140 +**
F111: c21s[F] c17s[2] c20s* c22d* c17s* c20g* c20s* c20v[2] c20s[2] c21s* c24g[3] **h–**
Mar 12]

    After enjoying a remarkable run of big-race victories, Barry Geraghty came
down to earth with a bump, both literally and metaphorically, on the first day
of the Punchestown Festival. He suffered a fall on one hot favourite, Barrow Drive,
in the Ellier Developments Novices' Chase, and was then unseated from another,
Moscow Flyer, in the BMW Chase. Geraghty walked away unscathed from both
incidents, blaming his misfortune on the Punchestown fences, which he claimed
were 'like stone walls', an appropriate analogy to use at a fixture where such an
obstacle has to be negotiated on its cross country course. Geraghty's analogy was
hardly a fair one, however. The fences at this Festival, as at those at Cheltenham
and Aintree which preceded it, weren't ones with which to take liberties, and nor
should they be, given that these meetings attract the cream of the steeplechasing
division. On this occasion both Barrow Drive and Moscow Flyer were caught out
by the fences, whereas all bar one of the other runners in the two races coped
perfectly well with them. Barrow Drive himself was still bang in contention when
he came down at the ninth, despite having not travelled or jumped with much zest
prior to that, and it's our view that he wouldn't have produced his best form had he
got round.

Dr P. J. Moriarty Novices' Chase, Leopardstown—
Barrow Drive is left clear at the last as odds-on Le Coudray falls

It was Barrow Drive's second fall, the first having occurred at Cork in June on his chasing debut. In between, he had jumped soundly in the main and shown himself a smart and admirably consistent novice chaser, winning six of his ten races and gaining a place in the four others. Five of those wins came in an unbeaten sequence from July to November, at Kilbeggan, Galway (two of them), Gowran and Punchestown, where he made nothing of the fences and all of the running when completing his five-timer in the Grade 3 Irish Field Novices' Chase. Good efforts when second to Le Coudray in a Grade 1 at Fairyhouse and Intelligent at Limerick were then followed by win number six, in the Grade 1 Dr P. J. Moriarty Novices' Chase at Leopardstown in February. Le Coudray started at odds on for this seven-runner contest, and he and Barrow Drive had it to themselves from a long way out. Barrow Drive, again making the running, was closely pressed by Le Coudray from the start and appeared not to be travelling so well as the favourite when joined three out. To his credit, Barrow Drive kept pulling out extra under pressure and was still disputing it at the last where Le Coudray came down, leaving Barrow Drive a long way clear. Le Coudray had just come off the bridle, and with Barrow Drive gamely sticking to his task the outcome was far from settled. It would have been very close had both remained on their feet. The performance was Barrow Drive's best over fences at that stage, though he ran to a similar level in defeat on his only subsequent completed start. Tried at three miles for the first time over fences, having won at the trip over hurdles, Barrow Drive finished third to One Knight and Jair du Cochet, beaten a length and three quarters and ten lengths, in the Royal & SunAlliance Chase at Cheltenham, one paced after two out having tracked the front-running winner. More testing conditions would have benefited Barrow Drive, who will stay a lot further than three miles.

Barrow Drive is another notable jumper sired by the recently-deceased Gunner B, whose career has been summarised in the essay on Iris's Gift. Barrow Drive is the tenth foal of Fille de Soleil and comfortably the best of them, the pick of her other winners being the one-time fairly useful chaser Lambrini Gold (by

		Royal Gunner	Royal Charger
	Gunner B	(ch 1962)	Levee
	(ch 1973)	Sweet Councillor	Privy Councillor
Barrow Drive		(b 1968)	Sugarstick
(b.g. 1996)		Sunyboy	Mourne
	Fille de Soleil	(b 1970)	Fair Bid
	(b 1979)	Panniers Premier	Pannier
		(gr 1964)	The Duchess of Berwick

Gildoran). Fille de Soleil, herself unraced, is a half-sister to the fairly useful hurdler Grimsby Town and the useful hurdler and fairly useful chaser Samuel Pepys. The next dam, Panniers Premier, also unraced, is a half-sister to the useful staying hurdler Whispering Grace. The sturdy Barrow Drive, who has raced only on good going or softer and acts on heavy, made only seven appearances before embarking on his chasing career, winning two of his three starts in bumpers and two of his four over hurdles. The chances are that he will go on to show even better form over fences and, although unlikely to be up to troubling the leading chasers on level terms, he looks the sort to pick up a valuable handicap over three miles or more in the next season. *Anthony Mullins, Ireland*

BARROW (SWI) 6 br.g. Caerleon (USA) – Bestow (Shirley Heights) [2002/3 h102: **h86** 16m 21m* Apr 21] angular gelding: modest hurdler: off nearly 2 years prior to reappearance: won maiden at Huntingdon in April: will stay 3m: acts on soft and good to firm going. *Ferdy Murphy*

BARRYSCOURT LAD (IRE) 9 b.g. Glacial Storm (USA) – Clonana (Le Bavard **c130** (FR)) [2002/3 c105p: c33g² c25sF c24d* Jan 25]
    For the first time in its fifty-five-year history the Great Yorkshire Chase went to a horse who hadn't previously won a steeplechase, Barryscourt Lad gaining his first win outside points when getting the better of Ryalux in a thrilling finish to this valuable three-mile handicap. In doing so, Barryscourt Lad also maintained the good recent record of novices in a competitive race contested mainly by seasoned campaigners, first-season chasers Young Hustler, Addington Boy and Beau all having won it in the previous ten years. At nine, Barryscourt Lad was older than that trio when they contested the Great Yorkshire and, strictly speaking, he was a second-season chaser, but he could hardly be said to have gained much more in the way of experience than his predecessors had done. Started off in points in Ireland, Barryscourt Lad won on the last of his three appearances there, in November 2001, and joined David Pipe shortly after, running eight times for him in a three-month spell early in 2002. As in Ireland, Barryscourt Lad was successful on the last of his three starts in points, while he also finished second in an amateur event at Sandown and in hunter chases at Warwick, Aintree and Cheltenham. Barryscourt Lad was ridden during this period by his owner, our reporter at Cheltenham coming to the conclusion that 'there is almost certainly plenty of untapped potential in him should the reins ever be handed over to a professional.'
    On his return from eight months off and now with David Pipe's father Martin, Barryscourt Lad had professional handling of the highest calibre in the shape of Tony McCoy and was backed as if defeat were out of the question in a novice handicap chase at Cheltenham. As things turned out McCoy failed where Barryscourt Lad's previous rider had always succeeded, in that he didn't complete the course on him. Had he done so, the gamble would have been landed. After moving up full of running three out, Barryscourt Lad was still poised and upsides when falling at the last. With McCoy opting to go to Cheltenham for its next meeting at the end of January, Rodi Greene, also based at Pipe's yard, was given the opportunity to grab the headlines on Barryscourt Lad at Doncaster, and he didn't let it slip. If strong handling was what Barryscourt Lad needed to bring out the best in him then Greene, who had first come to prominence as a 7-lb claimer in the late-'eighties when teaming up successfully with the useful staying chaser Midnight Madness, wasn't going to fail him in that respect. Installed as clear favourite when ante-post betting on the Great Yorkshire began, despite being set to race off a mark 7 lb higher than at Cheltenham, Barryscourt Lad eventually started second favourite after heavy support on the morning of the race for another novice Bold Investor. Bold Investor was tailed off when pulled up three out, one of six of the

skybet.com Great Yorkshire Chase (Handicap), Doncaster—
a first success outside points for Barryscourt Lad as he just prevails from Ryalux (noseband)

eighteen runners who failed to complete in a truly-run race. Barryscourt Lad was prominent from the off and took over at the eleventh, soon having his rivals on the stretch. Driven along turning for home, he was pressed by Ryalux two out and the pair had the race to themselves at the last, where Ryalux put in a quicker jump and went a length up. Barryscourt Lad was far from done with, though, and, with his rider asking for everything, he rallied most gamely to regain the advantage near the line and win by a head. Greene's joy would have been tempered by a three-day ban for having used his whip with excessive frequency, and the news that his mount had returned lame and would miss the remainder of the season. It is to be hoped Barryscourt Lad makes a full recovery and is able to complete a full season in 2003/4. If he does, there is every chance that he could pick up another valuable staying chase. A return to further than three miles will suit Barryscourt Lad, who showed when second over four miles and a furlong at Cheltenham that stamina is his forte. The Welsh National would be just the sort of race for him.

		Arctic Tern	Sea-Bird II
	Glacial Storm (USA)	(ch 1973)	Bubbling Beauty
	(b 1985)	Hortensia	Luthier
Barryscourt Lad (IRE)		(b 1977)	Helenouchka
(b.g. 1994)	Clonana	Le Bavard	Devon
	(b 1981)	(ch 1971)	Lueur Doree
		Arctic Freedom	Arctic Chevalier
		(b 1971)	Peggy French

Barryscourt Lad, a tall, workmanlike gelding who acts on good to firm and heavy going, is the second foal of Clonana. Like Barryscourt Lad and her first foal Barryscourt Castle (by Strong Gale), Clonana is a winning Irish pointer. However, Barryscourt Lad's success at Doncaster was virtually the first for the family outside points since grandam Arctic Freedom won a mile-and-a-quarter maiden at Phoenix Park in 1974. *M. C. Pipe*

BARTON 10 ch.g. Port Etienne (FR) – Peanuts (FR) (Mistigri) [2002/3 c154p, h–: c24d c20d³ c21g⁶ c25g⁶ Apr 3] tall, lengthy gelding: one of the best novice chasers in 2001/2: had reappearance delayed by torn ligament in foot and well below best in 2002/3: **c136** **h–**

effective at testing 2m and stays 25f: acts on heavy and good to firm going: has worn near-side pricker: found to have mucus on lungs final outing. *T. D. Easterby*

BARTON BANDIT 7 ch.g. Sula Bula – Yamrah (Milford) [2002/3 c76, h–: c16m⁵ c20g² c20m² c22mᵖᵘ c16mᵖᵘ c20d⁴ c26mᵖᵘ Aug 26] medium-sized gelding: poor maiden chaser: may prove better at 2½m than 2m: acts on good to firm going: tongue tied: sold £3,700 Ascot October Sales, failed to complete first 4 starts in points. *D. McCain*
   c76 h–

BARTON BARON (IRE) 5 b.g. Phardante (FR) – Boolavogue (IRE) (Torus) [2002/3 F16s F16g Apr 2] €9,000 4-y-o: well-made gelding: second foal: dam lightly-raced sister to useful staying chaser Flashthecash: well held in 2 bumpers. *D. P. Keane*
   F–

BARTON BOG (IRE) 9 gr.g. Roselier (FR) – Al's Niece (Al Sirat (USA)) [2002/3 c77§, h75§: c26m⁵ Nov 4] workmanlike gelding: winning pointer: poor maiden hurdler/chaser: will prove best at 3m+: acts on good to firm and heavy going: tried blinkered: moody. *J. R. Cornwall*
   c– § h– §

BARTON DANTE 6 b.m. Phardante (FR) – Cindie Girl (Orchestra) [2002/3 h106, F89: 16g³ 20gᵘʳ Mar 25] tall, unfurnished mare: fair hurdler: creditable third in handicap at Wetherby on belated reappearance: stays 21f: acts on good to firm and heavy going: has had tongue tied: often looks no easy ride. *M. W. Easterby*
   h104

BARTON DREAM (IRE) 7 b.g. Le Bavard (FR) – Tax Dream (IRE) (Electric) [2002/3 h–, F–: 22g⁶ 22mᶠ 24dᵖᵘ 19m⁵ 22mᶠ Jul 14] little worthwhile form over hurdles: should stay 3m. *John Allen*
   h79 ?

BARTON GATE 5 b.g. Rock Hopper – Ruth's River (Young Man (FR)) [2002/3 F17g⁵ F16d F17v³ 20g⁶ Mar 23] unraced second foal: half-brother to useful hunter chaser My Shout (by Nicholas Bill): dam, of little account, sister to very smart 2m chaser My Young Man and useful staying hurdler/fair chaser Cliffalda: modest form in bumpers: mistakes when well held in novice on hurdling debut: blinkered third start. *M. W. Easterby*
   h– F78

BARTON HILL 6 b.g. Nicholas Bill – Home From The Hill (IRE) (Jareer (USA)) [2002/3 F17d⁵ 20dᵖᵘ 19d 16s⁴ Mar 15] leggy gelding: first foal: dam fairly useful 2m hurdler, also won up to 1½m on Flat: fifth in maiden bumper on debut: easily best effort in novice hurdles when fourth at Uttoxeter: should stay beyond 2m. *T. D. Easterby*
   h95 F80

BARTON NIC 10 b.g. Nicholas Bill – Dutch Majesty (Homing) [2002/3 c83, h–: 20v⁵ 24v* 24v³ 16v* c26s⁵ Feb 26] workmanlike gelding: winning pointer: poor maiden chaser: modest hurdler: won conditional jockeys handicaps at Uttoxeter (novice) in December and Plumpton (subsequently tested positive for morphine) in February: effective at 2m given test, barely at 3¼m: acts on heavy going: wore cheekpieces first 3 starts, blinkered otherwise. *D. P. Keane*
   c66 + h95

BARTON SAINT (NZ) 8 ch.g. St Hilarion (USA) – Aquatramp (NZ) (Pevero) [2002/3 h–: c21g 25g⁵ c21g³ c21fᵖᵘ c21g² c19m⁴ c26g² c25mᵖᵘ c25mᵖᵘ Nov 5] leggy, angular gelding: poor form over hurdles: won maiden point in 2002: poor novice chaser: stays easy 3¼m: acts on good to firm and good to soft going: has had breathing problems (tongue tied on reappearance). *P. R. Rodford*
   c79 h–

BASFORD BOY 4 b.g. Tragic Role (USA) – Legatee (Risk Me (FR)) [2002/3 17g² Sep 28] well beaten in 2 maidens on Flat: second in juvenile seller at Market Rasen on hurdling debut: dead. *A. Streeter*
   h81

BASIL 10 br.g. Lighter – Thrupence (Royal Highway) [2002/3 c–, h–: 26g c22d⁵ c22v³ c26s* c23gᶠ Mar 18] tall gelding: winning pointer: no form over hurdles: poor handicap chaser, improved effort when winning at Warwick in January: stays 3¼m: best efforts on going softer than good (acts on heavy). *R. H. Buckler*
   c78 h–

BASSANO (USA) 9 b.g. Alwasmi (USA) – Marittima (USA) (L'Emigrant (USA)) [2002/3 c24d⁶ c26v³ c19d c24v⁴ Mar 10] stocky, lengthy gelding: modest form on chasing debut in 2000/1 but poor efforts since (missed 2001/2): should stay 3m: raced on good going or softer (acts on heavy): has found little. *S. C. Burrough*
   c– h–

BASSENHALLY 13 ch.g. Celtic Cone – Milly Kelly (Murrayfield) [2002/3 c97, h–: c24d⁴ c23g³ Nov 30] workmanlike gelding: modest handicap chaser nowadays: stays 25f: acts on good to firm and heavy going: has won 5 times at Fakenham: front runner. *Mrs P. Sly*
   c89 h–

BASSETT TIGER (IRE) 7 b.g. Shardari – Bassett Girl (Brigadier Gerard) [2002/3 h118: c22s⁴ c16s⁴ c20sᶠ c18v² c17d⁴ c20m² Apr 12] fairly useful hurdler: fair novice chaser: would have won maiden at Punchestown in February but for falling last: effective at 2m to 2¾m: acts on good to firm and heavy going: has had tongue tied: consistent. *W. P. Mullins, Ireland*
   c111 h–

BATHSHEBA 4 b.f. Overbury (IRE) – Winnow (Oats) [2002/3 F18v Feb 10] first **F–**
foal: dam, poor chaser, stayed 3m: no show in maiden bumper on debut. *J. Gallagher*

BATHWICK ANNIE 7 ch.m. Sula Bula – Lily Mab (FR) (Prince Mab (FR)) [2002/3 **h95**
20s² 20v⁴ 20v 21s³ 22d⁵ Mar 6] sixth foal: sister to winning pointer and half-sister to
several winners, including fairly useful hurdler Barton Ward (by Malaspina), stayed 3m:
dam winning 2m hurdler: completed once from 3 starts in maiden points: modest novice
hurdler: should stay 2¾m: acts on soft going. *D. P. Keane*

BATMAN SENORA (FR) 7 b.g. Chamberlin (FR) – Cartza (FR) (Carmarthen (FR)) **c152**
[2002/3 c151, h117: c22s⁴ c29s² c22d 20s³ 19s² c22s c27v⁴ 20v 20m* Apr 12] rangy ex- **h123**
French gelding: smart chaser: second in 2002 and 2003 runnings of Grand Steeple-Chase
de Paris at Auteuil, making much of running when beaten 10 lengths by Line Marine in
latest renewal in May: poor effort in Prix des Drags there following month: fairly useful
hurdler: first run since leaving P. Rago, only fair form when winning novice at Bangor on
good to firm going in April: ran well at Auteuil following month: stays 29f: raced mainly
on going softer than good (acts on heavy): usually blinkered: races prominently. *Ian
Williams*

BATOUTOFTHEBLUE 10 br.g. Batshoof – Action Belle (Auction Ring (USA)) **h–**
[2002/3 h101: 16mᵖᵘ Oct 4] quite good-topped gelding: fair hurdler: poor effort on
reappearance: will stay beyond 25f: acts on good to firm going: has hung/carried head
awkwardly under pressure and is not an easy ride: sold 500 gns Doncaster October Sales,
soundly beaten in point in April. *G. A. Swinbank*

BATSWING 8 b.g. Batshoof – Magic Milly (Simply Great (FR)) [2002/3 c132, h124: **c121**
c16d⁶ c20dᵖᵘ c16vʳᵒ c16d⁴ 16d c16g⁵ Apr 3] lengthy gelding: fairly useful handicap **h–**
hurdler: progressed into useful chaser in 2001/2, winning handicap at Punchestown final
start: generally out of sorts in 2002/3, respectable third in same race in early-May: raced
mainly around 2m (found stamina stretched at testing 21f): acts on good to firm and heavy
going: tried in cheekpieces: usually sound jumper. *B. Ellison*

BATTEN DOWN (IRE) 5 b.g. Glacial Storm (USA) – Dikler Gale (IRE) (Strong **h81 +**
Gale) [2002/3 F16g 25g 16g Mar 16] IR £17,000 3-y-o: rather leggy gelding: sixth foal: **F78**
half-brother to poor hurdler Cockpit Lady (by Commanche Run), stays 3m, and bumper
winner Ballynattin Buck (by Buckskin): dam unraced, from family of The Dikler: won
Irish point in 2002: modest form only run in bumper: better effort over hurdles when
seventh of 17 in maiden at Ludlow final outing: should be suited by further than 2m.
Jonjo O'Neill

BATTLE LINE 4 b.g. Brief Truce (USA) – Forest Heights (Slip Anchor) [2002/3 16v **h–**
16d 16vᵇᵈ 16s 16v Feb 13] compact gelding: modest and unreliable maiden on Flat (stays
1½m, tried blinkered/visored): showed little over hurdles. *E. McNamara, Ireland*

BATTLE WARNING 8 b.g. Warning – Royal Ballet (IRE) (Sadler's Wells (USA)) **h109**
[2002/3 19d² 24dᵖᵘ 19d* 20v² 22d² 21m⁴ 24mᵖᵘ Apr 16] angular gelding: fair on Flat
(stays 2¼m): fair novice hurdler: won at Doncaster in January: should stay beyond 2¾m:
acts on good to soft and good to firm going: blinkered sixth start. *P. Bowen*

BAY ISLAND (IRE) 7 b. or br.g. Treasure Hunter – Wild Deer (Royal Buck) [2002/3 **c94**
c–, h–: c24s* c26m* c23m* c24d³ c25d² c24dᵖᵘ Mar 19] tall gelding: has had wind **h–**
operation: modest chaser: improved form when winning handicaps at Bangor, Warwick
(amateurs) and Leicester in autumn: pulled up as if something amiss final outing: stays
3¼m: acts on soft and good to firm going: usually tongue tied: front runner: tends to jump
right. *Mrs H. Dalton*

BAY LEGEND (IRE) 5 b.g. Toulon – Kabarda (Relkino) [2002/3 F17m May 3] **F–**
seventh foal: dam unraced: favourite, ran as if amiss when tailed off in bumper on debut.
M. Pitman

BAY MAGIC (IRE) 10 b.g. Ela-Mana-Mou – Come In (Be My Guest (USA)) [2002/3 **c90**
h88: 20d³ c20v* c22vᶠ c21s⁵ c21v⁴ 24v² 24v⁴ 20d⁶ c25s² c24g⁵ Apr 23] plain gelding: **h87**
modest maiden hurdler: of similar standard over fences, left J. H. Johnson after winning
weak handicap at Hexham in November: effective at 2½m to 25f: acts on heavy and good
to firm going: effective blinkered or not, often wears cheekpieces: sometimes let down by
jumping. *Miss Lucinda V. Russell*

BAY OF DREAMS 4 ch.g. Salse (USA) – Cantico (Green Dancer (USA)) [2002/3 **h–**
16d⁴ 17d⁶ 16s 17d 17g Mar 16] brother to Supreme Novices' Hurdle winner Sausalito
Bay: poor maiden on Flat (should be suited by at least 1¼m) for I. Balding: showed little
over hurdles. *R. M. Stronge*

BAY OF PLENTY 9 b.m. Teenoso (USA) – Bara Peg (Random Shot) [2002/3 16m⁶ **h76**
19mᶠ Jun 4] lengthy, good-topped mare: poor maiden hurdler, off 13 months prior to
reappearance: stays 19f: acts on good to firm and heavy going. *P. J. Hobbs*

B B BOY 7 br.g. Arctic Lord – Belle Muguet (Bargello) [2002/3 F–: c25dᵖᵘ c16gᶠ c20g⁴ **c86**
c20m⁴ Mar 23] medium-sized gelding: modest novice chaser: stays 2½m: acts on good to
firm ground: sold 7,000 gns Doncaster May Sales. *K. C. Bailey*

BDELLIUM 5 b.m. Royal Vulcan – Kelly's Logic (Netherkelly) [2002/3 F16g F17g **F–**
Mar 15] third foal: dam unraced half-sister to fairly useful out-and-out staying chaser The
Malakarma: little show in 2 bumpers. *B. I. Case*

BE A BETTER BOY 7 b.g. Primitive Rising (USA) – Carat Stick (Gold Rod) [2002/3 **h–**
24dᵖᵘ Jun 6] fifth foal: brother to winning chaser Pillaging Pict, stays 3m: dam fair staying
hurdler/chaser: no show in novice hurdle: won maiden point in April. *J. B. Walton*

BEACHCOMBER BAY (IRE) 8 ch.g. Un Desperado (FR) – Beachcomber Lass **c130**
(Day Is Done) [2002/3 h130, F89: 20g* c20v³ c17s² c20sᵘʳ c17s⁵ c18d* c16d³ c20gᶠ Mar **h99 +**
30] lengthy gelding: useful hurdler: won novice at Gowran very early in season: useful
novice chaser: won easily at same course in February and Punchestown (by 3½ lengths
from Ground Ball) in early-May: stays 2½m when conditions aren't testing: raced on
good going or softer (acts on heavy). *N. Meade, Ireland*

BEACON HILL LASS 5 b.m. Reprimand – Wild Moon (USA) (Arctic Tern (USA)) **h–**
[2002/3 16mᵖᵘ 21mᵖᵘ 17dᵘʳ Aug 2] half-sister to modest hurdler up to 21f Wild Hadeer
(by Hadeer): well held in 2 sellers at 2 yrs for C. Fairhurst: failed to complete in 3 races
over hurdles, jumping poorly. *R. Ford*

BEACON VALE (IRE) 7 ch.g. Forest Wind (USA) – Pam Story (Sallust) [2002/3 **h–**
20dᵖᵘ Oct 12] medium-sized gelding: thrice-raced maiden on Flat, sold out of
M. Meagher's stable 1,000 gns Doncaster June (1999) Sales: none too fluent in novice on
hurdling debut. *G. Barnett*

BEAMISH (IRE) 9 ch.g. Caesar Imperator (FR) – Super Slaney (Brave Invader **c–**
(USA)) [2002/3 h–: c19vᵖᵘ c23dᵘʳ Jan 27] little sign of ability over hurdles or in 2 novice **h–**
chases: tried visored. *P. C. Ritchens*

BEANBOY 5 ch.g. Clantime – Lady Blues Singer (Chief Singer) [2002/3 17mᵖᵘ 20dᶠ **h–**
Oct 25] poor maiden on Flat (stays 1¼m): failed to complete both outings over hurdles.
Mrs S. Lamyman

BEAR ON BOARD (IRE) 8 b.g. Black Monday – Under The River (Over The River **c115**
(FR)) [2002/3 c24vᵖᵘ c25s³ c23s³ c24v* c26s² Mar 15] well-made gelding: fair hurdler: **h–**
missed 2001/2, reportedly with tendon trouble: fairly useful from over fences, winning
handicap at Bangor in March: stays 3¼m: acts on heavy going. *A. King*

BEASLEY 4 b.g. First Trump – Le Shuttle (Presidium) [2002/3 16sᶠ 18m⁴ 16f³ 16g **h77**
18d 16v⁴ Dec 20] poor and ungenuine maiden on Flat (stays 7f): poor juvenile hurdler:
acts on any going: has worn visor/cheekpieces: needs to improve jumping: sold 900 gns
Doncaster January Sales. *M. Pitman*

BEAT THE HEAT (IRE) 5 b.g. Salse (USA) – Summer Trysting (USA) (Alleged **h104**
(USA)) [2002/3 16d³ 17v² 16m³ 16g⁵ Jan 18] angular ex-Irish gelding: fairly useful on
Flat (stays 1½m), trained at 3 yrs by D. Weld: fair novice hurdler: will stay beyond 17f:
acts on heavy going: blinkered final start. *Jedd O'Keeffe*

BEAT THE RETREAT 8 b.g. Terimon – Carpet Slippers (Daring March) [2002/3 **c90**
h103: 22d³ 20dᵖᵘ 16dᵖᵘ 17d³ 16mᵖᵘ 17m c20m² Apr 21] medium-sized gelding: modest **h85**
novice hurdler: similar form when second of 3 in novice at Huntingdon on chasing debut:
probably stays 2½m: acts on good to soft ground, probably on good to firm: inconsistent.
A. King

BEAT THE RING (IRE) 5 br.g. Tagula (IRE) – Pursue (Auction Ring (USA)) **h92**
[2002/3 h88: 16m³ May 9] little form on Flat: improved effort over hurdles (not knocked
about first 3 starts) when third in handicap at Southwell: should stay beyond 2m.
C. A. Dwyer

BEAUANARROW (IRE) 8 b.g. Beau Sher – Ardnasagh Rose (Crash Course) **c–**
[2002/3 c93, h74, F99: c19gᶠ May 4] good-topped gelding: won Irish point in 2001: fairly **h–**
useful bumper winner: poor form on hurdling debut, modest form over fences: should
stay at least 2½m: acts on good to firm and heavy going. *N. M. Babbage*

BEAU BRUN (FR) 7 b. or br.g. Cadoudal (FR) – Atakaia (FR) (Ataxerxes (GER))   h–
[2002/3 h–: 22d^{pu} 24g^{pu} Sep 15] lengthy gelding: lightly raced and no form over hurdles:
joined G. Balding. *Graeme Roe*

BEAU CASTLE (IRE) 11 b.g. Castle Keep – Temba (Beau Chapeau) [2002/3 c20m^{ur} c92
c21m^4 c16d^{pu} c22m^{pu} Mar 21] compact gelding: winning hurdler: would have gone close   h–
to winning novice hunter chase at Huntingdon in May but for unseating last: stays 2¾m:
acts on good to firm going: has had tongue tied. *Mrs K. Lawther*

BEAUCHAMP MAGIC 8 b.g. Northern Park (USA) – Beauchamp Buzz (High Top)   h–
[2002/3 16g^6 19s 27s Mar 11] lengthy gelding: modest on Flat (stays 2m): little worthwhile form over hurdles: left M. Usher after reappearance: tried blinkered/tongue tied.
K. R. Burke

BEAUCHAMP NYX 7 b.m. Northern Park (USA) – Beauchamp Image (Midyan   h–
(USA)) [2002/3 24g^3 22s Nov 8] lengthy mare: of little account on Flat and well beaten
both starts over hurdles. *P. A. Pritchard*

BEAUCHAMP ORACLE 6 gr.g. Mystiko (USA) – Beauchamp Cactus (Niniski   F–
(USA)) [2002/3 F16m Oct 30] £5,300 5-y-o: lengthy, unfurnished gelding: fifth foal:
half-brother to winning 2¼m hurdler Beauchamp Noble (by Northern Park), later 1m
winner in Italy: dam 17.6f winner: soundly beaten in bumper on debut. *A. J. Chamberlain*

BEAUFORT ZERO 9 b.g. Strong Gale – Miss Roulette (Mummy's Game) [2002/3   h–
25g^5 24g^{pu} Apr 21] rangy gelding: lightly raced and little worthwhile form over hurdles.
C. P. Morlock

BEAU JAKE (IRE) 8 b.g. Jolly Jake (NZ) – Cool Mary (Beau Charmeur (FR))   c97 ?
[2002/3 h65, F88: c16s^5 c24s^5 c26s^F 26g^6 c24m^3 Apr 2] poor maiden hurdler: seemingly   h–
modest form in novice chases first 2 starts in 2002/3: probably stays 3¼m: acts on soft
going, bumper form on good to firm. *N. M. Babbage*

BEAULY (IRE) 8 b.g. Beau Sher – Woodland Theory (Sheer Grit) [2002/3 20v 20s   h63
20v 17f* 19m^3 Apr 15] IR 4,400 4-y-o: good-topped gelding: second foal: dam ran twice:
fell in maiden point on debut in 2002: poor form over hurdles last 2 starts, winning
conditional jockeys novice handicap at Exeter in March: stays 19f: acts on firm going,
possibly unsuited by soft/heavy. *J. G. M. O'Shea*

BEAU ROBERTO 9 b.g. Robellino (USA) – Night Jar (Night Shift (USA)) [2002/3   h79
22m^2 20s^5 Nov 16] poor on Flat (stays 2m) nowadays: lightly-raced novice hurdler,
modest form at best: reportedly lame final start. *J. S. Goldie*

BEAUSEJOUR (USA) 5 ch.m. Diesis – Libeccio (NZ) (Danzatore (CAN)) [2002/3   h70
16s^F 20v^5 16d 16g Mar 25] poor and unreliable maiden on Flat (stays 9.7f): poor form
over hurdles. *B. G. Powell*

BEAU TORERO (FR) 5 gr.g. True Brave (USA) – Brave Lola (FR) (Dom Pasquini   c75
(FR)) [2002/3 F16m^3 F12g 16d 16d 20v 16g c16d^5 Apr 9] lengthy, useful-looking   h–
gelding: first foal: dam ran once: close third in bumper on debut: poor form over hurdles   F92
and in novice on chasing debut: ran as if amiss second and fifth starts: sold 3,100 gns
Doncaster May Sales. *Mrs L. C. Taylor*

BEAU TUDOR (IRE) 9 b.g. Aragon – Sunley Silks (Formidable (USA)) [2002/3   h–
16d^{pu} Mar 5] little form on Flat and showed nothing on hurdling debut. *Miss L. C. Siddall*

BEAVER LODGE (IRE) 6 gr.g. Grand Lodge (USA) – Thistlewood (Kalamoun)   h114
[2002/3 h107: 21d^6 19s* 22d^4 20d 20g Mar 25] workmanlike gelding: fair handicap
hurdler: won at Market Rasen in December: stays 2¾m: acts on good to firm and heavy
going. *C. J. Mann*

BECKDALE 7 b.g. Perpendicular – Knocksharry (Palm Track) [2002/3 c–, h76: 16m^{pu} c–
16v^3 17s^6 17s^5 21v^{pu} Jan 21] strong gelding: winning hurdler: no worthwhile form in   h–
2002/3: tried blinkered: has flashed tail: possibly ungenuine. *Andrew Turnell*

BECKLEY (IRE) 7 b.g. Phardante (FR) – Baybush (Boreen (FR)) [2002/3 h75, F94:   h104 p
16d^4 20v^{pu} 20d* Apr 25] tall gelding: will make a chaser: much improved effort over
hurdles when winning novice handicap at Perth: stays 2½m: has pulled hard: type to keep
on progressing. *C. Grant*

BECKON 7 ch.m. Beveled (USA) – Carolynchristensen (Sweet Revenge) [2002/3   h70
16m^3 Oct 7] modest up to 1½m on Flat (not an easy ride): poor form when third of 5 in
claimer at Plumpton on hurdling debut: sold to join R. Wilman 2,200 gns Newmarket
Autumn Sales. *B. R. Johnson*

BED BUG (FR) 5 b.g. Double Bed (FR) – Cotation (FR) (Recitation (USA)) [2002/3 **h99** F16g F16d⁴ 19d⁵ 19d 16m³ 16m* Apr 21] 46,000 3-y-o: unfurnished gelding: half- **F93** brother to 3 winners in France, including Escroquerie (by Sicyos), successful up to 1m: dam won up to 1¼m at 2 yrs in France: fair form on second of 2 starts in bumpers: best effort over hurdles when winning novice handicap at Fakenham: may prove best around 2m: acts on good to firm going. *N. J. Henderson*

BEDE (IRE) 7 b.g. Spanish Place (USA) – Midnight Oil (Menelek) [2002/3 h86, F85: **c–** c19g May 1] workmanlike gelding: some promise in bumper/novice hurdles: folded **h–** tamely in novice handicap on chase debut: should stay 2½m: sold 7,000 gns Doncaster May Sales prior to showing little in points. *P. J. Hobbs*

BEDFORD LEADER 5 b.m. Bedford (USA) – Neladar (Ardar) [2002/3 F16s F18v **F–** Feb 10] first foal: dam poor maiden pointer: little show in 2 bumpers. *A. P. Jones*

BEE AN BEE (IRE) 6 b.g. Phardante (FR) – Portia's Delight (IRE) (The Parson) **h110** [2002/3 F95: 20d⁶ 22d⁴ 16s² 17d* 17s 20v² 21s⁴ 20gF Apr 2] well-made gelding: fair novice hurdler: won handicap at Exeter in December: stays 21f: raced on good going or softer (acts on heavy): visored last 2 starts. *P. Winkworth*

BEECHBROOK GALE (IRE) 7 b.g. Toulon – Swan Upping (Lord Gayle (USA)) **c–** [2002/3 c79: c25gF c21d⁶ Dec 5] lengthy gelding: in frame all completed starts in Irish points: signs of only a little ability in steeplechases. *John R. Upson*

BEECHCOURT 6 b.g. Son Pardo – Calametta (Oats) [2002/3 F110: 16s² 16s³ 16s² **h110** Dec 1] tall gelding: useful bumper winner: fair form when placed all 3 starts in maiden/ **F–** novice hurdles: raced at 2m on good to soft/soft going: has hung left and found little. *M. J. P. O'Brien, Ireland*

BEECHES GIRL 8 b.m. Lord Americo – Phyll-Tarquin (Tarqogan) [2002/3 c–, h–: **c– §** c19dpu 22m⁴ 17g⁴ 20s⁵ 21g² 21gpu 16s³ 16v³ 16d³ 17g⁴ Mar 22] good-topped mare: no form **h71 §** over fences: poor maiden hurdler: best efforts around 2m: acts on soft going: tried blinkered: ungenuine: claimed £3,000 final start. *R. Dickin*

BEECHWOOD 5 b.g. Fraam – Standard Rose (Ile de Bourbon (USA)) [2002/3 F16g⁴ **F95** F16g⁴ F16d³ F16g⁴ Mar 16] lengthy, good sort: second foal: half-brother to 8.5f winner El Pedro (by Piccolo) and winner in Germany by Interrex: dam, fair hurdler who stayed 3m, also won on Flat: fairly useful form in bumpers, in frame at Wincanton (twice), Doncaster and Ludlow. *Miss H. C. Knight*

BEEDULUP 8 br.g. Perpendicular – Biloela (Nicholas Bill) [2002/3 c21g⁵ c16gpu 21s **c–** 21g⁶ 22d⁴ 22m² 20g² 21g² 21f⁵ 20g⁴ Apr 21] leggy gelding: placed in 2 maiden points **h75** in 2002: no form in 2 novice chases: poor hurdler: won conditional jockeys selling handicap at Cartmel in August: sold out of J. A. Moore's stable 6,000 gns Doncaster November Sales before final start: stays 2¾m: acts on good to firm and good to soft going. *P. Wegmann*

BEEF OR SALMON (IRE) 7 ch.g. Cajetano (USA) – Farinella (IRE) (Salmon **c165 p** Leap (USA)) [2002/3 h133, F107: c20v* c16s* c24v* c24s* c26gF Mar 13] **h–**

Even in an era in which it has become the norm for good novice chasers to take their chance outside novice company, either in conditions races or top handicaps, the 2002/3 campaign set out for Beef Or Salmon took such a fighting policy to the ultimate extreme: Beef Or Salmon was the top novice chaser in 2002/3 but he never ran in a race restricted to novices. Instead, he won his first four starts in graded races open to all and then fell at the third when second favourite to Best Mate for the Tote Cheltenham Gold Cup in March. In form terms, his achievements don't quite match those of the best novices of recent years. Strong Promise, Danoli, Escartefigue, Florida Pearl (who didn't race outside novice company), Beau and Gloria Victis in the preceding six seasons all showed better form as a novice and Beef Or Salmon's early departure at Cheltenham left questions unanswered about whether he is a serious challenger to Best Mate or merely a horse that has made the very most of his opportunities under one set of conditions.

Much was made of Beef Or Salmon's lack of experience in the build-up to the Gold Cup, but there never seemed any doubt on the part of trainer Michael Hourigan that the Gold Cup rather than the Royal & SunAlliance Chase for novices should be the Cheltenham target. Hourigan had trained Dorans Pride to finish third in the 1997 Gold Cup on just his sixth start over fences and there were a few examples of horses who had won the blue riband with little more experience than

Beef Or Salmon—although not as a novice, Dawn Run won the 1986 Gold Cup on her fifth appearance over fences and Best Mate himself had had just six runs in chases before his success in 2002. The supposed dangers of running relatively inexperienced horses in the Gold Cup had been well aired after Gloria Victis' death in the 2000 renewal which he contested after just six appearances in chases. Just as that horse's performance in winning the Racing Post Chase on his previous outing had shown he was well worth his place in the line-up, Beef Or Salmon too had more business being in the line-up at Cheltenham than most. A race different in tempo to any other he had run in over fences may have played its part in his falling so early in the Gold Cup, but the same would have applied in the SunAlliance.

At the start of the season, any suggestion that Beef Or Salmon might start second favourite for the Cheltenham Gold Cup would have seemed fanciful in the extreme. It is true that he looks every inch a chaser—a strong gelding in appearance —but he had shown no more than useful form in nine races in bumpers and over hurdles in 2001/2 after winning one of his two starts in points and had not demonstrated that he stayed beyond two and a quarter miles. On his first appearance in a steeplechase, in the Grade 2 Morris Oil Chase at Clonmel in November, Beef Or Salmon beat a horse that a year earlier had been ante-post favourite for the Gold Cup, though an impressive three-and-a-half-length victory, in receipt of 13 lb from Sackville, wasn't quite the performance it would have been then. Three weeks later, in the Grade 3 O'Connell Transport Hilly Way Chase at Cork, Beef Or Salmon was dropped back to two miles and failed quite to repeat his debut form, a below-par effort from the favourite Fadoudal du Cochet leaving Beef Or Salmon the straightforward task of seeing off the outsider River Clodagh. Beef Or Salmon clearly had the potential to be a smart novice but reported plans about going for the Gold Cup seemed premature at the time. Twelve days later, success in the Ericsson put such claims in a different light.

The Ericsson has become one of the most significant chases run in Ireland, in recent seasons not far behind the Hennessy Cognac Gold Cup at Leopardstown and the more recently instituted Heineken Punchestown Gold Cup in terms of quality. The Hennessy Cognac was the Irish Grade 1 staying chase when the official Anglo-Irish pattern came into being and the Punchestown Gold Cup was accorded similar status when it was introduced in 1999. All told, in 2001/2, there were forty-five races with Grade 1 status scheduled in Britain and Ireland, twenty-five in Britain and twenty in Ireland, of which ten took place at the Punchestown Festival and another four at the Fairyhouse meeting in early-December. Similarly, in Britain, ten Grade 1 races are staged at the Cheltenham Festival, three at the King George meeting at Kempton and four at Aintree, three of those at Aintree in cate-

Ericsson Chase, Leopardstown—after the last and still all to play for;
Beef Or Salmon (nearest camera) produces the best finish to collar Colonel Braxton
with Harbour Pilot (far side) third and Foxchapel King fourth

Hennessy Cognac Gold Cup, Leopardstown—another steadily-run Grade 1, with Beef Or Salmon again winning from Colonel Braxton; only the fourth is different, Rince Ri (stripes) filling that spot

gories not catered for at Cheltenham. The aim of the pattern appeared to be to provide a limited number of championship races, at most four, in each category in the hope of bringing together the very best in Britain and Ireland. Things haven't worked so well as they might have. Conservative thinking on the part of trainers, Grade 1 races that fail to offer sufficiently richer rewards than supposedly lesser races closer to home and poor placement within the schedule have all contributed to this. The British Horseracing Board has also allowed Newbury and Sandown, with the AON Chase and the valuable conditions races at the end-of-season meeting, to stage races that detract from established Grade 1 races staged in Ireland, partly as a result of which the Irish authorities have taken the view that they are better promoting their own races, rather than trying to reach an accommodation with the British. Five new Grade 1 races, as well as increases in the numbers at lower levels, were created in 2002/3, the James Nicholson at Down Royal, the Deloitte And Touche Novices' Hurdle, the Dr P. J. Moriarty Novices' Chase, the December Festival Hurdle and the Ericsson. The Anglo-Irish pattern is to all intents and purposes dead. Ireland now has no fewer than four Grade 1 chases at around three miles, one of them clearly not a championship standard race, and with Britain having just two there may be pressure to promote other British events to Grade 1 status. It goes without saying that courses (and trainers) will want more, rather than fewer, with the clear danger that the pattern will become devalued. By definition, there can only be a finite number of championship races.

The first running of the Ericsson as a Grade 1 event, two days after the King George VI Chase at Kempton, attracted two top-class chasers on the comeback trail, the former King George winner First Gold and Rince Ri who had won the Ericsson in 1999 and 2000. Beef Or Salmon also faced the 2001 winner Foxchapel King as well as Sackville and two of the better Irish novices of the previous season, Colonel Braxton and Harbour Pilot. Beef Or Salmon, receiving 5 lb from all his rivals (a penalty scale in any supposed championship race is surely a contradiction), started third favourite behind First Gold and Rince Ri. On testing ground, Colonel Braxton and Foxchapel King set a steady pace, Beef Or Salmon, running over three miles for the first time, travelling well and jumping safely held up in rear. The race only really took shape after two out, Beef Or Salmon making good progress at that stage and impressing with his turn of foot as he pulled clear after the last, going on to beat Colonel Braxton by six lengths with Harbour Pilot staying on late for third.

With First Gold the first beaten and Rince Ri also well below his best, there were clear grounds for questioning the value of the form and single figure odds about Beef Or Salmon for Cheltenham seemed stingy, though it was still some performance from a horse having only his third start in steeplechases, the best by any novice at such an early stage of his career since Florida Pearl won the SunAlliance.

Six weeks after the Ericsson there was a rematch in the Hennessy Cognac Gold Cup with Colonel Braxton and Harbour Pilot, as well as Rince Ri, a field of five completed by Florida Pearl. It is a measure of the change in fortunes that, even on terms 5 lb worse, Beef Or Salmon started evens favourite and Rince Ri the outsider of the field at 9/1. The race was a virtual rerun of the Ericsson, though Harbour Pilot shared pacemaking with Colonel Braxton in the absence of Foxchapel King. The pace was again less than true and Beef Or Salmon, turning in another solid round of jumping, was once more able to quicken past his rivals, winning by four lengths from Colonel Braxton with a neck to Harbour Pilot and a further length to Rince Ri. Harbour Pilot came out best of the first three in the Gold Cup itself, finishing third, and Rince Ri ended the campaign showing himself as good as ever with a second-placing in the Punchestown Gold Cup. That was one of two important races Beef Or Salmon missed because of unsuitable ground in the spring, withdrawn on the day after his trainer disagreed with the official assessment of good to yielding. Beef Or Salmon had been due to make his first start in novice company at Fairyhouse earlier in April but missed the two-and-a-half-mile Powers Gold Cup for the same reason. Cheltenham wasn't, though, Beef Or Salmon's final outing in the spring as he won over two miles on the Flat at the Curragh, landing a minor event which Dorans Pride had won in 1999 (the two runnings in between had gone to Knife Edge and Ned Kelly).

Mr B. J. Craig's "Beef Or Salmon"

Beef Or Salmon (IRE)
(ch.g. 1996)

	Cajetano (USA) (b 1986)	Run The Gantlet (b 1968)	Tom Rolfe / First Feather
		Intensive (br 1979)	Sir Wiggle / Flying Legs
	Farinella (IRE) (ch 1988)	Salmon Leap (ch 1980)	Northern Dancer / Fish-Bar
		Boldella (b 1977)	Bold Lad / Ardelle

Beef Or Salmon's rise to the top could hardly have been predicted from his pedigree. His sire Cajetano was listed placed on the Flat, winning four times in France and Switzerland, and a useful handicap hurdler. A half-brother to three stakes winners in the States, he went to stud in Ireland in 1993 but is now based in Sardinia. Beef Or Salmon is the fourth foal out of the once-raced Farinella. Of the previous three, all by Project Manager, Ballyvelig Lady has raced without revealing any ability. More might be expected of Farinella's 2000 filly by Saddlers' Hall who made 52,000 guineas at the 2003 Doncaster May Sales. Beef Or Salmon's grandam Boldella, herself a winner on the Flat, produced four winners over jumps, including the fairly useful two-miler Wally Wallensky and the useful juvenile hurdler Lunulae who finished second to Royal Derbi in the Champion Four Year Old Hurdle at Punchestown. There are some fairly notable Flat winners a little further back in the family, including a couple of names familiar to followers of jumps breeding: the Prix Jean de Chaudenay winner Armos, the sire of Escartefigue's sire Start Fast and the maternal grandsire of Pistolet Bleu, and Phantom Breeze, the sire of Le Coudray and Bilboa. Beef Or Salmon's third dam Ardelle is the dam of Armos and third dam of Phantom Breeze. Beef Or Salmon isn't certain to be suited by a thorough test of stamina. He has raced almost always on soft or heavy going over jumps, making a bad mistake and being hampered on his only appearance on good to soft. He shaped quite well on good in a bumper but is clearly regarded as being ideally suited by softer going. Given the likelihood of finding suitable conditions near to home, not to mention less exacting opposition, it seems probable that Beef Or Salmon's full abilities may only finally be thoroughly tested at Cheltenham. Whether he can jump so fluently and show his turn of foot in a truly-run Gold Cup remains a fascinating question. *Michael Hourigan, Ireland*

BEEFY 7 ch.g. Shining Jewel – Cherry Sip (Nearly A Hand) [2002/3 F16m5 F16g Jul 10] fifth foal: half-brother to fair 2½m chaser Beefy Nova (by Ra Nova): dam pulled up in 2 points: poor form on first of 2 outings in bumpers. *J. R. Best* — **F66**

BEEFY NOVA 11 ch.g. Ra Nova – Cherry Sip (Nearly A Hand) [2002/3 c20s3 c20d6 c20s c20g4 c24g4 c24d c24m5 Apr 22] workmanlike gelding: fair handicap chaser in 2000/1, poor on return: best around 2½m: acts on good to firm and heavy going: has gone in snatches: sketchy jumper: none too consistent. *G. H. Yardley* — **c78 x h–**

BEETHOVEN (IRE) 7 b. or br.g. Yashgan – Adare Princess (Paico) [2002/3 h110, F92: 20s5 Dec 7] lengthy gelding: fairly useful hurdler: collapsed and died after fifth in handicap at Chepstow on reappearance: stayed 2½m: raced only on ground softer than good. *Noel T. Chance* — **h117**

BE FAIR 5 br.g. Blushing Flame (USA) – Tokyo (Mtoto) [2002/3 F97: F17d* F16g* F16g4 F16g F17g2 Apr 5] well-made gelding: useful bumper performer: won first 3 starts, including at Newton Abbot and Worcester in September: very good second to Classic Native, pair clear, in Grade 2 at Aintree final outing. *D. E. Cantillon* — **F114**

BEFORE THE MAST (IRE) 6 br.g. Broken Hearted – Kings Reserve (King's Ride) [2002/3 F108: F16d3 Oct 23] rangy, rather unfurnished gelding: promising second to Lord Sam in bumper at Sandown on debut in 2001/2: odds on, some way below that form when third at Chepstow 8 months later, and not seen out again. *Noel T. Chance* — **F93**

BEGSY'S BULLET 8 b.m. Primitive Rising (USA) – Seeker's Sister (Ashmore (FR)) [2002/3 16s c20sF 21v* 17v5 c20s c21s2 Mar 11] compact mare: poor hurdler/ chaser, missed 2001/2: made all in mares novice hurdle at Sedgefield in January: will stay beyond 21f: raced only on soft/heavy going. *D. McCain* — **c74 h77**

BEHARI (IRE) 9 b.g. Kahyasi – Berhala (IRE) (Doyoun) [2002/3 h–: 20g c19dpu c23d4 c21sur c23mpu 20g 21m4 20d 20m6 24gpu Sep 15] no longer of any account: often tongue tied. *F. M. Barton* — **c– h–**

Mrs Edward Cantillon's "Be Fair"

BEHAVINGBADLY (IRE)   8 b.g. Lord Americo – Audrey's Turn (Strong Gale)   **c110 x**
[2002/3 h122, F93: c20s c25v³ c24dᶠ c20s⁴ c25v³ c25s² c25s* c32g Mar 21] good-topped   **h–**
gelding: fairly useful hurdler: fair chaser: won 3-finisher handicap at Ayr in March by a
distance: often let down by jumping otherwise: should stay beyond 25f: raced on good
going or softer (acts on heavy). *A. Parker*

BEHRAJAN (IRE)   8 b. or br.g. Arazi (USA) – Behera (Mill Reef (USA)) [2002/3   **c168**
c166+, h158: c24s⁶ c24v* c25s* c26g⁵ c36d Apr 5]   **h–**
'I will keep dropping the marks of the better horses until they start
performing better,' the BHB's senior jumps handicapper Phil Smith was quoted as
saying after the latest Grand National. Handicap weights are usually allotted using
the centrally-stored assessments of the BHB handicapping team, but Smith enjoys
the freedom to produce a one-off for jumping's biggest prize and he has taken to
compressing the weights to favour the top horses. All of which should be good
news for connections of a horse like Behrajan who, even though he carried top
weight of 11-12 in the latest National, ran off a BHB mark 6 lb lower than he would
have had in a 'normal' race against similar opposition at the time. Seeing that
Behrajan came tenth of fourteen finishers at Aintree, seventy-eight lengths behind
the winner Monty's Pass, it seems he might be the subject of even more favourable
treatment in the 2004 National if Mr Smith stays true to his word. No horse carrying
more than 11-0 has won the National since Grittar (11-5) and Corbiere (11-4) in the
early-'eighties but the cracking performances of recent runners-up What's Up Boys
(under 11-6 in 2002) and Suny Bay (12-0 in 1998) should encourage the connections of more good staying chasers to have a tilt at the National, especially now they
look set to receive *relatively* even more favourable handicap marks.

cantorsport.co.uk Silver Cup (Handicap Chase), Ascot—
Behrajan (right) revels in the testing conditions and successfully concedes 20 lb to Exit To Wave

Both Suny Bay and What's Up Boys finished fifth in the Cheltenham Gold Cup before their respective weight-carrying efforts in the National. Behrajan, who incidentally went down to What's Up Boys in one of the closest finishes in the history of the Hennessy, has run in the last two Cheltenham Gold Cups, pulled up in 2002 and finishing a creditable fifth in the latest edition, close behind the horses who filled the minor placings. The big, angular Behrajan is a top-class chaser with the frame for carrying big weights and if his jumping can be made more reliable —he didn't jump well enough to stay in contention from halfway in the latest National—he could make a name for himself one day at Aintree. It is in his favour

Pillar Property Chase, Cheltenham—Behrajan makes the most of another good opportunity

that his programme in the next season is to be geared towards another Grand National challenge and he is unlikely to tackle the Gold Cup again. Behrajan has never fallen but he still takes too many liberties with his fences and will no doubt undergo further intensive reschooling with the ubiquitous Yogi Breisner. Former international three-day-event rider Breisner has enjoyed some notable successes with top chasers in his time and he was called in to tutor Behrajan after he put in a poor round of jumping when tailed off on his reappearance, conceding lumps of weight all round in the Troytown Handicap Chase at Navan in November.

Behrajan jumped better on his next two outings, picking up valuable prizes in the cantorsport.co.uk Silver Cup at Ascot in December and the Pillar Property Chase at Cheltenham in January. Shouldering top weight of 11-12, and conceding between 13 lb and 20 lb to his six rivals, Behrajan led or disputed the lead throughout on heavy going at Ascot and responded very gamely to hold the sustained challenge of runner-up Exit To Wave by a neck, with a distance back to third-placed Zafarabad. Behrajan again made all, being in no danger from the home turn, on soft ground at Cheltenham in a race marred by a fatal injury to the favourite Bacchanal, whose owner also has a share in Behrajan. Behrajan won the Pillar by fourteen lengths from Foly Pleasant but his victory caused barely a ripple in the ante-post market on the Cheltenham Gold Cup. He started at 14/1 in the Gold Cup and, under less testing conditions that were widely expected not to suit him, he stayed on again from the second last after being unable to hold his place among the leaders following a blunder at the eleventh and another mistake at the sixteenth. The Gold Cup was only Behrajan's second race on anything firmer than good to soft as a steeplechaser and his form was only a little below his best. Firmish going didn't seem to inconvenience him over hurdles, when placed efforts in the Stayers' Hurdle at Cheltenham and the Long Distance Hurdle at Haydock, both on good to firm, were as good as any he produced. One thing definitely hasn't changed since Behrajan's hurdling days: he is a thorough stayer who needs all of three miles to bring out the best in him.

The Behrajan Partnership's "Behrajan"

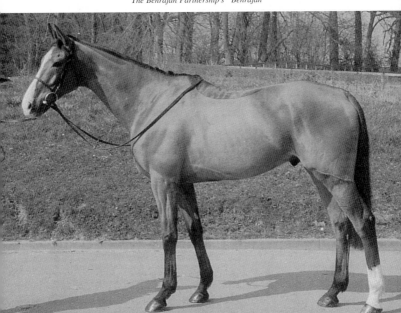

		Arazi (USA)		Blushing Groom		Red God

Behrajan (IRE)
(b. or br.g. 1995)

	Arazi (USA) (ch 1989)	Blushing Groom (ch 1974)	Red God / Runaway Bride
		Danseur Fabuleux (b 1982)	Northern Dancer / Fabuleux Jane
	Behera (b 1986)	Mill Reef (b 1968)	Never Bend / Milan Mill
		Borushka (b 1981)	Bustino / Valdavia

Behrajan's blue-blooded Flat pedigree has been discussed at length in previous Annuals. As was pointed out in *Chasers & Hurdlers 1999/2000*, Behrajan is the last horse you could imagine spinning round the tight turns of an American racetrack, where both his sire Arazi and his dam Behera distinguished themselves. Arazi won a Breeders' Cup Juvenile in breathtaking style, while Prix Saint-Alary winner and Arc runner-up Behera finished a close fourth in a Breeders' Cup Turf. Behera has bred three Flat winners so far for the Aga Khan's studs, the best of them the useful French staying filly Bayrika (by Khayasi). Sir Michael Stoute trained another, Behra (by Grand Lodge), to be placed in listed company in 2002. *H. D. Daly*

BEHZAD (IRE)   4 b.g. Kahyasi – Behriya (IRE) (Kenmare (FR)) [2002/3 F17g³ F17g Apr 5] €2,000 3-y-o: sturdy gelding: first foal: dam unraced half-sister to very smart hurdler/top-class chaser Behrajan, stays 3¼m: 16/1, keeping-on 2 lengths third of 8 to Alf Lauren in bumper at Bangor on debut: tailed off in Grade 2 at Aintree 2 weeks later: will be suited by further than 17f. *D. McCain*   **F84**

BEKSTAR   8 b.m. Nicholas Bill – Murex (Royalty) [2002/3 h82: 22f⁴ 22g* 22m² 17g⁵ 20s⁵ 24g 19f 20m Apr 12] lengthy, rather sparely-made mare: modest handicap hurdler: won at Newton Abbot in June: lost form after next outing, sweating badly on first occasion: stays 2¾m: acts on firm and good to soft going. *J. C. Tuck*   **h97 d**

BELARUS (IRE)   11 b.g. Waajib – Kavali (Blakeney) [2002/3 c25gᴿ Mar 18] fair pointer: novice hurdler/chaser, moody effort (refused eleventh) in hunter at Exeter in March: stays 25f: acts on good to soft going: often blinkered. *Mrs T. White*   **c– §** / **h–**

BELISARIO (IRE)   9 b. or br.g. Distinctly North (USA) – Bold Kate (Bold Lad (IRE)) [2002/3 c116, h–: c20d³ c24d Mar 15] big, leggy gelding: fair chaser: shaped encouragingly after year's absence on reappearance, but very disappointing next time: better around 3m than shorter: acts on heavy and good to firm going. *M. W. Easterby*   **c108** / **h–**

BELITLIR   11 b.m. Lir – Kimberley Ann (St Columbus) [2002/3 c–, h–: 22g c21g⁴ c26g⁵ c21g⁴ Jul 31] leggy mare: little form outside points. *Miss S. Young*   **c–** / **h–**

BELLA BRIO (IRE)   5 b.m. Shernazar – Spin A Coin (Torus) [2002/3 F17m F17m⁵ F16g Apr 1] seventh foal: half-sister to fair chaser Broguestown Breeze (by Montelimar), stays 3¼m, and bumper winner Native Coin (by Be My Native): dam unraced half-sister to high-class staying chaser Run For Free and smart staying hurdler/chaser Banker's Benefit: well held in 3 bumpers. *G. A. Harker*   **F–**

BELLACACCIA (IRE)   7 ch.m. Beau Sher – Game Gambler (IRE) (Long Pond) [2002/3 F84: 21m⁶ 16g⁴ 20sᵇᵈ 20sᶠ 20s 20g³ Apr 1] small, sparely-made mare: poor novice hurdler: will stay 3m: acts on soft going (bumper form on good to firm): jumps none too fluently. *C. W. Thornton*   **h79**

BELLAFICIENT (IRE)   4 b. or br.g. Revoque (IRE) – Efficient Funding (IRE) (Entitled) [2002/3 16s 16s⁶ 16s² 16s³ 16d⁴ Feb 15] no form at 2 yrs: fairly useful form in juvenile maiden hurdles, placed in large fields at Fairyhouse (second to Harchibald) and Naas (third to Smuggler's Song) prior to winning 20-runner event at Gowran comfortably by 2½ lengths from Laoch Na Mara: raced only on going softer than good. *M. Halford, Ireland*   **h112**

BELLA MARY   8 b.m. Derrylin – Pro-Token (Proverb) [2002/3 19g⁴ 20sᵖᵘ 16s³ 16s² 16v 16dᵖᵘ 21s 17mᵖᵘ Apr 26] workmanlike mare: novice hurdler, poor on balance: should stay 2½m: bled from nose sixth outing. *C. T. Pogson*   **h92 ?**

BELLA'S PRINCESS   9 b. or br.m. Broadsword (USA) – Kathy Cook (Glenstal (USA)) [2002/3 20d⁶ 20gᵖᵘ 24g⁶ Sep 15] little sign of ability, including in points. *R. J. Smith*   **h–**

BELLE D'ANJOU (FR)   6 b.m. Saint Cyrien (FR) – Epsibelle (IRE) (Darshaan) [2002/3 h126: 16f c16gᵖᵘ 17m⁶ 17g Mar 13] small, leggy mare: fairly useful hurdler in   **c–** / **h–**

first half of 2001/2: well beaten in handicaps in 2002/3, left M. Pipe after reappearance: reportedly struck into when pulled up after second on chasing debut: stays 19f when emphasis is on speed: has won on soft going, best efforts in Britain on good or firmer. *P. J. Hobbs*

BELLE DERRIERE   8 b.m. Kylian (USA) – Metannee (The Brianstan) [2002/3 h–: c24s^{bd} Mar 10] angular mare: winning 2m hurdler: third in point in March: brought down first in novice hunter chase at Stratford: tried blinkered. *J. A. Danahar*   **c– h–**

BELLE D'ORSINI (FR)   8 ch.m. Le Nain Jaune (FR) – Ma Belle (FR) (Lightning (FR)) [2002/3 h–: 19m^F Oct 19] leggy, angular mare: showed traces of stringhalt: fairly useful handicap hurdler at best in 2000/1: stayed 2½m: acted on heavy going: dead. *Jonjo O'Neill*   **h–**

BELLEFLEUR   6 b.m. Alflora (IRE) – Isabeau (Law Society (USA)) [2002/3 F70: 20v 20d⁴ 16d⁵ 25d^{pu} 20d³ Mar 6] sturdy mare: poor form in bumpers and over hurdles (possibly flattered final outing): has carried head awkwardly. *J. M. Jefferson*   **h75**

BELLINO EMPRESARIO (IRE)   5 b.g. Robellino (USA) – The Last Empress (IRE) (Last Tycoon) [2002/3 19g^{pu} Apr 19] angular gelding: modest on Flat (stays 11f), successful twice in 2002, sold out of I. Wood's stable 4,800 gns Doncaster September Sales: failed to settle on hurdling debut. *B. Llewellyn*   **h–**

BELLINO SPIRIT (IRE)   7 b.m. Robellino (USA) – Working Model (Ile de Bourbon (USA)) [2002/3 h71: 20d 20s² 20d c25v⁵ c21v* c21s^{pu} Mar 11] poor maiden hurdler: poor chaser: won mares novice at Sedgefield in February: should stay beyond 21f: raced on going softer than good (acts on heavy). *M. Todhunter*   **c73 h71**

BELL LANE LAD (IRE)   6 b.g. Wakashan – Busti Lass (IRE) (Bustineto) [2002/3 F–: F16d 22d 20v 22s^{pu} 20m* Apr 12] useful-looking gelding: modest form second start in bumpers: first run for 4 months and after leaving J. Jenkins, much improved effort over hurdles when winning 18-runner handicap at Bangor: should stay beyond 2½m: acts on good to firm going. *A. King*   **h79 F77**

BELLMANEAR   5 b.m. Alflora (IRE) – Mirthful (Will Somers) [2002/3 F16m F16m Apr 10] twelfth foal: half-sister to useful 2m hurdlers Simenon (by Oats) and State Jester (by Free State) and to bumper winner by Relkino: dam placed over hurdles/successful around 1¼m on Flat: well held in 2 bumpers. *M. F. Harris*   **F–**

BELLOC   8 gr.g. Arzanni – Princess Story (Prince de Galles) [2002/3 h62: 26s^{pu} Nov 23] workmanlike gelding: runner-up twice in bumpers: little form over hurdles: tongue tied both runs in 2001/2. *Mrs D. Haine*   **h–**

BELL TEX (IRE)   11 br.g. Orchestra – Lyngard (Balliol) [2002/3 h74: 19m Apr 15] poor novice hurdler, lightly raced: stays 2½m: acts on good to firm going. *J. C. Fox*   **h–**

BELL TOR (IRE)   6 b.m. King's Ride – Shannon Juliette (Julio Mariner) [2002/3 F77: 20v^{pu} 20d^{pu} 20v² 19m⁶ Mar 21] poor novice hurdler: will stay beyond 2½m: hung left third outing. *D. R. Gandolfo*   **h78**

BELSKI   10 br.g. Arctic Lord – Bellekino (Relkino) [2002/3 c25d² c26g^{pu} c21g² c16m² c20m² Aug 23] winning pointer: sold out of Mrs L. Young's stable £2,250 (privately) Ascot June Sales after second outing: modest form when runner-up in novice chases all 3 subsequent starts: likely to prove better around 2½m than shorter: acts on good to firm going. *C. Tizzard*   **c97**

BELVENTO (IRE)   11 b.g. Strong Gale – Salufair (Salluceva) [2002/3 c26m* c20s^{pu} c20g² c24d^{pu} c26m⁴ Apr 19] good sort: fairly useful pointer/hunter chaser: won novice hunter at Folkestone (for N. Gifford) in May: form after only on third start: stays 3¼m: best efforts on good/good to firm ground: none too consistent. *J. T. Gifford*   **c99 § h–**

BELVOIR (IRE)   8 b.g. Husyan (USA) – Coumeenoole Lady (The Parson) [2002/3 16s Nov 16] IR 16,000 4-y-o: first foal: dam, fair winning Irish 2½m hurdler, half-sister to useful Irish chaser up to 2¾m An Maineach: completed once from 4 starts in maiden Irish points: no show on hurdling debut. *Miss Lucinda V. Russell*   **h–**

BE MY ADELINA (IRE)   5 b.m. Be My Native (USA) – Adelinas Leader (IRE) (Supreme Leader) [2002/3 F17m³ Apr 15] IR £12,000 3-y-o, 19,000 4-y-o: first foal: dam, winning pointer, half-sister to high-class 2m to 2½m chaser Travado: 7/1 from 5/2, around 2 lengths third of 9 to demoted Mrs Philip in mares bumper at Exeter on debut. *P. F. Nicholls*   **F88**

*IAWS Thyestes Handicap Chase, Gowran—the front-running Be My Belle picks up this valuable prize;
Takagi and Kirmar are second and third respectively*

BE MY BELLE (IRE)   7 b.m. Be My Native (USA) – Boreen Belle (Boreen (FR))
[2002/3 h139, F81: c24s² c25s* c20s⁴ c24v* c21v³ c24s* c20s³ c22s² Mar 16] strong
mare: useful hurdler: similar level over fences: made all in maiden at Fairyhouse and
Grade 2 novice at Leopardstown in December and IAWS Thyestes Handicap Chase at
Gowran (beat Takagi 2½ lengths) in January: well below form last 2 starts, unable to
dominate after being reluctant to race on first occasion: better around 3m than shorter:
goes well on soft/heavy going. *S. J. Treacy, Ireland*   **c133 h–**

BE MY BETTER HALF (IRE)   8 b.g. Be My Native (USA) – The Mrs (Mandalus)
[2002/3 c114, h84p: c18d² c20v* Mar 8] seventh of 17 in maiden on hurdling debut in
2001/2: fair form in maiden chases, winning at Navan in March: will stay beyond 2¾m:
acts on heavy going. *A. L. T. Moore, Ireland*   **c114 h–**

BE MY DESTINY (IRE)   6 b.g. Be My Native (USA) – Miss Cali (Young Man (FR))
[2002/3 F90: 16g 17s² 17v* 17v² 20v⁵ Mar 8] tall gelding: chasing type: fair novice
hurdler: won at Folkestone in January easily by 7 lengths from What's The Count: second
to Hale Bopp there following month, better subsequent effort: should stay 2½m: raced on
good ground or softer (acts on heavy). *M. Pitman*   **h110**

BE MY DREAM (IRE)   8 b.g. Be My Native (USA) – Dream Toi (Carlburg) [2002/3
c87p, h101p: c23d² c24v* c24d² c26d² c25d² c27g⁵ c26d⁴ Mar 8] tall gelding: winning
hurdler: fair chaser: won novice at Uttoxeter in June: sold out of J. O'Neill's stable 18,500
gns Doncaster September Sales after fourth start: best effort in hunters on return from
6-month absence when second to impressive Macgeorge at Hereford: stays 25f: acts on
heavy going: may benefit from headgear. *R. J. Webb*   **c110 d h–**

BE MY FRIEND (IRE)   7 ch.g. Be My Native (USA) – Miss Lamb (Relkino)
[2002/3 17s³ 19g⁵ 17g* Mar 22] fourth foal: dam, fair hurdler who stayed 21f, half-sister
to useful 2m hurdler Burns: much improved effort in novice hurdles when winning at
Bangor comfortably by 9 lengths from Fair Question: may do better again. *Mrs H. Dalton*   **h106 +**

BE MY MANAGER (IRE)   8 b.g. Be My Native (USA) – Fahy Quay (Quayside)
[2002/3 c122?, h–: c21g⁵ c24d³ c25d c21v³ c21s c24g c21d Apr 4] tall gelding: fairly
useful handicap chaser: well held in competitive events last 3 starts: stays 3m: acts on soft
and firm going: has reportedly had leg trouble: sold 54,000 gns Doncaster May Sales.
Miss H. C. Knight   **c124 h–**

BE MY ROYAL (IRE)   9 b.g. Be My Native (USA) – Royal Rehearsal (Pamroy)
[2002/3 c113x, h134?: c16s* c21s³ c20d* c28s* c26g* Nov 30]   **c144 h–**
A serious tendon injury which seemed virtually certain to end the career of
the winner Be My Royal provided a sad postscript to the latest Hennessy Cognac
Gold Cup. But insult was later added to injury when Be My Royal became the most
high-profile victim of a rash of positive tests for morphine, mostly in November
and December. Traces of the prohibited substance were found in batches of feed
following testing at an Irish feedstuffs supplier. Contaminated feed from the
supplier was established as the source of the traces found in thirty-seven horses
which were tested positive in Britain, Be My Royal being one of sixteen winners
facing eventual disqualification. Two point-to-point winners also tested positive
and there were numerous cases in Ireland.

Be My Royal's albeit short-lived resurgence came as something of a surprise. After looking an interesting prospect when third in the Champion Bumper at the Cheltenham Festival as a six-year-old, and then developing into a smart novice hurdler the next season, Be My Royal's first campaign over fences in 2001/2 came as a considerable anti-climax. Badly let down by his jumping, he completed the course only once in seven steeplechases. Starting the latest season still eligible for novice events over fences, Be My Royal got off the mark in a maiden at Wexford in May and also finished third in a handicap at Cork in June before his summer break. He showed that he had put his jumping problems behind him when winning a conditions event on his return at Thurles in October, scoring with quite a bit in hand from Thari after making most of the running. Be My Royal then added the valuable City Life Cork Grand National, a competitive handicap over three and a half miles three weeks before the Hennessy, again making most and pulling clear with runner-up Golden Storm in the closing stages, sticking to his task very well and proving himself a thorough stayer.

Connections still had the option of mapping out a campaign for Be My Royal in the top staying events for novices, and their decision to allow him to take his chance at Newbury looked beforehand to be extremely ambitious. The outstanding field of twenty-five, the largest for the Hennessy in forty years, contained few who could be discounted altogether. The previous season's attheraces Gold Cup winner Bounce Back at 13/2 and the previous season's Royal & SunAlliance Chase winner Hussard Collonges at 9/1 were the only runners sent off at shorter than 11/1 in as competitive a handicap chase as you are ever likely to see. Be My Royal, down among the 10-0 brigade and carrying 9 lb more than his allotted handicap mark, was sent off at 33/1, though he was very much the pick of the paddock. Be My Royal was always well placed, jumping soundly, in an event not run at a particularly strong pace. Seven were still right in the firing line at the last fence, within a couple of lengths of the lead, Be My Royal hitting the front after the leader Harbour Pilot blundered. Be My Royal was ridden out to hold off the 2000 runner-up Gingembre by half a length with Harbour Pilot a length and a half further back in third; the rallying Whitenzo came fourth, Hussard Collonges fifth, Carbury Cross sixth and Gunther McBride seventh in a memorable climax to a race that fully lived up to its promise. It soon transpired, however, that Be My Royal had broken down,

Be My Royal is led in after passing the post first in the Hennessy

almost certainly very near the line, putting something of a damper on the celebration of a first Irish victory in the Hennessy since Bright Highway in 1980. With Gingembre eventually set to get the race after Be My Royal's virtually certain disqualification, Bright Highway remains the only Irish-trained winner of the Hennessy since Arkle's two victories under 12-7 in 1964 and 1965.

Be My Royal (IRE) (b.g. 1994)	Be My Native (USA) (br 1979)	Our Native (b or br 1970)	Exclusive Native
			Our Jackie
		Witchy Woman (ch 1972)	Strate Stuff
			Witchy Norma
	Royal Rehearsal (b 1980)	Pamroy (b 1969)	Pampered King
			Ten Above
		Last Alliance (br 1974)	Honour Bound
			Royal Alliance

The tall Be My Royal comes from an excellent jumping family which has produced two Champion Hurdle winners in Morley Street and Granville Again, both out of a half-sister to Be My Royal's grandam Last Alliance. Last Alliance is also a sister to the top-class chaser Royal Bond. Be My Royal's dam Royal Rehearsal, a lightly-raced pointer and a runner-up over hurdles, has yet to breed another winner. Further details of Be My Royal's pedigree can be found in *Chasers & Hurdlers 2000/01*. Be My Royal was best at three miles plus; he raced only on good going or softer over jumps, his only start on good to firm coinciding with his fine effort in the Champion Bumper. *W. P. Mullins, Ireland*

BENBECULA (IRE) 6 b.g. Glacial Storm (USA) – Lough View (Radical) [2002/3 **h114 +** F94: 16d⁵ 16s³ 19d² 21s² 20v³ Mar 8] rangy, angular gelding: chasing type: fair novice hurdler: visored first time (looked hard ride previous start), mistake last when good 10½ lengths third of 12 to Tana River in Grade 3 novice handicap at Sandown final outing: will stay beyond 21f: raced on good going or softer (acts on heavy). *P. R. Webber*

BENBOW 6 ch.g. Gunner B – Juno Away (Strong Gale) [2002/3 F16g 26g⁵ 24m³ 24m⁴ **h?** Apr 10] first foal: half-brother to bumper winner Shady Anne (by Derrylin): dam, modest **F—** winning 2m hurdler, half-sister to useful staying chaser Killusty: well held in bumper: probably flattered when fourth of 8 in steadily-run novice hurdle at Ludlow, first run for over 5 months. *F. Jordan*

BENBRADAGH (IRE) 9 b.g. Mister Lord (USA) – Meenia (Black Minstrel) [2002/3 **h—** h—: 24d^pu Jun 8] big, strong gelding: has been tubed: maiden hurdler, no form since 2000/1: tried visored (failed to settle): has had tongue tied. *B. W. Duke*

BENBYAS 6 b.g. Rambo Dancer (CAN) – Light The Way (Nicholas Bill) [2002/3 **h134** h125: 16d⁴ 16g 16s* 16v³ 17s² 16g⁵ 21g Mar 12] medium-sized gelding: useful handicap hurdler: better than ever when winning 5-runner event at Doncaster in December by 19 lengths from Full Irish: good efforts in much stronger races after, including third to Chauvinist in Ladbroke Hurdle at Ascot and fifth to Spirit Leader in Tote Gold Trophy at Newbury: raced mainly around 2m (failed to stay 21f) on good going or softer (acts on heavy): usually forces pace: superb jumper: most genuine and reliable. *D. Carroll*

BENEFIT 9 b.g. Primitive Rising (USA) – Sobriquet (Roan Rocket) [2002/3 h77: **c77** c25d^pu 24g c23d⁴ c20s³ c24v^pu c21v² c24g^F 22g* 22g 22g Apr 26] small, lengthy gelding: **h81** poor handicap hurdler/novice chaser: won over hurdles at Market Rasen in March: probably stays 23f: raced on good going or softer (acts on heavy). *Miss L. C. Siddall*

BEN EWAR 9 b.g. Old Vic – Sunset Reef (Mill Reef (USA)) [2002/3 h131: 16d⁴ 20s^pu **h111** 21d⁵ 16d^pu 20v 20g⁴ 16d² 16f³ Apr 25] leggy, angular gelding: fairly useful hurdler on balance: back to form last 3 outings, though possibly flattered when 21 lengths third of 6 to Santenay in valuable minor event at Sandown: stays 2½m: probably acts on any going: has had tongue tied: has broken blood vessels. *K. O. Cunningham-Brown*

BENGAL BOY 7 b.g. Gildoran – Bengal Lady (Celtic Cone) [2002/3 c87x, h80: c16d **c86 x** 16m³ c17d^ur 17d² 20s⁴ 17s⁶ 16v⁶ 16g⁴ 16d⁵ 19d⁶ 16g⁶ c21m⁴ Apr 26] good-topped **h91** gelding: modest chaser/novice hurdler, often let down by jumping over fences: probably stays 21f: acts on good to firm and heavy going: tried in tongue strap. *P. Beaumont*

BENICK (IRE) 10 b.g. Yashgan – Sounds Symphonic (Orchestra) [2002/3 c–, h–: **c—** c24s^pu c25g^pu Nov 9] strong gelding: winning staying hurdler: no form since 2000/1, **h—** including over fences: acts on heavy going: tried blinkered. *N. A. Twiston-Davies*

BENJAMIN (IRE) 5 b.g. Night Shift (USA) – Best Academy (USA) (Roberto (USA)) **h—** [2002/3 17f 16d 17v^pu 17s^pu 16d Mar 19] smallish gelding: poor maiden on Flat, sold out of P. Mitchell's stable 3,200 gns Newmarket July Sales: well held in novice hurdles: breathing problem third start, tongue tied after. *Jane Southcombe*

BEN MORE 5 b.g. Seymour Hicks (FR) – Stac-Pollaidh (Tina's Pet) [2002/3 F16m³ **h70** F17d⁵ 19d 19f⁴ 22f² Apr 24] rather unfurnished gelding: first foal: dam, winning hurdler **F82** who stayed 3m, from family of very smart chaser The Tsarevich: modest form in bumpers, poor over hurdles. *J. S. King*

BENNIE'S PRIDE (IRE) 7 b.g. Welsh Term – Mugs Away (Mugatpura) [2002/3 **c103** F16s* F17s 16s² 20d³ 20m* 22d 22g⁶ 22g³ 24s⁵ c24f² c20s* c20g⁴ c24v⁴ c24v c18s c24v^F **h103** Mar 8] well-made gelding: half-brother to several winners, including Irish Grand Nat- **F92** ional winner Glebe Lad (by Le Bavard) and fairly useful hurdler up to 2½m Stashedaway (by Treasure Hunter): dam lightly raced: won bumper at Clonmel in May: fair hurdler: won maiden at Ballinrobe in July: best effort over fences when winning maiden at

Clonmel in November: should stay beyond 2¾m: acts on good to firm and heavy going. *E. J. O'Grady, Ireland*

BENNY THE VICE (USA)   4 ch.g. Benny The Dip (USA) – Vice On Ice (USA)   **h–** (Vice Regent (CAN)) [2002/3 16d 16g Nov 23] fair on Flat (stays 1½m) for M. Johnston, winner in blinkers: dropped away tamely in juvenile hurdles at Ayr and Catterick (claimer, blinkered). *Mrs A. Duffield*

BENRAJAH (IRE)   6 b.g. Lord Americo – Andy's Fancy (IRE) (Andretti) [2002/3   **h105** F97p: 20d³ 20d³ 20v⁵ 21s 25g* 26m³ Apr 21] well-made gelding: largely disappointing over hurdles, though landed odds in novice at Warwick in March: may prove best around 3m: acts on good to soft going (second in bumper on soft): sold 20,000 gns Doncaster May Sales. *H. D. Daly*

BENS BIG   7 br.g. Vouchsafe – Strathdearn (Saritamer (USA)) [2002/3 c20sᵖᵘ c21vᵖᵘ   **c–** Nov 12] 3,000 5-y-o: half-brother to 3 winning hurdlers, including Might Move (by Town And Country), fairly useful at 2m: dam, won over hurdles, also 1½m winner on Flat: failed to complete in 3 maiden points in 2002 and in 2 novice chases (tongue tied). *Mrs S. J. Smith*

BENSON (IRE)   8 b. or br.g. Hawkstone (IRE) – Erin St Helen (IRE) (Seclude (USA))   **c103** [2002/3 h75: c19g⁴ c20s⁵ c20s³ c20s c20gᶠ c20g* c21mᵖᵘ Apr 17] workmanlike gelding: **h–** maiden hurdler: fair chaser: won handicaps at Hereford (novice) in October and Warwick in March: best efforts around 2½m on good going: sketchy jumper: sold 8,000 gns Doncaster May Sales. *H. D. Daly*

BENTYHEATH LANE   6 b.g. Puissance – Eye Sight (Roscoe Blake) [2002/3 h–:   **h65** 16dᵖᵘ 16m³ 17m² 16m² 20m 17m Oct 3] poor novice hurdler: raced mainly around 2m: acts on good to firm going. *M. Mullineaux*

BENVOLIO   6 br.g. Cidrax (FR) – Miss Capulet (Commanche Run) [2002/3 c–, h–:   **c–** c19d c23dᴿ c21s³ c23gᵖᵘ c21m⁵ c24vᵖᵘ c20v⁴ c20sᵖᵘ c23s⁵ c25dᵖᵘ c23gᵖᵘ c20m⁴ Mar 18]   **h–** smallish gelding: of little account. *C. N. Kellett*

BEREWOLF (IRE)   9 b.g. Commanche Run – Iron Star (General Ironside) [2002/3   **c–** c–, h85d: 22m May 6] lengthy gelding: disappointing maiden hurdler/chaser: blinkered   **h–** only outing in 2002/3: sold £1,000 Ascot June Sales. *J. T. Gifford*

BERGAMO   7 b.g. Robellino (USA) – Pretty Thing (Star Appeal) [2002/3 h103: 21g⁵   **h104 d** 16g² 16m⁶ 21d 20g⁵ 21m⁴ Apr 26] small gelding: fair handicap hurdler: largely below form in 2002/3: stays 2½m: acts on soft and good to firm going (ran poorly on heavy): tried visored/in cheekpieces, usually blinkered. *B. Ellison*

BERING GIFTS (IRE)   8 b.g. Bering – Bobbysoxer (Valiyar) [2002/3 h105: 18m   **c102 §** 17g⁴ 16m* 16m⁴ 16d 16g³ 16m⁴ c21g² c19f³ c21m⁵ Apr 21] workmanlike gelding: fair   **h113 §** handicap hurdler: won at Stratford in June: left C. Mann and off 5 months, placed first 2 starts in hunter chases: stays easy 21f: acts on firm going: needs waiting tactics: temperamental. *Mrs T. J. Hill*

BERKELEY FRONTIER (IRE)   10 ch.g. Imperial Frontier (USA) – Harristown   **c–** Rose (Miami Springs) [2002/3 c–, h90: 24sᵖᵘ 26gᵖᵘ Feb 22] sturdy gelding: maiden   **h–** chaser: modest handicap hurdler, ran poorly both outings in 2002/3: stays 3m: acts on good to firm and good to soft going, probably on heavy: tried visored: inconsistent. *N. A. Twiston-Davies*

BERKELEY HALL   6 b.m. Saddlers' Hall (IRE) – Serious Affair (Valiyar) [2002/3   **h82 ?** 16g⁶ 16m Apr 22] modest on Flat (barely stays 7f) for B. Palling: likely to have stamina problems over hurdles, seemingly better effort when sixth of 17 in maiden at Ludlow. *R. Lee*

BERLIN BLUE   10 b.g. Belmez (USA) – Blue Brocade (Reform) [2002/3 c–, h111+:   **c125** 21s c24m³ c25dᵖᵘ c33mᶠ Apr 12] compact gelding: winning hurdler: fairly useful   **h–** handicap chaser: showed he retained his ability when third to Eau de Cologne at Newbury in March: stiff task final start: stays 4m: acts on good to firm and good to soft going: usually sound jumper. *R. M. Stronge*

BERMUDA BAY (IRE)   6 b.m. Be My Native (USA) – Von Carty (IRE) (Supreme   **F–** Leader) [2002/3 F16d Aug 3] IR 20,000 4-y-o: second foal: sister to fair 2m hurdler Woodys Deep Ocean: dam, bumper winner/13f winner on Flat, granddaughter of useful 2m hurdler The Very Thing: 5/1, well held in bumper at Worcester on debut: joined R. Lee. *N. J. Henderson*

BERMUDA BLUE   7 gr.g. Arzanni – Calora (USA) (Private Account (USA)) [2002/3   **h82** 24v³ Jun 6] 17,500 4-y-o: second foal: dam, won on Flat and over jumps in France, half-sister to high-class chaser Chatam: successful twice in points in 2002: visored, looked temperamental when third in maiden at Uttoxeter on hurdling debut: sold to join Mrs F. Needham 2,000 gns Ascot July Sales, little show returned to points. *M. C. Pipe*

BERNARDON (GER)   7 b.g. Suave Dancer (USA) – Bejaria (GER) (Konigsstuhl   **h131 §** (GER)) [2002/3 h100+: 16s* 17m² 17m⁴ 16v 16d 16g 16dᵖᵘ 16v Mar 8] close-coupled gelding: useful hurdler: won handicap at Worcester in June: largely well below form after next outing: will prove best around 2m: acts on soft and good to firm going: visored 2 of last 3 starts (jumped slowly and to the right when pulled up in between). *M. C. Pipe*

BERRINGTON (NZ)   6 b.g. Fort Prospect (USA) – Calamity (NZ) (Bally Royal)   **h–** [2002/3 F–: 16mᵖᵘ Oct 5] no sign of ability. *B. P. J. Baugh*

BESEIGED (USA)   6 ch.g. Cadeaux Genereux – Munnaya (USA) (Nijinsky (CAN))   **h105 p** [2002/3 F88: F16m* 16d* 19m* Apr 21] fairly useful form in bumpers, won at Perth in   **F96** May: unbeaten in novice hurdles in small fields at same track in June and Market Rasen 10½ months later: stays 19f, at least when emphasis is on speed: yet to race on extremes of going: open to further improvement. *R. A. Fahey*

BESIDE HIMSELF (IRE)   10 b.g. Brush Aside (USA) – Lady Torsil (Torus)   **c–** [2002/3 c20dᵖᵘ Mar 4] sturdy gelding: winning pointer but possesses very little ability. *N. M. Lampard*

BESO MI RAPIDO   5 b.m. Alderbrook – Love You Madly (IRE) (Bob Back (USA))   **F–** [2002/3 F17d F16d Mar 6] second foal: dam, temperamental staying hurdler, sister to useful hurdler up to 3m Tarthooth: showed nothing in bumpers. *M. C. Pipe*

BESSIE BUNTER   7 b.m. Rakaposhi King – Black H'Penny (Town And Country)   **h83 d** [2002/3 h–, F65: 19s⁵ 16s⁵ 16v 24s 19vᵇ Mar 10] poor maiden hurdler: bred to be suited by 2½m+: raced only on soft/heavy going. *J. A. B. Old*

BEST AVAILABLE (IRE)   8 b.g. Accordion – Grangeshoon (Green Shoon) [2002/3   **c98** h98: c19g² c23dᶠ c21gᵖᵘ May 31] tall gelding: modest hurdler: similar form when second   **h–** in novice at Hereford on chasing debut: pulled up early final outing: stays 3m: raced on good going or softer: has carried head awkwardly/looked far from keen: placed in points in 2003. *P. J. Hobbs*

BEST GREY   7 gr.h. Ezzoud (IRE) – Best Girl Friend (Sharrood (USA)) [2002/3 h119:   **h112** 20s 20v⁶ 24s 22d 20d² Feb 15] fair hurdler: back to near best (off 15 months before reappearance) when 2 lengths second of 16 finishers to Back On Top in handicap at Gowran: stays 2½m: raced mainly on going softer than good (acts on heavy). *E. J. O'Grady, Ireland*

BEST MATE (IRE)   8 b.g. Un Desperado (FR) – Katday (FR) (Miller's Mate)   **c182** [2002/3 c173, h–: c20d* c24s* c26g* Mar 13]   **h–**

Henry Ford's popularly-remembered *Chicago Tribune* quote that 'History is more or less bunk' seems apt when applied to the welter of historical, statistical information published on horse-racing nowadays, particularly before big races at showpiece meetings. Ages and weights carried by previous winners, the races they had run in, the record of the top stables in the particular races or at the meeting, the position in the betting market of previous winners—the list goes on. Such facts may be of interest but the prominence they are sometimes given can create an impression that such statistics are a more fruitful avenue for research for a punter than a study of the ability of the individual runners, and how they might be suited by the prevailing conditions. Statistics are a poor substitute for form study. More horses win races because their form said they had a good chance at the weights than for any other reason. An unfortunate by-product of preoccupation with statistics is that when, in popular parlance, a horse 'defies the stats' it tends to earn a reputation out of proportion to the actual form-value of its performance.

Take the Cheltenham Gold Cup, for example. Until the latest season, no horse had won the race in successive years since L'Escargot in 1970 and 1971, statistical analysis illustrating, according to some, that, because of the often-gruelling nature of the race, 'Gold Cup winners are never the same again', a well-worn view which has tended to be preferred before each renewal in which the previous year's winner has taken part. The portents for the winner of the same season's King George VI Chase have also been regarded as anything but good, eleven of its winners having failed in the same season's Gold Cup since Desert Orchid completed the double in 1988/9, the only one to do so since Arkle. And then there were statistics showing the Gold Cup to be a 'bogey' race for favourites, the shorter the odds the worse the prospects apparently, the last eleven horses to start at 7/4 or shorter in the Gold Cup having been beaten. Not surprisingly, 'history' was portrayed as being stacked against 13/8-favourite Best Mate, winner not only of the previous year's Gold Cup but also of the current season's King George VI Chase. On a glorious spring day and on near-perfect going, Best Mate won his second Gold Cup in imperious style, as the form-book said he should, under a copybook ride from Jim Culloty, waited with and jumping flawlessly and economically before cruising into the lead on the bridle after three out and quickening clear from the last.

Best Mate's performance confirmed that he is a class apart from his contemporaries among the staying chasers, at least when conditions place the emphasis on speed. He was deserving of a good proportion of the praise he received afterwards, but to place him above Desert Orchid and some of the other champions of the last thirty years or so—let alone ahead of Arkle—was hardly justified on any rational appreciation of the actual performance. Almost everything written afterwards began with the fact that Best Mate had become the first to win successive Gold Cups for thirty-two years, closely followed in some reports by the fact that he had also become the first since Desert Orchid to win the King George VI Chase and the Gold Cup in the same season. More than one reviewer stated that Best Mate had 'overcome' or 'defied' history. 'Best is better than Arkle', 'Best Mate's Gold strike ranks him with Arkle', 'The best of all time? History beckons for Gold Cup hero' provide just a flavour of the exaggerated headlines in the national dailies. *The Independent* correspondent wrote 'If Arkle's memory is secure in the mists of time . . . it cannot any longer be said to be without challenge' and a specialist writer in the *Daily Telegraph* offered the view that 'To mention another horse in the same breath as Arkle was blasphemy. We may not have found his better but yesterday perhaps we found his equal in Best Mate.' The chief sports writer of the *Daily Express* thought that Best Mate had provided enough glory 'to last a whole year', just as well since the horse's connections announced almost immediately that he

McCallum Corporate Consulting Peterborough Chase, Huntingdon—
Best Mate makes a highly satisfactory return, defeating Douze Douze (left) and Geos

would not be seen out again and would have a similarly truncated campaign in 2003/4, his principal targets the King George and the Gold Cup.

Tiresome references to Arkle have dogged Best Mate's career since his hugely promising first season over fences in 2000/1 when his main target, the Arkle Trophy, did not take place, the Cheltenham Festival a casualty of the most serious foot and mouth outbreak the country has ever known. Best Mate was never seriously tested in three novice chases—he reverted to hurdling on his last start when beaten by Barton in the Aintree Hurdle—and he ended the campaign a tip-top prospect for the next season. He was seen out four times in 2001/2, all over fences, and, though beaten by Florida Pearl in the King George VI Chase at Kempton, he went on to win the Cheltenham Gold Cup—not seen out between the two races—in only his seventh steeplechase, making him the least experienced winner of the race since Dawn Run in 1986. It seemed reasonable to conclude that further improvement might be forthcoming and Best Mate's reappearance in the McCallum Corporate Consulting Peterborough Chase at Huntingdon in November was eagerly awaited. The Haldon Gold Cup at Exeter—where the going was eventually considered too firm—and the Edward Hanmer Chase at Haydock—where the owner couldn't be present—had previously been pencilled in for Best Mate's seasonal debut and his appearance at Huntingdon denied stable-mate Edredon Bleu (in the same ownership) the chance of a fifth successive win in the Peterborough Chase. Faced with four rivals, most notably the smart pair Douze Douze and Geos, both of whom received 10 lb, Best Mate made a highly satisfactory reappearance. Culloty had no hesitation in sending him on once it was clear none of his rivals was going to make the running, and Best Mate won by eight lengths and two and a half from Douze Douze and Geos, responding well to pressure in the closing stages after briefly looking as if he might have a fight on his hands after making the only semblance of a mistake two out.

Best Mate's participation in the Pertemps King George VI Chase at Kempton on Boxing Day was seemingly in some doubt for a time, his trainer calling the state of the Kempton chase course 'an absolute disgrace' when withdrawing three runners on the day at the track's end-of-October meeting—the withdrawal of one of them, Impek, resulting in a walkover. 'There's no grass here. It hasn't been properly looked after and it won't grow between now and the end of the year,' she said, adding that Best Mate wouldn't be running in the King George unless there was a dramatic improvement. Huntingdon's right-handed flat track has some similarities to Kempton, and the relative test of speed provided by the Peterborough Chase over an extended two and a half miles seemed to offer an ideal warm-up for the King George for Best Mate. Ground conditions, however, were softer at Kempton then they had been for any of Best Mate's races since his novice chasing campaign and his rather laboured winning performance does not rank highly in the King George's illustrious history. There was a rare double-figure field, Best Mate's nine opponents including Florida Pearl, who hadn't enjoyed an ideal preparation in his bid to follow up the previous year's victory, the previous year's third Bacchanal, the Punchestown Chase winner Native Upmanship, the reigning Queen Mother Champion Chase winner Flagship Uberalles, Douze Douze, and the Charlie Hall Chase winner Marlborough who had finished fourth to Best Mate in the Gold Cup. With his regular rider suspended, Best Mate was ridden for the second successive year at Kempton by Tony McCoy who completed the fastest two hundred winners ever by a jump jockey on Lord Sam earlier on the programme. Culloty's fairly quiet style contrasts with that of McCoy and seems to suit Best Mate whom Culloty himself says is 'so well balanced that he is a better horse if you sit still on him at a fence.'

McCoy had been convinced Best Mate would have won the previous year's King George had he not been given instructions to ride a waiting race—the more enterprisingly-ridden Florida Pearl held him off by three-quarters of a length—and he set out to ride Best Mate more forcefully in the latest edition. With Best Mate kept handy from the start and moving smoothly for much of the way, McCoy took the bull by the horns approaching five out, after being bumped at the previous fence, and sent Best Mate to the front. The middle part of the race had been particularly strongly run, the runners reaching the fifth last in a time over eight seconds faster than the novices had done in the earlier Feltham Chase, and, with Best Mate pressing on, the King George developed into a gruelling encounter. Only

Pertemps King George VI Chase, Kempton—
Best Mate and Marlborough are clear of Bacchanal at the last

Bacchanal and Marlborough were still in with a chance against Best Mate by the second last. Best Mate was actually joined by Marlborough going to the final fence but the cleaner jump kept him in front and he gamely held on to win all out by a length and a half, with Bacchanal filling third for the second year in a row, four lengths behind Marlborough and twelve in front of fourth-placed Florida Pearl; the principals finished tired and the race proved altogether too much of a test of stamina for the likes of Native Upmanship, a well-beaten fifth, and Flagship Uberalles, who was pulled up. Best Mate's final time for the course, incidentally, was only a second faster than that recorded by Jair du Cochet in the Feltham. For the record, the form shown by Best Mate at Kempton was certainly no improvement on his effort in the race, ridden more patiently, the previous year.

    Best Mate had plenty of time to recover from his exertions at Kempton. As in the previous season, he wasn't seen out again until the Tote Cheltenham Gold Cup in March. His main rival at Cheltenham was widely seen as the Irish novice Beef Or Salmon, though records showed that the Gold Cup had been waiting for another novice winner—Captain Christy being the last in 1974—almost as long as it had been waiting for a dual winner. Beef Or Salmon had actually never contested a novice event and, on two of his four starts over fences, had beaten established stayers in good style in the Ericsson Chase at Leopardstown in December and in the Hennessy Cognac Gold Cup over the same course in February. The second and third in the Irish Gold Cup, Colonel Braxton and Harbour Pilot, were also in the Cheltenham line-up. Both had contested the previous season's Royal &

SunAlliance Chase at the Festival, finishing fifth and unseating rider respectively. The first and third in that race, Hussard Collonges and Chives, and another faller Valley Henry, also contested the latest Gold Cup, as did the previous year's Arkle fourth Truckers Tavern, who had beaten Hussard Collonges in the Peter Marsh Chase in January. Valley Henry, Chives and Truckers Tavern had filled the first three places in the AON Chase at Newbury in February, while Hussard Collonges, who ran a cracker at Haydock going down by two and a half lengths conceding 15 lb to Truckers Tavern, had also looked a good prospect when a fine fifth, conceding weight to most, in a hotly-contested Hennessy Cognac Gold Cup at Newbury back in November. Five of the previous year's Gold Cup runners took the field again, Best Mate joined by the second, third and fourth Commanche Court, See More Business and Marlborough (a faller in the AON Chase on his only run since Kempton), and by Behrajan who failed to do himself justice on Gold Cup day but was back in good form, having won the Silver Cup at Ascot and the Pillar Property Chase at Cheltenham on his last two starts. On form, Best Mate's credentials were outstanding and, apart from him, only three others in the fifteen-strong field started at shorter than 14/1, 5/1-shot Beef Or Salmon and 8/1-shots Hussard Collonges and Commanche Court. The 2000 King George winner First Gold, who had been badly out of sorts, went off at 33/1.

Few championship races, let alone the Cheltenham Gold Cup, are as good as over so far from home. Best Mate made his task look easy, winning with great authority, moving best from a long way out. Nothing had the slightest chance with him as soon as he was sent effortlessly into the lead after three out. Just kept up his work after the last, with the race already well won, Best Mate passed the post ten lengths in front of runner-up Truckers Tavern, a margin of victory bettered only twice in the Gold Cup since Arkle won by a record-breaking thirty in 1966. Master Oats was a fifteen-length winner on soft going—which can accentuate superiority —in 1995 and Alverton won by twenty-five in 1979 after Tied Cottage fell when upsides him at the last. Both runner-up Truckers Tavern and third-placed Harbour Pilot, a further two and a half lengths back, stayed on strongly after being off the pace for most of the race. Both surpassed themselves, facing the stiffest test of stamina of their careers so far. Fourth-placed Valley Henry, who faded in the closing stages, was probably the second-best horse in the race on the day, looking the main danger to Best Mate until making a mistake four out, while Behrajan, whose front-running did so much to make the Gold Cup a true test, ran a good race to finish fifth, staying on again from the second last. Commanche Court filled sixth place, over fifteen lengths behind Best Mate. In a race remarkably short of incident,

Tote Cheltenham Gold Cup Chase—three out, and a close race still looks possible as Chives (centre) and Valley Henry jump with Best Mate . . .

. . . but it's all over by the next

Beef Or Salmon was the only faller, coming down at the third, while Hussard Collonges was well held when pulled up two out, a fence after First Gold, who gave little inkling of the form he was to show at Aintree and Punchestown.

Allowing that Truckers Tavern and Harbour Pilot appeared to run well above any form they had previously achieved and were almost certainly flattered by the result. Best Mate's superiority over the likes of Valley Henry, Behrajan and Commanche Court earned him a Timeform rating which puts him behind only Arkle (212), Flyingbolt (210), Mill House (191), Desert Orchid (187), Dunkirk (186), Burrough Hill Lad (184) and Master Oats (183) among the top jumpers in Timeform's experience. Arkle, Mill House, Desert Orchid and Burrough Hill Lad are among a fairly extensive list of horses who have won both the King George VI Chase—instituted in 1947—and the Gold Cup, the two most important weight-for-age chases in the British calendar. Best Mate became the fourteenth to win both races, the sixth to do so in the same season. Desert Orchid, with four King George wins and a Gold Cup, and Arkle and Cottage Rake, with three Gold Cups and a King George, have compiled the best combined records in the two races (Golden Miller won the Gold Cup five times between 1932 and 1936). Things never stand still for long in racing, but Best Mate is still only eight and could well go on to win both the King George VI Chase and the Gold Cup again. A victory at Kempton would make him the only horse to win both major staying championship races at least twice. The King George and the Gold Cup often call for different qualities, the Gold Cup, run over a slightly longer distance, placing more of a premium on stamina. Soft-ground Festivals are much rarer than they used to be but, under such conditions, the Gold Cup can provide a particularly severe test and a result that can make a mockery of form and judgement. The stayer with a slight deficiency in finishing speed is not at such a disadvantage under testing conditions against the speedier type of staying chaser like Best Mate. To that extent, a good ground Gold Cup would favour Best Mate, though he has shown himself effective on soft and heavy during his career (he has yet to race on firm).

117

Best Mate is one of the very best chasers of recent times, most genuine and consistent, and it was a pity that followers of jump racing were not able to see their new star in action again after the Gold Cup. A racehorse owner, of course, is perfectly entitled to campaign his horses in any way he wants, within the laws of the land and the rules of racing, but a valuable promotional opportunity for jumping was certainly lost when Best Mate's connections cold-shouldered Aintree and Punchestown. The decision was all the more puzzling given that Best Mate was clearly right at the top of his form and had had anything but a hard race at Cheltenham. Furthermore, this was a horse described by his trainer as 'a trainer's joy, such an easy horse to train'. By limiting Best Mate's appearances, connections evidently believe his career at the top will be more long-lasting. In that respect, an examination of the career of the last horse to win successive Gold Cups, L'Escargot, is illuminating. L'Escargot was curiously left out of the various comparisons after Best Mate's second victory at Cheltenham, yet he is the only horse, apart from Golden Miller, to have won both the Cheltenham Gold Cup and the Grand National and, although European-bred, he features in American racing's Hall of Fame. L'Escargot started his career in bumpers in Ireland and won a division of the Gloucestershire Hurdle by six lengths at the 1968 Cheltenham Festival. Sixth in the Champion Hurdle the next year, he went on to have a successful summer and autumn over fences in North America, winning the prestigious Meadow Brook Handicap Chase at Belmont and earning the title of US Champion Steeplechase Horse of the year. Returned to training in Ireland, he won the seventeen-runner Final of the newly-inaugurated WD & HO Wills Premier Chase at Haydock before going on to spring a 33/1 surprise in the Gold Cup. Sent back again to race in North America that summer, he began the build-up to his second Gold Cup when fourth to Persian War in the Sweeps Hurdle at Christmas, the last time a reigning Gold Cup winner and a reigning Champion Hurdle winner met in racecourse competition. The Leopardstown Chase, a handicap, was the race chosen as L'Escargot's Gold Cup warm-up (as it had been the previous season) and he finished a creditable third, carrying 12-2 and conceding 37 lb to the winner and 33 lb to the runner-up. After winning his second Gold Cup by ten lengths and fifteen from Leap Frog and The Dikler—on very heavy going incidentally—he shouldered a 5-lb penalty (bringing his weight to 12-7) in the Irish Grand National at Fairyhouse, failing by a length and a half and three quarters of a length to concede 36 lb to King's Sprite and 20 lb to Proud Tarquin.

L'Escargot continued to be campaigned mostly in big handicaps, carrying big weights, and he was saddled for his first Grand National in the year after his second Gold Cup victory—coming down at the third when favourite under 12-0. L'Escargot went on to run in four Gold Cups in all, finishing fourth in the two years after his victories, and came third and then second in the Grand National in successive seasons before finally triumphing under 11-3 at Aintree on his fourth attempt at the age of twelve in 1975. Though equipped with blinkers in his later years, L'Escargot never lost his appetite for racing. His owner Raymond Guest, a former United States ambassador to Ireland, gave him to the wife of the trainer Dan Moore after his Grand National win, on the understanding that he should not race again. L'Escargot was apparently in such good fettle the following September that the stable decided to run him in the Kerry National at Listowel. Carrying 12-0, he failed only by a head to concede 23 lb to the winner. It was the resulting controversy over that outing which reportedly led to L'Escargot being sent to live out his days at his owner's farm in Virginia. L'Escargot's Grand National win took him into fourth place at the time, behind Comedy of Errors, Arkle and Red Rum, in the list of jumping's leading money winners, but he failed to capture the public's imagination in quite the same way as some of the sport's other big names at around that time. He denied Red Rum what would have been a universally popular third successive Grand National and both his Gold Cups featured hard-luck stories. The favourite in 1970 was Kinloch Brae who was seemingly going really well when coming down three out; the commentary on L'Escargot in the final *Timeform* issue that season concluded its Gold Cup description with the words 'probably only winning because of Kinloch Brae's third-last fall'. L'Escargot's task in 1971 was again made easier by the fall of one of the leading fancies, Glencaraig Lady (who went on to success the following year) also going well when departing three out.

Most readers will need no reminding of Desert Orchid's monumental achievements—he won thirty-four races in a career spanning ten seasons—but it is probably worth reiterating that he earned his Timeform rating of 187, not in the Gold Cup or the King George VI Chase, but with a stunning performance in a handicap, in the Racing Post Chase, carrying 12-3 (including a penalty) to an eight-length victory in 1990. Desert Orchid was exceptional, his other big handicap victories including a Whitbread under 11-11 and an Irish Grand National under 12-0. He thoroughly merited the description *great* and deservedly became a symbol of so much that is good about National Hunt racing. Big handicaps offer more potential than weight-for-age championship events to find out how good the top horses really are. Arkle's Timeform rating came from his conceding lumps of weight in races such as the Leopardstown Chase, the Hennessy and the Whitbread. Best Mate's only crack at conceding lumps of weight all round ended in his failing to concede 20 lb, carrying 11-10, to Wahiba Sands in the First National Gold Cup at Ascot, a performance which, nonetheless, put him among a relatively small band of jumpers who have run to a Timeform rating of 170 or above in a handicap in recent years. Terry Biddlecombe, husband of Best Mate's trainer, was a champion jump jockey in Arkle's era and won the Gold Cup on Woodland Venture the year after Arkle's retirement. His tongue-in-cheek remarks after the latest Gold Cup about Arkle being 'just a galloper who beat old boats' were widely reported. Not reported was a later remark he made to the effect that his wife 'tends to wrap her horses up in cotton wool a little too much'. Arkle's achievements came in an era before 'cotton wool' was invented. For the record, he ran six times in the season when he won his second Gold Cup, his five victories including the Hennessy Gold Cup at Newbury

Mr Jim Lewis' "Best Mate"

by ten lengths under 12-7, after which he was beaten a short head and a length carrying 12-10, including a 3-lb penalty, in the following week's Massey-Ferguson Gold Cup at Cheltenham. Arkle was 'warmed up' for the Gold Cup in the Leopardstown Handicap Chase at the end of February which he won under 12-7, conceding 35 lb to the runner-up Scottish Memories who went on to land the odds in the Cathcart at the Cheltenham Festival. Arkle's season didn't end with the Gold Cup that year either. He carried 12-7 to a five-length victory in the Whitbread Gold Cup.

In the 1965/6 season, Arkle ran four times before his third Cheltenham Gold Cup victory, starting off with a twenty-length win under 12-7 in the Gallaher Gold Cup at Sandown in November, setting a time record of 5m 59sec that still stands for the course and distance. Later that month, Arkle took his second successive Hennessy under 12-7, winning by fifteen lengths from Freddie who received 32 lb. Arkle made it three wins from three starts with victory by a distance in the King George VI Chase before again winning the Leopardstown Chase on his way to Cheltenham. Arkle conceded 42 lb to the second and third at Leopardstown; runner-up Height o' Fashion, who went down by a neck, did most of her racing in Ireland but was worth a Timeform rating of 168+ while third-placed Splash, beaten a further fifteen lengths, had won the previous year's Irish Grand National with 10-13, earning a Timeform rating of 157. Arkle gave them a 43 lb and 55 lb beating respectively and was 10/1-on when making it five out of five for the season when taking the Gold Cup in a canter. If these reminiscences about Arkle conjure up strains of the theme from a brown bread commercial, we apologise—but if comparisons with Arkle had not been made we should not have had to refute them. Arkle's feats were extraordinary by the standards of his day, and nothing short of staggering by those of the present day. It is very difficult to envisage Best Mate or any other modern champion chaser—with the possible exception of Desert Orchid—arriving at the Gold Cup in circumstances even vaguely similar to those of Arkle.

Best Mate (IRE) (b.g. 1995)	Un Desperado (FR) (b 1983)	Top Ville (b 1976)	High Top
			Sega Ville
		White Lightning (gr 1970)	Baldric II
			Rough Sea
	Katday (FR) (br 1987)	Miller's Mate (b 1982)	Mill Reef
			Primatie
		Kanara (b 1973)	Hauban
			Alika

The big, rangy Best Mate usually takes the eye before his races and looked magnificent on Gold Cup day, dominating his rivals in the paddock as much as he did in the race itself. His pedigree was extensively discussed in last year's Annual though there are one or two updates. His dam Katday's third foal, like Best Mate a son of the deceased Un Desperado, reached the racecourse in the latest season after fetching IR £110,000 as an unraced four-year-old at the Derby Sale in 2001. Now named Cornish Rebel, he won a bumper on his debut at Newbury most impressively before finishing in the middle of the field in the Champion Bumper at the Festival. Katday's second foal Inca Trail joined his year-older brother Best Mate at West Lockinge in the latest season and developed into a useful novice hurdler; he was also in action at the Cheltenham Festival, finishing eighth of nineteen to Back In Front in the Supreme Novices'. Katday's fourth foal Inexorable (by Roselier), who broke the record for a National Hunt store when making 185,000 guineas as an unraced four-year-old at the Doncaster Spring Sales in 2002, won a maiden point in Ireland in the latest season. Katday's fifth foal, a filly by Oscar named Sidalcea, was in training with Edward O'Grady in the latest season but wasn't sent out. Katday was barren to Topanoora in 2000 but has a two-year-old filly by Un Desperado who has been named Flying Iris. There is a yearling colt by Pistolet Bleu but Katday slipped her foal to Bob Back in 2003. *Miss H. C. Knight*

BEST WAIT (IRE)   6 b.m. Insan (USA) – Greek Melody (IRE) (Trojan Fort) [2002/3   **h109**
h109, F85: 17g⁶ 16d* 16d⁴ 16m² 16m⁶ 16m³ Apr 11] rather unfurnished ex-Irish mare: fair handicap hurdler: won at Roscommon in September, final start for T. Hogan: found little final outing: raced around 2m: acts on soft and good to firm going (won bumper on firm): tongue tied. *P. F. Nicholls*

BESUTO (IRE)   6 br.g. Fourstars Allstar (USA) – Mabbots Own (Royal Trip) [2002/3   h–
F17s⁴ 20d⁵ 20v⁶ Dec 20] sixth known foal: half-brother to modest staying hurdler/chaser   **F77**
Exemplar (by Carlingford Castle) and to winning pointer by White Christmas: dam,
novice hurdler, sister to useful staying chaser Excursion: staying-on fourth in maiden
bumper at Taunton on debut: well beaten in 2 novice hurdles: sold £3,500 Ascot April
Sales. *A. King*

BETABATIM (IRE)   8 b.g. Alphabatim (USA) – Lucy Platter (FR) (Record Token)   c–
[2002/3 h80+: 16d* 16m⁵ 18g⁵ c17sᵘʳ c17dᵖᵘ Mar 1] modest hurdler: won maiden at   **h88**
Kelso in May: race still to take shape when unseating 2 out in intermediate at same
course on chasing debut after 5-month absence: off further 4 months, pulled up halfway
final outing: should stay beyond 2m: acts on good to firm and good to soft going.
J. E. Brockbank

BETTER DAYS (IRE)   7 b.g. Supreme Leader – Kilkilrun (Deep Run) [2002/3 h103:   c–
c21vᵖᵘ Dec 21] useful-looking gelding: won novice hurdle in 2001/2: shaped as if   h–
something amiss 2 of 3 starts since, including on chasing debut: should stay 2½m.
N. J. Henderson

BETTER MOMENT (IRE)   6 b.g. Turtle Island (IRE) – Snoozeandyoulose (IRE)   c84
(Scenic) [2002/3 h75: 20g² 16d⁴ 17s⁴ 16m* 20m⁶ 17m* c17m⁵ 17f³ 19m⁶ 16s⁴ Jan 3]   h90
smallish gelding: poor form only run over fences: modest hurdler: won seller at Worcester
in June and minor event at Newton Abbot in July: best around 2m: has form on heavy
going, probably ideally suited by good or firmer (acts on firm): blinkered/visored: has
had tongue tied: usually forces pace. *M. C. Pipe*

BETTER THYNE (IRE)   7 ch.g. Good Thyne (USA) – Cailin Cainnteach (Le   c111
Bavard (FR)) [2002/3 h94: 24s* c26vᵘʳ c23dᶠ 24g⁶ 24dᵖᵘ Feb 23] strong gelding: fair   h102
handicap hurdler: won at Taunton in December: ran as if amiss final outing: failed to
complete in novices both starts over fences, though showed plenty of promise (held in
second when falling 2 out at Exeter): best at 3m+: acts on heavy going. *V. R. A. Dartnall*

BE UPSTANDING   8 ch.g. Hubbly Bubbly (USA) – Two Travellers (Deep Run)   c112
[2002/3 h93: 16g⁶ c17s³ c21v³ c21v* c21s c24g² c24d* c24gˢᵘ Apr 25] big, useful-   h93
looking gelding: modest hurdler: fair novice chaser: won handicaps at Fakenham in
January and Uttoxeter (idled) in April: stays 3m: acts on heavy going: not an easy ride.
Ferdy Murphy

BEWLEYS HOTELS (IRE)   7 ch.g. Muharib (USA) – Alchymya (Cosmo) [2002/3   c88 p
F79: 16m³ 16d² c16g⁴ Nov 23] good-topped gelding: placed in maiden Irish point/   h96 p
bumper: better effort in novice hurdles at Haydock when 3 lengths second of 16 to Kalco
Mome: promising 12½ lengths fourth to Gralmano in novice at Catterick on chasing
debut, weakening soundly: will stay at least 2½m: open to improvement, particularly given
stiffer test of stamina. *Mrs M. Reveley*

BEYOND BORDERS (USA)   5 b.g. Pleasant Colony (USA) – Welcome Proposal   h89 §
(Be My Guest (USA)) [2002/3 h109: 17g 18d 16s³ 16f² 16d 16d⁶ 20v⁴ 16d 16d² 16g⁶
Mar 23] compact ex-Irish gelding: half-brother to fairly useful 2m hurdler Silvian Bliss
(by Green Forest): fairly useful on Flat (stays 1½m): modest maiden hurdler, left D. Weld
after fourth start: not sure to stay much beyond 2m: probably acts on any going: usually
blinkered: of doubtful temperament. *S. Gollings*

BEYOND CONTROL (IRE)   8 b.g. Supreme Leader – Bucktina (Buckskin (FR))   c–
[2002/3 c101p, h103: c26sᵖᵘ c23dᵘʳ 22s* 24s* 23s 22v* 24gᵖᵘ Apr 2] strong, useful-   h120
looking gelding: fair novice only completed outing in steeplechases (let down by jumping
otherwise): fairly useful hurdler: won seller at Folkestone (final start for P. Nicholls) and
handicap at Kempton in January, and handicap at Sandown (beat Haydens Field a length)
in March: very stiff task, pulled up eighth after losing action in Grade 2 at Ascot: stays
3¼m: raced mainly on going softer than good (acts on heavy). *C. Tizzard*

BEYOND THE PALE (IRE)   5 b.g. Be My Native (USA) – Cyrano Imperial (IRE)   h114 p
(Cyrano de Bergerac) [2002/3 F93: F17g* F16d⁵ 16s* Dec 28] tall, angular gelding: F103
fairly useful form in bumpers, won at Sedgefield in October easily by 4 lengths and fifth
to Rhinestone Cowboy in listed event at Cheltenham: good start over hurdles, winning
steadily-run novice at Newbury in December by 1¾ lengths from Derivative: not seen out
again, but useful hurdler in the making. *Noel T. Chance*

BEZWELL BLUE   4 ch.f. Bluebird (USA) – Willisa (Polar Falcon (USA)) [2002/3   F–
F16g Feb 12] 8,700Y, resold 23,000Y, 700 3-y-o: second foal: half-sister to fair 2000
2-y-o sprinter Waterpark (by Namaqualand), later won at 1m: dam, 7f winner, half-sister

to useful sprinters Alzianah and Return of Amin: no show in mares bumper on debut. *Mrs J. C. McGregor*

BHUTAN (IRE)   8 b.g. Polish Patriot (USA) – Bustinetta (Bustino) [2002/3 h119§: 18d⁵ 16v* 18d² 16d³ 16m⁵ Mar 20] neat gelding: fair hurdler: won seller at Chepstow (sold from Mrs M. Reveley 6,200 gns) in November: left D. Wintle after next outing, successful 3 times on Flat in February: best efforts around 2m: unraced on firm going, acts on any other: weak finisher, and best with delayed waiting tactics. *G. L. Moore*   **h106 §**

BICYCLE THIEF (IRE)   10 ch.g. Archway (IRE) – Push Bike (Ballad Rock) [2002/3 h126: c17s^F c21v³ c21d² c20d² c19s³ c24g* Mar 22] smallish gelding: fair handicap hurdler: similar form over fences, workmanlike in landing odds in 5-runner novice at Bangor: stays 3m: acts on heavy going: blinkered last 2 outings in 2001/2: has failed to impress with attitude/jumping over fences. *Miss Venetia Williams*   **c109 h–**

BID FOR FAME (USA)   6 b. or br.g. Quest For Fame – Shroud (USA) (Vaguely Noble) [2002/3 21d⁴ 21m³ Mar 21] leggy gelding: half-brother to fairly useful hurdler Westholme (by Lyphard's Wish), stayed 19f: useful on Flat (stays 2m), successful 3 times in 2002, sold out of T. Mills's stable 52,000 gns Newmarket Autumn Sales, good second in April: fair form in 2 starts over hurdles, jumping better in main than on debut and having run of race when third to Red Socialite in maiden at Newbury. *N. J. Henderson*   **h98**

BID ME WELCOME   7 b.g. Alzao (USA) – Blushing Barada (USA) (Blushing Groom (FR)) [2002/3 17m² Aug 26] one-time fairly useful on Flat (stays 2m), poor nowadays: runner-up in seller at Southwell on hurdling debut: sold £600 Ascot November Sales. *Mrs J. R. Ramsden*   **h79**

BIG JOE DAKARA   8 b.g. Akarad (FR) – Ruling Honor (USA) (Hero's Honor (USA)) [2002/3 20d^pu 24v^pu 20s⁴ 20m⁵ Jul 24] big, workmanlike gelding: has been tubed: little sign of ability. *J. Mackie*   **h–**

BIG MAX   8 b.g. Rakaposhi King – Edwina's Dawn (Space King) [2002/3 h98: c20s² 21d^pu c20d⁴ c24d^ur c24s⁵ c24d³ c24s^pu Feb 15] useful-looking gelding: modest handicap hurdler: similar form over fences, third in novice handicap at Ludlow: stays 3m: acts on good to firm and good to soft going, probably on soft. *Miss K. M. George*   **c92 h–**

BIGNOYSE (IRE)   10 b.g. Little Bighorn – Black River Lady (River Beauty) [2002/3 c–, h–: 24d^pu 20m⁶ 20d^pu May 23] of no account: visored/blinkered in 2002/3. *C. R. Wilson*   **c– h–**

BIG QUICK (IRE)   8 ch.g. Glacial Storm (USA) – Furryvale (Furry Glen) [2002/3 h85p, F84: 20m² 20g² 22m 20d 22d² 21m³ 24m* 27f⁴ Apr 24] modest novice hurdler: improved form to win 6-runner handicap at Exeter in April, 10 lengths clear when all but unseating last: best at 3m+: unraced on heavy going, acts on any other. *L. Wells*   **h98**

BIG STAR (IRE)   6 ro.g. Fourstars Allstar (USA) – Dame Blakeney (IRE) (Blakeney) [2002/3 F16v F16s Mar 8] well held in 3 bumpers. *J. S. Haldane*   **F–**

BIG WHEEL   8 ch.g. Mujtahid (USA) – Numuthej (USA) (Nureyev (USA)) [2002/3 c16d^F c16s⁵ 17g* 21m² Apr 26] angular gelding: modest hurdler, missed 2001/2: won conditional jockeys selling handicap at Sedgefield in March: good second to Brush A King in similar event there following month: well held completed start over fences: stays easy 21f: acts on firm and soft going: tried blinkered. *N. G. Richards*   **c87 h99**

BIGWIG (IRE)   10 ch.g. Thatching – Sabaah (USA) (Nureyev (USA)) [2002/3 h87§: 21g⁶ 19m 16s 22s⁵ 19s³ 21s 21v 21g 21m 21m⁴ Apr 19] rather sparely-made gelding: poor handicap hurdler: stays 21f: acts on any going: tried visored, blinkered nowadays: has won 5 times at Plumpton: has looked less than keen (ran out once), and not one to trust. *G. L. Moore*   **h83 §**

BILBOA (FR)   6 b.m. Phantom Breeze – Maisonnaise (FR) (Labus (FR)) [2002/3 h152: c19s* c19s^F Oct 8] smallish, leggy mare: smart hurdler, third in Champion Hurdle at Cheltenham in 2002: won on debut over fences at Enghien in September: still to be asked for effort when fell heavily 3 out there following month: would have stayed beyond 19f: acted on heavy going, probably on good to firm: held up: retired. *F. Doumen, France*   **c128 h–**

BILLESLEY BELLE   6 ch.m. Sula Bula – Tara VII (Damsire Unregistered) [2002/3 F17s F16g Mar 23] first foal: dam unraced: tailed off in 2 bumpers: headstrong. *A. J. Wilson*   **F–**

BILLIE JOHN (IRE)   8 ch.g. Boyne Valley – Lovestream (Sandy Creek) [2002/3 h99, F77: 16g* 20m⁴ 19m² 17g⁴ 17m* Sep 14] modest novice hurdler: won at Hexham in June and Bangor in September: takes strong hold, and probably better suited by 2m than 2½m: raced on good/good to firm going. *Mrs K. Walton*   **h94**

BILL OWEN 7 ch.g. Nicholas Bill – Pollys Owen (Master Owen) [2002/3 c21d^{pu} **c–** c19g^5 c24g^4 Apr 12] medium-sized gelding: half-brother to fair chaser Country Store (by Sunyboy), stays 27f, and winning 2m hurdler Relkowen (by Relkino): dam, winning hurdler/chaser, stayed well: runner-up on second of 2 starts in maiden points in 2002: little encouragement in 3 novice chases. *D. P. Keane*

BILL'S ECHO 4 br.g. Double Eclipse (IRE) – Bit On Edge (Henbit (USA)) [2002/3   **F75** F14d^5 F16v^5 F16d F16s^4 Mar 8] fourth foal: dam no sign of ability: poor form in bumpers at Ayr. *P. Monteith*

BILLY BALLBREAKER (IRE) 7 b.g. Good Thyne (USA) – Droichead Dhamhile   **h64** (IRE) (The Parson) [2002/3 F87: 17g^6 Mar 18] leggy gelding: fair form on first of 2 outings in bumpers: started slowly and pulled hard when sixth in novice selling hurdle at Exeter after 15-month absence: joined C. Tizzard. *P. F. Nicholls*

BILLY BONNIE (IRE) 6 ch.g. Anshan – Sinology (Rainbow Quest (USA)) [2002/3   **h124** h121: 22d^3 Aug 3] medium-sized gelding: fairly useful hurdler: good third to Vatirisk in handicap at Galway, only outing in 2002/3: stays 2¾m: raced on going softer than good (acts on heavy): tried tongue tied. *N. Meade, Ireland*

BILLY NOMAITE 9 ch.g. Komaite (USA) – Lucky Monashka (Lucky Wednesday)   **c108 +** [2002/3 c105, h–: c20s^2 c20d^F c20m* c20d^{ur} Jul 20] workmanlike gelding: winning   **h–** hurdler: fair chaser: won handicap at Market Rasen in June: stays 2½m: acts on soft and good to firm going: failed to complete 3 of last 5 outings and needs to improve his jumping. *Mrs S. J. Smith*

BILLY THE SNAKE (IRE) 10 b.g. Yashgan – Kathy's Trix (Callernish) [2002/3   **c113** c104p, h108: c17v c20s^6 c20s^4 c24v^5 c19s^4 c28s^{pu} Feb 2] good-topped gelding: fair   **h–** hurdler/chaser: best effort over fences when winning listed handicap at Leopardstown in January: should have stayed 3m+: raced on good going or softer (acted on heavy): dead. *P. Hughes, Ireland*

BINDAREE (IRE) 9 ch.g. Roselier (FR) – Flowing Tide (Main Reef) [2002/3 c146,   **c138** h–: 25d c27d^F c26g^{ur} c26s^2 c24d^4 c28d c36d^6 Apr 5] leggy gelding: winning hurdler: **h–** useful handicap chaser, won Martell Grand National at Aintree in 2002: left with too much to do after bad mistake sixth (Becher's) when sixth of 14 finishers to Monty's Pass in same race year on: best efforts in 2002/3 when in frame in valuable limited handicaps at Chepstow (second to See More Business) in December and at Haydock (fourth to Truckers Tavern) in January): stays 4½m: yet to race on firm going, acts on any other: blinkered last 3 outings in 2000/1: usually a sound jumper. *N. A. Twiston-Davies*

BINDY BONDY 6 b.m. Beveled (USA) – Rockmount Rose (Proverb) [2002/3 F17s   **h–** F16s F16g 16m^{pu} Mar 31] smallish mare: second foal: dam, modest chaser, stayed 3m: **F70** signs of only little ability in bumpers: showed nothing on hurdling debut. *J. R. Best*

BIN IT (IRE) 7 b.m. Supreme Leader – Castle Stream (Paddy's Stream) [2002/3 h114:   **h117** 24s^2 23v^5 Nov 19] medium-sized mare: fairly useful hurdler: much better effort in handicaps in 2002/3 on reappearance: stays 3m: raced on going softer than good (acts on heavy): patiently ridden: consistent: joined B. Pollock. *C. J. Mann*

BINNY BAY 7 b.m. Karinga Bay – Binny Grove (Sunyboy) [2002/3 h74, F65: 20s*   **c77** 26s^5 21v^6 c16s^2 c16v^3 c16v^4 c20g^4 c17m^3 Apr 12] leggy mare: modest hurdler: won   **h85** novice handicap at Bangor in May: poor novice chaser: stays 21f: acts on good to firm and heavy going: tongue tied. *D. McCain*

BINT ST JAMES 8 b.m. Shareef Dancer (USA) – St James's Antigua (IRE) (Law   **h–** Society (USA)) [2002/3 h70d: 20g 23v 16v^5 Nov 28] winning selling hurdler, no form for some time: tried in visor. *W. Clay*

BIRCHALL BELLE (IRE) 5 b.m. Presenting – Queenford Belle (Celtic Cone)   **F–** [2002/3 F16g Feb 22] second foal: dam, 2½m hurdle winner, half-sister to high-class staying chaser Couldnt Be Better: well beaten in bumper on debut. *Mrs H. Dalton*

BIRD KING 6 b.g. Rakaposhi King – Miss Wrensborough (Buckskin (FR)) [2002/3   **h–** F–: 21g^{ur} 21d^{pu} Nov 4] rather unfurnished gelding: no sign of ability in bumper/2 novice hurdles. *D. R. Gandolfo*

BIROTEX BOY (IRE) 10 b.g. Meneval (USA) – Ballymorris Belle (Laurence O)   **c–** [2002/3 c77, h–: c16s c16v^{pu} c17s^5 Nov 21] lengthy gelding: maiden jumper, no form in   **h–** handicap chases in 2002/3: should be suited by further than 2m: acts on soft and good to firm going: tried tongue tied. *M. W. Easterby*

BIRTH OF THE BLUES 7 ch.g. Efisio – Great Steps (Vaigly Great) [2002/3 18m   **h–** Sep 24] angular gelding: modest on Flat (stays 1½m): no form over hurdles. *A. Charlton*

BISHLIR 5 gr.g. Lir – Rose Park Dancer VII (Damsire Unregistered) [2002/3 F18d   F—
Feb 17] first foal: dam unraced: showed nothing in bumper on debut. *Miss K. M. George*

BISHOP'S BLADE 6 b.g. Sure Blade (USA) – Myrtilla (Beldale Flutter (USA))   h—
[2002/3 19d Jan 27] second foal: dam winning hurdler around 2m: well held on Flat for
J. King: 66/1 and blinkered, eighth of 11 finishers in novice at Exeter on hurdling debut.
M. Hill

BISHOP'S BRIDGE (IRE) 5 b.g. Norwich – River Swell (IRE) (Over The River   F74
(FR)) [2002/3 F16s Jan 27] 8,500 4-y-o: unfurnished gelding: second foal: half-brother to
winning hurdler around 2m Marcus William (by Roselier): dam unraced, out of half-sister
to smart staying hurdler Gillan Cove: 50/1, ninth of 20 in bumper at Kempton on debut.
C. P. Morlock

BISHOPSTONE BELLE 6 b.m. Formidable (USA) – Relatively Easy (Relkino)   h—
[2002/3 h–: 21gpu Sep 6] close-coupled mare: seems of no account. *J. A. Moore*

BISON KING (IRE) 6 b.g. King's Ride – Valantonia (IRE) (Over The River (FR))   F98
[2002/3 F16d2 F16g Dec 13] IR 120,000 3-y-o: big, rangy gelding: third foal: dam unraced half-sister to Champion Hurdle winners Morley Street and Granville Again: length
second of 18 to Musimaro in maiden at Ludlow, better effort in bumpers. *C. R. Egerton*

BISQUET-DE-BOUCHE 9 ch.m. Most Welcome – Larive (Blakeney) [2002/3 h89:   c—
20d 24g5 21spu c20s5 25dpu Mar 6] sparely-made mare: modest handicap hurdler: no form   h—
after lengthy absence in 2002/3, including over fences: stays 25f: acts on good to firm and
good to soft going. *A. W. Carroll*

BIT OF A GEM 7 b.m. Henbit (USA) – Krystle Saint (St Columbus) [2002/3 F16g   h—
F16g 20g 20mpu Apr 21] leggy mare: fourth foal: dam temperamental winning chaser   F—
who stayed 3m: no sign of ability. *K. A. Morgan*

BITOFAMIXUP (IRE) 12 br.g. Strong Gale – Geeaway (Gala Performance (USA))   c—
[2002/3 c–, h–: c24g c24m6 c25gur c21gur Apr 3] tall, rangy gelding: one-time very smart   h—
pointer/hunter chaser: won 3 times in points in 2003, but no form in steeplechases for
long time, mainly in handicaps: tried blinkered (unseated first): usually tongue tied.
M. J. Roberts

BIT OF A SNOB 12 b.g. St Columbus – Classey (Dubassoff (USA)) [2002/3 c93, h–:   c—
c19gpu c16gpu c16mpu 16m Jun 29] leggy gelding: winning hurdler/chaser, no form after   h—
lengthy absence early in 2002/3: best around 2m: acts on soft and firm going: sometimes
blinkered: front runner. *J. S. King*

BIT OF MINSTER 7 b.g. Minster Son – Bit On Edge (Henbit (USA)) [2002/3 c75,   c—
h56: c25gpu May 11] poor maiden jumper: stays 25f: acts on soft going. *P. Monteith*   h—

BIT O' GOLD 5 b.g. Henbit (USA) – Run of Gold (Deep Run) [2002/3 F16g F16m   F—
F17m F17g Apr 21] 1,000 3-y-o: fourth foal: dam lightly raced and little sign of ability:
well beaten in bumpers, left D. Smith after third start. *Mrs K. B. Mactaggart*

BIT O MAGIC (IRE) 11 ch.g. Henbit (USA) – Arpal Magic (Master Owen) [2002/3   c98
c89, h–: c17d3 c17g2 c16d3 c16g c19g3 c19s c20gF c20g* c17d2 c17g2 c20gF Apr 23]   h—
workmanlike gelding: modest handicap chaser: won at Musselburgh in January: good
efforts all 3 subsequent starts: stays easy 2½m: yet to race on heavy going, acts on any
other: tried blinkered. *Ferdy Murphy*

BIT O'SPEED (IRE) 12 b.g. Henbit (USA) – Speedy Debbie (Pollerton) [2002/3   c92
c24g* c21g3 Apr 19] rangy, useful-looking gelding: fair hunter chaser: made all jumping   h—
boldly when winning at Stratford in April: stays 3m: acts on firm and good to soft going:
has had tongue tied. *Mrs S. Richardson*

BITTER SWEET 7 gr.m. Deploy – Julia Flyte (Drone (USA)) [2002/3 h73+: 16g2   h98
16g2 17g2 17d4 16m* 16s3 16g5 Apr 12] sparely-made mare: modest handicap hurdler:
much improved in 2002/3, won at Warwick in November: raced around 2m: acts on soft
and good to firm going: consistent. *J. L. Spearing*

BIVACASTLE 7 ch.m. Carlingford Castle – Bivadell (Bivouac) [2002/3 20gpu Apr   h—
21] third foal: dam maiden pointer: failed to complete in 3 maiden points and mares
novice hurdle. *B. N. Pollock*

BLACK BEATLE 8 b.g. Roscoe Blake – Rose Albertine (Record Token) [2002/3   h—
22gpu Oct 19] third foal: brother to 3¼m chase winner Running Mute: dam well beaten in
2-y-o maidens: failed to complete in 4 maiden points in 2002 and on hurdling debut.
S. H. Shirley-Beavan

BLACKBERRY WAY   9 ch.m. Almoojid – Prickly Path (Royal Match) [2002/3 h73:   **c87**
c20m* c25d³ c24s⁴ c22m³ c24m⁵ Apr 10] tall mare: lightly raced: winning pointer: fair   **h–**
hunter chaser, won novice at Huntingdon in May: stays 3m: acts on soft and good to firm
going. *Ms Louise Cullen*

BLACK BULLET (NZ)   10 br.g. Silver Pistol (AUS) – Monte d'Oro (NZ) (Cache of   **c116**
Gold (USA)) [2002/3 c–, h–: c16d³ c16g² c16v³ c19g⁵ c16d* c16d* c16vᵖᵘ c16d⁵ c16g⁵   **h–**
c16s* Mar 7] tall, angular gelding: fairly useful handicap chaser: left A. Streeter after
third outing: won at Newcastle in November, Haydock in December and Hereford (best
effort, beat Athnowen 2½ lengths after flashing tail and mistakes last 2) in March: stays
2½m: acts on good to firm and heavy going: has been early to post: has bled from nose/
had breathing problems: races prominently. *Mrs J. Candlish*

BLACKCHURCH MIST (IRE)   6 b.m. Erins Isle – Diandra (Shardari) [2002/3 F–:   **h102**
F18g F16m³ F16d F16f³ 20m³ 22d² 21dᵖᵘ 22d* 20g* 20mᵖᵘ 21m⁵ Apr 17] angular mare: **F81**
modest form in bumpers: fair novice hurdler: won handicap at Wincanton in December
and mares event at Folkestone in March: dictated pace and improved form when fifth of 9
to Blue Ride in listed mares race at Cheltenham (6 lb out of handicap): will stay 3m: acts
on good to soft and good to firm going (bumper form on firm): tongue tied over hurdles:
front runner. *B. W. Duke*

BLACKCOUNTRY LAD   8 b.g. Henbit (USA) – Cupids Bower (Owen Dudley)   **h–**
[2002/3 19dᵖᵘ 17sᵖᵘ Dec 18] good-topped gelding: no sign of ability. *A. P. James*

BLACK DANTE (IRE)   9 b.g. Phardante (FR) – Orchardstown (Pollerton) [2002/3   **c103**
c26sᵖᵘ c24sᴿ Jan 27] lengthy gelding: fairly useful hurdler in 2000/1: showed more than   **h–**
on steeplechasing debut/first run for 20 months when refusing last in steadily-run novice
won by Hersov at Kempton, around 2 lengths behind eventual third at time (dismounted
and reportedly lame): likely to prove best at 3m+: acts on heavy going. *P. J. Hobbs*

BLACK FROST (IRE)   7 ch.g. Glacial Storm (USA) – Black Tulip (Pals Passage)   **h116**
[2002/3 h–: 20d³ 16d⁵ 20s* 20sᵖᵘ 20g* Apr 21] sturdy gelding: easily best effort over
hurdles when winning 15-runner novice at Haydock in January by 2½ lengths from Palua:
simple task when successful at Carlisle final outing: will stay beyond 2½m: raced on
good going or softer (acts on heavy): bled from nose both starts in 2001/2. *Mrs S. J. Smith*

BLACKJACK LIR   9 b.g. Lir – Miss Black Glama (Derrylin) [2002/3 h–: 22gᵖᵘ May   **h–**
25] no show in 2 novice hurdles. *P. R. Rodford*

BLACK KITE (IRE)   4 br.g. Desert King (IRE) – Snoozeandyoulose (IRE) (Scenic)   **h–**
[2002/3 F16g 21sᵖᵘ Feb 24] compact gelding: third foal: half-brother to modest hurdler   **F–**
around 2m Better Moment (by Turtle Island): dam fair 7f winner: no show in bumper/
novice hurdle. *H. J. Manners*

BLACKOUT (IRE)   8 b.g. Black Monday – Fine Bess (Fine Blade (USA)) [2002/3   **c–**
c21d⁴ c21d⁵ c25v⁴ c20v³ c16s⁵ Mar 8] poor maiden hurdler/chaser: stays 3m: raced   **h–**
mainly on going softer than good (acts on heavy). *J. Barclay*

BLACK RAINBOW (IRE)   5 br.m. Definite Article – Inonder (Belfort (FR)) [2002/3   **h75**
F78: F16d F17s³ 19d 16v 16m Mar 23] sturdy mare: modest form in bumpers for   **F78**
A. Dickman: first form over hurdles when eighth of 17 in maiden at Huntingdon final
start (pulled hard): sold 4,800 gns Doncaster May Sales. *T. J. Etherington*

BLACK SECRET   10 br.m. Gildoran – Polypodium (Politico (USA)) [2002/3 h77?:   **h–**
20g³ Jul 10] lengthy mare: bumper winner: lightly-raced maiden hurdler, reportedly lame
only outing in 2002/3. *R. J. Baker*

BLACK STRIPE LADY   5 b.m. Karinga Bay – Garvenish (Balinger) [2002/3 F16d⁴   **F65**
F16g⁴ Apr 14] €8,000 4-y-o: fifth foal: dam, novice hurdler/chaser, half-sister to useful
2½m chaser Wayward King: poor form in bumpers. *M. Todhunter*

BLAKENEY COAST (IRE)   6 b.g. Satco (FR) – Up To More Trix (IRE) (Torus)   **c80**
[2002/3 F86: 20d 20d⁵ c16g⁶ c16gᵖᵘ c21sᵖᵘ c16g³ c20g² Apr 14] good sort: well beaten in   **h–**
2 novice hurdles: poor novice chaser: should stay beyond 2½m. *Mrs M. Reveley*

BLAKENEY HILL   8 ch.m. Baron Blakeney – Hillgate Lady (Rustingo) [2002/3 h–,   **h–**
F–: 26gᵖᵘ May 4] no show in bumpers or novice hurdles. *Mrs N. S. Sharpe*

BLAKEY (IRE)   7 b.g. Maledetto (IRE) – Villars (Home Guard (USA)) [2002/3 20gᵖᵘ   **h–**
20mᵖᵘ Jun 19] no sign of ability: tried tongue tied. *Mrs N. S. Sharpe*

BLANK CHEQUE   13 b.g. Idiot's Delight – Quickapenny (Espresso) [2002/3 c–, h–:   **c70**
c25d⁵ May 13] fairly useful pointer: maiden hunter chaser, never dangerous at Towcester   **h–**
in May. *J. J. Coates*

BLASKET SOUND (IRE) 11 b.g. Lancastrian – June's Friend (Laurence O) **c–** **§**
[2002/3 c–§, h99§: 27g 26s 22s² 22v⁵ 25s³ Mar 10] rather sparely-made gelding: modest **h86** **§**
hurdler: stays 27f: acts on good to firm and heavy going: tried blinkered: unreliable.
D. J. Wintle

BLAYNEY DANCER 6 b.g. Contract Law (USA) – Lady Poly (Dunbeath (USA)) **h–**
[2002/3 h–: 17m Jun 22] sparely-made gelding: modest 2m winner over hurdles: well
beaten in 2 handicaps only starts since 2000. *Jonjo O'Neill*

BLAZING BATMAN 10 ch.g. Shaab – Cottage Blaze (Sunyboy) [2002/3 c83: c20d⁴ **c67**
c23s⁴ 17d⁴ 24d⁶ 17s³ 25d² 24s³ 26m⁶ 27g Apr 19] sturdy gelding: poor chaser/novice **h81**
hurdler: stays 29f: acts on any going: blinkered (pulled up) once: has broken blood
vessels. *Dr P. Pritchard*

BLAZING COURT (IRE) 6 ch.g. Roselier (FR) – The Blazing Star (Proverb) **F–**
[2002/3 F16s Jan 27] IR £17,000 4-y-o: leggy gelding: brother to fairly useful staying
chaser Rossi Novae and half-brother to fair staying jumper Jupiter's Glory (by Derring
Rose): dam winning Irish pointer: behind in bumper at Kempton on debut. *D. J. Wintle*

BLAZING LISS (IRE) 4 b.f. Supreme Leader – Liss de Paor (IRE) (Phardante (FR))] **F100 p**
[2002/3 NR] small, stocky filly: first foal: dam, fairly useful 2½m hurdler, half-sister to
very smart hurdler Liss A Paoraigh: looked smart prospect when winning 4-y-o bumper
at Punchestown on debut in early-May by 2 lengths from Brutto Facie, travelling strongly
and quickening well: bred to stay at least 2½m but clearly not short of speed. *J. E. Kiely,
Ireland*

BLAZING MIRACLE 11 b.m. Shaab – Cottage Blaze (Sunyboy) [2002/3 c26s* **c86**
May 28] angular mare: novice hurdler: modest hunter chaser: won at Newton Abbot in **h–**
May, having still been virtually tailed off 3 out: stays 3¼m: acts on soft and good to firm
going. *G. Chambers*

BLAZING SADDLES (IRE) 4 b.g. Sadler's Wells (USA) – Dalawara (IRE) (Top **h71**
Ville) [2002/3 18d 17g 16m² Apr 21] disappointing maiden on Flat (should stay at least
1½m), sold out of I. Balding's stable 4,500 gns Newmarket Autumn Sales: poor form in
juvenile hurdles, runner-up in weak 2-finisher event at Plumpton (wore cheekpieces).
P. R. Hedger

BLESS YOURSELF (IRE) 7 b.g. Shardari – Wee Madge (Apollo Eight) [2002/3 **h–**
F–: 16d 20v⁶ 17sᵖᵘ Feb 7] useful-looking gelding: little sign of ability. *D. McCain*

BLEU SUPERBE (FR) 8 b.g. Epervier Bleu – Brett's Dream (FR) (Pharly (FR)) **c136**
[2002/3 c116x, h–: c16g* c16g* c20dᵖᵘ c20gᵖᵘ c17g* c16d* c16sᵖᵘ c16gᵖᵘ c16gᵖᵘ Apr 3] **h–**
rather sparely-made gelding: useful handicap chaser: successful all 4 completed starts
(saddle slipped on fourth) in 2002/3, at Aintree and Towcester in May, Newbury in
November and Doncaster (by 1¾ lengths from Abalvino) in January: poor efforts last 3
outings: ideally suited by 2m with emphasis on speed: acts on good to firm and heavy
going: front runner/races prominently: sometimes let down by jumping. *Miss Venetia
Williams*

BLOOD SUB (IRE) 6 b.g. Roselier (FR) – Clearwater Glen (Furry Glen) [2002/3 **h106 P**
F17s² 22d⁵ 20s* Mar 15] 25,000 3-y-o: medium-sized gelding: fifth foal: half-brother to **F95**
useful but thoroughly ungenuine chaser Montana Glen (by Montelimar), stays 3m: dam
unraced, out of useful 2m hurdler The Very Thing: runner-up in bumper at Folkestone on
debut: favourite, confirmed promise of hurdling bow (reportedly had breathing problem)
when impressive winner of novice at Uttoxeter, leading on bridle last and not extended
to beat Longshanks a length: will prove suited by further than 2½m: open to plenty of
improvement, sure to win more races. *Jonjo O'Neill*

BLOOMING AMAZING 9 b.g. Mazilier (USA) – Cornflower Blue (Tyrnavos) **h–**
[2002/3 17g 16m 16m Jun 29] good-topped gelding: showed traces of stringhalt: modest
on Flat (stayed 1½m), well held in 2002: well held all 4 starts over hurdles: dead.
D. Burchell

BLOSSOM WHISPERS 6 b.m. Ezzoud (IRE) – Springs Welcome (Blakeney) **h70 §**
[2002/3 19s 16v⁵ 17v³ 21d 20s 27s⁶ 23mᶠ Apr 21] smallish mare: dam half-sister to
useful staying chaser Capability Brown: staying maiden on Flat, claimed from C. Cyzer
£6,000 in August: poor maiden hurdler: should stay 3m: acts on heavy and good to
firm going: wore cheekpieces final outing: temperamental (tends to go in snatches).
Mrs M. Reveley

BLOWING AWAY (IRE) 9 b. or br.m. Last Tycoon – Taken By Force (Persian **c–**
Bold) [2002/3 c–, h55: c16g⁶ 17g⁶ 18m⁴ 24f³ 20g 17g Mar 15] poor on Flat, won in July: **h55**

bad hurdler: showed nothing in 2 novice chases for J. Long: probably stays 3m: acts on firm and soft going: tongue tied final start. *Julian Poulton*

BLOWING KISSES   4 b.f. Missed Flight – Blowing Bubbles (Native Admiral (USA))   F–
[2002/3 F12g Dec 18] eighth foal: half-sister to useful sprinter Blessingindisguise (by Kala Shikari): dam won 5 times from 7f to 8.3f: 50/1, tailed off in bumper at Newbury on debut. *M. Mullineaux*

BLOWING ROCK (IRE)   11 b.g. Strong Gale – Poor Elsie (Crash Course) [2002/3   c–
c120, h–: c23g6 c21m4 c26m4 c25dpu Nov 21] lengthy gelding: fairly useful handicap   h–
chaser, out of sorts in 2002/3: stays 25f: best form on good going or firmer: races prominently: sound jumper. *Miss H. C. Knight*

BLOWING WIND (FR)   10 b. or br.g. Fabulous Dancer (USA) – Bassita (Bustino)   c120
[2002/3 c149, h–: c27d3 c21v6 c21s c20g c36d Apr 5] lengthy gelding: smart handicap   h–
chaser: well below best in 2002/3, eighth of 14 finishers to Monty's Pass in Grand National at Aintree (placed in previous 2 renewals): best form up to 25f: acts on heavy and good to firm going: tried blinkered, not since 1998/9. *M. C. Pipe*

BLOW WIND BLOW (IRE)   9 b. or br.g. Strong Gale – Phargara (IRE) (Phardante   c–
(FR)) [2002/3 25s 20s 24d Feb 23] sturdy gelding: fair handicap hurdler in 2000/1: let   h–
down by jumping and no form over fences: left C. Roche, mistakes and well held back over hurdles after 19-month absence: reportedly had breathing problem final outing: stays 3m: acts on firm and soft going, possibly not heavy. *Jonjo O'Neill*

BLUE AMERICO (IRE)   5 br.g. Lord Americo – Princess Menelek (Menelek)   F77 +
[2002/3 F16m Mar 22] IR £58,000 3-y-o: useful-looking gelding: half-brother to several winners, notably top-class chaser Imperial Call (by Callernish), stayed 3¼m: dam winning pointer: odds on, failed to settle when eighth of 18 in bumper at Newbury on debut: clearly thought capable of better. *P. F. Nicholls*

BLUEBELL HILL   6 b.m. Puget (USA) – Fooling With Fire (Idiot's Delight) [2002/3   h–
F17v6 F17v 19gpu 17g Mar 22] lengthy mare: second foal: dam, bumper winner, out of   F–
half-sister to top-class 2m hurdler/smart chaser Prideaux Boy: no form in bumpers or over hurdles. *Mrs L. Williamson*

BLUEBELL WEDDING   8 b.m. Henbit (USA) – Ina's Farewell (Random Shot)   h–
[2002/3 20mpu Jun 21] no sign of ability (has run out in points). *J. Barclay*

BLUE CANYON (IRE)   5 b.g. Phardante (FR) – Miss Gosling (Prince Bee) [2002/3   F79
F16d F16g Mar 14] strong gelding: fourth foal: half-brother to modest 2m hurdler Hidden Ability (by Alphabatim): dam, winning hurdler who stayed 2½m, half-sister to dam of useful 2m hurdler Lady Arpel: better effort in bumpers (failed to settle on debut) when tenth of 19 at Warwick. *B. De Haan*

BLUE DERBY (IRE)   5 b.g. Supreme Leader – Minigirls Niece (IRE) (Strong Gale)   F87
[2002/3 F16s F17f* Mar 24] IR £34,000 3-y-o: second foal: dam, placed in bumpers/over hurdles, closely related to smart hurdler Minorettes Girl, dam of Shotgun Willy and Mini Sensation: made all in falsely-run 5-runner bumper at Taunton, despite tending to hang left. *P. J. Hobbs*

BLUE ENDEAVOUR (IRE)   5 b.g. Endeavour (USA) – Jingle Bells (FR) (In The   F86
Mood (FR)) [2002/3 F17g4 Apr 19] €46,000 4-y-o: ninth foal: half-brother to 4 winners in France, including 15f hurdle winner Djort (by Pebble): dam won 15f hurdle in France: 3/1, 10¾ lengths fourth of 14 in maiden bumper at Newton Abbot on debut. *P. F. Nicholls*

BLUE IRISH (IRE)   12 gr.g. Roselier (FR) – Grannie No (Brave Invader (USA))   c–
[2002/3 c–, h–: c25m4 27d2 24d6 27s 27v2 24v6 27s2 Mar 11] workmanlike gelding: h84
shows traces of stringhalt: poor maiden hurdler: one-time fairly useful handicap chaser, little form since 1999/00 reappearance: stays 27f: acts on heavy going: sometimes blinkered, wears cheekpieces nowadays: sketchy jumper of fences. *Ferdy Murphy*

BLUE JAR   5 b.g. Royal Abjar (USA) – Artist's Glory (Rarity) [2002/3 F–: 20vpu 16gbd   h–
16dpu 17gpu Mar 22] of little account. *M. Mullineaux*

BLUE LEADER (IRE)   4 b.c. Cadeaux Genereux – Blue Duster (USA) (Danzig   h–
(USA)) [2002/3 16v 16d 16d 17fpu Mar 27] tall colt: fairly useful on Flat (stays 1¼m), sold out of E. Dunlop's stable 14,000 gns Newmarket Autumn Sales): no show over hurdles. *G. Brown*

BLUE LEGEND (IRE)   6 b.m. Blues Traveller (IRE) – Swoon Along (Dunphy)   h–
[2002/3 16gpu 16gF 22g Oct 19] 7f winner on Flat, no form in 2001: tongue tied, no show over hurdles. *B. Mactaggart*

BLUE LIZARD (IRE)   6 b.g. Roselier (FR) – Rathsallagh Tartan (Strong Gale)   **h70**
[2002/3 23s⁴ 24s Feb 24] IR 20,000 3-y-o, IR £50,000 4-y-o: good-bodied gelding: fourth
foal: brother to winning hurdler/one-time fairly useful chaser Knight Templar, stays 21f:
dam unraced half-sister to top-class 2m hurdler/chaser Buck House: poor form on first of
2 starts over hurdles. *Ferdy Murphy*

BLUE MOMMA (IRE)   4 b.f. Petardia – Heads We Called (IRE) (Bluebird (USA))   **h71**
[2002/3 16vᵖᵘ 17s² 19v 17g Apr 21] half-sister to winning 2¾m hurdler Seeking Destiny
(by Two Timing): well held in two 1¼m maidens at 3 yrs for P. Webber: best effort over
hurdles when second in seller at Taunton. *M. C. Pipe*

BLUE MORNING   5 b.m. Balnibarbi – Bad Start (USA) (Bold Bidder) [2002/3 F16v   **F–**
F17g Mar 28] eighth foal: half-sister to minor French 1¼m winner Susy Star (by
Brustolon): dam, unplaced on 6 starts in France, daughter of smart French 9f and 10.5f
winner North Sea: no show in 2 bumpers. *Mrs J. C. McGregor*

BLUE NATIVE   6 br.m. Be My Native (USA) – Supreme Wings (IRE) (Supreme   **F–**
Leader) [2002/3 F16g Mar 14] 26,000 4-y-o: first foal: dam unraced, out of half-sister to
top-class 2m hurdler Ekbalco: well held in bumper on debut. *R. J. Hodges*

BLUE PLANET (IRE)   5 b.g. Bluebird (USA) – Millie Musique (Miller's Mate)   **h92 +**
[2002/3 h78: 21g⁴ 20d⁴ 20s² Mar 2] workmanlike gelding: fairly useful at one time on
Flat: modest form over hurdles, generally progressive: stays 21f: acts on soft going.
P. G. Murphy

BLUE RIDE (IRE)   6 b.m. King's Ride – Charmere's Beauty (IRE) (Phardante (FR))   **h129**
[2002/3 F88: 19s² 16d* 22d* 21m³ 21m*] Apr 17] lengthy, rather unfurnished mare:
bumper winner: successful on 3 of 5 starts in mares hurdles, in novices at Wincanton in
December and February and listed handicap at Cheltenham in April: useful form when
beating Deep Sunset 11 lengths at latter, clear when blundering last: stays 2¾m: acts on
good to firm and good to soft going, probably soft: has her quirks. *P. F. Nicholls*

BLUESHAAN (IRE)   10 b.g. Darshaan – Pale Blue (Kris) [2002/3 h–: 17g* c16g3   **c71**
c19m⁶ c19m Oct 3] useful-looking gelding: tumbled in weights, won selling handicap   **h75**
hurdle at Hereford (sold from Dr P. Pritchard 4,200 gns) in May: similar form on first of 3
starts over fences: stays 2½m: acts on heavy going: races freely. *Mrs A. M. Thorpe*

BLUE SHANNON (IRE)   5 b.m. Be My Native (USA) – Shannon Foam (Le Bavard   **F80**
(FR)) [2002/3 F16m² F17m F17g⁴ Apr 21] IR £75,000 3-y-o: leggy mare: half-sister to
fairly useful hurdler/chaser Bunratty Castle (by Supreme Leader), stays 25f, and winning
pointer by Royal Fountain: dam, well held in bumper/over hurdles, sister to useful hurdler
Shannon Spray who stayed 2¾m: 1½ lengths second of 4 in bumper at Ludlow on debut:
well beaten subsequently. *P. F. Nicholls*

BLUES OF THE NIGHT   7 gr.m. Petong – Candane (Danehill (USA)) [2002/3 16g   **h–**
16sᵖᵘ Nov 2] no form over hurdles. *R. Johnson*

BLUES STORY (FR)   5 b.g. Pistolet Bleu (IRE) – Herbe Sucree (FR) (Tiffauges)   **h–**
[2002/3 F–: F18v⁴ 16v⁴ Mar 8] lengthy gelding: best effort (poor form) in bumpers on   **F75**
reappearance: remote fourth of 5 in novice at Sandown on hurdling debut. *P. R. Webber*

BLUE STREAK (IRE)   6 ch.g. Bluebird (USA) – Fleet Amour (USA) (Afleet (CAN))   **h97**
[2002/3 16m⁴ 16m* 16g⁶ 16d² 16s* 16s⁶ 18v Mar 3] angular gelding: modest on Flat
(stays easy 1½m): similar standard over hurdles, won weak claimer in October and
amateur handicap in November, both at Plumpton: raced mainly at 2m: acts on good to
firm and soft going, poor efforts on heavy. *G. L. Moore*

BLUE STYLE (IRE)   7 ch.g. Bluebird (USA) – Style For Life (IRE) (Law Society   **h81**
(USA)) [2002/3 19s 18m² 16m 17s Nov 14] poor on Flat (should stay at least 1¾m): form
over hurdles only when second in seller at Fontwell: looked to down tools when blinkered
final outing. *P. Burgoyne*

BLUNHAM HILL (IRE)   5 ch.g. Over The River (FR) – Bronach (Beau Charmeur   **h91**
(FR)) [2002/3 20s⁵ 20d³ 20d³ 20sᵖᵘ 24s⁵ Feb 27] quite good-topped gelding: sixth foal: half-
brother to bumper winner Crossbar (by Lord Americo): dam winning pointer: easily best
effort in novice hurdles when third at Haydock: should be suited by 3m+. *John R. Upson*

BLUSHING SPUR   5 b.g. Flying Spur (AUS) – Bogus John (CAN) (Blushing John   **h–**
(USA)) [2002/3 16gᵘʳ 16vᵖᵘ Dec 21] workmanlike gelding: fair on Flat (stays 7f),
successful in February: not fluent and failed to complete in 2 starts over hurdles: wore
visor/cheekpieces: joined A. Charlton. *D. Shaw*

BLYTH BROOK   11 b.g. Meadowbrook – The Bean-Goose (King Sitric) [2002/3   **c105 x**
c94, h–: c20m c24g³ c25gᵖᵘ Apr 5] leggy gelding: fair pointer/hunter chaser, trained by   **h–**

Miss S. Forster on reappearance: stays 27f: acts on good to firm going, probably on good to soft: not a fluent jumper. *W. T. Reed*

BLYTHE LADY 9 b.m. Warrshan (USA) – Aldwick Colonnade (Kind of Hush) [2002/3 h68: 16s⁴ 16m 20gᵖᵘ 16m³ c20f⁵ c24sᵖᵘ c16v⁵ c20sᵖᵘ 16d 16sᵖᵘ 20gᵖᵘ Apr 21] leggy mare: poor maiden hurdler: little form in 2002/3, including over fences (reportedly bled from nose on debut): stays 3m: acts on any going: blinkered last 4 starts. *T. Wall*
c–
h–

BNEYA (FR) 6 b.m. Hero's Honor (USA) – Khariyada (FR) (Akarad (FR)) [2002/3 23sᵖᵘ Dec 7] fairly useful maiden on Flat, lightly raced: fair maiden hurdler in 2001/2 for J. Bertran de Balanda: fatally injured on British debut: stayed 19f: raced on going softer than good. *Mrs M. Reveley*
h–

BOARDROOM DANCER (IRE) 6 b.g. Executive Perk – Dancing Course (IRE) (Crash Course) [2002/3 F18s⁴ F16s⁶ 20d⁶ Apr 9] IR 13,000 3-y-o, 17,000 4-y-o: third foal: dam 19f hurdle winner: signs of a little ability in 2 bumpers: well held in novice on hurdling debut. *D. J. Caro*
h–
F71

BOARD WALK (IRE) 8 b.g. Commanche Run – Swift Tide (Hardboy) [2002/3 c86: c22m³ c22d² Nov 17] big gelding: modest handicap chaser, lightly raced: should prove best at 3m+: acts on soft and good to firm going: patiently ridden: has been let down by jumping. *Mrs M. Reveley*
c98

BOARDWALK KNIGHT (IRE) 6 b.g. Shardari – Takhiyra (Vayrann) [2002/3 16d 16d* 16d 16g 16gᵖᵘ Nov 23] IR 15,500 3-y-o: ex-Irish gelding: half-brother to fairly useful sprinter Roblexie (by Dominion): dam unraced half-sister to Princess Royal Stakes winner Tashtiya and to dam of smart stayer Tiraaz: twice-raced in bumpers: modest over hurdles, won maiden at Wexford in August: sold out of D. Hughes's stable 8,000 gns Doncaster October Sales after fourth start: broke blood vessel on British debut: raced at 2m on good going or softer. *M. Todhunter*
h90

BOATER 9 b.g. Batshoof – Velvet Beret (IRE) (Dominion) [2002/3 h100§: 17g* 16s⁶ 22mᶠ 17g⁴ Apr 19] sturdy gelding: fair handicap hurdler: gained third course win at Newton Abbot in May: stays 19f: acts on any going: blinkered: carries head high/has found little: not one to rely on. *R. J. Baker*
h102 §

BOBALONG (IRE) 6 b.g. Bob's Return (IRE) – Northern Wind (Northfields (USA)) [2002/3 F17d Feb 23] half-brother to 3 winners, including fairly useful 2m hurdler/fair chaser Common Sound (by Common Grounds): dam unraced: 50/1, well-held eighth of 15 in bumper at Exeter on debut. *C. P. Morlock*
F72

BOBANVI 5 b.m. Timeless Times (USA) – Bobanlyn (IRE) (Dance of Life (USA)) [2002/3 h67: 20dᵖᵘ 16g² 16s⁴ 16d 16d 17g 16g⁶ 23m³ Apr 21] smallish mare: poor maiden hurdler: raced mainly at 2m: acts on good to soft going: usually wears cheek-pieces: none too genuine. *J. S. Wainwright*
h67 §

BOB AR AGHAIDH (IRE) 7 b.g. Bob Back (USA) – Shuil Ar Aghaidh (The Parson) [2002/3 F91: 22s⁵ 20v² 22s³ 24v² Jan 17] sturdy gelding: fair form over hurdles, placed in novice/maidens 3 of 4 starts: stays 3m: raced on going softer than good (acts on heavy). *A. J. Lidderdale*
h106

BOBAWAY (IRE) 6 br.g. Bob Back (USA) – Baybush (Boreen (FR)) [2002/3 F–: F17s 21sᵖᵘ Jan 3] unfurnished gelding: no form in 2 bumpers or maiden hurdle. *A. J. Lidderdale*
h–
F–

BOBAYARO (IRE) 7 b.g. Bob Back (USA) – Instanter (Morston (FR)) [2002/3 h104, F91: 20g² c20d³ c24g² c24gᶠ c25s⁴ c25g² c24g* Apr 23] tall gelding: fair hurdler: similar form over fences, didn't need to be at best to win 6-runner novice at Perth in April, making all and jumping soundly: stays 25f: acts on soft going (won bumper on good to firm): blinkered once in bumpers. *N. G. Richards*
c109
h104

BOBBIE JAMES (IRE) 7 ch.g. Roselier (FR) – Brown Forest (Brave Invader (USA)) [2002/3 F16m F16d Nov 7] workmanlike gelding: eighth foal: half-brother to several winners, including fair chaser Brown Buck (by Buckskin), stays 21f, and 2¾m hurdle winner Forest Musk (by Strong Gale): dam unraced, out of sister to Irish National winner Garoupe: well held in bumpers. *J. Mackie*
F–

BOBBI ROSE RED 6 ch.m. Bob Back (USA) – Lady Rosanna (Kind of Hush) [2002/3 F68: F16d⁶ F16s 19d⁵ 24sᶠ 25g⁴ Mar 14] signs of a little ability in mares bumpers and novice hurdles. *P. T. Dalton*
h70 ?
F–

BOBBY BLAKENEY 8 gr.g. Baron Blakeney – Coming Out (Fair Season) [2002/3 20dᵖᵘ Apr 9] no sign of ability, even in points. *Miss L. V. Davis*
h–

BOBBY GRANT 12 ch.g. Gunner B – Goldaw (Gala Performance (USA)) [2002/3 **c134**
c–, h–: c24d[3] c24d[2] c28v[4] c28d Mar 1] close-coupled gelding: high-class chaser at best: **h–**
showed himself still capable of useful form after nearly another year off first 2 starts in
2002/3, 1½ lengths second of 4 to Sackville in Grade 2 at Haydock: stayed 25f: raced on
good going or softer (acted on heavy): retired. *P. Beaumont*

BOB JUSTICE (IRE) 7 b.g. Bob Back (USA) – Bramdean (Niniski (USA)) [2002/3 **c123**
h139: c17s* c20s[F] 16v[2] c16v[5] c16s[4] c20s[2] c21v[pu] c20d[F] c24v[3] Mar 8] useful hurdler at **h–**
best: fairly useful novice chaser: impressive when winning maiden at Navan in May:
largely disappointing subsequently: effective at 2m to easy 3m: acts on heavy going:
usually races prominently. *T. M. Walsh, Ireland*

BOB LE GAOTH (IRE) 7 br.g. Bob Back (USA) – Shuil Le Gaoth (IRE) (Strong **h–**
Gale) [2002/3 h73: 21d[F] Nov 4] useful bumper winner: off a year after hurdling debut,
disputing lead when falling sixth in novice at Plumpton: will prove suited by 2½m+.
A. J. Lidderdale

BOBOSH 7 b.g. Devil's Jump – Jane Craig (Rapid Pass) [2002/3 h86: 16d 21m[5] 19m **h90**
26g[4] 18m[4] 16m[4] 21d Nov 15] leggy gelding: modest hurdler: stays 21f: acts on soft and
good to firm going: visored once (tried to run out): usually front runner. *R. Dickin*

BOBSBEST (IRE) 7 b.g. Lashkari – Bobs (Warpath) [2002/3 h71: 17g[5] 20g[2] 16d 19s **c–**
26s[pu] c19d c16g[F] 22g* 22g[pu] 22g[2] Apr 26] angular gelding: no form in 2 starts over **h75**
fences (fell when visored): poor handicap hurdler: won novice at Market Rasen in March:
stays 2¾m: acts on soft and good to firm going. *R. Dickin*

BOB'S BUSTER 7 b.g. Bob's Return (IRE) – Saltina (Bustino) [2002/3 c78, h85: **c85**
16g[3] 16g 16v[4] c16g[5] Nov 23] sturdy gelding: modest handicap hurdler/novice chaser: **h85**
raced around 2m: acts on soft and good to firm going: held up: headstrong. *R. Johnson*

BOB'S GONE (IRE) 5 ch.g. Eurobus – Bob's Girl (IRE) (Bob Back (USA)) [2002/3 **h92**
20g[ur] 22g 24m[4] 21m[4] Apr 21] ex-Irish gelding: 2m winner on Flat: modest hurdler, won
maiden at Limerick in 2001/2: sold out of Miss F. Crowley's stable 6,000 gns Doncaster
November Sales after third outing: should stay beyond 2m: acts on soft and good to firm
going. *R. J. Smith*

BOB THE PILER 7 b.g. Jendali (USA) – Laxay (Laxton) [2002/3 17s[4] Nov 28] **h78 p**
medium-sized gelding: fair bumper winner in 2000/1: off 20 months, kept on without
reaching leaders when around 16 lengths fourth in novice hurdle at Carlisle: will stay at
least 2½m: raced only on soft/heavy going: should improve. *N. G. Richards*

BOB WHAT (IRE) 9 b.g. Bob Back (USA) – Whatyawant (Auction Ring (USA)) **h130**
[2002/3 h114: 16g[2] 17m* 16d[5] 17g* 16m[2] 16m Apr 22] good-topped gelding: useful
hurdler: in good form in 2002/3, winning handicaps at Bellewstown in July and Tralee
(listed event) in August: very good second to Intersky Falcon in Grade 2 at Tipperary in
October: effective at 2m and should stay beyond 2½m: probably acts on any going:
tongue tied: sometimes none too fluent. *Patrick Mullins, Ireland*

BO DANCER (IRE) 9 ch.g. Magical Wonder (USA) – Pitty Pal (USA) (Caracolero **h87**
(USA)) [2002/3 h80: 20d[4] 24g[2] 27g[2] 17d* 16m* 21m[3] 27g[3] 17d[4] 20f[3] 24g[3] 22m[4] Oct 6]
tall gelding: modest handicap hurdler: won at Cartmel and Hexham in June: effective at
2m to 27f: acts on any going: consistent. *Mrs E. Slack*

BODFARI CREEK 6 ch.g. In The Wings – Cormorant Creek (Gorytus (USA)) **h91**
[2002/3 F95: 17d[2] 16g[F] Aug 26] fair bumper winner: also showed ability both starts
over hurdles, in third when fell last in maiden at Huntingdon: will stay beyond 17f.
P. R. Webber

BODFARI ROSE 4 ch.f. Indian Ridge – Royale Rose (FR) (Bering) [2002/3 17s[3] **h87**
16s[3] 17d[2] 16s[pu] Mar 8] modest maiden on Flat (stays 1¼m): similar form when placed
in juvenile hurdles: looked reluctant and jumped poorly when blinkered (reportedly
distressed) final outing. *A. Bailey*

BODFARI SIGNET 7 ch.g. King's Signet (USA) – Darakah (Doulab (USA)) [2002/3 **h96**
h100: 20d[2] 20m* 16d[2] 24g[4] 16g[5] 20g[5] 16g 22d[6] 20g[5] 20g[2] 20m[3] 20g[3] Apr 24]
leggy gelding: modest handicap hurdler: won at Perth in May: stays easy 2½m: acts on
firm and soft going: tried blinkered/visored/in cheekpieces: usually waited with. *Mrs
S. C. Bradburne*

BOHEIDEL (GER) 5 b.h. Dashing Blade – Birthday Party (FR) (Windwurf (GER)) **h–**
[2002/3 16d Oct 23] leggy horse: half-brother to 2m hurdle winner Birthplace (by
Top Ville): useful on Flat in Germany, successful over 1m (at 3 yrs) and 9f (at 4 yrs) for

W. Kujath: favourite, pulled hard and weakened quickly after fourth in novice at Chepstow on hurdling debut. *M. C. Pipe*

BOHILL LAD (IRE)   9 b.g. Contract Law (USA) – La Sass (Sassafras (FR)) [2002/3 c107, h107: c16d⁵ c16g* 17m³ c16dᵖᵘ 19sᵖᵘ 16d⁶ 16d 16d⁵ 17g 19m* Apr 15] lengthy gelding: fair handicap hurdler/chaser: won over fences at Newton Abbot in July and hurdles at Exeter in April: best form up to 19f: acts on firm and soft going: tried blinkered. *J. D. Frost* **c116 h111**

BOLD BISHOP (IRE)   6 b.g. Religiously (USA) – Ladybojangles (IRE) (Buckskin (FR)) [2002/3 F95: F16d⁴ F16g F16g⁴ Mar 12] rangy gelding: generally progressive in bumpers, left J. I. A. Charlton after reappearance: smart form in first-time blinkers when close fourth of 25 to Liberman in Champion Bumper at Cheltenham: will stay beyond 2m: should do well in novice hurdles in 2003/4. *Jonjo O'Neill* **F117**

BOLD CARDOWAN (IRE)   7 br.g. Persian Bold – Moving Trend (IRE) (Be My Guest (USA)) [2002/3 h86: 20d* 24d* 20g³ c20dᵖᵘ 20d 25g 19d³ 21s 22g⁵ Mar 17] small gelding: modest hurdler: won minor event at Newcastle and novice at Hexham early in season: jumped poorly on chasing debut: stays 3m: acts on heavy going: tends to carry head high. *John Berry* **c– h88**

BOLD DECISION   5 ch.g. Bold Arrangement – Cap That (Derek H) [2002/3 F16g F16d Feb 1] big, strong gelding: fourth foal: half-brother to poor chaser Garbo's Boy (by Silly Prices), stays 27f: dam bumper winner: backward, well held in bumpers at Catterick and Wetherby. *J. R. Turner* **F–**

BOLD DOLL (IRE)   4 b.f. Dolphin Street (FR) – Bold Miss (Bold Lad (IRE)) [2002/3 17mᵘʳ 16g 17f³ Oct 1] half-sister to winning pointer by Salmon Leap: modest maiden on Flat: well held both completed starts in juvenile hurdles. *Mrs P. N. Dutfield* **h–**

Mrs G. Smith's "Bold Bishop"

BOLDER ALEXANDER (IRE) 6 b.g. Persian Bold – Be Yourself (USA) (Noalcoholic (FR)) [2002/3 h–: 22m^{pu} 20m Jul 17] small, angular gelding: no form over hurdles: sold £1,100 Ascot November Sales. *F. Jordan* **h–**

BOLD HUNTER 9 b.g. Polish Precedent (USA) – Pumpona (USA) (Sharpen Up) [2002/3 c72, h–: c17g* c17m³ c19g⁵ c16s³ c17v^F c16v⁵ c17v^{pu} c16g⁵ Mar 17] sturdy gelding: winning hurdler: poor chaser: won novice handicap at Bangor in May: stays easy 21f: acts on any going: tried blinkered, not since early-2000/1. *M. J. M. Evans* **c74**
h–

BOLD INVESTOR 6 b.g. Anshan – Shirlstar Investor (Some Hand) [2002/3 h116: c20s* c24g* c24s³ c24d^{pu} c24m c20g² Apr 3] workmanlike gelding: fairly useful handicap hurdler: made good start to chasing career, winning novices at Carlisle in October and Kempton (beat Iris Royal 7 lengths) in November and third to Jair du Cochet in Grade 1 novice at Kempton in December: back to form after 2 poor runs when 2½ lengths second of 16 to Midland Flame in valuable novice handicap at Aintree: stays 3m: raced mainly on good going or softer (acts on soft): sound jumper. *Jonjo O'Neill* **c141**
h–

BOLD JOGGER (IRE) 6 b.g. Persian Bold – Mouette (FR) (Fabulous Dancer (USA)) [2002/3 16g 16d 19g Feb 28] good-topped gelding: maiden on Flat in Hong Kong, well held on British debut: well held in 3 starts over hurdles: sold £1,100 Ascot April Sales. *N. A. Graham* **h–**

BOLD KING (FR) 8 gr.g. Turgeon (USA) – Vanila Fudge (USA) (Bold Bidder) [2002/3 c102, h116: c25d³ c24f^{pu} 24g² c28s³ c27g 24g 26g 21g* c24f³ c26g⁴ c26g* Apr 21] tall gelding: fair handicap chaser, won 3-finisher event at Uttoxeter in April: fair hurdler, didn't need to be near best to win claimer at Warwick previous month: stays easy 3¼m: acts on firm and soft going: tried visored: carries head awkwardly under pressure, and often looks less than keen. *Ian Williams* **c106 §**
h105 §

European Breeders Fund Novices' Chase, Kempton—
Bold Investor gains a second success of the season

BOLD MCLAUGHLAN   5 b.g. Mind Games – Stoneydale (Tickled Pink) [2002/3   h–
h–: 19m^pu Oct 3] no form in 3 novice hurdles. *Miss M. Bragg*

BOLD MOMENTO   4 b.g. Never So Bold – Native of Huppel (IRE) (Be My Native   F–
(USA)) [2002/3 F16m Mar 22] 13,000 3-y-o: useful-looking gelding: first foal: dam
unraced: 33/1, needed race and experience when eleventh of 18 in bumper at Newbury on
debut. *B. De Haan*

BOLD NAVIGATOR   13 b.g. Lighter – Drummond Lass (Peacock (FR)) [2002/3 c–:   c94
c20g^pu c25g* c24v^4 c24s* c25g^ur Apr 14] modest chaser, lightly raced: won novice at
Hexham in October and handicap at Carlisle in March: stays 25f: acts on soft going.
A. M. Crow

BOLD PRECEDENT   6 b.g. Polish Precedent (USA) – Shining Water (USA) (River-   h–
man (USA)) [2002/3 20g^pu Oct 9] modest on Flat (stays 13f): jumped badly in seller on
hurdling debut. *J. R. Best*

BOLD RAIDER   6 b.g. Rudimentary (USA) – Spanish Heart (King of Spain) [2002/3   h–
16s^pu Dec 7] useful on Flat (stays 1¼m): pulled way to front then pulled up lame before
fourth on hurdling debut. *I. A. Balding*

BOLD STATEMENT   11 ch.g. Kris – Bold Fantasy (Bold Lad (IRE)) [2002/3 c25d^ur   c– x
c24m Apr 2] strong, workmanlike gelding: one-time fair chaser, lightly raced nowadays: h–
stays 3m: successful on soft/heavy, ideally suited by less testing ground (acts on firm):
sketchy jumper: sold £1,500 Ascot June Sales: successful twice in points in 2003.
S. Flook

BOLD TACTICS (IRE)   7 br.g. Jurado (USA) – Bold Lyndsey (Be My Native (USA))   c99
[2002/3 c25s^2 c23d^3 c25g^5 Mar 18] fourth foal: half-brother to Irish bumper winner
Park's Pet (by Bob Back): dam won over hurdles around 2m: won both completed starts
in points in 2002: easily best effort in hunter chases when second to Paddy For Paddy at
Folkestone: best by jumping next time: may prove best short of 25f. *F. A. Hutsby*

BOLEYKNOWSBEST (IRE)   5 b.g. Camden Town – Barrys Best (IRE) (King   h97 +
Luthier) [2002/3 16s^3 F16v^2 Dec 1] IR £11,000 3-y-o: strong gelding: first foal: dam   F102
unraced half-sister to useful hurdler up to 21f Bo Knows Best: modest form on hurdling
debut: much better effort in bumpers when second of 29 to G V A Ireland at Fairyhouse.
R. P. Burns, Ireland

BOLSHIE BARON   14 b.g. Baron Blakeney – Contrary Lady (Conwyn) [2002/3   c84 x
c84x, h–: c33g^bhd c25g^6 c30m^pu May 11] small, sturdy gelding: modest hunter chaser on   h–
his day: won point in April: stays 31f: acts on good to firm and good to soft going: tried
blinkered: tongue tied: often makes mistakes. *M. Harris*

BOLSHOI BALLET   5 b.g. Dancing Spree (USA) – Broom Isle (Damister (USA))   h95
[2002/3 16s 16v^5 16d 20s^pu 16d* Mar 1] quite good-topped gelding: first foal: dam
modest 2m to 2½m hurdler: fair on Flat (probably stays 2m): won modest novice hurdle:
won handicap at Newbury by 5 lengths from Polish Cloud: should stay at least 2½m. *J. Mackie*

BOLT ACTION (IRE)   7 br.g. Phardante (FR) – Ebony Jane (Roselier (FR)) [2002/3   h111
20v* 22d^pu Jan 18] first foal: dam, useful staying chaser, won Irish Grand National: won
maiden point on debut in 2002: impressively won novice at Chepstow on hurdling debut,
easily beating Brewster by 4 lengths: fatally injured at Wincanton following month.
P. F. Nicholls

BOLTON BARRIE (IRE)   5 b.g. Broken Hearted – Ballyduggan Queen (IRE) (King   F89
Luthier) [2002/3 F16d F16d^6 F16g^3 F16d Apr 25] 5,000 4-y-o: first foal: dam unraced
sister to one-time fairly useful hurdler short of 3m Scoring Pedigree: best effort in
bumpers when close third in maiden at Hexham. *R. C. Guest*

BOLTON FOREST (IRE)   10 b.g. Be My Native (USA) – Tickenor Wood (Le   c–
Bavard (FR)) [2002/3 c77, h–: c25g^5 c25m May 29] tall gelding: winning hurdler/chaser: h–
well held in 2 hunters in May: stays 3m: acts on firm and soft going: tried in tongue strap.
C. Storey

BOLTOUTOFTHEBLUE   4 ch.g. Bluegrass Prince (IRE) – Forget To Remindme   h–
(Forzando) [2002/3 18m^5 17d^6 Sep 4] disappointing maiden on Flat: visored, well held in
2 juvenile hurdles. *J. S. Moore*

BOMBA CHARGER   11 b.g. Prince of Peace – Lady Guinevere (Tormento) [2002/3   c90
c26s^2 c23d^4 Mar 4] fairly useful pointer/hunter chaser nowadays, successful in 3 points   h–
in March and April: suited by good test of stamina. *Mrs R. Welch*

BOMB ALASKA   8 br.g. Polar Falcon (USA) – So True (So Blessed) [2002/3 h–: 16g^{pu} Nov 30] lengthy gelding: has reportedly had wind operation: useful at one time up to 1¼m on Flat: little show in 3 starts over hurdles: has had tongue tied. *G. B. Balding*   **h–**

BONEYARROW (IRE)   7 ch.g. Over The River (FR) – Apicat (Buckskin (FR)) [2002/3 h136, F102: c17s^2 c20v^F Dec 1] sturdy gelding: developed into useful novice hurdler in 2001/2: encouraging start to chasing career when 1½ lengths second to The Premier Cat in maiden at Clonmel: fell tenth following month (sustained cervical vertebrae fracture and missed rest of season): needs good test around 2m and should stay 3m: raced on good going or softer (acts on heavy): consistent: should still improve over fences. *W. P. Mullins, Ireland*   **c123 p**   **h–**

BONFIRE NIGHT (IRE)   7 b.m. Air Display (USA) – Smokey Path (IRE) (Scallywag) [2002/3 F16g May 22] third foal: half-sister to fair hurdler/fairly useful chaser Merry Path (by Alphabatim), stays 3¼m: dam unraced, from family of top-class 2m hurdler Royal Vulcan: behind in bumper on debut: joined R. Dickin. *D. J. Wintle*   **F–**

BONGO FURY (FR)   4 b.f. Sillery (USA) – Nativelee (FR) (Giboulee (CAN)) [2002/3 16g^2 17f^2 16f* 16d* 16d^2 16s* 16v^2 16s* 16d Mar 6] sparely-made ex-French filly: half-sister to 3 winning jumpers, notably very smart 4-y-o hurdler Denham Red (by Pampabird), stayed 19f, and 5 Flat winners: dam unraced: fairly useful on Flat, claimed from J. Pease €31,000 after second in 1¼m claimer in May: fairly useful juvenile hurdler: won at Ludlow (maiden) and Stratford (novice handicap) in October and Sandown in December and February: made all when easily beating Zilarator 13 lengths in last-named: raced around 2m: has won on firm going, best efforts on softer than good (acts on heavy): visored after debut. *M. C. Pipe*   **h113**

BONNY BOY (IRE)   8 b.g. Bustino – Dingle Bay (Petingo) [2002/3 24v c26s^3 c32g^{pu} Mar 12] sturdy gelding: successful 4 times in points in 2002: has looked ungenuine all starts over hurdles/in novice chases: visored. *D. A. Rees*   **c– §**   **h– §**

BONNYBRIDGE (IRE)   6 ch.m. Zaffaran (USA) – Oralee (Prominer) [2002/3 F16g F16f F18m^4 F16g 18s c20g^5 Apr 2] half-sister to smart chaser up to 3m Promalee (by Homo Sapien) and useful hurdler/chaser up to 3m Michael Mor (by Denel): dam unraced, out of half-sister to Cheltenham Gold Cup winner Little Owl: won only completed start in maiden points: poor form in bumpers: well held in maidens over hurdles and fences. *Liam Lennon, Ireland*   **c–**   **h–**   **F68**

BONUS BRIDGE (IRE)   8 b.g. Executive Perk – Corivia (Over The River (FR)) [2002/3 h99: c16m^2 c16g^5 c19d^2 c19s^2 c24g^2 Apr 2] tall gelding: winning hurdler: fairly useful novice chaser, runner-up 4 out of 5 starts, though below form final one: should stay 3m: acts on soft and good to firm going. *H. D. Daly*   **c116**   **h–**

BONUS TRIX (IRE)   7 b.g. Executive Perk – Black Trix (Peacock (FR)) [2002/3 F94: 16d 17s^6 20s^{pu} Jan 18] good-topped gelding: bumper winner: best effort in novice hurdles when sixth of 17 at Bangor: should stay at least 2½m. *A. J. Lidderdale*   **h90**

BOOGY WOOGY   7 ch.g. Rock Hopper – Primulette (Mummy's Pet) [2002/3 c91§, h–§: c21m^3 c21m^3 c23m^2 c25d^4 c24s^3 Mar 10] leggy, lengthy gelding: winning hurdler: maiden chaser: sold out of T. Easterby's stable 13,000 gns Doncaster October Sales after third outing: better effort in novice hunters when fourth to Hazel Reilly at Kelso: stays 25f: acts on soft and good to firm going: blinkered: ungenuine. *Robert Bowling*   **c91 §**   **h– §**

BOOKS LAW   5 b.g. Contract Law (USA) – In A Whirl (USA) (Island Whirl (USA)) [2002/3 17m^{pu} 16m^{pu} Oct 19] half-brother to winning pointer Book's Way (by Afzal): well held in 3 maidens on Flat for J. M. Bradley: no show both starts over hurdles, jumped poorly on debut. *Mrs D. A. Hamer*   **h–**

BOOK'S WAY   7 br.g. Afzal – In A Whirl (USA) (Island Whirl (USA)) [2002/3 22m^{pu} c24m^{pu} Apr 22] sparely-made gelding: winning pointer: no form over hurdles or in hunter chase: tried visored. *Paul Hamer*   **c–**   **h–**

BOOM OR BUST (IRE)   4 ch.g. Entrepreneur – Classic Affair (USA) (Trempolino (USA)) [2002/3 16m^5 17s^{pu} 17f^3 16m^F 16g^{pu} Apr 19] angular gelding: modest on Flat (seems to stay 1¾m): best effort in juvenile hurdles (held in second) when falling last in race won by Penny Pictures at Ludlow: wore cheekpieces last 3 starts. *Miss K. M. George*   **h81**

BORANI   8 b.g. Shirley Heights – Ower (IRE) (Lomond (USA)) [2002/3 h112: 17d Jul 20] medium-sized gelding: much improved hurdler in 2001/2 for J. O'Neill: well held in valuable handicap at Market Rasen only outing in 2002/3: will prove best around 2m: raced on good ground or softer (acts on soft). *S. Gollings*   **h–**

BORDER BURN   9 ch.g. Safawan – Burning Ryme (Rymer) [2002/3 c73: c25d⁴ c25g   **c85**
May 11] workmanlike gelding: modest pointer/hunter chaser: stays 25f: well held when
blinkered. *N. M. L. Ewart*

BORDER FARMER (IRE)   10 b.g. Riverhead (USA) – Double Figures (FR) (Double   **c–**
Form) [2002/3 c79, h–: c24mᵘʳ Apr 10] winning pointer: poor novice hurdler/steeple-   **h–**
chaser: stays 3m: acts on good to firm going. *James Richardson*

BORDER GLEN   7 b.g. Selkirk (USA) – Sulitelma (USA) (The Minstrel (CAN))   **h–**
[2002/3 17sᵖᵘ 17sᵖᵘ 17g 16m⁶ 19g Apr 19] compact, plain gelding: modest on all-
weather, poor on turf on Flat (stays easy 1m): sold out of J. Bridger's stable 1,400 gns
Ascot August Sales: no form over hurdles: blinkered/visored except on debut.
P. Wegmann

BORDER LIGHT   10 ch.g. Lighter – Border Cherry (Deep Run) [2002/3 c87: c26s³   **c–**
c25gᵖᵘ Apr 5] lengthy gelding: modest pointer/maiden hunter chaser: stays 3¼m: often
none too fluent. *H. J. Manners*

BORDER NATIVE   7 ch.g. Distinct Native – Sanjo (Kafu) [2002/3 24vᵖᵘ 20gᵖᵘ Apr   **h–**
1] fifth foal: dam of little account: winning pointer: no show in 2 runs over hurdles.
A. Parker

BORDER NOMAD   9 b.m. Nomadic Way (USA) – Ascot Lass (Touching Wood   **h–**
(USA)) [2002/3 17g⁵ 17d 20m⁵ 22s Nov 2] small mare: third foal: half-sister to useful
hurdler Surprising (by Primitive Rising), stays 25f: dam unraced half-sister to useful
sprinter Our Dynasty: well held over hurdles: takes strong hold. *M. A. Barnes*

BORDER RUN   6 b.g. Missed Flight – Edraianthus (Windjammer (USA)) [2002/3 c–,   **c–**
h–: c17gᵖᵘ c16m c16s c17vᵖᵘ 16d 20g 21g Mar 12] leggy gelding: winning hurdler in   **h–**
2000/1: no form since, including over fences: wore blinkers/cheekpieces last 4 starts.
M. Mullineaux

BORDER STAR (IRE)   6 b.g. Parthian Springs – Tengello (Bargello) [2002/3 h68,   **h86**
F–: 16m⁴ 18g⁶ 16s* 16m⁴ 16d³ 20s⁶ Dec 7] lengthy gelding: modest hurdler: won
conditional jockeys handicap at Stratford in August: should stay beyond 2m: acts on soft
and good to firm going. *J. M. Jefferson*

BOREHILL JOKER   7 ch.g. Pure Melody (USA) – Queen Matilda (Castle Keep)   **c–**
[2002/3 c87, h98: 16d⁶ 16d* 16g⁴ 17s 17sᵖᵘ 16s 16v³ 16g Mar 12] sparely-made gelding: **h99**
not fluent only start over fences: modest handicap hurdler: won amateur event at
Towcester in May: below form all 5 starts after 8-month absence: barely stays 2½m: raced
mainly on good going or softer (acts on heavy): tongue tied: often makes running.
E. Haddock

BORING GORING (IRE)   9 b.g. Aristocracy – Coolrusk (IRE) (Millfontaine)   **c89 x**
[2002/3 c–x, h99?: 24g c20gᵇᵈ 20g⁴ c20m³ c25m² 21m Mar 31] rangy gelding: poor   **h–**
hurdler: modest maiden chaser: stays 25f: acts on soft and good to firm ground: tongue
tied: sketchy jumper. *Miss A. M. Newton-Smith*

BORN FLYER (IRE)   8 b.m. Jurado (USA) – Gentle Flight (Furry Glen) [2002/3   **c110**
16s⁶ 16g* 17m³ 16s⁵ 16m⁴ 16f c18s³ c17s c18v⁴ c17d³ c18gF Apr 21] good-topped mare: **h104**
fourth living foal: half-sister to Irish 2m hurdle winner Friendly Flyer (by Corvaro): dam
lightly-raced maiden jumper: fair handicap hurdler: won at Down Royal in June: similar
form in maiden chases: raced around 2m: acts on soft and good to firm going: has had
tongue tied. *J. A. O'Connell, Ireland*

BORN OF FUBAR   9 gr.g. North Col – Scallykath (Scallywag) [2002/3 h76?: 16mᵖᵘ   **h–**
Jun 19] angular gelding: novice hurdler: sold £500 Ascot October Sales: failed to
complete in points in 2003: headstrong. *B. J. M. Ryall*

BORORA   4 gr.g. Shareef Dancer (USA) – Bustling Nelly (Bustino) [2002/3 16s Nov   **h– p**
27] close-coupled gelding: half-brother to fair 2m hurdler Fitness Fanatic (by Nishapour),
fairly useful hurdler/chaser at 2m to 3m Silk Degrees (by Dunbeath) and winning jumper
in Germany by Kalaglow: fair maiden on Flat (stays 12.4f), sold out of I. Balding's stable
9,000 gns Newmarket Autumn Sales: better than ninth of 15 suggests in juvenile hurdle
at Wetherby (reportedly bled from nose) won by Mistanoora, travelling powerfully until
2 out, eased once beaten. *D. E. Cantillon*

BORRISHEEN BAY   8 b.g. Arctic Lord – Soraway (Choral Society) [2002/3 h80?:   **h–**
21gᵖᵘ May 3] poor maiden hurdler: stays 25f: acts on good to firm going: often tongue
tied. *Mrs Richard Arthur*

BOSPHORUS   4 b.g. Polish Precedent (USA) – Ancara (Dancing Brave (USA))   **F–**
[2002/3 F12g Dec 18] 3,000 3-y-o: third foal: half-brother to fairly useful 1¼m winners

Anamore (by Sanglamore) and Monolith (by Bigstone): dam, French 1¼m and 1½m winner, from very good middle-distance family: behind in bumper at Newbury on debut: poor form on first of 2 starts in maidens on Flat. *D. G. Bridgwater*

BO SQUIDLEY   6 b.m. Karinga Bay – Martins Lottee (Martinmas) [2002/3 F16s^ur 22g^R Jun 22] 500 4-y-o: medium-sized mare: third foal: dam unraced: tailed off when unseated in bumper: refused third in novice on hurdling debut. *Mrs S. Gardner*   **h–**
F–

BOSS DOYLE (IRE)   11 b.g. Lapierre – Prolific Scot (Northern Guest (USA)) [2002/3 c–, h150: 25d² 24g⁴ 24s² Dec 28] sturdy gelding: winning chaser: smart hurdler: runner-up in Grade 2 events at Wetherby (when attempting hat-trick in race) in November and Leopardstown (behind Limestone Lad) in December: stayed 3¼m: raced mainly on good going or softer (acted on heavy): effective blinkered or not: usually soon off bridle: sketchy jumper of fences: has been retired. *M. F. Morris, Ireland*   **c–**
h150

BOSS MORTON (IRE)   12 b.g. Tremblant – Sandy Kelly (Ovac (ITY)) [2002/3 c–, h–: 17s³ 19g 20m² 23m² Apr 21] neat gelding: poor handicap hurdler: stays 23f: acts on soft and good to firm going: tongue tied in 2002/3: has shown signs of temperament. *S. G. Chadwick*   **c–**
h60

BOSS ROYAL   6 ch.g. Afzal – Born Bossy (Eborneezer) [2002/3 h85: 22f^pu c19d^F c16g^ur Mar 23] workmanlike gelding: winning hurdler: trained by G. Ham until after reappearance: let down by jumping both starts over fences, left S. Sherwood after chasing debut: stays 2½m, at least when conditions aren't testing: acts on soft and good to firm going: tongue tied: races prominently. *S. T. Lewis*   **c69 x**
h–

BOSS TWEED (IRE)   6 b.g. Persian Bold – Betty Kenwood (Dominion) [2002/3 h86?: 16g⁴ 16g⁶ Apr 24] set steady pace and probably flattered when fourth of 7 in intermediate hurdle at Kelso in May: off nearly a year, ran as if in need of race when sixth in novice at Perth: tongue tied since hurdling debut. *B. Mactaggart*   **h82 +**

BOSTON LASS   6 br.m. Terimon – Larksmore (Royal Fountain) [2002/3 h72, F63: 24g 25m⁴ 24d⁵ 21v² 27s³ 20s 21v² c21s^pu Mar 15] close-coupled mare: poor maiden hurdler: similar form when second in mares novice at Sedgefield on chasing debut, stiff task next time: seems to stay 27f: acts on heavy and good to firm going: effective with or without cheekpieces. *R. D. E. Woodhouse*   **c72**
h63

BOSUNS MATE   10 ch.g. Yachtsman (USA) – Langton Lass (Nearly A Hand) [2002/3 c114x, h–: c20s* c23d² c26d³ Mar 8] useful-looking gelding: fair chaser nowadays: won 3-finisher hunter at Sandown in February: suited by 3m+: acts on heavy and good to firm going: tried visored, effective blinkered or not: often forces pace: usually let down by jumping. *M. Keighley*   **c107 x**
h–

BOSWORTH BOY   5 b.g. Deploy – Krill (Kris) [2002/3 F87: 17s Dec 5] good-topped gelding: placed once from 3 starts in bumpers: well held on more testing ground in novice at Market Rasen on hurdling debut. *Ian Williams*   **h–**

BOUCHASSON (FR)   10 b.g. Big John (FR) – Kizil Ayak (FR) (Stratege (USA)) [2002/3 c125, h–: c24g² c26d^ur c24d² c23g⁶ c24f⁶ Oct 17] workmanlike gelding: fairly useful handicap chaser: in-and-out form in 2002/3: stays 25f: acts on soft and good to firm going: blinkered/visored: usually races prominently: has jumped markedly right: not to be trusted. *P. J. Hobbs*   **c125 §**
h–

BOULEVARD BAY (IRE)   12 b.g. Royal Fountain – Cairita (Pitcairn) [2002/3 c76: c16d² May 6] well-made gelding: poor handicap chaser: stays 2½m: raced on good going or softer (acts on heavy): blinkered: has had tongue tied: races prominently. *Mrs P. Robeson*   **c82**
h–

BOULTA (IRE)   9 ch.g. Commanche Run – Boulta View (Beau Chapeau) [2002/3 c–: c20m² c25m⁵ c26d c20m^pu c25d c25g² Apr 7] fair pointer: easily best efforts in hunter chases when runner-up at Perth and Kelso (wore cheekpieces): stays 25f: acts on good to firm ground: breathing problem only start in tongue tie. *Mrs Clare Moore*   **c90**

BOUNCE BACK (USA)   7 ch.g. Trempolino (USA) – Lattaquie (FR) (Fast Topaze (USA)) [2002/3 c155, h150: c26g c29v^pu c29m⁶ Apr 26] tall gelding: smart hurdler/chaser in 2001/2: easily best effort of 2002/3 when sixth, attempting repeat win in race, to Ad Hoc in attheraces Gold Cup Chase (Handicap) at Sandown, jumping far from fluently: stays 29f: acts on heavy and good to firm going: tried blinkered/visored. *M. C. Pipe*   **c143**
h–

BOUND   5 b.g. Kris – Tender Moment (IRE) (Caerleon (USA)) [2002/3 h115: 16m³ 16m 16m² 17d³ 16d 16v 16m Mar 22] tall gelding: fair handicap hurdler: will prove best around 2m: acts on soft and good to firm going: tongue tied: races freely, has found little. *Mrs L. Wadham*   **h113**

BOUNDTOHONOUR (IRE)   11 b.g. Rashar (USA) – Densidal (Tanfirion) [2002/3   c–
c–, h–: 27d 26s c20g c25gᵖᵘ Mar 29] strong gelding: winning hurdler/chaser, no form   h–
since 2000/1: sometimes blinkered/visored. *Ian Williams*

BOURBON MANHATTAN   5 b.g. Alflora (IRE) – Vanina II (FR) (Italic (FR))   F111
[2002/3 F17s* F16d* F16g⁶ Mar 12] useful-looking gelding: second reported foal; dam,
French middle-distance maiden, sister to very smart staying chaser Antonin: useful
bumper performer: won at Taunton in November and Newbury in March, beating
Moscow Fields by 13 lengths at latter course: ran well when sixth of 25 to Liberman in
Grade 1 at Cheltenham final start: will stay at least 2½m: interesting hurdling prospect.
A. King

BOWCLIFFE COURT (IRE)   11 b.g. Slip Anchor – Res Nova (USA) (Blushing   h–
Groom (FR)) [2002/3 h–: 17g May 4] sparely-made gelding: fairly useful 2m hurdler in
1997/8: no sign of retaining ability: tongue tied only run in 2002/3 (reportedly finished
lame). *G. H. Jones*

BOWDEN VULCAN   5 b.g. Royal Vulcan – No Grandad (Strong Gale) [2002/3   F–
F17g Mar 22] third foal: dam fair staying chaser: showed little in maiden bumper on
debut. *B. N. Pollock*

BOWLEAZE (IRE)   4 br.g. Right Win (IRE) – Mrs Cullen (Over The River (FR))   F101
[2002/3 F17m* Apr 15] €4,600 3-y-o: fourth foal: half-brother to 3 poor performers: dam
unraced half-sister to dam of useful chaser Saxophone: created good impression when
winning bumper at Exeter on debut by 5 lengths from Classify, not fully extended to
assert. *R. H. Alner*

BOWLES PATROL (IRE)   11 gr.g. Roselier (FR) – Another Dud (Le Bavard (FR))   c90
[2002/3 c97, h–: c24d⁵ c27s⁴ c25g⁵ c27dꟳ Mar 18] leggy gelding: winning hurdler: h–
modest handicap chaser: stays 27f: acts on good to firm and heavy going. *John R. Upson*

BOWLING BEAUTY   5 bl.m. Alderbrook – Bowling Fort (Bowling Pin) [2002/3   F72
F16g⁶ Mar 29] 800 4-y-o: fourth foal: half-sister to fairly useful but temperamental
staying hurdler/chaser King Pin (by King's Ride): dam unraced, from family of very
smart staying chaser Fort Fox: sixth of 13 in maiden bumper at Hexham on debut.
Miss S. E. Forster

BOW ROCKY   10 b.g. Failiq (FR) – Just Maunby (Derek H) [2002/3 c16m⁴ Nov 4]   c–
poor maiden pointer: bled from nose on steeplechase debut. *Mrs J. A. Saunders*

BOW STRADA   6 ch.g. Rainbow Quest (USA) – La Strada (Niniski (USA)) [2002/3   c128
h124+: 20m² c17g² c19g³ c16m* 21g c19g* c20m⁴ Apr 12] angular, close-coupled   h131
gelding: useful hurdler: good second in handicap at Uttoxeter on reappearance: fairly
useful novice chaser: won at Leicester in November and Ascot (beat Ins And Outs 10
lengths) in March: reportedly distressed when tailed off final start: stays 21f: acts on firm
and good to soft going: hung left under pressure on chasing debut: consistent. *P. J. Hobbs*

BOX BUILDER   6 ch.g. Fraam – Ena Olley (Le Moss) [2002/3 h104: 20g* 20d² 24m²   c–
c23g⁴ 22fꟳ 21d c26sᵖᵘ Dec 7] close-coupled gelding: has reportedly had breathing   h104
operation: fair novice hurdler: won at Aintree in May and Newton Abbot in August: no
encouragement either start over fences: stays 3m: acts on firm and good to soft going:
tongue tied. *B. G. Powell*

BOXER'S DOUBLE   6 b.g. Petoski – Grayrose Double (Celtic Cone) [2002/3 h–,   c–
F71: 20mᵖᵘ 20g 19f⁵ 19f³ 19g⁴ 16d 16v 19s⁶ c24f c21gꟳ Apr 19] lengthy gelding: bad   h–
maiden hurdler: reportedly lame on chasing debut, not fluent and behind when refusing
next time: has worn blinkers/visor/cheekpieces. *G. A. Ham*

BOYNE BANKS (IRE)   8 ch.g. Boyne Valley – Pallatess (Pall Mall) [2002/3 h–:   c79
c24d⁶ c16s⁴ c20s c26sᵖᵘ Feb 26] won only completed start in maiden Irish points: pulled   h–
up on hurdling debut: signs of only a little ability in steeplechases. *N. A. Twiston-Davies*

BOYZONTOOWA (IRE)   11 b.g. Beau Sher – Lindabell (Over The River (FR))   c–
[2002/3 c95, h–: c16dᵖᵘ Nov 25] smallish gelding: modest handicap chaser: winning   h–
hurdler: showed little only start in 2002/3: stays 3¼m: successful on good to firm going,
raced mainly on softer (acts on heavy). *W. Storey*

BOZO (IRE)   12 b.g. Kefaah (USA) – Hossvend (Malinowski (USA)) [2002/3 c98§,   c– §
h–: c19g c19fᵖᵘ c24gꟳ Apr 12] workmanlike gelding: modest chaser: left B. Ryall prior to   h– §
showing little in 2 hunters: stays 2¾m: acts on heavy and good to firm going: tried
blinkered/visored: lazy: unreliable. *N. Parker*

BRACEY RUN (IRE)   13 b.g. The Parson – Outdoor Ivy (Deep Run) [2002/3 c–x,   c– x
h110: 17s⁴ 20d* 20s⁴ 20d² 22d⁶ Nov 11] good-bodied gelding: let down by jumping all 4   h101

starts over fences: fair handicap hurdler: won conditional jockeys race at Southwell in May: should stay beyond 21f: acts on good to firm and heavy going: visored (ran in snatches) once: has found little. *A. J. Lidderdale*

BRACEYS GIRL (IRE)   6 b. or br.m. Be My Native (USA) – Minigirls Niece (IRE)   c–
(Strong Gale) [2002/3 h63, F69: 20s^{pu} 20m Aug 17] poor maiden hurdler: successful in   h–
points in February and March: likely to stay 3m: has had tongue tied. *D. Brace*

BRACKEN FIRE   9 b.m. Jupiter Island – Dragon Fire (Dragonara Palace (USA))   h–
[2002/3 19s^{F} 16d^{6} 19d^{pu} 17s 17d^{pu} Feb 23] workmanlike mare: half-sister to winning 2m
selling hurdler Set-Em-Alight (by Relkino) and bumper winner Fooling With Fire (by
Idiot's Delight): dam, modest 1m/1¼m winner, half-sister to top-class 2m hurdler/smart
chaser Prideaux Boy: no sign of ability over hurdles. *G. F. H. Charles-Jones*

BRACKENHEATH (IRE)   12 b.g. Le Moss – Stable Lass (Golden Love) [2002/3   c86 x
c97x, h–: c21m^{3} c25s^{pu} Feb 11] sturdy gelding: fair pointer/hunter chaser nowadays: h–
stays 27f: acts on heavy going, probably good to firm: effective with or without blinkers:
often let down by jumping. *Mrs D. M. Grissell*

BRACKNEY BOY (IRE)   9 b.g. Zaffaran (USA) – Donard Lily (Master Buck)   c– x
[2002/3 c16g^{F} c20v^{6} c25s c18v^{F} c25s^{F3} 24d Mar 22] fourth foal: half-brother to winning   h–
pointer by Torus: dam winning pointer: didn't take to chasing: fair hurdler: well held in
handicap final start: likely to stay beyond 3m: acts on soft going. *I. A. Duncan, Ireland*

BRAD   5 b.g. Deploy – Celia Brady (Last Tycoon) [2002/3 F92: F16v^{5} Nov 27] lengthy   F92
gelding: fair form in bumpers: fifth at Chepstow only start in 2002/3: seems a stayer.
P. R. Webber

BRADLEY MY BOY (IRE)   7 ch.g. Treasure Hunter – Clonaslee Baby (Konigssee)   c–
[2002/3 h98, F83: 16s 16s 16m c18g^{F} 20g^{pu} 17m^{5} Apr 19] bumper winner: little form   h78
over hurdles and behind when falling on chasing debut (final outing for V. Bowens): has
had tongue tied. *Mrs A. M. Naughton*

BRADLEY WOOD   8 b.g. Primitive Rising (USA) – Synonymous (New Member)   h–
[2002/3 18m 18g^{pu} 17f^{ur} 17v^{pu} Nov 6] second foal: dam, winning pointer, half-sister to
fairly useful staying jumper Squire Jim: failed to complete in 5 maiden points in 2002: no
form over hurdles: blinkered last 2 starts. *Mrs Jane Galpin*

BRADOGUE (IRE)   6 b.g. Nucleon (USA) – Waweewawoo (IRE) (Rusticaro (FR))   h–
[2002/3 17s^{pu} Dec 18] sturdy gelding: third foal: dam of little account: showed nothing in
novice hurdle (tongue tied) on debut. *F. Lloyd*

BRADY BOYS (USA)   6 b.g. Cozzene (USA) – Elvia (USA) (Roberto (USA))   h76
[2002/3 h69: 17d^{4} 17s 16v^{4} 16s^{2} 16d 17v* 21m Apr 2] modest and lightly-raced maiden
on Flat (stays 11f): poor hurdler: off bridle by halfway when winning seller at Taunton in
March: should stay beyond 17f: acts on heavy going, reportedly lost action when well
held on good to firm final start. *J. G. M. O'Shea*

BRAEBURN   8 b.g. Petoski – Great Granny Smith (Fine Blue) [2002/3 c93: c16s^{F} c93 ?
c18m^{pu} Mar 22] useful-looking gelding: very lightly raced: runner-up on first of 2 starts
in novice chases in 2001/2 for N. Henderson: shaped as if retaining ability on return,
fourth when falling last on reappearance, lame on second occasion. *R. T. Phillips*

BRAMBLEHILL DUKE (IRE)   11 b.g. Kambalda – Scat-Cat (Furry Glen) [2002/3   c130 x
c123x, h–: c24g^{3} c24v* c25d^{2} c26s c24s c24g c36d^{F} Apr 5] medium-sized gelding: useful   h–
handicap chaser: won at Bangor in November: stays 3¼m: acts on good to firm and heavy
going: takes strong hold and possibly best held up: often let down by jumping: none too
consistent. *Miss Venetia Williams*

BRAMLYNN BROOK (FR)   5 ch.g. Apple Tree (FR) – Sainte Lys (FR) (Don   F97
Roberto (USA)) [2002/3 F12d^{5} F17s^{2} F18v^{2} Feb 10] big, lengthy gelding: has scope:
sixth foal: half-brother to 2 winners, notably smart French chaser up to 2¾m Garde
d'Estruval (by Garde Royale): dam placed up to 1½m in France: fairly useful form in
bumpers, length second to Were In Touch in maiden at Plumpton final start. *Miss Venetia
Williams*

BRAND NEW DANCE   9 b.g. Gildoran – Starawak (Star Appeal) [2002/3 h–: 17d^{pu} h–
May 14] fair form in 2 maiden hurdles in 2000/1 in Ireland: no encouragement in 2 runs
in Britain, tongue tied on second occasion: third in point in April. *D. J. Wintle*

BRANDSBY STRIPE   8 ch.g. Nomadic Way (USA) – I'm Fine (Fitzwilliam (USA))   h67
[2002/3 17s^{6} 19s 20v^{pu} 17s^{4} Mar 11] well held in bumper in 1999/00: poor form over
hurdles: best efforts around 2m. *P. Beaumont*

BRANKLEY BOY 5 ch.g. Afzal – Needwood Fortune (Tycoon II) [2002/3 F16d* **F96**
Feb 15] rather unfurnished gelding: fifth foal: half-brother to 2 winners by Rolfe, notably
top-class hurdler around 2½m Lady Rebecca: dam unraced sister to useful staying
chasers Tartan Takeover and Tartan Tyrant: won bumper at Wincanton on debut by ½
length from Mister Flint: will stay 2½m. *N. J. Henderson*

BRASSIS HILL (IRE) 12 b.g. Marktingo – Mystery Woman (Tula Rocket) [2002/3 **c67**
c69, h–: c16m⁶ May 3] poor maiden chaser: pulled up in 3 points after reappearance: **h–**
stays 21f (reportedly finished distressed at 25f): acts on firm and soft going: tongue tied.
Miss A. M. Newton-Smith

BRAVE CARADOC (IRE) 5 b.g. Un Desperado (FR) – Drivers Bureau (Proverb) **F79**
[2002/3 F16v³ Mar 8] €20,000 4-y-o: tall, rather unfurnished gelding with scope: sixth
foal: brother to winning hurdler up to 25f The Kew Tour and half-brother to winning
pointer by Town And Country: dam ran once: shaped like a stayer when remote third of 8
in bumper at Sandown on debut. *G. L. Moore*

BRAVE EFFECT (IRE) 7 br.g. Bravefoot – Crupney Lass (Ardoon) [2002/3 h99p: **h86**
16g 20vᵖᵘ 19d⁴ 16d⁴ 16g 20m* Apr 19] winning Irish pointer: modest hurdler: best effort
in 2002/3 when winning novice handicap at Carlisle: stays 2½m: acts on good to firm and
good to soft going: tongue tied fifth start. *M. Todhunter*

BRAVE INCA (IRE) 5 b.g. Good Thyne (USA) – Wigwam Mam (IRE) (Com- **h79 p**
manche Run) [2002/3 16s 16s F16v* F16d* Mar 22] **F117**
　　　With four starts over hurdles, starting at 20/1 three times and 33/1 once, and the
best of his efforts a seventh in a maiden at Wexford in March 2002 and a remote
eighth in a minor event at Naas eight months later, it was hardly surprising that
Brave Inca started an unconsidered 25/1-chance on his first appearance in a
bumper, at Fairyhouse in March. Not quite so surprising, though, as the style of his

Novices Syndicate's "Brave Inca"

victory—he cruised through the race and galloped on strongly in the straight to win by sixteen lengths (officially twenty) from the fairly useful Mitchelstown. The margin possibly flattered Brave Inca a little, as the runner-up tired after setting the pace, but this still ranked as one of the best performances in a bumper in Ireland during the whole season. Three weeks later at Navan, Brave Inca repeated the form when, in a more steadily-run race on less testing ground, he quickened in good style to beat the Fairyhouse third Doors To Manual seven lengths. Quite a few of those behind went on to uphold the form and Brave Inca himself was an intended runner in the Grade 1 bumper at Punchestown shortly after the end of the British season but was withdrawn when the ground was considered firmer than ideal. Clearly, the level of form shown in bumpers strongly suggests Brave Inca should be well up to winning races over hurdles when he is tried again, particularly given a lowly handicap mark. Bought for IR 14,000 guineas as a three-year-old, Brave Inca is by Good Thyne out of an unraced Commanche Run mare, Wigwam Mam, who is from the family of the top-class chaser Merry Gale. Brave Inca has been raced at two miles so far but is bred to stay at least two and a half. He has done all his racing so far on going softer than good. *C. A. Murphy, Ireland*

BRAVE KING (IRE) 10 b.g. King's Ride – Arumah (Arapaho) [2002/3 h71: 16g Dec 13] rangy, good sort: very lightly raced and only poor form over hurdles: should stay beyond 2m: raced on good going or softer. *Ronald Thompson* — **h70**

BRAVE KNIGHT 6 b.g. Presidium – Agnes Jane (Sweet Monday) [2002/3 h–: c17d^2 c16g^{pu} c16v^{pu} Jan 1] leggy gelding: poor maiden on Flat (stays 1¼m): little sign of ability over jumps (including in point), distant second in novice chase on reappearance. *N. Bycroft* — **c?** **h–**

BRAVE LORD (IRE) 6 ch.g. Mister Lord (USA) – Artic Squaw (IRE) (Buckskin (FR)) [2002/3 F17s^6 Mar 6] IR 16,000 4-y-o: fourth foal: brother to fair pointer Lively Lord: dam unraced, out of half-sister to very smart staying chaser Arctic Call: sixth of 8 to Drombeag in bumper at Carlisle on debut. *L. Lungo* — **F83**

BRAVE SPIRIT (FR) 5 b.g. Legend of France (USA) – Guerre Ou Paix (FR) (Comrade In Arms) [2002/3 F16d 20g Apr 2] rather leggy gelding: third foal: half-brother to 1¼m and 1½m winner Treve Ou Paix (by Cricket Ball): dam, 11f winner, half-sister to useful hurdler/chaser up to 2½m Grand Souvenir: well held in bumper and novice hurdle. *Ian Williams* — **h–** **F—**

BRAVE THOUGHT (IRE) 8 b.g. Commanche Run – Bristol Fairy (Smartset) [2002/3 18d^F 16s 16s^6 16s^3 16d* 18s^3 16s^4 16s^3 16d^5 Feb 27] fourth foal: dam, 2m hurdle winner, half-sister to useful hurdler/chaser up to 3m Templemore: bumper winner: fairly useful novice hurdler: won minor event at Thurles in December: raced around 2m on going softer than good (acts on heavy): not a straightforward ride. *M. Purcell, Ireland* — **h118**

BRAVE VISION 7 b.g. Clantime – Kinlet Vision (IRE) (Vision (USA)) [2002/3 h84: 16g* 16m^6 20d^3 16v 17v^5 22d^5 Mar 1] sturdy gelding: modest handicap hurdler: won conditional jockeys event at Kelso in May: couldn't repeat the form: will prove best around 2m: acts on good to firm and heavy going. *A. C. Whillans* — **h95**

BRAVO 5 b. or br.g. Efisio – Apache Squaw (Be My Guest (USA)) [2002/3 h67: 16s 19s^4 17s 20s 20m* Mar 23] leggy gelding: modest hurdler: improved form when winning novice handicap at Huntingdon: stays 2½m, at least when conditions aren't testing: acts on good to firm going: visored last 2 starts. *J. Mackie* — **h86 +**

BRAZIL (IRE) 5 b.g. Germany (USA) – Alberta Rose (IRE) (Phardante (FR)) [2002/3 F12g F16g 16g Apr 25] second foal: dam, 7f/9f winner, modest maiden hurdler: looked non-stayer in bumpers and maiden hurdle. *T. R. George* — **h–** **F69**

BREA HILL 10 b.g. Brotherly (USA) – Top Feather (High Top) [2002/3 c68x, h–: c25g^{pu} Apr 30] tall, rangy gelding: poor maiden chaser: well held in point in February: stays 27f: raced on good going or softer (acts on soft): tongue tied: often let down by jumping. *Ferdy Murphy* — **c– x** **h–**

BREAK DANCER (IRE) 4 b.g. Danehill Dancer (IRE) – Peep of Day (USA) (Lypheor) [2002/3 18d^{pu} 17s^{pu} 17g^{pu} Mar 16] little show in 1¼m maiden on Flat: pulled up all 3 starts in juvenile hurdles, virtually refused to race tried in blinkers final one. *M. J. Roberts* — **h– §**

BREAKING BREEZE (IRE) 8 b.g. Mandalus – Knockacool Breeze (Buckskin (FR)) [2002/3 h93: 19d c20m* c21m⁴ c21g³ c20g* c19m* Sep 11] modest hurdler: fair chaser: won novices at Huntingdon in June and August and handicap at Hereford in September: barely stays 21f: acts on soft and good to firm going: free-going sort who usually races up with pace. *J. S. King* **c104 h–**

BREATHTAKING VIEW (USA) 7 b.g. Country Pine (USA) – Lituya Bay (USA) (Empery (USA)) [2002/3 17v⁵ 19d 20g 16m³ Apr 21] leggy gelding: smart at one time on Flat, successful 3 times up to 1½m in UAE at 4/5 yrs: sold out of E. Charpy's stable 26,000 gns Newmarket July Sales, well held 3 starts in Britain: poor novice hurdler: wore cheekpieces third outing. *G. Prodromou* **h74**

BREGOGUE (IRE) 9 ch.g. Alphabatim (USA) – Sandra's Joy (Pollerton) [2002/3 c16g* c22dF 16m c16f⁵ c20m c16gF c20m* Apr 19] plain gelding: winning hurdler: fair handicap chaser: won at Tramore in June and Cork in April: effective at 2m to 3m: acts on heavy and good to firm going: none too consistent. *Ms Helen Mary O'Keeffe, Ireland* **c113 h–**

BRENDA'S DELIGHT (IRE) 5 b.m. Blues Traveller (IRE) – Tara's Delight (Dunbeath (USA)) [2002/3 h–: 16g⁵ 18gur 16g 17dpu Nov 5] little sign of ability, including on Flat: has worn cheekpieces. *P. Butler* **h–**

BRERETON (IRE) 7 b.g. Be My Native (USA) – Society News (Law Society (USA)) [2002/3 F96: 20v⁴ 21s 24m Apr 16] useful-looking gelding: modest novice hurdler: stays 21f: acts on heavy going. *N. J. Henderson* **h90**

BRETECHE (FR) 8 b.m. Fijar Tango (FR) – Foinery (Reference Point) [2002/3 c–§, h65§: c25fpu May 15] leggy mare: temperamental winning hurdler/chaser: fair pointer, successful in March: very best form around 2m: acts on any going: usually blinkered/visored: has had tongue tied. *Miss C. Newman* **c– § h– §**

BREUDDWYD LYN 5 br.g. Awesome – Royal Resort (King of Spain) [2002/3 F16g 16spu 16gF Mar 16] fourth foal: dam 7f seller winner who stayed 1¼m: no show in bumper or 2 hurdles: poor maiden on Flat up to 1½m. *D. Burchell* **h– F–**

BREWSTER (IRE) 6 b.g. Roselier (FR) – Aelia Paetina (Buckskin (FR)) [2002/3 F16v* 20s³ 20d² 20v² Dec 27] IR £22,000 4-y-o: rather leggy gelding: sixth foal: half-brother to winning pointer by Mandalus: dam, placed in point, sister to smart staying chaser Buck Rogers: fairly useful form when winning bumper at Sligo in April on debut for I. Buchanan: fair form when placed all 3 starts in novice hurdles: will be suited by 3m+: raced on going softer than good (acts on heavy). *Ian Williams* **h106 F100**

BRIAN JAMES 9 ch.g. River God (USA) – Rose Orchard (Rouser) [2002/3 c–, h93: c21d 27v⁴ 25s 24vpu 27vpu 27s³ 27gpu Mar 25] sturdy gelding: well beaten in 2 novice chases: poor handicap hurdler: largely out of form in 2002/3: stays 27f: raced on good going or softer (acts on heavy): has worn blinkers/cheekpieces: often soon off bridle and not to be trusted. *F. P. Murtagh* **c– § h80 §**

BRIAR (CZE) 4 b.c. House Rules (USA) – Bright Angel (AUT) (Antuco (GER)) [2002/3 16m 16s⁴ 17s* 16s⁴ 17s³ 21d⁴ 20v² 19m Mar 22] leggy, close-coupled colt: in frame once from 4 starts up to around 7f on Flat in Czech Republic at 2/3 yrs for J. Votavova: modest juvenile hurdler: won maiden at Folkestone in November: stays 2½m: acts on heavy going, well held both starts on good to firm: wore cheekpieces last 4 outings. *M. Pitman* **h91 +**

BRIAR ROSE (IRE) 8 gr.m. Roselier (FR) – Born Lucky (Deep Run) [2002/3 c21vpu c25v⁶ c21vpu c24s c32v² c25g³ Mar 29] lengthy mare: winning pointer but has little ability. *N. M. L. Ewart* **c– h–**

BRIAR'S MIST (IRE) 6 gr.g. Roselier (FR) – Claycastle (IRE) (Carlingford Castle) [2002/3 h101p, F84: c21v⁴ c26sF c19vpu c24g³ Mar 22] good-topped gelding: twice-raced hurdler: modest form in novice chases: stays 3m: raced on good going or softer (acts on heavy). *Miss H. C. Knight* **c94 h–**

BRIC A BRAC 6 ch.m. Minster Son – Greenhill's Girl (Radetzky) [2002/3 F–: 16g Apr 25] small mare: no sign of ability. *W. G. Young* **h–**

BRIDAL WHITE 7 b.m. Robellino (USA) – Alwatar (USA) (Caerleon (USA)) [2002/3 c–, h–: 16dpu Dec 4] smallish mare: one-time fair maiden on Flat: has shown little over jumps. *M. Wigham* **c– h–**

BRIDGEND BLUE (IRE) 7 b.g. Up And At 'em – Sperrin Mist (Camden Town) [2002/3 h–: 16d 17g 16f⁵ 22m 21g⁵ Oct 15] no worthwhile form over hurdles: tried blinkered: has had tongue tied. *J. S. Hubbuck* **h–**

BRIEF DANCE (IRE) 6 b.g. Brief Truce (USA) – Serenad Dancer (FR) (Antheus **h110** (USA)) [2002/3 16d* 17s[F] 16s[F] 16g* 16f² 16m 16d³ Dec 5] compact ex-Irish gelding: fairly useful 11f winner on Flat: fair hurdler: won novices at Ballinrobe in May and Tramore in June: left P. Hughes before final start: raced around 2m: acted on soft and firm ground: tried tongue tied: dead. *P. J. Hobbs*

BRIGADE CHARGE (USA) 8 b.g. Affirmed (USA) – Fairy Footsteps (Mill Reef **c116 +** (USA)) [2002/3 c116p, h–: c20g⁶ c19s³ Jan 26] well-made gelding: fairly useful handicap **h–** hurdler/chaser: shaped well both starts in 2002/3: should stay beyond 19f: acts on good to firm and heavy ground: consistent. *C. Roche, Ireland*

BRIGADIER DU BOIS (FR) 4 gr.g. Apeldoorn (FR) – Artic Night (FR) (Kaldoun **h–** (FR)) [2002/3 16d² 16v 17v³ 16g Apr 3] ex-French gelding: fourth foal: half-brother to winning hurdlers up to 2¼m Spechled Band (by Nashamaa) and Diamont Royale (by Diamond Prospect): dam ran once: runner-up over 11f on Flat: placed twice in 3 starts in juvenile hurdles at Pau for C. Diard: stiff task in Grade 2 juvenile at Aintree final outing. *Mrs L. Wadham*

BRIGANTE GIRL (IRE) 5 b.m. Old Vic – Strong Winds (IRE) (Strong Gale) **F87** [2002/3 F17d² F14d³ Dec 9] lengthy, unfurnished mare: first foal: dam unraced, out of useful 2m hurdler/chaser Ballychorus Dream: fair form when placed in bumpers at Bangor (mares) and Ayr. *N. G. Richards*

BRIGGS TURN 9 b.g. Rudimentary (USA) – Turnabout (Tyrnavos) [2002/3 h109: **h–** 16d Mar 10] big, good-bodied gelding: fair handicap hurdler: well below form only start in 2002/3: stays 19f: raced on good going or softer (acts on heavy). *Mrs Merrita Jones*

BRIGHT APPROACH (IRE) 10 gr.g. Roselier (FR) – Dysart Lady (King's Ride) **c126** [2002/3 c106: c33g* c31m² c27g* c26g² c24m² Apr 2] smallish gelding: smart hunter chaser: won at Cheltenham in May and Ludlow in February: very good 2½ lengths second of 24 to Kingscliff in Foxhunter at Cheltenham fourth start: suited by thorough test of stamina: acts on good to firm going. *Mrs O. Bush*

BRIGHT BEACON 9 br.g. Lighter – Pennulli (Sir Nulli) [2002/3 c24s⁴ Mar 10] fair **c–** pointer: off nearly a year, last of 4 finishers in novice hunter chase at Stratford. *Evan Williams*

BRIGHT DESTINY 12 br.g. Destroyer – Bright Suggestion (Magnate) [2002/3 c84? **c–** , h–: c25d c25s⁴ c20v[pu] c24v⁵ c25v[pu] c25s[pu] Feb 23] lengthy gelding: handicap chaser, **h–** very much on the downgrade: stays 4m: has form on firm going, races on softer than good nowadays (acts on heavy): sometimes visored, tried in cheekpieces. *J. S. Goldie*

BRIGHTER SHADE (IRE) 13 b.g. Sheer Grit – Shady Doorknocker (Mon Capi- **c86** taine) [2002/3 c25m³ May 8] strong, sturdy gelding: fair pointer/hunter chaser: stays 3m: acts on good to firm and heavy going. *Mrs Sarah L. Dent*

BRIGHT NOVEMBER 12 b.g. Niniski (USA) – Brigata (Brigadier Gerard) [2002/3 **c–** c116d, h–: c16g[F] May 24] tall, leggy gelding: one-time fairly useful chaser: let down by **h–** jumping and below best since 2000/1: ran out in point in April: stays 2½m: acts on soft and good to firm going: 6 of 7 wins on right-handed courses: usually front runner. *D. R. Gandolfo*

BRIGHT QUESTION 6 ch.g. Nashwan (USA) – Ozone Friendly (USA) (Green **h–** Forest (USA)) [2002/3 h–: 16m[pu] Jun 1] angular gelding: signs of only a little ability over hurdles, reportedly lame only outing in 2002/3. *Mrs Merrita Jones*

BRIGHT STEEL (IRE) 6 gr.g. Roselier (FR) – Ikeathy (Be Friendly) [2002/3 F–: **h–** 16v 16d Mar 7] well held in bumper and 2 maiden hurdles. *A. Parker*

BRILLIANT STAR (NZ) 11 b.g. Star Way – Karman Gal (Persian Bold) [2002/3 **c–** c107, h–: c22d[pu] c17d Aug 2] workmanlike gelding: fair handicap chaser: went off too **h–** fast in valuable event at Galway on reappearance: well held there 2 days later: stays 2½m: acts on soft and good to firm going: has reportedly bled from nose: unbeaten in 3 completed starts for A. McCoy. *S. A. Brookshaw*

BRITANNIA MILLS 12 gr.m. Nordico (USA) – May Fox (Healaugh Fox) [2002/3 **h–** h–: 22d[pu] 17d[pu] 21m 22g⁵ Oct 6] of no account nowadays: usually blinkered. *D. Burchell*

BRITISH VOLUNTEER (IRE) 7 br.g. Executive Perk – Dante Light (IRE) (Phar- **h91** dante (FR)) [2002/3 h83: 21d³ Nov 25] sturdy gelding: modest novice hurdler: stays 21f: raced on good going or softer. *C. J. Mann*

BROADBROOK LASS   9 ch.m. Broadsword (USA) – Netherbrook Lass (Netherkelly) [2002/3 c24v² c21s* c24mᶠ c20d* c25mᵖᵘ Apr 5] has been to stud and had 2 foals: winning pointer: won novice chases at Uttoxeter in June and Bangor in August: off 8 months, jumped markedly left in handicap at Hereford final outing: stays 3m: acts on good to firm and heavy ground: front runner: tail flasher. *Mrs H. Dalton*   **c101**

BROADGATE FLYER (IRE)   9 b.g. Silver Kite (USA) – Fabulous Pet (Somethingfabulous (USA)) [2002/3 c71, h–: 17m⁵ c16m³ c16g³ c16d c16mᵘʳ c20g⁴ c20g⁴ c20m* Apr 19] medium-sized gelding: winning hurdler: modest handicap chaser: left D. Lamb, improved form to win at Carlisle in April: stays 2½m: acts on firm going, not on soft/ heavy: blinkered once (jumped poorly): tongue tied. *Miss Lucinda V. Russell*   **c89 h76**

BROADNARD   9 b.g. Ardross – Broadhurst (Workboy) [2002/3 20s⁴ 24d³ Nov 30] smallish gelding: modest handicap hurdler: off 2½ years before reappearance: stays 3m: acts on soft going. *Mrs P. Sly*   **h86**

BROCKTON MIST (IRE)   8 ch.g. Mister Lord (USA) – Glens Princess (Prince Hansel) [2002/3 F86: 20m² 23d* 24g* c24d² c24d² c26dᶠ c23d³ c24gᵘʳ 24m³ Apr 15] strong, lengthy gelding: fair hurdler: won novices at Wetherby in May and Perth in September: encouraging second first 2 starts in novice chases, but badly let down by jumping well subsequently: will prove best at 3m+: acts on good to firm and good to soft going. *P. J. Hobbs*   **c119 h100**

BROCTUNE LINE   9 ch.g. Safawan – Ra Ra (Lord Gayle (USA)) [2002/3 c–, h–: 16dᵖᵘ May 6] leggy gelding: no show on chasing debut: maiden hurdler: tried blinkered. *Mrs P. Ford*   **c– h–**

BROGUESTOWN BREEZE (IRE)   10 b.g. Montelimar (USA) – Spin A Coin (Torus) [2002/3 c–, h81: c26g² Oct 21] workmanlike gelding: lightly-raced maiden hurdler: modest handicap chaser: went in snatches when second at Plumpton on return from 17-month absence, not seen out again: stays 3¼m: acts on good to firm and heavy going. *L. A. Dace*   **c91 h–**

BROKEN ARROW (IRE)   6 b.g. Sri Pekan (USA) – Domniga (IRE) (Be My Guest (USA)) [2002/3 h91, F79: 17s 17m⁶ Jun 1] sturdy gelding: bumper winner: some promise on hurdling debut in 2001/2 but failed to progress, well beaten on Flat debut in August: tongue tied. *A. J. Lidderdale*   **h–**

BROKEN DREAM (IRE)   6 b.g. Broken Hearted – A Little Further (Mandalus) [2002/3 h101p: c20v² c20d³ c19dᵘʳ c24gᵖᵘ Apr 12] fair novice hurdler: similar form in novice chases, though went with no zest last 2 outings: stays 2½m: raced on good going or softer (acts on heavy). *Miss H. C. Knight*   **c100 h–**

BROKEN KNIGHTS (IRE)   6 ch.g. Broken Hearted – Knight's Row (Le Bavard (FR)) [2002/3 F16d* F16g² 20v* 20g* Apr 14] IR £13,000 4-y-o: well-made gelding: fifth foal: dam maiden placed over hurdles/in points: won bumper at Ayr in November: created good impression when winning novice hurdles at Ayr in January and Hexham in April: reportedly finished lame at latter course but likely to continue to progress. *N. G. Richards*   **h117 p F107**

BROKE ROAD (IRE)   7 b.g. Deploy – Shamaka (Kris) [2002/3 h102: c16g* c16s² c16d⁶ c16g* 16g² 17m⁴ 17m⁴ Sep 13] leggy gelding: fair handicap hurdler: won novice chases at Fakenham (fourth course success) in May and Worcester in July: at least respectable efforts back over hurdles last 3 starts: raced around 2m: acts on soft and good to firm going (pulled up on heavy): visored once: has had tongue tied. *Mrs H. Dalton*   **c93 h102**

BROMLEY'S DAUGHTER   7 b.m. Minster Son – Bromley Rose (Rubor) [2002/3 F16m 16d 17d 20d 20m Apr 19] half-sister to fairly useful 2m hurdler Little Bromley (by Riberetto): dam unraced: little sign of ability. *R. Ford*   **h– F–**

BRONHALLOW   10 b.g. Belmez (USA) – Grey Twig (Godswalk (USA)) [2002/3 24d 24s 20vᵖᵘ 23v 21s 22v c20d⁶ c24m³ c25m⁴ Apr 5] angular gelding: poor handicap hurdler in 2000/1: first sign of retaining ability when third in maiden chase at Huntingdon in March: stays 3m: probably acts on any going: tried visored/blinkered: tongue tied. *Mrs Barbara Waring*   **c83 h–**

BRONZE LIGHT   5 ch.m. Moscow Society (USA) – Barton Bay (IRE) (Kambalda) [2002/3 F12d F16d 20gᵖᵘ 20g Mar 16] plain, shallow-girthed mare: fourth foal: halfsister to 2m hurdle winner Yesyes (by Supreme Leader): dam unraced, out of half-sister to top-class staying chaser Barton Bank: showed little in bumpers/novice hurdles. *M. J. Roberts*   **h– F–**

Royal Bank of Scotland 'National Hunt' Novices' Hurdle, Ayr—Brooklyn Breeze looks a good prospect

BRONZESMITH 7 b.g. Greensmith – Bronze Age (Celtic Cone) [2002/3 h98: c16g³ c19sᶠ c16d² c19g⁴ Mar 25] lengthy gelding: modest hurdler: fair maiden chaser, makes mistakes: likely to prove best at 2½m+: acts on soft going (won poor race over hurdles on good to firm). *B. J. M. Ryall*   **c112 x** **h–**

BROOK BEE 11 br.g. Meadowbrook – Brown Bee III (Marcus Superbus) [2002/3 c24s⁶ c25mᵖᵘ Jun 1] strong, lengthy gelding: has been hobdayed: modest chaser at best: very lightly raced outside points nowadays: best at 3m+: acts on good to soft going, possibly not on softer: blinkered once: sold 1,000 gns Doncaster November Sales. *T. H. Caldwell*   **c–** **h–**

BROOKLANDS LAD 6 b.g. North Col – Sancal (Whistlefield) [2002/3 F16g⁴ F17d 19d 19g² Apr 19] 3,800 4-y-o: workmanlike gelding: fourth foal: dam well beaten in novice hurdles: fair form on first of 2 starts in bumpers: much better effort over hurdles when second in maiden at Stratford: will stay beyond 19f. *J. W. Mullins*   **h87** **F85**

BROOKLYN BOY 6 ch.h. Meadowbrook – Blue Ivory VII (Damsire Unregistered) [2002/3 F17d⁶ F17m F17s Nov 21] first foal: dam never ran: well held in 3 bumpers. *J. C. Tuck*   **F–**

BROOKLYN BREEZE (IRE) 6 b. or br.g. Be My Native (USA) – Moss Gale (Strong Gale) [2002/3 F92: F17d* 16g* 20m* 24g* Apr 24] useful-looking gelding: type to make a chaser: won at Aintree in November on second of 2 starts in bumpers: unbeaten in 3 novice hurdles, landing odds at Musselburgh (by 9 lengths from The Kew Tour) in April: stays 3m: capable of better still. *L. Lungo*   **h127 p** **F99**

BROOKLYN'S GOLD (USA) 8 b.g. Seeking The Gold (USA) – Brooklyn's Dance (FR) (Shirley Heights) [2002/3 h103: 17g* 16d² 16s* 16g⁴ 16d⁴ 16m* 16m³ 16g³ Apr 5] close-coupled, quite good-topped gelding: fairly useful handicap hurdler: much improved in 2002/3, winning at Hereford in October, Huntingdon in November and Kempton in February: ran really well when third last 2 starts: raced around 2m: has won on soft going, best efforts on good or firmer: genuine and consistent. *Ian Williams*   **h124**

BROOKSBY WHORLTON (IRE) 9 b.g. Commanche Run – Superlee (IRE) (Le Moss) [2002/3 h70§: 20d 21s* 21vᵖᵘ 20gᵖᵘ 21d⁶ Apr 8] angular gelding: poor hurdler: won minor event at Sedgefield in December: stays 21f: acts on soft going: usually blinkered/in cheekpieces: has bled from nose: not one to trust. *G. A. Harker*   **h84 §**

144

BROOKSIE　8 b.g. Efisio – Elkie Brooks (Relkino) [2002/3 h94§: 17g² 17g⁵ 16g* **h100**
17m* Jul 15] angular gelding: fair handicap hurdler: won at Worcester and Newton Abbot
in July: barely stays 2¾m: acts on any going: visored/blinkered: has had tongue tied: has
found little. *Miss K. M. George*

BROOK STREET　6 b.g. Cruise Missile – Sweet Spice (Native Bazaar) [2002/3 F77: **h66**
F18g⁵ F16g 21s⁶ Nov 24] workmanlike gelding: modest form in bumpers: didn't jump **F77**
fluently when well held in novice at Plumpton on hurdling debut: should stay at least
2½m: has looked hard ride. *C. Tizzard*

BROOK TEAN　9 b.m. River God (USA) – Saucy Eater (Saucy Kit) [2002/3 17g⁵ **h–**
20dᵖᵘ Apr 9] medium-sized mare: second in mares bumper on debut in 2000/1: little show
since, including over hurdles. *W. M. Brisbourne*

BROOM CLOSE (IRE)　9 b.g. Yashgan – Pick Nine (Tumble Wind (USA)) [2002/3 **c87 ?**
c–, h–: 20d* 20d² c20s⁶ c16v⁵ c16v⁴ 20s* 24v⁴ Mar 13] lengthy gelding: poor hurdler/ **h78**
maiden chaser: won handicaps at Carlisle (novice) in October and Newcastle in February:
stays 2½m, possibly not 3m: acts on heavy going. *R. Johnson*

BROTHER ERNEST　8 b.g. Phardante (FR) – Minerstown (IRE) (Miner's Lamp) **c–**
[2002/3 c–, h–: 21gᵖᵘ May 30] well-made gelding: little encouragement over jumps: tried **h–**
blinkered/visored/tongue tied. *Ferdy Murphy*

BROTHER JOE (NZ)　9 ch.g. Hula Town (NZ) – Olivia Rose (NZ) (Travolta (FR)) **h154 §**
[2002/3 h146x: 25d* 24g⁶ 25vᵖᵘ 24g 24g⁵ 21mᵖᵘ Apr 16] smallish gelding: smart
hurdler on his day: impressive winner of Grade 2 John Smith's West Yorkshire Hurdle at
Wetherby in November: very disappointing subsequently: stays 25f: acts on any going:
blinkered fourth start: reportedly had breathing problem third outing: free-going sort

John Smith's West Yorkshire Hurdle, Wetherby—an impressive success for the frustrating Brother Joe

(held up) and suited by strong gallop: often let down by jumping: not one to trust. *P. J. Hobbs*

BROTHER TED   6 b.g. Henbit (USA) – Will Be Wanton (Palm Track) [2002/3 F17m   F–
F16m⁵ F17d F16d Mar 6] leggy gelding: ninth foal: half-brother to 3 winners, including modest 2m chaser The Secret Seven (by Balidar): dam won 2m selling hurdle: signs of only a little ability in bumpers: tongue tied final start. *J. K. Cresswell*

BROWJOSHY (IRE)   10 b.g. Zaffaran (USA) – Keeping Company (King's Com-   c– §
pany) [2002/3 c107§, h100§: 27g c27dᶠ c28s⁵ c31dᵖᵘ Dec 13] rangy gelding: winning   h– §
hurdler: useful staying chaser at best: no encouragement in 2002/3, leaving M. Pitman after reappearance: often blinkered/visored: ungenuine. *K. C. Bailey*

BROWN CHIEFTAIN (IRE)   10 b.g. Meneval (USA) – Brown Trout (IRE) (Beau   c–
Charmeur (FR)) [2002/3 c26sᵖᵘ May 28] ex-Irish gelding: fair pointer, won in March: no form in steeplechases: tried blinkered. *A. W. G. Geering*

BROWN ESQUIRE   12 b.g. Broadleaf – Ana Brown (Souvran) [2002/3 c87, h–:   c–
c24g⁶ c25dᵖᵘ Feb 10] lengthy gelding: winning pointer: modest form at best in hunter   h–
chases: stays 3m: acts on good to firm going. *Miss G. Dewhurst*

BROWNE STREET (IRE)   8 b. or br.g. Supreme Leader – Greencloyne Girl (Deep   c112
Run) [2002/3 h100, F106: c24dᵘʳ c17s c20s⁵ c22v² c24v* c25sᶠ Jan 19] fair form over   h–
hurdles: bit better over fences, won maiden at Limerick in December: stayed 3m: raced on good going or softer (acted on heavy): dead. *Anthony Mullins, Ireland*

BROWNIE RETURNS (IRE)   10 b.g. Dry Dock – What A Brownie (Strong Gale)   c94
[2002/3 25g c22d c25s⁴ c25m* c24g c28s⁶ c24s⁴ c25d* c24sᵖᵘ c24v c24d* c25g² Apr 20]   h–
angular gelding: maiden hurdler: modest handicap chaser: won at Kilbeggan in August, Folkestone in December and Limerick in March: stays 25f: acts on any going: usually blinkered. *M. F. Morris, Ireland*

BROWN OWL   9 b.m. Petoski – Laura Grey (Cantab) [2002/3 c21mᵖᵘ Jul 15] lightly   c–
raced and no sign of ability: has shown signs of temperament. *W. G. M. Turner*   h–

BROWNS DELIGHT   6 b.m. Runnett – Fearless Princess (Tyrnavos) [2002/3 h–:   h–
17g May 1] no form over hurdles: tried blinkered. *Mrs A. C. Tate*

BROWN TEDDY   6 b.g. Afzal – Quadrapol (Pollerton) [2002/3 F88: F17d 17s⁴ 16m⁴   h95
16g* 16g* 20g⁵ Apr 1] lengthy gelding: fair form on first of 2 starts in bumpers: modest   F73
form over hurdles: won novice at Musselburgh in January and ladies handicap at Huntingdon in March: should stay at least 2½m (badly let down by jumping final outing). *R. Ford*

BRUERN (IRE)   6 b.g. Aahsaylad – Bob's Girl (IRE) (Bob Back (USA)) [2002/3   F–
F16g Feb 8] IR £33,000 4-y-o: good-topped gelding: third foal: half-brother to 3 winners, including modest hurdler around 2m Bob's Gone (by Eurobus) and bumper winner Jumbo Gunner (by Houmayoun): dam, placed over hurdles, half-sister to useful French jumper Norlero: well held in Grade 2 bumper on debut. *Mrs Mary Hambro*

BRUMALIS (NZ)   11 b.g. High Ice (USA) – Kerry Sue (NZ) (Knighthood (NZ))   c–
[2002/3 c–, h–: c34gᵘʳ May 22] tall gelding: of little account nowadays: tried blinkered/   h–
visored: has been ridden in spurs. *Miss Laura Cottam*

BRUNO PAILLARD   6 ch.g. Minster Son – Chasers' Bar (Oats) [2002/3 F17m Jun   F–
22] third foal: brother to winning pointer and half-brother to useful chaser Noble Lord (by Lord Bud), stays 33f: dam, modest hurdler, stayed 3m: failed to complete in 3 points in 2002: well beaten in bumper: sold 1,300 gns Doncaster August Sales. *J. R. Turner*

BRUSH A KING   8 b.g. Derrylin – Colonial Princess (Roscoe Blake) [2002/3 h–:   h83
20m³ 21mᵖᵘ 20gᵖᵘ 19s 24v⁴ 24v⁶ 19d* 21g⁵ 21m* Apr 26] plain gelding: poor handicap hurdler: won sellers at Catterick in February and Sedgefield in April: stays 21f, probably not 3m: acts on good to firm going, probably on heavy: usually ridden by claimer (wasn't at Sedgefield). *C. T. Pogson*

BRUSH THE ARK   9 b.m. Brush Aside (USA) – Expensive Lark (Sir Lark) [2002/3   h83
h81: 26g³ 23d² 26g² 22g² Nov 9] small, lengthy mare: bumper winner: poor maiden hurdler: good placed efforts all 4 starts in 2002/3: stays 3¼m: raced on good going or softer (acts on soft). *J. S. Smith*

BRUSH WITH FAME (IRE)   11 b.g. Brush Aside (USA) – Cheeney's Gift (Quay-   c–
side) [2002/3 c–, h–: 24m 26mᵖᵘ Aug 12] close-coupled gelding: winning hurdler/chaser,   h–
retains little ability: tried blinkered. *G. J. Smith*

146

Quinns of Baltinglass Chase For The La Touche Cup, Punchestown—
Buailtes And Fadas leads the field over the first bank; twenty set out but only five completed

BRUTHUINNE (IRE) 8 ch.g. Vaquillo (USA) – Portane Miss (Salluceva) [2002/3 **c102**
c98, h–: c25m* c26g* c26d⁴ c25d^F Dec 2] strong gelding: fair chaser: won novice at **h–**
Hereford (simple task) and handicap at Plumpton in October: stays easy 3¼m: acts on
soft and good to firm going: front runner. *B. G. Powell*

BRYANTS ROONEY 7 ch.g. Prince Rooney (IRE) – Forever Blushing (Blushing **F–**
Scribe (USA)) [2002/3 F16m Jun 3] first foal: dam 2-y-o 7f winner: well held in bumper
on debut. *Miss M. P. Bryant*

B SO BOLD 9 b.g. Never So Bold – Gunner Girl (Gunner B) [2002/3 24g^pu May 3] big **h–**
gelding: very lightly raced: signs of a little ability in bumpers: pulled up early on hurdling
debut: joined Mrs S. Williams. *J. Neville*

BUADHACH (IRE) 7 b.g. Petoski – Viking Rocket (Viking (USA)) [2002/3 h72§, **c– §**
F–: c19m Apr 21] lengthy, angular gelding: poor and temperamental hurdler: sold out of **h– §**
A. Parker's stable 750 gns Doncaster October Sales: well held in hunter chase on return:
should stay beyond 2½m: acts on good to soft going, bumper form on firm: has had
tongue tied. *M. A. Hill*

BUAILTES AND FADAS (IRE) 8 b. or br.g. Be My Native (USA) – Ballyline **c108 +**
Dancer (Giolla Mear)) [2002/3 NR] IR 33,000 4-y-o: workmanlike gelding: fifth foal:
brother to winning 21f hurdler Native Eire: dam, won bumper in Ireland, half-sister to
useful hurdler Dawlish: winning pointer: won cross-country races at Punchestown on
consecutive days, beating Galapiat du Mesnil a distance in Quinns of Baltinglass Chase
(La Touche Cup) on second occasion: stays 33f. *E. Bolger, Ireland*

BUALADHBOS (IRE) 4 b.g. Royal Applause – Goodnight Girl (IRE) (Alzao (USA)) **h–**
[2002/3 16d⁶ Nov 12] workmanlike gelding: modest maiden on Flat (may prove best
around 1¼m): well behind in juvenile on hurdling debut. *F. Jordan*

BUCCANEER BOY (IRE) 10 b.g. Buckskin (FR) – Shady Miss (Mandamus) **c101 §**
[2002/3 c30d³ c30v⁵ Feb 7] good sort: has reportedly had soft palate operation: fairly
useful chaser in 2000/1 for P. Nicholls: well below form both starts on return, running
moody race on first occasion: should stay beyond 3m: raced on going softer than good
(acts on heavy): blinkered/visored: races prominently: tends to jump right: needs treating
with caution. *Ian Williams*

BUCKBY LANE 7 b.g. Nomadic Way (USA) – Buckby Folly (Netherkelly) [2002/3 **h119 +**
h83: 21s² 21v^ur 21s³ 21s* 21m* Apr 16] useful-looking gelding: will make a chaser:

147

Telectronics Systems 'National Hunt' Auction Novices Hurdle, Cheltenham—
Buckby Lane dominates the closing stages

fairly useful novice hurdler: best efforts last 2 starts, winning at Plumpton (easily) in March and Cheltenham (by 13 lengths from Fantasmic) in April: should stay 3m: acts on soft and good to firm going. *P. R. Webber*

BUCKLAND BOY   6 b.g. Rakaposhi King – Lichen Moss (Le Moss) [2002/3 c24mpu   **c–**
Apr 22] 3,000 4-y-o: third foal: dam never ran: fair pointer: no show in hunter on steeplechase debut. *P. Haskins*

BUCKLAND KNIGHT (IRE)   7 b. or br.g. Commanche Run – Myra Gaye (Buck-   **h–**
skin (FR)) [2002/3 h105?: 17m 21dpu 22ssur 19s5 20vpu Jan 6] lengthy gelding: 100/1-winner of novice hurdle in 2001/2: little show since: should stay at least 2½m: acts on heavy going: blinkered last 3 starts. *D. M. Grissell*

BUCKSKIN LAD (IRE)   8 b. or br.g. Buckskin (FR) – Loverush (Golden Love)   **h83**
[2002/3 24g6 22gpu 20vpu 25d* 26s2 25m6 Mar 31] first form over hurdles when winning novice handicap at Catterick in February: ran at least as well in similar event at Hereford next time: stays 3¼m: acts on soft going: wore cheekpieces third start. *C. Roberts*

BUCK'S PALACE   10 ch.g. Buckley – Lady Geneva (Royalty) [2002/3 c–§, h–§:   **c– §**
c20vpu c23gpu Mar 23] strong gelding: fair chaser at best: lightly raced and of little   **h– §**
account nowadays: tried in blinkers/cheekpieces: temperamental. *B. Mactaggart*

BUCKS VIEW (IRE)   13 b.g. Buckskin (FR) – Our View (Our Mirage) [2002/3 c–:   **c92**
c24sF c28gur May 31] lengthy gelding: fair pointer: third start in hunter chases, disputing second when unseating 2 out in valuable novice at Stratford. *G. D. Hanmer*

BUDDHI (IRE)   5 b.g. Be My Native (USA) – Paean Express (IRE) (Paean) [2002/3   **F–**
F17dpu Nov 24] leggy gelding: first foal: dam never ran: shaped well until pulled up over 3f out (presumably amiss) in 20-runner bumper at Aintree on debut. *M. Pitman*

BUDDY DIVER   10 br.g. Revlow – Rely-On-Pearl (Deep Diver) [2002/3 h–: 16s Feb   **h–**
26] lengthy gelding: of little account. *C. J. Gray*

BUDDY GIRIE   10 b.g. Lord Bud – Hatsu-Girie (Ascertain (USA)) [2002/3 c27d4   **c90**
Mar 18] fair pointer, successful in March and April: similar form when fourth to Son of   **h–**
Anshan in hunter at Sedgefield. *P. Cornforth*

BUDE 4 gr.g. Environment Friend – Gay Da Cheen (IRE) (Tenby) [2002/3 17m⁵ 16f² **h82**
17g⁴ 16m⁶ 20d⁶ 16g 16s 16g* 19mᵖᵘ 16m² 17m³ Apr 19] angular gelding: disappointing
maiden on Flat: modest juvenile hurdler: won handicap at Ludlow in March: best around
2m on good going or firmer: blinkered last 6 starts: usually races prominently: tricky ride.
S. A. Brookshaw

BUFFALO BILL (IRE) 7 ch.g. Be My Native (USA) – Sylvia Fox (Deep Run) **F107**
[2002/3 F16f* F16m* Oct 6] IR 40,000 3-y-o: angular gelding: second foal: brother to
smart bumper winner/promising hurdler Masteroffoxhounds and half-brother to bumper
winner Back Nine (by Bob Back): dam, 2m winner over hurdles/on Flat, half-sister to
fairly useful 2m chaser Belstone Fox: off 2 years after debut: won bumpers at Listowel
and Tipperary in autumn, useful form when showing good turn of foot to beat Ruff Justice
2½ lengths at latter: left A. O'Brien, didn't take eye when only ninth in Grade 1 bumper
at Punchestown in late-April. *D. Wachman, Ireland*

BUGSY MALONE 5 b.g. Sir Harry Lewis (USA) – Aisholt (Avocat) [2002/3 F16m **F–**
F16d F12g Dec 18] second foal: dam winning pointer: behind in 3 bumpers, visored final
outing. *M. R. Bosley*

BUILDERS MATE 9 b.g. Cruise Missile – Crossing Star VII (Damsire Unregistered) **c–**
[2002/3 c25sᵖᵘ c27vᵖᵘ Jan 21] good-topped gelding: fourth foal: dam never ran: showed
nothing in 2 maiden chases at Sedgefield. *S. J. Marshall*

BULLET 8 b.g. Alhijaz – Beacon (High Top) [2002/3 19d Oct 19] leggy gelding: fairly **h–**
useful on Flat (stayed 1¾m) at 4 yrs, well below form both starts in 2001 (for M. Pipe):
tailed off only outing over hurdles: dead. *Mrs H. Dalton*

BULLFINCH 10 ch.g. Anshan – Lambay (Lorenzaccio) [2002/3 c–, h111d: 27g⁴ 22g⁵ **c–**
27g⁴ 27m³ 26g⁶ Aug 26] sparely-made gelding: poor handicap hurdler nowadays: stays **h83**
27f: acts on firm and soft going. *R. T. Phillips*

BULOUGUN (FR) 4 ch.f. Pistolet Bleu (IRE) – Buloula (FR) (Bikala (FR)) [2002/3 **h132**
15v* 18v* 18s 19v² Apr 26] third foal: half-sister to useful hurdler up to 21f Domloula
(by Dom Pasquini): dam placed on Flat: won over 1½m only start on Flat: useful hurdler:
raced exclusively at Auteuil in 2002/3, winning fillies races in October (newcomers) and
November and Group 3 Prix de Longchamp (dictated pace when beating Katoune 3
lengths) in May: again made running when good second to Nickname in Group 1 Prix
Alain du Breil in June, headed when mistake last: will stay beyond 19f: raced on going
softer than good (acts on heavy): has worn a hood. *M. Rolland, France*

BUNBURY 10 ch.g. Gildoran – Metaxa (Khalkis) [2002/3 c17v² c20vᵖᵘ 16s⁵ Feb 26] **c83**
tall gelding: lightly raced: maiden hurdler: off 2 years, best effort in 2002/3 when second **h–**
in novice handicap at Bangor on chasing debut: probably stays 2¾m: raced on going
softer than good (acts on heavy). *E. L. James*

BUNGEE JUMPER 13 b.g. Idiot's Delight – Catherine Bridge (Pitpan) [2002/3 c–§, **c– §**
h–§: 20gᵖᵘ Apr 21] sturdy gelding: winning 2m hurdler/chaser, very lightly raced nowa- **h– §**
days: acts on firm going: tried blinkered/in cheekpieces: has found little. *P. L. Clinton*

BUNKUM 5 b.g. Robellino (USA) – Spinning Mouse (Bustino) [2002/3 h112: 20v* **h115**
Feb 4] good-topped gelding: fairly useful hurdler: off over 10 months, won handicap at
Chepstow in February: will probably stay beyond 2½m: acts on heavy ground. *R. Lee*

BUNRATTY CASTLE (IRE) 8 b.g. Supreme Leader – Shannon Foam (Le Bavard **c121**
(FR)) [2002/3 c111, h108: c20d* c21gᵘʳ c25d* Dec 5] rather leggy, lengthy gelding: **h–**
winning hurdler: fairly useful chaser: won novice at Stratford in October and handicap at
Wincanton (finished lame when beating Dear Deal 2½ lengths) in December: stays 25f:
acts on any going: may be capable of further improvement over fences if able to return in
2003/4. *P. F. Nicholls*

BURCOT GIRL (IRE) 6 b.m. Petardia – Phoenix Forli (USA) (Forli (ARG)) **h–**
[2002/3 h–: 16f 16dᵖᵘ 16dᵖᵘ 17d Dec 3] of little account. *Mrs A. C. Tate*

BURDENS GIRL 6 ch.m. Alflora (IRE) – Dalbeattie (Phardante (FR)) [2002/3 F78: **h–**
F16d⁴ 21d 19g Feb 28] modest form in bumper on debut: well held both starts over **F–**
hurdles. *H. D. Daly*

BURGUNDY LACE (USA) 4 b.f. Lord Avie (USA) – Oro Bianco (USA) (Lyphard's **h89**
Wish (FR)) [2002/3 16s⁴ 16v⁶ 16vᵖᵘ Feb 10] medium-sized ex-French filly: half-sister to
poor hurdler Straffan Gold (by Lear Fan), stays 2½m: fairly useful on Flat (stays 1¼m),
successful in October, sold out of J. Pease's stable 15,000 gns Newmarket December
Sales: best effort over hurdles when fourth in juvenile at Kempton: failed to settle/made
mistakes final start. *Mrs L. Wadham*

BURLU (FR) 9 ch.g. Garde Royale – Acquevillaise (FR) (Un Prince) [2002/3 c24g^{pu} c–
c36d^F c29m^{pu} Apr 26] medium-sized ex-French gelding: twice-raced over hurdles at 3 h–
yrs: useful form over fences for J-P. Daireaux in 2001/2: failed to complete all 3 starts in
valuable handicaps in Britain, taking little interest final one: stays 23f: acts on heavy
going: sometimes blinkered, including when successful. *M. C. Pipe*

BURNING TRUTH (USA) 9 ch.g. Known Fact (USA) – Galega (Sure Blade h107
(USA)) [2002/3 16m⁴ 16g⁵ 17m* 16f² 16f* 16g* 16g⁴ Apr 19] good-topped gelding: fair
at best on Flat (stays easy 1½m): lightly raced over hurdles, sold out of Mrs A. Duffield's
stable 2,200 gns Doncaster August Sales after reappearance: did well after, making all or
most when winning handicaps at Hereford (novice) and Ludlow in October and Stratford
in April: unable to dominate final start: will prove best around 2m: acts on firm going.
M. Sheppard

BURRA SAHIB 7 b.g. First Trump – Old Flower (Persian Bold) [2002/3 h–: 22g c–
c21g³ c26g⁴ c26f^{pu} Aug 13] tall, angular gelding: no sign of ability over jumps: has had h–
tongue tied: sold £500 Ascot October Sales. *P. C. Ritchens*

BURRY BRAVE 4 b.g. Presidium – Keep Mum (Mummy's Pet) [2002/3 16g^{pu} Dec h–
28] half-brother to poor hurdler Keep Battling (by Hard Fought), stays 21f: little form on
Flat: showed nothing on hurdling debut. *J. S. Goldie*

BURUNDI (IRE) 9 b.g. Danehill (USA) – Sofala (Home Guard (USA)) [2002/3 c94
h116: 17m* 19d³ c16v c16d⁵ c19g^F 16v 20d* 20d² 20g 21m⁵ Apr 16] tall gelding: modest h118
form at best in 3 novice chases: fairly useful handicap hurdler: won at Folkestone in May
and Wetherby (beat After Me Boys 5 lengths) in February: stays 2½m: acts on soft and
good to firm going, possibly not on heavy: fell only run in blinkers: held up. *A. W. Carroll*

BURWOOD BREEZE (IRE) 7 b.g. Fresh Breeze (USA) – Shuil Le Cheile (Quay- c98
side) [2002/3 h94, F84: c20v^F c25s⁵ c20g⁵ c20s² Mar 10] workmanlike gelding: modest h–
novice hurdler: easily best effort over fences when second to Villair in handicap at
Plumpton: should stay 3m: acts on soft going. *T. R. George*

BUS 8 ch.g. Weld – Roaring Breeze (Roaring Riva) [2002/3 17g³ c16s⁴ c17m^F c16g² Jul c90 ?
15] angular gelding: poor hurdler: off 20 months, running best race over fences (reluctant h–
to race on debut) when falling 2 out in novice won by Canadiane at Stratford: raced
mainly around 2m: best efforts on good to firm ground: tried tongue tied. *Mrs
L. Williamson*

BUSHEHR (IRE) 11 b.g. Persian Bold – Shejrah (USA) (Northjet) [2002/3 c73, h–: c70 x
c16m^{ur} c16m³ c16g^{ur} 22d² 20g² 20g³ Aug 26] small, lengthy gelding: poor form over h85
fences (often let down by jumping): modest maiden hurdler: stays 2¾m: acts on good to
firm and heavy going: tried tongue tied early in career. *Mrs A. M. Thorpe*

BUSH HILL BANDIT (IRE) 8 b. or br.g. Executive Perk – Baby Isle (Menelek) c92
[2002/3 h–: c24m* Apr 21] novice hurdler: fair pointer: won at Fakenham on hunter h–
chase debut: stays 3m: acts on good to firm going. *Mrs Anne-Marie Hays*

BUSHIDO (IRE) 4 br.g. Brief Truce (USA) – Pheopotstown (Henbit (USA)) [2002/3 h108
16m 16g² 16d² 17d* 17d² 16g* 16g³ Apr 19] small gelding: fair maiden on Flat (tried
blinkered), stays 9f: fair juvenile hurdler, sold out of D. Weld's stable 2,200 gns
Doncaster September Sales after debut: won at Carlisle (maiden) and Hexham (made all)
in March: raced around 2m: acts on good to soft going: not an easy ride (has hung left) but
is consistent. *Mrs S. J. Smith*

BUSH PARK (IRE) 8 b.g. Be My Native (USA) – By All Means (Pitpan) [2002/3 c117 ?
c105, h99: 24g c21m* c19d⁴ c20d^{bd} c20d³ c20v* c20m c21g^F Apr 21] strong, lengthy h–
gelding: winning hurdler: fair handicap chaser: won at Uttoxeter in October and Plump-
ton (probably flattered in 4-runner race) in December: should stay beyond 21f: acts on
any going. *R. H. Alner*

BUSINESS 4 br.c. Bluegrass Prince (IRE) – Dancing Doll (USA) (Buckfinder (USA)) h– §
[2002/3 18m^{pu} 16d^{pu} 16s^R Jan 23] leggy colt: no form on Flat or over hurdles: refused in
visor final start: ungenuine. *G. A. Ham*

BUSINESS CLASS (NZ) 11 b.g. Accountant (NZ) – Fury's Princess (NZ) (Our c104
Kungfu (NZ)) [2002/3 c90: c20d² c22g* c22m² c24d^F 16d 19d⁶ c20g³ c21d^{pu} c20g³ Apr h–
26] lengthy gelding: former eventer: twice-raced hurdler: fair handicap chaser: won at
Market Rasen in June: should stay 3m: acts on good to firm and good to soft going.
Mrs M. Reveley

BUSKY GORSE 7 gr.m. Scallywag – Miss Anax (Anax) [2002/3 F–§: 17d 17g^{pu} Jun h–
12] workmanlike mare: no form in bumpers or novice hurdles: has refused to race.
P. Beaumont

BUSTAMANTE 7 ch.g. Sir Harry Lewis (USA) – Carribean Sound (Good Times (ITY)) [2002/3 h–: c16d^{ur} Nov 17] no show in maiden hurdle or novice chase (bled from nose). *P. Monteith*

c–
h–

BUSTED FLAT (IRE) 10 br.g. Bustino – Trailing Rose (Undulate (USA)) [2002/3 c–, h–: 20d 20s^{pu} 19s 23d* 26g⁶ Feb 22] strong, good-bodied gelding: not fluent only outing over fences: poor handicap hurdler nowadays: first form for long time when winning at Wetherby in February: probably stays 3¼m: acts on soft going. *Mrs M. Reveley*

c–
h84

BUSTER CLYDE (IRE) 6 b.g. Bustomi – The Red Mare (Sagaro) [2002/3 F16s Dec 16] fifth foal: dam unraced, out of very smart staying chaser Lesley Ann: well held in bumper on debut. *J. R. Bewley*

F–

BUSTISU 6 b.m. Rakaposhi King – Tasmin Gayle (IRE) (Strong Gale) [2002/3 F16m⁶ F17s³ Dec 2] 1,500 4-y-o: second foal: dam, lightly-raced hurdler, half-sister to fairly useful staying chaser Dont Tell The Wife: better effort in mares bumpers when third at Folkestone, taking strong hold early. *D. J. Wintle*

F71

BUSTLING RIO (IRE) 7 b.g. Up And At 'em – Une Venitienne (FR) (Green Dancer (USA)) [2002/3 c100p, h116: 20d Nov 2] good-topped gelding: fairly useful hurdler, ran poorly only outing in 2002/3: successful on 2 of 3 starts over fences: stays 3m: acts on heavy and good to firm going: usually held up, and tends to idle: runner-up on Flat in January. *P. C. Haslam*

c–
h–

BUST OUT 7 ch.g. Bustino – Nordic Beauty (USA) (Northjet) [2002/3 h147: c18s* c17v² c17s* Jan 26]

c142
h–

The stop-start career of Bust Out ground to a halt again in March when it was announced that a recurrence of a leg injury would condemn him to another lengthy spell on the sidelines, trainer Jessica Harrington indicating that he could be off for between a year and eighteen months. Bust Out has twice come back from similar injuries to show himself at least as good as ever and it is to be hoped he does so again, because he showed smart form in a novice chase campaign spanning three races and just over six weeks. He would have needed to improve to reach a place behind Azertyuiop in the Arkle, but had certainly appealed as an interesting prospect for Cheltenham.

Bust Out's reappearance in a maiden chase at Fairyhouse in December was his first run for almost a year, but he went off favourite and made a fine start over fences, making only one serious mistake. Bust Out drew clear with Canary Wharf

Baileys Arkle Perpetual Challenge Cup Novices' Chase, Leopardstown—
Bust Out survives an awkward jump at the last; eventual fourth Ricardo is also in shot

and was going the better of the pair when that horse took a crashing fall at the last which necessitated his being destroyed. Barry Geraghty is the regular rider of both Bust Out and Le Coudray, and he chose the latter when the pair clashed in the Denny Gold Medal Novices' Chase at Leopardstown less than two weeks later. Ridden by Paul Carberry on this occasion, Bust Out went very close to giving Geraghty cause to regret his decision. Again, Bust Out made only one notable error and kept up a strong challenge to the more experienced winner on the run-in, eventually going down by half a length. Geraghty was back on board Bust Out for the Grade 1 Baileys Arkle Perpetual Challenge Cup at Leopardstown the following month and the 11/10 favourite didn't need to match the form he'd shown behind Le Coudray. Travelling strongly as usual under a patient ride, Bust Out tended to fiddle and jump left but looked poised to win in good style when stretching clear after the last. In the end, he needed firm handling as he drifted right and idled, before holding the staying-on Native Scout by a length, with Rathgar Beau two lengths back in third.

The only season in which Bust Out has appeared on the racecourse beyond January was his first, in 1999/00 when, having finished runner-up in a maiden hurdle on his debut in February, he landed a couple of bumpers. With his novice status still intact, Bust Out reverted to hurdling the following season, winning two of his four starts between November and January, though injury ended any hopes of running him in the Supreme Novices' Hurdle before foot and mouth put paid to the meeting. Bust Out was restricted to just a couple of outings in his next season as a hurdler, but on the second of those he very nearly became one of those rare horses to inflict defeat on Istabraq, going down by a head in the December Festival Hurdle at Leopardstown.

	Bustino (b 1971)	Busted (b 1963)	Crepello
			Sans Le Sou
		Ship Yard (ch 1963)	Doutelle
Bust Out (ch.g. 1996)			Paving Stone
	Nordic Beauty (USA) (ch 1987)	Northjet (ch 1977)	Northfields
			Jellatina
		Comely (ch 1966)	Boran
			Comnene

The strong, workmanlike Bust Out has reportedly been fired and hobdayed. His dam Nordic Beauty has also produced a winner on the Flat in Hungary by Most Welcome. The unraced Nordic Beauty is a half-sister to Pharly and Melyno, both top-class performers on the Flat at around a mile to a mile and a quarter, as well as the high-class French two-year-old Comeram, later second in the Irish Two Thousand Guineas. Bust Out has done all of his racing at around two miles and his sire, the now-deceased Bustino, has been responsible for high-class winners over the minimum trip over jumps, including the Tote Gold Trophy winners Decoupage and Mysilv. His trainer has regularly expressed the opinion that Bust Out, who has been raced only on going softer than good to date, will be suited by less testing conditions, though given his history of leg trouble, there would have to be some doubt on that score, not to mention how he would handle the undulations of Cheltenham should he finally get the chance to race there. *Mrs J. Harrington, Ireland*

BUTTERWICK CHIEF 6 b.g. Be My Chief (USA) – Swift Return (Double Form) **h–**
[2002/3 h–: 18v^{pu} 17s^3 Dec 26] good-topped gelding: temperamental maiden on Flat: signs of only a little ability over hurdles. *R. A. Fahey*

BUZ KIRI (USA) 5 b.g. Gulch (USA) – White Corners (USA) (Caro) [2002/3 16g **h71**
Feb 27] poor maiden stayer on Flat: tongue tied, never-dangerous ninth of 15 finishers in novice at Ludlow on hurdling debut. *A. W. Carroll*

BUZYBAKSON (IRE) 6 b. or br.g. Bob Back (USA) – Middle Verde (USA) (Sham **h101**
(USA)) [2002/3 F16g F16m^6 20s^F 19s* 22v^3 Jan 6] 1,400 3-y-o: brother to bumper **F83**
winner Back To Hong Kong and half-brother to several winners, including modest hurdler Teejay'n'aitch (by Maelstrom Lake), stays 2½m: dam Irish maiden: mid-division in 2 bumpers: won maiden hurdle at Market Rasen in December: better form when third to Cowboyboots in novice at Fontwell: will stay 3m: acts on heavy going: sold 10,500 gns Doncaster May Sales. *A. M. Hales*

BY DEFINITION (IRE) 5 gr. or b.m. Definite Article – Miss Goodbody (Castle **h–**
Keep) [2002/3 16d^pu 16g 17s^pu Dec 26] poor maiden on Flat (stays 1m): doubtful stayer
and no form over hurdles: wore cheekpieces second start. *J. M. Bradley*

BY DEGREE (IRE) 7 gr.g. Roselier (FR) – Decent Enough (Decent Fellow) [2002/3 **h114**
F16g^5 22d^F 22d^2 24v^2 24v* Mar 4] IR 30,000 3-y-o, IR 45,000 4-y-o: sturdy gelding: fifth **F86**
foal: half-brother to 2½m hurdle winner Mallardstown (by Buckskin): dam dual bumper
winner: won maiden Irish point in 2002: third outing in bumpers (first since leaving
P. Cashman) when fifth at Wincanton in November: fair form when runner-up in novice
hurdles, beaten 3½ lengths by Murphy's Cardinal at Ascot on second occasion: simple
task at Exeter following month: will probably prove best at 3m+: acts on heavy going:
takes good hold. *R. J. Hodges*

BYGONE 5 b.g. Past Glories – Meltonby (Sayf El Arab (USA)) [2002/3 F17m^2 Jul 25] **F84**
second foal: dam fair 6f to 1m winner: beaten 3½ lengths by eased Sahem in bumper at
Sedgefield on debut. *J. Hetherton*

BY N BY (IRE) 7 b.g. Un Desperado (FR) – Andonova (Prince Tenderfoot (USA)) **F–**
[2002/3 F84: F18g Apr 29] good-topped gelding: mid-division on first of 2 starts in
bumpers. *Miss Venetia Williams*

BYRON LAMB 6 b.g. Rambo Dancer (CAN) – Caroline Lamb (Hotfoot) [2002/3 **c126 p**
h115p, F100: c16d* c21s^2 c16v* c17d^2 c16g* Mar 29] leggy, unfurnished gelding: fairly **h–**
useful form over hurdles: took well to chasing, landed odds in novices at Ayr in December
and January and Hexham in March: better form when runner-up to Vol Solitaire at Kelso
penultimate start, though not always fluent: raced mainly around 2m, should prove as
effective around 2½m: raced on good going or softer (acts on heavy): reliable, and
probably hasn't finished improving. *N. G. Richards*

C

CABALLE (USA) 6 ch.m. Opening Verse (USA) – Attirance (FR) (Crowned Prince **h99 d**
(USA)) [2002/3 h104d: 16d* 16s^4 16d 21d^5 17d 19g 17g 17g^5 Apr 19] workmanlike
mare: fair hurdler: won handicap at Huntingdon in November: well held last 3 starts, sold
out of N. Henderson's stable 5,600 gns Doncaster March Sales after first one: should stay
2½m: acts on heavy going: tried blinkered. *Dr P. Pritchard*

CABARET QUEST 7 ch.g. Pursuit of Love – Cabaret Artiste (Shareef Dancer (USA)) **c–**
[2002/3 h61: 16g c16g^F c16m^pu Jun 29] good-topped gelding: poor on Flat (barely stays **h–**
1¼m): little form over hurdles: failed to complete in 2 starts over fences: tried tongue
tied: joined R. C. Guest. *J. M. Bradley*

CABILLE (FR) 11 ch.g. Lesotho (USA) – Ironique (FR) (Riverman (USA)) [2002/3 **c–**
c20s^pu c23g^ur Feb 25] workmanlike gelding: winning pointer: no form in steeplechases **h–**
for long time, off 3 years before reappearance: tried blinkered/visored. *H. H. G. Owen*

CADES BAY 12 b.g. Unfuwain (USA) – Antilla (Averof) [2002/3 c–, h–: c21g May 1] **c–**
poor pointer/maiden steeplechaser: stays 2½m: acts on good to firm and good to soft **h–**
going: tried blinkered. *Miss L. Gardner*

CADOUGOLD (FR) 12 b.g. Cadoudal (FR) – Fontaine Aux Faons (FR) (Nadjar **c–**
(FR)) [2002/3 c129, h–: c23g^4 c22f^5 18m^5 c21g^F Sep 12] leggy gelding: one-time smart **h–**
hurdler/useful chaser: claimed from M. Pipe £6,000 after dismal effort third outing:
won point in March: stays 3m: acts on any going: visored second start: jumps none too
fluently. *Miss K. Marks*

CADOU ROYAL (FR) 7 b.g. Cadoudal (FR) – Leonie Des Champs (FR) (Crystal **c118**
Palace) [2002/3 h116: c17s^3 c16s^3 c20s^2 c19s c16v* c17d Mar 22] good-topped gelding: **h–**
fairly useful hurdler: similar form over fences, won handicap at Naas in March: stays
2½m: raced on going softer than good (acts on heavy): has found little and may prove
best in truly-run races. *A. L. T. Moore, Ireland*

CADRILLON (FR) 13 br.g. Le Pontet (FR) – Jenvraie (FR) (Night And Day) [2002/3 **c86**
c–, h–: c25m^5 c26d^2 c27d^pu Mar 18] smallish, sparely-made gelding: fair pointer/hunter **h–**
chaser: stays 3¾m: acts on soft going: sometimes blinkered. *Miss J. E. Foster*

CADW (IRE) 8 b.g. Cadeaux Genereux – Night Jar (Night Shift (USA)) [2002/3 h–: **c–**
16s^6 16d c16g^6 Mar 17] angular gelding: no form. *R. Dickin* **h–**

CAERNOMORE 5 b.g. Caerleon (USA) – Nuryana (Nureyev (USA)) [2002/3 17m^{pu} **h–**
Apr 21] half-brother to winning 2¾m hurdler Mystic Hill (by Shirley Heights): poor
maiden on Flat (probably stays 1¼m) for P. Haslam: showed nothing in seller on hurdling
debut. *W. G. M. Turner*

CAESAR'S PALACE (GER) 6 ch.g. Lomitas – Caraveine (FR) (Nikos) [2002/3 **h118 d**
h120: 24g* 24d² 24d³ 22d* 24g⁶ 24s² 22v⁶ 23v 22d² 20m⁴ Apr 19] workmanlike gelding:
fairly useful hurdler: won amateur handicap at Chepstow in May and claimer at Stratford
(unimpressive in face of easy task, claimed from M. Pipe £8,000) in August: below best
subsequently: stays 3m: acts on soft and good to firm going: tried blinkered/in cheekpieces, best form when visored: races prominently: hard ride (usually soon off bridle).
Miss Lucinda V. Russell

CAGE AUX FOLLES (IRE) 8 b.g. Kenmare (FR) – Ivory Thread (USA) (Sir Ivor) **h72**
[2002/3 h–: 17v 19d 16d 16m⁵ Mar 19] lengthy gelding: handicap hurdler, little form
since 2000/1: probably best short of 2¾m: acts on any going: tried blinkered/visored:
usually tongue tied. *R. Lee*

CAHER SOCIETY (IRE) 11 ch.g. Moscow Society (USA) – Dame's Delight **c94 x**
(Ballymoss) [2002/3 c107x, h–: c16d⁴ c28g May 31] lengthy gelding: fairly useful hunter **h–**
chaser: best efforts at 2½m to 3m: acts on heavy going: sketchy jumper. *Paul Morris*

CAHORS (IRE) 10 b.g. Mandalus – Croom River (IRE) (Over The River (FR)) **c–**
[2002/3 c22m⁶ Mar 21] lengthy gelding: fairly useful hunter chaser at best: lacklustre
effort at Newbury in March: stays 3¼m: acts on heavy going: blinkered. *J. J. Boulter*

CAILIN'S PERK (IRE) 9 ch.m. Executive Perk – Cailin Run (Deep Run) [2002/3 **h127 §**
h109, F94: 16s* 17d² 16s⁵ 16s⁶ 16d⁵ 16d² Feb 23] lengthy, angular mare: fairly useful
hurdler: won handicap at Tipperary in May: ran well most starts after, though became
temperamental (virtually refused to race in Grade 1 at Punchestown in early-May): best
around 2m: raced on good going or softer (acts on heavy): has had tongue tied: best
treated with caution. *James Morrissey, Ireland*

CAISHILL (IRE) 4 b. or br.g. Dolphin Street (FR) – Pretonic (Precocious) [2002/3 **h119**
16g 16v 16s² 16v⁴ 16v* 16s⁴ 16d⁵ 16g² 16g³ Apr 21] useful-looking gelding: fair on Flat
(stays 11f): fairly useful juvenile hurdler: won maiden at Clonmel in December: consistent after until poor effort in well-contested minor event at Punchestown in late-April:
raced at 2m: acts on heavy going. *Miss F. M. Crowley, Ireland*

CAITRIONA'S CHOICE (IRE) 12 b.g. Carmelite House (USA) – Muligatawny **c109**
(Malacate (USA)) [2002/3 c17s* c16v⁶ c17v c20s⁶ c16v² c16v^{pu} c16g Apr 24] tall **h–**
ex-Irish gelding: fair handicap chaser: won at Navan in June: creditable effort after only
on fifth start (final one for M. Cunningham): raced mainly around 2m: acts on any going:
tongue held up: inconsistent. *P. Monteith*

CALAMINT 4 gr.g. Kaldoun (FR) – Coigach (Niniski (USA)) [2002/3 16d 17s 16s^{pu} **h–**
Feb 12] half-brother to winning 2½m hurdler Aston Mara (by Bering): fair maiden on
Flat (bred to be suited by 1½m+), sold out of J. Fanshawe's stable 8,000 gns Newmarket
Autumn Sales: no form over hurdles. *K. C. Bailey*

CALATAGAN (IRE) 4 ch.g. Danzig Connection (USA) – Calachuchi (Martinmas) **h109**
[2002/3 16d* 16g^F Dec 28] fair maiden on Flat (stays 1½m) for Miss J. Camacho:
favourite, won juvenile at Catterick on hurdling debut in December, soon clear and
unchallenged: disputing lead (though not travelling so well as winner Far Pavilions) when
fell 3 out at Musselburgh later in month. *J. M. Jefferson*

CALCOT FLYER 5 br.g. Anshan – Lady Catcher (Free Boy) [2002/3 F16s F16d Mar **F80**
10] fifth foal: half-brother to 2 poor performers: dam, poor novice hurdler/chaser,
daughter of dual Grand National third Eyecatcher: better effort in bumpers when eighth
of 20 at Haydock on debut. *A. King*

CALDAMUS 11 gr.g. Scallywag – Portodamus (Porto Bello) [2002/3 c96, h–: c25d* **c98**
Mar 6] workmanlike gelding: fair hunter chaser: won at Wincanton in March: stays 25f: **h–**
acts on good to soft going: front runner. *Miss S. Waugh*

CALFSTOWN LORD 11 b.g. Arctic Lord – Calfstown Maid (Master Buck) [2002/3 **c– x**
c73x, h–: c22d^{ur} c23f May 15] lengthy gelding: winning pointer: poor maiden chaser: **h–**
stays 25f: acts on any going: tried visored/blinkered: has had tongue tied: sketchy jumper.
C. J. Gray

CALIBAN (IRE) 5 ch.g. Rainbows For Life (CAN) – Amour Toujours (IRE) (Law **h103**
Society (USA)) [2002/3 h90: 20d⁶ 16d* 16m² Apr 21] neat gelding: modest on Flat (stays

2m), successful in March: fair hurdler: won 6-runner handicap at Haydock in November: stays 2½m: acts on soft and good to firm going: visored once: carries head high. *Ian Williams*

CALINASH (IRE) 9 b.g. Insan (USA) – Hi Cal (Callernish) [2002/3 20d^{pu} c16m^5 c17s^4 c21v^{pu} c17v^3 c20s Jan 3] IR 6,000 4-y-o: workmanlike gelding: fourth foal: half-brother to 2 winning pointers: dam unraced: little sign of ability. *Mrs L. Williamson* c–
h–

CALITAS (FR) 4 b.g. Solido (FR) – Callistine (FR) (Arctic Tern (USA)) [2002/3 15m^3 16g* c17v^4 16g^{pu} Feb 12] seventh foal: dam French 11f to 1¾m winner: won juvenile hurdle at Fontainebleau in October: fourth of 7 finishers in 3-y-o chase at Enghien following month (final outing for G. Macaire): fatally injured on British debut. *G. A. Harker* c104
h?

CALIWAG (IRE) 7 b.g. Lahib (USA) – Mitsubishi Style (Try My Best (USA)) [2002/3 h66: c16v^3 Mar 8] lengthy gelding: modest maiden on Flat (stays easy 1½m): only poor form over hurdles, looking a non-stayer: out of depth in 3-runner novice at Sandown on chasing debut. *Jamie Poulton* c–
h–

CALKO 6 ch.g. Timeless Times (USA) – Jeethgaya (USA) (Critique (USA)) [2002/3 16s^6 17m^5 Aug 26] poor on Flat (stays 11f) nowadays: well held in 2 selling hurdles. *R. Wilman* h–

CALLADINE (IRE) 7 b.g. Erins Isle – Motus (Anfield) [2002/3 h135+: 24s^4 16g^{ur} 16d^3 Feb 15] close-coupled gelding: useful hurdler: 14½ lengths third of 6 to Sacundai in Grade 2 at Gowran: ideally suited by 2½m+: acts on soft going (pulled too hard on good to firm). *C. Roche, Ireland* h135

CALLED TO THE BAR 10 b.g. Legal Bwana – Miss Gaylord (Cavo Doro) [2002/3 24d^{pu} 22d^2 Mar 6] workmanlike gelding: poor hurdler, off over 2½ years before reappearance: stays 3½m: acts on good to firm and good to soft going. *P. M. Rich* c–
h82

CALLEVA STAR (IRE) 12 b.g. Over The River (FR) – Ask The Madam (Strong Gale) [2002/3 c90, h–: c25d^6 c30m^{pu} May 11] good-topped gelding: fair hunter chaser on his day: won 2-runner point in March: should stay beyond 27f: acts on good to firm and heavy going: inconsistent: often let down by jumping. *Mrs F. E. Needham* c– x
h–

CALLFOURSEASONS (IRE) 11 b.g. Euphemism – Home And Dry (Crash Course) [2002/3 c–§, h–: c20d^{pu} c24s^{ur} c20d^{pu} 22m^{pu} Jul 14] workmanlike gelding: one-time fairly useful handicap chaser, no form for long time, including over hurdles: stays 25f: acts on good to firm and heavy going: has found little. *M. Mullineaux* c– §
h–

CALLING BRAVE (IRE) 7 ch.g. Bob Back (USA) – Queenie Kelly (The Parson) [2002/3 F109: 16g^8 20s^{ur} 19g* 21s^2 21m^2 21g 24g Apr 3] well-made gelding: will make a chaser: bumper winner: fairly useful novice hurdler: successful at Kempton in November and Newbury in December: further improvement when second, beaten 6 lengths by Foreman at Kempton on second occasion: well held in Grade 1 at Cheltenham and valuable handicap at Aintree last 2 starts: likely to prove best at 2½m+: acts on soft and good to firm going. *N. J. Henderson* h125

CALL ME JACK (IRE) 7 b.g. Lord Americo – Tawney Rose (Tarqogan) [2002/3 c88p, h93: 16g^{pu} 17v^3 20d^F c16d^2 Mar 18] rangy gelding: modest handicap hurdler: similar form when second in novice at Sedgefield on completed start over fences: raced mainly around 2m on going softer than good (acts on heavy): usually tongue tied: front runner. *J. Hetherton* c91
h89

CALL ME SONIC 7 b.g. Henbit (USA) – Call-Me-Dinky (Mart Lane) [2002/3 h93?, F71: 22f^3 c20d^{pu} c16g^5 Apr 21] poor novice hurdler/chaser on balance of form, trained second start only by C. Fuller: probably stays 2¾m. *R. H. Alner* c–
h82

CALL MY GUEST (IRE) 13 b.g. Be My Guest (USA) – Overcall (Bustino) [2002/3 h102: 21d^{pu} Oct 26] smallish, leggy gelding: fair handicap hurdler, well held only start in 2002/3: stays 21f: acts on good to firm and heavy going. *R. E. Peacock* h–

CALL THE SHOTS (IRE) 14 br.g. Callernish – Golden Strings (Perspex) [2002/3 c85, h–: c22m^{pu} Jul 7] workmanlike gelding: modest handicap chaser, lightly raced nowadays: stays 3½m: acts on firm and soft ground. *J. Wade* c–
h–

CALON LAN (IRE) 12 b.g. Bustineto – Cherish (Bargello) [2002/3 c–§, h–: 17g^{pu} c20m^{pu} c21m^2 c21f^4 Aug 13] winning hurdler/chaser: form for long time only when second of 5 from 19 lb out of handicap at Newton Abbot: stays 21f: acts on any going: tried blinkered: has bled from nose: temperamental. *R. Williams* c88 §
h–

CAMADERRY (IRE)   5 ch.g. Dr Devious (IRE) – Rathvindon (Realm) [2002/3 **h83** 18m⁶ 16g³ May 30] ex-Irish gelding: fair maiden on Flat (stays 1¼m), sold out of D. Weld's stable IR £17,000 Goffs October (2001) Sale: poor form in 2 early-season events over hurdles: likely to prove best over sharp 2m. *Noel T. Chance*

CAMAIR COMMANDER (IRE)   5 b.g. Beau Sher – Miss Josephine (IRE)   **h–** (Kemal (FR)) [2002/3 F–: 16d 20v 24s 20sᵖᵘ 17s⁶ 17d Mar 18] little sign of ability: tried   **F–** blinkered. *W. McKeown*

CAMAIR CRUSADER (IRE)   9 br.g. Jolly Jake (NZ) – Sigrid's Dream (USA)   **c– §** (Triple Bend (USA)) [2002/3 c–§, h75§: 16d* 16d 19g 21g 21g³ 16s Feb 24] leggy   **h78 §** gelding: no form over fences: poor hurdler: won selling handicap at Newcastle in April: stays 21f: acts on soft and good to firm going: usually held up: has been reluctant to race/ found little: not to be trusted. *F. P. Murtagh*

CAMARADERIE   7 b.g. Most Welcome – Secret Valentine (Wollow) [2002/3 h74:   **h83 §** 16g² 16m² 16d* 16m⁴ Apr 2] poor hurdler: left Mrs M. Reveley, jumped better than usual when winning seller at Chepstow in March: raced around 2m: acts on good to firm and good to soft going: effective blinkered or not: held up: unreliable. *A. G. Juckes*

CAMBIO (IRE)   5 b.g. Turtle Island (IRE) – Motley (Rainbow Quest (USA)) [2002/3   **h89** h81: 17m⁶ 20s* 16d Nov 16] angular gelding: modest maiden on Flat (stays easy 19f): similar level over hurdles, won handicap at Worcester in June: likely to prove better at 2½m than shorter: acts on soft and good to firm going. *B. R. Johnson*

CAMBRIAN DAWN   9 b.g. Danehill (USA) – Welsh Daylight (Welsh Pageant)   **c115 p** [2002/3 h114: 20d c25dᶠ c24sᵘʳ Jan 27] sturdy gelding: fair hurdler, ran as if in need of   **h–** race on reappearance: would almost certainly have made successful chasing debut but for falling 2 out in novice at Hereford, around 3 lengths up at time: blundered and unseated second in novice at Kempton: stays 25f: raced on good going or softer (acts on heavy): tongue tied once in bumpers: will win races over fences if brushing up his jumping. *Jonjo O'Neill*

CAMDENATION (IRE)   7 b.g. Camden Town – Out The Nav (IRE) (Over The   **h93** River (FR)) [2002/3 F90: 16m 22d* 22s² 20s³ 22d Feb 17] modest novice hurdler: won at Folkestone in November: likely to stay 3m: acts on soft going. *J. T. Gifford*

CAMDEN DOLPHIN (IRE)   6 gr.m. Camden Town – Ackle Backle (Furry Glen)   **h–** [2002/3 F–: F16g 18gᵖᵘ Mar 17] well beaten in 2 bumpers 11 months apart: reportedly   **F–** lame on hurdling debut. *B. A. Pearce*

CAMDEN KING (IRE)   8 br. or b.g. Camden Town – Valerie Owens (IRE) (Lancas-   **c–** trian) [2002/3 h–: 16d⁴ c21fᵖᵘ May 10] sparely-made gelding: poor novice hurdler: no   **h57** show on chasing debut. *T. P. McGovern*

CAMDEN TANNER (IRE)   7 b.g. Camden Town – Poor Elsie (Crash Course)   **h128 +** [2002/3 h120: 24v² 16s³ 22v² 21g Mar 12] good-topped gelding: fairly useful handicap hurdler: good efforts when placed in valuable events won by Xenophon at Leopardstown and Chopneyev at Sandown on second and third starts: far from discredited when twelfth of 27 to Xenophon in Coral Cup at Cheltenham: effective at 2m to 3m: acts on heavy ground: patiently ridden: consistent. *Robert Tyner, Ireland*

CAMDEN WEST (IRE)   9 b.g. Camden Town – Wedding Gift (Glen Quaich) [2002/3   **c110** c24sˢᵘ c24sᵘʳ c24d c24v² c28sᵖᵘ 24d³ c24d³ Mar 17] medium-sized gelding: second foal: **h101** brother to winning pointer Baile An Daingin: dam unraced: winning hurdler: fair handicap chaser: should stay beyond 3m: acts on heavy ground: tongue tied. *E. Sheehy, Ireland*

CAMERON BRIDGE (IRE)   7 b.g. Camden Town – Arctic Raheen (Over The   **c114 x** River (FR)) [2002/3 h102: 17gᶠ 16m³ c20d⁶ c19s³ c16g⁵ c16d⁴ c19s* c16g⁴ c19m* c20fᶠ⁴   **h102** Apr 25] useful-looking gelding: fair hurdler: fairly useful novice chaser: won at Exeter in March and Hereford (didn't need to be anywhere near best) in April: let down by jumping most other starts over fences: stays 19f: acts on soft and good to firm going. *P. J. Hobbs*

CAMERON JACK   8 b.g. Elmaamul (USA) – Ile de Reine (Ile de Bourbon (USA))   **c75 x** [2002/3 17g⁵ 22gᵘʳ c16v³ c24g⁶ c20vᵖᵘ c21g² Mar 25] lengthy, angular gelding: poor   **h–** novice hurdler/chaser, lightly raced: possibly best around 2m: acts on heavy going: makes mistakes over fences. *Miss Kate Milligan*

CAMEROSA   7 b.g. Risk Me (FR) – High Heather (Shirley Heights) [2002/3 16s   **h–** 17vᵖᵘ Dec 28] no show on Flat or in 2 starts over hurdles. *A. D. Smith*

CAMITROV (FR) 13 b.g. Sharken (FR) – Emitrovna (FR) (Buisson d'Or) [2002/3 **c79** c84, h–: c24m⁶ May 11] leggy gelding: one-time smart chaser, but not easy to train and **h–** retains only a little ability: stays 3m: acts on any going. *G. R. Kerr*

CAMPAIGN TRAIL (IRE) 5 b.g. Sadler's Wells (USA) – Campestral (USA) **h127 p** (Alleged (USA)) [2002/3 h103+: 17d* 20s* Jan 30] good-topped gelding: confirmed promise in juvenile hurdles when easily winning handicap at Carlisle (by 5 lengths from Totally Scottish) in October and novice at Southwell in January: will stay 3m: acts on soft going: capable of better still. *Jonjo O'Neill*

CAMP HILL 9 gr.g. Ra Nova – Baytino (Neltino) [2002/3 c76, h80: c25dᵖᵘ 18s⁶ 20d **c93** c21d⁴ c20s* c25v² c24vᵘʳ c20v² c21s³ Feb 23] angular gelding: maiden hurdler: modest **h–** novice chaser: 50/1-winner of weak minor event at Ayr in December: barely stays testing 25f: acts on heavy going. *J. S. Haldane*

CAMP NOU (IRE) 6 b.g. Sadler's Wells (USA) – Campestral (USA) (Alleged (USA)) **h112** [2002/3 h90, F73: 20d⁴ 24d* 22v* 24g 24d³ Mar 2] good-topped gelding: fair handicap hurdler: won at Southwell and Newton Abbot in November: blinkered then tongue tied, laboured efforts last 2 outings: stays 3m well: raced mainly on going softer than good (acts on heavy): temperament under suspicion. *Jonjo O'Neill*

CAMUS DES MOTTES (FR) 7 b.g. Africanus (FR) – Camille Des Mottes (FR) **c–** (Abdonski (FR)) [2002/3 c–, h–: 22dᵖᵘ Jun 1] good-topped gelding: no form **h–** over fences/hurdles in Britain: tried blinkered. *Dr P. Pritchard*

CANADA 5 b.g. Ezzoud (IRE) – Chancel (USA) (Al Nasr (FR)) [2002/3 h97+: 16s² **h124** 16v⁴ 20d³ Apr 4] leggy, useful-looking gelding: fairly useful hurdler: good 6½ lengths third of 16 to Patriot Games in listed handicap at Aintree: stays 2½m: acts on heavy going. *M. C. Pipe*

CANADA ROAD (IRE) 5 b.g. Great Marquess – New Technique (FR) (Formidable **F81** (USA)) [2002/3 F16m⁵ Apr 21] 8,000 4-y-o: first foal: dam no form on Flat: around 14 lengths fifth of 8 in bumper at Huntingdon on debut. *R. J. Smith*

CANADIANE (FR) 8 ch.m. Nikos – Carmonera (FR) (Carmont (FR)) [2002/3 c–, **c117** h112: c17g³ c20m* c20d² c19m* c17m² c17m* c21m³ c16g² c17d³ c20m* c23g³ c19m³ **h116** c21g² c20g⁴ c16d⁴ 17d* c18s² c16f* c21dᵘʳ 19m⁵ Apr 15] sparely-made mare: fairly useful handicap hurdler: won at Taunton in January: similar form over fences: won novices at Ludlow, Hereford, Stratford and Fontwell early in season and handicap at Haydock (beat Chergan 1½ lengths) in March: will prove best up to 21f: acts on firm and soft going: consistent. *M. C. Pipe*

CANAL END (IRE) 6 b.g. Montelimar (USA) – Miss Cripps (IRE) (Lafontaine **h85** (USA)) [2002/3 18s 18s 18s 20s 25g² 20m⁶ Apr 12] IR 19,000 3-y-o, 20,000 4-y-o: ex-Irish gelding: first foal: dam won bumper: best efforts over hurdles (trained by C. Roche first 2 starts) last 2 outings: stays 25f. *Jonjo O'Neill*

CANARY WHARF (IRE) 7 ch.g. Accordion – Avida Dancer (Ballymore) [2002/3 **c126** h129: c18sᶠ c18sᶠ Dec 14] lengthy gelding: fairly useful hurdler: fell both starts in **h–** maiden chases, fatally injured when holding every chance at last in well-contested event won by Bust Out at Fairyhouse: would have stayed beyond 2½m: raced on good going or softer (acted on heavy): raced prominently. *J. Bleahen, Ireland*

CAN CORTANA (IRE) 7 b.g. Supreme Leader – Glen Boosh (Furry Glen) [2002/3 **h–** h76, F67: 20mᵖᵘ 25m⁵ Oct 16] angular gelding: poor novice hurdler: should stay at least 2½m: sold 3,400 gns Doncaster November Sales: third in point in April. *T. D. Easterby*

CANCUN CARIBE (IRE) 6 ch.g. Port Lucaya – Miss Tuko (Good Times (ITY)) **h90** [2002/3 17s 19d 19g* Mar 17] fair on Flat (stays 1¼m) for K. McAuliffe: dropped in class and well-backed favourite, easily won novice selling hurdle at Hereford: stays 19f, should prove as effective at 2m. *J. D. Frost*

CANDARLI (IRE) 7 ch.g. Polish Precedent (USA) – Calounia (IRE) (Pharly (FR)) **h114** [2002/3 h97: 16d³ 16s 17g² 16mᵖᵘ Apr 2] rather sparely-made gelding: fair handicap hurdler: best effort when ¾-length second to Quabmatic (pair clear) at Exeter in March: reportedly bled from nose final start: likely to prove best given test of speed around 2m. *D. R. Gandolfo*

CANDOUR 4 b.f. So Factual (USA) – Outward's Gal (Ashmore (FR)) [2002/3 16d **h–** 16d Dec 14] half-sister to fair hurdler The Robe (by Robellino), stays 2½m, and bumper winner Hell of A Guy (by Absalom): well held in maidens on Flat and 2 juvenile hurdles: joined M. Wallace. *Mrs D. Haine*

CANDY ANCHOR (FR) 4 b.f. Slip Anchor – Kandavu (Safawan) [2002/3 17s⁵ **h–**
18dᵖᵘ 16vᵖᵘ Dec 20] modest maiden on Flat (stays 1½m): signs of ability over hurdles
only on debut. *Andrew Reid*

CA NE FAIT RIEN (IRE) 7 ch.g. Denel (FR) – Fairytale-Ending (Sweet Story) **F82**
[2002/3 F74: F16m⁴ May 11] best effort in bumpers when fourth at Worcester in May:
will be suited by much further than 2m. *M. N. Babbage*

CANNON BRIDGE (IRE) 5 ch.g. Definite Article – Hit For Six (Tap On Wood) **h81**
[2002/3 F70: 16s² Jun 13] poor form in bumper and maiden hurdle (made several errors):
well held in maidens on Flat in between: likely to prove best around 2m: sold 4,500 gns
Doncaster August Sales, resold £3,400 Ascot October Sales. *D. Shaw*

CANNY CHIFTANE 7 b.g. Be My Chief (USA) – Prudence (Grundy) [2002/3 h69§: **h– §**
20dᵖᵘ May 4] stocky gelding: poor hurdler: stays 2½m: acts on heavy and good to firm
going: usually blinkered/visored: not one to trust. *Miss C. J. E. Caroe*

CANON BARNEY (IRE) 8 b. or br.g. Salluceva – Debbies Candy (Candy Cane) **c111 x**
[2002/3 c99, h107, F107: c17s³ c20sᵘʳ c17s⁴ c26s* Mar 15] sturdy gelding: winning **h–**
hurdler for T. Hogan in 2001/2: fair novice chaser: upped in trip, good effort when winning
handicap at Uttoxeter (jumped right throughout) in March: stays 3¼m: raced on going
softer than good: reportedly distressed third start: poor jumper of fences. *Jonjo O'Neill*

CANON MCCARTHY (IRE) 7 ch.g. Be My Native (USA) – Archetype (Over The **c81**
River (FR)) [2002/3 c82, h–: c25g² c20s⁴ c24d⁶ Jan 24] tall gelding: has run tubed: poor **h–**
maiden hurdler/chaser: likely to prove suited by 3m+: acts on soft ground (bumper form
on firm): has had tongue tied: sold £3,000 Ascot April Sales. *A. W. Carroll*

CANOVAS KINGDOM 5 ch.g. Aragon – Joan's Venture (Beldale Flutter (USA)) **h–**
[2002/3 16dᵖᵘ Nov 12] rather sparely-made gelding: modest maiden on Flat (stays 1m):
doubtful stayer over hurdles, pulled up in novice on debut: sold 1,600 gns Doncaster
November Sales. *Bob Jones*

CANTARINHO 5 b.g. Alderbrook – Hot Hostess (Silly Season) [2002/3 c21m² Apr **c72**
21] 8,400 4-y-o: fifth foal: half-brother to winning pointer by Broadsword: dam, placed
in 2 points, from good jumping family: won point on debut: short-head second to Grand
Ambition in novice hunter chase at Fakenham. *M. A. Kemp*

CAN'T BE SCRABBLE 10 b.g. Gargoor – Scribble Along (Supergrey) [2002/3 **c–**
c16mᶠ Apr 5] fair pointer: fell second on hunter chase debut. *R. J. Down*

CANTENAC BROWN (IRE) 8 ch.g. Ikdam – Mossbrook (Le Moss) [2002/3 c27m⁶ **c–**
Apr 11] 6,000 4-y-o: half-brother to winning chaser Fern Leader (by Supreme Leader),
stays 25f: dam unraced: winning pointer: well beaten on hunter chase debut. *J. J. Boulter*

CANTERBURY (IRE) 10 b.g. King's Ride – Private Dancer (Deep Run) [2002/3 **h–**
h–: 20m⁴ 22mᵖᵘ Aug 5] strong gelding: poor maiden hurdler, lightly raced: lame final
start. *R. J. Baker*

CANTERBURY JACK (IRE) 6 b.g. Supreme Leader – Crest of The Hill (Prince **h101**
Regent (FR)) [2002/3 24g² 22f² 22f³ Oct 10] IR 15,000 3-y-o: seventh foal: half-brother
to winning pointer by Husyan: dam unraced, from family of very smart hurdler/useful
staying chaser Henry Mann: well held in bumper: won last of 4 starts in maiden Irish
points in 2002, sold 15,000 gns Doncaster May Sales: fair form when second in maiden
at Worcester on hurdling debut: disappointing both subsequent starts, looked less than
keen in visor second time: will stay beyond 3m. *M. C. Pipe*

CANTYS BRIG (IRE) 6 gr.g. Roselier (FR) – Call Catherine (IRE) (Strong Gale) **h–**
[2002/3 F16g F16s⁶ F16s F16v 25d³ 20g Apr 1] IR £16,000 4-y-o: first foal: dam placed **F–**
in points: well held in bumpers (reluctant to set off on debut) and 2 novice hurdles.
Miss L. C. Siddall

CANYOUBATIM (IRE) 9 b.g. Alphabatim (USA) – Boat Whistle (Amoristic **c67**
(USA)) [2002/3 c–, h–: c21m⁵ c24mᵖᵘ c26m² c26m³ c24m⁴ c24m⁴ c20d⁶ c16v⁶ c21d⁵ **h–**
c19v⁴ 22sᵖᵘ Mar 2] workmanlike gelding: little worthwhile form: tried in blinkers/cheek-
pieces. *Dr P. Pritchard*

CAPACOOSTIC 6 ch.m. Savahra Sound – Cocked Hat Girl (Ballacashtal (CAN)) **h–**
[2002/3 16g 17g Mar 22] poor maiden on Flat (probably best up to 7f), sold out of
S. R. Bowring's stable 1,300 gns Doncaster August Sales: well held in 2 claiming hurdles.
A. G. Juckes

CAPE CANAVERAL (IRE) 4 b.g. Sadler's Wells (USA) – Emmaline (USA) **h114 d**
(Affirmed (USA)) [2002/3 18d² 16d 16v⁵ 16d⁵ 19m⁵ Mar 22] rangy, good sort: fairly

useful form when runner-up over 1½m only outing on Flat (for A. O'Brien): second to Old California in juvenile at Fontwell on hurdling debut but regressed, never travelling or jumping with any fluency final outing: will stay 2½m: may benefit from headgear. *G. L. Moore*

CAPE CORAL   6 ch.m. Henbit (USA) – Celtic Deep (Celtic Cone) [2002/3 F17g Oct 11] first foal: dam unraced: well held in bumper on debut. *A. Parker*   **F–**

CAPE STORMER (IRE)   8 b.g. Be My Native (USA) – My Sunny South (Strong Gale) [2002/3 h90, F76: 20m* c19m² c20m* c25g³ c20g* c24g⁶ c22m* c20g 22f² Apr 21] workmanlike gelding: fair novice hurdler: won at Fontwell in May: sold out of Miss H. Knight's stable 27,000 gns Doncaster Sales later in month: better over fences, won handicaps at Cheltenham (novice) in October, Ludlow (amateurs) in December and Newbury (improved effort, beat Elenas River 3½ lengths in 4-finisher novice) in March: best short of 3m: raced mainly on good going or firmer (acts on firm): reliable. *P. F. Nicholls*   **c119 h110**

CAP IN HAND   11 ch.g. Nearly A Hand – Beringa Bee (Sunley Builds) [2002/3 20m⁴ 20g 20g 20g Apr 21] leggy, lengthy gelding: poor handicap hurdler, lightly raced: stays easy 21f: acts on good to firm and good to soft going: races freely. *Mrs S. J. Smith*   **h–**

CAPITAL LAD (IRE)   5 b.g. Charnwood Forest (IRE) – Casla (Lomond (USA)) [2002/3 16mᶠ 16m Jun 28] maiden on Flat, little form at 3 yrs: no encouragement either outing over hurdles. *G. Brown*   **h–**

CAP IT IF YOU CAN (IRE)   10 b.m. Capitano – Lady of Tara (Deep Run) [2002/3 c–, h87d: 21m² 24s² 22mᵖᵘ 19d 20gᵖᵘ 20mᵖᵘ Apr 12] sturdy mare: twice-raced over fences: poor handicap hurdler, lost form after second start: stays 3m: acts on good to firm and heavy going: often amateur ridden. *T. H. Caldwell*   **c– h76 d**

CAPPADRUMMIN (IRE)   6 ch.g. Bob Back (USA) – Out And About (Orchestra) [2002/3 F104p: 16g⁵ 19dᶠ Feb 28] rather leggy, useful-looking gelding: won bumper on debut: fair form when fifth of 18 to Keltic Bard in novice at Newbury on hurdling bow: evens, no impression in fourth when falling 2 out in similar event won by Backbeat there 3 months later: should be suited by further than 2m. *N. J. Henderson*   **h100**

CAPPA HILL (IRE)   7 ch.g. Dromod Hill – Swatter (IRE) (Over The River (FR)) [2002/3 24sᵖᵘ 24gᵖᵘ 25gᵖᵘ Mar 23] 4,400 3-y-o: first foal: dam unraced half-sister to fair but inconsistent chaser Zambezi Spirit, stayed 25f: in frame in maiden Irish points in 2002: sold 2,500 gns Doncaster May Sales, resold 3,600 gns Doncaster November Sales: pulled up in 3 novice hurdles. *Mrs A. M. Thorpe*   **h–**

CAPRICORN   5 b.g. Minster Son – Loch Scavaig (IRE) (The Parson) [2002/3 F83: 20v⁵ 24s² 24s³ 25g² Mar 17] leggy gelding: modest form over hurdles, second to easy winner Florries Son in novice at Wetherby final start: stays 25f: acts on heavy going: wears cheekpieces/blinkers. *W. McKeown*   **h98**

CAPRICORN PRINCESS   9 b.m. Nicholas Bill – Yamrah (Milford) [2002/3 h97: 16d* Apr 9] angular mare: handicap hurdler, formerly with A. Streeter: off 19 months, much improved when winning at Uttoxeter on return, leading going well before 3 out and beating Ben Ewar 18 lengths: best form around 2m: acts on good to firm and good to soft going. *B. D. Leavy*   **h114**

CAPRIOLO (IRE)   7 ch.g. Priolo (USA) – Carroll's Canyon (IRE) (Hatim (USA)) [2002/3 h81: 17g⁴ 16g² 16d* 18d³ 21v² 20v³ 18s⁵ 21v 21d⁵ 21m Mar 31] sturdy gelding: modest hurdler, left J. Fox after reappearance: won novice claimer at Plumpton in November: stays 21f: raced mainly on good going or softer: tried blinkered, wears cheekpieces nowadays: irresolute. *P. G. Murphy*   **h97 §**

CAPTAIN BRAVADO (IRE)   9 b.g. Torus – Miss Bavard (Le Bavard (FR)) [2002/3 h–: 22d May 4] slipped up only start in points: no show in 2 novice hurdles. *D. J. Caro*   **h–**

CAPTAIN CLOONEY (IRE)   10 b.g. Supreme Leader – Capincur Lady (Over The River (FR)) [2002/3 c?, h–: c26v* c25sᶠ c26vᵖᵘ Feb 10] winning hurdler: poor chaser: won amateur handicap at Plumpton in December, only completion in Britain: stays 3¼m: raced on good going or softer (acts on heavy). *N. R. Mitchell*   **c81 h–**

CAPTAIN FLINDERS (IRE)   6 b.g. Satco (FR) – Auburn Queen (Kinglet) [2002/3 F16d F16d² Dec 12] rangy gelding with scope: half-brother to useful staying chasers General Rusty (by General Ironside) and Sheer Ability (by Carlingford Castle): dam never ran: better effort in bumpers when second at Huntingdon: will stay at least 2½m. *C. J. Mann*   **F96**

CAPTAIN JAKE   8 b.g. Phardante (FR) – Cherry Crest (Pollerton) [2002/3 c22dᵖᵘ c24sᵖᵘ Feb 26] big gelding: twice-raced hurdler: pulled up in 2 novice chases. *H. D. Daly*   **c– h–**

CAPTAIN O'NEILL 9 b.g. Welsh Captain – The Last Tune (Gunner B) [2002/3 h85: 17g⁵ 20g* 24g c20d³ c16m⁴ c21m⁴ c23m³ c24s² c20g³ c23gᵖᵘ 24v 17sᶠ 19s 16d 16v² Feb 4] lengthy, angular gelding: modest maiden chaser: poor handicap hurdler: won seller at Chepstow in May: effective at 2m to 3m: acts on any going: visored final start: joined A. Carroll. *J. G. M. O'Shea* **c85 h81**

CAPTAIN ROBIN (IRE) 9 b.g. Supreme Leader – Gentle Madam (Camden Town) [2002/3 20v 24v⁴ 24vᵖᵘ Feb 15] well-made gelding: useful bumper winner in 1999/00: poor form over hurdles on return: likely to prove best at 2½m+. *N. A. Twiston-Davies* **h80**

CAPTAIN RON (IRE) 7 b.g. Marju (IRE) – Callas Star (Chief Singer) [2002/3 h–: c19m Apr 21] once-raced over hurdles: winning pointer, including in March: no show in hunter chase at Hereford. *S. Lloyd* **c– h–**

CAPTAIN SCOTTLAND 4 b.g. Beveled (USA) – Little Egret (Carwhite) [2002/3 16s Nov 9] no form on Flat or on hurdling debut. *D. J. S. ffrench Davis* **h–**

CAPTAIN'S LEAP (IRE) 7 ch.g. Grand Plaisir (IRE) – Ballingowan Star (Le Moss) [2002/3 F94: 16d⁵ Nov 25] well-made gelding: fair bumper winner: fifth of 20 in maiden at Newcastle on hurdling debut, only outing in 2002/3: will be suited by further than 2m: should do better. *L. Lungo* **h80 p**

CAPTAINS TABLE 10 b.g. Welsh Captain – Wensum Girl (Ballymoss) [2002/3 c83: c16m² c16g* c20sᵖᵘ c16d² c16g² c20g³ c17gᶠ Apr 19] workmanlike gelding: fairly useful chaser: made all in maiden at Doncaster in December: good efforts when runner-up: should stay 2½m: acts on good to firm and good to soft going. *R. Dickin* **c116**

CAPTAIN'S WALK 7 b.g. Seymour Hicks (FR) – Mayina (Idiot's Delight) [2002/3 h78, F84: 24sᵖᵘ 21s⁶ Mar 10] modest form in bumpers: broke down on hurdling debut in 2001/2, no sign of retaining ability on return. *P. Bowen* **h–**

CAPTAINTWOTHOUSAND 8 b.g. Milieu – Royal Scarlet (Royal Fountain) [2002/3 h85: c20d⁵ c17s² c21v⁵ c16v⁶ c16g⁶ Jan 18] good-topped gelding: modest hurdler: similar form in novice chases: stays 19f: acts on heavy going: has had tongue tied. *C. W. Fairhurst* **c92 h–**

CAPTAIN VALIANT (IRE) 5 b.g. Supreme Leader – Anna Valley (Gleason (USA)) [2002/3 F13s F16g³ F16m² Apr 10] second foal: dam, fair staying hurdler, half-sister to useful hurdlers Robin Goodfellow, stayed 2½m, and The Decent Thing, stayed 2¾m: fairly useful form when placed at Ludlow last 2 starts in bumpers. *G. B. Balding* **F92**

CAPTAIN ZINZAN (NZ) 8 b.g. Zabeel (NZ) – Lady Springfield (NZ) (Sharivari (USA)) [2002/3 c102, h–: c16m³ c20d³ c20sᶠ c18m⁵ 16d⁴ 16g³ Apr 19] leggy gelding: modest hurdler/novice chaser: left Mrs A. Perrett after fourth start: probably stays 2½m: acts on good to firm going: has finished weakly. *L. A. Dace* **c96 h92**

CARACCIOLA (GER) 6 b.g. Lando (GER) – Capitolina (FR) (Empery (USA)) [2002/3 16v² 16g⁴ 16s³ 16g* 16m³ 16dᵖᵘ Apr 4] leggy ex-German gelding: half-brother to very smart Flat stayer Camp David (by Surumu): useful winner around 1½m in 2001 in Germany for P. Rau: fairly useful novice hurdler: won at Newbury in December (maiden) and February: below form in better company last 2 starts, particularly so on final one: raced at 2m: best effort on good going. *N. J. Henderson* **h123**

CARACCIOLA (NZ) 7 ch.g. Fiesta Star (AUS) – Striking Princess (NZ) (Straight Strike (USA)) [2002/3 h–: 16gᵖᵘ 16v² 17d 26sᵖᵘ 24f Apr 3] probably flattered when runner-up in novice claimer at Leicester in January, no other form over hurdles. *J. L. Spearing* **h69 ?**

CARAMELLE (IRE) 7 ch.m. Be My Guest (USA) – Lobbino (Bustino) [2002/3 17sᵖᵘ 16gᵖᵘ May 31] lengthy mare: lightly raced and little sign of ability. *J. D. Czerpak* **h–**

CARANDREW (FR) 10 b.g. Saint Andrews (FR) – Cara Maria (FR) (Cadoudal (FR)) [2002/3 c–x, h124: 16d 22s³ 21vᶠ Jan 23] rangy gelding: fairly useful hurdler, won 6 times in 2001/2: sold out of M. Pipe's stable for 2,600 gns Ascot July Sales, well below best on return: successful at 23f, best form up to 2½m: acts on any going. *D. M. Lloyd* **c– h81 +**

CARAPUCE (FR) 4 ch.g. Bigstone (IRE) – Treasure City (FR) (Moulin) [2002/3 16g⁵ 16g 16dᵇᵈ 20g Apr 14] lengthy ex-French gelding: fairly useful at best on Flat, winning twice up to 1¼m in French Provinces at 2 yrs: sold out of H.-A. Pantall's stable €60,000 Goffs July Sale: best effort over hurdles (wore cheekpieces) when fifth in juvenile at Musselburgh: pulls hard. *L. Lungo* **h87**

CARBONADO 9 b.g. Anshan – Virevoite (Shareef Dancer (USA)) [2002/3 c99, h–: c21g⁴ c24m² c25dᵖᵘ c25dᵖᵘ c24m⁵ Apr 2] well-made gelding: fair hunter chaser: won point in March: stays 3m: acts on good to firm going. *H. R. Tuck* **c99 h–**

CARBURY CROSS (IRE) 9 b. or br.g. Mandalus – Brickey Gazette (Fine Blade (USA)) [2002/3 c157, h115: c25gᵖᵘ c26g⁶ c24vᵖᵘ c24m c28d c24gᵖᵘ c36d Apr 5] smallish, close-coupled gelding: smart handicap chaser: form in 2002/3 only when sixth to Be My Royal in Hennessy at Newbury in November: should stay beyond 3¼m: best form on good/good to firm going (ran poorly on heavy): usually blinkered: possibly best on left-handed tracks: one to treat with caution. *Jonjo O'Neill* **c148 § h–**

CARDINAL ERROR 5 ch.g. Pure Melody (USA) – Shy Marianet (IRE) (Shy Groom (USA)) [2002/3 F16g F16m Mar 18] first foal: dam unraced: tailed off in 2 bumpers. *John A. Harris* **F–**

CARDINAL MARK (IRE) 9 b.g. Ardross – Sister of Gold (The Parson) [2002/3 c26v⁴ c27s⁶ c25d⁴ c24v³ c20s Feb 24] IR 42,000 4-y-o: leggy ex-Irish gelding: third foal: half-brother to 2 winners by Arctic Lord, including 19f chase winner Twotensforafive: dam unraced sister to useful hurdler Book of Gold: winning hurdler/chaser: sold out of E. O'Grady's stable 14,500 gns Doncaster May Sales: largely disappointing over fences in 2002/3: stays 3¼m: acts on good to firm and heavy going: tried blinkered. *Mrs S. J. Smith* **c88 h–**

CARDINAL WAY (IRE) 10 b. or br.g. Cardinal Flower – Loving Way (Golden Love) [2002/3 c–, h–: c20mᵖᵘ May 11] maiden pointer: no form in 2 hunter chases. *Mrs Julie Read* **c– h–**

CAREW 7 b.g. Minster Son – The White Lion (Flying Tyke) [2002/3 F75: 17d 17g 21m⁴ Oct 1] leggy gelding: signs of ability in bumpers but little encouragement over hurdles. *C. Grant* **h–**

CAREW LAD 7 b.g. Arzanni – Miss Skindles (Taufan (USA)) [2002/3 F16g⁶ Jul 10] 1,100 3-y-o, 2,000 5-y-o: sixth foal: dam, 7f winner, from family of very smart 1¼m winner Homme de Loi and very smart sprinter Mister Majestic: refused in maiden point on debut, runner-up in March: sixth of 15 in bumper at Worcester. *Mrs D. A. Hamer* **F77**

CAREYSVILLE (IRE) 12 b.g. Carmelite House (USA) – Kavali (Blakeney) [2002/3 c104, h–: c24s⁵ c24s² c31gᵖᵘ Apr 24] tall gelding: fair chaser, lightly raced nowadays: stays 3¼m: acts on good to firm and heavy going. *Miss Venetia Williams* **c104 h–**

CARIAD PRESELI (IRE) 8 b.m. Jurado (USA) – Big Sally (Salluceva) [2002/3 19m⁶ 19g⁵ 17g Mar 22] angular mare: little sign of ability, including in points: has had tongue tied. *S. G. Griffiths* **h–**

CARIBBEAN COVE (IRE) 5 gr.g. Norwich – Peaceful Rose (Roselier (FR)) [2002/3 F16d F16v 16d 19d³ 20m* Apr 12] close-coupled gelding: tenth foal: half-brother to 19f hurdle winner Desert Captain (by Asir): dam unraced half-sister to smart 3m chaser Johnny Setaside: poor form in bumpers: best effort in novice hurdles when landing odds with plenty to spare at Bangor: will stay beyond 2½m: capable of better still. *Miss H. C. Knight* **h99 p F73**

CARIBBEAN SUMMER 6 b.g. Bold Arrangement – Poppadom (Rapid River) [2002/3 17g⁶ 24dᵖᵘ Oct 26] half-brother to poor chaser Indian Viceroy (by Lord Bud), stays 21f, and 2m hurdle winner Four On The Trot (by Totem): dam, half-sister to dam of high-class middle-distance stayer User Friendly, won 2½m hurdle: no sign of ability in 2 starts on Flat or 2 novice hurdles: sold 950 gns Doncaster November Sales. *J. R. Turner* **h–**

CARIBEAN DREAM 8 ch.m. Afzal – Lovelek (Golden Love) [2002/3 19sᵖᵘ Mar 7] fourth foal: half-sister to smart hunter chaser Knight of Passion (by Arctic Lord), stays 3¼m: dam winning pointer: unseated in point in 2000: no show in novice hurdle 3 years later. *G. E. Jones* **h–**

CARLESIMO (IRE) 5 b. or br.g. Erins Isle – Diamond Display (IRE) (Shardari) [2002/3 16d³ 16d² 16s⁵ 16s* 17m* 16d² 16f² 16g³ Apr 21] fair on Flat (stays 2m): fairly useful novice hurdler: won at Kilbeggan in June and Bellewstown and Tipperary in July: off 7 months after seventh start: raced around 2m: acts on any going. *N. Meade, Ireland* **h121**

CARLINGBROOK 9 ch.g. Carlingford Castle – Siliferous (Sandy Creek) [2002/3 h70: 16vᵖᵘ Nov 28] workmanlike gelding: lightly raced: fair form in bumpers, poor form over hurdles. *T. R. George* **h–**

CARLING ELECT 7 ch.m. Carlingford Castle – Electress (Baron Blakeney) [2002/3 c–, h–: c24mᵘʳ Apr 22] won 2-finisher maiden point in April, no worthwhile form otherwise: has had tongue tied. *R. H. P. Williams* **c– h–**

Martell Cognac Nisa Today's Handicap Hurdle, Aintree—
Carlovent gains a second win in the race, at the chief expense of the grey Rostropovich

CARLOVENT (FR) 8 b.g. Cadoudal (FR) – Carlaya (FR) (Carmarthen (FR))
[2002/3 c–x, h143x: 24s⁵ 25d 20v³ 22d⁴ 22vᵖᵘ 20v⁵ 25g 24g* 24m³ 24m³ Apr 26] angular
gelding: reportedly blind in one eye: useful hurdler/chaser, raced only over hurdles since
2000/1: won valuable handicap at Aintree in April by 1½ lengths from Rostropovich:
stays 25f: acts on heavy and good to firm going (looked ill at ease on firm): blinkered
once, visored last 4 starts: sketchy jumper: difficult ride. *M. C. Pipe* **c– x h133 x**

CARL'S BOY 7 ch.g. Itsu (USA) – Adelbaran (FR) (No Pass No Sale) [2002/3 c20g³
c16mᵖᵘ 16m² c16m⁵ Apr 5] small, angular gelding: poor maiden hurdler/chaser: left
B. Llewellyn after third start: won point in April: raced mainly around 2m: acts on good
to firm and heavy going. *F. H. Williams* **c64 h79**

CARLTON CLIMBER 5 b.g. Carlton (GER) – High Climber (Mandrake Major)
[2002/3 F16v* Jan 29] 2,800 4-y-o: sixth foal: half-brother to 1993 4-y-o 6f/7f winner
Perusal (by Sizzling Melody) and winners in Sweden and Italy: dam poor maiden who
stayed 7f: collapsed and died after winning bumper at Newcastle on debut by 3½ lengths
from Tom Fruit. *Mrs S. J. Smith* **F102**

CARLY BAY 5 b.m. Carlton (GER) – Polly Minor (Sunley Builds) [2002/3 F18g
F17d⁴ 17s⁴ 18s⁴ 16v* 20v⁵ Mar 3] first foal: dam modest hurdler up to 2¾m: better effort
in bumpers when fourth at Folkestone: modest novice hurdler: easily best effort when
winning mares event at Plumpton in February: should stay 2½m: raced on good going or
softer (acts on heavy). *G. P. Enright* **h94 F79**

CARLYTA 7 ch.m. Carlingford Castle – Baryta (Nishapour (FR)) [2002/3 h–, F–: 17d⁵
16d³ Nov 21] tall mare: first sign of ability when close third in mares novice handicap
hurdle at Wincanton: raced mainly around 2m: has looked wayward. *J. T. Gifford* **h72**

CARNACRACK 9 b.g. Le Coq d'Or – Carney (New Brig) [2002/3 c22m² c26d*
c27d c28v² c25v* c30dᶠ c24s⁴ c26s c25g³ c25g³ Apr 7] half-sister to fair staying
hurdler Carnetto (by Le Coq d'Or): dam once-raced sister to fairly useful staying chaser
Solo Sam: won all 3 starts in points in 2002: modest novice chaser: won at Cartmel in
June and Kelso (handicap) in November: no form last 3 starts: thorough stayer: acts on
heavy going, probably on good to firm: races prominently. *Miss S. E. Forster* **c87**

CARNAGE (IRE) 6 b.g. Catrail (USA) – Caranina (USA) (Caro) [2002/3 20m⁵ 16m⁴
Apr 22] half-brother to fair hurdler/winning chaser Total Joy (by Persian Bold), stayed
25f, and winning 2m hurdler Misniuil (by Unblest): formerly modest up to 2m on Flat:
sold out of C. Drew's stable £2,000 Ascot February Sales: better effort over hurdles when
fourth in maiden at Chepstow. *P. Bowen* **h85**

162

CARNA TOO   6 br.m. Afzal – H And K Punter (Mandalus) [2002/3 F–: 16d 18s 19v^{pu}   **h–**
22m Mar 20] no sign of ability. *C. J. Drewe*

CARNOUSTIE (USA)   5 gr.m. Ezzoud (IRE) – Sarba (USA) (Persepolis (FR))   **h91 §**
[2002/3 h86: 17g³ 16v⁴ 17g* 19m² 22m⁴ 17m 17d³ 16d⁵ 19s² 19d* Mar 10] modest
novice hurdler: won at Newton Abbot in June and Stratford (seller) in March: should stay
beyond 19f: acts on good to firm and good to soft going: has worn cheekpieces, including
when successful: ungenuine. *R. T. Phillips*

CAROLE'S DOVE   7 b.m. Manhal – Nimble Dove (Starch Reduced) [2002/3 h66:   **h–**
17s 24v Dec 28] quite good-topped mare: poor maiden hurdler: stays 19f: raced on good
going or softer. *C. J. Price*

CAROLINE'S ROSE   5 bl. or br.m. Fraam – Just Rosie (Sula Bula) [2002/3 F16g   **F–**
Sep 15] second foal: dam fair hurdler up to 21f: well held in bumper and on Flat.
A. P. Jones

CAROUSING   6 b.g. Selkirk (USA) – Moon Carnival (Be My Guest (USA)) [2002/3   **h71 §**
h102§: 20s⁶ 16v⁴ 20m Dec 17] small, rather sparely-made gelding: maiden hurdler, only
poor form in 2002/3: stays 2½m: acts on heavy going: has failed to impress with finishing
effort more than once. *Mrs J. C. McGregor*

CARPET PRINCESS (IRE)   5 gr. or ro.m. Prince of Birds (USA) – Krayyalei (IRE)   **h82**
(Krayyan) [2002/3 20m* 24m³ 17f² 20s⁶ 16d⁴ 19v Dec 28] rather leggy mare: poor
maiden on Flat (stays 15f): poor novice hurdler: won maiden at Bangor in August: may
prove best up to easy 2½m: acts on firm and good to soft going, possibly unsuited by
softer. *Mrs P. N. Dutfield*

CARRACA (IRE)   5 b.g. Alzao (USA) – Honey Bun (Unfuwain (USA)) [2002/3 19g⁶   **h– §**
16m^{rtr} 17g^{pu} Jun 29] temperamental maiden on Flat (should stay 1½m), sold out of
J. Bethell's stable 1,300 gns Newmarket Autumn (2001) Sales: signs of more temperament than ability over hurdles. *Mrs A. M. Thorpe*

CARRADIUM   7 b.g. Presidium – Carrapateira (Gunner B) [2002/3 h–: 20d⁴ 16g⁴   **c–**
16m 16g 16s c21v^{pu} Nov 12] signs of only a little ability: tongue tied. *R. Shiels*   **h–**

CARRIAGE RIDE (IRE)   5 b.g. Tidaro (USA) – Casakurali (Gleason (USA))   **h–**
[2002/3 20g Apr 23] 4,000 4-y-o: fourth known foal: dam lightly raced in bumpers/over
hurdles: always behind in maiden hurdle on debut. *N. G. Richards*

CARRICK TROOP (IRE)   10 gr.g. Roselier (FR) – Over The Pond (IRE) (Over The   **c118**
River (FR)) [2002/3 c115: c16g* c16s⁴ c16d³ c20g c16d⁵ c16d c17d⁴ Feb 28] tall gelding:
fairly useful handicap chaser: won at Wetherby in November: not at best after third start:
successful at 27f but best up to 2½m: acts on good to firm and heavy going: held up, and
suited by well-run race: sound jumper. *Mrs M. Reveley*

CARRIED INTEREST (IRE)   9 br.g. Celio Rufo – Laurie Belle (Boreen (FR))   **c–**
[2002/3 c106d, h–: c24d^{pu} Oct 25] well-made gelding: fair handicap chaser, below form   **h–**
since second start in 2001/2: stays 3m: acts on soft and firm going: tried blinkered: sold
8,000 gns Doncaster May Sales, won point in March. *D. J. Caro*

CARRIGAFOYLE   8 b.g. Young Senor (USA) – Miss Skindles (Taufan (USA))   **h87**
[2002/3 h–, F–: 17v 16s² 19s 16d⁵ 19g 17g^{pu} 16m^{pu} Apr 21] sturdy gelding: modest
novice hurdler: should stay 2½m: acts on soft ground: inconsistent. *O. Brennan*

CARROLL'S DOVE   5 ch.m. Carroll House – Dancing Dove (IRE) (Denel (FR))   **h–**
[2002/3 F16g³ F17s 22s^{pu} Jan 14] first foal: dam, fairly useful hurdler from 2m to 2¾m,   **F76**
half-sister to smart staying chaser Niki Dee: third in mares bumper on debut: very
disappointing subsequently, including on hurdling debut: should stay beyond 2m: sold
1,600 gns Doncaster May Sales. *M. C. Pipe*

CARROLL'S GOLD (IRE)   5 br.g. Carroll House – Missfethard-On-Sea (Deep   **F91**
Run) [2002/3 F17f⁵ F16d F12g Dec 18] IR £13,000 3-y-o: sixth foal: half-brother to
winning pointer by Over The River: dam third in bumper: some promise when fifth of
18 in maiden bumper at Exeter on debut: well held both starts after 6-month absence.
E. L. James

CARRYONHARRY (IRE)   9 gr.g. Roselier (FR) – Bluebell Avenue (Boreen Beag)   **c128 x**
[2002/3 c118+, h–: c25d^{pu} c24s* c24d c24s^{pu} c24m⁴ c24g⁶ c33m^{pu} Apr 12] leggy   **h–**
gelding: fairly useful handicap chaser: won at Kempton in December: should stay beyond
3m: acts on good to firm and heavy going: visored last 3 starts: usually held up/sometimes
idles: often let down by jumping. *M. C. Pipe*

CASE OF POTEEN (IRE) 7 b. or br.m. Witness Box (USA) – On The Hooch (Over **h82** The River (FR)) [2002/3 h80: 20g^F 24m^{co} 24v^4 20d^2 22d^3 22g Mar 21] medium-sized mare: poor maiden hurdler: stays 3m: acts on heavy going. *Mrs S. C. Bradburne*

CASHABAN 10 ch.g. Ballacashtal (CAN) – Portway Anna (Hot Brandy) [2002/3 c–, **c–** h67: 16g 17s Jun 3] medium-sized gelding: well held on chasing debut: poor maiden **h–** hurdler: stays 19f: best efforts on good/good to firm going: tried blinkered: pulls hard. *J. S. Smith*

CASHAPLENTY 10 ch.g. Ballacashtal (CAN) – Storm of Plenty (Billion (USA)) **c–** [2002/3 16g May 26] tall, angular gelding: let down by jumping in 2 novice chases: **h–** one-time fair hurdler: well held in point and selling handicap hurdle, only outings in 2002: best around 2m: acts on soft going: usually held up. *J. W. Unett*

CASHEL DANCER 4 b.f. Bishop of Cashel – Dancing Debut (Polar Falcon (USA)) **h77** [2002/3 16g^4 16f^4 16d Nov 7] lengthy, angular filly: poor maiden on Flat: similar form in juvenile hurdles. *S. A. Brookshaw*

CASHEW KID (IRE) 6 b.g. Persian Mews – No Honey (Dual) [2002/3 F–: F17f **h–** 20m^{pu} 21m^{pu} Mar 19] no sign of ability: left Miss K. Marks after second start. **F–** *S. E. H. Sherwood*

CASH FOR QUESTIONS (IRE) 11 b.g. Supreme Leader – Deep Dollar (Deep **c–** Run) [2002/3 c–, h–: 16d 20m^5 20s^3 19d* 20d^{pu} 20g 23m^4 Apr 21] workmanlike gelding: **h84** unseated early only outing over fences: poor handicap hurdler nowadays: won at Doncaster in January: should stay beyond 2½m: acts on firm and good to soft going. *R. A. Fahey*

CASH 'N CARROTS 4 b.g. Missed Flight – Rhiannon (Welsh Pageant) [2002/3 **h–** F13s F16s F16s 16d Mar 19] 500 3-y-o: leggy gelding: eleventh foal: half-brother to **F–** several winners, including modest 3m hurdler Alcian Blue (by Tina's Pet) and modest hurdler/chaser up to 3m King of Shadows (by Connaught): dam maiden who stayed 1m at 2 yrs: no form in 3 bumpers and selling hurdle. *R. C. Harper*

CASH 'N' CREDIT 5 b.m. Homo Sapien – Not Enough (Balinger) [2002/3 F–: 16s^5 **h68** 16m^3 19g^4 Apr 19] leggy mare: well held in bumpers: poor form first 2 starts over hurdles. *R. Dickin*

CASH RETURN 4 b.f. Bob's Return (IRE) – We're In The Money (Billion (USA)) **h–** [2002/3 F14d F12g 19d 22d 22d Feb 17] lengthy filly: second foal: dam, winning hurdler/ **F–** chaser who stayed 25f, out of half-sister to smart colt up to 7f Superlative: no form in bumpers or novice hurdles. *B. G. Powell*

CASING (IRE) 5 gr.m. Case Law – Singhana (IRE) (Mouktar) [2002/3 16d^{pu} Nov 26] **h–** compact mare: poor sprint maiden on Flat: jumped poorly and showed nothing on hurdling debut: sold £1,500 Ascot April Sales. *F. Jordan*

CASPAR'S DATE 6 ch.g. Afzal – Rabdanna (Rabdan) [2002/3 F71: F16d^6 F17m Oct **F73** 3] poor form in bumpers: would probably have been placed but for going lame final start. *J. Gallagher*

CASSIA GREEN 9 gr.g. Scallywag – Casa's Star (Top Star) [2002/3 c–: c19d^6 c21d^F **c85 +** c20g^3 c16g* Mar 14] modest novice chaser: left R. Bevis and off 9 months after second start: won handicap at Warwick in March: probably stays 21f: sound jumper. *Mrs H. Dalton*

CASSIA HEIGHTS 8 b.g. Montelimar (USA) – Cloncoose (IRE) (Remainder Man) **c105** [2002/3 c100, h69: c24d^2 c22m^2 c24d^4 c24s^2 c27g^2 c24v^4 c24g^2 c24m^6 c24f^3 c21d c24m^4 **h–** Apr 19] tall gelding: fair handicap chaser: stays 27f: acts on soft and good to firm going: tongue tied: usually sound jumper: consistent. *S. A. Brookshaw*

CASTANET 4 b.f. Pennekamp (USA) – Addaya (IRE) (Persian Bold) [2002/3 17s^2 16f^4 **h81** 17m^6 Apr 16] lengthy filly: modest maiden on Flat (stays 1½m), sold out of W. Haggas' stable 5,500 gns Newmarket Autumn Sales: modest form all 3 starts in juvenile hurdles. *A. E. Price*

CASTLEBRIDGE 6 b.g. Batshoof – Super Sisters (AUS) (Call Report (USA)) **h–** [2002/3 h–: 16g 20v^3 21v 16s Feb 26] leggy gelding: poor and unreliable on Flat (stays 10.5f), left M. Usher in October: signs of only a little ability over hurdles: usually visored/ blinkered: has found little. *K. R. Burke*

CASTLE CLEAR (IRE) 10 b.g. Castle Keep – Rose of Allendale (Green Shoon) **c–** [2002/3 c73, h88: 20m^3 c20d^2 22m 22g 22s c20s^F 20d 20s^2 20g Jan 17] sturdy, lengthy **h87** gelding: winning chaser, though often let down by jumping: modest hurdler, lame final start: stays 2¾m: acts on soft and good to firm going: tried blinkered/in cheekpieces: often finds little: inconsistent. *Mrs S. C. Bradburne*

CASTLE FOLLY (IRE) 11 b.g. Carlingford Castle – Air Plane (Arratos (FR)) **c97**
[2002/3 c68: c21s^F c21m^3 c26m^2 c21m* c22g* Oct 6] modest chaser: made most when winning maiden at Southwell in September and novice handicap at Fontwell in October: stays 3¼m, at least when conditions aren't testing: acts on good to firm going, probably on soft: usually blinkered. *J. White*

CASTLEFORD (IRE) 5 b.g. Be My Native (USA) – Commanche Bay (IRE) (Com- **F96**
manche Run) [2002/3 F16m F16d^5 Mar 19] medium-sized gelding: first foal: dam unraced half-sister to smart staying chaser Topsham Bay and useful hurdler Mixed Blends: better effort in bumpers when fifth at Chepstow: likely to benefit from greater test of stamina. *P. J. Hobbs*

CASTLE FRIEND 8 b.g. Durgam (USA) – Furry Friend (USA) (Bold Bidder) **h69**
[2002/3 h68: 16g^pu 16m^5 17m^5 17g^4 Aug 1] poor maiden hurdler: best around 2m: acts on firm going: sweating badly third start. *F. S. Storey*

CASTLEHALE (IRE) 10 ch.g. Over The River (FR) – Anns Fancy (River Knight **c81**
(FR)) [2002/3 c19f^2 c28g^pu May 31] ex-Irish gelding: winning pointer: modest form at **h–**
best in hunter chases: stays 25f: acts on any going: tried blinkered: reportedly lame final outing. *A. W. Congdon*

CASTLEMORE (IRE) 5 b.g. Be My Native (USA) – Parsonetta (The Parson) **F95**
[2002/3 F16d^4 F16d^4 Mar 6] IR £78,000 3-y-o: sixth foal: half-brother to winning 2¼m hurdler Supreme Being (by Supreme Leader): dam unraced half-sister to useful hurdler up to 2½m Atteses and useful hurdler/chaser up to 3m Native Estates: fourth in bumpers at Ludlow and Wincanton: will stay 2½m. *P. J. Hobbs*

CASTLE OWEN (IRE) 11 b.g. Castle Keep – Lady Owenette (IRE) (Salluceva) **c102**
[2002/3 16g c16d^2 16g c16g^ur c16m^4 Oct 4] useful-looking gelding: one-time fairly **h–**
useful hurdler: fair chaser: stays 25f: acts on heavy going, probably on good to firm: headstrong. *Mrs A. C. Hamilton*

CASTLE PRINCE (IRE) 9 b.g. Homo Sapien – Lisaleen Lady (Miner's Lamp) **c111**
[2002/3 c101+, h–: c16f^2 c16f^3 c17g^4 c16d^5 c20d^5 c16d^ur c21d^3 c17g^4 c16d c16g c16f^2 **h–**
Apr 21] tall gelding: fair chaser, often highly tried: best around 2m: acts on firm and soft going: has looked tricky ride. *R. J. Hodges*

CASTLE RICHARD (IRE) 6 gr.g. Sexton Blake – Miss McCormick (IRE) (Rose- **h110**
lier (FR)) [2002/3 F17d^6 20d^5 21s* 20v^2 24s^pu Mar 6] IR 7,000 3-y-o: first foal: dam **F76**
lightly-raced hurdler: unseated in maiden Irish point on debut in 2002: sixth of 14 in maiden bumper: fair form in novice hurdles, won at Sedgefield in December: ran as if amiss final start: should stay 3m: raced on going softer than good (acts on heavy). *G. M. Moore*

CASTLE RIVER (USA) 4 b.g. Irish River (FR) – Castellina (USA) (Danzig Connec- **h–**
tion (USA)) [2002/3 16g Dec 18] close-coupled gelding: fairly useful on Flat (stays 1¼m), sold out of B. Hills's stable 27,000 gns Newmarket Autumn Sales: well held in juvenile on hurdling debut. *B. G. Powell*

CASTLESHANE (IRE) 6 b.g. Kris – Ahbab (IRE) (Ajdal (USA)) [2002/3 h118: **h130**
16g^2 16d^5 17g 16m* Apr 22] tall, quite good-topped gelding: should make a chaser: useful hurdler: won handicap at Chepstow in April by 10 lengths from Murray River: raced mainly around 2m: acts on firm and good to soft going: blinkered once: free-going front runner: genuine. *S. Gollings*

CATALPA CARGO (IRE) 9 b.g. Buckskin (FR) – Money For Honey (New Brig) **h115**
[2002/3 20v^2 Mar 1] fairly useful hurdler, very lightly raced: good second to Mullacash in minor event at Fairyhouse after 18-month absence: will stay 3m: acts on heavy going (won bumper on good to firm). *C. Roche, Ireland*

CATCHATAN (IRE) 8 b.g. Cataldi – Snowtan (IRE) (Tanfirion) [2002/3 c20d^pu **c92**
c23g^2 c16d^4 c20s c16g^4 c20g^5 Mar 12] lengthy, useful-looking gelding: winning pointer: **h–**
poor form on second of 2 starts in novice hurdles in 2000/1: modest novice chaser: won handicap at Leicester in December: effective at 2m to 23f: acts on good to soft going: tongue tied after reappearance: jumped poorly final start. *P. R. Webber*

CATCH BALL 7 ch.m. Prince Sabo – Canoodle (Warpath) [2002/3 h134?: 20s^6 24g **h116**
24s^5 24s^5 24s^5 Jan 23] sparely-made mare: useful hurdler at best: largely out of sorts since 2000/1: stays 3m: acts on good to firm and heavy going. *W. P. Mullins, Ireland*

CATCH THEM ALL (IRE) 6 br.g. Mandalus – Only Flower (Warpath) [2002/3 **h66** F16d F19s 16d 24g 17v⁵ 20sᵖᵘ 25dᵖᵘ Feb 25] smallish, sturdy ex-Irish gelding: half-**F—** brother to poor hurdler Island Warrior (by Warcraft), stays 2¾m: dam, winning hurdler/chaser up to 2¾m, sister to smart hurdler up to 2½m Path of Peace and to dam of smart 2m hurdler Satin Lover: form only when fifth in novice hurdle at Sedgefield (first start after leaving C. Swan): tried blinkered. *J. Howard Johnson*

CATCH THE PERK (IRE) 6 b.g. Executive Perk – Kilbally Quilty (IRE) (Monte-**h—** limar (USA)) [2002/3 F16g⁶ F16m⁴ F16m² F16g⁵ 16g 20m⁴ 17g⁶ Apr 21] IR 9,800 3-y-o: **F86** workmanlike gelding: first foal: dam unraced, out of half-sister to smart staying chasers Seskin Bridge and Comeragh King: fair form in bumpers: well held in novice hurdles: should be suited by further than 2m. *Miss Lucinda V. Russell*

CATEEL BAY 5 ch.m. Most Welcome – Calachuchi (Martinmas) [2002/3 17d 16g⁶ **h—** 16mᵘʳ 17s 16g⁶ 16dᵖᵘ 16d 16g Mar 14] half-sister to winning 2m hurdler Calatagan (by Danzig Connection): poor on Flat: has shown little over hurdles. *H. Alexander*

CAT FIVE 4 b.g. Catrail (USA) – Wassl This Then (IRE) (Wassl) [2002/3 16g 16g⁴ **h111** Apr 21] half-brother to winning hurdler Hannah Park (by Lycius), stays 2½m: fairly useful around 1m on Flat: better effort in juvenile hurdles when fourth at Fairyhouse: tongue tied on debut. *G. M. Lyons, Ireland*

CATHERINE'S WAY (IRE) 11 b.g. Mandalus – Sharp Approach (Crash Course) **c—** [2002/3 c90, h—: c16dᵖᵘ c21sᵖᵘ May 28] compact gelding: fair chaser at best: sold 1,000 **h—** gns Ascot July Sales, subsequently unplaced in points: stays 2¾m: acts on heavy going: has broken blood vessel: often front runner. *Neil King*

CAUCASIAN (IRE) 5 gr.g. Leading Counsel (USA) – Kemal's Princess (Kemal **F—** (FR)) [2002/3 F16g Mar 2] €25,000 4-y-o: rather unfurnished gelding: fifth foal: brother to fair hurdler/fairly useful chaser Kemal's Council, stays 25f: dam unraced, out of half-sister to very smart 2m to 2½m hurdler Fane Ranger: backward when tenth of 19 in maiden bumper at Huntingdon on debut. *Ian Williams*

CAUGHT'N THE SLIPS (IRE) 7 b.m. Roselier (FR) – Bold Glen (Bold Owl) **F—** [2002/3 F16m Jul 4] IR 1,600 4-y-o: third foal: dam unraced, from family of useful hurdler up to 3m William Crump: well held in maiden bumper on debut. *D. J. Caro*

CAVERSFIELD 8 ch.g. Tina's Pet – Canoodle (Warpath) [2002/3 16s Feb 26] small **h—** gelding: poor on Flat (best at 7f/1m): tailed off in selling handicap on first hurdles start for 3 years: sold £1,100 Ascot April Sales. *J. M. Bradley*

CAVVIES NIECE 5 b.m. Ballet Royal (USA) – Cavisoir (Afzal) [2002/3 F16d 18mᵖᵘ **h—** Aug 23] first foal: dam unraced, out of half-sister to high-class hunter chaser Cavalero: **F—** no show in bumper or selling hurdle (tongue tied). *H. J. Manners*

CAYMAN WENT 4 b.g. Bering – Bonne Ile (Ile de Bourbon (USA)) [2002/3 F12g³ **F90** F16g⁵ F16g Apr 2] 25,000 3-y-o: close-coupled gelding: eighth foal: half-brother to several winners, including leading American hurdler All Gong (by Kris), stays 21f, and fairly useful 1m and 1¼m winner Bonne Etoile (by Diesis): dam middle-distance stayer, later Grade 1 1¼m winner in USA: third in bumper at Newbury on debut: raced too freely when well held both subsequent starts. *C. C. Bealby*

CEAD MILE FAILTE 8 ch.g. Most Welcome – Avionne (Derrylin) [2002/3 h—: 19f **h—** Oct 9] winning pointer: poor on Flat: no form over hurdles: has worn cheekpieces. *B. J. Llewellyn*

CEANANNAS MOR (IRE) 9 b. or br.g. Strong Gale – Game Sunset (Menelek) **c123 §** [2002/3 c127, h—: c31d⁵ c24s⁴ c24mᵖᵘ c21dᵖᵘ Apr 4] useful-looking gelding: fairly useful **h—** handicap chaser: badly out of sorts after second start, including in Topham Chase at Aintree in April and cross-country event at Punchestown in early-May: stays 3m: acts on soft going, probably on good to firm: weak finisher. *N. J. Henderson*

CEARNACH 5 b.g. Night Shift (USA) – High Matinee (Shirley Heights) [2002/3 **h—** 16dᵖᵘ 16gᵖᵘ 17s⁵ 21v⁵ 16vᵖᵘ 17s 16s 19g Mar 17] poor maiden on Flat (stays 1m): signs of only a little ability over hurdles: blinkered second start. *J. M. Bradley*

CEDAR 6 gr.g. Absalom – Setai's Palace (Royal Palace) [2002/3 20mᶠ 22g⁴ Apr 12] **h73** second foal: dam, modest hurdler, stayed 2¾m: fourth of 12 in novice at Stratford, second start over hurdles. *R. Dickin*

CEDAR BROOM (IRE) 10 b.g. Brush Aside (USA) – Flash 'n' Run (Record Run) **c67** [2002/3 20sᵖᵘ c16m⁶ c21mᶠ c20g⁴ c20sᵖᵘ c20g³ c19mᵖᵘ Sep 11] sparely-made gelding: **h—** poor hurdler in 2000/1, no show on reappearance: showed only a little over fences: stays 2½m: acts on firm and good to soft going: often none too fluent. *E. R. Clough*

CEDAR CHIEF 6 b.g. Saddlers' Hall (IRE) – Dame Ashfield (Grundy) [2002/3 c–, h75§: c26m⁶ c23gᵘʳ 22m Jun 30] well held only completed start over fences: poor hurdler: won point in April: probably stays 3m: acts on any going: needs blinkers: hard ride. *R. J. O'Sullivan*

**c– §
h– §**

CEDAR FLAG (IRE) 9 br.g. Jareer (USA) – Sasha Lea (Cawston's Clown) [2002/3 h–: 20mᵖᵘ 18f Jun 3] little form over hurdles: has had tongue tied. *L. A. Dace*

h–

CEDAR GREEN 9 br.g. Bustino – Explosiva (USA) (Explodent (USA)) [2002/3 c116: c25v³ c29s⁵ c26d⁴ c30s² Mar 4] rangy gelding: fairly useful handicap chaser: won at Fontwell in February: thorough stayer: acts on heavy ground: blinkered. *K. C. Bailey*

c119

CEDAR GROVE 6 b.g. Shirley Heights – Trojan Desert (Troy) [2002/3 16s 16s Dec 27] smallish, good-topped gelding: modest maiden on Flat (stays 1¾m): little show in 2 races over hurdles. *John A. Harris*

h–

CEDAR MASTER (IRE) 6 b.g. Soviet Lad (USA) – Samriah (IRE) (Wassl) [2002/3 17m 16g³ 20m² 16m⁴ 19s⁶ Aug 1] fairly useful on Flat (stays 2m): modest novice hurdler: likely to prove best around 2m: acts on good to firm going: blinkered final start: not one to trust implicitly. *R. J. O'Sullivan*

h94

CEDAR SQUARE (IRE) 12 b.g. Dancing Dissident (USA) – Friendly Ann (Artaius (USA)) [2002/3 c100, h–: c25g² c21g² c24d³ c22m³ Aug 23] sturdy gelding: modest handicap chaser: stays 25f: acts on soft and good to firm going: blinkered second/third starts: usually races prominently: prone to the odd mistake: sometimes finds little. *V. R. A. Dartnall*

**c99
h–**

CELEBRATION TOWN (IRE) 6 b. or br.g. Case Law – Battle Queen (Kind of Hush) [2002/3 16d 16g Apr 24] half-brother to Czech chaser St Roger (by Prince Rupert), successful up to 29f: fairly useful on Flat (probably best up to 1m, has refused to race) for D. Morris: poor form in 2 novice hurdles: will prove best at 2m: withdrawn after refusing to line up on intended hurdling debut. *N. G. Richards*

h80

CELIBATE (IRE) 12 ch.g. Shy Groom (USA) – Dance Alone (USA) (Monteverdi) [2002/3 c133, h–: c21m³ c20g⁴ Nov 20] sparely-made gelding: smart chaser at best, on downgrade: never dangerous in 2 handicaps in 2002/3: stays 21f: acts on any going: tried blinkered: usually races prominently: sound jumper. *C. J. Mann*

**c124
h–**

CELIOSO (IRE) 6 b.g. Celio Rufo – Bettons Rose (Roselier (FR)) [2002/3 h–, F67: 21gᵖᵘ 17s⁴ 25g⁴ 24g* 24g⁴ Apr 21] lengthy gelding: chasing type: poor hurdler, sold out of A. Crook's stable 3,000 gns Doncaster May Sales after reappearance: won novice handicap at Carlisle in March: suited by 3m+: raced on good going or softer. *Mrs S. J. Smith*

h80

CELONY 6 b.m. Primitive Rising (USA) – Lapopie (Deep Run) [2002/3 h–, F–: 20g⁴ May 8] leggy, unfurnished mare: signs of only a little ability. *C. P. Morlock*

h–

CELTIC BLAZE (IRE) 4 b.f. Charente River (IRE) – Firdaunt (Tanfirion) [2002/3 16s² 16g² Dec 28] small, sturdy ex-Irish filly: fair on Flat (stays 1¾m), won in March: modest form when second in juvenile hurdles at Wetherby and Musselburgh. *B. S. Rothwell*

h88

CELTIC BOUNTY (IRE) 7 b.g. Treasure Hunter – Welsh Glen (Furry Glen) [2002/3 h–, F–: 16sᵖᵘ c19dᵖᵘ Jan 27] tall gelding: little sign of ability. *R. J. Hodges*

**c–
h–**

CELTIC DANCER (IRE) 4 b.g. Sadler's Wells (USA) – Noora Abu (Ahonoora) [2002/3 16s⁵ 16g 16d 17d 21sᵖᵘ Feb 28] sturdy, useful-looking gelding: dam half-sister to very smart 2m hurdler Condor Pan and useful 2m hurdler Vestris Abu: better effort in maidens on Flat at 3 yrs when fifth in 1½m event: sold out of J. Bolger's stable 20,000 gns Newmarket July Sales: signs of only a little ability over hurdles: blinkered and tongue tied final start: sold 2,600 gns Doncaster March Sales. *Jonjo O'Neill*

h82

CELTIC DUKE 11 b.g. Strong Gale – Celtic Cygnet (Celtic Cone) [2002/3 c24m² Apr 21] sturdy gelding: fair chaser at best: successful in points in February and April: creditable second in hunter at Fakenham: stays 3½m: acts on firm and good to soft going, possibly not on heavy. *J. M. Turner*

**c96
h–**

CELTIC FLOW 5 b.m. Primitive Rising (USA) – Celtic Lane (Welsh Captain) [2002/3 F17v⁵ 16d 24s 21s⁶ Mar 11] leggy mare: first foal: dam poor pointer: no sign of ability. *C. R. Wilson*

**h–
F–**

CELTIC JUSTICE (IRE) 8 br.g. Mister Lord (USA) – Just Ginger (The Parson) [2002/3 h103, F82: 19d⁵ 17s* 20d Jun 3] leggy gelding: winning pointer: fair hurdler:

h103

back to form when winning seller at Newton Abbot in May: should stay 2½m: acts on soft going. *R. J. Hodges*

CELTIC LEGEND (FR) 4 br.g. Celtic Swing – Another Legend (USA) (Lyphard's Wish (FR)) [2002/3 16d 17d[6] 18g[4] Mar 21] tall, leggy ex-French gelding: fairly useful maiden on Flat (stays 1½m), left Mme C. Head-Maarek and well below form on British debut: poor form in juvenile hurdles: tongue tied final start. *Mrs M. Reveley* **h76**

CELTIC PRIDE (IRE) 8 gr.g. Roselier (FR) – Grannie No (Brave Invader (USA)) [2002/3 h129: c24d[3] Nov 7] tall gelding: fairly useful hurdler: favourite, last of 3 finishers to Cracking Dawn in novice at Haydock on chasing debut, reportedly distressed: should be suited by 3m+: raced on good going or softer (acts well on heavy). *Jonjo O'Neill* **c–** **h–**

CELTIC ROVER 5 b.g. Celtic Swing – Lady Sabo (Prince Sabo) [2002/3 h–: 16d[pu] Nov 12] sparely-made gelding: of little account on Flat: no show over hurdles. *C. R. Dore* **h–**

CELTIC SEASON 11 b.g. Vital Season – Welsh Flower (Welsh Saint) [2002/3 c106, h–: c21g[5] c25d[pu] c24m Jun 1] tall gelding: has reportedly had wind operation and been freeze-fired: fair hunter chaser: stays 3m: acts on good to firm and heavy going: effective with or without blinkers: tongue tied. *C. W. Loggin* **c92** **h–**

CELTIC SONG (IRE) 7 b.g. Cataldi – Iron Mariner (IRE) (Mandalus) [2002/3 22f* 17f Mar 27] fair form in bumpers: reportedly injured knee when falling on hurdling debut in late-2000/1: off 18 months, won novice at Wincanton in October: ran no sort of race 5 months later. *P. F. Nicholls* **h82**

CELTIC STAR (IRE) 5 b.g. Celtic Swing – Recherchee (Rainbow Quest (USA)) [2002/3 h92: 16s 17m[3] 18m* 18g[3] 19d[pu] 16m[6] 24s[6] Nov 14] lengthy gelding: modest hurdler: won novice at Fontwell in September: should stay beyond 2¼m: acts on firm and soft going: tried visored, including when successful. *Nick Williams* **h99**

CELTIC TANNER (IRE) 4 b.g. Royal Abjar (USA) – Mills Pride (IRE) (Posen (USA)) [2002/3 F16m Feb 22] £6,000 3-y-o: third foal: dam, winning 2m hurdler, half-sister to dam of Grande Course de Haies winner Nobody Told Me: in need of race, fifteenth of 19 in bumper at Kempton on debut. *D. J. Wintle* **F–**

CELTIC VISION (IRE) 7 b.g. Be My Native (USA) – Dream Run (Deep Run) [2002/3 F109: 17d[2] 20d* 20s[2] 20v[pu] 18g* Mar 21] rather leggy gelding: fairly useful novice hurdler: won at Southwell in November and Kelso (handicap) in March: will stay beyond 2½m: acts on heavy going: has won with/without tongue strap: reportedly choked on reappearance, lame fourth start. *Jonjo O'Neill* **h121**

CENKOS (FR) 9 ch.g. Nikos – Vincenza (Grundy) [2002/3 c163+, h–: c16s* c17g[2] c16g[3] c20d[4] c16m[2] Apr 26] **c163** **h–**
    The latest season started as the previous one had ended for Cenkos—with a wide-margin win at Sandown. The Mitsubishi Shogun Tingle Creek Trophy in December looked a race to savour beforehand, with Flagship Uberalles and Moscow Flyer, winner of the Champion Chase and Arkle respectively at Cheltenham the previous March, meeting for the first time. Experience was marginally preferred over potential in the betting, with Flagship Uberalles, bidding for his fourth successive win in the race, starting favourite at 15/8, just ahead of Moscow

Mitsubishi Shogun Tingle Creek Trophy Chase, Sandown—
Cenkos leads the riderless Moscow Flyer at the second last

Mrs J. Stewart's "Cenkos"

Flyer at 2/1, with Cenkos next in the betting at 6/1. However, things didn't go to plan for the market leaders. Flagship Uberalles overjumped and lost his footing at the fifth fence, losing ground and also baulking Moscow Flyer, causing that horse to unseat Barry Geraghty. With the market leaders effectively out of the contest, Cenkos, who had managed only fourth in the two previous renewals, took full advantage, jumping into the lead at the sixth, clear by three out and ridden out after a mistake at the final fence. Rider Ruby Walsh, clearly unaware of the exact nature of the incident at the fifth, reportedly thought that Cenkos was being pressed by Flagship Uberalles on the run-in, rather than by the riderless Moscow Flyer. Walsh needn't have worried, as Cenkos passed the post fourteen lengths ahead of runner-up Edredon Bleu, with Wahiba Sands fifteen lengths back in third and Flagship Uberalles completing to beat the outsider Get Real. The Tingle Creek confirmed that Cenkos was still a high-class chaser, though the failure of any of his rivals to give their true running—Edredon Bleu and Wahiba Sands performed below their best—cast doubts on the value of the form, and so too did the time, around a second and a half slower than that recorded by Impek in the novice chase earlier on the card.

The best of four subsequent efforts by Cenkos came when he was returned to Sandown in April to attempt a repeat win in the Queen Elizabeth The Queen Mother Celebration Chase. He had defeated a below-par Flagship Uberalles by fourteen lengths the year before but, even with that horse (who missed Sandown because of the ground) and Moscow Flyer running instead in the BMW Chase at Punchestown three days later, Cenkos still had a bit on his plate conceding 4 lb to Seebald. The free-running Cenkos looked for nearly all the race as if he was going to do it, outjumping his rivals in front, striking for home after four out but faltering going to the last. Cenkos was unable to hold off Seebald on the run-in, going down by a length and a quarter. It's unusual for a horse to be sent for home in earnest on

169

the long run from four out rather than into the turn after three out at Sandown, and it's possible that had his jockey made his move a fence later Cenkos would have prevailed. Typically for Cenkos, he was unable to sustain that level of form for the whole season. He was beaten at odds on by stable-companion Kadarann in the Game Spirit Chase at Newbury in February—trainer Paul Nicholls revealing: 'He needed a gallop and he might as well have had one around here'—then was far from discredited when third in the Champion Chase at Cheltenham for the second successive year. Cenkos is generally a fluent jumper, though he makes the occasional bad mistake as he did on his only other outing, when a blunder four out ended what chance he might have had over a trip beyond his best in the Melling Chase at Aintree.

		Nonoalco	Nearctic
Cenkos (FR) (ch.g. 1994)	Nikos (br 1981)	(b 1971)	Seximee
		No No Nanette (ro 1973)	Sovereign Path
			Nuclea
	Vincenza (ch 1979)	Grundy (ch 1972)	Great Nephew
			Word From Lundy
		Lady Vincent (ch 1967)	High Hat
			Almsgiver

The strong, lengthy Cenkos will no doubt be campaigned at the highest level again in 2003/4, and will have to be taken seriously in the best races, though he was exposed in the Champion Chase as being a little removed from a top performer like Moscow Flyer. Cenkos might even have his work cut out just to maintain his position as the leading two-mile chaser in his own stable, with the up-and-coming pair Azertyuiop and Le Roi Miguel (in the same ownership as Cenkos) likely to push him hard for that spot. The pedigree of French-bred Cenkos has been dealt with in previous editions of this Annual—his most notable relative is his dam's half-sister Vincent, a very smart stayer who finished third behind Le Moss and Ardross in the 1980 Gold Cup at Royal Ascot. Best at around two miles, despite having plenty of stamina in his pedigree, Cenkos has yet to race on firm going but acts on any other. *P. F. Nicholls*

CENTAUR EXPRESS 11 b.g. Siberian Express (USA) – Gay Twenties (Lord Gayle (USA)) [2002/3 c–, h83: c20g[pu] c17s[6] Nov 21] small gelding: fairly useful handicap hurdler/chaser at best: retains little ability: left A. Streeter after reappearance: best around 2m: best efforts on soft/heavy going: front runner. *Mrs J. Candlish*   **c–** **h–**

CENTAUR SPIRIT 6 b.g. Distant Relative – Winnie Reckless (Local Suitor (USA)) [2002/3 h67: 17d[pu] Oct 19] angular gelding: modest on Flat (stays 1¼m): poor form over hurdles: lame only start in 2002/3: joined Mrs J. Candlish. *A. Streeter*   **h–**

CENTAX (CZE) 9 ch.g. Lincoln (CZE) – Centaurea (CZE) (Chiavari) [2002/3 c22g* c29g c25s[2] c34v[4] c31d Nov 15] angular gelding: successful 3 times over fences in Czech Republic, including at Pardubice in May: 25/1, tailed off in cross-country event at Cheltenham in November: stays well. *Z. Semenka, Czech Republic*   **c?**

CENTRAL COMMITTEE (IRE) 8 ch.g. Royal Academy (USA) – Idle Chat (USA) (Assert) [2002/3 22g[5] 20m[6] 20m* 21d* 24d[3] 19d[3] 22d* 24g[4] Mar 3] leggy gelding: has had wind operation: fair handicap hurdler: off 2 years prior to reappearance: won at Bangor in September, Sedgefield in October and Fontwell (idled) in February: stays 3m: acts on firm and good to soft going (unproven on softer): blinkered once: formerly tongue tied. *R. T. Phillips*   **h106**

CENTRAL HOUSE 6 b.g. Alflora (IRE) – Fantasy World (Kemal (FR)) [2002/3 h99p, F102: F16s* 16s* 16s* 16v[2] 16s[2] 20d[3] 16m[2] Apr 22] tall gelding: will make a chaser: useful team in bumpers, winning at Punchestown in November: fairly useful hurdler: won maiden at Clonmel later in November and novice at Cork in December: ran well last 3 starts: probably stays 2½m: acts on soft and good to firm going: effective with or without tongue tie: consistent. *D. T. Hughes, Ireland*   **h121** **F106**

CERESFIELD (NZ) 7 br.m. Westminster (NZ) – Audrey Rose (NZ) (Blue Razor (USA)) [2002/3 14f[2] 13v[4] c20f[5] 16v 16d[5] 16m[2] Apr 21] leggy mare: winner twice around 1¼m on Flat: won once from 7 starts over hurdles in New Zealand, easily best effort in Britain when second in amateur handicap at Wetherby: last of 5 on chasing debut: likely to prove best around 2m. *R. C. Guest*   **c–** **h89 +**

CEREUS (USA)   4 ch.g. Gilded Time (USA) – Dayflower (USA) (Majestic Light   h–
(USA)) [2002/3 16s^{pu} 16d^{pu} Feb 28] sturdy gelding: fair on Flat (probably stays 1m), sold
out of B. Hills's stable 6,000 gns Newmarket July Sales: pulled up in 2 juvenile hurdles,
trained by I. Williams on first occasion. *Miss J. S. Davis*

CERILLY (FR)   6 b.g. Sassanian (USA) – Wilhelmine (FR) (Trenel (FR)) [2002/3   c141
c21s c22s* 20s^2 c22s^4 c27v^2 18v^5 19s^3 Mar 23] seventh foal: half-brother to 1½m winner   h141
Philibert (by Iron Duke): dam winning hurdler/chaser around 2m: useful hurdler/chaser:
raced exclusively at Auteuil in 2002/3, winning Prix Rigoletto in July: good placed
efforts subsequently, second over fences in Prix La Haye Jousselin (beaten 5 lengths by
Sunny Flight) in November and Prix des Drags (blinkered, 2½ lengths behind Ty Benjam)
in May and close third to Great Love in slowly-run Group 3 hurdle in March: stays 27f:
raced on going softer than good (acts on heavy). *J. Bertran de Balanda, France*

CERULEAN   5 ch.g. Polar Falcon (USA) – Billie Blue (Ballad Rock) [2002/3 F18g   F–
Apr 29] half-brother to several winners on Flat, notably smart performer up to 7f
Tumbleweed Ridge: dam second over 7f on only start: well held in bumper on debut: no
form on Flat. *Dr J. D. Scargill*

CERULEAN ROSE   4 ch.f. Bluegrass Prince (IRE) – Elegant Rose (Noalto) [2002/3   h–
16d Nov 13] half-sister to modest 2m hurdler Dancing Pearl (by Dancing Spree) and poor
hurdler Bowden Rose (by Sharrood), stays 2½m: well beaten on Flat: tongue tied, tailed
off in juvenile on hurdling debut. *A. W. Carroll*

CESARIA (FR)   6 b.m. Highest Honor (FR) – Cat Storm (CAN) (Storm Cat (USA))   c75
[2002/3 h112: 16s^2 18d^4 c19d^5 25s^{pu} Jan 23] angular mare: fairly useful hurdler: good   h117
second in handicap at Huntingdon on reappearance: disappointing subsequently, only
poor form on chasing debut: best efforts around 2m: acts on heavy going: tried visored.
M. C. Pipe

C'EST DEJA VU (IRE)   7 b.g. Phardante (FR) – Quayside Romance (Quayside)   h71
[2002/3 h81, F87: 27m^4 May 7] sturdy gelding: poor form over hurdles: sold 8,000 gns
Doncaster May Sales, runner-up on completed start in points. *P. F. Nicholls*

CETTI'S WARBLER   5 gr.m. Sir Harry Lewis (USA) – Sedge Warbler (Scallywag)   F–
[2002/3 F16s Dec 7] second foal: dam, modest maiden hurdler/chaser up to 3m,
half-sister to useful staying hurdler Arctic Teal: soundly beaten in bumper on debut.
Mrs P. Robeson

CHABIBI   4 br.f. Mark of Esteem (IRE) – Nunsharpa (Sharpo) [2002/3 16s^{pu} Jan 30]   h–
poor maiden on Flat (seems to stay 10.5f): no show in novice on hurdling debut: sold
3,000 gns Newmarket February Sales. *T. H. Caldwell*

CHABRIMAL MINSTER   6 b.g. Minster Son – Bromley Rose (Rubor) [2002/3   h92
20s^2 Mar 6] seventh known foal: half-brother to fairly useful 2m hurdler Little Bromley
(by Riberetto): dam unraced: second in novice hurdle at Carlisle on debut: likely to stay
beyond 2½m. *R. Ford*

CHADSWELL (IRE)   10 b.g. Lord Americo – Marita Ann (Crozier) [2002/3 c94,   c96
h93: 26s* c28v^{pu} c27s^2 c26v^{pu} 24s c26s^3 Mar 6] sturdy gelding: modest handicap hurdler/   h98
chaser: won over hurdles at Cartmel in June: stays 3½m: acts on heavy going: has worn
cheekpieces: has gone in snatches. *R. Ford*

CHAIN LINE   13 br.g. Relkino – Housemistress (New Member) [2002/3 c–, h–: 16g   c–
16m^F 16g^{pu} 16d^{pu} 19d^{pu} 19d^{pu} Mar 5] big, rangy gelding: winning hurdler, retains little   h–
ability. *J. W. F. Aynsley*

CHALCEDONY   7 ch.g. Highest Honor (FR) – Sweet Holland (USA) (Alydar   c113
(USA)) [2002/3 c89, h–: c20f* c20m^3 c20m^2 c20m^3 c20m* c16m* Oct 29] strong   h–
gelding: winning hurdler: fair novice chaser: won at Fontwell in June and in small fields
at Plumpton and Cheltenham in October: stays 2½m: acts on any going: blinkered once,
wore cheekpieces last 2 outings: reportedly died from nose second start. *R. Rowe*

CHALFORD OAKS   6 ch.g. High Adventure – Soulieana (Manado) [2002/3 19s^{pu} h–
16v^{ro} Jan 29] lengthy, unfurnished gelding: no form over hurdles. *T. R. Greathead*

CHALLENOR   5 ch.g. Casteddu – Expletive (Shiny Tenth) [2002/3 16d 16s 20g^{pu} h–
Mar 2] lengthy gelding: half-brother to winning pointer by Lochnager: modest on Flat
(stays easy 11f): no show in novice hurdles: lame final start. *Ian Williams*

CHAMPAGNE HARRY   5 b.g. Sir Harry Lewis (USA) – Sparkling Cinders (Nether-   h–
kelly) [2002/3 F17s^3 F16d 19g^{ur} Apr 19] workmanlike gelding: half-brother to several   F82
winners, including winning hurdler/chaser Prancing Blade (by Broadsword), stays 3m,
and fairly useful hurdler/winning chaser up to 21f Razer Blade (by Teenoso): dam, poor

staying maiden hurdler/chaser, sister to useful 2½m chaser Fu's Lady: shaped like a stayer in 2 bumpers: unseated second on hurdling debut. *N. A. Twiston-Davies*

CHAMPAGNE LIL 6 gr.m. Terimon – Sparkling Cinders (Netherkelly) [2002/3 h81, F89: 17g⁶ 20s 22d⁴ 21d² 21sᵖᵘ 24g³ Apr 23] leggy mare: bumper winner: modest maiden hurdler: stays 3m: acts on good to soft and good to firm going, possibly unsuited by soft. *N. A. Twiston-Davies* **h85**

CHAMPAGNE NATIVE (IRE) 9 b.g. Be My Native (USA) – The Race Fly (Pollerton) [2002/3 c124, h–: c20sᵖᵘ 20s 20d 24dF c21v⁵ c20s c20d c20m⁴ Apr 12] tall, useful-looking gelding: winning hurdler/fairly useful chaser, largely well below form in 2002/3: should stay beyond 21f: acts on heavy going: tried blinkered/in cheekpieces: inconsistent. *Miss I. T. Oakes, Ireland* **c113 h102**

CHANCE INVESTMENT 6 b.m. Homo Sapien – Edithmead (IRE) (Shardari) [2002/3 h71?, F–: 16m³ 17d Aug 26] angular mare: poor maiden hurdler: sold 500 gns Doncaster September Sales. *R. Ford* **h62**

CHANCERS DANTE (IRE) 7 b.g. Phardante (FR) – Own Acre (Linacre) [2002/3 h82, F95: 23d 26s⁶ 25vᵖᵘ 20d Mar 15] angular gelding: poor maiden hurdler: stays 27f: acts on heavy going (won bumper on good to firm). *Ferdy Murphy* **h75**

CHANCIT 4 b.f. Piccolo – Polly Worth (Wolver Hollow) [2002/3 17g 16dᵖᵘ Dec 4] disappointing maiden in Flat, sold out of A. Reid's stable 2,000 gns Doncaster August Sales: no show either outing over hurdles. *M. E. Sowersby* **h–**

CHANCY CHARLY (IRE) 10 b.g. King's Ride – Lady Siobhan (Laurence O) [2002/3 22dᵖᵘ 24dᵖᵘ c24sᵖᵘ Jun 13] strong gelding: fair chaser in 1999/00: no sign of retaining ability: stays 3m: acts on soft and good to firm going. *S. Gollings* **c– h–**

CHANGE OF IMAGE 5 b.m. Spectrum (IRE) – Reveuse du Soir (Vision (USA)) [2002/3 19g Nov 23] modest 9.7f winner on Flat, well below form since leaving H. Cecil: showed nothing on hurdling debut. *J. R. Weymes* **h–**

CHAN MOVE 11 b.g. Move Off – Kanisa (Chantro) [2002/3 h–: 20s⁵ Dec 16] leggy gelding: maiden hurdler: no form for long time: tried blinkered/in cheekpieces. *W. J. Smith* **h–**

CHANNAHRLIE (IRE) 9 gr.g. Celio Rufo – Derravarragh Lady (IRE) (Radical) [2002/3 c81, h82: c25g 24g² c24f² c26m² c23m² c23g² c24s² c24m* c24gᵖᵘ c31gᵖᵘ Apr 24] tall, angular gelding: modest handicap hurdler/chaser: won over fences at Southwell in March: probably best at 3m+: acts on soft and firm going: usually wears cheeekpieces. *R. Dickin* **c86 h94**

CHANOUD 7 b.g. Ezzoud (IRE) – Chandni (IRE) (Ahonoora) [2002/3 h124: 17d⁶ 18d⁵ 17g² 16s Oct 11] useful-looking gelding: fairly useful handicap hurdler: best effort in 2002/3 when short-head second to Bob What in listed event at Tralee in August: best around 2m: acts on soft and firm going. *M. Halford, Ireland* **h123**

CHANTESSA SIOUX 5 b.m. Paley Prince (USA) – Legendary Lady (Reprimand) [2002/3 16gᵖᵘ May 17] half-sister to fair hurdler Saspys Lad (by Faustus), stays 19f: no form on Flat: showed nothing on hurdling debut. *W. G. M. Turner* **h–**

CHANTICLIER 6 b.g. Roselier (FR) – Cherry Crest (Pollerton) [2002/3 F109p: 21d⁶ 24d⁵ Dec 14] well-made gelding: second of 19 in bumper at Sandown on debut in 2001/2: much better effort in novice hurdles at Cheltenham when sixth to Taming: not fluent in Grade 2 month later. *K. C. Bailey* **h105**

CHANTILLY LADY 10 ch.m. Rising – Ladiz (Persian Bold) [2002/3 16dᵖᵘ 22d Dec 5] tall mare: lightly raced over hurdles, no show in 2002/3. *M. J. Weeden* **h–**

CHAOS THEORY 8 b.g. Jupiter Island – Indian Orchid (Warpath) [2002/3 c102x, h113: 16s⁶ 16d⁶ 16g 20g Mar 23] rangy gelding: winning chaser but generally let down by jumping: handicap hurdler: failed to impress with attitude in 2002/3, showing modest form: should stay beyond 2½m: acts on heavy going (bumper form on good to firm): blinkered first 3 starts: one to treat with caution. *Mrs M. Reveley* **c– x h98 §**

CHAPARRO AMARGOSO (IRE) 10 b.g. Ela-Mana-Mou – Champanera (Top Ville) [2002/3 c89, h74: c16m* c16g² c16g³ c16d³ c21g⁴ Aug 9] has stringhalt: maiden hurdler: fair handicap chaser: won at Wetherby in May: seems ideally suited by 2m: acts on firm and good to soft ground: visored twice: has had tongue tied: sketchy jumper of fences: seemed not to go through with effort third start. *B. Ellison* **c103 h–**

CHAPEL ROYALE (IRE) 6 gr.g. College Chapel – Merci Royale (Fairy King (USA)) [2002/3 16s 16d 16d Mar 5] leggy gelding: second foal: dam ran once in Irish **h79**

bumper: fair on Flat (stays easy 9f) for D. Nicholls: poor form in novice hurdles. *Jedd O'Keeffe*

CHAPELTOWN (IRE)   11 b.g. Denel (FR) – Lady Dunsford (Torus) [2002/3 h136: 16m^{ur} Mar 22] well-made gelding: useful handicap hurdler: clipped heels and unseated home turn on belated reappearance, beginning to struggle at time: stays 19f: acts on soft and good to firm going. *N. J. Henderson*   **h–**

CHARALAMBOUS (USA)   6 b.g. Hermitage (USA) – Hula Lei (USA) (State Dinner (USA)) [2002/3 16s^4 16g^6 Sep 14] sturdy gelding: poor maiden hurdler: off 18 months, not discredited at Worcester both starts on return: raced around 2m on good going or softer (acts on heavy): joined C. Down. *C. L. Popham*   **h78**

CHARGE CARD   5 b.h. Zafonic (USA) – Prophecy (IRE) (Warning) [2002/3 F17m Jun 1] third foal: brother to useful sprinters Threat and Arabesque: dam, Cheveley Park winner who stayed 1m, out of Lancashire Oaks winner Andaleeb: sold unraced out of H. Cecil's stable only 3,500 gns Newmarket Autumn (2001) Sales: no show in maiden bumper and 2 races on Flat. *Miss M. E. Rowland*   **F–**

CHARLATAN (IRE)   5 b.g. Charnwood Forest (IRE) – Taajreh (IRE) (Mtoto) [2002/3 16d 16s 20g Feb 22] little form on Flat for Mrs C. Dunnett: soundly beaten over hurdles. *M. J. Gingell*   **h–**

CHARLES SPENCELAYH (IRE)   7 b.g. Tenby – Legit (IRE) (Runnett) [2002/3 h79: 20g^{pu} 16v^5 Nov 27] rather sparely-made gelding: fair on Flat (stays 17f), won in June: poor form over hurdles, left M. Pipe after reappearance: tried visored. *J. G. M. O'Shea*   **h–**

CHARLIEADAMS (IRE)   13 b.g. Carlingford Castle – Lucy Platter (FR) (Record Token) [2002/3 c98x: c21g^2 c16d^F c20m^{ur} c21m* c21g* c20g* c24g^2 c25g^2 c21d^2 c27d^6 Mar 18] workmanlike gelding: fair chaser: joined L. Lungo fourth to eighth starts and won handicaps at Sedgefield (2) and Perth in summer: nowhere near that form completed outings in hunters: effective at 2½m to 3¼m: acts on good to firm and heavy going: largely fluent for A. Dobbin fourth to eighth outings, sketchy jumper otherwise. *J. F. W. Muir*   **c108 x**

CHARLIE BUBBLES (IRE)   6 b.g. Un Desperado (FR) – Bounty (IRE) (Cataldi) [2002/3 F17g Jun 10] IR £7,000 4-y-o: first foal: dam unraced: 10/1 from 25/1, well held in bumper on debut. *B. De Haan*   **F–**

CHARLIE CHANG (IRE)   10 b.g. Don't Forget Me – East River (FR) (Arctic Tern (USA)) [2002/3 c83?, h–: c25d^F May 6] close-coupled gelding: winning hurdler/chaser: fell second over fences in May, not seen out again: stays 3m: seems best on soft/heavy going: often blinkered. *A. G. Juckes*   **c–**
h–

CHARLIE HAWES (IRE)   14 b.g. Euphemism – Eyecap (King's Ride) [2002/3 c24s^{pu} c22m^{ur} Mar 21] sturdy gelding: winning pointer: little worthwhile form over hurdles/in steeplechases: tried visored/blinkered. *Miss Gillian A. Russell*   **c–**
h–

CHARLIE KENNET   5 b.g. Pyramus (USA) – Evaporate (Insan (USA)) [2002/3 F16m^2 F17m^2 F16f^4 F16d^4 16d 20d Dec 14] plain gelding: first foal: dam 11.8f winner: fair form all 4 starts in bumpers: bit disappointing both runs in novice hurdles, failing to improve as expected for longer trip on second occasion. *D. G. Bridgwater*   **h83**
F89

CHARLIEMOORE   7 ch.g. Karinga Bay – Your Care (FR) (Caerwent) [2002/3 F82: F18g 16d 19g 21m Feb 22] strong, lengthy gelding: bumper winner: modest form over hurdles, looking none too keen final start. *G. L. Moore*   **h86**
F82

CHARLIE PICKLE (USA)   5 b.g. Ghazi (USA) – Dancing Vaguely (USA) (Vaguely Noble) [2002/3 F16m^2 F16d^2 F16d^4 19d^4 Jan 13] 4,000 4-y-o: smallish, sturdy gelding: brother to winning sprinter in USA and half-brother to fairly useful hurdler/temperamental winning chaser Reve de Valse (by Conquistador Cielo), effective at 2m to 27f, and winning 2m hurdler Daphnis (by Lead On Time): dam listed 1½m winner in France: fair form when second in bumpers: some encouragement when fourth in novice at Doncaster on hurdling debut: may prove best around 2m. *C. C. Bealby*   **h95**
F94

CHARLIES FUTURE   5 b.g. Democratic (USA) – Faustelerie (Faustus (USA)) [2002/3 h94: 24s 22s^6 19d^4 22v 19s^2 19v* 20g^5 Apr 2] tall gelding: fair handicap hurdler: won at Taunton in March by 8 lengths from Compton Amica: good fifth to Rosco in 20-runner event at Ascot 3 weeks later: stays 2¾m: acts on heavy ground. *S. C. Burrough*   **h107**

CHARLIE SIDDLE   9 b.g. Thowra (FR) – Figrant (USA) (L'Emigrant (USA)) [2002/3 c63, h61: c17g c21f^{pu} May 10] poor maiden hurdler/chaser: no show either   **c–**
h–

outing over fences very early in 2002/3: stays 2½m: acts on soft and good to firm going: tried blinkered/visored: sketchy jumper of fences. *Miss K. M. George*

CHARLIESMEDARLIN 12 b.g. Macmillan – Top Cover (High Top) [2002/3 c24g^{ur} Apr 19] workmanlike gelding: much improved chaser in early-2000/1: held when unseating 4 out in handicap at Stratford on return: stays 23f: acts on firm going: visored once: has had tongue tied. *Mrs Barbara Waring* c– h–

CHARLIE STRONG (IRE) 10 b.g. Strong Gale – The Village Vixen (Buckskin (FR)) [2002/3 c102: c21f* c28m^{pu} Jun 1] fairly useful hunter chaser: won at Wincanton in May: failed to get beyond halfway in valuable event at Stratford next time: should stay beyond 23f: acts on firm and soft going. *R. Kelvin-Hughes* c99

CHARLIE TAYLOR (IRE) 7 ch.g. Insan (USA) – Gusserane Lark (Napoleon Bonaparte) [2002/3 h–: 16s 16v Nov 28] big, lengthy, angular gelding: little sign of ability: sold 500 gns Doncaster January Sales. *C. N. Kellett* h–

CHARMING ADMIRAL (IRE) 10 b.g. Shareef Dancer (USA) – Lilac Charm (Bustino) [2002/3 c–, h–: 17s^5 c25d* c27v^{pu} c26s^6 c20v* Mar 13] sturdy gelding: winning hurdler: modest handicap chaser: won at Catterick (subsequently tested positive for morphine) in December and Hexham in March: stays 25f: raced mainly on going softer than good (acts on heavy): usually races prominently: moody and one to treat with some caution. *Mrs A. Duffield* c93 § h80 §

CHARMING JACK 6 b.g. Charmer – No Fizz (Broadsword (USA)) [2002/3 F17d 16d^F 21s^{pu} Feb 24] first foal: dam fairly useful hunter chaser: no sign of ability, including in point: tongue tied final start. *D. M. Grissell* h– F–

CHARM OFFENSIVE 5 b.m. Zieten (USA) – Shoag (USA) (Affirmed (USA)) [2002/3 17v^5 17s 19d Feb 23] half-sister to winning hurdler Zaaheyah (by Irish River), stayed easy 3m: modest on Flat (stays 2m), sold out of S. R. Bowring's stable 5,200 gns Doncaster August Sales: best effort over hurdles when fifth in novice at Taunton. *C. J. Gray* h72

CHARMOUTH FOREST 7 ch.g. Lir – Crimson Lady (Crimson Beau) [2002/3 h76, F65: 19d^5 19s^5 17d^5 22g^6 22g^4 Apr 19] poor maiden hurdler: barely stays 2¾m: raced on good going or softer (acts on soft). *C. J. Gray* h75

CHARNWOOD STREET (IRE) 4 b.g. Charnwood Forest (IRE) – La Vigie (King of Clubs) [2002/3 16d 16d 17g^5 Mar 15] modest on Flat (stays 2m): poor form in 3 juvenile hurdles. *D. Shaw* h71

CHARTER RIDGE (IRE) 10 b.g. Glacial Storm (USA) – Pure Spec (Fine Blade (USA)) [2002/3 c–, h–: c24d^{pu} Nov 2] tall gelding: useful chaser at best: stayed 25f: possibly unsuited by soft/heavy going, acted on any other: often raced up with pace: dead. *Jonjo O'Neill* c– h–

CHARTER ROYAL (FR) 8 gr.g. Royal Charter (FR) – Tadjmine (FR) (Tadj (FR)) [2002/3 c74§, h–: c20d^{pu} 20d^6 c16s^3 c21s^{pu} 20g c24g 20s^{pu} Feb 24] compact gelding: maiden hurdler: poor handicap chaser: effective at 2m to 3m: acts on good to firm and heavy going: tried blinkered: unreliable. *A. R. Dicken* c66 § h– §

CHASE THE SUNSET (IRE) 5 ch.g. Un Desperado (FR) – Cherry Chase (IRE) (Red Sunset) [2002/3 F17d 17s^4 Nov 28] useful-looking gelding: first foal: dam, bumper winner, half-sister to useful staying hurdler Turnpole: mid-field in bumper on debut: promising fourth in maiden hurdle at Taunton following month, still looking green and not at all knocked about once held: likely to improve. *Miss H. C. Knight* h83 p F–

CHASING THE WIND 8 b.m. Henbit (USA) – Deep In The Arctic (Deep Run) [2002/3 16d^{pu} 21m Sep 13] second foal: dam temperamental winning pointer: no sign of ability, even in points. *Mrs L. Wadham* h–

CHATEAU BURF 7 ch.g. Cruise Missile – Headstrong Miss (Le Bavard (FR)) [2002/3 F17d F17g Jun 12] third foal: dam Irish bumper winner: well held in 2 bumpers. *D. G. Bridgwater* F–

CHATEAU ROSE (IRE) 7 b.g. Roselier (FR) – Claycastle (IRE) (Carlingford Castle) [2002/3 h103+: 22d^4 26v^3 c23s^4 c26v^3 c24s^3 c22m^{ur} Mar 21] compact gelding: fair maiden hurdler: similar form over fences, winning maiden at Leicester in January: likely to prove best at 3m+: raced mainly on going softer than good (acts on heavy). *N. A. Gaselee* c110 h94

CHATER FLAIR 6 b.g. Efisio – Native Flair (Be My Native (USA)) [2002/3 h87: 24m^{ur} 22m^2 20d Dec 14] modest on Flat (should stay beyond 2m): similar form when h93 runner-up twice from 4 starts over hurdles: sold out of C. Mann's stable 7,000 gns Doncaster September Sales prior to final start: should prove best at 2½m+. *D. Burchell*

CHATERGOLD (IRE) 11 b.g. Posen (USA) – Fiodoir (Weavers' Hall) [2002/3 c92§, h–§: 22d c20d^{pu} 20g^3 20d 22d^4 24g^4 Aug 24] sturdy, workmanlike gelding: winning chaser/maiden hurdler, poor form in 2002/3: stays 3¼m: acts on any going: tried blinkered/visored: usually takes little interest. *P. Wegmann*

c– §
h72 §

CHAUVINIST (IRE) 8 b.g. Roselier (FR) – Sacajawea (Tanfirion) [2002/3 h109: 16d* 16v* 21d^3 16g 16g^3 Mar 11]

h139

It seems unlikely that Ladbrokes will have cause to regret their decision to end their sponsorship of one very valuable two-mile handicap hurdle at Leopardstown, and institute another at Ascot's December fixture. The new contest already looks as though it could, given time, establish itself just as firmly in the racing calendar. Sixteen contested the first edition of the listed Ladbroke Hurdle in 2001, won by subsequent Champion Hurdle runner-up Marble Arch; and the second attracted a useful field of twenty, of which four were from Ireland. That in itself bodes well for the race's future. British trainers have hardly been falling over themselves to send their horses for the Leopardstown race in recent years, and just three took part in the most recent renewal, which was still the best tally since 1999. Admittedly, three of those Irish challengers for the latest Ladbroke were from the Willie Mullins' yard, including the favourite Holy Orders; and with Martin Pipe responsible for four of the entries and Nicky Henderson for three, just three trainers were responsible for half of the runners. Henderson himself had the second favourite Chauvinist, one of the oldest in the field yet paradoxically the one with the least racing experience.

Marked down by many as one to follow when sent over hurdles after making an impressive winning debut in a bumper at Kempton in February, 2001, Chauvinist failed to justify favouritism in three runs over timber the following season, but he put that matter right with the minimum of fuss again favourite in a maiden at Newbury in November on his return. The Ladbroke Hurdle, in which Chauvinist was the only one of the four carrying bottom weight of 10-0 to race off his proper mark, provided a far sterner test, although Chauvinist's performance in

Ladbroke Hurdle (Handicap), Ascot—Chauvinist emerges from the fog well clear at the last

Mrs E. Roberts & Nick Roberts' "Chauvinist"

winning what beforehand had looked a very competitive handicap didn't make it appear so. With so many unable to cope with a well-run race in very testing ground, only five were still properly in contention turning for home, Chauvinist the last of the quintet and pushed along. He could hardly be named the winner at this stage but the picture changed markedly shortly after. Responding very well to pressure and taking a narrow advantage two out, Chauvinist was left clear when Whistling Dixie, who was still travelling strongly, fell at this flight. Chauvinist pulled further away as he continued to run on strongly kept up to his work and at the line had fifteen lengths to spare over his nearest pursuer Idaho d'Ox, outsider of the Pipe quartet. Chauvinist was ridden by Norman Williamson as stable-jockey Mick Fitzgerald was unable to do the weight, though as things turned out it would have taken more than a few pounds overweight to have stopped Chauvinist from winning. Chauvinist had three more runs and ran up to his Ascot form only in the last of them, the Supreme Novices' Hurdle at Cheltenham; and that despite the far less-testing conditions not showing him to best advantage. Flat out at the fourth, Chauvinist was outpaced down the hill but stayed on well in the straight to take third behind Back In Front and Kicking King, beaten fourteen lengths by the winner.

		Misti IV	Medium
	Roselier (FR)	(br 1958)	Mist
	(b 1973)	Peace Rose	Fastnet Rock
Chauvinist (IRE)		(gr 1959)	La Paix
(b.g. 1995)		Tanfirion	Habitat
	Sacajawea	(b 1974)	Tingitana
	(b 1986)	Sun Spray	Nice Guy
		(ch 1969)	Sunbow

Both the Ladbroke Handicap and the Supreme Novices' are run over two miles, but Chauvinist has had four outings at distances ranging from two and a half miles to two and three quarter miles, including one in the latest season. That was in a twenty-one-furlong novice event at Kempton in which he finished third behind the smart pair Lord Sam and Sh Boom (who received 4 lb from the other two), proving one paced from two out. By Roselier out of an unraced half-sister to the smart hurdler and useful chaser at up to three miles Forest Sun, and from the family of Mr Mulligan, Chauvinist has a pedigree which suggests that he should prove at least as effective at around two and a half miles as he is at two. Sacajawea's other winning half-brothers included the useful hurdler/chaser Young Lover and the fairly useful chaser Bright Intervals who both stayed two and a half miles. There are few clues to be gained from Sacajawea's other produce, as apart from Chauvinist, her fourth foal, the only one to have shown any form is Summer In The Sun (by Shardari) who won a maiden point in April as a nine-year-old. Chauvinist, who has raced only on good going or softer and acts well on heavy, could well be tried over fences in the next season. He is not obviously a chaser on looks, being on the small side and lacking in substance, but is in very good hands and won't necessarily be held back by his physique. *N. J. Henderson*

CHELSEA BRIDGE (IRE) 5 b.g. Over The River (FR) – Anguillita (IRE) (King of Clubs) [2002/3 F16m* Feb 22] tall, good sort: third foal: dam, maiden, out of half-sister to useful hurdlers Seldom Dry and Native Friend: created good impression when winning bumper at Kempton on debut by neck from Trabolgan: will stay 2½m: good jumping prospect. *Miss H. C. Knight* **F105 p**

CHEM'S TRUCE (IRE) 6 b.g. Brief Truce (USA) – In The Rigging (USA) (Topsider (USA)) [2002/3 h91: 16m* 17s² 16g² 16d⁶ Nov 16] leggy, close-coupled gelding: useful on Flat (stays 1½m): fair hurdler: won conditional jockeys handicap at Haydock in October: at least creditable efforts subsequently: likely to prove best around 2m: acts on soft and good to firm going. *Miss Venetia Williams* **h104**

The Earl Cadogan's "Chelsea Bridge"

CHEQUERED FLAG 8 ch.m. Deploy – Monza (Hotfoot) [2002/3 h96: c17m^F Jun 22] modest hurdler: off 8½ months, would have shown similar form but for falling last (held in fourth at time) in novice chase at Market Rasen, only outing in 2002/3: stays 2½m: acts on good to firm and good to soft going: whipped round start on hurdling debut: may need exaggerated waiting tactics. *P. R. Webber* **c96**
h–

CHERCHER L'AMOUR (FR) 4 b.f. Charnwood Forest (IRE) – Recherchee (Rainbow Quest (USA)) [2002/3 16g^5 16d 16d 17d Mar 18] ex-French filly: half-sister to modest 2m hurdler Celtic Star (by Celtic Swing): well beaten in 4 starts on Flat for Mme C. Head-Maarek: little form over hurdles: sold 4,200 gns Doncaster May Sales. *Mrs M. Reveley* **h–**

CHERGAN (IRE) 10 b.g. Yashgan – Cherry Bright (IRE) (Miner's Lamp) [2002/3 c106, h–: c16g^5 c16g* c20m* c16d^5 c24m^2 c24g^3 c20d^6 c20g c16f^2 c21d c16g^2 Apr 24] lengthy gelding: fairly useful handicap chaser: won at Perth in September and Wetherby in October: effective at 2m, barely stays 25f: acts on any going: has won/been placed all 13 completed outings at Musselburgh: very sound jumper. *Mrs S. C. Bradburne* **c115**
h–

CHERMESINA (IRE) 9 ch.m. Be My Native (USA) – Annabrook Lass (Laurence O) [2002/3 h116, F91: 16s^2 20s^5 16g^6 20d 22d 16m 22v 20v 20s Jan 11] fair handicap hurdler: regressed after reappearance: stays 2½m: probably acts on any going, though seems ideally suited by softer than good. *Timothy Doyle, Ireland* **h114 d**

CHEROKEE BOY 11 gr.g. Mirror Boy – Cherry Side (General Ironside) [2002/3 c115§: c25f^pu c32m^pu Jun 30] workmanlike gelding: handicap chaser, dropped himself out both starts in 2002/3: subsequently in frame several times in points: stays 4m: has form on soft going, best efforts on good or firmer: blinkered once (looked ungenuine): usually races prominently: sound jumper: unreliable. *B. J. M. Ryall* **c– §**

CHERRY BRANDY 7 ch.g. Elmaamul (USA) – Brand (Shareef Dancer (USA)) [2002/3 19g^pu 21d^6 Jan 18] lengthy, useful-looking gelding: bumper winner in early-2000/1: modest form on second of 2 starts in novice hurdles on return. *Miss H. C. Knight* **h87**

CHERRY GOLD 9 b.g. Rakaposhi King – Merry Cherry (Deep Run) [2002/3 c24m* Apr 22] fairly useful pointer, successful in March: made most to win hunter at Chepstow following month despite trying to run out stable bend: stays 3m: acts on good to firm ground. *Evan Williams* **c108**

CHERRY HUNTER (IRE) 7 b.g. Treasure Hunter – Clever Cherry (Decent Fellow) [2002/3 h113p, F97: 20g* 20v^3 20s Mar 16] tall gelding: fair hurdler: won novice at Gowran in May: will stay beyond 2½m: acts on heavy going. *J. T. R. Dreaper, Ireland* **h111**

CHERRY TART (IRE) 9 b.m. Persian Mews – Cherry Avenue (King's Ride) [2002/3 c99, h92: 16g^2 20m^6 c20d* 21g^3 Oct 15] rather sparely-made mare: modest handicap hurdler/chaser: won over fences at Perth in June: best form up to 2½m: acts on any going: tried blinkered: usually makes running. *R. Ford* **c99**
h92

CHESNUT WOOD 9 ch.g. Tigerwood – Sally Haven (Haven) [2002/3 c24m^F Apr 22] modest pointer: in rear when falling fourth in hunter on steeplechase debut. *Miss Beth Roberts* **c–**

CHESTER PARK 5 ch.g. King's Signet (USA) – Good Skills (Bustino) [2002/3 F17g Apr 19] fourth foal: half-brother to fair hurdler Quabmatic (by Pragmatic), stays 2½m: dam bad maiden hurdler: always behind in maiden bumper on debut. *K. Bishop* **F–**

CHEVALIER BAYARD 10 br.g. Strong Gale – Flying Pegus (Beau Chapeau) [2002/3 c77, h–: c22m^2 c24m^4 c21g* c20m^2 c20m c20s^3 c20g** c20g^3 c19m^4 c20g^6 Mar 28] rangy gelding: poor handicap chaser: won at Southwell in September and Mussel-burgh in January, idling both times: best around 2½m: acts on soft and good to firm going: blinkered/visored after second start. *J. R. Adam* **c83**
h–

CHEVALIER ERRANT (IRE) 10 b. or br.g. Strong Gale – Luminous Run (Deep Run) [2002/3 c121, h–: c21m* c20m^ur c24f c24f^5 c20d^F c20d^6 c24d c24g^5 Feb 27] tall, good sort: fairly useful handicap chaser: won at Stratford in June: below form subsequently: stays 21f: acts on good to firm and heavy going, possibly unsuited by firm. *J. R. Adam* **c125 d**
h–

CHEVET BOY (IRE) 5 b.g. Welsh Term – Sizzle (High Line) [2002/3 20g^F Mar 17] €21,000 4-y-o: tall, angular gelding: half-brother to several winners, including useful hurdler/winning chaser up to 2½m Hot Stuff (by Satco): dam, once-raced hurdler, half-sister to smart staying chaser Brown Windsor: well behind when falling 3 out in maiden hurdle on debut. *J. Howard Johnson* **h–**

CHEVET GIRL (IRE) 8 ch.m. Roselier (FR) – Vulcash (IRE) (Callernish) [2002/3 **c97 p**
h95: 16g* 16dᵖᵘ c16gᶠ 16g 16g 17g³ Apr 21] plain mare: held in third when falling 2 out **h106**
in novice on chasing debut (should do better): fair handicap hurdler: improved form when
winning intermediate at Wetherby in November: best form around 2m: acts on good to
firm and good to soft going: free-going front runner. *J. Howard Johnson*

CHEYENNE CHIEF 4 b.g. Be My Chief (USA) – Cartuccia (IRE) (Doyoun) **h96**
[2002/3 17g⁵ 17m² 17d⁴ 20gᶠ 16d* 16d⁴ 16s⁴ 24g 25gᵖᵘ Mar 17] leggy gelding: modest
maiden on Flat (stays 1¾m): fair juvenile hurdler: made virtually all at Newcastle in
November: should prove suited by 2½m+: acts on good to soft going, probably on good
to firm: blinkered fourth start, wore cheekpieces last 3. *G. M. Moore*

CHICAGO BULLS (IRE) 5 b.g. Darshaan – Celestial Melody (USA) (The Minstrel **h119**
(CAN)) [2002/3 h118: 20s² 22v³ 20s² 20s⁴ 22v 21g Mar 12] good-topped gelding: fairly
useful hurdler: good efforts in handicaps first 4 starts (sweating first occasion): will be
suited by 3m+: acts on heavy going. *A. King*

CHICUELO (FR) 7 b.g. Mansonnien (FR) – Dovapas (FR) (Paseo (FR)) [2002/3 **c136**
c114, h–: c20d* c20dᵖᵘ c19v* c24d* c24mᵖᵘ 21g c25f* Mar 27] **h–**
The rise in popularity of summer jumping continued apace in 2002/3:
trainers, responding to increased prize money and generally better ground than is
usually found in late-summer and early-autumn, kept more and better horses on the
go into June and July. Champion trainer Martin Pipe is at the forefront of those
targeting the best races and he landed three of the most valuable, the Summer
National at Uttoxeter with Stormez, the Summer Hurdle at Market Rasen with
Puntal and the Tote Scoop6 Summer Plate at the latter venue with Chicuelo. It's
some measure of the advance in prize-money on offer for summer jumping that the
Plate has gone from less than £14,000 to the winner in 1998 to £37,700 in the latest
season, when it was the equal-fifth most valuable chase in Britain from the start of
the season to Christmas Day. Only the Hennessy, the Thomas Pink, the Tripleprint
and the Tingle Creek were worth more, while the Becher was worth the same. The
realisation that jumping, as well as Flat racing, is now a year-round sport hasn't

Tote Scoop6 Summer Plate (Handicap Chase), Market Rasen—Chicuelo lands a gamble on his
first start for Martin Pipe, chased home by Star Jack in the biggest race of the summer in Britain

been reflected so far in the racing media and Chicuelo's success didn't receive the coverage it deserved.

Chicuelo was having his first start for Pipe's yard when landing a huge gamble in good style at Market Rasen. He had been a useful hurdler/maiden chaser when trained in France by Marcel Rolland in 2000/1, finishing third to Douze Douze and Sleeping Night in the top chase for four-year-olds, but had lost his way when trained by Ian Williams in his first season in Britain, his jumping letting him down somewhat over British-style fences. Chicuelo jumped rather better at Market Rasen and could be named the winner a long way out, eventually beating Star Jack with something in hand by five lengths. The rest of Chicuelo's season was something of an anticlimax, though he showed form on a par with his best French form and won three of his five subsequent chases. However, they were uncompetitive affairs, a five-runner handicap at Ascot in December and a couple of four-runner novice chases for which he started odds on, at Huntingdon in January and Exeter in March. Chicuelo's performances in two runs in competitive handicap chases were littered with mistakes and he was pulled up in both the Thomas Pink at Cheltenham (for which he started 2/1 favourite, despite a rise of 16 lb for his Market Rasen win) and the Racing Post Chase at Kempton. He also cut little ice when a 33/1-chance for the Coral Cup at the Cheltenham Festival on his first start over hurdles in Britain. Chicuelo might well be more difficult to place in 2003/4, uncompetitive handicap chases which place least pressure on his jumping likely to prove his connections' best options. Chicuelo stays an easy twenty-five furlongs and, though he has won on firm going, his best efforts have been on softer than good. He is visored nowadays. A compact gelding, Chicuelo comes from a fairly undistinguished family. He is the best of six winners out of his dam Dovapas, who won over jumps and at up to nearly two miles on the Flat. Chicuelo's maternal grandam Dovannah won at up to a mile on the Flat and bred a couple of fair hurdlers. *M. C. Pipe*

CHIEF CASHIER 8 b.g. Persian Bold – Kentfield (Busted) [2002/3 16d³ 16d² 16s⁶ 16s⁴ 16s* 16d* 17s 16m⁵ 16d 16m* 17m⁴ Apr 16] smallish, good-topped gelding: fairly useful hurdler: much improved in 2002/3, winning handicaps at Ludlow (amateur novice) and Wincanton in January and at Ludlow again in April: raced around 2m: acts on soft and good to firm going. *G. B. Balding*   **h119**

CHIEF CHIPPIE 10 b.g. Mandalus – Little Katrina (Little Buskins) [2002/3 c–, h68: c23d⁶ c25mᵖᵘ c25m⁶ Jun 21] plain gelding: poor handicap hurdler: little form in steeplechases (placed in 2 points in March): effective at 19f to 3m: acts on heavy going, looked ill at ease on firm: sometimes blinkered, though not for win. *P. Needham*   **c–** **h–**

CHIEF MONTE (IRE) 8 b.g. Montelimar (USA) – Giollaretta (Giolla Mear) [2002/3 h–: 19m⁴ 25m⁶ c16s⁵ c16gᵖᵘ Nov 23] tall gelding: little sign of ability: has hinted at temperament. *Mrs S. J. Smith*   **c–** **h–**

CHIEF MOUSE 10 b.g. Be My Chief (USA) – Top Mouse (High Top) [2002/3 c–, h–: c20d c20m³ c24m⁵ c24m 21m⁶ c26m³ Sep 13] workmanlike gelding: winning hurdler: modest handicap chaser: little form since 2000/1: stays 3m: acts on firm and good to soft going (poor efforts on soft): tried blinkered/tongue tied: moody sort. *B. D. Leavy*   **c94 d** **h–**

CHIEFTAIN'S CROWN (USA) 12 ch.g. Chief's Crown (USA) – Simple Taste (USA) (Sharpen Up) [2002/3 h–: 20m⁵ 21m May 11] leggy gelding: winning hurdler: no worthwhile form since 1997/8, including in points: stays 2½m: acts on any ground: tried blinkered. *Mrs H. M. Bridges*   **h–**

CHIEF WITNESS (IRE) 7 b.g. Witness Box (USA) – Rosies Sister (IRE) (Deep Run) [2002/3 23v* 22d* 25g* Mar 14] IR 13,500 4-y-o: second foal: dam, lightly raced in bumpers, half-sister to fairly useful hurdler/chaser up to 2½m Bruton Street: won once from 5 starts in Irish points in 2002 (refused once): created good impression when winning all 3 starts over hurdles, amateur maiden at Fakenham in January, novice at Fontwell (comfortably beat Wintertide 4 lengths) in February and novice at Warwick (left with simple task) in March: likely to prove suited by 3m+: remains open to improvement. *Noel T. Chance*   **h116 p**

CHILI PEPPER 6 b.m. Chilibang – Game Germaine (Mummy's Game) [2002/3 16vᵖᵘ 17v 16dᵖᵘ 16dᵖᵘ Feb 25] small mare: poor on Flat (stays 1m) nowadays: no show over hurdles: most unlikely to stay 2m. *P. R. Wood*   **h–**

CHILLI JO 11 b.g. Latest Model – Arctic Caper (Pardigras) [2002/3 c–: c23f^{pu} c16s^{pu} **c–**
c16g^6 c21g c16m^R Jul 28] leggy gelding: no form outside points: has had tongue tied.
D. D. Scott

CHINESE CRACKER 5 b.g. King's Signet (USA) – Heart Broken (Bustino) **h–**
[2002/3 16s^{pu} Dec 16] always behind in 1¼m maiden at 3 yrs for N. Tinkler: no show in
novice on hurdling debut. *J. R. Norton*

CHIVES (IRE) 8 b.g. Good Thyne (USA) – Chatty Actress (Le Bavard (FR)) **c166**
[2002/3 c148, h–: c24d^2 c29v^2 c24g^2 c26g c36d^{pu} Apr 5] **h–**
    Chives has always looked the part but a big-race victory still eludes him.
The improvement he showed when third in the Royal & SunAlliance Chase at the
2002 Cheltenham Festival continued well into the latest season, but he failed to get
his head in front in five starts. Five wins from fifteen career starts is a more than
respectable haul but Chives has never won a first prize of more than £5,155. His
best performance was a victory of strictly the moral variety, a cracking run in the
Gold Cup that yielded no prize money at all. Hopes and best-laid plans for the
Grand National, the main target for Chives in the latest season, have a habit of
melting into thin air and he proved a sorry disappointment, his effort over almost
before it started. Neither was this the mere indignity of most early casualties in
the Grand National, a first-fence fall, as Chives ended the day among the walking
wounded, jumping with increasing hesitancy until he was pulled up after the
eleventh, the reason readily apparent as he was bleeding from the nose, from both
nostrils. Two of owner Trevor Hemmings' other National contenders have suffered
far more cruel fates in the last two runnings, of course, and hopefully Chives can
resume his career none the worse in 2003/4.
    Chives has bled before, on his reappearance in 2001/2. On that occasion,
though, he completed the race, despite one bad mistake, and was staying on at the
finish, and his absence from the racecourse lasted all of five weeks. Jumping errors
were more of a problem in that novice season but he was much more assured by his
final start, which brought that third place—at 33/1—in the Royal & SunAlliance
Chase. Soon finding his stride in the latest season, Chives was runner-up in the
Edward Hanmer Memorial at Haydock, the Welsh Grand National at Chepstow and
the AON Chase at Newbury. On heavy going at Chepstow, he carried top weight
but duly improved for the stiffer test of stamina, given a shrewd ride by Richard
Guest, who bided his time in the straight as the leaders went for home too soon, but
somewhat unlucky to encounter a very well-handicapped Mini Sensation who did
the same and was enjoying one of his good days. Back over three miles on good
ground at Newbury in February, Chives was ridden more prominently but could not
keep tabs on Valley Henry.
    One measure of Chives's improvement was that he was now being talked of
in connection with the Gold Cup as well as the National. Chives received 6 lb from
Valley Henry at Newbury and his owner's Aintree ambitions were well known, as
was the fact that trainer Henrietta Knight had another string to her bow for the
Gold Cup, but Chives lined up at Cheltenham nevertheless. It had been said by
connections that he would do so only if the ground was on the soft side, but he was
still allowed to take his chance even though the going was good. Chives started at
25/1 but showed the best form of his career and did so with a most eye-catching
performance. Guest, who has ridden Chives in all his races since the Royal &
SunAlliance, is not well known for his forcing tactics but he gave Chives an almost
Tony McCoy-style ride in the Gold Cup and sent him on at the last open ditch, six
from home, holding a four-length lead as the field turned downhill. Joined at the
third last, however, Chives was a clear third entering the straight and faded into
seventh, beaten about twenty lengths by the winner, his stable-mate Best Mate, and
around ten lengths by the runner-up. 'He ran a good race in the Gold Cup but I was
disappointed where he finished,' reported the trainer later. 'If he was held up he
could have been placed. Richard usually does hold him up but didn't for some
reason at Cheltenham.' Unfortunately, tactical nuances played no part in Chives's
performance at Aintree. After disputing favouritism in ante-post lists for much of
the winter, he was sent off at 10/1 and his backers knew quickly that they were on
a loser.

Mr Trevor Hemmings' "Chives"

Chives (IRE) (b.g. 1995)	Good Thyne (USA) (br 1977)	Herbager (b 1956)	Vandale II Flagette
		Foreseer (b or br 1969)	Round Table Regal Gleam
	Chatty Actress (b 1981)	Le Bavard (ch 1971)	Devon Lueur Doree
		Southern Actress (b 1977)	Menelek Southern Slave

Chives is a well-made gelding who usually impresses in appearance. He should stay beyond three miles five furlongs and he acts on heavy going, having also run well on good to firm in his younger days in the Champion Bumper. He is now a good jumper of fences, though you would not have known it in the Grand National, the burst blood vessel presumably the explanation. Chives's pedigree, which was detailed in last year's Annual, backs up the assertion that he would stay well. His unraced dam Chatty Actress was also represented in the latest season by the year-younger I'm Home (by Good Thyne) who showed only poor form in Ireland. *Miss H. C. Knight*

CHIVITE (IRE) 4 b.g. Alhaarth (IRE) – Laura Margaret (Persian Bold) [2002/3 16d **h92** 16d² 16g³ Mar 14] fair maiden on Flat (probably stays 1¾m), sold out of Mrs A. Perrett's stable 17,000 gns Newmarket Autumn Sales and gelded: modest form over hurdles, placed in juvenile at Kelso and conditional jockeys maiden at Fakenham: will stay 2½m: joined P. Hobbs. *K. R. Burke*

CHIVVY CHARVER (IRE) 6 ch.g. Commanche Run – Claddagh Pride (Bargello) **h–** [2002/3 F78: 16g 20g 22spu Jun 3] signs of only a little ability in bumpers and over hurdles: bred to stay 2½m+: joined A. Whillans. *G. A. Swinbank*

CHOCOLATE SOLDIER (IRE)   5 ch.g. Mister Lord (USA) – Traditional Lady   F–
(Carlingford Castle) [2002/3 F16g F16g⁵ Apr 14] fourth foal: brother to winning pointer
Lord of The Realm: dam unraced: showed little in 2 bumpers and failed to complete in 3
points in between: sold 1,600 gns Doncaster May Sales. *T. P. Tate*

CHOICE CUT (IRE)   10 b.g. Tirol – Lancette (Double Jump) [2002/3 c23dᵖᵘ Mar 4]   c–
rather sparely-made gelding: winning hurdler: off 2 years, no sign of retaining ability in   h–
hunter on chasing debut. *T. H. Caldwell*

CHOISTY (IRE)   13 ch.g. Callernish – Rosemount Rose (Ashmore (FR)) [2002/3   c–
c113, h–: 24sᵖᵘ c29d⁴ Mar 8] close-coupled gelding: very lightly raced over hurdles: h–
winning chaser, on the downgrade: stays 29f: acts on soft and good to firm going.
H. E. Haynes

CHOP-CHOP (IRE)   9 b. or br.g. Be My Native (USA) – Arctic Bavard (Le Bavard   c–
(FR)) [2002/3 c–, h67: 17m³ 17dᵖᵘ 17fᶠ 17f⁶ Oct 17] tailed off only start in a steeplechase: h–
maiden hurdler, no worthwhile form in 2002/3: failed to complete in points in February
and March: tongue tied. *D. C. Turner*

CHOPNEYEV (FR)   5 b.g. Goldneyev (USA) – Pierre de Soleil (FR) (Jefferson)   h137 +
[2002/3 h111: 20v² 20v* 24v* 22v* 20v² 25g Mar 11]
   The novice Chopneyev was one of the most progressive performers in handicap
hurdles in 2002/3 and it will be no surprise if he is able to resume his
rise in the next winter after a poor final run of the season in the Pertemps Final at
Cheltenham. Chopneyev started his career in handicaps off a lenient-looking mark
when justifying short odds at Uttoxeter in December after being beaten at odds on
in a novice at Hexham on his reappearance (he'd been second in fairly useful
company on the first of two starts at the end of the 2001/2 season). Chopneyev won

Tote Scoop6 Sandown Handicap Hurdle—
the unexposed Chopneyev gets the better of Camden Tanner (right) to complete a hat-trick

off a mark 12 lb higher when beating Camden Tanner by three-quarters of a length in the Tote Scoop6 Sandown Handicap six weeks later (having hacked up when facing an easy task in a novice at Ayr in the meantime). He then narrowly failed to defy a further 11 lb increase against another unexposed young hurdler Korelo in another valuable handicap, at Ascot later in February, the pair having the remainder well strung out. Despite another sizeable step up, putting him off a mark 31 lb higher than at Uttoxeter, Chopneyev started second favourite in a field of twenty-four for the Pertemps Final but failed to run his race, beaten a long way out and finishing twenty lengths behind the second-last horse to complete. Chopneyev had been running on heavy ground until Cheltenham and much less testing conditions at the Festival may explain, in part at least, his effort there, though it was such a poor showing that there was almost certainly more to it than that. Chopneyev had been well held on good going at Aintree on his final start in 2001/2, but a sharp two miles in top juvenile company at such a stage of his career was unlikely to show him to best advantage.

Chopneyev isn't bred for jumping—he had shown himself a useful middle-distance stayer on the Flat in France—and as a leggy, close-coupled gelding he doesn't look like a jumper either. He has shaped as if he should stay three miles and will be worth another try over that sort of trip. He held entries in both the Royal & SunAlliance Novices' Hurdle and the Stayers' Hurdle at Cheltenham but would have had to improve to reach the first six in a strong renewal of the former and wouldn't have been nearly good enough for the latter. At least to start with, valuable handicaps are likely to be his obvious targets in 2003/4. *R. T. Phillips*

Mrs Claire Smith's "Chopneyev"

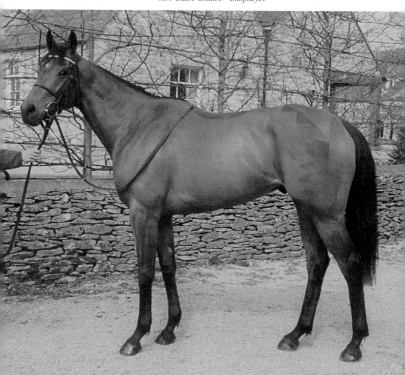

CHO POLU (IRE) 6 ch.g. Un Desperado (FR) – Rainbow Alliance (IRE) (Golden **h102**
Love) [2002/3 F–: 17d² 21d⁵ 16s² 17s² 17s Jan 25] good-topped gelding: fair novice
hurdler: runner-up 3 times: should stay 21f: raced only on good to soft/soft going:
blinkered last 2 starts: has looked tricky ride. *P. J. Hobbs*

CHOPWELL FABRICS (IRE) 5 b.g. Thatching – Maridana (USA) (Nijinsky **h–**
(CAN)) [2002/3 h–: 16m⁵ 17g 27vᵖᵘ 16d Dec 4] sturdy, lengthy gelding: no form over
hurdles: has worn cheekpieces/had tongue tied. *J. Howard Johnson*

CHOTAPEG 6 b.g. Sulaafah (USA) – Totally Tiddly (French Vine) [2002/3 F17g **h–**
F17dᵖᵘ 16gᵖᵘ 19d Mar 10] 1,000 4-y-o: half-brother to winning pointers by Afzal and **F–**
Relief Pitcher: dam winning pointer: probably of little account: sold out of J. A. Moore's
stable £3,500 Ascot December Sales after second start. *P. Wegmann*

CHRIS AND RYAN (IRE) 5 b.g. Goldmark (USA) – Beautyofthepeace (IRE) **F–**
(Exactly Sharp (USA)) [2002/3 F16g Sep 26] half-brother to 3 winners on Flat up to 2m:
dam unraced: always behind in bumper on debut. *R. Allan*

CHRISTMAS TRUCE (IRE) 4 b.g. Brief Truce (USA) – Superflash (Superlative) **h83 p**
[2002/3 17g⁴ Mar 15] fairly useful on Flat (stays 13f), won twice in 2002: fourth in
juvenile at Market Rasen on hurdling debut, not fluent: should improve. *M. H. Tompkins*

CHRISTOPHER 6 gr.g. Arzanni – Forest Nymph (NZ) (Oak Ridge (FR)) [2002/3 **h112**
h93, F100: 17f* 20g* 20d⁴ 21dᶠ 19s Nov 28] close-coupled gelding: fair hurdler: won
novices at Exeter and Uttoxeter in May: shaped as if possibly amiss last 2 starts: should
stay beyond 2½m: acts on any going. *P. J. Hobbs*

CHRISTY JNR (IRE) 9 b.g. Andretti – Rare Currency (Rarity) [2002/3 17d 20d **h–**
24m⁴ 23m⁵ Apr 21] lengthy ex-Irish gelding: third foal: half-brother to fairly useful
chaser up to 2¾m Shekels (by Orchestra): dam unraced, from family of top-class chaser
up to 25f Fifty Dollars More: well beaten in maiden point: signs of only a little ability
over hurdles: has hung left. *C. J. Teague*

CHRISTY'S PRIDE (IRE) 11 ch.m. Kambalda – Caddy Shack (Precipice Wood) **c–**
[2002/3 c–, h95: c20d⁴ c32g Mar 12] smallish, workmanlike mare: fair hurdler: little **h–**
show in 3 races over fences, not impressing with jumping: stays 3¼m: acts on heavy
going. *C. Weedon*

CHUNITO 8 b.g. Beveled (USA) – Wasimah (Caerleon (USA)) [2002/3 h–: 16s 24f **h–**
20gᵖᵘ Apr 21] maiden hurdler, no form since early-2000/1: stays 2¾m: acts on firm
going. *D. M. Lloyd*

CHURCHTOWN GLEN (IRE) 10 b. or br.g. Be My Native (USA) – Hill Side Glen **c83 §**
(Goldhill) [2002/3 c86, h–: c25g⁵ c25s⁴ c23g⁶ c24g⁵ c24g⁴ Mar 23] rangy, good-topped **h–**
gelding: poor handicap chaser: stays 3¼m: acts on good to firm and heavy going:
blinkered twice: has had tongue tied: usually races prominently, and often finds little:
inconsistent. *Ian Williams*

CHURLISH LAD (IRE) 6 b.g. Commanche Run – Pennyala (Skyliner) [2002/3 **F86**
F18g* F17dᵘʳ May 14] IR 10,000 3-y-o: half-brother to 2 winning hurdlers up to 2½m:
dam maiden half-sister to high-class hurdler up to 2½m Corporal Clinger: 7/1 from 16/1,
won bumper at Plumpton on debut in fairly good style: whipped round and unseated start
following month. *M. Bradstock*

CILLAMON 6 b.m. Terimon – Dubacilla (Dubassoff (USA)) [2002/3 F16g⁶ May 8] **F73**
first foal: dam top-class staying chaser: sixth of 16 in bumper at Chepstow on debut: won
maiden point in February. *L. G. Cottrell*

CILL CHURNAIN (IRE) 10 b.g. Arctic Cider (USA) – The Dozer (IRE) (Bulldozer) **c–**
[2002/3 c89§, h86§: 24d⁴ 26d² 24m* 21m* 21g³ 21g* 20g* 20d² 21dᵈ Nov 17] small, **h119**
plain gelding: modest chaser: fairly useful hurdler: much improved in 2002/3, winning
novice at Worcester and handicaps at Sedgefield, Southwell and Worcester between June
and September: best form up to 3m: acts on heavy and good to firm going: has refused to
race/run out, but did little wrong in 2002/3. *Mrs S. J. Smith*

CIMARRONE COVE (IRE) 8 gr.g. Roselier (FR) – Sugarstown (Sassafras (FR)) **c113 §**
[2002/3 c120d, h–: c25g⁵ c24v³ c24s² c27dᶠ c26vᵖᵘ Feb 4] well-made gelding: fair **h–**
handicap chaser: left M. Pitman after reappearance: should stay beyond 3¼m: acts on
heavy going: tried blinkered/visored: unreliable: sold 10,500 gns Doncaster May Sales.
N. J. Henderson

CINDESTI (IRE) 7 b.g. Barathea (IRE) – Niamh Cinn Oir (IRE) (King of Clubs) **c– x**
[2002/3 c78x, h–: 21sᵖᵘ Nov 21] good-topped gelding: let down by jumping in novice **h–**

chases (poor form): winning hurdler: showed nothing in selling handicap only start in 2002/3: stays 2½m: acts on good to firm going. *C. N. Kellett*

CINNAMON CLUB 11 b.m. Derrylin – Cinnamon Run (Deep Run) [2002/3 c21g^{pu} Mar 14] workmanlike mare: poor 2m hurdler: fair pointer nowadays, successful 4 times in 2003: tongue tied, no show in novice hunter on steeplechasing debut: acts on good to soft ground: tried blinkered. *Mrs Ruth Hayter*   c– h–

CINNAMON LINE 7 ch.g. Derrylin – Cinnamon Run (Deep Run) [2002/3 h87: 22d⁶ 24v^F 24s³ 22g⁵ Mar 18] tall, good sort: type to make a chaser: modest maiden hurdler: stays 3m: raced mainly on going softer than good (acts on heavy): has bled from nose. *R. H. Alner*   h98

CIONN MHALANNA (IRE) 5 b.g. Corrouge (USA) – Pennyland (Le Bavard (FR)) [2002/3 F17d F16g⁵ Apr 14] sixth foal: half-brother to 3 winning pointers, including fair maiden hurdler/chaser Penncaler (by Callernish): dam, won 2¼m chase, out of sister to useful 3m chaser Kilkilwell: modest form in 2 bumpers. *P. Beaumont*   F83

CIRCLE OF WOLVES 5 ch.g. Wolfhound (USA) – Misty Halo (High Top) [2002/3 h90+: 19d⁵ 22s⁴ 16d⁵ 16d 20s⁵ 16g 20m 22g³ Apr 12] close-coupled gelding: modest maiden hurdler: left B. Jones after seventh start: likely to prove best up to 2½m: acts on soft going: has worn cheekpieces. *M. J. Gingell*   h90

CIRCUMSTANCE 5 ch.m. Beveled (USA) – Instant Pleasure (Bairn (USA)) [2002/3 17m^{ur} 20g^{pu} May 26] tailed off in 6f maiden at 3 yrs for A. Reid: no aptitude for hurdling: joined Miss J. Feilden. *N. A. Graham*   h–

CIRCUS MAXIMUS (USA) 6 b.g. Pleasant Colony (USA) – Crockadore (USA) (Nijinsky (CAN)) [2002/3 h117: 17m 16d 24d⁶ 22v⁶ 24s^{pu} Nov 17] compact gelding: fair on Flat (stays 2m): fair handicap hurdler: should stay beyond 2¾m: raced on going softer than good (acts on heavy): often blinkered: joined I. Williams. *D. K. Weld, Ireland*   h110

CISCO 5 b.g. Shambo – School Run (Deep Run) [2002/3 h66+, F–: 16d⁵ 20d⁶ 20s^{ur} 17s⁵ 20d Mar 15] well-made gelding: poor maiden hurdler: best efforts at 2m: tried blinkered. *Andrew Turnell*   h–

CITA VERDA (FR) 5 b.m. Take Risks (FR) – Mossita (FR) (Tip Moss (FR)) [2002/3 h109: 16g³ 16m[*] 20d⁵ 17d⁵ 20g⁴ 16v[*] 16m[*] Apr 11] well-made mare: chasing type: successful on Flat in March: fairly useful hurdler: won mares intermediate at Perth in May and mares handicaps at Ayr in January and April: best efforts around 2m: acts on good to firm and heavy going: free-going sort: genuine. *P. Monteith*   h116 +

CITIUS (IRE) 7 b.g. Supreme Leader – Fancy Me Not (IRE) (Bulldozer) [2002/3 c99, h–: c22g^{pu} Dec 18] rangy gelding: winning hurdler: modest chaser: reportedly lost action only start in 2002/3: should stay beyond 21f: acts on heavy going, possibly not on good to firm. *R. Rowe*   c– h–

CITY GENT 9 b.g. Primitive Rising (USA) – Classy Lassy (Class Distinction) [2002/3 c84d, h–: 16d⁵ c20g⁵ c16s³ c17g⁴ c20g^{ur} c17m⁴ c20g² Apr 26] well-made gelding: maiden hurdler: poor handicap chaser: seems best around 2m: acts on good to firm and heavy going: tried blinkered/in cheekpieces: has had tongue tied: idles, and best held up: sometimes let down by jumping. *N. Wilson*   c86 h–

CITY KID (DEN) 11 ch.g. Village Star (FR) – Irish Lute (Luthier) [2002/3 c21s⁴ c22g⁴ c21v³ c31d⁵ Dec 13] lengthy, angular gelding: winning hurdler/chaser: returning from long absence when 6½ lengths last of 4 finishers to Berthram in Norsk Grand National at Ovrevoll in September: in frame at Taby and Bremen after, well beaten in cross-country race at Cheltenham: stays 21f: acts on soft going. *R. Haugen, Norway*   c? h–

CITY POSER (IRE) 8 b.g. Posen (USA) – Citissima (Simbir) [2002/3 h99: 24m² 27g^f 24d⁴ c24g² Oct 19] close-coupled gelding: fair handicap hurdler: similar form when second in novice at Stratford on chasing debut: stays 25f: acts on soft and good to firm going, probably heavy: has had tongue tied. *Simon Earle*   c108 h111

CITY REACH 7 b.g. Petong – Azola (IRE) (Alzao (USA)) [2002/3 17v^{pu} 17d^{pu} Jan 16] modest on Flat (barely stays 1¼m), won in October, sold out of P. Makin's stable 3,800 gns Doncaster November Sales: tongue tied, no encouragement in 2 novice hurdles. *Miss M. Bragg*   h–

CITY STANDARD (IRE) 7 b.g. Rainbow Quest (USA) – City Fortress (Troy) [2002/3 h82: 19d^{pu} 25d^{pu} Feb 25] fair maiden at best on Flat (stays 1½m): poor form first 2 starts over hurdles in 2001/2, no show since: has looked difficult ride. *M. F. Harris*   h–

Martell Cognac Sainsbury's Topham Chase (Handicap), Aintree—the leaders at Bechers Brook; the winner Clan Royal (No.20) is poised to take over

CIVIL GENT (IRE)   4 ch.g. Flying Spur (AUS) – Calamity Kate (IRE) (Fairy King   h–
(USA)) [2002/3 16d 16s^F 17s^{pu} 19g Feb 28] 1,000 3-y-o: compact gelding: first foal: dam,
maiden who stayed 1¼m, half-sister to one-time fairly useful chaser Weaver George: not
fluent and no show in 4 starts over hurdles. *M. E. Sowersby*

CLAIRE'S NOMAD   7 b.g. Nomadic Way (USA) – Clairet (Sagaro) [2002/3 20d⁶   h–
Jun 8] third foal: half-brother to winning pointer by Primitive Rising: dam winning
pointer: poor pointer: soon tailed off on hurdling debut. *J. S. Wainwright*

CLAIR VALLEY   9 b.m. Ardross – Annicombe Run (Deep Run) [2002/3 h76: 25d*   **h79**
27m⁵ Jul 17] small mare: poor hurdler: off a year prior to winning weak maiden at
Wolverhampton in July: reportedly lame later in month: stays 27f: acts on firm and good
to soft going. *Ferdy Murphy*

CLAN ROYAL (FR)   8 b.g. Chef de Clan II (FR) – Allee du Roy (FR) (Rex Magna   **c123**
(FR)) [2002/3 c19d³ c16d⁵ c18s* c16d⁴ c20s* c21d* Apr 4] leggy ex-Irish gelding: ninth   **h–**
foal: half-brother to 3 winners, including fairly useful hurdler/chaser around 2m Robo-
ratif (by Robore): dam unraced: winning hurdler: fairly useful handicap chaser: trained in
2001/2 by A. Moore: won at Fontwell in February, Newbury (signs of reluctance and left
clear last) in March and Aintree (29-runner Martell Cognac Sainsbury's Topham Chase)
in April: beat Macs Gildoran 2½ lengths in last named: will stay beyond 21f: acts on soft
and good to firm ground: tends to jump less than fluently, but only one mistake of note at
Aintree. *Jonjo O'Neill*

CLARAS PRIDE (IRE)   11 b.g. Be My Native (USA) – Our Hollow (Wolver   **c–**
Hollow) [2002/3 c68, h–: c23d⁵ Jun 8] ex-Irish gelding: fourth brother to winning   **h–**
pointer: dam winning hurdler: poor form over hurdles and fences: won point in March:
stays 2½m. *M. S. Wilesmith*

CLARENDON (IRE)   7 ch.g. Forest Wind (USA) – Sparkish (IRE) (Persian Bold)   **h113**
[2002/3 h105: 16m* 16d 16d 16m Feb 21] sturdy gelding: fair handicap hurdler: off a
year, won at Stratford in July: disappointing all 3 subsequent starts, leaving impression
all wasn't well: raced around 2m: acts on good to firm going. *P. J. Hobbs*

CLASHBRIDANE (IRE)   11 b.g. Lancastrian – Castleview Rose (Master Buck)   **c77**
[2002/3 c82: c26d⁵ Jun 8] smallish, workmanlike gelding: winning pointer: modest
hunter chaser: stays 3¼m: acts on soft going, probably on heavy. *Mrs G. B. Walford*

CLASSICAL BEN   5 ch.g. Most Welcome – Stoproveritate (Scorpio (FR)) [2002/3   **F91**
F16d³ F16g* Apr 14] lengthy gelding: second foal: half-brother to fair hurdler Exstoto
(by Mtoto), stays 21f: dam fair 2m hurdler: fair form in bumpers, won at Hexham in
April. *R. A. Fahey*

CLASSIC CHINA   6 ch.m. Karinga Bay – Chanelle (The Parson) [2002/3 F18s²   **F88**
F17s² Jan 14] seventh foal: half-sister to useful hurdler/fair chaser Country Beau (by
Town And Country), stays 3m, and to 2 winning pointers: dam, winning pointer, half-
sister to useful hurdler/fairly useful staying chaser Arabian Music: shaped like a stayer

187

when second both starts in bumpers, wearing cheekpieces on second occasion: will stay at least 2½m. *J. W. Mullins*

CLASSIC CONKERS (IRE)   9 b.g. Conquering Hero (USA) – Erck (Sun Prince) **h84**
[2002/3 20d² 20v³ 20d⁴ Dec 14] modest on Flat (stays 2m): poor novice hurdler: stays 2½m: acts on heavy going: amateur ridden. *Miss J. Feilden*

CLASSIC EAGLE   10 b.g. Unfuwain (USA) – La Lutine (My Swallow) [2002/3 c–, **c–**
h–: 20v⁴ Jun 6] lengthy gelding: twice-raced chaser: winning hurdler: little form since **h–**
1998/9: blinkered once. *Miss J. Feilden*

CLASSIC EXAMPLE   4 ch.c. Mark of Esteem (IRE) – Classic Form (IRE) (Alzao **h–**
(USA)) [2002/3 16dᵖᵘ 17gᶠ Mar 22] stocky colt: fair maiden on Flat (stays 1½m): beaten some way out in juvenile on hurdling debut: fell fifth next time. *Miss S. J. Wilton*

CLASSIC FABLE (IRE)   11 b.m. Lafontaine (USA) – Rathmill Syke (True Song) **c–**
[2002/3 c–, h–: 27mᵖᵘ May 7] of little account: tongue tied. *J. L. Needham* **h–**

CLASSIC JAZZ (NZ)   8 br.g. Paris Opera (AUS) – Johnny Loves Jazz (NZ) (Virginia **h–**
Privateer (USA)) [2002/3 h114: 17sᵖᵘ Jan 25] strong, rangy, good sort: successful at 1¼m on Flat in New Zealand: created good impression when winning novice at Worcester in June 2001 on hurdling debut: off bridle long way out in handicap at Cheltenham when next seen almost 20 months later: sold only 2,200 gns Doncaster May Sales. *N. J. Henderson*

CLASSIC LASH (IRE)   7 b.g. Classic Cheer (IRE) – Khaiylasha (IRE) (Kahyasi) **c95**
[2002/3 h82: 20vᵖᵘ 24s 20m⁵ 20g⁵ 22m 24g² 22m* 24g* 20s⁴ 27sᵖᵘ c21s³ c16d⁵ c21g³ **h81**
c21d* c20g² Apr 21] poor handicap hurdler, won at Downpatrick and Limerick in October: sold out of P. Rothwell's stable 4,500 gns (privately) Doncaster November Sales after ninth start: better form over fences: won novice at Sedgefield in April: stays 3m: acts on firm and soft going: blinkered once (below form). *P. Needham*

CLASSIC NATIVE (IRE)   5 b. or br.g. Be My Native (USA) – Thats Irish (Furry **F116**
Glen) [2002/3 F16s* F16g F17g* Apr 5]
  In winning the Martell Champion Standard National Hunt Flat race at Aintree in April, Classic Native went one better than his stable-companion Iris's Gift had done in the same event twelve months earlier. Iris's Gift was runner-up to Kickham; and the fortunes of that pair when they were sent over hurdles in the latest season could hardly have been more contrasting, with the former proving himself an outstanding novice and the latter failing to win any of his four starts. While it is most unlikely that Classic Native will be capable of emulating Iris's Gift's achievements when he goes over hurdles in the next season, it will be a major surprise if he doesn't fare a great deal better than Kickham.
  Classic Native ran to a similar level of form to Kickham in winning at Aintree, his performance a smart one in this Grade 2 event which sometimes falls short compared to the Champion Bumper at Cheltenham. Three of the twenty-one that lined-up at Aintree had taken part in the Cheltenham race, including Classic Native who had fared much the best of the trio in finishing eleventh. Classic Native was also one of fourteen who had already been successful in bumpers, having won at Warwick in December on his debut, but plenty of those were preferred to him in the betting and he went off at 25/1. It did look a competitive and open renewal, but a furious pace on well-watered ground proved far too much for the majority of the runners and the field was well strung out going into the home turn, where Be Fair moved smoothly to the front pressed by Classic Native. Held up in the early stages, Classic Native had come off the bridle after being hampered before halfway and

Martell Champion Standard National Hunt Flat Race, Aintree—
Classic Native (left) and Be Fair are well clear of the riderless Vodka Bleu

was now under stronger pressure, but he never stopped responding as he pulled away from the remainder with Be Fair, staying on the stronger to forge clear in the final furlong and win by two and a half lengths. Third-placed Tighten Your Belt was a further seventeen lengths behind. The emphasis had been very much on stamina, which played to the strengths of Classic Native, who has a pedigree chock-full of stamina. It is only to be hoped that such a hard race hasn't left its mark.

			Our Native	Exclusive Native
	Be My Native (USA)		(b or br 1970)	Our Jackie
	(br 1979)		Witchy Woman	Strate Stuff
Classic Native (IRE)			(ch 1972)	Witchy Norma
(b. or br.g. 1998)			Furry Glen	Wolver Hollow
	Thats Irish		(b 1971)	Cleftess
	(br 1985)		Kilbricken Money	Even Money
			(b 1971)	Clonroche

Classic Native, a tall, good sort, was one of the most imposing individuals we saw in bumpers in the latest season, and he no doubt attracted plenty of attention when he went through the sale-ring as a three-year-old, a bid of 52,000 guineas needed to secure him. He certainly looks the part for jumping, and is bred for it, too. Sired by Be My Native, he is out of a once-raced daughter of Kilbricken Money, a fairly useful performer who carried the Dawn Run colours to victory in the valuable Guinness Handicap Chase at Punchestown in 1980. Classic Native's third dam Clonroche won a bumper and three hurdle races in Ireland, also coming third in the three-mile handicap hurdle at the Cheltenham Festival in 1967. Clonroche is also the grandam of the smart staying hurdler and useful chaser Birkdale, while Kilbricken Money is also the grandam of the useful hurdler/chaser St Mellion Fairway, who was fourth in Earth Summit's Grand National. Thats Irish, the dam of Classic Native, is also responsible for a couple of winning pointers from five earlier foals, namely Paddy Clyde (by Royal Fountain) and Irish Money (by Mandalus). Classic Native is going to need at least two and a half miles when sent over hurdles and, like Iris's Gift, probably won't really come into his own until he tackles distances of three miles or more. He looks a good prospect. *Jonjo O'Neill*

CLASSIC NOTE (IRE) 8 b.m. Classic Secret (USA) – Fovea (IRE) (Sarab) [2002/3 **h99** 16d* 19v 16s 16m⁵ Apr 22] sister to modest 2m hurdler Classic Mix: bumper winner: fair maiden on Flat (stays 1¾m): well-backed favourite, best effort over hurdles when winning 28-runner novice handicap at Cheltenham in November by 1½ lengths from Bongo Fury (subsequently tested positive for morphine): creditable efforts in other big-field handicaps at Fairyhouse (fifth to High Prospect) in April and Punchestown (fourth to Sabadilla) in early-May: should stay 2½m: acts on good to firm and good to soft going. *A. J. Martin, Ireland*

CLASSIC ROCK 4 b.g. Classic Cliche (IRE) – Ruby Vision (IRE) (Vision (USA)) **F74** [2002/3 F12d F16s Jan 18] lengthy gelding: first foal: dam, modest hurdler who stayed 3m, half-sister to fairly useful French hurdler Mt Speculation: poor form on first of 2 starts in bumpers, when seventh of 23 to Enitsag at Newbury. *J. W. Unett*

CLASSIFIED (IRE) 7 b.g. Roselier (FR) – Treidlia (Mandalus) [2002/3 h147, **h157** F114: 21d² 21s* 20d* 24g⁴ Mar 13]

With the likelihood of Stayers' Hurdle runner-up Iris's Gift being kept over hurdles for another season, Classified is the best British prospect for longer-distance novice chases in 2003/4. The temptation to send Classified over fences in the latest season, which was only his second, must have been strong, but he gave connections no cause to regret the decision to keep him over hurdles, as he won a Grade 1 and a Grade 2 event and picked up almost £80,000 in win and place prize-money. Classified's record over hurdles—he has also won a couple of bumpers—is highly commendable, standing at seven wins from ten starts, and his win and place prize-money total all told is nigh on £160,000. As the good-topped Classified looks the type who will prove even more effective over fences, it is hard to be any other than very enthusiastic about his prospects.

Classified, who had won the Martell Mersey Novices' Hurdle at Aintree from Eternal Spring on his final start in 2001/2, shaped encouragingly when second to that horse at Cheltenham in December on his return, and it was a different story

Byrne Bros Cleeve Hurdle, Cheltenham—
Classified does well to catch stable-companion Mr Cool after still having plenty to do at the last

when the pair met again in the Byrne Bros Cleeve Hurdle over the same course and distance the following month. A Grade 1 race which is seldom of true championship class, the latest renewal of the Cleeve Hurdle looked particularly weak and Classified, meeting Eternal Spring on more favourable terms, started at odds on. Eternal Spring didn't give Classified any problems this time, but the latter's stable-companion Mr Cool certainly did. Mr Cool, dictating at a stop-start pace, was sent for home in earnest two out, where Eternal Spring fell when looking held. Classified had been waited with and was left with a fair amount of ground to make up, but he gradually reduced the deficit, caught Mr Cool in the last seventy-five yards and went on to win by a length. Classified also had to work quite hard to land the odds on his next start, in the upgraded Collins Stewart National Spirit Hurdle at Fontwell. A race enjoying Grade 2 status for the first time, it wasn't run to suit Classified who, having been held up initially, increased the pace after jumping to the front at the seventh. His stamina came into play after the second last, where he was being pressed by both Telimar Prince and Comex Flyer, and he stayed on well under pressure to win by a length and a half from the former. The step up to three miles in the Stayers' Hurdle seemed sure to suit Classified, and so it proved. He simply wasn't up to beating three top-class performers in Baracouda, Iris's Gift and Limestone Lad, staying on without being able to land a serious blow.

Classified (IRE) (b.g. 1996)	Roselier (FR) (gr 1973)	Misti IV (br 1958)	Medium	
			Mist	
		Peace Rose (gr 1959)	Fastnet Rock	
			La Paix	
	Treidlia (b 1987)	Mandalus (b or br 1974)	Mandamus	
			Laminate	
		Gold Fellina (b 1981)	Decent Fellow	
			Crock of Gold	

Classified is the second foal of Treidlia. Her first, Tourniquet (by Torus), won a maiden point in Ireland in 2002 and was placed over hurdles in Britain in the latest season. The three dams at the bottom of the pedigree achieved little: Treidlia showed little in bumpers, her dam Gold Fellina was unraced and her grandam Crock of Gold managed a place from five starts in bumpers. However, there are other notable jumpers to be found elsewhere in Classified's family, such as Another City, Better Times Ahead and The Man Himself. The tough and consistent Classified has been raced only on good ground or softer, and gained one of his wins in bumpers on heavy going. He will stay beyond three miles. *M. C. Pipe*

CLASSIFY 4 b.g. Classic Cliche (IRE) – Slmaat (Sharpo) [2002/3 F16m³ F17m² Apr **F91** 15] first foal: dam fair 7f to 1½m winner: favourite, fair form when placed both starts in bumpers, 5 lengths second of 6 to Bowleaze at Exeter. *P. F. Nicholls*

CLASS OF NINETYTWO (IRE)   14 b.g. Lancastrian – Lothian Lassie (Precipice Wood) [2002/3 c99, h–: c34g² c26d³ c24vᵖᵘ Mar 5] workmanlike gelding: fair hunter chaser nowadays: stays 4¼m: acts on soft and good to firm going: has had tongue tied. *S. Wynne*   **c99 h–**

CLASSY CLARE   5 b.m. Nicholas Bill – Clare's Choice (Pragmatic) [2002/3 17sᵖᵘ 17gᵖᵘ Apr 19] half-sister to fair hurdler Nick's Choice (by Sula Bula), stays 2¾m: no form on Flat or in 2 starts over hurdles. *J. M. Bradley*   **h–**

CLASSY CLARENCE (IRE)   6 ch.g. Un Desperado (FR) – Winscarlet North (Garland Knight) [2002/3 F16g Mar 14] IR £67,000 4-y-o: brother to winning 3m chaser Lotto Lolly and half-brother to modest hurdler up to 2¾m Gypsy (by Distinctly North): dam unraced half-sister to dual Two Mile Champion Chase winner Hilly Way: well held in bumper at Warwick on debut. *A. J. Lidderdale*   **F–**

CLAUDE GREENGRASS   7 ch.g. Shalford (IRE) – Rainbow Brite (BEL) (Captain's Treasure) [2002/3 16v 16s 16g² 16d* 20s⁵ 16dᶠ 16v² Mar 7] sturdy gelding: 9f winner on Flat at 5 yrs: no form over hurdles for E. Berry: much improved in 5 handicaps in Britain, winning 18-runner conditional jockeys event at Doncaster (idled) in January: had race at his mercy when falling last at Wetherby: probably stays 2½m: raced on good going or softer (acts on heavy): travelled better in blinkers last 2 outings: not a fluent jumper: may do better yet. *Jonjo O'Neill*   **h96**

CLAUDE (IRE)   5 b.g. Hamas (IRE) – Tigora (Ahonoora) [2002/3 F17g Jun 12] sixth foal: half-brother to modest hurdlers by Barbarolli and Marju: dam never ran: no show in bumper, Flat maiden or in point. *B. Palling*   **F–**

CLAUDIAS RAINBOW   6 br.m. Alflora (IRE) – By The Lake (Tyrant (USA)) [2002/3 F16g 19dᵖᵘ 16d 20pᵖᵘ Feb 26] leggy mare: eighth foal: half-sister to fair chaser Jokers Charm (by Idiot's Delight), stays 3m, and modest hurdler Southend Scallywag (by Tina's Pet), stays 2½m: dam poor staying maiden: no sign of ability. *R. C. Guest*   **h– F–**

CLAUDIUS TERTIUS   6 b.g. Rudimentary (USA) – Sanctuary Cove (Habitat) [2002/3 h55: 16dᵖᵘ 11m⁶ 17g* 21g³ 22d Aug 24] sturdy gelding: poor hurdler: won selling handicap at Sedgefield in August: stays 21f: probably acts on any going: sometimes blinkered/tongue tied: sold 500 gns Doncaster September Sales. *N. B. Mason*   **h64**

CLAYMORE (IRE)   7 b.g. Broadsword (USA) – Mazza (Mazilier (USA)) [2002/3 h117, F102: c20d³ c16v* c16d⁴ c19v* c22d³ c22d* c18sᵘʳ c21sᵖᵘ Mar 15] leggy, lengthy gelding: winning hurdler: useful chaser: won maiden at Uttoxeter in November, 3-runner handicap at Chepstow in December and novice at Haydock (easily from Full Minty) in February: stays 3m: acts on heavy going: races prominently. *O. Sherwood*   **c132 h–**

CLEAR AWAY (IRE)   6 b.g. Clearly Bust – Twinkle Bright (USA) (Star de Naskra (USA)) [2002/3 24g⁴ Sep 15] IR 5,200 3-y-o: first foal: dam 7f winner: third in Irish point in 2002: bought 580 gns Doncaster August Sales: fourth of 5 finishers in maiden hurdle at Worcester. *P. G. Murphy*   **h–**

CLEAR DAWN (IRE)   8 b.g. Clearly Bust – Cobra Queen (Dawn Review) [2002/3 c97, h–: c24m⁶ c24g² c20g³ c24s c24d Apr 9] well-made gelding: winning hurdler: fair handicap chaser: best efforts when placed at Musselburgh, though none too fluent closing stages each time: should stay beyond 3m: unraced on firm going, acts on any other. *J. M. Jefferson*   **c102 h–**

CLEAR SKIES (IRE)   10 b.g. Phardante (FR) – Fighting Doleila (Humdoleila) [2002/3 c110, h–: c20dᵘʳ c20d Nov 23] workmanlike gelding: fair chaser: well held on completed start in 2002/3: best around 2m: raced on good going or softer (acts on soft): consistent. *N. A. Gaselee*   **c– h–**

CLEOPATRAS THERAPY (IRE)   6 b.g. Gone Fishin – Nec Precario (Krayyan) [2002/3 F16s* F16d⁵ F16g² F16g² Mar 12] third foal: dam, Irish 1m winner, half-sister to useful 2m hurdler Dick's Folly: fair form in bumpers, won 17-runner conditional jockeys event at Ludlow in January: 12 lengths second of 16 to Eric's Charm at Huntingdon: sold 20,000 gns Doncaster May Sales. *Ian Williams*   **F94**

CLEVER FELLA   4 ch.g. Elmaamul (USA) – Festival of Magic (USA) (Clever Trick (USA)) [2002/3 F16g Jan 17] half-brother to winning hurdler/chaser Afrostar (by Soviet Lad), stays 2½m, and to 2 winners on Flat: dam 1m winner on Flat: eighth of 15 in bumper at Musselburgh. *M. Dods*   **F–**

CLEVER THYNE (IRE)   6 b.g. Good Thyne (USA) – Clever Milly (Precipice Wood) [2002/3 h79+, F84: 22d² c24gᶠ 21d² 21g³ 21gᶠ 24g⁴ Mar 22] medium-sized   **c– p h98**

gelding: fell twelfth on chasing debut: modest novice hurdler: should stay 3m: raced on good going or softer: has had tongue tied. *H. D. Daly*

CLEYMOR HOUSE (IRE)   5 ch.g. Duky – Deise Lady (Le Bavard (FR)) [2002/3   h–
21s 16v 19s Feb 27] lengthy gelding: chasing type: fourth foal: half-brother to winning
pointer by Balinger: dam winning pointer: well held in 3 races over hurdles. *John
R. Upson*

CLIFTON FOX   11 b.g. Deploy – Loveskate (USA) (Overskate (CAN)) [2002/3 16d   h113
20v² Feb 4] small gelding: useful up to 1½m on Flat at one time: lightly raced over
hurdles, impressive winner of novice in 1999/00: much better effort in handicaps on
return from 3-year lay-off when second to Bunkum at Chepstow: stays 2½m: acts on
heavy going. *Jonjo O'Neill*

CLIFTON MIST   7 gr.m. Lyphento (USA) – Brave Maiden (Three Legs) [2002/3   h83
h67§: 19f* 19s^pu 19v* 21d 21m Apr 16] lengthy, angular mare: poor hurdler: won
handicaps at Taunton in October (conditional jockeys seller) and December (novice):
may prove best up to 21f: acts on any going: has taken strong hold. *H. S. Howe*

CLINGSTONE   7 b.m. Henbit (USA) – Linen Leaf (Bold Owl) [2002/3 F64: 16d²   h84
20g⁵ 17s^pu Mar 5] useful-looking mare: best effort in mares novice hurdles when
short-head second to Blue Ride at Wincanton: breathing problem next start, reportedly
broke blood vessel last one: bred to stay at least 2½m. *T. R. George*

CLODAGH VALLEY (IRE)   8 b.g. Doubletour (USA) – Raise A Princess (USA)   c–
(Raise A Native) [2002/3 c–, h–: c24g^pu c22d May 13] of little account nowadays: tried   h–
blinkered. *R. J. Bevis*

CLOD HOPPER (IRE)   13 gr.g. Roselier (FR) – Clodagh Lady (Boreen (FR))   c–
[2002/3 c24m^pu Jul 4] angular gelding: winning hurdler: modest handicap chaser: pulled   h–
up after mistake ninth on return from 18-month absence: stays 25f: acts on firm and good
to soft going. *Ian Williams*

CLODOALD (FR)   6 b.g. Beaudelaire (USA) – Mint Stick (FR) (Tropular) [2002/3   c– §
c109, h93§: 16g² 20s^pu 22f⁴ 16m* 20d* 20m³ 20m³ 21d^bd Nov 15] leggy gelding: fair   h106 §
hurdler: won sellers at Uttoxeter (handicap) and Worcester and handicap at Huntingdon
before end of September: stays 2½m: acts on good to firm and heavy going: visored after
reappearance: tongue tied: usually soon off bridle. *M. C. Pipe*

CLONMEL'S MINELLA (IRE)   12 b.g. Strong Gale – Martones Chance (Golden   c105
Love) [2002/3 c21m² c19f* c22g* c18s^F c24v³ c19s² c32g c20m^ur Apr 12] medium-sized   h–
gelding: one-time fairly useful hurdler: fair chaser, off nearly 2 years prior to reappearance: won handicaps at Listowel in September and Cork in October: ran best race over
fences when fourth to Rule Supreme in valuable novice handicap at Punchestown in
late-April: probably stays 4m, effective at much shorter: acts on any going. *Michael
Hourigan, Ireland*

CLONROCHE VINYLS (IRE)   8 ch.m. Rashar (USA) – Clonroche Beggar   h78
(Pauper) [2002/3 h95, F85: 24s⁶ 16v³ 20d 22g⁶ 22g 24g⁵ Apr 23] lengthy mare: bumper
winner: poor novice hurdler on balance: probably stays 3m: raced on good going or softer.
Ferdy Murphy

CLONSHIRE PADDY (IRE)   7 gr.g. Roselier (FR) – Gusserane Princess (Paddy's   c91
Stream) [2002/3 c–, h–: 23d c25v³ c22v² c27s^ur c25v⁵ c25s^F 22d 24v Mar 13] good-   h80
topped gelding: novice hurdler/chaser, modest at best: should stay beyond 25f: raced
mainly on going softer than good (acts on heavy): visored sixth outing: has been let down
by jumping over fences. *C. Grant*

CLOONE RIVER (IRE)   7 b. or br.g. Un Desperado (FR) – Grangemills (Strong   h118
Gale) [2002/3 h77p, F101: 16d² 16f* 20g⁴ 16s* 16s⁶ Nov 30] fairly useful hurdler: won
maiden in September and handicap in November, both at Punchestown: best form at 2m:
acts on firm and soft ground. *Paul Nolan, Ireland*

CLOTH OF GOLD   6 b.g. Barathea (IRE) – Bustinetta (Bustino) [2002/3 h112:   h120
22m* Jun 14] lightly raced on Flat (maiden) and over hurdles: well backed, fairly useful
form when winning handicap at Newton Abbot in June: will stay 3m. *Lady Herries*

CLOUDKICKER (IRE)   10 b.g. Dry Dock – Last Sprite (Tug of War) [2002/3 c76,   c– x
h–: c26v^F c21d^ur 22d 19v^pu Dec 28] medium-sized gelding: error-prone maiden jumper: h– x
sold 600 gns Doncaster May Sales. *Miss Venetia Williams*

CLOUDY BAYS (IRE)   6 ch.g. Hubbly Bubbly (USA) – Bellteen (Strong Gale)   c110 x
[2002/3 F16s 16s* 20d 24m^F 20g^F c16g³ c17m c22f* c19f^F c20g² c20d³ c20g^pu c20m^ur   h89 x
c20m^ur Apr 19] fell in point: third on first of 3 starts in bumpers: form over hurdles only   F–

192

when winning maiden at Wexford in June: fair chaser: won maiden at Listowel in September: effective at 2m to 2¾m: acts on firm going, probably on soft: tried blinkered: has had tongue tied: often let down by jumping. *C. Byrnes, Ireland*

CLOUDY CREEK (IRE) 9 gr.g. Roselier (FR) – Jacob's Creek (IRE) (Buckskin (FR)) [2002/3 h85: c24s⁴ c24dᶠ c20d⁶ c24sᵖᵘ Feb 27] strong, well-made gelding: winning pointer/hurdler: possibly flattered when 17 lengths fourth of 8 to Tales of Bounty in novice chase at Taunton on reappearance: well held only completed subsequent start: will prove suited by 3m+. *Miss H. C. Knight* **c110 ? h–**

CLOUDY GREY (IRE) 6 gr.g. Roselier (FR) – Dear Limousin (Pollerton) [2002/3 F16s⁴ F17d* F16s* F16g² Feb 8] **F115**

There were few more exciting prospects for jumping seen in bumpers in 2002/3 than Cloudy Grey. After hanging left in the home straight at Sandown, when an eye-catching fourth on his debut in November, he went on to gain impressive wins at Hereford and Haydock and ran a good second to Cornish Rebel in the Grade 2 bumper at Newbury's Tote Gold Trophy meeting, just about the best bumper apart from the Champion Bumper run all season. Cloudy Grey didn't take his chance at Cheltenham, his trainer fearing the experience might be all too much for him at this stage of his career, but that patience should pay off when Cloudy Grey goes over jumps. Although he'll presumably be sent hurdling first, he has the physique, demeanour and pedigree to suggest he will make an even better chaser. A big, lengthy gelding, Cloudy Grey travelled strongly in his races and showed a lot more speed than is usually associated with a son of Roselier when winning by six lengths from subsequent winner Tom Fruit at Haydock, quickening away on the soft ground in the final two furlongs. At Newbury he put up another useful effort and acquitted

Mrs J. R. Lavelle & Mrs A. Hepworth's "Cloudy Grey"

himself really well in a well-run event on less testing ground than he had previously encountered. Although he had no answer to Cornish Rebel in the straight, going down by eleven lengths, Cloudy Grey was conceding 7 lb to the winner and had some of the best bumper horses in Britain behind him: the fourth Be Fair finished second at Aintree, the fifth and sixth Control Man and He's The Boss had fought out the Grade 2 bumper at the Welsh National meeting and the eighth Bold Bishop went on to finish a close fourth in the Champion Bumper itself.

Cloudy Grey was bought for IR16,000 guineas as a three-year-old at the Derby Sale. He doesn't come from a particularly distinguished family, being the fourth foal and first winner out of his dam Dear Limousin, herself a winning pointer and half-sister to several winners, including the one-time fairly useful hurdler and error-prone winning chaser Pealings, who stays three and a quarter miles. Dear Limousin is also half-sister to the dam of the useful hurdler at up to three miles Mr Red Banner. Cloudy Grey is bred to stay three miles, though it seems likely he will be effective at much shorter trips. He has so far raced on good going or softer. *Miss E. C. Lavelle*

CLUB ROYAL 6 b.g. Alflora (IRE) – Miss Club Royal (Avocat) [2002/3 17m^{pu} 16d⁶ 17s⁴ 17s 17g² Apr 21] fourth foal: half-brother to winning 27f chaser Master Club Royal (by Teenoso): dam fair staying hurdler/chaser: poor novice hurdler: will be suited by further than 17f. *D. McCain*   **h76**

COACHMAN (IRE) 5 b.g. King's Ride – Royal Shares (IRE) (Royal Fountain) [2002/3 F17g Apr 21] €3,000 4-y-o: first foal: dam unraced, out of sister to useful hurdler Book of Gold: well beaten in bumper at Carlisle on debut. *J. Howard Johnson*   **F–**

COASTGUARD (IRE) 9 b.g. Satco (FR) – Godlike (Godswalk (USA)) [2002/3 c100, h–: c24s³ c22d^{ur} c21d³ 22d c24d c22d³ c31g^{pu} Apr 24] compact gelding: winning hurdler: handicap chaser, fair at best: out of sorts in 2002/3: should stay beyond 3m: raced on good going or softer (acts on heavy): blinkered: sometimes let down by jumping. *C. J. Mann*   **c85 x** **h–**

COASTWARD (IRE) 7 b.g. Scenic – Sarakarta (USA) (Trempolino (USA)) [2002/3 17m^{pu} May 3] narrow gelding: fair form in bumpers in 1999/00: tailed off quickly fifth in maiden hurdle, only subsequent outing. *P. R. Hedger*   **h–**

COBBET (CHR) 7 b.g. Favoured Nations (IRE) – Creace (CZE) (Sirano (CZE)) [2002/3 h112: 17g⁶ c16m² c16m³ c16d³ c16m* Apr 17] leggy gelding: fair hurdler: improved effort over fences when winning handicap at Cheltenham by 12 lengths from Korakor: barely stays 21f: acts on firm and good to soft going: genuine and consistent. *T. R. George*   **c120** **h–**

COBRECES 5 b.g. Environment Friend – Oleada (IRE) (Tirol) [2002/3 c18v* c17d³ c20s c20d 18v⁵ c16s² c20g* c20m* Mar 19] tall, useful-looking gelding: 1m winner on Flat: fairly useful juvenile hurdler in 2001/2, successful twice at Auteuil: similar form over fences, won 4-y-o event at Auteuil in May and novices at Warwick (second start since leaving M. Rolland, beat Lodestar 12 lengths) and Fontwell (3 ran) in March: stays 2½m: yet to race on firm going, acts on any other. *P. F. Nicholls*   **c120 +** **h112 +**

COCK A HOOP 9 b.g. Roscoe Blake – Rose Delight (Idiot's Delight) [2002/3 c–, h–: 24g² 22g² 27g^{pu} 26m⁴ Sep 11] rangy gelding: winning pointer, pulled up in 2 steeplechases: poor hurdler: stays 3¼m: acts on good to firm going: sold 2,500 gns Doncaster September Sales. *C. J. Mann*   **c–** **h82**

COCKATOO RIDGE 6 ch.g. Riverwise (USA) – Came Cottage (Nearly A Hand) [2002/3 F16s F16d⁵ F18f* Apr 24] fifth foal: brother to Champion Hurdle winner Rooster Booster: dam fairly useful pointer: improved effort in bumpers when winning at Fontwell. *N. R. Mitchell*   **F90**

COCKNEY RAINBOW (IRE) 6 b.m. Rainbows For Life (CAN) – Cockney Ground (IRE) (Common Grounds) [2002/3 20s⁴ 22g^{pu} 20d⁴ 16d⁴ Dec 26] first foal: half-sister to 5f winner in Italy by Fayruz: dam unraced: won mares maiden Irish point on debut in 2002: bought €21,000 Goffs June Sale: poor form over hurdles: sold 2,400 gns Doncaster May Sales. *R. H. Alner*   **h72**

COCK OF THE NORTH (IRE) 6 b.g. Supreme Leader – Our Quest (Private Walk) [2002/3 19s² Dec 26] 25,000 4-y-o: half-brother to top-class staying chaser Rough Quest (by Crash Course): dam ran once: 14/1, 14 lengths second of 12 to Keep On Running in novice hurdle at Hereford on debut: should do better. *C. R. Egerton*   **h98 p**

COCK OF THE ROOST (IRE)   6 b.g. Executive Perk – Sly Maid (Rapid River)   **h–**
[2002/3 F16d F16g F16g F17m⁵ 17g 20dpu 16s 20spu 20v⁶ Jan 29] IR 21,000 3-y-o: **F–**
lengthy gelding: sixth foal: half-brother to winning pointer Shylock (by Bustino): dam 5f
winner in Britain, later successful in Italy: pulled up in Irish point in 2002, bought £4,100
Ascot April Sales: no form in bumpers/novice hurdles: tried tongue tied: headstrong.
S. T. Lewis

COCKSURE (IRE)   8 b.g. Nomination – Hens Grove (Alias Smith (USA)) [2002/3   **c–**
16spu Aug 9] ex-Irish gelding: 1½m winner on Flat: second in 2m juvenile hurdle at   **h–**
Fairyhouse in November 1998: little other form (well held on chasing debut): tried
blinkered/tongue tied. *B. J. Llewellyn*

CODE SIGN (USA)   4 b.g. Gulch (USA) – Karasavina (IRE) (Sadler's Wells (USA))   **h63 +**
[2002/3 17s⁶ 17s 17d Feb 23] leggy gelding: fairly useful maiden on Flat (stays 1¼m),
sold out of J. Gosden's stable 22,000 gns Newmarket Autumn Sales: well held in 3 runs
over hurdles. *P. J. Hobbs*

CODY   4 ch.c. Zilzal (USA) – Ibtihaj (USA) (Raja Baba (USA)) [2002/3 16d 17d 17d   **h–**
16g 19m 22g Apr 19] modest maiden on Flat (stays 1½m): no form over hurdles.
G. A. Ham

COLD COMFORT   11 b.g. Arctic Lord – Main Brand (Main Reef) [2002/3 h71: 19gF   **h– x**
Jun 12] not fluent all 3 starts in novice hurdles. *I. R. Brown*

COLEHAM   5 b.m. Saddlers' Hall (IRE) – Katie Scarlett (Lochnager) [2002/3 F92:   **F91**
F16m² Jun 3] fair form in bumpers, second at Huntingdon, only start in 2002/3.
W. M. Brisbourne

COLETTE (IRE)   6 b.m. Nicolotte – Ascensiontide (Ela-Mana-Mou) [2002/3 h82:   **h–**
20gpu May 3] rather leggy, lengthy mare: poor hurdler: stayed easy 21f: acted on good to
firm and heavy going: dead. *S. T. Lewis*

COLIN'S HOPE   5 b.g. Then Again – Bahawir Pour (USA) (Green Dancer (USA))   **h–**
[2002/3 F70: F17g F17d F18v⁶ 22spu 16g Feb 22] poor form in bumpers, sold out of   **F–**
M. Easterby's stable 2,750 gns Doncaster November Sales after second start: no encouragement in seller or novice over hurdles. *M. J. Gingell*

COLLECTIVE DREAM   8 b.g. North Col – Toumanova (High Line) [2002/3 24dpu   **h–**
Mar 1] 2,600 3-y-o: deep-girthed gelding: ninth foal: half-brother to modest staying
chaser Baroncelli (by Baron Blakeney): dam, poor maiden hurdler, out of half-sister to
top-class staying chaser Spanish Steps: no show in novice hurdle at Newbury on debut.
R. Curtis

COLLEGE CITY (IRE)   4 b.g. College Chapel – Polish Crack (IRE) (Polish Patriot   **h78**
(USA)) [2002/3 16d 16g 16g 16s* 19d² Mar 5] poor maiden on Flat (seems to stay 1m),
sold out of S. Magnier's stable 1,400 gns Doncaster September Sales: poor hurdler: won
selling handicap at Newcastle in February: stays 19f: acts on soft going. *R. C. Guest*

COLLIERS COURT   6 b.g. Puget (USA) – Rag Time Belle (Raga Navarro (ITY))   **F74**
[2002/3 F16v⁶ F16s F17v Feb 11] second foal: dam modest 2m hurdler/chaser: poor form
on first of 3 starts in bumpers. *Mrs L. Williamson*

COLLIERS QUAY (IRE)   7 b.g. Warcraft (USA) – Francois's Crumpet (IRE)   **h106**
(Strong Gale) [2002/3 18s F16s 24m* 20d⁴ 26g* 21g² 21d 24s⁵ 24d Jan 16] 11,500 4-y-o: **F–**
first foal: dam, maiden hurdler, half-sister to useful 25f hurdle winner Crumpet Delite:
little form in bumpers: fair hurdler: won minor event at Cork in July and novice at
Southwell (first outing since leaving M. O'Brien, very simple task) in September: stays
3¼m: acts on soft and good to firm going: has had tongue tied. *Miss Venetia Williams*

COLLINE DE FEU   6 ch.m. Sabrehill (USA) – Band of Fire (USA) (Chief's Crown   **h94**
(USA)) [2002/3 h86: 16s² 19d⁴ 16s⁵ 16s³ 21d³ Jan 15] leggy mare: modest hurdler: stays
2½m: raced on good going or softer over hurdles (acts on heavy). *Mrs P. Sly*

COLNEL RAYBURN (IRE)   7 b.g. Un Desperado (FR) – Super Boreen (Boreen   **h114**
(FR)) [2002/3 h–p, F108: 16v² 16s* 16s 17s* 16d² 20d Feb 23] tall gelding: fair hurdler:
improved efforts when winning handicaps at Gowran in December and January: best
around 2m: acts well on soft/heavy going: has failed to impress with attitude. *Paul Nolan,
Ireland*

COLNSIDE BONNIE   5 ch.m. Afzal – Armagnac Messenger (Pony Express)   **h83**
[2002/3 F16d² F16g⁵ F17m⁴ F17s 19dF 22dpu 17s² 19v⁵ 16m* 17f² 19mF Apr 8] fifth   **F82**
foal: half-sister to winning pointers by Vital Season and Lyphento: dam winning pointer:

modest form first 3 starts in bumpers, when trained by H. Haynes: poor novice hurdler: won handicap at Wincanton in March: should stay beyond 17f: acts on firm and soft going: front runner. *B. G. Powell*

COLOMBE D'OR   6 gr.g. Petong – Deep Divide (Nashwan (USA)) [2002/3 h73: 16m 17m 17m 16m[5] 17d[6] Aug 4] poor maiden hurdler: likely to prove best around 2m: acts on soft going, probably on good to firm: blinkered third start: has carried head high: sold to join I. Williams 1,200 gns Doncaster August Sales. *M. C. Chapman*   **h– §**

COLOMBIAN GREEN (IRE)   9 b.g. Sadler's Wells (USA) – Sharaya (USA) (Youth (USA)) [2002/3 c–, h114: 16d[3] 16v[6] c17d[3] c20s[4] c20d[pu] c16v[4] Mar 8] useful-looking gelding: fair handicap hurdler: best effort over fences (let down by jumping twice) when third in novice at Exeter: stays easy 21f: raced on good going or softer over jumps (acts on heavy): often weak finisher. *D. R. Gandolfo*   **c107 §** **h114 §**

COLONEL BRAXTON (IRE)   8 b.g. Buckskin (FR) – Light The Lamp (Miner's Lamp) [2002/3 c139p, h–: 20v[4] c24v[2] c17s* c24s[2] 26g Mar 13] well-made gelding: smart hurdler, backward on reappearance: very smart chaser: twice good second to impressive Beef Or Salmon in Grade 1 events at Leopardstown, beaten 6 lengths in Ericsson Chase in December and 4 lengths in Hennessy Cognac Gold Cup in February: won listed race at Fairyhouse in between: well beaten in Gold Cup at Cheltenham final start: successful around 2m, should stay 3¼m: raced on good going or softer (acts on heavy): usually races up with pace. *D. T. Hughes, Ireland*   **c156** **h–**

COLONEL BROWN (IRE)   7 b.g. Scenic – Musical Smoke (IRE) (Orchestra) [2002/3 c90, h90: 17m[pu] 16g[6] c17s[pu] Aug 1] sturdy gelding: modest maiden hurdler/winning chaser in Ireland: no form in Britain: tried blinkered/tongue tied. *O. O'Neill*   **c–** **h–**

COLONEL CUSTER   8 ch.g. Komaite (USA) – Mohican (Great Nephew) [2002/3 h–: 20g May 8] modest on all-weather Flat (stays 1½m), little form on turf: no show in 2 novice hurdles. *R. Brotherton*   **h–**

Mrs John Magnier's "Colonel Braxton"

COLONEL FRANK 6 b.g. Toulon – Fit For Firing (FR) (In Fijar (USA)) [2002/3 **h113 p** F82: F17d³ 16d⁴ 19g⁶ 18g* 20d² Apr 9] useful-looking gelding: better effort in bumpers **F90** when third at Folkestone on reappearance: fair novice hurdler: held on by a short head (despite broken stirrup leather) at Fontwell in March: improved again when second to Fair Prospect at Uttoxeter, again making running: likely to stay beyond 2½m: type to progress further. *B. G. Powell*

COLONEL KURTZ (USA) 5 b.g. Slip Anchor – Rustaka (USA) (Riverman (USA)) **h–** [2002/3 21mᵖᵘ Jul 17] poor maiden on Flat (stays 1¾m): showed little in novice on hurdling debut: sold £2,800 Ascot August Sales. *John Berry*

COLONEL MONROE (IRE) 6 b. or br.g. Lord Americo – Fairy Blaze (IRE) (Good **h119** Thyne (USA)) [2002/3 F16g³ F16d* 20g* 22s² 24s³ 20v* 22v* 24s⁶ 20g⁵ Apr 20] IR **F92** 40,000 3-y-o: well-made gelding: will make a chaser: second foal: half-brother to promising hurdler Kicking King (by Old Vic) and modest chaser who stays 2½m Glenfarclas Boy (by Montelimar): dam unraced: fair form in bumpers, winning at Clonmel in May: fairly useful hurdler: won novice at Limerick in October and 2 other events (within 3 days) there in December: stays 3m: acts on heavy going. *E. J. O'Grady, Ireland*

COLONEL MUSTARD 7 ch.g. Keen – Juliet Bravo (Glow (USA)) [2002/3 16m **h–** 16g 17s 22g Mar 17] workmanlike gelding: fair on Flat (stays 11.6f): no form over hurdles: sold out of P. Murphy's stable 5,000 gns Doncaster August Sales after reappearance. *Mrs H. E. Rees*

COLONEL NORTH (IRE) 7 b.g. Distinctly North (USA) – Tricky (Song) [2002/3 **c–** 20d 16d 20d 17s c16d⁶ Jan 24] sturdy gelding: novice hurdler: well held in 2002/3, **h–** including on chasing debut: sold 2,000 gns Doncaster May Sales. *D. Pearson*

COLONIAL RULE (USA) 6 b.g. Pleasant Colony (USA) – Musicale (USA) (The **h83 §** Minstrel (CAN)) [2002/3 h–: 20d 22g² 21sᵖᵘ 21s⁴ 22v³ 26g³ 22gᵖᵘ 24gᵖᵘ 21m Apr 26] close-coupled gelding: poor handicap hurdler: left J. O'Neill after eighth start: stays 3¼m: raced mainly on good going or softer (acts on heavy): tried blinkered/visored/tongue tied: moody. *Mrs L. B. Normile*

COLONIAL SUNRISE (USA) 6 b.g. Pleasant Colony (USA) – Dancing Reef **h79** (USA) (Danzig (USA)) [2002/3 h77+: 16d³ 16g 16v² Nov 16] useful-looking gelding: poor novice hurdler: likely to prove best around 2m: raced on good going or softer (acts on heavy). *T. D. Easterby*

COLONIAL SUNSET (IRE) 9 b.g. Lancastrian – Thai Nang (Tap On Wood) **c103** [2002/3 21g² 24gᵖᵘ c20g⁵ 20d 24g 18m⁵ 17f⁵ c16g² c16m³ c17v² c20m c18s² c16v³ **h70** c20m⁶ Mar 31] plain sparely-made gelding: half-brother to 4 winners, including fair staying hurdler Thai Electric (by Electric): dam lightly-raced maiden: sold out of T. Stack's stable 1,200 gns Doncaster November (2001) Sales: fair hurdler at best, only poor nowadays: fair novice chaser: stays 21f: acts on heavy going: tried blinkered/tongue tied. *Dr P. Pritchard*

COLORADO FALLS (IRE) 5 b.g. Nashwan (USA) – Ballet Shoes (IRE) (Ela- **h103** Mana-Mou) [2002/3 17s* Jun 3] fairly useful on Flat (probably stays 15f): winning debut over hurdles in 6-runner 4-y-o novice at Cartmel, beating Westernmost comfortably by 2½ lengths: looked sure to progress, but wasn't seen out over hurdles again. *P. Monteith*

COLOURFUL LIFE (IRE) 7 ch.g. Rainbows For Life (CAN) – Rasmara (Kala- **c– x** glow) [2002/3 c105x, h108: 16v⁵ 21d 16s² 16s² 20v⁶ 16m 20d⁶ Apr 4] big, lengthy **h121** gelding: winning chaser but often let down by jumping: fairly useful handicap hurdler: good efforts 3 of last 4 starts, second to Xenophon in Pierse Hurdle at Leopardstown in January on first occasion: best form up to 2½m: acts on good to firm and heavy going: held up, and carries head awkwardly under pressure. *Mrs M. Reveley*

COLQUHOUN 9 b.g. Rakaposhi King – Red Rambler (Rymer) [2002/3 c19dF c20d² **c103** c18mᵘʳ Mar 21] good-topped gelding: lightly raced: fair hurdler: similar form when **h–** runner-up both completed starts over fences (often let down by jumping): possibly best short of 3m: acts on good to soft going, probably on good to firm. *T. R. George*

COLUMBA (IRE) 7 b.g. Lord Americo – Jackson Miss (Condorcet (FR)) [2002/3 **h125** h124, F97: 16s³ 18s⁴ Nov 30] angular gelding: fairly useful hurdler: much better effort in 2002/3 when third in handicap at Naas: stays 2½m: acts on heavy going. *D. T. Hughes, Ireland*

COLUMBUS (IRE) 6 b.g. Sadler's Wells (USA) – Northern Script (USA) (Arts And **h110** Letters (USA)) [2002/3 17g⁴ 19s² 20s⁶ 19d² 19s² 22f² 24m² Apr 12] angular gelding: fair handicap hurdler: trained until after reappearance by C. Grant: ran well without winning all bar one subsequent outing, including at Punchestown in early-May: stays 3m: acts on firm and soft going: blinkered/visored: often looks none too keen. *Mrs J. Candlish*

COLVADA 7 b.m. North Col – Prevada (Soldier Rose) [2002/3 h79?: c20d^{pu} 22s^{pu} Feb 3] useful-looking mare: would have been placed but for falling in novice hurdle on debut but no form since (jumped ponderously on chasing debut): left A. King after reappearance. *P. G. Murphy*   c– h–

COMANCHE WAR PAINT (IRE) 6 b.g. Commanche Run – Galeshula (Strong Gale) [2002/3 22s^6 23v^2 c24s^F Feb 13] IR 12,000 4-y-o: seventh foal: half-brother to fair chaser Ridgewood Water (by Over The River), up to 2¾m: dam unraced sister to useful chaser up to 3m Edberg: won last of 4 starts in maiden Irish points in 2002: bought 15,000 gns Doncaster May Sales: better effort in maiden hurdles when 24 lengths second to Chief Witness in amateur event at Fakenham: fell fifth on steeplechasing debut: will be suited by 3m+. *P. F. Nicholls*   c– h87

COMBE CASTLE 8 gr.g. Carlingford Castle – Silver Cirrus (General Ironside) [2002/3 h–: c23g^{ur} c24d c24v^R c23v^6 c21s^{pu} Jan 14] lengthy gelding: of little account: has worn cheekpieces. *K. C. Bailey*   c– h–

COMBINED VENTURE (IRE) 7 b.h. Dolphin Street (FR) – Centinela (Caerleon (USA)) [2002/3 h–: 16g^{pu} 17m^{pu} 17g 17d^5 17s^{pu} 20d^{pu} 17s Dec 26] sparely-made horse: little form over hurdles: often tongue tied. *G. J. Smith*   h–

COMEDY GAYLE 16 b.g. Lir – Follifoot's Folly (Comedy Star (USA)) [2002/3 c99, h–: c21g^{pu} May 1] workmanlike gelding: one-time useful hunter chaser: pulled up at Cheltenham in May: stays 25f: acts on firm and soft going. *Ms Sue Willcock*   c– h–

COME IN MOSCOW (IRE) 7 ch.m. Over The River (FR) – Kiria Mou (USA) (To-Agori-Mou) [2002/3 c20s^2 c20v^{pu} c20s^6 c24v^{pu} c17s^3 c20s* c24v^R c21d^F c24m^4 Apr 20] lengthy, angular mare: sister to modest chaser Meandering By, stays 2¾m, and half-sister to fairly useful chaser up to 2¾m Lord Heavens (by Lord Americo): dam lightly-raced maiden: winning hurdler: fair chaser: won valuable listed mares novice at Thurles in January: let down by jumping next 2 starts (fell first in Topham Chase at Aintree): stays 3m, effective at much shorter: raced mainly on soft/heavy ground. *John Joseph Murphy, Ireland*   c109 h–

COME ON BOY 9 ch.g. Henbit (USA) – Miss Rewarde (Andy Rew) [2002/3 c25s^{pu} Mar 7] maiden pointer: showed nothing on hunter chase debut. *Mark Doyle*   c–

COME ON GEORGE (IRE) 7 b.g. Barathea (IRE) – Lacovia (USA) (Majestic Light (USA)) [2002/3 c24g^{pu} May 30] angular gelding: successful twice in points in 2002: has made mistakes over hurdles/in hunter chase. *Mark Doyle*   c– h–

COMEOUTOFTHEFOG (IRE) 8 b.g. Mujadil (USA) – Local Belle (Ballymore) [2002/3 16d^{pu} Jul 5] poor on Flat (stays 1m): showed nothing in seller on hurdling debut. *Mrs P. Ford*   h–

COMERAGH GALE (IRE) 10 b.g. Strong Gale – Comeragh Princess (Le Moss) [2002/3 h74: 22g* 22f^{ur} 22g^{pu} 22g^4 Jun 29] poor hurdler: won amateur novice at Exeter in May: reportedly lame third outing: stays 2¾m: acts on good to soft going: blinkered last 5 starts. *V. R. A. Dartnall*   h86

COMETE DU LAC (FR) 6 b.m. Comte du Bourg (FR) – Line du Nord (FR) (Esprit du Nord (USA)) [2002/3 c17g^2 c18s* c21s^3 c21s^F c17s^2 c16d^4 c16s^R 20g Dec 28] leggy mare: third foal: sister to winning Italian hurdler/chaser around 2m Febus du Lac: dam unraced half-sister to useful 4-y-o chaser Little Point: winning hurdler: fairly useful chaser: won minor event at Auteuil in June: left J. Ortet, no encouragement all 3 starts in Britain (well held when refused 4 out second time): stays 21f: acts on any going: usually blinkered, visored final start. *M. D. Hammond*   c120 § h– §

COMEX FLYER (IRE) 6 ch.g. Prince of Birds (USA) – Smashing Pet (Mummy's Pet) [2002/3 h127: c16m^3 c16g* c16f^{wo} c19m^4 20s^3 21d^{2} 22d^3 20s^2 21s^5 20d^3 20d^2 17g^F Mar 13] rather leggy gelding: easily won novice chase at Fakenham in October: walked over at Kempton later in month: useful hurdler: won handicap at Warwick in December: stayed 2¾m: acted on soft and good to firm going: tongue tied all starts bar one over hurdles: dead. *P. F. Nicholls*   c110 h137

COMFORTABLE CALL 5 ch.g. Nashwan (USA) – High Standard (Kris) [2002/3 26d^6 17g^{pu} 19m 16g 16s^4 17g^3 17g* Apr 26] lengthy gelding: fair maiden on Flat (stays 1¾m) at 3 yrs, sold out of E. Dunlop's stable 5,000 gns Newmarket (2001) Autumn   h69

Sales: poor hurdler: fortunate to win selling handicap at Market Rasen, not always fluent and held when left in front at last: should stay beyond 2m: tongue tied last 3 starts. *H. Alexander*

COMING THROUGH (IRE) 11 ch.g. Le Bavard (FR) – Gay Countess (Master **c–** Buck) [2002/3 c–: c17g⁴ c21dᵖᵘ c16mᵖᵘ c21mᵖᵘ c23mᵖᵘ c20d³ c20m⁵ Aug 17] winning pointer: usually fails to complete in steeplechases: visored once. *T. Wall*

COMMANCHE COURT (IRE) 10 ch.g. Commanche Run – Sorceress (FR) **c163** (Fabulous Dancer (USA)) [2002/3 c171, h140: c16s³ c20d* c26g⁶ c25g³ Apr 3] lengthy, **h129** good sort: top-class chaser: excelled himself when second to Best Mate in Cheltenham Gold Cup in 2002: three subsequent efforts when sixth in same race and staying-on 14¾ lengths third of 7 to First Gold in Martell Cognac Gold Cup at Aintree: earlier won very weak 4-runner handicap at Navan: lightly raced over hurdles nowadays, fifth of 6 in Grade 1 event at Punchestown in early-May: best at 3m+ on good going or softer (acts on heavy): usually held up: usually sound jumper. *T. M. Walsh, Ireland*

COMMANCHE DRUMS (IRE) 9 b.g. Commanche Run – Mabbots Own (Royal **h84** Trip) [2002/3 h83: 19g⁵ 17g⁶ 20m³ Mar 29] workmanlike gelding: poor novice hurdler: probably stays 2¾m: acts on good to firm going (bumper form on soft). *O. Brennan*

COMMANCHE GENERAL (IRE) 6 b.g. Commanche Run – Shannon Amber **h84** (IRE) (Phardante (FR)) [2002/3 F79: F17g⁴ F16d⁴ 22d³ 20vᵖᵘ 19d 24d⁶ 21g* 21m⁴ Apr **F91** 2] lengthy, angular gelding: best effort in bumpers when fourth at Newton Abbot on reappearance: poor novice hurdler: won 16-runner conditional jockeys race at Market Rasen in March: probably stays 3m: acts on good to soft going, not discredited on good to firm. *J. F. Panvert*

COMMANCHE HERO (IRE) 10 ch.g. Cardinal Flower – Fair Bavard (Le Bavard **c88** (FR)) [2002/3 c–§, h81§: 22m³ 22fᵖᵘ 24d c17v⁵ c20g c24g* c24d² c24g³ Apr 19] work- **h81** manlike gelding: poor handicap chaser/maiden hurdler: gained first win at Huntingdon in March: stays 3m: acts on heavy and good to firm going: has found little. *R. J. Price*

COMMANCHE JIM (IRE) 7 b.g. Commanche Run – On A Dream (Balinger) **c106** [2002/3 h97, F–: 24f⁴ c21sᶠ c26v² c21d* 26s⁵ c24s* c26s* c26s⁶ Mar 15] sturdy gelding: **h–** fair chaser: won handicaps at Folkestone (novice) in December, Taunton in February and Fontwell (best effort when beating Irish Option 11 lengths) in March: below form both outings over hurdles in 2002/3: should stay beyond 3¼m: acts on heavy going: often less than fluent over hurdles but better jumper of fences. *R. H. Alner*

COMMANCHE PRIDE (IRE) 9 b.g. Commanche Run – Galla's Pride (Quayside) **c69** [2002/3 22g 20d c20m³ c16g⁶ Aug 27] 6,000 4-y-o: workmanlike gelding: third foal: **h–** half-brother to bumper winner D'Ygrande (by Good Thyne) and winning pointer by Carlingford Castle: dam ran twice in points: poor maiden hurdler/chaser: stays 2½m: acts on good to firm and heavy going: tried blinkered. *E. McNamara, Ireland*

COMMANCHE QUEST (IRE) 7 b.g. Commanche Run – Conna Dodger (IRE) **c103** (Kemal (FR)) [2002/3 h92, F73: 20s³ 20s⁵ c25vᶠ 20s⁶ 20sᵖᵘ c25s³ c20s⁴ Mar 2] lengthy **h94** gelding: modest novice hurdler: fair form both completed starts over fences but let down by jumping in latter stages: stays 25f: raced on going softer than good: blinkered fifth start (ran poorly). *Mrs M. Reveley*

COMMANCHE SUMMER (IRE) 9 b.m. Commanche Run – Royal Typhoon (Royal **c68** Fountain) [2002/3 c66, h–: 22d 22d⁴ 24v⁶ 17v³ c25s³ c21g Apr 19] leggy mare: poor **h75** maiden hurdler/chaser: effective at testing 2m to 3¼m: acts on good to firm and heavy going: didn't impress with attitude last 2 starts. *J. D. Frost*

COMMANCHE WIND (IRE) 8 b.g. Commanche Run – Delko (Decent Fellow) **h99** [2002/3 h–: 21g* 24g 20d* 19g³ 21m² 21g* 20dᵖᵘ Apr 25] lengthy gelding: modest hurdler: won maiden at Sedgefield and handicap at Wetherby (wandered under pressure) in May: off over 8 months before final outing: stays 21f: acts on good to firm and good to soft going: tends to jump right. *E. W. Tuer*

COMMANDANT (IRE) 10 b.g. Good Thyne (USA) – Slave Run (Deep Run) **c–** [2002/3 c21mᵘʳ c21gᵖᵘ Oct 15] well-made gelding: little form since hurdling debut, **h–** including in points: tried blinkered. *C. C. Bealby*

COMMANDER GLEN (IRE) 11 b.g. Glenstal (USA) – Une Parisienne (FR) (Bol- **c– §** konski) [2002/3 c71§, h–: c27mᵘʳ Apr 11] workmanlike gelding: one-time modest chaser: **h–**

unseated third on hunter debut: stays 27f: acts on firm and good to soft going: usually visored/blinkered: has had tongue tied: ungenuine. *J. W. Hughes*

COMMASARRIS 11 gr.g. Joli Wasfi (USA) – Lucy Aura (Free State) [2002/3 c22d^{pu} **c93** c21m^2 May 22] fair pointer: tongue tied, first form in hunter chases when second in maiden at Folkestone. *Mrs S. Wall*

COMMISSAR (IRE) 4 b.g. Common Grounds – Trescalini (IRE) (Sadler's Wells **h–** (USA)) [2002/3 16d^F Feb 7] workmanlike gelding: half-brother to modest chaser Macha-lini (by Machiavellian), stays 27f: fair 1¼m winner on Flat, sold out of R. Charlton's stable 22,000 gns Doncaster November Sales: behind when falling fifth in juvenile at Kempton on hurdling debut. *J. J. Bridger*

COMMONCHERO (IRE) 6 b.g. Desert of Wind (USA) – Douala (GER) (Non- **h109** Thoroughbred) [2002/3 F16g^5 F16g^6 F16s^2 F16s 18s^4 F16s* 16s* 16d^3 Feb 27] IR 7,600 **F104** 3-y-o: half-brother to five winners, including fair staying hurdler/chaser Matts Dilemma (by Pitskelly): dam won at 3 yrs in Germany: fairly useful in bumpers: won maiden at Tramore in January: fair form over hurdles: won maiden at Punchestown in February: raced around 2m on good going or softer (acts on soft). *M. J. P. O'Brien, Ireland*

COMMON GIRL (IRE) 5 gr.m. Roselier (FR) – Rumups Debut (IRE) (Good Thyne **F85** (USA)) [2002/3 F16m^5 F16m^3 Apr 21] IR £18,000 3-y-o: third foal: dam unraced: better effort in mares maiden bumpers when third to Waterlily at Fakenham. *O. Brennan*

COMPADRE 5 gr.g. Environment Friend – Cardinal Press (Sharrood (USA)) [2002/3 **h–** 20g^{pu} Apr 14] 6,000Y: second living foal: half-brother to fair 7f to 11f winner Supreme Salutation (by Most Welcome) and fairly useful 2002 2-y-o 6f winner Queen of Night (by Piccolo): dam maiden half-sister to smart sprinter Coquitos Friend, from family of smart 6f to 1m performer Muchea: 40/1, weakened after 3 out in novice hurdle at Hexham on debut. *P. Beaumont*

COMPOSTELLO (IRE) 8 ch.g. Erins Isle – Your Mine (Push On) [2002/3 F113: **h113** 16d^3 17g^4 16m* 20s Nov 17] workmanlike gelding: will make a chaser: bumper winner: fair form over hurdles, won maiden at Tralee in August and novice at Limerick in October: raced mainly around 2m (beaten before stamina became an issue over 2½m final outing): acts on good to firm and good to soft going: successful only start in blinkers. *N. Meade, Ireland*

COMPTON AMICA (IRE) 7 gr.m. High Estate – Nephrite (Godswalk (USA)) **h84** [2002/3 h80: 24d^4 16g^5 19d^5 16s^3 17s^3 19d 17d 19v^2 Mar 10] neat mare: poor handicap hurdler: stays 19f: acts on heavy going: has looked tricky ride. *K. Bishop*

COMPTON CHICK (IRE) 5 b.m. Dolphin Street (FR) – Cecina (Welsh Saint) **h97** [2002/3 h81: 18m^4 18f^2 16g^5 22d^4 20s^2 22d 20s^4 18f^4 Apr 24] modest maiden hurdler: tongue tied, well below form last 3 starts, off 4 months before final one (also wore cheek-pieces): stays 2½m: acts on firm and soft going. *J. W. Mullins*

COMTE DE CHAMBORD 7 gr.g. Baron Blakeney – Show Rose (Coliseum) **F78** [2002/3 F16s^3 F16g F17m^5 Jul 25] 6,500 4-y-o: medium-sized gelding: seventh foal: half-brother to fair jumper up to 3m Impale (by Crash Course): dam, winning jumper suited by 2½m, sister to smart chaser up to 3m Cancello: best effort in bumpers when third in weakly-contested event at Worcester on debut: looks very much a stayer. *Mark Campion*

CONCERTO COLLONGES (FR) 13 br.g. El Badr – Mariane Collonge (FR) (Cap **c–** Martin (FR)) [2002/3 c–: c25m^6 May 8] fairly useful hunter chaser: well held at Wetherby in May: thorough stayer: acts on heavy going: ran creditably when blinkered final 2000/1 start. *Miss A. Armitage*

CONCHITA 6 b.m. St Ninian – Carnetto (Le Coq d'Or) [2002/3 F16v^3 F17d^3 F16g* **F95 +** Mar 29] first foal: dam fair staying hurdler: fair form in bumpers, won maiden at Hexham in March: will stay beyond 2m. *G. A. Harker*

CONDOYLE (IRE) 10 b.g. Rare One – Worthy Gale (Strong Gale) [2002/3 h74: c20g^6 **c62** c25m^4 c25g^{pu} c19d^2 Oct 23] lengthy gelding: poor maiden hurdler: hasn't convinced with **h–** jumping all 4 starts in steeplechases: barely stays 2¾m: acts on good to firm and good to soft ground: tried blinkered: has pulled hard. *R. J. Baker*

CONQUER (IRE) 8 b.g. Phardante (FR) – Tullow Performance (Gala Performance **c–** (USA)) [2002/3 c100, h–: c24g^{ur} c24d^{pu} Jan 16] lengthy gelding: winning pointer in **h–** 2000: lightly raced over hurdles/fences, ran as if amiss final start: stays 25f: acts on good to firm and heavy going. *H. D. Daly*

CONROY 4 b.g. Greensmith – Highland Spirit (Scottish Reel) [2002/3 F12d⁴ F14d⁵ **F84**
F16m³ Apr 10] 500Y: leggy gelding: fourth foal: half-brother to 2 winning hurdlers by
Never So Bold, including fair 2-miler Langwaki River: dam 2-y-o 6f/7f winner, also
fairly useful hurdler: fair form in bumpers, third to Hartest Rose at Ludlow. *F. Jordan*

CONTACT (IRE) 6 br.g. Grand Lodge (USA) – Pink Cashmere (IRE) (Polar Falcon **h88**
(USA)) [2002/3 16s⁵ Dec 26] good-topped gelding: fair on Flat (stays 7f): 66/1, pulled
hard when well-held fifth of 8 in novice hurdle at Kempton: sold 500 gns Doncaster
January Sales. *M. Wigham*

CONTES (IRE) 11 b.g. Lafontaine (USA) – Dara's Diocese (Bishop of Orange) **c101**
[2002/3 c–, h86: c20m³ c20s⁺ c22f* c20d⁴ c21g^pu Jun 22] sparely-made gelding: maiden **h–**
hurdler: fair handicap chaser: won at Fontwell in June: clear when fell last previous start:
best form up to 2¾m: acts on soft and firm going: blinkered in 2002/3: none too
consistent. *P. R. Hedger*

CONTI D'ESTRUVAL (FR) 13 b.g. Synefos (USA) – Barbara Conti (ITY) (Teodoro **c–**
Trivulzio) [2002/3 c21g^pu c16d^pu May 13] lengthy gelding: tubed: fair hunter chaser in **h–**
1998/9: no show in 4 starts since: stays 21f: acts on firm going: has worn blinkers/visor.
Mrs P. Smith

CONTRACT SCOTLAND (IRE) 8 br.g. Religiously (USA) – Stroked Again (On **c93**
Your Mark) [2002/3 h86+, F–: 20d* 27g* 22s⁵ 22d⁶ c20g² Mar 23] deep-girthed gelding: **h93**
modest handicap hurdler: successful at Newcastle (novice) and Kelso early in season:
second to King's Bounty in maiden at Wetherby on chasing debut, jumping soundly:
effective at 2½m to 27f: raced mainly on good going or softer: may improve over fences.
L. Lungo

CONTROL MAN (IRE) 5 ch.g. Glacial Storm (USA) – Got To Fly (IRE) (Kemal **F118**
(FR)) [2002/3 F18v* F16v* F16g⁵ Feb 8] angular gelding: sixth foal: half-brother to
modest hurdler up to 3m Indian Wings and 2¾m chase winner in Switzerland (both by
Commanche Run): dam unraced: created good impression first 2 starts in bumpers,
winning at Plumpton and Chepstow (stayed on really well to beat He's The Boss in Grade
2 event) in December: probably unsuited by less testing conditions when fifth to
impressive Cornish Rebel in another Grade 2 at Newbury: will be suited by further than
2m: useful prospect. *M. C. Pipe*

COOKIES BANK 5 b.g. Broadsword (USA) – Kitty Come Home (Monsanto (FR)) **F–**
[2002/3 F17f⁵ Mar 24] 5,800 4-y-o: eighth foal: half-brother to several winners, notably
useful 2m chaser Nearly An Eye (by Nearly A Hand): dam, modest hurdler, stayed 21f:
last of 5 in steadily-run bumper at Taunton on debut. *Mrs S. D. Williams*

COOK O'HAWICK (IRE) 6 b.g. King's Ride – Miners Yank (Miner's Lamp) **h65 p**
[2002/3 F16g 16d⁵ 16g Apr 7] 23,000 4-y-o: fourth foal: dam, placed in bumper/points, **F69**
half-sister to fairly useful 2m chaser Yank Brown, from family of top-class chaser
Waterloo Boy: signs of ability in bumper and 2 starts over hurdles, not given hard time:
likely to prove capable of better in due course. *L. Lungo*

COOL ARCHIE 10 b.g. Roscoe Blake – Echo Lake (Tycoon II) [2002/3 h–: c20f⁶ **c–**
Oct 24] little sign of ability, including in points. *M. Mullineaux* **h–**

COOL BORDER 8 gr.m. Grey Desire – Irish Orchid (Free State) [2002/3 h75, F71: **c§§**
20s 22s⁶ 20d c24g^rtr Feb 22] compact mare: poor form first 2 starts over hurdles: has **h§§**
become thoroughly temperamental, twice reluctant to set off prior to refusing to race final
outing: tried blinkered/in cheekpieces: one to avoid. *M. Bradstock*

COOL CHILLI 5 gr.g. Gran Alba (USA) – Miss Flossa (FR) (Big John (FR)) [2002/3 **h–**
F–: 16d^ur 19s^pu 16d 17g 16d⁶ 16m Apr 21] workmanlike gelding: little sign of ability:
tongue tied last 3 starts. *N. J. Pomfret*

COOL COSSACK (IRE) 6 ch.g. Moscow Society (USA) – Knockacool Breeze **F94**
(Buckskin (FR)) [2002/3 F17g² Apr 21] fourth foal: half-brother to fair chaser around
2½m Breaking Breeze (by Mandalus): dam, placed in 2m maiden hurdles, from family of
very smart staying chaser Cogent: 8/1, encouraging debut when 4 lengths second to
Random Native in 14-runner bumper at Carlisle. *Mrs S. J. Smith*

COOL DEGREE (IRE) 5 br.g. Arctic Lord – Ballyfin Maid (IRE) (Boreen (FR)) **F85**
[2002/3 F17s⁴ F16m⁴ Apr 21] third foal: dam unraced, from family of high-class 2½m
chaser Half-Free: fair form in bumpers at Carlisle and Huntingdon: will stay at least 2½m.
Ferdy Murphy

COOLE ABBEY (IRE) 11 b.g. Viteric (FR) – Eleanors Joy (Sheer Grit) [2002/3 **c112**
c107: c25d³ c25g² c22m² c24g* c24d* Mar 15] rangy, good sort: fairly useful hunter

chaser: off 8 months, won at Musselburgh (third win in race) in February and Newcastle (beat Hazel Reilly 3 lengths in 3-runner event) in March: stays 25f: acts on soft and firm going: sound-jumping front runner: excitable sort. *Mrs Clare Moore*

COOLE SPIRIT (IRE)   10 b.g. All Haste (USA) – Chocolate Biscuit (Biskrah) [2002/3 c117, h–: c24s* c34s^{pu} Mar 15] small gelding: winning hurdler: fairly useful chaser: off 14 months, improved effort when winning handicap at Kempton in January by 5 lengths from Merchants Friend: favourite, pulled up in valuable event at Uttoxeter 2 months later: should stay beyond 3¼m: raced on good going or softer (acts on heavy). *Miss E. C. Lavelle*   **c127 h–**

COOL FROLIC (IRE)   9 br.g. Strong Gale – Delia Murphy (Golden Love) [2002/3 c23d^{pu} May 23] big gelding: won Irish point in 1999: no show in novice hurdle and chase (net muzzle) 19 months apart. *O. Brennan*   **c– h–**

COOLING OFF (IRE)   6 b.m. Brief Truce (USA) – Lovers' Parlour (Beldale Flutter (USA)) [2002/3 h88: 16d^{pu} 20g^6 16v^{pu} 20d^{pu} 18d* 16s^5 16g^5 18g Mar 17] sturdy mare: modest hurdler: had run of race when winning seller at Fontwell in December: effective at 2m, likely to stay beyond 2½m: acts on soft going: usually visored: front runner: not one to trust. *J. R. Jenkins*   **h86 §**

COOL INVESTMENT (IRE)   6 b.g. Prince of Birds (USA) – Superb Investment (IRE) (Hatim (USA)) [2002/3 h92: 20s^4 21d c20v^2 c24d* c22s* Dec 28] leggy, close-coupled gelding: fair maiden hurdler: better form over fences, winning novices at Warwick and Newbury (handicap, drawing further clear after last) in December: stays 3m: acts on heavy going: has had tongue tied: sound jumper. *R. M. Stronge*   **c115 h101**

COOL MILLION   10 ch.g. Derrylin – Goldaw (Gala Performance (USA)) [2002/3 c–: c22d^5 c25d^{pu} c23d^{pu} Dec 19] poor pointer: has worn cheekpieces. *Mrs H. M. Bridges*   **c–**

COOL MINER (IRE)   11 b.g. Miner's Lamp – Coolafinka (IRE) (Strong Statement (USA)) [2002/3 h–: 20d 24m Jul 7] lengthy gelding: winning hurdler: out of form since 2000/1: blinkered once: has had tongue tied. *J. Wade*   **h–**

COOL MONTY (IRE)   9 ch.g. Montelimar (USA) – Rose Ground (Over The River (FR)) [2002/3 h103: 16v^{pu} c17s* c20s^{pu} Dec 27] close-coupled gelding: fair maiden hurdler: made all in novice at Market Rasen on chase debut: ran no sort of race later in month: stays 21f: acts on soft going: made mistakes over hurdles. *I. A. Balding*   **c98 h–**

COOLNAGORNA (IRE)   6 b. or br.g. Warcraft (USA) – Mandalaw (IRE) (Mandalus) [2002/3 h89p, F96: 22s^2 20v* 20s* 21s* 21g^{2d} 20g^F Apr 3]   **h151**

Coolnagorna's career, and his life, ended at the third-last flight in the Mersey Novices' Hurdle at Aintree in April, when an awkward fall resulted in a broken near-hind leg that necessitated his being put down. He was in front and going well at the time, looking set to justify short-priced favouritism and confirm his status as one of the best of the season's novices. Indeed for much of the winter he was *the* leading novice, appearing a really bright prospect, better even than his stable-companion Iris's Gift. Coolnagorna had a record of three wins from his first five starts over hurdles, including the Grade 1 Stan James Challow Hurdle at Newbury, though jumping was not initially Coolnagorna's strongest point, and he lost his reappearance race at Uttoxeter in November for that reason. Favourite in a fifteen-runner maiden on the strength of two bumper successes at Cork (for Tom Hogan) in November 2001 and an eye-catching debut over hurdles three months later, he made a couple of mistakes at the second last, and went down by a head to Silken Thyne, the pair well clear. A foot-perfect performance followed at Chepstow later in the month, when Coolnagorna made most of the running and scored by seventeen lengths. He briefly returned to bad habits in the Grade 2 GQ Winter Novices' Hurdle at Sandown early in December. Going off in front, he jumped sloppily and lost the lead after a bad blunder three from home. Entering the straight, Coolnagorna did not look to be going so well as those around him, but superior stamina enabled him to regain the advantage and stay on very strongly to win by five lengths (value ten, as he was eased) from Thisthatandtother with the subsequent Champion Hurdle fourth Self Defense back in third.

With his star in the ascendancy, Coolnagorna started 6/4-on for the Challow Hurdle at the end of the month. All but one of his six opponents had won, with

GQ Winter Novices' Hurdle, Sandown—Coolnagorna gallops his rivals into the ground

Texas Ranger and Yorkshire both multiple scorers early in the season and Maybe The Business, Calling Brave and No Collusion apparently useful performers in the making. However, they were not a strong collection overall and Coolnagorna crushed them, making the running as usual and striding clear in the straight to beat Calling Brave by twenty-nine lengths. Here was a horse going from strength to strength, giving an impressive display in a race whose most recent winners— King's Road, Bindaree and Classified—had all landed big races subsequently. Given that staying was clearly his forte, Coolnagorna might reasonably have been aimed at the Stayers' Hurdle at the Cheltenham Festival, following the route eventually chosen for Iris's Gift. However, although entered for the race, he was kept over the same trip as in the Challow and lined up for the Royal & SunAlliance Hurdle. All his previous starts had been on going softer than good, and heavy posed no problem, so the ground at Cheltenham probably was not ideal in so far as it failed to place sufficient emphasis on stamina. Coolnagorna was sent off second favourite and battled on stoutly when challenged by Hardy Eustace before losing out by a length and a quarter after mistakes at the third- and second-last flights. At the latter he hampered the eventual fourth Lord Sam, resulting in disqualification and a seven-day ban for his rider Tony Dobbin for causing intentional interference—a harsh verdict when the fault lay at least as much with the rider of Lord Sam.

		Ack Ack	Battle Joined
	Warcraft (USA)	(b 1966)	Fast Turn
	(b 1987)	Became A Lark	TV Lark
Coolnagorna (IRE)		(b 1974)	Blow Up
(b. or br.g. 1997)		Mandalus	Mandamus
	Mandalaw (IRE)	(b or br 1974)	Laminate
	(b 1989)	Dawskin	Buckskin
		(ch 1984)	Bowdaw

 Coolnagorna cost 2,800 guineas as a foal in Ireland. He was the best offspring so far of his sire Warcraft who showed smart form in twenty-one starts at around a mile in the States, including winning the Grade 3 Native Diver Handicap and running second in a Grade 1. The dam Mandalaw did not race and none of her

Mrs G. Smith's "Coolnagorna"

other progeny, two of them also by Warcraft, has made a mark. The best the next dam Dawskin, also unraced, managed at stud was a winning point-to-pointer but, on the plus side, she was a half-sister to the dam of Bobby Grant, a high-class staying chaser who twice won the Tommy Whittle Chase. *Jonjo O'Neill*

COOL ROXY   6 b.g. Environment Friend – Roxy River (Ardross) [2002/3 h81?, F–: 16m^{pu} 16g^4 16m^4 16g^4 16g^4 16d* 20d^2 21s^2 16g* 21m^6 Apr 16] stocky gelding: modest novice hurdler: won handicaps at Fakenham in November and March: stays 21f: acts on soft and good to firm going: reportedly lame on reappearance. *A. G. Blackmore*   **h97**

COOLSAN (IRE)   8 b.g. Insan (USA) – Coolreagh Princess (Raise You Ten) [2002/3 h87, F98: 22d^2 21d* 25d* 24d^{pu} 24g^{pu} Feb 8] well-made gelding: type to make a chaser: fair hurdler: won novices at Plumpton in November and Warwick in December: ran as though something amiss both subsequent starts: stays 25f: raced on good going or softer (won bumper on soft): tongue tied once. *R. H. Alner*   **h110**

COOL SONG   7 ch.g. Michelozzo (USA) – Vi's Delight (New Member) [2002/3 F79: F17d^5 17s^5 Nov 18] strong gelding: modest form in bumpers: fifth of 6 in conditional jockeys novice on hurdling debut. *D. J. Caro*   **h–**
  F78

COOL SPOT (IRE)   15 ch.g. Boyne Valley – Beagle Bay (Deep Run) [2002/3 17m Jul 7] plain gelding: fairly useful handicap chaser in 2000/1: always behind in novice handicap hurdle at Folkestone on return: stays 21f: acts on soft going: best form on right-handed tracks. *J. R. Best*   **c–**
  h–

COOLTEEN HERO (IRE)   13 b.g. King Luthier – Running Stream (Paddy's Stream) [2002/3 c82: c19g c25g c24m^F c25f^3 c24m^2 c25m^4 c23m^3 c23g* c22d^F c26s^F Dec 26] tall gelding: poor handicap chaser: won conditional jockeys event at Leicester in November: probably stays 25f: acts on any going: usually races prominently. *R. H. Alner*   **c75**

COOMBS SPINNEY 6 b.g. Homo Sapien – Woodram Delight (Idiot's Delight) **h–**
[2002/3 F–: 16d Nov 29] strong, good-bodied gelding: well beaten in 2 bumpers and a
maiden hurdle. *Mrs P. Sly*

CO OPTIMIST 6 b.g. Homo Sapien – Tapua Taranata (IRE) (Mandalus) [2002/3 h70, **h96**
F97: 17g⁵ 22d³ 26s² 24g⁵ Feb 8] good-topped gelding: bumper winner: modest maiden
hurdler: stays 3¼m: raced on good going or softer (acts on soft). *N. A. Twiston-Davies*

COOTEHILL BOY (IRE) 9 br.g. Strong Gale – Orospring (Tesoro Mio) [2002/3 **c–**
h80: 20d² 24mᵖᵘ c22mᵘʳ c20gᶠ Jun 15] good-topped gelding: poor hurdler: failed to **h83**
complete in 2 chases: stayed 3m: acted on soft and good to firm going: tongue tied: dead.
W. Storey

COPELAND 8 b.g. Generous (IRE) – Whitehaven (Top Ville) [2002/3 h157: 16g 16gᶠ **h144 +**
20g⁶ 16f² Apr 25] smallish, sturdy gelding: very smart hurdler, shaped as if retaining all
his ability in Champion Hurdle at Cheltenham, close second and pushed along when fell
3 out: useful form at best all 3 completed starts: stays 2½m: raced mainly over shorter:
acts on heavy and good to firm going, seemed unsuited by firm final outing: formerly
blinkered, visored nowadays: often races up with pace. *M. C. Pipe*

COPERNICUS 8 b.g. Polish Precedent (USA) – Oxslip (Owen Dudley) [2002/3 c130, **c134**
h128: 16s c16s* c16s⁴ c17v⁴ c16s² c16d⁵ c17s³ Mar 16] good-topped gelding: fairly **h–**
useful hurdler: useful chaser: won minor event at Naas in November: best subsequent
efforts when in frame behind Moscow Flyer in graded events at Leopardstown and
Punchestown fourth and fifth starts: effective at 2m to 3m: yet to race on firm going,
probably acts on any other: reportedly lame final start. *P. Hughes, Ireland*

COPPEEN SAM (IRE) 8 ch.g. Samhoi (USA) – Castleview Rose (Master Buck) **c–**
[2002/3 h–: c22s⁵ Dec 28] rangy gelding: disappointing maiden hurdler: soundly beaten **h–**
in novice handicap on chasing debut: stays 23f: acts on soft going: tried blinkered. *Miss
Jacqueline S. Doyle*

Professor D. B. A. Silk & Mrs Heather Silk's "Copeland"

COPPERBEECH (IRE) 9 ch.m. Common Grounds – Caimanite (Tap On Wood) **h–**
[2002/3 16mᵖᵘ Jun 19] maiden on Flat: no sign of ability over hurdles. *H. H. G. Owen*

COPPERMALT (USA) 5 b.g. Affirmed (USA) – Poppy Carew (IRE) (Danehill **h84**
(USA)) [2002/3 16m³ Jul 24] fair maiden on Flat (stays 1¼m) for P. Harris: poor form
when third in novice at Worcester on hurdling debut: sold 2,500 gns Newmarket Autumn
Sales: runner-up in point in April. *P. J. Hobbs*

COPPER MOSS 5 ch.g. Le Moss – Shiona Anne (Royal Fountain) [2002/3 F–: F14d **h86**
F16v 20vᵖᵘ 20d⁴ 16d² 20m⁵ Apr 11] well held in bumpers: modest novice hurdler: raced **F–**
only at Ayr, best effort when second in maiden in March: bred to be suited by 2½m+.
N. W. Alexander

COPPERPOT (IRE) 6 ch.g. Treasure Hunter – Merillion (Touch Paper) [2002/3 **h77**
h77: 20d⁵ Apr 29] rather leggy gelding: poor form over hurdles: will be suited by further
than 2½m: acts on good to soft going. *N. G. Richards*

COPPER SHELL 9 ch.g. Beveled – Luly My Love (Hello Gorgeous (USA)) **c80 x**
[2002/3 c91x, h–: c16m³ c16g⁴ 16s c21s³ c16v² c20g Mar 2] leggy, plain gelding: maiden **h–**
hurdler: poor handicap chaser: stays 21f: possibly best nowadays on going softer than
good (acts on heavy): has worn cheekpieces: tongue tied: not a fluent jumper. *Miss
A. M. Newton-Smith*

COPPLESTONE (IRE) 7 b.g. Second Set (IRE) – Queen of The Brush (Averof) **h77**
[2002/3 h79: 16s⁴ 17s⁶ 16d* 16s² 21vᵘʳ 19d⁵ 19d⁴ 17dᵖᵘ Mar 18] modest on Flat (stays
2m): poor hurdler: won selling handicap at Catterick in December: stays 19f: acts on soft
going: wears cheekpieces: has failed to impress with finishing effort. *W. Storey*

COPSALE LAD 6 ch.g. Karinga Bay – Squeaky Cottage (True Song) [2002/3 16d⁵ **h97**
20vᵖᵘ Dec 20] strong, lengthy gelding: chasing type: fifth foal: mare ran once: burly,
shaped well when fifth in maiden hurdle at Newbury on debut, green early but staying on
very strongly: reared smart, pulled hard and folded tamely in novice at Ascot next time,
possibly amiss: should stay 2½m. *Miss H. C. Knight*

COQ HARDI DIAMOND (IRE) 9 b.g. King's Ride – Snoqualmie (Warpath) **c115**
[2002/3 c24sᶠ c20s⁴ c24v* Dec 29] good sort: fairly useful hurdler/chaser: won very **h–**
valuable Paddy Power Handicap Chase at Leopardstown in December by 7 lengths from
Satcoslam, staying on strongly despite blunder last: should be well suited by long
distances: acts well on heavy going: has worn near-side pricker. *N. Meade, Ireland*

COQUELLES (FR) 7 b.m. In The Wings – La Toja (FR) (Gift Card (FR)) [2002/3 **c83**
h82: 24d⁵ c20d⁴ 19sᶠ 19d* c20g⁴ c21sᵖᵘ Mar 15] good-topped mare: modest handicap **h95**
hurdler: won at Hereford in February: failed to convince with jumping all 3 starts over
fences, virtually refusing on last occasion: stays 21f: acts on heavy going. *R. M. Stronge*

CORALINGA 6 b.m. Terimon – Kintra (Sunyboy) [2002/3 F70?: 19sᵖᵘ 26g 22mᵖᵘ **h–**
Apr 15] sturdy mare: second of 4 in bumper on debut: no form in 3 starts over hurdles,
jumping poorly. *Miss E. C. Lavelle*

CORAL ISLAND 9 b.g. Charmer – Misowni (Niniski (USA)) [2002/3 c112, h89: **c112**
c20d⁵ c31dᵘʳ c16s⁶ c24s⁶ c20s³ c24sᵖᵘ c18m* Mar 21] useful-looking gelding: winning **h–**
hurdler: fair chaser: returned to form when winning handicap at Newbury: stays 2¾m:
acts on firm and soft going: tried blinkered, not since early-1999/00. *R. M. Stronge*

CORBIE ABBEY (IRE) 8 b.g. Glacial Storm (USA) – Dromoland Lady (Pollerton) **c–**
[2002/3 c–, h83: 19dᵖᵘ Oct 19] rangy gelding: poor maiden hurdler/chaser: best efforts at **h–**
2m: acts on good to firm and good to soft going. *P. Beaumont*

CORBIE'S GLEN 9 b.m. Broadsword (USA) – Celestial Bride (Godswalk (USA)) **c78**
[2002/3 h–: c25m² Oct 6] workmanlike mare: poor maiden hurdler: second of 8 in novice **h–**
at Kelso on chasing debut: stays 25f: acts on good to firm ground. *B. Mactaggart*

CORDILLA (IRE) 5 b.g. Accordion – Tumble Heather (Tumble Wind (USA)) [2002/3 **F91**
F16s² Mar 8] eleventh foal: half-brother to winning jumper Ballyfin Lake (by Smooth
Stepper) and winning 2½m hurdler Keiths Choice (by Aristocracy): dam unraced sister to
smart 2m to 3m chaser Pounentes: seemed in need of experience when second of 7 in
bumper at Ayr on debut. *N. G. Richards*

CORE OF SILVER (IRE) 4 b.g. Nucleon (USA) – My Silversmith (IRE) (Cyrano **F–**
de Bergerac) [2002/3 F16d Apr 25] third foal: dam of no account: ninth of 17 in bumper
at Perth on debut. *P. Monteith*

CORKAN (IRE) 9 b.g. Torus – Broad Tab (Cantab) [2002/3 c77+, h–: c26m* c24m² c24m⁵ c27gᵖᵘ Sep 6] rather sparely-made gelding: modest handicap chaser: won at Fontwell in May: stays 3¼m: acts on good to firm going: front runner. *J. Cullinan* **c86 h–**

CORK HARBOUR (FR) 7 ch.g. Grand Lodge (USA) – Irish Sea (Irish River (FR)) [2002/3 17v 17s Feb 13] fair on Flat (stays 1m), sold out of Mrs N. Smith's stable £7,500 Ascot November Sales: little show over hurdles, distressed final start: blinkered. *P. Bowen* **h–**

CORLETTO (POL) 6 b.g. Professional (IRE) – Cortesia (POL) (Who Knows) [2002/3 h80: c17g³ c16m² c17s* c16v³ c16gᵖᵘ Mar 14] good-topped gelding: poor hurdler: modest chaser: won handicap at Market Rasen in November (subsequently tested positive for morphine): let down by jumping last 2 starts: stays 21f: acts on soft and good to firm going. *T. R. George* **c94 h–**

CORNISH GALE (IRE) 9 br.g. Strong Gale – Seanaphobal Lady (Kambalda) [2002/3 c128, h78: c20mᵖᵘ c18mᶠ c16m Apr 17] well-made gelding: fairly useful chaser: off 14 months before reappearance: ran as if retaining all his ability in handicap at Newbury second start, but well held in similar race at Cheltenham month later: stays 2½m: best efforts on good/good to firm going: has had tongue tied: of suspect temperament (reluctant to race on chasing debut). *P. F. Nicholls* **c109 + h–**

CORNISH REBEL (IRE) 6 br.g. Un Desperado (FR) – Katday (FR) (Miller's Mate) [2002/3 F16g* F16g Mar 12] **F118**

    'You only get what you pay for' is not a saying that could ever be applied to the inexact art of purchasing horses to go jumping. Duds with experience come at prices to suit all pockets, whether they're claimed out of a seller off the Flat or possess pattern-class form. Buying an unraced horse at auction is even more precarious: it may look like a Porsche, and have the pedigree of one, but the engine is just as likely to be that of a second-hand Reliant Robin. When a Good Thyne gelding from the celebrated Shuil family went for 100,000 guineas at the Doncaster Spring Sales in 2000, owner Graham Roach must have hoped for rather better than a fifth placing from two outings in bumpers and a wayward display in a selling hurdle at Exeter for such an outlay. Perhaps the name chosen—Billy Ballbreaker —was tempting providence. Roach enjoyed his biggest successes with the top-

AON Standard Open National Hunt Flat Race, Newbury—Cornish Rebel makes a striking debut

notch two-mile hurdler Prideaux Boy and crack chaser Viking Flagship, and he has had a bit more luck so far with another recent big-money purchase: he splashed out 110,000 punts for a brother to Best Mate (then a highly promising chaser just out of novice class) at the Derby Sale in 2001, the highest-priced lot at the sale. Carrying the rather classier name of Cornish Rebel, he has run twice in bumpers and, in winning a Grade 2 on his debut at Newbury in February, put up one of the best efforts in this sphere all season.

Cornish Rebel (IRE) (br.g. 1997)	Un Desperado (FR) (b 1983)	Top Ville (b 1976)	High Top
			Sega Ville
		White Lightning (gr 1970)	Baldric II
			Rough Sea
	Katday (FR) (br 1987)	Miller's Mate (b 1982)	Mill Reef
			Primatie
		Kanara (b 1973)	Hauban
			Alika

The AON Standard Open National Hunt Flat on Tote Gold Trophy day attracted a field which, but for the lack of Irish challengers, would have graced the Champion Bumper itself. The nine previous winners in a field of twenty-three included some of the best seen in Britain to that point, which wasn't a surprise given the £75,000 bonus if the winner went on to success in the Champion Bumper at Cheltenham. Cornish Rebel went off a 12/1-chance and made a most impressive first appearance, coming from behind in the straight in a well-run race to lead with little more than a furlong to run before storming clear, putting eleven lengths between himself and runner-up Cloudy Grey. The effort was all the more impressive as Cornish Rebel showed distinct signs of inexperience, hanging badly all the way up the straight. Cornish Rebel was in receipt of 7 lb but, as the runner-up had already shown himself good enough to reach the frame at Cheltenham, this was clearly form out of the top drawer. Not much happened afterwards to dispel that view. The fourth Be Fair went on to finish a clear second in the Grade 2 bumper at Aintree, while the eighth Bold Bishop ran fourth in the Champion Bumper. In all, seven of the first eight ended the season rated 110 or more. Cornish Rebel did not, however, go on to repeat the form. He looked to hold an excellent chance at Cheltenham but failed to reproduce his Newbury running. Whereas he looked most imposing beforehand at Newbury, a rangy, good sort if rather unfurnished at present, he looked in the paddock at Cheltenham as if Newbury had taken a lot out of him physically. After briefly improving at the top of the hill, he could not hold his position when the pace increased, finishing twelfth, the best part of twenty lengths behind the winner Liberman. It is to be hoped that Cornish Rebel's exertions at the Festival haven't set him back too much—he wasn't made available to our photographer when he visited the stable to take posed portraits in April—as he has the potential to be among the leading novice hurdlers in 2003/4. Details of Cornish Rebel's family have appeared in various essays on Best Mate in *Chasers & Hurdlers*. *P. F. Nicholls*

CORPORATE PLAYER (IRE) 5 b.g. Zaffaran (USA) – Khazna (Stanford) [2002/3 **F81** F17g⁶ Mar 16] sixth foal: half-brother to fairly useful hurdler/winning chaser Sentosa Star (by Reasonable), stays 2¾m: dam never ran: odds on and tongue tied, sixth of 11 in maiden bumper at Folkestone on debut, reportedly having breathing problem. *Noel T. Chance*

CORRARE (IRE) 6 b.m. Corrouge (USA) – Granig Rarity (Rarity) [2002/3 16s **h61** 20vᵖᵘ 20g 21m³ Apr 19] €800 5-y-o: fifth foal: half-sister to one-time smart hurdler/ winning chaser Rash Remark (by Rashar), stays 3m: dam unraced: blinkered, first sign of ability over hurdles when third in conditional jockeys selling handicap at Plumpton. *J. R. Boyle*

CORRECT AND RIGHT (IRE) 4 b.f. Great Commotion (USA) – Miss Hawkins **h86** (Modern Dancer) [2002/3 16m³ 16d 17s² 17s 22d⁵ 19v 16g* 17m⁴ Apr 8] angular filly: third reported foal: dam placed in bumper: modest hurdler: landed odds in mares maiden at Warwick in March: may prove best short of 2¾m: acts on soft and good to firm going: wore cheekpieces last 2 starts. *J. W. Mullins*

CORRIB LAD (IRE) 5 b. or br.g. Supreme Leader – Nun So Game (The Parson) **F97** [2002/3 F16s F16g³ Mar 14] well-made gelding: second foal: dam, bad novice hurdler, out of half-sister to useful staying chaser Secret Progress: better effort in bumpers (virtually ran off course on debut) when close third at Warwick, hanging right final 1f. *P. J. Hobbs*

CORRIB SUPREME (IRE)   8 b.g. Supreme Leader – Black Pit (Black Minstrel) [2002/3 16d 16v⁵ 16g Apr 25] second foal: half-brother to modest hurdler That's The Goose (by Be My Native), stays 2½m: dam winning pointer: fair form in bumpers: best effort over hurdles when seventh in steadily-run maiden at Perth final start. *A. J. Martin, Ireland*   **h91 ?**

CORROBOREE (IRE)   6 b.g. Corrouge (USA) – Laura's Toi (Quayside) [2002/3 h77, F89: 16v* 21d Nov 15] leggy, rather sparely-made gelding: modest hurdler: improved form when winning conditional jockeys handicap at Kempton in November: badly hampered later in month: should stay beyond 2m: raced mainly on going softer than good (acts on heavy). *N. A. Twiston-Davies*   **h95 +**

CORSTON JOKER   13 b.g. Idiot's Delight – Corston Lass (Menelek) [2002/3 c24g* c31mʳᵗʳ May 22] sturdy gelding: useful handicap chaser in prime: fair hunter nowadays: won at Fakenham in May: walked over in point in March: stays 3m: acts on good to firm going: tried blinkered: not always a fluent jumper: has refused to race 5 times and not one to rely on. *J. M. Turner*   **c96 §**
h§§

CORUNDUM (USA)   4 b. or br.g. Benny The Dip (USA) – Santi Sana (Formidable (USA)) [2002/3 16dᵖᵘ Oct 26] angular gelding: half-brother to modest 2m hurdler Minnesota (by Danehill): modest maiden on Flat (seems to stay 2m): tongue tied, no encouragement in juvenile on hurdling debut. *D. E. Cantillon*   **h–**

CORUNNA   6 b.g. Puissance – Kind of Shy (Kind of Hush) [2002/3 17gᵖᵘ 16gᵖᵘ Apr 1] modest on Flat (probably stays 1m), sold out of A. Berry's stable 1,800 gns Doncaster November Sales: showed nothing in 2 runs over hurdles, wearing cheekpieces on second occasion. *R. Johnson*   **h–**

COSI FAN TUTTE   5 b.g. Inchinor – Bumpkin (Free State) [2002/3 17s⁵ Nov 28] fairly useful on Flat (stays 1½m), successful in October: visored, didn't jump well when fifth in maiden at Taunton on hurdling debut. *M. C. Pipe*   **h85**

COSMIC CASE   8 b.m. Casteddu – La Fontainova (IRE) (Lafontaine (USA)) [2002/3 16s* 20d² 20mᵇᵈ 16g* 16m* 20d 19s⁶ 20g⁶ 16g⁵ Apr 23] angular mare: modest on Flat (best form at 1½m/1¾m): fair handicap hurdler: won at Perth in August and September (fortunate) and Kelso in October: at least as effective at well-run 2m as 2½m: acts on good to firm and heavy going: has won with/without visor: tough and genuine. *J. S. Goldie*   **h100**

COSMIC FLIGHT (IRE)   7 b.g. Torus – Palatine Lady (Pauper) [2002/3 F76: F16m³ 20g 16mᵖᵘ Sep 7] rangy gelding: modest form at best in bumpers: still on weak side and no form in 2 starts over hurdles: joined N. Babbage. *Noel T. Chance*   **h–**
F70

COSMIC RANGER   5 b.g. Magic Ring (IRE) – Lismore (Relkino) [2002/3 19m⁶ 16vᵖᵘ 16g 17v⁴ 16d 17d Mar 18] workmanlike gelding: bad maiden hurdler. *H. Alexander*   **h55**

COSMIC SONG   6 b.m. Cosmonaut – Hotaria (Sizzling Melody) [2002/3 16sᵖᵘ 16s⁴ Jan 30] poor on Flat (stays 1¼m), won seller in July: poor form on second of 2 starts in mares novice hurdles at Southwell. *R. M. Whitaker*   **h66**

COSMOCRAT   5 b.g. Cosmonaut – Bella Coola (Northern State (USA)) [2002/3 h92+: 16s² 16v 17s 16dᶠ Mar 1] rangy gelding: fair on Flat (should stay 1¼m): modest maiden hurdler: will prove best around 2m: acts on soft going: sold 8,000 gns Doncaster May Sales. *C. G. Cox*   **h95**

COSMO JACK (IRE)   7 b.g. Balla Cove – Foolish Law (IRE) (Law Society (USA)) [2002/3 c97?, h–: c24mᶠ May 6] sparely-made gelding: fair hurdler at best: only one completion in hunter chases: best around 2m: acts on good to firm and heavy going: tried blinkered/visored: has looked temperamental. *S. Flook*   **c–**
h–

COSMOSONIC   4 ch.f. Cosmonaut – Double Birthday (Cavo Doro) [2002/3 16gᵖᵘ 17dᵖᵘ Apr 8] half-sister to fair hurdler up to 25f Moonshine Dancer (by Northern State) and winning 2m hurdler Major Ivor (by Mandrake Major), latter fairly useful up to 1m on Flat: dam ran once: no show in 2 juvenile hurdles. *W. Storey*   **h–**

COTEBROOK   4 ch.g. First Trump – Chantelys (Ballacashtal (CAN)) [2002/3 16dᵖᵘ Nov 7] leggy gelding: poor maiden on Flat (barely stays 1¾m): showed little on hurdling debut. *J. M. Jefferson*   **h–**

COTOPAXI (IRE)   7 b.g. Turtle Island (IRE) – Ullapool (Dominion) [2002/3 16s 16s⁵ 20gᵖᵘ 17d³ 19d* 17m* 20s⁴ Nov 9] rather leggy ex-Irish gelding: fairly useful handi-   **h125**

cap hurdler: left M. Cunningham after reappearance: won at Wolverhampton in July and Market Rasen and Southwell in August: barely stays testing 2½m: acts on good to firm and heavy going: effective blinkered or not. *Miss Venetia Williams*

COTTSTOWN BOY (IRE)   12 ch.g. King Luthier – Ballyanihan (Le Moss) [2002/3   **c– x**
c85x, h98: 24m³ May 15] leggy gelding: winning hurdler/chaser: poor effort only outing   **h–**
in 2002/3: stays 3m: acts on good to firm and heavy going: visored once: usually races
prominently: not a fluent jumper of fences. *Mrs S. C. Bradburne*

COULD BE ANYTHING   6 b.m. Homo Sapien – Our Chrisy (Carlburg) [2002/3   **h–**
F16d 21d^{ur} Jan 16] 3,900 (privately) 4-y-o: eleventh foal: half-sister to winning Irish   **F–**
pointer by Lancastrian: dam unraced half-sister to Cheltenham Gold Cup winner Captain
Christy: well beaten in maiden bumper on debut: mid-division when unseating 5 out in
mares maiden hurdle: dead. *R. T. Phillips*

COULD IT BE LEGAL   6 b.g. Roviris – Miss Gaylord (Cavo Doro) [2002/3 F16s   **F–**
Dec 7] fourth foal: half-brother to poor hurdler Called To The Bar (by Legal Bwana),
stays 3½m: dam modest 1¼m winner: well held in bumper on debut. *P. M. Rich*

COULDN'T BE PHAR (IRE)   6 ch.g. Phardante (FR) – Queenford Belle (Celtic   **F–**
Cone) [2002/3 F18d F18d Feb 17] first foal: dam, won 2½m hurdle, half-sister to high-
class staying chaser Couldnt Be Better: showed very little in 2 bumpers. *D. R. Gandolfo*

COULOIR   7 gr.m. Gran Alba (USA) – Hollow Creek (Tarqogan) [2002/3 h86: c16g⁵   **c93**
c20s^{pu} c20g^{pu} 16g⁵ 17m⁴ 22g^{bd} Apr 26] sturdy mare: last of 5 only completed start in   **h90**
novice chases: modest handicap hurdler: best efforts at 2m, should stay further: acts on
soft and good to firm going. *H. Morrison*

COULTERS CANDY   5 ch.g. Clantime – Heldigvis (Hot Grove) [2002/3 F16g²   **h92 ?**
F17v F16d F16g⁵ 16g 16g⁶ Apr 25] 500 3-y-o: ninth foal: half-brother to several winners,   **F90**
including fairly useful staying hurdler/chaser Fast Thoughts (by Feelings) and fair 2m
chaser Grouse-N-Heather (by Grey Desire): dam modest 2-y-o 7f/1m winner: runner-up
in bumper on debut: best subsequent effort when sixth in maiden hurdle at Perth, possibly
flattered in steadily-run race. *A. C. Whillans*

COULTHARD (IRE)   10 ch.g. Glenstal (USA) – Royal Aunt (Martinmas) [2002/3   **c– §**
c102d, h114d: 16s³ 16v³ 17d c16v⁴ 16v² c16g² Feb 22] angular gelding: fair handicap   **h109 §**
hurdler: maiden chase, poor efforts both starts in 2002/3: stays around 2m: acts on heavy
going, possibly not on good to firm: has had tongue tied: held up, and best in strongly-run
race: irresolute and needs treating with caution. *Mrs P. Sly*

COUNTBACK (FR)   4 b.g. Anabaa (USA) – Count Me Out (FR) (Kaldoun (FR))   **F78**
[2002/3 F17g⁶ Apr 26] 1,400,000 francs Y: third foal: dam useful French performer up to
2m: sold unraced out of G. Wragg's stable 3,500 gns Newmarket Autumn Sales: pulled
hard when sixth of 14 in bumper at Market Rasen on debut. *C. C. Bealby*

COUNT CAN DO (IRE)   4 br.c. Doyoun – Countess Candy (Great Nephew) [2002/3   **h112**
16v* 17v⁵ 16g³ 17g 19s^F Apr 4] half-brother to modest hurdler Kanooz (by Wassl),
stayed 2¾m: fair on Flat (stayed 2m), successful in October: fairly useful juvenile
hurdler: won at Enghien in November: good third of 20 to impressive Saintsaire at
Newbury in December: acted on heavy going: blinkered: dead. *F. Doumen, France*

COUNTESS CAMILLA   6 b.rm. Bob's Return (IRE) – Forest Pride (IRE) (Be My   **F104**
Native (USA)) [2002/3 F16s⁴ F17s* Feb 22] 9,000 4-y-o: good-topped mare:
second foal: dam modest 2m hurdler: won mares bumpers at Folkestone (maiden) in
January and Huntingdon in February: will stay 2½m. *K. C. Bailey*

COUNT KENI   8 ch.g. Formidable (USA) – Flying Amy (Norwick (USA)) [2002/3   **c–**
c71, h–: c22m c25g³ c25d⁶ c20g⁶ Apr 21] winning pointer: poor form in steeplechases: **h–**
left Miss K. Roncoroni after reappearance. *Mrs K. B. Mactaggart*

COUNT OSKI   7 b.g. Petoski – Sea Countess (Ercolano (USA)) [2002/3 h85?, F64:   **c93**
19d c21d^F c17s^F c25d⁵ c24g⁴ c24g* c21m^{pu} Apr 17] tall gelding: poor maiden hurdler: **h–**
modest novice chaser: won handicap at Ascot in March: should stay beyond 3m.
M. J. Ryan

COUNTRY BOY   12 b.g. Town And Country – Hollomoore (Mooresstyle) [2002/3   **c75**
c65, h–: c21g^{pu} c26m c24g² May 30] workmanlike gelding: winning pointer: poor   **h–**
maiden hurdler/chaser: probably stays 3¼m: acts on soft and good to firm going:
blinkered (dropped away tamely) once. *Steve Cheatle*

COUNTRY CHEF   7 b.g. Henbit (USA) – Witney Girl (Le Bavard (FR)) [2002/3   **h–**
h–, F74: 16d^{pu} 21d^{pu} 21g^{pu} Dec 12] good-topped gelding: no form over hurdles: dead.
John Allen

COUNTRY KRIS 11 b.g. Town And Country – Mariban (Mummy's Pet) [2002/3 c–, h95: 21g 19s 17v Mar 4] workmanlike gelding: handicap hurdler, no form in 2002/3: stays 3m: acts on good to firm and heavy going: no show in blinkers/visor, also tried in cheekpieces: usually front runner. *B. J. M. Ryall* **c–**
h–

COUNTRY ROSE 7 ch.m. Carlingford Castle – Clover Song (True Song) [2002/3 F–: 17m c17s[6] Nov 24] smallish, plain mare: no sign of ability: tried tongue tied. *Mrs P. Townsley* **c–**
h–

COUNTRYWIDE STAR (IRE) 5 ch.g. Common Grounds – Silver Slipper (Indian Ridge) [2002/3 h–: 18m 16m[3] 16s 16s[pu] Dec 27] sturdy gelding: form over hurdles only when third in ladies handicap at Stratford in October, carrying head high: will prove best around 2m: jumped badly final outing. *C. N. Kellett* **h62**

COUNT TALLAHASSEE 6 ch.g. Dervish – Give Me An Answer (True Song) [2002/3 h–, F–: c17g May 8] no sign of ability. *J. Parkes* **c–**
h–

COUNT TONY 9 ch.g. Keen – Turtle Dove (Gyr (USA)) [2002/3 h102: 19d[pu] May 14] close-coupled gelding: fair handicap hurdler at best: lame only start in 2002/3: unlikely to stay beyond 2½m: acts on any going: blinkered once (ran poorly): usually races prominently: joined J. Gallagher. *P. Bowen* **h–**

COUNTY CLASSIC 4 b.f. Noble Patriarch – Cumbrian Rhapsody (Sharrood (USA)) [2002/3 F14d[2] Nov 25] leggy filly: fourth foal: dam fair 2m hurdler: second in bumper at Newcastle on debut. *T. D. Easterby* **F82**

COUNTY DERRY 10 b.g. Derrylin – Colonial Princess (Roscoe Blake) [2002/3 c117: c25d* c28m[4] c26v[F2] c26g[5] Mar 13] strong gelding: smart hunter chaser: won quite valuable event at Towcester in May: won points in January and February: fifth in last 2 renewals of Foxhunter at Cheltenham, beaten 8¾ lengths by Kingscliff in latest: raced at 3m+: acts on good to firm and heavy going: sometimes makes mistakes. *J. Scott* **c129**

COUNTY FLYER 10 b.g. Cruise Missile – Random Select (Random Shot) [2002/3 c83, h–: c24g[pu] c19g[5] c24d[6] Apr 9] lengthy, plain gelding: modest chaser: reportedly finished lame final start in 2001/2, subsequently off 14 months: stays 3m: acts on firm and soft going: blinkered once. *J. S. Smith* **c86**
h–

COURAGE UNDER FIRE 8 b.g. Risk Me (FR) – Dreamtime Quest (Blakeney) [2002/3 c97, h78: c25d* c24d[2] c26d* c25s[3] c33v[pu] Dec 26] good-topped gelding: fair handicap chaser: better than ever in 2002/3, winning at Market Rasen in October and Fontwell in November: stays 3¼m: acts on good going or softer (acts on heavy): blinkered: usually races prominently. *C. C. Bealby* **c114**
h–

COURSER'S COVE 6 b.g. Sir Harry Lewis (USA) – Pearl Cove (Town And Country) [2002/3 F89: F16d[4] 21m[pu] Mar 19] sturdy gelding: runner-up from 4 starts in bumpers: appeared to break down in novice at Ludlow on hurdling debut, held in fourth when pulled up run-in. *Mrs P. Robeson* **h86**
F73

COURSING RUN (IRE) 7 ch.g. Glacial Storm (USA) – Let The Hare Run (IRE) (Tale Quale) [2002/3 h106: c24d* Nov 12] smallish, angular gelding: fair hurdler: won novice chase at Southwell only start in 2002/3: stays 3m: raced only on good to soft going: open to improvement over fences. *H. D. Daly* **c109 p**
h–

COURTCARD 4 b.f. Persian Bold – Hafhafah (Shirley Heights) [2002/3 16s[pu] Aug 10] well held on Flat debut (withdrawn after giving trouble before start intended runs either side): reluctant to race on hurdling debut: clearly needs treating with caution. *Mrs Lucinda Featherstone* **h–**

COURT CHAMPAGNE 7 b.m. Batshoof – Fairfield's Breeze (Buckskin (FR)) [2002/3 h86: 16d[bd] 19s[6] 17g 20m[F] 20g[2] Apr 21] modest handicap hurdler: form in 2002/3 only when second at Uttoxeter: stays easy 2½m: acts on firm and good to soft going: has worn cheekpieces. *R. J. Price* **h85**

COURT DREAMING 6 b.m. Alflora (IRE) – Court Town (Camden Town) [2002/3 F16d F17s[pu] Jan 14] fourth foal: half-sister to winning 2m hurdler Russian Court (by Soviet Lad): dam, modest 1m winner on Flat, half-sister to very smart sprinter Broxted: no form in 2 mares bumpers, raced far too freely having bolted to post on second occasion. *D. R. Gandolfo* **F–**

COURT EMPRESS 6 ch.m. Emperor Fountain – Tudor Sunset (Sunyboy) [2002/3 F16g Mar 1] fourth foal: dam no sign of ability: well held in maiden bumper on debut. *P. D. Purdy* **F–**

COURT IN THE ACT (IRE) 7 b.m. Commanche Run – Princess Andromeda (Corvaro (USA)) [2002/3 h82: 17g⁶ 26g⁶ 22m⁴ 22g³ 21m* Jul 19] compact mare: poor hurdler: won novice seller at Southwell in July: stays 2¾m: acts on good to firm going. *J. W. Mullins* **h73**

COURTLEDGE 8 b.g. Unfuwain (USA) – Tremellick (Mummy's Pet) [2002/3 c90, h–: c20g³ c21g³ c20d* c21m⁴ c24gᵖᵘ c22gᵖᵘ c24dᵖᵘ c24dᵖᵘ Nov 24] lengthy gelding: modest handicap chaser: won at Wolverhampton in July: ran poorly last 4 starts: stays 3m: acts on good to firm and heavy going. *M. J. Gingell* **c93** **h–**

COURT NANNY 9 ch.m. Nicholas Bill – Tudor Sunset (Sunyboy) [2002/3 h–: 24sᵖᵘ Jan 28] lengthy mare: has stringhalt: possesses more temperament than ability. *P. D. Purdy* **h– §**

COURT OF APPEAL 6 ch.g. Bering – Hiawatha's Song (USA) (Chief's Crown (USA)) [2002/3 h96: 17d Jul 20] fairly useful on Flat (stays 1¾m): won on hurdling debut in 2001/2: well held all 3 starts since: tried tongue tied. *B. Ellison* **h–**

COURT OF JUSTICE (USA) 7 b.g. Alleged (USA) – Captive Island (Northfields (USA)) [2002/3 h106: 16s* 20v⁴ 16d³ Mar 6] leggy, angular gelding: modest hurdler: won seller at Leicester in December: stays 2½m: acts on heavy going: has worn cheekpieces. *K. A. Morgan* **h97**

COVENT GARDEN 5 b.g. Sadler's Wells (USA) – Temple Row (Ardross) [2002/3 h74: 16f* 20g* 20d* 24m* 18d* Mar 1] sturdy gelding: unbeaten in 5 starts over hurdles in 2002/3, in handicaps at Hexham in September, Carlisle in October (both novices, easily), Aintree in November and Musselburgh in December, and Grade 2 Tote Exacta Premier Kelso Hurdle in March: beat Talarive a head in last-named, battling well: effective at 2m to easy 3m: acts on firm and good to soft going, unraced on soft/heavy: hasn't finished improving. *J. Howard Johnson* **h128 p**

COWBOYBOOTS (IRE) 5 b.g. Lord Americo – Little Welly (Little Buskins) [2002/3 F91: 21g³ 21d² 22v* 24d³ 24vᵖᵘ Feb 15] well-made gelding: best effort over hurdles when winning novice at Fontwell in January by 19 lengths from Slooghy: laboured efforts last 2 starts: should be suited by 3m: acts on heavy going: temperament under suspicion. *L. Wells* **h119**

COXWELL FOOTMAN 7 b.g. Infantry – Coxwell Quick Step (Balinger) [2002/3 h–, F68: 17s c19dᵖᵘ Feb 23] little sign of ability: tried visored. *Mrs L. C. Taylor* **c–** **h–**

COY LAD (IRE) 6 ch.g. Be My Native (USA) – Don't Tutch Me (The Parson) [2002/3 F92: F16d⁶ F16g⁴ Dec 28] useful-looking gelding: fair form in bumpers in 2001/2: well below that in 2002/3, pulling hard on reappearance. *J. G. FitzGerald* **F69**

CRACKING DAWN (IRE) 8 b.g. Be My Native (USA) – Rare Coin (Kemal (FR)) [2002/3 h112, F–: c24d* Nov 7] well-made gelding: successful in 3 Irish points: won first of 2 outings in novice hurdles in 2001/2: again created good impression when winning novice at Haydock on steeplechase debut, running on strongly to beat Brockton Mist 7 lengths: will stay beyond 3m: useful chaser in the making. *R. H. Alner* **c125 p** **h–**

CRACKRATTLE (IRE) 9 ch.g. Montelimar (USA) – Gaye Le Moss (Le Moss) [2002/3 c–: c17g⁶ c21d Apr 8] fair pointer, won in February: no form in 3 steeplechases, jumped badly on first occasion: has had tongue tied. *B. N. Pollock* **c–**

CRACK REGIMENT (IRE) 11 b.g. Lafontaine (USA) – Princess Crack (IRE) (Buckskin (FR)) [2002/3 c–, h–: 26g⁴ 24g² 24v² 20s⁴ 24g² 26m⁶ c24d³ c24d⁵ 22s 26s⁵ Mar 7] lengthy gelding: modest maiden hurdler: no form after firth start, including back over fences: probably stays 3¼m: yet to race on firm going, acts on any other: sketchy jumper. *R. H. Buckler* **c–** **h85**

CRACOW (IRE) 6 b.g. Polish Precedent (USA) – Height of Secrecy (Shirley Heights) [2002/3 h68: 16g c16m² c16g 17g⁵ Jul 31] smallish, angular gelding: formerly useful on Flat: poor maiden hurdler/chaser: tried blinkered: often none too fluent: ungenuine. *N. J. Hawke* **c76 §** **h– §**

CRAFTY MONKEY (IRE) 6 b.g. Warcraft (USA) – Mikey's Monkey (Monksfield) [2002/3 F16d⁶ Oct 25] 20,000 4-y-o: fourth foal: half-brother to modest chaser Monkey Island (by Jupiter Island), stays 3m: dam, poor maiden jumper, half-sister to smart 2m to 3m chaser Egypt Mill Prince: favourite, sixth of 12 in bumper at Fakenham on debut. *M. Pitman* **F78**

CRAIGARY 12 b.g. Dunbeath (USA) – Velvet Pearl (Record Token) [2002/3 c64d, h65d: c21gᵖᵘ 16m May 15] compact gelding: winning hurdler: of little account nowadays: tried blinkered. *D. A. Nolan* **c–** **h–**

CRAMOND (IRE)   5 br.g. Lord Americo – Rullahola (Bluerullah) [2002/3 F16m[6] Apr 12] IR 14,000 3-y-o: thirteenth foal: half-brother to winning pointer by Satco: dam, placed over hurdles, sister to very smart jumper up to 3m Chinrullah: backward, never a factor when sixth of 7 in bumper at Ayr on debut. *A. Parker*   **F85 ?**

CRANBORNE (IRE)   6 b.m. King's Ride – Random Wind (Random Shot) [2002/3 F18v F17d Jan 16] third foal: half-sister to fairly useful bumper winner Random Native (by Be My Guest): dam, winning hurdler/poor novice chaser, stayed 2½m: no show in 2 bumpers: joined A. Mactaggart. *B. G. Powell*   **F–**

CRANE BEACH   5 b.m. Afzal – Indian Cruise (Cruise Missile) [2002/3 F16s F16m Mar 23] third foal: half-sister to fairly useful pointer Bengal Bullet (by Infantry): dam, winning chaser, stayed 2¾m: well held in 2 bumpers. *B. W. Duke*   **F–**

CRARAE JACK   5 gr.g. Gran Alba (USA) – Double Dose (Al Sirat (USA)) [2002/3 F16m Apr 12] smallish, leggy gelding: fourth foal: dam, poor novice hurdler, half-sister to useful staying chaser Bishops Island: tongue tied, last of 7 in bumper on debut. *H. P. Hogarth*   **F–**

CRAZY HORSE (IRE)   10 b.g. Little Bighorn – Our Dorcet (Condorcet (FR)) [2002/3 c–, h155: 20s[pu] 20d[6] 24g[pu] Mar 13] smallish, leggy, plain gelding: very smart hurdler: off nearly 2 years due to leg injury, showed little in 2002/3: stays easy 23f: acts on good to firm and heavy going: hard ride (often finds less than seems likely and has hung badly right more than once). *L. Lungo*   **c–**
h–

CRAZY LIKE A FOOL (IRE)   4 b.g. Charnwood Forest (IRE) – Shanghai Girl (Distant Relative) [2002/3 F16g[pu] Mar 29] second foal: dam, useful sprinter, half-sister to useful French hurdler Generous Libra: breathing problem when pulled up in maiden bumper on debut. *B. Mactaggart*   **F–**

CRAZY MAZIE   6 b.m. Risk Me (FR) – Post Impressionist (IRE) (Ahonoora) [2002/3 F76: 16d 21g 20g[4] 22g[F] Apr 26] poor novice hurdler: stays 2½m. *K. A. Morgan*   **h66**

CREAM GORSE   7 ch.m. Alflora (IRE) – Celtic Slave (Celtic Cone) [2002/3 h79: c25g[F] c24d[F] c25d[6] c25d[pu] Feb 23] lengthy mare: poor maiden hurdler: failed to complete 3 out of 4 starts over fences, seemingly running easily best race when falling 2 out in novice at Hereford on reappearance: should prove better around 3m than shorter. *H. D. Daly*   **c96 ?**
h–

CREATIVE TIME (IRE)   7 b.g. Houmayoun (FR) – Creative Princess (IRE) (Creative Plan (USA)) [2002/3 c102, h74: c24s[2] c24d c24g[pu] Feb 27] rangy gelding: fair maiden chaser: creditable effort in 2002/3 only on reappearance: likely to stay beyond 3m: acts on soft going. *Miss H. C. Knight*   **c105**
h–

CREDENZA MOMENT   5 b.g. Pyramus (USA) – Mystoski (Petoski) [2002/3 h–§: 16v 24v[pu] 17v[pu] Mar 10] has shown more temperament than ability over hurdles: tried blinkered. *M. Madgwick*   **h– §**

CREEK TOWER   6 b.g. Rainbow Quest (USA) – Pass The Peace (Alzao (USA)) [2002/3 F70: F16g[pu] Sep 15] signs of only a little ability in bumpers: looked wayward only run in 2002/3. *C. J. Price*   **F–**

CREGG HOUSE (IRE)   8 ch.g. King Persian – Loyal River (Over The River (FR)) [2002/3 c143§: c16d[3] 16g* 16g 20f[3] c20g[2] c16s[4] c24s[5] c20v[3] 16d[2] c24v[pu] c24s 22v[6] 20v c20g[4] c36d[R] 18g[5] Apr 21] tall gelding: fair hurdler: won novice at Navan in June: useful chaser: some creditable efforts in 2002/3, nearest finish when fourth to Young Spartacus in Mildmay of Flete Handicap Chase at Cheltenham in March: effective at 2m to 25f (held when refusing both starts over further): acts on heavy going: tried tongue tied: inconsistent and temperamental. *Patrick Mullins, Ireland*   **c135 §**
h114 §

CREON   8 b.g. Saddlers' Hall (IRE) – Creake (Derring-Do) [2002/3 c93x, h104§: 24s 24v* 25g[6] Mar 11] leggy gelding: modest chaser: fairly useful handicap hurdler: confirmed promise of reappearance when easily winning at Chepstow in November: creditable never-nearer sixth to Inching Closer in valuable event at Cheltenham over 3 months later: stays 3¼m: acts on heavy and good to firm going: tried blinkered/tongue tied: usually held up and often finds little: sketchy jumper of fences. *Jonjo O'Neill*   **c– x**
h120

CRESSWELL CHERRY (IRE)   8 b.m. Camden Town – Cherry Country (Town And Country) [2002/3 h89: 21d[2] 24d[2] 20s[4] c24s[pu] 24g Feb 27] angular mare: modest handicap hurdler: no show on chasing debut: needed thorough test at 2m and stayed 3m: probably acted on any going, though went particularly well on softer than good (acted on heavy): dead. *N. A. Twiston-Davies*   **c–**
h95

CRESSWELL GOLD   6 b.m. Homo Sapien – Running For Gold (Rymer) [2002/3   **h–**
F–: F16d 16g⁵ 20dᵖᵘ 20s⁶ 22dᵖᵘ 20vᵖᵘ 20sᵖᵘ Mar 2] winning pointer: no worthwhile form   **F–**
in bumpers or over hurdles. *D. A. Rees*

CRESSWELL QUAY   10 ch.g. Bold Fox – Karatina (FR) (Dilettante II) [2002/3 c–,   **c103**
h–: c26v* c26d* c22d* c24v² c25s* Jan 14] sturdy gelding: fair handicap chaser: won 4   **h–**
of 5 starts in 2002/3, at Newton Abbot (novice) and Warwick in November, Fontwell in
December and Folkestone in January: stays 3¼m: acts on any going: held up. *P. Bowen*

CREWSKI   8 br.g. Newski (USA) – Darlin' Again (Jolly Me) [2002/3 c21gᵖᵘ May 1]   **c–**
first foal: dam of little account over hurdles: poor pointer. *H. J. Manners*

CRIMINAL SILK   8 b.m. Tragic Role (USA) – See You In Court (London Gazette)   **h–**
[2002/3 h–, F69: 16m 24gᵖᵘ May 24] rather leggy mare: no worthwhile form over
hurdles: has raced freely. *S. J. Gilmore*

CRIMSON BROCADE   12 b.m. Daring March – Stellaris (Star Appeal) [2002/3 c–:   **c–**
c20m May 8] big, rangy mare: won points in February and March: little show in steeplechases. *Mrs K. J. Tutty*

CRIMSON PIRATE (IRE)   6 b.g. Phardante (FR) – Stroked Again (On Your Mark)   **h103 p**
[2002/3 F–: 16g² 16g* Mar 12] strong gelding: type to make a chaser: well held in
bumper: fair form in 2 starts over hurdles, well-backed favourite when making all in
maiden at Huntingdon: will be suited by 2½m: should continue to progress. *B. De Haan*

CRINAN (IRE)   5 ch.g. Carroll House – Esther (Persian Bold) [2002/3 F16m F17g   **F–**
Apr 26] 10,000 4-y-o: sturdy gelding: fourth foal: half-brother to fair hurdler Barrelbio
(by Elbio), stays 3m, and winner in Belgium by Tirol: dam unraced, out of half-sister to
Bustino: well held in 2 bumpers. *Mrs P. Sly*

CRISTAL LADY   5 b.m. Broadsword (USA) – Lots of Luck (Neltino) [2002/3 F16m   **F–**
Mar 23] 2,000 (privately) 4-y-o: fourth foal: half-sister to poor 2m hurdler Fortune
Hopper (by Rock Hopper): dam modest 2m hurdler/1m to 1¼m winner on Flat: showed
nothing in bumper on debut. *R. Wilman*

CRISTOFORO (IRE)   6 b.g. Perugino (USA) – Red Barons Lady (IRE) (Electric)   **h–**
[2002/3 h–: 16d Oct 31] lengthy, good-topped gelding: well held in novice hurdles: won
3 times up to 13f on Flat in December. *B. J. Curley*

CRISTOPHE   5 b.g. Kris – Our Shirley (Shirley Heights) [2002/3 h–: 21v³ 20s⁶ 19d   **h68**
17d² 17g² 21d⁴ Apr 8] lengthy gelding: poor maiden hurdler: stays 21f: acts on heavy
going: tried visored: consistent. *Mrs B. K. Thomson*

CRISTYS PICNIC (IRE)   13 b.g. Tremblant – My Maizey (Buckskin (FR)) [2002/3   **c–**
c–, h–: c21gᵖᵘ c24m⁴ May 6] winning chaser: no longer of much account. *G. M. Spencer*   **h–**

CROAGHNACREE (IRE)   6 b.m. Mister Lord (USA) – Castle Flame (IRE)   **h–**
(Carlingford Castle) [2002/3 F16s F16v 17dᵖᵘ Mar 2] workmanlike mare: fourth foal: **F–**
half-sister to winning 3m hunter chaser Boss Murphy (by Supreme Leader): dam
unraced: no show in 2 bumpers or novice hurdle. *S. J. Marshall*

CROCADEE   10 b.g. Rakaposhi King – Raise The Dawn (Rymer) [2002/3 c26gᶠ Nov   **c–**
30] tall, useful-looking gelding: one-time useful hurdler/chaser: had good first season   **h–**
over fences in 2000/1, winning 3 novices (including 2 Grade 2 events): missed 2001/2
reportedly due to tendon injury: fell sixth in Hennessy at Newbury on return: may prove
best around 2½m: acts on good to firm and heavy going: has run well when sweating:
races freely. *Miss Venetia Williams*

CROC AN OIR (IRE)   6 ch.g. Treasure Hunter – Cool Mary (Beau Charmeur (FR))   **c–**
[2002/3 F16s c20s³ Mar 3] fifth foal: dam unraced: won last of 3 starts in maiden Irish   **F–**
points in 2002: signs of only a little ability in bumper/weak novice chase. *Miss Venetia
Williams*

CROC EN BOUCHE (USA)   4 b.g. Broad Brush (USA) – Super Cook (USA) (Best   **F–**
Turn (USA)) [2002/3 F16m F16m Apr 10] eighth foal: half-brother to 3 winners on Flat,
including 7f winner El Comendador (by Crafty Prospector): dam, Grade 3 winner in
USA, half-sister to Park Hill Stakes winner Niodini: signs of only a little ability in 2
bumpers. *Mrs H. Dalton*

CROCODILES DEN (IRE)   7 b.g. Alphabatim (USA) – Misty Gold (Arizona   **c–**
Duke) [2002/3 c20f³ c24dᵘʳ 23vᵖᵘ Jan 22] 5,000 3-y-o: ex-Irish gelding: second foal: **h–**

half-brother to winning pointer by Boreen: dam, lightly raced on Flat, sister to winning hurdler Blaze Gold, dam of top-class hurdler/chaser Danoli: well held in 2 bumpers in early-2001/2 for G. Cully: placed both starts in maiden Irish points in 2002: showed nothing in steeplechases or on hurdling debut. *R. Wilman*

CROKER (IRE) 8 ch.g. Rainbows For Life (CAN) – Almagest (Dike (USA)) [2002/3 **h85** h77§: 17m³ 16s* 17s* 16s² 19d 16s Feb 12] workmanlike gelding: modest handicap hurdler: won at Leicester and Bangor (conditional jockeys) in December: stays 2½m: acts on good to firm and heavy going: tried blinkered/visored: has looked difficult ride. *S. T. Lewis*

CROMARTY RULES 6 b.g. Anshan – Cromarty (Shareef Dancer (USA)) [2002/3 **h–** 16m 16g 21gᵖᵘ Sep 8] 3,000 4-y-o: second foal: dam, fairly useful hurdler who stayed 2½m, half-sister to smart 3m chaser River Lossie: no form over hurdles: tongue tied first 2 starts: sold 500 gns Doncaster September Sales. *N. B. Mason*

CROMER PIER 8 b.g. Reprimand – Fleur du Val (Valiyar) [2002/3 h–: 17g 16v Nov **h–** 28] leggy gelding: winning 17f hurdler: lightly raced and no form since 2000/1: tried visored. *G. Fierro*

CROMWELL (IRE) 8 b.g. Last Tycoon – Catherine Parr (USA) (Riverman (USA)) **c–** [2002/3 c99, h–: c24vᵘʳ c33vᵖᵘ c22gᵖᵘ Mar 29] workmanlike gelding: handicap chaser, **h–** failed to complete in 2002/3: stays 3¼m: acts on any going: usually blinkered: has won 7 times at Market Rasen. *M. C. Chapman*

CROSBY DON 8 b.g. Alhijaz – Evening Star (Red Sunset) [2002/3 16v⁵ 20sᵘʳ 20s **c72 ?** 19d c16g c20g² Apr 26] leggy gelding: maiden hurdler: little form over fences: stays **h–** 2¾m: acts on firm and soft going. *J. R. Weymes*

CROSBY DONJOHN 6 ch.g. Magic Ring (IRE) – Ovideo (Domynsky) [2002/3 16g **h–** 19dᵖᵘ 16dᵖᵘ Mar 5] smallish gelding: modest and unreliable on Flat (stays 1¼m): showed little in novice hurdles. *J. R. Weymes*

CROSSBOW CREEK 5 b.g. Lugana Beach – Roxy River (Ardross) [2002/3 F16d* **F106** F16g Mar 12] rangy gelding: second foal: half-brother to winning 2m hurdler Cool Roxy (by Environment Friend): dam, fair 2m hurdler, half-sister to dam of Bacchanal: won bumper at Wetherby on debut by 1½ lengths from Diamond Sal, pair clear: never in contention in Grade 1 at Cheltenham following month. *M. G. Rimell*

CROSS THE RUBICON (IRE) 12 ch.g. Over The River (FR) – One Way Only **c–** (Le Bavard (FR)) [2002/3 c–, h–: c25gᵖᵘ c25gᵖᵘ May 11] staying maiden chaser, retains **h–** little ability: blinkered. *G. A. Harker*

CROW CREEK (IRE) 5 br.g. Presenting – Rossacrowe Gale (IRE) (Strong Gale) **F64** [2002/3 F16m³ Apr 12] IR £4,000 3-y-o: first foal: dam unraced: third of 7 in conditional jockeys bumper at Chepstow on debut. *B. N. Doran*

CROWNFIELD 4 b.g. Blushing Flame (USA) – Chief Island (Be My Chief (USA)) **h103** [2002/3 16v 16d⁴ 20dᵖᵘ 16g 16g² Apr 19] workmanlike gelding: thrice-raced on Flat at 2 yrs for W. Turner: fair juvenile hurdler: every chance penultimate start when saddle slipped: good 3½ lengths second to impressive Unleash in handicap at Stratford: likely to prove best around 2m. *Mrs M. Reveley*

CROWNING GLORY 9 b.m. Rakaposhi King – Miss Lizzie (Push On) [2002/3 h–: **h–** 17dᵖᵘ 19m⁶ Jun 4] lightly raced and no form over hurdles. *Mrs D. A. Hamer*

CRUAGH EXPRESS (IRE) 7 b.g. Unblest – Cry In The Dark (Godswalk (USA)) **h81 §** [2002/3 h88§: 16m² Oct 19] modest on Flat (stays 1¼m): lightly-raced winning hurdler: will prove best at 2m: tongue tied: has looked less than resolute: sold £600 Ascot December Sales. *G. L. Moore*

CRUISE AROUND 11 b.g. Cruise Missile – New Cherry (New Brig) [2002/3 20f⁶ **h–** Sep 15] lightly-raced gelding: has shown more temperament than ability in points and on hurdling debut. *A. R. Dicken*

CRUNCHY (IRE) 5 ch.g. Common Grounds – Credit Crunch (IRE) (Caerleon (USA)) **h93** [2002/3 16s 16d⁴ 20g⁴ 17g⁴ Mar 22] small gelding: fair on Flat, improved in 2003 (successful twice over 11f on all-weather): modest form in novice hurdles, not fluent final start: tongue tied. *B. Ellison*

CRUSOE (IRE) 6 b.g. Turtle Island (IRE) – Self Reliance (Never So Bold) [2002/3 **h–** h–: 17s Nov 21] fair on Flat (stays 9.4f), successful 4 times on all-weather early in 2003: no form over hurdles: tried blinkered/tongue tied. *A. Sadik*

Weatherbys Travel 'National Hunt' Novices' Hurdle, Uttoxeter—Crystal d'Ainay is out on his own

CRUZ SANTA   10 b.m. Lord Bud – Linpac Mapleleaf (Dominion) [2002/3 h95: 22d³ 22m* 24g² 20sᶠ 22s⁵ 19g Feb 28] light-framed mare: fair hurdler: won seller at Stratford in July: ran poorly last 2 starts: stays 3m: acts on heavy and good to firm going, below form on firm: held up: not an easy ride (failed to go through with effort third start) and one to treat with caution. *Mrs M. Reveley*   **h107 §**

CRYSTAL D'AINAY (IRE)   4 b.g. Saint Preuil (FR) – Guendale (FR) (Cadoudal (FR)) [2002/3 16d⁴ 18s* c18s* c17s² 16d² 16s* 20g² Apr 3] good-topped gelding: second foal: brother to 2¼m hurdle winner Guendoline d'Ainay: dam lightly-raced maiden over hurdles: left G. Macaire after fourth start: fairly useful hurdler: won juvenile at Bordeaux in November and novice at Uttoxeter in March: also ran well both other outings in Britain, second to Far Pavilions in falsely-run minor event at Haydock and Leinster in Grade 2 novice at Aintree: twice-raced over fences, won 5-runner 3-y-o race at Angers: stays 2½m: acts on soft going. *A. King*   **c?** **h125**

CRYSTAL VEIN   5 gr.g. Miner's Lamp – Crystal Comet (Cosmo) [2002/3 F–: 19gᵖᵘ 19dᵖᵘ 16dᵖᵘ Jan 18] good-topped gelding: no form in bumpers: pulled up all starts in novice hurdles. *B. G. Powell*   **h–**

CUDLIC CANDYFLOSS   10 b.m. Abutammam – Cudlic Cream (No Evil) [2002/3 c70, h65: c20dᵘʳ May 4] poor maiden hurdler: let down by jumping over fences: stays 3m: acts on firm and good to soft going. *P. Bowen*   **c–** **h–**

CULLEN ROAD (IRE)   5 b.g. Wakashan – My Wings (Erin's Hope) [2002/3 F16m⁶ F16d 16v 20s⁵ 16gᶠ 17g⁵ Mar 16] IR 580 3-y-o: leggy gelding: third foal: dam unraced: probably flattered in bumper on debut: little other form, mainly over hurdles. *J. R. Jenkins*   **h63** **F87 ?**

CULLIAN   6 b.m. Missed Flight – Diamond Gig (Pitskelly) [2002/3 F73: 17d* 18sᵖᵘ 19d 21s* Feb 24] modest hurdler: won mares events at Folkestone (novice) in November and Plumpton (handicap, wore cheekpieces) in February: should stay beyond 21f: acts on soft going. *Mrs N. Smith*   **h91**

CULMINATE   6 ch.g. Afzal – Straw Blade (Final Straw) [2002/3 17s 17s Dec 17] of little account on Flat: well held both starts over hurdles. *J. E. Long*   **h–**

CUMBRIAN KNIGHT (IRE)   5 b.g. Presenting – Crashrun (Crash Course) [2002/3 F16m⁴ F16g² F17g³ F16d* 16d⁴ 16s⁴ 19d Feb 25] IR £22,000 3-y-o: good-topped gelding: sixth foal: dam unraced: progressive form in bumpers, won at Haydock in November: best effort in novice hurdles when fourth of 19 to Hey Ref at same course sixth start: will stay at least 2½m: may still improve over hurdles. *J. M. Jefferson*   **h100** **F96**

CUPBOARD LOVER   7 ch.g. Risk Me (FR) – Galejade (Sharrood (USA)) [2002/3 h118: 16s³ 16m³ Feb 21] rather leggy gelding: better than ever on Flat in 2002, winning 3   **h124**

times up to 2m: fairly useful handicap hurdler: ran well both starts in 2002/3, third to Brooklyn's Gold at Kempton (got worked up at start) on return from 6-month absence on second occasion: stays easy 21f: acts on soft and good to firm going. *N. J. Henderson*

CURLY SPENCER (IRE) 9 br.g. Yashgan – Tim's Brief (Avocat) [2002/3 c98, h–: c24m⁵ 20d* c20d* c20v* c22d⁴ Mar 1] leggy, quite good-topped gelding: fair handicap hurdler/chaser: successful first 3 starts after 6-month break, over hurdles at Carlisle (novice, easily) in November and over fences at Newcastle later in month and Ayr in January: creditable fourth of 6 to Pillaging Pict at Kelso: should stay 3m: best efforts on going softer than good (acts on heavy). *A. Parker*   **c109 h107**

CURTINS HILL (IRE) 9 b.g. Roi Guillaume (FR) – Kinallen Lady (IRE) (Abednego) [2002/3 16v⁶ 21g* 17s* 24g⁴ 18s 22g² Apr 21] IR 500 4-y-o: lengthy gelding: second foal: dam unraced: successful 3 times in Irish points, including twice in 2002: fair hurdler, trained in early-2001/2 by D. Dorgan: won novice handicaps at Ludlow and Cheltenham (hung left run-in) in December: good second to progressive Therealbandit in handicap at Newton Abbot: stays 2¾m: acts on soft going. *T. R. George*   **h104**

CUTHILL HOPE (IRE) 12 gr.g. Peacock (FR) – Sicilian Princess (Sicilian Prince) [2002/3 c113, h–: c25d⁵ c25m³ c22s* Nov 2] good-topped gelding: fair handicap chaser: gained first win at Kelso when making all to beat Ardent Scout 10 lengths on return from 5-month absence in November: stays 25f: acts on heavy going, probably on good to firm: effective visored or not: usually races prominently: none too consistent. *A. C. Whillans*   **c113 h–**

CYANARA 7 b.m. Jupiter Island – Shamana (Broadsword (USA)) [2002/3 h67: 16d 16v 17vʳᵒ 22g Apr 21] compact mare: winning 2m hurdler, no form in 2002/3. *Dr P. Pritchard*   **h–**

CYBELE ERIA (FR) 6 b.m. Johann Quatz (FR) – Money Can't Buy (Thatching) [2002/3 h112: 17sᶠ 17g² 16d⁵ 16d 17d c17v³ c16g² c16g* c17m² Apr 21] close-coupled mare: fair handicap hurdler: modest novice chaser: made heavy weather of straight-forward task in maiden at Warwick in March: raced around 2m, mainly on good going or softer: often weak finisher. *N. J. Henderson*   **c94 h112 §**

CYFOR MALTA (FR) 10 b.g. Cyborg (FR) – Force Nine (FR) (Luthier) [2002/3 c153, h–: c20d* c21d⁴ c25sᵘʳ Jan 25]   **c166 h–**

The title of the feature event at Cheltenham's Open meeting is to undergo another change, but the name of the trainer of the horse most likely to win it remains the same, with Martin Pipe sure to be pulling out all the stops in an attempt to improve his already remarkable record in this two-and-a-half-mile handicap chase. He is the only trainer to win it under its three guises to date, beginning in 1987 when Beau Ranger took the Mackeson Gold Cup, the race's title from its inception in 1960 until 1995. For the next four years it was known as the Murphy's Gold Cup and Pipe won the first and third editions with Challenger du Luc and Cyfor Malta respectively; while all three runnings as the Thomas Pink Gold Cup went to Pipe-trained horses, namely Lady Cricket, Shooting Light and Cyfor Malta again. Dual winners of this prestigious event aren't uncommon, with Fortria, Gay Trip, Half Free and Bradbury Star having also achieved the same feat, but, whereas that quartet either did the double in consecutive years or after a one-year gap, there were four years between Cyfor Malta's victories. Given that Cyfor Malta had had his physical problems and run only seven times in between, to win such a competitive race for a second time, recapturing the top-class form he showed in the 1998/9 season in the process, speaks volumes for Pipe's skill.

Cyfor Malta's first win in the contest followed victories in the previous season's Cathcart Chase and John Hughes Trophy and preceded that in the Pillar Property Chase. At that stage of his career the sky seemed the limit for the six-year-old, but leg trouble kept him off the course for two years and when Cyfor Malta finished a distant last of three finishers in the 2001 Pillar Property Chase on his return it appeared that his best days were well behind him. That Cyfor Malta was able to run five times and produce smart form in the 2001/2 season, winning a handicap at Newbury and finishing second to Florida Pearl in the Martell Cup at Aintree, showed that he was far from a back number, though not even Pipe himself expected him to make a winning reappearance in the Thomas Pink. Racing off a mark 4 lb higher than when successful in the Murphy's in 1998, Cyfor Malta had to concede weight to all bar Foly Pleasant in a fifteen-runner field which also included his shorter-priced stable companions Exit Swinger and Chicuelo, the last-named

217

Thomas Pink Gold Cup Chase (Handicap), Cheltenham—Cyfor Malta challenges
the front-running Korakor two out with second and third Poliantas (right) and Wave Rock just behind

the mount of stable-jockey Tony McCoy who, in order to make the weight of 10-1, reportedly survived on the days leading up to the race on a diet of vitamin pills, a piece of chicken, a jaffa cake and lots of sweetened tea. Unlike McCoy, whose mount was badly let down by his jumping and was eventually pulled up, Cyfor Malta's rider Barry Geraghty would have enjoyed the build-up to the Thomas Pink—he had won the previous contest on the card on Stormez, McCoy having chosen to ride the other Pipe runner Shooting Light—and particularly the race itself, with Cyfor Malta giving a smooth performance. He didn't look to be going all that well before three out but led at the next, quickened into the straight and was in no danger from thereon, winning by seven lengths from Poliantas. Despite having to race off a mark 10 lb higher, Cyfor Malta started favourite when returned to Cheltenham the following month for the Tripleprint Gold Cup, but this time he managed only fourth, eighteen lengths behind the winner Fondmort. A fourth attempt at the Pillar Property Chase—he had also run in it the previous year, finishing fourth—was Cyfor Malta's only subsequent appearance. This time he failed to complete, unseating his rider at the fourteenth when still going well enough.

    Cyfor Malta is a half-brother to two winning jumpers in France, including the six-year-old Royal Origny (by Royal Charter) who also finished third in a novice chase at Wetherby in the 2001/2 season. Their dam Force Nine, a winner over a mile and a half in France, is a half-sister to the dams of the high-class mile-and-a-quarter winner and jumps sire Un Desperado and the Coronation Cup winner Saint Estephe. Cyfor Malta, a tall, lengthy gelding, stays twenty-five furlongs and acts on soft and good to firm going. He was visored on his last two starts in 2001/2, including in the Martell Cup. Cyfor Malta looked a fine Grand National prospect after his runaway success in the John Hughes at the age of five but, for various

218

Mr D. A. Johnson's "Cyfor Malta"

Cyfor Malta (FR) (b.g. 1993)	Cyborg (FR) (ch 1982)	Arctic Tern (ch 1973)	Sea-Bird II
			Bubbling Beauty
		Cadair (b 1970)	Sadair
			Blarney Castle
	Force Nine (FR) (b 1977)	Luthier (br 1965)	Klairon
			Flute Enchantee
		Rough Sea (gr 1964)	Herbager
			Sea Nymph II

reasons, he has been unable to take part in the big race. He did hold an entry for the latest edition until the five-day stage, having also been withdrawn from the Cheltenham Gold Cup at the overnight stage. Cyfor Malta has a tendency to jump left and has run only on left-handed courses; nine of his fifteen races in Britain have been at Cheltenham, where he has won four times. *M. C. Pipe*

CYFRINACH LYN   5 b.m. Awesome – Blue Corn (Henbit (USA)) [2002/3 F16g Mar   **F–**
16] second known foal: dam unraced half-sister to Irish St Leger winner Opale: 100/1 and green, well beaten in bumper at Ludlow on debut. *D. Burchell*

CYINDIEN (FR)   6 b. or br.g. Cyborg (FR) – Indiana Rose (FR) (Cadoudal (FR))   **h102**
[2002/3 F90p: 22d² 17s² 25d² Dec 21] once-raced in bumpers: runner-up all 3 starts over hurdles, beaten 1¼ lengths by Coolsan in novice at Warwick on last occasion: stays 25f: raced on going softer than good. *Miss Venetia Williams*

CYNARA 5 b.m. Imp Society (USA) – Reina (Homeboy) [2002/3 h92: 27d^{ur} Oct 31]   h–
angular mare: modest juvenile hurdler in 2001/2: ducked left and unseated first on return,
not seen out again: stays 21f: raced on good going or softer over hurdles (form on good to
firm on Flat): visored last 2 starts in 2001/2. *G. M. Moore*

CYNOSURE 6 b.g. Runnett – Polly Two (Reesh) [2002/3 16d^5 16m^{pu} Jun 21] no form   h–
on Flat: well beaten in novice company over hurdles at Hexham: sold 800 gns Doncaster
August Sales. *J. R. Weymes*

CYRIUM (IRE) 4 b.g. Woodborough (USA) – Jarmar Moon (Unfuwain (USA))   F–
[2002/3 F17g Apr 26] IR 10,000Y: half-brother to winning hurdler/fair chaser around 2m
Moon Glow (by Fayruz) and fairly useful 2000 2-y-o 5f/6f winner Ash Moon (by General
Monash): dam, lightly-raced maiden, out of sister to dam of sprinters Prince Sabo and
Millyant: raced freely when tenth of 14 in bumper at Market Rasen on debut. *R. F. Fisher*

CZAR OF PEACE (IRE) 5 ch.g. Brief Truce (USA) – Metroella (IRE) (Entitled)   h116
[2002/3 h118: 16d 16g^2 16f^4 16g^5 16v^4 16v^{pu} 20s Jan 11] smallish gelding: fairly useful
handicap hurdler: creditable efforts in 2002/3 when in frame: should stay beyond 2m (lost
chance when blundering 4 out over 2½m final outing): acts on any going: has flashed tail.
W. P. Mullins, Ireland

D

DABARPOUR (IRE) 7 b. or br.g. Alzao (USA) – Dabara (IRE) (Shardari) [2002/3   h101
h97: 16f* 16m^4 16m^6 16m^2 16f^4 Oct 24] good-topped gelding: fair handicap hurdler:
won 5-runner contest at Warwick in May: best effort after when neck second to Infini at
Worcester: raced around 2m: acts on firm and good to soft ground: usually tongue tied
(not last 2 starts): goes well fresh: sold to join J. O'Shea 6,000 gns Doncaster November
Sales. *Ian Williams*

DA BUICK (IRE) 5 b.g. Turtle Island (IRE) – Kindness Itself (IRE) (Ahonoora)   h–
[2002/3 17v^{pu} Nov 12] third foal: half-brother to 1m to 1½m winner Pirro (by Persian
Bold) and 7f winner Calamella (by Brief Truce), both fairly useful: dam, 7f winner,
half-sister to smart miler Mediation: always behind in novice hurdle at Sedgefield on
debut. *S. J. Magnier*

DABUS 8 b.g. Kris – Licorne (Sadler's Wells (USA)) [2002/3 17d^3 17m^2 17m 19g^2 c–
17g^3 16m 16m^3 c17v^F Dec 26] medium-sized gelding: modest hurdler: fell second on   h91
chasing debut: barely stays 19f: acts on firm and good to soft going: takes good hold.
M. C. Chapman

DADDY DANCER (FR) 12 b.g. Italic (FR) – Tresse d'Or (FR) (Northern Treat   c–
(USA)) [2002/3 c101, h–: c33g^{pu} c34g^{pu} May 22] compact gelding: modest handicap   h–
chaser/novice hurdler: has failed to complete all 3 starts in hunter chases, though running
well when falling on first occasion: probably stays 31f: acts on heavy going: tried
blinkered. *Martin Jones*

DADS LAD (IRE) 9 b.g. Supreme Leader – Furryvale (Furry Glen) [2002/3 c93: c25g   c86
c24d^3 c24s^F c25s^4 c25s^{bd} c24v^3 Mar 10] modest handicap chaser: sold out of H. Daly's
stable 6,000 gns Doncaster May Sales after reappearance: little subsequent form:
thorough stayer: raced on good going or softer (acts on heavy): often blinkered: difficult
ride. *Miss Suzy Smith*

DAFFANARC 5 b.m. Weld – Flower of Tintern (Free State) [2002/3 F17m Apr 15]   F–
sixth foal: half-sister to winning pointer See More Sense (by Seymour Hicks): dam
winning 2m hurdler/fairly useful up to 1¼m on Flat: 7/1 from 10/1, needed experience
when seventh of 9 in mares bumper at Exeter on debut, hanging left off home turn.
P. F. Nicholls

DAIMAJIN (IRE) 4 b.g. Dr Devious (IRE) – Arrow Field (USA) (Sunshine Forever   h–
(USA)) [2002/3 16d 16d Mar 19] fairly useful on Flat (stays 1¼m), successful in September for B. Meehan: well held both starts over hurdles, mistakes first time. *R. H. Alner*

DAINTY MAN (IRE) 11 b. or br.g. Cardinal Flower – Web of Gold (Bustineto)   c–
[2002/3 c20d c24m^6 Apr 10] modest pointer: little form in hunter chases (not fluent both
starts in 2002/3). *Mrs A. R. Hewitt*

DAISY LEIGH 9 b.m. Crested Lark – Mrs Pepperpot (Kinglet) [2002/3 c24s c23d^{pu} c–
c25d^{pu} Feb 6] lengthy mare: first foal: dam, winning pointer, half-sister to useful 2m
chaser Our Fun: poor pointer: no show in 3 novice chases. *G. B. Balding*

DAJAZAR (IRE)   7 b.g. Seattle Dancer (USA) – Dajarra (IRE) (Blushing Groom (FR)) [2002/3 16m 19s³ 16m 16m 22g* c20m² 24mᵖᵘ 22g 27g Apr 25] maiden on Flat: fair handicap hurdler, won at Tralee in August: second in maiden at Kilbeggan on chasing debut: sold out of P. Rothwell's stable 900 gns Doncaster November Sales, tailed off both subsequent starts: stays 2¾m: acts on any going: usually blinkered in Ireland: has had tongue tied. *Miss V. Scott*   **c98 h102**

DALBY OF YORK   7 ch.g. Polar Falcon (USA) – Miller's Creek (USA) (Star de Naskra (USA)) [2002/3 h–: 23v⁵ 27sᵖᵘ Nov 26] fair on Flat (stays 15.4f) at one time: no form in 3 starts over hurdles. *M. E. Sowersby*   **h–**

DALCASSIAN BUCK (IRE)   9 ch.g. Buckskin (FR) – Menebeans (IRE) (Duky) [2002/3 c–, h88: 16d* 21m⁴ 22d⁶ 22dᵖᵘ 22dᵖᵘ c19d⁴ c25dᶠ Feb 6] workmanlike gelding: modest hurdler: won novice at Towcester in April: sold out of K. Bailey's stable 3,000 gns Doncaster May Sales after third start: often let down by jumping in steeple-chases: effective at 2m to 3m: acts on good to soft going. *C. L. Popham*   **c69 x h88**

DALE CREEK (IRE)   8 b.g. Mandalus – Typhoon Signal (Aristocracy) [2002/3 c24mᶠ c25sᵖᵘ c22mᵖᵘ c25mᵘʳ c24g c24v⁴ c25d² Jan 27] IR 5,900 3-y-o: third foal: dam, placed over hurdles, out of half-sister to useful hurdler/chaser up to 25f Gallaher: winning pointer: modest chaser, won maiden at Kilbeggan in 2001/2: second outing since leaving H. de Bromhead, back form when second in handicap at Taunton: stays 25f: acts on good to soft going. *R. H. Alner*   **c92 h–**

DALLIGAN (IRE)   9 b.g. Executive Perk – Comeragh Queen (The Parson) [2002/3 c84: c20m⁴ c24g* c24v³ Jun 6] former hunter chaser: left N. Pewter and 22 lb wrong at weights, improved form to win handicap at Fakenham in May: stays 3m: possibly unsuited by heavy going: ridden by 7-lb claiming amateur. *D. E. Cantillon*   **c94 + h–**

DALUS PARK (IRE)   8 b.g. Mandalus – Pollerton Park (Pollerton) [2002/3 c96: c22d² c28g May 31] winning pointer: fair form when second in hunter chases, not helped by loose horse on run-in at Towcester in May. *Mrs Antonia Bealby*   **c96**

DAME FONTEYN   6 b.m. Suave Dancer (USA) – Her Honour (Teenoso (USA)) [2002/3 h84: 22f 19s⁴ 16s⁴ 16v² 21d⁶ 17d 22m⁵ Mar 20] leggy mare: poor maiden hurdler: needs good test at 2m and stays 2¾m: acts on heavy going, below form on firmer than good: ran creditably only try in blinkers. *C. Tizzard*   **h84**

DAMIEN'S CHOICE (IRE)   11 b.g. Erin's Hope – Reenoga (Tug of War) [2002/3 c101, h89: 16g⁶ c17g⁵ c17d² c16gᵘʳ c20dᶠ c16d⁵ c17d⁵ c16m² c17g* c16g* Apr 24] tall gelding: winning hurdler: left F. Murphy after reappearance: fair handicap chaser: ended season well, winning at Kelso and Perth in April: stays 2½m, raced mainly at shorter: acts on soft and good to firm going: has worn visor/cheekpieces, effective without: held up: has been reluctant to race/found little. *G. A. Swinbank*   **c106 h–**

DAMIENS PRIDE (IRE)   13 b.g. Bulldozer – Riopoless (Royal And Regal (USA)) [2002/3 c102: c21g² c19f* c21s³ c19fᶠ Mar 27] fairly useful hunter chaser: won novice at Exeter in May: stays 3¼m: acts on firm going, possibly unsuited by soft. *Mrs S. J. Batchelor*   **c103 d**

DAM THE BREEZE   10 b.g. Ikdam – Cool Breeze (Windjammer (USA)) [2002/3 c105, h98: c24s c21gᶠ Apr 3] lengthy gelding: winning hurdler: fair chaser: close third going well when falling thirteenth in Fox Hunters' at Aintree: stays 3¼m: acts on firm and good to soft going: visored once: jumps right, and probably best on right-handed tracks: genuine front runner. *Evan Williams*   **c105 h–**

DAMUS (GER)   9 b.g. Surumu (GER) – Dawn Side (CAN) (Bold Forbes (USA)) [2002/3 c127, h111+: c17mᶠ 16m⁶ 16f² c16g⁴ c19d⁴ c18m⁴ c20g³ Apr 12] leggy gelding: fair hurdler: fairly useful handicap chaser: off 4 months after fourth start, generally below best on return: stays easy 2½m: acts on any going: races prominently. *Ian Williams*   **c125 d h110**

DANAEVE (IRE)   8 b.g. Camden Town – Niagara Belle (Beau Charmeur (FR)) [2002/3 c126, h103: c20s³ 20m* c22d 20g c17v⁵ c20s c19s⁵ Jan 26] leggy gelding: fair hurdler: won minor event at Tipperary in July: fairly useful chaser, mostly well below form in 2002/3: stays 21f: acts on firm and soft going: tried tongue tied. *G. Keane, Ireland*   **c118 h106**

DANCE FREE (USA)   5 b.g. Fly So Free (USA) – Dances With Music (USA) (Sovereign Dancer (USA)) [2002/3 16s⁵ 16m 19f Mar 24] ex-Irish gelding: fair maiden (stays 1½m) on Flat: little form over hurdles, sold out of M. Grassick's stable €4,800 Goffs October Sale after second start. *I. R. Brown*   **h–**

DANCE IN TUNE   6 ch.g. Mujtahid (USA) – Dancing Prize (IRE) (Sadler's Wells (USA)) [2002/3 17m* 16g* 16m⁶ 17f⁴ 17g³ Apr 19] half-brother to winning 2m hurdler   **h100**

Dancing Phantom (by Darshaan): fairly useful at 2 yrs, well beaten only start on Flat at 3 yrs, sold out of Sir Mark Prescott's stable 25,000 gns Newmarket Autumn (2000) Sales: won first 2 starts over hurdles, novices at Newton Abbot and Worcester in August: best effort in handicaps after 7-month absence when third of 6 to Enitsag at Newton Abbot: will prove best around 2m: acts on good to firm going. *P. J. Hobbs*

DANCE OF LIFE   4 b.f. Shareef Dancer (USA) – Regan (USA) (Lear Fan (USA))   **h72 +**
[2002/3 17s^{pu} 16d^6 16s 16d 17g^F Apr 26] second foal: dam winning hurdler/chaser up to 25f: little form over hurdles: first form over hurdles when falling last in selling handicap at Market Rasen, 5 lengths clear and in command: raced around 2m: has worn cheekpieces, blinkered last 3 starts: needs to improve jumping. *S. Gollings*

DANCER POLISH (POL)   5 b.g. Professional (IRE) – Doloreska (POL) (Who   **h89**
Knows) [2002/3 16m^4 16g^2 16m* 20d^3 16m* 16s^5 Nov 13] close-coupled gelding: successful twice from 9 starts on Flat in Poland, including over 1m at 3 yrs: modest novice hurdler: won at Uttoxeter in October: stays 2½m: acts on soft and good to firm going. *A. Sadik*

DANCES WITH RIVERS   4 b.f. River Falls – Make Merry (IRE) (Dunbeath   **F–**
(USA)) [2002/3 F16g Feb 12] second foal: dam unraced: well held in mares bumper at Musselburgh on debut. *Mrs M. Reveley*

DANCETILLYOUDROP (IRE)   12 b.g. Clearly Bust – Keep Dancing (Lord Gayle   **c112**
(USA)) [2002/3 c116, h–: c31m^3 c26g* c32m^{ur} c26m^3 c25s^{pu} c27g^{pu} Feb 27] good-   **h–**
topped gelding: has had wind operation: maiden hurdler: fair chaser: made all in hunter at Folkestone in May and handicap at Newton Abbot in June: pulled up with breathing problems both starts after 7-month absence, tongue tied second occasion: best at 3m+: acts on any going: sometimes none too fluent. *P. F. Nicholls*

DANCING BAY   6 b.g. Suave Dancer (USA) – Kabayil (Dancing Brave (USA))   **h117**
[2002/3 h112p: 16s* 16d^4 21s* 16v Mar 8] sturdy gelding: useful on Flat (stays 2m, has gone in snatches/hung): fairly useful novice hurdler: landed odds at Plumpton in January and February (couple of mistakes and driven out to beat Benbecula a length): found little when well beaten in valuable handicap at Sandown final start: stays 21f: acts on soft going: held up. *N. J. Henderson*

DANCING DOLPHIN (IRE)   4 b.f. Dolphin Street (FR) – Dance Model (Unfuwain   **h69**
(USA)) [2002/3 16g^3 16m 16d Oct 26] lengthy filly: poor maiden on Flat (stays 1¼m): well held in juvenile hurdles after third in weak maiden at Uttoxeter on debut. *Julian Poulton*

DANCING FOSENBY   7 b.g. Terimon – Wave Dancer (Dance In Time (CAN))   **c–**
[2002/3 h62: 20g^6 17s c16g^4 Jul 15] bad novice hurdler (tried blinkered): jumped poorly   **h–**
after hampered first on chasing debut: sold £2,000 Ascot October Sales, won 3 times in points in February and March. *D. McCain*

DANCING PEARL   5 ch.m. Dancing Spree (USA) – Elegant Rose (Noalto) [2002/3   **h96**
F90: 16s^4 17s^4 16s* 16m* 16m^6 Apr 11] leggy mare: modest hurdler: won novices at Southwell in January and March, weak event on latter occasion: raced around 2m: acts on soft going, probably on good to firm. *C. J. Price*

DANCING SHIRLEY   5 b.m. Dancing Spree (USA) – High Heather (Shirley   **h–**
Heights) [2002/3 F70: 21g Oct 21] poor form on first of 2 starts in bumpers: well held in novice on hurdling debut. *T. P. McGovern*

DANCING WATER   4 gr.g. Halling (USA) – Gleaming Water (Kalaglow) [2002/3   **h105**
16s 16s 16d^3 Mar 10] fair maiden on Flat (stays 1½m, blinkered nowadays), sold out of F. J. Houghton's stable 11,000 gns Newmarket Autumn Sales: fair form in juvenile hurdles (highly tried second start), 5¼ lengths third of 15 to East Tycoon at Stratford. *Patrick O. Brady, Ireland*

DAN DE LION   4 b.c. Danzig Connection (USA) – Fiorini (Formidable (USA))   **h–**
[2002/3 16g^{pu} Sep 26] no sign of ability on Flat or on hurdling debut. *Jedd O'Keeffe*

DAN DE MAN (IRE)   12 br.g. Phardante (FR) – Slave De (Arctic Slave) [2002/3   **c68 §**
c81§, h81§: c16m^{pu} 16d 20d^{pu} 20d c22d^6 c20s^5 c20v^{pu} c16d^2 Mar 15] lengthy gelding: **h– §**
poor handicap chaser/hurdler: stays 2½m: acts on heavy going, probably on good to firm: best held up: unreliable. *Miss L. C. Siddall*

DANDE'S RAMBO   6 gr.g. Rambo Dancer (CAN) – Kajetana (FR) (Caro) [2002/3   **c–**
h90: c20d^F Feb 7] modest maiden on Flat at 3 yrs: fifth in 4-y-o novice hurdle in May   **h–**
2001: fell tenth on chasing debut: dead. *P. R. Hedger*

DANDONELL (IRE) 9 b.g. Ajraas (USA) – Courtown Bay (Don) [2002/3 h87: 22g⁴ c25f^F May 15] winning hurdler: fell fatally on chasing debut: stayed 25f: acted on firm and good to soft going: blinkered twice: occasionally broke blood vessels. *J. C. Tuck* **c– h78**

DANDY LAD (IRE) 6 b.g. Zaffaran (USA) – Gerdando Lady (IRE) (Exhibitioner) [2002/3 F16g⁶ F18m⁵ Mar 31] 16,000 4-y-o: first foal: dam lightly-raced half-sister to fairly useful chaser up to 3¼m Harristown Lady: sixth of 19 to Majestic Moonbeam at Warwick, better effort in bumpers. *O. Sherwood* **F86**

DANDY REGENT 9 b.g. Green Desert (USA) – Tahilla (Moorestyle) [2002/3 17s^pu Dec 26] modest on Flat (probably best at 7f/1m), sold out of J. Harris' stable £1,000 Ascot November Sales: failed to settle in novice selling hurdle at Hereford. *C. J. Price* **h–**

DANESWOOD 4 b.g. Be My Chief (USA) – Floria Tosca (Petong) [2002/3 16m⁴ Sep 29] modest and ungenuine on Flat (stays 1¼m): fourth in juvenile at Huntingdon on hurdling debut: sold 2,000 gns Doncaster May Sales. *P. W. D'Arcy* **h65**

DANGEROUSDANMAGRU (IRE) 7 b.g. Forest Wind (USA) – Blue Bell Girl (Blakeney) [2002/3 20s* 20s 17g⁵ 20s⁴ 16s 20s⁶ 20v⁴ Dec 21] half-brother to several winners, including fair hurdler/winning chaser Winn's Pride (by Indian Ridge), effective at 2m to 3m: fair on Flat (stays 1¾m): fair handicap hurdler: won at Cork in May: respectable fourth to Chopneyev at Uttoxeter final start: stays 2½m: raced on good going or softer (acts on heavy). *N. F. Glynn, Ireland* **h108**

DANGEROUS DEPLOY 6 b.g. Deploy – Emily-Mou (IRE) (Cadeaux Genereux) [2002/3 h62: 19d 16v c20s^F Mar 3] leggy gelding: poor maiden hurdler: behind when falling 5 out in weak novice on chasing debut: stays 2¾m: raced mainly on going softer than good (acts on heavy): tried visored: has had tongue tied: often jumps none too fluently. *Miss K. M. George* **c– h–**

DANGEROUSLY GOOD 5 b.g. Shareef Dancer (USA) – Ecologically Kind (Alleged (USA)) [2002/3 19d⁵ 16g Mar 11] leggy gelding: half-brother to winning 2m hurdler Mysterious Ecology (by Mystiko): ran once on Flat in Britain at 3 yrs for D. Morris, sent to Spain and successful over 1½m at Mijas in June and San Sebastian in August for J. Brown: 66/1 and visored, thirteenth of 19 to Back In Front in Grade 1 novice at Cheltenham on second start over hurdles, still travelling well towards rear after 3 out: likely to prove best at 2m: wore cheekpieces on debut: carried head awkwardly both starts: capable of winning a race over hurdles. *R. C. Guest* **h117**

DANIELS HYMN 8 b.g. Prince Daniel (USA) – French Spirit (FR) (On Your Mark) [2002/3 18d³ 22s⁴ 21d⁴ 24s^pu 16g² 20m* Apr 20] well-made gelding: second reported foal: dam unraced: fair hurdler: favourite, won 19-runner maiden at Cork, beating Lord Ajus a length: stays 21f: acts on good to soft and good to firm going (won bumper on firm). *Miss F. M. Crowley, Ireland* **h110**

DANIMAS (IRE) 6 b.g. Foxhound (USA) – Cerosia (Pitskelly) [2002/3 18s⁴ 16s 16g* c18v⁶ 17v³ 19m^F Mar 21] ex-Irish gelding: half-brother to fair hurdler Segala (by Petorius), stayed 2½m: modest maiden on Flat (stays 1¾m): 9 lb out of handicap, improved effort over hurdles to win at Musselburgh in February: well held in maiden at Fairyhouse on chasing debut: left C. Swan after next start: best form at 2m on good going. *B. G. Powell* **c– h96**

DANNY'S CHAPEL (IRE) 4 b.g. College Chapel – Blue Sioux (Indian Ridge) [2002/3 F16g Mar 2] second foal: dam 5f winner: tailed off in bumper at Huntingdon. *J. Neville* **F–**

DANSE SLAVE (FR) 4 b.f. Broadway Flyer (USA) – Snow Girl (FR) (River Mist (USA)) [2002/3 F12d 16d² 17d⁴ 17d 17g² 19m* Apr 8] second foal: half-sister to winner up to 1½m Soleil Boreal (by Showbrook): dam middle-distance winner: mid-division in bumper on debut: modest form over hurdles, won mares novice at Exeter: stays 19f: acts on good to firm and good to soft going. *R. H. Alner* **h87 F–**

DANTECO 8 gr.g. Phardante (FR) – Up Cooke (Deep Run) [2002/3 h–: c16d^ro c20m* c20m^F c21m^F 21g* 22d⁴ 21g² 20f* c21m² c21d^pu c20m⁴ Apr 19] big gelding: modest hurdler/chaser: made all in maiden chase at Hexham in June, novice handicap hurdle at Sedgefield in August and handicap chase at Hexham in September: badly let down by jumping final outing: stays 21f: possibly needs good going or firmer (acts on firm): headstrong. *Miss Kate Milligan* **c97 h90**

DANTE'S BATTLE (IRE) 11 b.g. Phardante (FR) – No Battle (Khalkis) [2002/3 c124, h–: 16g⁴ c17d⁵ 17m⁵ c21m^pu Aug 27] ex-Irish gelding: fairly useful hurdler/chaser at best, sold out of N. Meade's stable 13,500 gns Doncaster August Sales after second **c114 x h113**

start: stays 21f: acts on good to soft and good to firm going: often let down by jumping over fences: reportedly bled from nose final outing. *Miss K. Marks*

DANTE'S BROOK (IRE) 9 ch.g. Phardante (FR) – Arborfield Brook (Over The River (FR)) [2002/3 c16g³ c16g³ c17g⁴ c25gᵖᵘ Nov 1] strong, lengthy gelding: winning pointer: poor maiden hurdler/chaser: seems best around 2m: acts on firm going: tongue tied. *B. Mactaggart*   **c77 h–**

DANTES REEF (IRE) 7 b.g. Phardante (FR) – Thousand Flowers (Take A Reef) [2002/3 F16m² 16s 16s³ F16s² 19v⁴ 16d* 22g Apr 21] fifth foal: dam winning hurdler/chaser, stayed 2½m: fairly useful form in bumpers: fair hurdler: won maiden at Down Royal in March: stays 2½m: acts on heavy going, probably on good to firm. *A. J. Martin, Ireland*   **h101 F101**

DANTES VENTURE (IRE) 6 b.g. Phardante (FR) – Fast Adventure (Deep Run) [2002/3 F73: 17g² 21v² 20v³ 21g 24g² 24m Apr 12] sturdy gelding: modest novice hurdler, best efforts on first 2 starts: stays 3m: acts on heavy going, well held on good to firm. *D. J. Caro*   **h98**

DANTES WAGER (IRE) 7 b.g. Phardante (FR) – Gales Wager (Strong Gale) [2002/3 F16s⁵ 22d⁵ 24mᵖᵘ Mar 21] well-made gelding: third foal: dam winning chaser, stayed 2¾m: poor form in bumper and novice hurdles. *Miss G. Browne*   **h77 F71**

DANTIE BOY (IRE) 7 br.g. Phardante (FR) – Ballybride Gale (IRE) (Strong Gale) [2002/3 h109: 22d⁵ 20g* c19f² c19m* c21g³ 19f² 21m⁶ c21m⁶ Apr 17] lengthy gelding: fair hurdler: simple task in novice at Worcester in September: best effort over fences (usually let down by jumping) when winning novice at Taunton in October: stays 2¾m: acts on firm going. *P. J. Hobbs*   **c101 h110**

DANTON (IRE) 5 ch.g. Cadeaux Genereux – Royal Circle (Sadler's Wells (USA)) [2002/3 16d⁶ 16v⁴ 16d* Jan 24] angular gelding: fair on Flat (stays 1¼m): best effort in novice hurdles when 13 lengths fourth to Domenico at Uttoxeter: will prove best at 2m. *Miss S. J. Wilton*   **h94**

DANZIG FLYER (IRE) 8 b.g. Roi Danzig (USA) – Fenland Express (IRE) (Reasonable (FR)) [2002/3 h–: 16m 21sᶠ Jul 20] of little account. *M. Mullineaux*   **h–**

DANZIG ISLAND (IRE) 12 b.g. Roi Danzig (USA) – Island Morn (USA) (Our Native (USA)) [2002/3 c89, h95: c24g May 26] close-coupled gelding: modest handicap hurdler/chaser: stays 25f: acts on soft and good to firm going: tried blinkered/visored. *Mrs H. Dalton*   **c– h–**

DAPRIKA (FR) 5 b.m. Epervier Bleu – Kaprika (FR) (Cadoudal (FR)) [2002/3 c17s* 16s⁵ 16d⁴ Jan 15] leggy ex-French mare: fourth foal: half-sister to 3 winners, including very smart hurdler/smart chaser Geos (by Pistolet Bleu), stays 2½m, and promising 4-y-o Kapgarde (by Garde Royale): dam, minor 15f hurdle winner, also 1¼m winner on Flat: 11f winner on Flat: fair novice hurdler: won 4-y-o event at Enghien in September on chasing debut, jumping fluently and making all (final start for J. Bertran de Balanda): raced around 2m on ground softer than good: should do better over fences. *N. J. Henderson*   **c91 p h102**

DARAK (IRE) 7 b.g. Doyoun – Dararita (IRE) (Halo (USA)) [2002/3 h72d: 17gᵇᵈ 16g 27m 21gᶠ 21g⁴ Oct 15] sturdy gelding: poor handicap hurdler, little form for long time, left F. Murphy after second start: has had tongue tied. *Mrs K. J. Tutty*   **h–**

DARAPOUR (IRE) 9 b.g. Fairy King (USA) – Dawala (IRE) (Lashkari) [2002/3 h128§: 20sᵖᵘ 20s* 24dᵇᵈ Dec 13] small gelding: fairly useful handicap hurdler: easily won at Southwell in December: brought down ninth at Cheltenham week later: effective at 2m to 3¼m: acted on good to firm and heavy going: blinkered once: tried tongue tied: usually found little: dead. *Jonjo O'Neill*   **h128 §**

DARAYDAN (IRE) 11 b.g. Kahyasi – Delsy (FR) (Abdos) [2002/3 c–§, h112: c34gᵘʳ May 22] leggy gelding: one-time smart hurdler/winning chaser: fairly useful pointer nowadays, successful in 2-finisher event in March: stays 27f: probably acts on any going: blinkered once (mulish and ran poorly): none too trustworthy. *D. Pipe*   **c– § h–**

DARDANUS 5 ch.g. Komaite (USA) – Dance On A Cloud (Capote (USA)) [2002/3 18m* 19m⁴ 18m² 18g² 16m Oct 30] medium-sized gelding: fair on Flat (stays 1½m, sometimes visored), sold out of R. J. White's stable 14,000 gns Newmarket July Sales: fair form over hurdles: won 6-runner novice at Fontwell in August: ran poorly in blinkers final start: raced mainly on good to firm going: seems suited by front-running tactics. *C. J. Mann*   **h103**

DARE 8 b.g. Beveled (USA) – Run Amber Run (Run The Gantlet (USA)) [2002/3 c–, h102§: 17g c16s⁴ c20s³ c16v⁶ 16d⁵ 16s 19d 21d Mar 8] leggy gelding: fair handicap   **c– h90 §**

hurdler, below best in 2002/3: little aptitude for chasing: stays easy 2½m: acts on heavy going: effective visored/blinkered or not, wore cheekpieces final outing: tongue tied: weak finisher. *R. Lee*

DARETOBEDIFFERENT (IRE)   5 ch.g. Aristocracy – Telmary (Guillaume Tell   h–
(USA)) [2002/3 21d 21s 22dᶠ 24mᵖᵘ Mar 21] IR £12,000 3-y-o: chasing type: eleventh
foal: half-brother to winning hurdlers up to 21f Marys Madera (by Toca Madera) and Call
Mary (by Young Man): dam lightly-raced maiden on Flat: runner-up in Irish point in
2002: signs of ability over hurdles: pulled up lame final outing. *Miss H. C. Knight*

D'ARGENT (IRE)   6 gr.g. Roselier (FR) – Money Galore (IRE) (Monksfield) [2002/3   h–
h118p, F78: 20d 20g Apr 2] leggy, useful-looking gelding: will make a chaser: progressive in novice hurdles in 2001/2, won 2 of 3 starts: disappointing both starts in handicaps
5 months apart in 2002/3 (reportedly bled from nose second time): will stay 3m: acts on
good to soft going. *A. King*

DARIALANN (IRE)   8 b.g. Kahyasi – Delsy (FR) (Abdos) [2002/3 c98p, h130:   c92
c17sᵘʳ 16dᶠ c17dᶠ c17m³ c16s⁵ c18sᵖᵘ 16dᵖᵘ Apr 9] compact gelding: useful hurdler: won   h130 d
minor event at Galway in July: only modest form over fences: sold out of A. Moore's
stable 13,000 gns Doncaster November Sales after sixth start: no encouragement on
return in spring: raced mainly around 2m (should be suited by further): acts on soft going:
often blinkered: tongue tied once (well beaten). *O. Brennan*

DARIEN   9 b.g. Sadler's Wells (USA) – Aryenne (FR) (Green Dancer (USA)) [2002/3   h–
19s⁴ 16d 16d 24] close-coupled gelding: modest form over hurdles in 1998/9 for
R. Dickin: little encouragement on 2 outings after lengthy absence: should stay 2½m: has
had tongue tied. *R. J. Price*

DARINA'S BOY   7 b.g. Sula Bula – Glebelands Girl (Burslem) [2002/3 F18s³ 21s*   h110
24d² 24s* 27m² 24m 24m⁶ Apr 26] workmanlike gelding: will make a chaser: second   F83
foal: dam winning hurdler, stayed 3m: won maiden on second of 2 starts in Irish points in
2002: bought 5,600 gns Doncaster August Sales: third of 9 in bumper at Fontwell: fair
novice hurdler: won at Plumpton in January and Bangor (handicap) in March: best
effort second of 5 to Howdydoody in handicap at Fontwell, flashing tail under pressure
(dismounted after line): out of depth final outing: stays 27f: acts on soft and good to firm
going: usually front runner. *L. Wells*

DARINGLY   14 b.g. Daring March – Leylandia (Wolver Hollow) [2002/3 c73, h–:   c–
c25gᵖᵘ c21g⁵ c22f⁴ c24mᵖᵘ c21g c26m c26mᵖᵘ Aug 27] lengthy gelding: winning   h–
hurdler/chaser, retains little ability: left M. Appleby after first start: tried blinkered.
G. F. Bridgwater

DARING NATIVE (IRE)   10 b. or br.g. Be My Native (USA) – Scarlet Tina (Dusky   c–
Boy) [2002/3 c–, h–: c26d Jun 8] poor pointer/novice chaser: tried blinkered/visored: h–
usually tongue tied. *J. M. Ratcliffe*

DARING NEWS   8 b.g. Risk Me (FR) – Hot Sunday Sport (Star Appeal) [2002/3 h–:   h–
19s 19d 16m 16gᵖᵘ Apr 12] good-topped gelding: winning hurdler, little worthwhile
form since early-1999/00. *O. O'Neill*

DARING THOMAS   8 b.g. Derrylin – Dawn Encounter (Rymer) [2002/3 h86: 20sᵖᵘ   h–
Nov 2] leggy gelding: novice hurdler, ran as if amiss only start since May 2001.
D. M. Grissell

DARIOLE (IRE)   7 b.g. Priolo (USA) – Dance Land (IRE) (Nordance (USA))   h129
[2002/3 h118: 17m² 16m* 20f* 20f² Sep 28] fairly useful handicap hurdler: won at Tralee
in August and Tipperary in September: good second at Listowel final start: stays 2½m:
acts on any going. *M. Halford, Ireland*

DARK BUCCANEER   5 b.g. Sovereign Water (FR) – Some Cherry (Some Hand)   F–
[2002/3 F16v Nov 16] tall gelding: seventh foal: half-brother to bumper winner Free
Native (by Escapism): dam, half-sister to several winners, of little account: pulled hard
when last of 14 in bumper at Wetherby on debut. *J. Wade*

DARK CHARACTER   4 b.g. Reprimand – Poyle Jezebelle (Sharpo) [2002/3 F16d²   F95
F16m* F17g⁶ Apr 5] second foal: dam, 6f winner, sister to smart sprinter Poyle George:
fair form in bumpers: odds on, won at Southwell in March: sixth in Grade 2 at Aintree
following month. *G. A. Swinbank*

DARK CRUSADER (IRE)   8 br.g. Cajetano (USA) – Glissade (Furry Glen) [2002/3   c– §
c79§, h–§: 24mᵖᵘ Aug 27] tall gelding: winning hurdler/maiden chaser: stays 21f: acts   h– §
on heavy going: sometimes blinkered, including for both wins: not to be trusted. *Miss
Lucinda V. Russell*

DARK FAIRY 5 br.m. Tragic Role (USA) – Sharp Fairy (Sharpo) [2002/3 h109: 16d³ **h115**
16m³ 20g³ 22m* 20m⁴ Oct 5] leggy, angular mare: fair handicap hurdler: won steadily-run 4-runner race at Newton Abbot in July: ran as if amiss only subsequent start: stays 2¾m, at least when emphasis is firmly on speed: acts on good to firm and heavy going. *M. C. Pipe*

DARK ISLAND 8 b.g. Silver Season – Isle Maree (Star Appeal) [2002/3 24dᵖᵘ Mar **h–**
1] lengthy, rather sparely-made gelding: sixth foal: half-brother to winning hurdlers by Rakaposhi King and Stalker: dam ran once: showed nothing in novice hurdle at Newbury on debut. *Mary Meek*

DARK MAGIC (IRE) 12 br.g. Over The River (FR) – Mwanamio (Sole Mio (USA)) **c115**
[2002/3 c111, h–: c22v⁵ c16s c24v* c24vᶠ Jan 12] fairly useful handicap chaser: won at **h–**
Wexford in November: stayed 3m: acted on heavy going: dead. *Paddy Fennelly, Ireland*

DARK MANDATE (IRE) 5 b. or br.m. Mandalus – Ceoltoir Dubh (Black Minstrel) **h–**
[2002/3 16gᵖᵘ Apr 7] eighth foal: half-sister to Irish bumper winner Phardubh (by Phardante): dam unraced half-sister to Galway Plate winner Master Player, from family of high-class 2½m chaser Half Free: 100/1, no show in novice hurdle on debut. *J. S. Haldane*

DARK'N SHARP (GER) 8 b.g. Sharpo – Daytona Beach (GER) (Konigsstuhl **c151**
(GER)) [2002/3 h94, h–: 16d³ c16vᶠ c16g³ c16g³ c16g² c21mᵘʳ Apr 16] sturdy gelding: **h133 +**
useful hurdler: smart handicap chaser: good efforts when placed in valuable events at Kempton (third to Young Devereaux), Cheltenham (third to Palarshan in Grand Annual) and Aintree (second of 16 to Golden Alpha): upped in trip, held when unseating 2 out in Grade 2 limited event won by Poliantas at Cheltenham: should stay beyond 2m: acts on soft and good to firm going: patiently ridden. *R. T. Phillips*

DARK ROOM (IRE) 6 b.g. Toulon – Maudlin Bridge (IRE) (Strong Gale) [2002/3 **c109**
c20s⁶ c22dᵘʳ c21v⁵ c25v* c24d² c24d² c22s³ c32gᵖᵘ c32g Mar 21] IR 30,000 3-y-o: lengthy gelding: first foal: dam unraced half-sister to dam of useful 2½m to 3m chaser Dun Belle: won 4-y-o maiden Irish point in 2001: fair chaser, trained by E. Bolger only start in 2001/2: improved form when winning novice at Market Rasen on handicap debut in December: good placed efforts in similar events next 3 starts: stays 25f: acts on heavy going: jumps none too fluently: usually claimer ridden. *Jonjo O'Neill*

DARK SHADOWS 8 b.g. Machiavellian (USA) – Instant Desire (USA) (Northern **h94**
Dancer) [2002/3 h94: 16d² 16dᵖᵘ 16dᵖᵘ 20g² Mar 17] modest maiden hurdler: stays 2½m: acts on good to soft going. *W. Storey*

DARK SOCIETY 5 b.g. Imp Society (USA) – No Candles Tonight (Star Appeal) **h– §**
[2002/3 h83§: 16v⁴ 17sᵖᵘ Feb 13] sturdy gelding: poor maiden hurdler: raced around 2m: acts on heavy going: weak finisher. *A. W. Carroll*

DARK VICTOR (IRE) 7 b.g. Cadeaux Genereux – Dimmer (Kalaglow) [2002/3 16s **h77**
16s⁵ 16v 16g⁵ 16d Feb 8] leggy gelding: fair but quirky on Flat (stays 1¾m): only poor over hurdles. *D. Shaw*

DARMIL (IRE) 10 br.g. Welsh Term – Ballinkillen (Levmoss) [2002/3 c106x, h–: **c– x**
c20gᵖᵘ Jan 28] tall gelding: winning hurdler/chaser, fair on his day: stays 25f: acts on soft **h–**
going: often let down by jumping over fences. *I. A. Duncan, Ireland*

DARNLEY 6 b. or br.g. Henbit (USA) – Reeling (Relkino) [2002/3 F–: F16d 17sᵖᵘ **h95**
16dᶠ 16m³ 16g⁴ Apr 25] tall gelding: modest form over hurdles, over 15 lengths third to **F–**
Laouen in 5-runner novice at Ayr in April. *J. N. R. Billinge*

DARRELL BOY (IRE) 8 b.g. Commanche Run – Free For Ever (Little Buskins) **h– §**
[2002/3 h67§, F75: 20s⁶ 20v⁵ Jan 15] workmanlike gelding: poor hurdler: stays 27f: acts on heavy going: blinkered/visored: ungenuine. *J. R. Norton*

DASH FOR GOLD 4 br.f. Highest Honor (FR) – Dashing Water (Dashing Blade) **h–**
[2002/3 16m 16dᵖᵘ 16d⁴ 16g 17s⁴ 21v⁴ 20s 17d 17d Mar 18] maiden on Flat: little form over hurdles: blinkered last 2 starts. *J. Hetherton*

DASHING DOLLAR (IRE) 12 b.g. Lord Americo – Cora Swan (Tarqogan) [2002/3 **h–**
h107d: 22g⁵ 27sᵖᵘ 22gᶠ 19d 24dᵖᵘ 22g⁵ Apr 21] smallish, workmanlike gelding: fair handicap hurdler at best, no form in 2002/3: stays 2¾m: possibly needs good going or softer (acts on heavy): has been mounted on track. *J. R. Payne*

DASHING HOME (IRE) 4 b.g. Lahib (USA) – Dashing Rose (Mashhor Dancer **h127**
(USA)) [2002/3 16g² 16v* 16s³ 16v³ 17g 16g* Apr 21] tall gelding: will make a chaser: dam fair 2m hurdler: fairly useful on Flat up to 1¼m: useful juvenile hurdler: won maiden at Down Royal in November and minor event at Fairyhouse in April, odds on when

Mrs P. Towey's "Dashing Home"

beating Harchibald 3 lengths in latter: badly impeded 3 out when keeping-on tenth of 27 to Spectroscope in Triumph Hurdle at Cheltenham: creditable sixth, despite not fully applying himself, to Sporazene in Grade 1 at Punchestown in early-May: not sure to stay beyond 2m: acts on heavy going. *N. Meade, Ireland*

DASHING STEVE 4 b.g. Danzig Connection (USA) – Blazing Sunset (Blazing **h–** Saddles (AUS)) [2002/3 16g 16d 16m^pu Apr 22] poor sprint maiden on Flat: no form over hurdles: sold out of M. Hammond's stable 1,000 gns Doncaster January Sales after second start. *Mrs A. M. Thorpe*

DASH OF MAGIC 5 b.m. Magic Ring (IRE) – Praglia (IRE) (Darshaan) [2002/3 16d **h–** Feb 26] leggy mare: modest up to 1½m on Flat, successful on all-weather in January: no encouragement in novice at Wetherby on hurdling debut. *J. Hetherton*

DAT MY HORSE (IRE) 9 b.g. All Haste (USA) – Toposki (FR) (Top Ville) [2002/3 **cxx** c106x, h–: 26g* 24g* 24g* 24g 25m² 19g³ 22v c23d³ c20d⁴ c24g^pu Feb 27] big, work- **h113** manlike gelding: not a good walker: fair novice hurdler: easily won at Hereford (maiden), Towcester and Market Rasen early in season: badly let down by jumping in steeplechases: effective around 2½m to 3¼m: best form on good going: sometimes finishes tamely. *P. G. Murphy*

DAUGHTER IN LAW (IRE) 10 b.m. Law Society (USA) – Colonial Line (USA) **h56** (Plenty Old (USA)) [2002/3 h61: 21d^pu 21g⁶ 19g 24g⁴ 20m^pu Jul 17] lengthy, angular mare: bad maiden hurdler: stays 21f: acts on soft and good to firm going: tongue tied. *Miss C. J. E. Caroe*

DAVENPORT DEMOCRAT (IRE) 5 ch.g. Fourstars Allstar (USA) – Storm **F105 +** Court (IRE) (Glacial Storm (USA)) [2002/3 F16s F16s* F16g Mar 12] tall, rather

227

unfurnished gelding: first foal: dam unraced, from family of smart 2m to 2½m chaser Brockley Court and smart 3m chaser Glyde Court: easily best effort in bumpers when winning 15-runner event at Fairyhouse in February: in rear in Grade 1 at Cheltenham. *W. P. Mullins, Ireland*

DAVENPORT MILENIUM (IRE) 7 b.g. Insan (USA) – Society Belle (Callernish) [2002/3 h147p: 16s³ Dec 26] useful-looking gelding: progressive novice hurdler in 2001/2, successful 4 times, notably in Grade 1 events at Punchestown last 2 starts: 9 lengths third of 6 to Intersky Falcon in Christmas Hurdle at Kempton on return, no extra in straight (missed rest of season reportedly due to strained tendon): will stay beyond 2½m: raced on good going or softer (won bumper on heavy). *W. P. Mullins, Ireland*   **h149**

DAVE THE BANK 8 ch.g. Desert Dirham (USA) – L'Ancressaan (Dalsaan) [2002/3 20sᵖᵘ Jan 30] workmanlike gelding: probably of little account: sold 1,700 gns Doncaster May Sales. *T. H. Caldwell*   **h–**

DAVIDS LAD (IRE) 9 b.g. Yashgan – Cool Nora (IRE) (Lafontaine (USA)) [2002/3 c152², h–: c25s⁴ c16d c29g⁴ Apr 21] strong, lengthy gelding: smart chaser: easily best effort in 2002/3 when fourth under top weight to Timbera in Irish Grand National at Fairyhouse: reportedly distressed on reappearance, always behind in Grade 2 at Naas (horse banned for 42 days, jockey for 7 and trainer fined €1,000 under schooling in public rule) next time: best at 2½m+ (stays 29f): acts on any going: tongue tied: held up: usually sound jumper: game. *A. J. Martin, Ireland*   **c148**   **h–**

DAVOSKI 9 b.g. Niniski (USA) – Pamela Peach (Habitat) [2002/3 c142, h–: c16d* c16d³ c16v⁴ c16v³ 16g Feb 8] angular gelding: one-time useful hurdler, well held in very valuable handicap at Newbury final start: smart chaser: favourite, won quite valuable handicap at Ascot in November by 4 lengths from Just Jasmine: successful at 21f, best efforts at 2m: acts on good to firm and heavy going: still prone to mistakes. *Miss Venetia Williams*   **c148**   **h–**

DAVY'S IMAGE 9 ch.g. Milieu – Reigate Head (Timber King) [2002/3 h–: 16gᵖᵘ Nov 23] sturdy, plain gelding: no sign of ability: tongue tied in 2001/2. *B. Bousfield*   **h–**

DAWN COURT 6 b.m. Rakaposhi King – Herald The Dawn (Dubassoff (USA)) [2002/3 F–: 19sᵖᵘ 19d 22m Mar 20] no form in bumper or 3 novice hurdles: sold £1,700 Ascot April Sales. *R. H. Alner*   **h–**

DAWN FOX (IRE) 7 ch.m. Phardante (FR) – Golden Vixen (Goldhill) [2002/3 h–, F–: 17sᵖᵘ 19g⁶ 17m 17gᵖᵘ Nov 7] stocky mare: of little account. *N. G. Ayliffe*   **h–**

DAWN'S COGNAC (IRE) 10 b.g. Glacial Storm (USA) – Misty Venture (Foggy Bell) [2002/3 c24dᵖᵘ c26dᵖᵘ Feb 17] rangy gelding: fair pointer, successful in February: let down by jumping in hunter chases. *D. Brace*   **c– x**

DAY DU ROY (FR) 5 b.g. Ajdayt (USA) – Rose Pomme (FR) (Rose Laurel) [2002/3 18d c17s c19s* c19dᵖᵘ c16vᵖᵘ Feb 4] rather leggy ex-French gelding: third foal: half-brother to French middle-distance winner Star du Roy (by Dalal): dam maiden on Flat/ over hurdles: won 4-y-o chase at Fontainebleau in November, final start for F. Danloux: pulled up in 2 novices in Britain, losing action on first occasion and reportedly distressed on second. *Jonjo O'Neill*   **c?**   **h?**

DAY LEWIS 7 b.g. Golden Heights – Darling Dianne (IRE) (Burslem) [2002/3 F17f 20dꟳ Oct 23] good-topped gelding: first foal: dam 2-y-o 6f winner: little encouragement in bumper or novice hurdle. *Jonjo O'Neill*   **h–**   **F–**

DAYTIME DAWN (IRE) 12 b.g. Rashar (USA) – Ard Clos (Ardoon) [2002/3 c?, h–: c17mᵖᵘ c20mᵖᵘ Mar 19] one-time useful pointer/hunter chaser: lightly raced in recent years and appears to retain little ability, left Mrs P. Robeson after reappearance. *R. N. C. Wale*   **c–**   **h–**

DAZZLING RIO (IRE) 4 b.g. Ashkalani (IRE) – Dazzling Fire (IRE) (Bluebird (USA)) [2002/3 16mᵖᵘ 16g² 16m⁶ 16g³ 16g⁴ Dec 13] lengthy gelding: modest on Flat (stays 11f): modest juvenile hurdler: likely to stay beyond 2m: jumps none too fluently. *P. C. Haslam*   **h87**

DB MY SON 7 b.g. Gildoran – Rolling Dice (Balinger) [2002/3 c24sꟳ c16m c16m² c20g* c17s⁴ c24g⁶ c19fꟳ c19v* c20d Jan 16] 4,200 4-y-o: fifth foal: half-brother to winning 2½m chaser Pitchthedice (by Relief Pitcher): dam, modest 2½m chaser, half-sister to smart hunter chaser Risk A Bet: no form over hurdles: modest chaser: won maiden at Tralee in August and novice handicap at Taunton (first outing since leaving V. Bowens) in December: stays 2½m: acts on good to firm and heavy going: needs to improve jumping. *P. F. Nicholls*   **c98**   **h–**

D-DAY-SMOKE 9 ch.g. Cigar – Little Pockthorpe (Morston (FR)) [2002/3 16gpu Sep **h–**
12] no show both starts on Flat or in seller on hurdling debut (pulled hard). *A. Streeter*

DD'S GLENALLA (IRE) 6 b.m. Be My Native (USA) – Willowho Pride (Arapaho) **F81**
[2002/3 F16g F17s⁶ F18s² F16d F17mpu Apr 17] leggy mare: seventh live foal: half-sister
to winning pointer by Fidel: dam unraced: best effort in bumpers (trained by I. Ferguson
on debut, subsequently runner-up in Irish point) when second in mares event at Fontwell: shaped as if something amiss final start: will stay at least 2½m: has flashed tail.
N. A. Twiston-Davies

DEAD AIM (IRE) 9 b.g. Sadler's Wells (USA) – Dead Certain (Absalom) [2002/3 **c–**
17vpu 17g⁶ 20g c25gF Apr 14] has reportedly had wind operation: maiden hurdler: little **h–**
sign of retaining ability (well behind when falling on chasing debut). *N. Wilson*

DEAD-EYED DICK (IRE) 7 b.g. Un Desperado (FR) – Glendale Charmer (Down **c89**
The Hatch) [2002/3 h–: 24g c23d* c21dF c22spu c24s⁶ c24vpu Mar 10] tall, quite good- **h–**
topped gelding: hinted at temperament over hurdles: first run for 5 months, easily won
novice handicap at Exeter in December on chasing debut: ran as if amiss last 3 starts:
stays 23f: acts on good to soft going. *Nick Williams*

DEADLY DORIS 9 b.m. Ron's Victory (USA) – Camp Chair (Ela-Mana-Mou) **h– §**
[2002/3 h69§: 16d⁴ 16s 20mpu Apr 12] sturdy mare: poor hurdler: stays 2½m: acts on
good to firm and heavy going: tried blinkered: ungenuine. *N. A. Smith*

DEALER DEL 9 b.g. Deltic (USA) – No Deal (Sharp Deal) [2002/3 c71: c21g⁵ c22d* **c97**
c28gpu c24s² c32gur c25mpu Apr 5] big, rangy gelding: modest chaser: easily best effort
when winning novice hunter at Towcester in May despite again making mistakes, and
flashing tail: probably stays 3m: acts on soft ground, possibly unsuited by firmer than
good. *C. J. Down*

DEALER'S CHOICE (IRE) 9 gr.g. Roselier (FR) – Cam Flower VII (Damsire **c115**
Unregistered) [2002/3 c111, h88: 22d² c21d* c24spu c20dF c20gur Apr 12] rather leggy, **h99**
quite good-topped gelding: fair maiden hurdler, very unruly in preliminaries but ran well
on reappearance: fairly useful handicap chaser: won at Folkestone in December: left at
start next time: should stays 3m: acts on soft going: blinkered once. *M. Pitman*

DEANO'S BEENO 11 b.g. Far North (CAN) – Sans Dot (Busted) [2002/3 c–, **c–**
h144: 23f² 24g³ 25v* 23s² 24m* 24g⁶ 24g* 24m² Apr 26] **h167 d**
'Will the real Deano's Beeno step forward please.' The Anglo-Irish Hurdle
Classification for 2002/3, published in the *Racing Calender* in May, ranked him
only joint-ninth in the two-and-a-half-miles-plus category. Deano's Beeno is
assessed at 154, 16 lb behind Stayers' Hurdle winner Baracouda who beat him into
sixth place at Cheltenham. However, the pair also met in the Cantor Sport Long

*Cantor Sport Long Walk Hurdle, Ascot—finally victorious after three seconds in the race,
Deano's Beeno holds off Baracouda close home*

betfair.com Rendlesham Hurdle, Kempton—Deano's Beeno is much too good for a substandard field

Walk Hurdle at Ascot in December, the form of which—astonishingly for a Grade 1 championship event—has been completely ignored by the BHB and Turf Club handicappers. Deano's Beeno inflicted the first defeat in eleven starts on Baracouda and is the only horse to beat him for the best part of three seasons. On any logical reading of the form-book, Deano's Beeno produced a top-class performance that day, one bettered over the distance during the season—by our reckoning—only by Baracouda, Iris's Gift and Limestone Lad, the three who filled the places in a vintage Stayers' Hurdle. Deano's Beeno has now contested three editions of the Stayers' Hurdle, finishing ninth and eighth on his two previous appearances, and has never finished closer than twenty-five lengths to the winner. It is wrong to judge him on those performances, however, and he is certainly slighted by his latest Classification assessment. For all his well-documented quirks and physical problems, Deano's Beeno is capable of top-class form on his day and proved himself still too good in the latest season for most of the leading staying hurdlers in training. In a busier campaign than usual, he also won two other graded events, the Rendlesham at Kempton in February and the Long Distance Hurdle at Ascot in April.

Deano's Beeno is a hard ride and his jockey—usually Tony McCoy—sometimes has his work cut out to keep his mind on racing. He is a tricky customer and can be unpredictable, and is not one to take a short price about as he showed when twice beaten at odds on in the latest season. The progressive Lord Transcend beat him a neck in the Premier Stayers' Hurdle at Haydock in January and, facing a relatively simple task in a conditions event at Sandown in April, Deano's Beeno was unable to shake off Rostropovich and was caught close home, beaten a short head. Deano's Beeno attempted to duck out passing the stables at Haydock where he was off the bridle a long way from home. There had been no such antics when Deano's Beeno had come second, responding well despite having to be driven along from early on the final circuit, under top weight in the Long Distance Handicap Hurdle at Haydock back in May. That performance indicated that Deano's Beeno was no back number, despite the fact that he had been seen out only twice the previous season—having 'lots of problems' according to his trainer—and had been off the course for nine months before an appearance in the Stayers' Hurdle. Deano's Beeno reappeared after the summer in the Long Distance Hurdle at Newbury on Hennessy day. He had won the race twice before but managed only third this time behind Bacchanal and Native Emperor. It was then on to fog-shrouded Ascot for the Long Walk Hurdle, in which Deano's Beeno had finished second three times. Emulating that placing looked the best connections could hope for against Baracouda who started at 11/4-on, seeking his third successive win in the event. Jumping fast and fluently, and racing with more enthusiasm than he sometimes shows, Deano's Beeno made all. Baracouda gradually reduced the gap after Deano's Beeno, the best part of twenty clear of third-placed Baracouda in Swinley Bottom, had held a ten-length advantage over him three out. Baracouda was almost upsides at the last but Deano's Beeno pulled out more close home under a determined ride from McCoy to hold on by a length. It was some measure of the performances of the first two that the smart Native Emperor, sent after Deano's Beeno four out but unable to make an impression, finished a distance behind in third.

sportingoptions.co.uk Long Distance Hurdle, Ascot—
Deano's Beeno makes it three wins in a season for the first time since 1997/8

Deano's Beeno didn't reproduce his Long Walk form in subsequent races but he was too good for the opposition in the betfair.com Rendlesham Hurdle at Kempton in which, after turning mulish when kicked at the start, he raced lazily in front before forging clear from the home turn to beat Palua by twelve lengths. The sportingoptions.co.uk Long Distance Hurdle at Ascot looked another fairly straightforward opportunity and Deano's Beeno didn't have to be near his best to win by eight lengths from Frosty Canyon; Deano's Beeno was typically indolent and needed to be ridden along at around halfway, passing the stabling area.

Deano's Beeno (b.g. 1992)	Far North (CAN) (b 1973)	Northern Dancer (b 1961)	Nearctic
			Natalma
		Fleur (b 1964)	Victoria Park
			Flaming Page
	Sans Dot (b 1978)	Busted (b 1963)	Crepello
			Sans Le Sou
		Juliette Marny (b 1972)	Blakeney
			Set Free

At the advanced age of eleven, there must be a doubt about whether Deano's Beeno will enjoy another season as successful as the latest one, but, despite his fairly limited appearances, he has been a fine servant to his stable over the years since being bought off the Flat as a four-year-old. He also reflects great credit on those who have handled him at Pond House. Difficult to keep sound, Deano's Beeno was also hobdayed and had a tie-back operation to alleviate a wind infirmity before his 1999/00 campaign. The leggy Deano's Beeno and ill-fated top-class hurdler French Holly (by Sir Ivor) are the best of several winners produced by Sans Dot, a daughter of Oaks winner Juliette Marny. Sans Dot had a stamina-packed pedigree—she was by Busted—and it is no surprise that front-running Deano's Beeno, who acts on any going and is a fluent jumper, is a thorough stayer, best at

Axom's "Deano's Beeno"

three miles plus. A career over fences—in which sphere Deano's Beeno won his only start—might be thought unlikely to be resurrected at this late stage, although he was declared at the overnight stage for the subsequently abandoned Eider Chase. For the record, Deano's Beeno has been tried once in blinkers. *M. C. Pipe*

DEAR DEAL   10 b.g. Sharp Deal – The Deer Hound (Cash And Carry) [2002/3 c109, h–: c26m² c23f² c26g² c32m c26mˢᵘ c26s² c25d² c23dᵘʳ Dec 19] lengthy gelding: winning hurdler: fair maiden chaser: should stay beyond 3¼m: acts on soft and firm going: blinkered fourth/fifth outings. *C. Tizzard*   **c112 h–**

DEAR LORD (IRE)   6 ch.g. Mister Lord (USA) – Carange (Known Fact (USA)) [2002/3 25d c19dᵖᵘ 20g 22vᵖᵘ Mar 3] 2,000 5-y-o: half-brother to several winners, including fairly useful 2½m bumper winner Keltech Warrior (by Glacial Storm): dam, maiden, out of half-sister to Irish Derby winner Weavers' Hall: little sign of ability, saddle slipped final outing: joined B. Smart. *Mrs A. M. Thorpe*   **c– h–**

DEB'S SON   6 b.g. Minster Son – Deb's Ball (Glenstal (USA)) [2002/3 h104?: 17d⁶ 22vᵖᵘ 21d 21d* Apr 8] sparely-made gelding: poor hurdler: visored, first form of season when winning selling handicap at Sedgefield in April: stays 27f: acts on heavy going: tried in cheekpieces: not a fluent jumper. *James Moffatt*   **h80**

DECISIVE   4 b.g. Alhaarth (IRE) – Alys (Blakeney) [2002/3 16v Feb 1] half-brother to modest staying hurdler Warfield (by Glint of Gold) and winning 2m hurdler Dawaam (by Young Generation): fair on Flat (stays 2m), successful in March: jumped sluggishly when well held in juvenile at Sandown on hurdling debut. *P. R. Webber*   **h–**

DECISIVE ACTION (USA)   8 br.g. Alleged (USA) – Maria Balastiere (USA) **h119**
(Majestic Light (USA)) [2002/3 h122: 16s⁴ 16s⁵ 16s Feb 9] fairly useful handicap
hurdler: races mainly at 2m on good going or softer (acts on heavy): reportedly lame
second start. *Andrew Slattery, Ireland*

DECKIE (IRE)   8 b.g. Be My Native (USA) – Shannon Spray (Le Bavard (FR)) [2002/3 **c102**
24s 22g⁶ c22d³ c23f³ c20m* c16g c16s³ c25d⁵ c16s³ Dec 8] angular gelding: fourth foal: **h–**
half-brother to useful chaser Eirespray (by Executive Perk), stays 25f, and fairly useful
chaser Shannon Gale (by Strong Gale), stays 3m: dam, smart hurdler up to 2¾m, half-
sister to dam of Royal & SunAlliance Chase winner One Knight: bumper winner/winning
hurdler: fair chaser: won maiden at Kilbeggan in September: effective at 2m to easy 23f:
acts on firm and soft going: effective tongue tied or not. *C. Roche, Ireland*

DECODED   7 ch.g. Deploy – Golden Panda (Music Boy) [2002/3 c79, h–: c25m* **c83**
c27v⁴ c25g^pu Jan 18] compact gelding: winning hurdler: poor chaser: first run for 6 **h–**
months and after leaving J. O'Keeffe, won novice at Kelso in October: stays 3¼m: acts
on good to firm and heavy going: wore cheekpieces in 2002/3. *C. Grant*

DEEP KING (IRE)   8 b. or br.g. King's Ride – Splendid Run (Deep Run) [2002/3 **c99 d**
c20m* c23f⁴ c17s³ c20v^pu c20s^ur c25d^pu c17m³ Apr 19] lengthy gelding: maiden pointer:
modest form in steeplechases, won maiden at Wexford in July: left M. Treacy after third
start, well beaten only completed subsequent outing: stays 23f: acts on firm going: has
had tongue tied (including when successful). *J. W. Mullins*

DEEPRITIVE   6 b.m. Primitive Rising (USA) – Last of The Deep (IRE) (Deep Run) **h–**
[2002/3 F67: 19g^pu Apr 19] angular mare: little sign of ability in bumpers or maiden
hurdle. *R. Hollinshead*

DEEP SIGH   6 b.g. Weld – At Long Last (John French) [2002/3 F17v⁵ F18v 19d^pu **h–**
Feb 23] sixth foal: half-brother to 2 winners by Gunner B, including winning hurdler/ **F77**
fairly useful chaser Gunnerblong, stays 2¾m: dam, closely related to fairly useful 3m
chaser Baluchi, never ran: modest form in first of 2 bumpers: no show in maiden hurdle.
D. R. Gandolfo

DEEP SUNSET (IRE)   7 b.m. Supreme Leader – Twinkle Sunset (Deep Run) **c113**
[2002/3 h119: 16v⁴ 16s⁴ 16d⁵ c20g* c21s^F 16m² 21m² Apr 17] workmanlike mare: fairly **h122**
useful handicap hurdler: creditable efforts all starts in 2002/3, second to Blue Ride in
listed mares event at Cheltenham final one: landed odds in mares novice at Ludlow in
February on completed start over fences: stayed 21f: acted on heavy and good to firm
going: stud. *N. J. Henderson*

DEEP WATER (USA)   9 b.g. Diesis – Water Course (USA) (Irish River (FR)) [2002/3 **c118**
c–, h121: 20d⁴ 20d 16s³ 16s² 20s⁴ c17d* c16g* Mar 17] leggy gelding: fair handicap **h113**
hurdler: fairly useful chaser: won handicaps at Market Rasen and Wetherby in March:
barely stays 2¾m: acts on heavy going, probably on good to firm: visored twice (won
once) over fences in 2000/1. *M. D. Hammond*

DEER DOLLY (IRE)   6 b.m. Welsh Term – Wild Deer (Royal Buck) [2002/3 20m^pu **h–**
Mar 19] IR 8,000 4-y-o: half-sister to modest staying chasers Matta Mia Flyer (by
Boreen) and Bay Island (by Treasure Hunter) and fair hurdler Dearborn Tec (by Sexton
Blake), stays 2½m: dam, winning pointer, half-sister to fairly useful staying chaser
General Symons: jumped poorly and soon detached in novice hurdle on debut. *P. Butler*

DEER PARK LASS (IRE)   11 ch.m. Mister Lord (USA) – Adare Flore (IRE) (Fair- **c–**
bairn) [2002/3 c72, h64: c16d⁴ 21v^pu 19g c16d Dec 4] tall mare: poor maiden hurdler/ **h–**
chaser: stays 2¾m: acts on heavy going, probably on good to firm: has worn blinkers/
cheekpieces: has had tongue tied: has refused twice over fences. *R. Johnson*

DEFERLANT (FR)   6 ch.g. Bering – Sail Storm (USA) (Topsider (USA)) [2002/3 **c111 §**
h123§: c17m³ c17m⁴ c21m² c17g* c16d* c20s* c16g^F 16d⁴ 17s 19d 16g⁴ c16f c16m^F **h111 §**
Apr 21] close-coupled gelding: fair handicap hurdler/novice chaser: won over fences at
Stratford, Perth and Worcester in summer: stays 21f: acts on soft and good to firm going:
visored: prone to finishing weakly. *Mrs H. Dalton*

DEFINITE FLASH (IRE)   5 b.m. Definite Article – Superflash (Superlative) [2002/3 **h–**
16s 19g^pu Feb 28] maiden on Flat, no form since 3 yrs, sold out of G. Bravery's stable
£670 Ascot April (2002) Sales: no show in 2 starts over hurdles. *M. Wellings*

DEFINITE RETURN (IRE)   5 ch.m. Definite Article – Keen Note (Sharpo) [2002/3 **h–**
17s^pu Mar 7] lightly raced and little form on Flat: showed nothing on hurdling debut.
D. J. Wintle

DELAWARE BAY 4 ch.g. Karinga Bay – Galacia (IRE) (Gallic League) [2002/3 17g 16s⁵ 16d⁴ 19v⁵ Dec 28] useful-looking gelding: fair maiden at 2 yrs for W. Turner: poor form over hurdles: likely to prove better around 2½m than shorter. *R. H. Alner* **h82**

DELAWARE (FR) 7 b.g. Garde Royale – L'Indienne (FR) (Le Nain Jaune (FR)) [2002/3 c126, h–: 17f 20g³ 17s² 17m² 22g* 22s* 24m² 21g³ 18d 21v⁴ Dec 4] leggy, angular gelding: fairly useful chaser: fair hurdler: won handicap at Newton Abbot in June and weak novice at Stratford in August: ran moodily last 3 starts: effective around 2m to easy 3m: acts on heavy and good to firm going: has won when blinkered, visored nowadays: often let down by jumping over fences: not one to trust. *M. C. Pipe* **c– h106 §**

DELGANY ROYAL (IRE) 11 b.g. Denel (FR) – Glen of Erin (Furry Glen) [2002/3 c123, h102: c16s⁶ c24s⁴ 22s³ c24v⁶ c24v⁴ c24dᵘʳ c28s⁴ c28s⁵ 20s⁶ 24d c24g Mar 30] tall, angular gelding: fairly useful handicap chaser, generally below form in 2002/3: lightly-raced maiden hurdler: probably stays 29f: acts on heavy going, possibly not on good to firm. *D. T. Hughes, Ireland* **c121 h101**

DELICEO (IRE) 10 b.g. Roselier (FR) – Grey's Delight (Decent Fellow) [2002/3 c77§, h73§: c25dᵖᵘ c24sᵘʳ c19g* c20m⁴ 19s c20g* c20g Mar 16] leggy gelding: maiden hurdler: modest handicap chaser: won at Hereford in November and Leicester in February: needs thorough test at 2m and stays 25f: acts on any going: unreliable. *M. Sheppard* **c87 § h– §**

DELILAH BLUE (NZ) 10 b.m. High Ice (USA) – Calamity (NZ) (Bally Royal) [2002/3 c95, h–: c20d² May 4] rangy mare: winning hurdler: modest handicap chaser: stays 21f: acts on firm and good to soft going, probably not on soft. *S. A. Brookshaw* **c95 h–**

DELLONE 11 b.g. Gunner B – Coire Vannich (Celtic Cone) [2002/3 c–x, h85: 17v 16s c16dᵘʳ 19s⁴ 16v⁴ 16gᵘʳ Mar 12] sturdy gelding: poor handicap hurdler, below form in 2002/3: error-prone maiden chaser: form only around 2m: acts on heavy going: races prominently. *T. R. George* **c– x h67**

DELMONTE (IRE) 7 b.g. Montekin – Delway (Fidel) [2002/3 20g 24d 22f 20f c20vᵖᵘ Nov 8] third foal: half-brother to fair 2¼m hurdle winner Munster (by Zaffaran): dam twice-raced sister to very smart 2m hurdler Fidway: little sign of ability, left H. Smyth after third start: blinkered on chasing debut. *J. J. Lambe, Ireland* **c– h–**

DELPHI 7 ch.g. Grand Lodge (USA) – Euridice (IRE) (Woodman (USA)) [2002/3 16g⁴ 20g⁵ 20g 16f 20g 19d 22d 21s 21m³ Apr 21] smallish ex-Irish gelding: modest stayer on Flat: maiden hurdler: modest form at best in 2002/3, left C. Collins after fifth start: should stay beyond 2½m: acts on soft and good to firm going: tried blinkered, visored last 2 starts: has looked none too keen. *B. G. Powell* **h98 d**

DELTAS FIRST 7 b.g. Nile Delta (IRE) – Shalabia (Fast Topaze (USA)) [2002/3 h–: c22g³ c21gᵖᵘ 16dᵖᵘ c19sᵖᵘ Mar 4] good-topped gelding: little sign of ability: sold out of R. Woodhouse's stable £1,100 Ascot December Sales after third start. *D. C. Turner* **c– h–**

DEL TROTTER (IRE) 8 b.g. King Luthier – Arctic Alice (Brave Invader (USA)) [2002/3 c17sᵘʳ c16v* 17s⁶ 17s³ 16g⁴ 16g³ 21m⁵ Apr 20] half-brother to 4 winning hurdlers, including fair Alices Run (by Deep Run), stayed 2½m: dam won 2 bumpers: bumper winner: fair chaser/modest maiden hurdler: bought out of M. Cullen's stable 6,500 gns (privately) Doncaster May Sales: won handicap at Sedgefield in November: raced mainly around 2m: acts on heavy going: sold 3,000 gns Doncaster May Sales. *J. Howard Johnson* **c107 h90**

DEMASTA (NZ) 12 ch.g. Northerly Native (USA) – Hit It Gold (AUS) (Hit It Benny (AUS)) [2002/3 c139p, h–: c16f* c20dᵖᵘ c16dᵖᵘ c16g⁴ c16m⁴ c16m⁵ Apr 17] compact gelding: winning hurdler: useful chaser: won minor event at Warwick in May: easily best effort after fourth when fourth to Young Devereaux in Grade 2 handicap at Kempton fourth start: best around 2m: possibly needs good going or firmer (acts on firm): bold-jumping front runner. *N. J. Henderson* **c135 h–**

DEMI BEAU 5 b.g. Dr Devious (IRE) – Charming Life (NZ) (Sir Tristram) [2002/3 16d⁴ 16m⁴ 16m⁴ Apr 11] tall gelding: half-brother to winning 2m hurdler Rajati (by Chief's Crown), successful 3 times in 2002, sold out of W. Jarvis' stable 18,000 gns Newmarket Autumn Sales: impressive on hurdling debut, winning 16-runner novice at Doncaster in January by 6 lengths from Mythical King: shaped as if something amiss both outings after, dropping out tamely each time. *C. J. Mann* **h109**

DEMPSEY (IRE) 5 b.g. Lord Americo – Kyle Cailin (Over The River (FR)) [2002/3 F16m³ F16gᵖᵘ F17g Apr 5] good-topped gelding: fourth foal: brother to useful chaser Puget Blue, stayed 3m: dam, winning pointer, sister to fairly useful hunter Overheard: **F101**

failed to settle but shaped well when third of 19 to Chelsea Bridge in bumper at Kempton on debut: highly tried after, pulled up presumably amiss in Grade 1 at Cheltenham and tailed off in Grade 2 at Aintree. *M. Pitman*

DENADA 7 ch.g. Bob Back (USA) – Alavie (FR) (Quart de Vin (FR)) [2002/3 c26s² c24dF c24g³ c25dpu Feb 26] IR 26,000 3-y-o: lengthy gelding: first foal: dam won around 2m over fences in France: won Irish point in 2002: fair form when placed in novice chases at Warwick and Newbury: reportedly lost action final outing: likely to prove best at 3m+. *Mrs Susan Nock* **c115**

DENARIUS (USA) 8 b.g. Silver Hawk (USA) – Ambrosine (USA) (Mr Prospector (USA)) [2002/3 c–, h106: 17d 16d 16v⁴ 25g 17s⁵ 16s³ 21v* Dec 26] good-topped gelding: modest handicap hurdler: wearing cheekpieces, won at Sedgefield in December: stays 21f (beaten long before stamina became an issue over 25f): acts on heavy going: has had tongue tied (has reportedly had breathing problems, including only start over fences): ungenuine. *G. A. Swinbank* **c– §** **h98 §**

DENEISES BLOSSOM (IRE) 10 b.m. Beau Sher – Lindabell (Over The River (FR)) [2002/3 c–§, h76§: 20d³ 24g 16g⁶ 17s² 22d³ 20g⁴ c16g⁶ c17s³ c27d² c24g 27s⁴ c27d⁶d c20g Apr 14] angular mare: poor maiden hurdler/chaser: effective around 2m to 27f: best efforts on going softer than good (acts on soft): usually finds little. *W. Storey* **c66 §** **h69 §**

DENEL LADY (IRE) 9 ch.m. Denel (FR) – Lough Hill Lady (Cantab) [2002/3 c20m⁴ 16gpu May 17] no form outside points (won in January and March): tried blinkered: sold 500 gns Ascot July Sales. *R. Dickin* **c–** **h–**

DENE VIEW (IRE) 8 br.g. Good Thyne (USA) – The Furnituremaker (Mandalus) [2002/3 c–, h86: 19d³ 21s³ c16d* c19m² c18mpu 20m³ Apr 21] sturdy gelding: modest handicap hurdler/chaser: won over hurdles at Catterick (conditional jockeys) in December and fences at Doncaster (novice, went in snatches) in January: stays 21f: acts on good to soft and good to firm going: ran sour race in blinkers fifth start. *R. A. Fahey* **c98** **h94**

DENISE BEST (IRE) 5 ch.m. Goldmark (USA) – Titchwell Lass (Lead On Time (USA)) [2002/3 20m² 17m⁶ Apr 26] poor maiden on Flat (stays 1½m): found little when second in weakly-contested maiden at Bangor on hurdling debut: well held at Sedgefield 8 months later. *Miss K. M. George* **h80 ?**

DENNETT LOUGH (IRE) 12 b.g. Torus – Monica's Pet (Sovereign Gleam) [2002/3 c81: c25dF May 4] rangy gelding: modest hunter chaser: stays 27f: acts on firm and good to soft going. *C. Storey* **c–**

DENNEY'S WELL (IRE) 8 ch.g. Good Thyne (USA) – Julias Well (Golden Love) [2002/3 c26d³ c24v⁵ Nov 29] third foal: brother to winning Irish pointer Castle Thyne and half-brother to another: dam placed in points: modest pointer, successful twice in 2002: respectable third in maiden hunter at Cartmel (trained by G. Hanmer), outclassed in novice nearly 6 months later: sold 2,800 gns Doncaster May Sales. *H. D. Daly* **c82**

DEOCH AN DORAIS (IRE) 8 b.g. Supreme Leader – General Rain (General Ironside) [2002/3 h98: c16g² c20vur c23s² c16s² c22mur c24gpu Apr 2] tall, good sort: modest maiden hurdler: similar form when runner-up all 3 completed starts in maiden chases (let down by jumping otherwise): effective at 2m to 23f: acts on soft going. *N. J. Henderson* **c98** **h–**

DE ORALIE (IRE) 10 ch.g. Tremblant – Tsing Tao (He Loves Me) [2002/3 c–, h–: 17m 17g 17m³ Jun 22] poor maiden hurdler/chaser: best around 2m: tried in tongue strap: headstrong. *A. J. Lockwood* **c–** **h62**

DEPUTY LEADER (IRE) 11 b.g. Florida Son – Larne (Giolla Mear) [2002/3 c20m⁴ c20mur c16m⁶ 21g⁶ c16g c21dF Aug 26] rangy gelding: modest pointer: novice hurdler/chaser, left K. Hunter after first start. *K. S. Thomas* **c78** **h–**

DERBY HEIGHTS 10 br.g. Golden Heights – Elvonera (Elvis) [2002/3 16d 16gpu Dec 12] lengthy gelding: modest form in 3 starts on Flat in 2002: no show in 2 starts over hurdles (wore cheekpieces on second). *R. J. Smith* **h–**

DEREK TROTTER 4 b.g. Cosmonaut – Cinderella Derek (Hittite Glory) [2002/3 F18f Apr 24] sixth foal: half-brother to winning hurdler/chaser Pertemps Cindrella (by Almoojid), stays 2¾m: dam successful over hurdles, also winning sprinter: tailed off in bumper on debut. *A. D. Smith* **F–**

DERE LYN 5 b.g. Awesome – Our Resolution (Caerleon (USA)) [2002/3 h72: 16m 22g⁸ 22d⁶ Jun 8] smallish, rather leggy gelding: modest maiden on Flat: poor hurdler: upped in trip, 25/1-winner of 17-runner selling handicap at Newton Abbot in May: will stay beyond 2¾m: tried blinkered. *D. Burchell* **h80**

DERIVATIVE (IRE)   5 b. or br.g. Erins Isle – Our Hope (Dancing Brave (USA))   h105
[2002/3 h117: 16v³ 16s² 17s⁶ 20v* 20v⁵ Mar 7] smallish gelding: useful on Flat at 3 yrs:
fair novice hurdler: idled when winning at Ayr in February: stays 2½m: acts on heavy
going: edgy and sweating when well held final 2001/2 outing: not an easy ride. *Miss
Venetia Williams*

DERRING BRIDGE   13 b.g. Derring Rose – Bridge Ash (Normandy) [2002/3 c91,   c– §
h95: 24d³ 24d* 24mʳᵗʳ 26mᵖᵘ Sep 11] leggy gelding: modest handicap hurdler/chaser: h98 §
gained sixth course success at Worcester over hurdles in August: refused to race/very
reluctant to do so last 2 starts: stays 4m: acts on firm and soft going: has had tongue tied:
races lazily and needs strong handling. *Mrs S. M. Johnson*

DERRING DOVE   11 b.g. Derring Rose – Shadey Dove (Deadly Nightshade) [2002/3   c94 §
c97, h–: c26vᵖᵘ c25s² c24d³ c24m³ Apr 10] angular gelding: winning pointer: modest   h–
maiden chaser: no form over hurdles: stays 3¼m: acts on good to firm and heavy going:
jumped markedly left final outing: inconsistent. *H. W. Lavis*

DERRINTOGHER YANK (IRE)   9 b.g. Lord Americo – Glenmalur (Black Mins-   c115
trel) [2002/3 c21dᵖᵘ c24d* Nov 25] rangy gelding: formerly fairly useful hurdler: only   h–
second outing in over 2 years, won novice chase at Ludlow by 8 lengths from Ballycassidy: stays 3m: raced mainly on good going or softer: front runner. *S. E. H. Sherwood*

DERRY ANN   7 b.m. Derrylin – Ancat Girl (Politico (USA)) [2002/3 F80: F16g³ 16d³   h61
19g Nov 23] modest form in bumpers: only poor form on first of 2 starts over hurdles: F80
should stay beyond 2m. *G. P. Kelly*

DERRY DICE   7 b.g. Derrylin – Paper Dice (Le Dauphin) [2002/3 F16v F16d F16g⁴   h–
F16s⁶ 20g 21mᵘʳ Apr 21] lengthy gelding: chasing type: sixth foal: half-brother to   F83
winning pointer by Rakaposhi King: dam behind in bumpers: modest form in bumpers:
eighth of 13 in slowly-run maiden at Wetherby on completed outing over hurdles:
blinkered after debut. *C. T. Pogson*

DERRYQUIN   8 b.g. Lion Cavern (USA) – Top Berry (High Top) [2002/3 17m* 17g⁴   h87
17m² Sep 13] half-brother to winning 2m hurdler Mr Micky (by Rudimentary): fair on
Flat (best around 1m, usually blinkered): modest form over hurdles, won weak novice at
Newton Abbot in July, making virtually all: will prove best at sharp 2m: raced freely in
blinkers final outing. *P. L. Gilligan*

DERRYROSE   10 br.g. Derrylin – Levantine Rose (Levanter) [2002/3 c83, h–: c25d⁵   c99 ?
c25g* May 8] strong gelding: novice hurdler: beat some below-par rivals and probably   h–
flattered when winning hunter chase at Kelso in May: stays 27f: acts on soft and good to
firm going: blinkered twice in 2000/1 (ran well on first occasion). *R. J. Kyle*

DERVALLOC (IRE)   6 b.g. Zaffaran (USA) – Keeping Company (King's Company)   h–
[2002/3 F16s 24v⁴ Mar 4] 21,000 4-y-o: tall gelding with scope: eleventh foal: brother to   F–
one-time useful but ungenuine staying hurdler/chaser Browjoshy and half-brother to
winner in Austria by Kampala: dam, Irish middle-distance winner, half-sister to smart 2m
hurdler/useful chaser Pearlstone: never a danger in bumper on debut: tailed off in novice
hurdle. *P. Winkworth*

DESAILLY   9 ch.g. Teamster – G W Superstar (Rymer) [2002/3 c111, h–: c22d² c25d²   c119
c24s⁵ c23s⁶ c21d⁴ Mar 6] strong, lengthy gelding: fairly useful handicap chaser: good   h–
second at Newbury and Exeter: poor efforts last 2 starts: best at 2¾m+: raced on good
going or softer (acts on soft): weak finisher: needs treating with caution. *M. C. Pipe*

DESERT AIR (JPN)   4 ch.g. Desert King (IRE) – Greek Air (IRE) (Ela-Mana-Mou)   h117
[2002/3 16d² 17s* 16d³ Feb 7] angular gelding: third foal: dam 1m winner, sister to very
smart French performer up to 1¼m Grecian Urn, herself dam of useful hurdlers Grecian
Dart and Dark Shell: fair on Flat (stays easy 1½m) for P. Cole, successful in July: made
all in novice hurdle at Taunton in January: better form when third to Bareme in juvenile at
Kempton, forcing pace until 2 out despite wandering at several flights: will prove best
around 2m: visored last 2 starts. *M. C. Pipe*

DESERT ARC (IRE)   5 b.g. Spectrum (IRE) – Bint Albadou (IRE) (Green Desert   F97
(USA)) [2002/3 F16mᵘ F17d Mar 2] good-topped gelding: third foal: half-brother to 1½m
winner in France by Mujtahid: dam fairly useful 2-y-o 6f winner, half-sister to useful 2m
hurdler Danegold, out of very smart filly up to 1¼m Cistus: fairly useful form when close
fourth to Patriarch Express in bumper at Cheltenham on debut: disappointing at Carlisle
(found little) 4 months later: fair form over 8.5f and 6f on Flat in spring for A. Balding.
Jonjo O'Neill

236

DESERT BOOT   8 gr.g. High Kicker (USA) – Desert Mist (Sharrood (USA)) [2002/3   c–
c–, h–: c23m⁴ c24mᵖᵘ 26mᵖᵘ Aug 12] big, strong gelding: of little account: sold 1,200 gns   h–
Doncaster November Sales. *T. H. Caldwell*

DESERT CITY   4 b.g. Darnay – Oasis (Valiyar) [2002/3 16d 16d 16m³ Apr 10]   h75
good-topped gelding: half-brother to fair but ungenuine 2m hurdler Jaguar (by Barathea):
fair maiden on the Flat (stays 11f), sold out of R. Hannon's stable 13,500 gns Newmarket
Autumn Sales: easily best effort in juvenile hurdles when eighth at Doncaster on debut.
P. R. Webber

DESERT MOSS   6 b.g. Le Moss – Super Gambler (Lighter) [2002/3 20gʳᵒ May 17]   h–
fifth foal: half-brother to winning 2½m hurdler Icefire Dancer (by Arctic Lord): dam
maiden on Flat/over hurdles: very green in novice hurdle at Aintree on debut: sold 1,000
gns Doncaster September Sales. *N. B. Mason*

DESERT TRAVELLER (IRE)   5 b.g. Desert Style (IRE) – Cellatica (USA) (Sir   h–
Ivor) [2002/3 h–: 22m 22f⁴ Oct 1] no worthwhile form over hurdles: sometimes
blinkered. *R. J. Baker*

DESIR D'UN SOIR (FR)   5 b.h. Assessor (IRE) – Mystere d'Un Soir (FR) (Mistigri)   h142 +
[2002/3 18s* 18s* 19v* 19s² Mar 23] first foal: dam won 19f chase: won over 1¼m at 3
yrs on Flat: progressive form over hurdles, winning 4-y-o handicaps at Auteuil in
September and October and Group 3 Prix Leopold d'Orsetti at Enghien in November,
beating Great Love impressively by 8 lengths at latter after challenging Tiger Groom fell
last: neck second to Great Love in slowly-run Group 3 at Auteuil in March: raced around
19f on soft/heavy going. *M. Rolland, France*

DESIRE ME   5 b.m. Silca Blanka (IRE) – Dazzle Me (Kalaglow) [2002/3 17g May 1]   h–
poor maiden on Flat (stays 7f): showed nothing on hurdling debut. *A. D. Smith*

DESMOND TUTU (IRE)   6 b.g. Be My Native (USA) – Amy Fairy (The Parson)   h106
[2002/3 F105: F16d* 17s² 16d² 19s³ 18g² 19f* 22m² 22f* Apr 21] workmanlike gelding: F107
unbeaten in 2 bumpers, including at Chepstow in October: fair novice hurdler: didn't
have to run to best to win at Exeter in March and Wincanton in April: stays 2¾m: successful on firm going, at least as effective on good or softer. *P. F. Nicholls*

DESPERATE MEASURES   7 ch.m. Kasakov – Precious Ballerina (Ballacashtal   h63 §
(CAN)) [2002/3 h–, F79?: 16mᵘʳ 20d³ 17m⁶ 16s³ 17sᵖᵘ Aug 24] bad maiden hurdler,
reportedly lame final outing: has looked temperamental. *Miss Lucinda V. Russell*

DESTIN D'ESTRUVAL (FR)   12 b.g. Port Etienne (FR) – Vocation (FR) (Toujours   c–
Pret (USA)) [2002/3 c19f Mar 27] tall gelding: one-time useful chaser, retains little   h–
ability: blinkered once. *A. W. Congdon*

DESTINY CALLS   13 ch.g. Lord Avie (USA) – Miss Renege (USA) (Riva Ridge   c– §
(USA)) [2002/3 c–§, h–§: c20g⁶ c21g⁴ c23mᵖᵘ Jul 17] rangy, good-topped gelding: h– §
formerly useful chaser, little worthwhile form since 2000: held up: has refused to race 3
times, and not to be trusted. *N. A. Gaselee*

DESTRUCTIVE (USA)   5 b. or br.g. Dehere (USA) – Respectability (USA) (His   h–
Majesty (USA)) [2002/3 19dᵖᵘ 20g 19gᶠ 21gᵖᵘ Mar 12] lengthy gelding: disappointing
maiden on Flat: no encouragement over hurdles: blinkered after debut: sold £2,400 Ascot
April Sales. *J. Mackie*

DETONATEUR (FR)   5 b.g. Pistolet Bleu (IRE) – Soviet Princess (IRE) (Soviet Lad   h105
(USA)) [2002/3 h113: 16d 16d⁵ 16v⁴ 16d³ 16g 16g² Apr 20] leggy gelding: fair maiden
hurdler: unlikely to stay beyond 19f: acts on heavy going. *Ian Williams*

DETROIT DAVY (IRE)   12 b.g. Detroit Sam (FR) – Pretty Damsel (Prince Hansel)   c– x
[2002/3 c21gᵖᵘ May 1] sparely-made gelding: winning pointer: novice chaser: stays   h–
3¼m: acts on heavy going: has had tongue tied: often fails to impress with jumping.
D. W. Oakes

DEVIL'S RUN (IRE)   7 b.g. Commanche Run – She Devil (Le Moss) [2002/3 h106:   c111
21d⁶ c20sᶠ c21s⁴ c20v² c27v³ c20s² c21s* c20g² Mar 28] strong gelding: fair handicap   h–
hurdler: similar form over fences, jumped better than usual when winning 6-runner
handicap at Sedgefield in March: best form around 2½m, should stay further: raced on
good going or softer (probably acts on heavy): reliable. *J. Wade*

DEVON ABBOT   5 br.g. Bishop of Cashel – Final Attraction (Jalmood (USA))   F–
[2002/3 F17s F13s Dec 6] seventh foal: half-brother to useful bumper winner Bodfari
Queen (by Rudimentary): dam once-raced half-sister to smart 1m to 1¼m performer
Gussy Marlowe: well held in 2 bumpers. *R. J. Hodges*

DEVON DREAM (IRE) 7 b.g. Paris House – Share The Vision (Vision (USA)) **h–**
[2002/3 20g 17v^pu Nov 6] poor on Flat (stays 1¼m) nowadays: no show in 2 starts over
hurdles (blinkered second time). *R. J. Baker*

DEVONSHIRE (IRE) 10 b. or br.g. King's Ride – Lispatrick Lass (Kambalda) **c98**
[2002/3 c27g² c25s⁴ Mar 7] lengthy, angular gelding: winning hurdler: fair hunter chaser **h–**
nowadays: made mistakes when second to Bright Approach at Ludlow in February: stays
27f: raced on good going or softer (acts on heavy). *D. Lowe*

DEVON VIEW (IRE) 9 b.g. Jolly Jake (NZ) – Skipaside (Quayside) [2002/3 c123: **c132**
c19d³ c16s* c16s* c16s³ c16d^ur c19d³ c20m² Apr 26] tall gelding: useful handicap
chaser: won at Chepstow in November and Warwick (by 3½ lengths from Shampooed)
following month: ran well when second to Skycab in 7-runner quite valuable event at
Sandown, left in front 2 out and might well have won but for jockey dropping whip: stays
2½m: unraced on firm going, acts on any other. *P. F. Nicholls*

DEVOTE 5 b.g. Pennekamp (USA) – Radiant Bride (USA) (Blushing Groom (FR)) **h83**
[2002/3 h97: 19s 22s 17s³ 19s⁴ 17v² 16d² Mar 19] close-coupled gelding: winning hurdler, in frame in sellers in 2002/3: stays 19f: acts on heavy going: blinkered: has looked
none too easy a ride. *B. J. Llewellyn*

DIAMANT NOIR 5 b.m. Sir Harry Lewis (USA) – Free Travel (Royalty) [2002/3 **F100**
F16g² F16d* F16f* Mar 29] 18,500 4-y-o: third foal: dam, fair 2m hurdler, half-sister to
top-class 2½m chaser Dublin Flyer: fairly useful form in bumpers, won mares events at
Warwick (maiden, beat Entree easily by 5 lengths) and Haydock (by short head from
Flame of Zara) in March: will stay beyond 2m: type to do well in mares novice hurdles.
Jonjo O'Neill

DIAMOND COTTAGE (IRE) 8 b.g. Peacock (FR) – Sea Bright (IRE) (King's **h73**
Ride) [2002/3 h70: 24d² 25d⁵ 24d⁴ Nov 1] good-topped gelding: poor novice hurdler:
suited by 3m+: raced on good to soft/soft going: tongue tied second start. *R. Johnson*

DIAMOND DARREN (IRE) 4 ch.g. Dolphin Street (FR) – Deerussa (IRE) (Jareer **h81**
(USA)) [2002/3 17s⁴ 17g³ 17d⁴ 16m² 16f³ 16g Nov 23] half-brother to 15f hurdle winner
in Italy by Archway: poor maiden on Flat (stays 1m): modest juvenile hurdler: needs
sharp 2m: acts on firm going: claimed £3,000 final start, to join R. Woodhouse. *John
Berry*

DIAMOND DAZZLER 5 br.g. Sula Bula – Dancing Diamond (IRE) (Alzao (USA)) **F–**
[2002/3 F16d F17s Feb 11] second foal: dam 9.7f to 2m winner out of half-sister to smart
French miler King James: well held in bumpers (tongue tied, failed to settle second time).
D. P. Keane

DIAMOND DYNASTY 6 b.g. Son Pardo – Reperage (USA) (Key To Content (USA)) **h–**
[2002/3 h–, F–: 16d^pu 16g 16g 16g Apr 25] workmanlike gelding: probably of little
account. *J. N. R. Billinge*

DIAMOND HALL 10 b.g. Lapierre – Willitwin (Majestic Maharaj) [2002/3 c78, h98: **c83**
c17g^ur c16m^pu 24g⁵ c19m² c19g³ c20d⁵ c16g c16s⁵ c20s c17v³ c20g c21m³ Apr 17] good- **h85**
topped gelding: modest handicap hurdler: poor maiden chaser: left N. Twiston-Davies
after sixth outing: probably best short of 3m: acts on heavy and good to firm going (won
bumper on firm). *R. D. Tudor*

DIAMOND JOBE (IRE) 4 ch.g. College Chapel – Dazzling Maid (IRE) (Tate **h71**
Gallery (USA)) [2002/3 16g⁶ Feb 12] modest maiden on Flat (probably stays 7f): doubtful stayer over hurdles and not fluent when 16 lengths sixth in juvenile at Musselburgh on
debut. *J. Hetherton*

DIAMOND JOSHUA (IRE) 5 b.g. Mujadil (USA) – Elminya (IRE) (Sure Blade **h102**
(USA)) [2002/3 h135?: 21d⁶ 17v 16d⁴ 16d 20d^pu 20g³ Mar 23] smallish gelding: fair
hurdler on balance, almost certainly flattered when third in Triumph Hurdle at Cheltenham in 2001/2: stays 2½m: acts on good to soft going, ran no sort of race on good to firm:
tongue tied last 4 outings. *M. E. Sowersby*

DIAMOND MAX (IRE) 5 b.g. Nicolotte – Kawther (Tap On Wood) [2002/3 16d⁴ **h94 p**
Dec 14] fairly useful around 1m on Flat: around 7 lengths fourth in novice at Haydock on
hurdling debut, jumping far from fluently: will do better provided his jumping improves.
P. D. Evans

DIAMOND MONROE (IRE) 7 ch.g. Treasure Hunter – Star of Monroe (Derring **h80 +**
Rose) [2002/3 21d⁵ 21s 24d⁵ 19m⁵ 24g² Apr 21] IR 3,000 4-y-o: lengthy, angular gelding:
fourth foal: half-brother to winning pointer by Celio Rufo: dam unraced: won Irish point
in 2002: poor form over hurdles: stays 3m. *N. J. Henderson*

DIAMOND SAL   5 b.m. Bob Back (USA) – Fortune's Girl (Ardross) [2002/3 F16d²   **F100 p**
Feb 1] close-coupled mare: second foal: dam, fair hurdler who stayed 27f, also 1½m winner on Flat: shaped well when 1½ lengths second of 16 to Crossbow Creek in bumper at Wetherby on debut, running on strongly from mid-field to pull clear of remainder: will stay at least 2½m: should improve and win a similar event. *Mrs M. Reveley*

DIAMONDS WILL DO (IRE)   6 b.m. Bigstone (IRE) – Clear Ability (IRE) (Be   **h99**
My Guest (USA)) [2002/3 19m 19m⁵ 21d⁴ 17s² 16d³ 21s³ 21v 22g Mar 15] rather leggy mare: fair maiden on Flat: fair hurdler, won maiden at Down Royal in 2001/2: sold out of M. O'Brien's stable 12,000 gns Doncaster August Sales after reappearance: creditable placed efforts in handicaps subsequently: stays 21f: acts on soft going. *Miss Venetia Williams*

DIAMOND TIPPED   5 ch.m. Sure Blade (USA) – Locket (Precocious) [2002/3 F17s   **F–**
F17m Jul 15] sturdy mare: first foal: dam no sign of ability: tailed off in 2 bumpers: sold £500 Ascot November Sales. *M. R. Bosley*

DIAMOND VEIN   4 b.c. Green Dancer (USA) – Blushing Sunrise (USA) (Cox's   **F85**
Ridge (USA)) [2002/3 F14d F16s F17v* F16d Mar 19] first foal: dam, winner in USA at 4 yrs, out of half-sister to US 2-y-o Grade 1 1m winner Senor Pete (by Green Dancer), from family of Affirmed: easily best effort in bumpers when winning maiden at Sedgefield in February: trained by A. Dickman on debut, next 2 starts by R. Wilman. *P. A. Blockley*

DICEMAN (IRE)   8 b.g. Supreme Leader – Henry's Gamble (IRE) (Carlingford   **c112**
Castle) [2002/3 h–: 19g* c19d² c22d³ c20s* c20d* Mar 15] lengthy gelding: sold out of   **h107**
Mrs H. Dalton's stable 6,000 gns Doncaster May Sales: easily best effort over hurdles when winning novice at Doncaster in December by 1½ lengths from Il Cavaliere: similar form over fences, won maiden at Carlisle and novice at Newcastle (beat You're Special 1¾ lengths) in March: should stay beyond 2½m: raced on good going or softer (acts on soft): let down by jumping third start and at Punchestown in late-April. *Mrs S. J. Smith*

DICK MCCARTHY (IRE)   11 b.g. Lancastrian – Waltzing Shoon (Green Shoon)   **c92 §**
[2002/3 c101, h–: c26g³ c24d³ c24v⁵ c26dᵖᵘ c26s⁵ c21m² c26f² Apr 24] medium-sized   **h–**
gelding: modest handicap chaser: stays 3¼m: acts on any going: tried blinkered (jumped with no fluency)/in cheekpieces. *R. Rowe*

DICK THE TAXI   9 b.g. Karlinsky (USA) – Another Galaxy (IRE) (Anita's Prince)   **h113**
[2002/3 h–: 16g⁶ 16m* 16sᵖᵘ Jun 9] useful-looking gelding: fair on Flat (stays 1½m), successful in February: fair handicap hurdler: easily best effort early in season when winning 5-runner race at Stratford: acts around 2m: acts on heavy and good to firm going: races freely. *R. J. Smith*

DICK TURPIN (USA)   9 br.g. Red Ransom (USA) – Turn To Money (USA) (Turn   **h102**
To Mars (USA)) [2002/3 20d³ 20d* 16d⁶ 19d 16s² 16g⁴ 17g* 16m² Apr 21] fairly useful at one time on Flat: fair hurdler, off over 3 years before reappearance: won novice at Fakenham in December and handicap at Market Rasen (by 3½ lengths from Gudlage) in March: effective at 2m to 2½m: acts on soft and good to firm going. *Mrs L. Wadham*

DIDIFON   8 b.g. Zafonic (USA) – Didicoy (USA) (Danzig (USA)) [2002/3 h115d: **c96**
16d⁶ 16d c16d³ c16v³ c16g* c16g² Apr 1] compact ex-Irish gelding: one-time fairly   **h–**
useful handicap hurdler, sold out of N. Meade's stable €3,000 Goffs October Sale before reappearance: modest form in novice chases: won 3-finisher event at Sedgefield in March, held when left clear by The French Furze's fall at last: should stay 2½m: raced on good going or softer (acts on heavy): tried blinkered, wore cheekpieces last 2 starts: usually held up. *N. P. McCormack*

DIDN'TSLEEPAWINK (IRE)   7 b.g. Dromod Hill – Kamalee (Kambalda) [2002/3   **h–**
17d⁵ 16d 16d⁵ 16g Dec 13] compact gelding: sixth living foal: dam, winning Irish pointer, sister to fairly useful hurdler up to 2¾m Kamadoor: once-raced on Flat: easily best effort in bumpers when second final outing in 2001/2 when with P. Mullins: fifth in 2¾m maiden on hurdling debut, no subsequent form: acts on heavy going. *Jonjo O'Neill*

DIE FLEDERMAUS (IRE)   9 b.g. Batshoof – Top Mouse (High Top) [2002/3 c98§,   **c104 §**
h–§: c20m² c25g* 24d⁴ c20dᵖᵘ c20d c25d⁴ c20vᵖᵘ Dec 21] leggy gelding: winning   **h– §**
hurdler: fair handicap chaser: under pressure throughout final circuit when winning at Wolverhampton in July: stays 25f: acts on firm going, probably on soft: sometimes blinkered: ungenuine. *D. J. Wintle*

DIGDAGA (USA)   4 b. or br.f. Machiavellian (USA) – Baaderah (IRE) (Cadeaux   **h–**
Genereux) [2002/3 16vᵖᵘ Jan 22] modest maiden at best on Flat (stays 1½m): wearing tongue strap and cheekpieces, no show in juvenile on hurdling debut. *Mrs S. Lamyman*

DIHATJUM   6 b.g. Mujtahid (USA) – Rosie Potts (Shareef Dancer (USA)) [2002/3   **h98**
h96: 17m⁵ 18f³ 16m³ 16g⁵ 16m⁵ Oct 11] leggy gelding: modest hurdler: best at sharp 2m:
raced mainly on good going or firmer (acts on firm). *R. M. Flower*

DILETIA   6 b.m. Dilum (USA) – Miss Laetitia (IRE) (Entitled) [2002/3 h85: 24g³   **h95**
20m² 22f* 19f* 25g³ 22dᵇᵈ 22d⁵ 24s 22g* 24m² 24m² Apr 15] leggy mare: modest
hurdler: won 2 novices in October and 17-runner handicap in March, all at Exeter: stays
25f: best efforts on good going or firmer (acts on firm): often soon off bridle. *R. H. Alner*

DILLY   5 br.m. Dilum (USA) – Princess Rosananti (IRE) (Shareef Dancer (USA))   **h–**
[2002/3 18f⁴ 16mᵖᵘ 18m⁵ 16g¹ᵖ Sep 14] half-sister to 2m hurdle winner Indira (by Indian
Ridge): fair at best on Flat (stays easy 1¼m): signs of ability over hurdles only on debut:
sold £320 Ascot December Sales. *P. R. Chamings*

DIM BYD   4 ch.g. So Factual (USA) – Time Clash (Timeless Times (USA)) [2002/3   **h–**
16mᵖᵘ Oct 5] compact gelding: last in maiden at 2 yrs for Mrs M. Jones: showed nothing
in juvenile on hurdling debut. *P. D. Williams*

DINGO DANCER   10 b.g. Dancing High – Some Shiela (Remainder Man) [2002/3   **c95**
c89, h–: c17g* c22m⁵ c16gᵖᵘ c17m³ c21m⁵ c19g* c16d³ Dec 4] tall gelding: modest   **h–**
chaser: won novice at Kelso in May and handicap at Catterick in November: effective
around 2m to easy 2¾m: acts on good to firm and good to soft going, possibly not on soft:
lung infection third start. *J. P. Dodds*

DINKY DORA   10 ch.m. Gunner B – Will Be Wanton (Palm Track) [2002/3 h80: 22d⁵   **h–**
22mᵖᵘ 20d 21s Nov 21] small mare: winning hurdler, no form in 2002/3 after lengthy
absence: stays 27f: acts on firm and soft going. *J. K. Cresswell*

DINOFELIS   5 b.g. Rainbow Quest (USA) – Revonda (IRE) (Sadler's Wells (USA))   **h71**
[2002/3 16f⁶ 16mᵖᵘ 16dᵖᵘ 16dᵖᵘ 16d 16m² Apr 21] modest on Flat (should stay 2m): first
form over hurdles when second in selling handicap at Fakenham: raced at 2m: acts on
good to firm ground: tongue tied second start (reportedly hung badly): wore cheekpieces
last 2 outings. *W. M. Brisbourne*

DINSEY FINNEGAN (IRE)   8 b.g. Fresh Breeze (USA) – Rose of Solway (Derring   **c71**
Rose) [2002/3 c21mᵖᵘ c20d⁴ Mar 4] fourth foal: brother to fair 2m chaser Skinsey   **h–**
Finnegan and half-brother to winning pointer by Jolly Jake: dam pulled up in 3 Irish
points: well held in bumper/novice hurdle for G. Cully: raced freely both starts in hunter
chases, sold out of N. Padfield's stable 6,200 gns Doncaster August Sales prior to remote
fourth in maiden at Leicester: better form in points, successful later in March and in April:
tried visored/in cheekpieces. *Simon Bloss*

DIONN RIGH (IRE)   8 b.g. Asir – Happy Eliza (Laurence O) [2002/3 c25gᵖᵘ c27s*   **c107**
c27v* c32gᵖᵘ c27m² Apr 26] big, lengthy gelding: first foal: half-brother to winning
pointer by Lord Americo: dam, winning pointer, half-sister to useful 2½m to 3m chaser
Dun Belle: won maiden point in 2002, fourth on completed start in hunter chases: sold
out of P. Fahy's stable 20,000 gns Doncaster May Sales: fair form over fences in Britain,
won twice at Sedgefield, maiden in December and novice in February: should stay
beyond 27f (stiff task over 4m): acts on heavy going, below form on good to firm. *J.
Howard Johnson*

DIORAMA (GER)   8 b.m. Bakharoff (USA) – Dosha (FR) (Sharpman) [2002/3 21d*   **h83**
22d⁶ 24v 22vᵖᵘ 21s 21g⁴ 25mᶠ Mar 31] angular mare: 9f winner in Germany at 3 yrs: poor
hurdler: left A. Martin after final start in 2001/2: easily best effort when landing gamble
in conditional jockeys handicap at Plumpton in November: idling markedly: should stay
beyond 21f: acts on good to soft going: tried blinkered/tongue tied. *L. A. Dace*

DIRECT ACCESS (IRE)   8 ch.g. Roselier (FR) – Spanish Flame (IRE) (Spanish   **c137**
Place (USA)) [2002/3 c128, h–: c25v* c26gᵖᵘ Nov 30] tall, rangy, angular gelding: useful   **h–**
chaser: won handicap at Kelso in November, jumping soundly and barely needing to
come off bridle to beat Interdit 3½ lengths: pulled up in very valuable handicap at
Newbury later in month, and not seen out again: will prove best at 3m+: acts on heavy
going, not discredited on good to firm. *L. Lungo*

DIRECT BEARING (IRE)   6 b.g. Polish Precedent (USA) – Uncertain Affair (IRE)   **h132**
(Darshaan) [2002/3 h126: 16d² 16s 20s 17g⁶ Mar 13] well-made gelding: useful on Flat,
best effort when second to Miss Fara in Tote Cesarewitch at Newmarket: useful hurdler:
blinkered first time, not discredited when sixth of 28 to Spirit Leader in valuable handicap
at Cheltenham: should prove suited by 2½m+: acts on heavy going. *D. K. Weld, Ireland*

DIRECT DESCENDANT (IRE)   4 ch.g. Be My Guest (USA) – Prague Spring (Salse   **h83**
(USA)) [2002/3 17g* 16m 16g 16g³ Dec 13] workmanlike gelding: modest maiden on

Flat (seems to stay 12.4f): modest juvenile hurdler: won seller at Market Rasen in September. *J. J. Quinn*

DIRECTION 5 b.m. Lahib (USA) – Theme (IRE) (Sadler's Wells (USA)) [2002/3 **F88** F94p: F17s F16g² F17g⁴ F17m Apr 17] medium-sized mare: fair form in bumpers, in frame in 2002/3 at Ludlow and Market Rasen. *K. A. Morgan*

DIRECT ROUTE (IRE) 12 b.g. Executive Perk – Mursuma (Rarity) [2002/3 16sᵖᵘ **c–** Dec 14] lengthy, good-topped gelding: top-class chaser at best, won Mumm Melling **h–** Chase at Aintree in 1999 and 2000, and placed in Champion Chase at Cheltenham same years: off 20 months, showed little in handicap hurdle, only start in 2002/3: stayed 2½m: acted on good to firm and heavy going: travelled strongly, and was suited by exaggerated waiting tactics: has been retired. *J. Howard Johnson*

DIRK COVE (IRE) 9 ch.g. Montelimar (USA) – Another Miller (Gala Performance **c100** (USA)) [2002/3 c106, h–: c24g³ c26d³ c26s⁴ c24gᵖᵘ 24s⁴ 21v c24g⁵ c25g³ c24g⁴ c22f* **h–** Apr 24] angular gelding: fair handicap hurdler at best: generally well below that level over fences, though won novice at Fontwell in April: should stay beyond 3m: acts on any going: usually wore blinkers/cheekpieces in 2002/3. *R. Rowe*

DIRTY SANCHEZ 5 b.g. Manhal – Lady Poly (Dunbeath (USA)) [2002/3 F18m 16m **h–** Jul 14] second foal: half-brother to winning 2m hurdler Blayney Dancer (by Contract **F–** Law): dam winning hurdler up to 2½m: tailed off in bumper (unseated and bolted before start) and novice selling hurdle. *Jamie Poulton*

DISCERNING AIR 7 b.m. Ezzoud (IRE) – Jhansi Ki Rani (USA) (Far North (CAN)) **c106** [2002/3 c106, h115: c20s* c20gᵘʳ 17g³ 22d Aug 3] close-coupled mare: fair hurdler/ **h111** chaser: won mares novice over fences at Cork in May: effective at 2m (given good test) to 2¾m: acts on any going: usually blinkered: sold €60,000 Fairyhouse January Sale. *Michael Hourigan, Ireland*

DISCREET GIRL 4 b.f. Mistertopogigo (IRE) – Pillow Talk (IRE) (Taufan (USA)) **F–** [2002/3 F14d F17g F16mᵖᵘ Apr 21] lengthy filly: second foal: dam, 8.5f winner on Flat, modest maiden hurdler: no form in bumpers: very unlikely to stay 2m. *Mrs S. Lamyman*

DI'S DILEMMA 5 b.m. Teenoso (USA) – Reve En Rose (Revlow) [2002/3 F17g³ **F83** F16m Apr 21] 4,600 4-y-o: first foal: dam, modest hurdler/fair chaser, stayed 2¾m: easily better effort in mares bumpers when close third to True Destiny at Market Rasen. *C. C. Bealby*

DISPOL FOXTROT 5 ch.m. Alhijaz – Foxtrot Pie (Shernazar) [2002/3 16vᵖᵘ 19d **h–** Feb 25] sturdy mare: fair on Flat (stays 11f), successful 3 times in 2002 for T. D. Barron: no promise either outing over hurdles. *A. Scott*

DISPOL ROCK (IRE) 7 b.g. Ballad Rock – Havana Moon (Ela-Mana-Mou) [2002/3 **h90** 21g⁵ 18gᵘʳ 16m 16m 16vᶠ 16v⁵ 16d⁴ 16v³ 16s³ 17v* 17m Apr 5] angular gelding: modest and temperamental on Flat (stays 1½m), sold out of T. D. Barron's stable 1,400 gns Doncaster August Sales: modest hurdler: well backed, easily won weak novice handicap at Taunton in March: raced mainly around 2m: acts on heavy going, possibly unsuited by good to firm. *Dr P. Pritchard*

DISTANT ROMANCE 6 br.m. Phardante (FR) – Rhine Aria (Workboy) [2002/3 **h–** F16s 16dᵖᵘ Nov 30] seventh foal: dam 2m novice hurdler: no show in bumper or mares **F–** novice hurdle. *Miss Z. C. Davison*

DISTANT SKY (USA) 6 ch.g. Distant View (USA) – Nijinsky Star (USA) (Nijinsky **h–** (CAN)) [2002/3 17sᵇᵈ 16s 21d Jan 18] compact gelding: fair maiden at best on Flat (stays 13f): well held both completed outings in novice hurdles: sold 1,800 gns Doncaster March Sales. *P. Mitchell*

DISTANT STORM 10 ch.g. Pharly (FR) – Candle In The Wind (Thatching) [2002/3 **h91** h97: 19d⁴ 19m⁵ 22g⁶ 22m³ 18m* 19m 16m⁴ 19d⁶ 22d⁵ 20d² 16s 21g³ 20m⁵ Apr 21] small, sturdy gelding: modest hurdler: won seller at Fontwell in August: stays 2¾m: acts on any going: tried visored, blinkered nowadays: tongue tied: not an easy ride (usually ridden by Miss E. J. Jones): none too consistent. *B. J. Llewellyn*

DISTANT THUNDER (IRE) 5 b.g. Phardante (FR) – Park Breeze (IRE) (Strong **F97** Gale) [2002/3 F16s² F16m⁴ Feb 22] lengthy gelding: fifth foal: half-brother to fairly useful but temperamental chaser/winning hurdler Moving Earth (by Brush Aside), stays 21f, and fairly useful hurdler up to 3m Fork Lightning (by Roselier): dam unraced sister to useful staying chaser Risk of Thunder: fairly useful form when in frame in bumpers at Kempton, second to Hawk's Landing and fourth to Chelsea Bridge. *R. H. Alner*

DISTILLERY (USA) 5 ch.g. Mister Baileys – Respectable (USA) (Northrop (USA)) h–
[2002/3 16m⁶ 16sᵖᵘ Aug 1] some promise on debut at 2 yrs for P. Cole, but no form on Flat in 2002: no show in 2 selling hurdles at Stratford, visored second time. *J. G. M. O'Shea*

DISTINCTIVE (IRE) 14 ch.g. Orchestra – Zimuletta (Distinctly (USA)) [2002/3 c–
c105, h–: c21gᵖᵘ May 1] angular gelding: fairly useful hunter chaser: disappointing at h–
Cheltenham in May, not seen out again: stays 3¼m: acts on soft and good to firm going: suited by forcing tactics. *Mrs Caroline Chadney*

DISTINCTLY WELL (IRE) 6 b.g. Distinctly North (USA) – Brandywell (Skyliner) h–
[2002/3 16d 16s 16d Jan 24] leggy gelding: half-brother to winning hurdler/chaser Yakareem (by Rainbows For Life), stays easy 3m: modest on Flat (stays 11.6f): well held in novice hurdles, pulling hard. *B. A. McMahon*

DISTINGO (FR) 6 b. or br.g. Courtroom (FR) – Quinte Au Roi (FR) (Prince Regent h106
(FR)) [2002/3 16d² 17s³ 16sᵖᵘ Feb 24] leggy gelding: eighth foal: half-brother to 3 winners on Flat: dam won around 1¼m: successful 4 times up to 1½m on Flat at 3/4 yrs, in frame twice in 2002, sold out of J. F. Bernard's stable €35,500 Goffs July Sale: fair form when placed first 2 starts over hurdles: dead. *Mrs L. Wadham*

DIVA 6 b.m. Exit To Nowhere (USA) – Opera Lover (IRE) (Sadler's Wells (USA)) h115
[2002/3 h94: 17mᵖᵘ 16m⁴ 16m* Oct 11] leggy mare: fairly useful handicap hurdler: won at Huntingdon by 8 lengths from Monte Cristo, easily best effort in 2002/3: raced around 2m: acts on good to firm and good to soft going: headstrong. *A. King*

DIVET HILL 9 b.g. Milieu – Bargello's Lady (Bargello) [2002/3 c117, h–: c25d* c122
c20m* c25m² c16g² c20m³ 21m* 21m* 20d* 21g⁴ c25m* c22d⁵ c21g⁴ Apr 19] h104
leggy, quite good-topped gelding: fair hurdler, won novices at Sedgefield (2) in July and Perth in August: fairly useful chaser: won hunter at Hexham and handicap at Perth in May, handicap at Kelso in October and Martell Cognac Golden Cross Inn Fox Hunters' Chase at Aintree (beat General Wolfe 11 lengths) in April: effective at 2m to 25f: acts on firm and good to soft going: front runner: usually jumps well: genuine: a credit to connections. *Mrs A. Hamilton*

DIVINE MIST (IRE) 6 br.g. Roselier (FR) – Tate Divinity (IRE) (Tate Gallery h–
(USA)) [2002/3 F71: F16d² 19d 22dᶠ Feb 23] lengthy gelding: best effort in bumpers F83
when second in maiden at Fakenham on reappearance: jumped poorly on hurdling debut, disputing fourth when falling 2 out in maiden at Exeter next time. *Jonjo O'Neill*

DIVORCE ACTION (IRE) 7 b.g. Common Grounds – Overdue Reaction (Be My c–
Guest (USA)) [2002/3 c–, h100: 16f⁵ 20d³ 19m³ 20s 17m⁴ Jul 19] sturdy gelding: well h86
held on chasing debut: modest handicap hurdler: stays 19f when conditions aren't testing: best form on good going or firmer (acts on firm): has had tongue tied: sold £1,500 Ascot August Sales. *R. M. Stronge*

Martell Cognac Golden Cross Inn Fox Hunters' Chase, Aintree—
Divet Hill follows Dam The Breeze over Bechers

DIVULGE (USA)   6 b.g. Diesis – Avira (Dancing Brave (USA)) [2002/3 h80: 16d^F **c67**
16m^{ur} 16m^4 17g^2 16s^5 c17s^5 c17m^3 17g Sep 28] leggy gelding: modest maiden hurdler: **h85**
poor form both starts over fences: needs sharp 2m: acts on soft and good to firm going:
tends to find little: sketchy jumper. *A. Crook*

DIX BAY   8 b.g. Teenoso (USA) – Cooks Lawn (The Parson) [2002/3 h107: c19g^{ur} **c– x**
c16d^5 c20s^{pu} Feb 24] quite good-topped gelding: fair handicap hurdler: jumped poorly   **h–**
in 3 novice chases: likely to stay beyond 2½m: acts on soft and good to firm going.
M. W. Easterby

DIXCART VALLEY   7 b.g. Carlingford Castle – Renshaw Wood (Ascertain (USA))   **c–**
[2002/3 19d^{pu} 27v^{pu} 25g^5 25d^5 25d 20d c25g^{pu} Apr 14] quite good-topped gelding: **h–**
second foal: dam, poor hurdler/chaser, stayed 3m: signs of only a little ability over
hurdles: no show on chasing debut. *P. Beaumont*

DIXON VARNER (IRE)   13 b.g. Sheer Grit – Raise The Bells (Belfalas) [2002/3   **c94**
c26m^2 May 3] workmanlike ex-Irish gelding: one-time leading hunter chaser for
E. Bolger: off 3 years prior to no match for Noyan at Folkestone in May: subsequently
placed several times in points: stays 3¼m: acts on heavy going, probably on good to firm:
usually held up. *Mrs D. M. Grissell*

DIZZY LAD (IRE)   7 b.g. Alphabatim (USA) – Court Session (Seymour Hicks (FR))   **h–**
[2002/3 21m^4 Apr 19] maiden pointer: poor form in 2 starts over hurdles. *J. S. King*

DIZZY'S DREAM (IRE)   5 b.g. Shernazar – Balingale (Balinger) [2002/3 F16s*   **F110**
F16g Mar 12] €15,000 4-y-o: tall gelding: sixth foal: half-brother to fair hurdler/chaser
up to 3m Heavy Hustler and winning chaser up to 2½m Ceannairceach (both by Strong
Gale): dam, point/bumper winner, from family of smart 2m hurdler Bootlaces: created
good impression when winning bumper at Leopardstown on debut by 8 lengths from
Farranfore: well held in Grade 1 at Cheltenham month later. *N. Meade, Ireland*

DIZZY TART (IRE)   4 b.f. Definite Article – Tizzy (Formidable (USA)) [2002/3   **h89**
17d^2 16g^3 16m* 16d 16d^2 16d 17d^3 16g^5 Apr 12] leggy, close-coupled filly: half-sister to
useful hurdler/chaser Chief's Song (by Chief Singer), stayed 21f, and winning 17f hurdler
In A Tizzy (by Sizzling Melody): modest and inconsistent maiden on Flat (seems to stay
easy 1¼m): modest juvenile hurdler: won at Huntingdon in September: generally creditable efforts otherwise: raced around 2m: acts on good to firm and good to soft going.
Mrs P. N. Dutfield

DJC THE BLUE (IRE)   10 gr.g. Young Man (FR) – Polocracy (IRE) (Aristocracy)   **h–**
[2002/3 24d^{pu} 25d^{pu} May 30] ex-Irish gelding: won maiden Irish point in 2000, little show
otherwise. *J. Hetherton*

DJEDDAH (FR)   12 b.g. Shafoun (FR) – Union Jack III (FR) (Mister Jack (FR))   **c130 §**
[2002/3 c142§, h–: c29s^{pu} c22d^3 c22s^4 20d^2 c22s c25g^5 c25d c24g^5 c36d Apr 5] tall   **h108 §**
gelding: winning hurdler, second in minor event at Compiegne in October: useful chaser:
few worthwhile efforts in 2002/3, fifth in valuable 3m handicap at Cheltenham: stays 29f:
acts on good to firm and heavy going, blinkered: usually sound jumper: inconsistent and
irresolute. *F. Doumen, France*

D J FLIPPANCE (IRE)   8 b.g. Orchestra – Jane Bond (Good Bond) [2002/3 c83,   **c109**
h85: 24d^3 c28v* c30d* Nov 30] rangy gelding: maiden hurdler: fair handicap chaser: **h98**
improved form when winning at Kelso and Newcastle in November: stays 3¾m: raced
mainly on going softer than good (acts on heavy). *A. Parker*

DOBBIESGARDENWORLD (IRE)   6 b.g. Great Marquess – Rosy Posy (IRE)   **F99**
(Roselier (FR)) [2002/3 F16s* F16v^3 F17s^3 Mar 6] 35,000 4-y-o: quite good-topped
gelding: fifth foal: half-brother to fairly useful bumper winner Go White Lightning and
winning 25f chaser Greyton (both by Zaffaran): dam unraced half-sister to smart 2m
hurdler Honeygrove Banker: fairly useful form in bumpers, won at Newcastle in
December: will be suited by further than 2m. *L. Lungo*

DOBERMAN (IRE)   8 br.g. Dilum (USA) – Switch Blade (IRE) (Robellino (USA))   **h73**
[2002/3 16s^4 16d^3 Jan 16] poor on Flat (stays easy 1¼m): poor maiden hurdler: raced at
2m: acts on soft going: visored/blinkered. *W. M. Brisbourne*

DOCKLANDS LIMO   10 b.h. Most Welcome – Bugle Sound (Bustino) [2002/3 h134:   **h–**
16d 17d 22v^{pu} Feb 1] leggy horse: useful handicap hurdler on his day: left N. Twiston-
Davies and off 18 months, showed little on return: stays 2½m: acts on good to firm and
heavy going. *G. F. Bridgwater*

DOC RYAN'S   9 b.g. Damister (USA) – Jolimo (Fortissimo) [2002/3 20d^6 Aug 3]   **h76**
medium-sized gelding: fair hurdler in 1999/00 for M. Ryan: runner-up only completed

start in points in 2002: sixth in seller back over hurdles: stays 2½m: acts on good to firm and heavy going: blinkered. *B. J. Llewellyn*

DOCTOR BRAVIOUS (IRE) 10 b.g. Priolo (USA) – Sharp Slipper (Sharpo) [2002/3 c–, h–: 21g^{pu} Apr 29] medium-sized gelding: winning hurdler/once-raced chaser, no form for long time: tried visored, blinkered nowadays: not an easy ride. *Jamie Poulton* **c– h–**

DOCTOR DOVE 9 ch.g. St Enodoc – Saucy Dove (Saucy Kit) [2002/3 h–: 20g^{pu} Jul 15] little sign of ability, including in points. *C. J. Price* **h–**

DOCTOR GREEN (FR) 10 b.g. Green Desert (USA) – Highbrow (Shirley Heights) [2002/3 c–, h91§: 16s 22f^{pu} Aug 13] neat gelding: winning hurdler: no encouragement in 2 selling handicaps in 2002/3: visored: jumps none too fluently: none too keen. *M. C. Pipe* **c– § h– §**

DOCTOR JOHN 6 ch.g. Handsome Sailor – Bollin Sophie (Efisio) [2002/3 h–: 16d 19d^5 22g Mar 18] workmanlike gelding: modest novice hurdler: may prove best short of 2¾m. *Andrew Turnell* **h88**

DOCTOR WOOD 8 b.g. Joligeneration – Ladywood (Doctor Wall) [2002/3 h–, F78: 17g^5 17m 22d 19v^3 17d^2 Feb 10] leggy gelding: bumper winner: poor novice hurdler: stays 19f: acts on heavy going: amateur ridden. *Miss V. A. Stephens* **h77**

DOE NAL RUA (IRE) 6 b.g. Mister Lord (USA) – Phardante Girl (IRE) (Phardante (FR)) [2002/3 F16v^3 F16s 16d 19d 21v^3 Feb 11] 10,500 4-y-o: big, rangy gelding: first foal: dam won 2m hurdle: better effort in bumpers when third at Wetherby: easily best effort in novice hurdles when third at Sedgefield: will stay 3m: raced only on going softer than good (acts well on heavy). *T. D. Easterby* **h92 F94**

DOES IT MATTER 6 b.g. Carlingford Castle – Flopsy Mopsy (Full of Hope) [2002/3 F17f F17m F16m 19d^{pu} Feb 28] has scope: sixth foal: half-brother to modest chaser Dubelle (by Dubassoff), stays 21f: useful hurdler half-sister to very smart 2m hurdler Sula Bula and to useful hurdler around 2½m Permabos: little sign of ability: pulls hard. *P. C. Ritchens* **h– F–**

DOIGTS D'OR (FR) 8 b.g. Sanglamore (USA) – Doigts de Fee (USA) (L'Emigrant (USA)) [2002/3 c16v^4 c20s^4 Jan 3] big, lengthy gelding: modest hurdler: promising fifth on chasing debut in 2000/1: shaped as if retaining all his ability on second of 2 starts on return: will prove best short of 2½m: acts on soft and good to firm going: headstrong. *P. R. Webber* **c85 + h–**

DOIRE-CHRINN (IRE) 7 b. or br.m. Unblest – Princess Monarch (IRE) (Fairy King (USA)) [2002/3 16s^4 16d 16v^6 16s^4 16v^6 Mar 2] small mare: fair on Flat (stays 1¼m, has won when blinkered): modest maiden hurdler: raced at 2m on good going or softer (acts on soft). *D. P. Kelly, Ireland* **h93**

DO IT ON DANI 8 br.m. Weld – Dark City (Sweet Monday) [2002/3 h73: 26g^2 26g^3 27g* 27g^2 22d^2 24m* 22d^4 24g* 25g* 25d 24v^{pu} 24g^6 24m^4 Apr 17] small, leggy mare: fair hurdler: much improved in 2002/3, winning handicaps at Newton Abbot, Market Rasen and Plumpton and novice at Uttoxeter between June and October: thorough stayer: acts on good to firm and good to soft going (well below best all runs on heavy): genuine and consistent. *Mrs A. M. Thorpe* **h111**

DO KEEP UP 6 b.g. Missed Flight – Aimee Jane (USA) (Our Native (USA)) [2002/3 F–: 20s^{pu} 20s 16g 16m Mar 20] leggy gelding: little sign of ability. *N. P. Littmoden* **h–**

DO L'ENFANT D'EAU (FR) 4 ch.g. Minds Music (USA) – L'Eau Sauvage (Saumarez) [2002/3 17v^3 17s* 16s^3 17s* 19d^2 20s^3 17d* 16d* 16g* 16g Apr 3] compact ex-French gelding: first foal: dam ran once: thrice-raced on Flat: useful juvenile hurdler: placed twice at Auteuil for J-P. Totain: won at Hereford in November, Folkestone (novice) in December, and handicaps at Hereford in February and Newbury and Warwick (beat Indien Royal 7 lengths in valuable event) in March: ran no sort of race in Grade 2 at Aintree final start: stays 2½m: raced only on good going or softer. *P. J. Hobbs* **h130**

DOLI CYGNUS 5 gr.m. Bedford (USA) – Damsong (Petong) [2002/3 F16d^5 F17s^3 Nov 21] medium-sized mare: fifth foal: dam unraced half-sister to top-class 2m hurdler/smart chaser Nohalmdun: modest form in 2 bumpers, shaping like a stayer when third in mares event at Hereford. *E. L. James* **F84**

DOLLAR LAW 7 ch.g. Selkirk (USA) – Western Heights (Shirley Heights) [2002/3 16d^4 16s^3 16v^3 17s^3 17s^2 16v^3 16s^4 16d^4 16d* 17g^{ur} Mar 22] angular gelding: fair up to 1¼m on Flat: fair novice hurdler: in frame all 9 completed starts, winning at Chepstow in March: may prove best around 2m: acts on heavy going: wore cheekpieces after third appearance: tongue tied: waited with: reliable. *R. J. Price* **h107**

DOLLY MOP 7 b.m. Nearly A Hand – Roving Seal (Privy Seal) [2002/3 F–: 17s⁵ 20s⁶ **h–**
20g Mar 25] signs of only a little ability. *B. J. M. Ryall*

DOLPHINELLE (IRE) 7 b.g. Dolphin Street (FR) – Mamie's Joy (Prince Tender- **h77 §**
foot (USA)) [2002/3 h74: 16m⁴ᵈ 16m 16d 16s 16s⁶ Feb 24] strong gelding: poor maiden
hurdler: raced around 2m: acts on soft and good to firm going: tried blinkered: unreliable.
Jamie Poulton

DOMAPPEL 11 b.g. Domynsky – Appelania (Star Appeal) [2002/3 c94, h–: c20mᵖᵘ **c–**
c20gᶠ May 24] tall, workmanlike gelding: winning hurdler: modest maiden chaser: failed **h–**
to complete both starts in early-2002/3: stays easy 3m: acts on firm and good to soft
going. *M. C. Banks*

DOME 5 b.g. Be My Chief (USA) – Round Tower (High Top) [2002/3 h–: 18f³ 20m **h90 ?**
22m⁶ Jun 28] useful-looking gelding: modest maiden on Flat (stays 12.6f): apparently
easily best effort over hurdles when third in 4-y-o novice at Fontwell in June: should stay
2½m: sometimes tongue tied. *S. Dow*

DOMENICO (IRE) 5 b.g. Sadler's Wells (USA) – Russian Ballet (USA) (Nijinsky **h107**
(CAN)) [2002/3 h102: 16v* 20s⁵ 16d³ 16s⁵ Mar 10] good-topped gelding: fairly useful
on Flat (stays 2½m), sold out of P. Webber's stable 16,000 gns Newmarket Autumn Sales:
fair novice hurdler: won at Uttoxeter in November: should stay beyond 2m: acts on heavy
ground: jumped poorly second start. *J. R. Jenkins*

DOMINIKUS 6 b.g. Second Set (IRE) – Dolce Vita (GER) (Windwurf (GER)) [2002/3 **c105**
h103: c16g⁵ c20m² c20m* c20d² Aug 2] leggy gelding: fair hurdler: similar form in **h–**
novice chases, won at Market Rasen in July: stays 21f: acts on firm and good to soft
going. *Ferdy Murphy*

DOMINION PRINCE 5 b.g. First Trump – Lammastide (Martinmas) [2002/3 16m **h–**
Mar 23] maiden on Flat: tongue tied, showed nothing on hurdling debut. *D. Mullarkey*

Mr Terry Warner's "Do L'Enfant d'Eau"

DOMQUISTA D'OR   6 b.g. Superpower – Gild The Lily (Ile de Bourbon (USA)) [2002/3 h73: 20g^{pu} 17g 16m^3 16s^2 17d^{pu} 19m^{pu} 19g^5 21m Apr 2] leggy, plain gelding: poor maiden hurdler: best around 2m: acts on soft (well beaten only start on heavy) and good to firm going: blinkered second and sixth starts. *G. A. Ham*   **h72**

DOM SHADEED   8 b.g. Shadeed (USA) – Fair Dominion (Dominion) [2002/3 16s 17g^{ttr} Mar 18] modest on Flat (should stay 1¾m): little show over hurdles: refused to race final start. *R. J. Baker*   **h– §**

DONADINO (IRE)   10 br.g. Be My Native (USA) – Atteses (Smooth Stepper) [2002/3 c119, h–: 20s^3 c20d^{pu} c17d* c16f c20m^3 Sep 29] tall ex-Irish gelding: winning hurdler: fairly useful handicap chaser: back to form when winning at Galway in August: first outing since leaving C. Swan, found less than seemed likely final start: successful at 21f, very best efforts around 2m: has won on soft going, best efforts on firmer. *Jonjo O'Neill*   **c115 h94**

DONA FERENTIS (IRE)   8 b.m. Homo Sapien – Greek Tan (Pitpan) [2002/3 c–, h72: c16d^{pu} Mar 4] poor maiden hurdler: won maiden point in 2002, yet to complete in steeplechases: tried blinkered and tongue tied. *S. Flook*   **c– h–**

DONALLACH MOR (IRE)   11 b.g. Phardante (FR) – Panalee (Pitpan) [2002/3 c108x: c25g^{pu} c24s^4 c25g^{pu} Apr 7] strong gelding: winning chaser: little show in 2002/3: second in point in March: stays 3½m: acts on firm and good to soft going: makes mistakes. *Mrs S. H. Shirley-Beavan*   **c– x**

DONATUS (IRE)   7 b.g. Royal Academy (USA) – La Dame du Lac (USA) (Round Table) [2002/3 h91: 16g^F 16m^2 17g^4 20m^6 16g^3 20m^{pu} Jul 17] neat gelding: modest hurdler: left S. Dow after reappearance: stays easy 2½m: acts on soft and good to firm going, probably on firmer: tried visored: often finds little. *Miss K. M. George*   **h96**

DONEGAL SHORE (IRE)   4 b.c. Mujadil (USA) – Distant Shore (IRE) (Jareer (USA)) [2002/3 16d 19d 17d 16d^{pu} Apr 9] fairly useful at best on Flat (best efforts at 6f), sold out of B. Hills's stable 800 gns Newmarket Autumn Sales and well held subsequently: no form over hurdles: tongue tied last 2 starts. *Mrs J. Candlish*   **h–**

DON FERNANDO   4 b.c. Zilzal (USA) – Teulada (USA) (Riverman (USA)) [2002/3 16d* 17d* 17s^2 17g^{bd} 16d Apr 4] leggy juvenile colt: fairly useful on Flat (stays 1¼m) for E. Dunlop: useful juvenile hurdler: won at Cheltenham in November and December (Grade 2, got on top close home to beat dead-heaters Lilium de Cotte and Nas Na Riogh ¾ length): close up when brought down 3 out in Triumph Hurdle at Cheltenham: disappointing favourite in Grade 2 novice at Aintree final start: raced on good ground or softer. *M. C. Pipe*   **h131**

Tripleprint Juvenile Novices' Hurdle, Cheltenham—Don Fernando is all out to land the odds after jumping the last between Lilium de Cotte and Nas Na Riogh (right) who dead-heated for second

Lucayan Stud's "Don Fernando"

DON IDO (ARG) 7 b.g. Lazy Boy (ARG) – She's Got You (ARG) (Indalecio (ARG)) **h77**
[2002/3 h–p: 17f⁴ 16m³ 16m⁵ Oct 29] good-topped gelding: successful 3 times at 1m/
9f on Flat in Argentina: poor form over hurdles: will probably prove best around 2m:
headstrong. *J. A. B. Old*

DONIE DOOLEY (IRE) 5 ch.g. Be My Native (USA) – Bridgeofallen (IRE) (Torus) **F–**
[2002/3 F16d Mar 1] workmanlike ex-Irish gelding: third foal: dam won Irish point:
modest form in 2 bumpers for P. O'Keeffe in 2001/2: tailed off on British debut.
P. T. Dalton

DONNABELLA 6 b.m. Bustino – Howanever (Buckskin (FR)) [2002/3 F17d 20g **h–**
Mar 16] angular mare: third foal: dam won Irish point: well held in bumper for R. Hodges **F–**
and mares novice hurdle. *John R. Upson*

DONNINI (IRE) 6 ch.g. Kris – La Luna (USA) (Lyphard (USA)) [2002/3 17d² 17m³ **h95 d**
16sᶠ 18m⁶ 16g⁵ 16gᵖᵘ 16d 17d 16dᵖᵘ Apr 9] leggy gelding: half-brother to fairly useful
2m hurdler Moon Shot (by Pistolet Bleu): well held in 2 maidens on Flat for P. Harris:
placed in 2 early-season novice hurdles: sold out of P. Hobbs's stable 4,000 gns Doncaster
August Sales and lost his form: sold out of Miss K. Marks' stable 2,200 gns Doncaster
October Sales after sixth start: may prove best around 2m: has had tongue tied.
B. D. Leavy

DONNYBROOK (IRE) 10 ch.g. Riot Helmet – Evening Bun (Baragoi) [2002/3 c106, **c115**
h–: c16m c25g⁴ c20s⁵ c20d* c20d⁴ c24d⁴ c20d c21s⁴ Mar 15] tall gelding: fairly useful **h–**

247

handicap chaser: won at Haydock in November: let down by jumping last 2 starts: stays 3m: acts on good to firm and heavy going: effective blinkered or not. *R. D. E. Woodhouse*

DON ROYAL 9 b.g. Rakaposhi King – Donna Farina (Little Buskins) [2002/3 c25d³ c20sᵖᵘ c25gᵖᵘ Apr 5] tall gelding: fair pointer, successful in March: best effort in hunter chases when third at Towcester in May: saddle slipped next time. *J. Scott* **c88**

DON'T SIOUX ME (IRE) 5 b.g. Sadler's Wells (USA) – Commanche Belle (Shirley Heights) [2002/3 16g⁶ 16m² 16d³ Apr 9] half-brother to fair 2m hurdler Persian Brave (by Persian Heights): lightly raced on Flat, useful form up to 1¾m, disappointing both starts in 2002 and sold out of H. Cecil's stable only 8,000 gns Newmarket Autumn Sales: modest form over hurdles: will stay beyond 2m: has pulled hard/carried head awkwardly/jumped less than fluently. *C. R. Dore* **h92**

DON'T TELL JR (IRE) 9 b.g. Mister Lord (USA) – Middle Third (Miner's Lamp) [2002/3 c91+, h–: c24d³ c29d² Nov 24] tall gelding: modest chaser: raced on good going or softer (acts on heavy): has been let down by jumping. *Ferdy Murphy* **c91**
h–

DON VALENTINO (POL) 4 ch.g. Duke Valentino – Dona (POL) (Dakota) [2002/3 17d Feb 23] ex-Polish gelding: ran 11 times on Flat, winning 4 times up to 1¼m, left D. Kaluba in September: showed little in juvenile maiden on hurdling debut. *T. R. George* **h–**

DOOLEY GATE 6 b.g. Petoski – High 'b' (Gunner B) [2002/3 F16s Dec 16] 1,800 4-y-o: workmanlike gelding: first foal: dam unraced: well held in bumper on debut. *F. P. Murtagh* **F–**

DOON RUN (IRE) 9 ch.g. Commanche Run – Paupers Spring (Pauper) [2002/3 24d 25v³ c22dᵖᵘ Nov 29] workmanlike ex-Irish gelding: fair hurdler/maiden chaser: sold out of M. Hourigan's stable 6,000 gns Doncaster May Sales after reappearance: possibly amiss final outing: stays 3m: acts on soft and good to firm going, probably on heavy: has run creditably in blinkers. *B. G. Powell* **c–**
h96

DOORS TO MANUAL (FR) 5 b. or br.g. Saumarez – Filigree (FR) (Great Nephew) [2002/3 F16g² F16s⁵ F16v³ F16d² Mar 22] tenth foal: half-brother to 6 winners on Flat, in France, Italy and Morocco: dam unraced: fairly useful bumper winner: good second to Brave Inca at Navan in March and fifth to Kim Fontaine in quite valuable event at Punchestown in early-May. *Charles O'Brien, Ireland* **F105**

DORAN'S DAY (IRE) 6 b.g. Gildoran – Inverdonan (Our Mirage) [2002/3 F85: 19g³ 22dᵖᵘ Nov 5] modest in bumpers, looking very much a stayer: third in novice at Hereford on hurdling debut: again finished lame 6 months later. *Mrs H. Dalton* **h85**

DORANS GOLD 9 b.g. Gildoran – Cindie Girl (Orchestra) [2002/3 c120, h–: c20s* c20gᵖᵘ c20d* c20d² c24g Mar 11] lengthy, useful-looking gelding: fairly useful handicap chaser: won at Bangor (first start for nearly 12 months) in October and Warwick in December: stays 3m: acts on soft and good to firm going. *P. F. Nicholls* **c125**
h–

DORANS PRIDE (IRE) 14 ch.g. Orchestra – Marians Pride (Pry) [2002/3 c129, h129: c24s² c26gᶠ Mar 13] leggy gelding: top-class hurdler/chaser in his prime, won 1995 Stayers' Hurdle and twice third in Gold Cup: won 3 points prior to 10 lengths second of 4 finishers to Sheltering in hunter chase at Leopardstown: fell second and broke leg in Foxhunter at Cheltenham: stayed 3¼m: unraced on firm going, acted on any other: thoroughly game and genuine: dead. *Michael Hourigan, Ireland* **c128**
h–

DOREEN'S DREAM (IRE) 5 ch.m. Moscow Society (USA) – Sister Gabrielle (IRE) (Buckskin (FR)) [2002/3 F16s 16vᵖᵘ Feb 10] first foal: dam unraced, out of half-sister to useful staying hurdler/chaser Deep Gale and Fox Hunters winner Gayle Warning: no show in bumper or mares novice hurdle. *G. B. Balding* **h–**
F–

DORSET FERN (IRE) 7 b.m. Tirol – La Duse (Junius (USA)) [2002/3 h–: 17gᵖᵘ 17s² 19s 19s³ 16v 19s c16g⁴ Mar 17] lengthy mare: poor maiden hurdler: no show on chasing debut: stays 19f: acts on soft going. *G. B. Balding* **c–**
h66

DOTTIE DIGGER (IRE) 4 b.f. Catrail (USA) – Hint-Of-Romance (IRE) (Treasure Kay) [2002/3 16g 16g 16bᵈ 18g⁶ 16gᵖᵘ Apr 24] modest maiden on Flat (barely stays 1¼m) for I. Semple: no form over hurdles: wore cheekpieces after debut. *Miss Lucinda V. Russell* **h–**

DOUBLE ACCOUNT (FR) 8 b.g. Sillery (USA) – Fabulous Account (USA) (Private Account (USA)) [2002/3 c96, h–: 21m* 22v 22m⁵ Apr 11] sturdy gelding: modest chaser: fair handicap hurdler: off 17 months, won at Kempton in February: poor efforts **c–**
h115

both subsequent starts: stays 2¾m: acts on good to firm and heavy going: blinkered once. *C. J. Mann*

DOUBLE AGENT   10 ch.g. Niniski (USA) – Rexana (Relko) [2002/3 c–, h92: 27m^{pu} May 7] sturdy gelding: maiden chaser: modest hurdler: should stay beyond 3m: acts on soft and good to firm going: tried blinkered. *Miss A. M. Newton-Smith*   c– h–

DOUBLE BID   6 b.g. Rudimentary (USA) – Bidweaya (USA) (Lear Fan (USA)) [2002/3 h–: 17g^{pu} 16m^{pu} 17g^{pu} 17g⁵ 24d Nov 25] leggy gelding: winning hurdler, showed nothing in 2002/3: tried blinkered/in cheekpieces: tongue tied: has reportedly broken blood vessels. *Mrs N. S. Sharpe*   h–

DOUBLE BLADE   8 b.g. Kris – Sesame (Derrylin) [2002/3 h120: 16g⁵ 16g* 17m* 16m³ Oct 16] strong, lengthy gelding: fairly useful hurdler: won claimers at Perth in September and Sedgefield (very easily) in October: better form when beaten in handicaps first and final starts: suited by strongly-run 2m: acts on firm and good to soft going: held up: carries head high. *Mrs M. Reveley*   h118

DOUBLE BOGEY BLUES (IRE)   7 b.g. Celio Rufo – Belmount Star (IRE) (Good Thyne (USA)) [2002/3 c101, h112: c24s⁵ c26s⁶ c24v⁵ c25d* c25s² c24m* c24f^{pu} Mar 29] angular ex-Irish gelding: fair hurdler: modest chaser: sold out of M. Morris' stable 36,000 gns Doncaster May Sales after reappearance: won novices at Hereford (handicap, despite numerous mistakes) in February and Ludlow (weak 3-runner event) in March: stays 25f: acts on soft and good to firm going: races prominently: often let down by jumping. *M. Mullineaux*   c97 x h–

DOUBLE BUBBLE (IRE)   5 b. or br.g. Mandalus – Double Talk (Dublin Taxi) [2002/3 F17d Dec 3] IR £10,000 3-y-o, 6,000 4-y-o: fifth foal: brother to winning pointer Mandy Chat: dam, placed once over 5f at 2 yrs, out of half-sister to smart 2m to 3m chaser Clear Cut: tailed off in bumper on debut. *C. N. Kellett*   F–

DOUBLE CAR (FR)   7 b.g. Sleeping Car (FR) – Double Roots (FR) (Deep Roots) [2002/3 c160, h137: c29s*^{dis} 19v* c22s³ c22s^{pu} Apr 13] good-topped gelding: useful hurdler, didn't need to be at best to win in minor event at Bordeaux in March: very smart chaser: disqualified on technical grounds after passing post first in Grand Steeple-Chase de Paris at Auteuil in 2002: shaped as if retaining plenty of ability when third to Rouge-noir in Prix Troytown there in March: ran as if amiss following month: ideally suited by a test of stamina: raced mainly on soft/heavy going. *B. de Watrigant, France*   c158 h118 +

DOUBLE DESTINY   7 b.g. Anshan – Double Gift (Cragador) [2002/3 16m 17m² 16m⁵ Apr 22] modest on Flat (stays 1m), left D. Ivory after final start in 2002: modest form over hurdles. *Miss E. C. Lavelle*   h85

DOUBLE DIPLOMACY   7 b.g. State Diplomacy (USA) – Malmo (Free State) [2002/3 21s^{pu} 19s^{pu} 20g^{pu} Jan 17] eighth foal: brother to fair staying chaser Twin States and half-brother to winning staying hurdler/chaser Movie Man (by Move Off): dam barely stayed 2m over hurdles: showed little over hurdles: blinkered final start. *P. Beaumont*   h–

DOUBLE EM   4 b.g. Balnibarbi – Something Speedy (IRE) (Sayf El Arab (USA)) [2002/3 17s^{pu} 17g 17g Sep 28] modest maiden on Flat (should stay 1¼m): no form in 3 juvenile hurdles, pulling hard. *C. W. Fairhurst*   h–

DOUBLE EMBLEM (IRE)   6 ch.m. Weld – Sultry (Sula Bula) [2002/3 F16g Aug 24] fourth foal: dam maiden hurdler/pointer: failed to complete in 2 points in 2002: didn't look easy ride when seventh of 12 in bumper at Worcester. *W. M. Brisbourne*   F–

DOUBLE FUN (HOL)   4 b.c. Bretigny (FR) – Rising Stream (Pharly (FR)) [2002/3 16s² 16d 16d⁶ Mar 10] small colt: successful 6 times on Flat (stays 1¾m) in Holland/Germany, including on sand at Neuss in January: best effort in juvenile hurdles when ½-length second of 11 to Star Protector at Ascot in November. *C. Von Der Recke, Germany*   h100

DOUBLE HONOUR (FR)   5 gr.g. Highest Honor (FR) – Silver Cobra (USA) (Silver Hawk (USA)) [2002/3 16d* 19d* 21m³ 21g 17m* Apr 8] smart on Flat (stays 2¾m) for M. Johnston: fairly useful novice hurdler: won at Huntingdon and Exeter in January and Exeter again in April: tenth to Hardy Eustace in Grade 1 event at Cheltenham in March: will stay beyond 21f: has room for improvement in his jumping. *P. J. Hobbs*   h123

DOUBLE RICH   10 ch.g. Rich Charlie – Spartona (Cisto (FR)) [2002/3 c25g^{ur} c27d^{pu} Mar 18] modest pointer: failed to complete in 2 hunter chases in March, though travelled   c–

well until approaching 3 out at Sedgefield (reportedly distressed) on second occasion. *David M. Easterby*

DOUBLE SPEY   4 b.g. Atraf – Yankee Special (Bold Lad (IRE)) [2002/3 16m⁴ 16d   h94
Mar 1] workmanlike gelding: half-brother to winning 2m hurdler Yankee Flyer (by
Henbit): modest maiden on Flat (should stay 1¼m): shaped quite well when fourth in
juvenile at Wetherby on hurdling debut: jumped poorly in similar event next time.
P. C. Haslam

DOUBLE TEE (IRE)   7 br.g. Jurado (USA) – Monkeylane (Monksfield) [2002/3 c–,   c–
h61: c24m 22fᵖᵘ May 15] angular, close-coupled gelding: of little account nowadays: h–
tried visored. *N. J. Hawke*

DOUBLE WISH (IRE)   5 b.h. Barathea (IRE) – Love Bateta (IRE) (Caerleon (USA))   h–
[2002/3 21vᵖᵘ 17m Apr 5] ex-French horse: fairly useful maiden on Flat (stays 1½m),
sold out of Mme C. Head-Maarek's stable 3,000 gns Newmarket Autumn (2001) Sales:
no show either outing over hurdles: tried visored. *Miss M. E. Rowland*

DOUBLE YOU CUBED   9 b.g. Destroyer – Bright Suggestion (Magnate) [2002/3   c–
h–: c25g⁵ c25gᵘʳ Apr 14] leggy gelding: no worthwhile form, even in points. *J. S. Goldie*   h–

DOUCEUR DES SONGES (FR)   6 b.m. Art Francais (USA) – Ma Poetesse (FR)   c– §
(Sorrento (FR)) [2002/3 c96, h91: 16v³ 16g² 17m³ 19m² 17g⁴ c24m⁵ c21sᵖᵘ 16v² 18d³   h105 §
24sᵖᵘ 21s 21m⁶ Apr 21] leggy, lengthy mare: maiden chaser: fair hurdler: won mares
novice at Uttoxeter in June: badly out of sorts last 4 starts: best efforts around 2m: acts on
heavy going: tried visored/in cheekpieces: ungenuine. *M. C. Pipe*

DOUZE DOUZE (FR)   7 ch.g. Saint Cyrien (FR) – Kitkelly (FR) (Tamelo (FR))   c154
[2002/3 18s* c20d² c24sᵖᵘ c19sᵘʳ 18s* Mar 9] big gelding: smart hurdler/chaser: h146
won minor events over hurdles at Cholet (having been off 2 years with leg injury) in
November and Auteuil (led again close home when beating El Paradiso a short head) in
March: second of 5 to Best Mate in Grade 2 at Huntingdon on completed outing over
fences in between: effective around 2m and should stay 3m: acts on good to firm and
heavy going: has had tongue tied: has room for improvement in his jumping over fences.
G. Macaire, France

DOVE FROM ABOVE   10 b.g. Henbit (USA) – Sally's Dove (Celtic Cone) [2002/3   c–
c–, h–: 26g 22m⁴ 26m 22dᵖᵘ Nov 5] angular gelding: winning hurdler: no form since   h–
1999/00, including over fences (none too fluent): often blinkered. *R. J. Price*

DOVETTO   14 ch.g. Riberetto – Shadey Dove (Deadly Nightshade) [2002/3 c72d, h–:   c–
c25dᵖᵘ May 6] sparely-made gelding: poor chaser: stays easy 3m: acts on any going: none   h–
too consistent. *C. J. Price*

DOW JONES (GER)   5 b.g. Temporal (GER) – Dahsa's Dream (IRE) (Pitpan) [2002/3   h112
16s 16s 18v 16m* Apr 6] won twice around 1¼m at 4 yrs on Flat in Germany for
R. Rohne: easily best effort over hurdles when winning maiden at Tramore in April:
possibly unsuited by soft/heavy going. *M. Halford, Ireland*

DOWN (FR)   12 b.g. Le Nain Jaune (FR) – Izoba (FR) (Bamako III) [2002/3 c33g   c80
c26vᵖᵘ c21g Apr 3] lengthy gelding: half-brother to useful chaser Elzoba (by Un Desperado), stayed 2½m: dam won on Flat and over jumps in France: winning chaser for
G. Cherel, including in cross country events: fairly useful form in points in Britain,
successful 5 times: well held in hunters (stiff task final outing): failed to stay 33f: raced
on good going or softer (acts on heavy): effective with/without blinkers. *R. Waley-Cohen*

DOWNPOUR (USA)   5 b.g. Torrential (USA) – Juliac (USA) (Accipiter (USA))   h106
[2002/3 h87p: 19g⁸ 16g 19d³ Mar 1] useful-looking gelding: fair hurdler: won novice at
Hereford in May: best effort when third in similar event at Doncaster final start: stays 19f:
raced on good/good to soft going. *Ian Williams*

DO YE KNOW WHA (IRE)   11 b. or br.g. Ajraas (USA) – Norton Princess (Wolver   c–
Hollow) [2002/3 c–, h120: 20g⁵ 22m 22gᵖᵘ Jul 27] rangy gelding: winning chaser (often   h99
let down by jumping): fairly useful hurdler at best: out of form early in 2002/3: stays 3m,
at least when conditions aren't testing: acts on firm and soft going (well beaten only start
on heavy): sometimes blinkered, best form when not: looking increasingly temperamental: sold £1,800 Ascot November Sales, won point in March. *R. Curtis*

DOYENNE   9 gr.m. Mystiko (USA) – No Chili (Glint of Gold) [2002/3 22m² 22m Sep   h74
7] leggy mare: modest form in points: winning hurdler, poor form on first of 2 starts in
2002/3: stays 2¾m: acts on good to firm going: tried blinkered: tongue tied in 2002/3.
J. Neville

DRAGON HUNTER (IRE)   8 b.g. Welsh Term – Sahob (Roselier (FR)) [2002/3   **c– p** h100: c26s^F Dec 7] fair hurdler: fell twelfth in novice chase at Warwick only run in   **h–** 2002/3: best at 3m+: raced only on soft/good to soft going. *C. R. Egerton*

DRAGON KING   11 b.g. Rakaposhi King – Dunsilly Bell (London Bells (CAN))   **c95** [2002/3 c83, h–: c20g⁴ c22g c26g⁴ c21m² c21g* c26v⁴ c22v² c20s⁴ c22s* c20g⁴ c21g^F   **h–** c26f* Apr 24] sturdy gelding: modest chaser: won minor event at Newton Abbot in July and handicaps at Fontwell in February (amateurs) and April: stays easy 3¼m: acts on any going: effective visored/blinkered/in cheekpieces or not: front runner: tough. *P. Bowen*

DRAGON LORD   9 b.g. Warning – Cockatoo Island (High Top) [2002/3 c21m^F May   **c– x** 22] close-coupled gelding: bumper winner: error-prone maiden hurdler: placed several   **h– x** times in points but badly let down by jumping on hunter chase debut: stays 2½m: acts on soft and good to firm going. *Mrs Alison Hickman*

DRAGUT TORGHOUD (IRE)   7 b.g. Persian Mews – Artist's Jewel (Le Moss)   **h82 +** [2002/3 F16d⁴ 22d^{pu} 20v⁴ 20s⁶ 21m² Apr 2] IR 4,500 3-y-o: fifth foal: dam unraced, from   **F77** family of top-class 2m to 3m hurdler Gaye Brief and very smart staying jumper Gaye Chance: fourth in bumper on debut: poor form in novice hurdles: will prove best at 2½m+. *N. M. Babbage*

DRAKESTONE   12 b.g. Motivate – Lyricist (Averof) [2002/3 c–, h97: 17d Feb 10]   **c–** workmanlike gelding: maiden chaser (let down by jumping): modest handicap hurdler: **h–** reportedly lame last 2 starts in 2001/2 and shaped as if possibly amiss on return: stays 23f: acts on soft and good to firm going: blinkered twice. *R. L. Brown*

DRAMA KING   11 b.g. Tragic Role (USA) – Consistent Queen (Queen's Hussar)   **h76** [2002/3 h88: 20g 20g⁵ 22g^{pu} 16v* 17s⁵ 21v 16v⁴ 16s Feb 26] small gelding: poor handicap hurdler: first outing for 6 months, won conditional jockeys seller at Uttoxeter in November (subsequently tested positive for morphine): effective at 2m to 2¾m: acts on any going: usually blinkered/visored: inconsistent. *B. J. Llewellyn*

DRAMATIC MISS   8 b.m. Deploy – Stos (IRE) (Bluebird (USA)) [2002/3 F–: 16s   **h–** 16g^{pu} Sep 14] no sign of ability. *R. J. Price*

DRAMATIC QUEST   6 b.g. Zafonic (USA) – Ultra Finesse (USA) (Rahy (USA))   **h105 d** [2002/3 h104: 19s⁵ 20v^{pu} 20g² 24g Apr 23] good-topped gelding: fair on Flat nowadays: fair hurdler: below form after reappearance: stays 19f, not 3m: acts on soft going: tried blinkered. *Ian Williams*

DR BILLY (IRE)   9 b.g. Dry Dock – Carrigconeen (Beau Charmeur (FR)) [2002/3   **c81 ?** c25g⁶ Apr 7] ex-Irish gelding: no form over hurdles for J. P. Whelan or in points: sixth in   **h–** maiden hunter chase at Kelso, possibly flattered: tried blinkered/tongue tied. *A. Kirtley*

DR CHARLIE   5 ch.g. Dr Devious (IRE) – Miss Toot (Ardross) [2002/3 h98p: 19d⁵   **h98** 22s⁵ 20v⁴ 19d 22g⁴ Mar 15] angular gelding: modest handicap hurdler: stays 2¾m: acts on good to firm and heavy going: hung left off bridle third start. *C. J. Mann*

DR DEDUCTIBLE   11 b.g. Derrylin – Tantrum (Leading Man) [2002/3 c20m⁵ Jun 1]   **c77** modest pointer: fifth in hunter at Hexham in June. *J. E. Brockbank*

DREAM A DREAM   4 b.f. Emperor Jones (USA) – Thornbury (IRE) (Tender King)   **h–** [2002/3 16m Sep 29] modest maiden on Flat (stays 9f): well held in juvenile on hurdling debut. *Mrs D. Haine*

DREAMIE BATTLE   5 br.m. Makbul – Highland Rossie (Pablond) [2002/3 h82:   **h58** 16g⁵ 16d³ 16s⁴ 16m⁵ 16d⁵ 16m^{ur} 17m Apr 5] poor maiden on Flat (best form up to 1m): bad maiden hurdler: unlikely to stay beyond 2m: races freely. *R. Hollinshead*

DREAM OF NURMI   9 ch.g. Pursuit of Love – Finlandaise (FR) (Arctic Tern (USA))   **c–** [2002/3 c116, h112: 20d³ c24g^{pu} May 17] workmanlike gelding: fairly useful chaser/fair   **h106** hurdler: broke leg at Stratford in May: seemed to stay 3m: acted on firm and soft going: tried blinkered: refused to race/showed reluctance at start on several occasions: dead. *Mrs S. J. Smith*

DREAM ON THEN   7 ch.m. Royal Vulcan – Dreamside (Quayside) [2002/3 16g   **h–** May 17] second foal: dam little sign of ability: whipped round start and showed nothing in mares novice seller on hurdling debut: fell in point in February. *John R. Upson*

DREAM ON WILLIE (IRE)   6 b.g. Synefos (USA) – Mrs Mahon's Toy (IRE)   **h90** (Roselier (FR)) [2002/3 22s⁶ 20s² 20g 20d³ 22g⁵ Mar 15] second foal: dam unraced: in frame all 3 starts in maiden Irish points in 2002: bought 18,000 gns Doncaster May Sales: best effort over hurdles when second in novice at Carlisle in November: probably stays 2¾m: raced on good going or softer (acts on soft). *E. A. Elliott*

United House PFI Handicap Hurdle, Ascot—Dream With Me makes it five in a row

DREAM WITH ME (FR) 6 b.g. Johann Quatz (FR) – Midnight Ride (FR) (Fast Topaze (USA)) [2002/3 h93: 16m* 16m* 19m* 17d* 16d* 16d⁶ 21gᵖᵘ 16g Apr 5] sturdy gelding: fairly useful hurdler: successful first 5 starts in 2002/3, in novice handicap at Stratford, novices at Uttoxeter and Hereford and handicaps at Bangor and Ascot between June and November: stays 19f: acts on good to firm and good to soft going: blinkered (found little) once: usually tongue tied. *M. C. Pipe* **h125**

DR JAZZ (NZ) 11 ch.g. First Norman (USA) – Almacenista (NZ) (Nuage d'Or (USA)) [2002/3 c–, h86d: 17m Jun 14] close-coupled gelding: maiden chaser: one-time useful hurdler, has deteriorated considerably: stays 2½m: acts on heavy going: tried blinkered/visored: difficult ride: sold 600 gns Ascot July Sales, pulled up in point in January. *M. C. Pipe* **c– h–**

DROMBEAG (IRE) 5 b.g. Presenting – Bula Beag (IRE) (Brush Aside (USA)) [2002/3 F17d³ F17s* Mar 6] IR £10,000 3-y-o: first foal: dam unraced: won maiden Irish point on debut in 2002: fairly useful form in 2 bumpers, beating Baron Monty a head at Carlisle: will stay 2½m. *Jonjo O'Neill* **F97**

DROMOD POINT (IRE) 14 ch.g. Dromod Hill – Bright Point (Shackleton) [2002/3 c21fᵖᵘ May 10] poor maiden hurdler/chaser: pulled up in novice hunter at Wincanton in May: probably stays 25f: acts on good to firm and good to soft going: usually blinkered. *Mrs N. K. Case* **c– h–**

DROM WOOD (IRE) 7 ch.g. Be My Native (USA) – Try Your Case (Proverb) [2002/3 h91, F87: c16v 22gᶠ Apr 19] lengthy gelding: bumper winner: generally well held over hurdles and on chasing debut: has had tongue tied. *T. R. George* **c– h–**

DR RAJ 4 ch.g. In The Wings – Tawaaded (IRE) (Nashwan (USA)) [2002/3 F16d Mar 1] 1,500Y: strong, lengthy, dipped-backed gelding: half-brother to useful French 1m **F–**

winner who stays 1¼m Sahaat (by Machiavellian): dam, 7f winner who stayed 1m, from family of Singspiel (by In The Wings): tailed off in bumper on debut. *B. A. McMahon*

DR STRANGELOVE (IRE) 5 ch.g. Dr Devious (IRE) – Renzola (Dragonara Palace (USA)) [2002/3 h–: 17dᵖᵘ 16s Jan 3] quite good-topped gelding: disappointing maiden on Flat, sold out of M. Hammond's stable 600 gns Doncaster October Sales: no form over hurdles: tried in blinkers/cheekpieces. *P. R. Johnson*   **h–**

DRUID'S GLEN (IRE) 7 br.g. Un Desperado (FR) – Fais Vite (USA) (Sharpen Up) [2002/3 c–p, h109, F89: c25s* c24s* c20dᵖᵘ c20m² c32g c25g² Mar 29] tall, attractive gelding: fair hurdler: useful novice chaser: won at Market Rasen in November and Southwell in December: excellent second to Hand Inn Hand in Grade 2 at Kempton fourth start: stays 25f (failed to stay 4m in National Hunt Chase at Cheltenham): acts on soft and good to firm going: usually races prominently: not straightforward (has hung/flashed tail). *Jonjo O'Neill*   **c132 h–**

DRUM BATTLE 11 ch.g. Bold Arrangement – Cannon Boy (USA) (Canonero (USA)) [2002/3 c96x, h–: c26d³ c28g⁵ c26g⁶ Apr 19] leggy gelding: won point impressively in January for R. Barber: only modest form back in handicaps subsequently: suited by 3m+: acts on any going: usually tongue tied: races prominently: sketchy jumper. *P. F. Nicholls*   **c93 x h–**

DRUMDONEY (IRE) 8 br.g. Dromod Hill – Stradbally Bay (Shackleton) [2002/3 c–, F83: c25m³ c24gᵖᵘ Nov 20] won maiden point on debut in 2001: modest form only completion in steeplechases. *R. H. Alner*   **c89**

DRUMLIN (IRE) 8 b.g. Glacial Storm (USA) – Shannon Lough (IRE) (Deep Run) [2002/3 c–, h–: c21m⁶ Apr 21] sturdy gelding: winning hurdler: no form in steeplechases: blinkered once: has looked difficult ride. *J. M. Turner*   **c– h–**

DRUM MAJORETTE 8 ch.m. Infantry – Smart Chick (True Song) [2002/3 F83: 22g⁵ 22s⁵ 22s* Feb 3] smallish, sparely-made mare: in frame in 2 bumpers in 2001/2: improved effort over hurdles when winning seller at Fontwell: likely to stay 3m: raced on good going or softer (acts on soft). *B. G. Powell*   **h98**

DRY HIGHLINE (IRE) 11 b.g. Dry Dock – Fandango Girl (Last Fandango) [2002/3 c–, h–: c24mᶠ May 11] useful pointer on his day: would probably have won novice hunter chase at Huntingdon in May but for falling last: headstrong front-runner who needs to improve his jumping. *Mrs Ruth Hayter*   **c96 x h–**

DUAL STAR (IRE) 8 b.g. Warning – Sizes Vary (Be My Guest (USA)) [2002/3 c20d c16m* c16m* c16mᵖᵘ c16g⁵ c16g³ 19m c19s⁴ c25s⁶ Nov 21] sparely-made ex-Irish gelding: half-brother to useful 2m hurdler Just Little (by Mtoto) and poor chaser Upward Surge (by Kris), stays 2½m: winning hurdler: modest chaser: left S. Donohoe, successful in handicaps at Newton Abbot in July and August: stays 19f: acts on soft and good to firm going: tried blinkered: tongue tied: has gone in snatches. *P. J. Hobbs*   **c94 h83**

DUBAI SEVEN STARS 5 ch.m. Suave Dancer (USA) – Her Honour (Teenoso (USA)) [2002/3 h122?: 24s² 21d⁴ 25g 20d Apr 4] leggy mare: fairly useful handicap hurdler: failed to go through with effort when good second to Springfield Scally at Chepstow on reappearance, best effort in 2002/3: also found nothing second/third starts: stays 3m: raced on good going or softer (acts on soft): one to treat with caution. *M. C. Pipe*   **h126 §**

DUBLIN LIGHTS (IRE) 8 b. or br.g. Electric – Whosview (Fine Blade (USA)) [2002/3 c–, h–: 24dᵖᵘ May 4] little sign of ability. *J. I. A. Charlton*   **c– h–**

DUC DE COIGNY 8 b.g. Damister (USA) – Shercol (Monseigneur (USA)) [2002/3 F–: 20sᶠ c16sᵖᵘ c19dᵖᵘ c16dᵘʳ Mar 5] no sign of ability. *M. Mullineaux*   **c– h–**

DUCHAMP (USA) 6 b.g. Pine Bluff (USA) – Higher Learning (USA) (Fappiano (USA)) [2002/3 c113+, h104: 21g⁵ c20d⁴ c20g² c16s⁵ c21vᵘʳ c19d c20m⁴ c19dᶠ c18m² Mar 21] tall, leggy gelding: winning hurdler: fairly useful handicap chaser: best form up to 2½m: acts on good to firm and heavy ground: usually visored: front runner. *A. M. Balding*   **c122 h–**

DUCHAS MACNAS (IRE) 8 b.g. Be My Native (USA) – Soda Fountain (Lafontaine (USA)) [2002/3 16v² Mar 2] rangy gelding: fairly useful bumper winner: fair form over hurdles, second in maiden at Fairyhouse in March on return from long absence: stays 2½m: acts on heavy going. *M. J. P. O'Brien, Ireland*   **h111**

DUDLEYS DELIGHT 4 b.f. Makbul – Steadfast Elite (IRE) (Glenstal (USA)) [2002/3 17sᵖᵘ Nov 21] fair on Flat (seems to stay 1m), successful 3 times in autumn: **h–**

weakened quickly after racing freely in clear lead in juvenile at Hereford on hurdling debut. *M. C. Pipe*

DUDS (IRE) 4 ch.g. Definite Article – Domino's Nurse (Dom Racine (FR)) [2002/3 **h–** 17mᵖᵘ Sep 14] third in 6f maiden on debut but no worthwhile form on Flat since (trained at 2 yrs by P. Cole): showed nothing in juvenile (led in) on hurdling debut. *F. P. Murtagh*

DUKEEN (FR) 8 ch.g. Iron Duke (FR) – Oliver's Queen (FR) (King Cyrus (USA)) **c141** [2002/3 c148, h–: c22s⁵ c29sᵖᵘ 22d⁴ 18d² 18s² c21v⁴ c22v⁵ Dec 1] compact gelding: **h148** smart hurdler: second in minor events at Cholet in October and November, apparently good effort behind Douze Douze on second occasion: smart chaser at best, mostly well below form in Group company at Auteuil in 2002/3: stays 2¾m: raced on good going or softer (acts on heavy). *G. Margogne, France*

DUKE OF BUCKINGHAM (IRE) 7 b.g. Phardante (FR) – Deselby's Choice **c102** (Crash Course) [2002/3 F94: c19m² c20d³ c21d⁴ c16s⁴ Dec 31] rangy gelding: placed both starts in bumpers: won 2½m maiden point in 2002: fair novice chaser: may prove best up to 2½m: acts on soft and good to firm going. *P. R. Webber*

DUKE OF EARL (IRE) 4 ch.c. Ali-Royal (IRE) – Faye (Monsanto (FR)) [2002/3 **h119** 16s⁸ 17d⁵ 16v³ 16m³ 17g Mar 13] small, leggy colt: half-brother to fair 2m hurdler Wray (by Sharp Victor) and winning 2¼m chaser Owen Roe (by Blues Traveller): fairly useful on Flat (stays 1¾m): fairly useful juvenile hurdler: won at Huntingdon in November: creditable efforts in Grade 2 events at Cheltenham and Kempton second and fourth starts: will stay beyond 17f: acts on good to firm and heavy ground. *S. Kirk*

DULAS BAY 9 b.g. Selkirk (USA) – Ivory Gull (USA) (Storm Bird (CAN)) [2002/3 **c–** c120, h–: c20d⁴ Nov 9] tall gelding: fairly useful handicap chaser: badly hampered **h–** first and 2 bad mistakes when trying to recover, only outing in 2002/3: stays 3m, at least when conditions aren't testing: acts on good to firm and heavy going: sometimes runs in snatches. *M. Pitman*

DUMADIC 6 b.g. Nomadic Way (USA) – Duright (Dubassoff (USA)) [2002/3 h–, **h–** F76: 16m May 9] lengthy gelding: no show in 2 novice hurdles: successful in point in February. *T. D. Walford*

DUMARAN (IRE) 5 b.g. Be My Chief (USA) – Pine Needle (Kris) [2002/3 16g 16s⁸ **h113** 16v⁵ 17sᵖᵘ Jan 25] leggy gelding: useful on Flat (stays 9f), won 3 times in 2002: easily best effort over hurdles when winning 22-runner novice at Warwick in December by 6 lengths from Cho Polu: conditions too testing next time: likely to prove best at 2m: races freely. *A. M. Balding*

DUMA TAU (IRE) 7 gr.g. Executive Perk – Di's Wag (Scallywag) [2002/3 h–: 21s **h–** 19d Feb 28] workmanlike gelding: no sign of ability. *J. T. Gifford*

DUN AN DORAS (IRE) 7 b.g. Glacial Storm (USA) – Doorslammer (Avocat) **h93** [2002/3 17m⁵ 20v 17s² 19d³ 20v⁵ 22g⁴ Mar 18] IR 8,000 4-y-o: leggy ex-Irish gelding: third foal: brother to winning pointer: dam, winning hurdler/chaser around 2½m, from family of high-class staying chaser Door Latch: won maiden Irish point in 2002: modest novice hurdler: will stay 3m: acts on heavy going. *J. D. Frost*

DUNCRIEVIE GALE 6 gr.g. Gildoran – The Whirlie Weevil (Scallywag) [2002/3 **h–** F–: 24dᵖᵘ Oct 26] big gelding: no show in bumper or novice hurdle. *Mrs L. B. Normile*

DUN DISTINCTLY (IRE) 6 b.g. Distinctly North (USA) – Dunbally (Dunphy) **c–** [2002/3 h–: c16g⁶ c17s Jun 3] leggy gelding: winnng hurdler: no form for long time, **h–** including over fences: form only around 2m: acts on good to soft going. *P. C. Haslam*

DUNDONALD 4 ch.g. Magic Ring (IRE) – Cal Norma's Lady (IRE) (Lyphard's **h–** Special (USA)) [2002/3 16f 17d Apr 8] strong, workmanlike gelding: fair on Flat (stays 8.5f), won in November: well held in 2 juvenile hurdles, not fluent on debut. *P. D. Niven*

DUNGARVANS CHOICE (IRE) 8 ch.g. Orchestra – Marys Gift (Monksfield) **c122** [2002/3 h122: c19s² c19vᵖᵘ 21s* 22s² Mar 15] sturdy, useful-looking gelding: tempera- **h132** mental efforts in 2 novice chases at Chepstow, though fairly useful form on first occasion: improved form returned to hurdling, won handicap at Newbury in February and second to Valleymore in similar event at Uttoxeter in March: likely to stay 3m: raced on good going or softer (acts on soft): edgy sort. *N. J. Henderson*

DUNKERRON 6 b.g. Pursuit of Love – Top Berry (High Top) [2002/3 h71: 16g⁵ 16g **h68** 20s 16g² 16m⁵ 20m³ 17m 16dᵖᵘ Oct 31] compact gelding: poor maiden hurdler: stays

2½m: acts on good to firm and good to soft going: went off too fast when blinkered second outing. *J. Joseph*

DUNLEA (IRE) 7 b.g. Common Grounds – No Distractions (Tap On Wood) [2002/3   **h93**
16g⁶ 21d⁴ 22s 18s Jan 15] angular gelding: fair winning hurdler, largely well held since
1999/00: should stay beyond 21f: acts on soft going. *J. G. Carr, Ireland*

DUNMANUS BAY (IRE) 6 gr.g. Mandalus – Baby Fane (Buckskin (FR))   **c–**
[2002/3 22d 22g³ 22g³ 23g c24dᶠ c24g⁶ Mar 25] IR 1,750 3-y-o: fourth foal: half-   **h86**
brother to 3m hurdle winner Lord Fane (by Lord Americo): dam unraced, from family of
very smart 2m to 2½m hurdler Fane Ranger: second in 2 maiden Irish points in 2001:
showed some ability in novice hurdles, but none in 3 runs over fences, left B. Powell
before final one (jumped poorly). *R. H. Alner*

DUNNICKS CHANCE 8 b.m. Greensmith – Field Chance (Whistlefield) [2002/3   **h65**
h–: 19sᵖᵘ 16d³ 16vᵖᵘ 22d⁶ 19d 22m 17g² Apr 19] maiden hurdler: first form when second
in weak mares maiden at Newton Abbot. *F. G. Tucker*

DUNNICKS FIELD 7 b.g. Greensmith – Field Chance (Whistlefield) [2002/3 h–,   **h–**
F73: 17s⁶ 19dᵖᵘ Apr 7] plain gelding: little sign of ability. *F. G. Tucker*

DUNNICKS TRUST 5 b.g. Greensmith – Country Magic (National Trust) [2002/3   **F–**
F16d F16d Mar 6] good-bodied gelding: fifth living foal: half-brother to staying chaser
Dunnicks View (by Sula Bula): dam winning pointer: well beaten in bumpers at
Wincanton. *F. G. Tucker*

DUNNICKS VIEW 14 b.g. Sula Bula – Country Magic (National Trust) [2002/3 c83,   **c78**
h–: c26d⁶ c19s³ c25g⁵ c26g⁵ Apr 19] lengthy gelding: poor handicap chaser: stays 3¼m: **h–**
acts on good to firm and good to soft going. *F. G. Tucker*

DUNOWEN (IRE) 8 b.g. Be My Native (USA) – Lulu Buck (Buckskin (FR)) [2002/3   **c88**
20v³ 20s² c20s² c20s* c32gᶠ Mar 12] winning pointer: maiden hurdler: modest chaser: **h84**
won handicap at Limerick in February: very stiff task at Cheltenham following month:
should stay beyond 2½m: raced on good going or softer over jumps (acts on heavy):
blinkered last 3 starts. *T. Hyde, Ireland*

DUNRAVEN 8 b.g. Perpendicular – Politique (Politico (USA)) [2002/3: 25g 16g⁴   **c80**
16g 17g* 16d⁴ 20s 16d⁴ 16g c16v³ 16v³ c16dᵘʳ c16m³ Apr 21] workmanlike gelding: **h76**
poor handicap hurdler: won at Southwell (seller) and Fakenham in October: similar form
on first of 2 completed outings over fences: stays 2½m, at least as effective at 2m: acts on
heavy going. *M. J. Gingell*

DUNRIG (IRE) 8 b.g. King's Ride – Belon Brig (New Brig) [2002/3 c24sᵖᵘ c25d²   **c94**
c25g² c25g* Apr 7] ex-Irish gelding: fifth foal: dam, winning chaser, stayed 3m: winning
pointer: behind when pulled up on hunter chase debut for J. P. Berry: off 10 months, did
well in 3 similar events at Kelso, landing odds in maiden in April: stays 25f. *L. Lungo*

DUNSFOLD DAZZLER 11 b.m. Phardante (FR) – Rositary (FR) (Trenel) [2002/3   **c–**
c33gᵖᵘ May 1] first foal: dam useful staying hurdler/winning pointer: winning pointer:
very stiff task only outing in hunter chase. *Mrs Mair Hughes*

DUNSFORD HALL (IRE) 9 gr.g. Top of The World – Dark Fluff (Mandalus)   **h–**
[2002/3 26gᵖᵘ 24gᵖᵘ Sep 15] sixth foal: dam, placed over hurdles, half-sister to fairly
useful 2m hurdler Granville Hotel: no sign of ability, mainly in Irish points. *R. N. Bevis*

DUNSTER CASTLE 8 ch.g. Carlingford Castle – Gay Edition (New Member)   **c105**
[2002/3 c–p, h95: c24d³ c24gᵖᵘ c21d² c24m* Apr 2] workmanlike gelding: modest   **h–**
hurdler: allowed to dictate and jumped better when winning 3-runner novice at Ludlow,
left well clear when in control last and seemingly best effort over fences: stays 3m: acts
on soft and good to firm going: free-going sort, and often looks awkward/finds less than
expected under pressure. *P. J. Hobbs*

DUNSTON ACE 9 b.g. Sizzling Melody – Miss Vaigly Blue (Vaigly Great) [2002/3   **c–**
c–, h–: c21mᵖᵘ Jul 4] no form. *B. D. Leavy*   **h–**

DUNSTON BILL 9 b.g. Sizzling Melody – Fardella (ITY) (Molvedo) [2002/3 c115,   **c115**
h–: c20d² c22s* c20sᵘʳ c20d² c20v³ c21sᵖᵘ Mar 15] workmanlike gelding: fair handicap   **h–**
chaser: won 5-runner event at Market Rasen in November, clear much of way and in
control when left well ahead last: stays 2¾m: acts on heavy and good to firm going:
blinkered. *C. J. Mann*

DUNSTON DURGAM (IRE) 9 b.g. Durgam (USA) – Blazing Sunset (Blazing   **h–**
Saddles (AUS)) [2002/3 22gᶠ 22dᵖᵘ 16m 16g Sep 12] of little account. *R. Hollinshead*

DUNSTON GOLD 9 ch.g. Risk Me (FR) – Maria Whittaker (Cure The Blues (USA)) **c60**
[2002/3 h–: 22d c21d² c25gᶠ 26mᵖᵘ Aug 12] bad maiden jumper. *G. Barnett* **h–**

DUNSTON HEATH (IRE) 10 b.g. Durgam (USA) – Yola (IRE) (Last Tycoon) **c–**
[2002/3 h68: 22g⁴ c24sᵖᵘ 21g Mar 12] sparely-made gelding: poor hurdler: no show in **h64**
novice on chasing debut: stays 3m: acts on soft going: blinkered once: has had tongue
tied. *B. D. Leavy*

DUNSTON SLICK 10 ch.g. Weld – Havrin Princess (Scallywag) [2002/3 c–, h–: **c–**
16m Jun 29] tall gelding: of little account: tried visored/tongue tied. *W. Clay* **h–**

DURHAM GLINT 12 b.g. Glint of Gold – Jem Jen (Great Nephew) [2002/3 c26dᵖᵘ **c–**
Jun 8] sturdy gelding: poor pointer: has failed to complete both starts in hunter chases.
Mrs J. E. Speight

DURINGTHENIGHT (IRE) 4 b.g. Namaqualand (USA) – Legend of Spain (USA) **F102**
(Alleged (USA)) [2002/3 F17d⁶ F16g² F16g² F16d² Apr 25] seventh foal: brother to 2
winners on Flat, including fair Irish stayer Goldnblues and half-brother to 2 others: dam
unraced: fairly useful form in bumpers, best effort when 1¼ lengths second to Flight
Command in 17-runner race at Perth final outing. *G. A. Swinbank*

DURLSTON BAY 6 b.g. Welsh Captain – Nelliellamay (Super Splash (USA)) [2002/3 **h103**
h87: 17m³ 17f² 22m* Jun 1] sturdy gelding: fair hurdler: won novice at Stratford (reportedly finished lame) in June: effective around 2m to 2¾m: best form on going firmer than
good. *S. Dow*

DUSHAAN 8 ch.g. Anshan – Soon To Be (Hot Spark) [2002/3 h87: 17s Nov 26] good- **h–**
topped gelding: modest 2m hurdler, disappointing all 3 starts since winning on 2001/2
reappearance: acts on heavy going (bumper form on good to firm): tried blinkered/tongue
tied: has looked ungenuine. *Mrs L. B. Normile*

DUSK DUEL (USA) 8 b.g. Kris – Night Secret (Nijinsky (CAN)) [2002/3 c148, h–: **c–**
16m Mar 22] rangy gelding: smart chaser: little encouragement over hurdles on return **h–**
from 15-month absence: should stay beyond 21f: acts on soft and good to firm going.
N. J. Henderson

DUSKY BLUE (IRE) 4 b.g. Bluebird (USA) – Massada (Most Welcome) [2002/3 **h72**
17sᵖᵘ 17d³ Aug 2] well held on Flat: blinkered and tongue tied, well-held third in juvenile
hurdle at Bangor. *Jonjo O'Neill*

DUSKY LIGHT 5 b.m. Gildoran – Starawak (Star Appeal) [2002/3 F17s³ 19s⁴ Nov **h81 p**
28] half-sister to several winners on Flat, including fairly useful 6f to 1m winner Fame **F77**
Again (by Then Again) and useful 1¼m to 15f winner Army of Stars (by Posse): dam,
1½m winner, half-sister to smart miler Spring In Deepsea and Chester Vase winner
Kaytu: in frame in bumper and mares novice hurdle at Taunton in November, still looked
green when just over 20 lengths fourth to Fragrant Rose in latter. *P. F. Nicholls*

DUSTY DEMOCRAT 5 b.g. Democratic (USA) – Two Shots (Dom Racine (FR)) **h65**
[2002/3 h68: 17m⁴ 17m⁶ 16g 16f² 19f⁴ Oct 17] poor maiden hurdler: raced mainly around
2m (left with too much to do over 19f): acts on firm going: effective visored or not: has
had tongue tied. *W. G. M. Turner*

DUSTY STAR 4 b.f. Danzig Connection (USA) – Sindos (Busted) [2002/3 17fᵘʳ 16f **h–**
Oct 24] half-sister to modest 2m hurdler Hold Court (by The Noble Player): no sign of
ability on Flat or over hurdles. *W. G. M. Turner*

DUSTY TOO 5 gr.m. Terimon – Princess Florine (USA) (Our Native (USA)) [2002/3 **h–**
F16d* F16g* F16g⁴ 19g Dec 18] leggy mare: fourth foal: half-sister to bumper winner **F90**
Fine de Claire (by Teenoso) and fairly useful 2½m to 2¾m hurdler Wright (by Broadsword): dam unraced: out of half-sister to Poule d'Essai des Poulains winner In Fijar: fair
form in bumpers at Worcester, successful twice in August: off 3 months, never dangerous
in novice at Newbury on hurdling debut. *Mrs A. J. Perrett*

DUTCH DYANE 10 b.m. Midyan (USA) – Double Dutch (Nicholas Bill) [2002/3 h–: **h80**
22m 20s 21mᵖᵘ 22s* 24gᵖᵘ Nov 20] leggy mare: fair handicap hurdler at best: 25/1, first
form for long time when winning conditional jockeys event at Sandown in November:
reportedly finished lame later in month: stays 2¾m: raced mainly on good going or
softer (acts on heavy): has had tongue tied: has worn near-side pricker/cheekpieces.
G. P. Enright

DUTSDALE DANCER (IRE) 9 b.g. Commanche Run – Miss Polymer (Doulab **c124**
(USA)) [2002/3 h126: 20s c17s² c20s* c20s* c21vᵖᵘ c24dᵖᵘ Feb 16] lengthy, rather **h–**
sparely-made gelding: fairly useful handicap hurdler: similar form over fences, won at

Navan in November (maiden) and December (novice, beat Bob Justice 1½ lengths): reportedly lost action fifth outing: stays 2½m: acts on any going: tried tongue tied. *A. J. Whelan, Ireland*

DYNAMIC LIFTER (IRE) 5 ch.g. Be My Native (USA) – Best Trump (Le Bavard (FR)) [2002/3 F16d 21s 21s⁶ 20v 25d³ 24m² Mar 18] 25,000 3-y-o: third foal: dam winning pointer: eighth of 13 in bumper at Southwell: modest form over hurdles: better around 3m than shorter: acts on good to soft and good to firm going: blinkered final start: has looked tricky ride. *Jonjo O'Neill*　　**h84 F75**

DYRICK DAYBREAK (IRE) 4 ch.f. Ali-Royal (IRE) – Lovely Deise (IRE) (Tate Gallery (USA)) [2002/3 16g⁴ 16s⁴ 16v³ 16s³ 16s Feb 9] angular filly: half-sister to fairly useful 2m hurdler Tate Tirol (by Tirol): successful on 2 of 4 starts on Flat (at 1¾m/2m), showing fairly useful form: fairly useful juvenile hurdler: third in graded races at Leopardstown in December and Punchestown in January: tongue tied: wandered markedly on hurdling debut. *David A. Kiely, Ireland*　　**h115**

E

EARL SIGURD (IRE) 5 ch.g. High Kicker (USA) – My Kind (Mon Tresor) [2002/3 h97: 16d 20g 16gᵖᵘ Apr 14] leggy gelding: fair juvenile hurdler in 2001/2 (returned with gash to near-hind fetlock final start): caught the eye on second outing back but ran no sort of race following month: should stay beyond 2m: acts on good to firm and good to soft going. *L. Lungo*　　**h86 +**

EARL'S KITCHEN 6 ch.g. Karinga Bay – Rempstone (Coronash) [2002/3 F16v² F18v* F16g F18d Feb 17] deep-girthed gelding: will make a chaser: first foal: dam poor pointer: last of 4 finishers on completed start in maiden points in 2002: fairly useful form in bumpers: won at Fontwell in January: reportedly finished lame final outing: will be suited by 2½m+. *C. Tizzard*　　**F100**

EARL TOKEN 7 b.g. Primitive Rising (USA) – Lady Token (Roscoe Blake) [2002/3 c26gᵖᵘ c20dᵖᵘ May 30] 3,400 4-y-o: second foal: dam, modest chaser who stayed 3¼m, out of half-sister to Sun Alliance Chase winner Envopak Token: has failed to complete in 2 novice chases and most points. *R. J. Armson*　　**c–**

EARLY DAWN 9 ch.m. Rakaposhi King – Early Run (Deep Run) [2002/3 h–: c21g* c20d⁴ c17s c20dᵖᵘ c20mᵖᵘ c19f Mar 27] poor pointer, successful in 2-runner race in April: made all in weak early-season novice chase at Sedgefield, only form in steeplechases: sold out of C. Grant's stable 4,000 gns Doncaster August Sales after third outing. *Miss T. McCurrich*　　**c67 h–**

EARLY EDITION 7 b.g. Primitive Rising (USA) – Ottery News (Pony Express) [2002/3 c22mᵖᵘ c20mᶠ Apr 12] tall gelding: half-brother to 2¼m hurdle winner Precis (by Pitpan): dam smart staying chaser: signs of ability in hunter chase at Newbury on debut: mistakes when out of depth next time. *O. J. Carter*　　**c– p**

EARLY MORNING CALL (IRE) 11 ch.g. Henbit (USA) – Golonig (Goldhill) [2002/3 c83: c33gᵖᵘ c26fᵖᵘ Apr 24] winning pointer, won in January (later tested positive for morphine): poor chaser: stays 3m: acts on heavy going: has had tongue tied. *D. P. Keane*　　**c–**

EARLY RISER 5 b.m. Primitive Rising (USA) – Coneygree (Northern State (USA)) [2002/3 F–: 17mᵖᵘ Jun 1] no form in 2 bumpers or maiden hurdle. *C. C. Bealby*　　**h–**

EARLY START 5 ch.m. Husyan (USA) – Gipsy Dawn (Lighter) [2002/3 F18s* F17m³ Apr 17] lengthy, rather unfurnished mare: second foal: half-sister to bumper winner Alfa Sunrise (by Alflora): dam winning hurdler, stayed 2½m: easily won maiden bumper at Fontwell on debut in February: better form when 6 lengths third of 17 to Amorello in listed mares event at Cheltenham. *J. W. Mullins*　　**F98**

EARTHMOVER (IRE) 12 ch.g. Mister Lord (USA) – Clare's Crystal (Tekoah) [2002/3 c146, h–: c24dᵖᵘ c25d* c26v* c26g⁴ c27m* c26m* Apr 17] rangy gelding: smart handicap chaser in 2001/2: did well returned to hunters (former winner of Foxhunter at Cheltenham), successful at Wetherby and Chepstow (fifth course win) within 4 days in　　**c136 h–**

Wilmot-Smith Memorial Cup (Hunters' Chase), Wetherby—
Earthmover (right) makes a successful return to hunter chase company

February and Ayr (by distance) and Cheltenham (beat Macgeorge 6 lengths, pair well clear) within 7 days in April: best at 3m+: acts on any going: prone to mistakes in competitive company (early casualty in 2 Grand Nationals): usually races prominently: game. *P. F. Nicholls*

EASIBROOK JANE   5 b.m. Alderbrook – Relatively Easy (Relkino) [2002/3 F13s F17s⁵ 16v³ 19v² 20g Mar 16] 7,800 4-y-o: tall mare: sixth foal: half-sister to 5f and 1m winner Beats Working (by Aragon) and 2m winner Uplift (by Bustino): dam, fair hurdler/chaser who stayed 3¼m, half-sister to useful 2m to 21f chaser Just Jasmine: poor form in bumpers: best effort in 3 mares novice hurdles when second to Jenga at Exeter: should stay beyond 19f. *C. Tizzard*   **h89 F72**

EASTERNKING   4 ch.f. Sabrehill (USA) – Kshessinskaya (Hadeer) [2002/3 16d 16s 17s⁵ 16v⁶ 16v⁵ 19d² 22g Mar 29] little form on Flat: poor juvenile hurdler: jumped poorly/looked less than keen final outing: likely to prove best up to 19f: acts on good to soft going: wore cheekpieces/visor after second start. *J. S. Wainwright*   **h73 §**

EASTERN PROPHETS   10 b.g. Emarati (USA) – Four Love (Pas de Seul) [2002/3 16m Jun 29] poor on Flat (stays 7f, often blinkered/visored), no form in 2002: well held in seller on hurdling debut. *Jedd O'Keeffe*   **h–**

EASTERN RED   5 b.m. Contract Law (USA) – Gagajulu (Al Hareb (USA)) [2002/3 h–: 17s Feb 13] poor maiden on Flat at 3 yrs: no sign of ability over hurdles. *Miss M. Bragg*   **h–**

EASTERN TRIBUTE (USA)   7 b.g. Affirmed (USA) – Mia Duchessa (USA) (Nijinsky (CAN)) [2002/3 h107: 18d* 16dᵘʳ 22s⁴ 16v² 20d⁶ 16s 20v* 20sᶠ 20sᵖᵘ Mar 8] sturdy gelding: fair handicap hurdler: won at Kelso in May and Ayr (beat Polish Flame 4 lengths) in January: barely stays 2¾m: raced on good going or softer (acts on heavy). *A. C. Whillans*   **h112**

EASTER PRESENT (IRE)   4 br.g. Presenting – Spring Fiddler (IRE) (Fidel) [2002/3 F16d³ Mar 6] second foal: dam unraced half-sister to fairly useful chaser up to 21f Cuban Question: well-backed favourite: 2½ lengths third of 16 to Sargasso Sea in bumper at Wincanton on debut. *Miss H. C. Knight*   **F96**

EAST HILL (IRE)   7 b.g. Satco (FR) – Sharmalyne (FR) (Melyno) [2002/3 h97: 16g⁴ 22s 21s⁴ 21g⁵ 19m² Mar 21] workmanlike gelding: chasing type: modest maiden hurdler: should stay 3m: best efforts on good/good to firm going. *G. B. Balding*   **h99**

EASTON GALE   9 b.g. Strong Gale – Laurello (Bargello) [2002/3 c120, h–: c24fᵖᵘ c24d* c24d³ Dec 14] rangy, useful-looking gelding: fairly useful handicap chaser, lightly raced nowadays: won 5-runner event at Fakenham (fourth course success) in November: should stay beyond 3m: acts on good to firm and heavy going: has broken blood vessel. *Ferdy Murphy*   **c125 h–**

EAST TYCOON (IRE)   4 ch.g. Bigstone (IRE) – Princesse Sharpo (USA) (Trempolino (USA)) [2002/3 16d* 16m⁴ 16d* Mar 10] tall, angular ex-Irish gelding: 9f winner on Flat debut at 3 yrs, useful form when runner-up both subsequent starts then left M. Grassick: fairly useful form in juvenile hurdles, successful on 2 of 3 starts, at Doncaster (beat Mirant 2 lengths) in January and Stratford (blinkered, beat Golden Flight 1¼ lengths in 15-runner event) in March, patiently ridden and easing clear on bridle from last on both occasions: failed to settle and didn't jump fluently when fourth to Well Chief in slowly-run Grade 2 at Kempton in between: will prove best around 2m: open to further improvement in handicaps in 2003/4. *Jonjo O'Neill*   **h121 p**

EASTWELL MANOR   5 b.g. Dancing Spree (USA) – Kinchenjunga (Darshaan) [2002/3 h–: 17m³ 16gF Aug 24] poor form only completed outing over hurdles: pulled hard in blinkers on debut. *Miss M. Bragg*   **h72 ?**

EASTWOOD DRIFTER (USA)   6 ch.g. Woodman (USA) – Mandarina (USA) (El Gran Senor (USA)) [2002/3 h69: 16m⁶ 16s³ 22m² 22mᵖᵘ c23g⁶ Sep 15] leggy gelding: poor maiden hurdler: well held on chasing debut: stays 2¾m: acts on firm and soft going: tried tongue tied. *B. G. Powell*   **c–**
h76

EASY COMPANY (IRE)   7 ch.g. Commanche Run – Thistle Chat (Le Bavard (FR)) [2002/3 F16m 20s³ 19mᵖᵘ Jul 4] IR 5,600 3-y-o: fifth foal: half-brother to bumper winner Parkdota (by Good Thyne) and winning pointer by Phardante: dam maiden on Flat/over hurdles: signs of only a little ability in bumper and novice hurdles early in season. *H. E. Haynes*   **h–**
F–

EASY SQUEEZY   6 b.g. Alflora (IRE) – Easy Horse (FR) (Carmarthen (FR)) [2002/3 F16s⁵ 22d 20g Apr 23] eighth known foal: half-brother to several winners, including fair hurdler Sau-Mynde (by Saumarez), stays 27f: dam, winning French jumper, half-sister to smart French hurdlers Sweet Virginia and Dazzling Horse, former dam of very smart staying hurdler Sweet Duke: fifth of 13 in bumper at Southwell: well held in novice company over hurdles. *N. A. Twiston-Davies*   **h62**
F85

EASY TIGER (FR)   5 ch.g. Sillery (USA) – Extreme Dream (FR) (Zino) [2002/3 F–: F17m⁵ May 3] has scope: pulled hard both starts in bumpers, poor form on second occasion. *N. J. Henderson*   **F67**

EAU DE COLOGNE   11 b.g. Persian Bold – No More Rosies (Warpath) [2002/3 c145, h–: c24f⁶ c25g⁶ c25d³ c25d⁴ c24s c25d⁵ c24g c21d² c24m* c24f* c25m² Apr 21] good-topped gelding: useful handicap chaser: dropped considerably in weights prior to winning at Newbury and Haydock (made all to beat Lord Rapier 9 lengths) in March: neck second of 6 to Tonoco at Wetherby, worn down only after last: stays 25f: acts on any going: usually wears headgear nowadays: ridden by promising conditional J. Davies last 3 starts. *B. G. Powell*   **c134**
h–

EAU SO SLOE   12 b.g. Baron Blakeney – Final Attraction (Jalmood (USA)) [2002/3 c–, h–: c16g c34gᵖᵘ c27gᵖᵘ c16m c19m Apr 21] compact gelding: of no account: usually blinkered. *F. L. Matthews*   **c–**
h–

EBINZAYD (IRE)   7 b.g. Tenby – Sharakawa (IRE) (Darshaan) [2002/3 c–p, h122: 18d² 16g 20d⁵ 20v 20d Feb 26] angular gelding: unseated early only run over fences: fairly useful handicap hurdler: out of form after reappearance: stays 2½m: acts on any going: sometimes let down by jumping. *L. Lungo*   **c–**
h118

Stan James Handicap Chase, Newbury—Eau de Cologne takes advantage of a drop in the weights; he leads Cassia Heights and runner-up Montifault in the back straight

William Hill Haldon Gold Cup (Limited Handicap), Exeter—Edredon Bleu is on song first time out, beating below-par rivals for the first of his three wins in 2002/3

EBONY LIGHT (IRE) 7 br.g. Buckskin (FR) – Amelioras Daughter (General Ironside) [2002/3 h97, F85: 20d³ 25d³ 20s³ 20s⁴ c20sF c20v* c25vF c20s* c20s* c26s⁴ Mar 15] tall gelding: modest hurdler: better form in novice chases: won at Newcastle in January and February (jumped badly right) and Carlisle (seemingly best effort when beating Joly Bey ½ length) in March: effective at testing 2½m and stays 27f: acts on good to firm and heavy going: consistent. *D. McCain* **c115 h99**

ECHO DU LAC (FR) 7 b.g. Matahawk – Love Dream (FR) (Platonic Love) [2002/3 h106: c20dF c24s⁴ c25spu c24d² c24s³ c22m⁴ Mar 21] sturdy gelding: has reportedly had breathing operation: fair handicap hurdler: fair chaser: won handicap at Southwell in December: good placed efforts in similar events twice after: stays 3m: acts on heavy going: sometimes tongue tied: not easy ride. *A. King* **c110 h–**

ECHO'S OF DAWN (IRE) 11 ch.g. Duky – Nicenames (IRE) (Decent Fellow) [2002/3 c115: c24v³ c24v* c28vpu c24s c21spu Mar 15] tall gelding: fair handicap chaser: made all in 6-runner event at Uttoxeter in December, only form of season: should stay beyond 3m: acts on good to firm and heavy going. *John R. Upson* **c113**

ECKLEYS PRIDE 6 b.g. Michelozzo (USA) – Marnie's Girl (Crooner) [2002/3 F17m⁵ F17m⁴ 19g⁵ Oct 6] unfurnished gelding: half-brother to poor chaser Mischievous Girl (by Funny Man), stays 27f: dam little worthwhile form: poor form in bumpers: showed nothing on hurdling debut. *C. W. Thornton* **h– F74**

ECUYER DU ROI (FR) 7 b.g. Roi de Rome (USA) – Mill's Cambric (FR) (Iron Duke (FR)) [2002/3 c108, h–: c25fpu May 15] big, workmanlike gelding: fairly useful hurdler at best (disappointing in Britain): fair chaser, lame only outing in 2002/3: stays 29f: acts on firm and soft going: tongue tied. *M. C. Pipe* **c– h–**

EDE'IFF 6 b.m. Tragic Role (USA) – Flying Amy (Norwick (USA)) [2002/3 h71: 16g⁶ 16m⁵ 16d⁶ 17sur 17d³ 16g* 17s⁴ 16s* 16s* 16d³ 16m Mar 19] leggy mare: modest hurdler: won at Ludlow in December (novice claimer) and January (seller) and at Leicester (claimer) in February: likely to prove best around 2m: acts on firm and soft going: tongue tied for all wins: takes good hold: temperamental display fourth outing. *W. G. M. Turner* **h87**

260

EDEN DANCER 11 b.g. Shareef Dancer (USA) – Dash (Connaught) [2002/3 c122d, h–: c20m^pu c16g^3 c21m^pu 20s^pu 21g^5 16g^4 17m 16d c22s^ur Dec 5] stocky gelding: winning hurdler/chaser, has lost his way completely: left M. Pipe after fourth start: stays 2½m: acts on any going: tried blinkered, not since 1998/9: usually front runner. *B. Ellison* **c–** **h–**

EDGAR GINK (IRE) 9 ch.g. Step Together (USA) – Turbo Run (Deep Run) [2002/3 c86x, h82: c24f^2 c25g^3 Apr 5] lengthy gelding: once-raced hurdler: sold out of S. Sherwood's stable £2,800 Ascot June Sales: winning pointer: fair form in 2 hunter chases, distant third to impressive Lord Atterbury in quite valuable novice at Aintree: stays 25f: acts on firm going: has had tongue tied: improved jumper. *L. Corcoran* **c95** **h–**

EDGATORIUS (IRE) 7 b.g. Phardante (FR) – Silent Shot (Random Shot) [2002/3 F83: 19d^pu Jan 24] workmanlike gelding: fell in Irish point: eighth only outing in bumpers: showed little in novice on hurdling debut. *B. Smart* **h–**

EDGELY (IRE) 8 b.g. Warcraft (USA) – Clodagh's Treasure (Tarqogan) [2002/3 h–: 21g^pu 17m^pu 24g^pu Apr 21] winning Irish pointer: no form over hurdles: tried blinkered. *K. G. Wingrove* **h–**

EDGINSWELL LASS 5 b.m. Morpeth – Oribi Gorge (IRE) (Heraldiste (USA)) [2002/3 F16m F17d Oct 22] sturdy mare: first foal: dam winning pointer: last in 2 bumpers. *J. D. Frost* **F–**

EDMO HEIGHTS 7 ch.g. Keen – Bodham (Bustino) [2002/3 16g^4 16s^pu 19d^2 16d^* 16g^* 16d^* 16g^5 16g^4 16g^ro Apr 23] smallish, leggy gelding: off 19 months before reappearance: developed into fairly useful handicap hurdler, won at Haydock in December and Catterick in January and February: good fourth to Risky Reef in valuable event at Aintree: in front when running out 3 out at Perth: races mainly around 2m: acts on good to firm and good to soft going: races prominently: genuine and consistent. *T. D. Easterby* **h116 +**

EDREDON BLEU (FR) 11 b.g. Grand Tresor (FR) – Nuit Bleue III (FR) (Le Pontet (FR)) [2002/3 c166, h–: c17g^* c16s^2 c21d^* c21d^* c16g^6 c20d^6 Apr 4] tall, useful-looking gelding: top-class chaser at best: successful in Peterborough Chase at Huntingdon for fourth consecutive year in 2001/2: won William Hill Haldon Gold Cup (Handicap) at Exeter on reappearance in November, beating Seebald 10 lengths: didn't look quite the same force after, though won 2 minor events in small fields at Wincanton: well-held sixth in Champion Chase at Cheltenham, turned in moody display (also did so final start in 2001/2) when tailed off in Grade 1 at Aintree: stays 21f: acts on good to firm and good to soft going: tongue tied: bold-jumping front runner. *Miss H. C. Knight* **c167** **h–**

EFFECTUAL 10 b.g. Efisio – Moharabuiee (Pas de Seul) [2002/3 h131: 23f^3 c25d^5 21d^5 23s c26s^* Mar 2] compact gelding: one-time smart hurdler, on the downgrade: second outing over fences, easily landed odds in weak 3¼m novice at Fontwell: acts on any going: sometimes swishes tail: capable of better over fences. *Miss Venetia Williams* **c105 p** **h124**

EFFIE GRAY 4 b.f. Sri Pekan (USA) – Rose Bouquet (General Assembly (USA)) [2002/3 16g 16m 16v^4 16d^6 Dec 4] fair maiden at best on Flat (stays 1½m): well held over hurdles, including in seller. *P. Monteith* **h–**

Connaught plc John Bull Chase, Wincanton—Edredon Bleu is found another good opportunity in Somerset for his third win; below-form Poliantas is second

EFFRONTERY (IRE) 10 ch.g. Lanfranco – Arctic Raheen (Over The River (FR))   **h–**
[2002/3 16s^{pu} Jun 9] sturdy gelding: very lightly raced and little sign of ability, including
in a point. *A. J. Chamberlain*

EFFUSIVE 10 b.g. Phardante (FR) – Bubbling (Tremblant) [2002/3 c–p, h123: 16s^5 **c–**
16d^{pu} Dec 5] useful-looking ex-Irish gelding: departed early both starts over fences: fairly   **h–**
useful handicap hurdler on his day: left T. Stack, well below form both starts in 2002/3:
raced mainly around 2m: acts on firm and good to soft going. *Jonjo O'Neill*

EGYPT 5 b.g. Green Desert (USA) – Just You Wait (Nonoalco (USA)) [2002/3 h84:   **h83**
17g 16m^5 16v* 16m^5 16g^{pu} 16g^3 16m^4 16s^4 20m* 19m^2 19m^F Oct 3] tall, quite
good-topped gelding: poor hurdler: won handicaps at Uttoxeter (ladies) in June and
Fontwell (novice) in August: stays 2½m: acts on heavy and good to firm going: visored
third to fifth starts. *Miss K. Marks*

EGYPT POINT (IRE) 6 b.g. Jurado (USA) – Cherry Jubilee (Le Bavard (FR))   **h–**
[2002/3 F–: 20v^6 Nov 28] lengthy gelding: well beaten in bumper and novice hurdle.
D. G. Bridgwater

EIBH'N ABBIE 4 b.g. Forzando – Brookhead Lady (Petong) [2002/3 17d^6 Aug 2]   **h–**
poor on Flat (stays easy 7f): looked non-stayer on hurdling debut. *P. D. Evans*

EI EI 8 b.g. North Briton – Branitska (Mummy's Pet) [2002/3 c121, h92: c20m^3 c20g^5 **c133**
c17d* c20m^2 c16d^4 c20d^6 c17d^3 c17m^5 c16g* c17g^4 c17d^2 c16d* c16v^5 16d* 16s* c16d^3 **h108**
16d 16d^6 c16f* Apr 25] sturdy gelding: useful handicap chaser: had another highly
successful season, won at Cartmel in June, Worcester in September, Southwell in November and Sandown (showed more resolution than 3 rivals, beat Ivanoph 2 lengths) in
April: took advantage of much lower handicap mark when also winning over hurdles at
Huntingdon and Southwell around turn of year: stays 2½m when emphasis is on speed:
acts on firm and soft going: headstrong front runner who jumps boldly: tremendously
tough, genuine and consistent. *M. C. Chapman*

EIGHT (IRE) 7 ch.g. Thatching – Up To You (Sallust) [2002/3 h–: 16d 16g Mar 16]   **h–**
compact gelding: modest on Flat (stays 1¾m): little encouragement in 3 races over
hurdles. *C. G. Cox*

Heathorns Handicap Chase, Sandown—
Ei Ei (left) gains a sixth win from nineteen starts in 2002/3; Ivanoph is second

EILEAN 5 b.m. Jurado (USA) – Upper Mount Street (IRE) (Strong Gale) [2002/3 F16g **F–** F17g F16m Jun 29] first foal: dam Irish bumper winner: little worthwhile form in bumpers: blinkered final outing. *C. P. Morlock*

EILEEN ALANNA (IRE) 11 b.m. Rashar (USA) – Kilcotty Wonder (Peacock (FR)) **h72 §** [2002/3 h73: 27d⁶ 27v² 26sᵖᵘ 22d 24v⁴ 22v 24f 27g⁶ Apr 19] lengthy mare: poor handicap hurdler: stays 27f: acts on heavy going: tried blinkered/in cheekpieces: unreliable. *G. F. Edwards*

ELA AGAPI MOU (USA) 10 b.g. Storm Bird (CAN) – Vaguar (USA) (Vaguely **c– §** Noble) [2002/3 c–§, h86§: 20g 24g⁶ c23dᵖᵘ Jun 8] close-coupled gelding: poor handicap **h73 §** hurdler nowadays: has failed to complete in 2 novice chases: in frame in points in 2003: stays 25f: acts on any going: tried visored, usually blinkered: lazy and unreliable. *R. S. Brookhouse*

ELAANDO 8 b.g. Darshaan – Evocatrice (Persepolis (FR)) [2002/3 h98: 16dᵖᵘ c20mᵖᵘ **c79** c22m³ 19f³ 21dᵖᵘ Oct 26] well-made gelding: seemed not to stay on completed start in **h–** novice hurdles: winning hurdler, out of form in 2002/3: stays 19f: acts on firm and good to soft going. *Mrs Merrita Jones*

ELA D'ARGENT (IRE) 4 b.f. Ela-Mana-Mou – Petite-D-Argent (Noalto) [2002/3 **h99** 17dᶠ 16g* 16m* 16d 16s⁵ 16m* Mar 31] sparely-made filly: fair on Flat (barely stays 1½m) for M. Johnston/P. Monteith: fair juvenile hurdler: won at Perth in September, Chepstow in October and Plumpton (claimer) in March, favourite each time: will prove best at 2m: acts on good to firm going: front runner. *M. C. Pipe*

ELA JAY 4 b.f. Double Eclipse (IRE) – Papirusa (IRE) (Pennine Walk) [2002/3 16dᵘʳ **h–** Dec 21] modest maiden on Flat (stays 2¼m): hampered and unseated first on hurdling debut. *H. Morrison*

ELA LA SENZA (IRE) 6 b.g. Lord Americo – Diamond Glow (Kalaglow) [2002/3 **h77 x** 17d⁴ 16d⁵ 17s⁵ 17s⁶ 17s 20vᵘʳ Feb 13] 10,000 4-y-o: rather unfurnished gelding: seventh foal: half-brother to winning pointers by Boyne Valley, Corvaro and Over The River: dam, once-raced on Flat, from family of 1000 Guineas winner Quick As Lightning: poor form over hurdles: should stay 2½m: not a fluent jumper. *N. A. Twiston-Davies*

ELA RE 4 ch.g. Sabrehill (USA) – Lucia Tarditi (FR) (Crystal Glitters (USA)) [2002/3 **h102** 16d 17g² 16gʳᵒ 17g³ 16g Apr 19] sparely-made gelding: modest maiden on Flat up to 1¼m: best effort over hurdles (trained by G. Prodromou on debut) when third to Our Armageddon in novice at Market Rasen: likely to prove best around 2m: difficult ride (ran out third start, bolted going down final outing). *C. R. Dore*

EL BANDITO (IRE) 9 ch.g. Un Desperado (FR) – Red Marble (Le Bavard (FR)) **c99 +** [2002/3 c–, h75: c21gᵖᵘ c20dᵖᵘ c20g* c19d* Mar 19] well-made gelding: modest chaser: **h–** sold out of J. H. Johnson's stable 6,500 gns Doncaster May Sales after reappearance: much improved last 2 starts, winning novice handicaps at Leicester in February and Chepstow in March: stays 2½m: acts on good to soft going (bumper winner on firm): has reportedly broken blood vessels. *R. Lee*

EL CORDOBES (IRE) 12 b.g. Torus – Queens Tricks (Le Bavard (FR)) [2002/3 **c95** c85, h–: c21g* c19g⁴ c21gᵖᵘ c21d⁴ c20d² c22s* c16vᶠ c17d³ c20g⁴ c22g³ c21m³ Apr 21] **h–** lengthy gelding: modest handicap chaser: won at Fakenham in May and Market Rasen in December: successful at 2¾m, effective over much shorter: acts on firm and soft going: headstrong, usually front runner. *Mrs J. R. Buckley*

EL DIVINO (GER) 8 b.g. Platini (GER) – Eivissa (GER) (Frontal) [2002/3 h88: 16s **h– §** Jun 13] compact gelding: useful on Flat (stays 8.5f) in Germany, well held only start in Britain: modest form at best over hurdles: has looked none too keen. *Ian Williams*

EL DON 11 b.g. High Kicker (USA) – Madam Gerard (Brigadier Gerard) [2002/3 c–x, **c– x** h–: 17gᵖᵘ 17m 17gᵖᵘ Apr 21] tall gelding: let down by jumping over fences: one-time **h–** fairly useful handicap hurdler, no longer of any account: tried blinkered. *B. Scriven*

ELECTRIC NELLIE 6 gr.m. Neltino – Alternation (FR) (Electric) [2002/3 F17dᵘʳ **F73** F16m⁵ F16s F16g³ F17m Apr 17] sturdy mare: first foal: dam 2¾m hurdles winner, also successful on Flat: poor form in bumpers. *S. Gollings*

ELEGANT CLUTTER (IRE) 5 b.g. Petorius – Mountain Hop (IRE) (Tirol) **h–** [2002/3 16d 16dᵖᵘ Apr 9] ex-Irish gelding: third living foal: half-brother to fairly useful German 7.5f and 1¼m winner Poccino (by Desert King): dam poor half-sister to very smart Flat stayer Mr Dinos: once-raced on Flat: maiden hurdler, modest form at best: no show both starts in 2002/3: raced at 2m on going softer than good: tongue tied on debut. *R. N. Bevis*

ELEGANT FAN (USA) 8 b. or br.g. Lear Fan (USA) – Elegance (USA) (Providential) [2002/3 h–: 20d^{pu} 16g 20g Jun 15] of no account: tried blinkered/tongue tied. *Mrs K. M. Lamb*   **h–**

ELEGANT KNIGHT 6 ch.g. Elegant Monarch – Night Bloomer (USA) (Told (USA)) [2002/3 F16g F17d 16d Mar 19] fourth foal: dam signs of ability on Flat/none over hurdles: well held in 2 bumpers (left Mrs S. Gardner after first) and novice hurdle. *R. H. Alner*   **h–** **F–**

ELENAS RIVER (IRE) 7 br.g. Over The River (FR) – Elenas Beauty (Tarqogan) [2002/3 c114p, h100: c24g^F c20s^{ur} c24g⁴ c23s c22m² 24m³ Apr 8] rather sparely-made gelding: fair hurdler/novice chaser: stays 3m: has won on soft going, best form under less testing conditions. *Miss H. C. Knight*   **c111** **h105**

ELFEET BAY (IRE) 8 b.g. Yashgan – Marjoram (Warpath) [2002/3 17g⁶ 20m Apr 12] ex-Irish gelding: half-brother to winning pointer Elfeet Castle (by Carlingford Castle): dam modest 2m hurdler: modest in bumpers: little worthwhile form over hurdles: tried blinkered. *Mrs L. Williamson*   **h–**

EL FUEGO (FR) 11 b.g. Dauphin du Bourg (FR) – Norade (FR) (Shafaraz (FR)) [2002/3 c–, h152: 21s⁵ 25d⁴ 19s⁶ 20s 24v³ 20v⁴ 19d³ 21s^F 18v⁶ 19s⁶ Mar 23] sturdy gelding: winning chaser: smart hurdler: hasn't won since 2000/1, usually contesting Group contests at Auteuil, best efforts in 2002/3 when in frame second, fifth (third to Laveron in Grand Prix d'Automne) and sixth (fourth to Katiki in Prix Leon Olry-Roederer) starts: below best last 2 outings: effective around 2½m and stays 25f: raced on good going or softer (acts on heavy): usually blinkered. *B. Barbier, France*   **c–** **h152**

ELGAR 6 ch.g. Alflora (IRE) – School Run (Deep Run) [2002/3 h100p, F–: 20g Mar 2] big, strong gelding: type to make a chaser: promising second in novice on hurdling debut when trained by N. Twiston-Davies: well beaten in similar event at Huntingdon 11 months later: staying type. *G. H. Yardley*   **h–**

EL HAMRA (IRE) 5 gr.g. Royal Abjar (USA) – Cherlinoa (FR) (Crystal Palace (FR)) [2002/3 17v Feb 11] fair on Flat (probably stays 9.4f), lost form in 2002, sold out of B. McMahon's stable 7,000 gns Newmarket Autumn Sales: no show in novice on hurdling debut. *M. J. Haynes*   **h–**

EL HOMBRE 5 b.g. Afzal – Dunsilly Bell (London Bells (CAN)) [2002/3 F14d F16d³ Dec 14] 5,500 4-y-o: good-topped gelding: eighth foal: half-brother to 3 winners, including modest hurdler/chaser Dragon King (by Rakaposhi King), stays 3¼m: dam, Irish maiden best up to 7f, ran once over hurdles: modest form both starts in bumpers, third to Radcliffe in maiden at Fakenham. *C. C. Bealby*   **F82**

EL HOMBRE DEL RIO (IRE) 6 ch.g. Over The River (FR) – Hug In A Fog (IRE) (Strong Gale) [2002/3 F91: 17v² 24s⁴ 24s² 24d² 26d³ 24m² Mar 21] rangy gelding: fair maiden hurdler: should stay beyond 3m: yet to race on firm going, acts on any other: has got on edge: often looks hard ride (may benefit from headgear). *R. H. Alner*   **h104**

ELJAY'S BOY 5 b.g. Sir Harry Lewis (USA) – Woodland Flower (Furry Glen) [2002/3 F16d F17g² Apr 19] 18,000 4-y-o: tall, useful-looking gelding: third foal: half-brother to fair hurdler/fairly useful chaser up to 2½m Stamparland Hill (by Gildoran): dam winning staying hurdler/chaser: better effort in bumpers (green on debut) when second to Special Conquest in maiden at Newton Abbot. *P. F. Nicholls*   **F91**

ELJUTAN (IRE) 5 b.g. Namaqualand (USA) – Camarat (Ahonoora) [2002/3 h100: 18s Feb 3] workmanlike gelding: fair form in juvenile hurdles in 2001/2 for R. O'Sullivan, well held after 14-month absence, only outing in 2002/3: raced around 2m: acts on good to firm going. *J. Joseph*   **h–**

ELLA CARISA 4 b.f. Elmaamul (USA) – Salty Girl (IRE) (Scenic) [2002/3 16d⁶ 18d Dec 10] leggy filly: modest maiden on Flat (stays 2m): showed nothing in 2 juvenile hurdles. *A. Charlton*   **h–**

ELLAMINE 9 b.m. Warrshan (USA) – Anhaar (Ela-Mana-Mou) [2002/3 c84, h93: 22g* 16m³ 20m 17f² 17f² 17m² 19s^{pu} 17s 19m⁵ Apr 8] sparely-made mare: poor form on completed outing over fences: modest handicap hurdler: won seller at Newton Abbot in June: effective at 2m to 2¾m: acts on firm and good to soft going, possibly not on softer: ran creditably when visored fifth/sixth starts: often tongue tied. *M. C. Pipe*   **c–** **h95**

ELL-EMM-ESS 8 b.m. Golden Heights – Four M'S (Majestic Maharaj) [2002/3 h–: 24m^{pu} 20d^F 20g^{pu} Aug 24] plain, sparely-made mare: no form: headstrong. *Mrs N. S. Sharpe*   **h–**

ELLEN'S ROCK 5 b.m. Rock Hopper – Hellene (Dominion) [2002/3 F14d Nov 25] **F–**
600Y: small mare: half-sister to 6f winner Sideloader Special (by Song) and 5f winner
D'Marti (by Emarati): dam unraced: well held in bumper on debut. *Paul Johnson*

ELLE ROSEADOR 4 b.f. El Conquistador – The Hon Rose (Baron Blakeney) **F85**
[2002/3 F16m⁴ F18f² Apr 24] first foal: dam unraced: fair form when in frame in bumpers
at Wincanton and Fontwell. *M. Madgwick*

ELLE ROYAL (IRE) 4 br.f. Ali-Royal (IRE) – Silvretta (IRE) (Tirol) [2002/3 17s **h–**
16v⁵ 18sᵘʳ 17g Mar 16] disappointing maiden on Flat: little show over hurdles.
T. P. McGovern

ELLIE MOSS 5 b.m. Le Moss – Kayella (Fine Blade (USA)) [2002/3 F16d Mar 8] **F71**
fifth foal by thoroughbred stallion: half-sister to fairly useful chaser around 2m Fine
Harvest and winning pointer Just Ben (both by Oats): dam maiden half-sister to dam of
useful 2m chaser Mister Oddy: 24 lengths seventh of 13 in mares maiden bumper at
Warwick on debut. *R. Dickin*

ELLO OLLIE (IRE) 8 b.g. Roselier (FR) – Kayanna (Torenaga) [2002/3 c78x, h91: **c– x**
20d² 24g⁵ May 11] close-coupled gelding: modest handicap hurdler: poor chaser: stays **h89**
3¼m: raced on good going or softer (acts on soft): effective blinkered or not: makes
mistakes over fences. *Andrew Turnell*

EL MONTY (IRE) 8 b.g. Montelimar (USA) – Tax Code (Workboy) [2002/3 h126: **h–**
22sᵖᵘ Dec 7] useful-looking gelding: fairly useful hurdler, lightly raced (has reportedly
had leg trouble and been fired): pulled up and dismounted seventh only outing in 2002/3:
better suited by 2½m than shorter: acts on good to soft going. *R. H. Alner*

EL PASO III (FR) 11 br.g. Video Rock (FR) – La Salamandre (FR) (Pot d'Or (FR)) **c159 §**
[2002/3 c159, h154: c22s² c29s* c22d* 20s* c22s* c27vᵖᵘ 19s⁴ c22s³ Apr 13] tall, rangy **h139 §**
gelding: useful hurdler nowadays, won minor event at Auteuil in September: one-time
top-class chaser, very smart at best in 2002/3: won Grand Steeple-Chase de Paris
(finished second to Double Car, later awarded race) in May, Prix des Drags in June and
Group 3 Prix Heros XII (beat Fustrien du Paon 2 lengths) in October, all at Auteuil:
increasingly temperamental and mostly well below best subsequently: stays 29f: raced on
good ground or softer (acts on heavy): tried blinkered. *B. Secly, France*

EL PEDRO 4 b.g. Piccolo – Standard Rose (Ile de Bourbon (USA)) [2002/3 16d 16g **h83**
17s Jan 14] leggy, lengthy gelding: half-brother to winning hurdler in Germany by
Interrex: dam fair hurdler, stayed 3m: modest on Flat (stays easy 1½m): mid-division at
best in 3 juvenile hurdles: likely to need sharp 2m: may yet do better. *M. R. Channon*

EL PENYON 6 b.g. Rock Hopper – Capel Lass (The Brianstan) [2002/3 F16g F17s **F–**
F16g Apr 2] 1,200 3-y-o, £4,000 5-y-o: unfurnished gelding: half-brother to 1990 2-y-o
5f winner Midnight Lass (by Today And Tomorrow): dam never ran: no sign of ability in
bumpers. *J. W. Mullins*

ELSARONI 9 ch.g. Primitive Rising (USA) – Malmo (Free State) [2002/3 h89: c20m⁶ **c–**
May 8] workmanlike gelding: modest novice hurdler: well held only start over fences: **h–**
best efforts at 2½m: blinkered last 2 starts in 2001/2: dead. *P. Beaumont*

ELTIGRI (FR) 11 b.g. Mistigri – Obepine II (FR) (Quart de Vin (FR)) [2002/3 c24s⁵ **c116**
c24s* Dec 28] rather leggy gelding: fairly useful handicap chaser, lightly raced (missed **h–**
2001/2): probably needed reappearance, back to best to win at Newbury by 4 lengths
from Midnight Gunner: should stay beyond 3¼m: raced on going softer than good (acts
on heavy): less than reliable. *A. Ennis*

ELUNA 5 ch.m. Unfuwain (USA) – Elisha (GER) (Konigsstuhl (GER)) [2002/3 h118: **c83 p**
c16d⁴ c19d⁵ 19m⁶ 21m⁶ Apr 17] lengthy, sparely-made mare: fairly useful hurdler **h115**
respectable sixth to Blue Ride in listed mares handicap at Cheltenham (tongue tied):
shaped better than distance beaten suggests in 2 novice chases: stays 21f: acts on good to
firm and heavy going: edgy sort: capable of better over fences. *Ian Williams*

EL VAQUERO (IRE) 5 ch.g. Un Desperado (FR) – Marble Fontaine (Lafontaine **F98**
(USA)) [2002/3 F16d* F17g Apr 5] rangy gelding: third foal: dam, placed in 2m Irish
hurdle, from family of useful 2m hurdler Unarmed (by Un Desperado): 9/2, won 20-
runner bumper at Huntingdon on debut in December by 2½ lengths from Captain
Flinders: under pressure by halfway when below that form in Grade 2 at Aintree.
Miss H. C. Knight

ELVERA 5 b.m. Elmaamul (USA) – Bewitch (Idiot's Delight) [2002/3 F16g F17m Apr **F–**
15] first foal: dam, second in bumper, half-sister to useful chaser up to 21f First Love, out
of half-sister to high-class staying chaser Spanish Steps: signs of ability on first of 2
outings in bumpers. *J. M. Bradley*

McCabe Builders Ltd Boyne Hurdle, Navan—Emotional Moment leads at the last, outpacing No Discount and runner-up Over The Bar in a steadily-run contest

EL VIEJO (IRE)   6 b.g. Norwich – Shuil Na Gale (Strong Gale) [2002/3 h116, F101:   **h116** 21g³ 24gᵖᵘ Sep 28] rangy, useful-looking gelding: fairly useful bumper winner/winning hurdler: reportedly struck into himself when pulled up at Market Rasen: should stay beyond 21f: raced on good going or softer. *L. Wells*

ELVIS   10 b.g. Southern Music – Tyqueen (Tycoon II) [2002/3 c95, h95: c20dF 21v⁴ 18s   **c–** 18v⁶ 18gᵇᵈ 16m 16m² Apr 19] strong, lengthy gelding: modest form on second completed   **h87 +** outing over fences: modest hurdler: best around 2m: acts on firm and soft going: tried blinkered/visored: headstrong (has been early to post). *L. Wells*

ELVIS (FR)   7 ch.g. Red Paradise – Safari Liz (USA) (Hawaii) [2002/3 c21s² c24m²   **c93** Jun 28] ex-French gelding: runner-up over 2m on second of 2 starts on Flat: modest form   **h–** over hurdles, in frame twice at Enghien in 1999/00 for T. Civel: easily won only start in points in May: runner-up in 2 novice chases, modest form on second occasion: stays 3m: acts on heavy and good to firm going. *R. Waley-Cohen*

ELVIS REIGNS   7 b.g. Rock City – Free Rein (Sagaro) [2002/3 c–, h–: 16m c17s*   **c97** c20s³ c20v⁵ c16d⁶ c16v² c16d⁴ c16v⁴ c16g c16d³ c16s⁵ c16f³ c16m³ Apr 21] sturdy   **h–** gelding: winning hurdler in France: modest chaser: won novice handicap at Cartmel in June: in-and-out form subsequently, left F. Murphy after eighth start: stays 2½m: acts on any going: tried blinkered/in cheekpieces: of suspect temperament. *M. D. Hammond*

EL ZITO (IRE)   6 b.g. Mukaddamah (USA) – Samite (FR) (Tennyson (FR)) [2002/3   **h–** h116: 19sᵖᵘ 16d Dec 21] workmanlike gelding: fairly useful hurdler: off 19 months, little show both starts on return: should stay beyond 17f: acts on soft going: usually tongue tied: front runner. *R. Brotherton*

EMALI   6 b.g. Emarati (USA) – Princess Poquito (Hard Fought) [2002/3 h–: 17fᵖᵘ   **c–** c16sᵖᵘ c19f⁴ Apr 3] good-bodied gelding: winning pointer: no form over hurdles or in   **h–** novice chases, reportedly lame last 2 starts: tongue tied. *Mrs H. E. Rees*

EMERALD MIST (IRE)   4 b.f. Sacrament – Jade's Gem (Sulaafah (USA)) [2002/3   **h61** 17s⁵ 19d 18s⁶ 19g⁶ 21mʳᵒ Apr 19] poor maiden on Flat (seems to stay 1½m): poor novice hurdler: probably stays 21f (would have performed creditably but for running out last final start). *G. B. Balding*

EMLEY   7 b.m. Safawan – Bit of A State (Free State) [2002/3 17m Jul 17] no longer of   **h–** any account on Flat: no show on hurdling debut. *N. Wilson*

EMMA HAMILTON   6 b.m. Karinga Bay – Tharita (Thatch (USA)) [2002/3 F16m⁶   **h–** F17m F16d 19fᵖᵘ Mar 27] 1,400 4-y-o: sixth foal: half-sister to winning pointer   **F–** Childsway (by Salmon Leap): dam lightly-raced daughter of useful sprinter Mi Favorita: little sign of ability. *C. J. Gray*

EMMET (IRE)   5 b.g. Supreme Leader – Virginia Ironside (General Ironside) [2002/3   **h110** 18s* 22s* 22v⁵ 22d Mar 22] fourth known living foal: half-brother to 2½m bumper winner/winning 2¾m hurdler Miss Information (by Commanche Run): dam maiden: successful on completed start in point: well held in bumper: successful first 2 starts over hurdles, in 5-y-o maiden at Fairyhouse (dead-heated) and novice at Thurles in January: below best last 2 starts, looking ill at ease on course at Clonmel on first occasion: stays 2¾m: acts on soft ground. *E. J. O'Grady, Ireland*

EMOTIONAL MOMENT (IRE) 6 b.g. Religiously (USA) – Rosceen Bui (IRE)   **h140**
(Phardante (FR)) [2002/3 16s* 16v* 16s* 16s⁴ 24d* 21g⁴ 20d⁴ Apr 4] leggy gelding: first
foal: dam, maiden hurdler, half-sister to useful hurdler up to 3¼m Crank Shaft: useful
hurdler: had excellent season, winning handicaps at Wexford in October, Down Royal
(valuable event) in November and Navan in December, and Grade 2 McCabe Builders
Ltd Boyne Hurdle at Navan (showed best turn of foot in steadily-run race when beating
Over The Bar 5 lengths) in February: creditable fourth in valuable handicaps at
Cheltenham and Aintree last 2 outings, getting very agitated when having shoe removed
prior to start at latter course: effective at 2m to 3m: raced on good going or softer (acts on
heavy): tough and consistent. *T. J. Taaffe, Ireland*

EMPEREUR RIVER (FR) 11 b.g. Riverquest (FR) – Nuit Des Fanges (FR) (Trac)   **c?**
[2002/3 c26dF c29s⁴ c25g² c30s⁵ c25d* c28v⁵ c31v⁴ c23d³ c36dpu Apr 5] smallish,
angular gelding: leading cross-country chaser in France, won at Pau in December: 250/1,
not fluent and soon trailing in Grand National at Aintree final start: stays long distances:
raced on good going or softer (acts on heavy): usually front runner. *J. Ortet, France*

EMPEROR ROSS (IRE) 8 b. or br.g. Roselier (FR) – Gilded Empress (Menelek)   **c122 +**
[2002/3 c85+, h92: c25d* c24d* c20m* c32mF c27m* c24dpu c20g² Apr 23] useful-   **h–**
looking gelding: reportedly had 3 wind operations: fairly useful novice chaser: won at
Hexham (twice), Perth (handicap) and Sedgefield between May and July: will prove best
at 2¾m+: acts on good to firm and good to soft going: tongue tied: usually jumps well.
N. G. Richards.

EMPERORS GUEST 5 b.g. Emperor Jones (USA) – Intimate Guest (Be My Guest   **h118**
(USA)) [2002/3 h124: 16d 16s⁵ 16sF 16d 16g 16m Apr 22] tall gelding: fairly useful
hurdler, generally below form in handicaps in 2002/3 (best effort on second start): raced
at 2m: acts on heavy going: tried in cheekpieces. *Patrick Mullins, Ireland*

EMPEROR'S MAGIC (IRE) 12 ch.g. Over The River (FR) – Sengirrefcha   **c119**
(Reformed Character) [2002/3 c108, h–: c24dF c22s⁶ c24d* c19g⁴ c25d³ c20g* c22g²   **h–**
c24m³ c24g⁵ Apr 25] lengthy gelding: fairly useful handicap chaser: won at Newcastle in
November and Market Rasen in March: effective at 2½m to 25f: acts on good to firm
and heavy going: tried visored, usually wears cheekpieces: effective tongue tied or not:
patiently ridden: consistent. *R. C. Guest*

Watercork Syndicate's "Emotional Moment"

EMPHATIC (IRE)   8 ch.g. Ela-Mana-Mou – Sally Rose (Sallust) [2002/3 22d² 22s³   h102
22d⁴ 26g* 26m² 27f⁵ Apr 24] small gelding: fair handicap hurdler: won at Huntingdon in
March: stays 3¼m: acts on heavy and good to firm going: usually blinkered/visored, has
also won when not: usually makes running: lazy. *J. G. Portman*

EMPIRE PARK   8 b.g. Tragic Role (USA) – Millaine (Formidable (USA)) [2002/3   c–
c–, h108: 21m³ 20s* 26m* 22v* 22s⁶ 24d 21d* 22vᵖᵘ 24g 24d 24g⁵ Mar 3] smallish   h112
gelding: fair hurdler: won claimers at Worcester and Southwell in August and handicaps
at Newton Abbot in November and Huntingdon in January: well below form subsequently: won at 3¼m, best form up to 2¾m: acted on any going: wore blinkers (visored
once): dead. *C. R. Egerton*

EMPRESS ALICE   6 b.m. Petoski – Blue Empress (Blue Cashmere) [2002/3 h–:   c–
16mᴿ 16mᵖᵘ Nov 9] no sign of ability, including on Flat: left R. Peacock before   h–
final start: headstrong. *Dr P. Pritchard*

EMPRESS STREAMLINE   7 b.m. Emperor Fountain – Judys Line (Capricorn   h–
Line) [2002/3 17sᵘʳ 16dᵖᵘ 22dᵖᵘ Feb 6] no sign of ability. *R. H. Alner*

EM'S ROYALTY   6 b.g. Royal Fountain – Gaelic Empress (Regular Guy) [2002/3   h100 p
20v³ Feb 8] third foal: dam winning pointer: shaped encouragingly when third in novice
hurdle at Ayr on debut: should improve. *A. Parker*

ENCHANTED COTTAGE   11 b.g. Governor General – Mitsubishi Colour (Cut   c–
Above) [2002/3 c–, h71: 21m⁵ 20sᵖᵘ 22s 21m 21mⁿʳ Apr 19] lengthy gelding: poor   h– §
handicap hurdler: became temperamental in 2002/3: best around 2½m: acts on any going:
visored/blinkered once: one to avoid. *D. M. Grissell*

ENCHANTED FLIGHT   7 b.m. Access Travel – Fair Enchantress (Enchantment)   h–
[2002/3 16d 20sᵖᵘ 19m⁵ 22mᵖᵘ Jul 14] first foal: dam 5f/point winner: no form over
hurdles or in points: tried blinkered: has looked temperamental. *C. N. Kellett*

ENCORE CADOUDAL (FR)   5 b.g. Cadoudal (FR) – Maousse (FR) (Labus (FR))   h101
[2002/3 F91: 20d⁶ 16d³ 19d 16m⁵ Mar 20] leggy gelding: fair novice hurdler: will prove
best around 2m: will try to race on extremes of going. *M. C. Pipe*

ENDLESS MAGIC (IRE)   8 br.g. Zaffaran (USA) – Merillion (Touch Paper)   h122
[2002/3 h124d: 19v 16s⁵ 20s³ 20m* Apr 19] good sort: chasing type: winning pointer:
fairly useful handicap hurdler: back to best when winning at Cork in April: stays 2½m:
acts on soft and firm going, well beaten on heavy. *E. J. O'Grady, Ireland*

END OF AN ERROR   4 b.f. Charmer – Needwood Poppy (Rolfe (USA)) [2002/3 16s   h67
16d 17m⁴ Apr 21] modest 1m winner at 2 yrs for B. McMahon, below form on Flat since:
poor form over hurdles. *M. C. Chapman*

EN EL EM FLYER   8 b.g. Seymour Hicks (FR) – Sound 'n' Rhythm (Tudor Rhythm)   h67
[2002/3 h–, F73: 22s 25v² 24v³ Dec 20] poor maiden hurdler: stays 25f: acts on heavy
ground. *R. Curtis*

ENGAGED   8 b.g. St Ninian – Betrothed (Aglojo) [2002/3 c–: c20sᵘʳ c20dᶠ Mar 15]   c–
well-made gelding: runner-up in maiden point in 2001: yet to complete in steeplechases:
has worn cheekpieces. *T. D. Walford*

ENHANCER   5 b.g. Zafonic (USA) – Ypha (USA) (Lyphard (USA)) [2002/3 F87+:   F103 +
F16f* F16g* Mar 17] good-topped gelding: fairly useful in bumpers, successful all 3
starts, including at Hexham in September and Wetherby (beat Sir Rowland Hill 8 lengths)
in March: sold to join Mrs L. Jewell 67,000 gns Doncaster May Sales. *G. A. Swinbank*

ENITSAG (FR)   4 ch.g. Pistolet Bleu (IRE) – Rosala (FR) (Lashkari) [2002/3 F12d*   h104
F13s* 17s* 17d⁶ 16g 17g* Apr 19] leggy gelding: first foal: dam 7.5f to 1½m winner in   F93
France: successful both starts in bumpers, at Newbury in November and Exeter in
December: fair form over hurdles: won novice at Bangor in February and handicap at
Newton Abbot (hung right) in April: unlikely to stay beyond 2m: acts on soft going.
M. C. Pipe

ENNEL BOY (IRE)   10 ch.g. Torus – Golden Symphony (Le Moss) [2002/3 c–, h88:   c–
24d² 27m³ 24mᵖᵘ 24m⁵ Apr 26] close-coupled gelding: no form in steeplechases: fair   h106
hurdler: best at 3m+: acts on firm and good to soft going. *N. M. Babbage*

ENRIQUE (GER)   8 ch.g. Niniski (USA) – Eicidora (GER) (Surumu (GER)) [2002/3   c–
c140, h–: c33mᵖᵘ Apr 12] tall gelding: useful handicap chaser in 2001/2: off a year but fit,   h–
pulled up long way out in Scottish Grand National at Ayr: stays 33f when conditions
aren't testing: has won on soft going, best form on good/good to firm: well below form
only outing in blinkers: no easy ride, and usually held up: has made mistakes. *P. J. Hobbs*

ENTERTAINER (IRE) 7 b.g. Be My Guest (USA) – Green Wings (General Assembly (USA)) [2002/3 c–, h126: 24s 20s c20d⁵ 21v² 20s⁶ 18g⁴ 16g⁶ Apr 23] good-topped gelding: has reportedly had surgery for sinus problem: well held both starts over fences: formerly fairly useful handicap hurdler: well below best in 2002/3, leaving P. Nicholls after fourth start: stays 2½m: acts on soft and good to firm going: tried blinkered: of suspect temperament. *A. R. Dicken*   **c–** **h109**

ENTREE (FR) 4 b.f. Ela-Mana-Mou – Easter Baby (Derrylin) [2002/3 F12d⁶ F16d² Mar 8] fourth known foal: half-sister to 2m winner Kintbury (by Kylian): dam winning 2m hurdler: better effort in bumpers when second in mares maiden at Warwick. *P. D. Cundell*   **F87**

ENVIOUS 4 ch.g. Hernando (FR) – Prima Verde (Leading Counsel (USA)) [2002/3 16g⁶ 16m 16d Nov 15] good-topped gelding: modest maiden on Flat (stays 1¼m): poor form in juvenile hurdles. *R. Allan*   **h67**

ENVIRONMENT AUDIT 4 ch.g. Kris – Bold And Beautiful (Bold Lad (IRE)) [2002/3 16d 16s⁴ 16d⁴ 16s² 17s 16v⁶ 16g⁴ Mar 2] good-topped gelding: bad mover: fairly useful on Flat (stays 1½m), sold out of B. Hills's stable 19,000 gns Newmarket July Sales: modest juvenile hurdler: will stay beyond 2m: acts on soft ground. *J. R. Jenkins*   **h88**

ENZO DE BAUNE (FR) 6 b.g. En Calcat (FR) – Pure Moon (FR) (Pure Flight (USA)) [2002/3 c17g c18v⁶ c21vᵖᵘ c24s⁴ c20s⁴ c16d⁴ c16v⁴ c16gᵘʳ c21d² c20g* Apr 21] good-topped ex-French gelding: tenth foal: brother to winning cross-country chaser Fee de Baune and half-brother to 3 winners, including fairly useful chaser up to 2¾m Tenor de Baune (by Shafaraz): dam winning hurdler around 2m, also won over 11f on Flat: thrice-raced on Flat: modest novice chaser, trained by P. Cottin until after fourth start: made all in handicap at Carlisle: raced up to 21f in Britain: acts on good to soft going: tried blinkered: races freely: has jumped right. *G. A. Harker*   **c98**

EOINS PRIDE (IRE) 8 b.g. Houmayoun (FR) – Cheeky Chic (Laurence O) [2002/3 c24s⁶ c20d⁴ 16g c21m⁶ c24f c31d⁴ c31d² c18vᶠ c24s c20sᵖᵘ Mar 16] lengthy gelding: fourth foal: half-brother to fair hurdler/fairly useful chaser Linda's Boy (by Phardante), stays 3m, and fair hurdler Coolamill (by Millfontaine), stays 21f: dam 2½m bumper winner: once-raced hurdler: winning hunter chaser: apparently improved efforts when in frame in cross-country events at Cheltenham sixth and seventh starts: well below that level when second in similar contest at Punchestown in late-April: stays 31f: acts on heavy ground: has had tongue tied. *E. Bolger, Ireland*   **c120 ?** **h–**

EPERVIER D'OR (FR) 5 b.g. Epervier Bleu – Magdor (FR) (Magwal (FR)) [2002/3 c16g* c17d* c16s* c16g² c20m⁵ Feb 22] big, leggy, rather raw-boned ex-French gelding: first foal: dam fairly useful hurdler/chaser around 2m in France: placed twice around 11f on Flat: fair form in 2 juvenile hurdles for G. Cherel in 2001/2, winning at Enghien: fairly useful novice chaser: won at Wetherby in November and Exeter and Kempton in December: good second of 5 to Farmer Jack at last-named track in January: should have stayed 2½m: raced mainly on good going or softer (acted on heavy): tongue tied last 4 starts: broke blood vessel final outing: jumped fluently: dead. *P. F. Nicholls*   **c127** **h–**

EPICURE (FR) 6 b. or br.g. Northern Crystal – L'Epicurienne (FR) (Rex Magna (FR)) [2002/3 h–, F–: 17s* 17g* 20d* 17m² 20gᵖᵘ 16s⁵ 17s 17d 19sᵖᵘ 17sᵖᵘ Feb 27] unfurnished gelding: fair hurdler: much improved early in season, won novice at Newton Abbot in May and handicaps there in June and Bangor in August: lost his form after fourth start: stays 2½m: acts on soft and good to firm going. *M. C. Pipe*   **h114 d**

EPITRE (FR) 6 b.g. Common Grounds – Epistolienne (Law Society (USA)) [2002/3 16s⁶ 16s 24vᵖᵘ Feb 15] leggy ex-French gelding: half-brother to useful French chaser Chante Reve (by Dancing Spree): smart on Flat (stays 15f), successful in minor event at Longchamp in October, left A. Fabre later in month: well beaten over hurdles: visored final outing. *M. F. Harris*   **h–**

EPOP (IRE) 6 b.g. Religiously (USA) – General Rain (General Ironside) [2002/3 22s 20d 16s 24vᵖᵘ 25dᵖᵘ Feb 25] 10,000 3-y-o: lengthy gelding: sixth foal: half-brother to bumper winner Deoch An Dorais (by Supreme Leader): dam, winning pointer, half-sister to fairly useful staying jumper Wee Windy: no sign of ability over hurdles. *J. Howard Johnson*   **h–**

EPSILO DE LA RONCE (FR) 11 b. or br.g. Le Riverain (FR) – India Rosa (FR) (Carnaval) [2002/3 c113§, h–: c21g* c20f* c21s² c22d⁶ c20d² c20m* c21g⁵ c19m⁴ Apr 21] medium-sized gelding: fairly useful hunter chaser: won well-run races at Cheltenham and Warwick in May and Ludlow in March: effective at 2½m to 3m: acts on any going: blinkered once: has found little: needs things to go his way. *S. Flook*   **c107** **h–**

EQUAL BALANCE 5 ch.g. Pivotal – Thatcher's Era (IRE) (Never So Bold) [2002/3 h–
19m^F 16m 16d Oct 23] rather leggy gelding: signs of only a little ability at 2 yrs for
M. Blanshard: tailed off both completed starts over hurdles. *C. J. Hemsley*

EQUINAME 6 b.g. Rock Hopper – Bayrouge (IRE) (Gorytus (USA)) [2002/3 F91: h64
20v 17s 24v^pu 16s 21g^6 Mar 12] lengthy gelding: poor novice hurdler: visored last 3
starts: reportedly lame final outing. *J. G. M. O'Shea*

EQUIVOCAL (IRE) 7 ch.g. Roselier (FR) – Coral Cluster (Jasmine Star) [2002/3 h99
20g^5 16s^4 19s^ur 16d 17s^3 22s^2 24s^3 24s 18s^*dis 24d^d Mar 20] IR 12,000 4-y-o: smallish,
close-coupled gelding: fourth foal: dam Irish bumper winner: modest hurdler: won maiden at Thurles
(subsequently disqualified on
technical grounds) in March: effective at 2m to 3m: acts on soft going. *M. F. Morris,
Ireland*

ERCON (IRE) 5 ch.g. Thatching – Certain Impression (USA) (Forli (ARG)) [2002/3 h–
F17g F17g^6 19g^pu 16s^pu Feb 8] workmanlike gelding: fourth foal: half-brother to useful F68
sprinter Impressive Flight (by Flying Spur) and 1m winner in Italy by Petardia: dam
unraced: signs of only a little ability in 2 bumpers: no show both starts over hurdles: sold
to join L. Waring £1,300 Ascot April Sales. *R. Hollinshead*

ERIC'S CHARM (FR) 5 b.g. Nikos – Ladoun (FR) (Kaldoun (FR)) [2002/3 F18d* F113 +
F16g* F17g^5 Apr 5] 7,200 3-y-o, 40,000 4-y-o: sixth foal: half-brother to fairly useful
hurdler/chaser around 2m Monkerhostin (by Shining Steel) and 4 winners on Flat in
France and Belgium: dam middle-distance stayer: useful form when winning bumpers
at Fontwell in February and Huntingdon (made all) in March: better than distance
beaten suggests when fifth to Classic Native in Grade 2 at Aintree, setting strong pace.
O. Sherwood

ERICS WAY 6 b.g. Man Among Men (IRE) – Gypsy Crystal (USA) (Flying Saucer) h–
[2002/3 F–: 22g^pu 20s^5 22d^5 Sep 4] lengthy gelding: no worthwhile form outside points.
P. R. Rodford

ERIN ALLEY (IRE) 10 ch.g. Be My Native (USA) – Cousin Flo (True Song) [2002/3 c74
c85, h–: c19d^5 c21s^5 c20s^3 Mar 10] sparely-made gelding: poor handicap chaser: stays h–
21f: acts on heavy going: has broken blood vessel. *D. J. Wintle*

ERINS LASS (IRE) 6 b.m. Erins Isle – Amative (Beau Charmeur (FR)) [2002/3 h66: h71
19m 17m^2 19g^2 23d 19d^6 Nov 26] rather leggy, workmanlike mare: poor maiden hurdler:
stays 19f: acts on good to firm and good to soft going. *R. Dickin*

ERNE LADY (IRE) 6 b.m. Mandalus – Clonalig Lady (Deep Run) [2002/3 24d^pu h–
Feb 7] IR £2,000 4-y-o: lengthy, unfurnished mare: fourth foal: sister to winning pointer:
dam lightly raced in bumpers: runner-up in Irish point on debut in 2002: little encouragement in novice on hurdling debut. *Mrs L. C. Taylor*

ERNEST LLEWELLYN 6 b.g. Afzal – Little Gift (Broadsword (USA)) [2002/3 F–
F16m Apr 10] second foal: dam unraced: tailed off in bumper on debut. *O. O'Neill*

ERNEST WILLIAM (IRE) 11 b. or br.g. Phardante (FR) – Minerstown (IRE) c98
(Miner's Lamp) [2002/3 c117, h–: c16g^pu 21g^3 21d^pu c20d^pu c20d^4 21d^4 c22g^6 c21m^2 Apr h96
21] well-made gelding: modest hurdler/chaser nowadays: left F. Murphy after sixth start:
should stay beyond 2¾m: acts on good to firm and heavy going: has worn cheekpieces.
J. A. Supple

ERRAND BOY 9 b.g. Ardross – Love Match (USA) (Affiliate (USA)) [2002/3 c105x, c– x
h–: c26d^F May 4] strong gelding: winning hurdler: fair maiden chaser, often let down h–
by jumping: effective at testing 17f to easy 3m: acts on heavy and good to firm going.
Mrs S. J. Smith

ERRIGAL (FR) 8 ch.g. Murmure (FR) – Miss Big John (FR) (Big John (FR)) [2002/3 c–
c–, h–: 16s 22s 24d 26g^pu Feb 22] useful-looking gelding: winning hurdler, no form since h–
2000/1: tried blinkered/in cheekpieces: temperament under suspicion. *K. C. Bailey*

ERRIS EXPRESS (IRE) 5 ch.h. Definite Article – Postie (Sharpo) [2002/3 F16v h–
16d 16d Feb 26] useful-looking horse: seventh foal: brother to fairly useful 1m winner F–
Spy Game and half-brother to 5f winner Post Mistress and 6f/7f winner Posted Abroad
(both by Cyrano de Bergerac): dam unraced half-sister to useful sprinter Case Law:
shaped like a non-stayer in bumper and 2 novice hurdles. *J. J. Quinn*

ERRO CODIGO 8 b.g. Formidable (USA) – Home Wrecker (DEN) (Affiliation h55
Order (USA)) [2002/3 h57: 17s 17d^5 16m^5 17s 17d^F 16f 16m^4 17d^pu 16d Dec 4] small,
sturdy gelding: bad maiden hurdler. *F. P. Murtagh*

ESCORT 7 b.g. Most Welcome – Benazir (High Top) [2002/3 h92: 24g 20d 22m⁴ 24m⁴ 16m⁶ 20d⁴ Aug 3] sturdy gelding: poor hurdler: stays 3m: acts on good to firm and heavy going: usually visored. *W. Clay* — **h78**

ESCORT BOY (USA) 5 b.g. Dare And Go (USA) – Exactly Like You (Sassafras (FR)) [2002/3 c20sʳ c20s⁴ 17g² 18v* c20v* c23v² c26v* 19s* 17s³ c21g Apr 19] half-brother to 4 winners on Flat in USA: dam, ungenuine maiden, half-sister to smart 6f and 1¼m winner Sarania: smart hurdler: won at Lyon Villeurbane in November and Pau (well-contested minor event, beat Fustrien du Paon and Rougenoir) in January, improved form in latter: smart chaser: apparently much improved when beating Line Marine 20 lengths in 3¼m Grand Prix de Pau in January: earlier won Group 3 Prix Morgex at Auteuil (4-y-o event): effective at 2¼m given test, stays 3¼m well: raced mainly on soft/heavy going (almost certainly found conditions against him in Nakayama Grand Jump final start). *J. Ortet, France* — **c150 +** **h149**

ESENDI 8 b.g. Buckley – Cagaleena (Cagirama) [2002/3 h85: c22vᵘʳ 22d Mar 6] bought out of G. McCourt's stable 12,000 gns Doncaster August Sales: unseated third in handicap on chasing debut: modest form at best over hurdles: well held in handicap 2 months later: likely to prove best at 2½m+: acts on soft going. *Miss Venetia Williams* — **c–** **h–**

ESHBRAN LAD 6 b.g. Golden Lahab (USA) – Lansdowne Lady (Orange Bay) [2002/3 F16g⁵ F17g Apr 26] leggy gelding: fourth foal: dam unraced: better effort in bumpers when fifth of 9 at Wetherby on debut, pulled hard next time. *R. C. Guest* — **F84**

ESHER COMMON (IRE) 5 b.g. Common Grounds – Alsahah (IRE) (Unfuwain (USA)) [2002/3 16s 16d Jan 15] fair on Flat (stays 11.6f), sold out of D. Cantillon's stable £6,200 Ascot August Sales: tongue tied, raced freely both starts over hurdles, ninth of 12 in steadily-run novice at Newbury on debut. *C. J. Price* — **h78**

ESKIMO JACK (IRE) 7 ch.g. Glacial Storm (USA) – Covette (Master Owen) [2002/3 h117: c20s³ c18s* c20s* c24v³ c21s⁴ c20d² c29g Apr 21] useful-looking gelding: fairly useful hurdler: useful novice chaser: easily won maiden at Thurles in November and handicap at Navan in December: placed subsequently in valuable handicap at Leopardstown (third to Youlneverwalkalone) and novices at Naas (Grade 2) and Punchestown (in early-May, third to Beachcomber Bay): likely to prove best at 2½m+ (stays 3m): acts on heavy going. *A. L. T. Moore, Ireland* — **c131** **h–**

ESKLEYBROOK 10 b.g. Arzanni – Crystal Run VII (Damsire Unregistered) [2002/3 c138§, h76: c16s* c16m* c16gᵖᵘ Mar 13] tall gelding: smart chaser: back to best in 2002/3, won handicap at Sandown (beat Tiutchev by 2 lengths) and minor event at Kempton (by 1¼ lengths from Turgeonev) in February: best around 2m: acts on soft and — **c145** **h–**

Elmbridge Handicap Chase, Sandown—
50/1-chance Eskleybrook (centre) and Mr Dave Mansell spring one of the shocks of the season;
Tiutchev (right) is the beaten favourite, while Redemption is about to fall two out

good to firm going: tried blinkered: best making running/racing prominently (unable to dominate final outing): amateur ridden nowadays. *V. Y. Gethin*

ESPERANZA IV (FR)   11 b.m. Quart de Vin (FR) – Relizane III (FR) (Diaghilev) [2002/3 c94, h–: 24d^{pu} c24g^2 c28g^3 c24s^3 Jun 13] medium-sized mare: winning hurdler: modest handicap chaser: probably stays 3½m: acts on soft and good to firm going: blinkered twice: idles, and best with waiting tactics. *M. J. Roberts*   **c94 h–**

ESP HILL   5 ch.m. Moscow Society (USA) – Heatheridge (IRE) (Carlingford Castle) [2002/3 F17g^5 F16g^6 Apr 14] first foal: dam, of little account, from family of useful staying jumpers Sommelier and Coq Hardi Affair: signs of ability in bumpers. *L. Lungo*   **F62**

ESPRIT DE COTTE (FR)   11 b.g. Lute Antique (FR) – Rafale de Cotte (FR) (Italic (FR)) [2002/3 c26m^4 c24f^5 c21g Apr 3] round-barrelled gelding: type to carry condition: useful chaser at best: very much on downgrade, left R. Parker after reappearance: won point in April: stays 25f: acts on soft going: sometimes blinkered. *R. Gurney*   **c82 h–**

ESSIE   6 b.m. Ezzoud (IRE) – Safari Park (Absalom) [2002/3 17m Jun 1] disappointing maiden on Flat and no show on hurdling debut. *Miss M. E. Rowland*   **h–**

ESS OF NORWAY (FR)   4 gr.g. Linamix (FR) – Tres de Cem (NOR) (Rainbow Quest (USA)) [2002/3 16d^6 16g Mar 16] good-topped gelding: third foal: half-brother to French middle-distance winners Ess Express (by Subotica) and Sandra Mia (by Homme de Loi): dam unraced: much better effort over hurdles when sixth in juvenile at Newbury. *J. C. Tuck*   **h94**

ESTABELLA (IRE)   6 ch.m. Mujtahid (USA) – Lady In Green (Shareef Dancer (USA)) [2002/3 22g^{pu} 16g Dec 13] no worthwhile form over hurdles. *M. Wellings*   **h–**

ESTERS BOY   5 b.g. Sure Blade (USA) – Moheli (Ardross) [2002/3 F16g F17d 16m Apr 2] unfurnished gelding: third foal: half-brother to 2¾m hurdle winner La Mola Sun (by Henbit): dam, modest hurdler up to 2¾m, out of smart staying hurdler Mayotte, herself dam of smart hurdler/chaser Arctic Camper: signs of ability in bumpers and novice hurdle. *P. G. Murphy*   **h73 F70**

ESTUARY (USA)   8 ch.g. Riverman (USA) – Ocean Ballad (Grundy) [2002/3 h87: 16m^6 16m^3 16g^2 17m^3 Sep 13] workmanlike gelding: modest maiden hurdler: raced mainly around 2m: yet to race on extremes of going. *Ms A. E. Embiricos*   **h87**

ESTUPENDO (IRE)   6 b.g. Tidaro (USA) – Spendapromise (Goldhill) [2002/3 h–, F71: 20d 22s^4 21s^{pu} 24s^{ur} Feb 26] apparently easily best effort over hurdles when fourth in maiden at Folkestone: will stay beyond 2¾m: wore cheekpieces/blinkers last 2 outings. *L. Wells*   **h99 ?**

ETERNAL SPRING (IRE)   6 b.g. Persian Bold – Emerald Waters (Kings Lake (USA)) [2002/3 h140p: 16d^F 21d^4 24s^4 21s^F 16d^F Feb 15] workmanlike gelding: useful hurdler: won minor event at Cheltenham in December, making most in falsely-run affair to beat Classified 5 lengths: fell 3 out of other 4 starts in 2002/3: stays 21f (found little and finished very tired at 3m): acts on heavy going: tongue tied final outing. *J. R. Fanshawe*   **h140**

ETTRICK (NZ)   8 b.g. Hereward The Wake (NZ) – Kardinia (NZ) (Creag-An-Sgor) [2002/3 c–, h82: 17g* 16g^4 17m^2 17m Jun 22] workmanlike gelding: little encouragement only outing over fences: poor hurdler: won novice handicap at Hereford in May: raced mainly around 2m, should stay further: acts on soft and good to firm going, possibly unsuited by heavy: blinkered (found little) once: temperament under suspicion. *Mrs Barbara Waring*   **c– h81**

EURO BLEU (FR)   5 b.g. Franc Bleu Argent (USA) – Princess Card (FR) (Gift Card (FR)) [2002/3 18d 16v^5 17s* 20g Apr 3] useful-looking ex-French gelding: fifth foal: half-brother to winning cross-country chaser Starcom (by Come As You Are): dam maiden: thrice-raced over hurdles for E. Lemartinel, winning 5-y-o event at Pau in January: looked an excitable sort (on toes, pulled hard) when well held in Grade 2 novice at Aintree on British debut. *Mrs L. Wadham*   **h?**

EUROPA   7 b.g. Jupiter Island – Dublin Ferry (Celtic Cone) [2002/3 c128, h–: c16m* c19s* c16d^3 c19d* c20g^F Mar 12] big, well-made gelding: useful chaser: won intermediate at Perth in May and handicaps at Doncaster in December and March (beat Mr Bossman 7 lengths): let down by jumping in competitive handicap final start: should stay beyond 2½m: acts on heavy going, probably on good to firm. *T. P. Tate*   **c144 h–**

EVEIES BOY (IRE)   8 b.g. Shardari – Bloomfield (IRE) (Alzao (USA)) [2002/3 c–, h–: c16m^3 Apr 5] winning pointer, including in 2002: bought 2,200 gns Ascot July Sales: **c71 h–**

probably needed run when third in hunter chase at Hereford: tried blinkered. *Richard Mathias*

EVENING OUT   6 b.g. Charmer – Princess Dancer (Alzao (USA)) [2002/3 F16m Jul   F—
24] 650 3-y-o: fourth foal: brother to fairly useful Flat performer up to 1½m Northern
Sun: dam ran once at 2 yrs: failed to complete in 3 maiden points in 2002: showed nothing
in bumper. *P. D. Williams*

EVENING SCENT   7 b.m. Ardkinglass – Fresh Line (High Line) [2002/3 16s 16v⁴   **h121**
16v* 16s² 16s 24s³ Jan 23] sparely-made mare: fairly useful on Flat (stays 2m): fairly
useful hurdler: easily won handicap at Fairyhouse in December: good efforts when placed
in handicap at Leopardstown and Grade 3 at Gowran (third to Satco Express): effective at
2m to 3m: acts on heavy going: not a fluent jumper (made mistakes in very competitive
event fifth start). *Mrs J. Harrington, Ireland*

EVENING SPLASH (IRE)   7 b.m. Royal Fountain – Red Dusk (Deep Run) [2002/3   **h—**
F79?: F17d 22s 17s 22vᵖᵘ Jan 2] signs of a little ability in bumpers: no form in novice   **F—**
hurdles. *Mrs J. K. M. Oliver*

EVEN MORE (IRE)   8 b.g. Husyan (USA) – Milan Moss (Le Moss) [2002/3 c23d   **c98**
c25d² c32gᵖᵘ c25f³ c24g³ Apr 2] workmanlike gelding: modest pointer (has run out),
successful twice in 2002: modest novice chaser: stays 25f: acts on good to soft going.
R. H. Alner

EVER BLESSED (IRE)   11 b.g. Lafontaine (USA) – Sanctify (Joshua) [2002/3 c–,   **c—**
h–: c24dᵘʳ c26g Nov 30] well-made gelding: smart staying chaser in 1999/00: lightly   **h—**
raced and little show since. *P. J. Hobbs*

EVER PRESENT (IRE)   5 ch.g. Presenting – My Grand Rose (IRE) (Executive   **h117**
Perk) [2002/3 F18d⁵ 17s* 17s² 17s⁴ 19s⁵ Feb 27] unfurnished gelding: fourth foal: dam,   **F90**
unraced half-sister to fairly useful 2½m chaser Washingtoncrossing, from family of very
smart 1m winner Irish Minstrel: some promise in bumper on debut: good start to hurdling
career when winning novice at Bangor in November: fairly useful form next 2 starts,
disappointing final one: should be suited by further than 17f. *A. King*

Auckley Handicap Chase, Doncaster—Europa out on his own

EVERREADY 5 b.g. Afzal – Sister Shot (Celtic Cone) [2002/3 F18d⁴ F16d³ Mar 10] **F94**
ex-Irish gelding: third foal: dam once-raced sister to top-class 2m to 3m hurdler/chaser
Celtic Shot: thrice-raced in bumpers (trained by D. J. Barry when well held on debut), fair
form when in frame in 2002/3. *P. J. Hobbs*

EVIYRN (IRE) 7 b.g. In The Wings – Evrana (USA) (Nureyev (USA)) [2002/3 h74§: **h– §**
16s 22d 22gᵖᵘ Mar 17] medium-sized gelding: poor handicap hurdler: barely stays 2¾m:
acts on heavy going: sometimes visored: irresolute. *J. R. Jenkins*

EVOLUTION (IRE) 6 b.m. Phardante (FR) – Cape Breeze (IRE) (Strong Gale) **h–**
[2002/3 h65: 20s⁶ 21d 19s⁶ 23v⁶ 22v 20m⁵ 25m Mar 31] poor maiden hurdler: trained by
G. Yardley first to third starts: stays 3¼m: acts on good to firm going (bumper form on
heavy): tried blinkered. *M. J. Gingell*

EVOLUTION LAD (IRE) 7 b.g. Sharp Charter – Neatly Does It (IRE) (Camden **h–**
Town) [2002/3 h–, F82: 19mᵖᵘ 21f 17s⁶ Nov 11] bumper winner: no form over hurdles.
D. J. Caro

EWAR BOLD 10 b.g. Bold Arrangement – Monaneigue Lady (Julio Mariner) [2002/3 **h90**
h79: 21d* 16d² 24g⁶ 19m⁴ 25g⁶ 25gᵖᵘ Mar 23] leggy gelding: won novice seller at
Towcester in April by a distance, poor form over hurdles otherwise: stays 2¾m: acts on
firm and good to soft going: tried blinkered: tongue tied. *K. G. Wingrove*

EXACT (FR) 11 ch.g. Beyssac (FR) – Valse de Sienne (FR) (Petit Montmorency **c70**
(USA)) [2002/3 c78, h–: c25g⁵ Apr 7] lengthy gelding: modest hunter chaser nowadays: **h–**
stays 3m: acts on soft and good to firm going: often blinkered: has had tongue tied: has
shown signs of temperament. *Mrs R. L. Elliot*

EXALTED (IRE) 10 b.g. High Estate – Heavenward (USA) (Conquistador Cielo **c– §**
(USA)) [2002/3 c–, h103§: 24d* 20g 20d Apr 4] leggy gelding: winning hurdler, largely **h– §**
out of form since 2000/1: stays 3m: acts on good to firm and heavy going: blinkered once
(refused to race): irresolute. *T. A. K. Cuthbert*

EXCELLENT VIBES (IRE) 5 b.g. Doyoun – Hawait Al Barr (Green Desert **h–**
(USA)) [2002/3 F16s 19f⁶ 24m Apr 10] 3,000 3-y-o: half-brother to useful 1m/9f winner **F–**
Equity Princess (by Warning): dam useful up to 2m on Flat: no form in bumper or 2
novice hurdles: visored final outing. *J. L. Spearing*

EXECUTIVE CHOICE (IRE) 9 b.g. Don't Forget Me – Shadia (USA) (Naskra **h57**
(USA)) [2002/3 h93d: 16d⁶ 19g 21gᵖᵘ 22d 17g⁴ 17dᵖᵘ Oct 31] leggy gelding: winning
hurdler, retains only a little ability: left Miss V. Haigh after reappearance: tried visored,
blinkered last 3 starts: tongue tied: has looked less than keen. *B. Ellison*

EXECUTIVE DECISION (IRE) 9 ch.g. Classic Music (USA) – Bengala (FR) **c116 §**
(Hard To Beat) [2002/3 c109§, h113§: 20dᵖᵘ 16dᵖᵘ 16d² 16s⁶ 17v³ c16g* c16v³ c16m³ **h107 §**
Apr 17] rangy gelding: has had wind operation: fair handicap hurdler: left P. Hobbs after
second outing: fairly useful handicap chaser: won strongly-run event at Huntingdon in
February: best around 2m: acts on heavy and good to firm going: usually blinkered/
visored: held up: usually finds little, and not one to trust. *Mrs L. Wadham*

EXECUTIVE FLYER (IRE) 12 ch.g. Executive Perk – Luton Flyer (Condorcet **c–**
(FR)) [2002/3 17m c16m⁶ c17m⁶ c20g⁵ Aug 24] ex-Irish gelding: modest hurdler at **h–**
best: left D. O'Connell prior to reappearance: no form since 2000/1, including over
fences: raced mainly around 2m: acts on soft and good to firm going: tried tongue tied.
Mrs A. M. Thorpe

EXECUTIVE MISTRESS (IRE) 6 ch.m. Executive Perk – Buckland Filleigh **F–**
(IRE) (Buckskin (FR)) [2002/3 F16g May 22] first foal: dam won 17f maiden hurdle:
showed little in bumper on debut. *P. R. Rodford*

EXECUTIVE NETWORK 5 b.g. Silca Blanka (IRE) – Scene Stealer (Scenic) **h–**
[2002/3 17gᵖᵘ Mar 18] little form on Flat: tailed off when pulled up lame in novice seller
on hurdling debut. *A. D. Smith*

EXECUTIVE OFFICE (IRE) 10 bl.g. Executive Perk – Lilly's Pride (IRE) (Long **c86**
Pond) [2002/3 c–, h–: 25vᵖᵘ c20s* c20s* c20g⁴ c24vᵖᵘ Mar 5] leggy gelding: maiden **h–**
hurdler: modest chaser: improved efforts when winning handicaps at Warwick in January
and Leicester in February: stays easy 25f: acts on soft and good to firm going. *S. T. Lewis*

EXECUTIVE QUESTION (IRE) 5 ch.g. Executive Perk – Fair Survival (IRE) **F–**
(Le Moss) [2002/3 F16d Apr 25] first foal: dam maiden Irish pointer: well beaten in
bumper on debut. *A. Robson*

EXHIBIT (IRE) 5 b.g. Royal Academy (USA) – Juno Madonna (IRE) (Sadler's Wells (USA)) [2002/3 16d^{pu} Mar 6] fair maiden at best on Flat (stays 1m) for R. Hannon: no promise on hurdling debut. *N. J. Hawke*   **h–**

EXISTENTIAL (FR) 8 b.g. Exit To Nowhere (USA) – Lyceana (USA) (Super Concorde (USA)) [2002/3 c94, h–: c21d* c20d³ c22d⁵ c24v² c24d* c22d⁵ Mar 1] lengthy gelding: fair handicap chaser: won at Fakenham in October and Kempton (conditional jockeys) in February: stays 3m: acts on good to firm and heavy going: blinkered twice. *P. F. Nicholls*   **c113 h–**

EXIT SWINGER (FR) 8 b.g. Exit To Nowhere (USA) – Morganella (FR) (D'Arras (FR)) [2002/3 c152, h125: c20d^{ur} c21d c21v⁴ c16g c21d³ Apr 4] angular gelding: fairly useful hurdler: useful handicap chaser: back in some form last 3 starts, third of 29 to Clan Royal in Topham Chase at Aintree: stays 21f: acts on good to firm and heavy going: usually held up. *M. C. Pipe*   **c142 h–**

EXIT TO WAVE (FR) 7 ch.g. Exit To Nowhere (USA) – Hereke (Blakeney) [2002/3 c144, h–: c24d⁴ c20g³ c24v² c24m c34s^{pu} c21d^{ur} c33m^{pu} Apr 12] small, strong, compact gelding: useful handicap chaser: best efforts in 2002/3 when placed: had wind operation after third start: stays 3m: acts on heavy going, seemingly not on good to firm: blinkered final outing: tongue tied. *P. F. Nicholls*   **c141 h–**

EXODUS (ARG) 7 ch.g. Equalize (USA) – Empire Glory (ARG) (Good Manners (USA)) [2002/3 h90?: 16s³ 16m 16g³ Mar 25] angular gelding: modest novice hurdler: raced at 2m. *J. A. B. Old*   **h95**

EXOTIC PROFILES 9 ch.m. Minster Son – Ragroyal (Royal Palace) [2002/3 c17g^{pu} 22f^{ttr} May 10] light-framed mare: winning hurdler/pointer: no show on steeplechasing debut: raced mainly around 2m: acts on soft going: refused to race final start (has also done so in points) and best avoided. *Miss K. M. George*   **c– § h– §**

EXPENSE ACCOUNT (IRE) 9 b.m. Executive Perk – Cranagh Lady (Le Bavard (FR)) [2002/3 c–, h–: c20m^{ur} c25d^{pu} May 14] medium-sized mare: of little account: tried blinkered. *Mrs H. Dalton*   **c– h–**

EXSTOTO 6 b.g. Mtoto – Stoproveritate (Scorpio (FR)) [2002/3 h105, F96: 20d⁵ 21s² 19d³ 20v^{pu} 20g² 22f⁶ 20m³ Apr 21] angular gelding: fair handicap hurdler: will stay 3m: acts on firm and soft going (pulled up only run on heavy): genuine. *R. A. Fahey*   **h110**

EXTERIOR PROFILES (IRE) 13 b.g. Good Thyne (USA) – Best of Kin (Pry) [2002/3 h–, h94: 19s⁵ 19s^{pu} 16d 19d 22d⁵ 22v^F Mar 3] rangy gelding: generally let down by jumping over fences: modest hurdler: stays 27f: acts on firm and soft going: races prominently. *Miss K. M. George*   **c– h86**

EXTRA CACHE (NZ) 10 br.g. Cache of Gold (USA) – Gizmo (NZ) (Jubilee Wine (USA)) [2002/3 h107: c16f⁴ c21v² c21s^{ur} c19s* c19d⁴ c23d² c20g* c20m* Apr 21] leggy gelding: winning hurdler: fair novice chaser: won in small fields at Doncaster in December and Huntingdon in March and April: stays 21f: acts on any going: sound jumper. *O. Brennan*   **c109 h–**

EXTRA JACK (FR) 11 b.g. Neustrien (FR) – Union Jack III (FR) (Mister Jack (FR)) [2002/3 c145, h–: 20s⁵ c20g⁴ c20v² c20g⁵ c16s⁵ c17d⁵ c21d Apr 4] tall gelding: winning hurdler: useful handicap chaser, below best in 2002/3: raced around 2½m: acts on good going or softer (acts on heavy): blinkered. *P. F. Nicholls*   **c133 h–**

EXTRA PROUD 9 ch.g. Dancing High – Spring Onion (King Sitric) [2002/3 h90: c24m^{ur} c22m* c21m^{ur} c21m* c20g⁴ c24g³ c20g² c20m² Apr 19] winning hurdler: fair chaser: won novices at Kelso in May and Stratford (handicap) in July: often let down by jumping otherwise over fences: should stay 3m: acts on soft and good to firm going: tongue tied. *W. Amos*   **c111 h–**

EXTRA STOUT (IRE) 11 ch.g. Buckskin (FR) – Bold Strike (FR) (Bold Lad (USA)) [2002/3 c78, h–: c25g Apr 7] rangy gelding: winning hunter chaser, largely disappointing outside points since 1998/9: stays 25f: acts on good to soft going: has had tongue tied. *Miss J. M. Furness*   **c– h–**

EYE OF THE TIGER (IRE) 7 ch.g. Regular Guy – Banner Lady (Milan) [2002/3 16v 18s⁴ 20s 20s³ 24s 24d 22m Apr 11] eighth foal: brother to useful hurdler up to 3m Mr Red Banner and fairly useful 2m chaser/winning hurdler Irregular Planting and half-brother to winning pointer by Millfontaine and to dam of Cloudy Grey: dam unraced: fair handicap hurdler: generally well below best after second outing: should stay 2½m: acts on soft going. *S. A. Kirk, Ireland*   **h102**

EYES DONT LIE (IRE) 5 b.g. Namaqualand (USA) – Avidal Park (Horage) [2002/3 **h–**
h78?: 17s⁶ 20s⁵ 22m⁴ 22g 20m Dec 17] sturdy gelding: poor maiden hurdler: stays 2¾m:
acts on soft and good to firm going: tried blinkered/visored: has had tongue tied.
D. A. Nolan

EYES TO THE RIGHT (IRE) 4 ch.g. Eagle Eyed (USA) – Capable Kate (IRE) **h68**
(Alzao (USA)) [2002/3 16d⁶ 16sᵖᵘ 16s 16g⁶ 16g⁴ 16m⁵ 16mᵘʳ Apr 21] leggy gelding:
poor on Flat (stays 1¼m): poor juvenile hurdler: sold out of P. McEntee's stable £1,500
Ascot April Sales before final start: likely to prove best at sharp 2m. *A. J. Chamberlain*

EYZE (IRE) 7 b.g. Lord Americo – Another Raheen (IRE) (Sandalay) [2002/3 c17sᵘʳ **c–**
16s⁶ c20mᵖᵘ 16g⁶ c20mᶠ 24vᵖᵘ 22d Mar 1] IR 8,000 3-y-o: ex-Irish gelding: first foal: **h86 d**
dam unraced: won maiden Irish point in 2001: little form over hurdles and in steeplechases, left E. O'Grady after fifth start. *B. Mactaggart*

F

FABLE (USA) 7 b.g. Hansel (USA) – Aragon (Raconteur (USA)) [2002/3 16g⁴ c17m **c73**
c16f⁴ c17sᵖᵘ c17sᶠ Nov 3] strong gelding: carries condition: missed 2001/2: useful **h120**
hurdler at best, fourth in handicap at Gowran: only poor form over fences: raced around
2m: acts on soft and good to firm going: tongue tied last 3 starts. *N. Meade, Ireland*

FABREZAN (FR) 4 b.g. Nikos – Fabulous Secret (FR) (Fabulous Dancer (USA)) **h93**
[2002/3 17mᵖᵘ 17d³ 16d⁶ 16g³ 19s³ 19vᵖᵘ Dec 28] smallish gelding: well beaten in 3
maidens at 2 yrs: modest juvenile hurdler: stays 19f: acts on soft going, possibly not on
heavy. *Nick Williams*

FACTS NOT FICTION (IRE) 9 b. or br.g. Phardante (FR) – Facts 'n Fancies **c–**
(Furry Glen) [2002/3 c127, h135: 20g* c21gᵖᵘ 20v 24d 20s 19s Mar 16] lengthy gelding: **h114 §**
has been hobdayed: useful hurdler: fairly useful chaser: won minor hurdle at Baden-
Baden in May: below form afterwards, looked none too keen at Cheltenham and
Sandown 2 outings before final one: stays 3m: acts on heavy going: effective blinkered or
not: has worn tongue strap. *F. Doumen, France*

FADALKO (FR) 10 b.g. Cadoudal (FR) – Kalliste (FR) (Calicot (FR)) [2002/3 c161, **c151 d**
h–: c21d⁵ c21d² c19s⁵ c20g c36dᵘʳ c21m⁶ Apr 16] good-topped gelding: usually looks **h–**
very well: has been pin-fired near fore: top-class chaser at best: disappointing in 2002/3:
best up to 21f: ran poorly on firm going, acts on any other: blinkered final start: usually
sound jumper (unseated sixth in Grand National). *P. F. Nicholls*

FADDAD (USA) 7 b.g. Irish River (FR) – Miss Mistletoes (IRE) (The Minstrel (CAN)) **h90 ?**
[2002/3 h–: 17m⁵ 16g 17gᵖᵘ Mar 16] angular gelding: apparently best effort over hurdles
when fifth in steadily-run maiden at Folkestone in May. *D. C. O'Brien*

FADOUDAL DU COCHET (FR) 10 b.g. Cadoudal (FR) – Eau de Vie (FR) (Dhau- **c138**
devi (FR)) [2002/3 c139, h139: c16s³ c16s³ c16g c16d² c16gᵖᵘ Mar 13] well-made **h–**
gelding: useful hurdler/chaser: largely out of sorts over fences in 2002/3: creditable effort
only when second to Arctic Copper in Grade 2 at Naas: raced mainly around 2m, only on
good going or softer (acts on heavy). *A. L. T. Moore, Ireland*

FAIR ENOUGH (IRE) 8 b.m. Phardante (FR) – Woodford Princess (Menelek) **h75**
[2002/3 17d⁶ 16d 21d 27f³ Apr 24] IR 9,500 3-y-o: sturdy ex-Irish mare: eighth foal:
half-sister to 3 winners, including winning 2½m chaser Woodford Gale (by Strong Gale):
dam, sister to useful hurdler Woodford Prince, won over hurdles in Ireland: first form
over hurdles (trained in 2001/2 by A. J. Kennedy) when third to Muharib Lady in
handicap at Fontwell: stays 27f. *R. Rowe*

FAIR EXCHANGE 10 b.g. Bustino – Sharp Vixen (Laurence O) [2002/3 c25g* Mar **c89 +**
29] non-thoroughbred gelding: fairly useful pointer, won 3 times in 2002 and once in
2003: won hunter chase at Market Rasen in March, running on strongly to beat Ridgeway
1½ lengths. *Mrs M. G. Sheppard*

FAIRMEAD PRINCESS 5 b.m. Rudimentary (USA) – Lessons Lass (IRE) **h–**
(Doyoun) [2002/3 h–: 16gᵖᵘ Apr 29] leggy mare: no sign of ability: sold £650 Ascot June
Sales. *M. J. Gingell*

FAIR PROSPECT 7 b.g. Sir Harry Lewis (USA) – Fair Sara (McIndoe) [2002/3 F91: **h109 +**
16dᶠ 16d⁴ 20d* Apr 9] useful-looking gelding: bumper winner: first run since leaving

J. Glover, best effort in novice hurdles when winning at Uttoxeter: stays 2½m: yet to race on extremes of going. *P. F. Nicholls*

FAIR QUESTION (IRE)   5 b.g. Rainbow Quest (USA) – Fair of The Furze (Ela-Mana-Mou) [2002/3 16d^pu 16s^6 17g^4 17g^2 Mar 22] leggy, useful-looking gelding: useful on Flat (stays 1¾m), sold out of J. Dunlop's stable 52,000 gns Newmarket July Sales: fair form over hurdles: raced around 2m. *Miss Venetia Williams*   **h100**

FAIR SPRITE (IRE)   6 ch.g. Over The River (FR) – Saucy Sprite (Balliol) [2002/3 c23d^5 c26v^pu Jan 17] ninth foal: half-brother to fair staying chaser Laundry Lady's Lad (by Ardross) and winning pointer by Royal Match: dam winning hurdler, stayed 2½m: won 2 of his 3 starts in points in 2002, including 2½m event: better effort in novice chases when fifth at Exeter. *R. H. Alner*   **c83**

FAIRTOTO   7 b.g. Mtoto – Fairy Feet (Sadler's Wells (USA)) [2002/3 h95: 21d 20v^6 24g Feb 27] good-topped gelding: modest handicap hurdler: well held all 3 starts in 2002/3: should stay beyond 2¾m: acts on firm and good to soft going: tongue tied: held up and takes strong hold. *D. J. Wintle*   **h–**

FAIR WIND (IRE)   11 b.g. Strong Gale – Corcomroe (Busted) [2002/3 c113: c26g^2 c26v^pu c24s^R c26g^pu Mar 13] workmanlike gelding: useful hunter chaser: lacklustre efforts after first outing: stays 3¼m: acts on heavy going: tried blinkered: usually held up. *Mrs H. Bartlett*   **c113 d**

FAIRWOOD HEART (IRE)   6 b. or br.g. Broken Hearted – Bowery Lass (IRE) (Abednego) [2002/3 16s^8 16s^2 17g^3 16f^3 20v^3 16s 22d^8 24s^5 23s^2 24g^4 Apr 3] IR 4,800 3-y-o: workmanlike gelding: second foal: dam unraced: fairly useful hurdler: won novice at Ballinrobe in June and handicap at Leopardstown in January: good efforts in handicaps last 3 starts, fourth to Carlovent at Aintree: stays 3m: acts on soft going (won bumper on good to firm). *P. J. Rothwell, Ireland*   **h119**

FAIT LE JOJO (FR)   6 b.g. Pistolet Bleu (IRE) – Pretty Davis (USA) (Trempolino (USA)) [2002/3 h134: 16f c16m* c17d^ur c16d^4 c16s* c16g* c20g^F c16m^F Apr 11] rather leggy gelding: useful handicap hurdler: fairly useful novice chaser: won at Uttoxeter in October and Ludlow in January (best effort, beat Regal Exit 2 lengths) and March: let down by jumping all other starts over fences: raced mainly around 2m: acts on firm and soft going: races freely. *P. J. Hobbs*   **c126 x** **h–**

FALCHION   8 b.g. Broadsword (USA) – Fastlass (Celtic Cone) [2002/3 h90: 20d^3 c21v^2 c16v^3 c20v^3 c20v^F c20d^2 c25g^ur Mar 21] quite good-topped gelding: modest hurdler: fair novice chaser: would have won at Ayr in February but for falling last: should stay 3m: raced mainly on going softer than good (acts on heavy): tongue tied: reliable. *J. R. Bewley*   **c107** **h96**

FALCON DU COTEAU (FR)   10 b. or br.g. Apeldoorn (FR) – Ifrika (FR) (Bamako III) [2002/3 c108, h–: 16s 20s c19s c18v c17d c21d^5 c29g Apr 21] small gelding: winning hurdler: fair handicap chaser: easily best effort in 2002/3 when fifth in Topham Chase at Aintree in April: stays 21f: acts on heavy going: often blinkered (wasn't at Aintree), including for all wins: sold 7,500 gns Doncaster May Sales. *A. J. Martin, Ireland*   **c112** **h–**

FALCON GEORGIE   4 b.f. Sri Pekan (USA) – Georgia Stephens (USA) (The Minstrel (CAN)) [2002/3 18s^4 17g^pu 18f^5 Apr 24] poor maiden on Flat: no worthwhile form over hurdles. *Miss B. Sanders*   **h–**

FALCON RIDGE   9 ch.g. Seven Hearts – Glen Kella Manx (Tickled Pink) [2002/3 c90?, h–: c16g^3 c16m^pu Jul 15] lengthy, plain gelding: modest hurdler/maiden chaser: pulled up lame at Newton Abbot in July: stays 21f: probably acts on any going. *Miss E. C. Lavelle*   **c84** **h–**

FALMER FOR ALL (IRE)   5 b.g. Warcraft (USA) – Sunset Walk (Le Bavard (FR)) [2002/3 F18d^5 F16g^5 Mar 23] €13,000 4-y-o: sixth foal: dam unraced half-sister to smart 2m to 2¾m chaser Gale Again: looked a stayer when fifth in bumper at Fontwell on debut: unsuited by less of a test of stamina in similar event next time. *T. P. McGovern*   **F81**

FALSE TAIL (IRE)   11 b.g. Roselier (FR) – Its Good Ere (Import) [2002/3 c25s^pu c26g^F c24m^ur Apr 9] sturdy gelding: successful 4 times in points in 2002/3: winning hunter chaser, has poor completion record. *J. J. Lambe, Ireland*   **c– x**

FAMFONI (FR)   10 b.g. Pamponi (FR) – India Rosa (FR) (Carnaval) [2002/3 c105x, h–: 27g^3 c28g^4 c31d^F Nov 15] quite good-topped gelding: winning hurdler: fairly useful chaser: best effort in 2002/3 when winning Sporting Index Chase (Cross Country) at   **c122 x** **h96**

Sporting Index Chase (Cross Country), Cheltenham—Famfoni (right) jumps alongside Galapiat du Mesnil while Czech raiders Red Dancer and Centax follow Lucky Clover on the left

Cheltenham by 2 lengths from The Quads: stays 31f: acts on any going: tried visored/ blinkered: far from fluent jumper of conventional fences: has looked less than keen. *K. C. Bailey*

FAMI (FR)   10 ch.g. Le Nain Jaune (FR) – Quimie II (FR) (Barbotan (FR)) [2002/3 c94x, h–: 27g^pu May 17] plain gelding: winning hurdler/chaser: effective at 19f to 3¼m: acts on soft and good to firm going: usually let down by jumping over fences: sold 2,800 gns Doncaster May Sales, won point in April. *Miss Venetia Williams*   **c– x**
  h–

FAMILIE FOOTSTEPS   9 b.g. Primitive Rising (USA) – Ramilie (Rambah) [2002/3 h100: 16m^5 May 8] good-topped gelding: fair hurdler, showed little on first start for 8 months in handicap in May: should stay 2½m: acts on firm going. *G. A. Swinbank*   **h–**

FAMILY BUSINESS (IRE)   7 ch.g. Over The River (FR) – Morego (Way Up North) [2002/3 c106x, h91p: c24m^4 c25d^2 c24s^3 c24s^F c26g^bd c21g^ur c26m^F Apr 17] lengthy gelding: best effort in steeplechases when runner-up to Kingscliff in hunter at Wincanton: successful in points in January and March (twice): likely to prove better around 3m than shorter (seemed not to stay 4m): acts on soft and good to firm going, probably on heavy: visored/blinkered last 3 starts: has worn near-side pricker: often let down by jumping. *D. Pipe*   **c119 x**
  h–

FAMILY VENTURE (IRE)   6 br.g. Montelimar (USA) – Well Honey (Al Sirat (USA)) [2002/3 16m 24d^3 19d^6 24g* 24g^3 24g^2 Feb 12] IR 5,200 3-y-o: has scope: sixth foal: half-brother to poor hurdler Sorely Missed (by Yashgan), stays 25f: dam, winning 2m hurdler, half-sister to useful staying chaser Musthaveaswig: won maiden Irish point in 2002: modest novice hurdler: won handicap at Musselburgh in January: better suited by 3m than shorter: tongue tied final start. *Ferdy Murphy*   **h97**

FANDANGO DE CHASSY (FR)　10 b.g. Brezzo (FR) – Laita de Mercurey (FR)　**c96**
(Dom Luc (FR)) [2002/3 c96, h107: c25d^{pu} c26s^2 c26v^5 c30d^2 24d c33v^{pu} 25s^3 26g^4　**h101**
24m^{pu} Apr 12] good-topped gelding: fair hurdler: modest chaser: thorough stayer: ideally
suited by going softer than good (acts on heavy): tried blinkered/visored, often wore
cheekpieces in 2002/3: has had tongue tied. *Mrs L. Wadham*

FANFARON (FR)　10 b.g. Sarpedon (FR) – Ocana IV (FR) (Monsieur X) [2002/3　**c97 §**
c111§, h–: c25g^2 c25d^6 c24s c25g^F Mar 18] good-topped gelding: fair hunter chaser: stays　**h–**
25f: acts on soft and good to firm going: tried blinkered: races up with pace: often finishes
weakly. *Paul Phillips*

FANION DE NOURRY (FR)　10 ch.g. Bad Conduct (USA) – Ottomane (FR) (Quart　**c–**
de Vin (FR)) [2002/3 c–, h–: c33g^F c25d^6 c34g^{pu} May 22] workmanlike gelding: winning　**h–**
hunter chaser, little show since 2000: stays 4¼m: acts on good to firm going. *E. Haddock*

FANTASMIC　7 ch.g. Broadsword (USA) – Squeaky Cottage (True Song) [2002/3　**h99 +**
F88: 19d^{pu} 16s^3 16s 16d* 21m^2 Apr 16] good-topped gelding: modest novice hurdler:
won at Uttoxeter in April: stays 21f: acts on soft and good to firm going: takes good hold.
A. M. Hales

FANTASTIC CHAMPION (IRE)　4 b.g. Entrepreneur – Reine Mathilde (USA)　**h120**
(Vaguely Noble) [2002/3 16g 16d^2 16d^2 Feb 7] strong, close-coupled gelding: fairly
useful on Flat (stays 11.6f), sold out of P. d'Arcy's stable 37,000 gns Newmarket July
Sales: fairly useful form when second at Kempton last 2 starts in juvenile hurdles: sure to
win a race. *Mrs L. Wadham*

FAR AHEAD　11 b.g. Soviet Star (USA) – Cut Ahead (Kalaglow) [2002/3 16d^{pu} 16s　**h–**
17v Feb 11] rather leggy gelding: fairly useful hurdler in 1996/7: showed nothing in 3
handicaps on return. *D. Carroll*

FARAWAY JOHN (IRE)　5 b.g. Farhaan – Indiana Dancer (Hallgate) [2002/3 16v^{pu}　**h–**
Dec 4] half-brother to fair hurdler/chaser Indiana Journey (by Eurobus), stays 2¾m:
modest at best on Flat (should stay beyond 1½m): not fluent in novice at Plumpton on
hurdling debut. *G. P. Enright*

FAR BRIDGE　8 ch.g. Phardante (FR) – Droichidin (Good Thyne (USA))　**c–**
[2002/3 c–, h–: c17m^6 c21g^{pu} Apr 21] strong, workmanlike gelding: little sign of ability.　**h–**
P. Wegmann

FAR DAWN (USA)　10 b.g. Sunshine Forever (USA) – Dawn's Reality (USA) (In　**c98**
Reality) [2002/3 c23g^6 c24m* c25d^{pu} c24m^2 Apr 22] strong, workmanlike gelding:　**h–**
winning hurdler: modest chaser nowadays, off 2 years before reappearance: won novice
at Southwell in March: stays 3m: acts on good to firm and good to soft going: tried
blinkered: has had tongue tied. *J. Gallagher*

FARD DU MOULIN MAS (FR)　10 b. or br.g. Morespeed – Soiree d'Ex (FR)　**c–**
(Kashtan (FR)) [2002/3 c–, h–: c21g^F c20d^5 c22g^{pu} Dec 18] good-topped gelding: useful　**h–**
handicap hurdler/chaser in 1999/00: injured when falling final outing that season and
little worthwhile form since: stays 3m: acts on soft going. *M. E. D. Francis*

FARE DEALING (IRE)　10 b.g. Tremblant – Charming Whisper (Deep Run) [2002/3　**c89**
c–, h100: 18g* 18m 22f^5 16g^6 c17m^2 c16g^2 c20m 22d 20s^3 Dec 6] leggy gelding: modest　**h95**
handicap hurdler, won amateur event at Plumpton in April: similar standard when
runner-up 2 out of 3 completed starts in novice chases: stays 2¾m: probably acts on any
going: seems to go well with forcing tactics. *M. J. Gingell*

FARFIELDS PRINCE　11 b.g. Weldnaas (USA) – Coca (Levmoss) [2002/3 c96§,　**c– §**
h–: 16m 19m 20s 16m Jun 29] leggy gelding: winning hurdler/chaser, no form early in　**h– §**
2002/3: stays easy 2½m: acts on firm and soft going: often blinkered/visored: one to treat
with caution. *K. G. Wingrove*

FAR GLEN (IRE)　8 b.g. Phardante (FR) – Asigh Glen (Furry Glen) [2002/3 c–, h94:　**c104**
21g^2 c25d^F c27m^2 Apr 11] big, angular gelding: maiden hurdler, often ran as if amiss in　**h68 §**
2001/2: fairly useful form on completed start in hunter chases: stays 27f: best efforts on
good/good to firm going: has had tongue tied: races freely: unreliable. *R. D. E. Woodhouse*

FAR HORIZON (IRE)　9 b.g. Phardante (FR) – Polly Puttens (Pollerton) [2002/3　**h123**
16d^2 20v* 21d^3 20g^{pu} Apr 2] lengthy, useful-looking gelding: lightly raced: improved
hurdler in 2002/3, winning novice at Ascot in December: running well when bad mistake
2 out and pulled up and dismounted before last final start: will prove better around 2½m
than 2m: raced on good going or softer (acts on heavy). *N. J. Henderson*

FARINEL 7 b.g. In The Wings – Dame de L'Oise (USA) (Riverman (USA)) [2002/3 **c94**
h126: 24s³ c20s⁶ c20s 16d 25g 20d Apr 4] good-topped gelding: fairly useful handicap **h125 d**
hurdler: creditable third to Springfield Scally at Chepstow on reappearance: disappointing subsequently, including over fences: will stay beyond 3m: acts on soft and good
to firm going: blinkered final start. *A. L. T. Moore, Ireland*

FARINGTON LODGE (IRE) 5 b.g. Simply Great (FR) – Lodge Party (IRE) (Strong **F71**
Gale) [2002/3 F12g Dec 18] leggy, useful-looking gelding: second foal: dam maiden
half-sister to dams of high-class 2m hurdler King Credo and smart 2m to 3m chaser
Comeragh King: shaped as if in need of stiffer test of stamina when eleventh of 22 in
bumper at Newbury on debut. *Jonjo O'Neill*

FARMER JACK 7 b.g. Alflora (IRE) – Cheryls Pet (IRE) (General Ironside) **c143**
[2002/3 h128: c19g⁴ c19s* c16d* c16g* c20s² c16g⁴ c20m³ Apr 12] **h–**
Much improved over hurdles after joining his present stable in 2001/2,
Farmer Jack continued to progress when sent chasing in the latest season. He jumps
fences well and owed at least some of his success as a novice to his jumping. His
sound technique should stand him in good stead against more experienced opponents in handicaps in the next season and he could run well in races like the Paddy

HBLB Twickenham Novices Chase, Kempton—
Farmer Jack leads Epervier d'Or early on

Mr Peter Partridge's "Farmer Jack"

Power Gold Cup (former Thomas Pink) at Cheltenham and the First National Gold Cup at Ascot. Farmer Jack wasn't right up there with the top novices, his fourth in the Arkle exposing his limitations, though he still held every chance that day when making a rare bad mistake at the second last. Farmer Jack won three times before the Cheltenham Festival. After a pipe-opener at Exeter in early-November, he scored unextended at Taunton later that month, put up a useful performance to give weight and a beating to Vol Solitaire at Haydock in December and coasted home from Epervier d'Or at Kempton in January. Farmer Jack put in an assured round of jumping on each occasion, as he did when losing nothing in defeat, despite his rider losing an iron, when going down to Tarxien in the Scilly Isles Novices' Chase at Sandown in February. Farmer Jack finished behind Tarxien again when the pair filled the minor placings behind Vol Solitaire in the Future Champion Novices' Chase at Ayr in April, Farmer Jack being niggled along some way from home and shaping as if possibly past his best for the season.

The workmanlike Farmer Jack is the first foal of the modest hurdler Cheryls Pet who won at up to twenty-one furlongs and showed signs of only a little ability tried over fences at up to three and a quarter miles. She was also represented on the racecourse in the latest season by Farmer Jack's brother Harry's Dream, a winning pointer and modest maiden hurdler. Their grandam the unraced Kilmanahan was a half-sister to the smart Irish hurdler Troyswood. The reliable Farmer Jack is effective at up to two and a half miles and acts on soft going (won bumper on firm). *J. W. Mullins*

FARMER JOSH   9 b.g. Dancing High – Millie Duffer (Furry Glen) [2002/3 16g 20g   **c–** Apr 21] of little account: tried blinkered. *Miss L. V. Davis*   **h–**

Victor Ludorum Juvenile Novices' Hurdle, Haydock—the laurels go to Far Pavilions (left), gaining his fourth win in a row at the main expense of Crystal d'Ainay

FARNE ISLE 4 ch.f. Midnight Legend – Biloela (Nicholas Bill) [2002/3 F17v* F16g⁶ F17g⁵ F17m Apr 17] smallish, sparely-made filly: third foal: half-sister to winning 2¾m hurdler Beedulup (by Perpendicular): dam, 1¼m winner, half-sister to dam of useful hurdler/chaser up to 2¾m Northern Starlight: fair form in bumpers, made all in mares event at Sedgefield on debut in January. *G. A. Harker* **F91**

FAR PAVILIONS 4 b.g. Halling (USA) – Flambera (FR) (Akarad (FR)) [2002/3 16d* 16g* 16g* 16d* 16gᵖᵘ Apr 3] useful-looking gelding, unfurnished at present: fairly useful on Flat (stays 10.5f) for Mrs J. Ramsden: made excellent start to hurdling career, won juveniles at Catterick and Musselburgh in December, Musselburgh again in February and Haydock (by neck from Crystal d'Ainay) in March: never going well in Grade 2 at Aintree final start: likely to prove best at 2m: raced on good/good to soft going. *G. A. Swinbank* **h129**

FARRAGO 5 b.m. Bold Arrangement – Farah (Lead On Time (USA)) [2002/3 F17d⁶ F16v⁶ Nov 8] unfurnished mare: second foal: dam once-raced half-sister to high-class staying hurdler Anzum and high-class 2m hurdler Jazilah: well held in mares bumpers: sold £500 Ascot December Sales. *J. R. Turner* **F—**

FARRANFORE (IRE) 5 b.g. Be My Native (USA) – Mandy's Treasure (IRE) (Mandalus) [2002/3 F16s² Feb 9] IR £100,000 3-y-o: good sort: first foal: dam winning pointer: created good impression when second to Dizzy's Dream in maiden bumper at Leopardstown on debut: will stay at least 2½m: sure to improve and win similar event. *E. J. O'Grady, Ireland* **F102 p**

FAS 7 ch.g. Weldnaas (USA) – Polly's Teahouse (Shack (USA)) [2002/3 h–: 16g 16gᵖᵘ Jan 28] no worthwhile form over hurdles, left C. Fairhurst after reappearance. *Mrs K. Walton* **h–**

FASGO (IRE) 8 b.g. Montelimar (USA) – Action Plan (Creative Plan (USA)) [2002/3 c111, h99: c25d² c30dᶠ c29s² c26s³ c26v⁵ Feb 4] tall, leggy gelding: fair handicap chaser: stays 29f: raced on good going or softer (acts on soft): blinkered final start: has idled/gone in snatches: often none too fluent. *P. F. Nicholls* **c114 h–**

FASHION HOUSE   7 b.m. Homo Sapien – High Heels (IRE) (Supreme Leader) [2002/3 F65: 17g 22f⁵ 22m⁵ c24m² Apr 10] poor form over hurdles: fair pointer in 2003, successful twice in March: second at Ludlow on hunter chase debut, would have won but for being hampered twice in latter stages: stays 3m. *S. Pike*   **c89 +** **h73**

FASHION VICTIM   8 b.g. High Estate – Kirkby Belle (Bay Express) [2002/3 h83: 16m 16g 17g 17gᵖᵘ 16g 19m* 21f⁴ 17m⁶ 16dʳᵗʳ Nov 12] medium-sized gelding: has reportedly had breathing operation: poor handicap hurdler: made all at Hereford in October: acts easy 19f: acts on good to firm and heavy going: tongue tied fourth outing: pulls hard: refused to race final start. *Mrs A. C. Tate*   **h83 §**

FASSAN (IRE)   11 br.g. Contract Law (USA) – Persian Susan (USA) (Herbager) [2002/3 c66§, h–§: c21dᵖᵘ c28d⁶ Feb 8] big gelding: poor chaser: left A. Crook after reappearance: third in point in April: stays 21f: acts on heavy going, probably on good to firm: tried visored/blinkered: unenthusiastic. *Mrs K. J. Tutty*   **c– §** **h– §**

FAST FLOWING   5 b.m. Sovereign Water (FR) – Spartona (Cisto (FR)) [2002/3 F17g 20vᵖᵘ Nov 8] third foal: half-sister to winning pointer by Rich Charlie: dam placed over hurdles, stayed 3m: no form in bumper or novice hurdle. *J. Wade*   **h–** **F–**

FAST KING (IRE)   5 b.g. Housamix (FR) – Fast Girl (FR) (Gay Minstrel (FR)) [2002/3 h90: 20d 17v⁵ 19s* 19s 17s c16gᶠ Apr 21] leggy gelding: modest handicap hurdler: won at Taunton in December: fell fifth on chasing debut: stays 19f: raced mainly on going softer than good: blinkered: no easy ride: inconsistent. *P. J. Hobbs*   **c–** **h97**

FAST MIX (FR)   4 gr.g. Linamix (FR) – Fascinating Hill (FR) (Danehill (USA)) [2002/3 16d* 16vᵖᵘ 16v² 20vᶠ 17f² Mar 24] angular gelding: first foal: dam unraced half-sister to very smart middle-distance colt Fragrant Mix: fairly useful maiden on Flat, in frame all 3 starts around 1½m at 3 yrs for A. Fabre: fair juvenile hurdler: easily won weak event at Newbury in November: may prove best around 2m: probably acts on any going: has room for improvement in his jumping. *M. C. Pipe*   **h101**

FATAL FLAW (USA)   6 b.g. Hansel (USA) – Fateful (USA) (Topsider (USA)) [2002/3 16dᵖᵘ c16m⁵ c16g⁶ c18m⁴ Mar 19] useful-looking ex-French gelding: successful 3 times at 1m at 3 yrs: won 5-y-o hurdle at Pau in 2001/2 for J. Ortet: little worthwhile form over jumps in Britain, though won on Flat in February for D. Shaw: stays 19f: has worn cheekpieces: breathing problem second start, tongue tied otherwise in 2002/3. *A. Ennis*   **c–** **h–**

FATE A COMPLI (IRE)   8 ch.g. Over The River (FR) – Oh Clare (Laurence O) [2002/3 c26gᵖᵘ Apr 29] tall, lengthy gelding: winning pointer: no show in 2 steeplechases: sold 1,600 gns Doncaster May Sales, resold £400 Ascot November Sales. *R. H. Alner*   **c–**

FATEHALKHAIR (IRE)   11 ch.g. Kris – Midway Lady (USA) (Alleged (USA)) [2002/3 c126, h118: 21m* c24d³ 24g c25d⁴ c33mᵖᵘ c28m⁵ Apr 26] sparely-made gelding: fairly useful handicap hurdler/chaser: won over hurdles at Sedgefield in July: stays easy 3½m, effective at much shorter: acts on any going: a credit to connections. *B. Ellison*   **c126** **h115**

FATHER D (IRE)   8 b.g. Mister Lord (USA) – Abrahams Cross (IRE) (Bustomi) [2002/3 h91, F93: 17gᶠ 16m 17s 17g 19m* 16m⁴ Apr 19] rangy gelding: in frame in Irish points in 2001: modest hurdler: won handicap at Exeter in April, wandering under pressure: stays 19f: acts on good to firm and heavy going: headstrong. *R. H. Buckler*   **h87**

FATHERLY CHAT (IRE)   7 b.g. Supreme Leader – Frozen Ground (Arctic Slave) [2002/3 F16d 24vᵖᵘ Jan 17] IR 6,400 3-y-o: half-brother to 3 winners, including fair staying chaser Frozen Drop (by Le Bavard): dam, winning hurdler who stayed 3m, from family of top-class staying chaser Alexander Banquet: showed little in bumper and maiden hurdle. *R. T. Phillips*   **h–** **F–**

FATHER MULCAHY   7 b.g. Safawan – Constant Delight (Never So Bold) [2002/3 h91?: 20gᵖᵘ c17vᵖᵘ c16v³ c16v⁴ c17vᵖᵘ Feb 7] workmanlike gelding: maiden hurdler, little worthwhile form since 1999/00, including over fences: blinkered last 2 starts: has had tongue tied. *D. McCain*   **c–** **h–**

FATHER PADDY   8 ch.g. Minster Son – Sister Claire (Quayside) [2002/3 h90: c19g³ 21d² Mar 18] good-topped gelding: modest maiden hurdler: similar form when third in novice at Catterick on chasing debut: stays 21f: acts on good to firm going, bumper form on soft. *T. J. Fitzgerald*   **c90** **h97**

FATHER RECTOR (IRE)   14 b.g. The Parson – Mwanamio (Sole Mio (USA)) [2002/3 c105, h–: c25m* c22m* c20m⁶ c24mᶠ Jul 4] angular gelding: fair chaser: won   **c105** **h–**

hunters at Wetherby in May and Market Rasen in June, then left Mrs F. Needham: won point in April: stays 25f: acts on any going: has looked none too keen. *R. Tate*

FATHOM   5 ch.g. Zafonic (USA) – River Lullaby (USA) (Riverman (USA)) [2002/3   **F71**
F17g F16d Apr 25] sturdy gelding: eighth foal: brother to 1m winner Torch Song and half-brother to several winners, including useful French middle-distance performer Berceau (by Alleged) and very smart 1m/9f performer Wixim (by Diesis): dam, Irish 2-y-o 6f winner, third in 1¼m listed race at 3 yrs: signs of ability on second start in bumpers. *Mrs L. B. Normile*

FAUGERE   7 ch.g. Jupiter Island – Pinch (Ardross) [2002/3 20v² 24m⁶ Mar 21] 13,000   **h111**
3-y-o: lengthy gelding: first foal: dam, second over 1½m in France/poor novice hurdler in Britain, half-sister to useful hurdler/chaser up to 3m Heist: third on first of 2 starts in maiden points in 2002: second to Palua in maiden at Folkestone on hurdling debut, having run of race and flattered by proximity to idling winner: possibly unsuited by much firmer ground next time: should stay beyond 2½m. *P. F. Nicholls*

FAUSTINO   11 b.g. Faustus (USA) – Hot Case (Upper Case (USA)) [2002/3 c80§, h–:   **c80 §**
c26m³ May 7] sturdy, workmanlike gelding: has been hobdayed: poor handicap chaser: **h–**
probably bled from nose: ungenuine (tends to go in snatches). *D. M. Grissell*

FAVOURED OPTION (IRE)   8 ch.g. Glacial Storm (USA) – Hot House Flower   **c113**
(Derring Rose) [2002/3 c99x, h–: c25dᵖᵘ c23gᵘʳ c25m⁵ c24d² c25d² c25d² c23g² c29g²   **h–**
c25m* c24m* Apr 19] strong gelding: fair handicap chaser: won at Hereford and Carlisle in April: stays 29f: acts on heavy and good to firm going: often makes mistakes: consistent. *Ian Williams*

FAWN PRINCE (IRE)   10 b.g. Electric – Regent Star (Prince Regent (FR)) [2002/3   **c–**
c–, h74d: 16dᵖᵘ Mar 5] close-coupled gelding: sold out of M. Gingell's stable 700 gns   **h–**
Doncaster November Sales: winning hurdler, well held in seller only outing in 2002/3: once-raced over fences: raced around 2m: acts on soft and good to firm going: raced too freely only start in visor. *S. G. Chadwick*

FAYALIE (IRE)   8 b.m. Classic Memory – Much Obliged (Crash Course) [2002/3   **c–**
c27dᵖᵘ Mar 18] won maiden from 4 starts in Irish points in 2002: bought 2,800 gns   **h–**
Doncaster May Sales: no other form. *Miss V. J. Parvin*

FAYRWAY RHYTHM (IRE)   6 b.g. Fayruz – The Way She Moves (North Stoke)   **h– §**
[2002/3 h92§: 22g 17g⁶ Apr 21] modest handicap hurdler: well beaten both outings in 2002/3: seems barely to stay 2½m: acts on soft and good to firm going: blinkered/visored: has been tongue tied: ungenuine. *Ian Emmerson*

FEANOR   5 b.m. Presidium – Nouvelle Cuisine (Yawa) [2002/3 h91: 16dᵘʳ 16dᵖᵘ 16vᵖᵘ   **h–**
16gᵖᵘ 16m Apr 21] leggy mare: winning hurdler: no form in 2002/3: raced around 2m: acts on soft going. *Mrs S. A. Watt*

FEARLESS MEL (IRE)   9 b.g. Mandalus – Milan Pride (Northern Guest (USA))   **c99**
[2002/3 c20d³ c24g² Mar 22] behind in bumper in 2000/1: much better effort in steeplechases on return when second of 5 in novice at Bangor. *Mrs H. Dalton*

FEAR SIUIL (IRE)   10 b.g. Strong Gale – Astral River (Over The River (FR)) [2002/3   **c110**
c100, h–: c16m⁴ c16g² c20m* c17d² c21mᵖᵘ c17g³ c16f⁴ Oct 26] lengthy gelding: fair   **h–**
handicap chaser: sold out of D. Forster's stable 12,000 gns Doncaster May Sales after reappearance: won at Stratford in July: stays 21f: acts on good to firm and good to soft going: usually tongue tied: has been let down by jumping: game. *Nick Williams*

FEELING FIZZICAL   5 b.g. Feelings (FR) – Stepdaughter (Relkino) [2002/3 24vᵖᵘ   **h–**
27dᵖᵘ Mar 25] first foal: dam, lightly-raced novice hurdler, stayed 3m: no show either outing over hurdles. *Mrs J. C. McGregor*

FEEL THE PRIDE (IRE)   5 b.m. Persian Bold – Nordic Pride (Horage) [2002/3   **h96 p**
19d³ Nov 5] ex-Irish mare: closely related to winning 2m hurdler Dignified (by Pennine Walk) and half-sister to another by Vision: fair on Flat (stays 1¾m): sold out of J. Bolger's stable €34,000 Goffs International June Sale: weak 16/1, caught the eye when third in novice at Exeter on hurdling debut, patiently ridden and considerably handled at all stages: reportedly fractured cannon bone, but should still improve. *Jonjo O'Neill*

FELIX DARBY (IRE)   8 b.g. Buckskin (FR) – Cool Anne (Orchardist) [2002/3 21s⁴   **c86**
20v⁴ 24d⁵ c29g⁴ c24m² Apr 22] IR 23,000 5-y-o: workmanlike gelding: fourth foal: **h82**
brother to useful hurdler Anne's Buckskin, stayed 2¾m, and bumper winner Annes Brown: dam 2m hurdle winner: in frame all 3 completed starts in maiden Irish points in

2002: poor form over hurdles: better effort in handicap chases when second at Chepstow: likely to prove suited by thorough test of stamina. *Miss G. Browne*

FELIX RANDAL (IRE)   7 ch.g. Be My Native (USA) – Odd Sox (FR) (Main Reef) [2002/3 c–, h95+, F–: 23m³ 24d 22dᵖᵘ c25g² Mar 17] workmanlike gelding: modest handicap hurdler: much better effort over fences when second in handicap at Hereford: stays 25f: best form on good/good to firm going: blinkered and tongue tied third outing (looked less than keen): sold only 1,200 gns Doncaster May Sales. *Jonjo O'Neill*   **c85 h95**

FELLOO (IRE)   14 br.g. Decent Fellow – Cuckaloo (Master Buck) [2002/3 c26gᵖᵘ May 22] workmanlike gelding: modest pointer, successful twice in March: maiden hunter chaser: stays 25f: acts on soft and good to firm going: tried blinkered: has looked reluctant. *Mrs R. E. Walker*   **c– § h– §**

FELONY (IRE)   8 ch.g. Pharly (FR) – Scales of Justice (Final Straw) [2002/3 h–: 20d 17g 17dᵖᵘ 26sᵖᵘ 16d⁴ 21g⁵ Mar 14] winning hurdler, retains little ability: sometimes tongue tied, including when looking temperamental last 2 starts. *L. P. Grassick*   **h–**

FEN GYPSY   5 b.g. Nashwan (USA) – Didicoy (USA) (Danzig (USA)) [2002/3 16g 16g Dec 18] lengthy gelding: half-brother to fairly useful 2m hurdler/winning chaser Didifon (by Zafonic): disappointing maiden on Flat: well held both starts over hurdles: tongue tied. *P. D. Evans*   **h–**

FERBET JUNIOR (FR)   10 gr.g. Royal Charter – Matuvu (FR) (Trenel) [2002/3 c137d, h–: c20g⁴ Oct 10] lengthy gelding: smart chaser at best: fourth of 6 to Barrow Drive in minor event at Gowran, only start in 2002/3: probably best up to 2½m: raced on good going or softer (acts on heavy): headstrong when tried in blinkers: headstrong (has been early to post) and forces pace: carefree jumper. *Mrs J. Harrington, Ireland*   **c133 ? h–**

FERNLEIGH   6 b.g. Another Sam – Price of Sentiment (IRE) (Trojan Fen) [2002/3 F16s 19mᵖᵘ Jul 7] smallish, leggy gelding: second foal: dam unraced: no show in bumper or novice hurdle. *M. J. Gingell*   **h– F–**

FERN LORD (IRE)   6 ch.h. Mister Lord (USA) – Deep Fern (Deep Run) [2002/3 24d 21m⁵ 24dᵖ Mar 1] big horse: half-brother to several winners, including useful staying chaser Mossy Fern (by Le Moss) and useful hurdler/fairly useful chaser Coq Hardi Affair (by The Parson), stayed 25f: dam, bumper winner, half-sister to useful staying chaser Sommelier and useful 2m to 3m hurdler/chaser Bective Road: third in Irish point in 2002: progressive form in novice hurdles, winning at Newbury by 21 lengths from Stack The Pack: will stay beyond 3m: open to further improvement. *Jonjo O'Neill*   **h115 p**

FERRETS HILL (IRE)   7 br.g. Good Thyne (USA) – Doolin Lake (IRE) (Salluceva) [2002/3 h–, F89: 20m⁴ 20dᵖᵘ 20d³ 23v⁴ 25dᵖᵘ c25d⁴ c20d⁵ Mar 15] well-made gelding: poor maiden hurdler: similar form when fifth at Newcastle on second of 2 starts in novice chases: probably stays 23f: acts on good to firm and heavy going. *Ferdy Murphy*   **c76 h79**

FERZAO (IRE)   6 b.g. Alzao (USA) – Fer de Lance (IRE) (Diesis) [2002/3 17m⁵ 17g² 16m² Jun 28] useful on Flat (free-going sort, stays easy 1¼m), sold out of Mrs A. Perrett's stable 17,000 gns Newmarket Autumn Sales: fair form when second in novice hurdles at Newton Abbot and Stratford: will prove best around 2m: tongue tied. *C. J. Mann*   **h110**

FESTIVAL FLYER   8 b.g. Alhijaz – Odilese (Mummy's Pet) [2002/3 h86: 22m 24m* Apr 8] modest handicap hurdler, lightly raced: off 9 months, allowed to dictate when winning steadily-run event at Exeter: stays 3¼m: acts on firm and soft ground. *Miss M. Bragg*   **h90**

FEY MACHA (IRE)   8 b.m. Phardante (FR) – West Lodge (Deep Run) [2002/3 22g 20m⁶ 24g* 20g² 19m* 20f² 21d Nov 17] strong, lengthy, good sort: fourth foal: dam well beaten in bumper: fair hurdler: won maiden at Cork and mares novice at Kilbeggan in August: stays 3m: acts on firm ground (bumper winner on good to soft). *Paul A. Roche, Ireland*   **h110**

FICHE AND CHIPS   4 b.c. Distant Relative – Moorefield Girl (IRE) (Gorytus (USA)) [2002/3 16m 16m Oct 16] good-topped colt: half-brother to fairly useful up to 2½m Zsarabak (by Soviet Lad): dam fair staying hurdler: no worthwhile form on Flat or in 2 juvenile hurdles: tried visored: sold 500 gns Doncaster January Sales. *A. Dickman*   **h–**

FIDDLERS BAR (IRE)   7 ch.m. Un Desperado (FR) – Theyllallwin (IRE) (Le Bavard (FR)) [2002/3 20s 22s F20m* Apr 13] third foal: dam unraced: won point in 2002: no form in 2 races over hurdles: won maiden bumper at Listowel by 15 lengths from Uptotrixagain, always prominent. *L. Young, Ireland*   **h– F100**

FIDDLERS ELBOW   7 ch.g. Jester – Swallow This (Town Crier) [2002/3 F16mʳᵒ F17d 16sᶠ Nov 18] fourth foal: dam never ran: no sign of ability. *J. R. Jenkins*   **h– F–**

FIELDING'S HAY (IRE) 7 b.m. Supreme Leader – Kates Fling (USA) (Quiet Fling (USA)) [2002/3 h78, F88: 20g c22d^{pu} c20s c25s^6 c24d^4 c26g^2 Apr 21] good-topped mare: bumper winner: little form over hurdles for A. Streeter: modest form over fences last 2 starts: stays 3¼m: acts on good to soft and good to firm going: tried visored. *Mrs J. Candlish* **c89** **h–**

FIELD MASTER (IRE) 6 ch.g. Foxhound (USA) – Bold Avril (IRE) (Persian Bold) [2002/3 h81: 16g^5 16f^3 19m* 19s* 19s^2 20v^{pu} 22f^4 Mar 27] modest handicap hurdler: won amateur events at Taunton in October and November: stays 21f: acts on firm and soft going. *C. J. Gray* **h95**

FIERCE MONEY 7 b.g. Nicholas Bill – Nut Tree (King of Spain) [2002/3 F87: F16g 22m^{pu} Apr 15] twice-raced in bumpers, well held on reappearance: not fluent and always behind in novice at Exeter on hurdling debut. *R. T. Phillips* **h–** **F–**

FIER GOUMIER (FR) 8 b.g. Chef de Clan II (FR) – Azilal (FR) (Rex Magna (FR)) [2002/3 c22d c20m c20m Feb 22] leggy ex-Irish gelding: third foal: dam, won twice around 11f on Flat in France, half-sister to fairly useful 2m hurdler Turkestan: modest form at best over hurdles: fair handicap chaser: no form in 2002/3 (left A. Moore after second start), though shaped better than finishing position suggests final outing: stays 2½m: acts on firm going. *Jonjo O'Neill* **c–** **h–**

FIERY CREEK 6 ch.m. Moscow Society (USA) – Deep Creek (Deep Run) [2002/3 F78: F16d F17d 20v Feb 4] big, workmanlike mare: third in mares maiden bumper on debut in 2001/2: well held since, including over hurdles. *D. J. Wintle* **h–** **F–**

FIERY PEACE 6 ch.g. Tina's Pet – Burning Mirage (Pamroy) [2002/3 h–, F79: 17g^6 16g^5 16g^F 16s Jan 3] good-topped gelding: poor maiden hurdler: raced mainly around 2m. *H. D. Daly* **h76**

FIERY RING (IRE) 8 b.g. Torus – Kakemona (Kambalda) [2002/3 h110: c17s^3 c17d* c16m^3 c17g* c18s^3 c20v^3 c16s^5 c17s^2 c17g^5 Apr 20] lengthy gelding: fair hurdler: fairly useful novice chaser: won at Limerick in June (maiden) and October (listed event, allowed to race in clear lead when beating Ansar 7 lengths): ridden with more restraint than usual when good second in handicap at Punchestown in early-May: stays 2½m: acts on good to firm and heavy going: has had tongue tied: front runner. *J. R. H. Fowler, Ireland* **c124 +** **h–**

FIFE AND DRUM (USA) 6 b. or br.g. Rahy (USA) – Fife (IRE) (Lomond (USA)) [2002/3 h–: 16m^{pu} Jun 1] angular gelding: fair on Flat (better at 1¼m than 1½m): no form over hurdles. *J. Akehurst* **h–**

FIFTEEN REDS 8 b.g. Jumbo Hirt (USA) – Dominance (Dominion) [2002/3 h79?: 21m^2 17g^5 20f^5 21m^3 24m^{ro} 24g* 20d^5 27v^5 20g Apr 14] leggy gelding: poor hurdler: won 3-runner handicap at Hexham in October: stays 3m: races mainly on firmer nowadays (probably acts on firm): tried visored: none too reliable (ran out fifth start). *F. S. Storey* **h84**

FIFTH GENERATION (IRE) 13 b.g. Bulldozer – Fragrant's Last (Little Buskins) [2002/3 c73, h94: 16d^5 16f^3 17g^6 17g 22m^2 16g* 17d 19s^3 16s 16d^4 16s 17g 16g^2 17g Apr 21] workmanlike gelding: winning chaser: modest handicap hurdler: made all at Stratford in July: effective at 2m to 3¼m: seems to act on any going: tried blinkered, not since 1999/00: front runner. *Dr P. Pritchard* **c–** **h91**

FIFTYSEVENCHANNELS (IRE) 14 b.g. Bustineto – Allitess (Mugatpura) [2002/3 c–: c25m^F c26d^{pu} Jun 5] sturdy gelding: one-time useful chaser, deteriorated considerably after 1998/9: barely stayed 3m on a conventional course: acted on good to firm and heavy going: effective with or without blinkers: usually a sound jumper: dead. *Miss A. Armitage* **c–**

FIGAWIN 8 b.g. Rudimentary (USA) – Dear Person (Rainbow Quest (USA)) [2002/3 c91, h–: c22s^5 c27v Nov 12] leggy gelding: modest handicap chaser: showed little either start in 2002/3: stays 3m: acts on soft and good to firm going. *R. Wilman* **c–** **h–**

FILLE D'ARGENT (IRE) 4 gr.f. Desert Style (IRE) – Talina (General Assembly (USA)) [2002/3 17m Aug 17] half-sister to fairly useful 2m hurdler Talina's Law (by Law Society): modest maiden on Flat (should stay 1m): always behind in juvenile on hurdling debut. *Mrs P. N. Dutfield* **h–**

FILOU DU BOIS (FR) 10 b.g. Shafoun (FR) – Jamaica (FR) (Tryptic) [2002/3 c26g^{pu} May 22] good-topped gelding: poor maiden hurdler/steeplechaser: won maiden point in February: stays 2½m: acts on heavy and good to firm going: tried blinkered. *Ms A. E. Embiricos* **c–** **h–**

FILSCOT   11 b.g. Scottish Reel – Fililode (Mossberry) [2002/3 c89, h–: c25d⁴ c25d* **c101**
c20g² c25m⁴ c20m³ c23m⁶ c24g* c24d⁴ c23d⁴ c22mᵖᵘ c21g² Apr 19] compact gelding: **h–**
fair chaser: won handicaps at Hereford in May and Stratford in July: left C. Morlock after
eighth start: stays 25f: acts on firm and soft going: tried blinkered/visored, all wins when
not: none too consistent. *Mrs S. S. Harbour*

FILS DE CRESSON (IRE)   13 b.g. Torus – Hellfire Hostess (Lucifer (USA)) [2002/3 **c85**
c92, h–: c16d⁴ c17dᵖᵘ Oct 12] angular gelding: modest handicap chaser: reportedly lame **h–**
at Bangor in October: best around 2m: acts on soft and good to firm going: tried
blinkered: tongue tied. *J. R. Adam*

FINAL CHANCE   9 ch.m. Nader – Milly's Chance (Mljet) [2002/3 h–: 19f 19f⁶ c19f⁴ **c–**
c19mᵘʳ Oct 30] no worthwhile form over hurdles or fences. *C. Tizzard* **h–**

FINAL ESCAPADE   10 ch.g. St Columbus – Country Princess (Country Retreat) **c–**
[2002/3 c–: c20d Mar 4] little sign of ability, even in points. *C. Wadland*

FINAL LAP   7 b.g. Batshoof – Lap of Honour (Final Straw) [2002/3 h58x: 17s⁶ 19m **h67**
16m 20gᵖᵘ 16s* 16s⁵ 16gᵖᵘ 17f 19f² 16m³ 16d³ 17g³ 17s⁵ 17d 16s 17m Apr 5] smallish
gelding: poor hurdler: won weak seller at Stratford in August: stays 19f: acts on soft and
firm going: visored/blinkered first 4 outings: sometimes makes mistakes. *S. T. Lewis*

FINAL MATCH   5 b.m. Derrylin – Furstin (Furry Glen) [2002/3 F16s F16m Jun 29] **F–**
smallish mare: half-sister to 2 winners, including fair hurdler First Crack (by Scallywag),
stayed 3m: dam, 1m winner, poor plater over hurdles: well tailed off in 2 bumpers. *T. Wall*

FINAL VIEW (FR)   4 b.g. Distant View (USA) – Unafurtivalagrima (USA) (Quest **h–**
For Fame)) [2002/3 17s Nov 21] ex-French gelding: first foal: dam placed on Flat in USA:
twice-raced around 1½m on Flat in 2002, sold out of M. Zilber's stable 24,000 gns
Doncaster August Sales: tailed off in juvenile on hurdling debut. *T. Wall*

FINBAR'S LAW   6 b.g. Contract Law (USA) – De Valera (Faustus (USA)) [2002/3 **h82**
h–, F–: 16gᵖᵘ 16d 21g⁴ 24vᵖᵘ 22g 16g* Mar 29] poor hurdler: best effort when winning
2m novice at Hexham: tongue tied: races freely. *R. Johnson*

FIN BEC (FR)   10 b.g. Tip Moss (FR) – Tourbrune (FR) (Pamponi (FR)) [2002/3 c99x, **c101 x**
h–: c23g³ c20dᵘʳ c22dᵖᵘ c21dᵖᵘ c24sᵖᵘ c20s* c23s⁵ c22g⁴ c25m* Apr 21] strong, lengthy **h–**
gelding: fair chaser: won handicap at Leicester in January and minor event at Market
Rasen in April: stays 3¼m: acts on any going: usually blinkered (wore cheekpieces fourth
outing): front runner: poor jumper. *A. P. Jones*

FIND THE KING (IRE)   5 b.g. King's Theatre (IRE) – Undiscovered (Tap On Wood) **h122**
[2002/3 h128: 20g* 16f 22g 22g Apr 21] good-topped gelding: fairly useful on Flat (stays
2m), successful twice in October: fairly useful hurdler: easily won minor event at Tralee
in August: long way below form in handicaps both subsequent starts: stays 2½m: acts on
soft going: usually tongue tied: has been led in. *E. J. O'Grady, Ireland*

FIND THE LADY (IRE)   9 b.m. Montelimar (USA) – Run Lizzy Run (IRE) (Dun- **c–**
beath (USA)) [2002/3 c21mᵖᵘ c24gᵖᵘ May 31] ex-Irish mare: first foal: sister to fair 2½m **h–**
and 3m hurdle winner Just Ask Me: dam winning hurdler: winning pointer, no other form.
Stephen McCormick

FINEST OF MEN   7 b.g. Tina's Pet – Merry Missus (Bargello) [2002/3 c–, F62: c25d **c–**
May 4] no form in 2 steeplechases: won maiden point in March. *J. B. Walton*

FINE TIMES   9 b.g. Timeless Times (USA) – Marfen (Lochnager) [2002/3 c90, h–: **c–**
c21g⁵ May 3] compact gelding: winning hunter chaser: stays 25f: tongue tied. *Milson* **h–**
Robinson

FINNIGAN'S LOT (IRE)   9 b.g. Lancastrian – Light Bidder (Auction Ring (USA)) **c–**
[2002/3 c21gᵖᵘ c26mᵖᵘ May 22] workmanlike gelding: fair pointer at best: pulled up in 2 **h–**
hunter chases: tried blinkered: sold 1,000 gns Ascot July Sales. *E. L. James*

FINZI (IRE)   5 b.g. Zaffaran (USA) – Sporting Talent (IRE) (Seymour Hicks (FR)) **F–**
[2002/3 F16v F16g Apr 2] 24,000 4-y-o: good-topped gelding: first foal: dam unraced
half-sister to useful chaser Latent Talent, stayed 25f: showed more temperament than
ability in 2 bumpers at Ascot (whipped round start on debut). *D. J. Caro*

FIOLINO (FR)   10 b.g. Bayolidaan (FR) – Vellea (FR) (Cap Martin (FR)) [2002/3 **c–**
c92, h88: 20sᵖᵘ c24sᶠ c25gᵖᵘ 25d Feb 8] rather leggy gelding: maiden hurdler/winning **h–**
chaser, out of sorts in 2002/3. *M. W. Easterby*

FIONNULA'S RAINBOW (IRE)   8 ch.m. Rainbows For Life (CAN) – Bon Retour **c– §**
(Sallust) [2002/3 c109§, h108§: c20s⁶ 24dᵖᵘ 20m⁶ 16m⁴ 19m³ 19s 19d 22d⁶ 20s² 21s 24s⁵ **h84 §**

287

Feb 13] close-coupled mare: winning chaser: poor handicap hurdler nowadays: stays 21f: acts on any going: tried blinkered: moody and inconsistent. *S. T. Lewis*

FIORI 7 b.g. Anshan – Fen Princess (IRE) (Trojan Fen) [2002/3 h129: c17g* c17s²ᵈ c16g c16d² c17v³ c20gᶠ Apr 25] close-coupled gelding: impresses in appearance: useful handicap hurdler: easily won novice at Kelso in October on chasing debut: running best race over fences when falling last in novice handicap at Perth, upsides winner at time: probably stays 2½m: raced on good going or softer over jumps (acts on heavy): usually races prominently. *P. C. Haslam* **c117 h–**

FIRE ANGEL 6 ch.m. Henbit (USA) – Stane Street (IRE) (Gorytus (USA)) [2002/3 F16s 21dᵖᵘ Jan 16] first foal: dam winning hurdler, stayed 2¾m: no show in bumper or mares maiden hurdle (pulled hard). *R. T. Phillips* **h– F–**

FIREAWAY 9 b.g. Infantry – Handymouse (Nearly A Hand) [2002/3 h106: c19s⁴ Dec 14] fair hurdler: fourth in novice at Doncaster on chasing debut, not seen out again: should be suited by 2½m: acts on firm and soft going: has hung/jumped left under pressure. *O. Brennan* **c95 h–**

FIREBALL MACNAMARA (IRE) 7 b.g. Lord Americo – Glint of Baron (Glint of Gold) [2002/3 h108: c16g² c21d² c19s² c19d* c19d² c20sᵖᵘ c20gᵖᵘ Apr 3] useful-looking gelding: fair hurdler: fairly useful novice chaser: improved round of jumping when winning at Doncaster in January: ran as if amiss last 2 starts: effective at 2m to 2¾m: acts on firm and soft going. *M. Pitman* **c116 h–**

FIRE IN ICE 4 b.f. Missed Flight – Boulabas (IRE) (Nashamaa) [2002/3 17sᵖᵘ 17gᶠ 17fᵘʳ 16fᵘʳ 16mᵘʳ Apr 10] poor maiden on Flat: showed more temperament than ability in juvenile hurdles: banned from racing. *B. P. J. Baugh* **h– §**

FIRE RANGER 7 ch.m. Presidium – Regal Flame (Royalty) [2002/3 F17g⁵ F17m² F16m⁴ 19v⁴ 17g⁵ Mar 17] fifth foal: dam, bumper winner, half-sister to high-class 2m hurdler/smart chaser Prideaux Boy: modest form in 3 bumpers: not given hard time when well held in mares novice/maiden hurdles. *J. D. Frost* **h– p F82**

FIRESIDE LEGEND (IRE) 4 b.g. College Chapel – Miss Sandman (Manacle) [2002/3 16g 16d 16g⁵ 16vʳᵒ 16v⁴ 16v⁴ 17s⁶ 16s⁵ 22g 16mᵇᵈ Apr 21] leggy gelding: half-brother to winning chaser in Italy by Salmon Leap: modest on Flat (stays 1¼m): poor juvenile hurdler, trained until after seventh start by W. Turner: will prove best around 2m: acts on soft going: usually blinkered: has had tongue tied: has shown signs of temperament (ran out fourth start). *Miss M. P. Bryant* **h67**

FIRESTONE (GER) 6 b.g. Dictator's Song (USA) – Fatinizza (IRE) (Niniski (USA)) [2002/3 h102: 16d⁵ 16d 16s 16g³ 16d⁶ 16d² 16m⁴ 17g² Apr 19] leggy gelding: modest handicap hurdler: seems best around 2m: acts on heavy going: tongue tied last 5 outings: has broken blood vessels. *A. W. Carroll* **h93**

FIREY SENORITA (IRE) 6 b.m. Great Commotion (USA) – Spanish Rose (Belmez (USA)) [2002/3 23dᵖᵘ 18f Jun 3] ex-Irish mare: poor maiden on Flat (stays 1¼m): poor maiden hurdler: tried blinkered. *L. A. Dace* **h–**

FIREY STEEL (IRE) 6 gr.g. Roselier (FR) – Charming Mo (IRE) (Callernish) [2002/3 20s⁵ 16s 22s⁵ 24s⁴ 20s⁶ Feb 8] smallish gelding: second foal: half-brother to fairly useful bumper winner Northern Native (by Be My Native): dam unraced half-sister to Supreme Novices' Hurdle winner Tourist Attraction: modest novice hurdler: stays 3m: raced on good to soft/soft ground. *A. J. Martin, Ireland* **h95**

FIRINN 8 b.g. Phardante (FR) – Viking Rocket (Viking (USA)) [2002/3 24d² 25gᵖᵘ Jan 18] angular gelding: signs of ability in bumpers in 2000/1: distant second of 4 finishers in novice hurdle at Carlisle on return: tried to run out next time. *A. M. Crow* **h84**

FIRST ALLIANCE (IRE) 6 b.g. Caerleon (USA) – Lady Liberty (NZ) (Noble Bijou (USA)) [2002/3 h–: 20gᵖᵘ 20m Jun 21] sturdy gelding: no form over hurdles: sold out of K. Morgan's stable 4,200 gns Doncaster May Sales after reappearance: tried visored: has had tongue tied: has looked temperamental. *E. W. Tuer* **h–**

FIRST BASE 4 ch.g. First Trump – Rose Music (Luthier) [2002/3 16d 16gᵖᵘ 17d³ Apr 8] poor maiden on Flat (probably stays 1m): tried in cheekpieces, first form in juvenile hurdles when third at Sedgefield. *R. E. Barr* **h76**

FIRST DAY COVER (IRE) 7 b.g. Toulon – Bilberry (Nicholas Bill) [2002/3 F90: 17v⁴ 20v⁶ 21m 22g⁴ Mar 17] better effort in bumpers in 2001/2 when winning at Plumpton: modest form over hurdles on return: stays 2½m: acts on heavy going, seemed ill at ease on good to firm. *Noel T. Chance* **h94**

FIRST EMBRACE 7 b.g. Faustus (USA) – Legal Embrace (CAN) (Legal Bid (USA)) **h74**
[2002/3 h85: 24g 24f⁵ Oct 17] leggy gelding: poor maiden hurdler: probably stays 3m:
acts on firm and good to soft going: has had tongue tied. *K. Bell*

FIRST FLIGHT 7 br.g. Neltino – The Beginning (Goldhill) [2002/3 h112: c19dᶠ **c– p**
25gᵖᵘ Mar 14] close-coupled gelding: fair novice hurdler in 2001/2: off 10½ months, yet **h–**
to be asked for effort when falling 4 out in novice at Exeter on chasing debut (open to
improvement): jumped poorly back over hurdles: stays 3m: raced on good going or softer.
K. C. Bailey

FIRST GOLD (FR) 10 b.g. Shafoun (FR) – Nuit d'Or II (FR) (Pot d'Or (FR)) **c171**
[2002/3 c164+, h148+: c20s³ c24v c25d³ c26gᵖᵘ c25g* Apr 3] **h–**
    First Gold's essay in last year's Annual began with the forecast that, follow-
ing injury, he could face an uphill task to re-establish himself as the best staying
chaser in training. His task was certainly an arduous one in the latest season, made
even more so after performances for much of the campaign which suggested his
career was on a slippery slope. Things hit rock-bottom for First Gold in the
Cheltenham Gold Cup but sparkling victories at the two other spring Festival
meetings gave the firm impression that, if not quite the best staying chaser around
these days, he would be among the best placed to profit in the absence of Best Mate,
or should the reigning champion have an off day.
    First Gold had been sidelined for the best part of twelve months before his
return to action at Punchestown in December. A problem with a leg after the
previous season's King George VI Chase at Kempton, in which he had finished a
well-beaten fourth when favourite behind Florida Pearl, had brought a premature
end to his 2001/2 campaign. After a period of recuperation at his owner's stud, First
Gold returned to Francois Doumen's stable in August and became his trainer's first
runner over jumps in Ireland when reappearing in the Punchestown Chase. Given
his absence, and the inadequate trip, First Gold's running-on third behind two-and-
a-half-mile specialist Native Upmanship looked a most encouraging comeback.
But it turned out to be a false dawn and, despite his trainer's insistence to the
contrary, First Gold's next three outings suggested his best days were in the past.
The first of those came at Christmas time in Ireland in the Ericsson Chase at
Leopardstown, tackled in preference to an attempt to regain the King George crown
which he had won so impressively in 2000/1. Back at three miles, First Gold started

Martell Cognac Cup Chase, Aintree—First Gold, in blinkers first time, shows he's still a top-class chaser

favourite against most of Ireland's leading stayers but was the first beaten and finished last behind rising star Beef Or Salmon. Tests revealed that First Gold was suffering from a respiratory tract infection at Leopardstown, a valid excuse, but his next appearance, in the Country Gentlemen's Association Chase—the former Jim Ford—at Wincanton, hardly boosted his Gold Cup claims. Still looking some way off peak fitness, he was ridden with an eye to the future, closing gradually to half-way after being dropped out in rear but unable to quicken, eventually finishing third to another former King George winner See More Business, three years his senior. Mistakes at the last three fences, as well as lack of fitness, meant First Gold didn't even finish second, losing that place to the Agfa Diamond winner Iris Bleu.

There were, therefore, plenty with better recent form when First Gold lined up for the Cheltenham Gold Cup, his first outing of any sort at the track. Denied the chance to run in the 2002 Gold Cup by injury, he had been ante-post favourite for the Gold Cup that never was in 2001. First Gold held an alternative entry at the Festival in the National Hunt Handicap Chase but after pleasing in his work with Baracouda—'we think we have the real horse back'—First Gold was allowed to take his chance in the Gold Cup. Only Harbour Pilot, You're Agoodun and no-hoper Modulor started at longer odds than 33/1-shot First Gold and, whilst stripping fitter than at Wincanton, he did not stand out in the paddock and looked a shadow of his former self in the race. A mistake at the thirteenth consigned him to the rear division and he was well held when pulled up before three out.

But so much for the doom and gloom. There was none of that after the Martell Cognac Cup Chase three weeks later at Aintree. First Gold's only previous success in ten starts in the J. P. McManus colours had come in the same race two years earlier when he had routed a good field with an exuberant display of fast and accurate jumping. Blinkered for the first time and receiving weight from all six of his rivals, First Gold scored a second success in the race, showing not only all his zest of old, but also something like the top-notch form of his younger days. Starting at 14/1 (only Irish challenger More Than A Stroll started at longer odds), First Gold faced three others seeking compensation for defeat in the Gold Cup in Valley Henry, Commanche Court and Marlborough who had finished fourth, sixth and eleventh respectively. Completing the line-up were the top-class mare Lady Cricket and another ten-year-old with something to prove after injury, Barton, a course-and-distance winner as a novice. Looking very well this time, First Gold jumped well in front, quickening the tempo with a circuit to go, giving the slip to his nearest pursuer Marlborough from the home turn and galloping on strongly to win unchallenged. Lady Cricket stayed on from the rear to finish fourteen lengths back in second, just ahead of Commanche Court, while the other finishers, favourite Valley Henry, Marlborough and Barton were all soundly beaten.

Francois Doumen expanded afterwards on the problems that First Gold had evidently shrugged off by Aintree. 'He's been very tight in his muscles and ligaments, particularly around his shoulders. I thought he was right when he went to Cheltenham and he was going very well, just behind Best Mate, when he made a bad mistake going out on the second circuit. Thierry thought the best thing to do was to pull him up . . . and he then told me the horse was still not quite right in his shoulders.'

First Gold had been allotted 12-0 in the Irish National, though that represented a mark 5 lb lower than his re-assessed BHB assessment after Aintree, in line with the weights being compressed 'Aintree-style' to attract a better quality and more competitive Irish National field. Meanwhile, First Gold could still run off his old BHB mark in the attheraces Gold Cup and was made ante-post favourite for the Sandown race in which he now looked well treated. But, in the event, he ran in neither of those handicaps, instead adding to what promised to be one of the year's best staying chases, the Punchestown Heineken Gold Cup shortly after the end of the British season. First Gold was denied a further meeting with Gold Cup casualty Beef Or Salmon, as well as Cheltenham third Harbour Pilot, when both were taken out of the race due to concerns about the state of the ground. An early fall from Hussard Collonges and lacklustre efforts from both Native Upmanship and Florida Pearl also made the race less competitive than it had looked on paper. But, blinkered again, First Gold turned in another top-class effort to justify favouritism this time, making just about all and stretching his rivals four out to win by six lengths and seven from Rince Ri and Native Upmanship.

Mr J. P. McManus' "First Gold"

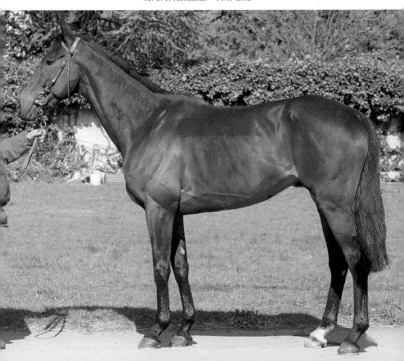

First Gold has been at the top for a long time, longer perhaps than many in Britain might appreciate. He won the Grand Steeple-Chase de Paris as a five-year-old and two and a half years later denied the twelve-year-old Al Capone II an eighth consecutive win in the Prix La Haye Jousselin. Now it is First Gold who is in the position of having to contend with a younger brigade of chasers. Best Mate and the four who followed him home in the Gold Cup are all eight-year-olds, Beef Or Salmon a year younger still. An eleven-year-old First Gold will struggle to win a Gold Cup, but a clash in the King George between Best Mate and a First Gold in the sort of form he ended the latest season would be a race to savour.

First Gold (FR) (b.g. 1993)	Shafoun (FR) (b 1979)	Labus (b or br 1971)	Busted
			Cordovilla
		Cephira (b 1975)	Abdos
			Jamira
	Nuit d'Or II (FR) (b 1979)	Pot d'Or (b 1966)	Buisson d'Or
			Appo
		Fyrole II (b 1971)	Le Tyrol
			Verveine VII

The tall First Gold stays twenty-nine furlongs and has raced only on good ground or softer. He usually jumps well, and zestful fencing has been a feature of his best performances. Whether his quick, rather low style of jumping would be suited to the National fences is another matter though. First Gold was entered for the Grand National in the latest season and his owner was keen to let him take his chance, though his trainer and jockey had the final say in opting for the Martell Cup instead. 'It probably wasn't a wise idea to throw him around over the National fences,' remarked Thierry Doumen. 'He's not that easy to manoeuvre and I had to ask him to change legs on the bends well in advance. I wouldn't be sure about going round the Canal Turn.' First Gold is another fine advertisement for the skills of his trainer, already demonstrated with the likes of The Fellow, and Jim And Tonic on the Flat, at handling a horse able to compete successfully at the top level over a number of seasons. First Gold has now made a successful return from injury not once, but twice; he was off for nearly two years after his win in the Grand Steeple-Chase with a tendon injury. However he fares from now on, First Gold has now won chases at the highest grade in France, Britain and (no doubt, most importantly for his current owner) Ireland, a feat that while not totally without precedent—Tied Cottage won valuable prizes over fences in all three countries and Dawn Run won championship races over hurdles in each of the three—could hardly be bettered and will be very difficult to equal. *F. Doumen, France*

FIRST GREY   4 gr.f. Environment Friend – Myrtilla (Beldale Flutter (USA)) [2002/3   **F79** F14d F16v⁴ F17v² F17d Mar 2] tall filly: third foal: dam winning hurdler around 2m: modest form in bumpers. *E. W. Tuer*

FIRST JUDGEMENT (IRE)   7 b.g. Leading Counsel (USA) – Star Gold (Bonne   **h81** Noel) [2002/3 F75: 22d⁵ Oct 22] good-topped gelding: modest form on first of 2 starts in bumpers: fifth of 13 in amateur novice at Exeter on hurdling debut: shapes like a thorough stayer. *J. W. Mullins*

FIRST LOVE   7 br.g. Bustino – First Romance (Royalty) [2002/3 h125: c16v² c18s²   **c130 +** c21s* c16v² Mar 8] good sort: fairly useful hurdler: odds on all 4 starts over fences, only   **h–** success when impressively making all in novice at Folkestone in February: will probably stay 3m: raced on going softer than good (acts on heavy): free-going sort, probably best allowed to stride on. *N. J. Henderson*

FIRST OFFICER (USA)   6 b.g. Lear Fan (USA) – Trampoli (USA) (Trempolino   **c83** (USA)) [2002/3 16d⁶ 20d⁵ 20s 19s⁵ c20gᵖᵘ c25g³ c26m² Apr 19] well-made gelding: **h87** modest maiden hurdler: first form over fences when second of 4 finishers in novice handicap at Plumpton, jumping right throughout: probably stays 3¼m: acts on good to soft going, probably on good to firm: tried blinkered: has reportedly broken blood vessels. *C. C. Bealby*

FIRST TOUCH (IRE)   9 br.g. Montelimar (USA) – Jennycomequick (Furry Glen)   **h–** [2002/3 21sᵖᵘ 16gᵖᵘ Dec 18] tall, angular gelding: seventh of 20 in above-average bumper at Cheltenham in 2000/1: no show in 2 maiden hurdles on return, tongue tied on second occasion. *M. R. Bosley*

FIRST TRUTH   6 b.g. Rudimentary (USA) – Pursuit of Truth (USA) (Irish River (FR)) [2002/3 h87: 17g³ 17s* May 18] smallish gelding: fair hurdler: improved form when winning handicap at Bangor in May: raced around 2m on good going or softer (acts on soft). *Mrs H. Dalton* **h100**

FISHER STREET   8 gr.g. Tigani – Pricket Walk (Amboise) [2002/3 c92, h64: c20m⁴ c25m* May 29] leggy gelding: maiden hurdler: modest chaser: visored, won handicap at Kelso: stays 25f: acts on good to firm and heavy going. *Mrs S. C. Bradburne* **c96** **h–**

FISHKI'S LAD   8 b.g. Casteddu – Fishki (Niniski (USA)) [2002/3 c–§, h–§: 20d² 24d* 25g³ 19d 24v² 22g⁴ Apr 7] leggy, lengthy gelding: modest form on completed start over fences: modest handicap hurdler, won at Hexham in June for A. Crook: sold out of M. Hammond's stable 8,400 gns Doncaster August Sales after next start: stays 3m: acts on heavy and good to firm going: usually visored/blinkered, not last 3 outings: has looked ungenuine. *E. W. Tuer* **c–** **h99**

FIVE PENCE   7 b.g. Henbit (USA) – Le Saule d'Or (Sonnen Gold) [2002/3 16d 19d Dec 19] rather lightly-made gelding: second foal: half-brother to 10.2f winner Talents Little Gem (by Democratic): dam, fair 2-y-o 1m winner who stayed 1¼m, half-sister to fairly useful hurdler at 2½m+ Rich Desire: no show in maiden or novice hurdle. *P. Winkworth* **h–**

FLAG FEN (USA)   12 b. or br.g. Riverman (USA) – Damascus Flag (USA) (Damascus (USA)) [2002/3 h92: 16d⁴ 16d⁵ 16g⁶ 16m⁵ Apr 21] good-topped gelding: modest handicap hurdler: best around 2m: acts on soft and good to firm going, possibly not on heavy. *H. J. Collingridge* **h88**

FLAGSHIP UBERALLES (IRE)   9 br.g. Accordion – Fourth Degree (Oats) [2002/3 c170, h–: c16s⁴ c24sᵖᵘ c16g⁵ Mar 12] **c164** **h–**

After three seasons as the top two-mile chaser, Flagship Uberalles lost his crown to the young pretender Moscow Flyer, though none of their three encounters was an entirely satisfactory contest and a close race was on the cards when Moscow Flyer lost his rider two out in the BMW Chase at Punchestown shortly after the end of the British season. Although time favours the younger horse, it is not a foregone conclusion, if they meet when both are on song, that Moscow Flyer will come out on top. Prior to Punchestown, Flagship Uberalles hadn't given his running in either the Tingle Creek Chase at Sandown or the Queen Mother Champion Chase at Cheltenham, though he had an excuse in the Tingle Creek. He also made an abortive attempt at the King George VI Chase over three miles at Kempton on Boxing Day when soft ground and a strongly-run race proved altogether too much of a test of stamina; he was beaten a long way out and eventually pulled up.

BMW Chase, Punchestown—
Flagship Uberalles is poised to take advantage of Moscow Flyer's blunder two out

Mr J. P. McManus' "Flagship Uberalles"

Flagship Uberalles made his now-customary return at Sandown for the Tingle Creek, and for once he hadn't changed stables over the summer. He had won the three previous renewals, in both 2000/1 (when the race was run at Cheltenham) and 2001/2 putting up his best performance of the campaign. Flagship Uberalles started at shorter odds for the latest edition than in previous years, though he only just shaded favouritism over the 2002 Arkle Chase winner Moscow Flyer, who had the benefit of a run at Down Royal the previous month. The match between champion and challenger dominated the build-up to the race but the contest ended in a 'knockout' at the fifth, Flagship Uberalles overjumping and losing his footing, in the process ending his own chance and that of the baulked Moscow Flyer whose rider was dislodged. Flagship Uberalles started 7/4 favourite for the 2002 renewal of the Queen Mother Champion Chase but, three months on from Kempton, he went to Cheltenham an unconsidered 12/1 chance. It was only four outings, but a whole year, since Flagship Uberalles had shown anything like his best form and the application of blinkers for the first time was hardly an encouraging sign. He was running for the first time in the colours of J. P. McManus (his previous American-based owners having sold him reportedly because they were no longer able to travel to Britain) and Flagship Uberalles hardly looked one of his new owner's shrewder purchases as he trailed in twenty lengths behind Moscow Flyer. Flagship Uberalles looked extremely well but produced a laboured effort and, despite a lengthening list of excuses, appeared a long way removed from the top-class chaser he was in his prime.

Punchestown caused a revision of that view. The field for the BMW wasn't so strong as the Champion Chase by any means, Latalomne the only other in a

294

seven-horse line-up, apart from Moscow Flyer and Flagship Uberalles, with pretensions to winning a championship race. As in the previous year, the Celebration Chase at Sandown the previous weekend weakened the line-up—Cenkos had been an intended runner in both but missed Punchestown after defeat at Sandown. Flagship Uberalles himself was initially going to run at Sandown but was withdrawn on account of the firmish ground. After Moscow Flyer was sent for home four out, only Flagship Uberalles looked to have any prospect of getting close to him and, despite a slow jump at the next, he had closed right up when the favourite again parted company with Barry Geraghty, this time following a mistake of his own two from home. Flagship Uberalles was far from certain to have won but a close race was on the cards and Flagship Uberalles was shaping into the first two-mile chaser to make a race of it with Moscow Flyer during the season. Flagship Uberalles went on to gain a six-length victory over the useful Arctic Copper, which, on bare reading, is hardly top-class form, though Flagship Uberalles had certainly raced with much of his old zest. Hopefully, the 2003 Tingle Creek, with Azertyuiop adding extra spice, will provide a clear-cut verdict on the relative standing of the top two-milers.

Flagship Uberalles (IRE) (br.g. 1994)	Accordion (b 1986)	Sadler's Wells (b 1981)	Northern Dancer, Fairy Bridge
		Sound of Success (ch 1969)	Successor, Belle Musique
	Fourth Degree (br 1949)	Oats (b 1973)	Northfields, Arctic Lace
		Puzzes Times (b 1969)	Olden Times, Puzzesca

Flagship Uberalles' pedigree has been much discussed in previous Annuals and doesn't require much reprising. His illustrious half-brother Viking Flagship (by Viking) also won the BMW Chase, as a novice when it was a limited handicap. That horse's owner Graham Roach purchased through an agent a foal by Supreme Leader out of Flagship Uberalles's sister Queen's Flagship, a two-mile hurdle winner, for €90,000 at the 2002 Fairyhouse November Sale, which was, for about a week, a record price for a NH-bred foal, the same owner surpassing the figure at Doncaster a week later when paying 70,000 guineas for a son of Saddlers' Hall. Two years previously, at the same Fairyhouse Sale, Roach had also paid a then-record figure at an Irish sale for a NH-bred yearling when paying IR 56,000 guineas for Pirate Flagship, an as-yet unraced French-foaled gelding from this family. The rangy Flagship Uberalles should stay beyond two miles, though seems unlikely to be given many more chances over further. He is ideally suited by good going or softer and acts on soft. Usually a sound jumper, he carries his head awkwardly but is perfectly genuine. *P. J. Hobbs*

FLAHIVE'S FIRST   9 ch.g. Interrex (CAN) – Striking Image (IRE) (Flash of Steel) [2002/3 c73+, h79: c17g² c17s² c17s² c16s³ c16g⁵ c16m² c20g⁵ c20s³ c17s* c17d* c16d⁴ c16s c19s⁴ c21d^ur c19s^pu c17v c16s³ c18s⁶ 19v⁶ c20g⁴ 17m⁶ c19m⁴ Apr 21] sparely-made gelding: poor hurdler: modest handicap chaser: won twice within 3 days at Cartmel (first a novice) in August: stays 21f: acts on soft and good to firm going. *D. Burchell*   **c90 h–**

FLAMEBIRD (IRE)   6 b.m. Mukaddamah (USA) – Flamenco (USA) (Dance Spell (USA)) [2002/3 17g^F 16f³ May 10] bad maiden on Flat for Mrs A. King: showed more on completed outing over hurdles, third to Inn Antique in novice at Wincanton. *Jonjo O'Neill*   **h80**

FLAME CREEK (IRE)   7 b.g. Shardari – Sheila's Pet (IRE) (Welsh Term) [2002/3 h120p: 16g² 17v* 16s* 16g 16m^pu Apr 12]   **h154**

    'He won't run again before Cheltenham. Nothing would tempt me to go for the Tote Gold Trophy—you're better going to the Champion Hurdle fit and fresh.' So said trainer Noel Chance after Flame Creek's success in the seven-runner Red Square Vodka Champion Hurdle Trial at Haydock in January. Flame Creek would have picked up a 4-lb penalty for Newbury and, as he was already ante-post favourite, he might well have started very short odds after a much improved effort at Haydock. Not surprisingly, he also shortened quite a bit in the market for the Champion itself, in to 14/1 or shorter after being available at 33/1 immediately after winning a handicap at Cheltenham less than three weeks previously. It clearly

Red Square Vodka Champion Hurdle Trial, Haydock—Flame Creek safely over the last

wasn't difficult for Chance to make his mind up between the two races, after all winning the Champion is worth £100,000 more than winning the Tote Gold Trophy. That also assumes, though, that the chance of winning the respective races was roughly equal and, furthermore, that this was really an either/or option. It wasn't and it isn't. Make A Stand and Flakey Dove were Champion Hurdle winners in the 'nineties who contested the Tote Gold Trophy. Make A Stand won at Newbury, while Flakey Dove finished third having also won the same Haydock race as Flame Creek, and then, for good measure, winning the Cleeve Hurdle at Cheltenham between Haydock and Newbury and the Berkshire Hurdle at Newbury between the Tote Gold Trophy and the Champion. King Credo, Large Action, Oh So Risky, For Auction and Within The Law are all among those to have made the frame in both races in the same season. Not all horses would stand up nearly so well to a busy campaign as Flakey Dove did, but a sizeable number would stand up a good deal better to a more ambitious campaign than some of the leading lights of the training profession would evidently have you believe.

As for which race provided Flame Creek's connections with the prospect of a big pay-day, there's no argument—the way we see it at least—that his chance in the Tote Gold Trophy was much better than his chance in the Champion. Had he taken his place in the field at Newbury Flame Creek would have been clear top-rated on Timeform ratings, whereas at Cheltenham he was rated behind seven of his sixteen rivals with two others, including the favourite Rhinestone Cowboy, who had much greater potential for improvement, within a couple of pounds. Flame Creek failed to give his running in the Champion anyway, trailing in last but one of the fourteen finishers, and was later reported to have an infection. Even accounting for those with better form who failed to give their running, Flame Creek's Haydock form would have entitled him to finish only fifth to Rooster Booster. He would not have had to improve much to take a place but he wouldn't have been able to get near the winner. As it is, there's some doubt whether Flame Creek could have matched his Haydock form under the conditions which prevailed on Champion Hurdle day.

The Champion Hurdle Trial was just the sixth race of Flame Creek's career and confirmed his marked progress in the twenty-one months since he had made a winning debut in a bumper at Wincanton. He had needed the experience when beaten on his hurdling debut in January 2002 but won a novice at Cheltenham and an intermediate at Kelso (beating the useful Monkerhostin half a length at level weights) shortly before and shortly after the end of the 2001/2 season, and had already been talked of by his trainer as a Champion Hurdle possible when putting up a useful effort to win at Cheltenham on New Year's Day. Beating the frustrating

Sonevafushi six lengths was hardly championship form and the third Westender, who was conceding the winner 15 lb, was the best horse at the weights (and, much improved, went on to finish runner-up in the Champion itself). Flame Creek needed to jump more fluently for one thing and a tendency to hang left (also shown when winning his novice) needed ironing out as well. Flame Creek started second favourite at Haydock, in a race where the field hardly lived up to the race title. The clear form pick was the favourite Ilnamar, making his first appearance since winning the Aintree Hurdle the previous April, none of the five others in the line-up having any realistic Cheltenham claims. Flame Creek could hardly be blamed for Ilnamar's moderate showing and he beat the useful October Mist convincingly enough by thirteen lengths, surviving a blunder two out and seeing out his race really well on the testing ground. Flame Creek was a horse going the right way but, so far as Cheltenham was concerned, there remained doubts about his jumping prowess and whether he had the speed for the Champion, doubts that remain. Flame Creek's jumping let him down badly on his only start after Cheltenham, in the Scottish Champion Hurdle at Ayr, where he met Westender at level weights but was pulled up two out. The race went to In Contrast, who was receiving 11 lb from Flame Creek having been set to give him weight in the original handicap for the Tote Gold Trophy.

Flame Creek (IRE) (b.g. 1996)	Shardari (b 1982)	Top Ville (b 1976)	High Top
			Sega Ville
		Sharmada (gr 1978)	Zeddaan
			Shireen
	Sheila's Pet (IRE) (b 1991)	Welsh Term (b 1979)	Welsh Pageant
			Trinity Term
		Sheila's Flame (b 1977)	Reformed Character
			Lady Flame

Martin Wesson Partners' "Flame Creek"

Flame Creek looks the part for chasing—he is a tall gelding in appearance —and made a successful if not altogether convincing start over fences shortly after the end of the British season, though at the time of writing a return to hurdling in the autumn is on the agenda. He is likely to be well worth trying over further than two miles. Despite repeated assertions that he needs good ground to show his best form (it's even been suggested that he wants firm), he's shown himself fully effective on soft and heavy and has yet to match those efforts under less testing conditions. Flame Creek doesn't come from that distinguished a family and those of note in it have been stayers. His unraced dam Sheila's Pet, whose first foal he is, is a half-sister to the fairly useful staying chaser Full of Fire and the winning hurdler/pointer The Bird O'Donnell, who was suited by three miles or more. The third dam Lady Flame was half-sister to the dour staying jumper Fort Knight, who ran in the 1968 Grand National. Flame Creek is the best jumper so far sired by the top-class middle-distance horse Shardari, who is also responsible for the useful staying chaser Shardam and the successful French hurdler Walk On Seas, who has raced at up to twenty-one furlongs. *Noel T. Chance*

FLAMENCA (USA) 4 b.f. Diesis – Highland Ceilidh (IRE) (Scottish Reel) [2002/3 17g 17d³ 16m² 16d⁶ 16sᵖᵘ 16d 16d⁶ 18g⁵ 16g⁴ 17m³ Apr 26] poor maiden on Flat (probably stays 13f): poor novice hurdler: appeared to sulk after hampered first final outing: will stay 2½m: acts on good to firm and good to soft going: wore visor/cheekpieces 6 of last 7 starts. *R. Allan* **h81 §**

FLAME OF ZARA 4 ch.f. Blushing Flame (USA) – Sierra Madrona (USA) (Woodman (USA)) [2002/3 F12g⁴ F16s² F16f² F17m² Apr 17] angular filly: second foal: dam ungenuine staying hurdler: progressive form in bumpers, 2 lengths second of 17 to Amorello in valuable mares listed event at Cheltenham final start: will stay beyond 2m: carries head awkwardly. *Mrs M. Reveley* **F98**

FLAMING CHEEK 5 b.g. Blushing Flame (USA) – Rueful Lady (Streetfighter) [2002/3 F17s⁴ F16d F16v⁴ F16g⁵ 16g⁶ Mar 14] seventh foal: half-brother to winning hurdler/chaser around 2m Thistle Princess (by Belfort): dam, winning hurdler, stayed 21f: modest form in bumpers: 28 lengths sixth in conditional jockeys maiden at Fakenham on hurdling debut. *A. G. Blackmore* **h76** **F83**

FLAMING HECK 6 b.g. Dancing High – Heckley Spark (Electric) [2002/3 F16g³ Apr 30] 6,600 4-y-o: second foal: dam lightly-raced maiden: 18½ lengths third to Abzuson in bumper at Hexham on debut. *Mrs L. B. Normile* **F70**

FLAMING SPIRT 4 b.f. Blushing Flame (USA) – Fair Test (Fair Season) [2002/3 16gᵘʳ 16vᵖᵘ Dec 27] lengthy filly: fair but unreliable on Flat (stays 11f): in touch when unseating 3 out in juvenile won by Saintsaire at Newbury on hurdling debut: very stiff task at Chepstow 9 days later. *J. S. Moore* **h100**

FLASHANT 8 ch.g. Henbit (USA) – La Furze (Winden) [2002/3 h–: 16d 24dF 20m⁵ 17d⁴ Aug 4] winning hurdler, no form for long time: blinkered final outing. *A. W. Carroll* **h–**

FLASH GORDON 9 ch.g. Gildoran – Florence May (Grange Melody) [2002/3 c104: c20sF c21dᵖᵘ c24gᵘʳ Apr 19] tall gelding: lightly raced: fair chaser: failed to complete in 2002/3, though would have been placed but for unseating last in handicap at Stratford: stays 3m: acts on firm going: has given trouble in preliminaries/at start: clearly difficult to keep sound. *Mrs S. Richardson* **c93**

FLASH OF MEMORY 6 b.m. Rock Hopper – Mystic Memory (Ela-Mana-Mou) [2002/3 F89: 20m³ 16d Nov 2] bumper winner: modest on Flat (stayed 2¼m), successful in June for R. Fahey: poor form in 2 novice hurdles at Wetherby: would have proved suited by further than 2m: dead. *P. D. Niven* **h77**

FLAT MATE (IRE) 6 br.g. Supreme Leader – Lady Nethertown (Windjammer (USA)) [2002/3 F16d 20sᵖᵘ 19d c20sF Mar 2] tall gelding: seventh foal: half-brother to several winners, including useful chaser Glemot (by Strong Gale), probably stayed 27f, and fair 2m chaser Rash Decision (by Rashar): dam, won at 2m over hurdles, half-sister to smart 3m chaser Johnny Setaside: no sign of ability, fell fatally on chasing debut. *Mrs S. J. Smith* **c–** **h–** **F–**

FLAT STANLEY 4 b.g. Celtic Swing – Cool Grey (Absalom) [2002/3 19dᵖᵘ Jan 13] poor maiden on Flat (stays 1½m): no show in novice on hurdling debut. *R. Bastiman* **h–**

FLAT TOP 12 b.g. Blakeney – New Edition (Great Nephew) [2002/3 c109, h–: c20d⁵ c25dᵘʳ c25sᵘʳ c24v Jan 29] small, sturdy gelding: fair handicap chaser: needs test at 2½m **c102** **h–**

and stays 3¼m: acts on heavy going, probably on good to firm: blinkered once: has reportedly broken blood vessel: probably ideally suited by waiting tactics in well-run race. *M. W. Easterby*

FLAT TOP (USA) 10 b. or br.g. Alleged (USA) – Lady of The Light (USA) (The Minstrel (CAN)) [2002/3 24f³ 19s³ 21s* 22d* Nov 17] leading American hurdler, successful on 9 of 17 starts: off 2 years before April 2002: contested only Grade 1 events on return, winning Breeders Cup Chase at Far Hills (made all) in October and Colonial Cup at Camden (by 6¼ lengths) in November, beating Tres Touche each time: stays 2¾m: acts on firm and soft going. *Janet E. Elliot, USA*   **h?**

FLAVIATORE 5 b.h. Deploy – Trundley Wood (Wassl) [2002/3 16d 16g^pu 17g⁴ Apr 13] angular horse: successful at 1m and 1¼m on Flat in Germany: poor form on first of 2 starts over hurdles in Britain: well held at Munich final outing: takes good hold. *M. Hofer, Germany*   **h80**

FLAXLEY ABBEY 6 gr.m. Arzanni – Dunbrody Abbey (Proverb) [2002/3 F–: F17g F17m 19v^pu 17m⁵ 22m Apr 15] worthwhile form only when seventh in maiden bumper at Newton Abbot, second start. *J. D. Frost*   **h–**
F72

FLAXLEY WOOD 12 b. or br.g. Kambalda – Coolbawn Run (Deep Run) [2002/3 c121, h–: c22f² c21m* c24m Oct 5] compact gelding: winning hurdler: fairly useful handicap chaser: won at Uttoxeter in August: well held in stronger race at Chepstow 6 weeks later: effective at 2½m to 3m: probably acts on any going: races prominently: usually jumps well: game. *R. H. Buckler*   **c117**
h–

FLECTHEFAWNA (IRE) 7 b.h. Glacial Storm (USA) – Lady Sperrin (Abednego) [2002/3 F17s F18v 21s⁴ Jan 27] fourth foal: half-brother to Amid Birds of Prey (by Over The River), won 19f hurdle in Ireland: dam unraced, from family of top-class staying chaser Alexander Banquet: placed several times in maiden Irish points in 2002: well held in 2 bumpers: modest form when around 27 lengths fourth of 21 to Fork Lightning in novice at Kempton on hurdling debut: will stay beyond 21f. *L. A. Dace*   **h91**
F–

FLEET LAD (USA) 8 b.g. Afleet (CAN) – Temperence Cordial (USA) (Temperence Hill (USA)) [2002/3 h–: 17g^pu Jun 22] useful-looking gelding: no form over hurdles. *J. D. Frost*   **h–**

FLEMMING (USA) 6 ch.g. Green Dancer (USA) – La Groupie (FR) (Groom Dancer (USA)) [2002/3 17d^pu 20g⁶ 19m⁶ Sep 11] second foal: brother to fair hurdler around 2m Green Fan and middle-distance winner Groupinsky: dam 1m winner: modest maiden on Flat (stays 1¼m), placed 5 times in France at 4 yrs, claimed from M. Rolland €12,100: little encouragement in 3 starts over hurdles, blinkered last 2. *A. G. Juckes*   **h–**

FLEUR 7 b.m. Petoski – Mizzie Lizzie (Netherkelly) [2002/3 F–: F16d 16g 16s^pu 21d^pu Nov 26] lengthy, rather sparely-made mare: no form: headstrong. *J. Gallagher*   **h–**
F–

FLEUR DE MARECHAL 8 br.m. Greensmith – Welsh Flower (Welsh Saint) [2002/3 c63, h63: c20d³ c21g^F c25g² c23g^pu c21m^F c22m³ c25m^pu Sep 11] lengthy mare: maiden hurdler: poor novice chaser, often let down by jumping: lame final outing: stays 25f: acts on firm and good to soft going: visored second to fifth starts. *J. W. Mullins*   **c68 x**
h–

FLEXIBLE ACTION (IRE) 5 b. or br.g. Brief Truce (USA) – Uncertain Affair (IRE) (Darshaan) [2002/3 F16f* F16g² Apr 20] IR 12,000 2-y-o: angular gelding: fourth foal: half-brother to 4 winners, including useful 2m hurdler/Flat stayer Direct Bearing by Polish Precedent) and fairly useful 2m hurdler Brief Decline (by Alzao): dam, fair Irish 1¾m winner, out of half-sister to dam of Slip Anchor: won bumper at Listowel in September on debut: much better form when next seen out in spring, second of 15 to Royal Alphabet at Fairyhouse and fifth to Royal Rosa in Grade 1 at Punchestown. *J. E. Kiely, Ireland*   **F114**

FLEXIBLE CONCIENCE (IRE) 8 br.g. Glacial Storm (USA) – Philly Athletic (Sit In The Corner (USA)) [2002/3 h87, F81: 21d^pu Nov 29] good-topped gelding: lightly raced, has shown some ability over hurdles: will be suited by 3m. *J. A. B. Old*   **h78**

FLIGHT COMMAND 5 ch.g. Gunner B – Wing On (Quayside) [2002/3 F16d* Apr 25] 25,000 4-y-o: brother to useful 2m jumper Crack On, and half-brother to several other winners, including fairly useful 2m hurdler/chaser Captain Khedive (by Deep Run) and fair staying hurdler Richmond Lady (by Broadsword): dam unraced: 20/1, won 17-runner bumper at Perth on debut by 1¼ lengths from Duringthenight, patiently ridden and finding plenty after leading 1f out: useful prospect. *P. Beaumont*   **F103 p**

FLIGHT TO TUSCANY 5 b.m. Bonny Scot (IRE) – Tuscan Butterfly (Beldale Flutter (USA)) [2002/3 16g Sep 14] poor maiden on Flat (stays 1¾m): well held in maiden on hurdling debut. *J. M. Bradley*   **h–**

FLIGHTY LEADER (IRE)   11 b.g. Supreme Leader – Flighty Ann (The Parson)   c–
[2002/3 c–, h82d: 27g 24d⁴ 20m Jun 21] smallish, lengthy gelding: winning hurdler/   h–
maiden chaser, no worthwhile form since reappearance in 2001/2: stays 3¼m. *P. Spottiswood*

FLINDERS   8 b.m. Henbit (USA) – Stupid Cupid (Idiot's Delight) [2002/3 c69, h75:   c78
c17g⁵ c25g* c22d c24f² c26mᵖᵘ Apr 21] leggy mare: maiden hurdler: poor chaser: won   h–
novice handicap at Folkestone in November: stays 25f: acts on firm and good to soft
going: broke blood vessel final outing. *R. Rowe*

FLINDERS CHASE   8 gr.g. Terimon – Proverbial Rose (Proverb) [2002/3 c97p, h–:   c102 §
c17d³ c16g³ c20v³ c18g³ c16s² c20s² c24d³ c21dᵘʳ Mar 6] workmanlike gelding: won   h–
only outing over hurdles: fair novice chaser: stays 3m: raced on good going or softer (acts
on heavy): consistent, but usually finds little (may benefit from headgear). *C. J. Mann*

FLINSKI (IRE)   8 b.g. Warcraft (USA) – Rose Almond (Stanford) [2002/3 16s 18s   h75
16s⁵ 16d 16v 20d² 20f⁵ 20m Apr 13] fifth foal: dam placed on Flat and over hurdles: fair
maiden in bumpers: poor maiden hurdler: stays 2½m: acts on firm and soft going: has had
tongue tied, including last 3 starts. *J. P. Broderick, Ireland*

FLINT KNAPPER   9 ch.g. Kris – Circe's Isle (Be My Guest (USA)) [2002/3 20s*   h124
16d Aug 1] one-time useful 1¼m winner on Flat, modest nowadays: improved form over
hurdles when winning minor event at Navan in June: soundly beaten in valuable handicap
at Galway 2 months later: stays 2½m: acts on soft ground. *Patrick O. Brady, Ireland*

FLITE OF ARABY   6 b.g. Green Desert (USA) – Allegedly Blue (USA) (Alleged   h–
(USA)) [2002/3 17sᵖᵘ 17s Jan 28] sturdy gelding: half-brother to winning hurdler up to
21f Milady Ana (by Generous): modest maiden on Flat (stays 1½m) at 4 yrs for W. Muir:
bought £1,800 Ascot October Sales: little show in novice hurdles at Taunton. *N. J. Hawke*

FLOOD'S FANCY   10 gr.m. Then Again – Port Na Blath (On Your Mark) [2002/3   h–
16mᵖᵘ Apr 2] sparely-made mare: maiden hurdler, no form for long time: blinkered/
tongue tied. *B. R. Foster*

FLORAL LEADER   7 b.m. Alflora (IRE) – Inch Ahead (IRE) (Over The River (FR))   h–
[2002/3 h–, F–: 24gᵘʳ May 3] small mare: no sign of ability. *C. N. Kellett*

FLORA MUCK   7 b.m. Alflora (IRE) – Muckertoo (Sagaro) [2002/3 h63, F80: 24d*   c–
22v² c25d³ c19dᶠ c26sᵘʳ c25s⁵ Mar 7] tall mare: poor hurdler: won handicap at Towcester   h79
in May: generally let down by jumping over fences, well held both completed starts: will
prove best at 3m+: raced on good going or softer (acts on heavy). *N. A. Twiston-Davies*

FLORA POSTE   7 ch.m. Alflora (IRE) – Preachers Popsy (The Parson) [2002/3 h–,   h–
F–: 17s 16d⁵ 22g Mar 18] sturdy mare: well held over hurdles. *J. C. Tuck*

FLORA PRINCESS   6 b.m. Alflora (IRE) – Rakaposhi Queen (Rakaposhi King)   c–
[2002/3 h87: 22g c21d³ c20d Dec 10] unfurnished mare: modest maiden hurdler: not   h–
fluent and well held in 2 novice chases: stays 2½m: acts on soft going: tends to carry head
awkwardly under pressure: temperament under suspicion. *A. King*

FLORENZAR (IRE)   5 b.m. Inzar (USA) – Nurse Tyra (USA) (Dr Blum (USA))   h–
[2002/3 18f⁶ Jun 3] thrice-raced maiden on Flat, seemingly best effort over 11.9f: raced
too freely in 4-y-o novice on hurdling debut. *Miss S. West*

FLORIDA COAST (IRE)   8 b.g. Florida Son – Deep Peace (Deep Run) [2002/3   h121 ?
24s* 20v² 16s⁵ 20d⁵ Feb 23] third known foal: half-brother to smart novice hurdler
Solerina (by Toulon): dam maiden hurdler, probably stayed 2¾m: fairly useful form in 2
bumpers in 2001: won 2m maiden on Flat debut in October: easily won novice at
Fairyhouse on hurdling bow in January: seemingly best effort when 4 lengths second to
Sacundai in slowly-run minor event at Naas week later: will probably prove better around
3m than shorter: acts on heavy going. *James Bowe, Ireland*

FLORIDA (IRE)   5 b.m. Sri Pekan (USA) – Florinda (CAN) (Vice Regent (CAN))   h–
[2002/3 h–: 17sᵖᵘ Dec 26] poor stayer on Flat: no form in 3 runs over hurdles: saddle
slipped only start in 2002/3. *I. A. Wood*

FLORIDA PEARL (IRE)   11 b.g. Florida Son – Ice Pearl (Flatbush) [2002/3   c156
c173: c24s⁴ c24s⁴ c24sᵖᵘ c16g Mar 12]
     Spring heralded a revival in the fortunes of two of the best chasers of recent
times, First Gold and Flagship Uberalles, but for a third, Florida Pearl, there was no
such turnaround after a season in which nothing went to plan. He had a disappointing season after such a productive time in 2001/2, when three Grade 1 successes,
including one in the King George VI Chase, as well as victory in the Grade 2

Martell Cup, came his way. Trainer Willie Mullins was talking optimistically, after Florida Pearl's final run, behind First Gold at Punchestown, of better things to come in 2003/4. It's to be hoped, however, that Florida Pearl isn't asked to race on in obvious decline.

Florida Pearl's season comprised five below-par efforts, four of them in races he'd won at least once before and the other in the Queen Mother Champion Chase over two miles at Cheltenham. There was also a whole list of missed engagements due to one setback or another. Florida Pearl made his now-customary reappearance in the Championship Chase at Down Royal, a race elevated to Grade 1 status for the first time in 2002. Florida Pearl won the race in 1999 but invariably gives the impression he needs his first outing and a particularly gruelling race this time round, forcing the pace from after halfway, took a lot out of him. He was reportedly stiff and sore afterwards and missed an intended outing in the Punchestown Chase at the start of December after disappointing in his work. Florida Pearl made the line-up for the King George at Kempton, bidding to follow up his 2001 success after being second to First Gold the year before. He failed to match those efforts but ran as well as he did all season, shaping as if he retained all his ability. Florida Pearl was travelling as well as the winner Best Mate going to three out but soon came under pressure and weakened at the next, finishing fourth, over seventeen lengths behind the winner. The King George proved a false dawn. Florida Pearl was entered for the replacement race at Kempton for the Victor Chandler and another two-mile event at Fairyhouse in January but missed both due to another minor setback. It was reported that Florida Pearl might go straight to Cheltenham after that but, despite not pleasing totally, he was sent to Leopardstown for the Hennessy Cognac Gold Cup in early-February (after the Ascot Chase was considered as an alternative) and turned in just about the worst performance of his career, looking a shadow of himself and pulled up before the last. Cheltenham had to be in doubt after such a display but, as the Mullins' yard's form after a poor winter began to pick up entering March (it had a total of nine winners in December,

Mrs Violet O'Leary's "Florida Pearl"

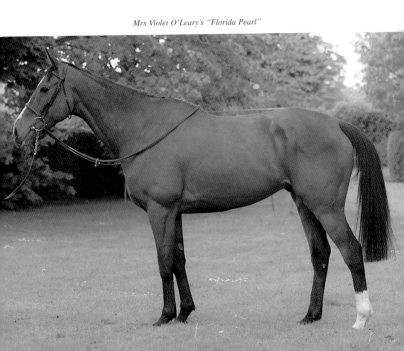

January and February compared to eighteen in each of the previous two seasons), so Florida Pearl seemed to revive on the gallops and was added to the Cheltenham team, a run in the Champion Chase rather than the Gold Cup (in which he'd twice been placed) preferred because of his troubled preparation. Not surprisingly given his pedigree, he found the trip against him and, jumping more ponderously than usual, never got into contention, trailing in last of eight finishers, over thirty lengths behind the winner Moscow Flyer. A plan to run in the Martell Grand National at Aintree was scrapped, indeed Aintree was abandoned altogether in favour of a repeat bid—shortly after the end of the British season—in the Punchestown Heineken Gold Cup, which he'd won in style in 2002. For the first time in the campaign, Florida Pearl had his optimum conditions, the ground much less testing than it had been previously, but his performance mirrored his King George effort—he travelled well but didn't see his race out, fading in the straight and being beaten over twenty lengths by First Gold.

		Florida Son (b 1979)	Busted (b 1963)	Crepello
Florida Pearl (IRE) (b.g. 1992)				Sans Le Sou
			Peach Stone (b 1968)	Mourne
				La Melba
		Ice Pearl (b 1984)	Flatbush (b 1963)	Dumbarnie
				Golden Pride
			Ice Blossom (b 1969)	Spartan General
				Arctic Pearl

Kempton, and to a lesser extent Punchestown, suggest Florida Pearl still retains much of his old ability. A better preparation and a drier winter could work to his advantage, but it's hard to envisage him making a major impact at the very highest level. More performances like the one at Leopardstown should surely bring a deserved retirement. Florida Pearl should stay beyond three and a quarter miles and acts on heavy and good to firm going, though is probably best on going around good these days. A strong, well-made gelding, Florida Pearl has featured extensively in previous Annuals and there is nothing to add to details of his pedigree. *W. P. Mullins, Ireland*

FLORIDA RAIN (IRE) 7 b.g. Florida Son – Ameretto (Stetchworth (USA)) [2002/3 F93: 16d 19d* Dec 4] big, rangy gelding: fair form in bumpers: caught eye on hurdling debut, then won 15-runner novice at Catterick, drifting left but staying on well to get on top after last and beat Another Dude a neck: will be suited by 2½m+: should continue to progress. *Mrs M. Reveley*   **h111 p**

FLORRIES SON 8 b.g. Minster Son – Florrie Palmer (Deadly Nightshade) [2002/3 20g² 24m* 22g* 23d* 20s³ 25g* 22m² Apr 11] tall gelding: chasing type: sixth foal: dam winning pointer: progressed really well over hurdles in his first season, won novices at Hexham, Kelso and Wetherby in autumn (last 2 for conditional jockeys, both handicaps) and Wetherby again in March: best form when second to Mirjan in handicap at Ayr final start: stays 25f: acts on good to soft and good to firm going: genuine. *M. Todhunter*   **h121**

FLOSSY TOPS 5 b.m. Gildoran – Right You Be (Sunyboy) [2002/3 F72: F17d⁵ F17d 20v* 20d 20d⁵ Mar 6] leggy, lengthy mare: form in bumpers only in weak race on debut: 25/1, won amateur maiden at Wetherby in November on hurdling bow: well held there both subsequent starts: will stay beyond 2½m: acts on heavy going: sold 3,800 gns Doncaster May Sales. *R. D. E. Woodhouse*   **h85 F—**

FLOWER OF PITCUR 6 b.g. Alflora (IRE) – Coire Vannich (Celtic Cone) [2002/3 F16g* F17gᵖᵘ F16d Apr 25] sturdy gelding: fifth foal: half-brother to winning hurdler around 2m Dellone (by Gunner B): dam, winning hurdler, stayed 2½m: fair form in bumpers, won at Huntingdon on debut in March by length from Imperial Dream and seventh to Flight Command at Perth: tailed off in Grade 2 at Aintree in between: will stay beyond 2m. *T. R. George*   **F93**

FLUFF 'N' PUFF 9 ch.g. Nicholas Bill – Puff Puff (All Systems Go) [2002/3 c86, h–: c21g³ c24d* c24d² c25s⁴ c25dᵖᵘ c21d² c24g² c21m³ c21m⁵ Apr 17] strong gelding: maiden hurdler: modest chaser: fortunate to win handicap at Ludlow in November: stays 3m: acts on good to firm and heavy going: blinkered once: reportedly broke blood vessel fourth start: usually races prominently: consistent. *J. S. King*   **c95 h—**

FLUSH (FR) 8 b. or br.m. Warning – Garden Pink (FR) (Bellypha) [2002/3 16d 17d² 16g⁴ c20s⁵ c17g³ c16d⁴ Apr 9] angular mare: one-time fair handicap hurdler, off 2½ years before reappearance: barely stayed 2½m: acted on good to firm and heavy going: dead. *Miss S. J. Wilton*   **c82 + h83**

FLY BUY DUBAI 4 b.g. Salse (USA) – Her Honour (Teenoso (USA)) [2002/3 19f⁵ **h–**
17f⁶ Apr 3] half-brother to fairly useful but irresolute hurdler Dubai Seven Stars (by
Suave Dancer), stays 3m: signs of ability on Flat: visored, little aptitude for hurdling in
novice and maiden at Taunton. *M. C. Pipe*

FLY FOR PADDY 5 b.g. Michelozzo (USA) – Tirley Pop Eye (Cruise Missile) **F70**
[2002/3 F70: F17s⁴ F17d Dec 3] unfurnished gelding: poor form in bumpers. *Mrs
H. Dalton*

FLYING BOLD (IRE) 8 ch.g. Persian Bold – Princess Reema (USA) (Affirmed **h76**
(USA)) [2002/3 h70: 20g⁶ 17m⁴ 17m 22f* 26g⁵ 19s Dec 12] angular gelding: poor
hurdler: won selling handicap at Newton Abbot (quickly dismounted after line) in
August: off 3 months and well held both starts after: stays 2¾m: acts on any going: tried
blinkered, including first 3 starts: has looked difficult ride. *N. G. Ayliffe*

FLYING FIRST (IRE) 8 b.g. Executive Perk – Rule The Waves (Deep Run) [2002/3 **h–**
20d^pu 18s^pu Mar 2] lightly-raced gelding: runner-up in bumper: no sign of retaining
ability over hurdles in 2002/3, distressed second outing. *T. D. McCarthy*

FLYING FORTRESS 6 b.g. Petoski – Misty Fort (Menelek) [2002/3 h–p, F–: 16d³ **c81**
21d 17s 17d c16g³ c19d^pu Mar 19] sturdy gelding: poor novice hurdler: similar form on **h81**
chasing debut: lame final outing: should be suited by at least 2½m. *H. D. Daly*

FLYING FORTUNE (IRE) 7 b.g. Jolly Jake (NZ) – Dynamite Flyer (USA) (Explod- **h105**
ent (USA)) [2002/3 h105, F–: 22m* 24s⁴ 24m³ 24m² Apr 16] tall gelding: fair novice
hurdler: won at Wincanton in October: might well have won handicap at Cheltenham
final outing but for bit slipping through mouth (hung left): stays 3m: acts on good to soft
going: takes good hold. *N. M. Babbage*

FLYING GUNNER 12 ch.g. Gunner B – Dans Le Vent (Pollerton) [2002/3 c–§, h–: **c– §**
24s 24s⁴ 25s⁵ 24g Feb 8] tall gelding: didn't take to chasing: useful handicap hurdler at **h105**
best, capable of only fair form nowadays: best at 3m+: acts on soft going: often soon off
bridle. *A. King*

FLYING HIGH (IRE) 8 b.g. Fayruz – Shayista (Tap On Wood) [2002/3 c81, h74: **c82**
c20d³ c16m³ c21g⁵ c21m⁵ 17g 16f Sep 15] compact gelding: poor chaser/maiden hurdler: **h–**
barely stays 2½m: acts on firm and good to soft going: well held in blinkers/visor.
M. Todhunter

FLYING MARIA 12 gr.m. Neltino – Flying Mistress (Lear Jet) [2002/3 c–: c21f^pu **c–**
May 10] lengthy, sparely-made mare: fairly useful hunter chaser in 2000: pulled up all 3
starts outside points since: stays 21f: acts on soft and good to firm going. *J. S. Papworth*

FLYING SPIRIT (IRE) 4 b.g. Flying Spur (AUS) – All Laughter (Vision (USA)) **h76**
[2002/3 16g⁵ 17m⁶ Apr 21] half-brother to fair hurdler Gabby Hayes (by Tirol), stays 21f:
fair on Flat (stays 1¼m), looks difficult ride: poor form both starts over hurdles, second a
seller. *M. H. Tompkins*

FLYING VEIL 9 gr.g. Neltino – Take The Veil (Monksfield) [2002/3 h–: c26m^F May **c–**
22] workmanlike gelding: progressive pointer in 2002, successful twice: fell fatally on **h–**
hunter chase debut. *Mrs D. M. Grissell*

FLY KICKER 6 ch.g. High Kicker (USA) – Double Birthday (Cavo Doro) [2002/3 **h67**
17g³ 17v 16d 25d^pu 17g³ 20g Apr 1] half-brother to fair hurdler up to 25f Moonshine
Dancer (by Northern State) and winning 2m hurdler Major Ivor (by Mandrake Major):
dam ran once: poor maiden hurdler: will prove best around 2m. *W. Storey*

FLYOFF (IRE) 6 b.g. Mtoto – Flyleaf (FR) (Persian Bold) [2002/3 h–: 16m⁶ 16g Sep **h–**
14] well held all 3 outings over hurdles, reluctant at start second one in 2002/3: takes
good hold. *K. A. Morgan*

FLYOVER 6 b.m. Presidium – Flash-By (Ilium) [2002/3 16g 16d 20g 16d⁵ 17g⁶ Apr **h66**
21] half-sister to poor hurdler by Sure Blade: fair on Flat (stays 1½m) at 3 yrs, only poor
form in 2001: sold out of B. R. Millman's stable £3,500 Ascot October Sales: poor novice
hurdler. *J. C. Fox*

FNAN 7 b.g. Generous (IRE) – Rafha (Kris) [2002/3 c85, h131: c23s c22d^pu c22m* **c115**
c20m* c24f 20d Apr 4] small, strong gelding: useful hurdler, fourth of 6 to Holy Orders **h131 +**
in 3m Grade 1 at Punchestown in early-May: not so good over fences, but won handicaps
at Tramore and Tralee in August: no luck in running when seventh to Monty's Pass in
Kerry National at Listowel following month: stays easy 3m, effective at much shorter:
unraced on heavy going, acts on any other: has had tongue tied (not for some time).
N. Meade, Ireland

Jim Lewis & Friends' "Foly Pleasant"

FOGGY (IRE)   10 gr.g. Merrymount – Rosy Waters (Roselier (FR)) [2002/3 c–, h–: 23v⁶ 21s⁵ 20sᵖᵘ Feb 24] leggy gelding: one-time modest staying hurdler, no form (including over fences) since 2000/1: tried blinkered/visored. *J. R. Norton*   c– h–

FOLLOW DE CALL   13 b.g. Callernish – Designer (Celtic Cone) [2002/3 c73, h–: c20f May 11] compact gelding: poor chaser: stays easy 2½m: probably acts on any going: tried blinkered: tongue tied last 3 starts. *Michael Blake*   c– h–

FOLLOW JEAN   7 b.m. Perpendicular – Ask Jean (Ascertain (USA)) [2002/3 h–, F–: 20gᵖᵘ Apr 30] no sign of ability. *M. E. Sowersby*   h–

FOLLOW ME   7 ch.g. Keen – Fairlead (Slip Anchor) [2002/3 h104§: 25v⁵ 21d 24d 21d Mar 18] angular gelding: fair handicap hurdler at best: below form in 2002/3, left J. O'Neill after second start: stays 3m: acts on good to firm and heavy going: wore cheekpieces final outing: temperamental. *F. P. Murtagh*   h92 §

FOLLOW THE FLOW (IRE)   7 ch.g. Over The River (FR) – October Lady (Lucifer (USA)) [2002/3 c24v⁴ c24mᵖᵘ c25s³ c27gᵖᵘ c26s c32v⁴ Mar 13] fourth foal: half-brother to winning hurdlers around 2m C D Boy and An Seabhac (both by Lord Americo): dam unraced: maiden Irish pointer: no form in steeplechases. *P. A. Pritchard*   c–

FOLLOW THE TREND (IRE)   9 br.g. Beau Sher – Newgate Princess (Prince Regent (FR)) [2002/3 c90, h–: 21g⁶ 21d⁴ c20v* c24d c20d⁴ c20m⁴ Apr 19] smallish gelding: maiden hurdler: modest handicap chaser: won at Leicester in January: ran poorly 3 subsequent outings: stays 2¾m: acts on heavy going (possibly not good to firm): blinkered once, wears cheekpieces nowadays: formerly sketchy jumper. *Miss A. M. Newton-Smith*   c94 h–

FOLLOW UP   5 b.g. Phardante (FR) – Dashing March (Daring March) [2002/3 F16g⁴ F12d² Nov 13] 22,000 3-y-o: good-topped gelding: third foal: dam, poor novice hurdler around 2m, half-sister to very smart 2m hurdler Ra Nova: better effort in bumpers when   F101 keeping-on 7 lengths second of 23 to Enitsag at Newbury: will prove at least as effective back at 2m. *N. J. Henderson*

FOLLOW YOUR STAR   5 ch.g. Pursuit of Love – Possessive Artiste (Shareef Dancer (USA)) [2002/3 16m^pu Jul 18] fair maiden on Flat (stays 1¼m), sold out of P. Harris' stable 3,200 gns Newmarket Autumn Sales: reportedly lost action on hurdling debut: joined F. Beluschi, Italy (fifth on Flat in February). *P. J. Hobbs*   **h–**

FOLLY ROAD (IRE)   13 b.g. Mister Lord (USA) – Lady Can (Cantab) [2002/3 c105§, h–: c25d⁴ c24s⁴ c24s⁶ c22m² c21g Apr 3] big, rangy gelding: fair hunter chaser nowadays: best at 3m+: acts on heavy and good to firm going: sometimes visored, also tried in blinkers/cheekpieces: not one to trust. *D. L. Williams*   **c95 §**
h– §

FOLY PLEASANT (FR)   9 ch.g. Vaguely Pleasant (FR) – Jeffologie (FR) (Jefferson) [2002/3 c159, h–: c20d⁴ c21d² c25s² c24g Mar 11] lengthy gelding: very smart chaser: good efforts at Cheltenham first 3 starts, fourth to Cyfor Malta and second to Fondmort in very valuable handicaps and second to Behrajan in Grade 2: ran poorly there final outing: barely stays 25f under testing conditions: acts on heavy and good to firm going: tongue tied: edgy sort: sound jumper: genuine. *Miss H. C. Knight*   **c158**
h–

FOND FAREWELL (IRE)   8 b.m. Phardante (FR) – Doorslammer (Avocat) [2002/3 h79: c25g⁴ Nov 9] poor maiden hurdler: first outing for 7 months, fourth of 6 in novice handicap at Wincanton on chasing debut: better around 3m than shorter: acts on soft going, probably on good to firm. *K. C. Bailey*   **c73**
h–

FONDMORT (FR)   7 b.g. Cyborg (FR) – Hansie (FR) (Sukawa (FR)) [2002/3 c142, h–: c21d³ c21d* c16g^F c24m c20g² c21m² Apr 16]   **c154**
h–

A Cheltenham Festival without at least one Nicky Henderson-trained winner is a rare occurrence but the stable drew a blank at the meeting in the latest season. It did not, however, leave completely empty-handed. Of the stable's twenty-one runners, Trabolgan and Irish Hussar finished runner-up in the Champion Bumper and the Cathcart respectively, there were third places for Chauvinist in the Supreme Novices' Hurdle and Isio in the Arkle, while Fondmort and Scots Grey were both placed in the Mildmay of Flete. Starting second favourite at 11/2, Fondmort was the shortest-priced of the Henderson stable's Festival runners and he ran a good race to finish four lengths behind Young Spartacus, creeping into contention to be almost upsides the eventual winner two out but unable to stay on to quite such good effect after a slightly awkward jump at the last.

Fondmort ran his three very best races at Cheltenham in the latest season. A month after the Festival, he was second there again, this time to Poliantas, carrying top weight in the Silver Trophy Chase (the race was run as a limited handicap rather

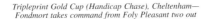

Tripleprint Gold Cup (Handicap Chase), Cheltenham—
Fondmort takes command from Foly Pleasant two out

Mr W. J. Brown's "Fondmort"

than a conditions chase for the first time) but gave the impression that, by that stage of the season, the handicapper had his measure. Earlier in the campaign though, Fondmort had taken one of Cheltenham's major handicaps, the Tripleprint Gold Cup in December, in the manner of an improving young chaser. As a novice over fences, Fondmort had raced exclusively at two miles but his stamina for the twenty-one furlong Tripleprint had been tested in a promising reappearance over the same trip, albeit at an easier track, Wincanton, nine days earlier. On that occasion Fondmort finished third to Poliantas in a limited handicap run as a substitute for the abandoned First National Gold Cup at Ascot, though the concerns about the longer trip meant that Fondmort's effort was delayed, allowing the winner first run. Fondmort was ridden more positively at Cheltenham and, after travelling strongly and making progress from four out, was sent on two from home, clearing the final fence with an extravagant leap. Course regular Foly Pleasant followed him home six lengths back, with the same distances separating the future Festival winner Youlneverwalkalone and the Thomas Pink winner Cyfor Malta in third and fourth. Fondmort ran twice more before the Festival, both times at Kempton, a track where he had won twice as a novice. But the drop back to two miles for the Tote Exacta Chase ended with a crashing fall three out, while an attempt over three miles in the Racing Post Trophy, in which he finished a respectable seventh under top weight, seemed to reveal the limits of his stamina, though again he made a bad mistake three out.

Fondmort's sire Cyborg first made his name in Britain with the Stayers' Hurdle winner Cyborgo and, while he has also been represented here by the staying chaser Historg, the likes of Hors La Loi III, Cyfor Malta and Fondmort have all proven effective at shorter distances. The dam's side of Fondmort's pedigree is essentially Flat-oriented and all three of the mares on his bottom line were successful in France. His dam Hansie won an amateur riders event in the Provinces over a mile and three quarters and is out of a half-sister to Ex-Libris, winner of the Group 2 Prix du Conseil Municipal at Longchamp. Fondmort is his dam's fifth reported foal, the only other to have raced being Pinceloup (by Mont Basile) who has been placed over hurdles in France.

Fondmort (FR) (b.g. 1996)	Cyborg (FR) (ch 1982)	Arctic Tern (ch 1973)	Sea-Bird / Bubbling Beauty
		Cadair (b 1970)	Sadair / Blarney Castle
	Hansie (FR) (b 1985)	Sukawa (br 1969)	Sodium / Serge de Nimes
		Hobanty (b 1970)	Hauban / Hayati

Given his good record at Cheltenham, and that two and a half miles or thereabouts seems his optimum trip, the Paddy Power Gold Cup (formerly known as the Thomas Pink) would seem a likely starting point for Fondmort in his next campaign, though he is going to be vulnerable to more progressive and lightly-weighted rivals in handicaps from now on. His consistency and usually sound jumping will stand him in good stead though, and he is not dependent on the state of the ground, having shown his form on heavy and good to firm. Fondmort began his career in France, where he was a useful juvenile hurdler, incidentally wearing blinkers. *N. J. Henderson*

FOOTBALL CRAZY (IRE)   4 b.g. Mujadil (USA) – Schonbein (IRE) (Persian   **h68 p** Heights) [2002/3 16d⁵ Nov 24] useful on Flat (stays 1¼m), successful 4 times in 2002: favourite, none too fluent and just poor form when fifth of 12 in juvenile at Fakenham on hurdling debut: should do better. *N. A. Callaghan*

FORBES PARK   8 b.g. Alzao (USA) – Rose Alto (Adonijah) [2002/3 h–: 23gᵖᵘ 16m³   **h77** Jun 19] lightly-raced gelding: maiden on Flat: poor form when third in novice claimer at Worcester, best effort over hurdles: headstrong. *M. J. Coombe*

FOR CATHAL (IRE)   12 b.g. Legal Circles (USA) – Noble For Stamps (Deep Run)   **c85** [2002/3 c100, h–: c25d⁴ c25m⁴ May 8] rangy gelding: winning hurdler: modest hunter/   **h–** pointer nowadays: stays 3½m: acts on good to firm and heavy going: difficult ride. *Mrs Sarah L. Dent*

FOREMAN (GER)   5 ch.h. Monsun (GER) – Fleurie (GER) (Dashing Blade) [2002/3   **h143** 17m* 16g* 19s³ 18s² 19s³ 20v² 16v³ 21m* 21g⁴ 19s* Apr 14] angular horse: first foal: dam once raced sister to smart miler Faberger: useful on Flat (stays 1½m) in Germany:

Frank Pengelly Novices' Hurdle, Kempton—Foreman, defeating Calling Brave (right) and Double Honour, gives Thierry Doumen his first winner as a trainer in Britain

useful hurdler: won maiden at Folkestone and minor event at Baden-Baden (final start for C. Von Der Recke) in May, novice at Kempton in February and listed race at Enghien in April: good second to Karly Flight in Group 1 4-y-o event at Auteuil sixth outing, creditable fifth (promoted) to Hardy Eustace in Grade 1 novice at Cheltenham penultimate one: stays 21f: acts on heavy and good to firm going. *T. Doumen, France*

FORESHORE MAN 12 b.g. Derrylin – Royal Birthday (St Paddy) [2002/3 c79, h–: c16s⁶ Nov 26] sturdy, workmanlike gelding: maiden hurdler: poor handicap chaser: stays 3m: raced on good going or softer (acts on heavy): usually visored: has broken blood vessel. *B. S. Rothwell*   c– h–

FOREST DANTE (IRE) 10 ch.g. Phardante (FR) – Mossy Mistress (IRE) (Le Moss) [2002/3 c109: c22gʳ c19g⁶ c22s³ c19d 21dᵖᵘ c20g⁵ c20gʳ c28m⁴ Apr 26] big, lengthy gelding: fair handicap chaser: out of form in 2002/3 (including over hurdles), though shaped bit better over too long a trip final outing: stays 2¾m: acts on good to firm and heavy going: blinkered once: often let down by jumping. *F. Kirby*   c83 h–

FOREST FLORA 9 b.m. King's Ride – Celtic Flora (Celtic Cone) [2002/3 c–, h–: c21f c20g⁵ c23d⁴ c21g⁴ c23m c21g⁵ c25m⁶ 21m⁶ Sep 28] sturdy mare: winning hurdler/ maiden chaser, little form for some time: visored final outing. *J. W. Mullins*   c– h–

FOREST FOUNTAIN (IRE) 12 b. or br.g. Royal Fountain – Forest Gale (Strong Gale) [2002/3 c107d: c33g⁵ c30m⁴ c34g⁵ May 22] workmanlike gelding: fairly useful hunter chaser at best, on the downgrade: stays 33f: acts on good to firm going. *Mrs H. L. Needham*   c88

FOREST GREEN FLYER 7 b.m. Syrtos – Bolton Flyer (Aragon) [2002/3 h83d: 21dᵖᵘ 19g 16d5 17s* 16v² 16v 24m 16d 16v⁵ 17vᵖᵘ Mar 4] angular mare: poor hurdler: fortunate to win selling handicap at Taunton in November: raced mainly around 2m (doesn't stay 3m): acts on heavy going: tried blinkered/visored: has had tongue tied: unreliable. *Ö. O'Neill*   h69 §

FOREST GUNNER 9 ch.g. Gunner B – Gouly Duff (Party Mink) [2002/3 h109: c21dᵖᵘ c21d* c24d² Dec 14] leggy gelding: fair hurdler: quickly showed himself better over fences (jumps well), won novices at Sedgefield and Fakenham in autumn and good second of 3 finishers to Kemal's Council in similar event at latter: stays 3m: raced on good going or softer (acts on soft): usually makes running/races prominently: amateur ridden for all but one of his wins. *R. Ford*   c117 h–

FOREST HEATH (IRE) 6 gr.g. Common Grounds – Caroline Lady (JPN) (Caro) [2002/3 h–: 16d 16m⁵ 16g⁶ Apr 12] temperamental and on downgrade on Flat (usually wears headgear): poor form over hurdles. *H. J. Collingridge*   h84

FOREST IVORY (NZ) 12 b.g. Ivory Hunter (USA) – Fair And Square (NZ) (Crown Lease) [2002/3 c–, h126?: 24s 25g 27s² 23v⁴ 27v⁵ 26g 24v 24m⁵ 21m⁶ Apr 16] leggy gelding: one-time useful handicap hurdler/chaser, very much on the downgrade: sold out of R. Wylie's stable 1,700 gns Doncaster March Sales after seventh start: stays 4¼m: ideally suited by soft/heavy going: tried blinkered/visored: usually soon off bridle: often let down by jumping over fences. *Dr P. Pritchard*   c– h101 ?

FORESTRY 9 b.g. Highest Honor (FR) – Arboretum (IRE) (Green Desert (USA)) [2002/3 17g⁶ 22gᵖᵘ 19mᵖᵘ c21mᵖᵘ c16g³ Jul 15] leggy gelding: poor maiden hurdler in 1998/9, little sign of retaining ability (including over fences): visored third outing. *J. G. M. O'Shea*   c– h–

FOREST THYNE (IRE) 9 ch.g. Good Thyne (USA) – Tullow Performance (Gala Performance (USA)) [2002/3 c–, h–: 23g⁴ May 8] smallish gelding: novice hurdler: winning pointer: no form in steeplechases: should stay beyond 3m: acts on soft going, possibly not on good to firm: tried blinkered/visored: usually soon off bridle: sold 2,200 gns Doncaster October Sales. *J. R. Jenkins*   c– h–

FOREST TUNE (IRE) 5 b.g. Charnwood Forest (IRE) – Swift Chorus (Music Boy) [2002/3 16d² 16g 16s² 16m* 16m² Apr 2] tall, angular gelding: fairly useful on all-weather, fair on turf on Flat (stays 1¼m): confirmed earlier promise over hurdles when winning handicap at Ludlow in March by 3½ lengths from Generous Ways: good second to Alvino in novice there 2 weeks later: likely to prove best around 2m: acts on good to firm going, probably on soft. *B. Hanbury*   h108

FOREVER DREAM 5 b.g. Afzal – Quadrapol (Pollerton) [2002/3 F17s⁶ F16s² F16d⁵ F16m* Mar 20] useful-looking gelding: second foal: brother to 2m hurdle winner Brown Teddy: dam bumper winner: fairly useful hurdler in bumpers, won at Wincanton by 2½ lengths from Spread The Dream, running on strongly despite hanging right: looked reluctant second start. *P. J. Hobbs*   F96

FOREVER NOBLE (IRE) 10 b.g. Forzando – Pagan Queen (Vaguely Noble) [2002/3 c89x, h–: c17g Apr 7] sparely-made gelding: fair hurdler/chaser at best: never   c– x h–

dangerous over inadequate trip only start in 2002/3: stays 3m: acts on good to firm and heavy going: blinkered once: sketchy jumper. *R. Allan*

FOREVER POSH   6 b.m. Rakaposhi King – B Final (Gunner B) [2002/3 F16g Feb 27] second foal: dam unraced out of half-sister to Champion Hurdle winner Royal Gait (by Gunner B): tailed off in mares bumper on debut. *Mrs S. M. Johnson*   **F–**

FORK LIGHTNING (IRE)   7 gr.g. Roselier (FR) – Park Breeze (IRE) (Strong Gale) [2002/3 20v⁴ 19d⁴ 21s* 22d³ 20g² 24m* Apr 16] IR 15,000 4-y-o: workmanlike gelding: fourth foal: half-brother to winning hurdler/fairly useful but temperamental chaser Moving Earth (by Brush Aside), stays 21f: dam unraced sister to useful staying chaser Risk of Thunder: won maiden Irish point in 2002: quickly developed into fairly useful novice hurdler, won at Kempton in January and Cheltenham (handicap, beat Flying Fortune 1¼ lengths, tending to wander under pressure but responding well) in April: good second to impressive Isard III at Ascot earlier in April: stays 3m: acts on soft and good to firm going: interesting prospect for novice chases in 2003/4. *A. King*   **h117**

FORLORN HOPE   6 b.g. Tragic Role (USA) – Rum N Raisin (Rakaposhi King) [2002/3 16dᵖᵘ 16d Apr 9] little form at 2 yrs, including in sellers: little sign of ability in 2 novice hurdles. *B. D. Leavy*   **h–**

FORMAL BID (USA)   6 b. or br.g. Dynaformer (USA) – Fantastic Bid (USA) (Auction Ring (USA)) [2002/3 h96: 16d³ 16d³ 19d* 20d³ 16s 20s* 19s² 20v² 20v³ Feb 15] medium-sized gelding: fairly useful hurdler, much improved: won maiden at Market Rasen in October and novice at Leicester in December: good placed efforts in handicaps after, third to Korelo in valuable event at Ascot in February and Blue Away in competitive race at Punchestown in late-April: stays 2½m: raced on good going or softer (acts on heavy): patiently ridden: reliable. *C. C. Bealby*   **h115**

FORMAL INVITATION (IRE)   14 ch.g. Be My Guest (USA) – Clarista (USA) (Riva Ridge (USA)) [2002/3 c76, h–: c24mᶠ Jun 1] tall, lengthy gelding: one-time useful chaser, retains little ability. *David Maybury*   **c70**
h–

FORMIDABLE FLAME   10 ch.g. Formidable (USA) – Madiyla (Darshaan) [2002/3 17m 22m⁴ 22fᵖᵘ Aug 13] sturdy gelding: poor maiden hurdler, no form in 2002/3: hampered first and soon pulled up only outing in steeplechases: tried visored/blinkered. *C. Tizzard*   **c–**
h–

FORMIDABLE STELLA   7 b.m. Formidable (USA) – Stellajoe (Le Dauphin) [2002/3 F17m F17f F16m Jun 3] third foal: half-sister to 2 poor performers: dam, winning hurdler, stayed 2½m: no sign of ability in bumpers or on Flat. *Miss Z. C. Davison*   **F–**

FORNAUGHT ALLIANCE (IRE)   10 br.g. Zaffaran (USA) – Carrick Shannon (Green Shoon) [2002/3 c94, h87: c21d³ c27d² c25g Apr 7] workmanlike gelding: modest hurdler/chaser: best effort in hunters when second to stable-companion Son of Anshan at Sedgefield: won point later in March: stays 27f: seems to need going softer than good (acts on heavy): usually blinkered/visored: none too consistent. *G. Tuer*   **c99**
h–

FORREST TRIBE (IRE)   10 b. or br.g. Be My Native (USA) – Island Bridge (Mandalus) [2002/3 c90§, h–§: c25g³ May 4] tall, lengthy gelding: modest handicap chaser: stays 3½m: acts on good to firm and heavy going: usually blinkered: has worn tongue strap: irresolute. *W. Jenks*   **c89 §**
h– §

FORTHECHOP   6 b.g. Minshaanshu Amad (USA) – Cousin Jenny (Midyan (USA)) [2002/3 h–: 17s⁴ 16sᵖᵘ 16v⁶ 16v⁵ Feb 10] of little account. *R. C. Harper*   **h–**

FORTUNATE DAVE (USA)   4 b.g. Lear Fan (USA) – Lady Ameriflora (USA) (Lord Avie (USA)) [2002/3 16m* 16d 17s² 18d³ 16g² 16g⁴ 17d² 20d Apr 25] angular gelding: fair on Flat (stays 1¾m): fair juvenile hurdler: won at Warwick in November: generally creditable efforts in frame after: should stay 2½m: acts on soft and good to firm going: room for improvement in his jumping. *Ian Williams*   **h101**

FORTUNE ISLAND (IRE)   4 b.g. Turtle Island (IRE) – Blue Kestrel (IRE) (Bluebird (USA)) [2002/3 16dᵖᵘ 17d* 17g 17g Mar 13] good-topped gelding: 13f winner on Flat at 3 yrs for C. Wall: fair form over hurdles, won juvenile maiden at Exeter in February by 3½ lengths from King Solomon: much stiffer task, never-dangerous twelfth of 27 in Triumph Hurdle at Cheltenham: improved form on Flat when winning over 2m in April: should still do better. *M. C. Pipe*   **h111 p**

FORTUNE'S FOOL   4 b.g. Zilzal (USA) – Peryllys (Warning) [2002/3 16dᵖᵘ 17g⁶ 17d 17g⁴ Apr 26] modest form at 2 yrs, sold out of B. Smart's stable 600 gns Doncaster October (2001) Sales: poor form over hurdles: headstrong. *I. A. Brown*   **h65**

FORTY LOVE (IRE)   8 b.g. Second Set (IRE) – Pharjoy (FR) (Pharly (FR)) [2002/3 c20mᶠ May 16] winning hurdler: fairly useful pointer, successful twice in 2002: broke   **c–**
h–

leg in hunter chase at Perth: stayed 2½m: acted on good to soft going: tired visored. *Miss J. Fisher*

FORUM CHRIS (IRE)   6 ch.g. Trempolino (USA) – Memory Green (USA) (Green Forest (USA)) [2002/3 22s* 20m* 20m* Jul 24] fairly useful on Flat (will stay beyond 1¾m) at 3 yrs for M. Johnston: successful all 3 starts over hurdles, in maiden at Cartmel and novice at Hexham in June and novice at Worcester in July: will stay 3m: front runner: tail swisher. *Mrs S. J. Smith*   **h112**

FOR WILLIAM   17 b.g. Whistling Deer – Pampered Sue (Pampered King) [2002/3 c25m^{pu} May 22] ex-Irish gelding: one-time useful staying chaser: won point in 2000: no show in hunter on return. *Mrs M. Rigg*   **c–** **h–**

FOR YOUR EARS ONLY (IRE)   7 b.g. Be My Native (USA) – Sister Ida (Bustino) [2002/3 F75: F16m^3 20m Dec 17] rangy gelding: fair form in bumpers, third to Gastornis at Hexham in October: not given unduly hard time when eighth in maiden on hurdling debut: takes strong hold: should do better over hurdles, particularly back around 2m. *A. Parker*   **h– p** **F91**

FORZACURITY   4 ch.g. Forzando – Nice Lady (Connaught) [2002/3 17g^6 17s^5 Nov 29] leggy gelding: fair on Flat (stays 1m), successful twice in first half of 2002: poor form in 2 juvenile hurdles: has worn cheekpieces. *J. L. Spearing*   **h77**

FORZA GLORY   4 ch.f. Forzando – Glory Isle (Hittite Glory) [2002/3 17s^3 16d 16d^5 16v^4 Jan 23] small filly: half-sister to fair hurdler/winning chaser Blasket Hero (by Kalaglow), stayed 27f: modest maiden on Flat (stays 1m): poor form over hurdles, including in handicap: will prove best at 2m: races freely. *Miss B. Sanders*   **h76**

FOSSE HILL   6 b.g. Bustino – Amber's Image (Billion (USA)) [2002/3 F99: 16f^6 May 10] good sort: fairly useful bumper winner: only sixth of 13 in novice at Wincanton on hurdling debut, and not seen out again. *Miss H. C. Knight*   **h82**

FOSSY BEAR   11 br.m. Lir – Full Spirit (Bay Spirit) [2002/3 c25g^4 Mar 18] fair pointer, successful in February and March: first form in hunter chases when fourth to Aller Moor at Exeter. *Miss S. Young*   **c87**

FOSTER   4 b.g. Teenoso (USA) – Glorious Jane (Hittite Glory) [2002/3 F16g F16m^{pu} Apr 22] half-brother to fairly useful hurdler/chaser Auburn Castle (by Good Times), stays 21f, and winning pointer by Pablond: dam fairly useful Irish hurdler around 2m: no show in bumpers: dead. *M. F. Harris*   **F–**

FOSTON SECOND (IRE)   6 ch.m. Lycius (USA) – Gentle Guest (IRE) (Be My Guest (USA)) [2002/3 h–: 16g Apr 29] poor maiden on Flat: little sign of ability over hurdles: sold £750 Ascot June Sales, resold 700 gns Doncaster October Sales. *C. Weedon*   **h–**

FOTA ISLAND (IRE)   7 b.g. Supreme Leader – Mary Kate Finn (Saher) [2002/3 F106: c22s^{ur} c17s^3 c20s^4 20s^3 16s^2 19v^2 16v* 16s* Mar 16] well-made gelding: promising third in strongly-contested maiden at Fairyhouse, but let down by jumping both other starts over fences: fairly useful novice hurdler: won at Leopardstown (maiden) and Punchestown in March, beating Talking Tactics 7 lengths at latter: creditable third to Back In Front in Grade 1 at Punchestown in late-April: stays 2½m: acts on heavy going: sometimes jumps none too fluently. *M. F. Morris, Ireland*   **c116 p** **h127**

FOU DOUX (FR)   7 b.g. Le Grillon II (FR) – Folie Douce (FR) (Fast (FR)) [2002/3 c–, h–: 16d^3 c20g^{pu} c16v^{ur} 16d c25s^{pu} 20g Feb 22] winning hurdler: no form in Britain, including over fences: trained until after second start by D. Bridgwater: tried blinkered/visored/tongue tied. *P. W. Hiatt*   **c–** **h–**

FOUETTE   5 b.m. Saddlers' Hall (IRE) – Tight Spin (High Top) [2002/3 h–: 16d^{pu} May 4] smallish mare: no form over hurdles. *J. Howard Johnson*   **h–**

FOUNTAIN BANK (IRE)   10 b.g. Lafontaine (USA) – Clogrecon Lass (Raise You Ten) [2002/3 h104: c24g^{ur} c24g^5 20m^6 c23g* c26m^3 c23g^4 22m c23m^{pu} c21d^{pu} 21m^{pu} 20g^3 Apr 21] good-topped gelding: fair handicap hurdler, below form in 2002/3: modest chaser: won maiden at Worcester in August: stays 3m: best form on good going or firmer: usually wears headgear: has looked difficult ride. *M. J. Gingell*   **c96** **h83**

FOUNTAIN BID (IRE)   11 b.g. Royal Fountain – Lilford Castle (Carlingford Castle) [2002/3 c26m^{pu} May 22] good-topped gelding: poor hurdler/novice chaser: no form in points and hunter in 2002: stays 27f: acts on heavy going, probably on good to firm: usually blinkered: difficult ride. *R. Dean*   **c–** **h–**

FOUNTAIN BRIG   7 b. or br.g. Royal Fountain – Lillies Brig (New Brig) [2002/3 h77?, F–: 20d 24v^{pu} 24v^3 20v^3 c21s^6 Feb 23] poor novice hurdler: similar form on chasing debut: stays 3m: raced on going softer than good (acts on heavy). *N. W. Alexander*   **c71 ?** **h69 ?**

FOUR ACES   6 b.g. Forzando – Anhaar (Ela-Mana-Mou) [2002/3 h128: 20g* 20s* 20d⁴ 22g⁴ Aug 12] fairly useful hurdler: won novices at Gowran and Clonmel in May: at least respectable efforts in handicaps last 2 starts: stays 2¾m: acts on soft going: had had tongue tied. *Mrs J. Harrington, Ireland*   **h125**

FOURLOCH (IRE)   5 b.m. Fourstars Allstar (USA) – Loch Wee (IRE) (Colmore Row) [2002/3 17d Jun 5] poor maiden on Flat at 3 yrs: no show on hurdling debut. *N. G. Richards*   **h–**

FOUR MEN (IRE)   6 b.g. Nicolotte – Sound Pet (Runnett) [2002/3 h–: 17mᵖᵘ Aug 26] poor maiden on Flat: pulled up both starts over hurdles. *Miss K. M. George*   **h–**

FOUR MILE CLUMP   9 b.g. Petoski – Rare Luck (Rare One) [2002/3 c96, h84: c25d⁴ c26v³ c25sᵖᵘ c24sᵖᵘ c25g 27f Apr 24] workmanlike gelding: maiden hurdler: handicap chaser: off a year, poor form in 2002/3: stays 3¼m: acts on good to firm and good to soft going: tried in visor/cheekpieces/tongue strap. *P. J. Jones*   **c81 §** **h–**

FOUR OF A KIND   5 b.g. Most Welcome – Pegs (Mandrake Major) [2002/3 F–: F16g Apr 30] good-topped gelding: no promise in bumpers or on Flat: sold 1,600 gns Doncaster May Sales. *C. W. Thornton*   **F–**

FOURS ARE WILD (IRE)   10 ch.g. Montelimar (USA) – Lousion (Lucifer (USA)) [2002/3 c–x, h–: c25g Jun 12] well-made gelding: fair 2½m chaser in 1999/00: badly let down by jumping and no form since, including in points. *K. C. Bailey*   **c– x** **h–**

FOURSPICE ALLSPICE (IRE)   5 b.m. Fourstars Allstar (USA) – A'Dhahirah (Beldale Flutter (USA)) [2002/3 F18m⁵ F17g⁵ F16m⁴ 16m⁶ 22gᵖᵘ 19dᵘʳ 17s Feb 13] IR £30,000 3-y-o: eighth foal: half-sister to winning hunter by Ballacashtal and to bumper/ 1½m Flat winner Row Ree (by Ore): dam unraced half-sister to smart 7f to 1¼m performer Beau Sher and smart 2m hurdler Bold Boss: poor form in bumpers: little encouragement over hurdles, left J. Mullins after fifth start. *B. R. Millman*   **h64** **F75**

FOUR TO WIN (IRE)   7 b.g. Tremblant – Ballybeg Rose (IRE) (Roselier (FR)) [2002/3 h81, F76: c20dꟳ c21dᵖᵘ c16gꟳ Apr 21] rangy gelding: poor form in novice hurdles: failed to complete in 3 chases, blinkered last 2. *Miss Jacqueline S. Doyle*   **c–** **h–**

FOXCHAPEL KING (IRE)   10 b.g. Jolly Jake (NZ) – Monatrim (Le Moss) [2002/3 c164, h–: c24sᵖᵘ c25s* c24v⁴ c24v² c24s⁴ c24gᵘʳ c24g c29m Apr 26] strong, compact gelding: high-class chaser: didn't have to be near best to win weakly-contested 5-runner

Duggan Brothers Porterstown Handicap Chase, Fairyhouse—
Foxchapel King shows he can jump fluently on his day

handicap at Fairyhouse in November: looking very well, creditable seventh to Ad Hoc in very valuable handicap at Sandown in April, though finished tamely: stayed 29f: acted on good to firm and heavy going: often made mistakes: reportedly retired after injuring off-fore suspensory in Grade 1 event at Punchestown in late-April. *M. F. Morris, Ireland*

FOXCHAPEL QUEEN (IRE) 5 b.m. Over The River (FR) – Glencairn Lass (Buckskin (FR)) [2002/3 F18v² F16f³ F17m⁵ Apr 17] IR 6,500 3-y-o: leggy mare: half-sister to fair hurdler up to 2½m Go Go Henry (by Roselier) and modest 2m to 3m jumper Beeper's Gale (by Strong Gale), and to dam of Foxchapel King: dam twice-raced half-sister to dam of useful Irish jumper New Co: fair form in bumpers (trained by Mrs E. Finn on debut): took good hold and wandered under pressure when 8 lengths fifth of 17 to Amorello in listed mares event at Cheltenham: will be suited by 2½m+. *N. J. Henderson* **F92**

FOXES FANDANGO 6 br.g. Munjarid – The Pride of Pokey (Uncle Pokey) [2002/3 F16d 16g Mar 12] 9,500 4-y-o: big gelding: third foal: dam, winning pointer, from family of high-class hunter Grimley Gale: little show in bumper and maiden hurdle. *N. A. Gaselee* **h–** / **F80 ?**

FOXHALL LADY 6 gr.m. Lyphento (USA) – Carmel (Malaspina) [2002/3 F17d 19d 17g Mar 17] first foal: dam unraced: no sign of ability. *J. C. Tuck* **h–** / **F–**

FOXIES LAD 12 b.g. Then Again – Arctic Sands (Riboboy (USA)) [2002/3 19v c20s⁵ c22sᵘʳ c24s c21g⁶ c19mᵘʳ Apr 22] strong, lengthy gelding: modest chaser in 2000/1 for B. Scriven: below that level on return, not always impressing with jumping (unseated sixth in first-time blinkers final outing): stays 21f: acts on heavy going: has been early to post: has reportedly broken blood vessels. *C. J. Gray* **c79** / **h–**

FOX IN THE BOX 6 b. or gr.g. Supreme Leader – Charlotte Gray (Rolfe (USA)) [2002/3 F93: 22d⁴ 20s* 20sᵖᵘ 20g⁵ Apr 2] strong gelding: modest novice hurdler: won at Chepstow in December by short head from Moscow Tradition: will be suited by 3m: acts on soft going: ran as if something amiss third start: not a fluent jumper. *R. H. Alner* **h96**

FOXMEADE DANCER 5 b.g. Lyphento (USA) – Georgian Quickstep (Dubassoff (USA)) [2002/3 F16g 19sᵖᵘ 16mᵖᵘ 19g⁶ 17sᶠ Nov 21] good-topped gelding: third known foal: dam poor novice hurdler: ninth of 16 in bumper: no form over hurdles. *P. C. Ritchens* **h–** / **F–**

FOXS SHADOW 8 gr.m. Neltino – Change of Fortune (Broadsword (USA)) [2002/3 16dᵖᵘ 20sᵖᵘ 16d Jan 13] first foal: dam unraced: no sign of ability in novice hurdles: tried in cheekpieces: sold £800 Ascot February Sales. *John A. Harris* **h–**

FOXY LAD 7 ch.g. Bob's Return (IRE) – Shy Hiker (Netherkelly) [2002/3 F65: 16gᵖᵘ 22dᵖᵘ 20g 21d Dec 12] sturdy gelding: no form over hurdles: tried visored. *Graeme Roe* **h–**

FRAAMTASTIC 6 b.m. Fraam – Fading (Pharly (FR)) [2002/3 17s⁵ 16s 16v⁶ Feb 10] medium-sized mare: no form over hurdles: may still do better under less testing conditions (raced only on soft/heavy going): wears cheekpieces. *B. A. Pearce* **h–**

FRAGRANT ROSE 7 b.m. Alflora (IRE) – Levantine Rose (Levanter) [2002/3 F100: 17g⁸ 19s* 19s³ 21m⁶ 19m² 20g* Apr 21] leggy mare: fair novice hurdler: won mares events at Hereford and Taunton in November and Uttoxeter (simple task) in April: stays 2½m: acts on soft going, possibly not on good to firm: usually races prominently: consistent. *Miss H. C. Knight* **h104**

FRANCES BERTHA 6 ch.m. Dervish – Glenside Charley (Chas Sawyer) [2002/3 F16g F16g Sep 15] first reported foal: dam never ran: little show in 2 bumpers. *Mrs H. Dalton* **F–**

FRANCINES-BOY (IRE) 7 b.g. Namaqualand (USA) – Nancy Drew (Sexton Blake) [2002/3 c111, h–: c20d⁴ c21v² c18s Feb 20] sturdy gelding: one-time useful hurdler: modest chaser: stays 21f: acts on good to firm and heavy going. *C. Roche, Ireland* **c95** / **h–**

FRANCOLINO (FR) 10 b.g. Useful (FR) – Quintefeuille II (FR) (Kashtan (FR)) [2002/3 c–, h77: 22d 22dᵖᵘ c20m⁵ c20m³ Apr 19] well-made gelding: most disappointing since winning handicap chase in 2000/1, including over hurdles: stays 2¾m: acts on heavy going: effective blinkered or not, has worn cheekpieces. *N. A. Gaselee* **c– §** / **h– §**

FRANCOSKID (IRE) 11 ch.g. Kambalda – Serocco Wind (Roi Guillaume (FR)) [2002/3 c20g³ c20s c20s* c24s⁵ c24g* c28s⁶ c24g⁶ Mar 26] small, angular gelding: modest handicap chaser: won at Down Royal in December and Musselburgh in February: stays 3m: acts on good to firm and heavy going: blinkered twice in 2001/2: inconsistent. *Liam Lennon, Ireland* **c98** / **h–**

FRANKIE ANSON 6 b.g. Anshan – Smilingatstrangers (Macmillion) [2002/3 F75: F16f⁴ F17g* 16d 19s⁴ 16s 16g 16d⁴ 23m* Apr 21] leggy gelding: fair form in bumpers, won at Market Rasen in October: left M. Easterby after sixth start: upped markedly in trip, easily best effort over hurdles when winning selling handicap at Wetherby: likely to stay beyond 23f: acts on good to firm going. *M. D. Hammond* **h79 F89**

FRANKIE'S RIVER 6 b.g. Over The River (FR) – Up The Junction (IRE) (Treasure Kay) [2002/3 h82, F84: 20g² 24v⁴ Jun 6] poor form over hurdles: dead. *R. H. Alner* **h79**

FRANKINCENSE (IRE) 7 gr.g. Paris House – Mistral Wood (USA) (Far North (CAN)) [2002/3 h98d: 16d 17s⁵ 21s⁶ 21v* 25d⁶ 21dᵖᵘ 21mᵖᵘ Apr 26] leggy gelding: modest hurdler: best effort in 2002/3 when winning selling handicap at Sedgefield in January: stays 21f: acts on heavy going: races prominently: has pulled hard. *A. J. Lockwood* **h89**

FRANKLIN-D 7 ch.g. Democratic (USA) – English Mint (Jalmood (USA)) [2002/3 16dᵖᵘ Jul 5] poor maiden on Flat: tailed off from halfway in novice on hurdling debut. *J. R. Jenkins* **h–**

FRANTIC TAN (IRE) 11 ch.g. Zaffaran (USA) – Brownskin (Buckskin (FR)) [2002/3 c–x, h–: c24d⁴ c29v⁶ c26vᵖᵘ c30dᵖᵘ c24sᶠ Mar 10] rangy, well-made gelding: has been tubed: one-time smart chaser: fairly useful at best nowadays, retains little enthusiasm: should stay beyond 3½m: tried blinkered: usually races prominently: makes mistakes: one to leave alone. *D. J. Caro* **c122 § h–**

FRATERNIZE 5 ch.g. Spectrum (IRE) – Proud Titania (IRE) (Fairy King (USA)) [2002/3 16d⁴ 17d 19s⁵ 16s⁴ 16d⁵ 16vʳᵗʳ 17dʳᵗʳ 17vᵖᵘ Mar 10] fair on Flat (stays 1½m), sold from S. Dow 6,000 gns after winning weak seller in August: poor novice hurdler: thoroughly temperamental: visored after debut. *M. C. Pipe* **h§§**

FRAZER ISLAND (IRE) 14 br.g. Phardante (FR) – Avransha (Random Shot) [2002/3 c98, h–: c24dᵖᵘ c26vᵖᵘ Dec 4] veteran chaser: won 2 points in 2002: stays 3½m: acts on soft going: visored once. *M. A. Allen* **c– h–**

FRAZER'S LAD 6 b.g. Whittingham (IRE) – Loch Tain (Lochnager) [2002/3 h–: 21gᵖᵘ 16g² 16d* 16g⁵ 17m* 17m⁶ 16m⁴ 17g³ Apr 26] good-topped gelding: poor handicap hurdler: won at Hexham (novice, made all) and Market Rasen (seller) in June: should stay 2½m: acts on good to firm and good to soft going: blinkered/visored: races prominently. *M. E. Sowersby* **h74**

FREDDIE'S COMET (IRE) 7 b.g. Freddie's Star – Baltimore Bay (Bishop of Orange) [2002/3 h79: 16d³ 17m* 17m⁶ 17m 19mᵖᵘ Sep 11] compact gelding: poor hurdler: won handicap at Market Rasen in June: stays 19f: acts on good to firm going, probably on good to soft. *John R. Upson* **h78**

FREDDIE TAYLOR 6 b.g. Sula Bula – Clowater Lady (IRE) (Orchestra) [2002/3 h–: 17mᵖᵘ 20dᵖᵘ Jun 8] angular gelding: no form over hurdles. *J. C. McConnochie* **h–**

FREDDY FLINTSTONE 6 b.g. Bigstone (IRE) – Daring Ditty (Daring March) [2002/3 h93: c16g Dec 12] one-time fairly useful maiden on Flat (best around 1m), on the downgrade: twice-raced over hurdles: never dangerous after mistake second when seventh in well-contested novice at Ludlow on chasing debut. *D. W. P. Arbuthnot* **c87 h–**

FREDERIC FOREVER (IRE) 5 b.g. Exit To Nowhere (USA) – Sarooh's Love (USA) (Nureyev (USA)) [2002/3 h109: 16m² 16m² Oct 5] compact gelding: fair hurdler: raced around 2m: acts on soft and good to firm going: blinkered (ran poorly) once: not an easy ride. *P. J. Hobbs* **h112**

FRED'S IN THE KNOW 8 ch.g. Interrex (CAN) – Lady Vynz (Whitstead) [2002/3 h116: 20d² 20d⁴ c16d² c16d* c20sᵘʳ Mar 13] tall gelding: fair handicap hurdler: similar form in novice chases, won at Wetherby in February and Hexham in March: stays 21f: raced mainly on going softer than good (acts on heavy): held up: open to further improvement over fences. *N. Waggott* **c112 p h113**

FREECOM NET (IRE) 5 b.g. Zieten (USA) – Radiance (IRE) (Thatching) [2002/3 16d 16d 16gᵖᵘ Apr 1] fair on Flat (stays easy 1¼m), successful for A. Jarvis in September: no show in 3 starts over hurdles, wore cheekpieces last 2. *A. Crook* **h–**

FREEDOM FIGHTER 12 b.g. Fearless Action (USA) – Zuleika Hill (Yellow River) [2002/3 c94: c26gᵖᵘ c24mᵖᵘ c23dᵖᵘ Mar 4] sturdy gelding: fair hunter chaser at best, but runs more bad races than good ones nowadays: best at 3m+: acts on soft and good to firm going: not one to trust. *Mrs Rosemary Gasson* **c– §**

FREEDOM QUEST (IRE) 8 b.g. Polish Patriot (USA) – Recherchee (Rainbow Quest (USA)) [2002/3 16dᵖᵘ Nov 12] workmanlike gelding: fair on Flat (stays 1¾m) at **h–**

5 yrs for B. Rothwell: second start over hurdles, pulled up early as if amiss on return. *Mrs P. Robeson*

FREE GIFT 5 b.g. Presenting – Gladtogetit (Green Shoon) [2002/3 F16d F16m Mar 22] €18,000 4-y-o: lengthy gelding: has scope: fourth foal: half-brother to fair staying chasers Little Brown Bear (by Strong Gale) and Swincombe (by Good Thyne): dam modest chaser, stayed 3m: pulled hard and well held in 2 bumpers at Newbury. *R. H. Alner*
  F—

FREELINE FANTASY (IRE) 6 ch.g. Shernazar – Lollia Paulina (IRE) (Phardante (FR)) [2002/3 F90: 20s⁴ 20v⁴ Dec 27] angular gelding: third in bumper: modest form when fourth in novice hurdles at Chepstow: bred to stay well. *P. R. Webber*
  h90

FREE RETURN (IRE) 8 ch.g. Magical Wonder (USA) – Free Reserve (USA) (Tom Rolfe) [2002/3 19m³ 20m³ 22g⁸ 25g⁵ 17d* c16v⁵ c19d³ c20s³ c21m⁵ Mar 20] fair hurdler: generally disappointing for P. Lowry in Ireland in 2001/2: improved form after rejoining previous trainer, winning handicaps at Fontwell in October and Hereford (amateur novice) in December: modest form over fences: effective at 17f to 2¾m: acts on firm going, probably on soft: didn't impress with finishing effort fourth start. *Noel T. Chance*
  c98
  h102

FREE TO RUN (IRE) 9 b.g. Satco (FR) – Lady Oats (Oats) [2002/3 c78, h–: c25g⁴ c21s* c20d² c25m* c22m³ c27m² c21g³ c26d* c24d³ c24m⁴ c22d* c24s² c24v³ Dec 28] workmanlike gelding: modest chaser: won novices at Cartmel (2) and at Hexham (handicap) in summer and handicap at Haydock in November: stays 27f: acts on soft and good to firm going: genuine and consistent. *Mrs S. J. Smith*
  c99

FREETOWN (IRE) 7 b.g. Shirley Heights – Pageantry (Welsh Pageant) [2002/3 c108p, h148: 23f May 4] tall, leggy gelding: successful once from 2 starts over fences: smart handicap hurdler: won Pertemps Final at Cheltenham in 2001/2: well held at Haydock in May, not seen out again: suited by 3m+: raced mainly on good going or softer (acts on heavy), probably unsuited by firm. *L. Lungo*
  c–
  h–

FREE WILL 6 ch.g. Indian Ridge – Free Guest (Be My Guest (USA)) [2002/3 h76: 16g⁵ c16g^pu Aug 9] rather leggy gelding: fair on Flat (stays 1¼m): poor novice hurdler: soon struggling on chasing debut: will prove best around 2m: has bled from nose. *A. Scott*
  c–
  h70

FRENCH CONNECTION 8 b.g. Tirol – Heaven-Liegh-Grey (Grey Desire) [2002/3 c–, h65d: c16g⁴ c17s 16m c17s⁴ c21m^pu c17s² c17g⁴ c16g⁶ c16m c16d⁴ c16d^pu 17s² 16g Jan 18] lengthy gelding: poor hurdler/maiden chaser: best around 2m: acts on heavy and good to firm going: usually blinkered: often tongue tied. *B. D. Leavy*
  c65
  h65

FRENCH EXECUTIVE (IRE) 8 br.g. Beau Sher – Executive Move (IRE) (Executive Perk) [2002/3 h99§: c26d* c29s⁴ c24v³ c26v^pu c26m³ c26m² c22f² Apr 24] lengthy, angular gelding: modest hurdler: fair chaser: won novice handicap at Plumpton in November: should stay beyond 3¼m: acts on any going: blinkered: consistent, but often looks none too keen. *P. F. Nicholls*
  c114 §
  h– §

FRENCH GUEST 4 ch.g. Most Welcome – Laleston (Junius (USA)) [2002/3 17s^pu 17s 17v^rtr 17g 17g Apr 21] poor maiden on Flat (should stay 7f) for M. Jarvis: no worthwhile form over hurdles: refused to race third outing: sold 1,800 gns Doncaster May Sales. *P. J. Hobbs*
  h–

FRENCH MANNEQUIN (IRE) 4 gr.f. Key of Luck (USA) – Paris Model (IRE) (Thatching) [2002/3 16d⁶ 16d³ 17g* 16m* 16g Apr 12] angular, workmanlike filly: fair on Flat (stays 1¼m, usually visored), sold out of R. Beckett's stable 11,000 gns Newmarket Autumn Sales: modest juvenile hurdler: won maiden at Folkestone and mares novice at Plumpton in March: likely to prove best around 2m: acts on good to firm and good to soft going: front runner. *Mrs A. J. Hamilton-Fairley*
  h92

FRENCH MASTER (IRE) 6 b.g. Petardia – Reasonably French (Reasonable (FR)) [2002/3 h–§: 16m 22g^pu 20d^pu Jun 8] medium-sized gelding: little form over hurdles: visored twice: ungenuine. *Miss T. M. Ide*
  h– §

FRENCH TUNE (FR) 5 ch.g. Green Tune (USA) – Guerre de Troie (Risk Me (FR)) [2002/3 20s⁴ 16d Mar 5] ex-French gelding: fourth foal: half-brother to 3 winners on Flat in France: dam placed over 1¼m: fairly useful on Flat (stays 1¾m), sold out of Mme C. Head-Maarek's stable 150,000 francs Goffs Arc (2001) Sale, mostly well held in Britain: little show in novice company over hurdles. *Miss S. E. Hall*
  h–

FRENTZEN 6 b.g. Golden Heights – Milly Black (IRE) (Double Schwartz) [2002/3 22d^F 24s^pu 26g⁶ 26m³ 25m^ur 27f² Apr 24] workmanlike ex-Irish gelding: fifth in claimer
  h76

at 3 yrs for A. Leahy, only start on Flat: poor novice hurdler: thorough stayer: acts on firm going: tongue tied third start: has looked unwilling. *Miss E. C. Lavelle*

FRETEVAL (FR) 6 b.g. Valanjou (FR) – La Beaumont (FR) (Hellios (USA)) [2002/3 **c93 +** c20d* Mar 4] ex-French gelding: second foal: half-brother to 7.5f winner by Kaldou- **h–** nevees: dam placed up to 11f on Flat in France: novice hurdler/chaser for E. Chevalier du Fau: won 2½m maiden point in February and maiden hunter chase at Leicester (created good impression) in March: likely to stay beyond 2½m: raced on going softer than good. *Mrs K. J. Gilmore*

FREYDIS (IRE) 5 b.m. Supreme Leader – Lulu Buck (Buckskin (FR)) [2002/3 F17g **F75** Mar 15] IR £7,200 3-y-o: seventh foal: half-sister to winning pointers by Phardante and Be My Native: dam unraced half-sister to useful staying chaser Highfrith, from family of high-class 2m chaser I'm A Driver: seventh of 14 in mares bumper at Market Rasen on debut. *S. Gollings*

FRIAR WADDON 10 b.g. Pablond – Looking Swell (Simbir) [2002/3 c102, h72: **c103 x** c21g³ c22mF c19gᵖᵘ Apr 2] tall gelding: fairly useful pointer, won in March: similar form **h–** when third twice in hunters, let down by jumping most other starts: stays 23f: raced only on good/good to firm going. *K. Cumings*

FRIEDHELMO (GER) 7 ch.g. Dashing Blade – Fox For Gold (Glint of Gold) **c108** [2002/3 h–: 16g 17d c16g⁴ c16s* c16gᵘʳ c20sᵖᵘ c19d⁵ c16m⁵ Mar 23] strong, lengthy **h–** gelding: winning hurdler: fair form first 2 starts over fences, easily winning handicap at Southwell in December: shaped as if having problem subsequently: likely to prove best at 2m: acts on soft and good to firm going: usually tongue tied: not a fluent jumper of hurdles. *Miss Venetia Williams*

FRIENDLY REQUEST 4 b.f. Environment Friend – Who Tells Jan (Royal Fountain) **h–** [2002/3 16d 21d Jan 16] first foal: dam thrice-raced sister to fairly useful staying chaser Norman Conqueror: no show in 2 starts over hurdles, not fluent on second occasion. *Mrs P. Ford*

FRIEND'S AMIGO (IRE) 6 b.g. Accordion – Lady Sipash (Erin's Hope) [2002/3 **h120** F103: 16s* 16v⁶ 16v* 20g⁶ Apr 3] big, well-made gelding: will make a chaser: fairly useful novice hurdler: won at Punchestown (maiden) in November and Naas in March: should stay beyond 2m (beaten before stamina became issue over 2½m): acts on heavy going. *P. M. J. Doyle, Ireland*

FRILEUX ROYAL (FR) 10 br.g. Sarpedon (FR) – La Frileuse (FR) (El Toro (FR)) **c§§** [2002/3 c§§, h90§: 24g May 8] sturdy gelding: winning hurdler/cross-country chaser: **h– §** completely lost his way over fences in 2001/2, refusing 3 times: second in point in April: best at 3m+: acts on soft and good to firm going: tried blinkered/visored: one to leave alone. *T. R. George*

FROM LITTLE ACORNS (IRE) 7 b.g. Denel (FR) – Mount Gawn (Harwell) **h96 +** [2002/3 h81: 21g³ 20g* 20m* Jun 1] small gelding: winning pointer: modest hurdler: won maiden in May and handicap in June, both at Hexham: should stay 2¾m: acts on good to firm going: not always a fluent jumper. *Ferdy Murphy*

FROSTY CANYON 10 b.g. Arctic Lord – Rose Ravine (Deep Run) [2002/3 c145, **c140** h–: 25d⁴ c26g c29v⁴ c24s² c28d⁶ 24g² c29m⁴ Apr 26] tall gelding: useful hurdler, runner- **h136** up to Deano's Beeno in Grade 2 at Ascot in April: useful handicap chaser: largely creditable efforts in defeat in valuable events in 2002/3, fourth to Mini Sensation in Welsh National at Chepstow and Ad Hoc in attheraces Gold Cup at Sandown: best at 3m+: acts on heavy and good to firm going: usually visored/blinkered, tried in cheekpieces: consistent, though often takes plenty of driving. *P. R. Webber*

FROSTY RUN (IRE) 5 b.g. Commanche Run – Here To-Day (King's Equity) [2002/3 **F80** F16d⁶ Mar 10] 11,000 4-y-o: sixth foal: dam, behind in bumpers/novice hurdles, half-sister to fairly useful staying chaser Shoon Wind: sixth of 9 in maiden bumper at Stratford on debut. *Mrs H. Dalton*

FRYUP BOOSTER 6 ch.g. Bollin William – Comedy Imp (Import) [2002/3 17sᵖᵘ **h–** 20gᵖᵘ 16d Jan 24] leggy gelding: fourth foal: half-brother to winning hurdler/pointer Fryup Satellite (by Leading Star), effective up to 25f: dam lightly-raced maiden pointer: fell in point on debut in 2002: no show in novice company over hurdles: has had tongue tied. *P. D. Niven*

FRYUP SATELLITE 12 br.g. Leading Star – Comedy Imp (Import) [2002/3 c25m² **c94** May 8] good-topped gelding: winning hurdler/maiden chaser: won point in April: stays **h–** 25f: acts on good to soft and good to firm going. *Miss Freya Hartley*

FUERO REAL (FR) 8 b.g. Highest Honor (FR) – Highest Pleasure (USA) (Foolish Pleasure (USA)) [2002/3 h–: 24g^{pu} c23f^{pu} 24f^{pu} 25m 26g^{pu} 24s^{pu} Nov 14] sturdy gelding: of little account nowadays: tried blinkered. *S. T. Lewis* **c– h–**

FULLARDS 5 b.g. Alderbrook – Milly Kelly (Murrayfield) [2002/3 19d 21g^{pu} Mar 3] sturdy gelding: half-brother to several winners (all of whom stay at least 2½m), including one-time fair staying chaser Bassenhally (by Celtic Cone): dam won 2m hurdle: no show in 2 novice hurdles, jumping poorly on second occasion. *Mrs P. Sly* **h–**

FULL EGALITE 7 gr.g. Ezzoud (IRE) – Milva (Jellaby) [2002/3 h83?: 16d 16g^{6} 16m 21g^{pu} Mar 12] poor on Flat (stays 2m): no worthwhile form over hurdles: blinkered. *B. A. Pearce* **h–**

FULL IRISH (IRE) 7 ch.g. Rashar (USA) – Ross Gale (Strong Gale) [2002/3 h128p, F111: 21v* 16s^{2} 17g 16g Apr 5] sturdy gelding: fairly useful handicap hurdler: landed odds in 3-runner race at Sedgefield in November: creditable efforts next 2 starts: stays 21f: raced on good ground or softer (acts on heavy). *L. Lungo* **h126**

FULL MINTY 8 br.g. Phardante (FR) – Jouvencelle (Rusticaro (FR)) [2002/3 c24v^{pu} c22d^{2} Feb 8] fair hurdler in 2000/1: much better effort in novice chases on return when second at Haydock: should stay 3m: acts on soft and good to firm going. *N. A. Twiston-Davies* **c108 h–**

FULL ON 6 b.g. Le Moss – Flighty Dove (Cruise Missile) [2002/3 F–: F18d^{4} 21s^{2} 25v^{pu} 20s^{pu} Mar 15] useful-looking gelding: much better effort in bumpers when fourth at Plumpton on reappearance: promising second in novice there on hurdling debut, shaped as if something amiss both subsequent starts: bred to stay beyond 21f: raced on going softer than good. *A. M. Hales* **h91 F90**

FULLOPEP 9 b.g. Dunbeath (USA) – Suggia (Alzao (USA)) [2002/3 c127, h–: c17m^{pu} Jun 1] sturdy gelding: fairly useful handicap chaser: never travelling or jumping well on reappearance: won point in March: effective at 2m to 3m: acts on good to firm and good to soft going. *Mrs M. Reveley* **c– h–**

FULL SUIT 7 b.m. Local Suitor (USA) – Dereks Daughter (Derek H) [2002/3 F–: 16d^{pu} 16g^{pu} Jun 15] no sign of ability. *C. E. N. Smith* **h–**

FULWELL HILL 5 b.m. Anshan – Finkin (Fine Blue) [2002/3 F16g Mar 2] lengthy mare: chasing type: sixth foal: dam winning pointer: eighth of 19 in maiden bumper at Huntingdon on debut. *Ian Williams* **F69**

FUNDAMENTAL 4 ch.g. Rudimentary (USA) – I'll Try (Try My Best (USA)) [2002/3 16d^{3} 16v^{2} 16d* 16s^{4} Mar 8] half-brother to high-class 2m hurdler Intersky Falcon (by Polar Falcon) and fairly useful hurdler/chaser up to 25f Steel Mirror (by Slip Anchor): lightly-raced maiden up to 1½m on Flat: best effort over hurdles when making all in novice at Ayr in February: should stay beyond 2m: pulled hard second start. *T. P. Tate* **h95**

FUNNY FARM 13 ch.g. Funny Man – Ba Ba Belle (Petit Instant) [2002/3 c–: c25d^{6} Feb 10] fair pointer: jumped sloppily in hunter at Hereford in February. *Alan Walter* **c77**

FUNNY GENIE (FR) 10 b.g. Genereux Genie – Sauteuse de Retz (FR) (Funny Hobby) [2002/3 c–, h–: c19m^{pu} Apr 21] angular gelding: winning hurdler/chaser: of little account nowadays: blinkered/visored. *Miss H. M. Irving* **c– h–**

FUTONA 11 ch.m. Fearless Action (USA) – Chaise Longue (Full of Hope) [2002/3 c78, h–: c21f^{pu} c20g May 30] compact mare: winning hurdler: probably of little account nowadays. *A. J. Wilson* **c– h–**

G

GABIDIA 6 br.m. Bin Ajwaad (IRE) – Diabaig (Precocious) [2002/3 16g Apr 24] poor maiden on Flat (seems to stay 13f): well beaten in 3 races over hurdles. *A. J. Martin, Ireland* **h–**

GABOR 4 b.g. Danzig Connection (USA) – Kiomi (Niniski (USA)) [2002/3 16m* 16m^{2} 16m^{2} 16g^{pu} Apr 3] good-topped gelding: fairly useful on Flat (stays 1½m): winning debut over hurdles in juvenile at Plumpton in September: runner-up in similar events next 2 starts, out of depth final one (reportedly lost action). *G. L. Moore* **h102**

GADZ'ART (FR) 9 b.g. Art Bleu – Naftane (FR) (Trac) [2002/3 c135d, h114: c20g⁴ c–
May 3] workmanlike gelding: one-time very smart chaser in France, very much on the h–
downgrade: stays 25f: raced on good going or softer (acts on heavy): usually blinkered:
has had tongue tied. *A. King*

GAIA GREY 7 gr.m. Environment Friend – Princess David (USA) (Irish River (FR)) h86
[2002/3 F90: 20mᵖᵘ 23d² 25d² 24g⁰ᵘ 24m* Jul 17] tall, lengthy mare: modest novice
hurdler: won at Worcester in July, idling: stays 25f: acts on good to soft and good to firm
going: joined R. Ford. *T. P. Tate*

GAINFUL 4 ch.f. Elmaamul (USA) – Regain (Relko) [2002/3 16m⁴ 16d 17sᶠ 17s h–
17dᵖᵘ 17g Apr 21] leggy filly: half-sister to winning 2m hurdler White River (by Pharly),
winning Italian chaser around 2m Print Rate (by Primo Dominie) and winning pointer by
Elegant Air: maiden on Flat: no worthwhile form over hurdles. *G. F. H. Charles-Jones*

GALADHRIM (IRE) 6 b.g. Glacial Storm (USA) – La Mode Lady (Mandalus) F81
[2002/3 F16s F17s⁶ Feb 11] IR £25,000 4-y-o: tall gelding: has scope: first foal: dam
modest 2m chaser: better effort in bumpers when sixth of 14 at Folkestone, setting steady
pace. *Edward Butler, Ireland*

GALA DU MOULIN MAS (FR) 9 b.g. Le Riverain (FR) – Soiree d'Ex (FR) c73
(Kashtan (FR)) [2002/3 c65, h–: c16m² c16g c17mᵘʳ 16g c19s⁴ c22v⁴ c20sᵖᵘ c22sᵖᵘ Feb h–
3] rangy gelding: poor chaser/maiden hurdler: probably stays 2¾m: acts on good to firm
and heavy going: tried blinkered/in cheekpieces. *M. E. D. Francis*

GALANT EYE (IRE) 4 ch.g. Eagle Eyed (USA) – Galandria (Sharpo) [2002/3 18m³ h80
16m⁴ 18m³ 16m³ 18d⁶ 16s⁵ 22vᵖᵘ Feb 11] compact gelding: poor maiden on Flat (stays
1½m): modest juvenile hurdler: raced mainly around 2m: acts on good to firm going.
F. Jordan

GALANT MOSS (FR) 9 br.g. Tip Moss (FR) – Tchela (FR) (Le Nain Jaune (FR)) c120
[2002/3 c129, h156: 20v² 25d³ 19s⁵ 20s² 20v⁵ c19v³ c24s⁶ c20gᵖᵘ c24sᵖᵘ 23s 18vᵖᵘ 21g h156 d
20g Mar 25] leggy gelding: fairly useful chaser, often let down by jumping: very smart
hurdler: best effort in 2002/3 (first 5 outings all at Auteuil) when third to Laveron in
Grande Course de Haies d'Auteuil second start: out of sorts after turn of year: barely stays
25f: acts on any going: tried blinkered/visored: has idled, and best held up. *M. C. Pipe*

GALA PERFORMANCE (USA) 5 b.g. Theatrical – Claxton's Slew (USA) (Seattle h94
Slew (USA)) [2002/3 F17v³ F16v 16d⁵ 17s⁵ 16s⁴ Feb 14] $2,000,000Y: useful-looking F90
gelding: seventh foal: brother to smart 1¾m Flat winner/useful 2m hurdler Humbel and 2
Flat winners in USA, and half-brother to Breeders' Cup Distaff winner Escena (by
Strawberry Road): dam Irish 7f/9f winner: unraced on Flat for A. O'Brien: tongue tied,
fair form in 2 bumpers: caught the eye when fifth in novice at Haydock on hurdling debut,
travelling easily under restraint long way (trainer fined £800, jockey banned for 5 days
and horse for 30 days under non-triers rule): disappointing in similar events subsequently.
Jonjo O'Neill

GALAPIAT DU MESNIL (FR) 9 b.g. Sarpedon – Polka de Montrin (FR) (Danoso) c132 d
[2002/3 c130, h–: c24g* c25d⁶ c31d 20v c34sᵖᵘ Mar 15] leggy, angular gelding: useful h–
chaser: won handicap at Chepstow in May: disappointing otherwise in 2002/3, including
over hurdles: distant second in cross country chase at Punchestown in early-May:
effective at 19f (given test) to 31f: acts on good to firm and heavy going: usually races
prominently: sound jumper. *P. F. Nicholls*

GALAXY SAM (USA) 4 ch.g. Royal Academy (USA) – Istiska (FR) (Irish River h74
(FR)) [2002/3 16s 16v 16vᵖᵘ 16g Mar 25] tall gelding: half-brother to useful hunter chaser
Noyan (by Northern Baby), stays 3¼m, and fair hurdler Terdad (by Lomond), stays 3m:
modest maiden on Flat (probably stays 11.5f) for A. Berry/W. Haggas: poor form over
hurdles. *S. Dow*

GALEAWAY (IRE) 9 b.g. Strong Gale – Geeaway (Gala Performance (USA)) c73
[2002/3 c–, h–: c25dᵖᵘ c25dᵖᵘ c24m⁴ c26f³ Apr 24] tall, angular gelding: winning pointer: h–
poor chaser: stays 3¼m: acts on good to firm going: blinkered second outing (breathing
problem): has had tongue tied. *M. J. Roberts*

GALESHAN (IRE) 11 b.g. Strong Gale – Shan's Pal (Pals Passage) [2002/3 c22m⁵ c87
c21m c20g* c19m³ c26m² c23gᵖᵘ Oct 22] rangy gelding: modest handicap chaser: easily h–
best effort in 2002/3 when winning at Worcester in August: stays 2½m: acts on good to
firm going: tongue tied. *Mrs H. Dalton*

GALILEO (POL) 7 b.g. Jape (USA) – Goldika (POL) (Dakota) [2002/3 h150p: 24g h–
24g⁶ Apr 2] workmanlike gelding: made excellent start to hurdling career when winning

317

both starts in 2001/2, novice at Kempton and Royal & SunAlliance Novices' Hurdle at Cheltenham: off 12 months (reportedly injured sesamoid), well held in Stayers' Hurdle at Cheltenham and Grade 2 at Ascot on return: should stay beyond 21f: acts on soft ground. *T. R. George*

GALLANT GLEN (IRE) 10 b.g. Zaffaran (USA) – Furmore (Furry Glen) [2002/3 c110: c20d⁴ c20d c22sᵖᵘ c21g⁶ Apr 3] good-topped ex-Irish gelding: fair chaser: left J. J. Costello after third start: successful in points subsequently: stays 25f: acts on soft going. *Perry Harding-Jones* **c104**

GALLIK DAWN 5 ch.g. Anshan – Sticky Money (Relkino) [2002/3 F16d Mar 10] 22,000 (privately) 4-y-o: first foal: dam, modest hurdler/fair chaser who stayed 3m, half-sister to 2001 Grand National winner Red Marauder: tailed off in maiden bumper on debut. *A. Hollingsworth* **F–**

GALLILEO STRIKE (IRE) 7 b.g. Magical Strike (USA) – Dame Daffodil (IRE) (Petorius) [2002/3 h95: 19s 16s 17g 16g⁴ 16d 21d Nov 15] small gelding: modest on Flat (stays 2¼m): modest handicap hurdler: creditable effort in 2002/3 only on fourth outing: should stay beyond 2m: acts on good to firm going. *T. Cooper, Ireland* **h95**

GALLION'S REACH (IRE) 8 b.g. Good Thyne (USA) – Raise Our Hopes (IRE) (Salluceva) [2002/3 c70, h–: c24m² c21mᵘʳ c24m² c24gᶠ c24s* c25d⁴ c24dᵘʳ c25s³ c29sᵖᵘ c21d³ 24dᵖᵘ c21v⁴ c25s c24g² Mar 23] workmanlike gelding: winning hurdler: modest chaser: sold out of N. Twiston-Davies' stable 7,000 gns Doncaster May Sales after reappearance: won novice handicap at Stratford in August: generally out of sorts subsequently: stays 3m: acts on good to firm and heavy going: tried blinkered: usually tongue tied: makes mistakes over fences: probably ungenuine. *M. F. Harris* **c85 x h–**

GALLIUM 6 gr.m. Terimon – Genie Spirit (Nishapour (FR)) [2002/3 F16g⁶ 16s⁵ 19d⁴ Feb 10] third foal: dam, poor maiden hurdler, from family of smart 2m hurdler Bold Boss and smart 7f to 1¼m performer Beau Sher: fell in point on debut: well held in bumper and 2 mares novice hurdles. *D. J. Caro* **h– F–**

GALLOP RHYTHM (IRE) 7 ch.g. Mister Lord (USA) – Kiltannon (Dalsaan) [2002/3 h84, F–: 19dᵖᵘ c19mᵖᵘ Apr 5] big, angular gelding: form only when second in novice hurdle in 2001/2: looked temperamental on chasing debut. *R. J. Baker* **c– h–**

GALWAYBAY STAN (IRE) 5 b.g. Safety Catch (USA) – Crook Lady (Croghan Hill) [2002/3 F18v³ F17d⁴ Feb 23] 24,000 4-y-o: seventh foal: half-brother to winning pointer by Sharp Charter: dam unraced half-sister to smart staying chaser The Ellier: won maiden on first of 2 starts in Irish points in 2002: shaped very much like a stayer when in frame in bumpers at Plumpton (maiden) and Exeter. *L. Wells* **F96**

GALWAY (IRE) 10 b.g. Jurado (USA) – Solanum (Green Shoon) [2002/3 c–, h–: c26gᵖᵘ Mar 13] lengthy gelding: useful hunter chaser in 2001: first start since, gave impression amiss in Foxhunter at Cheltenham: should stay beyond 3m: acts on good to firm and heavy going: often forces pace. *Mrs Marilyn Scudamore* **c– h–**

GAME GUNNER 11 b.g. Gunner B – The Waiting Game (Cruise Missile) [2002/3 c92: c25dᵖᵘ Feb 10] rangy gelding: fair hunter chaser: no show at Hereford in February: stays 3m: acts on good to firm and good to soft going. *Miss B. Lewis* **c–**

GAME ON (IRE) 7 b.g. Terimon – Nun So Game (The Parson) [2002/3 h89, F89: c21gᵘʳ c16d⁶ Apr 9] modest form over hurdles: runner-up twice in points: well held in novice chase at Uttoxeter: stays 19f: acts on soft ground: tried tongue tied: races freely. *B. N. Pollock* **c– h–**

GANDON 6 ch.g. Hernando (FR) – Severine (USA) (Trempolino (USA)) [2002/3 h69: 20g 18fᵇ 19f⁵ 22d 19s 22d 18v⁴ Mar 3] poor maiden hurdler: should stay beyond 19f: probably acts on any going: tried visored: has had tongue tied. *P. G. Murphy* **h72**

GANGSTERS R US (IRE) 7 br.g. Treasure Hunter – Our Mare Mick (Choral Society) [2002/3 h89?: c16s⁶ c21d³ 20v* 22d Mar 7] tall gelding: poor form in 2 novice handicaps over fences: best effort over hurdles when winning amateur handicap at Ayr in February: should stay 2¾m: raced mainly on going softer than good (acts on heavy). *A. Parker* **c74 h91**

GARDEN FEATURE 5 b.m. Minster Son – Super Fountain (Royal Fountain) [2002/3 F16g⁵ F16v⁶ F16g⁵ 20g Apr 14] workmanlike mare: third foal: dam winning staying chaser: modest form in bumpers: well held in novice on hurdling debut. *J. B. Walton* **h– F76**

GARDEN PARTY II (FR)   9 br.g. Argument (FR) – Betty Royale (FR) (Royal **c84 d**
Charter (FR)) [2002/3 c81, h–: c17g³ c17s³ c16d⁴ c20m⁵ c16g⁶ c20v⁴ c16s⁴ c16d³ Mar **h–**
15] strong gelding: poor maiden chaser: probably stays 2½m: acts on heavy and good to
firm going. *Mrs J. C. McGregor*

GARDOR (FR)   5 b.g. Kendor (FR) – Garboesque (Priolo (USA)) [2002/3 h93: 16d **h–**
16s⁵ 16g 16g Apr 14] leggy gelding: modest juvenile hurdler in 2001/2: no worthwhile
form on return. *T. J. Fitzgerald*

GARE HILL (IRE)   9 ch.g. Aristocracy – Morning Jane (IRE) (Over The River (FR)) **c74**
[2002/3 c88, h–: c26v³ Dec 4] strong gelding: modest chaser in 2001/2: below best only **h–**
run in 2002/3: stays 3¼m: raced on good going or softer (acts on soft). *J. T. Gifford*

GARETHSON (IRE)   12 b.g. Cataldi – Tartan Sash (Crofter (USA)) [2002/3 c107, **c85**
h–: c20g³ c19gᵖᵘ Apr 2] good-bodied gelding: fair hunter chaser: probably stays 3m: acts **h–**
on good to firm and heavy going. *O. W. King*

GARGOYLE GIRL   6 b.m. Be My Chief (USA) – May Hills Legacy (IRE) (Be My **h82**
Guest (USA)) [2002/3 h76: 16m² 16d* 16g⁴ Oct 19] good-topped mare: fair on Flat (stays
2m), successful 4 times in 2002: improved form over hurdles when winning mares
handicap at Perth in June: should stay beyond 2m: acts on good to firm and good to soft
going. *J. S. Goldie*

GAROLO (FR)   13 b.g. Garde Royale – Valgoya (FR) (Valdingran (FR)) [2002/3 **c– x**
c90x, h–: c26gᵖᵘ Mar 13] strong, close-coupled gelding: fairly useful pointer nowadays, **h–**
successful in February and March: no show in Foxhunter at Cheltenham: stays 25f: acts
on soft going: often blinkered: has had tongue tied: sketchy jumper. *Mrs F. Browne*

GAROLSA (FR)   9 b.g. Rivelago (FR) – Rols du Chatelier (FR) (Diaghilev) [2002/3 **c85**
c?, h–: c21m² c26m² c26fᵘʳ c26g⁴ c25fᵘʳ c25m⁴ c25gᵖᵘ Nov 9] useful-looking gelding: **h–**
modest maiden chaser: stays 3¼m: acts on good to firm and heavy going: blinkered first
4 starts, also tried visored/in cheekpieces: has had tongue tied: has broken blood vessels:
not a fluent jumper. *C. Tizzard*

GARRAHEEN LUCY (IRE)   7 br. or b.m. Alphabatim (USA) – Ravaleen (IRE) **h–**
(Executive Perk) [2002/3 16s 20v 16d F16d⁴ F16s⁵ 17gᵖᵘ Apr 21] ex-Irish mare: second **F80**
foal: sister to fair hurdler up to 2½m Alphazar: dam unraced half-sister to fairly useful
hurdler up to 2½m Coralpha: modest form in bumpers: little show over hurdles, left
P. Fahy before final outing (reportedly broke blood vessel). *B. J. Llewellyn*

GARRISON FRIENDLY (IRE)   10 b.g. Buckskin (FR) – Ikeathy (Be Friendly) **c87 §**
[2002/3 c31m⁵ May 22] fair pointer/hunter chaser nowadays: won point in January:
thorough stayer: acts on soft going: blinkered: poor jumper: not one to trust. *Mrs
S. J. Hickman*

GARRUTH (IRE)   9 gr.g. Good Thyne (USA) – Lady Sipash (Erin's Hope) [2002/3 **c117 §**
c118§, h–: c28d⁵ c26dᵖᵘ 24g c24s² c30sᵖᵘ Mar 4] medium-sized gelding: has had wind **h–**
operation: useful hurdler at best: fairly useful handicap chaser: form in 2002/3 only when
second at Taunton: reportedly lame final start: best at 3m+: successful on good to firm
going, best form on more testing ground (acts on heavy): has won with/without blinkers:
tried tongue tied: not a fluent jumper of fences: lazy, and one to be wary of. *P. F. Nicholls*

GARSINGTON (IRE)   6 ch.g. Over The River (FR) – Apicat (Buckskin (FR)) **c68**
[2002/3 F17g⁴ 22vᵖᵘ 22s 18d⁴ 24s c17sᶠ c18d c22s c20vᵖᵘ c20g F19m⁴ Apr 19] brother **h89**
to useful hurdler/promising chaser Boneyarrow, stays 2½m, and half-brother to several **F92**
winners, including useful staying hurdler Friendship (by Strong Gale): dam unraced
half-sister to high-class staying chaser Simon Legree: maiden hurdler/chaser: better effort
in bumpers when fourth at Cork final start: should stay 3m. *Michael Hourigan, Ireland*

GARTH POOL (IRE)   6 b.g. Sri Pekan (USA) – Millionetta (IRE) (Danehill (USA)) **h–**
[2002/3 17mᵖᵘ 17m⁵ Aug 5] useful sprinter on Flat for T. D. Barron in 2000, only modest
at best in 2002, sold out of I. Wood's stable £650 Ascot June Sales: no show in 2 novice
hurdles: dead. *G. F. Edwards*

GARVIVONNIAN (IRE)   8 b.g. Spanish Place (USA) – Garvivonne (Belfalas) **c126**
[2002/3 20v⁵ c17sᵘʳ 18s* 19s² 16d 19s² 22g 20s 16s c17s⁵ c18s⁶ c22s² c21s² c20s² c20s* **h118**
c18s² c20s* c24m² Apr 20] fairly useful handicap hurdler: won at Wexford in June: fairly
useful novice chaser: won at Tramore in January (maiden) and March (minor event):
good second to Kadoun in listed intermediate at Cork final start: effective at 2m to easy
3m: acts on good to firm and heavy going: tough and consistent. *Edward P. Mitchell,
Ireland*

GARY'S PIMPERNEL 4 b.g. Shaddad (USA) – Pennine Star (IRE) (Pennine Walk) **F97**
[2002/3 F16d* F16g² Mar 23] fifth foal: half-brother to 1m winner Faraude (by Farfelu):
dam, 1½m winner, from family of Star Appeal and Strong Gale: won bumper at Catterick
on debut: better form when second to Paddy The Piper in similar event at Wetherby later
in month. *M. W. Easterby*

GASTORNIS 5 ch.g. Primitive Rising (USA) – Meggies Dene (Apollo Eight) [2002/3 **h113 p**
F67: F16f² F16m* F17d² 20g¹⁵ 16g² 20m* Apr 21] lengthy, angular gelding: fairly useful **F97**
bumper form, won at Hexham in October: successful twice at Wetherby from 3 starts over
hurdles, in maiden in March and novice (made all, beat Smiths Landing ½ length) in
April: will prove best at 2½m+: tongue tied after second outing: likely to progress further.
M. W. Easterby

GATE EXPECTATIONS 5 b.m. Alflora (IRE) – Dorazine (Kalaglow) [2002/3 F–: **h–**
F16g F17m⁶ 16d 16d⁶ 16g 16v Jan 17] little sign of ability: has worn cheekpieces. **F–**
R. J. Price

GATEJUMPER (IRE) 5 b.g. Zaffaran (USA) – Nelly Don (Shackleton) [2002/3 **F–**
F17d Feb 23] brother to Irish bumper winner Mum And I and half-brother to fairly useful
chaser Jamalade (by Carlingford Castle), stayed 3¼m: dam, lightly-raced maiden, sister
to useful chaser up to 2½m State Case: well held in bumper on debut. *R. H. Alner*

GATFLAX (IRE) 11 b.g. Supreme Leader – Polly's Slipper (Pollerton) [2002/3 c96, **c87**
h78: c16g^pu c17m⁵ c17s* c20m^pu c17g² c16d^bd Nov 15] good-topped gelding: has had **h–**
wind operation: modest handicap chaser: won at Stratford in August: best around 2m:
acts on soft and good to firm going: tried blinkered/visored, not since 2000/1: has used
tongue tied: has broken blood vessel: tends to jump right. *Andrew Turnell*

GATORADE (NZ) 11 ch.g. Dahar (USA) – Ribena (NZ) (Battle-Waggon) [2002/3 **c106**
c102, h–: c20d* c20m² 20g⁴ c20m⁵ 20m² c20m c24g² c19m^pu Apr 21] leggy gelding: fair **h103**
hurdler/chaser: won handicap over fences at Worcester in June: left I. Williams after fifth
start: stays easy 3m: acts on firm and good to soft going: wore cheekpieces last 2
appearances: has broken blood vessels. *N. H. Oliver*

GAUDI PARC 5 ch.g. King's Signet (USA) – Witch (Risk Me (FR)) [2002/3 16d^pu **h–**
16g^ro 16d 17m⁶ Apr 19] strong, lengthy gelding: tailed off in two 1¼m maidens at 3 yrs
for J. Hetherton: no worthwhile form over hurdles: ran out second start. *Mrs S. J. Smith*

GAULTIER GALE (IRE) 9 b.g. Ajraas (USA) – David's Pleasure (Welsh Saint) **c–**
[2002/3 c87d, h–: c20m⁶ c24d^ur May 26] rather leggy gelding: winning chaser: tried **h–**
visored/blinkered: sold 2,600 gns Doncaster August Sales, won point in March. *Mrs
L. B. Normile*

GAY ABANDON 8 ch.m. Risk Me (FR) – School Dinners (Sharpo) [2002/3 c20m^pu **c– x**
Mar 19] no worthwhile form on Flat: jumped poorly in points and hunter chase.
C. R. Johnson

GAYBLE 5 b.g. Good Times (ITY) – High Kabour (Kabour) [2002/3 F16m⁴ Oct 5] **F77 ?**
workmanlike gelding: second living foal: half-brother to winning 2m hurdler Gaynor (by
Almoojid): dam poor 2m maiden hurdler: fourth of 6 in steadily-run bumper at Chepstow
on debut. *P. F. Nicholls*

GAYE DREAM 5 b.g. Gildoran – Gaye Fame (Ardross) [2002/3 F16s⁵ F16s Jan 18] **F91**
49,000 4-y-o: first foal: dam, modest hurdler who stayed 3m, from family of top-class 2m
to 3m hurdler Gaye Brief and very smart staying jumper Gaye Chance: fifth of 22 in
bumper at Warwick on debut, veering violently left just after start: well held in similar
event next time. *D. J. Caro*

GAYLES AND SHOWERS (IRE) 9 b.g. Lord Americo – Decent Shower (Decent **c93**
Fellow) [2002/3 c93, h–: c24m³ c20g² c22s⁴ c16s² c25s⁶ c20v³ c16v⁴ c20d^pu Mar 7] quite **h–**
good-topped gelding: modest handicap chaser: barely stays 3m, effective at much shorter:
acts on good to firm and heavy going: visored twice. *Mrs S. C. Bradburne*

GAYLING 8 ch.m. Carlingford Castle – Gay Ticket (New Member) [2002/3 19m **c–**
c19v^pu Dec 28] little form over hurdles (off over 2 years before reappearance): no show **h–**
on chasing debut. *P. J. Hobbs*

GAYNOR 7 b.m. Almoojid – High Kabour (Kabour) [2002/3 h70: 17g⁶ c16m⁵ Jul 17] **c71**
poor hurdler: fifth in novice handicap at Worcester on chasing debut, again racing freely: **h75**
likely to prove best around 2m. *P. F. Nicholls*

GAYSUN 11 b.g. Lir – Indomitable (FR) (Indian King (USA)) [2002/3 c115, h106: c26g³ c26m* 24d² c24m² c26m³ c24m Oct 5] leggy gelding: fair hurdler: fairly useful handicap chaser: won at Newton Abbot in July: stays 3¼m: acts on firm and good to soft going: effective held up or making running: genuine and consistent. *P. F. Nicholls*

c116
h103

GAZEILA 4 b.f. Makbul – Liberatrice (FR) (Assert) [2002/3 16d 17f 18f⁶ Apr 24] small, leggy filly: poor maiden on Flat (stays 1m): well beaten over hurdles. *J. J. Bridger*

h–

GAZUMP (FR) 5 b.g. Iris Noir (FR) – Viva Sacree (FR) (Maiymad) [2002/3 F17d³ F12g F16g Feb 8] 30,000 4-y-o: rangy gelding: fourth foal: half-brother to winning French jumper up to 21f Iowa Sacree (by Trebrook): dam maiden on Flat/over jumps in France: third to Brooklyn Breeze in bumper at Aintree on debut: well held both subsequent starts, failing to settle on second occasion. *N. A. Twiston-Davies*

F88

GEBORA (FR) 4 ch.g. Villez (USA) – Sitapanoki (FR) (Houston (FR)) [2002/3 F17s* F17d⁶ F18m² Mar 31] fifth foal: half-brother to 2 winners, notably smart hurdler/chaser Nousha (by Air du Nord), stays 23f: dam unraced: fairly useful form in bumpers, won at Folkestone in February. *M. C. Pipe*

F97

GEE A TWO (IRE) 6 gr.h. Roselier (FR) – Miss Doogles (Beau Charmeur (FR)) [2002/3 F–: F16v 24s Feb 24] leggy horse: no sign of ability: sold 3,500 gns Doncaster May Sales. *Ferdy Murphy*

h–
F–

GEE BEE BOY 9 ch.g. Beveled (USA) – Blue And White (Busted) [2002/3 c–§, h78§: 17m 21g 16s 16m 19d Nov 26] compact gelding: winning hurdler: showed nothing in 2002/3: tried visored: has had tongue tied: ungenuine. *G. F. Bridgwater*

c– §
h– §

GEMI BED (FR) 8 b.g. Double Bed (FR) – Gemia (FR) (King of Macedon) [2002/3 h77: 16m² 17m 16s 16m³ Apr 19] modest on Flat, won twice in March: modest novice hurdler: likely to stay beyond 2m: acts on good to firm going: blinkered. *G. L. Moore*

h90

GEMINEYE LORD (IRE) 6 b.g. Mister Lord (USA) – Mum's Eyes (Al Sirat (USA)) [2002/3 F16d F17d 20mᵖᵘ Apr 21] IR £6,000 4-y-o: rangy gelding: fourth foal: dam winning pointer: no show in 2 bumpers or novice hurdle. *Mrs S. J. Smith*

h–
F–

GEM OF HOLLY 10 b.m. Holly Buoy – Stuart's Gem (Meldrum) [2002/3 h57: 24dᵖᵘ May 26] lengthy, angular mare: winning hurdler, no longer of much account: tongue tied. *R. S. Wood*

h–

GEMOLLY (IRE) 10 b.m. Be My Native (USA) – Hayhurst (Sandhurst Prince) [2002/3 c–§, h–§: c25dᵖᵘ c23g⁵ c25gᵖᵘ c21m³ c19d c25d⁴ c21g Apr 19] angular mare: bad maiden hurdler/chaser: winning pointer: tried visored/blinkered: temperamental. *T. Needham*

c– §
h– §

GENERAL 6 b.g. Cadeaux Genereux – Bareilly (USA) (Lyphard (USA)) [2002/3 h116: 16s⁵ 16g 16v* 17v⁵ 20v 16s⁵ Feb 26] good-topped gelding: fairly useful handicap hurdler: won at Chepstow in December: best around 2m: raced on good going or softer (acts well on heavy): often front runner. *Mrs N. Smith*

h119

GENERAL ASSEMBLY (IRE) 11 b.g. Pharly (FR) – Hastening (Shirley Heights) [2002/3 c24gᶠ May 8] good-topped gelding: maiden hurdler: fair pointer nowadays: stays 2½m: acts on good to firm and heavy ground: tried blinkered. *Mrs Peter Hall*

c–
h–

GENERAL CLAREMONT (IRE) 10 gr.g. Strong Gale – Kasam (General Ironside) [2002/3 c116, h–: c28g² c32m² c23s* c24f⁶ c24m⁵ c31dᵘʳ c31d⁴ c28mᵘʳ Apr 26] workmanlike gelding: fairly useful handicap chaser: won 3-runner event at Worcester in August: stays 4m: acts on soft and firm going: below form when blinkered fifth start: has finished weakly: consistent. *P. F. Nicholls*

c122
h–

GENERAL DOMINION 6 b.g. Governor General – Innocent Princess (NZ) (Full On Aces (AUS)) [2002/3 h–: 17dᵖᵘ May 14] no worthwhile form over hurdles. *Mrs A. M. Thorpe*

h–

GENERAL DUROC (IRE) 7 ch.g. Un Desperado (FR) – Satula (Deep Run) [2002/3 F89: F16d⁶ 16d 20v⁴ 24s* 24s* 22g² Mar 21] well-made gelding: type to make a chaser: best effort in bumpers when second on debut: progressive form over hurdles: successful in maiden at Newcastle in February and 4-runner handicap at Ayr and novice at Kelso in March, fairly useful form when beating Wise Man by 3 lengths at last-named: stays 3m: raced on good ground or softer over hurdles (bumper form on firm): genuine. *R. T. Phillips*

h117 +
F83

GENERAL GOSSIP (IRE) 7 b. or br.g. Supreme Leader – Sno-Sleigh (Bargello) [2002/3 h84, F94: 16gᶠ 21vᵖᵘ 21dᵖᵘ Nov 25] sturdy gelding: fair form in bumpers: failed

h100

to complete over hurdles in 2002/3, running best race when falling last in novice at Towcester (final start for J. Old): should stay 21f: tongue tied final outing: joined R. Phillips. *Miss H. C. Knight*

GENERAL JACKSON 6 ch.g. Cadeaux Genereux – Moidart (Electric) [2002/3 h– 22m 24s^{pu} 24g^{pu} Mar 16] compact gelding: modest maiden at best on Flat (best at 2m+), well held since 2001: no show in 3 runs over hurdles. *Jane Southcombe*

GENERAL O'KEEFFE 6 b.g. Alflora (IRE) – Rosie O'Keeffe (IRE) (Royal h– Fountain) [2002/3 F16s 19d^{pu} Jan 16] 4,000 4-y-o, 8,000 5-y-o: second foal: dam unraced F– half-sister to useful staying chaser Highfrith, from family of high-class 2m chaser I'm A Driver: won 2½m maiden on last of 4 starts in points in 2002: virtually carried out around halfway when well beaten in bumper at Warwick: no show on hurdling debut. *J. D. Frost*

GENERAL SEYMOUR 8 ch.g. Seymour Hicks (FR) – Madge Hill (Spartan General) c– [2002/3 17s 20d c20v c25s Feb 11] seems of little account. *R. Ford* h–

GENERALS LASTSTAND (IRE) 5 b.g. Little Bighorn – Our Dorcet (Condorcet F86 (FR)) [2002/3 F18s* F16s Jan 18] IR £14,000 3-y-o: eighth foal: brother to one-time useful smart hurdler Crazy Horse, stays 23f, and fairly useful bumper winner Powder Creek: dam unraced half-sister to fairly useful chaser up to 3m Baptismal Fire: won 9-runner bumper at Fontwell on debut in December: well held in similar event at Haydock 3 weeks later: will stay at least 2½m. *Miss G. Browne*

GENERAL TANTRUM (IRE) 6 b.g. Ilium – Barna Havna (Crash Course) [2002/3 h– 21s^{pu} 16g 19d 17d^{pu} Feb 10] IR £19,000 4-y-o: strong, lengthy gelding: seventh foal: half-brother to fair hurdler/useful chaser General Crack (by Lancastrian), stayed 3¼m: dam placed in bumpers/2m maiden hurdles in Ireland: little sign of ability over hurdles. *A. Ennis*

GENERAL TYPHOON 12 ch.g. Nearly A Hand – Steel Typhoon (General Iron- c– side) [2002/3 c25d^{ur} May 14] modest pointer, successful in 2002: made mistakes and well held when unseated 4 out in hunter at Hereford. *Mrs H. M. Tory*

GENERAL WOLFE 14 ch.g. Rolfe (USA) – Pillbox (Spartan General) [2002/3 c106 c120, h–: c21g^2 Apr 3] rangy gelding: shows traces of stringhalt: one-time high-class h– chaser: veteran nowadays, still able to finish 11 lengths second to Divet Hill in Fox Hunters' at Aintree: stays 31f: acts on heavy going. *T. W. Dennis*

GENERATION POWER 7 gr.m. Arzanni – Hallowed (Wolver Hollow) [2002/3 F– F16m F16g Dec 12] sixth foal: half-sister to 5 bad performers: dam winning 2½m selling hurdler: tailed off in 2 bumpers. *P. A. Pritchard*

GENEREUX 10 ch.g. Generous (IRE) – Flo Russell (USA) (Round Table) [2002/3 c–, c– h–: c25s^6 c24m^4 Apr 10] maiden hurdler: winning pointer: little show in hunter chases: h– stays 3m: acts on good to firm and good to soft going: usually wears visor/cheekpieces: has had tongue tied. *Mrs A. Price*

GENEROUS WAYS 8 ch.g. Generous (IRE) – Clara Bow (USA) (Coastal (USA)) h90 [2002/3 20s^{pu} 21s^{pu} 16d 16m^2 17m* Apr 15] fair on Flat (stays 2m), sold out of E. Alston's stable 3,000 gns Doncaster September (2001) Sales: improved form over hurdles last 2 starts, won 7-runner novice handicap at Exeter: should stay beyond 17f: tongue tied after hurdling debut. *R. Lee*

GENETIC 8 b.g. Syrtos – Abdera (Ahonoora) [2002/3 c92, h–: c25g^{pu} May 4] work- c– manlike gelding: winning chaser/novice hurdler, modest at best: stays 3m: raced on good h– going or softer (acts on heavy). *D. G. Bridgwater*

GENETIC GEORGE (IRE) 11 b.g. King's Ride – Ballyea Jacki (Straight Lad) c– [2002/3 c92, h–: c17g^5 c20d^F May 26] winning hurdler: novice chaser: not fluent h– both starts in 2002/3: stays 2½m: acts on good to firm and heavy going: races freely. *Dr P. Pritchard*

GENTLE BEAU 5 b.g. Homo Sapien – Tapua Taranata (IRE) (Mandalus) [2002/3 F98 F17d^2 Feb 23] fourth foal: brother to fairly useful bumper winner Co Optimist: dam unraced from family of useful 2½m chaser Snowtown Boy: 8 lengths second of 15 to Tragic Ohio in bumper at Exeter on debut, tending to wander under pressure. *P. J. Hobbs*

GENTLE RIVAGE (FR) 9 b.g. Rose Laurel – Silverado Trail (USA) (Greinton) c104 x [2002/3 c108, h–: c20d^3 c20s^3 c19s^4 c26s^3 Dec 7] useful-looking gelding: one-time h– useful hurdler: fair novice chaser, often let down by jumping: reportedly finished lame final outing: should stay beyond 3m: acts on good to firm and heavy going: often forces pace. *N. A. Twiston-Davies*

GEOMAR 10 ch.g. Lord Bud – Pretty Soon (Tina's Pet) [2002/3 c17s³ c20m³ c22g c20mᵖᵘ c16m⁴ c17m² Aug 12] winning pointer: poor novice hurdler/chaser: stays 2½m: acts on good to firm going, probably on soft: tricky ride. *P. Beaumont* — **c83 h–**

GEORDIES EXPRESS 11 b.g. Tina's Pet – Maestroes Beauty (Music Maestro) [2002/3 c94: c25d⁵ c24gᵖᵘ c25gᵘʳ c25g* Apr 7] leggy, lengthy gelding: fairly useful hunter chaser: won point in March and at Kelso (not extended to beat Go Nomadic 10 lengths) in April: stays 27f: acts on good to firm and heavy going. *G. T. Bewley* — **c110**

GEORGES GIRL (IRE) 5 b.m. Montelimar (USA) – Keshia (Buckskin (FR)) [2002/3 16s 17m 16v F16d⁶ 20s⁴ F18v⁴ 16s⁴ 16s⁴ Feb 2] fifth foal: half-sister to fair maiden staying jumper Aren't We Lucky (by Project Manager): dam, middle-distance winner on Flat, half-sister to fairly useful 2m hurdler Megabucks: successful both starts in bumpers, at Roscommon in September and Wexford (mares) in November: best efforts over hurdles last 2 starts, easily won 24-runner handicap at Leopardstown and 16 lengths fourth to Kicking King in Grade 2 novice at Punchestown: should be suited by 2½m+: acts on heavy going. *F. Flood, Ireland* — **h107 + F99**

GEORGE STREET (IRE) 5 b.g. Danehill (USA) – Sweet Justice (Law Society (USA)) [2002/3 17f 22dᵖᵘ 19d 16vᵖᵘ Feb 4] compact gelding: modest maiden on Flat (stays 1½m), sold out of J. Gosden's stable 16,000 gns Newmarket Autumn (2001) Sales, well beaten both starts in 2002: no encouragement over hurdles. *M. C. Pipe* — **h–**

GEORGIA PEACH (IRE) 5 b.g. Pennekamp (USA) – Across The Ice (USA) (General Holme (USA)) [2002/3 h–p: 16d⁴ Jun 6] useful-looking ex-Irish gelding: fair on Flat (stays 1¼m): only poor form in 3 starts over hurdles, but has left impression capable of better: will prove best around 2m. *L. Lungo* — **h83**

GEORGIAS GIFT 8 b.g. Genuine Gift (CAN) – Georgias Fancy (Montreal Boy) [2002/3 20gᵖᵘ Apr 14] brother to winning pointer Hopies Delight: dam unraced: no show in novice hurdle on debut. *A. M. Crow* — **h–**

GEORGIC BLAZE 9 b.g. Petoski – Pooka (Dominion) [2002/3 h83?: c19sᵘʳ 19d 16v 17d c19dᵘʳ 17g³ Apr 21] sparely-made gelding: unseated second both starts over fences: 33/1-winner of seller in 2001/2, little other worthwhile form over hurdles: poor jumper. *G. A. Ham* — **c– h61 x**

GEOS (FR) 8 b. or br.g. Pistolet Bleu (IRE) – Kaprika (FR) (Cadoudal (FR)) [2002/3 c152, h157: c20d³ 17d³ 16v* c19s² c16g⁴ 20g c16m⁵ Apr 26] smallish, strong gelding: smart hurdler/chaser: won 4-runner skybet.com Castleford Chase at Wetherby in December by 8 lengths from Armaturk: creditable efforts otherwise until last 2 outings, jumped — **c152 h147**

skybet.com Castleford Chase, Wetherby—
Geos makes hard work of defeating Armaturk in a substandard renewal

Thurloe Finsbury's "Geos"

none too fluently when 15 lengths fourth to Moscow Flyer in Champion Chase at Cheltenham: stays 2½m, at least with emphasis on speed: acts on heavy going, possibly unsuited by good to firm. *N. J. Henderson*

GET REAL (IRE) 12 br.g. Executive Perk – Lisa's Music (Abwah) [2002/3 c147d, h86: c16v⁴ c16s⁵ c16vᶠ Dec 21] tall gelding: high-class 2m chaser at best: fell fatally at Ascot (winner there 4 times): acted on soft going, probably on heavy: raced almost exclusively right-handed over fences: jumped boldly, and at his best when allowed to stride on: often finished weakly. *N. J. Henderson*   **c140 h–**

GET THE POINT 9 b.g. Sadler's Wells (USA) – Tolmi (Great Nephew) [2002/3 c16s² c19d c17v⁵ c16g⁶ Mar 16] compact gelding: one-time fairly useful hurdler: well held over fences after 2-year absence: raced mainly around 2m: acts on good to firm and heavy going. *R. M. Stronge*   **c– h–**

GET UP AND GO GO (IRE) 6 ch.g. Mister Lord (USA) – Monadante (IRE) (Phardante (FR)) [2002/3 F17d Oct 22] 16,000 4-y-o: well-made gelding: first foal: dam, placed in point, half-sister to useful staying chaser Plenty Crack: well held in bumper on debut. *K. C. Bailey*   **F–**

GET WISE (USA) 7 b.g. Silver Hawk (USA) – Wising Up (USA) (Smarten (USA)) [2002/3 19m Jul 7] good-bodied gelding: fair bumper winner in 2000/1: soon well behind in novice hurdle on return: should stay at least 2½m. *R. Allan*   **h–**

GHAAZI 7 ch.g. Lahib (USA) – Shurooq (USA) (Affirmed (USA)) [2002/3 h89: 19m 17g c16g c16m c21g² c21f⁴ Aug 13] lengthy gelding: maiden hurdler: easily best effort over fences when second in minor event at Newton Abbot, not finding much: finished feelingly final outing: stays 21f, at least as effective over shorter: acts on good to soft and good to firm going: usually visored/blinkered nowadays: sold 4,000 gns Doncaster October Sales. *M. Hill*   **c86 h–**

GHADAMES (FR)   9 b.g. Synefos (USA) – Ouargla (FR) (Armos) [2002/3 c115, h–: **c120 d** c20d* c20m^F c22d c21m^{pu} Aug 27] winning hurdler: fairly useful handicap chaser: **h–** first outing for 10 months, completed hat-trick at Southwell in May: sold out of M. Todhunter's stable 38,000 gns Doncaster Sales later in month: let down by jumping next 2 starts, reportedly lame final one: probably best around 2½m: acts on firm and good to soft going: has broken blood vessels. *W. M. Brisbourne*

GHALI (USA)   8 b.g. Alleged (USA) – Kareema (USA) (Coastal (USA)) [2002/3 c–, **c–** h–: 23g^{pu} 24g^{pu} 20d May 23] useful-looking gelding: jumped badly only outing over **h–** fences: maiden hurdler, no longer of much account: tried blinkered: usually tongue tied. *J. F. Coupland*

GHOST MOON   8 b.g. Cadeaux Genereux – Sickle Moon (Shirley Heights) [2002/3 **c65 x** c–, h–: 19s c16d^5 c19v^2 c17v^5 c19d^F c18s^{ur} c20d c24f Mar 24] no form over hurdles: poor **h–** novice chaser, usually let down by jumping. *R. J. Hodges*

GHUTAH   9 ch.g. Lycius (USA) – Barada (USA) (Damascus (USA)) [2002/3 h81: **c91** 16m^5 c16m* c17m^5 c16g^{pu} c16m^4 16d^6 c20g^F 16g 17f^9 19f^3 16g^4 17m^F Oct 30] leggy **h87** gelding: modest handicap hurdler: won seller at Exeter in October: best effort over fences when winning handicap on chasing debut in June: ideally suited by around 2m: goes particularly well on going firmer than good: below form only start in blinkers: best held up. *Mrs A. M. Thorpe*

GIANLUCA (IRE)   9 br.g. Un Desperado (FR) – Belwood Girl (Ballymore) [2002/3 **h90** h113: 16s Aug 4] impressive when winning bumper in 1999: sustained leg injury and raced just twice since, won novice on hurdling debut but well held in handicap. *C. R. Egerton*

GIELGUD   6 b.g. Faustus (USA) – Shirl (Shirley Heights) [2002/3 h92, F90: 24d 20v **h99** 20g 19m^2 Apr 21] strong, sturdy gelding: has reportedly had hairline fracture of cannon bone: modest maiden hurdler: stays 2½m: acts on soft and good to firm going: tongue tied last 2 starts. *P. R. Webber*

GIFTNEYEV (FR)   4 b. or br.g. Goldneyev (USA) – Girl's Gift (FR) (Gairloch) **h–** [2002/3 20m^5 Apr 12] fifth foal: half-brother to winning chaser Cadeau Texan (by Houston): dam won over hurdles/fences up to 2m at 3 yrs in France: fifth of 11 to easy winner Caribbean Cove in novice hurdle at Bangor on debut. *C. P. Morlock*

GIGHA   4 b.f. Never So Bold – Racing Brenda (Faustus (USA)) [2002/3 17m^{pu} Apr 21] **h–** second foal: dam, 7f and 8.3f winner, half-sister to useful 2m hurdler Have Merci: showed nothing in selling hurdle on debut. *Simon Earle*

GIG HARBOR   4 b.c. Efisio – Petonica (IRE) (Petoski) [2002/3 16s Dec 27] compact **h– p** colt: useful on Flat (stays 1½m), sold out of B. Hills's stable 12,000 gns Newmarket Autumn Sales, successful on polytrack in winter: not knocked about after slow jump 3 out when well beaten in juvenile at Kempton on hurdling debut: should do better. *Miss E. C. Lavelle*

GIGI BEACH (IRE)   12 ch.g. Roselier (FR) – Cranagh Lady (Le Bavard (FR)) **c–** [2002/3 c96d, h93: 22g^6 May 1] lengthy gelding: one-time fairly useful chaser, modest at **h–** best in 2001/2: went with little enthusiasm only second outing over hurdles: stays 4m: acts on good to firm and heavy going: tried blinkered/visored: races prominently: often makes mistakes. *Ian Williams*

GIGS BOUNTY   5 ch.g. Weld – City's Sister (Maystreak) [2002/3 F14g^4 F16m^4 Apr **F82** 10] 17,000 4-y-o: half-brother to several winners, including smart staying jumper Better Times Ahead (by Scallywag) and fair staying hurdler/winning 2m chaser Sweet City (by Sweet Monday): dam, winner up to 13f on Flat, half-sister to useful chaser Another City: fair form when fourth in bumpers at Hereford and Ludlow: likely to be suited by stiffer test of stamina. *M. Pitman*

GIGS GAMBIT (IRE)   6 ch.g. Hubbly Bubbly (USA) – Music Slipper (Orchestra) **c–** [2002/3 F90: 16m^2 16d^5 24s^5 c16v^F Dec 20] well-made gelding: modest form in novice **h85** hurdles: weakening when falling heavily 4 out in novice handicap at Ascot on chasing debut: may prove best short of 3m: acts on soft and good to firm going: looked hard ride second start and may benefit from headgear. *M. Pitman*

GILBERT WHITE   10 b.g. Little Wolf – Caribs Love (Caliban) [2002/3 h–: 16s^4 **h–** 19d^{pu} 16m^5 Apr 21] rather sparely-made gelding: little form over hurdles: pulls hard. *R. Lee*

GILDEN MAGIC   5 b.g. Magic Ring (IRE) – Have Form (Haveroid) [2002/3 16d **h–** Nov 26] smallish gelding: half-brother to winning pointer by Then Again: modest on Flat (stays 8.5f), successful in February: 100/1, eleventh of 22 in novice at Warwick on hurdling debut. *P. W. Hiatt*

Hennessy Cognac Gold Cup Chase (Handicap), Newbury—
Harbour Pilot (noseband) and Hussard Collonges are caught by Gingembre (far side)
and Be My Royal (hooped sleeves), who subsequently tested positive for morphine

GILDORANS SPICE 5 gr.m. Gildoran – Sea Spice (Precipice Wood) [2002/3 F17s 17vᵖᵘ Jan 24] sixth foal: half-sister to bumper winner Sargasso Sea (by Greensmith): dam, useful hurdler/fairly useful novice chaser up to 3¼m, out of sister to useful hurdler up to 3m Sea Empress: no encouragement in bumper or novice hurdle. *G. Brown*   **h–**
  F–

GILFOOT BREEZE (IRE) 6 b.g. Forest Wind (USA) – Ma Bella Luna (Jalmood (USA)) [2002/3 h–: 16d⁴ 20g⁵ 16g⁴ Apr 7] compact gelding: poor maiden hurdler: seems best around 2m: raced on good going or softer: reportedly had breathing problem last 2 starts. *A. Robson*   **h75**

GILLEEN LAD 11 ch.g. Gildoran – Miss Colleen (Joshua) [2002/3 c16gᵘʳ c20mᵖᵘ May 11] of little account: has broken blood vessel. *Mrs K. J. Gilmore*   **c–**
  h–

GILLMAN'S POINT (IRE) 7 ch.g. Persian Mews – Davidmoss (IRE) (Le Moss) [2002/3 F16m 22gᵖᵘ Mar 21] IR 1,800 5-y-o: first foal: dam unraced half-sister to fairly useful 2½m chaser Shining Light: showed nothing in bumper or novice hurdle: dead. *Mrs L. B. Normile*   **h–**
  F–

GILL'MAR (FR) 9 b.g. Le Nain Jaune (FR) – Lolomar (FR) (Midnight Sun) [2002/3 c25d⁴ Feb 10] good-topped gelding: winning chaser: fairly useful pointer, successful in January and April: stays 23f. *Mrs L. B. Normile*   **c86**
  h–

GILL THE TILL (IRE) 4 ch.f. Anshan – Bilander (High Line) [2002/3 17d⁵ 17mᶠ 18m⁵ 17g 22g Apr 12] half-sister to smart 1996/7 juvenile hurdler White Sea (by Soviet Lad): poor maiden at 2 yrs for M. Channon: no form over hurdles. *R. J. Baker*   **h–**

GILLYMOSS 9 b.m. Gildoran – Mossy Morning (Le Moss) [2002/3 c–, h63: 22d 24sᵖᵘ 21sᵖᵘ 22gᵖᵘ Mar 18] lengthy mare: of little account: sold 500 gns Doncaster May Sales. *J. C. Tuck*   **c–**
  h–

GILOU 7 b.m. Midyan (USA) – Lunagraphe (USA) (Time For A Change (USA)) [2002/3 16m² 22m² 26m Jul 19] poor novice hurdler, off 2 years before reappearance: stays 3m: acts on good to firm going. *C. W. Fairhurst*   **h77**

GILSTON LAD 10 b.g. Broadsword (USA) – Cannes Beach (Canadel II) [2002/3 16gᵖᵘ May 8] half-brother to winning staying chasers Gilston Lass (by Majestic Streak) and Lauderdale Lad (by Politico): dam lightly-raced half-sister to fairly useful staying chaser Pongee Boy and daughter of very useful hunter Bright Beach: soon well behind on belated debut: dead. *J. M. Dun*   **h–**

GILZINE 7 b.g. Gildoran – Sherzine (Gorytus (USA)) [2002/3 h–, F75: 22g⁴ 22m 20s⁶ Aug 9] poor form over hurdles, not fluent: sold £2,400 Ascot October Sales: won maiden point in February. *M. Hill*   **h72**

GIMME SHELTER (IRE)   9 ch.m. Glacial Storm (USA) – Glen Dieu (Furry Glen) **c98**
[2002/3 c–, h–: 20d^{pu} 22v^3 27v* 22v^4 27s 27v^{pu} 25d^4 24g^4 c24s^2 c32v* c31g^2 Apr 24] **h73**
lengthy, sparely-made mare: poor handicap hurdler: made all at Kelso in November:
improved chaser: won handicap at Hexham in March by distance: good second to Rockcliffe Gossip in similar event at Perth following month: suited by thorough test of
stamina: acts on heavy going. *S. J. Marshall*

GIMMICK (FR)   9 b.g. Chamberlin (FR) – Jaida (FR) (Alfaro) [2002/3 21d 22v^F **c106**
c16v^2 c16g^6 c16s^F c16v^2 16v 16d^{pu} 16g^2 Apr 12] good-topped gelding: fairly useful **h104**
novice hurdler in 2000/1 for Miss V. Williams: easily best effort in handicaps when
second to Burning Truth at Stratford: similar form all 3 completed outings in novice
chases: stays 19f: yet to race on firm going, acts on any other: blinkered eighth outing:
needs to brush up jumping over fences. *Jonjo O'Neill*

GIN AND TERIMONIC   5 gr.m. Terimon – Genie Spirit (Nishapour (FR)) [2002/3 **F70**
F16m^4 Apr 21] fourth foal: dam, poor maiden hurdler, from family of smart 2m hurdler
Bold Boss and smart 7f to 1¼m performer Beau Sher: over 20 lengths fourth of 13 in
mares maiden bumper at Fakenham on debut. *P. Winkworth*

GINGEMBRE (FR)   9 ch.g. Le Nain Jaune (FR) – Teuphaine (FR) (Barbotan (FR)) **c157**
[2002/3 c25d^3 c26g^2 c25s^3 c36d^{pu} Apr 5] workmanlike gelding: has reportedly been **h–**
fired: very smart handicap chaser: off 18 months before reappearance (encouraging third
in Grade 2 at Wetherby), better than ever when ½-length second to Be My Royal (who
tested positive for morphine and faces disqualification) in Hennessy Cognac Gold Cup at
Newbury, rallying well after mistake 3 out: shaped as if not right both starts after, behind
when pulled up 7 out in Grand National at Aintree (subsequently reportedly treated for
tendon damage): stays 33f: acts on soft and good to firm going. *Mrs L. C. Taylor*

Mrs L. C. Taylor's "Gingembre"

GINGERBREAD MAN 8 ch.g. Derrylin – Red Rambler (Rymer) [2002/3 h–: c24mᵖᵘ Mar 23] good-topped gelding: probably of little account. *J. A. Moore*   c– h–

GINGKO 6 b.g. Pursuit of Love – Arboretum (IRE) (Green Desert (USA)) [2002/3 16s 16vᵖᵘ 17g³ 16d⁴ Apr 9] well-made gelding: fair on Flat (stays 1½m), successful in February: modest form in novice hurdles last 2 starts. *P. R. Webber*   h88

GINNER MORRIS 8 b.g. Emarati (USA) – Just Run (IRE) (Runnett) [2002/3 17vᵖᵘ 16d² 16s⁵ 16d⁶ 16sᶠ Feb 24] smallish, deep-girthed gelding: poor maiden hurdler: unlikely to stay much beyond 2m: acts on soft ground. *J. Hetherton*   h67

GIN N ICE (IRE) 10 gr.g. Glacial Storm (USA) – Theo's Gin (Teofane) [2002/3 c57x, h–: c24m³ c21s⁴ c16gᵖᵘ c21gᶠ c24mᶠ 17gᵖᵘ Oct 12] sturdy gelding: winning hurdler: bad and error-prone maiden chaser: stays 25f: acts on soft and good to firm going: tried visored, blinkered nowadays. *J. R. Cornwall*   c57 x h–

GIN PALACE (IRE) 5 gr.g. King's Theatre (IRE) – Ikala (Lashkari) [2002/3 h110: 17s² 16d⁶ 17s⁵ 16s* 16m* Mar 22] good-topped gelding: fairly useful hurdler: won maiden at Plumpton (easily landed odds) in February and handicap at Newbury (favourite, off bridle long way but led close home to beat Murray River a neck) in March: raced around 2m, likely to stay further: acts on soft and good to firm going: not an easy ride. *G. L. Moore*   h120

GINSKI 7 b.g. Petoski – Upham Lass (Sula Bula) [2002/3 h–, F–: 17d 18s 16m 22g⁶ Apr 12] rather dipped-backed gelding: little sign of ability: sometimes tongue tied. *C. J. Drewe*   h–

GIOCOMO (IRE) 5 ch.g. Indian Ridge – Karri Valley (USA) (Storm Bird (CAN)) [2002/3 h127: 20s 16g⁶ 20s* 16vᵖᵘ 16g 18g Mar 21] sturdy gelding: fairly useful hurdler: won handicap at Chepstow in December by ¾ length from Chicago Bulls: ran poorly after, left J. O'Neill before final outing: stays 2½m: raced on good going or softer (acts on soft): blinkered once: has weakened tamely. *P. Monteith*   h128

GIOLLA VALLEY (IRE) 9 b.g. Boyne Valley – Bean Giolla (Giolla Mear) [2002/3 c88, h–: c16s Oct 26] rangy gelding: maiden hurdler: modest novice chaser: should have proved better at 2½m than 2m: raced on good going or softer (acted on soft): dead. *Mrs M. Reveley*   c– h–

GIPSY CRICKETER 7 b.g. Anshan – Tinkers Fairy (Myjinski (USA)) [2002/3 c–, h–: c16g⁶ c20f⁴ c16m² c16m* c17sᵖᵘ c19mᵖᵘ Sep 11] leggy, sparely-made gelding: maiden hurdler: poor chaser, left Mrs M. Scudamore after second outing: made all in novice handicap at Worcester in July: stays 2½m: probably needs good going or firmer: has had tongue tied: headstrong. *D. J. Caro*   c79 h–

GIPSY GEOF (IRE) 12 b.g. Miner's Lamp – Princess Menelek (Menelek) [2002/3 c80+, h103: c16m* May 3] leggy gelding: fair handicap hurdler: best effort over fences for long time when winning minor event at Folkestone in May: raced mainly around 2m (probably stays 21f): acts on any going: sketchy jumper. *Ferdy Murphy*   c89 h–

GIPSY GIRL 8 b.m. Motivate – Young Gipsy (The Brianstan) [2002/3 21s 24vᵖᵘ Jan 17] third known foal: dam modest pointer: runner-up in maiden points in 2002: well beaten on completed outing in maiden hurdles. *L. J. Williams*   h–

GIPSY WOOD 7 gr.m. Rakaposhi King – Silva Linda (Precipice Wood) [2002/3 20d⁶ Mar 6] seventh foal: half-sister to fairly useful hurdler Rosco (by Roscoe Blake), stays 25f, and fairly useful chaser up to 3m Linwood (by Ardross): dam, fairly useful 2m chaser, half-sister to top-class staying chaser Brown Chamberlin: in need of experience when sixth in mares novice hurdle at Wetherby on debut, not knocked about. *P. Beaumont*   h–

GIRL BAND (IRE) 5 b.m. Bluebird (USA) – Bandit Girl (Robellino (USA)) [2002/3 h–: 17d Mar 2] poor form on Flat at 2 yrs: no show in 2 novice hurdles. *E. A. Elliott*   h–

GIRL OF PLEASURE (IRE) 4 b.f. Namaqualand (USA) – Shrewd Girl (USA) (Sagace (FR)) [2002/3 16g* 16s² 16mᶠ 16s Nov 2] leggy filly: half-sister to winning hurdler Rainbow River (by Rainbows For Life), stays 21f: modest maiden on Flat (best around 1½m): won juvenile at Stratford on hurdling debut in July despite several mistakes: better form when clear second to Red Halo at same course: tailed off in stronger race final outing. *Mrs P. N. Dutfield*   h91

GIRL'S BEST FRIEND 6 b.m. Nicolotte – Diamond Princess (Horage) [2002/3 -h–: 16g⁶ Apr 29] fair on Flat (stays easy 1¼m): no form in 3 races over hurdles. *N. J. Henderson*   h–

GIRSON GIRL (IRE) 4 b.f. Kadeed (IRE) – Hill's Proposal (IRE) (Posen (USA)) F–
[2002/3 F17g Apr 21] first foal: half-sister to French 2002 2-y-o 1m winner Zaturi (by
Ali-Royale): dam unraced: tailed off in bumper on debut. *Mrs H. O. Graham*

GISMO 6 ch.g. Arazi (USA) – Gisarne (USA) (Diesis) [2002/3 F96: 16s⁶ 16d 19d 19gᶠ h92 +
Apr 19] stocky gelding: bumper winner: first form over hurdles when falling last in
maiden at Stratford, 4 lengths clear and in command at time: whipped round start hurdling
debut. *Miss Jacqueline S. Doyle*

GIVE AN INCH (IRE) 8 b.m. Inchinor – Top Heights (High Top) [2002/3 16vᵖᵘ h–
20dᵖᵘ Feb 23] half-sister to modest 2m hurdler Marzocco (by Formidable): fair on Flat
(stays 2¼m) at best in 2000: no show in 2 novice hurdles: sold 1,000 gns Doncaster
March Sales. *W. Storey*

GIVEAWAY 8 ch.g. Generous (IRE) – Radiant Bride (USA) (Blushing Groom (FR)) c– §
[2002/3 h86§: c19g⁵ c19g 24gᵖᵘ 19sᵖᵘ Dec 12] lengthy gelding: poor handicap hurdler: h– §
no form in 2002/3, including over fences: stays 2½m: raced mainly on good going or
softer (acts on soft): usually tongue tied: unenthusiastic. *D. J. Wintle*

GIVENDALE 5 b.g. Perpendicular – Knocksharry (Palm Track) [2002/3 F16g F16d F–
Mar 6] brother to winning 2m hurdler Beckdale and half-brother to another by
Lochnager: dam sprint winner: well held in 2 bumpers. *J. R. Turner*

GIVE OVER (IRE) 10 b.g. Lord Americo – Romany River (Over The River (FR)) c133
[2002/3 c137, h–: 20s² c24s³ c26g 24v² 24s Jan 12] compact gelding: useful hurdler/ h133
chaser: creditable efforts in 2002/3 until final start: stays 29f: best efforts on going softer
than good (acts on heavy): effective held up or ridden prominently. *E. U. Hales, Ireland*

GIVE US A PRICE 8 b.m. Silly Prices – Give Us A Treat (Cree Song) [2002/3 h–: h–
16g 22sᵖᵘ Jun 3] no show in 3 runs over hurdles. *John A. Harris*

GLACIAL ENTERPRISE (IRE) 10 ch.g. Glacial Storm (USA) – Miss Shamrock c– §
(Saritamer (USA)) [2002/3 c104§, h–: c26g³ c26dᵖᵘ Feb 17] fair chaser on his day, left h–
P. Hobbs after reappearance: numerous mistakes on hunter debut: stays 3¼m: acts
on heavy going, possibly not on good to firm: has won in blinkers: not one to trust.
Mrs H. J. Cobb

GLACIAL EVENING (IRE) 7 b. or br.g. Glacial Storm (USA) – Cold Evening h–
(IRE) (Strong Gale) [2002/3 F16d F16d 21sᵖᵘ Jan 27] sturdy gelding: bought 12,500 gns F–
Doncaster May Sales: little sign of ability. *R. H. Buckler*

GLACIAL MISSILE (IRE) 10 ch.m. Glacial Storm (USA) – Trident Missile c–
(Vulgan Slave) [2002/3 c91, h–: c23mᵖᵘ c23gᵖᵘ 20m³ 21m* 19m³ Aug 31] small, angular h93
mare: winning chaser: modest handicap hurdler: won at Southwell in August: should stay
3m: acts on any going: blinkered last 2 starts: often let down by jumping over fences.
P. Bowen

GLACIAL RIVER (IRE) 10 ch.g. Glacial Storm (USA) – Lucky Trout (Beau c91
Charmeur (FR)) [2002/3 h82: c21dᵖᵘ c21s² c25d² c29s³ c26sᵖᵘ Dec 26] lengthy gelding: h–
novice hurdler: modest maiden chaser: stays 29f: acts on soft and good to firm going.
D. J. Caro

GLACIAL SUNSET (IRE) 8 ch.g. Glacial Storm (USA) – Twinkle Sunset (Deep h115 +
Run) [2002/3 h105+: 22f³ 20g² 26g* 24d* 24m⁴ Apr 26] workmanlike gelding: progressive hurdler: won handicap at Wincanton in May, conditional jockeys novice at Hereford
in June and competitive 14-runner handicap at Cheltenham (beat Ennel Boy 1½ lengths)
in December: stiff task after another absence final outing: stays 3¼m: acts on firm and
good to soft going. *A. J. Lidderdale*

GLACIAL TABHAIRNE (IRE) 9 ch.g. Glacial Storm (USA) – Taberna Lady h65
(Paddy's Stream) [2002/3 h–: 16m 26g⁵ 24d 19g⁶ Jun 12] little form over hurdles: won in
point in February: tried blinkered. *K. C. Bailey*

GLACIAL TRIAL (IRE) 10 b.m. Glacial Storm (USA) – Protrial (Proverb) [2002/3 c103
c24g* May 31] ex-Irish mare: second foal: half-sister to fair staying chaser Nativetrial
(by Be My Native): dam winning pointer: once-raced in bumpers: fairly useful pointer:
favourite, won mares hunter chase at Stratford, still travelling well and just in front when
left clear last. *P. Jones*

GLADIATEUR IV (FR) 9 b.g. Useful – Friga (FR) (Montevideo) [2002/3 c122, h–: c135 +
c20m³ c24g* 20m² c24fᶠ Sep 25] lengthy, rather sparely-made gelding: fair handicap chaser: h106
useful handicap chaser: better than ever early in season, won at Worcester and Stratford
(beat Hurricane Lamp by 1½ lengths): fell first final outing: effective at 2½m to 3m: has

won on heavy going, best form on good or firmer: visored once (looked none too keen): successful only start tongue tied. *P. J. Hobbs*

GLADTOKNOWYOU (IRE) 10 ch.g. Over The River (FR) – Jonsemma (IRE) (Denel (FR)) [2002/3 c20s* c24d⁵ Feb 14] lengthy gelding: very lightly raced: novice hurdler: off nearly 3 years, won novice handicap at Kempton in January on chasing debut by ¾ length from reluctant Flinders Chase: ran no sort of race following month: should stay 3m: acts on soft going. *R. Rowe*   **c98**

GLADYS MAY (IRE) 6 b.m. Moscow Society (USA) – Cashla (IRE) (Duky) [2002/3 F84: F16g F17g⁶ 17gᵖᵘ Jun 22] best effort in bumpers when third at Ludlow in 2001/2: no encouragement on hurdling debut (raced freely). *P. J. Hobbs*   **h–** **F75**

GLAMANGLITZ 13 ch.g. Town And Country – Pretty Useful (Firestreak) [2002/3 c107, h–: c20m⁵ c20m c21g⁵ c16g⁴ c21m³ Oct 5] leggy gelding: veteran handicap chaser, well held in 2002/3. *P. T. Dalton*   **c–** **h–**

GLAMOROUS LEADER (IRE) 7 b.m. Supreme Leader – Glamorous Gale (Strong Gale) [2002/3 F17g⁶ F16s* 19m³ 16g Dec 12] fourth foal: half-sister to 2m hurdle winner Phar Breeze (by Phardante): dam winning hurdler/chaser, stayed 2½m: modest form in bumpers, won at Kilbeggan in August: best effort over hurdles when third in mares novice there (tongue tied) later in month, sold out of C. Roche's stable 3,800 gns Doncaster September Sales: stays 19f: acts on good to firm going (bumper form on soft). *C. Weedon*   **h83** **F79**

GLAMOUR GIRL 7 b.m. Lord Americo – Money Galore (IRE) (Monksfield) [2002/3 h–: 16g 19s 21g⁴ 20s 25dᵖᵘ 26s⁶ Mar 7] compact mare: little sign of ability, left M. Wilkinson after reappearance. *F. Jordan*   **h–**

GLANAMANA (IRE) 7 b.g. Be My Native (USA) – Brides Choice (Cheval) [2002/3 c–, h86, F–: c25m⁶ c26d³ c24vᵘʳ c24d* Feb 14] rangy gelding: maiden hurdler: modest chaser: improved form over jumps when winning novice handicap at Sandown by 9 lengths from Secret Drinker: stays 3¼m: acts on soft going: type to improve further. *B. G. Powell*   **c99 p** **h–**

GLANMERIN (IRE) 12 b.g. Lomond (USA) – Abalvina (FR) (Abdos) [2002/3 c93, h–: c16dᵖᵘ c20g³ c20d c20vᵖᵘ c20d² c20g⁶ c20g² Mar 16] leggy gelding: modest handicap chaser: stays 2½m: acts on heavy going (won on good to firm on Flat): tried tongue tied earlier in career: inconsistent. *R. Lee*   **c88** **h–**

GLASHEDY ROCK (IRE) 6 b.g. Shernazar – Classical Lady (IRE) (Orchestra) [2002/3 16d⁴ 22dᶠ 19g⁶ 22m⁴ Apr 15] IR £10,000 4-y-o: lengthy gelding: first foal: dam, once-raced in points, from family of top-class 2m chaser Rathgorman: won maiden Irish point in 2002: modest form in novice hurdles: likely to stay 3m. *Miss H. C. Knight*   **h89**

GLASS BREAKER 9 b.g. Infantry – Bottle Basher (Le Soleil) [2002/3 c20gᵖᵘ May 17] poor pointer: blinkered only start in hunter chase. *T. D. Bryce*   **c–**

GLEBE BEAUTY (IRE) 7 b.m. Good Thyne (USA) – Le Bavellen (Le Bavard (FR)) [2002/3 h–, F–: 22s c20m⁶ Dec 17] winning Irish pointer: no form over hurdles or in novice chase (made mistakes). *Mrs L. B. Normile*   **c–** **h–**

GLENAHARY ROSE (IRE) 10 b.g. Roselier (FR) – Ara Go On (Sandalay) [2002/3 c24s⁴ c25s⁶ c24sᵖᵘ Mar 7] ex-Irish gelding: winning pointer: poor maiden chaser, sold out of M. McCullagh's stable €11,000 Goffs June Sale: stays 3m: acts on soft going: tried blinkered. *Mrs T. White*   **c74**

GLENALLA BRAES (IRE) 10 b.g. Roi Guillaume (FR) – Willowho Pride (Arapaho) [2002/3 h–: 20dᵖᵘ c21vᵖᵘ 26g 16g c24m Mar 23] workmanlike gelding: of little account: visored last 3 starts. *M. J. Gingell*   **c–** **h–**

GLENBURN (IRE) 5 br.g. Dr Devious (IRE) – Edwina (IRE) (Caerleon (USA)) [2002/3 16mᵖᵘ 16vᵖᵘ 16m 16gᵖᵘ Apr 24] modest maiden on Flat (stays 1m) at 3 yrs, below form for I. Semple in 2002: no form over hurdles: usually tongue tied. *Miss Lucinda V. Russell*   **h–**

GLEN CANYON (IRE) 6 b.g. Tidaro (USA) – Glenadore (Furry Glen) [2002/3 F16g F17g Jun 10] 2,000 4-y-o: seventh foal: dam poor maiden, sister to smart 2m hurdler Athy Spirit: well held in bumpers. *T. Needham*   **F–**

GLENDAMAH (IRE) 6 b.g. Mukaddamah (USA) – Sea Glen (IRE) (Glenstal (USA)) [2002/3 h71: 16d* 16g* 16d² 16m⁴ Jun 21] poor hurdler: won 2 sellers at Hexham in   **h79**

May, second a handicap: stays easy 21f: acts on good to firm and good to soft ground. *J. R. Weymes*

GLENELLY GALE (IRE)   9 b. or br.g. Strong Gale – Smart Fashion (Carlburg)   **c127** [2002/3 c130, h–: c20s⁴ c16gF c16d³ c17s* c16g c17g⁴ Apr 20] big, lengthy gelding: **h–** fairly useful chaser: won listed handicap at Limerick in March by neck from Fiery Ring, pair clear: creditable fourth of 6 to Killultagh Storm from 6 lb out of handicap at Fairyhouse final outing, finished rather tamely: stays 2½m: acts on good to firm and heavy going. *A. L. T. Moore, Ireland*

GLENFARCLAS BOY (IRE)   7 b.g. Montelimar (USA) – Fairy Blaze (IRE) (Good   **c90** Thyne (USA)) [2002/3 h78: c22mur c16d* c20dpu c16spu c16d² c16mF c16g⁵ c21s² c16s³   **h–** c20m³ c20gpu Apr 23] good-topped gelding: maiden hurdler: modest novice chaser: won at Perth in June: placed 4 times at Ayr after, considerably flattered from 49 lb out of handicap on final occasion: stays 21f: acts on soft and good to firm going: often let down by jumping. *Miss Lucinda V. Russell*

GLENGOLDEN (IRE)   10 ch.m. Glenstal (USA) – Talk Is Cheap (Le Bavard (FR))   **c74** [2002/3 c67, h–: c25d⁴ c24m⁵ May 15] poor novice chaser: raced mainly around 3m.   **h–** *Mrs S. C. Bradburne*

GLENGOOLEY FLYER (IRE)   11 b.g. Ore – Trim Hen (Trimmingham) [2002/3   **c–** c20m Jun 1] winning pointer: twice-raced hurdler: well held in hunter chase: likely to   **h–** stay at least 3m. *Mrs Lynne Ward*

GLENHAVEN NUGGET (IRE)   7 br.g. Supreme Leader – Jasmine Melody   **h122** (Jasmine Star) [2002/3 F114: 18d* 16s⁴ 16s³ 16d* 16d⁵ 16g* Apr 21] sturdy gelding: fairly useful hurdler: won novices at Thurles in October and February and Fairyhouse in April, improved effort when beating Mutakarrim a head in Grade 2 Menolly Homes Novices' Hurdle at latter: stiff task in Grade 1 event at Punchestown in early-May: raced around 2m on good going or softer: mistakes and found nothing fifth outing: has had tongue tied. *E. J. O'Grady, Ireland*

GLENMOSS TARA (IRE)   5 b.m. Zaffaran (USA) – Majestic Run (Deep Run)   **h122 +** [2002/3 F110: 19g* 20s* 20g* 21m² Mar 22] lengthy, rather unfurnished mare: has reportedly had minor wind operation: useful bumper winner: successful first 3 starts over hurdles, in mares maiden at Catterick in November and novices at Ayr in December and Musselburgh (mares) in January: much better form when 2½ lengths second of 16 to Ar Muin Na Muice in valuable mares novice handicap at Newbury, jumping better: will stay beyond 21f: acts on soft and good to firm going: tail swisher: does just enough, and may do better still. *N. G. Richards*

GLENSAN (IRE)   6 b.g. Insan (USA) – Strikes Glen (Le Moss) [2002/3 h–, F87: 16d⁶   **h–** 20s Nov 30] sturdy gelding: some promise in bumper: little show in 3 outings over hurdles: should be suited by further than 2m: sold 3,000 gns Doncaster May Sales. *Mrs H. Dalton*

Menolly Homes Novices' Hurdle, Fairyhouse—
Glenhaven Nugget (right) challenges Mutakarrim at the last

GLENS MUSIC (IRE) 10 b.m. Orchestra – Glen's Pride (Furry Glen) [2002/3 h131: **c127**
16s 20s⁴ 16s* 16s² 20s c16s³ c20d* c16v² Mar 9] workmanlike mare: useful handicap **h134**
hurdler: won at Naas in November: good second to Emotional Moment at Navan
following month: best effort over fences when winning Grade 2 Anglo Irish Bank Nas Na
Riogh Novices' Chase at former course in February by 4½ lengths from Eskimo Jack:
stays 2½m: acts on heavy going. *J. A. O'Connell, Ireland*

GLENTRUST 5 ch.g. Eastern Whisper (USA) – Esprit de Femme (FR) (Esprit du **h–**
Nord (USA)) [2002/3 F18d F18v 21sᵖᵘ Mar 10] first foal: dam fair hurdler, stayed 2¾m: **F–**
no sign of ability. *D. M. Grissell*

GLEN WARRIOR 7 b.g. Michelozzo (USA) – Mascara VII (Damsire Unregistered) **h98 p**
[2002/3 h–, F81: 16g³ 22s 19s² 19s² 24s* 24d³ Feb 23] tall gelding: chasing type:
progressive handicap hurdler, won at Taunton in January: good third to Lets Go Dutch at
Exeter following month: will stay beyond 3m: acts on soft going: capable of better yet.
J. S. Smith

GLINGER (IRE) 10 b.g. Remainder Man – Harilla (Sir Herbert) [2002/3 c92, h69+: **c102**
c20g³ c20m* c20g* c20m³ Oct 30] workmanlike gelding: maiden hurdler: fair chaser: in **h–**
good form in first half of season, won handicap at Market Rasen in August and novice at
Carlisle (odds on) in October: good third to Cape Stormer in handicap at Cheltenham,
tending to jump right closing stages: raced mainly at 2½m: yet to race on firm going, acts
on any other: sound jumper. *N. G. Richards*

GLOBE BEAUTY (IRE) 5 b.m. Shalford (IRE) – Pen Bal Duchess (Chaparly (FR)) **F–**
[2002/3 F16g Mar 29] first foal: dam unraced: well held in maiden bumper at Hexham on
debut. *A. Parker*

GLOBE QUEEN (IRE) 6 ch.m. River Falls – Kristar (Kris) [2002/3 16m⁵ 17dᵖᵘ **h–**
16gᵖᵘ 16d Feb 8] leggy mare: little sign of ability, including on Flat at 2 yrs for J. O'Neill.
D. McCain

GLORIOUS WELCOME 5 b.g. Past Glories – Rest And Welcome (Town And **h–**
Country) [2002/3 h–: 19d 24d 24s⁶ 26sᵖᵘ Mar 7] sparely-made gelding: of little account:
visored last 3 starts: usually tongue tied. *Jane Southcombe*

GLORY STOREY (IRE) 9 b.g. Tremblant – Boule de Soie (The Parson) [2002/3 **c99**
c97, h76: c24m* c25dᵖᵘ Oct 19] useful-looking gelding: modest handicap chaser: won **h–**
intermediate at Huntingdon in June: mistakes when running poorly 4½ months later:
better at 3m than shorter: acts on soft and good to firm going: sold 1,800 gns Doncaster
May Sales. *K. C. Bailey*

GLORY TRAIL (IRE) 9 b.g. Supreme Leader – Death Or Glory (Hasdrubal) **c–**
[2002/3 h71: c22d⁴ May 13] winning pointer: well-held fourth of 15 on hunter chase **h–**
debut at Towcester. *Mrs D. M. Grissell*

GLOVES OFF (IRE) 6 br.g. Naheez (USA) – River Dance View (IRE) (Orchestra) **c74**
[2002/3 c16g³ c20d⁶ c26vᵖᵘ Feb 10] IR 4,800 3-y-o: second foal: dam unraced, out of **h–**
half-sister to smart 2m hurdler/useful staying chaser Interview II: well beaten in bumpers
and over hurdles: poor form in maiden/novice chases, left J. J. Murphy after first outing.
Mrs A. J. Hamilton-Fairley

GLYNN DINGLE (IRE) 10 b.g. Millfontaine – Banner Lady (Milan) [2002/3 c24sᶠ **c100 +**
c24dᶠ 24d c17m⁶ c17m c16s² c18sᵖᵘ c20d⁵ c20g* Apr 25] workmanlike gelding: winning **h–**
pointer: twice-raced over hurdles: first run for 5 months, improved effort in steeplechases
when winning novice handicap at Perth by 6 lengths from Kandy Four despite numerous
mistakes, about to take command when left clear last: should stay beyond 2½m: acts on
soft ground. *A. J. Martin, Ireland*

GO BALLISTIC 14 br.g. Celtic Cone – National Clover (National Trust) [2002/3 **c138**
c148, h–: c25d⁶ c24gᵖᵘ Mar 11] strong, deep-girthed gelding: top-class chaser at best, **h–**
runner-up in Cheltenham Gold Cup and King George VI Chase at Kempton in 1999:
easily better effort in handicaps at Cheltenham in 2002/3 when sixth to Horus: stayed
3¼m: acted on good to firm and heavy going: prone to mistakes: has definitely been
retired. *R. T. Phillips*

GO BOY 5 b.g. Sovereign Water (FR) – Tinkle (Petoski) [2002/3 F–: 19m⁶ Aug 31] **h–**
lengthy gelding: well held in bumpers and novice hurdle: sold £600 Ascot October Sales:
placed in points. *R. D. E. Woodhouse*

GODFATHER (IRE) 5 ch.g. Insan (USA) – Lady Letitia (Le Bavard (FR)) [2002/3 **F–**
F16s F16v Mar 8] tall gelding: ninth foal: half-brother to modest chaser Whatashot (by

Gunner B), effective at 2½m to 27f, and fair pointer by Seymour Hicks: dam, winning Irish hurdler, half-sister to top-class chaser Wayward Lad: in rear in bumpers at Kempton and Sandown. *M. Pitman*

GODS TOKEN 5 gr.g. Gods Solution – Pro-Token (Proverb) [2002/3 F17m⁶ F17m* F17g² Sep 28] seventh foal: half-brother to winning pointer by Rakaposhi King: dam, winning pointer, sister to very smart staying chaser Envopak Token: progressive form in bumpers, won at Market Rasen in June: 1½ lengths second to Tickton Flyer there 3 months later: will stay beyond 2m. *G. P. Kelly* **F99**

GOFAGOLD 8 ch.g. Tina's Pet – Golden Della (Glint of Gold) [2002/3 h87: 16g² 18g² c16v² c20vᶠ Feb 8] modest novice hurdler: off 8 months, similar form when 19 lengths second of 5 to Byron Lamb in novice at Ayr on chasing debut: raced mainly around 2m, on good going or softer (acts on heavy). *A. C. Whillans* **c92** **h87**

GO GO BARNEY 8 gr.g. Sylvan Express – Elegant Mary (Grey Ghost) [2002/3 c16gᶠ 17mᵖᵘ Oct 1] no sign of ability. *G. A. Harker* **c–** **h–**

GOGUENARD (FR) 9 b.g. Gaspard de La Nuit (FR) – Laika III (FR) (El Toro (FR)) [2002/3 c126, h–: c20m² c25d⁴ c20d* c27dᵘʳ c20g⁵ c20v* c24d³ c20d* c20gᵘʳ c36dᵘʳ Apr 5] leggy, lengthy gelding: smart handicap chaser: left N. Henderson prior to winning at Wetherby in November and December and Haydock (improved effort in beating Red Striker 6 lengths) in March: also looked likely winner when unseating 2 out in Mildmay of Flete at Cheltenham, unseated nineteenth in Grand National following month: stayed 3m: acted on heavy going, probably on good to firm: visored once: dead. *Mrs S. J. Smith* **c147** **h–**

GOHH 7 ch.g. Alflora (IRE) – Lavenham's Last (Rymer) [2002/3 h83, F82: 20d 16v³ 20d c16d³ c25gᶠ Mar 17] tall, angular gelding: modest hurdler, stiff tasks in handicaps in 2002/3 when 7 lengths third to Fred's In The Know in novice at Wetherby on chasing debut: hampered thirteenth (still going well) and little impression when falling 4 out over 25f there next time: should stay at least 2½m: raced on good going or softer (acts on heavy): tongue tied. *M. W. Easterby* **c96** **h93**

Favourites Racing Handicap Chase, Haydock—
Goguenard about to take over from Il'Athou (No.2) two out; runner-up Red Striker is almost hidden

GOING GLOBAL (IRE) 6 ch.g. Bob Back (USA) – Ukraine Girl (Targowice (USA))   h–
[2002/3 h104: 19d⁶ 19s⁶ Nov 28] strong, compact gelding: has reportedly had soft palate
operation: fair hurdler in 2001/2, well held in handicaps in 2002/3: stays 21f: acts on
heavy going: has had tongue tied. *G. L. Moore*

GOING SOLO 7 ch.m. Sula Bula – Little Beaver (Privy Seal) [2002/3 F–: F17f 16sᵖᵘ   h–
17g⁶ Jun 22] medium-sized mare: won maiden point in April, no other form. *Mrs*   F–
S. Gardner

GOLA CHER (IRE) 9 b.g. Beau Sher – Owen Money (Master Owen) [2002/3   c131
c124+, h–: c25g² c26gᶠ c24v³ Mar 8] rangy gelding: useful handicap chaser: best effort   h–
when second to Swansea Bay in Badger Brewery Chase at Wincanton on reappearance:
should stay beyond 25f: raced on good going or softer (acts on heavy): blinkered second
start (reportedly struck into), wore cheekpieces final one: lazy. *A. King*

GOLA SUPREME (IRE) 8 gr.g. Supreme Leader – Coal Burn (King Sitric) [2002/3   c112
h105: c24v² c24vᵘʳ c24dᵖᵘ Jan 15] workmanlike gelding: winning pointer/hurdler: shaped   h–
encouragingly when 5 lengths second of 6 to The Villager in novice at Bangor on chasing
debut, jumping soundly in main: travelling comfortably when unseating 5 out in handicap
at Uttoxeter, broke blood vessel final start: will stay beyond 3m: acts on heavy going:
joined R. Lee. *A. King*

GOLDANZIG (IRE) 8 b.g. Posen (USA) – Sharp Invite (Sharpo) [2002/3 h–: 21dᵖᵘ   h–
Oct 26] compact gelding: fairly useful hurdler at best: behind when pulled up lame only
start in 2002/3: stays 19f: acts on soft going: tongue tied. *T. P. McGovern*

GOLDBRIDGE (IRE) 8 b.g. Distinctly North (USA) – Bold Kate (Bold Lad (IRE))   c89
[2002/3 c89, h–: c20d³ c21g³ May 31] good-topped gelding: winning hurdler: modest   h–
maiden chaser: stays 2¾m: acts on firm and good to soft going: tried blinkered.
T. P. McGovern

GOLDBROOK 5 b.g. Alderbrook – Miss Marigold (Norwick (USA)) [2002/3 17s²   h98
17s³ 17v³ 17s⁴ 20v² Mar 3] good-topped gelding: first foal: dam, unreliable winning
hurdler/chaser up to 3m, half-sister to smart hunter chaser What A Hand: well beaten on
Flat at 3 yrs: modest form when in frame all 5 starts over hurdles: stays 2½m: raced only
on soft/heavy going: usually races prominently. *R. J. Hodges*

GOLDEN ALPHA (IRE) 9 b.g. Alphabatim (USA) – Gina's Love (Golden Love)   c150
[2002/3 h124: c16f* c16s* c16g* c16g* c16d² c16dᵘʳ c16s² c16g⁴ c16gᶠ c16g*   h–
Apr 3]

    The Cheltenham Festival hasn't been a happy hunting ground for champion
jockey Tony McCoy in recent years. Five winners over the last four Festivals would
be a record most jockeys would be happy with—but not McCoy for whom expectations are always sky-high before the biggest three days of the jumping year.
McCoy's recent Festival achievements pale into insignificance compared to 1997,
when he landed the Champion Hurdle-Gold Cup double on Make A Stand and Mr
Mulligan, and 1998, when he rode five winners, equalling the record of Fred Winter
and Jamie Osborne. While riding honours at the latest Festival belonged to Barry
Geraghty, who also landed five victories (one more than Richard Johnson), McCoy
had to be content with a hard-fought win on Liberman in the Champion Bumper.
The opening day saw McCoy on the deck twice—at the third fence in the Arkle and
the third-last in the Champion Hurdle—and he was stood down later that afternoon
for dehydration, forced to give up his last two rides.
    Liberman's victory on the middle day, under a typically-determined McCoy
ride, came in the last race of another frustrating afternoon which included a fifth-
fence fall on second favourite Tiutchev in the Queen Mother Champion Chase.
Beaten a head on Well Chief in the Triumph Hurdle, the opening race of the final
day, was the closest McCoy came to another victory before he broke his left collar
bone in the fifth race, the Grand Annual, in a crashing fall from Golden Alpha.
McCoy had returned to race-riding only the week before Cheltenham after eight
days on the sidelines with a shoulder injury. The fall on Golden Alpha, still in front
when coming down three out, resulted in another absence, this time lasting nineteen
days. There had been talk of McCoy reaching three hundred winners for the
season—he had passed the two-hundred mark in record time at Kempton on Boxing
Day—but hopes were finally ended by his injuries. He still finished the season on

Martell Cognac Safeway Red Rum Chase (Handicap), Aintree—
a much improved effort from Golden Alpha

two hundred and fifty-seven, only thirty-two fewer than his phenomenal record set in 2001/2 and one hundred and ten more than Richard Johnson, runner-up in the championship for the sixth consecutive time.

Golden Alpha repaid McCoy with a victory at Aintree in the Martell Cognac Safeway Red Rum Handicap Chase. After riding two winners the previous day at Ascot on his return, McCoy landed a first-day double on Carlovent and Golden Alpha at the Grand National meeting. Golden Alpha was something of a revelation, jumping really well and putting up much his best effort to win by ten lengths, taking command down the back straight and running on strongly to slaughter a competitive field which included the first four from the previous year and several who had run well at the latest Cheltenham Festival, including the Grand Annual second and third Risk Accessor and Dark'N Sharp. Golden Alpha showed smart form which put him among the leading two-mile novices of the season. His Cheltenham target at the start of the campaign had been the Arkle but he hadn't progressed as expected in the build-up to the Festival. After strolling home at odds on over the summer in novice chases at Warwick, Newton Abbot (two) and Wolverhampton, Golden Alpha was no match for Azertyuiop in the November Novices' Chase at Cheltenham's Open meeting. Around three lengths up when blundering and unseating McCoy two out in a handicap at the same track in December, Golden Alpha found it tough going back in good novice company on his next two starts, beaten by Vol Solitaire later in the month at Cheltenham and managing only fourth to Farmer Jack at Kempton in January, his last race before the Festival. Golden Alpha's prospects in the first half of next season seem to be in the hands of the handicapper who raised him no less than 13 lb for his Aintree victory.

Mr D. A. Johnson's "Golden Alpha"

Golden Alpha (IRE) (b.g. 1994)	Alphabatim (USA) (b 1981)	Verbatim (b or br 1965)	Speak John
			Well Kept
		Morning Games (gr 1976)	Grey Dawn II
			Major Play
	Gina's Love (ch 1981)	Golden Love (b 1967)	Above Suspicion
			Syncopation
		Gina Rose (b 1969)	Prince Hansel
			Solbay Gina

A smart bumper performer back in 1998/9 when runner-up in the Champion Bumper, the well-made Golden Alpha missed the next two seasons before developing into a fairly useful novice hurdler on his return. He looked none too keen on occasions over hurdles and was visored on his last three starts, and McCoy described him after Aintree as 'a good jumper provided you let him do his own thing, but he isn't a very strong finisher.' Golden Alpha's dam Gina's Love, a sister to the useful two-and-a-half-mile chaser Gold Bearer, won a three-mile handicap chase in Ireland, but front-running Golden Alpha has shown his best form at around two miles. He possibly failed to stay twenty-one furlongs when favourite for the 2002 Coral Eurobet Cup. He acts on firm and soft going and won a bumper on heavy. *M. C. Pipe*

GOLDEN ARMS   4 ch.g. Blushing Flame (USA) – Beacon Hill (Bustino) [2002/3   **F–** F16g F16d Feb 1] half-brother to several winners, including useful 8.2f and (in UAE) 1½m winner Clever Cliche (by Danehill) and winning hurdlers Rhodes (by Pharly) and High Summer (by Green Desert), latter stayed 3m: dam, second over 1¼m from 3 starts, sister to Height of Fashion, herself dam of Nashwan, Unfuwain and Nayef: tongue tied, well held in 2 bumpers. *M. W. Easterby*

336

GOLDEN CHANCE (IRE)   6 b.g. Unfuwain (USA) – Golden Digger (USA) (Mr   h–
Prospector (USA)) [2002/3 h–: 20v^{pu} 19d Feb 25] sturdy gelding: poor on Flat (stays
1½m): no form over hurdles. *M. W. Easterby*

GOLDEN CHIMES (USA)   8 ch.g. Woodman (USA) – Russian Ballet (USA)   c88
(Nijinsky (CAN)) [2002/3 h104: c25d⁴ Mar 5] fair handicap hurdler: tongue tied, fourth   h–
in novice hunter chase at Catterick: won points in March and April: stays 21f, possibly
not 25f: acts on firm going, probably on soft. *G. Tuer*

GOLDEN COIN   7 ch.g. St Ninian – Legal Coin (Official) [2002/3 F76: F16d* F16s*   h74
F16s⁴ 20d⁵ 20s³ 17s³ 21g^{ur} Feb 27] strong gelding: fairly useful form when winning   F102
bumpers at Uttoxeter (maiden) and Southwell in May: only poor form over hurdles,
didn't impress with attitude final start: probably stays 2½m: raced on good going or softer
(acts on soft). *W. M. Brisbourne*

GOLDEN CROSS (IRE)   4 b.g. Goldmark (USA) – Fordes Cross (Ya Zaman   h130 p
(USA)) [2002/3 16s* 16v⁶ 16s² 16s* 17g³ Mar 13]
    Golden Cross was the best juvenile hurdler trained in Ireland in 2002/3. He
wasn't quite so good as the best of the British, having to settle for third place in both
the Grade 1 events in the spring but, had conditions been more testing, he might
have done even better. Golden Cross won twice from six starts over hurdles, both
Grade 3 events at Fairyhouse, having developed into a fairly useful performer on
the Flat as a three-year-old, winning three handicaps on the trot, all in the mud, the
last of them over a mile and a half at Leopardstown in November. Golden Cross
was clearly expected to do well over hurdles, as he started second favourite for the
betfair.com Juvenile Three-Year-Old Hurdle later that month and beat Mirpour and
Dashing Home, who had already shown potential over hurdles, by four lengths and
six. He had an excuse for a poor run when favourite for a Grade 2 event at
Leopardstown over Christmas (reported to have swallowed some dirt) and put

Mrs H. Johnson's "Golden Cross"

himself firmly in the Triumph Hurdle picture with a head second to Mutineer in the Spring Hurdle at Leopardstown followed by a four-length defeat of Statim in the Winning Fair Juvenile Hurdle later in February. Golden Cross was well supported for Cheltenham and was sent off 11/2 favourite for an open Triumph Hurdle in which less testing ground didn't play to his strengths; he stayed on all too late for third behind Spectroscope and Well Chief, around five lengths behind the close finishers. It was a good effort, all the same. Similar conditions prevailed in the IAWS Champion Four Year Old Hurdle at Punchestown—shortly after the end of the British season—but Golden Cross still got a length closer to Spectroscope who chased home the two-length winner Sporazene.

Golden Cross will plainly be well suited by a step up in trip, for all that there's nothing in his pedigree to suggest as much, though there's nothing to suggest he would make a jumper either. His unraced dam Fordes Cross has produced five other winners on the Flat, the best of them the useful Irish mare She's Our Girl (by Royal Abjar), who stays a mile and a quarter. Golden Cross is from the second crop of the Grand Criterium winner Goldmark, which also includes the fairly useful hurdler Newlands Gold, who finished seventh in the Triumph. The compact Golden Cross is a fluent jumper and all round a likeable type, who can be expected to do well again in 2003/4. *M. Halford, Ireland*

GOLDEN CRUSADER 6 b.g. Gildoran – Pusey Street (Native Bazaar) [2002/3 h–, F84?: 16s 16d^ro 16s^4 17v^3 17d^4 17v^3 Mar 10] tall gelding: poor maiden hurdler: likely to prove best around 2m: acts on good to firm and heavy ground: pulls hard. *J. W. Mullins* **h72**

GOLDEN DAWN 6 gr.g. Gran Alba (USA) – Golden Curd (FR) (Nice Havrais (USA)) [2002/3 h67: 20d c16m c17s^6 Jun 3] strong, good-bodied gelding: signs of only a little ability. *G. M. Moore* **c– h–**

GOLDEN FACT (USA) 9 b.g. Known Fact (USA) – Cosmic Sea Queen (USA) (Determined Cosmic (USA)) [2002/3 16m Apr 2] ex-Irish gelding: one-time useful around 1m on Flat, only fair nowadays: modest form in 2 maiden hurdles in 2001/2 for M. McElhone: well held in novice at Ludlow on return. *B. A. McMahon* **h70**

GOLDEN FLIGHT (FR) 4 b.g. Saint Cyrien (FR) – Sunday Flight (FR) (Johnny O'Day (USA)) [2002/3 17v* 16d^5 16d^2 18s^3 Mar 23] leggy, useful-looking gelding: brother to very smart French hurdler/chaser Sunny Flight (by Saint Cyrien), stays 27f, and half-brother to 3 winners: dam, half-sister to very smart hurdler Karly Flight, prolific winning jumper up to 2½m: fairly useful juvenile hurdler: won at Auteuil in May: creditable second to East Tycoon at Stratford: will be suited by 2½m+: acts on heavy going. *G. Macaire, France* **h115**

GOLDEN (FR) 5 ch.m. Sanglamore (USA) – Golden Sea (FR) (Saint Cyrien (FR)) [2002/3 h72: 16g^4 17f^5 17g Jun 22] sturdy mare: poor hurdler: will stay beyond 17f: acts on firm and good to soft going: sold 5,000 gns Newmarket December Sales. *N. A. Gaselee* **h77**

GOLDEN GENT (IRE) 8 ch.g. Ikdam – Golden Seekers (Manado) [2002/3 F20g c16g^6 c25g^pu Apr 14] ex-Irish gelding: won maiden point in 2002: last of 19 finishers in bumper (tongue tied) for L. Archdeacon: showed little in 2 points and 2 steeplechases subsequently. *T. D. Walford* **c– F–**

GOLDEN GOAL (GER) 7 br.g. Nebos (GER) – Goralin (GER) (La Tour (GER)) [2002/3 c132, h133: c21d^2 c21d^6 Dec 14] tall gelding: fairly useful hurdler: useful chaser: much better effort in handicaps in 2002/3 when good second of 6 to Poliantas in fairly valuable intermediate limited event at Wincanton: stayed 2¾m: acted on good to firm and heavy going: made the odd mistake: dead. *Miss Venetia Williams* **c140 h–**

GOLDEN GRAVEL (IRE) 10 ch.g. Domynsky – Whimbrel (Dara Monarch) [2002/3 h–: 17s 20s* 19d^5 26s^pu 16v^pu 26s^pu Mar 7] stocky gelding: won selling handicap hurdle at Leicester in December: no comparable form: blinkered twice, including when successful: poor jumper: dead. *S. T. Lewis* **h63 x**

GOLDENHALO (IRE) 6 b.g. Rainbows For Life (CAN) – Tangle Thorn (Thatching) [2002/3 c93, h116: 20s^2 c20m* c20m^2 c20g^3 c24m^3 Apr 20] compact gelding: fair hurdler: fair novice chaser: won maiden at Wexford in July: stays 3m: acts on firm and soft going: blinkered: mistakes final outing. *Miss F. M. Crowley, Ireland* **c107 h114**

GOLDEN HAWK (USA) 8 ch.g. Silver Hawk (USA) – Crockadore (USA) (Nijinsky (CAN)) [2002/3 h71: 16m^3 May 15] poor hurdler, lightly raced: will stay beyond 2m: acts on firm and good to soft going. *Mrs D. M. Ewart* **h73**

GOLDEN HAZE 6 ch.m. Safawan – Hazel Hill (Abednego) [2002/3 F17s F16m Jul 24] chunky mare: first foal: dam winning pointer: well beaten in 2 bumpers: sold 800 gns Doncaster January Sales. *J. K. Cresswell* **F–**

GOLDEN LEGEND (IRE) 6 b.g. Last Tycoon – Adjalisa (IRE) (Darshaan) [2002/3 16f^pu 16d^pu Oct 31] pulled up all 4 starts over hurdles: has had tongue tied: has bled from nose. *R. J. Price* **h–**

GOLDEN NOUGAT (IRE) 5 ch.g. Montelimar (USA) – Serenade Run (Deep Run) [2002/3 F16m* F17m⁴ Apr 15] 18,000 4-y-o: seventh foal: half-brother to several winners, including fair 2m hurdler Run Bavard (by Le Bavard) and fairly useful bumper winner Zero Risk (by Insan): dam unraced, out of half-sister to smart hurdler up to 3m Last Serenade: won 4-runner bumper at Ludlow on debut in March, given good tactical ride: fourth of 5 finishers in similar event at Exeter. *L. Wells* **F87**

GOLDEN ORION (IRE) 8 ch.g. Phardante (FR) – Raise The Bells (Belfalas) [2002/3 h79, F–: 24g^pu Sep 25] leggy gelding: modest maiden hurdler: looked likely winner when pulled up lame 2 out in novice at Perth: likely to prove suited by around 3m: raced on good going or softer. *Mrs J. C. McGregor* **h86**

GOLDEN RIVET 6 b.g. Weld – Golden Valley (Hotfoot) [2002/3 F17d Oct 19] lengthy gelding: eighth foal: brother to winning pointer and half-brother to 2 others: dam unraced half-sister to useful 2m to 2½m chaser Amber Rambler and fairly useful staying jumper Ambergate: well held in maiden bumper: runner-up in 2 points, including in April. *T. D. Walford* **F–**

GOLDEN ROD 6 ch.g. Rainbows For Life (CAN) – Noble Form (Double Form) [2002/3 16d⁵ 16s 16d 24g 20m 20m⁵ 20g* Apr 21] sturdy gelding: modest on all-weather, poor on turf on Flat (stays 1¾m) for P. Harris: poor novice hurdler: won handicap at Uttoxeter in April: stays 2½m, at least when conditions aren't testing: unraced on extremes of going: has worn cheekpieces, including at Uttoxeter. *K. C. Bailey* **h82**

GOLDEN ROSE (IRE) 11 br.m. Roselier (FR) – Lady Nethertown (Windjammer (USA)) [2002/3 c87, h88: c20m^ur c20d² c20d c20d^pu c20s⁵ c21s^pu Jan 14] small, light-framed mare: modest hurdler/maiden chaser: worthwhile form in handicap chases in 2002/3 only when second at Plumpton: should stay 3m: raced mainly on going softer than good (acts well on heavy): has worn cheekpieces. *T. P. McGovern* **c93 h–**

GOLDEN STORM (IRE) 6 ch.g. Magical Wonder (USA) – Independent Woman (IRE) (Carmelite House (USA)) [2002/3 c120, h120: c23s⁵ c22v³ c22v⁴ c28s² c24s⁴ c24v^R c28s² Feb 2] smallish, rather leggy gelding: fairly useful handicap chaser: good second to Be My Royal in listed event at Cork in November: stays 3½m: acts on heavy going. *Miss F. M. Crowley, Ireland* **c120 h–**

GOLDEN THUNDERBOLT (FR) 10 b.g. Persian Bold – Carmita (Caerleon (USA)) [2002/3 c81, h97: 20d⁴ 20m 22d³ 19d⁵ 17v² 20v⁶ 20s 19d 21d³ 16m³ 21m⁶ Apr 26] neat gelding: modest hurdler: effective at 2m to 3m: acts on any going: visored once: has had tongue tied: often races prominently: has looked irresolute. *H. Alexander* **c– h86 d**

GOLDEN THYNE (IRE) 9 ch.g. Alphabatim (USA) – Droichidin (Good Thyne (USA)) [2002/3 16g May 24] sixth in bumper on debut: off 2 years, showed nothing in novice hurdle. *Ms A. E. Embiricos* **h–**

GOLD MENELEK (IRE) 4 ch.g. Goldmark (USA) – Newlands Cross (Mandalus) [2002/3 F16g Mar 12] fourth foal: half-brother to winning hurdlers up to 2½m Lock And Load (by Red Sunset) and Didntearyea (by Supreme Leader): dam, bumper winner, half-sister to fairly useful chaser up to 25f Mr Frangipani: well held in bumper on debut. *T. P. McGovern* **F–**

GOLD MERIT (NZ) 12 ch.g. Gold Blend (USA) – Teresavari (NZ) (Godavari) [2002/3 20s⁶ Feb 8] sturdy gelding: developed into useful 2m novice hurdler in 1999/00 for S. Brookshaw, winning twice: tailed off in handicap on return: should stay 2½m: acts on good to firm and good to soft going. *P. T. Dalton* **h–**

GOLD NATIVE (IRE) 5 br.g. Be My Native (USA) – Goldiyana (FR) (Glint of Gold) [2002/3 F16m⁴ F16g³ Jan 17] fifth foal: half-brother to 2½m hurdle winner Golden Rambler (by Roselier): dam unraced from family of Prix du Jockey Club winner Mouktar: modest form when in frame in 2 bumpers at Musselburgh. *B. Ellison* **F83**

GOLDNECU (IRE) 8 b.g. Eurobus – Inchmarlo (USA) (Nashua) [2002/3 c–p, h114: c20s⁵ c16s² c17s⁶ Jan 19] fair hurdler: easily best effort over fences when second in maiden at Cork in January: effective at 2m and will stay 3m: raced on soft/heavy going. *Miss F. M. Crowley, Ireland* **c114 h–**

GOLDOAK 8 ch.g. Sunley Builds – Indian Election (Sula Bula) [2002/3 h–, F–: 22g^{pu} **h–**
May 1] angular gelding: fourth foal: half-brother to 2½m point winner Black Oak (by
Zambrano): dam unraced: little sign of ability over hurdles: runner-up in point in
February: tried blinkered. *R. E. Pocock*

GOLD QUEST (IRE) 6 ch.g. Rainbow Quest (USA) – My Potters (USA) (Irish **h–**
River (FR)) [2002/3 h105: 21d 19s 24s^{pu} Jan 27] tall, angular gelding: has reportedly had
soft palate operation: fair hurdler on his day: no worthwhile form in 2002/3: stays 21f:
acts on good to soft going: tongue tied: held up: sold 1,500 gns Doncaster March Sales.
C. J. Mann

GOLDSTONE 11 b.g. Precious Metal – Moon Chant (Humdoleila) [2002/3 c–: c24g^5 **c–**
May 8] poor pointer. *S. Flook*

GOLDSTREET (IRE) 6 b.g. Dolphin Street (FR) – Up To You (Sallust) [2002/3 **c121**
h121: c16s^3 c17s* c16v^4 c16s^4 20s^5 18s^5 c16d^2 c16v^5 c17d^2 Mar 22] good-topped geld- **h–**
ing: winning hurdler: fairly useful novice chaser: won maiden at Navan in November: ran
well but looked difficult ride seventh start: blinkered after, again good efforts when in
frame at Navan in March and Punchestown in early-May: raced mainly around 2m: has
won on good to firm going, best form on softer than good (acts on heavy): looked difficult
ride seventh start, blinkered last 2. *Miss F. M. Crowley, Ireland*

GOLFAGENT 5 b.g. Kris – Alusha (Soviet Star (USA)) [2002/3 16d^{pu} 16m^F 16m^2 **h99 §**
19s* 20m^2 18m^3 19d^2 21g^5 17d 17s 20s^2 19s^6 19s^3 22g^3 24m^{rtr} 24g* Apr 21] small,
close-coupled gelding: dam half-sister to high-class hurdler Pridwell and useful staying
chaser Inchcailloch: poor maiden on Flat (stays 17f): modest hurdler, sold out of
P. D. Evans's stable 18,000 gns Doncaster November Sales after seventh appearance: won
maiden at Stratford in August and novice handicap at Uttoxeter in April: stays easy 3m:
acts on soft and good to firm going: tongue tied: refused to race fifteenth start and one to
treat with caution. *Miss K. Marks*

GOLF LAND (IRE) 11 ch.g. Be My Native (USA) – Just Clara (Camden Town) **c–**
[2002/3 c25d^{pu} May 4] leggy gelding: maiden hurdler: showed nothing on chasing **h–**
debut: fair pointer, successful in February: stays 2½m: acts on good to soft going.
W. M. Aitchison

GOLLY (IRE) 7 b.g. Toulon – Tor-Na-Grena (Torus) [2002/3 F17m^{ur} May 3] IR **F–**
43,000 4-y-o: fourth foal: half-brother to 2 winning chasers by Orchestra, smart staying
chaser/useful hurdler Corket and fairly useful hurdler/chaser up to 25f Market Lass: dam
unraced: loose beforehand and unseated start in bumper on debut. *M. Pitman*

GO MAN (IRE) 9 b.g. Mandalus – Cherry Park (Netherkelly) [2002/3 h–: c16m Apr **c–**
5] workmanlike gelding: lightly raced and little worthwhile form, including in points. **h–**
C. Staley

GONE BONKERS (IRE) 8 b.g. Lord Americo – Lady Harrier (Some Hawk) **h–**
[2002/3 16s 17g 16g Mar 29] good-topped gelding: ninth foal: half-brother to winning
2m hurdler Johnjoes Pride (by Distinctly) and to 2 winning pointers by Deep Society:
dam unraced: no sign of ability in Irish point and 3 novice hurdles. *Mark Campion*

GONE FAR (USA) 6 b.g. Gone West (USA) – Vallee Dansante (USA) (Lyphard **h120 p**
(USA)) [2002/3 h120p: 17s^5 Jan 25] leggy gelding: fairly useful hurdler: stiff task, bit
better than result suggests when fifth in handicap at Cheltenham only run in 2002/3,
travelling easily long way: will stay beyond 17f: raced on going softer than good:
probably remains capable of better. *M. C. Pipe*

GO NOMADIC 9 br.g. Nomadic Way (USA) – Dreamago (Sir Mago) [2002/3 c92: **c97**
c28d^3 c24v^3 c27s^2 c25g^3 c25g^2 c31d* Apr 25] lengthy gelding: fair hunter chaser: won at
Perth in April: stays 31f: acts on heavy going (below best on good to firm): tongue tied:
consistent. *D. G. Atkinson*

GOODBYE GOLDSTONE 7 b.g. Mtoto – Shareehan (Dancing Brave (USA)) **h–**
[2002/3 h65: 16d 16v Jan 23] leggy, sparely-made gelding: fair on Flat (stays 1½m): poor
form over hurdles: has worn cheekpieces. *T. P. McGovern*

GOODBYE MRS CHIPS 4 ch.f. Zilzal (USA) – Happydrome (Ahonoora) [2002/3 **h–**
16s^{pu} 16g^{pu} Apr 24] modest maiden on Flat (will stay 1m) for J. Bethell: tongue tied,
pulled up in 2 outings over hurdles. *Mrs L. B. Normile*

GOOD GOOD (IRE) 9 ch.m. Good Thyne (USA) – Pinata (Deep Run) [2002/3 c77, **c–**
h–: c25g^6 Apr 5] workmanlike mare: winning pointer, including in February: out of depth **h–**
in quite valuable novice hunter at Aintree: stays 2¾m: tongue tied. *F. J. Brennan*

GOOD HEART (IRE) 8 ch.g. Be My Native (USA) – Johnstown Love (IRE) **c70**
(Golden Love) [2002/3 h74: c19d c20g^F 22f^4 Mar 29] sturdy, lengthy gelding: bumper **h–**
winner: poor maiden hurdler: little show in 2002/3, including over fences: best efforts
around 2m: acts on soft going: tried visored. *T. H. Caldwell*

GOOD LOOKING GUY 14 ch.g. Cruise Missile – Saxon Belle (Deep Run) [2002/3 **c–**
c86d, h–: c23f^pu May 15] lengthy gelding: winning pointer: inconsistent maiden chaser: **h–**
has had tongue tied. *Mrs J. A. Young*

GOOD LORD MURPHY (IRE) 11 br.g. Montelimar (USA) – Semiwild (USA) **c– §**
(Rumbo (USA)) [2002/3 c129§, h–: 21g c21g^6 c21m^F 24d 22s^6 c21d^pu 27g^4 Apr 19] **h90 §**
tall, useful-looking gelding: one-time fairly useful hurdler/useful staying handicap
chaser: has deteriorated considerably: acts on heavy going: blinkered once: irresolute.
Dr P. Pritchard

GOOD POTENTIAL (IRE) 7 b.g. Petardia – Steel Duchess (IRE) (Yashgan) **c–**
[2002/3 h86§: c21v^pu c17v^4 19d 21s^pu 19d 22d Mar 6] winning hurdler: out of sorts in **h– §**
2002/3, including over fences: stays 2¾m: acts on any going: tried blinkered/in cheekpieces: tongue tied: ungenuine. *D. J. Wintle*

GOOD SHUIL (IRE) 8 b.g. Good Thyne (USA) – Shuil Run (Deep Run) [2002/3 **c135**
c122+, h–: 16s c20g^5 c20d^4 c27d^3 c25d^pu c20d c36d^pu Apr 5] good sort: winning hurdler: **h–**
useful chaser: good third to Stormez in listed handicap at Cheltenham in November: well
below form last 3 starts, left T. Taaffe before final one: will prove best at 3m+: raced on
good going or softer (acts on heavy). *C. J. Mann*

GOOD THYNE JOHNNY (IRE) 9 b.g. Good Thyne (USA) – Wiasma (Ashmore **h84**
(FR)) [2002/3 20g 24g* 21g^2 22f 24m^pu 25g^2 27g^ur 24d^2 26g^5 24g^pu Sep 15] poor handicap hurdler: won at Uttoxeter in May: pulled up and dismounted final start: probably
stays 3¼m: acts on soft going, no form on firmer than good: takes good hold and usually
makes running. *L. A. Dace*

GOOD TIME BOBBY 6 b.g. Primitive Rising (USA) – Goodreda (Good Times **h–**
(ITY)) [2002/3 h–, F67: 16g Apr 7] small gelding: signs of only a little ability.
G. A. Swinbank

GOODTIME GEORGE (IRE) 10 b.g. Strong Gale – Game Sunset (Menelek) **c–**
[2002/3 c19d^6 Jan 25] strong gelding: useful hurdler in 1998/9: twice-raced over fences **h–**
since, well held in novice at Doncaster in January: stays 3m: acts on good to firm and
heavy going. *M. Pitman*

GOOD TIMING 5 bl.g. Timeless Times (USA) – Fort Vally (Belfort (FR)) [2002/3 **h–**
16d Mar 5] modest maiden on Flat (best at 7f/1m): no show in novice on hurdling debut.
J. J. Quinn

GOOD VINTAGE (IRE) 8 b.g. Lashkari – Furry Hope (Furry Glen) [2002/3 c101, **c113**
h110: c20m^2 20m^2 24g^2 c22d* c22v^5 c24s^2 c24v^R c24d^2 c29g Apr 21] modest maiden **h99**
hurdler: fair chaser: won maiden at Gowran in October: below form in valuable
handicaps at Fairyhouse in April and Punchestown late same month: stays 3m: acts on
soft and good to firm going, bumper winner on heavy: tried blinkered/in cheekpieces.
N. Meade, Ireland

GO-ONMYSON 10 b.g. Primitive Rising (USA) – Ice Lass (Heroic Air) [2002/3 h99: **h–**
22g^pu Jul 27] lengthy gelding: modest handicap hurdler: reportedly lame only start in
2002/3: stays 3m, at least when conditions aren't testing: acts on firm and soft going:
blinkered: has broken blood vessel: has dwelt/found little. *Mrs A. C. Tate*

GORDI (USA) 10 ch.g. Theatrical – Royal Alydar (USA) (Alydar (USA)) [2002/3 h–: **h–**
17m 22f 22g Jun 22] winning hurdler: retains very little ability. *Miss L. Bower*

GORDON HIGHLANDER 4 b.f. Master Willie – No Chili (Glint of Gold) [2002/3 **F79**
F16g F17g^6 F16g Apr 2] angular filly: sixth foal: half-sister to several winners, including
one-time fair hurdler Doyenne (by Mystiko), stays 2¾m, and 1½m winner Cut The Spice
(by Suave Dancer): dam 1½m winner, later successful in USA: modest form in bumpers.
Mrs P. Robeson

GORFOU DE MASPIE (FR) 4 b.c. Comte du Bourg (FR) – Mysgorfou (FR) **c135**
(Gorfou (USA)) [2002/3 15s* 15d^5 17s^6 c17s^5 c17s^2 c17v^F c17s^3 c17s^3 c20s^2 c20v* Apr **h116**
26] fifth foal: half-brother to 2 winners, including hurdler/middle-distance stayer on Flat
Fille de Maspie (by Saratogan): dam won over middle distances: won claiming hurdle at
Auteuil on debut in May, better form next 2 starts: much better over fences, raced
exclusively at Auteuil, winning Group 2 Prix Jean Stern in April by ½ length from Vesuve

despite wandering: good second to Ladykish, pair well clear, in Group 3 previous outing: stays 2½m: raced mainly on soft/heavy going: blinkered after chasing debut: not an easy ride (took little interest in Group 1 in late-May). *J-P. Bernhardt, France*

GO ROGER GO (IRE) 11 b.g. Phardante (FR) – Tonto's Girl (Strong Gale) [2002/3 c17v³ c17s² c16d³ c20g^ur c20d⁶ Mar 22] rangy, good sort: useful chaser, off 2 years prior to reappearance: placed behind Moscow Flyer in Grade 2 at Leopardstown and Colonel Braxton in listed race at Fairyhouse first 2 starts: will prove best up to 21f: acts on good to firm and heavy going: consistent. *E. J. O'Grady, Ireland* **c141 h–**

GORSEY BANK (IRE) 11 b.g. Lancastrian – Yankee's Princess (Yankee Gold) [2002/3 c–: c25g^pu Mar 18] workmanlike gelding: winning pointer: no worthwhile form in steeplechases: has had tongue tied. *E. A. Thomas* **c–**

GORTMORE MEWS (IRE) 9 b.g. Persian Mews – Flat Out (Random Shot) [2002/3 c99x, h107: c19d Dec 3] angular gelding: fairly useful hurdler at best: modest chaser: ran poorly only outing in 2002/3: stays 19f: acts on any going: tried blinkered: has reportedly bled from nose: often let down by jumping over fences. *Ferdy Murphy* **c– x h–**

GORT NA GCAPPILL 10 b.g. Presidium – Ranipa (Raga Navarro (ITY)) [2002/3 20d^pu Aug 3] no sign of ability in Flat claimer or selling hurdle. *O. O'Neill* **h–**

GORTROE GUY (IRE) 11 b.g. Carlingford Castle – Calfstown Night (Bargello) [2002/3 c–, h–: 25g⁶ 27g 21g 26g Jun 12] good-topped gelding: winning pointer: maiden hurdler/steeplechaser, retains very little ability: tried blinkered: has had tongue tied. *J. F. Panvert* **c– h–**

GOSH JOSH (IRE) 5 b.g. Blues Traveller (IRE) – Freedom's Flame (IRE) (Caerleon (USA)) [2002/3 F16m May 16] first foal: dam placed at 12.5f in Ireland: showed nothing in bumper on debut: sold 1,100 gns Doncaster May Sales, failed to complete in 2 points. *R. A. Fahey* **F–**

GOSPEL SONG 11 ch.g. King Among Kings – Market Blues (Porto Bello) [2002/3 h73: 17s³ 24d³ 16g⁴ 20v^pu 16s⁵ 22d⁵ 21d Mar 18] small gelding: modest handicap hurdler: won at Cartmel (seller) and Hexham in June: off 7 months, below form subsequently: stays 2½m: acts on heavy going: tried tongue tied: free-going front runner. *A. C. Whillans* **h85**

GOT ALOT ON (USA) 5 b. or br.g. Charnwood Forest (IRE) – Fleety Belle (GER) (Assert) [2002/3 h–: 19s 17v⁴ 17s⁵ 17d Feb 23] good-topped gelding: disappointing maiden on Flat: poor novice hurdler: raced mainly around 2m: acts on heavy going. *Miss M. Bragg* **h72**

GOTHAM ABBEY (IRE) 6 gr.m. Gothland (FR) – Abbeyside (Paddy's Stream) [2002/3 16s 20m 20v^pu 19s^pu 16m^F Mar 19] IR 5,800 3-y-o: leggy ex-Irish mare: half-sister to several winning pointers: dam winning 2m hurdler: no form in bumpers or over hurdles, left A. J. Kennedy after second outing. *B. Llewellyn* **h–**

GOTHAM (IRE) 6 gr.g. Gothland (FR) – Inchriver (IRE) (Over The River (FR)) [2002/3 h–, F71: 16m* 16m² Oct 27] rather unfurnished gelding: second outing over hurdles, won novice at Plumpton in October: shaped well when second in similar event at Wincanton later in month: not seen out again but remains open to improvement granted stiffer test of stamina. *R. H. Alner* **h101 p**

GOT NEWS FOR YOU 9 gr.g. Positive Statement (USA) – Madame Ruby (FR) (Homing) [2002/3 c99x, h–: c25f^f⁶ 24s³ 22d Jan 18] compact gelding: modest hurdler/chaser: stays 3m: acts on heavy going: visored on reappearance: usually let down by jumping over fences: inconsistent. *N. J. Hawke* **c– x h91**

GOT ONE TOO (FR) 6 ch.g. Green Tune (USA) – Gloria Mundi (FR) (Saint Cyrien (FR)) [2002/3 h136: c16g* c16s² c16d^ur c18s* c16g Mar 13] angular gelding: useful hurdler: useful novice chaser: won at Leicester (made all) in November and Newbury in March: running well (held in second behind Azertyuiop) when unseated last at Wincanton in February: stiffish task in handicap at Cheltenham final start: won on Flat in April: stays 19f: acts on good to firm and heavy going: usually races up with pace. *N. J. Henderson* **c131 h–**

GO TO SHUL 4 b.g. Runnett – Kopjes (Bay Express) [2002/3 F16d F16d Mar 6] good-topped gelding: sixth foal: brother to winner up to 1m in Denmark and half-brother to winning 2m hurdler Nautical Jewel (by Handsome Sailor): dam, poor maiden, half-sister to top-class American jumper Census and useful 2m to 2½m chaser Vicars Landing: well held in 2 bumpers. *M. W. Easterby* **F–**

GOTTABE 10 ch.g. Gunner B – Topsy Bee (Be Friendly) [2002/3 c91, h104: c20m* c20d² c23d* c25v* c25d³ c26s⁴ c25d⁵ c24dᶠ c23g⁴ Mar 23] workmanlike gelding: fair handicap hurdler: fair chaser: won novices at Wetherby (handicap) in May and Worcester in June and handicap at Wetherby in November: effective at 2½m to 25f: acts on heavy and good to firm going: has had tongue tied. *Mrs S. J. Smith*

c113 h–

GOVAMIX 5 gr.g. Linamix (FR) – Segovia (Groom Dancer (USA)) [2002/3 F101: F16v* F16g Mar 12] good sort: useful bumper performer: won at Leopardstown in December: best effort when seventh of 25 to Liberman in Grade 1 at Cheltenham: won 13f maiden on Flat debut in May. *D. K. Weld, Ireland*

F109

GOVERNOR DANIEL 12 b.g. Governor General – Princess Semele (Imperial Fling (USA)) [2002/3 c–, h–: 22m³ 20g* 17m* 20m* 21m⁴ 16d* 16d* 20d³ 21d³ c21g* 17m² Apr 21] sturdy gelding: fair hurdler/handicap chaser: had excellent season in 2002/3, won selling hurdles at Huntingdon (conditional jockeys) and Market Rasen in August and Ludlow (2 first conditional jockeys) in November and over fences at Fontwell in September and Newton Abbot (seller) in April: stays 21f with emphasis on speed: acts on firm and good to soft going: has had tongue tied: sometimes let down by jumping over fences: tough and consistent. *Ian Williams*

c102 h101

GO WHITE LIGHTNING (IRE) 8 gr.g. Zaffaran (USA) – Rosy Posy (IRE) (Roselier (FR)) [2002/3 h91: c19s³ c24sᵖᵘ c24d² c23s³ c22d⁴ Feb 8] leggy gelding: twice-raced hurdler: easily best effort over fences when second to Another General in novice at Doncaster in January: stays 3m: acts on good to firm and heavy going: races keenly. *M. Bradstock*

c109 h–

GRACEFUL DANCER 6 b.m. Old Vic – Its My Turn (Palm Track) [2002/3 F87: F17s⁵ 20s⁵ 20v⁶ 21d 24s* 21s² 26s* 28g² Mar 16] good-topped mare: fair at best in bumpers: modest hurdler: won mares amateur handicap at Taunton in February and novice handicap at Hereford in March: stays 3½m: raced on good going or softer (acts on soft): blinkered fourth start (looked unwilling), visored subsequently. *C. P. Morlock*

h92 F65

GRADY 4 ch.c. Bluegrass Prince (IRE) – Lady Sabina (Bairn (USA)) [2002/3 16dᵖᵘ Dec 5] close-coupled colt: modest maiden on Flat (probably stays 7f): showed nothing on hurdling debut. *Miss Jacqueline S. Doyle*

h–

GRALMANO (IRE) 8 b.g. Scenic – Llangollen (IRE) (Caerleon (USA)) [2002/3 h121p: 16f² 17dᵖᵘ c16g* c20m* 16g 20d² Apr 4] sturdy gelding: successful both starts in novice chases, at Catterick in November and Musselburgh in December: useful hurdler: best effort in valuable handicaps in 2002/3 when second of 16 to Patriot Games in listed event at Aintree final start: will probably stay beyond 2½m: acts on firm and soft going: open to improvement over fences. *K. A. Ryan*

c126 p h135

GRANBY BELL 12 b.g. Ballacashtal (CAN) – Betbellof (Averof) [2002/3 c103, h–: c20g* c20s⁴ c19g* c20m⁵ c19d² c20dᵖᵘ c19dᵘʳ c19s⁶ c20mᵖᵘ Mar 31] leggy gelding: fair handicap chaser: won at Plumpton in April and Hereford in June: stayed 21f: acted on good to firm and heavy going: tried in cheekpieces, usually visored: often made running: dead. *Miss E. C. Lavelle*

c113 h–

GRAN CLICQUOT 8 gr.m. Gran Alba (USA) – Tina's Beauty (Tina's Pet) [2002/3 16mᵖᵘ 16m⁵ Oct 7] poor on Flat (stays 1m): none too fluent and no worthwhile form over hurdles. *G. P. Enright*

h–

GRAND AMBITION (USA) 7 b.g. Lear Fan (USA) – Longing To Dance (USA) (Nureyev (USA)) [2002/3 h77: c16d⁴ c21sᶠ 20s c17m c22d 24s c21m* Apr 21] poor maiden hurdler: sold out of M. Hourigan's stable 500 gns Doncaster November Sales after sixth start: won novice hunter chase at Fakenham: stays 21f: acts on soft and good to firm going: tried blinkered. *Mrs P. Sly*

c78 h–

GRAND FINALE (IRE) 6 b.h. Sadler's Wells (USA) – Final Figure (USA) (Super Concorde (USA)) [2002/3 16vᵖᵘ 16d⁴ Feb 15] compact horse: half-brother to fair 2m hurdler Peerless Motion (by Caerleon) and fair hurdler/winning chaser Strong Boost (by Topsider), stayed 3m: smart up to 1½m on Flat at 3 yrs for D. Weld, subsequently well held in 2 starts in USA (reportedly sustained tendon injury after second one) and looked less than keen only start in Britain in 2002: much better effort over hurdles when fourth in novice at Wincanton, not unduly knocked about: should improve. *Miss Venetia Williams*

h91 p

GRAND FOUGERAY (FR) 9 b.g. Port Etienne (FR) – Poupee du Fougeray (FR) (Rigolo IV (FR)) [2002/3 c79?, h–: 16dᵖᵘ c21gᵘʳ 20d⁴ 16m c16mᵖᵘ Jul 15] lengthy gelding: winning chaser in France, including in cross-country events: has achieved very little in Britain, including over hurdles: tried blinkered. *A. W. Carroll*

c– h–

GRAND GOUSIER (FR) 9 b.g. Perrault – Tartifume II (FR) (Mistigri) [2002/3 c98
c17g² c20d⁴ c20g³ c20s⁵ Jan 29] good-topped gelding: modest handicap chaser: effective h–
around 2m, probably stays 3m: acts on heavy going, not fluent only outing on firm.
H. D. Daly

GRAND JURY (IRE) 6 ch.g. Grand Lodge (USA) – Scales of Justice (Final Straw) h–
[2002/3 19d 16d 19sᵖᵘ Dec 12] stocky gelding: half-brother to winning 19f selling
hurdler Felony (by Pharly): no sign of ability on Flat debut at 3 yrs or 3 starts over hurdles.
J. S. Smith

GRANDMERE 8 gr.m. Gran Alba (USA) – Cuckmere Grange (Floriana) [2002/3 16d h–
20dᵖᵘ 20d Mar 6] fourth foal: half-sister to one-time fairly useful staying chaser Mere
Class (by Class Distinction): dam never ran: little show in 3 mares novice hurdles.
P. Beaumont

GRAND PRAIRIE (SWE) 7 b.g. Prairie – Platonica (ITY) (Primo Dominie) h–
[2002/3 h–: 21mᵖᵘ Feb 22] successful several times up to 1m on Flat in Sweden and
Spain: little sign of ability in novice hurdles. *R. C. Guest*

GRAND PROMPT 4 ch.g. Grand Lodge (USA) – Prompting (Primo Dominie) h99
[2002/3 16d³ 17sᵖᵘ 16g 20m⁶ Apr 12] angular ex-French gelding: fair maiden up to 1¾m
on Flat, sold out of R. Gibson's stable 16,000 gns Newmarket Autumn Sales: seemingly
easily best effort over hurdles when eighth of 20 in competitive juvenile at Newbury third
outing: should stay beyond 2m: blinkered/visored last 3 starts. *Mrs L. Wadham*

GRAND SLAM (IRE) 8 b.g. Second Set (IRE) – Lady In The Park (IRE) (Last c86 §
Tycoon) [2002/3 c78, h94d: 16gᵖᵘ 16m 17m c16f² c20g⁵ Oct 11] good-bodied gelding: h– §
handicap hurdler, out of form first 3 starts in 2002/3 and sold out of L. Lungo's stable
3,100 gns Doncaster August Sales: best effort over fences when runner-up in novice at
Hexham: raced mainly around 2m: acts on firm and good to soft going: often takes little
interest and not one to trust. *A. C. Whillans*

GRANGE LEADER (IRE) 11 b.g. Supreme Leader – Deep Serenade (Deep Run) c113
[2002/3 c22d c20v⁶ c21s³ c24d⁵ c24v* c22v⁴ c24s c28s c20s² c24g c20mᶠ Apr 6] tall h–
gelding: fair chaser: won handicap at Limerick in December: stays 3m: acts on heavy
going. *S. J. Treacy, Ireland*

GRANGEWICK FLIGHT 9 b.g. Lighter – Feathery (Le Coq d'Or) [2002/3 c81: c105
c24dᵖᵘ c23mʳᵒ c21dᵖᵘ c20v² c24d² c21d² c20sᶠ c27v c20s* c22dᵘʳ c20vᵘʳ c20g² c24g³
c20g³ Apr 25] workmanlike gelding: fair handicap chaser: won at Newcastle in February:
stays 3m: acts on heavy going: has worn cheekpieces, including at Newcastle: sometimes
let down by jumping: ran out second outing. *N. Wilson*

GRANIT D'ESTRUVAL (FR) 9 b.g. Quart de Vin (FR) – Jalousie (FR) (Block- c–
haus) [2002/3 c133, h104+: c24vᵖᵘ Mar 8] tall, useful-looking gelding: winning hurdler/ h–
useful chaser: not fluent on reappearance: thorough stayer: raced on going softer than
good (acts on heavy). *Ferdy Murphy*

GRANITE STEPS 7 gr.g. Gran Alba (USA) – Pablena (Pablond) [2002/3 h100: c100 ?
c25sᶠ c24dᵘʳ c24v³ c25sᵖᵘ Feb 23] lengthy gelding: fair hurdler: only completion over h–
fences when last of 3 finishers in novice at Fakenham in January: stays 25f: raced on
going softer than good (acts on heavy). *Ferdy Murphy*

GRANNY DICK 8 ch.m. Broadsword (USA) – Penny's Colours (Hornet) [2002/3 h–
h–: 21d⁴ Apr 29] small, light-framed mare: bad novice hurdler: unplaced in points: tried
blinkered. *J. L. Spearing*

GRANNY RICH 9 ch.m. Ardross – Weareagrandmother (Prince Tenderfoot (USA)) h–
[2002/3 h95: 27sᵖᵘ 20d⁵ 19g Nov 7] angular mare: modest handicap hurdler: well below
form in 2002/3, off over 5 months after second start: should stay beyond 2½m: acts on
soft going: has had tongue tied. *P. M. Rich*

GRAN STATEMENT 6 b.g. Gran Alba (USA) – State Lady (IRE) (Strong Statement h–
(USA)) [2002/3 F–: 16d Nov 26] workmanlike gelding: well held in bumper and novice
hurdle 18 months apart: sold 900 gns Doncaster January Sales. *Ferdy Murphy*

GRATE DEEL (IRE) 13 ch.g. The Parson – Cahernane Girl (Bargello) [2002/3 c–, c103
h–: c25d* c30d* c24m⁴ c25d* c26d⁴ c26m* c25dᵖᵘ Oct 19] smallish, strong gelding: fair h–
handicap chaser: won at Wetherby in May, Cartmel in June, Market Rasen in August and
Uttoxeter (conditional jockeys) in October: best at 3m+: acts on soft going, raced on
firmer nowadays: tried blinkered, not for long time. *Mrs S. J. Smith*

GRATTAN LODGE (IRE) 6 gr.g. Roselier (FR) – Shallow Run (Deep Run) **h111**
[2002/3 h–: 20m⁶ 23d 20d* 20v* 27v* 24d* Mar 2] good-topped gelding: progressive
hurdler in 2002/3, won handicaps at Newcastle and Carlisle (amateurs) in November,
Sedgefield in January and Carlisle (by 8 lengths from Sireric with something in hand) in
March: effective at 2½m to 27f: raced mainly on going softer than good (acts on heavy).
J. Howard Johnson

GRAVE DOUBTS 7 ch.g. Karinga Bay – Redgrave Girl (Deep Run) [2002/3 F97: 16f **h121**
17g³ 17m 17d⁶ 16m* 17f* 17g* 16m* 16g^pu 17m^F Apr 16] good-topped gelding: fairly
useful novice hurdler: won at Plumpton in September and Exeter, Hereford and Cheltenham (handicap) in October: raced around 2m: acts on firm going, probably on good to
soft: tongue tied after third outing. *K. Bishop*

GRAY KNIGHT (IRE) 6 gr.g. Insan (USA) – Moohono (IRE) (Roselier (FR)) **h71**
[2002/3 h94: 17f⁶ 22d^pu 20s⁴ 20d Jan 15] sturdy gelding: modest form on hurdling debut
in 2001/2, failed by long way to repeat it in 2002/3: lame on reappearance: should be
suited by at least 2½m: sold £9,000 Ascot April Sales. *Miss H. C. Knight*

GRAY'S EULOGY 5 b.g. Presenting – Gray's Ellergy (Oats) [2002/3 16d Nov 24] **h79**
sturdy gelding: second foal: dam, fair staying hurdler, half-sister to Tolworth Hurdle
winner Hawkbarrow: eighth of 12 in novice hurdle at Aintree on debut. *D. R. Gandolfo*

GRAYSLAKE (IRE) 7 b.g. King's Ride – Castlegrace (IRE) (Kemal (FR)) [2002/3 **h86**
21s 22d 24g³ Mar 16] first foal: dam winning pointer: best effort over hurdles when third
in novice at Ludlow: stays 3m. *Miss H. C. Knight*

GREAT AS GOLD (IRE) 4 b.g. Goldmark (USA) – Great Land (USA) (Friend's **h94**
Choice (USA)) [2002/3 16d⁵ 16d² 17g³ Mar 3] fair on Flat (stays 2m): modest form all 3
starts over hurdles: will be suited by 2½m+: has worn cheekpieces. *B. Ellison*

GREAT CHAOS (IRE) 4 b.g. Great Commotion (USA) – Hassosi (IRE) (High **F87**
Estate) [2002/3 F16v² F16v⁵ Mar 2] first foal: dam of little account on Flat: second
in bumper at Ayr on debut: tailed off in similar event at Leopardstown 5 weeks later.
Michael Cunningham, Ireland

GREAT CRUSADER 11 ch.g. Deploy – Shannon Princess (Connaught) [2002/3 **c–**
c79?, h–: 22s³ 17s* 24v* 24d⁴ 21s⁵ 22v* 22v⁶ 28g* 24g* 27g⁴ Apr 25] small, sturdy **h111**
gelding: let down by jumping over fences: fair handicap hurdler: had good season in
2002/3, won at Folkestone and Taunton (idled) in December (both sellers), Folkestone in
February and March and Perth (amateurs) in April: suited by 3m+: acts on heavy going:
takes good hold. *M. J. Hogan*

GREAT LOVE (FR) 5 gr.h. Great Palm (USA) – Andrew's Love (FR) (Saint **c?**
Andrews (FR)) [2002/3 h139: 19s² 19d* 18v* 19v² c19d^F c19v* c20s^F 18v* 19s* 20s² **h151**
Apr 21] good-topped horse: smart hurdler: won competitive minor event at Enghien in
November and 3 times at Auteuil, Prix Alain du Breil in June, and Prix Juigne and Prix
Hypotheuse (beat Desir d'Un Soir a neck in slowly-run event) in March: no chance with
Karly Flight when good second in Prix Leon Rambaud and Prix La Barka in spring: won
5-y-o minor event at Pau in January impressively, only completed start over fences: stays
21f: raced on going softer than good (acts on heavy). *P. Boisgontier, France*

GREAT NEWS 8 b.g. Elmaamul (USA) – Amina (Brigadier Gerard) [2002/3 20v^pu **h–**
16d Dec 14] fair on Flat (stays 1¼m): looked non-stayer both starts over hurdles.
N. Tinkler

GREAT OAKS 9 b.g. Sylvan Express – Springdale Hall (USA) (Bates Motel (USA)) **h85**
[2002/3 22s⁴ 20m⁴ 20g⁶ Jan 28] lengthy gelding: modest maiden hurdler, lightly raced:
should be suited by further than 2½m: acts on good to firm and heavy going: has pulled
hard. *J. M. Jefferson*

GREAT OVATION (FR) 4 ch.f. Boston Two Step (USA) – Baldiloa (No Lute (FR)) **h80 ?**
[2002/3 16m 17d⁵ 16m Mar 22] lengthy ex-French filly: fifth foal: half-sister to winner
on Flat by Panoramic: dam, winning hurdler/chaser up to 21f, half-sister to useful
hurdler/fairly useful chaser Oa Baldixe, stays 29f: in frame once over 1¼m from 5 starts
on Flat in France for T. Trapenard: best effort in juvenile hurdles when fifth at Exeter,
though possibly flattered: tongue tied final start. *R. T. Phillips*

GRECIAN STAR 11 b.g. Crested Lark – Grecian Lace (Spartan General) [2002/3 **c100**
c100: c33g³ c25d² c26g^pu c23d⁶ Mar 4] strong, deep-girthed gelding: fair hunter chaser:
won point in March: stays 33f: acts on firm and good to soft going. *G. J. Tarry*

GREENACRES BOY 8 b.g. Roscoe Blake – Deep Goddess (Deep Run) [2002/3 **h–**
16s⁶ Jun 13] sixth foal: half-brother to winning 3m Irish hurdler Borrismore Flash (by Le

Moss) and winning pointer by Saxon Farm: dam unraced: well beaten in maiden hurdle on debut, subsequently pulled up in points. *C. N. Kellett*

GREENACRES MISS 6 b.m. Michelozzo (USA) – Royal Cause (Le Bavard (FR)) **h–**
[2002/3 F–: 17g^pu Mar 22] leggy mare: no sign of ability. *M. Mullineaux*

GREEN ADMIRAL 4 b.g. Slip Anchor – Jade Mistress (Damister (USA)) [2002/3 **F77** F16s^6 F17v Feb 11] smallish gelding: third foal: half-brother to 1¼m and 1½m winner Dion Dee (by Anshan): dam modest maiden who stayed 1½m, half-sister to smart miler Just A Flutter and smart middle-distance performer Slicious: sixth in bumper at Haydock on debut: carried head awkwardly and hung when well below that form in maiden next time. *J. J. Quinn*

GREENBACK (BEL) 12 b.g. Absalom – Batalya (BEL) (Boulou) [2002/3 c–, **c–** h105?: 19m* 19d^3 17f^4 21d Dec 12] smallish, angular gelding: winning chaser: modest **h98** hurdler nowadays: made all in seller at Hereford in June: stays 2½m: acts on any going: usually makes running: tended to jump left over fences: joined J. Joseph. *J. D. Frost*

GREENBOROUGH (IRE) 5 b.g. Dr Devious (IRE) – Port Isaac (USA) (Seattle **h–** Song (USA)) [2002/3 16g May 22] disappointing maiden on Flat: tailed off in novice on hurdling debut. *Mrs P. Ford*

GREENFIELD (IRE) 5 ch.g. Pleasant Tap (USA) – No Review (USA) (Nodouble **h109** (USA)) [2002/3 16d^3 16s^3 Feb 8] fairly useful on Flat (stays 1½m), successful for R. Guest/J. Fanshawe in 2002: fair form when third in novice hurdles at Huntingdon and Haydock: will probably stay beyond 2m. *R. T. Phillips*

GREENFIRE (FR) 5 ch.g. Ashkalani (IRE) – Greenvera (USA) (Riverman (USA)) **F–** [2002/3 F–: F17g F17g Oct 11] well held in 3 bumpers: has had tongue tied. *Mrs Dianne Sayer*

GREEN GO (GER) 5 ch.g. Secret 'n Classy (CAN) – Green Fee (GER) (Windwurf **c–** (GER)) [2002/3 16m^5 20m* 21m^3 18m^6 21g^4 c17m^pu Sep 28] third foal: half-brother to **h88** Flat winners by Goofalik and Al Nasr: dam won from 7.5f to around 9f on Flat in Germany: successful once over 1m from 8 starts on Flat in Czech Republic at 3 yrs: modest form over hurdles, won novice at Uttoxeter in July: reportedly broke blood vessel on chasing debut: may prove best short of 21f: acts on good to firm going. *A. Sadik*

GREENHOPE (IRE) 5 b.g. Definite Article – Unbidden Melody (USA) (Chieftain **h–** II) [2002/3 h112+: 16m Feb 21] leggy, useful-looking gelding: useful on Flat (stays 21f): fairly useful juvenile hurdler in 2001/2: heavily backed when sustaining overreach in handicap at Kempton only start in 2002/3: will be suited by 2½m+: unraced on extremes of going: usually races up with pace. *N. J. Henderson*

GREEN ICENI 4 br.g. Greensmith – Boadicea's Chariot (Commanche Run) [2002/3 **F88** F16m F17g^4 Mar 16] 6,200 3-y-o: lengthy, rather unfurnished gelding: fourth foal: half-brother to useful 7f winner Agrippina (by Timeless Times): dam winning hurdler, stayed 2½m: better effort in bumpers when fourth in maiden at Folkestone. *J. R. Best*

GREEN IDEAL 5 b.g. Mark of Esteem (IRE) – Emerald (USA) (El Gran Senor **h122** (USA)) [2002/3 h117: 16d 16d^2 16m^4 Apr 2] compact gelding: fairly useful hurdler: best effort when length second to heavily-eased Our Vic in handicap at Wincanton in February: raced around 2m: has had tongue tied: sold to join F. Murphy 32,000 gns Doncaster May Sales. *N. J. Henderson*

GREEN JACKET 8 b.g. Green Desert (USA) – Select Sale (Auction Ring (USA)) **h–** [2002/3 h–: 26m^pu Jul 19] of little account nowadays: tried blinkered. *J. Joseph*

GREENKEYS (AUS) 9 b.g. Bonhomie (USA) – Cindy Doll (AUS) (Cindy's Son) **c–** [2002/3 h–: c16g^5 Feb 22] compact gelding: lightly raced and little worthwhile form. **h–** *R. C. Guest*

GREEN PURSUIT 7 b.g. Green Desert (USA) – Vayavaig (Damister (USA)) [2002/3 **h–** h–: 16m^pu Oct 19] poor on Flat (stays 1m): no form in 3 starts over hurdles: tried visored: sold £550 Ascot November Sales. *W. M. Brisbourne*

GREENSMITH LANE 7 br.g. Greensmith – Handy Lane (Nearly A Hand) [2002/3 **h73** h–, F77: 17s^4 17m^6 17g^5 19v^pu 17d 17g^2 17m Apr 5] poor novice hurdler: raced mainly around 2m: well held on going softer than good. *N. J. Hawke*

GREEN SMOKE 7 gr.g. Green Adventure (USA) – Smoke (Rusticaro (FR)) [2002/3 **c86** h73: c16g^3 c16v^3 c20s^2 Feb 24] poor maiden hurdler: modest form over fences: stays **h–** 2¾m: acts on heavy going: wore cheekpieces final start. *J. M. Jefferson*

GREGORIO (FR) 9 b.g. Passing Sale (FR) – Apside (FR) (Mistigri) [2002/3 c120: 22s⁴ c20s² 24sᵘʳ Jan 19] fairly useful chaser: creditable second in handicap at Navan in December: just modest form on completed start over hurdles: stays 2½m: acts on good to firm and heavy going: none too consistent. *Mrs S. A. Bramall, Ireland* **c120 h97**

GREGS WAY 9 br.g. Nomadic Way (USA) – Gregory's Lady (Meldrum) [2002/3 h83: 17g⁵ c20m⁴ 24g 19g* c20d⁴ c16g* c20m² c16g* Oct 11] strong, lengthy gelding: poor hurdler: won novice handicap at Stratford in July: modest novice chaser: won at Perth in August and Carlisle (handicap) in October: stays 2½m: acts on good to firm going. *Mrs S. J. Smith* **c96 h84**

GRETTON 6 b.m. Terimon – Gulsha (Glint of Gold) [2002/3 F–p: F16s Jan 27] has scope: poor form in 2 bumpers, went off far too fast when tenth of 20 at Kempton in January. *Noel T. Chance* **F67 +**

GREY ABBEY (IRE) 9 gr.g. Nestor – Tacovaon (Avocat) [2002/3 c148, h–: c25d⁴ c24d⁵ c21v³ c20dᵖᵘ Feb 1] lengthy gelding: has had wind operation: useful chaser: creditable efforts when in frame at Wetherby (Grade 2, fourth of 5 finishers to Marlborough) and Cheltenham (handicap, third to Ballinclay King): stays 33f when conditions aren't testing: acts on good to firm and heavy going: tongue tied: found to have nasal discharge final outing: first past post 6 times at Ayr: bold-jumping front runner: genuine. *F. P. Murtagh* **c143 h–**

GREY BADGER 6 gr.g. Terimon – Tsarella (Mummy's Pet) [2002/3 F16g F17v Feb 11] 8,800 4-y-o: fourth foal: half-brother to fairly useful hurdler Mulligan Express (by Phardante), stays 2½m, and fairly useful bumper winner Alexander Nevsky (by Be My Native): dam, fair chaser up to 3m, sister to very smart chaser The Tsarevich, effective from 2½m to 4½m: well held both starts in bumpers. *J. Howard Johnson* **F–**

GREY BROTHER 5 gr.g. Morpeth – Pigeon Loft (IRE) (Bellypha) [2002/3 F17f F17d³ F17v² 19d³ 22d* Feb 23] sturdy gelding: fourth foal: half-brother to bumper winner Miss Woodpigeon (by Landyap): dam, poor maiden on Flat, runner-up in 17f seller only completed start over hurdles: fair form in bumpers: much better effort over hurdles when winning maiden at Exeter by 8 lengths from Supreme Piper, running on strongly: will stay at least 3m: should continue to progress. *J. D. Frost* **h111 p F90**

GREY CISEAUX (IRE) 8 gr.g. Mujtahid (USA) – Inisfail (Persian Bold) [2002/3 c25f³ c24m⁶ c26g⁵ c25g⁶ c24fᵖᵘ c24fᵖᵘ Apr 3] fair pointer, successful in February: largely below that level in steeplechases (left Miss L. Gardner after third outing): stays 25f: acts on firm ground: effective blinkered or not. *A. E. Jones* **c87 h–**

GREYCOAT 5 ch.g. Lion Cavern (USA) – It's Academic (Royal Academy (USA)) [2002/3 h80d: 16m⁴ 16mᵖᵘ 17mᵖᵘ Aug 26] poor form over hurdles: will prove best around 2m: raced only on going firmer than good over hurdles: raced freely in blinkers second outing. *Jean-Rene Auvray* **h65**

GREYFIELD (IRE) 7 b.g. Persian Bold – Noble Dust (USA) (Dust Commander (USA)) [2002/3 c103, h–: c16s³ c16s⁴ Jan 28] leggy gelding: one-time useful hurdler: fair form when in frame all 4 starts in novice chases: stays easy 19f: acts on firm and soft going. *K. Bishop* **c99 h–**

GREYTON (IRE) 10 gr.g. Zaffaran (USA) – Rosy Posy (IRE) (Roselier (FR)) [2002/3 c85, h–: c19s⁴ Feb 26] useful-looking gelding: modest handicap chaser, very lightly raced nowadays: best at 3m+: acts on any going. *R. Rowe* **c– h–**

GRIMALDI LASS 5 b.m. Factual (USA) – Carousel Zingira (Reesh) [2002/3 F17d Oct 19] workmanlike mare: third foal: half-sister to winning hurdler/fairly useful chaser Grimaldi Lad (by Lord Americo), stayed 2¾m, and poor hurdler Walter Plinge (by Theatrical Charmer), stays 21f: dam ran once: tailed off in bumper on debut. *M. D. Hammond* **F–**

GRIZZLY GOLFWEAR (IRE) 9 b.g. Commanche Run – Dunwellan (Tekoah) [2002/3 c–, h–: c24s² c24m³ c24mᶠ Apr 22] lengthy gelding: novice hurdler: winning pointer: placed in 2 hunter chases, running creditably when falling last in another: stays 3m: acts on soft and good to firm going. *Mrs S. E. Hughes* **c93 h–**

GROOVEJET 4 b.g. Emperor Jones (USA) – Sir Hollow (USA) (Sir Ivor) [2002/3 16sᵖᵘ Nov 2] leggy gelding: brother to fair 2m hurdler Moon Emperor: fair maiden on Flat (should stay at least 1¼m), lost his form in 2002: showed nothing on hurdling debut. *J. R. Jenkins* **h–**

GROUND BALL (IRE) 6 b. or br.g. Bob's Return (IRE) – Bettyhill (Ardross) **c125** [2002/3 h120: c16s^F c16g^2 c20s* c21v^2 c20s^3 c24d^F 20s^2 Mar 16] well-made gelding: **h110** winning hurdler, fair form when second in minor event at Punchestown in March: fairly useful novice chaser: won maiden at Navan in December: ran well next 2 starts, including when third of 4 to Tarxien in Grade 1 at Sandown, and when second to Beachcomber Bay at Punchestown in early-May: needs good test around 2m and stays 21f: acts on heavy going: front runner/races prominently: reliable. *C. F. Swan, Ireland*

GROUP ONE'S HOPE 7 b.m. Absalom – Hopeful Waters (Forlorn River) [2002/3 **c–** F–: 5f6^pu 16m c16m^F c16s^pu Nov 21] medium-sized mare: no sign of ability. **h–** *A. W. Carroll*

GROUSE HALL 9 ch.g. Primitive Rising (USA) – Em-Kay-Em (Slim Jim) [2002/3 **c85** c79, h–: c20d^3 c19g^2 Nov 23] workmanlike gelding: poor novice hurdler/chaser: finished **h–** lame when second in handicap over fences at Catterick: stays 25f: acts on soft going. *M. Todhunter*

GROUSE MOOR (USA) 4 b.g. Distant View (USA) – Caithness (USA) (Roberto **F88** (USA)) [2002/3 F18v^4 F16m Feb 22] 22,000 3-y-o: sturdy gelding: sixth living foal: half-brother to several winners, including useful hurdler Stromness (by Trempolino), stays 3m: dam, French 11f winner, half-sister to very smart performer around 7f Condrillac: better effort in bumpers (needed race on debut) when eighth of 19 to Chelsea Bridge at Kempton. *P. Winkworth*

GROVE HOUSE 7 b.g. Hatim (USA) – Camden Grove (Uncle Pokey) [2002/3 F92: **h76** 24m^2 16g Apr 24] fair form in bumpers: poor form on second of 2 outings (seemed not to stay 3m on debut) over hurdles at Perth nearly a year apart. *A. Scott*

GRUMPY STUMPY 8 ch.g. Gunner B – Moaning Jenny (Privy Seal) [2002/3 c89, **c–** h78: c24d^4 Nov 13] good-topped gelding: well held both starts over hurdles: modest form **h–** over fences: raced freely and reported to have hung right at Newbury, only outing in 2002/3: should prove best at 3m+: best efforts on soft/heavy ground. *N. A. Twiston-Davies*

GUARD DUTY 6 b.g. Deploy – Hymne d'Amour (USA) (Dixieland Band (USA)) **h123 §** [2002/3 h123: 25d^5 24v 24d^F 23s^3 25g^5 24g Apr 3] leggy gelding: fairly useful handicap hurdler: creditable never-nearer fifth of 24 to Inching Closer in valuable event at Cheltenham fifth outing: stays 25f: raced on good going or softer (acts on heavy): tongue tied: held up, and is no easy ride (finds little). *M. C. Pipe*

GUDLAGE (USA) 7 b.g. Gulch (USA) – Triple Kiss (Shareef Dancer (USA)) **c–** [2002/3 c95, h95: 16d* 17g^2 Mar 29] workmanlike gelding: fair on Flat nowadays, **h105** successful over 1½m in August: fair handicap hurdler: won amateur event at Newcastle in November: improved effort when second to Dick Turpin at Market Rasen 4 months later: modest form only outing over fences (jumped less than fluently): will prove best around 2m: raced mainly on good/good to soft going over jumps: tongue tied. *M. W. Easterby*

GUE AU LOUP (FR) 9 gr.g. Royal Charter (FR) – Arche d'Alliance (FR) (Pamponi **c90** (FR)) [2002/3 c108, h–: c21g c16s^5 c16s^ur c20d^3 c20s^4 c20g^6 Mar 16] tall gelding: modest **h–** handicap chaser, little form in 2002/3: stays 2½m: acts on soft going: has broken blood vessel: often front runner. *H. D. Daly*

GUERNSEY BOB 5 ch.g. Beveled (USA) – Martian Melody (Enchantment) [2002/3 **F–** F17s Nov 14] brother to winners up to 6f Out of This World and Random and half-brother to 5f/6f winner Mister Raider (by Ballacashtal): dam best at 6f: showed nothing in maiden bumper or 7f seller on Flat. *R. J. Hodges*

GUEST LINE (FR) 4 ch.g. Ashkalani (IRE) – Double Line (FR) (What A Guest) **h78** [2002/3 16m^3 Sep 7] leggy gelding: headstrong maiden on Flat for B. Meehan: never-nearer third of 16 in juvenile at Stratford on hurdling debut: sold 4,000 gns Doncaster September Sales. *C. J. Mann*

GUID WILLIE WAUGHT (IRE) 8 ch.g. Montelimar (USA) – Drumdeels Star **c97** (IRE) (Le Bavard (FR)) [2002/3 c81, h76: c21g* c22m* c20m^2 c20d^5 Aug 4] lengthy, **h–** good-topped gelding: poor maiden hurdler: better form over fences, won novice handicaps at Stratford in May and Market Rasen in June: stays 2¾m: best efforts on good to firm going. *J. R. Adam*

GUIGNOL DU COCHET (FR) 9 ch.g. Secret of Success – Pasquita (FR) (Bour- **c87** bon (FR)) [2002/3 c16m c16s^2 c16d^2 c16v^4 c16g^F Feb 22] tall gelding: modest handicap **h–**

chaser, off 20 months before reappearance: best around 2m: acts on soft going: tried blinkered/visored/tongue tied, not since 1999/00. *Mrs L. Richards*

GUILSBOROUGH GORSE 8 b.g. Past Glories – Buckby Folly (Netherkelly) **c93** [2002/3 c90: c20m² c17m² c20mᵖᵘ c20g* c24d c23g⁵ c17g³ c20g³ c20g⁴ Apr 26] lengthy gelding: modest handicap chaser: won at Hexham in October: efective at 2½m to 25f: acts on soft and good to firm going: creditable effort only try in blinkers. *T. D. Walford*

GULCH KING (USA) 5 b.g. Gulch (USA) – Crockadore (USA) (Nijinsky (CAN)) **h–** [2002/3 h–: 16g Nov 20] good-topped gelding: modest maiden on Flat (stays 1½m) at 3 yrs for D. Weld: no form in 4 outings over hurdles. *G. L. Moore*

GUMLEY GALE 8 b.g. Greensmith – Clodaigh Gale (Strong Gale) [2002/3 h111: **h108** 20d* 20g⁴ 19g 22s⁶ 20v⁵ Dec 21] sturdy gelding: fair handicap hurdler: won at Uttoxeter in May: off 5½ months, well below form last 3 starts: stays 2¾m: acts on good to firm and good to soft going, seemingly not softer. *K. Bishop*

GUMPTION 5 b.g. Muhtarram (USA) – Dancing Spirit (IRE) (Ahonoora) [2002/3 **h112** 24s² Feb 27] fairly useful maiden on Flat (should stay 2m) for J. Dunlop: well clear of remainder when second to easy winner Strong Flow in novice at Taunton on hurdling debut. *K. C. Bailey*

GUNG HO (IRE) 6 b.g. Mister Lord (USA) – Deruma Lady (IRE) (Black Minstrel) **h81 ?** [2002/3 F16m 22m⁵ 19f² Mar 27] IR 24,000 3-y-o: first foal: dam unraced half-sister to **F–** useful hurdler/smart chaser up to 3¼m Lord Singapore (by Mister Lord): well held in bumper: left M. Pitman and off 7 months, 6 lengths second to Desmond Tutu in weak novice at Exeter, not fluent. *M. C. Pipe*

GUNNERBE POSH 9 ch.g. Rakaposhi King – Triggered (Gunner B) [2002/3 c–, **c–** h72: 20d 19d Jan 27] leggy gelding: poor novice hurdler, left with too much to do amateur **h71** ridden both outings in 2002/3: well beaten only start over fences: likely to prove best up to 2½m: raced mainly on good to soft going. *Noel T. Chance*

GUNNER B SPECIAL 10 ch.g. Gunner B – Sola Mia (Tolomeo) [2002/3 c72, h–: **c65** c19g⁵ May 1] workmanlike gelding: poor handicap chaser: stays 2½m: acts on good to **h–** soft going: tried visored/blinkered: has worn tongue strap: has broken blood vessels. *R. Lee*

GUNNER DREAM 7 b.g. Gunner B – Star Route (Owen Dudley) [2002/3 c24d⁵ **c–** c20v⁴ c25d³ Feb 26] 4,000 4-y-o: workmanlike gelding: fifth foal: half-brother to modest hurdler Owthorpe Borders (by Rolfe), stays 19f: dam fair hurdler up to 2½m: modest maiden pointer: well held in 3 novice chases. *C. Grant*

GUNNER SID 12 ch.g. Gunner B – At Long Last (John French) [2002/3 c20s⁶ c24d **c– §** c20g⁵ c19m⁵ Apr 22] sparely-made gelding: one-time modest hurdler: no form over **h– §** fences: tried blinkered: unreliable. *W. Jenks*

GUNNER WELBURN 11 ch.g. Gunner B – Vedra (IRE) (Carlingford Castle) **c136** [2002/3 c128: c24s* c29v³ c24d c24s* c36d⁴ Apr 5] strong, lengthy gelding: formerly smart hunter chaser: won handicaps at Chepstow in December and Newbury (easily, by 5 lengths from Moral Support) in March: in frame in Welsh Grand National at Chepstow (20 lengths third to Mini Sensation) in December and Grand National at Aintree, prominent most of final circuit when 28 lengths fourth of 14 finishers to Monty's Pass in latter, tiring only from 2 out: best form up to 3¼m: acts on heavy going (below form only outing on good to firm): usually sound jumper: genuine. *A. M. Balding*

GUN'N ROSES II (FR) 9 gr.g. Royal Charter (FR) – Offenbach II (FR) (Ermitage **c136 x** (FR)) [2002/3 c134x, h–: 21sᵖᵘ c20s* c24dᵖᵘ c20d⁶ Mar 1] rangy gelding: winning **h–** hurdler: useful handicap chaser: form in 2002/3 only when making all in 4-runner event at Wetherby in December, showing greater resolution than stable-companion Monarch's Pursuit: stays 3m: raced mainly on good going or softer (acts on heavy): blinkered final outing: front runner: often let down by jumping. *T. D. Easterby*

GUN SHOT 8 ch.m. Gunner B – Real Beauty (Kinglet) [2002/3 c–, h93: 21m⁶ 24d **c–** 24v⁶ c24s Jan 3] sturdy, plain mare: improved hurdler in 2001/2, successful 3 times: well **h–** beaten in 2002/3: let down by jumping both starts over fences: ideally suited by 3m+: acts on good to firm and heavy going: has had tongue tied. *N. M. Babbage*

GUNSMOKE 5 gr.g. Thethingaboutitis (USA) – Fairy Princess (IRE) (Fairy King **h–** (USA)) [2002/3 F16s 17gᵖᵘ Mar 22] first foal: dam twice-raced on Flat: showed nothing **F–** in bumper/novice hurdle. *D. McCain*

GUNSON HIGHT 6 b.g. Be My Chief (USA) – Glas Y Dorlan (Sexton Blake) [2002/3 F16g 16d Jan 13] sixth foal: half-brother to poor hurdler/chaser It's Not My Fault (by Red Sunset), stays 3¼m: dam 1½m winner: well beaten in bumper and novice hurdle. *M. Todhunter*

h–
F–

GUNTHER MCBRIDE (IRE) 8 b.g. Glacial Storm (USA) – What Side (General Ironside) [2002/3 c138, h111: 25v* c26g c24s⁵ c24m² c33mᵘʳ c29m³ Apr 26] good-topped gelding: fairly useful hurdler: won handicap at Kempton in November: useful handicap chaser: generally ran well in valuable events in 2002/3, second to La Landiere in Racing Post Chase at Kempton and third to Ad Hoc in attheraces Gold Cup at Sandown: still not far away when unseated 2 out in Scottish Grand National at Ayr: stays 33f: acts on good to firm and heavy going: usually a sound jumper: races prominently: game and consistent. *P. J. Hobbs*

c140
h119 +

GURU 5 b.g. Slip Anchor – Ower (IRE) (Lomond (USA)) [2002/3 h98: 17m³ 21dᵖᵘ 16v 16d 16s* 18g* Mar 17] leggy gelding: maiden on Flat: fair handicap hurdler: left S. Dow and off 2 months, back to form to win at Plumpton in February and Fontwell in March: may prove best short of 2½m: acts on soft and good to firm going: room for improvement in his jumping. *G. L. Moore*

h101

GUS BERRY (IRE) 10 ch.g. Montelimar (USA) – Eurolink Sea Baby (Deep Run) [2002/3 c79, h–: c27s³ c27d⁵ Mar 18] smallish, angular gelding: poor chaser: stays 27f: raced on good going or softer (acts on heavy): usually blinkered prior to 2002/3: has had tongue tied: none too consistent. *P. England*

c81
h–

GUS DES BOIS (FR) 9 ch.g. Lampon (FR) – Fiacina (FR) (Fiasco) [2002/3 c27sᵘʳ c24sᵖᵘ c16d⁴ c20d² c20v* c19s³ c21sᵖᵘ Mar 15] strong gelding: brother to 2 winners on Flat: dam won 1¾m hurdle at 3 yrs: won 13.5f non-thoroughbred race on Flat at 3 yrs: once-raced hurdler: successful in cross-country chase at Durtal in 1999/00: fair form in handicap chases in Britain: won 6-runner event at Plumpton in January: effective at 2m to 2¾m: acts on heavy going: tried blinkered, including last 3 starts: sound-jumping front runner. *R. H. Alner*

c108
h–

G V A IRELAND (IRE) 5 b.g. Beneficial – Dippers Daughter (Try My Best (USA)) [2002/3 17g F16s³ F16v* 18v² 19v² 20d 24s Feb 22] half-brother to useful 2m chaser Dines (by Phardante): dam unraced half-sister to very smart staying hurdler/useful chaser Henry Mann and smart hurdler/chaser up to 3m Royal Dipper: fairly useful form in bumpers, won at Fairyhouse in December: fair novice hurdler: should stay beyond 19f: acts on heavy going: reportedly had respiratory tract infection sixth start. *F. Flood, Ireland*

h102
F102

GWEN 4 ch.f. Beveled (USA) – Taffidale (Welsh Pageant) [2002/3 F16g Feb 22] seventh foal: dam maiden, stayed 1½m: tailed off in bumper on debut. *B. L. Lay*

F–

GWENN (FR) 9 gr.g. Montorselli – King Bar (FR) (King Cyrus (USA)) [2002/3 c18s* c23s* Apr 21] first foal: dam unraced: winning hurdler: useful chaser: off over 2½ years, won both starts at Auteuil on return in April, minor event and very valuable Prix du President de La Republique (handicap), in latter making all, tending to jump right, when beating Holy Joe 2 lengths: stays 23f: raced on good going or softer (acts on heavy). *A. Chaille-Chaille, France*

c130 +

GYPSY (IRE) 7 b.g. Distinctly North (USA) – Winscarlet North (Garland Knight) [2002/3 h97: 24g⁴ 20d⁶ 20d³ 22g³ 20d* 20g⁴ 20d 21d² 20d Nov 7] leggy gelding: modest handicap hurdler: left Miss V. Williams after third start: won at Wolverhampton in July: best short of 3m: raced on good going or softer (acts on soft). *Ian Williams*

h97

GYPSY MUSIC (IRE) 7 b.m. Treasure Kay – Mighty Special (IRE) (Head For Heights) [2002/3 17g Oct 11] lightly raced and well beaten on Flat since 2 yrs (has been to stud): last in novice on hurdling debut. *I. W. McInnes*

h–

H

HAAFEL (USA) 6 ch.g. Diesis – Dish Dash (Bustino) [2002/3 h92: 21gᵖᵘ 18dᵘʳ 21m² Mar 31] angular gelding: fair on Flat (stays 2m): fair hurdler: blinkered, best effort when second to Little Bud in amateur handicap at Plumpton: stays 21f: acts on good to soft and good to firm going, possibly unsuited by soft/heavy. *G. L. Moore*

h100

HACHTY BOY (FR) 7 br.g. Cadoudal (FR) – Hachty Girl (FR) (Ashtar) [2002/3 c102, h–: c23d*ᵈⁱˢ c23dᵖᵘ Jun 8] useful-looking gelding: fair novice chaser: won at

c105
h–

Wetherby (subsequently disqualified due to prohibitive substance) in May: stayed 23f: best efforts on good going or softer (acted on soft): jumped soundly: dead. *Miss H. C. Knight*

HADAWAY LAD 11 ch.g. Meadowbrook – Little Swinburn (Apollo Eight) [2002/3 c20m Jun 1] winning pointer: well held over hurdles and in hunter chase (blinkered). *R. A. Ross*

c–
h–

HADES DE SIENNE (FR) 8 b.g. Concorde Jr (USA) – Aube de Sienne (FR) (Cupids Dew) [2002/3 c97, h90: c25v^6 c28s^{pu} 27v c24s^2 c26s^2 Mar 6] workmanlike gelding: fair handicap chaser: maiden hurdler, took little interest third start: stays 4m: acts on heavy going: tried visored/in cheekpieces. *A. Parker*

c101
h–

HADITH 8 ch.h. Nashwan (USA) – Azyaa (Kris) [2002/3 16s 19d^6 16g^3 17g^{pu} Mar 3] rather leggy horse: half-brother to useful 2m to 3m hunter chaser Shafi (by Reference Point) and winning 2m hurdler Samsaam (by Sadler's Wells): fair on Flat (stays 1¼m), successful twice in UAE in 2001 for E. Sharpy: poor form in novice hurdles: badly injured final start. *Ferdy Murphy*

h78

HADITOVSKI 7 b.g. Hatim (USA) – Grand Occasion (Great Nephew) [2002/3 h122: 16v^5 16d^2 16v^4 16g 16d^5 Mar 1] compact gelding: fairly useful handicap hurdler: creditable efforts in 2002/3 on second and fourth outings, both at Newbury: best around 2m: goes well on ground softer than good: visored: usually ridden up with pace. *J. Mackie*

h122

HAIKAL 6 b.g. Owington – Magic Milly (Simply Great (FR)) [2002/3 h82: 21g^4 21v^4 16g^6 22g 20g Apr 1] strong, workmanlike gelding: poor handicap hurdler, little form in 2002/3: barely stays 2½m: acts on any going: blinkered final outing: sold 2,000 gns Doncaster May Sales. *E. W. Tuer*

h–

HAILSTORM (IRE) 10 ch.g. Glacial Storm (USA) – Sindys Gale (Strong Gale) [2002/3 c95d, h–: c20d c20g^3 c24d^2 c24m^3 c25m^2 c20v^{co} c24d^6 c20s^{pu} c20s c20g^6 Apr 14] smallish, angular gelding: poor handicap chaser, out of form in second half of season: stays easy 25f: acts on soft and good to firm going: usually makes mistakes. *Miss Lucinda V. Russell*

c83 x
h–

HAITHEM (IRE) 6 b.g. Mtoto – Wukk (IRE) (Glow (USA)) [2002/3 h–: 16g^{pu} Sep 12] poor and temperamental on Flat (stays 8.5f): showed little both starts over hurdles, tongue tied on first. *D. Shaw*

h–

HAKIM (NZ) 9 ch.g. Half Iced (USA) – Topitup (NZ) (Little Brown Jug (NZ)) [2002/3 h97: 16d^{pu} 16s^3 19d^5 17s 16s^2 17d^3 16d^5 Mar 1] sturdy gelding: poor maiden hurdler: may prove best around 2m: acts on soft and good to firm going: tends to race freely. *J. L. Spearing*

h84

HALE BOPP (GER) 6 b.h. Monsun (GER) – Heatherland (FR) (Be My Guest (USA)) [2002/3 18v^F 17s^4 17v^4 16s^2 Mar 10] seemingly useful on Flat (stays 1½m) in Germany, successful 3 times in 2000, placed 6 times since, including in 2002: fair novice hurdler: won at Folkestone in February: creditable second to Mister Putt at Plumpton: likely to stay beyond 17f: acts on heavy ground. *Frau E. Mader, Germany*

h111

HALEXY (FR) 8 b.g. Iron Duke (FR) – Tartifume II (FR) (Mistigri) [2002/3 c–, h–: c19d* c20d* c21v^{ur} c21s Jan 25] good sort: fairly useful chaser: off 17 months, won handicaps at Chepstow (impressive) in October and Cheltenham (left clear 2 out and idled when beating Strong Magic 5 lengths) in November: folded tamely final outing: has won at 3m, possibly better over shorter: raced mainly on good going or softer: bold jumper who races with plenty of zest. *Miss Venetia Williams*

c126
h–

HALF A CALF 6 ch.g. Jupiter Island – Chief Lady Nicola (Nicholas Bill) [2002/3 F18s^4 F16s 22d Feb 6] 4,000 4-y-o: well-made gelding: chasing type: second foal: dam, lightly raced in bumpers, half-sister to top-class 2m to 2½m hurdler Celtic Chief: modest form on first of 2 starts in bumpers: tailed off in novice on hurdling debut. *R. H. Buckler*

h–
F77

HALF AN HOUR 6 b.g. Alflora (IRE) – Country Mistress (Town And Country) [2002/3 F97: 16g 22d^4 24s^4 22f* 21m Apr 16] well-made gelding: will make a chaser: fair novice hurdler: easily won weak race at Haydock in March: tailed off in quite valuable event at Cheltenham following month: stays 2¾m: acts on firm and good to soft going (won bumper on soft). *A. King*

h100

HALF BARRELL (IRE) 11 br.g. Lord Americo – Araybeam VII (Damsire Unregistered) [2002/3 c114, h–: c20s^5 c21s^{pu} c23s^{pu} c17d^3 c22v^2 c22v c28s^{pu} Nov 10] fair handicap chaser: best effort in 2002/3 when second to Lord of The Turf in listed event at Galway in September: effective around 2m and stays 3m well: acts on heavy going. *V. T. O'Brien, Ireland*

c114
h–

HALF EACH 11 b.m. Weld – Golden Valley (Hotfoot) [2002/3 c25d^{pu} May 4] no form outside points: tried visored: has refused to race. *Mrs C. A. Watson* c– §
h– §

HALF NELSON 5 br.g. Be My Chief (USA) – Petindia (Petong) [2002/3 h–: 16g^4 16s^{pu} Jun 13] little worthwhile form over hurdles. *T. R. George* h80 ?

HALF THE POT (IRE) 8 b.g. Homo Sapien – Deep Green (Deep Run) [2002/3 h109: 25g^6 25v^6 22s^5 20v^4 20v^{pu} 17v* 18s^4 20v 22s* 18g^F Mar 17] leggy gelding: fair handicap hurdler: won at Folkestone in January and Fontwell (able to dominate and jumped better than usual) in March: fell fatally at Fontwell: effective around 2m under testing conditions, should have stayed 3m: acted well on soft/heavy going: made running. *R. Rowe* h106

HALLAND PARK LAD (IRE) 4 ch.g. Danehill Dancer (IRE) – Lassalia (Sallust) [2002/3 18d^4 Dec 10] half-brother to 3 winners over jumps, including fairly useful staying hurdler/winning chaser Snowy Lane (by Commanche Run): fair on Flat (stays easy 1½m): shaped with promise when fourth of 15 to Old California in juvenile at Fontwell on hurdling debut, improving to dispute lead 3 out but fading home turn: likely to benefit from more of a test of speed. *S. Kirk* h96 p

HALL'S MILL (IRE) 14 ch.g. Buckskin (FR) – Grainne Geal (General Ironside) [2002/3 c–: c21g^3 May 1] workmanlike gelding: veteran hunter chaser: would probably have troubled winner but for mistakes last 2 when third to Epsilo De La Ronce at Cheltenham: stays 3m: acts on good to firm and good to soft going: sometimes let down by jumping: genuine. *Miss S. Waugh* c95 +

HALLYARDS GAEL (IRE) 9 br.g. Strong Gale – Secret Ocean (Most Secret) [2002/3 c104, h105: c17g^3 c20d* c20d^{pu} c21s^3 c20g* c24m^{wo} Apr 19] strong, lengthy gelding: fairly useful novice chaser: won 4-runner events at Wetherby in May and Carlisle (first run since leaving Mrs M. Reveley, improved form to beat Devil's Run easily by 9 lengths) in March: also walked over at Carlisle: likely to stay 3m: raced on good going or softer: has reportedly had breathing problems (distressed third start). *L. Lungo* c124 h–

HAMADEENAH 5 ch.m. Alhijaz – Mahbob Dancer (FR) (Groom Dancer (USA)) [2002/3 h94: 16m^5 16d^5 17d^5 16g* 21m^4 16m^5 16m* 17m^2 Apr 26] leggy mare: modest hurdler, left K. Bailey after second start: won seller at Uttoxeter in September and claimer at Ludlow in March: best around 2m: acts on soft and good to firm going. *D. McCain* h91

HAMMOCK (IRE) 5 b. or br.g. Hamas (IRE) – Sure Victory (IRE) (Stalker) [2002/3 21d^{pu} 20g 16g Mar 14] sturdy gelding: temperamental maiden on Flat: no form over hurdles. *P. S. McEntee* h–

HAMUNAPTRA 4 ch.g. Alhijaz – Princess Dancer (Alzao (USA)) [2002/3 16d^5 16s^{pu} 16m^{pu} Mar 23] smallish, angular gelding: modest maiden on Flat (stays 7f), sold out of P. Gilligan's stable 1,700 gns Newmarket Autumn Sales: probably doesn't stay over hurdles. *M. Wigham* h–

HANAKHAM (IRE) 14 b.g. Phardante (FR) – Evas Charm (Carlburg) [2002/3 c100, h88: c20g^3 c25g^F 26d^5 c24v* c24m* Apr 12] big, strong, good sort: twice-raced hurdler: one-time smart chaser: still retains fair amount of ability, won hunters at Bangor in March and April (reportedly finished sore): stays 27f: acts on good to firm and heavy going. *D. McCain Jnr* c102 h–

HANBRIN ROSE 6 gr.m. Lancastrian – Rymolbreese (Rymer) [2002/3 F16s 19g^3 Apr 19] 8,000 4-y-o: leggy mare: second foal: half-sister to fair hurdler/chaser Seymour Breese (by Seymour Hicks), stays 3m: dam poor novice hurdler/chaser: well held in bumper: third of 13 to Quedex in maiden at Stratford on hurdling debut: will be suited by further. *R. Dickin* h72 F–

HANCOCK 11 b.g. Jester – Fresh Line (High Line) [2002/3 16d 21s^{pu} 17s^{pu} 19s^{pu} 16s 17s Dec 26] sparely-made gelding: maiden chaser: winning hurdler, little form for long time. *J. Hetherton* c– h–

HAND INN HAND 7 b.g. Alflora (IRE) – Deep Line (Deep Run) [2002/3 h122+: c19s^3 c19s* c20v* c16v* c20m* c16g^5 Mar 11] c141 p h–

Forty years after she was foaled, the tip-top hunter chaser Matchboard continues to have an influence on the jumping scene, the grandam of the brothers Granville Again and Morley Street appearing as the third dam in the pedigree of the smart novice chaser Hand Inn Hand. While unlikely to reach the heights attained by the two Champion Hurdle winners, the chances are that we still haven't seen the

Read The Racing Post Before You Bet Pendil Novices' Chase, Kempton—
Hand Inn Hand leads the field four out

best of Hand Inn Hand who appeals as the type to win a good race in the next season, at either two or two and a half miles. A creditable fifth in the Arkle Chase at the latest Cheltenham Festival, Hand Inn Hand could be a leading contender at the next one in either the Grand Annual or Mildmay of Flete, races won in 2003 by his stable-companions Palarshan and Young Spartacus respectively. Or perhaps he will be seen out in the Cathcart, a race overlooked by connections in favour of a tilt at the Arkle.

Hand Inn Hand went into the Arkle seeking a five-timer, after winning novice events in small fields at Chepstow and Haydock in December and Uttoxeter and Kempton in February. He had put up his best performance on the last-named course in the Pendil Novices' Chase, but it was still one which left him with plenty to find if he was to continue his winning run at Cheltenham. The Grade 2 Pendil Chase attracted eight runners and the betting suggested the race lay between three of them, with Epervier d'Or and Scots Grey joint-favourites at 9/4, Hand Inn Hand at 3/1 and 12/1 bar that trio. Hand Inn Hand had raced only on good ground or softer previously, and there were concerns about his ability to handle the good to firm ground at Kempton. In the event, such concerns proved totally unfounded. Hand Inn Hand jumped well apart from a mistake at the seventh, took up the running at the fourth and was ridden to go clear before two out, Druid's Glen and Scots Grey the only others still in touch at this point, Epervier d'Or having broken a blood vessel. Druid's Glen just got the better of the battle for the minor placings but had no chance with Hand Inn Hand, who was eased near the line and still won by five lengths. Back over two miles in the Arkle, Hand Inn Hand didn't jump well enough and was unable to land a blow but he still emerged from the race with plenty of credit, keeping on to finish fifth behind Azertyuiop, beaten twenty lengths.

Hand Inn Hand (b.g. 1996)	Alflora (IRE) (b 1989)	Niniski (b 1976)	Nijinsky
			Virginia Hills
		Adrana (ch 1980)	Bold Lad
			Le Melody
	Deep Line (b 1985)	Deep Run (ch 1966)	Pampered King
			Trial By Fire
		High Board (b 1977)	High Line
			Matchboard

The latest season was Hand In Hand's third, the first two having been spent over hurdles when he showed fairly useful form and won three of his six starts. He

Patrick Burling Developments Ltd's "Hand Inn Hand"

is the seventh foal of the unraced Deep Line, whose only other winner is the fairly useful hurdler and useful chaser at up to two and a half miles Tom Brodie (by Ardross). The next dam High Board, responsible for Granville Again and Morley Street, was also unraced. Hand Inn Hand, a close-coupled, workmanlike gelding, acts on heavy going as well as good to firm. *H. D. Daly*

HANDOVER 6 b.g. Nearly A Hand – Keylu (Sula Bula) [2002/3 F17f⁴ F16v 18vᵖᵘ Jan 6] first foal: dam fourth in bumper: probably flattered when fourth of 6 in steadily-run bumper at Taunton on debut, only sign of ability. *M. Madgwick* **h–** **F81 ?**

HANDSOME LAD (IRE) 5 ch.g. Inzar (USA) – Elite Exhibition (Exhibitioner) [2002/3 h–: 22dᵖᵘ 20g 17d⁶ Apr 8] no sign of ability. *A. Scott* **h–**

HANDYMAN (IRE) 9 b.g. Hollow Hand – Shady Ahan (Mon Capitaine) [2002/3 c110, h–: c23g* c23g² c25dᶠ c24s³ c24sᵖᵘ c26m³ Apr 16] leggy gelding: fairly useful handicap chaser: improved in 2002/3, won at Exeter in May: generally good efforts after, third of 7 to Midnight Gunner at Cheltenham final outing: stays 3¼m: acts on heavy and good to firm going: reliable. *P. J. Hobbs* **c126** **h–**

HANDY MONEY 6 b.g. Imperial Frontier (USA) – Cryptic Gold (Glint of Gold) [2002/3 F85: F17d⁴ 16g³ 17s² 16d⁵ 16v² 19g* 20v⁴ Mar 8] workmanlike gelding: signs of ability in bumpers: fair novice hurdler: won at Doncaster in February by ¾ length from Abzuson: better than distance beaten suggests when almost 20 lengths fourth of 12 to Tana River in Grade 3 novice handicap at Sandown final start: likely to stay 2½m under less extreme conditions: acts on heavy going. *M. J. Ryan* **h107** **F80**

HANG'EM HIGH   9 b.g. Supreme Leader – Culinary (Tower Walk) [2002/3 h115: **c80** 24d 22v 21d c16s c17s c16s c16d c20vF Dec 31] tall gelding: fair hurdler, well below **h95** form in handicaps in 2002/3 (badly hampered when blinkered third start): first sign of ability over fences when falling last in 6-runner novice handicap at Punchestown, weakening in third having made running: stays 2½m: probably acts on any going. *S. O'Farrell, Ireland*

HANG'EM OUT TO DRY (IRE)   12 b.g. Executive Perk – Obsession (Wolver **c–** Hollow) [2002/3 c97d, h–: c17dpu Oct 12] tall, attractive gelding: fairly useful 2m chaser **h–** at best, no form since 2001/2 reappearance: tried in tongue strap. *B. De Haan*

HANNAH PARK (IRE)   7 b.m. Lycius (USA) – Wassl This Then (IRE) (Wassl) **h–** [2002/3 h97: 20d5 Jun 6] small mare: modest hurdler, well beaten only outing in 2002/3: stays 2½m: best efforts on good going (possibly unsuited by heavy): sold 1,400 gns Doncaster January Sales. *P. Monteith*

HANNIBAL TWO   6 b.g. Rock City – Appealing (Star Appeal) [2002/3 F16s Jan 3] **F–** 1,100 4-y-o: brother to smart performer up to 1¾m Hannibal Lad: dam, 4-y-o 1¼m winner, half-sister to fairly useful 1m to 1½m winner Gifford: behind in bumper on debut. *P. D. Evans*

HANOI HANNA   7 b.m. Lancastrian – Farm Track (Saxon Farm) [2002/3 h–: 21gpu **h–** 16d Jun 4] no sign of ability. *R. Johnson*

HANOVER SQUARE   7 b.g. Le Moss – Hilly-Down Lass (Deep Run) [2002/3 h84, **c98** F–: c28d2 c26s5 c27s3 c30spu c24s4 c30s4 Mar 4] workmanlike gelding: maiden hurdler: **h–** modest novice chaser: thorough stayer: raced mainly on going softer than good: not a fluent jumper. *N. A. Twiston-Davies*

HANSBURY (IRE)   7 gr.g. Roselier (FR) – Ramble Bramble (Random Shot) [2002/3 **c106** c25d2 c26sF Feb 3] IR 50,000 3-y-o: brother to smart staying chaser Seven Towers: dam twice-raced half-sister to very smart staying chaser Deep Bramble: won second of 2 starts in maiden Irish points in 2002: runner-up at Hereford on novice chase debut: fell fatally at Fontwell. *P. F. Nicholls*

HANSEAT (GER)   6 b.g. Goofalik (USA) – Hanseatin (GER) (Pentathlon) [2002/3 **h?** 16v* 20sF 16s 17s2 Mar 15] successful 3 times up to 8.5f on Flat in Germany, including at Cologne in 2002: won minor hurdle at Bremen in October: second in similar event at Krefeld: well held in novice at Plumpton third outing: raced on soft/heavy going. *Frau E. Mader, Germany*

HAPPICAT (IRE)   8 gr.g. Cataldi – Gladonia (Godswalk (USA)) [2002/3 h113: 16f **c–** c16s6 c17m6 c17m Jul 4] good-topped gelding: fair hurdler: well held in 3 novice chases: **h109** will prove best around 2m: probably best on good going or firmer (acts on firm). *P. R. Webber*

HAPPY CHANGE (GER)   9 ch.g. Surumu (GER) – Happy Gini (USA) (Ginistrelli **c80** (USA)) [2002/3 h–: c20g3 c16g3 c16m2 c20spu c19spu Dec 26] good-topped gelding: **h–** winning hurdler: poor maiden chaser, left Miss V. Williams after second start: will need emphasis on speed to stay 2½m: jumps none too fluently: races freely. *Ian Williams*

HAPPY DAYS   8 b.g. Primitive Rising (USA) – Miami Dolphin (Derrylin) [2002/3 **h78** h78: 20g4 17d 20dpu 19dbd 20g2 Apr 1] leggy gelding: poor maiden hurdler: stays 2¾m: acts on heavy going: tried visored. *James Moffatt*

HAPPY HUSSAR (IRE)   10 b.g. Balinger – Merry Mirth (Menelek) [2002/3 c77x, **c73 x** h–: c26d3 c24d3 c23spu 26m2 22f2 25m 20d3 22d4* 17d2 23d5 24m4 Apr 16] workmanlike **h89** gelding: has stringhalt: poor chaser: modest hurdler: won amateur handicap at Exeter in December: effective around 2m given a test and stays 3¼m: acts on any going: has broken blood vessels (more than once in 2002/3): often makes mistakes over fences. *Dr P. Pritchard*

HAPPY MEDIUM (IRE)   10 b.g. Fairy King (USA) – Belle Origine (USA) (Exclu- **c–** sive Native (USA)) [2002/3 c21gur Mar 14] leggy gelding: winning pointer: unseated first **h–** in novice hunter chase: tried blinkered/visored over hurdles. *Mrs T. H. Hayward*

HARASARAH (FR)   8 b.g. Glaieul (USA) – Carasarah (FR) (Noir Et Or) [2002/3 **c– x** c16mF c21m4 c19dF Oct 23] lengthy gelding: useful hurdler in France: fairly useful **h–** chaser in 2000/1: well held over longer trip only completed start on return: best form around 2m: acts on heavy going: usually let down by jumping. *M. C. Pipe*

HARBOUR BELL   4 b.g. Bal Harbour – Bellara (Thowra (FR)) [2002/3 16d⁵ 16d   **h–**
Nov 29] modest on Flat (stays easy 2m): well held in 2 juvenile hurdles at Newbury.
J. White

HARBOUR PILOT (IRE)   8 b.g. Be My Native (USA) – Las-Cancellas (Monks-   **c164**
field) [2002/3 c148, h–: c26g³ c24v³ c24s³ c26g³ Mar 13]   **h–**
    Second-season chaser Harbour Pilot put up the performance of his life in the
Cheltenham Gold Cup, proving himself a thorough stayer and running way above
anything he had previously achieved. Labouring from an early stage in a race run at
a searching gallop on good going, he was flat out and quite a way behind the leaders
coming down the hill before making up ground hand over fist in the home straight.
He finished best of all, passing four horses from the second last to snatch third place
from Valley Henry close home, beaten ten lengths and two and a half lengths by
Best Mate and Truckers Tavern. Harbour Pilot started at 40/1 and hardly looked
good enough for the Gold Cup beforehand. His three victories as a novice had
included two Grade 1 events in Ireland, the Drinmore at Fairyhouse and the Dr
P.J. Moriarty at Leopardstown (in which Truckers Tavern was second), before he
unseated his rider at the twelfth when third favourite for the Royal & SunAlliance
at the Cheltenham Festival.
    Harbour Pilot's jumping technique was suspect in his first season over
fences and it continued to let him down in the latest one. He looked to be getting on
top in a very competitive Hennessy Gold Cup at Newbury on his reappearance in
late-November but a blunder at the last cost him his narrow lead and he passed

Kays Syndicate's "Harbour Pilot"

the post in third, half a length and a length and a half behind Be My Royal and Gingembre. Harbour Pilot made a number of other mistakes at Newbury and wasn't foot perfect on either of his subsequent outings before Cheltenham, both at Leopardstown, in the Ericsson Chase in December and the Hennessy Cognac Gold Cup in February. Harbour Pilot finished third behind Beef Or Salmon and Colonel Braxton on both occasions, making minor mistakes in the latter stages.

Harbour Pilot (IRE) (b.g. 1995)	Be My Native (USA) (br 1979)	Our Native (b or br 1970)	Exclusive Native
			Our Jackie
		Witchy Woman (ch 1972)	Strate Stuff
			Witchy Norma
	Las-Cancellas (b 1984)	Monksfield (b 1972)	Gala Performance
			Regina
		Synarria (br 1977)	Guillaume Tell
			Spinning Jenny

The rangy Harbour Pilot isn't bred to be so thoroughly well suited by a stamina-sapping test like the Gold Cup. His sire Be My Native is not a particularly strong influence for stamina and, though Harbour Pilot's dam Las-Cancellas is a sister to the dam of Grand National winner Monty's Pass, she herself won at a mile and a quarter and a mile and a half on the Flat and gained her only victory over hurdles at two miles. Las-Cancellas was represented on the racecourse in Britain by two other offspring in the latest season, Harbour Pilot's year-older half-brother the winning pointer Manolito (by Mandalus), who showed only poor form in handicap chases, and six-year-old half-brother Metal Detector (by Treasure Hunter) who showed himself a fairly useful novice hurdler, winning three times over distances ranging from twenty-one furlongs to three miles. Harbour Pilot, who was blinkered on his last two starts, has been raced only on good ground or softer (acts on heavy) and was a late withdrawal from the Punchestown Gold Cup shortly after the end of the British season because of worries about the going turning too firm. His trainer regards Harbour Pilot as a horse who goes best fresh and it is noticeable that his races in his latest campaign were fairly well spaced out, connections adhering almost to the letter to the programme mapped out for Harbour Pilot at the start of the season. *N. Meade, Ireland*

HARBOUR POINT (IRE) 7 b.g. Glacial Storm (USA) – Forest Jem (Croghan Hill) [2002/3 F–: F16d* 17s³ 19s⁶ 19mᵇᵈ 22g³ Apr 21] won bumper at Fakenham in October: poor form over hurdles, including on handicap debut. *D. J. Caro*   **h74 F94**

HARCAMONE (FR) 8 br.g. Passing Sale (FR) – Raise A Baby (FR) (Albert de Vongy) [2002/3 c87x, h–: 16dᶠ c16m⁶ c20m⁵ c16dᵖᵘ 20vᵖᵘ Dec 20] sparely-made gelding: winning hurdler/novice chaser: no form in 2002/3, left M. Sheppard after first outing: probably stays 2½m: suited by soft/heavy going: usually tongue tied: usually let down by jumping over fences: has shown signs of temperament. *A. G. Hobbs*   **c– x h–**

HARCHIBALD (FR) 4 b.g. Perugino (USA) – Dame d'Harvard (USA) (Quest For Fame) [2002/3 16s* 16v³ 16s 16s³ 16d² 16g⁵ 16g² Apr 21] rather leggy, useful-looking gelding: first foal: brother to 1m winner Jeu de Dame: dam French 2-y-o 5f winner: useful over middle distances on Flat in France, sold out of B. Goudot's stable €90,000 Goffs Arc Sale: fairly useful juvenile hurdler: won at Fairyhouse in December: better form most starts after, including when beating Master Papa by 1½ lengths in 4-y-o minor event at Punchestown in late-April: raced at 2m: acts on heavy ground: tongue tied after third outing: carries head high, and has failed to go through with effort. *N. Meade, Ireland*   **h124**

HARDEN GLEN 12 b.g. Respect – Polly Peril (Politico (USA)) [2002/3 c–: c25d May 1] workmanlike gelding: winning chaser: modest pointer nowadays, successful in April: stays 4m: acts on any going: tried blinkered. *C. Storey*   **c–**

HARDI DE CHALAMONT (FR) 8 gr.g. Royal Charter (FR) – Naita II (FR) (Dom Luc (FR)) [2002/3 c89, h–: 16g⁵ 16m⁵ 17d⁴ 18s² 18v³ c20s⁴ c16sᶠ 16g Apr 14] leggy gelding: winning chaser in France, largely let down by jumping over fences in Britain: poor hurdler: stays 19f: acts on soft and good to firm going: visored after reappearance. *A. Parker*   **c– h83**

HARD LINES (USA) 7 b.g. Silver Hawk (USA) – Arctic Eclipse (USA) (Northern Dancer) [2002/3 c87x, h–: c16d c16v* 16v* Nov 8] close-coupled gelding: poor and inconsistent hurdler: better form over fences, won 4-runner novice handicap at Hexham in March: raced around 2m: acts on heavy going. *M. D. Hammond*   **c98 h74**

HARD PRESSED (IRE)   7 b.g. Jurado (USA) – Valantonia (IRE) (Over The River   h–
(FR)) [2002/3 F16m⁴ F17v 17s 22dᵖᵘ Feb 23] 1,500 5-y-o: second foal: dam unraced   **F79**
half-sister to Champion Hurdle winners Morley Street and Granville Again: well-beaten
fourth of 17 in bumper at Worcester on debut: off 5 months, no show on more testing
ground after, including over hurdles. *B. J. Llewellyn*

HARD TO KNOW (IRE)   5 b.g. Common Grounds – Lady Fern (Old Vic) [2002/3   **h95 §**
h89: 16m* 17g 16mᵘʳ Jun 19] compact gelding: modest hurdler: won handicap at Ludlow
in May: likely to prove best around 2m: acts on firm going: blinkered in 2002/3: temperamental: sold 700 gns Doncaster August Sales. *P. J. Hobbs*

HARD TO LAY (IRE)   5 br.m. Dolphin Street (FR) – Yavarro (Raga Navarro   **h83**
(ITY)) [2002/3 17m⁴ 16m* 17g Jul 31] modest maiden on Flat (stays 1m) at 3 yrs for
D. Cosgrove: poor form over hurdles: won novice seller at Stratford in July: well held in
handicap later in month: likely to prove best at sharp 2m. *P. J. Hobbs*

HARDY BREEZE (IRE)   12 b.g. Henbit (USA) – Chake-Chake (Goldhill) [2002/3   **c72**
c64, h–: c25d³ c25g³ May 24] poor chaser/maiden hurdler: stays 3¼m: acts on heavy and   **h–**
good to firm going. *Miss A. M. Newton-Smith*

HARDY DUCKETT (IRE)   4 br.g. Key of Luck (USA) – Bramdean (Niniski   **h110**
(USA)) [2002/3 16s⁶ 16s F16s F16m² Apr 22] €41,000 3-y-o: half-brother to useful   **F96**
hurdler/winning chaser Bob Justice (by Bob Back), stays easy 3m, and winning 2m
hurdler Ah Gowan (by High Estate): dam 1¼m winner who stayed 1½m on Flat: better
effort in juvenile hurdles when seventh of 12 to Golden Cross in Grade 3 at Fairyhouse
second start: much better effort in bumpers when second to Newmill in valuable event at
same course in April. *D. T. Hughes, Ireland*

HARDY EUSTACE (IRE)   6 b.g. Archway (IRE) – Sterna Star (Corvaro (USA))   **h149**
[2002/3 F110: 16s* 16v* 20s* 18s² 21g* 24d⁵ Apr 4]
    The Royal & SunAlliance Novices' Hurdle was the strongest novice hurdle
of the season. Half a dozen of the nineteen runners had already shown enough
ability to suggest they could win an average renewal, while useful novices like
Calling Brave, Mossy Green and Saitensohn started at odds of 33/1. Only Rosslea
had yet to win a race over hurdles. The 2002 Champion Bumper winner Pizarro
started favourite at 2/1 after winning two of his three starts over hurdles, including
the only defeat suffered by the mare Solerina (who seemed, at the time, the one
notable absentee from the SunAlliance). The Challow Hurdle winner Coolnagorna
and the unbeaten Lord Sam headed the home team while the French-trained
Foreman and the Pipe inmate Puntal, rather surprisingly running here in preference
to the Supreme Novices' the day before, could also be given every chance on form.
Along with Pizarro, the Irish had another major contender in Hardy Eustace. He too
had made a mark in bumpers in 2002, winning the very valuable Goffs Land Rover
at Fairyhouse, and had encountered Solerina, meeting his only defeat in four starts
over hurdles when going down by two lengths to her in the Deloitte And Touche
Novices' Hurdle at Leopardstown, a performance which gave him every chance.
Running to two out, virtually all the main contenders were bang in contention.
Coolnagorna, who had been sent on at the fifth after the early pace wasn't that
strong, was driven along, with Pizarro, back on the bridle, and Lord Sam close
behind. Jumping, Lord Sam was short of room but blundered anyway and Pizarro
was soon flat out and hanging fire; meanwhile Hardy Eustace, who had been
making steady progress chased along, really began to stay on and went to the front
into the straight. He was untidy over the last, with a lead of over a length, and was
driven out to hold Coolnagorna by a length and a quarter with Pizarro third and
Lord Sam fourth past the post, though the runner-up was harshly disqualified after
the stewards decided his rider had impeded Lord Sam at the second last.
    Since it was introduced to the Festival as the Aldsworth Hurdle in 1971 (and
not even the course seems to know why it was given the name of a village some
way the other side of Cheltenham), the SunAlliance has had a distinguished list of
winners and, in recent times, it has consistently taken a better performance to win it
than the Supreme Novices'. Whereas the two-mile race in recent years has a rollcall
of the ill-fated and the infirm, the SunAlliance list includes several who went on
to show themselves out of the top drawer over either hurdles or fences, Danoli,
Istabraq, French Holly and Barton being among its winners in the last decade.
Whether Hardy Eustace has the ability to make up into a top-class performer in

*Royal & SunAlliance Novices' Hurdle, Cheltenham—Hardy Eustace holds a decisive lead over the last;
the subsequently-disqualified Coolnagorna (right), Pizarro and Lord Sam give chase*

open company remains to be seen. He was seen out once after Cheltenham, starting
second favourite to the Stayers' Hurdle second Iris's Gift—who had been a
SunAlliance entry—in the Sefton Novices' Hurdle over three miles at Aintree but
running as if he might not have been over his exertions at Cheltenham and
weakening quickly going to three out, finishing a distant fifth to the favourite.
Hardy Eustace is certainly worth a chance in the autumn to show himself a serious
Stayers' Hurdle candidate. Though he did well physically through the season, he
makes more appeal as a hurdling prospect than as a novice chaser.

As well as the Royal & SunAlliance, Hardy Eustace gained a Grade 1
success when winning the second of his three earlier wins over hurdles, in the
Boylesports Royal Bond Novices' Hurdle. Despite its position so early in the
season, the Royal Bond, run at Fairyhouse in early-December, has proved a good
guide to the best Irish novices (the race, along with the other Grade 1 events on an
excellent card, is almost always ignored by British stables) and the latest running
was no exception, with Hardy Eustace getting the better of the subsequent Supreme
Novices' winner Back In Front by a length and a half, the pair clear. Either side of
that success, Hardy Eustace won a maiden at Punchestown and a novice at
Leopardstown, in the latter beating Nil Desperandum by three quarters of a length.

Hardy Eustace (IRE) (b.g. 1997)	Archway (IRE) (ch 1988)	Thatching (b 1975)	Thatch Abella
		Rose of Jericho (b 1984)	Rose Red Vaguely Noble
	Sterna Star (b or br 1984)	Corvaro (b 1977)	Delmora Sovereign Gleam
		Star Girl (b 1973)	Sterna

Hardy Eustace was bought at the 2001 Goffs Land Rover Sale for IR
£21,000. Judged on pedigree, his appeal as a prospective jumper was not obvious.
He is from the last Irish crop of the smart sprinter Archway, who is a half-brother to

Mr Laurence Byrne's "Hardy Eustace"

the Derby winner Dr Devious and has since made more of an impact as a sire in Australia. Hardy Eustace's dam Sterna Star won a mile-and-a-half ladies race on the Flat at four and numbered a modest maiden on the Flat by Don't Forget Me and a maiden in Italy by Double Schwartz among four previous foals. The once-raced grandam Star Girl produced nine winners on the Flat. The most notable of them was the useful Irish one-mile winner Star Spartan, but they also included Star Player who was fairly useful on the Flat and over hurdles, where he finished second in the Imperial Cup. The third dam Sterna also foaled nine winners, including a couple of immediately recognisable names, the Arc and Eclipse Stakes winner Star Appeal and Sterntau. Sterntau was a minor Flat winner but appears numerous times in tabulated pedigrees in *Chasers & Hurdlers* as the dam of Strong Gale. Whatever the attraction of Hardy Eustace in the sale-ring, he has fully rewarded his owner's faith. A good-topped gelding, he shapes as if he will prove effective at three miles. He has raced on good going or softer, coping well with both good ground at Cheltenham and very testing conditions in the Royal Bond. *D. T. Hughes, Ireland*

HAREBELLE 6 b.m. Almoojid – Velvet Heart (IRE) (Damister (USA)) [2002/3 h–: 17dbd 24vur 16v 21d Feb 7] sparely-made mare: signs of only a little ability. *A. D. Smith*   h–

HAREM SCAREM (IRE) 12 b.g. Lord Americo – River Rescue (Over The River (FR)) [2002/3 c84, h–: c21g² c21g² c17v⁴ Nov 19] tall, workmanlike gelding: winning hurdler: poor handicap chaser: stays 21f: raced mainly on good going or softer (acts on heavy): tried in blinkers: usually races prominently. *Mrs L. Williamson*   c84
h–

HARFDECENT 12 b.g. Primitive Rising (USA) – Grand Queen (Grand Conde (FR)) [2002/3 c113, h–: c22g⁶ c20d⁶ c23sF c23sur c21m² Aug 26] small, sparely-made gelding: fair handicap chaser, reportedly suffers from breathing problem: stays 25f: acts on soft   c106 x
h–

360

and good to firm going: has had tongue tied: often let down by jumping: joined Miss J. Tremain. *Mrs M. Reveley*

HARIK 9 ch.g. Persian Bold – Yaqut (USA) (Northern Dancer) [2002/3 c102, h–: c20m² c16m³ c21d⁴ c18g⁴ c18m² c19f* c20m* c20g⁴ Apr 12] workmanlike gelding: fair handicap chaser: successful at Taunton and Plumpton in March: improved effort when beating Tambo by 11 lengths at latter: stays 2½m: acts on any going: usually blinkered/visored: tongue tied. *G. L. Moore*   **c111** **h–**

HARLEIDALUS (IRE) 9 b.g. Mandalus – Spartan Park (Scorpio (FR)) [2002/3 c88, h–: c24dᵖᵘ c25m⁶ c25g⁵ Oct 19] workmanlike gelding: lightly-raced winning 3m chaser: little sign of retaining ability. *Mrs L. B. Normile*   **c–** **h–**

HARLOV (FR) 8 ch.g. Garde Royale – Paulownia (FR) (Montevideo) [2002/3 c93, h96: c20v* c26v² Nov 28] well-made gelding: modest handicap hurdler/chaser: won intermediate chase at Carlisle on reappearance: good second of 5 to Le Cabro d'Or later in month: stays 27f: acts on heavy going: tried blinkered, has run well in cheek-pieces. *A. Parker*   **c99** **h–**

HARMONIC (USA) 6 b.m. Shadeed (USA) – Running Melody (Rheingold) [2002/3 h88: 16d² 16g⁵ 16g⁵ 16s* 16g* 20d⁴ 16d 16dᵖᵘ 16d Dec 14] leggy mare: modest hurdler: won maiden at Worcester in August and novice at Fakenham in October: out of form last 3 starts: likely to prove best around 2m: acts on heavy and good to firm going: joined H. Collingridge. *G. Prodromou*   **h90**

HARMONY HALL 9 ch.g. Music Boy – Fleeting Affair (Hotfoot) [2002/3 16f⁵ Oct 24] sturdy gelding: modest on Flat nowadays, raced around 1m: fairly useful hurdler in 1999/00: last of 5 in handicap at Ludlow on return: raced at 2m: acts on good to firm and good to soft going. *J. M. Bradley*   **h–**

HARPASGON DE L'OMBRE (FR) 8 b.g. Mbaiki (FR) – Undress (FR) (Signani (FR)) [2002/3 c95: c24gᵖᵘ c18mᶠ c20f* c22s⁴ c25d⁴ c22g Mar 29] sturdy gelding: modest chaser: left with simple task in novice at Ludlow in October: found very little when blinkered final outing: stays 2¾m: acts on firm and soft going. *O. Sherwood*   **c93**

HARPOON 7 b.g. Kris – Jezebel Monroe (USA) (Lyphard (USA)) [2002/3 22vᵖᵘ 16gᵖᵘ Feb 27] lengthy, useful-looking gelding: third in bumper on debut in 2000/1: beaten long way out in 2 novice hurdles. *P. R. Webber*   **h–**

HARROVIAN 6 b.g. Deploy – Homeoftheclassics (Tate Gallery (USA)) [2002/3 F94p: 16v⁵ 20s⁴ Nov 28] second in bumper at Newbury on debut in 2001/2: better effort in novice hurdles when fifth to Zamat at Kelso: should stay beyond 2m. *Ferdy Murphy*   **h88**

HARRY B 4 b.g. Midyan (USA) – Vilcabamba (USA) (Green Dancer (USA)) [2002/3 16f³ 16m³ Nov 4] modest on Flat (will prove best around 1½m), claimed from G. Bravery £5,000 after winning at Wolverhampton in September: modest form when third in juvenile hurdles at Ludlow and Warwick. *R. J. Price*   **h91**

HARRY COLLINS 5 ch.g. Sir Harry Lewis (USA) – Run Fast For Gold (Deep Run) [2002/3 F16s F17s 16g Mar 12] workmanlike gelding: third foal: dam, poor 2m hurdler, raced after birth of first foal: modest form when eighth in bumpers at Kempton and Folkestone: behind in maiden on hurdling debut. *B. I. Case*   **h–** **F76**

HARRYCONE LEWIS 5 b.g. Sir Harry Lewis (USA) – Rosie Cone (Celtic Cone) [2002/3 19d⁶ 20v Feb 11] unfurnished gelding: sixth foal: half-brother to winning hurdlers Molsum (by Lord Bud), stays 3¼m, and Standing Bloom (by Presidium): dam winning hurdler, probably stayed 3m: modest form on first of 2 outings over hurdles when sixth in novice at Doncaster: should be suited by 2½m+. *Mrs P. Sly*   **h90**

HARRY HOOLY 8 b.g. Lithgie-Brig – Drummond Lass (Peacock (FR)) [2002/3 h86: 22d 20d* 22m 17d⁶ 27d⁴ 27v⁶ Nov 19] leggy gelding: modest handicap hurdler: won at Hexham in May: below form after, reportedly lame final outing: effective at 2½m given test and stays 27f: raced mainly on going softer than good: usually ridden by Miss L. Hislop, including for all 4 wins. *Mrs H. O. Graham*   **h94**

HARRY JUNIOR 5 b.g. River Falls – Badger Bay (IRE) (Salt Dome (USA)) [2002/3 17mᵖᵘ Oct 1] temperamental maiden on Flat: no show in novice on hurdling debut. *J. S. Wainwright*   **h–**

HARRY'S ACE 5 b.g. Phountzi (USA) – Throw In Your Hand (Niniski (USA)) [2002/3 F17d F16d Mar 6] £1,800 4-y-o: fourth foal: dam unraced, from family of very smart Flat stayer Longboat: well held in 2 bumpers. *P. D. Williams*   **F–**

HARRY'S DREAM 6 b.g. Alflora (IRE) – Cheryls Pet (IRE) (General Ironside) **h93**
[2002/3 20vᵖᵘ 19g⁵ 21dᵖᵘ 19s 19m⁴ 22g Apr 19] leggy, workmanlike gelding: second
foal: brother to fairly useful hurdler/smart chaser Farmer Jack, stays 2½m: dam, modest
hurdler who stayed 21f, half-sister to dam of very smart chaser up to 25f Second
Schedual: won maiden from 2 starts in points in 2002: modest maiden hurdler: stays 19f
(shaped like non-stayer over 2¾m final start): easily best efforts on good going or firmer.
J. W. Mullins

HARRY THE EAR (IRE) 5 b.g. Definite Article – Kilboy Concorde (African Sky) **h110**
[2002/3 16s³ 16m* 16m* 16v⁶ 16s 16d 16g⁵ Mar 30] unfurnished gelding: half-brother to
several winners on Flat, including useful Lyford Law (by Contract Law), stayed 8.5f:
dam poor maiden on Flat: modest form at best in bumpers: fairly useful on Flat up to
1¾m, successful twice from 4 starts: fair hurdler: won twice at Kilbeggan, maiden in
August and 4-y-o novice in September: raced at 2m: acts on good to firm and heavy
going: tongue tied. *M. Halford, Ireland*

HARRY THE HORSE 5 b.g. Sir Harry Lewis (USA) – Miss Optimist (Relkino) **h–**
[2002/3 17sᵖᵘ Jan 28] £4,200 (priv) 4-y-o: workmanlike gelding: first foal: dam, fairly
useful hurdler, stayed 2½m: jumped poorly and tailed off when pulled up in novice hurdle
on debut. *Miss E. C. Lavelle*

HARTEST ROSE 4 b.f. Komaite (USA) – Plough Hill (North Briton) [2002/3 F16g **F87**
F16m* Apr 10] fourth foal: sister to winning 2m hurdler Plough Boy and 5f winner Robin
Hood: dam unraced: stepped up markedly on debut effort when winning 15-runner
bumper at Ludlow: likely to prove best at 2m with emphasis on speed. *D. E. Cantillon*

HARTSHEAD 4 b.g. Machiavellian (USA) – Zalitzine (USA) (Zilzal (USA)) [2002/3 **F74**
F17g Mar 22] 7,800 3-y-o: first foal: dam, 1m winner, daughter of smart French 7f
performer Bitooh: 3/1, seemed not to stay when seventh of 8 in bumper at Bangor on
debut, still travelling well in lead entering straight: placed over 11f on Flat debut in April.
G. A. Swinbank

HARVEY'S SISTER 7 ch.m. Le Moss – Wings Ground (Murrayfield) [2002/3 F17s **F–**
May 18] lengthy mare: seventh foal: sister to useful hurdler/winning chaser Moss
Harvey, stays 25f, and half-sister to winning pointer by Balinger: dam, winning hurdler/
chaser, stayed 2½m: backward and green, never dangerous in mares bumper on debut.
J. M. Jefferson

HARVIS (FR) 8 b.g. Djarvis (FR) – Tirana (FR) (Over) [2002/3 c121, h–: c24mᶠ **c123**
c20d³ c24d² c19v² 20s⁶ c16d* c16g c16g⁶ Apr 3] smallish, angular gelding: winning **h114**
hurdler: fairly useful handicap chaser: led close home when winning at Sandown in
February by ½ length from Abalvino: effective around 2m to easy 3m: acts on heavy
and good to firm going: often fails to impress with jumping and/or attitude. *Miss Venetia
Williams*

HARWELD 11 ch.g. Weld – Fruit Farm (Twiberry) [2002/3 c21gʳᵗʳ May 1] winning **c§§**
pointer, failed to complete in 5 starts in 2002: refused to race in maiden hunter chase: best
left alone. *Mrs Edward Crow*

HASARD SAISI (FR) 7 ch.g. Mill Pond (FR) – Askja (FR) (Jefferson) [2002/3 c105, **c–**
h–: c16g³ c18dᵖᵘ 17s Dec 17] novice hurdler: winning chaser in France: most disap- **h–**
pointing in Britain, left P. Nicholls before final outing: stays 2½m: acts on heavy and
good to firm going: has had tongue tied. *C. Tizzard*

HASARY (FR) 8 b.g. Marasali – Asterie L'Ermitage (FR) (Hamster (FR)) [2002/3 **c?**
c21g³ c21d² c21g c19s³ c26sᵖᵘ c19vᵖᵘ Dec 27] leggy gelding: first known foal: half- **h–**
brother to fairly useful hurdler Idiome (by Djarvis), stays 2½m, and Flat winner by Iris
Noir: dam, unplaced on Flat and over jumps, half-sister to smart 4-y-o chaser up to 2½m
Tamarix: winning hurdler: maiden chaser: third in non-thoroughbred event at Angers in
November (final start for J. M. Robin): let down by jumping after in novices at Plumpton
and Chepstow (blinkered): raced mainly up to 21f on good ground or softer. *G. Macaire,
France*

HASTEN BAK 10 ch.g. Shaab – Kirstins Pride (Silly Prices) [2002/3 c77x, h74x: 22f **c– x**
22g May 25] angular gelding: poor chaser/maiden hurdler: successful in points in March **h– x**
and April: stays 3¼m: acts on good to firm and heavy going: poor jumper. *Mrs S. Gardner*

HASTE YE BACK (IRE) 9 b.g. All Haste (USA) – Less Pressure (IRE) (Torus) **c70 x**
[2002/3 c24g⁴ c26m³ c29dᵖᵘ c24vᵖᵘ 26s⁴ c24dᵖᵘ 26g 26m⁴ Mar 23] useful-looking **h71**
gelding: poor hurdler/maiden chaser: should stay beyond 3¼m: acts on heavy going,
probably on good to firm: tried visored, often blinkered: usually soon off bridle: sketchy
jumper. *D. J. Caro*

Light Infantry Plate (Novices' Hurdle), Doncaster—Hasty Prince gains an easy success

HASTY PRINCE 5 ch.g. Halling (USA) – Sister Sophie (USA) (Effervescing (USA)) **h125 p**
[2002/3 16v² 16d* 16gᵇᵈ 19d* Mar 1] leggy, sparely-made gelding: useful on Flat (stays
1½m), sold out of B. Hanbury's stable 18,000 gns Newmarket Autumn Sales: fairly
useful form in novice hurdles, winning at Huntingdon in January and Doncaster (beat
Balladeer easily by 6 lengths) in March: every chance when brought down 3 out in
between: stays 19f: open to further improvement. *Jonjo O'Neill*

HATCHAM BOY (IRE) 13 br.g. Roselier (FR) – Auling (Tarqogan) [2002/3 c97x, **c89 x**
h–x: c30m² c31m³ May 22] rangy gelding: fair hunter chaser: stays 4¼m: acts on good to **h– x**
firm and heavy going: tried blinkered: sketchy jumper: consistent. *Mrs Ruth Hayter*

HATCH GATE 10 gr.g. Lighter – Yankee Silver (Yankee Gold) [2002/3 c21m⁴ May **c68**
22] fair pointer, successful twice in April: favourite, not fluent when fourth of 5 finishers
in novice at Folkestone on hunter chase debut. *P. York*

HAT OR HALO (IRE) 11 b.g. Hatim (USA) – Saintly Grove (Welsh Saint) [2002/3 **c–**
c96, h123: 17d 16v* 16g² 20s⁵ Nov 3] sturdy gelding: modest form over fences: useful **h135**
hurdler: won minor event at Navan in July by 20 lengths from Bob Justice: needs good
test at 2m and stays 2½m well: acts on heavy going: game. *Niall J. Donohoe, Ireland*

HATSNALL 5 b.g. Mtoto – Anna of Brunswick (Rainbow Quest (USA)) [2002/3 **c73**
16vᵖᵘ 16f 16d⁴ c16m³ c16g⁵ 22g 19g⁴ Apr 26] good-topped ex-Irish gelding: half- **h86**
brother to winner in Germany: dam, 9.7f winner who stayed 1¾m, half-sister to useful
2m hurdler/chaser Atlaal: modest maiden hurdler: twice-raced maiden chaser: sold out of
F. Flood's stable 13,000 gns (privately) Doncaster October Sales after fifth start: stays
19f: acts on heavy going, probably on good to firm. *Miss C. J. E. Caroe*

HATTON FARM BABE 12 b.m. Lochnager – Hatton Farm Girl (Humdoleila) **c91**
[2002/3 c91: c20mᶠ c22d⁵ c26g* c28mᵖᵘ Jun 1] fair pointer: back to form in hunter chases
when 25/1-winner of novice at Uttoxeter in May, tending to jump right: stays 3¼m: acts
on good to firm going. *Mrs Susan Norbury*

HAUT CERCY (FR) 8 b.g. Roi de Rome (USA) – Mamoussia (FR) (Laniste) [2002/3 **c139**
c110, h–: c24d* c22d⁴ c24s³ c25d* c25d³ c24g² Mar 11] leggy gelding: useful chaser: **h–**
won novice at Chepstow in October and handicap at Wincanton in January: in frame all

363

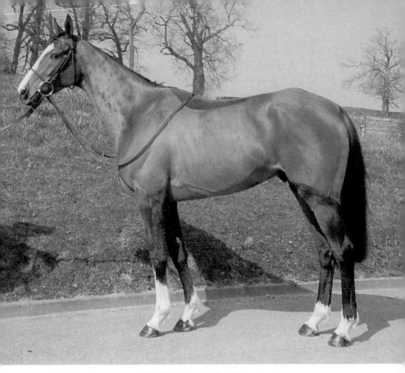

The Wiggin Partnership's "Haut Cercy"

other starts in 2002/3, particularly good effort when second to Youlneverwalkalone in National Hunt Handicap at Cheltenham: better around 3m than shorter (possibly failed to stay 4m): acts on soft going, probably on good to firm: usually sound jumper. *H. D. Daly*

HAVETWOTAKETWO (IRE) 9 b.g. Phardante (FR) – Arctic Tartan (Deep Run) **c– x**
[2002/3 c–, h–: c20d^ur Apr 29] little show over hurdles: fair pointer at best: still to be **h–**
asked for effort when unseating before straight in novice at Newcastle on hunter chase debut: has had tongue tied. *Michael Smith*

HAVOC 4 b.g. Hurricane Sky (AUS) – Padelia (Thatching) [2002/3 17s^pu Dec 5] **h–**
half-brother to winning 21f hurdler Pa d'Or (by Slew O'Gold): fair maiden on Flat (best form around 1m), sold out of E. Dunlop's stable 10,000 gns Newmarket July Sales, well held subsequently: no show in juvenile on hurdling debut. *N. Wilson*

HAWADETH 8 ch.g. Machiavellian (USA) – Ghzaalh (USA) (Northern Dancer) **h125**
[2002/3 h115: 16g³ 16s² 16v⁵ 16s³ 16d² 16v 17g^bd 16g Apr 5] compact gelding: fairly useful handicap hurdler: should stay beyond 17f: raced on good going or softer (acts on heavy): tried blinkered: consistent, though often soon off bridle. *V. R. A. Dartnall*

HAWICK 6 b.g. Toulon – Slave's Bangle (Prince Rheingold) [2002/3 F16v² F16s³ Mar **F99**
8] seventh foal: half-brother to several winners, including fairly useful hurdler/chaser Swansea Bay (by Jurado), stays 25f, and fairly useful chaser up to 3¼m Gower-Slave (by Mandalus): dam, lightly raced in Ireland, half-sister to useful staying hurdler Spaced Out: better effort in bumpers at Ayr when head second to Baron Monty. *D. W. Whillans*

HAWKES RUN 5 b.g. Hernando (FR) – Wise Speculation (USA) (Mr Prospector **h117**
(USA)) [2002/3 h120: 20s⁵ 22s^co 24s⁵ Dec 18] close-coupled gelding: poor walker: fairly

364

useful hurdler: best effort in handicaps in 2002/3 when fifth to Yeoman's Point at Chepstow on reappearance: stays 2½m: acts on soft going: tried blinkered. *C. J. Mann*

HAWK'S LANDING (IRE) 6 gr.g. Peacock (FR) – Lady Cheyenne (Stanford) [2002/3 F16d² F16s* F16s⁴ Feb 14] IR £5,000 4-y-o: has scope: second foal: brother to winning hurdler around 2m Norbrook: dam lightly-raced maiden: progressive form in bumpers, trained by Miss F. Crowley on debut: won at Kempton in January by 4 lengths from Distant Thunder and fourth to Patricksnineteenth at Sandown in February. *Jonjo O'Neill* **F104**

HAWTHORN 7 ch.g. Primo Dominie – Starr Danias (USA) (Sensitive Prince (USA)) [2002/3 h–: 17m⁵ 17mᵖᵘ Sep 14] tall gelding: no form in novice hurdles. *M. F. Harris* **h–**

HAWTHORN PRINCE (IRE) 8 ch.g. Black Monday – Goose Loose (Dual) [2002/3 16g 16dᵖᵘ F17gᵘʳ 20fᵘʳ F20f³ 21g Oct 15] ex-Irish gelding: half-brother to several winners, including fairly useful chaser Liver Bird (by Lafontaine), stayed 3m: dam poor Irish maiden: little worthwhile form in bumpers or over hurdles: blinkered last 4 outings: has looked far from resolute: sold 600 gns Doncaster November Sales, successful in 2 points in March. *Michael Hourigan, Ireland* **c–** **h–** **F84**

HAYAAIN 10 b.g. Shirley Heights – Littlefield (Bay Express) [2002/3 c–, h100: 18d 24m² 27g⁵ 26m² Sep 11] good-topped gelding: well beaten only outing over fences: fair handicap hurdler: left J. Barclay before final start: stays 3¼m: acts on good to firm and good to soft going: blinkered twice: has looked ungenuine. *P. G. Murphy* **c–** **h102**

HAYBURN VAULTS 5 b.m. Bettergeton – Agdistis (Petoski) [2002/3 F16d Mar 6] first foal: half-sister to 2002 5f winner in Greece: dam won 2m juvenile hurdle: well held in bumper on debut. *Mrs S. J. Smith* **F–**

HAY DANCE 12 b.g. Shareef Dancer (USA) – Hay Reef (Mill Reef (USA)) [2002/3 c20m³ c21gᵖᵘ Mar 14] good-topped gelding: fair pointer/hunter chaser nowadays: stays 2½m: acts on good to firm and good to soft going: held up. *J. Ibbott* **c88** **h–**

HAYDENS FIELD 9 b.g. Bedford (USA) – Releta (Relkino) [2002/3 h112+: 24g* 22g* 25d* 20sᵖᵘ 23sᵖᵘ 22v² 22s⁶ Mar 15] angular gelding: winning pointer: fairly useful hurdler: made all in novices at Bangor, Newton Abbot and Wetherby in May: easily best effort in handicaps subsequently when second at Sandown: stays 25f: raced on good going or softer (acts on heavy). *P. M. Rich* **h123**

HAYDN JAMES (USA) 9 ch.g. Danzig Connection (USA) – Royal Fi Fi (USA) (Conquistador Cielo (USA)) [2002/3 c111, h100: c20m* c20m⁴ c20m* c20m⁶ 22f* c21m³ c24m⁴ c22g⁴ c24f Oct 17] angular gelding: fairly useful handicap chaser: won at Fontwell in May and Uttoxeter in June: modest handicap hurdler: made all at Newton Abbot in August: generally let down by jumping over fences subsequently: stays 2¾m: probably needs good going or firmer (acts on firm): blinkered final start. *P. J. Hobbs* **c117 x** **h96**

HAYTON BOY 9 ch.g. Gypsy Castle – Young Christine VII (Damsire Unregistered) [2002/3 16dᵘʳ 26dᵖᵘ 20sꟳ Aug 4] second foal: dam never ran: no sign of ability in 3 starts over hurdles, tongue tied final one. *S. G. Chadwick* **h–**

HAZEL REILLY (IRE) 12 b.m. Mister Lord (USA) – Vickies Gold (Golden Love) [2002/3 c85: c25dᵖᵘ c28d* c25d* c24d² c25g⁴ c31d² Apr 25] smallish, lengthy, angular mare: fair hunter chaser: won at Catterick in February and Kelso (novice) in March: stays 31f: acts on heavy going: reliable. *Mrs Sarah L. Dent* **c94**

HEAD FOR HOME (IRE) 6 ch.m. Executive Perk – Lancastrian Rose (IRE) (Lancastrian) [2002/3 h–, F–: 16gᵖᵘ Oct 12] no form in bumpers or novice hurdles: has had tongue tied. *Mrs Dianne Sayer* **h–**

HEADS ONTHE GROUND (IRE) 6 br.g. Be My Native (USA) – Strong Wings (Deep Run) [2002/3 F20s⁴ 24v² 22s* 22s² 22d² Mar 22] IR 55,000 3-y-o: fourth live foal: dam unraced half-sister to dam of Marlborough: fair form on first of 2 starts in bumpers: fairly useful novice hurdler: won maiden at Navan in January: better form when second to Nil Desperandum at same course final outing: stays 3m: acts on heavy ground. *D. T. Hughes, Ireland* **h117** **F82**

HEALY'S PUB (IRE) 7 b.g. Accordion – Valary (Roman Warrior) [2002/3 18d⁴ F16s* 16v² 16s² 18v³ 16s* 16s* 16m⁴ Apr 22] 27,000 3-y-o: half-brother to several winners, including fair hurdler New Legislation (by Dominion Royale), stays 2½m: dam ran twice: won bumper at Gowran in October: progressed into a fairly useful hurdler, winning maiden at Wexford in November and handicaps at Leopardstown in February and Punchestown (led run-in when beating Greywell ½ length) in March: good fourth to **h120** **F101**

High Prospect in valuable handicap at Fairyhouse final outing: will stay 2½m: acts on heavy and good to firm ground. *Oliver McKiernan, Ireland*

HEAR MY SONG (IRE) 7 b.g. Commanche Run – Pampered Finch VII (Damsire Unregistered) [2002/3 h–, F–: c17g May 1] lengthy gelding: little sign of ability. *J. S. King* — c–, h–, F–

HEARTACHE 6 b.g. Jurado (USA) – Heresy (IRE) (Black Minstrel) [2002/3 h–: 19f³ 19gᵖᵘ 16m Apr 22] tall gelding: apparently easily best effort over hurdles when third of 4 finishers in novice at Exeter, probably flattered: has worn cheekpieces. *R. Mathew* — h80 ?

HEART MIDLOTHIAN (FR) 6 gr.g. Royal Charter – Pride of Queen (FR) (Saint Henri (FR)) [2002/3 18s* 19s² 20s² 20d⁵ 20g* 20g⁴ c16v⁴ 24sᵖᵘ c20fᶠ c22g* Apr 20] medium-sized, long-necked gelding: has reportedly had wind operation: first foal: dam, lightly raced on Flat, half-sister to fairly useful French chaser around 2m Again The Queen (by Royal Charter): fairly useful hurdler, won novice at Navan in May and minor event at Cork in August: fairly useful form over fences, winning maiden at Fairyhouse and Grade 3 novice at Punchestown (beat Joly Bey 4 lengths) in April: stays 2¾m: acts on soft going: reportedly gurgled on chasing debut, tongue tied for last 2 wins: open to further improvement over fences. *Seamus Neville, Ireland* — c126 p, h115

HEATHERJACK 6 b.m. Nalchik (USA) – Healaughs Pride (Healaugh Fox) [2002/3 F17g Apr 21] second foal: dam of no account: well beaten in bumper on debut. *B. Mactaggart* — F–

HEATHER LAD 10 ch.g. Highlands – Ragged Rose (Scallywag) [2002/3 c20mᵖᵘ Jun 1] modest pointer, successful in May: reportedly lost action in hunter chase. *C. B. Taylor* — c–

HEATHYARDS ELEMENT 7 ch.g. Henbit (USA) – Moment's Pleasure (USA) (What A Pleasure (USA)) [2002/3 c–, h74: 20mᵖᵘ 16d⁶ Jul 5] well held both runs over fences: poor maiden hurdler: looked to finish lame final start (blinkered): stays 2½m: acts on firm and good to soft going. *D. McCain* — c–, h–

HEATHYARDS FRIEND 4 b.g. Forest Wind (USA) – Heathyards Lady (USA) (Mining (USA)) [2002/3 17d² 16g* 17d 16d Apr 9] leggy gelding: little sign of ability on Flat at 2 yrs: poor form over hurdles, won seller at Doncaster in December: looked hard ride both subsequent starts. *R. Hollinshead* — h76

HEATHYARDS GUEST (IRE) 5 ch.g. Be My Guest (USA) – Noble Nadia (Thatching) [2002/3 h69: 16m³ 16d⁴ 19d 17d⁶ Mar 18] workmanlike gelding: poor maiden hurdler: tried in cheekpieces. *Mrs K. Walton* — h69

HEATHYARDS MATE 6 b.g. Timeless Times (USA) – Quenlyn (Welsh Pageant) [2002/3 16g⁵ 16f 16dᵖᵘ Oct 23] smallish gelding: half-brother to 3 winning jumpers: poor on Flat (probably stays 11f), sold out of R. Hollinshead's stable 500 gns Doncaster August Sales: no form over hurdles. *R. J. Baker* — h–

HEATHYARDS TIPPLE (IRE) 7 b.m. Marju (IRE) – Nikki's Groom (Shy Groom (USA)) [2002/3 h88: 16m* 16m³ 17mᵖᵘ Jul 19] neat mare: poor handicap hurdler: won mares event at Hexham in June: shaped as if amiss final start: raced mainly around 2m: acts on firm and soft going: effective blinkered or not: sometimes looks none too keen. *D. McCain* — h80

HEAVENLY HILL 6 b.m. Nomadic Way (USA) – Tees Gazette Girl (Kalaglow) [2002/3 F–: F16g³ F16m Apr 21] strong mare: best effort in mares bumpers when third at Musselburgh in February: sold out of Mrs M. Reveley's stable 5,500 gns (privately) Doncaster March Sales. *M. J. Gingell* — F85

HEAVENLY KING 5 b.g. Homo Sapien – Chapel Hill (IRE) (The Parson) [2002/3 F17g⁶ 20vᵖᵘ 16dᵖᵘ 19dᵖᵘ Jan 27] quite good-topped gelding: second foal: half-brother to winning hurdler/chaser around 2m Heavenly Stride: dam modest 2½m hurdle winner: poor form in bumper on debut: pulled up in 3 novice hurdles. *P. Bowen* — h–, F73

HEAVENLY STRIDE 7 b.g. Karinga Bay – Chapel Hill (IRE) (The Parson) [2002/3 c103, h103: c16vᶠ c20v³ c16v* c16gᶠ Apr 3] lengthy gelding: fair handicap chaser: won at Sandown in March: should stay beyond 2m: acts well on heavy going: still has room for improvement in his jumping. *D. McCain* — c108, h–

HEDGEHUNTER (IRE) 7 b.g. Montelimar (USA) – Aberedw (IRE) (Caerwent) [2002/3 h116, F95: c20s² c22s² c20s³ c28s* c32g Mar 12] useful-looking gelding: fair hurdler: useful chaser: upped in trip, made all in fairly valuable handicap at Punchestown in February: travelling like winner when all but unseating 2 out in valuable amateur event at Cheltenham in March: sweating, good second to Rule Supreme in valuable novice — c134, h–

handicap at Punchestown in late-April: should stay 4m: raced on good going or softer (acts on heavy): has found little/hung right under pressure. *W. P. Mullins, Ireland*

HEIDI III (FR) 8 b.g. Bayolidaan (FR) – Irlandaise (FR) (Or de Chine) [2002/3 c133, h–: 22s⁶ c27d c25s² Dec 7] close-coupled gelding: winning hurdler: fairly useful handicap chaser: fitted with cheekpieces, easily best effort in 2002/3 when second at Wetherby (usually goes well there): stays 25f: acts on good to firm and heavy going: races prominently. *Mrs L. Williamson* — **c123 h–**

HELICAL GIRL 5 b.m. Presidium – Oubeck (Mummy's Game) [2002/3 16gᵖᵘ Aug 26] poor maiden on Flat (stays 8.5f), sold out of T. Clement's stable 900 gns Ascot July Sales: showed nothing on hurdling debut. *P. S. McEntee* — **h–**

HELIXIR DU THEIL (FR) 8 ch.g. Aelan Hapi (USA) – Manolette (FR) (Signani (FR)) [2002/3 h103: 24g⁴ 26g³ c26m⁴ c21m² Sep 13] workmanlike gelding: modest maiden hurdler: better effort over fences (lost all chance with bad mistake on debut) when second to Castle Folly in maiden at Southwell: suited by 3m+: acts on soft and good to firm going. *R. H. Buckler* — **c97 h95**

HELLO DEE 5 b.m. Alflora (IRE) – Donna Farina (Little Buskins) [2002/3 F16g³ F17g² Mar 15] half-sister to one-time fairly useful chaser Mountain Path, stays 3¼m, and winning pointer Don Royal (both by Rakaposhi King): dam, winning hurdler/chaser who stayed 2½m, half-sister to smart staying hurdler/chaser Realt Na Nova and useful hurdler up to 2½m The Hacienderos: placed in mares bumpers at Huntingdon and Market Rasen (carried head high). *Jonjo O'Neill* — **F85**

HELLO DE VAUXBUIN (FR) 8 b.g. Le Nain Jaune (FR) – Quadrille de Cuy (FR) (Baraban) [2002/3 c72, h–§: c24d* c20g³ c24dᶠ c26mᴿ 21g Oct 15] good-topped gelding: maiden hurdler: modest chaser: soon clear when winning handicap at Newcastle very early in season: placed in 2 points in April: stays 3m: acts on good to soft going: tried blinkered: needs to improve jumping over fences: ungenuine. *R. Ford* — **c86 § h– §**

HELL-OF-A-SHINDY (IRE) 9 b.g. Phardante (FR) – Tonto's Girl (Strong Gale) [2002/3 c104: c21g* c24v² 24s⁵ c21dᵖᵘ c24mᵖᵘ Mar 22] sturdy gelding: fair handicap chaser: won at Wincanton in November: disappointing over hurdles third start, reportedly amiss last 2: stays 3m: acts on any going: has had tongue tied: held up. *Jonjo O'Neill* — **c107 h–**

HELLO STRANGER (IRE) 7 gr.g. Roselier (FR) – Emily Bishop (IRE) (The Parson) [2002/3 20d Oct 23] IR 11,000 3-y-o, IR 16,000 4-y-o: rather leggy gelding: brother to winning Irish pointer and half-brother to another (by Moscow Society) and to bumper winner Sally Webster (by Norwich): dam unraced: placed on first of 2 starts in Irish points in 2002: shaped quite well when seventh of 16 in novice at Chepstow on hurdling debut: should improve. *A. M. Hales* — **h92 p**

HELMSLEY FLIER 9 ch.g. Sula Bula – Penair (Good Times (ITY)) [2002/3 c20m⁵ May 11] strong, plain gelding: maiden hurdler: modest pointer, won in February: stays 2½m: acts on good to firm and heavy going: tried tongue tied. *Miss Jenny Garley* — **c77 h–**

HELP YOURSELF (IRE) 7 gr.m. Roselier (FR) – Sweet Run (Deep Run) [2002/3 F87: 16g 20v 19s⁵ 17v 16d Feb 25] smallish, plain mare: won mares bumper on debut in 2001/2: well held in novice hurdles. *L. Lungo* — **h–**

HELVETIUS 7 b.g. In The Wings – Hejraan (USA) (Alydar (USA)) [2002/3 h84: 20d⁵ c21g* c21f² c25g⁵ c20m⁴ c22s² c24vᵖᵘ c22sᵖᵘ c22f³ Apr 24] leggy gelding: poor hurdler: fair novice chaser: fortunate to win at Newton Abbot in July: stays 2¾m: acts on any going: has worn cheekpieces. *P. C. Ritchens* — **c104 h–**

HEMSWORTHY 8 ch.g. North Col – Look Back (Country Retreat) [2002/3 20v Nov 27] tall, lengthy gelding: signs of ability in bumpers and on hurdling debut in 2000/1: well held in novice hurdle on return. *Miss M. Bragg* — **h–**

HENBIT'S PARTY 6 ch.m. Henbit (USA) – Bantel Bouquet (Red Regent) [2002/3 F–: F17g⁵ 16dᵖᵘ Nov 14] smallish mare: little sign of ability. *B. A. McMahon* — **h– F–**

HENBRIDGE 7 ch.m. Henbit (USA) – Celtic Bridge (Celtic Cone) [2002/3 h–: 16m⁶ 16mᶠ Jun 29] plain mare: bad maiden hurdler. *Mrs S. M. Johnson* — **h–**

HENDERSON 4 br.g. Wesaam (USA) – Akatombo (Ilium) [2002/3 16dᶠ Oct 26] well held in 4 maidens on Flat: well beaten when falling 2 out in juvenile on hurdling debut. *D. E. Cantillon* — **h–**

HENNA 5 ch.m. Henbit (USA) – Celtic Chimes (Celtic Cone) [2002/3 F17s F16g F18mᵖᵘ Mar 31] second foal: half-sister to 1998 2-y-o 6f winner Welsh Assembly (by — **F–**

Presidium): dam, little sign of ability on Flat, won 2m hurdle: tailed off in bumpers: wore cheekpieces final start. *G. P. Enright*

HENNERWOOD IVY   8 b.m. Tina's Pet – Come On Clover (Oats) [2002/3 F–: 16g^F 16m^{pu} Sep 7] sparely-made mare: no sign of ability. *R. J. Price*   **h–**

HENRIANJAMES   8 b.g. Tina's Pet – Real Claire (Dreams To Reality (USA)) [2002/3 c81, h–, F–: c16d^6 16d^2 c16s^F c17m^4 c17m c17s c17g^3 c16f^F c16g* c16m^2 c17m^3 Apr 21] strong gelding: modest form on second of 2 starts over hurdles: improved effort over fences when winning novice at Perth in September: raced around 2m: acts on firm and good to soft going. *Mrs M. Reveley*   **c101 h87**

HENRY BRUCE   11 ch.g. Buckley – Booterstown (Master Owen) [2002/3 c25d Feb 10] workmanlike gelding: useful hunter chaser in 2000: ran moody race at Hereford in February: stays 3¼m: acts on good to soft going, probably on soft: often blinkered/ visored: inconsistent. *Miss R. S. Reynolds*   **c– §**

HENRY ISAIAH (IRE)   6 b.g. Corrouge (USA) – Maid In The Mist (Pry) [2002/3 h–: c17d^{pu} c16d^F Dec 17] of no account. *C. Tizzard*   **c– h–**

HENRY PEARSON (USA)   5 ch.g. Distant View (USA) – Lady Ellen (USA) (Explosive Bid (USA)) [2002/3 h–: 16m Dec 17] workmanlike gelding: modest maiden on Flat (stays 1¼m): better effort over hurdles 11 months apart when seventh of 15 in novice at Musselburgh (tongue tied) in December. *H. P. Hogarth*   **h79**

HERA   6 b.m. Thethingaboutitis (USA) – Zalina (Tyrnavos) [2002/3 F17d F16m Apr 10] first foal: dam poor maiden on Flat/novice hurdler: well held in 2 bumpers. *M. Wellings*   **F–**

HERACLES   7 b.g. Unfuwain (USA) – La Masse (High Top) [2002/3 c113, h112: 18m^3 c20d* 20d^5 c21g* c23m* c21m^3 c21g^3 21d^4 Oct 26] leggy gelding: fair hurdler: similar form in novice chases, winning at Southwell in May, Newton Abbot in June and Worcester in July: stays 23f: acts on soft and good to firm going: let down by jumping seventh start. *B. G. Powell*   **c112 h112**

HERACLITEAN FIRE (IRE)   6 b.g. Norwich – Mazovia (FR) (Taufan (USA)) [2002/3 F16s 19s 16s 17d 16d^6 16d^5 16d^5 F16s 20s^4 Dec 14] workmanlike gelding: half-brother to winner around 7f in Italy by Fayruz: dam placed on Flat and over hurdles: modest form on second of 2 runs in bumpers: modest maiden hurdler: stays 2½m: raced only on good to soft/soft going: joined J. Lambe. *S. O'Farrell, Ireland*   **h90 F78**

HERE COMES HENRY   9 ch.g. Dortino – Epryana (English Prince) [2002/3 c–: c23g^5 c24s^2 c20d^2 c21d^{ur} c24d c26d^2 c28g^3 c24m^{pu} c24g^4 Apr 19] sturdy gelding: fair handicap chaser: probably best at 3m+: acts on heavy going: blinkered fifth start: usually let down by jumping. *R. H. Alner*   **c105 x**

HERE COMES STEVE   6 b.g. Primitive Rising (USA) – Keldholme (Derek H) [2002/3 F–: 20s^4 24d^3 16s^6 24v^2 Jan 29] big gelding: modest novice hurdler: will stay beyond 3m: raced on going softer than good (acts on heavy). *A. Crook*   **h95**

HERECOMESTANLEY   4 b.g. Missed Flight – Moonspell (Batshoof) [2002/3 F16d Mar 10] first foal: dam, lightly-raced maiden on Flat/well beaten in juvenile hurdles, out of half-sister to dam of very smart miler Fly To The Stars: well held in maiden bumper on debut. *M. F. Harris*   **F–**

HERESTHETHING   7 b.g. Thethingaboutitis (USA) – Chocolate Ripple (Hasty Word) [2002/3 19d^{pu} c24s^{ur} c19s^{pu} Mar 4] no sign of ability. *J. S. King*   **c– h–**

HERMES III (FR)   8 b.g. Quart de Vin (FR) – Queenly (FR) (Pot d'Or (FR)) [2002/3 c–, h110p: 20d* 20d* c20s* c21s^3 c20g^{pu} Mar 12] useful-looking gelding: fairly useful novice hurdler: easily landed odds at Wetherby in May and Perth in June: first start over fences in Britain, much better form when winning 4-runner handicap at Sandown in December: good third to Lady Cricket in valuable handicap at Cheltenham next time, beaten long way out final start: will stay beyond 21f: raced on good going or softer (acts on soft). *N. J. Henderson*   **c141 h116 +**

HERMIT'S HIDEAWAY   6 b.g. Rock City – Adriya (Vayrann) [2002/3 16d^{pu} Oct 31] modest on all-weather, poor on turf on Flat (stays 1½m), sold out of T. D. Barron's stable 5,100 gns Doncaster August Sales: pulled up in seller on hurdling debut: dead. *Mrs A. M. Thorpe*   **h–**

HERNANDITA   5 b.m. Hernando (FR) – Dara Dee (Dara Monarch) [2002/3 h107: 19s 16s 25s^{pu} Jan 23] small, leggy mare: made all in juvenile and mares novice in 2001/2   **h–**

on first 2 starts over hurdles, disappointing since: should stay beyond 2m: acts on heavy going: visored (raced too freely) once: not an easy ride. *M. C. Pipe*

HEROICUS (NZ) 6 ch.g. Heroicity (AUS) – Glenford (NZ) (Sackford (USA)) [2002/3 **h–** h–, F68: 16m⁶ 17gᵖᵘ 16vᵖᵘ 16d 17d 16g Mar 29] no form over hurdles: headstrong. *F. Kirby*

HERON'S GHYLL (IRE) 6 b.g. Simply Great (FR) – Leisure Centre (IRE) (Tan- **F99** firion) [2002/3 F17s² F18s⁵ F17d* Feb 23] 7,500 3-y-o: has reportedly had wind operation: first foal: dam, placed in Irish bumpers, half-sister to smart hurdler/chaser up to 25f Castle Sweep: well-backed favourite, belatedly confirmed debut promise when winning maiden bumper at Hereford by short head from Krzyszkowiak. *Miss Venetia Williams*

HERONSTOWN (IRE) 4 b.g. Standiford (USA) – Eleckydo (Electric) [2002/3 F13s **h101** 16s² 16s⁴ Feb 26] third foal: dam, poor maiden on Flat/over hurdles, half-sister to useful **F–** sprinter Great Deeds and smart 1¼m winner Busaco: never dangerous in bumper on debut: fair form when in frame in 2 juvenile maiden hurdles. *William Coleman O'Brien, Ireland*

HERSELF 6 b.m. Hernando (FR) – Kirsten (Kris) [2002/3 h99: 24s⁵ Nov 8] leggy **h–** mare: modest handicap hurdler: stays 2¾m: acts on heavy going: usually tongue tied (not when well held only start in 2002/3): consistent. *J. Mackie*

HERSILIA (IRE) 12 br.m. Mandalus – Milan Pride (Northern Guest (USA)) [2002/3 **c79** c–, h79: 24g³ c24d² 27g³ 27m⁶ Jul 17] fair hurdler/chaser at best, poor nowadays: stays **h80** 27f: acts on soft going: tried blinkered. *R. Ford*

HERSOV (IRE) 7 gr.g. Roselier (FR) – Higher Again (IRE) (Strong Gale) [2002/3 **c115** h122p: c23g* c24s* c24g⁴ Feb 8] rangy gelding: fairly useful form in novice hurdles in **h–** 2001/2: successful first 2 outings over fences, in maiden at Leicester in December and novice at Kempton in January: ran as if all wasn't well final start: will stay beyond 3m: acts on soft ground. *N. J. Henderson*

HE'S A RASCAL (IRE) 5 b.g. Fumo di Londra (IRE) – Lovely Ali (IRE) (Dunbeath **c–** (USA)) [2002/3 16m 16d⁴ 16d 16d⁵ 22dᵖᵘ c21s c26sᶠ Mar 2] compact gelding: little form **h–** on Flat for H. Morrison: flattered when fourth in novice hurdle at Chepstow in October: no form otherwise over jumps: tried blinkered/in cheekpieces. *Jean-Rene Auvray*

HESK (FR) 8 b.g. Spoleto – Negrilla (FR) (Signani (FR)) [2002/3 c17mᵖᵘ Sep 7] **c–** lengthy gelding: successful in 4 novice chases in 2000/1: fell heavily final outing that **h–** season, pulled up in handicap on return: may prove best around 2m: acts on good to firm and heavy going: takes good hold. *M. C. Pipe*

HE'S MY UNCLE 8 ch.g. Phardante (FR) – Red Dusk (Deep Run) [2002/3 h–, F–: **h–** 16dᵖᵘ Mar 7] strong gelding: no sign of ability. *Mrs J. K. M. Oliver*

HE'S THE BIZ (FR) 4 b.g. Nikos – Irun (FR) (Son of Silver) [2002/3 F12d 16d **h72 ?** 16d⁶ 16v⁵ 17dᵖᵘ Feb 10] good-topped gelding: third foal: half-brother to winning hurdler/ **F–** chaser around 2m Irun Speed (by Mansonnien): dam winning hurdler: signs of only a little ability. *Nick Williams*

HE'S THE BOSS (IRE) 6 b.g. Supreme Leader – Attykee (IRE) (Le Moss) [2002/3 **F116** F104: F16v² F16g⁶ F16g Mar 12] workmanlike gelding: smart bumper performer: best effort when second to Control Man in Grade 2 at Chepstow on reappearance: unsuited by less testing conditions both subsequent starts: will be very well suited by further than 2m. *R. H. Buckler*

HETLAND HILL 7 ch.g. Secret Appeal – Mohibbah (USA) (Conquistador Cielo **F86** (USA)) [2002/3 F17d³ F16g⁶ Dec 28] sixth foal: brother to modest 2m hurdler Park Royal and 6f/7f winner Secret Conquest: dam fairly useful 2-y-o 5f winner: travelled comfort- ably long way both starts in bumpers, better effort when third in maiden at Sedgefield. *L. Lungo*

HEVER GOLF GLORY 9 b.g. Efisio – Zaius (Artaius (USA)) [2002/3 h65: 16m **h–** Apr 21] signs of only a little ability over hurdles, off nearly 2 years before reappearance: raced mainly around 2m. *C. N. Kellett*

HEYNESTOWN PRIDE (IRE) 6 ch.m. Zaffaran (USA) – Mayobridge (Our **h–** Mirage) [2002/3 F16s F18s F16s F16s 21s⁵ 20g⁶ Apr 23] ex-Irish mare: fourth foal: **F–** half-sister to Irish bumper winner Bridges Daughter (by Montelimar): dam useful hurdler, stayed 3m: no form in bumpers for P. Boyle: signs of a little ability in 2 races over hurdles. *N. G. Richards*

HEY REF (IRE) 6 b.g. King's Ride – Jeanarie (Reformed Character) [2002/3 F–: F17d* 20s⁴ 16s* Feb 8] good-bodied gelding: much better effort in bumpers when winning at Carlisle in October: dropped back in trip, impressive winner on second of 2 starts in novice hurdles at Haydock: open to further progress. *Jonjo O'Neill* **h114 p F101**

HI BUDDY 6 br.g. High Kicker (USA) – Star Thyme (Point North) [2002/3 h86: 16mᶠ 20s⁴ 16g 16v³ 17m Jun 22] tall gelding: poor maiden hurdler/pointer: likely to prove best around 2m: acts on heavy (below form all 3 starts on good or firmer): usually blinkered/visored. *J. Mackie* **h81**

HICKEY'S GIFT (IRE) 7 ch.g. Over The River (FR) – Chorabelle (Choral Society) [2002/3 h–, F78: 21f* 22m Jun 14] won weak novice at Warwick in May on second start over hurdles, carrying head awkwardly: well beaten in handicap month later. *R. H. Alner* **h87**

HICKLETON CLUB 5 b.g. Aragon – Honest Opinion (Free State) [2002/3 F16g Dec 28] half-brother to several winners on Flat, including 7f/1m winner Hickleton Lady (by Kala Shikiri): dam 5f 2-y-o winner: beaten long way in bumper on debut: not bred to stay 2m: sold 3,000 gns Doncaster January Sales. *G. A. Swinbank* **F–**

HI CLOY (IRE) 6 b.g. Be My Native (USA) – Thomastown Girl (Tekoah) [2002/3 F16s² F18s³ 16s* 20s* 18s⁴ 20d⁴ 21gᶠ Mar 12] rangy gelding: chasing type: half-brother to 4 winners, including fairly useful 2m hurdler/winning chaser Doran's Town Lad (by Tumble Gold) and fairly useful chaser up to 25f Hawaiian Sam (by Hawaiian Return): dam, bumper winner, half-sister to 1982 Champion Hurdle winner For Auction: won second of 2 outings in maiden points in 2002: useful at best in bumpers: won maiden at Leopardstown in December and minor event there in January on first 2 starts over hurdles: appeared to excel himself when fourth to Solerina in 2¼m Grade 1 novice at Leopardstown: just fairly useful form subsequently, fifth to Nobody Told Me in Grade 1 novice at Punchestown in early-May: will stay beyond 2½m: raced on good going or softer (acts on soft). *Michael Hourigan, Ireland* **h120 + F106**

HIDDEN AFFAIR (IRE) 7 b.g. Mandalus – Lovely Affair (IRE) (Roselier (FR)) [2002/3 22dᵖᵘ 20dᵖᵘ 22v⁶ 17d⁴ 17dᵖᵘ Feb 23] angular gelding: won maiden Irish point in 2000, let down by jumping on steeplechasing debut: poor novice hurdler: blinkered last 3 starts. *C. J. Mann* **c– h77**

HIDDEN EXIT 7 b.m. Landyap (USA) – Queen of The Nile (Hittite Glory) [2002/3 F–: F16m⁴ 16m⁵ 17m³ 16m⁴ 17d⁵ 17s⁶ Oct 28] leggy mare: signs of only a little ability in bumpers and over hurdles. *Mrs L. Williamson* **h– F–**

HIDDEN PEARL (IRE) 7 b.g. Posen (USA) – Cockney Miss (Camden Town) [2002/3 h–: 21d⁵ 23g⁵ 16d⁶ 19s³ 17s 22g Mar 29] big gelding: poor maiden hurdler: left F. Murphy before final start: probably stays 23f: acts on soft going: has worn cheekpieces. *J. A. Supple* **h60**

HIDDEN SMILE (USA) 6 b.m. Twilight Agenda (USA) – Smooth Edge (USA) (Meadowlake (USA)) [2002/3 20m 16dᵖᵘ Nov 12] tall mare: poor on Flat (stays 1m): no show in 2 novice hurdles. *F. Jordan* **h–**

HIDDEN VALLEY 11 b.g. St Columbus – Leven Valley (Ragstone) [2002/3 c107, h–: c23gᵖᵘ c23g⁶ c20d² c19s² c24sᵖᵘ Feb 13] leggy gelding: fair handicap chaser: good efforts when runner-up at Warwick in November and Taunton in January: stays 2¾m: has won on good to firm going, best efforts on soft/heavy: has won 4 times at Exeter. *J. D. Frost* **c107 h–**

HIERS DE BROUAGE (FR) 8 b.g. Neustrien (FR) – Thalandrezienne (FR) (Le Correzien (FR)) [2002/3 c91?, h–: c19s³ c21d* c24s c20sᵖᵘ c19g* Mar 18] tall, rangy gelding: fair handicap chaser: won at Wincanton in December and Exeter in March: stays 21f: raced on good going or softer (acts on soft). *J. G. Portman* **c105 h–**

HI FI 5 b.g. Homo Sapien – Baroness Orkzy (Baron Blakeney) [2002/3 F16g 17s⁴ 19d⁴ 19s 22g⁶ 19m⁵ Apr 21] third foal: dam winning chaser around 2m: eighth in bumper at Worcester on debut: poor novice hurdler: stays 19f: acts on soft ground. *Ian Williams* **h81 F81**

HIFINANBA 7 gr.m. Gran Alba (USA) – High Finesse (High Line) [2002/3 h–§, F73§: 16g³ 19m⁴ 16g² 19v⁶ c19dʳᵗʳ Jan 16] poor maiden hurdler: refused to race on chasing debut (did same once in bumpers): best form around 2m: acts on good to firm and heavy going: not one to trust. *J. W. Mullins* **c– § h73 §**

HIGH AND MIGHTY 8 b.g. Shirley Heights – Air Distingue (USA) (Sir Ivor) [2002/3 16d³ 19dᵖᵘ Jan 13] useful at best on Flat (stays 2½m well): not fluent when third in novice at Haydock on hurdling debut: wearing cheekpieces, ran no sort of race in similar event at Newcastle month later: should be suited by further than 2m. *G. Barnett* **h94**

HIGHBANK 11 b.g. Puissance – Highland Daisy (He Loves Me) [2002/3 c–§, h97§: 16m 19d 19s 17s 16d 19d³ 17g* 20g 17m³ Apr 21] workmanlike gelding: winning chaser: modest hurdler: won selling handicap at Market Rasen in March: stays 21f: acts on firm and soft going: effective with or without blinkers, below form when visored fifth and sixth starts: has looked reluctant: unreliable. *Mrs M. Reveley* **c– §** **h87 §**

HIGHBEATH 12 b.g. Dunbeath (USA) – Singing High (Julio Mariner) [2002/3 c89§, h–: c22m c21m c16m c21m^pu Aug 12] poor handicap chaser nowadays: stays 2¾m: acts on firm and good to soft going: none too keen. *N. Wilson* **c– §** **h–**

HIGH CHEVIOT 6 b.g. Shirley Heights – Cutleaf (Kris) [2002/3 h89: 16m⁴ 22s² 20m⁵ 20d 20m³ 19v⁵ 19d^pu 16g Mar 14] modest maiden hurdler: seems barely to stay 2¾m when conditions are testing: acts on soft and good to firm going: tried in blinkers/cheekpieces. *Ferdy Murphy* **h89**

HIGH COTTON (IRE) 8 gr.g. Ala Hounak – Planalife (Beau Charmeur (FR)) [2002/3 c115, h99: c19s² c24d⁴ c33v⁴ c24g² c25d⁴ c32g⁴ c24g^pu Apr 2] useful-looking gelding: fairly useful maiden chaser, often highly tried: suited by 3m+: raced on good going or softer (acts on heavy): blinkered fifth start: has looked ungenuine and one to treat with caution. *D. R. C. Elsworth* **c119 §** **h–**

HIGHCROFT BOY 8 gr.g. Silver Owl – Caroline Ranger (Pony Express) [2002/3 F82: 22f* c23d² 22f² Apr 21] runner-up only start in bumpers: off a year, won at Wincanton in May, better effort in novice hurdles: jumped right when second in novice at Worcester on chasing debut: presumably not easy to train. *P. J. Hobbs* **c89** **h102**

HIGH DRAMA 6 b.g. In The Wings – Maestrale (Top Ville) [2002/3 22f³ 17f³ 22m² 24s^pu 20d^pu 22d 21g* Mar 25] modest on Flat (seems best up to 2m), sold out of A. Crook's stable 2,700 gns Doncaster August Sales: fair novice hurdler: made all in amateur event at Sedgefield: stays 2¾m: acts on firm going. *P. Bowen* **h104**

HIGH EXPECTATIONS (IRE) 8 ch.g. Over The River (FR) – Andy's Fancy (IRE) (Andretti) [2002/3 c–: c25d c25g⁴ Apr 7] fair pointer, won in March: best effort in hunter chases when fourth in maiden at Kelso: stays 25f. *J. S. Haldane* **c83**

HIGH FIELDS 4 b.g. Sovereign Water (FR) – Once Bitten (Brave Invader (USA)) [2002/3 F16d³ F16m F17g Apr 21] eleventh foal: half-brother to fair hurdler Carrick Lanes (by Oats), stayed 3¼m, and bumper/point winner Celtic Park (by Celtic Cone): dam, winning hurdler, half-sister to useful chaser up to 3m Greenwood Lad: poor form in bumpers: looks a stayer. *M. W. Easterby* **F73**

HIGH GREEN 11 b.g. Green Adventure (USA) – High Affair (High Line) [2002/3 c–: c24m^pu Jun 3] lengthy gelding: winning pointer: no encouragement in steeplechases: tried blinkered. *J. L. Spearing* **c–**

HIGH HOPE (FR) 5 ch.h. Lomitas – Highness Lady (GER) (Cagliostro (GER)) [2002/3 16g⁴ 16g⁶ Feb 8] leggy ex-French horse: useful on Flat (stays 15f), successful twice in 2002 for R. Gibson: fair form over hurdles in maiden and novice at Newbury, pulling hard and less than fluent in latter. *G. L. Moore* **h107**

HIGHLAND DANCER (IRE) 4 b.g. Barathea (IRE) – Dancer Tully (USA) (Seattle Dancer (USA)) [2002/3 F12d 16d^pu 24v^pu 19d 26m^pu Apr 5] 10,000Y, 1,500 3-y-o: first foal: dam, Italian 9f to 11f winner, half-sister to Oaks third Crown of Light: no sign of ability: tried blinkered: sold 950 gns Doncaster May Sales. *C. N. Kellett* **h–** **F–**

HIGHLAND MONARCH 10 b.g. Super Sunrise – Highland Chance (Bronze Hill) [2002/3 c–: c20m^F c25d^pu Mar 1] modest pointer: no form in hunters: has had tongue tied. *C. Storey* **c–**

HIGHLAND ROSE (IRE) 7 b.m. Roselier (FR) – Carrick Grinder (Sheer Grit) [2002/3 h84, F62: c16m^pu 19d^F 22v 16d Feb 26] workmanlike mare: no show on chasing debut: modest hurdler: bred to stay at least 2½m: acts on good to soft going: inconsistent. *Ms A. E. Embiricos* **c–** **h91**

HIGH LEARIE 13 b.g. Petoski – Lady Doubloon (Pieces of Eight) [2002/3 c–, h–: c25m⁵ May 22] workmanlike gelding: winning chaser, little worthwhile form outside points since 1998/9: often blinkered. *Mrs D. M. Grissell* **c–** **h–**

HIGH MOOD 13 b.g. Jalmood (USA) – Copt Hall Princess (Crowned Prince (USA)) [2002/3 c100, h–: c22d^pu Feb 8] sturdy gelding: fair chaser at best: won point in April: stays 3¼m: acts on heavy going: makes mistakes. *Mrs J. A. Wall* **c–** **h–**

HIGH PADDY 4 b.g. Master Willie – Ivy Edith (Blakeney) [2002/3 17m⁴ Apr 16] lengthy, rather sparely-made gelding: dam fairly useful 2m hurdler: lightly-raced maiden **h90**

on Flat: nearest finish when fourth to Bal de Nuit in juvenile at Cheltenham on hurdling debut. *R. Ingram*

HIGH PEAK 6 b.g. Alflora (IRE) – High Heels (IRE) (Supreme Leader) [2002/3 h79, F80: 16g 17d6 20d 16g3 16g 20g2 19g4 22g Mar 29] sturdy gelding: poor maiden hurdler: probably stays 2½m: raced on good going or softer: visored last 3 starts. *C. Grant* **h83**

HIGH PLACES 5 b.g. Shirley Heights – Fajjoura (IRE) (Fairy King (USA)) [2002/3 F99: F16g F16g Apr 14] second in maiden bumper at Huntingdon on debut: off nearly a year, most disappointing in similar events on return. *G. A. Swinbank* **F–**

HIGHPOINT (GER) 5 b.m. Acatenango (GER) – Holly (GER) (Cortez (GER)) [2002/3 19d 20v 20v4 Mar 3] leggy, useful-looking ex-German mare: successful 3 times up to 1¼m on Flat in 2002, sold out of A. Wohler's stable 28,000 gns Newmarket Autumn Sales: best effort over hurdles when fourth in maiden at Fontwell: will be at least as effective given less of a test. *Mrs L. Wadham* **h86**

HIGH PROSPECT (IRE) 5 b.g. Lycius (USA) – Pay The Bank (High Top) [2002/3 18d4 17sF 16g6 18m* 16m* Apr 22] fair on Flat (stays 2m): fair hurdler: won maiden at Downpatrick in May and handicaps at Thurles and Fairyhouse (Powers Gold Label Handicap Hurdle, beat Junior Fontaine ½ length) in April: will stay 2½m: acts on good to firm and good to soft going. *Paul Nolan, Ireland* **h108 +**

HIGH RATIO (NZ) 7 b.g. Classic Fame (USA) – Ginevra (NZ) (Alvaro) [2002/3 h–: 16mpu Jun 1] useful-looking gelding: little form over hurdles: has bled from nose. *A. King* **h–**

HIGH ROCKER 5 b.g. First Trump – Wild Abandon (USA) (Graustark) [2002/3 F16d F16d Mar 6] compact gelding: half-brother to several winners, including fairly useful 9.4f winner Astronaut (by Sri Pekan) and Irish 7f winner Sweet Ciseaux (by Be My Guest), latter poor staying hurdler: dam, ran once in USA, from family of Shareef Dancer: seventh of 16 in bumper at Wincanton on debut: tongue tied: soundly beaten in similar event there next time. *M. C. Pipe* **F91**

HIGH STURT 9 b.m. Petoski – Barge Mistress (Bargello) [2002/3 c21mF May 22] poor pointer, successful in April: tried blinkered: has had tongue tied. *J. W. Dufosee* **c–**

HIGH SUN 7 b.g. High Estate – Clyde Goddess (IRE) (Scottish Reel) [2002/3 h–: 20gpu Sep 14] modest up to 1¼m on Flat, sold out of P. Monteith's stable 2,600 gns Doncaster August Sales: no form over hurdles. *Mrs A. M. Thorpe* **h–**

HIGH THYNE (IRE) 12 b.g. Good Thyne (USA) – Annie Buskins (Little Buskins) [2002/3 c25dpu May 13] lengthy gelding: temperamental maiden chaser: stays 25f: acts on soft and good to firm going: often blinkered: has had tongue tied: none too fluent a jumper. *P. C. Shires* **c– §**
h–

HIGHWAY ROBBERY 6 b.g. Un Desperado (FR) – Drivers Bureau (Proverb) [2002/3 F16d6 16d7 19gpu Dec 18] IR £26,000 4-y-o: useful-looking gelding, unfurnished at present: good walker: fifth foal: brother to winning hurdler up to 25f The Kew Tour and half-brother to winning pointer by Town And Country: dam placed in bumper: caught the eye when sixth of 16 in bumper at Chepstow on debut: failed to complete both outings over hurdles. *Miss E. C. Lavelle* **h–**
F85

HIJACKED 9 b.g. True Song – Scamper (Abwah) [2002/3 c23gpu c26vpu c19d6 c29g Mar 14] poor pointer. *A. Hollingsworth* **c–**

HI JAMIE (IRE) 11 b.g. Parliament – Lilo Lil (Dunphy) [2002/3 20d c24g c19f6 17s Nov 26] leggy ex-Irish gelding: maiden hurdler: winning chaser: no worthwhile form in 2002/3, left J. Cromwell prior to final start: tried blinkered. *F. P. Murtagh* **c–**
h–

HI LILY 7 b.m. Jupiter Island – By Line (High Line) [2002/3 F–: 16mpu 16g2 16v2 20m3 c21dpu 16d2 c20d2 c25vpu c20g c20m* c21gpu c20m2 Apr 19] tall mare: modest novice hurdler: poor chaser: won weakly-contested conditional jockeys handicap at Southwell in March: stays 2½m: unraced on firm going, acts on any other. *C. C. Bealby* **c81**
h85

HILL CHARM 5 ch.m. Minster Son – Snarry Hill (Vitiges (FR)) [2002/3 F–: F16g 16gpu Jun 15] little sign of ability in 2 bumpers and novice hurdle. *C. Grant* **h–**
F–

HILL FORTS HENRY 5 ch.g. Karinga Bay – Maggie Tee (Lepanto (GER)) [2002/3 F17s5 F18v 17sF 16d Mar 6] first foal: dam poor 2m novice hurdler: signs of only a little ability in bumpers and maiden hurdles. *J. W. Mullins* **h–**
F67

HILL MAGIC 8 br.g. Magic Ring (IRE) – Stock Hill Lass (Air Trooper) [2002/3 17s Nov 28] fair on Flat (stays 1m): shaped like non-stayer in maiden on hurdling debut: joined W. Kittow. *L. G. Cottrell* **h–**

HILLTOP HARRY (IRE) 6 b.g. Commanche Run – Whats In A Name (IRE) (Le Moss) [2002/3 F16v⁵ 24s⁵ 25g³ Mar 14] IR 4,800 3-y-o: sturdy gelding: fourth foal: brother to winning pointer and half-brother to fairly useful hurdler/promising chaser Another General (by Glacial Storm), stays 25f: dam unraced, from good jumping family: won second of 2 starts in maiden Irish points in 2002: bought 24,000 gns Doncaster May Sales: fifth in bumper at Uttoxeter: poor form in 2 novice hurdles. *Lady Connell* **h84 F82**

HIMALAYAN BLUE 11 b.g. Hallgate – Orange Parade (Dara Monarch) [2002/3 c–, h–: c20m² c20gᵘʳ c20mᵖᵘ c20sᵖᵘ Jul 20] sturdy gelding: very lightly raced and little worthwhile form over hurdles: second only completed start in novice chases: lame final outing: stays 2½m: acts on good to firm going. *P. Beaumont* **c90 h–**

HIM OF PRAISE (IRE) 13 b.g. Paean – Tamed (Rusticaro (FR)) [2002/3 c95§, h–: c26d⁴ Feb 17] lengthy gelding: one-time smart staying chaser, very difficult ride and nowhere near so good nowadays: tried visored/blinkered/in cheekpieces: ungenuine. *Simon Bloss* **c– § h–**

HINT OF MAGIC 6 b.g. Magic Ring (IRE) – Thames Glow (Kalaglow) [2002/3 h–: 19gᵖᵘ 17s⁶ 16d⁴ 16m Apr 2] good-topped gelding: fair but unreliable on Flat (stays 1¼m): no worthwhile form in selling hurdles. *H. W. Lavis* **h–**

HIP POCKET (IRE) 7 b.g. Ela-Mana-Mou – Ebony And Ivory (IRE) (Bob Back (USA)) [2002/3 20dᶠ 20s³ 21d⁵ Nov 15] close-coupled gelding: half-brother to winning Irish 2m hurdler Pianissimo (by Shernazar): modest stayer on Flat: fair hurdler: improved performer upped in trip in handicaps in 2002/3: will stay beyond 21f: acts on soft going: tried blinkered. *D. K. Weld, Ireland* **h114**

HIRAPOUR (IRE) 7 b.g. Kahyasi – Himaya (IRE) (Mouktar) [2002/3 16d⁴ 19d² 20v³ 21m⁴ 17m* 20g* Apr 24] workmanlike gelding: half-brother to one-time fairly useful 2m chaser Hisar (by Doyoun): useful at best on Flat (stays 2¼m), sold out of Mrs A. Perrett's stable 11,000 gns Newmarket Autumn Sales: progressive over hurdles, won conditional jockeys handicaps at Ludlow (novice), Exeter and Perth (eased when beating Scarletti 9 lengths, useful form) in April: will stay beyond 21f: acts on good to firm and good to soft going. *Ian Williams* **h130**

HIRAYNA 4 b.f. Doyoun – Himaya (IRE) (Mouktar) [2002/3 F14d Nov 26] leggy filly: sixth foal: sister to one-time fairly useful 2m chaser Hisar and half-sister to progressive hurdler Hirapour (by Kahyasi): dam, runner-up at 1½m from 2 starts in Ireland, daughter of Prix Vermeille winner Highest Hopes: ninth of 18 in bumper on debut. *W. M. Brisbourne* **F–**

HIRT LODGE 12 ch.g. Jumbo Hirt (USA) – Holly Lodge (Rubor) [2002/3 22g³ 22s 22d⁴ 22v⁶ 22v⁶ 24vᵖᵘ 20d Mar 2] modest hurdler, off 3 years before reappearance: won conditional jockeys novice handicap at Kelso in November: out of sorts subsequently: stays 3m: raced only on good going or softer (acts on heavy). *J. E. Dixon* **h90**

HI RUDOLF 8 b.g. Ballet Royal (USA) – Hi Darlin' (Prince de Galles) [2002/3 c83, h67: c25g⁵ c19d³ 22v⁵ c21vᶠ c17sᵖᵘ c20sᵖᵘ c20s* c19dᶠ Mar 19] small gelding: poor chaser/maiden hurdler: won weak novice over fences at Fontwell in March: still going well when falling 5 out at Chepstow later in month: stays 25f: acts on soft and good to firm going. *H. J. Manners* **c86 h–**

HIRVINE (FR) 5 ch.g. Snurge – Guadanella (FR) (Guadanini (FR)) [2002/3 27v³ 20vᶠ Feb 8] good-topped gelding: fair maiden on Flat (will stay at least 1¾m): poor form in 2 novice hurdles: may do better if jumping improves. *T. P. Tate* **h80**

HISAR (IRE) 10 br.g. Doyoun – Himaya (IRE) (Mouktar) [2002/3 c116, h–: c17m³ c20m³ c16d c16g⁴ c16f³ Apr 21] leggy gelding: winning hurdler: fairly useful handicap chaser in 2001/2, has lost his form: suited by sharp 2m: acts on soft and firm going: races freely up with pace. *P. C. Ritchens* **c– h–**

HIS NIBS (IRE) 6 b.g. Alflora (IRE) – Mrs Jennifer (River Knight (FR)) [2002/3 F101: 17s* 17s³ 21s³ 20vᵖᵘ Mar 8] medium-sized gelding: bumper winner: successful in novice at Folkestone on hurdling debut in December: similar form when third in handicaps at Cheltenham (novice) and Newbury: stays 21f: acts on soft ground, ran poorly on heavy. *Miss Venetia Williams* **h112**

HIS SONG (IRE) 10 ch.g. Accordion – Pampered Finch VII (Damsire Unregistered) [2002/3 c–, h–: 17d 24s³ 21d⁴ Jan 18] strong gelding: formerly useful chaser/smart hurdler: reportedly suffered hairline fracture final outing in 2000/1: showed himself still capable of fairly useful form over hurdles last 2 starts, including when fourth of 13 to Il Cavaliere in handicap at Kempton: stays 3m: best form on good going or softer (acts on heavy): blinkered once: usually tongue tied prior to 2002/3. *N. J. Henderson* **c– h122**

HISTORG (FR)   8 b.g. Cyborg (FR) – Kalliste (FR) (Calicot (FR)) [2002/3 c125, h–:   **c127** c25v³ c25d² c26s* c28v³ c24m⁶ c24g⁶ Mar 11] leggy, useful-looking gelding: fairly   **h–** useful handicap chaser: won at Cheltenham in December by 7 lengths from Southern Star: creditable efforts in valuable events at Kempton and Cheltenham last 2 starts, 5 lb out of weights when sixth to Youlneverwalkalone at latter: suited by 3m+: acts on heavy and good to firm going: sound jumper. *Ferdy Murphy*

HIT AND RUN (FR)   8 ch.g. River Mist (USA) – La Dunanerie (FR) (Guadanini   **c114 +** (FR)) [2002/3 c125, h–: c16f³ c16m* c20m⁵ 20mᵖᵘ Aug 26] leggy gelding: smart handi-   **h–** cap hurdler at best: fairly useful over fences: easily landed odds in 6-runner intermediate event at Hereford in June: reportedly lame final outing: best around 2m: has won on good to firm going, best efforts on good or softer (acts on soft): usually blinkered/visored, has won when not: has run well when sweating: usually forces pace: tends to jump right over fences. *M. C. Pipe*

HITCHHIKER   9 b.g. Picea – Lady Lax (Henbit (USA)) [2002/3 c–x, h–: c20mᵖᵘ   **c67 x** c21s² c24s⁴ c20g⁵ c24gᵘʳ c24s c20mᶠ Mar 18] plain gelding: poor chaser: stays 25f: acts   **h–** on good to firm and heavy going: tried blinkered: poor jumper: weak finisher. *R. Ford*

HI TECH   4 b.g. Polar Falcon (USA) – Just Speculation (IRE) (Ahonoora) [2002/3   **h69** 16m 16dᵖᵘ 17v⁶ 16v⁵ 17v⁴ 16dᵖᵘ Apr 9] smallish, angular gelding: poor form in 7f maidens on Flat, sold out of W. Jarvis' stable 900 gns Doncaster August Sales: whipped round and lost 10 lengths at start when fourth in seller at Taunton, only form over hurdles. *Dr P. Pritchard*

HI TEK   8 ch.m. Arzanni – Storm Foot (Import) [2002/3 h62: 26g⁶ 24mᵖᵘ Jun 29]   **h–** sparely-made mare: poor maiden hurdler: stays 2¾m: acts on firm going: tried blinkered. *Mrs A. C. Tate*

HITMAN HERONS (IRE)   7 ch.g. Glacial Storm (USA) – Popular View (Torus)   **F75** [2002/3 F16g⁵ F17g⁴ Oct 6] 4,000 4-y-o: sturdy gelding: sixth foal: dam unraced, out of half-sister to smart 2m hurdler/useful staying chaser Interview II: poor form in bumpers at Worcester and Market Rasen: joined M. Hammond. *J. L. Spearing*

HITMAN (IRE)   8 b.g. Contract Law (USA) – Loveville (USA) (Assert) [2002/3   **c112 x** h125: c18sᶠ c16v³ c16gᶠ c19gᵖᵘ 16m⁴ Apr 12] well-made gelding: impresses in   **h–** appearance: fairly useful hurdler, very stiff task final outing: fair novice chaser: made all in 3-finisher event at Warwick in January: let down by jumping otherwise over fences: not sure to stay much beyond 2m: raced mainly on good going or softer: blinkered fifth start. *M. Pitman*

HIT ROYAL (FR)   8 ch.g. Montorselli – Valse Royale (FR) (Cap Martin (FR))   **c106** [2002/3 c94, h90: c16g* c17g* c20d⁴ c18g⁵ Dec 18] workmanlike gelding: winning   **h–** hurdler: fair chaser: left G. McCourt, won handicaps at Huntingdon in August and Market Rasen (beat Mighty Strong short head) in September: struggled after off higher mark: successful at 3m, best form around 2m: raced on good going or softer (acts on heavy). *P. R. Webber*

HIT THE NET (IRE)   6 b. or br.h. Be My Native (USA) – Thetravellinglady (IRE)   **F104** (Callernish) [2002/3 F104: F16s* F16d² Feb 23] good sort: fairly useful form in bumpers, winning maiden at Limerick in December: 2 lengths second to John Oliver at Naas next time. *T. Stack, Ireland*

HIYAH (IRE)   4 ch.g. Petardia – Stairway To Heaven (IRE) (Godswalk (USA)) [2002/3   **h81** 16mᵖᵘ 17g 16m 16d 16m* Apr 21] good-topped gelding: has been hobdayed: fifth foal: half-brother to winning 17f selling hurdler Risky Flight (by Risk Me): dam, won on Flat up to 1m, half-sister to Supreme Novices' Hurdle winner Indefence: first form when winning 2-finisher juvenile hurdle at Plumpton: will prove best around 2m: blinkered last 3 starts (reportedly had breathing problem on first): has looked temperamental. *John R. Upson*

HOBART JUNCTION (IRE)   8 ch.g. Classic Secret (USA) – Art Duo (Artaius   **h67** (USA)) [2002/3 h74: 16m 20m³ 22dᵖᵘ 19f² 24fᵘʳ Apr 3] lengthy gelding: poor hurdler: stays 19f: acts on firm and good to soft going: tried blinkered: has broken blood vessels. *J. A. T. de Giles*

HOBBYCYR (FR)   8 b.g. Saint Cyrien (FR) – Sauteuse de Retz (FR) (Funny Hobby)   **c83** [2002/3 c96, h–: c16gᵖᵘ c25fᵖᵘ c26s⁴ May 28] tall gelding: winning hurdler/chaser, ran   **h–** as if amiss first 2 starts: fair pointer, successful in February: stays 3m: acts on soft going. *R. Kelvin-Hughes*

HOH INVADER (IRE)   11 b.g. Accordion – Newgate Fairy (Flair Path) [2002/3 c16m   **c–** 20sᵖᵘ 20g* 20g⁵ 19g 20g Apr 1] tall gelding: modest maiden on Flat: winning chaser: **h87**

modest hurdler nowadays: won seller at Musselburgh in January, easily best effort in 2002/3: stays 2½m, at least when conditions aren't testing: acts on firm and soft going: tried blinkered: has found little. *Mrs A. Duffield*

HOH NO 7 b.g. Efisio – Primetta (Precocious) [2002/3 h82: 16d⁴ 16s⁴ c21g⁶ c17m⁵ c17sᵘʳ 16s 24g⁵ 16g⁶ c17m³ c17m² Oct 7] compact gelding: poor maiden hurdler/chaser: best around 2m: acts on good to firm going: blinkered sixth start (ran poorly), tongue tied last 3. *R. M. Stronge* **c74** **h68**

HOH TEL (IRE) 9 ch.g. Montelimar (USA) – Party Dancer (Be My Guest (USA)) [2002/3 c25g⁵ Apr 7] lengthy gelding: novice hurdler/chaser: fair pointer, successful 3 times in March and April: probably stays 3m: acts on soft and good to firm going: usually blinkered/visored over fences: makes mistakes. *G. F. White* **c84 x** **h–**

HOLBORN HILL (IRE) 11 gr.g. Riberetto – Grey Tor (Ahonoora) [2002/3 c–, h–: 22vᵖᵘ 21m 21mᶠ Apr 16] strong gelding: let down by jumping in novice chases: one-time fairly useful handicap hurdler: stayed 3m: acted on heavy going: tried tongue tied: dead. *A. King* **c–** **h105**

HOLD THE FORT 12 b.g. Baron Blakeney – Mizpah (Lochnager) [2002/3 c20mᵘʳ Sep 28] good-topped gelding: no sign of ability. *T. Needham* **c–** **h–**

HOLLAND PARK (IRE) 6 gr.g. Roselier (FR) – Bluebell Avenue (Boreen Beag) [2002/3 17v³ 19d² 22d³ Feb 23] sixth foal: brother to fairly useful hurdler/chaser Carryonharry, stays 3m: dam unraced, out of half-sister to top-class hunter chaser Eliogarty: fair form in novice hurdles at Exeter last 2 starts, second to Tana River and third of 17 to Grey Brother: will stay at least 3m. *Mrs S. D. Williams* **h99**

HOLLAND'S NEPHEW 6 b.g. Nearly A Hand – Our Mrs'p (Idiot's Delight) [2002/3 F–: c20sᵖᵘ c21vᶠ c21sᴿ 26gᵘʳ Mar 2] tall gelding: no sign of ability. *P. R. Chamings* **c–** **h–**

HOLLOA AWAY (IRE) 11 b.g. Red Sunset – Lili Bengam (Welsh Saint) [2002/3 c–, h63: 22g⁶ Jun 22] sturdy gelding: once-raced over fences: poor handicap hurdler: stays 2¾m: acts on soft and good to firm going: well beaten both runs in blinkers. *J. A. T. de Giles* **c–** **h–**

HOLLOW LEGS 7 ch.m. Alflora (IRE) – Sayshar (Sayfar) [2002/3 h72: 16gʳᵗʳ 17dᵖᵘ Nov 5] sturdy mare: poor novice hurdler: may prove best around 2m: acts on soft going: races freely: refused to race on reappearance. *Miss Z. C. Davison* **h– §**

HOLLOWS MILL 7 b.g. Rudimentary (USA) – Strawberry Song (Final Straw) [2002/3 h75, F–: 16g⁴ 16g⁵ 17m³ 16g⁶ 17d⁵ 16g⁵ 17g* Apr 21] modest hurdler: off 5 months, won novice at Carlisle in April: unlikely to stay beyond 2m: often finishes weakly. *F. P. Murtagh* **h86** **F–**

HOLLYBUSH HYBRID 7 ch.m. Risk Me (FR) – Absent Lover (Nearly A Hand) [2002/3 F70: 19sᶠ 19dᵖᵘ 17sᵖᵘ Mar 7] failed to complete in 3 races over hurdles, blinkered last 2: dead. *S. E. H. Sherwood* **h–**

HOLME FARM BOY (IRE) 7 b.g. River Falls – Lady Conchita (IRE) (Whistling Deer) [2002/3 19m⁴ 26mᵖᵘ Jul 19] angular gelding: modest juvenile hurdler in 1999/00: little sign of retaining ability, including on Flat. *G. M. Moore* **h–**

HOLMESDALE (IRE) 5 b.g. Norwich – Sister Cecelia (Trombone) [2002/3 F16m F16v⁴ Mar 8] €38,000 4-y-o: has plenty of scope: fifth foal: half-brother to fairly useful staying hurdler Fuzzy Logic (by Buckskin) and fairly useful pointer Imperial Dawn (by Roselier): dam unraced sister to very smart hunter chaser False Note: bit backward, shaped well long way when seventh of 19 to Chelsea Bridge in bumper at Kempton on debut: well beaten under very testing conditions at Sandown just 2 weeks later, weakening closing stages having travelled well. *M. J. Ryan* **F92 +**

HOLY ORDERS (IRE) 6 b.g. Unblest – Shadowglow (Shaadi (USA)) [2002/3 16v 16s 16g 16g Mar 11] **h144 +**
   A smart hurdler, yes, but not the champion his curriculum vitae would have you believe. Holy Orders has now won two Grade 1 races with the word 'champion' in the title, the first the Champion Four Year Old Hurdle at Fairyhouse and, two years later, at the same meeting but back at its usual home of Punchestown, the Ballymore Properties Champion Stayers' Hurdle. There were six runners, all Irish-trained, for the Champion Stayers', none of whom had contested the Stayers' Hurdle at Cheltenham. With the possible exception of Sacundai, who started odds-on at Punchestown, none of the six would probably have been good enough to make the frame at Cheltenham. Sacundai had earned favouritism with a defeat of

the Champion Hurdle winner Rooster Booster at Aintree, while second-favourite Rostropovich had also won in Britain the time before, narrowly beating Deano's Beeno in a valuable event on the last day of the British season at Sandown just five days earlier. Holy Orders started at 6/1, along with the top-class chaser Commanche Court, with Fnan (third in the race the previous year) and the novice Colonel Monroe at long odds. Holy Orders had done all his racing over hurdles at two miles but had proven himself a smart stayer on the Flat, while Sacundai was also trying the three-mile trip for the first time. Sacundai's rider was the first to commit, quickening a couple of lengths clear two out, but Shay Barry, who had given Holy Orders a patient ride, was not panicked into going for his whip and coaxed his mount, who has not always looked the most genuine individual, into joining issue at the last before leading near the finish to win by half a length, the pair pulling thirteen lengths clear of Rostropovich.

The Punchestown race came after an otherwise barren campaign over hurdles for Holy Orders. He contested three of the season's most competitive handicaps, the Ladbroke at Ascot, the Pierse at Leopardstown and the Tote Gold Trophy at Newbury and finished well beaten each time. In the first of those races he was sent off favourite, though that was largely due to the improvement he had shown on the Flat in 2002; he had not run over hurdles since his juvenile days. As well as close second places in the Duke of Edinburgh Stakes at Royal Ascot and the Irish Cesarewitch, Holy Orders' five-year-old campaign on the Flat had included a couple of easy wins in minor events at Navan, in the second of them winning on the bridle from Limestone Lad (something he'd be unlikely to repeat if they met over hurdles) and the future Melbourne Cup winner Media Puzzle.

One race with the word 'champion' in the title that eluded Holy Orders was, not surprisingly, the Champion Hurdle itself. He lined up as one of the race's three 100/1-shots, looking sour beforehand and seemingly having half a mind to take his cue from Hors La Loi III and remain rooted to the spot when the tapes went up. Holy Orders actually ended up running his best race prior to Punchestown, well behind before staying on for eighth, some twenty-five lengths behind Rooster Booster. Holy Orders had a couple of starts back on the Flat in listed races between Cheltenham and Punchestown, booking his place in the Champion Stayers' field with another easy win at Navan just five days beforehand. He didn't take to French hurdles when sent over for the Prix La Barka at Auteuil in late-May and returned tailed off after downing tools a good way out.

Ballymore Properties Champion Stayers' Hurdle, Punchestown—
the blinkered Holy Orders, up in trip, upsets the odds on Sacundai

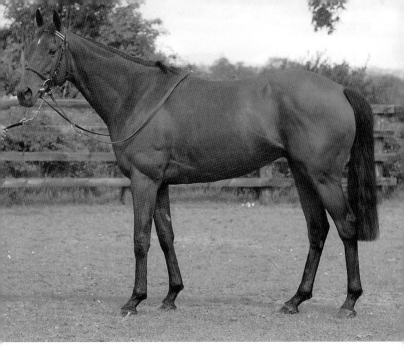

Mr A. McLuckie's "Holy Orders"

Holy Orders (IRE) (b.g. 1997)	Unblest (b 1991)	Alzao (b 1980)	Lyphard Lady Rebecca
		Missed Blessing (b 1977)	So Blessed Miss By Miles
	Shadowglow (b 1992)	Shaadi (b 1986)	Danzig Unfurled
		Aquaglow (b 1986)	Caerleon Light of Eire

As the appraisal of Holy Orders' pedigree in *Chasers & Hurdlers 2000/01* pointed out, there is little in his pedigree to suggest he would make a hurdler and, now it must be added, still less a staying one. His once-raced dam, Shadowglow, by the miler Shaadi, has had one other runner to date, the two-year-old seven-furlong winner Bamalko (by Royal Applause). Her two-year-old filly by Cape Cross made €20,000 at Goffs as a yearling and has joined the Mullins stable as well; she has been named Diaconate. A smallish, workmanlike gelding who is blinkered nowadays, Holy Orders has been successful on heavy ground, but is probably ideally suited by less testing conditions (the ground was good at Punchestown). *W. P. Mullins, Ireland*

HOLYROOD PRINCESS (IRE) 4 b.f. Moshaajir (USA) – Kawarau Queen (Taufan **h–**
(USA)) [2002/3 16v Nov 19] half-sister to winning 2m hurdler Robert The Bruce (by Distinct Native): tailed off in 2 maidens on Flat and novice selling hurdle. *A. R. Dicken*

HOLYWELL GIRL 6 b.m. Alhaatmi – Merry Maggie (Stanford) [2002/3 F–: 19d[pu] **h–**
Oct 19] angular mare: no sign of ability in bumpers or maiden hurdle: won maiden point in March. *John A. Harris*

HOMBRE 8 ch.g. Shernazar – Delray Jet (USA) (Northjet) [2002/3 c–, h–: c21s* **c76**
c24s³ c16v² c20s⁴ c21s³ c21mᵖᵘ Apr 21] leggy gelding: poor handicap chaser: won **h–**
at Sedgefield in December: effective at 2m to 3m: acts on any going: tried blinkered.
M. D. Hammond

HOME JAMES (IRE) 6 b.g. Commanche Run – Take Me Home (Amoristic (USA)) **h116 +**
[2002/3 F91: 22s³ 20v² 19d* 19g* Apr 26] sturdy gelding: bumper winner: confirmed
earlier promise over hurdles when winning maiden at Hereford (by 5 lengths from Hirapour) in February and novice at Market Rasen (odds on) in April: will stay 3m: raced on
good going or softer (acts on heavy): type to do well in novice chases in 2003/4. *A. King*

HOMELEIGH MOONCOIN 8 ch.g. Jamesmead – Super Sol (Rolfe (USA)) **h107**
[2002/3 20m⁶ 20g* 21g* 26g* 25m⁴ Nov 4] third foal: half-brother to fairly useful 1¼m/
1¾m winner Three Lions, useful stayer/fair 2½m hurdler Spunkie (both by Jupiter Island)
and modest chaser A Right Set Too (by Island Set), stays 3¼m: dam winning selling
hurdler, barely stayed 2½m: needed experience on debut: won maiden hurdle (50/1) at
Worcester in August and novices easily at Southwell in September and October: ran as if
amiss final start: stays 3¼m. *Mrs L. Wadham*

HOMELY SORT (IRE) 4 b.f. Petardia – Safe Home (Home Guard (USA)) [2002/3 **h–**
16dᵖᵘ 16vᵖᵘ 16vᵖᵘ Jan 22] half-sister to fair hurdler Home Counties (by Ela-Mana-Mou),
stayed 2¾m: no form on Flat at 2 yrs or over hurdles: wore cheekpieces final start. *Mrs
S. Lamyman*

HOME MADE 5 b.g. Homo Sapien – Inch Maid (Le Moss) [2002/3 F–: F16d May 4] **F–**
well held in 2 bumpers: won maiden point in April. *S. A. Brookshaw*

HOMEMAKER 13 b.m. Homeboy – Ganadora (Good Times (ITY)) [2002/3 16sᵖᵘ **h–**
22dᵖᵘ Dec 19] neat mare: one-time modest 2m hurdler: has been to stud and had 4 foals,
including a filly by Sure Blade in 2001: no sign of retaining ability. *A. E. Jones*

HOMER (IRE) 6 b.g. Sadler's Wells (USA) – Gravieres (FR) (Saint Estephe (FR)) **h98**
[2002/3 h112: 19gᵖᵘ 16m 20m² 19m Aug 31] modest hurdler: first start after leaving
N. Babbage, easily best effort in 2002/3 when second in amateur handicap at Bangor:
stays 2½m: acts on soft and good to firm going: tongue tied last 3 outings. *M. C. Pipe*

HOMESTEAD 9 ch.g. Indian Ridge – Bertrade (Homeboy) [2002/3 h100: 24d⁴ 20d⁵ **h96 d**
24d 20g 20f 20g⁵ 20s⁶ 21dˢᵘ Nov 15] angular gelding: handicap hurdler: blinkered, modest form at best in 2002/3: stays 3m: acts on heavy and good to firm going. *E. McNamara,
Ireland*

HOME TOR 6 b.g. Homo Sapien – Torus Queen (Torus) [2002/3 F17m F16f⁵ Oct 10] **F76 ?**
fifth foal: dam never ran: signs of ability in bumpers: runner-up in maiden point in April.
S. A. Brookshaw

HOMME DE FER 11 b.g. Arctic Lord – Florence May (Grange Melody) [2002/3 **c112**
c107, h–: c25f⁵ c24d* c27g⁶ c24g c24m² c24m³ Apr 21] medium-sized gelding: fair **h–**
handicap chaser: off 5 months, won at Ludlow in November: easily best efforts when
placed: stays 25f: acts on any going, races mainly on good or firmer nowadays: reportedly
bled from nose once in 2001/2. *K. C. Bailey*

HONEST HERBERT (IRE) 10 b.g. Salluceva – Bold And True (Sir Herbert) **c–**
[2002/3 c–, h–: c23gᵖᵘ Sep 15] workmanlike gelding: lightly-raced novice hurdler/chaser. **h–**
K. F. Clutterbuck

HONEYBUNCH (IRE) 5 b.m. Supreme Leader – Hunter's Pet (Cracksman) [2002/3 **F84**
F16g⁴ F16f⁴ Mar 29] sixth foal: sister to fairly useful hurdler Scenic Route, stayed 2½m,
and half-sister to winning 3m chaser Trader Tye (by Buckskin): dam unraced, from
family of top-class 2m to 3m hurdler Gaye Brief and very smart staying jumper Gaye
Chance: modest form when fourth in mares bumpers at Musselburgh and Down Royal.
C. F. Swan, Ireland

HONEY HONEY (FR) 8 gr.g. Djarvis (FR) – Urta (FR) (Le Pontet (FR)) [2002/3 **c–**
c–, h–: c21gᵖᵘ Apr 19] rather leggy gelding: winning chaser in France: little form in **h–**
varied events in Britain, including points, shaping as if he has a problem. *Ms Lisa Stock*

HONEY'S GIFT 4 b.f. Terimon – Honeycroft (Crofter (USA)) [2002/3 16sᵘʳ 17s **h79**
16dᵘʳ 16v³ 16g⁵ Mar 2] leggy filly: dam winning selling hurdler: modest maiden on
Flat (stays 1½m): poor juvenile hurdler: should stay 2½m: acts on heavy ground.
G. G. Margarson

HONEY THYME 5 ch.m. Palais de Danse – Forever₄Honey (Palm Track) [2002/3 **h–**
h–, F–: 17gᵖᵘ Mar 17] non-thoroughbred mare: no sign of ability: tried tongue tied.
R. Ford

HONEY TRADER 11 b.g. Beveled (USA) – Lizzie Bee (Kind of Hush) [2002/3 c72§, **c– §** h74§: c19g c16g[5] c18f[6] 16d[4] c16m[5] 17m Jul 28] good-topped gelding: poor hurdler/ **h71 §** chaser: barely stays 19f: acts on any going: tried blinkered/tongue tied: ungenuine. *C. L. Popham*

HONNEUR FONTENAIL (FR) 4 ch.g. Tel Quel (FR) – Fontanalia (FR) (Rex **h–** Magna (FR)) [2002/3 F12d 16d Jan 18] angular gelding: fifth foal: half-brother to modest **F–** hurdler/fair chaser around 2m Soeur Fontenail (by Turgeon) and winning hurdler Dame Fontenail (by Pampabird): dam unplaced over jumps in France: little show in bumper or novice hurdle. *N. J. Hawke*

HONOR'S LAD 4 ch.g. Sabrehill (USA) – Ackcontent (USA) (Key To Content **h–** (USA)) [2002/3 17s[pu] 16v[pu] 17g Mar 16] little form on Flat, sold out of C. Kellett's stable 500 gns Doncaster September Sales: no show in juvenile hurdles: tried in visor/cheekpieces: sold 700 gns Doncaster March Sales. *Mrs L. C. Jewell*

HONOURABLE CHIEF 6 b.g. Be My Chief (USA) – Magic Orb (Primo Dominie) **h–** [2002/3 16g 18g[6] 16d 16d[5] 18d Nov 11] sturdy gelding: signs of only a little ability on Flat and over hurdles (trained on debut by G. Prodromou): blinkered final start. *J. T. Gifford*

HOPBINE 7 ch.m. Gildoran – Haraka Sasa (Town And Country) [2002/3 h114, F–: **h106** 21d 21d[6] 20v 19d 22g[2] 20g Apr 2] small, sturdy mare: fair handicap hurdler: will be suited by 3m: acts on heavy going. *J. L. Spearing*

HOPE VALUE 8 b.g. Rock City – Folle Idee (USA) (Foolish Pleasure (USA)) [2002/3 **c–** c–, h–: 18v 17g Mar 18] good-topped gelding: winning hurdler: no form since 2000/1, **h–** including over fences: has broken blood vessels. *G. F. Edwards*

HOPPERTREE 7 b.g. Rock Hopper – Snow Tree (Welsh Pageant) [2002/3 h–, F91: **h–** 19d[ur] Jan 27] medium-sized gelding: fair in bumpers, hinting at temperament: failed to complete both starts over hurdles, yet to be asked for effort when unseating 4 out in novice at Exeter. *R. S. Brookhouse*

HOPPING MAD 10 b.m. Puget (USA) – Mapleline (Shy Groom (USA)) [2002/3 **c–** c25g[5] Mar 29] winning pointer: well held on hunter chase debut (tongue tied): tried blinkered. *B. G. Duke*

HORATIO (IRE) 7 b.g. Warcraft (USA) – Coolruss Quay (Quayside) [2002/3 F16s **h–** 17s 18s[5] Mar 2] fourth in bumper in May 2000: no sign of retaining ability. *R. J. Hodges* **F–**

HORIZON (FR) 6 ch.g. Arctic Tern (USA) – Furtchella (FR) (Dancing Spree (USA)) **c–** [2002/3 c?, h?: 21m[4] 19s[pu] Nov 21] rather leggy gelding: fair maiden hurdler/winning **h–** chaser in France: no form in Britain. *P. C. Ritchens*

HORNBILL 5 b.g. Sir Harry Lewis (USA) – Tangara (Town Crier) [2002/3 17s 20g[pu] **h–** Mar 2] lengthy, workmanlike gelding: sixth foal: half-brother to 19f hurdle winner Bellbird (by Bob's Return): dam unraced: no show in 2 novice hurdles. *Mrs P. Robeson*

HORNER ROCKS (IRE) 7 b.g. Phardante (FR) – Horner Water (IRE) (Over The **h109** River (FR)) [2002/3 20d* 16s 20s* 20v[5] 24s 19v[6] 20s 19v[3] Mar 9] smallish gelding: first foal: dam, winning hurdler who stayed 2¾m, half-sister to one-time smart chaser up to 2½m Mr Baxter Basics: fair handicap hurdler: won at Killarney in May and Clonmel in November: likely to stay beyond 2½m: acts on heavy going, well held only start on good to firm. *Michael Hourigan, Ireland*

HORS LA LOI (FR) 7 ch.g. Exit To Nowhere (USA) – Kernia (IRE) (Raise A Cup **h110** (USA)) [2002/3 16d 17s 16g[3] 16g[2] Apr 23] close-coupled gelding: fair handicap hurdler: off nearly 2 years before reappearance, gradually found his form: raced around 2m on good going or softer (acts on heavy). *Ian Williams*

HORS LA LOI III (FR) 8 b.g. Cyborg (FR) – Quintessence III (FR) (El Condor **h136 §** (FR)) [2002/3 h161: 17d[F] 16s[4] 16d[3] 16g[rtr] 20g Apr 5] leggy gelding: high-class hurdler on his day: long way below best in 2002/3 after falling on reappearance, refused to race when bidding to win Champion Hurdle at Cheltenham for second year in succession: raced mainly around 2m: acted on soft and good to firm going: tongue tied towards end of career: occasionally bled from nose: held up: has been retired. *J. R. Fanshawe*

HORTON DANCER 6 b.g. Rambo Dancer (CAN) – Horton Lady (Midyan (USA)) **h–** [2002/3 h81: 20g Mar 23] poor stayer on Flat: winning hurdler, well held in handicap only start in 2002/3: should stay 2½m: acts on soft going. *I. W. McInnes*

ladbrokes.com Handicap Chase, Newbury—a useful performance from Horus

HORUS (IRE) 8 b.g. Teenoso (USA) – Jennie's First (Idiot's Delight) [2002/3 c119+: c26g* c25d³ c24m* c20g* c25d* c26s⁴ c21s c20g⁶ c25dᵖᵘ Apr 4] good-topped gelding: winning pointer/hunter chaser for D. Pipe, including at Cheltenham in May: jumped more fluently and useful form in handicaps, winning at Stratford in June and valuable events at Newbury in November and Cheltenham (by 1¼ lengths from Bramblehill Duke) in December: disappointing last 3 starts: effective at 2½m to easy 3¼m: acts on soft and good to firm going: pulled too hard in visor second start. *M. C. Pipe* **c138**

HOT BUNNY (IRE) 7 b.m. Distinctly North (USA) – Debach Dust (Indian King (USA)) [2002/3 20d 19m 18d 18d 22g 20dᵖᵘ Aug 17] leggy mare: no form in 2 races over fences: winning hurdler, little form since 2000: best around 2m: acts on good to firm and good to soft going, probably on soft. *C. F. Swan, Ireland* **c– h87**

HOT CLASSIC 4 b.f. Classic Cliche (IRE) – White Heat (Last Tycoon) [2002/3 F16g Feb 27] third foal: half-sister to 2000 2-y-o 5f winner Media Mogul (by First Trump): dam maiden stayed 1m: tailed off in mares bumper at Ludlow on debut. *J. R. Best* **F–**

HOTELIERS' DREAM 5 b.m. Reprimand – Pride of Britain (CAN) (Linkage (USA)) [2002/3 17dᶠ 16vᵖᵘ 17g Mar 18] poor maiden on Flat (stays 11.8f): no form in 3 novice hurdles, including a seller. *W. S. Kittow* **h–**

HOT PRODUXION (USA) 4 ch.g. Tabasco Cat (USA) – Princess Harriet (USA) (Mt Livermore (USA)) [2002/3 17g 16d² 16d³ 16d³ 19m² Mar 22] compact gelding: fair maiden on Flat (stays 1¼m), sold out of Mrs A. Perrett's stable 19,500 gns Newmarket July Sales: fair juvenile hurdler: off nearly 4 months, improved effort when 9 lengths second to Silver Charmer in handicap at Newbury final start: stays 19f: acts on good to firm and good to soft going: visored last 3 starts: not an easy ride. *J. Mackie* **h100**

HOT SHOTS (FR) 8 b.g. Passing Sale (FR) – Uguette IV (FR) (Chamberlin (FR)) [2002/3 c124, h–: c16fᵖᵘ 16s⁵ 16d 16dᵘʳ 16dᵘʳ 16m* 16m² 16gᵖᵘ Apr 19] good-topped gelding: fairly useful chaser/handicap hurdler: won at Wincanton in March by 6 lengths from Best Wait: raced mainly around 2m: acts on good to firm and heavy going: usually held up. *M. Pitman* **c– h117**

HOTSPUR STREET 11 b.g. Cadeaux Genereux – Excellent Alibi (USA) (Exceller (USA)) [2002/3 c–, h73: 17m⁵ 22f May 10] smallish gelding: poor handicap hurdler: effective at 2m to 3m: probably acts on any going: blinkered/visored: reportedly bled from nose once in 2001/2. *E. L. James* **c– h65**

HOTTERS (IRE) 8 b.g. Be My Native (USA) – Siul Currach (Deep Run) [2002/3 h82, F84: 21d 23d c25g⁴ c23gᵘʳ c33vᶠ c26v⁵ 26g 27m⁵ Mar 19] bumper winner: poor **c84 h–**

380

maiden hurdler/novice chaser: stays 25f: acts on soft and good to firm going: wore cheek-pieces/blinkers last 6 starts: sketchy jumper. *M. Pitman*

HOT TO TROT (IRE) 10 b.g. Yashgan – La Tante (Bold Lad (IRE)) [2002/3 c–,   **c–**
h94: 27g² 22m³ Aug 5] sturdy gelding: modest hurdler: sold out of C. Mann's stable 2,800   **h94**
gns Doncaster May Sales: reportedly lame only subsequent outing: stays 27f: acts on soft
going: tried blinkered. *C. J. Gray*

HOT WELD 4 b.g. Weld – Deb's Ball (Glenstal (USA)) [2002/3 F17d² Mar 2] third   **F99 p**
foal: half-brother to modest hurdler Deb's Son (by Minster Son), stays 27f: dam useful
hurdler stayed 25f: 25/1, neck second of 15 to Riothamus in bumper at Carlisle on debut,
finishing well from rear without being knocked about: sold to join F. Murphy 47,000 gns
Doncaster May Sales: should do better. *T. P. Tate*

HOULIHANS CHOICE 6 ch.g. Norton Challenger – Model Lady (Le Bavard (FR))   **F–**
[2002/3 F82: F16d Dec 12] little encouragement in 2 bumpers 8½ months apart. *Ferdy
Murphy*

HOUSELOPE BECK 13 ch.g. Meadowbrook – Hallo Cheeky (Flatbush) [2002/3   **c–**
c27s⁵ Mar 11] fair pointer: has shown little in steeplechases: has had tongue tied. *Miss
C. Osborne*

HOUSEPARTY (IRE) 5 b. or br.g. Grand Lodge (USA) – Special Display (Welsh   **h–**
Pageant) [2002/3 16dᶠ Mar 6] brother to fairly useful 2m hurdler Berengarius: fairly useful on Flat (stays 1½m) at 3 yrs for Sir Michael Stoute, well held only 3 subsequent outings: well beaten when collapsing after 2 out in maiden hurdle at Wincanton. *J. A. B. Old*

HOWABOYS QUEST (USA) 6 b.g. Quest For Fame – Doctor Black (USA) (Family   **c–**
Doctor (USA)) [2002/3 h66: 20d⁶ 16d⁴ c16g Nov 23] poor maiden hurdler: showed   **h66**
nothing on chasing debut: stays 21f: acts on good to firm going, possibly not on heavy.
Ferdy Murphy

HOWAYA PET (IRE) 7 br.m. Montelimar (USA) – Sarahs Music (IRE) (Orchestra)   **h109**
[2002/3 F18s² F18s² F20s* F20s⁴ 22v⁴ 20s 19s³ 20v² 22s³ 24v⁴ 20s³ 22d⁴ 20s² 20d 20vᶠ 24v* 24d*   **F95**
Mar 22] IR 2,200 4-y-o: second foal: dam unraced, out of sister to top-class hurdler/
chaser up to 3m Daring Run: successful 3 times in Irish points, including twice in 2002:
won bumper at Wexford in June: fair hurdler: improved efforts when winning twice in
large-field handicaps at Navan in March: stays 3m: acts on heavy ground: usually tongue
tied, effective when not. *G. Keane, Ireland*

HOWDYDOODY (IRE) 7 b.g. Hawkstone (IRE) – Larry's Law (IRE) (Law Society   **h108**
(USA)) [2002/3 22d³ 24s³ 24s* 24g³ 27m* Mar 19] medium-sized gelding: fourth foal:
dam unraced: well behind in bumper: won twice in Irish points in 2002: bought 22,000
gns (privately) Doncaster May Sales: fair form over hurdles: won novice at Taunton in
January and handicap at Fontwell (off bridle some way out) in March: will prove best at
3m+: yet to race on extremes of going: tongue tied. *P. F. Nicholls*

HOWEY IN THE HILLS (IRE) 7 b.g. Phardante (FR) – Tacova (Avocat) [2002/3   **h–**
h–, F–: 20gᵖᵘ Apr 30] workmanlike gelding: no form in bumper or 2 novice hurdles: fell
first 3 starts in points. *D. McCain*

HOW GREAT THOU ART 7 b.g. Almoojid – Mamamere (Tres Gate) [2002/3 F86:   **h68**
F17d⁶ 20s⁶ 19d 19s 22g⁵ Apr 12] big, lengthy gelding: fair form at best in bumpers: first   **F83**
form over hurdles when fifth of 12 in novice at Stratford: stays 2¾m. *R. J. Baker*

HOW RAN ON (IRE) 12 br.g. Mandalus – Kelly's Bridge (Netherkelly) [2002/3   **c76 x**
c81, h–: c16s⁴ c17s² c16g⁶ c17g³ c16g⁶ c16m⁵ c16g² c16f* c16m* c18drᵒ c17v³ Nov 19]   **h–**
poor handicap chaser: won at Ludlow (seller) in October and Warwick in November:
stays 21f: acts on any going: tried tongue tied: front runner: often let down by jumping.
Mrs L. Williamson

HOWRWENOW (IRE) 5 b.g. Commanche Run – Maythefifth (Hardboy) [2002/3   **h101**
16d⁶ 19d² 20g⁴ Apr 2] rather leggy gelding: third foal: brother to winning pointer State In
Emergency: dam, maiden pointer, runner-up in 2½m steeplechase: won maiden Irish
point on debut in 2002: fair form when in frame in novice hurdles, flat out halfway when
20 lengths fourth of 15 to Isard III at Ascot: will be suited by 3m. *Miss H. C. Knight*

HUBBLY BUBBLY 5 b.g. Gildoran – Spinayab (King of Spain) [2002/3 F–: F17m⁵   **F–**
Apr 15] headstrong and well held in bumpers: unseated in point. *J. W. Mullins*

HUGE HEART (NZ) 7 b.g. T V Heart Throb (USA) – Christmas Lady (NZ) (Palm   **h–**
Beach (FR)) [2002/3 19dᵖᵘ 17s 19sᵖᵘ 16dᵘʳ 20m Apr 12] stocky gelding: ran 14 times up
to 1½m on Flat in New Zealand, winning 6f event on 2-y-o debut: bought 4,000 gns
Doncaster May Sales: has shown nothing over hurdles. *R. N. Bevis*

HUGH DANIELS   15 b.g. Adonijah – Golden Realm (Red Regent) [2002/3 c–, h–: c16g^{pu} c16g Jun 12] leggy gelding: winning hurdler/maiden chaser, no longer of any account. *C. J. Hemsley*   **c–ㅤh–**

HUGO DE GREZ (FR)   8 b.g. Useful (FR) – Piqua Des Gres (FR) (Waylay) [2002/3 c117, h–: c26s^{ur} c26v* c25v* c20v² c28d 24d⁵ Mar 15] rather leggy, close-coupled gelding: useful handicap chaser: better than ever in 2002/3, won at Carlisle (sixth course success) in November and Kelso (by ¾ length from Ryalux) in December: good second to A Piece of Cake in 4-finisher event at Ayr: labouring long way out on rare outing over hurdles: needs thorough test at 2½m and should stay beyond 3½m: acts very well on heavy going: effective tongue tied or not: sound jumper. *A. Parker*   **c136ㅤh93 +**

HUGO DE PERRO (FR)   8 b.g. Perrault – Fontaine Aux Faons (FR) (Nadjar (FR)) [2002/3 c100x, h117: 18d³ 22d* 21v³ 20d^{rtr} 22v* 20s⁵ 20v⁵ c20v^{pu} 20s* 24d² Mar 15] leggy gelding: badly let down by jumping over fences since winning on chasing debut: fairly useful hurdler: won handicaps at Cartmel in June and Kelso in December and claimer at Carlisle in March: stays 3m: acts on heavy and good to firm going: difficult ride (refused to race fourth outing, has found little). *P. Monteith*   **c– xㅤh128 §**

HUIC HOLLOA (IRE)   7 b.g. Denel (FR) – Buckalgo (IRE) (Buckskin (FR)) [2002/3 h72: 19d 25g⁵ Mar 23] lengthy gelding: poor form in bumpers: well held in 2 novice hurdles. *J. A. T. de Giles*   **h–**

HUISH (IRE)   12 br.g. Orchestra – Lysanders Lady (Saulingo) [2002/3 h–: 16g^{pu} Mar 12] maiden hurdler, very lightly raced nowadays. *Mrs N. Macauley*   **h–**

HUKA LODGE (IRE)   6 ch.g. Roselier (FR) – Derrella (Derrylin) [2002/3 20d 20s⁵ 16v³ 20d Mar 2] 30,000 4-y-o: fourth foal: dam unraced sister to high-class 2m hurdler Kesslin and half-sister to smart hurdler/useful chaser Rathconrath: poor form over hurdles, let down by jumping final outing. *L. Lungo*   **h69**

HUMMING   6 b.g. Bluebird (USA) – Risanda (Kris) [2002/3 F81: 19g^{pu} 19g² Mar 17] leggy gelding: modest form at best in bumpers: off over a year, much better effort over hurdles when second to impressive Cancun Caribe in novice seller at Hereford: will stay at least 2½m. *Miss M. E. Rowland*   **h77**

HUNTER GOLD (FR)   8 br.g. Chamberlin (FR) – Une de Mai IV (FR) (Ice Light (FR)) [2002/3 c–, h82: c21d^{pu} c16v³ c24g⁵ Mar 12] leggy gelding: winning chaser in France: lightly raced over hurdles/fences in Britain, weakened closing stages all 3 starts in 2000/3 (tongue tied final one): stays 21f: raced on good going or softer: sold £1,400 Ascot April Sales. *T. R. George*   **c–ㅤh–**

HUNTERS CREEK (IRE)   9 b.g. Persian Mews – Creek's Sister (King's Ride) [2002/3 c109: c19g⁵ 20d³ 20s² 20v⁶ 20g² c21m* Apr 26] leggy, useful-looking gelding: fair chaser: won 5-runner handicap at Sedgefield in April: modest form when placed 3 of 4 starts in novice hurdles: stays 2¾m: acts on soft and good to firm going: sometimes let down by jumping. *Mrs M. Reveley*   **c111ㅤh95**

HUNTERS TWEED   7 ch.g. Nashwan (USA) – Zorette (USA) (Zilzal (USA)) [2002/3 h125: c24m* c25g² c22d³ c24s³ c20v³ c24g² c22d* c20g^{ur} c20g* Apr 23] leggy gelding: fairly useful hurdler/chaser: won intermediate chase at Perth in May (changed hands 62,000 gns Doncaster August Sales) and handicaps at Haydock (much improved effort over fences, by 21 lengths from Joe di Capo) in March and Perth (by 3 lengths from Emperor Ross) in April: stays 25f: acts on heavy and good to firm going. *P. Beaumont*   **c124ㅤh–**

HUNTERSWAY (IRE)   6 ch.g. Treasure Hunter – Dunmanway (Le Bavard (FR)) [2002/3 24g^{pu} 19m⁵ Oct 3] 3,200 4-y-o: third foal: dam ran once: no form in 2 novice hurdles: has worn cheekpieces: won maiden point in April. *Mrs A. Price*   **h–**

HUNTERS WOOD (IRE)   8 gr.g. Wood Chanter – Barnmeen Lass (IRE) (Floriferous) [2002/3 h–: c26g⁴ Apr 21] no form over hurdles or in maiden chase: third in point in March. *R. J. Baker*   **c–ㅤh–**

HUNT IN PAIRS   4 b.g. Pursuit of Love – Emily-Mou (IRE) (Cadeaux Genereux) [2002/3 16s^{pu} 16s⁵ 16d 16s Dec 27] angular gelding: headstrong maiden on Flat: little show in juvenile hurdles. *R. H. York*   **h–**

HURDANTE (IRE)   13 ch.g. Phardante (FR) – Hurry (Deep Run) [2002/3 c81, h–: c21g^{pu} c16d May 13] well-made gelding: winning hurdler/pointer: poor novice chaser: stays 2½m: raced mainly on good going or softer. *Mrs L. A. Parker*   **c–ㅤh–**

HURLYBURLY (IRE)   6 ch.g. Hubbly Bubbly (USA) – Swans Leap (Swan's Rock) [2002/3 F70: F16g Mar 2] workmanlike gelding: signs of ability in bumpers, off 16 months before reappearance (sweating). *M. Pitman*   **F–**

HURRICANE BAY   7 ch.g. Karinga Bay – Clodaigh Gale (Strong Gale) [2002/3   **c–**
h–: 20d⁶ 26g² 24d⁵ 22m³ c23m Jul 17] poor novice hurdler: well held in handicap on   **h76**
chasing debut: stays 3¼m: acts on good to firm going: blinkered third/fourth outings.
Jonjo O'Neill

HURRICANE COAST   4 b.g. Hurricane Sky (AUS) – Tread Carefully (Sharpo)   **h–**
[2002/3 16mᵖᵘ 16dᵖᵘ Nov 7] lengthy, rather sparely-made gelding: fair on Flat (stays 7f),
won in September: no show in 2 juvenile hurdles. *T. D. Easterby*

HURRICANE DIPPER (IRE)   5 b.g. Glacial Storm (USA) – Minnies Dipper (Royal   **h–**
Captive) [2002/3 F16g 20g Apr 2] IR £17,000 3-y-o, 12,000 4-y-o: tall gelding: ninth   **F–**
foal: brother to winning pointer and half-brother to modest hurdler Woodstock Wanderer
(by Mandalus), stayed 2¾m: dam, of little account, sister to smart hurdler/chaser up to
3m Royal Dipper and half-sister to very smart staying hurdler/useful chaser Henry Mann:
tailed off in bumper (Grade 2) and novice hurdle. *Miss A. M. Newton-Smith*

HURRICANE GEORGES   7 b.g. Milieu – Miss Colonnette (Flatbush) [2002/3   **h–**
F82?: 22vᵖᵘ Jan 2] workmanlike gelding: probably flattered when showing only form in
bumpers: no show in novice hurdle. *J. N. R. Billinge*

HURRICANE LAMP   12 b.g. Derrylyn – Lampstone (Ragstone) [2002/3 c138x, h–:   **c136 x**
c24g² c21m² c20m² c20g* c19s² c20gᵖᵘ c20d c20g⁴ c26m² Apr 16] rangy, good sort: **h–**
useful handicap chaser: won at Kempton in November: stayed 3m: acted on soft and good
to firm going: usually held up: sketchy jumper: reportedly retired after injuring a tendon
at Cheltenham. *A. King*

HUSSARD COLLONGES (FR)   8 b.g. Video Rock – Ariane Collonges (FR)   **c167**
(Quart de Vin (FR)) [2002/3 c153, h–: c25d² c26g⁵ c24d² c26gᵖᵘ Mar 13]   **h–**
    The Yorkshire stable of Peter Beaumont gained its most famous victory
with Jodami in the 1993 Cheltenham Gold Cup, but the yard knew its fate soon
after halfway in the latest edition when Hussard Collonges attempted to emulate
Jodami's achievement. Hussard Collonges shaped up into a credible Gold Cup
contender through the season—looking one of the most likely to make a race of it
with Best Mate—and it was disappointing to see his being chased along behind the
leaders early on the final circuit. Hussard Collonges was out of contention when his
rider finally called it a day and pulled him up before the second last. Hussard
Collonges looked in magnificent shape—as he usually does—before the Gold Cup
but veterinary tests afterwards reportedly revealed that he had contracted a bacterial
infection which also affected some of the others in the yard. Still only eight, the
top-class Hussard Collonges has time on his side and his prospects of winning a
Gold Cup shouldn't be written off. He is very genuine and usually a fine jumper,
and was improving with every race leading up to the Gold Cup. He was an early
faller on his only outing after Cheltenham, in the Punchestown Gold Cup shortly
after the end of the British season, and it remains possible that he hasn't come to the
end of his improvement yet.
    Hussard Collonges was a 33/1-shot when winning a no-more-than-average
renewal of the Royal & SunAlliance Chase at the 2002 Cheltenham Festival, and
he looked to face a stiff task on his reappearance, up against the Gold Cup fourth,
fifth, seventh and tenth in the Charlie Hall Chase at Wetherby in early-November.
Hussard Collonges ran a fine race, despite being short of peak fitness, disputing
the lead—he usually races prominently—and jumping superbly throughout before
going down by two lengths to Marlborough. Hussard Collonges was conceding 5 lb
to Marlborough and the BHB handicapper put him up 8 lb after Wetherby, which
proved crucial in the Hennessy Gold Cup at Newbury later in the month. Jodami
just came off worse in a close finish to the Hennessy in his Gold Cup-winning
season and Hussard Collonges also ran a cracker in the race, carrying 11-4 and
receiving weight in a twenty-five-runner field only from Lord Noelie and Marlborough. As at Wetherby, Hussard Collonges led or disputed the lead virtually all
the way, again jumping really well until making a mistake two out. Headed at that
point, Hussard Collonges was still there with every chance at the final fence before
the weight began to tell and he eventually finished fifth, beaten five and a half
lengths by first-past-the-post Be My Royal. Hussard Collonges surpassed even that
effort on what turned out to be his final outing before Cheltenham, pulling clear in
the straight with Truckers Tavern and staying on very gamely, conceding 15 lb, to
be beaten two and a half lengths in the Peter Marsh Chase at Haydock in January,

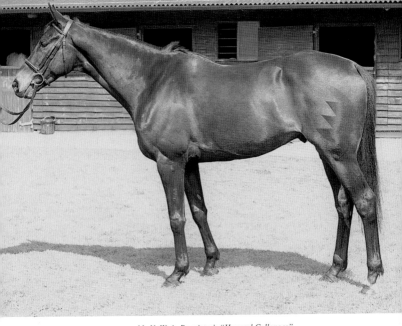

Mr N. W. A. Bannister's "Hussard Collonges"

a race Jodami had won on the way to his Gold Cup (Jodami also won the Hennessy Gold Cup at Leopardstown between Haydock and Cheltenham). If the Gold Cup performances of Truckers Tavern and Harbour Pilot are any guide, Hussard Collonges should have been very much involved in the finish at Cheltenham.

			No Lute	Luthier
	Video Rock		(b 1978)	Prudent Miss
	(b 1984)		Pauvresse	Home Guard
Hussard Collonges (FR)			(b 1978)	Misoptimist
(b.g. 1995)			Quart de Vin	Devon
	Ariane Collonges (FR)		(b 1972)	Quartelette
	(b 1988)		Exempte	Makalu
			(b 1970)	Penelope

Hussard Collonges is a useful-looking individual in appearance. His sire Video Rock, a smart middle-distance winner on the Flat in France, has made a name for himself as a sire of jumpers, represented, among others, by the top French chaser El Paso III. Video Rock's best-known offspring in Britain before Hussard Collonges was probably the Welsh National winner Edmond and, like him, Hussard Collonges—who was entered in the latest Grand National—will stay beyond three and a quarter miles. Ariane Collonges, the dam of Hussard Collonges, won over nine furlongs in the French Provinces and is a sister to Turf Collonges, a winning chaser at up to two miles five furlongs in France, and a half-sister to several other winning jumpers. Hussard Collonges is Ariane Collonges' first foal; her second and third, both by Lute Antique, have raced without success in France. Quart de Vin, the sire of Ariane Collonges and Turf Collonges, was a stayer on the Flat and a good hurdler who sired the 1991 Sun Alliance Chase winner Rolling Ball and the leading French chaser Ucello II. Hussard Collonges has only been raced on good going or softer and he acts on heavy. *P. Beaumont*

HUSSY　9 b.m. Broadsword (USA) – Smart Chick (True Song) [2002/3 h–: 21g⁴ 20g⁶ 20d May 23] lengthy, sparely-made mare: fell in 2 points in 2002: poor maiden hurdler: stays 21f: acts on good to soft going. *Mrs Sarah Horner-Harker*　**h67**

HYDEMILLA　13 b.m. Idiot's Delight – Bellaloo (Privy Seal) [2002/3 c24g May 31] smallish, close-coupled mare: winning pointer: poor maiden hurdler: well beaten completed start in steeplechases: stays 2½m: acts on any going. *Mrs C. J. A. Suthern*　**c–**　**h–**

HYPERACTIVE (IRE)　7 b.g. Perugino (USA) – Hyannis (FR) (Esprit du Nord (USA)) [2002/3 h70: 17d* Aug 26] leggy gelding: modest up to 1m on Flat: poor form over hurdles, made all in selling handicap at Cartmel: will prove best around 2m: acts on firm and good to soft going: races freely. *B. Ellison*　**h74**

HYPERION DU MOULIN II (FR)　8 b.g. Kedellic (FR) – Mipour (FR) (Shakapour) [2002/3 h–: 20mᵖᵘ 18f* 22mᵖᵘ Jun 28] tall gelding: form over hurdles only when winning handicap at Fontwell in June: reportedly had mucus on lungs final start: should be suited by 2½m+: acts on firm going: reportedly has broken blood vessels. *Lady Herries*　**h76**

HYPERSONIC　6 b.g. Marju (IRE) – Hi-Li (High Top) [2002/3 h–: 16gᵖᵘ Sep 14] compact gelding: poor on Flat (stays 1m) nowadays: little form over hurdles: sold £800 Ascot October Sales. *B. R. Millman*　**h–**

I

IACACIA (FR)　7 b. or br.g. Silver Rainbow – Palencia (FR) (Taj Dewan) [2002/3 c–, h91: 20s Mar 15] small, sparely-made gelding: winning chaser in France/novice hurdler: well held on return after near 2-year absence: stays 2¾m: acts on soft going. *Miss Venetia Williams*　**c–**　**h–**

IADORA　8 br.m. Gildoran – Combe Hill (Crozier) [2002/3 h74: 22d c19dᵖᵘ c25s⁴ Mar 7] rather leggy mare: poor maiden hurdler: well-held fourth in mares novice at Hereford on completed outing over fences: probably stays 25f. *J. A. B. Old*　**c66**　**h–**

IBAL (FR)　7 b.g. Balsamo (FR) – Quart d'Hekla (FR) (Quart de Vin (FR)) [2002/3 c114, h–: c16d³ c20v* c19v* c26v* c16v* Mar 8] big, useful-looking gelding: one-time　**c136**　**h–**

Sunderlands Bookmakers Novices' Chase, Sandown—
Ibal defeats odds-on First Love to gain a fourth win in a row

useful hurdler: useful over fences in 2002/3, won novices at Plumpton and Chepstow in December, Plumpton in January and Sandown (beat First Love 10 lengths in 3-runner event) in March: best form up to 2½m (finished very tired when winning at 3¼m): raced on good going or softer (acts well on heavy): sound-jumping front runner: genuine. *Mrs N. Smith*

IBERUS (GER) 5 b.g. Monsun (GER) – Iberica (GER) (Green Dancer (USA)) **h100 ?**
[2002/3 16s³ 16g^F 17g⁶ Mar 29] angular ex-German gelding: useful on Flat (stays 1½m), successful 3 times in 2002, left P. Schiergen after well held in Group 3 in late-June: odds on, looked less than straightforward when third in maiden at Plumpton (wore cheekpieces) on hurdling debut: tailed off when fell 3 out in Champion Hurdle (visored), well held in novice at Market Rasen final start. *M. C. Pipe*

IBIN ST JAMES 9 b.g. Salse (USA) – St James's Antigua (IRE) (Law Society **c98**
(USA)) [2002/3 c–, h87: c25d⁴ c29d* c32d c24g‡ Feb 22] sturdy gelding: one-time fairly **h–**
useful hurdler: successful over fences in handicaps at Fakenham in November and Huntingdon (amateurs) in February: stays 29f: acts on soft going: tried blinkered, including last 3 starts: has broken blood vessel. *M. Bradstock*

IBIS ROCHELAIS (FR) 7 b.g. Passing Sale (FR) – Ta Rochelaise (FR) (Carmont **c125**
(FR)) [2002/3 c114, h102: c20d² c24g‡ c20s² c21s² c24s* c24g² c25dᵖᵘ Apr 4] big, **h–**
lengthy gelding: fair hurdler: fairly useful chaser: won handicap at Sandown in February by 3 lengths from Spinofski: several other good placed efforts in 2002/3, second to Royal Predica in amateur handicap at Cheltenham following month: left impression amiss final start: stays 3m: acts on soft going: has reportedly broken blood vessels: sound jumper nowadays. *A. Ennis*

I CAN IMAGINE (IRE) 8 b.m. Husyan (USA) – Cyn Alley (The Parson) [2002/3 **c117**
c113+: 20v³ 20s⁶ 20s² c24v c28s² c24g⁵ Mar 30] angular mare: fair form on last of 3 runs **h105**
in novice hurdles: fairly useful novice chaser: good efforts last 2 starts, had plenty of use made of her when fifth to Native Jack at Cork final one: effective at 2½m to 3½m: raced on good going or softer (acts on heavy): tongue tied. *Robert Tyner, Ireland*

I CAN'T REMEMBER 9 br. or gr.g. Petong – Glenfield Portion (Mummy's Pet) **h–**
[2002/3 h–: 16mᵖᵘ 16d⁵ 20g⁵ Sep 26] poor on Flat: no form over hurdles. *Miss Lucinda V. Russell*

ICARE D'OUDAIRIES (FR) 7 ch.g. Port Etienne (FR) – Vellea (FR) (Cap Martin **h–**
(FR)) [2002/3 h104: 19m Oct 30] workmanlike gelding: fair hurdler: mid-division in amateur handicap only outing in 2002/3: stays 2½m: raced mainly on going softer than good (acts on heavy). *C. Tizzard*

ICEALION 5 b.g. Lion Cavern (USA) – Icecapped (Caerleon (USA)) [2002/3 h–: 16d **h–**
17v 17s 16d Dec 4] tall, leggy gelding: little sign of ability, including on Flat: has had tongue tied. *M. W. Easterby*

ICEBERGE (IRE) 7 b.g. Glacial Storm (USA) – Laura Daisy (Buckskin (FR)) **h97**
[2002/3 F94: 20m² 21s³ 20v⁵ 24v³ 26g* 24g* Mar 16] lengthy gelding: modest hurdler: won maiden at Huntingdon and novice at Ludlow (none too fluent) in March: stays 3¼m: acts on heavy going. *Ian Williams*

ICE COOL LAD (IRE) 9 b.g. Glacial Storm (USA) – My Serena (No Argument) **c76**
[2002/3 c86, h–: c20m⁶ c21m³ c22d⁵ c20sᵖᵘ c20s c28g* c26f⁵ Apr 24] sturdy gelding: **h–**
poor handicap chaser: won at Fontwell in March: stays easy 3½m: acts on heavy going: blinkered fifth start: inconsistent. *R. Rowe*

ICE CRYSTAL 6 b.g. Slip Anchor – Crystal Fountain (Great Nephew) [2002/3 h111: **h106**
22dᵖᵘ 20v* Jan 6] leggy gelding: fair handicap hurdler: 25/1-winner of 11-runner event at Fontwell, only second outing in a year: will be suited by 3m: acts on heavy going. *S. Woodman*

ICE CUBE 7 b.g. Rakaposhi King – Arctic Rymes (Rymer) [2002/3 c60, h–: c16g 22d **c–**
19v⁴ 16v 16v⁶ c20m⁵ 19m 16m Apr 21] close-coupled gelding: poor winning chaser/ **h64**
maiden hurdler: stays 21f: acts on good to firm and heavy going: tried blinkered/in cheekpieces: tongue tied second start. *Mrs L. Williamson*

ICELANDIC LORD 10 b.g. Arctic Lord – Arctic Ander (Leander) [2002/3 c–, h–: **c–**
c16dᵖᵘ 17m Aug 31] lengthy gelding: of no account. *Mrs L. B. Normile* **h–**

ICELANDIC SPRING 11 ch.g. Derrylin – Snow Time (Deep Run) [2002/3 c25d **c83**
c25m⁶ c25g³ c24g³ Apr 21] fair pointer: best effort in steeplechases when third to Dunrig in maiden hunter at Kelso third outing, off bridle some way out: blinkered last 2 starts. *J. E. Brockbank*

ICE MOOD (FR)   4 ch.g. Turgeon (USA) – Miss Mood (Bon Sang (FR)) [2002/3   **c139**
15v⁵ c17s c17s* Apr 10] eighth foal: half-brother to 7 winners, including fairly useful   **h85 p**
chaser up to 21f Mood Turk (by Baby Turk) and fair 2m to 2½m chaser Man Mood (by
Brinkmanship): dam 11f winner at 4 yrs on Flat: fifth in newcomers hurdle on debut: most
progressive hurdler, winning last 3 starts, all at Auteuil, minor events in April and
May and Group 1 Prix Ferdinand Dufaure later in May: always well placed in steadily-
run event when beating Kapgarde a neck in last-named: stays 2½m: raced on soft/heavy
going: may improve even further. *A. Chaille-Chaille, France*

ICENI QUEEN   5 b.m. Formidable (USA) – Queen Warrior (Daring March) [2002/3   **h–**
h–: 17gᵖᵘ May 1] seemingly of little account. *D. J. Minty*

ICE SAINT   8 gr.g. Ballacashtal (CAN) – Sylvan Song (Song) [2002/3 22m* 24gʳᵒ   **h82**
22m* 19g⁴ 22s³ 26g 22d Feb 17] good-topped gelding: winning pointer: bought 5,500
gns Doncaster May Sales: poor hurdler: won novices at Stratford in June (handicap) and
July: should stay 3m: acts on heavy and good to firm going. *M. J. Gingell*

ICHI BEAU (IRE)   9 b.g. Convinced – May As Well (Kemal (FR)) [2002/3 c140,   **c124**
h108: c16f⁵ c17g⁶ c16gᵖᵘ c20m² c16m² 16g² Apr 24] sturdy, deep-bodied gelding: useful   **h99**
chaser: below best in 2002/3, second to Kadarann and Korakor in weakly-contested
handicaps on consecutive days at Ayr: fair maiden over hurdles, no match for Laouen in
novice at Perth: best form at 2m: acts on heavy and good to firm going: tongue tied:
effective held up or making running: bold jumper, though inclined to make odd mistake.
Ferdy Murphy

ICKFORD OKEY   11 b.g. Broadsword (USA) – Running Kiss (Deep Run) [2002/3   **c89**
c96, h–: c25g⁵ c24m² c25dᵘʳ Mar 6] big, rangy gelding: fair pointer/hunter chaser: threw   **h–**
away winning chance after being left clear last at Huntingdon second outing, idling badly
and hanging left: stays 3m: acts on good to soft and good to firm going: unseated early
only outing in blinkers: sketchy jumper. *Mrs S. S. Harbour*

ICONIC   9 b.g. Reprimand – Miami Melody (Miami Springs) [2002/3 c–, h–: c21m⁵   **c–**
May 22] poor novice hurdler/chaser. *Darren Page*   **h–**

I CRIED FOR YOU (IRE)   8 b.g. Statoblest – Fall of The Hammer (IRE) (Auction   **h88**
Ring (USA)) [2002/3 16d 16d⁶ 16d⁶ Feb 26] sturdy gelding: useful on Flat (stays 1¼m),
several creditable efforts in 2002: modest form when sixth in novice hurdles: will prove
best with emphasis on speed at 2m. *J. G. Given*

ICY RIVER (IRE)   6 ch.g. Over The River (FR) – Icy Lou (Bluerullah) [2002/3 F16v⁵   **h73 p**
F16v⁶ 16d 20g⁶ Apr 1] strong, lengthy gelding: seventh foal: brother to fairly useful   **F80**
chaser Time of Flight, stays 2½m, and fair staying hurdler Ganpati: dam won Irish point:
better effort in bumpers when fifth of 14 at Newcastle on debut: never on terms and not
knocked about in novice hurdles at Wetherby and Newcastle: will prove suited by 2½m+:
capable of better. *Mrs M. Reveley*

IDAHO D'OX (FR)   7 b.g. Bad Conduct (USA) – Queseda (FR) (Quart de Vin (FR))   **c–**
[2002/3 c107, h127: c17gᵖᵘ 16v 16s 16v² 16d 16v 17g 16g⁵ Apr 5] sparely-made gelding: **h128**
fairly useful handicap hurdler: 50/1, best effort in 2002/3 when 15 lengths second of 20
to Chauvinist in valuable event at Ascot in December, keeping on late past beaten horses
and probably flattered: jumped appallingly only outing over fences in Britain: best form
around 2m: acts on any going: blinkered/visored: normally held up: probably doesn't
have ideal attitude. *M. C. Pipe*

IDBURY (IRE)   5 b.g. Zaffaran (USA) – Delcarrow (Roi Guillaume (FR)) [2002/3   **F–**
F16v F17s F16d⁵ Mar 1] 17,000 4-y-o: strong, good-topped gelding: sixth foal: dam unraced: well held in 3 bumpers. *N. A. Twiston-Davies*

IDEAL DU BOIS BEURY (FR)   7 b. or br.g. Useful (FR) – Pampa Star (FR) (Pampa-   **c104**
bird) [2002/3 h128: c16s² c19s² c16s⁴ c21sᵖᵘ 22v 21m 21g Mar 12] leggy gelding: fairly   **h–**
useful hurdler in 2001/2: fair form when runner-up first 2 starts in novice chases: no form
subsequently, including back in handicap hurdles: stays 2½m: acts on heavy going: tried
visored: held up: joined P. Monteith. *M. C. Pipe*

IDEAL JACK (FR)   7 b.g. Agent Bleu (FR) – Nuit Des Fanges (FR) (Trac) [2002/3   **c100 d**
c19d³ c17vᵖᵘ c19d³ c16g Apr 21] modest hurdler in 2000/1: third in novice handicap   **h–**
chase at Taunton on return from 2½-year absence: disappointing in 3 similar events
subsequently: stays 2¾m: probably acts on any going: visored. *M. C. Pipe*

IDEALKO (FR)   7 b.g. Kadalko (FR) – Belfaster (FR) (Royal Charter (FR)) [2002/3   **c101**
c–, h–: 20d⁴ 20s² 20sᵖᵘ 21gᵘʳ c20g* c20m³ c20m³ Apr 10] leggy gelding: modest maiden   **h90**
hurdler: fair chaser: won from handicap at Ludlow in March: stays 2½m: acts on soft and good
to firm going. *Ian Williams*

Tote Exacta Handicap Chase, Wetherby—bold-jumping front-runner Il'Athou in action

IDEAS MAN (IRE)   7 b.g. Executive Perk – Emmodee (Bowling Pin) [2002/3 F74: 17d^R 17m^5 c16m^4 c16m^4 c20d^F c21d^{pu} Apr 8] tall, sparely-made gelding: signs of ability in bumpers: no worthwhile form in novice hurdles or chases: blinkered second start (pulled hard). *D. McCain*

     c–
     h–

IDLEWILD (IRE)   8 br.g. Phardante (FR) – Delia Murphy (Golden Love) [2002/3 c–: 20m^5 20g^{pu} c16m^{pu} Apr 21] maiden pointer: no form in steeplechases or over hurdles (looked none too keen): tried blinkered. *M. J. Polglase*

     c–
     h–

IDOLE DES FONTAINES (FR)   7 b.g. Le Riverain (FR) – Dame d'Avril (FR) (Brezzo (FR)) [2002/3 c129, h?: 20s^4 c23s^5 c25s 18v^6 c26v^3 c21v^2 c22s^2 Apr 13] useful hurdler at best, better effort in 2002/3 when sixth in handicap at Auteuil: smart chaser: improved efforts there when second to Line Marine in Group 3 in March and to Jerico Vallis in Group 2 in April: pulled up in Grand Steeple-Chase de Paris there in May: best short of 3m: acts on heavy going: has worn blinkers/tongue strap. *C. Diard, France*

     c146
     h127

IFNI DU LUC (FR)   7 b. or br.m. Chamberlin (FR) – Acca du Luc (FR) (Djarvis (FR)) [2002/3 c125p, h–: c20g^2 c24s^F c24s^4 c24g c21d^{ur} c20m^6 Apr 26] leggy mare: useful handicap chaser: good short-head second of 5 to Sir Toby at Leicester on reappearance: barely stays testing 3m: acts on heavy going, well held on good to firm final start: has run creditably when sweating. *N. J. Henderson*

     c133
     h–

IFRANE BALIMA (FR)   7 ch.g. Video Rock (FR) – Balima Des Saccart (FR) (Quart de Vin (FR)) [2002/3 h65: 17d^3 16s* 16s* 16d^4 16v^6 18s 17g Mar 18] rather leggy gelding: modest hurdler: improved form when winning handicaps at Uttoxeter and Leicester in November: poor efforts last 3 outings: raced around 2m: acts on soft going: has pulled hard/hung right. *J. C. Tuck*

     h90

IFTIKHAR (USA)   4 b.g. Storm Cat (USA) – Muhbubh (USA) (Blushing Groom (FR)) [2002/3 F16g^2 Mar 16] 9,000 3-y-o: half-brother to several winners, including useful 1995 2-y-o 5f/6f winner Amaniy (by Dayjur) and smart 6f and 7f winner Kayrawan (by Mr Prospector): dam won Princess Margaret Stakes: second to She's Our Native in bumper at Ludlow on debut, tending to edge left. *W. M. Brisbourne*

     F96

I GOT RHYTHM   5 gr.m. Lycius (USA) – Eurythmic (Pharly (FR)) [2002/3 h94: 16m^4 20d^2 16d^2 16g^3 Feb 28] angular mare: modest hurdler: likely to be suited by 2½m: acts on good to firm and good to soft going. *Mrs M. Reveley*

     h97

I HAVNT A CENT (IRE)   6 b.g. Unfuwain (USA) – Miss Gris (USA) (Hail The Pirates (USA)) [2002/3 F16s F16s* F16d 18s 16d Mar 17] half-brother to several winners, including smart 7f to 1m winner Mahoob (by Marju), useful 1m to 1¾m winner in Britain/UAE Nabhaan (by In The Wings) and fairly useful 2m hurdler Elflaa (by Sure Blade): dam very smart 2-y-o, useful 1m and 10.5f winner at 3 yrs: easily best effort in bumpers when winning maiden at Down Royal in December: well held in 2 maiden hurdles. *D. Broad, Ireland*

     h–
     F104

I HEAR THUNDER (IRE)   5 b.g. Montelimar (USA) – Carrigeen Gala (Strong Gale) [2002/3 F16s F16s Jan 18] 29,000 4-y-o: fourth foal: dam winning pointer: well held in 2 bumpers. *R. H. Buckler*

     F–

IJIKA (FR)   7 ch.g. Aelan Hapi (USA) – Belle Des Airs (FR) (Saumon (FR)) [2002/3   **c–**
h95: c17d c16d^{pu} c19d^{pu} 20s^{pu} Feb 8] modest maiden hurdler: no show over fences first 3   **h–**
starts: ran no sort of race back over hurdles final appearance: should stay beyond 2m:
raced on good going or softer: reportedly lame second outing. *H. D. Daly*

IKRENEL ROYAL (FR)   7 b.g. Bricassar (USA) – Kreneldore (FR) (Trenel) [2002/3   **c115**
c24v^{pu} c20g^6 Jan 18] winning hurdler: successful first 2 starts over fences, useful form in   **h–**
quite valuable novice at Sandown on British debut in 2000/1: well below best on return
from 20-month absence: stays 2½m: acts on heavy going. *N. J. Henderson*

ILABON (FR)   7 ch.g. Secret Haunt (USA) – Ahuille (FR) (Haltea (FR)) [2002/3 19g^4 **h120**
18s^5 16v^3 16m^2 Mar 22] angular ex-French gelding: fourth known foal: brother to 13f
winner on Flat in France: dam never ran: won non-thoroughbred event around 11f on Flat
at 5 yrs: twice-raced over hurdles for L. Viel, sold €30,000 Goffs November Sale: better
effort in Britain when neck second to Pepe Galvez in novice at Newbury: sure to win a
race. *M. C. Pipe*

ILARE (FR)   7 gr.g. April Night (FR) – Vousseliere (FR) (Tourangeau (FR)) [2002/3   **c146**
18s^6 c23v^2 Apr 26] raced exclusively at Auteuil: unbeaten in first 6 starts over jumps, and   **h117**
6 lengths second to Kotkijet in Grand Steeple-Chase de Paris in May 2001: injured tendon
in October that year, smart form over fences on return, second to impressive Line Marine
in Prix William Head in April and fifth to same horse in latest renewal of Grand
Steeple-Chase: stays 29f: raced on going softer than good (acts on heavy). *E. Chevalier
du Fau, France*

IL'ATHOU (FR)   7 b.g. Lute Antique (FR) – Va Thou Line (FR) (El Badr) [2002/3   **c145**
c135, h–: c20d^F c20d^2 c20g^{pu} c20d* c20d^3 Mar 1] tall, lengthy gelding: smart handicap   **h–**
chaser: won at Wetherby in February by 13 lengths from Dorans Gold: good third to
Goguenard at Haydock final start: stays 2½m: acts on heavy going: tends to get on toes
and sometimes sweats: bold-jumping front runner who races freely. *S. E. H. Sherwood*

IL CAPITANO   6 ch.g. Be My Chief (USA) – Taza (Persian Bold) [2002/3 h110:   **c127**
c26m* c20m* c22f^3 24f* 20m* 19f* c19f* c24m^2 c19f* c25m^3 c20f* Apr 25] leggy   **h119 +**
gelding: fairly useful hurdler, won in small fields at Exeter (twice) and
Chepstow within 10 days in October: fairly useful novice chaser: again very well placed,
won at Fontwell (twice) in May, Taunton in October and April and Sandown (handicap)
later in April: effective at 19f to 27f: best efforts on good going or firmer (goes very well
on firm): tough and consistent. *P. F. Nicholls*

*Bet attheraces 0800 083 83 83 Novices' Handicap Chase, Sandown—Il Capitano (stripes) en route
to his eighth win of the season; runner-up Iris Royal is on the left*

IL CAVALIERE 8 b.g. Mtoto – Kalmia (Miller's Mate) [2002/3 h113: 20d² 19g² 20g* **h121** 21d* 21mᶠ Feb 22] sturdy gelding: fairly useful on Flat, below best in 2002: fairly novice hurdler: won maiden at Musselburgh (easily) in December and handicap at Kempton in January, improved form when beating Persian Waters ¾ length on latter course: will stay beyond 21f: acts on firm and good to soft going: held up. *Mrs M. Reveley*

ILE DE LIBRATE 9 b.g. Librate – Little Missile (Ile de Bourbon (USA)) [2002/3 **c98 ?** c98, h90: 22d 22s c24d c26fᵘʳ Apr 24] leggy gelding: modest hurdler/chaser: first sign of **h–** retaining ability in 2002/3 when unseating 4 out, yet to be asked for maximum effort, in handicap chase at Fontwell: stays 3¼m: acts on soft and firm going: tongue tied last 2 outings. *R. J. O'Sullivan*

ILE DISTINCT (IRE) 9 b.g. Dancing Dissident (USA) – Golden Sunlight (Ile de **c–** Bourbon (USA)) [2002/3 c–, h65: c16mᵖᵘ c21m⁶ Jul 14] angular gelding: poor maiden **h–** hurdler: little show over fences: probably stays 2½m: best efforts on going firmer than good (acts on firm). *K. R. Pearce*

ILEWIN JANINE (IRE) 12 b.m. Soughaan (USA) – Mystery Queen (Martinmas) **c–** [2002/3 c78, h85: c19d c18d³ Nov 11] leggy, long-backed mare: winning hurdler: poor **h–** handicap chaser: badly let down by jumping final start: stays 2½m when conditions aren't testing: acts on any going: visored once. *G. Brown*

I'LLEVEIT TOU (IRE) 7 b.g. King Luthier – Shady Jumbo (Callernish) [2002/3 **F81** F18g² Apr 29] fourth foal: half-brother to winning pointer by Brush Aside: dam unraced: second of 12 in bumper at Plumpton on debut. *R. Rowe*

ILLINEYLAD (IRE) 9 b.g. Whitehall Bridge – Illiney Girl (Lochnager) [2002/3 **c72** c68, h76: c24mᵖᵘ c23g² c24mᵖᵘ c22g³ Oct 6] sparely-made gelding: winning pointer: **h–** poor maiden hurdler/chaser: stays 25f: acts on good to firm and good to soft going: visored once: has broken blood vessel. *Mrs N. S. Sharpe*

ILL SWING BY (IRE) 9 b.m. Jurado (USA) – Big Sally (Salluceva) [2002/3 16g⁴ **c–** 21mᵖᵘ 20d⁶ 21v c16mᶠ 16s c16v⁵ Mar 13] winning pointer: little form otherwise. **h–** *Miss S. E. Forster*

ILLUMINATE 10 b.g. Marju (IRE) – Light Bee (USA) (Majestic Light (USA)) **h–** [2002/3 18v⁵ 21m Apr 19] leggy gelding: modest hurdler at best: off over 2 years prior to showing little in 2002/3: stays 2½m: acts on heavy going. *D. C. O'Brien*

ILNAMAR (FR) 7 b.g. Officiel (FR) – Quillemare (FR) (Le Pontet (FR)) [2002/3 **c–** c136, h156: 16s³ Jan 18] good-topped gelding: useful chaser: high-class hurdler: much **h145** improved last 2 starts in 2001/2, winning Coral Eurobet Cup at Cheltenham and Grade 1 Martell Aintree Hurdle: off 9 months, below-form third to Flame Creek in Grade 2 at Haydock on reappearance: reported following month to have suffered tendon strain and missed rest of season: likely to stay 3m: acts on good to firm and heavy going. *M. C. Pipe*

ILTON 4 ch.g. Dr Devious (IRE) – Madame Crecy (USA) (Al Nasr (FR)) [2002/3 16dᵖᵘ **h83** 16dᶠ 16s⁴ 20s⁵ 17v³ 16g 16gᵖᵘ Mar 23] workmanlike gelding: modest maiden on Flat (seems to stay 1½m), sold out of J. Bethell's stable 3,000 gns Doncaster September Sales: modest juvenile hurdler: best around 2m: acts on heavy going. *M. E. Sowersby*

IMAGE DE MARQUE II (FR) 7 b.m. Royal Charter (FR) – Tourbrune (FR) **c–** (Pamponi (FR)) [2002/3 c–, h131: 22d⁶ 20dᶠ 17g 16m Apr 11] small, angular mare: **h115 d** useful hurdler in 2001/2, nowhere near so good in 2002/3: stays 21f: acts on soft and good to firm going: tongue tied: held up. *M. C. Pipe*

IMAGINAIRE (USA) 8 b.g. Quest For Fame – Hail The Dancer (USA) (Green **c104** Dancer (USA)) [2002/3 c119, h–: c16m⁴ c16m³ c21dᵇᵈ c20d³ c20d⁴ Jan 16] angular **h–** gelding: fair chaser: effective at 2m to 23f: acts on heavy going, possibly unsuited by good to firm: has had tongue tied: jumps well: sometimes finds little. *Miss Venetia Williams*

IMAGO II (FR) 7 b.g. Chamberlin (FR) – Pensee d'Amour (FR) (Porto Rafti (FR)) **c101** [2002/3 h81: c22dᵖᵘ c24d c22s⁶ Dec 28] tall gelding: poor form in novice hurdles: let **h–** down by jumping all 3 starts over fences, likely to have shown fair form but for almost falling 3 out on reappearance: should be suited by further than 2½m: tried blinkered. *Jonjo O'Neill*

I'M DREAMING (IRE) 9 ch.g. White Christmas – Suffolk Bells (London Bells **c89** (CAN)) [2002/3 c69: c20s³ c24sᵖᵘ c20m⁵ c24g⁴ c26m⁶ Apr 17] medium-sized gelding: winning pointer: modest on balance of form in hunters: best around 2½m: acts on heavy going: has had tongue tied. *Andrew J. Martin*

I'M FOR WAITING 7 ch.g. Democratic (USA) – Fausterelie (Faustus (USA)) **h72** [2002/3 h59: 21g² Mar 14] small gelding: poor hurdler: stays 21f: acts on heavy going: blinkered once. *John Allen*

IMMOLA (FR)   7 b. or br.g. Quart de Vin (FR) – Jessica (FR) (Laniste) [2002/3 F16v   **h106 p**
F16s⁴ 16v⁵ 16v* Mar 8] tall, useful-looking gelding: chasing type: eleventh foal: brother   **F76**
to 25f chase winner Quazvin II and brother/half-brother to 6 winners on Flat: dam
maiden: modest form on second of 2 starts in bumpers: much better effort over hurdles
when winning novice at Sandown by distance, soon clear and galloping on strongly: will
stay well beyond 2m: raced only on soft/heavy going: should continue to progress.
Miss E. C. Lavelle

IMNOTALADY   5 ch.m. Shalford (IRE) – Lissahane Lass (Daring March) [2002/3   **h–**
F67: F13s⁶ 18s⁵ Dec 26] poor form in 2 bumpers: showed nothing on hurdling debut.   **F64**
P. R. Hedger

IMPALA   9 ch.g. Interrex (CAN) – Raleigh Gazelle (Absalom) [2002/3 16mᵇᵈ 16m   **h–**
16mᵖᵘ 17gᵖᵘ 17mᵖᵘ 17dᵖᵘ Sep 4] compact gelding: fair hurdler in 2000/1, no sign of
retaining ability: raced around 2m: acts on firm and good to soft going: has had tongue
tied. *W. G. M. Turner*

IMPEK (FR)   7 b.g. Lute Antique (FR) – Attualita (FR) (Master Thatch) [2002/3   **c152**
h147: c16g* c16g* c16s* c16g² c16g³ Apr 5]   **h–**
A Ludlow maiden hurdle worth little more than £3,000 was the only success
Impek had to his name after a couple of seasons over the smaller obstacles. That
was scant reward, considering he made into a smart hurdler in the 2001/2 season,
ending with a narrow defeat in the Imperial Cup at Sandown and a good third to
Copeland and Intersky Falcon in the Masai Hurdle at the same course. Impek's
chasing career, on the other hand, has proved much more lucrative and it has taken
only a handful of races for him to prove himself as good a chaser as he was a
hurdler. As a confidence booster, Impek made his chasing debut soon after the start
of the new season before being put away for the more serious winter campaign. As
might have been expected for a novice chase in May, a distinctly mixed bag took on

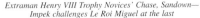

Extraman Henry VIII Trophy Novices' Chase, Sandown—
Impek challenges Le Roi Miguel at the last

Impek at Huntingdon and he landed the odds impressively, jumping increasingly fluently as the race went on and winning with any amount in hand. Unlikely as it seemed at the time, Impek took what turned out to be his biggest scalp of the season, inflicting the only defeat over fences on runner-up La Landiere whose seven subsequent wins included the Racing Post Chase and the Cathcart Chase.

Considered best when fresh, Impek was due to return at Kempton in late-October (and would have faced only one rival) but his trainer withdrew all her horses from the meeting, branding the state of the track 'an absolute disgrace'. Instead, Impek contributed to Hereford's hottest novice chase of the season when taking on Vol Solitaire and three others nearly a fortnight later. Impek's jumping was again impressive and, after odds-on Vol Solitaire fell when challenged two out, Impek needed only to be shaken up to assert on the home turn, having a good deal more in hand than the seven-length beating he gave Palarshan, a four-year-old receiving 19 lb from the winner. Impek had another four-year-old as his main rival the following month in Sandown's Extraman Trophy, better known as the Henry VIII Novices' Chase. Le Roi Miguel received 11 lb and looked like making that count when quickening three out, before Impek came with a strong challenge going to the last and showed plenty of resolution to overhaul him on the run-in, winning by a length and a half, with Tysou, the only other runner, well held. Impek's winning time was faster than that recorded by Cenkos in winning the Tingle Creek Chase just over half an hour later.

After Sandown, Impek was put aside for the Arkle Trophy at Cheltenham and, come March, he could still boast some of the best two-mile novice chase form around. Starting 6/1 second favourite, he beat all bar the favourite Azertyuiop, travelling smoothly into contention and battling on well after hitting the second last to take second place from Isio, eleven lengths behind the winner. Azertyuiop's

Mr Jim Lewis' "Impek"

absence from the Maghull Novices' Chase at Aintree seemed to give Impek a good opportunity of landing the Grade 1 prize that had eluded him at Cheltenham, particularly as his four rivals included the pair he had beaten at Sandown, Le Roi Miguel receiving only 3 lb this time. But Impek was already off the bridle in the back straight and was unable to take second after Le Roi Miguel had quickened away, finishing last of the three finishers, just behind runner-up Vol Solitaire. Impek did not altogether redeem his reputation when beaten a second time by Le Roi Miguel in the Swordlestown Cup at Punchestown after the end of the season in Britain, found wanting for pace and staying on to be beaten six lengths after being left second at the final fence.

For all his ability, Impek is an edgy type and, while at the finish of a race he has not done much wrong, he has proved troublesome at the start, at Hereford for example veering left when the tapes went up. His trainer also reported that he could not be coaxed out of his box or onto the gallops when he first arrived at the yard and she accompanied him to lead him in at the start of some of his races in the latest season. Miss Knight has done the trick so far, but the day may come when Impek declines to jump off.

Impek began his career in France with Francois Doumen, winning three Flat races for non-thoroughbreds at a mile and a half before joining his current stable for 1,700,000 francs at the 2000 Goffs Arc Sale. Impek's sire Lute Antique was one of the best four-year-old hurdlers of his generation in France and was a very good chaser too. Lute Antique has already got some good chasers in Britain, including Edelweis du Moulin and Il'Athou, both of whom, like Impek, lost unbeaten records over fences in previous editions of the Arkle. Impek's dam Attualita won twice at around a mile and a quarter in the French Provinces and produced one foal prior to Impek, a brother named Herton who has yet to win in France but has shown fairly useful form over fences. Their lightly-raced grandam Gaouri is also grandam of the smart French chasers Ceillac and D'Auteuil and of Hopeful, a fairly useful hurdler/winning chaser in Britain.

Impek (FR) (b.g. 1996)	Lute Antique (FR) (b 1985)	No Lute (b 1978)	Luthier
			Prudent Miss
		Sweet Annie (ch 1980)	Pharly
			Beronaire
	Attualita (FR) (b 1988)	Master Thatch (ch 1978)	Thatch
			Miss Sarah
		Gaouri (b 1972)	Pan
			Rieuse III

The rather leggy Impek has done all his racing at two miles but is due to be stepped up in trip in his second season over fences; he is likely to stay two and a half miles. He acts on good to firm ground and, despite his trainer's doubts about letting him take his chance there, proved every bit as effective on soft at Sandown. He was well held on his only start on heavy. Patiently ridden, Impek is a good jumper and his record of going well fresh is something to bear in mind when he reappears. He was disappointing when tried once in blinkers over hurdles. *Miss H. C. Knight*

IMPERIAL DE THAIX (FR) 7 b.g. Roi de Rome (USA) – Soiree d'Ete (FR) (Prove It Baby (USA)) [2002/3 c–, h129: 23f c23g³ c26v² c25dᵖᵘ 21s 24s 21m 22fᵖᵘ Mar 27] leggy, close-coupled gelding: fairly useful handicap hurdler/chaser: badly out of sorts after third start: stays 3¼m: acts on heavy and good to firm going: often tongue tied: has been let down by jumping. *M. C. Pipe*   c126 d h117 d

IMPERIAL DREAM (IRE) 5 b.g. Roselier (FR) – Royal Nora (IRE) (Dromod Hill) [2002/3 F16g² F17g² Mar 22] has scope: first foal: dam unraced half-sister to 1996 Cheltenham Gold Cup winner Imperial Call: second in maiden bumpers at Huntingdon and Bangor: will be suited by 2½m+. *Miss H. C. Knight*   F92

IMPERIAL EYE (IRE) 5 b.m. Eagle Eyed (USA) – Capellino (IRE) (Imperial Frontier (USA)) [2002/3 17sᵖᵘ Jul 20] ex-Irish mare: fair maiden on Flat (stays 1m) at 3 yrs for J. Bolger, no form in Britain: raced too freely and not fluent on hurdling debut. *John R. Upson*   h–

IMPERIAL HONORS (IRE) 12 ch.g. Crowning Honors (CAN) – Within A Whisper (Welsh Pageant) [2002/3 c16d c21g⁵ Mar 14] workmanlike gelding: poor pointer/hunter chaser: stays 2¾m. *N. M. Lampard*   c67 h–

Pertemps Final (Handicap Hurdle), Cheltenham—
Inching Closer challenges as the grey Royal Emperor fluffs the last

IMPERIAL LINE (IRE) 9 ch.g. Mac's Imp (USA) – Ellaline (Corvaro (USA)) **c89 ?**
[2002/3 c25m c20m6 c26d2 Jun 8] leggy gelding: modest hunter chaser: won point in **h–**
May: stays 3¼m: acts on good to firm and good to soft going: tongue tied last 2 outings.
Mrs P. A. Cowey

IMPERIAL MAN (IRE) 8 b.g. Mandalus – The Foalicule (Imperial Fling (USA)) **c–**
[2002/3 c–, h–, F84: 17m Apr 19] little form over hurdles or fences, sold out of **h–**
M. Gingell's stable 1,600 gns Doncaster May Sales: tried tongue tied. *P. Spottiswood*

IMPERIAL MIST (IRE) 9 br.g. Royal Fountain – Mossy Mistress (IRE) (Le Moss) **c69**
[2002/3 c26g3 May 22] fair pointer: last of 3 finishers in novice at Uttoxeter on chasing
debut. *K. F. Clutterbuck*

IMPERIAL SHO 4 ch.g. Royal Abjar (USA) – Magnetic Point (USA) (Bering) **F–**
[2002/3 F14d Nov 25] 1,000F, 2,500Y: strong gelding: sixth foal: half-brother to 7f
winner Just Magical (by Emperor Jones) and Slovak 2-y-o winner by Most Welcome:
dam, maiden who stayed 1¼m, half-sister to US 2-y-o Grade 1 6.5f winner Great Navigator, out of Poule d'Essai des Pouliches second Nonoalca: well beaten in bumper on
debut. *J. R. Weymes*

IMPERO 5 b.g. Emperor Jones (USA) – Fight Right (FR) (Crystal Glitters (USA)) **h–**
[2002/3 h–: 19dpu 19dpu 16dpu Apr 9] medium-sized gelding: little sign of ability over
hurdles. *R. J. Armson*

IMPERTIO 9 b.g. Primitive Rising (USA) – Silly Beggar (Silly Prices) [2002/3 **c105 §**
c108§, h–§: c26s4 c25v4 c27d c24v3 c24s3 c24v2 c24d3 c31gpu Apr 24] strong gelding: **h– §**
fair handicap chaser: lame final start: stays 3½m: acts on good to firm and heavy going:
has won with/without blinkers: jumps soundly in main: weak finisher. *P. Beaumont*

IMPETUS (GER) 7 b.g. Lomitas – Ile de Re (GER) (Readily (ARG)) [2002/3 h68: **h–**
16s 17m 16g Aug 26] leggy, angular gelding: maiden hurdler: no form in 2002/3: tried
blinkered: pulls hard and has looked none too keen. *P. Wegmann*

IMPINDA (IRE) 4 b.f. Idris (IRE) – Last Finale (USA) (Stop The Music (USA)) **F81**
[2002/3 F14d3 F16g F16d Feb 23] IR 5,000F, 9,000Y: smallish filly: third foal: dam
unraced daughter of multiple US Grade 1 winner Optimistic Gal: soon off bridle when
third in bumper at Newcastle on debut: tongue tied, well held subsequently, including on
Flat debut in April. *P. Monteith*

IMPISH JUDE 5 b.m. Imp Society (USA) – Miss Nanna (Vayrann) [2002/3 16d 16s3 **h86**
17s* 16d 17d2 16d Feb 25] rather leggy mare: modest maiden on Flat (stays 13f): modest
hurdler: won novice seller at Hereford in December: raced around 2m on good to soft/soft
going. *J. Mackie*

IMPISH LAD 5 b.g. Imp Society (USA) – Madonna Da Rossi (Mtoto) [2002/3 h–: **h–**
16g May 29] small gelding: little form over hurdles. *D. W. Whillans*

IMPORTANT BOY (ARG) 6 ch.g. Equalize (USA) – Important Girl (ARG) **h77**
(Candy Stripes (USA)) [2002/3 16f 17g6 16s 16f3 21fpu Oct 24] won 3 times on Flat in
Argentina from 1m to 10.5f in early-2001, runner-up once from 5 starts in Britain in 2002:
poor novice hurdler: may prove best around 2m: acts on firm ground: joined D. Scott.
J. A. B. Old

IMPREVUE (IRE) 9 ch.m. Priolo (USA) – Las Bela (Welsh Pageant) [2002/3 h–: **h72**
20m* 20m4 Aug 23] poor hurdler: best effort when winning selling handicap at Worcester

394

in July: stays 2½m: acts on good to firm going: usually blinkered: joined Miss S. Wilton. *R. J. O'Sullivan*

I'M THE MAN 12 ro.g. Say Primula – Vinovia (Ribston) [2002/3 c86§, h93§: c28d² c21g³ Apr 3] workmanlike gelding: winning hurdler: fair chaser: sold privately out of Mrs D. Sayer's stable 5,000 gns Doncaster November Sales: second in hunter at Catterick on reappearance: appeared to excel himself when never-nearer third in Fox Hunters' at Aintree 2 months later: stays 3¾m: acts on any going: inconsistent. *Mrs S. H. Shirley-Beavan* **c105 §** **h– §**

I'M WILLIE'S GIRL 7 br.m. Royal Fountain – Milton Lass (Scallywag) [2002/3 20g^pu Apr 30] third foal: dam signs of a little ability in points: showed nothing in novice hurdle on debut. *F. P. Murtagh* **h–**

INAKI (FR) 6 b.g. Dounba (FR) – Incredule (FR) (Concertino (FR)) [2002/3 c105d, h–: c17d⁵ c16g⁶ c20s* c20v⁵ c20g² c21g² Mar 14] leggy, useful-looking gelding: fair handicap chaser: won easily at Plumpton in January: stays 21f: acts on heavy going: tried blinkered, creditable efforts in visor last 2 starts. *P. Winkworth* **c103** **h–**

INCA TRAIL (IRE) 7 br.g. Un Desperado (FR) – Katday (FR) (Miller's Mate) [2002/3 F110p: F16d³ 16s² 21s* 16g 20g^pu Apr 3] tall, good sort: useful bumper winner: confirmed promise of hurdling debut when winning maiden at Ludlow in January, still looking green: best effort when eighth of 19 to Back In Front in Grade 1 novice at Cheltenham fourth start: found little when well below best at Aintree 3 weeks later: will stay beyond 21f: raced on good ground or softer (acts on soft): type to do well in novice chases in 2003/4. *Miss H. C. Knight* **h128** **F110**

INCHING CLOSER 6 b.g. Inchinor – Maiyaasah (Kris) [2002/3 h112: 20s* 25g* 24g Apr 3] tall, leggy gelding: reportedly had wind operation before reappearance: smart hurdler: much improved in 2002/3, won handicaps at Haydock in February and Cheltenham in March: best effort when beating Royal Emperor a short head in 24-runner Pertemps Final at latter: best at 2½m+ (stays 27f): acts on soft going: reportedly bled from nose final start. *Jonjo O'Neill* **h145**

Mrs N. L. Spence's "Inching Closer"

INCH PERFECT   8 b.g. Inchinor – Scarlet Veil (Tyrnavos) [2002/3 16g⁴ 16v² c16d* **c102**
c16g² 17d³ Apr 8] leggy, sparely-made gelding: fairly useful on Flat (stays 1¾m), won **h89**
twice in January: modest maiden hurdler: better form over fences, winning maiden at
Catterick in March: likely to prove best with emphasis on speed at 2m: acts on good to
soft going: found less than seemed likely final start. *R. A. Fahey*

INCH WAY (IRE)   11 br.g. Kambalda – Glenaveel (Furry Glen) [2002/3 c69, h–: **c64**
c24dᵖᵘ c25g⁶ Jan 18] neat gelding: poor handicap chaser: stays 3¼m: acts on heavy **h–**
going: tried blinkered/tongue tied: pulls hard. *A. J. Lockwood*

IN CONTRAST (IRE)   7 b. or br.g. Be My Native (USA) – Ballinamona Lady (IRE) **h149**
(Le Bavard (FR)) [2002/3 h144: 16m³ 16dᶠ 21d³ 16g⁴ 16g⁶ 16m* Apr 12] leggy gelding:
smart hurdler: won Samsung Electronics Scottish Champion Hurdle (Limited Handicap)
at Ayr by 2½ lengths from Thisthatandtother: mostly good efforts otherwise in 2002/3,
sixth to Rooster Booster in Champion Hurdle at Cheltenham previous outing: has won at
2½f but best form at 2m: acts on good to firm and good to soft going (well held on heavy
in bumpers): hangs left under pressure: held up and suited by truly-run race: sometimes
makes mistakes: consistent. *P. J. Hobbs*

INCORPORATION   4 b.g. In The Wings – Danishkada (Thatch (USA)) [2002/3 **h–**
17sᵖᵘ Nov 21] well held on Flat, sold out of R. Charlton's stable 2,400 gns Doncaster
August Sales: showed nothing on hurdling debut. *J. K. Price*

INDALO (IRE)   8 b.g. Lord Americo – Parson's Princess (The Parson) [2002/3 h126: **c121 x**
c16m* c22d² c17d⁴ c20s³ c19s* c20d* c21s⁵ c20g³ c20m³ Apr 26] compact gelding: **h–**
fairly useful hurdler: similar standard over fences: simple tasks in novices at Haydock in
October and Plumpton in February and also won handicap at Taunton in January: stays
2¾m: acts on heavy and good to firm going: takes strong hold: usually makes mistakes.
Miss Venetia Williams

INDECISIVE   8 ch.m. Then Again – Nine Hans (Prince Hansel) [2002/3 h–: 22s 24sᵖᵘ **h–**
Feb 27] no sign of ability. *M. J. Coombe*

Samsung Electronics Scottish Champion Hurdle (Limited Handicap), Ayr—
In Contrast makes the most of ideal conditions; Thisthatandtother is in pursuit at the last

Mr Tony Staple's "In Contrast"

INDEED (IRE) 8 ch.g. Camden Town – Pamrina (Pamroy) [2002/3 h103p: 18d c21d^F c20d^2 c20g^2 Mar 12] strong gelding: winning hurdler: chaser on looks and much better form when second to Scots Grey in novice at Kempton: let down by jumping both other starts over fences: should stay beyond 2½m: raced on good going or softer. *J. T. Gifford* — **c117 h–**

INDEED TO GOODNESS (IRE) 8 b.m. Welsh Term – Clare's Sheen (Choral Society) [2002/3 h99: 19d^3 20s^2 c26s* c19d^{ur} c20s^F c26v^3 c26v^{pu} Feb 10] tall mare: modest hurdler: similar form on completed starts in novice chases, won at Plumpton in November: stays 3¼m: acts on heavy going: tended to jump left final start. *J. W. Mullins* — **c99 h99**

INDEPENDENCE HALL (IRE) 6 b.g. Sadler's Wells (USA) – Fruition (Rheingold) [2002/3 17s^6 22s 22v 22v^5 22v Feb 11] half-brother to fairly useful staying hurdler Great Marquess (by Touching Wood): fairly useful 1½m winner at 3 yrs but has deteriorated on Flat since: poor novice hurdler: stays 2¾m: acts on heavy going. *J. E. Long* — **h75**

INDIANA JOURNEY (IRE) 8 b.m. Eurobus – Indiana Dancer (Hallgate) [2002/3 c76, h100: c22d^3 c16d^{ur} 16g^6 c20m^4 c18g* 16f^3 c16v^5 c18s Dec 11] easily best effort over fences when winning maiden at Downpatrick in September: probably found ground too testing when well held last 2 starts: stays 21f: acts on firm going. *A. J. Martin, Ireland* — **c106 h107**

INDIAN BEAT 6 ch.g. Indian Ridge – Rappa Tap Tap (FR) (Tap On Wood) [2002/3 h–: 16m^5 22d^{pu} Sep 4] little show in 3 races over hurdles: has looked none too keen. *C. L. Popham* — **h–**

INDIAN CHANCE 9 b.g. Teenoso (USA) – Icy Miss (Random Shot) [2002/3 c100, h–: c25d* c25d^{pu} c25d^4 c24s^6 Feb 1] useful-looking gelding: fairly useful handicap chaser: won at Towcester in April: stays 25f: acts on heavy going: usually sound jumper. *Dr J. R. J. Naylor* — **c115 h–**

INDIAN GUNNER 10 b.g. Gunner B – Icy Miss (Random Shot) [2002/3 c86, h–: c20g^3 c16d* c16v^{pu} c16g c21d* c25m* c21d Apr 4] tall, good-topped gelding: fairly — **c115 h–**

useful handicap chaser: won at Wincanton in December and twice in March: effective at 2m to easy 25f: acts on good to firm and good to soft going: has had tongue tied. *Dr J. R. J. Naylor*

INDIAN MISS 11 b.m. Idiot's Delight – Icy Miss (Random Shot) [2002/3 c–: c25f^{pu} May 15] lengthy, workmanlike mare: lightly raced: fair handicap chaser in 1999/00, no form since. *Dr J. R. J. Naylor*

c–

INDIAN SCOUT (IRE) 8 b.g. Phardante (FR) – Kemchee (Kemal (FR)) [2002/3 c20d* c21v^2 c24s^F Feb 15] rangy, good sort: fairly useful novice hurdler in 2000/1: off 21 months (reportedly due to severe bout of colic), similar form in novice chases on return, won at Haydock in November: stays 21f: raced on going softer than good (acts on heavy). *B. De Haan*

c123
h–

INDIAN STAR (GER) 5 b.g. Sternkoenig (IRE) – Indian Night (GER) (Windwurf (GER)) [2002/3 16g 16m 19g* Apr 19] leggy ex-German gelding: successful at 1m (at 2 yrs) and 11f (at 4 yrs) on Flat for P. Schiergen: best effort in maiden hurdles when winning at Stratford, held in second when left clear last. *J. C. Tuck*

h88 +

INDIAN SUN 6 ch.g. Indian Ridge – Star Tulip (Night Shift (USA)) [2002/3 h–: 16d 16d 17g^{pu} 17s^2 16g^5 16v^F 16m* Apr 2] compact gelding: modest on Flat (probably stays 2m): poor hurdler: won seller at Ludlow in April: should stay beyond 2m: acts on good to firm and heavy going: usually tongue tied. *R. L. Brown*

h71

INDIAN TEMPLE 12 ch.g. Minster Son – Indian Flower (Mansingh (USA)) [2002/3 c–, h–: c25d^{pu} c25g Jun 12] lengthy, angular gelding: winning chaser: of little account nowadays. *K. Bishop*

c–
h–

INDIAN VENTURE (IRE) 9 b.g. Commanche Run – Believe It Or Not (Quayside) [2002/3 h113: c16g^4 c20m^F c16g^4 c16g^2 c20s^5 c16d^F c17m^3 Apr 21] lengthy, angular gelding: fair hurdler: fair novice chaser: won at Sedgefield in March and Market Rasen in April: probably stays 2½m: acts on soft and good to firm going: tends to carry head rather high. *N. G. Richards*

c102
h–

INDIAN VICEROY 10 b.g. Lord Bud – Poppadom (Rapid River) [2002/3 c76, h–: c19d^{pu} c21m c16v^{pu} Jan 22] workmanlike gelding: poor handicap chaser, little form since 2000/1: blinkered once. *P. Winkworth*

c–
h–

INDIAN WINGS (IRE) 10 b.g. Commanche Run – Got To Fly (IRE) (Kemal (FR)) [2002/3 c–, h101: c16g^2 Aug 17] strong gelding: successful 3 times in Irish points: fair hurdler: easily best effort in novice chases when second at Perth only start in 2002/3: stays 3m: raced on good ground or softer (acts on soft). *A. Scott*

c94
h–

INDIEN DU BOULAY (FR) 7 ch.g. Chef de Clan II (FR) – Radesgirl (FR) (Radetzky Marsch (USA)) [2002/3 c106, h87+: c22g^4 c20m^F c20d^3 16v^4 c24g* 24g c22d^{pu} Mar 1] leggy, useful-looking gelding: winning hurdler: fair chaser: won handicap at Musselburgh in December: stays 3m: acts on good to firm and heavy going: tried blinkered/visored/in cheekpieces: often looks ungenuine. *P. Monteith*

c110 §
h– §

INDIEN ROYAL (FR) 4 b.g. Dauphin du Bourg (FR) – Royale Nabeysse (FR) (Beyssac (FR)) [2002/3 15v^5 16s 18s 18s^3 16s^2 16v^2 16d^2 16g^2 17m* Apr 16] good-topped ex-French gelding: first foal: dam twice-raced over hurdles: twice-raced over 1¼m on Flat: fairly useful juvenile hurdler: left B. Barbier after fourth start: won novice at Cheltenham, leading on bridle entering straight and soon quickening clear: likely to stay 2½m: acts on heavy and good to firm going: reliable. *P. F. Nicholls*

h115 +

INDIGO BEACH (IRE) 7 b.g. Rainbows For Life (CAN) – Sandy Maid (Sandy Creek) [2002/3 h66: 17m 16g* 16g* May 26] good-topped gelding: poor hurdler: won 2 sellers at Fakenham in May (second a handicap, sold 4,700 gns): best at 2m: acts on good to firm and good to soft going: blinkered: has had tongue tied, including for last 2 wins: front runner: no easy ride. *P. S. McEntee*

h84

INDISCRET (FR) 7 b.g. Garde Royale – Please (FR) (Le Pontet (FR)) [2002/3 h–, F–: c20d^4 c22d^F c16g^6 c20d^F c26d^F c22d^3 c24v^{ur} c22v c24g* Mar 23] medium-sized gelding: poor chaser: won handicap at Warwick in March: likely to stay 3¼m: raced only on good going or softer: usually a poor jumper. *F. Jordan*

c75 x
h–

INDIUM 9 b.g. Groom Dancer (USA) – Gold Bracelet (Golden Fleece (USA)) [2002/3 h–: 16m* 16g^{pu} May 31] form in 3 starts over hurdles only when winning amateur novice at Huntingdon in May, making most: will prove best at 2m. *D. E. Cantillon*

h103

INDOUX (FR) 7 b.g. Useful (FR) – Pin'hup (FR) (Signani (FR)) [2002/3 h83: 22d^6 24s 19s* 17d 19d 20v* 21s^6 22g^{pu} Mar 18] leggy gelding: modest hurdler: won novice handicaps at Exeter (conditional jockeys) in December and Sandown in February: probably stays 3m: acts on any going: unreliable. *R. J. Hodges*

h86 §

INDUCEMENT   7 ch.g. Sabrehill (USA) – Verchinina (Star Appeal) [2002/3 c–, h114: 18m² 16d² 16g³ 17d 20g³ Aug 24] strong, useful-looking gelding: let down by jumping only outing over fences: fair handicap hurdler: left Mrs A. Perrett after third start: stays 19f: acts on firm and soft going: sometimes finds little. *R. M. Stronge*   **c– h112**

INDULGE (IRE)   10 b.g. Mandalus – Phantom Thistle (Deep Run) [2002/3 20v c20g c20s^{pu} Mar 10] good-bodied gelding: maiden hurdler/winning chaser: off nearly 3 years, no show in 2002/3: has looked reluctant under pressure. *M. Pitman*   **c– h–**

IN EXTREMIS II (FR)   7 b.g. Useful (FR) – Princesa Real (FR) (Garde Royale) [2002/3 c–, h74: 21g* 20d² 22d⁵ 21m³ 21g² 21m³ 21g² 20g² 23m Oct 24] close-coupled gelding: no form over fences: modest hurdler: won novice handicap at Sedgefield in May: largely creditable efforts subsequently: stays 25f: acts on good to firm and good to soft ground: blinkered seventh outing, wore cheekpieces last 2: has had tongue tied. *G. M. Moore*   **c– h86**

INFAMELIA   7 b.m. Infantry – Incamelia (St Columbus) [2002/3 h65, F69: 24d Jun 8] won point in May: little worthwhile form over hurdles: tried blinkered. *N. J. Henderson*   **h–**

INFINI (FR)   7 gr.g. Le Nain Jaune (FR) – Contessina (FR) (Mistigri) [2002/3 c107, h103: c20g^{pu} c16g^{F} 16m* 18m 16v 16v⁵ Mar 7] tall, leggy gelding: fair hurdler/chaser: let down by jumping over fences first 2 starts: easily best effort in handicap hurdles subsequently when making all at Worcester in July: effective at 2m to 2¾m: acts on any going: visored second appearance: reportedly bled from nose fourth outing: sold 6,000 gns Doncaster May Sales. *M. C. Pipe*   **c– x h108**

INFINITE RISK   4 gr.g. Vettori (IRE) – Dolly Bevan (Another Realm) [2002/3 16s 17d 16g⁶ 16f⁵ 17g^{pu} Apr 21] modest maiden on Flat (seems to stay 1m), sold out of R. Hannon's stable 5,000 gns Doncaster May Sales: no worthwhile form over hurdles. *N. J. Hawke*   **h–**

INFLATION (FR)   7 b.m. Port Etienne (FR) – Ravenna III (FR) (Unoaprile) [2002/3 h72: 20d³ 25g⁶ 19g^{pu} 21m^{pu} Aug 12] leggy mare: poor hurdler: stays 21f: acts on firm and good to soft going (won bumper on soft): tried visored (including when successful)/ blinkered: not one to trust. *G. Prodromou*   **h81 §**

INFLUENCE PEDLER   10 b.g. Keen – La Vie En Primrose (Henbit (USA)) [2002/3 c92, h–: c25f² c24m³ c24m³ c24g³ c24f⁴ c28m⁶ Apr 26] smallish, well-made gelding: modest handicap chaser: stays 27f: acts on firm and soft going: has had tongue tied: races prominently: sound jumper. *Miss K. M. George*   **c95 h–**

INFRASONIQUE (FR)   7 b.g. Teresio – Quatalina III (FR) (Chateau du Diable (FR)) [2002/3 c125, h?: c20m⁵ c24d² c26g c26s⁶ c24s³ c24s⁴ c26m⁵ Mar 19] good-topped gelding: useful chaser: good second to You're Agoodun in handicap at Ascot: generally below form after, reportedly lame final start: stays easy 25f: acts on heavy and good to firm going: sound jumper. *Mrs L. C. Taylor*   **c130 h–**

INGENU (FR)   7 b.g. Royal Charter (FR) – Una Volta (FR) (Toujours Pret (USA)) [2002/3 c105, h–: c20d 20s* 20d⁴ 20s⁴ 24d 22g⁵ Apr 12] rather leggy gelding: fair handicap chaser: well held on reappearance: modest hurdler: won novice at Haydock in November: stays 21f: acts on good to firm and heavy going. *R. H. Alner*   **c– h99**

IN GOOD FAITH   11 b.g. Beveled (USA) – Dulcidene (Behistoun) [2002/3 16m 16d⁵ 16d⁵ 17m c16f⁴ c16g⁵ c21m⁴ c16g⁴ 16g 16v⁶ 16d⁵ 16s Dec 16] leggy gelding: fairly useful handicap hurdler at best: missed 2001/2 and little form in 2002/3 after second start, including over fences: best around 2m: acts on any going: has worn cheekpieces: held up. *R. E. Barr*   **c– h102 d**

INHERIT THE EARTH   9 b.m. Silver Season – Balayer (Balidar) [2002/3 16m^{pu} 16m^{pu} 17g^{pu} Apr 19] pulled up in point in 1999: no form in 3 starts over hurdles: has had tongue tied. *Mary Meek*   **h–**

INIGO JONES (IRE)   7 b.g. Alzao (USA) – Kindjal (Kris) [2002/3 h107?: c17m⁴ c19s^{pu} 18v³ 16m⁴ Mar 19] no form in 2 starts over fences: modest hurdler: raced mainly around 2m: acts on heavy and good to firm going: blinkered: headstrong: has looked difficult ride. *G. Brown*   **c– h98**

INIGO MONTOYA   11 b.g. Liberated – Darklands (Feelings (FR)) [2002/3 c83: c25d May 4] fair pointer: well held in maiden hunter chase at Hexham in May. *C. P. Dennis*   **c–**

INIS CARA (IRE)   11 b.g. Carlingford Castle – Good Sailing (Scorpio (FR)) [2002/3 c–, h–: c24g⁵ c25d⁵ c27g^{pu} Feb 27] good-topped gelding: formerly useful chaser: well below best since 2000/1, left Miss V. Williams after reappearance. *G. W. Thomas*   **c85 h–**

INIS EILE (IRE) 8 b.g. Peacock (FR) – Slippery Bell (No Argument) [2002/3 h–: 20d⁴ 24d c25m 20mᶠ 21g 24d² 22d⁵ 26g³ Sep 8] poor maiden hurdler: no show on chasing debut: looks thorough stayer: tried blinkered: sold 1,500 gns Doncaster September Sales, runner-up in point in April. *Mrs S. J. Smith*   **c–** **h61**

INITIATIVE 7 ch.g. Arazi (USA) – Dance Quest (FR) (Green Dancer (USA)) [2002/3 h–: 17s⁴ 17g⁵ 17g* 16fᵖᵘ 17m² 16g³ 16v³ 17s⁴ 17s* 17v⁵ 16d 17v Feb 11] smallish gelding: modest handicap hurdler: won at Sedgefield in September (seller) and December (novice): will prove best around 2m: acts on soft and good to firm going. *J. Hetherton*   **h91**

INJUN 4 ch.g. Efisio – Lassoo (Caerleon (USA)) [2002/3 16d 16s 17s 16g Mar 2] compact gelding: poor maiden on Flat: well held over hurdles: has had tongue tied. *Miss A. M. Newton-Smith*   **h–**

INLET (IRE) 6 ch.g. Insan (USA) – River Rescue (Over The River (FR)) [2002/3 F82: 16d⁶ 19g 19d 24m⁵ Mar 21] well-made gelding: some promise on hurdling debut but showed little in 3 subsequent starts. *J. T. Gifford*   **h81**

INN ANTIQUE (FR) 7 b.g. Lute Antique (FR) – Taghera (FR) (Toujours Pret (USA)) [2002/3 c–, h103§: 16f* 16s⁴ 17g² 17v* 16d² 17v* 16m Feb 21] tall gelding: fairly useful chaser, usually let down by jumping: fairly useful hurdler: won novices at Wincanton (made all) in May and Sedgefield in November (first start after leaving P. Nicholls) and January: raced mainly around 2m: acts on any going: often finds little. *Ferdy Murphy*   **c–** **h116 §**

INNER SANCTUM (IRE) 6 ch.g. Bob's Return (IRE) – Princess Wager (Pollerton) [2002/3 F18v³ F16g 20m⁴ Apr 12] IR 30,000 4-y-o: half-brother to fair jumpers Bone Setter (by Strong Gale), best up to 2½m, and Simber Hill (by Phardante), suited by 3m+: dam unraced: modest form in bumpers at Fontwell and Warwick: fourth of 11 in novice at Bangor on hurdling debut. *Miss Venetia Williams*   **h79** **F82**

INN FROM THE COLD (IRE) 7 ch.g. Glacial Storm (USA) – Silver Apollo (General Ironside) [2002/3 h–: 24dᵖᵘ 22g 22vᵖᵘ 20s 16v⁶ 16d Mar 7] strong gelding: little sign of ability. *L. Lungo*   **h–**

INNOVATE (IRE) 11 b.m. Posen (USA) – Innate (Be My Native (USA)) [2002/3 c83, h–: c24m² c26m³ c24dᵖᵘ c26g² Apr 21] poor handicap chaser: stays 3¼m: acts on firm and good to soft going: tongue tied: races prominently: no easy ride. *Miss Lucinda V. Russell*   **c81 d** **h–**

INNOX (FR) 7 b.g. Lute Antique (FR) – Savane III (FR) (Quart de Vin (FR)) [2002/3 c134: c21s c23s⁴ c27v³ c22v⁴ c24v⁴ c24sᵖᵘ c22s⁵ c22s Apr 13] good-topped gelding: useful chaser: in frame in group company at Auteuil third and fourth (2¾ lengths fourth to Jerico Vallis) starts, well below best after: probably stays 27f: acts on heavy going: usually sound jumper (fell only outing in blinkers). *F. Doumen, France*   **c134**

IN QUESTION 9 br. or b.g. Deploy – Questionable (Rainbow Quest (USA)) [2002/3 c114, h–: 20m² 21m³ 19gᶠ c20d Nov 23] well-made gelding: fair hurdler/chaser: probably best up to 2½m: acts on good to firm and good to soft going: has bled from nose: races prominently. *Ian Williams*   **c–** **h113**

INS AND OUTS (IRE) 9 ch.g. Insan (USA) – My Dear Good Woman (Lucifer (USA)) [2002/3 c16g⁴ c16vᶠ c16d* c21s⁴ c19g² Mar 25] good-bodied gelding: winning hurdler: fairly useful novice chaser: won at Huntingdon in January: may prove better around 2m than 2½m: acts on good to firm and heavy going: has carried head awkwardly. *J. T. Gifford*   **c122** **h–**

INSHALLAH 8 ch.m. Durgam (USA) – Kaliala (FR) (Pharly (FR)) [2002/3 17mᵖᵘ Apr 19] maiden on Flat, well beaten at 3 yrs: jumped poorly and soon detached in novice on hurdling debut. *Miss Lucinda V. Russell*   **h–**

INSHARANN (FR) 4 b.g. Sheyrann – My Last Chance (FR) (Tiffauges) [2002/3 F17mᵖᵘ Apr 15] 21,000 3-y-o: half-brother to 3 winners, including hurdler/chaser around 2m My Litane Chance (by Cosmopolitan): dam maiden half-sister to Prix du President de La Republique winner My Phil: went lame on home turn in bumper on debut. *N. J. Henderson*   **F–**

INSTANT APPEAL 6 gr.g. Terimon – Free Travel (Royalty) [2002/3 F17d⁶ 16s 22vᵖᵘ 20g² Mar 2] 36,000 4-y-o: stocky gelding: second foal: half-brother to bumper winner Diamant Noir (by Sir Harry Lewis): dam, fair 2m hurdler, half-sister to high-class 2½m chaser Dublin Flyer: well held in bumper: clearly best effort in novice hurdles when 3 lengths second to Sh Boom at Huntingdon final start: should stay beyond 2½m: possibly unsuited by heavy ground: capable of further improvement. *P. Winkworth*   **h101 p** **F–**

INSTANT JUSTICE (IRE)   7 gr.g. Roselier (FR) – Montekova (IRE) (Montekin)   **h–**
[2002/3 h79?, F–: 18v^{pu} 22v^{pu} 16g Apr 12] little sign of ability in bumper or novice hurdles. *D. M. Grissell*

INTELLIGENT (IRE)   7 b.g. Religiously (USA) – Culkeern (Master Buck)   **c138**
[2002/3 h118, F94: 24d² c17s^{pu} c20v* c24s² c20s* c21v⁶ c24v³ c24d² c34s*   **h118**
Mar 15]
There was quite a gulf in form between Beef Or Salmon and the best of the Irish-trained novice chasers in 2002/3. Bust Out, who missed out on the spring Festivals through injury, Le Coudray, Barrow Drive and Rathgar Beau all have claims to be regarded as second in the pecking order, as does the now-retired Be My Royal. However, with the latter's eventual disqualification from first place in the Hennessy at Newbury, the most valuable success gained by an Irish-trained novice apart from Beef Or Salmon will become Intelligent's in landing the John Smith's Midlands Grand National at Uttoxeter. Coming just two days after the end of the Cheltenham Festival, the value of this event is in danger of being overlooked (first prize was considerably more than for any of the handicaps at Cheltenham and only slightly less than the Hennessy). Raising awareness of the race could be even more of a problem for the Midlands track when a fourth day is added to the Festival and Saturday's racing coverage is dominated by what happened in the Gold Cup rather than what is taking place at Uttoxeter that afternoon. The latest Midlands National field was perhaps not quite so strong as might have been expected for the money, for all that seventeen went to post. It did include five last-time-out winners, among them the unexposed favourite Coole Spirit and the Pipe-trained novice Jurancon II, as well as the Welsh National winner Mini Sensation. There was a two-pronged Irish challenge with Silver Steel, not seen to best advantage in the Kim Muir earlier in the week, joining Intelligent. The last-named went off 6/1 second favourite, looking fairly treated on his form in novice company in Ireland, and probably didn't have to improve to win what developed into a slog through the

John Smith's Midlands Grand National Chase (Handicap), Uttoxeter—
Intelligent (nearer camera) and Akarus slug it out over the last

Norman Moore's "Intelligent"

mud, typical for the track. Soft or heavy going at Uttoxeter provides some of the most gruelling conditions around and, with a sound pace set over a marathon trip, few of the Midlands National field lasted the distance. Five were still in contention turning for home, where a slipped saddle ruined Silver Steel's chance. Jurancon II and River Bug also weakened soon after and a duel developed between Intelligent and 33/1-chance Akarus, the former getting on top at the last and ridden out as he idled in front to win by a length and a half, with twenty-eight lengths back to Jurancon. Intelligent was the fourth Irish-trained winner of the Midlands National in the last seven runnings and a second for Jessica Harrington's stable following Miss Orchestra in 1998. Like Intelligent, Miss Orchestra was a seven-year-old novice when successful. Connections will hope Intelligent doesn't follow any further in Miss Orchestra's footsteps as she failed to win again.

Intelligent didn't appear over fences in public until November, on his second start of the season, and after an unfortunate beginning (badly hampered at the first and third and then pulled up) he proved a consistent and reliable performer, one clearly a fair bit better than he was over hurdles. He won twice at two and a half miles, a maiden at Down Royal and the Grade 2 Guinness Greenmount Park Novices' Chase at Limerick, in which he beat Barrow Drive five lengths, and was placed in an intermediate at Sandown (no match for Valley Henry but still a good second) and Grade 3 novices at Naas and Navan. Despite Intelligent's good efforts at shorter, a well-run three miles at Navan, where he went down by four and a half lengths, conceding 5 lb, to The Premier Cat, looked to suit him well, and that trip or further is likely to bring out the best in him in handicaps in future. That may lead to limited opportunities in Ireland—the Thyestes is one possibility—and further trips to Britain will surely be on the agenda.

402

Intelligent (IRE) (b.g. 1996)	Religiously (USA) (b or br 1984)	Alleged (b 1974)	Hoist The Flag
			Princess Pout
		Pas de Nom (b 1968)	Admiral's Voyage
			Petitioner
	Culkeern (b 1979)	Master Buck (br 1961)	Buckhound
			Bezique
		Vulplume (ch 1968)	Vulgan
			Pengo

Intelligent is the most significant winner by his sire Religiously, an unraced Alleged half-brother to Danzig. The best of his other progeny since being moved from the States to Northern Ireland in 1994 are the useful hurdler Emotional Moment and the smart bumper performer Bold Bishop. Intelligent doesn't come from a distinguished family, names of any note being remotely connected. His dam Culkeern was unraced while the second dam Vulplume and third dam Pengo were maidens. Culkeern has produced just one other winner outside points in the fair chaser at two and a half miles or more Willchris (by Fidel). Vulplume's one winner was the fair staying chaser Weirpool but Pengo was rather more successful, producing five winners, including the useful staying hurdler/chaser Penvulgo, a brother to Vulplume and a durable performer in the 'sixties. The good-topped Intelligent acts well on soft and heavy going, though he ran creditably over hurdles on his only outing on good (yet to race on firmer). He was tried once in blinkers, running respectably in a competitive handicap hurdle. *Mrs J. Harrington, Ireland*

INTERDIT (FR) 7 b. or br.g. Shafoun (FR) – Solaine (FR) (Pot d'Or (FR)) [2002/3 **c109** c90, h–: c26m^2 c25f* c25m^2 c24m^F 24m^2 c23g^3 24f^3 c24f* c25v^2 c22v^2 c25s^2 c24g^4 **h97** c24d^5 c25v* c22d^3 24d^6 c32g^2 c24g^2 c25m^5 Apr 12] leggy gelding: winning hurdler: fair handicap chaser: won at Exeter in May, Ludlow (novice, sold out of P. Hobbs's stable 10,000 gns Doncaster Sales prior to next start) in October and Ayr in February: good second at Kelso and Carlisle in March: stays 4m: acts on any going: effective blinkered or not: tough. *Mrs B. K. Thomson*

INTER ROCK (FR) 7 b.g. Video Rock (FR) – Aniste (FR) (Brezzo (FR)) [2002/3 **c–** c–, h–: c25d^{pu} May 14] leggy gelding: winning hurdler: poor form on first of 2 starts in **h–** steeplechases: won point in March: stays 3m: acts on good to soft going: blinkered once. *R. C. Harper*

INTERSKY FALCON 6 ch.g. Polar Falcon (USA) – I'll Try (Try My Best **h161** (USA)) [2002/3 h152p, F99: 16f* 16m* 16d* 16s* 16g^5 Mar 11]
Intersky Falcon went into the Champion Hurdle with current-season form better than all except Rooster Booster but, starting third favourite at 5/1, he failed to run up to his best, beaten around seventeen lengths into fifth, Westender, Rhinestone Cowboy and Self Defense, in addition to Rooster Booster, finishing ahead of him. Intersky Falcon went down with a viral infection afterwards and missed possible engagements at Sandown and Punchestown, but, nevertheless, probably wasn't ridden to best advantage. He had a lot of use made of him which made an asset of his fine jumping but rather negated his equally fine turn of foot. After a rare mistake at the fifth he had little left once headed after two out. Cheltenham may not be Intersky Falcon's ideal course, but, along with stable-companion Rhinestone Cowboy, he remains as likely as any that win the 2003 field to make an impact in the Champion Hurdle twelve months on.
Intersky Falcon's latest campaign continued the excellent progress made in 2001/2. He was not kept nearly so busy as in his novice campaign, when his five wins included one in the Cordon Bleu Handicap at Aintree, but he won all four of his starts prior to the Festival. The first of those was virtually a coda to his novice campaign, the Merewood Homes Swinton Handicap Hurdle at Haydock coming just six days into the new season and a week after his final run of 2001/2 (narrowly beaten by Copeland in the Masai Hurdle at Sandown). Intersky Falcon's half-length defeat of Gralmano at Haydock under top weight, and off a mark fully 30 lb higher than he had won off at Aintree a month earlier, confirmed his position among the top two-mile hurdlers. Three successes in graded company followed in the last quarter of the year. None of the three races was entirely satisfactory in that, on each occasion, what appeared the principal opposition failed to run up to expectations. In the John James McManus Memorial Hurdle at Tipperary at the start of October,

two of Intersky Falcon's main rivals failed to give their running and another three failed to complete, the race being marred by fatal injuries to Timber King and Just Our Job. Intersky Falcon looked likely to beat the useful Bob What by much more than the final margin of a length and a half, lack of an outing a possible explanation. Nearly two months later, in the Pertemps 'Fighting Fifth' Hurdle at Newcastle, Intersky Falcon's main market rival, the 2002 Champion Hurdle runner-up Marble Arch, was a long way below his best, but a six-length defeat of The French Furze, barely coming off the bridle, was still impressive.

An appearance in the Bula Hurdle at Cheltenham seemed a possibility, and with it an informative clash with Rooster Booster and a test of Intersky Falcon's ability to handle an undulating track. Instead, however, connections opted for what always seemed a more suitable target, the Pertemps Christmas Hurdle at Kempton. Although a Grade 1 event, this was principally viewed as another potentially revealing Champion Hurdle trial. Intersky Falcon started even money, though the first and second in the 2002 Champion were in the line-up, Hors La Loi III joining Marble Arch, as was Davenport Milenium, making his first appearance since winning the Emo Oil Hurdle at the Punchestown Festival. Hors La Loi and Marble Arch were unable to cope with the soft ground, however, and Davenport Milenium proved short of fitness. The main threat to Intersky Falcon turned out to be essentially himself, as he idled badly in the straight after showing a scintillating turn of foot to have his race seemingly won after three from home. Challenged again at the last by the useful Santenay, Intersky Falcon had to be shaken up for a three-length victory, which hardly reflects his performance.

At the time it was run, the Christmas Hurdle, along with the Feltham Novices' Chase and the King George VI Chase, the other Grade 1 events on the Boxing Day card, looked as if it might be finding a new home in 2004. Plans to sacrifice the National Hunt course and turn Kempton into London's premier all-weather track were the subject of much discussion. The King George, and presumably the other Grade 1 events, were thought likely to move to sister track Sandown. London had been due to have a new all-weather track by the autumn of 2003 anyway, but plans for London City at Fairlop had become hopelessly mired in planning issues. There seems a risk that local objections might scupper any such plans at Kempton as well. At the time of writing, however, the preferred option of Kempton's owners, effectively Racecourse Holdings Trust, a subsidiary of the Jockey Club, seems less contentious, involving the ending of turf Flat racing but the continuation of jumping and, probably more importantly, adapting the existing grandstand rather than building a new one.

Supporters of National Hunt racing who campaigned to save the King George at Kempton appear to have gained a reprieve, but the threat to jumping in general has never been greater. RHT wants an all-weather venue, as does another major group Northern Racing. The difficulties of getting permission to build an all-weather track at Newcastle has led to the promotion of the same group's Sedgefield as a potential all-weather venue. It is hard to imagine a jumps track less suitable for such a circuit, but local authority support and the driving ambition of Sir Stanley Clarke may well bring the plan to reality. Newbury is also well on the way to installing an artificial surface for Flat racing, awaiting planning permission at the time of writing. While Kempton, Sedgefield and Newbury have all said they

John James McManus Memorial Hurdle, Tipperary—
Intersky Falcon reaches for the last as Bob What closes

Pertemps Christmas Hurdle, Kempton—a better jump this time is enough to see off Santenay

will remain dual-purpose venues, followers of jumping might like to reflect that Lingfield and Wolverhampton had similar plans. Lingfield is hardly functioning as a jumps track, with its one full day dropped from the calendar and the half day not staged in 2003, and Wolverhampton, whose turf track is too narrow, ceased jumping in July 2003. Southwell has survived as a jumps track, though with widely criticised portable obstacles and often unsatisfactory ground. To Lingfield and Wolverhampton can be added other tracks that have given up jumping to concentrate on less expensive and more profitable Flat fixtures. There were campaigns, similar to those fought over Kempton, when Nottingham and Windsor announced plans to drop jumping but they made not a ha'p'orth of difference.

With the Office of Fair Trading likely to give more freedom to courses (in the process almost certainly favouring the big groups over the small independent tracks, hence Bangor-on-Dee's recent move to join forces with Chester for financial protection) and bookmaker-led demands for two all-weather fixtures per day in the winter (squeezing out one levy-financed and otherwise uneconomic jumping card) jumping may well be further threatened. Perhaps no-one regretted the passing of Woore, where, in the wet, cars had to be towed *onto* the car park, or bleak and soulless Wye, but tracks like Stockton, Nottingham, Windsor, Lingfield and the old Wolverhampton all had something to offer. Not many more need to be added to the list to begin endangering the structure of jumping.

The British Horseracing Board's response has been limited, though some of the recommendations of the Racing Review committee merit serious consideration, while others do not. The committee concentrated on Flat racing and, in a report produced at the end of April, only a fraction of the content dealt with jump racing. The focus was on lots more low-grade Flat racing to meet the demands of the major bookmakers. Dubbed 'regional racing', which gives it a stigma from the start, this will be the horse-racing equivalent of BAGS greyhound racing, low-quality, high-margin betting shop fodder. The question of how to help jump racing, how to make more races more competitive and better supported was not fully addressed in the Racing Review committee's report, which did, however, acknowledge the danger that 'the foundations of jumping are likely to be undermined and the finances of jumping transferred to all-weather racing. An important part of the sport of racing would, in all probability, ultimately disappear.'

405

One problem that needs addressing is the quality of supporting races, particularly novice events, at tracks like Ascot and Sandown. Why do trainers prefer to run promising horses at tracks like Taunton and Exeter for half the money available at the metropolitan tracks? There is a well-founded perception that finishing third or fourth to a good novice at Ascot or Sandown can see a horse's handicap mark raised considerably for little or no reward. One answer would be to provide incentives to run in the races within the pattern. For example, being placed in the Supreme Novices' at Cheltenham could bring greater reward if the horse in question has contested one or more of the recognised trial races like the Kennel Gate and the Dovecote. There should be fewer opportunities, too, to avoid smart opposition. Once a horse has won a novice, it should be going on to face other winners, not being found further opportunities against inferior rivals; at the other end, horses which patently are not good enough to win a novice should be pushed into low-grade handicaps. Winners races (not just for novices), races restricted to horses which have not run more than three times over jumps, median auction races for progeny of sires whose stock is sold at the main NH sales and alternative races for horses perceived as badly treated in handicaps (possibly with a penalty structure based on prize money won) are among ideas to consider, along with appropriate use of appearance money, scandalously used to attract Flat failures to fill juvenile hurdle fields in the autumn. The Review Group acknowledged that unless the problems of abandonments and field sizes in jumping are addressed, it will be hard to resist the betting industry's wish to replace jumping fixtures with all-weather cards between November and March, the betting industry preferring all-weather racing anyway because it is more profitable for them. Some recommendations for

interskyracing.com & Mrs Jonjo O'Neill's "Intersky Falcon"

increasing the number of jumpers and encouraging jumpers to run more often did appear in the Racing Review committee's report but all are subject to BHB board approval. At the time of writing, the only recommendations implemented have been: the paying of appearance money to all mares in steeplechases; the proposed introduction of 25% owners' premiums, on top of prize money, in most races in Britain from January 2004 for British-bred horses, no age restriction applying to jumps premiums and the premium being 50% for fillies and mares in races over jumps; the conversion of some novice chases to beginners chasers (for horses who have not won over fences); and the requirement that novices should run in three steeplechases before being eligible for Class A or B handicaps. Among other ideas to come out of the Racing Review committee were: expansion of the race programme for horses which have not raced on the Flat and expansion of bumpers for three- and four-year-olds; introduction of all-weather bumpers; an appearance money scheme for chasers rated 140 and above based on the number of outings they have during the season; a Winter Triple Crown and Grand Slam; and the promotion of two more weekend jumping Festivals in addition to those at Cheltenham in November and March. As a response to criticism, the BHB announced in July that the NH pattern committee (which met twice a year) would have an enhanced role and a new title, the Jumping Racing Advisory Panel.

The concept of 'regional racing' suggests the BHB is looking for a structure for betting, rather than a structure that promotes the sport. The bookmakers offer 'virtual racing' as well as real racing, they offer racing from Newmarket in Suffolk and South Africa, numbers betting, BAGS greyhounds and slot machines, while at the same time crying crocodile tears about racing's falling share of the market. Most of the 'alternatives' offer higher profit margins than racing.

So far as the threat to jumping of all-weather racing is concerned, perhaps more could be done to build on the success of summer jumping, transferring fixtures away from winter Mondays and leaving those to the all-weather. Summer jumping, which has done well, offering good prize money and competitive racing, needs more promotion, instead of which it is set to suffer as a result of giving bookmakers more say in the fixture list. Through the winter there must be a strong programme every weekend centred on a major handicap with potential for ante-post betting from the Tuesday, and with good supporting contests. Newbury has generally worked hard to enhance its programmes—notably with the Tote Gold Trophy meeting—which makes the feeble card staged there on the first Saturday in March all the more puzzling. Cheltenham might be round the corner but if the course isn't prepared to try harder the fixture should go elsewhere. Favouritism towards the big tracks and big groups should not come into things. National Hunt racing has tremendous popular appeal and has all the elements that go to make up a viable competitive sport. But it cannot survive simply on three days in March and one in April. It needs a vibrant structure all the way through the year.

			Nureyev	Northern Dancer
	Polar Falcon (USA)		(b 1977)	Special
	(b or br 1987)		Marie d'Argonne	Jefferson
Intersky Falcon			(ch 1981)	Mohair
(ch.g. 1997)			Try My Best	Northern Dancer
	I'll Try		(b 1975)	Sex Appeal
	(ch 1982)		Polifontaine	Bold Lad
			(br 1976)	Mortefontaine

To return to Intersky Falcon, this leggy individual is by no means an imposing sort and not an obvious candidate to be sent over fences. He is bred for the Flat, though his half-brother Steel Mirror (by Slip Anchor) was a fairly useful hurdler/chaser up to twenty-five furlongs, while another, Fundamental (by Rudimentary), won a two-mile novice hurdle at Ayr in the latest season. Further details of Intersky Falcon's Flat relatives can be found in *Chasers & Hurdlers 2001/02*. He is best at around two miles, acts on soft and firm going and wears blinkers nowadays. Intersky Falcon remains likely to play a significant role in the top races. *Jonjo O'Neill*

INTERSKY NATIVE (IRE) 7 ch.g. Be My Native (USA) – Creative Music (Creative Plan (USA)) [2002/3 F96: 16d[6] 19g 20g[4] Apr 1] well-made gelding: fairly useful **h79**

form when second in bumper on debut: only poor form in novice hurdles: likely to stay 3m. *N. G. Richards*

INTERSKY SOVEREIGN (IRE)   5 b.g. Aristocracy – Queen's Prize (Random Shot) [2002/3 16d Mar 15] 23,000 4-y-o: sixth foal: half-brother to one-time fair hurdler/chaser Right'n'royal (by Good Thyne), stays 25f, and bumper winner Regal Gem (by Torus): dam unraced: no show in novice hurdle on debut. *J. Howard Johnson*   **h–**

INTHAAR   6 b.g. Nashwan (USA) – Twafeaj (USA) (Topsider (USA)) [2002/3 19g 16g May 22] poor on Flat (stays 1½m): well held in 2 novice hurdles. *R. Brotherton*   **h–**

IN THE FLOW (USA)   6 b.g. Irish River (FR) – In The Mood (USA) (Lyphard (USA)) [2002/3 h101: 16g 17d Sep 4] rather sparely-made gelding: fair handicap hurdler in 2001/2: well below form on return: will prove best around 2m: best form on good to firm going: held up. *P. J. Hobbs*   **h88**

IN THE FORGE   6 ch.g. Zilzal (USA) – Harir (Kris) [2002/3 h128p, F86: 16m³ Apr 22] tall gelding: progressive form over hurdles in 2001/2, winning twice (reportedly suffered overreach on second occasion): fit from Flat, third to Swordplay in minor event at Fairyhouse on reappearance: looking extremely well and again tongue tied, appeared to run very well when third to Quazar in Grade 1 at Punchestown following month, soon setting good pace: likely to prove best around 2m: acts on soft going, possibly not ideally suited by good to firm. *M. Halford, Ireland*   **h143**

IN THE ROUGH (IRE)   12 b.g. Strong Gale – Cherrydawn (Pollerton) [2002/3 c111x, h–: 25s² c30s Mar 4] lengthy gelding: fair handicap hurdler/chaser: ran creditably over hurdles on reappearance, poorly over fences next time: stays 29f: raced on good going or softer (acts on heavy): has looked less than keen: sketchy jumper of fences. *J. A. B. Old*   **c– x**
h103

INTOX III (FR)   7 ch.g. Garde Royale – Naftane (FR) (Trac) [2002/3 h118: 17m⁵ 20m⁴ 19dᵇᵈ 19s 17v⁴ 17dᵖᵘ 17s 16s Feb 24] compact gelding: fairly useful handicap hurdler: still moving comfortably when brought down 2 out at Newbury third March start, but disappointing otherwise in 2002/3: best around 2m: acts on any going: often visored. *M. C. Pipe*   **h105 d**

INTREPID MOGAL   6 b.g. Terimon – Padrigal (Paddy's Stream) [2002/3 h89?, F73: 22dᵖᵘ 16mᵖᵘ 20d² 24s² 25d² 22g⁶ Apr 26] workmanlike gelding: poor maiden hurdler: stays 25f: acts on soft going: bled from nose second start: races prominently. *N. J. Pomfret*   **h75**

INTYMCGINTY (IRE)   6 b.g. Port Lucaya – Mother Tongue (Montelimar (USA)) [2002/3 F90: F16s⁵ 19g³ 19d² 21m Mar 21] rangy gelding with scope: fair form in bumpers: not fluent when placed in 2 novice hurdles at Newbury: should be suited by further than 19f: ran poorly on good to firm going final start. *Noel T. Chance*   **h95**
F90

INVESTOR RELATIONS (IRE)   5 b.g. Goldmark (USA) – Debach Delight (Great Nephew) [2002/3 h78: 17g 17s³ 17m* 17g³ 16m² 17m⁵ 17m² 17d Sep 4] modest hurdler: won amateur selling handicap at Newton Abbot in June: will prove best around 2m: acts on firm and soft going. *N. J. Hawke*   **h86**

INVITADO (IRE)   4 ch.g. Be My Guest (USA) – Lady Dulcinea (ARG) (General (FR)) [2002/3 16d⁵ Dec 4] half-brother to winning 2m hurdler in Italy by Eagle Eyed: little form on Flat: well held in juvenile at Catterick on hurdling debut. *J. G. FitzGerald*   **h–**

INZARMOOD (IRE)   5 b.m. Inzar (USA) – Pepilin (Coquelin (USA)) [2002/3 17d³ 16m⁴ 16d 16g² 16g 16m Apr 21] poor maiden on Flat (stays 11f): poor novice hurdler: raced around 2m: acts on good to soft going: visored/blinkered last 5 starts: unreliable. *K. R. Burke*   **h63 §**

IOGA (FR)   7 b. or br.g. Video Rock (FR) – Valentia (FR) (Brezzo (FR)) [2002/3 c–, h–: 24g 20g⁶ May 22] first past post in 2 chases in France in early-2000/1 (subsequently disqualified from both on technical grounds): little show in 3 novice hurdles in Britain: stays 2½m. *Miss Venetia Williams*   **c–**
h–

IORANA (FR)   7 ch.g. Marignan (USA) – Fareham (FR) (Fast Topaze (USA)) [2002/3 c–, h–: 16g⁴ 19d³ 19m³ 16d* 16m* 16f* c16g* c16s⁴ c16d³ c16v⁴ 17d⁵ 16m² Mar 19] leggy gelding: fair hurdler: won handicap at Worcester in August and sellers at Uttoxeter and Ludlow in October: fairly useful handicap chaser: won at Hereford later in October: stays 2½m, at least when conditions aren't testing: acts on any going: has looked none too keen. *M. C. Pipe*   **c117**
h107

IPLEDGEALLEGIANCE (USA)   7 b.g. Alleged (USA) – Yafill (USA) (Nureyev (USA)) [2002/3 h100: 20m* 16g 16s 16dᵖᵘ Dec 14] sparely-made gelding: modest handicap hurdler: best around 2m: acts on heavy going: usually tongue tied. *K. A. Morgan*   **h86**

IRA HAYES (IRE)   8 b.g. Commanche Run – Parsons Glen (IRE) (Glen Quaich) **c107 x**
[2002/3 c20s^ur c21s^2 20m^4 c24d^2 c20d^F c20s^3 c25s^F c24d c25s^pu c21v^ur c20f^F Apr 13] IR **h106**
8,200 4-y-o: plain, good-topped gelding: third foal: dam unraced, from family of useful
staying hurdler Willie Wumpkins: twice-raced on Flat: fair hurdler: similar form on his
day over fences, though usually let down by jumping: probably stays 3m: acts on soft and
good to firm going. *John A. Codd, Ireland*

IRBEE   11 b.g. Gunner B – Cupids Bower (Owen Dudley) [2002/3 c135§, h107§: c20s^2 **c106 §**
c24s^2 c26s* c25g^3 c21g^4 Apr 3] tall, well-made gelding: useful chaser at best: fairly **h– §**
useful in hunters in 2002/3, won at Plumpton in March: stays 3¼m: acts on good to
firm and heavy going: blinkered: carries head high: irresolute. *P. F. Nicholls*

IRELAND'S EYE (IRE)   8 b.g. Shareef Dancer (USA) – So Romantic (IRE) **h100**
(Teenoso (USA)) [2002/3 h103: 20d^4 20v 20d^4 21d^4 Mar 18] small gelding: fair handicap
hurdler: will stay beyond 2½m: raced on going softer than good (acts well on soft/heavy):
sometimes hangs left under pressure. *J. R. Norton*

IRIS BLEU (FR)   7 ch.g. Beyssac (FR) – Dear Blue (FR) (Cyborg (FR)) [2002/3 **c152**
c129, h–: c24d* c24s* c25d^2 c28d^3 c36d^pu Apr 5] **h–**

These days, the Grand National spawns some peripheral betting opportunities to tempt the once-a-year punter seeking an easier alternative to finding the
winner of the race—number of finishers, number of fallers at the first, identity of
the favourite, and so on. Perhaps the most bizarre of these dreamt up by the
bookmakers in the latest season was the book opened on the star sign of the winning
horse. We cannot confirm that the horoscope for Monty's Pass for Grand National
week foretold that he would be going on a long and hazardous journey on Saturday,
or that he would come into a large amount of money soon afterwards, but as a
Taurean (one of a dozen in the race, apparently) his victory meant that the bookmakers had to pay out on a winning favourite in that particular market.

For Iris Bleu, who was pulled up lame at Aintree, the stars were evidently
less favourable, but only those armed with a crystal ball could have foreseen that a
horse who started as one of the three 100/1 outsiders—all from the Pipe stable
—when an early casualty in the 2002 Grand National would be vying for
favouritism in the race twelve months later. Iris Bleu's very different position in

*Agfa Diamond Handicap Chase,
Sandown—much improved Iris Bleu
is out on his own*

the Aintree betting in the latest season
was the result of sudden and spectacular
improvement which first manifested
itself in the Agfa Diamond Handicap
Chase at Sandown in February. On his
only previous run of the season, Iris Bleu
had won an amateur riders chase at Cheltenham in November, notching his trainer's hundredth winner of the season. It
was Iris Bleu's first success in Britain
after a couple of consistent but frustrating
seasons. The Sandown race looked well
contested, with the previous season's
Racing Post Chase winner Gunther
McBride heading the betting at 9/2. Iris
Bleu was a 12/1-chance under Tom Scudamore, with Tony McCoy favouring
stable-companion You're Agoodun.
Referring to Iris Bleu, Martin Pipe
remarked afterwards that 'We needed to
get him in the weights for the Grand
National.' It was mission accomplished,
but the plan worked a little too well. Iris
Bleu simply ran away with the race,
shooting clear after the last of the railway
fences and in no danger from the home
turn, eventually coasting home by
twenty-three lengths from Frosty Canyon, who came through to snatch second

from Lord Jack and Ifni du Luc. When the National weights were announced just days later, the concern for connections was now that Iris Bleu was too high in the handicap, rather than too low. Reacting to Iris Bleu's 16 lb higher mark after Sandown, Pipe said 'Obviously, he's got to go up, but it does seem rather harsh. It doesn't make sense to me. When he went to the National last year he was a 100/1-chance. I told the handicapper but he just walked away.' The horse's starting price in the race twelve months earlier was, of course, of no relevance to how he would be assessed, and the handicapper was soon vindicated when, in our view at least, Iris Bleu reproduced his Sandown form to the pound, not once, but twice more before Aintree. On the first occasion, Iris Bleu started favourite for the Country Gentlemen's Association Chase at Wincanton, taking on former King George winners See More Business and First Gold at level weights. He got the better of a battle with First Gold for second but found the veteran See More Business too strong from five out, going down by nine lengths. Back in handicap company, Iris Bleu started favourite off his new mark for the first time in the Red Square Vodka Gold Cup at Haydock in March. Creeping into contention on the final circuit, Iris Bleu ran a cracker, finding plenty under pressure before going down by three-quarters of a length and a short head to Shotgun Willy and You're Agoodun (on this occasion the longest priced of his stable's runners), Shotgun Willy being promoted to National favouritism.

A major factor in the odds of any Pipe-trained runner in a big handicap, where the stable is invariably represented by more than one horse, is the choice of ride made by Tony McCoy. The stable ran seven in the latest National, but they included the usual no-hopers, three starting at 200/1; Blowing Wind, on whom McCoy had finished third in the two previous Nationals, must have been the only realistic rival to Iris Bleu in his choice of mounts. With the support of office money, Iris Bleu was sent off the 8/1 joint second-favourite. Geed up in the preliminaries, he made a couple of bad mistakes and was pulled up immediately after the second one, at the Chair. Although lame, tests at the University of Liverpool revealed that Iris Bleu had not sustained any fractures.

		Paris Jour	Herbager
	Beyssac (FR)	(b 1962)	La Petite Hutte
	(ch 1978)	Dori	Nordiste
Iris Bleu (FR)		(ch 1966)	Paraphernalia
(ch.g. 1996)		Cyborg	Arctic Tern
	Dear Blue (FR)	(ch 1982)	Cadair
	(b 1991)	Olableue	Oarsman
		(b 1980)	Valse Bleue II

Already a winning chaser in France as a four-year-old, Iris Bleu, a stocky selle francais gelding, was not stepped up to three miles or more until well into the 2001/02 season. There were, however, enough elements in his pedigree to suggest staying would ultimately be his game. His sire Beyssac, best known in Britain for the smart staying chaser Banjo, himself stayed long distances on the Flat before becoming one of the best four-year-old hurdlers of his generation in France. Iris Bleu's dam Dear Blue (whose first foal he is) is an unraced half-sister to the Grande Steeple Chase di Milano winner Cate Bleue, while his grandam Olableue, lightly raced on the Flat, was a sister to the smart French staying chaser Lamie Bleue. The consistent Iris Bleu's fifth in the 2002 attheraces Gold Cup showed he stays at least twenty-nine furlongs. If he eventually returns, he will presumably be kept to three miles or more. He acts on any going, with the possible exception of firm. *M. C. Pipe*

IRIS COLLONGES (FR) 7 b.g. Luchiroverte (IRE) – Soubrette Collonge (FR) (Saumon (FR)) [2002/3 c103, h105: c19d² c19gᵖᵘ Mar 25] useful-looking gelding: fair hurdler on balance of form: in frame first 3 starts in novice chases, second at Hereford on belated reappearance: possibly amiss month later: stays 19f: acts on heavy going: has found little. *N. J. Henderson* **c105 h–**

IRIS D'ESTRUVAL (FR) 7 b.g. Quart de Vin (FR) – Claire d'Estruval (FR) (Misti-gri) [2002/3 c26gᵘʳ May 25] 320,000 francs 3-y-o: first foal: dam, French 11f winner, sister to top-class French chaser Sabre d'Estruval and useful staying chaser Granit d'Estruval: modest pointer: stumbled and unseated before fifteenth in hunter chase at Newton Abbot. *E. Retter* **c–**

IRISH BLESSING (USA)   6 b.g. Ghazi (USA) – Win For Leah (USA) (His Majesty   h–
(USA)) [2002/3 h–: 26g May 30] smallish gelding: poor on Flat nowadays: no form over
hurdles: tried blinkered. *F. Jordan*

IRISH CHAPEL (IRE)   7 b.g. College Chapel – Heart of Flame (Top Ville) [2002/3   F–
F–: F17g Jun 10] well held in 3 bumpers. *H. E. Haynes*

IRISH DISTINCTION (IRE)   5 b.g. Distinctly North (USA) – Shane's Girl (IRE)   h69
(Marktingo) [2002/3 16m^F 16g 16d 17f^3 Apr 3] leggy gelding: fair on Flat (stays 1½m),
successful in August and October, claimed from A. Jarvis £10,000 on latter occasion:
poor form on last of 4 starts over hurdles (left M. Pipe after first): headstrong.
T. R. George

IRISH FASHION (USA)   8 ch.g. Nashwan (USA) – L'Irlandaise (USA) (Irish River   c–
(FR)) [2002/3 h106: c19m^5 Oct 5] sturdy gelding: fair handicap hurdler: last of 5 in quite   h–
valuable novice at Chepstow on chasing debut, not seen out again: best around 2m: raced
mainly on good going or softer (acts on soft): races prominently: fluent jumper of hurdles.
Dr P. Pritchard

IRISH GOLD (IRE)   8 b.g. Good Thyne (USA) – Ardfallon (IRE) (Supreme Leader)   h–
[2002/3 21s^5 Mar 10] seventh in novice hurdle on debut in 2000/1: well held in similar
event on return. *P. Winkworth*

IRISH HUSSAR (IRE)   7 b.g. Supreme Leader – Shuil Ard (Quayside) [2002/3   c152 p
h130p: c21d* c21s^F c23g* c21g^2 c25d* Apr 4]   h–
    In stark contrast to the Cheltenham Festival, where he has enjoyed con-
siderable success over the years, Nicky Henderson won't have too many happy
memories of Aintree's Grand National meeting. So, having unusually drawn a
blank at the former in the latest season, Henderson would probably have been less
optimistic than usual about his prospects of ending a drought at the latter, where a
losing run of seventy-three had followed the victory of Thinking Twice in the 1995
Cordon Bleu Handicap Hurdle. That run had been extended to eighty-one by the
time Henderson's best opportunity of a winner at the fixture came along, Irish
Hussar in the Happy Shopper Mildmay Novices' Chase. Perhaps Henderson's

Happy Shopper Mildmay Novices' Chase, Aintree—Irish Hussar gets the better of It Takes Time

Major Christopher Hanbury's "Irish Hussar"

record had a bearing on the market formed on what was a weak renewal of this Grade 2 event. Irish Hussar was sent off only second favourite in a race for which he was entitled to start favourite, given his form and the fact that he was set to receive 5 lb from both It Takes Time and Joly Bey, his main rivals. This trio occupied the first three places, Irish Hussar jumping well as he dictated a fairly steady pace. His rider appeared unconcerned when the favourite It Takes Time took a narrow lead four out, and the confidence wasn't misplaced, Irish Hussar quickening to regain the upper hand approaching the last and going on to win by five lengths from It Takes Time, with Joly Bey a further seven lengths behind.

Irish Hussar has been brought along very steadily by his stable, the Aintree race being only his ninth in three seasons' racing, which have yielded five wins. Successful in a bumper at Sandown on his only start in his first season, Irish Hussar made just three appearances over hurdles in his second, showing useful form and winning a novice event at Newbury. He would have gone on to better things kept to hurdling but, always very much a chaser in appearance, was switched to fences in 2002/3. He took to steeplechasing quickly, winning novice events at Wincanton and Leicester on his first two completed starts. In the former he overcame his inexperience to beat Ask Henry by half a length, and in the latter he accomplished a simple task without fuss. Irish Hussar's jumping let him down on his only start in between, in a novice handicap won by La Landiere at Cheltenham, falling two out when keeping on in third. Irish Hussar wouldn't have troubled La Landiere, who was conceding him 5 lb, so his chance was far from obvious when the pair met again almost two months later over the same course and distance, in the Cathcart Chase. Irish Hussar, despite terms 7 lb worse, gave La Landiere a great deal more to do this time, though, helping force the pace and battling on well when headed by La Landiere two out, eventually beaten only a length and a half. The performance represented smart form, and Irish Hussar didn't need to step up on it to go one better at Aintree. He remains open to further improvement and should develop into a good-class handicapper in the next season.

Irish Hussar (IRE) (b.g. 1996)	Supreme Leader (b 1982)	Bustino (b 1971)	Busted
			Ship Yard
		Princess Zena (b 1975)	Habitat
			Guiding Light
	Shuil Ard (ch 1984)	Quayside (ch 1967)	London Gazette
			Wong
		Shuil Avanter (ch 1974)	Levanter
			Shuil Agragh

Irish Hussar is the last of eight foals produced by the unraced Shuil Ard and by far the best of them, her only other winners being the modest hurdler Knayton Prospect (by Strong Gale) and the lightly-raced pointer Native Isle (by Be My Native). The next two dams on the bottom line of Irish Hussar's pedigree, namely Shuil Avanter and Shuil Agragh, both won over hurdles, the former also over fences. Shuil Agragh is also the dam of the Scottish National winner Baronet and grandam of the very smart hurdler Liss A Paoraigh, while other recent notable jumpers in this family include the Welsh National winner Jocks Cross. There is plenty of stamina in Irish Hussar's pedigree and he will certainly stay beyond twenty-five furlongs, the distance of the Mildmay and the furthest he has tackled so far. Irish Hussar, a tall, useful-looking gelding, has raced only on good ground or softer and won his bumper on heavy. It is highly unlikely that he will be risked on ground firmer than good. 'He gets sore shins and must have some cut,' according to his trainer. *N. J. Henderson*

IRISHKAWA BELLEVUE (FR) 5 b. or br.g. Irish Prospector (FR) – Strakawa (FR) (Sukawa (FR)) [2002/3 F18s⁶ F17d⁴ F16g⁵ 22g 21m⁵ Apr 19] fifth foal: half-brother to winning cross-country chaser by Gaspard de La Nuit: dam winning hurdler/cross-country chaser: fair in bumpers: no encouragement in 2 novice hurdles, jumping poorly on first occasion: should stay at least 2½m. *Jean-Rene Auvray* **h– F89**

IRISHMAN (IRE) 9 b.g. Bob Back (USA) – Future Tense (USA) (Pretense) [2002/3 c16g 20d³ c24m* c22dᵘʳ 20gᶠ c24f³ 20s c24m³ c20gᵖᵘ c26g⁵ Apr 21] ex-Irish gelding: maiden hurdler: modest handicap chaser: won at Wexford in July: sold out of P. Roche's stable 9,000 gns Doncaster November Sales after sixth start, no form subsequently: stays 3m: acts on firm and good to soft ground: tried blinkered/in cheekpieces. *Miss I. E. Craig* **c86 d h84 d**

IRISH NATIVE (IRE) 6 br.g. Be My Native (USA) – Thats Irish (Furry Glen) [2002/3 h–, F–: c20dᵖᵘ Oct 31] tall, rather unfurnished gelding: has reportedly had breathing operation: no form in varied events. *Miss H. C. Knight* **c– h–**

IRISH OPTION (IRE) 10 ch.g. Executive Perk – Erins Treasure (Brave Invader (USA)) [2002/3 c20d⁴ c20d³ c21d² c24d⁴ c26dᶠ c26s² c24dᵖᵘ Apr 9] leggy gelding: fair handicap chaser: may prove best up to 3m: acts on good to firm and heavy going: consistent. *J. T. Gifford* **c100 h–**

IRISH PADDY (IRE) 4 b.g. Idris (IRE) – Ceili Queen (IRE) (Shareef Dancer (USA)) [2002/3 17g 16m 16g 16g 16g 17vᵖᵘ 16gᵖᵘ Mar 23] small gelding: tailed off in 2 maidens on Flat, sold out of K. McAuliffe's stable 500 gns Doncaster October (2001) Sales: no form over hurdles. *I. A. Brown* **h–**

IRISH PATRIARCH (IRE) 7 b.g. Mister Lord (USA) – Moon Lock (Lock And Load (USA)) [2002/3 F17s Nov 18] ninth foal: half-brother to winning Irish chaser Tourig Lady (by Proverb): dam never ran: last in bumper on debut. *P. G. Murphy* **F–**

IRISH PRINCE (IRE) 7 b.g. Fresh Breeze (USA) – Kilivarig (Crozier) [2002/3 F17d 19dᵖᵘ 25d² 20sᵖᵘ Mar 15] sturdy gelding: seventh foal: brother to fair Irish 2½m hurdler/chaser Irish Breeze: dam maiden 2m hurdler: tenth of 16 in bumper on debut for J. O'Shea: second in weak 3-finisher novice hurdle at Warwick in March: looked none too keen in visor final start: pulls hard. *D. Shaw* **h– F–**

IRISH SEA (USA) 10 b.g. Zilzal (USA) – Dunkellin (USA) (Irish River (FR)) [2002/3 c87, h76: c22dᶠ c16d³ c19g³ Apr 2] neat gelding: fair hunter chaser: stays 23f, effective at much shorter: acts on any going: blinkered once. *S. Flook* **c91 h–**

IRIS ROYAL (FR) 7 b.g. Garde Royale – Tchela (FR) (Le Nain Jaune (FR)) [2002/3 h133: c24g² c24g* c24m* c24gᵖᵘ c20gᵖᵘ c20f² Apr 25] smallish gelding: useful **c130 h–**

handicap hurdler: similar form over fences: won novices at Newbury in December and Doncaster (match) in February: creditable second to Il Capitano in novice handicap at Sandown final start: stays 3m: acts on any going: reportedly lost action fifth outing. *N. J. Henderson*

IRIS'S GIFT 6 gr.g. Gunner B – Shirley's Gift (Scallywag) [2002/3 F110: 20d* 25m* 24d* 20v* 23d* 24g2 24d* Apr 4] **h172**

The Stayers' Hurdle was the best race of the season, one of the most memorable horse-races of recent times, and it was a pity it took place in the shadow of Best Mate's second successive victory in the Gold Cup. The Stayers' had been anticipated with relish for weeks, featuring the first clash between the French-trained reigning champion Baracouda, winner of ten of his last eleven races, and Ireland's most popular jumper, the tough and genuine eleven-year-old Limestone Lad, carrying a weight of public sentiment. It was widely seen as a two-horse race, the pair starting 9/4 joint favourites, but the most abiding image of the race was provided by the British-trained novice Iris's Gift.

Turning down the hill towards the second last, in a race that had been run at a searching gallop from the off, Barry Geraghty was sitting up confidently as Iris's Gift, still on the bridle, stalked the front-running Limestone Lad, with Baracouda starting to move past Classified to get on terms with the two leaders. Iris's Gift seemed, just for a moment, to have reserves that neither of the pushed-along principals possessed. He still looked to be travelling best as the leaders rounded the home turn and began to straighten up for the final flight. Geraghty knew he had Limestone Lad covered and took a glance over his right shoulder to check on Baracouda but, as he did so, Baracouda loomed up alongside. There was little between Baracouda, Iris's Gift, now suddenly under pressure, and Limestone Lad going to the last but Baracouda forged into a narrow lead and was half a length in front of Iris's Gift jumping it, with Limestone Lad still close up in third. Baracouda and Iris's Gift pulled away on the run-in, Geraghty going for everything as Iris's Gift rallied very gamely. The combination of the resolute attention of Iris's Gift and the steep climb to the finish would have found out Baracouda had this been one of those days when his renowned tendency to idle had manifested itself. But Baracouda kept on pulling out more and, in a pulsating finish, held off Iris's Gift by three quarters of a length, with Limestone Lad five lengths further back in third and thirteen lengths clear of fourth-placed Classified who had been the only other runner in with a chance three out. The remainder crossed the line at well-spaced

Red Square Vodka Prestige Novices' Hurdle, Haydock—
Iris's Gift is pressed by Tees Components at the third from home

Martell Cognac Sefton Novices' Hurdle, Aintree—
an awkward jump at the last but Iris's Gift already has the race well won

intervals. Two established top-class hurdlers in Baracouda and Limestone Lad had been joined by a new one in Iris's Gift whose successful graduation straight from novice events to open championship company had been a revelation.

Iris's Gift had been one of the previous season's best bumper horses. He had won three times and run well at both the Cheltenham Festival (fifth to Pizarro) and at Aintree (second to Kickham) despite, on occasions, looking anything but an easy ride, displaying a tendency to hang. He had been schooled over hurdles but those who had handled him at Jackdaws Castle hadn't been able to get him jumping properly. He was not particularly fluent, and needed a couple of sharp reminders when in front, before landing the odds, pushed out, on his jumping debut in a run-of-the-mill novice hurdle at Bangor in October. Iris's Gift looked a better prospect, despite still taking a few liberties with his hurdles, when romping home by twenty-five lengths at Cheltenham later in the month, and showed further improvement when wearing down Ad Hoc—the pair a distance clear—to complete his hat-trick in the Bristol Novices' Hurdle at the same course in December. Iris's Gift looked in really good shape beforehand and was clearly thriving, though there were no thoughts as yet about his possibly proving good enough to take on the best in open company. In fact, a relentless display of galloping on heavy going at Uttoxeter in February, which saw him come home a distance in front in the Jacuzzi UK Classic Novices' Hurdle, prompted more speculation about his long-term chasing prospects which looked—and still look—excellent. Iris's Gift made it five out of five over hurdles when coasting home by seventeen lengths in the Red Square Vodka Prestige Novices' Hurdle at Haydock shortly before the Cheltenham Festival, his task made considerably easier by what seemed at the time the disappointing showing of main rival Tees Components. Iris's Gift held a number of engagements at the Festival and the Stayers' Hurdle supplanted the Pertemps Final as his target after the Haydock performance (Iris's Gift had 11-12—equivalent to

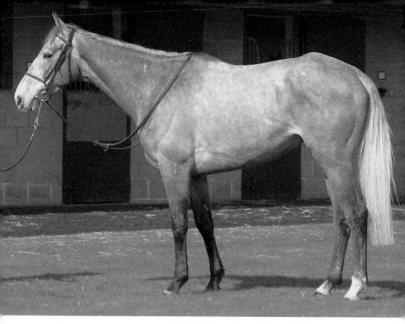

Mr Robert Lester's "Iris's Gift"

a BHB mark of only 142—in the Pertemps, for which he also escaped a penalty).
Incidentally, Iris's Gift was qualified for the Final after being entered for the
abandoned qualifier at Warwick in January, along with eleven other Jonjo O'Neill-
trained horses, who included the winner Inching Closer.

Iris's Gift had also been entered for the Royal & SunAlliance Hurdle at the
Festival and he met the first and third (promoted to second) in that—the Irish-
trained pair Hardy Eustace and Pizarro—at Aintree three weeks later. The Martell
Cognac Sefton Novices' Hurdle is the season's top event for the three-mile novice
hurdlers and odds-on Iris's Gift romped home, showing no ill-effects from his
Festival exertions and giving another tremendous display in a very strongly-run
affair, looking a class apart from most of his rivals from a very early stage and
winning by eight lengths and twelve from the Pertemps Final runner-up Royal
Emperor and the Royal & SunAlliance eighth Supreme Prince. Hardy Eustace was
well below form in fifth, presumably not over his race at Cheltenham, and Pizarro
fell early on. The only black mark against Iris's Gift was that, after being clear from
four out, he idled late in the race, jumped the last awkwardly and needed reminders
before racing away again to finish well on top. His victory completed an Aintree
treble on the day for trainer Jonjo O'Neill, successful earlier with Master Tern and
Clan Royal.

The big, workmanlike Iris's Gift is very much a chasing type in appearance
but, at the time of writing, with Baracouda set to be switched to fences, it seems that
Iris's Gift will be staying over hurdles for another season at least. The performance
of Iris's Gift in the Stayers' Hurdle was the best by a novice hurdler since Baracouda won the Long Walk Hurdle at an even earlier stage of his career, at Ascot in
December 2000. Additionally, only Golden Cygnet and Alderbrook have recorded
a higher Timeform rating as a novice since *Chasers & Hurdlers* began. Iris's Gift
looks the one to succeed to Baracouda's crown as king of the staying hurdlers. He
seems to thrive on racing and is likely to have a full campaign before tackling the

Stayers' Hurdle, which should be good news for racegoers at Wetherby (West York-shire Hurdle), Newbury (Long Distance Hurdle) and Ascot (Long Walk Hurdle) in the weeks leading up to Christmas. The grey Iris's Gift has all the makings of a jumper who could become one of the sport's most popular performers over the next few seasons, all being well. He is built to make a tremendous chaser one day.

Iris's Gift (gr.g. 1997)	Gunner B (ch 1973)	Royal Gunner (ch 1962)	Royal Charger
			Levee
		Sweet Councillor (b 1968)	Privy Councillor
			Sugarstick
	Shirley's Gift (gr 1986)	Scallywag (gr 1973)	Sea Hawk II
			Scammell
		Earlsgift (b 1976)	Dusky Boy
			Austrian Girl

Iris's Gift was originally sent to his trainer with instructions to 'send him back if he's no good', the owner having reportedly bought him for only 3,500 guineas. Iris's Gift was conceived when his sire Gunner B was already twenty-three but, remarkably, Gunner B was still covering around twenty mares a season in his late-'twenties. He died at the age of thirty in January, believed to be the oldest active thoroughbred stallion in Europe. His feats at stud had just been recognised for the fourth year in succession at the Thoroughbred Breeders' Association annual awards dinner in London. He had been the year's leading active British-based stallion, in terms of both prize-money earned over jumps and most individual steeplechase winners. Gunner B began his stud career as a Flat stallion in Lincolnshire after a racing career in which he showed himself a notably tough and genuine performer with a great zest for racing, his most important victories coming in the Eclipse Stakes and the Prince of Wales's Stakes. But his British-raced progeny proved somewhat disappointing at first and he was eventually exported to Germany before being repatriated in 1988 after the achievements of his son Royal Gait in 1987, notably in winning the Prix du Cadran and Prix Royal-Oak. Royal Gait was most controversially disqualified in the 1988 Ascot Gold Cup and, nearly four years later, after at one time being pensioned off because of leg trouble, he returned to action over jumps and won the Champion Hurdle while still a novice. Gunner B's switch to the Shade Oak Stud in Shropshire gave his career further impetus and he made a name for himself as principally a sire of chasers, his progeny including Grand National winner Red Marauder, the high-class Bobby Grant, Red Striker, Jim Thorpe, Gunner Welburn and Barrow Drive, one of Gunner B's few Irish winners, and the high-class hurdler Swingit Gunner, among others. Given the huge books covered by many of his Irish-based rivals, Gunner B's achievements are even more noteworthy given that he never sired a crop of foals at Shade Oak numbering more than fifty and his later crops were understandably fairly small. Though he sired a Grand National winner—and a Grand National fourth in Gunner Welburn —Gunner B hasn't been that strong an influence for stamina. Iris's Gift's pedigree has stamina on the dam's side, however. His dam Shirley's Gift was an unraced daughter of the St Leger third Scallywag, a grey who stood 17.2 hands and was so big that he could not be accommodated in an ordinary steeplechase stall (a special strap was made to replace the rear doors). Iris's Gift's grandam the winning pointer Earlsgift was a half-sister to the top-class hurdler Browne's Gazette out of Austrian Girl, an unraced half-sister to Ascot Gold Cup and Doncaster Cup winner Pandofell; one of Austrian Girl's half-sisters Pepe produced Grand National runner-up Young Driver. Shirley's Gift has produced just two foals apart from Iris's Gift, the unraced Cheeky Mare (by Derrylin), who is now at stud, and a 2001 filly by Bob's Return. Iris's Gift will stay beyond twenty-five furlongs, and acts on good to firm and heavy going. Despite idling in front on occasions, he is a thoroughly genuine racehorse, and a tough one too. *Jonjo O'Neill*

IRLANDAIS II (FR) 7 ch.g. Moon Madness – Platine III (FR) (Iveday (FR)) [2002/3 c79, h75: c16g^{pu} c16g c24d c27v^{pu} c20s^{pu} Feb 24] lengthy gelding: poor maiden hurdler/ chaser: no form in 2002/3: tried in cheekpieces: has had tongue tied: sketchy jumper of fences. *G. A. Harker*   c–h–

IRON DRAGON (IRE) 5 b.g. Royal Academy (USA) – Kerry Project (IRE) (Project Manager) [2002/3 16m^{ur} May 11] poor maiden on Flat (probably stays 1¼m): jinked and unseated second in 4-y-o novice on hurdling debut. *Mrs M. Reveley*   h–

IRON EXPRESS   7 b.g. Teenoso (USA) – Sylvia Beach (The Parson) [2002/3 h–: c21d³ c21v³ c19s⁵ c16g⁵ c25d³ c21d⁴ c25g³ Apr 14] sparely-made gelding: winning hurdler: modest novice chaser: stays 25f: acts on heavy going. *G. M. Moore* **c96 h–**

IRON MOUNTAIN (IRE)   8 b.g. Scenic – Merlannah (IRE) (Shy Groom (USA)) [2002/3 16d 16g^F 16s² Dec 5] good-topped gelding: poor maiden hurdler: likely to prove best at well-run 2m: acts on heavy going. *Mrs L. C. Jewell* **h80**

IRON N GOLD   11 b.g. Heights of Gold – Southern Dynasty (Gunner B) [2002/3 c89, h–: c20v^pu c21s c19m^pu Apr 22] good-topped gelding: modest handicap chaser in 2001/2: disappointing on return: stays 25f: acts on good to firm and heavy going: visored once: often finds little. *B. G. Powell* **c– h–**

IRON PRINCESS (IRE)   7 b.m. Insan (USA) – Mrs Cullen (Over The River (FR)) [2002/3 h–: c25d^pu May 4] lengthy mare: no sign of ability: tried visored/blinkered. *G. M. Moore* **c– h–**

IRON TROOPER (IRE)   5 ch.g. Glacial Storm (USA) – Iron Star (General Ironside) [2002/3 21v 19g^F Feb 28] half-brother to modest staying chaser Steel Moss and winning pointer She Devil (both by Le Moss): dam unraced: well held in 2 starts over hurdles. *J. Wade* **h–**

IRO ORIGNY (FR)   7 b.g. Saint Cyrien (FR) – Coralline (FR) (Iron Duke (FR)) [2002/3 22g^pu 20m⁶ c19m⁴ c19g³ c19g⁴ c20d^rtr c19v^rtr Dec 28] small gelding: poor maiden hurdler/chaser: seems best short of 2½m: acts on firm and soft going: usually tongue tied: refused to race last 2 starts and one to leave severely alone. *Miss Venetia Williams* **c§§ h§§**

ISAM TOP (FR)   7 b.g. Siam (USA) – Miss Sic Top (FR) (Mister Sic Top (FR)) [2002/3 c82, h93: c16m⁵ c21f^F 18f^pu 20s c16m^pu 22m 18m* 17d² 18g⁴ 17g³ Oct 18] compact gelding: poor maiden chaser: fair hurdler: back to form when winning handicap at Fontwell in August: best form around 2m: acts on soft and firm going: blinkered twice: races prominently: tends to jump right. *M. J. Hogan* **c– h101**

ISARD III (FR)   7 gr.g. Royal Charter (FR) – Aurore d'Ex (FR) (Mont Basile (FR)) [2002/3 c20g^F 20g* Apr 2] tall, angular gelding: won bumper at Newbury in late-2000/1: won point in 2002, fell first on novice chase debut: looked useful prospect when winning novice hurdle at Ascot by 6 lengths from Fork Lightning, in command when left clear 2 out and eased considerably: sure to improve and win more races if all is well with him. *M. C. Pipe* **c– p h127 p**

Rosling King 'National Hunt' Novices' Hurdle, Ascot—Isard III looks a bright prospect

ISCA MAIDEN 9 b.m. Full Extent (USA) – Sharp N' Easy (Swing Easy (USA)) **c66**
[2002/3 c–, h71: 19s⁶ c17v³ c16s 17dᵖᵘ Mar 18] angular mare: poor handicap hurdler/ **h–**
novice chaser: best around 2m: acts on heavy and good to firm going: none too consistent.
G. Brown

ISEFOUL DE BELLEVUE (FR) 7 b.g. Useful (FR) – Frika (FR) (Kashneb (FR)) **c–**
[2002/3 21sᵖᵘ 26dᵖᵘ c20gᵘʳ c16g⁴ c19m Apr 22] ex-Irish gelding: second foal: dam **h–**
unraced half-sister to smart French chaser Staff: little show in bumpers: modest maiden
hurdler at best: sold out of M. Hourigan's stable 3,000 gns Doncaster May Sales: no form
in Britain, including over fences: tried blinkered: tongue tied last 3 starts. *R. M. Stronge*

ISHANDRAZ (GER) 6 gr.g. Mondrian (GER) – Isla Limpia (GER) (Limbo (GER)) **h91**
[2002/3 17d⁵ 17s 16s 25m* 22g² Apr 19] ex-German gelding: lightly raced on Flat, won
over 1¼m in 2000, claimed from D. Fechner 161,000 francs later that year: upped in trip,
improved form over hurdles when winning novice handicap at Plumpton in March
despite mistakes: good second in similar event at Newton Abbot following month: stays
25f: acts on good to firm going: has pulled hard. *M. C. Pipe*

ISIO (FR) 7 b.g. Silver Rainbow – Swifty (FR) (Le Riverain (FR)) [2002/3 h129: **c146**
c16g* c16d* c16g* c16g³ Mar 11] **h–**

Some impressive records over fences were put on the line in the Arkle. The
top half-dozen in the betting had between them won seventeen of their twenty-one
starts in chases and three of the field were still unbeaten, Azertyuiop, Impek and
Isio each having won all three of their outings in novice chases. Unlike the first
two in the betting, Isio had not been tried in graded company over fences but his
performance in the Arkle fully confirmed the promise he had shown in lesser
events. It was only from the home turn at Cheltenham that Azertyuiop quickened
away from Isio, but until then Isio had kept close tabs on the favourite, jumping and
travelling well on the heels of the leaders until hitting the top of the second last. Isio
stuck on well but just found Impek too strong up the hill and lost out for second
place by a length, beaten a total of twelve lengths behind the very impressive
winner.

It had been the plan to test Isio's readiness for a race as hot as the Arkle by
contesting Warwick's Kingmaker Novices' Chase in February, but when that was
abandoned connections had to be content with a third easy win in an ordinary
novice chase at Huntingdon. As in his two other novice chases, at Kempton in

Doncaster Racecourse Sponsorship Club Novices' Chase—Isio gains an impressive victory

November and Doncaster in January, Isio impressed with the speed and fluency of his jumping and landed the odds with plenty in hand. None of the horses he beat in any of his three wins prior to the Arkle were anywhere near Festival standard, his most significant opponent probably being Midland Flame, third behind him at Doncaster, who went on to land a valuable novices handicap at Aintree.

Like the two who beat him at Cheltenham, Isio is a French non-thorough-bred. His sire Silver Rainbow, though, raced in Britain and was bred to win a Derby, something his brother Quest For Fame actually achieved. Silver Rainbow had just four starts for Guy Harwood, showing himself a smart if lazy stayer by making the frame in the Queen's Vase and Goodwood Cup. Isio's selle francais family is an unremarkable one. His dam Swifty was placed several times around a mile and a quarter on the Flat and is a half-sister to plenty of winners, including Enivrant (by Quart de Vin), a winning chaser for the Pipe stable. Grandam Miss Fany was an unraced half-sister to Vaddyto, a winner of Belgium's big jumps race, the Grand Steeple Chase des Flandres. Like his dam's other winner Dornes (by Balsamo), Isio was successful on the Flat in France (over a mile and a half), and he joined his current stable for 600,000 francs at the Goffs July Sale in 2001.

Isio (FR) (b.g. 1996)	Silver Rainbow (b 1988)	Rainbow Quest (b 1981)	Blushing Groom
			I Will Follow
		Aryenne (br 1977)	Green Dancer
			Americaine
	Swifty (FR) (b 1984)	Le Riverain (b 1975)	Riverman
			Fine II
		Miss Fany (ch 1978)	Ermitage
			Fany des Saccart

Isio has raced only at around two miles so far, though members of the selle francais breed are rarely lacking in stamina and his options would be greater in his

Sir Peter And Lady Gibbings' "Isio"

second season over fences were he to prove effective at around two and a half miles. He acts on soft and good to firm going. Isio has been a model of consistency to date, the Arkle being the first occasion that he has finished out of the first two for his current stable. He won three of his last four starts in his novice hurdle campaign and Nicky Henderson reported at the beginning of the latest season that 'We were tempted to keep him over hurdles, as we thought he might progress again, but as soon as we schooled him over fences, he told us categorically that this is what he ought to be doing.' An angular gelding who took the eye with his well-being on more than one occasion in the latest season, Isio looks sure to win more races over fences. *N. J. Henderson*

ISKAN (GER) 8 b.g. Perceive Arrogance (USA) – Ifakara (GER) (Athenagoras (GER)) [2002/3 c–, h79d: 17d 16v^{pu} 21s^{pu} Dec 10] tall, leggy gelding: winning 2½m hurdler: largely disappointing since 1999/00: fell early on chasing debut: tried visored: has had tongue tied: difficult ride (headstrong). *A. Parker* — c– h–

ISLAND FAITH (IRE) 6 b. or br.g. Turtle Island (IRE) – Keep The Faith (Furry Glen) [2002/3 F106: 20d⁶ 20d² 22v³ 20v* 21m 16d² Mar 7] strong, compact gelding: fair novice hurdler: won at Newcastle in January: may prove best up to 2½m: acts on heavy going, possibly unsuited by good to firm: has found little. *Ferdy Murphy* — h110

ISLAND FORTRESS 4 ch.f. Infantry – Misty Fort (Menelek) [2002/3 F17d⁵ F16g⁵ Feb 27] half-sister to fair chaser Island Mist (by Jupiter Island), stays 2½m: dam, useful chaser, stayed 2¾m: twice-raced in mares bumpers, lost all chance by running wide leaving back straight at Taunton on debut: failed to improve next time. *H. D. Daly* — F77

ISLAND SOUND 6 b.g. Turtle Island (IRE) – Ballet (Sharrood (USA)) [2002/3 h108§: c16s^{ur} c16d³ c16v² c16g^{ur} Mar 23] angular gelding: fair hurdler: shaped promisingly on chasing debut but failed to improve as expected, his not fluent: raced around 2m on good going or softer (acts on heavy): has failed to impress with attitude more than once over hurdles. *D. R. C. Elsworth* — c106 h– §

ISLAND STREAM (IRE) 4 b.g. Turtle Island (IRE) – Tilbrook (IRE) (Don't Forget Me) [2002/3 16d 16v* 16d 16g⁴ Mar 14] tall, close-coupled gelding: thrice-raced maiden at 2 yrs, showing modest form for J. L. Eyre: best effort over hurdles when fourth in juvenile at Sandown second start, possibly flattered: raced at 2m on good going or softer (acts on heavy): has pulled hard. *J. R. Jenkins* — h99

ISLAND WARRIOR (IRE) 8 b.g. Warcraft (USA) – Only Flower (Warpath) [2002/3 c–, h70: 22g³ 22m^F c16m^{pu} Jul 17] workmanlike gelding: poor hurdler: no show in 3 runs over fences: stays 2¾m: acts on firm going (bumper form on soft): blinkered once: has had tongue tied. *F. Jordan* — c– x h70

ISMENE (FR) 7 b.m. Bad Conduct (USA) – Athena de L'Isle (FR) (Quart de Vin (FR)) [2002/3 h92: 20v* 20d^{pu} c20d^F 20d* Mar 19] close-coupled mare: fell fifth on chasing debut: fair handicap hurdler: won at Uttoxeter in June and Chepstow in March, allowed to dictate at latter: should stay 3m: acts on heavy going: often looks temperamental. *Miss Venetia Williams* — c– h107 §

ISMENO 12 b.g. Ela-Mana-Mou – Seattle Siren (USA) (Seattle Slew (USA)) [2002/3 16s^{pu} 21s^{pu} Jan 13] compact gelding: useful handicap hurdler in 1998/9: showed little on return. *S. Dow* — h–

ISO BALD (FR) 7 ch.g. Cyborg (FR) – Renny (FR) (Diaghilev) [2002/3 h87, F77: c16f³ c20v⁶ c16v^{pu} c16g^{pu} 27g Apr 25] poor form in novice chases: modest hurdler: well beaten in handicap final outing: should stay 3m: best efforts over hurdles on good ground: has worn cheekpieces: often shapes as if amiss (jumped badly right final 2 runs over fences). *A. M. Crow* — c79 h–

ISOU (FR) 7 ch.g. Dom Alco (FR) – Aghate de Saisy (FR) (Rhapsodien) [2002/3 h102: c21v⁶ c26s⁴ c25s² Dec 26] sturdy gelding: fair hurdler: only modest form in novice chases: likely to prove best at 3m+: probably acts on any going. *V. R. A. Dartnall* — c85 h–

ITALIAN COUNSEL (IRE) 6 b.g. Leading Counsel (USA) – Mullaghroe (Tarboosh (USA)) [2002/3 16m⁵ 16m 17d* 18m² 17d³ 17g^{pu} c16g c16d³ c16v² c17v⁶ c16s⁵ c21m^{pu} Apr 21] angular ex-Irish gelding: no form on Flat: modest hurdler: won selling handicap at Market Rasen in August: poor novice chaser: should stay 2½m: acts on good to firm and heavy going: has worn cheekpieces: has had tongue tied. *B. J. Llewellyn* — c83 h85

ITCANBEDONE AGAIN (IRE) 4 b.c. Sri Pekan (USA) – Maradata (IRE) (Shardari) [2002/3 16s⁶ 16d Dec 14] fair on Flat (barely stays 1½m) for R. Hollinshead: well held both starts in juvenile hurdles. *Ian Williams* — h–

ITCH 8 b.g. Puissance – Panienka (POL) (Dom Racine (FR)) [2002/3 16s^{pu} 16v^4 16d^{pu} **h64** Feb 26] small gelding: poor on Flat (probably stays 9f) nowadays: poor form over hurdles: will need sharp 2m: pulls hard. *R. Bastiman*

ITCHEN MILL 6 b.m. Alflora (IRE) – Treble Chance (Balinger) [2002/3 F17m^5 Apr **F78 ?** 15] second foal: dam temperamental winning pointer: fifth of 9 in steadily-run mares maiden bumper at Exeter on debut. *R. H. Alner*

ITCHINTOGO (IRE) 5 b.g. Namaqualand (USA) – Lamp of Phoebus (USA) (Sun- **F–** shine Forever (USA)) [2002/3 F18v Dec 4] 1,000 4-y-o: second foal: dam twice-raced half-sister to smart French performer up to 10.5f Accomodating: tailed off in bumper on debut. *L. A. Dace*

I TINA 7 b.m. Lycius (USA) – Tintomara (IRE) (Niniski (USA)) [2002/3 17s 19s 17g^4 **h–** Apr 19] modest on Flat (best around 1¼m): little show over hurdles. *A. G. Juckes*

ITSALF 5 ch.g. Afzal – Sail On Sunday (Sunyboy) [2002/3 F16d F18m^6 F16m^6 Apr **F74 ?** 10] 4,500 4-y-o: angular gelding: first foal: dam ran only in points: signs of only a little ability in bumpers. *R. J. Smith*

IT'S ALL A CHANCE (IRE) 8 ch.g. Eve's Error – Butlers Pier (Good Thyne **c84** (USA)) [2002/3 c–, h92: 20d c20f^2 Sep 15] workmanlike gelding: modest handicap **h–** hurdler: distressed on reappearance: not fluent over fences, best effort when second in handicap at Hexham in September: stays 21f: acts on any going. *J. Howard Johnson*

ITSANOTHERGIRL 7 b.m. Reprimand – Tasmim (Be My Guest (USA)) [2002/3 **h85** 16v Dec 26] leggy mare: good walker: fair on Flat (stays 1½m): modest juvenile hurdler in 1999/00: well held in novice on return: likely to prove best at sharp 2m: acts on soft going: tried blinkered. *M. W. Easterby*

IT'S BEYOND BELIEF (IRE) 9 b.g. Supreme Leader – Rossacurra (Deep Run) **c114** [2002/3 c104: c26s* Mar 10] lightly-raced winning pointer: best effort in steeplechases when winning novice at Plumpton on return from 15-month absence, all out to beat Another Moose 1¾ lengths: stays 3¼m. *P. F. Nicholls*

ITSDEDFAST (IRE) 7 ch.g. Lashkari – Amazing Silks (Furry Glen) [2002/3 F17d* **h–** 20m^{pu} Dec 17] IR 30,000 3-y-o: second foal: dam winning 2m hurdler: comfortably won **F95** maiden bumper at Sedgefield on debut in October: couple of bad mistakes and beaten long way out in maiden hurdle at Musselburgh. *L. Lungo*

IT'S HARRY 5 b.g. Aragon – Andbracket (Import) [2002/3 F17m^2 F16g^4 Jul 10] **F86** 1,400 4-y-o: fifth foal: half-brother to modest 2m hurdler Disco Tex and fair 1m/9f winner Dispol Gem (both by Rambo Dancer): dam unraced: in frame in bumpers at Market Rasen and Worcester. *Mrs S. J. Smith*

IT'S HIMSELF 11 b.g. Rakaposhi King – Coole Pilate (Celtic Cone) [2002/3 c125, **c125 x** h–: c29v^F c24d^5 Feb 8] rangy gelding: fairly useful handicap chaser: stays 3½m: acts **h–** on good to firm and heavy going: tongue tied: usually waited with: sketchy jumper. *A. J. Martin, Ireland*

IT'S JUST SALLY 6 b.m. Kylian (USA) – Hush It Up (Tina's Pet) [2002/3 F79: 16s^5 **h–** 17f^5 Oct 9] poor form in mares bumpers in 2001/2: little encouragement in 2 outings over hurdles. *C. R. Egerton*

ITSMYTURNNOW (IRE) 8 b.g. Glacial Storm (USA) – Snuggle (Music Boy) **c78** [2002/3 c24m^6 c22f^5 Apr 24] third foal: dam, winner on Flat/fair all-weather hurdler, sister to very smart 2m chaser Young Snugfit: lightly raced in points, successful in January and March: soundly beaten in hunter and novice chase, jumping left in latter. *M. J. Roberts*

IT'SNOTSIMPLE (IRE) 11 b.m. Homo Sapien – Perpetue (Proverb) [2002/3 **c–** c26s^{pu} May 28] fair pointer, successful in March: little worthwhile form otherwise: tried **h–** blinkered. *H. Messer-Bennetts*

ITSONLYME (IRE) 10 b.g. Broken Hearted – Over The Arctic (Over The River **c119** (FR)) [2002/3 c122p, h–: c20d^7 c22d* c25g^3 c24s^F c24s^{pu} Feb 13] useful-looking **h–** gelding: fairly useful chaser: landed odds in novices at Towcester very early in season: let down by jumping in handicaps next 2 starts, ran as if amiss final one: stays 3m: acts on soft and good to firm going (won bumper on heavy). *Miss Venetia Williams*

ITS ONLY POLITE (IRE) 7 b.g. Roselier (FR) – Decent Debbie (Decent Fellow) **c91** [2002/3 h118, F88: c24s^2 c25s* c26v^5 Jan 17] workmanlike gelding: progressive form in **h–** novice hurdles in 2001/2: second outing in novice chases, won at Hereford in December:

ran poorly in better race at Chepstow following month: should stay beyond 25f: raced only on going softer than good. *A. J. Lidderdale*

ITS TIME FOR A WIN (IRE)   11 b.g. Lord Bud – Autumn Gift (Martinmas)   **c–** [2002/3 c142, h–: c16s⁵ c20dᶠ Nov 16] lengthy gelding: useful chaser at best: long way   **h–** below form in Grade 3 at Navan on reappearance: put down after falling at Cheltenham: effective at 2½m to 3m: acted on heavy and good to firm going: won only on left-handed tracks: not always a fluent jumper. *W. P. Mullins, Ireland*

ITS WALLACE JNR   4 b.g. Bedford (USA) – Built In Heaven (Sunley Builds)   **h105 ?** [2002/3 16d* 16s³ 17g 19m Mar 22] leggy gelding: modest maiden on Flat (stays 2m): 66/1, won juvenile at Wincanton on hurdling debut, left clear last: stiff tasks when well held last 2 starts, flattered in Triumph Hurdle on first occasion: should stay beyond 2m. *Miss S. West*

IT TAKES TIME (IRE)   9 b.g. Montelimar (USA) – Dysart Lady (King's Ride)   **c143 +** [2002/3 h154: 25d³ c25d² c22d* c24g⁶ c25d² Apr 4]   **h156**

    At a Festival where nearly every winner seemed either to be the favourite or a well-supported second or third choice, the Royal & SunAlliance Chase, the championship event for novices, bucked the trend. The favourite Keen Leader and his main market rival It Takes Time both failed to give their running. Keen Leader wasn't seen out again but It Takes Time went a fair way towards redeeming his reputation when second, conceding weight, to Irish Hussar in the Grade 2 Mildmay Novices' Chase at Aintree. It Takes Time went to Cheltenham with just two races in steeplechases under his belt—he had won a point in Ireland at the start of his career. He had been beaten half a length by Sir Rembrandt in a Grade 2 novice at Cheltenham in December on his debut over fences, then landed the odds in a four-runner novice at Haydock the following month, his three rivals, headed by The Bajan Bandit, all conceding him 8 lb. It Takes Time was impressive that day, jumping with more confidence than he had at Cheltenham and shaping as if he'd soon be reaching the level of form he had shown over hurdles. He had put up a

Isle of Skye Blended Whisky-Kelso Novices' Chase, Haydock—
It Takes Time gains his only success of the season

very smart performance when third to Baracouda in the 2002 Stayers' Hurdle and matched that effort when third to Native Emperor under top weight in a valuable handicap again at Cheltenham on his reappearance. Lack of experience over fences might have been a possible drawback in the SunAlliance, but it hardly appeared to concern connections who also left him in the Gold Cup until the final declaration stage. It couldn't be said that lack of experience had much to do with It Takes Time's disappointing effort. He was well placed four out but his response was very limited and he trailed in last of the six finishers behind One Knight. No explanation came to light for his poor effort but punters clearly weren't discouraged. He started favourite at Aintree and turned in a much better effort, jumping to the front four out but unable to get Irish Hussar, who was receiving 5 lb, off the bridle. It Takes Time was soon put in his place once headed at the last, trailing by five lengths at the line. It Takes Time is likely to benefit from a stiffer test of stamina than he has had so far over fences and there could well be better to come in handicaps in 2003/4. It Takes Time is set to start the season on an attractive mark and it would be no surprise if his stable has him primed for something like the Intervet Trophy at Cheltenham or even the Hennessy at Newbury on his reappearance. It Takes Time, an angular gelding in appearance, will stay beyond twenty-five furlongs and acts on good to firm and heavy going. He tends to idle in front but is consistent. *M. C. Pipe*

IVANOPH (FR) 7 b.g. Roi de Rome (USA) – Veronique IV (FR) (Mont Basile (FR)) [2002/3 c119, h101+: c16g² c16d* c17g⁴ 17s c17d² c16f² Apr 25] tall, sparely-made gelding: successful on first of 2 starts over hurdles: fairly useful handicap chaser: won at Wincanton in November: largely creditable efforts otherwise in 2002/3, though not for first time found less than seemed likely when second of 4 to Ei Ei at Sandown final start: stays 2½m: acts on any going: temperament under suspicion. *P. F. Nicholls*   **c124 h–**

I'VEHADIT (IRE) 9 ch.g. Treasure Hunter – Had Enough (Hadeer) [2002/3 h126, F96: 16f⁴ 24sᵖᵘ c17s⁵ c25sᵖᵘ c22v* c24v* c20v³ c20d³ c24d² c29g Apr 21] lengthy gelding: fairly useful hurdler: useful novice chaser: won maiden at Limerick in December and Grade 3 at Naas (by short head from The Premier Cat) in January: good second to Jenniferjo in listed race at former course: badly let down by jumping in Irish Grand National at Fairyhouse: light in condition, laboured effort when fourth in Grade 3 at Punchestown in late-April: stays 3m: acts on heavy going, poor efforts on firmer than good. *D. T. Hughes, Ireland*   **c135 h–**

IVERAIN (FR) 7 b.g. Le Riverain (FR) – Ursala (FR) (Toujours Pret (USA)) [2002/3 c–, h124: c25m* c20d² c25d⁴ c19v³ c21d⁴ c24m* Apr 22] good-topped gelding: fairly useful hurdler: similar form in novice chases, won at Wincanton in November and Chepstow (simple task) in April: stays 25f: acts on good to soft and good to firm going: well below form in blinkers fourth start: usually a sound jumper. *P. F. Nicholls*   **c119 h–**

IVORSAGOODUN 4 b.f. Piccolo – Malibasta (Auction Ring (USA)) [2002/3 17s⁵ 17s⁴ 17d⁴ 17v⁶ 16m³ 19m⁶ Apr 15] leggy filly: modest maiden on Flat (stays 1¾m) for Mrs P. N. Dutfield: modest juvenile hurdler: not fluent when visored final start: temperament under suspicion. *M. C. Pipe*   **h80**

IZNOGOUD (FR) 7 br.g. Shafoun (FR) – Vancia (FR) (Top Dancer (FR)) [2002/3 c151, h–: c26gᵖᵘ c24d⁵ c24gᵘʳ c21g c29m⁵ Apr 26] tall, leggy gelding: has a markedly round action: smart chaser: generally let down by jumping in 2002/3, more fluent when fifth to Ad Hoc in attheraces Gold Cup at Sandown (looked very well): well held in Group 1 hurdle at Auteuil in June: stays 29f: acts on good to firm and heavy going: visored twice (departed early on both occasions). *M. C. Pipe*   **c146 x h–**

J

JABIRU (IRE) 10 b. or br.g. Lafontaine (USA) – Country Glen (Furry Glen) [2002/3 c103, h–: c21g² c26g* c28m² c24s³ c26g c24f* c24f* c26m⁴ Apr 17] good-topped gelding: fairly useful hunter chaser: won at Newton Abbot in May and Taunton in March and April, jumping left last 2 occasions: stays 3½m: best efforts on good ground or firmer (acts on firm). *Mrs K. M. Sanderson*   **c107 h–**

JABO ORIGNY (FR) 6 gr.g. Royal Charter (FR) – Coralline (FR) (Iron Duke (FR)) [2002/3 F77: 20vF 16s⁶ 20m⁴ Apr 12] smallish gelding: best effort in novice hurdles when sixth of 8 finishers at Uttoxeter: seemed not to stay 2½m final start. *Miss Venetia Williams*   **h92**

JABOUNE (FR)   6 ch.g. Johann Quatz (FR) – Seasonal Pleasure (USA) (Graustark)   **h129**
[2002/3 h105+: 16g² 17m* 17g* 17m* 17dᵖᵘ 16d* 16d² 16g² 16s 16g³ 16m² 16g 17g⁵
16d Apr 4] compact gelding: type to carry condition: fairly useful hurdler: won novices at
Hereford and Newton Abbot and handicap at Market Rasen in June and novice at
Wetherby in November: generally ran well afterwards, twice second in Grade 2 novices
and seventh in Supreme Novices' at Cheltenham: raced around 2m: acts on good to firm
and good to soft going, possibly not soft: tongue tied first 5 starts: genuine and reliable.
A. King

JAC AN REE (IRE)   7 b.g. Supreme Leader – Nic An Ree (IRE) (King's Ride)   **h–**
[2002/3 F82: F16s⁶ 21s⁵ Jan 13] fair form in bumpers, sixth of 22 to Classic Native at   **F90**
Warwick: favourite, not fluent when tailed off in novice on hurdling debut. *D. M. Grissell*

JACDOR (IRE)   9 b.g. Be My Native (USA) – Bellalma (Belfalas) [2002/3 c–x, h100:   **c– x**
16m* 16s² 17d⁶ 25s* 24g² Mar 22] tall gelding: winning chaser, often let down by   **h118**
jumping: fairly useful handicap hurdler: won at Cheltenham (conditional jockeys) in
October and Warwick in January: effective around 2m to 25f: acts on good to firm and
heavy going: blinkered/visored: has had tongue tied. *R. Dickin*

JACK BE SMART   8 ch.g. Henbit (USA) – Trimar Gold (Goldhill) [2002/3 c–, h–:   **c–**
26gᵖᵘ c27vᵖᵘ c25dᵖᵘ Feb 25] workmanlike gelding: maiden hurdler/chaser: little worth-   **h–**
while form for long time, left F. Murphy after reappearance: tried blinkered/in cheekpieces. *J. Howard Johnson*

JACK DAWSON (IRE)   6 b.g. Persian Bold – Dream of Jenny (Caerleon (USA))   **h105**
[2002/3 h–p: 17m* 16m² Oct 7] fairly useful on Flat (stays 2m), successful twice in 2002:
second outing over hurdles, easily won novice at Southwell in September: finished lame
when beaten at long odds on in similar event at Plumpton: should stay beyond 17f. *John
Berry*

JACKEM (IRE)   9 b. or br.g. Lord Americo – Laurence Lady (Laurence O) [2002/3   **c85**
c–, h95, F87: 23g⁴ 23d³ 25d⁴ 24g³ 25m³ c27v⁴ c24g c24m² c25m² Apr 21] useful-looking   **h93**
gelding: modest hurdler: won novice at Fakenham in May: similar form, not fluent, over
fences: stays 25f: acts on heavy going, probably on good to firm. *Ian Williams*

JACK FRY (IRE)   6 gr.g. Lashkari – Most of All (Absalom) [2002/3 F79: F16d 16g   **h71**
19d⁶ 16g² 16m 20m⁴ Apr 21] leggy gelding: signs of ability in bumpers: generally well   **F72**
held over hurdles. *Noel T. Chance*

JACK FULLER (IRE)   6 b.g. Be My Native (USA) – Jacks Sister (IRE) (Entitled)   **h75**
[2002/3 F17m³ F16s 21s⁴ 22s 19d 17g³ Mar 16] 52,000 4-y-o: tall, angular gelding: **F84**
first foal: dam unraced half-sister to useful jumpers Joss Naylor, Native Mission and
Jack Doyle (all by Be My Native): third in bumper on debut: poor form over hurdles.
D. M. Grissell

JACK HIGH (IRE)   8 br.g. Erdelistan (FR) – Lyntim (Fidel) [2002/3 F105: 19g³ 16s   **h127**
24s³ 20m⁶ 19s* 24v* 24s⁵ 24s³ 24s³ 20s³ Mar 16] smallish gelding: first foal: dam, fair
hurdler/chaser who probably stayed 3m, sister to useful 2m hurdlers Eddie Wee and
Helynsar: bumper winner: fairly useful hurdler: won maiden at Naas in November and
handicaps at Leopardstown in December and Fairyhouse (novice, beat Poker Pal a
length) in February: good placed efforts in handicap at Punchestown in March and Grade
1 novice there (5 lengths second to Nobody Told Me) in early-May: likely to prove best at
3m+: acts well on going softer than good, probably unsuited by good to firm. *W. Rock,
Ireland*

JACKIE C (IRE)   8 b.g. Supreme Leader – Gloria St Julien (Duky) [2002/3 c102,   **c–**
h102: c20sᵘʳ Dec 18] workmanlike gelding: fair hurdler: fair novice chaser: unseated   **h–**
third only outing in 2002/3: likely to prove best up to 23f: raced on good ground or softer
(acts on heavy). *T. R. George*

JACKIE JARVIS (IRE)   6 b.m. Alphabatim (USA) – Miss Brantridge (Riboboy   **c103 p**
(USA)) [2002/3 F–§: c21mᵘʳ c21g* Mar 14] showed more temperament than ability in
bumpers (refused to race once): fair pointer, successful in February and March: won
novice at Fakenham on completed start in hunter chases: open to improvement. *P. York*

JACK (IRE)   11 br.g. Be My Native (USA) – Martialette (Welsh Saint) [2002/3 c–,   **c–**
h86: 16m Aug 27] tall, sparely-made gelding: maiden chaser: modest handicap hurdler: **h–**
off over 9 months, no encouragement only start in 2002/3: stays 2½m: acts on firm and
good to soft going, once visored or softer. *J. C. Tuck*

JACKLIGHTE BELLEVUE (FR)   6 b.g. Saint Cyrien (FR) – Kalighte (FR) (Light   **c91**
Butterfly) [2002/3 h111: c20g⁵ c19d c23g³ Feb 25] good-topped gelding: fair hurdler: **h–**
best effort over fences (finished distressed on reappearance) when third to Irish Hussar in

novice at Leicester: should stay beyond 21f: best form on going softer than good (acts on heavy). *Mrs H. Dalton*

JACK LYNCH 7 ch.g. Lancastrian – Troublewithjack (Sulaafah (USA)) [2002/3 **F82** F16g⁴ Jun 15] fourth foal: dam poor maiden, stayed 11f: twice-raced in points, runner-up in maiden in May: fourth of 12 in bumper at Hexham. *Ferdy Murphy*

JACK MARTIN (IRE) 6 ch.g. Erins Isle – Rolling Penny (IRE) (Le Moss) [2002/3 **F96** F16v³ F16v⁴ Dec 27] 2,400 5-y-o: leggy gelding: second foal: dam ran once: in frame in 2 bumpers at Chepstow, fairly useful form when third to Villa: sold to join S. Gollings 21,000 gns Doncaster January Sales. *M. Hill*

JACKOFALLTRADES (IRE) 5 b.g. Lord Americo – Wind Chimes (The Parson) **h–** [2002/3 F16v⁵ F16v 20sᵖᵘ Mar 6] seventh foal: half-brother to winning pointers by Pitpan **F–** and Insan: dam poor novice hurdler: no sign of ability. *A. C. Whillans*

JACK POT II (FR) 6 ch.g. Luchiroverte (IRE) – Roxane II (FR) (Signani (FR)) **h85** [2002/3 F16v³ F16v⁶ 20g⁴ Mar 17] 32,000 4-y-o: useful-looking gelding: half-brother to **F92** several winners, including fair hurdler/chaser Acajou III (by Cap Martin), stays 3m: dam once-raced half-sister to top-class French jumper El Paso III: better effort in bumpers when third at Ayr on debut: fourth in slowly-run maiden at Wetherby on hurdling debut, looking in need of experience. *L. Lungo*

JACKS BIRTHDAY (IRE) 5 b.g. Mukaddamah (USA) – High Concept (IRE) **h–** (Thatching) [2002/3 h76: 16d 19gᵖᵘ 17m Apr 5] poor form in 2 juvenile hurdles in 2001/2: showed little on return: tried blinkered. *D. J. Caro*

JACKS CRAIC (IRE) 4 b.g. Lord Americo – Boleree (IRE) (Mandalus) [2002/3 **F–** F16g Apr 2] €16,000 3-y-o: good-topped gelding: second foal: dam lightly-raced half-sister to fairly useful hurdler/fair chaser up to 3m Maneree: tenth of 19 in bumper at Ascot on debut. *C. Weedon*

JACKS JEWEL (IRE) 6 b.g. Welsh Term – September Daydream (IRE) (Phardante **F–** (FR)) [2002/3 F17f⁴ F17g Apr 19] 9,000 4-y-o: first foal: dam unraced half-sister to fair 2m hurdler Ask June: achieved little, pulling hard, in 2 bumpers. *M. Hill*

JACKSON (FR) 6 b.g. Passing Sale (FR) – Tynia (FR) (Djarvis (FR)) [2002/3 F–: **h68 ?** F17s 20s 17s⁵ Feb 7] sturdy gelding: signs of only a little ability in bumpers and over **F–** hurdles: tongue tied last 2 starts. *Mrs H. Dalton*

JACKSON'S BAY 5 b.m. Primitive Rising (USA) – Crammond Brig (New Brig) **h–** [2002/3 F17g* F16v⁵ F17v F16g 20dᵖᵘ 20g⁵ Mar 23] small mare: ninth foal: half-sister **F83** to useful 2m to 2½mile chaser Easthorpe (by Sweet Monday): dam fair staying hurdler: won bumper at Carlisle on debut in October: very disappointing subsequently, over hurdles last 2 starts: has looked less than keen: sold 2,000 gns Doncaster May Sales. *M. W. Easterby*

JACKSON'S HOLE 10 b.g. Brush Aside (USA) – Jack's The Girl (IRE) (Supreme **c–** Leader) [2002/3 c94, h94: c21d⁴ c25v⁶ c24vF c27v⁴ c20sᵖᵘ Feb 24] strong gelding: **h–** winning pointer: maiden hurdler/steeplechaser, well below best over fences in 2002/3: barely stays testing 3m: acts on heavy going. *M. W. Easterby*

JACKSONVILLE (FR) 6 b.g. Petit Montmorency (USA) – Quinine Des Aulnes **c87** (FR) (Air du Nord (USA)) [2002/3 h87, F–: c21d² Nov 17] sturdy gelding: modest **h–** maiden hurdler: second in novice handicap at Ayr on chasing debut, only start in 2002/3: should prove better at 3m than shorter: raced only on good going or softer (acts on heavy). *A. Parker*

JACK THE BEAR (IRE) 9 b. or br.g. Un Desperado (FR) – Vale of Peace (Wolver **c106** Hollow) [2002/3 c26s* c26v³ c32d³ Dec 6] tall gelding: fair chaser: missed 2001/2: won handicap at Newton Abbot on reappearance: thorough stayer: acts on heavy and good to firm going: consistent. *P. F. Nicholls*

JACK WEIGHELL 4 b.g. Accordion – Magic Bloom (Full of Hope) [2002/3 F16d **F–** Feb 25] good-topped gelding: first foal: dam fair chaser, stayed 25f: backward and in need of experience when well-held seventh of 19 in maiden bumper at Catterick on debut. *J. M. Jefferson*

JACK YEATS (IRE) 11 b.g. Don't Forget Me – Petty Session (Blakeney) [2002/3 **c–** § c86d, h–§: 26g Nov 7] leggy gelding: maiden hurdler: modest handicap chaser: no **h– §** form since winning at Perth in early-2001/2: blinkered once: has had tongue tied. *Ferdy Murphy*

JACOB'S WIFE   13 ro.m. Baron Blakeney – Vido (Vimadee) [2002/3 c24s⁴ May 18]   **c79**
leggy mare: fair chaser at best: winning pointer: well held when blundering last in hunter   **h–**
at Bangor in May: stays 25f: acts on firm and heavy going: blinkered once.
G. L. Edwards

JACOPO (FR)   6 b.g. Grand Tresor (FR) – Qolombine (FR) (Damsire Unregistered)   **h91**
[2002/3 h–, F–: 16d⁶ 16g⁶ 16s⁴ 19s² 20s² 21d⁴ 20m* 24m⁶ Apr 16] workmanlike gelding:
modest novice hurdler: simple task in weak maiden at Southwell in March: effective at
2m to 3m: acts on soft and good to firm going. R. Dickin

JAFFEG STORM (IRE)   7 b.g. Glacial Storm (USA) – She's A Monkey (Monksfield)   **h–**
[2002/3 h–: 20vᵖᵘ Nov 8] little show in 2 novice hurdles. Miss Lucinda V. Russell

JAGUAR   7 b.g. Barathea (IRE) – Oasis (Valiyar) [2002/3 c–, h99: 19d May 14] smal-   **c–**
lish, sturdy gelding: failed to complete in 2 chases: winning hurdler: on the downgrade: **h–**
tried blinkered: has looked ungenuine: sold 4,800 gns Doncaster May (2002) Sales,
subsequently well held on Flat for J. Best. N. A. Twiston-Davies

JAGUAR CLAW (IRE)   8 b.g. Sylvan Express – Sky Baloo (Skyliner) [2002/3 c16s²   **c110**
c16d* c20dᶠ c21s⁴ c20d⁵ c24v² c24sᶠ c24vᵖᵘ c20s⁴ c28sᵖᵘ c24d⁴ c20mᵖᵘ Apr 19]   **h–**
medium-sized gelding: second foal: dam, third in bumper, half-sister to useful hurdler
up to 2½m Lucky Baloo: bumper winner/winning hurdler: fair chaser: won maiden at
Ballinrobe in May: effective at 2m to 3m: acts on heavy going. Miss F. M. Crowley,
Ireland

JAGUAR (NZ)   10 b.g. St Hilarion (USA) – Saab (NZ) (Three Legs) [2002/3 h100:   **c–**
c23m⁵ c22mᵖᵘ 20m 22mᵖᵘ 20v⁶ Jan 15] no show both outings in novice chases, left   **h–**
P. Hobbs after first: one-time fair hurdler, no form in 2002/3: found little only run in
blinkers: sold 700 gns Doncaster March Sales. J. S. Wainwright

JAHASH   5 ch.g. Hernando (FR) – Jalsun (Jalmood (USA)) [2002/3 17s⁴ 19d² 17s²   **h118**
16d³ 24m* Apr 10] half-brother to winning hurdler in Italy by Muhtarram: modest on
Flat (stays 17f), sold out of Sir Mark Prescott's stable 15,000 gns Newmarket Autumn
Sales: fairly useful novice hurdler: won at Taunton (maiden) in November and Ludlow
in April: stays easy 3m, effective at much shorter: acts on soft and good to firm going.
P. J. Hobbs

JAIR DU COCHET (FR)   6 b.g. Rahotep (FR) – Dilaure (FR) (Rose Laurel)   **c150 p**
[2002/3 h163: c17d* c16m* c20g* c24s* c24sᵘʳ c24g² Mar 12]   **h–**
   Whatever you do, you can't please everyone. Jair du Cochet's regular
jockey Jacques Ricou will have found that out after riding the horse at two
successive Cheltenham Festivals. In 2002 Ricou incurred the wrath of his boss
Guillaume Macaire for making too much use of his mount in the Stayers' Hurdle,
while twelve months later he came in for criticism in the media for going to the
other extreme and giving the horse too much to do in the Royal & SunAlliance
Chase. After the Stayers' Hurdle, Macaire had been quoted as saying 'I'm not
happy with his riding, not at all . . . he was to take the first circuit quietly and
switched off, and not be in front . . . he rode badly and we will have to see if he rides
the horse again.' Ricou kept the ride but must have had those words—or the French
equivalent—ringing in his ears before the Royal & SunAlliance at the latest
Festival, though the critics—and Timeform must be counted among them—felt that
the waiting tactics were overdone this time. Dropped out in rear and travelling
strongly, Jair du Cochet jumped well in the main bar a mistake at the fence after the
stands at the start of the final circuit. Still some way off the pace when One Knight
was sent for home after four out, Jair du Cochet crept closer down the hill before
moving into second before the final fence. But instead of the front-running One
Knight coming back to him, Jair du Cochet found his rival had extra reserves once
he was asked for his own effort and he was unable to close the gap to less than a
length and three quarters at the line. This time, Guillaume Macaire had to defend
his jockey from brickbats rather than administer them himself. Whilst on this
occasion the criticism had some justification, Ricou had already come in for the
sort of treatment from the British media that seems to be reserved for overseas
jockeys, Adam Kondrat and Thierry Doumen being notable examples over jumps,
the Japanese Yutake Take on the Flat. Ricou's habit of 'calling a cab' at some of his
fences presumably offended some from a style point of view, though his thirty-six
per cent strike-rate in Britain (ten wins from twenty-eight rides here, plus eight
placings) speaks for itself, quite apart from his record in France.

Pertemps Aviation Resources Feltham Novices' Chase, Kempton—Jair du Cochet produces a flying leap

The partnership between Jacques Ricou and Jair du Cochet, described by Macaire in the latest season as 'a perfect wedding', had been forged in spectacular style over hurdles in the gelding's juvenile season when he looked an outstanding novice with wins in Britain at Chepstow and Cheltenham. His second season over hurdles did not bring quite the success his juvenile campaign had promised, but he showed high-class form when winning Haydock's Premier Hurdle. A fine jumper of the smaller obstacles, Jair du Cochet made an excellent transition to fences in the latest season, winning his first four outings. His route to Cheltenham had an unorthodox start with outings at Le Lion d'Angers in May and Folkestone in November. Guillaume Macaire had reasons for running him at these tracks though, at Le Lion d'Angers because 'three of the fences are like British obstacles', and at Folkestone 'because it was close to France'. Jair du Cochet jumped carefully on his chasing debut but was bolder at Folkestone where he landed the odds with any amount in hand. His first serious test came later in November in the Ballymore Properties Fulke Walwyn Novices' Chase at Newbury. Stepped up to two and a half miles, Jair du Cochet put in a good round of jumping on the whole (though tending to jump away to his left over the last three fences) to beat Scots Grey six lengths.

The performance promoted Jair du Cochet to ante-post favouritism for the Royal & SunAlliance Chase and his odds for the Cheltenham race shortened further after his next outing, in the Pertemps Aviation Resources Feltham Novices' Chase at Kempton. He did not start favourite at Kempton however, that honour going to Le Sauvignon who had even better hurdling form in France where he had won two editions of the Grande Course de Haies d'Auteuil. Back from injury and now with Paul Nicholls, Le Sauvignon had made a successful chasing debut in Britain nine days earlier, also at Folkestone. When Le Sauvignon slipped through on Jair du Cochet's inner rounding the home turn in the Feltham, it looked as though the market had got it right, but Jair du Cochet, who had jumped very fluently throughout, making much of the running, outjumped him three out to regain the lead and ran on to be well on top at the line. Le Sauvignon passed the post six lengths back in second but sadly collapsed and died shortly afterwards, while Bold Investor, also unbeaten over fences going into the race, finished well clear of the three other finishers in third. Jair du Cochet completed his preparation for Cheltenham in the Reynoldstown Novices' Chase at Ascot in February, though not in the way his connections would have wished. The four-runner race was billed as a match between Jair du Cochet (even money) and Keen Leader (11/10) who had emerged

428

as his main rival in the Royal & SunAlliance betting. Just as the race was starting to hot up, and with Jair du Cochet still travelling well, he left his hind legs in the ditch four out, giving his rider no chance of staying in the saddle and leaving Keen Leader to win by a distance.

Jair du Cochet (FR) (b.g. 1997)	Rahotep (FR) (b 1978)	Matahawk (br 1972)	Sea Hawk II / Carromata
		La Masure (b 1965)	Net / Miss Pink
	Dilaure (FR) (b 1984)	Rose Laurel (b 1970)	Klairon / Honeysuckle Rose
		Midice (ch 1974)	Dictus / Midas

Jair du Cochet's pedigree has been dealt with in the last two editions of *Chasers & Hurdlers*. The only update to it comes from the sales ring. His half-sister Gavotte du Cochet (a maiden on the Flat in France by the selle francais sire Urbain Minotiere) was sold in foal to Definite Article for 24,000 guineas at Doncaster in November, while her first foal, a colt by Classic Cliche, made 22,000 guineas at the same sale. Jair du Cochet is a good-topped gelding who was in outstanding shape at Kempton and looked very well again at Cheltenham. He stays three miles well and acts on heavy and good to firm going. He usually races prominently and his jumping is sound in the main. Jair du Cochet will need to improve to trouble the best staying chasers but he should make further progress, and, given his success at Kempton in the latest season, it would be no surprise to see him contesting the King George there in December. *G. Macaire, France*

JAKARI (FR) 6 b.g. Apeldoorn (FR) – Tartifume II (FR) (Mistigri) [2002/3 h100p: 17d³ c20s² c19d³ c19d* c20s* c25d^pu Apr 4] rather leggy gelding: successful on first of 2 starts over hurdles: fairly useful novice chaser: won at Hereford (maiden) in February and Stratford (improved effort to beat Lisaan 10 lengths) in March: will probably stay beyond 2½m: raced only on good to soft/soft going. *H. D. Daly* — **c121 h99**

JAKE THE JUMPER (IRE) 6 b.g. Jolly Jake (NZ) – Princess Tino (IRE) (Rontino) [2002/3 h86, F–: Oct 31] unfurnished gelding: modest form over hurdles, poor jumping costing him victory in weak novice at Warwick on reappearance: broke down next time: stays 21f: acts on firm and soft going. *Miss G. Browne* — **h86**

JALB (IRE) 9 b.g. Robellino (USA) – Adjacent (IRE) (Doulab (USA)) [2002/3 h88: 16g² 22f² Jun 3] compact gelding: modest handicap hurdler: effective at 2m to 2¾m: acted on soft and firm going: tried blinkered and tongue tied: dead. *P. G. Murphy* — **h94**

JALLASTEP (FR) 6 b.g. Boston Two Step (USA) – Balladine (FR) (Rivelago (FR)) [2002/3 h73: 20d 20g³ 22m² 22g* 21d 20d* Dec 10] lengthy, workmanlike gelding: fair handicap hurdler: won at Kelso in October and Ayr in December: will stay 3m: acts on good to firm and good to soft going. *J. S. Goldie* — **h100**

JALONS STAR (IRE) 5 b.g. Eagle Eyed (USA) – Regina St Cyr (IRE) (Doulab (USA)) [2002/3 h101: 20v 16v 21s⁶ 17g 16f⁵ Apr 25] workmanlike gelding: fair juvenile hurdler in 2001/2, mostly for G. McCourt: rejoined former trainer and little worthwhile form in 2002/3: raced mainly around 2m: acts on heavy going. *M. Quinn* — **h–**

JALOUX D'ESTRUVAL (FR) 6 b.g. Kadalko (FR) – Pommette III (FR) (Trac) [2002/3 c–, h72: c25d* c25s^F c24d³ c24g^F Feb 8] tall, unfurnished gelding: poor form on first of 2 starts over hurdles: fairly useful novice chaser: 100/1-winner at Hereford in December: stays 25f: raced on good going or softer: sometimes makes mistakes. *Mrs L. C. Taylor* — **c115 + h–**

JALPREUIL MALTA (FR) 6 gr.g. Saint Preuil (FR) – Alzira (FR) (Numbi (FR)) [2002/3 c21g³ c21v^pu c18s³ c20d² c20v* c25f² Mar 27] ex-French gelding: fourth foal: half-brother to winning hurdler/chaser around 2m Hiro Malta (by Lightning) and 2¼m hurdle winner Royal Malta (by Royal Charter): dam thrice-raced maiden: maiden hurdler: won cross-country chase at Pau in January, final start for P. H. Peltier: finished weakly when second of 4 to Chicuelo in novice chase at Exeter on British debut: may prove best short of 25f. *P. F. Nicholls* — **c103 + h–**

JAMAICAN FLIGHT (USA) 10 b.h. Sunshine Forever (USA) – Kalamona (USA) (Hawaii) [2002/3 h100: 19m⁴ 19g* 17g^pu 21d^pu 19s⁵ Dec 26] smallish horse: successful 3 times on Flat in 2003 before end of April: fair handicap hurdler: seventh course success — **h105**

when making all at Market Rasen in September: stays 21f: acts on any going: front runner: very tough. *Mrs S. Lamyman*

JAMES DEE (IRE) 7 b.g. Shalford (IRE) – Glendale Joy (IRE) (Glenstal (USA)) **h–**
[2002/3 16m 16s⁶ 16g 24gᵖᵘ 16m 16d⁴ 16g 16sᶠ Jan 3] poor on Flat (stays 1m) nowadays: showed little over hurdles: tried tongue tied. *Mrs P. Ford*

JAMES VICTOR (IRE) 5 b.g. Be My Guest (USA) – Antakiya (IRE) (Ela-Mana-Mou) [2002/3 F18v⁵ Jan 6] fourth foal: half-brother to middle-distance winners on Flat in France and Germany: dam, 1m winner in France, half-sister to useful staying hurdler Antapoura: took strong hold when distant fifth in maiden bumper on debut. *C. R. Egerton* **F–**

JAMIES FIRST (IRE) 10 ch.g. Commanche Run – Avionne (Derrylin) [2002/3 **c–**
c16dᵖᵘ Mar 4] winning pointer, retains no ability. *Mrs H. J. Cobb* **h–**

JAMORIN DANCER 8 b.g. Charmer – Geryea (USA) (Desert Wine (USA)) [2002/3 **c77 §**
c68, h72: c16m c16g³ c16d³ c16g³ c17m c17s⁶ 17g 16g³ c16m⁶ 17dᵖᵘ 16d 16g 17g⁴ 20g **h74 §**
c17g* Apr 26] sturdy gelding: poor hurdler/chaser: finally got off mark in weak handicap over fences at Market Rasen in April: raced mainly around 2m (beaten before stamina became issue over 2½m): acts on good to firm and good to soft going: wore blinkers/cheekpieces last 5 starts: irresolute. *R. C. Guest*

JANDAL 9 ch.g. Arazi (USA) – Littlefield (Bay Express) [2002/3 c–, h71: 17g May 4] **c–**
poor maiden hurdler. *Jane Southcombe* **h–**

JANE CORCORAN (IRE) 7 ch.m. Persian Mews – Back To Bahrain (Mandalus) **h–**
[2002/3 20d 16sᵖᵘ 21sᵖᵘ Nov 24] lengthy, plain ex-Irish mare: little sign of ability. *D. Burchell*

JANIDOU (FR) 7 b.g. Cadoudal (FR) – Majathen (FR) (Carmarthen (FR)) [2002/3 **h114 §**
h119: 17d 16s 16s³ 16v 16m Apr 22] good-topped gelding: fair handicap hurdler: bred to stay at least 2½m: acts on heavy going, possibly unsuited by good to firm: weak finisher. *A. L. T. Moore, Ireland*

JANITURE (FR) 6 gr.m. Turgeon (USA) – Majaway (FR) (Timmy's Way (FR)) **c124**
[2002/3 c–, h105: c17g³ c19s* c21dᶠ c21d³ c17m* c16f* Apr 21] rather leggy, lengthy **h–**
mare: has reportedly had breathing operation: fair hurdler: fairly useful chaser: won novice handicap at Taunton in November and 3-runner events at Plumpton (novice, easily) and Wincanton (handicap) within 3 days in April: stays 21f: probably acts on any going: has had tongue tied: has been let down by jumping. *P. F. Nicholls*

JAN'S DREAM (IRE) 9 ch.m. Executive Perk – Aunty Babs (Sexton Blake) [2002/3 **c94 x**
c92x, h–: c16sᵖᵘ c16s⁴ c16g² Mar 16] good-topped mare: winning hurdler: modest **h–**
maiden chaser: stays 2½m: acts on heavy going: has had tongue tied: sketchy jumper. *P. R. Webber*

JANSUE CHARLIE 9 ch.g. Ardar – Kincherinchee (Dunbeath (USA)) [2002/3 22s **h91**
22v² 20v 23dᵖᵘ 22dᵖᵘ Mar 1] lengthy gelding: fair handicap hurdler in 2000/1: easily best effort on return when second at Kelso in December: stays 2¾m: best form on going softer than good (acts on heavy): successful only start in blinkers, has also worn cheekpieces. *R. Nixon*

JANUARY SIXTEENTH 7 b.g. Presidium – Espanita (Riboboy (USA)) [2002/3 **h–**
h–: 17m May 3] of no account. *D. C. O'Brien*

JAPHET (FR) 6 b.g. Perrault – Una Volta (FR) (Toujours Pret (USA)) [2002/3 c141, **c128**
h–: 19vᵘʳ 17g² 18v* c21v⁶ Mar 2] tall, close-coupled gelding: won over 1½m on Flat in **h?**
October and November: fairly useful hurdler: won minor event at Bordeaux in February: useful novice chaser in 2001/2: disappointing in 3 starts at Auteuil in 2003, found nothing when second in amateur riders event in May: stays 3m: acts on heavy going, possibly not on good to firm: often a front runner: usually a fluent jumper. *G. Macaire, France*

JARDIN DE BEAULIEU (FR) 6 ch.g. Rough Magic (FR) – Emblem (FR) (Siberian **c103**
Express (USA)) [2002/3 c103+, h–p: c20dᵖᵘ c20s² c20v⁴ c19d⁵ Feb 23] well-made **h–**
gelding: fair maiden chaser: easily best effort in 2002/3 when head second to Skippers Cleuch in novice at Wetherby in December: stays 2½m: raced on good going or softer (acts on soft): often shapes as if amiss. *Ian Williams*

JARRO (FR) 7 b.g. Pistolet Bleu (IRE) – Junta (FR) (Cariellor (FR)) [2002/3 c107, **c121**
h–: c16gᶠ c16d² c16d⁴ c16v* c16vᵖᵘ c16v² c16g⁵ Mar 25] workmanlike gelding: fairly **h–**
useful handicap chaser: won at Uttoxeter in December: best around 2m: acts on good to firm and heavy going: free-going sort: jumps less than fluently. *Miss Venetia Williams*

JASEUR (USA)   10 b.g. Lear Fan (USA) – Spur Wing (USA) (Storm Bird (CAN))   c–
[2002/3 h105§: 24g⁴ 24d⁶ c21m 20d⁵ 20d³ 20s* 20v⁶ 19d⁵ 20s* 24m³ Apr 16] angular   **h110 §**
gelding: mistakes only start over fences: fair hurdler: won novice handicaps at Wetherby
in December and Bangor in February: stays 3m: acts on firm and soft going: wears headgear: not one to trust. *G. Barnett*

JASMIN D'OUDAIRIES (FR)   6 b.g. Apeldoorn (FR) – Vellea (FR) (Cap Martin   **c118 p**
(FR)) [2002/3 h110, F95: c17s⁶ c16s c20s⁵ c17d* Mar 22] fair hurdler: fairly useful form   **h–**
over fences, won novice at Navan in March by 1½ lengths from Goldstreet: should stay
2½m: acts on soft going: probably open to improvement. *W. P. Mullins, Ireland*

JASMIN GUICHOIS (FR)   6 ch.g. Dom Alco (FR) – Lady Belle (FR) (Or de Chine)   **c107**
[2002/3 c–, h–: 16d 20s* 20v c25d³ c24s³ c20sᶠ Mar 1] compact gelding: modest hurdler: **h96**
easily won conditional jockeys novice at Folkestone in December: narrow leader when
falling last in handicap chase at Newbury final outing: stays 2½m, not 3m: acts on heavy
going. *Miss Venetia Williams*

JASPER LAD   7 ch.g. Fearless Action (USA) – Last Shower (Town And Country)   **h–**
[2002/3 F–: 16dᵖᵘ Apr 29] no show in 2 bumpers and novice hurdle. *J. Gallagher*

JATO DANCER (IRE)   8 b.m. Mukaddamah (USA) – Que Tranquila (Dominion)   **h–**
[2002/3 h73: 19mᵖᵘ 16dᵖᵘ Jul 5] poor maiden hurdler. *R. Hollinshead*

JAVELOT D'OR (FR)   6 b. or br.g. Useful (FR) – Flika d'Or (FR) (Pot d'Or (FR))   **c–**
[2002/3 c19gᵖᵘ Apr 2] smallish, lengthy ex-French gelding: half-brother to fairly useful   **h–**
chaser Geant d'Or (by Le Nain Jaune), stayed 25f, and winning 2m hurdler Flic Royal
(by Royal Charter): dam maiden: successful 4 times from 6 starts over jumps in French
Provinces at 4 yrs for G. Macaire: off nearly 2 years, lost all chance with bad mistake
ninth in handicap chase at Ascot on British debut: raced mainly around 2m on good going
or softer (acts on heavy). *Miss Venetia Williams*

JAWLEYFORD COURT   4 b.f. Moshaajir (USA) – Mrs Jawleyford (USA) (Dixie-   **h–**
land Band (USA)) [2002/3 16dᵘʳ 17gᵖᵘ Mar 15] second foal: dam won over hurdles: little
form on Flat: failed to complete in juvenile hurdles at Warwick (unseated first) and
Market Rasen. *C. Smith*

JAWWALA (USA)   4 b.f. Green Dancer (USA) – Fetch N Carry (USA) (Alleged   **h88 §**
(USA)) [2002/3 16g 17s³ 16v² 16vᵖᵘ 17d⁶ 17s³ Mar 6] leggy filly: fair on Flat (stays
1¾m), sold out of J. W. Payne's stable 15,000 gns Newmarket Autumn Sales: modest
juvenile hurdler: will stay 2½m: acts on heavy going: reluctant to race 2 of last 3 outings:
one to treat with plenty of caution. *J. R. Jenkins*

JAYAS (FR)   6 b. or br.g. Rasi Brasak – Rigolette (FR) (Lychee (FR)) [2002/3 h–:   **c–**
c21gᵖᵘ c16mᵖᵘ 21m⁴ Aug 26] leggy gelding: fairly useful hurdler in France: very   **h–**
disappointing since British debut, including over fences: should stay beyond 2m: acts on
soft going: often visored: has had tongue tied. *M. C. Pipe*

JAYBEEDEE   7 b.g. Rudimentary (USA) – Meavy (Kalaglow) [2002/3 h109, F90:   **h–**
16v⁴ Nov 6] ex-Irish gelding: fair hurdler: tailed-off last of 4 finishers in handicap at
Kempton, only outing in 2002/3: best form at 2m: acts on heavy going. *K. C. Bailey*

JAY BEE ELL   6 b.g. Pursuit of Love – On Request (IRE) (Be My Guest (USA))   **h89 +**
[2002/3 F91: 16d⁵ 22g⁸ 22m⁴ Jun 1] sturdy gelding: modest form in novice hurdles, won
at Stratford in May: stays easy 2¾m. *A. King*

JAYBEJAY (NZ)   8 b.g. High Ice (USA) – Galaxy Light (NZ) (Balios) [2002/3 h117:   **c119**
20d c16g³ c21d* c20d⁵ c20mᵖᵘ c21dᶠ³ c19g³ c20g Apr 3] smallish gelding: fairly useful   **h–**
hurdler: similar standard in novice chases, won at Wincanton in January: not fluent after,
fell last when about 20 lengths clear at same course, remounted to finish distant third:
stays 21f: raced mainly on good going or softer. *M. C. Pipe*

JAYED (IRE)   5 b. or br.g. Marju (IRE) – Taqreem (IRE) (Nashwan (USA)) [2002/3   **h76 +**
17m³ 17s⁵ 16g⁴ 16g Apr 12] well held in 3 starts on Flat: best effort over hurdles (possibly
flattered) when 6 lengths fourth of 17 to Unleash in maiden at Ludlow: likely to prove
best at sharp 2m: headstrong. *M. Bradstock*

JAZZ BAND   5 b.g. Alhijaz – Little Preston (IRE) (Pennine Walk) [2002/3 F17g Oct   **F–**
6] workmanlike gelding: fifth foal: dam poor maiden, stayed 1¼m: showed nothing in
bumper on debut: sold 1,200 gns Doncaster November Sales. *Mrs L. C. Jewell*

JAZZ DU FOREZ (FR)   6 b.g. Video Rock (FR) – Ophyr du Forez (FR) (Fin Bon)   **c73**
[2002/3 h–, F–: 20gᵖᵘ 19g³ 22dᵇᵈ 21s² 25v³ 24s⁶ 25d⁶ c24m³ Mar 18] smallish gelding: **h60**
poor maiden hurdler: third of 4 in novice at Southwell on chasing debut: stays 25f: acts
on heavy and good to firm going: tried blinkered/in cheekpieces. *John Allen*

JAZZ DUKE　10 ch.g. Rising – Gone (Whistling Wind) [2002/3 c86§, h–§: c26d² c24d³ c25d Jan 27] leggy gelding: winning hurdler: poor maiden chaser: stays 27f: raced on good going or softer (acts on heavy): visored once: sometimes none too fluent: moody. *M. J. Weeden*　**c81 §**　**h– §**

JAZZ NIGHT　6 b.g. Alhijaz – Hen Night (Mummy's Game) [2002/3 h–: 16g² 16g 16d Nov 16] no form on Flat: 9 lengths second to Persian King in maiden at Worcester, easily best effort over hurdles. *N. A. Twiston-Davies*　**h91**

J DEE　10 ch.g. Rakaposhi King – Just Pam (Pamroy) [2002/3 c74, h–: c24mᵖᵘ c26mᵖᵘ c24g³ Oct 9] poor chaser, left J. McConnochie after reappearance: stays 3m. *John Allen*　**c65**　**h–**

JEAN D'AUTEUIL (FR)　7 b.g. River Sand (FR) – Santa Marta (FR) (Cadmus II) [2002/3 c115, h–: c22sᵖᵘ c19dᵖᵘ Jan 27] big, lengthy, good-topped gelding: fair hurdler: novice chaser at best: ran poorly both starts after 10-month absence (tongue tied in second): should stay beyond 19f: raced on good going or softer. *M. C. Pipe*　**c–**　**h–**

JEAN GUY (FR)　6 b.g. Passing Sale (FR) – Umea IV (FR) (Maiymad) [2002/3 c114d, h–: c24vᶠ c25d c23d c18vᵖᵘ Mar 2] sparely-made gelding: pulled up both runs over hurdles: disappointing over fences since winning 4-y-o event at Auteuil in early-2001/2, left P. Hobbs after second start: stays 2½m: acts on soft going: tried blinkered: sometimes makes mistakes. *G. Pannier, France*　**c– x**　**h–**

JEANNOT DE BEAUCHENE (FR)　6 b.g. En Calcat (FR) – Chipie d'Angron (FR) (Grand Tresor (FR)) [2002/3 h113: 21m² 20s² 20s 20d³ 22dᵖᵘ Dec 26] tall, rangy gelding: fairly useful hurdler: improved in 2002/3, placed in handicaps at Cheltenham and Haydock (2): struck into final outing: should have stayed 3m: acted on good to firm and heavy going: dead. *R. H. Alner*　**h127**

JEFERTITI (FR)　6 ch.g. Le Nain Jaune (FR) – Nefertiti (FR) (Tourangeau (FR)) [2002/3 c18v³ 16d⁵ c16v² 17m⁶ Apr 16] rangy, good sort: sixth foal: brother to 21f cross-country chase winner Canope and half-brother to winner on Flat by Mistigri: dam maiden half-sister to Sun Alliance Chase winner Rolling Ball: twice-raced on Flat at 4 yrs in France: third of 6 finishers in 5-y-o event at Auteuil on chasing debut for M. de Montfort: modest form over hurdles and fences in Britain, not knocked about: likely to be suited by 2½m: acts on heavy going: takes strong hold. *Miss H. C. Knight*　**c106**　**h94**

JEFF DE CHALAMONT (FR)　6 b.g. Abary (GER) – Clio de Chalamont (FR) (Milford) [2002/3 F16g⁴ 16v⁶ 20s³ 18s* 20s⁴ 22s⁴ 24s 20s* Mar 16] second foal: half-brother to winning chaser up to 2½m Ips de Chalamont (by Royal Charter): dam unraced: modest form only start in bumpers: fair hurdler: won maiden at Navan in December and minor event at Punchestown (tongue tied) in March, much improved when beating Ground Ball 2½ lengths at latter course: should stay beyond 2½m: acts on soft ground. *Mrs J. Harrington, Ireland*　**h112**　**F84**

JELALI (IRE)　10 b.g. Last Tycoon – Lautreamont (Auction Ring (USA)) [2002/3 c24sᵖᵘ May 18] workmanlike gelding: winning hurdler: poor form only completed start in steeplechases: should stay beyond 2½m: acts on good to soft going: tried blinkered/ tongue tied. *C. Moore*　**c–**　**h–**

JEMARO (IRE)　12 b.g. Tidaro (USA) – Jeremique (Sunny Way) [2002/3 c25d³ c25s³ c24m* c21gᵖᵘ Apr 19] smallish, good-topped gelding: fairly useful hunter chaser nowadays: won at Ludlow (fourth course success) in April by 12 lengths from below-par Bright Approach: best up to 25f: acts on good to firm and heavy going: usually jumps boldly (though makes the odd mistake) up with pace. *Mrs C. J. Robinson*　**c102**　**h–**

JENGA　6 ro.m. Minster Son – Maybe Daisy (Nicholas Bill) [2002/3 21d* 19v* Mar 4] first foal: dam unraced, out of half-sister to useful hurdler/chaser up to 3¼m Baron Blakeney: runner-up on completed start in maiden points in 2002, bought 15,000 gns (privately) Doncaster May Sales: successful both outings over hurdles, in 18-runner mares maiden at Ludlow in January and 4-finisher mares novice at Exeter (made all to beat Easibrook Jane 4 lengths) in March: will stay 3m: acts on heavy going. *K. C. Bailey*　**h99**

JENKO (FR)　6 b.g. Cadoubel (FR) – Maika d'Ores (FR) (Gaur) [2002/3 h79: c21m⁵ Oct 1] tall, unfurnished gelding: poor maiden hurdler: mistakes when last of 5 finishers in novice at Sedgefield on chasing debut: raced mainly around 2m: acts on soft ground: has had tongue tied. *M. Todhunter*　**c76**　**h–**

JENNIFERJO (IRE)　6 b. or br.m. Witness Box (USA) – Sweet Tune (Welsh Chanter) [2002/3 h122, F93: c20vᶠ c16s⁶ c22s* c24vᶠ c24v⁵ c18s³ c21v* c24d* Mar 17] has scope: fairly useful hurdler: useful chaser: won maiden at Downpatrick in December and listed handicap at Leopardstown and listed novice at Limerick (stayed on well to beat　**c131**　**h–**

I'vehadit a length) in March: will stay beyond 3m: best on going softer than good (acts on heavy). *P. A. Fahy, Ireland*

JENNY ROCKET   7 b.m. Minster Son – Jane's Affair (Alleging (USA)) [2002/3 h79:
16m³ 19m 16v² 16s* 20m³ 16g⁴ 24m³ 26mᵖᵘ Sep 11] leggy mare: poor handicap hurdler:
landed odds in weak conditional jockeys mares event at Uttoxeter in June: pulled up
amiss final outing: effective at 2m, seems to stay easy 3m: acts on heavy and good to firm
going: tried visored. *Miss K. Marks*   **h79**

JENSKI   8 b.g. Petoski – Mrs Jennifer (River Knight (FR)) [2002/3 h82: 21v* 22s⁶ 17s³
Mar 7] lightly-raced gelding: easily best effort over hurdles when making all in seller at
Plumpton in January: weakened quickly both subsequent starts: should stay beyond 21f:
acts on heavy going. *R. J. Hodges*   **h98**

JEREMY SPIDER   10 b.g. Nearly A Hand – Lucibella (Comedy Star (USA)) [2002/3
c111, h–: c29s³ c23g* c21d Apr 4] deep-girthed gelding: fair handicap chaser: at least as
good as ever when making all in 6-runner event at Leicester in February: couple of
mistakes when pulled up in Clan Royal in Topham Chase at Aintree: probably best short of
29f: acts on heavy going. *C. Tizzard*   **c113**
h–

JERICHO III (FR)   6 b.g. Lute Antique (FR) – La Salamandre (FR) (Pot d'Or (FR))
[2002/3 h100, F91: c19sᶠ c16v* c16dᶠ c16g⁴ Feb 25] leggy gelding: fair hurdler: odds
on, easily won at Leicester in January, second start in novice chases: may prove best
up to 2½m: acts on heavy going, bumper winner on good to firm: has worn crossed
noseband: exuberant when jumps boldly, though inclined to make odd mistake: joined
M. Todhunter. *N. J. Henderson*   **c107**
h–

JERICO VALLIS (FR)   6 b.g. Murmure (FR) – Bora Vallis (FR) (Le Pontet (FR))
[2002/3 c20d* c23s² c22v* c22s² c22s* Apr 13] third foal: half-brother to useful chaser/
fair hurdler Ipso Vallis (by Port Etienne), stays 2½m: dam unraced: raced exclusively at
Auteuil: twice-raced over hurdles, won only completed start: smart chaser: won
non-thoroughbred event in September and Group 2 events in December (Prix Georges
Courtois) and April (Prix Murat, beat Idole des Fontaines 2 lengths): good neck second to
Rougenoir in Group 3 in March: ran as if amiss when pulled up in Grand Steeple-Chase
de Paris in May: should stay beyond 23f: raced on good going or softer (acts on heavy):
races prominently. *J. Bertran de Balanda, France*   **c149**
h–

JERPAHNI   4 b.f. Distant Relative – Oublier L'Ennui (FR) (Bellman (FR)) [2002/3
17s 17dᵖᵘ 16f 16dᵖᵘ 17s⁶ 16vᵖᵘ Dec 20] poor maiden on Flat (stays 1m): showed more
temperament than ability in juvenile hurdles, left T. Wall after second start: tried blink-
ered/visored/in cheekpieces. *P. D. Evans*   **h– §**

JERROBOAM (FR)   6 b.g. Luchiroverte (IRE) – Banouda (FR) (Crin Noir II (FR))
[2002/3 F–: 22m 21sᵖᵘ Dec 7] no sign of ability. *S. E. H. Sherwood*   **h–**

JERUFLO (IRE)   8 b.m. Glacial Storm (USA) – Martiness (Martinmas) [2002/3 h88:
c21dᵖᵘ c20g⁵ c21s³ Mar 15] leggy mare: has reportedly had breathing problem: modest
hurdler: best effort over fences after 18-month absence when fifth of 6 finishers to Deep
Sunset in mares novice at Ludlow: should stay beyond 2½m: acts on soft and good to firm
going: tongue tied. *P. R. Webber*   **c80**
h–

JE SUIS (IRE)   7 b.m. Le Bavard (FR) – La Tortue (Lafontaine (USA)) [2002/3 F–:
17f Nov 7] angular mare: well held in 3 bumpers and mares novice hurdle. *B. J. Eckley*   **h–**

JET FILES (IRE)   12 ro.g. Roselier (FR) – Deepdecending (Deep Run) [2002/3 c96,
h–: c25f² May 15] lengthy, useful-looking gelding: winning hurdler: modest chaser,
lightly raced: would have been closer but for interference only outing in 2002/3: stays
25f: acts on firm and soft going. *M. Pitman*   **c99**
h–

JETOWA DU BOIS HUE (FR)   6 b.g. Kadrou (FR) – Vaika (FR) (Cosmopolitan
(FR)) [2002/3 h92: c16d³ c17v⁴ c16g* c16g⁴ Apr 21] modest maiden hurdler: similar
form over fences, won novice handicap at Hereford in March by 2 lengths from Macgyver: raced around 2m on good ground or softer. *T. R. George*   **c96**
h–

JEWEL FIGHTER   9 br.m. Good Times (ITY) – Duellist (Town Crier) [2002/3 h56:
21gᵖᵘ 16m⁵ Jun 3] bad maiden hurdler: best efforts around 2m. *J. L. Spearing*   **h52**

JEWEL OF INDIA   4 ch.g. Bijou d'Inde – Low Hill (Rousillon (USA)) [2002/3 17s⁴
Nov 29] fairly useful on Flat (stays 1¼m, usually blinkered), sold out of Sir Mark
Prescott's stable 17,000 gns Newmarket Autumn Sales: joint favourite, not fluent when
fourth of 6 in juvenile at Bangor on hurdling debut: will need sharp 2m. *P. J. Hobbs*   **h83**

JEXEL (FR)   6 b.g. Video Rock (FR) – Siesta (FR) (Prove It Baby (USA)) [2002/3
F94: 18g* 24d* 20d³ Nov 17] fair form over hurdles: won novices at Kelso in May and   **h102**

Perth (by neck from Knockholt) in June: likely to prove better at 3m than shorter: raced on good going or softer. *J. S. Goldie*

JIM BELL (IRE) 8 br.g. Supreme Leader – Mightyatom (Black Minstrel) [2002/3 **h103** h75, F75: 20v³ 21s³ 25d* 25d² 24v* Mar 13] strong, useful-looking gelding: fair hurdler: much improved, won handicaps at Catterick in February and Hexham in March: stays 25f: acts on heavy going (bumper form on good to firm): jumps none too fluently. *J. G. M. O'Shea*

JIM (FR) 6 b.g. Glaieul (USA) – Beautywal (FR) (Magwal (FR)) [2002/3 16s 16v⁴ 16s **h117** 16v* Mar 1] lengthy, well-made gelding: type to make a chaser: fourth foal: half-brother to fairly useful French hurdler Isle (by Cadoudal) and smart Gazelle Royale (by Garde Royale), stays 12.5f: dam, French 1¼m winner, half-sister to winning French jumper Chanson du Chenet: twice-raced in bumpers: best effort over hurdles when making all in 17-runner maiden at Fairyhouse, beating Leinster by 5 lengths: 18 lengths sixth to Nobody Told Me in 2½m Grade 1 novice at Punchestown in early-May: should stay beyond 2m: acts on heavy going. *J. T. R. Dreaper, Ireland*

JIM JAM JOEY (IRE) 10 ch.g. Big Sink Hope (USA) – Ascot Princess (Prince **c–** Hansel) [2002/3 c–, h110: 24d² 24s 25s 22d Feb 17] angular gelding: let down by jumping **h106** both outings over fences: fair handicap hurdler: form in 2002/3 only when second in weak race at Leicester: best at 3m+: acts on heavy going: blinkered (ran poorly) once: takes plenty of driving. *Miss Suzy Smith*

JIMMY BLUES 8 b.g. Durgam (USA) – Tibbi Blues (Cure The Blues (USA)) **c–** [2002/3 h72: 20gᵖᵘ c16m c20d⁶ c26d⁴ c20f⁵ Sep 15] useful-looking gelding: poor novice **h–** hurdler/chaser. *Ferdy Murphy*

JIMMY JUMBO (IRE) 10 ch.g. Dragon Palace (USA) – Sail On Lady (New **c–** Member) [2002/3 c–, h–: c24sᵖᵘ c26d Jun 8] workmanlike gelding: winning pointer: no **h–** form in steeplechases. *J. S. Swindells*

JIMMY MORSE 5 b.g. Chaddleworth (IRE) – Sea Crossing (FR) (Kala Shikari) **F–** [2002/3 F17d May 14] third known foal: dam won 1m seller: well held in bumper: poor form on Flat: dead. *J. White*

JIMMY'S CROSS (IRE) 13 ch.g. Phardante (FR) – Foredefine (Bonne Noel) **c–** [2002/3 c89, h–: c20f May 11] sturdy, lengthy gelding: fair hunter chaser, well held at **h–** Warwick in May: stays 25f: acts on firm and good to soft going: tried visored: held up. *Mrs Sue Maude*

JIMMY TENNIS (FR) 6 b. or br.g. Video Rock (FR) – Via Tennise (FR) (Brezzo **c– x** (FR)) [2002/3 c122, h–: c24dᵘʳ c26s⁵ Dec 7] leggy, lengthy ex-French gelding: fairly **h–** useful chaser, tailed off completing outing in 2002/3: effective around 2m to 3m: raced on good going or softer (acts on heavy): tried blinkered: early to post on reappearance: often let down by jumping. *Miss Venetia Williams*

JIMMY WISKERS (IRE) 8 b.g. Insan (USA) – Jackson Miss (Condorcet (FR)) **h–** [2002/3 h79: 20d 19s 21s⁴ Dec 10] leggy gelding: poor novice hurdler, well held in 2002/3: stays 23f: acts on any going: blinkered final outing. *Ferdy Murphy*

JINEFUL (FR) 6 b.g. Useful (FR) – Finegrila (FR) (Fin Bon) [2002/3 c–, h–: 20g⁶ **c67** 20gᵖᵘ c26m⁴ c22dᶠ Oct 19] tall gelding: running best race in Britain (no form over **h–** hurdles) when falling 3 out in novice handicap chase at Market Rasen. *N. J. Henderson*

JIVAROS (FR) 6 br.g. Video Rock (FR) – Rives (FR) (Reasonable Choice (USA)) **c104 p** [2002/3 h101+, F73: c25d⁶ c24dᵖᵘ c24g* Mar 2] leggy gelding: won second of 2 starts **h–** over hurdles: clearly best effort in novice chases when winning handicap at Huntingdon by 5 lengths from Fluff 'n' Puff: will prove best at 3m+: raced only on good/good to soft ground: should improve further. *H. D. Daly*

J J BABOO (IRE) 10 b.g. Be My Guest (USA) – Maricica (Ahonoora) [2002/3 c19g **c79 §** c25g c24g³ c25d* c24dᵖᵘ c31gᵖᵘ Apr 24] leggy, workmanlike gelding: poor handicap **h– §** chaser, off 2 years prior to reappearance: won at Wetherby in March: stays 25f: acts on any going: tried visored/blinkered/in cheekpieces: untrustworthy. *Jedd O'Keeffe*

JOB RAGE (IRE) 9 b. or br.g. Yashgan – Snatchingly (Thatch (USA)) [2002/3 h72: **c–** 20d* 22g 19m⁵ 22m³ 20mᵘʳ 17d⁴ 20f² 17g³ 19m c20d c20s c20mᵇᵈ Mar 23] angular **h87** gelding: modest handicap hurdler: won seller at Uttoxeter in May: not fluent and well held both completed starts over fences: barely stays 2¾m: acts on soft and firm going: tried visored/blinkered/tongue tied. *A. Bailey*

JOCKIE WELLS 5 b.g. Primitive Rising (USA) – Princess Maxine (IRE) (Horage) [2002/3 F16v⁶ F16d 16g Apr 25] first foal: dam fair up to 1m on Flat: well beaten in bumpers and maiden hurdle (proved intractable). *Miss Lucinda V. Russell* — **h–** **F—**

JOCKO GLASSES 6 ch.g. Inchinor – Corinthia (USA) (Empery (USA)) [2002/3 h113d: 16d³ 16mᵖᵘ Oct 16] strong, lengthy gelding: disappointing hurdler: pulled up lame final outing: likely to prove best at sharp 2m: acts on good to soft going: tried blinkered. *Mrs M. Reveley* — **h97**

JOCKS CROSS (IRE) 12 ch.g. Riberetto – Shuil Le Dia (Kabale) [2002/3 c142, h–: c27dᵖᵘ c28d⁵ c32gᵖᵘ Mar 21] lengthy gelding: useful handicap chaser: 66/1 on second outing in a year, led until 3 out when fifth of 17 to Shotgun Willy in valuable event at Haydock in March: stays 29f: probably best on good going or softer: prone to the odd bad mistake: genuine. *Miss Venetia Williams* — **c130 x** **h–**

JODANTE (IRE) 6 ch.g. Phardante (FR) – Crashtown Lucy (Crash Course) [2002/3 F74: F16d⁵ 16mᵖᵘ Dec 28] strong, lengthy gelding: better effort in bumpers when fifth in maiden at Uttoxeter on reappearance: 33/1, promising fourth of 7 to Temple Dog in novice at Haydock on hurdling debut, travelling well long way and not knocked about: likely to improve. *P. Beaumont* — **h83 p** **F83**

JOE BLAKE (IRE) 8 b.g. Jurado (USA) – I've No Idea (Nishapour (FR)) [2002/3 c124: c24s³ c24m* Apr 9] big, workmanlike gelding: useful hunter chaser: ran as if needing race on reappearance: won at Gowran 2 months later by 10 lengths from The Wipper: stays 3¼m: acts on good to firm and heavy going. *I. R. Ferguson, Ireland* — **c124**

JOE CRUMP 9 ch.g. Interrex (CAN) – Nellie O'Dowd (USA) (Diesis) [2002/3 h114: c20d⁵ c24g⁴ c19dᵘʳ Jan 25] big gelding: fair handicap hurdler: better effort on completed outings in novice chases when fifth to Supreme Catch at Huntingdon: should stay 3m: acts on heavy going: visored and tongue tied. *J. Mackie* — **c95** **h–**

JOE CULLEN (IRE) 8 ch.g. River Falls – Moycullen (Le Moss) [2002/3 h119+: 17d³ 16g 17g Mar 13] lengthy gelding: won 2000 Champion Bumper at Cheltenham: fairly useful hurdler: good third to Patsy Veale in valuable handicap at Killarney in May, final outing for W. Mullins: off 9 months, well held in similar events last 2 starts: will stay beyond 17f: acts on good to firm and heavy going. *Ian Williams* — **h123**

JOE DEANE (IRE) 7 ch.g. Alphabatim (USA) – Craic Go Leor (Deep Run) [2002/3 24v⁶ c16s³ 26d² c26sᵖᵘ Mar 15] sturdy, lengthy gelding: third foal: dam, placed in point, sister to useful staying chaser Plenty Crack: placed in 2 maiden Irish points in 2002: modest form when placed in maiden chase and novice hurdle: effective at 2m to 3¼m. *T. R. George* — **c93** **h89**

JOE DI CAPO (IRE) 8 b.g. Phardante (FR) – Supreme Glen (IRE) (Supreme Leader) [2002/3 h85: c23m⁴ c20d² c24d² c25sᶠ c24v² c24gᶠ c22d² c24d⁴ c24g⁴ Mar 28] lengthy, angular gelding: modest hurdler/novice chaser: will stay beyond 3m: acts on soft going: wears headgear: poor jumper of fences: inconsistent. *A. Crook* — **c95 x** **h–**

JOE LUKE (IRE) 11 b.g. Satco (FR) – Garden County (Ragapan) [2002/3 c105x, h119: 22s 24d 27s⁶ 27vᵖᵘ 23dᵘʳ Feb 1] big, angular gelding: winning chaser, usually let down by jumping: one-time fairly useful handicap hurdler, well below form in 2002/3 (looked none too keen final outing): stays 3m: acts on heavy going: has had tongue tied. *G. M. Moore* — **c– x** **h94**

JOELY GREEN 6 b.g. Binary Star (USA) – Comedy Lady (Comedy Star (USA)) [2002/3 h88: 16g* 17mᵖᵘ Sep 13] good-topped gelding: fair but rather moody on Flat (stays 2m), successful in February: modest form first 2 starts over hurdles, won maiden at Huntingdon in August: ran poorly in novice following month. *N. P. Littmoden* — **h88**

JOEY DUNLOP (IRE) 9 br.g. Maelstrom Lake – Middle Verde (USA) (Sham (USA)) [2002/3 c24m⁴ c20m⁴ c27m⁶ 20s 22dᵖᵘ Aug 26] successful in 3 Irish points, including twice in 2002: little form otherwise. *J. J. Lambe, Ireland* — **c–** **h–**

JOEY THE SCHNOZE 5 ch.g. Zilzal (USA) – Linda's Design (Persian Bold) [2002/3 h79: 17d⁴ 16v 16d Dec 4] leggy, close-coupled gelding: poor maiden hurdler: best at sharp 2m: raced on good going or softer: visored in 2002/3, also tongue tied final start: pulls hard. *S. J. Magnier* — **h82**

JOEY TRIBBIANI (IRE) 6 b.g. Foxhound (USA) – Mardi Gras Belle (USA) (Masked Dancer (USA)) [2002/3 16d 16m⁶ 17m³ c17sᶠ³ 16g⁵ c16d⁶ c16d² c16d* c16g² c16s³ c16m* c16m² Apr 21] leggy gelding: poor novice hurdler: fair chaser: won handicaps at Hereford in February and Huntingdon in March: will prove best at 2m: acts on soft and good to firm going: used to race freely. *Ian Williams* — **c105** **h74**

JOHANN DE VONNAS (FR) 6 b.g. Cadoudal (FR) – Diana de Vonnas (FR) (El **F86**
Badr) [2002/3 F–: F18m³ May 7] leggy gelding: better effort in bumpers when third in
slowly-run race at Fontwell. *N. J. Henderson*

JOHN BUSH (IRE) 9 b.g. Asir – Philosophical (Welsh Chanter) [2002/3 21m⁴ Jul **h–**
25] leggy gelding: winning hurdler in 1998/9 (pulled up lame final outing): poor form
only subsequent start (tended to hang right): stays 2½m: acts on good to firm and good to
soft going. *Ferdy Murphy*

JOHN FOLEY (IRE) 5 b.g. Petardia – Fast Bay (Bay Express) [2002/3 h82+: 16m⁶ **h–**
May 8] temperamental maiden on Flat: novice hurdler, no form on balance of form: will stay
beyond 2m: twice runner-up in points in March. *Mrs H. Dalton*

JOHN HUNTER (IRE) 6 b.g. Unfuwain (USA) – Aigue (High Top) [2002/3 h96p: **h99**
16m 17v 16d⁶ 17d⁴ 18s 17s⁴ 19f⁵ Mar 24] modest handicap hurdler: reportedly lame final
outing: raced mainly around 2m: acts on good to firm going, probably not ideally suited
by soft/heavy: tongue tied. *M. C. Pipe*

JOHNLEGOOD 7 ch.g. Karinga Bay – Dancing Years (USA) (Fred Astaire (USA)) **c92**
[2002/3 h103: 17m² c16g⁴ c24dᶠ c20sᵖᵘ c20v⁵ c19d² c18s⁵ c20m² c21m Apr 17] **h102**
workmanlike gelding: fair hurdler: modest novice chaser: stays 2½m: acts on heavy and
good to firm going: sometimes let down by jumping over fences. *G. L. Moore*

JOHNNY BRUSHASIDE (IRE) 10 b.g. Brush Aside (USA) – Flash Parade (Boreen **c112**
(FR)) [2002/3 c112, h–: c17s² Jun 9] well-made gelding: winning hurdler: fair handicap **h–**
chaser: effective around 2m to 3m: acts on good to firm and heavy going: tried blinkered/
tongue tied: none too consistent: sold 11,000 gns Doncaster October Sales, fifth in point
in January for D. Pipe. *N. Meade, Ireland*

JOHNNY GRAND 6 b.g. Kasakov – Richesse (FR) (Faraway Son (USA)) [2002/3 **c–**
20sᵘʳ 21d c20vᵖᵘ c25f⁴ Mar 27] 2,100 3-y-o: leggy gelding: half-brother to several **h–**
winners, including fairly useful hurdler Rich Desire (by Grey Desire), stays 25f: dam ran
once: no show in hurdles/novice chases: blinkered second start. *D. P. Keane*

JOHN OLIVER (IRE) 5 gr.g. Lure (USA) – Glitter Grey (Nishapour (FR)) [2002/3 **F107**
F16d* F16v* F17g Apr 5] tall gelding: third foal: half-brother to fair hurdler up to 2½m
John James (by Bravefoot) and bumper winner The Linen Hall (by Shernazar): dam,
winning hurdler/fair chaser over 2½m+, half-sister to high-class middle-distance horse
Oscar Schindler: won bumpers at Naas in February and Navan (useful form when beating
Kildare by 6 lengths) in March: favourite, failed to settle when soundly beaten in Grade 2
at Aintree. *E. J. O'Grady, Ireland*

JOHNSON'S POINT 5 ch.m. Sabrehill (USA) – Watership (USA) (Foolish Pleasure **h82 +**
(USA)) [2002/3 20mᵖᵘ 16sᵖᵘ 20gᶠ Mar 25] leggy mare: half-sister to several winning
hurdlers, notably smart Lanzerac (by Lycius), stays 21f: fair on Flat (stays 1¾m):
favourite, won mares novice at Haydock on hurdling debut in October: failed to complete
2 starts after, refusing to settle (blinkered) and held in fourth when falling last at Ascot:
should be as effective around 2m as 2½m. *M. W. Easterby*

JOHN STEED (IRE) 6 b.g. Thatching – Trinity Hall (Hallgate) [2002/3 h75?: 16m **h70**
19g* 19m 19s⁶ 19mᵖᵘ Apr 21] close-coupled gelding: poor hurdler: won weak conditional jockeys seller at Hereford (sold from J. Mullins 3,400 gns) in October: stays 19f.
Mrs A. C. Tate

JOHNSTON'S ART (IRE) 10 b.g. Law Society (USA) – Mirror of Flowers (Artaius **c– x**
(USA)) [2002/3 c–x, h87: 22d² 24m* 27g³ 24d* 24g² 22m 24sᵖᵘ 22v⁴ 24m⁴ 24gᵖᵘ 24d **h101 §**
27gᵖᵘ 22g 27g Apr 25] workmanlike gelding: let down by jumping over fences: fair
handicap hurdler: won handicaps at Perth in May and June (conditional jockeys): subsequently lost his form: stays 27f: yet to race on firm going, acts on any other: blinkered:
carries head high: ungenuine. *Mrs J. C. McGregor*

JOHN THE MOLE (IRE) 5 ch.g. Glacial Storm (USA) – City Dame (Golden Love) **h79**
[2002/3 F88: F16f³ 20m⁵ 16d 16d 20v³ 24g 22d Mar 1] compact gelding: fair form in **F84**
bumpers: poor novice hurdler: stays 2½m: probably acts on any going: hasn't looked easy
ride. *M. D. Hammond*

JOHN TUFTY 12 ch.g. Vin St Benet – Raffles Virginia (Whistling Deer) [2002/3 **c–**
c16dᵖᵘ c24gᵖᵘ May 30] sturdy gelding: long-standing maiden over fences: stays 2¾m: **h–**
acts on firm and good to soft going: tried blinkered/visored. *Miss C. Wolstenholme*

JOINT ACCOUNT 13 ch.g. Sayyaf – Dancing Clara (Billion (USA)) [2002/3 c116: **c124 x**
c25d* c23s² c20d⁵ c23s² c25d³ c25g⁵ c24dᵖᵘ Apr 9] plain gelding: fairly useful chaser,
better than ever when completing hat-trick in handicaps at Wetherby in May: sometimes

let down by jumping, including back in hunters (reportedly distressed final start): stays 27f: acts on firm and soft going. *R. Tate*

JOINT AUTHORITY (IRE) 8 b.g. Religiously (USA) – Highway's Last (Royal **h87** Highway) [2002/3 22d^{pu} 16d 20g^4 16g^4 20d^2 17g^3 Apr 21] lengthy gelding: fifth foal: half-brother to high-class chaser The Last Fling (by Avocat), stayed 3½m, and modest hurdler One More Fling (by Satco), stayed 2½m: dam winning Irish hurdler around 2m: successful 3 times in Irish points, including on both starts in 2002: best effort over hurdles when second to Almire du Lia in novice handicap at Newcastle: better suited by 2½m than 2m: free-going front runner. *L. Lungo*

JOJO (FR) 6 ch.g. Dadarissime (FR) – Belle Mome (FR) (Grand Tresor (FR)) [2002/3 **h–** c17g^4 c21g^5 c22d c20g^3 c21g^F c21g^{pu} c20g^3 c20g 20g^5 Apr 23] ex-French gelding: third foal: half-brother to 3 winners, including fairly useful 2m hurdler Kalca Mome (by En Calcat): dam unraced: maiden steeplechaser, raced mostly in cross-country events in Provinces when trained by P. Cottin: third on second of 3 starts in maiden points in Britain in 2003: fifth in maiden at Perth on second outing over hurdles: stays 2½m. *N. W. Alexander*

JOKERS CHARM 12 b.g. Idiot's Delight – By The Lake (Tyrant (USA)) [2002/3 **c95** c95, h–: c20g^{pu} c21d^6 20g^{pu} c16g* Oct 15] workmanlike gelding: maiden hurdler: **h–** modest handicap chaser: won at Sedgefield in October: has form at 3m, raced mainly over shorter: acts on any going, except possibly heavy: visored once, blinkered nowadays: tongue tied: sometimes let down by jumping. *N. B. Mason*

JOKESMITH (IRE) 5 b.g. Mujadil (USA) – Grinning (IRE) (Bellypha) [2002/3 **h–** 16v^{pu} Jan 14] useful at best on Flat (stays 1¼m), sold out of B. Meehan's stable 15,000 gns Doncaster November Sales: very tired in fourth when pulled up after 2 out (reportedly lost action) in maiden at Ayr on hurdling debut. *K. A. Ryan*

JOLIKA (FR) 6 b.m. Grand Tresor (FR) – Unika II (FR) (Rolling Bowl (FR)) [2002/3 **F90** F90: F17v^2 Jan 21] leggy mare: bumper winner: off 15 months, 14 lengths second to Farne Isle in mares event at Sedgefield in January. *L. Lungo*

JOLI POSH 6 ch.m. Rakaposhi King – Nunswalk (The Parson) [2002/3 F16s F17d **F–** Jan 16] 2,300 3-y-o: half-sister to 3 winning hurdlers, including modest up to 3¼m Nuns Jewel (by Julio Mariner): dam winning hurdler/chaser, stayed at least 2½m: well held in 2 bumpers. *R. J. Hodges*

JOLLANDS 5 b.g. Ezzoud (IRE) – Rainbow Fleet (Nomination) [2002/3 17g^4 24g^{pu} **h–** 16m^4 Oct 7] fair at best on Flat (stays 1¼m), well beaten in 2002: little encouragement over hurdles: unlikely to stay 3m. *R. Curtis*

JOLLIE BOLLIE (IRE) 8 b.m. Husyan (USA) – Jet Travel (Deep Run) [2002/3 **h126** h109p: 20s* 22s^2 22d* 22v 21m 20g 21m Apr 17] rather leggy, close-coupled mare: fairly useful handicap hurdler: won at Folkestone in November and Wincanton (by 3 lengths from Rum Pointer) in December: largely below form after: stays 2¾m: acts on soft going, possibly not on good to firm: races freely: jumps none too fluently. *Miss Venetia Williams*

JOLLY GIANT (IRE) 7 b.g. Jolly Jake (NZ) – Reve Clair (Deep Run) [2002/3 c81+: **c104** c26d^F c24d^3 c24s* c26v^{pu} c25d^F c25d* c25g^{ur} Mar 18] tall, useful-looking gelding: fair chaser: won handicaps at Chepstow in November and Exeter in January: stays 25f: acts on soft going: blinkered last 2 starts: has been let down by jumping. *P. F. Nicholls*

JOLLY GREEN GIANT (IRE) 10 b.g. Glacial Storm (USA) – Rambling Love **c– x** (Golden Love) [2002/3 c–x, h–: c25d^{pu} Feb 6] tall, angular gelding: one-time useful **h–** chaser, won 2 novices in 2000/1: pulled up all 5 starts since, usually jumping poorly: should stay beyond 3m: raced on good going or softer (acts on heavy). *P. R. Webber*

JOLLY HOPEFUL (IRE) 6 b.g. Glacial Storm (USA) – Tudor Lady (Green Shoon) **h–** [2002/3 h84, F88: 22d^{pu} Nov 5] once-raced in bumpers: looked a stayer when third in 2½m novice on hurdling debut: reportedly lame in similar event 7 months later. *C. P. Morlock*

JOLLY JOHN (IRE) 12 b.g. Jolly Jake (NZ) – Golden Seekers (Manado) [2002/3 **c–** c77, h89: 22f^3 23d^4 24d^2 24g^3 24m^4 Jul 24] angular gelding: poor handicap chaser/ **h81** maiden hurdler: stays 3m: acts on any going: ridden by Mrs C. Mann all starts in Britain. *C. J. Mann*

JOLLY MOONBEAM (IRE) 6 b.m. Jolly Jake (NZ) – Orient Moonbeam (Deep **h114** Run) [2002/3 F16g* 20d^3 16v* 16v* 20s^F 16s 16v* 16s^F 16d^3 Feb 23] tall mare: fifth **F98** foal: half-sister to useful pointer River Swilley (by Over The River) and bumper winner/ winning pointer Times Past (by Commanche Run): dam lightly-raced hurdler: successful twice from 4 starts in bumpers, including at Gowran in May: fair hurdler: won novices at Galway in October and Down Royal (mares) in November and intermediate at Limerick (beat Risky Reef by 1½ lengths) in December: best form at 2m: acts on heavy going. *Michael Hourigan, Ireland*

JOLLYOLLY   4 gr.g. Environment Friend – Off The Air (IRE) (Taufan (USA)) [2002/3 F18d F16d 19m² Apr 21] third foal: dam 8.5f (stayed 11f) winner on Flat: well held in bumpers: 4 lengths second of 4 to easy winner Besieged in slowly-run novice at Market Rasen on hurdling debut. *P. Bowen*   **h93** **F–**

JOLLYSHAU (IRE)   5 b.g. Jolly Jake (NZ) – Escheat (Torus) [2002/3 20v 21s⁴ 20g Apr 2] workmanlike gelding: first foal: dam, winning Irish pointer, out of half-sister to Whitbread Gold Cup winner Ushers Island: 100/1, apparently best effort over hurdles when seventh in novice at Ascot final start. *Miss A. M. Newton-Smith*   **h77 ?**

JOLLY SIDE (IRE)   10 b.g. Jolly Jake (NZ) – South Quay Lady (Quayside) [2002/3 16s⁶ c16d³ c16vᵖᵘ c16s⁴ c16g³ c16g Mar 16] lengthy gelding: maiden hurdler: one-time fairly useful chaser: sold out of A. Mullins' stable 26,000 gns Doncaster May (2000) Sales: only modest form in 2002/3 after 2½-year absence: stays 2¾m: acts on heavy and good to firm going: headstrong: sold 1,600 gns Doncaster May Sales. *C. J. Mann*   **c100** **h86**

JOLY BEY (FR)   6 ch.g. Beyssac (FR) – Rivolie (FR) (Mistigri) [2002/3 c112, h96, F–: c20s* c17d⁵ c21d² c21v* c24d² c24g³ c24v* c20d* 24s* c20s² c25d³ Apr 4] tall, angular gelding: useful novice chaser: won at Auteuil (non-thoroughbred event, left G. Macaire after next outing) in May, Newton Abbot in November, Fakenham in January and Sandown in February: in frame in graded events at Aintree and Punchestown in April,   **c137** **h100 p**

Million In Mind Partnership 12's "Joly Bey"

better effort when third to Irish Hussar at former: second start over hurdles, easily made all in amateur novice at Chepstow in February (open to improvement): stays 25f: raced on good going or softer (acts on heavy): fluent jumper: sold to join N. Gifford 240,000 gns Doncaster May Sales. *P. F. Nicholls*

JOLY BOIS (FR)   6 ch.g. Mister Sicy (FR) – Brindille Jolie (FR) (Lee (FR)) [2002/3   **h80** h78+: 19d⁵ 16s 22d 21m Mar 21] leggy gelding: poor maiden hurdler: stays 19f: acts on good to soft going: visored last 3 starts, jumped poorly first occasion. *M. C. Pipe*

JONAEM (IRE)   13 b.g. Mazaad – Priors Mistress (Sallust) [2002/3 c–, h–: c27g³   **c69** c25m³ c30d 20m 27m⁴ 17g² 21g* 22dᵖᵘ c20f³ c25m³ 22g c27d⁴ 27v* c27sᵖᵘ 21v⁵ 27sᵖᵘ   **h66** 27g* 21d c26g⁴ Apr 21] compact gelding: poor handicap hurdler/chaser, left Mrs E. Slack after fourteenth start: won over hurdles at Sedgefield in August, November and March, first 2 sellers: effective around 2m to 27f: acts on any going. *Mrs Dianne Sayer*

JONANAUD   4 b.g. Ballet Royal (USA) – Margaret Modes (Thatching) [2002/3 F16g   **F76** F16g F16g² Mar 23] leggy gelding: first foal: dam no form on Flat: modest form in bumpers, going in snatches when strong-finishing ½-length second of 7 to Romany Dream at Warwick. *H. J. Manners*

JONES LAD (IRE)   8 b.g. Posen (USA) – Dame's Folly (IRE) (Kings Lake (USA))   **c83** [2002/3 h74: 22f⁶ 20dᵖᵘ c16g² c16g² c16m³ c16m³ Jul 28] lengthy gelding: poor handicap   **h–** hurdler: similar form when placed all 4 starts over fences: stays 21f: acts on any going, races mainly on good or firmer nowadays: usually races prominently. *R. H. Buckler*

JONGLEUR COLLONGES (FR)   6 gr.g. Royal Charter (FR) – Soubrette Collonge   **h97** (FR) (Saumon (FR)) [2002/3 F93: 21v³ 21d⁴ 20g⁶ 24m⁵ Apr 16] tall, useful-looking gelding: chasing type: in frame in bumpers: modest form over hurdles: stays 3m: acts on good to firm and heavy going. *R. H. Alner*

JONJO   5 b.g. Charnwood Forest (IRE) – Katy-Q (IRE) (Taufan (USA)) [2002/3 16sᶠ   **h–** Feb 8] well held on Flat: behind when falling 4 out in novice on hurdling debut. *B. P. J. Baugh*

JORDAN'S RIDGE (IRE)   7 br. or b.g. Indian Ridge – Sadie Jordan (USA) (Hail   **c102** The Pirates (USA)) [2002/3 h92: 22g⁴ c16d* c16d² c16g⁴ c20m² Jul 7] sparely-made   **h–** gelding: winning hurdler: fair novice chaser: won at Hexham in June: best form up to 2½m: acts on any going: tried blinkered/tongue tied: often fails to impress with attitude. *P. Monteith*

JORN DU SOLEIL (FR)   6 ch.g. Murmure (FR) – Ina du Soleil (FR) (Or de Chine)   **c95** [2002/3 h104: c20sᵇᵈ c16d⁴ c16d³ Mar 5] well-made gelding: type to carry condition: fair   **h–** form over hurdles: best effort over fences when fourth in novice at Wetherby: raced mainly around 2m on going softer than good: found little final outing. *M. D. Hammond*

JORODAMA KING   9 b.g. Lighter – Princess Hecate (Autre Prince) [2002/3 c71x,   **c71 x** h–: c26g* c24m⁵ c24m⁴ c20g c26g³ c24f³ c24f³ c24m³ c27g c25gᵖᵘ c26mᵖᵘ c26mᵖᵘ   **h–** Apr 21] lengthy gelding: maiden hurdler: poor chaser: won weak novice at Plumpton in April: stays 3¼m: acts on firm and good to soft going: tried blinkered: often let down by jumping: of doubtful temperament. *O. Sherwood*

JOSANJAMIC   6 b.m. King Luthier – Ndita (Be My Native (USA)) [2002/3 F82:   **c–** F16g² F17d⁵ 22g 24v⁶ 22d c24g³ Apr 12] good-topped mare: modest form in bumpers: **h–** well held over hurdles and on chasing debut. *W. S. Kittow*   **F82**

JOSEPH WILLIAM (IRE)   4 b.g. College Chapel – Murroe Star (Glenstal (USA))   **h73** [2002/3 16g 17g 16m 16s⁴ 17d⁵ 24vᵖᵘ 16vᵖᵘ Jan 17] leggy gelding: half-brother to winning 2m hurdler The Staggery Boy (by Shalford) and winning hurdler/chaser Unforgotten Star (by Don't Forget Me), stays 25f: little form on Flat and over hurdles. *C. N. Kellett*

JOSHUA'S BAY   5 b.g. Karinga Bay – Bonita Blakeney (Baron Blakeney) [2002/3   **h79** F80: F17m F17m 16m 20mᵘʳ 16m⁶ 16g 16d³ 16v² 18s⁴ 17s* 16g⁴ Apr 12] sturdy   **F–** gelding: thrice-raced in bumpers, form only on debut: poor hurdler: won novice handicap at Sedgefield in March: raced mainly around 2m: acts on heavy going (second in bumper on good to firm). *J. R. Jenkins*

JOSHUA'S VISION (IRE)   12 b.g. Vision (USA) – Perle's Fashion (Sallust) [2002/3   **c–** c73, h–: c26vᵖᵘ c25sᵖᵘ Mar 7] workmanlike gelding: winning pointer: maiden hurdler/   **h–** steeplechaser: stays 25f: acts on firm and soft going: tried visored/in cheekpieces: often tongue tied: has bled from nose. *Lady Susan Brooke*

JOSS NAYLOR (IRE) 8 b.g. Be My Native (USA) – Sister Ida (Bustino) [2002/3 **c146**
h142, F102: c24s* c20s* c21v* c24g Mar 11] **h–**

Few sports come close to providing the sort of stamina test at which Joss
Naylor excelled. The Cumbrian sheep farmer was the outstanding long-distance
fell runner of the 'seventies and early-'eighties in his native lakelands. To help
quantify the term 'long distance', the Summer Jaunt 2000, a fundraising event
organised by Naylor, provides an interesting pointer, being a journey of approx-
imately ninety-five miles along the Wainwright memorial walk—hardly as short or
perhaps as pleasurable as the word 'jaunt' implies. The equine Joss Naylor is at his
best under less testing conditions—around three miles suits him ideally and, while
he doesn't possess quite the air of invincibility of his human namesake in his
heyday, he has certainly made a promising start to his chasing career.

Impressive when gaining his first success in bumpers and then in a six-race
campaign over hurdles, Joss Naylor continued the trend over fences, winning a
novice event at Uttoxeter in November on his debut. In truth the race turned into
something of a non-event with the modest Its Only Polite the only one of his four
rivals to complete, Joss Naylor sauntering home. His next outing at Bangor the
following month wasn't without incident either, three horses parting company with
their riders at the last, by which time Joss Naylor, who had taken a good hold, had
already asserted comfortably. Clearly Joss Naylor was ready for a step up in class,
or at least the chance to take on better quality opposition, which he met at Cheltenham on New Year's Day, when Tarxien was among his three rivals. Tarxien had
already shown himself a smart novice in winning his first two starts over fences,
including a Grade 2 at Ascot three days after Joss Naylor's Bangor success. The
Cheltenham race was essentially a match between the pair. Little should be read
into the proximity of the third horse Whereareyounow who, on heavy ground, was

Mr Darren C. Mercer's "Joss Naylor"

allowed to dictate a steady pace until after three out. The crucial moment came at
the next fence, where a mistake by Tarxien handed Joss Naylor a narrow advantage
and, in a driving finish, Joss Naylor kept on gamely to hold on by a short head. It's
possible that Tarxien would have shaded the verdict but for his mistake, though
there seemed little reason to doubt that Joss Naylor was also a smart novice,
particularly as the pair had been quite closely matched over hurdles. Smart maybe,
but Joss Naylor isn't up to championship standard and, for the second year running,
connections favoured running him in a handicap at the Cheltenham Festival rather
than a novice event. As a novice hurdler in 2001/2, Joss Naylor ran an excellent
race on soft ground to finish second to Ilnamar in the Coral Eurobet Cup from a
BHB mark of 132. On a mark of 140 for the National Hunt Handicap Chase, Joss
Naylor was sent off joint favourite with Ad Hoc but, with the ground good on this
occasion, Joss Naylor didn't run nearly so well, travelling smoothly enough but
folding tamely after four out, finishing eleventh.

The leggy, close-coupled Joss Naylor isn't an obvious chaser on looks,
though he jumps well enough and is certainly bred for the game, being a brother to
Native Mission and Jack Doyle, both useful chasers in the 'nineties. Something of a
nervy sort who got on his toes in the preliminaries before his victories at Bangor
and Cheltenham, Joss Naylor reportedly does most of his work at home on his own.
His best form has been on soft and heavy ground and, granted suitable conditions,
he should win a good handicap in 2003/4. *Jonjo O'Neill*

JOUEUR D'ESTRUVAL (FR) 6 gr.g. Perrault – Alrose (FR) (Kalyan (FR)) [2002/3 **h113**
F112: 16s⁵ 16s* 16g Mar 11] leggy, useful-looking gelding, still rather unfurnished:
bumper winner: fair form when winning maiden hurdle at Navan in January: well held
after in Grade 1 novices at Cheltenham and Punchestown: bred to stay beyond 2m: acts
on soft going: not yet a fluent jumper. *W. P. Mullins, Ireland*

JOUR J (FR) 6 b.g. Royal Charter (FR) – Ability (FR) (Olmeto) [2002/3 c116, h116: **c–**
c20dᵖᵘ Dec 21] leggy, lengthy gelding: fairly useful hurdler/chaser: pulled up lame only **h–**
outing in 2002/3: stays 21f: acts on soft going: reportedly bled once in 2001/2. *M. C. Pipe*

JOURNEY 10 ch.g. Tina's Pet – Lady Vynz (Whitstead) [2002/3 c21g⁶ May 3] lightly- **c–**
raced gelding: winning pointer: maiden hurdler: well held both starts in steeplechases. **h–**
Mrs Sarah Horner-Harker

JOWOODY 10 ch.m. Gunner B – Maskwood (Precipice Wood) [2002/3 c98, h94: **c106**
c25d* c22g² c24m² May 16] leggy mare: modest hurdler: fair handicap chaser: won at **h–**
Kelso in May: ran well facing barely adequate tests both outings in next 2 weeks: should
stay beyond 29f: acts on heavy and good to firm going: tried blinkered. *E. W. Tuer*

JOY AGAIN 5 ch.m. Then Again – Silver Spring (Silver Season) [2002/3 F16m May **F–**
16] first foal: dam unraced: well beaten in bumper on debut. *R. Allan*

JOYCE BEL (FR) 10 b.g. Rose Laurel – Jeanne de Laval (FR) (Gairloch) [2002/3 **c89**
17g c25dᵖᵘ c20mᶠ c17m² c22m⁴ c19m⁶ c16fᶠᵘʳ Oct 24] ex-Irish gelding: maiden hurdler: **h–**
modest handicap chaser: stays 3m, effective over much shorter: acts on heavy and good
to firm going: has worn cheekpieces. *Mrs H. Dalton*

JOY DE DISSE (FR) 6 b.g. Grand Tresor (FR) – Surprise de L'Isle (FR) (Rubloff **F–**
(USA)) [2002/3 F–: F16g Jan 17] last in 2 bumpers: sold 1,700 gns Doncaster May Sales.
N. G. Richards

JOYEUSE 5 b.m. Saddlers' Hall (IRE) – Jouvencelle (Rusticaro (FR)) [2002/3 F17d* **h90**
F16m² F16s³ 19s⁵ 20v⁶ 19dᶠ Feb 10] sturdy mare: half-sister to numerous winners, **F88**
including high-class 2m hurdler/winning chaser up to 2½m Land Afar (by Dominion)
and useful chaser up to 27f Valiant Warrior (by Valiyar): dam maiden, stayed 14.7f: fair
form in bumpers, won at Market Rasen in October: running best race over hurdles when
falling last in mares novice won by Scottish Dance at Hereford: dead. *N. A. Twiston-
Davies*

JOYEUX ROYAL (FR) 6 b.g. Cyborg (FR) – Samba du Cochet (FR) (Tanlas (FR)) **c114**
[2002/3 h102: c17g² c17d* c21gᶠ c20sᵖᵘ c16vᵖᵘ 16s⁶ Feb 26] tall gelding: winning **h–**
hurdler: fair form when winning handicap chase at Plumpton in November: poor efforts
last 3 starts, taking little interest in blinkers second occasion: probably stays 21f: acts on
soft and good to firm going: tongue tied. *P. F. Nicholls*

JOY FOR LIFE (IRE) 12 b.m. Satco (FR) – Joy's Toy (Wolverlife) [2002/3 c83, h–: **c–**
c30sᶠ c26sᵖᵘ c25dᵖᵘ c26d⁴ Feb 24] leggy, angular mare: poor handicap chaser: no form in **h–**
2002/3: stays 25f: acts on heavy and good to firm going. *R. M. Stronge*

Green Hammerton Novices' Chase, Wetherby—Jungle Jinks makes it four wins from five starts

JUBILEE GUNNER   8 b.g. Gunner B – Smokey Baby (Sagaro) [2002/3 c16m^{pu} Apr 5] no sign of ability. *A. P. Garland*   **c–**

J'UBIO   4 b.f. Bijou d'Inde – Eternal Triangle (USA) (Barachois (CAN)) [2002/3 16m^F 16s 17s Nov 28] leggy filly: poor maiden on Flat (stays 1m): well held both completed starts over hurdles. *B. A. Pearce*   **h–**

JUDAIC WAYS   9 b.g. Rudimentary (USA) – Judeah (Great Nephew) [2002/3 c94, h–: c24m^3 c19g c24s* c24g^3 c20m^3 c24g^{pu} Apr 19] lengthy gelding: maiden hurdler: modest handicap chaser: back to form when winning at Ludlow (third course success) in January: stays 3m: acts on firm and soft going: has shaped as if amiss more than once: prone to the odd bad mistake. *H. D. Daly*   **c96**   **h–**

JUDES LAW   5 gr.m. Contract Law (USA) – Linen Thread (Broxted) [2002/3 F16d Aug 3] 2,000 3-y-o: eighth foal: half-sister to 4 poor performers: dam, twice-raced hurdler, half-sister to top-class staying chaser Brown Chamberlin: tailed off in bumper on debut. *P. R. Rodford*   **F–**

JUDICIOUS (IRE)   6 b.g. Fairy King (USA) – Kama Tashoof (Mtoto) [2002/3 h–: 17m May 3] little aptitude for hurdling in 2 starts: sold 16,000 gns Doncaster May Sales: useful miler on Flat in 2002: dead. *C. J. Mann*   **h–**

JUDY GALE (IRE)   5 bl.m. Glacial Storm (USA) – Gale Choice (IRE) (Strong Gale) [2002/3 F17s 22d^{pu} Feb 17] first foal: dam unraced: no form in mares bumper or novice hurdle. *B. G. Powell*   **h–**   **F–**

JUICY LUCY   6 b.m. Bonny Scot (IRE) – Bijou Georgie (Rhodomantade) [2002/3 F18s^5 19v^{pu} 22m^{pu} 16m Mar 31] third foal: half-sister to fair 2m chaser Nick The Jewel (by Nicholas Bill): dam, winning hunter chaser, best around 2½m: no form in bumper or over hurdles. *J. S. King*   **h–**   **F–**

JULIA'S CHOICE   4 ch.f. Elmaamul (USA) – Daarat Alayaam (IRE) (Reference Point) [2002/3 F12g F17s^5 F16g 17s^3 16g^3 Mar 23] leggy filly: third foal: half-sister to 2000 2-y-o 7f winner Magic of You (by Magic Ring): dam unraced, from family of smart 2m hurdler For Reg: well held in bumpers: poor form when third in mares events over hurdles at Bangor and Warwick. *J. R. Jenkins*   **h72**   **F–**

JULIES BOY (IRE)   6 b.g. Toulon – Chickmo (IRE) (Seclude (USA)) [2002/3 F16s 16d^2 20g^{pu} 21m Apr 16] sturdy ex-Irish gelding: first foal: dam unraced: won maiden   **h88**   **F70**

442

Irish point in 2002: mid-division in bumper: head second of 17 in maiden hurdle at Thurles: left J. O'Callaghan, stiff tasks both starts in Britain. *T. R. George*

JULIE'S LEADER (IRE)   9 b.g. Supreme Leader – Parkavoureen (Deep Run) [2002/3 c104, h117: c26g^F 24v^4 c22g^pu c23s^pu 20m* 27g* Apr 19] workmanlike gelding: winning chaser, failed to complete all 3 starts in 2002/3: fair hurdler: didn't need to be at best to win seller at Fontwell in March and claimer at Newton Abbot in April: stays 27f: yet to race on firm going, acts on any other: reportedly lame third start. *P. F. Nicholls*   **c–** **h109**

JUMBO'S DREAM   12 b.g. Jumbo Hirt (USA) – Joyful Star (Rubor) [2002/3 c–, h–: 24g^6 27g^F May 29] deep-girthed gelding: winning 3m hurdler, little form for long time: tried blinkered. *J. E. Dixon*   **c–** **h–**

JUMBO'S FLYER   6 ch.g. Jumbo Hirt (USA) – Fragrant Princess (Germont) [2002/3 h–: 17g Aug 9] compact gelding: lightly raced and little form on Flat since 3 yrs: no show in novice company over hurdles. *F. P. Murtagh*   **h–**

JUMPTY DUMPTY (FR)   6 b.g. Chamberlin (FR) – Caryatide (FR) (Maiymad) [2002/3 c?, h?: 22f* 26g^4 20m^4 22d 19v 21m^6 Apr 10] tall gelding: winning cross-country chaser in France: poor hurdler: won novice handicap at Exeter in May: generally below form after, reportedly bled fifth outing: stays 2¾m: acts on firm and soft going. *J. C. Tuck*   **c–** **h84**

JUNE'S RIVER (IRE)   10 ch.g. Over The River (FR) – June Bug (Welsh Saint) [2002/3 c119x, h–: c17s^pu c20d^2 c16s^3 c16v^pu c24s^pu c16s^6 Mar 6] rather leggy gelding: handicap chaser, generally out of form in 2002/3: stays 2½m: raced on good going or softer (acts on heavy): held up: often let down by jumping: unreliable. *Mrs M. Reveley*   **c105 x** **h–**

JUNGLE JINKS (IRE)   8 b.g. Proud Panther (FR) – Three Ladies (Menelek) [2002/3 h118: c25g* c21s* c25v* c25d^2 c25d* Feb 26] smallish, workmanlike gelding: winning hurdler: fairly useful novice chaser: won at Wetherby (3 times) and Sedgefield (beat Lord Jack 9 lengths) between November and February: 24 lengths second of 6 to Keen Leader in Grade 2 at Wetherby: still to be asked for effort when brought down twelfth in valuable handicap at Punchestown in late-April: will stay beyond 25f: acts on heavy going: sound jumper: genuine and reliable. *G. M. Moore*   **c132 +** **h–**

JUNGLE JUICE   7 ch.g. Henbit (USA) – Deep In The Arctic (Deep Run) [2002/3 19d^6 Oct 19] workmanlike gelding: third foal: dam temperamental winning pointer: won last of 4 starts in maiden points in 2002: nearest finish when sixth in maiden at Market Rasen (reportedly had breathing problem) on hurdling debut: will stay beyond 19f. *Mrs L. Wadham*   **h87**

JUNGLE RUMBLER   4 b.f. Charnwood Forest (IRE) – Blueberry Walk (Green Desert (USA)) [2002/3 16v^pu 16v^F 16g Mar 14] ex-French filly: fairly useful on Flat (stays 1¼m), successful in June for R. Gibson: well held on completed start over hurdles. *P. Winkworth*   **h–**

JUNGLI (IRE)   10 b.g. Be My Native (USA) – Simple Mind (Decent Fellow) [2002/3 c141, h125: c20d^F Nov 2] lengthy, useful-looking gelding: fairly useful hurdler: useful handicap chaser: every chance when fell 2 out in race won by Goguenard at Wetherby, only outing in 2002/3: effective at 2m to 2½m: acts on good to firm and heavy going: usually jumps soundly up with pace: game and consistent. *P. R. Webber*   **c142 ?** **h–**

JUNIOR FONTAINE (FR)   6 b.g. Silver Rainbow – Blanche Fontaine (FR) (Oakland (FR)) [2002/3 17m^4 17g 16m^6 16f* 16s^2 16s 16m^2 Apr 22] workmanlike gelding: will make a chaser: third foal: brother to bumper winner Kim Fontaine: dam unraced: fairly useful handicap hurdler: won easily at Listowel in September: very good second to High Prospect at Fairyhouse final start: raced around 2m, likely to stay further: acts on any going. *A. L. T. Moore, Ireland*   **h118**

JUNKANOO   7 ch.g. Generous (IRE) – Lupescu (Dixieland Band (USA)) [2002/3 h100+: 20s* 20d^2 20d 23v^pu Dec 26] tall, workmanlike gelding: fairly useful handicap hurdler: won strongly-run race at Haydock in November by 13 lengths from Jeannot de Beauchene: should stay 3m+: raced mainly on going softer than good (acts on heavy): has 3 times reportedly finished distressed, including final outing: unreliable. *Mrs M. Reveley*   **h122 §**

JUPITER DE BUSSY (FR)   6 b. or br.g. Silver Rainbow – Tosca de Bussy (FR) (Le Riverain (FR)) [2002/3 F84: F17d^5 16v^4 16d* 16s* 20v^pu 16g^5 Apr 7] well-made gelding: chasing type: modest form in bumpers (raced quite freely): settled better and showed fair form over hurdles, winning novices at Aintree in November and Ayr (handicap, beat Workaway 3 lengths) in December: well below form last 2 starts: should stay beyond 2m: raced on good going or softer. *L. Lungo*   **h109** **F84**

JUPITER DIAMOND   8 b.g. Jupiter Island – Noire Small (USA) (Elocutionist   **h–** (USA)) [2002/3 h70, F–: 24g^{pu} May 22] form over hurdles only on final outing in 2001/2: stays 3¼m. *Ian Williams*

JUPITER JO   7 b.g. Jupiter Island – Marejo (Creetown) [2002/3 F–: c16d^4 c20m^{pu} **c74** Jun 21] little sign of ability in bumpers or novice chases: won maiden point in April. *J. B. Walton*

JUPITER'S FANCY   8 ch.m. Jupiter Island – Joe's Fancy (Apollo Eight) [2002/3 h–,   **c–** F76: c25d^{pu} Mar 5] won 3-runner maiden point in March: no form over hurdles or in   **h–** novice hunter chase. *A. Kirtley*

JUPON VERT (FR)   6 b.g. Lights Out (FR) – Danse Verte (FR) (Brezzo (FR)) [2002/3   **c88** c91, h–: c21f^5 c16m^4 c16s^6 19s* 19d^2 19d c16s* c16s^4 c16d^3 c19f^F c16g^3 Apr 21] modest   **h94** hurdler/chaser: won seller over hurdles at Taunton in December and novice handicap chase over fences there in February: stays 19f: acts on soft and firm ground: usually tongue tied. *P. F. Nicholls*

JURADO EXPRESS (IRE)   7 b.g. Jurado (USA) – Express Film (Ashmore (FR))   **c117** [2002/3 16g 16d^2 16d^2 16s^3 16f^3 16s* c16s* c16s* c17s^5 c16d^5 c17g^{pu} Apr 20] workman-   **h96** like gelding: seventh foal: brother to modest hurdler Jupiter Hollow and half-brother to 3 winning pointers: dam won 2m novice hurdle: modest hurdler: won maiden at Cork in November: fairly useful novice chaser: won at Thurles (maiden) and Cork (beat Rathgar Beau ½ length) in December: very stiff task when last of 5 in Grade 1 at Punchestown in early-May: raced around 2m: acts on soft going. *A. L. T. Moore, Ireland*

JURALAN (IRE)   8 b.g. Jurado (USA) – Boylan (Buckskin (FR)) [2002/3 c116p, h88+:   **c122** c21d^{pu} c20g^{pu} c20g^{pu} c16g^3 Mar 25] tall, good sort: twice-raced over hurdles (reportedly   **h–** distressed on second occasion): fairly useful chaser: form in handicaps in 2002/3 only when 4 lengths third of 6 to Lord York at Ascot: will stay beyond 21f. *Miss H. C. Knight*

JURANCON II (FR)   6 b.g. Scooter Bleu (IRE) – Volniste (FR) (Olmeto) [2002/3   **c118 p** h107: 21d* 21s^{pu} c21v* c34s^3 Mar 15] tall, leggy gelding: fairly useful handicap hurdler: **h125** in-and-out form, won 29-runner conditional jockeys event at Cheltenham in November: beat Indian Scout a length in 5-runner novice at Uttoxeter in December on chasing debut, though went in snatches and needed forceful ride from R. Greene: 29½ lengths third of 6 finishers to Intelligent in valuable handicap at latter course 3 months later, would have been closer but for mistake 3 out: should stay beyond 21f: acts on heavy going: should still do better over fences. *M. C. Pipe*

JURASSIC SCRATCH (IRE)   7 b.g. Jurado (USA) – On The Scratch (Le Bavard   **c74 §** (FR)) [2002/3 h66: c23g^F c26d^{pu} c23d c26s^{pu} c26v^2 c25s c26s^{pu} Feb 26] lengthy gelding: **h–** poor handicap chaser: suited by 3m+: raced on good going or softer (acts on heavy): has broken blood vessels: unreliable. *R. Rowe*

JURIST   9 b.g. Then Again – Forest Frolic (Celtic Cone) [2002/3 c–, h77: c25g^F Mar   **c–** 17] workmanlike gelding: poor form only outing over hurdles: no form over fences.   **h–** *B. S. Rothwell*

JUSFUL (FR)   6 b.g. Useful (FR) – Contesty (FR) (Sicyos (USA)) [2002/3 20m^{pu} **h–** 22g^{pu} 22m 20s^{pu} Aug 9] leggy gelding: blinkered, no form over hurdles. *M. C. Pipe*

JUST A MINUTE (FR)   6 b.m. Le Nain Jaune (FR) – Brave Again (FR) (Pot d'Or   **c97** (FR)) [2002/3 h89: 17g* 20g^3 22f 21m^3 21d^{pu} c25d^2 c19d* c19s^F Mar 4] useful-looking   **h93** mare: modest hurdler: won mares novice at Exeter in May: similar form over fences, successful in mares novice at same course in December: stayed 25f: acted on soft and good to firm going (below best on firm): dead. *R. H. Alner*

JUST A TOUCH   7 ch.g. Rakaposhi King – Minim (Rymer) [2002/3 h82, F–: 16s^{pu} **h90** 19d* 16d* 19d^5 17v^2 16s^4 Feb 24] workmanlike gelding: modest handicap hurdler: won at Warwick in November and December: barely stays 19f: raced on going softer than good (acts on heavy). *P. Winkworth*

JUST BARNEY BOY   6 b.g. Past Glories – Pablena (Pablond) [2002/3 c–, h–: c25d^{pu} **c–** c24m^{pu} c20m^{pu} c25d^{co} Mar 1] no form outside points (won 3 times in March and April).   **h–** *R. Nixon*

JUST BETH   7 ch.m. Carlingford Castle – One For The Road (Warpath) [2002/3 h–:   **h64** 21s^{pu} 24v^2 27v Jan 21] angular mare: form over hurdles only when second in conditional jockeys novice handicap at Uttoxeter: likely to prove better at 3m than shorter: acts on heavy going. *G. Fierro*

JUST CARAMEL   7 b.m. Montelimar (USA) – Cream By Post (Torus) [2002/3 h90,   **h84 d** F82: 22g^{pu} 22m^2 24m^3 22f^4 24m^4 22d^{pu} 26g^{pu} 21g Mar 14] small mare: maiden hurdler:

444

only poor in 2002/3, left P. Nicholls after fifth outing: stays 2¾m: best efforts on good going or firmer (acts on firm): possibly none too genuine. *A. G. Hobbs*

JUST ED   7 ch.g. Greensmith – Sovereign Maiden (Nearly A Hand) [2002/3 h69, F–: 16g⁶ 16g⁴ 22mᵖᵘ Oct 6] poor novice hurdler: should stay beyond 2m. *R. Nixon*   **h73**

JUST FOR FUN (IRE)   5 b.g. Kahyasi – Copper Breeze (IRE) (Strong Gale) [2002/3 F16d Mar 1] €33,000 4-y-o: smallish gelding: third foal: half-brother to winning pointer by Erins Isle: dam unraced half-sister to useful staying chaser Sir Leonard, from family of smart jumpers Boro Quarter and Boro Eight: well held in 9-runner bumper at Haydock on debut. *Ferdy Murphy*   **F–**

JUST FOR GER (IRE)   9 b.g. Beau Sher – Reasonar (Reasonable (FR)) [2002/3 c89, h–: 20d 19d c16s* c16d⁴ c20g⁴ Apr 14] leggy gelding: winning hurdler: modest handicap chaser: won at Ayr in March: effective at 2m to 3m: acts on soft going, probably on good to firm. *J. S. Goldie*   **c90 h75**

JUST GEORGE   9 b.g. Primitive Rising (USA) – Just Jessica (State Diplomacy (USA)) [2002/3 c68?, h–: c25mᵖᵘ 22dᵖᵘ c26mᵖᵘ Jul 19] good-topped gelding: little worthwhile form over hurdles or fences: runner-up in point in February: blinkered second start. *Ms Liz Harrison*   **c– h–**

JUST GOOD FRIENDS (IRE)   6 b.g. Shalford (IRE) – Sinfonietta (Foolish Pleasure (USA)) [2002/3 h–: 16f 17mᵖᵘ Oct 1] little form over hurdles: tried blinkered/tongue tied. *Denys Smith*   **h–**

JUST HENRY   6 b.g. Arzanni – Silk Touch (Lochnager) [2002/3 F–: F16d 22d Nov 21] useful-looking gelding: well held in 2 bumpers and novice hurdle. *A. King*   **h– F–**

JUST HOPING   10 b.g. Primitive Rising (USA) – Happy Penny (Tower Joy) [2002/3 c86: c20mᵖᵘ c16g² c16g c16mᵖᵘ Jun 29] good-topped gelding: modest chaser: best efforts at 2m: acts on good to firm ground: inconsistent. *Lady Susan Watson*   **c86**

JUST IN DEBT (IRE)   7 b. or br.g. Montelimar (USA) – No Debt (Oats) [2002/3 24f² 20g³ c22s* c24g⁶ Mar 30] useful-looking gelding: first foal: dam maiden jumper: fair form in novice company over hurdles: much better over fences, won maiden at Cork in November, left clear by Le Coudray's fall 2 out: stays 3m: acts on soft going, probably on firm. *P. M. J. Doyle, Ireland*   **c125 h102**

JUSTIN MAC (IRE)   12 br.g. Satco (FR) – Quantas (Roan Rocket) [2002/3 c111§, h–§: c16g⁴ c21s* c20d⁵ c20m² c20g c20g⁵ Mar 15] good-topped gelding: fair handicap chaser: won hunter at Newton Abbot in May by a distance: well held both starts after 8-month absence: stays 21f: acts on good to firm and heavy going: blinkered twice: often finds little: unreliable. *Mrs H. Dalton*   **c111 § h– §**

JUST IN TIME   8 b.g. Night Shift (USA) – Future Past (USA) (Super Concorde (USA)) [2002/3 h123: c17g* c17g* c20g* c19m³ c20gᶠ Nov 20] leggy gelding: fairly useful hurdler: successful first 3 starts in novice chases, at Exeter and Stratford in May and Perth in September, unimpressive in landing odds at last 2: partly let down by jumping last 2 outings: stays 21f: acts on soft and good to firm going. *P. J. Hobbs*   **c108 h–**

JUST JAKE   10 b.g. Jendali (USA) – Dohty Baby (Hittite Glory) [2002/3 c24g⁵ May 8] sturdy gelding: winning hurdler/chaser: fairly useful pointer in 2002, lost his form in 2003: barely stays 3m: acts on good to firm and heavy going: tried blinkered: held up. *Mrs C. M. Tinkler*   **c– h–**

JUST JASMINE   11 ch.m. Nicholas Bill – Linguistic (Porto Bello) [2002/3 c128, h–: c16d² c16d* c16v² c21s c17gᵘʳ Feb 8] good-topped mare: useful handicap chaser: in the form of her life in November, won quite valuable 5-runner event at Cheltenham by 6 lengths from Lady Cricket, coming from rear in strongly-run race: had far too much use made of her fourth start: effective at 2m to 21f: acts on any going: goes well for R. Greene: usually sound jumper: usually held up: reliable. *K. Bishop*   **c140 h–**

JUSTJIM   11 b.g. Derring Rose – Crystal Run VII (Damsire Unregistered) [2002/3 c103§, h–: c20g⁴ c24sᵖᵘ c23mᵖᵘ 24gᵖᵘ Sep 15] sparely-made gelding: fair handicap chaser on his day, poor efforts last 3 outings: stays 3¼m: acts on soft and good to firm going: tried blinkered/tongue tied: unreliable. *Mrs H. Dalton*   **c92 § h– §**

JUST JIMBO   7 ch.g. Karinga Bay – Ruby Green VII (Damsire Unregistered) [2002/3 17d 17d 16g 17v² 19f Mar 24] tall, angular gelding: poor novice hurdler: should stay beyond 17f: acts on heavy going. *W. G. M. Turner*   **h68**

JUST LIZZIE   10 b.m. Rakaposhi King – Kilglass (Fidel) [2002/3 h105: 23fᶠ May 4] leggy mare: fair handicap hurdler: stayed 2½m: acted on heavy going: none too consistent: dead. *R. Nixon*   **h–**

JUST MAYBE (IRE) 9 b.g. Glacial Storm (USA) – Purlace (Realm) [2002/3 h94: **c122**
c25g⁴ c22d³ c29s⁵ c32d⁵ c30s* c27d* c26v* c34sᵖᵘ Mar 15] good-bodied gelding: **h–**
modest novice hurdler: fairly useful chaser: progressed very well, won handicaps at
Bangor in December, Taunton in January and Uttoxeter (novice, beat News Maker 3½
lengths) in February: often none too fluent, particularly so in valuable event at Uttoxeter
final outing: suited by 3m+: acts on heavy going: best in blinkers: tongue tied and ridden
in spurs once in 2001/2: has carried head rather high. *Miss Venetia Williams*

JUST MIDAS 5 b.g. Merdon Melody – Thabeh (Shareef Dancer (USA)) [2002/3 h75: **h–**
16d 16m Apr 22] leggy, sparely-made gelding: little worthwhile form over hurdles, off
over 16 months before reappearance. *N. A. Smith*

JUST MUCKIN AROUND (IRE) 7 gr.g. Celio Rufo – Cousin Muck (IRE) (Henbit **c75**
(USA)) [2002/3 h–, F–: 22d⁴ 18m⁶ c19dᵇᵈ c20dᶠ 22vᵖᵘ 22v⁴ c17m² Apr 21] lengthy **h–**
gelding: signs of only a little ability over hurdles (shaped as if amiss more than once):
first completion in steeplechases when second in selling handicap at Plumpton: should
stay at least 2½m. *R. H. Buckler*

JUST MURPHY (IRE) 5 b.g. Namaqualand (USA) – Bui-Doi (IRE) (Dance of Life **h118**
(USA)) [2002/3 h116: 18m² 16d³ 16d³ 20g⁵ 20g Apr 2] leggy gelding: fairly useful
hurdler: stays 2½m: acts on soft and good to firm going: wore cheekpieces final outing
(below form): tends to carry head high under pressure: of suspect temperament.
N. J. Henderson

JUST NOBBY 8 b.g. Totem (USA) – Loving Doll (Godswalk (USA)) [2002/3 c23fᵖᵘ **c–**
May 15] angular gelding: little sign of ability. *A. E. Jones* **h–**

JUST OUR JOB (IRE) 8 b.g. Jolly Jake (NZ) – Kristellita (FR) (Crystal Palace **c–**
(FR)) [2002/3 c133, h141: 17d 16d³ 16mᵇᵈ Oct 6] sparely-made gelding: useful form at **h150**
best in novice company over fences: smart hurdler: 2 lengths third to Say Again in
24-runner Galway Hurdle (Handicap) in August: fatally injured in Grade 2 at Tipperary:
raced around 2m, mainly on good going or softer (acted on soft). *D. T. Hughes, Ireland*

JUST REUBEN (IRE) 8 gr.g. Roselier (FR) – Sharp Mama VII (Damsire Un- **c–**
registered) [2002/3 c–: c22sᶠ c20d² c23g⁵ c26m⁴ c25m⁵ c25f³ Apr 21] leggy gelding:
poor maiden chaser, form only in small-field novices. *C. Tizzard*

JUST SAL 7 b.m. Silly Prices – Hanim (IRE) (Hatim (USA)) [2002/3 h–, F75: 16g⁶ **h77**
20m⁴ 24dᵖᵘ 22s 22v² 22v³ 21v⁴ 20v⁵ 17v 16v* 20gᵖᵘ 24g⁶ Apr 23] poor hurdler: won
conditional jockeys mares handicap at Hexham in March: stays 2¾m: raced mainly on
good going or softer (acts on heavy): tried in cheekpieces: jumps none too fluently: has
shown signs of temperament. *R. Nixon*

JUST SALLY 5 b.m. Afzal – Hatherley (Deep Run) [2002/3 F–: F17f May 15] no **F–**
show in 2 bumpers: won maiden point in March. *J. D. Frost*

JUST SERENADE 4 ch.f. Factual – Thimbalina (Salmon Leap (USA)) **h87**
[2002/3 16m* Sep 7] medium-sized filly: half-sister to modest hurdler Northern Maestro
(by Rock Hopper), stayed 19f: modest maiden on Flat (stays 1m): 33/1, fortunate to win
juvenile at Stratford on hurdling debut, held when left clear 2 out, having been left in
contention following pile-up 4 out. *M. J. Ryan*

JUST SO JOLLY 9 b.g. Joligeneration – Military Star VII (Damsire Unregistered) **h–**
[2002/3 19dᵖᵘ 16d 16dᶠ 17d 16g Apr 14] lengthy gelding: of no account. *Lady Susan
Watson*

JUST SOOTY 8 br.g. Be My Native (USA) – March Fly (Sousa) [2002/3 c–, h84: **c–**
20d⁵ Aug 17] big, useful-looking gelding: poor novice hurdler, lightly raced: behind **h–**
when falling only outing over fences: stays 2½m: takes good hold. *N. G. Richards*

JUST STRONG (IRE) 10 b. or br.g. Strong Gale – Just Dont Know (Buckskin (FR)) **c92**
[2002/3 c92: c25d² c24s⁶ c24m⁴ c25d⁵ c20g³ c24m⁵ Apr 19] good-topped gelding: has
reportedly been hobdayed: modest handicap chaser: off 6 months and below form after
reappearance: stays 25f: acts on good to firm and good to soft going. *Mrs A. M. Naughton*

JUST SUPERB 4 ch.g. Superlative – Just Greenwich (Chilibang) [2002/3 16s 16vᵖᵘ **h–**
19g Apr 19] no sign of ability, including on Flat. *P. A. Pritchard*

JUST THE JOBE 5 b.g. Tragic Role (USA) – Southend Scallywag (Tina's Pet) **F86**
[2002/3 F16g² F16f⁶ F17d⁴ Oct 31] fifth foal: half-brother to fair hurdler Red Imp (by
Alflora), stayed 2½m: dam modest hurdler, stayed 2½m: fair form when in frame in
bumpers. *N. B. Mason*

JUST TOM   8 ch.g. Primitive Rising (USA) – Edenburt (Bargello) [2002/3 h86: c25m³ c21d^pu Nov 17] tall, quite good-topped gelding: modest form at best over hurdles: third in novice at Kelso on chasing debut: reportedly lame following month: should prove suited by further than 2m. *Jedd O'Keeffe*   **c81 h–**

JUST WHISKEY (IRE)   10 b.g. Satco (FR) – Illinois Belle (Le Bavard (FR)) [2002/3 c89, h–: c20v^pu c24d^pu Feb 7] rangy gelding: maiden hurdler/winning chaser: no show both outings after 14-month absence: stays 3¼m: acts on soft and firm going: has had tongue tied. *N. A. Twiston-Davies*   **c– h–**

K

KABEER   5 ch.g. Unfuwain (USA) – Ta Rib (USA) (Mr Prospector (USA)) [2002/3 F16m² Apr 21] 800 4-y-o: first foal: closely related to fairly useful 11f winner Mawaheb (by Nashwan): dam won Poule d'Essai des Pouliches: 5/1 from 14/1, 5 lengths second of 8 to Lord Perseus in bumper at Huntingdon on debut. *Julian Poulton*   **F89**

KADARA (IRE)   4 b.f. Slip Anchor – Kadassa (IRE) (Shardari) [2002/3 16s* 17s⁶ 16d^pu Feb 7] tall, useful-looking filly: half-sister to very smart chaser around 2m Kadarann (by Bigstone): thrice-raced maiden up to 1½m on Flat (fairly useful form), sold out of A. de Royer Dupre's stable €50,000 Goffs Arc Sale: won juvenile at Kempton on hurdling debut in December by 3½ lengths from Indien Royal: didn't go on as expected, reportedly broke blood vessel final outing: will stay beyond 2m: room for improvement in her jumping. *R. H. Alner*   **h111**

KADARANN (IRE)   6 b.g. Bigstone (IRE) – Kadassa (IRE) (Shardari) [2002/3 c138, h–: c16f^ur c18s² c16d* c17g* c16g c20d³ c20m* c16m³ Apr 12]   **c159 h–**

   'Maybe I should stick to training two-mile chasers,' was Paul Nicholls' wry response to seeing four of his five Grand National contenders, including Ad Hoc and Shotgun Willy, fail to complete at Aintree. The stable's record with chasers, stayers included, is one few yards can match, but Nicholls' comment alluded to the stable's currently considerable strength in depth in the two-mile chase division. Already housing Cenkos, Kadarann, Young Devereaux and Armaturk, they will be joined by the graduating novices Azertyuiop and Le Roi Miguel in 2003/4.

   Kadarann's place in the pecking order among the two-mile chasers at Manor Farm Stables was a fair bit higher at the end of the season than at the start,

Sodexho Prestige Game Spirit Chase, Newbury—Kadarann puts himself in the Champion Chase picture

Notalottery's "Kadarann"

though perhaps not so high as the defeat of Cenkos in the Game Spirit Chase at Newbury in February, taken at face value, would suggest. Cenkos started odds on for the Sodexho Prestige-sponsored event but it was Kadarann, receiving 6 lb from his stable companion, who was the pick of the five runners in the paddock. Always going well and jumping fluently, Kadarann led three out and just needed to be kept up to his work to beat a slightly below-par Cenkos by eight lengths, with the previous year's winner Lady Cricket, another not at her best on the day, third and 150/1-shot Castle Prince a remote last of the four finishers. Nicholls made it clear afterwards that Cenkos was still the stable's first string for the Queen Mother Champion Chase but Kadarann was only just behind him in the betting come the day, starting 9/1 fourth favourite ahead of the likes of Flagship Uberalles, Edredon Bleu, Florida Pearl, Native Upmanship and Seebald. Kadarann had been available at 40/1 for the Champion Chase a week before the Game Spirit, a gamble generated by a tipping line prior to his win at Newbury prompting much of the contraction in his ante-post odds for Cheltenham. The youngest runner in the Champion Chase line-up, Kadarann did not take the eye anything like so much as at Newbury and failed by some way to repeat that form, beating only Florida Pearl home among the eight finishers behind Moscow Flyer.

Kadarann also failed to match his Newbury form in his three remaining starts. He finished a well-held third to Native Upmanship and Seebald in the Melling Chase at Aintree, failing to stay the two and a half miles, though facing a stiff task against top-class rivals in any case. Just a week later, Kadarann was sent to Ayr to contest handicaps on consecutive days, having successfully run twice at the Scottish National fixture in 2001/2. Both were weak contests, with Kadarann facing just three rivals (all out of the handicap proper) in both races. On the Friday he managed to scramble home by half a length from Ichi Beau over two and a half miles (the race proved no sort of test at the trip) but the next day he finished last of three finishers to Korakor back at two miles, his effort the previous day possibly having left its mark.

Kadarann's efforts after the Game Spirit may have served to prove that he was flattered somewhat at Newbury, but there was enough other evidence in the latest season to show that he had improved since his novice chasing days. Kadarann unseated his rider in a minor event at Warwick shortly after the start of the season in May and was soundly beaten by Moscow Flyer on his return in the autumn in the three-runner Killultagh Properties Ltd Chase at Down Royal, but a win under top weight in a handicap at Cheltenham in December represented an improved performance. Whether Kadarann would have won if Golden Alpha had completed that day is another matter, though Kadarann was beginning to peg him back when Golden Alpha parted company with his rider two out, and he ran out a fifteen-length winner from Red Blazer.

Kadarann (IRE) (b.g. 1997)	Bigstone (IRE) (b 1990)	Last Tycoon (b 1983)	Try My Best
			Mill Princess
		Batave (ch 1982)	Posse
			Bon Appetit
	Kadassa (IRE) (b 1990)	Shardari (b 1982)	Top Ville
			Sharmada
		Kadissya (b 1979)	Blushing Groom
			Kalkeen

Kadarann is another name to add to the list of good jumpers produced as a by-product of the Aga Khan's studs. Kadarann comes from one of the best families in fact, his dam being a half-sister to the Derby and Irish Derby winner Kahyasi. The dam Kadassa was a fair maiden for John Oxx in Ireland, placed several times at a mile and a half and, as well as Kahyasi, is a half-sister to the St Simon Stakes winner Kaliana, the Park Hill runner-up Kadaka and to the dam of smart French pattern-race winners Kassani and Kassana and the one-time smart French chaser Kassiyan. Kassiyan gained his most notable success when winning the 2000 Prix Romati at Enghien from Or Jack. Kadarann's grandam Kadissya won at a mile and a quarter in France, including a listed race, while great grandam Kalkeen numbers St Leger winner Milan and Yorkshire Oaks winner Key Change among her other descendants. Kadassa was weeded out of the Aga Khan's broodmare band (she was sold for IR 27,000 guineas in 2001, in foal to Indian Ridge) with just one Flat winner up to then among her foals, Kabylia (by Brief Truce) being successful in France and later in the States. Kadassa's number of successful jumpers doubled in the latest season when Kadara (by Slip Anchor) won a juvenile hurdle for Robert Alner. Like his dam's other foals, Kadarann began his career with Alain du Royer Dupre, and showed fairly useful form in three starts at up to a mile and a half. After a successful juvenile hurdle campaign with Nicky Henderson, Kadarann joined his current stable for what now looks a bargain 15,000 guineas. The tall, close-coupled Kadarann is best at around two miles and acts on soft and good to firm ground. He is not going to prove so easy to place from now on, being high in the handicap but not quite good enough to beat the best two-milers at level weights. He has been led in at the start, including at Newbury. *P. F. Nicholls*

KADISKAR (IRE) 5 b.g. Ashkalani (IRE) – Kadissya (USA) (Blushing Groom (FR)) [2002/3 16g⁶ 16s² 18v*ᵈⁱˢ 18s⁵ Feb 9] lengthy, useful-looking gelding: half-brother to modest 2m hurdler Kariyadan (by Akarad) and to dam of Kadarann: fair form in 2 maidens at 3 yrs on Flat, sold out of Sir Michael Stoute's stable 62,000 gns Newmarket Autumn (2001) Sales: progressive form over hurdles: passed post first in maiden at Fairyhouse (subsequently disqualified due to prohibitive substance) in December, not extended to beat Pay It Forward 2½ lengths: fifth of 6 to Solerina in Grade 1 novice at Leopardstown final start: likely to stay beyond 2¼m: acts on heavy going: usually tongue tied (not at Fairyhouse). *C. Roche, Ireland*   h119 +

KADITO 7 b.g. Petoski – Kadastra (FR) (Stradavinsky) [2002/3 h80, F–: 19s* 19d* 17s 20v⁴ c19d* 19d³ c20g³ Mar 14] leggy gelding: modest hurdler: won novice handicaps at Hereford in November and Warwick (amateurs) in December: created good impression when winning 16-runner novice handicap at Hereford in February on chasing debut: nothing like so fluent when running poorly final start: should stay 2½m: acts on soft going. *R. Dickin*   c101 h96

KADLASS (FR) 8 b.g. Kadounor (FR) – Brave Lass (Ridan) [2002/3 17s² 17m* Apr **h89**
5] compact gelding: fell both starts in points: modest hurdler: off over a year, beaten neck
by Knightsbridge King in novice seller at Hereford: beat same horse by same margin in
similar event three month later, showing more resolution run-in: raced around 2m: acts
on soft and good to firm going. *Mrs D. A. Hamer*

KADOUKO (FR) 10 br.g. Cadoudal (FR) – Perle Bleue (FR) (Iron Duke (FR)) [2002/3 **c99**
c105d, h–: c17s⁵ c16v³ c16s* Mar 6] leggy, lengthy gelding: handicap chaser: best effort **h–**
for good while when winning at Carlisle: stays 2½m: acts on heavy ground: has had
tongue tied: bled from nose final 2001/2 outing: sold 7,200 gns Doncaster May Sales.
J. Howard Johnson

KADOUN (IRE) 6 b.g. Doyoun – Kumta (IRE) (Priolo (USA)) [2002/3 h139: 20s³ **c139**
24s⁴ 24s⁶ 24s⁴ c16s⁵ c20v² c22s* c21v* c24m* Apr 20] leggy gelding: useful hurdler: **h134**
similar form over fences, won maiden at Limerick in February, novice at Leopardstown
(beat Splendour 25 lengths) in March and listed event at Cork (didn't have to be at best to
beat Garvivonnian 2 lengths in 4-runner event) in April: fell twelfth in valuable novice
handicap at Punchestown in late-April: stays 3m: acts on heavy going, probably on good
to firm: often blinkered, as effective when not: formerly none too keen. *M. J. P. O'Brien,
Ireland*

KADOU NONANTAIS (FR) 10 b.g. Cadoudal (FR) – Belle Nonantaise (FR) (Char- **c–**
onville (FR)) [2002/3 c126, h–: c24dᶠ Nov 17] big, rangy gelding: fairly useful chaser: **h–**
12 lb out of handicap, just starting to weaken when falling 2 out in Grade 2 at Haydock,
only outing in 2002/3: probably stays 25f: acts on good to firm and heavy going: blink-
ered/visored: has worn near-side pricker: has sweated: free-going front runner: makes
odd bad mistake. *O. Sherwood*

KAFRI D'AIRY (FR) 5 b.m. Sheyrann – Afrika d'Airy (FR) (Marasali) [2002/3 **c100**
c17v⁴ 19d⁶ 20v⁶ Mar 3] ex-French mare: third foal: half-sister to fairly useful chaser/ **h–**
winning hurdler Ifrak d'Airy (by Laostic), stays 25f, and winning chaser around 2m:
Jikaly d'Airy (by Port Lyautey): dam lightly-raced maiden jumper: fair form over fences
for J. Ortet: little encouragement in 2 starts over hurdles in Britain: raced up to 2½m on
ground softer than good. *R. T. Phillips*

KAGRAM (IRE) 8 ch.g. Roi Danzig (USA) – Mexican Two Step (Gay Fandango **h– p**
(USA)) [2002/3 20g Apr 1] fair form in bumpers in 1999/00: first outing for over 2 years,
shaped as if retaining ability in novice hurdle at Newcastle. *Ferdy Murphy*

KAHUNA (IRE) 6 b.g. Mister Lord (USA) – My Baloo (On Your Mark) [2002/3 **F109**
F16v* F16d² F16g Mar 12] IR £14,000 4-y-o: tall, angular gelding: sixth foal: dam
unraced half-sister to useful hurdler up to 2½m Lucky Baloo: won maiden bumper at
Leopardstown on debut in December: better form when 2½ lengths second of 7 to Storm
Boxer three month later: well beaten in Grade 1 at Cheltenhan. *E. Sheehy, Ireland*

KAID (IRE) 8 b.g. Alzao (USA) – Very Charming (USA) (Vaguely Noble) [2002/3 **c82 §**
c88§, h–§: c17g³ 20d c21m² c20g² c19mᵖᵘ 17s* 19s⁶ 21g Mar 16] angular gelding: poor **h91 §**
maiden chaser: modest handicap hurdler: won seller at Hereford in November: stays 21f:
acts on good to firm and heavy going: visored once (went in snatches): unreliable. *R. Lee*

KAIKOVRA (IRE) 7 ch.g. Toulon – Drefflane Supreme (Rusticaro (FR)) [2002/3 **h103**
h97: 17m⁴ 16g 16g³ 16g² 17m² 16f² Apr 21] fair maiden hurdler: raced around 2m: acts
on good to firm going (won bumper on soft): pulls hard. *Noel T. Chance*

KAISERSTOLZ (GER) 10 b.g. Sure Blade (USA) – Kaisertreue (GER) (Luciano) **c–**
[2002/3 c–, h–: 16m⁵ 20m* 21m Aug 12] good-topped gelding: novice chaser (has been **h101 §**
let down by jumping): fair hurdler: won handicap at Worcester in June, only form since
2000: stays easy 2½m: acts on firm and soft going: tongue tied: unreliable. *Ian Williams*

KAKI CRAZY (FR) 8 b.g. Passing Sale (FR) – Radiante Rose (FR) (Akarad (FR)) **c103 §**
[2002/3 c124§, h–§: c30vᵖᵘ c30s⁵ Mar 4] leggy gelding: fairly useful handicap chaser in **h– §**
2001/2: well below best both starts on return, reluctant virtually from outset on second:
stays 4m: acts on good to firm and heavy going: has won with/without blinkers/visor: a
hard ride and not to be trusted: sold to join M. Hill £1,800 Ascot April Sales. *M. C. Pipe*

KALCA MOME (FR) 5 b.g. En Calcat (FR) – Belle Mome (FR) (Grand Tresor (FR)) **h123**
[2002/3 16m² 16d* 16s* 17s* 16v⁵ 16d* Mar 6] leggy ex-French gelding: fourth foal: half-
brother to 2 winners, including cross-country chaser Grande Mome (by Bright Dick):
dam unraced: twice-raced on Flat, won 1½m non-thoroughbred event (blinkered) at
Jallais for P. Bidon: fairly useful hurdler: won novices at Haydock in November and

Taunton in January and handicap at Wincanton (much best effort, came from last to beat Rainbows Aglitter by 6 lengths) in March: should stay beyond 17f: acts on soft ground: reportedly distressed third start. *P. J. Hobbs*

KALD RIVER (FR)　　4 b.g. River Mist (USA) – Komomo San (FR) (Niniski (USA))　　**F106 p**
[2002/3 F16s* Mar 16] fifth foal: half-brother to winning French 2m hurdler Gris Fer (by Prince Melchior): dam, maiden on Flat, out of smart chaser Furdanne: failed to complete in 2 points: looked useful prospect when winning 4-y-o bumper at Limerick in March by 12 lengths from Candy Girl. *P. M. J. Doyle, Ireland*

KALIC D'ALM (FR)　　5 b.g. Passing Sale (FR) – Bekaa II (FR) (Djarvis (FR))　　**F81**
[2002/3 F17s⁵ F17sᵖᵘ Jan 28] 6,560 4-y-o: tall gelding: second foal: dam maiden, from family of Stayers' Hurdle winner Cyborgo and Champion Hurdle winner Hors La Loi III: pulled hard when fifth of 9 in bumper at Folkestone on debut: tailed off when pulled up in similar event at Taunton 2 months later. *Miss Suzy Smith*

KALI DES OBEAUX (FR)　　5 b.m. Panoramic – Alpaga (FR) (Le Pontet (FR))　　**c100 +**
[2002/3 c18g⁴ c17g* c18d³ c20s* 16d² 16s³ 19d² 21d 16g 24m² Apr 10] compact mare: 　　**h103**
fifth foal: half-sister to winning cross-country chaser by Saint Cyrien: dam ran 3 times over hurdles in France: won 3 of 4 starts in non-thoroughbred events over fences, at Royan La Palmyre and Chalons-sur-Marne in May and Auteuil (final outing for G. Macaire) in June: fair novice hurdler: stays 3m: acts on soft and good to firm going: sold 20,000 gns Doncaster May Sales. *A. King*

KALIKO BOY　　7 b.g. Perpendicular – Reddy Girl (Doctor Wall) [2002/3 F17m Jun 1]　　**F—**
fourth foal: dam winning 2m hurdler: well held in maiden bumper on debut. *G. J. Smith*

KALINGALINGA　　6 b.g. Zafonic (USA) – Bell Toll (High Line) [2002/3 h–: 17dᵖᵘ　　**h—**
May 14] lengthy gelding: won over 1m at 4 yrs: showed nothing in 3 starts over hurdles. *B. J. Curley*

KALINNJAR (FR)　　6 b.g. Barathea (IRE) – Kalajana (USA) (Green Dancer (USA))　　**h86**
[2002/3 19s 17d⁶ 17d 17gᶠ 16g 18g² 20gᵘʳ 16m* 17g² 16m³ Oct 30] leggy gelding: runner-up 3 times around 1½m in France at 3 yrs for A. de Royer Dupre: bought €11,000 Goffs February (2002) Sale: modest novice hurdler: won seller at Hexham in October: may prove best around 2m: acts on good to firm going: blinkered last 7 starts: usually tongue tied: races freely. *G. J. McKeever, Ireland*

KALIVAR　　5 ch.m. Gunner B – Promitto (Roaring Riva) [2002/3 F73: F17s Oct 28]　　**F—**
poor form at best in bumpers. *Miss K. Marks*

KALKO DU CHARMIL (FR)　　6 b.g. Kadalko (FR) – Licada (FR) (A Tempo (FR))　　**c—**
[2002/3 h–, F88: c16gᵘʳ c19g⁶ c18gᶠ Apr 13] tall, leggy gelding: some promise on debut 　　**h—**
in bumper: let down by jumping over hurdles and fences: left Mrs M. Reveley after chasing debut. *G. Macaire, France*

KALLASSOR (FR)　　5 b.g. Assessor (IRE) – Balladine (FR) (Rivelago (FR)) [2002/3　　**h75**
h75: 16m 26gᵘʳ 22m³ 25d⁴ 21gᵖᵘ Mar 12] lengthy gelding: 13f winner on Flat: poor novice hurdler: stays 2¾m: acts on firm going: visored last 4 starts. *P. C. Ritchens*

KALOU (GER)　　5 b.g. Law Society (USA) – Kompetenz (IRE) (Be My Guest (USA))　　**h—**
[2002/3 20d⁶ 16d 20s Jan 30] useful at best on Flat (stays 1½m) in Germany for A. Trybuhl: well held in Britain, including in 3 novice hurdles. *B. J. Curley*

KALUGA (IRE)　　5 ch.m. Tagula (IRE) – Another Baileys (Deploy) [2002/3 h83: 19s　　**h—**
16d Dec 26] workmanlike mare: poor novice hurdler: stays 2¾m: acts on soft going. *P. R. Rodford*

KAMLOOPS (IRE)　　8 b.g. Insan (USA) – Furry Lady (Furry Glen) [2002/3 c16dᵖᵘ　　**c—**
Jan 24] rather sparely-made gelding: lightly-raced novice hurdler, modest at best: report-　　**h—**
edly lame on chasing debut: should stay beyond 2m. *Ferdy Murphy*

KANDJAR D'ALLIER (FR)　　5 gr.g. Royal Charter (FR) – Miss Akarad (FR) (Aka-　　**c141**
rad (FR)) [2002/3 c20vᶠ c17d⁴ c20s 18d² 18s c19sᶠ c17v* 18s³ 19s³ c21s⁵ Apr 4] fifth 　　**h122**
foal: half-brother to 2 winners, including hurdler Harmonie d'Allier (by Altayan): dam middle-distance winner in France: thrice-raced on Flat at 3 yrs: fairly useful maiden hurdler, improved form when third in minor event at Auteuil in March: useful chaser on his day, successful at same course in 4-y-o minor event in November and valuable Prix Saint Sauveur (handicap) in May, beating Saint Charles 6 lengths in latter: stays 21f: raced on going softer than good (acts on heavy): sometimes let down by his jumping: sold privately to join M. Harris. *J. Bertran de Balanda, France*

KANDLES-KORNER   9 b.g. Gold Dust – My Kizzy (The Ditton) [2002/3 c20g^{ur} c–
May 17] poor pointer: unseated first on hunter chase debut. *J. W. Tudor*

KANDY FOUR (NZ)   8 ch.g. Zeditave (AUS) – Executive Suite (NZ) (Western   c104
Symphony (USA)) [2002/3 c95, h–: c16m^2 c21m^2 c20s* c20d* c21m^F c20g^2 Apr 25]   h–
workmanlike gelding: fair chaser: won novices at Market Rasen (weak event) in July and
Perth (handicap) in August: first run for 8 months, good second to Glynn Dingle in novice
handicap at latter course final start: stays 2½m: acts on soft and good to firm going:
free-going sort: not always fluent jumper. *P. F. Nicholls*

KANONA   12 ch.g. Gunner B – Pugilistic (Hard Fought) [2002/3 c20m Jun 1] winning   c–
pointer: no form outside that sphere. *David F. Smith*   h–

KANSAS CITY (FR)   5 b.m. Lute Antique (FR) – Tenacity (FR) (Prove It Baby   c83
(USA)) [2002/3 c18g* c17d c18g5 c18g6 c16m^4 c16g^3 c16d^3 c21s^F c19v^3 16m^{pu} c17m^{pu} h–
Apr 21] lengthy mare: fourth foal: dam, 1½m winner, from family of Grand Steeple-
Chase de Paris winner Isopani: thrice-raced on Flat at 3 yrs: won non-thoroughbred event
at Cluny in May on chasing debut, left E. Vagne after fourth outing: poor form over fences
in Britain: no show on hurdling debut: stays 19f: acts on heavy going. *M. F. Harris*

KAOLIN DE PERCHE (FR)   5 b.g. Luchiroverte (IRE) – Craven II (FR) (Rhap-   h84 +
sodien) [2002/3 19d 25d^F Mar 8] 12,000 3-y-o: sturdy gelding: second foal: dam placed
over 9f: second start in novice hurdles, dictated pace and still every chance when fell 2
out in weak 4-runner event at Warwick. *C. P. Morlock*

KAPGARDE (FR)   4 b.c. Garde Royale – Kaprika (FR) (Cadoudal (FR)) [2002/3   c139 p
15v^4 15s* 17d^2 18s* 18s^6 19v^3 Apr 26] French-trained colt: fifth foal: half-brother to   h130
several winners, including very smart hurdler/smart chaser Geos (by Pistolet Bleu), stays
2½m, and fairly useful hurdler/chaser around 2m Cyborson (by Cyborg): dam, minor
15f hurdle winner, also 1¼m winner on Flat: useful hurdler, won juveniles at Auteuil in
November and March, beating Cheler ¾ length in Group 3 Prix Jacques d'Indy on second
occasion: good third to Nickname in Group 2 there in April: excellent start over fences at
Auteuil following month, winning minor event and neck second to Ice Mood in Group 1:
will stay beyond 2½m: raced mainly on soft/heavy going: good prospect for staying
novices chases in 2003/4. *G. Macaire, France*

KAPOK (FR)   7 b.g. Kaldoun (FR) – Karannja (USA) (Shahrastani (USA)) [2002/3   c122 §
h125§: 20g^2 16s^6 c17s^3 c17s c16s^5 20s 16s^2 16d Feb 23] leggy gelding: fairly useful   h122 §
handicap hurdler: similar form on first of 3 starts over fences: stays 2½m: acts on heavy
going: tried blinkered: often finds little: unreliable. *E. J. O'Grady, Ireland*

KAPPELHOFF (IRE)   6 b.g. Mukaddamah (USA) – Miss Penguin (General Assem-   h–
bly (USA)) [2002/3 F83: 20v^{ur} 18v 17v 22g 25m^{ur} Mar 31] unfurnished gelding: well
held all completed starts over hurdles. *Mrs L. Richards*

KAPSKA (FR)   5 b.g. Silver Rainbow – Chapska (FR) (Le Pontet (FR)) [2002/3 18s^{pu} h–
16m Apr 2] first foal: half-brother to middle-distance winner by Saint Preuil: dam little
sign of ability: no promise in 2 novice hurdles. *M. J. Roberts*

KARADIN (FR)   9 b.g. Akarad (FR) – In River (FR) (In Fijar (USA)) [2002/3 h97:   c102
c17g^{pu} c16s^2 c16g^4 c21m c21f* c24m^2 Mar 18] workmanlike gelding: winning hurdler: h–
fair novice chaser: won at Newton Abbot in August: probably best short of 3m: unraced
on heavy going, acts on any other: sold 7,000 gns Doncaster May Sales. *R. H. Buckler*

KARAHISAR (IRE)   4 b.g. Common Grounds – Karamiyna (IRE) (Shernazar)   F–
[2002/3 F16v Jan 29] IR £3,000 2-y-o: third foal: half-brother to 1¼m and 13f winner
Kariyfi (by Doyoun): dam, useful French 1m to 11f winner, sister to very smart 1¼m filly
Kartajana: tailed off in bumper on debut. *N. P. McCormack*

KARAJAN (IRE)   6 b.g. Fairy King (USA) – Dernier Cri (Slip Anchor) [2002/3 h90:   c90
c16v^2 c20v^3 c20s^5 Dec 16] angular gelding: modest hurdler: similar form in novice   h–
chases: stays 21f: acts on heavy and good to firm going: consistent. *G. M. Moore*

KARAKUM   4 b.g. Mtoto – Magongo (Be My Chief (USA)) [2002/3 16s 17m^5 16f^6 h–
Oct 24] fair form at best at 2 yrs: well held over hurdles. *A. J. Chamberlain*

KARENCY (FR)   5 ch.g. Video Rock (FR) – Reina Tennise (FR) (Quart de Vin (FR))   c71
[2002/3 17s c16g^4 Mar 2] angular gelding: half-brother to 5 winners, including chaser up
to 23f Harry Tennis (by Luchiroverte): dam maiden chaser: unplaced on Flat in French
Provinces at 4 yrs for F. Nicolle: well held on hurdling debut: 19 lengths fourth of 6 in
maiden chase at Huntingdon, disputing lead until 3 out: will be suited by 2½m+. *Miss
H. C. Knight*

KARISABAN   4 b.g. Hatim (USA) – Swiss Beauty (Ballacashtal (CAN)) [2002/3   **F—**
F17d F16g Apr 1] second foal: dam winning pointer 1½m winner on Flat: tailed off in 2
bumpers. *R. Johnson*

KARLY FLIGHT (FR)   5 b.m. Mansonnien (FR) – Karmyn Flight (FR) (Pure   **c133 p**
Flight (USA)) [2002/3 c132p, h123: c20s* 19d⁵ 18s* 18s* 19s* 20v* 20s* Apr 21]   **h153**
        He who hesitates is lost, so the old saw goes, and, judged on evidence in the
Grande Course de Haies d'Auteuil, he who changes his mind between the last two
flights is lost as well. Hot favourite Karly Flight, bidding for her eighth win in a
row, had led in customary fashion for much of the race until her rider allowed
Nobody Told Me to go on four from home; two out, Karly Flight was still going
well within herself, the only danger looking to be Nobody Told Me, those behind
having been seen off before the straight, but then Karly Flight's regular rider
Philippe Sourzac made a move, not forward but diagonally, switching Karly Flight
from behind Nobody Told Me across to the opposite side of the track. Realising too
late the threat Nobody Told Me posed, Sourzac's confidence dissolved into panic
soon after the last and he became unbalanced. Unable to claw back the ground
given away, Karly Flight went down by two lengths, performing well below the
form that had seen her win the two most important races in the build-up to the
Grande Course, form that established her as the top hurdler currently racing in
France (Baracouda being campaigned in Britain and Laveron retired to stud).
        After winning on her Flat debut in March, Karly Flight had gained impres-
sive victories in both the Prix Leon Rambaud in April and the Prix La Barka in
late-May, beating Great Love by fifteen and ten lengths respectively. Great Love
wasn't in the field for the Grande Course and Karly Flight's pari-mutuel odds—she
was paying €1.20 for a euro stake at the off—reflected her perceived superiority
over her rivals. The Grande Course was only the sixth defeat of Karly Flight's
career. She had been beaten four times over hurdles, twice in the first half of 2001
by the precocious Kotkita, and then at Pau in January 2002 and later that year in the
Group 1 Prix Alain du Breil, the top four-year-old hurdle, run on the same card as
the Grande Course. Whereas her defeat a year on was a shock, her fifth place behind
Great Love in the Alain du Breil was a good effort on her form over hurdles up to
that point. When Karly Flight was returned to Auteuil in the autumn, she was
clearly improved and won all her four starts, showing form verging on smart. She
beat Foreman in a minor event, then gained two victories over Saint des Saints in
Group 3 events before beating Foreman, Kotkita and Saint des Saints decisively in
the Group 1 Prix Renaud du Vivier the Grande Course de Haies des Quatre Ans.
        Before the Alain du Breil, Karly Flight had four outings over fences at
Auteuil, winning three times, including in the Group 2 Prix Jean Stern and the
Group 1 Prix Ferdinand Dufaure, showing useful form in the former but getting
away with jumping right and generally not being fluent when beating the same

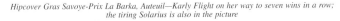

Hipcover Gras Savoye-Prix La Barka, Auteuil—Karly Flight on her way to seven wins in a row;
the tiring Solarius is also in the picture

rivals in the Dufaure. Karly Flight's jumping also let her down when meeting her only defeat over fences, in April 2002, though strangely a similar manoeuvre by Sourzac to that undertaken in the Grande Course played its part as well.

Karly Flight (FR) (b.m. 1998)	Mansonnien (FR) (ch 1984)	Tip Moss (ch 1972)	Luthier
			Top Twig
		Association (ch 1977)	Margouillat
			La Soupe
	Karmyn Flight (FR) (b 1980)	Pure Flight (b 1970)	Nearctic
			Maid of Flight
		Karmisyn (b 1974)	Baldric
			Embellie

Karly Flight isn't impressive to look at, being leggy and rather sparely made in appearance, and she seems unlikely to be sent back over fences. She is a more fluent jumper of hurdles than she used to be. Karly Flight is the best of the progeny of smart mile-and-a-half performer Mansonnien, his other notable winners including the leading 1999/00 juvenile Grand Seigneur and two winners of France's top handicap chase the Prix du President de La Republique, Le Cid and Subehargues. Karly Flight is the tenth foal of her dam, the six-furlong winner Karmyn Flight. Plenty of the others have made their mark over jumps, probably the best of them the useful hurdler/chaser up to two and a half miles King Flight (by General Assembly), a durable sort who finished second in one of Italy's top hurdle races, the Gran Corsa Siepi di Roma in February. Another foal Green Flight (by Galant Vert) was a fairly useful hurdler and winning chaser up to nineteen furlongs while yet another, Sunday Flight (by Johnny O'Day), won eleven times at up to two and a half miles in the Provinces, the most valuable of those successes coming at Loudeac. Karly Flight stays three miles and a furlong and it hardly needs adding that, as an Auteuil regular, she has raced exclusively on going softer than good. *A. Chaille-Chaille, France*

KARO DE VINDECY (FR) 5 b.g. Mollicone Junior (FR) – Preves du Forez (FR) **h68** (Quart de Vin (FR)) [2002/3 16d⁴ 17s⁶ 17s 16s 20g Mar 29] leggy gelding: second known foal: dam ran twice: thrice-raced on Flat: fourth of 8 finishers in non-thoroughbred event at Vichy on hurdling debut, final start for B. Barbier: soundly beaten all 4 outings in Britain: tongue tied. *M. D. Hammond*

KAROLENA BAY 6 ch.m. Karinga Bay – Owena Deep (Deep Run) [2002/3 F75: **h88** 16d⁶ 16g* 20dᵖᵘ 20mᶠ 26m* 23m⁵ 24gᵖᵘ Nov 20] angular mare: modest hurdler: won novices at Stratford (mares seller) in May and Southwell (handicap) in July: still in contention when pulled up (reportedly lame) final outing: stays 3¼m: acts on good to firm going: has hinted at temperament. *N. A. Twiston-Davies*

KARZHANG 11 b.g. Rakaposhi King – Smokey Baby (Sagaro) [2002/3 c–, h–: c20m⁶ **c75** Mar 19] workmanlike gelding: maiden hurdler: winning pointer: never a factor on **h–** completed start in hunter chases: has had tongue tied. *Mrs C. J. Robinson*

KASALAN (IRE) 5 br.m. Hawkstone (IRE) – Larry's Law (IRE) (Law Society **F–** (USA)) [2002/3 F16g Jan 18] sparely-made mare: fifth foal: sister to fair hurdler up to 27f Howdydoody: dam unraced: pulled very hard when well held in bumper on debut. *K. A. Ryan*

KASSALA (FR) 7 b.m. Phantom Breeze – Tip Land (FR) (Tip Moss (FR)) [2002/3 **c117 §** c105, h–: c16gᵖᵘ c17m* c16dᵖᵘ c16g³ c16m³ c17m³ c16g² c16m* c17g⁴ c17d⁴ Oct 31] **h–** well-made mare: winning hurdler: fairly useful handicap chaser: won at Stratford in June and Hereford in October: long way below form last 2 starts: raced around 2m: acts on heavy and good to firm going: sometimes let down by jumping: has failed to impress with attitude: one to treat with caution. *A. King*

KATAHOLIC 4 b.c. Bluegrass Prince (IRE) – Langton Herring (Nearly A Hand) **h–** [2002/3 17f⁶ 16m Apr 22] half-brother to 2 winning hurdlers, including modest Lago di Levico (by Pelder), stays 2¾m: no form on Flat or over hurdles. *G. A. Ham*

KATARINO (FR) 8 b.g. Pistolet Bleu (IRE) – Katevana (FR) (Cadoudal (FR)) [2002/3 **c139** c136, h–: c21v² c21s⁵ c24g⁵ c36dᵘʳ Apr 5] leggy gelding: has had breathing operation: **h–** one-time smart hurdler: useful handicap chaser: creditable efforts in valuable events at

Cheltenham first 3 starts: towards rear when unseating fifteenth (Chair) in Grand National at Aintree: stays 3m: acts on good to firm and heavy going. *N. J. Henderson*

KATE'S COTTAGE   7 b.m. Faustus (USA) – Try G'S (Hotfoot) [2002/3 F68: F16f[6] Oct 10] leggy mare: poor form in bumpers. *R. Ford*   **F–**

KATES IVY HILL (IRE)   9 b.m. King of Shannon – Raj Kumari (Vitiges (FR)) [2002/3 c–x, h–: c25s[pu] Mar 7] good-topped mare: no sign of ability. *Mark Doyle*   **c– x**   **h–**

KATES SON (IRE)   6 ch.g. Fayruz – Kates Choice (IRE) (Taufan (USA)) [2002/3 h–: 16m Jun 19] sturdy gelding: modest maiden on Flat (stays 1¼m): little form over hurdles: visored only outing in 2002/3: has raced freely. *Noel T. Chance*   **h–**

KATHAKALI (IRE)   6 b.g. Dancing Dissident (USA) – Shes A Dancer (IRE) (Alzao (USA)) [2002/3 16s 17s 16s 26s[pu] Mar 7] fair on all-weather, modest on turf on Flat (stays easy 1¼m), sold out of S. Dow's stable £5,500 Ascot June Sales: no form over hurdles: has worn cheekpieces. *C. J. Bennett*   **h–**

KATHELLA (IRE)   6 b.m. Fourstars Allstar (USA) – Niat Supreme (IRE) (Supreme Leader) [2002/3 F–: 17m 17m 16m 19s 19s[pu] 19m[pu] Apr 15] no sign of ability. *N. G. Ayliffe*   **h–**

KATIE BROON   6 ch.m. Minster Son – Gale Storm (Midland Gayle) [2002/3 F17d F16g Mar 29] second foal: dam winning pointer: behind in 2 bumpers. *Joseph Brown*   **F–**

KATIE BUCKERS (IRE)   9 ch.m. Yashgan – Glenkins (Furry Glen) [2002/3 c93, h–: c20d* c24s[4] c24v[4] c25s[pu] c25d c20s[pu] Feb 12] medium-sized mare: modest handicap chaser: won mares event at Uttoxeter in May: off 6 months and out of sorts after, reportedly broke blood vessel final outing: stays 3¼m: raced on good going or softer (acts on heavy). *K. C. Bailey*   **c96 d**   **h–**

KATIES DOLPHIN (IRE)   5 ch.m. Dolphin Street (FR) – Kuwah (IRE) (Be My Guest (USA)) [2002/3 16v[6] 16s 16g 16d[4] 21s[3] 20g[6] Mar 25] maiden on Flat, sold out of A. Berry's stable 1,500 gns Doncaster October Sales: poor maiden hurdler: tongue tied last 3 outings: has hung left under pressure. *R. Johnson*   **h77**

KATIES GENIE   5 b.m. Syrtos – Reine de La Chasse (FR) (Ti King (FR)) [2002/3 17g Mar 18] no form on Flat at 3 yrs for B. Doran: well held in novice seller on hurdling debut. *M. C. Pipe*   **h–**

KATIES HERO   5 b.g. Pontevecchio Notte – Kindly Lady (Kind of Hush) [2002/3 F17d F17g Apr 19] first foal: dam winning pointer: no show in 2 bumpers, blinkered in second. *J. D. Frost*   **F–**

KATIES TIGHT JEANS   9 b.m. Green Adventure (USA) – Haraka Sasa (Town And Country) [2002/3 h–, F–: 16s[pu] 16s[pu] Dec 6] no form over hurdles. *R. E. Peacock*   **h–**

KATIKI (FR)   6 b.g. Cadoudal (FR) – Tikiti Dancer (FR) (Fabulous Dancer (USA)) [2002/3 18s* 20s[5] 20v* 20s[rtr] Apr 21] compact gelding: useful juvenile hurdler in 2000/1: returned better than ever from year's absence in 2002/3, smart form when winning Group 2 Prix Leon Olry-Roederer at Auteuil in November by 4 lengths from Laveron: also successful in minor event there earlier in season: good third, staying on, to Nobody Told Me in Grande Course de Haies d'Auteuil in June: stays 25f: raced mainly on soft/heavy going: refused to race once, and not one to trust implicitly. *J-P. Gallorini, France*   **h146 §**

KATINKA   10 b.m. Rymer – Millymeeta (New Brig) [2002/3 h–: 20d[pu] Apr 21] lengthy mare: won 2 points in March (awarded race first occasion, 4 other finishers took wrong course): no form over hurdles: tried tongue tied. *A. M. Thomson*   **h–**

KATIYPOUR (IRE)   6 ch.g. Be My Guest (USA) – Katiyfa (Auction Ring (USA)) [2002/3 h73: 16f[5] 16m[pu] Jun 1] fair on Flat (stays 11f, carries head high): poor form over hurdles, visored final outing (failed to settle): raced at 2m: sold 10,000 gns Doncaster September Sales, in good form on all-weather for T. D. Barron subsequently. *P. R. Webber*   **h83**

KATTEGAT   7 b.g. Slip Anchor – Kirsten (Kris) [2002/3 c88, h104d: 16s[3] 19s[3] 20v[5] 20v[3] 21v[3] 24g[F] Feb 27] leggy gelding: novice chaser: fair handicap hurdler: should stay beyond 2½m: acts on heavy going: has broken blood vessel: not easiest of rides (has carried head awkwardly), ridden by 7-lb claiming amateur in 2002/3. *Mrs H. M. Bridges*   **c–**   **h101**

KATY THE DUCK (IRE)   8 br.m. Over The River (FR) – Zagliarelle (FR) (Rose Laurel) [2002/3 c–, h–: 17g[2] 21g[5] 21g 17g* 17m 20g[6] Apr 21] poor hurdler: won mares claimer at Bangor in March: probably stays 21f. *R. J. Price*   **c–**   **h69**

KAUROA MAIL (NZ)   9 b.g. First Norman (USA) – Penny Letter (NZ) (One Pound Sterling) [2002/3 h68: 22f[pu] Mar 29] leggy gelding: poor novice hurdler, very stiff task   **h–**

on return from 16-month absence: stays 2½m: acts on soft and good to firm going. *B. P. J. Baugh*

KAUSSE DE THAIX (FR)   5 ch.g. Iris Noir (FR) – Etoile de Thaix (FR) (Lute Anti-   **F92** que (FR)) [2002/3 F16s⁴ F16g Feb 8] useful-looking gelding: first foal: dam lightly-raced half-sister to fairly useful 2½m chaser Imperial de Thaix: easily better effort in bumpers (highly tried second start) when 9 lengths fourth of 20 to Hawk's Landing at Kempton. *A. M. Hales*

KAYTASH   4 b.f. Silverdale Knight – Lady Swift (Jalmood (USA)) [2002/3 17d⁵   **h–** 17mᵖᵘ 16g Sep 26] no sign of ability on Flat or over hurdles. *K. W. Hogg, Isle of Man*

KAYTEE DIAMOND   7 b.m. Afzal – Lasses Nightshade (Deadly Nightshade)   **h– x** [2002/3 22dᶠ 18sᶠ 16gᵖᵘ Mar 23] eighth foal: half-sister to several winners, including fair chaser Spinning Steel (by Kinglet), stays 3m, and 2m hurdler Nothingtodowithme (by Relkino): dam inconsistent winning pointer: yet to complete over hurdles, pulled up after virtually refusing at first 2 flights final one. *Dr P. Pritchard*

KEANEO (IRE)   8 b.g. Aristocracy – Nessa-Pride (IRE) (Balboa) [2002/3 c73, h85:   **c103 x** c16dᶠ c21gᵘʳ 19m⁶ c19m* c19g² 26g* c20d* Nov 12] workmanlike gelding: fair chaser: **h80 +** won selling handicap at Hereford in October and amateur minor event at Southwell (tended to jump right) in November: poor form over hurdles: won conditional jockeys minor event at Hereford in between: effective at 19f, and stays 3¼m: acts on good to firm and good to soft going: has broken blood vessel: often let down by jumping over fences. *N. A. Twiston-Davies*

KEDGE ANCHOR MAN   12 b.g. Bustino – Jenny Mere (Brigadier Gerard) [2002/3   **c–** c–, h100: 22s² 22s 22d³ 20s⁵ 26g⁵ Mar 12] lengthy gelding: modest hurdler, below form   **h100 d** after reappearance: stays 23f: raced mainly on good going or softer (acts on soft): races prominently: claimer ridden in 2002/3. *N. A. Gaselee*

KEDON (CZE)   8 gr.g. Mill Pond (FR) – Kelda (FR) (Northern Baby (CAN)) [2002/3   **c?** c21g³ c22g² c23g* c29s² c34v³ c31d Nov 15] medium-sized gelding: winning hurdler: **h–** successful several times over fences in Czech Republic, including at Svetla Hora in July: 16/1, ninth of 12 finishers in valuable cross-country event at Cheltenham final start: stays well. *Josef Vana II, Czech Republic*

KEEGAN BEARNAIS (FR)   5 b.g. Tropular – Sofyland (FR) (Kashneb (FR))   **c?** [2002/3 c19s⁴ 22dᵖᵘ 20m³ 16mᵖᵘ 20gᵖᵘ Apr 21] fourth foal: half-brother to 2 winners,   **h60** including useful chaser/winning hurdler Elan Bearnais (by Nellio): stayed 25f: dam won 21f chase/over middle distances on Flat: in frame 2 of 3 starts over fences in French Provinces, sold out of J-P. Totain's stable €24,000 Goffs July Sale after reappearance: maiden hurdler, found little only completed start in Britain: tried blinkered/in cheekpieces: sold 3,500 gns Doncaster May Sales. *A. M. Hales*

KEEN LEADER (IRE)   7 b.g. Supreme Leader – Keen Gale (IRE) (Strong Gale)   **c151 p** [2002/3 h146p: c24dᶠ c22d* c25d* c24s* c24g⁵ Mar 12]   **h–**

     Jackdaws Castle sent out three winners at the Cheltenham Festival and four at Aintree's Grand National meeting, but not everything went right for the stable, particularly at Cheltenham. A viral infection—which ultimately severely restricted operations, the stable having only one winner after Aintree—began to affect some of the horses in the build-up to the Festival. At least two of the stable's big-race hopes, Intersky Falcon in the Champion Hurdle and Keen Leader in the Royal & SunAlliance Chase, were found to be sick on their return from Cheltenham and neither was seen out again. Keen Leader started favourite for the Royal & SunAlliance but, after jumping sketchily, he was quickly in trouble after a mistake four out, his rider getting little response when the horse was asked for his effort. Keen Leader trailed home fifth of six finishers, almost forty lengths behind the winner One Knight. With the trainer unable to offer any explanation on the day, the Cheltenham stewards decided not to hold an inquiry into Keen Leader's running, but ordered him to be routine dope-tested.

     Keen Leader's switch to fences was eagerly anticipated after he developed into a very smart novice over hurdles the previous season, winning three races and suffering his only defeat when falling at the second last, still going well, in the Royal & SunAlliance Hurdle. Keen Leader, the winner of one of his two starts in points in Ireland in 2001, got off to an inauspicious start to his novice-chase career,

Weatherbys Towton Novices' Chase, Wetherby—Keen Leader puts up a smart performance

with another fall at Cheltenham when hot favourite in November. Keen Leader clipped the eighth fence and crumpled on landing but connections did not seem unduly perturbed—the horse had reportedly been schooling really well—and Keen Leader was turned out again only two days later in a similar event at Haydock. Keen Leader made amends in tremendous style, jumping well in the main and readily drawing clear to beat the fairly useful Indalo by twenty-six lengths. Keen Leader came back with a nicked artery in a hind leg which took time to heal. His next appearance was scheduled to be in the Dipper Chase in January, eventually abandoned because of frost after being transferred from waterlogged Newcastle to Haydock. He wasn't seen on a racecourse again until February when romping home again at odds on in the Weatherbys Towton Novices' Chase at Wetherby. Cruising to the front approaching four out, Keen Leader won by twenty-four lengths from Jungle Jinks, putting up a smart performance, though the impression was spoiled when Keen Leader's jumping became less fluent once he was ahead, particularly so at the last two fences where he failed to keep straight. Keen Leader made his final appearance before the Cheltenham Festival in the Amlin Reynoldstown Chase at Ascot, another course that takes plenty of jumping. The Reynoldstown carried bonuses totalling £100,000 if the winner went on to add the Royal & SunAlliance Chase (the £70,000 bonus for the winning owner, added to the winning prize-money for both races, would have nearly doubled the owner's prize-money haul). Keen Leader won the Reynoldstown by a distance from Whereareyounow, though the race was less informative than it would have been had French-trained Jair du

Cochet not departed four out, just as the race was about to start in earnest. The two principals seemed to be travelling equally well at the time and Jair du Cochet went on to finish second in the Royal & SunAlliance, a race in which he was over-confidently ridden and really should have won.

Keen Leader (IRE) (b.g. 1996)	Supreme Leader (b 1982)	Bustino (b 1971)	Busted
			Ship Yard
		Princess Zena (b 1975)	Habitat
			Guiding Light
	Keen Gale (IRE) (b 1989)	Strong Gale (br 1975)	Lord Gayle
			Sterntau
		Keening (b 1969)	Bally Joy
			Keenogue

The tall, angular, rather raw-boned Keen Leader, who has stringhalt, is a strapping chaser who looks the type to make his mark at championship level in the next season. He is clearly the apple of his trainer's eye and there was talk for a time after the Reynoldstown of his being saddled for the Gold Cup—for which he was priced at around 10/1 ante-post betting—rather than the SunAlliance. 'He was a bit weak in his days as a novice hurdler but I think he'll develop into a Gold Cup horse,' said O'Neill. 'He's very deceptive, lolloping along with his tongue hanging out, you think he's only walking until you see others off the bridle behind him.' Keen Leader remains the only winner so far for his dam, the unraced Keen Gale, who is out of Keening, a fairly useful hurdler effective at up to three miles and also a sister to a useful staying chaser in Tommy Joe and a half-sister to another useful chaser in Keengaddy. Keen Leader's great grandam Keenogue is a sister to a useful Irish chaser in King Vulgan, winner of the Leopardstown Chase and placed in the Irish Grand National. Keen Gale's 2000 gelding by Alphabatim fetched €38,000 at the 2003 Derby Sale and she had another colt by Supreme Leader in 2002. The strong-galloping Keen Leader will stay beyond twenty-five furlongs, the longest distance he has run over so far. He has yet to race on anything firmer than the good going he encountered at the latest Festival—his rider was inclined at first to blame the ground—and he may always need conditions on the soft side to be seen to best

Amlin Reynoldstown Novices' Chase, Ascot—
not so fluent four out, as Jair du Cochet (far side) is about to depart

Mrs Stewart Catherwood's "Keen Leader"

advantage. One silver lining to the cloud over his Cheltenham performance is that
Keen Leader will start the next season on a relatively handy mark for a horse of his
potential. The Hennessy Cognac Gold Cup at Newbury, where the galloping course
would suit him, might prove a tempting first target. *Jonjo O'Neill*

KEEN TO THE LAST (FR) 11 ch.g. Keen – Derniere Danse (Gay Mecene (USA))   **c99**
[2002/3 c101, h91: c24m* c25m² May 29] angular gelding: modest handicap hurdler: fair   **h–**
chaser: won handicap at Southwell in May: stays 25f: acts on heavy and good to firm
going: visored once. *Mrs S. J. Smith*

KEEPATEM (IRE)   7 ch.g. Be My Native (USA) – Ariannrun (Deep Run) [2002/3   **h122**
20s 20s 16s 22s⁵ 24s* 19v⁴ 24s* 24g³ Apr 3] workmanlike gelding: fairly useful handicap hurdler, off 20 months before reappearance: won at Leopardstown in January and
Punchestown (by head from Poker Pal) in February: in good shape, ran well when 2
lengths third of 22 to Carlovent in valuable event at Aintree, nearest finish: better at 3m
than shorter: raced mainly on soft/heavy going. *M. F. Morris, Ireland*

KEEPER'S CALL (IRE) 11 b.g. Mandalus – Thistletopper (Le Bavard (FR)) [2002/3   **c–**
c94: c31d⁵ Apr 25] good-topped gelding: useful hunter chaser in 1999: lightly raced and
fair form at best since: won 3-runner point in March: should stay beyond 3¼m: acts on
good to soft going. *Mrs V. J. Makin*

KEEPERS MEAD (IRE)   5 ch.g. Aahsaylad – Runaway Pilot (Cheval) [2002/3   **h68**
F18d⁶ 20sᶠ 18s⁶ 18gᵖᵘ Mar 17] second foal: dam maiden Irish pointer: sixth of 14 in   **F89**
maiden bumper at Plumpton on debut: well-beaten sixth to No Collusion at Fontwell on
completed start in novice hurdles: should be suited by at least 2½m. *R. H. Alner*

KEEP IKIS   9 ch.m. Anshan – Santee Sioux (Dancing Brave (USA)) [2002/3 19g⁴ 19g   **h66**
25g⁶ 24g Feb 12] angular mare: fair stayer on Flat: poor over hurdles: should stay well:
tried in cheekpieces/blinkers: sold 900 gns Doncaster March Sales. *Mrs M. Reveley*

KEEP ON RUNNING (FR) 5 ch.g. Beyssac (FR) – Kiruna V (FR) (Thalian) [2002/3 **h109** 19s* 20s 24mᵖᵘ Mar 21] lengthy gelding: half-brother to smart 4-y-o chaser Tamarix (by Kouban) and middle-distance winners by Le Frimas and Djarvis: dam winning chaser up to 2½m: won novice hurdle at Hereford in December on debut by 14 lengths: most disappointing both starts after, proving a handful either beforehand or during race. *A. King*

KEEP ON SKI 5 b.g. Petoski – Keep On Dancing (Crooner) [2002/3 F17d F17s **h–** 20mᵖᵘ 20dᵖᵘ Apr 9] sturdy gelding: second known foal: dam of little account: no sign **F–** of ability in bumpers (for A. Streeter) or over hurdles: tried visored. *Mrs J. Candlish*

KEEP OUT OF DEBT 6 b.m. Castle Keep – Deep In Debt (Deep Run) [2002/3 **h–** F16sᵖᵘ F16mᵖᵘ F17f⁶ 17gᵖᵘ Nov 7] smallish mare: eighth foal: sister to winning hurdler **F–** Keep Out of Debt, stayed 2¾m, and half-sister to fair hurdler Never In Debt (by Nicholas Bill), stays 3m: dam, 2m hurdle winner, out of half-sister to useful chaser The Lady's Master: showed more temperament than ability in bumpers and mares novice hurdle. *E. R. Clough*

KEEP RIGHT ON (IRE) 5 b.g. Be My Native (USA) – Mystery Woman (Tula **F71** Rocket) [2002/3 F16s Jan 27] IR £15,000 3-y-o: eighth foal: half-brother to 2 bumper winners by Marktingo and another by Roselier: dam won 2m hurdle: eleventh of 20 in bumper at Kempton on debut. *A. M. Hales*

KEEP SMILING (IRE) 7 b.g. Broken Hearted – Laugh Away (Furry Glen) [2002/3 **c109 x** h77: c18mᶠ c20d* c20dᵘʳ c20sᵘʳ c24gᵖᵘ Mar 2] tall, rather sparely-made gelding: poor **h–** form over hurdles: only completion in steeplechases when making all in 3-finisher novice at Bangor in October: should stay beyond 2½m: acts on good to soft going: poor jumper: sold 15,000 gns Doncaster May Sales. *Miss H. C. Knight*

KEETCHY (IRE) 4 b.g. Darshaan – Ezana (Ela-Mana-Mou) [2002/3 16d⁵ Mar 10] **h87** brother to winning staying hurdler Ezanak and half-brother to fairly useful hurdler Erzadjan (by Kahyasi), stayed 3¼m: fairly useful maiden on Flat (will be suited by further than 1¾m, has looked difficult ride), sold out of J. Dunlop's stable 15,000 gns Newmarket Autumn Sales: modest form when fifth of 15 to East Tycoon in juvenile at Stratford on hurdling debut: will be suited by further than 2m. *J. D. Frost*

KEFIR D'ANGRON (FR) 5 b.g. Panoramic – Wagama (FR) (Rigolo IV (FR)) **h116** [2002/3 17g* 18d² 17sᶠ 17g* 19d* 17v* 16g⁶ Nov 30] quite good-topped gelding: brother to winning chaser Iranica de Laulne and half-brother to 4 winners: dam never ran: 12.5f and 1¾m winner on Flat: fairly useful over hurdles, won at Chateaubriant, Cholet, Strasbourg and Enghien, beating After High a nose in €36,000 event at last-named in November: below form under less testing conditions at Newbury later in month: stays 19f: raced on good going or softer (acts on heavy). *G. Macaire, France*

KEIRAN (IRE) 9 b.g. Be My Native (USA) – Myra Gaye (Buckskin (FR)) [2002/3 **c119** h94: 16m² 16d⁶ c21g* c21d² c24d* c24m³ c24dᵖᵘ c22d⁴ c24d* c25m² Apr 12] sturdy **h94** gelding: modest handicap hurdler: left D. Forster after second start: fairly useful novice chaser: won at Sedgefield in October and Newcastle in November and March: blinkered, improved effort when second to Orswell Crest in valuable handicap at Ayr final start: stays 25f: acts on good to firm and good to soft going: reportedly had viral infection fourth outing. *H. P. Hogarth*

KELAMI (FR) 5 b.g. Lute Antique (FR) – Voltige de Nievre (FR) (Brezzo (FR)) **c127** [2002/3 h118: 17v⁴ c17s³ c20s c19s² c20v³ c17s* c23s⁵ Apr 21] tall gelding: has had soft **h101** palate operation: lightly-raced maiden over hurdles, fairly useful at best: better over fences, won handicap at Auteuil in March: good fifth to Gwenn in very valuable similar event there following month: effective at 17f to 23f: raced mainly on soft/heavy going: tried blinkered (failed to settle)/tongue tied. *F. Doumen, France*

KELANTAN 6 b.g. Kris – Surf Bird (Shareef Dancer (USA)) [2002/3 F16g⁶ May 22] **F84** much better effort in bumpers 13 months apart when sixth of 21 at Worcester in May. *K. C. Bailey*

KELLY CANYON 11 ch.g. Good Thyne (USA) – Kitty Castle (Rubor) [2002/3 c–, **c–** h–: c31dᵖᵘ Apr 25] fair pointer, successful in March: no show in 2 hunter chases: tried in **h–** cheekpieces: tongue tied. *A. M. Thomson*

KELLY PRIDE 6 b.g. Alflora (IRE) – Pearly-B (IRE) (Gunner B) [2002/3 h–: 24dᵖᵘ **h65** 16g⁵ 25d 21g³ Mar 3] poor maiden hurdler: sold out of J. H. Johnson's stable 3,000 gns Doncaster May Sales after reappearance: should stay 3m: raced on good ground or softer. *Mrs S. J. Smith*

KELNIK GLORY 7 b.g. Nalchik (USA) – Areal (IRE) (Roselier (FR)) [2002/3 h–: **h–** 19s⁵ 19s Dec 6] poor maiden hurdler: showed little in 2002/3: tried visored/blinkered. *Mrs S. M. Johnson*

M. Rowland, M. Collins & P. Cox's "Keltic Bard"

KELREV (FR) 5 ch.g. Video Rock (FR) – Bellile II (FR) (Brezzo (FR)) [2002/3 16d² **c108**
16g* c175F c17d* c18g* c19v* c16d³ c16v³ c20d³ Feb 14] leggy, angular ex-French **h?**
gelding: first known foal: dam cross-country chaser, won at up to 3¼m: won over hurdles
at Vichy in August: successful first 3 completed starts over fences, at Compiegne in
September, Le Pin Au Haras in October and Enghien (final outing for G. Macaire) in
November: last of 3 finishers in novices all 3 starts in Britain, not convincing with
jumping and leaving impression amiss: should stay beyond 19f: acts on heavy going.
Miss Venetia Williams

KELTECH GOLD (IRE) 6 b.g. Petorius – Creggan Vale Lass (Simply Great (FR)) **c69**
[2002/3 17f 16g⁶ 17m 16d 18s c20v c16d c16vur c16s⁴ c16mur c16m⁴ Apr 19] brother to **h–**
2m hurdle winner Room To Room Value: fairly useful miler on Flat: novice hurdler/
chaser (left B. Palling after third start), little form except when fourth in maiden chase at
Wexford ninth outing: best at 2m: has had tongue tied: takes strong hold. *S. J. Treacy,
Ireland*

KELTIC BARD 6 b.g. Emperor Jones (USA) – Broughton Singer (IRE) (Common **h134**
Grounds) [2002/3 h111: 16g* 16v 16d² 17s* 16dF 16g⁴ Mar 11] good-topped gelding:
useful novice hurdler: won in large fields at Newbury in November and Cheltenham
(handicap, beat Jahash a length) in January: best effort when fourth to Back In Front in
Grade 1 at Cheltenham final start: raced around 2m: acts on soft going: usually held up.
C. J. Mann

KELTIC FLUTE 4 b.g. Piccolo – Nanny Doon (Dominion) [2002/3 16m Sep 29] **h–**
poor maiden on Flat (likely to prove best up to 1m): well held in juvenile on hurdling
debut. *Mrs Lucinda Featherstone*

KELTIC HERITAGE (IRE) 9 gr.g. Roselier (FR) – Peek-A-Step (IRE) (Step **c118**
Together (USA)) [2002/3 h90: 22m⁴ c25g* c24dF c24d⁶ c20s³ c24g⁴ c24s² c25g* c25m* **h90**

461

c29m[pu] Apr 26] workmanlike gelding: modest hurdler: fairly useful novice chaser: won at Hereford in October, Market Rasen in March and Cheltenham (tended to idle) in April: should stay beyond 27f (stiff task at 29f final start): acts on soft and good to firm going: tongue tied: front runner: sound jumper of fences: genuine. *L. A. Dace*

KEMAL'S COUNCIL (IRE) 7 gr.g. Leading Counsel (USA) – Kemal's Princess (Kemal (FR)) [2002/3 h108: c25s* c24d* c28v[F] c34s[pu] Mar 15] workmanlike gelding: fair hurdler: won novices at Wetherby (impressive) in November and Fakenham (not so fluent) in December on first 2 runs over fences: failed to complete in valuable handicaps at Uttoxeter last 2 starts: should stay beyond 25f: raced on good going or softer (acts on heavy). *Jonjo O'Neill* **c117 h–**

KENILWORTH (USA) 4 b.c. Darshaan – Kerenza (Seattle Dancer (USA)) [2002/3 16s 16v[2] 16s[2] 16s* 16s[3] 17g 16d* Mar 22] leggy colt: fairly useful maiden on Flat (stays 1¾m), sold out of J. Oxx's stable 50,000 gns Newmarket Autumn Sales: useful juvenile hurdler: won at Punchestown (minor event, easily) in February and Navan (27-runner novice, beat Harchibald 1½ lengths) in March: tailed off, possibly amiss, in Grade 1 at Punchestown in early-May: raced around 2m: acts on heavy ground. *Patrick O. Brady, Ireland* **h125**

KENNYTHORPE BOPPY (IRE) 5 ch.g. Aragon – Spark (IRE) (Flash of Steel) [2002/3 h–: 16d Nov 2] leggy gelding: poor maiden on Flat (stays 1½m): tailed off on completed start over hurdles. *J. S. Wainwright* **h–**

KEN SCOTT (FR) 5 b.g. Kendor (FR) – Scottish Bride (FR) (Owen Dudley) [2002/3 16d* 16d[6] 17v[4] 18s[2] Feb 3] good-topped ex-French gelding: seventh foal: half-brother to several middle-distance winners in France: dam French winner up to 9.3f: successful around 1¼m on Flat for J. de Roualle: fair novice hurdler: won at Huntingdon in November: will prove best around 2m: acts on soft going: takes good hold. *P. Winkworth* **h108**

KEN'S DREAM 4 b.c. Bin Ajwaad (IRE) – Shoag (USA) (Affirmed (USA)) [2002/3 16s[2] 16s[5] 17s[5] 17g 16g Apr 3] workmanlike colt: half-brother to winning hurdler Zaaheyah (by Irish River), stayed easy 3m: fairly useful up to 11f on Flat, winning 3 times in 2002: fairly useful form in juvenile hurdles, fifth to Moneytrain in Grade 2 at Cheltenham third start: likely to stay 2½m: acts on soft ground. *Ms A. E. Embiricos* **h115**

KENTFORD BUSY B 9 b.m. Petoski – Busy Mittens (Nearly A Hand) [2002/3 c20m[6] May 11] angular mare: winning hurdler/pointer: not fluent when sixth in novice hunter chase at Huntingdon in May: acts on good to soft going. *M. F. Loggin* **c71 h–**

KENTFORD FERN 8 b.m. El Conquistador – Busy Mittens (Nearly A Hand) [2002/3 c91, h80: c25s[2] c20s* c24d[pu] c21s[2] c25m[pu] Apr 21] workmanlike mare: winning hurdler: fair chaser: made all in mares novice at Southwell in January: effective at 2½m to 3¼m: acts on heavy going, pulled up lame on good to firm final start: has been let down by jumping over fences. *J. W. Mullins* **c106 h–**

KENTFORD GREBE 4 b.f. Teenoso (USA) – Notinhand (Nearly A Hand) [2002/3 F14d[6] F12g 19d 22d[ur] 20v[3] Mar 3] rather unfurnished filly: seventh foal: half-sister to fair chaser The Land Agent (by Town And Country), stays 25f: dam unraced, out of half-sister to useful staying chasers Tartan Takeover and Tartan Tyrant and useful hurdler at 2½m+ Graphics Solar: poor form in bumpers and over hurdles. *J. W. Mullins* **h74 F69**

KENTISH WARRIER (IRE) 5 b.g. Warcraft (USA) – Garden County (Ragapan) [2002/3 F16m Mar 22] 21,000 4-y-o: workmanlike gelding: seventh foal: half-brother to one-time fairly useful hurdler/fair chaser Joe Luke (by Satco), stays 27f: dam unraced, out of fairly useful staying chaser Kylogue Lady, herself half-sister to Foxhunter winner Three Counties: badly in need of experience when well held in bumper on debut. *B. I. Case* **F–**

KEN'TUCKY (FR) 5 b.g. Video Rock (FR) – La Salamandre (FR) (Pot d'Or (FR)) [2002/3 F16s[3] F16g[4] F16m[3] Apr 12] leggy gelding: brother to top-class chaser/smart hurdler El Paso III, stays 29f, and half-brother to several winners, including useful hurdler/chaser up to 3m Hindiana (by Quart de Vin) and fair hurdler/chaser around 2m Jericho III (by Lute Antique): dam lightly-raced maiden: fairly useful form in frame in bumpers at Kempton, Warwick and Ayr: will stay beyond 2m. *N. J. Henderson* **F95**

KERCABELLEC (FR) 5 b. or br.g. Useful (FR) – Marie de Geneve (FR) (Nishapour (FR)) [2002/3 16s[5] Dec 28] seventh foal: half-brother to 2 winners, including modest hurdler/chaser around 2m Pornic (by Shining Steel): dam maiden: fair form both starts over hurdles, in minor event for G. Macaire and novice at Newbury (fifth to Beyond The Pale) in December. *N. J. Henderson* **h101**

KERRIGAND (FR) 5 gr.g. April Night (FR) – Gouerie (FR) (Cadoudal (FR)) [2002/3 **c102**
18s³ c17d⁵ 16s² 17v* 22v² 23s⁵ 25g Mar 11] sturdy, good-bodied ex-French gelding: **h120**
third foal: brother to winning Flat stayer Fleur d'Ajone and half-brother to winning cross-country chaser by Abdonski: dam unraced: 15f winner on Flat in France: fair form on chasing debut: fairly useful hurdler: sold out of M. Rolland's stable €72,000 Goffs July Sale after second start: won novice at Taunton in December: good second to Kimberley in handicap at Uttoxeter next time: should stay beyond 23f: raced on good going or softer (acts on heavy): tried blinkered/visored: often looks hard ride. *M. C. Pipe*

KERRY LADS (IRE) 8 ch.g. Mister Lord (USA) – Minstrel Top (Black Minstrel) **c126 x**
[2002/3 c115, h86: c26s³ c25s^F c25d³ c25v² c25s* c25s^F c33m⁴ Apr 12] workmanlike **h–**
gelding: maiden hurdler: fairly useful handicap chaser: won at Ayr in February: good fourth to Ryalux in Scottish Grand National there final start: stays 33f: acts on good to firm and heavy going: often let down by jumping over fences. *Miss Lucinda V. Russell*

KERRY SOLDIER BLUE 14 gr.g. Fine Blue – Kerry Maid (Maestoso) [2002/3 **c88**
c92: c24m^2dis Apr 22] fair hunter chaser: successful in point in March: creditable second in hunter at Chepstow in April (later disqualified on technical grounds): stays 3m: acts on good to firm and heavy going: races prominently. *D. O. Stephens*

KESTLE MILL (IRE) 7 ch.g. Be My Guest (USA) – Tatisha (Habitat) [2002/3 22d⁶ **h–**
22d Dec 5] workmanlike ex-Irish gelding: half-brother to several winners on Flat, including fairly useful middle-distance performer Grove Daffodil (by Salt Dome): dam, French 1m winner, half-sister to high-class sprinter Green God: generally well held in bumpers and over hurdles. *M. J. Coombe*

KETY STAR (FR) 5 b.g. Bojador (FR) – Danystar (FR) (Alycos (FR)) [2002/3 16m³ **h94**
19g^F 19d 16d⁶ Mar 1] leggy ex-French gelding: first foal: dam middle-distance winner: third both starts around 13f on Flat at 3 yrs for W. Delalande: encouraging third in novice hurdle at Worcester in May: failed to last home in similar events subsequently: will prove best at sharp 2m. *Miss Venetia Williams*

KEW 4 b.g. Royal Applause – Cutleaf (Kris) [2002/3 16s^pu 16d 16m^F Apr 21] small **h–**
gelding: poor maiden on Flat (probably stays 1½m): no form, pulling hard, in 3 juvenile hurdles. *J. J. Bridger*

KEYNOTE (IRE) 11 ch.g. Orchestra – St Moritz (Linacre) [2002/3 c–x, h–: c20m^bd **c– x**
Jun 28] rangy gelding: no longer of much account: sketchy jumper. *R. Rowe* **h–**

KEYSSAC (FR) 5 b.g. Beyssac (FR) – Dhop La (FR) (Son of Silver) [2002/3 h–: 17m **h–**
Aug 12] no form over hurdles: sold 1,000 gns Doncaster September Sales. *A. M. Hales*

KEZ 7 b.g. Polar Falcon (USA) – Briggsmaid (Elegant Air) [2002/3 16m⁵ Oct 5] fairly **h74**
useful on Flat (stays 1½m): only second start over hurdles when fifth of 7 in novice at Uttoxeter in October, pulling hard. *P. R. Webber*

KHALADJISTAN (IRE) 5 br.g. Tirol – Khaladja (IRE) (Akarad (FR)) [2002/3 F86: **h86**
16m⁶ 17g⁴ Oct 18] small-looking gelding: fair form in bumpers: not knocked about in novice on hurdling debut, sold out of N. Henderson's stable 20,000 gns Doncaster May Sales: hinted at temperament when fourth in similar event at Hereford 5 months later. *P. F. Nicholls*

KHAN KICKER (IRE) 7 b.g. Husyan (USA) – Orient Conquest (Dual) [2002/3 **h115**
h127: 20g 20s 16d 16g³ Feb 12] sparely-made gelding: fairly useful hurdler: tried in cheekpieces, best effort in 2002/3 when third in handicap at Musselburgh final start: should stay 2½m: acts on soft and good to firm going. *Ferdy Murphy*

KHARAK (FR) 4 gr.g. Danehill (USA) – Khariyda (FR) (Shakapour) [2002/3 16s* **h98**
16f³ 16m² 16g⁴ Apr 24] good-bodied ex-French gelding: half-brother to 4 winners, notably smart middle-distance stayer Kharizmi (by Lashkari): dam smart middle-distance filly: unplaced in 4 outings at 3 yrs on Flat for A. de Royer Dupre: fair juvenile hurdler: won at Ayr in March: ran creditably in cheekpieces final start. *Mrs S. C. Bradburne*

KHATANI (IRE) 8 b.g. Kahyasi – Khanata (USA) (Riverman (USA)) [2002/3 c121, **c119**
h–: c20g* c21m³ 20m⁴ c19g⁶ Apr 2] sturdy gelding: winning hurdler: fairly useful **h–**
handicap chaser: back to form when winning at Bangor in May: poor efforts last 2 starts, over hurdles on first occasion: should stay beyond 21f: raced on good going or firmer (acts on firm): has had tongue tied. *D. R. Gandolfo*

KHAYALI (IRE) 9 b.g. Unfuwain (USA) – Coven (Sassafras (FR)) [2002/3 c65, h70: **c72**
c20m* Aug 17] medium-sized gelding: maiden hurdler: poor chaser: won weakly- **h–**
contested handicap at Bangor in August, not seen out again: will prove best up to 21f: acts on soft and good to firm going, possibly not on heavy. *A. R. Dicken*

KHAYAL (USA) 9 b.g. Green Dancer (USA) – Look Who's Dancing (USA) (Affirmed (USA)) [2002/3 c–, h72: c24m⁶ May 6] sturdy gelding: maiden hurdler: well held in 2 handicaps over fences: runner-up in 2 points in March: should stay 3m: acts on firm going: tried visored. *P. J. Hobbs* c–
h–

KHAYSAR (IRE) 5 b.g. Pennekamp (USA) – Khaytada (IRE) (Doyoun) [2002/3 h96: 18d Dec 10] angular gelding: handicap hurdler, well held only outing in 2002/3: likely to prove best around 2m: acts on good to soft going. *Mrs L. Wadham* h–

KHETAAM (IRE) 5 b.g. Machiavellian (USA) – Ghassak (IRE) (Persian Bold) [2002/3 16g³ 16s² 18s* 16s² 16s³ 20v* 20g⁴ Apr 20] lengthy gelding: fairly useful on Flat (stays 1½m): similar standard over hurdles: won 4-y-o maiden at Gowran (easily) in December and intermediate at Fairyhouse (by ¾ length from Catalpa Cargo) in March: blinkered, stiff task when well held in Grade 1 novice at Punchestown in late-April: stays 2½m, at least as effective around 2m: acts on heavy going. *N. Meade, Ireland* h118

KHUZDAR (IRE) 4 ch.g. Definite Article – Mariyda (IRE) (Vayrann) [2002/3 16d⁵ 17d Feb 23] leggy, sparely-made gelding: half-brother to modest 2m hurdler Spontaneity (by Shalford): fair on Flat (stays 2m): fifth of 15 in novice at Wincanton, easily better effort over hurdles. *M. R. Channon* h86

KICK FOR TOUCH (IRE) 6 ch.g. Insan (USA) – Anns Run (Deep Run) [2002/3 h98: c20dF c21d³ c20v² c24m² c24m* c24g* Apr 12] rangy gelding: twice-raced hurdler: fair chaser: won maiden at Huntingdon in March and novice at Stratford (fortunate) in April: stays 3m: acts on good to firm and good to soft going. *Miss H. C. Knight* c109
h–

KICKHAM (IRE) 7 b.g. Supreme Leader – Knocknagow (Buckskin (FR)) [2002/3 F113: 16s 16s² 18v³ 16s Feb 9] tall gelding: useful bumper winner: easily best effort over hurdles (ran as if amiss on reappearance) when ¾-length second of 29 to Plenty of Ice in maiden at Navan in November: didn't find much next time, and soundly beaten in handicap in February: useful in bumpers, bit below best when seventh in Grade 1 at Punchestown in late-April: will stay 2½m. *E. J. O'Grady, Ireland* h117
F106

KICKING BEAR (IRE) 5 b.g. Little Bighorn – Rongo (IRE) (Tumble Gold) [2002/3 F18v^ro F17s⁵ 20v Mar 7] rangy gelding: fourth foal: brother to Irish bumper winner Out The Gap: dam unraced half-sister to Champion Hurdle winner For Auction: modest form on completed start in bumpers: jumped poorly when well held in novice on hurdling debut. *D. M. Grissell* h–
F82

KICKING KING (IRE) 5 b.g. Old Vic – Fairy Blaze (IRE) (Good Thyne (USA)) [2002/3 16s* 20s² 18s* 16s* 16g² Mar 11] h141 p
The three-year-olds of 1989 were a memorable bunch, with two outstanding middle-distance colts in Nashwan and Old Vic and two top-class milers in Zilzal and Polish Precedent, the quartet between them mopping up most of the races of consequence at seven furlongs or more that season. For much of that summer, argument raged as to which of the two Derby-winning colts was the better, and as they never met the subject can be debated to this day; the milers did meet, in a showdown in the Queen Elizabeth II Stakes at Ascot in September, with Zilzal emerging victorious. Great things might have been expected of the four top colts at stud, but none has enjoyed anything like the success of their contemporaries Danehill (a good sprinter who scraped into the top twenty three-year-olds in *Racehorses of 1989*) and the late-developing In The Wings (who didn't even manage that). Nashwan (Swain) and Polish Precedent (Pilsudski) at least sired horses near to or equal in merit to themselves, but Old Vic, a tremendous racehorse but probably too much of a stayer for modern commercial tastes, sired just a handful of useful or better performers over middle distances or further before gradually being switched to covering jumping mares in the mid-'nineties. His first wholly jumping crop, foaled in 1998, suggests he could belatedly make a significant impact as a stallion. It includes the very promising Our Vic, the potentially useful Were In Touch, a couple of fair hurdlers and the leading novice hurdler Kicking King. The last-named won three of his five starts over hurdles and found only Back In Front too good for him in the Supreme Novices' Hurdle at Cheltenham, and he looks a leading candidate for novice chasing honours in 2003/4.
Kicking King, successful at Leopardstown on the first of two starts in bumpers in 2001/2, didn't need to show better than fairly useful form in his first

Byrne Group plc Novices' Hurdle, Punchestown—the progressive Kicking King wins convincingly

four starts over hurdles, winning minor events at Naas in November and Cork in January and the Grade 2 Byrne Group Plc Novices' Hurdle at Punchestown in February. He was soon well on top after quickening two out when beating fairly useful handicapper The Dark Flasher to land the odds at Cork and responded really well when getting the better of Central House by four lengths at Punchestown. Kicking King's defeat on his second start—he went down by eight lengths to Solerina who was giving him 6 lb into the bargain—seemed to owe something to lack of experience, though it was also his only outing at two and a half miles and it's possible he lacked sufficient stamina at that stage of his career. Kicking King lined up at Cheltenham as the 13/2 third favourite in a field of nineteen. It wasn't the strongest renewal of the Supreme with several of the better two-mile novices aimed elsewhere and no more than two or three of the runners having shown form good enough to figure in the finish in an average year. In addition, Kicking King looked one of only a handful with the potential to improve enough to make an impact. Although no match for the favourite Back In Front, Kicking King acquitted himself really well, putting up a smart novice performance. Always well placed, he still held every chance when not fluent two out and, though soon outpaced by the winner, kept on to hold second in the straight, finishing ten lengths down.

		Sadler's Wells (b 1981)	Northern Dancer
	Old Vic (b 1986)		Fairy Bridge
		Cockade (b 1973)	Derring-Do
Kicking King (IRE) (b.g. 1998)			Camenae
		Good Thyne (br 1977)	Herbager
	Fairy Blaze (IRE) (b 1991)		Foreseer
		Fairy Tree (ch 1970)	Varano
			Precision Time

The rangy, well-made Kicking King has 'chaser' written all over him and it will be no surprise if he returns to the next Cheltenham Festival as a leading contender for the Arkle or Cathcart. Although he didn't quite see out his race at Navan, there's no reason on pedigree why Kicking King shouldn't prove every bit as effective over two and a half miles or further. Two earlier foals out of his unraced dam Fairy Blaze have stayed at least that far, the modest chaser Glenfarclas Boy (by Montelimar) and the fairly useful hurdler Colonel Monroe (by Lord Americo). Fairy Blaze was out of the nine-furlong winner Fairy Tree but is sister to a winning

Mr Conor Clarkson's "Kicking King"

pointer and a half-sister to five winners on the Flat, two of which, Carousel Rocket and Carousel Calypso, were later fair staying jumpers. Kicking King was bought for IR 21,000 guineas as a yearling. He raced solely on soft going over hurdles prior to Cheltenham, but proved every bit as effective on good ground there. *T. J. Taaffe, Ireland*

KIDITHOU (FR) 5 b.g. Royal Charter (FR) – De Thou (FR) (Trebrook (FR)) [2002/3 F16m² 20s³ 22vᵖᵘ 20v⁴ 20d⁶ Feb 23] first known foal: dam once-raced, from family of top-class staying chaser Otage du Perche: second to Beseiged in bumper at Perth on debut: best effort in novice hurdles when fourth of 7 to Broken Knights at Ayr, jumping more fluently than previously and keeping on without being given anything like a hard time: remains capable of better. *L. Lungo*   **h98 p**
F95

KIDS INHERITANCE (IRE) 5 b.g. Presenting – Princess Tino (IRE) (Rontino) [2002/3 F17d³ F16d⁵ F16s² F16v Jan 29] IR £37,000 3-y-o: good-topped gelding: second foal: dam unraced half-sister to smart hurdler/useful chaser up to 25f Toureen Prince: fair form when placed in bumpers at Carlisle and Newcastle: poor effort final start. *J. M. Jefferson*   **F94**

KID'Z'PLAY (IRE) 7 b.g. Rudimentary (USA) – Saka Saka (Camden Town) [2002/3 16d³ 16v⁶ 16d Jan 24] fair on Flat (stays 1½m): modest form over hurdles: temperamental. *J. S. Goldie*   **h95 §**

KILBRAGH KHAN 7 br.g. Rakaposhi King – Kilbragh Dreamer (IRE) (Decent Fellow) [2002/3 F82: c21vᵖᵘ c16v⁵ c24gᵖᵘ Apr 12] little sign of ability. *A. J. Wilson*   **c–**

KILCAROON (IRE) 8 b.g. Jurado (USA) – Alfuraat (Auction Ring (USA)) [2002/3 c79: c23mᶠ c25dᵘʳ 20m Dec 17] strong gelding: poor novice chaser, departed early first 2 starts: inadequate test on hurdling debut: stays 25f. *J. Howard Johnson*   **c–**
h–

KILCASH CASTLE (IRE) 9 b.g. Strong Gale – Cooleogan (Proverb) [2002/3 c107, h138: c16m² c17d³ c16fᶠ Sep 29] well-made gelding: useful hurdler: fair maiden   **c114**
h–

466

chaser, best effort when 1½ lengths second to Albatros in novice at Wexford on reappearance: stays 2½m: probably acts on any going. *A. P. O'Brien, Ireland*

KILCASKIN GOLD (IRE)   8 ch.g. Ore – Maypole Gayle (Strong Gale) [2002/3   c–
c25g^{pu} Apr 14] ex-Irish gelding: third foal: half-brother to winning pointer by Royal Fountain: dam unraced: bought 3,800 gns Doncaster August Sales: fair pointer, successful in April: no form in steeplechases: usually blinkered. *R. A. Ross*

KILDARE CHILLER (IRE)   9 b.g. Shahrastani (USA) – Ballycuirke (Taufan   h99
(USA)) [2002/3 h100: 17m^6 18m^6 17s^5 22f 18d^3 20v^5 18s 19s^4 18v^2 18g^6 Mar 17] leggy gelding: modest handicap hurdler: stays 21f: has won on good to firm going, best efforts on good or softer (acts on heavy): wore cheekpieces eighth start. *P. R. Hedger*

KILDARE (IRE)   6 br.g. Supreme Leader – Fairly Deep (Deep Run) [2002/3 F16d^5 F113
F16s^3 F16v^2 Mar 8] IR 50,000 3-y-o: tall gelding: half-brother to several winners, including fair hurdler Gale Star (by Strong Gale), stays 3m, and Land Rover Bumper winner Berkeley Run (by Montelimar): dam, winning 2m hurdler, from family of very smart 2m hurdler/chaser Wolf of Badenoch: progressive form in bumpers: best effort when 5 lengths third of 19 to Royal Rosa in Grade 1 at Punchestown in late-April, staying on well after getting tapped for foot: will stay 2½m: type to do well in novice hurdles in 2003/4. *D. T. Hughes, Ireland*

KILDEE LASS   4 gr.f. Morpeth – Pigeon Loft (IRE) (Bellypha) [2002/3 F14d^4 F13s   F81
F17s F14g Mar 17] leggy, angular filly: fifth foal: sister to 2¾m hurdle winner Grey Brother and half-sister to bumper winner Miss Woodpigeon (by Landyap): dam, poor maiden on Flat, runner-up in 17f seller only completed start over hurdles: easily best effort in bumpers when fourth of 18 to Rock Garden in 1¾m event at Warwick on debut: saddle slipped early next start. *J. D. Frost*

KILDORRAGH (IRE)   9 b.g. Glacial Storm (USA) – Take A Dare (Pragmatic)   c115
[2002/3 c124+: c26v^{pu} c26d^2 c24d^2 c34s^{pu} Mar 15] tall, useful-looking gelding: fairly useful handicap chaser, off 14 months before reappearance: respectable efforts when runner-up at Fontwell and Doncaster: should stay beyond 3½m: acts on good to firm and heavy going. *L. Wells*

KILDRUMMY CASTLE   11 b.g. Komaite (USA) – Khadine (Astec) [2002/3 c–,   c76
h–: c24d^2 c21g* c21g^6 c19g^{pu} Jun 12] strong gelding: poor handicap chaser: easily won   h–
at Fakenham in May, but return to form proved all too brief: stays 3m: acts on firm and soft going: has had tongue tied. *Ferdy Murphy*

KILLALA BAY (IRE)   8 b.m. Executive Perk – Killinure Point (Smooth Stepper)   c–
[2002/3 c16s^6 c20g^{pu} Mar 15] modest form in bumper in 2000/1, none in 2 starts over fences after long lay-off. *K. C. Bailey*

KILLALONGFORD (IRE)   6 b.g. Tenby – Queen Crab (Private Walk) [2002/3   h79
h91: 21d 22s 26s^{pu} 20s 17d^2 21g^2 20m^4 22g^4 Apr 26] poor maiden hurdler: seems best up to 2¾m: acts on soft and good to firm going. *Mrs S. M. Johnson*

KILLARNEY   5 gr.m. Pursuit of Love – Laune (AUS) (Kenmare (FR)) [2002/3 h–:   h66
16d^3 16g 17m^2 21g^4 17d Aug 26] sturdy mare: maiden on Flat: poor handicap hurdler: probably best around 2m: seems suited by good going or firmer. *Miss Kate Milligan*

KILLEANEY (IRE)   6 b.g. Classic Memory – Welsh Duchy (Welsh Saint) [2002/3   c76
F19s 16s^6 c20s Mar 15] IR 2,300 3-y-o: fourth foal: dam maiden: well held in bumper/   h–
novice hurdle: signs of ability after in points/hunter chase. *J. G. Carr, Ireland*   F–

KILLER (FR)   5 ch.g. Cupidon (FR) – Kaoutchka (FR) (Bakst (USA)) [2002/3 21d^{pu} h–
Nov 29] tall gelding: fourth foal: half-brother to 2 winners, including 2¼m hurdle winner Kaoutjack (by Mister Jack): dam 11.5f winner: runner-up twice up to 2m from 3 starts on Flat at 4 yrs, sold out of T. Civel's stable €50,000 Goffs July Sale: tongue tied, took good hold and weakened sixth in novice at Newbury on hurdling debut. *Jonjo O'Neill*

KILLERINE (FR)   8 br.g. Leading Counsel (USA) – Rose Petal (FR) (Pharly (FR))   c–
[2002/3 c106, h109: 20d^4 25d^{pu} 18s 19s* 19s^4 24v^6 18v^6 19s 20v Apr 26] close-coupled   h125
gelding: third over 11.5f on Flat in February: fair chaser: fairly useful hurdler on balance of form: left I. Williams after second start: enterprisingly ridden when winning conditional riders event at Auteuil in October: probably flattered in Group 1 event there sixth start: ran poorly after next outing: stays 3¼m: acts on heavy and good to firm going: has won with/without blinkers: has had tongue tied. *J-P. Delaporte, France*

KILLING TIME   12 b.g. Good Times (ITY) – Kelly's Bid (Pitskelly) [2002/3 c–, h–:   c–
16v^{pu} 19s^{pu} Feb 27] small gelding: winning hurdler, no longer of any account: tried   h–
visored. *S. T. Lewis*

Dan Moore Memorial Handicap Chase, Fairyhouse—
Killultagh Storm (nearer camera) gets his nose in front of Alcapone

KILLOUGH HILL (IRE) 6 b.g. Fourstars Allstar (USA) – Bristol Fairy (Smartset) **F–**
[2002/3 F–: F16m May 11] little sign of ability in bumpers or points. *C. J. Bennett*

KILLULTAGH STORM (IRE) 9 b.g. Mandalus – Rostrevor Lady (Kemal (FR)) **c139**
[2002/3 c140, h–: c16s^{pu} c20d^5 c21d c17s^5 c16s^4 c16d^6 c20d^4 c17g* Apr 20] strong **h–**
gelding: useful chaser: back to near best when winning 6-runner handicap at Fairyhouse
in April by head from Alcapone, racing lazily: blinkered, creditable third to Flagship
Uberalles in Grade 1 BMW Chase at Punchestown later in month, run best ignored there
3 days later: stays 2½m: acts on good to firm and heavy going: effective held up or ridden
prominently. *W. P. Mullins, Ireland*

KILLULTAGH THUNDER (IRE) 7 b. or br.g. Bravefoot – Rostrevor Lady **c111**
(Kemal (FR)) [2002/3 h117, F101: 17d^5 c20v^2 c20s^2 c20v^2 c24v^F c24d^{pu} Mar 17] lengthy **h117**
gelding: fairly useful hurdler: similar form on chasing debut: let down by jumping
subsequently, including when sixth to Rule Supreme in valuable novice handicap at
Punchestown in late-April: likely to prove best at 2½m+: acts on heavy going.
W. P. Mullins, Ireland

KILLUSTY (IRE) 9 b.g. Phardante (FR) – Lepida (Royal Match) [2002/3 c24v* **c140**
c36d^F c29m^{pu} Apr 26] tall gelding: winning hurdler: first past post all 5 completed starts **h–**
over fences, useful form when beating Lord Moose impressively by 10 lengths in
8-runner handicap at Sandown in March on return from 2-year absence: in touch when
falling twenty-second (Becher's) in Grand National at Aintree: broke down in very valuable handicap at Sandown: should stay beyond 3m: acts on heavy going. *C. R. Egerton*

KILLY BEACH 5 b.g. Kuwait Beach (USA) – Spiritual Lily (Brianston Zipper) **h81 ?**
[2002/3 F–: 22f^4 22m^4 Oct 27] leggy gelding: first sign of ability when 29 lengths fourth
of 8 finishers in novice hurdle at Wincanton, keeping on late past beaten horses and
possibly flattered: not seen out again. *J. W. Mullins*

KILMEADE PRINCE (IRE) 7 ch.g. Satco (FR) – Snowy Gunner (Gunner B) **h–**
[2002/3 17g^{pu} Nov 7] once-raced on Flat: fair form at best in bumpers, sold out of
P. J. Flynn's stable IR £4,000 Fairyhouse November (2001) Sale: no form over hurdles.
P. M. J. Doyle, Ireland

KILMEENA STAR 5 b.h. So Factual (USA) – Kilmeena Glen (Beveled (USA)) **h–**
[2002/3 16g^{pu} 16d^{ro} Mar 6] poor maiden on Flat (stays 7f): no aptitude for hurdles.
J. C. Fox

468

KILMENY (IRE) 5 b.m. Royal Abjar (USA) – Mouchez Le Nez (IRE) (Cyrano de Bergerac) [2002/3 16d 18s² 16s³ 17m² 17g^F Apr 19] modest on Flat (stayed 11f) in 2002, claimed from H. Morrison £8,000 in September: modest form over hurdles, would have won mares maiden at Newton Abbot (visored) but for falling fatally 2 out: raced around 2m: acted on soft and good to firm going. *M. C. Pipe* **h90**

KILMORE QUAY (IRE) 8 ch.g. Over The River (FR) – Sustenance (Torus) [2002/3 16d^pu 24v^pu Feb 1] workmanlike gelding: first foal: dam won 2¼m hurdle in Ireland: no show in 2 novice hurdles. *D. J. Wintle* **h–**

KILROSSANTY (IRE) 4 b. or br.g. Accordion – Baby Clair (Gulf Pearl) [2002/3 F16m* Apr 20] unfurnished gelding: half-brother to winning jumpers by Auction Ring and Nordico and to smart miler Cresta Auction (also by Auction Ring): dam fair 2-y-o 6f winner: won bumper at Cork on debut by 1½ lengths from Light des Mulottes, quickening well: rushed into lead after halfway when disappointing in Grade 1 at Punchestown later in month. *Henry De Bromhead, Ireland* **F95**

KILT (FR) 5 ch.g. Luchiroverte (IRE) – Unite II (FR) (Toujours Pret (USA)) [2002/3 h–: 16s 16s 16s^pu Jan 3] good-topped gelding: no form over hurdles: has had tongue tied. *Mrs L. Williamson* **h–**

KIMBERLEY 8 b.g. Shareef Dancer (USA) – Willowbank (Gay Fandango (USA)) [2002/3 c113, h130: 24v 24s⁶ 25s⁶ 22v* 24d⁴ Mar 1] compact gelding: one-time useful hurdler/winning chaser for P. Hughes: best effort over hurdles in 2002/3 when making all in handicap at Uttoxeter in February, gamely holding off Kerrigan by ½ length: probably stays 3m: raced mainly on good going or softer (acts on heavy): tried blinkered, visored last 3 starts: formerly tongue tied. *J. G. M. O'Shea* **c– h117**

KIMBI (IRE) 9 b.g. Kenmare (FR) – Troppo Cara (Sharpman (FR)) [2002/3 c–, h155: 21s⁶ 25d⁵ 19s⁴ 20s⁶ Oct 12] useful-looking gelding: top-class hurdler/smart chaser at best: smart form over hurdles in first half of 2002/3, behind Vic Toto in Group 3 events in September and October (5 lengths sixth of 8) on last 2 outings: stays 25f: raced mainly on soft/heavy going: often soon off bridle. *B. Secly, France* **c–h151**

easyodds.com The Price Is Right Handicap Chase, Sandown—
Killusty returns successfully from two years off, though Lord Moose leads at the last

KIMDALOO (IRE) 11 b.g. Mandalus – Kimin (Kibenka) [2002/3 c79, h–: c16d² **c92** c16g⁵ c16d³ c17m c21m 17g c17dᵖᵘ c17gᵇᵈ c16g⁴ c16m* c16g* c17s² c16d⁴ c17v² c16v⁵ **h–** c20g c16g Apr 24] lengthy gelding: maiden hurdler: modest chaser: won handicap and minor event at Hexham in October: raced mainly around 2m nowadays: acts on any going: usually tongue tied. *M. A. Barnes*

KIM FONTAINE (FR) 5 b. or br.g. Silver Rainbow – Blanche Fontaine (FR) **F108** (Oakland (FR)) [2002/3 F16s* F16g Mar 12] rather unfurnished gelding: fourth foal: brother to fairly useful hurdler around 2m Junior Fontaine: dam unraced: useful form in bumpers, won at Thurles on debut in January and 23-runner contest at Punchestown (by neck from Selby Road) in early-May: 11 lengths eighth of 25 to Liberman in Grade 1 at Cheltenham in between, unable to quicken straight. *W. P. Mullins, Ireland*

KIMOE WARRIOR 5 ch.g. Royal Abjar (USA) – Thewaari (USA) (Eskimo (USA)) **h75 §** [2002/3 h78: 16dᵖᵘ 16v³ 17v³ 17d 17v⁵ 17f³ Apr 3] leggy gelding: poor maiden hurdler: barely stays 19f: acts on any going: wore cheekpieces last 2 starts: tried tongue tied: not one to rely on. *M. Mullineaux*

KINCORA (IRE) 12 b.g. King Persian – Miss Noora (Ahonoora) [2002/3 c96, h–: **c83** c21m³ May 22] angular gelding: modest on balance of form in hunter chases, walked **h–** over in point in April: stays 3m: acts on good to firm and heavy ground. *Ms Lisa Stock*

KINDLE BALL (FR) 5 gr.m. Kaldounevees (FR) – Scala IV (FR) (Quart de Vin **F–** (FR)) [2002/3 F17g³ Apr 21] sixth foal: half-sister to 2 winners, including fair hurdler/useful chaser up to 2½m Fire Ball (by Perrault): dam, middle-distance winner, out of half-sister to smart 23f chase winner Martinet II: favourite, well-beaten third of 5 in mares bumper at Newton Abbot on debut. *Miss Venetia Williams*

KIND PRINCE 11 b.g. Kind of Hush – Silent Princess (King of Spain) [2002/3 17g **c–** May 4] leggy gelding: no promise in 2 novice chases: poor hurdler, off 2 years before **h–** only outing in 2002/3: best efforts around 2m: acts on soft and good to firm going: tried blinkered. *John A. Harris*

KIND SIR 7 b.g. Generous (IRE) – Noble Conquest (USA) (Vaguely Noble) [2002/3 **c107** c79, h87: 19mᵖᵘ c19g⁴ c16dᶠ³ c16s² c16d⁴ c16dᶠ c19s* c16v* c16g* c20sᵘʳ c20d² c16dᵖᵘ **h–** Feb 25] good-topped gelding: maiden hurdler: fair chaser: won 2 novice handicaps at Hereford in December, minor event at Leicester in January and novice handicap at Catterick (beat Risky Way 4 lengths) later in January: reportedly distressed final outing: best form up to 19f: acts on good to firm and heavy going: blinkered once: forces pace. *A. W. Carroll*

KINFAUNS LADY (IRE) 8 b.m. King's Ride – Dalkey Sound (Crash Course) **h76** [2002/3 h74: 21d³ 22v⁵ 24g³ 24gᶠ 24g³ Mar 25] poor maiden hurdler: stays 3m: raced on good going or softer (acts on soft). *D. W. Whillans*

KING BAVARD (IRE) 9 b.g. Jurado (USA) – Discerning Lady (Le Bavard (FR)) **c–** [2002/3 c73, h–: c25g May 11] workmanlike gelding: maiden hurdler/chaser: won points **h–** in January and February: stays 3m: acts on soft going. *J. I. A. Charlton*

KING BEE (IRE) 6 b.g. Supreme Leader – Honey Come Back (Master Owen) [2002/3 **h95** h81: 20s* 20s⁶ 20v⁶ 24v⁴ 20d⁵ Mar 2] medium-sized gelding: modest hurdler: won novice handicap at Ascot in November by 2 lengths from Putup Or Shutup: should stay beyond 2½m: raced on going softer than good. *H. D. Daly*

KING CAREW (IRE) 5 b.h. Fairy King (USA) – Kareena (Riverman (USA)) [2002/3 **c106 p** 16g⁶ 16s⁴ 18s³ 16s⁴ 16s 16s 16v⁴ 16d² 16g 16g³ c16m* Apr 19] useful-looking **h111** horse: fairly useful on Flat (probably stays 1½m, may not have ideal temperament) for M. Channon: fair hurdler: clear throughout when winning 4-y-o minor event at Limerick in December by distance: comfortably won maiden at Cork on chasing debut: raced around 2m: acts on heavy and good to firm going: effective with/without blinkers: open to improvement over fences. *Michael Hourigan, Ireland*

KING CLAUDIUS (IRE) 7 b.g. King's Ride – Lepida (Royal Match) [2002/3 F104: **h90** 21s 16g³ 21m⁵ 17m Apr 16] tall gelding: promising in bumpers in 2001/2, won at Kempton on debut: off 11 months and tongue tied, disappointing over hurdles, let down by jumping: stays 21f. *P. R. Webber*

KING DANTE (IRE) 6 b. or br.g. King's Ride – Tulladante (IRE) (Phardante (FR)) **h94 ?** [2002/3 F16g F16s⁵ 16g 16g⁵ Apr 25] IR £18,000 4-y-o: good-topped gelding: second **F84** foal: dam unraced half-sister to useful staying chaser Crank Shaft: modest form in bumpers: much better effort over hurdles when fifth to Vandas Choice in maiden at Perth, always prominent in steadily-run race: will be suited by further than 2m. *P. Beaumont*

KINGFISHER FLYER (IRE) 9 b.g. King's Ride – Melarka (Dara Monarch) [2002/3 **h78** 16d^{ur} 16s^4 21s^{pu} Jan 27] rangy, useful-looking gelding: fairly useful form in bumpers in 1998/9: well held on completed outing over hurdles after near 4-year lay-off: should stay beyond 2m. *P. R. Webber*

KINGFISHER STAR 8 ch.g. Derrylin – Legata (IRE) (Orchestra) [2002/3 c22d^6 **c68** c21m^3 May 22] first foal: dam well held in bumper/over hurdles: modest pointer: well held in 2 novice hunter chases. *S. R. Andrews*

KINGFISHER SUNSET 7 b.g. Alflora (IRE) – Jack It In (Derrylin) [2002/3 F16d **F—** F17m^4 F16m^5 F16m Oct 30] 5,000 4-y-o: good-bodied gelding: second foal: dam unraced half-sister to dam of useful hurdler/chaser around 2½m Crocadee: little sign of ability in bumpers. *J. G. M. O'Shea*

KING-FOR-LIFE (IRE) 5 ch.g. Rainbows For Life (CAN) – Fair Song (Pitskelly) **h—** [2002/3 F17d F16g^6 16d^2 F16d^2 19g^{pu} Apr 19] tall gelding: third foal: half-brother to **F91** winning 2m hurdler Clear Blue Water (by Dancing Dissident) and 2-y-o winner by Magical Wonder: dam unraced: fair form in bumpers for G. A. Swinbank, runner-up twice at Catterick (tended to hang left under pressure): shaped as if amiss on hurdling debut: sold 5,000 gns Doncaster May Sales. *J. R. Cornwall*

KING GEORGES (FR) 5 b.g. Kadalko (FR) – Djoumi (FR) (Brezzo (FR)) [2002/3 **h86** h—: 19d^{ur} 16s 16d^3 16s^5 19d^4 17d* 17v^6 Mar 4] tall, rather leggy gelding: type to make a chaser: modest hurdler: won handicaps at Wincanton (novice) in December and Exeter in February: best efforts around 2m on good to soft ground. *J. C. Tuck*

KING HARALD (IRE) 5 b.g. King's Ride – Cuilin Bui (IRE) (Kemal (FR)) [2002/3 **h114 +** 21m^3 19g^3 19d^3 19d^4 21s* Feb 28] IR £27,000 3-y-o: close-coupled gelding: third foal: brother to fair hurdler Prince Madoc, stays 21f: dam, fairly useful hurdler who stayed 3m, half-sister to useful staying hurdler Crank Shaft: fair novice hurdler: improved to win 17-runner conditional jockeys handicap at Newbury, quickening to beat Cool Roxy 6 lengths: will stay beyond 21f: acts on soft and good to firm going. *M. Bradstock*

KINGKOHLER (IRE) 4 b.g. King's Theatre (IRE) – Legit (IRE) (Runnett) [2002/3 **h87 p** 17g^3 Mar 15] ex-Irish gelding: lightly raced on Flat (stays 1½m), sold out of E. Lynam's stable €11,000 Goffs October Sale, well backed on British debut in February: well backed, 4¾ lengths third of 12 to Spainkris in juvenile at Market Rasen on hurdling debut, taking good hold in front and jumping none too fluently: open to improvement. *K. A. Morgan*

KINGLEY VALE 9 br.g. Neltino – Altaghaderry Run (Deep Run) [2002/3 c82, h–: **c—** c25m c26d^{pu} c24g Feb 22] workmanlike gelding: poor chaser: no form in 2002/3 (crack- **h—** ed bone in shoulder second start): stays 25f: acts on good to soft going. *Mrs L. Richards*

KING OF ARMS 5 b.g. Rakaposhi King – Herald The Dawn (Dubassoff (USA)) **h—** [2002/3 17v 21v 18d^{pu} 17s 22g^{pu} Mar 21] €28,000 4-y-o: medium-sized gelding: brother to fairly useful 2m hurdler Three Scholars and half-brother to fair pointer by Saxon Farm: dam unraced, from family of Dawn Run: no form over hurdles. *J. Howard Johnson*

KING OF BARBURY (IRE) 6 b.g. Moscow Society (USA) – Aine's Alice (IRE) **h92** (Drumalis) [2002/3 F94: 16s^3 16s^4 19d^3 22d^{pu} Mar 6] lengthy gelding: runner-up in bumper: modest form at best over hurdles: should stay beyond 2m. *A. King*

KING OF MOMMUR (IRE) 8 b.g. Fairy King (USA) – Monoglow (Kalaglow) **c106** [2002/3 c97, h–: 18f^5 c16g* c18m* c24m^4 Apr 21] leggy gelding: winning hurdler: fair **h84** chaser: won minor event at Leicester in February and handicap at Fontwell (best effort for long time, beat Harik 1¼ lengths) in March, making most in small fields each time: stays 2½m: acts on firm and good to soft going (below form on softer): tried blinkered. *B. G. Powell*

KING OF SPARTA 10 b.g. Kefaah (USA) – Khaizaraan (CAN) (Sham (USA)) **c101** [2002/3 c115, h–: c24s^{pu} c24d c24s^5 c22g* Mar 29] leggy, angular gelding: fair handicap **h—** chaser: dropped long way in weights prior to winning at Market Rasen: stays 3m: unraced on heavy going, acts on any other: formerly most temperamental and still has his quirks (tail swisher). *J. G. Portman*

KING OF THE BLUES 11 b.g. Rakaposhi King – Colonial Princess (Roscoe Blake) **c—** [2002/3 h58: 20d^{pu} 22d^{pu} c23g^{pu} 20g Oct 6] leggy gelding: maiden hurdler: little form for **h—** long time, including over fences: tried visored. *Graeme Roe*

KING OF THE CASTLE (IRE) 8 b.g. Cataldi – Monashuna (Boreen (FR)) [2002/3 **h94** h101: 16g^3 May 8] tall gelding: modest hurdler, raced only once since 2001: should stay beyond 19f: acts on firm ground: has bled from nose. *B. Mactaggart*

KING OF THE DAWN   12 b.g. Rakaposhi King – Dawn Encounter (Rymer) [2002/3   **c84 §**
c88§, h–: c22v* c21s² Jan 14] angular gelding: modest handicap chaser: won at Fontwell   **h–**
in January: stays 2¾m: acts on heavy and good to firm going: irresolute. *P. R. Hedger*

KING OF THE FOREST (IRE)   8 b.g. Good Thyne (USA) – Coolbawn Lady (Laur-   **c88**
ence O) [2002/3 F–: c25v² c24d⁴ c25v² Jan 14] lengthy gelding: unbeaten in 3 points in
2002: modest form when second in 2 maiden chases: stays 25f: acts on heavy going.
Miss S. E. Forster

KING OF THE SEA (IRE)   6 b.g. Gone Fishin – Reign of Swing (Star Appeal)   **F–**
[2002/3 F17d F17s Dec 26] IR £6,200 4-y-o: lengthy gelding: third foal: dam in frame up
to 1½m on Flat: well beaten in 2 bumpers, found to be lame on debut: sold £1,300 Ascot
April Sales. *V. R. A. Dartnall*

KING PLATO (IRE)   6 b.g. King's Ride – You Are A Lady (IRE) (Lord Americo)   **h84**
[2002/3 F76: 20g⁶ 17d⁵ 20m 24d* 20s* 23d⁵ 26g³ Nov 7] poor hurdler, left A. Crook after
second outing: improved efforts when winning handicap at Bangor (conditional jockeys,
easily) and Worcester (novice, idled) in August: should stay 3¼m: acts on soft going: has
shown signs of temperamant. *M. D. Hammond*

KING PLAYER (IRE)   6 b.g. King's Ride – West Along (Crash Course) [2002/3   **F101 p**
F16s² Dec 28] IR £105,000 4-y-o: sixth foal: half-brother to fair hurdler/chaser Duinin
(by Macmillion), stays 3m: dam unraced sister to top-class chaser Jodami: clear of remainder when 8 lengths second of 17 finishers to impressive Sixo in bumper at Newbury
on debut: promising. *N. J. Henderson*

KINGS AVENUE   6 b.g. Gran Alba (USA) – G W Supermare (Rymer) [2002/3 F–:   **c–**
21d^pu c19d Jan 27] workmanlike gelding: no show in varied events. *G. B. Balding*   **h–**

KING'S BANK (IRE)   6 b.g. King's Ride – Super Cailin (Brave Invader (USA))   **h–**
[2002/3 16d Nov 29] IR 32,000 3-y-o, IR £24,000 4-y-o: half-brother to several winners,
including staying hurdler Grace Moore (by Deep Run) and fairly useful chaser Pongo
Waring (by Strong Gale), stays 2¾m: dam unraced half-sister to useful chaser up to 21f
Freeline Finishing: always behind in maiden hurdle at Newbury on debut. *P. J. Hobbs*

KING'S BOUNTY   7 b.g. Le Moss – Fit For A King (Royalty) [2002/3 h101: 20d   **c100**
c20d³ c25s^F c21d c24d^bd c24d³ c27v² c25d² c20g* c25g* c25m⁴ Apr 21] rangy gelding: **h–**
fair hurdler: fair novice chaser: made running when winning weak races at Wetherby
(maiden) in March and Kelso in April: stiff task, good fourth of 6 to Tonoco in handicap
at Wetherby final start: stays 27f: acts on good to firm and heavy going: hasn't looked
straightforward ride. *T. D. Easterby*

KINGSBRIDGE (IRE)   9 b.g. Cataldi – Rockport Rosa (IRE) (Roselier (FR)) [2002/3   **c69**
c66, h62: 22g^pu c16m³ c16m⁵ Aug 5] fair pointer: maiden hurdler/chaser, often shapes as   **h–**
if having a problem: effective at 2m to 3¼m: acts on good to firm going: visored once
(reportedly distressed). *M. C. Pipe*

KING'S CHAMBERS   7 ch.g. Sabrehill (USA) – Flower Girl (Pharly (FR)) [2002/3   **h75**
h81: 17g⁵ Apr 21] sparely-made gelding: poor handicap hurdler: fell in point in February:
stays 19f: acts on good to firm and heavy going: tried blinkered: usually tongue tied: races
freely. *N. J. Hawke*

KINGS CHERRY (IRE)   15 b.g. King's Ride – Another Cherry (Le Bavard (FR))   **c–**
[2002/3 c–, h–: c16d May 6] close-coupled, workmanlike gelding: veteran chaser, retains   **h–**
little ability. *J. A. B. Old*

KINGSCLIFF (IRE)   6 b.g. Toulon – Pixies Glen (Furry Glen) [2002/3 c25d*   **c137 P**
c26g* Mar 13]
    Six-year-old winners of the Christie's Foxhunter Chase at Cheltenham are
few and far between and, by adding his name to a post-war list consisting of
Halloween (1951) and Attitude Adjuster (1986), Kingscliff staked a clear claim as
a horse to follow, receiving a quote of 33/1 for the next Cheltenham Gold Cup.
Although significant improvement is required for him to pose a threat to Best Mate
and others, his potential is obvious. The Foxhunter was only Kingscliff's second
start outside points after three victories in that sphere and, as a big, rangy individual
standing 17.2 hands, he has the make and shape of a horse likely to progress with
time and experience. Attitude Adjuster failed to win in twenty-three attempts over
the next five seasons and, although he completed the course three times in the
Grand National, he ended up rated with a squiggle, so it is to be hoped Kingscliff
does not follow his example. In contrast, if Kingscliff can emulate Halloween he
will make an even bigger name for himself, since, after falling on his first two

outings in open company, Halloween went on to win the King George VI Chase twice and be placed in four successive Gold Cups, from 1953 to 1956.

Kingscliff's connections were not entertaining an angel unawares, his owner reportedly backing him at 100/1 to win the latest Foxhunter after the gelding's easy successes in points at Badbury Rings (a maiden) and Larkhill (restricted) in 2002. After four weeks on the easy list in November and December on account of a hairline fracture on the edge of a pedal bone, Kingscliff's first outing in the new season came in a ten-runner hunter chase at Wincanton at the start of February. Starting 9/4 favourite ahead of Family Business, winner of a maiden chase the previous season and a point in January, and Red Brook Lad, successful in four of his last five outings in points, Kingscliff put up a smashing display, pulling his way to the front with a circuit to go and leaving the others toiling in his wake to score by thirty lengths from Family Business. Trainer Sally Alner said she chose Wincanton in part because the fences are pretty stiff. The experience was clearly salutary for Kingscliff who tended to jump left and made a couple of mistakes, including two out. Kingscliff was still ineligible for the Foxhunter Chase, for which a runner must have won two open point-to-points, or have finished first or second in two hunter chases, or have won one open point and finished first or second in a hunter chase during the previous two seasons and before February 23rd. The options to qualify Kingscliff were a hunter chase at Sandown or an open point at Milborne St Andrew; Kingscliff was sent for the latter and trotted up, and he duly appeared among forty-one entries for Cheltenham, reportedly a record for the race. Kingscliff's reputation was such that he started 11/4 favourite in a field of twenty-four, fifteen of whom were 33/1 or longer. The pick of the others on form were 1998 winner Earthmover, 2002 winner Last Option, leading Irish hunter chaser Sheltering and the useful Quetal, successful at Newbury in February; two fourteen-year-olds who had won at the Festival before, Dorans Pride and Nahthen Lad, also took part. The race was run at a searching gallop and the principals were well placed virtually throughout.

Christie's Foxhunter Chase Challenge Cup, Cheltenham—
exciting prospect Kingscliff is well clear at the final fence

Kingscliff, under a patient ride, led soon after the fourth last and quickened clear between the last two fences, having nine lengths in hand at the final fence before tiring a little on the run-in and getting home by only two and a half lengths from Bright Approach, who showed much improved form. Last Option and Earthmover were close up in third and fourth; Dorans Pride broke a leg at the second and was destroyed. If Kingscliff had been sent for home slightly later he might have won more impressively, though the Foxhunter still represented the best hunter-chase form of the season and Kingscliff deserves plenty of credit for putting up such a performance after so little experience. His Timeform rating, while some way behind that of ill-fated Castle Mane's 148 in 1999, is well up to standard for recent Foxhunter winners. Coincidentally, Teeton Mill, who bypassed the Cheltenham race, was rated 137p after his hunter-chase campaign in 1997/8 and went on to win the Hennessy Cognac Gold Cup, King George VI Chase and Ascot Chase, earning a rating of 173+, before injury intervened a year later. It is in Kingscliff's favour that he is joining Robert Alner, husband of Sally and responsible for a hunter chaser who won the Gold Cup in Cool Dawn, successful as a ten-year-old in 1998 two seasons after running second in the Foxhunter Chase. Alner stated: 'You would have to say [Kingscliff] is one of the most exciting horses I have had at this stage of his career', probably a tactful understatement. Whatever route is planned for Kingscliff in the next season the reappearance of this most exciting prospect should be anticipated with enthusiasm.

		Top Ville	High Top
	Toulon	(b 1976)	Sega Ville
	(b 1988)	Green Rock	Mill Reef
Kingscliff (IRE)		(ch 1981)	Infra Green
(b.g. 1997)		Furry Glen	Wolver Hollow
	Pixies Glen	(b 1971)	Cleftess
	(b 1985)	How Hostile	Tumble Wind
		(b 1977)	Pixie Hill

Mr A. J. Sendell's "Kingscliff"

The big, rangy Kingscliff stays well, which is no surprise given his pedigree, and if he fails to make up into a Gold Cup contender he might make an interesting candidate for the Grand National in the longer term. His sire Toulon put up his best performances in winning the St Leger and running on into fourth in the Prix de l'Arc de Triomphe, but he failed to add to his reputation thereafter, sent to race in the States, and was retired to stud in Ireland as a dual-purpose sire in 1995. Toulon's death at the age of ten, after covering a total of nearly three hundred mares with over sixty percent live foals, now looks a significant loss since his other runners include smart novice hurdler Solerina, Pierse Hurdle and Coral Cup victor Xenophon, and Too Forward, a Grade 2 winner over hurdles in 2001/2. All of those stay at least two and a half miles. Kingscliff fetched IR 2,400 guineas as a foal at Tattersalls (Ireland) November Sale and was withdrawn from the Goffs Land Rover Sale as a three-year-old. Kingscliff's dam Pixies Glen is a half-sister to useful chaser Fighting Words, who stayed well and gained his most important success in the Kim Muir Challenge Cup. Pixies Glen showed no form in bumpers but from four other foals she has produced a fairly useful winner in that sphere, Mister Felix (by Ore). *Mrs S. Alner*

KINGS COMMAND   6 b.g. Henbit (USA) – Country Festival (Town And Country) [2002/3 F16d F16g⁴ Mar 12] good-topped gelding: second foal: half-brother to fair hunter chaser Rustic Revelry (by Afzal), stays 2¾m: dam winning pointer: better effort in bumpers when eighth of 16 at Wincanton on debut. *A. King*   **F90**

KINGSCOTE THUNDER (IRE)   6 b.g. Montelimar (USA) – Sweet Thunder (Le Bavard (FR)) [2002/3 F80: F16d F16m* Apr 22] has scope: best effort in bumpers when winning 7-runner conditional jockeys event at Chepstow, settling better. *Noel T. Chance*   **F83**

KING'S COUNTRY (IRE)   11 b.g. King's Ride – Tatlock (Paico) [2002/3 c–x, h86: c16m² c24g⁵ Feb 12] useful-looking gelding: winning hurdler: poor maiden chaser, often let down by jumping: stays 21f: acts on heavy and good to firm going: usually tongue tied: has worn cheekpieces: sold 1,000 gns Doncaster May Sales. *N. B. Mason*   **c68 x**   **h–**

KINGS DELITE (IRE)   5 b.m. Rakaposhi King – Bella Delite (Uncle Pokey) [2002/3 F63: 21s 20vᵖᵘ 16g⁵ 19mᵖᵘ Apr 21] little sign of ability, trained first 2 starts by H. Daly: dead. *R. D. Tudor*   **h–**

KINGSDON (IRE)   6 b.g. Brief Truce (USA) – Richly Deserved (IRE) (Kings Lake (USA)) [2002/3 h–: 17v⁴ 16dᵖᵘ Nov 24] modest on Flat (stays 10.5f), successful 4 times in 2002: poor form in novice hurdles: visored in 2002/3: tongue tied. *J. G. FitzGerald*   **h67**

KINGSDOWN TRIX (IRE)   9 b.g. Contract Law (USA) – Three of Trumps (Tyrnavos) [2002/3 c–, h95: 24g⁵ 20s 24m³ c23m⁵ c23gᵖᵘ 26m 19g 26g⁴ 27g Apr 19] workmanlike gelding: no form over fences: modest hurdler, left R. Smith after sixth start: stays 27f: acts on soft and good to firm going: blinkered fifth outing: unreliable. *R. Dickin*   **c– §**   **h86 §**

KING'S ECHO   5 b.g. Rakaposhi King – Welgenco (Welsh Saint) [2002/3 F16d⁴ F16g⁴ Mar 23] good-topped gelding: half-brother to Irish bumper winner Trolly Dolly (by The Parson): dam won up to 2¾m over jumps: runner-up in maiden Irish point on debut in 2002: fourth in bumpers at Doncaster and Warwick, hanging right and finding little when odds on in weak race at latter. *S. Gollings*   **F75**

KING'S ENVOY (USA)   4 b.g. Royal Academy (USA) – Island of Silver (USA) (Forty Niner (USA)) [2002/3 16d 16dᵖᵘ 20gᵖᵘ Apr 23] leggy gelding: maiden on Flat, well held in 2002, sold out of E. Dunlop's stable 4,500 gns Doncaster May Sales: no form over hurdles. *Mrs J. C. McGregor*   **h–**

KINGSFOLD FREDDIE   5 ch.g. Rock City – Kingsfold Flame (No Loiterer) [2002/3 F14d F16s³ F16d 16g 20m Apr 12] IR £20,000 3-y-o: strong gelding: third foal: dam, useful up to 1¼m, half-sister to top-class staying chaser Flashing Steel and useful staying hurdler Miltonfield: modest form in bumpers: well held both starts over hurdles. *P. R. Webber*   **h–**   **F84**

KINGS GLEN (IRE)   7 b.g. King's Ride – Lady of Aherlow (Le Bavard (FR)) [2002/3 20vᵖᵘ 20s³ 24s* c17s² c20v* c21v³ Mar 2] rangy gelding: fourth foal: half-brother to 2¼m hurdle winner Otter Track Lady (by Strong Gale): dam unraced sister to fair jumper up to 3m Aherlow Glen: fair handicap hurdler: won at Punchestown in December: fairly useful form over fences, won maiden at Down Royal in February by 2 lengths from Kadoun: well behind same horse in novice at Leopardstown final start: effective around 2m to 3m: acts on heavy going. *Thomas Carberry, Ireland*   **c121**   **h107**

KINGS HIGHWAY (IRE)　8 b.g. King's Ride – Highways Daughter (IRE) (Phar-　h–
dante (FR)) [2002/3 16d^{ro} 17g^{pu} 17d^{pu} 17f⁶ 22d Oct 22] sturdy gelding: first foal: dam,
placed in Irish bumper, half-sister to fairly useful 2m chaser Knockbrack: fair form in
bumper on debut: very headstrong and no form over hurdles, sold out of N. Meade's
stable 10,000 gns Doncaster August (2001) Sales: tongue tied final start. *Dr P. Pritchard*

KING'S HUSSAR　8 b.g. Be My Chief (USA) – Croire (IRE) (Lomond (USA)) [2002/3　c– §
c–§, h–§: 24g⁴ Oct 6] leggy gelding: winning hurdler/maiden chaser, poor nowadays:　h67 §
stays 27f: tried visored/blinkered: has had tongue tied: ungenuine. *Mrs S. Lamyman*

KINGS KNIGHT (IRE)　8 b.g. King's Ride – Right Hand (Oats) [2002/3 16d² 16s⁴　c–
c16g^{pu} 19g Jul 27] IR 10,500 4-y-o: third foal: half-brother to winning pointer by Royal　h73
Fountain: dam unraced, out of fairly useful chaser up to 25f Chuckles Hansel: signs of
ability over hurdles and in points: soon toiling in novice chase. *H. M. Kavanagh*

KINGSLAND TAVERNER　12 ch.g. True Song – Princess Hecate (Autre Prince)　c86
[2002/3 c25g^{pu} c24m³ c26g^F May 22] stocky gelding: novice chaser: third of 6 in novice　h–
hunter at Huntingdon in May: stays 3¼m: acts on firm going, probably on good to soft:
has reportedly bled from nose. *M. Harris*

KINGS LINEN (IRE)　7 b.g. Persian Mews – Kings Princess (King's Ride) [2002/3　h72
F–: 19d 20s³ 20d 21g^F 22g⁶ 26m³ 24g⁶ Apr 21] poor novice hurdler: probably stays 3¼m:
acts on good to firm going. *B. I. Case*

KINGSMARK (IRE)　10 gr.g. Roselier (FR) – Gaye Le Moss (Le Moss) [2002/3　c163
c158, h–: c24d* c24d³ Dec 14]　h–

Haydock's Edward Hanmer Memorial Chase, formerly known as the Sun-
dew Chase and at one time a weight-for-age event, has built up an impressive roll
of honour in its forty-four-year history. Gold Cup winners L'Escargot, Forgive'N
Forget and Jodami have all won it, along with the likes of Pendil, Bula, Wayward
Lad and Beau Ranger. Bula, Forgive'N Forget and Beau Ranger won the race twice
in succession, but another Gold Cup winner, the Tony and Michael Dickinson-
trained Silver Buck, landed it twice as many times as those famous names, winning
consecutive editions between 1979 and 1982. Silver Buck produced some tip-top
handicap performances in the race: in 1979 he beat Night Nurse by a length and a
half receiving 1 lb; and in 1982 defeated future Gold Cup winner Burrough Hill
Lad comfortably by two and a half lengths, conceding him 21 lb. The very best
chasers appear in handicaps less frequently nowadays though, more recently, the
popular grey Suny Bay recorded a couple of fine performances when yet another
back-to-back winner of the Edward Hanmer in 1997 and 1998; for the second of
those successes, Suny Bay conceded 4 lb to Escartefigue and beat him by five
lengths, with another future Gold Cup winner, See More Business, conceding Suny
Bay just 2 lb, over a length further back in fourth. Silver Buck, Suny Bay . . . it
might conjure up images of something of a grey domination of the race, although
Silver Buck was brown, rather than the colour his moniker might suggest, his name
being taken from his sire Silver Cloud. Another who is most definitely grey,
Kingsmark, has made the Edward Hanmer his own in recent seasons. Kingsmark
has not won the race as often as Silver Buck, or produced a weight-carrying effort
so meritorious as Suny Bay's, but in November he became only the second
horse—after Silver Buck—to win it as many as three times, in doing so producing
one of the handicap performances of the latest season.

As one of the first three-mile pattern chases of the season, the Edward Hanmer Memorial is an ideal target for a horse like Kingsmark who goes particularly
well when fresh. He already had a couple of successes that autumn before taking
the Edward Hanmer from a BHB mark of 135 in 2000, but lined up on his seasonal
reappearance when gaining his second win from a mark 13 lb higher in 2001, and
also when taking the race from a BHB mark of 157 in the latest season, partnered,
as he had been for his earlier wins in the race, by David Dennis. The big chases at
Haydock often want for runners, though the latest Edward Hanmer had a relatively
large field of nine, four of which were out of the handicap. Carrying top weight
of 11-10, Kingsmark started second favourite at 100/30, just behind Chives, to
whom he was conceding 14 lb. Confirmed front runners Grey Abbey and Kadou
Nonantais ensured a truly-run race and, from the last, Kingsmark and Chives, both
having travelled well throughout, pulled clear, Kingsmark winning very gamely by
a length and a half, with Bobby Grant nineteen lengths back in third. The high-class

Edward Hanmer Memorial Chase (Limited Handicap), Haydock—pursuing a riderless horse at the last, the grey Kingsmark gains a third successive victory in the race; Chives fills the runner-up spot

effort, which showed Kingsmark to be better than ever, augured well for his prospects of bettering his previous season's second placing in the Tommy Whittle Chase at the same course the following month, particularly as he was 6 lb better off with Bobby Grant, who was going for his third win in that contest. However, as in the previous year, the race turned into a relative test of speed and Kingsmark, who failed to jump so fluently under pressure as usual, was beaten again, finishing only third of four behind Sackville and Bobby Grant. Kingsmark's campaign was all set to mirror that of 2001/2 when, following the Edward Hanmer and the Tommy Whittle, Kingsmark was given a four-month break before tackling the Grand National, in which he travelled strongly for a long way and finished fourth, despite reportedly losing his action. Unfortunately, however, after being among the final declarations for the latest National, for which he was around a 16/1-chance, Kingsmark was ruled out by a tendon injury. Assuming he makes a full recovery, Kingsmark will surely be back to try to emulate Silver Buck in the Edward Hanmer before another crack at the National. Perhaps he'll even make it third time lucky in the Tommy Whittle.

	Roselier (FR)	Misti IV	Medium
	(gr 1973)	(b 1958)	Mist
Kingsmark (IRE)		Peace Rose	Fastnet Rock
(gr.g. 1993)		(gr 1959)	La Paix
	Gaye Le Moss	Le Moss	Le Levanstell
	(ch 1982)	(ch 1975)	Feemoss
		Artiste Gaye	Artist's Son
		(b 1961)	Goldiane

    The pedigree of the smallish, sound-jumping Kingsmark was covered fully in *Chasers & Hurdlers 2000/01*. He remains proven only at up to three and a quarter miles, though is unlikely to fail for lack of stamina if tried beyond it again. Apart from his run in the National, Kingsmark has raced only on good going or softer and is particularly suited by testing conditions. *M. Todhunter*

KING'S MILL (IRE)   6 b.g. Doyoun – Adarika (Kings Lake (USA)) [2002/3 16s⁵ **h109** 16g² 16d Jan 15] leggy gelding: useful on Flat (best at 1¼m): easily best effort over hurdles (lost all chance when nearly brought down on debut) when 1½ lengths second of 25 to Caracciola in maiden at Newbury: broke blood vessel following month. *N. A. Graham*

KINGS MINSTRAL (IRE) 13 ch.g. Andretti – Tara Minstral VII (Damsire Unregistered) [2002/3 c64, h–: c25m c21m c25m[5] c27g[ur] c27d Oct 31] plain gelding: poor handicap chaser: stays 25f: acts on firm and good to soft going: usually races prominently. *D. A. Lamb*   c–
h–

KINGS MISTRAL (IRE) 10 b.g. Strong Gale – Mrs Simpson (Kinglet) [2002/3 c103, h–: c24v* c24s* c24s[4] c24s* Mar 7] rangy gelding: fair chaser: in form of his life in 2002/3, winning handicaps at Ascot in November and Sandown in December and amateur race at Sandown (beat Careysville 5 lengths) in March: stays 25f: acts on any going. *P. R. Chamings*   c113
h–

KINGSMOOR 7 b.g. Regal Embers (IRE) – Cupids Bower (Owen Dudley) [2002/3 h84: c24s[F] Feb 27] signs of ability on second of 2 outings in novice hurdles in spring 2001: soon struggling on chasing debut. *K. Bishop*   c–
h–

KING SOLOMON (FR) 4 gr.c. Simon du Desert (FR) – All Square (FR) (Holst (USA)) [2002/3 17d[2] 17g 16g Apr 3] close-coupled colt: useful on Flat (stays 1½m) at best, sold out of P. Cole's stable 88,000 gns Newmarket Autumn Sales: fairly useful form in juvenile hurdles, highly tried after debut, eleventh of 27 to Spectroscope in Triumph Hurdle at Cheltenham and ninth of 19 to Le Duc in Grade 2 at Aintree, weakened closing stages having travelled well both times. *Miss Venetia Williams*   h114

KING'S OPERA (IRE) 5 b.m. King's Theatre (IRE) – Thrifty's Best (Glenstal (USA)) [2002/3 16g[F] 16m* 16g* 16m[4] 16g[2] Mar 30] fair at 3 yrs on Flat (stays 1½m), well held only start in 2002: fairly useful hurdler: won maiden at Ballinrobe in August and minor event at Down Royal in September: good second to Stashedaway in handicap at Cork: likely to stay beyond 2m: acts on soft and good to firm going. *M. J. Grassick, Ireland*   h117

KINGS ORCHARD (IRE) 6 ch.g. Castle Keep – Orchardstown Lady (Paddy's Stream) [2002/3 F16s[2] F16f* F20d[3] 16s[5] 18s 20s* 20s 20g[2] Apr 20] medium-sized gelding: second foal: dam unraced half-sister to useful 2½m chase winner Haepenny Well, from family of Bula: fairly useful form in bumpers, won at Punchestown in September: fairly useful hurdler: won maiden at Limerick in February: very good length second to Pay It Forward in Grade 3 novice at Fairyhouse in April, ran moody race when well held at Punchestown in early-May: will stay beyond 2½m: acts on soft and firm going. *N. Meade, Ireland*   h117
F95

KINGS RAPID (IRE) 9 b.g. King's Ride – Smokey River (Over The River (FR)) [2002/3 c–, h–: c21d[pu] 20d[pu] 17s Nov 28] tall gelding: winning hurdler/maiden chaser, has shaped as if amiss since 2001/2 reappearance. *Mrs S. J. Smith*   c–
h–

KING'S REIGN (IRE) 7 ch.g. King's Ride – Lena's Reign (Quayside) [2002/3 h–, F–: 20d 19d 22d 20v Feb 13] lengthy gelding: little sign of ability. *N. A. Twiston-Davies*   h–

KING'S STRIDE (IRE) 11 b.g. King's Ride – Anavore (Darantus) [2002/3 c98d, h–: c20d Jun 4] workmanlike gelding: winning hurdler/chaser, has lost his form: tried visored/tongue tied. *P. Monteith*   c–
h–

KINGSTHORPE 15 ch.g. Brotherly (USA) – Miss Kewmill (Billion (USA)) [2002/3 c89, h–: c25g[pu] May 1] leggy, sparely-made gelding: veteran hunter chaser. *M. R. Daniell*   c–
h–

KINGSTON-BANKER 7 b.g. Teamster – Happy Manda (Mandamus) [2002/3 c101, h–: c24d[5] c21v[2] c24s[3] c24d[pu] c19d[2] c26m[F] Mar 31] sturdy gelding: fair novice chaser, often let down by jumping: stays 3m: acts on any ground. *R. H. Alner*   c102 x
h–

KINGSTON BILL 6 b.g. Then Again – Tricata (Electric) [2002/3 16d[3] 19d[5] 16s[6] 16s[pu] 16v[5] Jan 29] workmanlike gelding: probably flattered when never-nearer third of 16 in novice hurdle at Chepstow on reappearance: poor form otherwise. *W. G. M. Turner*   h77

KINGSTON GAME 4 b.g. Mind Games – Valmaranda (USA) (Sir Ivor) [2002/3 17s[pu] 16g[pu] 17m[pu] Aug 17] modest and unreliable on Flat (stays 9.4f): no show in 3 juvenile hurdles: visored final start. *Miss K. M. George*   h–

KINGSTON VENTURE 7 b.g. Interrex (CAN) – Tricata (Electric) [2002/3 h–: 20d[3] 24d 19s[2] 19d[4] c19s[4] c20s[pu] Jan 3] good-topped gelding: fair handicap hurdler: no form in 2 starts over fences: stays 2½m: acts on soft and good to firm going: effective visored/blinkered or not. *W. G. M. Turner*   c–
h101

KINGSTON WISH (IRE) 4 b.g. Mujadil (USA) – Well Wisher (USA) (Sanglamore (USA)) [2002/3 16g Feb 12] maiden on Flat: soundly beaten on hurdling debut. *Ian Emmerson*   h–

KINGS TO OPEN   6 b.g. First Trump – Shadiyama (Nishapour (FR)) [2002/3 h84:   h–
17s 17d 20m Mar 23] leggy gelding: maiden hurdler, well held in handicaps in 2002/3:
tried tongue tied. *R. Dickin*

KING'S TRAVEL (FR)   7 gr.g. Balleroy (USA) – Travel Free (Be My Guest (USA))   c–
[2002/3 h–: 17v⁵ 16s 16s⁶ c16s 17g* Apr 21] tall, angular gelding: bought 2,600 gns   h79
Ascot July Sales: best effort over hurdles when winning selling handicap at Newton
Abbot: well held on chasing debut: likely to prove best at sharp 2m. *J. D. Frost*

KINGS VALLEY (IRE)   9 b.g. Castle Keep – Boreen Bro (Boreen (FR)) [2002/3   c116
c126, h–: 22v 20s 24vᵖᵘ c20d² Feb 16] good-topped gelding: fair hurdler: fairly useful   h106
handicap chaser: ½-length second of 4 to Commanche Court from 14 lb out of handicap
at Navan in February: stays 29f: acts on good to firm and heavy going. *N. Meade, Ireland*

KINGTOBEE (IRE)   5 b.g. King's Ride – Zephyrelle (IRE) (Celio Rufo) [2002/3   F75
F16m Mar 22] rangy gelding: has scope: first foal: dam, fair form in bumpers, sister to
useful 2m hurdlers Winter Squall and Zephyrus and half-sister to smart 2m hurdler
Carobee and useful hurdler Alekhine: shaped as if in need of experience when tenth of 18
in bumper at Newbury on debut. *J. A. B. Old*

KING TORUS (IRE)   13 b.g. Torus – Kam A Dusk (Kambalda) [2002/3 c104§, h–:   c82 §
c21g c21d³ c21g² c21m⁵ c21gᵖᵘ Jul 31] leggy gelding: veteran chaser, on the downgrade: h–
stays 25f: acts on firm and soft going: usually blinkered: unreliable. *V. R. A. Dartnall*

KING TRITON (IRE)   6 br.g. Mister Lord (USA) – Deepwater Woman (The Parson)   h86
[2002/3 h75, F79: 24s 25v³ 22v² 27v² 25s* Mar 10] modest hurdler: soon off bridle when
winning handicap at Plumpton: thorough stayer: raced on going softer than good (acts on
heavy). *L. Wells*

KINNINO   9 b.g. Polish Precedent (USA) – On Tiptoes (Shareef Dancer (USA))   h66
[2002/3 h–: 16m 17m⁵ 16s 16vᵖᵘ 18vᵖᵘ Mar 3] small gelding: little form over hurdles: has
worn cheekpieces: races freely. *G. L. Moore*

KINO'S CROSS   14 b.g. Relkino – Coral Delight (Idiot's Delight) [2002/3 c–, h76:   c–
16gᵖᵘ May 21] sturdy gelding: veteran 2m hurdler. *A. J. Wilson*   h–

KIORA BAY   6 b.g. Karinga Bay – Equasion (IRE) (Cyrano de Bergerac) [2002/3   F–
F17d Dec 3] 12,000 4-y-o: first foal: dam, modest maiden on Flat who stayed 1½m,
half-sister to useful hurdler/chaser up to 21f Hawthorn Blaze: well held in bumper on
debut. *Jonjo O'Neill*

KIPLING   7 b.g. Rudimentary (USA) – Sharmood (USA) (Sharpen Up) [2002/3 F17s⁶   h86
F18v⁵ 21s 24vᵖᵘ 27v³ Mar 3] seventh foal: half-brother to fairly useful but irresolute   F81
hurdler King Kato (by Unfuwain), stays 3m, and 11.6f winner Brig O'Turk (by Inchinor):
dam maiden in USA: signs of ability in bumpers: seemingly better effort on completed
starts in novice hurdles when 10¾ lengths third of 4 finishers to Rosarian at Fontwell
final start (none too fluent): stays 27f. *Miss S. West*

KIPPANOUR (USA)   11 br.g. Alleged (USA) – Innsbruck (General Assembly   c– §
(USA)) [2002/3 c–§, h97§: 27m³ 27g⁵ 27s* 24gᵖᵘ 25g 24d⁶ 26s³ 26s³ 25s 26g⁵ 25d⁵ Mar   h90 §
6] smallish gelding: winning chaser: modest handicap hurdler: won at Newton Abbot in
May: stays 27f: acts on firm and soft going (below form only start on heavy): blinkered/
visored: ungenuine (takes plenty of driving). *A. G. Hobbs*

KIPPOUR (FR)   5 b.g. Luchiroverte (IRE) – Obole III (FR) (Signani (FR)) [2002/3   h73
F82p: F17d⁵ 19g 21gᵖᵘ Mar 3] close-coupled, quite attractive gelding: modest form in 2   F84
bumpers: dropped away in novice hurdles at Doncaster and Market Rasen. *H. D. Daly*

KIRDFORD (IRE)   9 b. or br.g. Miner's Lamp – Somelli (Candy Cane) [2002/3 h78:   h–
22sᶠ Nov 9] sturdy gelding: poor handicap hurdler: stayed 2¾m: acted on good to firm
and heavy going: dead. *R. H. Buckler*

KIRISNIPPA   8 b.g. Beveled (USA) – Kiri Te (Liboi (USA)) [2002/3 h–: 22gᵖᵘ May 1]   h–
lengthy gelding: modest on Flat (stays 2m): no show in 3 starts over hurdles. *A. P. Jones*

KIRKHARLE (IRE)   9 b.g. Commanche Run – Dardy Daughter (Side Track)   c–
[2002/3 c78, h–: c25d 19dᵖᵘ 24s⁶ c24d³ c24gᵖᵘ Feb 22] winning pointer: poor novice   h–
hurdler/chaser, left Mrs A. Hamilton after reappearance: stays 25f: has worn cheekpieces.
K. F. Clutterbuck

KIRMAR (IRE)   9 b.g. Montelimar (USA) – Winsome Doe (Buckskin (FR)) [2002/3   c127
c105, h115: c22v⁶ c24s³ c20s c24vᴿ c24s³ c28s c25sᶠ c24d⁵ c29g Apr 21] tall gelding: h–

fairly useful hurdler: winning chaser, much improved when third to Be My Belle in valuable handicap at Gowran fifth start: stays 3m: acts on heavy going (below form on good to firm): tongue tied third outing. *P. A. Fahy, Ireland*

KIRSTY LEA 4 b.f. Presidium – Adder Howe (Amboise) [2002/3 F14d Nov 25] fifth **F–** foal: dam well beaten in bumper and novice hurdles: behind in bumper on debut. *I. W. McInnes*

KISSED BY MOONLITE 7 gr.m. Petong – Rose Bouquet (General Assembly **h–** (USA)) [2002/3 20m^{pu} Jun 19] poor maiden on Flat: temperamental display on hurdling debut. *J. W. Unett*

KISS ME KATE 7 b.m. Aragon – Ingerence (FR) (Akarad (FR)) [2002/3 19d^2 Nov **h74** 26] leggy mare: one-time fair handicap hurdler: well backed on return from 20-month absence, 1½ lengths second of 16 at Warwick, staying on well from poor position: stays 2½m: acts on heavy and good to firm going. *Mrs P. Robeson*

KITIMAT 6 b.g. Then Again – Quago (New Member) [2002/3 F–: 22f^{pu} 19g^4 17g **c62** 22m^5 20s^6 c19d c25d^{pu} c18s^4 c18m^6 Mar 22] rangy gelding: poor novice hurdler/chaser: **h74** free-going sort. *R. H. Buckler*

KITLEY CREEK 8 b.g. Michelozzo (USA) – May Reef (IRE) (Simply Great (FR)) **h–** [2002/3 h78+: 22f^{pu} 17d^{pu} Oct 22] lengthy, rather sparely-made gelding: lightly raced over hurdles, pulled up both starts in 2002/3, lame final one: raced mainly around 2m on going firmer than good. *M. Hill*

KIT SMARTIE (IRE) 11 b.g. Be My Native (USA) – Smart Cookie (Lord Gayle **c125** (USA)) [2002/3 c125, h–: c25s^2 c28s* c25d^4 c28d^{pu} c33m Apr 12] angular gelding: **h–** winning hurdler: fairly useful handicap chaser: won 5-finisher event at Haydock in November by 11 lengths from Native Buck: stayed 3½m: acted on good to firm and heavy going: wore cheekpieces/blinkers late in career (often soon off bridle): usually tongue tied: dead. *D. M. Forster*

KITTENKAT 9 b.m. Riverwise (USA) – Cut Above The Rest (Indiaro) [2002/3 h106: **c90 x** c23m^3 c19s^5 c26s^3 c26d^3 c26v^F c24s^5 c26s^{ur} c24s^5 c24s^4 c26s^2 c32g c24g^6 Apr 2] lengthy, **h–** angular mare: fair handicap hurdler: modest novice chaser, often let down by jumping: stays 3¼m: acts on heavy going, possibly not on good to firm. *N. R. Mitchell*

KIVOTOS (USA) 5 gr.g. Trempolino (USA) – Authorized Staff (USA) (Relaunch **h102** (USA)) [2002/3 16v 16v* 18d^{pu} 20s^3 20d^2 Apr 25] leggy gelding: lightly-raced maiden on Flat: fair novice hurdler: awarded maiden at Ayr in January on technical grounds: good second to Beckley in 14-runner handicap at Perth: stays 2½m: raced on going softer than good. *A. C. Whillans*

KLONDIKE CHARGER (USA) 9 b.g. Crafty Prospector (USA) – Forever **c102 §** Waving (USA) (Hoist The Flag (USA)) [2002/3 c100, h–: c25f^3 c26d^{pu} c23m^{pu} c24g^2 **h–** c26m^{pu} c27g^5 c22g^2 c24f^2 c24d^5 c24d^2 c27g Dec 12] leggy gelding: fair handicap chaser, left P. Nicholls after second start: stays 3¼m: probably ideally suited by good going or firmer (acts on firm): blinkered once: unreliable. *Dr P. Pritchard*

KNIAZ (FR) 5 gr.g. Saint Preuil (FR) – Alberade (FR) (Deep Run) [2002/3 16s^3 16s* **h111 p** Mar 16] fifth foal: half-brother to 3 winners, including useful 2¼m hurdle winner Hyperiade (by Genereux Genie): dam won up to 1½m: fair form in 2 maiden hurdles at Punchestown, beating The Boys In Green ½ length on second occasion: may well prove best around 2m: useful prospect. *A. J. Martin, Ireland*

KNIFE EDGE (USA) 8 b. or br.g. Kris S (USA) – My Turbulent Miss (USA) (My **c148** Dad George (USA)) [2002/3 c154, h–: c16s 16s^3 c17v^2 c17s^3 c20d^2 Mar 22] tall gelding: **h–** very smart hurdler at best: smart chaser: best effort in 2002/3 when length second to Rince Ri in listed contest at Navan in March: sixth of 7 in Grade 1 at Punchestown in late-April: stays 2½m: acts on heavy going, possibly not on good to firm. *M. J. P. O'Brien, Ireland*

KNIGHT OF KILCASH (IRE) 8 ch.g. Buckskin (FR) – Lady Pauper (IRE) (Le **c–** Moss) [2002/3 c21m^{pu} May 22] IR 5,000 3-y-o: fourth foal: brother to winning pointer and half-brother to 2 others: dam unraced, from family of high-class 2m to 2½m hurdler King Credo: won maiden point in 2002: never a factor on hunter chase debut. *Mrs O. Bush*

KNIGHT OF PASSION 11 b.g. Arctic Lord – Lovelek (Golden Love) [2002/3 c–, **c–** h93: c24s^{pu} Mar 7] small, angular gelding: novice hurdler: one-time useful hunter chaser, **h–**

dropped right out in blinkers at Sandown in March: best at 3m+: acts on soft and good to firm going: sometimes makes mistakes. *Miss S. E. Robinson*

KNIGHT OF SILVER 6 gr.g. Presidium – Misty Rocket (Roan Rocket) [2002/3 **h66 §** h–§: 16g 16m 19m⁴ 20m 22s² 22d^pu 24g^pu 21m³ 20g² 16d³ 20d^pu 17s 17m² Apr 21] sparely-made gelding: poor maiden hurdler: sold out of M. Gingell's stable 1,700 gns Doncaster January Sales before final start: probably stays 2¾m: acts on soft and good to firm going: has worn blinkers/visor/cheekpieces: has been reluctant to race: not to be trusted. *R. Williams*

KNIGHTON STAR 7 b.m. Gildoran – Barrica (Main Reef) [2002/3 F–: 19g² Jun 12] **h78** lengthy mare: lightly raced: modest form on first of 2 starts in bumpers: 2 lengths second of 12 in novice at Hereford on hurdling debut: will stay beyond 19f. *R. T. Phillips*

KNIGHTSBRIDGE KING 7 ch.g. Michelozzo (USA) – Shahdjat (IRE) (Vayrann) **h89 §** [2002/3 h–, F89: 19m² 21g 16d³ 16g⁴ 19s⁵ 19d² 17s* 17m² Apr 5] rather sparely-made gelding: modest hurdler: won novice seller at Hereford in March: stays 19f: acts on soft and good to firm going: effective blinkered/visored or not: ungenuine. *A. King*

KNIGHT'S CREST (IRE) 13 ch.g. The Parson – Sno-Cat (Arctic Slave) [2002/3 **c–** c87, h–: c25d^pu Apr 29] tall, good-topped gelding: veteran staying chaser: acts on good to **h–** firm and good to soft going, possibly not softer. *R. Dickin*

KNIGHT'S EMPEROR (IRE) 6 b.g. Grand Lodge (USA) – So Kind (Kind of **c97** Hush) [2002/3 c88p, h97: 16m³ 16m⁵ 16m³ 16d² c17g* c16g^F Sep 14] good-topped **h99** gelding: modest handicap hurdler: similar form when landing odds in novice chase at Southwell in September: let down by jumping both other starts over fences, looking likely winner when falling 4 out at Worcester: likely to prove best at sharp 2m: acts on firm and good to soft going: consistent. *J. L. Spearing*

KNIGHT TEMPLAR (IRE) 10 b.g. Roselier (FR) – Rathsallagh Tartan (Strong **c–** Gale) [2002/3 c97, h–: c27d⁴ Apr 8] useful-looking gelding: winning hunter chaser: won **h–** point in March: well held at Sedgefield following month: stays 27f (beaten before stamina became an issue over 31f): probably acts on any going: tried visored/tongue tied. *C. P. Dennis*

KNOCKAUN WOOD (IRE) 9 ch.g. Be My Native (USA) – Misty Venture (Foggy **c–** Bell) [2002/3 h–: c23d^pu Mar 4] big, rather leggy gelding: very lightly raced and little **h–** worthwhile form. *C. A. Fuller*

KNOCKDOO (IRE) 10 ch.g. Be My Native (USA) – Ashken (Artaius (USA)) [2002/3 **c– §** c94§, h106§: 24d³ 24d c21d⁴ 24g² Apr 23] good-topped gelding: maiden chaser (doesn't **h104 §** jump fluently): fair handicap hurdler: left J. O'Neill after second start: stays 27f: acts on heavy going: visored once: has had tongue tied: often finds little. *J. S. Goldie*

KNOCKFIARNE MAGIC (IRE) 11 b.g. Buzzards Bay – Daisy Star (Star Appeal) **h–** [2002/3 20m^pu Jun 30] remote third of 4 finishers in maiden point in 2000: broke leg in maiden hurdle at Uttoxeter. *B. P. J. Baugh*

KNOCKHOLT 7 b.g. Be My Chief (USA) – Saffron Crocus (Shareef Dancer (USA)) **h96** [2002/3 h–: 24d² 20m² 21m⁴ 24d² Aug 17] useful but none too consistent on Flat (stays 2m): modest form when runner-up over hurdles: stays 3m: acts on good to firm and good to soft going: visored final start. *L. Lungo*

KNOCK KNOCK (IRE) 6 b.g. Executive Perk – Knockananig (Carlingford Castle) **c125** [2002/3 c20s⁶ c20v⁶ c22s c22s* c20s* c20g² c29g² Apr 21] fourth foal: half-brother to fair chaser Lurgoe (by Camden Town), stayed 3m, and winning pointer Mr Pistachio (by Royal Fountain): dam unraced half-sister to high-class 2m chaser I'm A Driver: in frame all 4 starts in points: most progressive form in steeplechases: won handicaps at Thurles and Limerick in March: very good second last 2 starts, beaten head by Timbera in Irish Grand National at Fairyhouse: stays 29f: acts on soft going. *D. Wachman, Ireland*

KNOCKOUT (IRE) 7 b.g. Persian Mews – Knockaville (Crozier) [2002/3 16m^pu **h–** 20g^pu 16g^pu Sep 14] IR 28,000 4-y-o: ex-Irish gelding: half-brother to several winners, including fairly useful hurdler up to 3m Henrietta Howard (by King's Ride) and fair staying chasers Bishop's Staff (by Monksfield) and Gay Moore (by Raise You Ten): dam unraced, out of sister to Irish Grand National winner Sweet Dreams: fair in bumpers and modest form over hurdles for M. Morris in 2001/2: no completions in points or over hurdles in Britain: tried visored. *Miss K. Marks*

KNOCKRIGG (IRE) 9 ch.g. Commanche Run – Gaiety Lass (Le Moss) [2002/3 **c–** c88, h–: 20s⁶ 22m⁶ 17m⁶ c16g 17v² 17s² 16v⁵ 17d⁵ 17g² Apr 21] good-bodied gelding: **h77** poor hurdler/chaser: stays 2½m: acts on any going: tried blinkered. *Dr P. Pritchard*

Gerrard Wealth Management Kennel Gate Novices' Hurdle, Ascot—
Kopeck (left) comes to wear down favourite Puntal after the last

KNOCKTOPHER ABBEY 6 ch.g. Pursuit of Love – Kukri (Kris) [2002/3 h97: **h97**
16m³ 16g⁴ 16m* Apr 22] medium-sized gelding: fair on Flat (stays 1¼m): modest
hurdler: trained until after reappearance (blinkered) by R. Millman: won maiden at
Chepstow: likely to prove best at sharp 2m. *Miss Venetia Williams*

KNOWHOW (IRE) 6 br.g. Mister Lord (USA) – Mossy Mistress (IRE) (Le Moss) **h74**
[2002/3 F93: 16g 19s⁶ 24d⁴ Mar 1] big, rangy, good sort: fair form only run in bumper:
poor form over hurdles. *M. Pitman*

KNOW THYNE (IRE) 9 ch.g. Good Thyne (USA) – Bail Out (Quayside) [2002/3 **h–**
h–, F88: 22mᵖᵘ 16m 20g 20mᵖᵘ Apr 12] lengthy gelding: won bumper on debut in May
2001: no worthwhile form over hurdles, left H. Daly after second start. *P. T. Dalton*

KOCK DE LA VESVRE (FR) 5 b.g. Sassanian (USA) – Csardas (FR) (Maiymad) **c111 §**
[2002/3 c17v⁶ c17d* c20s c20s² c16s³ c17v* c20gᶠ c17m² c16g* Apr 24] leggy, lengthy **h–**
ex-French gelding: first known foal: dam twice-raced on Flat/pulled up only start over
fences: won 1½m non-thoroughbred event on Flat at 3 yrs: in frame both starts over
hurdles: fair chaser: won 4-y-o event at Auteuil in May (sold out of T. Civel's stable
€60,000 Goffs July Sale after next start) and novices at Bangor in March and Perth (very
easily) in April: probably stays 2½m: acts on heavy going, probably on good to firm:
blinkered at Auteuil: has looked unwilling and is one to treat with caution. *Miss Venetia
Williams*

KOLPATCHEVA (FR) 6 b.m. Cricket Ball (USA) – Tosca de Bellouet (FR) (Olmeto) **c– x**
[2002/3 c–: 19dᶠ c16sᵘʳ c16dᶠ 17s 16vᶠ 17g Mar 25] close-coupled mare: little sign of **h–**
ability: poor jumper of fences. *G. Brown*

KOMBINACJA (POL) 5 ch.m. Jape (USA) – Komancza (POL) (Dakota) [2002/3 **h99 +**
16v 21m⁴ Feb 22] big, lengthy mare: successful 7 times from 12 starts up to 1¾m on Flat
in Poland, including in Derby and St Leger at 3 yrs for B. Mazurek: much better effort
over hurdles when fourth to Foreman in well-contested novice at Kempton. *T. R. George*

KOMORI (IRE) 13 b. or br.g. Rising – Pandos Pet (Dusky Boy) [2002/3 c73: c25g⁶ **c–**
c20s c27vᵖᵘ Nov 12] poor maiden pointer. *A. M. Crow*

KOMPLIMENT 5 ch.g. Komaite (USA) – Eladale (IRE) (Ela-Mana-Mou) [2002/3 **h–**
16mᵖᵘ Aug 27] half-brother to 17f hurdle winner Sharway Lady (by Shareef Dancer): fair

482

sprinter on Flat: pulled hard and jumped none too fluently in novice on hurdling debut. *Mrs H. Dalton*

KONFUZIUS (GER) 5 b.g. Motley (USA) – Katrina (GER) (Windwurf (GER)) [2002/3 16v⁶ 16m 24vᶠ 17v⁶ 16s 17d⁴ 20gᵖᵘ Apr 1] ex-German gelding: brother to 2 Flat winners in Germany, including Kolumbus, useful up to 1½m, and half-brother to another: dam 6f and 7f winner: won once from 5 starts up to 1¼m on Flat in 2002 for H. Blume: bad novice hurdler: best efforts around 2m: acts on heavy going: has worn cheekpieces. *P. Monteith* **h58**

KONKER 8 ch.g. Selkirk (USA) – Helens Dreamgirl (Caerleon (USA)) [2002/3 h121d: 17d² Nov 11] small, compact gelding: fairly useful handicap hurdler: creditable second in conditional jockeys event at Carlisle only start in 2002/3: best around 2m on soft/heavy going: held up. *Mrs M. Reveley* **h113**

KOPECK (IRE) 5 ch.g. Moscow Society (USA) – Cashla (IRE) (Duky) [2002/3 F88p: 16v* 16d⁵ Jan 18] well-made gelding: type to make a chaser: promising when second in bumper on debut in 2001/2: 33/1, useful form when winning 8-runner Grade 2 Gerrard Wealth Management Kennel Gate Novices' Hurdle at Ascot on reappearance, closing on Puntal in straight to win by 2 lengths: didn't run much of a race (had reportedly coughed earlier in week) when tailed off in Grade 1 novice at Wincanton following month: will stay 2½m. *J. T. Gifford* **h137**

KORAKOR (FR) 9 ch.g. Nikos – Aniflore (FR) (Satingo) [2002/3 c137, h–: c20mᵖᵘ c20dᵖᵘ c20d² c20d c19s³ c16g c16m* c16m² Apr 17] good-topped gelding: useful handicap chaser: 15 lb out of handicap when making all in 4-runner event at Ayr in April: probably best up to 21f: acts on good to firm and heavy going. *Ian Williams* **c137 h–**

KORELO (FR) 5 b.g. Cadoudal (FR) – Lora du Charmil (FR) (Panoramic) [2002/3 c20v² 17d⁵ c20s c22v⁵ 17d³ 17v* 16d⁴ 20v* 16v* 21g⁵ 20gᵖᵘ Apr 3] **c126 + h137**

Korelo became the fifth Martin Pipe-trained winner of the Sunderlands Imperial Cup at Sandown, fourteen years after the first, Travel Mystery. The other victories for Pond House stables came in 1993 with Olympian, 1998 with Blowing Wind and in 2002 with Polar Red. In common with the stable's other Imperial Cup winners, Korelo started a well-backed favourite, though with sixteen rivals (there were four withdrawals because of the heavy ground) it was a more competitive affair than the betting suggested; apart from Korelo (9/4), only Talarive (13/2), a good second at Kelso the week before, and the Lanzarote runner-up Hawadeth (8/1) started at shorter than 10/1. With the outsider Lawz forcing the pace, the test of stamina proved ideal for Korelo. Waited with, he seemed to be going nowhere

William Hill Handicap Hurdle, Ascot—progressive hurdlers Korelo and Chopneyev fight out the finish

under the whip early in the straight but, switched to the inside after the second last and still with half a dozen horses ahead of him, Korelo began to make ground. Jumping to the front at the last, past the tiring Lawz and another 33/1-shot Mercato, Korelo stayed on strongly to win by six lengths from the Irish mare Newhall, with Lawz third and one of Korelo's stable-companions Canada a staying-on fourth.

Victory in the Imperial Cup these days brings with it the prospect of a £60,000 bonus if the winner can follow up at the following week's Cheltenham Festival. A tough task, but not one that had proved beyond either Olympian or Blowing Wind who landed the bonus in the Coral Cup and County Hurdle in their respective years. Korelo had already been made ante-post favourite for the Coral Cup, the longer trip at Cheltenham looking likely to be in his favour, but under much less testing conditions than at Sandown he was always struggling to keep tabs on the leaders, though still emerged with plenty of credit under his penalty to finish fifth of the twenty-five finishers behind the well-backed Xenophon who had supplanted him as favourite—Korelo went off joint-third favourite. Two hard races within five days seemed to leave their mark and Korelo was pulled up in the Mersey Novices' Hurdle at Aintree on his only subsequent start.

Korelo's campaign for his current connections began in novice hurdles as well. He showed promise on his British debut when third to Rhinestone Cowboy in a four-runner event at Cheltenham, then made rather hard work of landing the odds in a weak contest at Taunton later in December, before coming fourth in an ordinary race at Wincanton. All those races were at around two miles, and it was no coincidence that Korelo showed marked improvement when stepped up to two and a half miles on his handicap debut at Ascot in February. The William Hill Handicap Hurdle was not so strong a race for the same amount of money (£29,000 to the winner) as the Imperial Cup, but was run in similarly testing conditions. Another novice, Chopneyev, shaded Korelo for favouritism at the off (Korelo had been strongly supported in the morning) and the market leaders had the race to themselves up the straight. In receipt of nearly a stone from his main rival, Korelo was ridden to get on top on the run-in and won by a length and a quarter from Chopneyev, the pair twelve lengths clear. Korelo's improved form meant he had to overcome a rise of 13 lb in his BHB mark to win at Sandown.

Korelo's future lies over fences, or to be more precise, back over fences. He had been mainly campaigned as a chaser by Guy Cherel in France before joining the Pipe stable. His novice status remains intact as he failed to win there, but he twice finished second at Auteuil, and on his final start in France came a close fifth in the Group 1 Prix Maurice Gillois, the top autumn race for four-year-old chasers, showing fairly useful form. The workmanlike Korelo has a fine jumping pedigree. His sire Cadoudal regularly tops the jumps sires tables in France and, despite relatively few runners, has made his mark in Britain too, Fadalko being his best representative this side of the Channel. Korelo's dam, Lora du Charmil, was second

Sunderlands Imperial Cup Hurdle (Handicap), Sandown—a second valuable success; third-placed Lawz and the weakening Mister McGoldrick are also in shot at the last

Mr D. A. Johnson's "Korelo"

Korelo (FR) (b.g. 1998)	Cadoudal (FR) (br 1979)	Green Dancer (b 1972)	Nijinsky Green Valley
		Come To Sea (gr 1971)	Sea Hawk II Camarilla
	Lora du Charmil (FR) (b 1993)	Panoramic (b 1987)	Rainbow Quest Immense
		Cartza (b 1977)	Carmarthen Tzara

on her only Flat outing before a brief hurdling career at Auteuil as a three-year-old which also yielded a second place. Much the most noteworthy of her siblings is Batman Senora, a smart chaser placed in successive editions of the Grand Steeple-Chase de Paris. Korelo's twice-raced grandam Cartza was a half-sister to the Grand Prix de Pau winner Vaquero and to that horse's brother Bokaro, another good French export to Britain. A smart hurdler, Bokaro was campaigned far and wide by Charlie Brooks, his wins including the Queen Mother Supreme Hurdle at Belmont and the Corsa Siepi di Milano, Italy's version of the Champion Hurdle. Korelo looks unlikely to be the last good jumper from this family. His three-year-old half-sister Cartzagrouas (by Esprit du Nord) began her career by winning a listed fillies hurdle for newcomers at Auteuil in May. Korelo will need a good test again back at two miles and will stay three miles. Raced only on good going or softer, all three of Korelo's wins have come on heavy. He ought to prove at least as good over fences. *M. C. Pipe*

KOSAMET (IRE) 6 b.g. Jurado (USA) – Liffey's Choice (Little Buskins) [2002/3 **h85** F–: F16m² 21m⁵ 19s⁵ 16s² 16g 16g⁶ 20m² 16m 17s⁴ Nov 18] leggy gelding: remote third **F83** only completed start in maiden points in 2002: much better effort in bumpers when

485

second in maiden at Stratford in July: poor novice hurdler: claimed from G. McCourt £5,200 second outing: stays 2½m: acts on soft and good to firm going. *M. J. Gingell*

KOSMIC LADY 6 b.m. Cosmonaut – Ktolo (Tolomeo) [2002/3 h–: 17s[6] 17d[5] 16d Jan 16] modest on Flat (barely stays 1¼m): poor maiden hurdler: will need sharp 2m: tongue tied. *P. W. Hiatt* — **h66**

KOSOVKO (FR) 4 b.g. Kadalko (FR) – Brumelli (FR) (Tip Moss (FR)) [2002/3 F12g F16s 22d[pu] Feb 23] smallish gelding: fifth foal: dam, lightly-raced maiden on Flat, runner-up in 15f hurdle on first of 2 starts over jumps: poor form both starts in bumpers: no show on hurdling debut. *M. C. Pipe* — **h– F74**

KOUMBA (FR) 5 b.g. Luchiroverte (IRE) – Agenore (FR) (Le Riverain (FR)) [2002/3 F16m[5] 20d Apr 9] first known foal: dam, ran twice, from family of top-class French chaser Jasmin II: well beaten in varied events, including points. *B. N. Pollock* — **h– F–**

KRABLOONIK (FR) 9 b.g. Bering – Key Role (Be My Guest (USA)) [2002/3 c119d, h–: c16d[2] c20d[6] c16g[4] c20d[pu] c19d Jan 24] tall gelding: winning hurdler: fair maiden chaser: stays 2½m: acts on good to firm and heavy going: visored once: tongue tied final start: held up: unreliable. *A. King* — **c112 § h–**

KRACH (FR) 5 b.g. Lute Antique (FR) – Voilette (FR) (Brezzo (FR)) [2002/3 24v[2] Nov 22] very tall, imposing gelding: third foal: half-brother to leading non-thoroughbred Flat performer Gloria IV (by Video Rock): dam, winner on Flat, from family of top-class staying hurdler/chaser Ubu III and smart hurdler/chaser up to 25f Corton: successful both starts in non-thoroughbred races on Flat: shaped with plenty of promise when second both starts over hurdles (changed hands in between), 27 lengths second of 5 to Ad Hoc in novice at Ascot in November, getting tired in very testing conditions: looked open to further improvement but not seen out again. *F. Doumen, France* — **h121 p**

KRACK DE L'ISLE (FR) 5 b.g. Kadalko (FR) – Ceres de L'Isle (FR) (Bad Conduct (USA)) [2002/3 F87: F16d[5] F16s[4] 22v* 20v[3] 24v[ur] Feb 8] fair form in bumpers: won novice at Ayr on hurdling debut in January: let down by jumping next time, still going well when stumbling and unseating 4 out final start: should stay 3m: raced on going softer than good (acts on heavy): sometimes takes strong hold. *A. C. Whillans* — **h111 F92**

KRISTINEAU 5 ch.m. Cadeaux Genereux – Kantikoy (Alzao (USA)) [2002/3 22m[6] Oct 6] modest maiden at best on Flat, sold out of C. Wall's stable 5,500 gns Newmarket Autumn (2001) Sales: sixth in novice at Kelso on hurdling debut, weakening after 3 out having pulled hard. *Mrs E. Slack* — **h–**

KROISOS (IRE) 5 b.g. Kris – Lydia Maria (Dancing Brave (USA)) [2002/3 22d[6] 16s 22s[6] 25v[4] 25s[2] Mar 10] workmanlike gelding: half-brother to 2 winning hurdlers, including fairly useful hurdler around 2m Premier Bay (by Primo Dominie): modest maiden on Flat (stays 1½m), sold out of P. Harris's stable 5,200 gns Newmarket Autumn (2001) Sales: first form over hurdles when second in 25f handicap at Plumpton. *R. Curtis* — **h71**

KROSNO 9 ch.g. Kris – Pastorale (Nureyev (USA)) [2002/3 17m[pu] 17g 20g 20g* 20g* 20m[5] 20s Nov 2] fair handicap hurdler: won at Tramore and Tralee in August: stays 2½m: acts on soft and good to firm going. *Miss I. T. Oakes, Ireland* — **h110**

KRZYSZKOWIAK (IRE) 5 b.g. Polish Precedent (USA) – Overdrive (Shirley Heights) [2002/3 F17d F18d[2] F17d[2] Feb 23] fifth foal: half-brother to 3 winners, including 1½m and 2m winner Endorsement (by Warning) and 6f (at 2 yrs)/7f winner Zugudi (by Night Shift), both useful: dam useful stayer on Flat: fairly useful form when second in bumpers at Fontwell and Hereford: sold 30,000 gns Doncaster May Sales. *C. R. Egerton* — **F95**

KUNG HEI FAT CHOI (IRE) 8 b.g. Roselier (FR) – Gallant Blade (Fine Blade (USA)) [2002/3 c87, h–: c25g[4] c20s[3] c25d[6] c25s[3] c25g* c25v[4] c20d[2] c24d[2] c25m[pu] Apr 21] modest handicap chaser: won at Catterick in January: stays 25f: acts on heavy going, probably unsuited by good to firm: poor jumper. *J. S. Goldie* — **c88 x h–**

KUSTOM KIT KEVIN 7 b.g. Local Suitor (USA) – Sweet Revival (Claude Monet (USA)) [2002/3 h–: 16d[pu] Jul 5] regressed on Flat: no show in 2 races over hurdles. *Miss L. V. Davis* — **h–**

KUWAIT MILLENNIUM 6 b.g. Salse (USA) – Lypharitissima (FR) (Lightning (FR)) [2002/3 h95§: 22g 17d[5] 22d 22v* 26g[2] Mar 17] angular gelding: modest hurdler: trained by J. Neville on reappearance: won selling handicap at Fontwell in March: stays 3¼m: acts on heavy and good to firm going: tried visored/blinkered, wore cheekpieces last 3 starts: has had tongue tied: formerly temperamental. *Mrs A. M. Thorpe* — **h93**

KUWAIT THUNDER (IRE) 7 ch.g. Mac's Imp (USA) – Romangoddess (IRE) **h82**
(Rhoman Rule (USA)) [2002/3 16s⁴ 19d 17s 17d 16m Apr 21] good-topped gelding: poor
on Flat (barely stays 1½m, weak finisher): poor novice hurdler: raced mainly around 2m:
tongue tied: races freely. *D. Carroll*

KWAY DE LA FORET (FR) 5 b. or br.g. Bobinski – Rose de La Foret (FR) (Ice **F–**
Light (FR)) [2002/3 F16m Oct 30] £2,000 4-y-o: medium-sized gelding: eighth foal:
half-brother to several winners, including French chasers up to 21f Espoir de La Foret (by
Shafoun) and Gitane de La Foret II (by Spoleto): dam never ran: tailed off in bumper on
debut. *R. J. Hodges*

KYLIE TIME (IRE) 6 ch.g. Good Thyne (USA) – Miss Kylogue (IRE) (Lancastrian) **h–**
[2002/3 F16s F16d F16g 20g^pu Apr 23] IR £30,000 4-y-o: lengthy gelding: second foal: **F79**
dam unraced, out of fairly useful staying chaser Kylogue Lady, herself half-sister to
Foxhunter winner Three Counties: modest form at best in bumpers: no show on hurdling
debut. *P. Beaumont*

KYLKENNY 8 b.g. Kylian (USA) – Fashion Flow (Balidar) [2002/3 16g Dec 18] good- **h89 p**
topped gelding: fairly useful on Flat (stays easy 1½m), successful in February (twice) and
March: well held 2 out of 3 starts over hurdles, though not knocked about in maiden at
Newbury on reappearance: should prove capable of better. *H. Morrison*

KYLMAX 4 b.g. Classic Cliche (IRE) – Dame Lorraine (Damister (USA)) [2002/3 **h–**
16m^pu Oct 16] tall gelding: signs of only a little ability on Flat: pulled up lame after early
mistake on hurdling debut: dead. *H. A. McWilliams*

KYMANI PRINCE (IRE) 7 b.g. Shernazar – Best of British (Young Generation) **h100**
[2002/3 F97: 16g² Apr 25] rather leggy gelding: third in bumper in 2001/2: second in
maiden hurdle at Perth on belated reappearance. *L. Lungo*

KYMBERLYA (FR) 5 ch.g. Esteem Ball (FR) – Catty Douce (FR) (Cadoudal (FR)) **h100**
[2002/3 20g^F 20d^pu 16m³ Apr 2] lengthy, angular ex-French gelding: third foal: half-
brother to 17f chase winner Isathis (by Chef de Clan II): dam unraced: won 15f non-
thoroughbred event on Flat at Durtal in June when trained by J. Barbe: dropped in trip,
best effort over hurdles when third in novice at Ludlow, jumping more fluently.
M. C. Pipe

KYPER DISCO (FR) 5 b.g. Epervier Bleu – Disconea (FR) (Bayolidaan (FR)) **h106**
[2002/3 F98: 16d³ 18v² 20v⁵ Feb 11] well-made gelding: fair form first 2 starts over
hurdles: failed to settle when upped further in trip in maiden at Folkestone final outing.
N. J. Henderson

L

LAAZIM AFOOZ 10 b.g. Mtoto – Balwa (USA) (Danzig (USA)) [2002/3 c98d, h99: **c83**
c23g³ c23m³ c26m² c26f² c26m³ c27g* c27d⁵ 22d⁶ 26g Mar 17] smallish gelding: poor **h94**
handicap chaser nowadays: won at Sedgefield in October: modest handicap hurdler: stays
27f: acts on firm and good to soft going (possibly unsuited by soft/heavy): usually wears
cheekpieces: tongue tied: not a fluent jumper of fences. *R. T. Phillips*

LABULA BAY 9 b.g. Sula Bula – Lady Barunbe (Deep Run) [2002/3 c105, h–: c26m³ **c85**
May 22] fairly useful pointer/hunter chaser at best: appeared to pull up feelingly when **h–**
third in novice at Folkestone in May, not seen out again: should stay 3m: acts on soft
going: tried blinkered. *Miss C. F. Elliott*

LA COLINA (IRE) 8 ch.g. Be My Native (USA) – Deep Stream (Deep Run) [2002/3 **c94**
c–, h–: c17s² c19s⁶ c20v^F c16d⁵ c16m⁴ Feb 28] tall, workmanlike gelding: winning hurd- **h–**
ler: modest form when second in handicap at Market Rasen on reappearance, nowhere
near that form all other starts over fences (let down by jumping): stays 2½m: acts on soft
going: sold 2,100 gns Doncaster March Sales. *C. J. Mann*

LADY ANGLESBY 6 b.m. Then Again – Moy Ran Lady (Black Minstrel) [2002/3 **F–**
F16g May 8] 700 3-y-o: sixth foal: half-sister to 21f chase winner Sir Norman (by Arctic
Lord): dam, winning pointer, half-sister to one-time fairly useful 2m to 21f hurdler/chaser
Dante's Battle: behind in bumper: little show in points. *C. J. Drewe*

LADY ARNICA 4 b.f. Ezzoud (IRE) – Brand (Shareef Dancer (USA)) [2002/3 16d³ **h78**
16d 16s 20g² Apr 21] lengthy filly: half-sister to fair hurdler around 2m Brandy Snap
(by Broadsword) and bumper winner by Elmaamul: no encouragement in 2 starts on Flat:

poor form over hurdles, second in mares novice at Uttoxeter final start: stays 2½m.
A. W. Carroll

LADY BLACKTHORN 5 br.m. Seymour Hicks (FR) – Myblackthorn (IRE)   h–
(Mandalus) [2002/3 F18d F16d 22m^pu Apr 15] first foal: dam fair chaser, stayed 2½m: no   F–
form in bumpers or novice hurdle. *B. J. M. Ryall*

LADY BOB BACK 6 br.m. Bob Back (USA) – Whimbrel (Dara Monarch) [2002/3   h79
h–, F76: 23d^5 25d^pu 20v^2 21v^5 24v^6 20d 20m^3 Apr 19] lengthy, unfurnished mare: poor
novice hurdler: left Mrs M. Reveley before final start: should be suited by 3m+: acts on
heavy going, probably on good to firm: temperament under suspicion. *M. A. Barnes*

LADY B WARNED (IRE) 6 b.m. Zaffaran (USA) – Frostbite (Prince Tenderfoot   h–
(USA)) [2002/3 h–, F71: 24d^pu May 6] poor form on first of 2 starts in bumpers: little
show over hurdles. *N. A. Twiston-Davies*

LADY CRICKET (FR) 9 ch.m. Cricket Ball (USA) – Lady Mariza (Dunbeath   c165
(USA)) [2002/3 c165, h–: c16d^2 c21s* c17g^3 c20g^5 c25g^2 Apr 3]   h–

Top-class mares over fences are rare creatures. Lady Cricket was one of
the best chasing mares since *Chasers & Hurdlers* began in 1975/6, her rating
bettered only by Anaglogs Daughter (171), Dawn Run (167) and Dubacilla (166).
The outstanding Irish mare Anaglogs Daughter was tough and genuine, as well as
being top class, contesting one hundred and seven races, sixty-four of them over
jumps. *Chasers & Hurdlers 1981/82* stated: 'Her enthusiasm, which manifested
itself in her bold, quick jumping, her natural front running and her battling finishing, was something to marvel at.' Anaglogs Daughter was the best novice chaser of
1979/80 when a tremendously impressive winner of the Arkle, and the following
season was runner-up in the King George VI Chase (to Silver Buck) and the Champion Chase, this in the days before the mares' sex allowance. Defeat in the latter
race, incidentally, ruled her out of an intended outing in the next day's Gold Cup.
Just as impressive were some of her performances in handicaps which make
modern-day complaints about weight assignments (a subject particularly relevant
where Lady Cricket is concerned) seem petty. For example, she won the Foxrock
Cup at Leopardstown under 12-5 (and that's even after taking her rider's 7 lb claim
into account), giving 40 lb to the runner-up Luska who won that year's Irish Grand
National.

In contrast to Anaglogs Daughter, her compatriot Dawn Run had only seven
races over fences, winning all five that she completed without mishap. Had her
chasing career not been cut short by a fatal fall over hurdles in France, Dawn Run
must have had a good chance of going on to prove better still over fences. By the
time Dawn Run won her Gold Cup in 1986, the 5-lb allowance for mares had been
brought in, an important factor in her being able to complete her unique Champion
Hurdle-Gold Cup double. Nine years later, Dubacilla put up the best performance
by a mare in the Gold Cup since Dawn Run when finishing second to Master Oats.
That represented the highlight of Dubacilla's career; she was fourth in the Grand
National on her only subsequent outing.

Lady Cricket, on the other hand, never contested a Cheltenham Gold Cup
—the trip would almost certainly have stretched her stamina. The Queen Mother
Champion Chase might have been a better opportunity for her to win a Grade 1
chase but she was not entered for the race in 2002 and conditions were probably
not testing enough for her to take on the top two-milers at the latest Festival. Cheltenham, though, was very much Lady Cricket's track, she found her niche there
in the top handicaps at around two and a half miles. She won the Thomas Pink
Gold Cup in 2000, and the following season carried a big weight into second in
both the Ladbroke Trophy and the Mildmay of Flete, putting up one of the best
performances of her career in the latter race when denied only by the late surge of
stable-companion Blowing Wind to whom she was conceding 17 lb.

Lady Cricket had a record of going well fresh but she did not go with much
zest on her reappearance in the latest season in a two-mile handicap at Cheltenham,
going down to another mare, Just Jasmine, who was getting 26 lb. But after a break
of more than two months Lady Cricket was back to her best when going one better
than the year before in the Ladbroke Trophy Chase at Cheltenham in January.
Giving upwards of 10 lb to her fourteen rivals, Lady Cricket was sent off the 9/2

Ladbroke Trophy Chase (Handicap), Cheltenham—a final success for top-class mare Lady Cricket;
Shamawan (hoops) and Hermes III (centre) take the places

favourite in an open and competitive renewal, ahead of stable-companion Horus and the Nicky Henderson-trained pair Hermes III and Katarino. Travelling much more smoothly this time under the softest conditions she encountered all season, Lady Cricket led before two out and ran on well, despite drifting left, to hold on by a neck and three and a half lengths from the lightly-weighted pair Shamawan and Hermes.

The previous season, Lady Cricket had won the Game Spirit Chase at Newbury, helped by her main rivals being out of sorts but, in the same race this time round, under conditions which were not soft enough for her, it was Lady Cricket who was among those to disappoint, clearly third best from some way out behind Kadarann and Cenkos. Maybe a second win in the Game Spirit would have persuaded connections to have a crack at the Champion Chase, but instead Lady Cricket's Festival target was the Mildmay of Flete once more. Off top weight, on a BHB mark of 164, Lady Cricket never looked like repeating her effort of twelve months earlier and finished only fifth of the thirteen finishers behind Young Spartacus. Three miles had always looked a bit further than ideal for Lady Cricket but, on what turned out to be her final start, she ran right up to her best over twenty-five furlongs in the Martell Cognac Cup at Aintree. She was never the remotest threat to a rejuvenated First Gold, being the first off the bridle, but she stayed on past tiring rivals to finish fourteen lengths behind the winner. Although this was a weight-for-age contest rather than a handicap, Lady Cricket was done no favours by the race conditions, having to give First Gold 5 lb rather than receive it.

Lady Cricket's retirement was announced after Aintree, and for good this time. Her owner had originally threatened to put her on the market as a broodmare during the 2001/2 season when he became frustrated at what he saw as harsh treatment of Lady Cricket at the hands of the BHB handicapper. With her new career in mind, it's as well to recap briefly on Lady Cricket's pedigree. It's essentially a Flat one, her third dam Lucyrowe being a high-class filly whose wins included the Coronation Stakes, Nassau Stakes and Sun Chariot Stakes. However, Lucyrowe did not pass on much of her ability to either daughter Edwinarowe (a Wolverhampton maiden winner over nine furlongs) or to her granddaughter Lady Mariza who failed to win on the Flat in France. Lady Mariza's two winners are by very different sires and the results were the opposite of what might have been expected: her Flat winner, Marizado, is by Best Mate's sire Un Desperado, while

Lady Cricket is by the very smart sprinter Cricket Ball. The lengthy, sparely-made Lady Cricket was a smart hurdler before she had her attentions switched to chasing and had won four times over hurdles in France before joining the Pipe yard. She wore blinkers on all her starts in Britain.

Lady Cricket (FR) (ch.m. 1994)	Cricket Ball (USA) (b 1983)	Olden Times (b 1958)	Relic
			Djenne
		Caterina (gr 1963)	Princely Gift
			Radiopye
	Lady Mariza (ch 1986)	Dunbeath (b 1980)	Grey Dawn II
			Priceless Fame
		Edwinarowe (b 1976)	Blakeney
			Lucyrowe

Ironically, Lady Cricket retires just as the mares' allowance is due to be increased in pattern races over jumps in the 2003/4 season. The allowance will be increased to 7 lb from 5 lb and could be extended to all weight-for-age races over jumps in due course if the move is considered a success. The increase was prompted by a BHB study which found that mares won proportionally fewer races over jumps than their numbers would lead one to expect, the shortfall being greater over fences than hurdles. But would the prospect of just a couple of pounds less weight really persuade owners to race more mares over jumps (and over fences in particular), and would an extra 2 lb have an appreciable effect on the proportion of races mares win against geldings? It has to be doubted. For one thing, the attractions of a stud career are always likely to outweigh the risks, real or imagined, inherent in a career over jumps, particularly in chases. Regardless of allowances, mares like Lady Cricket will always be few and far between. Top-class horses by definition make up a tiny proportion of the racing population, and because mares are in a minority over

Mr D. A. Johnson's "Lady Cricket"

jumps, top-class mares are rarer still. That said, Lady Cricket wasn't the only mare to enjoy a high profile over fences in the latest season. The novice La Landiere made into a very smart chaser in Britain, as did Line Marine in France, where she became the first mare to win the Grand Steeple-Chase de Paris for thirty-seven years. *M. C. Pipe*

LADY DOMITOR 8 b.m. Domitor (USA) – Dawn O'Er Kells (IRE) (Pitskelly) [2002/3 20m⁴ 22dᵖᵘ Sep 4] poor maiden hurdler: left W. Roper before reappearance: reportedly lame both starts in 2002/3. *Mrs D. A. Hamer*   **h–**

LADY FAUSTUS 6 b.m. Faustus (USA) – Princess Lucy (Local Suitor (USA)) [2002/3 F87p: F16s² F16v Dec 27] big, rangy mare: fair form in bumpers, better effort in 2002/3 when second in mares event at Wetherby in November. *Jonjo O'Neill*   **F90**

LADY FELIX 8 br.m. Batshoof – Volcalmeh (Lidhame) [2002/3 24g⁴ c24g² Apr 12] small mare: fair handicap hurdler: off 19 months before reappearance: second in novice at Stratford on chasing debut: better at 3m than shorter: acts on good to firm and good to soft going. *R. H. Alner*   **c85**
h83 +

LADY INCH 5 b.m. Inchinor – Head Turner (My Dad Tom (USA)) [2002/3 h–: 16gᵖᵘ 21sᵖᵘ 21dᵖᵘ Dec 12] little form on Flat, none over hurdles: tried visored. *S. L. Keightley*   **h–**

LADY JEANNIE 6 b.m. Emarati (USA) – Cottonwood (Teenoso (USA)) [2002/3 16v* 17s⁵ 16sᵖᵘ Jan 13] half-sister to fairly useful hurdler Calico Lady (by First Trump), stays 2½m: modest on Flat (stays 1¼m): poor form over hurdles, won novice at Plumpton in December. *M. J. Haynes*   **h79**

LADY JONES 6 b.m. Emperor Jones (USA) – So Beguiling (USA) (Woodman (USA)) [2002/3 h84: 19dᵖᵘ 16vᶠ 19dᶠ Feb 25] strong, compact mare: fair on Flat (stayed 1¾m): maiden hurdler: failed to complete in 2002/3: dead. *P. L. Gilligan*   **h–**

LADYKISH (FR) 4 b.f. Comte du Bourg (FR) – Turkish Lady (FR) (Baby Turk) [2002/3 17d² 17s* 18s² 18sᶠ 18v³ c18s* c20s* Apr 4] second foal: sister to useful chaser/ fairly useful hurdler Turkish Junior, stays 2½m: dam won over hurdles and fences up to 2½m: raced only at Auteuil: useful juvenile hurdler/chaser: won fillies hurdle in June and over fences in minor event in February and Group 3 Prix Fleuret (beat Gorfou de Maspie a neck) in April: good fourth to Ice Mood in Group 1 in May: stays 2½m: raced on going softer than good (acts on heavy). *Mlle F. Forneron, France*   **c129**
h127

LADY LAP DANCER 5 b.m. Shareef Dancer (USA) – Jelabna (Jalmood (USA)) [2002/3 16g⁴ 16s³ 16v⁶ 16v* 16vᵖᵘ 20g² 22g³ Apr 7] poor maiden stayer on Flat: modest novice hurdler: won weak seller at Kelso in November: ran well upped in trip last 2 starts: will stay 3m: raced on good going or softer over hurdles (acts on heavy). *Mrs M. Reveley*   **h85**

LADY LAUREATE 5 b.m. Sir Harry Lewis (USA) – Cyrillic (Rock City) [2002/3 h121: 16d 20s⁴ 21s³ 23vᵖᵘ 16gᵖᵘ Feb 28] small mare: fair on Flat (stays 17f): fair maiden hurdler: should stay 3m. *G. C. Bravery*   **h110 ?**

LADY LEWIS 7 b.m. Sir Harry Lewis (USA) – Gaygo Lady (Gay Fandango (USA)) [2002/3 F76: 19d⁶ 22m⁶ Apr 15] signs of only a little ability in bumper and 2 novice hurdles. *C. J. Down*   **h–**

LADY LIGHTHOUSE 5 b.m. Alhijaz – Fairfield's Breeze (Buckskin (FR)) [2002/3 F16d Aug 3] second foal: half-sister to modest 2m hurdler Court Champagne (by Batshoof): dam won 21f hunter chase: well beaten in bumper on debut. *R. J. Price*   **F–**

LADY MERCURY 5 b.m. Rock Hopper – Bellezza (Ardross) [2002/3 17sᵖᵘ 17sᵖᵘ 24sᵖᵘ 16m 17mᵖᵘ Apr 26] leggy mare: second foal: dam, fair hurdler, stayed 2½m: no form over hurdles: tried visored. *Miss K. M. George*   **h–**

LADY NETBETSPORTS (IRE) 4 b.f. In The Wings – Auntie Maureen (IRE) (Roi Danzig (USA)) [2002/3 16v⁶ 16dᶠ Mar 1] leggy filly: fair maiden on Flat (stays 1¾m): little show in 2 juvenile hurdles. *B. S. Rothwell*   **h–**

LADY OF LISLE 5 ch.m. Afzal – Holy Times (IRE) (The Parson) [2002/3 F16m 22d 19vᵖᵘ 20g Mar 25] sixth foal: half-sister to winning 3m hurdler The Holy Parson (by Satco) and bumper winner Oyster Bay (by Mandalus): dam unraced half-sister to useful hurdler up to 2½m Polar Bear: no sign of ability. *C. P. Morlock*   **h–**
F–

LADY OF TA'PINU 4 ch.f. Greensmith – Pitcairn Princess (Capricorn Line) [2002/3 16s 17d 16g 17gᵈ Sep 28] showed more temperament than ability on Flat and in juvenile hurdles and visored: sold 600 gns Doncaster January Sales. *C. N. Kellett*   **h– §**

LADY OF THE INN (IRE) 4 ch.f. Hamas (IRE) – Faakirah (Dragonara Palace **h88** (USA)) [2002/3 17m² 17f* 17d³ Dec 19] fair on Flat (will prove best around 1m), successful twice in May (for B. Meehan and D. Nicholls): second start over hurdles, easily won juvenile claimer at Taunton in October: better form when third in novice handicap at Exeter 2 months later: likely to prove best at 2m: wore cheekpieces last 2 starts: has been reluctant to post/at start. *M. C. Pipe*

LADY OF THE LAMP 8 b.m. Miner's Lamp – Lady Westgate (Welsh Chanter) **c–** [2002/3 c–, h82: 20v 23vᵖᵘ 24s Feb 13] tall mare: mistakes only start over fences: poor **h–** handicap hurdler, little show in 2002/3. *P. J. Jones*

LADY QC (IRE) 7 b.m. Leading Counsel (USA) – Tuesdaynightmare (Celtic Cone) **h–** [2002/3 h85d: 24dᶠ 20m Jun 21] lengthy mare: runner-up in mares maiden on hurdling debut in 2001/2, then lost her way: should stay 2½m: acts on good to firm going: blinkered on reappearance: joined H. Alexander. *L. Lungo*

LADY RACQUET (IRE) 4 b.f. Glacial Storm (USA) – Kindly Light (IRE) (Supreme **F–** Leader) [2002/3 F16g Feb 22] £36,000 3-y-o: first foal: dam, unplaced in 2 bumpers, half-sister to smart chaser up to 21f Native Charm: shaped as if probably in need of run when well held in bumper at Huntingdon on debut. *Mrs A. J. Bowlby*

LADY SANTANA (IRE) 6 b.m. Doyoun – Santana Lady (IRE) (Blakeney) [2002/3 **h–** h–: 16sᵖᵘ 16s⁴ Feb 24] lightly-raced maiden on Flat: no form in 3 outings over hurdles. *R. S. Brookhouse*

LADY SHREK 5 b.m. King's Signet (USA) – Come To Good (Swing Easy (USA)) **F–** [2002/3 F13s Dec 6] second foal: dam seemed of little account: tailed off in bumper on debut. *G. A. Ham*

LADY SOLRSKI 6 b.m. Petoski – Flaxen Tina (Beau Tudor) [2002/3 h–, F–: 20sᵖᵘ **h–** 20gᵖᵘ 24vᵖᵘ Feb 8] little sign of ability. *A. C. Whillans*

LADY STRATAGEM 4 gr.f. Mark of Esteem (IRE) – Grey Angel (Kenmare (FR)) **h82 d** [2002/3 16m* 16dᵖᵘ 16d 16d 17dᵖᵘ Mar 18] close-coupled filly: modest maiden on Flat (probably stays 9f): won juvenile at Kelso on hurdling debut in October: no form subsequently: likely to prove best around 2m. *E. W. Tuer*

LADY TEARAWAY 4 b.f. Arrasas (USA) – Manageress (Mandamus) [2002/3 F16m **F–** Feb 22] sparely-made filly: half-sister to several winners, including 7f/1m winner Dealers Delight (by Ballacashtal): dam 6f winner at 2 yrs: tailed off in bumper on debut. *J. E. Long*

LADY TERIMOND 6 br.m. Terimon – Kitty Come Home (Monsanto (FR)) [2002/3 **F84** F17d² F16s² F17s² Nov 21] 11,000 3-y-o: angular mare: seventh foal: half-sister to several winners, including useful 2m chaser Nearly An Eye (by Nearly A Hand): dam modest hurdler, stayed 21f: modest form when second in bumpers at Hereford (2) and Worcester. *N. J. Henderson*

LADY TILLY 6 b.m. Puissance – Lady of Itatiba (BEL) (King of Macedon) [2002/3 **h–** 16g⁵ Oct 12] no longer of much account on Flat: well held both starts over hurdles: has had tongue tied. *B. Mactaggart*

LADY TOULON (IRE) 5 b.m. Toulon – Orchard Lass (On Your Mark) [2002/3 **F105** F16m* F17s⁵ F17g F18g* Mar 26] unfurnished mare: half-sister to 2m hurdle winner Insan Magic (by Insan) and bumper winner That's Magic (by Lord Americo): dam unraced half-sister to smart staying hurdler Kristenson: won bumpers at Down Royal in May and Downpatrick in March: ran well but flashed tail and looked less than keen under pressure when fourth to Royal Rosa in Grade 1 at Punchestown in late-April: won 13f maiden on Flat in May. *D. M. Fogarty, Ireland*

LADY TURK (FR) 6 b.m. Baby Turk – Alyda (FR) (Dalal (FR)) [2002/3 c93, h108: **c93 x** c23gᵘʳ c24m³ c26vᵖᵘ 16d 20v⁶ 24s³ᶠ 24s³ 21s c22g* 20m³ c25m² Apr 21] leggy, narrow **h95** mare: modest hurdler: modest novice chaser (prone to mistakes): won mares event at Fontwell in March: probably stays 25f: acts on good to firm and heavy going: often blinkered/visored/tongue tied. *C. Tizzard*

LADY WARD (IRE) 5 b.m. Mujadil (USA) – Sans Ceriph (IRE) (Thatching) [2002/3 **h87 §** h67: 17m³ 16g² 16m² 16m³ 20m³ 17g² 20s² 16d 16v⁶ 19d 17s⁴ 17d Feb 23] modest handicap hurdler: sold out of Ms A. Embiricos' stable £3,500 Ascot June Sales after second start: stays 2½m: acts on soft and good to firm going: irresolute. *S. C. Burrough*

LADY WIDD (IRE) 5 ch.m. Commanche Run – Lady Geeno (IRE) (Cheval) [2002/3 **h–** F–: 16gᵘʳ 24d⁴ 24dᵖᵘ 20s Feb 24] lengthy mare: of little account. *S. J. Marshall*

LAFAYETTE (IRE)   5 b.h. General Monash (USA) – Bezee (Belmez (USA))   **h118**
[2002/3 h133p: 18s 16s Feb 9] good-topped horse: useful juvenile hurdler in 2001/2: well
held first 2 starts on return, third to Sabadilla in handicap at Punchestown in early-May:
raced around 2m: best efforts on good going. *R. J. Osborne, Ireland*

LA FEMME EN ROUGE   4 b.f. Slip Anchor – Bayrouge (IRE) (Gorytus (USA))   **F–**
[2002/3 F14d F16d Feb 25] rather leggy filly: third foal: dam, useful hurdler/fairly useful
chaser who stayed 25f, half-sister to smart hurdler up to 25f Ravaro: well held in 2
bumpers. *Mrs M. Reveley*

LAGANSIDE (IRE)   10 b.g. Montelimar (USA) – Ruby Girl (Crash Course) [2002/3   **c– §**
c110d, h–: c21g^pu Apr 3] lengthy gelding: fair chaser at best: won point (dead-heat) in   **h–**
March: hung badly right from start and tailed off when pulled up fourteenth in Fox
Hunters' at Aintree in April: stays 3m: unraced on firm going: acts on any other: tried
visored: has won with/without tongue tied: unreliable. *J. F. W. Muir*

LAGER DASH   5 b.g. Suave Dancer (USA) – Padelia (Thatching) [2002/3 F17s^pu   **F–**
Nov 21] half-brother to several winners, including winning 21f hurdler Pa d'Or (by Slew
O'Gold), useful miler Polar Boy (by Northern Baby) and fairly useful stayer Shining
High (by Shirley Heights): dam unraced: appeared to lose action and soon tailed off in
bumper on debut. *R. J. Price*

LAGO DI LEVICO   6 ch.g. Pelder (IRE) – Langton Herring (Nearly A Hand)   **h94 §**
[2002/3 h: 19m² 22d* 21d Nov 15] close-coupled gelding: modest hurdler: won weak
maiden at Stratford in October: stays 2¾m: acts on good to firm and good to soft going:
has been early to post: often looks temperamental. *C. J. Down*

LAKEFIELD LEADER (IRE)   12 b.g. Supreme Leader – Debonair Dolly (Cidrax   **c– x**
(FR)) [2002/3 c84x, h–: 21g⁵ 24g³ 27s⁴ 17g⁴ 22m Jul 14] sturdy gelding: winning chaser: **h100**
fair handicap hurdler: stays 27f: acts on good to firm and heavy going: often blinkered/
visored. *C. Tizzard*

LAKESIDE LAD   11 b.g. St Columbus – Beyond The Trimm (Trimmingham)   **c96**
[2002/3 c80, h–: c24g* c26g² c26m^pu Jul 18] tall gelding: modest chaser: fortunate to win   **h–**
novice at Fakenham in May: reportedly lame final start: stays 3¼m: acts on good to firm
and good to soft going: has run creditably in blinkers. *R. Wilman*

LA LANDIERE (FR)   8 b. or br.m. Synefos (USA) – As You Are (FR) (Saint   **c156**
Estephe (FR)) [2002/3 h114: c16g² c20m* c19m* c21d* c20s* c21s* c24m* c21g*   **h–**
Mar 13]

     After showing fairly useful form in her first ten outings over hurdles,
including winning three times and finishing second to Landing Light in a handicap
at Cheltenham, La Landiere lost her way completely, finishing much nearer last
than first in most of her next six races. Her performance in running odds-on Impek

Timeform Novices' Handicap Chase, Cheltenham—
La Landiere leads Whereareyounow and Irish Hussar two out

Racing Post Chase (Handicap), Kempton—six in a row and a very smart performance;
Gunther McBride and Ryalux (left) are left behind in her wake

to three lengths on her debut over fences at Huntingdon in May was much more encouraging. As a rangy mare who usually impresses in appearance, La Landiere had always had the physique to make a chaser, and the run led to the comment in *Timeform Perspective* that 'she should find a race if kept on the go'. For a race, read seven races, since La Landiere went through the rest of the campaign unbeaten, proving a nightmare for the BHB handicapper as she improved by around four stone in the space of four months and ended up winning the Racing Post Chase and Cathcart Chase on her last two appearances. Small wonder that she caught the imagination of the racing public, bringing deserved credit to herself and her trainer for the achievement.

La Landiere's first victory was not long in coming after her Huntingdon defeat, two days to be precise, when she landed the odds without being extended in a four-runner novice event at Market Rasen, a course which coincidentally also saw the first victory over fences of Azertyuiop. On her first two starts over fences, La Landiere's jumping was not entirely convincing but she was less hesitant next time at Chepstow in October, justifying favouritism by nine lengths from Cape Stormer, and from then on she rarely put a foot wrong. A mares only event at Wincanton in November proved easy pickings—La Landiere had the measure of the favourite Janiture when the latter fell three out—and novice handicaps at Kempton over Christmas and Cheltenham in January posed no problems either. In the Timeform Novices' Handicap Chase at Cheltenham, despite a 13 lb rise in the weights, she was holding Irish Hussar when he came a cropper at the second last; La Landiere then quickening clear after the final fence to account, eased down by six lengths, for Ibis Rochelais, who had also chased her home at Kempton.

All La Landiere's starts had been at up to around two and a half miles and her trainer did not enter her in the Royal & SunAlliance Chase because of stamina doubts. However, there was no reason to think she would find three miles beyond her on an easy track and the Racing Post Chase at Kempton at the end of February provided an opportunity to test the theory. The Grand National (£348,000 to the winner) is in a class of its own among handicap chases in prize-money, followed at a respectful distance by the attheraces Gold Cup (£87,000), after which there is close competition in the next group down. Since dropping away in the late 'nineties, the Racing Post Chase improved its position in the table in 2002/3, figuring alongside the Thomas Pink Gold Cup, Midlands Grand National and Tripleprint Gold Cup on £58,000 and not far adrift of the Red Square Vodka Gold Cup and the Scottish Grand National on £63,800 each and the Hennessy Cognac Gold Cup on £60,900 for the latest running. The abandoned Victor Chandler Chase would have been worth £69,600 to the winner. With the value of the former Thomas Pink set to rise ten percent under new sponsor Paddy Power, the pressure will be on the others to maintain their position in the pecking order.

Although the Racing Post Chase's prize money had been boosted, it failed to attract a top- or high-class chaser. Desert Orchid, Barton Bank, The Fellow, Algan and Docklands Express are among those to carry top weight off a Jockey Club or BHB mark of 158 or higher in the last fourteen runnings. In 2003 Fondmort was top weight with a BHB mark of 152. Although the first prize was about £12,000 ahead of the most valuable handicap chase at the Cheltenham Festival, Fondmort's mark was below that of the top weight in the Mildmay of Flete (Lady Cricket on 164), the National Hunt Handicap (Foxchapel King on 161) and the Grand Annual (Eskleybrook on 153). Another rise in the weights, by 12 lb, meant La Landiere carried second-top weight, 5 lb below Fondmort. The race, run on much firmer going than usual for the time of year, had fourteen runners and was highly competitive, with the leading stables all represented—Martin Pipe (Montreal, Carryonharry and Chicuelo), Philip Hobbs (Gunther McBride and Zafarabad), Paul Nicholls (Exit To Wave), Jonjo O'Neill (Bold Investor and Carbury Cross), Henrietta Knight (Maximize) and Nicky Henderson (Fondmort). La Landiere started joint favourite with the previous year's winner Gunther McBride, whose rider Richard Johnson, bidding for a fourth successive win in the race, had ridden La Landiere to four of her five successes during the season but reportedly turned her down this time out of loyalty to Hobbs, his main employer, but also because he believed she had risen too high in the weights. Not high enough for Johnson's purposes. With Warren Marston up, La Landiere, who looked extremely well, was always handy after taking a good hold—she usually races prominently—and went on from Gunther McBride three out, clear at the last and passing the post with three

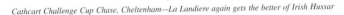

Cathcart Challenge Cup Chase, Cheltenham—La Landiere again gets the better of Irish Hussar

lengths to spare, proving conclusively that she stayed three miles. Ryalux was a length away third, clear of Carryonharry. This was La Landiere's best performance by some way—she clearly acts on good to firm going as well as soft—but talk of supplementing her for the Gold Cup came to nought and she concluded her campaign at the Festival in the easier Cathcart Challenge Cup. In what turned out to be a tactical race, with the outcome depending on speed over the last four fences, La Landiere led at the second last and kept on gamely to hold off Irish Hussar by a length and a half. La Landiere's form at Cheltenham was not quite so good as at Kempton and, although she is one of the best mares to have raced over fences in the last decade, she will probably need to improve to be in with a chance of landing a Grade 1 event. Given her rate of progress over fences so far, that's not out of the question, and she certainly deserves a chance at that level. An appropriate initial target, though, might be the aforementioned Paddy Power Gold Cup at Cheltenham's Open meeting.

		Irish River	Riverman
	Synefos (USA)	(ch 1976)	Irish Star
	(b 1982)	Salpinx	Northern Dancer
La Landiere (FR)		(b 1976)	Suprina
(b. or br.m. 1995)		Saint Estephe	Top Ville
	As You Are (FR)	(b 1982)	Une Tornade
	(b 1988)	Asania	Ace of Aces
		(b 1978)	Aurinette

La Landiere is French-bred, not selle francais or anglo-arab but a thoroughbred. Her sire Synefos was well bred, by Irish River out of high-class racemare Salpinx, and showed very useful form at up to a mile and a quarter, including when in the frame in the Poule d'Essai des Poulains. Retired to the Haras du Pin, he was fourth leading jump sire in France in 1993/4 before being sold for 220,000 francs in 1995 and transferred to The Glebe House in Northern Ireland. His fee is £650 and he has been covering progressively smaller books—thirty-five in 1998, twenty-

Mrs R. J. Skan's "La Landiere"

five in 1999, nine in 2000 and five in 2001. La Landiere, as genuine and consistent a performer as one could wish to find, is easily his best progeny. She is the first reported foal out of the twice-raced As You Are, whose dam was third in two pattern races at around nine furlongs on the Flat and foaled thirteen winners, including Astronomer, successful in eight races over jumps, highlighted by a win at Enghien in the most significant French hurdle race staged away from Auteuil. *R. T. Phillips*

LA LUNA (IRE) 6 b.m. Gothland (FR) – Diane's Glen (Furry Glen) [2002/3 F68: F17m² Aug 26] modest form at best in 3 bumpers. *Noel T. Chance*   **F75**

LA MAESTRA (FR) 5 b.m. Zayyani – Ginestra (USA) (L'Emigrant (USA)) [2002/3 h88: 17g 16s⁵ 20g Aug 26] winning hurdler, well held in 2002/3: probably ungenuine: sold £650 Ascot October Sales, subsequently showed little in points. *Miss S. J. Wilton*   **h– §**

LA MARETTE 5 ch.m. Karinga Bay – Persistent Gunner (Gunner B) [2002/3 F67: 17s⁵ 16d⁵ 16s⁵ 21d⁵ 20vᵖᵘ 17v⁵ 17g⁴ 17g* 22f³ Apr 21] sturdy mare: poor hurdler: fortunate to win weak mares maiden at Newton Abbot in April: stays 21f: acts on good to soft going: has had tongue tied. *R. J. Hodges*   **h74**

LAMBADORA 5 ch.m. Suave Dancer (USA) – Lust (Pursuit of Love) [2002/3 h84: 16g* 16m* 22fᵖᵘ 19mᵖᵘ 16dᵖᵘ Aug 3] poor hurdler: won mares novice at Plumpton in April and conditional jockeys seller (sold from J. O'Shea 10,000 gns) at Ludlow in May: pulled up all subsequent starts: should stay beyond 2m: acts on soft and good to firm going: tongue tied final outing in 2001/2. *Miss K. Marks*   **h81 d**

LAMBHILL STAKES (IRE) 5 gr.g. King's Ride – Summerhill Express (IRE) (Roselier (FR)) [2002/3 F–: F17g⁴ 23s² 25g² 24s⁵ Feb 24] rangy, rather unfurnished gelding: modest form on second of 2 starts in bumpers: easily best effort over hurdles when second in novice at Wetherby: stays 23f: acts on soft ground: races freely. *J. M. Jefferson*   **h100 F84**

LAMBRINI BIANCO (IRE) 5 br.g. Roselier (FR) – Darjoy (Darantus) [2002/3 F90: F16d F16g Mar 12] tall gelding: fair in bumpers, easily better effort in 2002/3 on reappearance: will be suited by 2½m+. *Mrs L. Williamson*   **F90**

LAMBRINI GOLD 9 b.g. Gildoran – Fille de Soleil (Sunyboy) [2002/3 c20v⁴ c19sᵖᵘ c20v² c21dᵖᵘ Apr 4] big gelding: fairly useful chaser at best: off over 2 years, form in handicaps on return only when second of 3 finishers at Hexham in March: will stay beyond 2½m: raced on going softer than good (acts on heavy): tongue tied final start: broke blood vessel second outing. *D. McCain*   **c99 h–**

LAMBRINI MIST 5 gr.g. Terimon – Miss Fern (Cruise Missile) [2002/3 F73?: F17s 20v Dec 20] third of 4 in bumper on debut in 2001/2: well held in similar event and novice hurdle on return. *Mrs L. Williamson*   **h– F–**

LA MINERA 5 b.m. Miner's Lamp – Bignor Girl (Torus) [2002/3 F–: F16d May 4] soundly beaten in 2 bumpers. *R. J. Armson*   **F—**

LA MOLA SUN 9 b.g. Henbit (USA) – Moheli (Ardross) [2002/3 22m³ 22g³ Oct 19] modest hurdler: winning pointer in 2002, sold 2,200 gns Doncaster May Sales: creditable third in 2 handicaps at Kelso on return to hurdling: stays 2¾m: acts on firm going: tried blinkered, including when successful: has run in snatches. *Mrs J. C. McGregor*   **h93**

LANCASHIRE LASS 7 b.m. Lancastrian – Chanelle (The Parson) [2002/3 h–: 22d² 19s 19s 20sᵖᵘ 22m 24f³ 21m⁶ Apr 19] bad maiden hurdler: stays 3m: acts on firm going. *J. S. King*   **h55**

LANCASTRIAN ISLAND 5 b.m. Lancastrian – Kelly's Island (Jupiter Island) [2002/3 F16g Dec 13] second foal: dam ran twice in points: showed little in bumper on debut. *John A. Harris*   **F—**

LANCASTRIAN JET (IRE) 12 b.g. Lancastrian – Kilmurray Jet (Le Bavard (FR)) [2002/3 c120: c26v² c32d² c24s c30s⁶ Mar 4] rangy gelding: fairly useful handicap chaser: stays 4m: acts on heavy going: raced right-handed nowadays: front runner: sound jumper. *H. D. Daly*   **c121**

LAND GIRL 5 b.m. General Monash (USA) – Charming Madam (General Holme (USA)) [2002/3 h–: 16g³ 16v⁵ 19fᵖᵘ Oct 9] well held on Flat: poor novice hurdler: reportedly lame final start. *J. G. M. O'Shea*   **h66**

LANDING LIGHT (IRE) 8 b.g. In The Wings – Gay Hellene (Ela-Mana-Mou) [2002/3 h157: 20v⁴ 17d² 16g 24g⁴ Apr 2] good-topped gelding: very smart hurdler: best   **h156**

effort in 2002/3 when 2½ lengths second to Rooster Booster in Grade 2 at Cheltenham in December: didn't impress with attitude 3 other starts: should stay 2½m: raced on good going or softer (acts on soft): tried in blinkers/cheekpieces last 3 appearances: reportedly had respiratory infection final outing in 2001/2: has awkward head carriage: useful form on Flat in 2003, second in Ascot Stakes in June. *N. J. Henderson*

LANDINGS 4 ch.f. Deploy – Sandblaster (Most Welcome) [2002/3 16d³ 16g⁶ 16v 16d⁶ 16g² Apr 1] angular filly: modest up to 1m at 2 yrs for W. Turner/Miss L. Perratt: poor juvenile hurdler: possibly unsuited by heavy going. *N. G. Richards*   **h73**

LANGCOURT JESTER 5 ch.m. Royal Vulcan – Singing Clown (True Song) [2002/3 F16d F16d Nov 25] first foal: dam winning pointer: in rear in 2 bumpers. *S. J. Gilmore*   **F–**

LANMIRE GLEN (IRE) 6 b.g. Jurado (USA) – Cool Glen (Furry Glen) [2002/3 c16s² c20s³ c32gᵖᵘ Mar 12] third foal: dam winning 2m hurdler: modest form in maiden hurdles: winning pointer: modest chaser: creditable placed efforts in handicaps first 2 starts: effective at 2m to 25f: acts on soft going, bumper form on good to firm. *E. Bolger, Ireland*   **c93** **h–**

LANMIRE LEADER (IRE) 8 b.g. Supreme Leader – Dark Fluff (Mandalus) [2002/3 c76, h94: c26m² 21f³ c21d³ c22dᵖᵘ 22s c20sᵖᵘ 22s⁵ Jan 14] poor maiden hurdler/chaser: stays 3¼m: acts on any going: wore cheekpieces final start. *A. Ennis*   **c77** **h73**

LANMIRE TOWER (IRE) 9 b.g. Celio Rufo – Lanigans Tower (The Parson) [2002/3 c123§, h–: c24g⁴ c28d³ c25d* c27g⁴ c24d⁴ c24g c32g⁵ c24m⁴ c28m² Apr 26] workmanlike gelding: fairly useful handicap chaser, trained on reappearance by J. O'Neill, next 3 starts by A. King: dead-heated with Satshoon at Wincanton in November, joined on line after idling: stays 4m: acts on heavy and good to firm going: usually blinkered/visored: has jumped markedly right: no easy ride. *S. Gollings*   **c122 §** **h–**

LANNKARAN (IRE) 10 b.g. Shardari – Lankarana (Auction Ring (USA)) [2002/3 c119, h–: c21s⁶ Mar 15] useful-looking gelding: fairly useful handicap chaser: showed little only start in 2002/3: stays 3m: acts on soft and good to firm going: tried blinkered: often runs as if amiss. *H. D. Daly*   **c–** **h–**

LANOSO (IRE) 5 b.g. Charnwood Forest (IRE) – Silver Spark (USA) (Silver Hawk (USA)) [2002/3 h–: 16mᵖᵘ May 11] angular gelding: no sign of ability on Flat or in 2 starts over hurdles, tongue tied on first occasion. *H. M. Kavanagh*   **h–**

LANOS (POL) 5 ch.g. Special Power – Lubeka (POL) (Milione (FR)) [2002/3 h81: 16m⁴ 16m 16d⁶ Oct 31] smallish, angular gelding: fair on Flat in Britain, sold 1,800 gns Doncaster November Sales, won in March for R. Ford: poor form over hurdles: raced around 2m: tried blinkered: has looked far from keen. *T. R. George*   **h78**

LANTERN LEADER (IRE) 8 b.g. Supreme Leader – Lantern Line (The Parson) [2002/3 19s⁴ 19s³ 22g* 24d* 24d² 22g c22fᵘʳ 20f³ 24d c20s c24d c22sᵖᵘ Nov 10] fairly useful handicap hurdler: won at Kilbeggan and Galway in summer: largely disappointing over fences: stays 3m: acts on firm and good to soft going: effective blinkered or not. *Michael Hourigan, Ireland*   **c106** **h117**

LANZLO (FR) 6 b. or br.g. Le Balafre (FR) – L'Eternite (FR) (Cariellor (FR)) [2002/3 h107: 16f² 19g² 20m 18m³ 16vᵖᵘ 24g⁴ 16g⁵ 17g⁴ Apr 21] small, angular gelding: fair handicap hurdler: below best after second start, sold out of P. Hobbs's stable 2,700 gns Doncaster October Sales after fourth: seems barely to stay 19f: acts on any going. *James Moffatt*   **h102 d**

LAOCH NA MARA (USA) 4 b.g. Sea Hero (USA) – Ceirseach (IRE) (Don't Forget Me) [2002/3 16s 16s⁴ 16d² 16vᶠ 16m² Apr 19] leggy gelding: fairly useful on Flat (stays 1¼m): similar form in juvenile hurdles, best effort when second in maiden at Gowran in February: blinkered, ran in snatches when well held in Grade 1 at Punchestown in early-May. *T. G. McCourt, Ireland*   **h113**

LAOUEN (FR) 5 br.g. Funny Baby (FR) – Olive Noire (FR) (Cadoudal (FR)) [2002/3 F109: F16d² 16s* 16g* 16m* 16g* Apr 24] leggy gelding: useful bumper winner: unbeaten in 4 novice hurdles, at Doncaster in December, Musselburgh in January and Ayr and Perth in April: impressive when beating Ichi Beau 7 lengths in 15-runner event at last-named: will stay 2½m: capable of better still. *L. Lungo*   **h124 p** **F109**

LAPLAND (IRE) 6 b.g. Arctic Lord – Ride of Honour (King's Ride) [2002/3 h84: 16d⁵ 19d 24v⁵ Dec 20] well-made gelding: poor maiden hurdler: probably stays 3m: acts on heavy going. *N. A. Callaghan*   **h77**

LARA'S DELIGHT 8 b.m. Then Again – Sarah Dream (IRE) (Strong Gale) [2002/3 h–: 17gᵖᵘ 16f 17g⁶ Jun 29] smallish mare: no sign of ability. *M. J. Weeden*   **h–**

LARAS GREY (IRE)   10 gr.g. Celio Rufo – Persian Winter (Persian Bold) [2002/3   **c85**
c25d c27g c26m⁵ Apr 17] workmanlike ex-Irish gelding: bumper winner: winning   **h–**
hurdler/pointer: modest steeplechaser on balance of form: probably stays 27f: probably
acts on any going. *S. Flook*

LARRY HOGAN (IRE)   7 b.g. Toulon – Tree Drops (Beau Charmeur (FR)) [2002/3   **h111**
h108, F93: 20g 25g² 19s⁵ 24s² 22g 24d 20s* 22s⁵ 24s 22v³ 24s 19vᶠ Jan 25] fair hurdler:
didn't need to be at best to win maiden at Clonmel in November: stays 25f: raced on good
going or softer (acts on heavy): blinkered final start: sometimes tongue tied, including at
Clonmel. *Patrick Sinnott, Ireland*

LAST GESTURE   4 b.g. Jester – Suile Mor (Satin Wood) [2002/3 16g⁴ 16s⁴ Aug 10]   **h–**
poor on Flat (stayed 1m): achieved little in 2 juvenile hurdles, not fluent in blinkers
second time: dead. *Jean-Rene Auvray*

LAST OPTION   11 br.g. Primitive Rising (USA) – Saint Motunde (Tyrant (USA))   **c126**
[2002/3 c126: c24g⁴ c28m³ c25d³ c22d³ c24g² c26g³ c33mᵖᵘ Apr 12] good-bodied
gelding: smart hunter chaser: won Christie's Foxhunter Chase at Cheltenham in 2001/2:
easily best effort in 2002/3 when 3 lengths third of 24 to Kingscliff in same race, always
well placed: suited by 3¼m+: acts on good to firm and heavy going: reportedly finished
lame second start, pulled up as if amiss final one: takes good hold. *R. Tate*

LAST REBEL (IRE)   4 b.g. Danehill (USA) – La Curamalal (IRE) (Rainbow Quest   **h–**
(USA)) [2002/3 17s⁶ 16d Jan 18] fairly useful 7f/1m winner at 2 yrs in Germany,
unplaced in 3 starts on Flat in 2002 for P. Schiergen: little impact both starts over hurdles,
failed to settle on debut. *R. T. Phillips*

LAST SYMPHONY   6 b.g. Last Tycoon – Dancing Heights (IRE) (High Estate)   **h–**
[2002/3 h–: 17v 17s 17sᶠ Feb 13] leggy gelding: has lost his way on Flat: bought out of
J. A. Moore's stable £1,700 Ascot April Sales. *W. J. Reed*

LAST THEATRE (IRE)   5 b.m. King's Theatre (IRE) – Last Flair (Busted) [2002/3   **h112 +**
16m⁴ 16d⁶ᵖᵘ 16g³ 20sᵖᵘ 16g* Feb 28] leggy mare: half-sister to fair staying hurdler/chaser
Il Trovatore (by Chief Singer): useful on Flat (stays 1¾m) for J. Bolger, won twice in
2002: fair hurdler: best effort when winning mares handicap at Doncaster, flicking tail
under whip but leading last and staying on well to beat Baby Gee 2 lengths: should stay
beyond 2m: reportedly distressed second start, also went as if amiss fourth start. *Jonjo
O'Neill*

LAST TRY (IRE)   12 ch.g. Try My Best (USA) – Alpenwind (Tumble Wind (USA))   **c–**
[2002/3 c92d, h–: c21gᵖᵘ c20d⁵ c23g⁴ c17m⁴ Jul 19] leggy, lengthy gelding: fair chaser at   **h–**
best, retains little ability: stays 21f: unraced on heavy going, acts on any other: blinkered
last 2 starts: tongue tied. *B. S. Rothwell*

LATALOMNE (USA)   9 ch.g. Zilzal (USA) – Sanctuary (Welsh Pageant) [2002/3   **c162**
c162, h123+: c17g⁵ 16d⁵ 17d c16gᶠ Mar 12]   **h119**
      No one died. They may have made another calamitous visit to the Chelten-
ham Festival, but Latalomne and Vinnie Keane live to fight another day. Though
possibly not so often as previously in each other's company. Their bad luck in the
latest Champion Chase was doubly unfortunate, after a virtually identical mishap
the previous year. The field was almost the same and Latalomne, with regular rider
Keane on board, was again close up on the outside from the start and disputing the
lead from before halfway. Disputing the lead until the second last. In 2002 they
were up there with Cenkos, and in 2003 it was Seebald. On the first occasion,
Latalomne got far too close and had no chance of keeping on his feet. Second time
around he made a far less serious mistake—but with the same result. Seebald also
fell. Crashing to the ground but almost immediately on his knees, as Latalomne and
the rest galloped away, Keane struck the ground twice with his whip and then threw
himself headlong to the turf, burying his face between his forearms and the grass.
With his whip raised above shoulder height, Keane provided one of the indelible
images of the 2003 Cheltenham Festival.
      Now for what was lost. In Latalomne's first Champion Chase, the conclu-
sion was that he would have finished somewhere near Cenkos, who was beaten
three and a half lengths into third. Latalomne had not been asked for absolutely
everything though, and the others were all off the bridle, so it was a calculated
guess. In the latest season, however, while it will be absolutely no consolation to
Keane and the horse's connections, it is possible to state with far more confidence
that Latalomne would not have won, one new factor in the equation being Moscow

Queen Mother Champion Chase, Cheltenham—Latalomne (centre) and Vinnie Keane suffer a repeat exit two out; Seebald (right) also falls, leaving Moscow Flyer clear

Flyer who was in close attendance and clearly travelling much the better. Lata-lomne and Seebald are rated as having finished five lengths behind the winner and two lengths in front of the eventual runner-up, Native Upmanship, who was hampered in the melee. That ought to be a high-class performance by any measure, though the compilers of the Anglo-Irish Classification gave Latalomne a mark of only 140, a figure at least 12 lb below any of his ten rivals in the latest Champion Chase

The third- and second-last fences on Cheltenham's Old Course and the third-last fence on the New Course are obstacles at which discretion is definitely the better part of valour and precision is vital. All are positioned on a quite steep and sustained downhill stretch, the severest on the course, when the field is usually travelling at its fastest. Even slight mistakes can make it very hard for some horses to keep their footing. The fences have been labelled unfair in the past, and it is not many years since the course management took measures to level the ground in the immediate vicinity of the third-last fence on the Old Course. Many horses are still found out, though few spring to mind as having fallen there two years running, let alone at the head of affairs like Latalomne and in a race like the Champion Chase. In another top race at the meeting, the Champion Hurdle, Land Afar was up with the leaders and still on the bridle when he fell at the second last in 1994; twelve months later, he was again close up, though apparently not travelling quite so well, when the third last found him out. Elsewhere, Travado fell seven out in both the 1993 and 1994 King George at Kempton, leaving his suspect stamina still untested. More famously, Golden Miller unseated his rider two fences after Valentine's in the 1935 Grand National, after trying to refuse, and then successfully refused at the very same fence in both 1936 (having already been brought down at the first) and 1937. Also in the Grand National, having been third in 1981, Royal Mail fell at first Becher's in both 1982 (when second favourite) and 1983.

Another major element of frustration with Latalomne's two falls at Chelten-ham is that the performances he was in the process of producing looked to be a long way in advance of anything else seen from him. In 2001/2 there was the compensa-tion of one victory, negotiating Cheltenham without mishap in a £14,219 handicap, but in 2002/3 there was not a bean in consolation. The Haldon Gold Cup at Exeter in November provided a dire reappearance effort, after which Latalomne was put back to hurdles for two valuable handicaps at Cheltenham before the end of the year, showing only fairly useful form and just out of the money. Given a break, Latalomne had a gallop on the Southwell all-weather track at the end of February in final preparation for Cheltenham. 'He is a horse who runs his best races when fresh,' said his trainer Brian Ellison. Latalomne's owners had their say on what might be best for the horse when they replaced Keane with Tony Dobbin for the Grade 1 BMW Chase at the Punchestown Festival shortly after the end of the British season but, even though Moscow Flyer blundered his way out at the second last, Latalomne could finish only fourth. Incidentally, he ran well below form for Richard Johnson at Aintree the previous April and for Mick Fitzgerald at Exeter. Perhaps Keane will get his chance after all to make it third time lucky in the Champion Chase.

			Northern Dancer
	Zilzal (USA)	Nureyev	Special
	(ch 1986)	(b 1977)	Le Fabuleux
Latalomne (USA)		French Charmer	Bold Example
(ch.g. 1994)		(ch 1978)	Tudor Melody
		Welsh Pageant	Picture Light
	Sanctuary	(b 1966)	Doutelle
	(ch 1979)	Hiding Place	Jojo
		(b 1963)	

Starting at 14/1 and 25/1 on his two appearances in the Champion Chase, the leggy Latalomne would be at many times those odds to excel over jumps if there was only a cursory glance at his pedigree to go on. He is a half-brother to the Breeders' Cup Sprint winner Sheikh Albadou (by Green Desert) and his sire is Zilzal, outstanding over seven furlongs and a mile. Latalomne's dam Sanctuary has, however, produced a couple of other winning jumpers in Durham (by Caerleon) and the stayer Captain Jack (by Salse). Latalomne has shown easily his best form is at around the minimum trip, but he did land the odds over an easy two miles and five furlongs as a novice. He acts on good to soft going, and the ground was soft when he made such a bold show in the 2002 Champion Chase, but his trainer maintains that Latalomne is suited by less testing conditions. *B. Ellison*

LATE HARVEST (NZ) 11 b.g. Tarrago (ITY) – Pamira (AUS) (Nassau (AUS))   **c–**
[2002/3 c67, h74: 17g^{pu} May 4] lengthy gelding: poor maiden hurdler/chaser: stays 2½m: **h–**
acts on good to firm and good to soft going: visored last of last 5 outings. *A. J. Deakin*

LATE NIGHT OUT 8 b.g. Lahib (USA) – Chain Dance (Shareef Dancer (USA))   **h78**
[2002/3 16g⁵ Oct 9] smart on Flat (barely stays 8.5f), generally below best in 2002:
favourite, not fluent last 2 having been poorly placed when only fifth of 10 in novice
at Fakenham on hurdling debut: likely to need sharp 2m: sold 24,000 gns Newmarket
Autumn Sales. *W. Jarvis*

LATENSAANI 5 b.g. Shaamit (IRE) – Intoxication (Great Nephew) [2002/3 21g^{ur} 20f*   **h113**
21m* 20m* 21m² 20d^{pu} Nov 24] leggy gelding: modest on Flat (stays 2m) for W. Haggas:
fair novice hurdler: won at Hexham in September and Sedgefield and Wetherby in
October, long odds on first 2 occasions: 11 lengths second of 4 to Taming at Cheltenham:
stays 21f: acts on firm going, ran poorly on good to soft final start. *G. M. Moore*

LATIMER'S PLACE 7 b.g. Teenoso (USA) – Pennethorne Place (Deep Run) [2002/3   **c88 +**
h111, F80: c21d⁵ c19d Jan 27] sturdy gelding: largely progressive form over hurdles in   **h–**
2001/2, won EBF National Hunt Novices' Handicap Hurdle Final at Sandown: shaped as
if badly in need of race on chasing debut, possibly found race coming too soon 9 days
later: should stay beyond 2½m: raced on good to soft/soft going. *G. B. Balding*

LAUDERDALE 7 b.g. Sula Bula – Miss Tullulah (Hubble Bubble) [2002/3 c70, h75:   **c109**
c17d* c16m⁶ c20m^F c21m^F 24g^{pu} c17g^F c17s² c17v* c16g² c20v⁵ c16v³ c17d³ c20g   **h–**
c17g⁵ Apr 7] good-topped gelding: winning hurdler: fair chaser: won at Kelso in May
(weak novice) and November (handicap): has won at 3m, seems best around 2m: acts on
heavy going: usually front runner. *Miss Lucinda V. Russell*

LAUNDMOWER 7 br.g. Perpendicular – Sound Work (Workboy) [2002/3 F86:   **h–**
20m⁵ Apr 21] useful-looking gelding: third in bumper at Catterick on debut: well behind
in novice hurdle at Wetherby over year later. *Mrs S. J. Smith*

LAURAS THEME (IRE) 5 ch.m. Nucleon (USA) – Lovely Leitrim (IRE) (Erin's   **h–**
Hope) [2002/3 16d 16m⁵ 20g 16d^{pu} Jun 7] third foal: dam little sign of ability: lightly-
raced maiden on Flat in Ireland: no form over hurdles. *L. Lungo*

LAURELDEAN (IRE) 5 b.g. Shernazar – Power Run (Deep Run) [2002/3 F16s*   **F100**
F16m⁴ Apr 22] €54,000 4-y-o: fourth live foal: dam, bumper winner, out of half-sister
to useful 3m chaser Arctic Beau: won maiden bumper at Tramore on debut: some improvement when fourth to Newmill in valuable event at Fairyhouse following month.
S. J. Treacy, Ireland

LAUREL PRINCE 7 b.g. Reprimand – Laurel Queen (IRE) (Viking (USA)) [2002/3   **h88**
h86: 16m⁴ 16d⁵ 16g 17d 20sᵖᵘ 16dᵘʳ 16d 16v* 16s* 17g⁴ Mar 18] good-bodied gelding:
modest handicap hurdler: trained second to fifth starts by F. Lloyd: back to form after
turn of year, won sellers at Leicester (for W. Clay) in January and Chepstow (claimed
from B. Leavy 7,200 gns) in February: stays 2½m: acts on good to firm and heavy going:
effective visored/blinkered or not: races prominently. *Mrs A. M. Thorpe*

LAUREL VIEW (IRE) 5 b.g. Arctic Lord – Solmus (IRE) (Sexton Blake) [2002/3   **h111 p**
F16m³ F16s² F16v² F16s² 16v³ Dec 29] second foal: dam, placed in bumper, half-sister   **F102**
to smart staying chaser Glyde Court: fairly useful in bumpers: third to Stacumny Bridge
in maiden at Leopardstown on hurdling debut: will stay at least 2½m: should improve.
N. Meade, Ireland

LAURIER ROSE (FR) 6 b.g. Subotica (FR) – Light of Realm (Realm) [2002/3   **c90**
c17s⁵ c17m³ c17d⁵ c20s² c20f* 20m 20s Mar 8] leggy ex-Irish gelding: half-brother to   **h–**
fair 2m jumper Flash of Realm, also useful on Flat: maiden on Flat: bumper winner/
winning hurdler: modest chaser: won maiden at Tipperary in August: sold out of
E. O'Grady's stable €3,800 Goffs December Sale after next outing: stays 2½m: acts on
any ground: has had tongue tied. *Lindsay Woods, Ireland*

LAVENDER LADY (IRE) 7 b. or br.m. Lord Americo – Polarogan (Tarqogan)   **c–**
[2002/3 h–, F74: 20g³ 20g⁴ 22s 16g⁵ 20m⁴ 16g⁶ 16d⁶ 16d⁴ c21dᶠ 24sᵖᵘ Dec 6] sturdy   **h79**
mare: poor maiden hurdler: left G. M. Moore after sixth start: behind when falling tenth
on chasing debut: stays 2½m: acts on good to firm and good to soft going: tried in cheekpieces. *M. J. Gingell*

LAVERON 8 b.h. Konigsstuhl (GER) –   **h161**
La Virginia (GER) (Surumu (GER)) [2002/3
h161: 21s* 25d* 20s³ 24v* 20v² Nov 24]
tall, angular horse: third foal: brother to
Deutsches Derby and Mehl-Muhlens Ren-
nen (2000 Guineas) winner Lavirco: dam,
winner twice in Germany at 1¼m, is from a
very good German classic family: pattern-
race performer on Flat, wins including
Deutsches St Leger, also third in Deutsches
Derby: fairly useful in novice hurdles in
Britain in 2001/2: considerably better form
after at Auteuil, successful in 2002/3 in
Group 2 Prix La Barka in May and 2 Group
1 events, Grande Course de Haies d'Auteuil
in June and Grand Prix d'Automne (length
ahead of Tiger Groom, pair clear) in November: good second, conceding weight all
round, to Katiki in Group 2 there final start:
stayed 25f: acted on heavy going: sometimes
jumped none too fluently: held up (set too
much to do third start): retired to Scarvagh
House Stud in Ireland. *F. Doumen, France*

*Grand Prix d'Automne, Auteuil—
leading French hurdler Laveron*

LAWAHIK 9 b.g. Lahib (USA) – Lightning Legacy (USA) (Super Concorde (USA))   **h–**
[2002/3 19sᵖᵘ 16sᵖᵘ Jan 30] smallish gelding: one-time fairly useful 2m handicap hurdler:
very lightly raced nowadays, no show both starts in 2002/3. *T. H. Caldwell*

LAWN 5 b.m. Contract Law (USA) – Pastures Green (Monksfield) [2002/3 F17sᵖᵘ   **F– §**
F17d Feb 23] second foal: dam lightly-raced half-sister to high-class staying chaser
Scotton Banks: showed more temperament than ability in 2 maiden bumpers. *P. Bowen*

LAW UNTO HIMSELF 5 b.g. Contract Law (USA) – Malacanang (Riboboy (USA))   **h–**
[2002/3 F70: 20dᵖᵘ 17s 19d Dec 19] signs of ability only on debut in bumper. *N. J. Hawke*

LAWZ (IRE) 9 br.g. Lahib (USA) – Sea Port (Averof) [2002/3 h122: 18d 16v³ 17d³ **h122**
18s* 16v³ Mar 8] leggy ex-Irish gelding: fairly useful handicap hurdler: back to best last
2 starts, winning at Fontwell in February in game fashion by 5 lengths from Ken Scott
and third of 17 to Korelo in valuable race at Sandown: raced around 2m on good going or
softer (acts on heavy): usually races up with pace. *C. J. Mann*

LA YOLAM 5 ch.m. Unfuwain (USA) – Massorah (FR) (Habitat) [2002/3 h88: 17g⁴ **h99**
16m³ Jun 1] fairly useful on Flat (stays 1¼m) at 3 yrs for B. Hanbury: best effort over
hurdles when third in novice handicap at Stratford: likely to prove best around 2m.
N. J. Henderson

LAZY BUT LIVELY (IRE) 7 br.g. Supreme Leader – Oriel Dream (Oats) [2002/3 **h117**
h110: 22s³ 24s³ 24dᵖᵘ Mar 15] medium-sized gelding: fairly useful handicap hurdler:
best effort when second to A Few Bob Back at Kelso on reappearance: off 4 months,
poor efforts last 2 starts: stays 3m well: raced on going softer than good (acts on heavy).
R. F. Fisher

LAZZAZ 5 b.g. Muhtarram (USA) – Astern (USA) (Polish Navy (USA)) [2002/3 h83: **h88**
16m 16g³ 17g⁶ 17sᶠ 17d⁶ Dec 3] fair on all-weather, modest on turf on Flat (stays 1¼m),
successful in February and March: modest form over hurdles, running best race when
falling last in selling handicap at Taunton: will prove best at 2m. *P. W. Hiatt*

LEADER SUPREME (IRE) 8 b.m. Supreme Leader – Country Daisy VII (Damsire **c–**
Unregistered) [2002/3 h84: 16s 21d 25vᵖᵘ 20d c20s³ 27v⁴ c24gᶠ c22g⁴ Mar 17] workman- **h–**
like mare: signs of ability only on hurdling debut. *J. R. Jenkins*

LEAD STORY (IRE) 8 b.g. Lead On Time (USA) – Mashmoon (USA) (Habitat) **c– §**
[2002/3 c112, h–: c25dᶠ c24fᵖᵘ Apr 3] strong gelding: useful hunter chaser on his day: **h–**
failed to complete both outings in 2002/3: won point in February: stays 3¼m: acts on soft
and good to firm going, probably on firm: tried blinkered: unreliable. *G. Chambers*

LEAD VOCALIST (IRE) 14 ch.g. Orchestra – Eternal Youth (Continuation) [2002/3 **c– x**
c–, h–: c25gᵖᵘ May 1] strong gelding: winning pointer/maiden steeplechaser (poor **h–**
jumper): stays 25f: acts on good to firm and heavy going: has found little. *Miss Lucy
Brack*

LEAGUES (NZ) 8 b.g. Kenfair (NZ) – Hidden Depths (NZ) (Beaufort Sea (USA)) **c96 x**
[2002/3 h87: c16dᵖᵘ c16g⁴ c16sᵖᵘ c16m⁶ c18m Mar 22] strong, lengthy gelding: maiden **h–**
hurdler: usually let down by jumping over fences, form only when fourth in maiden at
Doncaster: best efforts at 2m on good going: sold 2,900 gns Doncaster May Sales.
Mrs L. C. Taylor

LEARNED LAD (FR) 5 ch.g. Royal Academy (USA) – Blushing Storm (USA) **h–**
(Blushing Groom (FR)) [2002/3 16dᵖᵘ Nov 2] fair on Flat (stays 1¼m), won in March:
weakened very quickly in straight in novice at Ascot on hurdling debut. *Jamie Poulton*

LEARN THE LINGO 7 b.g. Teenoso (USA) – Charlotte Gray (Rolfe (USA)) **F–**
[2002/3 F80: F17mᵖᵘ Aug 26] best effort in bumpers when fourth at Ludlow on debut in
2001/2. *Mrs H. Dalton*

LEATHERBACK (IRE) 5 b.g. Turtle Island (IRE) – Phyllode (Pharly (FR)) [2002/3 **h–**
h100+: 16s 16d 16s Dec 27] compact gelding: fairly useful on Flat: winning hurdle,
well beaten in handicaps in 2002/3: likely to prove best around 2m: acts on soft going.
N. A. Callaghan

LE CABRO D'OR 9 b.g. Gildoran – Deirdre's Choice (Golden Love) [2002/3 c106: **c125**
c26v* c25dᵖᵘ Dec 19] good-topped gelding: fairly useful chaser: made all in 5-runner
handicap at Carlisle in November, beating Harlov 1¾ lengths despite mistakes: reportedly lame following month: should stay beyond 3¼m: acts on heavy going: front runner.
John R. Upson

LE CHABLIS (FR) 5 b.g. Sassanian (USA) – L'Aumance (FR) (Mont Basile (FR)) **c137**
[2002/3 c20s⁴ c20s* c20s² c20s* c22v* 18s⁵ c22s⁵ Apr 13] first foal: dam won up to 2¼m **h114**
over hurdles: maiden hurdler, fair form when fifth in minor event at Auteuil in March:
useful chaser: raced only at Auteuil in 2002/3, successful 3 times in 4-y-o group events,
notably Group 1 Prix Maurice Gillois in November, beating Kilefou of d'Airy ½ length: stiff
task, good fifth to Jerico Vallis in Group 2 in April: will stay beyond 2¾m: raced on soft/
heavy going: usually held up. *T. Trapenard, France*

LECKAMPTON 7 b.m. Bedford (USA) – I'm Unforgettable (Dublin Taxi) [2002/3 **h–**
F–: 17g⁶ Mar 17] smallish mare: once-raced in bumpers: well held in mares maiden
hurdle. *S. E. H. Sherwood*

LE COUDRAY (FR)   9 b.g. Phantom Breeze – Mos Lie (FR) (Tip Moss (FR))   **c142 +**
[2002/3 c22s^F c16s* c20v* c17v* c21s^F c21g^4 Mar 13]   **h–**

    Le Coudray enjoyed an excellent season in novice chases in Ireland in 2002/3, winning two Grade 1 events and falling at the last when in with every chance of landing a third. That he made it onto the track at all, however, was something of a miracle. A top-class staying hurdler, first in France and then for Aidan O'Brien, Le Coudray was out of action for a month short of three years before making his chasing debut in November. He had last been seen on the racecourse in a four-runner minor hurdle at Navan, where he started odds on to beat Limestone Lad at level weights, even though the latter had gained a famous victory over Istabraq less than a fortnight previously. Le Coudray failed to run to his best that day and was beaten twenty lengths. Two months later he was ruled out of the 2000 Stayers' Hurdle with injury and, in October of that year, was reported as set to miss the 2000/1 season. Switched to Christy Roche, Le Coudray was due to make his chasing debut in the Grade 1 Drinmore Novices' Chase at Fairyhouse in November 2001 but was taken out at the overnight stage and still hadn't made his return when injury to a sesamoid in January 2002 curtailed yet another campaign. Mind you, once Le Coudray stayed free of injury long enough to face the starter he quickly made up for lost time—having four races in barely six weeks and winning three races in little over a month. Le Coudray's form didn't reach the level of his best over hurdles, but it would have been unrealistic to expect it. His season ended in something of an anticlimax with fourth place in the Cathcart Chase at Cheltenham, but there may well be more to come from him in 2003/4 if he continues to steer clear of injury.

    The first of Le Coudray's Grade 1 novice victories came in the race he'd missed at the last minute in 2001, the Drinmore, sponsored by the Pierse Group. Barrow Drive, Native Scout and Boneyarrow, all useful novice hurdlers who had already shown they were likely to be at least as good over fences, were in the nine-runner line-up but Le Coudray started evens favourite on the strength of an impressive win in a maiden at Naas the previous week (he had fallen two out when still travelling strongly in a similar event at Cork on his comeback). On as inhospit-

Denny Gold Medal Novices Chase, Leopardstown—
Le Coudray gets the better of Bust Out to gain a second Grade 1 success

Mr J. P. McManus' "Le Coudray"

able a day as there was all winter, and on ground that was close to unraceable, Le Coudray and the experienced Barrow Drive, making his eighth start in a chase, coped much better than their rivals and had the race to themselves in the last mile, Le Coudray going the better and scoring impressively by six lengths after leading two out. Later in December, Le Coudray lined up for the Denny Gold Medal Novices' Chase at Leopardstown. He was odds on this time with just four opposing him, Bust Out, a smart hurdler who had made a winning debut over fences two weeks previously, appearing his most serious rival. Barry Geraghty was in the saddle, having turned down the chance to ride Florida Pearl in the King George VI Chase, and needed to be at his strongest as Bust Out pushed Le Coudray, making the running over the shorter trip, all the way to the line. Le Coudray stuck really well to his task and held on by half a length, the pair twenty clear of the third Ricardo.

A rematch with Bust Out in the Irish version of the Arkle was a possibility but, instead, connections waited for the Dr P. J. Moriarty Novices' Chase again at Leopardstown in early-February and a second clash with Barrow Drive. The pair dominated the closing stages, Le Coudray again travelling really well, and a much closer finish than at Fairyhouse was on the cards when Le Coudray, just in front, took a crashing fall at the last after appearing to jump the fence cleanly. Thankfully, he eventually got to his feet and was found to have suffered no serious injury, connections still able to plan for Cheltenham. Although Le Coudray was entered in both the SunAlliance Chase and the Gold Cup, the decision to go for the Cathcart was announced not long after the P. J. Moriarty, though warnings were issued that he wouldn't run at all if the ground was anything firmer than 'yielding to soft'. As it turned out, going that was officially good, good to soft in places, was yielding enough to allow Le Coudray to take his chance, but he failed to run quite to his best in finishing fourth, thirteen and a half lengths behind La Landiere. Le Coudray didn't jump so well as previously and couldn't quicken after travelling well and holding every chance three out. Perhaps he isn't going to be any better than his form over fences so far suggests, but there is a chance that a return to more testing ground will bring about improvement in open company, though, with his fragile nature, connections are likely to try to place him with particular care. The John Durkan Memorial at Punchestown could be a good race in which to start him off.

Le Coudray (FR) (b.g. 1994)	Phantom Breeze (b 1986)	Vision (b 1981)	Nijinsky
			Foreseer
		Ask The Wind (ch 1980)	Run The Gantlet
			Arburie
	Mos Lie (FR) (b 1989)	Tip Moss (ch 1972)	Luthier
			Top Twig
		Lestelie (br 1974)	Taj Dewan
			Leslie

Le Coudray is from the first crop of the smart Flat performer Phantom Breeze, who is also the sire of the smart hurdler Bilboa. Le Coudray is the first foal of his dam Mos Lie. Her only other reported foal, Le Coudray's sister Breeze Lie, was unplaced in four outings on the Flat in France. Mos Lie is related to a jumper raced in Britain in the latest season, being a half-sister to the dam of the fair hurdler/chaser Mercato, but further back this is a Flat-oriented family. The grandam Lestelie won at a mile and a half and was sister to the smart middle-distance colt Tajeslie and half-sister to another in Dhausli. She is also half-sister to the dam of the smart filly up to a mile and a quarter La Nana. The rangy, good-topped Le Coudray is effective at around two miles to three miles and has raced on good going or softer. He is unlikely to be risked on anything firmer and handles heavy particularly well. He wore a tongue strap on his first two starts and also in the Cathcart. *C. Roche, Ireland*

LE DIAMONT (FR) 4 ch.g. Broadway Flyer (USA) – Lady Diamond (FR) (Diamond Prospect (USA)) [2002/3 F16s⁵ F16m 19g Apr 19] angular gelding: fourth foal: half-brother to French middle-distance winner Ladonia (by Take Risks): dam never ran: modest form in bumpers at Kempton: well held in maiden on hurdling debut. *C. P. Morlock*   h–
F84

LE DUC (FR) 4 b.g. Villez (USA) – Beberova (FR) (Synefos (USA)) [2002/3 15v² 17g² 16d² 16s⁴ 16vᶠ 17s⁴ 17g⁶ 16g* Apr 3]   h133 §
Le Duc started at long odds for the top two juvenile hurdles in Britain at Cheltenham and Aintree. He was a 40/1-chance for the Triumph Hurdle and a 33/1-shot for the Ember Inns Anniversary Hurdle. Those odds were not so much a measure of Le Duc's chances on form, because he had shown plenty of ability, but more a reflection of his temperament, because he had shown plenty of that as well. Of course, if one day Le Duc consented to put his best foot forward he was an upset waiting to happen, and that is exactly what he did at Aintree.
Le Duc arrived from France with something of a reputation, but it did not take him long to acquire a very different one in Britain. He was beaten at 4/1-on on his British debut at Hereford in October, travelling like an odds-on shot for most of the race but hanging right at the last, ducking in behind the winner Short Change and not running on. Le Duc was similarly unenthusiastic on his subsequent outings, though for the most part showing better form as well. He ran second to Don Fernando at Cheltenham next time out in what was the best juvenile hurdle of the season up to that point, looked booked for second again when falling at the last in the Finale Hurdle at Chepstow in December, and came fourth to Moneytrain in the Wragge & Co Finesse Juvenile Hurdle at Cheltenham in January. The last time Le Duc was sent off favourite during the season was at Huntingdon in November when a noticeably reluctant display making the running saw him manage only fourth to Duke of Earl. Tried in blinkers at Chepstow and Cheltenham, with no significant change of attitude, Le Duc did not wear them when he belied his odds to finish sixth in the Triumph Hurdle, travelling well for a long way but typically finding little

once asked for more of an effort after two out, passing the post around fourteen lengths adrift of the winner Spectroscope.

Spectroscope was one of eight runners from the Triumph whom Le Duc reopposed at Aintree in a nineteen-strong field. Triumph runner-up Well Chief was made 2/1 favourite to reverse Cheltenham placings with Spectroscope, Mughas (fifth) was another rival who had finished ahead of Le Duc three weeks earlier, while Moneytrain (brought down) and Starzaan (hampered in the same incident) were both fancied to atone for their bad luck in the Triumph. With more than £63,000 on offer, Le Duc chose a good race in which finally to shed his maiden tag. Spectroscope and Well Chief looked set to fight out another finish but Le Duc was produced between them jumping the last. Finding more under pressure than previously, under a determined Ruby Walsh, Le Duc initially hung across Spectroscope after the final flight but thwarted that rival's renewed challenge to win by a head, with Well Chief two and a half lengths back in third and Starzaan fourth. Having the stand rail to race against may well have been instrumental in Le Duc's putting his best foot forward. A tendency to hang right had manifested itself in several of his previous races, so it is somewhat surprising that his two worst performances on form came when running right-handed at Hereford and Huntingdon.

Le Duc's effort at Aintree put him not far behind the best of a rather ordinary crop of juvenile hurdlers. It also turned out that he had met some of the best of his contemporaries on his debut against other newcomers at Auteuil in May on his only outing over hurdles (he'd had a couple of runs on the Flat) for Jean-Pierre Pelat. The winner Nickname, who beat Le Duc six lengths into second, developed into the top juvenile hurdler in Europe, while third-placed Lilium de Cotte went on to finish fourth in the Triumph. Incidentally, two more horses from the same race at Auteuil, Indien Royal and Bal de Nuit, joined Le Duc in Paul Nicholls' yard later in the season.

Unlike many juvenile hurdlers, Le Duc was bred for jumping rather than the Flat and, interestingly, both his sire and dam excelled as juvenile hurdlers in France. His sire Villez was the best of his generation, winning his first nine races over hurdles though, just as importantly where Le Duc is concerned, Villez was himself a tricky ride with a tendency to hang right. Le Duc's dam Beberova couldn't claim to be the best of her generation but she was not far off judging from her placed efforts in the Prix Cambaceres and Prix Renaud du Vivier, the autumn championship races at Auteuil for three- and four-year-old hurdlers respectively. She also won the Prix Pierre de Lassus and the Prix de Maisons-Laffitte, a couple of four-year-old hurdles which these days have pattern status. Beberova's two foals prior to Le Duc also showed precocity over jumps; both Cadourova (by Cadoudal) and Jackie Brown (by Mansonnien) did their winning as three-year-olds, the former over fences at Enghien and the latter over hurdles at Auteuil. Le Duc's next two dams, Ouargla and Quina, also won over jumps in France. The latter bred several

Ember Inns Anniversary 4-Y-O Novices' Hurdle, Aintree—Le Duc (noseband) finally gets off the mark; Spectroscope, making a mistake, and Well Chief are bang in contention over the last

good jumpers herself, including Jet Moon, winner of the Grande Steeple Chase di Milano, Quota, runner-up in the Grand Prix de Pau, and Rolling Horse who earned plenty of money in handicaps at Auteuil.

	Villez (USA) (ch 1992)	Lyphard's Wish (b 1976)	Lyphard / Sally's Wish
Le Duc (FR) (b.g. 1999)		Valhalla (ch 1974)	New Chapter / Varig
	Beberova (FR) (b 1989)	Synefos (b 1982)	Irish River / Salpinx
		Ouargla (b 1980)	Armos / Quina

As well as being bred for jumping, Le Duc looks the part too, being a tall, good-topped gelding, the sort to jump fences. Indeed, Le Duc is due to go chasing in the next season when his trainer feels he will come into his own. 'Someone said he had a Timeform squiggle but I haven't bothered to look. When he's a chaser they won't call him ungenuine.' We shall see. If he does become more resolute, or isn't fully tested (and it's not hard to imagine his being found some straightforward opportunities in novice chases), Le Duc should have no difficulty adding to his only win so far. He has raced only at around two miles on good going or softer. *P. F. Nicholls*

LEEFEN QUEEN (IRE) 6 b.m. King's Ride – Splendid Run (Deep Run) [2002/3 F16m³ F16m⁶ Apr 21] eighth foal: sister to winning 2½m chaser Deep King and half-sister to fair chaser Sigma Run (by The Parson), stays 2½m: dam unraced half-sister to useful 2m hurdler Hansel Rag: third of 4 in bumper at Ludlow on debut: well held in bigger field at Fakenham month later. *N. J. Henderson* **F79**

LEE'S ROSIE (IRE) 8 b.m. Zaffaran (USA) – Muse of Fire (Laurence O) [2002/3 h–: 20g c25g* Apr 14] workmanlike mare: no form over hurdles for N. Twiston-Davies: 25/1, won maiden hunter at Hexham on chasing debut, seeming to have measure of Star of Raven when left clear last. *Miss Bianca Dunk* **c79 +** **h–**

LEET BRIG 12 b.g. Pitpan – Gilzie Bank (New Brig) [2002/3 c25gᵖᵘ Apr 7] lightly raced and little sign of ability, including in point: poor jumper. *Miss Charlotte Mooney* **c– x** **h–**

LEFT BANK (IRE) 7 ch.g. Over The River (FR) – My Friend Fashion (Laurence O) [2002/3 c65, h71: c20m³ c21dᵖᵘ c23m* c20m⁶ c24d⁴ c21ᵘʳ c25g³ c24g c25g* c24g³ c21m Apr 17] sturdy gelding: maiden hurdler: poor chaser: won novice handicaps at Wetherby in October and March: stays 25f: needs good going or firmer: usually wears headgear: irresolute. *Mrs M. Reveley* **c79 §** **h– §**

LEGAL LUNCH (USA) 8 b.g. Alleged (USA) – Dinner Surprise (USA) (Lyphard (USA)) [2002/3 h124: 23s 24d⁵ 22sᵖᵘ 20g Apr 2] smallish, well-made gelding: fairly useful handicap hurdler at best: off 14 months before reappearance: signs of retaining ability second and final (visored) outings: stays 3m: raced on good going or softer over hurdles (well beaten on heavy). *R. M. Stronge* **h103**

LEGAL PERK (IRE) 9 b.m. Executive Perk – Running Valley (Buckskin (FR)) [2002/3 h–: 16dᵖᵘ Nov 12] workmanlike mare: no form over hurdles. *J. L. Needham* **h–**

LEGAL TENDER 6 b.g. Contract Law (USA) – Slip A Coin (Slip Anchor) [2002/3 19dᵖᵘ May 14] seems of little account. *Mrs D. A. Hamer* **h–**

LEG BEFORUM (IRE) 9 b.g. Distinctly North (USA) – Paulines Girl (Hello Gorgeous (USA)) [2002/3 c20mᵘʳ Jun 1] leggy, sparely-made gelding: fair pointer, successful 3 times in 2002: unseated eighth on hunter chase debut: sold £6,000 Ascot February Sales. *Mrs Sarah L. Dent* **c–** **h–**

LEGGIES LEGACY 12 b.g. Jupiter Island – Hit The Line (Saulingo) [2002/3 c–, h89: 22m 21d 22s 21s* 21v³ 22s Mar 2] poor handicap hurdler, left L. Wells after reappearance: easily best effort in 2002/3 when winning at Plumpton in January: stays 3m: best on soft/heavy going: found nothing only run in blinkers. *J. Gallagher* **c–** **h83**

LEGOLAS 4 b.c. Primitive Rising (USA) – Teddy's Bow (IRE) (Archway (IRE)) [2002/3 F17v⁴ F16d⁴ Feb 25] smallish colt: first foal: dam modest sprint maiden: poor form in bumpers at Sedgefield and Catterick. *M. W. Easterby* **F74**

LE GRAND GOUSIER (USA) 9 ch.g. Strawberry Road (AUS) – Sandy Baby (USA) (Al Hattab (USA)) [2002/3 c24gᵖᵘ 22gᵖᵘ Jun 22] leggy gelding: winning hurdler: **c–** **h–**

little show in points or hunter chase: barely stays 2½m: acts on firm going, probably on soft: formerly blinkered, visored in 2002/3. *R. J. Price*

LE GRAND ROCHER   6 ch.g. Factual (USA) – Honey Bridge (Crepello) [2002/3 F16s² Jun 9] workmanlike gelding: half-brother to several winners, notably St Leger winner Minster Son (by Niniski): dam 6f winner at 2 yrs: off bridle before halfway when second of 10 in bumper at Worcester on debut. *D. J. Caro*   F81

LE GRAND VIZIER   4 br.g. Doyoun – Just Visiting (Superlative) [2002/3 16sᵖᵘ Dec 5] no form on Flat or on hurdling debut. *J. R. Jenkins*   h–

LE GUVNOR   8 br.g. Le Moss – High Heels (IRE) (Supreme Leader) [2002/3 21fᵖᵘ 20gᵖᵘ 20dᵖᵘ 16s 21gᵖᵘ 27sᵖᵘ Mar 11] strong gelding: first foal: dam never ran: of no account. *G. J. Smith*   h–

LEINSTER (IRE)   6 br.g. Supreme Leader – Jennycomequick (Furry Glen) [2002/3 F110p: 18v² 16s⁴ 16d⁴ 16v² 20g* Apr 3]   h128 p
    Despite winning the St Austell Brewery Mersey Novices' Hurdle at Aintree in April, Leinster didn't quite fulfil the potential of his debut success in a bumper at the 2002 Punchestown Festival. The Mersey was his only victory as a novice over hurdles, and easily his best performance. Leinster's task was eased by below-form efforts from some of the leading contenders, and he might well not have won had the short-priced favourite Coolnagorna not met a cruel end three from home. Leinster himself was also going well at that stage and made the most of his opportunity, staying on well and beating the useful four-year-old Crystal d'Ainay by seven lengths with the remaining six finishers (all but one starting at 66/1 or longer) well strung out behind. Leinster's first four appearances over hurdles had been in maidens around two miles in Ireland. Each time he shaped as if the trip was on the short side, his jumping also lacking fluency. Leinster was clearly suited by the step up to two and a half but he couldn't repeat the form in the Grade 1 novice over the same trip at Punchestown in early-May (after the British season), again let down by his jumping when only seventh to Nobody Told Me.
    Leinster is the third foal out of Jennycomequick, who was also represented in the latest season by First Touch (by Montelimar), pulled up on both starts over hurdles, and by Theatre Call (by Old Vic), an encouraging fourth on his debut in a

St Austell Brewery Mersey Novices' Hurdle, Aintree—
Leinster survives a mistake at the last to defeat Crystal d'Ainay

Mr Cathal M. Ryan's "Leinster"

bumper. Jennycomequick herself was a useful hurdler and winning chaser who stayed two and three quarter miles. Leinster will probably be suited by three miles and has raced on good going or softer. A good sort in appearance, Leinster looks the sort to make more of an impact over fences. *D. T. Hughes, Ireland*

LEITH HILL STAR 7 ch.m. Comme L'Etoile – Sunnyday (Sunley Builds) [2002/3 h69: 16v⁴ c22sᶠ 21s⁶ 25s⁵ 25m⁴ 21m² Apr 21] angular mare: fell first on chasing debut: poor maiden hurdler: probably stays 25f: acts on good to firm and heavy going. *R. Rowe*   c–
h71

LEITH LYNX 6 ch.m. Minster Son – Pinkie Hill (Le Coq d'Or) [2002/3 h–: 18g 16g 21mᵖᵘ 21g⁵ 24dᵖᵘ Aug 17] lengthy, unfurnished mare: no form over hurdles: sold 900 gns Doncaster September Sales. *P. Monteith*   h–

LEIXLIP (IRE) 5 b.g. Jurado (USA) – The Parson's Filly (IRE) (The Parson) [2002/3 F16m⁶ Dec 17] IR £7,000 3-y-o: first foal: dam, winning 2¼m hurdler, out of half-sister to top-class chaser Wayward Lad: sixth of 11 in bumper at Musselburgh: dead. *Mrs K. B. Mactaggart*   F75

LE MILLENAIRE (FR) 4 b. or br.g. Ragmar (FR) – Ezaia (FR) (Iron Duke (FR)) [2002/3 F16d Feb 23] 7,000 (privately) 3-y-o: second foal: dam unraced, from family of Welsh National winner Edmond: well held in bumper on debut. *S. H. Shirley-Beavan*   F–

LEMON BRIDGE (IRE) 8 b.g. Shalford (IRE) – Sharply (Sharpman) [2002/3 19m* 19m⁵ Aug 31] sturdy gelding: well held on Flat in 2002, refused to race once: modest hurdler: blinkered and tongue tied, won amateur handicap at Stratford in June: never a danger at Market Rasen 3 months later: stays 19f: acts on good to firm and good to soft going. *Ian Williams*   h90

LE-MONDE (IRE) 5 br.g. Anabaa (USA) – Alexandra Fair (USA) (Green Dancer (USA)) [2002/3 16m⁴ 16d* 20s² 20s² 24v* c22s² 24v 22v⁴ 20v⁵ 24m⁴ Apr 13] modest on Flat (stays 2m), successful in July: promising second on chasing debut: fair hurdler: won   c97 p
h111

510

novice at Cork in October and handicap at Clonmel in November: effective at 2m to 3m: acts on good to firm and heavy going. *D. Wachman, Ireland*

LEOPARD SPOT (IRE) 5 b.g. Sadler's Wells (USA) – Savoureuse Lady (Caerleon (USA)) [2002/3 h97: 20s^{pu} 20d^2 Oct 26] quite good-topped gelding: fairly useful maiden on Flat at 3 yrs for A. O'Brien: best effort over hurdles when second in novice handicap at Carlisle: stays 2½m: raced on good going or softer (acts on good to soft). *Jonjo O'Neill* **h103**

LEOPHIN DANCER (USA) 5 b.g. Green Dancer (USA) – Happy Gal (FR) (Habitat) [2002/3 17s^{pu} 16g^6 16s Jan 3] modest maiden up to 2m on Flat: best effort over hurdles when sixth of 17 in novice claimer at Ludlow (tongue tied): reportedly lame on debut. *P. W. Hiatt* **h72**

LE PERO (FR) 5 b.h. Perrault – Nuit d'Ecajeul (FR) (Matahawk) [2002/3 F16s^3 17v^2 18s^6 18s* Apr 16] well-made horse: fifth foal: half-brother to Slovak middle-distance winner Erik d'Ecajeul (by Synefos): dam, won over 15f in France, half-sister to very smart French hurdler Roi d'Ecajeuil: tongue tied, third in bumper at Sandown on debut: fairly useful form over hurdles, won 5-y-o minor event at Auteuil by 8 lengths. *G. Macaire, France* **h127**
F98

L'EPICURIEN (FR) 7 ch.g. Chef de Clan II (FR) – L'Epicurienne (FR) (Rex Magna (FR)) [2002/3 c127, h–: c17s* c21g* c21m^4 c16v^2 c20v^2 c20m^5 c21s^{pu} c21g Apr 21] leggy gelding: fairly useful chaser: won at Bangor (intermediate) and Newton Abbot (handicap) in May: ran poorly last 3 outings: will stay beyond 21f: acts on heavy and good to firm going: blinkered: difficult ride. *M. C. Pipe* **c126 §**
h–

LE ROI MIGUEL (FR) 5 b.g. Point of No Return (FR) – Loumir (USA) (Bob's Dusty (USA)) [2002/3 h120+: c19s^2 c16s^2 c16g^F c16g* Apr 5] **c156 p**
h–

'He's only a baby but has lots of potential ... He's a two-miler through and through and the biggest problem I'm going to have is keeping him away from Azertyuiop.' So trainer Paul Nicholls told *The Irish Field* after Le Roi Miguel had won the Grade 1 Swordlestown Cup Novices' Chase at Punchestown shortly after

Martell Maghull Novices' Chase, Aintree—
five-year-olds Le Roi Miguel (right) and Vol Solitaire lead Impek early on

the end of the British season. The success meant a clean sweep for Nicholls in the three Grade 1 two-mile novice chases in the spring, Azertyuiop having won the Arkle at Cheltenham and Le Roi Miguel landing the Martell Maghull Novices' Chase at Aintree from another stable companion Vol Solitaire. Although the ill-fated Vol Solitaire won't be around in the autumn, the other pair, along with Cenkos and others, give Nicholls a very strong hand in the top two-mile chases. It was some measure of the regard in which he was held at the start of the season that Le Roi Miguel's first two appearances came in Grade 2 novices before Christmas. He was outstayed by One Knight over just short of two and a half miles when odds on for the Rising Stars at Chepstow in November and worn down after the last by Impek on testing ground in the three-runner Henry VIII at Sandown a month later, looking a certain future winner, with his sights lowered just slightly. But Le Roi Miguel wasn't seen out again until March and his remaining outings were all in Grade 1 events. He started an 11/1-chance for the Arkle at Cheltenham, seventh in the betting in a field of nine, but reached only the third before coming down.

Nearly a month after Cheltenham, Le Roi Miguel got his chance of revenge on Impek, the pair dominating the five-runner line-up for the Maghull. Impek was 8 lb better off compared to Sandown and started favourite, but the sharper track and less testing ground were all in Le Roi Miguel's favour. With Vol Solitaire making the running, Le Roi Miguel was able to sit comfortably in second and the race was as good as over when he was sent on three out. He beat his stable companion by eleven lengths, Impek a further head back in third after getting tapped for foot. Le Roi Miguel gave Nicholls his third win with a five-year-old in the race in the last five seasons, having been successful with Flagship Uberalles in 1999 and Armaturk in 2002. The Swordlestown Cup was a virtual rerun of the Maghull. Impek was again in the line-up and was 4 lb better off than at Aintree though, for the first time in three clashes, Le Roi Miguel started favourite. Rathgar Beau, a faller at Aintree when still in contention four out, was the other major contender in a field of five. With no Vol Solitaire to make the running this time, Ruby Walsh controlled the gallop on Le Roi Miguel. Despite the stiffer track, softer ground and some minor mistakes (excusable given the inhospitable conditions in which the race was run), the outcome was never in serious doubt, Le Roi Miguel kept up to his work to beat Impek by six lengths, Rathgar Beau having lost second place with a blunder at the last. Surprisingly, Le Roi Miguel is the first five-year-old to have won the Swordlestown Cup since it was introduced in 1992. It isn't always easy for good novices of his age to make an impact when they lose the weight allowance—Armaturk's sole win in 2002/3 came in a four-runner minor event—but Le Roi Miguel has shown form of a rather higher level and has the potential to improve further.

As top jumpers' pedigrees go, they don't come much less likely than Le Roi Miguel's. He is by Point of No Return, a middle-distance stayer and no more than useful hurdler in France who stood at a fee of just 5,000 francs. He has had a mere

Swordlestown Cup Novices' Chase, Punchestown—a second Grade 1 success

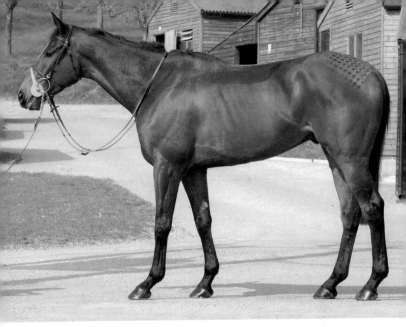

Mrs J. Stewart's "Le Roi Miguel"

			Pyjama Hunt (ch 1975)	Huntercombe
		Point of No Return (FR) (ch 1985)		Kamiyanna
			Pointe Rousse (ch 1977)	Margouillat
Le Roi Miguel (FR) (b.g. 1998)				Pointe d'Onyx
			Bob's Dusty (b 1974)	Bold Commander
	Loumir (USA) (b 1982)			Countess Alice
			Mai Ling (b 1975)	Icecapade
				Mia Lisa

handful of runners in France, including the fairly useful chaser Pointor, who won the Grand Steeple-Chase de Dieppe. Le Roi Miguel's dam Loumir has an American Flat background, though she herself won over a mile in France before gaining successes over hurdles and fences in both Ireland and France. Her two previous winners, Louvre Royale (by Garde Royale) and Lourale (by General Holme), were both successful on the Flat in France. The grandam Mai Ling and third dam Mia Lisa were both maidens who bred several Flat winners in the States, those out of Mai Ling including the fairly useful two-year-old five-furlong winner in Britain Steal The Show. Mia Lisa was a half-sister to three minor stakes winners out of a sister to the useful handicapper at up to a mile and a half Hinton Blewett. Le Roi Miguel will prove best at around two miles. He has been raced mainly on going softer than good, though clearly went very well on good at Aintree. A tall, useful-looking gelding, he showed fairly useful form as a juvenile hurdler but is clearly much better over fences. *P. F. Nicholls*

LE SAUVAGE (IRE)   8 b.g. Tirol – Cistus (Sun Prince) [2002/3 h–: 24g 21s^{pu} 20v^2 **h77** 20s^3 19d^5 20g^4 21m Apr 26] leggy gelding: fair hurdler at best, only poor nowadays: should stay 3m: best efforts on good going or softer (acts on heavy). *D. W. Barker*

Stone Street Novices' Chase, Folkestone—
dual winner of the Grande Course de Haies Le Sauvignon (left) makes a winning debut over fences

LE SAUVIGNON (FR) 9 b.g. Morespeed – Tarde (FR) (Kashtan (FR)) [2002/3 c25d* c24s² Dec 26] tall, angular gelding: top-class hurdler: won Prix La Barka and Grande Course de Haies d'Auteuil in 2001, both at Auteuil: subsequently off 18 months and left J. Bertran de Balanda: most impressive chasing debut when easily landing the odds in 4-runner novice at Folkestone in December, jumping well: 6 lengths second of 7 to Jair du Cochet in Grade 1 novice at Kempton later in month (collapsed and died after line): effective at 19f to 25f: acted on heavy going, well held on good to firm. *P. F. Nicholls*   **c145** **h–**

LESCER'S LAD 6 b.g. Perpendicular – Grange Gracie (Oats) [2002/3 F–: F16m F16g³ Apr 14] off 11 months and left B. Ellison, easily best effort in bumpers when third to Classical Ben in maiden at Hexham. *J. Hetherton*   **F85**

LESDREAM 6 b.g. Morpeth – Lesbet (Hotfoot) [2002/3 h–, F–: 19d 20v 20s² 17d* 17d* Feb 23] progressive form over hurdles: won novice handicaps at Hereford and Exeter in February: likely to prove better at 2½m than 2m: acts on soft ground. *J. D. Frost*   **h94**

LE SKI D'OR 7 b.g. Petoski – Page of Gold (Goldhill) [2002/3 F68: 20d Nov 11] poor form in bumpers: seventh of 11 finishers in maiden at Fontwell on hurdling debut. *D. R. Gandolfo*   **h72**

LESTER LONGFELLOW 7 b. or br.g. Riverwise (USA) – Cut Above The Rest (Indiaro) [2002/3 F–: 21sᵖᵘ Nov 24] no sign of ability in bumper or novice hurdle. *N. R. Mitchell*   **h–**

L'ETANG BLEU (FR) 5 gr.g. Graveron (FR) – Strawberry Jam (FR) (Fill My Hopes (FR)) [2002/3 h94§: 22f³ 19m⁵ 16g⁶ 19d 19m 19s 17d² 16v 17dˢᵘ 16d* Apr 9] leggy gelding: modest hurdler: back to form to win selling handicap at Uttoxeter: effective around 2m to easy 2¾m: acts on soft and firm going: often visored, tried blinkered/in cheekpieces: ungenuine. *M. C. Pipe*   **h91 §**

LETS DANCE 4 b.f. Master Willie – Quick Quick Sloe (Scallywag) [2002/3 F17m⁴ Apr 15] first foal: dam winning pointer: 25/1, under 4 lengths fourth of 9 to demoted Mrs Philip in steadily-run mares bumper at Exeter on debut: will be suited by greater test of stamina. *C. J. Down*   **F86**

LET'S FLY (FR) 8 b.g. Rose Laurel – Harpyes (FR) (Quart de Vin (FR)) [2002/3 h108: 16d³ 17dᵖᵘ c20d³ Aug 4] good-topped gelding: fair hurdler: won intermediate at Southwell in May: shaped as if amiss next time: disappointing last of 3 finishers in novice at Market Rasen on chasing debut: should stay at least 2½m: raced on going softer than good (acts on heavy): sold 7,800 gns Doncaster October Sales, runner-up in points in 2003. *Mrs M. Reveley*   **c–** **h97**

LETS GO DUTCH   7 b.m. Nicholas Bill – Dutch Majesty (Homing) [2002/3 h89: **h107** 24d⁶ 24s² 24d* 22v³ Mar 7] workmanlike mare: fair handicap hurdler: improved in 2002/3, won at Exeter in February by length from Darina's Boy, off bridle long way out and jinking badly approaching last: will prove best at 3m+: raced on going softer than good (acts on heavy). *K. Bishop*

LETZ BEE ON   5 b.g. Flying Tyke – Jacques Point (Jester) [2002/3 F17v F16d Feb **F–** 25] first live foal: dam poor maiden: well held in 2 bumpers. *P. R. Wood*

LEVALLOIS (IRE)   7 b.g. Trempolino (USA) – Broken Wave (Bustino) [2002/3 18dᶠ **c114** 18sᵖᵘ c21d³ 19s³ 18v⁴ 22d 22s Mar 15] smallish gelding: successful 3 times up to 15f on **h129** Flat, including twice in 2002: fairly useful hurdler/chaser: sold out of J-P. Gallorini's stable €24,000 Goffs November Sale after fifth start: little show in 2 handicaps in Britain: stays 21f: raced on good going or softer (acts on heavy). *P. J. Hobbs*

LEWIS ISLAND (IRE)   4 b.c. Turtle Island (IRE) – Phyllode (Pharly (FR)) [2002/3 **h119** 16d⁵ 16s* 16v² 16s³ 16s² 16g Apr 3] well-made colt: brother to fair 2m hurdler Leatherback: fairly useful on Flat (stays 1½m), sold out of T. Mills's stable 86,000 gns Newmarket Autumn Sales: fairly useful juvenile hurdler: made all at Leicester in December: didn't go on as expected, though second to Nas Na Riogh in Grade 1 at Chepstow and Visibility at Leicester: well held in Grade 2 at Aintree: will probably stay beyond 2m: acts on heavy going: front runner. *N. A. Twiston-Davies*

LEWIS MEAD   4 b.g. Sir Harry Lewis (USA) – Normead Lass (Norwick (USA)) **F–** [2002/3 F14g F16g⁶ Mar 23] first foal: dam poor maiden: well held in 2 bumpers. *Mrs S. A. Liddiard*

LIBERDAL (FR)   5 b.g. Cadoudal (FR) – Libertina (FR) (Balsamo (FR)) [2002/3 **h93** 17s² 18v³ 20v³ Dec 27] lengthy gelding: sixth foal: half-brother to fairly useful hurdler around 2¼m Liberthine (by Chamberlin) and middle-distance winner Aubrisquini (by Dom Pasquini): dam maiden half-sister to very smart hurdler up to 25f Full of Ambition and smart hurdler Aubisque: lightly-raced maiden hurdler, third to Bold Action in novice at Chepstow final start: tried blinkered. *G. Macaire, France*

LIBERMAN (IRE)   5 b.g. Standiford (USA) – Hail To You (USA) (Kirtling) **F119** [2002/3 F103: F17d* F16d² F16g* Mar 12]
Bookmakers took a caning at the Cheltenham Festival with a record number of winning favourites—ten in all—and one of the biggest gambles was landed by Liberman in the Weatherbys Champion Bumper, the final race on the middle day. Backed down from 3/1 to 2/1, Liberman attracted a string of huge bets, including a recorded £300,000-£100,000 and a £225,000-£100,000. In a close finish and under a typically determined ride by Tony McCoy, Liberman held off 50/1-shot Trabolgan, 33/1-shot Widemouth Bay and 50/1-shot Bold Bishop after being sent on at the top of the hill, five furlongs out. The distances were half a length, a length, and half a length again, the first four finishing clear of Miller's Bay and Bourbon Manhattan as British-trained runners dominated the twenty-five-runner race; Govamix and Kim Fontaine, seventh and eighth, were the first Irish finishers in an event they often dominate (eight of the ten previous editions had been won by Irish-trained horses).

Liberman had his first three races for Paddy Mullins in Ireland, beating a big field at the Punchestown Festival the previous season (with short-priced favourite Govamix third) and then winning at Bellewstown in July before being bought to carry the colours of leading British owner David Johnson. Liberman's

Weatherbys Champion Bumpers (Standard Open National Hunt Flat Race), Cheltenham— a game victory for Liberman, chased home by Trabolgan, Widemouth Bay and Bold Bishop

first appearance in the royal blue, emerald green sleeves, green-spotted white cap came in the Open Bumper, the final race at Cheltenham's three-day Open meeting in November. The Pipe stable was in tip-top form and Liberman would have made it an amazing eight winners at the fixture from twenty-two runners had he not come up against the unlucky runner-up in the previous season's Champion Bumper, Rhinestone Cowboy. Liberman went down by a length, conceding weight to the winner, with a further five lengths back to third-placed Inca Trail. The conditions for the Champion Bumper at the Festival in March stipulate that contenders must not have run in more than four bumpers. With Rhinestone Cowboy set to be switched to hurdling, Liberman's connections decided to put him by for the winter and keep him for the Champion Bumper. He couldn't have been made fitter and looked tuned up to run for his life at the Festival.

	Standiford (USA) (br 1989)	Lyphard (b 1969)	Northern Dancer / Goofed
Liberman (IRE) (b.g. 1998)		Louisville (b 1977)	Val de L'Orne / Laddisa
	Hail To You (USA) (br 1984)	Kirtling (b 1978)	Grundy / Silky
		High Hail (br 1968)	Hail To All / High Folly

For the latest edition of the Champion Bumper to prove such a rich source of jumpers as its immediate predecessor would be a very tall order. The winner Pizarro was promoted to second in the latest Royal & SunAlliance Hurdle, Rhinestone Cowboy won his first four races over hurdles and finished third when favourite for the Champion Hurdle, the third Back In Front ran away with the

Mr D. A. Johnson's "Liberman"

Supreme Novices' Hurdle, fourth-placed Thisthatandtother numbered the Grade 1 Tolworth Hurdle amongst his successes in the latest season, and the fifth Iris's Gift improved in leaps and bounds, winning six of his seven starts over hurdles and showing himself a top-class performer when runner-up to Baracouda in the Stayers' Hurdle. The form of the latest Champion Bumper is no better than average for the race, but Liberman is clearly a smart prospect though he looked rather unimposing in the paddock, overshadowed by some good-looking rivals. Medium-sized and rather unfurnished, he should fill out with another summer under his belt. Liberman's pedigree must have been of limited appeal to prospective purchasers. His sire the Lyphard stallion Standiford, who was raced in France and America (where he was second in the Grade 2 American Derby), stands in Ireland but has been poorly supported, his best winner before Liberman being the useful middle-distance Flat performer Rathkenny, twice a winner over hurdles in Ireland in the latest season. Liberman's dam Hail To You, a minor sprint winner in the States, has bred three other winners, all on the Flat, two minor winners in North America and the fair Un Parfum de Femme (by Mill Native), successful at up to a mile and a half. Liberman has yet to race on going firmer than good. *M. C. Pipe*

LIBERTY'S MELODY   6 ch.m. Gildoran – Music Interpreter (Kampala) [2002/3   **F—**
F16s Jun 9] lengthy, plain mare: sixth foal: half-sister to useful bumper/2¾m hurdle winner Maybe The Business (by Karinga Bay) and hunter chase winner Mr Collins (by Brush Aside): dam winning 2m hurdler/1¾m winner on Flat: tailed off in bumper on debut. *Mrs S. M. Johnson*

LIBIDO   8 b.g. Good Thyne (USA) – Country Mistress (Town And Country) [2002/3   **c—**
c91, h—: c24dᵖᵘ 24v 26d Feb 23] useful-looking gelding: novice hurdler/chaser, no form   **h—**
since reappearance in 2001/2: should stay beyond 2½m: acts on good to firm and heavy going: form only on left-handed tracks: tends to make mistakes. *H. D. Daly*

L'IDEFIX (IRE)   11 ch.g. Buckskin (FR) – Katty London (Camden Town) [2002/3   **c—**
c25d⁴ Oct 19] small, strong gelding: fair chaser in 2000/1: well held after shaping as if   **h—**
retaining ability only subsequent outing: stays 25f: raced mainly on good going or softer (acts on soft). *T. R. George*

LIGHT HEARTED LILY   4 b.f. Deploy – Darling Splodge (Elegant Air) [2002/3   **F—**
F16g Mar 12] fifth foal: sister to 2m winner Our Monogram and 1¼m winner Starry Mary: dam unraced half-sister to fairly useful middle-distance stayer Much Sought After: well held in bumper on debut. *R. M. Beckett*

LIGHTMOOR LADY   5 b.m. Puget (USA) – Dragon Fire (Dragonara Palace   **F—**
(USA)) [2002/3 F16m Apr 21] half-sister to winning 2m selling hurdler Set-Em-Alight (by Relkino) and bumper winner Fooling With Fire (by Idiot's Delight): dam, modest 1m to 1¼m winner, half-sister to top-class 2m hurdler/smart chaser Prideaux Boy: well held in mares maiden bumper on debut. *Mrs L. Williamson*

LIGHTNING GALE (IRE)   10 br.m. Strong Gale – Laurie Belle (Boreen (FR))   **c—**
[2002/3 c20sᶠ c17m c20f³ c16g c18d⁶ Oct 24] lengthy, rather sparely-made mare: no   **h—**
form over hurdles: poor maiden chaser: tongue tied. *J. McCaghy, Ireland*

LIGHTNING QUEST (IRE)   12 b.g. Rainbow Quest (USA) – Rare Roberta (USA)   **c107**
(Roberto (USA)) [2002/3 17m⁴ c20mᶠ c23m² 19d⁴ c20g² c21mᶠ c21gᶠ Oct 12] tall   **h91**
gelding: winning hurdler, off over 2 years before reappearance: fair handicap chaser: stays 23f: has won on good to soft going, best form on good or firmer: blinkered once (ran poorly). *Mrs S. J. Smith*

LIGHTNING STAR (USA)   8 b.g. El Gran Senor (USA) – Cuz's Star (USA) (Galaxy   **c—**
Libra) [2002/3 c—, h—: 25g 22dᵖᵘ 16s⁶ 16s² 21g Mar 12] angular gelding: winning hurdler,   **h89**
only modest at best nowadays: showed nothing only outing over fences: stays 2¾m: probably acts on any going: blinkered. *T. P. McGovern*

LIGHTNING STRIKES (IRE)   9 b.g. Zaffaran (USA) – Nimbi (Orchestra) [2002/3   **h105**
h—: 20g 19m* Apr 21] well-made gelding: fair hurdler, very lightly raced: improved form when winning 4-runner handicap at Market Rasen by 8 lengths from Rising Generation: should stay beyond 19f: acts on soft and good to firm going. *Mrs L. Wadham*

LIGHT-O-DAY   10 gr.g. Gods Solution – Brampton Lyn (Derrylin) [2002/3 21mᵖᵘ Jul   **h—**
17] second foal: dam winning 2m hurdler: no show in novice hurdle on belated debut. *C. Grant*

LIGHT ON THE BROOM (IRE)   7 b.g. Aristocracy – Montevelle (IRE) (Monte-   **h109**
limar) [2002/3 16v² F16v* 16d* 16s^pu 16d² 16d^F Mar 17] IR 6,000 4-y-o: first foal: dam   **F96**
unraced: won point in 2002: fairly useful form when winning bumper at Clonmel in
December: fair hurdler: won maiden at Thurles later in month: will stay beyond 2m: acts
on heavy going. *G. Stack, Ireland*

LIGHT PROGRAMME   9 b.g. El Gran Senor (USA) – Nashmeel (USA) (Blushing   **h66**
Groom (FR)) [2002/3 h–: 16g* 19g 22m^pu Sep 7] compact gelding: has had knee operation: won novice handicap at Wolverhampton in July, little other form over hurdles:
probably best around 2m: tongue tied once. *A. L. Forbes*

LIGHT REFLECTIONS   10 b.g. Rainbow Quest (USA) – Tajfah (USA) (Shadeed   **c–**
(USA)) [2002/3 c83, h–: c26m^F May 7] tall gelding: poor handicap chaser: stays 29f: **h–**
raced mainly on good going or softer (acts on soft): visored twice (jumped poorly).
P. G. Murphy

LIGHT SCENT (USA)   4 ch.g. Silver Hawk (USA) – Music Lane (USA) (Miswaki   **h76**
(USA)) [2002/3 16v 16d 17g⁵ Mar 16] good-topped gelding: fairly useful on Flat (stays
1¼m), sold out of Sir Michael Stoute's stable 38,000 gns Newmarket Autumn Sales: poor
form in juvenile hurdles. *J. Akehurst*

LIGHT THE FUSE (IRE)   11 b.g. Electric – Celtic Bombshell (Celtic Cone) [2002/3   **c–**
c–, h90: 22m 22g⁵ 24d^pu 22m 24g^pu 22s³ 24d 16s^pu Dec 7] sturdy gelding: fell only outing   **h71**
over fences: maiden hurdler, little form in 2002/3: stays 2¾m: acts on soft and good to
firm going. *B. G. Powell*

LIGHT THE SKY   10 b.g. Lighter – Saleander (Leander) [2002/3 c84?: c22d^pu   **c–**
c34g^pu May 22] strong gelding: fair pointer, won in March: little form in steeplechases:
has had tongue tied. *Ms A. E. Embiricos*

LIKE-A-BUTTERFLY (IRE)   9 b.m. Montelimar (USA) – Swifts Butterfly   **h152**
(Furry Glen) [2002/3 h145: 16d* 16g 20g³ Apr 5]

When C. F. Swan appears next to a horse's name on a race card from now
on it will be in the trainer's column only. Exultant shouts of 'come on Charlie'
which have reverberated from Clonmel to Cheltenham in a riding career spanning
twenty years will be heard no longer, Swan having announced his retirement after
winning the final race on the second day of Aintree's Grand National meeting on
Patriot Games, whom he also trains. Swan did go on to ride in a couple of races on
National day itself and, although he failed to win either of them, the tremendous
reception he received from the very large crowd would have made the occasion a
memorable one for him. Swan signed off after finishing third on Like-A-Butterfly
in the Aintree Hurdle and will now concentrate solely on his other profession as a
trainer, after combining both riding and training since 1998. 'I'm aiming to get
some better horses in my yard and felt that I needed to give it my full attention,'
said Swan. One of the horses he will be responsible for as a full-time trainer is the
three-year-old gelding by Alflora, a half-brother to See More Business, who, at
200,000 guineas, became the most expensive jumping store to pass through a public
sales ring when sold at the Doncaster May Sales. Swan's association with the
mighty Istabraq—he rode the triple Champion Hurdle winner in all twenty-nine of
his races over hurdles, winning twenty-three—would probably be enough in itself
to afford him legendary status in National Hunt racing. Yet even without Istabraq,
Swan would have had a riding career which surely exceeded all his expectations
when he started off as an apprentice on the Flat at the age of fifteen. A total of
1,312 winners for a start, 1,188 of them coming over jumps in Ireland where he was
champion for nine consecutive seasons. Swan's decision in 1998 to call a halt to
riding in steeplechases put paid to his chances of winning a tenth title. A host of
major races besides the Champion Hurdle came Swan's way, though not the Gold
Cup nor Grand National. His victory on Trapper John in the 1990 Stayers' Hurdle
was the first of seventeen at the Cheltenham Festival, with number seventeen
provided by Scolardy in the 2002 Triumph Hurdle, two days after he had won the
Supreme Novices' Hurdle on Like-A-Butterfly.

A highly polished and tactically-astute rider, Swan would have been entertaining thoughts of yet another Champion Hurdle victory after Like-A-Butterfly
made a successful reappearance in January in the AIG Europe Champion Hurdle at
Leopardstown, a race he had won four times on Istabraq. Despite having been off
the course for nine months, Like-A-Butterfly looked fit and was sent off favourite

at 6/4 for a Grade 1 contest which perhaps wasn't so strong a race as it might have been, lacking a British-trained runner, as well as Davenport Milenium and Ned Kelly who were both sidelined through injury, the former in the two days leading up to the race. Second favourite at 15/8 in a five-runner contest was Limestone Lad, reverting from three miles to two miles as he attempted to extend a run of seven straight wins. The two market leaders served up a memorable clash, the front-running Limestone Lad ensuring a strong pace which, coupled with the good to soft ground, placed the emphasis on stamina at the trip. Only Like-A-Butterfly was able to stay with Limestone Lad from after the second last. She moved alongside approaching the last and then proved every bit as game as her illustrious rival, initially edging left on the run-in but battling on splendidly to hold his rally by a head. Swan, even at the veteran stage, showed he still had the strength to go with his finesse. Like-A-Butterfly, whose jumping in her novice days had been on the sloppy side, looked much more assured in that department and the performance represented improved form from Like-A-Butterfly. But it was still short of that required to win a Champion Hurdle and, with good ground at Cheltenham placing less of an emphasis on stamina, Like-A-Butterfly always seemed likely to be up against it. Even so, she should have run better than she did. Calmer in the paddock than she had been at Leopardstown, Like-A-Butterfly turned in a rather lacklustre performance, weakening soon after the fifth and already held when hampered at the next, managing only tenth behind Rooster Booster. Westender, the horse she had touched off in the Supreme a year earlier, was runner-up. A return to two and a half miles in the Aintree Hurdle seemed sure to benefit Like-A-Butterfly, who had been successful on the first of her two attempts at the trip as a novice. She failed to improve on her Leopardstown form but did run a lot better than at Cheltenham in finishing seven lengths third behind close-finishers Sacundai and Rooster Booster, travelling smoothly held up then unable to quicken from two out. Like-A-Butterfly has been ridden in all of her races over hurdles by Swan, but the association would have come to an end even if the latter hadn't hung up his boots, as Like-A-Butterfly is to be tried over fences. She is a big mare, one that looks the part for chasing and

AIG Europe Champion Hurdle, Leopardstown—a thrilling finish
with Like-A-Butterfly (nearer camera) just getting the better of Limestone Lad

though time isn't on her side—she is rising ten—she can still be expected to do well.

	Montelimar (USA) (b 1981)	Alleged (b 1974)	Hoist The Flag Princess Pout
Like-A-Butterfly (IRE) (b.m. 1994)		L'Extravagante (br 1973)	Le Fabuleux Fanfreluche
	Swifts Butterfly (b 1985)	Furry Glen (b 1971)	Wolver Hollow Cleftess
		Baloney (ch 1974)	Balidar Bay Pearl

The latest season proved a most successful one for Like-A-Butterfly's sire Montelimar, who died in 1997, as he was also responsible for her stable-companion Youlneverwalkalone, winner of the National Hunt Handicap at Cheltenham, and the Grand National winner Monty's Pass. There is not much to shout about on the bottom line of Like-A-Butterfly's pedigree, though. All three of the mares in it failed to win a race. Swifts Butterfly was a poor novice hurdler, Baloney lightly raced on the Flat and over hurdles and Bay Pearl a poor two-year-old who showed no form at three. Shalaines Pride (by Yashgan), Swifts Butterfly's only previous foal, finished third on his one start in bumpers but has achieved very little over hurdles. Like-A-Butterfly has raced only on good going or softer and acts on heavy. She has sometimes idled in front but is as genuine as her record of nine wins from twelve starts suggests. *C. Roche, Ireland*

LILAC LADY   6 b.m. Weld – Lilac Wood (Precipice Wood) [2002/3 F17s^{pu} F16s May 26] lengthy, angular mare: third foal: dam, winning pointer, half-sister to smart chasers Clever Folly, stayed 21f, and Bishops Yarn, stayed 3m: tailed off on completed start in bumpers (saddle slipped on debut): runner-up in maiden point in April. *F. Jordan*   **F–**

LILARDO   6 b. or br.m. Son Pardo – Jimlil (Nicholas Bill) [2002/3 h–: 20g^{pu} 20g^{5} 19g^{3} Mar 17] leggy mare: poor maiden hurdler: stays 2½m: acts on heavy going: tongue tied last 2 starts. *B. Palling*   **h64**

LILIUM DE COTTE (FR)   4 b.g. Ragmar (FR) – Vanille de Cotte (FR) (Italic (FR)) [2002/3 15v^{3} 16g^{8} 16g^{2} 17d^{2} 16v^{4} 16v* 17g^{4} Mar 13] good-topped gelding: fourth foal: half-brother to 1½m winner Gamin de Cotte (by Quart de Vin): dam won up to 1½m on Flat, placed at 2¼m over hurdles: successful in 4 non-thoroughbred events around 1½m on Flat in 2002: useful juvenile hurdler: won at Vichy in August and Sandown in February: ran well when equal-second to Don Fernando in Grade 2 at Cheltenham fourth start and fourth of 27 to Spectroscope in Triumph Hurdle at same course: likely to stay beyond 2m: raced on good going or softer (acts on heavy). *G. Macaire, France*   **h128**

LILLIEPLANT (IRE)   11 b.m. Aristocracy – Canute Princess (Torenaga) [2002/3 h–: c21g^{F} May 1] lengthy, angular mare: well held over hurdles: winning pointer: fell first on hunter chase debut: races freely. *E. J. Ford*   **c–**
h–

LILY BROWN   8 br.m. Sula Bula – Lily Mab (FR) (Prince Mab (FR)) [2002/3 c16v^{4} c19d^{F} c19v^{pu} 19d^{pu} 18v c20s^{4} Mar 10] sturdy mare: fifth foal: half-sister to several winners, including fairly useful hurdler Barton Ward (by Malaspina), stayed 3m: dam winning 2m hurdler: won 2½m maiden point in 2002: little form otherwise. *D. P. Keane*   **c–**
h–

LILY PADS   5 b.m. Barrish – Ballyorney Girl (New Member) [2002/3 20d^{pu} 22d^{pu} Sep 4] fourth foal: half-sister to fair staying chaser Bally Lira (by Lir): dam novice selling hurdler, stayed 2½m: little show in 2 novice hurdles. *P. R. Rodford*   **h–**

LIMBO LAD   4 b.g. Millkom – Bumble Boogie (IRE) (Bluebird (USA)) [2002/3 16g^{2} 17m^{pu} 16g^{4} 17f^{4} 17d^{pu} Oct 31] modest on Flat (stays 1¼m): poor juvenile hurdler: has looked none too keen. *P. C. Haslam*   **h78**

LIMERICK BOY (GER)   5 b.h. Alwuhush (USA) – Limoges (GER) (Konigsstuhl (GER)) [2002/3 16d* 16g^{6} 16d* Apr 4]   **h132**
There were more ex-German horses than ever racing over jumps in Britain in the latest season. What began as a trickle has quickly turned into a steady stream of German imports, with the successes of Seebald, Dark'n Sharp, Sudden Shock, Auetaler, Samon, Miros and Golden Goal doing much to advertise German bloodstock to potential British jumps owners. The demand is there, and so is the supply. Germany's racing industry has experienced troubled times of late, so offers from Britain are particularly attractive. On top of the German imports, Cologne-based

trainer Christian Von Der Recke made several successful trips to Britain in the latest season, gaining ten wins at a strike rate of thirty-four percent and making a bit of history when Barito became the first German-trained horse to win a chase in Britain, at Plumpton in January. Plenty of the German imports have shown a good level of form on the Flat, with listed and even pattern winners among them. Of course, continental Flat form does not always translate into success over jumps in Britain. Iberus, for example, was a dual listed winner in Germany and third in the Derby Italiano but he was an odds-on flop on his British debut at Plumpton and was tailed off when falling in the Champion Hurdle. The former Deutsches Derby runner-up and smart pattern winner Subiaco was another notable disappointment on his two runs over hurdles.

Limerick Boy was another with smart form on the Flat in Germany, and he did make a successful transition to hurdling. Limerick Boy won a couple of Group 3 events as a three-year-old and was considered good enough to contest both the Derby Italiano and the Deutsches Derby. His new connections therefore had some justification in aiming high and entering him for the Supreme Novices' Hurdle, though at the five-day stage on the Thursday morning before Cheltenham he had yet to appear over hurdles. Later the same day he made his debut in a maiden hurdle at Wincanton, justifying good support in impressive fashion and booking his place at Cheltenham. Given his lack of experience and rather hurried preparation (his hurdling debut had reportedly been delayed by coughing), Limerick Boy's sixth to Back In Front in the Supreme Novices' was a fine effort.

Confirmation that Limerick Boy was a useful recruit to hurdling came in the Laurel Pub Company Top Novices' Hurdle at Aintree three weeks later. In the absence of any of the first five from the Supreme Novices', Limerick Boy started third favourite behind the only four-year-old in the field of twelve, Don Fernando (a casualty in the Triumph Hurdle) and Irish challenger Glenhaven Nugget. Incidentally, also in the line-up were two more imports from Germany, Caracciola and Ontos. Unlike his two previous outings (and his subsequent start as well), when

Laurel Pub Company Top Novices' Hurdle, Aintree—
Limerick Boy grinds out victory as Man O'Mystery goes left at the last

Limerick Boy had taken a good hold each time, he was off the bridle from an early stage at Aintree and well in arrears. However, he began to make ground from the home turn and, after Glenhaven Nugget found nothing off the bridle after going ominously well, Limerick Boy stayed on up the stand rail, leading approaching the last and running on to win by four lengths from Man O'Mystery. The front-running mare Lirfox stayed on again to take third from Ontos, with Glenhaven Nugget fifth and the remainder soundly beaten. Limerick Boy reopposed Back In Front in the Evening Herald Champion Novices' Hurdle at Punchestown at the end of April. Back In Front was 11/4-on to confirm his Cheltenham superiority over Limerick Boy, the 7/1 second favourite. There had been around twenty lengths between them in the Supreme Novices' but Limerick Boy cut the deficit to two and a half at Punchestown. He never looked a serious danger to the favourite who won readily, but drew away from the third on the run-in to record another useful performance.

			Nureyev (b 1977)	Northern Dancer Special
Limerick Boy (GER) (b.h. 1998)	Alwuhush (USA) (b 1985)		Beaming Bride (b 1975)	King Emperor Khazaeen
	Limoges (GER) (b 1989)		Konigsstuhl (br 1976)	Dschingis Khan Konigskronung
			Lohe (b 1978)	Caro Loisach

Limerick Boy proved a bargain buy for Andreas Schutz's stable as he cost the equivalent of less than 5,000 guineas as a yearling at Baden-Baden. His sire Alwuhush, a smart middle-distance horse, did most of his racing for John Dunlop, winning twice in Group 1 company in Italy as a four-year-old before a move to the States brought him a Grade 1 success at Santa Anita. Limerick Boy's dam Limoges

Favourites Racing's "Limerick Boy"

gained her only win in a maiden at Neuss over an extended mile and a quarter and has bred a couple of ordinary middle-distance winners in Germany besides Limerick Boy, the fillies Lupita (by Niniski) and Laureata (by Alwasmi). There are some much better fillies a bit further back in the pedigree though. Grandam Lohe was second in the German classic for middle-distance fillies, the Preis Der Diana, a race won by both her half-sister Las Vegas (also successful in the Deutsches St Leger) and her dam Loisach.

The close-coupled Limerick Boy, who is still an entire, is not an obvious chaser on looks and presumably handicap hurdles will be part of his programme in 2003/4. He will need to jump more fluently to make an impact, however. He will probably stay beyond two miles. It could be that Limerick Boy has yet to race on his ideal ground so far in Britain; he evidently revelled in the mud when winning those Group 3 races at Krefeld and Hoppegarten by seven and eight lengths respectively. *Miss Venetia Williams*

LIMERICK LEADER (IRE) 5 b.g. Supreme Leader – View of The Hills (Croghan Hill) [2002/3 F16d F16g F16g² Mar 14] IR £21,000 3-y-o: useful-looking gelding: fourth foal: brother to fairly useful hurdler/fair chaser Karratha, stays 3m: dam unraced: best effort in bumpers (highly tried first 2 starts) when ¾-length second of 19 to Majestic Moonbeam at Warwick, finishing strongly: will be suited by further than 2m. *P. J. Hobbs* **F96**

LIMESTONE LAD (IRE) 11 b.g. Aristocracy – Limestone Miss (Raise You Ten) [2002/3 c147, h167: 20s* 16s* 20v* 20s* 24s* 16d² 24g³ Mar 13] **c–**
h172

Limestone Lad had a quiet season by his standards in 2002/3, appearing just seven times and going for periods of more than a month without a run. He added five further successes to his tally, notably gaining a third win in the Hatton's Grace Hurdle at Fairyhouse, but his most memorable performances came in defeat on his last two starts when he went down by a head to Like-A-Butterfly in the AIG Europe

Morgiana Hurdle, Navan—Limestone Lad puts up one of the best performances of the season in a two-mile hurdle; Ballyhampshire Boy is about to fall

Ballymore Properties Hatton's Grace Hurdle, Fairyhouse—
a third success in this Grade 1 event for Limestone Lad

Champion Hurdle at Leopardstown and finished third to Baracouda and Iris's Gift in the Stayers' Hurdle at Cheltenham. Limestone Lad's chief assets, very accurate jumping and the ability to set and maintain a relentless gallop, mean that the majority of the more exciting races he's been involved in have been when he's been beaten. The appearance of Limestone Lad's running his heart out is somehow more admirable when it isn't quite enough. It isn't only God who loves a trier. Over two miles on good to soft ground at Leopardstown, Limestone Lad set a really good pace but still wasn't able to run the sting out of the reappearing Like-A-Butterfly, the pair involved in a tremendous tussle in the straight with the result in doubt virtually to the line. On good ground over three miles at Cheltenham, Limestone Lad played a full part in a race that will live long in the memory of anyone lucky enough to have seen it. However, after leading to before the last in the Stayers' Hurdle, he had nothing more to give and went down by three quarters of a length and five lengths.

Since winning a maiden hurdle at the fifth attempt, at Clonmel on April 23rd 1998, Limestone Lad has been beaten fourteen times over hurdles and twice over fences. Of those sixteen defeats, five were at two miles, seven at two and a half and four at three miles. There were races at each of those trips in which he had excuses and races where he wasn't good enough. More significant is the breakdown of the going on which they took place. Five defeats came on good or firmer, eight on good to soft and just three on soft or heavy. In the first of those three, Le Coudray beat him by twenty lengths over two and a half miles at Naas in January 1999, when Limestone Lad had still to show himself a top-class hurdler; in the second Istabraq beat him by seven lengths over two miles at Tipperary in October 1999; finally Bannow Bay, receiving 5 lb, beat him by five lengths over two and a half miles at Cork in October 2000 when Limestone Lad was having his first outing in seven months. Although Limestone Lad can show top-class form on good or good to soft, he is more vulnerable under those conditions. On soft or heavy, perhaps only Baracouda could be confidently expected to beat him at level weights among the current leading hurdlers, both two-milers and stayers.

Limestone Lad's five victories in the latest season took his tally under National Hunt rules to thirty-five, a phenomenal total for any horse, Flat or jumps, top class or merely very durable. Indeed, very durable isn't automatically enough. Sonny Somers, for example, the last eighteen-year-old to win a race in Britain, had a fourteen-year career but managed a mere twenty-six successes. The remarkable Flying Ace gained fifty-nine victories in the 'eighties but only twenty-three came in hunter chases while the rest were gained in points. At a higher level, Limestone Lad's tally takes a lot of beating, probably the best horse with a better score being the great dual-purpose horse Sea Pigeon who won twenty-one times over hurdles and sixteen times on the Flat for a total of thirty-seven. Thirty-five is one more win than Desert Orchid managed in a career that stretched over ten seasons while the top French jumper Or Jack was another to amass thirty-four victories (including two wins on the Flat). The best hurdler of all time Night Nurse, later good enough to finish second in the Cheltenham Gold Cup, managed thirty-two wins over jumps and when added to three wins on the Flat give him a career total matching Limestone Lad's. One other notable jumper to muster over thirty wins is Lochroe whose 1958 King George VI Chase win was one of thirty-two from sixty-one starts. For allcomers, the record since the start of the twentieth century is held by Crudwell who gained fifty wins (including seven on the Flat) in a twelve-year career between 1949 and 1960. That total is surpassed by The Admiral, who raced in Ireland at the end of the nineteenth century. His tally of wins, variously reported as fifty-two or fifty-three, included the 1894 Irish National.

The Hatton's Grace Hurdle, sponsored by Ballymore Properties, came on Limestone Lad's third start and was the one Grade 1 success among Limestone Lad's five victories, though it was hardly a victory to compare with his 1999 defeat of Istabraq or even his 2001 defeat of Liss A Paoraigh. Just four opposed Limestone Lad, the unfit Ned Kelly and Colonel Braxton (tuning up for fences), the no-hoper Balapour and the doubtful stayer Scottish Memories. The last-named provided the closest thing to serious opposition but a margin of eight lengths hardly told the tale of Limestone Lad's superiority. The woodiesdiy.com Christmas Hurdle at Leopardstown later in December, on his fifth start, seemed likely to provide a sterner test for Limestone Lad, featuring as it did a repeat of the 2001 running when he had gone down by a length to Bannow Bay in another memorable contest. There was no repeat: the ill-fated Bannow Bay was well below his best and Limestone Lad had little trouble seeing off Boss Doyle by nine lengths.

For his three other victories, all gained at Navan, Limestone Lad defeated his old rival Liss A Paoraigh, and they number among the best performances over hurdles all season. For the first two, Liss A Paoraigh received 5 lb. In the Philips Electronics Lismullen Hurdle in November, Limestone Lad, with the benefit of a run on the Flat, won by two lengths with the pair twenty-five lengths clear of the rest. Two weeks later, in the Morgiana Hurdle, Limestone Lad won by eleven lengths but only after Ballyhampshire Boy fell when holding a narrow lead at the

woodiesdiy.com Christmas Hurdle, Leopardstown—a seventh win in a row; Boss Doyle gives vain pursuit

last. Limestone Lad had a fight on his hands but was beginning to get the better of his rival and even a narrow defeat by a smart rival receiving 13 lb would have been a top-class effort. Limestone Lad's success in the 2001 renewal of the Morgiana Hurdle (at Punchestown) was the best performance by a hurdler over two miles in 2001/2 and Limestone Lad's latest form in winning the race was bettered at the trip in 2002/3 only by Rooster Booster. Limestone Lad's best performance, however, came in the least important of the five races he won, the Giltspur Scientific Hurdle. Starting at similar odds to the Hatton's Grace (he was odds on for all five wins), he faced a much stiffer task than in that race, trying to concede an extra 10 lb to Liss A Paoraigh in addition to the mares allowance. Coming to three out, defeat looked distinctly possible, but responding really well—as ever—when asked for extra, Limestone Lad had the mare's measure after the next and was six lengths up and well on top at the line. Even with Liss A Paoraigh considered to have run some way below her best, this rates one of Limestone Lad's very best performances.

		Aristocracy (b 1974)	Lord Gayle (b 1965)	Sir Gaylord
				Sticky Case
Limestone Lad (IRE) (b.g. 1992)			Roxboro (ch 1968)	Sheshoon
				Sally Stream
		Limestone Miss (b 1981)	Raise You Ten (br 1960)	Tehran
				Visor
			Miss Kiln (b 1967)	Sir Herbert
				Kinneagh

Limestone Lad wasn't seen out after Cheltenham. He was due to run at Punchestown shortly after the end of the British season but was reported off colour the week before the meeting and missed defending his crown in the Champion Stayers' Hurdle. He had also missed out on a prep run for Cheltenham, the Boyne

James Bowe's "Limestone Lad"

LIN

Hurdle at Navan, after being treated for a cough. He is set to return in the autumn for another campaign over hurdles and, with little sign of his being on the decline, he should be able to add further to his considerable tally. The strong, lengthy Limestone Lad's pedigree has been dealt with exhaustively in previous editions of *Chasers & Hurdlers*. It goes almost without saying that he is remarkably tough and genuine, deservedly one of the most celebrated horses of modern times. *James Bowe, Ireland*

LIMITED EDITION (IRE) 5 b.g. Parthian Springs – Rosemount Rose (Ashmore (FR)) [2002/3 F16s² 16d^F 19d⁵ 16d Apr 4] rangy gelding: seventh foal: half-brother to 3 winners, including one-time fairly useful staying chaser Choisty (by Callernish) and fair 2m hurdler Genuine Article (by Insan): dam ran 3 times: second of 22 to Classic Native in bumper at Warwick on debut: modest form when fifth of 18 to Backbeat in novice at Newbury (highly tried other 2 starts over hurdles): likely to stay beyond 19f. *M. Pitman* — **h81 F95**

LINCOLN CROSS (IRE) 8 b.g. Lord Americo – Keen Cross (IRE) (Black Minstrel) [2002/3 F98: 20d⁴ᵈ 16d 17g⁵ 22g³ Apr 19] leggy gelding: runner-up on second of 2 starts in bumpers: poor form over hurdles: stays 2¾m. *O. Sherwood* — **h84**

LINCOLN DEAN 7 b.g. Mtoto – Play With Me (IRE) (Alzao (USA)) [2002/3 h–: 16d^pu 17g^bd Sep 6] no form over hurdles: bled from nose when tongue tied once in 2001/2. *F. P. Murtagh* — **h–**

LINCOLN PLACE (IRE) 8 ch.g. Be My Native (USA) – Miss Lou (Levanter) [2002/3 c16m* c20g* c21m^F 17d⁴ c20m² c19m³ Apr 21] 12,000 3-y-o: ex-Irish gelding: seventh foal: half-brother to winning staying hurdler/hunter chaser Roskeen Bridge (by Black Minstrel) and winning pointer by Strong Gale: dam winning Irish pointer: winning pointer in 2002: fair chaser: won handicaps at Worcester in June and August: would have completed hat-trick but for falling heavily at last in similar event at Newton Abbot: easily best effort over hurdles when close fourth of 15 in handicap at latter: should stay beyond 21f: acts on good to firm and good to soft going. *P. J. Hobbs* — **c104 h96**

LINCOLN STAR 5 b.g. Lugana Beach – Esilam (Frimley Park) [2002/3 F–: F16d 16g^pu 16s^pu Jun 9] lengthy gelding: no sign of ability. *A. G. Hobbs* — **h– F–**

LINDAJANE (IRE) 11 b.m. Erin's Hope – Tempo Rose (Crash Course) [2002/3 c25g^F c22m³ c20d* c20g² c20v^ro c21d³ c20g c31g^pu Apr 24] winning hurdler: poor chaser: won handicap at Hexham in June: probably stays 23f: acts on heavy and good to firm going. *D. W. Whillans* — **c78 h–**

LINDIWE (IRE) 6 gr.m. Roselier (FR) – Sacajawea (Tanfirion) [2002/3 F17s May 18] IR £11,000 4-y-o: rather leggy mare: fifth foal: sister to useful hurdler Chauvinist, probably stays 21f: dam unraced half-sister to smart hurdler/useful chaser up to 3m Forest Sun: well held in mares bumper on debut. *N. J. Henderson* — **F–**

LINDON RUN 14 b.g. Cruise Missile – Trial Run (Deep Run) [2002/3 c20d c25d^pu May 4] winning pointer: little form in hunter chases: tongue tied. *K. Robson* — **c–**

LINE APPLE (FR) 6 b.m. Apple Tree (FR) – Cackle (USA) (Crow (FR)) [2002/3 c21g² c17d* c21g* c21g* c19s⁴ c21d c20v^F c24s⁵ c25g^F Apr 7] tenth foal: half-sister to several winners, notably useful hurdler/very smart chaser Grey Jack (by Bikala), stays 25f: dam 3-y-o 1½m winner in France: winning hurdler: fair chaser: won at Claire-fontaine and Vittel (twice) early in 2002/3: sold out of C. Aubert's stable €17,000 Goffs November Sale: let down by jumping in hunter chases: stays 21f: acts on soft going. *J. J. Boulter* — **c111 d h–**

LINE MARINE (FR) 6 ch.m. Agent Bleu (FR) – Line Saj (FR) (Dhaudevi (FR)) [2002/3 c114g, h139p: c18v² c20d* c26v² 19v* c21v* 18s* c23v* Apr 26] — **c159 + h139 p**

The 2003 spring and summer season at Auteuil was a notable one for fillies and mares, 'L'annee de la femme' as *Paris-Turf* put it. The Irish-trained mare Nobody Told Me became the first of her sex to win the Grande Course de Haies since Dawn Run in 1984, beating another mare Karly Flight into second, and, on a red letter day when three pattern races on the card fell to females, Line Marine ran out an easy winner of the biggest race of the year in France, the Grand Steeple-Chase de Paris at the end of May. Line Marine was the first mare to win that race since 1966, when the legendary Hyeres III gained her third successive win. Line Marine isn't yet a performer of that stature, nor does she compare with some of the best recent winners of the race, like Kotkijet, First Gold, Al Capone II, Ucello II

527

Gras Savoye Grand Steeple-Chase de Paris, Auteuil—over the Riviere des Tribunes with a circuit to go; the winner Line Marine leads runner-up Batman Senora, Jerico Vallis, El Paso III and Ilare

and Ubu III but a record of fifteen wins and three places from nineteen starts over hurdles and fences is not to be sneezed at.

Unusually, Line Marine hadn't contested either of the main trial races, the Group 3 Prix Ingre or the Group 2 Prix Murat, both over two and three quarter miles, earlier in the spring. Instead she had her preparatory race in the Prix William Head, a valuable non-pattern event over a trip nearer three miles. Line Marine gained an eight-length victory over Ilare, runner-up to Kotkijet in the 2001 Grand Steeple-Chase and having his second start back from injury, putting up an apparently very smart effort, though possibly flattered as the runner-up tired on testing ground. Line Marine was taken on again by Ilare in the Grand Steeple-Chase, with Jerico Vallis and Sunny Flight, the winners respectively of the Murat and the Ingre also in a field of eleven. The promoted first four from 2002, El Paso III, Batman Senora, Urga and Rougenoir again took their chance. El Paso's temperament got the better of him and neither Sunny Flight nor Jerico Vallis gave anything like their running. The front-running Batman Senora and Rougenoir were still on terms with Line Marine going to the last but once Christophe Pieux asked his mount to accelerate she did so to devastating effect, finishing ten lengths ahead with the jockey waving to the crowd at the line. The next three were in the same order as in 2002, Batman Senora a short head in front of Urga. Ilare failed to improve on his effort in the William Head and finished fifth. Pieux, who was gaining his first victory in France's top jumps race, dominates his contemporaries, numerically at least, every bit as much as Tony McCoy does in Britain. He became the winning-most jump jockey in France in October 2000 and has now ridden the winners of over thirteen hundred races. In the build-up to the Grand Steeple-Chase Pieux was presented with La Medaille d'Or de la Jeunesse et des Sports, the first jockey to receive the prestigious award. Pieux has been leading rider by number of winners every year bar one since 1990 (joint top on one occasion) and in 2002 rode one hundred and ten winners from four hundred and thirty-nine rides, thirty-six ahead of his nearest rival. Thierry Doumen rode eleven winners, ranked ninth in terms of prize money but outside the top thirty by number of winners.

Line Marine began the 2002/3 season with a rare defeat, in a mares chase at Auteuil in November, but as she was returning a year off and conditions were very testing she hardly needs an excuse. Her only other defeat of the season came on even worse ground, in the Group 3 Grand Prix de Pau in January when the effort of forcing the pace over three and a quarter miles proved too much. After galloping most of her rivals into the ground she weakened herself after two out and crossed

528

the line twenty lengths behind Escort Boy. Three of Line Marine's four other wins came in minor events, a chase at Pau in December designed for those unsuccessful during the year, and over hurdles at Pau in February and Auteuil in March in races framed for chasers. Her other victory came at the Paris track earlier in March, in the Group 3 Prix Robert de Clermont-Tonnerre. Line Marine had contested rather better races over hurdles as a four-year-old, when trained by Jacques Ortet, winning two pattern events, including the Group 1 Prix Renaud du Vivier, the top race for that age group.

Line Marine (FR) (ch.m. 1997)	Agent Bleu (FR) (b 1987)	Vacarme (ch 1981)	Lyphard	
			Virunga	
		Acoma (b 1973)	Rheffic	
			Almyre	
	Line Saj (FR) (b 1989)	Dhaudevi (ch 1965)	Dhaulagiri	
			Devivor	
		Assaj (b 1977)	Taj Dewan	
			As Blue	

Had Line Marine won the Grand Prix de Pau she would have emulated her dam Line Saj, a useful hurdler/chaser for Ortet whose sixteen wins included one in that race in 1995. Line Saj was also third to her top-class stable companion Or Jack in the 1995 Gran Premio di Merano. Line Marine is her first foal. The second Pom Jack (by Noir Et Or) has yet to make the first three in a handful of outings over jumps. There are a couple of other notable names in recent generations of this family as Line Saj is out of a half-sister to the smart mile-and-a-quarter filly Blue Tip, the grandam of the high-class Flat performer Grandera. Line Marine stays twenty-nine furlongs, the longest distance she is likely to be asked to tackle. She has raced only on going softer than good. *C. Aubert, France*

LINGERING FOG (IRE) 9 br.g. Over The River (FR) – Mandasari (Mandalus) **c–**
[2002/3 c20s 22d Oct 22] IR 10,400 4-y-o: sturdy gelding: third foal: dam lightly raced **h–**
over hurdles: modest pointer: no form otherwise: trained on reappearance by M. Higgins.
J. D. Frost

LINGHAM BRIDESMAID 7 b.m. Minster Son – Lingham Bride (Deep Run) **h81**
[2002/3 h63, F–: 16m² 16d² 20g³ 20g³ 20d⁴ 16s 20g² 20g⁴ 20d 16g³ 24g Apr 23] small,
sparely-made mare: poor maiden hurdler: stays 2½m: acts on good to firm and good to
soft going. *Mrs J. C. McGregor*

LINIYAN (IRE) 8 b.g. Kahyasi – Linnga (IRE) (Shardari) [2002/3 c87x, h–: c25dᵖᵘ **c– x**
Apr 29] lengthy gelding: winning hurdler/chaser, usually fails to complete over fences: **h–**
stays 3¼m: acts on good to firm and good to soft going (bumper form on soft/heavy):
tried tongue tied: poor jumper. *Miss Venetia Williams*

LINK COPPER 14 ch.g. Whistlefield – Letitica (Deep Run) [2002/3 c–, h–: c24f³ **c76**
Apr 3] sturdy gelding: one-time fairly useful pointer: modest form only 2 starts in hunter **h–**
chases since 1997. *Mrs E. J. Taplin*

LINNING WINE (IRE) 7 b.g. Scenic – Zallaka (IRE) (Shardari) [2002/3 h–: 16gᵖᵘ **h–**
May 17] good-topped gelding: has reportedly been fired: fairly useful bumper winner:
useful on Flat: dropped right out both starts in novice hurdles. *B. G. Powell*

LINUS 5 b.g. Bin Ajwaad (IRE) – Land Line (High Line) [2002/3 16gᴿ 19m 19d 19s* **h86**
17v* 17f⁶ Mar 27] modest maiden on Flat (stays 1¾m, none too keen), claimed £6,000
from S. Kirk in July: no show in 3 starts over hurdles for G. Ham, looking temperamental:
easily won handicaps at Taunton (seller, 8 lb out of weights) in February and Exeter
(amateur) in March: stays 19f: acts on heavy going, possibly unsuited by firm: wore
cheekpieces third start: joined C. Down. *M. C. Pipe*

LION GUEST (IRE) 6 ch.g. Lion Cavern (USA) – Decrescendo (IRE) (Polish **h78**
Precedent (USA)) [2002/3 16m 20gᵖᵘ 16g⁶ 16d 16g 16g⁴ Apr 14] modest maiden on Flat
(stays 1¼m) at 3 yrs for G. Margarson: poor form over hurdles. *Mrs S. C. Bradburne*

LIRFOX (FR) 6 b.m. Foxhound (USA) – Lirfa (USA) (Lear Fan (USA)) [2002/3 17d* **h120**
19s* 16g 16d³ 16m² Apr 11] angular ex-French mare: first foal: dam unraced: fairly
useful on Flat (stays 12.5f), successful 5 times in 2002: won both starts over hurdles in
France, 5-y-o event at Pau (by 10 lengths from Japhet) in December and minor event
there in January: fairly useful form in novices in Britain, 16 lengths third to Limerick Boy
in Grade 2 at Aintree: good head second to Laouen at Ayr week later, responding well
after tending to hang left early in straight: will stay at least 2½m: free-going front runner.
M. C. Pipe

Evening Herald December Festival Hurdle, Leopardstown—Liss A Paoraigh routs a substandard field

LIRSLEFTOVER   11 ch.g. Lir – Full Tan (Dairialatan) [2002/3 c80: c17g c21g⁵ c21g   **c–**
Jul 31] winning pointer: poor maiden steeplechaser. *Miss S. Young*

LISAAN (IRE)   6 ch.g. Bigstone (IRE) – Linnga (IRE) (Shardari) [2002/3 h123§: 16s⁶   **c109 §**
16v c18s⁵ c16s⁴ 18v 16s c20s⁵ c16s^pu c18d⁴ c16d⁴ c20s² Mar 10] workmanlike gelding: **h– §**
fairly useful handicap hurdler, well held in 2002/3: fair novice chaser: stays 2½m: acts
on heavy going: effective blinkered or not: often looks unwilling under pressure: joined
J. O'Neill. *W. Durkan, Ireland*

LISA-B (IRE)   6 b.m. Case Law – Nishiki (USA) (Brogan (USA)) [2002/3 h–: 27m^pu   **h67**
16d² 17d⁶ 16m 22m^pu 20g⁴ 21m³ 20m 26m^pu 19f 19g² 23m^pu Apr 21] quite good-topped
mare: poor maiden hurdler: stays 21f: acts on good to firm and good to soft going:
sometimes visored: has had tongue tied. *D. L. Williams*

LISA DU CHENET (FR)   4 b.f. Garde Royale – Tchela (FR) (Le Nain Jaune (FR))   **F78**
[2002/3 F16m⁷ Apr 17] 42,000 3-y-o: medium-sized filly: seventh foal:
sister to useful hurdler/chaser Iris Royal, stays 3m, and half-sister to 5 others, notably
very smart hurdler/useful chaser Galant Moss (by Tip Moss), stays 25f: dam placed
around 2m over jumps in France: modest form first 2 starts in bumpers, raced too freely
in stronger company final one. *Mrs Susan Nock*

LISCANNOR LAD (IRE)   5 b.g. Nicolette – Tinerana Memories (IRE) (Don't   **h119**
Forget Me) [2002/3 F16g* F16d* 16m 16s⁵ 18v² 18s* 20v⁵ 16d⁴ Mar 22] has scope: first   **F90**
reported foal: dam won bumper: fair form in bumpers, won at Naas in May and Galway
in August: dead-heated in 30-runner maiden hurdle at Fairyhouse in January: good fourth
of 27 to Kenilworth in novice at Navan final start: raced mainly around 2m: acts on heavy
going. *D. T. Hughes, Ireland*

LISCOMBE   7 b.m. Petoski – Take The Veil (Monksfield) [2002/3 16g^pu May 17] no   **h–**
show in maiden bumper and mares novice selling hurdle 15 months apart. *D. R. Stoddart*

LISDANTE (IRE)   10 b.g. Phardante (FR) – Shuil Eile (Deep Run) [2002/3 c92, h–:   **c114**
c25g* c28g* c32m^pu c24g^pu c23g⁴ c26g² c26s* c24d⁶ c28s³ c24s^pu Jan 30] sturdy   **h–**
gelding: fair handicap chaser: improved form in 2002/3, won at Aintree and Stratford in
May (shaped as if amiss next 2 starts) and Carlisle in October: dropped out quickly final

530

outing: stays 4m: acts on good to firm and heavy going: blinkered twice in 1999/00. *Mrs S. J. Smith*

LISLAUGHTIN ABBEY 11 ch.g. Nicholas Bill – Kates Fling (USA) (Quiet Fling (USA)) [2002/3 c99, h–: c24mᵖᵘ 16g c16v² c16s⁵ c16g⁵ c21m* Apr 21] lengthy, sparely-made gelding: novice hurdler: modest handicap chaser: won 3-finisher event at Fakenham (fifth course success) in April: effective at 2m to 3m: acts on any going: has sweated. *O. Brennan* **c95 h–**

LISMEENAN (IRE) 9 ch.g. Be My Native (USA) – Sakanda (IRE) (Vayrann) [2002/3 h90: 17m 16m 19m⁵ 20m⁴ c16d⁴ Dec 3] leggy gelding: poor handicap hurdler: off 5½ months, fourth of 14 in novice handicap at Hereford on chasing debut: barely stays 2½m: acts on soft and good to firm ground: has had tongue tied. *C. P. Morlock* **c86 h81**

LISS A PAORAIGH (IRE) 8 b.m. Husyan (USA) – Shuil Liss (Deep Run) [2002/3 h159: 20s² 16s² 20s² 16v* 16d² 24g⁵ Mar 13] rangy, useful-looking mare: very smart hurdler: clear throughout when winning Grade 1 Evening Herald December Festival Hurdle at Leopardstown by 25 lengths from Stage Affair: second to Limestone Lad in Grade 2 at Gowran on fifth: well-held fifth of 11 to Baracouda in Stayers' Hurdle at Cheltenham final one: effective at 2m given good test, should stay 3m: raced on good going or softer (acts on heavy). *J. E. Kiely, Ireland* **h158**

LISTEN UP 8 b.m. Good Thyne (USA) – Inbisat (Beldale Flutter (USA)) [2002/3 h92: 21v* Nov 12] useful-looking mare: bumper winner: modest form over hurdles, won handicap at Sedgefield in November by 5 lengths with something in hand: stays 21f: raced mainly on going softer than good (acts on heavy): takes good hold. *R. T. Phillips* **h93 +**

LITE THE WAY 6 b.m. Miner's Lamp – Polly Tix (Politico (USA)) [2002/3 F16d Mar 19] third foal: dam unraced: well held in bumper on debut. *P. D. Williams* **F–**

LITTLE ALFIE (IRE) 6 b.g. Shahanndeh – Debbies Scud (IRE) (Roselier (FR)) [2002/3 F–: 16dᵖᵘ 16d⁴ 17g 16fᶠ 17g 20g⁴ Oct 11] poor maiden hurdler: raced mainly around 2m: acts on firm and good to soft going. *B. S. Rothwell* **h62**

LITTLE BIG HORSE (IRE) 7 b.g. Little Bighorn – Little Gort (Roselier (FR)) [2002/3 h–, F92: 20m² 16g² 20s⁴ 19s² 16s⁴ 24g⁵ 20d² 21m³ Apr 16] leggy gelding: modest maiden hurdler: stays 3m: acts on soft and good to firm going: not an easy ride (tends to hang/run in snatches). *Mrs S. J. Smith* **h94**

LITTLE BLACKIE 6 br.m. Royal Fountain – Mother Machree (Bing II) [2002/3 24gᵖᵘ Apr 23] half-sister to temperamental winning staying chaser Donovans Reef (by Cool Guy): dam unraced: showed nothing in mares novice hurdle on debut. *F. P. Murtagh* **h–**

LITTLE BROWN BEAR (IRE) 9 br.g. Strong Gale – Gladtogetit (Green Shoon) [2002/3 c95, h–: c27g* c25g³ c28g³ c27g² c28g³ c27d² c28g² c28m³ Apr 26] workman-like gelding: fair handicap chaser: won at Sedgefield in May: placed all 7 starts after, generally running at least creditably: stays 3½m: acts on good to firm and good to soft going: sound jumper: consistent. *R. Ford* **c100 h–**

LITTLE BUD 9 br.m. Lord Bud – Sindur (Rolfe (USA)) [2002/3 h93: 21m⁶ 16v³ 16v³ 21vᵖᵘ 16g⁵ 21m* 21m* Apr 21] smallish, lengthy mare: modest handicap hurdler: won at Plumpton in March (amateurs) and April (fifth course win): stays 21f: acts on heavy and good to firm going: tried blinkered, not since 2000/1: usually races prominently. *Miss A. M. Newton-Smith* **h97**

LITTLE EM 8 ch.m. Rock City – Sleepline Princess (Royal Palace) [2002/3 17m 17gᶠ 21gᵖᵘ Sep 6] sister to very smart 2m to 2½m chaser Rockforce and half-sister to fairly useful 2m hurdler Sleepline Royale (by Buzzards Bay): dam fair 6f winner at 2 yrs, became thoroughly temperamental: of no account. *R. Johnson* **h–**

LITTLE ENAM (IRE) 7 gr.g. Un Desperado (FR) – Black Pheasant (IRE) (Sexton Blake) [2002/3 F16s⁶ 19d⁶ Jan 16] 14,000 4-y-o: third foal: dam unraced half-sister to Champion Bumper winner/useful hurdler Wither Or Which and to dam of top-class staying chaser Alexander Banquet: sixth of 17 finishers to Sixo in bumper at Newbury on debut: didn't jump well when well held in novice hurdle at Taunton. *C. R. Egerton* **h– F70**

LITTLE FLORA 7 ch.m. Alflora (IRE) – Sister's Choice (Lepanto (GER)) [2002/3 h94: 16g⁵ 20m⁵ 16m³ 16g⁵ Jul 10] compact mare: modest hurdler, below best early in 2002/3: stays 21f: acts on any going: has bled from nose: front runner. *A. Scott* **h85**

LITTLE HECK (IRE) 6 b.g. Executive Perk – Princess Andromeda (Corvaro (USA)) [2002/3 F16d Feb 25] 8,000 4-y-o: seventh live foal: half-brother to 21f hurdle winner Court In The Act (by Commanche Run) and to 2 winning pointers: dam, 9f winner, out of half-sister to Night Nurse: tailed off in bumper on debut. *T. D. Easterby* **F–**

LITTLE HERMAN (IRE)   7 b.g. Mandalus – Kilbricken Bay (Salluceva) [2002/3   c–
h86?, F–: 20v c20s Jan 23] well-made gelding: thrice-raced novice hurdler, modest form   **h70**
on debut: co-favourite, let down by jumping in handicap at Warwick on chasing debut:
will stay 3m. *J. A. B. Old*

LITTLE JOHN   7 b.g. Warrshan (USA) – Silver Venture (USA) (Silver Hawk (USA))   **h–**
[2002/3 17g⁵ Oct 11] poor maiden on Flat (stays easy 2m, weak finisher): lightly raced
over hurdles, let down by jumping at Carlisle in October. *Miss L. A. Perratt*

LITTLE KNOWLEDGE   5 b.m. Terimon – Madam-M (Tina's Pet) [2002/3 F16g   **F–**
May 22] fifth foal: half-sister to winning 3m hurdler Madam's Man (by Sir Harry Lewis):
dam, irresolute and of little account, half-sister to useful 2½m chase winner Loddon Lad:
well beaten in bumper on debut. *N. A. Twiston-Davies*

LITTLE LAURA   7 ch.m. Casteddu – At First Sight (He Loves Me) [2002/3 F16f   **F–**
F16g Sep 26] little sign of ability in bumpers. *K. W. Hogg, Isle of Man*

LITTLE LES   7 b.g. Jumbo Hirt (USA) – Hand On Heart (IRE) (Taufan (USA))   **h69**
[2002/3 h55: 16m⁶ 16d³ 16g² 20m³ 17mᵖᵘ Jul 25] lengthy gelding: poor maiden hurdler:
lame final outing: should stay 2½m: acts on good to soft going: tongue tied first 2 starts.
F. P. Murtagh

LITTLE MADAME   4 b.f. Faustus (USA) – Sprig Muslin (Ra Nova) [2002/3 17dᵖᵘ   **h–**
17m³ 16vᵖᵘ Dec 20] first foal: dam, winning 2¾m hurdler, half-sister to smart hurdler/
chaser up to 3m Trying Again: signs of only a little ability in juvenile hurdles: blinkered
after debut. *D. R. Gandolfo*

LITTLE MICKEY   5 ch.g. Rock Hopper – Sixslip (USA) (Diesis) [2002/3 F18v⁴   **h68**
F18s³ 21sᵘʳ 24vᵖᵘ 26g³ Mar 2] lengthy gelding: seventh foal: half-brother to fairly useful   **F79**
bumper winner Point (by Polish Precedent) and winning pointer by Belmez: dam, 1¼m
and 1¾m winner, half-sister to useful hurdler/chaser up to 3m Copernicus: in frame in 2
bumpers: poor form on completed outing over hurdles (wandered) in 3¼m maiden at
Huntingdon: visored last 2 starts. *N. A. Twiston-Davies*

LITTLE MICK (IRE)   6 b.g. Mister Lord (USA) – Strong Trump (IRE) (Strong   **h–**
Gale) [2002/3 F17s 20vᵖᵘ Dec 20] IR 4,000 3-y-o: first foal: dam unraced half-sister to   **F–**
useful chaser up to 3m Bell Staffboy: no show in maiden bumper or novice hurdle.
J. A. B. Old

LITTLE MISTER   7 ch.g. Gran Alba (USA) – Chrissytino (Baron Blakeney) [2002/3   **h–**
h–, F–: 18vᵖᵘ 24sᵖᵘ Jan 28] medium-sized gelding: no form in bumper or novice hurdles.   **F–**
N. R. Mitchell

LITTLE NOBBY   4 b.g. Makbul – Simply Style (Bairn (USA)) [2002/3 16g Sep 12]   **h–**
half-brother to poor hurdler Weet And See (by Lochnager), stays 2½m: poor maiden
on Flat (probably stays 1m): little impact in juvenile maiden on hurdling debut.
R. Hollinshead

LITTLE ROCK   7 b.h. Warning – Much Too Risky (Bustino) [2002/3 16g Dec 18]   **h88 p**
small, angular horse: half-brother to poor 2m hurdler Doubling Dice (by Jalmood): very
smart at one time on Flat (stays 1½m well) for Sir Michael Stoute, probably useful on
balance in France in 2002: joint favourite, not fluent and found little when seventh of 25
to Caracciola in maiden at Newbury on hurdling debut: should do better. *F. Doumen,
France*

LITTLE RORT (IRE)   4 b.g. Ali-Royal (IRE) – Florinda (Vice Regent (CAN))   **h113**
[2002/3 16v² 16s⁵ 16v* 16s⁵ 17g Mar 13] sturdy gelding: fair on Flat (stays 1½m): fairly
useful juvenile hurdler: won maiden at Limerick in December: best efforts when 7 lengths
fifth to impressive Golden Cross in Grade 3 at Fairyhouse in February and fourth to
Harchibald in 4-y-o novice at Punchestown in late-April: mid-field in Triumph Hurdle at
Cheltenham in between: will be suited by further than 2m: raced on good ground or softer
(acts on heavy): tongue tied after third outing. *M. J. Grassick, Ireland*

LITTLE ROSS   8 b.g. St Ninian – Little Katrina (Little Buskins) [2002/3 h79?: 21v³   **c80**
c20sᵘʳ c16s³ c18s⁴ c16g⁵ c20mᵖᵘ Mar 31] lengthy gelding: poor form over hurdles and   **h79**
fences: stays 21f: raced mainly on good going or softer (acts on heavy): tongue tied in
2002/3. *D. M. Grissell*

LITTLE SKY   6 gr.m. Terimon – Brown Coast (Oats) [2002/3 F–: F16s 16mᵘʳ 16mᵖᵘ   **h–**
Mar 31] no sign of ability. *D. Mullarkey*   **F–**

LITTLE SPORT (IRE)   6 ch.g. Moscow Society (USA) – Ath Dara (Duky) [2002/3   **h134**
F95: F17d² 20v³ 20d* 20d* 23v² 20s³ 20v² 24s* 21g 24g Apr 3] big gelding: chasing   **F96**
type: fairly useful in bumpers: useful hurdler: won 2 novices at Newcastle in November

and handicap at same course in February: best efforts when second to Royal Emperor in handicap at Wetherby fifth outing and mid-division in Grade 1 novice at Cheltenham on ninth: will prove suited by 3m+: acts on heavy ground: genuine and consistent. *A. Scott*

LITTLE TASK 5 b.g. Environment Friend – Lucky Thing (Green Desert (USA)) [2002/3 h93: 16d* 17d⁶ 20m 16m⁵ 16g⁶ 17m² 16m 16g c16g⁶ 17g 16m Apr 21] small gelding: modest hurdler: best after, including on chasing debut: raced mainly around 2m: acts on good to firm and good to soft going: tried visored/ in cheekpieces. *J. S. Wainwright* **c70 h93 d**

LITTLE TOBIAS (IRE) 4 ch.g. Millkom – Barbara Frietchie (IRE) (Try My Best (USA)) [2002/3 17f* Oct 1] poor maiden on Flat (probably stays 1m): won 5-runner juvenile at Exeter on hurdling debut, driven out to beat Bongo Fury 1½ lengths. *Andrew Turnell* **h92**

LITTLETON BOREAS (USA) 4 b. or br.c. Foxhound (USA) – Susita Song (USA) (Seattle Song (USA)) [2002/3 16dᵖᵘ Nov 24] poor maiden on Flat: broke down on hurdling debut: dead. *T. J. Naughton* **h–**

LITTLETON ZEUS (IRE) 4 ch.g. Woodborough (USA) – La Fandango (IRE) (Taufan (USA)) [2002/3 16g 17g Mar 15] poor maiden on Flat (probably stays 9.4f), sold out of R. White's stable 1,700 gns Newmarket July Sales: well held in 2 juvenile hurdles. *W. S. Cunningham* **h–**

LITTLE TUSKA (IRE) 13 gr.g. Step Together (USA) – Peek-A-Boo (Bustino) [2002/3 c70, h–: c16d⁶ c17m³ 17m⁴ c21m⁶ c20gᵖᵘ c21g⁴ 16v⁵ c16g⁵ c19m⁴ Apr 22] workmanlike gelding: poor handicap chaser/maiden hurdler, sold out of N. Mason's stable 800 gns Doncaster September Sales after sixth start: stays 21f: acts on any going: usually blinkered for former stable: tongue tied: not one to trust. *M. J. M. Evans* **c70 § h72 §**

LITTLE WORSALL (IRE) 10 ch.g. Broadsword (USA) – In My View (King's Ride) [2002/3 c–, h58: c25d c25g⁵ Apr 14] workmanlike gelding: maiden hurdler/chaser: let down by jumping in 2 hunters in 2003: won all 3 starts in points in between: should stay beyond 2m: acts on firm going. *Mrs K. J. Tutty* **c74 x h–**

LITUUS (USA) 10 gr. or ro.g. El Gran Senor (USA) – Liturgism (USA) (Native Charger) [2002/3 17g³ 18g³ 16gᵖᵘ c16gᵖᵘ Oct 9] won 7f maiden at Nad Al Sheba in 1997, twice well held on Flat in Britain in 2001: placed twice over hurdles for A. Chaille-Chaille: showed nothing on chasing debut. *Miss Gay Kelleway* **c– h?**

LIVELY DESSERT (IRE) 10 b.g. Be My Native (USA) – Liffey Travel (Le Bavard (FR)) [2002/3 c95, h–: c25d² c28vF c27s⁴ c24vᵖᵘ c24sᵖᵘ 24g⁵ c31gᵖᵘ Apr 24] lengthy gelding: modest handicap chaser: out of form after reappearance, including over hurdles: probably stays 4m: acts on good to firm and heavy going: tried visored/in cheekpieces. *F. P. Murtagh* **c95 d h–**

LIVENLEARNLAD 7 b.g. Norton Challenger – Welcoming Arms (Free State) [2002/3 F16d Oct 25] second foal: dam, modest 1¼m and 17f winner, half-sister to useful staying hurdler King's College Boy: showed little in bumper on debut. *B. De Haan* **F–**

LIVE THE DREAM 5 b.m. Exit To Nowhere (USA) – Inveraven (Alias Smith (USA)) [2002/3 h117: 16m⁶ 20d 20s 21d³ 24d⁴ 21s* Dec 31] leggy, unfurnished mare: fairly useful hurdler: gradually returned to form, won handicap at Cheltenham by 3 lengths from Monger Lane: stays 3m: acts on soft going: visored last 4 starts in 2001/2: has worn cheekpieces: used to force pace but held up last 4 starts (raced lazily on penultimate). *M. C. Pipe* **h115**

LIVINGSTONEBRAMBLE (IRE) 7 b.g. Supreme Leader – Killiney Side (General Ironside) [2002/3 h119p, F92: c24dF c20s² c16s c20vᵖᵘ Dec 31] compact gelding: shaped well both starts over hurdles in 2001/2, winning maiden at Fairyhouse: form over fences (let down by jumping first and third outings) only when 1½ lengths second to Dutsdale Dancer in maiden at Navan: reportedly had respiratory tract infection final start: likely to stay beyond 2½m: raced on good going or softer (acts on soft). *W. P. Mullins, Ireland* **c121 h–**

LIZZY LAMB 5 b.m. Bustino – Caroline Lamb (Hotfoot) [2002/3 F17m³ Jul 25] half-sister to several winners, including useful bumper winner/winning chaser Lord Lamb (by Dunbeath), stays 25f, useful hurdler Mr Lamb (by Deploy) and fairly useful hurdler/chaser Byron Lamb (by Rambo Dancer): dam, winning hurdler, half-sister to useful 2m hurdler Burns: third of 9 in bumper at Sedgefield on debut. *Miss S. E. Hall* **F70**

LIZZYS FIRST 11 b.g. Town And Country – Lizzy Longstocking (Jimsun) [2002/3 c– x c–x, h72: 19s³ 22s⁴ 19s* 19d⁶ 19s² 21g 24f* 24m⁵ Apr 15] workmanlike gelding: let h91 down by jumping over fences: modest handicap hurdler: won at Hereford in December and Taunton (seller) in April: effective at 19f to 3m: acts on any going: blinkered twice in 2000/1. C. J. Down

LOBLITE LEADER (IRE) 6 b.g. Tirol – Cyrano Beauty (IRE) (Cyrano de Bergerac) h95 [2002/3 16g⁵ 19d³ Feb 25] good-topped gelding: modest on Flat (stays 1¾m), well held in 2002: better effort over hurdles when third of 16 to Another Dude in novice at Catterick. G. A. Swinbank

LOBUCHE (IRE) 8 b.g. Petardia – Lhotse (IRE) (Shernazar) [2002/3 c71, h88: 17s⁶ c– c17s⁶ Dec 5] small gelding: modest handicap hurdler: poor novice chaser: well held both h– starts in 2002/3: stays 3m: acts on firm and good to soft going, probably on soft: usually tongue tied. M. C. Chapman

LOCHBUY JUNIOR (FR) 8 b.g. Saumarez – Chalabiah (Akarad (FR)) [2002/3 h104 h104: 20s* Mar 8] rather leggy gelding: fair handicap hurdler: first run for over 15 months, won at Ayr by 2 lengths from Robert The Bruce: likely to prove best up to around 2½m: best efforts on good going or softer (acts on soft). M. Todhunter

LOCHIEDUBS 8 br.g. Cragador – Linn Falls (Royal Fountain) [2002/3 h85, F85: h82 20v³ 25d Feb 25] lengthy gelding: poor maiden hurdler: should be suited by further than 2½m: acts on good to firm and heavy going. Mrs L. B. Normile

LOCH NA BPEISC (IRE) 6 b.g. Over The River (FR) – Ballyhire Lady (IRE) h– (Callernish) [2002/3 21d 20s 24vᵖᵘ Jan 17] stocky gelding: second known foal: dam, winning pointer, from family of Buck House: runner-up on first of 2 starts in maiden Irish points in 2002: no encouragement in 3 runs over hurdles. P. G. Murphy

LOCHNAGEN 9 b.g. Lochnager – Broken Paws (Busted) [2002/3 20gᵖᵘ May 8] h– pulled up in 2 maiden points in 2002 and novice hurdle. S. E. H. Sherwood

LOCH TORRIDON 4 b.g. Syrtos – Loch Scavaig (IRE) (The Parson) [2002/3 F16d F– Mar 5] third foal: dam useful staying hurdler who became uncooperative: looked badly in need of experience in bumper on debut. James Moffatt

LODESTAR (IRE) 6 br.g. Good Thyne (USA) – Let's Compromise (No Argument) c101 [2002/3 F–: c19gᵖᵘ c25s⁴ c24dᶠ c23g⁵ c20g² 22g* 26m² Apr 21] tall gelding: fair form h101 over fences: won novice at Stratford on hurdling debut in April: better form when second of 6 to The Lyme Volunteer in similar event at Hereford: stays 3¼m: acts on good to firm and good to soft going. Ian Williams

LOGICIAN (NZ) 12 b.g. Lord Ballina (AUS) – Thornton Lady (NZ) (Sound Reason c143 (CAN)) [2002/3 c136, h?: c16d* c20d³ c17g² Nov 30] well-made gelding: useful h– handicap chaser: won at Wolverhampton in July by ¾ length from Star Jack: probably best up to 2½m: acted on good to firm and heavy going: often tongue tied prior to 2002/3: raced up with pace and usually jumped well: genuine: reportedly retired. I. A. Balding

LOG ON INTERSKY (IRE) 7 ch.g. Insan (USA) – Arctic Mo (IRE) (Mandalus) c122 [2002/3 c–, h87: 21g³ 21g* 20g⁵ c21g² c16s* c16d* c19d⁴ c16d* c16g⁴ Apr 3] lengthy h90 gelding: has reportedly had wind operation: modest hurdler: fortunate to win novice at Sedgefield in September: considerably better over fences, won handicaps at Carlisle in October and Catterick in December and novice at Catterick in February: good fourth of 16 to Golden Alpha in valuable handicap at Aintree final start: effective at 2m to 21f: raced on good going or softer (acts on soft): often tongue tied over hurdles: sound jumper: front runner/races prominently. J. Howard Johnson

LOI DE MARTIALE (IRE) 5 br.g. Presenting – Thresa-Anita (IRE) (Over The F87 River (FR)) [2002/3 F16g² F16g Jan 17] IR 27,000 3-y-o: first foal: dam, winning 2¾m chaser, half-sister to useful chaser around 2½m Haki Saki: much better effort in bumpers at Musselburgh when staying-on second to Loopy Linda. J. M. Jefferson

LOLLY COPSE 5 b.m. Lancastrian – Game Spinney (Precipice Wood) [2002/3 F16s F– F16g Feb 22] medium-sized mare: seventh foal: dam ran twice: showed nothing in 2 bumpers. S. J. Gilmore

LONDOLOZI LAD (IRE) 4 b.g. Ali-Royal (IRE) – Ashdown (Pharly (FR)) [2002/3 h82 16mᶠ 16g* 16d Oct 31] leggy gelding: poor on Flat (stays 8.5f): won juvenile maiden hurdle at Uttoxeter in September: well held in novice handicap following month: likely to need sharp 2m. P. C. Haslam

LONER 5 b.g. Magic Ring (IRE) – Jolis Absent (Primo Dominie) [2002/3 17s⁶ Nov 14] modest on Flat (stays 7.5f): badly hampered first when well beaten in maiden on hurdling debut. *M. Wigham* **h?**

LONE SOLDIER (FR) 7 ch.g. Songlines (FR) – Caring Society (Caerleon (USA)) [2002/3 c92, h98: 16d⁶ 16g 24m Jul 7] compact gelding: winning 2m hurdler/chaser: well held after absence early in 2002/3: tongue tied: has found little. *S. B. Clark* **c– h–**

LONESOME DEALER (IRE) 7 b. or br.g. Supreme Leader – Slievenaree (IRE) (Lancastrian) [2002/3 c16m c17m⁴ c22gᵖᵘ c18d⁴ 24m Apr 12] IR 15,000 4-y-o: ex-Irish gelding: first foal: dam, winning pointer, out of half-sister to useful 2m hurdler/chaser Atone: modest hurdler: best effort over fences when fourth in handicap at Thurles: sold out of P. Doyle's stable 15,500 gns Doncaster November Sales before final start: should stay 2½m: acts on heavy ground. *B. G. Powell* **c87 h–**

LONE STAR (IRE) 11 b.g. Satco (FR) – Masterstown Lucy (Bargello) [2002/3 16dᵖᵘ 20m⁴ May 6] rangy gelding: novice hurdler/chaser: tried tongue tied: sold £650 Ascot June Sales: poor form in points in 2003. *A. M. Hales* **c– h–**

LONG JOURNEY (IRE) 4 b.c. Blues Traveller (IRE) – Pudgy Poppet (Danehill (USA)) [2002/3 16dᶠ Nov 16] lightly-raced maiden on Flat: blinkered and tongue tied, took good hold and just beginning to weaken when falling 2 out in 16-runner juvenile at Cheltenham on hurdling debut. *Edward Butler, Ireland* **h–**

LONGSHANKS 6 b.g. Broadsword (USA) – Brass Castle (IRE) (Carlingford Castle) [2002/3 20s⁴ c21d 20v² 20sᵖᵘ 20s² Mar 15] 5,000 3-y-o, 10,000 4-y-o: workmanlike gelding: fourth foal: dam unraced, from family of Teeton Mill, Celtic Ryde and Noddy's Ryde: won maiden Irish point on debut in 2002: bought 45,000 gns (privately) Doncaster May Sales: modest novice hurdler: no extra after a mistake 4 out when seventh of 8 finishers in valuable novice at Cheltenham on steeplechase debut (should do better): should stay beyond 2½m: raced on going softer than good. *K. C. Bailey* **c93 p h97**

LONG SHOT 6 b.m. Sir Harry Lewis (USA) – Kovalevskia (Ardross) [2002/3 F82: 17g 22g* 21d⁴ 22d³ 21mᶠ 24g² Apr 23] leggy mare: modest hurdler: made all in mares novice at Wincanton in November: stays 3m: raced mainly on good going or softer: flashes tail. *N. J. Henderson* **h93**

LONGSTONE BOY (IRE) 11 br.g. Mazaad – Inger-Lea (Record Run) [2002/3 c23d² c24m³ Apr 22] good-bodied gelding: fair hunter chaser: stays 3m: acts on firm and good to soft going. *E. R. Clough* **c88**

LONGSTONE LAD 11 b.g. Pittacus (USA) – Fatu Hiva (GER) (Marduk (GER)) [2002/3 c26g² c26vᵘʳ c24sᵖᵘ Feb 27] tall, workmanlike gelding: fair pointer: maiden steeplechaser: moody effort final start: stays 3¼m: raced on good going or softer over jumps (acts on heavy). *R. Rawle* **c97 h–**

LONGSTONE LADY (IRE) 6 b.m. Mister Lord (USA) – Monamandy (IRE) (Mandalus) [2002/3 F17m Jul 15] first foal: dam, winning Irish pointer, out of half-sister to high-class staying chaser Simon Legree: no show in mares maiden Irish point or maiden bumper. *J. D. Frost* **F–**

LONGSTONE LOCH (IRE) 6 b.g. Executive Perk – Lyre-Na-Gcloc (Le Moss) [2002/3 25g 20mᵖᵘ Apr 12] lengthy gelding: first foal: dam unraced: well held in 2 Irish points in 2002: bought 7,000 gns (privately) Doncaster November Sales: showed nothing both runs over hurdles (trained by T. Keddy on debut). *D. J. Caro* **h–**

LONGTERM (IRE) 6 b.g. Welsh Term – Sahob (Roselier (FR)) [2002/3 F17d* 20s² Nov 17] IR 28,000 3-y-o: good-topped gelding: fourth foal: brother to winning 27f hurdler Dragon Hunter and half-brother to winning pointer by Noalto: dam unraced half-sister to useful staying chaser Aston Express: second outing in bumpers (trained by S. Neville on debut), won 18-runner event at Exeter in October by 8 lengths from Priests Bridge despite wandering: upped in trip, 3½ lengths second to Simply Supreme in novice at Haydock on hurdling debut, travelling well and jumping soundly: will stay beyond 2½m: should improve. *Jonjo O'Neill* **h110 p F112**

LOOKING DEADLY 9 b.m. Neltino – Princess Constanza (Relkino) [2002/3 c–, h–: 17d² 16g c17s⁴ c17m⁵ c25mᵘʳ 27d⁵ c17v⁵ 18vᵖᵘ Dec 2] poor maiden hurdler/chaser: best efforts around 2m. *F. P. Murtagh* **c63 h63**

LOOKING FORWARD 7 b.g. Primitive Rising (USA) – Gilzie Bank (New Brig) [2002/3 c76: c22v⁴ c24vᵖᵘ c16sᶠ c21gᵘʳ c21d* Apr 8] good-topped gelding: modest chaser: improved last 2 starts, won handicap at Sedgefield by 5 lengths from Uncle Bert **c88**

despite not looking straightforward ride: stays 21f: raced mainly on good going or softer.
Ferdy Murphy

LOOK IN THE MIRROR 12 b.g. Rakaposhi King – Moaning Jenny (Privy Seal)   **c105**
[2002/3 c116, h–: c25f*dis c28mur Jun 1] leggy gelding: useful hunter chaser at best: won   **h–**
at Exeter in May (subsequently disqualified due to prohibited substance): still going well
enough in second when unseating thirteenth in valuable contest at Stratford (won 2001
renewal) 2 weeks later: stays 3½m: acts on firm and soft going: sound-jumping front
runner: genuine. *Fergal O'Brien*

LOOK SHARPE 12 b.g. Looking Glass – Washburn Flyer (Owen Dudley) [2002/3   **c83**
c–: c25m c20m4 c25g Apr 14] modest hunter chaser: should stay beyond 2½m: raced
mainly on good going or firmer. *T. S. Sharpe*

LOOK SHARP (FR) 6 b.g. Keen – Hunt The Thimble (FR) (Relkino) [2002/3 16dpu   **h–**
Oct 26] leggy ex-French gelding: third foal: half-brother to 2 winners, including fairly
useful hurdler/fair chaser Roi de La Chasse (by Royal Vulcan), stayed 3m: dam unraced:
twice-raced over hurdles in French Provinces at 4 yrs, winning at Compiegne: sold out of
T. Trapenard's stable 10,000 gns Doncaster May Sales: pulled up lame early on British
debut. *T. Wall*

LOOKSHARP LAD (IRE) 5 b.g. Simply Great (FR) – Merry Madness (Raise You   **F– p**
Ten) [2002/3 F16v6 Mar 8] €135,000 4-y-o: good sort: half-brother to several winners,
including smart hurdlers Over The Bar and Merry Masquerade (both by King's Ride) and
useful chaser Merry People (by Lafontaine), stayed 25f: dam winning pointer: remote
sixth of 8 in bumper at Sandown on debut on very testing ground: looks type to do better.
Mrs A. J. Bowlby

LOOKS LIKE MINE 6 b.g. Miner's Lamp – Glenisla (Sunyboy) [2002/3 F16m Jul   **F–**
4] first foal: dam lightly-raced pointer, resumed racing after birth of this foal: well held in
weak bumper on debut. *A. P. Jones*

LOOKS LIKE VALUE (IRE) 7 gr.g. Euphemism – Crossdrumrosie (IRE) (Roselier   **c–**
(FR)) [2002/3 F16d c20vpu c25spu c24m5 Mar 23] IR 2,000 4-y-o: workmanlike gelding: **F–**
first foal: dam unraced: in frame all 3 starts in maiden Irish points in 2002: bought 13,500
gns Doncaster May Sales: no form in bumper or maiden chases. *K. C. Bailey*

LOOK TO THE FUTURE (IRE) 9 b.g. Roselier (FR) – Toevarro (Raga Navarro   **c–**
(ITY)) [2002/3 19dpu 20d2 22dpu c19dpu 20v3 21g6 c25gpu 22m3 Apr 8] compact gelding: **h94**
brother to 4 winners, including fairly useful winner up to 3¼m Misty Class and fair
winner up to 25f Beatson: dam Irish bumper winner/maiden hurdler: modest maiden
hurdler: sold out of M. Morris' stable 6,800 gns Doncaster October (2001) Sales: no
promise in 2 runs over fences: stays 2¾m: acts on heavy going, possibly unsuited by good
to firm: inconsistent: sold 6,000 gns Doncaster May Sales. *C. J. Mann*

LOOP THE LOUP 7 b.g. Petit Loup (USA) – Mithi Al Gamar (USA) (Blushing   **h132**
Groom (FR)) [2002/3 h114+: 20g3 20d3 17d2 16dbd 22m3 20m* Apr 21] sturdy gelding:
fairly useful on Flat, successful in June: useful handicap hurdler: won 5-runner race at
Wetherby, leading last when beating Mirjan a neck: needs good test around 2m, stays
2¾m: acts on good to firm and good to soft going: effective blinkered or not: consistent.
Mrs M. Reveley

LOOPY LINDA (IRE) 5 b.g. Simply Great (FR) – Albane (Shirley Heights) [2002/3   **h– p**
F16v F16g* F16g* F16g2 20v4 Jan 29] leggy gelding: sixth foal: half-brother to winner   **F98**
in Germany by Tirol: dam placed twice in France: fairly useful in 4 bumpers: won at
Doncaster and Musselburgh (flashed tail, beat Loi de Martiale by 4 lengths) in December:
jumped poorly when well beaten in novice on hurdling debut: possibly unsuited by heavy
going: races up with pace: should do better over hurdles. *T. D. Easterby*

LORAMORE 6 ch.m. Alflora (IRE) – Apsimore (Touching Wood (USA)) [2002/3   **h–**
F17f 16dpu Dec 26] second foal: dam, modest hurdler up to 3m, won over 17f on Flat: **F74**
signs of ability in maiden bumper at Exeter: no show on hurdling debut. *J. C. Tuck*

LORD ALVINRU (IRE) 6 b.g. Lord Americo – Alvinru (Sandalay) [2002/3 h86,   **h74**
F–: 20g5 16mpu 20f6 17mur Oct 1] useful-looking gelding: maiden hurdler: shaped as if
amiss first 2 starts: stays 19f: acts on good to firm going: won maiden point in March.
G. A. Swinbank

LORD ALYN (IRE) 5 b.g. Topanoora – Glenstal Priory (Glenstal (USA)) [2002/3   **F–**
F16vpu Feb 15] useful-looking gelding: third reported foal: half-brother to 3 winners up
to 8.5f on Flat, including sweet Duke of Aston (by Shalford): dam poor maiden hurdler,
successful up to 2¼m on Flat: favourite, reportedly distressed in bumper at Ascot on
debut, tailed off when pulled up over 2f out. *C. R. Egerton*

LORD ATTERBURY (IRE) 7 ch.g. Mister Lord (USA) – Tammyiris (Arapahos   **c126 p**
(FR)) [2002/3 c23d* c25g* Apr 5]
    It's not like *Formcard*, the Irish point-to-point experts, to underestimate a
horse, so it's somewhat surprising that it was so wide of the mark with regard to
Lord Atterbury: 'had to wait until final day of season to forfeit maiden tag in hard
earned fashion . . . will possibly struggle to record a follow up.' In truth, that
seemed an honest verdict on a horse that was having his sixth start spread over eight
months. However, switched to David Pipe's pointing yard for 2003, Lord Atterbury
was beaten only once in completed starts in points and hunter chases and looked a
really exciting prospect. It was reported in the summer that he would be switched to
father Martin's stable in 2003/4, doubtless with some of the major handicaps on the
agenda. Lord Atterbury started the latest campaign in points, winning a restricted
and an intermediate on his first two appearances. He failed to negotiate the third on
his next outing but, campaigned in hunter chase class for the first time, was soon
back on track, winning a maiden at Leicester in March by twenty-eight lengths.
Lord Atterbury met his only defeat on a completed start back in point company later
in the month, but the horse that beat him, Mister Benjamin, went unbeaten on five
completed starts in points. His performance at Leicester had suggested he had the
makings of a useful hunter but it was his next appearance in that grade which really
marked him down as a potential star. The race after the Grand National isn't usually
one that gets much attention but the latest running of the Martell Reserve Novices'
Hunter Chase was notable for the way in which Lord Atterbury demolished the

Mr P. J. Finn's "Lord Atterbury"

opposition, jumping well in front and in no danger from a long way out. He won by a distance (actually, by around thirty-four lengths) from Arctic Times. The second, fourth and fifth all ran at least creditably next time out, which suggests Lord Atterbury was already close to showing useful form on just his second start outside points (he ran to a similar level when winning over four miles and a furlong at Cheltenham the week after the end of the British season). Although he has raced at three miles or more, Lord Atterbury doesn't look a sluggard and it wouldn't be a surprise if he is tried over shorter distances at some point. He is a sturdy gelding in appearance and is the first foal of a winning Irish pointer. *D. Pipe*

LORD BELFRY 7 ch.g. Baron Blakeney – Capricious Lady (IRE) (Capricorn Line) **h–**
[2002/3 20d^{pu} 21v^{pu} Dec 4] sturdy gelding: no sign of ability in bumpers or over hurdles. *A. Charlton*

LORDBERNIEBOUFFANT (IRE) 10 b.g. Denel (FR) – Noon Hunting (Green **c–**
Shoon) [2002/3 c116, h–: c24d^5 Dec 13] rather leggy gelding: fairly useful handicap **h125** chaser: ran about as well as he's ever done over hurdles when fifth to Glacial Sunset in competitive handicap at Cheltenham, only outing in 2002/3: suited by 3m+: acts on good to firm and heavy going: often sweating/edgy: has broken blood vessel. *J. T. Gifford*

LORD BREX (FR) 7 gr.g. Saint Estephe (FR) – Light Moon (FR) (Mendez (FR)) **h95 §**
[2002/3 h122: 17s* 19g^6 20s^2 16d^3 Mar 19] useful-looking gelding: has had breathing operation: one-time useful hurdler, modest nowadays: won seller at Taunton in February: stays 2½m: acts on soft and good to firm going: wears headgear: ungenuine. *J. G. M. O'Shea*

LORD BROADWAY (IRE) 7 b.g. Shardari – Country Course (IRE) (Crash Course) **c80**
[2002/3 c80, h–: c25g c23m^{pu} c21m^4 c23g^F c24d^3 c24g^2 c24g^2 c24g^2 c25m^4 Apr 17] very **h–** tall, angular gelding: poor maiden hurdler/chaser: probably flattered final outing: stays 25f: unraced on firm going, acts on any other. *N. M. Babbage*

LORD BUCKINGHAM 5 ch.g. Carroll House – Lady Buck (Pollerton) [2002/3 **F82**
F16d^5 F16m Mar 22] lengthy, unfurnished gelding: half-brother to several winners, including fairly useful chaser Shining Willow (by Strong Gale), stays 3m, and fair hurdler up to 2¾m Young Buck (by Glacial Storm): dam never ran: favourite, better effort in bumpers at Newbury when 22¾ lengths fifth of 13 to Bourbon Manhattan: tongue tied second outing. *N. J. Henderson*

LORD CAPITAINE (IRE) 9 b. or br.g. Mister Lord (USA) – Salvation Sue (Mon **c105**
Capitaine) [2002/3 c96: c25d^{pu} c24s^3 c26s^4 c27d* c28g* Mar 25] workmanlike gelding: fair handicap chaser: unbeaten in 5 starts at Sedgefield, winning twice there in March: stays 3½m: acts on soft going: tried blinkered: has had tongue tied: tends to jump right. *J. Howard Johnson*

LORD CONYERS (IRE) 4 b.f. Inzar (USA) – Primelta (Primo Dominie) [2002/3 **h–**
17g^5 Sep 28] poor maiden on Flat (stays 1¼m): fifth of 14 in juvenile seller at Market Rasen on hurdling debut. *B. Ellison*

LORD DAL (FR) 10 b.g. Cadoudal (FR) – Lady Corteira (FR) (Carvin) [2002/3 c–, **c–**
h–: 24d 19s 19d 20m^{pu} Apr 12] angular gelding: one-time useful hurdler/fairly useful **h–** chaser, no form outside points since 2000: tried blinkered. *A. J. Whitehead*

LORD DILROCK (IRE) 7 ch.g. Lord Americo – Dillrock Damsel (Over The River **h–**
(FR)) [2002/3 22g^{pu} May 17] IR 5,200 3-y-o: second foal: dam winning pointer: third in Irish point in 2000: pulled up in novice on hurdling debut. *Miss G. Browne*

LORD DIXON (IRE) 7 b. or br.g. Lord Americo – Dixons Dutchess (IRE) (Over **c–**
The River (FR)) [2002/3 h–, F86: c26s^F Mar 10] well held in 2 novice hurdles: successful **h–** twice in points in 2002: fell fatally on steeplechase debut: should have been suited by 2½m+. *C. J. Gray*

LORD DUNDANIEL (IRE) 6 b. or br.g. Arctic Lord – Killoskehan Queen (Busti- **h87**
neto) [2002/3 F16s 16s^6 19d^4 Feb 23] IR £12,000 4-y-o: second foal: dam won 2¾m **F–** hurdle: third in maiden Irish point in 2002: raced too freely in bumper: upped in trip, better effort in novice hurdles when fourth of 16 to Vanormix at Exeter: may do better again over further. *B. De Haan*

LORD ECTOR 7 b.g. Mon Tresor – Lady Ector (USA) (King Pellinore (USA)) **F–**
[2002/3 F16s^{pu} Jun 9] plain gelding: half-brother to 2m hurdle winner Greenway Lady (by Prince Daniel) and to winning middle-distance stayer in Italy by Stormy Fighter: dam

unraced daughter of half-sister to high-class 1m to 1½m performer Artaius: tongue tied, pulled up halfway (reportedly distressed) in bumper on debut. *G. F. Bridgwater*

LORD EDWARDS ARMY (IRE)   8 b.g. Warcraft (USA) – Celtic Bombshell (Celtic Cone) [2002/3 h110, F99: 25g 19s 24g⁵ 22g 19m 22d 20f² 21d 24v⁶ c20s⁴ c16s c18d⁵ c22g³ Apr 20] strong, lengthy gelding: fair hurdler, largely well held in handicaps in 2002/3: modest form in maiden chases: probably stays 3m: acts on firm and soft going. *Patrick Mullins, Ireland*   **c93 h102**

LORD FERNANDO   4 ch.g. Forzando – Lady Lacey (Kampala) [2002/3 16m 17s⁴ 16d 16d³ 16v 16v³ 17d⁴ 16g* 16g⁴ Mar 16] good-topped gelding: modest maiden on Flat (stays 1m): poor handicap hurdler: won juvenile at Huntingdon in March: unlikely to stay much beyond 17f: acts on soft going: visored after third outing (hung badly left). *G. B. Balding*   **h78**

LORD FLEET (IRE)   9 b.g. Aristocracy – Sweet And Fleet (Whistling Deer) [2002/3 c70, h101: c17m⁶ c20g² c22mᵖᵘ c22g² c20m⁴ c20m c16d⁶ c24dᵖᵘ c20g c20m² Mar 18] lengthy gelding: won completed start over hurdles: poor maiden chaser: stays 2¾m: acts on good to firm going: has had tongue tied: often forces pace. *J. R. Cornwall*   **c73 h–**

LORD GEORGE   11 ch.g. Lord Bud – Mini Gazette (London Gazette) [2002/3 c21g c24sᶠ c20m Mar 19] modest pointer, won twice in 2002: let down by jumping in 3 hunter chases: sold out of D. Atkinson's stable 2,000 gns Doncaster August Sales after first one. *G. C. Evans*   **c– x**

LORD GIZZMO   6 ch.g. Democratic (USA) – Figrant (USA) (L'Emigrant (USA)) [2002/3 16s⁵ 20v 16m 22g Apr 19] close-coupled gelding: half-brother to useful but temperamental 2m chaser Nipper Reed (by Celestial Storm): modest on Flat (stays 1½m), won at 4 yrs for R. Beckett: no form in 4 starts over hurdles. *J. Cullinan*   **h–**

LORD GREY (IRE)   10 gr.g. Celio Rufo – Clooragh Rose (Boreen (FR)) [2002/3 17g⁶ c16f* c16g² c16f* 16m* 16d⁴ c16g c16g Apr 3] workmanlike gelding: fairly useful chaser: won handicaps at Tipperary in August and Listowel (made all and jumped well when beating Mykon Gold 3 lengths) in September: well held at Cheltenham and Aintree last 2 starts: fair handicap hurdler, won at Tipperary in October: best form around 2m: goes particularly well on good going or firmer (acts on firm). *D. P. Kelly, Ireland*   **c125 h105**

LORD HARRY (IRE)   11 b.g. Mister Lord (USA) – Vickies Gold (Golden Love) [2002/3 c106: c26g³ c24s* c28mᵖᵘ Jun 1] rangy gelding: fairly useful hunter chaser: won at Bangor in May for third successive year, off bridle some way out but well on top at finish: ran poorly in valuable race at Stratford following month: stays 3½m: acts on soft and good to firm going: tried blinkered (lacklustre effort). *Mrs Edward Crow*   **c104**

LORD JACK (IRE)   7 ch.g. Mister Lord (USA) – Gentle Gill (Pollerton) [2002/3 h97: c21v* c21s² c21v* c20v* c24s³ c24g Mar 11] angular gelding: modest hurdler: useful over fences: successful in novices at Sedgefield in November and December, and in 6-runner handicap at Ayr (beat The Rile 5 lengths, eased run-in) in January: ran well when third of 14 to easy winner Iris Bleu in valuable handicap at Sandown: soon off bridle when well held in amateur handicap at Cheltenham final outing: will stay beyond 3m: probably best on going softer than good (acts on heavy): tongue tied: sound jumper. *N. G. Richards*   **c130 h–**

LORD JURADO (IRE)   7 b.g. Jurado (USA) – Via Del Tabacco (Ballymoss) [2002/3 21g⁶ 18m Sep 24] IR 7,800 3-y-o: ex-Irish gelding: half-brother to high-class hurdler Vicario di Bray (by Furry Glen), stayed 2½m, and to winners in Italy: dam won twice in Italy: well beaten in bumper and over hurdles: tried tongue tied. *T. P. McGovern*   **h–**

LORD KHALICE (IRE)   12 b.g. King's Ride – Khalice (Khalkis) [2002/3 c108, h–: c28dᵖᵘ 26s Nov 23] tall, sparely-made gelding: winning hurdler: fair handicap chaser: no show both starts in 2002/3: stays 3¼m: acts on good to firm and heavy going. *Ferdy Murphy*   **c– h–**

LORD KILPATRICK (IRE)   9 ch.g. Mister Lord (USA) – Running Frau (Deep Run) [2002/3 c24s² c24sᵖᵘ c22m⁴ Mar 21] lengthy, workmanlike gelding: winning pointer in Ireland: went with plenty of zest when second to Storm Damage in amateur event at Sandown in February, easily best effort in steeplechases: stays 3m: acts on soft going: races prominently. *Mrs Laura J. Young*   **c105**

LORD KNOX (IRE)   13 ch.g. Tale Quale – Lady Knox (Dalsaan) [2002/3 c67: c24g⁴ May 8] winning pointer: maiden hunter: tried blinkered. *Ms K. Clark*   **c72**

LORD LUPIN (IRE)   7 b.g. Sadler's Wells (USA) – Penza (Soviet Star (USA)) [2002/3 F–: 20d 20sᵖᵘ 20s⁴ 20s 26d⁴ 24s⁴ 24g² Mar 28] well-made gelding: poor novice hurdler: stays 3¼m: raced on good going or softer (acts on soft). *T. H. Caldwell*   **h83**

LORD MAIZEY (IRE)   6 b.g. Mister Lord (USA) – My Maizey (Buckskin (FR))   **c108 p**
[2002/3 F16s* c26v⁴ c16s* Feb 12] IR 17,000 3-y-o: ex-Irish gelding: half-brother to   **F100**
winning chaser up to 23f Christys Picnic (by Tremblant): dam unraced: won all 3 completed starts in Irish points: fairly useful form when winning bumper at Naas in
November for J. A. Berry: second outing in steeplechases, won maiden at Leicester by
20 lengths from Deoch An Dorais: should stay well beyond 2m: should improve again.
N. A. Twiston-Davies

LORD MISTRAL   4 b.g. Makbul – South Wind (Tina's Pet) [2002/3 16s 17mF 17g   **h70**
16d⁴ 16d 16g⁶ 16m⁵ Apr 10] angular gelding: never dangerous in 8.5f maiden on Flat,
sold out of B. R. Millman's stable £3,500 Ascot June Sales: poor juvenile hurdler: raced
around 2m: acts on good to soft going. *Mrs N. S. Sharpe*

LORD MOOSE (IRE)   9 b.g. Mister Lord (USA) – Moose (IRE) (Royal Fountain)   **c115**
[2002/3 c114p, h–: c20d* c22d³ c22g⁴ c24s³ c24v² Mar 8] rangy gelding: fairly useful   **h–**
handicap chaser: won at Sandown in November by 1¾ lengths from Dunston Bill:
creditable efforts all starts after, second to impressive Killusty on same course: stays 3m:
raced on good going or softer (acts on heavy): has shaped as if amiss more than once.
H. D. Daly

LORD NATIVE (IRE)   8 b.g. Be My Native (USA) – Whakapohane (Kampala)   **h–**
[2002/3 h105: 16dpu 16v⁶ Mar 7] rather sparely-made gelding: fair hurdler, very lightly
raced: no encouragement in 2 handicaps after lengthy absence: raced around 2m: acts on
soft going (won bumper on firm). *N. J. Henderson*

LORD NELLSSON   7 b.g. Arctic Lord – Miss Petronella (Petoski) [2002/3 h?: 16g²   **h89**
16s 17s³ 21g² 20vpu 21m Apr 2] compact gelding: modest novice hurdler: likely to stay
beyond 21f: best efforts on good going. *J. S. King*

LORD 'N' MASTER (IRE)   7 b.g. Lord Americo – Miss Good Night (Buckskin   **c107**
(FR)) [2002/3 h87: 22m⁶ 19d* 22d³ 24d⁴ c20s* c22s³ c20spu c24s* c26spu c20f⁵ Apr 25]   **h90**
useful-looking gelding: modest hurdler: won handicap at Exeter in October: fair novice
chaser: won handicaps at Sandown in December and March: stays 3m: acts on soft going,
seemingly unsuited by firmer than good: room for improvement in his jumping. *R. Rowe*

LORD NOELIE (IRE)   10 b.g. Lord Americo – Leallen (Le Bavard (FR)) [2002/3   **c150**
c167, h–: c25dur c26g c24spu Dec 26] useful-looking gelding: impresses in appearance: **h–**
not a good walker: top-class chaser on his day, though hasn't won since 2000 Royal &
SunAlliance: mid-division in very valuable handicap at Newbury on completed
outing in 2002/3: stays 3¼m well: acts on good to firm and heavy going: reportedly bled
from nose final start in 2001/2. *Miss H. C. Knight*

LORD NORTH (IRE)   8 b.g. Mister Lord (USA) – Mrs Hegarty (Decent Fellow)   **c121**
[2002/3 c102: c20g² c20s* c21mpu c20d* c24spu c23s⁴ c21dF c20gpu Mar 22] rangy, good   **h–**
sort: fairly useful handicap chaser: won at Bangor (fortunate) in May and Leicester in
December: improved form on return from 7-month absence at latter, long way below best
after: stays 2½m: acts on soft going, easy task on good to firm: tongue tied after third
outing: inconsistent. *P. R. Webber*

LORD O'ALL SEASONS (IRE)   10 b. or br.g. Mister Lord (USA) – Autumn News   **c–**
(Giolla Mear) [2002/3 c112: c25dpu Apr 29] rangy gelding: lightly-raced winning
chaser, ran poorly at Towcester very early in season: should stay beyond 3m: acts on
heavy going: sold 16,000 gns Doncaster May Sales: well beaten in point in January.
N. J. Henderson

LORD OF ILLUSION (IRE)   6 b.g. Mister Lord (USA) – Jellaride (IRE) (King's   **h103**
Ride) [2002/3 20v 16d 17s* 22g² 27g Apr 25] tall gelding: chasing type: first foal: dam,
in frame in point, sister to fairly useful chaser up to 3m Ounavarra Creek: runner-up on
second of 2 starts in maiden Irish points in 2002: fair hurdler: won novice at Bangor in
February: improved form when second of 17 to Diletia on handicap debut at Exeter:
dropped right out closing stages final start: should stay at least 3m: raced on good going
or softer. *T. R. George*

LORD OF LOVE   8 b.g. Noble Patriarch – Gymcrak Lovebird (Taufan (USA))   **c–**
[2002/3 c–, h105: 24m⁴ 24g⁶ 19m² 17gur Oct 18] good-topped gelding: fair handicap   **h88**
hurdler on his day, well below best in 2002/3: stays 27f: acts on good to firm and heavy
going: held up. *D. Burchell*

LORD OF THE HILL (IRE)   8 b.g. Dromod Hill – Telegram Mear (Giolla Mear)   **c–**
[2002/3 c18mF c20g⁴ May 30] tall gelding: winning Irish pointer: no form over hurdles   **h–**
or fences. *G. Brown*

LORD OF THE LAND   10 b.g. Lord Bud – Saint Motunde (Tyrant (USA)) [2002/3   **c–** c94, h–: 20g 21m Apr 26] leggy gelding: winning hurdler/chaser: well held in 2 handicap   **h–** hurdles after long lay-off: stays 25f: acts on firm and good to soft going. *Mrs E. Slack*

LORD OF THE LOCH (IRE)   12 b. or br.g. Lord Americo – Loughamaire (Brave   **h88** Invader (USA)) [2002/3 h101: 18d⁴ 20d⁶ 20d⁴ 20v⁴ 20d⁶ 24mᵘʳ 20g 24g⁶ Jan 17] leggy, rather plain gelding: has reportedly had tendon trouble: modest handicap hurdler: stays 2½m: acts on good to firm and heavy going. *W. G. Young*

LORD OF THE MANOR (SWE)   6 b.g. Spectacular Tide (USA) – Sobhiato   **c–** (AUS) (Motavato (USA)) [2002/3 h59: 22f 20g c16mᵖᵘ Jun 29] angular gelding: bad   **h58** maiden hurdler: blinkered, showed nothing on chasing debut: stays 3m: acts on good to firm going: tongue tied last 5 outings. *D. W. P. Arbuthnot*

LORD OF THE NORTH (IRE)   6 br.g. Arctic Lord – Ballyfin Maid (IRE) (Boreen   **h66** (FR)) [2002/3 F–: 17s⁵ 22sᵖᵘ 20m³ 25m 21m Apr 19] signs of only a little ability over hurdles. *M. R. Hoad*

LORD OF THE RIVER (IRE)   11 br.g. Lord Americo – Well Over (Over The River   **c112** (FR)) [2002/3 c128, h–: c24s⁶ c24s⁵ Mar 1] tall, close-coupled gelding: usually looks   **h–** well: one-time smart chaser, off 3 years before 2001/2: some encouragement on return from another absence, but ran poorly 2 weeks later: stays 25f: raced mainly on good going or softer (acts on heavy): usually a sound jumper. *N. J. Henderson*

LORD OF THE TURF (IRE)   10 b.g. Supreme Leader – Avida Dancer (Ballymore)   **c133** [2002/3 c–, h111: c17s² c22s³ c17s⁴ c20s³ c22d* c22v* c22v* c24s³ c24v⁴ c24dᵖᵘ c20dᶠ   **h–** c24d³ Mar 17] angular gelding: fair hurdler: progressed into useful chaser, won at Galway in August (maiden), September (listed handicap) and October (handicap): below best after next outing: stays 3m: raced on going softer than good (acts on heavy): tried blinkered. *J. Bleahen, Ireland*

LORD PAT (IRE)   12 ch.g. Mister Lord (USA) – Arianrhod (L'Homme Arme) [2002/3   **c65** c–, h84: 21g⁶ 21d 20dᶠ 21s³ 19s* 20sᵖᵘ c20m³ Mar 18] small gelding: poor handicap   **h72** hurdler: won conditional jockeys seller at Market Rasen in December: thrice-raced over fences, twice jumping poorly: probably stays 21f: acts on heavy going. *Miss Kate Milligan*

LORD PERSEUS (IRE)   6 ch.g. Mister Lord (USA) – Greek Empress (Royal Buck)   **F96** [2002/3 F96: F16m* Apr 21] rather unfurnished gelding: fairly useful form in bumpers: off a year before winning 8-runner event at Huntingdon: will stay beyond 2m. *M. Pitman*

LORD PIERCE   5 b.g. Tragic Role (USA) – Mirkan Honey (Ballymore) [2002/3 h93:   **h72 +** 17v³ 20g⁶ 17v⁶ 16g Apr 14] sturdy gelding: maiden hurdler, poor form in 2002/3: will prove best around 2m: tried in cheekpieces: has had tongue tied: races freely. *J. Howard Johnson*

LORD RAPIER   10 b.g. Broadsword (USA) – Doddycross (Deep Run) [2002/3 h107:   **c113** c21d⁴ c25s² c28sᵖᵘ c24vᶠ c30v² c25d* c26s³ c24f² c24mᵖᵘ Apr 12] lengthy gelding: **h–** winning hurdler: fair novice chaser: won at Market Rasen (reluctant to line up) in March by 4 lengths from Wild Spice despite idling markedly: stays 3¾m: acts on any going: blinkered last 3 outings: of suspect temperament. *D. J. Caro*

LORD RICHFIELD (NZ)   12 b.g. Kirmann – Lady Grange (NZ) (Sir Bart (NZ))   **c–** [2002/3 c93x, h–: c30d 24s⁴ 22m 24mᵖᵘ 24d⁴ Aug 2] good-bodied gelding: fair handicap   **h–** hurdler/modest maiden chaser at best: little form since early-2001/2: best up to 2½m: acts on any going: tried visored: usually let down by jumping over fences. *B. P. J. Baugh*

LORD ROCHESTER   7 b.g. Distant Relative – Kentfield (Busted) [2002/3 h117:   **c95 x** c23f⁴ c20g⁴ c24mᶠ c24m³ c23gᵖᵘ 20g⁶ 21g⁶ Oct 12] close-coupled gelding: modest form   **h–** at best over fences, usually let down by jumping: fairly useful handicap hurdler: long way below form both starts in 2002/3, sold out of C. Mann's stable 7,300 gns Doncaster September Sales in between: probably stays 3m: acts on firm going, probably on good to soft: blinkered: has pulled hard: front runner. *K. F. Clutterbuck*

LORD SAM (IRE)   7 b. or br.g. Supreme Leader – Russian Gale (IRE) (Strong   **h144** Gale) [2002/3 F116: 16s* 16s* 21d* 21g³ Mar 12]

A couple of well-above average novice hurdlers helped turn around the fortunes of Devon-based trainer Victor Dartnall in the latest season, Lord Sam and Rosarian picking up three races apiece after Dartnall, hampered by not having his all-weather gallop available for five weeks in the autumn, had gone seven months without a winner. Dartnall, who quickly made a name for himself on the point-to-point scene, has found it difficult to make much of an impact since taking out a professional licence in 1998/9, but with his small stable housing a jumper as promising as Lord Sam he has good reason to be optimistic about the future.

It was Lord Sam who brought to an end his trainer's lean spell, when winning at Sandown in December on his hurdling debut. He and Inca Trail, also running for the first time over hurdles, dominated both the market and the race itself, the latter at odds on despite Lord Sam having shown the better form in bumpers. Indeed, Lord Sam had been one of the best bumper horses in Britain in 2001/2, winning at Sandown and Newbury on his only starts. The pair pulled right away from their rivals when the race began in earnest two out, Lord Sam gaining the advantage when Inca Trail fluffed that flight and going on to win by three and a half lengths. Fluent jumping was one of the features of Lord Sam's performance, but that wasn't so on his three subsequent outings. His jumping wasn't enough of a hindrance to stop him justifying favouritism at Kempton on his next two starts, though. Testing ground helped show him to best advantage over two miles there on Boxing Day, Lord Sam taking the lead three out and staying on well to draw twenty lengths clear of his nearest pursuer Porak; incidentally, he was ridden for the only time by Tony McCoy, who was gaining his two-hundredth success of the season in record time. Lord Sam's stamina also came into play in the closing stages when stepped up to twenty-one furlongs over three weeks later. He did well to recover so quickly from a bad error three out on that occasion and kept on too strongly for Sh Boom and Chauvinist. Lord Sam was stepped up in class on his only subsequent start, in the Royal & SunAlliance Novices' Hurdle at Cheltenham, where he lost his unbeaten record but acquitted himself well, nonetheless. He began to work his way into contention going to four out, hit two out when unsighted as Coolnagorna drifted across him, and kept on until unable to find any extra in the final hundred yards. Lord Sam passed the post in fourth, five and three quarter lengths behind the winner Hardy Eustace, but was promoted to third on the disqualification of the runner-up Coolnagorna.

HBLB Middlesex Novices' Hurdle, Kempton—Lord Sam holds a narrow lead over Sh Boom at the last

Plain Peeps' "Lord Sam"

Lord Sam (IRE) (b. or br.g. 1996)	Supreme Leader (b 1982)	Bustino (b 1971)	Busted
			Ship Yard
		Princess Zena (b 1975)	Habitat
			Guiding Light
	Russian Gale (IRE) (br 1988)	Strong Gale (br 1975)	Lord Gayle
			Sterntau
		People (br 1983)	Al Sirat
			Hide Well

Lord Sam might be a sketchy jumper of hurdles, but too much attention shouldn't be paid to that fact when it comes to assessing his chasing prospects. There are numerous examples of horses who haven't impressed with their technique over hurdles and yet have proved accomplished jumpers of fences, one reason being that they treat the bigger obstacles with more respect. The stocky Lord Sam is a chasing type in appearance and is bred for the job, too, being by Supreme Leader out of a mare who won a three-mile chase, a handicap at Clonmel to be precise. Lord Sam is the second foal of Russian Gale. Her first, Rushing Bye (by Rontino), was a poor maiden hurdler in Ireland; and her third, Lord Sam's year-younger brother Dunshaughlin, who cost IR 51,000 guineas as a three-year-old, finished sixth of sixteen in a bumper at Newton Abbot in April, his only start to date. The next dam People is an unraced half-sister to the smart hurdler and Irish Cesarewitch winner Potato Merchant. Lord Sam, who will stay three miles, has raced only on good ground or softer and he acts on soft. *V. R. A. Dartnall*

LORD SANDROVITCH (IRE) 8 b.g. Be My Native (USA) – Killiney Side (General Ironside) [2002/3 c103x, h–: c16g[6] c24d[3] 21d[5] 20g[pu] Feb 22] useful-looking   **c– x**   **h93**

gelding: fair chaser, badly let down by jumping since winning novice in 2001/2: modest form on first of 2 starts back over hurdles, lame when blinkered on second: probably stays 3m: raced on good going or softer (acts on soft): has had tongue tied. *M. W. Easterby*

LORDS BEST (IRE)   7 b.g. Mister Lord (USA) – Ballinlonig Star (Black Minstrel) [2002/3 h107: 21v* 22d* 24d⁴ 24s³ Mar 22] workmanlike gelding: fairly useful hurdler: won novices at Kempton and Wincanton in November and handicap at Bangor in March, making all to beat Jacdor by 3 lengths for final success: will prove best at 3m+: acts on heavy going, probably on good to firm: has drifted/jumped right under pressure. *A. King*   **h122**

LORD SCROOP (IRE)   9 br.g. Supreme Leader – Henry Woman (IRE) (Mandalus) [2002/3 c78, h–: c24dᵖᵘ Apr 29] sturdy gelding: poor maiden hurdler/chaser : stays 3m: acts on good to firm and heavy going: tried blinkered/tongue tied: sold 4,200 gns Doncaster May Sales, subsequently placed several times in points. *Mrs K. Walton*   **c–**
h–

LORD SEAMUS   8 b.g. Arctic Lord – Erica Superba (Langton Heath) [2002/3 c123, h83: c23g⁵ c30dꟷ c24s³ c32g c24m³ Apr 19] compact gelding: fair chaser on balance of form: stays 4m: acts on firm and soft going. *K. C. Bailey*   **c106**
h–

LORD STRICKLAND   10 b.g. Strong Gale – Lady Rag (Ragapan) [2002/3 c103, h100: 22m c20d³ 22m³ c23m³ c21m* c21fꟷ Aug 13] good-topped gelding: fair handicap hurdler/chaser: several creditable efforts prior to winning over fences at Newton Abbot in July: stays 3m: acts on soft and firm going: makes mistakes. *P. J. Hobbs*   **c109 x**
h104 x

LORD THOMAS (IRE)   5 b.g. Grand Lodge (USA) – Noble Rocket (Reprimand) [2002/3 F16d Feb 1] €6,500 4-y-o: first foal: half-brother to useful sprinter Dragon Flyer (by Tagula): dam unraced sister to useful 7f winner Royal Rebuke: showed nothing in bumper on debut. *A. J. Wilson*   **F–**

LORD TOKEN   9 b.g. Lighter – Lady Token (Roscoe Blake) [2002/3 h–: c25dᵖᵘ 20d May 23] medium-sized gelding: no sign of ability. *Mrs S. J. Smith*   **c–**
h–

LORD TRANSCEND (IRE)   6 gr.g. Aristocracy – Capincur Lady (Over The River (FR)) [2002/3 h84p: 16v* 16d* 23s* 20g⁵ Apr 5]   **h148 p**

The fortunes of trainer Howard Johnson took a decided turn for the better in 2002/3. A total of thirty-three races won by his stable was more than double the previous season's haul, and his best since 1995/6, while total prize-money won was comfortably greater than the amount earned during the previous two seasons put together. Johnson has every reason to think that 2003/4 will prove even more

Premier Stayers' Hurdle, Haydock—
the grey Lord Transcend puts up a smart effort to defeat Deano's Beeno

successful, especially as he will have charge of Royal Rosa, who broke the record for a jumper at public auction when bought for 340,000 guineas at Doncaster in May. Royal Rosa, whose three wins in bumpers for Nicky Henderson included one in the Paddy Power Champion INH Flat race at Punchestown, is a very promising youngster, but no more promising than a six-year-old that Johnson has had in his care since he was bought for a mere IR £30,000 as an unraced four-year-old at the 2001 Derby Sale. This is Lord Transcend, the winner of the first four of his five starts, all of them over hurdles, and a horse Johnson holds in very high regard. 'I've had a lot of good horses, including Morceli, Direct Route and Ushers Island, and I don't often get carried away, but I really do think this could be the one,' said Johnson, after Lord Transcend had completed his hat-trick when making all in a handicap at Newcastle in November, his previous wins having been gained in a novice at the same course the previous season and a handicap at Hexham on his reappearance. Two months later, Lord Transcend showed that his trainer hadn't been guilty of overestimating his ability. Stepped up markedly in class and also in trip, from two miles to virtually three miles, Lord Transcend upset the odds laid on Deano's Beeno in the Grade 2 Premier Stayers' Hurdle at Haydock. It's true Deano's Beeno wasn't in one of his more co-operative moods, but it still required a smart performance from Lord Transcend to get the better of him. Lord Transcend, having taken over at the seventh, responded really well when challenged persistently by Deano's Beeno after two out, holding on by a neck as the pair pulled twenty lengths clear of third-placed Stromness. The contest provided a good test of stamina which brought out the best in Lord Transcend, unlike his only subsequent race. This was the Grade 1 Aintree Hurdle run over two and a half miles on ground much less testing than at Haydock, and in finishing fifth to Sacundai, beaten fourteen lengths, Lord Transcend lost little in defeat. The lengthy, angular Lord Transcend remains a good prospect, and he looks just the sort to take high rank among the staying novice chasers in 2003/4.

		Lord Gayle	Sir Gaylord
	Aristocracy	(b 1965)	Sticky Case
	(b 1974)	Roxboro	Sheshoon
Lord Transcend (IRE)		(ch 1968)	Sally Stream
(gr.g. 1997)		Over The River	Luthier
	Capincur Lady	(ch 1974)	Medenine
	(gr 1984)	All Put	Letricolore
		(gr 1968)	What Ever

Lord Transcend is the fifth foal of the two-mile hurdle winner Capincur Lady, whose other winners include the fair staying hurdler Captain Clooney (by Supreme Leader) and Lord Transcend's full brother Ardnataggle, a modest staying chaser. The next two dams both won over hurdles, and Lord Transcend's great grandam What Ever produced several other winners, including the fair staying chaser Willy What. Lord Transcend is by Limestone Lad's sire Aristocracy, so he certainly has plenty of stamina in his pedigree and will stay very long distances. He has so far raced only on good going or softer. *J. Howard Johnson*

LORD VILLE (FR)   4 b.g. Useful (FR) – Triaina (Lancastrian) [2002/3 16d⁶ 16d⁵ 17d⁶ 17v 17f⁵ 16f* Apr 21] leggy ex-French gelding: eighth foal: half-brother to 3 winners, including 2m hurdler Riviaina (by Riverval): dam never ran: thrice-raced on Flat, winning 11.5f non-thoroughbred event in May for T. Civel: modest form over hurdles in Britain, won 3-runner conditional jockeys handicap at Wincanton: raced around 2m: acts on firm going, ran poorly on heavy. *P. J. Hobbs*   **h98**

LORD WARFORD   8 b.g. Bustino – Jupiter's Message (Jupiter Island) [2002/3 h81: c21m⁵ c16s⁵ c19sᵖᵘ c21d⁴ c24m⁴ Mar 23] sturdy gelding: very disappointing since early-2000/1, including over fences: stays 2¾m: acts on good to soft going: has had tongue tied, including when successful. *C. L. Popham*   **c– h–**

LORD WHO (IRE)   6 b.g. Mister Lord (USA) – Le Bavellon (Le Bavard (FR)) [2002/3 F20s² F16s 16s⁵ 24d* Mar 17] second foal: half-brother to a winning pointer by Good Thyne: dam winning pointer: won point in 2002: fair form in bumpers: much better effort in maiden hurdles at Limerick when winning in March by 3 lengths from Satcoman: will stay beyond 3m. *P. M. J. Doyle, Ireland*   **h109 F94**

LORD YORK (IRE)   11 b. or br.g. Strong Gale – Bunkilla (Arctic Slave) [2002/3 c138, h109: c16g⁴ c21m⁵ c20dᵖᵘ 17m³ 21g⁴ c16g* c16g c16f³ Apr 25] rangy gelding: fair   **c125 § h110 §**

hurdler: handicap chaser, fairly useful form in 2002/3: back with former trainer (after 2 runs for M. Todhunter), won at Ascot in March by 3½ lengths from Super Nomad: taken on for lead and below form last 2 starts, downing tools on second occasion: best around 2m nowadays: has won on soft going, ideally suited by good or firmer (acts on firm): usually blinkered/visored: tongue tied third outing: best forcing pace: unreliable. *Ian Williams*

LORENZINO (IRE) 6 ch.g. Thunder Gulch (USA) – Russian Ballet (USA) (Nijinsky (CAN)) [2002/3 h126+: 23f⁶ 19mᶠ 24d 22v⁶ 22d 20dᵘʳ 22sᵖᵘ Mar 15] close-coupled gelding: fairly useful handicap hurdler, little worthwhile form after first outing: barely stays 3m: acts on firm and soft going: tongue tied last 2 starts: temperament under suspicion. *Jonjo O'Neill*   **h124 d**

LORGNETTE 9 b.m. Emperor Fountain – Speckyfoureyes (Blue Cashmere) [2002/3 h102: 22g⁴ c24d c24m² c19s² c24d⁴ 24s 22d² 22s⁵ 22d³ 22f² 22f³ Apr 21] rather sparsely-made mare: modest handicap hurdler/novice chaser, not convincing with jumping over fences: stays 3m: acts on firm and soft going. *R. H. Alner*   **c95**
h98

L'ORPHELIN 8 ch.g. Gildoran – Balula (Balinger) [2002/3 24sᵖᵘ 24s 16m⁴ Mar 20] small, rather plain gelding: poor maiden hurdler: should stay beyond 2m: acts on good to firm going (bumper winner on good to soft). *C. Tizzard*   **h71**

LOST DIRECTION 8 b.m. Heading North – Precis (Pitpan) [2002/3 c20gᵖᵘ c26gᵖᵘ 24m⁵ Jun 29] first known foal: dam, out of smart staying chaser Ottery News, won 17f hurdle: no sign of ability in 2 novice hunter chases or novice hurdle: whipped round start on debut. *O. J. Carter*   **c–**
h–

LOST IN NORMANDY (IRE) 6 b.g. Treasure Hunter – Auntie Honnie (IRE) (Radical) [2002/3 F17d⁵ F17d 16s 17sᵖᵘ 21v⁵ Feb 11] lengthy gelding: first foal: dam well beaten in Irish bumper: much better effort in bumpers when fifth at Hereford on debut for G. McCourt: first sign of ability over hurdles when fifth in novice at Sedgefield final start. *Mrs L. Williamson*   **h64**
F82

LOST IN THE RAIN (IRE) 4 b.g. King's Theatre (IRE) – Shanira (Shirley Heights) [2002/3 16g⁴ 16f* 16s⁵ Feb 9] sturdy gelding: useful on Flat (best effort at 1¼m): made good start to hurdling career, winning juveniles at Tralee in August and Listowel in September: tongue tied, below that form when fifth of 8 in Grade 2 at Leopardstown final start: may not do better. *N. Meade, Ireland*   **h114 +**

LOST THE PLOT 8 b.m. Lyphento (USA) – La Comedienne (Comedy Star (USA)) [2002/3 h86: 20m³ 21m* 22m* 21g² Oct 12] tall, leggy mare: modest hurdler: won mares maiden at Southwell and handicap at Fontwell in September: will stay 3m: acts on firm and good to soft going: shaped as if all wasn't well when tongue tied. *D. W. P. Arbuthnot*   **h96**

LOST TIME (IRE) 6 b.g. Glacial Storm (USA) – Overtime (IRE) (Executive Perk) [2002/3 h89p, F97p: F16s* 16d³ Jan 26] tall gelding: better effort in bumpers when winning at Navan in November: third start over hurdles and easily best effort when third to Back In Front in maiden at Leopardstown: will be suited by 2½m: room for improvement in his jumping but sure to win races over hurdles. *C. Roche, Ireland*   **h111 p**
F104

LOS VADOS (GER) 4 b.g. Dashing Blade – La Vega (GER) (Turfkonig (GER)) [2002/3 16m⁶ 16m⁴ 16mᵘʳ Apr 21] ex-German gelding: won over 9f at Hoppegarten at 3 yrs for A. Wohler: ridden by 7-lb claimer, signs of a little ability over hurdles. *Ian Williams*   **h72**

LOTHIAN EMERALD 6 ch.m. Greensmith – Lothian Rose (Roscoe Blake) [2002/3 F17s 17dᵖᵘ Jun 5] 1,500 (privately) 4-y-o: workmanlike mare: second foal: dam novice hurdler, stayed 3m: no show in mares bumper (pulled hard) or novice selling hurdle: sold 800 gns Ascot July Sales, subsequently pulled up in 2 points. *D. McCain*   **h–**
F–

LOTTERY LIL 8 ch.m. Petoski – Quarry Machine (Laurence O) [2002/3 c24gᵖᵘ May 31] sturdy mare: maiden pointer: mistakes in mares hunter chase at Stratford. *I. Hudson*   **c–**

LOTTERY TICKET (IRE) 14 b.g. The Parson – Beauty Run (Deep Run) [2002/3 c–x, h–: c26dᵘʳ Jun 5] tall gelding: winning hurdler/chaser: no form outside points for long time: tried blinkered: sketchy jumper. *S. J. Robinson*   **c– x**
h–

LOUDY ROWDY (IRE) 12 br.g. Strong Gale – Express Film (Ashmore (FR)) [2002/3 c–, h–: 22g⁵ c21dᵖᵘ 20g³ Apr 21] bumper winner: poor maiden hurdler/chaser: has had tongue tied. *Mrs J. K. M. Oliver*   **c–**
h–

LOUGAROO (FR) 4 ch.c. Snurge – Titian Queen (Sicyos (USA)) [2002/3 15dᶠ 16d* 17v² 18v* 16v³ 17s Jan 25] leggy colt: fourth foal: dam 1¼m winner in France: fairly useful form in juvenile hurdles, won at Bordeaux in October and Auteuil in December: **h113**

well held in graded company at Chepstow and Cheltenham last 2 starts: will stay beyond 2¼m: acts on heavy ground. *G. Macaire, France*

LOUGHBEG RAMBLER 8 ch.g. Weld – Rose Rambler (Scallywag) [2002/3 c24d6 c24s c16m2 c16g* c16g* c19f2 24g2 22d3 c20d4 Nov 17] lengthy gelding: half-brother to modest staying hurdler/chaser The Snow Burn (by River God): dam unraced sister to fairly useful promising chaser Naughty Future: winning pointer: poor maiden hurdler: modest chaser: won 2 handicaps at Tralee in August: effective at 2m to 3m: acts on firm and good to soft going: often tongue tied. *D. Hassett, Ireland*   **c93 h80**

LOUGHCREW (IRE) 7 ch.g. Good Thyne (USA) – Marys Course (Crash Course) [2002/3 24vpu Jan 29] ex-Irish gelding: second foal: half-brother to bumper winner Radcliffe (by Supreme Leader): dam fair hurdler/chaser up to 3m: modest hurdler: sold out of M. Hourigan's stable 18,000 gns Doncaster November (2001) Sales: well held since, leaving B. Jones before only outing in 2002/3: stays 3m: acts on good to firm ground. *L. Lungo*   **h–**

LOUGH LEIN LADY (IRE) 8 ch.m. Alphabatim (USA) – Cap Reform (IRE) (Phardante (FR)) [2002/3 c–, h–: c20dpu Apr 29] won maiden Irish point in 2000: no form in Britain: has had tongue tied. *A. W. Carroll*   **c– h–**

LOUGH RYNN (IRE) 5 b.g. Beneficial – Liffey Lady (Camden Town) [2002/3 F16d6 F17s5 19d Feb 28] tall, rather unfurnished gelding: seventh foal: half-brother to fairly useful staying hurdler/chaser Yeoman Sailor (by Roselier) and fair hurdler Cromwells Keep (by Castle Keep), stays 2¾m: dam lightly-raced maiden: modest form in 2 bumpers: well beaten in novice at Newbury on hurdling debut. *Miss H. C. Knight*   **h– F83**

LOUISES GLORY (IRE) 8 ch.g. Executive Perk – Ring-Em-All (Decent Fellow) [2002/3 18d6 19d Nov 26] lengthy, angular ex-Irish gelding: fifth foal: half-brother to fair hurdlers around 2½m April Seventh and Lisa's Storm (both by Glacial Storm): dam unraced half-sister to dam of very smart staying hurdler Splendid Thyne: modest hurdler/maiden chaser for E. Sheehy: well held over hurdles both starts in Britain: raced mainly around 2m on good ground or softer (acts on heavy): tried blinkered: usually tongue tied. *D. J. Wintle*   **c– h–**

LOUP BLEU (USA) 5 b.g. Nureyev (USA) – Louve Bleue (USA) (Irish River (FR)) [2002/3 19d4 17g4 17v2 Dec 28] ex-French gelding: 1¼m winner on Flat at 3 yrs: fairly useful maiden hurdler: sold out of J-P. Gallorini's stable €50,000 Goffs November Sale after second start: below best when second in novice at Taunton on British debut: raced up to 19f on good ground or softer (acts on heavy). *P. J. Hobbs*   **h107**

LOVE DIAMONDS (IRE) 7 b.g. Royal Academy (USA) – Baby Diamonds (Habitat) [2002/3 h74x: 17g 16mrtr 16g 16g4 16mpu 16g4 Jul 15] rather leggy gelding: poor maiden hurdler: has had tongue tied: pulls hard and makes mistakes: not one to trust. *Miss C. Dyson*   **h– §**

LOVE KISS (IRE) 8 b.g. Brief Truce (USA) – Pendulina (Prince Tenderfoot (USA)) [2002/3 h81: 16d3 20d4 16gpu 16d4 17gpu Mar 15] tall, rather leggy gelding: poor hurdler: left W. Storey after third start: best around 2m: raced on good going or softer (acts on soft): usually tongue tied. *M. Dods*   **h73**

LOVE POTION 8 br.m. Neltino – Celtic Honey (Celtic Cone) [2002/3 h83: 21d3 16gpu May 17] lengthy mare: poor maiden hurdler: well below form both starts in 2002/3: best at 2m: unraced on extremes of going. *E. L. James*   **h–**

LOVERS TALE 5 b.g. Pursuit of Love – Kintail (Kris) [2002/3 F–: F17s 17s 16g Mar 16] well held in bumpers or over hurdles. *H. M. Kavanagh*   **h– F–**

LOVE VENTURE 9 b.m. Pursuit of Love – Our Shirley (Shirley Heights) [2002/3 16gpu Dec 13] angular mare: maiden hurdler: off over 3 years, showed nothing on return. *Miss M. E. Rowland*   **h–**

LOWENA 5 ch.m. Carlingford Castle – Walnut Way (Gambling Debt) [2002/3 F18s 20gpu Mar 16] fifth foal: dam, fairly useful chaser, stayed 2¾m: no sign of ability in mares bumper/novice hurdle. *M. R. Hoad*   **h– F–**

LOWRY (USA) 5 b. or br.g. Gulch (USA) – Aviara (USA) (Cox's Ridge (USA)) [2002/3 16dpu Nov 12] tall gelding: half-brother to fairly useful but ungenuine hurdler up to 25f Prokofiev (by Nureyev): little sign of ability on Flat or in novice hurdle. *J. S. King*   **h–**

LOXLEY 4 b.g. Ezzoud (IRE) – Shewillifshewants (IRE) (Alzao (USA)) [2002/3 17spu 17g 17d6 Aug 24] little sign of ability on Flat for M. Buckley or in 3 juvenile hurdles: sold to join P. Monteith 1,100 gns Doncaster September Sales. *Mrs S. J. Smith*   **h–**

LOZZY LEE (IRE) 5 b.g. Zaffaran (USA) – Amazing Lee (IRE) (Amazing Bust) **F90**
[2002/3 F12d F18v² F17s⁴ Dec 26] 30,000 4-y-o: big, good-topped gelding: first foal:
dam unraced half-sister to smart chaser up to 3m Promalee and useful hurdler/chaser
Michael Mor, stays 3m: fair form in 3 bumpers. *D. J. Caro*

LUCIEN (IRE) 5 ch.g. Catrail (USA) – What A Candy (USA) (Key To The Mint **h–**
(USA)) [2002/3 F77: F16m³ F17g 16mᵖᵘ 17d 16d 16s 16vᵖᵘ 16d 19m Apr 8] angular **F82**
gelding: modest in bumpers: sold out of N. Henderson's stable 4,200 gns Doncaster
August Sales after reappearance: no form subsequently, mostly over hurdles. *M. F. Harris*

LUCKY BAY (IRE) 7 b.g. Convinced – Current Liability (Caribo) [2002/3 h100: **c126**
c23f⁵ c25m² c24d² c24d* c24s⁵ c32g⁶ c25dᵖᵘ Apr 4] well-made gelding: fair hurdler: **h–**
fairly useful novice chaser: best effort when winning Grade 2 Systems By Design
Worcester Novices' Chase at Newbury in November by 5 lengths from Joly Bey: likely
to prove best at 3m+: acts on firm and good to soft going. *Miss H. C. Knight*

LUCKY BRUSH (IRE) 9 b.g. Brush Aside (USA) – Luck Daughter (Lucky Brief) **c94**
[2002/3 c69: c26g⁶ c25d³ c25g⁵ Mar 21] winning pointer: easily best effort in hunter
chases when third in novice at Kelso (first start after leaving Miss C. Barclay) in March:
stays 25f. *N. W. Alexander*

LUCKY CATCH (IRE) 5 b.g. Safety Catch (USA) – Lucky Monday (Lucky **F74**
Wednesday) [2002/3 F17d Mar 2] IR £4,000 3-y-o: sixth foal: dam once-raced half-sister
to high-class hurdler Cockney Lad and smart 1¼m filly Cockney Lass: tenth of 15 in
bumper at Carlisle on debut: sold 7,000 gns Doncaster May Sales. *R. C. Guest*

LUCKY CLOVER 11 ch.g. Push On – Winning Clover (Winden) [2002/3 c123?, h–: **c119 §**
27gᵖᵘ c26d⁴ c24m c24f⁴ c31d c31d⁵ᵈⁱˢ Dec 13] well-made gelding: twice-raced hurdler: **h– §**
fairly useful chaser on his day: best efforts in 2002/3 in 31f cross-country races at
Cheltenham, disqualified after briefly going wrong way on second occasion: off nearly 5
months, ran poorly in similar race at Punchestown in early-May: stays 31f: acts on firm
and good to soft going: has won with/without blinkers: has broken blood vessel: often
front runner: temperamental. *C. Tizzard*

LUCKY DO (IRE) 6 b.g. Camden Town – Lane Baloo (Lucky Brief) [2002/3 F80: **h75**
21s 17s² 16g Feb 22] medium-sized gelding: modest in bumpers in 2001/2: poor form
over hurdles: should stay 2½m. *R. Dickin*

LUCKY DUCK 6 ch.g. Minster Son – Petroc Concert (Tina's Pet) [2002/3 F–: F17d **F77**
Oct 26] better effort in bumpers when seventh of 18 at Carlisle in October. *Mrs
A. Hamilton*

LUCKY HEATHER (IRE) 6 b.m. Soviet Lad (USA) – Idrak (Young Generation) **h53**
[2002/3 h–: 16g⁴ 16m 16m⁵ 16d⁴ 16s Jan 3] poor on Flat (stays 1¼m well): bad maiden
hurdler: raced at 2m: acts on good to firm and good to soft going. *R. J. Baker*

LUCKY JOE (IRE) 10 br.g. Denel (FR) – Breezy Dawn (Kemal (FR)) [2002/3 c–, **c70**
h65: c26m³ 22s⁶ Jun 3] winning pointer: poor form over hurdles or in steeplechases: stays **h71**
3¼m: acts on soft and good to firm going. *J. White*

Systems By Design Worcester Novices' Chase, Newbury—
Lucky Bay (left) holds a narrow lead two out over Joly Bey and One Knight (hidden)

LUCKY LEADER (IRE) 8 b.g. Supreme Leader – Lucky House (Pollerton) [2002/3 c17s^{pu} c24s^{pu} c24s^2 c26s^3 c24g^F Apr 2] lengthy ex-Irish gelding: winning pointer: seemingly modest form in steeplechases (left J. Brassil after reappearance) when placed in novices at Chepstow in February and Plumpton in March. *N. R. Mitchell*   c92 ?

LUCKY LUCKY BOB (USA) 6 b.g. Alleged (USA) – Alloy (FR) (Pharly (FR)) [2002/3 F–: 16v^3 17v^6 16s Jan 13] well held in 2 bumpers and on Flat: bought £1,000 Ascot April (2002) Sales: poor form in novice hurdles. *P. R. Chamings*   h75

LUCKY MASTER (IRE) 11 b.g. Roselier (FR) – Golden Chestnut (Green Shoon) [2002/3 c96, h87: 24d c29d^3 c30s^3 Dec 18] sturdy gelding: modest hurdler: poor handicap chaser nowadays: probably stays 3¾m: acts on soft and good to firm going. *John R. Upson*   c77 h–

LUCKY MICK (IRE) 8 b.g. Husyan (USA) – Kindly Go (IRE) (Buckley) [2002/3 h88: 20m^4 c25m^6 17v 20s^{pu} Mar 6] well-made gelding: well held on chasing debut: modest hurdler: form in 2002/3 only on reappearance in May: reportedly lame final start: should stay 3m: acts on firm and soft going: tongue tied. *J. I. A. Charlton*   c– h83

LUCKY NOMAD 7 br.g. Nomadic Way (USA) – Daleena (Dalesa) [2002/3 20m^{pu} 19m^4 17d^4 19g^6 19d^{pu} Oct 19] 2,000 4-y-o: medium-sized gelding: seventh foal: half-brother to poor 2m chaser Another Red (by Move Off) and winning hurdler Old Mill Stream (by Rapid River), probably stayed 25f: dam winning pointer: no form over hurdles: has worn cheekpieces: sold 2,000 gns Doncaster November Sales, subsequently showed nothing in points. *I. W. McInnes*   h–

LUCKY PENNY 7 ch.m. Karinga Bay – Redgrave Rose (Tug of War) [2002/3 F88: F16d 22g^6 Nov 9] workmanlike mare: fair form at best in bumpers: looked difficult ride when remote sixth of 13 in mares novice at Wincanton on hurdling debut. *K. Bishop*   h–

LUCKY SHAMROCK 9 b.m. Muqadar (USA) – Bonnie Wednesday (Lucky Wednesday) [2002/3 17s^{pu} Dec 26] no sign of ability in bumper or novice selling hurdle: joined K. Wingrove. *W. G. M. Turner*   h–

LUCKY SINNA (IRE) 7 b. or br.g. Insan (USA) – Bit of A Chance (Lord Ha Ha) [2002/3 h92+: 22f^2 May 10] rangy gelding: will make a chaser: modest maiden hurdler: stays 2¾m: acts on firm and good to soft going (third in bumper on soft): has had tongue tied. *J. T. Gifford*   h92

LUCKY TEENY (IRE) 6 ch.m. Phardante (FR) – Rusty Iron (General Ironside) [2002/3 F76: 22s^{pu} 20s^F 17g Nov 7] modest in mares bumpers: no form over hurdles: should stay at least 2½m. *D. G. Bridgwater*   h–

LUCKY TIME (IRE) 11 b.g. Phardante (FR) – Rock Ellie (Random Shot) [2002/3 c–: c16d^2 c19d* c25m^{pu} c25g^3 c25m^3 21m^{pu} c27m^4 Jul 25] modest chaser: won maiden at Hereford in May: ran no sort of race last 2 starts (hurdling debut on first occasion): stays 25f: acts on good to soft and good to firm going. *Ferdy Murphy*   c92 h–

LUCKY TYROL (IRE) 5 ch.g. Midhish – Tirol's Luck (IRE) (Tirol) [2002/3 19d^{pu} Dec 4] IR £3,400 3-y-o: first foal: dam placed at 7f/1m on Flat at 3 yrs: tongue tied, showed nothing in novice hurdle on debut. *N. B. Mason*   h–

LUCY LANCASTER 8 b.m. Elegant Monarch – Lancaster Rose (Canadel II) [2002/3 22g^{bd} Apr 12] half-sister to modest staying chaser Rose Lancaster and winning 21f hurdler Henry Lancaster (both by Oh Henry) and modest chaser up to 21f Benjamin Lancaster (by Dubassoff): dam unraced: towards rear when brought down fifth, having jumped poorly, in novice hurdle at Stratford on debut: withdrawn on vet's advice later in month. *Miss G. Browne*   h–

LUCYS LAD 9 b.g. Le Moss – Lucy Lastic (Tycoon II) [2002/3 c–x, h–: c25d* c25d^5 c24s^F c24m^2 c25g^{pu} c26s* c23v* c24s^{ur} c24s^{ur} c24s^4 c26d^{pu} c30s^{pu} Mar 4] angular gelding: fair chaser: won handicap at Towcester in May, minor event at Fontwell (first start for 5 months) in December and handicap at Leicester in January: stays 3¼m well: acted on heavy and good to firm going: made mistakes: dead. *Miss Venetia Williams*   c100 x h–

LUDERE (IRE) 8 ch.g. Desse Zenny (USA) – White Jasmin (Jalmood (USA)) [2002/3 h91: 20d 19g^5 22v^6 21d^6 20s* 24s 22s^3 24d^4 24s^2 26g^{pu} Mar 12] angular gelding: modest handicap hurdler: won at Leicester in December: stays 3m: acts on any going. *B. J. Llewellyn*   h91

LUFTIKUS (GER) 6 ch.g. Formidable (USA) – La Paz (GER) (Roi Dagobert) [2002/3 16d^3 20s 16g Mar 12] workmanlike ex-German gelding: half-brother to German middle-distance winner Ludwig (by Goofalik): dam winning hurdler: successful 4 times up to 1½m on Flat, including at Cologne for C. Von Der Recke in September: best effort   h80 over hurdles when third in novice at Huntingdon, finishing tired after pulling very hard early: may have stamina limitations. *A. G. Hobbs*

LUKE WARM   13 ch.g. Nearly A Hand – Hot 'n Scopey (Hot Brandy) [2002/3 c102, **c81** h–: c25gᵖᵘ c24d⁵ c24s⁴ c24v³ c26s⁵ c24d⁵ c26s³ c24d⁴ c24m⁴ Apr 22] compact gelding: **h–** fair handicap chaser at best: only poor in 2002/3: barely stays 3¼m: acts on good to firm and heavy going. *D. R. Gandolfo*

LUMACA (IRE)   8 b.g. Riberetto – Broken Mirror (Push On) [2002/3 h76: 26s⁶ **c66** c25dᵖᵘ c25s⁶ c25d³ Feb 23] workmanlike gelding: poor handicap hurdler: similar form **h–** over fences: best at 3m+: acts on heavy going (bumper form on good to firm). *J. Neville*

LUMBACK (IRE)   4 b.g. Desert Style (IRE) – Bellingham Jester (Jester) [2002/3 **F–** F14d Nov 25] sixth foal: half-brother to winner in Italy up to 10.5f by Archway and 6f winner in Singapore by Nordico: dam showed little on Flat and over hurdles: tailed off in bumper on debut. *N. Wilson*

LUNA NOVA   5 b.g. Aragon – Lucidity (Vision (USA)) [2002/3 h–: 17sᵖᵘ 17g⁶ 22d **h–** 17gᵖᵘ Sep 6] leggy gelding: of no account: tried tongue tied. *D. Moffatt*

LUNAR CRYSTAL (IRE)   5 b.g. Shirley Heights – Solar Crystal (IRE) (Alzao **h124** (USA)) [2002/3 h104: 16m² 18f* 16m* 17s* 17d* 17m* 16m⁵ 16m⁶ Feb 21] leggy gelding: fairly useful hurdler: made most when winning novices at Fontwell (4-y-o event), Stratford, Market Rasen, Bangor and Newton Abbot (handicap, swished tail) between June and August: raced around 2m: acts on firm and soft going: below form in visor seventh start. *M. C. Pipe*

LUNARDI (IRE)   5 b.g. Indian Ridge – Gold Tear (USA) (Tejano (USA)) [2002/3 **c72** h97: c25g³ 16m Apr 21] neat gelding: modest hurdler in 2001/2: third in hunter at Market **h–** Rasen on chasing debut: took little interest back over hurdles: probably stays 25f: acts on good to firm and heavy going: visored twice. *D. L. Williams*

LUNAR DRAM   5 ch.g. Cosmonaut – Moonshine Malt (Superlative) [2002/3 F16v **F–** F16s Dec 16] workmanlike gelding: first foal: dam unraced: signs of only a little ability in 2 bumpers. *M. Dods*

LUNAR LORD   7 b.g. Elmaamul (USA) – Cache (Bustino) [2002/3 h93+: 16s Jan 30] **h–** leggy gelding: modest handicap hurdler: fit from Flat, well held only start in 2002/3: will stay at least 2½m: possibly needs going softer than good. *D. Burchell*

LUNAR MAXWELL   8 b.g. Dancing High – Pauper Moon (Pauper) [2002/3 h90: **c94** c25g³ c25s² c25v⁴ c30d⁵ Feb 8] rather leggy, close-coupled gelding: modest hurdler: **h–** similar form over fences: stays 3¼m: acts on good to soft and good to firm going (bumper form on heavy): not an easy ride. *J. I. A. Charlton*

LUPIN (FR)   4 b.c. Luchiroverte (IRE) – Amarante II (FR) (Brezzo (FR)) [2002/3 **h104** F16m⁵ 18s 16s* 18s⁶ Apr 25] rather unfurnished colt: fourth foal: half-brother to useful **F92** 2m chase winner Incas (by Video Rock) and cross-country chase/Flat winner Jojo (by Kadalko): dam, successful around 1¼m, half-sister to smart 21f chase winner Gabion: fifth of 19 in maiden at Kempton: best effort in 4-y-o hurdles at Enghien when winning in April. *F. Doumen, France*

LURPAK LEGEND (IRE)   9 br.g. Castle Keep – Welsh Tan (Welsh Saint) [2002/3 **c70** c73, h83: 16d 20d 19g³ 24m 21s⁶ c20g² Aug 3] useful-looking gelding: poor hurdler/ **h73** maiden chaser: stays 2½m: acts on firm and good to soft going: held up and best in strongly-run race: none too fluent over fences: sold 3,300 gns Doncaster September Sales. *Mrs M. Reveley*

LUTIN VILLE (FR)   4 b.g. Rifapour (IRE) – Singing Rodney (Goldneyev (USA)) **c131** [2002/3 15s 15d 16s* c15s* c17s* 17v⁴ c17s* c20s⁴ c19s² Apr 25] first foal: dam won **h119** up to 19f over fences: fairly useful hurdler, won at Enghien in September: better over fences: successful twice there in autumn and in Group 3 Prix Duc d'Anjou at Auteuil (beat Vesuve 2 lengths) in March: good efforts in useful company at Auteuil and Enghien afterwards, poor one in Group 1 at former course in May: stays 2½m: raced on going softer than good (acts on heavy). *T. Civel, France*

LUXEMBOURG   4 b.g. Bigstone (IRE) – Princess Borghese (USA) (Nijinsky **h–** (CAN)) [2002/3 F12d 16dᵘʳ 16d Dec 21] 29,000 3-y-o: lengthy, angular gelding: fifth **F–** foal: half-brother to winning 2¾m hurdler Bauble (by Sanglamore): dam 1¼m winner: well held in bumper on debut: visored, looked hard ride when tailed off on completed start in juvenile hurdles. *N. A. Twiston-Davies*

LUZCADOU (FR)   10 b.g. Cadoudal (FR) – Luzenia (FR) (Armos) [2002/3 c124, **c124** h–: c20s* Nov 16] good-topped gelding: fairly useful handicap chaser: won weakly- **h–**

contested event at Ayr on only start in 2002/3, beating The Grey Dyer 6 lengths: best form around 2½m on soft/heavy going: usually blinkered/visored: sometimes let down by jumping. *Ferdy Murphy*

LYDIA'S ECHO 7 b.m. Backchat (USA) – Lydia's Well (Current Magic) [2002/3 F–: F16d 22fᵖᵘ 17s May 28] of little account. *J. W. Mullins* h–
F–

LYNCHAHAUN (IRE) 7 b. or br.g. Good Thyne (USA) – Smart Decision (IRE) (Le Moss) [2002/3 20g Apr 23] IR 7,200 4-y-o: first foal: dam, winning pointer, out of half-sister to very smart staying chaser Everett: pulled up all 4 starts in Irish points: showed little on hurdling debut. *P. Monteith* h–

LYNPHORD GIRL 12 ch.m. Lyphento (USA) – Woodlands Angel (Levanter) [2002/3 c20m² c21gᶠ c20m c20d² c20g⁴ Aug 26] temperamental winning pointer in 2000: seemingly poor form when runner-up in novice chases: stays 2½m: acts on good to firm and good to soft going: makes mistakes. *Dr J. R. J. Naylor* c75

LYNRICK LADY (IRE) 7 b.m. Un Desperado (FR) – Decent Lady (Decent Fellow) [2002/3 24sᵖᵘ 25s⁵ 20v* 20d⁴ 21m Mar 22] tall ex-Irish mare: half-sister to useful staying chaser Betty's Boy (by Cataldi) and fair bumper/hurdles winner (stays 21f) Water Stratford (by Jurado): dam, Irish bumper winner/2m maiden hurdler, half-sister to useful 2m chaser Springholm: no show in 2 bumpers, won maiden Irish point in 2002: modest novice hurdler: won mares event at Chepstow in February despite wandering: should stay beyond 2½m: acts on heavy going, possibly unsuited by good to firm. *J. G. Portman* h94

LYNWOOD LEGEND 5 ch.g. Gold Dust – Beths Wish (Rustingo) [2002/3 F14g F17g Apr 19] first foal: dam bad maiden hurdler: showed more temperament than ability in 2 bumpers. *B. J. Llewellyn* F–

LYPHARD'S FABLE (USA) 12 b.g. Al Nasr (FR) – Affirmative Fable (USA) (Affirmed (USA)) [2002/3 c–, h–: c24mᵖᵘ Jun 1] compact gelding: winning hurdler: poor maiden chaser/pointer: stays 21f: acts on any going: tried blinkered: not a fluent jumper. *Mrs David Plunkett* c–
h–

LYRINGO 9 b.m. Rustingo – Lyricist (Averof) [2002/3 h–: 16gᵖᵘ 24s 18v 21mᵖᵘ Mar 31] smallish mare: winning hurdler: no form since 2000/1: has worn cheekpieces. *B. J. Llewellyn* h–

LYSANDER'S QUEST (IRE) 5 br.g. King's Theatre (IRE) – Haramayda (FR) (Doyoun) [2002/3 16g 16g Mar 12] modest maiden on Flat (stays 1¾m): better effort in maiden hurdles when ninth of 25 at Newbury on debut: likely to be suited by further than 2m. *L. Montague Hall* h87

M

MAAS (IRE) 8 br.h. Elbio – Payne's Grey (Godswalk (USA)) [2002/3 h70: 16g⁶ 16g May 29] poor maiden hurdler: raced around 2m on good going or softer: sometimes tongue tied. *N. B. Mason* h–

MA BARNICLE (IRE) 10 ch.m. Al Hareb (USA) – Soltina (Sun Prince) [2002/3 c75, h–: c16m c16d⁵ c21m⁶ c18f² c16gᵖᵘ c16gᵖᵘ Mar 16] angular mare: poor hurdler/chaser: best around 2m: acts on firm and good to soft going: tried blinkered: has had tongue tied. *T. D. McCarthy* c81
h–

MACANILLO (GER) 5 gr.g. Acatenango (GER) – Midday Girl (GER) (Black Tie Affair) [2002/3 16dᵖᵘ 16sᵖᵘ Dec 14] good-topped ex-German gelding: won over 1m at Hanover in 2002 for S. Stokes, well held on Flat in 2003: pulled up in 2 novice hurdles. *Ian Williams* h–

MACEO (GER) 9 ch.g. Acatenango (GER) – Metropolitan Star (USA) (Lyphard (USA)) [2002/3 h103: 16g* 16g⁴ 16d⁴ 16s³ 16s⁴ 20d³ 16g⁶ Mar 17] angular gelding: fair handicap hurdler: won at Wetherby in November: took little interest final outing: stays 2½m: acts on soft going: held up. *Mrs M. Reveley* h109

MAC FIVE (IRE) 8 gr.g. Sharp Victor (USA) – Fine Flame (Le Prince) [2002/3 c–: c24mᶠ c26m³ Jul 28] sturdy, lengthy gelding: fair pointer: no form in novice chases, finished lame final start. *C. L. Popham* c–

MACGEORGE (IRE) 13 b.g. Mandalus – Colleen Donn (Le Moss) [2002/3 c130, h–: c25dᵖᵘ c26vᵖᵘ c25d* c26d* c25gᵘʳ c26m² Apr 17] lengthy gelding: useful chaser: c130
h–

did well in hunters in 2002/3, winning at Hereford in February and Warwick (easily) in March: good second to Earthmover at Cheltenham: stays 3¼m: acts on good to firm and heavy going: races prominently: prone to mistakes. *R. Lee*

MACGYVER (NZ) 7 b.g. Jahafil – Corazon (NZ) (Pag-Asa (AUS)) [2002/3 14f² 14s⁴ 13v 17m⁴ 16d⁵ 16d 16gᵖᵘ c16d³ c16d² c16s⁵ c16m⁵ c16g² Mar 17] medium-sized gelding: 7f winner in New Zealand: also won over hurdles at Wanganui in June: seemingly best effort over hurdles in Britain when fifth in novice at Chepstow in October: poor form in novice chases: will prove best around 2m: acts on soft going: headstrong front runner who jumps boldly: joined H. Kavanagh. *Mrs L. C. Taylor*   **c84 h86 ?**

MACHETE MAN 8 b.g. Broadsword (USA) – Ribo Melody (Riboboy (USA)) [2002/3 c–: c16mᵖᵘ Nov 5] strong, lengthy gelding: modest form in 2 bumpers in 2000/1: failed to complete both starts over fences: headstrong: joined J. de Giles. *P. R. Webber*   **c–**

MACH FOUR (IRE) 5 b.g. Bob Back (USA) – Tasmania Star (Captain James) [2002/3 F16s F16s F16m Feb 22] 13,500 4-y-o: tall gelding: ninth foal: half-brother to 3 winners, including modest hurdler/fair chaser Slingsby (by Heraldiste), stayed 2½m: dam won in Italy: best effort in bumpers when ninth of 19 at Kempton final start, twice running wide off bend. *N. A. Twiston-Davies*   **F90**

MAC HINE (IRE) 6 b.g. Eurobus – Zoe Baird (Aragon) [2002/3 F16s* 20v⁴ 16d² 16d 21m 17g Mar 29] tall gelding: first foal: dam, winning 2m hurdler, half-sister to fairly useful hurdler up to 3m Three Rivers: green, created good impression when winning bumper at Sandown on debut in November: best effort over hurdles when runner-up to Motcomb Jam in novice at Doncaster (hung left off bridle) in January: may prove best short of 21f: needs to learn to settle. *Jonjo O'Neill*   **h101 F96**

MACKINUS (IRE) 7 b.g. Tidaro (USA) – Tepukei River (Tepukei) [2002/3 c22d⁵ c20s² c22d F16d⁶ c24s⁴ c17s² c26s³ c18s² c16d⁴ c22vᵘʳ c24s² c20s⁴ c24s* c32g Mar 12] well-made gelding: sixth foal: half-brother to bumper winner Ask The Builder (by Salluceva) and fairly useful hurdler/fair chaser Duky's River (by Duky), stays 2½m: dam, won 2m hurdle, half-sister to dam of very smart staying hurdler Minella Lad: fair in bumpers: twice-raced hurdler: modest chaser: won amateur handicap at Clonmel in February: very stiff task final start: stays 3¼m: raced on good going or softer (acts on soft): sometimes tongue tied. *P. A. Fahy, Ireland*   **c85 h– F78**

MACKOY (IRE) 10 b.g. Riverhead (USA) – Urdite (FR) (Concertino (FR)) [2002/3 c24s Mar 7] sturdy gelding: modest maiden pointer. *M. J. Gingell*   **c–**

MACNANCE (IRE) 7 b.m. Mandalus – Colleen Donn (Le Moss) [2002/3 h87: 17g² 17g² 16d* 19d² 21mᵘʳ 20m² Apr 12] angular mare: fair novice hurdler: won mares event at Leicester in November: will stay beyond 2½m: acts on good to firm and heavy going: reliable. *R. Lee*   **h103**

MACONNOR (IRE) 6 b.g. Religiously (USA) – Door Belle (Fidel) [2002/3 F72: 25mᶠ 16s⁴ 16v 16v² 16s³ Mar 15] rangy gelding: fair form over hurdles: shaped as though capable of better when placed in novices at Chepstow and Uttoxeter last 2 starts: should be suited by further than 2m. *H. D. Daly*   **h106 p**

MACREATER 5 b.m. Mazaad – Gold Caste (USA) (Singh (USA)) [2002/3 F16d F16g⁴ F17v³ F16d⁵ F17m Apr 17] unfurnished mare: second foal: dam fairly useful staying chaser: poor form in bumpers. *K. A. Morgan*   **F73**

MAC'S DIAMOND (IRE) 7 b.m. Mac's Imp (USA) – Plunket's Choice (Home Guard (USA)) [2002/3 20m⁶ 16m Oct 19] ex-Irish mare: eighth foal: half-sister to 3 winners, including 1m winner Race To Time (by Runnett): dam never ran: little sign of ability, including in points: left M. Vaughan after reappearance. *D. J. Wintle*   **h–**

MACS GILDORAN 9 b.g. Gildoran – Shamrock Bridge (Golden Love) [2002/3 c118, h–: c17v* c24vᵖᵘ c21g³ c21d² Apr 4] good-topped gelding: useful chaser: won handicap at Fairyhouse in December by 2 lengths from Ballyamber: good efforts when placed in Cathcart Chase at Cheltenham (third to La Landiere) and Topham Chase (Handicap) at Aintree (second of 29 to Clan Royal), but let down by jumping in handicap at Punchestown (respiratory tract infection) in early-May: should stay 3m: raced on good going or softer (acts on heavy): reportedly lame second outing. *W. P. Mullins, Ireland*   **c143 h–**

MACS VALLEY (IRE) 6 b.g. Hubbly Bubbly (USA) – Black Valley (IRE) (Good Thyne (USA)) [2002/3 17d* 16d⁵ 16g* 20f* 16m² 16s⁶ Feb 2] useful-looking gelding: has scope: will make a chaser: third foal: dam, winning pointer, half-sister to useful hurdler/chaser up to 2½m Sean Ogue: twice-raced in bumpers: fairly useful novice   **h120**

hurdler: won at Bellewstown (maiden) in July and Tralee and Tipperary in September: good third to Hardy Eustace in Grade 1 at Fairyhouse: likely to prove better at 2½m than 2m: acts on any going. *W. P. Mullins, Ireland*

MADALYAR (IRE) 4 b.g. Darshaan – Madaniyya (USA) (Shahrastani (USA)) [2002/3 16d⁵ 16d⁵ 17dᶠ Jan 27] angular ex-Irish gelding: fairly useful on Flat (should stay 1¾m), successful twice in 2002, sold out of J. Oxx's stable 50,000 gns Newmarket Autumn Sales: modest form in juvenile hurdles: very much caught the eye when fifth at Fakenham second start, soon plenty to do and not at all knocked about (trainer fined £3,400, jockey suspended for 21 days and horse for 40 days under non-triers rule): didn't impress with attitude on debut and beaten when falling heavily last on final appearance. *Jonjo O'Neill*   **h82**

MADAME DERRY 11 ch.m. Derrylin – Teletex (Pollerton) [2002/3 h–: 22g 22fᵖᵘ May 10] maiden pointer: no form over hurdles. *Mrs K. Lundberg-Young*   **h–**

MADAME POULET 7 gr.m. Gold Dust – Came Cottage (Nearly A Hand) [2002/3 F–: F16s 24sᵖᵘ 18fᵖᵘ Apr 24] workmanlike mare: no sign of ability. *N. R. Mitchell*   **h–**   **F–**

MADAM FLORA 6 b.m. Alflora (IRE) – Madam's Choice (New Member) [2002/3 h84, F85: 16m 16d² 22d³ 16d* 16d³ 22d² 22m* Mar 20] unfurnished mare: fair novice hurdler: won mares events at Wincanton in December and March: effective at 2m to 2¾m: yet to race on extremes of going. *M. J. Weeden*   **h104**

MADAM MOSSO 7 b.m. Le Moss – Rochestown Lass (Deep Run) [2002/3 F–: 22g⁵ 22g² 24v* 22g⁴ 26m⁴ 25m⁴ 22s* 23v⁴ 21v⁵ 26g² c25s* Mar 7] workmanlike mare: modest hurdler: won maiden at Uttoxeter in June and handicap at Exeter in December: chaser on looks, and won mares novice at Hereford in March on debut over fences: will prove suited by 3m+: acts on good to firm and heavy going: genuine: open to improvement over fences. *Mrs A. M. Thorpe*   **c97 p**   **h97**

Mrs Margaret McManus' "Macs Gildoran"

MADAM'S MAN   7 b.g. Sir Harry Lewis (USA) – Madam-M (Tina's Pet) [2002/3 **c104** h100, F88: 24g³ 24d 24d* 26m³ c22sᶠ⁴ Nov 21] rangy gelding: fair hurdler: won **h100** novice handicap at Worcester in June: chasing type and running well when falling last (remounted) in handicap at Market Rasen on debut over fences, would have finished second: stays 3¼m: acts on soft and good to firm going: consistent. *N. A. Twiston-Davies*

MADDY'S SUPREME (IRE)   7 b.m. Supreme Leader – Shannon Lough (IRE) **h85** (Deep Run) [2002/3 h85, F69: 23d⁶ 21v⁴ 19g³ 20vᶠ Dec 26] good-topped mare: modest maiden hurdler: probably stays 23f: raced on good going or softer (acts on heavy). *T. D. Easterby*

MADEMIST SAM   11 b.g. Lord Bud – Mademist Susie (French Vine) [2002/3 c22d³ **c79** Nov 17] workmanlike gelding: modest chaser in 2000/1: only start since when close third **h–** in handicap at Haydock: seems to stay 3m: acts on soft and good to firm going: has won with/without blinkers. *P. Beaumont*

MADFORIT   5 b.g. Prince Sabo – Elusive (Little Current (USA)) [2002/3 F–: F12d **h–** 18vᵖᵘ 16m Apr 2] no sign of ability. *M. J. Roberts*   **F–**

MADGE CARROLL (IRE)   6 b.m. Hollow Hand – Spindle Tree (Laurence O) **h86** [2002/3 21d² 20d* 19d⁶ 21d Feb 7] IR £3,200 4-y-o: small, sturdy mare: ninth foal: half-sister to winning Irish pointer by Over The River: dam unraced half-sister to useful Irish chaser up to 3½m Riska's River: runner-up on second of 2 starts in Irish points in 2002: modest form over hurdles, making all in novice at Huntingdon in December: will stay 3m: raced only on good to soft going. *T. R. George*

MAD GENIUS   4 b.g. Makbul – Rinca (Unfuwain (USA)) [2002/3 16g 18m⁶ Sep 24] **h–** tailed off in maidens and claimer on Flat for T. Caldwell and in 2 juvenile hurdles. *Miss A. M. Newton-Smith*

MADHAZE (IRE)   12 ch.g. Zaffaran (USA) – Canhaar (Sparkler) [2002/3 c–, h–: **c–** c23fᵖᵘ c22mᶠ c17m⁴ Apr 21] lengthy gelding: lightly raced and no worthwhile form over **h–** jumps: trained on second start by Miss S. Parmentier. *A. E. Jones*

MADIBA   4 b.g. Emperor Jones (USA) – Priluki (Lycius (USA)) [2002/3 16s³ 16d Nov **h98** 16] leggy gelding: fairly useful maiden on Flat (stays 2m): better effort in juvenile hurdles when third at Ascot. *S. Dow*

MADISON AVENUE (GER)   6 b.g. Mondrian (GER) – Madly Noble (GER) (Irish **h99** River (FR)) [2002/3 21v³ 24vᵖᵘ 17v⁴ 16s⁵ 19d² Mar 10] leggy gelding: successful 5 times from 8.5f to 1¾m on Flat at 3/4 yrs, unplaced in France last 3 starts in 2002: won novice claimer at Plumpton (claimed from C. Von Der Recke £6,000) on hurdling debut: well below that form subsequently, blinkered final start. *T. M. Jones*

MAD JACK   8 b.g. Mazaad – Glazepta Final (Final Straw) [2002/3 h–, F–: c24dᵖᵘ **c–** c24dᵖᵘ c24vᵖᵘ Jan 22] lengthy gelding: placed in 2 maiden points in 2002: pulled up in 3 **h–** novice chases: has had tongue tied. *M. J. Ryan*

MAGENKO (IRE)   6 ch.g. Forest Wind (USA) – Bebe Auction (IRE) (Auction Ring **h–** (USA)) [2002/3 h78: 24gᵖᵘ 22g Oct 19] quite good-topped gelding: poor handicap hurdler: no form either start in 2002/3: stays 21f: acts on good to firm and heavy going: tried blinkered: inconsistent. *F. P. Murtagh*

MAGGIES BROTHER   10 b.g. Brotherly (USA) – Sallisses (Pamroy) [2002/3 c80: **c96** c25g⁸ c24m* c25m² c28g⁵ c26vᵖᵘ c27g⁶ c25sᶠ c26mᵖᵘ Apr 17] workmanlike gelding: fair hunter chaser: won at Cheltenham (idled) and Huntingdon (novice, somewhat fortunate) in May: stays 27f: acts on good to firm going. *R. Shail*

MAGGIE'S PET   6 b.m. Minshaanshu Amad (USA) – Run Fast For Gold (Deep Run) **h–** [2002/3 h–, F70: 16s⁶ Jun 6] medium-sized mare: little sign of ability in bumpers/over hurdles: has pulled hard: sold 2,200 gns Doncaster August Sales: modest form on Flat for K. Bell. *G. M. McCourt*

MAGGIES WELL   5 br.m. Royal Fountain – Ragged Rose (Scallywag) [2002/3 21s⁵ **h76** 27vᵖᵘ 21v² 21v 16vᵖᵘ 20gᵖᵘ Mar 23] leggy mare: sixth foal: half-sister to winning pointer by Highlands: dam failed to complete in 4 points: poor novice hurdler: should stay beyond 21f: acts on heavy going. *C. Grant*

MAGICAL APPROACH (IRE)   13 ch.g. Callernish – Farm Approach (Tug of **c90** War) [2002/3 c–: c24s⁶ c24sʳᵒ Mar 7] workmanlike gelding: fairly useful chaser at best: modest form on completed start in 2002/3: stays 3¼m: raced mainly on soft/heavy going. *Giles Smyly*

554

MAGICAL ATTRACTION (USA) 6 b. or br.g. Exbourne (USA) – Abeer (USA) **h–**
(Dewan (USA)) [2002/3 17g Oct 18] 6,500 2-y-o, £2,000 5-y-o: sturdy gelding: half-
brother to numerous winners, including useful sprinter In Fact (by Known Fact), useful
French miler Cloud Forest (by Green Forest), later successful up to 11f in USA, and fairly
useful chaser Spacial (by Star Appeal), stayed 23f: dam won Queen Mary and Flying
Childers Stakes: well held in novice hurdle on debut (reportedly lame): subsequently
pulled up in 2 points. *Mrs A. Price*

MAGICAL BAILIWICK (IRE) 7 ch.g. Magical Wonder (USA) – Alpine Dance **c–**
(USA) (Apalachee (USA)) [2002/3 h99: c21m^{pu} Aug 26] leggy, close-coupled gelding: **h–**
modest hurdler: no show in handicap on chasing debut, only outing in 2002/3: raced
mainly around 2m on good going or softer (acts on heavy): tried blinkered. *R. J. Baker*

MAGICAL DAY 4 ch.f. Halling (USA) – Ahla (Unfuwain (USA)) [2002/3 17d^4 17m^5 **h86**
17f^2 17d^2 16s^2 17s^4 16v^2 16d^2 19d* 21s 16s^3 Mar 10] modest maiden on Flat (should stay
1½m, one to have reservations about): modest juvenile hurdler: won maiden claimer at
Hereford in February: stays 19f: acts on any going: effective visored/blinkered or not: has
found little. *W. G. M. Turner*

MAGICAL FIELD 5 ch.m. Deploy – Ash Glade (Nashwan (USA)) [2002/3 16d^4 **h85**
16d^F 16d^4 Mar 15] lengthy mare: dam unraced half-sister to useful 2m hurdler Ulundi:
modest maiden on Flat (should stay beyond 1¼m), best efforts on all-weather: similar
standard over hurdles. *Mrs M. Reveley*

MAGICAL KNIGHT 5 b.g. Sir Harry Lewis (USA) – Formal Affair (Rousillon **h–**
(USA)) [2002/3 h–: 17g^F Jun 12] lengthy gelding: fair maiden on Flat: showed little only
completed start over hurdles: dead. *R. T. Phillips*

MAGICAL LIAISON (IRE) 5 b.g. Mujtahid (USA) – Instant Affair (USA) (Lyphard **F91**
(USA)) [2002/3 F16g^5 F16d^2 F16s^2 F17g^6 Mar 22] third foal: half-brother to 5f/6f winner
in Italy by Bob's Return: dam useful 7f and 1¼m winner: fair form in bumpers: runner-up
at Ludlow second and third starts. *W. Jenks*

MAGICAL POITIN (IRE) 10 ch.m. Magical Strike (USA) – Poitin Still (Royal **c–**
Match) [2002/3 c25g^{pu} Apr 7] winning pointer: no form otherwise, let down by jumping. **h–**
Ms Emma Anderson

MAGIC ARROW (USA) 7 b.g. Defensive Play (USA) – Magic Blue (USA) (Cure **h–**
The Blues (USA)) [2002/3 17g 21d^F Apr 8] of little account on Flat nowadays: little
worthwhile form over hurdles. *Ian Emmerson*

MAGIC BENGIE 4 b.g. Magic Ring (IRE) – Zinzi (Song) [2002/3 16g^{pu} 16d^F Dec 4] **h–**
little worthwhile form on Flat: sold out of Mrs L. Stubbs's stable 900 gns Doncaster May
Sales: showed nothing on hurdling debut, fell fourth next time. *F. Kirby*

MAGIC BOX 5 b.g. Magic Ring (IRE) – Princess Poquito (Hard Fought) [2002/3 h69: **h77**
16d^4 17m 16m 17m* 17s^5 17g^5 17g 16m^F Oct 24] angular gelding: poor handicap hurdler: won conditional jockeys event at Sedgefield in July: will prove best at sharp 2m: acts
on good to firm going, probably on good to soft (well below form on soft). *Miss Kate
Milligan*

MAGIC CHARM 5 b.m. Magic Ring (IRE) – Loch Clair (IRE) (Lomond (USA)) **h–**
[2002/3 16d 17s Nov 28] poor on Flat (stays 1½m): well held in 2 starts over hurdles.
A. G. Newcombe

MAGIC COMBINATION (IRE) 10 b.g. Scenic – Etage (Ile de Bourbon (USA)) **c–**
[2002/3 c–, h136: 20g^6 20d 17m 17d 20d* Aug 17] leggy gelding: successful on Flat in **h120**
July and September: useful handicap hurdler on his day: easily best effort in 2002/3 when
winning at Perth: stays 21f: acts on good to firm and heavy going: usually held up:
inconsistent. *L. Lungo*

MAGIC DANCER (IRE) 10 b.g. Carefree Dancer (USA) – Giveushope (Whistling **c81 d**
Deer) [2002/3 c104d, h–: c25d^6 c24m c25s^2 c26v^{pu} c31d^{pu} c25s^{pu} c24s c25g^4 Mar 17] **h–**
lengthy, rather sparely-made gelding: poor chaser nowadays: stays 25f: acts on any
going: tried in headgear: untrustworthy. *Capt. J. A. George*

MAGIC DRAGON (FR) 5 ch.g. Cyborg (FR) – Dix Huit Brumaire (FR) (General **F88**
Assembly (USA)) [2002/3 F16m^4 Apr 12] well-made gelding: first foal: dam unraced
half-sister to smart 2m hurdler Mounamara: looked in need of run when fourth of 7 in
bumper at Ayr on debut. *Mrs M. Reveley*

MAGICIEN (FR) 7 b.g. Muroto – French Look (FR) (Green River (FR)) [2002/3 **c–**
c19m^{pu} Jun 4] winning pointer: no show over hurdles: jumped poorly on steeplechasing **h–**
debut: has had tongue tied. *Miss K. Marks*

MAGIC MAID   4 b.f. Presidium – Mrs Magic (Magic Mirror) [2002/3 17d^{pu} Sep 4] no **h–**
sign of ability in 4 starts on Flat or in juvenile hurdle. *H. S. Howe*

MAGIC OF SYDNEY (IRE)   7 b.g. Broken Hearted – Chat Her Up (Proverb)   **c109**
[2002/3 h–: c21g* c21d^F c25d² Dec 17] sturdy gelding: not given hard time in 2 novice   **h–**
hurdles in 2001/2: fair form in steeplechases, far from fluent at times when making all in
novice at Folkestone in November: probably stays 25f. *R. Rowe*

MAGIC ROUTE (IRE)   6 b.g. Mr Confusion (IRE) – Another Chapter (Respect)   **c–**
[2002/3 h–, F–: 16m² 16m 16v^{pu} c16d⁵ 25g^{pu} Mar 17] tall, unfurnished gelding: poor   **h78**
form in novice hurdles: no show on chasing debut: should stay beyond 2m (ran no sort of
race over 25f final start): has worn cheekpieces. *J. Howard Johnson*

MAGIC SOUND   5 ch.g. Savahra Sound – Ace Girl (Stanford) [2002/3 17s 16g^F 17v   **h–**
19d^{pu} 19g^{pu} Feb 28] lengthy gelding: modest sprint maiden on Flat at 3 yrs for Mrs
A. Duffield, no form in 2002: no form over hurdles: likely to have stamina limitations.
Mrs S. J. Smith

MAGIC TO DO (IRE)   5 b.g. Spectrum (IRE) – Smouldering (IRE) (Caerleon   **h83**
(USA)) [2002/3 h76: 17m* 20m³ Jun 21] workmanlike gelding: twice-raced on Flat:
modest hurdler: won selling handicap at Folkestone in May: stays 2½m: acts on good to
firm going: blinkered: sold 900 gns Doncaster August Sales. *O. Sherwood*

MAGIC WATERS   5 b.g. Ezzoud (IRE) – Paradise Waters (Celestial Storm (USA))   **h98**
[2002/3 h98: 16s⁵ 23v^{pu} 19d 20d⁶ 26g³ Mar 12] leggy gelding: modest hurdler: probably
stays 2½m: acts on soft going: usually blinkered: not an easy ride. *T. D. Easterby*

MAGIQUE ETOILE (IRE)   7 b.m. Magical Wonder (USA) – Shes A Dancer (IRE)   **c–**
(Alzao (USA)) [2002/3 h66: 17m 16m⁴ 20m c17g^R 16s⁶ c20m^{pu} Aug 23] smallish mare: **h60**
poor maiden hurdler: failed to complete in 2 novice chases: best around 2m: acts on good
to firm going, probably not on softer than good: tongue tied after reappearance: sold £700
Ascot August Sales, no form in points subsequently. *Dr J. R. J. Naylor*

MAGNATISM   6 b.g. Charmer – Bright-One (Electric) [2002/3 F17m⁴ F16g F17d Oct   **F67**
19] lengthy gelding: seventh foal: half-brother to useful 2m hurdler Albrighton (by
Terimon) and 2¾m hurdle winner Mill-Dot (by Petoski): dam winning 2m hurdler: poor
form in bumpers. *C. W. Thornton*

MAGNUS (FR)   7 b.g. Roakarad – Volcania (FR) (Neustrien (FR)) [2002/3 h157:   **c106**
c21v³ c16d⁶ Dec 14] strong, stocky gelding: very smart hurdler: fair form on first of 2   **h–**
starts in novice chases when third to Joly Bey at Newton Abbot: stays 3m: raced on good
going or softer (acts on heavy): reportedly bled from nose last 2 starts in 2001/2: held up:
rejoined J. Ortet. *M. C. Pipe*

MAGS TWO   6 b.g. Jumbo Hirt (USA) – Welsh Diamond (High Top) [2002/3 F16g   **h–**
F17d 20d 20d 20s⁶ Dec 26] fifth live foal: brother to winning 21f hurdler Magslad: dam,   **F–**
maiden, best at 2 yrs: well held in bumpers and novice hurdles. *Ms Liz Harrison*

MAIDEN FLIGHT (IRE)   7 b.m. Jurado (USA) – Dream of Money (IRE) (Good   **h76**
Thyne (USA)) [2002/3 h76, F–: 20d^{pu} 20m⁴ 26m Jul 19] poor maiden hurdler: should
stay beyond 2½m. *P. R. Webber*

MAIDEN VOYAGE   5 b.m. Slip Anchor – Elaine Tully (IRE) (Persian Bold) [2002/3   **h95**
16d^F 17s 21d² 19v³ 20g² 20m³ Apr 12] good-topped mare: modest maiden on Flat (stays
2m), generally creditable efforts in 2002 for Mrs J. Ramsden: modest novice hurdler:
stays 21f. *P. R. Webber*

MAIDSTONE MAGIC (IRE)   8 b.g. Balinger – Anyone's Fancy (Callernish)   **c– x**
[2002/3 c–x: c26m⁵ Aug 5] signs of only a little ability over fences: poor jumper: joined
Miss A. M. Newton-Smith. *M. C. Pipe*

MAIDSTONE MONARCH (IRE)   10 b. or br.g. King's Ride – Curragh Breeze   **c– x**
(Furry Glen) [2002/3 c–, h–: c26s^{ur} c26v^{pu} c26v^{pu} Feb 10] big, workmanlike gelding: **h–**
bad maiden chaser: makes mistakes. *Miss A. M. Newton-Smith*

MAIDSTONE MONUMENT (IRE)   8 b.g. Jurado (USA) – Loreto Lady (Brave   **c106**
Invader (USA)) [2002/3 c93, h–: c24m³ c24d^{pu} c24m⁴ c26g* c26m² c26f⁴ c26d*   **h–**
c23g^{pu} c26m² c26m^{ur} c24d⁴ c27d^{pu} c24s^{pu} Nov 30] lengthy gelding: fair handicap chaser:
won at Newton Abbot in June (19 lb out of weights) and September: stays 3¼m: acts
on good to firm and good to soft going: well held only start in blinkers: front runner.
Mrs A. M. Thorpe

MAIDSTONE MOUNTIE 7 b.g. Royal Fountain – Millie Duffer (Furry Glen) **h–**
[2002/3 F18s 25v^{pu} 24s^{pu} Jan 28] 6,500 4-y-o: workmanlike gelding: third foal: dam poor **F–**
maiden: no sign of ability in bumper and 2 novice hurdles: visored last 2 starts. *M. C. Pipe*

MAID TO TALK 9 b.m. Arctic Lord – Chatty Lass (Le Bavard (FR)) [2002/3 c–, h–: **c–**
c16d^5 c17g^5 c20d^{pu} c16m^{pu} 20f^{pu} c20g^3 c20g^4 Oct 11] no worthwhile form: often tongue **h–**
tied. *W. S. Coltherd*

MAI POINT 10 b.m. Blakeney – Quilpee Mai (Pee Mai) [2002/3 c24g^F May 31] fairly **c–**
useful pointer, successful in March: fell first in hunter chase in May. *Mrs P. A. Twinn*

MAISEY DOWN 6 b.m. Rakaposhi King – Win Green Hill (National Trust) [2002/3 **F–**
F17s Dec 2] eleventh foal: half-sister to 1998 Grand National winner Earth Summit (by
Celtic Cone) and a winning pointer by Royal Match: dam winning 17f chaser: showed
little in mares bumper on debut. *J. A. B. Old*

MAISIEBEL 5 ch.m. Be My Native (USA) – High 'b' (Gunner B) [2002/3 F17s F16g **F–**
Feb 12] unfurnished mare: second foal: dam unraced: well held in 2 bumpers. *R. N. Bevis*

MAITRE DE MUSIQUE (FR) 12 ch.g. Quai Voltaire (USA) – Mativa (FR) (Sat- **c86**
ingo) [2002/3 c88, h–: c25d^4 c25m^3 c24v^5 Mar 5] tall gelding: fair hunter chaser: left **h–**
T. Walford after second start: won point in February: stays 27f: acts on good to firm and
heavy going: tongue tied: sound jumper: inconsistent. *Mrs F. E. Needham*

MAJADOU (FR) 9 b.g. Cadoudal (FR) – Majathen (FR) (Carmarthen (FR)) [2002/3 **c–**
c–, h–: c26m^{pu} Jul 15] rather leggy gelding: smart chaser at best: very lightly raced and **h–**
little show since 2000/1: well beaten in point in January: stays 21f: acts on heavy going:
below form only outing in blinkers. *M. C. Pipe*

MAJED (FR) 7 b.g. Fijar Tango (FR) – Full of Passion (USA) (Blushing Groom (FR)) **c104 +**
[2002/3 c–, h145: c32g c36d c36f Apr 5] compact gelding: progressed into smart handicap **h–**
hurdler in 2001/2: one-time fairly useful chaser in France: highly tried and well held over
fences in Britain: stays 3m (probably not 4m+): acts on good to firm and heavy going:
tried blinkered, visored in Britain. *M. C. Pipe*

MAJESTIC BAY (IRE) 7 b.g. Unfuwain (USA) – That'll Be The Day (IRE) (Thatch- **c118**
ing) [2002/3 h105: 19d^4 22d^3 22s^3 24v^4 c21v^2 c24s^3 c24g^4 Apr 2] sturdy gelding: fair **h101**
maiden hurdler: easily best effort over fences when winning novice at Ascot in April,
beating Bonus Bridge 19 lengths: stays 3m, at least when conditions aren't testing: raced
on good going or softer (acts on soft). *J. A. B. Old*

MAJESTIC (IRE) 8 b.g. Belmez (USA) – Noble Lily (USA) (Vaguely Noble) **c–**
[2002/3 c120, h136: 24g^3 21m^F 21g 24g^F 21m^2 Apr 16] smallish gelding: winning chaser: **h134**
useful handicap hurdler: best efforts in 2002/3 when placed at Market Rasen and
Cheltenham, second to See You Sometime at latter course: stays 3m: acts on soft and firm
going: blinkered and tongue tied: usually forces pace: often races lazily. *Ian Williams*

MAJESTIC MOONBEAM (IRE) 5 b.g. Supreme Leader – Magic Moonbeam **F97**
(IRE) (Decent Fellow) [2002/3 F16g* Mar 14] first foal: dam, Irish bumper winner, out
of half-sister to smart 2m to 2¾m hurdler Troyswood: won maiden bumper at Warwick
on debut by ¾ length from Limerick Leader, showing good attitude. *Jonjo O'Neill*

MAJESTIC STORM (IRE) 10 b.g. Glacial Storm (USA) – Grin And Bear It (Deep **c–**
Run) [2002/3 c–, h–: 22g 24m^{ro} May 16] rangy gelding: of no account. *Mrs L. B. Normile* **h–**

MAJLIS (IRE) 6 b.g. Caerleon (USA) – Ploy (Posse (USA)) [2002/3 h122: c16m^F **c–**
16v 17v^6 16g 16m 16g^{pu} Apr 12] strong, well-made gelding: fell fifth on chasing debut: **h–**
fairly useful hurdler in 2001/2, out of form in 2002/3: will stay 2½m: acts on soft going:
blinkered: joined R. Cowell. *T. R. George*

MAJOR ADVENTURE (IRE) 10 b.g. Glacial Storm (USA) – Dual Adventure **c99**
(Deep Run) [2002/3 c86, h–: c24m* c25d^F c25m^4 c25m^2 24g^5 Sep 28] sturdy gelding: **h90**
winning hurdler: modest chaser: won novice handicap at Ludlow in May: let down by
jumping subsequently: stays 25f: acts on good to firm going, probably on heavy: tried
visored. *Ian Williams*

MAJOR BENEFIT (IRE) 6 b.g. Executive Perk – Merendas Sister (Pauper) [2002/3 **c67 +**
c26v^3 Feb 4] IR 20,000 3-y-o: eleventh foal: half-brother to winning chasers Credo Is
King (by Le Moss), stays 25f, and Dunaree (by Lapierre), stays 3m, and several winning
pointers: dam unraced half-sister to dam of high-class 2m to 2½m hurdler King Credo:
won all 3 starts in points in 2002: last of 3 finishers to Earthmover at Chepstow on hunter
chase debut, travelling well but tiring badly in straight: should do better. *Mrs P. Grainger*

MAJOR BIT   7 b.g. Henbit (USA) – Cute Pam (Pamroy) [2002/3 c69, h70, F70: c24m   **c–**
c26g[pu] c25m3 Sep 11] deep-girthed gelding: poor maiden hurdler/chaser: stays 25f: acts   **h–**
on soft and good to firm going: tongue tied. *S. A. Brookshaw*

MAJOR BLADE (GER)   5 b.g. Dashing Blade – Misniniski (Niniski (USA))   **h90**
[2002/3 16s[pu] 16d5 16m5 Mar 22] good-topped gelding: fairly useful on Flat (stays 1¼m)
in Germany, well held in 2 handicaps in Britain in February: pulled up on hurdling debut
at Bremen in October for C. Von Der Recke: modest form when fifth in maiden at
Wincanton and novice at Newbury. *B. G. Powell*

MAJOR BLUE   8 ch.g. Scallywag – Town Blues (Charlottown) [2002/3 F88: 20v   **h90**
24v3 26d6 26m2 24m[pu] Apr 16] rangy gelding: novice hurdler, seemingly best effort on
second outing: better around 3m than shorter: acts on good to firm and heavy ground:
jumps none too fluently. *J. G. M. O'Shea*

MAJOR DRIVE (IRE)   5 b.g. Sadler's Wells (USA) – Puck's Castle (Shirley Heights)   **h99**
[2002/3 h–: 17g2 20m* 20d 19d 24g* Feb 12] modest hurdler: won novices at Hexham in
October and Musselburgh (handicap) in February: stays easy 3m: best efforts on good
going or firmer. *J. Howard Johnson*

MAJOR EURO (IRE)   6 b.g. Lord Americo – Gold Bank (Over The River (FR))   **F86**
[2002/3 F16g F16g Apr 2] IR 17,500 3-y-o, 2,600 4-y-o: good-topped gelding: eleventh
foal: half-brother to 3m chase winner Mandys Gold (by Mandalus) and to 2 winning
pointers: dam unraced: won maiden Irish point in 2002: fair form on first of 2 starts in
bumpers. *S. J. Gilmore*

MAJORITY VERDICT   7 b.g. Leading Counsel (USA) – Culm Valley (Port Corsair)   **h100 p**
[2002/3 h100p: 16s2 Mar 15] rangy gelding: chasing type: useful bumper winner: showed
promise when second in novice hurdles at Aintree and Uttoxeter 16 months apart, behind
impressive Crystal d'Ainay at latter course: will be suited by 2½m+: takes good hold:
should progress. *H. D. Daly*

MAJOR OPTION (IRE)   7 b.g. Doubletour (USA) – Dainty Dancer (Prince Tender-   **F89**
foot (USA)) [2002/3 F18m* F16d Aug 3] IR 12,500 3-y-o: ex-Irish gelding: half-brother
to 3 winners, including fair 2m chaser Nosuch Thing (by Executive Perk): dam maiden:
second in bumper at Sligo on debut, when trained by A. J. Martin: off a year, landed odds
in similar event at Fontwell in May: well held at Worcester 3 months later. *M. C. Pipe*

MAJOR SHARK (IRE)   5 b.g. Saint Preuil (FR) – Cindy Cad (FR) (Cadoudal (FR))   **h85**
[2002/3 F18d F17s3 20s5 20v 22d5 20s* 25s[pu] Mar 10] fourth foal: brother to fair chaser   **F83**
Bacchus du Berlais (by Saint Preuil), stays 2½m, and half-brother to winning chaser by
Mister Sicy: dam, won around 2m over hurdles in France, sister to very smart French
hurdler around 2½m Tenerific: modest form in bumpers: similar form over hurdles, won
novice handicap at Fontwell in March: lame final outing: probably stays 2¾m: raced on
going softer than good: wore cheekpieces last 2 starts. *L. A. Dace*

MAJOR SHARPE (IRE)   11 b.g. Phardante (FR) – Winsome Doe (Buckskin (FR))   **c94 x**
[2002/3 c–, h100: 25g3 c25d4 c25m* c26gF Jun 29] well-made gelding: poor maiden   **h83**
hurdler: modest chaser: made all in handicap at Hereford in June: stays 3¼m: acts on firm
going: often makes mistakes. *B. J. M. Ryall*

MAJOR SPONSOR (IRE)   11 b.g. Strong Gale – Hue 'n' Cry (IRE) (Denel (FR))   **c–**
[2002/3 c119, h–: c16m[pu] May 8] rangy gelding: fairly useful handicap chaser: reportedly   **h–**
distressed final start in 2001/2 and on reappearance: stays 21f: acts on any going: usually
races prominently. *G. M. Moore*

MAKE HASTE SLOWLY   6 b.g. Terimon – Henry's True Love (Random Shot)   **h102 p**
[2002/3 16d2 Nov 14] ninth foal: half-brother to several winners, including useful staying
chaser Sail By The Stars (by Celtic Cone) and fair hurdler/chaser up to 2½m Hearts Are
Wild (by Scallywag): dam, third in 2½m selling hurdles, half-sister to useful jumper
Dublin Express, the dam of Dublin Flyer: encouraging ¾-length second to Soho Fields
(pair clear) in novice hurdle at Ludlow on debut, patiently ridden and finishing strongly:
will stay beyond 2m: should improve. *H. D. Daly*

MAKHPIYA PATAHN (IRE)   11 g.g. Nestor – Our Mare Mick (Choral Society)   **c–**
[2002/3 c82, h–: c33g c26mF May 22] lengthy gelding: poor maiden steeplechaser: **h–**
walked over in point in April: has looked difficult ride. *J. H. Young*

MAKIN' DOO (IRE)   13 ch.g. Black Minstrel – Ariannrun (Deep Run) [2002/3   **c– §**
c75§, h78§: c22d[pu] May 13] sturdy gelding: maiden hurdler: veteran hunter chaser: often   **h– §**
makes mistakes/goes in snatches. *Mrs V. J. Makin*

MALAGA BOY (IRE) 6 b.g. Nordic Brave – Ardglass Mist (Black Minstrel) **F91** [2002/3 F17m³ F17s⁶ F16v² Feb 15] fifth foal: half-brother to winning pointer Royal Dew (by Royal Fountain): dam unraced, out of half-sister to smart 2½m chaser Coxswain: best effort in bumpers when second to Mister Mustard at Ascot. *C. Tizzard*

MALAKAL (IRE) 7 b.g. Shernazar – Malmada (USA) (Fappiano (USA)) [2002/3 **h89** h73: 17g* 17m² Oct 3] lengthy gelding: modest hurdler: fit from Flat (successful in July) and heavily backed, very easily won novice handicap at Market Rasen on reappearance: odds on, respectable second in similar event at Hereford 5 days later: likely to prove best around 2m. *B. J. Curley*

MALAKAND (IRE) 5 b.g. Dolphin Street (FR) – Malmada (USA) (Fappiano (USA)) [2002/3 F–: 23v² 24d⁶ 20sᵖᵘ Dec 16] form only when second in selling hurdle at Wetherby **h82** on reappearance. *D. Carroll*

MALANDRA 4 b.f. Mtoto – Nibabu (FR) (Nishapour (FR)) [2002/3 F16s Jan 27] **F–** 10,000Y: half-sister to several winners, notably smart 7f/1m performer Nijo (by Top Ville): dam, maiden, best at 7f/1m: achieved little in bumper on debut. *G. L. Moore*

MALARKEY 6 b.g. Mukaddamah (USA) – Malwiya (USA) (Shahrastani (USA)) **h81** [2002/3 h91: 16g⁴ 20s⁵ 17g 20s 16g⁶ Nov 20] rather angular gelding: fair on Flat (stays 17.2f), successful in August and September: poor maiden hurdler: should stay 2½m: acts on good to soft going, probably unsuited by soft: has worn cheekpieces. *P. R. Hedger*

MALBEC (IRE) 6 b.g. Lord Americo – Key-Door (IRE) (Beau Charmeur (FR)) **h–** [2002/3 h–: 26gᵖᵘ 21d⁴ 24sᵖᵘ Nov 14] little sign of ability in novice hurdles: has worn cheekpieces/blinkers. *Miss A. M. Newton-Smith*

MALCOM (FR) 4 b.g. Villez (USA) – La Musardiere (FR) (Cadoudal (FR)) [2002/3 **h134** 17s² 18s* 18s* 18vF 18s⁴ 19v⁴ Apr 26] fifth foal: half-brother to 3 winners, including useful hurdler/chaser Musardo (by Grand Tresor), stays 25f: dam in frame around 1¼m: useful on Flat, second over 1½m in March: useful hurdler, raced exclusively at Auteuil in 2002/3: won twice in autumn, minor event and Group 2 Prix Georges de Talhouet-Roy (beat Pyraleety 2½ lengths): length up when fell last in Group 1 won by same horse next time: better subsequent effort when fourth to Nickname in 2¼m Group 3 in April: should stay 19f: raced on soft/heavy going. *B. Secly, France*

MALEK (IRE) 7 b.g. Tremblant – Any Offers (Paddy's Stream) [2002/3 c89, F82: **c–** 20s* 20s⁵ Feb 8] angular gelding: lightly raced: successful on completed start over **h106** fences: fair form when winning novice at Haydock in November on first of 2 starts over hurdles: stays 3m: raced only on going softer than good (acts on heavy). *Mrs M. Reveley*

MALLORY 9 b.g. North Col – Veritate (Roman Warrior) [2002/3 h76: 24mᵖᵘ May 9] **h–** tall, angular gelding: poor novice hurdler: should stay beyond 2m: acts on good to soft going: joined T. George. *M. J. Wilkinson*

MALONE (FR) 5 gr.h. Celtic Arms (FR) – Nexia (FR) (Linamix (FR)) [2002/3 17dᵖᵘ **c–** 17d³ 18s² 18s² 18v³ 18v² 18v* 20v* Apr 26] 1½m winner at 3 yrs on Flat: lightly-raced **h134** maiden over fences: successful twice at Auteuil in spring, improved form when winning Group 3 Grande Course de Haies de Printemps by 2 lengths from Walk On Seas, coming from virtually last 3 out to lead last 50 metres and win going away: out of depth in Group 1 there in June: should stay beyond 2½m: raced on going softer than good (acts on heavy). *J. Bertran de Balanda, France*

MAMBOESQUE (USA) 5 b.g. Miesque's Son (USA) – Brawl (USA) (Fit To Fight **h77** (USA)) [2002/3 h85: 16m 20d 16d³ 19g³ 16s 16v 16g 19d* 16g⁶ Mar 12] leggy gelding: poor hurdler: won handicap at Catterick in March on first start after leaving W. Clay: stays 19f: acts on heavy going: often wears headgear: none too consistent. *J. Mackie*

MAMIDEOS (IRE) 6 br.g. Good Thyne (USA) – Heavenly Artist (IRE) (Heavenly **h97** Manna) [2002/3 F99: 24g* 20v 21g³ Feb 27] lengthy, useful-looking gelding: bumper winner: easily won weakly-contested novice at Market Rasen in October on hurdling debut, not for first time looking tricky ride (hung left): much better effort in novice handicaps subsequently when third at Ludlow: stays 3m: raced good going or softer (acts on soft). *T. R. George*

MAMMA'S BOY 8 b.g. Rock City – Henpot (IRE) (Alzao (USA)) [2002/3 17d Aug **h–** 26] chunky gelding: poor on Flat (probably stays 9f): showed no aptitude for hurdling on debut. *A. Berry*

MANA-MOU BAY (IRE) 6 b.g. Ela-Mana-Mou – Summerhill (Habitat) [2002/3 **h104 +** 16g⁴ 16d 16m 17d⁵ 17m* Apr 26] lengthy gelding: fairly useful at best on Flat (stays 1½m), successful twice in 2002 for D. Nicholls: jumped more fluently and easily best effort over hurdles when making all in conditional jockeys novice at Sedgefield: raced around 2m: acts on good to firm going: has worn cheekpieces. *B. Ellison*

MAN AT THE TOP 7 b.g. Northern Park (USA) – Kotsina (Top Ville) [2002/3 20m^{pu} **h–** Jun 1] 500 4-y-o: second foal: half-brother to winner abroad by Mujadil: dam placed in France and Ireland: no show in novice hurdle on debut: sold 4,000 gns Doncaster August Sales, no form in points subsequently. *R. Wilman*

MANAWANUI 5 b.g. Karinga Bay – Kiwi Velocity (NZ) (Veloso (NZ)) [2002/3 **h–** F16v^6 19d 22d Feb 23] sturdy gelding: first foal: dam fair hurdler/chaser, suited by test of **F86** stamina: sixth of 15 in bumper on debut: well held both starts over hurdles. *R. H. Alner*

MANBOW (IRE) 5 b.g. Mandalus – Treble Base (IRE) (Orchestra) [2002/3 F17g **F–** Mar 28] sixth foal: half-brother to winning 2¾m chaser Woodchester (by Buckskin): dam unraced: hung left and always behind in bumper on debut. *M. D. Hammond*

MANCHESTER (IRE) 4 b.g. Danehill Dancer (IRE) – Lils Fairy (Fairy King (USA)) **h–** [2002/3 16s^{pu} 16s 16m^{pu} Apr 19] angular ex-Irish gelding: fair maiden (stays 1m) on Flat at 2 yrs for A. O'Brien: no form over hurdles, trained first 2 starts by M. Croke: blinkered final outing. *Miss A. M. Newton-Smith*

MANDALIAS BOY 7 b.g. Henbit (USA) – Mandalia (Mansingh (USA)) [2002/3 **h–** 17s^{pu} Mar 22] seventh foal: dam fairly useful sprinter: no sign of ability in 2 novice hurdles. *Mrs L. Williamson*

MANDATE MAN (IRE) 9 b.g. Mandalus – Atalaya Park (King of Spain) [2002/3 **c66** c20d^4 Apr 29] ex-Irish gelding: third foal: dam, placed once in bumper, half-sister to **h–** smart chaser up to 21f Gold Options: winning Irish pointer: poor form over hurdles/in steeplechases: bought privately out of G. Stewart's stable 2,000 gns Doncaster August (2001) Sales. *Miss J. B. W. Monteith*

MANDOOB 6 b.g. Zafonic (USA) – Thaidah (CAN) (Vice Regent (CAN)) [2002/3 **h–** h88: 16d^3 Oct 26] leggy gelding: fair on Flat (stays 1¾m), successful twice in late-2002: modest form in 2 novice hurdles in 2001/2: out of depth only run in 2002/3: tongue tied. *B. R. Johnson*

MANDOWN 4 b.g. Danehill Dancer (IRE) – Golden Decoy (Decoy Boy) [2002/3 16d **h–** Mar 6] poor maiden on Flat (may prove best at 1m/1¼m): tailed off in maiden on hurdling debut. *J. S. Moore*

MANDY CHAT (IRE) 10 b.m. Mandalus – Double Talk (Dublin Taxi) [2002/3 c70, **c64** h–: c21g^{pu} c17m c16m^{pu} c16m^6 c17s c17g^5 c17m^2 c16m^{pu} c17g^{ur} Oct 12] poor maiden **h–** chaser: largely out of sorts in 2002/3: form only around 2m: acts on good to firm going: has had tongue tied. *P. T. Dalton*

MANDY'S ROSE (IRE) 7 b. or br.m. Mandalus – Rookery Lady (IRE) (Callernish) **h–** [2002/3 F17g^3 20m 20v^{pu} 17s^4 22g^F Mar 29] lengthy mare: second foal: dam unraced: **F65** successful in 2 Irish points: bought 12,000 gns Doncaster May Sales: third in bumper: no worthwhile form in novice hurdles, though close up and still to be asked for effort when falling 3 out in handicap final outing. *T. R. George*

MANE FRAME 8 b.g. Unfuwain (USA) – Moviegoer (Pharly (FR)) [2002/3 h99+: **h–** 22v 22d 21s^{pu} Feb 28] leggy gelding: fair hurdler: no form since winning handicap in 2001/2: stays 21f: acts on soft going, seemingly not on heavy (also ran poorly on firm): has had tongue tied: held up: has looked none too keen. *H. Morrison*

MAN FROM DELCARROW (IRE) 6 b.g. Zaffaran (USA) – Delcarrow (Roi **F91** Guillaume (FR)) [2002/3 F16g^6 F17g Apr 19] 26,000 4-y-o: sturdy gelding: fifth foal: brother to 2½m hurdle winner Pride of Caulry: dam unraced: close sixth of 18 in bumper at Doncaster on debut: again didn't see race out so well as seemed likely when favourite at Newton Abbot 4 months later: changed hands 3,500 gns Doncaster May Sales. *O. Sherwood*

MAN FROM HAVANA (USA) 4 b.g. Green Dancer (USA) – Charmie Carmie **h93 §** (USA) (Lyphard (USA)) [2002/3 16m^2 16d 16s^{ur} Dec 6] workmanlike gelding: fair maiden on Flat (stays 11.6f): best effort in juvenile hurdles when second to easy winner Gabor at Plumpton: off bridle long way out and no impression when ducking violently left and unseating approaching 2 out final start: needs treating with caution. *S. Dow*

MAN FROM HIGHWORTH 4 b.g. Ballet Royal (USA) – Cavisoir (Afzal) [2002/3 **F–** F16m^5 Apr 22] second foal: dam unraced, out of half-sister to high-class hunter chaser Cavalero: fifth of 7 in conditional jockeys bumper at Chepstow on debut. *H. J. Manners*

MANFUL 11 b.g. Efisio – Mandrian (Mandamus) [2002/3 20v^{pu} 17d Feb 10] sturdy **h–**
gelding: seems of little account nowadays: blinkered/visored. *M. J. M. Evans*

MANGO CHUTNEY 9 b.g. Safawan – Malacanang (Riboboy (USA)) [2002/3 17d^{pu} **h–**
May 14] third foal: dam modest 2m hurdler: showed nothing in novice hurdle on belated
debut. *T. Wall*

MANHATTAN CASTLE (IRE) 14 br.g. Strong Gale – Allamanda (FR) (Versailles **c87**
II) [2002/3 c107d, h–: c20f^3 c28m^{pu} Jun 1] good-topped gelding: one-time useful chaser: **h–**
won point in May: stayed 21f: acted on any going: found little on occasions: dead. *Miss
S. E. Cook*

MANHATTAN RAINBOW (IRE) 12 b.g. Mandalus – Clara Girl (Fine Blade **c77**
(USA)) [2002/3 c–: c25d^2 c25g^4 c25g^4 Apr 7] lengthy gelding: one-time fairly useful
hunter chaser: only modest nowadays: stays 25f: acts on heavy and good to firm going:
tried visored. *Mrs J. M. Hollands*

MANIATIS 6 b.h. Slip Anchor – Tamassos (Dance In Time (CAN)) [2002/3 16s^2 18d **h106**
Mar 1] good sort: half-brother to fairly useful 2m hurdler Rescue Time and fair hurdler/
chaser Porphyrios (both by Mtoto), stayed 2½m: useful on Flat (stays 1¾m), sold out of
Mrs A. Perrett's stable 16,000 gns Newmarket Autumn Sales: promising second to Hey
Ref in novice at Haydock on hurdling debut: very disappointing in Grade 2 novice at
Kelso, leaving impression probably amiss. *M. D. Hammond*

MANIKATO (USA) 9 b.g. Clever Trick (USA) – Pasampsi (USA) (Crow (FR)) **h–**
[2002/3 h–: 16g Sep 14] poor on Flat (stays 1½m): lightly raced and little show over
hurdles. *R. Curtis*

MANINGA 7 ch.m. Karinga Bay – Amberush (No Rush) [2002/3 h105, F–: 22v^5 24v **h100**
20v 21s^4 25s 21s^4 Feb 24] fair handicap hurdler: should stay 3m: raced on going softer
than good (acts on soft). *Mrs L. Richards*

MANKIND 12 b.g. Rakaposhi King – Mandarling (Mandalus) [2002/3 c–, h88: 22m **c– §**
c23g^{rtr} Oct 22] leggy gelding: modest hurdler, lightly raced since 1998/9: refused to race **h– §**
on chasing debut: stays 2¾m: acts on good to firm and good to soft going. *J. A. T. de Giles*

MAN MURPHY 7 b.g. Euphemism – Been About (IRE) (Remainder Man) **c128**
[2002/3 h123, F100: c17s* c20d* c20d* c20s* c22d^4 c20v* c20s^3 Mar 6] sturdy gelding: **h–**
fairly useful hurdler: of similar standard over fences, winning intermediate at Kelso and
2 novices at Newcastle in November and novices at Newcastle in December and Ayr
(fortunate) in February: should stay beyond 2½m: acts on soft going, possibly amiss only
start on good to firm: tends to idle: sound jumper. *Mrs M. Reveley*

MANODEE (IRE) 9 b.g. Mandalus – Emmodee (Bowling Pin) [2002/3 c20s^{pu} c25m **c81**
c24m* c23g^6 c25m^F c24d^3 Nov 25] ex-Irish gelding: second foal: dam winning pointer: **h–**
once-raced over hurdles: poor handicap chaser: first outing after leaving A. Moore, won
weak event at Huntingdon in September: stays 3m: acts on good to firm going, probably
on good to soft: folded dramatically/flashed tail final start. *Miss Venetia Williams*

MANOLITO (IRE) 9 b.g. Mandalus – Las-Cancellas (Monksfield) [2002/3 c20d^3 **c76**
c22m^{pu} c20m^6 c24m^F c24g^2 c21d^3 c24g^F Apr 19] smallish gelding: won maiden point in **h–**
2002: poor maiden chaser, left M. Wilkinson after third start: stays easy 3m: acts on soft
going. *B. I. Case*

MAN O'MYSTERY (USA) 6 b.g. Diesis – Eurostorm (USA) (Storm Bird (CAN)) **h128**
[2002/3 17s^2 17g* 16d^2 Apr 4] smallish gelding: smart around 1¼m on Flat for J. Noseda,
successful in 2002: second start over hurdles, landed odds in novice at Market Rasen
in March: much better form when 4 lengths second to Limerick Boy in Grade 2 novice
at Aintree following month: likely to prove best held up in well-run races around 2m.
P. R. Webber

MANORAM (GER) 4 ch.g. Zinaad – Mayada (USA) (The Minstrel (CAN)) [2002/3 **h73**
16d 17g^3 Mar 17] rather leggy ex-German gelding: successful over 11f on Flat for
S. Wegner: poor form on second of 2 starts in juvenile hurdles. *Ian Williams*

MANOR DOWN (IRE) 5 b.g. Moscow Society (USA) – Scalp Hunter (IRE) **h–**
(Commanche Run) [2002/3 16d F16d 21m^{pu} Mar 21] 25,000 4-y-o: lengthy, rather **F–**
unfurnished gelding: first foal: dam maiden pointer: more signs of temperament than
ability: blinkered second start. *P. J. Hobbs*

MANOR FROM HEAVEN 5 ch.m. Most Welcome – Manor Adventure (Smack- **h–**
over) [2002/3 16d^{pu} 16s^{pu} 17g^{pu} Mar 22] leggy mare: little sign of ability on Flat: pulled
up all 3 starts over hurdles. *P. T. Dalton*

MANOR STAR 4 b.f. Weld – Call Coup (IRE) (Callernish) [2002/3 F16g Feb 27] F—
first foal: dam remote third in point on only start: little show in mares bumper on debut.
B. D. Leavy

MANQUE NEUF 4 b.g. Cadeaux Genereux – Flying Squaw (Be My Chief (USA)) h—
[2002/3 16m Apr 22] fair maiden on Flat (stays 1½m), sold out of J. Bethell's stable
16,000 gns Newmarket Autumn Sales: never a factor in maiden on hurdling debut.
Mrs L. Richards

MANTELLO 8 ch.g. Mon Tresor – Laena (Roman Warrior) [2002/3 16dᵖᵘ 20gᵖᵘ 18f c—
c25gᵖᵘ Jun 12] workmanlike gelding: maiden hurdler: no show on chasing debut: visored/ h—
blinkered: usually tongue tied: dead. *B. G. Powell*

MANTEL MINI 4 b.f. Reprimand – Foretell (Tirol) [2002/3 F16g F17d Feb 23] F—
lengthy filly: first foal: dam unraced, out of sister to smart French sprinter Reasonable:
tailed off in 2 bumpers. *B. A. Pearce*

MANTILLA 6 b.m. Son Pardo – Well Tried (IRE) (Thatching) [2002/3 h82: 17g 17f³ h73
17d⁴ 24s 17g³ 17f 19m³ Apr 8] poor maiden hurdler: stays 19f: acts on firm and good to
soft going: blinkered final start. *J. D. Frost*

MANTLES PRINCE 9 ch.g. Emarati (USA) – Miami Mouse (Miami Springs) c118 §
[2002/3 c132, h156: c20s² c36dᵘʳ 16f⁶ Apr 25] sturdy gelding: one-time very smart h— §
hurdler/useful chaser, sold out of P. Hughes's stable 16,000 gns Doncaster October Sales
after reappearance: behind when unseating 6 out in Grand National at Aintree, ran moody
race back over hurdles final start: barely stays 2½m: acts on heavy and good to firm
going: best left alone nowadays. *A. G. Juckes*

MAOUSSE HONOR (FR) 8 b.m. Hero's Honor (USA) – Maousse (FR) (Labus c102
(FR)) [2002/3 h107: c16s* c16m* c16g² c17gᵖᵘ 16d* 17v* 17v⁴ 16v³ 24sᵖᵘ Dec 12] tall h92
mare: fair novice chaser: made all at Worcester in June and Newton Abbot in July: fair
hurdler: didn't need to be near best to make all in sellers at Stratford in October and
Newton Abbot in November: seems best at 2m: acts on good to firm and heavy going: has
worn cheekpieces: possibly needs left-handed track: not an easy ride. *M. C. Pipe*

MAPLETON 10 br.g. Skyliner – Maple Syrup (Charlottown) [2002/3 c88, h–: c24m³ c103
c24d* c20g* c23m⁴ c21g* c25m Aug 31] close-coupled gelding: fair handicap chaser: h—
better than ever in 2002/3, winning at Southwell in May, Hexham in June and Sedgefield
in August: stays 25f: probably acts on any going. *Mrs S. J. Smith*

MARABOUT (FR) 6 b.g. Baby Turk – Maria Bethania (FR) (Pharly (FR)) [2002/3 c—
17d Mar 2] ex-French gelding: fifth foal: brother to useful chaser/winning hurdler Beau h—
Turk, stayed 2¾m: dam won over 11f in France: fair form over hurdles/fences for
Y. Fouin: well held in novice at Carlisle (wore eyecover and eyeshields) on British debut:
stays 2½m: acts on heavy going. *Sir John Barlow Bt*

MARADAN (IRE) 7 b.g. Shernazar – Marmana (USA) (Blushing Groom (FR)) c—
[2002/3 c16sᶠ c21sᵖᵘ c22sᵘʳ 24g 21g 20gᵖᵘ Mar 28] workmanlike ex-Irish gelding: no h—
form over fences: one-time fair hurdler: no form for long time, sold out of T. O'Mara's
stable 3,000 gns Doncaster November Sales after fourth start: stays 2½m: acts on heavy
going. *Mrs J. C. McGregor*

MARAGUN (GER) 7 b.g. General Assembly (USA) – Marcelia (GER) (Priamos c– p
(GER)) [2002/3 h119: c16gᵖᵘ 16s² 21g⁶ 19f² 16d 17d² 17gᵇᵈ 16g 16m⁵ Apr 22] tall h119
gelding: made mistakes on chasing debut (should do better): fairly useful handicap
hurdler: best efforts in 2002/3 when second: stays 19f when conditions aren't testing: acts
on soft and firm going: visored twice: has had tongue tied: takes strong hold. *M. C. Pipe*

MARASCHINO 10 ch.m. Lycius (USA) – Mystery Ship (Decoy Boy) [2002/3 17dᵖᵘ h—
Aug 4] modest sprint maiden on Flat at 3 yrs for B. Meehan: has since produced 2 foals at
stud: showed nothing on belated hurdling debut. *K. W. Hogg, Isle of Man*

MARAUD 9 ch.g. Midyan (USA) – Peak Squaw (USA) (Icecapade (USA)) [2002/3 h89
h73: 24g⁴ 27gᵘʳ 24d³ 22m 24m⁵ 27m* 24g² 27dʳᵒ 24d² 25g* 27s⁴ 25d⁴ 24m⁶ 27gᶠ Mar
25] smallish gelding: modest handicap hurdler: won at Sedgefield in July and Catterick
in November: stays 27f: acts on firm and soft going: tried blinkered/in cheekpieces:
usually front runner. *M. E. Sowersby*

MARBLE ARCH 7 b.g. Rock Hopper – Mayfair Minx (St Columbus) [2002/3 h158: h145
16d³ 17d⁴ 16s⁵ 16g Mar 11] leggy gelding: very smart hurdler, second in 2002 Champion
Hurdle: best effort in 2002/3 when fourth to Rooster Booster in Bula Hurdle at Cheltenham in December: sweating, well held in Christmas Hurdle at Kempton and Champion
Hurdle at Cheltenham last 2 starts: raced mainly around 2m: has won on heavy going,

raced mainly under less testing conditions nowadays (acts on good to firm): held up, and travels strongly: has high head carriage: useful form at 1½m+ on Flat in 2003. *H. Morrison*

MARCH NORTH 8 b.g. Petoski – Coral Delight (Idiot's Delight) [2002/3 h105: 16m 16s 16d 17d 22d⁶ c20m² c24d³ Apr 9] compact gelding: modest handicap hurdler, well below best in 2002/3: modest form when placed both starts over fences: stays 3m: acts on soft going, probably on heavy: has worn cheekpieces. *Mrs P. Robeson* **c97 h–**

MARCUS DU BERLAIS (FR) 6 gr.g. Saint Previl (FR) – Rosacotte (FR) (Rose Laurel) [2002/3 h111: 20s 24s 19v* 20s* 20s* Mar 16] fairly useful hurdler: progressive form in handicap hurdles last 3 starts, won at Naas in January, Fairyhouse in February and Punchestown in March, rallying gamely when beating On The Jetty 1½ lengths for final success: stays 2¾m: raced on going softer than good (acts on heavy). *A. L. T. Moore, Ireland* **h128**

MARCUS MAXIMUS (USA) 8 ch.g. Woodman (USA) – Star Pastures (Northfields (USA)) [2002/3 h98: 16m* c20f² c16g² c16sᶠ c16g² Feb 22] angular gelding: fair hurdler: won intermediate at Ludlow in May: runner-up all 3 completed starts in novice chases, best effort when 1½ lengths behind Regal Exit there on second occasion: best form at 2m: acts on good to firm and good to soft going. *H. D. Daly* **c112 h107**

MARCUS WILLIAM (IRE) 6 ch.g. Roselier (FR) – River Swell (IRE) (Over The River (FR)) [2002/3 F86: F16d⁵ 17s⁶ 18v* 20d⁵ 20m³ Mar 19] good-topped gelding: signs of ability in bumpers: second start over hurdles, fair form when 66/1-winner of novice at Fontwell in January: helped set steady pace and probably flattered when fifth of 7 to Classified in Grade 2 there following month: should stay beyond 2¼m: acts on heavy going (disappointing on good to firm final outing). *B. G. Powell* **h106 F80**

MARDANI (IRE) 8 b.g. Fairy King (USA) – Marmana (USA) (Blushing Groom (FR)) [2002/3 h105: 24m* 21m* c21fᵖᵘ Aug 13] good-topped gelding: fair handicap hurdler: made most to win at Worcester in May and Huntingdon in June: shaping well, just behind winner, when pulled up lame before 2 out in novice at Newton Abbot on chasing debut: stays 3m: acts on firm and soft ground: blinkered in 2002/3. *R. S. Brookhouse* **c100 h114**

MARDELLO 5 b.m. Supreme Leader – Clonmello (Le Bavard (FR)) [2002/3 F16g Feb 22] seventh foal: sister to high-class hurdler up to 25f Marello and half-sister to fair hurdler/chaser Rockcliffe Gossip (by Phardante), stays 33f: dam unraced, out of half-sister to very smart French hurdler Highello: not knocked about when mid-field in bumper at Huntingdon on debut: bred to need much greater test of stamina. *N. J. Henderson* **F–**

MARE OF WETWANG 5 ch.m. River Falls – Kudos Blue (Elmaamul (USA)) [2002/3 16v 16vᵖᵘ 16d Feb 8] smallish mare: poor on Flat (probably stays 1¾m): no show over hurdles. *J. D. Bethell* **h–**

MARGOULIN (FR) 8 gr.g. Royal Charter (FR) – Marsaude (FR) (Tourangeau (FR)) [2002/3 c16s c20v⁵ c19s c16vᶠ c17v⁶ c17d c20g⁶ Apr 26] well-made ex-Irish gelding: one-time fair hurdler/chaser: showed little in 2002/3, left A. Moore prior to final start: should stay beyond 19f: raced on good going or softer (acts on heavy): has had tongue tied. *Mrs H. Dalton* **c– h–**

MARICO (IRE) 10 b.g. Lord Americo – Gilt Course (Crash Course) [2002/3 20d⁵ 22d⁶ 19m² 27vᵖᵘ Nov 12] sturdy ex-Irish gelding: modest in bumpers: fair pointer in Britain in 2002: poor maiden hurdler: stays 2¾m: acts on good to firm going, probably on heavy. *D. Brace* **h76**

MARIGLIANO (USA) 10 b.g. Riverman (USA) – Mount Holyoke (Golden Fleece (USA)) [2002/3 c100, h–: 16d³ 16s 16d* c16v² Jan 22] close-coupled, sparely-made gelding: modest handicap hurdler nowadays, won weak event at Fakenham in December: fair handicap chaser: raced around 2m: acts on good to firm and heavy going: has won in cheekpieces. *K. A. Morgan* **c100 h96**

MARINO WEST (IRE) 8 ch.g. Phardante (FR) – Seanaphobal Lady (Kambalda) [2002/3 h94: 20m c24mᵘʳ Jun 28] well-made gelding: winning pointer: form over hurdles only when winning novice in 2001/2, displaying awkward tail carriage throughout: hampered and unseated eleventh on steeplechasing debut: should stay beyond 2½m: acts on firm going. *N. M. Babbage* **c– h–**

MARINO WOOD (IRE) 4 ch.f. Woodpas (USA) – Forgren (IRE) (Thatching) [2002/3 16m Nov 4] poor maiden on Flat (stays 6f): slowly away and always behind in juvenile on hurdling debut: sold 700 gns Doncaster January Sales. *C. N. Kellett* **h–**

MARK-ANTONY (IRE)   9 ch.g. Phardante (FR) – Judysway (Deep Run) [2002/3 **c–**
c–, h–: 22g^{pu} 16m^{ur} Jun 30] of little account. *A. D. Smith* **h–**

MARKED MAN (IRE)   7 b.g. Grand Plaisir (IRE) – Teazle (Quayside) [2002/3 17v^6 **h99**
20d* 21g^5 21m^5 Apr 16] good-topped ex-Irish gelding: sixth foal: half-brother to fairly
useful hurdler/useful chaser Super Franky (by Lanfranco), stays 3m, and fairly useful
hunter Track O'Profit (by Kambalda), stays 3¼m: dam poor maiden hurdler: modest
hurdler: bought out of M. Morris's stable 13,000 gns Doncaster May Sales: won novice
handicap at Aintree in November: stays 21f: acts on soft and good to firm going. *R. Lee*

MARK EQUAL   7 b.g. Nicholas Bill – Dissolution (Henbit (USA)) [2002/3 h96, F85: **c96**
c16s^{F3} c19s c24d^{pu} c26g^{pu} Apr 19] winning hurdler: would have shown modest form but **h–**
for falling last (remounted) in novice at Warwick on chasing debut: shaped as if amiss all
3 subsequent starts, visored on final occasion: stays 19f: acts on firm and soft going.
M. C. Pipe

MARK IT   4 b.g. Botanic (USA) – Everdene (Bustino) [2002/3 16d^4 16m^4 16d* 16d* **h101**
17s^3 Dec 5] angular gelding: modest maiden on Flat (should stay 1¼m), sold out of
Mrs A. Perrett's stable 7,000 gns Newmarket July Sales: fair juvenile hurdler: won at
Huntingdon and Fakenham in November: acts on soft going. *D. E. Cantillon*

MARKSKEEPINGFAITH (IRE)   8 b.m. Ajraas (USA) – Felicitas (Mr Fluoro- **h–**
carbon) [2002/3 16d^{pu} May 30] ex-Irish mare: sister to fair hurdler/chaser up to 2½m
Keeping The Faith and half-sister to useful hurdler up to 21f Mystical City (by The Noble
Player): fairly useful on Flat (best around 1m): lightly raced over hurdles, modest form at
best. *N. B. Mason*

MARK THE MAN (IRE)   6 b.g. Supreme Leader – Nuala's Pet (Buckskin (FR)) **F110**
[2002/3 F16s^2 F16s* F20s^3 Dec 28] second foal: dam, won 2m chase, half-sister to fairly
useful 2m chaser Pantechnicon: useful form in bumpers, won at Fairyhouse in November
and Leopardstown in December, beating Property Partners 14 lengths in 2½m event at
latter course: interesting prospect for staying novice hurdles. *N. Meade, Ireland*

MARLBOROUGH (IRE)   11 br.g. Strong Gale – Wrekenogan (Tarqogan) [2002/3 **c169**
c160, h–: c25d* c26g c24s^2 c24g^F c26g c25g^5 Apr 3] **h–**
 The high point in a season which featured more downs than ups for Marlborough came in the King George VI Chase at Kempton, where he pushed Best
Mate closer than any other horse did in any of his three races in 2002/3. Marlborough has won a Grade 1 race, the Tote Gold Trophy Chase, billed as a substitute
Gold Cup at Sandown in 2000/1, though his short-head victory over twelve-
year-old Go Ballistic in that race, along with other runs, including a fourth in the
following season's Gold Cup, seemed to have exposed Marlborough as being just
short of true championship standard. He ran the race of his life on Boxing Day,
however, patiently ridden as suits him best, responding well to pressure, and
throwing down a strong challenge to Best Mate at the final fence; Marlborough
jumped it less well than Best Mate and was unable to close the gap on the flat, but
the winner was all out to hold him by a length and a half.
 Marlborough's one success from six starts in the latest season came in the
Peterhouse Group Charlie Hall Chase at Wetherby on his reappearance in November, when he re-opposed three horses who had finished behind him in the previous
season's Gold Cup, subsequent Grand National runner-up What's Up Boys,
Moscow Express and Lord Noelie, the eight-strong field completed by Hussard
Collonges, Grey Abbey, Gingembre and Whitenzo. Given such a high quality
line-up, the biggest surprise was that the Charlie Hall turned into one of the most
error-strewn races of the season. Gingembre made the first howler at the second,
but the main drama unfolded at the sixth, where Lord Noelie unseated his rider,
thereby failing to complete in the race for the second successive year, while What's
Up Boys took a crashing fall, in the process sustaining injuries which kept him off
the course for the remainder of the season. At the same fence, Marlborough and
Moscow Express were all but down, too, after bad mistakes, Marlborough looking
virtually out of the race after also being badly hampered. Meanwhile, the previous
season's Royal & SunAlliance winner Hussard Collonges was giving some more
experienced rivals a jumping lesson. Four out, by which time Moscow Express had
been pulled up, Whitenzo moved up strongly to dispute the lead, only to all but fall.
Marlborough, given plenty of time to recover from his error at the same fence on

Peterhouse Group Charlie Hall Chase, Wetherby—
Marlborough overcomes trouble in running to beat Hussard Collonges

the previous circuit, lost ground again by having to swerve to avoid Whitenzo. Hussard Collonges was clear by the next fence only to make a mistake himself, and he was soon being reeled in by both Grey Abbey and Marlborough. Grey Abbey completed the catalogue of errors in the race at the second last, but Marlborough continued to rally strongly, overhauling Hussard Collonges at the last and going on to record a two-length win, with Hussard Collonges all out to hold Gingembre for second in the end, and Grey Abbey fourth.

In between the Charlie Hall and the King George, Marlborough could finish only ninth, beaten eighteen and a half lengths, in the Hennessy at Newbury where, in the face of what was admittedly a stiff task, he was never in contention following early mistakes. Marlborough's jumping, which was sound in the main during the middle part of his career, became a cause for concern again in the latest season, as it had been back in 1999 when he failed to complete on four successive starts. Sent off favourite for the AON Chase at Newbury in February on the strength of his King George run, Marlborough fell at the last, though he was held in third at the time. He failed to take the eye before his last two runs, in the Gold Cup and the Martell Cognac Cup. At Cheltenham, he was a long way off reproducing the form of his fourth in the 2002 Gold Cup, let alone his King George second, his chance not helped by numerous mistakes. Marlborough had fallen at the first in the previous season's Grand National and, rather than carry top weight in the latest edition, he was saddled for the Gold Cup consolation race at the same meeting. Tried in cheek-pieces for the first time, Marlborough did at least go with much more zest than in the AON Chase or the Gold Cup, not fluent on a couple of occasions but disputing second behind First Gold until weakening before the last and eventually finishing a well-below-form fifth.

A strong gelding, Marlborough was operated on for a trapped epiglottis before his reappearance in 2001/2. He acts on good to firm and heavy going and stays three and a quarter miles, though he has twice weakened markedly in the

565

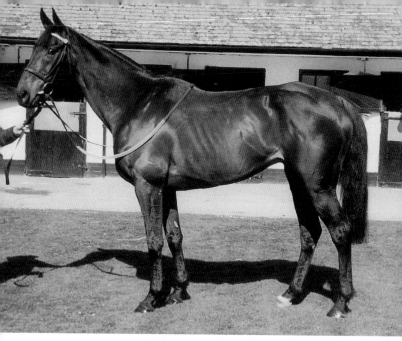

Sir Robert Ogden's "Marlborough"

Marlborough (IRE) (br.g. 1992)	Strong Gale (br 1975)	Lord Gayle (b 1965)	Sir Gaylord
			Sticky Case
		Sterntau (br 1969)	Tamerlane
			Sterna
	Wrekenogan (br 1980)	Tarqogan (br 1960)	Black Tarquin
			Rosyogan
		Wrekalong (ch 1971)	Wrekin Rambler
			Wingalong

closing stages of the Scottish National. His pedigree has been covered in earlier Annuals. Two other winners out of the unraced Wrekenogan, Marlborough's brothers Wrekengale, a fair hunter chaser nowadays, and Galeogan, who showed nothing on his return after a two-and-a-half-year lay-off, were also in action in the latest season. *N. J. Henderson*

MARMADUKE (IRE)   7 ch.g. Perugino (USA) – Sympathy (Precocious) [2002/3   **h114** h102: 17g² 17m² Jul 19] good-topped gelding: fair on Flat (seems to stay 2¼m), successful 3 times in 2002: fair handicap hurdler: good second at Hereford in June and Southwell in July: should stay beyond 17f: acts on good to firm and good to soft going: races freely/carries head awkwardly. *M. Pitman*

MARREL   5 b.g. Shareef Dancer (USA) – Upper Caen (High Top) [2002/3 20g⁶ 19d⁴   **h64** 19g⁵ Apr 26] half-brother to bumper winner Ambience Lady (by Batshoof): poor on Flat (stays 2m): signs of only a little ability in 3 starts over hurdles. *S. L. Keightley*

MARSHAL MURAT (IRE)   7 ch.g. Executive Perk – Magneeto (IRE) (Brush Aside   **F—** (USA)) [2002/3 F16d Nov 17] 21,000 4-y-o: well-made ex-Irish gelding: first foal: half-brother to useful bumper winner Watson Lake (by Be My Native): dam unraced

566

half-sister to useful hurdler Truth Be Told, stayed 3m: trained by E. Hales, fourth of 20 in bumper on debut in February 2001: well beaten in listed event at Cheltenham (reportedly finished slightly distressed) on return, pulling hard and soon eased once headed 4f out. *C. R. Egerton*

MARSH MARIGOLD 9 br.m. Tina's Pet – Pulga (Blakeney) [2002/3 h–: 17m 16s⁴ **h64** 16d Dec 14] leggy mare: winning hurdler, poor nowadays: best around 2m: acts on any going: tongue tied last 2 starts: usually held up. *G. Fierro*

MARTHA REILLY (IRE) 7 ch.m. Rainbows For Life (CAN) – Debach Delight **h88** (Great Nephew) [2002/3 h83: 24s³ 22v⁵ 23vF 23d⁴ 21d³ 24mF Mar 18] sturdy mare: modest handicap hurdler: stays 3m: acts on heavy going, probably on good to firm. *Mrs Barbara Waring*

MARTINEZ (IRE) 7 b.g. Tirol – Elka (USA) (Val de L'Orne (FR)) [2002/3 h–: 16s⁵ **c–** 20m c21mᵖᵘ Sep 13] leggy gelding: little form. *K. F. Clutterbuck* **h–**

MARTIN OSSIE 6 b.g. Bonny Scot (IRE) – So We Know (Daring March) [2002/3 **h–** F16g F16s F18v 18s⁶ 16g 16d Apr 9] 1,500 3-y-o: unfurnished gelding: first foal: dam **F–** bad maiden hurdler: well held in bumpers and over hurdles. *Dr P. Pritchard*

MARYLAND (IRE) 6 b.m. Executive Perk – Raven Night (IRE) (Mandalus) [2002/3 **F87** F17g F16m² Apr 21] first foal: dam ran once in point: better effort in mares bumpers when second to Waterlily at Fakenham. *O. Brennan*

MARZELLE (FR) 5 b.m. Sillery (USA) – Marzipan (IRE) (Green Desert (USA)) **h–** [2002/3 16m⁶ Sep 28] fair maiden on Flat (stays 11.7f), lost her form in 2002: well beaten in novice on hurdling debut. *S. Dow*

MA'S CONFUSION 5 b.m. Mr Confusion (IRE) – Spirited Lady VII (Damsire Unreg- **F–** istered) [2002/3 F16sᵖᵘ Jun 9] lengthy mare: first foal: dam unraced: well tailed off when pulled up 4f out in bumper on debut. *N. Tinkler*

MASHHOOR (USA) 5 b.g. Thunder Gulch (USA) – Memorive (USA) (Riverman **h61** (USA)) [2002/3 h–: 16d 16v³ 16s⁶ 16v⁵ 16d⁶ 19d⁶ Mar 10] leggy gelding: bad maiden hurdler: left B. Llewellyn after reappearance: blinkered: has found little. *Mrs Barbara Waring*

MASKUL (USA) 9 b.h. Lear Fan (USA) – Hooriah (USA) (Northern Dancer) [2002/3 **c?** c28g⁵ c28g³ c23g* c34v* Oct 13] won up to 1¾m on Flat at 3 yrs, third in Slovak Derby: **h–** successful 8 times over fences in Czech Republic and Slovakia since, gaining most notable win when beating Decent Fellow 7 lengths in Velka Pardubicka Ceske Pojistovny at Pardubice in October: successful on same course previous month: stays well. *R. Holcak, Czech Republic*

MASOURI SANA (IRE) 6 br.m. Broken Hearted – Say Thanks (Thatching) [2002/3 **F–** F17d Oct 12] tall, unfurnished mare: half-sister to 10.5f winner in Sweden by Taufan and 1m/11f winner in Hong Kong by Soviet Lad: dam unraced half-sister to Molecomb winner Hatta: showed nothing in mares bumper on debut. *Miss M. E. Rowland*

MASSENET (IRE) 8 b.g. Caerleon (USA) – Massawippi (Be My Native (USA)) **h–** [2002/3 h84: 19sᵘʳ Feb 27] good-topped gelding: lightly-raced hurdler, landed gamble in selling handicap in May 2001: again well backed, unseated fifth in similar event at Taunton only subsequent outing: will stay further than 2½m. *D. J. Wintle*

MASSIMO (CAN) 5 b.g. Numerous (USA) – Qui Bid (USA) (Spectacular Bid (USA)) **h–** [2002/3 h86?: 16m 20gᵖᵘ May 22] rangy, rather unfurnished gelding: form over hurdles only when second in juvenile (only start in tongue strap) in 2001/2. *Jonjo O'Neill*

MASTER BILLYBOY (IRE) 5 b.g. Old Vic – Clonodfoy (Strong Gale) [2002/3 **h109 p** F–: 16g⁵ 17s 19d* 19d² 21s² Feb 28] leggy gelding: fair form over hurdles, won novice at Exeter in December: good second to Dungarvans Choice in handicap at Newbury final start: raced on good going or softer (acts on soft): likely to improve further given another step up in trip. *Mrs S. D. Williams*

MASTER BILLY (IRE) 5 b.g. Parthian Springs – Curracloe Star (Over The River **F100** (FR)) [2002/3 F16v³ F18s² F18s* Mar 5] second foal: dam winning pointer: fairly useful form in bumpers, won maiden at Downpatrick in March by 6 lengths from Ballytobin. *Paul Nolan, Ireland*

MASTER BREW 5 b.g. Homo Sapien – Edithmead (IRE) (Shardari) [2002/3 F17s **F–** F18v Dec 4] 5,800 4-y-o: second foal: dam novice hurdler, stayed 2¾m: in trouble as soon as pace increased both starts in bumpers. *J. R. Best*

MASTER CHET (IRE)   13 b.g. Callernish – C C Meade (Paddy's Stream) [2002/3 c–, h74d: 26gᵖᵘ May 30] workmanlike gelding: novice hurdler/winning chaser, little form for long time: blinkered/tongue tied nowadays. *Miss Z. C. Davison* **c– h–**

MASTER CLUB ROYAL   8 b.g. Teenoso (USA) – Miss Club Royal (Avocat) [2002/3 c78, h–: c21s³ c24s³ c27s* c26vᵖᵘ c24v⁴ c22d⁶ c27d⁴ Mar 18] lengthy gelding: twice-raced hurdler: poor chaser: won amateur handicap at Sedgefield in November (subsequently tested positive for morphine), only form in 2002/3: stays 27f: raced on going softer than good (acts on heavy): has worn visor/cheekpieces, usually blinkered: unreliable. *D. McCain* **c78 § h–**

MASTER CRUISE   7 b.g. Zambrano – Miss Cruise (Cruise Missile) [2002/3 22dᵖᵘ Feb 17] first known foal: dam, sister to winning jumper Miss Fern, no sign of ability: no show in novice hurdle on debut. *N. M. Babbage* **h–**

MASTER ELECT (IRE)   6 ch.g. Phardante (FR) – Proud Polly (IRE) (Pollerton) [2002/3 F16d5 Aug 3] third foal: half-brother to winning pointer/poor hurdler Proud Fountain (by Royal Fountain), stays 3¼m: dam unraced half-sister to fairly useful staying hurdler/chaser Roundwood: fifth of 22 to Dusty Too in bumper at Worcester on debut. *M. Pitman* **F75**

MASTER ELLIS (IRE)   4 b.g. Turtle Island (IRE) – Take No Chances (IRE) (Thatching) [2002/3 17sᵖᵘ 16d 17s⁴ 16m² Apr 2] workmanlike gelding: lightly raced on Flat: best effort over hurdles when second in seller at Ludlow, racing freely early: probably suited by sharp 2m. *P. D. Evans* **h69**

MASTER FLORIAN (IRE)   6 gr.g. Roselier (FR) – Paddy's Well (Paddy's Stream) [2002/3 21s* 20s* 24s⁴ Jan 28] rather unfurnished gelding: third foal: dam, twice-raced in points, half-sister to Scottish National winner Moorcroft Boy: won maiden point on debut in 2002: fair form over hurdles: won novices at Plumpton in November and Fontwell (handicap, beat Lesdream ½ length) in December: favourite, not fluent when creditable fourth to Glen Warrior in handicap at Taunton: stays 3m: raced only on soft ground. *P. F. Nicholls* **h100 +**

MASTER GATEMAKER   5 b.g. Tragic Role (USA) – Girl At The Gate (Formidable (USA)) [2002/3 17gᶠ 16s 17gᵖᵘ 17s 16m Apr 21] poor maiden on Flat: no form over hurdles: tried in cheekpieces/tongue tied. *R. C. Guest* **h–**

MASTER GEORGE   6 b.g. Mtoto – Topwinder (USA) (Topsider (USA)) [2002/3 h115: 20v* 20s² 19d 20v⁶ 22d 24m⁴ Mar 21] close-coupled gelding: fairly useful hurdler: won novice at Ascot in November: disappointing subsequently, respectable effort only when sixth in handicap at Chepstow: stays 21f: acts on heavy going: blinkered final outing. *P. J. Hobbs* **h117**

MASTER GINGER POP   7 b.g. Supreme Leader – Ruckinge Girl (Eborneezer) [2002/3 h–: c23g⁴ c23d⁴ c23d⁴ c26vᵖᵘ c26sᵖᵘ c23g² c26g² Apr 21] lengthy, angular gelding: maiden hurdler/modest maiden chaser: stays 3¼m: blinkered last 5 outings. *Mrs S. D. Williams* **c86 h–**

MASTER JED (IRE)   6 br.g. Bob's Return (IRE) – Evan's Love (Master Owen) [2002/3 F16g F16m⁶ Mar 20] IR 17,000 3-y-o: thirteenth foal: half-brother to poor 2m hurdler Antiguan Smile (by Croghan Hill): dam unraced half-sister to dam of top-class chaser up to 3¼m Strong Promise: signs of ability in bumpers, 12 lengths sixth of 9 at Wincanton. *J. A. B. Old* **F84 ?**

MASTER JOCK   9 ch.g. Scottish Reel – Mistress Corrado (New Member) [2002/3 c26d⁴ Jun 8] first foal: dam maiden pointer: fair pointer, successful in January and April: keeping-on fourth in maiden hunter chase at Cartmel. *P. Jones* **c77**

MASTER JONES   6 b.g. Emperor Jones (USA) – Tight Spin (High Top) [2002/3 h–: 24m⁶ Jun 29] temperamental maiden on Flat: well held in 2 novice hurdles. *Mrs H. L. Walton* **h–**

MASTER MCGRATH (IRE)   5 b.g. Common Grounds – Darabaka (IRE) (Doyoun) [2002/3 25d⁴ 24v* 24d³ Feb 7] leggy gelding: half-brother to smart 2m hurdler Far Cry (by Pharly): fair on Flat (stays 17.5f): fair form over hurdles: jumped better when winning maiden at Chepstow in January by 5 lengths from Alleged Slave, looked less than willing under pressure: will stay beyond 3m: acts on heavy going: visored. *M. C. Pipe* **h108**

MASTER MILLFIELD (IRE)   11 b.g. Prince Rupert (FR) – Calash (Indian King (USA)) [2002/3 c–, h–: 16mᵖᵘ c19mᵖᵘ Apr 21] useful-looking gelding: one-time fairly **c– h–**

useful handicap hurdler, retains little ability: left R. Baker after reappearance: tried in cheekpieces. *Stephen Richard Griffiths*

MASTEROFFOXHOUNDS (IRE)   8 br.g. Be My Native (USA) – Sylvia Fox   **h117 p**
(Deep Run) [2002/3 F16s⁴ F16s* F16s* 16s* 16sᵖᵘ Feb 2]   **F116**

It's a pity Masteroffoxhounds was injured in the build-up to the Festival meetings in the spring. Judged on his initial efforts, he would have been well worth a place in one of the top novice hurdles. Although an eight-year-old, he was making just his fifth appearance when pulled up lame in a Grade 2 novice hurdle at Punchestown in February, for which he started second favourite behind Kicking King. Encouragingly, Masteroffoxhounds returned to action in the summer, winning a mile-and-three-quarter amateur riders maiden on the Flat, and can be expected to make an impact either over hurdles or in novice chase company in 2003/4. Masteroffoxhounds had won his three previous starts. After finishing a promising fourth in a bumper at Navan on his debut, he won two similar events at Cork. He had the field well strung out when landing the odds in December then put up a smart effort, one of the best in such a race all season in Ireland, when defeating Poker Pal and Rockstown Boy (later somewhat unfortunate in the Grade 1 bumper at Punchestown) in impressive style, showing a good turn of foot on testing ground, in January. A couple of weeks later he was odds on for his hurdling debut and barely came off the bridle to win by a length and a half from Lonesome Man. That represents just fairly useful form but there looked a good deal more to come. Masteroffoxhounds has so far raced only on soft going in bumpers and over hurdles (his Flat win was on firm), in contrast to his brother Buffalo Bill, a useful bumper winner who has yet to encounter softer than good. Buffalo Bill, who is also trained by David Wachman, and Masteroffoxhounds are the first two foals out of Sylvia Fox, a two-mile winner on the Flat and over hurdles in Ireland. Her third foal Back Nine (by Bob Back) also won a bumper in the latest season. Sylvia Fox is a half-sister to the useful two-mile chaser Belstone Fox. This is the family of the smart two-mile chaser Wild Fox, the County Hurdle winner Java Fox and the Champion Hurdle runner-up Farrney Fox. Whether Masteroffoxhounds, who was bought as a four-year-old for 50,000 guineas at the Doncaster May Sales, will prove best at two miles remains to be seen, but he certainly doesn't want for speed. *D. Wachman, Ireland*

MASTER OF ILLUSION (IRE)   10 ch.g. Castle Keep – Galloping Gold VII (Dam-   **c109**
sire Unregistered) [2002/3 c111, h–: c26s³ c25v² c24sᵘʳ c30s² c24s c24s* Mar 10] leggy,   **h–**
sparely-made gelding: fair handicap chaser: won at Stratford by a 1¾ lengths from Keltic Heritage: needs 3m+: acts on any going: effective visored or not. *R. Lee*

MASTER PAPA (IRE)   4 br.g. Key of Luck (USA) – Beguine (USA) (Green Dancer   **h117**
(USA)) [2002/3 16s⁴ 16s* 17d³ 16v⁵ 16m⁶ 17m³ Apr 16] angular gelding: fairly useful on Flat (stays 17f): fairly useful juvenile hurdler: won maiden at Thurles in November: sold out of K. Prendergast's stable €52,000 Goffs December Sale: best subsequent efforts when sixth in Grade 2 at Kempton in February and second to Harchibald in well-contested minor event at Punchestown in late-April: likely to stay beyond 17f: acts on good to firm and heavy going. *N. A. Twiston-Davies*

MASTER RIDE (IRE)   8 b.g. King's Ride – Cahore (Quayside) [2002/3 h–: 22g²   **c103**
c23d² c24s³ Feb 26] fair hurdler, lightly raced: similar form when 14 lengths second of 4   **h103**
finishers to One Knight in novice at Exeter on chasing debut: reportedly suffered heat exhaustion when well held following month: stays 23f: raced on good going or softer (acts on heavy). *A. J. Lidderdale*

MASTER RUSSELL (IRE)   9 b.g. Supreme Leader – Quality Suite (Prince Hansel)   **c– x**
[2002/3 c–x, h86: 22d³ 22s 21s⁴ 19dᶠ Dec 21] lengthy gelding: let down by jumping both   **h–**
starts over fences: maiden hurdler, little worthwhile form in 2002/3: best form up to 19f: acts on soft and firm going: tried visored. *P. A. Pritchard*

MASTER TERN (USA)   8 ch.g. Generous (IRE) – Young Hostess (FR) (Arctic Tern   **c140**
(USA)) [2002/3 c116p, h142: c20s⁴ c20gᵖᵘ c16d⁴ c20g² c25d* Apr 4] big, leggy gelding: **h–**
shows traces of stringhalt: has reportedly had wind operation: useful handicap hurdler/chaser: upped in trip, improved effort over fences when winning valuable 14-runner event at Aintree by 1¼ lengths from Shardam, making couple of mistakes but showing better

Martell Cognac V.S. Thresher Handicap Chase, Aintree—
Master Tern (right) proves too strong for Shardam and Ross Moff (noseband)

attitude than is sometimes the case: stays 25f: acts on good to firm and heavy going: patiently ridden: not fluent jumper of fences. *Jonjo O'Neill*

MASTER TRIX (IRE) 6 b.g. Lord Americo – Bannow Drive (IRE) (Miner's Lamp) **h108**
[2002/3 F99: 17s* 21d² 20v³ 22v² 20vᵖᵘ 24dᵘʳ Apr 4] compact gelding: bumper winner: fair novice hurdler: won conditional jockeys event at Folkestone in November: similar form when placed next 3 starts, but struggled when upped in class: should stay 3m: raced on going softer than good over hurdles. *M. Pitman*

MASTER TUMNUS (IRE) 7 b.g. Bob Back (USA) – Implicit View (Persian Bold) **h–**
[2002/3 16d 16dᶠ 16dᵖᵘ Mar 5] bumper winner in 1999/00: no sign of retaining ability over hurdles. *A. Dickman*

MASTER T (USA) 4 b.g. Trempolino (USA) – Our Little C (USA) (Marquetry **h102**
(USA)) [2002/3 17f* 16g² Apr 12] fair on Flat (stays 1¼m): won juvenile at Taunton on hurdling debut in March by 1½ lengths from Fast Mix, presented with lead 2 out and eased run-in: better form when neck second of 15 to Pirandello in novice handicap at Stratford, mistake last when looking sure to win: likely to prove best around 2m. *G. L. Moore*

MASTER WOOD 12 b.g. Wonderful Surprise – Miss Wood (Precipice Wood) **c112**
[2002/3 c–, h–: c25d⁴ c30d⁴ c25d² c22d* c25d* c21gᵘʳ c25mᵖᵘ Apr 21] sturdy gelding: **h–**
useful chaser at best: found some form again in hunters in 2003, won at Haydock in February and Wetherby (seventh course success) in March: stays 3¼m: acts on heavy going: often front runner. *C. Grant*

MATERIAL WORLD 5 b.m. Karinga Bay – Material Girl (Busted) [2002/3 F17g* **F103**
Apr 26] has only one eye (wears eyecover): third foal: dam, fairly useful hunter chaser, half-sister to very smart middle-distance performer Town And Country: 25/1, won bumper at Market Rasen on debut by 10 lengths from Prince of Slane. *Miss Suzy Smith*

MATRIX (AUS) 6 b.g. Centaine (AUS) – Iced Lass (NZ) (Half Iced (USA)) [2002/3 **h78**
F87: 19d 21s⁵ 16d 26m⁶ Mar 23] tall gelding: poor form over hurdles: failed to settle over 3¼m final start. *K. C. Bailey*

MATT HOLLAND 10 b.g. Makbul – Shirley Grove (Vulgan Slave) [2002/3 h94: **c– x**
c21sᶠ c23g c23dᵖᵘ Mar 6] workmanlike gelding: modest maiden hurdler: badly let down **h–**
by jumping over fences: should stay at least 3m: raced on good going or softer (acts on heavy). *Mrs L. Wadham*

570

MAUNBY ROLLER (IRE) 4 b.g. Flying Spur (AUS) – Brown Foam (Horage) **h–**
[2002/3 16d^{pu} 21g^{pu} Mar 25] half-brother to winning Irish pointer by Lafontaine: modest
on Flat (stays 9.4f), claimed from P. Haslam £4,000 after successful in January: pulled
up in 2 races over hurdles, jumped poorly on first occasion and blinkered on second.
P. A. Blockley

MAUNSELL'S ROAD (IRE) 4 b.g. Desert Style (IRE) – Zara's Birthday (IRE) **h85**
(Waajib) [2002/3 17d 18g^3 Mar 21] fair on Flat (stays 1½m), claimed from S. Kirk
£18,000 in October: caught the eye on hurdling debut, some improvement when 11
lengths third of 8 in juvenile at Kelso. *L. Lungo*

MAWTHOOK (USA) 5 ch.g. Silver Hawk (USA) – Zakiyya (USA) (Dayjur (USA)) **F–**
[2002/3 F–: F16s May 26] no show in 2 bumpers. *J. R. Turner*

MAXIE MCDONALD (IRE) 10 b.g. Homo Sapien – Lovely Sanara (Proverb) **c99**
[2002/3 c104, h–: c24m^3 c24d^{ur} c23g^4 c20d^2 c24s^{ur} Jan 27] lengthy gelding: modest **h–**
handicap chaser: effective at 2½m to 3m: acts on good to firm and good to soft going:
sometimes makes mistakes/soon off bridle. *N. A. Twiston-Davies*

MAXIMIZE (IRE) 9 b.g. Mandalus – Lone Run (Kemal (FR)) [2002/3 c134, h–: **c132**
c25g^4 c24s^4 c24m c24g^4 c36d^F Apr 5] strong gelding: useful chaser: creditable fourth to **h–**
Youlneverwalkalone in National Hunt Handicap Chase at Cheltenham: 16/1, had lost
place when falling nineteenth in Grand National at Aintree following month: should stay
beyond 25f: acts on good to firm and heavy going: races prominently: usually sound
jumper: sold to join M. Pipe 62,000 gns Doncaster May Sales. *Miss H. C. Knight*

MAXIMUS (IRE) 8 br.g. Un Desperado (FR) – Fais Vite (USA) (Sharpen Up) **c–**
[2002/3 c–, h114d: 16d 22f 17d 22s^2 22d^3 22v Mar 7] medium-sized gelding: let down **h92**
by jumping only outing in steeplechase: winning hurdler, modest nowadays: left
D. Grissell after second start: stays 2¾m: acts on soft going: tried blinkered/tongue tied.
C. P. Morlock

MAX PRIDE 8 br.g. Good Thyne (USA) – An Bothar Dubh (Strong Gale) [2002/3 **c115**
c100, h82: 22d* c22d^4 c29s* c30v* c29d^2 Mar 8] medium-sized gelding: easily best **h104**
effort over hurdles when winning novice handicap at Exeter in November: fairly useful
handicap chaser: won at Warwick in December and Bangor (made all) in February: better
than ever when 3½ lengths second of 5 to Ballybrophy at Warwick: thorough stayer: acts
on heavy going: genuine. *R. Dickin*

MAX'S MICRO (IRE) 4 b.g. Inzar (USA) – Guess Who (Be My Guest (USA)) **h80**
[2002/3 17g 16s^6 16d^{su} 16s^5 17s 16v^2 16v* 16s^3 Feb 12] medium-sized gelding: half-
brother to winning 2m hurdler Hazard A Guess (by Digamist): poor maiden on Flat for
P. D. Evans: poor hurdler: won novice claimer at Leicester in January: raced around 2m:
acts on heavy ground: has worn cheekpieces/visor. *John Allen*

MAYBE JUST MAYBE (IRE) 6 b.g. Tirol – Templemore (IRE) (Alzao (USA)) **h–**
[2002/3 F–: 19d^{pu} May 14] seemingly of no account. *Mrs A. M. Thorpe*

MAYBELLE 8 b.m. Royal Vulcan – Full of Love (Full of Hope) [2002/3 h–: 21d^{pu} **h–**
16g 20m^6 Mar 18] workmanlike mare: of little account. *J. S. King*

MAYBE'N 6 ch.g. Deploy – Travel Mystery (Godswalk (USA)) [2002/3 c–, h–: c19f^4 **c65**
May 15] poor maiden jumper: tried visored. *M. Ranger* **h–**

MAYBESEVEN 9 gr.g. Baron Blakeney – Ninth of May (Comedy Star (USA)) **c64**
[2002/3 c80d, h–: c26v^4 c20v^3 c22s^{pu} c26s^{pu} Feb 26] good-topped gelding: poor handicap **h–**
chaser: stays 3¼m: raced on good going or softer (acts on soft): blinkered final start
(made bad mistake): has broken blood vessel: inconsistent. *T. R. George*

MAYBE THE BUSINESS 7 ch.g. Karinga Bay – Music Interpreter (Kampala) **h118**
[2002/3 F112: 20s^F 16s^2 22s* 21s^4 24d^4 Jan 25] tall, angular gelding: winning pointer/
bumper winner: looked really promising first and third starts over hurdles, winning
maiden at Folkestone in December: disappointing otherwise, and collapsed and died after
fourth at Doncaster: should have stayed 3m: acted on soft going, won bumper on good to
firm. *P. F. Nicholls*

MAYB-MAYB 13 ch.g. Gunner B – Mayotte (Little Buskins) [2002/3 c–, h–§: 22g **c–**
May 25] tall gelding: winning hurdler, no form since 2000/1: blinkered/visored: tongue **h– §**
tied. *J. Neville*

MAYERLING 6 b.m. Old Vic – Manon Lescaut (Then Again) [2002/3 F–: 20d 20g^F **h–**
Mar 25] little sign of ability in bumper and novice hurdles. *Miss E. C. Lavelle*

MAYLANE   9 b.g. Mtoto – Possessive Dancer (Shareef Dancer (USA)) [2002/3 16m^rtr **h§§**
16m^rtr Jul 17] smart at best on Flat (stays 2½m) for A. Stewart, though thoroughly temperamental: refused to race both appearances over hurdles: one to avoid. *B. G. Powell*

MAZEED (IRE)   10 ch.g. Lycius (USA) – Maraatib (IRE) (Green Desert (USA)) **h–**
[2002/3 h77d: 22g 22m^6 20m 27g^6 22f^4 22m^pu Sep 7] sturdy gelding: winning hurdler,
out of form since early in 2001/2. *Miss K. M. George*

MAZILEO   10 b.g. Mazilier (USA) – Embroglio (USA) (Empery (USA)) [2002/3 **c121**
c111, h–: 24d^5 c24d^ur c24d* Nov 9] workmanlike gelding: winning hurdler: fairly useful **h–**
handicap chaser: won 6-runner event at Sandown convincingly from below-par rivals,
jumping boldly and in command some way out: barely stays 25f: acts on firm and soft
going: races freely, prone to odd blunder. *Ian Williams*

MAZRAM   4 b.f. Muhtarram (USA) – Royal Mazi (Kings Lake (USA)) [2002/3 F17g **F–**
F16g Mar 23] fourth foal: dam, ungenuine winning hurdler, half-sister to useful 2m
hurdler Executive Design: well beaten in 2 bumpers and in seller on Flat. *G. P. Kelly*

MAZURY (USA)   4 b.g. Langfuhr (CAN) – Assurgent (USA) (Damascus (USA)) **h–**
[2002/3 17d 16g 17f^5 16d^pu 17m^5 Apr 15] fair at best on Flat (stays 1m), sold out
of M. Johnston's stable 7,000 gns Newmarket July Sales: little form over hurdles.
Miss J. S. Davis

MAZZINI (IRE)   12 b.g. Celio Rufo – Dontellvi (The Parson) [2002/3 16g^pu 22m^3 **h93**
22m^5 26s^5 22d* 20s 22g* 27f^6 Apr 24] useful-looking gelding: modest handicap hurdler,
off 3 years prior to reappearance: won at Fontwell in December (left well clear when
Mithak fell 2 out) and March: stays 2¾m: acts on soft and firm going: has shown signs of
temperament. *R. Rowe*

MCCRINKLE (IRE)   6 b.g. Mandalus – Crinkle Lady (Buckskin (FR)) [2002/3 F16d **F–**
Apr 25] IR £3,200 4-y-o: fourth foal: brother to winning pointer: dam unraced half-sister
to smart chasers Another Coral and Raymylette: tailed off in bumper on debut. *Mrs
C. J. Kerr*

MCFARLINE (IRE)   7 b.g. Ela-Mana-Mou – Highland Ball (Bold Lad (IRE)) [2002/3 **c–**
19d^F 16d 17v^pu c19m^pu Apr 5] compact gelding: winning hurdler, no longer of any **h–**
account. *N. J. Hawke*

MCGINTY ALL STARS (IRE)   5 b.m. Fourstars Allstar (USA) – Dowdstown **F–**
Miss (Wolver Hollow) [2002/3 F16g Dec 12] sister to winning 2½m hurdler Dowdstown
Star and half-sister to winning 3m hurdler Bitofabuzz (by Electric) and fair jumper up to
3m Legal Artist (by Tate Gallery): dam, won up to 1½m in USA, half-sister to Strong
Gale: well beaten in mares bumper on debut. *R. J. Price*

MCGRUDERS CROSS (IRE)   5 b.g. Toulon – Kayanna (Torenaga) [2002/3 F16s* **F104**
F16d* F16g Mar 12] well-made gelding: fourth foal: half-brother to winning chaser Ello
Ollie (by Roselier), stays 3¼m: dam unraced: fairly useful form in bumpers: successful in
19-runner maiden at Fairyhouse in January and 6-runner event at Navan (made all) in
February, quickening well both times: failed to settle and never a threat in Grade 1 at
Cheltenham. *Anthony Mullins, Ireland*

MCSNAPPY   6 ch.g. Risk Me (FR) – Nannie Annie (Persian Bold) [2002/3 h87, F90: **h107**
24s^2 24v^3 Nov 22] leggy gelding: placed in bumpers: improved efforts over hurdles in
2002/3, stiff task when remote third of 5 to Ad Hoc in novice at Ascot: stays 3m: acts on
heavy going. *J. W. Mullins*

MEADOWS BOY   11 gr.g. Derrylin – What A Coup (Malicious) [2002/3 c§§, h§§: **c§§**
20g 19d^F 19g^2 20d* 23v Dec 28] workmanlike gelding: capable of fair form over **h106 §**
hurdles: won claimer at Haydock in November: stays 23f: probably acts on any going:
tried blinkered/in hood: often refuses to race: not to be trusted. *R. Lee*

MEAL TICKET   10 b.g. Henbit (USA) – Padykin (Bustino) [2002/3 c16d^4 c16g^6 **c–**
c17d^pu Aug 26] big gelding: winning pointer: modest form at best over fences, no show **h–**
in blinkers in 2002/3 (bled from nose final start): stays 2½m: acts on good to soft and
good to firm going: tongue tied. *J. G. Carr, Ireland*

MEANDER (IRE)   8 br.g. Mandalus – Lady Rerico (Pamroy) [2002/3 c97, h–: c24d^5 **c–**
c29s c28g^4 Mar 25] useful-looking gelding: winning 3m chaser: well held in handicaps **h–**
in 2002/3, left Miss H. Knight after second start: prone to breaking blood vessels. *Mrs
K. B. Mactaggart*

MEASURE OF THE MAN   5 b.g. Dr Devious (IRE) – Run Faster (IRE) (Comm- **h92**
anche Run) [2002/3 16d F17g^6 16d* 20d Nov 24] fifth foal: half-brother to several **F76**
winners on Flat, including 2001 5f winner Swiftly (by Cadeaux Genereux): dam Italian

1m/9f winner: once-raced in bumpers: modest hurdler: won handicap at Cork in October: weakened rapidly in similar event at Aintree following month: seems best at 2m: raced mainly on good/good to soft going: tongue tied last 2 starts. *C. Roche, Ireland*

MEDALLIST   4 b.g. Danehill (USA) – Obsessive (USA) (Seeking The Gold (USA)) **h73** [2002/3 16g 16d⁵ 16d 17d⁴ Mar 18] fairly useful on Flat (stays 1¼m), sold out of Sir Michael Stoute's stable 15,000 gns Newmarket Autumn Sales: poor form over hurdles: barely stays 2m. *B. Ellison*

MEDELAI   7 b.m. Marju (IRE) – No Islands (Lomond (USA)) [2002/3 h–: 17g⁴ 16mᵖᵘ **h54** 17d⁵ 16dᵖᵘ 16s³ 17m³ 16g 16s⁶ Dec 27] leggy mare: bad maiden hurdler: raced mainly around 2m: acts on good to firm and soft going: blinkered: takes strong hold. *A. G. Juckes*

MEDICI (FR)   5 bl.g. Cadoudal (FR) – Marie de Valois (FR) (Moulin) [2002/3 F16s⁴ **F92** Jan 18] leggy gelding: sixth foal: half-brother to 3 winners, including useful chaser/winning hurdler up to 25f Repere (by Rose Laurel): dam 9f winner in France: fair form when fourth of 20 to Cloudy Grey in well-contested bumper at Haydock on debut. *Jonjo O'Neill*

MEDIUM WAVE   11 b.g. Domynsky – Alumia (Great Nephew) [2002/3 c92, h–: **c87 §** c19g⁴ c16m⁴ c19gᵖᵘ Jun 12] leggy, quite good-topped gelding: winning hurdler: modest **h–** handicap chaser: stays 2¾m: acts on good and firm and soft going: blinkered/visored: usually tongue tied: not one to rely on. *S. E. H. Sherwood*

MEDKHAN (IRE)   6 ch.g. Lahib (USA) – Safayn (USA) (Lyphard (USA)) [2002/3 **h–** 16s 16m Jun 28] leggy gelding: disappointing maiden on Flat: always behind in 2 novice hurdles. *F. Jordan*

MEGABYTE (IRE)   9 b.m. Glacial Storm (USA) – Panalpina (Petorius) [2002/3 **c–** 16dᶠ Jul 5] workmanlike mare: winning hurdler/chaser: behind when fell in seller, only **h–** outing since early-2000/1: races freely. *Miss Lucinda V. Russell*

MEGA (IRE)   7 b.m. Petardia – Gobolino (Don) [2002/3 h78: 16m 24sᵖᵘ Jun 13] **h–** workmanlike mare: poor maiden hurdler: unlikely to stay 3m. *M. H. Tompkins*

MEGALEX   5 ch.m. Karinga Bay – Flaming Rose (IRE) (Roselier (FR)) [2002/3 **h78** F17g³ 20dᵖᵘ 18s⁴ 20v* Mar 3] first foal: dam no sign of ability: modest form when third **F79** of 17 in bumper at Hereford: left Miss G. Browne, best effort in mares novice hurdles when winning at Fontwell, though reportedly finished lame: stays 2½m: acts on heavy going. *G. L. Moore*

MEGAZINE   9 b.g. Shaab – Sherzine (Gorytus (USA)) [2002/3 c–, h–: 22g² 22g³ 17d⁵ **c–** 19d⁵ 22v⁴ 17v* 19s⁵ 17d⁵ 17v* Dec 28] pulled up only start over fences: modest handicap **h95** hurdler: won at Newton Abbot in November and Taunton (weak 5-runner event, by 17 lengths) in December: possibly best short of 2¾m: raced on good going or softer (acts on heavy): amateur ridden for both wins. *M. Hill*

MEGGIE'S BEAU (IRE)   7 ch.g. Good Thyne (USA) – Romantic Rose (IRE) (Strong **h112** Gale) [2002/3 24s⁵ 20v 19s² 20gᵖᵘ Apr 23] sturdy gelding: twice-raced in bumpers: easily best effort over hurdles (off 2 years before debut) when ½-length second to Nonantais in novice at Taunton: reportedly lame final start: should stay 3m: raced mainly on soft/heavy ground. *Miss Venetia Williams*

MEGGIES GAMBLE (IRE)   6 b.g. Zaffaran (USA) – Glaskerbeg Lady (IRE) **F94** (Radical) [2002/3 F18d³ Feb 17] second foal: dam unraced half-sister to dam of one-time useful staying hurdler Garruth: around 12 lengths third of 18 to easy winner Eric's Charm in bumper at Fontwell on debut. *Miss Venetia Williams*

MEGGIE'S LAD (IRE)   6 b.g. Beau Sher – Kambaya (IRE) (Kambalda) [2002/3 **F96** F16d* F16v⁵ Mar 8] IR 7,200 3-y-o: rather unfurnished gelding: second foal: dam unraced half-sister to smart hurdler/high-class chaser Boca Boca, stayed 25f: won bumper at Southwell on debut in November by 8 lengths from Nickel Suntoo: well held on more testing ground 4 months later: will stay beyond 2m. *Miss Venetia Williams*

MEILLEUR (NZ)   5 ch.g. Mellifont (USA) – Petite Cheval (NZ) (Engagement **F81** (USA)) [2002/3 F16s⁵ F16g Mar 2] unfurnished gelding: better effort in bumpers when fifth of 17 to Cleopatras Therapy in conditional jockeys event at Ludlow: raced far too freely next time. *A. J. Whitehead*

MELDRUM STAR (IRE)   6 ch.g. Fourstars Allstar (USA) – Meldrum Lass (Buck- **h86** skin (FR)) [2002/3 F16g⁶ 16m* 20dᵖᵘ Nov 12] sturdy gelding: third foal: half-brother to **F73** fairly useful hurdler up to 3m World Wide Web and a winning Irish pointer (both by Be My Native): dam unraced, from family of Irish National winner Sweet Dreams: pulled up in maiden Irish point on debut in 2002: sixth in bumper at Worcester: won novice at

573

Haydock on hurdling debut in October: weakened tamely at Southwell following month: should stay beyond 2m. *Mrs S. J. Smith*

MELFORD (IRE) 5 br.g. Presenting – Echo Creek (IRE) (Strong Gale) [2002/3 F16s⁶ 16d Nov 29] well-made gelding: third foal: half-brother to fair 2½m to 3m hurdler Over The Beck (by Over The River): dam lightly-raced maiden hurdler: shaped like a stayer when sixth of 12 to Mac Hine in bumper at Sandown on debut: soon in rear and less than fluent in maiden hurdle at Newbury later in month. *Miss H. C. Knight* **h– F86**

MELSTAIR 8 b.g. Terimon – Kevins Lady (Alzao (USA)) [2002/3 h–: c17dᵘʳ 20dᵖᵘ 20dᵖᵘ 20g⁵ 20g 20gᵖᵘ Apr 1] medium-sized gelding: poor maiden hurdler, little form since 2000/1: unseated first on chasing debut: bled from nose fifth outing. *A. R. Dicken* **c– h–**

MELTONIAN 6 ch.g. Past Glories – Meltonby (Sayf El Arab (USA)) [2002/3 h–, F88: 19g⁴ 17f 23d⁵ 24m⁶ 20d³ 21g² 20g³ 19dᵖᵘ Oct 19] compact gelding: modest novice hurdler, sold out of K. Bailey's stable 5,200 gns Doncaster May Sales after third start: may prove best short of 23f: acts on good to soft going: visored third outing. *K. F. Clutterbuck* **h86**

MELY MOSS (FR) 12 ch.g. Tip Moss (FR) – The Exception (FR) (Melyno)] [2002/3 NR] tall gelding: useful handicap chaser, very lightly raced: second to Papillon in Grand National in 2000: showed nothing in cross-country race at Punchestown after 13-month absence in early-May: stays 4½m: acts on soft going: usually sound jumper. *C. R. Egerton* **c– h–**

MEMORIAL ARCH 5 b.g. Meadowbrook – Sheer Luck (Shergar) [2002/3 F16g F16g³ F17g³ Sep 28] eighth foal: half-brother to 4 winners, including fairly useful hurdler up to 3m/Flat stayer Golden Arrow (by Glint of Gold): dam, 1¼m winner, half-sister to very smart 1m to 1¼m performer King of Clubs: modest form when third in bumpers. *I. A. Balding* **F84**

MEMORY LANE 8 ro.m. Baron Blakeney – Raise Memories (Skyliner) [2002/3 17gᵖᵘ Jun 10] little sign of ability, off 2 years before hurdling debut. *J. C. Tuck* **h–**

MEMSAHIB OFESTEEM 12 gr.m. Neltino – Occatillo (Maris Piper) [2002/3 h105: 20sᵖᵘ 19s³ 20v 21m⁴ Apr 17] strong, workmanlike mare: fair handicap hurdler: best effort in 2002/3 when fourth to Blue Ride in listed mares event at Cheltenham: probably finds 2½m a minimum, and stays 3m: acts on any going: not a straightforward ride: tough. *S. Gollings* **h102**

MENDIP MANOR 5 b.g. Rakaposhi King – Broughton Manor (Dubassoff (USA)) [2002/3 F16mᵘʳ F16g Apr 2] has scope: second foal: dam, fairly useful chaser, stayed 21f: tailed off on completed outing in bumpers (unseated after swerving right at start on debut). *S. C. Burrough* **F–**

MENELEK LORD (IRE) 9 b.g. Yashgan – Higcham (Le Moss) [2002/3 c92, h–: c24dᵖᵘ c24sᵖᵘ c30sᵖᵘ 25d³ 24s² 24v⁵ Mar 13] angular gelding: modest novice hurdler/ handicap chaser: left A. Streeter after first outing, ran poorly next 2 after break: stays 27f: acts on heavy going: wears headgear: sold 2,800 gns Doncaster May Sales. *R. Ford* **c– h85**

MENESONIC (IRE) 13 b.g. Meneval (USA) – Kandy Kate (Pry) [2002/3 c119, h–: c23g⁵ May 1] well-made gelding: veteran staying chaser, below form since 2001/2 reappearance: acts on any going: sound jumper: tends to go in snatches. *R. H. Alner* **c– h–**

MENSCH (IRE) 7 ch.g. Husyan (USA) – Floating Dollar (Master Owen) [2002/3 h61: c24f² c24m⁸ Apr 22] poor maiden hurdler: sold out of A. Hales's stable £750 Ascot June Sales: won both starts in points prior to distant second to Jabiru at Taunton, better effort in hunter chases: probably stays 3m: acts on firm going: tried blinkered/in cheek-pieces. *Paul Morgan* **c78 h–**

MERCATO (FR) 7 b.g. Mansonnien (FR) – Royal Lie (FR) (Garde Royale) [2002/3 h102: c19v⁴ c16s³ c16dᵘʳ c16g⁵ c16v² 21v* 20v 16v⁵ 18g⁵ Mar 17] good-topped gelding: fair form in novice chases, mostly highly tried: fair handicap hurdler: won at Plumpton in February by 1¾ lengths from What's The Count: stays 21f: acts on heavy going (won bumper on good to firm): has had tongue tied. *J. R. Best* **c110 h112**

MERCEDE (IRE) 6 b.m. Perugino (USA) – Miss Busybody (IRE) (Phardante (FR)) [2002/3 h66: 16m 17d* 16g³ Jun 15] poor hurdler: made all in mares seller at Cartmel in June: allowed to set up clear lead when third in mares novice at Hexham 10 days later: will prove best at 2m: acts on firm and good to soft going: tried tongue tied: headstrong. *N. Wilson* **h74**

MERCHANTS FRIEND (IRE) 8 b.g. Lord Americo – Buck Maid (Buckskin (FR)) [2002/3 20d 16s³ 19s 20v* c20d* c20d* c20g² c24s⁴ c24s² c23s² Feb 12] good-topped ex-Irish gelding: fifth foal: dam, poor Irish maiden hurdler, half-sister to **c122 h105**

Sun Alliance Chase winner The West Awake and smart staying hurdler Model Pupil: fair hurdler: left T. Taaffe after third start: easily won minor event at Pardubice in October: fairly useful handicap chaser: won at Plumpton and Newbury (held when left clear last) in November: effective at 2m to 3m: raced mainly on good going or softer (acts on heavy): held up: not a fluent jumper of fences: consistent. *C. J. Mann*

MERITOCRACY (IRE) 5 b.g. Lahib (USA) – Merry Devil (IRE) (Sadler's Wells (USA)) [2002/3 17s 16g 16d⁶ Mar 19] ex-Irish gelding: fair maiden on Flat (suited by 7f), generally below form in 2002, sold out of J. C. Hayden's stable 4,400 gns Newmarket July Sales: well held all 3 starts over hurdles: has pulled hard. *Miss A. E. Broyd* **h–**

MERLINS BAY (IRE) 9 b.g. Nearly A Nose (USA) – Kabarda (Relkino) [2002/3 20dᵖᵘ 16s Aug 9] tall gelding: little form. *J. F. Panvert* **c–**\
h–

MERRY MAJOR 10 br.g. K-Battery – Merry Missus (Bargello) [2002/3 c26d Jun 8] winning pointer: no form over hurdles/fences: sold 2,300 gns Doncaster August Sales. *J. B. Walton* **c–**\
h–

MERRY MASQUERADE (IRE) 12 b.g. King's Ride – Merry Madness (Raise You Ten) [2002/3 c103§, h–: c25d⁴ c26d² May 4] big, well-made gelding: one-time smart hurdler: not fluent and only fair form over fences: should stay 3½m+: needs going softer than good (acts on heavy): tried visored/blinkered: lazy. *Mrs M. Reveley* **c103 §**\
h–

MERRY MINSTREL (IRE) 10 b.g. Black Minstrel – Merry Lesa (Dalesa) [2002/3 c92: c21d² c19dᵖᵘ c20m² c16g³ Apr 24] tall gelding: fair handicap chaser: effective at 2m to 3m: acts on good to firm and good to soft going: lame second outing: has high head carriage. *C. J. Mann* **c101**

MERRY MOLE (IRE) 9 b.g. Good Thyne (USA) – Merry Miss (Deep Run) [2002/3 h–: 20g c20s⁵ c26dᵖᵘ Nov 26] lengthy gelding: no sign of ability. *J. A. B. Old* **c–**\
h–

MERRY SHOT (IRE) 11 b.g. Cataldi – Borgina (Boreen (FR)) [2002/3 c21f May 10] strong gelding: maiden chaser, poor at best: tried blinkered. *C. A. Green* **c–**\
h–

MERRY TINA 8 b.m. Tina's Pet – Merry Missus (Bargello) [2002/3 c20m c16v⁴ c21v⁶ c16v c21v⁵ c25dᵖᵘ c25g² c24g⁶ Apr 23] winning 2½m pointer: bad maiden steeplechaser. *J. B. Walton* **c53**\
h–

MERSEY BEAT 9 ch.g. Rock Hopper – Handy Dancer (Green God) [2002/3 c91, h–: c16d² c18m* c20f² c16m* c20m² Sep 28] well-made gelding: one-time useful hurdler: fair chaser: won weak maiden at Fontwell in May and handicap at Newton Abbot in June: barely stays 2½m: acts on firm and good to soft going: blinkered twice in 2001/2: has pulled hard. *G. L. Moore* **c112**\
h–

MERSEY SOUND (IRE) 5 b.g. Ela-Mana-Mou – Coral Sound (IRE) (Glow (USA)) [2002/3 16g⁶ 16s Dec 28] rather leggy gelding: fair on Flat (stays 1½m): modest form on first of 2 starts in novice company over hurdles at Newbury, possibly unsuited by soft ground second time. *D. R. C. Elsworth* **h89**

MESSAGE RECU (FR) 7 b.m. Luth Dancer (USA) – High Steppe (Petoski) [2002/3 19s⁶ 20d* 24d⁵ 20g⁴ 20s Oct 20] fair handicap hurdler: won at Limerick in July: stays 3m: raced on good going or softer (acts on heavy): sold to join S. Lewis only €4,000 Goffs February Sale. *E. J. O'Grady, Ireland* **h110**

METAL DETECTOR (IRE) 6 b.g. Treasure Hunter – Las-Cancellas (Monksfield) [2002/3 h93, F75: 22d³ 20s² 24s* 19s 21d* 24m⁵ Apr 12] fair hurdler: won novices at Uttoxeter in May and Taunton (beat The Lyme Volunteer ½ length) in November and handicap at Warwick in March: stays 3m: acts on soft going. *K. C. Bailey* **h112**

METICULOUS (USA) 5 b. or br.g. Theatrical – Sha Tha (USA) (Mr Prospector (USA)) [2002/3 16d 16s Dec 14] good-topped gelding: fourth foal: half-brother to very smart 1m to 1¼m winner State Shinto (by Pleasant Colony) and fair stayer Shastri (by Alleged): dam placed in Prix Marcel Boussac and Poule d'Essai des Pouliches, won Grade 2 over 9f in USA: fair 1¼m winner on dirt for K. McLaughlin in UAE: bought 14,000 gns Newmarket July Sales: well beaten both starts over hurdles (reluctant to go onto course on debut): sold to join Mrs A. Thorpe 2,200 gns Doncaster January Sales. *M. D. Hammond* **h–**

MEXICAN (USA) 4 b.c. Pine Bluff (USA) – Cuando Quiere (USA) (Affirmed (USA)) [2002/3 16g⁴ 16d⁴ 16f Mar 29] rather leggy colt: fairly useful maiden at best on Flat (barely stays 1½m), sold out of C. Brittain's stable 13,000 gns Newmarket Autumn Sales: best effort over hurdles when fourth to Far Pavilions in juvenile at Musselburgh: found little both subsequent starts. *M. D. Hammond* **h89**

MEZZO PRINCESS   11 b.m. Remezzo – Kam Tsin Princess (Prince Regent (FR)) c72
[2002/3 c75?, h–: c26g⁶ c24m⁴ c20d c21g⁶ c25g⁴ c24g⁵ Apr 12] poor maiden hunter h–
chaser: left Miss K. Thory after second start. *Mike Lurcock*

MICE DESIGN (IRE)   6 b.g. Presidium – Diplomatist (Dominion) [2002/3 h93: h–
17gᵖᵘ 17g⁶ Apr 26] winning hurdler: no encouragement in sellers in spring: stays 2½m:
acts on soft and good to firm going: tried blinkered. *S. B. Clark*

MICHAEL FINNEGAN (IRE)   10 b. or br.g. Phardante (FR) – Decent Slave c93
(Decent Fellow) [2002/3 h94: 16d 16s c16v² c16d c16v² Mar 13] sturdy gelding: modest h–
handicap hurdler: similar form when second in novice chases at Newcastle (handicap)
and Hexham: best around 2m: has won on good to firm going, best efforts on softer than
good: races freely. *Miss L. C. Siddall*

MICHAELMAS DAIZY   8 b.m. Michelozzo (USA) – Hals Lass (Halsall) [2002/3 h78
h77: 27dᵘʳ 24d³ 26s Nov 23] poor novice hurdler: stays 3¼m: acts on good to firm and
good to soft going. *S. E. H. Sherwood*

MICHAEL MOR (IRE)   9 ch.g. Denel (FR) – Oralee (Prominer) [2002/3 c132, h–: c128
c24s⁵ c24v⁵ c24s⁶ c20v⁴ 18g* Apr 21] workmanlike gelding: fairly useful hurdler/chaser: h124
awarded minor hurdle at Fairyhouse in April after finishing ½ length behind Moore's
Law: ran well when second to Torduff Bay in quite valuable handicap chase at Punchestown early following month, might well have won but for mistakes in closing stages:
stays 3m: acts on good to firm and heavy going: held up: has jumped left. *N. Meade,
Ireland*

MICHAELS JOY (IRE)   4 br.g. Presenting – Scarteen Lower (IRE) (Royal Fountain) F98
[2002/3 F17d⁴ Mar 2] second foal: dam never ran: ridden by 7-lb claimer, close fourth of
15 to Riothamus in bumper at Carlisle on debut. *G. M. Moore*

MICHAEL'S PRINCESS   8 b.m. King's Ride – Kathy Cook (Glenstal (USA)) c72
[2002/3 h82: 25g* 24d² 21m⁶ 24g² 24g 25m⁶ 24s⁴ 21d³ 25vᵖᵘ c23v³ 21s⁶ Jan 23] compact h82
mare: poor hurdler: won novice handicap at Plumpton very early in season: third of 9 to
Regal River in novice handicap at Leicester on chasing debut: stays 25f: acts on heavy
and good to firm going. *M. J. Gingell*

MICHIGAN BLUE   11 b.g. Rakaposhi King – Starquin (IRE) (Strong Gale) [2002/3 c98
c109, h–: c16g⁶ c19sᵖᵘ c16s⁴ Dec 7] good-topped gelding: maiden hurdler: fair handicap h–
chaser, won 4 times at Hereford in 2001/2: not at best in 2002/3, shaped as if amiss second
start: best form at 2m: acts on soft and good to firm going (probably unsuited by heavy):
bold-jumping front runner. *M. J. M. Evans*

MICKEY CROKE   6 b.g. Alflora (IRE) – Praise The Lord (Lord Gayle (USA)) F102
[2002/3 F17d⁶ F17s* Dec 26] fifth foal: half-brother to useful hurdler/chaser Whip Hand
(by Bob Back), stays 2½m, and fairly useful pointer Greenwich (by Handsome Sailor):
dam Irish maiden: promising start in bumpers, won 16-runner event at Hereford by neck
from Wrags To Riches. *C. R. Egerton*

MICKLEY (IRE)   6 b.g. Ezzoud (IRE) – Dawsha (IRE) (Slip Anchor) [2002/3 17d h76
21m² Oct 7] close-coupled gelding: fairly useful on Flat (barely stays 2m, tends to carry
head high under pressure), successful 4 times on all-weather in 2002: poor form over
hurdles: probably better around 2½m than 2m: tried in cheekpieces. *P. R. Hedger*

MICKLOW MINSTER   9 ch.g. Minster Son – Scotto's Regret (Celtic Cone) [2002/3 c–
c–, h–: 23m Apr 21] workmanlike gelding: twice-raced over fences: winning hurdler: h–
reportedly finished lame only outing in 2001/2: well held on return: stays 25f: acts on
good to firm and good to soft going. *C. Grant*

MICK MURPHY (IRE)   6 b.g. Jurado (USA) – Lee Ford Lady (Kemal (FR)) [2002/3 h–
F–: 16g May 11] tailed off in 2 bumpers and novice hurdle. *Mrs E. Slack*

MICKTHECUTAWAY (IRE)   11 b.g. Rontino – Le-Mu-Co (Varano) [2002/3 c122: c–
c24s⁴ c25sF c24mᵖᵘ Apr 12] workmanlike gelding: fairly useful handicap chaser in
2001/2: well beaten only completed outing on return: stays 25f: raced mainly on good
going or softer (acts on heavy): usually forces pace: jumps soundly in main. *Mrs
H. Dalton*

MICKTHETRICK   7 b.g. Henbit (USA) – Catherine Tudor (Tudor Wood) [2002/3 h–
F–: 21g 20gF Apr 14] quite good-topped gelding: no sign of ability. *Ian Emmerson*

MICKY MANSIONS (IRE)   9 gr.g. Phardante (FR) – Reneagh (Prince Regent c–
(FR)) [2002/3 c25dᵖᵘ May 4] winning pointer: showed nothing in maiden hunter chase.
W. M. Aitchison

MICMAC   5 br.g. Be My Native (USA) – Padykin (Bustino) [2002/3 F17m 16s^pu 17s^pu   **h–**
Dec 2] rather unfurnished gelding: half-brother to 3 winners, including winning hurdler   **F–**
up to 27f Silken Thyne (by Good Thyne) and fair staying chaser Committed Schedule
(by Saxon Farm): dam winning staying hurdler: no show in bumper or 2 novice hurdles.
P. Winkworth

MIDDLETHORPE   6 b.g. Noble Patriarch – Prime Property (IRE) (Tirol) [2002/3   **h103**
20v^4 16d^2 16d^2 16v^4 17v^2 16d* 16d* Mar 5] workmanlike gelding: half-brother to
winning 2m hurdler Property Zone (by Cool Jazz): fair on Flat (stays 1¾m): fair novice
hurdler: improved form last 2 outings, won in large fields at Wetherby (beat Tribal
Dispute 8 lengths) in February and Catterick (beat Crunchy ¾ length, pair clear) in
March: likely to prove best around 2m. *M. W. Easterby*

MIDDLEWAY   7 b.g. Milieu – Galway Gal (Proverb) [2002/3 h–, F–: 21m^pu 22g^2 20d   **h77 ?**
25d^pu 24g^4 20g^6 22g Apr 26] workmanlike gelding: signs of only a little ability over
hurdles. *Miss Kate Milligan*

MIDLAND FLAME (IRE)   8 b.g. Un Desperado (FR) – Lathanona (Reformed   **c128**
Character) [2002/3 h112: c17g^2 c19s^pu c16g^2 c16d^3 c20g* Apr 3] well-made gelding: **h–**
usually looks very well: fair hurdler: much improved when winning valuable 16-runner
novice handicap chase at Aintree by 2½ lengths from Bold Investor, helping force pace
and jumping well: stays 21f: acts on good to firm and good to soft going: takes strong
hold, and hasn't looked easy ride (usually held up). *Miss H. C. Knight*

MIDLEM MELODY   7 b.m. Syrtos – Singing Hills (Crash Course) [2002/3 h–, F71:   **c–**
18v^4 16s* 16v^5 17v 16d^4 c16v^6 c16d c16g^5 Mar 29] medium-sized mare: poor hurdler: **h60**
won selling handicap at Newcastle in December: well held in 3 novice chases: raced
mainly around 2m on going softer than good. *W. S. Coltherd*

MIDNIGHT COUP   7 br.g. First Trump – Anhaar (Ela-Mana-Mou) [2002/3 h–:   **c70 §**
c26m^5 c20g c18f^4 22g^3 21f^5 19d^5 22v 16f* Apr 21] poor hurdler/maiden chaser: won over   **h70 §**
hurdles in Jersey in April: stays 2¾m: acts on firm and soft going: tried blinkered/tongue
tied: temperamental. *B. G. Powell*

MIDNIGHT CREEK   5 b.g. Tragic Role (USA) – Greek Night Out (IRE) (Ela-   **h99 §**
Mana-Mou) [2002/3 16v* 16v^5 20v^3 20s^6 20d^3 22d^3 Mar 1] leggy gelding: fair on Flat
(barely stays 2¼m), sold out of Mrs A. Perrett's stable 8,500 gns Newmarket Autumn
Sales: modest novice hurdler: won maiden at Kelso in December: at least respectable
efforts all subsequent starts: effective at 2m to 2¾m: raced on going softer than good over
hurdles (acts on heavy): wore cheekpieces final outing: ungenuine. *G. A. Swinbank*

Martell Cognac Novices' Handicap Chase, Aintree—
a change of tactics and much improved form by 14/1-shot Midland Flame

Golden Miller Handicap Chase, Cheltenham—Midnight Gunner gains a third win of 2002/3

MIDNIGHT EXPRESS (IRE)   8 b.g. Orchestra – Loaker Lady (Furry Glen) [2002/3 c24s^ur Feb 13] workmanlike gelding: second foal: brother to winning 2m hurdler Earlshill Song: dam won around 2m over hurdles: no form in points or amateur chase. *G. J. Morgan*   **c– x**

MIDNIGHT GUNNER   9 b.g. Gunner B – Light Tonight (Lighter) [2002/3 c84, h90: c25g^2 c24d^2 c27g* c24s^2 c24g* c24m^4 c26m* Apr 16] well-made gelding: modest handicap hurdler: fairly useful handicap chaser: had excellent season, winning at Ludlow in December and February and at Cheltenham in April: beat Hurricane Lamp 8 lengths in quite valuable event for final success: best at 3m+: acts on any going: genuine. *A. E. Price*   **c117 +** **h–**

MIDNIGHT JAZZ (IRE)   13 b.g. Shardari – Round Midnight (Star Appeal) [2002/3 c–, h74^: 17g^pu 19s^pu 16m^3 Mar 19] good-topped gelding: poor hurdler nowadays: raced mainly around 2m: acts on soft and good to firm going: tried blinkered. *J. Harriman*   **c–** **h71**

MIDNIGHT MISSILE   6 b.g. Arms And The Man – Rewbell (Andy Rew) [2002/3 F–: 20g 17m Jul 28] leggy gelding: no sign of ability: sold £2,100 Ascot August Sales. *Mrs D. A. Hamer*   **h–**

MIDNIGHT MOON   8 b.g. Jupiter Island – Nunswalk (The Parson) [2002/3 h66: 20d Jun 3] leggy gelding: little sign of ability: has had tongue tied: sold 2,000 gns Doncaster August Sales. *B. D. Leavy*   **h–**

MIDNIGHT TANGO   6 ch.m. Milieu – Whistle Binkie (Slim Jim) [2002/3 F16f 22m 24d^pu Oct 26] second foal: dam winning pointer: no sign of ability. *Mrs H. O. Graham*   **h–** **F–**

MIDNIGHT WATCH (USA)   9 b.g. Capote (USA) – Midnight Air (USA) (Green Dancer (USA)) [2002/3 21m^pu May 11] lengthy, angular gelding: poor maiden hurdler in 1999/00, no sign of retaining ability only subsequent start: tried visored: tongue tied. *M. A. Allen*   **h–**

MIDY'S RISK (FR)   6 gr.g. Take Risks (FR) – Martine Midy (FR) (Lashkari) [2002/3 h99: 21g^4 16d^4 c17s^4 c20v^2 c17v^4 16s^6 c22f^4 Apr 24] lengthy, angular gelding: fair hurdler: hasn't shown much aptitude for chasing: probably stays 21f: acts on heavy going: wore blinkers/cheekpieces last 2 starts. *Mrs N. Smith*   **c90** **h103**

MI FAVORITA   5 b.m. Piccolo – Mistook (USA) (Phone Trick (USA)) [2002/3 16g 16d 16d 17g^6 17g^pu May 11] small mare: poor maiden on Flat (stays 1m) for Don Enrico Incisa: no show in selling hurdles. *Miss Kate Milligan*   **h–**

MIGHTY FINE   9 gr.g. Arzanni – Kate Kimberley (Sparkler) [2002/3 h–: 16f^3 17g c25m^4 c16s^3 c16v^2 c16s* c21s^ur c16v* c16d^ur c21g* c21d^3 Apr 8] rangy gelding: poor maiden hurdler: fair chaser: won handicaps at Sedgefield in November, December and March: stays 21f: acts on any going. *Mrs E. Slack*   **c101** **h71**

MIGHTY KILCASH (IRE)   10 ch.g. Black Minstrel – Any Wonder (Hardboy) [2002/3 18v^3 Jan 6] big, strong gelding: fair chaser in 2000/1: second start over hurdles, showed he retains ability when third in novice at Fontwell, only start on return: stays 3¼m: raced on good going or softer (acts on heavy). *K. C. Bailey*   **c–** **h92**

MIGHTY MAN (IRE) 8 b.g. Mandalus – Mossy Mistress (IRE) (Le Moss) [2002/3   c–
c–, h–: c23d^{pu} May 23] smallish, strong gelding: no sign of ability: tried visored.   h–
O. Brennan

MIGHTY MAX 5 b.g. Well Beloved – Jokers High (USA) (Vaguely Noble) [2002/3   h?
16m 17v^{pu} 17s^6 Nov 28] poor maiden on Flat (stays 1½m): tongue tied, apparently
best effort over hurdles when sixth in maiden at Taunton, though probably flattered.
G. A. Ham

MIGHTY MINSTER 6 ch.m. Minster Son – Mighty Fly (Comedy Star (USA))   h85
[2002/3 F16g^4 F17m^4 19g^5 19d^5 16s^4 16v^4 20s Feb 24] sparely-made mare: half-sister to   F78
several winners, including modest hurdler/chaser Ulusaba (by Alflora), stays 2½m: dam,
Lincoln and Royal Hunt Cup winner, out of half-sister to top-class chaser Kildimo, very
smart staying hurdler Baydon Star and Grand National winner Rubstic: modest form in
bumpers and over hurdles: stays 19f: acts on heavy going: has worn cheekpieces: has
carried head awkwardly. *R. C. Guest*

MIGHTY MONTEFALCO 7 b.g. Mtoto – Glendera (Glenstal (USA)) [2002/3   c117
h110, F81: 22g^2 22d* 24m* c24g* c24m* c25m^4 Apr 12] workmanlike gelding: has been   h115
freeze fired: fairly useful hurdler: won novice at Stratford and handicap at Uttoxeter in
August: jumped soundly and created good impression when winning novice chases in
small fields at Stratford and Cheltenham in October: off 5 months and odds on, bit
disappointing when fourth of 6 finishers in valuable novice handicap at Ayr: will prove
best at 3m+: acts on good to firm and good to soft going. *Jonjo O'Neill*

MIGHTY MOSS (IRE) 12 b.g. Moscow Society (USA) – Derry Girl (Rarity)   c102
[2002/3 c110, h–: c26s^2 Mar 10] lengthy gelding: usually looks very well: hunter chaser,   h–
on downgrade: stays 27f: acts on soft and good to firm going: usually jumps fluently:
genuine. *K. Hutsby*

MIGHTY MOUSE (IRE) 7 b.g. Roi Guillame (FR) – By Golly (Mandalus) [2002/3   c–
F18d c16g^{pu} 20g Sep 13] first foal: dam, winning Irish pointer, out of half-sister to useful   h–
chaser up to 25f Colonel In Chief: no sign of ability. *C. S. McKeever, Ireland*   F–

MIGHTY STRONG 9 b.g. Strong Gale – Muffet's Spider (Rymer) [2002/3 c95, h–:   c123
c19m^F c17g^2 c21g* c21g^F c20d^F c21d^4 c20d^3 c20s^{pu} Mar 1] sturdy, lengthy gelding: h–
fairly useful handicap chaser: won at Southwell in October: unlucky at Newbury (fell last
when in command) 2 starts later: stays 21f: acts on soft going: has broken blood vessel:
none too consistent. *N. J. Henderson*

MIGHTY SURPRISE 7 b.m. Sure Blade (USA) – Flash-By (Ilium) [2002/3 h81: 19m   h–
Jun 1] lengthy, angular mare: poor hurdler: twice-raced since 2000/1, always towards rear
on reappearance: stays 2¾m: acts on good to firm going: has gone in snatches: none too
consistent: sold 1,100 gns Doncaster August Sales. *P. J. Hobbs*

MIKE BASSETT (IRE) 7 b.g. Ballacashtal (CAN) – Lady Crusty (Golden Dipper) [2002/3   h91 §
h–: 24g^{pu} 19d^3 19s^4 19s^{pu} 21g Mar 16] leggy gelding: modest handicap hurdler: stays 21f:
acts on soft going: none too reliable. *L. P. Grassick*

MIKE STAN (IRE) 12 b.g. Rontino – Fair Pirouette (Fair Turn) [2002/3 c–, h–:   c–
c20g^{pu} Apr 23] lengthy gelding: handicap chaser, very lightly raced and no form of late: h–
stays 3¼m: acts on soft and good to firm going: makes the odd mistake. *L. Lungo*

MIKHAIL (USA) 6 ch.g. Nureyev (USA) – Rythmical (USA) (Fappiano (USA))   h–
[2002/3 h–, F–: 19g^F 17m Jun 14] sturdy gelding: little sign of ability. *N. J. Hawke*

MILAN KING (IRE) 10 b.g. King's Ride – Milan Moss (Le Moss) [2002/3 c71, h85:   c–
17m^5 16g 24m^{pu} 17g^5 17m^3 20f 17m^3 17d^{pu} 16g 17v^6 19d^{pu} 17g 21m^{ur} Apr 26] lengthy   h74 d
gelding: winning hurdler/maiden chaser, on the downgrade: stays 21f: acts on any going:
blinkered twice (pulled up both times). *A. J. Lockwood*

MILBRIG 7 b.m. Milieu – Meadow Brig (Meadowbrook) [2002/3 20v^{pu} 22g 24g^{pu} h–
Apr 23] first foal: dam unraced: no form in novice hurdles. *A. C. Whillans*

MILDON (IRE) 7 ch.g. Dolphin Street (FR) – Lycia (Targowice (USA)) [2002/3 h–:   h–
21g^6 17s^6 Aug 24] leggy gelding: maiden hurdler, no form since 2000/1: sometimes
tongue tied. *J. R. Weymes*

MILITAIRE (FR) 5 ch.g. Bering – Moon Review (USA) (Irish River (FR)) [2002/3   c–
18s 16d^5 20v^2 c16g^5 16d* 20d^{pu} 16g^{pu} Mar 17] close-coupled ex-French gelding: h111
half-brother to 2 winners over jumps, including fairly useful hurdler/chaser up to 19f
Mazalunna (by Sillery): 9f winner on Flat at 3 yrs for F. Head: fair novice hurdler, trained

until after reappearance by J. Bertran de Balanda: won handicap at Wetherby in February: tongue tied, poor efforts both subsequent starts: well held only outing over fences: best around 2m: acts on heavy going. *M. D. Hammond*

MILKAT (IRE) 5 b.g. Machiavellian (USA) – Desert Victory (Green Desert (USA)) [2002/3 16d 16g 16d* 16g⁵ 16f⁵ 16g* 16v² 16v 16s 22gᵖᵘ Apr 21] leggy gelding: fairly useful on Flat (stays 1¾m): fairly useful hurdler: won maiden at Wexford in August and minor event at Limerick in October: very good second to Emotional Moment in valuable handicap at Down Royal in November, disappointing subsequently: should stay beyond 2m: acts on heavy going: blinkered once. *W. P. Mullins, Ireland* **h121**

MILLCROFT REGATTA (IRE) 11 br.g. Miner's Lamp – Stradbally Bay (Shackleton) [2002/3 c21f³ c28gᵖᵘ May 31] compact gelding: maiden chaser: winning pointer: better effort in novice hunters in May when third at Wincanton: stays 3¼m: acts on firm and good to soft going: tried blinkered. *Mrs A. L. Tory* **c92 h–**

MILLCROFT SEASPRAY (IRE) 7 br.g. Good Thyne (USA) – Bucks Gift (IRE) (Buckley) [2002/3 h114: 22v² c24s³ 20d³ Mar 19] fairly useful handicap hurdler: shaped well when third to Tales of Bounty in novice at Taunton on chasing debut: should be well suited by 3m+: raced on good going or softer (acts on heavy): reliable: should improve over fences. *R. H. Alner* **c115 p h116**

MILLE ET UNE NUITS (FR) 4 b.f. Ecologist – Migre (FR) (Le Gregol (FR)) [2002/3 F17m⁶ Apr 15] 30,000 3-y-o: half-sister to numerous winners, including topclass hurdler Mister Banjo (by Mister Mat), stays 21f: dam placed once on Flat: in need of experience when sixth of 9 in mares bumper at Exeter on debut, hanging left off home turn and unable to be ridden out. *Miss K. Marks* **F–**

MILL EMERALD 6 b.m. Old Vic – Milinetta (Milford) [2002/3 h68: 20d* 20d* c20d³ c20s⁴ 20s³ 20g⁴ Mar 29] small mare: fair hurdler: won claimer at Wetherby in May and valuable selling handicap at Uttoxeter in June: showed little in 2 mares novice chases: stays 2½m: acts on soft and firm going. *Mrs M. Reveley* **c– h100**

MILLENIUM MOONBEAM (USA) 6 ch.g. Phone Trick (USA) – Shywing (USA) (Wing Out (USA)) [2002/3 16m 16g Sep 14] formerly useful on Flat (stays 1m) but very much on downgrade: shaped like non-stayer both starts over hurdles. *G. G. Margarson* **h–**

MILLENNIUM WAY (IRE) 9 ch.g. Ikdam – Fine Drapes (Le Bavard (FR)) [2002/3 c–, h–: c24m⁴ Apr 21] medium-sized gelding: maiden hurdler/chaser: winning pointer: should stay beyond 3m: acts on any going: blinkered (ran poorly) once. *J. M. Turner* **c73 h–**

MILLENNIUM GOLD 8 ch.g. Be My Chief (USA) – Forbearance (Bairn (USA)) [2002/3 c20m³ Jun 1] IR 10,500 4-y-o: ex-Irish gelding: second foal: half-brother to 2½m chase winner in Italy by Damister: dam, won at 2m over hurdles, sister to smart 2m hurdler Batabanoo: poor maiden hurdler for M. Hourigan: modest pointer: creditable third in hunter at Hexham in June: stays 2½m: acts on good to soft and good to firm ground: tried blinkered: sold £1,200 Ascot April Sales. *C. C. Pimlott* **c81 h–**

MILLENNIUM SUMMIT (IRE) 6 b.g. Apple Tree (FR) – Word of Honor (FR) (Highest Honor (FR)) [2002/3 16s³ 20s 20g 20g 24d⁴ 18d c23f⁵ 20s 22v 24g c18s Mar 5] good-topped gelding: maiden on Flat: poor maiden hurdler: well held in 2 chases: tried blinkered/visored/tongue tied. *T. G. McCourt, Ireland* **c– h84 d**

MILLER'S BAY 5 ch.g. Karinga Bay – Millers Action (Fearless Action (USA)) [2002/3 F16m² F17s* F16g⁵ Mar 12] rangy gelding: first foal: dam once-raced half-sister to useful 2m hurdler Bold Gait, out of half-sister to Champion Hurdle winner Royal Gait: useful form in bumpers: comfortably landed odds at Hereford in November: best effort when fifth of 25 to Liberman in Grade 1 at Cheltenham final start, nearest finish: will be very well suited by 2½m+: good jumping prospect. *Miss H. C. Knight* **F112**

MILLERSFORD 12 b.g. Meadowbrook – My Seer (Menelek) [2002/3 c97x, h–: c20g* c24s² c24mᵖᵘ c24m⁵ c22m² c23g³ c23gᵖᵘ c24dᵖᵘ Apr 9] rangy gelding: modest chaser: won minor event at Towcester in May: stays 3¼m: acts on soft and good to firm going: blinkered once: usually makes mistakes. *N. A. Gaselee* **c92 x h–**

MILLERS WAY 5 b.m. Nomadic Way (USA) – Keldholme (Derek H) [2002/3 F17d F16s⁶ 20d 20dᵖᵘ Feb 26] big, plain mare: seventh foal: half-sister to fair hurdler around 2m Marmaduke Jinks (by Primitive Rising): dam lightly-raced maiden pointer: signs of ability in bumpers: no form in 2 mares novice hurdles. *A. Crook* **h– F74**

MILLIESOME 5 b.m. Milieu – Some Shiela (Remainder Man) [2002/3 F16g Apr 1] fourth foal: half-sister to winning hurdler/chaser up to 2½m Dingo Dancer (by Dancing **F–**

High) and to winning pointer by Liberated: dam once-raced half-sister to useful staying chaser Toogood To Be True: took good hold when well held in bumpers at Newcastle. *J. P. Dodds*

MILLIGAN (FR)   8 b.g. Exit To Nowhere (USA) – Madigan Mill (Mill Reef (USA))   **h130** [2002/3 h147: 16f 20d⁴ 20d⁵ 16m Mar 22] close-coupled gelding: smart hurdler in 2001/2: below best in 2002/3, though trip too far second and third starts: best at 2m: acts on soft and good to firm going, possibly not ideally suited by heavy: usually patiently ridden. *Miss Venetia Williams*

MILLIONS   6 b.g. Bering – Miznah (IRE) (Sadler's Wells (USA)) [2002/3 h80§: 17dᵖᵘ   **h– §** 22m Aug 23] poor hurdler: stays 21f: acts on good to firm going: blinkered on reappearance: not one to trust. *Mrs H. Dalton*

MILLKOM ELEGANCE   4 b.f. Millkom – Premier Princess (Hard Fought) [2002/3   **h–** 16d Dec 4] poor maiden on Flat (stays 1¼m): tailed off in juvenile on hurdling debut. *K. A. Ryan*

MILL LORD (IRE)   10 b.g. Aristocracy – Millflower (Millfontaine) [2002/3 c62, h–:   **c–** c16dᵖᵘ c21f³ c24mᵖᵘ c21m⁴ c23g⁵ c22d c16dᵖᵘ 20sᵖᵘ c17m³ Apr 21] good-bodied   **h–** gelding: of little account nowadays: usually blinkered. *C. J. Drewe*

MILL O'THE RAGS (IRE)   14 b.g. Strong Gale – Lady Rag (Ragapan) [2002/3   **c–** c86, h–: c24g⁵ May 30] sturdy gelding: veteran hunter chaser: barely stays 3m: acts on   **h–** firm and good to soft going: tried blinkered. jumps well. *Neil King*

MILLYS FILLY   5 b.m. Polish Precedent (USA) – Lemon's Mill (USA) (Roberto   **h66** (USA)) [2002/3 17s 16g 20g⁵ 22fᵖᵘ Apr 21] first foal: dam smart hurdler/fairly useful chaser up to 3m: showed little in 2 maidens around 1½m at 3 yrs for R. Charlton: signs of just a little ability over hurdles. *O. Sherwood*

MIMAN JAMES (FR)   5 b.g. Montorselli – Kimolia (FR) (Prince Baladin) [2002/3   **F–** F17d F16d Oct 23] good-topped gelding: seventh known foal: half-brother to 3 winners, including fairly useful chaser up to 21f Brametot (by Maiymad): dam maiden on Flat and over jumps: well held both starts in bumpers: no form in points. *P. F. Nicholls*

MINCARLO   7 ch.m. Karinga Bay – Atlantic View (Crash Course) [2002/3 F86: 16d³   **h85** 21d³ 22dF Feb 6] sturdy mare: fair bumper winner: upped in trip, better completed effort over hurdles when never-nearer third in mares maiden at Ludlow: fell fatally at Wincanton: stayed 21f: tongue tied. *G. B. Balding*

MINDANAO   7 b.m. Most Welcome – Salala (Connaught) [2002/3 h99: 16d² 20g*   **h120** Mar 29] leggy mare: fair on Flat (stays 1¾m): fairly useful handicap hurdler: good second to Lord Transcend at Newcastle on reappearance, final outing for F. Murtagh: easily beat Tee-Jay 6 lengths at Hexham 4 months later: should stay 3m: acts on soft going: has been let down by jumping. *L. Lungo*

MINDEN ROSE   10 b.m. Lord Bud – Two Travellers (Deep Run) [2002/3 c–: c20d*   **c80 +** c20mᵖᵘ May 11] progressive pointer: first completion in hunter chases when winning weak event at Newcastle in April: lame in similar event at Huntingdon next time: should stay beyond 2½m. *Peter Maddison*

MIND HOW YOU GO (FR)   5 b.g. Hernando (FR) – Cos I Do (IRE) (Double   **h110** Schwartz) [2002/3 F99: 16d* 18s³ 17g² 21m Apr 16] sparely-made gelding: fair novice hurdler: won at Wincanton in January: placed at Fontwell and Market Rasen next 2 starts: should stay 2½m: acts on soft ground, well held on good to firm. *J. R. Best*

MIND OF MY OWN   4 ch.f. Master Willie – Come Dance With Me (IRE) (Rising)   **F–** [2002/3 F17m Apr 15] second living foal: dam modest 2m maiden hurdler: well held in mares maiden bumper on debut. *J. D. Frost*

MINDYER MILLIONS   7 b.g. Milieu – Mindyer Manners (Faustus (USA)) [2002/3   **c–** c20mᵖᵘ May 16] first foal: dam unraced: bad maiden pointer. *George R. Moscrop*

MINE FOREVER   4 br.g. Royal Academy (USA) – Overseas Romance (USA)   **h–** (Assert) [2002/3 17dᵖᵘ 17dᵖᵘ 16g Sep 12] poor maiden at 2 yrs for A. Berry: no form in juvenile hurdles: tried blinkered/tongue tied: sold £500 Ascot October Sales. *D. McCain*

MINELLA GOLD (IRE)   14 b.g. The Parson – Slieveglagh Queen (Proverb) [2002/3   **c87** c–, h–: c25d² c25g³ c25m⁴ c26d⁵ Jun 5] rangy gelding: modest chaser: best effort in   **h–** hunters in early-2002/3 when second at Kelso in May: stayed 27f: acted on good to firm and heavy going: tried blinkered: tongue tied: dead. *Alistair M. Brown*

MINELLA LEISURE (IRE)   9 b.g. Phardante (FR) – Mrs Minella (Deep Run)   **c116** [2002/3 20s* 20d* 24g³ 20vᵖᵘ 20g⁶ c17m* c19f* c21m² c17g⁴ c20d³ c21vᶠ c21sᶠ Feb 9]   **h110** lengthy, rather plain gelding: fair hurdler: won novice at Cork and handicap at Limerick in June: fairly useful novice chaser: successful in maiden at Killarney and handicap at Listowel in September: stays 3m, effective at much shorter: acts on soft and firm going. *Michael Hourigan, Ireland*

MINELLA SILVER (IRE)   10 gr.g. Roselier (FR) – Mrs Minella (Deep Run) [2002/3   **c104** c114+, h–: c24s³ c24v⁴ c24s⁴ Mar 7] workmanlike gelding: fair chaser: creditable efforts   **h–** in handicaps first 2 starts in 2002/3, went as if having a problem final one: stays 3m: acts on heavy going: front runner. *Mrs H. Dalton*

MINELLA STORM (IRE)   11 b.g. Strong Gale – Maul-More (Deep Run) [2002/3   **c81** c83, h–: 20d⁴ c23v⁴ c26v⁴ c24s Feb 13] good-bodied gelding: winning hurdler/chaser,   **h–** poor nowadays: stays 3m: acts on heavy and good to firm going: has won with/without blinkers: sold 4,200 gns Doncaster May Sales. *D. J. Wintle*

MINERS DANCE (IRE)   10 b.g. Miner's Lamp – Prudent Birdie (Lucifer (USA))   **c102** [2002/3 c33g⁴ May 1] angular gelding: winning hurdler/chaser: fair pointer nowadays: **h–** successful in April: stays 33f: raced on good going or softer (acts on heavy): tried blinkered. *J. W. Dufosee*

MINER'S GAMBLE   6 b.g. Miner's Lamp – Just Rosie (Sula Bula) [2002/3 h72, F–:   **c–** 20g⁴ c17gᶠ Oct 21] well-made gelding: little worthwhile form: tried tongue tied: dead.   **h–** *A. P. Jones*

MINIATURE ROSE   5 ch.m. Anshan – Rose Ravine (Deep Run) [2002/3 F12g⁵   **F91** F16g* F17m Apr 17] sparely-made mare: half-sister to several winners, including smart staying hurdler/chaser Frosty Canyon (by Arctic Lord) and smart bumper winner/ winning hurdler Alvino (by Afflora): dam won 1985 Stayers' Hurdle: confirmed debut promise when winning mares bumper at Ludlow in February: failed to settle and short of room 5f out when eighth of 17 in listed mares event at Cheltenham final outing. *H. Morrison*

MINIBALLIST (IRE)   5 b.m. Tragic Role (USA) – Herballistic (Rolfe (USA))   **h–** [2002/3 22mᵖᵘ 20gᵘʳ Jul 10] first foal: dam, behind in 2 bumpers, half-sister to one-time top-class staying chaser Go Ballistic: signs of ability when failing to complete in 2 novice hurdles. *Jonjo O'Neill*

MINI DARE   6 b.g. Derrylin – Minim (Rymer) [2002/3 F74: F18g³ 16d⁴ 19d⁶ 19s⁶   **h86** 24g² 26g⁵ Mar 17] modest form in bumpers and over hurdles: stays 3¼m: raced on good   **F80** going or softer. *O. Sherwood*

MINI MANDY   7 b.m. Petoski – Cindie Girl (Orchestra) [2002/3 F95: F16v 22d⁴ 16v⁴   **h93** 22d⁴ 21m Mar 22] good-topped mare: bumper winner: best effort over hurdles when   **F–** fourth of 17 in maiden at Exeter fourth outing: will stay beyond 2¾m (insufficient test of stamina when blinkered final start). *R. H. Buckler*

MINI SENSATION (IRE)   10 b.g. Be My Native (USA) – Minorettes Girl   **c149** (Strong Gale) [2002/3 c123, h–: c20s⁴ c29v* c28v* c28dᵖᵘ c34sᵖᵘ Mar 15]   **h–**

    A joint Jockey Club/BHB Security Review Group, set up in the wake of a series of allegations of corruption in racing, has made a number of recommendations for strengthening racing's security and integrity services. If the Group's report is acted upon, trainers and jockeys can expect, for one thing, a more robust approach to cases in which horses are 'schooled in public' or not allowed to run on their merits. The report referred to concerns that 'some trainers feel they are above the law' and that 'the likelihood of getting caught is low'. The Jockey Club has long been suspected of lacking the backbone to tackle the issue with the major yards, tending to target smaller trainers, partly as a way of sending out a general message about the limits. The charge could not be levelled in the latest season, however, when Jonjo O'Neill, who trains one of the strongest teams in the country at Jackdaws Castle, was called before the Jockey Club after three of the stable's runners were found guilty under the various so-called 'non-triers' rules, though the third offence was quashed on appeal. The first two offences took place on the same day, December 14th. In a sixteen-runner novice hurdle at Haydock the 14/1-chance Gala Performance, whose previous experience had come in bumpers, finished an eye-catching fifth, the rider Liam Cooper and the trainer both considered by the stewards to be in breach of various rules relating to the Jockey Club Instruction H2 'Schooling In Public'; Cooper was suspended for five days, O'Neill was fined £800 and Gala Performance was banned from racing for thirty days. More seriously, in a fourteen-runner juvenile hurdle at Fakenham, the 3/1 favourite Madalyar, who had shown some potential, though looking less than resolute, in a better race on his debut over hurdles, also finished fifth, nearest at the finish after losing ground at the start and being tenderly handled throughout; the trainer was found in breach of rules 155 (i) (which states that every horse shall be run on its merits) and 155 (ii) (dealing with a duty to give adequate instructions to a rider), while the rider Ron Flavin was found guilty under rule 157, which deals, among other things, with a jockey's 'intention of concealing the true ability of the horse or affecting the result of the race'. The Fakenham stewards suspended the rider for twenty-one days, banned Madalyar from racing for forty days and handed out a fine on O'Neill of £3,400, reportedly the highest penalty imposed by a local stewarding panel. The Jockey Club's director with responsibility in this area Malcolm Wallace described it as 'as bad a case as we've seen for quite some time'.

Less than two months later, O'Neill was in trouble again, over the running of Top of The Left in an eighteen-runner novice hurdle at Exeter. Having his third start over hurdles but his first in nearly two years, Top of The Left, a 10/1-chance, finished seventh, beaten around thirty-three lengths, and the stewards found O'Neill in breach of rule 150 (i) and (ii) and guilty of 'schooling in public'; the rider was found in breach of rule 158 (relating to the requirements for a horse to be given a full opportunity to win, but falling short of the stricter offence in rule 157). Since it was the trainer's third offence in less than a stipulated two-year period, the local stewards were required to refer the case to the stewards of the Jockey Club. Rider Tom Siddall told both the Exeter stewards (who heard his evidence confirmed by the trainer's representative) and the Disciplinary Panel that his instructions had been to settle the horse in, take his time, not to hit him behind the saddle, to do his best and not knock the horse about because he had been off the track for just short of two years. The rider admitted to the Panel that he had appeared to make insufficient effort in the straight and either should have pulled up or been more vigorous. The Panel found both rider and trainer guilty, though the trainer was not found guilty under rule 155 (i). Siddall's concern that the gelding was getting tired and hence he let it come home in its own time was not 'an adequate reason for not making more effort'. O'Neill's instructions to the rider, which seemed to have been very detailed, were nonetheless deemed inadequate ('Siddall might have ridden differently had O'Neill given instructions as to what to do if the horse got tired.'). O'Neill was fined £6,000 for breaching rule 152 (ii), this being his third offence under the rule. The possibility was inappropriately raised by the Jockey Club's public relations department that a more serious offence might have resulted in the loss or suspension of his licence.

O'Neill had little option but to take the Haydock and Fakenham fines on the chin ('I haven't appealed so what does that say? The buck stops with me') but did appeal against the Exeter verdict. In what he described as a very fair hearing, he had his penalty—and a thirty-day ban on the horse—overturned, the Appeal Board concluding that 'the reasons given by the Disciplinary Panel for not being satisfied that O'Neill had given adequate instructions were insufficient.' Jockey Club spokesman John Maxse expanded on the outcome: 'The culpability of the trainer where a jockey has made insufficient effort has always been a problem to determine. Rule 155, which deals with the situation, has always been difficult to apply. The rule was revised and simplified last month and we hope that, as a consequence, identifying trainers' responsibilities for giving adequate instructions to jockeys will be facilitated.' The new rule is more tightly drawn, containing, for one thing, a specific definition of what 'a horse shall be run on its merits' actually means. The rule states: 'For a horse to run on its merits the rider must take all reasonable and permissible measures throughout the race, however it develops, to ensure the horse is given a full opportunity to obtain the best possible placing.' The rule, which now no longer refers specifically to a horse being given a full opportunity to *win*, therefore imposes much wider responsibilities on trainers to give explicit instructions to cover all eventualities. How practical that will prove to be is a moot point.

Jackdaws Castle is owned by legendary punter J. P. McManus whose horses in the yard include Top of The Left. The stable is noted as much as any other major

*Coral Welsh National (Handicap Chase), Chepstow—Mini Sensation (right) and Chives
are about to collar Gunner Welburn (noseband) and Frosty Canyon (visored) 2 out*

yard for its ability to execute a perfectly legitimate betting coup. One notable
gamble landed is detailed in the essay on Ar Muin Na Muice, a heavily-backed
favourite at Newbury in March, while one that didn't quite come off involved the
ex-Irish Claude Greengrass. Claude Greengrass had shown nothing over hurdles
when trained by Frank Berry, now McManus's racing manager, though he had won
on the Flat. Making his debut for O'Neill, he was backed from 12/1 to 9/4 in a
handicap hurdle at Catterick in January but failed by a short head to get up. The
Coral Welsh National at Chepstow was one contest where a tilt at the ring went
rather more to plan after the McManus-owned Mini Sensation was backed from
25/1 the weekend before the race down to 8/1. Mini Sensation was having his

*Singer & Friedlander National Trial (Handicap Chase), Uttoxeter—
another valuable long-distance prize on barely raceable ground,
this time Mini Sensation wins at the expense of Ardent Scout (right)*

second outing of the season at Chepstow, having surprisingly been well backed when last of four on his reappearance over two and a half miles at Wetherby which was unlikely to provide a sufficient test of stamina. Mini Sensation's most convincing performances as a novice—when beating Hussard Collonges over three miles on soft going at Bangor and when second to The Bunny Boiler in the Midlands National on heavy—had come under very gruelling conditions such as prevailed at Chepstow. Mini Sensation showed just how effective he could be, brought with a well-timed run to lead before the last and soon clear, crossing the line with plenty of running still in him, seven lengths ahead of Chives. Raised 11 lb by the BHB handicapper, Mini Sensation struck again under similarly testing conditions in the Singer & Friedlander National Trial at Uttoxeter in February. The race attracted a field of only seven, a poor turnout for the money. Mini Sensation was again in front going to the final fence and needed no more than pushing out to beat Ardent Scout by twelve lengths. Mini Sensation was pulled up on both his subsequent appearances, on ground nowhere near testing enough in the Red Square Vodka Gold Cup at Haydock where his rider was quick to accept things and pulled him up early on the final circuit, and back at Uttoxeter for a second crack at the Midlands National, in which he only briefly looked likely to get in the shake up. The BHB handicapper decided to drop Mini Sensation's mark by 3 lb after these poor efforts. Mini Sensation held an entry for the Grand National but wouldn't have been suited at all by the conditions on the day. Indeed he would probably need close to the slog through the mud that prevailed in 2001 to be given much chance at Aintree. Mini Sensation's jumping was better in the latest season but may well not be up to the demands of the Grand National. A programme based around the Welsh National and the two Uttoxeter races would seem obvious for 2003/4, in the hope that ground conditions as usual come up very testing.

Mr J. P. McManus' "Mini Sensation"

Mini Sensation (IRE) (b.g. 1993)	Be My Native (USA) (br 1979)	Our Native (b or br 1970)	Exclusive Native Our Jackie
		Witchy Woman (ch 1972)	Strate Stuff Witchy Norma
	Minorettes Girl (b 1985)	Strong Gale (br 1975)	Lord Gayle Sterntau
		Minorette (b 1968)	Miralgo Quatre Bras

The medium-sized Mini Sensation was bought for 36,000 guineas at the Doncaster May Sales in 1997. He started his career with Arthur Moore in Ireland before joining O'Neill for the 2000/1 season, when he showed marked improvement to win both starts in handicap hurdles. Mini Sensation is by Be My Native out of Minorettes Girl and is a brother to Shotgun Willy in whose essay details of the pedigree can be found. *Jonjo O'Neill*

MINIVET 8 b.g. Midyan (USA) – Bronzewing (Beldale Flutter (USA)) [2002/3 c95, h112: 19d 16d* 16d* 20s³ 20g³ 22g* 27g⁶ Apr 25] close-coupled gelding: fair hurdler: won seller at Catterick and handicap at Wetherby in February and handicap at Kelso in April: effective at 2m to easy 2¾m: acts on soft and good to firm going, possibly not on heavy. *T. D. Easterby*   c– h107

MINSGILL GLEN 7 b.m. Minster Son – Gilmanscleuch (IRE) (Mandalus) [2002/3 F–: c20d^{pu} 20g^{pu} Apr 14] little sign of ability. *Mrs J. K. M. Oliver*   c– h–

MINSGILL MANS 5 b.g. Minster Son – Gilmanscleuch (IRE) (Mandalus) [2002/3 F17d F17s 19d 21s⁴ 24v³ 26d^{pu} Mar 7] 1,200 3-y-o, £1,100 4-y-o: medium-sized gelding: third foal: dam, poor maiden hurdler/chaser, half-sister to dam of very smart staying hurdler Splendid Thyne: twice-raced in bumpers: seemingly best effort when third of 16 to Bacardi Boy in maiden hurdle at Chepstow in January: likely to prove best at 3m+: raced on going softer than good (acts on heavy): tongue tied final start. *P. D. Williams*   h85 ? F–

MINSTER BAY 5 b.g. Minster Son – Melaura Belle (Meldrum) [2002/3 F17g² F17d² F17d Nov 24] fifth foal: half-brother to useful chaser Major Bell (by Silly Prices), stayed 25f: dam fair sprinter: fair form in bumpers, second twice at Sedgefield in October: well beaten at Aintree final outing. *W. Storey*   F90

MINSTER FAIR 5 b.m. Minster Son – Fair Echo (Quality Fair) [2002/3 F82: F17d⁴ 22v³ 16v⁴ 20v⁵ 20d⁵ 22g⁵ Mar 21] leggy, angular mare: best effort in bumpers when fourth at Carlisle on reappearance: modest novice hurdler: should be suited by 3m+: raced on good going or softer (acts on heavy). *A. C. Whillans*   h87 F87

MINSTER GLORY 12 b.g. Minster Son – Rapid Glory (Hittite Glory) [2002/3 c132, h–: c16d^{pu} c20d⁴ c16d² c17d c16g³ c17g Apr 7] tall gelding: formerly useful handicap chaser, fair at best in 2002/3: weakened quickly latter stages last 3 starts: best around 2m: acts on soft and good to firm going: usually races prominently. *M. W. Easterby*   c108 h–

MINSTER SUNSHINE 9 ch.g. Minster Son – Own Free Will (Nicholas Bill) [2002/3 c87, h–: c24s^{pu} c20d^{pu} c20v³ Jan 1] good-topped gelding: maiden chaser: well held on completed start in 2002/3: stays 3m: raced on good going or softer (acts on heavy). *K. C. Bailey*   c– h–

MINSTER YORK 9 ch.g. Minster Son – Another Treat (Derring-Do) [2002/3 c90, h73: c20g² c16g* c20m² c17m* c16m* c20m* c21m² c16g³ c16g⁴ c16f⁵ c16g⁶ Apr 24] smallish, angular gelding: fairly useful handicap chaser: much improved in 2002/3 (trained first 3 starts by A. Crook), won at Hexham in May, Market Rasen (idled) and Sedgefield in July and Bangor in August: stays 21f: best efforts on good ground or firmer: tongue tied on reappearance. *M. D. Hammond*   c120 h–

MINSTREL FAIR (IRE) 6 b.g. Roselier (FR) – Minstrel Park (Black Minstrel) [2002/3 F76: 20d^{pu} Nov 25] rather unfurnished gelding: modest in bumpers: showed little in novice on hurdling debut. *Mrs S. J. Smith*   h–

MINSTREL HALL 4 b.f. Saddlers' Hall (IRE) – Mindomica (Dominion) [2002/3 16v 16v⁴ 17d⁴ 16s³ 17d 16g⁴ Apr 1] modest on Flat (stays 1½m) for C. Thornton: modest juvenile hurdler: acts on soft ground: shaped as if amiss first 2 starts, subsequently tongue tied. *P. Monteith*   h82

MI ODDS 7 b.g. Sure Blade (USA) – Vado Via (Ardross) [2002/3 h79: 16v⁶ 16m³ 16m² Jun 29] fairly useful on all-weather, modest on turf on Flat (stays 1½m), successful   h81 in October and twice in February for Mrs N. Macauley: poor hurdler: best around 2m: acts on good to firm going, probably unsuited by heavy. *Ian Williams*

MIRACLE ISLAND 8 b.g. Jupiter Island – Running Game (Run The Gantlet (USA)) [2002/3 c–, h108: 16g² 20d May 23] tall gelding: modest on Flat (stays 2¼m): modest hurdler: should stay 2½m: acts on good to firm and heavy going: has had tongue tied. *K. R. Burke* — **c– h99**

MIRACLE KID (USA) 9 b.g. Red Ransom (USA) – Fan Mail (USA) (Zen (USA)) [2002/3 h102: 16m 16m Nov 4] quite good-topped gelding: fair handicap hurdler: creditable effort on first of 2 starts in 2002/3: best around 2m: acts on good to firm and good to soft going (unraced on soft/heavy). *N. J. Henderson* — **h105**

MIRANT 4 b.c. Danzig Connection (USA) – Ingerence (FR) (Akarad (FR)) [2002/3 16dᶠ 16d² 16d³ Mar 1] leggy, quite good-topped colt: half-brother to fair hurdler Kiss Me Kate (by Aragon), stays 2½m: fairly useful maiden on Flat (stays 1¾m) for E. Dunlop: fairly useful juvenile hurdler: would have made winning debut but for falling last at Wincanton: placed behind East Tycoon at Doncaster and Far Pavilions at Haydock: will stay beyond 2m: possibly not easiest of rides. *M. C. Pipe* — **h112**

MIRJAN (IRE) 7 b.g. Tenby – Mirana (IRE) (Ela-Mana-Mou) [2002/3 h127§: 21s⁵ 16s⁴ 16dᵖᵘ 16d⁶ 25g 22m³ 20m² Apr 21] angular gelding: useful handicap hurdler: won at Ayr in April: good neck second to Loop The Loup at Wetherby later in month: probably ideally suited by 2½m/2¾m nowadays: acts on good to firm and heavy going: tried visored/blinkered, in latter last 2 starts: unreliable. *L. Lungo* — **h130 §**

MIRPOUR (IRE) 4 b.g. Turtle Island (IRE) – Mirana (IRE) (Ela-Mana-Mou) [2002/3 16s² 16s² 16v² 16v⁵ Dec 26] good-topped gelding: half-brother to useful 2m to 2¾m hurdler Mirjan (by Tenby): useful up to 1¾m on Flat: sold out of J. Oxx's stable 115,000 gns Newmarket July Sales: fairly useful juvenile hurdler, best effort on debut: stiffish task, well held in Grade 1 at Punchestown in early-May: raced at 2m: acts on heavy going: wore blinkers/cheekpieces after hurdling debut. *E. Griffin, Ireland* — **h118**

MISBEHAVIOUR 4 b.g. Tragic Role (USA) – Exotic Forest (Dominion) [2002/3 16m 17sᵘʳ 17s* 16d 17d⁵ 16s² 16g⁵ 16m³ 21m⁵ Apr 19] modest maiden on Flat (should stay 1m): modest juvenile hurdler: won seller at Taunton in November: claimed from J. Portman £3,000 sixth start: not sure to stay beyond 2m: best efforts on going softer than good. *P. Butler* — **h88**

MISCONDUCT 9 gr.m. Risk Me (FR) – Grey Cree (Creetown) [2002/3 h108: 16v⁵ 16v 19d 20gᵘʳ Apr 2] medium-sized mare: fair hurdler: out of sorts in 2002/3: stays 19f: acts on good to firm and heavy going: has had tongue tied: races prominently. *J. G. Portman* — **h–**

MISE RAFTURAI (IRE) 5 b. or br.g. Erins Isle – Nordic Union (IRE) (Nordico (USA)) [2002/3 17s³ 16g* 17g* 16s* 16v 17gᵖᵘ 16m Apr 22] brother to fair 2m hurdle winner Consalvo: fair 11f winner on Flat (best efforts when blinkered): progressed really well in handicap hurdles in first half of 2002/3, won at Cork, Gowran (twice) and Killarney: below best subsequently, including when heavily-backed favourite for County Hurdle at Cheltenham sixth start: raced around 2m: acts on soft going. *Paul Nolan, Ireland* — **h119**

MISHEAD 5 ch.g. Unfuwain (USA) – Green Jannat (USA) (Alydar (USA)) [2002/3 h78: 17m³ 17gᵖᵘ 17m⁴ Jun 22] poor maiden hurdler: raced around 2m: acts on good to firm and good to soft ground. *M. C. Chapman* — **h84**

MISS ARAGONT 4 b.f. Aragon – Uninvited (Be My Guest (USA)) [2002/3 F16g Mar 23] 1,500 3-y-o: fifth foal: half-sister to winning 2m hurdler Miss All Alone (by Crofthall): dam won 2m hurdle: well held in bumper on debut. *S. G. Chadwick* — **F–**

MISS BLUE ICE 5 b.m. Michelozzo (USA) – Miss Vaigly Blue (Vaigly Great) [2002/3 F–: F16d May 4] no form in 2 bumpers. *P. Wegmann* — **F–**

MISS CASH 6 b.m. Rock Hopper – Miss Cashtal (IRE) (Ballacashtal (CAN)) [2002/3 h–: 27m Jul 17] strong, lengthy mare: poor maiden stayer on Flat: little worthwhile form over hurdles: tried blinkered: dead. *M. E. Sowersby* — **h–**

MISS COOL 7 b.m. Jupiter Island – Laurel Diver (Celtic Cone) [2002/3 h115p: 16m³ 16d³ 16d⁴ 17g 22f* 21m³ Apr 17] angular mare: useful handicap hurdler: upped in trip, improved form when winning at Haydock in March, not fully extended to beat Columbus 7 lengths: creditable third to Blue Ride in listed mares event at Cheltenham following month: stays easy 2¾m: acts on firm and soft going: visored after reappearance: often takes good hold. *M. C. Pipe* — **h131**

587

MISS COSPECTOR 4 ch.f. Emperor Fountain – Gypsy Race (IRE) (Good Thyne   F– (USA)) [2002/3 F17g Apr 21] first foal: dam modest novice hurdler/chaser: seventh of 14 in bumper at Carlisle on debut. *T. H. Caldwell*

MISSDMENA 4 br.f. Carlton (GER) – Menas Gold (Heights of Gold) [2002/3 F18v   F– F18f⁵ Apr 24] second foal: dam 2-y-o 7f/1m winner, stayed 1¼m: little worthwhile form in 2 bumpers. *G. P. Enright*

MISS ELLIE 7 b.m. Elmaamul (USA) – Jussoli (Don) [2002/3 h86: 16gᵖᵘ 22dᵖᵘ 16vᵖᵘ   h– Mar 13] workmanlike mare: modest handicap hurdler in 2001/2: showed nothing in 2002/3: barely stays 3m: acts on good to firm and good to soft going, probably unsuited by softer. *Mrs C. J. Kerr*

MISS FARA (FR) 8 ch.m. Galetto (FR) – Faracha (FR) (Kenmare (FR)) [2002/3 c–,   c– h134: 21sᵖᵘ 25g 24g Apr 3] leggy mare: useful on Flat, won Cesarewitch in October: h– useful handicap hurdler at best, ran poorly in 2002/3: stays 21f: acts on firm and soft going (well below form on heavy): usually held up. *M. C. Pipe*

MISS FENCOTE 7 b.m. Phardante (FR) – Jack's The Girl (IRE) (Supreme Leader)   h71 [2002/3 h74: 20m⁵ 23d⁶ 22s⁴ Jun 3] sturdy mare: poor maiden hurdler: barely stays 3m: acts on heavy going, possibly unsuited by good to firm. *P. Beaumont*

MISS GREEN 8 b.m. Greensmith – Miss Comedy (Comedy Star (USA)) [2002/3   h– h–: 17mᵖᵘ 16fᵖᵘ 17gᵖᵘ Jun 22] pulled up all 4 starts over hurdles: tried tongue tied. *Miss L. Bower*

MISS HONEYPENNY (IRE) 5 b.m. Old Vic – Honey Dream (Orchestra) [2002/3   F87 F16m² Mar 23] seventh foal: dam unraced: fair form when ¾-length second to Thanx Directory in mares maiden bumper at Huntingdon on debut. *B. G. Powell*

MISS JANICA 5 b.m. Sir Harry Lewis (USA) – Supreme Wonder (IRE) (Supreme   h73 Leader) [2002/3 F85: F16s F17g 20mᵘʳ 19s² 20m³ Aug 17] modest form at best in bump-   F68 ers: poor form when placed in maiden hurdles at Stratford and Bangor: stays 2½m. *Miss Venetia Williams*

MISS JEFF (FR) 5 ch.m. Mansonnien (FR) – Miss Jefferson (FR) (Jefferson) [2002/3   h93 h91: 19mᵇᵈ 16m⁵ Jul 18] angular mare: modest hurdler: good fifth in handicap at Uttox- eter in July, not seen out again: will probably prove best around 2m: acts on soft and good to firm going. *M. C. Pipe*

MISS KITZ 7 b.m. Cruise Missile – Frau Kitz (Master Buck) [2002/3 h–, F–: 21dᵖᵘ   c– c24vᵖᵘ Dec 20] leggy mare: no sign of ability: tried blinkered/visored. *Dr J. R. J. Naylor*   h–

MISS KOEN (IRE) 4 b.f. Barathea (IRE) – Fanny Blankers (IRE) (Persian Heights)   h– [2002/3 16d 16vᵖᵘ 16vᵖᵘ 16m 16g 27sᵖᵘ Mar 11] smallish, dipped-backed ex-Irish filly: fairly useful on Flat (stays 1½m), sold out of K. Prendergast's stable 8,000 gns New- market Autumn Sales: little show over hurdles. *D. L. Williams*

MISS LACROIX 8 b.m. Picea – Smartie Lee (Dominion) [2002/3 h79: 16m 19m³   h73 16m 22m* 22m⁶ 22s⁶ 16g³ 19s 17d 24g 21g Mar 16] compact mare: poor handicap hurdler: won conditional jockeys event at Fontwell in August: probably needs further than 2m, stays 2¾m: acts on good to firm and good to soft going: usually races promin- ently. *R. Hollinshead*

MISS LEWIS 5 b.m. Sir Harry Lewis (USA) – Teelyna (Teenoso (USA)) [2002/3   F77 F16m⁴ F16m² Apr 22] first known foal: dam unraced: modest form in frame in bumpers at Ludlow and Chepstow. *C. J. Down*

MISS MAILMIT 6 b.m. Rakaposhi King – Flora Louisa (Rymer) [2002/3 F16d⁶ Mar   F72 8] first foal: dam, novice hurdler who stayed 21f, half-sister to useful 2m to 2½m hurdler Winnie The Witch: sixth of 13 in mares maiden bumper at Warwick on debut. *J. A. B. Old*

MISS MATTIE ROSS 7 b.m. Milieu – Mother Machree (Bing II) [2002/3 h–:   h– 16d⁵ 16g 21g 24gᵖᵘ Apr 23] medium-sized mare: little sign of ability over hurdles. *S. J. Marshall*

MISS MELROSE 6 ch.m. Bob Back (USA) – Whatagale (Strong Gale) [2002/3 F–:   h– 16m⁵ 17d Jun 5] little sign of ability. *L. Lungo*

MISS NEL 8 b.m. Denel (FR) – Ice Lass (Heroic Air) [2002/3 h–: 24dᵖᵘ May 4] no   h– sign of ability. *R. H. Goldie*

MISS O'GRADY (IRE) 11 ch.m. Over The River (FR) – Polar Mistress (IRE)   c95 (Strong Gale) [2002/3 c97: c26g⁴ c25d² c20g* c19g² c21gᵖᵘ Apr 19] angular mare: won twice in points in February: fair form in hunter chases, won at Fontwell in March:

seems ideally suited by around 2½m: acts on good to soft going: sometimes let down by jumping: weak finisher (has reportedly broken blood vessels). *Mrs S. Alner*

MISS OPULENCE (IRE) 4 b.f. Kylian (USA) – Oriental Splendour (Runnett) [2002/3 16d³ 17s² 16v⁴ Jan 2] angular filly: half-sister to fairly useful 2m hurdler Really Chuffed (by Shavian): fairly useful on Flat (stays 1¼m), successful in April: modest form in juvenile hurdles, found conditions too testing when favourite at Ayr final start: will prove best at sharp 2m. *B. Ellison*   **h88**

MISS PORTCELLO 10 b.m. Bybicello – Port Mallaig (Royal Fountain) [2002/3 c80: c25d³ c20m³ c24g⁵ c25d³ c24g* Apr 21] fair hunter chaser: won maiden at Carlisle in April: will stay beyond 25f: unraced on extremes of going. *Mrs J. M. Hollands*   **c90**

MISS RENNENSKI 7 b.m. Petoski – Miss Wrensborough (Buckskin (FR)) [2002/3 h72: 22d² Aug 24] poor maiden hurdler: ran well when second in conditional jockeys selling handicap at Cartmel only start in 2002/3: will stay beyond 2¾m: raced on good going or softer. *D. R. Gandolfo*   **h77**

MISS SUTTON 5 b.m. Formidable (USA) – Saysana (Sayf El Arab (USA)) [2002/3 16g May 17] no longer of much account on Flat: visored, showed little on hurdling debut. *G. F. H. Charles-Jones*   **h–**

MISS TANGO 6 b.m. Batshoof – Spring Flyer (IRE) (Waajib) [2002/3 h114: 17d 18s 24dᵖᵘ 24mᵖᵘ Apr 8] sparely-made mare: fair hurdler: off 15 months, no form in handicaps in 2002/3: visored, lost action final start: stays 3m: best efforts on good going or firmer. *M. C. Pipe*   **h–**

MISS WOODPECKER 6 b.m. Morpeth – Pigeon Loft (IRE) (Bellypha) [2002/3 F17mⁿ⁶ Aug 26] third foal: sister to 2¾m hurdle winner Grey Brother and half-sister to bumper winner Miss Woodpigeon (by Landyap): dam runner-up in 17f seller only completed start over hurdles: favourite, well held in bumper at Newton Abbot on debut. *J. D. Frost*   **F–**

MISS WOODSTICK 7 b.m. Teenoso (USA) – Born Bossy (Eborneezer) [2002/3 c82, h89: 24g 24dᵖᵘ c24g c24g³ 28g⁴ c21mᶠ Apr 21] lengthy mare: poor hurdler/chaser: left J. Spearing after second start: stayed 3¼m: acted on good to firm and good to soft going: visored once: dead. *M. J. Gingell*   **c82 x**   **h79**

MISS WOODY 4 b.f. Bin Ajwaad (IRE) – Miss Doody (Gorytus (USA)) [2002/3 16mⁿ⁶ Sep 28] no worthwhile form on Flat: well held in juvenile on hurdling debut. *P. Butler*   **h–**

MISTANOORA 4 b.g. Topanoora – Mistinguett (IRE) (Doyoun) [2002/3 16g⁴ 16mⁿ⁶ 17g³ 16s² 16s* 16d⁵ 16v*16g 17mⁿ² Apr 16] small, leggy gelding: first foal: dam very smart hurdler up to 2¾m: fair form at best in 3 maidens at 2 yrs for M. Channon: useful juvenile hurdler, generally progressive: won at Wetherby in November and Sandown in February: good neck second to Bal de Nuit at Cheltenham final start: will be suited by further then 17f: acts on good to firm and heavy going: blinkered after second outing. *N. A. Twiston-Davies*   **h127**

MISTAWAY 5 b.m. Nomadic Way (USA) – Miss Puck (Tepukei) [2002/3 F17v F16g Mar 23] sixth foal: half-sister to poor pointer by Primitive Rising: dam tailed off in bumper: showed nothing in 2 bumpers. *I. A. Brown*   **F–**

MISTELLA 7 ch.m. Milieu – Streakella (Firestreak) [2002/3 F17g 22dᵖᵘ 19dᵖᵘ Dec 4] half-sister to several winners, including one-time fairly useful chaser Montrave (by Netherkelly), stays 2½m: dam 5f 2-y-o winner: no promise in bumper or novice hurdles. *Mrs J. C. McGregor*   **h–**   **F–**

MISTER BIGTIME (IRE) 9 br.g. Roselier (FR) – Cnoc An Oir (Goldhill) [2002/3 c118, h–: c25g⁴ c24sᵖᵘ c25d³ c24sᵖᵘ Mar 1] well-made gelding: fairly useful novice chaser, well below form in 2002/3: should stay beyond 3m: acts on heavy going. *B. G. Powell*   **c101**   **h–**

MISTER BROCK 8 b.g. Petoski – Romantic Run (Deep Run) [2002/3 c21gᵖᵘ May 1] lengthy gelding: poor pointer. *Miss E. J. Baker*   **c–**

MISTER CHISUM 7 b.g. Sabrehill (USA) – Anchor Inn (Be My Guest (USA)) [2002/3 16s² 17d³ 17g 17g² 16s² 16dᵘʳ 16s⁴ 16v⁴ 16d 17vᵖᵘ 16d* 16g* 16g* Apr 7] angular gelding: fair hurdler: left R. Bastiman after seventh outing: ridden from front and improved form when winning novice handicap at Ayr (first run after leaving Miss K. Key) in March and novice claimer at Newcastle and handicap at Kelso in April: raced around 2m on good going or softer (acts on heavy). *R. Allan*   **h103**

MISTER CLUB ROYAL   7 b.g. Alflora (IRE) – Miss Club Royal (Avocat) [2002/3 c58, h–, F–: c17g^{pu} c16s c20v^2 c17g^4 Mar 22] good-topped gelding: poor maiden chaser: will stay beyond 2½m. *D. McCain*   **c70 h–**

MISTER DAVE'S (IRE)   8 ch.g. Bluffer – Tacovaon (Avocat) [2002/3 h92, F67: 24g 25g c20s^F c25v^2 27g^2 Mar 25] tall, leggy gelding: modest hurdler: fair form when second in novice at Wetherby on completed outing over fences: stays 27f: acts on heavy and good to firm going: none too consistent. *Mrs S. J. Smith*   **c108 h90**

MISTER ERMYN   10 ch.g. Minster Son – Rosana Park (Music Boy) [2002/3 h–§: 16d^{pu} 20g^{pu} 22s^4 17s^6 Dec 17] tall, sparely-made gelding: winning hurdler: no longer of any account: visored/blinkered: temperamental. *L. Montague Hall*   **h– §**

MISTER FALCON (FR)   6 b.g. Passing Sale (FR) – Falcon Crest (FR) (Cadoudal (FR)) [2002/3 h103§: 22m^5 22m^{pu} Aug 5] sparely-made gelding: fair hurdler at best: only poor form on first of 2 starts in 2002/3: stays 27f: acts on soft and firm ground: visored: ungenuine: sold £2,000 Ascot August Sales. *M. C. Pipe*   **h81 §**

MISTER FELIX (IRE)   7 b.g. Ore – Pixies Glen (Furry Glen) [2002/3 F16v* 21s Jan 27] tall ex-Irish gelding: third foal: half-brother to Foxhunter winner Kingscliff (by Toulon): dam, well beaten in bumpers in Ireland, half-sister to useful staying chaser Fighting Words: trained by I. Gault when gamely winning bumper at Down Royal on debut in November: shaped as though in need of experience when seventh of 21 in novice at Kempton on hurdling debut: likely to do better. *Mrs Susan Nock*   **h83 p F95**

MISTER FLINT   5 b.g. Petoski – National Clover (National Trust) [2002/3 F16d^2 F16v^2 Mar 8] workmanlike gelding: half-brother to one-time top-class chaser Go Ballistic (by Celtic Cone), stays 3¼m: dam, very useful pointer, daughter of Welsh National winner Clover Bud: runner-up in bumpers at Wincanton (to Brankley Boy) and Sandown (behind Royal Rosa): will be suited by 2½m+. *P. J. Hobbs*   **F95**

MISTER FRIDAY (IRE)   6 b. or br.g. Mister Lord (USA) – Rebecca's Storm (IRE) (Strong Gale) [2002/3 20v^F 24v^2 20d* 24s^3 20m^F 27g^2 Apr 25] 22,000 4-y-o: leggy gelding: second foal: dam, lightly raced in bumpers, half-sister to useful staying hurdler What A Question: won maiden Irish point in 2002: fair novice hurdler: won at Ayr in February: stays 27f: unraced on firm going, acts on any other. *P. D. Niven*   **h106**

MISTER GRAHAM   8 b.g. Rock Hopper – Celestial Air (Rheingold) [2002/3 c80d, h–: c20m^2 c21m^4 c21m^5 c21d^{pu} 20d 16v^4 20g 16g^5 16m 16m Apr 21] strong, lengthy gelding: poor maiden hurdler/chaser: form in 2002/3 only on reappearance, sold out of Mrs S. Smith's stable 2,700 gns Doncaster September Sales after third start: stays 3m: acts on good to firm and good to soft going: tried blinkered, wore cheekpieces last 6 starts: sketchy jumper: ungenuine. *K. F. Clutterbuck*   **c63 § h– §**

MISTER KNIGHT (IRE)   4 ch.g. Mister Lord (USA) – Knights Bounty (IRE) (Henbit (USA)) [2002/3 F16d^6 Mar 1] tall, lengthy gelding: third foal: dam unraced: in need of race, well beaten in bumper on debut. *T. P. Tate*   **F–**

MISTER MAGNUM (IRE)   5 b.g. Be My Native (USA) – Miss Henrietta (IRE) (Step Together (USA)) [2002/3 F17s 17s^4 19s^4 Feb 27] 31,000 4-y-o: leggy gelding: fifth foal: half-brother to bumper winner Tollbrae (by Supreme Leader): dam, lightly-raced hurdler, from family of Buck House: seventh of 14 in bumper at Taunton on debut: modest form when fourth in maiden and novice there both starts over hurdles: likely to prove best at 2½m+. *M. C. Pipe*   **h85 F64**

MISTER MAGPIE   7 gr.g. Neltino – Magic (Sweet Revenge) [2002/3 h91p, F89: c16d^{pu} c16v^{ur} c16d^{pu} c16g^{pu} Feb 25] good-topped gelding: winning hurdler: no form in 4 chases: bred to stay well beyond 2m: blinkered final outing. *T. R. George*   **c– h–**

MISTER MCGOLDRICK   6 b.g. Sabrehill (USA) – Anchor Inn (Be My Guest (USA)) [2002/3 h101+: 16v* 16g 16s* 16s^4 20d^3 16v 16g 20m^4 Apr 21] workmanlike gelding: progressed into useful hurdler in 2002/3, winning handicaps at Wetherby in November and December: best effort when third to Quazar in similar event at Haydock: stays 2½m: seems to need going softer than good (acts on heavy): effective held up or ridden prominently: bold jumper: useful novice chase prospect for 2003/4. *Mrs S. J. Smith*   **h132**

MISTER MIMS (IRE)   7 b.g. Scenic – Miss Bagatelle (Mummy's Pet) [2002/3 20m^3 17m^2 Jul 15] ex-Irish gelding: half-brother to 2 winners on Flat abroad: dam, Irish 6f winner, half-sister to Ascot Gold Cup winner Arcadian Heights: fair maiden up to 1½m on Flat for J. Bolger: better effort over hurdles (pulled too hard on hurdling debut) when 1¼ lengths second to Bairon in novice at Newton Abbot: may prove best short of 2½m: sold 4,500 gns Doncaster September Sales. *C. J. Mann*   **h104**

MISTER MONTH (IRE) 6 ch.g. Roselier (FR) – Croghan Heather (Baragoi) **h112**
[2002/3 F16s* F20d² 20v² Oct 28] third foal: dam placed in bumpers/over hurdles: much **F114**
improved in bumpers first 2 starts, winning at Galway in September: useful form when
1½ lengths second to Rockstown Boy, pair clear, in 2½m event at Gowran in October: 1½
lengths second to Montayral in novice at Galway on hurdling debut: will be suited by 3m:
raced on ground softer than good: races prominently: looked sure to do better over
hurdles but not seen out again. *C. F. Swan, Ireland*

MISTER MOSS (IRE) 10 b.g. Don Tristan (USA) – Lindas Statement (IRE) (Strong **c–**
Statement (USA)) [2002/3 c21gᵖᵘ May 1] fair pointer, lightly raced: little show in maiden
hunter chase. *G. D. Hanmer*

MISTER MUDDYPAWS 13 b.g. Celtic Cone – Jane's Daughter (Pitpan) [2002/3 **c95**
c107?, h–: c27m⁴ Apr 11] lengthy gelding: fair handicap chaser on his day: first outing **h–**
for a year, never dangerous in hunter at Ayr won by Earthmover: stays 4m: acts on firm
and soft going: blinkered twice, successful on first occasion: tends to go in snatches.
C. P. Dennis

MISTER MUSTARD (IRE) 6 b.g. Norwich – Monalma (IRE) (Montekin) [2002/3 **F99**
F16v* F16m³ Mar 22] IR £11,000 4-y-o: good-bodied gelding: fourth foal: dam unraced
half-sister to high-class hurdler/useful chaser up to 2½m Bonalma: won 9-runner bumper
at Ascot on debut in February by 5 lengths from Malaga Boy: ran well when third of 18 to
Yardbird at Newbury following month: will stay beyond 2m. *Ian Williams*

MISTER ONE 12 b. or br.g. Buckley – Miss Redlands (Dubassoff (USA)) [2002/3 **c–**
c137, h–: c32m⁵ Jun 30] lengthy gelding: useful handicap chaser: below form in valuable **h–**
event at Uttoxeter in June: stays extreme distances: acts on good to firm going, probably
on soft: blinkered once: not an easy ride. *C. Tizzard*

MISTER PARTY 8 b.g. Henbit (USA) – Sally's Dove (Celtic Cone) [2002/3 h–: **c–**
c16dᵖᵘ Mar 4] won 3-finisher maiden point in February: yet to complete over hurdles and **h–**
in hunter chase. *Andrew J. Martin*

MISTER PICKWICK (IRE) 8 b.g. Commanche Run – Buckfast Lass (Buckskin **c– §**
(FR)) [2002/3 c69§, h81§: 21m⁵ 22f* c26m³ 21m* Sep 28] workmanlike gelding: poor **h83 §**
handicap hurdler/maiden chaser: successful at Fontwell in June and Plumpton (seller,
made all) in September: stays 25f: acts on any going: tried visored, usually blinkered:
often looks hard ride. *G. L. Moore*

MISTER PUTT (USA) 5 b. or br.g. Mister Baileys – Theresita (GER) (Surumu **h113**
(GER)) [2002/3 h99: 20d 17s 16v* 16s³ 16s* Mar 10] useful-looking gelding: fair hurdler: benefited from blinkers last 3 outings, winning twice in January and novice in March:
improved form when beating Hale Bopp 1¾ lengths in latter: raced mainly around 2m on going softer than good (acts on heavy): effective
tongue tied or not. *Mrs N. Smith*

MISTER SOOTY 5 b.g. Dilum (USA) – Spring Flyer (IRE) (Waajib) [2002/3 F16s **h–**
22dᵖᵘ Feb 23] third foal: half-brother to useful hurdler/fairly useful chaser up to 3m **F–**
Roveretto (by Robellino) and fair hurdler up to 3m Miss Tango (by Batshoof): dam, fair
7f to 9f winner, half-sister to smart sprinter A Prayer For Wings: behind in bumper on
debut: went as if amiss in maiden hurdle. *M. C. Pipe*

MISTER WEBB 6 b.g. Whittingham (IRE) – Ruda (FR) (Free Round (USA)) [2002/3 **c–**
h87: 21s 19d c20g⁶ c24gᵖᵘ 20m 19m⁴ Apr 21] poor novice hurdler: well held on com- **h65**
pleted start over fences. *Dr J. R. J. Naylor*

MISTER WELLARD 6 b.g. Sir Harry Lewis (USA) – Cream By Post (Torus) **h115**
[2002/3 F99p: F17f* 17vᶠ⁵ 17sᵖᵘ Dec 6] useful form in bumpers, easily landed odds **F104**
in weak race at Taunton in October: every chance when falling 2 out (remounted) in
novice at Newton Abbot on hurdling debut: fatally injured in similar event at Exeter.
P. F. Nicholls

MISTI HUNTER (IRE) 14 gr.g. Roselier (FR) – Lovely Stranger (Le Bavard (FR)) **c–**
[2002/3 c79, h–: c28d⁵ c27g c26dᶠ Mar 8] close-coupled gelding: modest hunter chaser: **h–**
fell fatally at Warwick: stayed 3¼m: acted on firm and good to soft going. *Mrs Carrie
Ford*

MISTLETOE (IRE) 9 gr.m. Montelimar (USA) – Nancy's Sister (The Parson) **c119**
[2002/3 c125, h–: c24dᶠ c24s c24v⁴ c24d³ c25sᵖᵘ Feb 23] workmanlike mare: fairly use- **h–**
ful chaser: respectable efforts in handicaps third and fourth outings: stays 3m: raced on
good going or softer (acts on heavy). *K. C. Bailey*

MISTRATO (GER) 9 b. or br.g. Surumu (GER) – Midnight Society (USA) (Imp   c–
Society (USA)) [2002/3 16s^pu 16g Sep 14] placed on chasing debut in Germany: no form   h–
over hurdles in Britain. *P. Wegmann*

MISTRESS MILLIE (IRE) 7 ch.m. St Ninian – Nearly Married (Nearly A Hand)   h72
[2002/3 F83: F16d³ F16s⁵ 20m^pu 16m 19m⁶ 20g² 20d⁴ Nov 24] modest in bumpers: poor   **F82**
novice hurdler: stays 2½m: raced on good/good to firm going over hurdles: blinkered last
2 outings. *A. W. Carroll*

MISTRESS OFTHEHALL 5 b.m. Son Pardo – Covent Garden Girl (Sizzling   h–
Melody) [2002/3 17s^pu Feb 13] well held in 3 maidens on Flat at 3 yrs for P. D. Evans:
always behind in maiden on hurdling debut. *Mrs N. S. Sharpe*

MISTY FUTURE 5 b.g. Sanglamore (USA) – Star of The Future (USA) (El Gran   h79
Senor (USA)) [2002/3 16d 17s⁶ 16s⁴ 16d² Mar 8] sturdy gelding: sixth foal: half-brother
to 2002 6f 2-y-o winner Latest Edition (by Charnwood Forest) and 7f winners fairly
useful Starry Eyed (by Warning) and useful Big Future (by Bigstone): dam, 7f and 1m
winner, half-sister to US Grade 2 9f winner Man From Eldorado: eighth of 16 on Flat
debut in France at 3 yrs, sold out of M. Zilber's stable 22,000 gns Newmarket Autumn
(2001) Sales: poor form over hurdles: raced around 2m: raced on good to soft/soft going.
Miss Venetia Williams

MISTY MEMORY 4 b.f. Alderbrook – Misty Sunset (Le Bavard (FR)) [2002/3 F16g   F–
Feb 27] seventh foal: half-sister to several winners, including fair staying hurdler Henry
Cone (by Celtic Cone) and smart chaser Percy Smollett (by Oats), stayed 25f: dam,
winning 2½m hurdler, half-sister to very smart 2m to 3m chaser Western Sunset: ran
green when eighth of 17 in mares bumper at Ludlow on debut. *R. F. Knipe*

MISTY RAMBLE (IRE) 8 b.g. Roselier (FR) – Ramble Bramble (Random Shot)   c88
[2002/3 c88, h–: c28v^ur c25s⁵ c27s² c27v² c27v³ c24s⁴ Mar 2] useful-looking gelding: h–
modest maiden chaser: stays 27f: acts on heavy going: tongue tied last 4 starts. *Ferdy
Murphy*

MISTY RIDGE (IRE) 8 b.g. Moscow Society (USA) – Abigail's Dream (Kalaglow)   c89 x
[2002/3 c–, h90: 16g⁵ 23d 20m² 19g⁴ 26m³ 20d³ c22m² c22g* c22d^F Oct 19] lengthy,   h92 x
angular gelding: modest hurdler: won handicap at Market Rasen in June: first form over
fences when second to Mount Gay in novice at same course: survived 2 bad mistakes
when beating 2 poor opponents there in October: stays 3¼m, at least when conditions
aren't testing: acts on firm going: effective blinkered or not: poor jumper. *Mrs S. J. Smith*

MITCHELDEAN (IRE) 7 b.g. Be My Native (USA) – Pil Eagle (FR) (Piling (USA))   c– x
[2002/3 c111, h–: c25d^pu c20d⁵ 20v^pu Dec 20] good-topped gelding: winning hurdler/   h–
chaser, no form in 2002/3: stays 3m: acts on heavy going: blinkered final outing: often
makes mistakes over fences. *M. Pitman*

MITCHELSTOWN (IRE) 5 b.g. Topanoora – Can't Afford It (IRE) (Glow (USA))   **F101**
[2002/3 F16s⁵ F16s³ F19v² F17d* F16d³ F16v² F16v³ F16d⁵ F16g Apr 20] second foal:
dam ran twice at 2 yrs, half-sister to useful sprinter Clever Caption (by Topanoora):
fairly useful in bumpers: won at Gowran in February: tongue tied: races prominently:
consistent. *C. Roche, Ireland*

MITHAK (USA) 9 b.g. Silver Hawk (USA) – Kapalua Butterfly (USA) (Stage Door   h111
Johnny) [2002/3 h81: 20d² 26s² 22d^F 23v* 24d* 24s² Jan 27] leggy gelding: fair handicap
hurdler: found some form again in 2002/3, winning at Haydock in December and Ludlow
in January: good second to Beyond Control at Kempton final start: stays 3¼m: acts on
good to firm and heavy going. *R. T. Phillips*

MITHRAIC (IRE) 11 b.g. Kefaah (USA) – Persian's Glory (Prince Tenderfoot (USA))   c–
[2002/3 c–, h85: 16d Apr 29] lengthy gelding: tubed: winning hurdler, very lightly raced   h–
nowadays: stays easy 2½m: acts on good to firm and heavy going. *W. S. Cunningham*

MIXED MARRIAGE (IRE) 5 ch.g. Indian Ridge – Marie de Flandre (FR) (Crystal   h102
Palace (FR)) [2002/3 16s* 16s⁴ 16g⁶ Mar 25] half-brother to 3 winning hurdlers, notably
useful 2½m performer Solo Mio (by Sadler's Wells), also very smart stayer on Flat:
modest maiden up to 13f on Flat: won 6-runner maiden at Plumpton on hurdling debut in
February: similar form other 2 starts, mistake last when sixth of 14 in novice handicap at
Ascot. *G. L. Moore*

MIXED OPINION (IRE) 10 b.g. Be My Guest (USA) – Outside Pressure (Sher-   h–
nazar) [2002/3 22m^pu 19g^pu 17m Aug 12] small gelding: maiden hurdler: showed nothing
in 2002/3 after 2-year absence, left C. Jackson after second start (blinkered): has had
tongue tied. *H. M. Kavanagh*

MIXSTERTHETRIXSTER (USA)   7 b.g. Alleged (USA) – Parliament House   **h121**
(USA) (General Assembly (USA)) [2002/3 16m⁵ 16s 19s² 16d* 16m 17gᶠ 16d⁵ Apr 9]
tall, angular gelding: useful hurdler in 1999/00 for T. Easterby, missed next 2 seasons:
bought 6,500 gns Doncaster May Sales: back to somewhere near best when winning
handicap at Doncaster in January impressively by 13 lengths from Tissifer: unable to
repeat the form: stays 19f: acts on soft and good to firm going: keen-going sort (has been
early to post): usually makes running/races prominently. *Miss T. M. Ide*

MOCHO WOOD   5 ch.g. Husyan (USA) – Dawn Call (Rymer) [2002/3 F16d Mar 6]   **F–**
second foal: dam well beaten both starts over hurdles: no show in bumper at Wetherby on
debut. *John Allen*

MODEL COUNTY (IRE)   6 b.g. Montelimar (USA) – Sedan Lady (IRE) (Sandalay)   **F–**
[2002/3 F16v Nov 27] second foal: dam pulled up in point: tailed off in bumper on debut.
Mrs H. Dalton

MODEM (NZ)   9 br.g. Omnicorp (NZ) – Replica (NZ) (Creag-An-Sgor) [2002/3   **c–**
h125: c20dᵖᵘ c19sᵖᵘ Dec 14] strong, compact gelding: fairly useful over hurdles at 2m,   **h–**
winner of 4 of his 6 starts: off 17 months, pulled up in novice chases at Huntingdon
(reportedly distressed) and Doncaster (reportedly broke blood vessel) in 2002/3: acts on
good to firm going. *S. E. H. Sherwood*

MODULOR (FR)   11 gr.g. Less Ice – Chaumontaise (FR) (Armos) [2002/3 c18d c21d   **c?**
c21d⁴ c23d⁶ c21gᵖᵘ c18v² c19v² c17s⁴ c19s⁵ c26g c21dᶠ Apr 4] small, plain gelding: **h–**
fairly useful hurdler/useful chaser in France for Y. Fertillet: prominent until halfway
when tailed off in Cheltenham Gold Cup on British debut, in rear when falling tenth in
Topham Chase (Handicap) at Aintree following month: stays 21f: probably acts on any
going: often blinkered, visored both starts in Britain. *M. C. Pipe*

MOHAWK BRAVE (IRE)   5 b.g. Be My Native (USA) – Aunty Dawn (IRE) (Strong   **F86**
Gale) [2002/3 F16d F16s⁴ Jan 16] good sort: second foal: half-brother to 2½m chase
winner Phar City (by Phardante): dam unraced, from family of Dawn Run: modest form
in bumpers, shaped as if stiffer test of stamina would suit when fourth of 17 in conditional
jockeys event at Ludlow. *K. C. Bailey*

MOHERA KING (IRE)   11 b.g. King's Ride – Kilbrien Star (Goldhill) [2002/3   **c105 §**
c25v⁴ c25s⁴ c21v³ c20g⁶ c25s³ c20d* c20g³ Mar 28] sturdy gelding: third foal: dam   **h–**
winning pointer: fair handicap hurdler in 1999/00: left J. J. Mangan, improved form
over fences in 2002/3, won 5-runner handicap at Ayr in March by 12 lengths from Kung
Hei Fat Choi: stays 25f: acts on good to firm and heavy going: often wears blinkers/
cheekpieces nowadays: moody. *Ferdy Murphy*

MOLLYCARRSBREKFAST   8 b.g. Presidium – Imperial Flame (Imperial Lantern)   **c–**
[2002/3 c23dᵖᵘ c24f⁴ c19m⁶ Apr 21] fair pointer: well held both starts in hunter chases:
trained on reappearance by K. Bishop. *Miss S. E. Robinson*

MOLLYCARRS GAMBUL   4 b.f. General Gambul – Emma's Vision (IRE) (Vision   **h–**
(USA)) [2002/3 17d 16s⁶ 17mᵖᵘ Sep 11] second foal: dam of no account: no form in 3
starts over hurdles. *W. G. M. Turner*

MOLLYCARRS VISION   6 b.g. Yaheeb (USA) – Emma's Vision (IRE) (Vision   **h–**
(USA)) [2002/3 F16g 17sᵖᵘ May 28] first foal: dam of no account: no sign of ability in   **F–**
bumper or selling hurdle. *P. R. Rodford*

MOMENT OF MADNESS (IRE)   5 ch.g. Treasure Hunter – Sip of Orange (Celtic   **F–**
Cone) [2002/3 F16d Feb 1] fifth foal: half-brother to 2 winners, including fair chaser
around 2½m Jaffa (by Kind of Hush): dam useful staying hurdler: burly, never a factor in
bumper at Wetherby on debut. *J. G. FitzGerald*

MOMENTOUS JONES   6 b.g. Emperor Jones (USA) – Ivory Moment (USA) (Sir   **c–**
Ivor) [2002/3 h95: 22d 16d⁵ 20v 20v² 24s⁶ c18sᵖᵘ 18g Mar 17] leggy gelding: modest   **h96**
handicap hurdler: pulled up after blundering fourth on chasing debut (bit slipped): stays
2½m: acts well on soft/heavy going: visored once: has folded tamely. *M. Madgwick*

MONARCH'S PURSUIT   9 b.g. Pursuit of Love – Last Detail (Dara Monarch)   **c118 §**
[2002/3 c119, h–: c16g³ c20dᶠ c16s³ c20s² c16d⁶ Dec 14] rangy, good sort: fairly useful   **h–**
handicap chaser: stays 2½m: yet to race on firm going, acts on any other: blinkered
nowadays: often tongue tied prior to 2002/3: weak finisher. *T. D. Easterby*

MONASH FREEWAY (IRE)   5 ch.h. General Monash (USA) – Pennine Pearl   **h–**
(IRE) (Pennine Walk) [2002/3 h99: 16s 19d Jan 27] fair form when placed both starts in
juvenile hurdles in 2001/2: well beaten in novices after more than year's absence. *Miss
Jacqueline S. Doyle*

MONDURU 6 b.g. Lion Cavern (USA) – Bint Albadou (IRE) (Green Desert (USA)) **h–**
[2002/3 17d 16d^{pu} Nov 12] rather leggy gelding: modest maiden on Flat (stays easy
1¼m): no encouragement in 2 novice hurdles, pulled hard in blinkers in second. *Miss
G. Browne*

MON ESPRIT 6 b.m. Terimon – Spartan Sprite (Country Retreat) [2002/3 F16d **F73**
F17v^4 Jan 21] rather leggy mare: second foal: dam winning hunter chaser: poor form in 2
bumpers: probably a stayer. *Ferdy Murphy*

MONET'S GARDEN (IRE) 5 gr.g. Roselier (FR) – Royal Remainder (IRE) (Rem- **F98 p**
ainder Man) [2002/3 F16d* Feb 23] IR £35,000 3-y-o: first foal: dam unraced: 7/2, won
18-runner bumper at Ayr on debut by ½ length from Dark Character, leading well over 1f
out and finding plenty when shaken up: promising. *N. G. Richards*

MONEY MAGIC 7 ch.m. Weld – Susie's Money (Seymour Hicks (FR)) [2002/3 **c–**
c27d^{pu} Apr 8] third foal: half-sister to winning hurdler/chaser The Sawdust Kid (by River
God), stays 3¼m: dam unraced: poor maiden pointer: showed nothing in hunter chase at
Sedgefield. *Miss S. E. Broadhurst*

MONEY MOUNTAIN 6 ch.g. Rakaposhi King – Black H'Penny (Town And Coun- **F–**
try) [2002/3 F16g Feb 8] workmanlike gelding: second foal: dam, won 2¾m hurdle,
half-sister to very smart staying hurdler Simpson: needed experience and never going
pace in Grade 2 bumper at Newbury on debut. *J. A. B. Old*

MONEYTRAIN (GER) 4 b.g. Platini (GER) – Miss Esther (GER) (Alkalde (GER)) **h124**
[2002/3 16d^4 16s^2 17s* 17g^{bd} 16g Apr 3] leggy, angular gelding: successful around 1¼m
on Flat for R. Suerland: 25/1, best effort in juvenile hurdles (bandaged behind/mistakes
on debut) when winning Grade 2 Wragg & Co Finesse Juvenile Hurdle at Cheltenham in
January, getting up near finish to beat Don Fernando 1½ lengths: not discredited when
seventh of 19 to Le Duc in Grade 2 at Aintree: raced around 2m: acts on soft going: sent
to USA. *C. Von Der Recke, Germany*

MONGER LANE 7 b.m. Karinga Bay – Grace Moore (Deep Run) [2002/3 h108, **h112**
F76: 21d 21s^2 24g 22s^4 Mar 15] tall, good sort: chasing type: fair handicap hurdler:
should be suited by 3m+: seems best on going softer than good: has looked tricky ride,
may benefit from headgear. *K. Bishop*

*Wragge & Co Finesse Juvenile Novices' Hurdle, Cheltenham—German-trained outsider Moneytrain
survives a mistake at the last to beat leading British juveniles Don Fernando (white cap),
Saintsaire (striped cap) and Le Duc (blinkers)*

MONICA GELLER 5 b.m. Komaite (USA) – Rion River (IRE) (Taufan (USA)) **h72**
[2002/3 26g 16g 16m Mar 23] lengthy mare: modest on Flat (stays 9f): mid-division at best in 3 maiden hurdles at Huntingdon. *J. W. Payne*

MONICASMAN (IRE) 13 br.g. Callernish – Sengirrefcha (Reformed Character) **c–**
[2002/3 c77d, h–: c34g⁶ c25m May 29] leggy, lengthy gelding: veteran staying chaser, **h–**
little form since 1999. *Miss Caroline Barclay*

MONITOR 9 ch.g. Machiavellian (USA) – Instant Desire (USA) (Northern Dancer) **c122**
[2002/3 c104, h–: 20g c20m* c20dᵖᵘ c22dᵖᵘ c22m² c20m⁶ Sep 1] workmanlike gelding: **h–**
winning hurdler: fairly useful chaser: won handicap at Wexford in July: good second to Fnan in similar event at Tramore: stays 2¾m: best form on good/good to firm going: tongue tied: inconsistent. *G. M. Lyons, Ireland*

MONKERHOSTIN (FR) 6 b.g. Shining Steel – Ladoun (FR) (Kaldoun (FR)) **c116**
[2002/3 c120, h126: 16f⁵ 16g² c16gᶠ c16m* c16g³ 16v⁵ 16d⁴ 16g⁶ 17g 16m⁵ 20d Apr 4] **h131**
lengthy gelding: fairly useful chaser, won novice at Warwick in November, but largely let down by jumping over fences: useful handicap hurdler: several good efforts in defeat in valuable events, fourth in Lanzarote Hurdle at Kempton and sixth to Spirit Leader in Tote Gold Trophy at Newbury: probably best around 2m: acts on any going: effective visored/ in cheekpieces or not: free-going sort, has found little: reportedly had breathing problem final outing. *O. Sherwood*

MONKEY ISLAND 8 b.g. Jupiter Island – Mikey's Monkey (Monksfield) [2002/3 **c90 d**
c86, h–: c20g* c20d⁵ c20d⁵ c24mᵘʳ c24gᵖᵘ c20gᵖᵘ Mar 28] tall gelding: modest chaser: **h–**
won intermediate at Hexham in April: off 6 months and out of sorts subsequently (lame final outing): stays 3m: raced mainly on good going or softer (acts on soft): usually blinkered: usually races prominently. *Ferdy Murphy*

MONKSFORD 4 b.g. Minster Son – Mortify (Prince Sabo) [2002/3 16v³ Jan 17] fair **h68 +**
on Flat (stays 9f), sold out of D. Smith's stable 8,000 gns Newmarket Autumn Sales: weakened 2 out when well-held third of 13 in juvenile claimer at Chepstow on hurdling debut: likely to benefit from less emphasis on stamina. *B. J. Llewellyn*

MONOLITH 5 b.g. Bigstone (IRE) – Ancara (Dancing Brave (USA)) [2002/3 17s 18g **h71 p**
17d⁶ Mar 2] compact gelding: fairly useful on Flat (should stay 1½m), sold out of Mrs A. Perrett's stable 25,000 gns Newmarket Autumn Sales: poor form in novice hurdles, though shaped as if capable of better on return from 9-month absence final outing. *L. Lungo*

MON PERFORMER 9 ch.g. Mon Tresor – Hot Performer (Hotfoot) [2002/3 17m⁶ **h57**
17d 17d³ 17s 16dᵖᵘ 17gᵖᵘ Mar 25] sturdy gelding: bad maiden hurdler: raced around 2m: tried blinkered. *D. W. Barker*

MONSIEUR DE RIEN (FR) 8 b. or br.g. Vorias (USA) – In Memoriam (IRE) (Buck- **c–**
skin (FR)) [2002/3 c–, h–: 20sᵖᵘ c24vᵘʳ c24dᵖᵘ Jan 16] leggy gelding: maiden hurdler: no **h–**
form since 2000/1, including over fences: tried blinkered/in cheekpieces. *M. Mullineaux*

MONSIEUR POIROT (IRE) 6 b.g. Lapierre – Mallia Miss (IRE) (Executive **h72**
Perk) [2002/3 F72: 16v³ 20s⁴ 16v 24g 20d Mar 2] signs of only a little ability. *Mrs S. C. Bradburne*

MONSIEUR TAGEL (FR) 7 b.g. Tagel (USA) – Miss Zonissa (FR) (Zino) [2002/3 **c110 §**
c102§, h–§: 21m³ 20d c20g² c24gᶠ c24sᵖᵘ c20gᵖᵘ Apr 12] good-topped gelding: fair **h106 §**
handicap hurdler/chaser on his day: stays 2¾m: acts on good to firm and heavy going: ran poorly only try in blinkers: sometimes let down by jumping over fences: weak finisher and not to be trusted. *Ian Williams*

MONT ACA (FR) 8 b.g. Phantom Breeze – Azuzuama (FR) (Cadoudal (FR)) [2002/3 **c75 x**
c–, h98: c20g⁵ Mar 17] leggy, workmanlike gelding: fair hurdler/chaser, fell both starts **h–**
over fences in 2001/2: left P. Hobbs, won in February: bad mistake eighth in hunter at Fontwell (reportedly lame): stays 2½m: acts on soft and good to firm going: blinkered once. *Miss Polly Curling*

MONTAGNETTE 9 ch.m. Gildoran – Deep Crevasse (Rolfe (USA)) [2002/3 h74: **h70**
26g² 24d⁴ 26sᵖᵘ 24sᵖᵘ Feb 13] sparely-made mare: poor hurdler: stays 3¼m: raced on good going or softer (acts on soft). *M. R. Bosley*

MONTALCINO (IRE) 7 b.g. Robellino (USA) – Only Gossip (USA) (Trempolino **c133**
(USA)) [2002/3 h145§: c18s* c16sᵖᵘ Jan 23] smallish, quite good-topped gelding: smart **h– §**
but error-prone hurdler for Miss V. Williams: impressive when winning 3-finisher novice at Newbury in December on chasing debut: broke leg following month: stayed 21f: acted on heavy going: blinkered once: often looked temperamental: dead. *M. C. Pipe*

MONTANA MOON (IRE)   4 b.g. Ajraas (USA) – Batilde (IRE) (Victory Piper   h–
(USA)) [2002/3 16g Nov 23] modest maiden at 2 yrs, well held on Flat in 2002: mid-
division in juvenile claimer at Catterick on hurdling debut. *R. A. Fahey*

MONTAYRAL (FR)   6 b.g. Lesotho (USA) – Demi Lune de Mars (FR) (Fast (FR))   c–
[2002/3 c117+, h–: 20v* 20s⁴ 24s⁴ c24vᶠ Dec 29] leggy gelding: fairly useful novice   h113
chaser for P. Nicholls in 2001/2: only second start over hurdles when making all in novice
at Galway in October: creditable fourth in Grade 3 novices at Navan and Cork next 2
starts: stays 3¼m: raced on good going or softer (acts on heavy): room for improvement
in his jumping over fences. *P. Hughes, Ireland*

MONTE CRISTO (FR)   5 ch.g. Bigstone (IRE) – El Quahirah (FR) (Cadoudal (FR))   c105
[2002/3 h103: 16m² 19m⁴ c19sᵘʳ c17s* c16v² c16d² c20m⁶ 16v⁴ c16m³ c18m² c16d²   h108
c20m³ Apr 21] big, useful-looking gelding: fair hurdler: of similar standard on his day
over fences, won maiden at Plumpton in November: should stay 2½m: acts on heavy
and good to firm going: effective blinkered/visored or not: temperament under suspicion.
Mrs L. C. Taylor

MONTEL GIRL (IRE)   7 ch.m. Montelimar (USA) – Grassed (Busted) [2002/3   h75
F16g⁶ 24m³ 22v⁵ 21s 21s Feb 24] small, angular ex-Irish mare: third foal: half-sister to   F80
bumper winner Hillcrest Girl (by Topanoora): dam, won 17f hurdle, placed up to 2m on
Flat: best effort in bumpers on reappearance: poor form over hurdles, left C. Roche after
debut. *T. P. McGovern*

MONTEMOSS (IRE)   6 ch.g. Montelimar (USA) – Gaye Le Moss (Le Moss) [2002/3   h81
F16g 23v⁵ 24g⁴ Mar 16] medium-sized gelding: ninth foal: half-brother to 2 winners by   F–
Roselier, notably high-class staying chaser Kingsmark: dam, bumper winner, half-sister
to top-class 2m to 3m hurdler Gaye Brief and very smart staying jumper Gaye Chance:
won point in 2002: well held in bumper: poor form in maiden/novice hurdles: likely to
prove best at 3m+. *M. G. Rimell*

MONTE ROUGE (IRE)   6 ch.g. Montelimar (USA) – Drumdeels Star (IRE) (Le   h–
Bavard (FR)) [2002/3 F88: 20d⁶ Dec 14] tall, quite good-topped gelding: fairly useful
form in bumpers, best effort on debut in 2000/1: never-dangerous sixth of 10 in novice at
Haydock on hurdling debut: bred to be stayed by 2½m+. *Miss L. C. Siddall*

MONTESINO   4 b.g. Bishop of Cashel – Sutosky (Great Nephew) [2002/3 F16d⁴ Mar   F84 ?
5] fifth living foal: closely related to useful 1¼m to 13f winner Montecristo (by Warning)
and half-brother to 3 winners, including fairly useful 7f winner Dancing Sioux (by Nabeel
Dancer): dam, suited by 1m to 1¼m, from family of Classic Cliche: dictated slow pace
when around 3 lengths fourth of 10 in bumper at Catterick on debut. *R. C. Guest*

MONTESSORI MIO (FR)   4 b.g. Robellino (USA) – Child's Play (USA) (Sharpen   h99 §
Up) [2002/3 16m⁵ 16m³ 16d⁴ 16d⁵ 17d³ 20d 16g⁴ 17d* 17m* Apr 19] rather angular
gelding: modest maiden on Flat (may prove best around 1¼m) for M. Johnston: fair
hurdler, won juvenile at Sedgefield and novice at Carlisle, both in April: likely to prove
best around 2m: yet to race on extremes of going: wore blinkers/cheekpieces after third
start: has failed to impress with attitude. *Mrs M. Reveley*

MONTE VISTA (IRE)   6 b.g. Montelimar (USA) – Tarqogan's Rose (Tarqogan)   F102 p
[2002/3 F16s³ Nov 30] IR £11,000 4-y-o: half-brother to 6 winners, notably smart
staying chaser River Tarquin (by Over The River): dam unraced, out of half-sister to dam
of smart staying chaser River Tarquin: showed signs of inexperience when promising
third to Mark The Man in bumper at Fairyhouse on debut: will stay beyond 2m.
Miss F. M. Crowley, Ireland

MONTEZUMA   10 br.m. Beveled (USA) – Miss Kuwait (The Brianstan) [2002/3   c65 x
c20d⁴ c21mᵖᵘ c16m³ c24sᵘʳ c21mᵖᵘ 17d Feb 10] smallish mare: no form over hurdles (ran   h– §
moody race final start): made mistakes and signs of only a little ability over fences: tried
blinkered. *N. A. Twiston-Davies*

MONTICELLO (IRE)   11 ch.g. Accordion – Erck (Sun Prince) [2002/3 h67: 17gᵖᵘ   c–
c17gᵖᵘ c19mᵖᵘ Jun 4] angular gelding: selling hurdler: showed nothing in 2 starts over   h–
fences (reportedly lame second time): stays 2½m: acts on good to firm and heavy going:
has been heavily bandaged. *G. F. Bridgwater*

MONTIFAULT (FR)   8 ch.g. Morespeed – Tarde (FR) (Kashtan (FR)) [2002/3 c138,   c138
h–: c25gᵖᵘ c24m² c36d⁵ c29mᵖᵘ Apr 26] lengthy, rather sparely-made gelding: has had   h–
soft palate operation: useful handicap chaser: back to form (has shaped as if amiss more
than once) when 7 lengths second to Eau de Cologne at Newbury in March: 33/1, close
up long way when fifth of 14 finishers to Monty's Pass in Grand National at Aintree:

lifeless display final start: stays 25f: acts on good to firm and heavy going: jumps well. *P. F. Nicholls*

MONTOYA (IRE)   4 b.g. Kylian (USA) – Saborinie (Prince Sabo) [2002/3 18d⁵ 16d 16d⁴ 19m³ Mar 22] close-coupled gelding: fair maiden on Flat (stays 1½m): modest form over hurdles: may prove best at 2m. *P. D. Cundell*   **h95 +**

MONTPELIER (IRE)   10 b.g. Montelimar (USA) – Liscarton (Le Bavard (FR)) [2002/3 c137, h–: c18m³ Mar 21] rangy gelding: useful handicap chaser in 2001/2: took little interest on return from 15-month absence: stays 21f: acts on good to firm and heavy going: sound jumper: idles markedly in front, and best with exaggerated waiting tactics. *N. J. Henderson*   **c—**
h—

MONTREAL (FR)   6 b. or br.g. Chamberlin (FR) – Massada (FR) (Kashtan (FR)) [2002/3 h133: c19g* c19v² c20d² c24m⁵ c24g⁴ c22f* c20g⁴ c16mᵘʳ c20f³ Apr 25] leggy, useful-looking gelding: useful handicap hurdler: quickly reached similar level over fences, won novices at Exeter in November and Haydock (2-runner race) in March: also 3 creditable efforts in well-contested handicaps, though let down by jumping when visored last 2 starts: stays 25f when conditions aren't testing: acts on any going: held up, and has idled in front/found little. *M. C. Pipe*   **c130**
h—

MONTU   6 ch.g. Gunner B – Promitto (Roaring Riva) [2002/3 F–: F16d F16d 20gᵖᵘ Apr 2] short-backed gelding: little sign of ability in bumpers or novice hurdle. *Miss K. M. George*   **h—**
F83 ?

MONTY BE QUICK   7 ch.g. Mon Tresor – Spartiquick (Spartan General) [2002/3 F78: F16d 16g 16g 19f³ 19mᶠ 16f³ Apr 21] leggy gelding: signs of a little ability in bumpers and over hurdles: tongue tied last 4 starts: has pulled hard. *J. M. Castle*   **h68**
F—

MONTY FLOOD (IRE)   6 b.g. Camden Town – Clonroche Artic (Pauper) [2002/3 16v⁶ 16d Feb 23] rather leggy gelding: seventh foal: half-brother to useful hurdler/chaser Ballinclay King (by Asir), stays 25f, and winning pointer by Tesoro Mio: dam, thrice-raced in Irish bumpers, refused to race once: well held in 2 novice hurdles. *Ferdy Murphy*   **h—**

MONTY'S DOUBLE (IRE)   6 b.g. Montelimar (USA) – Macamore Rose (Torus) [2002/3 h79p: 21d⁴ Nov 14] better effort over hurdles (green on debut) when fourth of 15 in maiden at Ludlow: will be suited by 3m. *O. Sherwood*   **h94**

MONTY'S PASS (IRE)   10 b.g. Montelimar (USA) – Friars Pass (Monksfield) [2002/3 c136, h111: 20g² 20s³ c20mᵖᵘ c22d⁶ c20m³ c24f* c24g³ 16v⁶ 16s⁴ c36d* Apr 5]   **c155**
h109
The Grand National remains far and away racing's biggest attraction—but the continuing fall in the domestic television audience, which slumped to its lowest since modern records began, is something of a worry. The figure of 7.8m, still representing a 65% share of the terrestrial audience at the time, comfortably out-stripped that a couple of months later for Flat racing's number-one attraction the Derby (3m watched the race, representing 33% of the audience) and compared favourably with another British sporting institution televised currently by the BBC, the FA Cup Final in May which drew 8.3m viewers, representing a 54% share. The 2003 FA Cup Final audience was higher than for the three previous years—7m (ITV) in 2000, 5m (ITV) in 2001 and 6.3m (BBC) in 2002—but below the 9.5m in 1999, and it is true to say that the trend for sporting television audiences in general is downwards. The FA Cup Final figures do not take into account a further million or so who watched the matches on satellite, but they do illustrate that live football is no longer the special event it once was. The fact that so many other top games are shown nowadays could partly explain the FA Cup Final audience figures, but there is no similarly ready explanation for the relative weakness of the Grand National's performance. Dry, spring-like weather, which has been enjoyed by most of the country on the last two Grand National days, is known to have an effect on the size of the television audience, and while this alone may go a long way to explaining a drop of 2.2m viewers—more than a fifth—over the last two years there may be other factors. The question was posed in *Chasers & Hurdlers 2000/01* about what the watching television audience had made of that year's mudbath National in which there were some horrific-looking falls and only two—Red Marauder and Smarty—completed the course without mishap. How many found the race such a sorry spectacle that they haven't watched since? Around ten million (also 65% of the available audience) watched the National in 2001, the figure having peaked

Guinness Kerry National Handicap Chase, Listowel—
Monty's Pass goes one better than in 2001; the novice Putsometnby takes second

for the 'nineties at 16.7m (87% share) in 1994, the year after two false starts led to a void race. The 1997 running—postponed to five o'clock on the Monday after a terrorist bomb scare—attracted 12m. Television audiences for sporting events can be influenced greatly by their timing, as the BBC's coverage of Tim Henman's fourth round victory at Wimbledon in June illustrated. The match was timed for early evening and attracted 12.7m viewers (Henman's matches in the early rounds had drawn fewer than 3m); the BBC delayed the start of its flagship soap *Eastenders* until the match was completed. If the National was staged at peak viewing time it would be guaranteed a bumper audience. But that's still not the whole story. Television viewing figures are difficult to trace for periods before the 'nineties but the National audience back in the 'seventies and 'eighties was regularly quoted as being around the 16.5m mark. As a TV draw, the race is still a monumental sporting attraction, but it ain't what it used to be.

The Grand National, of course, is more than simply a TV spectacle, and it was a much brighter picture on the racecourse and in the betting shops. There was a modern-day record Grand National crowd of 68,389, the three-day total for the meeting of 142,467 also setting a similar record. The total number of spectators on National day was nearly double those in attendance when Red Rum won his third National in 1977 during the troubled period when the very future of Aintree and the Grand National was in doubt. Off course bookmakers reported a record turnover of over £100m on the latest Martell-sponsored National, the second in a new era of

598

tax-free betting for off-course punters in which betting generally has boomed. As well as reporting record turnover, the big bookmakers also announced that the latest National had given them their 'best result in the race in recent years'. In a strong line-up, punters latched on to some of the in-form top weights from the big stables, sending the Red Square Vodka Gold Cup winner Shotgun Willy (11-9) off as a 7/1 favourite, with Agfa Diamond Chase winner (third to Shotgun Willy at Haydock) Iris Bleu (11-3) and National Hunt Handicap Chase winner Youlneverwalkalone (10-11) joint second-favourites at 8/1, ahead of 9/1-shot Ad Hoc (11-1), unlucky in the previous year's National and an encouraging third to Youlneverwalkalone at Cheltenham. The Gold Cup seventh Chives (11-5), runner-up earlier in the Welsh National, completed the top five in the betting at 10/1. The very lightly-raced nine-year-old Killusty, first past the post in all five of his races over fences, started at 12/1. He was on the minimum permitted bottom weight of 10-0, one of only four of the maximum forty runners carrying more than the weight allotted to them in the original handicap and the only horse in the bottom quarter to come in for strong support. The Hennessy runner-up, 14/1-shot Gingembre (11-9), who had bypassed the Cheltenham Festival to wait for the National, was the only other runner to start at shorter than 16/1. In the event, none of the market leaders completed the course, or even so much as showed with a chance on the second circuit, which undoubtedly contributed to the latest National turning into something of a muted affair. Any first-time racegoers or television watchers could have been excused for wondering what all the fuss had been about. The race was strangely lacking drama, particularly as a televisual experience, and especially so in the closing stages. The winner Monty's Pass, who drifted from 14/1 to 16/1 and was the subject of only two recorded major on-course bets, strolled home to a run-in reception that lacked the usual enthusiasm shown for the Grand National principals.

Early departures in the latest National were much lighter than usual, the first two fences claiming only The Bunny Boiler who, in the words of his jockey, 'was going all right until he went at the first', and 200/1 second-fence faller Bramblehill Duke, brought in as a reserve after the late withdrawal through injury of the

Martell Cognac Grand National Chase (Handicap), Aintree—
Ballinclay King is last of the forty runners away

previous year's fourth Kingsmark. Chives, Youlneverwalkalone and Iris Bleu had already been pulled up—the two last-named with career-threatening injuries—by the time no fewer than thirty survivors, most of them closely bunched, set out into the country for a second time. The stiff fences themselves had claimed only half a dozen victims on the first circuit, a fairly steady initial gallop playing its part after riders had been reminded that nine had fallen or been brought down at the first as the field went hell-for-leather the previous year. The effects of a fortnight's watering of the track to avoid firm going were probably also in the minds of the jockeys who were up against conditions more testing than average for a modern-day National; the second half of the race exacted its toll, though. Aintree has invested in new watering equipment and now has the facility to water each of its three courses (National, Mildmay and hurdles) during the same night. Faced with a spell of dry weather and little rain forecast for National week, the executive must have been in something of a quandary about the extent of watering. The clerk of the course placed himself in a difficult position by 'guaranteeing' trainers over a week before the meeting that the going would be 'no faster than good'. The going on the Mildmay and hurdles courses was described on the opening day as 'really soft' and 'very soft' by jockeys Charlie Swan and Mick Fitzgerald, though Timeform agreed with the official first-day description of good.

But unnecessary watering took place again on Thursday night, and the going on the Friday was bordering on soft for the Mildmay course. Strongly-run races on the last two days of the meeting were turned into too much of a test of endurance for most of the horses involved—the Sefton Novices' Hurdle on Friday and the Champion Bumper on Saturday being notable examples—and the effect on some of the Grand National runners was also pronounced. Unusually for a National, there were more casualties on the second circuit—sixteen in all—than on the first. The third fence, a big open ditch, sometimes catches out even the most reliable jumpers but, with some of the top dressing of spruce dislodged on the first circuit and the field more spread out, it is sometimes less of a hazard second time around, when it is the nineteenth of the thirty fences. In the latest National,

The second—Bramblehill Duke joins the sole first-fence casualty The Bunny Boiler out of the race

First Canal Turn—Monty's Pass (No.19) hugs the inner as he tracks early pacesetters (from left to right) Tremallt, Montifault, Torduff Express, Blowing Wind, Behrajan and Maximise

however, the nineteenth put paid to five runners down the field, including Ad Hoc, still going well enough but with plenty of ground to make up when blundering and unseating his rider. Goguenard also unseated his rider and was then knocked over by another horse, sustaining a hind-leg injury which meant he had to be put down, the race's only fatality but the second in a row in the race for owner Trevor Hemmings and trainer Sue Smith who lost The Last Fling in similar circumstances the year before. The 16/1-shot Maximise was knocked over at the same fence, where outsiders You're Agoodun and Robbo also departed in the pile-up. Killusty, making headway but still some way off the pace when blundering at the fence before Becher's, then fell at Becher's itself where Shotgun Willy, never in the hunt and now right out of touch, was finally pulled up. Gingembre, weakening after a blunder at the nineteenth, lasted two fences further than Shotgun Willy and Killusty before being pulled up at the second Canal Turn.

Monty's Pass was already clearly travelling better than anything at the second Canal Turn. He had established an early prominent position on the inner, cruised through the race just behind or up with the leaders and been foot perfect all the way. The always-prominent Gunner Welburn headed a small group who were putting daylight between themselves and the rest. Monty's Pass was followed by

The Chair—leader Gunner Welburn somehow clambers over; chasing him, along with Monty's Pass, are (from left to right) Royal Predica, Gingembre, Blowing Wind and Carbury Cross

Montifault, who had been up there most of the way, and the improving Amberleigh House, with a steadily widening gap back to Carbury Cross and Torduff Express who came next. 'From a long way out, it was a case of how far we would win, I couldn't believe how well he was going, he travelled like a dream the whole way,' reported Barry Geraghty, the rider of Monty's Pass. Monty's Pass stalked Gunner Welburn and had the race sewn up some time before Geraghty finally eased him into the lead two out. Monty's Pass quickly turned the National into a procession, soon stretching clear of Gunner Welburn and Amberleigh House. Monty's Pass brushed through the top of the last but drew further away on the run-in and still appeared full of running as he crossed the line, twelve lengths ahead of the staying-on Supreme Glory who had been only ninth at the second Canal Turn. Amberleigh House came a further two lengths behind in third, after jumping right at the last and losing second after the elbow, with Gunner Welburn, failing to see out the marathon trip, another fourteen lengths adrift in fourth. The next to finish in a field that was strung out were Montifault and the previous year's winner Bindaree, the latter doing pretty well considering his stable had been closed for over three weeks because of an outbreak of equine herpes and, in the race itself, he had sprawled on landing and nearly come down at first Becher's before narrowly avoiding being brought down at the nineteenth. Carbury Cross was seventh, ahead of Blowing Wind, a remote third in the two previous years, the bold-jumping first-circuit leader Tremallt and top weight and Gold Cup fifth Behrajan, the only finisher carrying 11-0 or more. Only fourteen completed the course, the slowish time of 9m 21.24sec (twelve and a half seconds off that of the previous year) an indication of the fairly testing conditions and relatively steady pace.

Predictions that the top weights would dominate the latest National—the BHB handicapper again compressed the weights to the benefit of the likes of Behrajan—proved wide of the mark. Concentrating on horses with proven form over the big, unusual Grand National fences would have been a better policy on this occasion. Experience of the National fences had, however, seemed less of an advantage than it sometimes did before the slight easing of some of the fences. Eight of the twelve National winners before Monty's Pass had been tackling the course for the first time and, of the four who had encountered the fences before, only Bindaree had actually got round, when fourth in the John Hughes (which has now reverted to its former identity as the Topham). Monty's Pass had finished second in the Topham Chase twelve months earlier, Amberleigh House had won a

The Water—the Paul Nicholls-trained pair Montifault and Torduff Express head the field

The nineteenth—Monty's Pass and Gunner Welburn retake the lead

Becher Chase and been runner-up in another one, and Gunner Welburn had been successful in one edition of the Fox Hunters' at Aintree and second in another. Amberleigh House and Gunner Welburn were controversially eliminated at the final forty-eight-hour declaration stage in Bindaree's National and the BHB handicapper was asked by the Aintree executive to place greater credence in the latest Grand National handicap on previous form over the fences (a study by a graduate at the University of Liverpool was produced to back up claims that the so-called 'Aintree factor' remained as strong as ever). Amberleigh House was given 8 lb more than he would have carried in a normal handicap and Gunner Welburn was also among a dozen whose marks were said by the handicapper to have been influenced by Aintree form. Both got into the latest National comfortably. The runner-up Supreme Glory was tackling the National fences for the first time, but had been the subject of strong ante-post support the previous year after winning the Welsh National, only to be ruled out of Aintree with a leg injury sustained in training two weeks before the big day.

The latest National was a triumph for three smaller stables. The yards of Jimmy Mangan, Pat Murphy and Ginger McCain, responsible for the first three, house between them fewer than a third the number of horses in champion trainer

The nineteenth—trouble further down the field as Robbo (cheekpieces), Goguenard (No.29), You're Agoodun (noseband) and Maximize join the fancied Ad Hoc (not in shot) out of the race

Two out—Amberleigh House will soon be left behind

Martin Pipe's string and less than half of the number in Paul Nicholls' yard. Pipe and Nicholls have dominated the jumping trainers' table in Britain for the past five years, filling first and second places respectively on each occasion. Pipe ran seven in the latest National, his team headed by Iris Bleu, and Nicholls ran five including Shotgun Willy and Ad Hoc. Pipe had three finishers, Blowing Wind, twelfth-placed Majed and thirteenth-placed Royal Predica, while Montifault was the only one of the Nicholls quintet to complete the course. Henrietta Knight, trainer of Chives, saddled three in the race, though stable-mate Best Mate was never entered; fourteenth and last Southern Star was the only one of her runners to finish. The only Irish-trained runner in the first five in the betting Youlneverwalkalone (a familiar chant on one half of Merseyside at least) hailed from the eighty-strong stable of Christy Roche and had been ridden by Barry Geraghty in the National Hunt Handicap Chase.

Geraghty was offered the mount on Youlneverwalkalone at Aintree but stayed loyal to Monty's Pass whose trainer Jimmy Mangan has around fifteen National Hunt horses in his yard at Conna in the backwoods of County Cork. Virtually unknown outside Ireland until the triumph of Monty's Pass, Mangan is probably seen as often in the sales rings as on the racecourse, having made his living principally from farming, and breeding and dealing in store horses (Bindaree passed through his hands as a yearling). Mangan's stable also houses a small string of point-to-pointers, in which sphere Monty's Pass began his career after joining the yard as an unraced four-year-old. He was pulled up after becoming tailed off on his racing debut in a maiden point at Dungarvan in January 1998, but got off the mark two weeks later in a similar event at Tallow and progressed well afterwards. Monty's Pass graduated to hunter chases towards the end of his second season when he twice finished runner-up to the leading Irish hunter Sheltering at Wexford and Gowran in between a deserved success at Cork. Once into handicapping company, Monty's Pass soon proved himself a tough and consistent chaser, finishing runner-up as a seven-year-old in the Galway Plate, a race his trainer won in 1997 with Stroll Home. The useful Monty's Pass had a busy campaign in 2001/2, winning twice and recording mostly good efforts otherwise, including on three visits to Britain. He finished third, under 11-10, to Shooting Light in a two-and-a-half-mile handicap at Cheltenham in the autumn and, after a winter break, was returned to contest the Mildmay of Flete at the Cheltenham Festival, running to his

604

best to finish fifth under 10-4, and a strong renewal of the Topham Chase over a circuit of the National course. Monty's Pass finished runner-up to Its Time For A Win at Aintree, having every chance and battling on well. Post-race discussion about a possible Grand National challenge focussed that day on the ill-fated Its Time For A Win, but connections of Monty's Pass apparently also decided there and then that the National would be their long-range target.

As in the previous year, Monty's Pass continued racing through that summer, partnered by Geraghty who had become his regular jockey and had had the mount in the Topham. Monty's Pass finished sixth under 11-10 in a typically competitive renewal of the Galway Plate and went on to win the valuable Guinness Kerry National at Listowel in September, carrying 11-9 and putting up one of the best performances of his career at up to that time, after which there was talk of another trip to Aintree in November for the Becher Chase. Connections evidently had a change of plan, however, and Monty's Pass was put by for the winter after a creditable third, off a mark 7 lb higher than at Listowel, in the Munster National at Limerick in mid-October. Monty's Pass wasn't seen over fences again until the Grand National, being warmed up for Aintree in novice hurdles at Naas and Punchestown in March. Two miles was inadequate for Monty's Pass and he failed to reach a place on either outing, showing just modest form without being given a hard time at Naas before running poorly at Punchestown. The performances had little bearing on his chance at Aintree but, even allowing for him to come on for the outings, he didn't look particularly well handicapped in the National and was unproven beyond three miles, having done most of his racing at shorter. Monty's Pass has now contested the Kerry National on three occasions, coming second to More Than A Stroll in 2001 and being pulled up when favourite for the race in 2000 after being impeded by two horses falling in front of him five out. But the Kerry National is a National in name only, three miles round Listowel's tight oval circuit (only a little over a mile in extent) presenting little in the way of a true test of stamina. One thing definitely in his favour as a Grand National candidate was that he was a sound jumper and had had plenty of racing experience (the National was his forty-seventh race outside points).

If the general public's reaction to the Grand National victory of Monty's Pass was somewhat half-hearted, the joy of his connections in the unsaddling enclosure afterwards was unrestrained, with the notable exception of the head of the successful Dee Racing Syndicate whose name appeared erroneously, but rather appropriately, in some of the press information as Mike Flutter. The word flutter is

The last—Monty's Pass completes a near foot-perfect round

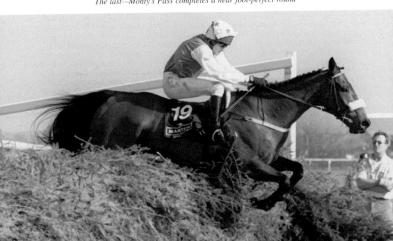

The run-in—Barry Geraghty is able to start the celebrations early;
Supreme Glory has snatched second from Amberleigh House

used to describe a bet made for excitement, rather than as a serious investment. The series of ante-post bets made by Northern Ireland-based bingo hall proprietor Mike Futter and his four co-owners reportedly landed a gamble of well over £1m. Hills alone reported that they paid out more than £400,000 on the ante-post gamble, laying £5,000 each-way at 33/1 in early-March and £10,000 each way at 20/1 shortly afterwards; Ladbrokes said the owners backed Monty's Pass with them to win £200,000. A spokesman for Hills described their liability as the biggest winning bet in the history of the National, but you'd hardly have thought it judging by the almost matter-of-fact manner in which Futter, who won the lion's share, fielded questions afterwards about the gamble. Asked how he felt when Monty's Pass crossed the winning line, Futter replied phlegmatically: 'A plan well executed, worked to perfection, a dream come true, that's about it.' Though Monty's Pass wasn't a strong public fancy on the day, Futter had apparently been urging his bingo hall customers to back the horse in the build-up to the race. If Monty's Pass is returned for another Grand National challenge in 2004 he is sure to receive more widespread support (straight after the latest edition he was quoted at 20/1 to follow up). His trainer's belief that he could have found 'the new Red Rum' may sound implausible given that Monty's Pass is now ten, but seldom can a National winner have had the race at his mercy from so far out, or looked so completely at home over the big Aintree fences.

Recent Irish-trained Grand National winners Bobbyjo and Papillon might be said to have parodied the old adage that you can wait an age for a bus, then two can come along at once. Their victories in 1999 and 2000 were the first for Ireland since L'Escargot back in 1975. The proximity of the victories of Bobbyjo and Papillon could have been passed off as coincidence, but three Irish-trained Grand National winners in five years cannot be. The strength of the Irish economy has led to more of that country's best stock being kept at home. The days when every Irish-bred store seemed to be on the market for export to Britain has become a thing of the past and Irish jumping is enjoying something of a golden age. Irish-trained horses enjoyed a splendid Aintree and another fine Cheltenham. Leinster(Mersey Novices' Hurdle), Native Upmanship (Melling Chase), Patriot Games (Clark's Brewery Handicap Hurdle), Risky Reef (Cordon Bleu Handicap Hurdle) and Sacundai (Aintree Hurdle) also won at the Grand National meeting, where the six Irish winners were all for different trainers. It was a similar story at the Cheltenham Festival where Back In Front (Supreme Novices' Hurdle), Youlneverwalkalone, Hardy Eustace (Royal & SunAlliance Hurdle), Moscow Flyer (Queen Mother Champion Chase), Xenophon (Coral Cup) and Spirit Leader (County Hurdle) also gave the Irish six winners, spread between five different trainers. Cheltenham was also memorable for Irish-based Barry Geraghty who rode five winners to equal the Festival record held jointly by Fred Winter, Jamie Osborne and Tony McCoy. Geraghty also won the Sefton Novices' Hurdle on the Friday at Aintree on Iris's Gift, while Ruby Walsh helped to make Grand National day even more memorable for the Irish by riding the first three winners on the card.

The sturdy Monty's Pass is by the now-deceased Montelimar, a big, rangy individual who showed very smart form in Ireland at a mile and a quarter and would have proved well suited by a mile and a half plus. Montelimar has been an influence for stamina and a very creditable proportion of his offspring over jumps have turned out to be useful or better, among them the Cheltenham Festival winners Montelado, Like-A-Butterfly and Youlneverwalkalone. On the distaff side, Monty's Pass is from the same immediate family as the Cheltenham Gold Cup third Harbour Pilot. Their dams Friars Pass and Las-Cancellas, the latter a winner on the Flat and over hurdles, are sisters, by the extremely game and genuine dual Champion Hurdle winner Monksfield out of the fairly useful hurdler Synarria who raced in the Monksfield colours.

Monty's Pass (IRE) (b.g. 1993)	Montelimar (USA) (b 1981)	Alleged (b 1974)	Hoist The Flag
			Princess Pout
		L'Extravagante (br 1973)	Le Fabuleux
			Fanfreleuche
	Friars Pass (b 1983)	Monksfield (b 1972)	Gala Performance
			Regina
		Synarria (br 1977)	Guillaume Tell
			Spinning Jenny

Synarria won at up to a mile and a half on the Flat in Ireland before being sent hurdling. She was successful four times in a lengthy juvenile campaign when she was a running-on seventh in Baron Blakeney's Triumph Hurdle on her eleventh outing. Synarria kept her form well the following season, raced at up to two and a half miles and winning a handicap over two and a quarter at Fairyhouse. Friars Pass showed little on the racecourse and hadn't bred a winner outside points when

Dee Racing Syndicate's "Monty's Pass"

Monty's Pass was offered as an unbroken four-year-old at the Derby Sale, fetching only IR 4,200 guineas. Friars Pass has bred a point-to-point winner in Magnum Bullum (by Cataldi) and has since bred another in Lord Knockemstiff (by Satco), as well as a bumper winner and fair maiden hurdler in Magic Maggan (by Lord Americo). Friars Pass was also represented in the latest season by the four-year-old filly Coppervega (by Toulon) who finished down the field in a bumper at Cork in April on her racecourse debut. Spinning Jenny, the great grandam of Monty's Pass, has a French background, being an unraced daughter of a winning French-bred mare Spinetta, imported into Ireland in 1971, who was a half-sister to the closely-related classic fillies Lastarria and Suvannee, the first-named runner-up in the Irish Oaks and fourth in the Prix de Diane and the latter runner-up in the Poule d'Essai des Pouliches. There are a few jumping connections in the family, mostly provided by another of Spinetta's half-sisters Alliance III, who was a very useful two-year-old in Ireland and is the grandam of some successful jumpers, notably Le Ronceray, winner of the Prix Leopold d'Orsetti, the Grande Course de Haies d'Enghien, and Manhattan Castle, winner of the Arkle at Leopardstown. Incidentally, Le Ronceray is also a Grand National winner, having landed the American version over hurdles later in his career. Another of Spinetta's half-sisters Saquebute was the dam of Imperial Cup winner Spy Net, as well as the Grand Criterium winner Satingo. The Grand National was the eighth win outside of points for the very smart Monty's Pass who is effective at two and a half miles to four and a half and acts on any going. He has been only lightly raced over hurdles and has shown fair form at best. For the record, he ran poorly when blinkered once in his hunter-chasing days. *James Joseph Mangan, Ireland*

MONTY'S QUEST (IRE) 8 b.g. Montelimar (USA) – A Bit of Luck (IRE) (Good Thyne (USA)) [2002/3 h77: 20g[5] c21s[4] c25d[F] c25g* c24g[4] Apr 23] tall gelding: poor form over hurdles: hasn't convinced with jumping over fences, showed more resolution than runner-up when winning novice at Hexham in April from The Grey Dyer: stays 25f: acts on good to soft going, probably on soft. *P. Beaumont* **c88 h85**

MONTYS TAG (IRE) 10 b.g. Montelimar (USA) – Herbal Lady (Good Thyne (USA)) [2002/3 c105: c24g[2] c25d* c28g* c22m* c19g[4] Apr 2] sturdy, lengthy gelding: fairly useful hunter chaser: won at Towcester and Stratford (valuable novice, left clear 2 out before idling badly run-in) in May and Newbury (made most to beat Folly Road 11 lengths) in March: unsuited by shorter trip final start: stays 3½m: acts on soft and good to firm going: sound jumper: reliable. *S. R. Andrews* **c104**

MONTY'S THEME (IRE) 9 b. or br.g. Montelimar (USA) – Theme Music (Tudor Music) [2002/3 c100d: c17g[4] c16g[5] c16m[6] c22g[5] c20s c24g[pu] Feb 22] winning chaser, has lost his form: tried visored. *P. Wegmann* **c–**

MONTY WOLLEY (IRE) 5 b.g. Turtle Island (IRE) – Sakanda (IRE) (Vayrann) [2002/3 16s 16d 16d[F] Mar 15] ex-Irish gelding: half-brother to 2 winning hurdlers, including fairly useful McCracken (by Scenic), stays 21f: fairly useful at best on Flat, 8.5f winner at 2 yrs, well held both starts in 2002: no form over hurdles, sold out of N. Meade's stable 5,000 gns Doncaster October Sales after reappearance. *C. Grant* **h–**

MON VILLEZ (FR) 4 ch.g. Villez (USA) – Europa Spa (FR) (Legend of France (USA)) [2002/3 c17s[3] c17s* c17s[3] c17s* c20s[5] c20v[3] Apr 26] fourth foal: half-brother to Flat winners up to 1½m by Saint Cyrien and Celtic Arms: dam unraced half-sister to top-class 1½m performer Epervier Bleu: lightly-raced on Flat: third both starts over hurdles: useful chaser, raced exclusively at Auteuil: won minor event in September and Group 2 Prix Congress in November by 1½ lengths from Vesuve: good third in spring in Group 2 (behind Gorfou de Maspie) and Group 1 (5¼ lengths behind Ice Mood): will stay beyond 2½m: raced mainly on soft/heavy going. *T. Civel, France* **c134**

MOODY BLUES (IRE) 9 ch.g. Orchestra – Blue Rainbow (Balinger) [2002/3 c101?: 24s[5] c25d[ur] c24d[6] c33v[pu] c25s[pu] Feb 11] medium-sized gelding: winning Irish pointer: disappointing in steeplechases: well held only outing over hurdles: blinkered final start. *A. M. Hales* **c– h78**

MOODY STYLE (IRE) 6 b.m. Desert Style (IRE) – Elle Meme (Ela-Mana-Mou) [2002/3 F17f[pu] May 15] first foal: dam, Irish maiden, out of half-sister to Danzig: showed nothing in maiden bumper on debut. *Mrs J. Scrivens* **F–**

MOON AT NIGHT 8 gr.g. Pursuit of Love – La Nureyeva (USA) (Nureyev (USA)) [2002/3 16s[pu] Dec 7] modest on Flat (stays 1m), successful in June, sold out of **h–**

W. Kittow's stable £1,400 Ascot October Sales: raced too freely on hurdling debut: sold 1,000 gns Doncaster March Sales. *Mrs P. Ford*

MOON COLONY   10 b.g. Top Ville – Honeymooning (USA) (Blushing Groom (FR)) [2002/3 h85: 16m⁶ 20g² 16g⁴ 21g⁵ 20mᵘʳ 24f³ Oct 10] angular gelding: modest maiden hurdler: stays 21f: acts on soft going, probably on good to firm. *A. L. Forbes*   **h90**

MOON GLOW (IRE)   7 b.g. Fayruz – Jarmar Moon (Unfuwain (USA)) [2002/3 h84: c17g⁴ c16f² c16g³ c16g³ c16m² c16gᵖᵘ c16m* c17m⁴ c17m* c16m⁴ c16d³ Apr 9] big, strong gelding: winning hurdler: fair chaser: won handicaps at Newton Abbot in August and Plumpton (novice) in September: raced mainly around 2m: acts on firm and good to soft going: effective blinkered or not: has been taken down early. *J. Gallagher*   **c103** **h–**

MOONING (IRE)   4 ch.f. Moonax (IRE) – Miss Ming (Tender King) [2002/3 F17g Apr 26] €2,800 3-y-o: seventh foal: half-sister to 2 winners abroad, including prolific sprinter Majestic Light (by Contract Law): dam, second over 1½m, half-sister to fairly useful hurdler up to 2¾m Nordic Breeze: in rear in bumper on debut. *S. Gollings*   **F–**

MOON ISLAND   9 b.m. Jupiter Island – Wild Moon (Belfalas) [2002/3 h–, F–: 16d⁶ 21m 20g 19m Jun 4] medium-sized mare: no sign of ability: visored/blinkered. *S. J. Gilmore*   **h–**

MOONLIGHTING   6 b.m. Lugana Beach – White Flash (Sure Blade (USA)) [2002/3 c–, h–: 16gᵖᵘ 16sᵖᵘ 17g⁴ 17v 19g⁴ 17m³ Apr 21] little worthwhile form over jumps, sold out of B. Johnson's stable £1,800 Ascot June Sales after reappearance: has stamina limitations: tried blinkered/tongue tied: wore cheekpieces last 3 starts. *Mrs N. S. Sharpe*   **c–** **h–**

MOONLITE MAGIC (IRE)   9 br.g. Phardante (FR) – Lucey Allen (Strong Gale) [2002/3 h81: c25gᵘʳ c21g⁶ c27d c27v⁴ c27s Nov 26] smallish, lengthy gelding: poor handicap hurdler: poor form over fences (makes mistakes), moody display final outing: stays 27f: acts on heavy ground: usually blinkered/visored (wore cheekpieces on reappearance): difficult ride and needs treating with caution. *Ferdy Murphy*   **c71 §** **h– §**

MOONLIT HARBOUR   4 b.g. Bal Harbour – Nuit de Lune (FR) (Crystal Palace (FR)) [2002/3 F16d* F16g³ F16g³ Apr 1] medium-sized gelding: tenth reported foal: half-brother to French 1¼m winner Night Watch (by Soviet Star) and middle-distance stayer Periode Bleue (by Pistolet Bleu), both useful: dam, French ½m winner, half-sister to high-class French stayer Soleil Noir: fair form in bumpers, won at Wetherby on debut in March: third to Enhancer on same course and Steppes of Gold at Newcastle. *M. W. Easterby*   **F89**

MOON RISING   11 b.g. Primitive Rising (USA) – Saucy Moon (Saucy Kit) [2002/3 c21mᵖᵘ May 22] maiden pointer: blinkered on hunter chase debut. *R. Dench*   **c–**

MOON ROYALE   5 ch.m. Royal Abjar (USA) – Ragged Moon (Raga Navarro (ITY)) [2002/3 h–: 17g Sep 6] poor form on Flat (probably best around 1m): well held in juvenile and novice hurdles at Sedgefield 12 months apart. *Denys Smith*   **h–**

MOONSHINE BAY (IRE)   9 b.g. Executive Perk – Sister of Slane (The Parson) [2002/3 c124+, h114: c20dᶠ 21m⁶ Feb 22] compact gelding: fairly useful hurdler/chaser at best: in touch when falling 6 out in handicap chase at Kempton on reappearance: effective at 2m to 2¾m: acts on heavy going, below best on good to firm: has been reluctant at start (refused to race on chasing debut). *J. T. Gifford*   **c–** **h–**

MOON SPINNER   6 b.m. Elmaamul (USA) – Lunabelle (Idiot's Delight) [2002/3 h89, F88: 20m 16m 16s³ 16g² 17d 16m² 24g³ 19s 19s 17d⁴ 19s 17s² 21g 19m⁶ 17m⁴ Apr 15] leggy mare: poor maiden hurdler: stays 21f: acts on soft and good to firm going: has had tongue tied: weak finisher. *J. M. Bradley*   **h79 §**

MOONZIE LAIRD (IRE)   5 b. or br.g. Good Thyne (USA) – Sweet Roselier (IRE) (Roselier (FR)) [2002/3 F16s* F16d Apr 25] 2,600 3-y-o: second foal: dam unraced, out of half-sister to useful staying jumpers Bective Road and Sommelier: 20/1, won 7-runner bumper at Ayr on debut in March by 3 lengths from Cordilla: well held in stronger race at Perth. *J. N. R. Billinge*   **F94**

MOORE'S LAW (USA)   5 b.g. Technology (USA) – Brass Needles (USA) (Twice Worthy (USA)) [2002/3 h126: 16g² 21d³ 20m* 20d² 21g 18g² Apr 21] leggy gelding: fairly useful hurdler: easily landed odds in maiden at Musselburgh in December: best effort of season when beating Michael Mor ½ length in minor event at Fairyhouse final start, subsequently demoted after drifting right and hampering rival: probably stays 21f: yet to race on extremes of going. *M. J. Grassick, Ireland*   **h126**

MOOR HALL HOPPER   7 gr.g. Rock Hopper – Forgiving (Jellaby) [2002/3 F16s F16m Jul 24] tall gelding: well held in 3 bumpers. *R. S. Brookhouse*   **F–**

MOORHALL (IRE) 4 b.g. Persian Bold – Never Told (IRE) (Classic Secret (USA)) **h77**
[2002/3 16g 16g 16m⁴ Apr 6] modest maiden on Flat (stays 8.5f), sold out of C. Collins'
stable €1,000 Goffs October Sale: poor form over hurdles, trained second start (tongue
tied) by G. McKeever: will prove best around 2m. *J. G. Cosgrave, Ireland*

MOOR HALL LADY 12 gr.m. Rambo Dancer (CAN) – Forgiving (Jellaby) [2002/3 **h–**
h78: 20m 20m 20g⁵ 22m⁶ 26mᵖᵘ 19m 19sᵖᵘ 24f⁵ 22gᵖᵘ Apr 26] small, sturdy mare:
winning hurdler, no form in 2002/3: tried visored. *R. S. Brookhouse*

MOOR HALL ROCK 8 b.g. Rock Hopper – Forgiving (Jellaby) [2002/3 c–, h77: **c–**
16g 20m³ c20mˢᵘ c21mᶠ Sep 13] poor maiden hurdler: no form over fences: best efforts **h–**
around 2m on good to firm going: blinkered last 3 outings. *R. S. Brookhouse*

MOORLAND HIGHFLYER 12 b. or br.g. Karlinsky (USA) – Moorland Heath VII **c– x**
(Damsire Unregistered) [2002/3 c–x: c34gᵖᵘ May 22] tall gelding: fair handicap chaser in
1998/9 (often made mistakes): little form since, including in points: tried blinkered/
tongue tied. *T. Long*

MOORLAND ROSE 8 br.m. Lir – Moorland Heath VII (Damsire Unregistered) **c–**
[2002/3 c26g⁵ May 25] half-sister to one-time fair chaser Moorland Highflyer (by
Karlinsky), stays 2¾m: modest pointer, successful 3 times in 2002: well held in hunter
chase at Newton Abbot. *Miss P. D. Mitchell*

MOORLANDS AGAIN 8 b.g. Then Again – Sandford Springs (USA) (Robellino **c116**
(USA)) [2002/3 h–: 25v² c26s* c26v² c24sᶠ c32g⁵ Mar 12] good-topped gelding: better **h87**
effort in novice hurdles when second of 6 at Plumpton on reappearance: fairly useful
novice chaser: made all in 3-finisher event at Fontwell in February: stays 4m: acts on
heavy going: tends to jump low and right. *C. Tizzard*

MOOR LANE 11 b.g. Primitive Rising (USA) – Navos (Tyrnavos) [2002/3 c131: **c125**
c24d⁴ c27dᶠ c26sᵖᵘ c26s⁶ c24m* c24gᵘʳ c24m Mar 22] tall gelding: fairly useful handicap
chaser: won weak amateur event at Kempton in February, little form otherwise in 2002/3:
should stay beyond 3m: acts on soft and good to firm going: visored second and third (ran
poorly) starts: races prominently. *A. M. Balding*

MOOR SPIRIT 6 b.g. Nomadic Way (USA) – Navos (Tyrnavos) [2002/3 F16d⁴ Mar **F74**
6] sixth foal: half-brother to fairly useful chaser Moor Lane (by Primitive Rising), stays
3m: dam, winning hurdler, best at 2m: 11¼ lengths fourth of 12 in bumper at Wetherby on
debut. *R. D. E. Woodhouse*

MOQUI MARBLE (GER) 7 b.g. Petit Loup (USA) – Margo's New Hope (USA) **h–**
(Cannonade (USA)) [2002/3 16g Mar 14] won 4 times on Flat in Germany: modest form
(stays 1¼m, has been visored) in Britain in 2002 for D. Cantillon: well held in 4 races
over hurdles (trained by R. O'Leary in Ireland first 3), looked non-stayer in selling
handicap at Fakenham (blinkered) in March. *B. J. Curley*

MORAL JUSTICE (IRE) 10 b.g. Lafontaine (USA) – Proven Right (IRE) (Kemal **c99**
(FR)) [2002/3 c107, h102, F88: c19g³ c20g² c21m* c21m* c25g² c21fᵖᵘ c20gᵖᵘ c19mᵖᵘ **h–**
Apr 21] good-topped gelding: winning hurdler: modest chaser: made all in novices at
Newton Abbot and Uttoxeter in June: pulled up last 3 starts, reportedly sore on first
occasion (visored): stays 25f: raced mainly on good going or firmer (acts on firm):
jumped left when racing right-handed second start. *S. J. Gilmore*

MORAL SUPPORT (IRE) 11 ch.g. Zaffaran (USA) – Marians Pride (Pry) [2002/3 **c113**
c126, h113: c26g c24vᵖᵘ c26v c24s² c32gᵖᵘ Mar 21] angular gelding: formerly useful **h–**
handicap chaser: form in 2002/3 only when second of 6 to easy winner Gunner Welburn
at Newbury: stays 3¾m: acts on heavy going: lazy. *J. S. Moore*

MORATORIUM (USA) 8 b.g. El Gran Senor (USA) – Substance (USA) (Diesis) **h122**
[2002/3 h121p: 16d 18g⁶ Apr 21] close-coupled gelding: progressive handicap hurdler in
2001/2, successful 3 times: shaped much better than result suggests when seventh of 24
to Say Again in very valuable event at Galway on reappearance: failed to settle and
reportedly choked when well beaten in minor event at Fairyhouse nearly 9 months later:
best around 2m: acts on firm and good to soft going: effective with or without blinkers/
tongue tied. *N. Meade, Ireland*

MORDON BOY (IRE) 11 ch.g. Persian Mews – Kindly (Tarqogan) [2002/3 c93x, **c– x**
h–: c24m⁴ c20mᵖᵘ Mar 19] modest chaser in 2001/2: no show both starts in 2002/3, off 9 **h–**
months in between: stays 3½m: acts on good to firm going: tried blinkered: sketchy
jumper. *D. Pearson*

MORE TEARS (IRE)   7 b.g. Witness Box (USA) – Anyone's Fancy (Callernish)   **c80**
[2002/3 h50: c23g^{ur} c21s^F c23d^3 c24v^F Dec 20] workmanlike gelding: bad maiden   **h–**
hurdler: better form when third of 9 in novice handicap at Exeter on completed start over
fences: stays 23f: raced mainly on good going or softer (acts on soft): sketchy jumper.
N. J. Hawke

MORE THAN A STROLL (IRE)   11 ch.g. Pennine Walk – Jenny's Child (Crash   **c144**
Course) [2002/3 c130§, h–§: c24g* c24s* c20s^4 c22v^2 c20d* c25g^{pu} Apr 3]   **h–**
        The fourth running of the James Nicholson Wine Merchant Championship
Chase, which takes place at Down Royal in November, produced the race's first
shock result when 20/1-shot More Than A Stroll accounted for six opponents,
including two of its previous winners Florida Pearl and Foxchapel King. The
betting had suggested that the race, run as a Grade 1 for the first time, lay between
the two last-named and the 1999 Cheltenham Gold Cup winner See More Business,
all three of whom were making their reappearance, unlike More Than A Stroll who
had returned a month earlier to win the Anglo Irish Bank Munster National at
Limerick. Rising eleven and seemingly fully exposed as a useful handicapper,
More Than A Stroll looked to face an extremely stiff task taking on, at level
weights, a trio who had shown either high-class or top-class form in the previous
season, and his victory seemingly came as much as a surprise to his trainer Arthur
Moore as anyone. 'I wasn't expecting him to win,' said Moore, having beforehand
described More Than A Stroll as 'a social runner'. As things turned out, More Than
A Stroll didn't need to show markedly improved form to capture the €84,000 first
prize, as the leading fancies were all well short of their best. In a race where those
up front, Florida Pearl and See More Business among them, were sent for home too
early in the very testing conditions, More Than A Stroll benefited from a very
patient ride from Conor O'Dwyer. Picking off the leaders after three out, More
Than A Stroll edged right between the last two but pulled out a bit more on the
run-in to win by five lengths from See More Business. More Than A Stroll went on
to run well in two of his next three starts, when fourth of five to Native Upmanship

James Nicholson Wine Merchant Championship Chase, Down Royal—20/1 outsider More Than A Stroll
takes advantage of some below-par rivals, including See More Business in second

in the John Durkan Memorial at Punchestown and when winning the Red Mills Danoli Chase at Gowran by half a length from Arctic Copper, and he seemed well on course for a tilt at the Grand National. He did turn up at Aintree in April, but, surprisingly, it was for the Martell Cognac Cup in which he faced a stiff task under a penalty for his Grade 1 win. One of the first in trouble when the pace increased on the final circuit, More Than A Stroll was already well held in fifth when blundering four out, and was pulled up before the second last. More Than A Stroll, normally a sound jumper, would have been a welcome addition to the National line-up. He'll be twelve by the time it comes round again, and perhaps the opportunity has passed him by. Interestingly, More Than A Stroll had Monty's Pass three and a half lengths behind him in third in the Munster National, and had also beaten him by the same margin when the pair took the first two places in the previous season's Kerry National at Listowel.

		Pennine Walk	Persian Bold	Bold Lad
More Than A Stroll (IRE) (ch.g. 1992)		(b 1982)	(br 1975)	Relkarunner
			Tifrums	Thatch
			(b 1977)	Persian Apple
		Jenny's Child	Crash Course	Busted
		(b 1983)	(b 1971)	Lucky Stream
			Nice Child	Narrator
			(ch 1959)	Fire Song

More Than A Stroll, who gained his sole win over hurdles in a maiden at Navan in 1998/9, has been successful on eight of his twenty-nine starts over fences and has made the frame on twelve of the others. Given his record, and his efforts in the latest season in particular, it seems harsh to point out that he did look irresolute at times in the 2001/2 season, though he also ran a moody race when pulled up in a

Mrs D. Grehan's "More Than A Stroll"

valuable handicap at Punchestown in early-May. More Than A Stroll's half-brother, the winning hurdler/pointer Chiappucci (by Doulab), didn't always look in love with the game, either. Their dam, Jenny's Child, who won three races over a mile and a half in Ireland, has produced one other winner, namely Newkidontheblock (by Be My Native), successful in a maiden point in Ireland and a bumper at Huntingdon. More Than A Stroll, by the miler Pennine Walk, gained his early victories at two miles, but he does all of his racing over two and a half miles and more nowadays and stays three miles well. A strong gelding, he acts on good to firm and heavy going. *A. L. T. Moore, Ireland*

MORLESS 4 b.f. Morpeth – Bush Radio (Hot Grove) [2002/3 17s^{pu} Nov 28] well beaten in seller at 2 yrs: showed nothing in juvenile seller on hurdling debut. *J. D. Frost* **h–**

MORNING FLIGHT (IRE) 7 b.m. Supreme Leader – Morning Jane (IRE) (Over The River (FR)) [2002/3 h–: 16g^5 Sep 14] signs of only a little ability over hurdles. *Noel T. Chance* **h67**

MORNING MELODY 5 b.m. Afzal – Pacific Overture (Southern Music) [2002/3 F17g Apr 19] first foal: dam bad novice hurdler: tailed off in maiden bumper on debut. *Mrs N. S. Sharpe* **F–**

MORNING MOVER (IRE) 10 b.g. White Christmas – More Tabs (Cantab) [2002/3 22m Sep 7] workmanlike gelding: of little account: tried blinkered/tongue tied. *John R. Upson* **h–**

MORPH 9 gr.g. Baron Blakeney – Amber Marsh (Arctic Kanda) [2002/3 h–: 24g^2 26m^{pu} Sep 29] tall gelding: runner-up only completed outing in points: form over hurdles only when second in very weak maiden at Worcester. *R. H. York* **h68**

MORSTOCK 13 gr.g. Beveled (USA) – Miss Melmore (Nishapour (FR)) [2002/3 c90, h–: c19g* c16s* c16m^6 c16m^{pu} Jul 15] sturdy gelding: modest handicap chaser: won at Exeter and Newton Abbot in May: effective at 2m, barely stays 2¾m: probably acts on any going: blinkered once: usually races prominently. *R. J. Hodges* **c92 h–**

MORTICIA 5 b.m. Rudimentary (USA) – Valkyrie (Bold Lad (IRE)) [2002/3 F–: F16g Dec 28] tongue tied, tailed off in 2 bumpers. *M. A. Barnes* **F–**

MOSCOW DANCER (IRE) 6 ch.g. Moscow Society (USA) – Cromhill Lady (Miner's Lamp) [2002/3 h–, F–: 19d^{pu} 17d^{pu} Feb 23] no show in bumper/over hurdles. *K. Bishop* **h–**

MOSCOW EXPRESS (IRE) 11 ch.g. Moscow Society (USA) – Corrielek (Menelek) [2002/3 c158x, h–: c20g^{pu} c25d^{pu} c20v^4 c20s^3 c20d^5 c20d^3 c24g^{pu} Mar 30] rangy gelding: very smart chaser at best, on the downgrade: stays 3¼m: acts on any going: effective tongue tied or not: often let down by jumping. *Miss F. M. Crowley, Ireland* **c142 x h–**

MOSCOW FIELDS (IRE) 5 ch.g. Moscow Society (USA) – Cloverlady (Decent Fellow) [2002/3 F16d^2 Mar 1] tall, unfurnished gelding: fourth foal: dam unraced, from family of useful staying chaser Ghia Gneuiagh: on toes, 13 lengths second to Bourbon Manhattan in bumper at Newbury on debut, looking a stayer. *Miss H. C. Knight* **F91**

MOSCOW FLYER (IRE) 9 b.g. Moscow Society (USA) – Meelick Lady (IRE) (Duky) [2002/3 c159p, h–: c18s* c16s^{ur} c17v* c16s* c16g* Mar 12] **c170 p h–**

Moscow Flyer had his ups and downs but the former decidedly outweighed the latter, and in winning the Queen Mother Champion Chase he lived up to the expectations created by his fine novice campaign, proving himself the best two-mile chaser in training. Oddly, though, for a horse who has run thirteen times over fences, there are still some unanswered questions, not least the matter of exactly how good he is. With luck, that will be revealed conclusively in the next season when he takes on such up-and-coming specialists as Azertyuiop and Le Roi Miguel, both of whose style of racing will suit Moscow Flyer down to the ground since he does best when coming from behind and tends to idle if in front for long.

To deal with Moscow Flyer's 'downs' first, they were as different as chalk and cheese, though both involved his failing to complete the course. In the Tingle Creek Chase at Sandown in December, he started second favourite and was in touch when colliding with favourite Flagship Uberalles after the latter stumbled in front of him at the fifth, giving Moscow Flyer's jockey no prospect of staying in the saddle. Whilst Sandown was entirely excusable, Moscow Flyer's departure two out

Paddy Power Dial-A-Bet Chase, Leopardstown—
Moscow Flyer, despite very testing ground, gains a convincing win

in the BMW Chase at Punchestown in May takes much more explaining. After taking up the running approaching four out, Moscow Flyer jumped that fence like a stag but then promptly went through the top of the second last and unseated Barry Geraghty. Geraghty claimed the horse took off too soon and 'paddled' the fence, though it looked very much as if he hardly took off at all. Such lapses are nothing new with Moscow Flyer—he had already done it at Punchestown two starts earlier. Blinkers might be worth considering as they often sharpen a horse up, but the most reliable safeguard for Moscow Flyer is likely to be continued alertness on the part of his jockey.

Moscow Flyer's record on his other starts was flawless, leaving him with a tally of nine wins from as many completed starts over fences. He had three races in Ireland before the Champion Chase, all on testing going and all at long odds on, as befitted a horse who had put up one of the best performances ever by an Arkle winner when defeating Seebald. The Killultagh Properties Ltd Chase at Down Royal in November attracted only two other runners, Kadarann, having his first outing since May, and Fiery Ring. Moscow Flyer treated them with contempt, leading at halfway after showing signs of rustiness and galloping home by twenty lengths from Kadarann despite tending to look around in front. After the Sandown debacle, Moscow Flyer had to cope with some of the worst conditions of the season in the Grade 2 Paddy Power Dial-A-Bet Chase at Leopardstown over Christmas. Irish racecourse executives sometimes race when their counterparts in Britain almost certainly would not. The reasons for this may include a wetter climate, fewer meetings, which makes the loss of any rather more damaging, and a greater acceptance among professionals, media and the public of the principle of carrying on if at all possible without feeling any reservations—it is difficult to imagine the sort of furore in Ireland which followed the running of the 2001 Grand National. Be that as it may, the going at Leopardstown was virtually bottomless, with two fences omitted and pools of water lying in the back straight. As an indication of how tough it was, in the seventeen-runner four-year-old maiden hurdle over two miles, the third horse finished a distance ahead of the fourth after as many as nine had still held a chance two out, and in the three-mile handicap chase only nine of the twenty-one runners completed, with the fourth home beaten thirty-five lengths. The best of Moscow Flyer's five opponents was Knife Edge and he had no difficulty dealing with him, jumping fluently, leading on the bridle entering the straight but idling noticeably on the run-in after going ten lengths up, eventually scoring by five. Afterwards, trainer Jessica Harrington revealingly admitted: 'The day he doesn't down tools at the end, with his ears pricked, will be the day something is wrong with him.' It was the same again when Moscow Flyer faced another simple task in the Byrne Group Plc Tied Cottage Chase at Punchestown in February, with Commanche Court, having his first run of the season and needing further than two miles nowadays, his only rival of mettle. Moscow Flyer jumped well until the last, where he began looking around, resulting in his making a bit of a hash of his jump. He had taken up the running five out, plenty soon enough, and idled on the run-in too before winning by nine lengths from Copernicus.

This succession of straightforward, some might say soft, races came to an end at Cheltenham. Moscow Flyer had been 4/1 favourite for the Queen Mother Champion Chase at the start of the season and was backed from 5/2 to 7/4 on the day, opposed by all the best two-mile chasers available. There were two of the old guard, Edredon Bleu and Flagship Uberalles, who had won the race in 2000 and 2002 respectively. The former had won three of his four starts in the current season, but two of those were in uncompetitive events, while Flagship Uberalles had not reproduced his Cheltenham form. The other members of the younger brigade were Arkle Trophy runner-up Seebald and Kadarann, winner last time out of the Game Spirit Chase in which he beat another contender, third favourite Cenkos, winner of the Tingle Creek. Second favourite Tiutchev had landed the Ascot Chase, Native Upmanship, runner-up in 2002, had been on the mark in a Grade 1 and a Grade 2 in Ireland and Latalomne, a faller when prominent two out the previous year, tried his luck again. The other runners were Florida Pearl, out of form and hardly likely to be suited by the distance, and Geos, winner of a weak renewal of the Castleford Chase. Held up as Edredon Bleu and Latalomne set a good pace followed by

Byrne Group plc Tied Cottage Chase, Punchestown—a tendency to idle prompts a last-fence mistake

Queen Mother Champion Chase, Cheltenham—
Moscow Flyer is far too good for the 2002 first three Flagship Uberalles (blinkers),
Native Upmanship (runner-up for the second year in a row) and Cenkos (almost hidden)

Cenkos, Moscow Flyer made a mistake four out but continued to travel well and was poised to take over in front when Seebald and Latalomne came a cropper independently at the second last. Neither faller was going so well as the favourite but their departure finished the race as a spectacle and Moscow Flyer was just kept up to his work to defeat the staying-on Native Upmanship by seven lengths, with Cenkos three lengths further back. In all probability the winner is better than he needed to show here, which is why a 'p' is retained on his rating. Whatever happens when Moscow Flyer defends his crown—the bookmakers make him 100/30 favourite with Azertyuiop 4/1 and Le Roi Miguel as big as 16/1—he should be in for another successful campaign, one which reportedly will start in the Fortria Chase at Navan in November.

		Nijinsky	Northern Dancer
	Moscow Society (USA)	(b 1967)	Flaming Page
	(ch 1985)	Afifa	Dewan
Moscow Flyer (IRE)		(ch 1974)	Hooplah
(b.g. 1994)		Duky	Midsummer Night II
	Meelick Lady (IRE)	(ch 1974)	Frondia
	(b 1988)	Quiet Life	No Argument
		(b 1972)	Brambling

Moscow Flyer's pedigree has been covered in detail in previous Annuals but there are one or two significant updates. His sister foaled in 1999 fetched a record price for a store filly when sold for €215,000 at the Derby Sale in June 2002 to a purchaser acting on J. P. McManus's behalf. His unraced dam Meelick Lady had a Luso foal withdrawn from auction in Ireland five months later. Moscow Society, Moscow Flyer's sire, had two above-average runners over hurdles during the season, Grade 2 winner Kopeck and Mossy Green, second in a race at that level at Naas. Moscow Society, who covered fifty-four mares in 1999 and forty-seven in 2000, has seen his popularity increase since then thanks to the achievements of his offspring, with totals of one hundred and thirty-five and one hundred and thirty-two in the next two years. This is not an untypical book for an Irish-based jumps stallion and the number of foals produced each year there, including in the North, is increasingly outstripping the number born in mainland Britain. In 1972 the foals born totalled 3,016 in the whole of Ireland and 4,724 in Britain, but in 2002 this had changed to 10,214 and 5,156. There are more than four times the number of officially designated jumps mares in Ireland, 3,000 against 700, compared with tallies of 1,700 and 850 when the designation was introduced by Weatherbys in 1995. With the mares available, and a favourable tax regime in the Irish Republic, if not in Northern Ireland, Irish-based jumps sires predictably cover much larger books. Of the twenty-eight jumps stallions who served one hundred mares or more in 2002, only four stood in Britain. The consequence of this, together with the importation of French-breds, was shown graphically at the Cheltenham Festival, where the runners in the twenty races counted by suffix consisted of one hundred and eighty-nine from Ireland, eighty-nine from France, seventy-seven from Britain and twenty-four from elsewhere, principally Germany and the United States. There were three victories for British-breds, compared to eleven for Irish-breds and five for French-breds, the British wins coming from Rooster Booster (by Riverwise) in the Champion Hurdle, Young Spartacus (by the deceased Teenoso) in the Mildmay of Flete and Inching Closer (Flat-bred, by Kris) in the Pertemps Final. The Queen Mother Champion Chase had five Irish-breds, three French-breds and just one British-bred, plus one each from Germany and the States. Depressing as this shift in the balance of power must be for British-based stallion owners and managers, it is having no damaging effect on the competitiveness of the top races, which can only be beneficial to punters and racegoers. To return to Moscow Flyer, he is a strong, lengthy gelding who looked very well at Cheltenham and has raced only on good going or softer, acting on heavy. Although he stays two and a half miles, his trainer says he will be kept at two for the foreseeable future, which seems a shade unfortunate given the lack of suitable Grade 1 opportunities for two-mile specialists and the relative weakness of some of the best chases over the longer trip. *Mrs J. Harrington, Ireland*

Mr Brian Kearney's "Moscow Flyer"

MOSCOW GOLD (IRE)   6 ch.g. Moscow Society (USA) – Vesper Time (The   h–
Parson) [2002/3 F–: 16g 22m 17s 24g⁵ Mar 16] big gelding: no form in bumpers or
over hurdles: trained until after second start by R. Smith: tried blinkered/tongue tied.
A. J. Wilson

MOSCOW LEADER (IRE)   5 ch.g. Moscow Society (USA) – Catrionas Castle   F79
(IRE) (Orchestra) [2002/3 F17d F17d⁵ F17g³ Mar 28] 5,500 4-y-o: sturdy gelding:
second foal: dam unraced: modest form in bumpers, over 7 lengths third of 10 to Reivers
Moon at Carlisle. *R. C. Guest*

MOSCOW TRADITION (IRE)   5 b.g. Moscow Society (USA) – Bucks Grove   h95
(IRE) (Buckskin (FR)) [2002/3 21d 20s² 21s⁶ 16v⁵ Feb 4] IR £12,000 3-y-o: strong, good
sort: second foal: brother to fair bumper winner Moscow Society Buck: dam unraced: modest
novice hurdler: stays 21f: not an easy ride. *Jonjo O'Neill*

MOSCOW WHISPER (IRE)   6 b.g. Moscow Society (USA) – Native Woodfire   h105 p
(IRE) (Mister Majestic) [2002/3 F17d³ 22m³ 20g* Apr 23] fourth foal: dam ran once: F85
third of 16 in bumper at Hereford: second outing over hurdles, won maiden at Perth by
1½ lengths from Salmon Ladder: probably capable of better again, particularly returned
to further. *P. J. Hobbs*

MOSE HARPER (IRE)   11 b.g. Supreme Leader – Miss Rockaway (Le Moss)   c68
[2002/3 20g c22dᶜᵒ c17s⁴ 20g⁵ c20mᵖᵘ c17v c18s c20s c24s c28s c20v⁶ c16d⁶ c17m⁴   h–
Apr 22] lengthy, sparely-made gelding: maiden hurdler/winning chaser, generally well
held in 2002/3: stays 3m: acts on soft and good to firm going: usually blinkered: has had
tongue tied. *T. O'Neill, Ireland*

MO'S KELIRO   11 b.m. Lir – Bossy Cleo (Proud Challenge) [2002/3 c–: c24gᵖᵘ May   c–
8] modest pointer: little show in hunter chases at Chepstow. *Mrs J. Marsh*

MOSS COTTAGE   7 b.m. Le Moss – Rodney's Sister (Leading Man) [2002/3 F17g   F–
F16d Oct 23] 800 4-y-o: lengthy mare: fourth foal: half-sister to bumper winner Bala
Pyjama (by Henbit): dam unraced half-sister to Triumph Hurdle winner Saxon Farm:
tailed off in 2 bumpers. *T. P. Walshe*

MOSS DEEPING   11 ch.g. Le Moss – Lady Run (Deep Run) [2002/3 h–: 21dᵘʳ 20d⁴   h–
27sᵖᵘ 26sᵖᵘ Dec 26] lengthy gelding: no form over hurdles: tongue tied. *R. N. Bevis*

MOSS HARVEY   8 ch.g. Le Moss – Wings Ground (Murrayfield) [2002/3 h135:   c121
c21d* c25v* c24d⁵ c25v³ 23s⁴ 25gᵖᵘ Mar 11] lengthy gelding: good start to chasing   h132
career when winning novices at Fakenham in October and Kelso in November: very disappointing at Newbury and Wetherby next 2 starts, jumping badly right: useful hurdler:
much better effort in handicaps last 2 outings when fourth to Royal Emperor at Haydock:
will stay beyond 25f: raced on good going or softer (acts on heavy). *J. M. Jefferson*

MOSS PAGEANT   13 b.g. Then Again – Water Pageant (Welsh Pageant) [2002/3   c74
c70, h–: c16d⁵ c16g² c16d⁴ c16g c16m⁶ c20g⁶ Aug 17] good-topped gelding: poor   h–
handicap chaser: best around 2m: probably acts on any going: tongue tied. *J. B. Walton*

MOSSPAT   4 b.g. Reprimand – Queen And Country (Town And Country) [2002/3   h–
17gᵖᵘ 16s⁶ 17s Nov 28] leggy, close-coupled gelding: poor maiden (barely stays 7f) at 2
yrs: showed little in 3 races over hurdles. *W. G. M. Turner*

MOSSTOWIE   7 b.m. Le Moss – Rowan Ville (Sexton Blake) [2002/3 F16d 20mᵖᵘ   h–
May 8] fourth foal: dam Irish 11f winner: no sign of ability in mares bumper and novice   F–
hurdle. *G. J. Smith*

MOSSY GREEN (IRE)   9 b.g. Moscow Society (USA) – Green Ajo (Green Shoon)   h127 +
[2002/3 20s² 19v* 20d² 21g Mar 12] has scope: useful in bumpers in 2000/1: fairly useful
form over hurdles on return, won maiden at Naas in January and 2 lengths second to
Rosaker in Grade 2 novice there following month: stiff task, weakened after 3 out when
well held in Grade 1 novice at Cheltenham final start: should stay beyond 2½m: raced on
good going or softer (acts on heavy). *W. P. Mullins, Ireland*

MOSTARSIL (USA)   5 ch.g. Kingmambo (USA) – Naazeq (Nashwan (USA)) [2002/3   h73
h84: 20m⁴ 17g³ 17m Sep 11] modest on Flat (stays 1½m): poor maiden hurdler: will
prove best around 2m: tried visored: sold to join G. L. Moore £4,000 Ascot December
Sales. *J. G. M. O'Shea*

MOSTYN   12 ch.g. Astral Master – Temple Rock (Melody Rock) [2002/3 c94: c25fᵖᵘ   c–
May 15] non-thoroughbred gelding: winning pointer/hunter chaser: taken on for lead and
appeared to sulk at Exeter in May: stays 19f: acts on firm going. *J. E. Tuck*

MOTAFAYEL 5 b.g. Unfuwain (USA) – Hamaya (USA) (Mr Prospector (USA)) **h98**
[2002/3 F82: F16d 16s^{bd} 16s 16v^3 16v 16d Mar 1] unfurnished gelding: fair form at best **F68**
in bumpers: would probably have been second but for being brought down last in novice
at Wetherby on hurdling debut: disappointing subsequently: not sure to stay beyond 2m:
raced on going softer than good. *Mrs S. J. Smith*

MOTCOMB JAM (IRE) 6 b.g. Frimaire – Flying Flo Jo (USA) (Aloma's Ruler **h102**
(USA)) [2002/3 F86: 16d^{bd} 16g 16d* 19g^3 20d^4 Apr 9] rather unfurnished gelding: fair
novice hurdler: won at Doncaster in January: may prove best short of 2½m: acts on good
to soft going: temperament under suspicion. *C. J. Mann*

MOTELLINO (IRE) 9 ch.g. Montelimar (USA) – Macamore Rose (Torus) [2002/3 **c–**
c–: c16d Mar 4] lengthy, dipped-backed gelding: winning Irish pointer: no form in
steeplechases: tried blinkered. *P. J. Millington*

MOTHER SAYS 7 b.g. Landyap (USA) – Miami Blues (Palm Track) [2002/3 F17m^3 **F70**
F17m^3 Oct 3] fifth foal: dam 1m and 1¼m seller winner: poor form when third in bumpers
at Newton Abbot and Hereford. *Jean-Rene Auvray*

MOTHERS HELP 8 b.m. Relief Pitcher – Laundry Maid (Forzando) [2002/3 c–, h–: **c114**
c20m^5 c17m^4 c24m^6 c21g c25m^5 c24m^4 c28g* c24f^3 c28d^4 c25m* c24d^3 c24s **h–**
c24g^{pu} c24v^4 c25m^4 Mar 20] workmanlike mare: fair handicap chaser: won at Market
Rasen in October and Folkestone and Huntingdon in November: below best subsequently: stays 3½m: acts on soft and firm going: effective tongue tied or not. *D. L. Williams*

MOTOWN MAN (IRE) 6 b.g. Detroit Sam (FR) – Hands Off (Nearly A Hand) **h–**
[2002/3 F16s 19d 19s Feb 27] 1,000 4-y-o: eighth foal: half-brother to bumper winner **F–**
Handy Julie (by Julio Mariner): dam, placed in point at 9 yrs: no sign of ability.
G. B. Balding

MOULOUYA (FR) 8 gr.m. Turgeon (USA) – Charabia (FR) (Bazin) [2002/3 c94, **c94**
h91: c24g^F May 8] smallish, sparely-made mare: modest hurdler: similar form over **h–**
fences (fell on 2 of 4 starts), in command when departing last at Fakenham in May:
probably stays easy 3m: acts on any going: sometimes races freely. *J. R. Best*

MOUNSEY CASTLE 6 ch.g. Carlingford Castle – Gay Ticket (New Member) **h104 +**
[2002/3 F93: F16g* 20g^2 21m^2 19m* 22g* Apr 12] good-topped gelding: fair form in **F89**
bumpers, winning at Chepstow in May: fair hurdler: didn't need to be at best to land odds
in maiden at Hereford (idled) and novice at Stratford in April: will stay 3m: acts on soft
and good to firm ground. *P. J. Hobbs*

MOUNTAIN DREAM 10 b.g. Batshoof – Echoing (Formidable (USA)) [2002/3 **c–**
20m 27m 20f^{pu} Sep 15] good-bodied gelding: winning hurdler: no form in 2002/3: tried **h–**
visored. *Miss S. E. Forster*

MOUNTAIN MAN (FR) 5 b.g. Cadoudal (FR) – Montagne Bleue (Legend of France **h79**
(USA)) [2002/3 F–: F16d^5 16s^4 Dec 14] lengthy gelding: poor form in bumpers and on **F72**
hurdling debut. *S. E. H. Sherwood*

MOUNTAIN NATIVE (IRE) 7 ch.g. Be My Native (USA) – Mountain Beauty (IRE) **h–**
(Executive Perk) [2002/3 F83: 20g^{pu} 22m^F Jun 1] workmanlike gelding: failed to
complete in 2 novice hurdles: sold £4,000 Ascot June Sales, won maiden point in April.
P. J. Hobbs

MOUNTAIN THYNE (IRE) 10 br.g. Good Thyne (USA) – Vanhalensdarling (Green **c93**
Shoon) [2002/3 c88: c25d* c25g^F c25g^6 Apr 7] fair pointer/hunter chaser: won maiden
hunter at Hexham in May and point in February: stays 25f: acts on good to firm and heavy
going. *Mrs R. L. Elliot*

MOUNT ALPHA (IRE) 7 ch.g. Alphabatim (USA) – Youthful Capitana (Hardboy) **c–**
[2002/3 F17d 20s^{pu} c27v^{pu} Jan 21] IR 4,500 4-y-o: workmanlike gelding: seventh foal: **h–**
dam, once-raced sister to useful chaser Pin's Pride, out of sister to top-class chaser **F–**
Captain Christy: little sign of ability. *D. McCain*

MOUNT GAY 10 ch.g. Montelimar (USA) – Candlebright (Lighter) [2002/3 20s^2 **c90**
c22m* c20m^{pu} Sep 14] lightly-raced winning pointer: first outing since 2000 when **h82**
second in maiden on hurdling debut: won novice at Market Rasen on steeplechasing
debut in August: behind when pulled up lame run-in in similar event at Bangor following
month: will stay 3m. *Mrs L. B. Normile*

MOUNT KARINGA 5 b.g. Karinga Bay – Candarela (Damister (USA)) [2002/3 **F98**
F16d* Mar 19] 4,200 3-y-o, 30,000 4-y-o: second foal: dam, poor maiden, half-sister to
useful 1¼m performer Game Ploy: fairly useful form when winning bumper at Chepstow
on debut by neck from Rooster's Reunion. *P. F. Nicholls*

MOUNT PRAGUE (IRE) 9 br.g. Lord Americo – Celtic Duchess (Ya Zaman (USA)) [2002/3 c112, h–: c20d³ c20s³ c20m⁶ c22gᵖᵘ c20g⁵ Apr 23] sturdy gelding: fairly useful handicap chaser: goes well fresh, best effort in 2002/3 when winning at Huntingdon on reappearance in November: barely stays 3m: acts on heavy going (well below form on good to firm): has found little. *K. C. Bailey* **c119 h–**

MOUNTRATH ROCK 6 b.m. Rock Hopper – Point of Law (Law Society (USA)) [2002/3 h80?: 18g⁴ 17d 16g 21m* Apr 19] small mare: poor and temperamental on Flat (stays easy 2m): poor hurdler: won conditional jockeys selling handicap at Plumpton despite looking far from straightforward under pressure: stays 21f: acts on firm going: tried visored/blinkered, including at Plumpton: tongue tied. *Miss B. Sanders* **h73**

MOUNTSORREL (IRE) 4 b.g. Charnwood Forest (IRE) – Play The Queen (IRE) (King of Clubs) [2002/3 17m 16f Oct 24] modest maiden at best on Flat (stays 1½m) for W. Muir/J. Best (twice claimed £6,000): well beaten in 2 juvenile hurdles: has worn cheekpieces. *T. Wall* **h–**

MOUNT VERNON (IRE) 7 b.g. Darshaan – Chellita (Habitat) [2002/3 h–: 17sᵖᵘ 17f⁵ 19g⁶ Apr 19] angular gelding: poor maiden hurdler: probably stays 19f: blinkered and tongue tied on debut. *P. Wegmann* **h–**

MOVING EARTH (IRE) 10 b.g. Brush Aside (USA) – Park Breeze (IRE) (Strong Gale) [2002/3 c120§: c20mᵖᵘ 24mʳᵗʳ 18d* 19g* c29mᵖᵘ Apr 26] lengthy gelding: has reportedly had soft palate operation: fairly useful handicap chaser on his day, pulled up both starts in 2002/3 (stiff task on final one): didn't need to run anywhere near that level to win claiming hurdles at Fontwell (claimed from P. Nicholls £5,000) in November and Doncaster in February: best form around 2½m: acts on soft and good to firm going: has had tongue tied: has refused to race several times (including second start) and remains best treated with plenty of caution. *A. W. Carroll* **c– § h103 §**

MOVING ON UP 9 b.g. Salse (USA) – Thundercloud (Electric) [2002/3 h129d: c16s³ c16v³ 16s² 16vᵖᵘ 16d 16g 24m⁵ 21g⁶ Mar 12] compact gelding: fair form on second of 3 starts in novice chases: fairly useful handicap hurdler: best effort in 2002/3 when runner-up to Spirit Leader in valuable listed event at Sandown in December: should stay beyond 21f: acts on heavy and good to firm going: visored once, blinkered nowadays: held up, and has found little. *C. J. Mann* **c102 h127**

MOWBRAY (USA) 8 b. or br.g. Opening Verse (USA) – Peppy Raja (USA) (Raja Baba (USA)) [2002/3 h106: 20d* Nov 11] good-topped gelding: fair hurdler: off over 16 months, showed he'd retained all his ability when winning maiden at Fontwell in November, not extended to beat Arctic Sky 7 lengths: not seen out again: will stay beyond 2½m: acts on good to firm and good to soft going. *G. L. Moore* **h106 +**

MOYKON (IRE) 6 b.g. Gothland (FR) – Yawa Prince (IRE) (Yawa) [2002/3 F74: 19g May 4] poor form on first of 2 starts in bumpers in 2001/2: tailed off in novice hurdle in May: placed twice from 5 runs in points subsequently. *Miss H. C. Knight* **h–**

MPLOY (IRE) 6 ch.g. Deploy – Sweet Quest (Rainbow Quest (USA)) [2002/3 h–, F75: 16m Oct 24] medium-sized gelding: poor form in bumper on debut: no show in 2 novice hurdles a year apart: sold 700 gns Doncaster March Sales. *Ferdy Murphy* **h–**

MR BABBAGE (IRE) 5 b.g. Carroll House – Winsome Doe (Buckskin (FR)) [2002/3 F18s* F16g Mar 12] big, rangy gelding: eighth foal: half-brother to several winners, including fairly useful hurdler/chaser Kirmar (by Montelimar), stays 3m: dam unraced half-sister to smart staying chaser Romany King: 6/4 favourite, won 20-runner bumper at Clonmel on debut in February readily by 4 lengths from Master Billy: insufficient test of stamina when well below that form in Grade 1 at Cheltenham in March and quite valuable event at Punchestown in early-May: will be suited by 2½m+. *W. P. Mullins, Ireland* **F102**

MR BAXTER BASICS 12 b.g. Lighter – Phyll-Tarquin (Tarqogan) [2002/3 c141, h–: c20d⁶ c20s² c19v² c24gᵘʳ c20g² c21dᶠ c24g² Apr 25] tall gelding: useful handicap chaser: runner-up 4 times in 2002/3: stays easy 3m: acts on heavy and good to firm going: weak finisher. *Miss Venetia Williams* **c129 h–**

MR BEN GUNN 11 ch.g. Newski (USA) – Long John Silvia (Celtic Cone) [2002/3 c82, h92d: 22gᵖᵘ c19mᵖᵘ 17m c20d* 19f³ c20m³ c23g³ c21sᵖᵘ Nov 6] strong gelding: poor maiden hurdler: modest chaser: won novice at Market Rasen in August: probably best at 2½m+: acts on firm and good to soft going. *J. D. Frost* **c90 h78**

MR BOSSMAN (IRE) 10 b.g. Jolly Jake (NZ) – Imperial Greeting (Be My Guest (USA)) [2002/3 c114, h–: c22sᵖᵘ c16d⁵ c16s⁶ 19d⁶ c20m* c19d² c21g* c21d⁴ c16m⁴ **c122 h–**

Apr 17] rangy gelding: fairly useful handicap chaser: won at Kempton in February and Fakenham in March: effective at 19f to 2¾m: acts on soft and good to firm going: tried blinkered, usually wears cheekpieces: often tongue tied. *R. C. Guest*

MR BUSBY 10 b.g. La Grange Music – Top-Anna (IRE) (Ela-Mana-Mou) [2002/3 c–, h85: 17m Jun 1] strong, lengthy gelding: maiden chaser: poor 2m hurdler, well held in handicap only start in 2002/3: acts on good to firm and heavy going. *John A. Harris* — c– h–

MR CAVALLO (IRE) 11 b.g. The Bart (USA) – Mrs Guru (Le Bavard (FR)) [2002/3 c70§, h87§: 22d 24g 20m² 24d⁶ 20d⁴ 27m² 21m⁵ 26g⁴ 26m² 20g 24g Apr 23] compact gelding: winning chaser: poor handicap hurdler: effective at 2½m to 27f: probably unsuited by heavy going, acts on any other: blinkered once: has looked none too keen. *Miss Lucinda V. Russell* — c– h79

MR CHATAWAY (IRE) 12 b.g. Le Bavard (FR) – Swift Invader (Brave Invader (USA)) [2002/3 c–, h–: c21mᵖᵘ May 22] of little account outside points nowadays. *Mrs D. M. Grissell* — c– h–

MR CHRISTIE 11 b.g. Doulab (USA) – Hi There (High Top) [2002/3 c–§, h87§: 23m 27v⁵ 24d⁶ 23v² 27v 24v 25d 24v Mar 13] sturdy gelding: poor handicap hurdler: largely well below form in 2002/3: needs thorough test of stamina: has form on good to firm going, all wins on softer than good (acts on heavy): tried visored/in cheekpieces: tongue tied: gets behind, and one to steer clear of. *Miss L. C. Siddall* — c– § h84 §

MR COLLINS 9 b.g. Brush Aside (USA) – Music Interpreter (Kampala) [2002/3 c–, h–: c21g* c20gᶠ c28gᶠ c23dᵖᵘ Jun 8] lengthy gelding: has been tubed: fair hunter chaser: won at Sedgefield in May: failed to complete subsequently: stays 3m: yet to race on extremes of going: has tongue tied. *R. Tate* — c86 h–

MR COOL 9 b.g. Jupiter Island – Laurel Diver (Celtic Cone) [2002/3 c128, h130: 16d² 20v² 16s⁵ 16v⁶ 21s² 16g 21g 20g Apr 5] workmanlike gelding: useful hurdler: second in minor event at Kempton, Grade 2 at Ascot (poached huge lead, beaten neck by Baracouda) and Grade 1 at Cheltenham (beaten length by Classified): poor efforts in 2 competitive handicaps and Grade 1 at Aintree last 3 starts: stays 21f: acts on any going: usually forces pace: game. *M. C. Pipe* — c– h144

MR COSPECTOR 6 b.g. Cosmonaut – L'Ancressaan (Dalsaan) [2002/3 h117: c20dʳᵒ c21s⁴ c26s* c24gᶠ Dec 18] lengthy, angular gelding: fairly useful hurdler: similar form in novice chases, winning at Warwick in December: would have been placed but for falling 3 out in race won by Iris Royal at Newbury later in month: stays 3¼m: raced on good going or softer (acts on heavy): consistent. *D. L. Williams* — c119 h–

MR CUSTARD 11 b.g. Newski (USA) – May Owen (Master Owen) [2002/3 c96: c25f⁴ May 15] workmanlike gelding: fair hunter chaser: well below best in May: won point in February: stays 3m: acts on firm going, pulled up on soft. *Miss L. J. C. Sweeting* — c–

MR DOW JONES (IRE) 11 b.g. The Bart (USA) – Roseowen (Derring Rose) [2002/3 c127: c25fᵖᵘ c22d⁵ c26d³ c24s² c26g Mar 13] medium-sized gelding: useful hunter chaser: creditable placed efforts at Fontwell and Newbury in February: stays 3¼m: acts on heavy going, probably on good to firm: jumps none too fluently. *K. Goldsworthy* — c110

MR ED (IRE) 5 ch.g. In The Wings – Center Moriches (IRE) (Magical Wonder (USA)) [2002/3 17s⁴ 17s² 19s⁴ Dec 26] fairly useful on Flat (stays 2m): modest form over hurdles: should stay at least 2½m: wears cheekpieces. *P. Bowen* — h92

MR EVANS 8 ch.g. Current Edition (IRE) – Manor Park Crumpet (True Song) [2002/3 F86: c22d² c20dᵖᵘ c23dᶠ Dec 19] easily best effort in bumpers in 2001/2 when winning steadily-run event on debut: seemingly modest form when second in novice at Fontwell on chasing debut: let down by jumping subsequently: stays 2¾m. *Miss E. C. Lavelle* — c96

MR FLUFFY 6 br.g. Charmer – Hinton Bairn (Balinger) [2002/3 h91p, F91: 20mᶠ 20d² 20m* 20d* 22d* Sep 4] leggy gelding: progressive hurdler: landed odds in maiden at Uttoxeter in June and novices at Worcester in August and Newton Abbot in September, winning easily last 2 occasions: will stay beyond 2¾m: acts on good to soft and good to firm going: open to further improvement. *P. J. Hobbs* — h113 p

MR GISBY (USA) 5 b. or br.g. Chief's Crown (USA) – Double Lock (Home Guard (USA)) [2002/3 h92: 19m⁵ Apr 5] sparely-made gelding: fairly useful on Flat (stays 2m), successful in February for S. Williams: modest form on 2 of 4 starts in juvenile hurdles in 2001/2 for D. Elsworth: below-form fifth in maiden at Hereford, only run in 2002/3. *Mrs L. Wadham* — h83

MR GRIMSDALE (IRE) 11 ch.g. Grimesgill (USA) – Lady Rose Walk (Sir Herbert) [2002/3 c–, h–: c19g^{pu} c25d^{pu} c16m Apr 5] strong, workmanlike gelding: winning hunter chaser: no longer of much account. *Mrs A. C. Tate* c– h–

MR HALF SHARP 10 ch.g. Mr Fluorocarbon – Star Shell (Queen's Hussar) [2002/3 c95, h–: c22d^{pu} May 13] angular gelding: winning hunter chaser: no show at Towcester in May: stays 3m: acts on firm ground. *Sidney J. Smith* c– h–

MR HAWKEYE (USA) 4 ch.g. Royal Academy (USA) – Port Plaisance (USA) (Woodman (USA)) [2002/3 16v^{pu} Feb 13] workmanlike gelding: disappointing maiden on Flat, sold out of W. Haggas' stable 2,500 gns Newmarket Autumn Sales: showed little on hurdling debut. *Ms A. E. Embiricos* h–

MR LAGGAN 8 b.g. Tina's Pet – Galway Gal (Proverb) [2002/3 c–, h72d: c25g^2 c25m^4 25m c27d^{pu} c25v^{pu} c25g^{pu} c20g^5 Apr 26] workmanlike gelding: poor maiden hurdler/chaser, largely out of sorts in 2002/3: stays 25f: acts on soft and good to firm going: has worn cheekpieces. *Miss Kate Milligan* c72 h–

MR LAMB 8 gr.g. Deploy – Caroline Lamb (Hotfoot) [2002/3 h–x: c21m^F Sep 7] lengthy gelding: useful hurdler at best: fell fatally on chasing debut: best form around 2m: acted on good to firm and good to soft going: took good hold. *S. Dow* c– h–

MR LEHMAN 6 ch.g. Presidium – Lehmans Lot (Oats) [2002/3 F16g^4 F16d^3 F16g Apr 1] workmanlike gelding: third foal: half-brother to poor hurdler Kilcreggan (by Landyap): dam, placed in bumper, half-sister to smart performer around 9f Mellottie: modest form first 2 starts in bumpers, showed nothing final one. *Mrs M. Reveley* F79

MR LEROI (IRE) 10 b.g. Camden Town – Black Tulip (Pals Passage) [2002/3 c21m^5 May 22] poor maiden hurdler: winning pointer: never a factor on hunter chase debut: raced mainly around 2m: acts on soft going. *R. A. Gadd* c64 h–

MR MAGNETIC (IRE) 12 b.g. Point North – Miss Ironside (General Ironside) [2002/3 c102, h–: c26g^5 c25d^{pu} Feb 6] medium-sized gelding: fair hunter chaser: suited by thorough test of stamina: acts on soft going: tried blinkered: poor jumper. *Dominic Harvey* c92 x h–

MR MAHDLO 9 b.g. Rakaposhi King – Fedelm (Celtic Cone) [2002/3 c–, h–: c25d^3 c24s* c24m^{pu} c26d^{pu} c27v* c30d^3 c24s^{pu} c30v^3 c25d^{pu} Mar 6] leggy, workmanlike gelding: modest handicap chaser: won at Uttoxeter in June and Sedgefield in November: suited by 3m+: acts on heavy going: blinkered once, usually wears cheekpieces nowadays: has had tongue tied: inconsistent. *R. D. E. Woodhouse* c94 § h–

MR MANN (IRE) 10 ch.g. Duky – Slan Abhaile (Trimmingham) [2002/3 c98d: c25d^{ur} Mar 1] modest pointer, successful in February: still close up but held when unseating last in novice hunter at Kelso in March: stays 3m: acts on good to firm and heavy going. *Mrs M. A. Kendall* c86

MR MARKHAM (IRE) 11 b.g. Naheez (USA) – Brighter Gail (Bustineto) [2002/3 c106, h132: c21g^4 c24d^{ur} c29s* c25d^5 c27d^F 20g Mar 25] workmanlike gelding: has been fired: fairly useful handicap chaser: won quite valuable event at Plumpton in November by 6 lengths from River Bug: below form otherwise in 2002/3, barely adequate test on return to hurdles final start: stays 29f: best form on going softer than good (acts on heavy): often blinkered, tried in cheekpieces: lazy. *J. T. Gifford* c116 h–

MR MCDUCK (IRE) 11 ch.g. Denel (FR) – Coldwater Morning (Laurence O) [2002/3 c21g^4 May 3] maiden hurdler: second start in steeplechases when well held in hunter at Sedgefield very early in season: won maiden point in April: stays 21f: acts on good to firm and good to soft going: tried blinkered. *Ms S. Duell* c– h–

MR MCDUFF (IRE) 7 b.g. Mandalus – Le Glen (Le Bavard (FR)) [2002/3 c–, h84: 19m^2 24m^5 20d^4 c20g^3 16g* 20g^4 20m^5 16m 20s 16g 16g Apr 12] tall gelding: let down by jumping in novice chases: modest hurdler: best effort when winning maiden at Worcester in September: no form last 5 starts: possibly best up to 2½m: acts on good to firm and good to soft going. *M. J. Gingell* c– h88 d

MR MICKY (IRE) 5 b.g. Rudimentary (USA) – Top Berry (High Top) [2002/3 h75: 16d 16v* 16v^3 17v Feb 11] workmanlike gelding: modest hurdler: improved effort when winning novice handicap at Wetherby in November, hanging left latter stages: raced around 2m on good going or softer (acts on heavy): sold 2,600 gns Doncaster May Sales. *T. D. Easterby* h85

MR MIDAZ 4 ch.g. Danzig Connection (USA) – Marmy (Midyan (USA)) [2002/3 **h83** 16m⁶ 17m⁴ 16g⁵ 16d 16d⁴ 17d* 16g Apr 7] sturdy gelding: modest maiden on Flat (should stay 1m): modest juvenile hurdler: sold out of J. O'Keeffe's stable 2,800 gns Doncaster October Sales after third start: best effort when winning handicap at Sedgefield in March: will prove best around 2m: acts on good to soft going. *D. W. Whillans*

MR MIGHTY (IRE) 7 br.g. Montelimar (USA) – Laurie Belle (Boreen (FR)) **c–** [2002/3 c24mʳᵒ Apr 21] IR 13,000 4-y-o: ex-Irish gelding: fourth foal: half-brother to fair chaser Carried Interest (by Celio Rufo), stays 3m: dam, winning hurdler around 2m, out of sister to high-class staying chaser Bright Highway: no form in bumpers in 2001/2 for M. Butler: won second of 2 starts in Irish points in early-2003: ran out in hunter at Fakenham. *N. J. Pewter*

MR MILLER (IRE) 11 b.g. The Bart (USA) – Celtic Connection (Martinmas) **c58** [2002/3 c–, h–: c23d⁶ c26s⁴ c25s⁴ c26sᵘʳ c25gᶠ c26gᵖᵘ Apr 21] tall, sparely-made gelding: **h–** unbeaten in points in 2002: bad maiden chaser: thorough stayer: acts on any going: often blinkered. *O. Sherwood*

MR MORRIS 7 ch.g. Current Edition (IRE) – Manor Park Crumpet (True Song) **h–** [2002/3 22dᵖᵘ 22m Apr 8] fifth foal: brother to fair bumper winner Mr Evans: dam ran once: showed little in 2 starts over hurdles. *Miss E. C. Lavelle*

MR MUSIC MAN (IRE) 10 b.g. Accordion – A New Rose (IRE) (Saher) [2002/3 **c–** 16g 16gᵖᵘ 20d⁵ 20m 17m c20s⁴ c22sᵖᵘ Dec 26] rangy, sparely-made gelding: bumper **h–** winner: disappointing over hurdles/fences: blinkered last 4 starts: has looked none too keen. *Miss G. Browne*

MR NO MAN 7 b.g. Cosmonaut – Christmas Show (Petorius) [2002/3 h87: 23dᵖᵘ **h–** 20dᵖᵘ 16g Apr 7] tall, strong gelding: winning hurdler: no form in 2002/3 after 21-month absence, tongue tied last 2 starts: should stay at least 2½m. *T. J. Fitzgerald*

MR PENDLEBERRY 9 ch.g. Symbolic – Antonoua (Anton Lad) [2002/3 c78, h86: **c–** 20dᵖᵘ May 4] leggy gelding: twice-raced chaser: winning hurdler: runner-up in points in **h–** February (2) and March: should stay beyond 2½m: acts on good to firm and heavy going. *A. Dickman*

MR PERRY (IRE) 7 br.g. Perugino (USA) – Elegant Tune (USA) (Alysheba (USA)) **c–** [2002/3 c–, h80: 20m 16s c20dᵖᵘ Nov 25] leggy gelding: winning hurdler/twice-raced **h–** maiden chaser: no form in 2002/3: raced mainly around 2m: acts on soft and good to firm going: visored once: sold 600 gns Ascot December Sales. *Mrs P. Ford*

MR PHIPPS 7 b.g. Shareef Dancer (USA) – Frost In Summer (Busted) [2002/3 18vᶠ **h78** 18s 19d⁶ 18g Mar 17] 3,200 3-y-o: workmanlike gelding: third foal: dam unraced: poor form in novice hurdles: dropped away tamely final start. *P. Winkworth*

MR PISTACHIO (IRE) 8 b.g. Royal Fountain – Knockananig (Pitpan) [2002/3 c94, **c–** h–: 26g⁵ c23d⁵ Mar 4] lengthy gelding: no form in 2 races over hurdles: fair pointer: **h–** similar form at best in hunters: shaped as if possibly amiss when well held in maiden at Leicester in March: should stay beyond 25f: tried blinkered/in cheekpieces. *Miss K. Marks*

MR PLAYFULL 13 br.g. Teamwork – Blue Nursery (Bluerullah) [2002/3 c–, h–: **c–** c26mᵖᵘ c25gᵖᵘ Jun 12] sturdy gelding: winning hurdler/chaser, retains no ability: tried **h–** blinkered. *Mrs L. C. Jewell*

MR RATHMORE (IRE) 9 gr.g. Valville (FR) – Lady Grasp (Ballad Rock) [2002/3 **c–** h76: c21sᵖᵘ c20dᵖᵘ Nov 25] lengthy gelding: poor maiden hurdler: no form in 2 runs over **h–** fences: stays 21f: acts on soft and good to firm going. *N. A. Twiston-Davies*

MRS DUF 9 b.m. Teenoso (USA) – Hatherley (Deep Run) [2002/3 h90: c25d⁴ 25s 21v **c82** 22d Mar 6] sturdy mare: winning hurdler: poor form in 2002/3, including on steeplechase **h82** debut: should stay 3m: acts on good to soft going. *R. H. Alner*

MRS I KNOW (IRE) 5 b.m. Presenting – Minerstown (IRE) (Miner's Lamp) **h–** [2002/3 F16d 20gᵖᵘ Mar 2] rather unfurnished mare: half-sister to fairly useful hurdler/ **F–** chaser Ernest William (by Phardante), stays 2¾m: dam unraced: no show in maiden bumper or novice hurdle. *Ferdy Murphy*

MRS JODI 7 b.m. Yaheeb (USA) – Knayton Lass (Presidium) [2002/3 h111: c16g⁴ **c–** c16g⁴ 16m 16v⁵ Nov 13] sparely-made mare: fair handicap hurdler: not fluent and well **h110** held both starts in novice chases: stays 2½m: acts on firm and soft going (none too fluent on heavy): looked less than keen in cheekpieces final outing. *J. M. Jefferson*

MR SMUDGE 11 ch.g. Fearless Action (USA) – Amerian County (Amerian (USA)) **c89 §**
[2002/3 c96: c25g² c25d⁵ c24sᵖᵘ c26gᵖᵘ Mar 13] workmanlike gelding: fair hunter chaser: successful in points in February and April: stays 25f: acts on good to firm going: none too consistent. *Mrs F. J. Marriott*

MR SNEAKY BOO (IRE) 7 b.g. Little Wolf – Florabalda (Kambalda) [2002/3 **c106 p** h108: 16d* 16s² 16s³ 16s³ 16s⁵ 20s* 16s 24s 16v 20s c16m* 22g⁵ Apr 21] lengthy **h125** gelding: fairly useful handicap hurdler: improved form in 2002/3, won at Limerick in May and Cork in January: won novice at Thurles on chasing debut in April (open to improvement): should stay beyond 2½m: acts on soft and good to firm going: tried blinkered: tough. *Michael Hourigan, Ireland*

MRS PHILIP 4 b.f. Puissance – Lightning Legacy (USA) (Super Concorde (USA)) **F89** [2002/3 F16g² F17m² Apr 15] half-sister to several winners, including fairly useful hurdler/chaser up to 3m Cabochon (by Jalmood) and fairly useful hurdler around 2m Lawahik (by Lahib): dam maiden, stayed 1m: confirmed debut promise when first past post in mares maiden bumper at Exeter in April, beating Scamp by short head but demoted due to interference caused by drifting left over 1f out (also wandered under pressure on debut). *P. J. Hobbs*

MRS PICKLES 8 gr.m. Northern Park (USA) – Able Mabel (Absalom) [2002/3 h81: **h94** 22s⁵ 26s⁴ 22d² 22d² 16v* 20v³ 24s⁴ 21sᵖᵘ Feb 24] workmanlike mare: modest handicap hurdler: trained by G. Brown third/fourth starts: won mares event at Chepstow in January: effective at 2m given thorough test and stays 3¼m: goes well on heavy going: usually needs plenty of driving. *M. D. I. Usher*

MRS POPPYFORD 5 b.m. Mistertopogigo (IRE) – Mrs Jawleyford (USA) (Dixie- **F–** land Band (USA)) [2002/3 F16d Aug 3] first foal: dam winning hurdler/2m winner on Flat: well held in bumper on debut. *C. Smith*

MRS RITCHIE 6 b.m. Teenoso (USA) – Material Girl (Busted) [2002/3 F71: F16d³ **F74** Apr 29] poor form in 2 mares bumpers. *M. Pitman*

MRS SHERMAN 8 b.m. Derrylin – Temporary Affair (Mandalus) [2002/3 c–, h–: **c–** c26g³ c25gᶠ c26gᵖᵘ c26d² Jun 8] sturdy mare: bad maiden steeplechaser: won maiden **h–** point in January: stays 3¼m: acts on heavy going: blinkered. *Mrs L. Williamson*

MR STITCH 6 br.g. Lancastrian – Hovian (Hotfoot) [2002/3 F17d 20mᵖᵘ c25sᵘʳ **c–** c25gᵖᵘ Mar 21] 4,200 4-y-o: eighth foal: dam maiden, stayed 1½m: of no account. **h–** *Mrs L. B. Normile* **F–**

MR TIMBROLOGY (IRE) 9 b.g. Insan (USA) – Mary Kate (Callernish) [2002/3 **c102** c96, h–: c19s² c25dᵘʳ c24sᵖᵘ Dec 28] strong, lengthy gelding: fair handicap chaser: ran **h–** as if amiss final outing: stays 3m: acts on any going: has reportedly bled from nose. *R. H. Alner*

MR WOODENTOP (IRE) 7 b.g. Roselier (FR) – Una's Polly (Pollerton) [2002/3 **c104 p** h119p, F98: 24s* c25v* c20sᵖᵘ Mar 6] leggy, close-coupled gelding: fairly useful form **h120** over hurdles, successful on all 4 completed starts, idling closing stages when beating Caesar's Palace 1¼ lengths in handicap at Ayr in November: promising start over fences when easily landing odds in weak maiden on same course on chasing debut in January: jumped badly final circuit and pulled up before 5 out in similar event at Carlisle: stays 25f: acts on heavy and good to firm going: should still do better over fences. *L. Lungo*

MR WOODLAND 9 br.g. Landyap (USA) – Wood Corner (Sit In The Corner (USA)) **c110** [2002/3 h106: c21m* c21m² c23g* c24m* c21v Nov 19] quite good-topped gelding: fair **h–** hurdler: good start to chasing career, winning novices at Newton Abbot in July, Worcester (tended to jump right) in September and Huntingdon (simple task) in October: well held final start: stays 3m: acts on firm and soft going. *J. D. Frost*

MS TRUDE (IRE) 6 b.m. Montelimar (USA) – Pencil (Crash Course) [2002/3 F85: **h–** 22vᴿ 19s⁶ 22v⁶ 21sᵖᵘ 26sᵖᵘ Mar 7] lengthy mare: fair at best in mares bumpers in 2001/2: no form over hurdles. *A. W. Carroll*

MUALLAF (IRE) 11 b.g. Unfuwain (USA) – Honourable Sheba (USA) (Roberto **h–** (USA)) [2002/3 h–: 16vᵖᵘ 16gᵖᵘ Nov 20] sturdy gelding: little form over hurdles. *Mrs A. M. Woodrow*

MUCKLE MAVIS 7 b.m. Nomadic Way (USA) – The Muckle Quine (Hubbly **c–** Bubbly (USA)) [2002/3 h84: 24dᵖᵘ 20d³ 20g 20d c21sᶠ 16v⁵ 24vᵖᵘ c21sᶠ Feb 23] poor **h77 §** maiden hurdler: fell both starts over fences: likely to prove best around 3m: acts on soft going: unreliable and often looks less than keen. *Miss Lucinda V. Russell*

MUCK SAVAGE 6 b.g. Homo Sapien – Rare Luck (Rare One) [2002/3 16d 20s⁶ 19s   **h115**
20d³ 24s² 21sᵘʳ 21s² 22vᵖᵘ 24d² Mar 1] IR 16,000 3-y-o: workmanlike ex-Irish gelding:
third foal: half-brother to modest chaser Four Mile Clump (by Petoski), stays 3¼m: dam
modest chaser, suited by test of stamina: fairly useful handicap hurdler: left A. Mullins
after third start: best effort when second to Springfield Scally at Doncaster final outing,
though none too fluent and wandered late on: stays 3m: raced on good going or softer
(acts on soft). *C. J. Mann*

MUDLARK 11 b.g. Salse (USA) – Mortal Sin (USA) (Green Forest (USA)) [2002/3   **c– x**
c–x, h–: 20d May 4] leggy gelding: of little account nowadays: blinkered/visored.   **h–**
J. R. Norton

MUGHAS (IRE) 4 b.g. Sadler's Wells (USA) – Quest of Passion (FR) (Saumarez)   **h124**
[2002/3 16s* 16v* 16m² 17g⁵ 16g⁶ Apr 3] good-topped ex-Irish gelding: fairly useful
maiden on Flat (stays 13f), sold out of K. Prendergast's stable 30,000 gns Newmarket
Autumn Sales: fairly useful juvenile hurdler: successful at Warwick in January and
Plumpton in February: good fifth of 27 to Spectroscope in Triumph Hurdle at Cheltenham: likely to prove suited by further than 17f: acts on good to firm and heavy ground:
carries head awkwardly. *A. King*

MUHAMI (IRE) 6 b.g. Phardante (FR) – The Vicarette (IRE) (The Parson) [2002/3   **h82**
h81, F77: 20sᵖᵘ 23d⁴ 20d⁴ 20g Dec 28] useful-looking gelding: poor maiden hurdler:
likely to prove best around 3m: raced on good going or softer (acts on soft). *Ferdy
Murphy*

MUHARIB LADY (IRE) 8 b.m. Muharib (USA) – Brickhill Lady (Le Bavard (FR))   **c80**
[2002/3 h73: 22d³ c23g³ c26m² c26m* c26d³ c25g 25v 24s⁶ 25m² 27f* Apr 24] sturdy   **h82**
mare: poor form over fences, won handicap at Plumpton in October: poor hurdler: best
effort when winning handicap at Fontwell in April: suited by 3m+: acts on firm and good
to soft going. *P. G. Murphy*

MUHTADI (IRE) 10 br.g. Marju (IRE) – Moon Parade (Welsh Pageant) [2002/3 c–,   **c–**
h77: 16d 16d 16g 16s Feb 24] workmanlike gelding: winning chaser/hurdler: well held   **h–**
over hurdles in 2002/3: raced mainly around 2m: acts on soft and good to firm going:
blinkered. *S. B. Clark*

MUJALIA (IRE) 5 b.g. Mujtahid (USA) – Danalia (IRE) (Danehill (USA)) [2002/3   **h–**
16gᴿ Apr 29] modest on Flat (stays easy 1¼m), showed considerable temperament last 2
outings: blinkered, all but refused to race in claimer on hurdling debut. *Jamie Poulton*

MUKDAR (USA) 9 b. or br.g. Gulch (USA) – Give Thanks (Relko) [2002/3 c–, h–:   **c–**
16d 16vᵖᵘ 16s² 16s⁶ 17g Mar 18] sturdy gelding: well held only outing over fences: **h82**
winning 2m hurdler: form for long time only when second in handicap at Leicester: acts
on firm and soft going. *K. C. Bailey*

MULHACEN (IRE) 7 br.m. Supreme Leader – Lancaster Lady (IRE) (Lancastrian)   **h89**
[2002/3 19m² 21mᵇᵈ 18f² Apr 24] leggy mare: signs of ability in bumpers in 2000/1: off
2½ years, runner-up at Hereford and Fontwell (mares) on completed starts in maiden
hurdles: will be suited by 2½m+. *Ian Williams*

MULKEV PRINCE (IRE) 12 b.g. Lancastrian – Waltzing Shoon (Green Shoon)   **c119**
[2002/3 c111, h–: c16d c20m c20m⁴ c17mᵖᵘ c20d² c20m* c20dᵘʳ c20s² c19d c20d*   **h–**
c20m* c21d Apr 4] stocky gelding: winning hurdler: fairly useful handicap chaser: maintained unbeaten record at Leicester when winning in November and March (amateurs),
also successful at Ludlow later in March: stays 2½m: acts on good to firm and heavy
going: has had tongue tied: has worn off-side pricker: headstrong front runner, prone to
the odd mistake. *D. Pearson*

MULLACASH (IRE) 5 b.g. Supreme Leader – The Parson's Line (The Parson)   **h111**
[2002/3 F16g* 18v⁵ 18v* 22s⁵ 20gᵖᵘ Apr 20] IR £26,000 3-y-o: rangy gelding: fifth foal: **F89**
dam winning pointer/placed in bumpers: second start in bumpers when winning at Cork
in May: fairly useful novice hurdler: won maiden at Leopardstown in December: better
form when length second to Aye Aye Popeye at Punchestown in late-April: should stay at
least 2½m: acts on heavy going. *N. Meade, Ireland*

MULLENSGROVE 9 b.g. Derrylin – Wedding Song (True Song) [2002/3 c78, h–:   **c99 §**
c24g* c27gᵖᵘ c24v⁶ c25g² c21gᵘʳ c24m Apr 12] good-topped gelding: fair hunter chaser: **h–**
won novice at Bangor in May: stays 25f: acts on good to soft going: reluctant to race final
start: one to treat with caution. *D. Lowe*

MULLIGAN EXPRESS 9 ch.g. Phardante (FR) – Tsarella (Mummy's Pet) [2002/3   **c100** c81, h–: c21d^ur^ c20s^6^ Mar 2] progressed into fairly useful novice hurdler in 2000/1:   **h–** lightly raced and fair form at best over fences since: will stay beyond 2½m: acts on heavy going. *Ferdy Murphy*

MULLIGATAWNY (IRE) 9 br.g. Abednego – Mullangale (Strong Gale) [2002/3   **h110** 16d 20v* 20s^3^ 22s^4^ Mar 2] lengthy, useful-looking gelding: fair handicap hurdler, off 2 years before reappearance: won at Ascot in December: good third to Taillefer at Sandown 2 months later: possibly amiss final start, travelling well but folding before 2 out: should stay beyond 2½m: acts on heavy and good to firm going. *J. T. Gifford*

MULLINTOR (IRE) 12 b.g. King Luthier – Latin Verses (Appiani II) [2002/3 c23g^pu^   **c–** Jul 10] strong, compact gelding: handicap chaser: lightly raced and no form since   **h–** 1999/00. *R. Rowe*

MULL'S NAG (IRE) 9 b.m. Lord Americo – Sue's A Lady (Le Moss) [2002/3 16d^3^   **h67** 17d 20g^5^ 25d^3^ 26m Aug 12] ex-Irish mare: poor maiden hurdler: stays 25f: acts on good to firm and good to soft going: usually tongue tied in Ireland. *Mrs S. J. Smith*

MULSANNE 5 b.g. Clantime – Prim Lass (Reprimand) [2002/3 h–: 16m^pu^ Jun 29] no   **h–** form on Flat or over hurdles: tried blinkered: has pulled hard. *P. A. Pritchard*

MULTEEN RIVER (IRE) 7 b.g. Supreme Leader – Blackwater Mist (IRE) (King's   **h118 p** Ride) [2002/3 16d^2^ 17s* Dec 18] 20,000 4-y-o: useful-looking ex-Irish gelding: third foal: dam unraced: won bumper at Thurles in 2001/2: shaped with great deal of promise when ¾-length second of 24 to Jaboune in well-contested novice at Wetherby on hurdling debut: landed odds by length from Ever Present in similar event at Bangor following month: likely to stay 2½m: acts on soft going: will go on to better things. *Jonjo O'Neill*

MULTI TALENTED (IRE) 7 b.g. Montelimar (USA) – Boro Glen (Furry Glen)   **c99** [2002/3 c22s^3^ c26v^2^ c25g* c26m^pu^ Mar 31] IR 20,000 3-y-o: fourth foal: dam, won 2½m hurdle, half-sister to useful 3m chaser Fair Is Fair: won maiden Irish point in 2002: bought 15,000 gns Doncaster May Sales: modest novice chaser: fortunate to land odds at Folkestone in March: reportedly bled 15 days later: looks a thorough stayer: sound jumper. *L. Wells*

MUMARIS (USA) 9 b. or br.g. Capote (USA) – Barakat (Bustino) [2002/3 c101,   **c102** h121d: c16d* c16d^2^ c16g^pu^ c16m^5^ c16g* c16g* c16d^5^ c20m^2^ c21d^pu^ Apr 8] workmanlike   **h–** gelding: fair novice chaser: won at Newcastle (idled) in April and Sedgefield (twice) in August: stays easy 2½m: acts on any going: usually sound jumper. *Mark Campion*

MUMBAI 7 b.g. Theatrical Charmer – Lehzen (Posse (USA)) [2002/3 c78, h61: c25d^6^   **c78** 20g c17s^3^ c17g^5^ c16v^4^ c16v^3^ c16d^2^ c16g c16s^6^ 17d^pu^ c16g c25g^pu^ Apr 14] angular   **h–** gelding: poor maiden hurdler/chaser: probably best around 2m on going softer than good (acts on heavy): tried blinkered: has had tongue tied: free-going sort. *M. A. Barnes*

MUMUQA (IRE) 11 ch.g. Noalto – Princess Isabella (Divine Gift) [2002/3 c101, h78:   **c94** c16m^3^ c19g^pu^ Apr 2] angular gelding: modest chaser: left B. Rothwell after reappearance,   **h–** little worthwhile form in points or hunter subsequently: best around 2m: acts on firm and good to soft going: blinkered once: usually races prominently. *Mrs A. L. Blanchard*

MUNADIL 5 ch.g. Nashwan (USA) – Bintalshaati (Kris) [2002/3 16m^6^ 16g^3^ 16g^3^ Sep   **h85** 14] fairly useful on Flat (stays 1¼m), sold out of M. Tregoning's stable 17,000 gns Newmarket Autumn (2001) Sales, bit below best in 2002: modest form in maiden hurdles: likely to prove best around 2m: tongue tied: headstrong. *P. R. Webber*

MUNDO RARO 8 b.g. Zafonic (USA) – Star Spectacle (Spectacular Bid (USA))   **h69** [2002/3 16d^3^ 17s 16v^5^ 17s 16v Jan 29] poor on Flat (stays 8.5f), sold out of J. FitzGerald's stable 1,200 gns Doncaster May Sales: similar standard over hurdles: likely to need sharp 2m: sold £400 Ascot February Sales. *R. M. Stronge*

MUQARRAR (IRE) 4 ch.c. Alhaarth (IRE) – Narjis (USA) (Blushing Groom (FR))   **F–** [2002/3 F16d Mar 1] 5,500 3-y-o: lengthy colt: closely related to 3 winners on Flat by Unfuwain, including 1994 May Hill winner Mamlakeh and 1996 Chesham winner Shamikh: dam 2-y-o 5f winner: well beaten in bumper (found to be setfast) on debut. *T. J. Fitzgerald*

MURAWA BELLEVUE (FR) 6 b.m. Murmure (FR) – Strakawa (FR) (Sukawa   **h–** (FR)) [2002/3 F16s 22s^pu^ Dec 17] fourth foal: half-sister to winning cross-country chaser   **F–** Titou de Beaulieu (by Gaspard de La Nuit): dam winning cross-country chaser: no sign of ability. *Jean-Rene Auvray*

Ascot United Football Club Novices' Hurdle, Ascot—
the promising Murphy's Cardinal maintains his unbeaten record

MURCHAN BENWOOD (IRE) 6 b.m. Ridgewood Ben – Ardnamurchan (Ardross) **h75**
[2002/3 h63, F77: 16s⁴ 20s⁴ 16v⁵ 20m Apr 12] lengthy, angular mare: poor maiden
hurdler: stays 2½m: acts on heavy going, possibly not on firmer than good: tried visored.
J. Mackie

MURDER MOSS (IRE) 13 ch.g. Doulab (USA) – Northern Wind (Northfields **c66**
(USA)) [2002/3 c75, h–: c16gᵖᵘ c24dᵘʳ c20fᶠᴿ 24g⁴ 24m³ c27d⁶ c28v⁵ Nov 13] no form **h–**
over hurdles: poor chaser: stays 27f: acts on good to firm and heavy going: visored last 2
starts (also tongue tied final one). *W. S. Colthred*

MURPHY'S CARDINAL (IRE) 7 b.g. Shernazar – Lady Swinford (Ardross) **h128 p**
[2002/3 F17s* 22s* 22v* 24v*] Feb 15] second living foal: dam won bumper and 2m **F97**
maiden hurdle: unbeaten in 4 starts, in bumper at Folkestone in November, maiden and
novice hurdles at same course in December and January and novice hurdle at Ascot in
February: fairly useful form when beating By Degree 3½ lengths (pair well clear) for
final success, travelling well, leading 3 out and holding on despite mistakes at last 2
flights: stays 3m: raced only on soft/heavy ground: open to further improvement.
Noel T. Chance

MURPHY'S NAILS (IRE) 6 b.g. Bob's Return (IRE) – Southern Run (Deep Run) **F74**
[2002/3 F16s Dec 7] IR £50,000 4-y-o: third foal: dam, winning pointer, half-sister
to dam of Chives: twelfth of 22 to Classic Native in bumper at Warwick on debut.
C. R. Egerton

MURPHY'S RETREAT (IRE) 6 b.g. Erins Isle – Mini Project (IRE) (Project **h– p**
Manager) [2002/3 F16s³ F16s* F20s⁵ 16v Mar 2] IR 11,500 3-y-o: first foal: dam, won at **F100**
2 yrs, half-sister to useful hurdler up to 3m Calladine (by Erins Isle): fairly useful form in
bumpers, winning at Punchestown in December: well beaten in maiden at Leopardstown
on hurdling debut: should stay beyond 2m: tongue tied after debut: should do better over
hurdles. *C. Roche, Ireland*

MURRAY RIVER (FR) 7 b.g. Esprit du Nord (USA) – Mulika (FR) (Procida **h125**
(USA)) [2002/3 16m² 20d 16m² Apr 22] lengthy gelding: fairly useful handicap hurdler:
ran well in 2002/3 after long absence, particularly good effort when second to Castleshane at Chepstow final start: may prove best around 2m: acts on soft and good to firm
going: blinkered once, visored nowadays: tongue tied last 2 outings. *M. C. Pipe*

MURRENDI (IRE) 5 b.g. Ashkalani (IRE) – Formaestre (IRE) (Formidable (USA)) **h83**
[2002/3 h79: 18m 16m² 16m⁴ 16m⁴ Jun 28] modest on Flat (stays 1¼m): poor maiden hurdler:
raced around 2m. *R. J. O'Sullivan*

MURT'S MAN (IRE) 9 b.g. Be My Native (USA) – Autumn Queen (Menelek) **c124**
[2002/3 c136: c27d⁶ c29v⁵ c24s Feb 13] good-topped gelding: useful handicap chaser in

627

2001/2: respectable efforts at best in valuable events first 2 starts in 2002/3: probably stays 29f: acts on heavy going: ran poorly when tried in blinkers: sometimes let down by jumping: has looked moody, including final outing. *P. F. Nicholls*

MUSALLY 6 ch.g. Muhtarram (USA) – Flourishing (IRE) (Trojan Fen) [2002/3 h65: 21m³ c20d⁶ 16m³ 17m⁵ 19m³ Apr 21] angular gelding: poor maiden hurdler: let down by jumping on chasing debut: stays 19f: acts on good to firm going: headstrong. *W. Jenks* — c– h75

MUSALSE 8 b.g. Salse (USA) – Musical Sally (USA) (The Minstrel (CAN)) [2002/3 h86: 24mᵖᵘ 23dᵖᵘ May 26] lightly-raced maiden hurdler: pulled up both starts early in 2002/3, seemingly lame on second occasion. *John R. Upson* — h–

MUSCADIN (FR) 5 br.g. Shaamit (IRE) – As Mustard (Keen) [2002/3 F–: F17g² 16dᵖᵘ Feb 23] unfurnished gelding: better effort in bumpers (pulled up amiss on debut) when second at Market Rasen: sold out of N. Richards' stable 9,200 gns Doncaster November Sales: no show in novice on hurdling debut. *A. C. Whillans* — h– F76

MUSICAL MAYHEM (IRE) 10 b.g. Shernazar – Minstrels Folly (USA) (The Minstrel (CAN)) [2002/3 h113: 22m² 25g⁸ 20s² Aug 9] leggy gelding: fair hurdler: won claimer at Wolverhampton in July: stays 25f: best form on good going or softer. *D. J. Wintle* — h108

MUSICAL SLING (IRE) 10 b.g. Orchestra – Coctail Bid (Mandalus) [2002/3 c–, h–: 22gᵖᵘ 16s c20m⁴ 16m 22m³ c17d⁴ c24dᶠ c29dᵖᵘ Nov 24] well-made gelding: winning hurdler/chaser, retains no ability. *Dr P. Pritchard* — c– h–

MUSIC THERAPY (IRE) 13 b.g. Roselier (FR) – Suny Salome (Sunyboy) [2002/3 c98, h–: c24vᵖᵘ Mar 5] workmanlike gelding: lightly raced: useful hunter chaser at best, very much on downgrade: raced on good going or softer (acts on heavy): tried tongue tied. *Mrs Polly Stockton* — c– h–

MUSIC TO MY EARS (IRE) 5 ch.g. Phardante (FR) – Evas Charm (Carlburg) [2002/3 F16s* F16d² Mar 1] 22,000 3-y-o: workmanlike gelding: fifth foal: brother to one-time smart chaser Hanakham, stays 27f, and half-brother to modest chaser Charming Gale (by Strong Gale), stays 25f: dam winning Irish pointer: fairly useful form in 2 bumpers, won at Southwell in January by head from Flame of Zara and second to impressive Tom Fruit at Doncaster: will stay well beyond 2m. *Jonjo O'Neill* — F98

MUSIMARO (FR) 5 b.g. Solid Illusion (USA) – Musimara (FR) (Margouillat (FR)) [2002/3 F18d³ F16d* 21s 18s³ Mar 2] IR 16,000 3-y-o: eighth foal: half-brother to several winners on Flat in France/Germany: dam 7f winner in France: confirmed debut promise when winning bumper at Ludlow in November: only poor form in 2 starts over hurdles (should improve): likely to prove best around 2m. *O. Sherwood* — h74 p F99

MUSKATSTURM (GER) 4 b.g. Lecroix (GER) – Myrthe (GER) (Konigsstuhl (GER)) [2002/3 16s² 16s⁶ 20g⁴ Mar 2] leggy ex-German gelding: useful on Flat (stays 1½m), successful 4 times in Hamburg, Bratislava (Slovak Derby) and Cologne in 2002: best effort in novice hurdles when fourth of 17 to Sh Boom at Huntingdon: possibly better at 2½m than 2m: blinkered last 2 starts. *B. J. Curley* — h89

MUSTANG MOLLY 11 br.m. Soldier Rose – Little 'n' Game (Convolvulus) [2002/3 c85: c21gᵖᵘ c17g⁴ c20m⁴ c20g² c21m² c21g³ c24f⁴ c21gᵖᵘ Apr 19] lengthy, rather sparely-made mare: winning pointer: poor maiden chaser: trained by P. Hiatt second to fifth starts: stays 3m: acts on firm going, probably on soft. *Andrew J. Martin* — c80

MUST BITE 7 b.g. Bustino – Once Bitten (Brave Invader (USA)) [2002/3 22g³ Mar 29] 33,000 3-y-o: eighth foal: half-brother to fair hurdler Carrick Lanes (by Oats), stayed 3¼m, and bumper/point winner Celtic Park (by Celtic Cone): dam, winning hurdler, half-sister to useful chaser up to 25f Greenwood Lad: little form over hurdles for J. Hassett: well-backed favourite, third in handicap at Market Rasen on British debut and first outing for 15 months, flashing tail and not seeming to go through with effort: stays 2¾m: raced on good ground or softer. *Jonjo O'Neill* — h91

MUTABARI (USA) 9 ch.g. Seeking The Gold (USA) – Cagey Exuberance (USA) (Exuberant (USA)) [2002/3 16f⁴ Oct 10] modest on Flat (barely stays 1¼m), successful in March: first form over hurdles when fourth in seller at Ludlow: needs sharp 2m: visored on debut. *J. L. Spearing* — h62

MUTADARRA (IRE) 10 ch.g. Mujtahid (USA) – Silver Echo (Caerleon (USA)) [2002/3 c69, h82: 22f² 19m² 17g⁵ 17g 22m 27g⁵ 16f* 16m* 16m⁴ 19s Nov 14] leggy, lengthy gelding: poor form on completed start over fences: modest handicap hurdler: won — c– h88 at Wincanton and Stratford (ladies) in October: effective at 2m to easy 2¾m: acts on firm and good to soft going, possibly not on softer: inconsistent. *J. W. Mullins*

MUTAKARRIM 6 ch.g. Mujtahid (USA) – Alyakkh (IRE) (Sadler's Wells (USA)) **h128**
[2002/3 h116: 16d* 16d² 16d* 16v⁴ 16g 16g² Apr 21] sturdy gelding: smart up to 1½m on Flat, well held at Nad Al Sheba in February: fairly useful novice hurdler: won maiden at Galway in July and Grade 2 Sharp Novices' Hurdle at Cheltenham (beat Jaboune 4 lengths) in November: creditable efforts last 2 starts, ninth of 19 to Back In Front in Grade 1 at Cheltenham (never nearer having looked none too keen) and head second to Glenhaven Nugget in Grade 2 at Fairyhouse: raced at 2m on good going or softer: blinkered. *D. K. Weld, Ireland*

MUTANASSIB (IRE) 10 b.g. Mtoto – Lightning Legacy (USA) (Super Concorde **h–**
(USA)) [2002/3 21d 20v^pu 19d^F Jan 16] angular gelding: fair hurdler in 1999/00: no sign of retaining ability after near-3-year lay-off: stays 3m: acts on soft and good to firm going: usually tongue tied: usually forces pace. *M. C. Pipe*

MUTASARRIF (IRE) 10 b.g. Polish Patriot (USA) – Bouffant (High Top) [2002/3 **c73**
c76, h–: c16d^pu 20m 22m^pu 17m⁵ c16g² c17d⁵ c16f^F Oct 24] angular gelding: winning **h–**
hurdler: poor maiden chaser: sold out of G. White's stable 1,100 gns Doncaster August Sales after fourth outing: probably best around 2m: acted on firm and good to soft going: often tongue tied: dead. *Miss L. V. Davis*

MUTED GIFT 5 ch.m. King's Signet (USA) – Ballet On Ice (FR) (Fijar Tango (FR)) **h–**
[2002/3 h–: 16v⁶ 16d 17s Dec 17] no form over hurdles. *W. G. M. Turner*

MUTINEER (IRE) 4 gr.g. Highest Honor (FR) – Miss Amy R (USA) (Deputy **h128**
Minister (CAN)) [2002/3 16v³ 16s³ 16s³ 16s³ 16v* 16s* 16s* 17g Mar 13] good-topped gelding: modest maiden on Flat (probably stays 1¾m): useful juvenile hurdler: won minor event at Leopardstown in December, Grade 3 at Punchestown in January and Grade 2 Cashmans Bookmakers Spring Juvenile Hurdle at Leopardstown (beat Golden Cross a head) in February, making all on last 2 occasions: at least respectable efforts when eighth of 27 in Triumph Hurdle at Cheltenham and fifth to Sporazene in Grade 1 at

Cashmans Bookmakers Spring Juvenile Hurdle, Leopardstown—
a second narrow win in graded company for Mutineer (blinkers), this time at the expense of Golden Cross

Seven To Eleven Syndicate's "Mutineer"

Punchestown in early-May: will stay 2½m: acts on heavy going: blinkered after fourth outing: usually tongue tied, effective when not: reliable. *D. T. Hughes, Ireland*

MUTINY 5 ch.g. Selkirk (USA) – Indian Love Song (Be My Guest (USA)) [2002/3 22d^{pu} 21s 25d 20v Dec 27] little sign of ability on Flat or over hurdles: wore cheekpieces last 3 starts. *B. W. Duke* — h–

MY ACE 5 b.m. Definite Article – Miss Springtime (Bluebird (USA)) [2002/3 F83: F17s^2 F16s^4 F17f^2 17g 16m^4 Mar 18] leggy mare: modest form in bumpers: not fluent when well held in mares novice hurdles: will prove best at 2m with emphasis on speed. *Mrs H. Dalton* — h– F83

MY BATON 8 ch.g. Orchestra – Laurello (Bargello) [2002/3 c101, h–: c20s^{ur} Oct 26] big, lengthy gelding: winning hurdler: fair novice chaser: stayed 3¼m: raced on good going or softer over jumps: didn't always impress with attitude: dead. *P. Beaumont* — c– h–

MY BOLD BOYO 8 b.g. Never So Bold – My Rosie (Forzando) [2002/3 h84: 16g 20m 17f* 17f* 19d 19s^6 c19s 19f 17m^F 19m^2 Apr 15] sturdy gelding: modest handicap hurdler: won twice in small fields at Exeter (all 4 wins there) in October: reportedly had breathing problem when well held on chasing debut: stays 19f: acts on firm and soft going. *K. Bishop* — c– h98

MYDANTE (IRE) 8 b.m. Phardante (FR) – Carminda (Proverb) [2002/3 h107: 24d* 27g^2 May 31] workmanlike mare: fair handicap hurdler: won at Towcester in May: stays 27f: acts on soft and firm going: tried visored: has flashed tail. *J. S. Moore* — h105

MY GALLIANO (IRE) 7 b.g. Muharib (USA) – Hogan Stand (Buckskin (FR)) [2002/3 c76, h90: 17m^4 c16g^5 16f^4 16m^2 19s^3 c16d^5 Dec 3] sparely-made gelding: modest hurdler/maiden chaser: best around 2m: acts on firm and soft going: runner-up on Flat in January and February. *B. G. Powell* — c86 h94

630

MY GOOD SON (NZ) 8 b.g. The Son (NZ) – Meadow Hall (NZ) (Pikehall (USA)) [2002/3 c93, h–: c24mF 20dpu 20dpu 27gpu 22m3 24m* 26g2 24m2 c26m3 c26mur Sep 28] fairly sparely-made gelding: modest handicap hurdler/chaser: won over hurdles at Worcester in July: stays 3¼m: acts on any going: effective blinkered or not: tongue tied once (pulled up). *Ian Williams* **c87 h97**

MYHEARTISBROKEN (IRE) 9 b.g. Broken Hearted – Lady Mearlane (Giolla Mear) [2002/3 20spu 20vpu 17gpu Apr 19] fairly useful hurdler in 1999/00: no sign of retaining ability, left D. Wachman after reappearance: let down by jumping both starts over fences: stays 2¾m: acts on heavy going: has had tongue tied: presumably difficult to train. *V. R. A. Dartnall* **c– h–**

MY JUNES MOON 5 b.m. Petoski – Peristyle (Tolomeo) [2002/3 F16m Jul 24] fifth foal: sister to modest hurdler Pertemps Profile, stays 3¼m: dam modest 2m hurdler: tailed off in bumper on debut. *A. D. Smith* **F–**

MY LEGAL EAGLE (IRE) 9 b.g. Law Society (USA) – Majestic Nurse (On Your Mark) [2002/3 h84: 17g4 16m* 17s2 16m2 Jun 1] rather sparely-made gelding: modest handicap hurdler: improved form when winning 18-runner event at Worcester in May: ran well both subsequent starts: should stay 2½m: acts on soft and good to firm going. *R. J. Price* **h100**

MY LINE 6 b.g. Perpendicular – My Desire (Grey Desire) [2002/3 h84P: 17s3 16d 16vF 16g6 Jan 17] sturdy gelding: fair on Flat (will stay beyond 2m), successful 3 times in 2002: modest form in novice hurdles: will be well suited by 2½m+. *Mrs M. Reveley* **h93 +**

MYLO 5 gr.g. Faustus (USA) – Bellifontaine (FR) (Bellypha) [2002/3 F96: F16d2 F16g2 17d2 19d4 16s 17v6 20v5 Feb 13] compact gelding: fairly useful form when second all 3 starts in bumpers: modest at best over hurdles, disappointing last 2 starts: likely to prove best short of 2½m. *Jonjo O'Neill* **h95 F100**

MY MATE WHITEY (IRE) 4 ch.g. Millkom – Imagery (Vision (USA)) [2002/3 16dpu 18d Dec 10] medium-sized gelding: no form, including on Flat for K. Bell. *M. A. Allen* **h–**

MY NAME'S NOT BIN (IRE) 6 b.m. Good Thyne (USA) – Crashrun (Crash Course) [2002/3 F16s5 18v 16s 20s4 22s* 20v2 24d6 24s3 24d* 20g3 Apr 20] fifth foal: half-sister to bumper winner Cumbrian Knight (by Presenting): dam unraced: poor form in 2 bumpers: fair novice hurdler: won maiden at Navan in January and minor event at Clonmel in March: stays 3m: raced on good going or softer (acts on heavy). *John P. A. Kenny, Ireland* **h108 F72**

MY NATIVE LAND (IRE) 8 b.g. Be My Native (USA) – Papukeena (Simbir) [2002/3 h91, F83: 24spu 24d 25v4 26spu 22v4 25s Mar 10] angular gelding: poor maiden hurdler: best at 2¾m+: raced mainly on going softer than good (acts on heavy): amateur ridden. *Miss T. M. Ide* **h79**

MY NATIVE MISS (IRE) 5 b.m. Be My Native (USA) – Explosive Missile (IRE) (Supreme Leader) [2002/3 F16d F16m Apr 21] IR £1,050 3-y-o, 4,500 4-y-o: second foal: dam, ran twice in points, from family of Spartan Missile: well held in maiden bumpers at Fakenham. *Mrs L. C. Jewell* **F–**

MY SHENANDOAH (IRE) 12 br.g. Derrylin – Edwina's Dawn (Space King) [2002/3 h115: 21s4 21d* 20gF 20g4 Jan 17] sturdy gelding: fair hurdler: won claimer at Huntingdon in December: lame final outing: barely stays 3m: acts on heavy and good to firm going: blinkered once: has won 4 times at Musselburgh: headstrong. *J. Howard Johnson* **h115**

MYSIE 8 ch.m. Weld – Saucy Eater (Saucy Kit) [2002/3 26spu Dec 26] winning 21f hurdler in 2000/1: showed little only subsequent start. *T. R. Greathead* **h–**

MYSON (IRE) 4 ch.g. Accordion – Ah Suzie (IRE) (King's Ride) [2002/3 F17s4 17gF Mar 16] second foal: dam never ran: fourth in bumper at Folkestone on debut: in second when falling 2 out in juvenile maiden hurdle there month later. *D. M. Grissell* **h97 F79**

MYSTERI DANCER 5 b.g. Rudimentary (USA) – Mystery Ship (Decoy Boy) [2002/3 16g2 16m4 16m4 Jul 18] fair on Flat (stays easy 1½m): modest form first 2 starts in novice hurdles. *R. J. O'Sullivan* **h86**

MYSTIC GLEN 4 b.f. Vettori (IRE) – Mystic Memory (Ela-Mana-Mou) [2002/3 F16f Mar 29] third foal: half-sister to fair bumper winner Flash of Memory (by Rock Hopper): dam, useful staying hurdler/winner up to 2m on Flat, half-sister to useful **F–**

staying hurdler/chaser Wain Mountain: held up and never a factor in mares bumper at Haydock on debut. *P. D. Niven*

MYSTIC HILL   12 b.g. Shirley Heights – Nuryana (Nureyev (USA)) [2002/3 h–: 22m* 21m⁵ 26s 22d 22v³ Mar 3] neat gelding: poor hurdler nowadays: dropped markedly in weights prior to 33/1-winner of 20-runner conditional jockeys selling handicap at Stratford in September: stays 2¾m: probably acts on any going. *J. Joseph*   **h67**

MYSTIC ISLE (IRE)   13 b.g. Callernish – Sleemana (Prince Hansel) [2002/3 c26gᵖᵘ Oct 21] lengthy gelding: one-time fairly useful staying chaser: little sign of retaining ability only start since 1999/00: acts on good to firm and heavy going: often blinkered: irresolute. *T. R. George*   **c– §**
h– §

MYSTIC LORD (IRE)   6 br.g. Roselier (FR) – Ash Dame (IRE) (Strong Gale) [2002/3 16v² 20s* 20s⁵ 24s⁵ 20v⁴ c25s* c24d⁴ Mar 17] unfurnished gelding: first foal: dam ran twice: fair hurdler: won maiden at Punchestown in December: fairly useful novice chaser: won at Fairyhouse in February: tongue tied, good fifth to Rule Supreme in valuable handicap at Punchestown in late-April: will stay beyond 25f: acts on soft going. *N. Meade, Ireland*   **c116**
h108

MYSTIC MAJOR   11 b.g. Wace (USA) – Mystic Mintet (King Log) [2002/3 c–: c24gᵖᵘ May 3] winning pointer: has failed to complete in 2 hunter chases. *Mrs I. Hughes*   **c–**

MYSTIC RIDGE   9 ch.g. Mystiko (USA) – Vallauris (Faustus (USA)) [2002/3 c78, h–: 16d 16m c17m⁴ Apr 12] good-bodied gelding: poor form over fences, none over hurdles: raced around 2m. *R. Lee*   **c–**
h–

MYTHICAL CHARM   4 b.f. Charnwood Forest (IRE) – Triple Tricks (IRE) (Royal Academy (USA)) [2002/3 16s⁴ 16m Mar 31] modest on Flat (stays 1½m), sold out of J. Gosden's stable 2,200 gns Newmarket Autumn Sales, successful in seller in April: well held in 2 claiming hurdles, looked none too keen second time. *B. R. Johnson*   **h60**

MYTHICAL KING (IRE)   6 b.g. Fairy King (USA) – Whatcombe (USA) (Alleged (USA)) [2002/3 16s³ 16v* 16d² 16s⁵ 16d* 16g Apr 5] workmanlike gelding: fair on Flat (stays 1½m) for B. Palling: fairly useful over hurdles: won novice at Uttoxeter (beat Hasty Prince ½ length) in December and handicap at Stratford (improved effort, led 2 out and quickened to beat Swan Knight 3 lengths) in March: ran poorly in valuable handicap at Aintree final start: likely to stay beyond 2m: raced on good ground or softer (acts on heavy): patiently ridden. *R. Lee*   **h117**

MYTIMIE (IRE)   8 b.g. Be My Native (USA) – Snoqualmie (Warpath) [2002/3 h106: c20s² c16v* c16d³ c16g³ c20s² Feb 24] rangy gelding: fair hurdler: similar form in novice chases: simple task at Carlisle in November: possibly best up to 2½m: acts on heavy and good to firm going: wore cheekpieces final outing (soon off bridle): occasionally runs as if amiss. *J. M. Jefferson*   **c105**
h–

MY TRUE LOVE (IRE)   4 b.g. Beneficial – Elfi (IRE) (Le Moss) [2002/3 F17g⁵ Apr 19] half-brother to Irish bumper winner by Castle Keep: dam unraced, from family of high-class 2m hurdler Supreme Halo: fifth of 14 to Special Conquest in maiden bumper at Newton Abbot on debut, pulling hard and carrying head awkwardly. *R. J. Baker*   **F84**

MY VERY OWN (IRE)   5 ch.g. Persian Bold – Cossack Princess (IRE) (Lomond (USA)) [2002/3 h–: 17m³ 17m Jun 14] angular gelding: fairly useful on Flat up to 1½m for N. Littmoden: much better effort over hurdles when third of 11 in novice at Newton Abbot: likely to stay 2½m. *K. C. Bailey*   **h91**

MY WAKASHAN (IRE)   8 b.m. Wakashan – My Wings (Erin's Hope) [2002/3 17d c16f⁶ Sep 15] sparely-made mare: poor maiden on Flat (stays 13f): no form in bumpers or over jumps. *J. J. Lambe, Ireland*   **c–**
h–

MY WHISPER (IRE)   4 b.f. Zaffaran (USA) – Floreamus (Quayside) [2002/3 F17g Apr 26] eighth foal: half-sister to winning pointer by Henbit: dam no form on Flat/only outing over hurdles: well held in bumper on debut. *A. King*   **F–**

N

NAGARA SOUND   12 b.g. Lochnager – Safe 'n' Sound (Good Investment (USA)) [2002/3 c19f⁵ May 15] workmanlike gelding: maiden jumper. *Mrs S. Warren*   **c–**
h–

NAHTHEN LAD (IRE)   14 b.g. Good Thyne (USA) – Current Call (Electrify) [2002/3 c87§, h–: c25dᵖᵘ c26g Mar 13] tall gelding: fair pointer/hunter chaser nowadays,   **c– §**
h–

out of depth in Foxhunter at Cheltenham: best short of 3½m: acts on good to firm and heavy going: usually blinkered/visored: often races lazily: inconsistent. *J. A. Danahar*

NAILBITER   4 b.g. Night Shift (USA) – Scylla (Rock City) [2002/3 F14d⁵ F14d h85 F16g³ 16sᶠ 16s⁵ 20g³ 16g² 17g⁵ Apr 26] 24,000Y, 4,500 2-y-o: quite good-topped F79 gelding: second foal: dam maiden half-sister to smart sprinter Northern Goddess (by Night Shift): modest form in bumpers and over hurdles: seems to stay 2½m: tongue tied final outing (below form): races prominently. *Mrs A. Duffield*

NAJ-DE   5 ch.g. Zafonic (USA) – River Jig (USA) (Irish River (FR)) [2002/3 h–: 18f⁵ h– 16mᵖᵘ Jun 19] close-coupled gelding: poor maiden on Flat (stays 1¼m): signs of ability over hurdles only when fifth of 7 in 4-y-o novice at Fontwell. *S. Dow*

NAMELESS WONDER (IRE)   7 b.g. Supreme Leader – Miss Kylogue (IRE) (Lan- h91 castrian) [2002/3 h100, F81: 20d 16d 22d⁴ 20d³ Jan 15] lengthy gelding: chasing type: modest form over hurdles: stays 2¾m: raced only on good to soft going: blinkered last 3 starts. *N. J. Henderson*

NAMPARA COVE   8 b. or br.g. Roscoe Blake – Lothian Lily (Alias Smith (USA)) c– [2002/3 c–: c26d Jun 8] won maiden point in 2002: no show in 2 hunter chases. *R. G. Russ*

NAMRON (IRE)   10 br.g. Strong Gale – Rigton Angle (Sit In The Corner (USA)) c– [2002/3 c21mᵖᵘ May 22] ex-Irish gelding: has run tubed: winning pointer: little form in h– steeplechases, went off too quickly when blinkered in hunter in May. *W. R. Hacking*

NAOMH PADRAIG (IRE)   7 b.g. Be My Native (USA) – Shirley's Dream (IRE) c102 (Mister Majestic) [2002/3 c20m* c21mᵖᵘ Jul 14] leggy ex-Irish gelding: first foal: dam h– unraced half-sister to useful juvenile hurdler Shirley's Delight (by Be My Native): bumper winner: maiden hurdler: fair form when winning maiden chase at Down Royal in May: sold out of N. Meade's stable 25,000 gns Doncaster Sales later in month: ran poorly in handicap, and subsequently made little impact in points: stays 3m: acts on soft and good to firm ground: tried blinkered. *C. C. Bealby*

NAPOLEON BONAPARTE (IRE)   6 b.g. Insan (USA) – Chiminee Fly (Proverb) h– [2002/3 F89: 16d 22gᶠ 19g⁶ Apr 19] well-made gelding: signs of ability in bumpers: no form over hurdles (not fluent): sold 7,000 gns Doncaster May Sales. *W. J. Musson*

NARROW WATER (IRE)   10 b.g. Mazaad – Miss Doogles (Beau Charmeur (FR)) c111 [2002/3 c–: c20d³ c24s⁶ Dec 7] workmanlike gelding: one-time useful chaser, largely disappointing since 2000/1, including at Punchestown in late-April (first start after leaving J. O'Neill): thorough stayer: raced on going softer than good (acts on heavy): often tongue tied. *T. Hogan, Ireland*

NARWHAL (IRE)   5 b. or br.g. Naheez (USA) – Well Why (IRE) (The Parson) [2002/3 h99 p F107: 16d³ Nov 29] close-coupled gelding: second in bumper in 2001/2: again shaped well when around 11 lengths third of 13 to eased Chauvinist in maiden hurdle at Newbury: bred to stay at least 2½m: should improve. *J. T. Gifford*

NASHVILLE STAR (USA)   12 ch.g. Star de Naskra (USA) – Mary Davies (Tyrn- c– § avos) [2002/3 c–§, h–: c21gᵖᵘ c20fᵖᵘ May 11] close-coupled gelding: one-time fair h– handicap chaser: little show since 1998/9, including over hurdles: wears visor: sometimes looks temperamental. *R. Mathew*

NAS NA RIOGH (IRE)   4 b.f. King's Theatre (IRE) – Abstraite (Groom Dancer h122 (USA)) [2002/3 16d² 16s* 16d² 17d² 16v* 18s* 17gᵘʳ Mar 13]
          Picking a winner can be difficult, but so can spelling it or pronouncing it, all the more so nowadays with the influx of French-breds, German-breds and even Polish-breds (usually with names in the local tongue) into the jumping game. Commentators almost need some qualification in modern languages, though few names present quite the difficulties, to English-only speakers at least, as those in Gaelic, where the cardinal rule seems to be that no word is pronounced anything like it looks. 2002/3 was a good year for Gaelic-named horses with Ar Muin Na Muice and Buailtes And Fadas to the fore, along with Nas Na Riogh. While it might be a puzzle to pronounce, Nas Na Riogh (the name of the main town in Kildare—Naas—and translated 'the assembly place of kings') is a name that will have been familiar to some readers with long memories. Nas Na Riogh was the dam of the magnificent chaser Mill House whose clashes with Arkle in the 'sixties became

legendary. The filly currently carrying the moniker came via the Goffs France July Sale (€36,000) from France, where she was a middle-distance maiden for Francois Rohaut. She is an interesting recruit to jumping, a tall filly who had much more about her physically than most of her contemporaries among the leading juvenile hurdlers. Her first season yielded three victories from eight starts and showed her well suited by testing conditions (probably best on going softer than good). She proved reliable too, winning at Sandown in November and, after good placed efforts at Newbury and Cheltenham (Grade 2 Tripleprint Juvenile Hurdle), revelling in the mud to win the Grade 1 Western Daily Press Finale Juvenile Hurdle at Chepstow in December by eleven lengths. Nas Na Riogh cruised to the front on the bridle after two out that day and had the race well won when her closest rival Le Duc came down at the last. The conditions in the Triumph Hurdle, Nas Na Riogh's Cheltenham target, provided much more of a test of speed than the Finale Juvenile Hurdle and Nas Na Riogh was a fair way off the leaders when she unseated her rider two out. On good ground in another Grade 1 at Punchestown in early-May, she was outpaced a long way out and finished a remote eleventh. She had been warmed up for the Festival in a fillies' only juvenile hurdle at Fontwell where she landed odds

Nas Na Riogh (IRE) (b.f. 1999)	King's Theatre (IRE) (b 1991)	Sadler's Wells (b 1981)	Northern Dancer Fairy Bridge
		Regal Beauty (b or br 1981)	Princely Native Dennis Belle
	Abstraite (ch 1990)	Groom Dancer (b 1984)	Blushing Groom Featherhill
		Absolute (ch 1979)	Luthier Artistically

Western Daily Press Finale Juvenile Hurdle, Chepstow—
Nas Na Riogh and the season's leading conditional jockey Marcus Foley are in command at the last

of 8/1-on in facile style. Nas Na Riogh is a half-sister to Bombardier Noir (by Turtle Island), a winning French hurdler at up to nineteen furlongs, and she will stay at least two and a half miles. For the record, she was tried blinkered in her Flat-racing days. *N. J. Henderson*

NASONE (IRE) 12 b.g. Nearly A Nose (USA) – Skateaway (Condorcet (FR)) [2002/3 c82, h–: c26m^{pu} c26g^{ur} c25g^{pu} Nov 18] tall gelding: long-standing maiden staying jumper: tried blinkered/in cheekpieces. *Miss M. P. Bryant*   c–
h–

NAT GOLD 7 b.g. Push On – April Airs (Grey Mirage) [2002/3 24v^4 24s^{pu} Jan 28] good-topped gelding: fourth foal: brother to highly successful pointer/winning hunter chaser Handsome Harvey and half-brother to fair staying hurdler/chaser Royal Barge (by Nearly A Hand): dam unraced: runner-up twice in points in 2002: poor form when fourth of 16 to Bacardi Boy in maiden at Chepstow, better effort over hurdles. *Mrs D. A. Hamer*   h77

NATIVA NEGRA (IRE) 6 br.m. Be My Native (USA) – Jayells Dream (Space King) [2002/3 F77: 19g^R 21m^{pu} Sep 13] runner-up in mares bumper on debut: no encouragement either start over hurdles: sold £1,100 Ascot October Sales. *A. King*   h–

NATIVE AFFAIR (IRE) 9 ch.g. Be My Native (USA) – Queens Romance (Imperial Fling (USA)) [2002/3 h98: 20m^F May 15] lengthy gelding: bumper winner: modest maiden hurdler: stays 2½m: acts on good to firm and good to soft going: has had tongue tied: prone to breaking blood vessels. *L. Lungo*   h–

NATIVE ALIBI (IRE) 6 b.g. Be My Native (USA) – Perfect Excuse (Certingo) [2002/3 c24g^5 c20v^{ur} c27v^5 Feb 11] IR £15,500 4-y-o: third foal: half-brother to winning chaser Salmon Cellar (by Roselier), stays 21f: dam bumper winner: runner-up in maiden point in 2002: little sign of ability in novice chases. *S. H. Shirley-Beavan*   c–

NATIVE APPROACH (IRE) 6 b.m. Be My Native (USA) – Castle Stream **h92**
(Paddy's Stream) [2002/3 F17g³ F16g* 19s³ 21d⁶ 19d³ 20d² 21m Mar 22] 25,000 4-y-o: **F87**
lengthy mare: sister to fairly useful hurdlers around 2½m Native Recruit and Native
Shore, former also fairly useful chaser, and half-sister to fair hurdler Bin It (by Supreme
Leader), stays 21f: dam unraced half-sister to useful hurdler Dutch Call: won bumper at
Worcester in July: modest form when placed in 3 mares novice hurdles, went rather in
snatches when runner-up to impressive Ar Muin Na Muice at Wetherby: stays 2½m: acts
on soft going: sold 14,000 gns Doncaster May Sales. *N. J. Henderson*

NATIVE BEAT (IRE) 8 b.g. Be My Native (USA) – Deeprunonthepound (IRE) **c106**
(Deep Run) [2002/3 c113, h108: c20d c20s⁵ c20s⁵ c19s⁴ c20d⁶ c24d⁶ c21d c25g³ Apr 20] **h–**
medium-sized gelding: fair chaser, largely below form in 2002/3: won cross-country
event at Punchestown in late-April: stays 3m: acts on any going. *J. R. H. Fowler, Ireland*

NATIVE BUCK (IRE) 10 ch.g. Be My Native (USA) – Buckskins Chat (Buckskin **c120**
(FR)) [2002/3 c115, h–: c28s² c29vᵖᵘ c30d* c34s⁶ Mar 15] leggy gelding: fairly useful **h–**
handicap chaser: won at Catterick in February by 3 lengths from Tribal Run: well held in
valuable events on starts either side: stays 3¾m: acts on heavy going (pulled up only start
on firmer than good). *T. R. George*

NATIVE COMMANDER (IRE) 8 b.g. Be My Native (USA) – The Better Half **c106**
(IRE) (Deep Run) [2002/3 c100, h–: c16s³ c16g c16s³ c17v⁴ c18s⁴ c16v² c16s* c19s **h–**
c16v⁵ c17v³ c17m* Apr 22] rangy gelding: maiden hurdler: fair staying chaser: won at
Punchestown in January and Fairyhouse (first start after leaving P. Morris, easily beat
Galway Breeze 7 lengths) in April: good fifth to Incas at Punchestown in early-May: best
around 2m: acts on good to firm and heavy going. *S. J. Mahon, Ireland*

NATIVE COVE (IRE) 11 b.g. Be My Native (USA) – Down All The Coves (Athen- **c96 §**
ius) [2002/3 c99: c24mᵖᵘ c24s² Mar 7] fair hunter chaser: creditable second to Rob Mine
at Sandown: stays 31f: acts on soft going: tried visored: unreliable. *E. Haddock*

NATIVE CUNNING 5 b.g. Be My Native (USA) – Icy Miss (Random Shot) [2002/3 **F83**
F13s F16m F16m Mar 22] 18,000 4-y-o: big, well-made gelding: chasing type: seventh
foal: half-brother to several winners, including fairly useful chaser Indian Chance (by
Teenoso), stays 25f: dam winning hurdler/chaser, stayed 3m: mid-division at best in 3
bumpers. *R. H. Buckler*

NATIVE DAISY (IRE) 8 b.m. Be My Native (USA) – Castleblagh (General Ironside) **c–**
[2002/3 c22dᵘʳ Feb 8] workmanlike mare: successful in points in Ireland, including in
April: twice-raced in hunter chases, well-held fourth to What Odds in valuable event at
Punchestown in late-April: stays 25f: has given trouble in preliminaries. *K. J. Burke,
Ireland*

NATIVE DESIGN (IRE) 6 br.m. Be My Native (USA) – Artist's Design (Precipice **h95**
Wood) [2002/3 F16s* 16s⁵ 20s⁵ 16s⁴ 16s² F16d 20g Apr 3] workmanlike mare: eighth **F93**
foal: half-sister to bumper winner Fisher's Cross (by Buckskin): dam unraced half-sister
to top-class 2m to 3m hurdler Gaye Brief and very smart staying jumper Gaye Chance:
won 24-runner bumper at Navan in May: modest form over hurdles: out of depth at Aintree final start: stays 2½m: acts on soft ground: tongue tied last 4 starts. *M. J. O'Connor,
Ireland*

NATIVE DRUM (IRE) 8 b.g. Be My Native (USA) – Lantern Lass (Monksfield) **c–**
[2002/3 20v⁵ 27vᵖᵘ c24gᵖᵘ Feb 22] strong, good-topped ex-Irish gelding: won 2 points in **h–**
Britain in 2002: no form over hurdles or on steeplechase debut (reportedly bled from
nose): blinkered last 2 starts: has had tongue tied: sold 3,100 gns Doncaster May Sales.
M. W. Easterby

NATIVE EIRE (IRE) 9 b.g. Be My Native (USA) – Ballyline Dancer (Giolla Mear) **c71**
[2002/3 c–, h92: c20g c20gᵇᵈ c20g³ Apr 26] tall, angular gelding: winning hurdler: poor **h–**
novice chaser: stays 21f: raced on good going or softer (acts on soft). *N. Wilson*

NATIVE EMPEROR 7 br.g. Be My Native (USA) – Fiona's Blue (Crash Course) **h147**
[2002/3 h130p: 25d* 24g² 25v³ 24gᵖᵘ Mar 13] tall, useful-looking gelding: will make a
chaser: smart hurdler: won listed handicap at Cheltenham in November by 1¼ lengths
from Yeoman's Point: improved again when 5 lengths second to Bacchanal in Grade 2 at
Newbury: lacklustre effort in Stayers' Hurdle at Cheltenham final outing: will stay
beyond 25f: raced on good going or softer (acts on heavy): patiently ridden. *Jonjo O'Neill*

NATIVE ESTATES (IRE) 11 b.g. Be My Native (USA) – Sesetta (Lucky Brief) **c–**
[2002/3 c–, h125: 24s⁴ 24s³ Jan 12] angular gelding: winning chaser: fairly useful **h126**
handicap hurdler: creditable efforts in big fields both outings in 2002/3, off 8 months in

between: effective at 2½m to 3¼m: acts on good to firm and heavy going: blinkered once.
N. Meade, Ireland

NATIVE FIELD (IRE) 14 b.g. Be My Native (USA) – Broomfield Ceili (North-   h86 §
fields (USA)) [2002/3 h84§: 27m² 21gᵖᵘ May 30] leggy gelding: modest hurdler: reportedly lame final start: stays 27f: acts on heavy going: tried blinkered: lazy. *D. J. Wintle*

NATIVE FLING (IRE) 11 b.g. Be My Native (USA) – Queens Romance (Imperial   c115
Fling (USA)) [2002/3 c119, h–: c20gᵖᵘ c17d³ c20g c16d⁶ c16v* c19g³ c20m⁴ c21g⁴ Apr   h–
21] angular gelding: winning hurdler: fairly useful handicap chaser: won at Chepstow in
January: best form short of 2½m: acts on good to firm and heavy going: tried blinkered,
often visored nowadays: of suspect temperament nowadays. *P. J. Hobbs*

NATIVE FOX 8 br.m. Be My Native (USA) – Leinthall Fox (Deep Run) [2002/3 h90:   h92
20m³ 19m² 19g* Jun 12] modest hurdler, off over 10 months before reappearance: won
novice at Hereford: possibly best up to 2½m: acts on good to firm going (won bumper on
good to soft). *J. L. Needham*

NATIVE GLEN (IRE) 9 b.g. Be My Native (USA) – The Gargle Monster (Furry   c–
Glen) [2002/3 c–, h–: c16dᵘʳ Mar 4] tall gelding: winning 2m hurdler: no form for long   h–
time, including over fences/in points: tongue tied. *S. Lloyd*

NATIVE HEATHER (IRE) 10 b.m. Be My Native (USA) – Pisa (IRE) (Carlingford   h–
Castle) [2002/3 16vᵖᵘ 20gᵖᵘ Apr 14] workmanlike ex-Irish mare: winning pointer:
modest in bumpers: no encouragement over hurdles: has had tongue tied. *N. Wilson*

NATIVE JACK (IRE) 9 br.g. Be My Native (USA) – Dorrha Daisy (Buckskin (FR))   c128
[2002/3 h126: c16v² 20s² c20s* c20s⁵ c24g* c29gᶠ Apr 21] tall, lengthy gelding: fairly   h119
useful hurdler: of similar level over fences, won maiden at Punchestown (most fortunate)
in February and handicap at Cork (by ¾ length from The Dell) in March: effective at 2m
to 3m: acts on heavy going. *A. L. T. Moore, Ireland*

NATIVE LADY 7 b.m. Distinct Native – Ladyville (Lord Nelson (FR)) [2002/3 21gᵖᵘ   c–
c25gᵖᵘ Apr 14] ninth foal: dam ran 4 times: pulled up in novice hurdle (flashed tail   h–
repeatedly)/chase. *F. P. Murtagh*

NATIVE LEGEND (IRE) 8 b.g. Be My Native (USA) – Tickhill (General Assembly   h99
(USA)) [2002/3 24dᶠ 20d² 24v* Jan 2] leggy, angular gelding: modest handicap hurdler:
improved in 2002/3 after 2-year absence, won at Ayr by 2 lengths from Savannah Mo
with something in hand: stays 3m: yet to race on firm going, acts on any other. *Ferdy
Murphy*

NATIVE MAN (IRE) 9 b.g. Be My Native (USA) – Try Your Case (Proverb) [2002/3   c–
c118, h–: c24s c23s c24gᵖᵘ c24mᵖᵘ Mar 18] rather sparely-made gelding: fairly useful   h–
chaser in 2001/2: badly out of sorts on return: stays 3m: acts on soft and good to firm
going: has broken blood vessel: usually tongue tied nowadays. *Jonjo O'Neill*

NATIVE NEW YORKER (IRE) 8 b.g. Be My Native (USA) – Sunbath (Krayyan)   h130
[2002/3 h99p: 18mᶠ 19m* 20sᶠ 16d 17s* 17gᵖᵘ Mar 13] rangy gelding: useful handicap
hurdler: much improved, successful at Stratford in October and, after shaping well on
previous start, Cheltenham in January: beat Benbyas by 7 lengths at latter, smooth headway to lead between last 2: pulled up reportedly lame final outing: should stay 2½m: acts
on soft and good to firm going: has had 2 handlers in paddock. *R. Rowe*

NATIVE PEACH (IRE) 8 ch.g. Be My Native (USA) – Larry's Peach (Laurence   c–
O) [2002/3 h100: c24g⁵ Mar 25] medium-sized gelding: fair hurdler, lightly raced: little   h–
encouragement on chase debut (mistakes early) after 12-month absence: will stay beyond
25f: acts on good to firm and good to soft going. *J. A. B. Old*

NATIVE PERFORMANCE (IRE) 8 b.g. Be My Native (USA) – Noon Perform-   c107
ance (Strong Gale) [2002/3 c20d⁵ c21s⁶ c20s c22d⁶ c22m³ c22m² c24f³ c24d⁶ Nov 15]   h–
tall, useful-looking gelding: fifth foal: dam unraced sister to fairly useful jumpers up to
3m Executive Options and Festival Dreams: maiden hurdler: fair chaser, won novice at
Downpatrick and handicap at Cork in 2001/2: generally creditable efforts in handicaps
in 2002/3: effective around 2½m to easy 3m: acts on firm and soft ground: consistent.
Michael Hourigan, Ireland

NATIVE SCOUT (IRE) 7 b.g. Be My Native (USA) – Carmels Castle (Deep Run)   c138
[2002/3 h136, F95: c16s* c16vᶠ c20vᵖᵘ c16v* c17s² c16g Mar 13] close-coupled gelding: h–
useful hurdler: similar level over fences: successful in maiden at Wexford in October and
6-runner novice at Uttoxeter in December: ran well last 2 starts when second, rallying
splendidly, to Bust Out in Grade 1 novice at Leopardstown and seventh to Palarshan in

valuable handicap at Cheltenham (hampered 3 out): should stay 2½m: raced on good going or softer (acts on heavy): usually tongue tied: consistent. *D. Hassett, Ireland*

NATIVE SESSIONS (IRE)   8 b.g. Be My Native (USA) – Weekly Sessions (Buckskin (FR)) [2002/3 h110: 20s* c22v* c20v^{pu} c20s^3 c24v^4 c24v^4 c24d^3 c21v^4 c24v* Mar 8] good sort: fairly useful hurdler, won minor event at Tipperary in May: useful chaser: won at Galway (maiden) in October and Navan in March: beat The Premier Cat by distance in 3-finisher novice handicap at latter: stays 3m: acts well on soft/heavy going (poor effort on good in valuable novice handicap at Punchestown in late-April): tongue tied last 2 starts. *N. Meade, Ireland*   **c129 h119**

NATIVE SPARKLE (IRE)   6 br.m. Be My Native (USA) – Star With A Glimmer (IRE) (Montekin) [2002/3 24d^F 22d^{ur} 20s^2 F19s* 20d^2 20d* 20d* 18d^5 24d 20v^F 16s* 20s^3 16v 18s^6 20d^6 21g 22d^5 20g^{pu} Apr 20] smallish, lengthy, angular mare: sixth foal: sister to fair hurdler Bardon Hill Boy, stays 2¾m, and half-sister to fairly useful chaser Star To The North (by Distinctly North), stayed 25f: dam never ran: dual bumper winner, including at Kilbeggan in June: fairly useful hurdler: won maiden at Killarney in July, novice at Galway in August and Grade 3 novice at Navan (made all) in November: generally well below best afterwards: possibly best up to 2½m: acts on soft going: has had tongue tied. *T. Hogan, Ireland*   **h117 F98**

NATIVE SPEAKER (IRE)   10 ch.g. Be My Native (USA) – My Wonder (Deep Run) [2002/3 c113, h–: c20d^3 Nov 9] rangy, useful-looking gelding: fair handicap chaser, very lightly raced: creditable third to Lord Moose at Sandown on only 2002/3 outing, went rather in snatches: probably best around 2½m: acts on soft going: often races prominently. *P. R. Webber*   **c113 h–**

NATIVE STAR (IRE)   5 b.g. Be My Native (USA) – Star Chamber (FR) (Tower Walk) [2002/3 F17d^4 F16g^6 F16m* Apr 12] leggy, angular gelding: fifth foal: dam, useful 1m winner, half-sister to useful 2m hurdler Freight Forwarder: improved effort in bumpers when winning 7-runner event at Ayr by neck from Noblefir. *P. J. Hobbs*   **F94**

NATIVE TASH (IRE)   7 b.g. Be My Native (USA) – Pallastown Gale (IRE) (Strong Gale) [2002/3 16v 18m^{ur} 20m 17d Aug 26] sturdy gelding: first foal: dam placed once over hurdles: poor maiden hurdler: tongue tied, no form in 2002/3: stays 2½m: acts on good to firm and good to soft ground. *Gerard McArdle, Ireland*   **h–**

NATIVETRIAL (IRE)   8 ch.g. Be My Native (USA) – Protrial (Proverb) [2002/3 c26d^4 c26d^2 c33v* c26v* c26v^2 c26d^{pu} Feb 24] sturdy ex-Irish gelding: third foal: dam winning pointer: modest hurdler: sold out of M. Morris' stable 22,000 gns Doncaster May (2001) Sales: fair handicap chaser: improved form after 18-month absence, won at Market Rasen (only one of 11 to complete) in December and Fontwell (beat New Rising 5 lengths) in January: never travelling or jumping with any fluency final outing: stays 33f: raced mainly on going softer than good (acts well on heavy): tried blinkered/tongue tied. *C. J. Mann*   **c108 h–**

NATIVE UPMANSHIP (IRE)   10 ch.g. Be My Native (USA) – Hi' Upham (Deep Run) [2002/3 c171, h–: c16s^2 c20s* c24s^5 c20s* c16g^2 c20d* Apr 4]   **c171 h–**

'I cannot remember a meeting when there was so much interest in all twenty races. Every one was of the highest quality and I thought the whole thing was exceptional on the racecourse. We have had some good meetings in the past, but I can't remember so many good horses winning in such style. It was just fabulous.' That summary of the latest Cheltenham Festival by Edward Gillespie, the racecourse's managing director, would be echoed by most followers of jumping. Which begs the question: if everything in the garden is rosy why meddle with it? The Cheltenham Festival provided a feast of racing and was a sell-out on all three days. But the meeting is set to become a victim of its own success following the decision of the Cheltenham board, sanctioned by the National Hunt Pattern Committee, to extend the fixture by another day from 2005. Cheltenham plays a crucial role within the Racecourse Holdings Trust group of tracks and it is estimated that a fourth day at the Festival, assuming a capacity 50,000 crowd, could increase profits by between £1.5m to £2m. Cheltenham has been addressing the operational issues for some time, including widening the racing surface to provide fresh ground for another day's racing on the inside of the New course, which is currently used only on Gold Cup day. The only decision that remains, seemingly, is the final composition of the programme, the Cheltenham executive having been asked to work

John Durkan Memorial Punchestown Chase—a second win in the race for Native Upmanship

towards four six-race cards with the Gold Cup moving to the Friday, and the Stayers' Hurdle becoming Thursday's principal feature.

Timeform is against the expansion of the Festival because the current overall quality of the racing at the meeting is unlikely to be maintained. From a purist's angle, there is simply no reason to add another day. However, commercial arguments always looked likely to prove decisive and, as part of Cheltenham's 'sounding out' of opinion, Timeform submitted a paper in October suggesting a programme that might minimize the inevitable watering down. Most of the existing races were left where regular racegoers and punters would expect them to be. The addition of a valuable two-mile handicap for juveniles, staged as a Final following a series of qualifiers at RHT courses, would provide much needed encouragement for owners to send more three-year-olds hurdling in preference to pursuing a winter Flat campaign on the all-weather; as it is, plans to build several new all-weather tracks and stage better racing on them may well lead to fewer juvenile hurdlers. Juveniles were to have a further opportunity in a new open conditions hurdle, along the lines of the current Cathcart for chasers, for four-year-olds and upwards over two and a half miles, though this event would probably take some runners from both the Champion Hurdle and the Stayers' Hurdle. Timeform believes there is some scope for introducing two novice handicaps at up to two and a half miles, one over hurdles and one over fences, without detracting too much from existing events at the Festival or elsewhere.

Three of these suggested events look likely to be in Cheltenham's final make-up, the novice handicap hurdle being created by switching the EBF Novices' Handicap Final from Sandown (though originally staged at Cheltenham's April meeting) and boosting its prize money. A two-and-a-half-mile novices chase—though not necessarily a handicap—is a possibility too, while the two-mile juvenile handicap hurdle, thought unlikely to be part of a series, looks a near-certainty. Cheltenham's choice for their fourth new race appears to be a cross-country chase, a weak betting event which would draw on a relatively small pool of mostly modest performers and, in our view, would be the crowning insult to those who have reservations about jumping's premier meeting becoming four days.

Timeform's suggested timetable also created opportunities for more of the better horses to run twice at the Festival and a large bonus was proposed for any horse winning two races over the four days. The only two horses to win twice at the same Cheltenham Festival are Solfen (winner of the Broadway Chase and the Spa

Martell Cognac Melling Chase, Aintree—
much easier than in 2002 as Native Upmanship gains a cheeky win over Seebald

Hurdle in 1960) and Inkslinger (Two-Mile Champion Chase and Cathcart in 1973). But there are more examples of the feat being attempted, including by Flyingbolt who won the Champion Chase and finished third in the Champion Hurdle on consecutive days in 1966. The 1980 Champion Chase winner, the subsequently disqualified Chinrullah, finished fifth in the Gold Cup day after, while the 1985 Arkle winner Boreen Prince went on to finish sixth in the Gold Cup. More recent examples are: My Young Man, who followed up his win in the 1992 Grand Annual with a third in the Cathcart; Or Royal, winner of the Arkle and third in the Cathcart in 1997; and Generosa, successful in the Stakis Casinos (now Pertemps) Final before coming third in the following day's Coral Cup in 1999. Sound Reveille won the 1995 Grand Annual after being pulled up after a bad mistake in the Arkle two days earlier. Also worthy of mention, though they didn't involve victories, are: Trapper John's second (subsequently disqualified) in the Stayers' Hurdle of 1992 which was followed by a creditable tenth, conceding lumps of weight all round, in the next day's Coral Golden Hurdle Final; Mysilv's sixth in the Champion Hurdle and second in the Stayers' in 1996; and Pridwell's double stints in 1994 (second in the Supreme Novices' and seventh in the Triumph) and 1997 (seventh in the Champion Hurdle and eighth in the Stayers'). There are sure to be even more examples when the Festival is expanded, and a bonus would attract publicity as well as providing another incentive. An earlier idea, discussed in *Chasers & Hurdlers 1996/97*, to amalgamate the Kim Muir and the National Hunt Handicap, which cater for the same type of horses, could create an opportunity for the Festival to stage a really valuable open handicap chase over four miles. Seasoned, out-and-out staying handicap chasers have no suitable Festival target at present, though such a race would obviously clash with the Midlands National at Uttoxeter and would clearly be to the detriment of it.

Debate about possible new races continued in the aftermath of the latest Cheltenham Festival when there was growing support for an event that had not appeared in Cheltenham's 'final' short-list of six published in mid-February (those already mentioned plus a mares' bumper and a three-mile conditions novices' hurdle). Cheltenham, it seems, is now considering staging a championship chase over two and a half miles in place of the Cathcart Chase, for which only novices and second-season chasers are eligible. Apart from coming close to the established Grade 1 Melling Chase over the same trip at Aintree, the new race would probably take runners from both the Queen Mother Champion Chase and the Gold Cup at the Cheltenham Festival. The failure to establish either the Newton Chase at Haydock or the Ascot Chase as genuine Grade 1 contests suggests there is a very limited pool of horses for such a race. Nevertheless, the focus was brought by the performances of Irish-trained Native Upmanship who, for the second year running, showed enough speed to come second in the Queen Mother Champion Chase at Cheltenham, over a trip short of his ideal, before winning his second successive Melling Chase. Native Upmanship has won at two miles and has shown at least high-class form from that distance right up to twenty-five furlongs (placed in successive editions of the Punchestown Gold Cup, the latest shortly after the end of the British season). But he has never won at much beyond two and a half miles. Native Upmanship has won eleven times over fences, all except two of those victories coming at around two and a half miles, over which trip he has been beaten only once in eleven outings in the course of his career (including a victory on his only start over two and a half in his hurdling days).

Native Upmanship's only defeat over two and a half miles came in the John Durkan Memorial Punchestown Chase in December 2001 when he went down by a short head to Florida Pearl. Native Upmanship has won the Punchestown Chase

Mrs John Magnier's "Native Upmanship"

in the years either side of the defeat, in the latest season quickening impressively, after jumping fluently throughout, to win from Rince Ri and First Gold. Native Upmanship was the beaten favourite in the Royal & SunAlliance Chase at the 2001 Cheltenham Festival, though his jumping let him down that day and a lack of stamina was not put forward at the time as a contributory factor. Native Upmanship's only other outing in Britain over a trip beyond two and a half miles came in the latest King George VI Chase at Kempton. The race proved too much a test of stamina for Native Upmanship in the gruelling conditions and he finished a well-beaten fifth. He was set to be entered in both the Queen Mother Champion Chase and the Gold Cup at the Cheltenham Festival (he wasn't eligible for the Cathcart), connections indicating that the state of the going could decide his target ('soft ground is a help to him over two miles, but not over the Gold Cup distance'). But, in the end, no entry was made for the Gold Cup and Native Upmanship was warmed up for the Champion Chase, as in the previous year, in the Kinloch Brae Chase over two and a half at Thurles at the end of January, when he had little trouble disposing of Arctic Copper and company. The going was good at Cheltenham and the consistent Native Upmanship ran his usual honest race, staying on but lacking the speed to trouble Moscow Flyer who beat him by seven lengths. The race illustrated that Native Upmanship ideally needs further than two miles to show his best form unless conditions are fairly testing.

Moscow Flyer didn't run at Aintree but four others who contested the Queen Mother Champion Chase were in the line-up for the Martell Cognac Melling Chase which was run on good to soft going. Starting 5/4 favourite, Native Upmanship looked really well in the paddock (he doesn't always take the eye and hadn't impressed in appearance at Cheltenham). Always going well and cruising into contention before leading on the bridle before the last, Native Upmanship won with his rider barely having to move a muscle. Seebald might have finished second to Moscow Flyer at Cheltenham had he not fallen two out, but Native Upmanship beat him really impressively at Aintree, the winning margin of a length considerably undervaluing his supremacy on the day. Third-placed Kadarann, a doubtful stayer, finished eighteen lengths further back with Cheltenham third Cenkos, another best at two miles, filling fourth. The presence of two doubtful stayers in the frame further indicates there is no necessity for another championship race over two and a half miles.

			Our Native		Exclusive Native
	Be My Native (USA)		(b or br 1970)		Our Jackie
	(br 1979)		Witchy Woman		Strate Stuff
Native Upmanship (IRE)			(ch 1972)		Witchy Norma
(ch.g. 1993)			Deep Run		Pampered King
	Hi' Upham		(ch 1966)		Trial By Fire
	(ch 1982)		Highly Acceptable		Immortality
			(ch 1964)		Token Gift

The tall Native Upmanship, who shows traces of stringhalt, is out of the modest maiden hurdler/chaser Hi' Upham, a close relative of Time For A Run, who was by Deep Run out of a half-sister to Hi' Upham. Time For A Run was a smart hurdler and useful chaser who was effective at around two and a half miles (won the Coral Cup) and stayed twenty-five furlongs. Hi' Upham is also a half-sister to another smart hurdler, the Sweeps Hurdle and Supreme Novices' Hurdle runner-up Glassilaun, who also won four races over fences but never became so good as he was over hurdles. Hi'Upham was also represented on the racecourse in the latest season by Native Upmanship's younger brother the maiden Dans Dealer (pulled up on his debut over fences and not seen out again) and by Tighten Your Belt (by Phardante), a successful ex-Irish pointer who won a bumper at Stratford and finished third in the Grade 2 bumper at Aintree. The versatile and reliable Native Upmanship acts on good to firm and heavy going and is usually held up. *A. L. T. Moore, Ireland*

NATURAL (IRE) 6 b.g. Bigstone (IRE) – You Make Me Real (USA) (Give Me **h92 d** Strength (USA)) [2002/3 h83: 17g² 17s* 17dᶠ 17s² 16d 16v 20g 20dᵖᵘ Apr 25] good-topped gelding: modest hurdler: won weak conditional jockeys novice handicap at Bangor in October: subsequently lost his form: should stay beyond 2m: acts on soft going: visored on debut: has looked less than keen. *F. P. Murtagh*

NAUGHTY DANDY (IRE)   10 gr.g. Celio Rufo – Annie Will Run (Deep Run) **c66**
[2002/3 c64, h65: c19d⁵ 23d c25g⁴ 24m Jul 7] workmanlike gelding: poor maiden **h–**
jumper: stays 25f: acts on good to firm and good to soft going, no form on soft/heavy: in
frame in points in 2003. *N. A. Twiston-Davies*

NAUNTON DOWNS   9 b.g. Teenoso (USA) – Kitty Come Home (Monsanto (FR)) **h–**
[2002/3 h–: 20gᵖᵘ 22m⁶ 20vᵖᵘ 20s Dec 7] lengthy, angular gelding: no form over hurdles
since debut in 2000: tried blinkered. *R. J. Smith*

NAUTICAL   5 ch. or gr.h. Lion Cavern (USA) – Russian Royal (USA) (Nureyev **h86**
(USA)) [2002/3 16dᵘ 16m 16m³ Apr 22] leggy, angular horse: fair on Flat (stays 1¼m),
successful 3 times in UAE at 4 yrs, sold out of E. Charpy's stable 30,000 gns Newmarket
July Sales: better completed start over hurdles when third of 16 in maiden at Chepstow,
not knocked about. *M. C. Pipe*

NAUTICAL STAR   8 b.g. Slip Anchor – Comic Talent (Pharly (FR)) [2002/3 h75: **h–**
18s 17s 20dᵖᵘ Dec 9] smallish gelding: poor on Flat (stays 2m): winning hurdler, no show
in 2002/3: should stay beyond 2m. *A. C. Whillans*

NAVALE (FR)   4 gr.f. Baryshnikov (AUS) – Nabita (FR) (Akarad (FR)) [2002/3 16d³ **h110**
17s⁴ 16d² 17d² 21m⁴ 17m⁵ Apr 16] angular filly: half-sister to 3 winning jumpers, including high-class chaser Nakir (by Nikos), barely stayed 2½m, and fair 2m hurdler Nawar
(by Kahyasi): fair maiden on Flat (stays 1½m) for J. Gosden: similar form when
runner-up in juvenile hurdles at Kempton and Hereford (handicap): should be suited by
2½m: possibly unsuited by good to firm ground: visored final outing. *A. King*

NAVAN PROJECT (IRE)   9 gr.g. Project Manager – Just Possible (Kalaglow) **c–**
[2002/3 c16d⁶ Jun 4] small gelding: poor 2m hurdler: well held in novice chase after **h–**
16-month lay-off. *A. R. Dicken*

NAVARONE   9 b.g. Gunner B – Anamasi (Idiot's Delight) [2002/3 c102, h–: c20m⁴ **c122**
c21g² c20d² c22g* c24dᵖᵘ c24m* c24g* Apr 25] tall gelding: fairly useful handicap **h–**
chaser: won at Newbury in December (left N. Twiston-Davies after next start) and
Bangor and Perth in April, improved form when beating Mr Baxter Basics 5 lengths in
quite valuable event at last-named: stays 3m: acts on good to firm and good to soft going:
has had tongue tied: usually bold-jumping front runner. *Ian Williams*

NAVARRE SAMSON (FR)   8 b. or br.g. Ganges (USA) – L'Eternite (FR) (Cariellor **h97**
(FR)) [2002/3 h99: 19d² 22m⁴ 22m² 26m* 22d² Sep 4] leggy gelding: modest hurdler:
won seller at Southwell in August: stays 3¼m: acts on firm and soft going: tried blinkered: tongue tied: carries head awkwardly: not easiest of rides. *P. J. Hobbs*

Press & Journal Handicap Chase, Perth—
Navarone confirms himself an improved performer for his new stable

NAWAMEES (IRE) 5 b.h. Darshaan – Truly Generous (IRE) (Generous (IRE)) **h117**
[2002/3 20d⁵ 16s⁴ 16m³ Mar 22] leggy horse: fairly useful on Flat (stays 12.5f), sold out
of J. Hammond's stable 40,000 gns Newmarket Autumn Sales: easily best effort over
hurdles (reportedly choked on debut) when third of 13 to Pepe Galvez in novice at
Newbury: sure to win a race. *G. L. Moore*

NDR'S CASH FOR FUN 10 b.g. Ballacashtal (CAN) – Basic Fun (Teenoso (USA)) **h–**
[2002/3 h70: 17s 24v 16v 19sᶠ 25s Mar 10] workmanlike gelding: poor hurdler, no show
in 2002/3: stays 3m: acts on heavy going, on good to firm. *A. W. Carroll*

NEARLY A GIMME (IRE) 7 gr.g. Roselier (FR) – Cosmicechoexpress (Deep Run) **h90**
[2002/3 24d 22v⁵ 24s⁴ 25g⁴ 24s 24g⁵ Jan 17] IR 17,500 4-y-o: ex-Irish gelding: second
foal: dam, maiden hurdler, half-sister to useful chaser up to 3m Tremallt: modest
handicap hurdler: won at Clonmel in 2001/2: stays 3m: raced on good going or softer
(acts on heavy): joined J. O'Neill. *C. F. Swan, Ireland*

NEARLY A MOOSE (IRE) 7 b.g. Supreme Leader – Miss Tarbow (Tarqogan) **c120**
[2002/3 c17sᶠ c16s⁵ c18s³ c20s* c24v³ c21v c18s⁶ c16v² c20g Mar 30] IR 7,000 4-y-o: **h–**
compact gelding: tenth foal: half-brother to fair hurdler Haveityourway (by Glacial
Storm), stays 2½m, and a winning pointer by Carlingford Castle: dam, maiden hurdler,
out of half-sister to useful staying chaser Rainbow Valley: winning hurdler: fairly useful
novice chaser: won maiden at Punchestown in December: good efforts after when placed,
including in Grade 3 at Punchestown in late-April: effective at testing 2m to 3m: raced on
good going or softer (acts on heavy): effective tongue tied or not: none too consistent.
Patrick Mullins, Ireland

NEARLY A SCORE 11 b.m. Nearly A Hand – Boherash (Boreen (FR)) [2002/3 **c– x**
c91x, h–: 22g⁵ Jun 22] good-topped mare: maiden chaser, often let down by jumping: **h–**
lightly raced over hurdles: stays 3¼m: acts on heavy going. *J. D. Frost*

NEARLY NOBLE (IRE) 10 b.g. The Bart (USA) – Crofter's Law (Furry Glen) **c–**
[2002/3 c24m⁴ Jun 28] ex-Irish gelding: lightly raced: failed to complete both starts over **h–**
hurdles: fair pointer, successful in March and April: well beaten in novice company over
fences. *K. R. Pearce*

NED DIVINE 8 br.g. Primitive Rising (USA) – Coral Princess (Imperial Fling (USA)) **c–**
[2002/3 c20s³ c20vᵖᵘ Nov 28] big, angular gelding: no sign of ability, including in point. **h–**
Mrs L. B. Normile

NED KELLY (IRE) 7 ch.g. Be My Native (USA) – Silent Run (Deep Run) [2002/3 **h–**
h163: 20v³ Dec 1] big, strong gelding: chasing type: high-class hurdler, successful 3
times in 2001/2, notably in Grade 1 AIG Europe Champion Hurdle at Leopardstown:
looked in need of race when distant third of 5 in Grade 1 at Fairyhouse (finished lame)
only outing in 2002/3: likely to prove best at 2m: acts on good to firm and heavy going:
reportedly bled once in 2001/2. *E. J. O'Grady, Ireland*

NEEDWOOD LEGEND 10 b. or br.g. Rolfe (USA) – Enchanting Kate (Enchant- **c–**
ment) [2002/3 c–, h–: 16g⁶ May 30] close-coupled gelding: poor maiden hurdler: no **h–**
form over fences: best at 2m: acts on firm going: tried visored/blinkered/tongue tied.
A. J. Wilson

NEEDWOOD LION 10 b.g. Rolfe (USA) – Arctic Lion (Arctic Slave) [2002/3 c103, **c120**
h95: c20s⁶ c19s⁴ c19d* c19s² c20s* c16v³ c20v⁴ c20m c21g³ Mar 14] well-made gelding: **h–**
winning hurdler: fairly useful handicap chaser: back to somewhere near best in 2002/3,
made all at Hereford and Kempton (beat Another Raleagh 8 lengths) in December: stays
21f: acts on heavy going, seemingly not on good to firm: free-going sort who usually
forces pace: sometimes makes mistakes. *Miss Venetia Williams*

NEEDWOOD MERLIN 7 b.g. Sizzling Melody – Enchanting Kate (Enchantment) **h–**
[2002/3 21mᵖᵘ 24dᵖᵘ Aug 4] modest maiden on Flat (should stay 1m) at 3 yrs for
B. Morgan, well beaten both starts in 2002: showed nothing in 2 novice hurdles.
K. W. Hogg, Isle of Man

NEEDWOOD MISSILE 7 b.g. Sizzling Melody – Sea Dart (Air Trooper) [2002/3 **h–**
F74: 16g Aug 26] lightly raced and little sign of ability. *J. L. Spearing*

NEEDWOOD SPIRIT 8 b.g. Rolfe (USA) – Needwood Nymph (Bold Owl) [2002/3 **h99**
h97: 17d⁴ 17s⁶ 16d² 16d Jan 25] close-coupled gelding: modest handicap hurdler:
effective around 2m, should stay beyond 2½m: acts on soft going. *A. M. Naughton*

NEGRESKO (FR) 4 gr.g. Great Palm (USA) – Negra (FR) (Tropular) [2002/3 15s **c?**
17sᵖᵘ 15g³ 16g* 16d* 15s* 17g* 17s* c17s³ 16d⁵ 20g⁵ 17m³ Apr 16] angular ex-French **h113**
gelding: first foal: dam 17f hurdle/chase winner, also successful on Flat: maiden on Flat:

fairly useful juvenile hurdler: successful at Divonne-Les-Bains (twice), Lyon Villeur-banne, Marseille Borely and Lyon Parilly between July and October: third of 7 in 3-y-o event at Lyon Parilly on chasing debut, final start for G. Blasco: easily best effort over hurdles in Britain when third to Indien Royal in novice at Cheltenham final start: raced mainly around 2m: acts on soft and good to firm going: effective with/without blinkers, also tried visored: has shown signs of temperament. *M. C. Pipe*

NEILSTONESIDE (IRE)   5 b.m. General Monash (USA) – Lady Counsel (IRE) **h–**
(Law Society (USA)) [2002/3 h–, F–: 21g^{pu} May 30] little sign of ability: tried visored/tongue tied. *M. J. Ryan*

NELLY MOSER   6 gr.m. Neltino – Boreen's Glory (Boreen (FR)) [2002/3 F82:   **F76**
F18m^4 F17g Mar 16] modest form at best in bumpers: sold out of Mrs D. Haine's stable 5,600 gns Doncaster August Sales after reappearance. *Mrs A. J. Hamilton-Fairley*

NELTINA   7 gr.m. Neltino – Mimizan (IRE) (Pennine Walk) [2002/3 F18m^2 F16m*   **h103**
F16m^4 F16m* 16d^4 18s^2 20g* Mar 25] workmanlike mare: should make a chaser: first   **F97**
foal: dam winning pointer: fairly useful form in bumpers, won at Stratford in July and Warwick in November: fair form over hurdles: first run for 3 months, won mares novice at Ascot in March by 9 lengths from Maiden Voyage: stays 2½m: takes strong hold. *Mrs J. E. Scrase*

NEMISTO   9 gr.g. Mystiko (USA) – Nemesia (Mill Reef (USA)) [2002/3 c99, h–:   **c–**
16m^4 16v^2 17s^2 20v^3 19d 17g^{pu} 24m^4 24m^6 Apr 15] good-topped gelding: modest maiden   **h101**
chaser: fair handicap hurdler: stays 21f: acts on good to firm and heavy going: effective tongue tied or not. *R. Lee*

NE M'OUBLIE PAS (FR)   7 b. or br.g. Shining Steel – Irish Lullaby (FR) (Prince   **c–**
Tenderfoot (USA)) [2002/3 c88, h–: c26f^{pu} Aug 13] useful-looking gelding: modest   **h–**
chaser: pulled up lame only outing in 2002/3: stays 3¼m: acts on any going: tried blinkered. *P. J. Hobbs*

NEPHITE (NZ)   9 b.g. Star Way – Te Akau Charmer (NZ) (Sir Tristram) [2002/3 c92,   **c98**
h–: 16m c16g^6 c17d^4 c21d^{pu} c17s^4 16v^3 c16v^5 c16s^2 c16d* c16m^6 c17g* Mar 29]   **h–**
workmanlike gelding: poor maiden hurdler: modest handicap chaser: made all at New-castle and Market Rasen in March: raced mainly around 2m: acts on heavy going, possibly unsuited by good to firm: usually wears cheekpieces: effective tongue tied or not: has carried head awkwardly under pressure: sound jumper. *R. C. Guest*

NEPTUNE   7 b.g. Dolphin Street (FR) – Seal Indigo (IRE) (Glenstal (USA)) [2002/3   **h75**
16g 16s 16g 17v^4 17g* Mar 18] lengthy gelding: poor on Flat (stays 2m): dropped in class, best effort over hurdles when winning novice seller at Exeter. *J. C. Fox*

NERINA PRINCESS (IRE)   4 b.f. Key of Luck (USA) – Finessing (Indian King   **h–**
(USA)) [2002/3 16m 16d^4 16g^{pu} Nov 23] small filly: poor form on Flat: signs of only a little ability over hurdles: sold to join K. Wingrove £600 Ascot December Sales. *J. S. Moore*

NERO'S PALACE   6 b.g. Emperor Jones (USA) – Sayulita (Habitat) [2002/3 h65, F75:   **h64**
20m^6 21m^5 24d^{pu} Aug 17] poor novice hurdler: should stay beyond 21f. *M. Todhunter*

NETHER ANOTHER   6 b.m. Another Sam – Poppy Kelly (Netherkelly) [2002/3   **h–**
F–: 16g^F 20d^{pu} 16s Nov 24] sturdy mare: no sign of ability. *M. J. Gingell*

NEUTRON (IRE)   6 ch.g. Nucleon (USA) – Balistic Princess (Lomond (USA))   **h121**
[2002/3 h112d: 16m* 16s^4 16d^2 21s^2 16m^F Feb 21] angular gelding: fairly useful handi-cap hurdler: won at Wincanton in October and December: good second to Protagonist at Kempton, though hung left under pressure: stays 21f: acts on soft and firm going: tried blinkered, effective visored or not: has looked difficult ride. *M. C. Pipe*

NEVA-AGREE   11 ch.g. St Columbus – Nee-Argee (Rymer) [2002/3 c–: c23d^{pu} Mar   **c–**
4] poor maiden chaser: stays 25f: acts on firm and good to soft going: blinkered. *Mrs P. J. Ikin*

NEVER CAN TELL   7 ch.g. Emarati (USA) – Farmer's Pet (Sharrood (USA))   **h82**
[2002/3 h83: 16s^5 17d^{pu} 19f^6 17f^2 Apr 3] workmanlike gelding: poor handicap hurdler: stays 19f: acts on firm and soft going: has worn cheekpieces: takes strong hold: has hung right: joined B. Leavy. *M. Mullineaux*

NEVER FORGET BOWIE   7 b.g. Superpower – Heldigvis (Hot Grove) [2002/3   **h–**
h–, F–: 16d 16m Jun 21] modest maiden on Flat (stays 9f): well beaten over hurdles: has been tongue tied. *R. Allan*

Sir Peter O'Sullevan's "Never"

NEVER (FR)   6 b.g. Vettori (IRE) – Neraida (USA) (Giboulee (CAN)) [2002/3 h126: 16g* 17d⁵ 17g 16g 19s* Apr 25] tall, sparely-made gelding: smart hurdler: won listed intermediate limited handicap at Newbury (Gerry Feilden, beat Jaboune 8 lengths) in November and minor event at Enghien (very easily) in April: good fifth to Rooster Booster in Grade 2 at Cheltenham in December: stays 19f: has won on heavy going, best efforts under less testing conditions. *F. Doumen, France*   **h146**

NEVER IN DEBT   11 ch.g. Nicholas Bill – Deep In Debt (Deep Run) [2002/3 c–, h–: 24g 22gᵖᵘ May 25] workmanlike gelding: winning hurdler/pointer: little form in steeplechases: tried visored. *E. R. Clough*   **c–**
h–

NEVER WONDER (IRE)   8 b.g. John French – Mistress Anna (Arapaho) [2002/3 c99, h–: c25gᵖᵘ c23g* c24s⁶ c24s c29g⁶ Mar 14] tall, useful-looking gelding: successful on second of 2 starts over hurdles: fair handicap chaser: off 5 months, form in 2002/3 only when winning at Exeter in October, jumping better than usual: stays 3¼m: raced on good going or softer (acts on soft): usually forces pace. *M. Bradstock*   **c103**
h–

NEW BIRD (GER)   8 b.g. Bluebird (USA) – Nouvelle Amour (GER) (Esclavo (FR)) [2002/3 c119, h–: c16mᵖᵘ c16g³ c16m⁵ c16m⁶ Apr 17] tall gelding: has had wind operation: fair handicap chaser: best form around 2m: acts on heavy and good to firm going: none too consistent. *Mrs H. Dalton*   **c107**
h–

NEWBY END (IRE)   9 br.g. Over The River (FR) – Comeallye (Kambalda) [2002/3 20dᵖᵘ c16v⁵ c22d² c24vᵖᵘ c25s³ c26s Feb 26] lengthy gelding: poor maiden hurdler/chaser: stays 25f: acts on soft going: blinkered once, visored last 2 starts: sold £3,000 Ascot April Sales.. *M. Madgwick*   **c74**
h–

NEW ERA (IRE)   9 b.g. Distinctly North (USA) – Vaguely Deesse (USA) (Vaguely Noble) [2002/3 c24v⁶ Mar 8] workmanlike gelding: fair chaser in 2000/1: weakened 3   **c–**
h–

out when last of 6 finishers in handicap at Sandown, only subsequent outing: stays 3m: acts on good to firm and heavy going: often races prominently. *B. De Haan*

NEWHALL (IRE) 5 b.m. Shernazar – Graffogue (IRE) (Red Sunset) [2002/3 h136: 16s 16s⁶ 16sᶠ 20v⁴ 16v² 16g⁶ 16m Apr 22] sturdy mare: fairly useful hurdler: best effort in 2002/3 when staying-on second to Korelo in Imperial Cup at Sandown in March: insufficient test of stamina last 2 starts: should stay 2½m: acts on heavy going. *F. Flood, Ireland* **h127**

NEW HORIZON (IRE) 5 b.g. General Monash (USA) – Gulf Craft (IRE) (Petorius) [2002/3 h75: 17d 16dᵖᵘ Oct 31] good-topped gelding: modest maiden on Flat (stays 1m) for J. Osborne: poor maiden hurdler: no show either start in 2002/3: tried blinkered: headstrong. *D. Brace* **h–**

NEWICK PARK 8 gr.g. Chilibang – Quilpee Mai (Pee Mai) [2002/3 c104, h–: c20d⁵ c21d³ c24s⁴ c21dᵖᵘ c18mᵖᵘ Mar 19] good-topped gelding: winning hurdler/chaser: badly out of sorts in 2002/3: stays 2½m: acts on heavy going: has worn cheekpieces. *D. M. Grissell* **c–** **h–**

NEWKIDONTHEBLOCK (IRE) 8 b.g. Be My Native (USA) – Jenny's Child (Crash Course) [2002/3 h73+: 20d² Jun 8] tall gelding: poor maiden hurdler: likely to stay beyond 21f: acts on good to firm and soft going. *J. R. Jenkins* **h70**

NEWLANDS GOLD (IRE) 4 ch.c. Goldmark (USA) – Persian Polly (Persian Bold) [2002/3 16s* 16v² 16v* 16s⁶ 17g Mar 13] good-topped colt: half-brother to winning hurdlers by Try My Best and Salmon Leap: thrice-raced maiden on Flat: fairly useful juvenile hurdler: won maiden at Navan in November and novice at Naas in January: creditable seventh of 27 to Spectroscope in Triumph Hurdle at Cheltenham in March: didn't look easy ride when running poorly at Punchestown in early May: acts on heavy going: usually blinkered. *M. J. P. O'Brien, Ireland* **h120**

NEW LEADER (IRE) 6 b.g. Supreme Leader – Two Spots (Deep Run) [2002/3 F17s F18s 21m 25g² 22m Apr 15] IR 18,000 3-y-o: fifth foal: half-brother to winning pointer by Lafontaine: dam, maiden, half-sister to top-class hurdler/chaser Danoli: form only when runner-up in novice hurdle at Warwick in March. *Mrs L. Richards* **h89** **F–**

NEW LEAF (IRE) 11 b.g. Brush Aside (USA) – Page of Gold (Goldhill) [2002/3 c–, h–: c24sᵖᵘ Feb 28] tall, good-bodied gelding: winning hurdler/chaser: first past post in point in 2002 (disqualified for taking wrong course): pulled up in hunter at Newbury in February: stays 25f: acts on good to soft going, probably on good to firm: blinkered once: not an easy ride. *J. S. Papworth* **c–** **h–**

NEWMILL (IRE) 5 br.g. Norwich – Lady Kas (Pollerton) [2002/3 F16m* Apr 22] €24,000 4-y-o: half-brother to 2 winning pointers and a bumper winner: dam, 2m hurdle winner, out of half-sister to top-class staying chaser The Dikler: won Goffs Land Rover Bumper at Fairyhouse on debut by 3½ lengths from Hardy Duckett, making most: useful prospect. *T. G. O'Leary, Ireland* **F103 p**

NEW MISCHIEF (IRE) 5 b.g. Accordion – Alone Party (IRE) (Phardante (FR)) [2002/3 F17v⁴ Nov 19] second foal: dam of little account: tongue tied, fourth of 9 in bumper at Newton Abbot on debut, carrying head shade awkwardly: sold 6,500 gns Doncaster May Sales. *Noel T. Chance* **F77**

NEW OPENINGS 4 b.c. Puissance – Moushka (Song) [2002/3 16gᵖᵘ Sep 12] 500 3-y-o: seventh foal: half-brother to several winners, including 1999 2-y-o 6f/7f winner Avezzano (by Most Welcome) and fairly useful 5f and 7f winner One Singer (by Anshan): dam unraced: soon struggling in juvenile maiden hurdle on debut. *I. W. McInnes* **h–**

NEW PERK (IRE) 5 b.g. Executive Perk – New Chello (IRE) (Orchestra) [2002/3 18g⁵ 20d⁵ 16s 18s² 16m⁶ Apr 19] 4,100 4-y-o: close-coupled gelding: first foal: dam, maiden pointer, half-sister to fairly useful chaser up to 25f Phar From A Fiddle, from family of very smart 2m chaser Wolf of Badenoch: poor novice hurdler: should stay beyond 2¼m: acts on soft going. *M. J. Gingell* **h81**

NEW RISING 11 b.g. Primitive Rising (USA) – Saucy (Saucy Kit) [2002/3 c95, h–: c23gᵖᵘ c25m³ c29d⁴ c26v² c26dᶠ c30sᵖᵘ Mar 4] strong, well-made gelding: modest handicap chaser: stays 29f: acts on heavy and good to firm going: once visored: unreliable. *P. Winkworth* **c92 §** **h–**

NEW ROSS (IRE) 11 gr.g. Roselier (FR) – Miss Lucille (Fine Blade (USA)) [2002/3 c26mᵖᵘ May 22] leggy gelding: poor pointer: successful in March and April: no form in steeplechases: tried blinkered/visored. *Mrs A. W. K. Merriam* **c–** **h–**

NEWRYMAN 8 ch.g. Statoblest – With Love (Be My Guest (USA)) [2002/3 c–, h–: c– 17m c17g⁶ 17gᵖᵘ 17m 16m⁵ Oct 4] lengthy gelding: of no account: has had tongue tied. h– *G. P. Kelly*

NEWS FLASH (IRE) 11 b.g. Strong Gale – Gale Flash (News Item) [2002/3 20g⁴ c76 24g⁵ 16m⁵ c19dꟳ c20dᵘʳ Nov 12] rangy gelding: poor maiden hurdler, lightly raced: h78 upsides winner when falling 3 out in selling handicap at Chepstow on chasing debut: stiff task and out of touch when unseating 3 out final start: stays 2½m: acts on good to soft going, probably on good to firm. *E. R. Clough*

NEWS MAKER (IRE) 7 b.g. Good Thyne (USA) – Announcement (Laurence O) c119 [2002/3 h99, F86: c24g² c24v* c26v² c23d* c26sᵖᵘ Mar 15] good-topped gelding: modest h– hurdler: fairly useful novice chaser: won at Haydock (handicap) in December and Wetherby (simple task) in March: pulled up early final outing: stays 3¼m: raced on good going or softer (acts on heavy): jumps soundly. *Mrs H. Dalton*

NEWSPLAYER (IRE) 7 br.g. Alphabatim (USA) – Another Tycoon (IRE) (Phar- h92 dante (FR)) [2002/3 F96: 16g⁵ 20d 16s 16d³ Mar 7] good sort: modest novice hurdler: caught eye on third start (jockey suspended): every chance when badly hampered 2 out final outing: likely to prove best around 2m. *R. T. Phillips*

NEWTON COMMANCHE (IRE) 6 b.m. Commanche Run – Ravens Way (Niels) h77 [2002/3 F80: 16m³ 20m⁴ Oct 24] sturdy mare: modest form in bumpers in 2001/2: better effort in novice hurdles when fourth in mares event at Haydock, appearing to lose action close home: stays 2½m. *K. C. Bailey*

NEWTOWN DANCER (IRE) 4 b.f. Danehill Dancer (IRE) – Patience of Angels h102 (IRE) (Distinctly North (USA)) [2002/3 16f² 16d* Nov 2] smallish, workmanlike filly: fair on Flat (stays 2¼m), successful in August: fair form both starts in juvenile hurdles, second to Lost In The Rain at Listowel and made all in Wensleydale Hurdle at Wetherby (beating Tunstall 2 lengths): will stay beyond 2m. *T. Hogan, Ireland*

NEWTOWNHEN (IRE) 8 b.m. Peacock (FR) – Cutty Sark (Strong Gale) [2002/3 c– c–: c25mᵖᵘ c20sᵖᵘ Oct 26] no form in novice chases: sold 2,400 gns Doncaster November Sales. *A. C. Whillans*

NEXT TO NOTHING (IRE) 6 b.g. Bob's Return (IRE) – Shuil Abhaile (Quayside) h– [2002/3 F17s⁵ 22gᵖᵘ Mar 21] IR 11,500 3-y-o: seventh foal: half-brother to winning F84 pointer by Roselier: dam unraced, from family of useful staying chaser Baronet and very smart staying hurdler Shuil Ar Aghaidh: some encouragement when fifth in bumper at Carlisle on debut, none when pulled up in novice hurdle at Kelso. *N. G. Richards*

NIAGARA (IRE) 6 b.g. Rainbows For Life (CAN) – Highbrook (USA) (Alphabatim h102 (USA)) [2002/3 h91p: 16m² 16dᵖᵘ 16g⁴ 17m Apr 16] medium-sized gelding: fair on Flat (seems to stay 13f): fair novice hurdler: raced around 2m: acts on good to firm going: reportedly distressed second start. *M. H. Tompkins*

NICE APPROACH (IRE) 10 ch.g. Over The River (FR) – Gayles Approach (Strong c– Gale) [2002/3 c82, h–: c21fᵖᵘ May 10] sturdy gelding: winning pointer: poor maiden h– steeplechaser: probably stays 2¾m: acts on heavy going: tried blinkered. *J. W. Dufosee*

NICELY PRESENTED (IRE) 6 b.g. Executive Perk – Minimum Choice (IRE) F91 (Miner's Lamp) [2002/3 F17d⁴ F17s³ F17s³ Jan 28] workmanlike gelding: fifth foal: half-brother to 19f hurdle winner Whether The Storm and 21f chase winner Tallow Bay (both by Glacial Storm): dam never ran: fair form when in frame in 3 bumpers. *Jonjo O'Neill*

NICE ONE TED (IRE) 7 b.g. Posen (USA) – Arburie (Exbury) [2002/3 F17m⁴ F16d h– F17s 19gᵖᵘ Apr 19] 1,650 3-y-o: lengthy gelding: tenth foal: half-brother to 2 winners on F69 Flat: dam, won around 13f, from family of Beef Or Salmon: poor form in bumpers: no show in maiden on hurdling debut. *Mrs Pippa Bickerton*

NICHOLAS PLANT 14 ch.g. Nicholas Bill – Bustilly (Busted) [2002/3 c76x, h56: c68 x c24d⁵ 27g⁴ c20d⁵ Jun 4] workmanlike gelding: poor hurdler/chaser nowadays: stays 29f: h66 acts on any going: blinkered once: poor jumper of fences. *J. S. Goldie*

NICHOL FIFTY 9 b.g. Old Vic – Jawaher (IRE) (Dancing Brave (USA)) [2002/3 h–: h77 21m³ 17d 21s⁵ Nov 21] angular gelding: modest on all-weather, poor on turf on Flat (stays 17f) nowadays: poor hurdler nowadays: should stay 2½m: acts on soft going: has had tongue tied. *N. Wilson*

NICHOLLS CROSS (IRE) 11 b.g. Mandalus – Milan Pride (Northern Guest c99 (USA)) [2002/3 c24mᵇᵈ c23s⁶ c24m⁵ c25s* c22m⁵ c25m c20d⁶ Mar 4] rangy ex-Irish h– gelding: winning hurdler: one-time useful chaser: modest nowadays: won handicap at

Kilbeggan in August: left E. O'Grady and off 6 months prior to well held in hunter final start: stays 25f: acts on any going: possibly none too genuine (has found little). *S. Wynne*

NICKEL SUNDANCER 7 b.g. Alflora (IRE) – Gunna Be Precious (Gunner B) **h69** [2002/3 h77?]: 19s 16v 25d⁵ 27g⁵ 20m⁶ Apr 19] poor maiden hurdler: probably stays 27f: acts on good to soft going. *Mrs S. J. Smith*

NICKEL SUN (IRE) 7 b.g. Phardante (FR) – Deep Green (Deep Run) [2002/3 h100, **h117** F94: 20m³ 20g* 22s 20d* 19d 20d⁴ 22f³ 21m³ Apr 16] sturdy gelding: fairly useful hurdler: won novice at Wetherby and handicap at Uttoxeter in May and quite valuable handicap at Haydock in December: stays 2¾m: acts on firm and good to soft going, won bumper on soft: has pulled hard: reliable. *Mrs S. J. Smith*

NICKEL SUNTOO (IRE) 6 b.g. Convinced – The Scarlet Dragon (Oats) [2002/3 **F88** F16d² F16g F16g Jan 18] IR £2,200 4-y-o: unfurnished gelding: third foal: dam of little account: second in bumper at Southwell on debut: disappointing in 2 similar events. *Mrs S. J. Smith*

NICKIT (IRE) 7 gr.g. Roselier (FR) – Run Trix (Deep Run) [2002/3 h–: c23d² c23vF **c75** c26s⁴ c22s³ c25sF 22g³ Mar 18] quite good-topped gelding: poor maiden hurdler/chaser: **h78** should stay beyond 23f: acts on soft going: blinkered final start: not a fluent jumper of fences. *Miss Venetia Williams*

NICKNAME (FR) 4 b.c. Lost World (IRE) – Newness (IRE) (Simply Great **h142** (FR)) [2002/3 15vª 17s* 17d³ 18v² 17v* 18s* 19v*] Apr 26]

There was no clear leader among the juvenile hurdlers in the British Isles, but, by contrast, one horse stood out among the same age-group in France. Nickname established himself there as the best of his generation over hurdles, winning six of his nine starts, culminating in the Group 1 Prix Alain du Breil, one of two outings which he had after the end of the season in Britain. Only four different horses finished ahead of him in the three races he lost, and he put the record straight by turning the tables on those same rivals in subsequent races.

Unraced on the Flat, Nickname's hurdling career began with a couple of wins at Auteuil, beating the future Paul Nicholls-trained Aintree winner Le Duc in a newcomers race and following up in a minor event later in May. Third in that minor event was Royaleety, meeting his first defeat in four starts over hurdles, but Nickname's early claims to being the top three-year-old hurdler at Auteuil took a knock when Royaleety won their next two encounters. In the first of those, Nickname was third in a minor event at June, and was then beaten four lengths into second in the Prix Cambaceres, the Group 1 three-year-old hurdle in November. Nickname's preparation for the latter race had not been ideal, as an injury in training had prevented him from having a prep race and he shaped as though in need of his first outing for nearly five months. The result could well have been different had Malcom (who had split Nickname and Royaleety in May) not fallen when holding a narrow lead at the last. Two weeks later, Nickname gained compensation on his only start away from Auteuil when winning the Group 3 Prix General de Saint-Didier at Enghien, showing a good turn of foot to come from last place and beat the Cambaceres fourth Sphinx du Berlais by three lengths.

It was April before Nickname was seen out again, in the Group 3 Prix de Pepinvast. Most of his rivals had the benefit of a more recent outing, as well as less weight, but Nickname showed he was still on the upgrade with a three-length defeat of Cheler who had been placed twice already in pattern company. The fact that Royaleety could finish only fifth this time suggested he might not have progressed since the autumn. Instead, the new challenge to Nickname in the spring came from the free-going filly Bulougun. She was only eighth in the Pepinvast, but got a lot closer when they met again in more testing conditions in the Group 2 Prix Amadou at the end of April, in which the confidently-ridden Nickname got the better of a sustained duel to win by a length. It was still a surprise though that Bulougun managed to come out on top in their third meeting in the Group 3 Prix de Longchamp in May. However, Nickname's jockey allowed the filly plenty of rope as she dictated in a small field, and Nickname was unable to respond when shaken up, eventually finishing only third. Despite the weights favouring Nickname a good deal more in the Prix Alain du Breil in June, it was Bulougun who shaded him for

Prix Alain du Breil-Course de Haies d'Ete des Quatre Ans, Auteuil—
Nickname gains his revenge on the hooded Bulougun

favouritism in Auteuil's top four-year-old hurdle of the first half of the year. The pair dominated the race, Bulougun setting the pace again, but Nickname was ridden in closer touch this time. At the last, a mistake from Bulougun allowed Nickname to jump to the front and he was soon well on top, going away to win by six lengths. The Prix de Longchamp runner-up Katoune was only third this time, with Cheler fourth.

By winning the Alain du Breil, Nickname was emulating his half-sister N'Avoue Jamais (by Marignan), winner of the race in 2000, while the following season their half-brother Nom d'Une Pipe (by Linamix) came third in the same contest. As well as these useful hurdlers (Nom d'Une Pipe has also won over fences), their excellent dam Newness has also produced the winning chasers Nagid (by Cadoudal) and Narkis (by Nickname's sire Lost World), the latter also successful over hurdles. Whereas Grand Criterium winner Lost World carried the familiar blue colours of the late Daniel Wildenstein, Newness, her offspring, and her own dam Neomenie all carried the green of Madame Wildenstein. Newness won once over hurdles and was near the top of her generation over fences, finishing third to Al Capone II in the top four-year-old chase, the Prix Maurice Gillois. Grandam Neomenie also won over both hurdles and fences and produced a couple more noteworthy jumpers besides Newness: Nile Prince was the winner of France's most prestigious handicap chase, the Prix du President de La Republique, while Nil Bleu, already a Group 3 winner on the Flat, also won the Prix de Pepinvast twelve years before Nickname.

Nickname (FR) (b.c. 1999)	Lost World (IRE) (b 1991)	Last Tycoon (b 1983)	Try My Best
			Mill Princess
		Last Tango (br 1973)	Luthier
			La Bamba
	Newness (IRE) (b 1988)	Simply Great (b 1979)	Mill Reef
			Seneca
		Neomenie (b 1978)	Rheffic
			Nordenberg

Still an entire, Nickname has the pedigree as well as the racing record to earn a place at stud in due course. That's not an unusual career move for the top juvenile hurdler in France, the previous season's holder of that title Saint des Saints having already begun stallion duties. There are clearly more races to be won with Nickname though, particularly as he'll be restricted to racing against fellow four-year-olds until the turn of the year. Raced only at up to nineteen furlongs so far, on ground softer than good, Nickname is a sound jumper who is held up and has a good turn of foot. *J-P. Gallorini, France*

NICK'S CHOICE   7 b.g. Sula Bula – Clare's Choice (Pragmatic) [2002/3 h109: 16v⁵   **h94**
16d 16v⁶ 22s 21g* Mar 16] compact gelding: modest handicap hurdler: best effort in
2002/3 when winning at Ludlow, tending to wander: stays 2¾m: acts on good to firm and
heavy going: tried blinkered: reportedly bled from nose second start: held up. *D. Burchell*

NICK THE JEWEL   8 b.g. Nicholas Bill – Bijou Georgie (Rhodomantade) [2002/3   **c105**
c80?, h–, F75: c19mᵖᵘ c16d* c16s* c16d* c16dᶠ c19sᵖᵘ c16g c16m³ Mar 23] tall, angular   **h–**
gelding: no form in novice hurdles: fair chaser: won handicaps at Ludlow and Hereford
(novices) in November and Huntingdon (conditional jockeys, hung right under pressure)
in December: bred to stay beyond 2m: acts on soft and good to firm going: reportedly
lame on reappearance: races prominently. *J. S. King*

NICODEMUS   9 br.g. St Ninian – Qurrat Al Ain (Wolver Hollow) [2002/3 c23gᵖᵘ   **c–**
24gᵖᵘ Sep 15] poor pointer. *K. F. Clutterbuck*   **h–**

NIGEL'S BOY   11 b.g. Bold Fort – Furnace Lass VII (Damsire Unregistered) [2002/3   **c88**
c25f² May 15] sturdy gelding: winning hurdler: fair pointer: creditable third in hunter at   **h–**
Exeter (later promoted on technical grounds) in May: should stay beyond 25f: acts on
firm and soft going. *Miss Victoria Scott*

NIGHT DIAMOND   6 b.g. Night Shift (USA) – Dashing Water (Dashing Blade)   **h–**
[2002/3 16fᵖᵘ 16m⁶ Oct 5] fair on Flat up to 1½m: showed little in 2 runs over hurdles,
visored and tongue tied on second occasion: sold 500 gns Doncaster November Sales.
M. C. Pipe

NIGHT DRIVER (IRE)   4 b.g. Night Shift (USA) – Highshaan (Pistolet Bleu (IRE))   **h93**
[2002/3 17s⁴ 16d⁴ Mar 6] fairly useful on all-weather, fair on turf on Flat (stays 1¼m),
sold out of B. Hills's stable 20,000 gns Newmarket Autumn Sales: fourth in maiden
hurdles at Taunton and Wincanton, better effort behind Limerick Boy at latter course.
P. J. Hobbs

NIGHT FIGHTER (GER)   8 b.g. Dashing Blade – Nouvelle (GER) (Nandino   **c102**
(GER)) [2002/3 h100: 20d³ 17m 17d* c20mᵖᵘ 16g² c17s³ c16d² c16g³ c16m* c20d⁴   **h107**
c20gᶠ c16m c16gᵘʳ Apr 24] sparely-made gelding: fair handicap hurdler, easily won at
Cartmel (finished lame) in August: fair chaser: easily won novice handicap at Doncaster
in February: probably better at 2m than 2½m: acts on firm and soft going: usually wears
cheekpieces: has had tongue tied. *R. C. Guest*

NIGHTGLADE (IRE)   7 b.g. Night Shift (USA) – Woodland Garden (Godswalk   **h–**
(USA)) [2002/3 16dᵖᵘ 16d 19mᵖᵘ Jul 7] half-brother to 1¾m bumper winner Rock Garden
(by Bigstone): of little account on Flat nowadays: showed little in 3 outings over hurdles,
tongue tied first 2. *B. W. Murray*

NIGHT MUSIC   6 br.m. Piccolo – Oribi (Top Ville) [2002/3 h63: 17sᶠ 19s³ 17fᵖᵘ 22g   **h67 ?**
Apr 19] poor maiden hurdler: stays 19f: acts on heavy going: has worn cheekpieces.
G. F. Edwards

NIJWAY   13 b.g. Nijin (USA) – Runaway Girl (FR) (Homeric) [2002/3 c–, h–: 24gᵖᵘ   **c–**
c20gᵖᵘ Mar 28] workmanlike gelding: winning hurdler/chaser, no longer of much   **h–**
account: tongue tied: has broken blood vessels. *M. A. Barnes*

NIKITA'S GIFT (IRE)   4 ch.g. Topanoora – Little Nikita (Lafontaine (USA)) [2002/3   **F–**
F16g Apr 1] third foal: dam poor maiden hurdler: showed nothing in bumper on debut.
C. F. Swan, Ireland

NIKSON (IRE)   7 b.g. Elbio – Goldkrone (EG) (Wildschutz (EG)) [2002/3 F16v 18s   **h–**
16g Feb 22] big, rangy gelding: chasing type: fourth foal: dam won on Flat/over hurdles   **F–**
in Germany: well held in bumper and 2 novice hurdles. *M. Pitman*

NIL DESPERANDUM (IRE)   6 b.g. Un Desperado (FR) – Still Hoping (Kambalda)   **h139**
[2002/3 F16g* F16d⁶ 16s* 20s² 16s* 18s³ 21g⁶ 22d* Mar 22] useful-looking gelding: **F101**
fifth foal: half-brother to 2½m hurdle winner Willoughby Joe (by Persian Mews): dam
winning Irish pointer: fairly useful form in 2 bumpers, winning at Roscommon in October: useful novice hurdler: won at Punchestown (maiden) in December and Navan in
January and March (beat Heads Onthe Ground 5 lengths): good promoted sixth to Hardy
Eustace in Royal & SunAlliance Novices' Hurdle at Cheltenham: will stay at least 3m:
raced on good going or softer (acts on soft): type to make mark in novice chases in
2003/4. *Miss F. M. Crowley, Ireland*

NILOUFER   12 br.m. Nader – Latanett (Dairialatan) [2002/3 c24g² May 31] modest   **c96**
pointer: ran well when second to Glacial Trial in mares hunter at Stratford in May.
Mrs C. Hobbs

NIMBUS STRATUS 10 br.g. Welsh Captain – Touching Clouds (Touching Wood (USA)) [2002/3 c–, h–: 19f⁶ 22d Oct 22] lengthy gelding: maiden hurdler/chaser: won point (match) in April: tried blinkered. *J. D. Frost* **c– h–**

NINE O THREE (IRE) 14 b.g. Supreme Leader – Grenache (Menelek) [2002/3 h106: 24m⁴ 27g³ 27g² 22m² Jul 28] small gelding: fair handicap hurdler: creditable efforts in frame all 4 starts in 2002/3: stays 27f: probably acts on any going: reliable. *Mrs S. D. Williams* **h103**

NIP ON 9 b.g. Dunbeath (USA) – Popping On (Sonnen Gold) [2002/3 c–, h90: 24dᵖᵘ 25g³ 21s² 24v³ 27g⁴ Mar 25] well beaten only outing over fences: poor hurdler: stays 27f: yet to race on firm going, acts on any other: blinkered once. *J. R. Turner* **c– h84**

NIPPER REED 13 b.g. Celestial Storm (USA) – Figrant (USA) (L'Emigrant (USA)) [2002/3 16d Apr 29] leggy, close-coupled gelding: winning hurdler: one-time useful 2m chaser: acts on heavy going: front runner: sound jumper: often gives trouble at start (has refused to race), and is one to treat with caution. *Miss K. M. George* **c– § h– §**

NISBET 9 b.g. Lithgie-Brig – Drummond Lass (Peacock (FR)) [2002/3 24d⁴ 24m⁴ 22s⁵ 22v⁵ 22vᵖᵘ c20m³ c24g³ c20gᵖᵘ c24g⁴ c24g⁵ c25g² c31g⁶ Apr 24] winning pointer: poor novice hurdler/chaser: stays 25f: acts on soft and good to firm going. *Miss Lucinda V. Russell* **c81 h77**

NIZAAL (USA) 12 ch.g. Diesis – Shicklah (USA) (The Minstrel (CAN)) [2002/3 c–, h–: c20g⁴ c16g c16m c16d Jun 4] workmanlike gelding: of little account nowadays: tried blinkered. *T. A. K. Cuthbert* **c– h–**

NOAFF (IRE) 9 b.g. Mandalus – Good Sailing (Scorpio (FR)) [2002/3 c24m c20sᵖᵘ c24m² Apr 22] no form over hurdles/fences in Ireland: fair pointer in Britain, successful in February and March: similar form when third at Chepstow (promoted a place) on hunter chase debut. *John Moore* **c91 + h–**

NOBIGSUPRISE (IRE) 4 b.f. Courtship – Pennine Sue (IRE) (Pennine Walk) [2002/3 17sᵖᵘ 17vᵖᵘ Mar 10] ex-Irish filly: no sign of ability on Flat or over hurdles. *W. G. M. Turner* **h–**

NOBLE BARON 7 gr.g. Karinga Bay – Grey Baroness (Baron Blakeney) [2002/3 F98: F16d 19d 22f³ Mar 29] workmanlike gelding: fairly useful bumper winner: only poor form in 2 novice hurdles: likely to stay beyond 2¾m. *C. G. Cox* **h79 F85**

NOBLE CAESAR (IRE) 5 b. or br.g. Montelimar (USA) – Timely Run (IRE) (Deep Run) [2002/3 20sᵖᵘ 20dᵖᵘ Feb 23] IR £41,000 3-y-o: fifth foal: brother and half-brother to winning pointers: dam, lightly raced in bumpers/over hurdles, sister to useful chaser up to 25f Deep Moment and half-sister to smart chaser up to 3m Harveystown: no show in 2 novice hurdles. *J. R. Adam* **h–**

NOBLE COMIC 12 b.g. Silly Prices – Barony (Ribston) [2002/3 c96, h–: c16g² c16s³ c16m² c16g* c20m³ c16g⁵ c16m² c17m⁶ c21f* c25m⁴ Oct 27] good-topped gelding: fair handicap chaser: won at Newton Abbot (fifth course success) in June and Wincanton (match) in October: stays 21f: acts on firm and good to soft going, probably not on softer: races prominently. *C. Tizzard* **c106 h–**

NOBLE DEED (IRE) 6 b.g. Lord Americo – Legal Statement (IRE) (Strong Statement (USA)) [2002/3 F73: 20dᵖᵘ 16v⁴ 19d Jan 16] well-made gelding: best effort over hurdles when fourth in novice at Plumpton in December. *Miss H. C. Knight* **h72**

NOBLEFIR (IRE) 5 b.g. Shernazar – Chrisali (IRE) (Strong Gale) [2002/3 F16d F16m² F17g³ Apr 21] lengthy, well-made gelding: chasing type: first foal: dam Irish bumper winner: won Irish point on debut in 2002: fair form when placed in bumpers at Ayr and Carlisle. *L. Lungo* **F94**

NOBLE HYMN 10 br.g. Arctic Lord – Soraway (Choral Society) [2002/3 c–, h–: c25d⁶ c25g² Apr 14] close-coupled gelding: modest hunter chaser: stays 25f: has had tongue tied: not a fluent jumper. *Mrs C. M. Mulhall* **c81 h–**

NOBLE JUSTICE (IRE) 7 b.g. Jurado (USA) – Furry Hope (Furry Glen) [2002/3 c104, h96, F67: c20dᵖᵘ 21gᵖᵘ Feb 27] tall gelding: lightly-raced hurdler/winning chaser: no encouragement either start on return (reportedly made noise on reappearance): will stay 3m: acts on firm going: has had tongue tied. *R. J. Hodges* **c– h–**

NOBLE LORD 10 ch.g. Lord Bud – Chasers' Bar (Oats) [2002/3 c27d Nov 16] good-topped gelding: useful handicap chaser: missed 2001/2 (reportedly due to broken pelvis), well held in valuable event at Cheltenham only run in 2002/3: best at 3m+ nowadays: acts on any going. *R. T. Phillips* **c– h–**

NOBLE SPY (IRE) 9 b.g. Lord Americo – Flashey Blond (Buckskin (FR)) [2002/3 **c–**
h100: 25s c24s^pu 24m Apr 12] good-topped gelding: modest hurdler: well held in 2 **h–**
handicaps in 2002/3, no show on chasing debut: better suited by 3m+ than shorter: acts
on soft and good to firm going. *Mrs D. A. Hamer*

NOBLE STAR 11 b.g. Jester – Mickley Spacetrail (Space King) [2002/3 c–: c16g^pu **c–**
May 1] poor pointer. *Mrs J. M. Bush*

NOBODY TOLD ME (IRE) 5 b.m. King's Theatre (IRE) – Thats Luck (IRE) **h140 p**
(Posen (USA)) [2002/3 16d* 16v² 16d* 20g* Apr 20]

'I felt she could be a different proposition over hurdles.' So trainer Willie
Mullins told *The Irish Field* about the mare Nobody Told Me after she had made a
winning hurdling debut in the Saggart Maiden Hurdle at Naas in February. Just how
different, perhaps even he did not know at that point. By the summer the mare, with
a Flat handicap mark of just 54, had won a further four races, including two after
the end of the British season, one of Ireland's top novice races, the Menolly Homes
Champion Novices' Hurdle over two and a half miles at the Punchestown Festival
and, famously, France's top hurdle race, the Grande Course de Haies d'Auteuil, in
which she caused one of the major upsets of recent times. *Paris-Turf* previewed
the race under the headline 'L'annee de la femme' but the femme referred to in
particular was not the unconsidered Nobody Told Me but the leading French
hurdler Karly Flight who was unbeaten in a year and had won the main trial race,
the Prix La Barka, in scintillating fashion. After another mare Line Marine had
gained a rare success for her sex when trotting up in the top chase, the Grand
Steeple-Chase de Paris three weeks earlier, the scene was set for a famous double.
Nobody Told Me had contested the La Barka along with her stable companion Holy
Orders, who had won the Champion Stayers' at Punchestown. Holy Orders had the
better form but did not take to the unusual French hurdles. Nobody Told Me, on the
other hand, adapted well and chased the pace for a long way before her jumping
became ragged late on and she was beaten over seventeen lengths by Karly Flight.
That still looked a good effort on form but Nobody Told Me seemed to have little
chance of reversing placings with the winner. Not many French connections
fancied their chances of overturning Karly Flight either, it seemed, and the field
would have been just five without Nobody Told Me and two Martin Pipe-trained
runners Iznogoud and Mr Cool.

With her supporters in the stands, holding aloft banners and decked out in
the green and yellow colours she carries, everything appeared set for Karly Flight.
She travelled smoothly in front and had most of her rivals in trouble going down the
back straight on the final circuit, though Nobody Told Me was still with her. Even
when Nobody Told Me went past four out, Karly Flight's rider still looked full of
confidence, and as he followed the Irish mare, now shaken up by David Casey, into

Menolly Homes Champion Novices' Hurdle, Punchestown—
Nobody Told Me is clear when she fluffs the last

*Grande Course de Haies d'Auteuil—winner Nobody Told Me (left)
and Karly Flight (No.8) are almost as wide apart at the start as they will be at the last;
British-trained Mr Cool (second left) and Iznogoud (crossbelts) still have every chance . . .*

the straight and then over the second last all seemed set fair for the expected victory. However, first indecision then panic overtook the unfortunate rider of Karly Flight. Having followed Nobody Told Me on the inside route into the straight, he changed his mind and switched his mount to where the remainder of the field was racing on the outside. This is often the best place to race at Auteuil, particularly when the ground is bad but, in veering across the track, Karly Flight forfeited valuable ground and, furthermore, the manoeuvre took Karly Flight across to race against horses which were no danger and away from one that clearly was. Jumping the last, the realisation must have set in that Nobody Told Me was still to be caught but Karly Flight's rider, who didn't shine, looking untidy in the finish, couldn't get his mount back in front. Nobody Told Me won by two lengths. 'Battue par l'irlandaise Nobody Told Me (Personne ne nous avait prevenus [*nobody told us*] dans la langue de Shakespeare)' as *Paris-Turf* poetically, if slightly inaccurately, put it.

Nobody Told Me's success was notable on several counts. Paying thirty-two euro for a one-euro stake, she was the longest-priced winner of the Grande Course since Goodea upset Marly River in 1988 at the equivalent of 33/1. More significantly, she was the first mare to win, and the first horse trained in Britain or Ireland to win, since Dawn Run triumphed for Mullins' father Paddy under brother Tony in 1984. Dawn Run was probably the greatest jumping mare of all time. *Chasers & Hurdlers 1983/84* described her as phenomenal. That season she won eight of her nine races, including the Champion Hurdle, the Wessel Cable Champion Hurdle (now the AIG Europe), the Christmas Hurdle, the Aintree Hurdle and the La Barka, as well as the Grande Course. She was the first mare to win the Champion Hurdle since 1939. After a season cut short by a setback, she returned in 1985/6 to win an epic Cheltenham Gold Cup from Wayward Lad on just her fifth start over fences, becoming the only horse to win both the Gold Cup and the Champion Hurdle. A tough and most genuine front runner, Dawn Run won three bumpers and eighteen races over hurdles and fences in a twenty-eight-race career cut short when she broke her neck in bidding for a second Grande Course in 1986. She was rated 173 over hurdles and 167, as a virtual novice, over fences.

. . . the post comes in time for Nobody Told Me as Karly Flight is unable to make up lost ground

Even if success in the Grande Course remains the only point of comparison between Dawn Run and Nobody Told Me as racehorses, the latter deserves praise for such a rare achievement. Earlier, back in Ireland, she had also overturned a hotpot to win the Champion Novices' Hurdle. This looked Pizarro's for the taking —he had easily the best form—but he failed to give his running, as did a couple of the other more fancied runners, Leinster and Rosaker, and Nobody Told Me quickened away after leading two out to beat Jack High by five lengths. The runner-up's form in handicaps suggested this was form below the usual standard for the race and Nobody Told Me's French form looks some way in advance of it. Nobody Told Me's other successes came in races restricted to fillies and mares. She won a novice at Clonmel by a length from Stashedaway, then beat the same rival twice as far in the quite valuable European Breeders Fund (Mares) Novices' Hurdle Championship Final at Fairyhouse in April. After her win in Paris, Mullins told the local paper that he would look for suitable opportunities back at Auteuil for the mare in the autumn and, as she has adapted so well to French hurdles, she may not be seen much at home.

Nobody Told Me (IRE) (b.m. 1998)	King's Theatre (IRE) (b 1991)	Sadler's Wells (b 1981)	Northern Dancer, Fairy Bridge
		Regal Beauty (b or br 1981)	Princely Native, Dennis Belle
	Thats Luck (IRE) (b 1993)	Posen (b 1985)	Danzig, Michelle Mon Amour
		Mill's Girl (b 1970)	Le Levanstell, Mill Baby

Amber Syndicate's "Nobody Told Me"

Although Irish-bred, the leggy Nobody Told Me began her career in France, racing on the Flat and disqualified after recording her only victory. She is the first foal of her unraced dam That's Luck, whose second Docklands Maximus (by Danehill Dancer) was a fairly useful two-year-old six-furlong winner in 2002. The grandam Mill's Girl produced seven winners, including two very smart performers, Quilted who won the Princess of Wales's Stakes over a mile and a half and Putty Road, a staying hurdler whose successes included the Sun Alliance Hurdle. Mill's Girl was also the dam of the smart seven-furlong to mile-and-three-quarter performer What A Riot and the fairly useful hurdler at up to three miles Robingo. She was half-sister to two high-class stayers on the Flat, Arctic Vale and Ragazzo. More remotely, the third dam Mill Baby is also third dam of another useful Irish jumper, Boyneside, who won the Munster National and was second in a County Hurdle and a Thyestes Chase. This is a family noted for its stayers and it came as little surprise that Nobody Told Me was well served by the step up to three miles plus at Auteuil. She has raced on good going or softer, her run on heavy appearing a creditable one at the time, though it's possible she'll prove ideally suited to less testing conditions. *W. P. Mullins, Ireland*

NOBRATINETTA (FR)   4 b.f. Celtic Swing – Bustinetta (Bustino) [2002/3 F12d³ F14d² F16v* F16g* F17m⁴ Apr 17] rather leggy filly: fourth foal: sister to useful 1½m performer Tomasino and half-sister to fairly useful hurdlers Bhutan (by Polish Patriot), best at 2m, and Cloth of Gold (by Barathea), stays 21f: dam, 11f winner, out of half-sister to very smart middle-distance colt Terimon: fairly useful form in bumpers, winning mares events at Newcastle in January and Musselburgh in February: good fourth to Amorello in listed mares event at Cheltenham final start: will stay beyond 17f. *Mrs M. Reveley*   **F100**

NO COLLUSION (IRE)   7 b.g. Buckskin (FR) – Miss Ironside (General Ironside) [2002/3 F97: 20d⁵ 19d* 21spu 19d² 18s* 18d³ 20g² 21m⁴ Apr 16] has scope: fairly useful novice hurdler: won at Hereford in December and Fontwell in February: very good head second to Anatar in handicap at Ascot seventh start: likely to prove best at 2½m+: acts on soft going: reportedly had mucus on lungs on reappearance, breathing problem when pulled up in Grade 1 at Newbury third outing. *Noel T. Chance*   **h123**

NODFORM RETURNS   5 ch.m. Minster Son – Gale Storm (Midland Gayle) [2002/3 F17g F16g F16g 24gpu Apr 23] third foal: dam winning pointer: little sign of ability. *D. Eddy*   **h–**
F–

NO DISCOUNT (IRE)   9 b.g. Be My Native (USA) – Flameing Run (Deep Run) [2002/3 c114, h–: 24vpu 24s 24s 24d³ 20s 25g Mar 11] tall gelding: fair chaser: useful hurdler at best: signs of retaining ability in 2002/3 only when third of 5 to Emotional Moment in steadily-run Grade 2 at Navan, flattered: stays 3m: acts on good to firm and heavy going. *T. M. Walsh, Ireland*   **c–**
h–

NOD'S NEPHEW   6 b.g. Efisio – Nordan Raider (Domynsky) [2002/3 16g Oct 9] fair on Flat (stays 9.4f): tongue tied, never dangerous after slow start (led in and reared up) in novice on hurdling debut. *D. E. Cantillon*   **h–**

NOD YA HEAD   7 ch.m. Minster Son – Little Mittens (Little Buskins) [2002/3 F16f Sep 15] fifth foal: half-sister to winning 3m hurdler Nite Sprite (by Silly Prices): dam fair staying hurdler: well behind in bumper on debut. *R. E. Barr*   **F–**

NOEL'S PRIDE   7 b.g. Good Thyne (USA) – Kavali (Blakeney) [2002/3 h104: 20d² c20m³ c20m 21m⁴ 21g* 20g* 24g* 24g² 21m⁵ 21v² 20g³ 20dpu Feb 26] angular gelding: modest form on first of 2 outings in novice chases: fairly useful handicap hurdler: won at Sedgefield and Worcester in August and Uttoxeter in September: ran as if amiss final start: effective at 2½m to 3m: acts on any going: has worn cheekpieces: game and consistent. *J. M. Jefferson*   **c90**
h119

NO FORECAST (IRE)   9 b.g. Executive Perk – Guess Twice (Deep Run) [2002/3 c110+, h–: c20d³ Nov 17] tall gelding: maiden hurdler/winning chaser, extremely lightly raced: third to Halexy in handicap at Cheltenham only run in 2002/3, would have gone very close but for losing footing 2 out when still holding narrow lead: stays 2¾m: raced on good going or softer (won bumper on heavy). *A. M. Hales*   **c109**
h–

NO GIMMICKS (IRE)   11 b.g. Lord Americo – Catspaw (Laurence O) [2002/3 c–, h87: 27d Oct 31] compact gelding: little encouragement over fences: modest handicap hurdler: folded tamely only start in 2002/3: stays 27f: acts on good to firm and heavy going: tried blinkered/visored. *J. G. FitzGerald*   **c–**
h–

NO IF'S OR BUT'S 5 b.g. Perpendicular – Tommys Dream (Le Bavard (FR)) [2002/3   **F–**
F17g⁶ F17d Oct 31] sixth foal: brother to winning 2½m hurdler Preston Brook: dam fair
hurdler, successful from 2m to 25f: well beaten in 2 bumpers. *J. Wade*

NOISETINE (FR) 5 ch.m. Mansonnien (FR) – Notabilite (FR) (No Pass No Sale)   **h103**
[2002/3 h104: 21d 20s⁶ 20v³ 20v 16g⁶ 20m² Apr 12] good-topped mare: fair handicap
hurdler: generally creditable efforts in 2002/3: will stay beyond 2¾m: acts on good to
firm and heavy going. *Miss Venetia Williams*

NO KIDDING 9 b.g. Teenoso (USA) – Vaigly Fine (Vaigly Great) [2002/3 c100x, h–:   **c101**
c16mᵖᵘ c25mᵖᵘ c19gᵖᵘ c16m* c20gᵖᵘ c17g⁶ c20g* c16g Apr 24] strong, lengthy gelding: **h–**
fair handicap chaser: easily best efforts in 2002/3 when winning at Musselburgh
(amateurs) in December and Hexham in April: stays 2½m: acts on firm and soft going:
sometimes makes mistakes. *J. I. A. Charlton*

NOKIMOVER 9 ch.g. Scallywag – Town Blues (Charlottown) [2002/3 c–p, h–:   **c100**
c26gᵘʳ c23d* c26g³ c24mᶠ c26mᵘʳ 24v c26v³ c25dᵖᵘ 19v⁵ 21m⁵ 24m⁴ Apr 15] rather   **h93**
sparsely-made gelding: fair novice chaser: won maiden at Uttoxeter in June: largely let
down by jumping over fences subsequently: modest hurdler: stays 3¼m: acts on heavy
going, probably on good to firm: has worn cheekpieces. *J. G. M. O'Shea*

NO LANGUAGE PLEASE (IRE) 9 ch.g. Arapahos (FR) – Strong Language   **c–**
(Formidable (USA)) [2002/3 c–, h64: 24g May 8] smallish gelding: winning pointer: **h–**
poor maiden hurdler/chaser: probably stays 3m and acts on any going: tried blinkered.
R. Curtis

NOLIFE (IRE) 7 b.g. Religiously (USA) – Garnerstown Lady (Pitpan) [2002/3 20d   **h–**
22d⁴ Nov 17] IR 3,100 4-y-o: leggy gelding: fifth foal: half-brother to modest hurdler The
Stitcher (by Denel), stayed 2½m: dam unraced, out of half-sister to 1973 Arkle winner
Denys Adventure: won maiden Irish point in 2002: bought 5,000 gns Doncaster August
Sales: well beaten in 2 novice hurdles. *Miss Lucinda V. Russell*

NOMADIC 9 gr.g. Kenmare (FR) – Legend of Arabia (Great Nephew) [2002/3 c18s²   **c111**
c16v³ c20s* c21s² c24dᵘʳ Feb 16] leggy gelding: very smart hurdler at best: missed   **h–**
2001/2: fair form over fences on return, winning novice at Gowran in January: should
stay beyond 2½m: acts on good to firm and heavy going: held up. *N. Meade, Ireland*

NOMADIC STAR 8 br.g. Nomadic Way (USA) – Dreamago (Sir Mago) [2002/3   **c80**
c25d⁵ Mar 1] brother to fair hunter chaser Go Nomadic, stays 3½m: modest pointer,
successful in February and March: tongue tied, fifth of 7 finishers in novice at Kelso on
hunter chase debut in between, making mistakes. *D. G. Atkinson*

NO MERCI (GER) 5 ch.m. General Assembly (USA) – Non Plus Ultra (GER) (Lord   **h–**
Udo (GER)) [2002/3 17sᵖᵘ Dec 17] useful on Flat for P. Remmert, 7f winner in Germany
at 2 yrs, placed several times up to 1m since, including in 2002: joint favourite, pulled up
before last in novice at Folkestone on hurdling debut (reportedly had breathing problem).
C. Von Der Recke, Germany

NO MERCY 7 ch.g. Faustus (USA) – Nashville Blues (IRE) (Try My Best (USA))   **h79 ?**
[2002/3 h–: 16v² 16d 16v Feb 4] angular gelding: poor maiden hurdler: raced mainly
around 2m: acts on good to firm and heavy going: tried blinkered, wears cheekpieces
nowadays: has had tongue tied. *B. A. Pearce*

NO MOORE BILLS 8 b.m. Nicholas Bill – Grace Moore (Deep Run) [2002/3 h71:   **h–**
22g⁶ 20mᵖᵘ Jul 17] poor maiden hurdler: stays 2½m: acts on good to soft going, no form
on firmer than good: has had tongue tied. *K. Bishop*

NO MORE HASSLE (IRE) 10 ch.g. Magical Wonder (USA) – Friendly Ann   **c111 §**
(Artaius (USA)) [2002/3 c115, h–: c26d² c32m c24g⁴ c24d⁴ c24v⁴ c21d⁴ c26m⁴ c24m⁵   **h–**
Apr 21] big, workmanlike gelding: fair handicap chaser, increasingly let down by
jumping nowadays: stays 3¼m: acts on any going: wore cheekpieces last 4 starts: lazy
and not one to trust. *J. Akehurst*

NONANTAIS (FR) 6 b.g. Nikos – Sanhia (FR) (Sanhedrin (USA)) [2002/3 F17d³   **h119 +**
19d⁶ 19d³ 17s* 19s* 20v² Mar 8] good-topped gelding: half-brother to winners on Flat   **F88**
and over jumps in France, including hurdler/chaser Mansonia (by Mansonnien): dam
won 3 times up to 1½m in France: third in bumper on debut: fairly useful form over
hurdles, making all in maiden and novice at Taunton in February: very much on toes,
forced good pace from fourth when good second to Tana River in Grade 3 novice
handicap at Sandown final start: stays 2½m: acts on heavy ground. *M. Bradstock*

NO NAY NEVER (IRE) 8 b.g. Tremblant – Monread (Le Tricolore) [2002/3 h–:   **h63**
17g⁴ Apr 21] medium-sized gelding: first form over hurdles when fourth in selling
handicap at Newton Abbot on return from 15-month absence. *J. W. Mullins*

Tote Scoop6 Lanzarote Hurdle (Handicap), Kempton—
J. P. McNamara takes full advantage of a chance ride on Non So

NONCHALANT (IRE)   5 ch.g. Magical Wonder (USA) – Look Nonchalant (IRE)   **h113**
(Fayruz) [2002/3 16s² 17g* 16g* 16s² 20s³ Nov 17] dam half-sister to useful 2m hurdlers
More Dash Thancash and Bolino Star: fairly useful on Flat (stays 1½m): fair novice
hurdler: won at Tralee (maiden) in September and Roscommon (made all when beating
Moore's Law 3 lengths) in October: creditable placed efforts in 2 Grade 3 events at Navan
in November: stays 2½m: acts on soft ground: blinkered last 3 starts. *Miss F. M. Crowley,
Ireland*

NO NEED FOR ALARM   8 ch.m. Romany Rye – Sunley Words (Sunley Builds)   **c126**
[2002/3 h120p, F90: c16s* c16v* c16vF c16v* c17vF c16mF c17g* Apr 19] rangy, useful-   **h–**
looking mare: fairly useful hurdler: unbeaten on completed starts in novice chases, at
Newton Abbot and Chepstow in November, Chepstow in February and Stratford
(fortunate) in April: bred to stay beyond 17f (weakened after 2 out over 21f): acts on
heavy going: free-going front runner, prone to mistakes when taken on for lead: sold
20,000 gns Doncaster May Sales. *P. F. Nicholls*

NON SO (FR)   5 b.g. Definite Article – Irish Woman (FR) (Assert) [2002/3 h116: 18d⁵   **h136**
16s* 16d* 16g² 17g⁴ 16g Apr 5] good-topped gelding: useful handicap hurdler: won at
Kempton in December and January (Tote Scoop6 Lanzarote Hurdle, quickly settled issue
when kicking for home 2 out and beat Hawadeth 2½ lengths): good efforts in frame
behind Spirit Leader in Tote Gold Trophy at Newbury and County Hurdle at Cheltenham
fourth and fifth starts, stable out of sorts when disappointing final one: will prove best
around 2m: raced on good going or softer (acts on soft): usually patiently ridden:
free-going sort. *N. J. Henderson*

NON VINTAGE (IRE)   12 ch.g. Shy Groom (USA) – Great Alexandra (Runnett)   **c– §**
[2002/3 c72, h61: 24m⁶ 26m⁶ c25mᵖᵘ c28g⁴ 17d 16d⁴ c23m⁴ Nov 18] workmanlike geld-   **h61 §**
ing: winning hurdler/chaser: poor nowadays: stays 3¼m: acts on any going: blinkered 3
times: has had tongue tied: looks none too keen. *M. C. Chapman*

NO PICNIC (IRE)   5 ch.g. Be My Native (USA) – Emmagreen (Green Shoon)   **h91**
[2002/3 F16g⁵ 16s 20m² 17d⁴ 20g Mar 29] seventh foal: half-brother to winning chaser   **F81**
around 2m Superb Leader (by Supreme Leader): dam won at 2½m over hurdles in Ireland: fifth in bumper on debut: modest form when in frame over hurdles: stays 2½m: acts
on good to firm and good to soft going: raced too freely final start. *Mrs S. C. Bradburne*

NO QUARTER (IRE) 10 ch.g. Persian Mews – Back To Bahrain (Mandalus) c–
[2002/3 h93: c24d^{pu} Nov 13] tall gelding: modest hurdler: pulled up in novice handicap h–
on chasing debut: stayed 2¾m: raced on going softer than good (acted on heavy): dead.
K. C. Bailey

NORBERT (IRE) 5 ch.g. Imperial Frontier (USA) – Glowing Reeds (Kalaglow) F–
[2002/3 F16m F17g Apr 19] first foal: dam little worthwhile form on Flat: no sign of
ability in 2 bumpers. *M. F. Harris*

NORDANCE PRINCE (IRE) 12 b.g. Nordance (USA) – Shirleys Princess (Sand- c130
hurst Prince) [2002/3 c130, h–: c20g^3 c20d^F Feb 7] angular gelding: useful chaser: h–
creditable third to Another Raleagh in handicap at Kempton on reappearance: fell heavily
fifth next time: stays 2½m: acts on firm and soft going. *Miss Venetia Williams*

NORDIC CREST (IRE) 9 b.g. Danehill (USA) – Feather Glen (Glenstal (USA)) c–
[2002/3 c114, h–: c20m^4 Oct 30] sturdy gelding: fair handicap chaser: off 16 months and h–
visored, mistakes when well-beaten last of 4 finishers at Cheltenham: won point in April:
stays 3m: acts on firm and good to soft going. *P. R. Webber*

NORDIC PRINCE (IRE) 12 b.g. Nordance (USA) – Royal Desire (Royal Match) c114
[2002/3 c108, h–: 24v^3 24s^2 c24v^{bd} c24s* c30v^4 20g* c24d^{pu} 21g^3 c24m^{pu} Apr 12] h107
compact gelding: fair hurdler/chaser: won handicap over fences at Southwell in January
and seller over hurdles at Huntingdon in February: effective around 2½m to 3¼m: acts on
any going: tried visored. *J. G. M. O'Shea*

NORLANDIC (NZ) 11 ch.g. First Norman (USA) – April Snow (NZ) (Icelandic) c100 x
[2002/3 c112x, h–: c25d^3 c24s^F c24s^{pu} c24v^3 Mar 5] good-topped gelding: fair handicap h–
chaser: form in 2002/3 when only third at Exeter on reappearance: best form up to 25f:
raced on good going or softer (acts on heavy): sketchy jumper. *P. J. Hobbs*

NORMANBY ROAD (NZ) 12 b.g. First Norman (USA) – Gladstone Lass (NZ) c–
(Silver Blaze (USA)) [2002/3 c–, h79: 17s^{pu} 17s^3 16d^4 c19d^F Feb 10] smallish, lengthy h79
gelding: maiden chaser: poor handicap hurdler nowadays: raced mainly around 2m: acts
on any going: wears cheekpieces: tongue tied once. *J. L. Spearing*

NORMANDY SANDS (IRE) 5 b. or br.g. Namaqualand (USA) – Buzz Along h–
(Prince Bee) [2002/3 F16s F18d^6 F16g^6 20d^5 Apr 9] tall gelding: third foal: dam won F78
Irish bumper: modest form in bumpers: well held in novice on hurdling debut. *L. A. Dace*

NORMANIA (NZ) 11 b.g. First Norman (USA) – Brigania (NZ) (Brigand (USA)) c95
[2002/3 c–x, h–: c21g^4 c21f^2 c22m^F Jun 1] workmanlike gelding: winning hurdler: fair h–
hunter chaser: stays 2¾m: acts on soft and firm going: has had tongue tied. *Miss S. West*

NORMANTON TURVILLE 7 b.g. Lancastrian – Royal Pocket (True Song) [2002/3 h–
20s^{pu} Nov 17] 1,000 6-y-o: second foal: dam winning pointer: showed nothing in novice
hurdle on debut. *Miss L. V. Davis*

NORMARANGE (IRE) 13 ch.g. Lancastrian – Perdeal (Perspex) [2002/3 c82, h–: c90 §
c25d^2 c25g* c25m^3 c23m^6 c23g^5 c31d c25d^5 c24s^{pu} Feb 13] sturdy gelding: modest h–
handicap chaser: won at Towcester in May: reportedly finished lame final start: probably
stays 31f: acts on soft and good to firm going: visored once: lazy. *S. C. Burrough*

NORMINS HUSSAR (IRE) 11 b.g. Glacial Storm (USA) – Little Slip (Super Slip) c–
[2002/3 20g^{pu} Jun 15] modest pointer: little sign of ability otherwise: tried blinkered. h–
C. Grant

NORSE 10 ch.g. Risk Me (FR) – Absent Lover (Nearly A Hand) [2002/3 c–: c17s^5 c–
c19m^4 Jun 4] lengthy gelding: little sign of ability: tongue tied both starts in 2002/3.
S. E. H. Sherwood

NORTHAW LAD (IRE) 5 ch.g. Executive Perk – Black Tulip (Pals Passage) [2002/3 F88
F16g^5 Apr 2] IR £31,000 3-y-o: sturdy gelding: twelfth foal: half-brother to several
winners, including fairly useful hurdler/maiden chaser Man On The Line (by Whistling
Deer): dam, winner on Flat and over hurdles in Ireland, from family of top-class staying
chaser Alexander Banquet: shaped quite well when fifth to Very Optimistic in bumper at
Ascot on debut. *A. J. Lidderdale*

NORTH CROFT 7 b.g. North Street – Sock Jinks (New Member) [2002/3 F–: F16m^5 h–
17m^4 20g^{pu} Aug 24] no sign of ability. *C. J. Gray* F–

NORTHERN BREEZE 5 ch.m. Lancastrian – The Mount (Le Moss) [2002/3 F16g h–
22g^{pu} Apr 12] third foal: half-sister to fair hurdler Kilgal (by Jupiter Island), stayed 27f: F–

dam unraced half-sister to fairly useful staying chaser Forest Ranger: showed nothing in maiden bumper and novice hurdle. *N. J. Pomfret*

NORTHERN ECHO 6 b.g. Pursuit of Love – Stop Press (USA) (Sharpen Up) [2002/3 h61§: 16d⁶ 20m 19mᵖᵘ 17m 17g³ 17g⁶ 17d 17g 17mᵘ⁴ 17dᵖᵘ 16m Apr 21] compact gelding: poor maiden hurdler: best around 2m: acts on firm going, possibly not on softer than good: tried blinkered/visored/tongue tied: refused to race once. *K. S. Thomas*   **h66 §**

NORTHERN FLASH 9 b.g. Rambo Dancer (CAN) – Spinster (Grundy) [2002/3 16vᵖᵘ 20dᵖᵘ 16d⁶ c16d c21g⁴ Mar 25] workmanlike gelding: of little account nowadays: usually blinkered/visored: has had tongue tied. *J. C. Haynes*   **c–** **h–**

NORTHERN FLEET 10 b.g. Slip Anchor – Kamkova (USA) (Northern Dancer) [2002/3 c72§, h–§: 21g³ 21s² 26gᵖᵘ Aug 26] poor hurdler nowadays: stays 3m: acts on soft and good to firm going: blinkered: difficult ride. *P. R. Hedger*   **c– §** **h73 §**

NORTHERN MINSTER 4 b.g. Minster Son – Hand On Heart (IRE) (Taufan (USA)) [2002/3 F16d⁵ F16g 17m Apr 19] third foal: dam modest 7f/1m winner: better effort in bumpers when fifth at Catterick on debut: well beaten in novice on hurdling debut. *F. P. Murtagh*   **h–** **F81**

NORTHERN MOTTO 10 b.g. Mtoto – Soulful (FR) (Zino) [2002/3 h–§: 22m⁵ 22m Jul 4] neat gelding: poor maiden hurdler: stays 25f: acts on any going: tried visored/blinkered: has broken blood vessel: has found little and not one to trust: sold £1,400 Ascot August Sales, won point in April. *C. Weedon*   **h70 §**

NORTHERN NATIVE (IRE) 7 br. or b.m. Be My Native (USA) – Charming Mo (IRE) (Callernish) [2002/3 F95+: F16s* 20d⁶ Feb 26] well-made mare: fairly useful in bumpers, successful twice, including in mares event at Wetherby in November: never a factor when sixth in mares novice there on hurdling debut, not fluent and off bridle long way out. *Mrs M. Reveley*   **h82** **F99**

NORTHERN RAIDER (IRE) 5 b.g. College Chapel – Pepper And Salt (IRE) (Double Schwartz) [2002/3 h74?: c25d⁵ Mar 5] sturdy gelding: form over hurdles only when winning weak juvenile seller in 2001/2: let down by jumping in novice hunter chase at Catterick in March: tried blinkered. *Miss T. Jackson*   **c71** **h–**

NORTHERN RAMBLER (IRE) 6 gr.g. Roselier (FR) – Ramble Bramble (Random Shot) [2002/3 F16s F16v⁵ 16d 16d⁶ 20g Apr 1] quite good-topped gelding: brother to smart staying chaser Seven Towers and half-brother to modest hurdler Pharrambling (by Phardante), stays 3m: dam twice-raced half-sister to very smart staying chaser Deep Bramble: looked short of pace in bumpers at Newcastle and Ayr: well held all 3 starts over hurdles: bred to need long distances. *Mrs M. Reveley*   **h–** **F83**

NORTHERN SOUND (IRE) 10 b.m. Montelimar (USA) – Castle Felda (Le Moss) [2002/3 c134?: c24s c20d⁴ c25s³ c24gᵖᵘ Mar 11] leggy mare: fairly useful chaser: form in 2002/3 only when fourth of 6 to More Than A Stroll in Grade 3 at Gowran in February: stays 29f: seems best on good going or softer (acts on heavy): tried blinkered: often less than fluent: inconsistent. *Paul A. Roche, Ireland*   **c120**

NORTHERN STARLIGHT 12 b.g. Northern State (USA) – Ganadora (Good Times (ITY)) [2002/3 c111+, h–: c20m c21d³ Mar 6] smallish, leggy gelding: one-time useful chaser, very lightly raced and little form since 1999/00: visored once: front runner. *M. C. Pipe*   **c–** **h–**

NORTHERN TENNESSEE (IRE) 8 ch.g. Muharib (USA) – Corun Girl (Apollo Eight) [2002/3 h94+, F100: 20m³ 17m² Sep 13] angular gelding: fair hurdler: best effort when second in handicap at Southwell in September: stays 2½m: acts on good to firm going. *B. G. Powell*   **h109**

NORTH FACE 6 ch.g. Factual (USA) – Northgate Dancer (Ile de Bourbon (USA)) [2002/3 h75: c17g May 8] leggy, lengthy gelding: poor hurdler: well held on chasing debut in May, not seen out again: raced around 2m: acts on firm ground, possibly not on softer than good: pulled hard only try in blinkers. *Miss Lucinda V. Russell*   **c–** **h–**

NORTH GOLD (IRE) 5 b.g. Distinctly North (USA) – Miss Goldie Locks (Dara Monarch) [2002/3 16s 16v 18s 20s³ 20g⁴ Apr 23] third living foal: half-brother to modest winner on Flat: dam, no form, half-sister to smart 5f performer Carol's Treasure: best effort in maiden hurdles when third at Punchestown in March: stays 2½m. *M. F. Morris, Ireland*   **h92**

NORTH (IRE) 5 br.g. Mukaddamah (USA) – Flamenco (USA) (Dance Spell (USA)) **h–**
[2002/3 16g 20v^{pu} Jan 29] little form on Flat for D. Chapman: no show in 2 novice
hurdles. *A. C. Wilson*

NORTH POINT (IRE) 5 b.g. Definite Article – Friendly Song (Song) [2002/3 16g* **h109**
16g 16m^4 16m* Apr 21] smallish, close-coupled gelding: fair on Flat up to 1¼m, sold out
of A. Jarvis' stable 14,500 gns Doncaster August Sales: similar level of form over
hurdles, won novices at Ludlow in February and Plumpton in April: likely to need sharp
2m: acts on good to firm going. *R. Curtis*

NORTON WOOD (IRE) 7 ch.g. Shardari – Colligan Forest (Strong Gale) [2002/3 **h–**
17d^F 17g Oct 18] £2,000 6-y-o: strong, workmanlike gelding: second foal: dam, winning
Irish pointer, sister to useful 2½m chaser Strong Medicine: none too fluent when well
held (reportedly lame) on completed start over hurdles: ran out in point in February.
Mrs A. Price

NORVIN (IRE) 6 b.g. Nashwan (USA) – Percy's Lass (Blakeney) [2002/3 F16d **d**
F17s^4 26g^{ro} 25d^5 25g^3 Mar 23] 14,000 3-y-o: good-topped gelding: half-brother to useful **F83**
1m/1¼m winner Blue Lion (by Lomond): dam, very smart performer up to 1½m but
temperamental, from family of 1983 Derby winner Teenoso: better effort in bumpers
when fourth at Bangor: poor form over hurdles, winning weak novice at Warwick in
March, jumping poorly and left clear 2 out: stays 25f. *Ian Williams*

NORWOOD PARK (NZ) 6 b.g. Centaine (AUS) – Janine (NZ) (Wharf (USA)) **h–**
[2002/3 F–: F17m 16g^{pu} Apr 1] no sign of ability. *Mrs M. Reveley* **F–**

NOSAM 13 b.g. Idiot's Delight – Socher (Anax) [2002/3 c116, h–: c25d^F c24d^{pu} c20g^5 **c116**
c21g^2 21g^4 c20m^6 c20d^3 c20s^3 c20d* c21d Apr 4] sparely-made, close-coupled gelding: **h–**
winning hurdler: fairly useful handicap chaser: won at Wetherby in February: effective at
19f to 25f: acts on any going: tongue tied: tough. *R. C. Guest*

NO SAM NO 5 b.m. Reprimand – Samjamalifran (Blakeney) [2002/3 h73: 22s^3 20m^4 **c–**
24m^{pu} 21g^2 22d^4 22g 19d^{pu} 21g^2 c21d c27m^4 Apr 26] leggy mare: poor maiden hurdler: **h73**
showed little in 2 novice chases: stays 2¾m: acts on soft going. *Mrs K. Walton*

NOSHINANNIKIN 9 ch.g. Anshan – Preziosa (Homing) [2002/3 c120x, h120: **c116 x**
c16g^4 16v 20d 19s 16d 16d^6 16d 16d^6 20g^4 16g^2 16g* 16m* Apr 21] big, strong gelding: **h105**
fairly useful chaser: fair handicap hurdler nowadays: dropped markedly in weights prior
to winning at Hexham and Wetherby (amateurs) in April: stays 2½m: acts on soft and
good to firm going: tried blinkered: tongue tied: sketchy jumper of fences. *M. W. Easterby*

NOTABLE EXCEPTION 14 b.g. Top Ville – Shorthouse (Habitat) [2002/3 20s^{pu} **c–**
Jun 9] leggy gelding: veteran hurdler/chaser: tried blinkered/visored. *R. Dickin* **h–**

NOT ATALL ATALL 6 b.g. Atall Atall – Paisley Park (Moor House) [2002/3 F16f^{pu} **F–**
Sep 15] first foal: dam runner-up in point: reportedly broke down in bumper on debut.
M. A. Barnes

NOT FADE AWAY 5 b.g. Ezzoud (IRE) – Green Flower (USA) (Fappiano (USA)) **h–**
[2002/3 h–: 22g^{pu} May 1] lengthy gelding: no worthwhile form over hurdles: tried
visored/tongue tied. *Miss E. C. Lavelle*

NOT FORGOTTEN (USA) 9 b.g. St Jovite (USA) – Past Remembered (USA) **h–**
(Solford (USA)) [2002/3 h61: 27m^{pu} May 7] poor handicap hurdler: lame only outing in
2002/3: stays 3¼m: acts on good to firm and heavy ground: sometimes visored (including
for win)/blinkered. *M. R. Hoad*

NOT FOR PARROT (IRE) 11 ch.g. Be My Native (USA) – Sugar Quay (Quayside) **c–**
[2002/3 c69, h62: c19m^{pu} Apr 21] sparely-made gelding: winning hurdler: poor maiden **h–**
chaser: stays 2½m: acts on soft and good to firm going (well beaten on heavy): tried
blinkered. *Gilbert Martin*

NOTHING DAUNTED 6 ch.g. Selkirk (USA) – Khubza (Green Desert (USA)) **h–**
[2002/3 16d 16m 16g Jan 17] no show in 3 novice hurdles: fairly useful at one time
around 7f on Flat, little show in 2 starts in February for J. Osborne: sold 1,200 gns
Doncaster March Sales. *P. Monteith*

NOT NOW GEORGE 4 b.g. Sovereign Water (FR) – Threads (Bedford (USA)) **F–**
[2002/3 F14d F16s Jan 18] medium-sized gelding: first foal: dam modest form in
bumpers: soundly beaten in 2 bumpers. *T. H. Caldwell*

NOT PROVEN 4 br.g. Mark of Esteem (IRE) – Free City (USA) (Danzig (USA)) **h–**
[2002/3 16d Nov 15] half-brother to winning hurdler around 2m in France/Belgium by

Suave Dancer: modest maiden on Flat at 2 yrs: well held in juvenile on hurdling debut. *J. G. FitzGerald*

NOT TO BE MISSED 5 gr.m. Missed Flight – Petinata (Petong) [2002/3 F12d F16g **h82** F17s 16d⁵ Apr 9] 2,100 3-y-o: unfurnished mare: third foal: half-sister to 7f winner **F81** Starlight (by King's Signet) and a winner around 6f in Sweden by Beveled: dam twice-raced half-sister to useful sprinter Peatswood Shooter: mid-division at best in bumpers: fifth in novice at Uttoxeter on hurdling debut: withdrawn after unseating rider and bolting before intended hurdling debut. *R. Dickin*

NOTTY 8 ch.m. Nicholas Bill – Silver Empress (Octavo (USA)) [2002/3 h–: 17m 24m⁴ **h–** 22g⁴ 20g 22mᵖᵘ 16d c19sᵖᵘ Nov 14] lengthy mare: no worthwhile form: has had tongue tied. *J. C. Fox*

NOTWHATSHEWANTED (IRE) 6 b.g. Supreme Leader – Wise Nellie (IRE) **h–** (Brush Aside (USA)) [2002/3 F16s F18d F17g 26mᵖᵘ Apr 21] IR 12,000 3-y-o, IR £7,000 **F–** 4-y-o: workmanlike gelding: first foal: dam runner-up in Irish bumper, only start: no sign of ability. *J. W. Mullins*

NOT YET DECENT (IRE) 10 gr.g. Decent Fellow – Yet (Last Fandango) [2002/3 **c86** c21f⁵ c26g⁴ c24g⁴ c26vᵖᵘ c25s⁵ c23dᵖᵘ c25gᵖᵘ Mar 29] fair form at best in hunter chases: possibly amiss last 2 starts (runner-up in point in between). *Mark Gillard*

NOUF 7 b.m. Efisio – Miss Witch (High Line) [2002/3 h106: 17g⁵ 16d³ 16d² Dec 12] **h109** angular mare: fair handicap hurdler: suited by sharp 2m: raced only on good/good to soft ground over hurdles. *K. C. Bailey*

NOUGHTYNOVA 6 b.m. Petoski – Nova Spirit (Electric) [2002/3 F90: F18v F16m⁵ **F79 ?** Mar 20] second in bumper on debut in 2001/2, below that form since. *M. S. Saunders*

NOUSAYRI (IRE) 8 b.g. Slip Anchor – Noufiyla (Top Ville) [2002/3 h82: 21m⁴ 24g **c–** 24m⁵ c16m⁵ c20f² c16f⁵ c21gᶠ Mar 14] leggy gelding: bumper winner: maiden hurdler: **h–** little form in 2002/3, including over fences: sold out of R. Hollinshead's stable 5,200 gns Doncaster November Sales before final start: stays 3m: acts on heavy going: has had tongue tied: reportedly bled from nose third outing. *Neil King*

NOUVEAU CHEVAL 8 b.m. Picea – Freeracer (Free State) [2002/3 h108: 16g³ **h107** 20m* 20m² Aug 26] sparely-made mare: fair hurdler: best effort in 2002/3 when winning claimer at Fontwell (claimed from M. Pipe £4,000) in May: effective at 2m, should stay beyond 2½m: acts on soft and good to firm going, possibly not on heavy: usually tongue tied nowadays. *S. Woodman*

NOVA GIRL 8 b.m. Vital Season – Sols Joker (Comedy Star (USA)) [2002/3 h–: **c83** 22gᵖᵘ 20g⁵ 20d⁵ 26g⁴ 21m² 20g³ 24f³ c21s* c21dᵘʳ c19d⁶ Dec 19] leggy mare: poor **h89** maiden hurdler: fortunate to win novice handicap at Newton Abbot on chasing debut: seems to stay 3m: acts on firm and soft going: tongue tied first 2 starts. *P. R. Rodford*

NOVI SAD (IRE) 5 b.g. Norwich – Shuil Na Gale (Strong Gale) [2002/3 F97: F17g⁵ **h95** F18d* 17s 21sᵖᵘ 21s⁵ 18g³ 16g* 16g³ 21m⁴ Apr 21] workmanlike gelding: fairly useful **F97** form in bumpers, won maiden at Plumpton in November: modest hurdler: won novice handicap at Ascot in March: should stay 2½m: acts on good to soft going. *L. Wells*

NO VISIBILITY (IRE) 8 b.g. Glacial Storm (USA) – Duhallow Lady (IRE) (Torus) **c130 p** [2002/3 c–, h97: 22s 17v³ c16s* c16v* c17gᶠ Apr 19] useful-looking gelding: modest **h–** maiden hurdler: much better over fences: made all in novices at Taunton in January and March (beat Island Sound 13 lengths): in command when falling 2 out in similar event won by No Need For Alarm at Stratford: stays 19f: acts on heavy going: races prominently: open to further improvement over fences. *R. H. Alner*

NOWATOR (POL) 6 ch.g. Jape (USA) – Naradka (POL) (Dakota) [2002/3 16g 16g⁴ **h83** 21m Mar 21] tall, sparely-made ex-Polish gelding: ran 14 times on Flat, winning 5 times from 7f to 13f, leaving M. Janikowski after fifth in Group 3 at Warsaw: poor form over hurdles in Britain: takes good hold. *T. R. George*

NOWELL HOUSE 7 ch.g. Polar Falcon (USA) – Langtry Lady (Pas de Seul) **h108** [2002/3 h96: 17s³ 16d⁵ 16v* 16d⁵ Feb 1] smallish, sparely-made gelding: useful at best on Flat (stays 13f): fair handicap hurdler: best effort when winning at Newcastle in January, settling better than usual: may prove best around 2m: raced on ground softer than good over hurdles (acts on heavy). *M. W. Easterby*

NO WIN NO FEE 8 gr.g. St Ninian – Nellie Bly (Dragonara Palace (USA)) [2002/3 **c–** c19gᶠ Apr 2] sturdy gelding: lightly raced and no sign of ability: dead. *K. D. Giles*

NOWORNEVER (IRE) 10 b.g. Tidaro (USA) – China Blake (Private Walk) [2002/3 c–
c30m^{pu} May 11] ex-Irish gelding: well beaten in bumper in 1999 for Miss F. Crowley:
modest pointer: stiff task, let down by jumping on hunter chase debut in May. *M. A. Kemp*

NOWT 6 b.m. Derrylin – Jolejester (Relkino) [2002/3 17s^{pu} Mar 5] fifth foal: dam, h–
bumper winner, half-sister to useful 2m hurdlers Simenon and State Jester: showed
nothing in mares novice hurdle on debut. *D. McCain*

NOW THEN SID 4 ch.g. Presidium – Callace (Royal Palace) [2002/3 F14d^4 F16g **h87**
16d^5 16d^6 Mar 15] leggy, lightly-made gelding: seventh foal: dam maiden, stayed 1m: **F82**
modest form in bumpers and over hurdles: sweating and edgy on hurdling debut.
Mrs S. A. Watt

NOYAN 13 ch.g. Northern Baby (CAN) – Istiska (FR) (Irish River (FR)) [2002/3 c113, **c113**
h–: c26m* c24m* c25g^{pu} c25m^{pu} c24g* c24m^2 c26m^{pu} Apr 17] lengthy gelding: useful **h–**
hunter chaser: easily won at Folkestone, Ludlow and Huntingdon in May: off 10½
months prior to running poorly final start: stays 3¼m: has won on good to soft going,
ideally suited by less testing ground (goes very well on firm): tends to sweat: probably
best forcing pace: fluent jumper. *D. L. Williams*

NUCLEON COUNT (IRE) 7 b.g. Nucleon (USA) – Clare's Hope (IRE) (Erin's **h71**
Hope) [2002/3 19m^3 Jul 7] lengthy gelding: little form on Flat for J. Given: poor form
when third in novice at Market Rasen on hurdling debut: has had tongue tied.
T. D. Easterby

NUMBERSIXVALVERDE (IRE) 7 b.g. Broken Hearted – Queens Tricks (Le **h119**
Bavard (FR)) [2002/3 F16s^2 F16s^4 16s^2 20s^2 18v* 24s^2 24s^3 Feb 22] fifth foal: half- **F91**
brother to modest chaser up to 2¾m El Cordobes (by Torus): dam unraced half-sister to
fairly useful 3m chaser Fatal Hesitation: fairly useful in bumpers: fairly useful novice
hurdler: won maiden at Punchestown in December: good third to Jack High in handicap
at Fairyhouse final start: effective around 2m and stays 3m: raced only on going softer
than good (acts on heavy). *Martin Brassil, Ireland*

NURSERYMAN (IRE) 6 b.g. Mandalus – The Mighty Midge (Hardgreen (USA)) **F–**
[2002/3 F16g Apr 2] good-bodied gelding: fifth foal: brother to winning 2½m hurdler
Mighty Mandy: dam, 1¼m/1½m winner at 3 yrs, half-sister to Night Nurse: in need of
race and experience when well held in bumper on debut. *P. Winkworth*

NURZYK (POL) 6 ch.g. Freedom's Choice (USA) – Numeria (POL) (Dakota) **h–**
[2002/3 22s^{pu} 19d 24m Mar 21] smallish ex-Polish gelding: successful 7 times from 1m
to 2m from 23 starts on Flat for K. Dorota: no form in novice company over hurdles.
T. R. George

NUTCRACKER LAD (IRE) 5 ch.g. Duky – Allercashin Moon (IRE) (Callernish) **F–**
[2002/3 F16m Apr 21] first foal: dam unraced half-sister to fairly useful 2m hurdler Jolly
Moonbeam: tailed off in bumper on debut. *M. J. Gingell*

NUTLEY KING (IRE) 4 b.g. Night Shift (USA) – Quintellina (Robellino (USA)) **h99**
[2002/3 16s^3 16d^6 16d^5 Feb 7] sturdy, close-coupled ex-Irish gelding: fairly useful on Flat
(stays 9.4f) for J. Gorman: best effort over hurdles when third in juvenile at Kempton:
likely to prove best at 2m with emphasis on speed: pulls hard. *M. C. Pipe*

NUZUM ROAD MAKERS (IRE) 12 b.g. Lafontaine (USA) – Dark Gold (Raise **c113**
You Ten) [2002/3 c112, h119: c24m* 20d 16s^2 c22d 20s Jan 11] rangy gelding: fairly **h117**
useful hurdler: fair handicap chaser: won at Down Royal in May: stays 25f: acts on good
to firm and heavy going: blinkered: has had tongue tied: not an easy ride. *Michael
Cunningham, Ireland*

O

OAKFORDS LAD 9 b.g. Syrtos – Dame Nellie (Dominion) [2002/3 19d 19f^{pu} Mar **h–**
27] half-brother to 3 winners, including modest staying hurdler Con Tricks (by El
Conquistador) and 2m hurdler St John's Hill (by Norwick): dam 2-y-o 7f winner: only
second outing, looked likely to finish second when breaking leg before 2 out in novice
hurdle at Exeter. *R. H. Alner*

OAKLANDS MILLIE (IRE) 10 b.m. Millfontaine – Milpe (Milan) [2002/3 h–: **h–**
16d^6 20g^6 17m^6 27d Oct 31] maiden pointer: no worthwhile form over hurdles. *I. Park*

OAKLEY CELLO 7 ch.g. Michelozzo (USA) – Susie Oakley VII (Damsire Un- F–
registered) [2002/3 F16g May 22] first foal: dam unraced: tailed off in bumper on debut.
M. Madgwick

OBOEDIRE (IRE) 10 br.g. Royal Fountain – Another Pride (Golden Love) [2002/3 c–
c84: c25d^{pu} c24f^4 Mar 29] good-topped gelding: won novice in 2001/2, no form
otherwise in steeplechases. *Sir John Barlow Bt*

OCCAM (IRE) 9 ch.g. Sharp Victor (USA) – Monterana (Sallust) [2002/3 h–: 16m^3 **c81 ?**
16m 16m^4 17m* 17s^3 16f 17g^3 16m 17m^4 16v^4 c16v^4 16d c17v^{pu} 17d c16g^2 c17g^3 Apr **h79**
26] leggy gelding: modest on Flat, won 1½m seller in January: poor hurdler, easily won
novice handicap at Bangor in August: tried in cheekpieces, form over fences only when
second of 5 finishers in maiden at Warwick in March: raced around 2m: acts on soft and
good to firm going. *A. Bailey*

OCCOLD (IRE) 12 b.g. Over The River (FR) – My Puttens (David Jack) [2002/3 **c130**
c130, h–: c23s^4 c24d^4 Aug 4] lengthy, shallow-girthed gelding: useful handicap chaser: **h–**
creditable fourth at Kilbeggan (valuable event, behind Keeponthesunnyside) in July and
Perth (to Aegean) in August on heavy going: stays 3¼m: acts on heavy going: tends to get very worked
up in preliminaries: not to be trusted implicitly. *Ferdy Murphy*

OCEAN DANCER 6 b.g. Primitive Rising (USA) – Bally Small (Sunyboy) [2002/3 **h92**
F17d^6 F17d 16d 19g^6 16d^2 Jan 13] tall gelding: sixth foal: dam unraced: modest form in 2 **F76**
bumpers: progressive form over hurdles, second to River City in novice at Doncaster:
will stay beyond 19f: raced only on good/good to soft going: type to do better over fences.
P. Beaumont

OCEAN LINE (IRE) 8 b.g. Kefaah (USA) – Tropic Sea (IRE) (Sure Blade (USA)) **h104**
[2002/3 h105: 16s^F 17m^6 20m* 21g^{pu} Sep 8] sparely-made gelding: fair hurdler: won
claimer at Fontwell in August: stays easy 2½m: best on good going or firmer: joined
M. Todhunter. *Jonjo O'Neill*

OCEAN LOVE (IRE) 5 b.m. Dolphin Street (FR) – Scuba Diver (Kings Lake **h–**
(USA)) [2002/3 h–: 16m Jun 1] close-coupled mare: little form over hurdles: has looked
less than keen. *C. Weedon*

OCEAN PEAK (NZ) 10 b.g. Gay Apollo – Red Sea (NZ) (Noble Bijou (USA)) **c–**
[2002/3 c–, h–: 19d 23d^{pu} 17s^5 16d^5 16m 16m^4 20g Apr 21] medium-sized gelding: **h65**
winning hurdler/chaser: little form since 2000/1: probably best around 2m: acts on good
to soft going: tongue tied last 2 starts. *B. P. J. Baugh*

OCEAN TIDE 6 b.g. Deploy – Dancing Tide (Pharly (FR)) [2002/3 h102: 22g* 22s^4 **h102 x**
24s^3 23v^5 24g^2 23d^{ur} 24g Feb 27] smallish gelding: fair hurdler: won intermediate at
Kelso in May: stays 3m: acts on soft and good to firm going, probably on heavy: visored:
jumps none too fluently. *R. Ford*

OCEAN TROUT 7 b.m. Sea Raven (IRE) – Rosa Trout (Goldhill) [2002/3 h–, F–: **h–**
23d^{pu} May 23] sturdy mare: little sign of ability. *R. D. E. Woodhouse*

OCKLEY FLYER 4 b.g. Sir Harry Lewis (USA) – Bewails (IRE) (Caerleon (USA)) **h–**
[2002/3 18d 17s^6 16v^3 20s 16m Mar 20] fifth foal: dam, twice-raced maiden, out of
daughter of Yorkshire Oaks and Park Hill Stakes winner Attica Meli: little form over
hurdles: tongue tied after debut. *A. Ennis*

OCTAGONAL (IRE) 6 b.g. Woods of Windsor (USA) – Strawberry Belle (IRE) **h97**
(Vision (USA)) [2002/3 20v^{pu} 16s^4 24s 17d^3 24s 20g* 20f* 24g^{pu} Feb 27] ex-Irish
gelding: dam fair maiden hurdler: maiden on Flat: modest hurdler: won at Roscommon
(maiden) and Clonmel (handicap) within 3 days in September: sold out of Miss
F. Crowley's stable 14,500 gns Doncaster November Sales: no show in handicap at
Ludlow on return from 5½-month absence: stays 2½m: acts on firm going, probably on
soft: blinkered last 5 starts. *Miss K. Marks*

OCTOBER MIST (IRE) 9 gr.g. Roselier (FR) – Bonny Joe (Derring Rose) [2002/3 **c–**
c116+, h–: 16d^4 20d^4 16s^2 16g 24m^4 Feb 21] stocky gelding: carries plenty of condition: **h137**
fairly useful novice chaser in 2001/2, became let down by jumping: useful hurdler:
creditable efforts at Haydock second and third starts, fourth to Nickel Sun in handicap
and staying-on second to Flame Creek in Grade 2: needs testing conditions at 2m and
should stay 3m: acts on heavy going, below form on good to firm. *Mrs M. Reveley*

ODAGH ODYSSEY (IRE) 9 ch.g. Ikdam – Riverside Willow (Callernish) [2002/3 **c124**
c132+, h–: c20d^5 c24v^F Mar 8] sturdy gelding: progressed into useful handicap chaser **h–**
in 2001/2, shaped well long way when fifth to Avalanche at Kempton on belated

reappearance: not fluent prior to falling seventeenth next time: should stay at least 3m: raced on good going or softer (acts on soft). *Miss E. C. Lavelle*

ODD JOB (IRE)   5 b. or br.g. Jolly Jake (NZ) – Kristellita (FR) (Crystal Palace (FR)) [2002/3 F17s F17g⁴ Apr 26] IR 20,000 3-y-o: ex-Irish gelding: fifth living foal: brother to useful hurdler around 2m Just Our Job and half-brother to winner in USA by Lear Fan: dam won over 1½m in France: better effort in bumpers (trained by D. Hughes on debut) when well-beaten fourth at Market Rasen, racing freely. *Jonjo O'Neill*   **F78**

ODDLYDODD (IRE)   7 b.g. Tremblant – Poor Times (IRE) (Roselier (FR)) [2002/3 h94, F–: c20dᵖᵘ c24d⁶ c24dᵖᵘ 19dᵖᵘ 16s 20g³ 22g⁶ 17g 21m³ Apr 21] workmanlike gelding: no encouragement over fences: modest handicap hurdler: stays 2¾m: acts on good to firm and heavy going: blinkered third start. *T. Keddy*   **c–**   **h89**

ODELL (IRE)   13 br.g. Torus – Indian Isle (Warpath) [2002/3 c20f⁶ c21gᵖᵘ c23mᵖᵘ Jun 29] rangy gelding: winning chaser, no longer of any account. *Miss A. E. Broyd*   **c– x**   **h–**

OFF BROADWAY (IRE)   5 b.g. Presenting – Mona Curra Gale (IRE) (Strong Gale) [2002/3 F16d² Mar 6] IR £26,000 3-y-o: second foal: dam, placed once over hurdles, out of sister to useful 2m hurdler Hansel Rag: second to Sargasso Sea in bumper at Wincanton on debut. *A. King*   **F99**

OFFLEY LUCIELASTIC   10 b.m. Tromeros – Village Pride (Quality Fair) [2002/3 c24gᵖᵘ May 3] poor pointer. *R. Hollinshead*   **c–**

OFFSHORE (IRE)   10 b.g. Over The River (FR) – Parson's Princess (The Parson) [2002/3 c–: c26sᵖᵘ c26s² c26sᵖᵘ c25gᵖᵘ Mar 16] winning pointer: signs of more temperament than ability in steeplechases: blinkered last 2 starts. *T. D. McCarthy*   **c–**

OFF THE WOOD   7 b. or gr.m. Baron Blakeney – Rocquelle (Coquelin (USA)) [2002/3 h–, F–: 16dᵖᵘ 17m Jun 4] small mare: no form. *Mrs Barbara Waring*   **h–**

O'FLAHERTY'S (IRE)   11 ch.g. Balinger – Deise Lady (Le Bavard (FR)) [2002/3 c20g³ c24g c21gᵘʳ Mar 14] ex-Irish gelding: well held in bumper: sold out of W. Mullins' stable 4,500 gns Doncaster May (2000) Sales: winning pointer: little show in hunters. *G. D. Blagbrough*   **c–**

OH NO NOT HIM   7 b.g. Reprimand – Lucky Mill (Midyan (USA)) [2002/3 16m 20gᵖᵘ Oct 12] poor and unreliable on Flat (stays 8.5f): no form over hurdles: tried blinkered. *W. M. Brisbourne*   **h–**

OH SO POSH   4 b.f. Overbury (IRE) – Sally Ho (Gildoran) [2002/3 F14d F17v F16d Feb 25] 2,000 3-y-o: workmanlike filly: second foal: dam unraced: well held in 3 bumpers: tongue tied final outing: sold to join Mrs A. Thorpe 4,000 gns Doncaster March Sales. *J. R. Bewley*   **F–**

OH SO WISLEY   8 b.g. Teenoso (USA) – Easy Horse (FR) (Carmarthen (FR)) [2002/3 h92+: c26vᵖᵘ c24s² c24v³ 24g Feb 8] modest hurdler/novice chaser: not fluent over fences. *N. A. Twiston-Davies*   **c95 x**   **h90**

OH TO BE   7 b.g. Weld – At Long Last (John French) [2002/3 19dᵖᵘ 16v Feb 13] workmanlike gelding: fifth foal: half-brother to 2 winners by Gunner B, including fairly useful hurdler/chaser Gunnerblong, stays 2¾m: dam, closely related to fairly useful 3m chaser Baluchi, never ran: carried out in maiden point on debut in 2002: no show in 2 novice hurdles. *G. B. Balding*   **h–**

OH WISE ONE   6 b.g. Homo Sapien – Bean Alainn (Candy Cane) [2002/3 F16d Aug 3] 20,000 4-y-o: fifth foal: half-brother to 3 winners, including 3m hurdle winner Gleann Alainn (by Teenoso) and 2m chaser Runner Bean (by Henbit): dam winning 3m chaser: completed once from 4 starts in points in 2002 (refused twice): well behind in bumper. *Miss K. Marks*   **F–**

OJAYS ALIBI (IRE)   7 b.g. Witness Box (USA) – Tinkers Lady (Sheer Grit) [2002/3 F18s⁶ 17s³ Feb 13] first foal: dam placed in maiden Irish points: in frame in maiden Irish points: sixth of 9 in bumper at Fontwell: modest form when third in maiden at Taunton on hurdling debut: will be suited by further. *J. D. Frost*   **h96**   **F75**

O J SELYM (IRE)   9 b.g. Be My Native (USA) – Myle Avenue (Push On) [2002/3 c–, h–: c16d* c16d⁶ c23g³ c23m³ c20gᵖᵘ Aug 3] strong gelding: modest chaser: went wrong way after winning novice handicap at Towcester very early in season: effective at 2m, should stay 3m: acts on heavy going: reportedly bled from nose second start. *H. D. Daly*   **c98 d**   **h–**

OK SO (IRE)   10 ch.g. Naheez (USA) – Flowering Moss (IRE) (Le Moss) [2002/3 c96, h–: c26m³ May 3] no form over hurdles: fair hunter chaser: reportedly finished lame   **c85**   **h–**

when third of 4 at Folkestone in May: stays 3¼m: acts on soft and good to firm going. *K. A. Nelmes*

OLABUD 11 ch.g. Lord Bud – Nugola (Derrylin) [2002/3 c80, h–: c16m^pu c19s^pu Nov 28] sturdy gelding: winning hurdler: poor maiden chaser. *P. Winkworth* c– h–

OLD BEAN (IRE) 7 b.g. Eurobus – Princess Petara (IRE) (Petorius) [2002/3 F99: 16m Mar 22] leggy, angular gelding: fairly useful bumper winner: not fluent when well held in novice hurdle on belated reappearance. *N. J. Henderson* h–

OLD CALIFORNIA (IRE) 4 b.c. Sadler's Wells (USA) – Turban (Glint of Gold) [2002/3 18d* 17g^F Mar 13] useful on Flat (stayed 15f), sold out of J. Dunlop's stable 85,000 gns Newmarket Autumn Sales: created very good impression when easily landing odds by 6 lengths from Cape Canaveral in juvenile at Fontwell on hurdling debut in December: still travelling well in share of lead when falling fatally 3 out in Triumph Hurdle at Cheltenham. *M. C. Pipe* h127

OLDE OAK 9 ch.g. Precocious – Quisissanno (Be My Guest (USA)) [2002/3 c–, h–: c16m c17s⁴ c17m^pu Jun 22] good-topped gelding: of little account: tongue tied. *B. Ellison* c– h–

OLD FEATHERS (IRE) 6 b.g. Hernando (FR) – Undiscovered (Tap On Wood) [2002/3 16m⁵ 20d^F 21d³ 22v* 24s Dec 18] workmanlike gelding: fair handicap hurdler: won at Uttoxeter in November: reportedly distressed when tailed off final start: should stay beyond 2¾m: acts on good to firm and heavy going: often goes in snatches. *Jonjo O'Neill* h99

OLD HUSH WING (IRE) 10 b.g. Tirol – Saneena (Kris) [2002/3 c–, h98: 19m⁴ Apr 21] rather sparely-made gelding: unseated eighth only outing over fences: modest hurdler: first run for a year, appeared to run creditably when last of 4 in handicap at Market Rasen in April: stays 25f: acts on any going: usually comes from well off pace (made running at Market Rasen). *Mrs S. J. Smith* c– h98

OLD KING COAL 7 b.g. Miner's Lamp – Mill Shine (Milan) [2002/3 F17s⁶ Oct 28] 10,000 3-y-o: eighth foal: half-brother to 3 winners, including hurdlers Konvekta Control (by Deep Run), stayed 2½m, and Oh So Bright (by Celtic Cone), stayed 2¾m: dam, winning hurdler up to 2½m, from family of one-time smart staying chaser Ever Blessed: no show in point or bumper. *R. M. Stronge* F–

OLD MARSH (IRE) 7 b.g. Grand Lodge (USA) – Lolly Dolly (Alleged (USA)) [2002/3 h110: 16g* 17s³ 16m* 16m* 16m² 16m⁵ 17s^co 20g^F 19d 16m⁴ Feb 21] strong, medium-sized gelding: fairly useful hurdler: won novices at Aintree in May and Uttoxeter and Worcester in July: good fourth to Brooklyn's Gold in handicap at Kempton final start: best around 2m: best efforts on good to firm ground: tried blinkered: has had tongue tied, including last 5 starts: usually makes running: prone to mistakes. *Miss Venetia Williams* h117

OLD NOSEY (IRE) 7 b.g. Muharib (USA) – Regent Star (Prince Regent (FR)) [2002/3 16d 16f⁵ 16d⁶ 16m⁶ F18f³ 20g⁶ 20d⁵ 20d^F 16s⁶ 20g 16g 20m² Apr 19] IR 3,000 3-y-o: ex-Irish gelding: half-brother to several winners, including useful but temperamental staying hurdler Loch Scavaig and fairly useful hurdler/winning chaser up to 3m Fairies Cross (both by The Parson): dam won up to 1m: modest form in bumpers: maiden maiden hurdler: sold out of D. Hughes's stable 1,200 gns Doncaster October Sales after sixth start: seems to stay 2½m: acts on firm and good to soft going: tried blinkered. *B. Mactaggart* h89 F77

OLD OPRY 6 b.g. Old Vic – Tina Rosa (Bustino) [2002/3 h119, F89: 17d 20s² 16v 16s Nov 30] good-topped gelding: fairly useful hurdler, not quite at best in 2002/3: should stay beyond 2m: raced on good going or softer (acts on heavy). *N. Meade, Ireland* h114

OLD ROLLA (IRE) 5 b.g. Old Vic – Criswood (IRE) (Chromite (USA)) [2002/3 F16v 16s 24v³ 24v³ 24s 24v 24g⁶ Apr 23] 11,000 4-y-o: lengthy gelding: second foal: dam unraced: well held in bumper on debut: poor novice hurdler: stays 3m: raced on good ground or softer (acts on heavy). *C. Grant* h82 F–

OLD ROUVEL (USA) 12 b.g. Riverman (USA) – Marie de Russy (FR) (Sassafras (FR)) [2002/3 h129: 23f 24s⁶ 24g Apr 3] close-coupled gelding: fairly useful handicap hurdler: well held last 2 outings: stays 3m: acts on heavy going: has reportedly broken blood vessel: held up, and sometimes finds little. *A. King* h122

OLD TIM (IRE) 10 b.g. Poet's Dream (IRE) – Settled (Blue Cashmere) [2002/3 21s* Nov 21] ex-Irish gelding: maiden pointer/once-raced in steeplechases: modest hurdler: first start for 14 months and after leaving D. Hassett, won selling handicap at Market Rasen: stays 3m: acts on soft and good to firm going. *S. Kirk* c– h90

OLE GUNNAR (IRE) 11 b.g. Le Bavard (FR) – Rareitess (Rarity) [2002/3 h–: 20d³ **h69** Jun 8] poor pointer, successful in May: similar level of form on second of 2 starts over hurdles: should stay beyond 2½m. *M. S. Wilesmith*

OLITHEAGA 8 ch.g. Safawan – Lyaaric (Privy Seal) [2002/3 h99, F93: 19dᵖᵘ 22g **h–** Apr 12] angular gelding: bumper winner: second in novice hurdle in 2001/2: off 16 months (reportedly sidelined by tendon injury, subsequently fired), no show both starts on return. *C. J. Mann*

OLIVER CROMWELL (IRE) 8 br.g. Mandalus – Gemini Gale (Strong Gale) **c115** [2002/3 h127: 23f c21g⁶ c23d³ 22s 24s⁵ c24g³ c19d c24s² Feb 13] workmanlike gelding: **h–** fairly useful handicap hurdler, below best in 2002/3: fairly useful novice chaser: probably better at 3m than shorter: acts on heavy going: tried in cheekpieces/blinkers: usually takes plenty of driving and temperament under suspicion. *P. R. Hedger*

OLIVETY 8 b.g. Lighter – Star of Tycoon (Tycoon II) [2002/3 h84: 22gˢ Oct 19] tall **h72** gelding: lightly raced: poor form over hurdles: bred to stay beyond 2½m: raced on good going or softer. *K. A. Ryan*

OLIVIER (USA) 5 ch.g. Theatrical – Izara (USA) (Blushing John (USA)) [2002/3 **h101** F97: F17d⁶ 21d³ Nov 14] better effort in bumpers when second on debut in 2001/2: off 6 **F78 +** months, third to Putup Or Shutup in maiden at Ludlow on hurdling debut: stays 21f, should prove at least as effective at shorter: has hung left. *Miss Venetia Williams*

OLLAR HOUSE (IRE) 12 b.g. Zaffaran (USA) – Lavengaddy (Balgaddy) [2002/3 **c–** c–, h–: 24m³ 27gᵖᵘ May 29] of little account. *J. Barclay* **h–**

OLLIE MAGERN 5 b.g. Alderbrook – Outfield (Monksfield) [2002/3 F17d F16d **h93 +** 16d 22g² Apr 12] smallish gelding: third foal: dam, modest 3m hurdler, from family **F–** of high-class 2½m chaser Townley Stone and 1991 Grand National third Auntie Dot: left F. Jordan, first form when second in novice hurdle at Stratford: stays 2¾m. *N. A. Twiston-Davies*

OLLIES BOY (IRE) 12 b.g. Electric – Kilcor Rose (Pitpan) [2002/3 c–x, h69: c20d³ **c70 x** Apr 29] strong gelding: poor maiden hurdler/chaser: stays 2¾m: acts on good to firm and **h–** heavy going: often let down by jumping over fences. *Miss Caroline Barclay*

OLNEY LAD 4 b.g. Democratic (USA) – Alipampa (IRE) (Glenstal (USA)) [2002/3 **h82** 16g⁵ 16f⁵ Mar 29] leggy gelding: half-brother to fair 2m hurdler Petuntse (by Phountzi): fair maiden on Flat (will stay 1½m) at 3 yrs for R. Guest: modest form in juvenile at Haydock on second of 2 starts over hurdles. *Mrs P. Robeson*

OMNI COSMO TOUCH (USA) 7 b.g. Trempolino (USA) – Wooden Pudden **c§§** (USA) (Top Ville) [2002/3 c§§, h§§: 24m⁶ 20dʳᵗʳ 17m⁶ 17dʳᵗʳ Oct 26] good-topped **h§§** gelding: fair hurdler on his day: runner-up on chasing debut in 2001/2: has become thoroughly temperamental (often refuses to race): sold out of O. Sherwood's stable 5,200 gns Doncaster May Sales after second start: won point in February: stays 2½m: acts on firm and good to soft going: tried blinkered: one to avoid. *Mrs S. J. Smith*

OMNISCIENT (IRE) 4 br.f. Distinctly North (USA) – Mystic Shadow (IRE) **h–** (Mtoto) [2002/3 16mᶠ Sep 28] modest on Flat (probably stays 1m): towards rear when falling fifth in juvenile on hurdling debut: sold 900 gns Doncaster October Sales. *Mrs P. N. Dutfield*

ON A DEAL 5 b.g. Teenoso (USA) – Gale Spring (IRE) (Strong Gale) [2002/3 F16s **F90** F17s⁴ F16dʳᵒ F17d⁵ Feb 23] long-backed gelding: first foal: dam no sign of ability: best effort in bumpers when close fourth at Taunton in January, pulling hard and making most until 2f out: close up when running out home turn at Wincanton next time. *R. J. Hodges*

ON A FULL WAGER 6 b.g. Homo Sapien – Ntombi (Trasi's Son) [2002/3 F17g⁴ **h–** F16m 16s 16d 20v 20dᵖᵘ Jan 15] angular, workmanlike gelding: third foal: half-brother **F78** to bumper winner Tirikumba (by Le Moss): dam won 2½m hurdle: signs of only a little ability in bumpers and over hurdles. *P. Bowen*

ON APPEAL (IRE) 7 b.g. Buckskin (FR) – Little Quince (Laurence O) [2002/3 F80: **h–** 22d Nov 5] sixth in bumper on debut in early-2001/2: no show in novice hurdle on return. *D. M. Grissell*

ON APPROVAL 4 b.g. First Trump – Gymcrak Lovebird (Taufan (USA)) [2002/3 **F–** F16d⁶ F16g F16g Apr 14] half-brother to fair hurdler Lord of Love (by Noble Patriarch), stays 27f, and 2 winning sprinters, including fair Dominelle (by Domynsky): dam fairly useful on Flat, stayed 1¼m: well held in 3 bumpers, looking unwilling in blinkers final start. *T. D. Easterby*

ONASSIS 6 b.g. Roselier (FR) – Jack's The Girl (IRE) (Supreme Leader) [2002/3 **h79** F16d³ 17s⁵ 21s² 24sᵖᵘ 21sᵖᵘ 20g³ Apr 21] 14,500 4-y-o: sturdy gelding: fourth foal: **F79** half-brother to winning pointer Jackson's Hole (by Brush Aside): dam unraced half-sister to smart staying chaser Lean Ar Aghaidh: third in bumper on debut: poor form when placed over hurdles: should stay beyond 21f: acts on soft going: blinkered final start. *O. Sherwood*

ONCOURSE (IRE) 7 b.g. Toulon – Slaney Jazz (Orchestra) [2002/3 24mᵖᵘ 17s Feb **h–** 13] IR 9,000 4-y-o: ex-Irish gelding: first foal: dam lightly raced in bumpers/points: won bumper at Dundalk in 2001/2: no show in 2 maiden hurdles, sold out of Miss F. Crowley's stable 800 gns Doncaster November Sales in between. *R. D. Tudor*

ONE A DACKIE 4 b.f. Lord Americo – Oriel Dream (Oats) [2002/3 F16f⁶ Mar 29] **F73** third foal: half-sister to fairly useful hurdler Lazy But Lively (by Supreme Leader), stays 3m: dam fair staying hurdler: never a factor in mares bumper at Haydock on debut. *Ferdy Murphy*

ONE FIVE EIGHT 4 b.g. Alflora (IRE) – Dark Nightingale (Strong Gale) [2002/3 **F–** F16g Apr 14] 6,200 3-y-o: second foal: dam fair hurdler up to 2½m: well beaten in maiden bumper on debut. *M. W. Easterby*

ONE FOR ME 5 br.m. Tragic Role (USA) – Chantallee's Pride (Mansooj) [2002/3 **h85** 16mᵐ 16vᵖᵘ Nov 6] modest on Flat (should stay 1¼m): won maiden at Stratford on hurdling debut in October: weakened quickly after 3 out in handicap under much more testing conditions at Kempton next time: will prove best around 2m. *Jean-Rene Auvray*

ONE FOR PHILIP 5 b.m. Blushing Flame (USA) – Ile de Danse (Ile de Bourbon **F83** (USA)) [2002/3 F17s⁴ F17m² F16m³ Dec 17] workmanlike mare: fifth foal: half-sister to winner in Spain by Blakeney: dam, French 10.5f winner at 4 yrs, from family of smart middle-distance performers Ile de Nisky and Bonne Ile, latter dam of useful American jumper All Gong: modest form in frame in 3 bumpers. *L. Lungo*

ONE FOR YOU (IRE) 6 b.m. Blues Traveller (IRE) – Steel Duchess (IRE) (Yash- **F–** gan) [2002/3 F17m Oct 3] lengthy mare: no sign of ability in 2 bumpers: sold £1,200 Ascot April Sales. *Jean-Rene Auvray*

ONEFOURSEVEN 10 b.g. Jumbo Hirt (USA) – Dominance (Dominion) [2002/3 **h–** h78: 23d Nov 1] smallish, sturdy gelding: poor maiden hurdler: stays 3m: acts on good to firm going, probably on soft. *P. C. Haslam*

ONE IN THE EYE 10 br.g. Arrasas (USA) – Mingalles (Prince de Galles) [2002/3 **h–** 16gᵖᵘ 21dᵖᵘ Nov 4] small gelding: poor hurdler in 1999/00: tongue tied, little sign of retaining ability. *Jamie Poulton*

ONE KNIGHT (IRE) 7 ch.g. Roselier (FR) – Midnights Daughter (IRE) (Long **c150 p** Pond) [2002/3 h120: c19s* c24d³ c23d* c23d* c24g* Mar 12] **h–**

'A slow old boat'. Possibly an extreme attempt to fool the BHB handicapper, but, whether in jest or not, this was Philip Hobbs's description of One Knight just after he had landed the championship event for staying novice chasers, the Royal & SunAlliance Chase at the Cheltenham Festival. The SunAlliance has a rather undeserved reputation as a race for plodders. Like any race of its nature, the SunAlliance has its vintage years and those a little less sparkling, winners who go on to make their mark in the biggest prizes in the sport and those that never win again. One Knight's form in winning isn't on a par with the best recent victors of the SunAlliance, Florida Pearl and Looks Like Trouble, but he's thereabouts with most of the rest and he could just be underestimated, as the main focus after the race seemed to be on the runner-up Jair du Cochet and the poor performances of the market leaders. In the period since *Chasers & Hurdlers* started, with the 1975/6 edition, the SunAlliance compares well with the championship event for two-mile novice chasers, the Arkle Trophy. Six winners of the Arkle Trophy have ended the season rated the top novice chaser—Anaglogs Daughter, Clayside, Bobsline, Danish Flight, Remittance Man and Moscow Flyer—compared to five winners of the SunAlliance—Brown Chamberlin, Kildimo, Miinnehoma, Monsieur Le Cure and Brief Gale. SunAlliance winners who weren't rated top novice chaser but who made a major impact include, in addition to Florida Pearl and Looks Like Trouble, Tied Cottage, Gay Spartan, Master Smudge and Garrison Savannah. Not many boats there.

Royal & SunAlliance Chase, Cheltenham—One Knight enjoys the run of things and holds off the patiently-ridden Jair du Cochet (noseband); the other horse pictured is third-placed Barrow Drive

One Knight, who joined his trainer as an unbroken three-year-old, was forward enough as a youngster to do well in bumpers, winning at Wincanton as a four-year-old and at Newbury early on at five. He did fairly well over hurdles the following season, scoring a couple of times at Chepstow including in the Grade 2 Persian War Novices' Hurdle before twice running as if amiss. As a tall gelding, he always looked the sort to do better over fences and it did not take him long to prove the point, upsetting the odds laid on Le Roi Miguel (also making his chasing debut) by five lengths in the seven-runner Grade 2 Tote Exacta Rising Stars Novices' Chase at Chepstow in November. The two-and-a-half-mile trip was too far for the runner-up, but well-regarded Hand Inn Hand was four lengths away third and there was no denying One Knight's promise in jumping fluently as he made all—a standard tactic with him by now, given a poor effort when restrained once over hurdles. Given his proficiency over the Chepstow fences, One Knight's performance when favourite for another Grade 2 at Newbury later in November, the Systems By Design Worcester Novices' Chase, came as a surprise. He all but fell five out and made another mistake two fences later, ending up seventeen lengths behind Lucky Bay in third. Easy odds-on successes at Exeter in December and January doubtless helped restore his confidence—he jumped slightly left on the first occasion but was bold and fluent on the second.

Even in the absence of such significant novices as Beef Or Salmon, La Landiere, Tarxien, Le Coudray and Stormez, One Knight was still only fourth favourite of the nine runners for the Royal & SunAlliance Chase. The first two in the betting, Keen Leader and It Takes Time, had both been possible Gold Cup runners; the latter's position in the market was based as much on his potential (he had finished third in the 2002 Stayers' Hurdle) and the fact that he represented the Pipe-McCoy combination as on form, but Keen Leader had put up fine displays to win important events at Wetherby and Ascot. Third favourite Jair du Cochet, the outstanding juvenile hurdler of 2000/1, had won four of his five starts over fences headed by the Grade 1 Feltham Novices' Chase at Kempton. There was just one Irish challenger, Barrow Drive, successful in a Grade 1 at Leopardstown, and the pick of the others looked to be dual winner Iris Royal. The race was unsatisfactory for several reasons. Keen Leader jumped indifferently and ran way below form in fifth and Jair du Cochet's jockey seemingly was guilty of over-confidence in holding his mount up and, as a result, setting him to make up eight lengths on the leader after the fourth last. The leader was One Knight, who had not jumped with much flair but had been allowed to make the running without being harried and certainly wasn't stopping when Jair du Cochet tried to peg him back. Far from it, since One Knight increased the pace and galloped on strongly all the way to the line to win by a length and three quarters from Jair du Cochet, with Barrow Drive ten lengths further back and It Takes Time last of the six finishers. One Knight is quoted at 33/1 for the 2004 Gold Cup, which seems a fair reflection of his chance. He is unlikely to be given so much rope in a top race again, but it is in his favour that he has been lightly campaigned, having only twelve runs in three seasons, so probably has improvement in him and is with a trainer who can be guaranteed to get the best out of him. One Knight isn't likely to start the season on a particularly favourable mark in handicaps, but races which play to his strengths, such as the Rehearsal and

Mr R. Gibbs' "One Knight"

the Welsh National (he will stay long distances), could provide the ideal start to his campaign.

One Knight (IRE) (ch.g. 1996)	Roselier (FR) (gr 1973)	Misti IV (br 1958)	Medium
			Mist
		Peace Rose (gr 1959)	Fastnet Rock
			La Paix
	Midnights Daughter (IRE) (ch 1991)	Long Pond (ch 1981)	Rarity
			Raindrops
		Midnight Oil (ch 1976)	Menelek
			Ballinacree

It was not just One Knight's looks that suggested he would make a chaser. His pedigree turned likelihood into probability. Roselier sires winners of all types of races—by dint of his large number of offspring—but is essentially a sire of chasers. Around forty per cent of his runners over fences win races and most of his horses do best given a test of stamina. One Knight, who has raced entirely on good going or softer and acts on soft, is suited by three miles and will stay further. The unraced dam Midnights Daughter comes from a splendid jumping family, that of Champion Chase victor Lough Inagh. She is a half-sister to four winners over jumps, headed by Shannon Spray, a smart and game front-running hurdler who won seven races plus one over fences and is dam of an above-average chaser in Eire-spray. Another sibling Renagown won a listed chase, and two others respectively have produced the useful staying hurdler/chaser Direct Access (by Roselier) and Sunset Lodge, a useful hurdler/chaser at up to two and a half miles. Incidentally, a three-year-old store by Spanish Place out of Midnights Daughter fetched €62,000 at the 2003 Derby Sale. *P. J. Hobbs*

ONE MORE NATIVE (IRE) 6 ch.g. Be My Native (USA) – Romany Fortune **F85**
(Sunyboy) [2002/3 F16d³ F16s⁴ Jan 30] fourth foal: half-brother to fairly useful bumper
winner For Paddy's Day (by Supreme Leader): dam unraced half-sister to smart staying
chaser Romany King: in frame both starts in bumpers at Southwell. *J. L. Needham*

ONE MORE STRIDE 7 ch.g. Beveled (USA) – Gem of Gold (Jellaby) [2002/3 **c–**
c16g^pu 17d⁶ 19d 19d Feb 10] workmanlike gelding: little sign of ability: left C. Cox after **h–**
reappearance: tried blinkered. *H. E. Haynes*

ONE NATION (IRE) 8 br.g. Be My Native (USA) – Diklers Run (Deep Run) **c–**
[2002/3 c97p, h–: c19s^pu 21s³ 21d 17s Jan 25] big, strong gelding: modest form at best in **h110**
novice chases, lacklustre effort on reappearance: one-time fairly useful hurdler, below
form in 2002/3: stays 21f: acts on heavy going (placed in bumper on good to firm):
free-going sort. *Miss H. C. Knight*

ONE NIGHT OUT (IRE) 7 b. or br.g. Jamesmead – Deladeuce (Le Bavard (FR)) **c122**
[2002/3 h133, F107: c17s* c24s⁴ c17s⁶ c18s^F c20g⁶ c29g^F c20m² Apr 22] sturdy gelding: **h–**
useful hurdler: fairly useful novice chaser: won maiden at Fairyhouse in November: none
too fluent subsequently, 3 lengths behind only other finisher Thari in weakly-contested
Grade 1 there final start: effective around 2m to 3m: acts on heavy going, probably on
good to firm. *W. P. Mullins, Ireland*

ONEOFOUROWN (IRE) 12 ch.g. Varshan – Twinkling (Star Appeal) [2002/3 **c88 x**
c24m⁵ c24s⁶ c24m³ c24m⁶ c24g⁵ c25f⁶ c24m³ c26s^ur c28v⁴ c24g* c25g^ur Apr 20] angular **h–**
gelding: modest handicap chaser: best effort in 2002/3 when winning at Downpatrick in
March: best at 3m+: acts on any going: blinkered: usually tongue tied but effective when
not: poor jumper. *S. Donohoe, Ireland*

ONE OF THE NATIVES (IRE) 9 b.g. Be My Native (USA) – Take Me Home **c–**
(Amoristic (USA)) [2002/3 c86: c24m c19d^pu May 14] lengthy gelding: winning pointer:
modest form at best in steeplechases, sometimes shapes as if amiss. *Miss H. C. Knight*

ONEOFTWO 6 ch.m. Bold Arrangement – Celtic Waters (Celtic Cone) [2002/3 F16g **h–**
22m^pu Oct 6] first foal: dam maiden staying hurdler/chaser: no sign of ability in bumper **F–**
and novice hurdle. *Mrs J. C. McGregor*

ONETHREESIXSQADRON 5 b.g. Bandmaster (USA) – Paprika (IRE) (The Par- **F–**
son) [2002/3 F17m Jul 15] first foal: dam runner-up in 17f hurdle: looked ungenuine
when tailed off in maiden bumper on debut. *A. G. Newcombe*

ONE UP (IRE) 5 b.m. Bob Back (USA) – Strong Desire (IRE) (Strong Gale) [2002/3 **h–**
16s 16s 17g⁵ Apr 21] ex-Irish mare: second foal: dam, won up to 3m over fences, out
of half-sister to good French jumper Cyborg: well held in 3 starts over hurdles, left
C. McCarthy after second. *M. Todhunter*

ONEWAY (IRE) 6 b.g. Bob's Return (IRE) – Rendezvous (Lorenzaccio) [2002/3 **h94**
F17d 19d⁵ 17s² 19d⁴ 25g⁵ Mar 17] 20,000 4-y-o: workmanlike gelding: has scope: ninth **F–**
foal: half-brother to fair hurdler/chaser Countess Verushka (by Strong Gale), stayed 25f:
dam, placed over hurdles, half-sister to useful juvenile hurdler Tenth of October, from
family of Lanzarote: placed once in maiden points in 2002: well held in bumper: modest
form first 3 starts in novice hurdles: should be suited by 2½m+. *M. G. Rimell*

ON ICE (IRE) 7 ch.g. Pursuit of Love – Ice Chocolate (USA) (Icecapade (USA)) **h–**
[2002/3 h–, F–: 17g^pu Oct 15] lengthy gelding: of no account: has had tongue tied.
F. P. Murtagh

ONLY LITTLE 5 ch.m. Sula Bula – Chicory (Vaigly Great) [2002/3 16s^pu 17s^pu Nov **h–**
28] small mare: half-sister to 2 poor hurdlers: dam twice-raced half-sister to useful Flat
performers/winning hurdlers Macmillion and Baz Bombati: showed nothing in 2 races
over hurdles. *D. P. Keane*

ONLY ONCE 8 b.g. King's Ride – Rambling Gold (Little Buskins) [2002/3 c27v* **c117 p**
c25g* Mar 21] IR 27,500 4-y-o: rather leggy gelding: sixth foal: half-brother to
high-class chaser Senor El Betrutti (by Roselier), stays 3¼m, and to winning pointer by
Strong Gale: dam, winning 2m hurdler, sister to very smart staying chaser Drumadowney
and useful staying hurdler Inish Glora: won second of 2 starts in maiden Irish points in
2001: successful both starts in steeplechases, in maiden at Sedgefield in January and
novice at Kelso in March: made all and jumped soundly to beat Bobayaro 2 lengths at
latter course, despite saddle slipping after 2 out and finishing lame (later reported sound):
stays 27f: acts on heavy going: open to further improvement. *L. Lungo*

ONLY ONE MATTY (IRE)   6 b.g. Satco (FR) – Poundworld (IRE) (Orchestra)   **h93**
[2002/3 16s³ 24s³ 18m⁴ 22g 16d Nov 25] IR 8,500 3-y-o: ex-Irish gelding: second foal:
dam lightly-raced maiden: modest maiden hurdler: sold out of C. Roche's stable 8,000
gns Doncaster September Sales after fourth outing: never dangerous but not at all
knocked about on British debut: effective at 2m to 3m: acts on soft and good to firm
ground: tongue tied second to fourth (also blinkered) starts. *Mrs K. Walton*

ONLY WHEN PROVOKED (IRE)   5 b.g. General Monash (USA) – Lyzia (IRE)   **h70**
(Lycius (USA)) [2002/3 h70: 16d³ 20d⁵ 19gᵖᵘ Jun 12] poor maiden hurdler: stays 2½m:
yet to race on extremes of going: blinkered/visored nowadays. *A. Streeter*

ONLY WORDS (USA)   6 ch.g. Shuailaan (USA) – Conversation Piece (USA)   **h74**
(Seeking The Gold (USA)) [2002/3 h69: 16d² 16g 20f² 17g 21g 17d* 16v² 16d⁵ 17s² 17v⁴
16g 17v² 19dᵖᵘ 21d Mar 18] workmanlike gelding: poor handicap hurdler: won seller at
Sedgefield in October: barely stays 2½m: acts on any going: well below form in blinkers
second outing. *A. J. Lockwood*

ONLY YOU   7 b.g. Gildoran – Outfield (Monksfield) [2002/3 h70§: 20g³ 20g⁵ May   **h70 §**
22] leggy, angular gelding: poor maiden hurdler: stays 21f: acts on good to firm and good   **F–**
to soft going: consistent, but finishes weakly. *N. A. Twiston-Davies*

ON THE BONE   11 b.m. Lyphento (USA) – Lydia Languish (Hotfoot) [2002/3 c–:   **c–**
c24gᵖᵘ May 3] modest maiden pointer. *R. Harvey*

ON THE DAY (IRE)   6 ch.g. Roselier (FR) – Solar Jet (Mandalus) [2002/3 h91p: **h91**
20d³ 27v² 24vᵖᵘ 24g³ Mar 28] lengthy gelding: modest form over hurdles: stays 27f: acts
on heavy going: reportedly distressed third start. *L. Lungo*

ON THE GAME   8 b.m. Unfuwain (USA) – All Glorious (Crowned Prince (USA))   **h–**
[2002/3 h–: 22sᶠ Dec 2] no form over hurdles. *D. C. O'Brien*

ON THE LUCE   6 b.g. Karinga Bay – Lirchur (Lir) [2002/3 F74: 16dᵖᵘ May 1]   **c–**
good-topped gelding: won maiden point in March, little other sign of ability. *L. Lungo*   **h–**

ON THE MEND (IRE)   10 ch.g. Broken Hearted – Mugs Away (Mugatpura) [2002/3   **c117**
c113, h116: c22g³ c18sᵖᵘ 20s* 20s² c19sᶠ c18s* c21v⁶ 24d c20mᵘʳ Apr 12] lengthy   **h113**
gelding: fair handicap hurdler: won at Cork in December: best effort
when winning minor event at Clonmel in February by 6 lengths from Garvivonnian:
effective around 2m to 2¾m: acts on soft and good to firm going: tried blinkered in
bumpers. *M. J. P. O'Brien, Ireland*

ON THE RUN (IRE)   9 ch.m. Don't Forget Me – Chepstow House (USA) (Northern   **c81**
Baby (CAN)) [2002/3 h79: 16m² 16d² 17m³ c16g⁴ c19m² c20m⁴ c20fᵘʳ c19gᵖᵘ Oct 18]   **h79**
lengthy, angular mare: poor hurdler/novice chaser: stays 2½m: acts on firm and good to
soft going: tongue tied. *D. J. Wintle*

ONTOS (GER)   7 b. or br.g. Super Abound (USA) – Onestep (GER) (Konigsstuhl   **h116**
(GER)) [2002/3 17sᶠ 16s⁴ 16sᶠ 16d⁵ 16m⁵ 16g* 17g* 16g* 16m⁴ 16g⁵ 16v* 17s⁴ 17d
16g⁴ 20v³ 16d³ 18d⁴ 18g³ 16d⁴ Apr 4] leggy, short-backed gelding: successful 4 times up
to 11f on Flat in Germany for Frau E. Schnakenberg: fairly useful hurdler: won maiden at
Huntingdon in August, novices at Sedgefield (final outing for R. O'Leary) and Perth in
September and handicap at Kelso in November: ran at least creditably most other starts,
fourth of 12 to Limerick Boy in Grade 2 novice at Aintree final one: barely stays testing
2½m: acts on heavy and good to firm going: has finished weakly, but is consistent.
A. Scott

ONWARDSANDUPWARDS (IRE)   4 b. or br.g. Un Desperado (FR) – Kalifornia   **F89 p**
Katie (IRE) (Sharp Charter) [2002/3 F17s* Jan 28] useful-looking gelding: first foal: dam
unraced: favourite, overcame inexperience to win bumper at Taunton on debut by neck
from Ramirez: sure to improve. *P. F. Nicholls*

OODACHEE   4 b.g. Marju (IRE) – Lady Marguerrite (Blakeney) [2002/3 F16g²   **F100**
F16m³ Apr 20] €27,000 3-y-o: fourth foal: dam, twice-raced on Flat, from family of St
Leger and Gold Cup winner Classic Cliche and smart 1½m filly My Emma: fairly useful
form when placed in 2 bumpers, second to Steppes of Gold at Newcastle and third to
Kilrossanty in 4-y-o event at Cork. *C. F. Swan, Ireland*

OO EE BE   7 b.g. Whittingham (IRE) – Miss Derby (USA) (Master Derby (USA))   **c73**
[2002/3 h69: c16d⁵ c20m Mar 19] leggy, angular gelding: poor maiden hurdler: sold out   **h–**
of M. Evans' stable £2,000 Ascot June Sales: poor form in points and hunter chases:
probably stays 2½m: acts on good to firm and heavy going. *Mrs N. J. Hughes*

OOPS (IRE) 4 b.g. In The Wings – Atsuko (IRE) (Mtoto) [2002/3 17d Jan 27] fair **h–**
maiden on Flat (should stay 1¾m) for J. Given: gelded and off 5½ months, seventh of 10
in juvenile at Exeter on hurdling debut: joined T. Easterby. *A. J. Lidderdale*

OPAL'LOU (FR) 7 b.m. Garde Royale – Calligraphie (FR) (R B Chesne) [2002/3 **c89 §**
c90, h?: c19d² c19d⁵ c20g³ c22g³ c25f² Apr 21] in frame over hurdles in France: modest **h–**
novice chaser: probably stays easy 25f: acts on firm and good to soft going: weak finisher,
and not to be trusted. *P. F. Nicholls*

OPAL RIDGE 6 ch.g. Jupiter Island – The Beginning (Goldhill) [2002/3 F16v⁴ Dec **F82**
21] half-brother to useful 21f hunter chase winner Itsgoneoff (by Neltino): dam winning
2m selling hurdler: won maiden from 3 starts in points in 2002: modest form when fourth
of 14 to Plastic Paddy in bumper at Uttoxeter: will stay beyond 2m. *P. R. Webber*

OPEN GROUND (IRE) 6 ch.g. Common Grounds – Poplina (USA) (Roberto (USA)) **h95 d**
[2002/3 h108: 20s⁴ 16sᵖᵘ 16v 16d 16dᶠ Mar 10] compact gelding: handicap hurdler, out
of sorts in 2002/3: should stay 2½m: acts on heavy going: usually blinkered/visored:
often makes running. *Ian Williams*

OPENING BAT 7 b.g. Batshoof – Absalantra (Absalom) [2002/3 F–: 16dᵖᵘ May 6] **h–**
no sign of ability. *Miss Z. C. Davison*

OPEN INVITATION (IRE) 9 b.g. Hollow Hand – Nohoval Jane (Amoristic (USA)) **c–**
[2002/3 c–: c24mᵖᵘ 20d⁴ 20m c20gᵖᵘ Sep 26] of little account. *Mrs J. C. McGregor* **h–**

OPTIMISM (FR) 5 b.g. Roakarad – Miss Daisy (FR) (Shirley Heights) [2002/3 F16d **F84 ?**
F17f³ Mar 24] third foal: half-brother to 1m winner by Solar One: dam maiden half-sister
to smart 1m to 1¼m performer Marrast: seemingly made better effort in bumpers when
third of 5 to Blue Derby in falsely-run event at Taunton. *R. H. Alner*

OPTIMISTIC CHRIS 8 b.g. Pharly (FR) – Gay Twenties (Lord Gayle (USA)) **c116**
[2002/3 c97, h95: c21g⁴ c17g³ c20s² c20d⁶ c16gᵖᵘ Dec 13] leggy gelding: winning **h–**
hurdler: fair handicap chaser: ran well when placed at Market Rasen and Bangor: left
A. Streeter, poor efforts last 2 starts: stays 2½m: acts on good to firm and heavy going:
effective visored or not: usually races up with pace. *Mrs J. Candlish*

OPTIMISTIC THINKER 9 ch.g. Beveled (USA) – Racemosa (Town Crier) **c– §**
[2002/3 c102§, h93§: c16m⁴ c16vᵖᵘ c16sᵖᵘ c17gᵖᵘ 17gᵖᵘ Apr 21] lengthy gelding: has **h– §**
reportedly had soft palate operation: winning hurdler/chaser, fair at best: out of sorts in
2002/3: raced mainly around 2m: acts on any going: has won with/without blinkers: has
had tongue tied: none too keen. *T. R. George*

OPTIMUM NIGHT 4 b.g. Superlative – Black Bess (Hasty Word) [2002/3 F16d **F–**
Mar 5] 2,500 3-y-o: second foal: dam unraced: little show in bumper or maidens on Flat.
P. D. Niven

ORACLE DES MOTTES (FR) 4 b.g. Signe Divin (USA) – Daisy Des Mottes (FR) **h104**
(Abdonski (FR)) [2002/3 17s² 16d³ 17dʳᵒ 17d³ Jan 27] tall ex-French gelding: third foal:
dam French 1993 2-y-o 1m winner: twice-raced on Flat, won 1½m event at Cluny in
September (final start for C. Diard): best effort over hurdles when third to Andy Gin in
juvenile at Exeter final outing: raced around 2m on good to soft/soft going: ran out third
start. *P. F. Nicholls*

ORAKE PRINCE 4 b.g. Bluegrass Prince (IRE) – Kiri Te (Liboi (USA)) [2002/3 **h–**
16dᵖᵘ 19gᵖᵘ Mar 17] modest maiden on Flat (should stay 1¼m): showed nothing in 2 runs
over hurdles. *J. G. Portman*

ORANGE ORDER (IRE) 10 ch.g. Generous (IRE) – Fleur d'Oranger (Northfields **c92**
(USA)) [2002/3 c94, h–: 20dᵖᵘ c20g⁵ c22mᵖᵘ c21m³ c21g³ c21gᵖᵘ c26mᵖᵘ c27g³ c21m³ **h–**
21gᵖᵘ 21m Apr 26] leggy, sparely-made gelding: winning hurdler: modest handicap
chaser, generally below form in 2002/3: stays 21f: acts on any going, though raced mainly
on good or firmer nowadays: successful 5 times at Sedgefield: races prominently.
G. M. Moore

ORANGERIE (IRE) 5 b.g. Darshaan – Fleur d'Oranger (Northfields (USA)) [2002/3 **h109 §**
h97p: 16m* 22d² 24s⁴ᵈ 20v⁴ 18sᵘʳ 16s² 19d³ 20g⁶ 20d⁵ Apr 25] good-topped gelding: fair
hurdler: won maiden at Cheltenham in October: effective at 2m to 2¾m: acts on soft and
good to firm going: blinkered after second outing: tends to find little. *P. J. Hobbs*

ORANGE TREE LAD 5 b.g. Tragic Role (USA) – Adorable Cherub (USA) (Halo **h74**
(USA)) [2002/3 16sᵖᵘ 16d 17v³ 17s³ 17d⁴ 19s⁴ 16s³ 17s⁵ 16s 17m⁶ 16dᵘʳ Apr 9] leggy
gelding: modest maiden on Flat (stays 9.4f), sold out of P. Hedger's stable 3,500 gns
Doncaster March (2002) Sales: poor novice hurdler: seems best around 2m: raced mainly
on going softer than good. *Mrs Jane Galpin*

ORAPA 4 b.g. Spectrum (IRE) – African Dance (USA) (El Gran Senor (USA)) [2002/3 **h–** 16d Feb 26] leggy, lengthy gelding: little sign of ability on Flat, sold out of Sir Michael Stoute's stable 500 gns Doncaster September Sales: tailed off in novice on hurdling debut. *Julian Poulton*

ORBICULARIS (IRE) 7 b.g. Supreme Leader – Liffey Travel (Le Bavard (FR)) **h–** [2002/3 h–, F–: 16m 22s 20s Nov 16] little sign of ability. *R. F. Fisher*

ORCHARD FIELDS (IRE) 6 b.g. Lord Americo – Art Lover (IRE) (Over The **h102** River (FR)) [2002/3 F84: 20d⁴ 20s⁴ 23d⁵ 20d 22g Apr 26] good-topped gelding: modest form in bumpers: 20/1, won 5-runner novice at Leicester in November on hurdling debut by head from Brewster: well below that form subsequently, let down by jumping more than once: should stay beyond 2½m: raced on good going or softer. *Mrs P. Sly*

ORCHESTRA'S BOY (IRE) 8 b.g. Homo Sapien – Ballycurnane Lady (Orchestra) **h75** [2002/3 h–, F89: 22m² 24m² Oct 30] runner-up on second of 3 outings in bumpers: poor form in small fields over hurdles: sold 6,000 gns Doncaster November Sales. *Mrs A. M. Thorpe*

ORIENTAL STYLE (IRE) 9 ro.g. Indian Ridge – Bazaar Promise (Native Bazaar) **c97 §** [2002/3 c90§, h–: c27s² c20v* c26v⁴ c25d 28g Mar 16] close-coupled gelding: modest **h– §** handicap chaser: won at Uttoxeter in December: ran poorly after, including over hurdles (first run after leaving P. Rodford): effective at testing 2½m to 27f: acts on heavy going: visored/blinkered: ungenuine. *M. R. Hoad*

ORIENT BAY (IRE) 8 b.g. Commanche Run – East Link (IRE) (Over The River **c80 ?** (FR)) [2002/3 c–: c24dᵖᵘ c25dᴿ c25s⁴ c24d⁴ c25dᵖᵘ c24m³ c25m³ c24gᵘʳ Apr 19] strong gelding: winning pointer: bought out of T. Tate's stable 15,000 gns Doncaster August Sales: little form in steeplechases (has had jumping problems): has worn cheekpieces. *M. Sheppard*

ORIENT EXPRESS (IRE) 6 b.g. Blues Traveller (IRE) – Oriental Splendour **c86 §** (Runnett) [2002/3 16m 16m 18m³ c16d³ c18m² c18dᵖᵘ c16vᵖᵘ Dec 20] half-brother to **h86 §** fairly useful 2m hurdler Really Chuffed (by Shavian): modest maiden on Flat (stays 9f) at 3 yrs for B. Meehan: apparently modest form in novice hurdle third start and maiden chase one: sold out of J. Gifford's stable £3,700 Ascot October Sales, reluctant to race both subsequent starts: best left alone. *Mrs L. Richards*

ORLANDO SUNRISE (IRE) 6 ch.m. Dolphin Street (FR) – Miss Belgravia (USA) **h–** (Smarten (USA)) [2002/3 h77: 16m 19g Jul 27] lengthy mare: maiden on Flat: poor novice hurdler: tried blinkered: joined R. Dickin. *Ian Williams*

ORLEANS (IRE) 8 b.g. Scenic – Guest House (What A Guest) [2002/3 h76: c27sᶠ **c–** Mar 11] tall gelding: poor maiden hurdler: first completion in points/hunter chase when **h–** successful in March (has refused twice): tried visored/blinkered: has also been reluctant to race. *S. J. Robinson*

ORSWELL CREST 9 b.g. Crested Lark – Slave's Bangle (Prince Rheingold) **c105** [2002/3 c86, h–: c25g* c25d* c24s³ c25s³ c23g³ c25m* c31g⁴ Apr 24] lengthy gelding: **h–** fair novice chaser: won handicaps at Wincanton and Aintree (comfortably) in November and Ayr in April, beat Keiran 2½ lengths in valuable 7-runner event at last-named: stays 3¼m (seemingly not 31f): acts on soft and good to firm going: races up with pace. *P. J. Hobbs*

OSCAIL AN DORAS (IRE) 14 ch.g. Avocat – Candora (Cantab) [2002/3 c23m **c–** c21m Jul 19] good-topped gelding: one-time fair chaser up to 2½m: successful 3 times in **h–** points in 2002, and in March: acts on any going: tried blinkered. *P. Bowen*

OSCAR MAC 4 b.g. Double Eclipse (IRE) – Stravano (Handsome Sailor) [2002/3 **h–** F16d F17d 17sᵖᵘ 17gᵖᵘ Mar 17] leggy, lengthy gelding: first foal: dam no form on Flat: no **F–** sign of ability. *Mrs L. Williamson*

OSCAR PERFORMANCE (IRE) 8 gr.g. Roselier (FR) – Miss Iverk (Torus) **c105** [2002/3 h–, F–: 16g*ᵈⁱˢ 20s* 23m² c24s³ c24mᵖᵘ Feb 21] lengthy gelding: fair hurdler: **h105** won novices at Towcester (subsequently disqualified on technical grounds) in May and Uttoxeter (made hard work of landing odds in very weak race) in June: off 6 months, 5¼ lengths last of 3 finishers to Hersov in steadily-run novice chase at Kempton: seemed to go amiss on handicap debut: stays 3m: acts on soft going. *R. H. Buckler*

OSCARSEXPRESS 6 ch.m. Gunner B – Anchor Express (Carlingford Castle) **h–** [2002/3 F66: 26gᵖᵘ May 4] poor form in bumpers, shaping like a stayer: jumped poorly on hurdling debut: won maiden point in April. *D. Burchell*

OSCAR WILDE 11 b.g. Arctic Lord – Topsy Bee (Be Friendly) [2002/3 c78: c16m May 3] tall gelding: winning chaser: fairly useful pointer nowadays, successful 3 times in 2003 before end of April: barely stays 25f: tends to make mistakes. *R. H. Alner*   **c– x**

O SO BOSSY 13 ch.g. Sousa – Bubbling Spirit (Hubble Bubble) [2002/3 c92x: c26s³ May 28] fair pointer: generally let down by jumping in hunter chases: stays 3¼m. *A. W. Congdon*   **c89 x**

OSOSHOT 10 b.g. Teenoso (USA) – Duckdown (Blast) [2002/3 h107: 16d 22dF 23d² 22d 22v 24g³ Mar 22] workmanlike gelding: fair handicap hurdler: easily best effort in 2002/3 on third outing: stays 23f: acts on soft going: has jumped poorly/looked hard ride. *A. J. Wilson*   **h104 x**

OTAHUNA 7 b.g. Selkirk (USA) – Stara (Star Appeal) [2002/3 16sᵖᵘ 17g 17d² 17g² 17g Sep 28] leggy gelding: poor 2m novice hurdler: sold 1,800 gns Doncaster October Sales, resold £2,000 (privately) Ascot November Sales. *J. A. Moore*   **h69**

OTTERINGTON GIRL 7 b.m. Noble Patriarch – Bidweaya (USA) (Lear Fan (USA)) [2002/3 17m 17m Apr 26] of little account. *Miss S. E. Hall*   **h–**

OTTOMAN (IRE) 6 b.g. Sadler's Wells (USA) – Morning Devotion (USA) (Affirmed (USA)) [2002/3 F16g May 22] 6,000 3-y-o: brother to useful 1m/9f winner First Night and winning 2m hurdler Vandas Choice, and closely related to several winners, including Oaks and Irish Derby winner Balanchine (by Storm Bird) and smart winner up to 1½m Romanov (by Nureyev): dam, 2-y-o 6f winner, stayed 1½m: seventh of 21 in bumper at Worcester on debut very early in season, hanging right and carrying head awkwardly when ridden: sold 5,000 gns Doncaster May Sales, resold 2,400 gns Doncaster September Sales. *G. A. Swinbank*   **F84**

OUDALMUTEENA (IRE) 8 b.g. Lahib (USA) – Roxy Music (IRE) (Song) [2002/3 h71+: c17g May 1] sturdy gelding: poor hurdler: no show on chasing debut: stays 21f: raced mainly on good going or softer (acts on heavy): inconsistent. *C. J. Gray*   **c– h– §**

OULTON BROAD 7 b.g. Midyan (USA) – Lady Quachita (USA) (Sovereign Dancer (USA)) [2002/3 h80: 17m⁶ 19d⁴ 20d* 22m⁴ 20g² c16dᵘʳ 20d⁶ 20m³ 23m* Oct 24] sparely-made gelding: won on Flat in July: one-time fairly useful hurdler: claimed from M. Ewer-Hoad £5,000 after second start: won handicaps at Perth and Uttoxeter in June and Haydock in October: unseated second on chasing debut: stays 23f: acts on soft and good to firm ground: wears cheekpieces. *R. Ford*   **c– h101**

OUR ARMAGEDDON (NZ) 6 b.g. Sky Chase (NZ) – Monte d'Oro (NZ) (Cache of Gold (USA)) [2002/3 17s² 16s* 16d³ 17d* 17g* Mar 29] rather leggy gelding: half-brother to fairly useful 2m chaser Black Bullet (by Silver Pistol): thrice-raced on Flat in New Zealand, won over 1m at 4 yrs: fairly useful novice hurdler: progressed well, winning novices at Newcastle in December and Carlisle and Market Rasen in March: again made all and jumped fluently when beating Mind How You Go 3½ lengths at last-named: likely to stay beyond 17f: raced on good going or softer over hurdles: may do better yet. *R. C. Guest*   **h118 +**

OUR BARRICK (IRE) 7 b.g. Sharp Charter – Mimmsie Starr (Pitskelly) [2002/3 c21mᵖᵘ Jul 4] big gelding: of little account. *J. Neville*   **c– h–**

OUR BOY (IRE) 8 b.g. Convinced – Miss Polymer (Doulab (USA)) [2002/3 c99, h–: c26g c25m² Apr 22] good-topped gelding: won point in February: fair hunter chaser: 11 lengths second of 6 finishers to Polaris Flame at Fairyhouse: stays 25f: acts on good to firm going: tongue tied. *J. G. Cromwell, Ireland*   **c94 h–**

OUR DESTINY 5 b.g. Mujadil (USA) – Superspring (Superlative) [2002/3 16d Jun 3] modest on Flat (stays 11f): no show on hurdling debut: sold to join D. Burchell 1,400 gns Doncaster August Sales: successful on all-weather in January and March. *M. A. Buckley*   **h–**

OUR DREAM (IRE) 4 b.f. Bob Back (USA) – Baybush (Boreen (FR)) [2002/3 F16g⁵ Feb 22] tenth foal: half-sister to several winners, notably one-time smart chaser up to 25f Sparky Gayle (by Strong Gale): dam, winning 2m hurdler, half-sister to high-class chaser up to 3m Golden Freeze: travelled comfortably long way when fifth of 20 to Countess Camilla in mares bumper at Huntingdon on debut. *Mrs M. Reveley*   **F81**

OUR ETHEL 5 ch.m. Be My Chief (USA) – Annes Gift (Ballymoss) [2002/3 F85: F16g F16g Mar 23] leggy mare: won mares bumper on debut in 2001/2: well held all 3 subsequent starts. *Mrs M. Reveley*   **F74**

OUR IMPERIAL BAY (USA) 4 b.g. Smart Strike (CAN) – Heat Lightning (USA) (Summer Squall (USA)) [2002/3 16g⁶ 16s⁵ Feb 24] tall gelding: fair on Flat (best form   **h101**

around 1½m): around 19 lengths sixth of 20 to Saintsaire in juvenile at Newbury on hurdling debut: went off too fast next time: blinkered both starts: joined R. Stronge. *Mrs A. J. Perrett*

OUR JOLLY SWAGMAN   8 b.g. Thowra (FR) – Queens Dowry (Dominion) [2002/3 c95, h–: c26s^{pu} c29s^{pu} c26v^{pu} c20s³ c26s c25s* c26s² c24d^{pu} c26g* Apr 19] sturdy gelding: fair handicap chaser: won at Folkestone in February and Newton Abbot (better than ever, beat Son of Light 15 lengths) in April: effective at 2½m (given test) to 3¼m: raced mainly on good going or softer (acts on heavy): wore cheekpieces/visor last 4 starts: has won 4 times at Plumpton. *J. W. Mullins*   c108 h–

OUR KEV (IRE)   7 b.g. Be My Native (USA) – Sunbath (Krayyan) [2002/3 h101: 21v^{pu} Nov 6] tall gelding: won Irish point in 2001: novice hurdler, pulled up only start in 2002/3. *B. G. Powell*   h–

OUR KRIS   11 b.g. Kris – Our Reverie (USA) (J O Tobin (USA)) [2002/3 24g Feb 27] tall gelding: winning hurdler/maiden chaser: no form for long time, including in points. *C. J. Bennett*   c– h–

OUR MAN FLIN (IRE)   10 br.g. Mandalus – Flinging (Good Times (ITY)) [2002/3 c–, h–: c21g May 1] workmanlike gelding: winning pointer: novice hurdler/chaser: tried in hood and blinkers. *Miss E. C. M. Neyens*   c– h–

OURMAN (IRE)   7 b.g. Good Thyne (USA) – Magic Minstrel (Pitpan) [2002/3 c100, h–: c26d^F c27d³ c24g^{ur} Apr 12] useful-looking gelding: fair handicap chaser: sold out of T. Tate's stable 17,000 gns Doncaster August Sales after reappearance: won point in March: likely to prove best at 3m+: raced on good going or softer (acts on heavy): has had tongue tied: often races up with pace: has raced lazily. *Mrs A. Bell*   c98 h–

OUR OSCA (IRE)   7 b.g. Supreme Leader – Mayrhofen (Don) [2002/3 20d^{pu} 21d^{pu} Nov 25] 7,800 5-y-o, 900 6-y-o: fourth foal: half-brother to useful chaser Hollybank Buck (by Buckskin), stays 4¼m: dam poor maiden: pulled up in 2 novice hurdles. *P. R. Johnson*   h–

OUR TOMMY   10 ch.g. Ardross – Ina's Farewell (Random Shot) [2002/3 c89: c24s⁶ c20s² c20s² c20d³ c20m^{pu} c24d^{pu} Apr 9] modest handicap chaser: best short of 3m: raced mainly on good going or softer (acts on soft): usually races prominently: sound jumper. *A. E. Price*   c90

OUR VIC (IRE)   5 b.g. Old Vic – Shabra Princess (Buckskin (FR)) [2002/3 17s* 19d* 16d* Feb 6]   h140 p
      Our Vic created such an impression in winning all three starts over hurdles in 2002/3 that he is quoted as short as 25/1 for the 2004 Champion Hurdle. Whether that is the ideal long-term target for him is debatable, but there are few horses whose return is so eagerly awaited. Our Vic had made just one appearance prior to joining Martin Pipe's stable in the autumn, winning a four-runner two-and-a-half-mile four-year-old maiden point in Ireland early in 2002 in impressive fashion. His first two appearances over hurdles came in European Breeders Fund qualifiers at Exeter and Taunton. At Exeter in December he overcame some sloppy jumping to defeat modest opposition convincingly and still wasn't foot perfect when landing the odds with a good deal in hand at Taunton the following month. Our Vic showed himself a strong galloper and had plenty of use made of him in those races but, dropped back to a bare two miles in a handicap at Wincanton on his final start, he showed he was potentially a smart hurdler, coasting through an otherwise competitive race, jumping more fluently than previously and winning with consummate ease. He was only a length ahead of Green Ideal at the line but the BHB handicapper was among those not taken in by the margin, raising him by 19 lb afterwards. Connections reportedly felt aggrieved and Our Vic, who hadn't been entered for the novice events at Cheltenham, wasn't given any handicap entries either. The good-topped Our Vic is clearly effective at two miles and is bred to stay beyond nineteen furlongs. His demeanour and pedigree suggest he could be at least as good over fences as hurdles, so his connections clearly have plenty of options. There isn't much to be said about his immediate relations. He is the fourth foal and first winner out of his dam Shabra Princess, a maiden over fences. Her dam Random View won over hurdles in Ireland and is a half-sister to the useful staying hurdler and winning

Mr D. A. Johnson's "Our Vic"

chaser Real View, who finished second in the Saddle of Gold Final, as well as to the dam of a fairly useful performer of more recent times, the staying chaser Radiation. *M. C. Pipe*

OUT OF THE SHADOWS   7 gr.m. Rock Hopper – Shadows of Silver (Carwhite) [2002/3 h101: 16m³ 16d 16m⁵ 16g³ 16d* 16d³ 16d⁴ 19dᵖᵘ 16g⁴ 16g² 16m⁴ Apr 11] strong, lengthy mare: carries condition: should make a chaser: fair handicap hurdler: won at Haydock in November: should stay beyond 2m (went as if amiss tried at 19f): unraced on extremes of going: wore cheekpieces last 3 starts: consistent, but not easiest of rides. *Mrs M. Reveley*   **h107**

OUZEL (IRE)   7 b.m. Mandalus – Dipper's Gift (IRE) (Salluceva) [2002/3 16d⁴ Nov 7] tall mare: lightly raced: 100/1, first form over hurdles when fourth to Kalca Mome in 16-runner novice at Haydock: should stay beyond 2m. *C. W. Thornton*   **h75**

OVER ANXIOUS (IRE)   7 ch.g. Over The River (FR) – Legal Statement (IRE) (Strong Statement (USA)) [2002/3 h109: 19d² Nov 13] tall gelding: chasing type: won maiden Irish point in 2002: thrice-raced hurdler, trained by R. Alner in 2001/2: best effort when 5 lengths second of 18 to Saitensohn in novice at Newbury: will prove better at 3m than shorter: open to further improvement and sure to win races provided all is well with him. *Jonjo O'Neill*   **h118 p**

OVER BRIDGE   5 b.g. Overbury (IRE) – Celtic Bridge (Celtic Cone) [2002/3 F16g F16m F17m⁵ 16d 17s 19sᵖᵘ 17dʳᵗʳ 17d 21g Mar 16] third foal: dam, no promise over hurdles, half-sister to one-time fairly useful staying jumper Derring Bridge: modest in bumpers: little show over hurdles, refusing to race once. *Mrs S. M. Johnson*   **h– §**   **F79**

OVER CHARGED (IRE)   6 b.g. Over The River (FR) – Rookery Lady (IRE) (Caller-nish) [2002/3 h–, F–: 21gᵖᵘ May 3] lengthy gelding: no sign of ability. *J. M. Jefferson*   **h–**

OVER EASY (IRE) 9 ch.g. Tremblant – Tell A Tale (Le Bavard (FR)) [2002/3 c16dᵖᵘ **c–**
Mar 4] IR 4,500 4-y-o: first foal: dam winning hurdler: little form over hurdles for **h–**
A. J. Kennedy: failed to complete in points and hunter chase. *G. C. Evans*

OVERLORD (IRE) 6 b.g. Lord America – Straddler's Hill (IRE) (Torus) [2002/3 **h66**
F16g 16s 22d Feb 23] IR £9,800 4-y-o: sturdy gelding: third foal: dam, unraced half-sister **F–**
to fairly useful chaser up to 27f Rifle Range, from family of Wayward Lad: signs of
ability in bumper and over hurdles: veered badly left once headed final outing. *B. De
Haan*

OVERSMAN 10 b.g. Keen – Jamaican Punch (IRE) (Shareef Dancer (USA)) [2002/3 **c– §**
c–, h71§: 16m⁴ c16g⁶ c16m⁶ 20sᵖᵘ Jun 9] workmanlike gelding: poor hurdler: no **h– §**
form over fences (makes mistakes): stays 2¾m: acts on good to firm and heavy going:
blinkered: usually tongue tied: irresolute. *M. J. M. Evans*

OVERSTRAND (IRE) 4 b.g. In The Wings – Vaison La Romaine (Arctic Tern **h107**
(USA)) [2002/3 16d³ 16d⁶ 17g Mar 13] lengthy gelding: half-brother to 2 poor winners
over jumps: dam, modest maiden on Flat (should stay 1¾m), sold out of Mrs A. Perrett's
stable 24,000 gns Newmarket Autumn Sales: fair juvenile hurdler: 4 lengths third of 14 to East
Tycoon at Doncaster on debut: refused to settle next time, outclassed when sixteenth of
27 in Triumph Hurdle at Cheltenham: likely to stay 2½m. *Mrs M. Reveley*

OVER THE BAR (IRE) 7 b. or br.g. King's Ride – Merry Madness (Raise You Ten) **c– p**
[2002/3 h145: c17sᵖᵘ c20sᵖᵘ 24d² Feb 16] lengthy, attractive gelding: useful hurdler: 5 **h138**
lengths second of 5 to Emotional Moment in Grade 2 at Navan: let down by jumping both
starts over fences, running as if amiss on second occasion: should prove suited by 3m+:
raced on good to soft/soft going. *E. J. O'Grady, Ireland*

OVER THE BURN 11 b.g. Over The River (FR) – Sharp Vixen (Laurence O) **c85**
[2002/3 c–, h–: c25d³ c25g³ c25mᵖᵘ Oct 6] strong gelding: poor hurdler/novice chaser: **h–**
stays 25f: acts on soft going. *B. Mactaggart*

OVER THE COUNTER (IRE) 7 b.m. Persian Bold – Scotia Rose (Tap On Wood) **h–**
[2002/3 16g Feb 28] fair 2m hurdler in early-2000/1: showed nothing on return from near
3-year absence: usually tongue tied: races freely. *E. A. Elliott*

OVER THE FIRST (IRE) 8 b. or br.g. Orchestra – Ruby Lodge (Peacock (FR)) **c120**
[2002/3 c118, h–: 16s 16sᵘʳ 20s² 16v* 16s* 16s⁴ 20s* c19sᶠ 16v⁴ 19v Mar 9] rangy **h122**
gelding: fairly useful hurdler/chaser: won handicap hurdles at Clonmel and Fairyhouse in
November and Navan (listed race, by short head from On The Mend) in January: good
third to Torduff Boy in valuable handicap over fences at Punchestown in early-May: stays
2½m: acts on heavy going, possibly not on good to firm: usually races up with pace:
game. *C. F. Swan, Ireland*

Ladbroke Racing Handicap Hurdle, Fairyhouse—
Over The First (nearer camera) lands this fairly valuable prize from Junior Fontaine

OVER THE HILL (IRE)   11 b.g. Over The River (FR) – Joint Equity (Callernish) **c– x**
[2002/3 27g⁵ 22d² 22m⁶ 21g* 27d* 27v³ 27s 21d² 21m³ Apr 26] small gelding: one-time **h79**
fairly useful hunter chaser, often let down by jumping: poor handicap hurdler: won
conditional jockeys seller and amateur event at Sedgefield in October: stays 27f: acts on
good to firm and good to soft going: usually blinkered over hurdles: has had tongue tied.
S. J. Magnier

OVER THE STORM (IRE)   6 b.g. Over The River (FR) – Naas (Ballymore) **c121**
[2002/3 c24g* c24s² c24s³ c32g Mar 12] workmanlike gelding: half-brother to 2 fairly
useful jumpers by Corvaro, Granvillewaterford, stayed 3m, and Corvassio, stayed 2½m:
dam unraced half-sister to very smart middle-distance stayer Novius: won maiden Irish
point in 2002: edgy, won novice at Doncaster on steeplechasing debut in December by 8
lengths from News Maker: better form when placed in steadily-run similar events at
Kempton and Taunton: well backed when tailed off in valuable amateur race at Cheltenham: should stay beyond 3m: acts on soft going. *Miss H. C. Knight*

OVER THE WATER (IRE)   11 gr.g. Over The River (FR) – Shanacloon Lass **c87**
(General Ironside) [2002/3 c105d, h–: c25f³ May 10] workmanlike gelding: fair handicap **h–**
chaser, well below best since second start in 2001/2: effective at 2½m to 3m: acts on soft
and good to firm going: usually races up with pace: usually sound jumper. *R. H. Alner*

OVER TO YOU BERT   4 b.g. Overbury (IRE) – Silvers Era (Balidar) [2002/3 F13s **F–**
Dec 6] half-brother to several winners on Flat: dam 2-y-o 5f winner: well held in bumper
on debut: signs of ability up to 1¼m on Flat. *Mrs P. N. Dutfield*

OVER ZEALOUS (IRE)   11 ch.g. Over The River (FR) – Chatty Di (Le Bavard **c101 +**
(FR) [2002/3 c93§, h–§: c25dᵖᵘ c27v³ c30d² c26s² c24v⁴ c26s* c29g* Mar 14] leggy **h–**
gelding: fair handicap chaser: successful in 22-runner event at Chepstow (made all to beat
Our Jolly Swagman ½ length) in February and 8-runner contest at Warwick (best effort,
rallied to beat Favoured Option 3½ lengths) in March: thorough stayer: raced on good
going or softer (acts on heavy): blinkered nowadays: often looks moody. *John R. Upson*

OWAY (FR)   5 b.g. Epervier Bleu – Lointaine (USA) (Lyphard's Wish (FR)) [2002/3 **c123**
17s² c17g² 17g* c17g* c19s⁴ 18s² 17d* 17d² 19s² 20s* c17v Mar 5] sixth foal: half- **h137**
brother to winning jumpers by Oblat and Sky Lawyer: dam winning hurdler/chaser up to
19f: fairly useful chaser: won 4-y-o event at Lyon Villeurbanne in October: useful
hurdler: won minor events at Mont-de-Marsan in September and Pau in December and
Grande Course de Haies de Pau in January, best effort when beating Gun 'N Roses and
Rougenoir in close finish in last-named: stays 2½m: raced on good going or softer (acts
on soft). *J. Ortet, France*

OWEN ROE (IRE)   6 b.g. Blues Traveller (IRE) – Faye (Monsanto (FR)) [2002/3 **c92**
c18m* c21mᵖᵘ 17d² c21dᵘʳ Dec 14] ex-Irish gelding: half-brother to fair 2m hurdler Wray **h99**
(by Sharp Victor): modest maiden up to 2m on Flat: modest maiden hurdler (trained in
2001/2 by L. Browne): left in front ninth when winning 3-finisher maiden at Fontwell in
September on chasing debut, let down by jumping both other starts over fences: should
stay 2½m: acts on soft and good to firm going. *Mrs H. Dalton*

OWEN'S PET (IRE)   9 b.g. Alphabatim (USA) – Ballinlovane (Le Moss) [2002/3 **c–**
c90, h–: c25d⁶ May 6] lengthy gelding: winning Irish pointer: modest form over hurdles **h–**
and fences: stays 3¼m: raced on good going or softer: sold 1,200 gns Doncaster January
Sales. *R. T. Phillips*

OWTHORPE HILL   9 br.g. Scorpio (FR) – Star Route (Owen Dudley) [2002/3 h–: **h–**
22dᵖᵘ May 4] big, rangy gelding: very lightly raced and no sign of ability. *John A. Harris*

OXENDALE   10 ch.g. Primitive Rising (USA) – Saucy Moon (Saucy Kit) [2002/3 **c–**
c26m May 22] fair pointer, successful in April: blinkered, well held in novice hunter
chase. *R. Dench*

OXIDOR (IRE)   8 br.g. Be My Native (USA) – Euroblend (IRE) (The Parson) [2002/3 **h79 §**
h79§: 22g³ 24g 27s⁵ 24d³ 26s Nov 23] poor handicap hurdler: stays 3¼m: acts on heavy
and good to firm going: blinkered/tongue tied: moody. *C. P. Morlock*

OYSTER BAY   7 b.m. Mandalus – Holy Times (IRE) (The Parson) [2002/3 h62, F89: **h62**
16d⁴ May 6] medium-sized mare: poor form over hurdles: should stay beyond 2m:
visored twice in 2001/2: last of 3 finishers on first completed start in points. *A. Streeter*

OYSTER SHELL (IRE)   6 b.g. Be My Native (USA) – Judys View (King's Ride) **h72 p**
[2002/3 2d²d⁶ Feb 23] 7,500 3-y-o: fourth foal: brother to winning 2m hurdler Native
View: dam, Irish bumper winner, half-sister to dam of very smart chaser up to 3m Gales
Cavalier: won last of 3 starts in maiden Irish points in 2002: sixth of 17 in maiden at

Exeter on hurdling debut, close up until tiring home turn and eased: likely to improve. *N. J. Henderson*

OZZIE JONES 12 b.g. Formidable (USA) – Distant Relation (Great Nephew) [2002/3   **c109** c113, h–: c25g⁴ c24m* c24m³ c26m² Jul 15] good-topped gelding: fair chaser: won ladies   **h–** hunter at Stratford in June: stays 27f: needs good going or firmer (acts on firm): visored once, effective with or without blinkers: often races prominently. *K. R. Pearce*

P

PACHINCO 5 ch.g. Bluebird (USA) – Lady Philippa (IRE) (Taufan (USA)) [2002/3   **h–** 17sᵖᵘ 17d 16mᵖᵘ 17mᵖᵘ Apr 16] tall, angular gelding: showed nothing in 2 maidens on Flat for P. Mitchell, sold £650 Ascot February (2002) Sales: little sign of ability over hurdles. *J. G. M. O'Shea*

PACIFIC ALLIANCE (IRE) 7 b.g. Fayruz – La Gravotte (FR) (Habitat) [2002/3   **h71** 16g⁵ 16m³ 16f⁵ 17d* 17m⁵ Oct 30] leggy gelding: half-brother to 2m hurdle winner Departure (by Gorytus): fairly useful on Flat (best around 1m) at 4 yrs, well held in 2002: poor form over hurdles: jumped more fluently when winning selling handicap at Market Rasen in October: will prove best around 2m: acts on good to soft going: blinkered second outing. *M. Wigham*

PACIFYC (IRE) 8 b.g. Brief Truce (USA) – Ocean Blue (IRE) (Bluebird (USA))   **h84 §** [2002/3 h81: 19g² 20m⁴ 22m 17d² 19m 17d⁶ Oct 19] rather leggy gelding: poor handicap hurdler: stays 2½m: acts on good to firm and good to soft ground: tongue tied: temperamental. *John A. Harris*

PACK LEADER (IRE) 7 b.g. Muharib (USA) – Royal Broderick (IRE) (Lancastrian) [2002/3 24d 22sᵖᵘ 20s 28g⁵ 22g Apr 26] IR 5,500 4-y-o: medium-sized gelding: **h83** first foal: dam unraced, out of half-sister to 1977 Cheltenham Gold Cup winner Davy Lad: won 2 Irish points in 2002: poor form over hurdles: has reportedly had breathing problems (tongue tied third and fourth outings). *Jonjo O'Neill*

PACO VENTURE (IRE) 8 b.g. Supreme Leader – Ethel's Daughter (Deep Run)   **h109** [2002/3 19g 20g³ 20s⁵ 16s⁵ 24g* 22m* 23m² 24m* 20s² 24s* 21s⁵ 22s Mar 15] 25,000 3-y-o: rangy gelding: type to make a chaser: fourth foal: half-brother to winning 3m chaser Artemis (by Strong Gale): dam unraced half-sister to smart staying chaser Plundering and smart staying hurdler Triple Witching: fair hurdler: left G. Lyons after fourth start: won maiden at Worcester in September, novices (odds on) at Uttoxeter and Taunton in October and handicap at Bangor in December: didn't look keen (swished tail under pressure) final outing: effective at 2½m and stays 3m well: acts on soft and good to firm going: tends to make mistakes. *Miss Venetia Williams*

PADDIES BOY (IRE) 8 ch.g. Astronef – Bushfield Lady (Le Bavard (FR)) [2002/3   **c92** c24d² c24s³ c24dᵖᵘ c20s⁶ 21m⁴ 21gᵖᵘ 17d c24s* c25g⁵ c24m* Apr 9] leggy gelding: **h74** winning pointer: poor maiden hurdler: modest chaser: won hunter at Downpatrick in March and handicap at Gowran in April: stays 3m: acts on soft and good to firm going: tried blinkered: none too easy ride. *J. J. Lambe, Ireland*

PADDY FOR PADDY (IRE) 9 b.g. Mandalus – Lady Rerico (Pamroy) [2002/3   **c105** c25s* c25g² c25gᵖᵘ Apr 5] IR 28,000 4-y-o: brother to fairly useful chaser Tyndarius, stays 25f, and half-brother to winning 3m chaser Meander (by Mandalus): dam winning pointer: winning pointer: fairly useful hunter chaser: won at Folkestone in February: better form when short-head second to Aller Moor at Exeter: ran poorly in quite valuable event at Aintree: stays 25f. *G. L. Landau*

PADDY MAGUIRE (IRE) 10 b.g. Mazaad – Knocknagow (Buckskin (FR)) [2002/3   **c–** 22d³ 20v⁵ c20sᵖᵘ 21g⁶ Mar 25] workmanlike gelding: maiden hurdler: no sign of   **h–** retaining ability after long absence, including over fences. *Mrs A. M. Naughton*

PADDYSPEARL 9 b.g. Henbit (USA) – La Furze (Winden) [2002/3 c–, h–: c16d³   **c–** c16gᶠ c16dᵖᵘ c17mᵖᵘ Jul 4] strong gelding: of little account: tried tongue tied.   **h–** *A. W. Carroll*

PADDY'S PROFILES (IRE) 9 b.g. Euphemism – Dame Niamh (IRE) (Buckskin   **h–** (FR)) [2002/3 h74: 19d 17d 21m 17m⁵ Apr 8] lengthy gelding: poor maiden hurdler: stays 2¾m: acts on firm going. *Miss K. M. George*

680

PADDY'S RETURN (IRE)   11 b.g. Kahyasi – Bayazida (Bustino) [2002/3 c124, h–: c–
c25f³ c25g Sep 29] close-coupled gelding: one-time top-class hurdler: fairly useful   h–
chaser in 2001/2: well held since at Pardubice and Merano (Grade 1): stays 4m: acts on
good to firm and heavy going: effective blinkered/visored or not. *Ferdy Murphy*

PADDY'S THYME (IRE)   7 gr.g. Good Thyne (USA) – Nanny Kehoe (IRE) (Sexton   c–
Blake) [2002/3 16d c23gᶠ c16gᵘʳ 27g² Mar 25] workmanlike gelding: failed to complete   h71
in 2 chases: best effort over hurdles when second in maiden at Sedgefield: stays 27f.
Ferdy Murphy

PADDY'S WOLF   12 b.g. Little Wolf – Paddy's Delight (Paddy's Birthday) [2002/3   c–
c–, h–: c21mᵖᵘ May 22] of little account. *Grahame A. Dedman*   h–

PADDY THE DRIVER (IRE)   7 b.g. Grand Plaisir (IRE) – Jude's Hollow (IRE)   h76
(Hollow Hand) [2002/3 h84: 17m⁶ Jul 15] poor maiden hurdler: probably stays 2¾m: acts
on good to firm going. *J. D. Frost*

PADDY THE OPTIMIST (IRE)   7 b.g. Leading Counsel (USA) – Erne Duchess   h74
(IRE) (Duky) [2002/3 F71: 16s⁶ 17s⁶ Dec 17] sturdy gelding: poor form in bumper and
novice hurdles: has raced freely. *T. R. George*

PADDY THE PIPER (IRE)   6 b.g. Witness Box (USA) – Divine Dibs (Raise You   F101
Ten) [2002/3 F92p: F16v² F16d* F16g* Mar 23] quite good-topped gelding: fairly useful
form in bumpers: won at Catterick in February and Wetherby (beat Gary's Pimpernel 2
lengths in 17-runner race) in March: will stay well beyond 2m: type to make his mark in
novice hurdles in 2003/4. *L. Lungo*

PAGAN LEADER (IRE)   10 b.g. Supreme Leader – Dawning Glory (Hittite Glory)   c–
[2002/3 c24dᵖᵘ Jan 13] lengthy gelding: of little account: tried blinkered. *P. T. Dalton*   h–

PAILITAS (GER)   6 b.g. Lomitas – Pradera (GER) (Abary (GER)) [2002/3 h–: 16m*   h75
16m² 16m 17mʳᵒ 17m⁶ 16g Apr 12] rather leggy gelding: first past post in handicaps at
Huntingdon (conditional jockeys seller) and Uttoxeter (novice, demoted to second after
hanging left and causing interference) in June: no other form over hurdles: will prove best
at sharp 2m: acts on good to firm going: headstrong. *Ian Williams*

PAKOCHINO (IRE)   11 ch.g. Moscow Society (USA) – Tossy Lass (Le Bavard   h66
(FR)) [2002/3 24s 22g⁵ 20g 16dʳᵒ Oct 25] poor maiden hurdler: in contention when ran
out 3 out in conditional jockeys selling handicap at Fakenham: stays 2¾m: tried blinkered: well held in points in 2003. *R. J. Osborne, Ireland*

PALACE PARADE (USA)   13 ch.g. Cure The Blues (USA) – Parasail (USA) (In   c–
Reality) [2002/3 c–, h–: c26gᵖᵘ Jun 29] angular gelding: winning pointer: no form in   h–
steeplechases since winning hunter in 2002: tried blinkered. *A. G. Hobbs*

PALACIO (IRE)   6 ch.g. Erins Isle – Gayle Gal (Lord Gayle (USA)) [2002/3 17s 20m   h–
17m Aug 29] modest maiden on Flat (stays 2¼m) at 4 yrs: well held in novice/maiden
hurdles. *E. McNamara, Ireland*

PALADIN (FR)   8 b.g. Risen Star (USA) – Allatum (USA) (Alleged (USA)) [2002/3   c139
c156, h–: c21s³ c21v³ 19v² 19v² c26v c21v⁴ Mar 2] very smart chaser in 2001/2, just use-   h136
ful form in 2002/3: fourth of 8 finishers to Line Marine in Group 3 at Auteuil final start:
useful hurdler, second in quite valuable events at Bordeaux and Pau in December: stays
3¼m: acts on heavy going: effective blinkered or not. *J. Ortet, France*

PALAIS (IRE)   8 b.g. Darshaan – Dance Festival (Nureyev (USA)) [2002/3 h–: 24d*   h79
26g 22g² 22g Apr 26] leggy gelding: poor hurdler: made all in weak novice at Market
Rasen in August: stays 3m: acts on good to firm and good to soft going. *John A. Harris*

PALARSHAN (FR)   5 b. or br.g. Darshaan – Palavera (FR) (Bikala) [2002/3   c140 p
h122p: c16g² c16d² c19v³ c16g* c16g* Mar 13]   h–
   Palarshan might have just turned five, but it is fair to say that his racing career is already worthy of the description colourful. While many jumpers of his age
are still finding their feet, Palarshan, to use a popular expression, has been there,
done that and got the T-shirt. A little more than eighteen months after he had made
a successful debut over hurdles, in the Czech Republic, he triumphed over fences at
the Cheltenham Festival; and he also won on the Flat there and in France in
between. Where next for Palarshan? Well, it has to be doubted whether he'll be
travelling too far from his current abode at Henry Daly's yard in Shropshire from
now on. Nor will he have to in order to pick up more good prizes. There will be
plenty of suitable races fairly near to home for a progressive young chaser who is
going to prove as effective over two and a half miles as he is at two, with the re-

Cheltenham Grand Annual Chase Challenge Cup (Handicap)—Palarshan kicks for home two out from fellow novice Vol Solitaire (right), Dark'n Sharp and Ross Moff (noseband)

named Paddy Power Gold Cup at Cheltenham's Open meeting in November looking a suitable target in the first part of next season.

Palarshan followed up his win over hurdles at Pardubice with a victory on the Flat at Velka Chuchle, the racecourse in Prague, before joining Daly after winning a fifteen-furlong event on the Flat at Mont-de-Marsan in February 2002, when trained in France by Jean-Luc Pelletan. His first appearance for his new trainer came in a juvenile hurdle at Cheltenham two months later, and it proved a winning one, with Palarshan creating a very favourable impression. Palarshan did look to have a bright future over hurdles but, as with his mentor the late Tim Forster, Daly regards hurdling as merely a stepping stone to chasing, so it was hardly a surprise when Palarshan's attentions were switched to fences in the latest season. It took Palarshan four attempts to get off the mark over fences, after he had the misfortune on his first three to come up against Impek at Hereford, Vol Solitaire at Warwick and Tarxien in a Grade 2 at Ascot. With nothing remotely of that calibre in opposition in a five-runner event at Leicester in February, Palarshan had no difficulty landing the odds. All four chases mentioned were novice events with small fields, and the tests they provided were far removed from the one which faced Palarshan on his fifth start over fences, on his handicap debut in the Grand Annual Chase at Cheltenham. Here Palarshan was up against twenty rivals, the majority of whom were seasoned handicappers, on a demanding course which would be sure to find out any flaws in his jumping technique. As things turned out, Palarshan, from 4 lb out of the weights, gave little indication that he was the least experienced chaser in the field. Indeed, he hardly put a foot wrong. Well, not until all of the fences had been safely negotiated, anyway. Palarshan was settled off a strong pace which eventually took its toll on those who raced prominently, and he was kept wide as he made progress in the second half of the race, thus avoiding the trouble which occurred when Golden Alpha and Wave Rock fell three out. Sweeping into the lead shortly after, Palarshan never looked like being pegged back, giving his supporters their only cause for concern when hanging right halfway up the hill and ending up close to the stand rail. Palarshan continued to run on strongly once straightened out, though, and passed the post three lengths ahead of his nearest pursuer Risk Accessor, with Dark'n Sharp three quarters of a length further back in third. The victory provided Daly with his second winner of the meeting, Young Spartacus having been successful for the stable the previous day in the Mildmay of Flete Chase. With Richard Johnson opting to ride Dark'n Sharp, Mark Bradburne, who had been an amateur when gaining his only previous Cheltenham Festival success three years earlier, on the Daly-trained Relaxation in the National Hunt Chase, came in for the mount on Palarshan. It says much for Bradburne that he was able to take full advantage of the opportunity, having broken a collarbone in a fall at Ludlow exactly two weeks earlier.

		Darshaan (br 1981)	Shirley Heights (b 1975)	Mill Reef
Palarshan (FR)				Hardiemma
(b. or br.g. 1998)			Delsy (br 1972)	Abdos
				Kelty
		Palavera (FR) (b or br 1987)	Bikala (b 1978)	Kalamoun
				Irish Bird
			Paulistana (ch 1980)	Pretense
				Near Me Now

Palarshan is by one Prix du Jockey Club winner, Darshaan, out of a sister to another in Polytain. The dam Palavera, a fairly useful winner over a mile in France, has bred several other winners, including three useful performers. Palafairia (by Always Fair) won a couple of listed events over a mile at Evry, Palacoona (by Last Tycoon) was successful in a nine-furlong listed race at Maisons-Laffitte, while Palinisa (by Night Shift) won over seven furlongs at two years and was placed in listed and Group company at three. Palarshan's grandam Paulistana ran six times in France without success, though she finished in the frame over seven furlongs and a mile. The tall, good-topped Palarshan, who is open to further improvement, has form on heavy going but is possibly better under less testing conditions, and he acts on good to firm. Palarshan finished slightly stiff when winning over hurdles at Cheltenham and was dismounted on the return to the winner's enclosure after the

Mrs A. L. Wood's "Palarshan"

Grand Annual. His trainer reported him to be very sore through his back the next morning but he suffered no long-term damage and was back in training in the summer. All continuing to be well, Palarshan should make up into a smart chaser at the very least. *H. D. Daly*

PALLINGHAM LAD (IRE) 13 b.g. Torenaga – Star Mill (Milan) [2002/3 c26g^{pu} May 25] fair pointer, successful 3 times in 2002: tongue tied, jumped poorly in hunter chase at Newton Abbot. *Miss Emma Oliver* c– h–

PALM BEACH (IRE) 4 ch.c. Pennekamp (USA) – Crystal Bright (Bold Lad (IRE)) [2002/3 16m^F 16m^{pu} Nov 4] no show in maiden on Flat or in juvenile hurdles: tried tongue tied. *D. J. S. Cosgrove* h–

PALUA 6 b.g. Sri Pekan (USA) – Reticent Bride (IRE) (Shy Groom (USA)) [2002/3 h98p: 20s^2 20v* 24m^2 24g Mar 13] useful-looking gelding: fairly useful but ungenerous stayer on Flat, sold out of I. Balding's stable 11,000 gns Newmarket Autumn Sales: idled when winning maiden hurdle at Folkestone in February: appeared to improve considerably when 12 lengths second to Deano's Beeno in 5-runner Grade 2 at Kempton 10 days later: stiff task, tailed off in Stayers' Hurdle at Cheltenham: stays 3m: acts on good to firm and heavy ground: found little on reappearance. *Miss E. C. Lavelle* h131

PAMELA ANSHAN 6 b.m. Anshan – Have Form (Haveroid) [2002/3 h64: 16d^6 17d c19d^6 c19d^{pu} c19s^4 c19f^2 Mar 24] angular mare: poor maiden hurdler: much better form over fences, second to Harik in handicap at Taunton: stays 19f: acts on firm going, probably on soft. *S. C. Burrough* c95 h–

PAMPERED GALE (IRE) 9 b.g. Strong Gale – Pampered Russian (Deep Run) [2002/3 c26m^6 May 22] useful-looking gelding: novice hurdler/chaser: fair pointer, successful 4 times in 2002: stays 3m: acts on firm going. *J. M. Turner* c– h–

Mark Barrett And Partners' "Palua"

PANGERAN (USA)   11 b.g. Forty Niner (USA) – Smart Heiress (USA) (Vaguely   c88 §
Noble) [2002/3 c97, h–: c24m⁵ c22m³ Jun 1] leggy gelding: fair hunter chaser: stays   h–
3¼m, effective at much shorter: acts on firm and soft going: sometimes let down by jumping: unreliable. *Neil King*

PANMURE (IRE)   7 b.g. Alphabatim (USA) – Serjitak (Saher) [2002/3 h70, F94: 19d   c– §
19d⁴ 17d c20vᵖᵘ 22g 20dᵘʳ Apr 25] good-topped gelding: disappointing over hurdles: h82 §
tried in tongue strap final outing (slipped and unseated after fifth): reportedly had breathing problem on chasing debut, final start for N. Henderson: tried blinkered (looked far
from keen). *P. D. Niven*

PANOORAS LORD (IRE)   9 b.g. Topanoora – Ladyship (Windjammer (USA))   h65
[2002/3 h–: 16d⁵ 16gF 17m⁵ 22m Jun 30] compact gelding: poor handicap hurdler:
best around 2m: acts on soft and good to firm going: visored once: has pulled hard.
J. S. Wainwright

PANTO   6 b.g. Lepanto (GER) – Sherzine (Gorytus (USA)) [2002/3 F16s Dec 7] fourth   F–
foal: half-brother to winning 17f hurdler Megazine (by Shaab): dam modest 2m hurdler/
1½m winner on Flat: tailed off in bumper on debut. *M. Hill*

PAPERISING   11 b.g. Primitive Rising (USA) – Eye Bee Aitch (Move Off) [2002/3   c141
c137, h121: c22g* c25d² 20d⁵ Dec 14] tall gelding: fairly useful handicap hurdler: useful   h120
handicap chaser: won at Kelso in May, beating Jowoody easily by 4 lengths: good second
to Joint Account at Wetherby later in month: off 7 months, considerably handled final
start: stays 25f: acts on good to firm and heavy going: usually jumps soundly: has found
little. *N. G. Richards*

PAPERPROPHET   5 b.g. Glory of Dancer – Living Legend (ITY) (Archway (IRE))   h114 p
[2002/3 F16d³ 17d* 20s* 20g² Dec 28] leggy gelding: first foal: dam unraced half-sister   F91
to very smart 6f to 1m winner Missed Flight: third of 22 in bumper at Worcester on debut:
progressed well over hurdles, won novices at Bangor in October and Ayr (handicap) in
November: 7 lengths second to Plutocrat, pair clear, in handicap at Musselburgh, under
pressure long way out: will stay beyond 2½m: acts on soft going: probably hasn't finished
improving. *N. G. Richards*

PAPERWEIGHT   7 b.m. In The Wings – Crystal Reay (Sovereign Dancer (USA))   h–
[2002/3 22m Jun 14] modest on Flat (stays 1½m): poor novice hurdler: unlikely to stay
2¾m: visored final start in 2000/1. *Miss K. M. George*

PAPHIAN BAY   5 b.g. Karinga Bay – Bichette (Lidhame) [2002/3 F16g Feb 8] rangy   F–
gelding: has scope: third foal: half-brother to 1m/9f winner Soller Bay (by Contract Law):
dam 7f winner, including at 2 yrs: in need of experience when well held in Grade 2 bumper at Newbury on debut. *Ferdy Murphy*

PAPILLON (IRE)   12 b.g. Lafontaine (USA) – Glens Princess (Prince Hansel) [2002/3   c–
c125, h–: c20d⁴ c25s⁴ 20s Mar 16] good-bodied gelding: impressed in appearance: smart   h–
chaser at best, won 2000 Martell Grand National at Aintree: generally went with little
zest after 2000/1, including over hurdles: stayed 4½m: acted on good to firm and heavy
going: blinkered (well held) once: tried in near-side pricker: sometimes looked none too
keen: reportedly retired. *T. M. Walsh, Ireland*

PARABLE   7 b.g. Midyan (USA) – Top Table (Shirley Heights) [2002/3 16d 16s⁶ Dec   h69
14] good-topped gelding: fair on all-weather, poor on turf on Flat (stays 1½m) at 4 yrs for
D. Barker: well held in novice hurdles at Warwick and Doncaster. *Mrs P. Sly*

PARADE RACER   12 b.g. Derring Rose – Dusky Damsel (Sahib) [2002/3 c102, h–:   c106
c25d* c20m* c27sᵖᵘ Mar 11] sturdy gelding: fairly useful hunter chaser: won at Kelso   h–
and Perth in May: fit from pointing (successful in March), disappointing at Sedgefield:
stays 25f: acts on heavy and good to firm going. *Tim Butt*

PARADISIO (FR)   7 b.g. Albert du Berlais (FR) – Pretty Lady (FR) (Le Gregol (FR))   c76
[2002/3 c24m⁵ Apr 21] ex-French gelding: half-brother to 3 Flat winners in France and   h–
another in Morocco: dam unraced: 1¼m winner on Flat: won over hurdles and fences in
2000 for J-P. Totain: fair form in points and hunter chase after 2-year absence: stays 3m.
W. J. Tolhurst

PARAHANDY (IRE)   13 b.g. Lancastrian – Dishcloth (Fury Royal) [2002/3 c112:   c103
c33g c26d² c24m⁵ Apr 12] workmanlike gelding: one-time fairly useful handicap chaser
for J. Mullins: won 3 points in 2002: best effort in hunter chases when second of 7 to
Macgeorge at Warwick: effective at 3m (given test) to 29f: acts on heavy and good to firm
going: tried blinkered. *Giles Smyly*

PARDINI (USA)   4 b.g. Quest For Fame – Noblissima (IRE) (Sadler's Wells (USA))   h87 p
[2002/3 16d⁴ Mar 10] ex-French gelding: third foal: dam, 13.4f winner, out of half-sister

to Grand Prix de Paris and Melbourne Cup winner At Talaq: in frame up to 15f from 10 starts on Flat in French Provinces for J-L. Pelletan: never a factor when fourth of 15 to East Tycoon in juvenile at Stratford on hurdling debut: should progress. *M. F. Harris*

PARDISHAR (IRE)   5 b.g. Kahyasi – Parapa (IRE) (Akarad (FR)) [2002/3 h–p: 16g⁵ May 17] well-made gelding: useful on Flat (should stay 1½m) for Sir Michael Stoute at 3 yrs, well beaten in 2002: tongue tied, better effort over hurdles at Aintree when fifth of 10 in novice in May, hanging left between last 2: sold 2,500 gns Newmarket Autumn Sales. *G. L. Moore*   **h96**

PARDON WHAT   7 b.g. Theatrical Charmer – Tree Poppy (Rolfe (USA)) [2002/3 F16g³ F16s⁴ 25mᵘʳ 20s⁵ 20v⁵ 21s⁴ 20v c20v* c19d⁴ c24dᵖᵘ Apr 9] leggy gelding: second foal: dam fairly useful hurdler/winning chaser up to 3m: fairly useful form in bumpers at Worcester, won weakly-contested event in June: won novice handicap at Bangor on chasing debut in March: generally let down by jumping otherwise, including over hurdles: stays 2½m: acts on heavy going: wore cheekpieces last 4 starts. *B. G. Powell*   **c84 x**\
h79 x\
F95

PARDUS (FR)   7 b.g. Unfuwain (USA) – Provacatrice (USA) (Irish River (FR)) [2002/3 19v* 19v⁵ 17vF Jan 24] useful on Flat, successful 7 times from 7.5f to 1½m in Germany: won minor race at Strasbourg on hurdling debut in November: fairly useful form when fifth of 20 to Caballo Raptor in similar event at Auteuil: weak in market, held in fourth when fell heavily last in novice at Folkestone. *M. Hofer, Germany*   **h118**

PARISH OAK   8 b.g. Rakaposhi King – Poppy's Pride (Uncle Pokey) [2002/3 h–: 16d* 20sᵖᵘ c21sᵖᵘ c20g c20d* c20mᵘʳ c20g* Apr 26] useful-looking gelding: form over hurdles only when 33/1-winner of handicap at Towcester very early in season: bit better over fences, won handicaps at Warwick (novice) in March and Market Rasen in April: saddle slipped in between: stays 2½m: acts on good to soft going: effective tongue tied or not. *Ian Williams*   **c86**\
h75

PARISIAN EIRE (IRE)   4 gr.g. Paris House – La Fille de Feu (Never So Bold) [2002/3 16sᵖᵘ 16dᵖᵘ 16s 16s 20gᵖᵘ Mar 2] leggy, sparely-made gelding: no form on Flat or over hurdles: tried blinkered. *N. A. Smith*   **h–**

PARIS LATINO (FR)   4 b.g. Nikos – Tarbelissima (FR) (Tarbes (FR)) [2002/3 F12d F12g Dec 18] 20,000 3-y-o: twelfth foal: half-brother to several winners, including a 3-y-o hurdler Pourcentage (by Katowice): dam won around 1m at 2 yrs in France: well held in 2 bumpers at Newbury. *C. Tizzard*   **F–**

PARIS PIKE (IRE)   11 b.g. Satco (FR) – Bouise (Royal Buck) [2002/3 c147?, h–: c24dF 20d⁵ 24d Mar 15] workmanlike gelding: impressed in appearance: winning hurdler: one-time smart chaser, won 2000 Scottish Grand National at Ayr: missed following season, and not the same force again: stayed 33f: acted on good to firm and heavy going: reportedly retired. *Ferdy Murphy*   **c–**\
h115

PARK CITY   4 b.g. Slip Anchor – Cryptal (Persian Bold) [2002/3 16mᵇᵈ 16m³ 16d 16g² 16s* 19dᵖᵘ 16d⁵ 17m 16g³ Apr 12] rather leggy gelding: modest maiden on Flat, sold out of P. Howling's stable 10,000 gns Newmarket July Sales: modest handicap hurdler: won conditional jockeys event at Warwick in December: best effort when third to Pirandello in novice handicap at Stratford final start: will stay 2½m: acts on soft going. *P. J. Hobbs*   **h92**

PARK END   11 ch.g. Bairn (USA) – Abdera (Ahonoora) [2002/3 c19f Mar 27] lengthy gelding: fair pointer, successful 3 times in 2002: well beaten in hunter chase at Exeter. *N. J. Legg*   **c–**

PARK LANE FREDDIE   5 b.g. Nalchik (USA) – Kathy's Role (Rolfe (USA)) [2002/3 F17d F16d F17s⁶ 19m 20m Apr 12] leggy gelding: fourth foal: dam unraced: mid-division at best in bumpers: well held in 2 runs over hurdles: tongue tied final start. *J. Mackie*   **h–**\
F78

PARK LEADER (IRE)   10 b.g. Supreme Leader – Parkavoureen (Deep Run) [2002/3 c20dᵖᵘ 16m c16s* c16g* 16s c19sᵖᵘ Jan 26] fair hurdler/chaser: won handicaps over fences at Gowran and Cork in October: stays 2¾m: acts on soft and good to firm going. *Paul Nolan, Ireland*   **c112**\
h–

PARK PLACE (IRE)   8 gr.g. Husyan (USA) – Iron Mermaid (General Ironside) [2002/3 h80, F89: c16g 20s⁴ 25g⁴ 20d⁴ Apr 25] workmanlike gelding: bumper winner: not fluent and well beaten only start over fences: upped in trip, best effort over hurdles when third in novice at Wetherby: stays 25f. *J. I. A. Charlton*   **c–**\
h87

PARLOUR GAME   7 br.m. Petoski – Henry's True Love (Random Shot) [2002/3 h102?: c20dF c20d⁴ c20dᵘʳ c19d³ c20s² c20gᵖᵘ c25s² Mar 7] lengthy, angular mare: fair   **c93**\
h–

hurdler at best: modest form on completed starts in novice chases: stays 25f: raced on good going or softer (acts on heavy). *H. D. Daly*

PARSIFAL 4 b.g. Sadler's Wells (USA) – Moss (USA) (Woodman (USA)) [2002/3 **h–** 16g 17d 16d^{pu} 17d⁶ Apr 8] fair maiden on Flat (stays 10.5f), sold out of J. Given's stable 7,500 gns Newmarket Autumn Sales: showed more temperament than ability in 4 races over hurdles (reluctant to race on debut, pulled hard subsequently). *J. Howard Johnson*

PARSONS BOY 14 ch.g. The Parson – Kylogue Daisy (Little Buskins) [2002/3 c107, **c–** h–: c22d Feb 8] stocky, short-backed gelding: one-time fairly useful chaser: well held in **h–** hunter on return from 16-month absence: stays 3¾m: raced on good going or softer (acts on heavy): pulled up all 3 starts in blinkers. *P. H. Morris*

PARSONS PRIDE (IRE) 7 b.g. Persian Mews – First Prize (IRE) (The Parson) **h–** [2002/3 F16g³ F16d 24d^{pu} 18s^{pu} Mar 2] 9,000 (privately) 5-y-o: angular gelding: third **F85** foal: brother to winning pointer Shes The Reason: dam unraced: 8 lengths third of 14 to impressive Be Fair in bumper at Worcester on debut: no show in 3 subsequent starts, last 2 over hurdles: sold 3,200 gns Doncaster May Sales. *C. Weedon*

PARTY AIRS (USA) 4 b.g. Geri (USA) – Elegant Champagne (USA) (Alleged **h124** (USA)) [2002/3 16g* 16s* 16v* 16s⁴ 16s⁴ Feb 22] angular gelding: lightly raced and fairly useful form on Flat (stays 1½m): successful first 3 starts in juvenile hurdles, at Gowran in October and Thurles and Leopardstown (beat Kenilworth 3½ lengths in Grade 2 Denny Juvenile Hurdle) in December: failed to progress further, seventh in Grade 1 at Punchestown in early-May: acts on heavy going: has looked less than keen. *D. K. Weld, Ireland*

PARTY ANIMAL (IRE) 11 b.g. Buckskin (FR) – More Chat (Torenaga) [2002/3 **c–** c96, h–: c26s^{pu} Feb 26] rangy gelding: modest chaser, lightly raced: reportedly bled **h–** from nose only outing in 2002/3: stays 3¼m: raced on good going or softer (acts on soft). *K. C. Bailey*

PARTY GAMES (IRE) 6 b.g. King's Ride – Shady Miss (Mandamus) [2002/3 F18g⁴ **h80** 21g⁵ Oct 21] fifth foal: half-brother to fairly useful chaser Buccaneer Boy (by Buckskin), **F77** stays 3m: dam, winning pointer, from family of top-class staying chaser Royal Bond: fourth of 12 in bumper at Plumpton on debut: 23½ lengths fifth of 14 in novice there on hurdling debut 6 months later, shaping like a stayer. *D. M. Grissell*

PARTY LAD (IRE) 10 b.g. King's Ride – Lantern Lass (Monksfield) [2002/3 c84d, **c–** h–: c25d^{pu} May 6] good sort: winning hurdler/chaser, modest at best: stays 25f: probably **h–** acts on any going: has shown signs of temperament: sketchy jumper. *N. A. Twiston-Davies*

PASO FINO (IRE) 4 b.g. Alzao (USA) – Kentucky Fall (FR) (Lead On Time (USA)) **F–** [2002/3 F16d F17g Apr 26] first foal: dam, fair 6f winner, half-sister to very smart miler Tillerman: behind in 2 bumpers. *J. R. Norton*

PASSENGER OMAR (IRE) 5 b.g. Safety Catch (USA) – Princess Douglas (Bishop **F–** of Orange) [2002/3 F16s^{rtr} F16g Feb 8] IR £650 3-y-o: rather unfurnished gelding: fifth foal: half-brother to winning pointer by The Bart: dam winning pointer: runner-up in 2½m maiden Irish point on debut in 2002: well held in Grade 2 bumper at Newbury: refused to race there 6 weeks earlier. *Noel T. Chance*

PASSEREAU (FR) 7 b.g. Fijar Tango (FR) – Becebege (FR) (Iron Duke (FR)) [2002/3 **c115** c94§, h–: c20s^{pu} c17m^{ur} c20g⁶ c17m² c17s^{F2} c20m² c16g³ c17g⁶ c17d* c16s³ c16v* c16d **h–** c16g^{pu} c20g² Mar 23] strong, lengthy gelding: fairly useful handicap chaser: improved form in 2002/3, won at Bangor in October and Fakenham (beat Marigliano 8 lengths) in January: stays 2½m when conditions aren't testing: acts on good to firm and heavy going: tried visored/tongue tied: formerly moody. *C. N. Kellett*

PASS ME BY 4 b.g. Balnibarbi – Errol Emerald (Dom Racine (FR)) [2002/3 F16g* **F96** F17d F16g⁴ Mar 17] tall, angular gelding: half-brother to 1991 2-y-o 5f winner Jiggerak (by Belfort) and winner up to 1¾m in Sweden by Safawan: dam rather temperamental middle-distance winner: fair form in bumpers: won at Musselburgh on debut in January by 3 lengths from Loopy Linda. *T. D. Walford*

PASTEUR (IRE) 5 b.g. Eagle Eyed (USA) – Life Support (IRE) (High Estate) [2002/3 **h118 §** h120§: 16g 16f* 18f^F Mar 9] good-bodied gelding: fairly useful on Flat (stays 2m): fairly useful hurdler: much better effort in 4-y-o handicaps first 2 outings when winning at Listowel in September by head from Carlesimo (final start for N. Meade): should stay beyond 2m: acts on firm and good to soft going: well held both starts in blinkers: has had tongue tied: has been reluctant to race: not to be trusted. *R. J. Hendricks, USA*

Clark's Brewery Handicap Hurdle, Aintree—
Patriot Games provides Charlie Swan with his final win in the saddle

PATELEY (IRE) 9 b.g. Cataldi – Suir Venture (Roselier (FR)) [2002/3 c93x, h–: c24m^{pu} 16m Jul 24] compact gelding: fair hurdler/chaser at best, has lost his form: tried blinkered: poor jumper of fences: ungenuine. *John R. Upson*　**c– x h– §**

PATRIARCH EXPRESS 6 b.g. Noble Patriarch – Jaydeeglen (Bay Express) [2002/3 F80: F16g* F16m* F16g F16g Mar 12] lengthy gelding: useful form in bumpers: won at Perth (easily, by 8 lengths from Cumbrian Knight) in September and Cheltenham (got up close home to beat Miller's Bay by head) in October: creditable seventh to impressive Cornish Rebel at Newbury, first and better effort in graded events: likely to make an impact in novice hurdles in 2003/4. *G. A. Harker*　**F106**

PATRIARCH (IRE) 7 b.g. Alphabatim (USA) – Strong Language (Formidable (USA)) [2002/3 23s^{pu} Feb 8] good sort: fairly useful hurdler in 2000/1: no sign of retaining ability after near 2-year absence: should stay 3m: acts on heavy and good to firm going. *M. Pitman*　**h–**

PATRICKSNINETEENTH (IRE) 6 b.g. Mister Lord (USA) – Many Miracles (Le Moss) [2002/3 F16s^3 F16s* F17g Apr 5] IR £32,000 4-y-o: well-made gelding: fifth foal: half-brother to 3 winners, including fair hurdler/winning chaser up to 3m Amy Johnson (by Ore) and fair 2¾m chaser Dunboy Castle (by Carlingford Castle): dam unraced half-sister to useful staying hurdler Final Run: confirmed debut promise when winning bumper at Sandown in February by 3½ lengths from Plastic Paddy: soon off bridle under less testing conditions when tailed off in Grade 2 at Aintree: stoutly bred. *P. R. Webber*　**F101**

PATRIOT GAMES (IRE) 9 b.g. Polish Patriot (USA) – It's Now Or Never (High Line) [2002/3 h126: 17d^4 17d 20g^3 16f* 16m^6 20d* Apr 4] good-topped gelding: useful hurdler: won 4-runner minor event at Punchestown in September and valuable 16-runner listed handicap at Aintree in April: looking in good shape after 6-month absence, beat Gralmano 1½ lengths at latter, leading on bridle 2 out and idling run-in (finished lame): stays 2½m: acts on soft and firm going. *C. F. Swan, Ireland*　**h137**

PATS FUTURE 4 ch.f. King's Signet (USA) – Bedelia (Mr Fluorocarbon) [2002/3 F17s F17d Feb 23] smallish filly: fifth foal: half-sister to Desperazione (by Interrex), winner up to 11f in Italy: dam twice-raced, out of half-sister to useful 2½m chaser Mr Peapock: well held in bumpers at Taunton and Exeter. *S. C. Burrough*　**F–**

PATSY VEALE (IRE) 8 b.g. Accordion – Bermuda Castle (Carlingford Castle) [2002/3 h119: 17d* 16d 16f^2 Sep 29] lengthy, angular gelding: fairly useful hurdler: won quite valuable handicap at Killarney in May by ¾ length from Cailin's Perk: stays 21f, at least as effective around 2m: acts on firm and soft going. *J. Queally, Ireland*　**h125**

PAULS DREAM (IRE) 8 ch.g. Deep Society – Pampered Sally (Paddy's Stream) [2002/3 h–: 22d^{pu} Nov 17] no sign of ability in 3 runs over hurdles. *P. Monteith*　**h–**

PAULS LEGACY   7 ch.g. Nicholas Bill – Extremity (Quayside) [2002/3 22m Apr 8]   h–
fifth foal: dam winning pointer: tailed off in maiden hurdle on debut. *J. D. Frost*

PAULTON   10 b.g. Lugana Beach – Runcina (Runnett) [2002/3 h82§: 20d^{pu} May 4]   h– §
close-coupled gelding: poor handicap hurdler: stays 2¾m: acts on soft and good to firm
going: blinkered: moody, and not to be trusted. *K. Bishop*

PAUNTLEY GOFA   7 b.g. Afzal – Gotageton (Oats) [2002/3 c–p, h116: 16m^4 c16g^3 c106
c17m* c20m^3 Jul 7] tall gelding: fairly useful hurdler at best: fair form in novice chases,   h101
won at Market Rasen in June: disputing lead and finding plenty for pressure when bad
mistake last there 2 weeks later: probably stays 2½m: acts on good to soft and good to
firm going (bumper form on firm): usually makes running. *J. L. Spearing*

PAVEY ARK (IRE)   5 b.g. King's Ride – Splendid Run (Deep Run) [2002/3 F16v   F85
F17g^5 F16g^2 Apr 14] 24,000 4-y-o: ninth foal: brother to winning 2½m chaser Deep King
and half-brother to fair chaser Sigma Run (by The Parson), stays 2½m: dam unraced half-
sister to useful 2m hurdler Hansel Rag: best effort in bumpers when second to Classical
Ben in maiden at Hexham. *James Moffatt*

PAWN BROKER   6 ch.g. Selkirk (USA) – Dime Bag (High Line) [2002/3 16s^6 Dec   h88 p
28] useful over middle distances on Flat (tends to find little), successful in March: some
promise when sixth of 12 to Beyond The Pale in steadily-run novice at Newbury on
hurdling debut, eased after tiring last: sure to do better. *D. R. C. Elsworth*

PAXFORD JACK   7 ch.g. Alflora (IRE) – Rakajack (Rakaposhi King) [2002/3 h93d: c112
16g^5 c21d^5 c24d^2 c21d* c25s^2 c24d^5 c24d* c32g c21d^{pu} Apr 4] lengthy gelding: modest   h–
hurdler: took well to chasing, won valuable novice at Cheltenham in December and
handicap at Haydock (beat Tonoco 2½ lengths) in February: should stay beyond 25f:
raced mainly on going softer than good (acts on heavy): sound-jumping front runner.
M. F. Harris

PAXFORD LADY   6 b.m. Alflora (IRE) – Rakajack (Rakaposhi King) [2002/3 h–,   h–
F–: 19g^{pu} May 4] no sign of ability: blinkered last 2 starts. *M. Harris*

PAXFORD TROOPER   9 b.g. Gunner B – Say Shanaz (Tickled Pink) [2002/3 h–:   h–
22g^{pu} May 17] winning pointer: no show in 3 races over hurdles. *M. Harris*

PAY IT FORWARD   5 b.g. Anshan – Kellsboro Kate (Paddy's Stream) [2002/3 F16d^4 h124
F16d F16s^5 18v* 18s^2 16s^3 16s^2 20s^4 20g^{pu} Apr 20] IR £9,000 3-y-o: rather unfurnished   F82
gelding: third foal: half-brother to modest hurdler Silver Gift (by Rakaposhi King), stays
27f: dam ran once: modest form in bumpers: fairly useful novice hurdler: won maiden at
Fairyhouse (awarded race) in December and Grade 3 Festival Novices' Hurdle there (beat
Kings Orchard a length) in April: further improvement when 8 lengths third to Nobody
Told Me in Grade 1 at Punchestown in early-May: stays 2½m: acts on heavy going. *Mrs
J. Harrington, Ireland*

PAYLANDER   7 ch.g. Karinga Bay – Bichette (Lidhame) [2002/3 16m^6 16d^4 20m^2 h87
Mar 19] lightly-raced maiden on Flat: easily best effort over hurdles when second of 5 in
seller at Fontwell: stays 2½m. *G. L. Moore*

*Doncaster Bloodstock Sales Future Champions Novices' Chase, Cheltenham—
an ordinary race despite its lofty title; bold-jumping front runner Paxford Jack springs a 33/1 surprise*

PAYMASTER (NZ) 8 ch.g. Norman Pentaquad (USA) – Tivy (NZ) (Noble Bijou (USA)) [2002/3 h95: c20m² c16g^{pu} c20m^F Oct 30] good-topped gelding: modest hurdler: every chance when bad mistake last when second of 6 in novice at Huntingdon on chasing debut: let down by jumping next 2 starts: successful in points in March and April: barely stays 21f: acts on good to firm going: sometimes tongue tied. *Miss H. C. Knight* **c88 h–**

PAYNESTOWN LAD (IRE) 7 b.g. Bravefoot – Athy Lady (Welsh Captain) [2002/3 16m 16d 16s⁶ 16v^{pu} 20m⁶ 22g^{ur} 21m* Apr 19] half-brother to 2¼m hurdle winner Doc Morrissey (by Le Bavard): ran in Ireland prior to winning 5 times on Flat in Spain at 5/6 yrs: bought 4,200 gns Doncaster August Sales: modest hurdler: 16/1, much improved when winning 6-runner novice at Plumpton: stays 21f: acts on good to firm ground: edged right and found little fifth start. *Miss C. J. E. Caroe* **h86**

PC'S EUROCRUISER (IRE) 7 b.g. Fayruz – Kuwait Night (Morston (FR)) [2002/3 h77: 16m⁴ 16g³ May 26] compact gelding: poor handicap hurdler: failed to complete in 4 points in 2003: needs sharp 2m: acts on soft and good to firm going: joined Mrs D. Sayer. *A. Crook* **h75**

PEACEMAKER (IRE) 11 br.g. Strong Gale – Gamonda (Gala Performance (USA)) [2002/3 c91, h–: c20g c24g c21g⁵ c24g^{pu} c25m³ Apr 21] sturdy gelding: modest handicap chaser at best, little show in 2002/3 after 15-month absence: stays 25f: acts on firm and soft going: tried blinkered/tongue tied. *J. R. Cornwall* **c– h–**

PEACOCK THEATRE 5 b.g. Red Rainbow – Fine Art (IRE) (Tate Gallery (USA)) [2002/3 h79: 20d³ 20d⁶ 24s^{pu} 22m 16s 20s Dec 26] sturdy gelding: poor handicap hurdler: sold out of A. Streeter's stable 2,400 gns Doncaster September Sales: well held both subsequent starts: should stay beyond 2½m: acts on soft going: usually visored/blinkered: none too keen. *Edward Sexton, Ireland* **h78 d**

PEALINGS (IRE) 11 gr.g. Wood Chanter – Ten-Cents (Taste of Honey) [2002/3 c110x, h–: c21g⁴ c24d⁵ Oct 25] tall gelding: fair chaser: stays 3¼m: acts on good to firm and heavy going: tried visored, wears cheekpieces nowadays: has been ridden in spurs: often let down by jumping. *Ferdy Murphy* **c101 x h–**

PEARLIWHIRL 4 b.f. Alflora (IRE) – Pearlossa (Teenoso (USA)) [2002/3 F16f Mar 29] first foal: dam unraced, from family of top-class 2m chaser Pearlyman: seventh of 11 in mares bumper at Haydock on debut: sold 24,000 gns Doncaster May Sales. *W. Jenks* **F73**

PEARTREE HOUSE (IRE) 9 b.g. Simply Majestic (USA) – Fashion Front (Habitat) [2002/3 h106: 16d⁴ 16m⁵ 16d^{ur} 16d Nov 25] modest on Flat nowadays: modest hurdler: soon clear when winning seller at Perth in August: needs sharp 2m: acts on firm and good to soft going: free-going sort: temperament under suspicion: sold to join D. Chapman 2,000 gns Doncaster January Sales. *Mrs M. Reveley* **h97**

PEASEDOWN TOFANA 10 b.m. Teenoso (USA) – Hatherley (Deep Run) [2002/3 25g^{pu} c23g² c23m^{pu} c25g Oct 18] compact mare: winning pointer: poor maiden hurdler: probably flattered when second to Stormez at Worcester, only form in novice chases. *R. H. Alner* **c66 h–**

PEBBLE MOON 7 gr.g. Efisio – Jazz (Sharrood (USA)) [2002/3 c99d, h85: c20g^{pu} Apr 30] medium-sized gelding: modest hurdler: winning chaser, looked less than keen at Hexham in April: stays 2¾m: raced on good going or softer (acts on heavy): usually blinkered/visored. *Miss Lucinda V. Russell* **c– h–**

PECCADILLO (IRE) 9 br.g. Un Desperado (FR) – First Mistake (Posse (USA)) [2002/3 c124, h–: c21g⁸ c20m* c21m⁴ c20g³ c20m c21d^{pu} c19g* c20m⁵ Apr 26] big, rangy gelding: fairly useful handicap chaser: won at Uttoxeter and Huntingdon in September and Ascot (beat Poly Amanshaa ¾ length) in April: no other form on last 4 starts: stays easy 21f: acts on firm and good to soft going (possibly unsuited by soft): has run well when sweating: races prominently: usually jumps soundly. *R. H. Alner* **c127 h–**

PEEJAY HOBBS 5 ch.g. Alhijaz – Hicklam Millie (Absalom) [2002/3 h74: 21d^F 22f 22g² 16m⁵ 20g* 20m² 22m* 24m⁶ Aug 27] modest hurdler, left P. Murphy after third start: improved subsequently, won novice seller at Wolverhampton in July and claimer at Newton Abbot in August: ran as if amiss final start: should stay 3m: acts on firm and soft going: consistent. *C. J. Gray* **h95**

PEEWIT BRIDGE 11 ch.g. Gildoran – Electric Panic (Chukaroo) [2002/3 c20f^{pu} c25d^{pu} c21d^{pu} Jun 3] big, lengthy gelding: one-time fair chaser up to 3m: has lost his way completely: has tended to hang and carry head high. *S. A. Brookshaw* **c– h–**

PEEYOUTWO 8 b.g. Golden Heights – Nyika (Town And Country) [2002/3 h–, F88: 22d Feb 23] fair mare in bumpers: well held in novice on completed start over hurdles after 14-month lay-off. *Mrs D. A. Hamer* **h–**

PEGGY HACKET (IRE)   6 b.m. Alflora (IRE) – Radical Lady (Radical) [2002/3   **h–**
F16v⁴ 20v 20d 19dᵖᵘ Jan 24] medium-sized mare: fourth foal: half-sister to useful staying   **F–**
hurdler Tyneandthyneagain (by Good Thyne) and winning chaser up to 3¼m Sabi Sand
(by Minster Son): dam fairly useful staying chaser: well beaten in mares bumper and novice hurdle. *N. B. Mason*

PEGGYS DELIGHT   8 ch.m. Minster Son – Chasers' Bar (Oats) [2002/3 h65: 20d   **h77**
May 23] winning pointer: poor novice hurdler: probably better at 2½m than shorter: tried
tongue tied. *J. R. Turner*

PEGGY SIOUX (IRE)   6 b.m. Little Bighorn – Gayable (Gay Fandango (USA))   **h76 p**
[2002/3 F82: F16v² 20m⁵ Dec 17] modest form when placed in mares bumpers: 26½   **F82**
lengths fifth of 15 in maiden at Musselburgh on hurdling debut, left with plenty to do and
not given hard time: bred to stay 2½m+: should do better. *J. I. A. Charlton*

PEGGY'S PRINCE   5 b.g. Morpeth – Prudent Peggy (Kambalda) [2002/3 F17m³ Apr   **F88**
15] first foal: dam, modest staying chaser, half-sister to fairly useful 2m hurdler Cotton
Call: 9 lengths third of 5 finishers in bumper at Exeter on debut: will be suited by greater
test of stamina. *J. D. Frost*

PEGO   5 b.m. Syrtos – Romantic Melody (Battle Hymn) [2002/3 F–: F16m Jul 4]   **F–**
behind in bumpers. *G. F. Bridgwater*

PELE MELE   7 b. or br.g. Milieu – Hiltie Skiltie (Liberated) [2002/3 F76: 20g c16gᵖᵘ   **c–**
20gᵖᵘ 24d 16sᵖᵘ Nov 2] no form over hurdles or fences. *A. M. Crow*   **h–**

PELE MELE (FR)   8 b. or br.g. Tel Quel (FR) – Star System (FR) (Northern Treat   **h–**
(USA)) [2002/3 h77: 17vᵘʳ 16s 17d Dec 19] sturdy gelding: little form over hurdles:
tongue tied/reportedly bled from nose once in 2001/2. *Miss Venetia Williams*

PELOTA VASCA   7 b.m. Relief Pitcher – Valls d'Andorra (Free State) [2002/3 F16d   **h– §**
F17g 20mᵖᵘ Jul 18] well beaten in bumpers: looked less than keen on hurdling debut.   **F–**
M. R. Bosley

PEN-ALMOZON   7 ch.h. Almoojid – Cornish Mona Lisa (Damsire Unregistered)   **c–**
[2002/3 F17v 19d 22v 24v c25dᶠ 24d c23g⁴ Mar 18] third reported foal: dam unraced: no   **h–**
form: tried in cheekpieces. *N. J. Hawke*   **F–**

PENDANT   8 b.g. Warning – Emerald (USA) (El Gran Senor (USA)) [2002/3 c–, h–:   **c–**
20mᵖᵘ c21g³ Apr 21] compact gelding: winning hurdler: no form over fences: tried   **h–**
visored/blinkered: often tongue tied. *Mrs J. Candlish*

PENDLE HILL   8 gr.g. Roscoe Blake – Pendle Princess (Broxted) [2002/3 c25v⁵ c20v²   **c105**
c20s² c24d⁴ c21s⁶ c20d⁴ c20g Apr 25] useful-looking gelding: winning hurdler: fair nov-   **h–**
ice chaser: poor efforts last 3 starts: stays 3m: best form on going softer than good (acts
on heavy): usually races prominently. *P. Beaumont*

PENDRAGON   11 b.g. Bold Fox – Celtic Royale (Celtic Cone) [2002/3 c85: c33gᶠ   **c–**
May 1] rangy gelding: modest pointer: let down by jumping 2 of 3 starts in hunter chases.
Mrs Sarah Faulks

PENGE POINT (IRE)   6 br.g. Lord Americo – Broken Boots (IRE) (King's Ride)   **h70**
[2002/3 F16g² F16v 19g 19d Feb 23] close-coupled gelding: first foal: dam unraced half-   **F89**
sister to very smart chaser Harcon: 9 lengths second of 16 to Widemouth Bay in bumper
at Wincanton on debut: well held all 3 starts after, 2 of them over hurdles: bred to stay
2½m+. *A. King*

PENGUIN BAY   7 b.g. Rock Hopper – Corn Lily (Aragon) [2002/3 c–, h86, F91: 20d⁵   **c– §**
16m 21m⁶ c16g 17m⁴ 16f² 16g 16m Apr 21] workmanlike gelding: maiden hurdler, left   **h85 §**
Mrs M. Reveley after fourth start: well held over fences: best form at 2m: acts on firm
going: tried blinkered: ungenuine. *N. Wilson*

PENNELESS DANCER   4 b.g. Pennekamp (USA) – Villella (Sadler's Wells (USA))   **h–**
[2002/3 16g 16d Dec 4] half-brother to modest hurdler Ennoble (by Highest Honor), stays
2¾m: modest maiden on Flat (stays 7f): sold second of M. Blanshard's stable £4,500 Ascot
August Sales: shaped like a non-stayer in 2 juvenile hurdles at Catterick. *M. E. Sowersby*

PENNINOIR   7 br.m. Royal Fountain – The Pride of Pokey (Uncle Pokey) [2002/3 h–,   **c–**
F–: c17gᶠ c21dᵖᵘ c24g⁵ c16gᵖᵘ c25sᵖᵘ Feb 23] workmanlike mare: of little account: tried   **h–**
visored/in cheekpieces. *Mrs S. C. Bradburne*

PENNYAGO (IRE)   6 b.g. Good Thyne (USA) – Boro Penny (Normandy) [2002/3   **F–**
F16d Feb 1] IR £50,000 4-y-o: sturdy gelding: half-brother to several winners, including
useful chaser up to 3m Sir Leonard (by Strong Gale) and fairly useful hurdler/winning
chaser Boro Sovereign (by King's Ride), stayed 3m: dam, poor middle-distance maiden/

bumper performer, sister to Galway Plate winner Boro Quarter and half-sister to smart 2m to 2½m hurdler Boro Eight: beginning to struggle when hampered over 5f out in bumper at Wetherby on debut: sold 4,500 gns Doncaster May Sales. *Mrs H. Dalton*

PENNYAHEI   12 b.m. Malaspina – Pennyazena (Pamroy) [2002/3 c–, h–: c25s⁵ Mar 7] angular mare: winning chaser: fairly useful pointer nowadays, successful twice in April: stays 3¼m: acts on good to firm and heavy going. *S. A. Brookshaw*   c– §
h– §

PENNY FICTION (IRE)   6 b.m. Welsh Term – First Edition (Le Bavard (FR)) [2002/3 F16m* Apr 22] good-topped mare: third foal: half-sister to 2m hurdle winner Boy Scout (by Bravefoot) and bumper winner First Print (by Jurado): dam lightly-raced maiden pointer: won bumper at Fairyhouse on debut by 4 lengths from Celestial Light: failed to improve as expected when mid-field in Grade 1 at Punchestown 8 days later. *D. M. Leigh, Ireland*   F93

PENNY PASS (IRE)   4 b.g. Pennekamp (USA) – Belle Etoile (FR) (Lead On Time (USA)) [2002/3 16mᵖᵘ 16vᵖᵘ Jan 17] signs of ability on Flat for Sir Mark Prescott: pulled up both starts in juvenile hurdles, reportedly lame on first occasion. *M. C. Pipe*   h–

PENNY PICTURES (IRE)   4 b.c. Theatrical – Copper Creek (Habitat) [2002/3 16d³ 17s* 16m* Apr 10] small colt: useful on Flat (stays 1½m), sold out of J. Given's stable 50,000 gns Newmarket Autumn Sales: favourite, soon clear when 3 lengths third to Spectroscope in juvenile at Kempton on hurdling debut: long odds on when easily making all in lesser events at Bangor (maiden) in March and Ludlow in April: will prove best around 2m for time being: free-going sort: remains open to improvement. *M. C. Pipe*   h115 p

PENNYS FROM HEAVEN   9 gr.g. Generous (IRE) – Heavenly Cause (USA) (Grey Dawn II) [2002/3 h74§: 17d⁵ 17g³ 17m⁴ 17g³ 20m 19m³ 17m² 19d⁶ Aug 4] compact gelding: poor maiden hurdler: best around 2m: acts on soft and good to firm going: tried blinkered: headstrong and irresolute. *Miss T. M. Ide*   h83 §

PENTHOUSE MINSTREL   9 b. or br.g. Seven Hearts – Pentameron (Heres) [2002/3 h91: 22mᵖᵘ c25dᵖᵘ Feb 6] lengthy gelding: maiden hurdler, left C. Gray after reappearance: pulled up on hunter chase debut: won maiden point in April. *Miss N. Stephens*   c–
h–

PENTLAND SQUIRE   12 b.g. Belfort (FR) – Sparkler Superb (Grisaille) [2002/3 h–: 16m 16g 16v⁵ 16gᵖᵘ Mar 14] rangy gelding: winning hurdler: lightly raced and no form since 2000/1. *Miss C. J. E. Caroe*   h–

PEPE GALVEZ (SWE)   6 br.g. Mango Express – Mango Sampaquita (SWE) (Colombian Friend (USA)) [2002/3 16m² 17s* 17s³ 16g² 16m⁵ Apr 16] sturdy gelding: brother to modest hurdler/fair chaser around 2m Antonio Mariano: fairly useful maiden on Flat (stays 1½m) at 3 yrs for B. Hanbury: fairly useful novice hurdler: won at Taunton (maiden) in November and Newbury (improved form, showed plenty of resolution to beat Ilabon a neck) in March: let down by jumping final start: raced around 2m: has won on soft going, best efforts on good/good to firm. *Mrs L. C. Taylor*   h126

PEPPERCORN (GER)   6 b.g. Big Shuffle (USA) – Pasca (GER) (Lagunas) [2002/3 16g³ 16s⁶ 16sᵖᵘ Feb 14] small, angular gelding: smart on Flat at 4 yrs, successful 5 times from 6f to 8.5f in Germany for U. Ostmann: not quite so good in 2002, successful in amateur event at Fontainebleau: encouraging effort over hurdles when third of 18 to Keltic Bard in novice at Newbury: pulled hard and dropped right out in similar events under more testing conditions at Kempton (blinkered) and Sandown: rejoined former stable. *F. Doumen, France*   h112

PEPPERCORN PRINCE   6 b.g. General Wade – Lady Regent (Wolver Hollow) [2002/3 F18fᵖᵘ Apr 24] half-brother to 6f/7f winner Trojan General (by Trojan Fen) and 9f/1¼m winner in Germany by Deploy: dam, Irish 7f winner, half-sister to high-class middle-distance filly Infamy, herself dam of useful staying hurdler Rostopovish: favourite, seemed to go amiss in bumper at Fontwell on debut. *Miss E. C. Lavelle*   F–

PER AMORE (IRE)   5 ch.g. General Monash (USA) – Danny's Miracle (Superlative) [2002/3 h101: 16s² 16f² 16d* 17v 16g 16m³ Apr 22] medium-sized gelding: fairly useful hurdler: improved form after break second and third starts, won 6-runner handicap at Wincanton in November: raced around 2m: acts on any going: wears blinkers/cheekpieces. *P. J. Hobbs*   h116

PERANGE (FR)   7 ch.g. Perrault – La Mesange (FR) (Olmeto) [2002/3 c117, h–: c19s⁵ c26d⁴ c21dᶠ c21g* Apr 21] close-coupled, workmanlike gelding: fairly useful handicap chaser: back to form last 2 starts, won at Newton Abbot by ¾ length from Athnowen: stays 21f: acts on heavy going. *P. F. Nicholls*   c122
h–

PERCHANCER (IRE) 7 ch.g. Perugino (USA) – Irish Hope (Nishapour (FR)) **h–**
[2002/3 h113: 16g⁵ Sep 25] fair but untrustworthy on Flat (stays easy 11f), successful in
May: winning hurdler: ran poorly only outing in 2002/3: likely to prove best up to 2½m:
acts on heavy going. *P. C. Haslam*

PERCHING (IRE) 9 b.g. Strong Gale – Fiona's Blue (Crash Course) [2002/3 c–, h–: **c70**
c25m c26m² Apr 21] strong gelding: winning chaser: lightly raced and only poor nowa- **h–**
days: stays 3¼m: acts on good to firm going: has worn cheekpieces. *P. Butler*

PERCIPIENT 5 b.g. Pennekamp (USA) – Annie Albright (USA) (Verbatim (USA)) **F69**
[2002/3 F17s⁵ Oct 28] seventh foal: half-brother to French 11.5f winner Belmontee (by
Belmez) and useful 5f (at 2 yrs) and 6f winner who stayed 7f Shamanic (by Fairy King):
dam, Irish sprint maiden, half-sister to fairly useful hurdler/chaser up to 3¼m Staunch
Rival: raced freely in front to 4f out when fifth of 9 in bumper at Bangor on debut.
G. Thorner

PERCY BASIL 4 b.g. Petoski – Madam-M (Tina's Pet) [2002/3 F17d Feb 23] sixth **F–**
foal: half-brother to winning 3m hurdler Madam's Man (by Sir Harry Lewis): dam, irresolute and of little account, half-sister to useful chaser up to 25f Loddon Lad: well held in
maiden bumper on debut. *Ian Williams*

PERCY BECK 7 ch.g. Minster Son – Kate O'Kirkham (Le Bavard (FR)) [2002/3 h–: **c–**
17g² 16g⁵ 16d* 16g⁴ 17m⁶ 16g c20sʳ Mar 2] poor handicap hurdler: won at Wetherby in **h77**
May: off 4 months, in rear when unseating 5 out in maiden on chasing debut: raced mainly
around 2m: acts on good to soft going. *P. Needham*

PERCY BRAITHWAITE (IRE) 11 b.g. Kahyasi – Nasseem (FR) (Zeddaan) **c–**
[2002/3 c77, h88: 26g⁶ 24d 19s⁶ Dec 28] small, angular gelding: winning hurdler/chaser, **h–**
no form in 2002/3: stays 21f: acts on firm and soft going. *Mrs P. Ford*

PERCY PARKEEPER 10 b.g. Teenoso (USA) – True Clown (True Song) [2002/3 **c122**
c111, h–: c17m* c16g² c20m⁴ c20g³ c24m³ c24g³ Apr 25] useful-looking gelding: fairly **h–**
useful handicap chaser: improved when winning at Stratford in September: ran well again
next time, but made mistakes most starts after, reportedly sustained cut to near hind fifth
one: effective around 2m, seems barely to stay 3m: unraced on firm going, acts on any
other: blinkered twice in 2001/2: usually front runner. *N. A. Twiston-Davies*

PERFECT FELLOW 9 b.g. Teamster – G W Supermare (Rymer) [2002/3 c132p, h–: **c122 +**
c20m* c20dᶠ Nov 16] smallish, sturdy gelding: useful chaser: won uncompetitive handi- **h–**
cap at Cheltenham in October by 9 lengths from Hurricane Lamp: fifth and weakening
when fell 2 out in very valuable event on same course following month: should stay 3m:
acts on good to firm and heavy going: usually sound jumper: doesn't stand much racing,
and went as if all wasn't well at Punchestown in early-May. *Miss H. C. Knight*

PERFECT LIAISON 6 b.g. Alflora (IRE) – Connie's Pet (National Trust) [2002/3 **F86**
F17d F16g⁶ Apr 2] tall gelding: second foal: dam once-raced half-sister to useful 2m
chaser Prize Asset: better effort in bumpers when sixth of 19 to Very Optimistic at Ascot.
R. H. Alner

PERIWINKLE LAD (IRE) 6 b.g. Perugino (USA) – Bold Kate (Bold Lad (IRE)) **c81**
[2002/3 16s 17s² 16s⁶ 16mᵘʳ 17m c16g 16m³ 16f 16f³ 16d 22s⁴ 20s³ 22v² 20v* 20s⁶ **h98**
22d⁶ 20s c18s² c22d 24mᵘ 22g³ Apr 21] angular gelding: half-brother to several winners,
including fair chaser Belisario (by Distinctly North): stays 3m: modest maiden on Flat:
modest handicap hurdler: won at Thurles in November, Tramore (easily) in December
and Listowel in April: good third to April Allegro at Fairyhouse final start: easily best
effort in maiden chases when second at Downpatrick: stays 3m: acts on any going: sometimes blinkered (not when successful): held up: tough: sold 15,000 gns Doncaster May
Sales. *E. McNamara, Ireland*

PERK ALERT (IRE) 9 b.g. Executive Perk – Clondo Blue (IRE) (Miner's Lamp) **c70**
[2002/3 c22sᵖᵘ c24d c23s⁶ c25gᶠ Mar 17] angular gelding: one-time fair maiden hurdler: **h–**
first form over fences after lengthy absence when winning handicap at Hereford, giving
improved display of jumping: stays 25f: acts on good to soft going. *A. King*

PERKYS PRIDE (IRE) 7 b.g. Executive Perk – Josie Mac (Pitpan) [2002/3 h130, **h114**
F105: 16s⁵ 16d 17d 22dᵖᵘ 17d 17g⁶ 22m⁴ Apr 11] lengthy ex-Irish gelding: useful hurdler
at best, left M. Cunningham after reappearance: little encouragement until stepped
back up in trip final outing: stays 2¾m: acts on soft going, probably good to firm.
M. C. Pipe

PEROUSE 5 ch.g. Alderbrook – Track Angel (Ardoon) [2002/3 F104: 16d 16d² 17f* **h104**
16f* Apr 21] fairly useful form in bumpers: reportedly distressed on hurdling debut, final

start for L. Lungo: landed odds in weakly-contested maiden at Taunton and 4-runner novice at Wincanton in April: will stay beyond 2m. *P. F. Nicholls*

PERSIAN BANDIT (IRE)   5 b.g. Idris (IRE) – Ce Soir (Northern Baby (CAN))   h–
[2002/3 h–: 16gpu Apr 29] fair at best on Flat (stays 1m), won twice in Spain in 2001, poor in Britain in 2002: no show either outing over hurdles, visored second occasion. *J. R. Jenkins*

PERSIAN KING (IRE)   6 ch.g. Persian Bold – Queen's Share (Main Reef) [2002/3   **h110**
h71: 17g² 17m³ 16g* 16m* 16m Oct 30] good-topped gelding: useful on Flat (probably stays 1¾m): much improved over hurdles, winning maiden at Worcester in September and novice at Chepstow (beat Old Marsh ½ length) in October: never a factor in handicap final outing: likely to stay beyond 2m: raced on good/good to firm going. *J. A. B. Old*

PERSIAN POINT   7 ch.g. Persian Bold – Kind Thoughts (Kashmir II) [2002/3 16d⁴   h–
19m⁶ Jul 7] little show in 3 starts over hurdles, taking strong hold: sold 2,700 gns Doncaster November Sales: successful in points in February and March. *Mrs A. Duffield*

PERSIAN PRIDE (IRE)   5 ch.g. Barathea (IRE) – Glenarff (USA) (Irish River (FR))   **h94**
[2002/3 17g² Jun 10] fairly useful on Flat (stays 1½m) for P. Harris: second to easy winner Jaboune in novice at Newton Abbot on hurdling debut, held when mistake 2 out: looked open to improvement but not seen out again. *P. J. Hobbs*

PERSIAN WATERS (IRE)   7 b.g. Persian Bold – Emerald Waters (Kings Lake   **h124**
(USA)) [2002/3 21d² 22d³ 21g Mar 12] leggy gelding: fairly useful handicap hurdler: returned about as good as ever, eighth of 27 to Xenophon in Coral Cup at Cheltenham: should stay 3m: raced on good going or softer over hurdles: reportedly bled from nose on reappearance. *J. R. Fanshawe*

PERSONAL ASSURANCE   6 b.g. Un Desperado (FR) – Steel Typhoon (General   **h110**
Ironside) [2002/3 F17d³ F17d² F16d³ 21s³ 16v* 16s⁵ 21m⁴ Apr 16] 15,000 4-y-o: rather   **F95**
unfurnished gelding: fifth foal: half-brother to 2 winners, including staying hurdler/chaser Tactix (by Nearly A Hand): dam, behind in bumper, sister to very smart 2m to 2½m chaser Blitzkreig: placed all 3 starts in bumpers: fair novice hurdler: won at Sandown in February by 3 lengths from Handy Money: creditable fourth to Buckby Lane in quite valuable event at Cheltenham: likely to stay 3m: acts on good to firm and heavy going. *Jonjo O'Neill*

PERSONA PRIDE   9 gr.g. St Enodoc – Le Jour Fortune (Twilight Alley) [2002/3 c86:   c–
c24spu c25spu Mar 7] angular gelding: modest pointer, successful twice in 2002: little worthwhile form in hunter chases. *Mrs B. Brown*

PERSUETS (IRE)   5 b.m. Gildoran – Furry Queen (Furry Glen) [2002/3 F17g⁴ Apr   **F88**
21] third known foal: dam, placed in bumper on Flat, out of half-sister to dam of top-class 2m chaser Badsworth Boy: around 5 lengths fourth to Random Native in bumper at Carlisle on debut. *J. I. A. Charlton*

PERTEMPS BOYCOTT (IRE)   5 b.g. Indian Ridge – Coupe d'Hebe (Ile de Bour-   h66
bon (USA)) [2002/3 h73: 16g³ 16mpu 19g 20m* 21s⁴ 22dpu 20f 20gpu 21d⁵ Apr 8] leggy gelding: poor hurdler: won conditional jockeys selling handicap at Hexham in June: possibly best up to 2½m: acts on soft and good to firm going. *H. Alexander*

PERTEMPS CINDERELLA   8 ch.m. Almoojid – Cinderella Derek (Hittite Glory)   **c82**
[2002/3 h73: 20d² 16s 20v⁴ 16v³ 16s⁶ c22d* Mar 3] plain, sparely-made mare: poor   **h73**
hurdler: fortunate to win 3-finisher handicap at Market Rasen on chasing debut, not fluent at times and left clear when 5-length leader Grangewick Flight unseated 2 out: stays 2¾m: acts on heavy going: ran poorly when blinkered fifth outing. *B. D. Leavy*

PERTEMPS FLASH   5 gr.g. Silca Blanka (IRE) – Fast Market (Petong) [2002/3 F16m   F–
F16mpu Jul 24] seventh foal: dam modest 1¼m winner: no show in 2 bumpers, pulled up and dismounted around halfway second occasion. *A. D. Smith*

PERTEMPS (IRE)   10 ch.g. Good Thyne (USA) – Julia's Pauper (Pauper) [2002/3   c–
c81, h–: c24g Mar 12] angular gelding: poor chaser/novice hurdler: no sign of retaining   h–
ability on return after 21-month absence: blinkered/ visored: none too genuine. *Ian Williams*

PERTEMPS JARDINE (IRE)   5 b. or br.g. General Monash (USA) – Indescent   h–
Blue (Bluebird (USA)) [2002/3 16gur 21d 16vpu Nov 27] workmanlike gelding: modest maiden on Flat (stays 7f) at 3 yrs for R. Fahey: no show in 3 outings over hurdles. *Mrs A. M. Thorpe*

PERTEMPS MACHINE 4 b.g. Danzig Connection (USA) – Shamrock Dancer (IRE) **h–**
(Dance of Life (USA)) [2002/3 16s^{pu} Aug 10] 800Y: second foal: dam third at 8.5f: soon
struggling in juvenile hurdle on debut. *A. D. Smith*

PERTEMPS SILENUS 5 b.g. Silca Blanka (IRE) – Silvie (Kind of Hush) [2002/3 **h–**
F–: F18d 17s^{pu} 17s^{pu} Feb 13] sturdy gelding: no sign of ability: headstrong. *A. D. Smith* **F–**

PERTEMPS SUSIE 7 b.m. Gildoran – Brilliant Future (Welsh Saint) [2002/3 h78, **h84**
F88: 17s 19s^5 17f^3 19m^2 21m^5 Apr 21] lengthy mare: bumper winner: poor novice
hurdler: stays 19f: acts on firm going, possibly unsuited by soft. *Ian Williams*

PERTEMPS TIMMY 5 b.g. Petoski – Brilliant Future (Welsh Saint) [2002/3 F79: **F77**
F16s^3 Jun 9] angular gelding: modest form when third in bumpers at Huntingdon and
Worcester. *A. Streeter*

PERTINO 7 b.g. Terimon – Persian Fountain (IRE) (Persian Heights) [2002/3 h108: **c108**
18d^5 16m^4 c16f* c16m^2 c17g* c17g^2 c16d Apr 9] good-topped gelding: fair handicap **h107**
hurdler/novice chaser: won easily over fences at Hexham in September and Southwell in
October: ran poorly final outing after 6-month absence: stays 2½m: acts on any going:
usually wears cheekpieces. *J. M. Jefferson*

PESCETTO LADY (IRE) 5 b.m. Toulon – Glenpatrick Peach (IRE) (Lafontaine **h100**
(USA)) [2002/3 F16d^{su} 16m^2 16f* 16d^F Nov 16] angular mare: second foal: dam, thrice- **F87**
raced in bumpers, half-sister to very smart 2m hurdler/chaser Space Trucker: fair on flat
(stays 1¾m), successful at Thurles in October: won maiden hurdle at Listowel month
earlier: improved form when fourth in novice at Punchestown in late-April: should stay
beyond 2m: acts on firm going. *Mrs J. Harrington, Ireland*

PESSIMISTIC DICK 10 b.g. Derrylin – Tycoon Moon (Tycoon II) [2002/3 c69, h–: **c111**
c23m* c23m^4 c26f^5 c26d* c27g* c26g* c24m* c24d^5 c32g^{pu} c26m^5 Apr 16] sturdy geld- **h–**
ing: fair handicap chaser: much improved in first half of season, winning at Worcester,
Cartmel, Sedgefield, Carlisle and Cheltenham (amateurs): stays 27f: has form on heavy
going, races on firmer nowadays (acts on firm): tried blinkered, not since 2000/1: usually
races prominently: sound jumper: genuine. *H. Morrison*

PETANQUE (IRE) 7 b.g. King's Ride – Phargara (IRE) (Phardante (FR)) [2002/3 **h112**
F97^p: F16g^5 19d* 16v* 16m^6 Mar 22] tall gelding: fairly useful form in bumpers, **F100**
successful on debut in 2001/2: won 20-runner novice at Doncaster in January on hurdling
debut by 2 lengths from Benbecula: well beaten over shorter both subsequent starts.
N. J. Henderson

PETARA (IRE) 8 ch.g. Petardia – Romangoddess (IRE) (Rhoman Rule (USA)) **h–**
[2002/3 17d 17g^{pu} Mar 29] good-topped gelding: won up to 1¼m on Flat: lightly raced
and no form over hurdles. *J. S. Wainwright*

PETERSHAM 6 b.h. Petardia – Hayhurst (Sandhurst Prince) [2002/3 h125: c16f^2 **c125 p**
c17s* c16v* Nov 17] fairly useful hurdler: already as good over fences, won Grade 3 **h–**
Craddockstown Novices' Chase at Wexford (tongue tied) comfortably by 4½ lengths
from Albatros: earlier won maiden at Gowran: jumped fluently in main on both occasions: should stay beyond 2m: acts on heavy going: likely to improve again over fences
provided all is well with him. *M. J. P. O'Brien, Ireland*

PETERSON'S CAY (IRE) 5 b.g. Grand Lodge (USA) – Columbian Sand (IRE) **h84**
(Salmon Leap (USA)) [2002/3 F83: F16d^4 F16g^3 16g^5 19g^{pu} 20g^4 Mar 23] fair form in **F86**
bumpers: best effort in novice hurdles when fifth to Laouen at Musselburgh: should stay
beyond 2m: blinkered second start: hasn't looked straightforward ride. *Mrs M. Reveley*

PETER'S TWO FUN (FR) 6 b.g. Funambule (USA) – Spinner's Mate (FR) (Miller's **h93 §**
Mate) [2002/3 h108: 22g^2 22f^3 20d* 22g^2 22m 26m^2 19m 22f^3 25g^4 20s^5 21g^2 22d 21s^{pu}
Jan 23] leggy gelding: modest hurdler: made all in maiden at Worcester in June: temperamental display final outing: stays 3¼m: acts on firm and soft going: visored after second
start: usually makes running: sold £1,200 Ascot April Sales. *M. C. Pipe*

PETE THE PARSON (IRE) 14 b.g. The Parson – Gemelek (Menelek) [2002/3 c96, **c–**
h–: c20g^{pu} c18g c21v^5 c20s^{pu} Feb 12] rather leggy gelding: one-time useful chaser up to **h–**
21f, in decline since 1998/9. *J. A. B. Old*

PETEURESQUE (USA) 6 ch.g. Peteski (CAN) – Miss Ultimo (USA) (Screen King **h88**
(USA)) [2002/3 h84: 16s^{pu} 16v^6 Feb 4] lightly-raced over hurdles, modest form at best:
reportedly lost action on reappearance. *R. H. Buckler*

PETITE AIMEE (IRE) 5 b.m. Toulon – Midnight Seeker (Status Seeker) [2002/3 **F–**
F16d^{pu} Apr 25] fourth foal: dam placed over jumps in Ireland: tailed off when pulled up
in bumper on debut. *J. S. Haldane*

PETITE RISK 9 ch.m. Risk Me (FR) – Technology (FR) (Top Ville) [2002/3 h94: **h–**
20sʳ Dec 7] leggy, angular mare: modest hurdler: unseated sixth in handicap, only start
in 2002/3: best around 2m: acts on soft and good to firm going: blinkered twice (well
beaten) in 2000/1. *D. M. Lloyd*

PETOLINSKI 5 b.g. Petoski – Olnistar (FR) (Balsamo (FR)) [2002/3 F81: 20d 20v **h101**
20s* 20s³ 25s 22gᵖᵘ Mar 18] fair novice hurdler: much improved form when 33/1-winner
at Chepstow in December: easily best other effort on next outing: should be suited by
3m+: acts on soft going: soon off bridle last 2 starts, and may benefit from headgear.
J. S. King

PETONGSKI 5 b.g. Petong – Madam Petoski (Petoski) [2002/3 16g Dec 13] good- **h–**
bodied gelding: unreliable on Flat: very unlikely to stay over hurdles. *D. W. Barker*

PETREA 8 b.m. St Ninian – Polypodium (Politico (USA)) [2002/3 h–: c24g³ May 31] **c94**
smallish mare: fair pointer, successful twice in 2002: made mistakes when third to Glacial **h–**
Trial in mares hunter chase at Stratford: tried blinkered over hurdles. *W. M. Burnell*

PETROS CHIEF 6 b.g. Factual (USA) – Dancing Ballerina (Record Run) [2002/3 **h–**
F16g 20vᵖᵘ 19gᵖᵘ Dec 13] fourth foal: dam winning chaser, stayed 2½m: little sign of **F–**
ability. *Miss M. E. Rowland*

PETTICOAT LIL (IRE) 7 b.m. Petoski – Heresy (IRE) (Black Minstrel) [2002/3 **h–**
16dᵖᵘ 16d 17s⁵ 17g⁶ Mar 22] sparely-made mare: no form over hurdles: visored final outing. *R. Mathew*

PETTREE (IRE) 9 ch.g. King Persian – Whackers World (Whistling Deer) [2002/3 **c94 x**
c98, h–: c20d⁶ c20d⁴ c26s c24s⁵ c24g² Apr 19] tall gelding: modest handicap chaser: **h–**
effective at 2½m to 3m: raced mainly on good going or softer: blinkered second start: has
gone in snatches: often let down by jumping. *N. A. Twiston-Davies*

PEVERIL PENDRAGON 9 b.g. Emarati (USA) – Princess Siham (Chabrias (FR)) **c–**
[2002/3 c17vᵖᵘ c16dᵖᵘ Feb 10] tall gelding: one-time fair 2m handicap hurdler: novice **h–**
chaser, no sign of retaining ability after nearly 4 years off: has had tongue tied.
G. B. Balding

PEWTER LIGHT (IRE) 6 gr.g. Roselier (FR) – Luminous Light (Cardinal Flower) **h–**
[2002/3 24vᵖᵘ 22dᵖᵘ 21m Mar 21] 20,000 4-y-o: rather unfurnished gelding: second foal:
dam, winning hurdler/pointer, half-sister to smart 2m to 3m hurdler Derrymoyle: little
show in maiden hurdles. *B. J. M. Ryall*

PHANTOM MIST 7 b.m. Opera Ghost – Titian Mist (Town And Country) [2002/3 F–: **F–**
F17mᵘʳ Jul 15] twice-raced in bumpers, unseated early on second occasion. *M. Salaman*

PHARAGON (IRE) 5 b.g. Phardante (FR) – Hogan (IRE) (Black Minstrel) [2002/3 **h–**
F14d F16g 16g Apr 25] €23,000 4-y-o: first foal: dam, lightly raced in points, from **F–**
family of useful 2m chaser Dan The Millar: no sign of ability. *Mrs C. J. Kerr*

PHARAILDE 5 ch.m. Phardante (FR) – Canal Street (Oats) [2002/3 F18m F18s 20g **h–**
22f³ Apr 24] lengthy, angular mare: second foal: dam twice-raced in bumpers/over **F–**
hurdles: little sign of ability. *M. J. Roberts*

PHARAOH HATSHEPSUT (IRE) 5 b.m. Definite Article – Maid of Mourne **h–**
(Fairy King (USA)) [2002/3 16vᵖᵘ Dec 2] poor on Flat (stays easy 1m): no encouragement in maiden in hurdling debut. *R. A. Fahey*

PHARAWAY CITIZEN (IRE) 8 ch.g. Phardante (FR) – Boreen Citizen (Boreen **c105**
(FR)) [2002/3 h97: 23v³ 24dᵖᵘ c25dᵖᵘ c22s* c23gᵖᵘ c22g⁵ c26g³ Apr 19] useful-looking **h78 +**
gelding: modest maiden hurdler: fair novice chaser: won handicap at Newbury in February: let down by jumping most other starts: barely stays 3¼m: raced on good going or
softer (acts on soft). *T. R. George*

PHARBEITFROME (IRE) 9 b.g. Phardante (FR) – Asigh Glen (Furry Glen) **c86**
[2002/3 c76, h–: c16d³ c17m* 19gᵖᵘ c19gᵖᵘ c16m³ c20gᶠ c16v* c16sᵘʳ c16v c17m⁵ Apr **h–**
21] lengthy, workmanlike gelding: modest handicap chaser: won at Market Rasen in June
and Sedgefield in January: second outing over hurdles when pulled up in novice, only run
for D. Cantillon: stays 2½m: acts on heavy and good to firm going: tongue tied: poor
jumper. *N. Wilson*

PHARBEIT (IRE) 6 b.g. King's Ride – Phargara (IRE) (Phardante (FR)) [2002/3 F16v **h70**
F16d⁶ 20g Apr 2] IR £16,000 4-y-o: rather unfurnished gelding: fifth foal: brother to **F72**
bumper/19f hurdle winner Petanque and half-brother to fair hurdler Blow Wind Blow (by
Strong Gale), stays 3m: dam unraced half-sister to high-class staying chaser Cahervillahow: poor form in 2 bumpers and novice hurdle (blinkered): has hung right. *E. L. James*

PHAR BREEZE (IRE)   8 b.m. Phardante (FR) – Glamorous Gale (Strong Gale)   **h75 §**
[2002/3 h71§, F–: 20g⁵ 16d* 17sᵖᵘ 16d 22dᵇᵈ 20dᵖᵘ Feb 26] small, angular mare: poor
hurdler: won weak mares maiden at Southwell in November: probably stays 2¾m: acts
on soft going: moody (often reluctant to race) and not one to trust. *Mrs J. M. Mann*

PHAR CITY (IRE)   6 b.g. Phardante (FR) – Aunty Dawn (IRE) (Strong Gale) [2002/3   **c101**
F16m⁵ 21d 20s³ 24vᵖᵘ 24v⁵ 22d 21s² c20m* Apr 21] strong, well-made gelding: winning   **h93**
pointer: fair form on second of 2 starts in bumpers: modest novice hurdler: won 3-runner   **r93**
maiden at Plumpton on chasing debut by 22 lengths from Phildari: unseated eighth in
handicap at Punchestown week later: stays 21f: acts on soft and good to firm going.
R. H. Buckler

PHARDANTE FLYER (IRE)   9 b.g. Phardante (FR) – Shannon Lek (Menelek)   **c–**
[2002/3 c112, h–: 17g 20g⁴ Apr 24] good-topped gelding: useful hurdler at best: off over   **h–**
14 months having reportedly suffered suspensory problem, tailed off in 2 handicaps: let
down by jumping both starts over fences: should stay 2½m: acts on soft and good to firm
going: has shown tendency to hang. *P. J. Hobbs*

PHAR ECHO (IRE)   12 b.g. Phardante (FR) – Borecca (Boreen (FR)) [2002/3 c71x,   **c73 x**
h–: c25g* c25mᵘʳ c30d⁶ c20gᵖᵘ c27d c27v⁶ c27s⁵ Nov 26] good-topped gelding: poor   **h–**
chaser: won intermediate at Hexham in April: well held after: thorough stayer: acts on
heavy and good to firm going: usually blinkered, has worn cheekpieces: often makes
mistakes. *Mrs H. O. Graham*

PHAR FROM A FIDDLE (IRE)   7 b. or br.g. Phardante (FR) – Lucycello (Monks-   **c121**
field) [2002/3 c123, h99: c20d⁴ c24d⁵ Aug 4] well-made gelding: modest maiden hurdler: **h–**
fairly useful handicap chaser: better effort in 2002/3 when fourth to Chicuelo in valuable
event at Market Rasen: effective around 2½m to 25f: acts on good to firm and heavy
going: often races up with pace: sometimes makes mistakes: consistent. *P. F. Nicholls*

PHAR FROM CHANCE   8 ch.g. Phardante (FR) – Chancer's Last (Foggy Bell)   **c90**
[2002/3 c78: c20fᵖᵘ c21g³ c26m³ c26f* c26mᶠ c25fᵘʳ c24f⁵ c24fᶠ c24m Oct 30] rangy
gelding: winning pointer: modest chaser: won handicap at Newton Abbot in August: no
form afterwards, though still in front when falling 4 out in amateur handicap at Ludlow
penultimate start: stays 3¼m: raced on good or firmer (acts on firm): broke blood
vessel on reappearance: reportedly lame fifth start: has carried head awkwardly: joined
T. W. Donnelly. *P. F. Nicholls*

PHAR FROM FAIR (IRE)   6 b.g. Phardante (FR) – Wintry Shower (Strong Gale)   **h91**
[2002/3 F83: F17m* F17m* F16d 17s² 18v⁴ Jan 6] good sort: confirmed debut promise   **F89**
when landing odds in bumpers at Hereford in September and October: better effort over
hurdles when 1½ lengths second of 13 to Do L'Enfant d'Eau in novice at Folkestone: will
probably stay 2½m. *L. Wells*

PHAR FROM FROSTY (IRE)   6 br.g. Phardante (FR) – Cold Evening (IRE)   **h90**
(Strong Gale) [2002/3 F17d F16d* 19g⁴ 19sᶠ Dec 26] useful-looking gelding: fourth foal: **F92**
half-brother to 21f hurdle winner Alpheus (by Alphabatim): dam unraced sister to high-
class hurdler/smart chaser Cab On Target: won bumper at Ludlow in November by short
head from Magical Liaison: better effort over hurdles when around 18 lengths fourth out
of 16 to Diceman in novice at Doncaster: likely to be suited by greater test of stamina.
C. R. Egerton

PHAR GLORY (IRE)   8 b.g. Phardante (FR) – Prudent Rose (IRE) (Strong Gale)   **h88**
[2002/3 h84+: 22f² May 15] rangy gelding: won novice hurdle in April 2002: better form
when second to Jumpty Dumpty in novice handicap at Exeter following month: stays
2¾m: acts on firm going. *A. J. Lidderdale*

PHARLEN'S DREAM (IRE)   7 b.m. Phardante (FR) – Local Dream (Deep Run)   **h–**
[2002/3 F–: F16d 18sᵖᵘ 21dᵖᵘ 20vᵘʳ 16d⁶ Mar 19] no sign of ability: tried blinkered.   **F–**
R. H. Buckler

PHARLY REEF   11 b.g. Pharly (FR) – Hay Reef (Mill Reef (USA)) [2002/3 h90: 17g⁶   **h98**
16d* 16m 16m² Jul 14] small gelding: modest handicap hurdler: best effort for long time
when winning at Uttoxeter in June: best around 2m: acts on firm and soft going.
D. Burchell

PHARMISTICE (IRE)   12 b.g. Phardante (FR) – Lucylet (Kinglet) [2002/3 c93, h–:   **c104**
c25m* c25g³ Apr 7] sparely-made gelding: winning hurdler: fairly useful hunter chaser: **h–**
won at Kelso by 2 lengths from Divet Hill in May: bit below best when third to Geordies
Express there 10 months later: won 2-finisher point later in April: should stay beyond
25f: acts on good to firm going. *Miss N. Stirling*

PHARPOST (IRE) 8 b.g. Phardante (FR) – Branstown Lady (Deep Run) [2002/3 **c111 §** h99: c25g² c25dᶠ c24s³ c21sᶠ c21d⁴ c22s² c19g⁴ Mar 18] lengthy, deep-girthed gelding: **h–** winning hurdler: fair novice chaser: stays 25f: acts on soft going: finds little, and one to treat with caution: changed hands 30,000 gns Doncaster May Sales. *Miss Venetia Williams*

PHAR TO COMFY (IRE) 8 b.m. Phardante (FR) – Roseowen (Derring Rose) **c–** [2002/3 c24mᶠ Apr 10] IR 550 4-y-o: third foal: half-sister to useful hunter Mr Dow Jones (by The Bart), stays 3¼m: dam unraced: fell seventh in hunter chase at Ludlow: runner-up in 3-finisher point later in month. *K. Goldsworthy*

PHARTODANTE (IRE) 6 b.m. Phardante (FR) – Hennywood (IRE) (Henbit (USA)) **h–** [2002/3 F16m 21mᵖᵘ Apr 19] 1,000 5-y-o: second foal: dam unraced: showed nothing in **F–** mares bumper and novice hurdle. *Mrs L. C. Jewell*

PHASE EIGHT GIRL 7 b.m. Warrshan (USA) – Bugsy's Sister (Aragon) [2002/3 **h76** h69: 20g³ 26g* 21g³ Sep 6] small mare: poor handicap hurdler: won at Huntingdon in August: best effort at 3¼m: acts on firm going. *J. Hetherton*

PHILDARI (IRE) 7 b.g. Shardari – Philosophical (Welsh Chanter) [2002/3 h106, F–: **c91** 20m³ 20d⁴ 21vᵖᵘ c16g⁵ c24m² c24m⁴ c20m² Apr 21] lengthy gelding: fair maiden hurd- **h104** ler: modest form over fences: stays 3m: acts on soft going, probably on good to firm: has worn cheekpieces: tongue tied: temperament under suspicion (has carried head high). *P. R. Webber*

PHILTRE (IRE) 9 b.g. Phardante (FR) – Forest Gale (Strong Gale) [2002/3 c107: **c–** c28mᵖᵘ Jun 1] tall, angular gelding: fair chaser in 2001/2: pulled up in valuable hunter at Stratford in June: won points in January and April: stays 3½m: acts on good to firm going: races prominently. *Mrs H. L. Needham*

PHINDA FOREST (IRE) 4 br.f. Charnwood Forest (IRE) – Shatalia (USA) (Shah- **h–** rastani (USA)) [2002/3 16g 16d 17dᵖᵘ Apr 8] modest maiden on Flat (should be suited by 1½m+) for I. Balding: no form in 3 juvenile hurdles, not knocked about final start. *W. Storey*

PHOENIX PHLYER 9 b.g. Ardross – Brown Coast (Oats) [2002/3 c86, h–: c21g **c–** May 1] maiden hurdler: fair pointer, successful first 4 starts in 2003: below that form in 2 **h–** hunter chases: should stay beyond 19f: acts on soft and good to firm going: sometimes blinkered/visored: usually races up with pace. *D. Pipe*

PHOTOGRAPHER (USA) 5 b. or br.g. Mountain Cat (USA) – Clickety Click (USA) **h94** (Sovereign Dancer (USA)) [2002/3 h95: 18m⁵ May 6] leggy gelding: modest form over hurdles: not certain to stay beyond 2¼m: has raced freely. *Mrs N. Smith*

PHYLOZZO 7 ch.m. Michelozzo (USA) – Phyllida Fox (Healaugh Fox) [2002/3 h–: **h–** 20dᵖᵘ Aug 3] poor maiden on Flat: little show in 2 outings over hurdles. *C. J. Price*

PHYSICAL FORCE 5 b.g. Casteddu – Kaiserlinde (GER) (Frontal) [2002/3 20mᵖᵘ **h–** Oct 11] half-brother to winning hurdler around 2m Doodle Bug (by Missed Flight): poor on Flat (stays 2m) nowadays: jumped very slowly first 2 and soon well tailed off in novice at Huntingdon on hurdling debut: sold to join D. Chapman 1,000 gns Doncaster Novem- ber Sales. *J. R. Best*

PHYSICAL GRAFFITI (USA) 6 b.g. Mister Baileys – Gleaming Water (USA) **h88** (Pago Pago) [2002/3 h68: 19dᶠ 16s* 19v⁴ Mar 4] compact gelding: modest hurdler: won handicap at Leicester in February: well held in similar event at Exeter following month: raced mainly around 2m: acts on heavy going. *J. A. B. Old*

PICCADILLY 8 ch.m. Belmez – Polly's Pear (Sassafras (USA)) [2002/3 **c83** c79, h83: 24m* c22g⁵ c25d² c25m³ c26mᶠ Sep 13] angular mare: modest hurdler: won **h85** handicap at Southwell in May: poor maiden chaser: stayed 25f: acted on firm and good to soft going: dead. *Miss Kate Milligan*

PICCOLINA 11 ch.m. Phardante (FR) – Highland Chain (Furry Glen) [2002/3 20m⁵ **h–** 21mᶠ Sep 13] angular mare: placed in points, little sign of ability otherwise. *G. J. Smith*

PICCOLO LADY 4 b.f. Piccolo – Tonic Chord (La Grange Music) [2002/3 16dᵖᵘ Oct **h–** 26] tall, angular filly: no form on Flat since debut: showed nothing on hurdling debut. *M. Wigham*

PICKET PIECE 12 br.g. Shareef Dancer (USA) – Jouvencelle (Rusticaro (FR)) **c–** [2002/3 c110, h–: c25d Apr 29] smallish, sturdy gelding: fair handicap chaser: tailed off **h–** only outing in 2002/3: stays 25f: acts on good to firm and heavy going. *N. A. Twiston-Davies*

PICTURE MEE 5 b.m. Aragon – Heemee (On Your Mark) [2002/3 h–: 16d^{pu} 16m^{pu} **h–**
Jun 21] small mare: modest on Flat (stays 9f): no form over hurdles: jumped erratically
and looked far from keen final outing (tongue tied). *M. A. Barnes*

PICTURE PALACE 5 ch.g. Salse (USA) – Moviegoer (Pharly (FR)) [2002/3 h103§: **h95 §**
16s^{pu} 21s^5 19d^4 16d^3 26g* Mar 17] workmanlike gelding: modest handicap hurdler: won
conditional jockeys event at Hereford: stays easy 3¼m: acts on soft and good to firm
going: blinkered: sometimes hangs right/finds little: not one to trust. *T. R. George*

PIERRE PRECIEUSE 4 ch.f. Bijou d'Inde – Time Or Never (FR) (Dowsing **F82**
(USA)) [2002/3 F16d F16s^6 F16d^6 Apr 25] second foal: half-sister to ungenuine winning
hurdler Sungio (by Halling), stays 2½m: dam won up to 1¼m, also placed at 3 yrs over
jumps: first form in bumpers when sixth to 17 to Flight Command at Perth, hanging left
off home turn: pulled hard first 2 starts. *J. S. Goldie*

PIETRO BEMBO (IRE) 9 b.g. Midyan (USA) – Cut No Ice (Great Nephew) [2002/3 **c–**
c111, h–: 16g^6 16s Dec 7] close-coupled gelding: one-time fairly useful handicap hurdler: **h–**
jumped soundly in main when in frame in 2 novice chases in 2001/2: fractured pelvis and
off a year, well held on return over hurdles at Wincanton (final start for Miss E. Lavelle)
and Sandown: stays 19f: acts on good to firm and heavy going: front runner: makes mistakes over hurdles. *P. C. Ritchens*

PIKESTAFF (USA) 5 ch.g. Diesis – Navarene (USA) (Known Fact (USA)) [2002/3 **h75**
22g 16v 16s 17m^2 Apr 19] small gelding: modest and inconsistent on Flat (stays 1½m),
sold out of T. D. Barron's stable 3,000 gns Doncaster August Sales: first form over
hurdles when second to Montessori Mio in novice at Carlisle. *M. A. Barnes*

PILGRIM GOOSE (IRE) 5 ch.g. Rainbows For Life (CAN) – Across The Ring **h–**
(IRE) (Auction Ring (USA)) [2002/3 16g Dec 13] smallish, sturdy gelding: poor maiden
on Flat (stays 1½m) for M. Tompkins/J. Best: well beaten in seller on hurdling debut.
Jedd O'Keeffe

PILLAGING PICT 8 ch.g. Primitive Rising (USA) – Carat Stick (Gold Rod) [2002/3 **c114**
c103: c22g^3 c17s* c16d^3 c20d^5 c22d* c20g^{pu} Apr 23] lengthy gelding: fair handicap
chaser: won at Kelso in November and March, best effort when beating Scotmail Lad 6
lengths in latter: mistakes when running poorly final outing: effective at 2m to 2¾m:
raced on good going or softer (acts on soft). *J. B. Walton*

PILLAR OF FIRE (IRE) 9 gr.g. Roselier (FR) – Cousin Flo (True Song) [2002/3 **c– §**
c88§, h–§: 20d^{ro} 20s 21d* 22s 22g Mar 15] leggy gelding: modest hurdler: won handicap **h97 §**
at Market Rasen in October: modest form when completing over fences in 2001/2: stays
2¾m: acts on good to soft going: well below form when tried in visor: ungenuine. *Ian
Williams*

PILLAR ROCK (USA) 7 b.g. Alysheba (USA) – Butterscotch Sauce (USA) (Clever **h112**
Trick (USA)) [2002/3 16d 16m^3 16g 16m Apr 22] leggy gelding: fair handicap hurdler:
easily best effort in 2002/3 when third at Tipperary in October: raced around 2m: acts on
any going: has had tongue tied: sometimes makes mistakes. *C. F. Swan, Ireland*

PILTDOWN CHIMES 8 b.m. Arctic Lord – Houston Belle (Milford) [2002/3 h–: **h–**
20m^{pu} Jun 3] no sign of ability. *J. R. Best*

PIMLICO (IRE) 5 ch.g. Imp Society (USA) – Willow Gale (Strong Gale) [2002/3 **F84**
F17d^5 F16d Nov 17] strong gelding: second foal: dam staying chaser: modest form in
2 bumpers, thirteenth of 24 to Rhinestone Cowboy in listed event at Cheltenham.
J. T. Gifford

PINGO HILL (IRE) 11 ch.g. Salt Dome (USA) – Andarta (Ballymore) [2002/3 c–, **c–**
h–: 19g* 20g^4 Aug 26] leggy gelding: poor hurdler: won selling handicap at Market **h71**
Rasen in June: stays 21f: acts on firm and good to soft going, unsuited by softer. *J. Mackie*

PIPERS LAMENT 4 ch.g. Hamas (IRE) – Highland Rhapsody (IRE) (Kris) [2002/3 **F–**
F16m^4 Mar 18] second foal: half-brother to fairly useful sprinter Muja Farewell (by
Mujtahid): dam 6f winner: well held in bumper at Southwell on debut, weakening having
raced in clear lead: sold 2,000 gns Doncaster May Sales. *R. Ford*

PIP MOSS 8 ch.g. Le Moss – My Aisling (John de Coombe) [2002/3 h–, F84: 16d 16d **h76**
22d^6 19v^3 Mar 10] lengthy, workmanlike gelding: poor form over hurdles: should stay at
least 2½m: raced on ground softer than good. *J. A. B. Old*

PIP'S BRAVE 7 b.g. Be My Chief (USA) – Pipistrelle (Shareef Dancer (USA)) [2002/3 **h–**
18d Nov 11] no form on Flat for long time or in 2 starts over hurdles more than 2 years
apart: tried tongue tied. *L. A. Dace*

PIRANDELLO (IRE) 5 ch.g. Shalford (IRE) – Scenic Villa (Top Ville) [2002/3 16g⁶ **h103**
16m* 16g* Apr 12] half-brother to fairly useful hurdler Globe Runner (by Adbass), stayed 2¾m: modest maiden on Flat (stays easy 1½m) for Miss K. Boutflower: progressive
form over hurdles, won maiden at Huntingdon in March and 15-runner novice handicap
at Stratford in April: likely to prove best around 2m. *K. C. Bailey*

PIRATE KING (IRE) 6 ch.g. Eurobus – Shakie Lady (Tug of War) [2002/3 16g **h–**
21sᵖᵘ 19dᵖᵘ Jan 24] IR 58,000 3-y-o, 13,000 4-y-o: rangy gelding: sixth foal: brother to
winning pointer Tower of Lloyd and half-brother to 2 winners, including fair hurdler/
prolific winning pointer Pharare (by Phardante): dam unraced: has shown nothing over
hurdles. *C. P. Morlock*

PIZARRO (IRE) 6 ch.g. Broken Hearted – Our Swan Lady (Swan's Rock) **h147**
[2002/3 F123: 20s* 20s³ 20v* 21g² 24dᶠ Apr 4]

Going to the second last in the Royal & SunAlliance Novices' Hurdle at the
Cheltenham Festival, Pizarro looked set for a second successive win at the meeting.
He had passed the post first in the Champion Bumper the year before, narrowly in
front of Rhinestone Cowboy, and controversially survived a stewards' inquiry.
Twelve months on, and he was poised behind the leader Coolnagorna, back on the
bridle after being chivvied along to close on the pacemakers at the top of the hill.
That, however, was as close as he got. When asked to step it up again, Pizarro hung
left and, though keeping on in the straight, was unable to peg back Coolnagorna or
the winner Hardy Eustace, beaten a length and a quarter and a length into third. As
things turned out, Pizarro was again the beneficiary of the stewards' deliberations,
albeit indirectly, as Coolnagorna was thrown out after causing marginal interference to the fourth Lord Sam. Although starting 2/1 favourite at Cheltenham, Pizarro
wasn't entitled to the position judged on his previous efforts over hurdles. At least
five of a strong field of nineteen—the three mentioned as well as Foreman and
Puntal—had shown a fair bit better form. Pizarro's effort at Cheltenham was his
best over hurdles. His efforts after Cheltenham were an anti-climax. He fell at the
fifth when third favourite (behind the Stayers' Hurdle runner-up Iris's Gift and
Hardy Eustace) in the three-mile Sefton Novices' Hurdle at Aintree and was part-

Tote Exacta 'Monksfield' Novices' Hurdle, Navan—
Pizarro inflicts the hidden Solerina's only defeat over hurdles as he makes a winning start

icularly disappointing when favourite for the Menolly Homes Champion Novices' Hurdle at Punchestown shortly after the end of the British season. This time his market position looked fully justified, but he was clearly in trouble a fair way out and tapped for foot after three out, eventually beaten ten and a half lengths by Nobody Told Me.

Pizarro had won two of his three races in the build-up to Cheltenham. He made a particularly promising debut in the Tote Exacta 'Monksfield' Novices' Hurdle at Navan in November when he put up a useful performance in inflicting the only defeat over hurdles on the mare Solerina, winning by two lengths, with twenty back to the third. It looks bizarre in hindsight but Pizarro started 4/1 second favourite with Solerina at 7/1, the fairly useful chaser Montayral starting favourite. Pizarro and Solerina met again at Navan a month later, with Pizarro odds on, but he failed by a long way to give his running and was later found to have mucus in his lungs. Given plenty of time to recover, Pizarro had his Cheltenham preparatory outing in a winners-of-one event at Down Royal against some motley opposition. Only three started shorter than 25/1, and they included an eleven-year-old having his first run in two and a half years, with Pizarro 9/2-on. Pizarro beat his only half-serious opponent My Name's Not Bin easily by twenty lengths (a mistake at the last the only blemish).

		Dara Monarch (b 1979)	Realm
	Broken Hearted (b 1984)		Sardara
		Smash (b 1976)	Busted
Pizarro (IRE)			Ash Lawn
(ch.g. 1997)		Swan's Rock (b 1977)	Tyrant
	Our Swan Lady (ch 1987)		Miss Cossie
		Our Day (b 1970)	Conte Grande
			Ding Dong Day

Mr Edward Wallace's "Pizarro"

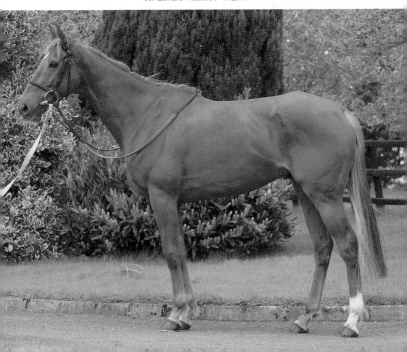

When he returns in 2003/4, Pizarro will have something to prove and it isn't easy to see where connections will go with him. He is workmanlike in appearance though not much over medium sized and he doesn't make obvious appeal as a potential chaser. There may be more to come from him over hurdles, and conditions hurdles may prove the best starting point, though there is a question mark against his resolution in the highest company. Pizarro has done most of his racing at two and a half miles but is likely to prove at least as effective over three. He has raced on good going or softer and acts on heavy. There isn't much to add to the details given about his pedigree in *Chasers & Hurdlers 2001/02*. His year-younger sister Lady Devonvale made her debut in the Goffs Land Rover Bumper at Fairyhouse, starting among the market leaders at 8/1 but finishing down the field. Pizarro remains the best jumper sired by Broken Hearted, though he had several fairly useful winners in 2002/3, including the chaser Ballybough Rasher and the hurdlers Fairwood Heart and Numbersixvalverde. *E. J. O'Grady, Ireland*

PLACE ABOVE (IRE) 7 b.g. Alphabatim (USA) – Lucky Pit (Pitpan) [2002/3 20d h–
24s⁵ Mar 6] second foal: dam lightly raced in points: won maiden Irish point in 2002:
bought 15,000 gns (privately) Doncaster May (2002) Sales: well beaten in 2 novice
hurdles, taking strong hold first occasion. *E. A. Elliott*

PLACID MAN (IRE) 9 br.g. Un Desperado (FR) – Sparkling Gale (Strong Gale) c113 p
[2002/3 c19vᵖᵘ c20v* Jan 6] big, rangy gelding: winning pointer: third in novice on hur- h–
dling debut in 2000/1: off nearly 2 years, better effort in steeplechases when winning
maiden at Fontwell by 26 lengths from Midy's Risk: bred to stay beyond 2½m: capable
of better still, but clearly difficult to train. *N. J. Henderson*

PLAIN CHANT 6 b.g. Doyoun – Sing Softly (Luthier) [2002/3 h–: 16dᵖᵘ May 13] h–
leggy gelding: no form over hurdles. *B. J. Llewellyn*

PLAISANCE (GER) 4 b.f. Monsun (GER) – Pariana (USA) (Bering) [2002/3 16sᶠ h87
18s² 17g³ 16gᵖᵘ Apr 19] sturdy filly: in frame 3 times from 5 starts up to around 1¼m on
Flat in Germany at 3 yrs for C. Von Der Recke: modest form when placed in juvenile
hurdles at Fontwell and Folkestone: possibly amiss final start: will prove best around 2m.
J. R. Jenkins

PLANET IRELAND (IRE) 11 b.g. Mandalus – Seapatrick (The Parson) [2002/3 c–
c76?, h–: c20d⁶ c20m⁵ May 16] strong gelding: poor pointer: tried blinkered (looked h–
ungenuine). *Mrs J. M. Hollands*

PLANTAGANET (FR) 5 br.g. Cadoudal (FR) – Ever Young (FR) (Royal Charter F89
(FR)) [2002/3 F16m F16g Apr 2] useful-looking gelding: second foal: half-brother to
2½m chase winner Ruyu River (by Nikos): dam won up to 2½m over jumps in France:
mid-division in bumpers at Kempton and Ascot. *Ian Williams*

PLANTAGEANT 6 ch.g. Superlative – International Star (IRE) (Astronef) [2002/3 h–
16d Apr 29] no sign of ability: tongue tied only outing in 2002/3. *N. B. Mason*

PLASTIC PADDY (IRE) 6 b.g. Beau Sher – Vultang Lady (Le Bavard (FR)) [2002/3 F105
F16v* F16s² Feb 14] IR £3,800 4-y-o: rangy gelding: has reportedly been hobdayed:
sixth foal: half-brother to winning 3m chaser Belhabour (by Lancastrian): dam unraced
sister to dam of high-class staying chaser Couldnt Be Better and half-sister to smart
chaser up to 3m Kilkilowen: won bumper at Uttoxeter on debut in December form when
3½ lengths second to Patricksnineteenth in similar event at Sandown, dictating pace: will
stay beyond 2m. *D. P. Keane*

PLATONIC-MY-EYE (IRE) 10 ch.g. Over The River (FR) – Love-In-A-Mist c– x
(Paddy's Stream) [2002/3 c105x, h101: c105x, h101] well-made gelding: fair handicap h103
hurdler/chaser: won 3 times early in 2001/2: shaped as though retaining his ability when
fourth to Wild Spice at Stratford only outing in 2002/3: stays 27f: acts on any going:
makes mistakes over fences. *Jonjo O'Neill*

PLAYAWAY (IRE) 9 b.g. Black Minstrel – Actually Stell (Deep Run) [2002/3 h68: h–
17m 17gᵖᵘ Jun 12] workmanlike gelding: very lightly raced: fair form on first of 2 starts
in bumpers: off a year, never dangerous in novice company over hurdles: sold 500 gns
Doncaster September Sales, pulled up both subsequent starts in points. *O. Brennan*

PLAYING AWAY 8 ch.m. Northern Game – Ottery News (Pony Express) [2002/3 h–: h–
25dᵖᵘ Jul 5] no sign of ability. *O. J. Carter*

PLENTY COURAGE 9 ch.g. Gildoran – Fastlass (Celtic Cone) [2002/3 c68, h101: c68
c21g² 20m⁴ 21d⁶ 17s 20d 19d 21d⁵ 22g² 20m⁵ Apr 19] small gelding: let down by **h91**
jumping in novices chases: modest handicap hurdler nowadays: should stay 3m: acts on
heavy going (bumper winner on good to firm): has worn cheekpieces: races prominently.
F. S. Storey

PLENTY INN HAND 7 b.g. Alflora (IRE) – Shean Deas (Le Moss) [2002/3 20v³ 20v **h100 ?**
20v³ 16dᵖᵘ 21g Mar 16] sturdy gelding: first foal: dam, fair pointer, out of half-sister to
smart 2½m chaser Winter Rain: failed to complete in 4 points in 2002, refusing twice:
flattered on hurdling debut, little other form: sold 2,500 gns Doncaster May Sales.
H. D. Daly

PLENTY OF ICE (IRE) 6 b.g. Camden Town – Salmoosky (IRE) (Salmon Leap **h121**
(USA)) [2002/3 F16s* 16s* 16s² 20sᶠ 16v³ Mar 9] IR 23,300 3-y-o: rather unfurnished **F101**
gelding: second foal: dam showed little in bumpers: won bumper at Naas in June: fairly
useful novice hurdler: won maiden at Navan in November: good efforts next 2 outings:
will prove best at 2½m+: raced only on soft/heavy going. *C. Roche, Ireland*

PLUMBOB (IRE) 14 br.g. Bob Back (USA) – Naujella (Malinowski (USA)) [2002/3 **c– x**
c88x, h–: c33gᵘʳ May 1] small, leggy gelding: veteran chaser, retains little ability: blink- **h–**
ered once: poor jumper of fences. *Mrs F. Browne*

PLUMIER (FR) 5 b.g. Beyssac (FR) – Plume Rose (FR) (Rose Laurel) [2002/3 F16v⁵ **h–**
26gᵖᵘ Mar 2] tall, useful-looking gelding: fifth foal: brother to fairly useful French **F–**
hurdler/chaser Belle Plume, stays 21f, and half-brother to winning chaser by Mistigri in
France and Italy: dam, 1¾m hurdle/17f chase winner at 3 yrs, out of half-sister to Grande
Course de Haies winner Le Pontet: well-held fifth of 9 in bumper at Ascot: hung right and
made mistakes when pulled up on hurdling debut. *Jonjo O'Neill*

PLUTO 8 b.g. Sharpo – No More Rosies (Warpath) [2002/3 c–, h–: 22d⁶ 21g⁴ 20f⁴ **c–**
22m⁵ 24g³ Oct 12] chunky gelding: well beaten only completed start in steeplechases: **h66**
poor maiden hurdler: stays 2¾m: acts on firm and soft going: blinkered in 2002/3: has
had tongue tied. *A. Robson*

PLUTOCRAT 7 b.g. Polar Falcon (USA) – Choire Mhor (Dominion) [2002/3 h113: **h117**
16g² 16g 22v 24m² 20g* 18g⁵ 20m² Apr 19] smallish, angular gelding: fairly useful handicap hurdler: best effort when winning quite valuable event at Musselburgh (has good
record there) in December by 7 lengths from Paperprophet: effective at 2m, barely stays
3m: acts on good to firm and good to soft going (possibly not on softer): usually patiently
ridden. *L. Lungo*

POACHERS RUN (IRE) 8 b.m. Executive Perk – Rugged Run (Deep Run) [2002/3 **c–**
c–, h83: c25gᵖᵘ 24m³ 20dᵖᵘ 21m* 21gᵘʳ 21v⁵ 19s Dec 14] angular mare: little aptitude for **h84**
chasing: poor handicap hurdler: won 4-runner event at Sedgefield in October: stays 3m:
acts on good to firm and heavy going: effective blinkered or not. *G. M. Moore*

POACHIN AGAIN (IRE) 6 b.g. Supreme Leader – Ariannrun (Deep Run) [2002/3 **h109 p**
F98p: 16s 18v² Dec 26] won bumper on debut in 2001/2: easily better effort over hurdles
when 6 lengths second to Thaix in maiden at Leopardstown, though didn't find much
having looked a danger on bridle approaching last: bred to stay well beyond 2¼m: should
improve. *A. L. T. Moore, Ireland*

POACHING (IRE) 5 b.g. Gone Fishin – Riveress (Dunphy) [2002/3 F17d F16g Apr **F–**
1] sixth foal: half-brother to a winner in Macau: dam won 1½m maiden on Flat in Ireland:
well held in 2 bumpers: sold 1,800 gns Doncaster May Sales. *Mrs A. Duffield*

POINT 6 b.g. Polish Precedent (USA) – Sixslip (USA) (Diesis) [2002/3 F96: 16d 20s² **h102**
Nov 17] lengthy gelding: fairly useful in bumpers: much better effort over hurdles (ran as
if amiss on debut, hanging right) when second to Malek in novice at Haydock: should
prove at least as effective back at 2m. *W. Jenks*

POINT OF ORIGIN (IRE) 6 b.h. Caerleon (USA) – Aptostar (USA) (Fappiano **h–**
(USA)) [2002/3 20g⁴ 24d⁵ 20gᵖᵘ 20sᵖᵘ Oct 28] signs of some ability on hurdling debut
(tongue tied) in 2000/1 but none all 4 starts since. *K. A. Morgan*

POKER PAL (IRE) 6 b.g. Hollow Hand – Lady Dee (Kambalda) [2002/3 F16g* 16d **h113**
F16s² 20s F16s² 24s³ 24s² 24s² 24v⁶ Mar 9] IR 8,500 3-y-o: sixth foal: half-brother to a **F111**
winning pointer by Grand Plaisir: dam, bumper winner/winning hurdler, from family of
very smart chaser up to 3m Bachelor's Hall and smart staying chaser Aquilifer: once-
raced pointer: won bumper at Down Royal in June: much better form when second at
Fairyhouse (to Mark The Man) and Cork (to Masteroffoxhounds): fair novice hurdler:

good second in handicaps at Punchestown and Fairyhouse: stays 3m: acts on soft going: usually tongue tied (well held when not second outing). *D. T. Hughes, Ireland*

POLAR CHAMP   10 b.g. Polar Falcon (USA) – Ceramic (USA) (Raja Baba (USA))   **c132**
[2002/3 h125: 24m³ c26g* c24m* c26m* c26m² c23g* 24s⁴ c33v² c34sᵖᵘ c36dᵘʳ 27g³   **h130**
Apr 19] sturdy gelding: useful chaser: won novices at Newton Abbot and Stratford in
June, Newton Abbot in July and Exeter in October: good second to Sir Frosty in handicap
at Cheltenham in January: useful hurdler: easily best effort in 2002/3 on reappearance:
stays 27f: acts on any going: blinkered twice in 1999/00, usually visored nowadays.
M. C. Pipe

POLAR GUNNER   6 b.g. Gunner B – Polar Belle (Arctic Lord) [2002/3 F16g⁴ 22g   **h–**
16s 19d Feb 25] 10,500 4-y-o: good-topped gelding: first foal: dam unraced half-sister to   **F69**
smart chaser up to 3m Mr Moonraker and useful staying hurdler/chaser Greenhil Tare
Away: poor form in bumper at Hexham on debut: well held in novice hurdles: tongue tied
first 2 starts. *J. M. Jefferson*

POLARIS FLAME (IRE)   10 b.m. Mandalus – Polar Crash (Crash Course) [2002/3   **c105**
c123: c25s* c25s³ c24s c25s² c26g c24m³ c25m* Apr 22] compact mare: fairly useful
hunter chaser: won at Kilbeggan early in season and Fairyhouse (beat Our Boy 11
lengths) in April: good short-head second at Punchestown in early-May: out of depth in
Foxhunter at Cheltenham: effective at 2½m to 25f: acts on soft and good to firm going:
effective with or without cheekpieces. *Mrs D. Foster, Ireland*

POLAR RED   6 ch.g. Polar Falcon (USA) – Sharp Top (Sharpo) [2002/3 h149: 16vᵖᵘ   **h141**
16g 17g 16g Apr 5] angular gelding: smart on Flat (very best form around 1¼m): also
smart over hurdles in 2001/2, won Imperial Cup at Sandown: below best in valuable
handicaps in 2002/3: probably best around 2m: acts on heavy going: visored nowadays.
M. C. Pipe

POLIANTAS (FR)   6 b.g. Rasi Brasak – Popie d'Ecorcei (FR) (Balsamo (FR))   **c151**
[2002/3 c125, h?: c20d² c21d* c21d² c21s⁶ c21g⁵ c21m* Apr 16]   **h–**
    While he hasn't yet hit the headlines with a victory in a really big race,
Poliantas did well in his first season out of novice company and may yet have
further improvement in him, so don't be surprised if a top handicap comes his way
in 2003/4. Poliantas won three of his five races in novice company after coming
from France in the summer of 2001 and landed a couple of quite valuable limited
handicaps from six outings in the latest season. On his second start he picked up the
Tote Exacta Levy Board Intermediate Chase at Wincanton in December and on the
sixth the Faucets For Mira Showers Silver Trophy Chase at Cheltenham in April.
Both successes owed something to the more dynamic approach to race planning
adopted in recent seasons by the British Horseracing Board. The Wincanton race
was put on after the First National Gold Cup at Ascot, a valuable prize aimed at the
previous season's better novices, was lost to the weather. Five of the six that lined
up had been intended runners at Ascot but Poliantas hadn't been. He had run the
weekend before Ascot was scheduled to take place, much improved in finishing a
seven-length second to Cyfor Malta in the Thomas Pink Gold Cup at Cheltenham.
The extra twelve days before Wincanton meant he could be added to the line-up. In
a closely-fought finish, Poliantas didn't look the likely winner into the straight but
gradually got on top after the last, beating the ill-fated Golden Goal by a length and
a half with the considerately-handled Fondmort a further length and a quarter away
in third.
    In the Silver Trophy, a change in the race conditions worked in Poliantas'
favour. The five most recent runnings of the race at Cheltenham's April fixture had
attracted either three or four runners, usually with an odds-on favourite, so the race
was changed from a conditions event to a limited handicap for 2003 with the result
that a competitive seven-runner field went to post. Poliantas again faced Fondmort
but, whereas they had met at level weights at Wincanton, Poliantas was set to
receive 9 lb at Cheltenham, the difference a reflection of Fondmort's progress in the
meantime. Poliantas, on the other hand, hadn't progressed quite as expected since
Wincanton. He proved no match for Edredon Bleu back there in the John Bull
Chase in January then produced a couple of rather lacklustre efforts at Cheltenham,
beaten a little over seventeen lengths when sixth to Lady Cricket in the Ladbroke
Trophy and fifth to La Landiere in the Cathcart. The form of the latter race had,

Faucets For Mira Showers Silver Trophy Chase (Limited Handicap), Cheltenham—
Poliantas heads 2002 winner Fadalko with a circuit to go in the inaugural running as a handicap

however, started to work out well and Poliantas, with a change of tactics, gave it a further boost by running his best race. He made all in the Silver Trophy, was pressed at the top of the hill but quickened after three out and soon had his race won, excellent jumps at the last two fences just extending his margin of victory. He won by ten lengths from Fondmort, who had started joint favourite with Dark'n Sharp, who was held in third when unseating two out. All of Poliantas' races in 2002/3 were at around twenty-one furlongs, but he has already won over three miles (he beat Maximise in a four-runner race on good to firm ground at Sandown on his final start as a novice) and he shapes as if he will prove at least as effective over that distance and further. Although he has won on soft going, his best efforts have been on less testing ground.

Poliantas (FR) (b.g. 1997)	Rasi Brasak (b 1986)	Kenmare (gr 1975)	Kalamoun
			Belle of Ireland
		Gay Hostess (b 1978)	Direct Flight
			So Gay
	Popie d'Ecorcei (FR) (b 1985)	Balsamo (b 1974)	Kashmir II
			Reine Helaine
		Sarais (b 1967)	Le Francais
			Sardes

Poliantas' pedigree is unlikely to ring any bells outside France, or possibly even inside it, but he is a thoroughbred from a successful jumping family. His little-known sire Rasi Brasak was a smart performer on the Flat and finished second in the Prix La Force over a mile and a quarter. Poliantas is one of three winners out of his dam Popie d'Ecorcei, the others, confusingly called Lucky des As (by Melypro) and Lucky d'As (by Sheyrann), winning at around two miles over hurdles. Popie d'Ecorcei herself was the last of ten winning jumpers out of her twice-raced dam Sarais, her three victories including the two-and-three-quarter-mile Grand Steeple-Chase de Vittel. The pick of Sarais' winners were the durable Fialster, who won

705

Mr Mark Tincknell's "Poliantas"

thirteen races, and the useful Saphiro, who finished fourth in the Gran Premio di Merano. Sarais was a half-sister to the dams of a couple of noteworthy four-year-old chasers in the early 'eighties, Ouiton who was useful and Louitonne who was even better, finishing second in the Prix Ferdinand Dufaure, which is now a Group 1 event. Poliantas is a leggy sort in appearance. He showed fair form over hurdles in the French Provinces when trained by Marc Boudot, winning three times, but he has not been raced over hurdles in Britain. *P. F. Nicholls*

POLICASTRO 5 b.g. Anabaa (USA) – Belle Arrivee (Bustino) [2002/3 20v^{pu} Mar 3] modest maiden on Flat (should stay beyond 1¾m), no form in 2003: sold out of P. Mitchell's stable 1,600 gns Newmarket February Sales: raced freely in maiden on hurdling debut. *Miss K. M. George*   **h–**

POLISH BARON (IRE) 6 b.g. Barathea (IRE) – Polish Mission (Polish Precedent (USA)) [2002/3 h108: 20m^3 May 6] close-coupled gelding: fair on Flat (barely stays 2m), successful 3 times on fibresand in 2002: fair hurdler in 2001/2: well below form in claimer at Fontwell only outing in 2002/3: stays 2½m: acts on firm and soft ground. *J. White*   **h84**

POLISH CLOUD (FR) 6 gr.g. Bering – Batchelor's Button (FR) (Kenmare (FR)) [2002/3 16s* 19d 16d^2 19m^4 20d^3 Apr 25] medium-sized gelding: fifth foal: half-brother to 4 winners on Flat, including useful 1¼m winner Speedfriend (by Unfuwain): dam 7.5f 3-y-o winner: successful 4 times from 6f to 2m on Flat in Poland: modest form over hurdles: won novice at Doncaster in December: best efforts afterwards when placed in novice handicaps at Newbury and Perth: stays 2½m: acts on soft going, below form on good to firm. *T. R. George*   **h98**

POLISHED 4 ch.g. Danzig Connection (USA) – Glitter (FR) (Reliance II) [2002/3 16g^5 Mar 29] brother to winning hurdler King Ubad (by Trempolino), stayed 19f: last of   **h76**

9 in 1¼m maiden at 3 yrs for K. Cunningham-Brown: last of 5 finishers in juvenile on hurdling debut. *R. C. Guest*

POLISH FLAME 5 b.g. Blushing Flame (USA) – Lady Emm (Emarati (USA)) **h117** [2002/3 h120p: 20d⁶ 20s 20v² 23s 24d Mar 15] leggy, useful-looking gelding: fair on Flat (stays 17f), won twice in 2002: fairly useful handicap hurdler: easily best effort in 2002/3 when second to Eastern Tribute at Ayr: should stay beyond 2½m: raced on good going or softer (acts on heavy). *Mrs M. Reveley*

POLISH LEGEND 4 b.g. Polish Precedent (USA) – Chita Rivera (Chief Singer) **h67** [2002/3 17s 17f⁴ 17m⁴ Apr 8] modest maiden on Flat (should stay 1½m): signs of only a little ability over hurdles. *R. J. Baker*

POLISH PADDY (IRE) 5 b.g. Priolo (USA) – Polish Widow (Polish Precedent **h87** (USA)) [2002/3 h80: 25g⁴ 21g* May 30] compact gelding: modest handicap hurdler: won seller at Huntingdon in May: stays 25f: acts on good to soft going, seems unsuited by soft: blinkered/visored last 3 starts: sold to join A. Hobbs £5,700 Ascot June Sales. *J. W. Mullins*

POLISH PILOT (IRE) 8 b.g. Polish Patriot (USA) – Va Toujours (Alzao (USA)) **c73** [2002/3 c70, h65: c16m² c17sᵖᵘ c16g⁴ c16mᵖᵘ c17m c17m³ c17m c16m⁴ 20d⁵ c16d⁵ **h–** c16s³ c16g⁴ c17g⁴ c17g⁵ c17m⁴ Apr 21] smallish gelding: poor hurdler/maiden chaser: best around 2m: acts on good to firm and heavy going: tried blinkered: has had tongue tied: none too consistent. *J. R. Cornwall*

POLISH SPIRIT 8 b.g. Emarati (USA) – Gentle Star (Comedy Star (USA)) [2002/3 **c91** h90: 17g² c21m* c21m³ Jul 14] rather sparely-made gelding: modest maiden hurdler: **h90** won maiden at Stratford on chasing debut in July: stays 21f: acts on good to soft and good to firm ground: blinkered last 3 starts: possibly none too genuine: sold to rejoin B. R. Millman 5,400 gns Doncaster October Sales, fifth in minor event on Flat in April. *P. J. Hobbs*

POLITBURO 8 b.g. Presidium – Kitty Come Home (Monsanto (FR)) [2002/3 c81, **c72** h65: c16m⁴ c20gᵖᵘ c20mᵖᵘ Mar 31] lengthy gelding: little form over hurdles: winning **h–** chaser: disappointing in 2002/3: raced mainly around 2m: best form on good to firm/firm ground. *J. T. Gifford*

POLITELY 5 b.m. Tragic Role (USA) – Polly Worth (Wolver Hollow) [2002/3 F16g **F–** Mar 16] half-sister to several winners, including 1993 2-y-o 5f/6f winner Culsyth Flyer (by Nomination) and 1995 2-y-o 7f seller winner Sizzling Symphony (by Sizzling Melody): dam maiden stayed 1m: tailed off in bumper on debut. *H. Morrison*

POLITICAL CRUISE 5 b.g. Royal Fountain – Political Mill (Politico (USA)) **F–** [2002/3 F16s F16v⁴ F16v Feb 8] smallish gelding: seventh foal: half-brother to modest hurdler Political Sox (by Mirror Boy): dam unraced sister to one-time fairly useful 2m chaser Political Tower: little sign of ability in bumpers: blinkered, gave trouble in preliminaries final start. *R. Nixon*

POLITICAL SOX 9 br.g. Mirror Boy – Political Mill (Politico (USA)) [2002/3 h68§: **c–** 16g⁴ c17g⁶ c22m⁴ c24d³ c17sᵖᵘ 20d 18v* 20s* 16v² 17v 16d 22d⁴ 20s⁴ 20g³ 22g⁶ **h91** 24g⁴ Apr 23] compact gelding: maiden chaser: modest handicap hurdler: won at Kelso (amateurs) and Newcastle (claimer) in December: effective at 2m to 27f: acts on good to firm and heavy going: tried blinkered/in cheekpieces: formerly ungenuine. *R. Nixon*

POLKA 8 b.g. Slip Anchor – Peace Dance (Bikala) [2002/3 h74: 17s 22gᵖᵘ Jun 22] **h–** poor form over hurdles: won 2-finisher maiden point in February. *V. G. Greenway*

POLLIGANA 7 b.g. Lugana Beach – Pollibrig (Politico (USA)) [2002/3 h93, F–: **h85** 24vᵖᵘ 17d 22g² 22g⁵ Apr 19] poor novice hurdler on balance of form: stays 2¾m: acts on good to firm going. *V. R. A. Dartnall*

POLLY LIVE WIRE 9 b.m. El Conquistador – Flash Wire (Flatbush) [2002/3 c–x: **c– x** c34gᵖᵘ May 22] leggy mare: modest pointer: has shown little in steeplechases (not fluent). *Mrs K. D. Day*

POLY AMANSHAA (IRE) 11 b. or br.g. Nashamaa – Mombones (Lord Gayle **c108 §** (USA)) [2002/3 c–, h89: c16g* c21g⁴ c19g² c20gᵖᵘ Apr 12] workmanlike gelding: win- **h–** ning hurdler: fair handicap chaser: won at Doncaster in December: stays 21f: acts on firm and soft going: unreliable. *M. C. Banks*

POLYDAMAS 11 b.g. Last Tycoon – Graecia Magna (USA) (Private Account (USA)) **c–** [2002/3 c–, h–: 24gᵖᵘ May 8] big, good-bodied gelding: winning hurdler/chaser: mostly **h–** disappointing since 1999/00: has worn blinkers: tried tongue tied. *Dr P. Pritchard*

POLYPHONY (USA) 9 b.g. Cox's Ridge (USA) – Populi (USA) (Star Envoy (USA)) **c–**
[2002/3 c–, h–: 22v² 28g⁶ Mar 16] lengthy gelding: poor maiden hurdler/chaser: stays **h67**
2¾m: raced on good going or softer (acts on heavy): visored once. *D. C. O'Brien*

PONTIUS 6 b.g. Terimon – Coole Pilate (Celtic Cone) [2002/3 h87: 20d⁵ 23d³ c24dᶠ **c84 x**
c25dᶠ c23g³ c21dᵇᵈ c20sᵖᵘ c22d³ 27g* Apr 25] tall, leggy gelding: modest novice chaser: **h104**
fair hurdler: won handicap at Perth in April: best at 3m+: acts on good to soft going: poor
jumper of fences. *N. A. Twiston-Davies*

PONTYPOOL 9 gr.g. Absalom – Girl's Brigade (Brigadier Gerard) [2002/3 20g **h–**
20dᵖᵘ 17s Dec 18] big, plain gelding: little sign of ability. *R. E. Peacock*

POPPET 7 gr.m. Terimon – Combe Hill (Crozier) [2002/3 19s 17g* Mar 17] eighth **h93**
foal: half-sister to winning pointer by Stanford: dam winning hurdler/chaser, barely
stayed 3m: much better effort over hurdles when winning mares maiden at Hereford, left
clear when length leader Tisho fell last: should stay at least 2½m. *N. J. Henderson*

POPPY'S PROGRESS 6 ch.m. Carlton (GER) – Countess Blakeney (Baron Blak- **F–**
eney) [2002/3 F16d F18s⁶ Feb 3] first foal: dam winning chaser, probably stayed 2¾m:
showed little in 2 bumpers. *T. D. McCarthy*

POPSI'S CLOGGS 11 ch.g. Joli Wasfi (USA) – Popsi's Poppet (Hill Clown (USA)) **c–**
[2002/3 c90, h–: c25mᵖᵘ Nov 5] big, leggy gelding: modest handicap chaser: reportedly **h–**
lame only outing in 2002/3: stays 25f: raced only on good/good to firm going. *R. Curtis*

PORAK (IRE) 6 ch.g. Perugino (USA) – Gayla Orchestra (Lord Gayle (USA)) **h116**
[2002/3 h97: 16d* 16s² 16d Jan 18] close-coupled gelding: fairly useful hurdler: fit from
Flat (successful in September), won novice at Ascot in November: raced at 2m: acts on
soft going (winner on good to firm on Flat). *G. L. Moore*

PORLOCK CASTLE 10 b.g. Thowra (FR) – Miss Melmore (Nishapour (FR)) **c–**
[2002/3 c18fᵖᵘ c19dᵖᵘ Oct 23] good-topped gelding: won on chasing debut in 1998/9: **h–**
pulled up all 4 starts since. *P. C. Ritchens*

PORLOCK HILL 9 b.g. Petoski – Gay Ticket (New Member) [2002/3 c56, h–: c24gᵘʳ **c– x**
c25gᵖᵘ Apr 5] tall, angular gelding: poor pointer, successful in February and April: very **h–**
little form over hurdles/in steeplechases (let down by jumping). *J. Scott*

PORNIC (FR) 9 b.g. Shining Steel – Marie de Geneve (FR) (Nishapour (FR)) [2002/3 **c– §**
c79§, h–§: 17d* 16d⁴ 17s³ 16d³ 16c² Jan 15] workmanlike gelding: winning chaser: **h96 §**
modest handicap hurdler: won conditional jockeys event at Carlisle in November: best
around 2m: acts on good to firm and heavy going: tried visored: often finds little and not
one to trust. *A. Crook*

PORT MORESBY (IRE) 5 b.g. Tagula (IRE) – Santana Lady (IRE) (Blakeney) **h85 +**
[2002/3 h–: 16sᵖᵘ 16d⁵ Dec 26] sturdy gelding: useful on Flat (stays easy 1½m): first form
over hurdles when fifth to King Georges in novice handicap at Wincanton, travelling best
into straight but folding tamely after mistake 2 out: will prove best at sharp 2m: has had
tongue tied. *N. A. Callaghan*

PORTOBELLO KING (IRE) 8 br.g. King's Ride – Raw Courage (IRE) (The Par- **h–**
son) [2002/3 19dᵖᵘ Jan 27] modest form in bumpers in 1999/00: unseated in point in
2001: no show in novice hurdle on return. *D. J. Wintle*

PORT VALENSKA (IRE) 10 b.g. Roi Danzig (USA) – Silvera (Ribero) [2002/3 c–, **c–**
h–: c19f Mar 27] angular gelding: of little account: tried blinkered/visored/tongue tied. **h–**
Matthew Vick

POSH PEARL 8 b.m. Rakaposhi King – Rim of Pearl (Rymer) [2002/3 19vᶠ 20g³ **h91 +**
Mar 25] leggy mare: useful in bumpers in 2000/1: off nearly 2 years, modest form when
third in mares novice at Ascot on completed start over hurdles: may prove best short of
2½m. *Miss Venetia Williams*

POSH STICK 6 b.m. Rakaposhi King – Carat Stick (Gold Rod) [2002/3 F–: F16g **h65**
17dᵖᵘ 27vᵖᵘ 21v 16d² 17s⁵ 24g Apr 23] sturdy mare: well held in bumpers: poor form **F–**
over hurdles: best effort at 2m: acts on good to soft going. *J. B. Walton*

POSITIVE PROFILE (IRE) 5 b.g. Definite Article – Leyete Gulf (IRE) (Slip **h83**
Anchor) [2002/3 16s³ 19g Dec 13] rather sparely-made gelding: fairly useful stayer on
Flat, successful in February: only poor form in 2 novice hurdles: will stay beyond 19f.
P. C. Haslam

POSSIBLE PARDON (NZ) 9 b.g. Iades (FR) – Wonderful Excuse (NZ) (Alibhai **c119 x**
(NZ)) [2002/3 c108: c26d² c27s* c29s⁵ c24v* c30s Mar 4] medium-sized gelding:
fairly useful handicap chaser: won at Taunton (jumped left) in November and Chepstow
(improved form when making virtually all to beat Tom's Prize 5 lengths) in January:

should stay beyond 27f: raced on going softer than good (acts on heavy): blinkered: takes plenty of driving: often less than fluent. *P. J. Hobbs*

POTENTATE (USA)   12 b. or br.g. Capote (USA) – Gay Fantastic (Ela-Mana-Mou) [2002/3 c–§, h119§: 16g* 16f⁴ May 11] tall gelding: one-time very smart hurdler/useful chaser: still capable of fair form over hurdles, won claimer at Plumpton very early in season: effective at 2m to 3m: acts on heavy and good to firm going: not one to rely on. *M. C. Pipe*   **c– §**   **h106 §**

POTOFFAIRIES (IRE)   8 ch.g. Montelimar (USA) – Ladycastle (Pitpan) [2002/3 h106: 19g 20gᵖᵘ 20d 24s³ c24v³ c24v Jan 25] fair handicap hurdler: not fluent when remote third of 5 finishers to The Villager in novice at Bangor on chasing debut: out of depth next time: should stay beyond 3m: acts on heavy going: effective blinkered or not. *Mrs S. A. Bramall, Ireland*   **c92**   **h107**

POT RED   13 ch.g. Noalto – Frieda's Joy (Proverb) [2002/3 c25m c21m c21g⁵ c21mᵖᵘ Sep 13] well-made gelding: of little account: poor jumper. *R. Johnson*   **c– x**

POUSSIN BLEU   6 b.m. Henbit (USA) – Blue Point (IRE) (On Your Mark) [2002/3 F17dˢᵘ Oct 12] medium-sized mare: second foal: dam, no worthwhile form, out of half-sister to Champion Hurdle winner Kribensis: slipped up after 5f in mares bumper on debut. *J. Mackie*   **F–**

POWDER CREEK (IRE)   6 b.g. Little Bighorn – Our Dorcet (Condorcet (FR)) [2002/3 F92: F16g* May 22] well-made gelding: easily best effort in bumpers when winning at Worcester in May, ridden more prominently and running on well to beat Mylo by 2½ lengths. *Mrs M. Reveley*   **F104**

POWER AND DEMAND   6 b.g. Formidable (USA) – Mazurkanova (Song) [2002/3 h–: 17m 17mᵖᵘ 17dᵖᵘ 17f⁶ 19f⁶ Oct 17] good-topped gelding: little worthwhile form over hurdles: has worn cheekpieces: has been reluctant to race: sold £1,300 Ascot December Sales, little show in points subsequently. *Miss M. Bragg*   **h–**

POWER HIT (USA)   7 b.g. Leo Castelli (USA) – Rajana (USA) (Rajab (USA)) [2002/3 24sᵖᵘ 17dᵖᵘ 24f Apr 3] compact gelding: modest maiden hurdler at best: off 2½ years, showed nothing in 2002/3: usually blinkered/visored. *K. Bishop*   **h–**

POWERNGLORY (IRE)   12 ch.g. Accordion – Fairfield Springs (Miami Springs) [2002/3 c84: 25dᵖᵘ Jul 5] winning pointer but little form otherwise: tried visored: tongue tied. *J. Neville*   **c–**   **h–**

POWER UNIT   8 ch.g. Risk Me (FR) – Hazel Bee (Starch Reduced) [2002/3 h90, F88: 17f³ 16g⁵ c19d⁴ c16v⁴ c20s⁴ c21m Apr 17] workmanlike gelding: modest form over hurdles: off 8 months, won novice handicap at Taunton on steeplechasing debut in January: let down by jumping last 2 starts: may prove best up to 2½m: probably acts on any going: has worn cheekpieces. *Mrs D. A. Hamer*   **c100**   **h90**

POYNDER PARK (IRE)   12 b.g. Mandalus – So Deep (Deep Run) [2002/3 c24g² Apr 21] fair pointer, won in April: wearing cheekpieces, similar form when second in 4-runner maiden hunter at Carlisle. *Mrs J. Williamson*   **c87**

PRAH SANDS   10 b.g. Henbit (USA) – Minor Furlong (Native Bazaar) [2002/3 c81: c19g c21f² c20m⁵ c26gᵖᵘ Jun 29] workmanlike gelding: poor maiden chaser: stays 21f: unraced on heavy going, acts on any other: blinkered/visored. *C. Tizzard*   **c81**

PRAIRIE MINSTREL (USA)   9 b.g. Regal Intention (CAN) – Prairie Sky (USA) (Gone West (USA)) [2002/3 c–, h–: c20d c19g c20m² c20g* c20gᵖᵘ c19m⁶ c20g Apr 26] sturdy, close-coupled gelding: modest handicap chaser: won at Leicester in December: badly out of sorts subsequently: stays 3m: acts on any going. *R. Dickin*   **c98**   **h–**

PRAIRIE RUN (IRE)   7 ch.m. Montelimar (USA) – Lady Leona (Leander) [2002/3 h80, F75: 21g² 16d* 16g² Jun 15] leggy mare: modest hurdler: didn't need to be at best to win maiden at Hexham in June: stays 21f: raced only on good going or softer. *L. Lungo*   **h86**

PRAIRIE STAR   8 br.g. Landyap (USA) – Stars And Stripes (Royalty) [2002/3 17s 19d³ 22d 22g Mar 18] sixth foal: half-brother to winning pointer by Newski: dam, fairly useful hurdler up to 2½m, half-sister to smart hurdler up to 3m Mount Harvard: apparently best effort over hurdles when third in novice at Exeter: should stay beyond 19f (beaten before stamina became an issue last 2 outings). *R. H. Buckler*   **h84 ?**

PRANCING BLADE   10 b.g. Broadsword (USA) – Sparkling Cinders (Netherkelly) [2002/3 c–, h–: c20g² c24g⁴ c23s³ c24m⁴ c23g² c24g* c24m⁴ c24dᶠ c24dᵖᵘ c25dᵖᵘ c24s c24s c24gᵖᵘ Feb 27] rather leggy gelding: fairly useful chaser: back to best when winning handicap at Perth in September: out of sorts subsequently: stays 3m: acts on firm and good to soft going. *N. A. Twiston-Davies*   **c119**   **h–**

PRATE BOX (IRE) 13 b.g. Ela-Mana-Mou – Prattle On (Ballymore) [2002/3 c–, h–: c21g^{pu} May 1] angular gelding: veteran hurdler/chaser, little form since 1997/8: won point in March: prone to mistakes. *Mrs P. Chamings*   c– h–

PRAYERFUL 4 b.f. Syrtos – Pure Formality (Forzando) [2002/3 16d 21d^{ur} 19d Mar 10] half-sister to fair chaser Ritual (by Selkirk), stays 2½m: poor maiden on Flat: no show both completed starts over hurdles. *B. N. Doran*   h–

PRECIOUS BANE (IRE) 5 b.g. Bigstone (IRE) – Heavenward (USA) (Conquistador Cielo (USA)) [2002/3 h84?, F78?: 17g 20m^6 F16d^5 22f^5 Oct 9] leggy, sparely-made gelding: modest form in 2 bumpers: little worthwhile form over hurdles: should stay beyond 2m. *B. P. J. Baugh*   h– F78

PRECIOUS MOMENTS 7 b.m. Polar Falcon (USA) – Brassy Nell (Dunbeath (USA)) [2002/3 F79: F17m Jun 1] modest in bumpers. *J. A. Moore*   F74

PRECIOUS MUSIC (IRE) 10 br.g. Orchestra – Precious Petra (Bing II) [2002/3 c111, h–: c24s* c24s* c24v^F c24v c24d c28s^{pu} Feb 2] fair handicap chaser: won at Naas in November and Navan (made all) in December: below best subsequently: stays 3m: acts on heavy going. *Gerard Farrell, Ireland*   c110 h–

PREFERRED (IRE) 5 b.g. Distant Relative – Fruhlingserwachen (USA) (Irish River (FR)) [2002/3 17m^3 16m^3 16m^5 19g 18m^3 16g^6 Aug 26] fair on Flat (stays 1¼m) for R. Hannon: poor novice hurdler: likely to prove much better around 2m: acts on good to firm going: blinkered fourth and final starts. *O. Sherwood*   h80

PRELOTTE (IRE) 4 b.g. Nicolotte – Prepare (IRE) (Millfontaine) [2002/3 F14d Nov 26] sturdy gelding: fourth foal: half-brother to 5f/6f winner Make Ready (by Beveled): dam, 7f winner, half-sister to high-class sprinter Anita's Prince: tailed off in bumper on debut. *J. Neville*   F–

PRELUDE TO FAME (USA) 10 b.g. Affirmed (USA) – Dance Call (USA) (Nijinsky (CAN)) [2002/3 h95: 16m Nov 4] smallish gelding: modest hurdler: reportedly lame only start in 2002/3: stays 3m: acts on soft and good to firm going: tried blinkered/visored. *Mrs A. C. Tate*   h–

PREMIER AMBITIONS 5 b.g. Bin Ajwaad (IRE) – Good Thinking (USA) (Raja Baba (USA)) [2002/3 17d^{ur} 16d 20v 17s 16d^6 16g^4 17g 17g^5 Mar 25] leggy, sparely-made gelding: half-brother to one-time useful hurdler Thinking Twice (by Kris), stays 21f: modest on all-weather, poor on turf on Flat (stays 1m), sold out of W. Haggas' stable 4,700 gns Newmarket July Sales: best effort over hurdles when fourth in selling handicap at Catterick in January: likely to prove best around 2m. *M. E. Sowersby*   h63

PREMIER BOY (IRE) 5 b.g. Blues Traveller (IRE) – Little Min (Nebbiolo) [2002/3 h–: 16g 17d^6 Jun 8] sturdy gelding: of little account over hurdles: tried blinkered/tongue tied. *B. S. Rothwell*   h–

PREMIER DRIVE (IRE) 10 ch.g. Black Minstrel – Ballyanihan (Le Moss) [2002/3 c111, h104: c20d^F c16s^5 c20v^3 c20v^3 c20v^F c20d Feb 26] workmanlike gelding: fair chaser: largely let down by jumping in handicaps in 2002/3: effective at 2m and should stay 3m: raced on good going or softer (acts on heavy): has had tongue tied: usually front runner. *G. M. Moore*   c111 h–

PREMIERE FOULEE (FR) 8 ch.m. Sillery (USA) – Dee (Caerleon (USA)) [2002/3 h69: 20m 18m^2 25m^{pu} 24f^2 19s^{pu} 18d^4 24v Dec 28] light-framed mare: poor maiden hurdler: barely stays 3m: acts on firm and soft going: tried blinkered: has finished weakly. *F. Jordan*   h69

PREMIER ESTATE (IRE) 6 b.g. Satco (FR) – Kettleby (IRE) (Tale Quale) [2002/3 F80: 21g 21v^5 21s^3 20s^3 20s^4 17g^{ur} Mar 16] tall gelding: poor novice hurdler: likely to be suited by 3m+: acts on soft going: failed to go through with effort (attempted to run out) fourth start: temperament under suspicion. *R. Rowe*   h79

PREMIER GENERATION (IRE) 10 b.g. Cadeaux Genereux – Bristle (Thatch (USA)) [2002/3 c104?, h81: c16g^4 c20m^{pu} c21m^4 Jul 28] leggy gelding: winning hurdler, poor form in 2001/2: fair chaser: raced mainly around 2m: acts on good to firm and heavy going: has won with/without blinkers: has had tongue tied. *Dr P. Pritchard*   c100 h–

PRESENT BLEU (FR) 8 b.g. Epervier Bleu – Lointaine (USA) (Lyphard's Wish (FR)) [2002/3 c123, h131: c17g^3 19g^2 c21g* c19d* c21d^2 c21g* 20g^4 c25g* 17d^5 20g Feb 16] leggy gelding: trained by M. Pipe in 2001/2: useful hurdler, probably best effort in 2002/3 when fourth in Corsa Siepi di Merano: in excellent form over fences in summer, won at Questembert and Clairefontaine in July, Grand Steeple-Chase de Deauville (handicap) at latter in August (final start for J. P. J. Dubois) and Gran Premio di Merano   c125 + h?

(in close finish from Repere and Ty Benjam) in September: stays 25f: acts on firm and soft going, possibly not on heavy: tried blinkered/visored. *E. de la Motte, Italy*

PRESENTING HENRY (IRE) 5 b.g. Presenting – Sleeven Lady (Crash Course) **h–**
[2002/3 F17d⁴ 21s Jan 27] lengthy gelding: fourth foal: half-brother to 2½m hurdle win- **F88**
ner Shade Me Shauny and 2½m bumper winner Henno's Quest (both by Phardante): dam
maiden Irish pointer: shaped like a stayer when fourth to Longterm in bumper at Exeter
on debut: well held in novice on hurdling debut. *P. J. Hobbs*

PRESENTING MIST (IRE) 5 ch.m. Presenting – Blackwater Mist (IRE) (King's **F–**
Ride) [2002/3 F16s F16d⁶ F16f Mar 29] €18,000 4-y-o: fifth foal: half-sister to fairly
useful hurdler around 2m Multeen River (by Supreme Leader) and 2½m hurdle winner
Maria Pia (by Bob's Return): dam unraced: well held in bumpers. *C. F. Swan, Ireland*

PRESSIONAGE 4 b.f. Puissance – My Girl (Mon Tresor) [2002/3 7fᵖᵘ Oct 1] poor **h–**
maiden on Flat (probably stays 7f): tongue tied, looked none too keen and pulled up early
on hurdling debut: sold £400 Ascot December Sales. *H. S. Howe*

PRESS TO STING 14 b.g. Scorpio (FR) – Olive Press (Ragapan) [2002/3 c87, h–: **c81**
c24mᵖᵘ c20fᶠ c25m⁴ c25g⁶ Oct 19] workmanlike gelding: poor chaser: stays 25f: acts on **h–**
firm going: has broken blood vessels. *A. H. Mactaggart*

PRESTIGE LORD (IRE) 11 b.g. Lord Americo – Fiona's Wish (Wishing Star) **c–**
[2002/3 c25g May 1] fair pointer: none too fluent when well held on hunter chase debut.
Miss L. J. C. Sweeting

PRESTO 6 b.g. Namaqualand (USA) – Polish Dancer (USA) (Malinowski (USA)) **h– §**
[2002/3 h85§: 22fᵖᵘ 16d⁴ 16g Mar 25] leggy gelding: maiden hurdler: showed little in
handicaps in 2002/3: raced mainly around 2m: acts on soft and good to firm going:
blinkered: tongue tied last 2 outings: not one to trust. *Mrs Merrita Jones*

PRESUMING ED (IRE) 10 b.g. Nordico (USA) – Top Knot (High Top) [2002/3 c94: **c–**
c25g⁶ May 1] fairly useful pointer: twice-raced in hunters, jumped poorly at Cheltenham
in May: stays 25f. *James R. Tuck*

PRICELESS SAM 12 b.m. Silly Prices – Samonia (Rolfe (USA)) [2002/3 c25d² Mar **c94**
5] lightly raced in points, winning twice: second to Ridgeway in novice hunter chase at
Catterick in March: stays 25f. *Mrs S. M. Barker*

PRIDE OF PENNKER (IRE) 10 b.m. Glacial Storm (USA) – Quitrentina (Green **c60**
Shoon) [2002/3 c24sᵖᵘ c18m³ c21m⁴ c19m⁵ c22d⁴ c24vᵖᵘ Dec 28] lengthy mare: winning **h–**
hurdler: poor maiden chaser: stays 2¾m: acts on firm and soft going. *G. A. Ham*

PRIDE OF THE PARK (FR) 4 b.g. Marju (IRE) – Taj Victory (Final Straw) [2002/3 **h–**
16m⁶ Sep 29] modest on Flat (stays 11f) for P. Haslam: blinkered, soundly beaten in
juvenile on hurdling debut. *Mrs N. Macauley*

PRIDEWOOD FUGGLE 13 b.g. Little Wolf – Quick Reply (Tarqogan) [2002/3 c–, **c–**
h80: 20gᶠ 19d⁶ 22g⁵ 19m⁴ 20s² 17g 22mᵖᵘ 19d c19dᶠ c20gᵖᵘ Feb 25] compact gelding: **h80**
poor handicap hurdler: won seller at Bangor in May: no form over fences (reportedly
lame final outing): probably stays 2¾m: acts on good to firm and heavy going. *R. J. Price*

PRIESTFIELD BOY (IRE) 6 b.g. Un Desperado (FR) – Sandbank (IRE) (Kam- **h–**
balda) [2002/3 Fᶠ 20mᶠ 16m⁵ 16g 20dᵖᵘ Nov 24] good-topped gelding: little sign of
ability: tried blinkered/tongue tied. *C. P. Morlock*

PRIESTS BRIDGE (IRE) 7 ch.m. Mr Ditton – Paddys Gale (Strong Gale) [2002/3 **h120**
F17d* F17d² 20s² 20v* 24d³ 20s 24d* 23d² 24gᵇᵈ Apr 3] sparely-made mare: fourth foal: **F106**
half-sister to winning pointer by Good Thyne: dam unraced: successful in 3 Irish points
in 2002: useful form in bumpers, making all in mares race at Bangor in October: fairly
useful novice hurdler: won at Uttoxeter in November and Kempton (soon long way clear
when beating El Hombre Del Rio 14 lengths) in February: second to impressive Iris's Gift
in Grade 2 at Haydock in March: likely to stay beyond 3m: raced on good going or softer
(acts on heavy): front runner. *N. A. Twiston-Davies*

PRIMAROSA 4 ch.f. Atraf – Prim Lass (Reprimand) [2002/3 17g Sep 28] modest on **h–**
Flat (seems to stay 1½m): none too fluent and well held in juvenile seller on hurdling
debut: sold £600 Ascot November Sales. *John A. Harris*

PRIMATICCIO (IRE) 8 b.g. Priolo (USA) – Martinova (Martinmas) [2002/3 c96, **c111 +**
h–: c21g* c21f* c21m* c28m* Jun 1] progressed into useful hunter chaser in 2002, winn- **h–**
ing at Cheltenham (competitive maiden), Wincanton (novice, final outing for V. Hughes)
and Folkestone in May, and Stratford (Intrum Justitia Cup Champion Hunters' Chase,
kept on bravely to beat Jabiru 3 lengths) in June: effective around 2½m and stays 3½m:

acts on firm going: visored last 2 starts: races prominently: often idles: missed rest of season reportedly due to leg injury. *D. L. Williams*

PRIME ATTRACTION   6 gr.m. Primitive Rising (USA) – My Friend Melody (Sizzling Melody) [2002/3 F89: F16g* 16g² 20m^ur Oct 24] leggy mare: fair in bumpers: won at Hexham in June: modest form on Flat: second in mares novice at Hexham on completed start over hurdles. *W. M. Brisbourne*   **h81**
F93

PRIME MINISTER   9 ch.g. Be My Chief (USA) – Classic Design (Busted) [2002/3 h63: 17g³ 16g³ 16s^pu 16m 17m⁴ Apr 5] angular gelding: poor maiden hurdler: raced mainly around 2m: acts on soft and good to firm going: races up with pace: has pulled hard/looked less than keen. *G. E. Jones*   **h70**

PRIMERO (IRE)   9 b.g. Lycius (USA) – Pipitina (Bustino) [2002/3 c85x, h–: c26m^ur c21g⁵ c23m c26m^F Aug 5] modest chaser: no form in handicaps in 2002/3, though runner-up in point in April: stays 3¼m: acts on good to firm ground: tried in blinkers: tongue tied: sketchy jumper: has looked less than keen. *P. F. Nicholls*   **c– x**
h–

PRIMITIVE SATIN   8 ch.g. Primitive Rising (USA) – Satinanda (Leander) [2002/3 c89: c25d² c26g⁵ May 22] fair hunter chaser: stays 25f: acts on good to soft going: wears blinkers. *R. Tate*   **c89**

PRIMITIVE SON   6 b.g. Primitive Rising (USA) – Bramcote Centenary (Alleging (USA)) [2002/3 F17g⁵ 23s⁶ 21g 20g⁶ 20m⁴ Apr 21] medium-sized gelding: third foal: dam unraced half-sister to fairly useful hurdler up to 2½m Pondering: signs of ability in bumper/over hurdles. *N. Wilson*   **h80 ?**
F–

PRIMITIVE WAY   11 b.g. Primitive Rising (USA) – Potterway (Velvet Prince) [2002/3 c94: c25g² c24m⁴ c25m⁴ c27m Apr 11] sturdy gelding: modest chaser: left Miss S. Forster after third start, below form in points and hunter subsequently: stays 25f: acts on soft and good to firm going, possibly not on heavy: wears blinkers/cheekpieces. *C. Storey*   **c94**

PRINCE ALBERT   5 ch.g. Rock City – Russell Creek (Sandy Creek) [2002/3 h67: 16g² Oct 9] modest maiden on Flat (stays 1¼m): much better effort over hurdles when second to Harmonic in novice at Fakenham in October: may prove best around 2m. *J. R. Jenkins*   **h86**

PRINCE AMONG MEN   6 b.g. Robellino (USA) – Forelino (USA) (Trempolino (USA)) [2002/3 h105: 17g* 16d² 16s³ 16d⁴ 17m* Apr 21] angular gelding: won sellers at Hereford in November and Market Rasen in April: will stay 2½m: acts on any going: effective visored or not: has found little. *N. G. Richards*   **h101**

PRINCE ATRAF   4 b.g. Atraf – Forest Fantasy (Rambo Dancer (CAN)) [2002/3 16d Dec 5] lengthy gelding: fair on Flat (likely to prove best at 7f/1m): soundly beaten in juvenile on hurdling debut, jumping poorly: sold 1,000 gns Doncaster March Sales. *B. R. Millman*   **h–**

PRINCE DE BERRY   12 ch.g. Ballacashtal (CAN) – Hoonah (FR) (Luthier) [2002/3 c–, h?: 22g May 1] lengthy gelding: bad hurdler/chaser, successful only in Jersey. *G. A. Ham*   **c–**
h–

PRINCE DE GALLES   10 b.g. Prince Des Coeurs (USA) – Royal Brush (King of Spain) [2002/3 c–, h68: 24m⁵ 24g 24s* 24m^pu 24g⁴ 25s⁴ 24f^pu Apr 3] angular gelding: fell early on chasing debut: poor handicap hurdler: back to form when winning at Uttoxeter in June: best at 3m+: acts on any going: blinkered at Uttoxeter and last 3 starts. *P. Bowen*   **c–**
h84

PRINCE DIMITRI   4 ch.g. Desert King (IRE) – Pinta (IRE) (Ahonoora) [2002/3 16d* 16s^F 16g 16d² 16g⁴ Apr 19] leggy gelding: modest on Flat (stays 9f), left D. Nicholls in August: fair juvenile hurdler: easily won at Warwick in December: running well when falling 2 out there next time: will prove best at 2m with emphasis on speed: raced on good going or softer over hurdles, won on good to firm on Flat: visored last 2 starts. *M. C. Pipe*   **h108 +**

PRINCE DORCET (IRE)   7 b.g. Asir – Lady Dorcet (Condorcet (FR)) [2002/3 F17g³ F16d 16g 17g Apr 21] ninth foal: half-brother to 3 winners, including very smart 2m chaser Lord Dorcet (by Remainder Man) and useful chaser up to 2¾m Go Universal (by Teofane): dam won over 9f in Ireland: third in bumper at Carlisle on debut: showed little after, including over hurdles. *J. I. A. Charlton*   **h–**
F71

PRINCE DUNDEE (FR)   8 ch.g. Ecossais (FR) – Princesse Normande (FR) (Belgio (FR)) [2002/3 c88x, h–: 17g^pu 20g 20d^pu 16m 22m 20m⁴ Jul 17] angular gelding: winning hurdler/maiden chaser: has deteriorated considerably: usually blinkered/visored: has had tongue tied: makes mistakes over fences: ungenerous. *J. Neville*   **c–**
h67 §

PRINCE HIGHLIGHT (IRE)   8 b.g. Lord Americo – Madamme Highlights (Andretti) [2002/3 h101: 18d c20d² c20mᵖᵘ c21v⁴ c16gᶠ c16m³ c21d³ c21mᶠ Apr 17] sturdy gelding: fair handicap hurdler, well held on reappearance: modest novice chaser: effective at 2m to 2¾m: acts on heavy and good to firm going: blinkered final start: has found little: sold 10,500 gns Doncaster May Sales. *Ferdy Murphy*   **c95**
h–

PRINCE MINATA (IRE)   8 b.g. Machiavellian (USA) – Aminata (Glenstal (USA)) [2002/3 h70: 16g Sep 14] modest on Flat (barely stays 1¼m), successful in June and February: form over hurdles only when third in novice in 2001/2: will prove best at sharp 2m: tried blinkered/tongue tied. *P. W. Hiatt*   **h–**

PRINCE NICHOLAS   8 ch.g. Midyan (USA) – Its My Turn (Palm Track) [2002/3 h90: 26d* 22d³ 24gᵖᵘ Sep 25] leggy gelding: modest hurdler: won novice at Cartmel in June: stays 3¼m: acts on soft going: has twice collapsed after race and needed oxygen: none too fluent. *K. W. Hogg, Isle of Man*   **h90**

PRINCE OF ARAGON   7 b.g. Aragon – Queens Welcome (Northfields (USA)) [2002/3 h75: 16m May 11] leggy gelding: poor maiden hurdler: stays easy 2½m: acts on good to firm going: joined Miss S. Smith. *D. M. Grissell*   **h71**

PRINCE OF PLEASURE (IRE)   9 b.g. Spanish Place (USA) – Oronocco Gift (Camden Town) [2002/3 c20d* c21s⁵ 20m² c22d⁵ c24gᶠ Oct 13] winning pointer: fair form on second of 2 starts over hurdles: fair handicap chaser: won at Limerick in May: effective at 2m to 2¾m: acts on good to firm and heavy ground. *D. Broad, Ireland*   **c110**
h105

PRINCE OF SLANE   4 b.g. Prince Daniel (USA) – Singing Slane (Cree Song) [2002/3 F17g² Apr 26] fourth foal: half-brother to fairly useful hurdler Hunting Slane (by Move Off), stays 25f: dam unraced half-sister to useful staying hurdler Tewit Castle: second to Material World in bumper at Market Rasen on debut, staying on from off pace. *C. Grant*   **F98**

PRINCE OMID (USA)   6 b.g. Shuailaan (USA) – Matilda The Hun (USA) (Young Bob (USA)) [2002/3 16m May 9] no longer of much account on Flat: well beaten in novice on hurdling debut. *Mrs Merrita Jones*   **h–**

PRINCE ON THE TER   8 b.g. Terimon – Princess Constanza (Relkino) [2002/3 c–, h87d, F70: 16m c21m⁵ c21g⁶ 26mᵖᵘ Aug 12] smallish gelding: little form over hurdles or in steeplechases: won point in April: has had tongue tied. *C. L. Popham*   **c–**
h–

PRINCE SANDROVITCH (IRE)   9 b.g. Camden Town – Devon Royale (Le Prince) [2002/3 c21gᵖᵘ May 1] useful-looking gelding: winning hurdler: fair pointer: never going well on hunter chase debut in May: stays 21f: acts on soft going: none too fluent a jumper over hurdles. *Mrs Jane Galpin*   **c–**
h–

PRINCE SHAAMAAL   5 b.g. Shaamit (IRE) – Princess Alaska (Northern State (USA)) [2002/3 19gᵘ 19d 17s⁵ Feb 13] won at 2 yrs, disappointing on Flat (should stay 1¼m) in 2001: poor form over hurdles: will prove best around 2m. *K. Bell*   **h72 +**

PRINCE SKYBURD   12 b.g. Domynsky – Burntwood Lady (Royal Buck) [2002/3 c76, h–: c17mᵖᵘ Jul 7] angular gelding: modest chaser at best: effective at 2m to 3m: acted on firm and soft going: best tongue tied: dead. *Mrs P. M. A. Avison*   **c–**
h–

PRINCE SLAYER   7 b.g. Batshoof – Top Sovereign (High Top) [2002/3 h–: 16s⁶ 16s³ Feb 24] modest maiden hurdler: likely to prove best at 2m: acts on heavy going: has worn cheekpieces. *T. P. McGovern*   **h86**

PRINCE SORINIERES (FR)   8 br.g. Valanjou (FR) – Somewhat Better (Rheingold) [2002/3 c–, h–: c25d⁵ c24vᵖᵘ c24f* Apr 3] workmanlike gelding: fairly useful chaser: dropped in weights, won weakly-contested handicap at Taunton by head from Un Jour A Vassy: stays 25f: acts on soft and firm going: tried blinkered/visored. *M. C. Pipe*   **c116**
h–

PRINCESS CLAUDIA (IRE)   5 b.m. Kahyasi – Shamarra (FR) (Zayyani) [2002/3 16m² 19m⁴ 19g⁴ Apr 19] small, leggy mare: poor form over hurdles: will stay beyond 19f. *M. F. Harris*   **h83**

PRINCESSE GREC (FR)   5 b.m. Grand Tresor (FR) – Perimele (FR) (Mon Fils) [2002/3 h–: 20d⁴ 16s² 20m⁵ 24g⁶ 16s² 16m c16d c21sᵖᵘ c18sᵖᵘ c32gᵘʳ c19m⁵ c16g⁶ Apr 21] plain mare: poor maiden hurdler: no form over fences: form only at 2m: acts on soft going: has flashed tail under pressure. *Dr P. Pritchard*   **c–**
h78

PRINCESS HATIE   4 b.f. Petoski – Culm Country (Town And Country) [2002/3 F18d Feb 17] first foal: dam, well beaten in 2 bumpers, out of fairly useful staying chaser Culm Port: showed nothing in bumper on debut. *P. R. Hedger*   **F–**

PRINCESS PUSHY 6 b.m. Broadsword (USA) – Phrase'n Cold (IRE) (Strong Statement (USA)) [2002/3 F17d F16m Jun 3] second foal: dam ran in 3 Irish points: well held in 2 bumpers. *D. L. Williams* **F—**

PRINCESS RIA (IRE) 6 b.m. Petong – Walking Saint (Godswalk (USA)) [2002/3 h68: 17v^{pu} 19g^{pu} Nov 23] poor on Flat: little show over hurdles. *M. E. Sowersby* **h—**

PRINCESS SOPHIE 5 b.m. Tragic Role (USA) – Octavia (Sallust) [2002/3 h–: 17d^4 16g 17m^5 17m^F Apr 26] angular mare: poor maiden hurdler around 2m: fell fatally at Sedgefield: acted on good to firm going. *K. W. Hogg, Isle of Man* **h71**

PRINCESS STEPHANIE 5 b.m. Shaab – Waterloo Princess (IRE) (Le Moss) [2002/3 F16m Apr 21] first foal: dam maiden Irish pointer: well beaten in mares maiden bumper on debut. *M. J. Gingell* **F—**

PRINCESS SYMPHONY (IRE) 7 ch.m. Lashkari – Hemmingford Grey (Sexton Blake) [2002/3 20g 24s* 24s^2 c22v^F c25s^3 c20v* c20s^2 c20s^2 c24d^{pu} c22s* c29g Apr 21] IR 3,500 3-y-o: leggy mare: sixth foal: dam, twice-raced on Flat, half-sister to smart middle-distance stayer and leading NH sire Orchestra: bumper winner: modest hurdler: won novice at Kilbeggan in May: fairly useful novice chaser: won mares events at Limerick in December (maiden) and March, beating Be My Belle 14 lengths in Grade 3 in latter: stays 25f: acts on good to firm and heavy going: tried blinkered: jumped badly right ninth start. *E. Sheehy, Ireland* **c117 h98**

PRINCE WOT A MESS (IRE) 12 ch.g. Buckskin (FR) – Valary (Roman Warrior) [2002/3 c24m^2 c20m c25m^{ur} c27g^{pu} c25f^2 Sep 29] strong gelding: poor handicap chaser: stays 25f: acts on firm and soft ground. *D. Broad, Ireland* **c79 h—**

PRIORY GARDENS (IRE) 9 b.g. Broken Hearted – Rosy O'Leary (Majetta) [2002/3 F17d^{pu} Mar 7] leggy gelding: no show either outing over hurdles (failed to complete in 2 points in between). *Mrs N. S. Sharpe* **h—**

PRIORY WOOD 7 ch.m. Gunner B – Penlea Lady (Leading Man) [2002/3 h–, F82: 19g^{pu} Nov 23] good-topped mare: won mares bumper on debut in 2001/2: disappointing in similar event and 2 mares maiden hurdles: has had tongue tied. *Mrs H. Dalton* **h—**

PRIVATE PERCIVAL 10 b.g. Arrasas (USA) – Romacina (Roman Warrior) [2002/3 c–, h–: c20d^6 c17s^3 Nov 24] rangy gelding: maiden chaser, modest form at best: stays 2½m: raced on good going or softer (acts on soft). *Jamie Poulton* **c90 h—**

PRIVATE PETE 10 ch.g. Gunner B – Vedra (IRE) (Carlingford Castle) [2002/3 c97: c25s^3 c21g Apr 3] sturdy gelding: successful in points in January and March: fairly useful hunter chaser: good third to Paddy For Paddy at Folkestone in February: well held in Fox Hunters' at Aintree: stays 25f: acts on soft going. *Lady Connell* **c104**

PRIVATE SEAL 8 b.g. King's Signet (USA) – Slender (Aragon) [2002/3 17g Oct 12] angular gelding: poor and ungenuine on Flat (stays 11.6f): no form over hurdles: tongue tied. *Julian Poulton* **h—**

PRIVATE TREATY 5 b.m. Contract Law (USA) – Inbisat (Beldale Flutter (USA)) [2002/3 F17d F16d 16g^{pu} Dec 12] 1,750 3-y-o: leggy mare: fifth foal: half-sister to 21f hurdle winner Listen Up (by Good Thyne): dam, disqualified winner on Flat/suited to 1¾m, half-sister to useful hurdlers Docklands Limo, stayed 2½m, and Major Bugler, raced mainly around 2m: no form in bumpers or novice claiming hurdle: tongue tied last 2 starts. *S. A. Brookshaw* **h— F—**

PRIZE DANCER (FR) 5 ch.g. Suave Dancer (USA) – Spot Prize (USA) (Seattle Dancer (USA)) [2002/3 h–: 24g^{pu} 16d Nov 2] leggy gelding: one-time fairly useful stayer on Flat: little show over hurdles: sold 2,500 gns Doncaster November Sales. *M. E. Sowersby* **h—**

PRO BONO (IRE) 13 ch.g. Tale Quale – Quality Suite (Prince Hansel) [2002/3 c102§, h–: c25d^{pu} c24s^{pu} c26d^{pu} Mar 8] lengthy gelding: winning chaser: no form in 2002/3: tends to make mistakes: unreliable. *M. G. Hazell* **c— § h—**

PROBUS LADY 6 ch.m. Good Times (ITY) – Decoyanne (Decoy Boy) [2002/3 22g^{pu} May 25] half-sister to fair staying chaser Cantoris Frater (by Brotherly) and to 2 winning pointers: dam never ran: showed nothing in novice hurdle on debut: joined C. Down. *K. Bishop* **h—**

PROBUS LORD 8 b.g. Rough Stones – Decoyanne (Decoy Boy) [2002/3 h–: 24g 20d^{pu} Jun 8] quite good-topped gelding: no form over hurdles: joined C. Down. *K. Bishop* **h—**

PROCEDURE (USA) 7 b. or br.g. Strolling Along (USA) – Bold Courtesan (USA) (Bold Bidder) [2002/3 h96: c16g^3 Feb 25] good-topped gelding: novice hurdler: off 11 months, never-dangerous third of 5 in novice on chasing debut: raced around 2m: acts on soft ground: takes good hold. *J. A. B. Old* **c87 h—**

714

PRO DANCER (USA) 5 b. or br.g. Pleasant Tap (USA) – Shihama (USA) (Shadeed **h109**
(USA)) [2002/3 16m^F 16m^3 16d^4 16d^6 16d 16m* Apr 13] sturdy gelding: lightly-raced
maiden on Flat: fair hurdler: won maiden at Listowel: unlikely to stay much beyond 2m:
acts on any going. *P. M. J. Doyle, Ireland*

PROFESSOR COOL (IRE) 10 b.g. Cataldi – Frostbite (Prince Tenderfoot (USA)) **h–**
[2002/3 24g^{pu} May 8] strong, lengthy gelding: fair hurdler in 1998/9: failed to complete
in points and handicap since. *R. J. Price*

PROFILER (USA) 8 b.g. Capote (USA) – Magnificent Star (USA) (Silver Hawk **c–**
(USA)) [2002/3 c89, h–: c16v^6 c19g^{pu} c21s^F c16v^3 c24g^{bd} c22d^{pu} c20g Apr 14] big, rangy **h–**
gelding: winning hurdler/chaser: little form in 2002/3: stays 2½m: probably acts on any
going: usually wears headgear: has broken blood vessel: sketchy jumper: has looked reluctant. *Ferdy Murphy*

PROKOFIEV (USA) 7 br.g. Nureyev (USA) – Aviara (USA) (Cox's Ridge (USA)) **c– §**
[2002/3 c97§, h113§: 24s^6 22s* 21s^6 22v^3 20v 21m^5 22s^{pu} 24m* Apr 12] angular gelding: **h121 §**
fairly useful handicap hurdler: won at Sandown in December and Bangor in April, eased
when beating Columbus 2 lengths in latter: below form otherwise in 2002/3: stays 25f:
acts on good to firm and heavy going: usually blinkered: has had tongue tied: has hung
under pressure: unreliable. *Jonjo O'Neill*

PROLOGUE (IRE) 12 b.g. Mandalus – Advance Notice (Le Bavard (FR)) [2002/3 **c72**
c23d^3 c20g^5 c22m^5 c22m^{pu} Jul 19] ex-Irish gelding: little sign of ability over hurdles for **h–**
Mrs J. Harrington: successful in point in May: poor form in steeplechases: sold 2,500 gns
Doncaster August Sales. *Mrs L. Williamson*

PROMINENT PROFILE (IRE) 10 ch.g. Mazaad – Nakuru (IRE) (Mandalus) **c96**
[2002/3 c–, h–: c22m^{ur} c18g^4 c20s^{pu} c20s^4 Mar 1] angular gelding: modest handicap **h–**
chaser nowadays: worthwhile form since 1999/00 only when making all at Newbury in
December, jumping better than usual: stays 2½m: acts on good to firm and heavy going:
tried blinkered. *N. A. Twiston-Davies*

PROMISING (FR) 5 ch.m. Ashkalani (IRE) – Sea Thunder (Salse (USA)) [2002/3 **h66**
16g^4 16g^6 16d^2 17s 17g^F 16d Apr 9] modest maiden on Flat (stays 7f): poor novice hurdler: likely to prove best around 2m: tongue tied after second start. *M. C. Chapman*

PROPER SQUIRE (USA) 6 b.g. Bien Bien (USA) – La Cumbre (Sadler's Wells **h116**
(USA)) [2002/3 h110: 22m* 21d^3 24g* 24d^3 24g^4 25g 24g Apr 3] sturdy gelding: fairly
useful handicap hurdler: won at Fontwell in May and Kempton in November: should stay
beyond 3m: acts on soft and good to firm going: blinkered last 2 starts. *C. J. Mann*

PROPERTY ZONE 5 b.g. Cool Jazz – Prime Property (IRE) (Tirol) [2002/3 h80: 16f **c–**
17g^6 c17d^F 16g^3 16d^3 16d^2 16d* 16g^4 16g* Apr 23] tall, leggy gelding: fell second on **h100**
chasing debut (final start for M. Easterby): fair hurdler: won handicaps at Doncaster
(novice) in March and Perth in April: raced around 2m: acts on good to firm and heavy
going: has found little. *C. Grant*

PROSPECTOR'S COVE 10 b.g. Dowsing (USA) – Pearl Cove (Town And Country) **h–**
[2002/3 16g Sep 14] angular gelding: poor on Flat (stays 11f) nowadays: thrice-raced
over hurdles in 1997/8, well held only start since: has found little. *J. M. Bradley*

PROTAGONIST 5 b. or br.g. In The Wings – Fatah Flare (USA) (Alydar (USA)) **h104**
[2002/3 h99: 16m^6 17d 21s* 21d 19d^{pu} Jan 25] good-topped gelding: fair handicap
hurdler: form in 2002/3 only when winning at Kempton in December: will stay beyond
21f: acts on soft going. *P. R. Webber*

PROTOCOL (IRE) 9 b.g. Taufan (USA) – Ukraine's Affair (USA) (The Minstrel **h86**
(CAN)) [2002/3 17d^2 16d^4 16d^6 16d 17s* 16v^5 16d^5 16s 17g Mar 15] compact gelding:
modest handicap hurdler: won seller at Market Rasen in December: should stay 2½m:
best efforts on good going or softer (acts on heavy): tried visored: tongue tied: less than
reliable. *Mrs S. Lamyman*

PROUD CAVALIER 7 b.g. Pharly (FR) – Midnight Flit (Bold Lad (IRE)) [2002/3 **h–**
16m^{pu} 16m^F Jun 19] no longer of much account on Flat: no form over hurdles. *Jean-Rene
Auvray*

PROUD FOUNTAIN (IRE) 10 br.g. Royal Fountain – Proud Polly (IRE) (Pollerton) **c–**
[2002/3 c–, h73: c25g Apr 7] strong, compact gelding: winning pointer: poor hurdler: **h–**
little show in hunter in April: stays 3¼m. *J. W. Hughes*

PROUD MONK 10 gr.g. Aragon – Silent Sister (Kind of Hush) [2002/3 16d 16g May **h–**
22] poor on Flat nowadays: little worthwhile form over hurdles: has had tongue tied.
Jean-Rene Auvray

PROUD PEER (IRE) 5 ch.g. Mister Lord (USA) – Raffeen Pride (Shackleton) **F84**
[2002/3 F16s⁵ F18v⁵ Feb 10] 17,500 4-y-o: fourth foal: dam unraced half-sister to smart
hunter chaser Animahron and useful staying hurdler Cash Is King: much better effort in
bumpers when fifth at Kempton on debut, shaping like a stayer. *M. Pitman*

PROUD WESTERN (USA) 5 b.g. Gone West (USA) – Proud Lou (USA) (Proud **h–**
Clarion) [2002/3 h–: 16g Jan 17] modest maiden on Flat (stays 1m): well held over
hurdles. *B. Ellison*

PROVENCE DREAMER 6 b.g. Alflora (IRE) – Kilbragh Dreamer (IRE) (Decent **h85**
Fellow) [2002/3 F17d² F17s² 24vᵖᵘ 21g⁵ 20g³ Mar 23] well-made gelding: second foal: **F91**
dam winning pointer: second in 2 bumpers: just poor form over hurdles: folded tamely
final start. *Jonjo O'Neill*

PROVERBIAL GRAY 6 ro.m. Norton Challenger – Clove Bud (Beau Charmeur **h63**
(FR)) [2002/3 F63: 16s⁵ 17d 17s⁶ 17s⁴ 17f 16d³ 16mˢᵘ Apr 21] poor maiden hurdler:
raced around 2m: acts on good to soft going. *D. R. Gandolfo*

PROVOCATIVE (FR) 5 b. or br.g. Useful (FR) – All Blue (FR) (Noir Et Or) [2002/3 **F102**
F16d² F16g³ Mar 29] fourth foal: brother to winning middle-distance stayer Idole du
Boulay and half-brother to 11f winner by Dadarissime: dam 1¾m hurdle winner, also
won around 1¼m on Flat: encouraging debut when head second to Vodka Bleu in bumper
at Haydock: odds on, only third in maiden at Hexham next time, looking all over winner
3f out but unable to quicken. *M. Todhunter*

PRUDISH LASS 6 b.m. Warcraft (USA) – Bella Delite (Uncle Pokey) [2002/3 F16s **F–**
Jan 18] fifth foal: dam, lightly-raced maiden, out of half-sister to top-class chaser Wayward Lad: showed nothing in bumper on debut. *A. J. Lidderdale*

PTARMIGAN 6 ch.g. Rock Hopper – Tee Gee Jay (Northern Tempest (USA)) [2002/3 **F–**
F–: F16g Mar 12] well held in 2 bumpers at Huntingdon 17 months apart. *T. T. Clement*

PTOLOMY 6 ch.g. Presidium – Moonwalker (Night Shift (USA)) [2002/3 F16m⁶ **F–**
May 11] fourth foal: brother to 7.5f to 1¼m winner Moonlight Flit: dam unraced: sixth of
11 in bumper at Worcester on debut. *J. G. FitzGerald*

PUCKS COURT 6 b.g. Nomadic Way (USA) – Miss Puck (Tepukei) [2002/3 F17gᵖᵘ **F–**
F17g F17d Oct 31] fifth foal: half-brother to poor pointer by Primitive Rising: dam tailed
off in bumper: showed nothing in 3 bumpers. *I. A. Brown*

PUCKS WAY 4 b.g. Nomadic Way (USA) – Adventurous Lady (Roman Warrior) **h–**
[2002/3 16f⁵ Oct 10] second foal: dam never ran: showed nothing in juvenile hurdle on
debut. *D. G. Bridgwater*

PUDLICOTT MILL (IRE) 4 b.g. Definite Article – Mimining (Tower Walk) **h–**
[2002/3 16gᵖᵘ Jul 27] fifth foal: half-brother to 9.3f and 11.9f winner Wellcome Inn (by
Most Welcome): dam fair sprinter: showed little in juvenile hurdle on debut. *M. F. Harris*

PUNTAL (FR) 7 b.g. Bering – Saveur (Ardross) [2002/3 c134, h134: 16m* 17d* **c–**
16g* 16g* 18dᵇᵈ 17d* 16v² 16d² 16g 16m* 21g 20gᵖᵘ Apr 3] **h142**
    Puntal effectively had two seasons in one. He made hay while the sun shone
in the summer, doing well enough to warrant support in the ante-post market on the
Champion Hurdle. In the colder light of winter he confirmed himself a smart novice
hurdler, but no better than that, and well short of Champion Hurdle standard. Puntal
had made his debut for the Pipe stable in the Grade 1 Sefton Novices' Hurdle over
three miles at Aintree at the end of the 2001/2 season. His seventh place meant his
novice status was preserved for the following season, whilst also indicating promise. That was confirmed at the start of the latest season when Puntal rattled off a
four-timer in novice hurdles in May at around two miles. He landed the odds each
time, making all at Southwell, Hereford, Worcester and Stratford. Three of those
wins were gained by wide margins, but his Worcester success, although less clear-
cut, was the most praiseworthy as he was giving a stone or more to his rivals,
including the fairly useful runner-up Jaboune. Puntal had found it hard to win at
Auteuil over both hurdles and fences when trained in France by Francois Belmont,
though he had no luck when sent back there for a handicap on his next start, being
brought down on the flat. That proved only a temporary setback as Puntal returned
to winning ways in the McCallum Corporate Consulting Summer Hurdle at Market
Rasen in July. The handicap, worth £23,200 to the winner, attracted a field of sixteen. They included Jaboune again, as well as the first two in the race the previous
year Magic Combination and Whistling Dixie, and the Irish-trained favourite

Gerrard Wealth Management Dovecote Novices' Hurdle, Kempton—
Tony McCoy is made to work hard for Puntal's sixth win of 2002/3

Patriot Games. Puntal routed his field with an impressive performance under top weight, taking a definite advantage from the third and soon having most of the field in trouble as he opened up a clear lead. Kept up to his work after the last, Puntal beat the 14/1-shots Loop The Loup and Cotopaxi by four lengths and the same. It was Puntal's best effort yet, one that promised to make him a novice to reckon with later in the season and, if the support that came for him in the Champion Hurdle betting during the autumn was anything to go by, some clearly saw him as having the potential to go right to the top.

A busy early-season campaign such as Puntal's is by no means prejudicial to a horse's form in the main part of the season. Indeed, Martin Pipe, in particular, is a master at exploiting the easier pickings of the summer months with above-average novices (including Seebald, Westender, Tarxien and Stormez), those horses gaining experience and confidence against modest opposition before going on to run with credit much later in the season, right up to and beyond the Cheltenham Festival. By the time Puntal got to Cheltenham in the spring though, the Champion Hurdle was off the agenda and Puntal had clearly gone off the boil. He ran poorly there in the Royal & SunAlliance Novices' Hurdle and was pulled up at Aintree in the Mersey Novices' three weeks later. Before then, Puntal had been beaten at odds on in his first two starts back from a five-month break, running to a similar level of form to Market Rasen both times. He went down by two lengths to 33/1-shot Kopeck in the Kennel Gate Novices' Hurdle at Ascot where the effort of forcing the pace in heavy ground seemed to take its toll in the closing stages; Puntal seemed beaten on merit however, again after making the running, when two and a half lengths behind Thisthatandtother in the rescheduled Tolworth Hurdle at Wincanton. Those efforts did not really justify his starting fourth favourite back in handicap company in the Tote Gold Trophy at Newbury (he was Tony McCoy's pick among five Pipe-trained runners) and Puntal finished well down the field, flat out turning into the straight. Puntal's winter campaign was not entirely without success because he won the Grade 2 Dovecote Novices' Hurdle at Kempton in February, landing the odds by eleven lengths from Jaboune again, the enthusiasm of his early-season efforts less evident as he had to be driven along to go clear again after being headed three out.

Mr Terry Neill's "Puntal"

Puntal (FR) (b.g. 1996)	Bering (ch 1983)	Arctic Tern (ch 1973)	Sea Bird
			Bubbling Beauty
		Beaune (ch 1974)	Lyphard
			Barbra
	Saveur (b 1988)	Ardross (b 1976)	Run The Gantlet
			Le Melody
		Youthful (b 1980)	Green Dancer
			First Bloom

Puntal was bred for the Flat and was successful twice on the level when trained in Spain as a three-year-old, winning across the French border at Toulouse over a mile and a quarter and then over eleven furlongs at San Sebastian. His year-younger brother Zenno Adria has won in Japan, while his half-sister Inimitable (by Polish Precedent) won closer to home, taking a mile-and-a-quarter maiden handicap at Salisbury. Their dam Saveur never ran but it's a fair bet she would have stayed well. Out of the French mile-and-a-half-winner Youthful, Saveur is a half-sister to Beneficial and Jeune who completed a pattern-race double at Royal Ascot in 1993, winning the King Edward VII and Hardwicke Stakes respectively. Jeune went on to make even more of a name for himself in Australia, winning the Melbourne Cup, while Saveur joined him down under in 1997 on the back of that success. Great grandam First Bloom was the best of her age and sex in Europe at two when she won the Prix Thomas Bryon. Her other descendants include the Grand Prix de Deauville winner First Prayer (son) and the US Grade 1 winner Talinum (grandson), while, as well as Puntal, another of her great-grandsons to have done well over jumps in Britain is the useful handicap hurdler/winning chaser Majestic.

The medium-sized Puntal seems to have had his limitations exposed over hurdles, but he had already shown useful form without winning over fences in

France and he is well worth another try over the larger obstacles. A few novice chases should be at his mercy at least. Puntal probably stays twenty-one furlongs, and he acts on heavy and good to firm going. *M. C. Pipe*

PURBECK WONDER 7 ro.g. Riverwise (USA) – Blue Wonder (Idiot's Delight) [2002/3 F–: F16m^{pu} May 11] leggy gelding: pulled up in 2 bumpers. *N. R. Mitchell*   **F—**

PURE BRIEF (IRE) 6 b.g. Brief Truce (USA) – Epure (Bellypha) [2002/3 h–: 16m* 16s^{pu} 17m^5 17m^5 17g^3 17g^5 Oct 12] angular gelding: modest hurdler: fortunate to win handicap at Uttoxeter in July: unable to repeat that form: raced mainly around 2m: acts on good to firm going (no form on soft): blinkered/visored. *A. Streeter*   **h86**

PURE FUN (IRE) 6 b.g. Lord Americo – Rath Caola (Neltino) [2002/3 h90, F95: 22f 19m^4 24f* 24f^4 20s 19s^4 21m^2 22f^m Apr 21] compact gelding: fair handicap hurdler: won 3-runner event at Ludlow in October: off 5 months, better than ever last 2 starts, successful in 5-runner event at Wincanton by 1¼ lengths from Cape Stormer: stays easy 3m: acts on firm and soft going. *P. J. Hobbs*   **h107**

PURE GRIT (IRE) 13 b.g. Sheer Grit – Shuil Eile (Deep Run) [2002/3 c26d^6 Jun 8] poor pointer: apparently improved effort in maiden at Cartmel on hunter chase debut, probably flattered. *G. D. Hanmer*   **c71 ?**   **h—**

PURE MISCHIEF (IRE) 4 b.g. Alhaarth (IRE) – Bellissi (IRE) (Bluebird (USA)) [2002/3 16d^3 16d^{ur} 16s^6 16s* 16g Apr 19] angular gelding: maiden on Flat (stays 1¼m), modest form in 2002: dropped in class, won juvenile claiming hurdle at Plumpton in March: well held in handicap following month: unsure to stay beyond 2m: amateur ridden. *Miss J. Feilden*   **h86**

PURSER PETE (IRE) 7 b.g. Jurado (USA) – Roselita (Deep Run) [2002/3 F16g F16m^5 Nov 17] IR 5,000 4-y-o: half-brother to several winners, including fair chaser Rocket Run (by Orchestra), stayed 3¼m: dam won over 5f at 2 yrs: no show in 2 bumpers: tongue tied on debut. *Miss Lucinda V. Russell*   **F—**

PUSEY SANCE 5 br.g. Puissance – Pusey Street (Native Bazaar) [2002/3 16d^{pu} 17g^{ur} Nov 7] half-brother to fairly useful hurdler/chaser Regal Holly (by Gildoran), stays 25f, and winning 2m hurdler Pusey Street Boy (by Vaigly Great): well beaten on Flat at 3 yrs for M. Bosley: failed to complete both starts over hurdles. *B. L. Lay*   **h—**

PUTSOMETNBY (IRE) 7 ch.g. Phardante (FR) – Bobs My Uncle (Deep Run) [2002/3 h114?, F96: 20d 24g^2 20s^2 22d^F 22d^2 25m* 20m^3 24f^2 20g* 27g^3 24d^2 24d^{ur} c32g^5 Mar 21] sturdy, lengthy ex-Irish gelding: fair hurdler: fairly useful chaser: won at Kilbeggan (maiden) in August and Limerick (4-runner novice) in October when trained by K. O'Brien: improved in handicaps last 2 starts, though jumping let him down both times, unseating when well clear last in quite valuable event at Doncaster: should stay beyond 27f: acts on firm and soft going: blinkered final outing. *Jonjo O'Neill*   **c124 x**   **h106**

PUTUP OR SHUTUP (IRE) 7 br.g. Religiously (USA) – Nights Crack (Callernish) [2002/3 h96, F96: 22d^4 20s^2 21d* 25d^5 24d^3 Jan 16] medium-sized gelding: bumper winner: modest hurdler: won maiden at Ludlow in November: stays 3m: raced on going softer than good. *K. C. Bailey*   **h99**

PUZZLEMAN 10 ch.g. Henbit (USA) – Floreamus (Quayside) [2002/3 c–, h–: 21m^{pu} May 6] lengthy gelding: maiden hurdler: no form in steeplechases: stays 2¾m: acts on firm going: tried blinkered: sold £3,000 Ascot June Sales, won points in January (only rival pulled up) and February. *D. J. Caro*   **c—**   **h—**

PYTHAGORAS 6 ch.g. Kris – Tricorne (Green Desert (USA)) [2002/3 h72: 16s^6 16d^4 Apr 9] sturdy gelding: disappointing maiden on Flat: poor form over hurdles, off 14 months before reappearance. *M. Sheppard*   **h71**

Q

QANDIL (USA) 7 ch.g. Riverman (USA) – Confirmed Affair (USA) (Affirmed (USA)) [2002/3 16g^{pu} Nov 30] poor on all-weather Flat (stays 7f): no show in novice on hurdling debut. *Miss J. Feilden*   **h—**

QOBTAAN (USA) 4 b.g. Capote (USA) – Queen's Gallery (USA) (Forty Niner (USA)) [2002/3 16d 16s Dec 7] good-topped gelding: modest maiden on Flat (barely   **h—**

stays 9.4f): well held both starts over hurdles, left A. Chamberlain before second (blinkered). *M. R. Bosley*

QUABMATIC 10 b.g. Pragmatic – Good Skills (Bustino) [2002/3 h91: 19dᵖᵘ 19sᵖᵘ **h101**
20v 19d³ 19d³ 19s* 17g* Mar 18] leggy gelding: fair handicap hurdler: back to best last 2
starts, won at Taunton in February and Exeter in March: stays 2½m: raced mainly on
good going or softer (acts on soft): tried blinkered, not since 1999/00. *K. Bishop*

QUADCO (IRE) 9 b.g. Be My Native (USA) – Anega (Run The Gantlet (USA)) **c116**
[2002/3 h117: 20m⁴ 16s* c18s² c20sᶠ c17v⁵ c17s Jan 19] leggy gelding: fair hurdler: won **h113**
handicap at Galway in September: shaped quite well when second to Eskimo Jack in
maiden at Thurles on chasing debut: disappointing subsequently, generally let down by
jumping: stays 2½m: acts on firm and soft going (won bumper on heavy): has found little.
P. A. Fahy, Ireland

QUAINTON HILLS 9 b.g. Gildoran – Spin Again (Royalty) [2002/3 c101, h–: 21vᵖᵘ **c–**
24vᵖᵘ 19g Feb 28] medium-sized gelding: fair handicap chaser in 2001/2: novice hurdler, **h–**
well held only completed outing in 2002/3: should be suited by further than 23f: acts on
good to firm and heavy going: sometimes makes mistakes. *D. R. Stoddart*

QUALITY FIRST (IRE) 10 b.g. Un Desperado (FR) – Vipsania (General Ironside) **c128**
[2002/3 c–, h109: 20v⁴ 20g⁴ c24sᵇᵈ c21s² c17sᶠ 16m c21v* c24d c20d⁴ c21s² c20g* **h106**
c21d⁶ c25m³ Apr 21] good-topped ex-Irish gelding: fair handicap
chaser: won at Cheltenham (first outing since leaving P. Nolan) in January and Bangor
(beat Mr Baxter Basics 1¼ lengths) in March: creditable sixth of 29 to Clan Royal in
Topham Chase at Aintree: probably best up to 21f: acts on heavy and good to firm going:
has been led in at start. *Mrs H. Dalton*

QUANTUM LADY 5 b.m. Mujadil (USA) – Folly Finnesse (Joligeneration) [2002/3 **h65**
16g 17v² Nov 6] fair at best on Flat (best around 6f), little form early in 2002: achieved
little in 2 selling hurdles, pulled hard when well-held second in weak event at Newton
Abbot. *J. D. Frost*

QUARTER MASTERS (IRE) 4 b.g. Mujadil (USA) – Kentucky Wildcat (Be My **h84**
Guest (USA)) [2002/3 17dᵖᵘ 17m⁶ 16m 16d* 20s³ 16v 17s 20sᵖᵘ Feb 7] lengthy gelding:
half-brother to useful hurdler Alpine Panther (by Tirol), stays 3m: poor on Flat (stays
11f): modest juvenile hurdler: had run of race when winning at Ayr in November: stays
2½m: acts on soft going. *G. M. Moore*

QUARTERSTAFF 9 b.g. Charmer – Quaranta (Hotfoot) [2002/3 c87: c20g² c21g³ **c101**
c25gᵘʳ c25g² c24g* Mar 28] lengthy gelding: fair novice chaser: let down by jumping in **h–**
latter stages 2 starts prior to winning 5-runner handicap at Carlisle: stays 25f: acts on
heavy going. *C. R. Wilson*

QUATERMASS 7 b.g. Karinga Bay – Panchellita (USA) (Pancho Villa (USA)) **h–**
[2002/3 h–, F–: 22gᵖᵘ May 17] no sign of ability outside points. *A. Hollingsworth*

QUAZAR (IRE) 5 b.g. Inzar (USA) – Evictress (IRE) (Sharp Victor (USA)) **h152**
[2002/3 h137: 16g³ 16d² 16s 20s* 16g 20d* 21g 20g⁴ Apr 5]
Quazar did it again in his second season over hurdles, proving tough,
reliable and better than ever, a credit to himself and to his stable. As a juvenile he
continually surpassed expectations, winning seven of his ten starts, and wound up
his campaign winning major races at Aintree and Punchestown. Those two meetings again saw his best performances of the latest campaign which brought him
three more wins, including another Grade 1 success. Quazar's aforementioned
qualities were always going to stand him in good stead, but after a busy juvenile
campaign there was a doubt whether he would be able to find the necessary
improvement to continue thriving in handicaps.

Those doubts were partly dispelled when Quazar was placed in his first two
starts of the season, finishing third to Santenay in the Elite Hurdle at Wincanton
(carrying top weight in the limited handicap) and then finding only Rooster Booster
nine lengths too good in the Rehabilitation of Racehorses Hurdle at Cheltenham.
Quazar was below form on his next start in another valuable race, the William Hill
Handicap Hurdle at Sandown, but was back to winning ways when successful at
Haydock on two of his next three outings. Both those wins were over two and a half
miles, a trip he had seemed far from sure to stay. On the first occasion, in January,
he stayed on well on the long run-in to beat Comex Flyer three lengths, justifying

Emo Oil Champion Hurdle, Punchestown—
Quazar (right) gains a second successive win at the Punchestown Festival,
upsetting the odds-on Back In Front (centre); also pictured is third-placed In The Forge

favouritism and not having to improve on his efforts in better handicaps at two miles. Following a creditable seventh back at two miles in the Tote Gold Trophy at Newbury, Quazar returned to Haydock in March, starting favourite once more. Comex Flyer was weighted to turn the tables this time but again had to settle for second place, a length and a half behind Quazar. This success earned Quazar a penalty for the Coral Cup at Cheltenham, bringing his weight to 12-1, minus his rider's 3 lb claim. Not surprisingly, the task proved beyond him in the much more competitive event and Quazar was never a threat.

Having crept up the handicap, Quazar was now tried outside handicap company for the first time since the previous season. He started as one of the outsiders for the Aintree Hurdle but excelled himself in finishing around eight lengths fourth to Sacundai, leading from three out until just after the next. On that effort, Quazar looked the chief rival to the Supreme Novices' Hurdle winner Back In Front in the Emo Oil Champion Hurdle at Punchestown in early-May. There was little to choose on form between Quazar and Back In Front, who had also won the Evening Herald Champion Novices' Hurdle at the same meeting three days earlier, but the more progressive Back In Front was 11/8-on and Quazar 7/2. In a disappointing turnout for a Grade 1 event, their four rivals were just fairly useful performers: Risky Reef had won the Cordon Bleu Handicap Hurdle at Aintree, Glenhaven Nugget had taken a substandard Grade 2 novice at Fairyhouse and In The Forge had had one run since a promising novice campaign in 2001/2. The remaining runner and outsider of the party Cailin's Perk effectively took no part after virtually refusing to race. After In The Forge had set a good pace for most of the way, the race boiled down to the expected duel between the market leaders but not with the expected outcome. Niggled along to close after the sixth, Quazar challenged at the last and gradually wore down Back In Front to win by a length, the latter possibly feeling the effects of a second race in four days. Incidentally, Quazar was ridden at Punchestown by Tony Dobbin who has been beaten on him only twice in nine outings together.

There's little to add to the pedigree details relayed about Quazar in last year's Annual. His year-younger half-brother Hereforagoodtime (by Petardia) has now embarked on a hurdling career in Ireland, though without showing any ability so far. A yearling half-brother to Quazar by Danetime was sold for €26,000 at Tattersalls (Ireland) in November. Quazar ended the latest season with form that would entitle him to a place in any of the best hurdles from now on, though, with the Champion Hurdle in mind, his stable already has the high-class Intersky Falcon, and Rhinestone Cowboy who could prove better still. It would be dangerous to rule

Mr C. D. Carr's "Quazar"

	Inzar (USA) (b 1992)	Warning (b 1985)	Known Fact
Quazar (IRE) (b.g. 1998)			Slightly Dangerous
		Czar's Bride (b 1979)	Northern Dancer
			American Legacy
	Evictress (IRE) (ch 1991)	Sharp Victor (ch 1984)	Sharpen Up
			Elegant Victress
		Nurse Jo (b 1982)	Jo Tobin
			Native Nurse

out further progress from Quazar judged on his career so far, though he's plenty
high enough in the handicap now and could be switched to fences if he doesn't
prove up to beating the top hurdlers in conditions events. The strong, compact
Quazar acts on good to firm and heavy going, and he is tongue tied nowadays. *Jonjo
O'Neill*

QUEDEX 7 b.g. Deploy – Alwal (Pharly (FR)) [2002/3 17s² 17d² 24v⁵ 21s⁴ 19m³ 19g* **h94**
Apr 19] smallish, angular gelding: fairly useful on Flat (probably stays 2¼m), sold out of
E. James's stable only £1,700 Ascot October Sales: modest novice hurdler: odds on, won
maiden at Stratford, rallying to beat Brooklands Lad ¾ length: stays 19f: acts on good to
firm and good to soft going: has worn cheekpieces. *R. J. Price*

QUEEN OF ARAGHTY 6 ch.m. Phardante (FR) – Queen's Darling (Le Moss) **h–**
[2002/3 F74: F16g⁶ 20m⁵ 22s Jun 3] well-made mare: poor in bumpers: well held both **F–**
starts over hurdles: second in 2-finisher maiden point in April. *M. Todhunter*

QUEEN OF JAZZ 6 b.m. Sovereign Water (FR) – When The Saints (Bay Express) **F–**
[2002/3 F17s F17g Jun 12] leggy mare: half-sister to 3 winners, including modest hurdler
The President (by Yaheeb), probably stays 2¾m: dam 6f winner at 3 yrs in Ireland: well
held in 2 bumpers. *Mrs H. Dalton*

QUEEN'S BANQUET 6 b.m. Glacial Storm (USA) – Culinary (Tower Walk) [2002/3 **F85** F17d³ F16g F16g F17m^rm Apr 17] unfurnished mare: sixth foal: half-sister to 3 winners, including fairly useful hurdler up to 2½m Hang'em High and fair hurdler/chaser up to 3m Kings Banquet (both by Supreme Leader): dam, 2m hurdle winner, from family of high-class jumpers Young Hustler and River Ceiriog: modest form in bumpers, but has looked temperamental: hung badly right and ran out over 1f out in listed mares event at Cheltenham. *P. R. Webber*

QUEENS HARBOUR (IRE) 9 b.g. Brush Aside (USA) – Queenie Kelly (The **h86** Parson) [2002/3 16d 20s⁶ Mar 15] well-made gelding: smart in bumpers in 1998/9: very lightly raced over hurdles, signs of retaining ability when seventh in novice at Doncaster on first outing for over 2 years: should stay at least 21f. *N. J. Henderson*

QUEENSLAND BAY 4 ch.f. Primitive Rising (USA) – Hysteria (Prince Bee) [2002/3 **F–** F16v F17v⁶ Feb 11] tall filly: eighth foal: half-sister to fairly useful hurdler Jackson Park (by Domynsky), stays 25f, and useful bumper winner/fairly useful hurdler Silver Knight (by Simply Great), stays 25f: dam unraced half-sister to fairly useful 2m hurdler Kaldan Khan: well held in 2 bumpers. *T. D. Easterby*

QUEEN'S PAGEANT 9 ch.m. Risk Me (FR) – Mistral's Dancer (Shareef Dancer **h104 §** (USA)) [2002/3 h92+: 19d⁵ 21d⁵ 19s* 20s 19s 20s² 22s Mar 15] compact mare: fair handicap hurdler: won at Taunton in November: ridden by A. McCoy, best effort when ½-length second to Taillefer at Sandown: stays 2½m: acts on soft going: wore cheekpieces last 2 starts: none too reliable. *J. L. Spearing*

QUEENSWAY (IRE) 11 b.g. Pennine Walk – Polaregina (FR) (Rex Magna (FR)) **c70** [2002/3 c96d, h–: c17m^pu c17s⁵ c16g² c17d^pu Nov 4] sturdy gelding: handicap chaser, **h–** poor form in 2002/3: stays easy 21f: acts on firm and good to soft going: tongue tied. *R. M. Carson*

QUETAL (IRE) 10 ch.g. Buckskin (FR) – Cantafleur (Cantab) [2002/3 c106+, h–: **c117** c24s* c26g Mar 13] rather sparely-made gelding: useful hunter chaser: beat Mr Dow **h–** Jones 9 lengths in 3-finisher event at Newbury in February: soundly beaten in Foxhunter at Cheltenham: will stay beyond 3¼m: acts on good to firm and soft going, probably on heavy: tends to make mistakes. *Mrs Laura J. Young*

Claydon Horse Exercisers Maiden Hurdle, Stratford—
Quedex (cheekpieces) provides Richard Johnson with his thousandth winner

QUIBBLE 6 ch.g. Lammtarra (USA) – Bloudan (USA) (Damascus (USA)) [2002/3 h–
16s 16s⁶ Nov 27] maiden on Flat (stays 12.5f), modest form at best in Britain: no show
both starts over hurdles. *A. Bailey*

QUICKSWOOD (IRE) 10 b.g. Yashgan – Up To Trix (Over The River (FR)) [2002/3 c–
c–, h94: 27g^pu May 17] workmanlike gelding: yet to complete in steeplechases: modest h–
handicap hurdler: stays 27f: acts on heavy going, possibly not on good to firm: usually
visored: won point in February. *C. R. Barwell*

QUIET CELEBRATION 6 b.m. Superpower – Quiet Amusement (USA) (Regal h–
And Royal (USA)) [2002/3 F16m 16m^pu Jul 17] 1,500 5-y-o: first foal: dam, modest 2m F–
hurdler, half-sister to smart 7f to 1¼m performer Calling Collect: no show in bumper and
maiden hurdle. *Miss K. M. George*

QUIET MOMENTS (IRE) 10 b.g. Ron's Victory (USA) – Saint Cynthia (Welsh c–
Saint) [2002/3 c25d⁴ c25d^pu May 13] angular gelding: poor chaser: no show in 2 hunters: h–
earlier won 3-runner point: stays 3¼m: acts on good to firm and heavy going: tried blinkered, often visored. *Miss P. Fitton*

QUIET WATER (IRE) 7 br.g. Lord Americo – Sirana (Al Sirat (USA)) [2002/3 h81: h98
21m* 19v 19s³ 21g* 19m* 20g Apr 2] leggy gelding: modest handicap hurdler: won at
Huntingdon (amateurs, subsequently sold out of M. Wilkinson's stable 14,000 gns Doncaster August Sales) in May, Ludlow (novice) in February and Newbury (improved form,
beat East Hill by 5 lengths in conditional jockeys novice) in March: stays 21f: acts on soft
and good to firm going. *P. J. Hobbs*

QUINTA LAD 5 b.g. Alhijaz – Jersey Belle (Distant Relative) [2002/3 17v 16s 16g^ro h–
Dec 13] quite good-topped gelding: poor maiden on Flat (stays 7f): no show over hurdles.
J. R. Norton

QUINTRELL DOWNS 8 b.g. Efisio – Nineteenth of May (Homing) [2002/3 17g³ h93
Oct 18] useful on all-weather on Flat (stays 1½m) for R. Cowell, successful twice in
January 2000: winning hurdler: first outing for over 3 years, shaped as if retaining much
of his ability when third of 6 finishers in handicap at Hereford: likely to prove best around
2m: acts on good to firm going. *T. R. George*

QUIT THE PACK (IRE) 5 b. or br.g. Grand Lodge (USA) – Treasure (IRE) (Treas- h–
ure Kay) [2002/3 h–: 16d^pu Nov 25] no form over hurdles. *R. N. Bevis*

QUIZZICAL 5 ch.g. Indian Ridge – Mount Row (Alzao (USA)) [2002/3 17g 20m⁶ h77
20s³ 16d² 16f 21d 21d 20s Mar 17] smallish, angular gelding: little form on Flat: poor
maiden hurdler: probably stays 2½m: acts on soft and good to firm going: tried in cheekpieces. *J. G. Carr, Ireland*

R

RACINGFORMCLUB BOY 4 ch.g. Blushing Flame (USA) – Sonoco (Song) h–
[2002/3 16d^pu 16d 17s^pu Dec 5] leggy gelding: poor maiden on Flat (stays 11.6f): no show
in juvenile hurdles, visored last 2 starts. *P. S. McEntee*

RADAR (IRE) 8 b.g. Petardia – Soignee (Night Shift (USA)) [2002/3 c106, h–: c16m⁵ c106
16g³ 21d⁵ c16v⁴ c16v* Feb 11] angular gelding: winning hurdler: fair chaser: back to best h84
when winning handicap at Sedgefield (third win over course and distance): raced around
2m: acts on any going. *Miss S. E. Forster*

RADBROOK HALL 4 b.g. Teenoso (USA) – Sarah's Venture (Averof) [2002/3 F16d F–
Mar 1] big, workmanlike gelding: half-brother to winning staying chaser Who Dares
Wins (by Kala Shikari): dam, won two 2m novice hurdles, also fair around 1½m on Flat:
burly, well held in bumper on debut. *M. W. Easterby*

RADCLIFFE (IRE) 6 b.g. Supreme Leader – Marys Course (Crash Course) [2002/3 h–
F16g⁶ F16d* F16s 19d⁶ Feb 23] IR 24,000 4-y-o: third foal: half-brother to modest hurd- F96
ler Loughcrew (by Good Thyne), stays 3m: dam fair hurdler/chaser up to 3m: favourite,
won maiden bumper at Fakenham in December: disappointing both subsequent starts, not
fluent on hurdling debut. *Miss Venetia Williams*

RADICAL JACK 6 b.g. Presidium – Luckifosome (Smackover) [2002/3 h–: 16g^pu c–
c20s^pu c16g^ur Mar 23] of no account. *C. W. Fairhurst* h–

RADLETT (IRE) 8 b.g. Supreme Leader – Classical Friend (IRE) (Lidhame) [2002/3 h–
16v^F Dec 21] tall gelding: well held in 2 bumpers: fell first on hurdling debut. *A. M. Hales*

RADLEY PARK (IRE) 4 b.g. Vettori (IRE) – Livry (USA) (Lyphard (USA)) [2002/3 **h–**
16d 17g Mar 15] easily best effort on Flat on debut, sold out of P. Makin's stable 7,500
gns Newmarket Autumn Sales: well held in juvenile hurdles: dead. *E. W. Tuer*

RAFFLES ROOSTER 11 ch.g. Galetto (FR) – Singapore Girl (FR) (Lyphard (USA)) **c120 x**
[2002/3 c120, h–: c25s⁵ c24v² c24v² c24d² Jan 13] good-topped gelding: fairly useful **h–**
handicap chaser: stays 3¼m: acts on good to firm and heavy going: often finds less than
expected, and best with exaggerated waiting tactics: often let down by jumping. *Miss
Venetia Williams*

RAGASAH 5 b.m. Glory of Dancer – Slight Risk (Risk Me (FR)) [2002/3 16g⁵ Oct 9] **h–**
poor on Flat (probably stays easy 1½m): fell second on hurdling debut. *Miss Gay
Kelleway*

RAGDALE HALL (USA) 6 b.g. Bien Bien (USA) – Gift of Dance (USA) (Trem- **h115**
polino (USA)) [2002/3 h100p: 16f² 16d* 16m³ 17m² 16d⁴ 18m² 17m² 19m* 20g⁴ 16g*
Apr 19] medium-sized gelding: fair novice hurdler: trained until after eighth start by
P. Hobbs: won at Uttoxeter (simple task) in June, Hereford in September and Stratford
(handicap, improved form when beating Ballykettrail 1½ lengths) in April: stays 2½m:
acts on firm and good to soft going: blinkered fifth/sixth outings (found less than seemed
likely): tongue tied fourth/fifth starts. *J. Joseph*

RAGLAN NIGHTFIRE 5 ch.g. New Reputation – Ophiuchus (Nader) [2002/3 F16s⁵ **F–**
F16d F18d F17v Nov 19] compact gelding: second foal: dam unraced: signs of only a
little ability in bumpers. *K. O. Cunningham-Brown*

RAGU 5 b.m. Contract Law (USA) – Marnworth (Funny Man) [2002/3 F79: 16d⁵ 20d⁴ **h88**
20g³ 21v² 16d 21m 17m⁴ Apr 19] leggy, unfurnished mare: modest novice hurdler: well
below form last 3 starts: stays 21f: acts on heavy going. *Ferdy Murphy*

RAINBOW CHASE (IRE) 5 b.g. Rainbow Quest (USA) – Fayrooz (USA) (Gulch **h83**
(USA)) [2002/3 h74: 16v⁵ 16d⁴ 16g⁶ 16d³ 17d 16gᵖᵘ Apr 14] tall, leggy gelding: maiden
on Flat: poor maiden hurdler: raced mainly around 2m: acts on good to soft going: tried in
cheekpieces/tongue strap. *S. J. Magnier*

RAINBOW DANCE (IRE) 7 ch.g. Rainbows For Life (CAN) – Nishila (USA) **c93**
(Green Dancer (USA)) [2002/3 h87+, F91: 25g² 21m* 24m² 20d* c20d² c21d³ c20d³ **h114**
c20d⁵ Nov 14] sturdy gelding: fair handicap hurdler: won at Ludlow (novice) in May and
Worcester in June: second of 3 finishers to Keep Smiling in novice at Bangor on chasing
debut, disappointing after: effective at 2½m to 25f: acts on good to firm and heavy going:
usually blinkered in 2002/3: has had tongue tied. *Jonjo O'Neill*

RAINBOW RIVER (IRE) 5 ch.g. Rainbows For Life (CAN) – Shrewd Girl (USA) **h104**
(Sagace (FR)) [2002/3 17g² 16g* 21m* 17g⁴ Mar 29] half-brother to winning 2m hurdler
Girl of Pleasure (by Namaqualand): modest on Flat (stays 1½m): started well over hurdles, won conditional jockeys maiden at Fakenham and novice at Ludlow (odds on) within
6 days in March: well-held fourth in more competitive novice at Market Rasen later in
month: stays 21f. *M. C. Chapman*

RAINBOWS AGLITTER 6 b.g. Rainbows For Life (CAN) – Chalet Waldegg **h112**
(Monsanto (FR)) [2002/3 h100: 17d² 21d² 16g³ 17d 16d² 16m Mar 22] angular gelding:
fair handicap hurdler: stays 21f: acts on soft and good to firm going: edgy sort: held up,
tends to find little. *D. R. Gandolfo*

RAINBOW SPIRIT (IRE) 6 b.g. Rainbows For Life (CAN) – Merrie Moment (IRE) **h–**
(Taufan (USA)) [2002/3 h90: 22dᵖᵘ 24m⁴ 19gᵖᵘ Jun 12] winning hurdler: no form in
handicaps early in 2002/3, reportedly lame final start: will prove best at 3m+: tongue tied
last 2 outings. *H. Alexander*

RAINBOW STAR (FR) 9 b. or br.g. Saumarez – In The Star (FR) (In Fijar (USA)) **c– §**
[2002/3 c–§, h–§: 16sʳᵗʳ 20m 26m³ c26gᵖᵘ Sep 12] tall gelding: winning hurdler, little **h– §**
form since 2000, including in steeplechases/points: usually blinkered/visored: has had
tongue tied: has refused/been reluctant to race. *Mrs P. Ford*

RAINBOW SUN 7 ch.g. Minster Son – Rilin (Ribston) [2002/3 F77: 19g 16m 21vᵖᵘ **h–**
24m Apr 10] no form in novice hurdles: hung badly right second start: has worn cheekpieces. *N. M. Babbage*

RAINCHECK 12 b.g. Mtoto – Lashing (USA) (Storm Bird (CAN)) [2002/3 c21mᵖᵘ **c–**
May 22] leggy gelding: one-time fair hunter chaser: no sign of retaining ability in 2002: **h–**
tongue tied. *Mrs Georgina Worsley*

RAIN DOCTOR 9 ch.g. Lycius (USA) – Rain Date (USA) (Blushing Groom (FR)) **c–**
[2002/3 c20dᵘʳ Apr 29] no form over jumps, even in points: tongue tied. *K. Robson* **h–**

RAINFOREST (IRE)   8 b. or br.g. Be My Native (USA) – Nanny Kehoe (IRE)   c–
(Sexton Blake) [2002/3 c16g Nov 30] useful-looking gelding: fair form in 2 bumpers in
1999/00: off over 2½ years, well held in novice chase: will be suited by further than 2m.
P. R. Webber

RAINTON   7 gr.g. Kasakov – Strathleven (My Swanee) [2002/3 c–, h–: c25g Apr 7]   **c81 ?**
leggy gelding: little form over hurdles: winning pointer: let down by jumping both starts   **h–**
in steeplechases: tried blinkered. *Miss N. Stirling*

RAISA'S GOLD (IRE)   5 b.m. Goldmark (USA) – Princess Raisa (Indian King   **h–**
(USA)) [2002/3 h–: 16g^{pu} Jun 15] poor maiden on Flat: signs of ability on first of 2 outings over hurdles. *B. S. Rothwell*

RAISE A GALE (IRE)   9 b.m. Strong Gale – Raise A Rose (IRE) (Cardinal Flower)   **c101**
[2002/3 c24g^F c23m* c24m² c24f³ Mar 24] useful-looking ex-Irish mare: maiden hurd-   **h–**
ler: successful in 2 points in Britain in 2002: trained by S. Sherwood second and third
starts, won novice chase at Worcester in June: below best back in hunter after 8-month
absence final outing: likely to stay beyond 3m: acts on good to firm and good to soft
going. *Mrs E. Hill*

RAISE A MCGREGOR   7 br.g. Perpendicular – Gregory's Lady (Meldrum) [2002/3   **h–**
h76, F–: 16d^{pu} 20v 16g Nov 23] maiden hurdler, no form in 2002/3: looked none too keen
final outing. *Mrs S. J. Smith*

RAISEAPEARL   8 b. or br.g. Pocketed (USA) – Little Anthem (True Song) [2002/3   **h–**
20d 20v⁶ Dec 28] third foal: dam poor pointer: ran out first in point in 2002: well held in
2 novice hurdles at Haydock. *R. D. Wylie*

RAISE A STORM (IRE)   6 b.g. Fourstars Allstar (USA) – Tipperary Tartan (Rarity)   **h–**
[2002/3 16v 16d⁶ F16g³ Apr 20] good-topped gelding: half-brother to several winners,   **F102**
including high-class hurdler Destriero (by Ile de Bourbon): dam, won at 1¼m on only
start, half-sister to dam of useful hurdler/chaser up to 3m Palette: fairly useful bumper
winner: fair form on hurdling debut in 2001/2, disappointing both starts very early in
2002/3: stays 2½m. *D. Wachman, Ireland*

RAISE YOUR GLASS (IRE)   4 b. or br.g. Namaqualand (USA) – Toast And Honey   **F–**
(IRE) (Glow (USA)) [2002/3 F14d F16g⁶ F16d Apr 25] third foal: dam 2m winner over
hurdles/1½m winner on Flat: little encouragement in bumpers. *C. W. Thornton*

RAJAH EMAN (IRE)   5 b.g. Sri Pekan (USA) – Jungle Book (IRE) (Ballad Rock)   **h–**
[2002/3 16s^F 17g^{pu} Sep 6] fairly useful on Flat (stays 11f) at 3 yrs for S. Woods, no form
for C. Dwyer in 2002: failed to complete both starts over hurdles. *R. Allan*

RAJATI (USA)   8 b.g. Chief's Crown (USA) – Charming Life (NZ) (Sir Tristram)   **c– §**
[2002/3 c24m Apr 22] angular gelding: novice chaser/winning hurdler: fair pointer, suc-   **h–**
cessful twice in 2002: stays 21f: acts on heavy going: tried blinkered/visored: has had
tongue tied: has looked none too keen over fences. *R. J. Rowsell*

RAKALACKEY   5 br.g. Rakaposhi King – Celtic Slave (Celtic Cone) [2002/3 F17s⁵   **F95**
F16g⁵ Mar 14] medium-sized gelding: half-brother to smart hurdler/chaser Young Spartacus (by Teenoso), barely stays 25f, and winning 2¼m hurdler Alpine Slave (by Alflora):
dam fair hurdler/fairly useful chaser, stayed well: better effort in bumpers when fifth of
19 to Majestic Moonbeam at Warwick, still looking green. *H. D. Daly*

RAKAPOSHI LASS   7 b.m. Rakaposhi King – Ballysax Lass (Main Reef) [2002/3   **h97 p**
F17g* F16m* F16m* 22m* Aug 26] 8,000 4-y-o: second foal: sister to useful 2m hurdler   **F116 +**
Chai-Yo: dam maiden half-sister to Supreme Novices' winner Sondrio: successful once
from 3 outings in points in 2002: created excellent impression when unbeaten in bumpers
at Newton Abbot and Worcester (2) early in season: long odds on, won 6-runner maiden
at Newton Abbot on hurdling debut, jumping left (overjumped first and rider lost iron)
but readily quickening clear from last: looked open to considerable improvement, but
wasn't seen out again. *M. C. Pipe*

RAKAPOSHI RAID   7 b.m. Rakaposhi King – Minty Muncher (Idiot's Delight)   **c–**
[2002/3 h70: c21g⁵ 24d⁴ Aug 17] poor maiden hurdler: well held on chasing debut: stays   **h70**
25f: acts on soft and good to firm ground: tried blinkered/visored: has had tongue tied:
sold 1,200 gns Doncaster September Sales. *N. B. Mason*

RAKASSA   5 ch.m. Ballet Royal (USA) – Shafayif (Ela-Mana-Mou) [2002/3 F16g   **F78**
F16g F16d⁵ F14g³ F17g Apr 5] lengthy, plain mare: third foal: dam, untrustworthy win-
ning 2m selling hurdler, out of smart miler Rare Roberta: modest form in bumpers.
H. J. Manners

RALEAGH NATIVE (IRE) 10 ch.g. Be My Native (USA) – Lagan Valley Rose **c104 x**
(Avocat) [2002/3 c104x, h–: c20g² c20s² c20vur c20s⁶ c20sF 20g Apr 2] tall gelding: fair **h–**
handicap chaser: winning hurdler: well held in cheekpieces final start: stays 21f: acts on
soft going: often let down by jumping over fences. *Miss A. M. Newton-Smith*

RAMBLEES HOLLY 5 ch.g. Alfie Dickins – Lucky Holly (General David) [2002/3 **h83**
F72: F16s F16f⁶ 19g³ 16d 20vpu 16g⁶ 17s⁵ 16m Apr 21] angular gelding: poor in bum- **F76**
pers: poor form over hurdles: should stay beyond 19f. *R. S. Wood*

RAMBLING HOME (IRE) 11 br.g. Orchestra – Rambling Ivy (Mandalus) [2002/3 **c–**
c20dpu Mar 4] successful 4 times in Irish points: bought 5,000 gns Doncaster May (2000)
Sales: no sign of retaining ability in maiden hunter chase at Leicester after nearly 4 years
off. *T. R. George*

RAMIREZ (IRE) 5 ch.g. Royal Abjar (USA) – Flooding (USA) (Irish River (FR)) **F91**
[2002/3 F17s² F17s F16g Apr 2] 5,200 3-y-o: strong gelding: half-brother to several winners, including fairly useful 1998 2-y-o 6f and 7f winner Lough Swilly (by Mukaddamah)
and fair 2001 2-y-o 5f winner Water Baby (by Tagula): dam unraced: best effort in bumpers when neck second to Onwardsandupwards at Taunton on debut: tended to hang left
second outing. *M. Pitman*

RANDOM HARVEST (IRE) 14 br.g. Strong Gale – Bavello (Le Bavard (FR)) **c118**
[2002/3 c121, h–: c20m c20dpu c26s² c24d³ c24dpu c25s⁴ c24d⁶ c23g* c24g³ c25m⁵ **h–**
c28m* Apr 26] tall, leggy gelding: has been fired: won only start over hurdles: fairly useful handicap chaser: won at Wetherby (seventh course win) in March and Sedgefield
(made most to beat Lanmire Tower a length) in April: stays 3½m: acts on good to firm
and heavy going: none too reliable. *Mrs M. Reveley*

RANDOM NATIVE (IRE) 5 br.g. Be My Native (USA) – Random Wind (Random **F98**
Shot) [2002/3 F–: F16g* F16g³ F17g* Apr 21] rather leggy gelding: fairly useful form in
bumpers: won at Catterick (maiden) in January and Carlisle (by 4 lengths from Cool
Cossack) in April: will stay beyond 2m. *T. J. Fitzgerald*

RANDRICH 6 b.m. Alflora (IRE) – Randama (Akarad (FR)) [2002/3 h–: 20vpu Nov **h–**
27] no show in novice hurdles 13 months apart. *P. M. Rich*

RANDY (GER) 5 gr.g. Neshad (USA) – Regal Beauty (GER) (Windwurf (GER)) **h–**
[2002/3 19dpu 19s 16spu 16vpu Feb 4] unplaced in 3 starts in Germany at 2 yrs for P. Rau:
not fluent and little sign of ability over hurdles. *M. C. Pipe*

RANEEN NASHWAN 7 b.g. Nashwan (USA) – Raneen Alwatar (Sadler's Wells **h83 §**
(USA)) [2002/3 h83§: 16f⁴ 20g 17g⁶ 17g³ Jun 29] lengthy gelding: fairly useful on Flat
(stays 1½m): poor maiden hurdler: best efforts around 2m: acts on firm and good to soft
going: raced freely in blinkers final outing: irresolute. *R. J. Baker*

RANELAGH GRAY (IRE) 6 gr.g. Roselier (FR) – Bea Marie (IRE) (King's Ride) **h83**
[2002/3 F18d F16d⁵ 21spu 16g⁵ 21m Mar 21] IR £17,500 4-y-o: leggy gelding: second **F83**
foal: brother to modest staying jumper One More: dam, winning pointer, out of sister to
dam of smart chaser up to 25f Tipping Tim (by King's Ride): modest form in bumpers:
best effort over hurdles (saddle slipped on debut) when fifth in novice at Huntingdon:
bred to stay well beyond 2m: takes strong hold. *Miss Venetia Williams*

RANGER SLOANE 11 ch.g. Gunner B – Lucky Amy (Lucky Wednesday) [2002/3 **c–**
16spu Nov 8] leggy gelding: winning hurdler: broke down on return from 2-year lay-off: **h–**
blinkered once. *G. Fierro*

RAPID DEPLOYMENT 6 b.g. Deploy – City Times (IRE) (Last Tycoon) [2002/3 **h118**
h115p: 20sF 20v⁴ 24sF 24s⁴ 16g Mar 30] compact gelding: fairly useful on Flat (probably
stays 2¼m): fairly useful handicap hurdler: good fourth to Keepatem at Punchestown
fourth outing: needs further than 2m and stays 3m: acts on heavy going: sometimes let
down by jumping. *P. Hughes, Ireland*

RAPID LINER 10 b.g. Skyliner – Stellaris (Star Appeal) [2002/3 c–, h–: 16m⁶ 19m **c–**
21m² Apr 19] bad maiden jumper, left J. Gallagher after reappearance: stays 21f: tried **h57**
blinkered. *B. G. Powell*

RAPIER 9 b.g. Sharpo – Sahara Breeze (Ela-Mana-Mou) [2002/3 h85: 20g⁵ May 3] **h78**
leggy gelding: winning hurdler, very lightly raced: best form around 2m: raced on good
going or softer: has bled from nose. *A. Streeter*

RAPT (IRE) 5 b.g. Septieme Ciel (USA) – Dream Play (USA) (Blushing Groom (FR)) **h–**
[2002/3 17m 16vpu 16d 16g Apr 7] leggy gelding: half-brother to 2¼m hurdle winner
Hello Excuse Me (by Storm Bird): fair on Flat (stays 7f), sold out of P. d'Arcy's stable
£3,600 Ascot June Sales: no aptitude for hurdles. *M. A. Barnes*

RARCHNAMARA (IRE)   8 b.g. Commanche Run – Knollwood Court (Le Jean) **c80**
[2002/3 h102§: c20m⁴ c27vᵘʳ Feb 11] tall, leggy gelding: fair hurdler: jumped deliber- **h– §**
ately when fourth in novice at Musselburgh on chasing debut: unseated twelfth next time:
stays 27f: raced mainly on good going or softer (acts on soft): effective blinkered/visored
or not: ungenuine. *Ferdy Murphy*

RARE GENIUS (USA)   7 ch.g. Beau Genius (CAN) – Aunt Nola (USA) (Olden **h–**
Times) [2002/3 h98: 19d Nov 13] one-time fair maiden on Flat (stays 2m): second in
maiden on hurdling debut: tailed off in novice at Newbury 16 months later: will stay
further than 19f. *Ian Williams*

RARE OCCURANCE   13 b.g. Damister (USA) – Superior Quality (Star Appeal) **c–**
[2002/3 c20mᵖᵘ c21dᵖᵘ Jun 3] strong, workmanlike gelding: winning 2½m chaser: no **h–**
sign of retaining ability after 3-year absence: has worn tongue strap. *A. W. Carroll*

RARE OUZEL (IRE)   7 b.g. Be My Native (USA) – Ring Ouzel (Deep Run) [2002/3 **h108 p**
F16d* 20s 21d² 18v* 16sᶠ Jan 12] useful-looking gelding: third foal: brother to bumper **F87**
winner Homebird: dam unraced half-sister to dam of useful chaser up to 3m Saxophone:
won bumper at Ballinrobe in May: much improved over hurdles in handicaps last 2 completed starts, second of 29 to Jurancon II at Cheltenham (conditional jockeys) in November
and won at Leopardstown in December by length from G V A Ireland: stays 21f: raced
on going softer than good (acts on heavy): open to further improvement. *A. J. Martin,
Ireland*

RARE PRESENCE (IRE)   4 b.g. Sadler's Wells (USA) – Celebrity Style (USA) **h79**
(Seeking The Gold (USA)) [2002/3 16v 17d 17g⁴ Mar 16] leggy ex-Irish gelding: fair
maiden on Flat (stays 1½m), sold out of D. Weld's stable 30,000 gns Newmarket Autumn
Sales: blinkered, first form over hurdles when fourth of 12 in juvenile maiden at Folkestone. *C. P. Morlock*

RASKO (FR)   7 gr.g. Kadalko (FR) – Fagaras (FR) (Kenmare (FR)) [2002/3 20s⁵ 19v* **c90 p**
18v³ 19v⁴ c24g⁴ Dec 18] seventh foal: closely related to 2 winning 2m hurdlers by **h134**
Cadoudal and half-brother to 2 winners, including French hurdle/Italian cross-country
chase winner Triple Saut (by Passing Sale): dam maiden on Flat: useful hurdler:
won at Lyon Parilly in October: under pressure when badly hampered 3 out in novice won
by Iris Royal at Newbury on chasing debut: stays 2½m: raced mainly on soft/heavy
ground. *T. Doumen, France*

RATHBAWN PRINCE (IRE)   11 ch.g. All Haste (USA) – Ellis Town (Camden **c140**
Town) [2002/3 c148, h–: 22d c16sᶠ c16d⁴ c24g³ c25dᵖᵘ c29g Apr 21] good-bodied **h–**
gelding: smart chaser/useful hurdler at best: long way below that in 2002/3, except when
third to Royal Predica in well-contested amateur handicap chase at Cheltenham in March:
stays 29f: acts on good to firm and heavy going. *D. T. Hughes, Ireland*

RATHGAR BEAU (IRE)   7 b. or br.g. Beau Sher – Salerina (Orchestra) [2002/3 **c145**
h133: c16s² c17sᵇᵈ c17s⁴ c16s³ c16s² c17v* c17s³ c16d² c16d* c16v* c16gᶠ Apr 5] **h–**
   The Deloitte And Touche Novices' Hurdle at Leopardstown was granted
Grade 1 status for the first time in 2002/3, which comes as little surprise when the
subsequent exploits of the 2002 field are examined. Five of the ten runners have
since won at least once at Grade 1 level—Like-A-Butterfly, Sacundai, Thari (albeit
fortuitously), Beef Or Salmon and Scottish Memories—while another Adamant
Approach has twice fallen when poised to land such a contest. Rathgar Beau, who
faded into fifth over a testing two and a quarter miles that day, has yet to win in
three attempts at Grade 1 level and may struggle to do so now, given that the
Champion Chase, the Tingle Creek and the BMW provide probably his only viable
opportunities, but he showed himself a smart novice chaser in 2002/3 and can be
expected to add to his tally of victories just below the highest level. Rathgar Beau
had been kept busy as a novice over hurdles (the Deloitte And Touche one of ten
appearances) and was seen even more frequently over fences, turned out twelve
times in all. Although never worse than fourth in ten completions, it took him six
starts to get off the mark, in a weak maiden at Limerick in December. He added two
more victories, in novices at Thurles in February, when he would have won very
easily but for trying to demolish the last, and at Naas in March. At Naas, in a well-
contested event, Rathgar Beau finally showed form on a par with his efforts over
hurdles in beating the useful Glens Music and Schwartzhalle four lengths and the
same. His four other outings were in graded company, paired either side of his
novice wins. Before them, he finished three lengths third to Bust Out in the Grade 1

Kilcock Novices' Chase, Naas—Rathgar Beau proves too strong for Glens Music

Arkle at Leopardstown and half a length behind Schwartzhalle in the Grade 2 Flyingbolt Novices' Chase at Navan, where a mistake two out may well have made the difference. Rathgar Beau's jumping was also a significant factor in the subsequent outings. He fell four out when bang in contention in the Maghull Novices' Chase at Aintree and, in a virtual rerun of that race, finished third to Le Roi Miguel and Impek in the Swordlestown Cup at Punchestown shortly after the end of the British season, when a blunder at the final fence cost him the runner-up spot. Rathgar Beau is best waited with and could show improved form tried in a well-run handicap, though his tendency to make the odd bad mistake would be severely tested in such circumstances. It will be no surprise if he is campaigned instead in the plethora of fairly valuable conditions races which provide ample opportunities for the better horses in Ireland. The useful-looking Rathgar Beau is the only foal out of the bumper winner Salerina. Best at around two miles, he has raced mainly on going softer than good and acts on heavy. *E. Sheehy, Ireland*

RATHGIBBON (IRE) 12 br.g. Phardante (FR) – Harp Song (Auction Ring (USA)) [2002/3 c87, h–: c16dpu c21mpu c24gpu c21d5 Oct 25] compact gelding: one-time fair chaser, retains little ability: sold out of N. King's stable 2,100 gns Ascot July Sales after third outing: tried blinkered: visored/tongue tied first 3 starts. *Mrs L. C. Jewell*   c– h–

RATIFIED 6 b.g. Not In Doubt (USA) – Festival of Magic (USA) (Clever Trick (USA)) [2002/3 c73, h77: c16m c17s5 17d2 17m 17s 17g 24g2 20m4 22d5 21s 16g 17s Dec 26] good-topped gelding: poor maiden hurdler/chaser: seems to stay 2¾m: acts on heavy going. *M. C. Chapman*   c– h77

RAUNCHY (IRE) 9 br.g. Be My Native (USA) – Dirty Diana (Boreen (FR)) [2002/3 c87, h114: 24s3 24m 22d2 Aug 26] ex-Irish gelding: modest form over fences: disappointing maiden hurdler, left J. Mulhern after second outing: stays 3m: acts on soft going. *Jonjo O'Neill*   c– h87

RAVEN ROCK (IRE) 7 b.g. Supreme Leader – Atteses (Smooth Stepper) [2002/3 h98p, F101: 22sdis 20s* 24s2 Dec 15] fairly useful form over hurdles: won novice at Cork   h117

729

in December: good second to Satco Express in Grade 3 novice at same course 2 weeks later: took wrong course on reappearance: stays 3m: raced only on soft/heavy going. *N. Meade, Ireland*

RAVENSWOOD (IRE) 6 b.g. Warning – Green Lucia (Green Dancer (USA)) [2002/3 h130p: 24s^{pu} 22s 21s^6 24g^2 25g^4 Mar 11] rather leggy, useful-looking gelding: useful handicap hurdler: back to form last 2 starts, neck second of 17 to Slooghy at Newbury and around 14 lengths fourth of 24 to Inching Closer in Pertemps Final at Cheltenham: stays 25f: acts on good to firm and good to soft going, seemingly not on soft: tongue tied. *M. C. Pipe*   **h133 +**

RAVING LORD (IRE) 6 b.g. Lord Americo – Miss Kertina (IRE) (Orchestra) [2002/3 F16m^6 F17m^5 F16g^5 F16d^4 19d 16g^{pu} Jan 28] IR £9,500 4-y-o: first foal: dam unraced, out of half-sister to top-class hurdler Daring Run: modest form in bumpers: well held both starts over hurdles, looked difficult ride on second occasion. *J. P. Dodds*   **h–** **F83**

RAW SILK 5 b.g. Rudimentary (USA) – Misty Silks (Scottish Reel) [2002/3 h93: 16g^3 17d^4 20s^4 17d 16m^2 18s^3 16d^2 Nov 7] good-bodied gelding: modest hurdler: left J. O'Neill, good second in handicaps at Haydock 2 of last 3 starts: probably best around 2m: acts on any going: wears blinkers/cheekpieces: tongue tied fourth start. *M. Todhunter*   **h98**

RAYBAAN (IRE) 4 b.g. Flying Spur (AUS) – Genetta (Green Desert (USA)) [2002/3 17m Apr 16] compact gelding: fairly useful on Flat (stays easy 1½m): well held in juvenile at Cheltenham on hurdling debut. *M. H. Tompkins*   **h–**

RAYBROOK (IRE) 8 ch.g. Moscow Society (USA) – Vesper Time (The Parson) [2002/3 F72: 20m^{pu} 18g^{pu} May 29] second in bumper on debut: pulled up both outings over hurdles: usually tongue tied: dead. *Mrs L. B. Normile*   **h–**

RAY RIVER 11 b.g. Waki River (FR) – Mrs Feathers (Pyjama Hunt) [2002/3 h–: 20g 19m^6 22m^2 25g c23m^F c20g^{pu} c25m^3 Oct 3] sparely-made gelding: bad hurdler nowadays: no form in 3 races over fences (poor jumper): stays 3¼m: acts on soft and good to firm going: sometimes blinkered: has worn cheekpieces. *K. G. Wingrove*   **c– x** **h59**

RAYWARE BOY (IRE) 7 b.g. Scenic – Amata (Nodouble (USA)) [2002/3 h83: 16d 16g^6 17m^2 16s^3 16g 16d^{rtr} 17g Mar 15] sparely-made gelding: poor handicap hurdler: likely to stay beyond 17f: acts on good to firm and good to soft going: blinkered/visored: refused to race sixth start (reluctant to do so time before): one to leave alone. *D. Shaw*   **h75 §**

RAZER BLADE 8 b.g. Teenoso (USA) – Sparkling Cinders (Netherkelly) [2002/3 c100, h–: c21d* c22m^3 c24g^F Apr 12] lengthy gelding: fairly useful hurdler in 2000/1: off 16 months after chasing debut, fortunate to win 6-runner novice at Wincanton on return in March, around 20 lengths down when left in front last: let down by jumping both starts after, tended to go right but still length ahead of Kick For Touch when fell last in novice at Stratford: stays 3m: acts on soft going (won bumper on good to firm): takes good hold, and has got on edge. *N. J. Henderson*   **c103** **h–**

RAZZMATAZZ (IRE) 9 br.g. Camden Town – Sallys Wish (Proverb) [2002/3 17g Mar 25] tall ex-Irish gelding: half-brother to 3 winners, including fair Irish 19f hurdle winner Celtic Gale (by Strong Gale): dam ran twice on Flat: little form in bumpers and over hurdles, off over 2 years before only outing in 2002/3. *J. Howard Johnson*   **h–**

REACHFORTHESTARS 7 b.m. Royal Fountain – China's Way (USA) (Native Uproar (USA)) [2002/3 16d^{pu} Feb 26] leggy mare: no show in 2 bumpers and novice hurdle. *J. Mackie*   **h–**

REACH THE CLOUDS (IRE) 11 b.g. Lord Americo – Dusky Stream (Paddy's Stream) [2002/3 c104, h87: c20g^5 c17g^F c17d^4 c20v^2 c16g^2 c19m^3 c16d^2 Mar 19] good-topped gelding: modest chaser, on long losing run: barely stays 2½m when conditions are testing: acts on heavy and good to firm going: blinkered twice: probably best on left-handed course: sometimes finds little. *John R. Upson*   **c95** **h–**

REAL CHIEF (IRE) 5 b.g. Caerleon (USA) – Greek Air (IRE) (Ela-Mana-Mou) [2002/3 F17d F16s F16g^{su} Jul 10] 1,300,000 francs £, 5,000 3-y-o: second living foal: half-brother to winning 17f hurdler Desert Air (by Desert King): dam, French 1m listed winner, sister to very smart French performer up to 1¼m Grecian Urn, herself dam of useful hurdlers Grecian Dart and Dark Shell: mid-division first 2 starts in bumpers, chasing pace when slipped up on home turn at Worcester final start. *Miss M. E. Rowland*   **F73**

REAL ESTATE 9 b.g. High Estate – Haitienne (FR) (Green Dancer (USA)) [2002/3 c84, h92: 16m^6 19s c20d^{ur} c20g^4 c20g^2 c20g 21m^3 21m^5 Apr 21] compact gelding: modest handicap hurdler: poor handicap chaser: stays 2½m: acts on soft and good to firm going, probably on firm: tried blinkered. *J. S. King*   **c82** **h92**

REAL FIRE (IRE)   9 b.g. Astronef – Golden Arum (Home Guard (USA)) [2002/3   c– §
h70: 16d 16g 27g^{pu} 20m³ 19g c21g⁴ c21d 27v⁴ 21s 16d⁴ c21s³ 24g 21v⁴ 16s² 27s c16g⁴   **h65 §**
Apr 1] small gelding: poor handicap hurdler/novice chaser: stays 21f: acts on heavy and
good to firm going: wears headgear and tongue strap nowadays: irresolute. *R. Johnson*

REAL SHADY   6 b.g. Bob's Return (IRE) – Madam Margeaux (IRE) (Ardross)   **h82**
[2002/3 F95: 19d^{pu} 16d^{pu} 16g² Mar 29] tall gelding: bumper winner: first form over
hurdles (saddle slipped on debut) when ½-length second in weak novice at Hexham.
M. W. Easterby

REAL SHARP (IRE)   5 br.g. Son of Sharp Shot (IRE) – Lady By Chance (IRE)   **h–**
(Never Got A Chance) [2002/3 F16d⁶ 19d 19s⁴ 20d Apr 9] IR £2,500 3-y-o: first foal: **F72**
dam unraced: sixth of 11 in bumper at Ludlow on debut: well held in novice hurdles.
S. E. H. Sherwood

REALSLIM SHADY   5 gr.g. Gran Alba (USA) – Shy Hiker (Netherkelly) [2002/3   **h–**
20g Apr 23] €6,500 4-y-o, 6,200 5-y-o: fifth foal: half-brother to winning hurdler up to
2½m Helm Wind (by North Col): dam 2½m winner over hurdles: no show on hurdling
debut. *A. C. Whillans*

REAL VALUE (IRE)   12 b.g. Matching Pair – Silent Verb (Proverb) [2002/3 c124d: **c109**
c25d c26d² c23d* c26m^F Apr 17] sturdy gelding: hunter chaser, useful nowadays: 2½
lengths second of 6 to Torduff Express at Fontwell in February: didn't need to match that
form when winning at Leicester in March: stays 3½m: acts on soft and good to firm going,
probably on heavy. *Mrs D. M. Grissell*

REASONABLE RESERVE (IRE)   6 ch.g. Fourstars Allstar (USA) – Alice   **h81**
O'Malley (The Parson) [2002/3 F20s⁴ F20d 24d₃³ Aug 17] IR 10,000 4-y-o: third foal: **F81**
half-brother to bumper/17f chase winner Intacta Print (by Glacial Storm): dam unraced
half-sister to top-class staying chaser Chives: modest form in bumpers: first form over
hurdles when third of 7 in novice handicap at Perth, jumped badly and off bridle long way
out: blinkered second start. *C. F. Swan, Ireland*

REASONING   5 ch.m. Selkirk (USA) – Attribute (Warning) [2002/3 19d^{pu} Oct 19]   **h–**
good-topped mare: modest on Flat (stays 1¼m): reportedly bled from nose on hurdling
debut. *B. S. Rothwell*

REBEL CLOWN   5 gr.g. King's Signet (USA) – Castle Cary (Castle Keep) [2002/3   **F–**
F17g F17m Jul 15] third foal: half-brother to 5f winner Blazing Castle (by Vague Shot):
dam 6f winner: well beaten in bumpers and on Flat: sold £600 Ascot October Sales.
N. J. Hawke

REBEL RAIDER (IRE)   4 b.g. Mujadil (USA) – Emily's Pride (Shirley Heights)   **h–**
[2002/3 16m^{co} Apr 10] ex-Irish gelding: fair maiden on Flat (stays 9f) for P. Flynn: fading
when carried out by loose horse 3 out in juvenile at Ludlow on hurdling debut.
B. N. Pollock

REBEL REPRIEVE (IRE)   7 b.g. Rich Rebel (USA) – Reprieved Run (Deep Run)   **c–**
[2002/3 c24v^{pu} Jun 6] third known foal: brother to winning pointer and half-brother to
winning chaser Moonvoor (by Duca di Busted), stays 2¾m: dam never ran: maiden
pointer: pulled up in novice chase. *S. A. Brookshaw*

REBEL'S GIFT   10 b.g. Genuine Gift (CAN) – Princess Veronica (Rebel Prince)   **c–**
[2002/3 c–, h69: 22m 20v^{pu} 20s^{pu} 20g⁵ Apr 1] leggy gelding: handicap hurdler, no form   **h–**
in 2002/3: visored once. *F. P. Murtagh*

RECESS (IRE)   7 b. or br.g. Approach The Bench (IRE) – Storms-Of-Life (Strong   **h95**
Gale) [2002/3 F16g⁵ F16s⁴ F16s⁴ 16s 16s 16d⁴ 18v⁵ 16s 16s^F 16g^F Mar 30] fifth foal: **F86**
dam unraced: fair form in bumpers: modest novice hurdler: one of better efforts when
fourth of 28 in handicap at Cheltenham: raced around 2m: acts on heavy going: often
blinkered. *J. T. Gorman, Ireland*

RED ADHERE   8 b.g. Insan (USA) – By The Lake (Tyrant (USA)) [2002/3 c–, h–:   **c–**
20d⁵ Apr 29] lengthy gelding: no sign of ability: tried blinkered. *N. B. Mason*   **h–**

RED AFGEM   6 ch.m. Afzal – Preacher's Gem (The Parson) [2002/3 F16g F16s³ F17g   **F–**
Jun 12] sixth foal: half-sister to fairly useful hurdler/winning chaser Joliver (by Strong
Gale), stayed 3¼m, and winning staying hurdler Kind Cleric (by Supreme Leader): dam,
modest 2½m hurdler, half-sister to good hunter Rolls Rambler and Eider Chase winner
David's Duky: well held in 3 bumpers: very stoutly bred. *Mrs S. M. Johnson*

RED ALERT MAN (IRE)   7 ch.g. Sharp Charter – Tukurua (Noalto) [2002/3 c–,   **c74 ?**
h76: c16s⁴ c16v⁴ c16d^{pu} c16v^{pu} c16s⁵ c16s⁶ c20v³ c17g^{ur} c21g* Apr 21] workmanlike   **h–**
gelding: poor novice chaser: won weak event at Uttoxeter in April: stays easy 21f: raced

on good going or softer (acts on heavy): wore blinkers/cheekpieces after third outing. *Mrs L. Williamson*

RED AND DANGEROUS   8 b.g. Afzal – Flori Wonder (Floriana) [2002/3 h–, F–: 20g^{pu} 19m^{pu} Sep 11] no sign of ability. *Mrs D. A. Hamer*   h–

RED ARK   10 ch.g. Gunner B – Minim (Rymer) [2002/3 c133, h–: c20d c16d^6 c24m c16g^6 c36d^{pu} Apr 5] good-bodied gelding: has been hobdayed: useful handicap chaser: ran creditably when sixth at Sandown in February and Cheltenham (valuable event, behind Palarshan) in March: jumped badly in Grand National at Aintree final outing: effective at 2m to 23f: yet to race on firm going, acts on any other: has worn cheekpieces: tongue tied. *R. C. Guest*   c131 h–

RED BLAZER   12 ch.g. Bustino – Klewraye (Lord Gayle (USA)) [2002/3 c126, h–: c20d* c16d^2 c21d^3 c16m^5 Feb 21] rangy, useful-looking gelding: useful chaser: best effort in 2002/3 when winning handicap at Huntingdon in November by short head from Il'athou: stays 2½m (finished sore only try at 3m): raced mainly on good going or softer (won bumper on heavy): has broken blood vessel: sound jumper. *Miss H. C. Knight*   c133 h–

RED BLOODED (IRE)   6 b.g. River Falls – Volkova (Green Desert (USA)) [2002/3 16s c20d^{pu} c16g^5 Mar 2] leggy gelding: modest maiden at best on Flat: signs of only a little ability over jumps: tried tongue tied. *Mrs L. C. Jewell*   c– h–

RED BRAE   6 b.g. Rakaposhi King – Sayshar (Sayfar) [2002/3 F85: 20d^{pu} Dec 14] lengthy gelding: fair form in bumpers: blinkered, hit first and never going well in novice at Haydock on hurdling debut: should stay at least 2½m. *Jonjo O'Neill*   h–

RED BROOK LAD   8 ch.g. Nomadic Way (USA) – Silently Yours (USA) (Silent Screen (USA)) [2002/3 c22d^{ur} c25d^F c19f^2 Mar 27] leggy gelding: fairly useful pointer, successful in January and February: first completion in hunter chases when second to Sol Music at Exeter: tried blinkered over hurdles. *C. St V. Fox*   c104 h–

RED CANYON (IRE)   6 b.g. Zieten (USA) – Bayazida (Bustino) [2002/3 h73: 25g^{pu} 20g 21g 20m* 22m* 22m* 22m^4 24g^4 24f^2 21d^5 Oct 26] sturdy gelding: modest handicap hurdler: sold out of B. Case's stable 5,200 gns Ascot June Sales after third outing: won next 3 races, at Worcester in June, Stratford in July and Newton Abbot in August: stays 3m: best efforts on going firmer than good: blinkered second start. *A. G. Hobbs*   h92

RED DANCER (FR)   7 b.g. Red Paradise – Majestic Dancer (FR) (What A Guest) [2002/3 c21g^2 c25g* c25f^F c19g^2 c25g c26g^2 c31d^6 Nov 15] leggy gelding: fair form over hurdles and fences at 4 yrs for T. Civel in France: has since won 3 times over fences in Czech Republic and Slovakia, including at Slusovice in June: well held in Grade 1 at Merano fifth start, close sixth to Famfoni in valuable cross-country event at Cheltenham final one: stays 31f: acts on heavy going. *C. Olehla, Czech Republic*   c112 ? h–

REDDE (IRE)   8 ch.g. Classic Memory – Stoney Broke (Pauper) [2002/3 h120: 24d^{pu} May 6] deep-girthed gelding: fairly useful hurdler: lacklustre effort in handicap at Towcester in May, not seen out again: should stay beyond 2½m: acts on soft going, won bumper on heavy: races prominently. *R. J. Smith*   h–

RED DIAMOND   4 b.g. Mind Games – Sandicroft Jewel (Grey Desire) [2002/3 16m^{pu} Nov 4] modest maiden at 2 yrs, well held on Flat in 2002: in cheekpieces, no show in juvenile on hurdling debut: sold £700 Ascot December Sales. *Miss K. M. George*   h–

RED EMPEROR   9 b.g. Emperor Fountain – Golden Curd (FR) (Nice Havrais (USA)) [2002/3 c90, h–: c24d^6 c24g^3 c26s^5 c28v^3 c24d^u c28s^{pu} c24s^5 c24d Mar 15] lengthy gelding: modest handicap chaser: won at Newcastle (for third consecutive year) in November: below form otherwise in 2002/3: stays 3¾m: acts on heavy going: tried visored, blinkered nowadays: often tongue tied: none too consistent: sold 3,000 gns Doncaster May Sales. *R. C. Guest*   c90 h–

REDEMPTION   8 b.g. Sanglamore (USA) – Ypha (USA) (Lyphard (USA)) [2002/3 c143, h–: c16v^3 c16v^F c16g^5 c16s^F c21m^4 Apr 16] workmanlike gelding: useful handicap chaser: looked back to best in race won by Eskleybrook at Sandown fourth start, coming from last place to dispute lead when falling 2 out: left P. Webber, not seen to best advantage in limited handicap at Cheltenham final outing: stays 2½m: acts on heavy and good to firm going: went in snatches in blinkers third appearance. *N. A. Twiston-Davies*   c141 h–

RED ENSIGN   6 ch.g. Lancastrian – Medway Queen (Pitpan) [2002/3 F18s F18m Mar 31] first foal: dam lightly raced: well held in 2 bumpers. *Mrs L. C. Jewell*   F–

RED FLYER (IRE)   4 br.g. Catrail (USA) – Marostica (ITY) (Stone) [2002/3 16d* 16d^2 16g^2 18g^F 16g^{pu} Apr 12] leggy, quite good-topped gelding: modest maiden on Flat   h94 (probably stays 11f): modest juvenile hurdler: won at Newcastle in November: will prove best at 2m. *P. C. Haslam*

RED FOREST (IRE)   4 b.g. Charnwood Forest (IRE) – High Atlas (Shirley Heights) [2002/3 16m^{pu} 16g^{pu} Sep 12] smallish gelding: fair on Flat (probably stays 1¼m), left B. Hills 8,500 gns after winning seller in July: pulled up in 2 juvenile hurdles. *W. Clay*   **h–**

RED GAUNTLET   10 b.g. Wonderful Surprise – Border Minstrel (Menelek) [2002/3 c25g^F Mar 21] fair pointer: successful in February and March: just in front when falling 2 out in hunter won by Trade Dispute at Kelso on steeplechasing debut. *Mrs A. C. Hamilton*   **c?**

RED GENIE   5 ch.g. Primitive Rising (USA) – Marsden Rock (Tina's Pet) [2002/3 F16f^3 F17g^4 F16d F16g^4 Mar 29] first foal: dam modest hurdler, stayed 21f: modest form in bumpers: wore cheekpieces final outing. *R. C. Guest*   **F85**

RED GOLD   9 ch.g. Sula Bula – Ruby Celebration (New Member) [2002/3 c83x, h–: c24s^{pu} Mar 2] workmanlike gelding: poor maiden chaser: often let down by jumping. *Andrew Turnell*   **c– x**
   h–

REDGRAVE WOLF   10 ch.m. Little Wolf – Redgrave Rose (Tug of War) [2002/3 c–, h–: c25d^2 c25g^4 c24s^4 c26d^{pu} Nov 26] leggy, angular mare: poor maiden chaser: stays 25f: acts on firm and soft going: well held only start in blinkers. *K. Bishop*   **c70**
   h–

RED GUARD   9 ch.g. Soviet Star (USA) – Zinzara (USA) (Stage Door Johnny) [2002/3 c110§, h–§: c20m^2 18g^F 19m^5 20d^{pu} c25d^3 c22g^3 c24d^F c24m^F c24m^2 Apr 21] workmanlike gelding: one-time useful hurdler, well held on completed start in 2002/3: fairly useful handicap chaser: won at Huntingdon in January: effective around 2m to 25f: acts on firm and soft going: has worn cheekpieces, including when successful: best held up: often fails to go through with effort and not one to trust. *J. T. Gifford*   **c117 §**
   h– §

RED HALO   4 b.c. Be My Guest (USA) – Pray (IRE) (Priolo (USA)) [2002/3 17d* 16s* 17m^2 16m^{pu} 17m Apr 16] angular colt: fair maiden on Flat (barely stays 1¾m) for R. Hannon: odds on when winning juvenile hurdles at Bangor (2) and Stratford in August: very disappointing last 2 starts, off over 6 months in between: usually front runner (unable to lead final outing). *M. C. Pipe*   **h102**

RED HARE (NZ)   9 ch.g. Famous Star – Mutual Belle (NZ) (Western Bay (NZ)) [2002/3 h88: 22m^F c26m^3 c23g^2 c25g^6 c24m* c25d^{pu} c28g^{pu} c21g^2 Apr 21] compact gelding: winning hurdler: best effort over fences when winning handicap at Taunton in October: sold out of N. Henderson's stable 15,000 gns Doncaster November Sales before next start: form subsequently only when second of 3 finishers in weak novice at Uttoxeter final outing: stays 3m: probably acts on any going: tried blinkered: unreliable. *Miss K. Marks*   **c94 §**
   h– §

RED HOT INDIAN (IRE)   10 b.g. Little Bighorn – Pepper Cannister (Lord Gayle (USA)) [2002/3 c78§, h87§: 18d^6 16d c20d c21d* c17g^F c17m^6 c20g^4 c20d^4 Nov 2] workmanlike gelding: winning hurdler: poor chaser: won handicap at Cartmel in August: stays 21f: acts on heavy and good to firm going: usually blinkered nowadays: often tongue tied: ungenuine. *N. B. Mason*   **c81 §**
   h– §

RED HOT ROBBIE   10 ch.g. Gildoran – Quarry Machine (Laurence O) [2002/3 24g^{pu} 20g^6 22d^3 24s^{pu} Dec 6] winning pointer in Ireland: maiden hurdler, sold out of Miss C. Johnsey's stable 1,250 gns Doncaster September (2001) Sales: best effort when third at Stratford in October: seemingly lame final outing: should stay 3m. *Mrs N. S. Sharpe*   **h81**

REDHOUSE CHEVALIER   4 b.g. Pursuit of Love – Trampolo (USA) (Trempolino (USA)) [2002/3 F16g F16d 18g^{pu} Mar 21] first foal: dam unraced half-sister to fairly useful hurdler Prokofiev, stays 25f: no show in 2 bumpers and juvenile hurdle. *J. R. Adam*   **h–**
   F–

RED HUSTLER (IRE)   7 ch.g. Husyan (USA) – Isoldes Tower (Balliol) [2002/3 h–, F–: c20v^5 c16g^F c16d^2 c16g^3 c16m* Apr 21] workmanlike gelding: modest novice chaser: edged left under pressure when winning at Wetherby in April: best efforts at 2m: acts on good to firm and good to soft going. *C. Grant*   **c92**
   h–

RED JUPITER   6 b.g. Jupiter Island – Glen Dancer (Furry Glen) [2002/3 F–: 20m^6 20g^{pu} 21g 20d^6 22v^6 c20g^{pu} Mar 23] no sign of ability: tried in blinkers/cheekpieces: sold 1,500 gns Doncaster May Sales. *R. C. Guest*   **c–**
   h–

RED KNIGHT (IRE)   5 b. or br.g. Goldmark (USA) – Dafwan (Nashwan (USA)) [2002/3 F18d* F17g Apr 5] rather unfurnished gelding: first foal: dam middle-distance maiden: won bumper at Clonmel on debut: well held in Grade 2 at Aintree following month. *C. Roche, Ireland*   **F95 +**

RED LION (FR) 6 ch.g. Lion Cavern (USA) – Mahogany River (Irish River (FR)) **h95**
[2002/3 16d³ 20v 16g³ 21m⁴ 24g Apr 23] good-topped gelding: fair on Flat (stays 2m) for
B. Meehan: modest novice hurdler: stays 21f: acts on good to firm ground (well held on
heavy): tongue tied last 2 outings. *N. J. Henderson*

RED MAGIC (FR) 5 b. or br.h. Grand Lodge (USA) – Ma Priere (FR) (Highest **h–**
Honor (FR)) [2002/3 16gᵖᵘ Dec 12] useful on Flat at 2 yrs, raced mainly for C. Clement
in USA at 3 yrs, showed little both starts back in Britain in 2002: visored, beaten by
halfway in novice claimer on hurdling debut. *M. C. Pipe*

RED MAIL (USA) 5 b.g. Red Ransom (USA) – Seattle Byline (USA) (Slew City **c–**
Slew (USA)) [2002/3 h–: 16v⁵ 16sᵖᵘ 16s 17g c21d⁵ c20g³ Apr 21] workmanlike gelding: **h–**
poor maiden on Flat: little form over hurdles and fences. *M. A. Barnes*

RED MAN (IRE) 6 ch.g. Toulon – Jamie's Lady (Ashmore (FR)) [2002/3 16d⁵ 21v **h88**
20d Feb 23] IR £25,000 4-y-o: seventh foal: half-brother to useful 2m hurdler Major
Jamie (by Welsh Term) and to several winning pointers: dam won up to 1¾m: fifth, never
a factor, in novice hurdle at Ayr on debut: well held in similar events both subsequent
starts. *M. Todhunter*

RED MARAUDER 13 ch.g. Gunner B – Cover Your Money (Precipice Wood) [2002/3 **c–**
24s⁴ Feb 24] rangy gelding: winning hurdler: smart handicap chaser: won 2001 Martell **h113**
Grand National at Aintree: first run since, shaped as if retaining plenty of ability when
never-dangerous fourth in handicap hurdle at Newcastle (not given at all a hard time,
reported to have gurgled): effective at 2½m and apparently stayed 4½m: acted on heavy
going, probably on good to firm: reportedly retired. *R. C. Guest*

RED MARSALA 5 b.g. Roselier (FR) – Radical Lady (Radical) [2002/3 F16d Mar 6] **F– p**
fifth foal: half-brother to useful staying hurdler Tyneandthyneagain (by Good Thyne) and
winning chaser up to 3¼m Sabi Sand (by Minster Son): dam fairly useful staying chaser:
shaped as if outing was needed when seventh of 12 in bumper at Wetherby on debut:
should do better. *R. C. Guest*

RED MINSTER 6 b.g. Minster Son – Minty Muncher (Idiot's Delight) [2002/3 h–: **c87**
22g c16s c16v³ c16v⁴ c24dᵖᵘ c20s³ c25d³ Mar 6] sturdy, lengthy gelding: no form over **h–**
hurdles: modest form over fences, making all in novice handicap at Newcastle in January:
stays 2½m: acts on heavy going: wears cheekpieces: sold 3,500 gns Doncaster May Sales.
R. C. Guest

REDMIRE 9 b.m. Nomadic Way (USA) – Decent Sort (Decent Fellow) [2002/3 c70: **c–**
c25d May 4] modest pointer: well held in hunter in May. *Miss V. J. Parvin*

RED NECK 12 ch.g. Nishapour (FR) – Roda Haxan (Huntercombe) [2002/3 c84, h–: **c93**
c24g² c19g⁵ c24mᵖᵘ Apr 22] stocky gelding: fair hunter chaser: stays 3m: acts on soft and **h–**
good to firm going: tongue tied: has looked difficult ride. *John Moore*

RED NOSE LADY 6 b.m. Teenoso (USA) – Red Rambler (Rymer) [2002/3 F84: **h87 §**
F16drᵘ 20m⁵ 20v⁴ 20s⁶ 20vᵖᵘ Dec 26] lengthy mare: has scope: modest in bumpers, hung **F–**
badly left on reappearance: best effort over hurdles when fourth in novice at Hexham in
November: stays 2½m: possibly best on soft/heavy going: ungenuine. *J. M. Jefferson*

RED OASSIS 12 ch.g. Rymer – Heron's Mirage (Grey Mirage) [2002/3 c77, h–: c20v⁵ **c74**
c16d⁴ c20gᵘʳ c16d* Mar 19] compact gelding: poor handicap chaser: won 3-runner race **h–**
at Chepstow in March: best form at 2m: acts on heavy going. *M. J. M. Evans*

REDOUBLE 7 b.g. First Trump – Sunflower Seed (Mummy's Pet) [2002/3 h78: 21f² **h83 §**
20s⁵ 20m⁴ 22g 22m 19f⁴ 20g⁴ 19m⁴ 20v⁴ 19s⁵ 21g⁵ 21m Mar 31] compact gelding: poor
maiden hurdler: sold out of B. R. Millman's stable 5,000 gns Ascot July Sales after fourth
start: stays 21f: acts on firm and soft going: effective blinkered/visored or not, also tried
in cheekpieces: has had tongue tied: not one to trust. *E. L. James*

RED PERK (IRE) 6 b.g. Executive Perk – Supreme View (Supreme Leader) [2002/3 **h61 +**
F–: 20m⁵ 26g² Sep 8] first sign of ability when remote second of 6 in novice hurdle at **F–**
Southwell in September. *N. B. Mason*

RED RAJA 10 b.g. Persian Heights – Jenny Splendid (John Splendid) [2002/3 c16dᵖᵘ **c–**
c16g³ c16d Apr 9] close-coupled gelding: one-time useful hurdler: no sign of retaining **h–**
ability in chases: left C. Cox after first start, has rejoined him. *H. J. Manners*

RED RAMPAGE 8 b.g. King's Ride – Mighty Fly (Comedy Star (USA)) [2002/3 **c101**
c90, h75: c21g⁵ c20vᶜᵒ c20v³ c25vᶠ c24s* c33vᵖᵘ c24vᶜᵒ c30d³ c26s* c31gᵖᵘ Apr 24] **h–**
poor maiden hurdler: modest handicap chaser: won at Newcastle (amateurs, made all) in
December and Carlisle in March, idling at latter course: seems to stay 3¾m (exhausted

when pulled up over 33f): acts on heavy and good to firm going: blinkered/visored: usually tongue tied: has carried head awkwardly/wandered under pressure. *R. C. Guest*

RED REBEL 11 gr.g. Scallywag – Little Red Flower (Blakeney) [2002/3 c–§: c24m* c24g[F] c16d* c19g Apr 2] fair hunter chaser: won at Huntingdon (despite idling) in May and Leicester in March: won point in April: effective at 2m to 3¼m: acts on soft and good to firm going: unreliable (has refused). *Mrs Caroline Bailey* — **c99 §**

RED RETURN (IRE) 6 ch.g. Bob's Return (IRE) – Kerrie's Pearl (Proverb) [2002/3 F16m⁵ F16g Sep 15] eleventh foal: dam unraced half-sister to very smart Irish staying chaser Garamycin: modest form on first of 2 starts in bumpers. *L. A. Dace* — **F78**

RED ROONEY 4 b.g. Astronef – Mica Male (ITY) (Law Society (USA)) [2002/3 16d[pu] Jan 18] little form on Flat: no show in juvenile hurdle. *P. Butler* — **h–**

REDSKIN RAIDER (IRE) 7 b.g. Commanche Run – Sheltered (IRE) (Strong Gale) [2002/3 h101, F–: c23s[pu] Jan 29] lengthy gelding: fair maiden hurdler: pulled up, reportedly distressed, in maiden at Leicester on chasing debut (withdrawn on veterinary advice on intended reappearance): should stay 3m: best effort on good to firm going. *T. R. George* — **c–** **h–**

RED SOCIALITE (IRE) 6 ch.g. Moscow Society (USA) – Dees Darling (IRE) (King Persian) [2002/3 F84p: 17v⁴ 21s 21m* Mar 21] angular gelding: much improved effort over hurdles (not knocked about on much softer ground first 2 starts) when winning maiden at Newbury by 3½ lengths from Mounsey Castle, smooth run to lead after 2 out and ridden clear: capable of better again. *D. R. Gandolfo* — **h107 p**

RED SQUARE DAWN 7 b.m. Derrylin – Raise The Dawn (Rymer) [2002/3 h74: 25g 20g 20s² 20m 20m² 21m 22m⁵ 20g³ Apr 21] smallish mare: poor maiden hurdler: stays 2¾m: acts on firm and soft going: usually blinkered/visored: prone to mistakes: none too consistent (has looked none too keen). *Mrs L. Williamson* — **h68**

RED SQUARE ICE 8 b.g. Scallywag – Arctic Rymes (Rymer) [2002/3 22s 21d⁶ Nov 25] 3,600 5-y-o: strong gelding: third foal: half-brother to poor chaser Ice Cube (by Rakaposhi King), stays 21f: dam winning pointer: better effort in novice company over hurdles when sixth at Ludlow, not knocked about. *G. Barnett* — **h69 +**

RED SQUARE ISLAND 8 ch.g. Jupiter Island – Queen of The Nile (Hittite Glory) [2002/3 h–: 16g[pu] May 11] no form over hurdles: tried blinkered: sold 600 gns Doncaster May Sales. *Mrs L. Williamson* — **h–**

RED SQUARE KING 5 ch.g. Sure Blade (USA) – Patscilla (Squill (USA)) [2002/3 h–: 16d⁵ 16g 17m⁵ 21f[pu] Oct 24] little sign of ability. *Mrs L. Williamson* — **h–**

RED SQUARE MAN (IRE) 8 b.g. Rashar (USA) – November Tide (Laurence O) [2002/3 17m⁴ 17d[pu] 16m⁶ 20s⁶ 17d³ 16s[pu] Jan 3] tall gelding: temperamental maiden hurdler. *Mrs L. Williamson* — **h– §**

RED STRANGER (FR) 6 b.g. Le Balafre (FR) – Abeille Royale (USA) (Turn To Mars (USA)) [2002/3 h§§, F86§: 25g[pu] Apr 29] rather leggy gelding: thoroughly ungenuine maiden hurdler: tried visored: has had tongue tied. *M. C. Pipe* — **h§§**

RED STRIKER 9 ch.g. Gunner B – Cover Your Money (Precipice Wood) [2002/3 c142, h–: c20d⁵ c26g c20v² c20d² c36d[ur] Apr 5] workmanlike gelding: useful handicap chaser: good efforts when runner-up at Ayr (beaten 1½ lengths by A Piece of Cake) in January and Haydock (6 lengths behind Goguenard) in March: should stay 3¼m: best form on going softer than good (acts on heavy): tongue tied: patiently ridden. *R. C. Guest* — **c144** **h–**

RED SUN 6 b.g. Foxhound (USA) – Superetta (Superlative) [2002/3 h100: 16g² 17g* 17m⁶ 16m² 16m³ 19s* 17s 17g⁴ 19m³ Apr 21] small, leggy gelding: fair hurdler: won novice at Market Rasen in June and handicap at Doncaster (first outing after leaving A. Streeter) in December: stays 19f: acts on soft and good to firm going. *J. Mackie* — **h108**

RED TYRANT 5 b.g. Minster Son – By The Lake (Tyrant (USA)) [2002/3 F16d⁵ F16s F16v F16d⁶ 20g 16g³ 20g⁴ Apr 14] lengthy gelding: ninth foal: half-brother to fair chaser Jokers Charm (by Idiot's Delight), stays 3m, and to modest hurdler Southend Scallywag (by Tina's Pet), stays 2½m: dam poor staying maiden: fair form at best in bumpers: poor form in novice hurdles: will probably stay 3m. *R. C. Guest* — **h81** **F87**

RED UNO (IRE) 6 ch.g. Executive Perk – Hogan's Cherry (General Ironside) [2002/3 F16g F17d Nov 24] half-brother to winning pointers by Le Moss and Lancastrian: dam unraced, from family of useful chaser Cherrynut: tongue tied, little sign of ability in 2 bumpers: sold 2,200 gns Doncaster May Sales. *N. B. Mason* — **F–**

REDUSKI 8 b.g. Thethingaboutitis (USA) – Call Me Daisy (Callernish) [2002/3 22g^pu h–
16d^5 16s 25d^pu 17d Aug 4] dipped-backed gelding: third foal: dam behind in novice
hurdles: no worthwhile form over hurdles. *A. J. Deakin*

RED WILL DANAGHER (IRE) 6 b.g. Glacial Storm (USA) – Clodas Pet (IRE) h88 §
(Andretti) [2002/3 22d^pu 20s 20v^2 20v Feb 13] IR 6,000 4-y-o: workmanlike gelding:
second foal: dam 17f hurdle/point winner: runner-up once from 4 starts in maiden Irish
points in 2002: form over hurdles only when second to Tana River in novice at Leicester
in January: temperamental display following month: one to treat with caution. *John Allen*

RED WINE 4 b.g. Hamas (IRE) – Red Bouquet (Reference Point) [2002/3 16s^3 16d* h123
17g Mar 13] angular gelding: useful on Flat (stays 1½m), successful on 5 occasions in
2002 including in November Handicap: fairly useful form in juvenile hurdles: won at
Newbury in February by 8 lengths from Indien Royal: ninth of 27 to Spectroscope in
Triumph Hurdle at Cheltenham following month. *J. A. Osborne*

REDWOOD GROVE (USA) 7 b.g. Woodman (USA) – Ikebana (IRE) (Sadler's c–
Wells (USA)) [2002/3 c–, h104d: 24g^pu 16s^4 16d 20v 16s 24d^pu Feb 23] tall, useful- h– §
looking gelding: not fluent and no show in 2 novice chases: handicap hurdler, has lost his
form: left N. Gaselee after second start: stays 2¾m: acts on good to firm and heavy going:
tried blinkered: has had tongue tied: far from keen. *Miss G. Browne*

REEL DANCER 6 b.g. Minshaanshu Amad (USA) – Sister Rosarii (USA) (Proper- h80
antes (USA)) [2002/3 F98: 20s^2 16v^6 Feb 13] sturdy gelding: fairly useful in bumpers:
well beaten in 2 novice hurdles, distant second of 3 finishers in conditional jockeys event
at Folkestone. *B. De Haan*

REEL HANDSOME 11 ch.g. Handsome Sailor – Reel Chance (Proverb) [2002/3 c71
c75: c16m^3 c17m c16g c21m^4 c22g^3 c17g^2 c17d^4 c21v^pu c20m^ur Mar 18] big, lengthy
gelding: poor maiden chaser: effective at 2m to 2¾m: acts on good to firm and heavy
going: tongue tied. *C. T. Pogson*

REFLECTIVE WAY 10 ch.m. Mirror Boy – Craigie Way (Palm Track) [2002/3 c77, c84
h–: c25g* c24d* c25m^pu Jun 21] tongue tied, no show only outing over hurdles: poor h–
chaser: won novices at Hexham (handicap) in May and Perth in June: pulled up as if
amiss final outing: stays 3¼m: probably acts on soft going. *A. C. Whillans*

REFLEX BLUE 6 b.g. Ezzoud (IRE) – Briggsmaid (Elegant Air) [2002/3 h74: 16g^2 h81 §
17m^3 21f^3 21f^4 19s^4 Nov 21] angular gelding: poor maiden hurdler: stays easy 21f: acts
on firm going: visored: temperamental. *R. J. Price*

REFLEX COURIER (IRE) 11 b.g. Over The River (FR) – Thornpark Lady c91
(Mandalus) [2002/3 c89: c22s^pu c22d^4 c24s* c24v^3 c23g^5 c24d Mar 15] good-bodied
gelding: modest handicap chaser: won at Haydock in November, idling run-in: stays 25f:
raced on good going or softer (acts on heavy). *John R. Upson*

REFLEX REACTION (IRE) 8 b.g. Arapahos (FR) – Beswick Paper Lady (Giolla c–
Mear) [2002/3 c–, h63: c26m^pu 26m^pu Jul 19] tall gelding: maiden hurdler: no form over h–
fences: should stay 3m: acts on good to firm going. *John R. Upson*

REGAL ALI (IRE) 4 ch.g. Ali-Royal (IRE) – Depeche (FR) (Kings Lake (USA)) h–
[2002/3 16v 17g^pu 17f Apr 3] poor maiden on Flat (barely stays 1¾m): showed nothing
over hurdles, left John Berry after debut. *G. A. Ham*

REGAL APPLAUSE 4 b.f. Royal Applause – Panchellita (USA) (Pancho Villa h–
(USA)) [2002/3 17s 18d Dec 10] no sign of ability on Flat, sold out of G. L. Moore's
stable £1,800 Ascot August Sales: well held in 2 juvenile hurdles. *M. R. Hoad*

REGAL CHANCE 10 b.g. Cisto (FR) – Regal Flutter (Henry The Seventh) [2002/3 c89
c19d^F c19s^pu c16v^2 c19d c16s c20g* Mar 2] good-bodied gelding: once-raced hurdler: h–
modest chaser: won handicap at Huntingdon in March: stays 2½m: acts on heavy going:
reportedly broke blood vessel on reappearance. *A. King*

REGAL EXIT (FR) 7 ch.g. Exit To Nowhere (USA) – Regalante (Gairloch) [2002/3 c124
h120: c16g* c16s^2 16g c19d^4 c21g c16g^pu Apr 3] good-topped gelding: shows traces of h120
stringhalt: useful hurdler at best: fairly useful novice chaser: won at Ludlow in December
and Doncaster in March: probably stays 21f: acts on good to firm and heavy going: jumps
fences soundly: has found little. *N. J. Henderson*

REGAL GALE (IRE) 9 b.g. Strong Gale – Diklers Queen (IRE) (The Parson) [2002/3 c–
c21d^pu Oct 31] useful-looking gelding: fair form at best in novice hurdles: pulled up in 2 h–
novice chases, reportedly having breathing problem on both occasions: winning pointer
in between: should stay 3m: raced on good going or softer. *J. Wade*

Tattersalls (Ireland) European Breeders Fund Mares' Novices' Chase, Uttoxeter—
Regal Holly and Noel Fehily make all

REGAL HOLLY 8 b.m. Gildoran – Pusey Street (Native Bazaar) [2002/3 h102: **c115**
c21d² c25d* c22s² c24v² c20g² c21s* Mar 15] angular mare: winning hurdler: fairly use- **h–**
ful chaser: won mares events at Folkestone (maiden, easily) in December and Uttoxeter
(valuable novice handicap, made all to beat Kentford Fern a length) in March: stays 25f:
raced on good going or softer over jumps (acts on heavy): sometimes blinkered, including
last 5 starts. *C. J. Mann*

REGAL HYMN 8 b.g. Regal Embers (IRE) – It's Only Her (French Marny) [2002/3 **h–**
21f^{pu} May 11] fourth foal: dam unraced half-sister to fairly useful staying chaser Late
Night Extra: showed nothing in novice hurdle on debut: pulled up in point in February.
Mrs Barbara Waring

REGAL LIGHT 8 gr.g. Gran Alba (USA) – Light of Zion (Pieces of Eight) [2002/3 **h–**
19d 20v^{pu} 19d^{pu} 20m⁶ Apr 12] strong gelding: sixth foal: half-brother to winning hurdler/
chaser Artful Arthur (by Rolfe) and winning staying hurdler Its Grand (by Sula Bula):
dam poor plater on Flat and over hurdles: little show in novice hurdles. *J. C. Tuck*

REGAL RIVER (IRE) 6 b.g. Over The River (FR) – My Friend Fashion (Laurence **c93**
O) [2002/3 h73: c20s^F c26v² c24v³ c23v* c26s^{pu} Jan 23] close-coupled gelding: winning **h–**
hurdler: modest chaser: won novice handicap at Leicester in January despite numerous
minor mistakes: ran in snatches at Warwick final start (reportedly choked): will prove
best at 3m+: raced on good going or softer (acts on heavy). *John R. Upson*

REGAL STATESMAN (NZ) 10 br.g. Vice Regal (NZ) – Hykit (NZ) (Swinging **c–**
Junior) [2002/3 c–, h89§: 20m⁴ c17g⁴ c24d c20m⁵ Mar 23] rangy gelding: modest hurd- **h89 §**
ler: little worthwhile form over fences: stays 25f when conditions aren't testing: acts on
firm ground, unsuited by softer than good: has found nothing: one to treat with caution.
O. Brennan

REGAL TERM (IRE) 5 b.g. Welsh Term – Regal Hostess (King's Ride) [2002/3 **F–**
F16s Jan 3] IR £8,500 3-y-o: fifth foal: half-brother to 2m hurdle winner Ithastobesaid
(by Lanfranco) and fair hurdler/chaser Star of Caulry (by Grand Plaisir): stayed 3m: dam
unraced: reportedly finished lame when well held in bumper on debut. *R. Dickin*

737

*Bewley Hotels & EBF National Hunt Fillies Championship Bumper, Punchestown—
the word championship can scarcely have been more ill-used
as Reine des Reines (in front) wins this extravagant prize*

REGAL TRIBUTE 5 b.g. Tragic Role (USA) – Hushlet (Governor General) [2002/3
F16d F16g Mar 23] first foal: dam unraced half-sister to very smart 2m hurdler Shadow
Leader: tailed off in 2 bumpers: sold 600 gns Doncaster May Sales. *R. C. Guest* **F—**

REGAL VISION (IRE) 6 b.g. Emperor Jones (USA) – Shining Eyes (USA) (Mr
Prospector (USA)) [2002/3 h100: 19g⁵ 19s⁴ 24g⁶ 21g⁴ 20g Apr 2] leggy gelding: modest
handicap hurdler: stays 2¾m: acts on good to firm going, probably on soft: usually
blinkered; sometimes races freely/shows little interest: none too reliable. *C. G. Cox* **h97 §**

REGARDEZ-MOI 6 b.m. Distinctly North (USA) – Tomard (Thatching) [2002/3
17v⁶ 17d^bd 19d⁵ 17d⁶ 22m⁶ 19m⁶ 17g⁵ Apr 19] disappointing maiden on Flat, sold out of
A. Carroll's stable 500 gns Doncaster September (2001) Sales: poor novice hurdler: may
prove best around 2m. *Miss M. Bragg* **h62**

REGAR (IRE) 11 b.g. Buckskin (FR) – Pass Thurn (Trimmingham) [2002/3 c20d^F
c20m^ur c20m² Jun 1] modest form when second at Hexham on completed start in hunter
chases: tried blinkered. *Brian McNichol* **c82
h—**

REGENCY RED (IRE) 5 ch.g. Dolphin Street (FR) – Future Romance (Distant
Relative) [2002/3 20d³ 16s Nov 2] modest on Flat (seems suited by 2m), left M. Usher
prior to winning seller in August: third of 6 in novice at Perth on hurdling debut: twice
ran badly on Flat before disappointing in novice seller. *R. Ford* **h89**

REGENTS WALK (IRE) 5 b.g. Phardante (FR) – Raw Courage (IRE) (The Parson)
[2002/3 F16m³ Mar 18] €5,500 4-y-o: fourth foal: dam winning pointer: looked green
under pressure when third to Dark Character in maiden bumper at Southwell on debut.
B. De Haan **F91**

738

REGGAE RHYTHM (IRE)   9 b.g. Be My Native (USA) – Invery Lady (Sharpen Up) [2002/3 c–, h105: 18m 17s⁵ 19s 21sᵖᵘ 16g² 20mᵖᵘ Apr 12] angular gelding: maiden chaser: winning hurdler, on the downgrade: left N. Chance after reappearance: stays 2½m: acts on heavy going: wore cheekpieces last 3 starts: not a fluent jumper. *R. N. Bevis*   **c–** **h74**

REGGIE BUCK (USA)   9 b. or br.g. Alleged (USA) – Hello Memphis (USA) (Super Concorde (USA)) [2002/3 h110: 17g 17s⁶ 17d⁶ 16m⁵ 16v⁶ 16s 16d 17m³ Apr 5] angular gelding: fair handicap hurdler at best: largely out of sorts in 2002/3: best around 2m: acts on soft and good to firm going: tried blinkered. *J. Mackie*   **h94**

REIGN DANCE   12 ch.g. Kinglet – Gay Criselle (Decoy Boy) [2002/3 c–: c25mᵖᵘ May 22] lengthy gelding: winning hunter chaser: retains little ability: has broken blood vessels. *Mrs D. H. McCarthy*   **c–**

REINE DES REINES (IRE)   5 b.m. Supreme Leader – La Grande Dame (Niniski (USA)) [2002/3 F16m⁵ Apr 21] 15,000 4-y-o, resold €27,000: lengthy mare: eighth foal: half-sister to fair hurdler/chaser Conagher Boy (by Le Moss) and fair hurdler We Three (by Brush Aside), both stay 21f: dam winning hurdler, stayed 2½m: better effort in bumpers when winning Bewleys Hotels And EBF National Hunt Fillies Championship Bumper at Punchestown in late-April by length from Deanery Nellie: will stay at least 2½m. *J. E. Kiely, Ireland*   **F90**

REISK SUPERMAN (IRE)   5 b.g. Naheez (USA) – Forward Gal (The Parson) [2002/3 F16m⁶ Apr 22] €16,000 4-y-o: fifth foal: half-brother to a winning pointer by Supreme Leader: dam winning pointer/hunter chaser: better effort in bumpers (in need of experience on debut) when sixth to Kim Fontaine at Punchestown in early-May. *Paul A. Roche, Ireland*   **F97**

REIVERS MOON   4 b. or br.f. Midnight Legend – Here Comes Tibby (Royal Fountain) [2002/3 F14d F17g* F17g⁶ Apr 21] smallish, leggy filly: third foal: dam poor hurdler/chaser, stayed 2¾m: modest form in bumpers, won at Carlisle in March by 7 lengths from River Mist. *W. Amos*   **F83**

RELATIVE DELIGHT   5 b.m. Distant Relative – Pasja (IRE) (Posen (USA)) [2002/3 h–: 16s 19s 17s Dec 26] leggy mare: little worthwhile form on Flat and over hurdles: has worn cheekpieces: sold 500 gns Doncaster January Sales. *John A. Harris*   **h–**

RELIANCE LEADER   7 ch.g. Weld – Swift Messenger (Giolla Mear) [2002/3 h–: 20vᵖᵘ 21m 22g Apr 12] strong gelding: no sign of ability over hurdles or in point. *D. L. Williams*   **h–**

RELIGIOUS LASS (IRE)   5 b.m. Religiously (USA) – Carolin Lass (IRE) (Carlingford Castle) [2002/3 20m⁶ Oct 4] second foal: dam unraced, from family of top-class staying chaser Brown Chamberlin: well held in bumper and 2 novice hurdles. *C. S. McKeever, Ireland*   **h–**

REMEMBER STAR   10 ch.m. Don't Forget Me – Star Girl Gay (Lord Gayle (USA)) [2002/3 c66, h75: 17g c21gᵖᵘ 16g 16m Jul 24] angular mare: winning hurdler/chaser: no form in 2002/3: has has tongue tied: has won 5 times at Exeter. *A. D. Smith*   **c–** **h–**

REMINGTON (IRE)   5 ch.g. Indian Ridge – Sea Harrier (Grundy) [2002/3 F78: F16m⁵ F16s 16g³ 16g² Mar 16] smallish gelding: modest in bumpers: placed over hurdles at Ludlow in February and maiden (second to Unleash) in March: likely to stay 2½m. *Mrs A. M. Thorpe*   **h100** **F78**

RENALOO (IRE)   8 gr.g. Tremblant – Rare Flower (Decent Fellow) [2002/3 c65, h–: c20d⁵ c20d⁵ c16d² c16s* c16vᶠ c18s³ c18s³ c16g* c19fᵖᵘ Mar 24] workmanlike gelding: modest handicap chaser: won at Folkestone in January (novice) and March (made all): probably best around 2m: acts on soft going: has found little and not one to trust. *R. Rowe*   **c85 §** **h–**

RENZO (IRE)   10 b.g. Alzao (USA) – Watership (USA) (Foolish Pleasure (USA)) [2002/3 h101§: 16d⁴ 19m* 19d 16s⁴ 19s Dec 26] good-topped gelding: fair handicap hurdler: made all under good ride from P. Flynn at Market Rasen in June: poor efforts last 3 starts: likely to stay beyond 19f: acts on soft and good to firm ground: jumps none too fluently: carries head high: ungenuine. *John A. Harris*   **h103 §**

REPLACEMENT PET (IRE)   6 b.m. Petardia – Richardstown Lass (IRE) (Muscatite) [2002/3 17g Jun 10] poor on Flat (stays 1¼m): pulled hard when tailed off in novice on hurdling debut. *H. S. Howe*   **h–**

REPULSE BAY (IRE)   5 b.g. Barathea (IRE) – Bourbon Topsy (Ile de Bourbon (USA)) [2002/3 h–: 16g 16d Mar 7] good-bodied gelding: modest and untrustworthy maiden on Flat (stays 1¼m): no worthwhile form over hurdles: has had tongue tied. *J. S. Goldie*   **h–**

REPUNZEL 8 b.m. Carlingford Castle – Hi-Rise Lady (Sunyboy) [2002/3 c80, h83: **c84** c17s^F c16d c17v* c18s^5 c16g^2 Mar 14] tall mare: poor hurdler/chaser: won novice handi- **h–** cap chase at Plumpton (all 3 wins there) in January, blundering last and idling: should stay beyond 17f: yet to race on firm going, acts on any other: inconsistent. *N. A. Gaselee*

REPUTE 5 b.g. Unfuwain (USA) – Someone Special (Habitat) [2002/3 F16v F16d **F–** F16d Mar 1] 170,000Y, 6,800 3-y-o: half-brother to several winners, including very smart 7f to 1¼m winner One So Wonderful (by Nashwan) and Relatively Special (by Alzao), smart up to 1¼m: dam, 7f winner who stayed 1m, half-sister to top-class miler Milligram, from family of smart 2m to 3m hurdler Her Honour: well held in 3 bumpers: tongue tied final start. *G. A. Swinbank*

REQUESTOR 8 br.g. Distinctly North (USA) – Bebe Altesse (GER) (Alpenkonig **h90** (GER) [2002/3 16v 16d 20g^4 20d^6 20g* Apr 1] half-brother to useful hurdler/fair chaser Angelo's Double (by M Double M), stayed 25f: fair at best on Flat (stays 9f): tongue tied, improved effort over hurdles when winning conditional jockeys selling handicap at Newcastle in April: stays 2½m. *T. J. Fitzgerald*

RESCATOR (FR) 7 b.g. Saint Estephe (FR) – La Narquoise (FR) (Al Nasr (FR)) **h84** [2002/3 23d^6 21g^6 20d^4 19g^3 Apr 19] workmanlike gelding: type to make a chaser: won once from 6 starts in points in 2002 for D. Pipe: poor maiden hurdler: lame final start: stays 21f: acts on soft going: has looked temperamental. *Mrs S. J. Smith*

RESCINDO (IRE) 4 b.g. Revoque (IRE) – Mystic Dispute (IRE) (Magical Strike **h100** (USA)) [2002/3 16d^2 16g^2 17f^4 Apr 3] medium-sized gelding: well beaten in maidens at 2 yrs for N. Littmoden: fair form when runner-up first 2 starts over hurdles: saddle slipped on final one. *M. C. Pipe*

RESEARCHER 4 ch.f. Cosmonaut – Rest (Dance In Time (CAN)) [2002/3 16d^6 17s^2 **h93** 16s^2 16g^6 Mar 14] fair on Flat (stays 1½m), sold out of R. Beckett's stable 11,500 gns Doncaster August Sales: modest juvenile hurdler: second at Southwell and Folkestone (mares novice) in January: acts on soft going: found little final start. *Miss Venetia Williams*

RESEDA (IRE) 6 b.g. Rock Hopper – Sweet Mignonette (Tina's Pet) [2002/3 F17f* **F99** F16m* Jun 3] first foal: dam, fairly useful 2m hurdler, half-sister to useful 2m hurdler Cardinal Flower: sold unraced out of Mrs M. Reveley's stable 11,500 gns Doncaster May (2001) Sales: created good impression when winning bumpers at Exeter (maiden, drifted badly left late on) in May and Huntingdon (beat Coleham 3 lengths) in June. *R. T. Phillips*

RESISTANCE (IRE) 6 br.g. Phardante (FR) – Shean Hill (IRE) (Bar Dexter (USA)) **h84** [2002/3 h–, F95: 19d^4 20v^F 17d^6 Dec 19] lengthy gelding: bumper winner: poor novice hurdler: seems to stay 19f. *G. A. Ham*

RESSOURCE (FR) 4 b.c. Broadway Flyer (USA) – Rayonne (Sadler's Wells (USA)) **h89** [2002/3 16d 16s^5 17s^4 17s^2 16v^F4 16s^3 16g 16s^6 Mar 10] leggy colt: well held on Flat in France (for A. Spanu) and on British debut: modest juvenile hurdler: raced around 2m: probably suited by going softer than good (acts on heavy): looked none too keen final outing. *G. L. Moore*

RESTLESS WIND (IRE) 11 b.g. Celio Rufo – Trulos (Three Dons) [2002/3 c98+: **c109** c23g^4 c24d^4 c24d^3 c27s^5 c25m^2 c24m* Apr 21] lengthy chaser: fair handicap chaser: won at Kempton in November and Huntingdon in April: stays 25f: acts on soft and good to firm going: patiently ridden, and sometimes finds less than expected. *G. B. Balding*

RET FREM (IRE) 10 b.g. Posen (USA) – New Light (Reform) [2002/3 c63x, h–: **c– x** c24g^2 May 8] sturdy gelding: poor hurdler/maiden chaser: distant second in novice chase **h–** at Fakenham in May: probably stays 3m: acts on soft and firm going: tried visored: makes mistakes. *A. G. Blackmore*

RETURNING 7 b.m. Bob's Return (IRE) – Buck Comtess (USA) (Spend A Buck **c116** (USA)) [2002/3 c125, h–: c16d^4 c20s^3 21d^pu Jan 18] tall mare: usually looks well: **h–** winning hurdler: fairly useful chaser, not so good in 2002/3: stays 2½m: acts on any going: usually jumps well. *Miss H. C. Knight*

RETURN THE CALL (IRE) 6 b.g. Bob Back (USA) – Ring Four (IRE) (Supreme **h–** Leader) [2002/3 F–: 22m Oct 27] well held in bumper and novice hurdle: won maiden point in March. *Miss H. C. Knight*

REVELINO (IRE) 4 b.g. Revoque (IRE) – Forelino (USA) (Trempolino (USA)) **h73** [2002/3 16d 16d 17g^4 Mar 17] useful-looking gelding: half-brother to fair hurdler around 2m Prince Among Men (by Robellino) and one-time useful hurdler up to 2½m Tough Act (by Be My Chief), became temperamental: fairly useful on Flat (stays 1¼m), sold out of

E. Dunlop's stable 26,000 gns Newmarket Autumn Sales: disappointing in 3 juvenile hurdles, again finding little when last of 4 finishers at Hereford final start. *Miss S. J. Wilton*

REVERSE CHARGE 11 b.g. Teenoso (USA) – Ebb And Flo (Forlorn River) [2002/3 **c88** c84, h112: 22s c25s³ c33vᵖᵘ c25v³ c24vᶠ 23s Feb 8] lengthy gelding: fair hurdler, well **h–** held in 2002/3: modest maiden chaser: probably stays 3¼m: acts on good to firm and heavy going: wore cheekpieces third start, visored last 2: tongue tied fourth appearance. *C. Grant*

REVERSE SWING 6 b.m. Charmer – Milly Kelly (Murrayfield) [2002/3 h–: 17m⁵ **h77** 17m 20g⁵ 16d* 16gᶠ 17d 16m 16m⁶ Apr 21] good-topped mare: poor hurdler: left Mrs P. Sly, won mares novice handicap at Wincanton in November: may prove best around 2m: acts on good to soft going: races keenly. *Mrs H. Dalton*

REVIEWER (IRE) 5 b.g. Sadler's Wells (USA) – Clandestina (USA) (Secretariat **h121** (USA)) [2002/3 h122: 17s 16d³ 16d² 16m Mar 22] neat gelding: fairly useful handicap hurdler: easily best effort in 2002/3 when second to Do L'Enfant d'Eau at Newbury in March: will stay 2½m: acts on soft going. *H. Morrison*

REVITALIZE 5 b.g. Lion Cavern (USA) – Belle Et Deluree (USA) (The Minstrel **h69** (CAN)) [2002/3 16v 19d 17d⁴ 16m⁶ 20sᵖᵘ 18d Nov 7] leggy gelding: maiden hurdler, only poor form in 2002/3: raced mainly around 2m: acts on heavy going: tried visored/ blinkered. *D. G. McArdle, Ireland*

REYNOLDS HOUSE (IRE) 9 br.g. Glacial Storm (USA) – Lucky House (Pollerton) **c–** [2002/3 h–: 17gᵖᵘ c16sᵖᵘ Jan 14] strong gelding: of little account: tried blinkered: sold **h–** £550 Ascot February Sales. *A. E. Jessop*

RHAPSODY IN BLUE (IRE) 8 b.g. Magical Strike (USA) – Palace Blue (IRE) **c70** (Dara Monarch) [2002/3 c61, h72: c21dᶠ 20v* c24g² c24s Mar 2] good-topped gelding: **h92** poor handicap chaser: modest handicap hurdler: easily won conditional jockeys event at Newcastle in January: stays 3m: acts on any going: tongue tied. *R. Ford*

RHEINDROSS (IRE) 8 gr.g. Ala Hounak – Ardcarn Girl (Ardross) [2002/3 c22v² **c111** c24s⁶ c20s² c21v* c16v⁴ c20s² c21v³ Mar 2] fair handicap chaser: won at Leopardstown in December: stays 2¾m: raced on ground softer than good (acts on heavy): usually held up: refused to race once. *A. L. T. Moore, Ireland*

RHETORIC (IRE) 4 b.g. Desert King (IRE) – Squaw Talk (USA) (Gulch (USA)) **h63** [2002/3 16m⁶ 16d 17sᵖᵘ 16s⁶ 26sᵖᵘ 24f⁴ 21m Apr 19] angular gelding: modest maiden on Flat (should stay 1½m), sold out of J. Gosden's stable 7,500 gns Newmarket July Sales: poor novice hurdler: stays easy 3m: acts on firm going: tongue tied once. *D. G. Bridgwater*

RHINESTONE COWBOY (IRE) 7 b.g. Be My Native (USA) – Monumental **h156 p** Gesture (Head For Heights) [2002/3 F123: F16d* 16d* 17d* 16d* 16d* 16g³ **F123** Mar 11]

What would Rhinestone Cowboy find off the bridle? During the latest season, this question must have been asked more often than any other. When one, two, three and then four 'races' over timber all failed to provide the answer, Rhinestone Cowboy was made favourite for the Champion Hurdle. 'We won't ever be able to replace him,' had been Aidan O'Brien's fair tribute on the retirement of Istabraq, but, if the betting for the first Champion Hurdle in a post-Istabraq era was to be believed, the next major force in hurdling, if not quite Istabraq's replacement, was a horse that had not long ago resided in O'Brien's own stables. In a former incarnation Rhinestone Cowboy had been a lead horse on the gallops at Ballydoyle, but allowed to do the pursuing rather than the pace-setting by his new stable, first in bumpers and then as a hurdler, he became National Hunt racing's hottest prospect. The likes of

Betfair Open Bumper, Cheltenham— amateur-ridden Rhinestone Cowboy starts off his season beating subsequent Champion Bumper winner Liberman

Rooster Booster and Intersky Falcon could mop up as many races as they liked but, when they all turned up at Cheltenham in March, it was Rhinestone Cowboy who appeared to many observers likely to provide the star material.

There were two highly persuasive factors that helped to create Rhinestone Cowboy's exalted status. Firstly, it was already known that he was a very good horse after his second in the Champion Bumper at Cheltenham in 2002, a race he looked particularly unlucky not to win both on the track and in the stewards' room. Secondly, he had given the unmistakeable impression of being potentially a very good horse indeed over hurdles. A maiden at Newbury in November and novice events at Cheltenham in December and Wetherby in February all fell to him with what might be described as the minimum of fuss, were it not that he plummeted to odds of 6/1 for the Champion Hurdle in the process. Yet he did not show more than useful form in any of them. Not only did the opposition not amount to much, but Rhinestone Cowboy won, respectively, by just three quarters of a length, a neck and a length and three quarters. These particular races were almost entirely cases of 'seeing is believing', the sight being a striking one as Rhinestone Cowboy passed the post being heavily restrained and seemingly having the proverbial ton in hand. What would Rhinestone Cowboy find off the bridle? As a Grade 2, the Wetherby race might in theory have helped clear up the issue, but it was a Grade 2 in name only and even when it did promise to provide enlightenment, after Rhinestone Cowboy fluffed the second last, it was only for a moment.

Two weeks later, the Axminster Kingwell Hurdle at Wincanton looked likely to supply the answer. In a six-runner field, Tolworth Hurdle winner Thisthat-andtother was easily the best novice to take on Rhinestone Cowboy and, more strikingly, the pair were also pitted against the reigning Champion Hurdle winner Hors La Loi III. Hors La Loi had won the Wincanton race twice before but, unimpressive in appearance, he was very weak in the betting following some downbeat comments from his connections. Rhinestone Cowboy, the unproven novice, was sent off at 11/8-on and the Champion Hurdle winner, conceding him just 4 lb, was at 100/30. The 7/2-shot Thisthatandtother went on with Rhinestone Cowboy when stable-mates Hors La Loi and Eternal Spring dropped away tamely early in the straight. Norman Williamson was not motionless by any means on Rhinestone Cowboy at this stage and matters weren't made any easier for him when Rhinestone Cowboy wasn't fluent at the second last either. Soon afterwards, though, Rhinestone Cowboy was suddenly cantering all over his rival. His winning margin—a length and three quarters—gave as little indication of his true superiority as the three that preceded it in greatly inferior company.

Gerrard Wealth Management Rossington Main Novices' Hurdle, Wetherby—
Rhinestone Cowboy's unbeaten record over hurdles is never in danger
despite the step up to Grade 2 company

Axminster Kingwell Hurdle, Wincanton—a hugely impressive win over Thisthatandtother (noseband)

After this, there was no doubt that Rhinestone Cowboy was worth his place in the Champion, 2/1 being the most common odds against him. And Norman Williamson's response to the question on everybody's lips? It proved as hard to decipher as the performance on the racecourse. 'If I answered you, the whole public would know,' said the jockey. 'I have an idea and Jonjo O'Neill has an idea, and that's enough.' Some might have read something sinister into the statement, but most spotted the humour. Amid the widespread acclaim, not to say amazement, at the style of Rhinestone Cowboy's victory, Jonjo O'Neill's was a rare voice of caution. This is not at all an unusual response from O'Neill when one of his horses has just won easily—particularly one who might be running in a handicap next time out—but his view that the Supreme Novices' rather than the Champion Hurdle would be the best option for Rhinestone Cowboy at Cheltenham was one he had stated several times before. He repeated it on occasions afterwards. 'I don't like taking two strides at a time going up a steep ladder,' said the trainer. With Williamson intent on keeping him hard held, Rhinestone Cowboy would have learned next to nothing about racing off the bridle from his first four hurdle races. O'Neill was more concerned that Rhinestone Cowboy learn some lessons about jumping hurdles at speed, which is why he ran in the Wincanton race, and still wasn't totally convinced. 'His jumping is still a bit novicey,' he observed, 'and you can't afford to make a single mistake at Cheltenham.'

The choice of Festival engagement for owner Sue Magnier was probably not hard to make. She is more used to winning classics on the Flat than jumps races, and a challenge for the Champion Hurdle understandably held more appeal to her than one for the Supreme Novices', a race she won in 1998 with French Ballerina. Despite O'Neill again stating that he preferred the chance of battle-hardened stable-mate Intersky Falcon, the public kept their faith that, when push came to shove in the closing stages, as it surely would this time, Rhinestone Cowboy would deliver. Rhinestone Cowboy started 5/2 favourite and there was consternation in the grandstands when he came under strong pressure around halfway. Jumping, as O'Neill feared, was the problem, Rhinestone Cowboy blundering at the second and being generally far from fluent. In the circumstances Rhinestone Cowboy gave a gutsy performance to move from eighth at the top of the hill to fourth turning for home and in the end he beat Intersky Falcon as well, keeping on past his tiring stable companion to finish third, albeit fourteen lengths behind runaway winner Rooster Booster. What would Rhinestone Cowboy find off the bridle? After such a long wait, the question had had to be answered an awful lot earlier than anticipated in the Champion. The race did produce a top-class horse, but it wasn't Rhinestone Cowboy.

Rhinestone Cowboy (IRE) (b.g. 1996)	Be My Native (USA) (br 1979)	Our Native (b or br 1970)	Exclusive Native
			Our Jackie
		Witchy Woman (ch 1972)	Strate Stuff
			Witchy Norma
	Monumental Gesture (b 1987)	Head For Heights (b 1981)	Shirley Heights
			Vivante
		Temporary Lull (ch 1980)	Super Concorde
			Magazine

A medium-sized, well-made gelding, Rhinestone Cowboy comes from a very good family whose jumping celebrities are dual Champion Chase winner Barnbrook Again, who is out of a close relative to third dam Magazine, and Triumph Hurdle winner Rare Holiday, a half-brother to Rhinestone Cowboy's dam Monumental Gesture. Rhinestone Cowboy was purchased for IR 82,000 guineas as a three-year-old before doing his stint at Ballydoyle. He will stay beyond two miles and has raced only on good ground or softer. To jump so indifferently as he did in the early stages at Cheltenham and still finish third indicates that Rhinestone Cowboy is still a horse of considerable potential. He may yet emerge as a Champ-

Mrs John Magnier's "Rhinestone Cowboy"

ion Hurdle winner but, strange as it may seem with that illustrious placing, he was not the season's top novice. Another stable companion, the stayer Iris's Gift, is well clear, though the pair are unlikely ever to meet again on the racecourse. They did in the 2002 Champion Bumper, when Iris's Gift was just under seventeen lengths back in fifth. A good race at the time, what a race that was in hindsight, with Pizarro first past the post and Back In Front third. The first three all started favourite over hurdles at the Festival twelve months later. Before his hurdling debut, Rhinestone Cowboy kicked off the latest season by beating subsequent Champion Bumper victor Liberman in the listed Betfair Open Bumper at Cheltenham in November, a race won in the three previous years by Back In Front, In Contrast and none other than Best Mate. Although he was receiving weight from the four-year-old Liberman, Rhinestone Cowboy won with so much in hand that, in our view at least, this represented the best bumper form of 2002/3. He was ridden by the owner's teenage son J. P. Magnier, who was registering a Cheltenham victory on just his seventh racecourse appearance as a jockey. The young man belied his inexperience, obeying instructions to the letter as he kept a good hold on the 9/4 favourite until well up the final straight and then went on to beat the Tony McCoy-ridden Liberman by a length. Who knows, that might just be worth something to Jonjo O'Neill when the Magniers are deciding what to do with some of the other Ballydoyle inmates that turn out to be surplus to requirements. *Jonjo O'Neill*

RHYTHM HILL (IRE) 8 b.m. Orchestra – Cantafleur (Cantab) [2002/3 F20d 20g⁶ 20d⁵ Feb 26] sturdy ex-Irish mare: little worthwhile form in bumpers: 100/1 and first outing after leaving G. Stewart, easily best effort over hurdles when fifth of 7 finishers in mares novice at Wetherby: will stay beyond 2½m: raced on good going or softer: has had tongue tied. *Mrs S. J. Smith* **h85 F—**

RHYTHM KING 8 b.g. Rakaposhi King – Minim (Rymer) [2002/3 h68: 19dᵘʳ c16g c16gᶠ c20dᵘʳ c16g Mar 14] lengthy gelding: poor maiden hurdler: well held both completed starts over fences: should stay 2½m: raced on good going or softer. *J. A. B. Old* **c— h—**

RIANATTA (IRE) 4 b.f. Nicolotte – Asturiana (Julio Mariner) [2002/3 16d 16v 18s Mar 2] half-sister to 2 winners over jumps: modest maiden on Flat (barely stays 1m): well held in 3 juvenile hurdles. *P. Butler* **h—**

RIBBON OF LIGHT 5 b.g. Spectrum (IRE) – Brush Away (Ahonoora) [2002/3 h–: 17sᵖᵘ Jul 20] close-coupled gelding: poor maiden on Flat (stays 11.5f): twice-raced over hurdles, ran moody race in visor only start in 2002/3. *Ian Williams* **h—**

RICARDO 9 b.g. Sanglamore (USA) – Nurica (USA) (Nureyev (USA)) [2002/3 h123: c16s² c17v³ c16sᵘʳ c17s⁴ c16d⁴ c16g 16g Mar 30] good-topped gelding: fairly useful hurdler, no show only run in 2002/3: useful novice chaser, fourth to Bust Out in Grade 1 at Leopardstown fourth outing: best around 2m: raced on good going or softer (acts on heavy): twice blinkered. *Brian Nolan, Ireland* **c129 h—**

RICCARTON 10 b.g. Nomination – Legendary Dancer (Shareef Dancer (USA)) [2002/3 c84?, h63: 17m⁴ c16m³ c16m² c16d² c19f⁵ c17g³ c21g⁵ Apr 19] leggy gelding: poor hurdler/maiden chaser: stays 19f: acts on any going: has had tongue tied. *D. C. Turner* **c84 h76**

RICE POINT 10 b.g. Gold Dust – My Kizzy (The Ditton) [2002/3 c–: c16gᵖᵘ May 1] modest pointer: pulled up both starts in hunters. *John Squire* **c—**

RICHIE'S DELIGHT (IRE) 10 br.g. Phardante (FR) – Johnstown Love (IRE) (Golden Love) [2002/3 c105, h92: 16mᵘʳ 20d⁴ 20s³ 20m⁴ 20d² 20s³ 20g² 20m² 21m⁴ c21d² c24dᵖᵘ 19d Nov 26] well-made gelding: modest hurdler/handicap chaser: best form around 2½m: acts on soft and firm going: not an easy ride (has worn cheekpieces). *Ferdy Murphy* **c94 h96**

RICKHAM GLORY 5 b.g. Past Glories – Rickham Bay (Snow Warning) [2002/3 F16s F16s F16m Apr 10] leggy gelding: first live foal: dam unraced: no show in bumpers. *H. E. Haynes* **F—**

RICKO (NZ) 9 b.g. Defensive Play (USA) – Native Hawk (NZ) (War Hawk) [2002/3 h–: c16s³ c17m⁶ c21m⁴ c21gᶠ c20s³ c21m* c21m* c21mᶠ c20m⁵ Oct 30] workmanlike gelding: winning hurdler in New Zealand: fair novice chaser: won 6-runner events at Newton Abbot (handicap, held when left clear last) in August and Stratford (not extended) in September: stays 21f: acts on soft and good to firm going: front runner. *B. G. Powell* **c103 h—**

RICKY B   7 b.g. Rakaposhi King – Fililode (Mossberry) [2002/3 h–: 20d⁴ 16g 19m Oct   h–
30] no form over hurdles: won maiden point in March. *M. Wellings*

RIDAPOUR (IRE)   4 b.g. Kahyasi – Ridiyara (IRE) (Persian Bold) [2002/3 20m³ Apr   h81 +
12] ex-French gelding: fairly useful maiden on Flat (stays 15f) at 3 yrs for A. de Royer
Dupre: less than fluent when third to easy winner Caribbean Cove in novice at Bangor on
hurdling debut. *D. J. Wintle*

RIDERS REVENGE (IRE)   5 b.g. Norwich – Paico Ana (Paico) [2002/3 F16d³   F86
F16d F16v Dec 1] IR £22,000 3-y-o: sturdy gelding: half-brother to winning hurdler/
pointer Ballyedward (by Roselier), stays well: dam unraced half-sister to smart chaser at
2½m+ Givus A Buck: showed some ability in bumpers, third of 18 to The Norwich Fly at
Thurles on debut: highly tried next time: joined Miss V. Williams. *P. M. J. Doyle, Ireland*

RIDGEWAY (IRE)   8 b.g. Indian Ridge – Regal Promise (Pitskelly) [2002/3 h85:   c101
17g⁴ 17g⁴ c25d* c25g² Mar 29] lengthy gelding: modest maiden hurdler for M. Easterby: h89
better form in novice hunter chases, won at Catterick in March: stays 25f: acts on heavy
going: has worn cheekpieces: has broken blood vessel. *Miss J. E. Foster*

RIDGEWAY LAD   5 ch.g. Primo Dominie – Phyliel (Lyphard (USA)) [2002/3   h80
17m⁴ Jun 1] fair maiden on Flat (stays 7.5f): reportedly had breathing problem when
fourth in maiden at Market Rasen on hurdling debut: sold 2,800 gns Newmarket July
Sales. *T. D. Easterby*

RIDING HIGH   4 ch.f. Afzal – Upper Mount Street (IRE) (Strong Gale) [2002/3   F–
F17s⁶ F18s Feb 3] second foal: dam Irish bumper winner: well held in 2 mares bumpers.
C. P. Morlock

RIFT VALLEY (IRE)   8 b.g. Good Thyne (USA) – Necochea (Julio Mariner) [2002/3   h104
h112: 22s 21d 24gᵘʳ 22d 22f* 20g⁶ Apr 2] good-topped gelding: fair handicap hurdler:
returned to near best to win 6-runner event at Exeter (made all, very easily) in March:
stays 3m: best on good going or firmer (acts on firm): best in visor. *P. J. Hobbs*

RIGADOON (IRE)   7 b.g. Be My Chief (USA) – Loucoum (FR) (Iron Duke (FR))   c89 §
[2002/3 c88, h–: c20m⁴ c25mᵖᵘ c25m² c23m³ c20d² c27s³ c24d* c25vᵖᵘ c25dᵖᵘ c28g⁵   h–
c25mᵖᵘ Apr 21] big, close-coupled gelding: winning hurdler: modest chaser: won novice
handicap at Huntingdon in December: poor efforts last 4 starts: stays 25f: acts on good to
firm and good to soft going, possibly not at best on soft/heavy: blinkered: reportedly
distressed second start: untrustworthy. *M. W. Easterby*

RIGHT   8 b.m. Teenoso (USA) – Left (Remainder Man) [2002/3 h76, F–: 17sᶠ 17s²   c–
c16vᵖᵘ c21v³ 20sᵖᵘ 17g² Mar 22] sturdy mare: showed little both starts over fences: poor   h89
hurdler: should stay 2½m: acts on heavy going: blinkered final outing (looked reluctant
time before). *D. McCain*

RIGHT JOB (IRE)   8 ch.g. Sharp Victor (USA) – Mlle Le Fabuleux (USA) (Le   h120
Fabuleux) [2002/3 16s 17s⁵ 16d* 16m⁶ Apr 22] good-topped gelding: fairly useful on
Flat (stays 9f): fairly useful handicap hurdler: easily won at Navan in February: better
effort in valuable events subsequently (didn't have run of race at Punchestown in
early-May) when sixth to High Prospect at Fairyhouse: raced around 2m: acts on soft and
good to firm ground. *P. J. Flynn, Ireland*

RIGHTSAIDFRED   15 b.g. Lighter – Ladybank (Dear Gazelle) [2002/3 c108: c25m*   c104
May 22] rangy gelding: one-time useful chaser: still retained plenty of ability in 2002,
successful in hunter at Folkestone in May: stays 3¾m: acts on good to firm and heavy
going: races prominently: sound jumper: genuine and reliable. *Miss A. M. Newton-Smith*

RIGMAROLE   5 b.g. Fairy King (USA) – Cattermole (USA) (Roberto (USA)) [2002/3   h120
h113: 18m³ 17d 16g² 16d 16d 16m² Feb 21] compact gelding: fairly useful handicap
hurdler: best efforts when second at Wetherby (first start since wind operation) in November and Kempton (beaten ½ length by Brooklyn's Gold) in February: will prove best
around 2m: acts on soft and good to firm going: usually tongue tied (wasn't at Wetherby):
often finds little. *P. F. Nicholls*

RIGOLADE (USA)   7 b.g. Dayjur (USA) – Arewehavingfunyet (USA) (Sham (USA))   c97
[2002/3 24g² 20m* 20g 20g c26g* c24f* c24dᵖᵘ Nov 15] useful-looking gelding: half-   h81
brother to 6 winners on Flat in France and USA, one of them dam of very smart middle-
distance stayer Mons: dam high-class 2-y-o in USA: poor hurdler: won amateur handicap
at Bangor in August: better over fences, won novice at Uttoxeter and handicap at Listowel
in September: stays 3¼m: acts on firm going: blinkered after reappearance: has had
tongue tied. *N. F. Glynn, Ireland*

Mr F. M. Moriarty's "Rince Ri"

RIMOSA   8 b.m. Miner's Lamp – Crosa (Crozier) [2002/3 h79, F–: 17g⁵ 16g⁶ 19mᵖᵘ 17m⁴ Jul 7] angular mare: poor novice hurdler: raced mainly around 2m: acts on good to firm going, probably on soft. *A. P. Jones*   **h74**

RINCE RI (IRE)   10 ch.g. Orchestra – Mildred's Ball (Blue Refrain) [2002/3 c163, h–: c20s² c24v⁶ c24v⁶ 20v³ c24s⁴ c25s* c20d* Mar 22] strong gelding: winning hurdler: top-class chaser: reportedly had surgery for colic after final outing in 2001/2: won Grade 2 Bobbyjo Chase at Fairyhouse (didn't need to be at best to beat Takagi 6 lengths) in February and listed race at Navan (beat Knife Edge a length) in March: best efforts when second to Native Upmanship in John Durkan Memorial Punchestown Chase in December and to First Gold in Punchestown Heineken Gold Cup in late-April: best form at 3m+: acts on heavy going, probably on good to firm: blinkered fifth start: formerly tongue tied. *T. M. Walsh, Ireland*   **c165 h117 ?**

RING DE SOU (FR)   6 b.g. Ajdayt (USA) – Ring Ann (IRE) (Auction Ring (USA)) [2002/3 c110§, h–§: 17m Jun 14] novice hurdler/winning chaser: blinkered/visored last 4 outings: ungenuine: sold 1,400 gns Doncaster September Sales. *M. C. Pipe*   **c– § h– §**

RIO GRANDE (IRE)   9 b.g. Un Desperado (FR) – Liffey's Choice (Little Buskins) [2002/3 h–: 22g³ May 1] rangy gelding: has been hobdayed: winning pointer: lightly raced over hurdles, first form when third in amateur novice at Exeter: tried tongue tied. *C. R. Barwell*   **h64**

RIO REAL (IRE)   7 b.g. Case Law – Fine Flame (Le Prince) [2002/3 16d* 16s⁶ 16m³ 16s⁴ Nov 8] good-topped gelding: modest hurdler: off 1½ years, won amateur seller at Towcester in May: probably flattered when third to Chem's Truce in conditional jockeys handicap at Haydock: may prove best at 2m: acts on soft and good to firm going: blinkered/visored. *J. Mackie*   **h95 ?**

Cordon Bleu Handicap Hurdle, Aintree—
Risky Reef lands the first leg of a 688/1-treble on Grand National day for Ruby Walsh;
Altay (noseband) takes second

RIOTHAMUS (IRE) 5 b.g. Supreme Leader – Kemchee (Kemal (FR)) [2002/3 **F101**
F17d* Mar 2] IR £38,000 3-y-o: seventh foal: half-brother to fairly useful hurdler/chaser
Indian Scout (by Phardante), stays 21f, and 2 winning chasers by Strong Gale: dam,
winning 2m hurdler, sister to smart jumper up to 3m Kissane: easy to back, won 15-runner
bumper at Carlisle on debut by neck from Hot Weld. *Ferdy Murphy*

RIO TINTO 8 gr.g. Gran Alba (USA) – Hollow Creek (Tarqogan) [2002/3 h90: 22g^pu **h–**
May 1] workmanlike gelding: modest handicap hurdler: reportedly lame at Exeter in
May: stays 3¼m: raced on good going or softer (acts on heavy): blinkered/visored last 4
starts. *W. Jenks*

RISE ABOVE (IRE) 9 b.m. Simply Great (FR) – La Tanque (USA) (Last Raise **h–**
(USA)) [2002/3 h–: 21g^pu May 30] sparely-made mare: maiden hurdler, no show only 2
outings since 1999. *J. Cullinan*

RISING GENERATION (FR) 6 ch.g. Risen Star (USA) – Queen's Victory (FR) **c– §**
(Carmarthen (FR)) [2002/3 c113, h107: 17d^5 19g^4 c20v^pu 16g^5 19m^2 Apr 21] fair hurdler/ **h103 §**
chaser, rather disappointing since winning on British debut in 2001/2: stays 19f: acts on
heavy and good to firm going: often finds little. *N. G. Richards*

RISK ACCESSOR (IRE) 8 b.g. Commanche Run – Bellatollah (Bellman (FR)) **c137**
[2002/3 c129, h144: c22d^4 c20d c20v^2 c16g^2 c16g^3 Apr 3] tall gelding: useful hurdler/ **h–**
chaser: good efforts over fences last 3 starts, second to The Premier Cat in minor event at
Clonmel and Palarshan in Grand Annual Chase (Handicap) at Cheltenham (denied a run),
and third of 16 to Golden Alpha in valuable handicap at Aintree: effective at 2m and
probably best short of 3m: acts on heavy going: tongue tied on reappearance: usually held
up (often finds little), but is effective making running. *C. Roche, Ireland*

RISKER (USA) 4 b.g. Gone West (USA) – Trampoli (USA) (Trempolino (USA)) **h82**
[2002/3 17d^F 16g 16m^5 16g^6 Apr 19] smallish gelding: fair on Flat (stays 1½m), sold out
of M. Johnston's stable 10,000 gns Newmarket July Sales: held in third when fell 2 out in
juvenile at Newton Abbot on hurdling debut: well beaten after, left P. Hobbs following
third outing (blinkered). *J. Joseph*

RISK OF LIGHTNING 7 ch.m. Risk Me (FR) – Lightning Legend (Lord Gayle **F–**
(USA)) [2002/3 F16g Feb 22] sister to several selling race winners on Flat, including
1994 2-y-o 6f winner Bitch: dam 2-y-o 7f winner: tailed off in bumper on debut.
Miss Z. C. Davison

RISKY GIRL 8 ro.m. Risk Me (FR) – Jove's Voodoo (USA) (Northern Jove (CAN)) [2002/3 h–: 17s May 28] very lightly-raced winning hurdler: well held only 2 starts since 1998. *H. J. Manners* — **h–**

RISKY REEF 6 ch.g. Risk Me (FR) – Pas de Reef (Pas de Seul) [2002/3 h127p: 16v³ 16v² 16s* 16g* Apr 5] lengthy gelding: fairly useful hurdler: won 18-runner minor event at Thurles in January and valuable 19-runner handicap at Aintree in April: confidently ridden and travelled strongly throughout when beating Altay by 1¾ lengths at latter: stiff task in Grade 1 at Punchestown in early-May: will prove best over easy 2m: raced on good going or softer. *Andrew Lee, Ireland* — **h129**

RISKY WAY 7 b.g. Risk Me (FR) – Hot Sunday Sport (Star Appeal) [2002/3 c88, h–: c16dur c16g² c16d* c17g² Apr 26] leggy, close-coupled gelding: modest novice chaser: enterprisingly ridden when winning handicap at Catterick in February: often let down by jumping otherwise over fences: stays 2½m: acts on good to firm and good to soft going: visored once in 2001/2. *B. S. Rothwell* — **c90 h–**

RITH DUBH (IRE) 11 b.g. Black Minstrel – Deep Bonnie (Deep Run) [2002/3 c134, h–: c25d c24gpu Mar 11] workmanlike gelding: winning hurdler: useful chaser, won National Hunt Chase at Cheltenham in 2001/2: well held in handicaps there both starts in 2002/3: stays 4m: acts on good to firm and heavy going: blinkered: held up, and often finds little. *Jonjo O'Neill* — **c– h–**

RITUAL 8 ch.g. Selkirk (USA) – Pure Formality (Forzando) [2002/3 c106+, h74: c16g* c16s³ c16dpu Dec 14] tall, lengthy gelding: fair handicap chaser: won at Folkestone (gamely from Ivanoph) in November: lame final start: stays 2½m: acts on soft and good to firm going. *Miss Jacqueline S. Doyle* — **c106 h–**

RIVER AMORA (IRE) 8 b.g. Willie Joe (IRE) – That's Amora (Paddy's Stream) [2002/3 c81, h–: c20g⁴ c20m³ c20g c20f⁵ c22m⁶ c20m³ c20m⁵ c26m³ c19d⁵ c21mpu 18d⁵ c20s³ c22v⁶ Jan 6] stocky gelding: maiden hurdler: poor chaser: stays 21f: acts on firm and soft going: visored last 2 starts: prone to mistakes. *P. Butler* — **c74 x h–**

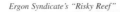

Ergon Syndicate's "Risky Reef"

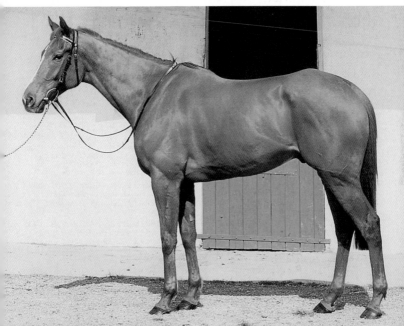

RIVER BAILIFF (IRE) 7 ch.g. Over The River (FR) – Rath Caola (Neltino) [2002/3   **c77**
c26m⁴ c16d⁶ c21s⁴ c16g⁶ c16g⁵ c20g⁵ Apr 21] useful-looking gelding: first foal: half-
brother to fair hurdler Pure Fun (by Lord Americo), stays easy 3m: dam winning pointer:
won maiden Irish point in 2001: bought 11,500 gns Doncaster May (2001) Sales: poor
form in steeplechases (trained by S. Garrott on debut): stays 3¼m: raced too freely in
blinkers fourth start. *J. Howard Johnson*

RIVER BANN (USA) 6 ch.g. Irish River (FR) – Spiritual Star (USA) (Soviet Star   **h89**
(USA)) [2002/3 17s⁴ 19d⁶ 17d⁴ 19d² 17s³ Feb 27] fairly useful on Flat (stays 1½m) at 3
yrs for P. Cole: bought £5,800 Ascot June Sales: modest novice hurdler: stays 19f: raced
on good to soft/soft going. *Mrs Jane Galpin*

RIVERBLUE (IRE) 7 b.g. Bluebird (USA) – La Riveraine (USA) (Riverman   **h–**
(USA)) [2002/3 h93+: 17vᵖᵘ Jan 24] fair on Flat (stays 1½m): lightly raced over hurdles,
second in novice on debut: pulled up on heavy going both starts since: likely to prove best
around 2m. *D. J. Wintle*

RIVER BUG (IRE) 9 ch.g. Over The River (FR) – Fiona's Wish (Wishing Star)   **c114**
[2002/3 c99: c24d³ c29s² c32d c26vᵖᵘ c26f* c34s⁴ Mar 15] sturdy gelding: fair
handicap chaser: won at Folkestone in January (under strong pressure long way out) and
Plumpton (amateur event, much improved in blinkers when beating Here Comes Henry
20 lengths) in February: thorough stayer: acts on heavy going: also blinkered final outing:
none too reliable. *Jamie Poulton*

RIVER CAPTAIN (USA) 10 ch.g. Riverman (USA) – Katsura (USA) (Northern   **c– p**
Dancer) [2002/3 21m⁵ 20d⁵ c17gᶠ Oct 19] compact gelding: modest hurdler: in front   **h100 ?**
and still going well when falling 3 out in novice at Kelso on chasing debut: probably stays
2½m: acts on soft going. *A. Scott*

RIVER CITY (IRE) 6 b.g. Norwich – Shuil Na Lee (IRE) (Phardante (FR)) [2002/3   **h115**
F95: 19g² 20g⁵ 17v* 16d⁴ 16dᵖᵘ 16m⁴ Mar 22] rather unfurnished gelding: bumper winner: fair novice hurdler: won at Newton Abbot in November and Doncaster (beat Ocean
Dancer 1½ lengths) in January: shaped as if possibly has a problem last 2 starts, running
well but throwing race away by hanging badly left run-in when close fourth to Gin Palace
in handicap at Newbury: should stay at least 2½m: acts on any going. *Noel T. Chance*

RIVER CLODAGH (IRE) 9 ch.g. Over The River (FR) – Polly Ringling (Pollerton)   **c121 §**
[2002/3 c121?, h–: 20g 20s 18d⁶ 20s c16s² c17s⁶ c20vᵖᵘ c17sᴿ Mar 16] smallish, sturdy   **h95 §**
gelding: modest hurdler: fairly useful chaser: second to Beef Or Salmon in Grade 3 at
Cork in December: effective at 2m to 3m: raced mainly on going softer than good (acts
on heavy): usually blinkered: inconsistent and not to be trusted. *Henry De Bromhead,
Ireland*

RIVER GOLD 9 ch.g. River God (USA) – Lady St Clair (Young Generation) [2002/3   **c71**
c–, h–: c20g⁵ c24m⁴ Mar 18] sturdy gelding: novice hurdler: poor form over fences: left   **h–**
J. Gifford and off 22 months prior to reappearance: should stay 3m: tried tongue tied.
M. Pitman

RIVER JOY (IRE) 5 b.g. Norwich – Vanessa's Palace (Quayside) [2002/3 F16s F17s   **F–**
F17d Feb 23] lengthy, unfurnished gelding: second foal: dam ran once in bumper: little
sign of ability in bumpers: tongue tied: went as if amiss on debut. *Noel T. Chance*

RIVERLORD 9 b.g. River God (USA) – Sultry (Sula Bula) [2002/3 c–: 20g c23g⁴   **c–**
c23m⁴ c21mᵖᵘ Jul 15] little sign of ability. *P. R. Rodford*   **h–**

RIVER MARSHAL (IRE) 5 b.g. Synefos (USA) – Marshallstown (Callernish)   **F95**
[2002/3 F14d⁶ F16g² F16d³ Feb 1] 4,500 4-y-o: workmanlike gelding: fifth foal: dam
bumper winner/winning hurdler: fair form when placed in bumpers at Catterick (blinkered, hung right throughout) and Wetherby (third to Crossbow Creek). *M. W. Easterby*

RIVER MERE 9 b.g. River God (USA) – Rupert's Daughter (Rupert Bear) [2002/3   **h89 ?**
h–: 16m 16m⁵ 16m⁴ Apr 21] workmanlike gelding: little worthwhile form over hurdles:
almost certainly flattered when fifth in novice at Ludlow, soon in clear lead: free-going
sort. *Mrs L. Williamson*

RIVER MIST (IRE) 4 ch.f. Over The River (FR) – Minature Miss (Move Off) [2002/3   **F73**
F17g² Mar 28] tenth foal: half-sister to fair hurdler The Mickletonian (by K-Battery),
stayed 21f: dam, winning hurdler, stayed 3¼m: 7 lengths second to Reivers Moon in
bumper at Carlisle on debut. *D. Eddy*

RIVER NESS 7 br.m. Buckskin (FR) – Stubbin Moor (Kinglet) [2002/3 h96: 22d²   **c–**
21g² 20s⁵ 16v² c21v⁴ 21dᵖᵘ 27g⁵ Apr 25] fair handicap hurdler: below form last 2 starts: **h102**

odds on, well beaten in mares novice at Sedgefield on chasing debut: stays 3m: raced on good going or softer (acts on heavy): held up. *N. G. Richards*

RIVER OF WISHES   5 b.m. Riverwise (USA) – Wishful Dream (Crawter) [2002/3   F–
F16v Feb 15] third known foal: dam pulled up only start: always behind in bumper at
Ascot on debut. *C. W. Mitchell*

RIVER PILOT   9 b.g. Unfuwain (USA) – Cut Ahead (Kalaglow) [2002/3 c111, h–:   c103
c16dF c20g c20m5 c16v4 c16g4 Feb 22] useful-looking gelding: one-time fairly useful   h–
hurdler: fair chaser: sold out of N. Meade's stable €16,000 Goffs October Sale after third
outing: stays 21f: acts on heavy and good to firm going: has found little. *C. J. Mann*

RIVER PIRATE (IRE)   6 b.g. Un Desperado (FR) – Kigali (IRE) (Torus) [2002/3   h104
F16d3 F16s3 16v3 16v5 Mar 8] IR £31,000 4-y-o: tall, unfurnished gelding: first foal: F97
dam, twice-raced in bumpers, out of half-sister to Grand National second Zongalero and
to dam of Cheltenham Gold Cup winner Garrison Savannah: fairly useful form when
third in 2 bumpers at Ludlow: 6 lengths third of 8 to Personal Assurance in novice at
Sandown on hurdling debut: favourite, not fluent and found little when tailed-off last of 5
in similar event there 3 weeks later: needs to learn to settle. *N. J. Henderson*

RIVER RAMBLER   4 ch.f. River Falls – Horsepower (Superpower) [2002/3 F16g   F–
Mar 23] first foal: dam unraced, out of half-sister to high-class 2m hurdler Past Glories:
well held in bumper on debut. *J. R. Norton*

RIVER REINE (IRE)   4 br.f. Lahib (USA) – Talahari (IRE) (Roi Danzig (USA))   h–
[2002/3 16s Nov 27] leggy, quite good-topped filly: fairly useful at best on Flat (stays
1½m), sold out of B. Hills's stable 8,000 gns Newmarket Autumn Sales: well held in
juvenile at Wetherby on hurdling debut: sold 2,600 gns Doncaster May Sales. *E. W. Tuer*

RIVER RISING   9 br.g. Primitive Rising (USA) – Dragons Daughter (Mandrake   h–
Major) [2002/3 h80: 20g Mar 17] long-backed gelding: failed to complete in points: poor
form over hurdles. *C. R. Wilson*

RIVER SHAMROCK (IRE)   9 ch.g. Alphabatim (USA) – High Feather (Nishapour   c72
(FR)) [2002/3 24s 24s4 c24d3 c24s5 c25s c24d c20f6 Apr 13] sturdy gelding: maiden   h74
hurdler: off nearly 6 months, best efforts over fences when third of 4 finishers to Super
Fellow in novice at Cheltenham on debut: stays 3m: acts on soft and good to firm going:
often blinkered over hurdles. *S. O'Farrell, Ireland*

RIVERSIDE LODGE (IRE)   9 b.g. Riverhead (USA) – Huricane Dodo (Sexton   c– x
Blake) [2002/3 c62x, h–: c27gpu May 3] leggy, quite good-topped gelding: poor handicap   h–
chaser, usually fails to complete: probably stays 21f: form only on good/good to firm
going: sketchy jumper: sold £3,000 Ascot June Sales. *R. D. E. Woodhouse*

RIVER SLAVE (IRE)   9 b. or br.g. Over The River (FR) – Sally Slave (Paddy's   c85
Stream) [2002/3 c21sF3 c26v3 c23v3 c20s3 c24dpu Feb 14] lengthy gelding: pulled up only   h–
start over hurdles: poor novice chaser: effective at 2½m to 25f: raced mainly on soft/
heavy going. *T. R. George*

RIVER STYX (IRE)   8 ch.g. Over The River (FR) – Money For Honey (New Brig)   c80
[2002/3 c72, h–: c17spu 17d3 c16m3 c16d2 c16g* c16m2 c16g4 Mar 23] workmanlike   h72
gelding: maiden hurdler: poor novice chaser: won handicap at Musselburgh in February:
reportedly injured back final outing: should stay 2½m: acts on firm and good to soft
going: usually blinkered over fences: often tongue tied. *D. McCain*

RIVER SURPRISE (IRE)   10 b.g. Over The River (FR) – Reelin Surprise (Royal   c–
Match) [2002/3 c16mpu Apr 5] maiden pointer, usually fails to complete. *Mike Lurcock*

RIVER TRIX (IRE)   9 b.g. Riverhead (USA) – Game Trix (Buckskin (FR)) [2002/3   c92
c–, h86: c24d 20s5 20d c19m3 Apr 22] useful-looking gelding: novice hurdler, modest at   h–
best: first form over fences when third to Wellie in selling handicap at Chepstow: should
stay 3m: acts on good to soft and good to firm going: tried in tongue strap. *D. J. Caro*

RIVER WYE (IRE)   11 b.g. Jareer (USA) – Sun Gift (Guillaume Tell (USA)) [2002/3   c–
c106, h–: c20spu Oct 28] good-topped gelding: one-time useful handicap chaser around   h–
2½m: well below best since 2000/1, shaping as if amiss more than once: acts on soft and
good to firm going: tongue tied. *G. H. Yardley*

RIVIERE   8 ch.m. Meadowbrook – Cimarron (Carnival Dancer) [2002/3 h–: 24v* Mar   h94
13] bumper winner: very lightly raced over hurdles: first run for 22 months, won novice
at Hexham, confidently ridden in slowly-run race and quickening to lead near line: stays
3m: acts on heavy going. *E. W. Tuer*

ROAMING RONAN (IRE) 5 b.g. Sri Pekan (USA) – Maradata (IRE) (Shardari) **h–**
[2002/3 h74: 20d^{pu} 16m^{pu} May 15] poor novice hurdler: looked none too keen final
outing: blinkered once. *R. W. Thomson*

ROBBER BARON (IRE) 6 ch.g. Un Desperado (FR) – N T Nad (Welsh Pageant) **h109 +**
[2002/3 h109, F104: 19d* 16d^{pu} Nov 15] strong, well-made gelding: chasing type: bumper winner: fair form over hurdles: easily landed odds in 17-runner novice at Exeter in
November by 5 lengths from Whispering John: favourite, pulled up lame 3 out in Grade 2
novice at Cheltenham later in month: will probably stay beyond 19f: acts on soft going
(bumper form on good to firm): may still do better. *Miss H. C. Knight*

ROBBER (IRE) 6 ch.g. Un Desperado (FR) – Christy's Girl (IRE) (Buckskin (FR)) **h85**
[2002/3 F88: 21s^5 20v 19d^3 24g 22g^F 24m Apr 16] leggy gelding: poor novice hurdler:
found very little final outing: should stay 3m: acts on good to firm and good to soft going.
P. J. Hobbs

ROBBIE CAN CAN 4 b.g. Robellino (USA) – Can Can Lady (Anshan) [2002/3 17s^5 **h90**
16d^4 16v* 16s Feb 12] fair maiden on Flat (stays easy 2m) for J. Given: easily best effort
in juvenile hurdles when winning claimer at Chepstow in January, making most: likely to
be suited by further than 2m: acts on heavy going. *A. W. Carroll*

ROBBIE'S ADVENTURE 9 ch.g. Le Coq d'Or – Mendick Adventure (Mandrake **c66 x**
Major) [2002/3 c70, h–: c24m^{pu} c26m^4 c27s^F c26v^3 c26v^{pu} c22s^{pu} c25s c26s c25g^3 c25g^{pu} **h–**
c26m^4 Apr 21] close-coupled gelding: poor handicap chaser, often let down by jumping:
stays 3¼m: acts on heavy and good to firm going: usually wears visor/cheekpieces.
D. L. Williams

ROBBO 9 b.g. Robellino (USA) – Basha (USA) (Chief's Crown (USA)) [2002/3 c138§, **c129 §**
h–: c25v 20d* 22v^3 23v^3 c24d* c24d 24s^5 24d^4 c34s^{pu} c36d^{ur} Apr 5] strong, close- **h124 §**
coupled gelding: fairly useful hurdler, won handicap at Newcastle in November: useful
handicap chaser, not quite at best in 2002/3, though won at Doncaster in January by 14
lengths from Raffles Rooster: disappointing otherwise in 2002/3, behind when hampered
and unseated nineteenth in Grand National at Aintree: should stay beyond 3¼m: acts on
heavy going: usually wears headgear: often looks unwilling. *Mrs M. Reveley*

ROBELLA 7 ch.m. Keen – Afrabela (African Sky) [2002/3 h61, F–: c16g^F Oct 9] **c–**
workmanlike mare: poor form over hurdles: fell fifth on chasing debut: raced mainly **h–**
around 2m: acts on heavy going. *K. A. Morgan*

ROBERT THE BRUCE 8 ch.g. Distinct Native – Kawarau Queen (Taufan (USA)) **h111**
[2002/3 h99: 20s^2 Mar 8] good-topped gelding: winning hurdler, very lightly raced: much
improved when second to Lochbuy Junior in handicap at Ayr in March: stays 2½m: acts
on soft and good to firm going: clearly difficult to train. *L. Lungo*

ROBERTY BOB (IRE) 8 ch.g. Bob Back (USA) – Inesdela (Wolver Hollow) **c122**
[2002/3 c127p, h–: c26d* c24d^4 c24v^2 24v^3 c26s^5 c26v^3 c29d^3 Mar 8] good-topped **h84**
gelding: maiden hurdler: fairly useful chaser: won intermediate at Uttoxeter in May:
didn't make expected further improvement: suited by 3m+: raced mainly on going softer
than good (acts on heavy). *H. D. Daly*

ROBINS MEG 7 b.m. Skyliner – Home Dove (Homeboy) [2002/3 F78: F17m F16d **h–**
19m^{ur} Apr 21] form in bumpers only on debut: tailed off when unseated 2 out in 4-runner **F–**
novice on hurdling bow. *M. E. Sowersby*

ROBINS PRIDE (IRE) 13 b.g. Treasure Hunter – Barney's Sister (Abednego) **c66 §**
[2002/3 c71§, h–§: c24s^5 c21d^5 c22v c26s^{pu} c16g^4 c19f^3 c21g^4 c19m^2 Apr 22] tall **h– §**
gelding: poor handicap chaser: stays 3m, effective at much shorter: acts on any going:
blinkered: prone to the odd mistake: unreliable. *C. L. Popham*

ROB LEACH 6 b.g. Robellino (USA) – Arc Empress Jane (IRE) (Rainbow Quest **h122**
(USA)) [2002/3 h118: 16d^5 16v* 16g Nov 30] smallish gelding: fairly useful handicap
hurdler: looking very well, won muddling event at Ascot in November, outpaced 3 out
before rallying strongly run-in to beat Under The Sand ½ length: possibly hadn't got over
that race when well held at Newbury 8 days later: should be suited by further than 2m:
acts on heavy going, probably on good to firm: effective blinkered or not: consistent.
G. L. Moore

ROB MINE (IRE) 11 b.g. Roselier (FR) – Noddi Fliw (Jasmine Star) [2002/3 c24s* **c98**
Mar 7] tall gelding: returned from 2-year absence in good form, successful twice in points **h–**
and in hunter chase at Sandown by 3 lengths from Native Cove, jumping fluently: stays
3m: acts on soft going. *C. Sporborg*

ROBOASTAR (USA)   6 b. or br.g. Green Dancer (USA) – Sweet Alabastar (USA)   **h81 §**
(Gulch (USA)) [2002/3 h79§: 20g⁴ 24dʳʳ Jun 8] leggy gelding: poor maiden hurdler:
stays easy 2½m: acts on soft going: has refused to race twice and one to treat with plenty
of caution: sold 1,000 gns Doncaster August Sales, little show in points in 2003.
P. G. Murphy

ROBSAND (IRE)   14 b.g. Sandalay – Remindful (Bargello) [2002/3 c25dᶠ May 14]   **c–**
workmanlike gelding: maiden chaser: tried visored. *A. L. Shaw*   **h–**

ROB THE FIVE (IRE)   6 b.g. Supreme Leader – Derravarragh Lady (IRE) (Radical)   **h109**
[2002/3 16s² 16s F16s* Feb 19] third foal: half-brother to modest hurdler/chaser   **F97**
Channahrlie (by Celio Rufo), probably best at 3m+: dam unraced half-sister to useful
chaser up to 3m Greenwood Lad: fairly useful form in bumpers, runner-up 3 of 4 starts:
fair form over hurdles: didn't need to be at best to win maiden at Limerick in February:
likely to stay 2½m: raced only on soft ground. *A. L. T. Moore, Ireland*

ROBYN ALEXANDER (IRE)   5 ch.m. Sharifabad (IRE) – Flagship Ahoy (IRE)   **h101 +**
(Accordion) [2002/3 F16g⁵ F16s² F16s⁵ 16d³ 18s* 17s 16gᶠ 17g³ 19f* Mar 24]   **F90**
lengthy, unfurnished mare: first foal: dam maiden sister to fairly useful hurdlers Flagship
Colm, stays 2¾m, and Flagship Therese, stayed 3¼m: fair form at best in Irish bumpers
for V. Bowens: fair novice hurdler: won mares event at Fontwell in December and
handicap at Taunton (easily by 2 lengths from Dantie Boy) in March: stays 19f: acts on
firm and soft going. *P. F. Nicholls*

ROCASTLE LAD (IRE)   7 gr.g. Roselier (FR) – Ivory Queen (Teenoso (USA))   **h–**
[2002/3 F–: F16m 17sᵖᵘ 19sᵖᵘ Dec 12] compact gelding: no sign of ability. *N. J. Hawke*   **F–**

ROCCIOSO   6 br.g. Pelder (IRE) – Priory Bay (Petong) [2002/3 h–: 16d 17s May 28]   **h–**
leggy gelding: bad maiden hurdler. *J. C. Fox*

ROCK BLEU (FR)   5 ch.g. Epervier Bleu – Egeria (FR) (Baly Rockette) [2002/3   **F–**
F14d F17s F17g⁶ Mar 28] fourth foal: half-brother to French middle-distance winner
Royal Rocket (by Garde Royale): dam won on Flat in France: little encouragement in
bumpers: sold 2,200 gns Doncaster May Sales. *A. Parker*

ROCKCLIFFE GOSSIP   11 ch.g. Phardante (FR) – Clonmello (Le Bavard (FR))   **c105 §**
[2002/3 c102§, h–: c25g⁴ c24d⁷ c24m⁶ c24v⁵ c32d⁶ c24s c31g* Apr 24] lengthy gelding: **h–**
fair handicap chaser: travelled more sweetly than usual when winning at Bangor in
October and Perth in April: best at 3m+: acts on good to firm and heavy going: effective
blinkered or not: lazy. *N. A. Twiston-Davies*

ROCK CRYSTAL   4 b.g. Joligeneration – Rusty Rock (Ayres Rock) [2002/3 F16s   **F–**
F17d F16m Apr 10] first foal: dam unraced: no form in bumpers. *J. L. Spearing*

ROCKET RADAR   12 b.g. Vouchsafe – Courtney Pennant (Angus) [2002/3 c106:   **c106**
c25d* c28m⁵ c27g³ Feb 27] sturdy gelding: fairly useful pointer/hunter chaser: won at
Hereford in May: respectable third of 14 to Bright Approach at Ludlow on return from
9-month absence: stays 27f: acts on good to firm and good to soft going: has had tongue
tied. *Mrs J. Hughes*

ROCKETTE   8 ch.m. Rock Hopper – Primulette (Mummy's Pet) [2002/3 16s Aug 1]   **h–**
sparely-made mare: lightly raced and little sign of ability over hurdles (has looked less
than keen). *A. J. Chamberlain*

ROCKFIELD LANE (IRE)   7 b. or br.g. Sharifabad (IRE) – Suir Surprise (Rusticaro   **h89**
(FR)) [2002/3 F16s 16s⁴ 16m⁵ F16f⁵ F16m 21dᵖᵘ 16s 17d 16d Dec 26] IR 3,200   **F80**
3-y-o: good-topped ex-Irish gelding: third foal: dam, 8.5f winner, out of half-sister to
high-class middle-distance colt Carwhite: runner-up in point in 2000: modest form at best
in bumpers/over hurdles, left P. Doyle after sixth outing: no form in Britain: has pulled
hard/found little. *G. F. Bridgwater*

ROCKFORD (IRE)   7 b.g. King's Ride – Pampered Russian (Deep Run) [2002/3   **h94 ?**
21sᵖᵘ 25d⁶ 24d⁴ 26g⁵ 26m Apr 5] tall gelding: chasing type: placed on second of 2 starts
in bumpers in 2000/1: apparently easily best effort over hurdles when 26 lengths fourth
of 16 to Priests Bridge in novice at Kempton: should stay beyond 3m: looked no easy ride
in visor final outing. *A. King*

ROCK GARDEN (IRE)   4 br.f. Bigstone (IRE) – Woodland Garden (Godswalk   **F96**
(USA) [2002/3 F14d* F13s³ F16f⁴ F17m Apr 17] smallish, angular filly: sixth foal: half-
sister to fair performer Forest Light (by Rainbow Quest), stays 1¾m, and fairly useful
1994 Irish 2-y-o 7f winner Boscabel (by Fairy King): dam unraced half-sister to useful
2½m to 3m hurdler Mister Lord: won 1¾m bumper at Warwick in November on debut by

neck from Samby: best effort when fourth to Diamont Noir in mares race at Haydock. *R. F. Johnson Houghton*

ROCKHOLM BOY (IRE) 10 b.g. Eve's Error – Rockholm Rosie (Tudor Rocket) **c129**
[2002/3 c117, h–: c22s* c22d* 20g c24f^bd c24g^4 c24s^ur 24d Mar 22] compact gelding: **h–**
maiden hurdler: fairly useful handicap chaser: won at Limerick in June and Hewlett
Packard Galway Plate (by 3½ lengths from Wotsitooya) in July: good fourth of 6 to More
Than A Stroll in another valuable event at former course in September: stays 3m: acts on
any ground. *Michael Hourigan, Ireland*

ROCK'N COLD (IRE) 5 b.g. Bigstone (IRE) – Unalaska (IRE) (High Estate) [2002/3 **h103**
h106: 16s^pu 20v^pu 16d* 17g^3 17m* Apr 21] lengthy gelding: fair hurdler: won sellers at
Catterick (first run since leaving T. George) in March and Hereford (simple task, sold
9,000 gns) in April: may prove best around 2m: acts on good to firm and heavy ground:
tried visored, wore cheekpieces last 3 starts. *R. M. H. Cowell*

ROCK ROSE 10 b.m. Arctic Lord – Ovington Court (Prefairy) [2002/3 c90, h76: **c77**
22g^4 c27s^6 c19s^5 c24s^4 c25m^5 Mar 20] workmanlike mare: poor chaser/novice hurdler: **h75**
left C. Tizzard after third outing: stays 3m: acts on good to firm and heavy going.
B. J. M. Ryall

ROCK SPRINGS 5 b.g. Rock City – Riva La Belle (Ron's Victory (USA)) [2002/3 **h–**
F–: F16g 25g^pu Jan 18] no sign of ability. *C. W. Fairhurst* **F–**

ROCKSTOWN BOY (IRE) 5 b.g. Toulon – Palatine Lady (Pauper) [2002/3 F20d* **F116**
F16s^2 F16s^3 F20d* Mar 17] rangy, useful-looking gelding: half-brother to winning 2½m
chaser Bens Dilemma (by Torus) and 19f bumper winner Quarter Marker (by Celio
Rufo): dam maiden pointer: useful form in bumpers: won 2½m events at Gowran (by 1½
lengths from Mister Month, pair clear) in October and Limerick (very easily) in March:
placed both starts in between, 6 lengths third to Masteroffoxhounds at Cork: unlucky
sixth, nearly knocked over into straight, to Royal Rosa in Grade 1 at Punchestown in late-
April: will stay beyond 2½m: exciting prospect for novice hurdles in 2003/4. *C. Byrnes,
Ireland*

ROCKVIEW (IRE) 8 b.g. Mandalus – Saltee Star (Arapaho) [2002/3 c64§, h–: **c64 §**
c16m^4 c18f^pu c16m^5 c16g^R 16m^6 c23g^R c21g^F Sep 6] workmanlike form over hurdles: **h– §**
poor maiden chaser: left G. McCourt after second start, sold out of R. York's stable
£2,600 March Ascot August Sales after sixth: best form around 2m: acts on good to firm going:
has refused on 4 occasions: best left alone. *M. E. Sowersby*

ROCKY BALBOA 11 b.g. Buckley – Midnight Pansy (Deadly Nightshade) [2002/3 **c–**
c23g^pu c24s^pu 27v^pu Nov 12] temperamental winning pointer: no sign of ability other- **h–**
wise. *W. Davies*

ROCKY ISLAND 6 b.g. Rock Hopper – Queen's Eyot (Grundy) [2002/3 h102: 20d^pu **h95**
20d^4 21d Nov 15] rather leggy, useful-looking gelding: modest handicap hurdler: stays
2½m: raced on good going or softer (acts on heavy): blinkered once. *J. Mackie*

RODALKO (FR) 5 b.g. Kadalko (FR) – Darling Rose (FR) (Rose Laurel) [2002/3 **h102**
F89: 21d^F 21d* 19g^4 22d^pu 21g 22g^pu Apr 21] good-topped gelding: confirmed promise
of hurdling debut when winning novice at Ludlow in November, making most: ran poorly
last 3 starts: should stay beyond 21f: raced on good/good to soft going. *O. Sherwood*

RODBER (USA) 7 ch.g. Rodrigo de Triano (USA) – Berceau (USA) (Alleged (USA)) **h93**
[2002/3 F16d^3 20d^pu 20v^4 20d^pu Feb 23] ex-Irish gelding: second foal: half-brother to **F95**
fairly useful hurdler Borazon (by Lyphard), stays 3m: dam French 1¼m/1½m winner:
fair form in bumpers, bought out of J. Fowler's stable 31,000 gns Doncaster May Sales:
best effort in novice hurdles (reportedly broke blood vessels other 2 starts) when fourth
of 12 to Derivative at Ayr. *Mrs L. B. Normile*

RODDY THE VET (IRE) 5 ch.g. Be My Native (USA) – Caronia (IRE) (Cardinal **h91**
Flower) [2002/3 F16g* 16d^6 21s 22d^4 21d Mar 8] sturdy gelding: second foal: dam un- **F89**
raced: fair form in bumpers: left S. O'Brien after winning 20-runner event at Gowran in
October: easily best effort over hurdles when fourth of 16 to Chief Witness in novice at
Fontwell: stays 2¾m. *A. Ennis*

RODIAK 4 b.g. Distant Relative – Misty Silks (Scottish Reel) [2002/3 16s^3 18m^2 16m^2 **h81**
17m^4 Oct 3] half-brother to modest hurdler around 2m Raw Silk (by Rudimentary):
modest on Flat (stays 11.5f), successful in October: modest form when placed in juvenile
hurdles: visored last 2 starts. *Bob Jones*

RODOLFO 5 b.g. Tragic Role (USA) – Be Discreet (Junius (USA)) [2002/3 F98: F16d **F98**
F16g^6 F17g^3 Apr 26] tall gelding: fairly useful in bumpers: likely to prove best around
2m. *O. Sherwood*

RODRIGO (IRE) 10 b.g. Good Thyne (USA) – Magic Minstrel (Pitpan) [2002/3 c–, h–§: c20g^pu May 24] leggy gelding: one-time fairly useful hurdler/maiden chaser, little form since 1998/9: temperamental display on debut for British stable in 2001/2: reportedly broke blood vessel following month: tried blinkered. *Ian Williams* **c–**
h– §

RODY (IRE) 6 b. or br.g. Foxhound (USA) – Capable Kate (IRE) (Alzao (USA)) [2002/3 h–: 17m^6 19g 20g^5 24d^pu 24g^pu 18m 17m^pu Apr 21] of little account: sold out of F. Jordan's stable £900 Ascot November Sales before final start (broke blood vessel). *I. R. Brown* **h–**

ROEBUCKS WAY 5 b.g. Shaamit (IRE) – Alwal (Pharly (FR)) [2002/3 F14d Nov 25] tall, unfurnished gelding: third foal: half-brother to fairly useful stayer on Flat/19f hurdle winner Quedex (by Deploy) and 7.5f winner in Italy by Ardkinglass: dam won 4 races in Holland, including Dutch Oaks: well held in bumper on debut. *D. Shaw* **F–**

ROGUE SPIRIT 7 b.g. Petong – Quick Profit (Formidable (USA)) [2002/3 h87§: 17m^4 16d^5 May 6] modest on Flat (seems to stay easy 2m): modest novice hurdler: raced mainly around 2m: acts on good to firm and good to soft going: usually blinkered: unreliable. *R. M. Stronge* **h90 §**

ROHAN 7 gr.g. Norton Challenger – Acushla Macree (Mansingh (USA)) [2002/3 F78: 16g 20m^2 Mar 19] sturdy gelding: fair form in bumpers: better effort in novice hurdles after 20-month absence when second of 5 at Fontwell: should stay beyond 2½m. *R. F. Johnson Houghton* **h87**

ROI DE DANSE 8 ch.g. Komaite (USA) – Princess Lucy (Local Suitor (USA)) [2002/3 h–: 17m May 3] modest up to 1¼m on Flat at 6 yrs: no form in 3 runs over hurdles. *Miss Z. C. Davison* **h–**

ROKY STAR (FR) 6 b.g. Start Fast (FR) – Rosydolie (FR) (Dhausli (FR)) [2002/3 h88, F99: 16g 19s^3 22v^4 22v^4 Jan 24] rather unfurnished gelding: bumper winner: modest novice hurdler: probably stays 2¾m: acts on heavy ground: tongue tied on reappearance. *M. R. Bosley* **h95**

ROLE MODEL 7 b.m. Tragic Role (USA) – Emerald Gulf (IRE) (Wassl) [2002/3 20d^3 Aug 3] poor form over hurdles, very lightly raced: stays 2½m: tongue tied only start in 2002/3: unseated in point in March. *J. Neville* **h70**

ROLEX FREE (ARG) 5 ch.g. Friul (ARG) – Karolera (ARG) (Kaljerry (ARG)) [2002/3 16m^6 Feb 21] leggy gelding: won at 1m and 1¼m on Flat in Argentina, seemingly fair form on first 2 of 3 starts in Britain: 66/1, jumped less than fluently and tailed off in Grade 2 novice at Kempton on hurdling debut. *Mrs L. C. Taylor* **h–**

ROLFE (NZ) 13 b.g. Tom's Shu (USA) – Tredia (NZ) (Mussorgsky) [2002/3 c–§, h74§: 24d^pu May 26] workmanlike gelding: poor hurdler: little form over fences: stays 21f: acts on any going: effective with or without blinkers: unreliable. *Dr P. Pritchard* **c– §**
h– §

ROLFES DELIGHT 11 b.g. Rolfe (USA) – Idiot's Run (Idiot's Delight) [2002/3 c–: c21f* c24d^F 20s 22m^5 c25f* c24m^5 c25d^pu c24s^pu Feb 27] workmanlike gelding: little show both starts over hurdles: poor chaser: won 2 handicaps at Wincanton, novice in May and conditional jockeys event in October: pulled up in hunters last 2 starts (tongue tied final one): stays 25f: acts on firm going: unreliable. *A. E. Jones* **c84 §**
h–

ROLLER BLADE 9 b.g. Broadsword (USA) – Sparkling Cinders (Netherkelly) [2002/3 c16d^F c16m* c25g^5 c20d^pu c22m^ur c17s^3 c25m* c24f^4 c25g^pu c21d^F c24d^R Mar 1] lengthy, angular gelding: winning hurdler: fair novice chaser, off 17 months before reappearance: won handicaps at Southwell in May and Hereford (jumped much better than usual, made all to beat Major Adventure easily by 9 lengths) in September: effective at 2m to 25f: acts on firm and good to soft going: often none too fluent: inconsistent. *N. A. Twiston-Davies* **c111**
h–

ROLLING MAUL (IRE) 8 b.g. Simply Great (FR) – Soyez Sage (FR) (Grundy) [2002/3 c80d, h–: c20m^5 c20g c24m^pu c24g^3 c25g^4 c26m^3 Apr 19] rangy gelding: winning hurdler/maiden chaser, little worthwhile form for long time: sometimes blinkered/visored. *Miss C. J. E. Caroe* **c–**
h–

ROLLING RIVER (IRE) 6 b.g. Over The River (FR) – Paddy's Dancer (Paddy's Stream) [2002/3 20m 27s^5 c24g^3 Dec 13] IR £5,400 4-y-o: workmanlike gelding: sixth foal: dam placed in points: won last of 3 starts in maiden points in 2002: well held in 2 novice hurdles: seemed to show modest form when third of 7 to Over The Storm in novice at Doncaster on steeplechasing debut. *J. Wade* **c95 ?**
h–

ROLLING TIDE (IRE) 7 b.g. Alphabatim (USA) – St Cristoph (The Parson) [2002/3   h–
h107p: 16d 21s^pu Dec 26] angular gelding: created good impression when winning novice
hurdle only outing in 2001/2: took strong hold and dropped right out in handicaps on
return: should stay beyond 2m. *N. J. Henderson*

ROLL WITH IT (IRE) 10 b.g. Royal Fountain – Deirdre Elizabeth (Salluceva)   c90
[2002/3 c24g^3 c24g^3 May 8] maiden hunter chaser: modest novice hunter chaser: stays 3m: acts   h–
on firm and good to soft going: blinkered once. *I. Anderson*

ROMAN CANDLE (IRE) 7 b.g. Sabrehill (USA) – Penny Banger (IRE) (Pennine   h80
Walk) [2002/3 h–: 16s^6 17m^ur 16m 19g^5 17m^2 16g^2 17g 16f^F 16m^5 Apr 21] lengthy,
workmanlike gelding: poor maiden hurdler: best given test of speed around 2m. *Mrs
Lucinda Featherstone*

ROMAN COURT (IRE) 5 b.g. Witness Box (USA) – Small Iron (General Ironside)   h80
[2002/3 F16d^6 22m^2 Apr 8] fifth foal: half-brother to winning pointer by Duky: dam, win-   F84
ning hurdler/pointer, half-sister to dual Foxhunter winner Fantus: sixth of 10 in bumper at
Chepstow on debut: 23 lengths second to Another Diamond in maiden hurdle at Exeter
following month, shaping like a stayer. *R. H. Alner*

ROMAN KING (IRE) 8 b.g. Sadler's Wells (USA) – Romantic Feeling (Shirley   h93
Heights) [2002/3 17s^F 17g^3 20d^4 16s^5 16d^2 16v^2 16d^6 16v^* 16s^6 16d^6 20s^F Mar 15] leggy
gelding: fairly useful on Flat (best around 1¼m) for J. Gosden/M. Johnston, below best in
2002: modest novice hurdler: trained by Mrs M. Reveley first 3 starts: won seller at
Uttoxeter (sold from P. Nicholls 8,600 gns) in February: best around 2m: acts on heavy
going: takes good hold. *Mrs J. Candlish*

ROMANNIE (BEL) 4 b.f. Piccolo – Green Land (BEL) (Hero's Honor (USA))   h–
[2002/3 17m^pu 16m 16d 17s Nov 26] close-coupled filly: poor maiden on Flat (stays
1½m), claimed from S. C. Williams £3,000 in August: no show over hurdles. *Mrs
S. A. Watt*

ROMAN OUTLAW 11 gr.g. Alias Smith (USA) – Roman Moor (Owen Anthony)   c95 x
[2002/3 c96x, h–: c27v^pu c24v^* c24v^6 c25v^5 c24s c32v^ur c20g^pu c24g^* c31g^pu Apr 24]   h–
strong, workmanlike gelding: modest handicap chaser: has won 4 times at Newcastle,
including in January and April: stays 3¾m: acts on good to firm and heavy going: wears
blinkers/cheekpieces: sketchy jumper: unreliable. *Mrs K. Walton*

ROMANTIC HERO (IRE) 7 b.g. Supreme Leader – Right Love (Golden Love)   c100
[2002/3 c93p, h–: c22d^F c18g^pu c21s^pu c20s^2 c24d^* Mar 19] big, strong gelding: fair   h–
handicap chaser: benefited from blinkers last 2 starts, making running and well clear from
home turn when winning at Chepstow: stays 3m: acts on soft going: free-going sort, probably best allowed to stride on. *N. A. Gaselee*

ROMAN WAY 7 ch.g. Gildoran – Olympian Princess (Master Owen) [2002/3 c25g^pu   c?
Apr 7] tenth foal: half-brother to several winners, including fair hurdler/chaser Banga-
bunny (by Gunner B), successful at 2m to 3½m: dam, useful Irish hurdler/chaser, half-
sister to smart staying jumper Bob Tisdall: maiden pointer: in with chance of making
frame when pulled up lame run-in in maiden hunter chase at Kelso. *R. W. Powell*

ROMANY CHAT 11 b.g. Backchat (USA) – Ranee's Song (True Song) [2002/3 c95:   c88
c21g^6 c25d^4 c28m^pu Jun 1] good-topped gelding: fair hunter chaser: won point in March:
stays 3m: acts on good to firm going. *Mrs Rosemary Gasson*

ROMANY DREAM 5 b.m. Nomadic Way (USA) – Half Asleep (Quiet Fling (USA))   h–
[2002/3 F16g^* 16m Apr 22] 3,800 4-y-o: sixth foal: half-sister to useful 2m chaser B   F74
The One and bumper winner Twenty Winks (both by Gunner B): dam fair 2½m hurdler:
won bumper at Warwick on debut in March: ninth of 16 in maiden hurdle at Chepstow.
R. Dickin

ROMANY FAIR (IRE) 4 b.g. Blues Traveller (IRE) – Fantasticus (IRE) (Lycius   h–
(USA)) [2002/3 17s^pu Jul 20] little form on Flat: no show on hurdling debut. *C. E. N.
Smith*

ROMANY HILL 8 b.m. Nomadic Way (USA) – Snarry Hill (Vitiges (FR)) [2002/3   c–
c–, h–: 19s^4 22d^3 26g^3 21m^4 20g^4 c20g^pu 16d Feb 25] lengthy mare: poor hurdler: made   h84
all in amateur handicap at Perth in September: no form over fences: stays 3¼m: acts on
good to firm and good to soft going: visored fourth outing (ran creditably). *J. M. Jefferson*

ROMANY LASS 7 br.m. Romany Rye – Furnace Lass VII (Damsire Unregistered)   h–
[2002/3 h–, F–: 16g 17d^4 Jun 5] little sign of ability. *W. Storey*

ROMA ROAD   7 b.g. Syrtos – Fair Cruise (Cruise Missile) [2002/3 F16g² F16v⁵ F16g **F89**
Jan 18] lengthy gelding: first foal: dam, sister to winning pointer, no sign of ability: fair
form in bumpers: short-head second of 16 to Mounsey Castle at Chepstow on debut,
hanging persistently left after leading over 2f out. *R. J. Smith*

ROME (IRE)   4 br.g. Singspiel (IRE) – Ela Romara (Ela-Mana-Mou) [2002/3 F16m⁶ **F89**
F14g* F17g⁵ Apr 26] 8,500 3-y-o: good-topped gelding: eighth foal: closely related to
smart 1m to 12.5f winner Earlene (by In The Wings) and half-brother to 2 winners,
notably smart 10.4f/1½m winner Foyer (by Sadler's Wells): dam won Lowther and
Nassau Stakes: fair form in bumpers, won 10-runner 1¾m event at Hereford in March.
G. P. Enright

ROMERO   7 b.g. Robellino (USA) – Casamarate (Be My Guest (USA)) [2002/3 h122§: **c112 §**
24d⁴ c16g⁴ 17d⁶ c19s³ c22d⁵ c22d* c22gᵘʳ c27d⁴ c22s⁴ c24m Mar 22] compact gelding: **h103 §**
winning hurdler, well below best in 2002/3: fair novice chaser: won handicap at Newbury
in November: below form last 3 starts, looking increasingly ungenuine: effective at 2m
(given good test) to 2¾m: probably acts on any going: often visored: has won 4 times at
Ascot: usually races prominently: not one to rely on. *Miss E. C. Lavelle*

ROMIL STAR (GER)   6 b.g. Chief's Crown (USA) – Romelia (USA) (Woodman **h88**
(USA)) [2002/3 h83: 16m* 16g May 29] fair on Flat (stays 1¾m), successful in February:
modest hurdler: made all in intermediate handicap at Perth in May: below form later in
month: raced around 2m: acts on good to firm going: tried tongue tied. *R. D. Wylie*

RONANS CHOICE (IRE)   10 b.g. Yashgan – Petite Port (Decent Fellow) **c–**
[2002/3 c75: c25dᵖᵘ c23mᵖᵘ c21mᵖᵘ Jul 14] workmanlike gelding: won 3¼m handicap in
2001/2, only form in steeplechases: blinkered last 4 starts (also tongue tied final one):
sold 4,500 gns Doncaster August Sales. *G. M. McCourt*

RON MIEL (IRE)   9 b.g. Brush Aside (USA) – Try Le Reste (IRE) (Le Moss) [2002/3 **c–**
c25dᵖᵘ May 14] poor maiden pointer. *M. Rodda*

ROOBIHOO (IRE)   4 b.g. Norwich – Griffinstown Lady (Over The River (FR)) **F88**
[2002/3 F16g⁵ F16d⁵ Apr 25] second foal: dam lightly raced in bumpers/points in Ireland:
better for debut experience, fifth of 17 to Flight Command in bumper at Perth. *C. Grant*

ROOFER (IRE)   5 b.m. Barathea (IRE) – Castlerahan (IRE) (Thatching) [2002/3 16d **h–**
21sᵖᵘ Jan 3] leggy mare: fair maiden on Flat (stays 10.8f), on downgrade in 2002: showed
more temperament than ability in 2 starts over hurdles. *Miss K. M. George*

ROOFTOP   7 b.g. Thatching – Top Berry (High Top) [2002/3 16dᵖᵘ Apr 29] strong **h–**
gelding: maiden hurdler, no form in Britain: tried visored. *W. Storey*

ROOKERY LAD   5 b.g. Makbul – Wayzgoose (USA) (Diesis) [2002/3 F16g 17m **h72**
16m⁶ 16g 16m 16g⁴ 22g 16m² Apr 21] fourth foal: dam once-raced daughter of very **F–**
smart French 10.5f winner Indoor: behind in bumper: poor maiden hurdler: left B. Leavy
after fifth start: best at 2m: raced on good/good to firm going: has been slowly away.
C. N. Kellett

ROOSTER   8 b.g. Roi Danzig (USA) – Jussoli (Don) [2002/3 c–, h–: c16dᵖᵘ c21g⁴ **c71**
c21m³ Apr 21] good-topped gelding: winning hurdler: off 20 months prior to reappear- **h–**
ance: poor form in novice hunters at Fakenham last 2 outings: stays 21f: acts on good to
firm and good to soft going. *Mrs Julie Read*

ROOSTER BOOSTER   9 gr.g. Riverwise (USA) – Came Cottage (Nearly A **h170**
Hand) [2002/3 h152: 16d* 16d* 17d* 16v* 16g* 20g² Apr 5]
      Continuous improvement reached its logical conclusion. That's not to say
that Rooster Booster cannot improve any further—rash in the extreme given how
he has progressed in the last four seasons—but there is not that much scope for
further enhancement now he has won the Champion Hurdle by eleven lengths. The
horse who earned praise the previous season for his improvement in the face of
honourable defeats facing stiffer and stiffer tasks as a handicapper, now did so for
being the best two-mile hurdler around and well-nigh unbeatable. The perpetual
bridesmaid turned into a serial bigamist. Here are Rooster Booster's ratings in
Chasers & Hurdlers: 94 after two bumper starts in 1998/9, 124 in 1999/00, 143
in 2000/1, 152 in 2001/2 and now 170 in 2002/3. The Champion Hurdle was his
twenty-sixth start over hurdles. This sort of steady build-up is not unprecedented—
Flakey Dove's 1994 Champion Hurdle triumph, for instance, came after twenty-
eight previous hurdles starts—but it is certainly unusual, as a look at the last ten

Rehabilitation of Racehorses Hurdle (Handicap), Cheltenham—
the grey Rooster Booster confirms himself a much improved performer; Quazar is second

other Champion Hurdle winners indicates. Hors La Loi III won it after eighteen jumps outings, Istabraq after ten, Make A Stand eleven, Collier Bay nine, Alderbrook two, Granville Again fifteen, Royal Gait three, Morley Street sixteen, Kribensis ten and Beech Road twenty-two. Flakey Dove was an eight-year-old when she won. At the age of nine or more, no Champion Hurdle winner has ever made the sort of progress that Rooster Booster did. Hatton's Grace is the closest example, winning the first of his three Champions as a nine-year-old in 1949, undoubtedly much improved after joining Vincent O'Brien the previous summer but having already finished fifth in that year's Champion. Four other nine-year-olds have taken the race: Free Fare (1937) and Our Hope (1938), who had both already been runner-up; Solford (1940), who fell at the last when holding every chance twelve months earlier; and Royal Gait (1992), who had been a high-class performer on the Flat. The incredible Sea Pigeon was already a Champion Hurdle veteran when he won the race for the first time at the age of ten in 1980—after, incidentally, thirty-one jumps outings and plenty more on the Flat.

To mention Rooster Booster in the same breath as Sea Pigeon would have seemed like blasphemy at the end of the 2001/2 season. Rooster Booster won at the Cheltenham Festival during that campaign, but did so in the County Handicap Hurdle. Masking the substantial improvement made up to that point, the County Hurdle was only his second victory and came on the back of sixteen consecutive defeats. In his only race after the County, however, came a hint of what Rooster Booster might be capable of: in the Grade 1 two-and-a-half-mile Aintree Hurdle, his first venture into pattern events, he travelled as strongly as anything into the straight before finishing fourth.

Back over two miles or thereabouts in the latest season, Rooster Booster reappeared at the Festival in the Champion Hurdle after four consecutive victories. An £8,151 event at Kempton in October, Rooster Booster's first port of call, did not, strictly speaking, see improved form, but he was pulling double all the way up the straight in winning by seven lengths from Mr Cool, a smart rival sent off at 6/4-on to beat him. Concentrating on the form, rather than the startling new manner of the Kempton victory, the bookmakers quoted Rooster Booster at 25/1 for the

Champion. A comprehensive reappraisal took place when he won his next outing in not dissimilar style, despite stepping back into handicap company and carrying top weight (off a BHB mark of 155) in the normally fiercely competitive Rehabilitation of Racehorses Hurdle at the Cheltenham Open meeting. The presence of the Supreme Novices' third and fourth, In Contrast and Eternal Spring, gave the race a considerable lustre beforehand, as did that of the previous season's Grade 1-winning juvenile Quazar, classy chasers Latalomne and Dark'n Sharp, and an easy last-time-out winner trained by Martin Pipe in Dream With Me, who was made favourite. Rooster Booster drifted from 11/2 to 7/1 in on-course betting but he trotted up; always travelling and jumping well, he went on after the second last and ran right away from his rivals—a race description that was going to be equally applicable later on. The final margin of victory over Quazar (who received 18 lb) was nine lengths, Rooster Booster recording a performance so outstanding that— the way we read the form-book—it would have won him the previous season's Champion.

Rooster Booster was now available at no bigger than 10/1 for the 2003 Champion, joint favourite in places, and his next appearance came back at Chelt-

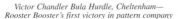

Victor Chandler Bula Hurdle, Cheltenham—
Rooster Booster's first victory in pattern company

Agfa Hurdle, Sandown—novice Self Defense pushes 7/2-on Rooster Booster surprisingly close

enham in a more conventional trial of his championship credentials, the Victor Chandler Bula Hurdle in December. With the previous season's Champion Hurdle first, second, fourth and fifth all in opposition it promised to be a good test. Rooster Booster was made the 11/8 favourite with doubts of one sort or another hanging over the aforementioned Hors La Loi, Marble Arch, Geos and Landing Light when compared to the conspicuously in-form Rooster Booster. The cramped odds were fully justified, as Rooster Booster won, but he did not actually enhance his Champion case, though his Champion odds were cut, of course, to 4/1 as the bookmakers gave nothing away. At the second last, it seemed that Rooster Booster might be about to win much as he had done four weeks earlier, but he did not assert his superiority this time, passing the post two and a half lengths ahead of Landing Light and Geos. With Landing Light conceding 4 lb, a strict interpretation of the result did not even make Rooster Booster the best horse in the race. Disappointment in his performance was not at all widely expressed, however, but was after his next start when he scraped home by just half a length from the unheralded novice Self Defense in the Agfa Hurdle at Sandown at the start of February. Once again, there was everything to admire in Rooster Booster's performance up to the second last, but after that he seemed to idle markedly in the heavy ground. Some thought he was not fully tuned up for this final start before the Champion, but trainer Philip Hobbs later speculated that perhaps it was just an 'off day'.

For the following month's Smurfit Champion Hurdle, Rooster Booster had an 'on day', the style of his victory so exalted that it again had his trainer and others groping in the dark for explanations. One week earlier, in fact, Hobbs had stated that 'If the ground is on the fast side, I could see [stable-mate] In Contrast finishing in front of Rooster Booster.' Watering and late rainfall made the ground good. Rooster Booster's handicap victory over the course in November was still the best form of the season and he ended up the 9/2 second favourite. Favourite, at 5/2, was a contrasting sort in novice hurdler Rhinestone Cowboy, the unlucky 2002 Champion Bumper runner-up who was fresh from four facile victories over hurdles. Also from Jonjo O'Neill's yard was 5/1 third favourite Intersky Falcon, the tough front runner who had won four in a row, including the Fighting Fifth at Newcastle and Christmas Hurdle at Kempton. Any late rain apparently boosted the chances of 2002 Supreme Novices' winner Like-A-Butterfly (13/2), whose latest start saw her get the better of a head-to-head with Limestone Lad in the AIG Europe Champion at Leopardstown. From the previous year's substandard running, only Hors La Loi (14/1), Marble Arch (25/1) and the blinkered Landing Light (14/1) did battle again, none of them having enhanced or even maintained their reputations in the meantime. Haydock Trial winner Flame Creek (14/1) was the only other runner to start at odds shorter than 25/1 in a seventeen-strong field. Although none of them had put up a hurdling performance right from the top drawer. the field that lined up was fully representative and produced a seemingly highly competitive edition of the championship in which the first five in ante-post lists (Rhinestone Cowboy, Intersky Falcon, Rooster Booster, Like-A-Butterfly and Flame Creek) had had a total of seventeen races during the season and won them all.

None of the other fancied horses lived up to expectations as Rooster Booster gloriously exceeded those held for him. A one-sided contest it may have been, but there was drama with thoroughly unforeseen events at the beginning, before half-way and at the finish. First, after a widespread reluctance by the jockeys to obey the orders of the starter when the seventeen lined up, the defending champion Hors La Loi III refused to race, the fact that his jockey was the only one to escape a caution from the stewards afterwards being scant consolation. Among those that did set off, the first surprise came from Rhinestone Cowboy. Tucked away on the inside, he was initially just ahead of Rooster Booster and then racing alongside him, but the two market leaders were soon travelling in starkly contrasting styles as shoddy jumping put the novice under pressure. Rhinestone Cowboy was supposed to challenge late and on the bridle, but the game was up for him an awful lot sooner

Smurfit Champion Hurdle Challenge Trophy, Cheltenham—
a brilliant performance by Rooster Booster, with a near-record eleven-length winning margin in the race;
the blinkered pair Westender and Intersky Falcon (right), followed by Rhinestone Cowboy (dark colours),
are his closest pursuers at the last

Mr Terry Warner's "Rooster Booster"

than that. It was a common story in the race. The field was hardly past halfway before the searching gallop set by Intersky Falcon had all of his opponents ridden along, all except one—Rooster Booster was pulling double, and still was when finally allowed to go on from the flagging Intersky Falcon turning into the final straight. There were no conceivable dangers bar a fall. Copeland had already fallen when disputing second with him three out, after which 33/1-shot Westender and the sticking-to-their-guns stable-companions Intersky Falcon and Rhinestone Cowboy were the only others theoretically still in touch, but Rooster Booster was four lengths clear by the last and continued his surge to score by a massive margin. The official eleven lengths has been exceeded only twice in Champion Hurdle history, when Istabraq won by twelve lengths in 1998 to match the record set by Insurance in the fifth Champion Hurdle, back in 1932. Just a year after Istabraq's retirement, the two-mile division had another champion who was streets ahead of the rest. How long could Rooster Booster remain at the top? It took less than four weeks for him to be beaten, but that was over two and a half miles in the Aintree Hurdle. Travelling strongly again, he quickened up, seemingly decisively, to go a length ahead approaching the last. This time, in contrast to his appearances over two miles, he did not go clear but might still have won had his now-regular jockey Richard Johnson not dropped his whip shortly after the final flight; Irish-trained Sacundai rallied to get his head in front just before the post.

    Rooster Booster is best at around two miles and the bare form of his Champion Hurdle triumph was better than that for either of Istabraq's second or third victories in the race, though not quite on a par with Istabraq's first or with some of Istabraq's other performances. Rooster Booster probably acts on any going and takes his hurdles fast and accurately nowadays, as well as being splendidly tough and consistent. To look at him, a sparely-made gelding, the substantial and sustained improvement he has made has to be a surprise. No single answer emerged as to how he was able to make such startling progress, but Hobbs observed that he was 'more relaxed and physically stronger than last year'. Rooster Booster's groom, Carol Burnett, described how 'the longer Rooster has been here, the happier and more relaxed he has become. He loves his work. When you're happy you do things better, don't you?' The installation of a three-furlong polytrack gallop has apparently helped with the horse's home work and he reportedly has daily visits from the physio Mary Bromiley. Rooster Booster's owner Terry Warner, a veteran of ownership in the National Hunt game who celebrated his two-hundredth winner in February, reflected that his star had thrived during his latest summer break. One thing that didn't make Rooster Booster happy was being schooled over fences—'he hated it,' reported Hobbs.

		Riverman	Never Bend
	Riverwise (USA)	(b 1969)	River Lady
	(b 1988)	Village Sass	Sassafras
Rooster Booster		(1982)	Village Beauty
(gr.g. 1994)		Nearly A Hand	Busted
	Came Cottage	(ch 1974)	Petite Chou
	(gr 1980)	Maybelle	Perhapsburg
		(gr 1965)	Tinkling

Warner acquired Rooster Booster in March 2000. 'I saw him run third at Chepstow and I wanted to buy a grey horse,' said the owner. 'I offered £50,000 but Richard Mitchell said it was £60,000 or no deal. I said I would pay it subject to the vet, but when the vet went down he said Rooster Booster was so wild he couldn't get near him in the box. I thought that the horse clearly had a bit of spirit, so I would buy him and I did.' As detailed in last year's Annual, West Country trainer Mitchell also bred Rooster Booster, from his own stallion Riverwise and broodmare Came Cottage. Riverwise was a well-bred failure as a racehorse, initially intended to run in the colours of Sheikh Mohammed. Came Cottage was a modest novice hurdler but fairly useful winning pointer. She now has a second winner, Rooster Booster's six-year-old chestnut brother Cockatoo Ridge who won a bumper at Fontwell in April, but their seven-year-old half-sister Madame Poulet (by Gold Dust) was well beaten, for the fourth time in as many starts, on the same card. There are further offspring by Riverwise out of Came Cottage on their way, four-year-old and yearling fillies who are with Mitchell and a two-year-old filly for whom he received an offer he couldn't refuse after the Champion Hurdle. The Champion result has also boosted the popularity of Riverwise, who had six outside mares booked before the race and, at the time of writing, another twenty-eight added after it. Tullons Lane was a third winner from nine runners for Riverwise during the latest season, the only one not trained by a Mitchell being Rooster Booster. Thanks to Rooster Booster's extraordinary rise to the top, Riverwise is no longer a family secret. Far from it. *P. J. Hobbs*

ROOSTER'S REUNION 4 gr.g. Presenting – Court Town (Camden Town) [2002/3 F14d F16d² Mar 19] useful-looking gelding: fifth foal: half-brother to poor 2m hurdler Russian Court (by Soviet Lad): dam, modest 1m winner on Flat, half-sister to very smart sprinter Broxted: patiently ridden, much better effort in bumpers when neck second to Mount Karinga at Chepstow. *D. R. Gandolfo* **F97 +**

ROPPONGI DANCER 4 b.f. Mtoto – Ice Chocolate (USA) (Icecapade (USA)) [2002/3 17s⁵ 17g⁶ 16g 16g Dec 13] small filly: poor maiden on Flat (stays 1½m): poor juvenile hurdler: will be suited by further than 17f. *Mrs M. Reveley* **h71**

ROSA GALLICA 7 ch.m. Sula Bula – Armonit (Town Crier) [2002/3 F16g May 8] sixth foal: half-sister to useful staying hurdler/chaser Gaelstrom (by Strong Gale) and poor 2m hurdler Vintage Red (by Sulaafah): dam won 5 races up to 2½m over hurdles: behind in bumper on debut. *Miss H. C. Knight* **F—**

ROSAKER (USA) 6 b.g. Pleasant Tap (USA) – Rose Crescent (USA) (Nijinsky (CAN)) [2002/3 16v⁵ 16s* 20d* 16g Mar 11] leggy, rather sparely-made gelding: half-brother to numerous minor winners in USA: dam, US Grade 3 11f winner, sister to Ile de Bourbon and half-sister to Rose Bowl, both top class: won handicaps at Jebel Ali (9f) and Abu Dhabi (1¼m) at 4 yrs for J. Sadler: bought 47,000 gns Newmarket July Sales: fairly **h129**

High Street Ceather Syndicate's "Rosaker"

useful novice hurdler: won maiden at Fairyhouse in December and Grade 2 Woodlands Park 100 Johnstown Novices' Hurdle at Naas (by 2 lengths from Mossy Green) in February: not discredited when tenth of 19 in Grade 1 at Cheltenham, disappointing in similar event at Punchestown in early-May: stays 2½m: raced on good ground or softer. *N. Meade, Ireland*

ROSALEE ROYALE 11 ch.m. Out of Hand – Miss Ark Royal (Broadsword (USA)) [2002/3 c16m⁶ Apr 5] workmanlike mare: poor maiden pointer. *Mrs S. Kittow*   c– h–

ROSALYONS (IRE) 9 gr.g. Roselier (FR) – Coffee Shop (Bargello) [2002/3 c–, h95: 21g 22g⁵ 21d c22v³ c25s⁵ c25v³ c24s⁶ 22d* 22d⁴ c25gᵖᵘ Mar 21] leggy gelding: has stringhalt: modest handicap hurdler: won at Kelso in March: little worthwhile form over fences, often let down by jumping: stays 25f: acts on heavy going: tried blinkered: takes plenty of driving. *Mrs H. O. Graham*   c82 h87

ROSARIAN (IRE) 6 b.g. Fourstars Allstar (USA) – Only A Rose (Glint of Gold) [2002/3 F106: 22s⁴ 24v⁴ 19d³ 22d* 24g³ 27v* 24m* 24mᶠ Apr 17] unfurnished gelding: fairly useful hurdler: won handicap at Wincanton in January and novices at Fontwell (simple task) and Newbury (improved form when beating El Hombre Del Rio 14 lengths) in March: visored, fell seventh final outing: will prove best at 3m+: acts on good to firm and heavy going: looked very well last 2 starts. *V. R. A. Dartnall*   h127

ROSCO 9 b.g. Roscoe Blake – Silva Linda (Precipice Wood) [2002/3 c–, h109: 20s⁴ 22v⁵ 20g* 24m² Apr 17] good sort: maiden chaser: fairly useful handicap hurdler: best efforts in 2002/3 in cheekpieces last 2 starts, winning 20-runner event at Ascot in April by 2 lengths from Samsaam and 11 lengths second to Tribal Venture at Cheltenham: stays 25f: acts on soft and good to firm going: none too fluent over fences. *J. T. Gifford*   c– h119

ROSE BOWL BOY (IRE) 5 ch.g. Lahib (USA) – Danita (IRE) (Roi Danzig (USA))   **F–**
[2002/3 F16s F16s F16d Mar 1] IR 25,000 3-y-o: unfurnished gelding: third foal: half-brother to 9f/1¼m winner in Japan by Namaqualand: dam 9f winner: well held in bumpers. *C. J. Mann*

ROSECHARMER 6 ch.m. Charmer – Rosie Cone (Celtic Cone) [2002/3 F64: 21d⁶   **h66**
20d⁶ 19d 22v⁶ 20dᵖᵘ Feb 26] medium-sized mare: signs of only a little ability in mares bumpers and novice hurdles: has pulled hard. *Mrs P. Sly*

ROSE D'APRIL (FR) 6 gr.g. April Night (FR) – Rose de Hoc (FR) (Rose Laurel)   **h103**
[2002/3 F100: 17s* 16s⁵ 20g* 20dᵖᵘ 22g Mar 21] rangy gelding: bumper winner: fair form over hurdles, won novices at Carlisle in November and Musselburgh (handicap) in January: twice badly let down by jumping, including final outing (wore cheekpieces): stays easy 2½m: acts on soft ground: ran as if amiss fourth start. *L. Lungo*

ROSEGROVE ROOSTER 6 b.g. Henbit (USA) – Cornbelt (Oats) [2002/3 F–:   **h–**
20mᵖᵘ Apr 12] little sign of ability in 2 bumpers and novice hurdle. *D. J. Caro*

ROSELIER BELL (IRE) 10 b.g. Roselier (FR) – Bell Walks Fancy (Entrechat)   **c–**
[2002/3 h–: 24v 22sᵖᵘ c27vᵖᵘ Jan 21] compact gelding: maiden hurdler: no form since   **h–**
2000, including on chasing debut: tried blinkered/in cheekpieces. *B. J. Llewellyn*

ROSEMEAD TYE 7 b.m. Kasakov – Nouvelle Cuisine (Yawa) [2002/3 F16s 20mᵖᵘ   **h–**
16d 16dᵖᵘ 16m Apr 21] first foal: half-sister to 2m hurdle winner Feanor (by Presidium):   **F–**
dam won around 2m over hurdles/winner at 1½m/2m on Flat: no form, including in points: tongue tied last 3 starts. *J. A. Moore*

ROSENCRANTZ (IRE) 11 b.g. Sadler's Wells (USA) – Rosananti (Blushing   **c106**
Groom (FR)) [2002/3 c80, h–: c16d* c20m³ c16v* c20d² c20mᵖᵘ c17d⁵ Aug 10] fair   **h–**
handicap chaser: won at Towcester in May and Uttoxeter (easily landed odds in 3-runner event) in June: reportedly lame final outing: stays 21f: acts on any going: has reportedly broken blood vessels: none too consistent. *Miss Venetia Williams*

ROSETA PEARL (IRE) 7 gr.m. Roselier (FR) – Brown Pearl (Tap On Wood) [2002/3   **c–**
c26s³ c25sᶠ c22g⁵ Mar 17] third foal: dam, 11f winner on Flat, out of half-sister to top-class jumper Lanzarote: no encouragement both completed outings in novice chases: tongue tied last 2 starts. *Mrs S. Wall*

ROSE TINA 6 b.m. Tina's Pet – Rosevear (IRE) (Contract Law (USA)) [2002/3 h72:   **c90**
16s 21s 21d³ c20g⁶ c22g² c19f² 19m⁴ Apr 15] leggy mare: poor novice hurdler, left   **h71**
E. Wheeler after reappearance: modet form over fences, hasn't convinced with jumping: stays easy 2¾m: acts on firm and soft going: takes good hold. *B. G. Powell*

ROSEWOOD (GER) 4 ch.f. Eagle Eyed (USA) – Rhode Island (GER) (Waajib)   **h89**
[2002/3 16dᶠ Dec 21] fairly useful on Flat, won over 11f in September for H. Remmert: ridden and looking set for third at best when falling 2 out in 21-runner juvenile at Warwick on hurdling debut. *C. Von Der Recke, Germany*

ROSEY BOY (IRE) 10 gr.g. Roselier (FR) – Rossian (Silent Spring) [2002/3 24d⁵   **c– §**
26s* 24g c25dᵘʳ 26gᶠ Mar 12] tall gelding: fair handicap hurdler, off 3½ years before   **h104**
reappearance: won 17-runner event at Hereford in December: failed to impress with attitude both starts over fences, hanging badly left: best at 3m+, seemingly on going softer than good: tried blinkered: sold 3,000 gns Doncaster May Sales. *H. Morrison*

ROSIDAVIS (IRE) 5 ch.g. Roselier (FR) – Zalara (Zalazl (USA)) [2002/3 F17m²   **F87**
F16f² F16mᵖᵘ Oct 4] first foal: dam 1¼m winner in Ireland, stayed 1½m: runner-up in bumpers at Sedgefield and Hexham: dead. *R. F. Fisher*

ROSIE REDMAN (IRE) 6 gr.m. Roselier (FR) – Carbia's Last (Palm Track) [2002/3   **h84**
F86: 16s⁵ 22v⁴ 20g⁴ 24v⁵ 20g⁴ Mar 29] leggy mare: poor novice hurdler: didn't seem to stay testing 3m: raced on good going or softer. *J. R. Turner*

ROSPO 7 b. or br.g. Tromeros – East Gale (Oats) [2002/3 F–: 16dᶠ 16vᵖᵘ Nov 13]   **h–**
tall, rather sparely-made gelding: no form in bumper or novice hurdles: headstrong. *Mrs L. B. Normile*

ROSSCARBERY GREY (IRE) 5 gr.g. Gothland (FR) – Millroad (Buckskin (FR))   **F–**
[2002/3 F16g F14g Mar 17] €5,000 4-y-o: fourth live foal: dam winning pointer: in rear in 2 bumpers. *S. T. Lewis*

ROSS COTTAGE 11 b.g. Hyrossi – Flavias Cottage (Marcus Superbus) [2002/3 c26g³   **c86 +**
c28g⁶ May 31] fair pointer: better effort in novice hunter chases when third to Hatton Farm Babe at Uttoxeter (would have finished closer but for almost unseating 4 out). *T. Long*

'Press The Red Button To Bet attheraces' Hurdle, Sandown—
cheekpieces and Norman Williamson conjure a win for Rostropovich over Deano's Beeno

ROSSLEA (IRE) 5 b.g. Roselier (FR) – Burren Gale (IRE) (Strong Gale) [2002/3 **h112 +**
20vᵖᵘ 20v² 22d³ 21g Mar 12] good-topped gelding: type to make a chaser: third foal: half-
brother to fairly useful hurdler/chaser Russell Road (by Phardante), stays 3m: dam
unraced: won maiden Irish point on debut in 2002: fair novice hurdler: 4 lengths second
to Sh Boom, pair clear, at Uttoxeter in December: stiff task, well beaten in Grade 1 at
Cheltenham final start: will stay 3m: acts on heavy going. *Miss H. C. Knight*

ROSS MINSTER (IRE) 9 br. or b.g. Roselier (FR) – Face To Face (The Parson) **c–**
[2002/3 c125, h–: c25gᵖᵘ Nov 9] medium-sized gelding: fairly useful handicap chaser: **h–**
weakening when all but coming down 2 out in valuable race at Wincanton, only outing in
2002/3: stays 4m: raced on good going or softer (acts on heavy): effective blinkered or
not: usually races prominently: sometimes none too fluent: usually takes plenty of
driving. *P. J. Hobbs*

ROSS MOFF (IRE) 10 b.g. Good Thyne (USA) – Miss Kamsy (Kambalda) [2002/3 **c132 x**
c17vᶠ c25d⁵ c20vᶠ c16g⁵ c25d³ c29gᶠ Apr 21] good-topped gelding: useful chaser, off **h–**
nearly 2 years before reappearance: creditable efforts in valuable handicaps at Cheltenham (fifth of 21 to Palarshan) in March and Aintree (made several mistakes when third of
14 to Master Tern) in April: fell on 3 other occasions in 2002/3, every chance when
departing last on first and third outings: needs good test at 2m, stays 25f: acts on good to
firm and heavy going: tongue tied: often makes mistakes. *A. J. Martin, Ireland*

ROSS PARK (IRE) 7 b.g. Roselier (FR) – La Christyana (IRE) (The Parson) [2002/3 **h66**
h74p: 24d 20v⁶ 25gᶠ Nov 23] poor novice hurdler: stays 3m: tongue tied final start.
J. Howard Johnson

ROSS WILL (IRE) 9 b.g. Satco (FR) – Jayells Dream (Space King) [2002/3 24vᵖᵘ **h70**
16d 20v 22gᵖᵘ Apr 26] IR 15,000 4-y-o: second foal: half-brother to fair maiden chaser
No Lives Lost (by Strong Gale): dam, modest hurdler up to 2¾m, half-sister to useful
staying chaser Sam Wrekin: runner-up in bumper for G. Stewart in 1999/00: poor form
over hurdles: dead. *Ian Williams*

766

ROSTROPOVICH (IRE)   6 gr.g. Sadler's Wells (USA) – Infamy (Shirley Heights)   **h141**
[2002/3 h131: 16m⁴ 24g⁵ 24s² 24s⁴ 24s² 24d⁴ 25g 24g² 24m* Apr 26] well-made gelding:
useful hurdler: in cheekpieces, well ridden to win 6-runner valuable minor event at
Sandown by short head from Deano's Beeno: not discredited most starts earlier in season
and, again in cheekpieces, when third to Holly Orders in Grade 1 at Punchestown in
early-May: stays 3m well: acts on soft and good to firm going: usually tongue tied:
possibly best ridden up with pace: has hung left. *M. F. Morris, Ireland*

ROTUMA (IRE)   4 b.g. Tagula (IRE) – Cross Question (USA) (Alleged (USA))   **h88**
[2002/3 16m⁵ 16d⁶ 16d³ 16d⁴ 17d³ 16g³ Mar 23] neat gelding: modest on Flat (stays
1¼m): modest juvenile hurdler: likely to prove best around 2m: blinkered third start,
visored last 2: consistent. *M. Dods*

ROUGENOIR (FR)   10 b.g. Nerio (FR) – Madame Rana (FR) (Sir Ribot) [2002/3   **c155**
c156, h137: c29s⁴ c22d² 19s² 20s⁴ 24v 20s³ 19s³ 18v³ c22s* c22s Apr 13] strong gelding: **h147**
smart hurdler: best efforts when in frame in Group 3 events won by Vic Toto at Auteuil
third and fourth starts and in well-contested minor event at Pau (third to Escort Boy)
seventh one: very smart chaser: won Group 3 Prix Troytown at Auteuil in March by neck
from Jerico Vallis, just holding on after finding little: faded late on when fourth to
impressive Line Marine in Grand Steeple-Chase de Paris there in May: ideally suited by
up to 2¾m: raced mainly on going softer than good (possibly not ideally suited by heavy):
blinkered nowadays: weak finisher. *R. E. Lecomte, France*

ROUGH TIGER (IRE)   10 ch.g. Glacial Storm (USA) – Mourne Trix (Golden Love)   **c94**
[2002/3 c23dᶠ Mar 4] fair pointer, successful in February/March: would have made frame
but for falling last at Leicester on hunter chase debut. *F. A. Hutsby*

ROUND THE BEND   11 b.g. Revolutionary (USA) – No Love (Bustiki) [2002/3   **c90**
c20m² c22m⁵ Jun 1] successful in points in February and March: fair form both starts in
hunter chases. *Miss Louise Allan*

ROUTE BARREE (FR)   5 ch.g. Exit To Nowhere (USA) – Star Des Evees (FR)   **h–**
(Moulin) [2002/3 h82: 16d⁶ Mar 5] leggy gelding: fair on Flat (stays 2m, carries head
awkwardly), successful in July: poor form over hurdles: has looked temperamental.
S. Dow

ROUTE ONE (IRE)   10 br.g. Welsh Term – Skylin (Skyliner) [2002/3 c16g c16d²   **c92**
c20v³ c16d² c20m² c19g* Apr 2] rather sparely-made gelding: winning hurdler: fair   **h–**
hunter chaser nowadays: beat Miss O'Grady 5 lengths in 17-runner event at Ascot:
effective at 2m to easy 2½m: acts on good to firm and good to soft going: has been let
down by jumping: best on right-handed tracks. *D. Frankland*

ROUTE SIXTY SIX (IRE)   7 b.m. Brief Truce (USA) – Lyphards Goddess (IRE)   **c82**
(Lyphard's Special (USA)) [2002/3 h100: c17gᵘʳ c16d* c16g c16gᵖᵘ 16gᵖᵘ Feb 28]   **h–**
compact mare: fair handicap hurdler in 2001/2: not fluent in novice chases, fortunate to
win at Ayr in November: will prove best at sharp 2m: acts on good to soft going. *Jedd
O'Keeffe*

ROVERETTO   8 b.g. Robellino (USA) – Spring Flyer (IRE) (Waajib) [2002/3 h126:   **c124**
23f⁵ 25d⁶ 22s² 24d⁶ c16g* c16g* c20d³ c20m⁴ Feb 22] sturdy gelding: fairly useful hand-   **h126**
icap hurdler: won novices at Musselburgh in January on first 2 starts over fences: easily
better effort at Kempton after (mistakes in Grade 2) when third of 8 to Scots Grey: stays
easy 3m: acts on soft and good to firm going. *Mrs M. Reveley*

ROVESTAR   12 b.g. Le Solaret (FR) – Gilberts Choice (My Swanee) [2002/3 c102§,   **c– §**
h–: c16s c27sᵖᵘ c24v c19s⁶ c24s c24d Apr 9] sparely-made gelding: fair but unreliable   **h– §**
handicap chaser in 2001/2, very much on downgrade: stays 3m: acts on good to firm and
heavy going: has worn cheekpieces, usually blinkered. *C. L. Popham*

ROXBY EXPLORER   7 b.g. Aragon – Super Blues (Welsh Captain) [2002/3 h91,   **c–**
F93: c16m⁴ c20dᶠ c21dᶠ 20sᵖᵘ 16s 16dᵖᵘ 17g² 21m⁵ 21mᵖᵘ Apr 21] sturdy gelding: bump-   **h76**
er winner: maiden hurdler/chaser, only poor form in 2002/3: blinkered last 5 outings:
dead. *O. Sherwood*

ROYAL ALLEGIANCE   8 ch.g. Kris – Wilayif (USA) (Danzig (USA)) [2002/3 h–:   **c–**
16dᵖᵘ c17m⁵ c17g³ Apr 19] compact gelding: poor 2m hurdler: no form since 2000/1,   **h–**
including over fences: tried visored/blinkered. *P. Wegmann*

ROYAL ALPHABET (IRE)   5 b.g. King's Theatre (IRE) – A-To-Z (IRE) (Ahonoora)   **F117**
[2002/3 F16d* F16g F16g* Apr 20] unfurnished gelding: fourth foal: half-brother to
fairly useful 8.3f winner Alphabet (by Saddlers' Hall): dam Nell Gwyn winner: smart in
bumpers, won 26-runner event at Galway in August and 15-runner race at Fairyhouse

Dr T. Mahony's "Royal Alphabet"

(quickened well once in clear to beat Flexible Action 2½ lengths) in April: easily better effort in Grade 1 events when 3½ lengths second to Royal Rosa at Punchestown in late-April: fairly useful form in 2 starts on Flat in June: will probably stay 2½m: interesting hurdling prospect. *W. P. Mullins, Ireland*

ROYAL ARROW (USA) 7 b.g. Dayjur (USA) – Buy The Firm (USA) (Affirmed (USA)) [2002/3 h66: 16g² 17s⁴ 16m Oct 4] poor maiden hurdler: raced around 2m: probably acts on any going. *Ferdy Murphy*   **h70**

ROYAL ARTIST 7 b.g. Royal Academy (USA) – Council Rock (General Assembly (USA)) [2002/3 17m⁶ Oct 1] modest on Flat (stays easy 8.5f, has proved mulish at start): looked non-stayer on hurdling debut. *M. Brittain*   **h65**

ROYAL AUCLAIR (FR) 6 ch.g. Garde Royale – Carmonera (FR) (Carmont (FR)) [2002/3 c140p, h–: c21d⁴ c24g⁴ c24g Mar 11] good-topped gelding: smart chaser, won Cathcart Challenge Cup at Cheltenham in 2001/2: best effort when fourth of 5 finishers to Valley Henry in Grade 2 at Newbury: made mistakes other 2 starts in 2002/3: will prove best at 2½m+: raced on good going or softer (acts on heavy): front runner. *M. C. Pipe*   **c151** **h–**

ROYAL BARGE 13 b.g. Nearly A Hand – April Airs (Grey Mirage) [2002/3 c–, h–: 20m⁴ c25m* 24d⁴ c24s³ Nov 14] good-topped gelding: winning hurdler: handicap chaser, still capable of fair form: won at Market Rasen in August: suited by 3m+: acts on any going: has jumped right. *P. Bowen*   **c101** **h92**

ROYAL BELUGA (USA) 6 b.g. Rahy (USA) – Navratilovna (USA) (Nureyev (USA)) [2002/3 h99: 16m³ 17m² 17g 16d c17v* c20s* c20d⁵ c20g³ c20s² c18m* c20g⁵ c21m² Apr 17] smallish gelding: modest maiden hurdler (has hinted at temperament): better over fences, won novice handicaps at Bangor (subsequently tested positive for morphine) in November, Ludlow in January and Newbury in March: excellent ½-length   **c116** **h89**

768

second of 15 to Banjo Hill in similar event at Cheltenham final start: stays 21f: acts on good to firm and heavy going: tried visored/tongue tied. *T. R. George*

ROYAL BUCKINGHAM (IRE) 8 b.g. Erdelistan (FR) – French Class (The Parson) **h–**
[2002/3 h–: 16g⁰ᵘ 16g⁰ᵘ 16m⁰ᵘ Jul 18] lengthy gelding: won bumper on debut in 1999/00: disappointing since, mainly over hurdles: has broken blood vessel. *J. A. Moore*

ROYAL CASCADE (IRE) 9 b.g. River Falls – Relative Stranger (Cragador) [2002/3 **h–**
16d⁰ᵘ Jan 24] modest on Flat (stays 9.4f): no show in novice at Doncaster on hurdling debut. *B. A. McMahon*

ROYAL CASINO (IRE) 6 b.g. Kasmayo – Gambling Princess VII (Damsire Unreg- **F–**
istered) [2002/3 F16g⁶ F16g Apr 14] workmanlike gelding: sixth foal: dam never ran: well held in 2 bumpers. *O. Brennan*

ROYAL CASTLE (IRE) 9 b.g. Caerleon (USA) – Sun Princess (English Prince) **h109**
[2002/3 h–: 24g 21g⁹ 20d 24m⁰ᵘ Apr 12] workmanlike gelding: fair hurdler: bought out of M. Tompkins' stable 6,000 gns Newmarket July Sales: easily best effort in handicaps in 2002/3 when winning 6-runner race at Sedgefield in October: should stay 3m: acts on firm and good to soft going: blinkered twice in 1999/00: successful on Flat in April. *Mrs K. Walton*

ROYAL CETI (FR) 6 b. or br.g. Garde Royale – Mira Ceti (FR) (Carvin) [2002/3 **h110**
18s* 18sᶠ 17dᶠ Jan 16] useful on Flat up to 15f: fair form when winning minor event over hurdles at Auteuil in September: left E. Lellouche after next start: fell fatally on British debut. *M. C. Pipe*

ROYAL CHARLIE 6 br.g. Royal Fountain – Cool View (Kinglet) [2002/3 F16s Jan **F–**
18] first foal: dam lightly-raced maiden pointer: never a threat when twelfth of 20 in bumper at Haydock on debut. *L. Lungo*

ROYAL CHINA (IRE) 5 b.g. Aristocracy – Luan Causca (Pampapaul) [2002/3 F17d **h83**
17d⁴ 21d 22m⁵ Apr 15] leggy, unfurnished gelding: half-brother to 7f winner Tite Spot **F74**
(by Muscatite): dam fair 2-y-o 5f winner: failed to settle in bumper on debut: best effort over hurdles when fifth of 11 in novice at Exeter, travelling strongly long way: may prove best short of 2¾m. *Miss H. C. Knight*

ROYAL COUNTY BUCK (IRE) 8 b.g. Good Thyne (USA) – Little Quince (Laur- **c80**
ence O) [2002/3 c17s⁶ c20v c17s c18s⁵ c16d c20v⁴ c24dᶠ Jan 16] IR 11,000 4-y-o: half- **h–**
brother to useful hurdler/hunter chaser Little Buck (by Buckskin) stayed 3¼m: dam unraced: runner-up on second of 2 starts in points in 2000: bumper winner: modest novice hurdler in 2001/2: poor over fences: stays 3m: acts on firm going: sometimes tongue tied. *A. J. Martin, Ireland*

ROYAL CRIMSON 12 b.g. Danehill (USA) – Fine Honey (USA) (Drone (USA)) **c68 §**
[2002/3 c24s³ c31dᵖᵘ Apr 25] lengthy gelding: fair handicap chaser in 2000/1 for **h–**
M. Hammond: successful in point in April, little show both starts in hunters: barely stays 3m: acts on soft and good to firm going: blinkered/visored: often looks less than keen. *Mrs F. E. Needham*

ROYAL DESTINY (IRE) 6 b.g. King's Ride – Kouron (Pauper) [2002/3 16d³ 16f* **h116**
16d² 16g³ 16m³ Sep 16] second foal: dam fair 2m hurdler: fairly useful novice hurdler: won at Tipperary in July: reportedly lame final start: raced at 2m: acts on firm and good to soft going: consistent. *T. J. Taaffe, Ireland*

ROYALE ANGELA (FR) 11 ch.g. Garde Royale – Santa Angela (FR) (Son of **c–**
Silver) [2002/3 24dᵖᵘ 24dᵖᵘ May 26] neat gelding: has been hobdayed: thrice-raced **h–**
novice chaser: fairly useful staying hurdler in 2000/1: no sign of retaining ability on belated return: visored once. *J. Neville*

ROYALE DE VASSY (FR) 9 b.m. Royal Charter (FR) – Bayalika (FR) (Kashtan **c126**
(FR)) [2002/3 c134, h–: c24dᵖᵘ c24dᶠ c24d⁶ c24g Mar 11] leggy mare: useful handicap **h–**
chaser: not quite at best in 2002/3, off 8 months after reappearance: stays 3¼m: acts on heavy going, possibly not on good to firm: sound jumper. *Miss Venetia Williams*

ROYALEETY (FR) 4 b.g. Garde Royale – La Grive (FR) (Pharly (FR)) [2002/3 15s* **h133**
17s³ 17d* 18s³ 18s² 18v* 18s³ 18v* 18s 18s⁵ 19vᵖᵘ Apr 26] sixth foal: half-brother to fairly useful hurdler/chaser Freecod (by Freedom Cry), stays 2½m, and to Flat winners up to 1½m in France and Morocco: dam won at 7.5f and 11f in Belgium: twice-raced maiden on Flat: raced exclusively at Auteuil over hurdles: won 6 of 9 starts in 2002, including in May, June (Prix Aguado, beat Black Honor and Nickname), September and November (Group 1 Prix Cambaceres, by 4 lengths from Nickname, left in lead last): below that form in 3 outings in 2003: should stay beyond 19f: raced mainly on soft/heavy going. *T. Civel, France*

ROYAL EMPEROR (IRE)   7 gr.g. Roselier (FR) – Boreen Bro (Boreen (FR))   **h152**
[2002/3 h90: 24d* 24d* 24d² 23v* 23s* 25g² 24d² Apr 4]

Few horses made more progress in the course of the latest campaign than
Royal Emperor, a cast-off picked up the previous season for only 4,200 guineas at
the Doncaster January Sales. Royal Emperor was still a maiden when he came
under the hammer, never having lived up to the promise of his racecourse debut as
a four-year-old when third in the usually informative listed bumper at Newbury's
February meeting. Royal Emperor showed only modest form in eight further starts
in bumpers and over hurdles for Ron Hodges and had one outing for Jonjo
O'Neill—an encouraging third in a novice handicap hurdle at Carlisle—before
being despatched to the sales. That outing for O'Neill was over two and a half
miles, the longest distance Royal Emperor had tackled, and when he reappeared for
Sue Smith back at Carlisle at the end of October, after eleven months off the course,
it was over three miles. Royal Emperor made all, relishing the stiffer test of stamina
and stepping up on the form he had shown for his previous trainers. Kept to
distances around three miles, Royal Emperor suffered his only defeat in his first
five starts at the hands of Tees Components, a smart bumper performer to whom
Royal Emperor, who had followed up in another novice event at Carlisle in the in-
terim, had to concede 12 lb in a novice hurdle at Newcastle at the end of November.

Back in handicap company at Wetherby on Boxing Day, Royal Emperor ran
his rivals ragged, winning by ten lengths from the favourite Little Sport. A nine-
length victory followed in a qualifier in the Pertemps Handicap series at Haydock
in February, Royal Emperor making light of an 11 lb rise in his BHB mark, taking
up the running before five out and forging clear. By now, Royal Emperor was estab-
lishing a reputation as a progressive novice who revelled in testing conditions (it
had been heavy at Wetherby and very soft at Haydock). But the theory that he might
have needed the mud to bring out the best in him was firmly scotched by a cracking
performance for a novice in the Pertemps Final at the Cheltenham Festival, where
Royal Emperor encountered ground firmer than good to soft for the first time
during the season, four of his runs over hurdles for Hodges having come on firmer
than good. Raised a further 12 lb by the handicapper after Haydock, Royal Emperor
started at 14/1 at Cheltenham but, taking over at the eighth, had seen off all his
rivals bar the O'Neill-trained Inching Closer going to the last. Royal Emperor
fluffed his jump but responded very gamely, going down by a short head after a

Pertemps Handicap Hurdle (Qualifier), Haydock—
Royal Emperor warms up for Cheltenham with his fourth win of the campaign

ding-dong battle up the steep climb to the finish, the first two pulling a dozen lengths clear of a big field. Royal Emperor was one of only two runners at the Festival for his stable, the other being Goguenard, who unseated his rider two out when looking the likely winner of the Mildmay of Flete.

Royal Emperor's stable sent out a regular flow of winners through the season, totalling seventy-four in all, and made the top ten in the trainers' prize-money tables for the first time (with a smaller string than any of the others in the top ten). Craiglands Farm was, in fact, the season's leading northern stable, Mrs Smith finishing over £120,000 in 1, 2, 3 earnings ahead of another top-ten trainer Mary Reveley; the pair of them joining Henrietta Knight and Venetia Williams to make a quartet of lady trainers among the season's top ten. The tough and genuine Royal Emperor wasn't done with for the season after Cheltenham and turned in another fine effort at Aintree, where the stable sadly lost Goguenard, its second fatality in the Grand National in as many years. Royal Emperor stuck to his task really well in the season's top three-mile hurdle for novices, the Sefton Novices' Hurdle, and finished eight lengths second to the outstanding Iris's Gift, pulling twelve lengths clear of third-placed Supreme Prince in a very good renewal.

	Roselier (FR)	Misti IV	Medium
	(gr 1973)	(or b 1958)	Mist
		Peace Rose	Fastnet Rock
Royal Emperor (IRE)		(gr 1959)	La Paix
(gr.g. 1996)		Boreen	Tamerlane
	Boreen Bro	(b 1968)	Scyllinda
	(b 1985)	Miss Bro	Rigi
		(br 1970)	Reynoldstown's Niece

The workmanlike Royal Emperor is set to go chasing in the next season and, if he turns out to be typical of his sire Roselier's offspring, he will prove at least as good over fences as hurdles. Roselier is principally a sire of chasers and has sired two Grand National winners in Royal Athlete and Bindaree, in addition to three winners of the Scottish National (Baronet, Moorcroft Boy and Take Control), two winners of the Welsh National (Carvill's Hill and Kendal Cavalier) and an Irish National winner (Ebony Jane). The distaff side of Royal Emperor's pedigree also has a Grand National connection, his third dam the point-to-point winner Reynoldstown's Niece, as her name implies, coming from the family of dual Aintree winner Reynoldstown. The biggest claim to fame of Reynoldstown's Niece is that she was the dam of the top-class chaser Kinloch Brae. Royal Emperor's grandam Miss Bro and his dam Boreen Bro, who do not appear in the *General Stud Book*, were only lightly raced and showed nothing on the racecourse, but Boreen Bro has done well at stud. Royal Emperor's brother, the useful chaser A Piece of Cake, has been a fine servant to the Reveley stable and won three times in the latest season, including the valuable Scottish Borders National over four miles at Kelso. Royal Emperor is also a half-brother to the fairly useful Irish chaser Kings Valley (by Castle Keep), a good fourth in the 2002 Irish Grand National. With all these references to Grand Nationals, it would surely be no surprise to see Royal Emperor win a National of some type in due course. He will have no difficulty staying beyond three miles and is a most genuine and reliable performer. *Mrs S. J. Smith*

ROYAL ENCLOSURE (IRE)   5 b.g. Royal Academy (USA) – Hi Bettina (Henbit (USA)) [2002/3 h65: 16m Mar 19] sparely-made gelding: modest on Flat (stays 1¼m) in 2002: little form over hurdles: usually visored/tongue tied. *Mrs S. M. Johnson*   **h–**

ROYAL ENTRANCE (IRE)   10 b.g. Don't Forget Me – Royal Miami (Miami Springs) [2002/3 c24d^{pu} Apr 9] ex-Irish gelding: won maiden Irish point in 1998: little show in steeplechases. *M. Rodda*   **c–**

ROYAL EVENT   12 ch.g. Rakaposhi King – Upham Reunion (Paridel) [2002/3 c98, h–: c20g^{pu} c21g⁴ May 25] medium-sized gelding: modest handicap chaser: stays 21f: acts on soft and good to firm going: has worn cheekpieces: usually a sound jumper: none too consistent. *D. R. Gandolfo*   **c– h–**

ROYAL FEELINGS   9 b.g. Feelings (FR) – Wedderburn (Royalty) [2002/3 h75: c24m⁴ c24d² c25m² c20m⁴ c20d^F Aug 4] small gelding: poor maiden hurdler/chaser: should stay beyond 25f: acts on good to firm and good to soft going. *Mrs D. Thomson*   **c79 h–**

Fulke Walwyn Kim Muir Challenge Cup Handicap Chase, Cheltenham—
Royal Predica springs a 33/1 shock on his reappearance

ROYAL GILLIE 6 br.m. Royal Fountain – Gilmanscleuch (IRE) (Mandalus) [2002/3   **F–**
F16g Apr 14] second foal: dam, poor maiden hurdler/chaser, from family of very smart
staying hurdler Splendid Thyne: seventh of 12 in maiden bumper at Hexham on debut.
Mrs J. K. M. Oliver

ROYAL HAND 13 b.g. Nearly A Hand – Royal Rushes (Royal Palace) [2002/3 c20gᵖᵘ   **c–**
Jun 12] workmanlike gelding: selling hurdler: no form in steeplechases or points: stays   **h– §**
21f: acts on firm and soft going: usually blinkered/visored: often tongue tied: unreliable.
C. N. Kellett

ROYAL HECTOR (GER) 4 b.g. Hector Protector (USA) – Rudolfina (CAN) (Pleas-   **h102**
ant Colony (USA)) [2002/3 16d² 16g⁵ 16d⁵ 16g 16g Mar 14] good-topped gelding:
successful twice around 9f at Cologne in 2002: fair form over hurdles (trained on debut
by C. Von Der Recke), best effort when fifth of 20 to Saintsaire in juvenile at Newbury
second outing: likely to prove best around 2m: jumped poorly final start. *A. G. Hobbs*

ROYAL JAKE (IRE) 9 b.g. Jolly Jake (NZ) – Wee Mite (Menelek) [2002/3 c118+,   **c124**
h109: c20s* c22d c22v⁶ c17m* c17v³ c16s² c24v c16g c21d Apr 4] well-made gelding: **h–**
fairly useful chaser: won minor events at Killarney in May and Cork (amateurs) in September: good placed efforts in handicaps, but never a factor in valuable events at
Cheltenham, Aintree and Punchestown: effective at 2m, barely stays 25f: acts on good to
firm and heavy going: effective blinkered or not: sold 20,000 gns Doncaster May Sales.
N. Meade, Ireland

ROYAL MEG 5 b. or br.m. Emperor Jones (USA) – Queen's Eyot (Grundy) [2002/3   **F–**
F16s F14d Dec 9] leggy mare: half-sister to several winners, including fairly useful 2m
hurdler Persuasive (by Sharpo) and bumper winner Ardarroch Prince (by Chief Singer):
dam, fair at 1¼m, out of half-sister to Stayers' Hurdle winner Lighter: last in 2 bumpers.
Mrs M. Reveley

ROYAL MYSTERY 4 ch.f. King's Signet (USA) – Miss Caradon (IRE) (Prince   **h–**
Rupert (FR)) [2002/3 16s 17sᵖᵘ Nov 28] poor maiden on Flat (stays 1¼m): no show in 2
juvenile hurdles. *H. S. Howe*

ROYALOUTLOOK 6 br.g. Royal Fountain – Broad Outlook (Broadsword (USA))   **h–**
[2002/3 F16v⁴ F16d F17g⁴ 20gᵖᵘ Apr 21] first foal: dam won 2m hurdle: poor form in   **F74**
bumpers: pulled up in novice on hurdling debut: should be suited by further than 2m.
G. A. Harker

ROYAL PARTNERSHIP (IRE) 7 b.g. Royal Academy (USA) – Go Honey Go   **c–**
(General Assembly (USA)) [2002/3 h77: c24mᵖᵘ c20gᵖᵘ c16gᵖᵘ 17m Aug 31] poor on   **h–**
Flat (stays 15f): poor novice hurdler: no form over fences: best efforts around 2m: tried
visored/blinkered: has had tongue tied. *D. L. Williams*

ROYAL PLAISIR (IRE) 8 b.g. Grand Plaisir (IRE) – Royal Well (Royal Vulcan)   **c107 p**
[2002/3 h121: c16g* c16s* Dec 8] fairly useful hurdler: successful both starts over   **h–**
fences, in maiden at Cork in May and intermediate handicap at Punchestown (by 2½

772

lengths from Royal Jake) in December: raced at 2m: acts on heavy going: prone to odd mistake over hurdles: likely to improve over fences. *A. L. T. Moore, Ireland*

ROYAL PLUM 7 ch.g. Inchinor – Miss Plum (Ardross) [2002/3 h83§: 23m Oct 24] leggy gelding: poor handicap hurdler: stays 3¼m: acts on soft and good to firm going: often visored/blinkered: irresolute: sold 2,300 gns Doncaster May Sales. *Mrs M. Reveley*   h– §

ROYAL PREDICA (FR) 9 ch.g. Tip Moss (FR) – Girl Vamp (FR) (Kaldoun (FR)) [2002/3 c140x, h–: c24g* c36d c29mᵖᵘ Apr 26] leggy gelding: useful handicap chaser: 33/1, improved form when winning Fulke Walwyn Kim Muir Challenge Cup at Cheltenham in March after 10½-month absence by 10 lengths from Ibis Rochelais: well held (for second year running) in Grand National at Aintree, ran no sort of race final outing: stays 25f: acts on any going: formerly blinkered/visored: tongue tied: often let down by jumping. *M. C. Pipe*   c144
h–

ROYAL PRETENCE 6 b.m. Royal Fountain – Just Pretend (Sayyaf) [2002/3 F–: 20mᵖᵘ 22mᵖᵘ 22g⁵ Jul 31] no sign of ability (tried blinkered): sold out of Miss L. Russell's stable 1,200 gns Doncaster May Sales after reappearance, resold £1,500 Ascot August Sales. *G. F. Edwards*   h–

ROYAL RACER (FR) 5 b.g. Danehill (USA) – Green Rosy (USA) (Green Dancer (USA)) [2002/3 16s 16vᵖᵘ 16d⁶ 16g 16m Apr 21] half-brother to winning hurdler Genseric (by Groom Dancer), stays 2¾m: fair at best on Flat (stays 1½m) in Britain, on downgrade in 2002: poor form over hurdles, not always fluent. *J. R. Best*   h82

ROYAL RAPPORT 10 ch.g. Rich Charlie – Miss Camellia (Sonnen Gold) [2002/3 c–, h–: c24mᵖᵘ c20sᵖᵘ c21dᵖᵘ c16s⁴ Jun 9] compact gelding: winning hurdler: little form over fences: best efforts around 2m: acts on firm going: often visored/blinkered. *T. Wall*   c–
h–

Mr P. A. Deal, J. S. Dale & A. Stennett's "Royal Predica"

ROYAL REWARD (IRE)   9 b.g. King's Ride – Fatima Rose (The Parson) [2002/3   **c–**
c–, h65: 20d Apr 29] sturdy gelding: unseated in 2 novice chases: poor maiden hurdler: **h–**
effective at 2m to 3m: acts on good to firm and good to soft going. *M. Todhunter*

ROYAL ROCKET (IRE)   6 b.m. King's Ride – Carols Cracker (IRE) (Persian   **F75**
Mews) [2002/3 F16f⁵ Mar 29] IR 10,000 3-y-o, 12,000 4-y-o: first foal: dam unraced
half-sister to useful 3m chaser King Lucifer (by King's Ride): fifth of 11 to Diamant Noir
in mares bumper at Haydock on debut. *Miss Venetia Williams*

ROYAL ROSA (FR)   4 ch.g. Garde Royale – Crystalza (FR) (Crystal Palace (FR))   **F118**
[2002/3 F12g* F16s⁶ F16v* Mar 8]

Whoever thought up the name of the Million In Mind syndicate might have
been accused of wishful thinking at the time, but the idea doesn't look nearly so
optimistic twelve seasons on. It isn't so much that the horses that run in the red,
green and white colours of the syndicate have won hatfuls of the top races but that
the end-of-season dispersal, required under the terms of the syndication and undertaken at Doncaster each May, has become something of a bonanza. Three times
Million In Mind-owned horses have set a British record for a jumper sold at
auction, Mysilv in 1994 went for 155,000 guineas, Mister Banjo in 2000 made
240,000 guineas and Royal Rosa in 2003 fetched 340,000 guineas. The last sale
came just one lot after another Million In Mind graduate Joly Bey had matched the
figure set by Mister Banjo. Two others in recent years, Tysou in 2001 and
Montayral in 2002, have brought up six figures as well. The Triumph Hurdle
winner Mysilv, Mister Banjo and Tysou made their mark at the sale after a season
in juvenile hurdles while Joly Bey and Montayral were above-average novice
chasers for the syndicate. Royal Rosa, a French-bred, like all those except Mysilv,
made his mark in bumpers, winning three of his four starts, including the Paddy
Power Champion National Hunt Flat Race at Punchestown.

Royal Rosa also has the distinction of winning one of the first so-called
junior bumpers, races over a distance of around a mile and a half, run in November
and December and open to three-year-olds, bumpers traditionally being open to
them only when they turn four on January 1st. While a study of tendon and bone
injuries had shown that consistent exercise of horses at a younger age made them
less prone to leg trouble later on, the main idea behind these new bumpers is
supposedly to encourage British breeders of jumping stock, though quite how is not
explained, a generous weight allowance to three-year-olds along with the shorter
trip making them ideal races for Flat breds and French breds. Royal Rosa, for
example, was chased home when he won at Newbury by a daughter of Selkirk and
a son of Bering out of a mile-and-a-quarter Grade 1 winner. That the races were
generally well subscribed and that Royal Rosa went on to be a leading bumper
performer do not of themselves prove the experiment to be a success. In 2003/4,
junior bumpers are set to be restricted to three-year-olds only. Royal Rosa's next

Paddy Power Champion INH Flat, Punchestown—
sole British raider Royal Rosa boosts his value with a third win

Million In Mind Partnership 12's "Royal Rosa"

two races came at Sandown. After seeming beaten on merit there in February he made the most of an easier opportunity and barely raceable conditions the following month, scoring by twenty-three lengths. It is perhaps a measure of how testing conditions were that day that none of the eight-runner field reappeared before the end of the British season, Royal Rosa's appearance at Punchestown coming shortly after it.

Royal Rosa was the sole British challenger for the Paddy Power and was an unconsidered 14/1-chance despite British domination of the bumpers at both Cheltenham and Aintree. Kickham, winner of the 2002 Grade 2 bumper at Aintree, started a short-priced favourite despite a fairly lacklustre campaign over hurdles in the meantime. Royal Alphabet, a flop in the Champion Bumper, and Flexible Action, first and second at Fairyhouse in April, disputed second favouritism. Buffalo Bill, Zum See (whose form looked nowhere near good enough) and the previous year's second Alexander Milenium, another flop over jumps, were also at shorter odds than Royal Rosa. In short, this didn't look a vintage renewal and the outcome confirmed the unusual dominance of British-trained bumper horses. Always well placed in a truly-run race, Royal Rosa went to the front flat to the boards three furlongs out, but he responded, and in the end stayed on too stoutly for his pursuers. Royal Alphabet had to give a generous 7 lb to the winner, more than he would have had to do in Britain, but was beaten on merit, three and a half lengths back in second, with the outsider Kildare, successful just once from five previous starts in bumpers, in third. The unlucky horse of the race was the fast-finishing sixth Rockstown Boy who was travelling strongly when all but knocked over turning into the straight. Royal Alphabet was one of three of the first five to win on the Flat shortly afterwards.

Although Royal Rosa is a half-brother to several above-average French jumpers, his background is essentially a Flat one, and a pretty good one at that. His third dam La Bamba was a high-class filly, winning the Prix Jacques le Marois and finishing third in the Arc and the Oaks and she is the grandam of two Grand Criterium winners, Lost World and Fijar Tango, the latter later a high-class middle-distance performer. The grandam Aldonza won on the Flat, as did four of her five winners, notable among them the smart middle-distance colt Dom Aldo. Another of her winners Aldo King was fair on the Flat and over jumps in Britain. Royal Rosa's dam Crystalza didn't have a lot of ability and managed a place just once from eleven starts on the Flat, but she has done a lot better at stud. The pick of her six winners before Royal Rosa are the smart hurdler Crylza Royal (by Northern Fashion), who was placed in the Prix La Barka and the Prix Leon Olry-Roederer and Ytalsa Royale (by Arokar), who won the top four-year-old chase the Prix Ferdinand Dufaure. Royal Rosa is closely related to another of Crystalza's winners, the fairly useful hurdler/chaser around two and a half miles Sylver Dargent (by Miller's Mate).

	Garde Royale (br 1980)	Mill Reef (b 1968)	Never Bend
			Milan Mill
Royal Rosa (FR)		Royal Way (gr 1969)	Sicambre
(ch.g. 1999)			Right Away
	Crystalza (FR) (gr 1982)	Crystal Palace (gr 1974)	Caro
			Hermieres
		Aldonza (b 1969)	Exbury
			La Bamba

The rather leggy Royal Rosa will be trained in the 2003/4 season by Howard Johnson, a new patron for his County Durham yard reportedly having bought the horse as a wedding present for his wife-to-be. It is to be hoped for marital harmony that Royal Rosa makes the sort of impact he should do in novice hurdles. After all, not all of Million In Mind's high-profile disposals have lived up to their billing or come close to recouping the sums paid for them. Readers can be forgiven for not being familiar with the career of Jacklighte Bellevue. He was sold by Million In Mind for an unlikely 68,000 guineas at the 2002 Doncaster May Sales and has so far picked up an £860 third prize in a novice chase at Leicester. *N. J. Henderson*

ROYAL SNOOPY (IRE) 10 b. or br.g. Royal Fountain – Lovely Snoopy (IRE) (Phardante (FR)) [2002/3 c110, h–: c24m³ c20d⁶ c24mᶠ c22m² c27d² Apr 8] lengthy gelding: fair chaser, sold out of C. Mann's stable 6,000 gns Doncaster September Sales after fourth start: fit from points, second of 5 to easy winner Trade Dispute in hunter at Sedgefield final outing: stays 27f: acts on any going: blinkered: front runner: usually jumps right. *Mrs F. E. Needham*   **c112 x** **h–**

ROYALTINO (IRE) 11 b.g. Neltino – Royal Well (Royal Vulcan) [2002/3 c24sᵖᵘ c24v² Mar 5] angular gelding: one-time fairly useful hurdler/useful chaser for F. Doumen: much better effort in hunter chases after over 3 years off (jumped poorly on comeback) when 4 lengths second to Hanakham at Bangor: stays 25f: acts on heavy going, probably on good to firm. *Miss T. McCurrich*   **c100** **h–**

ROYAL TIR (FR) 7 b.g. Royal Charter (FR) – Tirtaine (FR) (Mad Captain) [2002/3 19g⁵ 19g³ 19g³ c21s* c22s⁵ c21v 17d* 19s³ c23v³ 19g⁶ c21d* c22s Apr 25] workmanlike gelding: useful hurdler, won minor event at Pau in December: top-class chaser in 2000/1, no more than useful nowadays, successful in Prix Richard Et Robert Hennessy at Auteuil (beat Gondleen 6 lengths) in September and minor event at Nancy in April: effective at 17f to 3¼m: raced on good ground or softer (acts on heavy): effective blinkered or not. *C. Aubert, France*   **c141** **h135**

ROYAL TOMMY (IRE) 11 b.g. Royal Fountain – Cherry Token (Prince Hansel) [2002/3 c124: c31dᵖᵘ c24s⁵ c29v c33v⁶ c26v⁶ c30sᵖᵘ Mar 4] deep-girthed gelding: fairly useful handicap chaser at best: totally out of sorts in 2002/3 (didn't take to cross-country course on reappearance): thorough stayer: tried blinkered/visored. *R. H. Buckler*   **c–**

ROYAL WANDERER (IRE) 5 ch.g. Royal Abjar (USA) – Rose 'n Reason (IRE) (Reasonable (FR)) [2002/3 16d⁶ 19m⁵ 17m³ 17g³ 17d* 17g⁴ 16m⁴ 16d 19d⁶ 16g³ 16g⁴ 16g³ 16mᵖᵘ Apr 21] stocky gelding: well held on Flat for Mrs A. Duffield: modest hurdler: won maiden at Cartmel in August: ran at least creditably most subsequent starts: raced mainly around 2m: yet to race on extremes of going. *C. R. Wilson*   **h90**

ROYMILLON (GER) 9 b.g. Milesius (USA) – Royal Slope (USA) (His Majesty **h76 §**
(USA)) [2002/3 h79§: 22m⁵ 26m* 26g⁴ Nov 7] leggy gelding: poor handicap hurdler:
won at Huntingdon in September: best at 3m+: acts on firm going: blinkered once: often
gets behind, and one to treat with caution. *D. J. Wintle*

ROYRACE 11 b.g. Wace (USA) – Royal Tycoon (Tycoon II) [2002/3 c–, h–: c20dᵖᵘ **c–**
Aug 2] tall gelding: maiden jumper: visored once: has bled from nose. *W. M. Brisbourne* **h–**

RUBON PRINCE (IRE) 12 ch.g. Kambalda – Oh Clare (Laurence O) [2002/3 c–, **c–**
h–: c23gᵖᵘ Aug 24] workmanlike gelding: maiden hurdler/chaser: blinkered once. **h–**
N. B. Mason

RUBY GALE (IRE) 7 b.g. Lord Americo – Well Over (Over The River (FR)) [2002/3 **c118**
h116, F95: c17gᶠ c19g⁶ Nov 5] sturdy gelding: fairly useful hurdler: much better effort in **h–**
novice chases at Exeter when falling 2 out in race won by Stars Out Tonight, in with every
chance at time: likely to prove better at 2½m than 2m: raced on good/good to soft going.
P. F. Nicholls

RUDETSKI 6 b.g. Rudimentary (USA) – Butosky (Busted) [2002/3 16d 16d 16m⁵ **h83**
Dec 17] lengthy gelding: half-brother to 3 winning hurdlers: modest on Flat (stays 1¼m):
best effort over hurdles when fifth of 15 in novice at Musselburgh. *M. Dods*

RUDGE HILL 7 b.g. Almushmmir – Time After Time (High Award) [2002/3 F–: **c–**
c19sᵖᵘ Nov 28] workmanlike gelding: no sign of ability in bumpers or novice chase.
G. A. Ham

RUDI KNIGHT 8 ch.g. Rudimentary (USA) – Fleeting Affair (Hotfoot) [2002/3 h123: **c104**
20d⁵ c19s³ c19d³ Jan 27] angular gelding: one-time useful handicap hurdler, well held **h–**
since reappearance in 2001/2: fair form when third in novice chases at Chepstow and
Exeter: best form up to 19f: acts on heavy and good to firm going: often none too fluent
over hurdles. *Miss Venetia Williams*

RUDI'S CHARM 6 b.g. Rudimentary (USA) – Irene's Charter (Persian Bold) [2002/3 **F78**
F16m⁵ F16g Jan 17] seventh foal: half-brother to 3 winners, including fairly useful 7f and
1¼m winner Master Charter (by Master Willie): dam 7f to 1¼m winner: better effort in
bumpers at Musselburgh when fifth of 11 to Autumn Stroll. *J. A. Moore*

RUDI'S PLEASURE (IRE) 8 ch.g. Buckskin (FR) – Kind Sir She Said (Decent **c94**
Fellow) [2002/3 h99: 24d² 22g⁴ 20d² 22g⁴ 24f² 21d⁶ 24v⁴ c20v² c20s⁴ c24v⁴ c24d⁴ c22gᶠ **h100**
Apr 21] leggy, workmanlike gelding: fair handicap hurdler: modest form over fences:
stays 3m: acts on any going: usually held up: consistent. *E. McNamara, Ireland*

RUDOLF RASSENDYLL (IRE) 8 b.g. Supreme Leader – Chantel Rouge (Boreen **c103**
(FR)) [2002/3 h–, F–: 19d⁵ 20d* c20s⁴ c19s* c24s² Mar 7] workmanlike gelding: fair **h101**
hurdler/chaser: won novice handicaps at Huntingdon (hurdles, by ½ length from Intrepid
Mogal) in January and Chepstow (fences, eased run-in when beating Stormhill Stag 4
lengths) in February: effective around 2½m to 3m: acts on soft going. *Miss Venetia
Williams*

RUFF JUSTICE (IRE) 7 b. or br.g. Cashel Court – Rugged View (Rugged Man) **F100**
[2002/3 F–: F16s⁶ F20f* F16d³ F17g³ F16f² F16m² Oct 6] rangy gelding: steady progress
in bumpers in 2002/3 (looked wayward in 2001/2), won at Tipperary in July: second at
Listowel and Tipperary (beaten 2½ lengths by Buffalo Bill) last 2 starts. *Patrick Mullins,
Ireland*

RUFIUS (IRE) 10 b.g. Celio Rufo – In View Lass (Tepukei) [2002/3 c92§, h–: c23g² **c99**
c24m* c20m² c20d⁴ c20g² c25s* c23g⁶ c22sᵖᵘ c21m Apr 17] workmanlike gelding: **h–**
modest chaser: won novice at Huntingdon (simple task) in September and novice handicap at Cheltenham in December: ran poorly last 3 outings: stays 25f: acts on firm and
soft going: blinkered once (raced too freely): held up: often fails to impress with attitude.
P. Kelsall

RUGGED JACKET (IRE) 6 b.g. Bob Back (USA) – First Strike (IRE) (Magical **h105 +**
Strike (USA)) [2002/3 16d² 18s² F16d⁶ Mar 22] first foal: dam ran once: bumper winner: **F107**
fair form when second in maiden hurdles at Limerick and Navan in May, sold out of
P. O'Leary's stable €130,000 Fairyhouse August Sale: better effort in bumpers subsequently when fourth to Kim Fontaine at Punchestown in early-May: raced around 2m on
good going or softer. *D. T. Hughes, Ireland*

RUGGED MAN (IRE) 5 b.g. Topanoora – The Grey (GER) (Pentathlon) [2002/3 **h90**
17s³ 17d⁵ 16g 20d 21g⁴ 19m³ 16g Sep 25] half-brother to winning hurdler Grey Sonata
(by Horage), stayed 2½m: modest maiden on Flat (stays 1½m): sold out of M. Grassick's
stable €26,000 Goffs February (2002) Sale: poor maiden hurdler on balance of form:

should stay beyond 17f: blinkered last 3 starts, also tongue tied last 2: hasn't always impressed with attitude. *G. J. McKeever, Ireland*

RUGGED RIVER (IRE) 8 b.g. Over The River (FR) – Early Dalus (IRE) (Mand- **c135**
alus) [2002/3 c26v* c26s³ c29vᵖᵘ c24sᵖᵘ c24s³ Mar 1] lengthy gelding: useful handicap
chaser: won at Newton Abbot in November on first start for nearly 2 years: ran very well
when third of 5 to See More Business in quite valuable event at Chepstow next time, but
disappointed afterwards: stays 3¼m: acts on heavy going. *R. H. Alner*

RUGGED RUBEN 6 b.g. Minshaanshu Amad (USA) – Kiri Te (Liboi (USA)) [2002/3 **h–**
F17m⁵ 20gᵖᵘ 21gᵖᵘ Oct 21] £900 5-y-o: third foal: half-brother to 7f/1m winner Kanawa **F76 ?**
and modest middle-distance winner Kirisnippa (both by Beveled): dam unraced: fifth of
7 in steadily-run bumper at Hereford on debut: showed nothing in 2 novice hurdles (first
a claimer). *J. W. Mullins*

RULE SUPREME (IRE) 7 b.g. Supreme Leader – Book of Rules (IRE) (Phar- **c135 p**
dante (FR)) [2002/3 h130: c21v⁴ c20g⁵ Mar 30] **h–**
  After the machinations in the build-up the previous year, when its very
future was thought to be in doubt, the Punchestown Festival in 2003 was simply
about the racing. In November, Punchestown's owners, the members of the Kildare
Hunt Club, accepted a rescue package drawn up by Horse Racing Ireland which
safeguards the future of the track. Financial problems exacerbated by the loss of the
2001 Festival meant that, at the point the agreement was concluded, there was
possibly not enough money to pay staff wages that week. Efforts to turn round the
decline in the number of British runners in 2002 resulted in a numerically much
stronger overseas challenge, and British-trained horses landed five Grade 1 events,
with France also responsible for a Grade 1 winner. Attendances were also buoyant,
with a reported record paying attendance of 22,000 on the second day of the four-
day fixture. There were several changes to the programme, some of them more
welcome and successful than others. The first running of the ridiculously valuable
mares and fillies bumper (worth approaching three times as much to the winner as
the Grade 1 bumper at the meeting) attracted a predictably dismal field. One of the
best changes was the decision to restore the valuable novices handicap chase to a
prominent position at the meeting. Once the centrepiece of the whole festival—it
was the most valuable race of the three days until as recently as 1998—in the last
few years it has been run towards the end of the extra day. With a new sponsor and
change of title to the Colm McEvoy Auctioneers Novices' Handicap Chase, it was

Colm McEvoy Auctioneers Novices' Handicap Chase, Punchestown—preceded by a riderless horse,
Rule Supreme gets the better of favourite and stable-companion Hedgehunter at the last

Mr John P. Lynch's "Rule Supreme"

back on the second day and drew a competitive eighteen-runner field, with top weight carried by the useful Kadoun, winner of his last three races. Noel Meade's stable was numerically well represented with five runners, and there were four raiders from Britain, but the key yard turned out to be that of Willie Mullins. He ran three. Hedgehunter, possibly unfortunate when all but falling two out in the National Hunt Chase at Cheltenham, looked favourably weighted and was a well-supported favourite but had to give best in the race to the unexposed Rule Supreme.

Rule Supreme was having just his third race over fences in the Colm McEvoy. He had shown generally progressive form as a novice over hurdles when with Pat Hughes in 2001/2 but was unconsidered at 16/1 in a Grade 3 novice at Leopardstown on his chasing debut in January. He finished fourth to the shock winner Ten Poundsworth, doing remarkably well to get round after making numerous mistakes, but staying on strongly after travelling well off the pace. It was eleven weeks before Rule Supreme was seen again, when finishing well adrift of his odds-on stable companion Adamant Approach at Cork, a boost in his confidence seeming an important objective of the outing. Rule Supreme jumped much better at Punchestown and, after again travelling well held up, came late to head Hedgehunter at the last and win going away by three and a half lengths. Turn Two came out best of the Meade team in third while none of the British completed, the well-supported Shardam losing his rider at the second when slightly hampered and Tribal Dancer, from Venetia Williams' stable which gained the last British victory in the race with Jocks Cross in 1999, falling when still well in contention two out. The subsequent record of winners of this race has been patchy to say the least, but Rule Supreme looks the sort to make an impact in open handicap company, given that he is almost certainly open to further improvement and is unexposed beyond three miles or so.

	Supreme Leader (b 1982)	Bustino (b 1971)	Busted
			Ship Yard
		Princess Zena (b 1975)	Habitat
Rule Supreme (IRE) (b.g. 1996)			Guiding Light
	Book of Rules (IRE) (b 1989)	Phardante (b 1982)	Pharly
			Pallante
		Chapter Four (ch 1971)	Shackleton
			First Edition

It is no surprise, looking at his pedigree, that the well-made Rule Supreme has developed into a staying chaser. He is the first foal of the unraced Book of Rules who is half-sister to six winners, five effective at three miles or more over fences and the other prevented from following suit largely due to frailty. The last is the lightly-raced Sarsfield The Man, a useful hurdler and fairly useful chaser, who failed to give his running the only time he was raced beyond twenty-one furlongs. Two of the others were useful performers, Book of Kells and Scribbler, the latter down the field in the 1994 running of the Punchestown race. Another half-brother, the fair performer Professor Strong, won at the 1996 Punchestown Festival. Rule Supreme's grandam Chapter Four was a fairly useful hurdler while the third dam First Edition landed a novice chase though, as she won by two and a half lengths from a remounted runner-up, it's fair to say she was fortunate. First Edition produced five winners, easily the most notable the smart chaser Our Edition, who was placed in the 1977 Scottish National and Whitbread Gold Cup. Rule Supreme has raced on good going or softer, the ground being heavy when he made his chasing debut and good at Punchestown. *W. P. Mullins, Ireland*

RUM POINTER (IRE)   7 b.g. Turtle Island (IRE) – Osmunda (Mill Reef (USA)) [2002/3 h–: 20s⁴ 22d² 24s² 23s⁶ 22v 25gᶠ Mar 11] small gelding: fairly useful hurdler: running well when last (challenging for fourth) in valuable handicap at Cheltenham won by Inching Closer: stays 3m: raced on good going or softer (acts on heavy). *R. H. Buckler*   **h123**

RUNAWAY BISHOP (USA)   8 b. or br.g. Lear Fan (USA) – Valid Linda (USA) (Valid Appeal (USA)) [2002/3 c–, h85: 24d³ 17m⁴ 24m² 21s³ 17g³ c25s³ c24d⁴ Dec 14] lengthy gelding: modest chaser/maiden hurdler: sold out of Mrs A. Duffield's stable 4,200 gns Doncaster October Sales after fifth start: needs further than 2m and stays 25f: acts on any going: blinkered/visored 6 starts prior to last 2 (finished lame final one): has shown signs of temperament. *J. R. Cornwall*   **c91** **h84**

RUNAWAY RALPH   9 ch.g. Rolfe (USA) – Swift Messenger (Giolla Mear) [2002/3 c20m⁴ c19dᵖᵘ 26dᵘʳ Jun 5] little show in varied company: tried to refuse and unseated second in novice hurdle. *D. L. Williams*   **c–** **h–**

RUN FOR EILEEN (IRE)   8 b.m. Cataldi – Deep Dawn Run (Deep Run) [2002/3 20sᶠ 17gᵖᵘ Nov 7] first foal: dam bad novice hurdler: twice-raced over hurdles: fell early on debut, beaten by halfway in mares novice 10 days later: sold £650 Ascot December Sales. *A. Sadik*   **h–**

RUN FOR PADDY   7 b.g. Michelozzo (USA) – Deep Selection (IRE) (Deep Run) [2002/3 c125, h138: c24m* c21sᵖᵘ c25dᵖᵘ Apr 4] useful-looking gelding: useful hurdler/chaser: improved effort over fences when winning handicap at Chepstow in October by 1¾ lengths from Village King, pair clear: lacklustre efforts in quite valuable handicaps at Cheltenham and Aintree last 2 starts, over 2 months apart: stays 25f: acts on soft and good to firm going: unreliable. *Mrs H. Dalton*   **c140 §** **h–**

RUN FOR THE BOYS   7 ch.g. Michelozzo (USA) – Horns Lodge (High Line) [2002/3 F–: F16d 22sᵖᵘ Dec 17] lengthy gelding: no sign of ability in bumpers and maiden hurdle (failed to settle). *C. J. Mann*   **h–** **F–**

RUNNER BEAN   9 b. or br.g. Henbit (USA) – Bean Alainn (Candy Cane) [2002/3 h–: c16s⁴ c19s² c16s⁴ c16dᵖᵘ c17g² c16m* Apr 21] lengthy gelding: maiden hurdler: modest novice chaser: won 3-finisher handicap at Huntingdon: stays 2½m: acts on soft and good to firm going: blinkered once (reportedly bled) in 2001/2: sketchy jumper. *R. Lee*   **c93 x** **h–**

RUNNING BATTLE   7 br.m. Lepanto (GER) – Running Cool (Record Run) [2002/3 h–, F–: 22gᵖᵘ May 1] no show in bumper and 2 novice hurdles. *N. J. Hawke*   **h–**

RUNNING DE CERISY (FR)   9 ch.g. Lightning (FR) – Niloq (FR) (Nikos) [2002/3 c97x, h102: c20gᵖᵘ c17gᵖᵘ Mar 29] tall, lengthy gelding: fair hurdler/modest handicap chaser in 2001/2: off 11 months, twice pulled up at Market Rasen on return (reportedly   **c– x** **h–**

broke blood vessel second time): best around 2m: acts on any going: blinkered twice (failed to settle second occasion): not a fluent jumper of fences: sometimes finds little. *Miss S. J. Wilton*

RUNNING MACHINE (IRE)   6 b.g. Classic Memory – Foxborough Lady (Crash Course) [2002/3 19d 21d³ 27s^F 24s³ 24v^F c23d³ c21s³ c24g⁶ Mar 2] 6,200 4-y-o: lengthy, good sort: sixth known foal: half-brother to winning pointer by Husyan: dam maiden: in frame both completed outings in maiden Irish points in 2002: fair novice hurdler/chaser: stays 3m: raced on good going or softer (acts on soft): tongue tied after debut: sketchy jumper. *A. M. Hales*   **c100 x h96 x**

RUNNING MAN (FR)   9 ch.g. General Holme (USA) – Rudolfina (Pharly (FR)) [2002/3 16g⁴ c16g^F c16f³ 16g⁵ c16f⁴ Apr 25] angular gelding: fairly useful handicap hurdler/chaser: better than ever after 2-year lay-off, winning over hurdles at Huntingdon in August and fences at Kempton (jumped fluently, beat Damus 16 lengths) in October: ran poorly when last of 4 in handicap chase at Sandown after further 5½-month absence: raced at 2m: acts on firm and soft going: free-going front runner. *P. R. Webber*   **c123 h123**

RUNNING MOSS   11 ch.g. Le Moss – Run'n Fly (Deep Run) [2002/3 c104, h–: c22s³ c28v^pu c25v⁴ Dec 2] lengthy gelding: fair handicap chaser: stays 4m: raced on good going or softer (acts on heavy). *A. H. Mactaggart*   **c107 h–**

RUNNING MUTE   9 b.g. Roscoe Blake – Rose Albertine (Record Token) [2002/3 c26d* Jun 8] won maiden at Cartmel on hunter chase debut: in good form in points in 2003, won in February and April. *Mrs S. H. Shirley-Beavan*   **c90**

RUNNING TIMES (USA)   6 b.g. Brocco (USA) – Concert Peace (USA) (Hold Your Peace (USA)) [2002/3 h109: 19d* c16g^pu Mar 23] workmanlike gelding: fair hurdler: won seller (sold from M. Pipe 7,750 gns) at Hereford in May: well beaten completed start in points, and showed nothing on steeplechasing debut: stays 2¾m: acts on soft and good to firm going: visored last 3 starts: races prominently. *H. J. Manners*   **c– h106**

RUNNINGWITHTHEMOON   7 b.g. Homo Sapien – Ardeal (Ardross) [2002/3 F16m⁶ 20d^pu Nov 12] first foal: dam, winning pointer/poor novice chaser, out of sister to Arkle Chase winner Danish Flight: showed little in bumper and novice hurdle. *C. C. Bealby*   **h– F–**

RUPERT   6 ch.g. Arzanni – High Affair (High Line) [2002/3 F16m⁶ F16d Oct 23] 3,000 3-y-o: sturdy gelding: eighth foal: half-brother to modest staying hurdler Wedding Feast (by Oats) and winning pointer by Green Adventure: dam once-raced on Flat: well held in 2 bumpers at Chepstow. *S. G. Griffiths*   **F–**

RUSHEN RAIDER   11 br.g. Reprimand – Travel Storm (Lord Gayle (USA)) [2002/3 h82: 24g³ 21d Oct 31] leggy gelding: poor handicap hurdler nowadays: stays 27f: acts on firm and soft going: ran out final start in 2001/2: has broken blood vessel. *P. Needham*   **h70**

RUSHING AGAIN   8 br.g. Rushmere – Saunders Grove (IRE) (Sunyboy) [2002/3 h91: c20s^pu c26m⁴ c24m² c24m³ c24d⁴ c25d^ur c21v⁴ c26s^pu c26s^pu c24f⁴ c21g^pu Apr 19] workmanlike gelding: winning pointer: runner-up on first of 2 starts over hurdles for P. Nicholls: little worthwhile form in novice chases: stays 27f. *Dr P. Pritchard*   **c– h–**

RUSH'N'RUN   4 b.g. Kasakov – Runfawit Pet (Welsh Saint) [2002/3 F16g F17v F16g Mar 23] seventh foal: brother to 1m winner Zechariah: dam maiden at 2 yrs, only season to race: mid-division at best in bumpers. *D. Carroll*   **F71**

RUSH 'N TEAR   12 b.g. Rushmere – May Singer (Record Run) [2002/3 c26m May 22] modest pointer, successful in March: well held in novice hunter chase at Folkestone. *Mrs A. A. Hawkins*   **c–**

RUSSELL HOUSE (IRE)   7 b. or br.g. Roselier (FR) – Salufair (Salluceva) [2002/3 h94: c25g² c30d^F c29s^pu c24d* c24s^pu c25m⁶ Apr 12] useful-looking gelding: modest novice hurdler: fair form over fences, won novice handicap at Doncaster in January by length from Putsometnby: disappointed starts either side (blinkered first occasion, mucus on lungs second): should be suited by thorough test of stamina: raced mainly on good going or softer (well held on good to firm): sold 13,000 gns Doncaster May Sales. *A. King*   **c105 h–**

RUSSELL ROAD (IRE)   11 br.g. Phardante (FR) – Burren Gale (IRE) (Strong Gale) [2002/3 c25d c22g^pu c24d³ c24d³ c20d^pu Feb 26] big, good-bodied gelding: winning hurdler: fairly useful chaser at best: off 2 years, form on return only when third to Existential in conditional jockeys handicap at Kempton (found little): stayed 3m: raced on good going or softer (won bumper on heavy): dead. *A. King*   **c105 h–**

RUSSIAN COURT   7 b.g. Soviet Lad (USA) – Court Town (Camden Town) [2002/3 h77: 17g⁵ 16v⁴ 22g 16d* 17s³ 17s* 16d^F Mar 10] poor handicap hurdler: won at Ludlow   **h84**

(20-runner seller, bought from D. Gandolfo 4,600 gns) in January and Taunton in February: probably best around 2m: acts on heavy and good to firm going: headstrong, and has found little. *S. E. H. Sherwood*

RUSSIAN DANCER 7 b.g. Petoski – Merry Minuet (Trumpeter) [2002/3 h–: c21s⁵ **c71**
Feb 23] leggy, close-coupled gelding: poor form in novice hurdles: off 21 months, similar **h–**
form when fifth of 11 in novice handicap at Ayr on chasing debut. *Jedd O'Keeffe*

RUSSIAN GIGOLO (IRE) 6 b. or br.g. Toulon – Nanogan (Tarqogan) [2002/3 F89: **h97**
20d² 20s⁵ 19g² 22v³ 20s 20vᵖᵘ 24g⁴ Apr 24] lengthy, workmanlike gelding: modest novice hurdler: probably stays 3m: acts on heavy going. *N. A. Twiston-Davies*

RUSSIAN PRINCE (IRE) 8 b.g. Soviet Lad (USA) – Sweet Goodbye (Petorius) **c87 ?**
[2002/3 21dᶠ 20mᵖᵘ c22m⁶ Jun 1] lengthy gelding: little form in varied events: left **h–**
B. Rothwell after second start. *S. R. Bolton*

RUSSIAN RIVER 11 b.g. Sulaafah (USA) – Ninotchka (Niniski (USA)) [2002/3 h–: **h–**
18dᶠ 16s Nov 24] big gelding: poor 2m handicap hurdler, lightly raced and no form since 2000. *J. J. Bridger*

RUST EN VREDE 4 b.g. Royal Applause – Souveniers (Relko) [2002/3 16g³ 17d 16g⁵ **h81**
16g Apr 12] half-brother to several winners, notably smart hurdler/fairly useful chaser
Simply Gifted (by Simply Great), probably stays 2½m: modest maiden on Flat (stays
1¼m): modest juvenile hurdler: likely to prove best around 2m. *D. Carroll*

RUSTIC REVELRY 10 b.g. Afzal – Country Festival (Town And Country) [2002/3 **c87**
c93, h–: c16gᵇᵈ c16d⁶ c21m² c16s⁵ c21m³ c22m⁶ Jul 7] tall gelding: modest chaser: won **h–**
points in February and April: should stay beyond 21f: acts on good to firm going, possibly
unsuited by softer than good: blinkered last 4 starts. *R. H. York*

RUSTY ALNTYNE (IRE) 5 ch.g. Rashar (USA) – Sky Rainbow (IRE) (Henbit **h–**
(USA)) [2002/3 F72: F16m F17d 24d⁵ 25gᵖᵘ 16dᵖᵘ Mar 5] close-coupled gelding: mid- **F–**
division at best in bumpers: no form in novice hurdles. *G. M. Moore*

RUSTY FELLOW 13 b.g. Rustingo – Sallisses (Pamroy) [2002/3 c93§: c33g⁶ c30m* **c96 §**
c31m May 22] workmanlike gelding: fair hunter chaser: dictated pace when winning at
Huntingdon (for second year running) in May: stays 4¼m: acts on soft and good to firm
going: very difficult ride (usually soon off bridle) and needs things to go his way. *Mrs
G. M. Shail*

RUTLEDGE RED (IRE) 7 gr.g. Roselier (FR) – Katebeaujolais (Politico (USA)) **h102**
[2002/3 h99, F82: 20g 19m* 19g⁸ 20d* 20d² Nov 12] tall gelding: fair novice hurdler:
won at Market Rasen in August (wandered) and October (unimpressive when odds on),
and at Fakenham (seemed to idle) later in October: will probably stay 3m: acts on soft and
good to firm going. *J. M. Jefferson*

RYALUX (IRE) 10 b.g. Riverhead (USA) – Kings de Lema (IRE) (King's Ride) **c146**
[2002/3 c126, h111: c24f³ c25s* c25v² c24d² c24m³ c33m* Apr 12] **h–**
Ryalux finally won the big race he deserved when getting up close home to
land the Gala Casinos Daily Record Scottish National in April. The Ayr race was
the twenty-fifth completed start of his career and he had either won or been placed
in every one of them. For all his consistency though, the placings have tended to
outnumber the wins and, in his two races prior to the Scottish National Ryalux only
just missed out on a couple of other good prizes. At Doncaster in January he went
down by a head to Barryscourt Lad in the Great Yorkshire Chase after edging in
front on the run-in, and at Kempton the following month he ran another cracker to
finish four lengths third behind La Landiere and Gunther McBride in the Racing
Post Chase. Ryalux had also finished third at Kempton on his reappearance, despite
an uncharacteristically poor round of jumping on very firm ground, and there was
another narrow defeat when beaten three-quarters of a length by Hugo de Grez in a
£13,000 handicap at Kelso in December. Amid all these placed efforts, Ryalux's
fortunes had changed briefly but dramatically for the better when he was handed a
four-runner race, also at Ayr, in November; with Ryalux seemingly held in third
place at the last, the leader Kerry Lads fell, hampering Ballinclay King in the
process and leaving Ryalux to run out a four-length winner from the other runner
Kit Smartie.

The Scottish National drew a large field as usual, though, coming just a
week after Aintree, only one Grand National participant took his chance, Shotgun
Willy's presence at the top of the weights putting the majority of the nineteen

Gala Casinos Daily Record Scottish Grand National Chase (Handicap), Ayr—
the ultra-consistent Ryalux (noseband) rallies to deny Stormez an eighth win of the season

runners out of the handicap. Gunther McBride, third the year before, was sent off the 7/2 favourite, ahead of the National Hunt Chase first and second, Sudden Shock and Stormez on 6/1, Ryalux on 15/2 and Shotgun Willy on 8/1. Running over a mile further than he had tackled before, Ryalux made steady headway to get into contention on the final circuit and battled it out from two out with Stormez, who'd taken over in front from Gunther McBride. It was Stormez who got away from the last the quicker but, after looking held halfway up the run-in, Ryalux rallied splendidly up the rail to win by a neck. Gunther McBride had been just behind the leaders when unseating two out, leaving Spendid to take third place twenty lengths back, ahead of Kerry Lads, who had still been bang there two out, and Shotgun Willy, only eight completing in total. Ryalux's victory was a popular one for his small stable. Former head lad Andy Crook had taken over the training of Micky Hammond's horses, including Ryalux, when the latter quit training in 2001 but, when Hammond resumed, Ryalux was one of the horses Crook was able to retain for his own training operation. Ryalux's owner, incidentally, came by the horse in unusual circumstances, Ryalux being part of the package when he purchased the carpet firm of the same name.

		Riverman (b 1969)	Never Bend / River Lady
	Riverhead (USA) (b 1984)		
		Tertiary (ch 1976)	Vaguely Noble / Goofed
Ryalux (IRE) (b.g. 1993)			
		King's Ride (b 1976)	Rarity / Ride
	Kings de Lema (IRE) (b 1988)		
		Rose de Lema (ch 1973)	Beau Tudor / The Seventh Sister

Ryalux is by the well-bred but little-used Riverhead (who is out of a sister to the high-class filly Nobiliary and a half-sister to Lyphard), a winner on the Flat in France before becoming a smart two-mile hurdler for David Elsworth. Ryalux is the second, and seemingly final foal, out of his unraced dam Kings de Lema, the first, Helperby (by Brush Aside), being a poor maiden hurdler. This is a modest branch of a family which does not appear in the *General Stud Book* but nonetheless has some illustrious names a bit further back. The 1956 Champion Hurdle winner Doorknocker was a brother to Ryalux's third dam The Seventh Sister, and this is also the family of those high-class chasers Buck House and Door Latch.

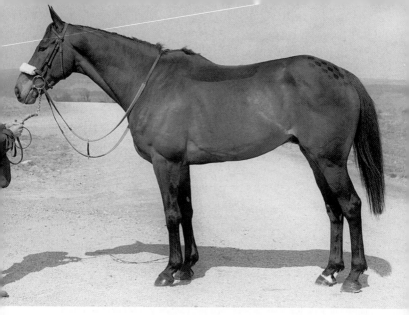

The lengthy Ryalux's stamina over extreme distances is now proven, he usually jumps soundly, and he probably acts on any ground, so connections can legitimately look forward to a tilt at Aintree in 2004. His trainer has stated that Ryalux will be campaigned over hurdles in the next season, at least until after the National weights have been announced, in order to prevent his chase rating rising any further before Aintree. This ploy was also adopted by Ad Hoc's connections in the latest season and, whilst trainers are free to campaign their horses however they choose within the rules, it is to be hoped this does not become common practice for National-bound chasers; if it did, the top staying chases that take place earlier in the season, such as the Welsh National, would suffer as a result. Unlike Ad Hoc, Ryalux has already won over hurdles so will be running in handicaps rather than novice events. He could still turn out to be very well treated over hurdles judged on his improved chasing form. It bears repeating that Ryalux is tremendously game and consistent. *A. Crook*

RYAN'S GOLD (IRE) 5 b.g. Distant View (USA) – Kathleen's Dream (USA) (Last Tycoon) [2002/3 16s^{pu} 16m 20g Dec 28] fair maiden at best on Flat (stays 1m), little form in 2002: no show over hurdles: wore cheekpieces last 2 starts. *B. Mactaggart*   **h–**

RYDERS STORM (USA) 4 b. or br.g. Dynaformer (USA) – Justicara (Rusticaro (FR)) [2002/3 18m* 17m* 18m* 16m⁴ 16g^{pu} Apr 3] leggy gelding: fairly useful 7f winner at 2 yrs for M. Johnston, well held all 3 starts in 2002 for P. Cole: odds on, successful first 3 starts in juvenile hurdles, at Fontwell (2) and Bangor in summer: unimpressive for last win and jumped poorly when very laboured in first-time visor fourth start: left M. Pipe, out of depth on return in spring: front runner. *T. R. George*   **h101 §**

RYDON LANE (IRE) 7 br.g. Toca Madera – Polocracy (IRE) (Aristocracy) [2002/3 h87, F73: 19d⁴ c21v^F 22d⁵ 19d* 24d^{pu} Feb 23] useful-looking gelding: modest hurdler: won handicap at Exeter in January: in contention when blundering 3 out there month later: fell second on chasing debut: stays 2¾m: raced on good going or softer. *Mrs S. D. Williams*   **c–** **h91**

RYE RUM (IRE) 12 br.g. Strong Gale – Eimers Pet (Paddy's Stream) [2002/3 c–§, h–: c20m⁵ c20gᵖᵘ c25mᵖᵘ Jun 21] small gelding: of no account: often visored/blinkered. *J. W. F. Aynsley* **c–§ h–**

S

SAAFEND ROCKET (IRE) 5 b.g. Distinctly North (USA) – Simple Annie (Simply Great (FR)) [2002/3 16d⁶ 16dᶠ Nov 25] modest on Flat (stays 8.5f): second outing over hurdles, would have been placed but for falling 3 out in seller at Ludlow: will need sharp 2m. *R. Lee* **h74**

SABADILLA (USA) 9 b.g. Sadler's Wells (USA) – Jasmina (USA) (Forli (ARG)) [2002/3 16g 19d⁵ 17v⁵ 16g⁶ 16m* Apr 20] leggy gelding: smart at one time on Flat (stays 1½m), lightly raced nowadays: fair hurdler, left M. Bosley after third start: improved subsequently, won handicaps at Cork in April and at Punchestown (led near finish when beating Peace In Ireland a neck) early following month: likely to prove best around 2m: acts on good to firm going: held up: bled from nose third outing. *Patrick Michael Verling, Ireland* **h105**

SABI SAND 7 b.m. Minster Son – Radical Lady (Radical) [2002/3 h64: c22d² 23d c26v* c24d⁴ c25v⁴ c24s* c25d* c21sᵖᵘ Mar 15] lengthy, sparely-made mare: poor maiden hurdler: modest handicap chaser: won at Uttoxeter in November, Newcastle in February and Catterick (beat Supreme Breeze by ½ length in novice event) in March: best at 3m+: raced on good going or softer (acts on heavy): wears cheekpieces, also tongue tied last 2 starts: usually sound jumper: sold 5,000 gns Doncaster May Sales. *R. C. Guest* **c88 h–**

SABY (FR) 5 b. or br.g. Sassanian (USA) – Valy Flett (FR) (Pietru (FR)) [2002/3 17v³ 17s⁶ 16v 19m c16g² Apr 21] tall gelding: fourth foal: dam little sign of ability: in frame over hurdles (for M. Boudot) and in 4-y-o chases (for G. Macaire) in France: poor form over hurdles in Britain: fair form when short-head second to Sandoran in novice handicap chase at Newton Abbot: raced up to 19f. *P. J. Hobbs* **c108 h79**

SACKVILLE (IRE) 10 b.g. Satco (FR) – Sackville Street (Ete Indien (USA)) [2002/3 c158, h135: c20v² c24d* c24v⁵ c22v* Jan 1] strong, good sort: smart chaser: won two 4-runner races in 2002/3, Tommy Whittle Chase at Haydock (beat Bobby Grant 1½ **c148 h–**

Tommy Whittle Chase, Haydock—
Sackville holds off course specialists Bobby Grant and Kingsmark (grey) in a muddling race

lengths) in December and minor event at Tramore (didn't need to be near best to beat below-form More Than A Stroll) in January, tending to jump left both times: reportedly injured while schooling later in month: should stay at least 3¼m: yet to race on firm going, acts on any other. *Miss F. M. Crowley, Ireland*

SACRIFICE   8 b.g. Arctic Lord – Kellyann (Jellaby) [2002/3 c89: c16g³ c20f² c16d⁴ **c99**
c20m³ c16m* c19m³ Apr 21] fair hunter chaser: both wins at Hereford, beating Alpha Romana by ¾ length, pair clear, in April: stays 2½m: acts on firm going. *T. Long*

SACUNDAI (IRE)   6 b.g. Hernando (FR) – Shahdiza (USA) (Blushing Groom **h159**
(FR)) [2002/3 h139: 20s⁴ 20v* 16d* 16d* 20g* Apr 5]
Sacundai holds the distinction of being the only horse to beat Champion Hurdle winner Rooster Booster in 2002/3. He did it at level weights too, though needed all of the run-in at Aintree to turn round a deficit of a length and a quarter at the last in the two-and-a-half-mile Martell Cognac Aintree Hurdle. Rooster Booster's rider Richard Johnson lost his whip, which might well have made the difference with a head the margin of victory, but the pair still finished seven lengths clear of Like-A-Butterfly, form which represented an improved effort on the part of Sacundai, one that puts him at the head of the second rank of hurdlers, behind the top stayers and Rooster Booster. Although Sacundai won his three races before Aintree he was relatively unconsidered at 9/1, the build-up dominated by Rooster Booster, attempting to follow up his Festival victory, and Like-A-Butterfly, whose jockey Charlie Swan was having his final ride. In a well-run race, the promising Lord Transcend took up the running at halfway and was still in front into the straight, with as many as seven others in with a chance. Copeland, Geos and Hors La Loi III were beaten by three out with Like-A-Butterfly tapped for foot and Lord Transcend one paced once headed. Quazar briefly took over as Sacundai, who had raced in mid-division, was ridden to keep up before Rooster Booster made his apparently decisive move for home. Two features of Sacundai's performance were that he jumped fluently and showed plenty of resolution under pressure.

It might be hard to imagine on the evidence of Aintree that Sacundai would have much chance of beating Rooster Booster in a Champion Hurdle on good ground—trainer Edward O'Grady commented wryly that he might get lapped under such circumstances—but two of Sacundai's three wins before Aintree were gained at two miles. In the Red Mills Trial Hurdle at Gowran in February he beat

Red Mills Trial Hurdle, Gowran—
Sacundai (far side) challenges odds-on shot Liss A Paoraigh at the last

*Martell Cognac Aintree Hurdle—the colours of Champion Hurdle winner Rooster Booster
are lowered after the latter's jockey drops his whip on the run-in*

the odds-on Liss A Paoraigh a length and a half in a virtual match then, connections
having failed to take up entries in either the Coral Cup or County Hurdle at Cheltenham, Sacundai landed a minor event at Limerick by a distance at odds of 9/2-on.
His winning run had begun with a minor hurdle at Naas in January when he showed
the best turn of foot in a slowly-run race to defeat odds-on Florida Coast by four
lengths.

Sacundai began and ended his campaign with a defeat. He picked up a
minor injury when a remote fourth to Limestone Lad in the Lismullen Hurdle at
Navan on his reappearance and was off nearly three months afterwards. A month
after Aintree, shortly after the end of the British season, he lined up for the Ballymore Properties Champion Stayers' Hurdle at Punchestown, starting odds on in the
absence of Limestone Lad. Sacundai went down by half a length to Holy Orders
after quickening two lengths clear two out but being unable to get the enigmatic
winner off the bridle. In hindsight, Sacundai might have done better had he been
sent for home sooner. There are more races to be won with Sacundai over hurdles,
and he could have further improvement in him, though his prospects in the very
best races almost certainly depend on plans for the likes of Baracouda and Iris's
Gift and on old age catching up with Limestone Lad.

		Niniski	Nijinsky
Sacundai (IRE) (b.g. 1997)	Hernando (FR) (b 1990)	(b 1976)	Virginia Hills
		Whakilyric	Miswaki
		(b 1984)	Lyrism
	Shahdiza (USA) (ch 1982)	Blushing Groom	Red God
		(ch 1974)	Runaway Bride
		Shahneez	St Paddy
		(b 1977)	Tazeem

Sacundai had been around a stone behind the best novice hurdlers in 2001/2,
finishing fifth in the Supreme Novices' at Cheltenham, and he progressed to a similar margin behind the very best hurdlers in 2002/3. Before joining O'Grady's
stable, Sacundai was trained by Pascal Bary in France and showed fairly useful
form in a handful of outings on the Flat, including finishing ninth in the Derby
Italiano. Details of Sacundai's pedigree were contained in *Chasers & Hurdlers*

Malm Syndicate's "Sacundai"

2001/02 and there is nothing to add. A medium-sized gelding, Sacundai is likely to prove best at two and a half miles or more and should be fully effective at three. He won on good to firm on his hurdling debut but has since raced on good going or softer and acts on heavy. *E. J. O'Grady, Ireland*

SADDLERS BOY 5 b.g. Saddlers' Hall (IRE) – Miss Poll Flinders (Swing Easy (USA)) [2002/3 F12d Nov 13] lengthy gelding: half-brother to several winners, including 19f hurdle winner Chilly Lad and fairly useful 5f to 7f winner Duffertoes (both by High Kicker): dam tailed off only start at 2 yrs: never better than mid-division in 23-runner bumper at Newbury on debut. *K. C. Bailey* **F–**

SADDLER'S QUEST 6 b.g. Saddlers' Hall (IRE) – Seren Quest (Rainbow Quest (USA)) [2002/3 16g Feb 27] smart on Flat (should stay at least 2m) at 3 yrs for G. Butler, well held in 2001 after stress fracture of cannon bone: little encouragement in novice at Ludlow on hurdling debut. *C. P. Morlock* **h73**

SADLER'S COVE (FR) 5 b.g. King's Theatre (IRE) – Mine d'Or (FR) (Posse (USA)) [2002/3 21m 19m 20m Apr 12] 30,000Y, 1,700 4-y-o: compact gelding: half-brother to several winners, including French hurdler Manilora (by Crystal Glitters): dam French maiden half-sister to Prix Royal-Oak winner Mersey and Prix Saint-Alary winner Muncie: signs of ability in 3 runs over hurdles only when never-dangerous seventh of 16 in maiden at Hereford second start (probably flattered). *B. G. Powell* **h–**

SADLER'S REALM 10 b.g. Sadler's Wells (USA) – Rensaler (USA) (Stop The Music (USA)) [2002/3 c119, h–: c19v⁴ c19sᵖᵘ c21dᶠ Feb 15] smallish, leggy gelding: has had leg problems: one-time useful hurdler/fairly useful handicap chaser: often let down by jumping over fences, including last 2 starts: stays 2½m: raced on good going or softer (acts on heavy). *P. J. Hobbs* **c–** **h–**

SADLER'S SECRET (IRE) 8 b.g. Sadler's Wells (USA) – Athyka (USA) (Secretariat (USA)) [2002/3 c–§, h103§: 27s³ 20d 22m^pu 24f² 20d* 24d² 27s³ 23v³ 24d² 24s 26g⁴ Feb 22] workmanlike gelding: fair handicap hurdler, sold out of M. Pipe's stable £1,600 Ascot August Sales after third start: largely ran well after, left clear last when winning at Haydock in November: stays 27f: acts on any going: formerly blinkered/visored: has had tongue tied: not a fluent jumper/often goes in snatches. *A. J. Deakin*
c–
h105

SAD MAD BAD (USA) 9 b.g. Sunny's Halo (CAN) – Quite Attractive (USA) (Well Decorated (USA)) [2002/3 c122, h–: c24d⁴ c25s* c25s* c26s 24s 24d c34s^pu c33m^pu Apr 12] workmanlike gelding: winning hurdler: fairly useful handicap chaser: won weak 4-runner event at Wetherby in November, lost his form subsequently: stays at least 29f: acts on good to firm and heavy going: effective blinkered/visored or not. *Mrs M. Reveley*
c120 d
h–

SAFARI PARADISE (FR) 6 ch.g. Red Paradise – Safari Liz (USA) (Hawaii) [2002/3 c21s^F c22s c23s 19d⁶ 16s⁴ 17s 21m³ 22v 24m Apr 16] lengthy gelding: third foal: brother to winning pointer Elvis: dam placed up to 1¼m on Flat: lightly raced on Flat/fairly useful maiden chaser in France, sold out of T. Civel's stable €110,000 Goffs November Sale after third outing: fair form at best over hurdles in Britain, soundly beaten in handicaps last 2 starts (visored final one): should stay beyond 2¾m: acts on heavy going: hard ride. *M. C. Pipe*
c119
h109

SAFE ENOUGH (IRE) 7 ch.g. Safety Catch (USA) – Godfreys Cross (IRE) (Fine Blade (USA)) [2002/3 h76: 16f 21m* Oct 7] medium-sized gelding: lightly-raced hurdler: won handicap at Plumpton: stays 21f: acts on soft and good to firm going. *J. T. Gifford*
h85

SAFE SHOT 4 b.g. Salse (USA) – Optaria (Song) [2002/3 16g 17d 20g Apr 23] half-brother to very smart hurdler/winning chaser up to 19f Grey Shot (by Sharrood): little show on Flat: no form over hurdles. *Mrs J. C. McGregor*
h–

SAFFRON SUN 8 b.g. Landyap (USA) – Saffron Bun (Sit In The Corner (USA)) [2002/3 h98: c23f⁶ c19d c24s^pu c23g* c23f² c21m⁴ c20f^F Apr 25] tall, workmanlike gelding: winning hurdler: fair chaser: won novice handicap at Exeter in March: stays 23f: best form on good going or firmer (acts on firm): possibly ideally suited by right-handed tracks. *J. D. Frost*
c106
h–

SAFI 8 b.g. Generous (IRE) – Jasarah (IRE) (Green Desert (USA)) [2002/3 c–, h–: 16m⁶ 19f Oct 17] leggy gelding: poor hurdler/maiden chaser: runner-up in point in March: usually blinkered: tongue tied. *D. McCain*
c–
h–

SAGA ROYALE (FR) 7 b.m. Garde Royale – Passionnante (FR) (Dike (USA)) [2002/3 h55: 21s⁵ 17g^R Mar 16] angular mare: poor maiden hurdler: possibly flattered from 13 lb out of weights when fifth in mares handicap at Plumpton on reappearance: tailed off when refusing sixth next time: stays 21f: acts on soft going: tried visored. *D. C. O'Brien*
h73

SAGE DANCER (USA) 6 b.g. Green Dancer (USA) – Sophonisbe (Wollow) [2002/3 16d² 16g* 16m⁵ c17d⁴ c16d^pu Mar 18] tall ex-Irish gelding: has scope: half-brother to several winners, including Irish Derby winner Zagreb (by Theatrical) and winner over fences in Italy by Shareef Dancer: dam, French listed 11f winner, half-sister to high-class Steinlen, best up to 1¼m: fairly useful on Flat (stays 2m, usually blinkered): fair form over hurdles: won maiden at Cork in August: sold out of D. Weld's stable 4,500 gns Doncaster November Sales: fourth to Vol Solitaire in novice at Kelso on chasing debut in March: shaped as if amiss later in month: likely to stay 2½m. *C. Grant*
c92
h107

SAHEM (IRE) 6 b.g. Sadler's Wells (USA) – Sumava (IRE) (Sure Blade (USA)) [2002/3 F16g² F16m² F17m* F16g⁴ 22s² 20d⁴ 16d⁶ 21s Dec 10] 400,000Y: well-made gelding: first living foal: dam unraced half-sister to Ela Romara, very smart up to 1¼m: fair form in bumpers: won at Sedgefield in July: modest form over hurdles: in frame in novices at Kelso and Newcastle in November: will probably prove better at 2½m+ than shorter: acts on soft and good to firm going: runner-up on Flat debut in April. *D. Eddy*
h91
F90

SAHHAR 10 ch.g. Sayf El Arab (USA) – Native Magic (Be My Native (USA)) [2002/3 h77: 16d⁶ 16d 19d⁴ 16g⁶ 20g⁵ Apr 21] small gelding: has reportedly had leg problems: poor hurdler: barely stays 19f: acts on firm and good to soft going. *B. D. Leavy*
h80

SAIDAI (IRE) 5 b.g. Roselier (FR) – V'Soske Gale (IRE) (Strong Gale) [2002/3 F17d⁶ Feb 23] 40,000 4-y-o: first foal: dam fair hurdler/chaser, stayed 2¾m: shaped like a stayer when sixth in maiden bumper at Hereford on debut. *Jonjo O'Neill*
F71

SAILOR JACK (USA) 7 b.g. Green Dancer (USA) – Chateaubrook (USA) (Alleged (USA)) [2002/3 h90: 21m⁵ 20d⁴ Aug 2] close-coupled gelding: modest handicap hurdler:
h–

off over a year, showed little both starts in 2002/3: stays 3m: acts on firm going, probably on soft: usually blinkered. *D. McCain*

SAINT DES SAINTS (FR)   5 b.h. Cadoudal (FR) – Chamisene (FR) (Pharly (FR)) [2002/3 c112, h145: 19s* 19d² 18s² 19s² 20v⁴ Nov 10] a leading 4-y-o hurdler at Auteuil in 2002, completing 5-timer when winning Group 3 Prix de Longchamp in May by 4 lengths from Great Love: at least respectable efforts subsequently, good neck second to Karly Flight (rec 9 lb) in Group 3 on third outing: stayed 19f: raced on going softer than good, very best form on soft: stud. *G. Macaire, France*   **c–**
h145

SAINT JOSEPH   13 ch.g. Lir – Kimberley Ann (St Columbus) [2002/3 c101: c19gᵖᵘ May 1] compact gelding: fairly useful hunter chaser: insufficient test when well held in handicap in May: stays 3¼m: acts well on going softer than good, probably unsuited by good to firm. *Miss S. Young*   **c–**

SAINT PAR (FR)   5 gr.g. Saint Preuil (FR) – Paris Or (FR) (Noir Et Or) [2002/3 c104, h116: 20dᵖᵘ 20s 20s⁴ c19d⁴ c21s² c24g⁴ c26g³ Apr 21] medium-sized gelding: fairly useful hurdler, poor efforts in handicaps first 2 starts: fair form over fences: stays 21f: acts on good to firm and heavy going: blinkered last 4 outings: none too consistent. *P. F. Nicholls*   **c107**
h–

SAINT ROMBLE (FR)   6 b.g. Sassanian (USA) – Limatge (FR) (Trac) [2002/3 c–, h–: c21fᵖᵘ c16d² c16v* c19d³ c18sᵖᵘ c18m⁴ Mar 22] leggy gelding: modest chaser: won novice handicap at Ascot in December, left well clear when Ins And Outs fell last: stays 19f: best efforts on going softer than good (acts on heavy). *P. J. Hobbs*   **c92**
h–

SAINTSAIRE (FR)   4 b.g. Apeldoorn (FR) – Pro Wonder (FR) (The Wonder (FR)) [2002/3 16g* 17s³ 16m⁵ 17g Mar 13] leggy, useful-looking ex-French gelding: successful 3 times up to 11.6f on Flat in 2002 for P. Lefevre: created very good impression when winning juvenile at Newbury on hurdling debut, quickening in fine style to beat Vanormix 8 lengths: failed to progress as expected, and folded tamely after 2 out when fifteenth of 27 in Triumph Hurdle at Cheltenham final start (reportedly suffered overreach). *N. J. Henderson*   **h125**

SAITENSOHN (GER)   5 b.h. Monsun (GER) – Saite (GER) (Marduk (GER)) [2002/3 c17s⁵ c17s² 19d* 21d* 22v* 21g Mar 12] quite good-topped horse: useful on Flat (stays 1¾m) in Germany, successful 4 times: twice-raced over fences in October, second in 4-y-o event at Krefeld: fairly useful form when winning 2 novice hurdles at Newbury in November: made heavy weather of accomplishing simple-looking task in similar event at Sandown in February on final start for C. Von Der Recke: stiff task, well held in Grade 1 at Cheltenham following month: stays 2¾m: acts on heavy ground: sent to USA. *Jonjo O'Neill*   **c?**
h124

SALAMAN (FR)   11 b.g. Saumarez – Merry Sharp (Sharpen Up) [2002/3 h–: 27m⁵ 22f⁶ 22d⁴ 22sᵖᵘ 22vᵖᵘ 28g³ 24f² Apr 3] sparely-made gelding: poor hurdler: stays 3½m: acts on any going: often blinkered/visored/tongue tied: ungenuine. *D. C. O'Brien*   **h67 §**

SALER SAL   6 ch.m. Primitive Rising (USA) – Portonia (Ascertain (USA)) [2002/3 24gᵖᵘ 21mᵖᵘ c21mᵖᵘ Oct 1] 5,000 4-y-o: second foal: dam fairly useful staying hurdler/chaser: no sign of ability, including in points: left J. O'Neill after hurdling debut. *P. D. Niven*   **c–**
h–

SALFORD   8 ch.g. Salse (USA) – Bustellina (Busted) [2002/3 c90, h–: 22dᵘʳ c24g⁴ c24vᵖᵘ c21m* c25m² c21g² Apr 19] strong gelding: winning hurdler: modest handicap chaser: won amateur event at Wincanton in March: probably stays 25f: best on good going or firmer: tried visored: usually races prominently: makes mistakes: unreliable. *N. J. Hawke*   **c85 §**
h–

SALGRADO (NZ)   7 ch.g. Prince Salieri (AUS) – Musing (Music Maestro) [2002/3 16s 16m Mar 22] angular gelding: won twice up to 1¼m on Flat in New Zealand: well held both starts in novice hurdles, poor form on second occasion. *Jonjo O'Neill*   **h77**

SALHOOD   4 b.g. Capote (USA) – Princess Haifa (USA) (Mr Prospector (USA)) [2002/3 F16m² F17g Apr 5] big gelding: third foal: half-brother to UAE 7f winner Kondoty (by Mtoto) and 11.5f winner Zeyaarah (by Rahy), both fairly useful: dam, 1m winner later successful up to 9f in USA, out of sister to top-class 2-y-o Storm Bird: bought unraced out of M. Tregoning's stable 11,000 gns Newmarket July Sales: second to Dark Character in maiden bumper at Southwell on debut: mid-field in Grade 2 at Aintree following month. *S. Gollings*   **F91**

SALIENT POINT (IRE)   6 gr.m. Sri Pekan (USA) – Tajarib (IRE) (Last Tycoon) [2002/3 16gᵖᵘ May 8] fair maiden at best on Flat (should stay 1¼m) at 3 yrs, sold out of   **h–**

S. Wood's stable 2,500 gns Newmarket Autumn (2000) Sales: no show on hurdling debut. *Mrs K. M. Lamb*

SALIERIOUS (NZ) 8 ch.g. Prince Salieri (AUS) – Analaw (NZ) (Diplomatic Agent (USA)) [2002/3 h63: 20d 21g^{pu} 22g^{pu} 16m 19g Jul 27] angular gelding: of little account nowadays: tried blinkered/visored: has had tongue tied. *J. C. Tuck*   h–

SALIM 6 b.g. Salse (USA) – Moviegoer (Pharly (FR)) [2002/3 17s 16s^{pu} Dec 27] brother to 3¼m hurdle winner Picture Palace and half-brother to 2 other winning hurdlers: modest on Flat (stays easy 1¼m), successful in March: no promise in 2 runs over hurdles. *J. E. Long*   h–

SALIX BAY 7 b.g. Karinga Bay – Willow Gale (Strong Gale) [2002/3 20v^6 c21s^6 c23g Feb 25] first foal: dam staying chaser: no sign of ability. *P. Butler*   c–
h–

SALIX DANCER 6 b.g. Shareef Dancer (USA) – Willowbank (Gay Fandango (USA)) [2002/3 h95: 16s^3 Nov 18] close-coupled gelding: modest maiden on Flat (stays 2¼m): similar form when placed 2 out of 3 starts over hurdles, third to Tim's The Man in novice at Leicester only run in 2000/3: will stay beyond 2m. *H. J. Collingridge*   h90

SALLIEMAK 5 b.m. Makbul – Glenbrook Fort (Fort Nayef) [2002/3 F17d Nov 24] first foal: dam, poor maiden staying hurdler, half-sister to Midlands National winner Glenbrook d'Or: well beaten in bumper on debut. *A. J. Wilson*   F–

SALLY SCALLY 11 ch.m. Scallywag – Petite Cone (Celtic Cone) [2002/3 c77, h–: c21g^3 c27s^{pu} c25g^4 Apr 14] smallish mare: fair pointer, successful in March: below that form in hunter chases: acts on firm going, possibly unsuited by soft: blinkered once: takes good hold, and is a weak finisher. *Miss T. Jackson*   c77
h–

SALLY'S PRIDE 6 gr.m. Norton Challenger – Another Scally (Scallywag) [2002/3 F16d^6 Dec 14] second reported foal: dam poor maiden all-weather hurdler: never dangerous when sixth of 10 in maiden bumper at Fakenham on debut. *Mrs H. Dalton*   F71

SALLY'S TWINS 10 b.m. Dowsing (USA) – Bird of Love (Ela-Mana-Mou) [2002/3 c56, h–: c21m 21g 21g^5 c21g^{pu} 24g^3 24m^2 c25g^2 c20v^2 c21s^F 24v 20g^6 21v^2 24g 25d^4 Feb 25] leggy mare: winning pointer: poor maiden hurdler/chaser: stays 25f: acts on good to firm and heavy going: visored once. *A. R. Dicken*   c64
h64

SALMON LADDER (USA) 11 b.g. Bering – Ballerina Princess (USA) (Mr Prospector (USA)) [2002/3 18s^3 20s^5 16s 20g^2 Apr 23] smart at one time on Flat: modest maiden hurdler: stays 2½m: acts on good to firm and heavy going: has had tongue tied. *A. J. Martin, Ireland*   h90

SALOUP 5 b.m. Wolfhound (USA) – Sarcita (Primo Dominie) [2002/3 h85: 16d May 23] leggy mare: modest form at best over hurdles: pulled hard when disappointing in handicap in May, not seen out again: likely to prove best at sharp 2m. *O. Sherwood*   h–

SALT HILL KING 6 b.g. Rakaposhi King – Domtony (Martinmas) [2002/3 h–: 19s 20d Jan 15] little worthwhile form over hurdles. *Ferdy Murphy*   h–

SALTIS (IRE) 11 ch.g. Salt Dome (USA) – Mrs Tittlemouse (Nonoalco (USA)) [2002/3 c78, h–: c16g c21f^6 c16m^{ur} c20d 20m 20d^{pu} Aug 3] angular gelding: poor pointer/steeplechaser/maiden hurdler: stays 3m: acts on firm going: tried blinkered: sometimes let down by jumping. *Mrs Jane Galpin*   c67
h–

SALTON MARE (IRE) 5 b.m. Houmayoun (FR) – Cygnet Wood (IRE) (Toca Madera) [2002/3 F17m^6 Jul 25] first foal: dam never ran: showed little in bumper on debut. *A. J. Lockwood*   F–

SALVAGE 8 b.g. Kahyasi – Storm Weaver (USA) (Storm Bird (CAN)) [2002/3 h92: 18d^{pu} c16m^3 16v c17d^5 c20d^6 c20g^4 c16g^2 c20g^5 Apr 25] angular gelding: modest handicap hurdler, below best both starts over hurdles in 2002/3: third to Europa in intermediate at Perth on chasing debut, below that form subsequently: should stay 2½m: acts on heavy and good to firm going: has had tongue tied. *Mrs J. C. McGregor*   c89
h–

SAM ADAMSON 8 br.g. Domitor (USA) – Sardine (Saritamer (USA)) [2002/3 19m^4 19g^5 Apr 19] sturdy gelding: signs of only a little ability over hurdles. *J. W. Mullins*   h–

SAMARARDO 6 b.g. Son Pardo – Kinlet Vision (IRE) (Vision (USA)) [2002/3 h–: 18f 22m^{pu} Jul 4] close-coupled gelding: no worthwhile form over hurdles: dead. *N. A. Dunger*   h–

SAMARA SONG 10 ch.g. Savahra Sound – Hosting (Thatching) [2002/3 16g Sep 14] small gelding: poor nowadays on Flat (best at 7f/1m): little worthwhile form over hurdles. *Ian Williams*   h–

SAMASAKHAN (IRE) 7 b.h. Slip Anchor – Samarzana (USA) (Blushing Groom (FR)) [2002/3 20s⁵ 20d³ 22s* 19m² 24s 21d² 24s 24s⁴ 24m⁵ Apr 13] workmanlike gelding: half-brother to useful 2m to 2½m chaser Samakaan (by Darshaan) and fairly useful 2m hurdler Samanid (by Shardari): formerly useful on Flat (stays 1¾m): fair hurdler: won maiden at Kilbeggan in July: in-and-out form subsequently: stays 3m: acts on soft and good to firm going: has jumped poorly/looked ungenuine. *P. Hughes, Ireland* **h110 §**

SAMBY 5 ch.g. Anshan – Mossy Fern (Le Moss) [2002/3 F14d² F18s² F17g* Mar 16] big, chunky gelding: second foal: half-brother to fair hurdler Mossy Bay (by Phardante), stays 3¼m: dam, useful chaser up to 3¼m, half-sister to useful jumper up to 25f Coq Hardi Affair: fairly useful form in bumpers, making all and holding on gamely by ½ length from Victory Gunner in maiden at Folkestone. *O. Sherwood* **F99**

SAMMAGEFROMTENESSE (IRE) 6 b.g. Petardia – Canoora (Ahonoora) [2002/3 16sᵖᵘ 16g³ 20m⁶ 17s 16vᵖᵘ 16g Apr 2] angular gelding: fairly useful at best on Flat, poor nowadays: poor maiden hurdler: best efforts at 2m when conditions aren't testing: tried blinkered: has had tongue tied. *N. F. Glynn, Ireland* **h75**

SAMMY SAMBA 5 b.g. Be My Chief (USA) – Peggy Spencer (Formidable (USA)) [2002/3 F88: F17m* 20sᵖᵘ 20g⁵ 16m⁶ 19f* 22f² 21f² 22dᵇᵈ Nov 5] leggy gelding: fair form in 2 bumpers, winning maiden at Newton Abbot in July: modest hurdler: successful in 2 novice handicaps at Exeter (amateurs on first occasion) in October: will stay 3m: acts on firm ground: tongue tied fourth and fifth starts: has hung. *P. J. Hobbs* **h101** **F88**

SAMON (GER) 6 ch.g. Monsun (GER) – Savanna (GER) (Sassafras (FR)) [2002/3 h132: 16s 20s³ 21g² 20d⁵ Apr 4] angular gelding: useful handicap hurdler, lightly raced: good efforts last 2 starts, in Coral Cup at Cheltenham (3½ lengths second of 27 to Xenophon) and listed event at Aintree (fifth of 16 to Patriot Games): stays 21f: acts on soft ground: usually races prominently. *M. C. Pipe* **h139**

SAM QUALE (IRE) 11 ch.g. Tale Quale – Samanthabrownthorn (Mandalus) [2002/3 c106, h–: c25d⁶ c24mᵖᵘ c20d³ May 26] workmanlike gelding: modest handicap chaser: stays 3m: acts on heavy going: usually visored/blinkered: often let down by jumping: sold 7,000 gns Doncaster May Sales, subsequently pulled up in 2 points. *B. Ellison* **c93** **h–**

SAM ROCKETT 10 b.g. Petong – Art Deco (Artaius (USA)) [2002/3 c–, h85§: 22g⁴ 22m 27g⁵ 27g³ Jul 31] small gelding: poor handicap hurdler: stays 27f: acts on firm going: usually blinkered: a hard ride (tends to get behind). *P. J. Hobbs* **c–** **h91 §**

SAMSAAM (IRE) 6 b.g. Sadler's Wells (USA) – Azyaa (Kris) [2002/3 h101: 17d 20v⁵ 20g² Apr 2] lengthy gelding: fairly useful handicap hurdler: good second to Rosco at Ascot final start: hung right and looked none too keen previous start: stays 2½m: blinkered: tongue tied last 2 starts. *M. C. Pipe* **h117**

SAMSON DES GALAS (FR) 5 b. or br.g. Agent Bleu (FR) – Sarema (FR) (Primo Dominie) [2002/3 F16d⁶ Feb 1] fourth foal: half-brother to winners around 9f by Lights Out and Luchiroverte: dam maiden: sixth to Crossbow Creek in bumper at Wetherby on debut. *R. Ford* **F89**

SAM'S PROFILES 9 b.g. Infantry – Lady De-Lacy (Pitpan) [2002/3 h–: 21dᵖᵘ c21mᵖᵘ 20g² Apr 21] sturdy gelding: poor maiden hurdler: pulled up on steeplechasing debut: won maiden point in April: stays 2½m: tried visored. *Miss K. M. George* **c–** **h66**

SAMUEL CHARLES 5 b.g. Green Desert (USA) – Hejraan (USA) (Alydar (USA)) [2002/3 F17s⁵ F16g 17s 18g⁶ Mar 17] 2,000 3-y-o, 20,000 4-y-o: third foal: closely related to 6f winner Haajra (by Polish Precedent) and half-brother to poor hurdler/fair chaser Helvetius (by In The Wings): dam, lightly-raced maiden, out of smart performer up to 1m Top Socialite: better effort in bumpers when fifth in maiden at Hereford on debut: well held in 2 novice hurdles. *Miss Venetia Williams* **h–** **F85**

SAMUEL WILDERSPIN 11 b.g. Henbit (USA) – Littoral (Crash Course) [2002/3 c136, h–: c24d² c26s³ c33v⁵ c24d⁴ c24g c26mᵖᵘ Apr 16] rangy gelding: useful handicap chaser: some creditable efforts in 2002/3, second to Iris Bleu at Cheltenham (amateurs) and fourth to Paxford Jack at Haydock: should stay beyond 3¼m: acts on heavy going, possibly not good to firm: tongue tied: has broken blood vessels: carries head awkwardly under pressure: sound jumper. *R. Lee* **c132** **h–**

SAMULE 13 gr.g. Another Realm – Dancing Kathleen (Green God) [2002/3 c20g* c22mᵖᵘ Jun 1] angular gelding: fair hunter chaser at best: only second outing after 4-year absence, won novice at Stratford in May: lame next time: tongue tied. *Mrs A. E. Harding* **c83**

SANDERSTEAD 4 b.g. So Factual (USA) – Charnwood Queen (Cadeaux Genereux) **h–**
[2002/3 16m 19d^{pu} Feb 10] leggy gelding: poor maiden on Flat (stays 1¼m/usually
blinkered): never a factor in juvenile and maiden claiming hurdles, blinkered on second
occasion: sold out of K. Morgan's stable 2,500 gns Doncaster September Sales in
between. *K. G. Wingrove*

SANDHOLES (IRE) 7 gr.m. Tirol – Caroline Lady (JPN) (Caro) [2002/3 h81: 20m^2 **h97**
20d^2 16d* Jun 7] fair handicap hurdler: won at Perth in June on second run there in 2
days: at least as effective at 2m as 2½m: acts on soft and good to firm going. *Miss Lucinda
V. Russell*

SAN DIMAS (USA) 6 gr.g. Distant View (USA) – Chrystophard (USA) (Lypheor) **h80**
[2002/3 h90?: 17m 22m^3 22g^3 16s^5 22v^{pu} 20m^4 Apr 19] poor hurdler: won novice at
Kelso in October: will stay 3m: acts on firm and good to soft going, possibly unsuited by
soft/heavy: usually visored, tried blinkered/in cheekpieces. *R. Allan*

SANDORAN 10 b.g. Gildoran – Party Miss (West Partisan) [2002/3 c95, h87: 16s^{pu} **c96**
c16g* Apr 21] workmanlike gelding: modest handicap hurdler/chaser: off a year before **h–**
reappearance: won novice chase at Newton Abbot in April: effective at 2m to 3m:
acts on good to firm and heavy going: visored twice. *M. Hill*

SANDS RISING 6 b.g. Primitive Rising (USA) – Celtic Sands (Celtic Cone) [2002/3 **h91**
F70: 16d 21s^3 16d 20v^4 24s^3 22g^4 Mar 21] quite good-topped gelding: modest novice
hurdler: stays 3m: raced on good going or softer (acts on soft). *R. Johnson*

SANDY DUFF 9 ch.g. Scottish Reel – Not Enough (Balinger) [2002/3 c115, h–: c19g^F **c–**
c21g^5 Apr 21] tall, lengthy gelding: fairly useful chaser: well held on completed **h–**
start in handicaps on belated return: raced mainly around 2m: acts on good to firm and
heavy going: tried visored: has shaped as if amiss more than once. *J. D. Frost*

SANDYWELL GEORGE 8 ch.g. Zambrano – Farmcote Air (True Song) [2002/3 **h–**
h–: 27g^6 22m^{ur} 19d 24v^{pu} 22g^{pu} 24g^5 Apr 21] good-topped gelding: of little account over
hurdles: has had tongue tied. *L. P. Grassick*

SAN FRANCISCO 9 b.g. Aragon – Sirene Bleu Marine (USA) (Secreto (USA)) **c82**
[2002/3 c92, h–: 16d^5 c20d^{pu} c25d^5 c20s^{pu} c20v^4 c20v^4 c20s^6 c20d^3 c16s^2 c16g^5 Apr 24] **h–**
tall gelding: poor handicap chaser: stays 2½m: acts on heavy going: effective tongue tied
or not: races prominently. *A. C. Whillans*

SAN GIORGIO 14 b.g. Lighter – Gold Willow (Goldfella) [2002/3 c–, h82§: 26g **c–**
24g^5 26m^6 24d^{pu} Nov 5] rangy gelding: veteran hurdler, retains little ability: sometimes **h– §**
blinkered: unreliable. *P. Kelsall*

SAN MARCO (IRE) 5 b.g. Brief Truce (USA) – Nuit Des Temps (Sadler's Wells **h–**
(USA)) [2002/3 20d^{pu} Oct 25] ex-Irish gelding: fair on Flat (stays 1½m), successful in
January: modest form at best over hurdles, leaving C. Collins before reappearance.
Mrs P. Sly

SAN MARINO (IRE) 7 b.g. Torus – Lousion (Lucifer (USA)) [2002/3 F77: c21v^3 **c67**
c16s^F c19d^F Feb 23] winning pointer: modest form in bumper: poor form on completed
start in steeplechases: needs to improve jumping. *Miss Venetia Williams*

SAN PEIRE (FR) 6 b.g. Cyborg (FR) – Shakapoura (FR) (Shakapour) [2002/3 h74, **h86 +**
F–: 20g^3 19d^{pu} 19d 16d^2 27g* Mar 25] modest hurdler: best effort when easily winning
maiden at Sedgefield by 19 lengths from Paddy's Thyme: stays 27f: raced only on good/
good to soft going: ran poorly in cheekpieces third start. *J. Howard Johnson*

SAN SURU (GER) 9 ch.h. Surumu (GER) – Sweet Virtue (USA) (Halo (USA)) **h?**
[2002/3 20g^6 20s^3 17s^3 16d^5 Feb 15] lengthy horse: useful on Flat (stays 1½m), successful 3 times in 2002: prolific winning hurdler in Germany, successful at Baden-Baden in
2001/2, placed twice in 2002/3: pulled hard and no form all 3 starts in Britain: stays 2½m:
acts on soft going: tried blinkered. *M. Hofer, Germany*

SANTA LUCIA 7 b.m. Namaqualand (USA) – Villasanta (Corvaro (USA)) [2002/3 **h93**
h93: 16m 20s^4 20g^2 19g^3 21d^3 22g^5 Apr 7] staying mare: modest hurdler: probably best up
to 21f: acts on good going: patiently ridden: consistent. *M. Dods*

SANTELLA BOY (USA) 11 b.g. Turkoman (USA) – Dream Creek (USA) (The **c73**
Minstrel (CAN)) [2002/3 c69, h–: c23m c26m* c26m^4 Aug 23] leggy gelding: poor **h–**
handicap hurdler/chaser: form in 2002/3 only when winning over fences at
Newton Abbot (dismounted soon after line) in August: jumped poorly final start: stays
27f: acts on firm and good to soft going: effective blinkered or not. *Miss C. Dyson*

Concept Hurdle, Sandown—
Santenay beats 2002 winner Copeland (visor) to land his third valuable prize of the campaign

SANTENAY (FR) 5 b.g. Mister Mat (FR) – Guigone (FR) (Esprit du Nord (USA)) **h155**
[2002/3 h111: 16m* 16g* 16s² 16g 16f* Apr 25] tall gelding: has scope: very smart hurdler: won 4-y-o handicap at Chepstow in October, K J Pike & Sons Elite Hurdle (Limited
Handicap) at Wincanton (by ½ length from Castleshane) in November and valuable
minor event at Sandown (beat Copeland 7 lengths) in April: better form when runner-up
to Intersky Falcon in Grade 1 event at Kempton in between: raced around 2m: acts on
firm and soft going: type to do well over fences in 2003/4. *P. F. Nicholls*

SAONE ET LOIRE (FR) 6 b.m. Always Fair (USA) – Saone (USA) (Bering) **h– §**
[2002/3 h83§: 16g^pu 17s Nov 14] poor hurdler: well below form both starts in 2002/3,
taking no interest on second occasion: raced around 2m on good going or softer (acts on
heavy): visored: tongue tied: temperamental. *M. C. Pipe*

SAORSIE 5 b.g. Emperor Jones (USA) – Exclusive Lottery (Presidium) [2002/3 h66: **h93**
16m^bd 17g* 16d 17v⁶ 16d⁴ 17g⁴ Mar 16] leggy gelding: best effort over hurdles when
winning handicap at Newton Abbot in July: raced around 2m: tried blinkered, not for win.
J. C. Fox

SARAGANN (IRE) 8 b.g. Danehill (USA) – Sarliya (IRE) (Doyoun) [2002/3 c–, **c129**
h128: 16s 20m² 20d^pu c17d* c17m² c16g^ur c20m^F c16d³ c19s⁴ c21v⁵ c20g Jan 18] leggy **h127**
gelding: fairly useful handicap hurdler/chaser: won over fences at Stratford in August:
barely stays testing 21f: acts on good to firm and heavy going: sometimes let down by
jumping over fences. *P. J. Hobbs*

SARAH'S SON (IRE) 8 b.g. Be My Native (USA) – Call Me Ruby (IRE) (Callernish) **h–**
[2002/3 21m^pu Jul 25] no sign of ability, even in points: has had tongue tied. *Miss Kate
Milligan*

SARAS DELIGHT 11 b.g. Idiot's Delight – Lady Bess (Straight Lad) [2002/3 c–, h–: **c–**
c25g^pu c27m^pu c31d³ Apr 25] rangy gelding: winning pointer: below that form in hunters: **h–**
thorough stayer: acts on soft going. *Major General C. A. Ramsay*

SARASOTA (IRE) 8 b.g. Lord Americo – Ceoltoir Dubh (Black Minstrel) [2002/3 **h–**
h77: 22g^{pu} Mar 29] angular gelding: poor maiden hurdler: off 18 months, pulled up in
handicap only outing in 2002/3: raced mainly around 2m: acts on firm going. *P. Bowen*

SARASOTA STORM 11 b.g. Petoski – Challanging (Mill Reef (USA)) [2002/3 h85: **h86**
22f² Aug 13] modest handicap hurdler: off a year, ran well when second of 3 at Newton
Abbot only start in 2002/3: not certain to stay beyond 2¾m: form only on good going or
firmer (acts on firm). *J. D. Frost*

SARATOV 5 b.g. Rudimentary (USA) – Sarabah (IRE) (Ela-Mana-Mou) [2002/3 17g³ **h92**
Jun 12] closely related to fair 2m hurdler Ice (by Polar Falcon): fairly useful on Flat (stays
10.4f): third to Red Sun in novice at Market Rasen on hurdling debut: sold 28,000 gns
Newmarket Autumn Sales. *G. A. Swinbank*

SARATOV (GER) 4 b.g. Acatenango (GER) – Sovereign Touch (IRE) (Pennine **h112 p**
Walk) [2002/3 16s^F Jan 23] maiden on Flat, in frame 6 times from 8.5f to 11f in Germany
at 3 yrs for S. Smrczek: shaped encouragingly in juvenile at Warwick won by Murghas on
hurdling debut, travelling well waited with and still every chance when falling last:
should improve. *Jonjo O'Neill*

SARENA SPECIAL 6 b.g. Lucky Guest – Lariston Gale (Pas de Seul) [2002/3 h–: **h–**
17s^{pu} May 28] neat gelding: 6f winner on Flat: no show in 3 runs over hurdles. *J. D. Frost*

SARGASSO SEA 6 gr.g. Greensmith – Sea Spice (Precipice Wood) [2002/3 F16s³ **F102**
F16d⁴ F16d* Mar 6] strong gelding: fifth foal: dam, useful hurdler/fairly useful novice
chaser up to 3¼m, out of sister to useful hurdler up to 3m Sea Empress: fairly useful form
in bumpers, winning maiden at Wincanton by 2½ lengths from Off Broadway: likely to
prove suited by at least 2½m. *J. A. B. Old*

The Hon Mrs Townshend's "Santenay"

SARN 4 b.g. Atraf – Covent Garden Girl (Sizzling Melody) [2002/3 16d[5] 16s[pu] Nov 27] **h–**
modest on Flat (stays 1m): well held in 2 juvenile hurdles, racing freely in cheekpieces on
second occasion: will prove best at sharp 2m. *A. Bailey*

SARTEANO 9 ch.m. Anshan – Daisy Girl (Main Reef) [2002/3 20m 20m[pu] Jun 30] **h–**
poor pointer, won maiden in May: showed little in 2 maiden hurdles. *G. J. Smith*

SASHA STAR (IRE) 5 b.g. Namaqualand (USA) – Trojan Relation (Trojan Fen) **h55**
[2002/3 h55: 16m[3] 16m 22g[4] 21d[pu] Nov 4] bad maiden hurdler: effective at 2m to 2¾m:
acts on soft and good to firm going: usually blinkered. *G. Brown*

SASPYS LAD 6 b.g. Faustus (USA) – Legendary Lady (Reprimand) [2002/3 h81: **h110**
17g[*] 17g[2] 16m[F] 18d 16m[*] 17m[*] Sep 13] fair maiden on Flat: progressive handicap
hurdler: won at Newton Abbot in June, Uttoxeter in August and Southwell in September,
and travelling well in clear lead when falling last at Uttoxeter in July: best around 2m: has
won on soft going, best form on good to firm. *W. M. Brisbourne*

SATANAS (FR) 5 b.g. Dress Parade – Oiseau Noir (FR) (Rex Magna (FR)) [2002/3 **h81**
F83: 17s[pu] 19d[6] 18s[5] 25m[pu] Mar 31] close-coupled gelding: poor form over hurdles:
probably failed to stay 25f final start. *O. Sherwood*

SATANTA 6 b.g. Cosmonaut – Expensive Gift (Record Token) [2002/3 h–, F–: 21d[pu] **h–**
19m Jun 4] little sign of ability. *J. W. Mullins*

SATCHMO (IRE) 11 b.g. Satco (FR) – Taradale (Torus) [2002/3 c139: c20d[3] c24g **c127**
Mar 11] big gelding, often impresses in appearance: useful chaser at best: off 15 months
and left D. Grissell, shaped as though retaining plenty of ability when third of 6 to More
Than A Stroll in Grade 3 at Gowran on reappearance: well held in valuable handicaps at
Cheltenham and Punchestown subsequently: effective at 2½m to 25f: acts on firm and
soft going: races prominently: bold jumper. *E. J. O'Grady, Ireland*

SATCO EXPRESS (IRE) 7 b.g. Satco (FR) – Rosel Chris (Roselier (FR)) [2002/3 **h132**
h106, F102: 20g[4] 20g[6] 20g[*] 18d[5] 22s[*] 24s[*] 24s[*] 20s[4] 24s[*] Jan 23]
The tough and genuine Satco Express is one to watch out for if sent novice
chasing in the next season. He had an excellent campaign over hurdles in 2002/3
until it was cut short by a leg infection picked up when recording a useful performance, on his first run outside novice company, to beat Rostropovich at Gowran in
January. Satco Express started favourite for the Gouldings Richland Galmoy
Hurdle, a Grade 3 event over three miles, and made all in typical style, keeping on
really gamely to win by a length and a half. Returning an improved performer after
a summer break, Satco Express, who had shown fairly useful form in bumpers, had
opened his account over hurdles at the same course in October, winning by five
lengths with a fair bit in hand. Stepped up further in trip the following month, he
again had plenty of use made of him when winning similar events—by fifteen

Gouldings Richland Galmoy Hurdle, Gowran—
Satco Express gains his fifth and most important win of 2002/3

lengths and nine—at Punchestown and Cork. Satco Express made it win number four in the Grade 3 O'Connell Warehousing Cork Stayers' Novice Hurdle in December, finding plenty when challenged after being waited with in front. Back at two and a half miles at Leopardstown's Christmas meeting, Satco Express was pushed along some way from home and couldn't quicken when a still creditable fourth to Hardy Eustace, a performance which confirmed that he ideally needs three miles plus. The well-made Satco Express is easily the most successful foal out of unraced Rosel Chris who is also the dam of a bumper winner in Abbey Prince (by Tanfirion). Satco Express has raced only on good going or softer (acts on soft). *E. Sheehy, Ireland*

SATCOSLAM (IRE) 8 b.g. Satco (FR) – Candy Slam (Candy Cane) [2002/3 c117, h–: c16s⁵ c21sᶠ c24v² c28s⁵ c24dᶠ c24g c29gᵖᵘ Apr 21] tall gelding: fairly useful handicap chaser: best effort in 2002/3 when second to Coq Hardi Diamond in very valuable event at Leopardstown in December: likely to prove best around 3m: raced on good ground or softer (acts on heavy): blinkered once: inconsistent. *L. Whitmore, Ireland* **c117 h–**

SATSHOON (IRE) 10 b.g. Satco (FR) – Tudor Lady (Green Shoon) [2002/3 c117: c23g* c25dᶠ c25d⁶ c25d c24s⁴ c24s Mar 7] tall, useful-looking gelding: fairly useful chaser: won handicaps at Exeter and Wincanton (fourth course success, stayed on strongly to dead-heat with Lanmire Tower) in November: below form over fences subsequently and just modest form when fourth in novice at Taunton on hurdling debut: should stay beyond 25f: raced on good going or softer (acts on heavy): blinkered. *P. F. Nicholls* **c126 h93**

SAUCY KIRINA 6 b.m. Regal Embers (IRE) – Eleri (Rolfe (USA)) [2002/3 h–, F–: 16g 19m Jun 4] of little account: sold £1,800 Ascot October Sales. *Mrs P. Ford* **h–**

SAUCY NIGHT 7 ch.g. Anshan – Kiss In The Dark (Starry Night (USA)) [2002/3 h–: c16m 26gᵖᵘ May 30] lengthy gelding: no sign of ability: joined S. Earle. *C. C. Bealby* **c– h–**

SAUMAREZ PARK 5 b.g. Magic Ring (IRE) – Rocquaine Bay (Morston (FR)) [2002/3 F12d Nov 13] first foal: dam, 1½m winner, half-sister to fairly useful hurdler/chaser The Quads, stays 31f: well held in bumper on debut. *G. L. Moore* **F–**

SAVANNAH MO (IRE) 8 ch.m. Husyan (USA) – Sweet Start (Candy Cane) [2002/3 24s 27vᵖᵘ 27s 24v² 27v⁶ 20s² 22d* Mar 7] leggy, lengthy mare: poor handicap hurdler: won at Ayr in March: stays 3m: acts on heavy going. *J. N. R. Billinge* **h79**

SAVE THE PLANET 6 b.m. Environment Friend – Geoffreys Bird (Master Willie) [2002/3 h–: 16g May 11] poor maiden on Flat (seems to stay 2m): no worthwhile form over hurdles: tried blinkered, visored nowadays. *P. Monteith* **h–**

SAWA-ID 10 b. or br.g. Anshan – Bermuda Lily (Dunbeath (USA)) [2002/3 c24mʳᵗʳ Apr 12] compact gelding: useful 2m hurdler/fairly useful chaser at best: won point in March: acts on good to firm and heavy going: tried visored/blinkered: has had tongue tied: often refuses to race: one to leave severely alone. *Mrs Caroline Bailey* **c§§ h§§**

SAWLAJAN (USA) 12 ch.g. Woodman (USA) – Crafty Satin (USA) (Crimson Satan) [2002/3 h–: 22mᵖᵘ Jul 14] compact gelding: one-time fairly useful handicap hurdler: well below form both starts in early-2001/2, broke down only outing in 2002/3: stays 2¾m, at least when conditions aren't testing: acts on firm and good to soft going: has had tongue tied: held up. *Mrs T. J. McInnes Skinner* **h–**

SAXON DUKE 12 b.g. Saxon Farm – Bucks Princess (Buckskin (FR)) [2002/3 c113, h–: c24s Feb 27] tall gelding: fairly useful handicap chaser in 2001/2: well held in hunter only start in 2002/3: stays 29f: acts on good to firm and heavy going: effective blinkered/visored or not. *Mrs M. J. McGuinness* **c– h–**

SAXON MILL 8 ch.g. Saxon Farm – Djellaba (Decoy Boy) [2002/3 h79§: 17s* 19s³ 16d Jan 24] workmanlike gelding: improved effort over hurdles when winning novice at Market Rasen in December (subsequently tested positive for morphine): stays 2½m: acts on heavy going: inconsistent. *Mrs Pippa Bickerton* **h95 §**

SAXON QUEEN 9 b.m. Lord Bud – Saxon Slave (Be Friendly) [2002/3 c–, h75: 20g* 19gᵖᵘ 20g⁶ 16g⁴ Oct 9] leggy mare: winning pointer: no promise in 2 steeplechases: modest hurdler: won mares handicap at Fakenham in May but badly out of sorts subsequently: stays 2½m: acts on soft and good to firm going: often races prominently. *G. Prodromou* **c– h85**

SAXON SPIRIT 7 ch.g. Saxon Farm – Miss Date (Mandamus) [2002/3 F–: F16g F17s 16s 19mᵖᵘ Apr 5] sturdy gelding: little sign of ability: reportedly lame final start. *I. R. Brown* **h– F–**

797

Guinness Galway Hurdle (Handicap)—
Say Again survives a mistake at the last to beat Mutakarrim (noseband)

SAY AGAIN (IRE)　7 gr.g. Celio Rufo – Tricia's Pet (Mandalus) [2002/3 h113: 16s* **c122**
16s² 16d* c16s² c17v⁴ c20s² 17g Mar 13] good-topped gelding: useful handicap hurdler: **h131**
much improved in first half of 2002/3, winning at Navan in May and Guinness Galway
Hurdle (beat Mutakarrim 2 lengths in 24-runner event) in August: fairly useful form at
best over fences, fourth of 5 to Le Coudray in Grade 1 novice at Leopardstown in December: best around 2m: acts on any going. *Paul Nolan, Ireland*

SAYWHEN　11 br.g. Say Primula – Practicality (Weavers' Hall) [2002/3 c63x: c24m⁴ **c– x**
c23gᶠ c23g c24f⁴ c20f⁴ Oct 24] largely let down by jumping and little form in steeplechases: runner-up in point in March: tried visored: tongue tied. *Mrs A. Price*

SCALLYBUCK (IRE)　11 br.g. Scallywag – Miss McNight (Master Buck) [2002/3 **c96**
c25s² c22s⁴ c20s⁴ 24s⁵ c22d c25sᶠ c22m c22m⁶ c25m⁵ c25m³ c24d⁶ c21d⁴ c26sᵖᵘ Dec 26] **h86**
workmanlike ex-Irish gelding: third foal: dam won 2m hurdle: modest maiden hurdler/
handicap chaser: left M. Hourigan after ninth start: below best subsequently: stays 25f:
acts on any going: tried blinkered. *R. H. Buckler*

SCALLY TAG　10 gr.m. Scallywag – Miss Mo Jo (Vaigly Great) [2002/3 h–: 16dᵖᵘ Jun **h– §**
4] of no account. *M. Smith*

SCAMP　4 b.f. Selkirk (USA) – Cut And Run (Slip Anchor) [2002/3 F12g² F16g F17m* **F90**
Apr 15] 7,000 4-y-o: leggy filly: third foal: half-sister to smart stayer Ski Run (by
Petoski): dam no worthwhile form on Flat: fair form 2 out of 3 starts in bumpers (trained

on debut by D. Cantillon), hampered 1f out and finishing strongly when beaten short head by Mrs Philip in mares maiden at Exeter (awarded race): raced too freely second start. *H. D. Daly*

SCARBOROUGH FAIR (IRE)   6 b.g. Synefos (USA) – Hue 'n' Cry (IRE) (Denel (FR)) [2002/3 h–p: 24s³ 21d 24v^{pu} Jan 17] rangy gelding, unfurnished at present: best effort over hurdles when third to Shardam in maiden at Chepstow on reappearance: pulled up lame after being hampered final start: will prove best at 3m+. *Jonjo O'Neill*   **h98**

SCARFACE   6 ch.h. Hernando (FR) – Scarlatine (IRE) (Alzao (USA)) [2002/3 16s 20s^{pu} 16d⁶ 19s 22g Mar 18] successful 5 times up to 1¾m on Flat in Germany and Holland for C. Von Der Recke: form over hurdles only when sixth in novice at Huntingdon in January: should stay beyond 2m. *A. G. Hobbs*   **h78**

SCARLETTI (GER)   6 ch.g. Master Willie – Solidago (USA) (Decies) [2002/3 16d² 16m² 16g² 16s* 17m⁴ 16g* 16m² 20g² Apr 24] stocky gelding: won 3 times on Flat (stays 9f) in Germany for B. Hellier: fair novice hurdler: won at Perth in August and Worcester (handicap) in September: may prove best in strongly-run races around 2m: has won on soft going, best efforts on good/good to firm: effective tongue tied or not: pulled hard final outing: found little second one. *Jonjo O'Neill*   **h110**

SCARTHY LAD (IRE)   5 ch.g. Magical Wonder (USA) – Grangeclare Rose (IRE) (Jaazeiro (USA)) [2002/3 F101: 16s* 16s* Dec 21] fairly useful bumper winner: made good start over hurdles, winning maiden at Thurles (easily) in November and novice at Navan (beat Khetaam a head after both had travelled strongly to before last) in December: will stay beyond 2m: remains open to improvement. *T. G. O'Leary, Ireland*   **h118 p**

SCATTIEHATTIE   8 gr.m. Arzanni – Kiki Star (Some Hand) [2002/3 22m^{pu} Jun 14] sixth foal: half-sister to smart hunter chaser What A Hand (by Nearly A Hand), stayed 29f, and winning hurdler/chaser Miss Marigold (by Norwick), stays 3m: dam won sellers at 1¼m and 1½m: showed nothing in maiden hurdle on debut. *M. Hill*   **h–**

Sean Duggan's "Say Again"

SCENIC STORM (IRE) 8 b.g. Scenic – Sit Elnaas (USA) (Sir Ivor) [2002/3 c70, c–
h–: c24dpu Nov 25] well-made gelding: poor maiden chaser: stiff task but still ran badly h–
in handicap at Ludlow only start in 2002/3: stays 3m: raced on good going or softer (acts
on soft). *Ferdy Murphy*

SCENTED AIR 6 b.m. Lion Cavern (USA) – Jungle Rose (Shirley Heights) [2002/3 h93 +
16m* 16d2 16d 16g* 16g 16f4 Apr 25] lengthy, rather sparely-made mare: half-sister to
one-time fairly useful hurdler Desert Fighter (by Green Desert), stays 2½m: modest on
Flat (stays easy 1¼m), successful in July, January (twice) and April: modest form over
hurdles: won seller at Stratford in October and mares handicap at Ludlow (made all) in
December: sold out of P. Hiatt's stable £9,000 Ascot April Sales, almost certainly flattered when fourth of 6 to Santenay in minor event at Sandown final start: needs sharp 2m:
acts on firm and good to soft going: not a fluent jumper. *J. D. Czerpak*

SCHEDULE B 5 ch.g. Dancing Spree (USA) – Jolizal (Good Times (ITY)) [2002/3 h–
20m5 Aug 17] poor maiden on Flat (seems to stay 1½m): showed little on hurdling debut.
R. Hollinshead

SCHEMER (IRE) 8 ch.g. Samhoi (USA) – Gambling Princess VII (Damsire Unreg- c–
istered) [2002/3 h–, F–: 20dpu 21m2 c16gpu 20m Aug 17] form over jumps only when h75 ?
second in novice selling handicap chase at Southwell in July. *Mrs S. J. Smith*

SCHOOLHOUSE WALK 5 b.g. Mistertopogigo (IRE) – Restandbejoyful (Taka- F75
chiho) [2002/3 F17m4 F16g F17g F16d Oct 25] first foal: dam behind in mares bumpers:
fourth in bumper at Market Rasen on debut, failed to progress: won point in April.
Mrs S. Lamyman

SCHUH VENTURE (IRE) 8 b.g. Little Bighorn – Elegant Miss (Prince Tenderfoot h86 ?
(USA)) [2002/3 22mpu 20s5 16s6 19d6 22dpu Mar 6] leggy gelding: modest maiden
hurdler: off 21 months prior to reappearance: seemed to run creditably when sixth in
maiden at Chepstow in December, no other form in 2002/3: should be suited by further
than 2m: acts on heavy going: has had tongue tied. *Dr P. Pritchard*

SCHWARTZHALLE (IRE) 6 b.g. Magical Wonder (USA) – Liams Flash (IRE) c128
(Callernish) [2002/3 20gpu 19s 16s6 17m6 20d 20s 20v3 16v 24s5 20s4 c17s* c20sF c16d* h97
c16v3 c17d5 Mar 22] workmanlike gelding: first foal: dam once-raced, out of half-sister
to useful staying chaser Perris Valley: winning hurdler: did well when switched to chasing, winning maiden at Fairyhouse in January and Grade 2 novice at Navan (able to
dominate when beating Rathgar Beau ½ length) in February: easily better subsequent
effort when third to same horse in novice at Naas: effective at 2m, probably stays 3m:
probably acts on any going. *D. Harvey, Ireland*

SCOLA GRAVACA (IRE) 5 ch.g. Petardia – Mystery Bid (Auction Ring (USA)) h–
[2002/3 F71: F16m 17v 16g Mar 12] little sign of ability, leaving K. Morgan after reap- F–
pearance (visored). *Mrs L. Wadham*

SCOLARDY (IRE) 5 b.h. Turtle Island (IRE) – Emerald Pendant (Nebos (GER)) h–
[2002/3 h147: 16g 16g Mar 11] good-topped horse: top juvenile hurdler in 2001/2, much
improved when landing JCB Triumph Hurdle at Cheltenham: off due to tendon injury
until well held in valuable handicap at Newbury in February and Champion Hurdle at
Cheltenham in March: will stay beyond 17f: raced on good going or softer (acts on heavy)
over hurdles. *W. P. Mullins, Ireland*

SCOLBOA (IRE) 6 gr.m. Bob's Return (IRE) – Dont Rough It (Pragmatic) [2002/3 h78
F16s5 20s5 20v6 18d 24v 20d5 22g2 27g Apr 25] fifth foal: half-sister to poor hurdler F71
Offtheroad (by King's Ride), stays 3m: dam, winning hurdler up to 2½m, half-sister to
useful chaser Thyne Will Tell: poor form in bumper on debut: poor maiden hurdler: stays
2¾m: raced on good ground or softer. *I. R. Ferguson, Ireland*

SCOOP (IRE) 7 b.m. Scenic – Big Story (Cadeaux Genereux) [2002/3 h89: c16g May c–
11] compact mare: modest hurdler: well held in handicap on chasing debut, not seen out h–
again: should stay beyond 2m: acts on firm and good to soft going. *G. M. Moore*

SCOOP THIRTY NINE 5 b.m. Petoski – Welsh Clover (Cruise Missile) [2002/3 h65
h–: 21g6 20dpu 17d* 16m6 Apr 21] leggy, unfurnished mare: 12/1 from 33/1, first form
over hurdles when winning selling handicap at Sedgefield in March, idling: failed to settle final start: bred to be suited by further than 17f. *Mrs E. Slack*

SCORING PEDIGREE (IRE) 11 b.g. King Luthier – Quick Romance (Lucky c101
Brief) [2002/3 c99, h–: c20m4 c24g6 c21g2 c23mF Nov 18] lengthy gelding: fair handicap h–
chaser: off 5½ months, best effort in 2002/3 when second of 3 finishers at Wincanton in

November: barely stays 3m: acts on soft and firm going: effective visored or not. *J. W. Mullins*

SCOTIA NOSTRA (IRE)   11 b.g. High Estate – Crown Witness (Crowned Prince (USA)) [2002/3 c24s³ c24mᶠ Mar 22] compact gelding: fairly useful handicap chaser at best: off 3 years, shaped as if in need of race on return, fell first next time: stays 3m: acts on heavy going. *Miss Venetia Williams*   **c92** **h–**

SCOTISH LAW (IRE)   5 ch.g. Case Law – Scotia Rose (Tap On Wood) [2002/3 16d 19s² 21m³ Mar 19] workmanlike gelding: half-brother to winning 2m hurdler Over The Counter (by Persian Bold): fair on Flat (stays 1¼m): modest form when placed twice from 3 starts in novice hurdles: stays easy 21f. *P. R. Chamings*   **h87**

SCOTMAIL BOY (IRE)   10 b.g. Over The River (FR) – Princess Paula (Smoggy) [2002/3 c117?, h–: c24d c30d⁴ c20d⁵ c32v³ c21d⁴ c26g² Apr 21] lengthy gelding: handicap chaser, only modest nowadays: stays 27f: acts on any going: tried blinkered/in cheekpieces. *J. Howard Johnson*   **c96** **h–**

SCOTMAIL LAD (IRE)   9 b.g. Ilium – Nicholas Ferry (Floriferous) [2002/3 c110, h–: c20s³ c20v⁶ c20v³ c22d² c24g⁴ Apr 1] leggy, workmanlike gelding: fair handicap chaser: stays 3m: raced on good going or softer (acts on heavy): effective blinkered/visored or not: front runner. *G. M. Moore*   **c110** **h–**

SCOTMAIL PARK   4 b.g. Presidium – Miss Tri Colour (Shavian) [2002/3 16dᵖᵘ 17dᵖᵘ Mar 2] poor maiden on Flat (seems to stay 1¼m): no form in 2 juvenile hurdles. *G. M. Moore*   **h–**

SCOTS GREY   8 gr.g. Terimon – Misowni (Niniski (USA)) [2002/3 h126: c20d* c20g² c19v² c20d* c20m³ c20g³ c33mᶠ Apr 12] sturdy gelding: fairly useful hurdler: did well in novice chases, won at Huntingdon in November and Kempton in February: placed in better company other completed starts, good third to Young Spartacus in Mildmay of Flete Handicap Chase at Cheltenham sixth outing: may prove best up to 2½m: acts on any going: races prominently. *N. J. Henderson*   **c138** **h–**

SCOTTIE YORK   7 b.g. Noble Patriarch – Devon Dancer (Shareef Dancer (USA)) [2002/3 16m 20d⁵ Jun 4] tall gelding: modest maiden on Flat (stays 2m): well held all starts over hurdles: should be suited by further than 2m. *P. Monteith*   **h–**

SCOTTISH CLOVER   10 ch.m. Scottish Reel – National Clover (National Trust) [2002/3 c23g⁴ c25sᵖᵘ c23sᵖᵘ Jan 29] half-sister to top-class chaser Go Ballistic (by Celtic Cone), stayed 3¼m: dam, very useful pointer, daughter of Welsh Grand National winner Clover Bud: won maiden on completed start in points in 2000: showed little in 3 steeplechases, not impressing with jumping: tongue tied final start. *Mrs H. Dalton*   **c–**

SCOTTISH DANCE   6 ch.m. Bustino – Highland Lyric (Rymer) [2002/3 F88: 19s 16d⁶ 19d* 21m Mar 22] angular mare: best effort over hurdles (had shaped as if amiss first 2 starts) when winning mares novice at Hereford in February by ½ length from Macnance: better around 2½m than shorter: tongue tied final start. *N. J. Henderson*   **h93**

SCOTTISH MEMORIES (IRE)   7 ch.g. Houmayoun (FR) – Interj (Salmon Leap (USA)) [2002/3 h149p: 16m⁵ 16v* 20v² 16d⁴ 16g Mar 11] good-topped gelding: smart hurdler: won quite valuable intermediate at Down Royal in November: travelled strongly long way when 8 lengths second to Limestone Lad in Grade 1 at Fairyhouse third start: below form last 2 outings: will prove best around 2m: acts on heavy going: has had tongue tied. *N. Meade, Ireland*   **h145**

SCOTTISH ROOTS   8 b.g. Roscoe Blake – Lothian Queen (Scorpio (FR)) [2002/3 h–, F93: 23gᵖᵘ 23dᵖᵘ May 23] angular gelding: fair form in bumpers: no form in novice hurdles, shaping as if all wasn't well: won points in February and April: tried blinkered. *C. R. Egerton*   **c–** **h–**

SCOTTISH SONG   10 b.g. Niniski (USA) – Miss Saint-Cloud (Nonoalco (USA)) [2002/3 16d 20d³ Mar 15] quite good-topped gelding: poor maiden hurdler, lightly raced: should stay beyond 2½m: acts on good to soft going. *Mrs M. Reveley*   **h80**

SCOTTON GREEN   12 ch.g. Ardross – Grange Hill Girl (Workboy) [2002/3 c119, h–: c26sᵖᵘ c25v⁵ c27d c31dᶠ c33vᴿ c24d⁴ Jan 13] lengthy, angular gelding: modest handicap chaser nowadays: stays 4¼m: acts on good to firm and heavy going: usually blinkered: often makes mistakes. *T. D. Easterby*   **c97** **h–**

SCOWLIN BRIG   7 ch.g. Minster Son – Gideonscleuch (Beverley Boy) [2002/3 h–: 21m⁶ c21g³ c24mᵖᵘ c27g³ c25v⁵ c25s³ Dec 10] compact gelding: maiden hurdler: poor novice chaser: probably stays 27f: acts on heavy going. *F. P. Murtagh*   **c61** **h–**

SCRAPMAN 10 ch.g. Backchat (USA) – Saila Thims (Alias Smith (USA)) [2002/3 16g **h–**
17d⁴ 20m Jun 21] once-raced in bumpers: signs of ability returning from long absence
only when fourth of 9 finishers in novice hurdle at Cartmel in June, almost certainly
flattered. *G. A. Swinbank*

SCRATCH THE DOVE 6 ch.m. Henbit (USA) – Coney Dove (Celtic Cone) [2002/3 **h91**
h76: 20s² 19mᵖᵘ 20s* 16g⁵ 21d⁴ 21g³ Mar 16] sturdy mare: modest handicap hurdler:
won mares novice at Leicester in November: stays 21f: acts on soft going, possibly not on
good to firm: has room for improvement in her jumping. *C. J. Price*

SCRAVELS 4 ch.g. Elmaamul (USA) – Defined Feature (IRE) (Nabeel Dancer (USA)) **h–**
[2002/3 16v 19d⁶ 17sᶠ Mar 7] modest maiden on Flat (stays 1¼m) for Dr J. Scargill: well
held in claimers on completed starts over hurdles. *J. K. Price*

SCRUMPY 4 b.g. Sir Harry Lewis (USA) – Superfina (USA) (Fluorescent Light **F–**
(USA)) [2002/3 F16g Mar 12] ninth foal: half-brother to fair 2m hurdler Josifina (by
Master Willie): dam unraced: well held in bumper on debut. *S. E. H. Sherwood*

SCRUTON 9 b.g. Cruise Missile – My Martina (My Swallow) [2002/3 c26dᵖᵘ Jun 8] **c–**
fair pointer, successful in May: pulled up in maiden hunter at Cartmel. *R. Ford*

SCULPTOR 4 b.g. Salse (USA) – Classic Colleen (IRE) (Sadler's Wells (USA)) **h78**
[2002/3 17s Jan 25] good-topped gelding: fair on Flat (should stay 1½m), successful in
July, sold out of G. Butler's stable 15,000 gns Newmarket Autumn Sales: always behind
in Grade 2 juvenile at Cheltenham on hurdling debut. *C. J. Mann*

SCURRA 4 b.g. Spectrum (IRE) – Tamnia (Green Desert (USA)) [2002/3 16dᵖᵘ 16dᵖᵘ **h–**
Feb 23] modest maiden on Flat (should stay 1¼m), sold out of R. Wilman's stable 1,200
gns Doncaster November Sales: no show in 2 starts over hurdles. *A. C. Whillans*

SEABROOK LAD 12 b.g. Derrylin – Moll (Rugantino) [2002/3 c–, h–: c24m² c24g³ **c91 x**
c24m³ Apr 2] good-topped gelding: fair hunter chaser: stays 3m: acts on soft and good to **h–**
firm going: sketchy jumper. *Mrs F. Kehoe*

SEA DRIFTING 6 b.g. Slip Anchor – Theme (IRE) (Sadler's Wells (USA)) [2002/3 **c127**
h119: c20dᶠ c21s³ c20s³ c24g* c21s³ c24g⁴ c22f² c25d⁵ c25m² Apr 17] good-topped **h–**
gelding: fairly useful hurdler: fairly useful novice chaser: won at Musselburgh in December: left F. Murphy after fifth start: stays 3m: acts on firm and soft going, seemingly
not on heavy: tried in cheekpieces. *K. A. Morgan*

SEA FERRY (IRE) 7 b.g. Ilium – Nicholas Ferry (Floriferous) [2002/3 h104: 24s⁴ **c– p**
c22s⁵ Dec 26] fair handicap hurdler: last of 5 finishers in novice on chasing **h105**
debut: will prove suited by 3m+: acts on going softer than good (acts on heavy): consistent: should improve over fences. *Noel T. Chance*

SEA HAITCH EM 8 ch.g. Norton Challenger – One Way Circuit (Windjammer **c87**
(USA)) [2002/3 h–: c20d² Mar 4] workmanlike gelding: no form over hurdles: sold out of **h–**
K. Morgan's stable 2,200 gns Doncaster August Sales: won points in January and Feb-
ruary: fair form when second to Freteval in maiden at Leicester on hunter chase debut.
Miss Lisa Llewellyn

SEAHORSE BOY (IRE) 6 b.g. Petardia – Million At Dawn (IRE) (Fayruz) [2002/3 **h–**
h–: 16dᵖᵘ Oct 31] no form over hurdles. *Mrs A. C. Tate*

SEALED ORDERS 6 ch.m. Bustino – Royal Seal (Privy Seal) [2002/3 20gᵖᵘ Mar **h–**
23] seventh foal: sister to bumper winner Hot Plunge: dam unraced: no encouragement in
novice hurdle on debut. *Mrs S. Lamyman*

SEA MAIZE 5 b.m. Sea Raven (IRE) – Dragons Daughter (Mandrake Major) [2002/3 **F–**
F16g F16m Apr 21] lengthy mare: third foal: dam unraced daughter of fairly useful
staying chaser River Sirene: well held in 2 bumpers. *C. R. Wilson*

SEA MARK 7 gr.g. Warning – Mettlesome (Lomond (USA)) [2002/3 h100: 16g⁴ **h100**
17m* 17gᵖᵘ 17m⁴ Jul 17] sturdy gelding: type to carry condition: fair hurdler: improved
effort when winning maiden at Market Rasen in June: reportedly lame next time, and
weakened rather tamely when running poorly final outing: likely to prove best around
2m: acts on good to firm going: blinkered last 3 starts: joined B. Ellison. *C. Grant*

SEAN AT THE IVY (FR) 4 b.g. Nikos – Matelica (FR) (R B Chesne) [2002/3 F18dᵖᵘ **F–**
Feb 17] 40,000 3-y-o: fourth foal: half-brother to fair 2m hurdle winner Ma Melissa (by
Fabulous Dancer): dam, winner twice around 1m in France, half-sister to top-class French

staying hurdler Matchou: favourite, failed to settle and beaten early on final circuit in bumper at Fontwell (reportedly lost action) on debut. *P. F. Nicholls*

SEAN'S MINSTREL (IRE)   10 gr.g. Black Minstrel – Gala Star (Gail Star) [2002/3 c–
c24g⁶ May 30] winning pointer, including in March: no show in 3 steeplechases.
Mrs D. M. Grissell

SEA PEARL   9 b.m. Derring Rose – Tillside Brig (New Brig) [2002/3 h–: 22g⁶ 26gᵖᵘ   h–
Jun 12] no form over hurdles. *Mrs S. P. Stretton*

SEA PRINCESS   6 b.m. Sea Raven (IRE) – Mighty Miss (Doc Marten) [2002/3 F–:   F–
F16sᵖᵘ May 26] no encouragement in 2 bumpers. *M. E. Sowersby*

SEARCH AND DESTROY (USA)   5 b. or br.g. Sky Classic (CAN) – Hunt The   h102
Thimble (USA) (Turn And Count (USA)) [2002/3 h98+: 16g* 16s 16g³ 16d Feb 15]
useful-looking gelding: fair hurdler: won conditional jockeys handicap at Doncaster in
December: raced around 2m: acts on good to firm and good to soft going, possibly unsuited by soft. *T. R. George*

SEARCH N' DESTROY (NZ)   8 b.g. Heroicity (AUS) – Nassa Charm (NZ) (Nassi-   h–
pour (USA)) [2002/3 F–: 17mᵖᵘ Aug 12] little promise in bumper and novice hurdle.
Lady Connell

SEASMITH   8 ch. or gr.g. Greensmith – Sea Spice (Precipice Wood) [2002/3 h84: 26d⁴   c–
20v⁶ c16vF 16d 16g Apr 14] tall, angular gelding: fell third on chasing debut: maiden   h–
hurdler, no show in 2002/3: sold 3,700 gns Doncaster May Sales. *L. Lungo*

SEASON EXPRESS   8 ch.g. Vital Season – Coach Rd Express (Pony Express) [2002/3   h–
20m⁴ 22m⁶ 22fᵘ Apr 21] first foal: dam maiden pointer: fell both starts in points in 2001:
signs of only a little ability in 3 starts over hurdles. *C. Tizzard*

SEA SPIRIT   11 gr.m. Nearly A Hand – Uncornered (USA) (Silver Series (USA))   c–
[2002/3 c26g⁴ May 25] modest pointer: well held in hunter chase in May. *Miss Emma
Kelley*

SEASQUILL (AUS)   8 bl.g. Squill (USA) – Sea Surge (AUS) (Rolle) [2002/3 16s⁴   h80
17s 16m⁶ 16g⁶ 17v 20mᵖᵘ Mar 23] useful on Flat (stays 12.5f) in Australasia at 3/4 yrs:
subsequently placed several times in UAE for E. Sharpy: poor form over hurdles, travelling comfortably but finding little most times: lame final outing. *Ferdy Murphy*

SEA TARTH   12 gr.m. Nicholas Bill – Seajan (Mandamus) [2002/3 c–, h75: 24g May   c–
22] has been hobdayed: winning hurdler/chaser: little show in handicap hurdle in May: h–
won points in March and April: stays 27f: acts on firm and soft going. *T. R. Kinsey*

SEATTLE ART (USA)   9 b.g. Seattle Slew (USA) – Artiste (Artaius (USA)) [2002/3   c83 §
c84§, h–: c16d c20g⁴ c22m* c21m⁴ c24d Aug 4] strong gelding: poor handicap chaser: h–
won at Market Rasen in July: stays 2¾m: acts on firm and good to soft going, seems
unsuited by softer: tried blinkered (raced too freely): unreliable: sold 3,000 gns Doncaster
September Sales. *P. Monteith*

SEATTLE LAD (IRE)   11 ch.g. Krayyan – Zedosa's Pet (Prince Bee) [2002/3 h–:   h–
27mᵖᵘ May 7] of no account. *M. A. Allen*

SEA URCHIN   10 b.g. Scallywag – Sailor's Shanty (Dubassoff (USA)) [2002/3 c19fᵖᵘ   c– §
May 15] modest pointer, successful in May: all but refused to race in novice hunter chase
at Exeter. *Mrs H. J. Wiegersma*

SECOND PICK (IRE)   7 b.g. Doubletour (USA) – Wurli (Wolver Hollow) [2002/3   c– §
F–§: 21dᵖᵘ 16mᵖᵘ 20dᵖᵘ 20dᵖᵘ c23dᵖᵘ Jun 3] smallish gelding: more temperament than   h– §
ability: sold £900 Ascot June Sales, runner-up in point in March. *R. J. Armson*

SECOND TENOR (IRE)   6 b.m. Glacial Storm (USA) – Rustic Path (Proverb)   h77 ?
[2002/3 20m³ Aug 17] IR £1,100 4-y-o: fourth live foal: sister to winning chaser First
Tenor, stayed 3m: dam winning hurdler/chaser, stayed 2¾m: fourth in mares maiden
point on debut: third of 6 in weakly-contested maiden at Bangor on hurdling debut, still
looking inexperienced: will stay 3m. *D. Brace*

SECRET ALLIANCE (IRE)   11 b.g. Royal Fountain – Hardy Polly (Polleron)   c89
[2002/3 c–: c21g* Apr 19] lengthy gelding: fair pointer, won in April: much better effort
in hunter chases when winning at Stratford later in month by neck from Filscot: stayed
21f: dead. *P. C. Handley*

SECRET CONQUEST   6 b.m. Secret Appeal – Mohibbah (USA) (Conquistador   h76
Cielo (USA)) [2002/3 17g⁴ 17m 16dᵖᵘ Mar 5] sister to modest 2m hurdler Park Royal:

modest on Flat (barely stays 1m): best effort over hurdles when fourth in novice at Sedgefield: will prove best at sharp 2m. *G. M. Moore*

SECRET DRINKER (IRE) 7 b.g. Husyan (USA) – Try Le Reste (IRE) (Le Moss) [2002/3 h74: c24d⁵ c23v⁵ c26s³ c24d² c29g³ c24gᵖᵘ Apr 2] useful-looking gelding: poor hurdler/novice chaser: stays 29f: raced on good going or softer (acts on soft): wore cheekpieces after second start. *O. Sherwood*   **c82 h–**

SECRETE CONTRACT 5 b.g. Contract Law (USA) – Secret Account (Blakeney) [2002/3 h–: 17m 18m May 6] workmanlike gelding: no form over hurdles: tried blinkered: has had tongue tied. *Miss A. M. Newton-Smith*   **h–**

SECRET FLUTTER (IRE) 4 b.f. Entrepreneur – Spend A Rubble (USA) (Spend A Buck (USA)) [2002/3 17s³ 18d 16v* 16v Jan 17] well held on Flat since debut: best effort in juvenile hurdles when winning seller at Uttoxeter in December: sweating badly, not fluent when well beaten in claimer at Chepstow following month: sold 1,200 gns Doncaster March Sales. *J. G. Portman*   **h89**

SECRET MISSION 7 b.m. Infantry – Scudding (Cruise Missile) [2002/3 F16m F16g⁵ Aug 24] first foal: dam lightly-raced maiden pointer: poor form in 2 bumpers. *Ms A. E. Embiricos*   **F72**

SECRET PROGRESS (IRE) 7 ch.g. Safety Catch (USA) – Lady Progress (Proverb) [2002/3 h85, F–: 18d⁴ 20s c22sᶠ c20s² c24g³ Jan 28] modest form at best over hurdles: fair novice chaser: likely to stay 2¾m: acts on soft going. *I. A. Duncan, Ireland*   **c100 h72**

SECRET SENTIMENT 5 b.m. Mark of Esteem (IRE) – Sahara Baladee (USA) (Shadeed (USA)) [2002/3 h–: 17mᵖᵘ 17m Jun 1] leggy mare: poor maiden on Flat (should stay 1¼m): no worthwhile form over hurdles: saddle slipped on reappearance. *A. B. Coogan*   **h–**

SECRET'S OUT 7 b.g. Polish Precedent (USA) – Secret Obsession (USA) (Secretariat (USA)) [2002/3 h81: 19s 16g³ 16g⁴ 16m² 16d⁵ Oct 31] leggy gelding: poor maiden hurdler: best at sharp 2m: acts on good to soft and good to firm going: effective visored or not: edgy type, takes good hold. *F. Lloyd*   **h81**

SECRET TRUTH 14 ch.m. Nestor – Another Nitty (Country Retreat) [2002/3 c89§: c16gᵖᵘ c24g⁴ May 31] rather sparely-made mare: fair hunter chaser: stays 3m: acts on firm and good to soft going: blinkered (pulled up) once: inconsistent. *Andrew J. Martin*   **c97 §**

SECURON DANCER 5 b.m. Emperor Jones (USA) – Gena Ivor (USA) (Sir Ivor) [2002/3 18f Jun 3] poor maiden on Flat, seems to stay 9.7f: showed nothing on hurdling debut. *R. Rowe*   **h–**

SECURON ROSE (IRE) 7 gr.m. Roselier (FR) – Hand Me Down (Cheval) [2002/3 h68x: 25gʳᵒ Apr 29] sturdy mare: poor maiden hurdler: ran out only outing in 2002/3: bred to stay 3m+: raced on good going or softer (acts on soft): needs to improve jumping: one to treat with caution. *R. Rowe*   **h– §**

SEEBALD (GER) 8 b.g. Mulberry (FR) – Spartina (USA) (Northern Baby (CAN)) [2002/3 c155, h–: c17g² c16v² c16g² c16gᶠ c20d² c16m* Apr 26]   **c167 h–**

For Seebald's owners international footballers Robbie Fowler and Steve McManaman, the gelding's triumph in the Queen Elizabeth The Queen Mother Celebration Chase at Sandown might be seen as the equivalent of them scoring a last-minute winner. Not only did the event take place on the final day of the season but, for much of the race, Seebald looked likely to end up in the familiar second place he had occupied on four previous completed starts in the latest campaign.

The Celebration Chase is the only one of the new events at Sandown's end-of-season fixture which, so far, has appeared worthwhile (albeit at the expense of an established Grade 1 two-mile chase at Punchestown) and it attracted the two best British-trained two-mile chasers at the time in Seebald and Cenkos, the pair dominating both the betting and the race itself. The weights favoured Seebald, who along with the three other runners was set to receive 4 lb from Cenkos, but it was the latter who shaded favouritism at 5/4, with Seebald at 11/8 and 7/1 bar the pair. Cenkos set out to make all and outjumped his rivals, all of whom were off the bridle by the end of the back straight. Seebald, only third at this stage, had moved into second by three out but was still almost four lengths down; and he had made no further impression by the next, where once again he wasn't fluent. The picture

*Queen Elizabeth The Queen Mother Celebration Chase, Sandown—
the battling Seebald is closing on 2002 winner Cenkos (No.1)*

began to change going to the last, though. Seebald, responding gamely to Tony
McCoy's urgings, closed the gap as Cenkos faltered, and a sustained effort edged
him ahead halfway up the run-in. Seebald won going away by a length and a
quarter. That his stable-companion Wahiba Sands was just over ten lengths behind
him in third suggests Seebald didn't quite run to his best, but his victory was well
deserved nonetheless. His most recent win had come over fifteen months earlier in
a novice chase at Warwick, where he completed a seven-timer. In between the
Warwick and Sandown victories, Seebald finished runner-up on all six of his
completed starts, defeats at the hands of Moscow Flyer in the Arkle Chase at
Cheltenham and Armaturk in the Maghull Chase at Aintree completing his first
season over fences. Seebald wasn't at his best behind Edredon Bleu at Exeter on his
reappearance but he ran very well on his next two starts, going down by a length to
Young Devereaux in valuable handicaps at Ascot and Kempton, conceding the
winner 25 lb and 15 lb in the respective races; and he also ran well on his
penultimate outing when beaten the same distance by Native Upmanship in the
Melling Chase at Aintree. Whereas Seebald made Young Devereaux work for his
victories, he wasn't able to make Native Upmanship break sweat and the margin
between them flattered Seebald considerably. Unlike in his hurdling days when his
jumping technique left a great deal to be desired, Seebald has made very few errors
of note over fences and has failed to complete only once in fifteen starts. That was
in the Queen Mother Champion Chase at Cheltenham, where he fell two out when
still in with every chance, although not travelling nearly so well as the winner
Moscow Flyer. Seebald probably would have had to settle, at best, for the runner-up
spot yet again, had he got round.

Seebald is the second foal out of the maiden Spartina and was bred in
Germany where he won on the Flat, as has his brother Salita, successful at up to
eleven furlongs, and half-brother Spreewald (by Dulcero). The four-year-old

The Macca & Growler Partnership's "Seebald"

Seebald (GER) (b.g. 1995)	Mulberry (FR) (ch 1977)	Mill Reef (b 1968)	Never Bend
			Milan Mill
		Lady Berry (ch 1970)	Violon d'Ingres
			Moss Rose
	Spartina (USA) (b 1987)	Northern Baby (b 1976)	Northern Dancer
			Two Rings
		Satin (b 1969)	Forli
			Lea Moon

Spreewald won a mile maiden at Hanover in September. So far, the major prizes have eluded Seebald, and Moscow Flyer and Native Upmanship, to name but two, will continue to make it difficult for him in the next season, when he will also have to contend with the latest season's leading novices. At least Seebald won't be short of opportunities, having shown himself effective at two miles to two and a half and on any ground. Visored once over hurdles, Seebald is a consistent sort and thoroughly genuine. *M. C. Pipe*

SEEF 9 b.g. Slip Anchor – Compton Lady (USA) (Sovereign Dancer (USA)) [2002/3 c75x, h–: c26m* c24m^{pu} c23g^{pu} c25m^5 c23m^5 c25g^6 c26m^{ur} Apr 21] compact gelding: poor chaser: won novice at Folkestone in May: stays 3¼m: acts on firm going (placed in bumper on heavy): sketchy jumper. *J. S. King*   **c75 x** **h–**

SEEM OF GOLD 7 b.m. Gold Dust – Shepani (New Member) [2002/3 h77, F83: 22f^6 24d^6 21f Oct 24] bumper winner: poor maiden hurdler: probably stays 2¾m: acts on firm and good to soft going. *J. W. Mullins*   **h68**

SEE MORE BUSINESS (IRE)   13 b.g. Seymour Hicks (FR) – Miss Redlands   **c162**
(Dubassoff (USA)) [2002/3 c164, h–: c24s² c26s* c25d* c26g Mar 13]   **h–**

Retirement isn't beckoning for See More Business just yet it seems and, in view of his performances in the latest season, it isn't difficult to understand why connections are happy to keep him on the go. At the age of thirteen See More Business is still among the top dozen staying chasers trained in Britain and, while he won't be picking up a second Gold Cup or a third King George VI Chase, a fourth Rehearsal Chase or a hat-trick of victories in Wincanton's Country Gentlemen's Association Chase might well be achievable. Judged on the rousing reception he received after winning the latter on his local course in February, his many admirers will no doubt be hoping that he will still retain his form at the age of fourteen.

See More Business began the latest season with a trip across the Irish Sea and, as on the first two occasions he made that journey, he had to settle for second. Dorans Pride proved the stumbling block when See More Business turned up at Fairyhouse and Leopardstown in his days as a novice chaser way back in 1996/7, and this time it was More Than A Stroll who came between just and victory, in the Grade 1 Championship Chase at Down Royal in November. See More Business, all the sharper for that run, was at the top of his form a month later for a fourth crack at Chepstow's Rehearsal Chase which he had won in 1997 and 1998 and held every chance when falling two out in 2001. The four who lined up against him in the latest edition, each receiving 20 lb, included Bindaree and Supreme Glory, respective winners of the previous season's Grand National and Welsh National. Bindaree did best of the quartet but gave See More Business very few problems, the latter showing admirable enthusiasm in making virtually all to win by seven lengths. Two no-hopers plus Iris Bleu and First Gold took on See More Business at Wincanton in February for the listed Country Gentlemen's Association Chase, formerly known as the Jim Ford Chase. There wasn't much to choose between the principals in the betting, Iris Bleu, fresh from his runaway win in Sandown's Agfa Diamond Chase, sent off favourite at 13/8, with See More Business at 7/4 and First Gold at 9/4. It was a different story in the race itself, though, See More Business making all, jumping well and, after upping the tempo at the seventeenth, running on strongly in the straight to win by nine lengths from Iris Bleu. It was a high-class performance

Country Gentlemen's Association Chase, Wincanton—a second successive win in the race for evergreen See More Business; Iris Bleu (white face) and First Gold take the places

from See More Business, who had taken the eye in the paddock, one which raised hopes that he might make the frame for a fourth time in the Gold Cup, having won it in 1999, finished fourth the following year and third in 2002. See More Business did lead briefly at the twelfth at Cheltenham in March but, on ground less testing than was ideal for him, he was ridden and outpaced at the fifteenth and well held when hitting three out. At least See More Business was none the worse for his exertions and lives to fight another day. Less than an hour after See More Business had passed the post in eighth place in the Gold Cup, his former adversary Dorans Pride broke a hind leg when falling at the second in the Foxhunter Chase and had to be destroyed.

See More Business (IRE) (b.g. 1990)	Seymour Hicks (FR) (b 1980)	Ballymore (b 1969)	Ragusa
			Paddy's Sister
		Sarah Siddons (b 1973)	Le Levanstell
			Mariel
	Miss Redlands (b or br 1983)	Dubassoff (b 1969)	Sea-Bird II
			Love Lyric
		Tartan Eve (b 1971)	Even Money
			Scotch Tune

See More Business' pedigree has been dealt with fully in several editions of *Chasers & Hurdlers*, but to bring it up to date it's worth mentioning that his half-brother Blue Business (by Roselier) is also in training with Paul Nicholls. The five-year-old made an encouraging debut when second in a bumper at Chepstow shortly after the 2002/3 season had ended and, shortly before, another half-brother, a three-year-old by Alflora, became the most expensive store to pass through a public sales ring when he fetched 200,000 guineas at Doncaster. The gelding's new owner is to place him with Charlie Swan, who has now given up race-riding to concentrate solely on training. A year-older half-brother by Flemensfirth made €130,000 at the 2002 Derby Sale and is in training with David Wachman. If either one of that pair does only half as well as See More Business he'll be worth the money paid for him. See More Business has won eighteen races, as well as two points, and earned virtually £700,000 in win and place money. The lengthy See More Business stays

Mr Paul K. Barber & Sir Robert Ogden's "See More Business"

three and a quarter miles and has shown his form on ground ranging from good to firm through to soft, though he is probably unsuited by heavy. He does need blinkers, and has worn them on all but one of his starts since they were fitted for the first time in the 1999 Gold Cup. He also needs to be ridden prominently. *P. F. Nicholls*

SEE MORE SNOW 6 b.g. Seymour Hicks (FR) – Snow Child (Mandrake Major) **h79**
[2002/3 F–: 17f⁴ 16m³ 20d⁵ 19d 17d³ 16m³ Mar 20] smallish gelding: poor novice hurdler on balance of form: should stay 2½m: acts on firm and good to soft going: wandered under pressure when running creditable in visor final start. *W. G. M. Turner*

SEE MORE STARS 6 b.g. Seymour Hicks (FR) – China's Way (USA) (Native Uproar **h–**
(USA)) [2002/3 h–: 20mᵖᵘ 17s⁵ 16d May 30] angular gelding: little sign of ability: has achieved little in 4 starts over hurdles. *J. Mackie*

SEE MY GIRL 5 gr.m. Terimon – Nessfield (Tumble Wind (USA)) [2002/3 F16g **F–**
F16d Feb 23] third foal: dam, fair hurdler/winning chaser who stayed 3¼m, out of half-sister to very smart middle-distance stayer Knockroe: well held in 2 bumpers: failed to settle on debut. *M. A. Barnes*

SEE YOU AROUND 8 b.g. Sharp Deal – Seeborg (Lepanto (GER)) [2002/3 c89, h–: **c91**
c21d² c16d⁵ c20v⁶ c20s c25d⁵ c26s³ c24d² Mar 19] compact gelding: modest maiden **h–**
hurdler/chaser: stays 3¼m: acts on heavy going: tried visored, usually blinkered. *C. Tizzard*

SEE YOU MAN 5 b.g. Young Freeman (USA) – Shepani (New Member) [2002/3 **F–**
F16m Mar 20] fifth foal: half-brother to useful hurdler See You Sometime (by Sharp Deal), stays 3¼m, and bumper winner Seem of Gold (by Gold Dust): dam, maiden Irish pointer, half-sister to Rendlesham Hurdle winner See Enough: well held in bumper on debut. *C. Tizzard*

SEE YOU SOMETIME 8 b.g. Sharp Deal – Shepani (New Member) [2002/3 h126: **h136**
21s⁴ 22d³ 21g 21m³ Apr 16] medium-sized gelding: useful handicap hurdler: better than ever in 2002/3, winning at Wincanton (made all) in February and Cheltenham (beat Majestic 1¼ lengths) in April: effective around 2½m, probably stays 3¼m: acts on good to firm and good to soft going (bumper form on heavy): genuine. *J. W. Mullins*

SEFTON BLAKE 9 b.g. Roscoe Blake – Rainbow Lady (Jaazeiro (USA)) [2002/3 **c–**
c–, h–: 23m⁶ Apr 21] workmanlike gelding: winning hurdler/chaser: little show since **h–**
2000/1: tried visored/blinkered: usually races prominently. *R. D. Wylie*

SEFTON LODGE 4 b.g. Barathea (IRE) – Pine Needle (Kris) [2002/3 17sᵖᵘ 16d Dec **h–**
14] half-brother to winning 2m hurdler Dumaran (by Be My Chief): modest maiden on Flat (raced at 6f/7f): no form in 2 juvenile hurdles. *M. J. Ryan*

SEIXO BRANCO 7 b.g. Saddlers' Hall (IRE) – Gift of Glory (FR) (Niniski (USA)) **c115**
[2002/3 16d c17v* c16g² Jan 17] angular gelding: lightly raced: fairly useful handicap **h–**
hurdler in 2000/1, well beaten on reappearance: won weakly-contested novice at Market Rasen on chasing debut by a distance from only other finisher: second to Roveretto in stronger race at Musselburgh following month, tending to jump left: effective at 2m, will stay beyond 2½m: acts on heavy going. *C. R. Egerton*

SEIZE THE DAY (IRE) 15 b.g. Lomond (USA) – Cheerful Heart (Petingo) [2002/3 **h–**
h–: 24g 24s Dec 12] lengthy gelding: veteran hurdler, no sign of retaining ability. *M. J. Coombe*

SEKWANA (POL) 4 b.f. Duke Valentino – Surmia (POL) (Demon Club (POL)) **h–**
[2002/3 16gᵖᵘ Mar 14] ex-Polish filly: ran 13 times on Flat, winning at 5f and 6f at 2 yrs, and in frame up to 1½m at 3 yrs, leaving D. Kaluba after seventh in Group 3 at Warsaw in September: no show in conditional jockeys maiden on hurdling debut. *Miss A. M. Newton-Smith*

SEL 5 b.m. Salse (USA) – Frog (Akarad (FR)) [2002/3 h90: 16g² 16d⁶ 17d² 20s³ 16s⁶ **h83**
Dec 6] leggy mare: poor maiden hurdler: best around 2m: acts on good to firm and good to soft ground: blinkered: sold £1,300 Ascot February Sales. *G. L. Moore*

SELBY ROAD (IRE) 4 b.g. Erins Isle – Motus (Anfield) [2002/3 F16s⁵ F16v* Mar **F104**
2] brother to useful hurdler at 2½m+ Calladine and half-brother to 3 winners on Flat: dam Irish 1½m winner: fairly useful form when winning 4-y-o bumper at Leopardstown in March by 20 lengths from Accordion Etoile, driven clear 2f out and hanging badly right: neck second to Kim Fontaine at Punchestown in early-May. *C. Roche, Ireland*

SELF DEFENSE   6 b.h. Warning – Dansara (Dancing Brave (USA)) [2002/3   **h155**
16g⁴ 20s³ 16d³ 16v² 16g⁴ 20gᵖᵘ Apr 5]

Until Sacundai beat him narrowly in the Aintree Hurdle over a trip beyond
his best, Rooster Booster's unbeaten record for the season came closest to being
threatened by Self Defense in the Agfa Hurdle at Sandown. A novice with just three
runs over hurdles to his name, yet to win a race and with no better than fairly useful
form to his name, Self Defense was an unlikely-looking candidate to threaten the
Champion Hurdle favourite's unblemished record, but conditions at Sandown were
ripe for an upset. The meeting only went ahead after several inspections, with the
ground particularly heavy on the hurdles course. Giving weight to all his rivals,
7/2-on Rooster Booster idled markedly after the last as Self Defense put in a
sustained challenge up the rail, causing the favourite to work a lot harder than
expected to win only by half a length. Self Defense's effort was easy to dismiss as
the sort of unexpected result which can occur in a steadily-run Champion Hurdle
trial run on heavy ground. Self Defense was dismissed as a Champion Hurdle
candidate himself. So much so that he had the dubious distinction of appearing in a
feature in the *Racing Post* on the biggest outsiders at the Cheltenham Festival, his
odds for the Champion at that time (late-February) quoted at 200/1. Half those odds
on the day of the race, Self Defense belied his market position with another very
smart performance behind Rooster Booster, beaten just under fifteen lengths in
fourth. Although never the remotest threat on this occasion, it was a good effort
from Self Defense at level weights against a top-form Rooster Booster. Struggling
at halfway after some less than fluent jumping, Self Defense still had a dozen rivals
in front of him at the top of the hill but stayed on really well from two out to run into

Fraser Miller Racing's "Self Defense"

the frame after the last. The extra half mile of the Aintree Hurdle looked likely to suit Self Defense in his third clash with Rooster Booster but he ran no sort of race and was pulled up, reportedly lame, on the run-in. Before his meetings with Rooster Booster, Self Defense had shown progressive form in novice company, though even at that level he was highly tried. A promising fourth on his debut at Newbury, he was then a remote third behind two of the season's best novices, Coolnagorna and Thisthatandtother, in the Winter Novices' Hurdle at Sandown, and then third to the latter in the rescheduled Tolworth Hurdle at Wincanton.

Given his form on the Flat in France, it should not have come as too much of a surprise that Self Defense has made a name for himself over hurdles too. He was a smart performer for Maurice Zilber's stable from a mile and a half to fifteen furlongs and won a listed race at Maisons-Laffitte as a three-year-old. Self Defense changed ownership (from Khalid Abdulla to Michael Watt), but not stables, for 65,000 guineas at the 2001 Autumn Sales at Newmarket after he had failed to win as a four-year-old, but he made only 22,000 guineas at the same venue a year later when joining his current yard. Self Defense's five-year-old season had begun with a win in an amateur event at Longchamp, but talk of his contesting the Gold Cup at Royal Ascot, and even the Melbourne Cup, came to nothing.

		Known Fact (b 1977)	In Reality
	Warning (b 1985)		Tamerett
		Slightly Dangerous (b 1979)	Roberto
Self Defense (b.h. 1997)			Where You Lead
		Dancing Brave (b 1983)	Lyphard
	Dansara (b 1990)		Navajo Princess
		Sarah Siddons (b 1973)	Le Levanstell
			Mariel

Although from an excellent Flat family, Self Defense has a couple of relatives who have done well in the jumping game. Upgrade, out of a half-sister to Self Defense's dam Dansara, was considered good enough to contest the Champion Hurdle—a year after his Triumph Hurdle success—though temperament tended to overshadow his ability in the latest season. The other, who has made his name as the sire of See More Business, is Seymour Hicks who won the Great Voltigeur Stakes. Dansara herself was unraced but has numerous winning siblings. They include the fair hurdlers Java Sea (like Self Defense, by Warning) and Star Quest, but this is predominantly a top-class family of Flat performers. Self Defense's grandam Sarah Siddons won the Irish One Thousand Guineas and Yorkshire Oaks and great grandam Mariel won the Pretty Polly Stakes at the Curragh, as well as making the frame in the Irish One Thousand Guineas, Oaks and Irish Oaks. Apart from Seymour Hicks, Sarah Siddons' other Flat performer of note is the Irish Oaks winner Princess Pati. Incidentally, two of Princess Pati's sons, the Cambridgeshire winner Pasternak and the Yorkshire Cup runner-up Parthian Springs, have themselves embarked on careers as National Hunt stallions and, still an entire, that avenue remains open to Self Defense. He is the best of his dam's three winners so far, the others being his sister Answer, a nine-furlong winner in France, and close relative Epping (by Charnwood Forest), a seven-furlong winner on the all-weather. Self Defense's three-year-old half-brother Dance World (by Spectrum) has shown promise for Zilber in a couple of starts at the time of writing, while his two-year-old half-sister Top Forty (by Rainbow Quest) has yet to race.

Losing his maiden status over hurdles ought to prove a formality for Self Defense and, whilst still eligible for novice events, his performances in open company will surely give connections every encouragement for further tilts at Rooster Booster and company in the top hurdling events. The sturdy Self Defense, who should stay two and a half miles, acts on heavy ground. Along with Tana River and Cloudy Grey in particular, Self Defense raised his stable's profile considerably in the latest season and should help to keep it in the limelight again in the next season. *Miss E. C. Lavelle*

SEMAH'S PARC 5 b.g. Pure Melody (USA) – Semah's Dream (Gunner B) [2002/3 F– F16f Sep 15] second foal: dam maiden who probably stayed 7f: well held in bumper and maidens on Flat. *Mrs A. M. Naughton*

SEMLIKI 10 b.g. Nearly A Hand – River Culm (Royal Salmon) [2002/3 c–: c26d^{pu} **c–**
Mar 8] poor pointer, successful in March: no show in 2 hunters chases: has worn cheekpieces. *A. D. Peachey*

SENORA HONORIA 5 b.m. Perpendicular – Star Thyme (Point North) [2002/3 **F–**
F16d Nov 12] second foal: dam poor novice hurdler: well beaten in bumper on debut.
J. Mackie

SENOR EDUARDO 6 gr.g. Terimon – Jasmin Path (Warpath) [2002/3 F81: F16d⁵ **F77**
Dec 14] modest in bumpers. *S. Gollings*

SENOR GIGO 5 b.g. Mistertopogigo (IRE) – Lady Carol (Lord Gayle (USA)) [2002/3 **F–**
F17g F16v Nov 16] half-brother to 11f and 1½m winner Carol Again (by Kind of Hush)
and fair sprinter Craigie Boy (by Crofthall): dam 1m winner: shaped like doubtful stayer
when well held in 2 bumpers. *A. Scott*

SENOR HURST 8 b.g. Young Senor (USA) – Broadhurst (Workboy) [2002/3 17m **h–**
17m Jul 7] angular gelding: poor maiden hurdler in 2000/1: well held in 2 handicaps on
return: stays 2½m, at least when emphasis is on speed: acts on soft and good to firm
going. *Mrs P. Sly*

SENSE OF ADVENTURE 10 ch.g. Lord Bud – Mistral Magic (Crofter (USA)) **c–**
[2002/3 c24m^{pu} Apr 21] won last of 4 starts in Irish points in 1999: lightly raced in
Britain, though successful 3 times, including in March: ran no sort of race on hunter chase
debut. *H. B. Hodge*

SENTO (IRE) 5 ch.g. Persian Bold – Esclava (USA) (Nureyev (USA)) [2002/3 F17m* **h103**
F16d 16s 16d⁶ 16d 20m⁴ 22g* Apr 19] IR £38,000 3-y-o: good-topped gelding: fourth **F96**
foal: half-brother to winners in Japan by Warning, Indian Ridge and Shirley Heights:
dam, third in France at 1¼m, daughter of Prix de Diane winner Escaline: won bumper at
Newton Abbot on debut: best effort in novice hurdles when winning handicap at same
course, staying on to beat Ishandraz 6 lengths: will stay 3m: acts on good to firm going.
A. King

SEPTEMBER HARVEST (USA) 7 ch.g. Mujtahid (USA) – Shawgatny (USA) **c–**
(Danzig Connection (USA)) [2002/3 c–, h–: 17g^{pu} 16d⁶ Oct 25] lengthy gelding: of little **h–**
account nowadays: tried blinkered: sold £900 Ascot November Sales. *Mrs S. Lamyman*

SEPTEMBER MOON 5 b.m. Bustino – Lunabelle (Idiot's Delight) [2002/3 F17d⁴ **h92 +**
F16m 21d 20v 22m* 22f^F Apr 24] angular mare: third foal: closely related to bumper **F–**
winner Sorrento (by Neltino) and half-sister to another Moon Spinner (by Elmaamul): when win-
dam winning 2m hurdler/chaser: first form (trained previously by J. Neville) when winning novice hurdle at Exeter in April: yet to be asked for effort when falling 4 out final
start: will stay 3m: acts on good to firm going. *Mrs A. M. Thorpe*

SERENDIPITY (FR) 10 b.g. Mtoto – Bint Damascus (USA) (Damascus (USA)) **h–**
[2002/3 24f^{pu} Oct 24] close-coupled gelding: won 2m maiden hurdle for M. Pipe in
1997/8: no chance of staying trip on return from 4-year absence: headstrong. *Miss
L. V. Davis*

SERENUS (USA) 10 b.g. Sunshine Forever (USA) – Curl And Set (USA) (Nijinsky **c–**
(CAN)) [2002/3 c113, h130: 19d 16d 19s² 16s² 21d 21m 16v 19f³ 19m⁴ Apr 15] **h117**
smallish, workmanlike gelding: one-time useful hurdler/chaser: best effort over hurdles
in 2002/3 when second to Non So at Kempton fourth start: effective at 2m to easy 25f:
acts on soft and good to firm going, probably on firm: amateur ridden after reappearance.
D. R. C. Elsworth

SERIOUS POSITION (IRE) 8 ch.g. Orchestra – Lady Temba (Callernish) [2002/3 **h84**
h84: 16m⁵ 16m⁴ 16d⁴ Nov 12] workmanlike gelding: poor maiden hurdler: best efforts
around 2m: acts on good to soft and good to firm going: sometimes races freely.
D. R. Stoddart

SERIOUS TRUST 10 b.g. Alzao (USA) – Mill Line (Mill Reef (USA)) [2002/3 h59: **h–**
21s⁵ 24d⁶ Aug 4] small gelding: lightly raced and little form over hurdles: tried visored.
Mrs L. C. Jewell

SEROTONIN 4 b.g. Barathea (IRE) – Serotina (IRE) (Mtoto) [2002/3 17v² 16v^F Feb **h96**
13] useful-looking gelding: useful on Flat (stayed 1½m), successful twice in 2002, sold
out of R. Charlton's stable 68,000 gns Newmarket Autumn Sales: 17 lengths second to
The Last Cast in juvenile at Cheltenham on hurdling debut: fell fatally at Sandown. *Jonjo
O'Neill*

SERRAVAL (FR) 5 ch.m. Sanglamore (USA) – Saone (USA) (Bering) [2002/3 h82+: **h82**
16m² 17g³ 17m⁶ 16g⁴ Aug 26] fairly useful on Flat (stays 10.5f) at 3 yrs in France, succes-

sful in Britain in 2002: poor novice hurdler: raced around 2m on good/good to firm going. *B. S. Rothwell*

SERTORIUS (IRE)   6 b.g. Sharifabad (IRE) – Nomun Nofun (Creative Plan (USA)) c– [2002/3 h–: 20m^{pu} 21g^{pu} 20s c16g c24d^{pu} c20m^F c16d c21g^{pu} Apr 21] medium-sized h– gelding: no form: has had tongue tied. *P. T. Dalton*

SESKIN-VIEW (IRE)   8 b. or br.m. Buckskin (FR) – Honey View (IRE) (Forties Field h– (FR)) [2002/3 16s^6 21d Nov 25] leggy mare: well held in bumpers in Ireland in 1999 and in 2 runs over hurdles. *Ferdy Murphy*

SET DANCE (IRE)   7 b.g. Suave Dancer (USA) – La Courant (USA) (Little Current h66 (USA)) [2002/3 h–, F–: 17m^2 22f^{pu} 16m 17m Jun 22] leggy gelding: form only when second in selling handicap hurdle at Folkestone: tried blinkered. *E. L. James*

SETTING SUN   10 ch.g. Generous (IRE) – Suntrap (USA) (Roberto (USA)) [2002/3 h89 16s^4 20d^4 22g^4 20d^5 20g Jan 17] sturdy gelding: modest handicap hurdler, missed 2001/2: poor efforts last 2 starts: stays 3m: acts on good to firm and good to soft going, probably on soft: usually races up with pace. *N. Waggott*

SEVEN MILE GALE (IRE)   11 b.g. Strong Gale – Moonlight Romance (Teenoso c– (USA)) [2002/3 c20g^F Jun 15] rangy gelding: made very good start over fences early in h– 1999/00, winning 3 times: favourite, just headed when falling 3 out in handicap at Hexham, only subsequent outing: stays 2½m: acts on firm going: front runner. *N. G. Richards*

SEVENSIDER (IRE)   5 b. or br.g. Satco (FR) – Pretty Beau (IRE) (Beau Charmeur h– (FR)) [2002/3 F16d F16v^6 16d 19d 16s 25d 17s^{pu} Mar 11] rangy, rather unfurnished F– gelding: second foal: dam, lightly-raced maiden, out of half-sister to dam of Pizarro: little sign of ability: tried blinkered. *M. W. Easterby*

SEVERN AIR   5 b.m. Alderbrook – Mariner's Air (Julio Mariner) [2002/3 F16g^6 F16d F73 Mar 8] second foal: dam, fairly useful hurdler, stayed 2½m: sixth of 20 in mares event at Huntingdon, better effort in bumpers. *J. L. Spearing*

SEVERN MAGIC   10 b.m. Buckley – La Margarite (Bonne Noel) [2002/3 c–: c24g^5 c– May 3] fair pointer: well held completed start in hunter chases. *D. Thomas*

SEYMOUR CHANCE   7 ch.m. Seymour Hicks (FR) – City's Sister (Maystreak) h– [2002/3 F–: F16s^4 F17m^6 F16m^3 16m 16s^4 16d 21g 20s^{pu} Feb 7] lengthy, angular mare: F66 signs of only a little ability in bumpers and over hurdles: visored final start. *Mrs G. S. Rees*

SHAADIVA   5 b.m. Shaamit (IRE) – Kristal Diva (Kris) [2002/3 16s F16g 16m^4 18f^3 h83 Apr 24] second foal: dam lightly-raced maiden, half-sister to smart 1½m performer Fight F67 Your Corner: never dangerous in bumpers: poor form when in frame in mares hurdles at Plumpton and Fontwell. *A. King*

SHADED (IRE)   9 b.g. Night Shift (USA) – Sarsaparilla (FR) (Shirley Heights) [2002/3 c– h74: c19v^F 16v^{pu} 19v^{pu} 17g Apr 21] good-topped gelding: poor hurdler, no form in h– 2002/3: fell sixth on chasing debut: stays 19f: acts on firm and good to soft going. *D. J. Minty*

SHADE LUCKY   7 ch.g. Gildoran – Snowy Autumn (Deep Run) [2002/3 F–: 19d^{pu} h– 22d^{pu} Nov 21] workmanlike gelding: no sign of ability. *B. J. M. Ryall*

SHADOW CATCHER   6 b.g. Missed Flight – Welgenco (Welsh Saint) [2002/3 h–, h– F–: 17g^5 16g 16g Nov 23] no form: headstrong. *E. W. Tuer*

SHADY AFFAIR (IRE)   12 b.g. Black Minstrel – Golden Ice (Golden Love) [2002/3 c– c75, h–: 20d^5 20d c24g^{pu} 25d Feb 25] poor chaser/novice hurdler: no form in 2002/3. h– *R. N. Bevis*

SHADY ANNE   5 ch.m. Derrylin – Juno Away (Strong Gale) [2002/3 F16d* F17g^6 h76 F17s* F16v 20v^5 21s 19v^{pu} Mar 10] smallish mare: second foal: dam, modest 2m hurdler, F96 half-sister to useful staying chaser Killusty: seemed suited by good test of stamina when winning bumpers at Towcester (mares, drifted left) in April and Bangor in October: poor form only on first of 3 outings over hurdles: will stay beyond 2½m. *F. Jordan*

SHADY GREY   5 gr.m. Minster Son – Yemaail (IRE) (Shaadi (USA)) [2002/3 F16v^6 F65 F16g F17s Mar 6] second foal: dam unraced half-sister to useful chaser up to 25f Gallateen: poor form in bumpers. *Miss S. E. Forster*

SHADY MAN   5 b.g. Shaamit (IRE) – Miss Hardy (Formidable (USA)) [2002/3 F70: h77 17d^{pu} 16s^6 16d 16v^2 Jan 29] chunky gelding: poor form over hurdles, best effort when second in handicap at Newcastle: raced around 2m: acts on heavy going. *N. G. Richards*

SHAFFISHAYES   11 ch.g. Clantime – Mischievous Miss (Niniski (USA)) [2002/3 **h80** h84: 16d 16d⁴ 16s³ 16v³ 16s³ 16dᵘʳ 17g² 16gᶠ Apr 1] lengthy gelding: has been hobdayed: modest on Flat (stays 1¾m): poor novice hurdler: raced around 2m on good ground or softer: often finds little. *Mrs M. Reveley*

SHAHBOOR (USA)   9 b.g. Zilzal (USA) – Iva Reputation (USA) (Sir Ivor) [2002/3 **c101** c94, h118: c17g² c16d* Apr 9] close-coupled, sparely-made gelding: fairly useful handi- **h–** cap hurdler: fair novice chaser, off 15 months before reappearance: won at Uttoxeter by 10 lengths from Monte Cristo: stays 2½m: acts on soft and good to firm going: has looked none too keen. *Mrs P. Robeson*

SHAH (IRE)   10 b.g. King Persian – Gay And Sharp (Fine Blade (USA)) [2002/3 c75, **c82** h–: c16dᵖᵘ c16g* May 22] angular gelding: poor chaser, lightly raced: won handicap at **h–** Worcester in May: effective from 2m to 2½m: acts on firm and good to soft ground. *P. Kelsall*

SHAKE EDDIE SHAKE (IRE)   6 b.g. Blues Traveller (IRE) – Fortune Teller **h–** (Troy) [2002/3 h–: 19dᵖᵘ 17s 19fⁱ⁴ 17g Apr 21] sturdy gelding: little form: tried blinkered. *H. S. Howe*

SHAKWAA   4 ch.f. Lion Cavern (USA) – Shadha (USA) (Devil's Bag (USA)) [2002/3 **h–** 17d 17g Mar 15] modest form in 1½m maidens at 3 yrs, sold out of M. Channon's stable 11,000 gns Newmarket July Sales: well held in 2 juvenile hurdles. *E. A. Elliott*

SHALAAL (USA)   9 b.g. Sheikh Albadou – One Fine Day (USA) (Quadratic (USA)) **c–** [2002/3 c87?, h–: c16s⁴ c16sᵖᵘ Jan 30] sturdy gelding: one-time fair 2m handicap hurdler: **h–** little form since chasing debut in 2000/1, off 14 months prior to reappearance: acts on soft and good to firm going. *M. C. Chapman*

SHALAINES PRIDE (IRE)   10 b.g. Yashgan – Swifts Butterfly (Furry Glen) **c–** [2002/3 19g⁴ 20mᵖᵘ c21gᵖᵘ 21dᶠ 25mᵖᵘ Mar 31] lengthy gelding: novice hurdler, off over **h67** 3 years prior to reappearance: pulled up after bad mistake third on chasing debut: tongue tied last 3 starts. *T. P. McGovern*

SHALAKO (IRE)   5 ch.g. Kingmambo (USA) – Sporades (USA) (Vaguely Noble) **h110** [2002/3 17s* 16v⁴ 17d* Jan 16] half-brother to leading 4-y-o hurdler Sporazene (by Cozzene): won 4 times up to 1½m on Flat in Germany at 3 yrs for P. Schiergen: successful on 2 of 3 starts over hurdles, in maiden in November and novice in January, both at Taunton: favourite, fortunate when beating Quedex 1¼ lengths in latter, held when left clear last then looking very reluctant. *P. J. Hobbs*

SHALBEBLUE (IRE)   6 b.g. Shalford (IRE) – Alberjas (IRE) (Sure Blade (USA)) **c96** [2002/3 h101: 16g⁶ 17s³ 20g 16g² c16d³ c16g² c16g³ c21mᵖᵘ Apr 26] neat gelding: fair **h102** handicap hurdler: not fluent and modest form over fences: barely stays 21f: acts on heavy and good to firm going: blinkered/visored: no easy ride. *B. Ellison*

SHALUJI (IRE)   6 b.m. Montelimar (USA) – Shuil Alanna (Furry Glen) [2002/3 **F77** F16s⁵ F16s F16gᵖᵘ Jan 18] IR 9,400 3-y-o: angular mare: fourth foal: dam, winning hurdler, from family of Scottish National winner Baronet and Welsh National winner Jock's Cross: best effort in bumpers when fifth in mares event at Wetherby: dead. *Mrs M. Reveley*

SHAMAN   6 b.g. Fraam – Magic Maggie (Beveled (USA)) [2002/3 17sᵖᵘ 16s⁶ 16m Apr **h66** 22] modest up to 1½m on Flat, successful in January: poor form over hurdles. *G. L. Moore*

SHAMAWAN (IRE)   8 b.g. Kris – Shamawna (IRE) (Darshaan) [2002/3 c120, h–: **c143** c16dᶠ c16v* c16v³ c21s² Jan 25] leggy gelding: useful handicap chaser: progressed in **h–** 2002/3, not fully extended when beating Just Jasmine 5 lengths in 5-runner event at Ascot in November: good neck second of 15 to Lady Cricket in quite valuable event at Chelt- enham: effective around 2m to 21f: acts on heavy going: has had tongue tied (not since early-2000/1): takes good hold, and is patiently ridden. *Jonjo O'Neill*

SHAMEL   7 b.g. Unfuwain (USA) – Narjis (USA) (Blushing Groom (FR)) [2002/3 **h–** 20sᵖᵘ Jan 18] strong gelding: fair 1¾m winner at 3 yrs for J. Dunlop: showed nothing on hurdling debut. *C. J. Price*

SHAMELESS   6 ch.g. Prince Daniel (USA) – Level Edge (Beveled (USA)) [2002/3 **h–** F78: 21sᵖᵘ 27vᵖᵘ 17vᵖᵘ 24sᵖᵘ 16d 23mᵖᵘ Apr 21] leggy gelding: no form over hurdles. *H. Alexander*

SHAMPOOED (IRE)   9 b.m. Law Society (USA) – White Caps (Shirley Heights) **c110** [2002/3 c100, h–: c20dᵖᵘ c16m* c17d⁶ c16s² c18g² c19d⁵ c16d Feb 14] workmanlike **h–** mare: winning hurdler: fair handicap chaser: won at Worcester in May: stays 19f: acts on heavy and good to firm going: usually visored nowadays (ran poorly when blinkered): races prominently. *R. Dickin*

SHAMSAN (IRE) 6 ch.g. Night Shift (USA) – Awayil (USA) (Woodman (USA)) c98
[2002/3 h108: 16d² 16d² 17g* 16m² 20m² c21g² c20m³ c20m* c20m² c24d² 16g⁴ 16m⁶ **h116**
Apr 22] small, sturdy gelding: fair handicap hurdler: won at Hereford in June: not fluent and only modest form in novice chases: won at Plumpton in September: left P. Hobbs after tenth outing: stays easy 2½m: acts on firm and good to soft ground: blinkered last 3 outings over fences: has had tongue tied: has idled and usually held up. *J. Joseph*

SHANE 5 ch.g. Aragon – Angel Fire (Nashwan (USA)) [2002/3 h–: 17d Aug 26] **h–**
maiden on Flat, well held in 2002: no form over hurdles. *F. P. Murtagh*

SHANESIA (IRE) 4 b.f. Erins Isle – Canadian Project (IRE) (Project Manager) **h110**
[2002/3 16d 16s 16d 16s⁶ 16g* Apr 2] lightly-raced 11f winner on Flat: best effort over hurdles when winning novice at Clonmel in April by 3 lengths from Caishill: will stay beyond 2m. *Paul Nolan, Ireland*

SHANNON GALE (IRE) 11 b.g. Strong Gale – Shannon Spray (Le Bavard (FR)) c–
[2002/3 c125, h–: c27dᵖᵘ c28sᵖᵘ c21vᵖᵘ 20s 24d c21d Apr 4] tall gelding: useful hurdler/ **h–**
chaser at best, has lost his form: stays 3¼m: acts on heavy and good to firm going. *C. Roche, Ireland*

SHANNON LIGHT (IRE) 11 b. or br.g. Electric – Shannon Lass (Callernish) **h95**
[2002/3 h95: 27s² 22mᵖᵘ Jun 14] compact gelding: modest hurdler: needs 3m+: acts well on soft going. *N. R. Mitchell*

SHANNON QUEST (IRE) 7 b. or br.g. Zaffaran (USA) – Carrick Shannon (Green c86
Shoon) [2002/3 c–, h86, F–: c16m² c16mᵖᵘ c16g⁵ c16g⁴ c16g² c16g³ c20mᶠ c20m⁵ 17mᵖᵘ **h–**
Apr 15] lengthy gelding: modest maiden hurdler/chaser: ran moody race final start: probably stays 19f: acts on soft and good to firm going: usually blinkered: sometimes finds little/let down by jumping. *O. Sherwood*

SHANNON'S DREAM 7 b.m. Anshan – Jenny's Call (Petong) [2002/3 h–: 17s **h–**
20sᵖᵘ Dec 5] of no account. *Mrs Barbara Waring*

SHANNON'S PRIDE (IRE) 7 gr.g. Roselier (FR) – Spanish Flame (IRE) (Spanish **h113 +**
Place (USA)) [2002/3 h83p: 22d* 20d* 22g³ Mar 21] well-made gelding: type to make a chaser: created good impression when winning novice hurdles at Ayr in November and December: odds on, didn't find much when third to General Duroc in similar event at Kelso: bred to stay at least 3m: may still do better. *N. G. Richards*

SHARDAM (IRE) 6 b.g. Shardari – Knockea Hill (Buckskin (FR)) [2002/3 h104, c131
F89: 19d³ 24s* c24dᵘʳ c19d² c22s* c24d⁵ c24s* c25d² Apr 4] leggy gelding: fair hurdler: **h102**
won maiden at Chepstow in November: useful chaser: justified favouritism in novice events at Fontwell in December and Chepstow in February: not take eye, best effort when 1¼ lengths second of 14 to Master Tern in valuable handicap at Aintree in April: unseated second in valuable novice handicap at Punchestown later in month: stays 25f: acts on soft going, runner-up in bumper on good to firm: consistent. *N. A. Twiston-Davies*

SHARED-INTEREST 9 ch.m. Interrex (CAN) – La Campagnola (Hubble Bubble) **h–**
[2002/3 h–: 19vᵖᵘ Mar 4] angular mare: no form outside points. *K. Bishop*

SHAREEF (FR) 6 b.g. Port Lyautey (FR) – Saralik (Salse (USA)) [2002/3 h102, F93: c119
20dᵖᵘ 19d³ 22fᵘʳ c19g² c16g² Nov 20] good-topped gelding: fair hurdler: first start since **h98**
leaving J. Mullins, fairly useful form when 3½ lengths second to Montreal in novice at Exeter on chasing debut: seemed unsuited by step back in trip later in month: will stay 3m: acts on good to firm and good to soft going (won bumper on soft). *A. King*

SHARE OPTIONS (IRE) 12 b. or br.g. Executive Perk – Shannon Belle (Pollerton) c–
[2002/3 c27gᵖᵘ Feb 27] lengthy gelding: one-time fairly useful handicap chaser: pulled **h–**
up in hunter on return from 2-year absence: stays 3¼m: acts on good to firm and heavy going: blinkered once: often races lazily. *P. Jones*

SHARIMAGE (IRE) 12 ch.g. Luxury Image – Even Fort (Even Money) [2002/3 c–
c25dᵖᵘ Feb 10] one-time fairly useful hunter chaser: lightly raced nowadays, successful **h–**
once from 2 starts in points in 2002: stays 3m: acts on any going. *Miss A. Nolan*

SHARLOM (IRE) 6 br.g. Shardari – Sarahs Music (IRE) (Orchestra) [2002/3 h–, F–: c59 x
20dᵖᵘ c21mᵖᵘ c21m⁶ c21mᵘʳ c22m⁴ c24m⁴ 16m³ Oct 5] workmanlike gelding: poor **h70**
maiden hurdler/chaser, left Mrs M. Stirk after reappearance: likely to prove best up to 2½m: tried blinkered: makes mistakes over fences. *R. D. E. Woodhouse*

SHARMADAN (FR)   7 ch.g. Zayyani – Sharmada (FR) (Zeddaan) [2002/3 F–: F16g   **F–**
Jan 18] close-coupled gelding: little worthwhile form in bumpers. *K. A. Morgan*

SHARMY (IRE)   7 b.g. Caerleon (USA) – Petticoat Lane (Ela-Mana-Mou) [2002/3   **h103**
h111: 16d³ 16d* 16dF 16m⁵ Apr 2] close-coupled gelding: useful on Flat (stays 1½m),
successful in January and February: fair novice hurdler: didn't need to be at best to win at
Huntingdon in November: likely to prove best around 2m: acts on soft and good to firm
going: reportedly hung left final outing. *Ian Williams*

SHARPAMAN   8 b.g. Mandalus – Sharp Glance (IRE) (Deep Run) [2002/3 c26dF Jun   **c–**
8] 5,000 4-y-o: second foal: half-brother to fair hurdler Digup St Edmunds (by Bustino),
stays 3m: dam unraced: fair pointer, won maiden in February: fell twelfth in novice chase
at Cartmel. *S. H. Shirley-Beavan*

SHARPASTRIZAM (NZ)   8 b.g. Try To Stop Me – Atristazam (NZ) (Zamazaan   **c107**
(FR)) [2002/3 c112, h–: c16d⁴ c16g⁴ c19d c16d⁴ c16g⁴ Apr 24] good-topped gelding: fair   **h–**
handicap chaser: stays 2½m: best form on good/good to firm going (yet to race on firm):
usually sound jumper. *P. Beaumont*

SHARPATEN (IRE)   8 b.g. Scenic – Sloane Ranger (Sharpen Up) [2002/3 c114,   **c–**
h132: c21s 16g³ 16d 16f 16s⁵ 19m³ 16d² 16d⁴ 16m Feb 21] leggy, angular ex-Irish   **h124**
gelding: winning chaser: useful handicap hurdler at best: not quite so good in 2002/3,
sold out of P. Hughes's stable 14,500 gns Doncaster October Sales after sixth outing: best
form at 2m, should stay further: acts on good to firm and heavy going. *C. J. Mann*

SHARP BELLINE (IRE)   6 b.g. Robellino (USA) – Moon Watch (Night Shift   **h103**
(USA)) [2002/3 h98: 24d* 26s² 24g⁴ 24g Sep 28] small, close-coupled gelding: fair
handicap hurdler: won at Southwell in May: best at 3m+: acts on firm and soft going:
lazy. *John A. Harris*

SHARP CITY   4 b.g. Rock City – Mary Miller (Sharpo) [2002/3 16dpu Nov 7] rather   **h–**
sparely-made gelding: little form on Flat: no show on hurdling debut. *A. C. Whillans*

SHARP EMBRACE   10 ch.g. Broadsword (USA) – Running Kiss (Deep Run)   **c–**
[2002/3 c80, h–: c24gpu c24m⁵ May 11] maiden staying jumper: often blinkered/visored.   **h–**
Miss Susan Rodman

SHARP GOSSIP (IRE)   7 b.g. College Chapel – Idle Gossip (Runnett) [2002/3 16spu   **h–**
Nov 27] plain gelding: modest and unreliable on Flat (stays 1m), sold out of J. Toller's
stable 6,500 gns Newmarket Autumn Sales, successful in January: no show on hurdling
debut. *J. R. Weymes*

SHARP HAND   7 ch.g. Handsome Sailor – Sharp Glance (IRE) (Deep Run) [2002/3   **h69**
F17s F17s 19dpu 17g⁵ 16m³ 17m⁵ Apr 5] big, plain gelding: third foal: half-brother   **F73**
to a winning pointer by Mandalus and fair hurdler Digup St Edmunds (by Bustino), stays
3m: dam unraced: poor form in bumpers and over hurdles: should stay 2½m.
J. G. M. O'Shea

SHARP SEAL   9 b.g. Broadsword (USA) – Little Beaver (Privy Seal) [2002/3 h–:   **c78**
c19f³ c22dur c21d⁴ c20s² c22vF c22spu c24f⁵ Mar 24] poor novice chaser: probably stays   **h–**
3m: acts on firm and soft going: sold £2,500 Ascot April Sales. *M. Madgwick*

SHARP SINGLE (IRE)   7 b.m. Supreme Leader – Pollyville (Pollerton) [2002/3   **h–**
20gpu 16dpu 16dpu 17spu Mar 5] 23,000 4-y-o: workmanlike mare: fifth foal: sister to
winning 2½m hurdler Cullen Bay and half-sister to modest 2m hurdler Roses Niece (by
Jeu de Paille): dam, placed in bumpers, half-sister to smart staying hurdler Rose Ravine,
herself dam of Frosty Canyon and Cardinal Red: pulled up all 4 starts in novice hurdles.
P. Beaumont

SHARP SOPRANO   4 b.f. Mon Tresor – Gentle Star (Comedy Star (USA)) [2002/3   **h–**
16fur Oct 10] half-sister to winning 21f chasers Lodestone Lad (by Norwick) and Polish
Spirit (by Emarati): little form on Flat: well held when unseated 2 out in juvenile on
hurdling debut (tended to hang left): sold £650 Ascot October Sales. *B. R. Millman*

SHARP STEEL   8 ch.g. Beveled (USA) – Shift Over (USA) (Night Shift (USA))   **c76**
[2002/3 h73: 16m⁵ 16gpu 16d⁶ c16d⁵ c17g³ Mar 22] poor maiden hurdler: similar form   **h81**
in 2 races over fences: raced around 2m: acts on good to soft going: headstrong.
Miss S. J. Wilton

SHARP WORD (IRE)   4 br.g. Needle Gun (IRE) – Pas de Mot (Tender King) [2002/3   **F62 +**
F14d⁶ Dec 9] fifth foal: half-brother to fair 2m hurdler Loquacious (by Distinctly North),
also 1½m winner on Flat: dam winning hurdler/chaser, stayed 2½m: possibly made
ground too soon when around 30 lengths sixth of 15 in bumper at Ayr on debut. *T. P. Tate*

SHARVIE 6 b.g. Rock Hopper – Heresheis (Free State) [2002/3 16m⁶ 22s 21d 16s h–
16dᵖᵘ 17m⁴ Apr 21] close-coupled gelding: modest at best on Flat (stays 2m) for Mrs
L. Pearce: no form over hurdles: blinkered final start. *C. J. Hemsley*

SHAYDEYLAYDEH (IRE) 4 b.f. Shaddad (USA) – Spirito Libro (USA) (Lear Fan h–
(USA)) [2002/3 16d Nov 12] angular filly: modest maiden on Flat (stays 11.5f): wearing
cheekpieces, took good hold and made mistakes when well held in juvenile at Huntingdon on hurdling debut. *C. N. Allen*

SHAYS LANE (IRE) 9 b.g. The Bart (USA) – Continuity Lass (Continuation) [2002/3 c–
h73: c25d⁵ c25g⁴ Apr 7] rangy, useful-looking gelding: lightly raced and little form over h–
hurdles or fences. *Ferdy Murphy*

SHAZAL 6 b.m. Afzal – Isolationist (Welsh Pageant) [2002/3 F–: 16v 16g 16dᶠ 16g⁶ h63
Apr 7] smallish, leggy mare: signs of only a little ability over hurdles. *J. N. R. Billinge*

SH BOOM 5 b.g. Alderbrook – Muznah (Royal And Regal (USA)) [2002/3 F102: h141
F16v* 20v* 21d² 20g* 21g⁵ 20gᵖᵘ Apr 3] F104
In a strong field for the latest Royal & SunAlliance Novices' Hurdle, none
appeals more as a prospective chaser than the sixth across the line Sh Boom. Later
promoted a place, Sh Boom found twenty-one furlongs on good ground in top
novice company barely enough of a test of stamina but, after being flat out at the
sixth, he stuck to his task well, finishing six and a half lengths behind the winner
Hardy Eustace. The Grade 1 Sefton Novices' Hurdle at Aintree over three miles
would have seemed the obvious target for Sh Boom after that, but with his stable
aiming Iris's Gift at the race he was dropped back slightly in trip for the Grade 2
Mersey Novices' Hurdle. Good ground and a sharp track proved far from ideal once
again for Sh Boom and, unable to hold his place four out as the leader kicked on, he
was pulled up two out. Although briefly loose before the start it made little difference to Sh Boom's performance. Sh Boom won all but one of his races before

TGK Construction Ltd's "Sh Boom"

Cheltenham and Aintree. He gained a game success in a bumper at Wetherby (his second such win, having scored at Towcester when with Kim Bailey in 2001/2) and was impressive when landing novice hurdles at Uttoxeter and Huntingdon. Between the last two victories, Sh Boom split the useful pair Lord Sam (two places and less than a length in front of him at Cheltenham) and Chauvinist at Kempton. Sh Boom is the best horse so far sired by the 1995 Champion Hurdle winner Alderbrook but he isn't yet the best of his dam Muznah's progeny. She has produced two high-class hurdlers in the two-miler Jazilah (by Persian Bold) and Sh Boom's close relative Anzum (by Ardross), who won the 1999 Stayers' Hurdle. Muznah's other winners include the useful hurdler at up to twenty-one furlongs Nahar (by Known Fact) and the fairly useful juvenile hurdler Formal Affair (by Rousillon). The useful-looking Sh Boom still looked unfurnished in the spring but can be expected to fill out over the summer. He has raced on good going or softer. With three miles sure to bring him into his own, he could well be back at Cheltenham in 2004 with the Royal & SunAlliance Chase on the agenda. *Jonjo O'Neill*

SHEEP STEALER 15 gr.g. Absalom – Kilroe's Calin (Be Friendly) [2002/3 20g c17m Jul 4] workmanlike gelding: winning hurdler/novice chaser, has gone to the pack. *R. E. Peacock* | c– h–

SHEILA MCKENZIE 6 b.m. Aragon – Lady Quachita (USA) (Sovereign Dancer (USA)) [2002/3 c–: c24s[pu] Mar 10] successful twice in points in 2002: pulled up in 2 hunter chases. *C. O. King* | c–

SHELLIN HILL (IRE) 9 ch.g. Sharp Victor (USA) – Queenspay (Sandhurst Prince) [2002/3 c89, h82: c17g[6] c17g[2] c17m[3] c16m[F] c19g[pu] c16m[3] c16d[pu] c20d c16v[4] c19s[3] c16v[F] c19f[4] c21m[pu] Apr 17] strong, lengthy gelding: modest handicap chaser: won novice at Southwell in September: little form after, lame final outing: probably best around 2m: acts on firm and soft going: has had tongue tied: none too hearty. *R. J. Price* | c89 d h–

SHELTERING (IRE) 11 b.g. Strong Gale – Mandy Brenda (IRE) (Crash Course) [2002/3 c127, h–: c25s* c24s* c26g c21g[F] Apr 3] lengthy, good sort: had several wind operations, one after 2001/2: high-class hunter chaser: won at Punchestown (second successive victory in race) in January and Leopardstown (made all to beat Dorans Pride 10 lengths) in February: well below best in Foxhunter at Cheltenham and in Champion Hunter Chase at Punchestown (second to What Odds) in late-April, fell third at Aintree in between: stayed 29f: acted on good to firm and heavy going: tried tongue tied: usually raced prominently: dead. *E. J. O'Grady, Ireland* | c136 h–

SHELU 5 b.g. Good Thyne (USA) – Nearly Married (Nearly A Hand) [2002/3 F–: F16d 26g 24v[3] 20g[pu] Apr 14] good-bodied gelding: form only when third of 8 in slowly-run novice hurdle at Hexham: reportedly lame next time: thorough stayer. *Ferdy Murphy* | h88 ? F–

SHEMARDI 6 b.g. Jumbo Hirt (USA) – Masirah (Dunphy) [2002/3 h68: 20d 22d c19v[F] c20v[4] c17v[ur] 20s 22g[2] Mar 17] good-topped gelding: poor maiden hurdler: well beaten only completed start over fences: stays 2¾m: acts on soft going: often visored (looked less than keen fifth outing): sold £4,600 Ascot April Sales. *M. Madgwick* | c– h67

SHEMDANI (IRE) 6 b.g. Unfuwain (USA) – Shemaka (IRE) (Nishapour (FR)) [2002/3 h113p: 16d[6] 16v* Feb 15] leggy gelding: fairly useful hurdler: much better effort in 2002/3 when winning 13-runner handicap at Ascot, jumping with more fluency than usual and beating Coulthard 2½ lengths: raced around 2m: acts on any going: lightly raced, and may be capable of further improvement. *M. C. Pipe* | h118 +

SHEMILL 5 b.g. Spectrum (IRE) – Shemaleyah (Lomond (USA)) [2002/3 F–: F16m F16g Jan 18] smallish, sturdy gelding: well held in bumpers. *D. Eddy* | F–

SHENANDOAH (IRE) 7 b.m. Supreme Leader – Gold Label (Deep Run) [2002/3 20d[2] 22m[3] 24g[3] 22d[ur] Nov 5] lengthy, workmanlike mare: twice-raced in bumpers in 2000/1: regressed over hurdles after second to very easy winner Mr Fluffy in novice at Worcester: should stay 3m. *P. J. Hobbs* | h82

SHENOSO 8 b.m. Teenoso (USA) – Mossy Morning (Le Moss) [2002/3 16d[pu] Jun 4] third foal: dam poor novice hurdler: pulled up in 3 points in 2000, and in maiden on hurdling debut. *M. A. Barnes* | h–

SHEPHERDS REST (IRE) 11 b.g. Accordion – Mandy's Last (Krayyan) [2002/3 c98, h–: c27g[F] c26d* c26g[2] 24d[5] c25m[2] c24d[pu] c24d[5] Dec 14] angular gelding: fair handicap chaser: won weak event at Uttoxeter in June: ran poorly 3 of last 4 starts, includ- | c103 h–

ing over hurdles: stays 3¼m: acts on good to firm and heavy going: visored: often finds little. *C. P. Morlock*

SHERBET LAD (IRE)　7 b.g. Cataldi – She's Foolish (IRE) (Callernish) [2002/3 **h102** F87: 16d 20v* Mar 7] workmanlike gelding: fair form in bumpers in 2001/2: bettered debut effort over hurdles when winning novice at Sandown by 5 lengths from Briar: well held in handicap at Punchestown in early-May: should stay beyond 2½m: acts on heavy going. *V. R. A. Dartnall*

SHERFIELD LASS　5 b.m. Tina's Pet – Mindyerownbusiness (IRE (Roselier (FR)) **F–** [2002/3 F16f Mar 29] first foal: dam, winning Irish pointer, half-sister to useful 6f and 7f filly The Bean Sidhe: last of 11 in mares bumper at Haydock on debut. *Mrs H. Dalton*

SHERNGOLD (IRE)　5 b.m. Shernazar – Portanob (IRE) (Be My Native (USA)) **h69** [2002/3 F16v 16dF 22d 17g³ 16m⁶ Mar 31] IR £6,200 3-y-o, 7,000 4-y-o: rather leggy **F–** mare: first foal: dam unraced, from family of very smart chaser up to 3m Gales Cavalier: behind in bumper: form over hurdles only when 24 lengths third in mares maiden at Hereford: will prove suited by further than 17f. *R. H. Alner*

SHERWOOD ROSE (IRE)　7 gr.m. Mandalus – Cronlier (Roselier (FR)) [2002/3 **h–** F60: 22g Nov 9] sturdy mare: well held in bumpers and mares novice hurdle. *K. C. Bailey*

SHE'S A CORKER (IRE)　8 br. or b.m. Jurado (USA) – Lean Over (Over The River **c–** (FR) [2002/3 c24gᵘʳ c26dᵖᵘ 22d* 26gᵖᵘ Nov 7] IR 1,000 3-y-o, 5,200 5-y-o: fifth foal: **h79** half-sister to 2 poor maiden jumpers by Lancastrian: dam, lightly-raced Irish maiden, placed in 2m hurdle: successful both starts in points in 2002: failed to complete in 2 hunters for Miss C. Elliott: poor hurdler (trained in 2000/1 by M. Hourigan), best effort when winning weak maiden at Stratford in October: held in fourth when went amiss in conditional jockeys minor event at Hereford: should stay beyond 2¾m: raced on good going or softer. *D. L. Williams*

SHESGOTTOHAVEIT (IRE)　4 b.f. Flying Spur (AUS) – Carousel Mall (IRE) **h–** (Soughaan (USA)) [2002/3 16m 16sᵖᵘ Nov 18] poor maiden on Flat (stays easy 1¼m): no show in 2 starts over hurdles: sold £300 Ascot December Sales. *P. Mitchell*

SHESKINQUEEN (IRE)　8 b.m. Black Monday – Our Lady Sofie (Ile de Bourbon **h–** (USA)) [2002/3 h94, F82: 16s 16s F68 12] angular mare: modest hurdler in 2001/2: bought out of M. Quinlan's stable 3,500 gns Doncaster August Sales: tailed off on return: will prove best around 2m: acts on good to soft going: has had tongue tied. *R. Wilman*

SHE'S OUR NATIVE (IRE)　5 b.m. Be My Native (USA) – More Dash (IRE) **F95** (Strong Gale) [2002/3 F17d² F16g* Mar 16] third foal: dam, bumper winner/winning pointer, half-sister to fairly useful chaser up to 25f Royal Jake and fairly useful hurdler up to 3m Aimees Mark: improved on debut form when winning bumper at Ludlow by 1¾ lengths from Iftikhar: will stay at least 2½m. *P. J. Hobbs*

SHE'S YOURS　4 ch.f. Whittingham (IRE) – Flood's Hot Stuff (Chilibang) [2002/3 **F–** F12d F16m⁶ Apr 22] first foal: dam 1m winner: tailed off in bumpers at Newbury (for B. Powell) and Chepstow. *A. J. Chamberlain*

SHE WONT SCREAM　5 b.m. Desert Dirham (USA) – Silent Scream (IRE) (Lahib **h– §** (USA)) [2002/3 F16dᵖᵘ 16mᵘʳ 24gʳᵗʳ Sep 15] leggy mare: first foal: dam unraced, out **F–** of half-sister to Derby third Mashkour: no sign of ability, trained on debut by Mrs J. Saunders: refused to race second start over hurdles. *C. J. Hemsley*

SHIFTING MOON　11 b.g. Night Shift (USA) – Moonscape (Ribero) [2002/3 c–§, **c– §** h98§: 16d⁴ 20m 22m⁴ 22g* 20d² 20m⁵ 24m³ 20m⁵ 22m 23mᵘʳ 20d Nov 7] compact **h84 §** gelding: not fluent and no form over fences: poor handicap hurdler: won weak race at Stratford in July: possibly best up to 2¾m: acts on any going: effective blinkered or not: tongue tied: none too genuine. *F. Jordan*

SHII-TAKE'S GIRL　5 ch.m. Deploy – Super Sally (Superlative) [2002/3 h–: 21mᵖᵘ **h–** Jul 17] lengthy mare: fair at best on Flat (stays 1½m), on downgrade in 2002: no form over hurdles: sold 800 gns Doncaster November Sales. *M. E. Sowersby*

SHILO (IRE)　9 ch.g. Roselier (FR) – Cathedral Street (Boreen Beag) [2002/3 c23mᵖᵘ **c–** Jul 24] compact gelding: well held in 2 bumpers in 1999/00: runner-up on 3 completed starts in maiden points in 2002: reportedly lame on steeplechase debut. *P. D. Williams*

SHINDA MONDIAL　5 b.h. French Gondolier (USA) – Off And On (Touching Wood **F81** (USA)) [2002/3 F16f⁵ F16m⁵ F17g⁶ Oct 11] fifth foal: dam, of little account, half-sister to useful juvenile hurdler Urizen: best effort (modest form) in bumpers on debut. *A. R. Dicken*

SHINING LEADER (IRE)   12 b.g. Supreme Leader – Shining Run (Deep Run) [2002/3 c20m⁶ c16g^F 24d⁴ 16g⁵ c18m³ c17m^pu Sep 28] winning pointer: little form otherwise: dead. *M. J. Gingell* **c– h–**

SHINING TYNE   9 b.g. Primitive Rising (USA) – Shining Bann (Bargello) [2002/3 c91?, h–: c20d⁴ c20d⁴ c24g⁵ c24d⁶ c24s⁵ c22d² c20d³ c24g² c24g² Apr 23] lengthy gelding: modest maiden chaser: stays 3m: acts on soft going: wore cheekpieces last 5 starts: has had tongue tied: ungenuine. *R. Johnson* **c91 § h–**

SHIPLEY MILL   7 b.g. St Ninian – Shipley Bridge (Town And Country) [2002/3 h–, F80: 17m^F 21g May 30] no form over hurdles (bled from nose on debut): well held completed start in points. *J. T. Gifford* **h–**

SHOBROOKE MILL   10 ch.g. Shaab – Jubilee Leigh (Hubble Bubble) [2002/3 c102: c21g⁶ c28g^ur May 31] fairly useful hunter chaser on his day: won point in March: stays 3¼m: acts on good to firm going. *Mrs S. Prouse* **c87**

SHOOTING LIGHT (IRE)   10 b.g. Shernazar – Church Light (Caerleon (USA)) [2002/3 c160, h–: c27d⁵ c24s^pu Dec 26] sturdy, workmanlike gelding: improved into a high-class chaser in 2001/2, winning 2 handicaps at Cheltenham (including Thomas Pink Gold Cup) and Tote Silver Cup at Ascot: tied up run-in when fifth in another valuable handicap at Cheltenham on reappearance: stiff task, laboured effort even so in King George VI Chase at Kempton: missed rest of season with tendon injury: stays 3m: acts on soft and good to firm going (probably on heavy): blinkered/visored. *M. C. Pipe* **c149 h–**

SHORT CHANGE   4 b.g. Revoque (IRE) – Maafi Esm (Polish Precedent (USA)) [2002/3 17g* 16f² 16d^bd 16d Dec 5] workmanlike gelding: modest on Flat (barely stays 1½m): fair form in juvenile hurdles: won maiden at Hereford in October by 1¾ lengths from Le Duc: ran poorly final start. *A. W. Carroll* **h98**

SHOSHONI WARRIOR (IRE)   7 b.g. Commanche Run – Delko (Decent Fellow) [2002/3 F16g* 19d^pu 24s³ 24v⁴ 20d^pu Mar 2] lengthy ex-Irish gelding: second foal: brother to modest hurdler Commanche Wind, stays 21f: dam unraced: fair form in bumpers, dead-heated with Curragh Gem in 20-runner event at Gowran in May (final outing for Ms C. Hutchinson): in frame twice in 3m novice hurdles, though found little both times: dead. *Jonjo O'Neill* **h96 F93**

SHOTGUN WILLY (IRE)   9 ch.g. Be My Native (USA) – Minorettes Girl (Strong Gale) [2002/3 c159, h–: c28d* c36d^pu c33m⁵ Apr 12] **c159 h–**

Training facilities have never been better, with all-weather gallops, swimming pools, indoor schools and other means of supplementing or replacing work on the traditional grass gallops. If there ever were, there is no longer any excuse for a horse not being fit enough to do itself justice on the racecourse. Granted, there are gross individuals who really need a race to put them spot-on, and lazy animals who won't do enough at home but, apart from these, and possibly one or two other cases, punters and racegoers really should be able to rely on trainers to do their job. Allowing horses simply to be 'schooled' round, even on their first outing after a lengthy absence, is unacceptable and stewards are to be applauded when they take action to stamp out such practices. An increasingly litigious society does mean, however, that stewards need to be sure of their ground and must be aware that they might face a challenge in the courts. The turf authorities in Ireland were dragged through protracted legal proceedings after the Naas stewards banned the strongly-fancied Grand National contender Davids Lad from racing for forty-two days—effectively ruling him out of Aintree (ante-post bets were lost)—after he had been allowed to come home in his own time, last of seven finishers, in the Newlands Chase over two miles on February 23rd. The jockey Timmy Murphy was suspended for seven days and a €1,000 fine was imposed on trainer Tony Martin, who had warned the public that Davids Lad would need the race after three months off following his finishing distressed on his reappearance.

The owners of Davids Lad were so incensed when the decision to ban Davids Lad was upheld on appeal that they took the case to the Dublin High Court to try to have the verdict quashed. The owners reportedly argued that they should not be held liable for the actions of their trainer and should have been invited to attend the Naas inquiry. They were initially granted an injunction against the Turf

Club but, after being contested by the Turf Club, this was lifted on the opening day of the Cheltenham Festival, ruling Davids Lad out of his intended target the Mildmay of Flete Handicap. The owners were also given leave to bring judicial review proceedings against the Turf Club but eventually admitted defeat in their legal battle at the end of March after a Supreme Court judge ruled that Davids Lad's ban should stand pending a full hearing at a later date. There was no chance such a hearing would be held in time for Davids Lad to run at Aintree. The court dismissed an appeal for a stay on the ban, Mr Justice Geoghegan saying that the obvious hardship of the owners—denied the chance to run their horse in the Grand National—had to be balanced with the implications for the Turf Club and the integrity of racing if the perception was created that the Turf Club's authority had been successfully challenged. He also pointed out that the rules of the Turf Club placed all responsibility on the trainer and that the owners had contractually agreed to those rules and were bound by them. Interestingly, a judge at an earlier stage had pointed out: 'It must not be forgotten that racing is a sport, and there is no question of the appellants' livelihood being involved here.'

Contrast the Aintree preparation of Davids Lad with that of another leading contender who had been off the course for even longer, the Paul Nicholls-trained Shotgun Willy. When he lined up for the Red Square Vodka Gold Cup at Haydock in early-March, the high-class Shotgun Willy was having his first outing for over ten months. He had been brought along slowly—not put back into training until January—after recovering from a leg injury sustained when second in the previous season's Scottish Grand National. His trainer pointed out before Haydock that Shotgun Willy's campaign was being geared towards the Grand National, but he reiterated that the horse had 'done enough work to run well'. In a fine field that was worthy of the prize money (£63,800 to the winner), most of Shotgun Willy's sixteen rivals had been in good form during the season. Carrying top weight of 11-12 and looking trained to the minute, Shotgun Willy started at 10/1 in a very open betting race. Pushed along from five out and looking held early in the home straight, Shotgun Willy produced a memorable late rally under a persistent ride from Ruby Walsh. As can happen on Haydock's long run-in, the picture changed dramatically as Shotgun Willy, only fourth soon after jumping the last, stayed on resolutely to snatch the race close home from the Pipe-trained pair You're Agoodun and 13/2 favourite Iris Bleu by three quarters of a length and a short head. Shotgun Willy was one of five Manor Farm runners in the Grand National line-up five weeks later. With Ruby Walsh electing to ride him in preference to the stable's other leading fancy Ad Hoc, Shotgun Willy started 7/1 favourite, carrying 11-9, at Aintree. Walsh rode the first three winners on the Grand National day programme but Shotgun Willy ran a stinker for him in the National, never in the hunt and pulled up before second Becher's having lost touch. It was rather surprising to see Shotgun Willy turned out a week later under top weight for the Scottish National at Ayr, but connections had been unable to find anything amiss after Aintree and concluded that Shotgun Willy had 'not tried too hard' after getting behind. He was fitted with blinkers for the first time at Ayr and ran well for a long way before fading in the home straight to finish a below-form fifth of the eight to complete.

Red Square Vodka Gold Cup Chase (Handicap), Haydock—top weight Shotgun Willy (star cap) still has plenty to do at the last as he chases You're Agoodun (visor), Wonder Weasel (cheekpieces) and Iris Bleu

Mr C. G. Roach's "Shotgun Willy"

Shotgun Willy (IRE) (ch.g. 1994)	Be My Native (USA) (br 1979)	Our Native (b or br 1970)	Exclusive Native
			Our Jackie
		Witchy Woman (2000)	Strate Stuff
			Witchy Norma
	Minorettes Girl (b 1985)	Strong Gale (br 1975)	Lord Gayle
			Sterntau
		Minorette (b 1968)	Miralgo
			Quatre Bras

Shotgun Willy is probably not a particularly hard horse to get fit, being tall and rather sparely made, and he has won first time out in three of the four seasons that he has been with Nicholls, to whom he was sent after showing promise in bumpers for David Nicholson. Stamina was quickly identified as one of Shotgun Willy's main assets and he has been raced almost exclusively at three miles or more since his novice hurdling days. Racegoers shouldn't be put off him in the paddock where he is readily picked out because he has stringhalt, a condition affecting one or both of a horse's hind legs causing exaggerated, involuntary bending of the hock. Stringhalt doesn't affect Shotgun Willy's racing performance and he is by no means the only good jumper to be affected by it, the Melling Chase winner Native Upmanship being another notable example. Shotgun Willy is a brother to another successful long-distance chaser, the Welsh National and Singer & Friedlander National Trial winner Mini Sensation, who was pulled up at Haydock. Their dam Minorettes Girl was a very smart hurdler, runner-up in the Sun Alliance Hurdle at

822

Cheltenham and the Aintree Hurdle and a half-sister to the high-class chaser Observe, the useful but in-and-out Espy and the fair Irish jumper Sub-Editor. Shotgun Willy's grandam Minorette won on the Flat and over hurdles and fences in France and Italy. Shotgun Willy acts on good to firm and heavy going. He has hung and jumped left on occasions and is thought by connections to be best on a left-handed track (he has won twice at Wincanton but hasn't run on a right-handed course since jumping left and running abysmally when favourite for the Feltham at Kempton in his novice chasing days). *P. F. Nicholls*

SHOULD BE FUN   6 ch.m. Milieu – Our Dessa (Derek H) [2002/3 F16g F16f 24d Oct 26] first known foal: dam, lightly-raced maiden hurdler/chaser, half-sister to fairly useful hurdler up to 2½m Brodessa: well held in 2 bumpers and novice hurdle: last of 3 finishers on points debut. *Miss S. E. Forster*   h– F–

SHOULTON (IRE)   6 br.g. Aristocracy – Jay Joy (Double-U-Jay) [2002/3 F–: F16s 24v 24d c24g^{ur} Mar 22] medium-sized gelding: little sign of ability in varied events. *G. H. Yardley*   c– h– F–

SHOWPIECE   5 b.g. Selkirk (USA) – Hawayah (IRE) (Shareef Dancer (USA)) [2002/3 16g^4 Feb 8] rather leggy, useful-looking gelding: fair on Flat (stays 13f), successful twice in 2002, sold out of W. Haggas' stable 13,000 gns Newmarket Autumn Sales: 10¾ lengths fourth of 14 to Caracciola in novice hurdle at Newbury, running on well having been caught flat-footed when pace increased: sure to do better. *C. J. Mann*   h107 p

SHOW THE WAY   5 ch.g. Hernando (FR) – Severine (USA) (Trempolino (USA)) [2002/3 h77: 17m 16m^3 16g^3 20g^{pu} 16d^2 16g Mar 14] poor maiden on Flat and over hurdles: should stay beyond 2m: acts on good to firm and good to soft going: visored/blinkered. *J. R. Jenkins*   h79

SHOWTIME SHIRLEY   5 ch.m. First Trump – Wollow Maid (Wollow) [2002/3 h–: 16g May 17] poor on Flat (seems to stay easy 2m): well beaten over hurdles, looking none too keen when visored. *A. Bailey*   h–

SHRILANKA (IRE)   7 b.m. Lashkari – Lady Nerak (Pitpan) [2002/3 21d 20v^5 19d^5 c24g^5 Apr 19] IR 5,000 4-y-o: sturdy mare: third foal: half-sister to a winning pointer by Un Desperado: dam unraced: in frame in Irish point/mares bumper: poor form over hurdles: always behind after bad mistake first on steeplechasing debut. *P. J. Hobbs*   c– h67

SHU GAA (IRE)   10 ch.g. Salse (USA) – River Reem (USA) (Irish River (FR)) [2002/3 c–, h–: c21m^{pu} May 22] compact gelding: formerly fair chaser on his day, beaten long way out in hunter in May: stays 3m: acts on soft and good to firm going: has run well visored/blinkered. *C. Goulding*   c– h–

SHUIL BACK (IRE)   6 b.m. Bob Back (USA) – Shuil Ar Aghaidh (The Parson) [2002/3 F82: 20d^{pu} Apr 9] some promise when third in bumper on debut: jumped poorly and pulled up in novice hurdle year later. *A. J. Lidderdale*   h–

SHUIL TSARINA (IRE)   5 b.m. King's Ride – Shuil Realt (IRE) (Jolly Jake (NZ)) [2002/3 F16g F16v^3 Nov 8] IR £28,000 3-y-o: first foal: dam unraced, from family of very smart hurdler Liss A Paoraigh and Scottish National winner Baronet: better effort in bumpers at Hexham when third of 7 in mares event. *J. M. Jefferson*   F77

SHUTTLEWORTH (IRE)   9 br.g. Be My Native (USA) – Cool Princess (Proverb) [2002/3 c98, h–: c22s^2 c24d^6 c24s^5 c22d^{pu} Mar 3] winning hurdler: modest chaser: lame final outing: stays 25f: acts on heavy ground. *C. C. Bealby*   c98 h–

SHYLOCK (IRE)   9 b.g. Buckskin (FR) – Sly Maid (Rapid River) [2002/3 c24g^4 Apr 21] poor pointer: last of 4 in maiden hunter chase at Carlisle. *T. H. Caldwell*   c– h–

SIAMO DISPERATI   5 ch.g. Aragon – Jambo (Rambo Dancer (CAN)) [2002/3 16d 19d^{pu} Feb 23] workmanlike gelding: fair maiden at 2 yrs for C. Booth: raced freely and no form in novice hurdles. *Miss M. Bragg*   h–

SIGMA DOTCOMM (IRE)   7 b.g. Safety Catch (USA) – Dream Academy (Town And Country) [2002/3 c116, h–: c20s c20s^3 c19s^{pu} c20d^3 c16v Mar 9] good-topped gelding: fair handicap chaser: stays 3m: raced on good going or softer (acts on heavy): tried blinkered/in cheekpieces. *N. Meade, Ireland*   c112 h–

SIGMA RUN (IRE)   14 b.g. The Parson – Splendid Run (Deep Run) [2002/3 c84, h–: c16m^{pu} May 3] rangy gelding: winning hurdler: poor chaser: reportedly struck into at   c– h–

Folkestone in May: stays 2½m: acts on firm and soft going: usually visored/blinkered prior to 2001/2. *Dr P. Pritchard*

SIGNED AND DATED (USA) 4 b.g. Red Ransom (USA) – Libeccio (NZ) (Danzatore (CAN)) [2002/3 16g^{pu} 17d 17m^F Apr 26] modest maiden (should stay 1¼m) at 2 yrs, sold out of P. Cole's stable 7,200 gns Doncaster October (2001) Sales: jumped badly all 3 starts over hurdles. *Mrs E. Slack*   **h– x**

SIJUJAMA (IRE) 8 b.g. Torus – Knights Bounty (IRE) (Henbit (USA)) [2002/3 c75, h–: c16d² c16g³ c20m⁴ c20g⁴ c23m^{pu} c21d^{pu} Dec 9] good-topped gelding: poor novice chaser: stays 2½m: acts on good to firm and good to soft going. *Miss Lucinda V. Russell*   **c71 h–**

SIKASSO (USA) 7 b. or br.g. Silver Hawk (USA) – Silken Doll (USA) (Chieftain II) [2002/3 16s³ 16g 17d³ 16d³ 16g³ Apr 14] good-topped gelding: fairly useful in bumpers and on Flat (will stay 2m): only modest form over hurdles: will stay beyond 2m: acts on soft going (bumper form on firm). *G. A. Swinbank*   **h98 +**

SILCHESTER DREAM 5 ch.m. Karinga Bay – Raghill Hannah (Buckskin (FR)) [2002/3 F12g F16g 17g⁴ Mar 17] first foal: dam unraced: well held in 2 bumpers and mares maiden hurdle. *C. G. Cox*   **h– F70**

SILENCE REIGNS 9 b.g. Saddlers' Hall (IRE) – Rensaler (USA) (Stop The Music (USA)) [2002/3 c128, h–: c20d^F c20g^{ur} 22m⁶ Apr 11] sturdy gelding: useful hurdler/chaser: off a year before reappearance, went as if having a problem final start: stays 2½m: acts on good to firm and good to soft going: often let down by jumping over fences. *P. F. Nicholls*   **c– h–**

SILENT ACTION (USA) 11 b.g. Greinton – Heather Bee (USA) (Drone (USA)) [2002/3 c–, h–: 20d⁵ 20g^{pu} 22m⁵ 20m 26m⁴ 26m⁴ Aug 26] angular gelding: maiden hurdler: no form in steeplechases: won points in March and April: tongue tied. *N. A. Smith*   **c– h–**

SILENT APPEAL 6 b.m. Alflora (IRE) – Silent Surrender (Nearly A Hand) [2002/3 F17s² F17s⁴ Jan 14] fourth foal: half-sister to fairly useful chaser Silent Cracker (by Teenoso), stays 21f: dam, fair hurdler/chaser who stayed 3m, half-sister to useful staying chaser ANC Express: better effort in mares bumpers at Folkestone when second to Ask Me What. *Simon Earle*   **F85**

SILENT GUEST (IRE) 10 b.g. Don't Forget Me – Guest House (What A Guest) [2002/3 h–: 16s Feb 26] leggy gelding: winning hurdler, lightly raced nowadays: stays 3m: acts on firm and good to soft going. *J. D. Frost*   **h–**

SILENT GUNNER 5 ch.g. Gunner B – Quiet Dawn (Lighter) [2002/3 F16d Mar 19] first foal: dam, winning hurdler/chaser who stayed 3¼m, half-sister to useful staying chaser ANC Express: showed nothing in bumper on debut. *J. S. King*   **F–**

SILENT HUNTER 7 ch.g. Lion Cavern (USA) – Zealous Kitten (USA) (The Minstrel (CAN)) [2002/3 c–, h–, F–: c26g^F Apr 29] workmanlike gelding: of no account: tried blinkered/tongue tied. *M. J. Ryan*   **c– h–**

SILENT SNIPE 10 ch.g. Jendali (USA) – Sasol (Bustino) [2002/3 c70, h–: c25g^{ur} c25g c25m* c25m⁴ c23g^{pu} 26m c25m* c27d c26g^{pu} Apr 21] leggy gelding: no form over hurdles: poor chaser: has gained all 3 wins at Hexham, including handicaps in June and October: stays 25f: acts on good to firm going: has had tongue tied: inconsistent. *Miss L. C. Siddall*   **c73 h–**

SILENT SOUND (IRE) 7 b.g. Be My Guest (USA) – Whist Awhile (Caerleon (USA)) [2002/3 19d 16m² 16m⁶ Apr 22] half-brother to modest chaser Qualitair Memory (by Don't Forget Me), stayed 3¼m: poor and unreliable on Flat (stays 2m), had 3 trainers in 2002, sold out of Mrs S. Liddiard's stable £1,000 Ascot December Sales: poor form over hurdles. *C. Tizzard*   **h79**

SILENT VOICE (IRE) 6 ch.g. Unfuwain (USA) – Symeterie (USA) (Seattle Song (USA)) [2002/3 h–: 20g^{pu} May 17] well held in 2 novice hurdles. *Sir John Barlow Bt*   **h–**

SILKEN MEMORIES 8 b.g. Past Glories – Ribonny (FR) (Fast Hilarious (USA)) [2002/3 21m^{pu} Jul 17] angular gelding: signs of some ability in bumpers in 1999/00: failed to complete in 3 maiden points in 2002, and on hurdling debut. *R. Shiels*   **h–**

SILKEN PEARLS 7 b.m. Leading Counsel (USA) – River Pearl (Oats) [2002/3 F91: F16v* 22v* 21v Jan 21] good-topped mare: confirmed debut promise when winning mares bumper at Hexham on reappearance: won weak mares novice at Kelso on hurdling   **h72 + F92 +**

debut later in November despite saddle slipping and rider losing irons: very disappointing in similar event at Sedgefield final start: will stay 3m: acts on heavy going. *L. Lungo*

SILKEN THYNE   7 b.g. Good Thyne (USA) – Padykin (Bustino) [2002/3 19g² 22s* 23s* 24vᵖᵘ Dec 21] rangy, useful-looking ex-Irish gelding: fifth foal: brother to bumper winner Barrier Express and half-brother to fair chaser up to 3¼m Committed Schedule (by Saxon Farm) and winning pointer by Henbit: dam winning staying hurdler: poor form in bumper in 2000/1 for P. Cashman: won point in 2002: fairly useful hurdler: won maiden at Uttoxeter (gamely beat Coolnagorna a head) in November and novice at Wetherby (simple task, made all to beat Lambhill Stakes 15 lengths despite mistakes) in December: sweating and on toes, lame at Ascot final start: should stay 3m: acts on soft going: needs to brush up jumping. *C. C. Bealby*   **h123 p**

SILK ST BRIDGET   6 b.m. Rock Hopper – Silk St James (Pas de Seul) [2002/3 16dᵖᵘ Nov 30] poor maiden on Flat (stays 1¼m): no show in mares novice on hurdling debut. *W. M. Brisbourne*   **h–**

SILK ST JOHN   9 b.g. Damister (USA) – Silk St James (Pas de Seul) [2002/3 h87: 16v Nov 28] compact gelding: fairly useful on Flat (stays 1¼m) at 7 yrs, well held all 3 starts in 2002: thrice-raced in novice hurdles, well beaten only run in 2002/3. *W. M. Brisbourne*   **h–**

SILK TRADER   8 b.g. Nomadic Way (USA) – Money Run (Deep Run) [2002/3 h106: 16s⁵ 16d 16v⁴ 16s⁴ 16v* 16m⁴ Apr 22] leggy gelding: fair handicap hurdler: won amateur event at Sandown in March for second successive year: stays easy 2½m, races over shorter nowadays: acts on heavy and good to firm going: has had tongue tied: genuine. *J. Mackie*   **h109**

SILLY BOY   8 ch.g. Crested Lark – Sutton Lass (Politico (USA)) [2002/3 c20dᵖᵘ c17vᶠ Dec 26] lengthy, workmanlike gelding: poor pointer. *R. C. Harper*   **c–**

SILOGUE (IRE)   6 b. or br.g. Distinctly North (USA) – African Bloom (African Sky) [2002/3 19m⁵ Aug 31] half-brother to 19f hurdle winner African Dante (by Phardante): poor maiden on Flat (stays 2m): tailed off in novice on hurdling debut. *O. Brennan*   **h–**

SILVA VENTURE (IRE)   6 b.m. Mandalus – Miss The Post (Bustino) [2002/3 F–: F16s 17d 16g Mar 29] well held in bumpers and novice hurdles. *L. Lungo*   **h–**
F–

SILVER BIRCH (IRE)   6 b.g. Clearly Bust – All Gone (Giolla Mear) [2002/3 24s⁴ 20v* 25v* 24v³ Mar 4] workmanlike gelding: fifth foal: half-brother to winning pointer by King's Ride: dam lightly raced in bumpers: won last of 3 starts in maiden Irish points in 2002: best effort over hurdles when winning novice at Chepstow in November by 6 lengths from Bob Ar Aghaidh: made hard work of landing odds in weak similar event at Plumpton 2 months later, and well-beaten third of 4 at Exeter final start: should prove as effective around 3m as 2½m: raced on soft/heavy going. *P. F. Nicholls*   **h111**

SILVER BUZZARD (USA)   4 b. or br.g. Silver Hawk (USA) – Stellarina (USA) (Pleasant Colony (USA)) [2002/3 16m⁵ 18m² 16d* 16v⁴ 22v⁴ 19m⁶ Mar 22] workmanlike gelding: modest form in 2 maidens on Flat (will stay 1½m): fair juvenile hurdler: left J. Hills after second start and M. Channon after winning at Haydock in November: effective at 2m given test and stays 2¾m: acts on heavy going. *Jonjo O'Neill*   **h108**

SILVER CHARMER   4 b.f. Charmer – Sea Dart (Air Trooper) [2002/3 16mᶠ 16d³ 16d⁴ 17d 17v⁴ 19m* 20gᶠ 21m Apr 17] close-coupled filly: half-sister to several winners over jumps, including useful staying hurdler Mr Kermit (by Rolfe): modest sprint maiden on Flat: fairly useful juvenile hurdler: not fluent when winning handicap at Newbury in March: 100/1, excelling herself when falling 2 out (close third and staying on well) in Grade 2 novice won by Leinster at Aintree next time: only seventh of 9 in listed mares handicap at Cheltenham final outing: should stay 2½m+: acts on good to firm and good to soft going. *H. S. Howe*   **h117 ?**

SILVER CHARTER (USA)   4 b.g. Silver Hawk (USA) – Pride of Darby (USA) (Danzig (USA)) [2002/3 16d² 16s⁶ 16g 19m⁴ 21m Apr 2] workmanlike gelding: fair on Flat (should be suited by 1¼m+): modest juvenile hurdler: stays 19f: acts on good to firm and good to soft going: makes mistakes. *G. B. Balding*   **h82 x**

SILVER CHEVALIER (IRE)   5 gr.g. Petong – Princess Eurolink (Be My Guest (USA)) [2002/3 h78?: 16m 19mᵖᵘ 20sᵖᵘ 16s 24gᵖᵘ Aug 24] angular gelding: little sign of ability over hurdles, leaving B. Llewellyn before final start: joined D. Burchell. *Mrs D. A. Hamer*   **h–**

SILVER CHIEFTAIN (IRE) 5 gr.g. Be My Native (USA) – Mystery Rose (Roselier **F78**
(FR)) [2002/3 F16m Mar 22] €75,000 4-y-o: tall, angular gelding: sixth foal: brother to
smart bumper winner Ingonish and fair hurdler Native Rosie, stays 2½m: dam, winning
staying hurdler/chaser, half-sister to useful staying chaser Daring Prince: seventh of 18 in
bumper at Newbury on debut. *P. J. Hobbs*

SILVER DANCER (IRE) 7 gr.g. Roselier (FR) – Fancy Step (Step Together (USA)) **h–**
[2002/3 F16s 20v⁵ 26d 20gᵘʳ Mar 17] IR 16,500 4-y-o: leggy gelding: second foal: half- **F–**
brother to 2m hurdle winner Yash Can Step (by Yashgan): dam fair hurdler around 2m:
no sign of ability, including in points. *M. G. Rimell*

SILVER GIFT 6 b.m. Rakaposhi King – Kellsboro Kate (Paddy's Stream) [2002/3 **c–**
h71: 20g c21dF 19gᵖᵘ 22m⁵ 24g² 26m² 27g* 24g* 26mᵇᵈ 24g* 22m⁴ 26m* 24sᵖᵘ 27sᵖᵘ **h88**
26g 27m⁴ 26m* 24m 27f Apr 24] leggy mare: behind when falling on chasing debut:
modest handicap hurdler: won at Sedgefield and Worcester (conditional jockeys novice)
in August, Worcester again in September, Huntingdon in October and Hereford (conditional jockeys novice) in April: stays 27f: acts on good to firm and good to soft going,
probably unsuited by softer: held up. *G. Fierro*

SILVER GROOM (IRE) 13 gr.g. Shy Groom (USA) – Rustic Lawn (Rusticaro **c82**
(FR)) [2002/3 c–, h–: c24m³ Jun 1] small gelding: fair pointer, successful in April: best **h–**
effort in steeplechases when third in ladies hunter at Stratford in June: acts on soft and
good to firm going. *David M. Easterby*

SILVER HOWE 10 gr.g. Move Off – Vinovia (Ribston) [2002/3 h91§: 22g² 22d⁴ 16g **h78 d**
20dᵖᵘ 17d⁵ Aug 26] workmanlike gelding: modest hurdler at best: below form in 2002/3:
stays 2¾m: acts on heavy and good to firm going: effective visored or not: often soon off
bridle: unreliable. *D. Moffatt*

SILVER JACK (IRE) 5 gr.g. Roselier (FR) – Consharon (IRE) (Strong Gale) [2002/3 **F86**
F16d⁶ Feb 23] first foal: dam fairly useful hurdler/winning chaser, stayed 3m: sixth of 18
to Monet's Garden in bumper at Ayr on debut. *M. Todhunter*

SILVER KNIGHT 5 gr.g. Simply Great (FR) – Hysteria (Prince Bee) [2002/3 F107: **h118**
16m 20v* 20d² 21s² 25g* 24d⁶ 20s³ 24d³ 24g 24g³ Apr 24] tall, useful-looking gelding,
rather unfurnished at present: fairly useful novice hurdler: won at Hexham in November
and Catterick in January: will prove best at 3m+: acts on heavy going: found little when
blinkered sixth start: has been early to post: jumps far from fluently: not the easiest of
rides (has run in snatches). *T. D. Easterby*

SILVER MAN 9 gr.g. Silver Owl – What An Experiance (Chance Meeting) [2002/3 **c–**
c21fᵖᵘ c16d⁴ Sep 4] winning pointer, lightly raced: no show in 2 novice chases.
D. C. Turner

SILVER POT BLACK 8 gr.g. Ron's Victory (USA) – Haunting (Lord Gayle (USA)) **c–**
[2002/3 c–, h–: c24gᵖᵘ May 8] leggy gelding: maiden hurdler: winning pointer: no show **h–**
in 2 runs in steeplechases: stays 3m: acts on soft going: looks a tricky ride and temperament under suspicion. *Miss L. Day*

SILVER RISKS (IRE) 5 gr.m. Take Risks (FR) – Turkansa (FR) (Baby Turk) [2002/3 **h–**
h–: 17g 20m 20d 16s Dec 7] won at 1¼m on Flat in Ireland at 3 yrs: little show over
hurdles: blinkered final start. *D. R. Gandolfo*

SILVER SLEEVE (IRE) 11 b.g. Taufan (USA) – Sable Coated (Caerleon (USA)) **c68**
[2002/3 c89, h–: c19g⁶ c20mᵘʳ 19mF 17f⁴ 16m 17s⁴ 20s² 17s³ 18s 17v⁴ 16g Mar 12] rather **h57**
leggy gelding: modest hunter chaser: bad hurdler: stays 2½m: acts on any going: usually
wears headgear: has had tongue tied: none too genuine. *Mrs H. M. Bridges*

SILVER SOCKS 6 gr.g. Petong – Tasmim (Be My Guest (USA)) [2002/3 h108+: **c84**
c16g³ c16vᵖᵘ Nov 16] close-coupled gelding: fair hurdler: let down by jumping both **h–**
starts in novice chases, fatally injured on second occasion: barely stayed 2½m: acted on
soft going. *M. W. Easterby*

SILVER STEEL 8 b.g. Shernazar – Yldizlar (Star Appeal) [2002/3 c128, h116: 24s* **c–**
22s² c24g c34s⁵ Mar 15] big, well-made gelding: fairly useful hurdler: won handicap at **h122**
Navan in November: of similar level over fences, had excuses when well held in valuable
handicaps at Cheltenham (conditions insufficiently testing) and Uttoxeter (saddle slipped): may prove best short of 4m: raced mainly on going softer than good (acts on heavy):
usually races prominently. *C. Roche, Ireland*

SILVER STREAK (IRE) 9 gr.g. Roselier (FR) – Vulcash (IRE) (Callernish) [2002/3 **c–**
c122, h–: 21mᵖᵘ Oct 29] tall, good-topped gelding: winning hurdler: fairly useful chaser: **h–**

won 2 novices in 2001/2: needed race in handicap hurdle only start in 2002/3: will stay beyond 25f: acts on soft and good to firm going: sound jumper. *J. T. Gifford*

SILVER STUD (FR) 4 b.c. Double Bed (FR) – Pointe Argentee (Pas de Seul) [2002/3   **h110**
15s³ 16s² 18v² 18v 16v² 18s⁶ 19sᶠ Apr 4] leggy colt: half-brother to winning hurdlers around 2m in France by Linamix and Germany by Homme de Loi: maiden on Flat, placed once at 11f: fair form in juvenile hurdles: acts on heavy going. *F. Doumen, France*

SILVER TARN (IRE) 5 gr. or ro.m. Parthian Springs – Mary Kate (Callernish)   **h70 +**
[2002/3 20vᵖᵘ 19dᵖᵘ 16d⁴ Mar 19] good-topped mare: sixth foal: half-sister to fair chaser Mr Timbrology (by Insan), stays 3m: dam unraced: form over hurdles only when remote fourth in novice at Chepstow final start: should be suited by further than 2m. *R. H. Alner*

SILVER THYNE (IRE) 11 br.g. Good Thyne (USA) – Fitz's Buck (Master Buck)   **h72**
[2002/3 16m² May 6] good-bodied gelding: fairly useful hurdler at best: off 3 years, poor form when second in conditional jockeys seller at Ludlow in May: stays 2½m: acts on good to firm going: blinkered once (ran well despite carrying head high): not an easy ride. *R. J. Hodges*

SILVER TONIC 7 gr.g. Petong – Princess Eurolink (Be My Guest (USA)) [2002/3   **h–**
22sᵖᵘ 16d 16gᵖᵘ Dec 12] modest form in 2 maidens around 7f on Flat at 4 yrs for K. Mahdi: failed to complete in 4 points in 2002: no form over hurdles, trained on debut by A. Hobbs. *J. M. Bradley*

SILVERTOWN 8 b.g. Danehill (USA) – Docklands (USA) (Theatrical) [2002/3 h97:   **h125 p**
19s 21v³ 19d 20g* 17m* 17g* Apr 21] sturdy, lengthy gelding: much improved in handicap hurdles last 3 starts, winning at Hereford (flashed tail) and Carlisle (easily) in April, making most or all: stays 2½m: seems best on good going or firmer: open to further improvement. *L. Lungo*

SIMBER HILL (IRE) 9 ch.g. Phardante (FR) – Princess Wager (Pollerton) [2002/3   **c115**
c89, h–: c25d⁵ c25d³ c24m* c24m* c23m³ c26d² c25g² c24m* c24s⁵ c24fᶠ c24g³ Apr 23]   **h–**
lengthy gelding: fairly useful chaser: sold out of A. King's stable 10,000 gns Doncaster May Sales after second appearance: won handicaps at Stratford and Uttoxeter in July and novice at Taunton (idled) in October: let down by jumping next 2 starts, found little final one: suited by 3m+: acts on good to firm and good to soft going: effective blinkered or not: temperament under suspicion. *P. J. Hobbs*

SIMONS CASTLE (IRE) 10 b.g. Scenic – Miss Toot (Ardross) [2002/3 c76§, h–:   **c71 §**
c19g 22m⁵ Jul 4] well-made gelding: poor maiden chaser: one-time fairly useful hurdler,   **h–**
well held in seller in July: well beaten in point in March for A. Farrant: stays 21f: acts on heavy going: blinkered once (reportedly distressed): none too keen. *J. D. Frost*

SIMOSKI 6 b.g. Petoski – Miss Simone (Ile de Bourbon (USA)) [2002/3 F–: 16m   **c–**
19m³ 19gᶠ c16dᵘʳ 16s Jan 3] smallish, angular gelding: unseated fourth on chasing debut: **h65**
poor maiden hurdler: stays 19f: acts on good to firm going: races prominently. *N. A. Twiston-Davies*

SIMPLY BETTER 10 b.g. Roscoe Blake – Pure-Lite (Imperial Fling (USA)) [2002/3   **c–**
c21g May 1] ex-Irish gelding: modest form in bumpers: poor form over hurdles: sold out   **h–**
of A. Martin's stable IR £1,500 Fairyhouse November (2001) Sale: winning pointer: well beaten in maiden at Cheltenham in May on hunter chase debut. *Mrs G. M. Shail*

SIMPLY DA BEST (IRE) 5 b.g. Lake Coniston (IRE) – Sakala (NZ) (Gold And   **F98**
Ivory (USA)) [2002/3 F88: F16g⁶ F16g⁵ Apr 20] fairly useful form in bumpers, winning weak event in 2001/2: left S. Magnier after reappearance (tongue tied): fair form on Flat debut prior to good fifth to Royal Alphabet at Fairyhouse. *Mrs J. Harrington, Ireland*

SIMPLY REMY 5 ch.g. Chaddleworth (IRE) – Exemplaire (FR) (Polish Precedent   **h–**
(USA)) [2002/3 19g Apr 19] small gelding: modest maiden on Flat (stays 1¾m): well held in maiden at Stratford on hurdling debut. *John Berry*

SIMPLY SUPREME (IRE) 6 b.g. Supreme Leader – Some Gift (Avocat) [2002/3   **h125**
F100: 22s* 20s* 20v* 20s² 23d⁴ 24d⁴ Apr 4] leggy gelding: fairly useful novice hurdler: won at Kelso in November and Haydock later in month and in December: stiff task, ran well when 42 lengths fourth of 9 to Iris's Gift in Grade 1 at Aintree final start: stays 3m: acts on heavy going: usually front runner (refused to settle when held up fifth outing). *Mrs S. J. Smith*

SIMPLY THE ONE (IRE) 6 ch.g. Simply Great (FR) – Lady Mearlane (Giolla Mear)   **c–**
[2002/3 h78: 16d⁴ c24d² c19s⁵ c24gᶠ c21mᵖᵘ c26gᵖᵘ Apr 21] close-coupled gelding: poor   **h72**
form in novice hurdles: no form over fences (let down by jumping): tried blinkered. *Mrs H. Dalton*

SINALCO (USA) 5 b.g. Quest For Fame – Sin Lucha (USA) (Northfields (USA)) F–
[2002/3 F16v[6] F16d F16s[5] Mar 8] half-brother to several winners, including 1996 2-y-o
5f/6f winner Stygian (by Irish River) and fairly useful 1½m winner Summer Splendour
(by Summer Squal): dam unraced sister to top-class miler Northjet: well held in 3
bumpers. *Mrs L. B. Normile*

SINGING SAND 13 b.g. Orchestra – Noss Head (New Brig) [2002/3 c96, h–: c20m[5] **c95**
c17d[6] c17m[6] c16g[5] Sep 26] compact gelding: modest handicap chaser nowadays: raced **h–**
mainly around 2m: acts on any going: takes good hold. *P. Monteith*

SINGLE SOURCING (IRE) 12 b.g. Good Thyne (USA) – Lady Albron (Royal **c–**
Match) [2002/3 c93, h–: c25s[3] Mar 8] rangy gelding: modest handicap chaser: tailed off **h–**
only start in 2002/3 after 14-month absence: stays 3¾m: acts on heavy going: has
reportedly bled from nose. *A. C. Whillans*

SINGLE TRIGGER (IRE) 5 ch.m. Ela-Mana-Mou – Tycoon Aly (IRE) (Last F–
Tycoon) [2002/3 F16m F16m F16d F14g[6] Mar 17] second foal: half-sister to 11.5f winner
Chez Benito (by Persian Bold): dam third over 1m in Ireland on only start: poor form in
bumpers: visored third start, blinkered final one. *H. E. Haynes*

SINGOVERTHESEA 7 b.g. Sea Raven (IRE) – Pentland Beauty (Remainder Man) **h–**
[2002/3 16g[ur] Feb 22] fourth foal: half-brother to 2½m chase winner If Only (by Lightning Dealer): dam maiden, stayed 1m: unseated first in novice hurdle on debut: dead.
J. R. Jenkins

SING SOLO (IRE) 8 ch.g. Be My Native (USA) – Caesonia (Buckskin (FR)) [2002/3 **c– §**
c100§, h–: c19m c21f[2] Oct 10] tall gelding: maiden hurdler: won novice handicap in **h–**
2001/2, no other form over fences: stays 21f: acts on heavy going: temperamental and one
to leave alone: sold 1,050 gns Doncaster October Sales, no show in 2 points subsequently.
P. J. Hobbs

SINNERMAN (IRE) 7 gr.g. Roselier (FR) – Madam Beau (Le Tricolore) [2002/3 **h–**
21m Mar 21] IR 7,500 4-y-o: good-topped gelding: eleventh foal: dam ran once in points:
runner-up on second of 2 starts in maiden Irish points in 2002: bought 15,000 gns
(privately) Doncaster August Sales: in need of run, always behind in maiden on hurdling
debut. *C. J. Hemsley*

SIP OF BRANDY (IRE) 10 ch.g. Sharp Charter – Manhattan Brandy (Frankincense) **c93**
[2002/3 c24m* Apr 10] angular gelding: fair hunter chaser: won at Ludlow in April: stays
25f: acts on good to firm and heavy going: tried blinkered. *W. J. G. Hughes*

SIR ALBERT (GER) 4 b.c. Dashing Blade – Santa Augusta (Esclavo (FR)) [2002/3 **h104**
17s* 16d[2] 16s[5] 16s[3] Nov 1] German-trained colt: in frame up to 10.5f on Flat, won on
sand in November: created very good impression when winning juvenile at Market Rasen
on hurdling debut, not at all extended in beating Almnadia 8 lengths: raced in Germany
subsequently, placed at Bremen and Munich: raced around 2m on soft/good to soft going.
C. Von Der Recke, Germany

SIR ALFRED 4 b.g. Royal Academy (USA) – Magnificent Star (USA) (Silver Hawk **h94**
(USA)) [2002/3 16d[pu] 16g[5] 16f* 16m[4] Apr 12] leggy gelding: half-brother to winning
hurdler/chaser Profiler (by Capote), stays 2½m: fair on Flat (should stay 1½m) for
B. R. Millman: best effort over hurdles when winning juvenile at Haydock in March,
leading close home under patient ride: finished distressed when well beaten final start:
will prove best with emphasis on speed around 2m: has been early to post: excitable sort.
A. King

SIR BOB (IRE) 11 br.g. Aristocracy – Wilden (Will Somers) [2002/3 c110x, h–: **c112**
c26d[pu] c24s[2] c23g[3] Feb 25] tall gelding: fair chaser: left K. Bailey and off 9 months, **h–**
creditable placed efforts in handicaps last 2 starts: should stay beyond 3m: raced on good
going or softer (acts on heavy): blinkered on reappearance: often none too fluent: lazy.
Mrs H. Dalton

SIR CUMFERENCE 7 b.g. Sir Harry Lewis (USA) – Puki Puki (Roselier (FR)) **c94**
[2002/3 c23d[6] c24d[pu] c24s[5] c24m* c24g* Apr 19] rangy gelding: second foal: dam, winning pointer, out of half-sister to useful staying jumpers Bective Road and Sommelier:
won twice from 5 runs in points in 2002: improved form in steeplechases in handicaps
last 2 starts, winning at Ludlow (novice) and Stratford: will prove best at 3m+: acts on
good to firm going. *Miss H. C. Knight*

SIR EDWARD BURROW (IRE) 5 b.g. Distinctly North (USA) – Alalja (IRE) **h85 +**
(Entitled) [2002/3 h89: 19d[pu] 16d[6] 20d[F] Mar 15] strong, good-topped gelding: modest
maiden hurdler: running easily best race in 2002/3 when falling 3 out in novice handicap
at Newcastle final start: likely to stay 2½m. *W. Storey*

SIRERIC (IRE) 13 b.g. Asir – Twice Regal (Royal Prerogative) [2002/3 c91, h–: c27g² c30d c27v⁵ c30d⁴ 27s* c27v* c24v² 27v⁴ c24v* 24s² 24d² 24d Mar 15] leggy, angular gelding: modest handicap hurdler/chaser: had good season, won over hurdles and fences at Sedgefield in December and over fences at Newcastle in January: stays 4m: acts well on soft/heavy going: front runner: tough. *R. Johnson* **c97 h98**

SIR FROSTY 10 b.g. Arctic Lord – Snowy Autumn (Deep Run) [2002/3 c112: c32d* c33v* c33mᵘʳ Apr 12] lengthy gelding: successful 4 times from 7 starts in steeplechases, including handicaps at Exeter in December and Cheltenham (beat Polar Champ a neck in quite valuable event) in January: stays 33f: acts on heavy going: tongue tied. *B. J. M. Ryall* **c123**

SIR HAMELIN (IRE) 6 b.g. Hernando (FR) – Georgia Stephens (USA) (The Minstrel (CAN)) [2002/3 h83: 20mᵖᵘ Jul 17] lengthy, useful-looking gelding: off a year, well held in selling handicap only start in 2002/3: visored and tongue tied most appearances: possibly none too genuine. *M. C. Pipe* **h–**

SIR HENBUE 7 ch.g. Henbit (USA) – Owena Deep (Deep Run) [2002/3 F66: F16g 21gᵖᵘ Mar 3] big, lengthy gelding: signs of only a little ability. *Mark Campion* **h– F–**

SIR HOMO (IRE) 9 b.g. Homo Sapien – Deise Lady (Le Bavard (FR)) [2002/3 h–: 21sᵖᵘ 17v Dec 26] no form for long time: tried blinkered. *E. W. Tuer* **h–**

SIRINNDI (IRE) 9 b.g. Shahrastani (USA) – Sinntara (IRE) (Lashkari) [2002/3 c–, h–: 16vᵖᵘ 20s³ 16v⁶ Feb 4] small gelding: no show on chasing debut: poor hurdler: stays 21f: acts on heavy going: has had tongue tied: inconsistent. *Miss K. Marks* **c– h65**

SIR LAMB 7 gr.g. Rambo Dancer (CAN) – Caroline Lamb (Hotfoot) [2002/3 h83, F–: 20m* Jun 1] strong gelding: visored, best effort over hurdles when winning novice at Hexham only start in 2002/3: stays 2½m: acts on good to firm going, probably on soft. *Miss S. E. Hall* **h98**

SIR MOUSE 7 gr.g. Phardante (FR) – Place Stephanie (IRE) (Hatim (USA)) [2002/3 h81: 20v³ 24mᵖᵘ Mar 21] sturdy gelding: best effort over hurdles when third in maiden at Fontwell on return from 16-month absence: soon struggling on very different ground 3 weeks later: bred to stay beyond 2½m. *R. Rowe* **h92**

SIR NINJA (IRE) 6 b.g. Turtle Island (IRE) – The Poachers Lady (IRE) (Salmon Leap (USA)) [2002/3 h90: c16f⁵ c16s⁵ May 28] modest maiden hurdler: showed little in 2 runs over fences, jumping badly on second occasion: subsequently placed once from 5 starts on Flat for S. Kirk: likely to prove best around 2m: pulled too hard only try in blinkers. *G. Brown* **c– h–**

SIR NORMAN 8 b.g. Arctic Lord – Moy Ran Lady (Black Minstrel) [2002/3 h–, F–: c25m⁵ c23m⁵ c21d* c20s² c20s² c16d³ c16m² Apr 21] tall gelding: maiden hurdler: modest novice chaser: made all in handicap at Ayr in November: placed all 4 subsequent starts: best up to 21f: acts on soft and good to firm going: usually tongue tied: front runner: bold jumper. *R. D. E. Woodhouse* **c98 h–**

SIR PELINORE 8 b.g. Caerleon (USA) – Soemba (General Assembly (USA)) [2002/3 F–: 24dᵖᵘ 16gᵇᵈ 20g Mar 2] no sign of ability: has had tongue tied. *Mrs A. M. Woodrow* **h– F–**

SIR REMBRANDT (IRE) 7 b.g. Mandalus – Sue's A Lady (Le Moss) [2002/3 h122p, F94: c22d* c25d* Dec 13] **c138 p h–**

A promising season in novice chases was cut short for Sir Rembrandt, his campaign curtailed prematurely by heat in a foreleg. His second race—in which his injury was probably sustained—established him as a useful novice. Sent off the 7/2 second favourite for the Ian Williams' Owners Novices' Chase at Cheltenham in December (a race awarded Grade 2 status as a result of the loss of a similar event at Lingfield), Sir Rembrandt upset the favourite It Takes Time, a very smart hurdler making his steeplechasing debut. In a field of seven, only the two mattered in the closing stages, Sir Rembrandt putting the seal on a round of sound jumping with a superb leap at the final fence and battling splendidly to hold off It Takes Time by half a length, with The Villager twenty-three lengths back in third. Sir Rembrandt was second favourite on the strength of his winning debut over fences in a novice at Newbury a month earlier when, caught flat-footed in a race run at an unsuitably steady pace most of the way, he stayed on strongly to prevail in a close finish also involving Ask Henry, Young Ottoman and Haut Cercy, the quartet separated by little more than half a length at the line.

Ian Williams' Owners Novices' Chase, Cheltenham—
Sir Rembrandt (right) looks a smart prospect as he touches off chase debutant It Takes Time

The big, strong, lengthy Sir Rembrandt is the fourth foal of the Irish bumper winner Sue's A Lady, her only other winner being the stayer Audacter (by Strong Gale), a useful hurdler in his prime who showed fairly useful form in handicap chases in the latest season before suffering a fatal fall at Folkestone four days after Sir Rembrandt's Cheltenham success. Sir Rembrandt, who is expected to return to action in the autumn, is essentially a stayer and will prove best at three miles and upwards. He has raced only on good and good to soft going so far and, when his stamina is brought more into play, should be capable of showing smart form at least. *R. H. Alner*

SIR RISKY (IRE) 10 b.g. Treasure Kay – Social Butterfly (USA) (Sir Ivor) [2002/3 c16m⁴ c17m⁶ c16g c17mᶠ 17f³ 19fⁱ⁴ c16fⁱ⁴ Oct 24] ex-Irish gelding: third foal: dam never ran: poor hurdler/maiden chaser, trained in 2001/2 by W. Burke: best around 2m: acts on soft and firm going: has had tongue tied. *B. J. Llewellyn*   **c73 h67**

SIR ROBBO (IRE) 9 b.g. Glacial Storm (USA) – Polly's Slipper (Pollerton) [2002/3 c92, h–: c25gᵍ c25dᵖᵘ May 14] workmanlike gelding: modest chaser: has gained all 4 wins at Hereford, including in handicap in May: ran poorly there later in month, not seen out again: stays 3¼m: acts on good to firm and good to soft going (pulled up feelingly only start on firm). *N. A. Twiston-Davies*   **c92 h–**

SIR ROWLAND HILL (IRE) 4 b.g. Kahyasi – Zaila (IRE) (Darshaan) [2002/3 F16g² F16g* Apr 14] sturdy gelding: fifth foal: brother to smart French middle-distance performer Zainta and half-brother to fairly useful but temperamental hurdler Zahari (by Shernazar), stays 21f, and 9f winner Zainabi (by Thatching): dam, French 10.5f and 11f winner, granddaughter of Petite Etoile: second in bumper at Wetherby on debut: showed   **F89**

good attitude to win maiden at Hexham following month, patiently ridden and leading close home when beating Duringthenight a neck. *Ferdy Murphy*

SIR RUSCOTT (IRE) 9 b.g. Mister Lord (USA) – Clash Moss (Le Moss) [2002/3 h91: 25g 24d* 27s 24v⁵ 24d⁵ 24v⁶ Mar 13] lengthy gelding: pulled up in 2 points in 2000: modest handicap hurdler: 25/1 and ridden in spurs, won weakly-contested event at Leicester in November despite again looking far from easy ride (idled): best at 3m+: acts on soft going: visored: one to treat with caution. *J. R. Norton*   **h87 §**

SIR STORM (IRE) 7 b.g. Ore – Yonder Bay (IRE) (Trimmingham) [2002/3 h108, F71: c17s² c16v* c20d² c16d³ c16v² c16v³ c16d⁵ Feb 26] lengthy gelding: fair hurdler: fair novice chaser: won handicap at Wetherby in November: stays 19f: raced on good going or softer (acts on heavy): sound jumper. *G. M. Moore*   **c108 h–**

SIR TOBY (IRE) 10 bl.g. Strong Gale – Cure The Blues (USA)) [2002/3 c101, h–: c20m* c20d* c20g* c20d⁴ Dec 27] rangy gelding: fair chaser: better than ever in 2002/3, winning novices at Huntingdon (handicap) in October and Kempton (made all to beat Ibis Rochelais a neck) in November and handicap at Leicester (beat Ifni du Luc a short head, pair clear) later in November: ran badly final start: likely to prove best short of 3m: acts on good to firm and good to soft going: usually sound jumper. *R. Rowe*   **c112 h–**

SIR VALENTINE (IRE) 9 b.g. Be My Native (USA) – Tumvella (Tumble Wind (USA)) [2002/3 c92, h–: c30dᵘʳ c32d c26s³ Dec 26] modest handicap chaser in 2001/2: below best on return: stays 3½m: acts on good to firm and heavy going: has worn cheek-pieces. *R. Rowe*   **c82 h–**

SIR WALTER (IRE) 10 b.g. The Bart (USA) – Glenbalda (Kambalda) [2002/3 c–, h97: c16m⁶ c16g² c17m⁴ 20s Jun 9] leggy gelding: modest hurdler: less than fluent and below that form in steeplechases: pulled up in 3 points in March and April: stays 19f: acts on good to firm and heavy going: effective tongue tied or not: held up: used to find little/look ungenuine. *A. G. Hobbs*   **c73 h–**

SIR WILLIAMWALLACE (IRE) 10 br.g. Strong Gale – Kemchee (Kemal (FR)) [2002/3 c–, h–: c25gᵖᵘ c20m c23m⁶ c25g³ c23m c26m⁴ c19m⁵ c24m² c25mᵖᵘ c26m² c19d⁶ c28dᵖᵘ Oct 31] lengthy gelding: poor handicap chaser: won point in April: stays 3¼m: acts on firm and good to soft going: sometimes wears headgear: has had tongue tied: reportedly bled from nose on reappearance: has hinted at temperament. *J. G. M. O'Shea*   **c77 d h–**

SISSINGHURST STAR (IRE) 8 b.g. Moscow Society (USA) – Raplist (Arapaho) [2002/3 c–, h–: c16f³ c16m⁵ c16mᵖᵘ c21mᵖᵘ 24m⁵ Aug 27] leggy gelding: poor maiden hurdler/chaser, little worthwhile form since 1999/0: won maiden point in February: raced mainly at 2m: acts on firm and soft going: blinkered/visored: far from fluent over fences. *R. Dickin*   **c– h–**

SISSINGHURST STORM (IRE) 5 b. or br.m. Good Thyne (USA) – Mrs Hill (Strong Gale) [2002/3 F17d 22g³ Apr 12] 10,000 4-y-o: sixth foal: half-sister to fair chaser Wap (by Be My Native), stays 3m: dam unraced half-sister to useful staying jumpers Sommelier and Bective Road and to dam of useful staying jumper Coq Hardi Affair: well held in maiden bumper on debut: poor form when third in novice hurdle at Stratford: will stay 3m. *R. Dickin*   **h69 F–**

SISTER AMY 6 gr.m. Gods Solution – Amys Sister (Silly Prices) [2002/3 F16g F16g Apr 14] first foal: dam never ran: refused in point: achieved little in 2 bumpers. *J. R. Turner*   **F–**

SISTER ANNA 5 br.m. Gildoran – Take The Veil (Monksfield) [2002/3 F16d² F17g 16d⁶ Apr 9] fifth foal: half-sister to fair pointer Flying Veil (by Neltino): dam, showed no aptitude for jumping, half-sister to dam of very smart staying chaser Party Politics: runner-up on first of 2 starts in bumpers: poor form in novice on hurdling debut: likely to be suited by further than 2m. *T. D. Walford*   **h66 F77**

SISTER CHARLOTTE 8 ch.m. Gildoran – Sharlinda (Deep Run) [2002/3 h–, F–: 22gᵖᵘ May 17] lengthy mare: no sign of ability. *J. C. Tuck*   **h– F–**

SISTER SUPERIOR (IRE) 8 b.m. Supreme Leader – Nicat (Wolver Hollow) [2002/3 h92§: 19d² 20v² 20d⁵ 20s c19d³ c21sᵖᵘ c25g⁵ Mar 29] good-topped mare: modest handicap hurdler: no worthwhile form in 3 novice chases: stays 2¾m: acts on heavy going (bumper form on firm): hard ride (needs plenty of driving). *S. Gollings*   **c– h92 §**

SISTER VALENTHYNE (IRE) 6 ch.m. Good Thyne (USA) – Coteri Run (Deep Run) [2002/3 F–: F17d³ Oct 12] unfurnished mare: signs of more temperament than ability in 3 mares bumpers, distant third only start in 2002/3: sold 5,000 gns Doncaster November Sales. *S. Gollings*   **F–**

attheraces.co.uk Handicap Chase, Sandown—Skycab (striped sleeves) overhauls Devon View to provide trainer Josh Gifford with a rousing last winner with his last runner

SIX CLERKS (IRE) 10 b.g. Shadeed (USA) – Skidmore Girl (USA) (Vaguely Noble) [2002/3 c83, h–: c16g² c22d c24spu c19gpu Apr 2] leggy gelding: modest hunter chaser, pulled up both starts in 2003: effective at 2m to 3m: acts on firm and good to soft going: blinkered once, visored nowadays: has looked ungenuine. *Mrs S. M. Odell*   **c81 h–**

SIX OF ONE 5 b.g. Kahyasi – Ten To Six (Night Shift (USA)) [2002/3 17v⁶ 21m⁶ 20v⁶ 16g Mar 25] useful-looking ex-French gelding: successful twice up to 14.5f on Flat at 4 yrs, sold out of E. Danel's stable €68,000 Goffs November Sale: poor form in novice hurdles: reported to have bled from nose when tailed off final start. *R. Rowe*   **h83**

SIXO (IRE) 6 gr.g. Roselier (FR) – Miss Mangaroo (Oats) [2002/3 F17v* F16s* F16g³ Feb 8] 15,000 4-y-o: leggy gelding: third foal: dam, winning 2½m hurdler, from family of top-class hurdler/chaser Celtic Shot: created good impression when winning bumpers at Newton Abbot in November and Newbury in December, making all when beating King Player 8 lengths in latter: creditable third to Cornish Rebel in Grade 2 at latter course final start: front runner: will stay at least 2½m. *M. C. Pipe*   **F114**

SIX PACK (IRE) 5 ch.g. Royal Abjar (USA) – Regal Entrance (Be My Guest (USA)) [2002/3 17m⁵ 16v Nov 28] good-topped gelding: half-brother to 2 winning 2m hurdlers: fair on Flat (stays 1m): well held in 2 novice hurdles. *Andrew Turnell*   **h–**

SKENFRITH 4 b.g. Atraf – Hobbs Choice (Superpower) [2002/3 16d 16g 16d³ 17d 20g² Apr 21] modest maiden on Flat, well beaten both starts in 2002 for A. Berry: upped in trip, best effort over hurdles when second in weak novice at Carlisle final start. *Miss S. E. Forster*   **h86**

SKIBB (IRE) 6 b.g. Be My Native (USA) – Inch Lady (Bulldozer) [2002/3 17d³ 16s 18s* 16s⁴ 16d⁴ 20s³ 20g⁴ Apr 3] rangy gelding: chasing type: second foal: dam fairly useful chaser, stayed 3m: poor form only start in bumper: fair hurdler: won 24-runner minor event at Punchestown in January: stays 2½m: acts on soft ground. *M. F. Morris, Ireland*   **h108**

SKIDDAW GALE 9 b.g. Strong Gale – Whimbrel (Dara Monarch) [2002/3 c–, h–: c20mpu c16d⁵ Jun 4] of little account: tried blinkered/tongue tied. *M. A. Barnes*   **c– h–**

SKIDDAW ROSE (IRE) 7 gr.m. Terimon – Whimbrel (Dara Monarch) [2002/3 h–, F–: 16m⁴ 16m⁴ 17g 16g³ 17m 16g³ 17d 16g Nov 23] small mare: poor maiden hurdler: form only around 2m: best efforts on good ground: makes mistakes. *M. A. Barnes*   **h66 x**

SKILLWISE 11 b.g. Buckley – Calametta (Oats) [2002/3 c121§, h–: c25d^{pu} c25d^{pu} c24d^5 c27d^6 c26s^5 Dec 14] big, workmanlike gelding: handicap chaser: well below form in 2002/3: stays 3¼m: acts on good to firm and heavy going: sometimes finds little: sold 6,000 gns Doncaster May Sales. *T. D. Easterby* **c– §** **h–**

SKINSEY FINNEGAN (IRE) 9 b.g. Fresh Breeze (USA) – Rose of Solway (Derring Rose) [2002/3 c16g^3 c19s^4 c21d^3 c16d^2 c16s^2 c16v^5 c16m^4 c17m^2 c18f^3 Apr 24] lengthy gelding: fair chaser: won novice handicap at Folkestone in December: probably best around 2m: acts on soft and good to firm going: tongue tied after third start: has been led in: has failed to impress with attitude. *C. A. Dwyer* **c104**

SKIORA 6 br.m. Petoski – Coral Delight (Idiot's Delight) [2002/3 F–: F16m^3 16d^{ur} 16d 16g^4 17s^{pu} Apr 19] leggy, angular mare: much better effort in bumpers when third at Worcester in May: showed more temperament than ability over hurdles: reportedly broke blood vessel when blinkered final start: one to treat with caution. *A. J. Wilson* **h– §** **F79**

SKIPMANTOO (IRE) 8 ch.g. Pips Pride – Sports Post Lady (IRE) (M Double M (USA)) [2002/3 F–: 17s^{pu} Dec 18] workmanlike gelding: well beaten on completed outing in bumpers (whipped round and unseated start on debut): showed nothing on hurdling debut (tongue tied): most unlikely to stay 2m. *Miss C. Dyson* **h–**

SKIPPERS CLEUCH (IRE) 9 b.g. Be My Native (USA) – Cloughoola Lady (Black Minstrel) [2002/3 c22v* c20s* c20v^{ur} c24g Mar 11] big, good-topped gelding: useful hurdler: missed 2001/2 (reportedly had operation on spine): won novice chases in small fields in workmanlike style at Kelso in November and Wetherby in December: unseated tenth in handicap at Ayr third start, weakened quickly after blunder 3 out when tailed off in strongly-contested amateur handicap at Cheltenham final one: should stay beyond 2¾m: raced on good going or softer (acts on heavy): has room for improvement in his jumping. *L. Lungo* **c109** **h–**

SKRAM 10 b.g. Rambo Dancer (CAN) – Skarberg (FR) (Noir Et Or) [2002/3 c104, h–: c20g^5 c20g^{pu} May 22] leggy gelding: winning hurdler: fair handicap chaser in 2001/2: twice ran poorly in May: lame on second occasion: stays 2¾m: acts on any going: ran respectably only start in blinkers: has had tongue tied: usually races prominently: none too consistent. *R. Dickin* **c–** **h–**

SKYCAB (IRE) 11 b.g. Montelimar (USA) – Sams Money (Pry) [2002/3 c118, h–: c20d^3 c19v^3 c24d* c24s^{pu} c25d^3 c20g* c20m* Apr 26] useful-looking gelding: useful handicap chaser: won at Fakenham (made all) in December and Stratford and Sandown in April, beating Devon View 2 lengths in quite valuable event at last-named course (looked extremely well): effective at 2½m to 25f: acts on soft and good to firm going: usually races prominently. *J. T. Gifford* **c130** **h–**

SKYLANDER 7 b.g. Thethingaboutitis (USA) – Mesembryanthemum (Warpath) [2002/3 F–: F18g^6 17m^5 Jun 4] good-bodied gelding: much better effort in bumpers when sixth at Plumpton very early in season: remote fifth in novice on hurdling debut: races freely and looks a difficult ride: joined Mrs M. Jones. *B. J. Llewellyn* **h–** **F76**

SKYLARKER (USA) 5 b.g. Sky Classic (CAN) – O My Darling (USA) (Mr Prospector (USA)) [2002/3 17v^5 16d^5 Mar 19] fairly useful on Flat (stays 1½m), sold out of C. Wall's stable 14,000 gns Newmarket Autumn Sales: poor form when fifth in novice hurdles at Taunton and Chepstow, taking very strong hold at latter course: should be capable of better. *W. S. Kittow* **h74 p**

SKY TO SEA (FR) 5 b.g. Adieu Au Roi (IRE) – Urban Sky (FR) (Groom Dancer (USA)) [2002/3 16m^2 Dec 17] fairly useful on Flat (stays 1¼m), successful in late-October: second to Altay in novice at Musselburgh on hurdling debut, running on without matching speed of winner: should improve. *M. J. Grassick, Ireland* **h105 p**

SLANEY FOX (IRE) 6 b.m. Foxhound (USA) – Mean To Me (Homing) [2002/3 F16s F16g^2 16m^3 16g 16g^5 16d Nov 16] smallish mare: half-sister to smart hurdler/chaser Slaney Native (by Be My Native), effective at 2½m to 3m: dam lightly-raced maiden on Flat: fair in bumpers, won mares event at Tralee in August: modest form over hurdles: raced at 2m: acts on good to firm going. *Mrs J. Harrington, Ireland* **h92** **F89**

SLASHER JACK (IRE) 12 b.g. Alzao (USA) – Sherkraine (Shergar) [2002/3 c64, h–: c17d^5 c25g^{pu} May 11] smallish gelding: winning hurdler: poor maiden chaser: no show in 2 novices in May: tried tongue tied. *Mrs D. Thomson* **c–** **h–**

SLEDMERE (IRE) 8 ch.g. Shalford (IRE) – Jazirah (Main Reef) [2002/3 c–, h–: c25d^{ur} c20m^{ur} May 16] winning pointer, little form otherwise: has had tongue tied. *George R. Moscrop* **c–** **h–**

SLEEPING MUSIC (FR) 6 b.g. Sleeping Car (FR) – Music Sobre (FR) (Crowned c–
Music (USA)) [2002/3 c?, h–: c16m⁴ c21m^pu c22m^pu 20g⁶ Oct 9] maiden hurdler/chaser: h–
little worthwhile form in Britain: usually blinkered. *J. R. Best*

SLEEPY RIVER (IRE) 12 ch.g. Over The River (FR) – Shreelane (Laurence O) **c87 d**
[2002/3 c95, h–: c24d³ c24m^F c24d^pu c28g^pu Mar 25] compact gelding: modest handicap h–
chaser: no show both outings after 10-month absence: stays 3½m: acts on heavy going.
Miss Kate Milligan

SLEEPYTIME TIM 7 b.g. Henbit (USA) – Cloncoose (IRE) (Remainder Man) F–
[2002/3 F–: F16g F16m^pu Jul 4] lengthy gelding: no show in 3 bumpers: seemingly amiss
when tongue tied final outing: very unruly going down when withdrawn second intended
start. *J. A. Moore*

SLEETING 10 ch.g. Lycius (USA) – Pluvial (Habat) [2002/3 c60, h78d: c21m c16m^pu c–
17g 22f² 21m² 24f⁴ Oct 24] compact gelding: poor handicap hurdler/maiden chaser: stays h62
2¾m: acts on firm and good to soft going: tried visored: not an easy ride. *J. Gallagher*

SLEIGHT 4 ch.f. Bob's Return (IRE) – Jolejester (Relkino) [2002/3 F16d⁴ F16m⁴ Mar F80
23] seventh foal: half-sister to winning pointer Oh So Droll (by Teenoso): dam, bumper
winner, half-sister to winning 2m hurdlers State Jester and Simenon: modest form when
fourth in mares maiden bumpers at Warwick and Huntingdon. *W. Jenks*

SLEIGHT OF HAND (IRE) 10 b.g. Hollow Hand – Marand (Damsire Unknown) c–
[2002/3 c–, h–: c20m^F c20d^pu c23g⁵ c19d⁵ 20g Feb 22] lengthy gelding: of little account h–
nowadays: has had tongue tied. *J. S. King*

SLEWMORE (IRE) 12 br.g. Mister Majestic – Lola's Pet (Ahonoora) [2002/3 c20f⁵ c69
c19m³ c17d⁶ c16f³ c19m Apr 21] angular ex-Irish gelding: winning hurdler: poor chaser: h–
left Mrs D. Hamer before final start: stays 2½m, at least when conditions aren't testing:
acts on firm and soft going: tried blinkered: has had tongue tied. *Richard Mathias*

SLIEMA CREEK 9 gr.g. Beveled (USA) – Sea Farer Lake (Gairloch) [2002/3 c–, c–
h–: c25d^pu May 4] leggy gelding: winning hurdler/chaser: of little account nowadays: h–
sometimes blinkered. *V. Thompson*

SLIEMA (IRE) 5 b.g. Desert Style (IRE) – Ascoli (Skyliner) [2002/3 F75: 17f May h–
15] signs of only a little ability in bumpers: well held on hurdling debut: subsequently
pulled up in 2 points: unlikely to stay 2m. *O. Sherwood*

SLINGSHOT 7 b.g. Seymour Hicks (FR) – Flower of Tintern (Free State) [2002/3 h–
F16v F16s 19d^pu Feb 23] 15,000 4-y-o: sturdy gelding: fourth foal: brother to winning F–
pointer: dam winning 2m hurdler/fairly useful up to 1¼m on Flat: no sign of ability.
M. G. Rimell

SLIP AWAY 10 gr.g. Jumbo Hirt (USA) – Au Pair (Runnymede) [2002/3 c–: c26d⁴ c–
c25m⁵ 27m c27m⁵ Jul 25] good-topped gelding: winning pointer: little worthwhile form h–
otherwise: tried blinkered. *Ms Liz Harrison*

SLIP THE NET (IRE) 9 b.g. Slip Anchor – Circus Ring (High Top) [2002/3 19s⁶ h–
Dec 6] compact gelding: runner-up once from 5 outings in maiden points in 2002: bought
£1,600 Ascot August Sales: signs of only a little ability in 4 starts over hurdles.
M. J. Weeden

SLIP THE RING 9 ch.g. Belmez (USA) – Sixslip (USA) (Diesis) [2002/3 h72: c20d^F c–
c26g^pu Apr 21] compact gelding: poor maiden hurdler: winning pointer, no show in 2 h–
handicap chases: stays 3m: acts on soft going. *Miss K. Marks*

SLOANE STREET (FR) 4 b.g. Sadler's Wells (USA) – Shy Danceuse (FR) (Groom h77
Dancer (USA)) [2002/3 16m^F 16d^pu 16d 16s 17v⁵ 16g³ 16g² 20m Apr 12] close-coupled
gelding: thrice-raced on Flat, leaving A. Fabre after runner-up around 1¼m in June: poor
juvenile hurdler: best around 2m: acts on heavy going: visored fourth start: sometimes
none too fluent. *D. J. Caro*

SLOOGHY (FR) 7 br.g. Missolonghi (USA) – Lady Charrecey (FR) (Fin Bon) h123
[2002/3 h–: 21d³ 22s² 22s² 22v² 24g* 24d^hd Mar 1] good-topped gelding: fairly useful hurdler:
improved form when winning handicap at Newbury in February by neck from Ravenswood, pair clear: seems better at 3m than shorter: raced on good going or softer.
N. J. Henderson

SMALL SHOTS 6 br.g. Roselier (FR) – My Adventure (IRE) (Strong Gale) [2002/3 h–
19g Dec 13] IR £5,400 4-y-o: smallish, leggy gelding: first foal: dam modest staying

hurdler: won maiden Irish point on debut in 2002: ninth of 16 in novice at Doncaster on hurdling debut. *C. R. Egerton*

SMART GUY　11 ch.g. Gildoran – Talahache Bridge (New Brig) [2002/3 c71, h–: c21g^pu c19g^pu c24g^5 c21d^F c18d^ro c22d^6 c20s* c20s^pu c22s^2 c16d^pu c20g^3 c24g c20m^pu c18f^2 Apr 24] workmanlike gelding: poor handicap chaser: won at Fontwell in December: stays 3m: acts on any going: usually wears cheekpieces: prone to mistakes: unreliable. *Mrs L. C. Jewell*　**c72 §** **h–**

SMART LORD　12 br.g. Arctic Lord – Lady Catcher (Free Boy) [2002/3 c68, h–: 20g 17d^5 17s^5 c16d^4 Dec 12] angular gelding: poor maiden hurdler/chaser: stays 21f: acts on firm and soft going: visored last 2 starts: effective tongue tied or not. *M. R. Bosley*　**c64** **h61**

SMART PLAY (USA)　10 gr.g. Sovereign Dancer (USA) – Casessa (USA) (Caro) [2002/3 21g^pu Oct 21] useful on Flat (stays 1½m) at 3 yrs, left Lord Huntingdon after showing little at 4 yrs: no show on belated hurdling debut. *A. J. Lidderdale*　**h–**

SMART SQUALL (USA)　8 b.h. Summer Squall (USA) – Greek Wedding (USA) (Blushing Groom (FR)) [2002/3 19d 24s^pu Jan 28] smallish horse: maiden hurdler, no show either start in 2002/3: stays 19f. *A. J. Lidderdale*　**h–**

SMARTY (IRE)　10 b. or br.g. Royal Fountain – Cahernane Girl (Bargello) [2002/3 c129, h101: c31d c27d^5 Nov 24] tall, close-coupled gelding: winning hurdler: one-time useful handicap chaser, well below form since second in Becher Chase at Aintree in 2001/2: stays 3½m: acts on heavy and good to firm going: often blinkered, also tried in visor/cheekpieces: sound jumper. *M. Pitman*　**c–** **h–**

SMASHING TIME (USA)　5 b.m. Smart Strike (CAN) – Broken Peace (USA) (Devil's Bag (USA)) [2002/3 17g^pu 17g Mar 29] poor maiden on Flat (stays 1m): no show in 2 novice hurdles. *M. C. Chapman*　**h–**

SMETHERDS TOM　9 b.g. Dortino – Nellie's Joy VII (Damsire Unregistered) [2002/3 c16s^6 c22s^ur c20v^pu c16s^pu c19f^3 c16g Apr 21] workmanlike gelding: poor maiden pointer: has worn cheekpieces. *N. R. Mitchell*　**c–**

SMILE PLEEZE (IRE)　11 b.g. Naheez (USA) – Harkin Park (Pollerton) [2002/3 c97§, h–: c25g^4 May 1] fair hunter chaser: won point in April: probably stays 3¼m: acts on soft going: usually gets behind: one to treat with caution. *M. R. Daniell*　**c86 §** **h–**

SMILING THRU　11 b.g. Reference Point – Ever Genial (Brigadier Gerard) [2002/3 h–: c26d^pu c24m^pu Sep 29] lengthy gelding: poor maiden pointer. *P. Grindey*　**c–** **h–**

SMITHS LANDING　6 b.g. Primitive Rising (USA) – Landing Power (Hill's Forecast) [2002/3 F16d^6 19d^4 16v^6 19d^4 20d^5 20g* 20m^2 Apr 21] medium-sized gelding: half-brother to fair hurdler around 2m Willy Star (by Minstrel Star): dam won twice in Belgium: sixth in bumper on debut: fair novice hurdler: improved form when winning handicap at Hexham in March: good second to Gastornis at Wetherby final outing: will stay beyond 2½m: acts on good to firm and good to soft going. *Mrs S. J. Smith*　**h112** **F83**

SMITH'S PERK (IRE)　10 b.g. Executive Perk – Sister of Slane (The Parson) [2002/3 21v^5 20s^pu c25g^pu c20m^6 Mar 23] tall gelding: bumper winner: largely very disappointing over hurdles/fences: tongue tied. *Mrs L. C. Jewell*　**c–** **h–**

SMITHS WYND　11 gr.g. Alias Smith (USA) – Carrapateira (Gunner B) [2002/3 c20d^2 c20m Jun 1] modest maiden pointer/hunter chaser: probably stays 3m: acts on good to firm and good to soft going. *R. Shiels*　**c75**

SMOKESTACK (IRE)　7 b.g. Lord Americo – Chiminee Fly (Proverb) [2002/3 h86?, F76: 16s^3 22g Mar 18] sturdy gelding: modest maiden hurdler: should prove better around 2½m than 2m: acts on soft going. *J. A. B. Old*　**h94 ?**

SMOOTH PASSAGE　4 b.g. Suave Dancer (USA) – Flagship (Rainbow Quest (USA)) [2002/3 16d Mar 10] poor maiden on Flat (seems to stay easy 1¼m): well held in juvenile on hurdling debut. *J. Gallagher*　**h–**

SMOOTH SAILING　8 gr.g. Beveled (USA) – Sea Farer Lake (Gairloch) [2002/3 h97: 16m^2 16g^2 May 22] leggy gelding: fairly useful at best up to 1¼m on Flat: modest hurdler: best around 2m with emphasis on speed: acted on soft and good to firm going: dead. *K. McAuliffe*　**h99**

SMUDGE (IRE)　6 br.g. Be My Native (USA) – Crash Call (Crash Course) [2002/3 F–: 16d^pu 19d 16d^6 Dec 14] well held in bumper: 66/1, easily best effort over hurdles　**h93**

when never-nearer sixth of 12 finishers in novice at Haydock: bred to be suited by further than 2m. *R. Ford*

SMUGGLER'S SONG (IRE)   4 b.g. Dr Devious (IRE) – Liberty Song (IRE) (Last   **h117** Tycoon) [2002/3 16s⁵ 16s* Feb 8] well-made gelding: useful on Flat (stays 1½m) for C. O'Brien: jumped more fluently than on hurdling debut when winning 24-runner juvenile maiden at Naas, getting back up to beat irresolute Statim by neck: again favourite, only sixth of 20 in 4-y-o novice at Punchestown in late-April. *C. Roche, Ireland*

SMYSLOV   5 b.g. Rainbow Quest (USA) – Vlaanderen (IRE) (In The Wings) [2002/3   **h–** h89: 16m Jun 30] fairly useful on Flat (stays 1½m) at 3 yrs for J. Dunlop: modest form in juvenile hurdles: visored, well held on handicap debut. *P. R. Webber*

SNAILS CASTLE (IRE)   4 b.g. Danehill (USA) – Bean Island (USA) (Afleet (CAN))   **h86** [2002/3 16g 16m³ Oct 6] fair maiden at 2 yrs, well held on Flat in 2002: better effort in juvenile hurdles when third to stable-companion Lady Stratagem at Kelso: looked open to further improvement, but not seen out again. *E. W. Tuer*

SNAKE GODDESS   5 b.m. Primo Dominie – Shoshone (Be My Chief (USA)) [2002/3   **h–** h–: 20dᵖᵘ May 23] maiden on Flat, well held in 2002: no form over hurdles: has worn hood and blinkers/visor. *D. W. P. Arbuthnot*

SNAPPER   12 b.g. Gunner B – Fortalice (Saucy Kit) [2002/3 c–, h–: 22g⁵ 24m* c24d⁴   **c–** Jun 7] workmanlike gelding: winning chaser, retains little ability: very lucky to win 4-   **h60 ?** finisher intermediate hurdle at Perth in May, off bridle in rear 4 out then left second when clear leader was carried out last: reportedly lame following month: stays 29f: acts on good to firm and heavy going: usually blinkered. *Mrs L. B. Normile*

SNIPE   5 ch.g. Anshan – Flexwing (Electric) [2002/3 F16s F16m⁴ Mar 22] lengthy,   **F87** angular gelding: first foal: dam modest form in bumpers: better effort in bumpers when 6¾ lengths fourth of 18 to Yardbird at Newbury. *G. A. Butler*

SNIPER   11 ch.g. Gunner B – Highfrith (Deep Run) [2002/3 c72§, h–§: c27gᵖᵘ c21d³   **c69 §** c27d c25v⁵ c25gᵖᵘ Mar 29] close-coupled gelding: poor handicap chaser: stays 27f: acts   **h– §** on heavy going: tried blinkered/tongue tied: has bled from nose: moody and unreliable. *F. P. Murtagh*

SNIZORT (USA)   5 b.g. Bahri (USA) – Ava Singstheblues (USA) (Dixieland Band   **h–** (USA)) [2002/3 24dᵖᵘ 17m 24g⁴ Oct 6] leggy gelding: modest maiden on Flat (stays 1½m): no show over hurdles: has worn cheekpieces. *M. E. Sowersby*

SNOB WELLS (IRE)   6 b.g. Sadler's Wells (USA) – Galitizine (USA) (Riverman   **c114** (USA)) [2002/3 h119: c17d* c17sF c16f² c17g³ c16v³ c17vᵖᵘ Dec 1] useful-looking   **h–** gelding: fairly useful hurdler: fairly useful novice chaser: won maiden at Galway in August: better form when third in listed event at Limerick and Grade 3 at Wexford: raced around 2m: acts on good to firm and heavy going: sometimes blinkered/tongue tied: has looked none too keen. *N. Meade, Ireland*

SNOWBOY (IRE)   11 br.g. Celio Rufo – Laurestown Rose (Derring Rose) [2002/3   **c82** c66, h–: c21m² May 22] compact gelding: poor maiden hurdler/steeplechaser: won 3-   **h–** runner maiden point in April: stays 21f: best efforts on good to firm/firm going. *Mrs J. M. Bailey*

SNOW CLOUD   9 b.m. Today And Tomorrow – Fancy Pages (Touch Paper) [2002/3   **h–** 17sᵖᵘ Dec 18] shallow-girthed mare: little sign of ability, including in points. *R. Brotherton*

SNOWMORE   7 ch.m. Glacial Storm (USA) – Royal Typhoon (Royal Fountain)   **h107** [2002/3 h81, F76: 21m² 21m* 21g* 21d 20s⁴ 19s⁴ 24g² 27gᵖᵘ Apr 25] angular mare: modest handicap hurdler: made all at Southwell in August and October: good 3 lengths second of 5 to Wagner at Market Rasen: stays 3m (not beaten by longer trip final start): acts on good to firm and heavy going: usually races prominently. *Mrs S. J. Smith*

SNOW PARTRIDGE (USA)   9 ch.g. Arctic Tern (USA) – Lady Sharp (FR) (Sharp-   **c76** man) [2002/3 22dF 19sᵖᵘ c20s⁵ c19d³ c20g c20m³ c24m⁵ c26mF Apr 19] smallish,   **h–** workmanlike gelding: one-time fair hurdler: poor novice chaser: should stay beyond 2½m: acts on good to firm going, probably soft: blinkered final start (fell eighth): has gone in snatches. *Mrs L. C. Taylor*

SNOWTRE (IRE)   6 b.g. Glacial Storm (USA) – Forest Gale (Strong Gale) [2002/3   **F–** F16m Jun 29] sixth foal: half-brother to fair staying chasers Forest Fountain (by Royal Fountain), Philtre (by Phardante) and Wishing William (by Riot Helmet): dam unraced: modest maiden pointer: well held in bumper at Worcester. *Mrs H. L. Needham*

SNOWY FORD (IRE) 6 b.g. Be My Native (USA) – Monalee Stream (Paddy's **h117**
Stream) [2002/3 20s 20s 18s 20s* 20d⁴ 24d Feb 23] medium-sized gelding: fairly useful
handicap hurdler: won at Punchestown in February: stays 2½m: acts on heavy going:
races prominently. *Paul Nolan, Ireland*

SOAP STONE 8 b.m. Gunner B – Tzarina (USA) (Gallant Romeo (USA)) [2002/3 **h§§**
20gʳᵗʳ 16m 21m 16m⁵ Apr 21] lengthy, rather sparely-made mare: very temperamental
maiden hurdler: usually blinkered: tongue tied. *Miss A. M. Newton-Smith*

SOARING MONARCH 8 b.g. Rakaposhi King – Flying Faith (Rymer) [2002/3 **c–**
h96: c19sᵘʳ c22dᶠ c21dᶠ 20d⁶ 24dᵖᵘ 22g 22g Apr 12] sturdy gelding: maiden hurdler, little **h78**
worthwhile form in 2002/3: let down by jumping all 3 starts over fences: stays 21f: acts
on soft going. *J. T. Gifford*

SOBER HILL 5 b.g. Komaite (USA) – Mamoda (Good Times (ITY)) [2002/3 h78: **h78**
16g⁴ 16s 17s² 17d⁶ Aug 26] angular, plain gelding: poor novice hurdler, reportedly lame
final outing: likely to prove best around 2m: acts on soft going: tongue tied last 2 starts.
N. B. Mason

SOCIALIST (USA) 7 b.g. Hermitage (USA) – Social Missy (USA) (Raised Socially **c–**
(USA)) [2002/3 c–, h–: 16g⁵ Apr 29] of little account: tried blinkered. *G. Brown* **h–**

SOCIETY BUCK (IRE) 6 b.g. Moscow Society (USA) – Bucks Grove (IRE) **h71**
(Buckskin (FR)) [2002/3 F76: F17m* F17d 16s⁴ 17v Jan 21] smallish, lengthy gelding: **F88**
fair form when winning bumper at Sedgefield in July: well held in 2 novice hurdles on
much more testing ground: bred to stay beyond 17f: sold 7,800 gns Doncaster May Sales.
M. W. Easterby

SOCUTE 8 b.m. Tina's Pet – Cute Pam (Pamroy) [2002/3 24v⁵ Jun 6] fourth foal: dam **h–**
winning pointer: won maiden point in March (has twice run out): showed nothing in poor
race on hurdling debut. *J. W. Mullins*

SODELK 9 ch.m. Interrex (CAN) – Summoned By Bells (Stanford) [2002/3 h§§: 16d **c§§**
c16gᵘʳ 20g⁵ 19f² 16g 22dʳᵗʳ 18dᵖᵘ 16s⁵ 21vʳᵗʳ Dec 4] leggy, sparely-made mare: unseated **h§§**
second on chasing debut: poor maiden hurdler: stays 19f: acts on firm and soft going:
tried blinkered/tongue tied: has refused to race several times and one to leave well alone.
J. E. Long

SOEUR FONTENAIL (FR) 6 b.m. Turgeon (USA) – Fontanalia (FR) (Rex Magna **c114**
(FR)) [2002/3 c87, h89: c17g³ c17g* c17d² c16d² c19d⁴ c19d³ c17v* c16g⁶ c20gᵖᵘ Apr **h–**
12] big, lengthy mare: modest hurdler: fair novice chaser: won at Plumpton in October
(handicap) and February: ran well when placed in between: stays 19f: raced mainly on
good ground or softer (acts on heavy): tried in cheekpieces: sound jumper: front runner/
races prominently. *N. J. Hawke*

SOFISIO 6 ch.g. Efisio – Legal Embrace (CAN) (Legal Bid (USA)) [2002/3 h83: 17g⁶ **h82**
16m⁵ 16g 16m² Jul 18] leggy gelding: fair on all-weather Flat (stays 1½m), successful in
June: poor maiden hurdler: barely stays 17f: acts on soft and good to firm going: blinkered last 2 starts: often tongue tied. *Miss S. J. Wilton*

SOHO FIELDS (IRE) 6 b.g. Good Thyne (USA) – Rosie Owen (IRE) (Roselier (FR)) **h103**
[2002/3 16d* 19g 17s⁵ 21g⁴ Feb 27] IR 28,000 3-y-o: leggy, useful-looking gelding: third
foal: half-brother to winning hurdler up to 2½m Stop The Gossip (by Cataldi): dam
placed over hurdles, half-sister to useful staying hurdler/chaser Gola Cher: favourite, won
novice hurdle at Ludlow on debut in November: rather disappointing after: should stay
beyond 2m. *Miss H. C. Knight*

SOL CHANCE 4 ch.g. Jupiter Island – Super Sol (Rolfe (USA)) [2002/3 F16d⁶ Feb **F87**
15] 22,000 3-y-o: rather unfurnished gelding: fifth foal: brother to winning 17f hurdler
Three Lions, fairly useful on Flat, and half-brother to 3 winners, including fair 2½m
hurdle winner Spunkie (by Jupiter Island), also useful 1¾m/2m winner: dam winning selling hurdler: never-nearer sixth of 16 in bumper at Wincanton on debut. *R. S. Brookhouse*

SOLDERSHIRE 6 b.g. Weld – Dishcloth (Fury Royal) [2002/3 F18g 18g³ 21vᵖᵘ Nov **h83 ?**
6] half-brother to fairly useful chaser Parahandy (by Lancastrian), stays 3¼m: dam fairly **F–**
useful 2m hurdler/winning chaser: well held in bumper: off 5 months, apparently better
effort in novice hurdles when third of 10 at Fontwell. *S. Dow*

SOLDIER OF ROME (IRE) 6 b.g. Satco (FR) – Queens Tricks (Le Bavard (FR)) **h89**
[2002/3 h106, F–: 21vᵖᵘ 16g 22s Dec 6] strong, lengthy gelding: disappointing maiden
hurdler: should stay beyond 2½m: sold £8,200 Ascot February Sales. *P. R. Hedger*

SOLDIER'S SONG 10 b.m. Infantry – Top Soprano (High Top) [2002/3 h–: c17gᵖᵘ **c–**
May 1] lengthy mare: of little account. *R. J. Hodges* **h–**

SOLERINA (IRE)   6 b.m. Toulon – Deep Peace (Deep Run) [2002/3 F20d⁵ 16d* **h146 p**
20s² 22s* 16s* 20s* 16v* 20d* 18s* Feb 9]   **F87**

Solerina's absence from the Royal & SunAlliance Hurdle was a cause for
regret, since she had shown herself one of the top novices in Ireland with seven
victories from eight starts before falling foul of an infection close to the cannon
bone in a near-hind leg three weeks before the Festival. Apparently the problem
went back to a scratch she picked up at Thurles early in the season, which for some
reason had been lying dormant during her victory roll. With a defeat of Hardy
Eustace in the Grade 1 Deloitte & Touche Novices' Hurdle at Leopardstown
already in the bag, her form bore the closest inspection and looked even better after
Hardy Eustace's Cheltenham victory. Though it was curtailed, front-running
Solerina's campaign certainly captured the hearts of the Irish racing public.
Solerina takes her flights with verve, is as tough as old boots, lacks nothing in
courage and determination and is based in a stable of only four horses, alongside an
even better front runner and role model for never-say-die jumping, Limestone Lad.
Both horses are a credit to themselves and their connections—Solerina was bred by
one of trainer James Bowe's sons and is owned by another—and the Bowes must
be hopeful that one day the mare might be able to pick up the baton from their stable
star, now rising twelve and by rights ready to start feeling the effects of increasing
age before long.

Solerina contested five bumpers before having her attentions turned to
hurdles, winning at Naas in March 2002 when trained by Thomas Foley but finishing nearly twenty-five lengths adrift on her reappearance at Gowran Park in
October. Her hurdling on her debut in an eighteen-runner maiden event at Thurles
early in November was stylish as she beat Windfall readily. But then came
Solerina's only defeat so far, against Pizarro in the Grade 3 Monksfield Novices'
Hurdle at Navan later in the month. After taking it up entering the straight she went
down by two lengths, the pair clear. Connections argued that not sending the mare
to the front from the off contributed to her defeat, and there is no doubt she is suited
by making her own running, but Pizarro, having his first run over hurdles, is a smart

*INH Stallion Owners EBF Novices' Hurdle, Punchestown—
conditional Gary Hutchinson gains a second win on Solerina*

performer. Solerina proceeded to chalk up six straight wins after Navan. Races at Thurles again at the end of November and Punchestown ten days later were fairly simple tasks and she justified short-priced favouritism by twenty-five lengths and five lengths respectively. The Grade 3 Barry & Sandra Kelly Memorial Novices' Hurdle at Navan in mid-December posed a greater test as Solerina's four opponents again included Pizarro, who started at odds on. In the event, Pizarro ran poorly due to sickness and Solerina hacked up by eight lengths from Kicking King. Characteristically not letting the grass grow under the feet of any of his team, Bowe next ran the mare at Leopardstown over Christmas, when very testing going resulted in three non-runners in the Grade 2 paddypower.com Future Champions Novices' Hurdle and left the race as a match between Solerina and Central House, successful on two of his three starts over hurdles. Much better suited by the conditions, Solerina landed odds of 9/4-on by a distance. Another easy odds-on victory, by six lengths from Moore's Law, in the weakly-contested Grade 3 betfair.com Golden Cygnet Novices' Hurdle at Leopardstown late in January preceded Solerina's toughest test—the six-runner Deloitte and Touche Novices' Hurdle, run as a Grade 1 for the first time, on the same course in February. By this stage, Solerina's fans appeared to think her invincible and her starting price of 11/10 looked a shade ungenerous against second favourite Hardy Eustace, successful in all his three races over hurdles including the Royal Bond at Fairyhouse. Another runner Nil Desperandum had shown useful form but the finish concerned the two market leaders, Solerina, who looked in very good shape, jumping really well in the main and keeping on tenaciously after being ridden entering the straight to hold Hardy Eustace by two lengths. An untidy jump at the final flight possibly helped her cause, since the runner-up was hit on the shin by the hurdle flying back after Solerina caught it, but this was still a grand performance.

In stamina and versatility, Solerina looks a carbon copy of Limestone Lad, because she is effective at two miles and will stay three. This increases the options available to her trainer, who has gone on the record to say she will not be tried over fences due to her lack of stature. In make and shape she is as far removed from Kingscliff, another good runner by her sire Toulon, as it is possible to be. He is built on the grand scale, she is leggy and light-framed, standing only 15.3 hands.

John P. Bowe's "Solerina"

Solerina (IRE) (b.m. 1997)	Toulon (b 1988)	Top Ville (b 1976)	High Top
			Sega Ville
		Green Rock (ch 1981)	Mill Reef
			Infra Green
	Deep Peace (ch 1984)	Deep Run (ch 1966)	Pampered King
			Trial By Fire
		Bargy Music (ch 1971)	Tudor Music
			Patsy Brown

Solerina's non-thoroughbred dam Deep Peace is by Deep Run and showed some ability over hurdles, gaining places at around two miles and indicating she probably stayed two and three quarters. Deep Peace's other progeny include Solerina's eight-year-old stable-companion Florida Coast (by Florida Son), successful in a three-mile novice hurdle at Fairyhouse, as well as a two-mile maiden on the Flat, and second to Sacundai at Naas in January. Deep Peace foaled a gelding by Beneficial in 2000 and a filly by Taipan in 2002. Neither of the next two dams reached the track. Solerina has raced only on going softer than good and acts on heavy. She looks set for an other successful season since it will surely be difficult keeping such a tough and enthusiastic performer out of the winner's enclosure for long. *James Bowe, Ireland*

SOLID LAND (FR)   4 b.f. Solid Illusion (USA) – Tip Land (FR) (Tip Moss (FR))   **h104**
[2002/3 15v⁶ 18s³ 16dᶠ 16v⁴ Jan 22] ex-French filly: fourth foal: half-sister to fairly useful chaser around 2m Kassala (by Phantom Breeze): dam maiden: fair form in juvenile hurdles, left A. Hosselet after third at Auteuil in September: 6 lengths down in second when fell heavily last at Warwick on British debut: found little at Fakenham month later. *P. F. Nicholls*

SOL MUSIC 11 ch.g. Southern Music – Tyqueen (Tycoon II) [2002/3 c105, h–: c21g c16d* c20d* c19f* Mar 27] lengthy gelding: useful hunter chaser: back to near best in 2002/3, won at Towcester very early in season and at Leicester and Exeter (for second year in succession, by ½ length from Red Brook Lad) in March: stays 2½m: acts on any going: front runner: genuine. *Mrs V. M. Graham*
  c112 h–

SOLO DANCER 5 ch.m. Sayaarr (USA) – Oiseval (National Trust) [2002/3 h69: 22m⁶ 24sᵖᵘ 17dᶠ 17dᶠ 16vᵖᵘ 17g³ Apr 19] rather sparely-made mare: poor maiden hurdler, usually let down by jumping: stays 3m: has worn cheekpieces. *Mrs H. M. Bridges*
  h59 x

SOLSGIRTH 12 br.g. Ardross – Lillies Brig (New Brig) [2002/3 c77, h–: c21dᵖᵘ Mar 7] tall gelding: poor chaser nowadays: won 2-finisher point in April: stays 25f: raced mainly on going softer than good (acts on heavy): tried tongue tied. *N. W. Alexander*
  c– h–

SOLTERO (IRE) 7 ch.g. Good Thyne (USA) – Golden Ambition (Torus) [2002/3 h129: c18sᶠ c16vᶠ c16s* c17s⁴ c17sᶠ Jan 26] workmanlike gelding: fairly useful hurdler: won maiden chase at Cork in January: appeared to show useful form when 3½ lengths fourth of 7 to Colonel Braxton in listed race at Fairyhouse: fell fatally at Leopardstown: stayed 2½m: raced on good going or softer (acted on heavy). *Mrs J. Harrington, Ireland*
  c140 h–

SOLVANG (IRE) 11 b.g. Carlingford Castle – Bramble Bird (Pitpan) [2002/3 c–, h–: 20sᵖᵘ c23mᵖᵘ c22m⁵ c19mᵖᵘ Sep 11] smallish gelding: fairly useful handicap chaser in 1999/00, has deteriorated considerably, placed in point in March: tongue tied. *F. Jordan*
  c– h–

SOLWAY BREEZE (IRE) 10 b.m. King's Ride – Spicey Cut (Cut Above) [2002/3 c88, h–: c24sᵘʳ c25gᵖᵘ c31gᵖᵘ Apr 24] sparely-made mare: modest chaser, out of sorts in 2002/3: stays 3¼m: raced on good going or softer (acts on heavy): blinkered 3 times, including when successful. *Ms Liz Harrison*
  c– h–

SOLWAY COASTER 10 b.g. Jumbo Hirt (USA) – Lady Mag (Silver Season) [2002/3 c20m⁴ c20m⁶ 20s Aug 4] little sign of ability, even in points: has had tongue tied. *Ms Liz Harrison*
  c– h–

SOLWAY DONAL (IRE) 10 b.m. Celio Rufo – Knockaville (Crozier) [2002/3 c76x, h–: c20fᵘʳ c24gᵖᵘ c20dᵖᵘ c21m⁵ Apr 26] medium-sized mare: winning chaser, no form in 2002/3: sketchy jumper. *Ms Liz Harrison*
  c– x h–

SOLWAY GALE (IRE) 6 b.m. Husyan (USA) – Some Gale (Strong Gale) [2002/3 F68: 20m 20g⁶ 16d³ 16d 20s⁵ 24g⁶ Mar 28] angular mare: races freely and signs of only a little ability. *Ms Liz Harrison*
  h–

SOLWAY GORGE 7 ch.g. Jumbo Hirt (USA) – Kilkenny Gorge (Deep Run) [2002/3 F16f F16g 27gᵖᵘ Mar 25] second known foal: dam poor pointer: no sign of ability. *Ms Liz Harrison*
  h– F–

SOLWAY MINSTREL 6 ch.g. Jumbo Hirt (USA) – Spicey Cut (Cut Above) [2002/3 F16f Sep 15] third foal: half-brother to modest hurdler/chaser Solway Breeze (by King's Ride), stays 3¼m: dam unraced, out of half-sister to smart 3m hurdler Maelkar: showed nothing in bumper on debut. *Ms Liz Harrison*
  F–

SOLWAY PLAIN 9 b.g. King's Ride – Oh Dear (Paico) [2002/3 h67: c25d⁵ c24mᵖᵘ c22mᵖᵘ c20dᵖᵘ Aug 4] poor novice hurdler: no form in steeplechases (runner-up in points): stays 25f: acts on heavy going. *Ms Liz Harrison*
  c– h–

SOLWAY ROSE 9 ch.m. Minster Son – Lady Mag (Silver Season) [2002/3 c95, h–: c26sᵖᵘ c24d² c26v⁴ c25d⁴ c24vᵘʳ Jan 15] lengthy, angular mare: modest handicap chaser: best at 3m+: acts on heavy and good to firm going: races prominently: inconsistent. *Ms Liz Harrison*
  c95 § h–

SOMAYDA (IRE) 8 b.g. Last Tycoon – Flame of Tara (Artaius (USA)) [2002/3 h–: 16gᵖᵘ 16dᵖᵘ Dec 26] leggy gelding: useful at one time on Flat, well held in 2002: no show over hurdles. *Miss Jacqueline S. Doyle*
  h–

SOME BUZZ (IRE) 8 b. or br.g. Rashar (USA) – Tourin Neofa (Teofane) [2002/3 16s³ 16s 19m 16s⁶ 16s 16s 16s⁴ 16s⁴ 16s* 16s c16s² 16m Apr 22] useful-looking gelding: second foal: half-brother to a winning pointer by Phardante: dam unraced: winning pointer: fair handicap hurdler: improved form when winning at Leopardstown in December: fairly useful form when 2½ lengths second to Turn Two in maiden at Naas on steeplechasing debut: best at 2m: acts on soft going. *T. M. Walsh, Ireland*
  c122 h107

SOME GO WEST (IRE) 9 b.g. Un Desperado (FR) – Costly Lady (Bold Lad (IRE)) [2002/3 h–: c24gᵘʳ c25mᵖᵘ May 22] angular gelding: fair hunter chaser in 2001: failed to complete following year, including in point: stays 25f: acts on firm and soft going: raced freely when tried in blinkers: has worn tongue strap. *Neil King*
  c– h–

SOMEMANFORONEMAN (IRE)   9 b.g. Asir – Wintry Shower (Strong Gale) [2002/3 c124, h–: c27d^{pu} c24v^4 c24v^F 24d^6 24m^{pu} Apr 17] rangy gelding: useful chaser at best up to 3m, very disappointing overall in 2002/3, including over hurdles: left C. Mann after third start: usually blinkered (wore cheekpieces third outing): has worn near-side pricker: often makes mistakes: one to leave alone. *R. S. Brookhouse*   **c– §**
h95 §

SOME OPERATOR (IRE)   9 b.g. Lord Americo – Rathvilly Flier (Peacock (FR)) [2002/3 h72x: 16m 19g^2 Apr 19] sturdy gelding: poor novice hurdler: stays 19f: acts on firm going: often let down by jumping. *T. Wall*   **h84 x**

SOMERTON (POL)   5 b.g. Saphir (GER) – Sobota (POL) (Pawiment (POL)) [2002/3 19d^{pu} 17d^{pu} Jan 16] ex-Polish gelding: won 4 of 10 starts on Flat, from 5f to 1¼m: no show in novice hurdles at Newbury and Taunton. *T. R. George*   **h–**

SOME STORY (IRE)   7 b.g. Mandalus – April Lilly (Deep Run) [2002/3 24m 16g 22s^{ur} Nov 8] IR 10,000 4-y-o: smallish gelding: fourth foal: dam, bumper winner, half-sister to fairly useful staying chaser Valigan: no sign of ability in point or over hurdles. *Mrs V. J. Makin*   **h–**

SOMETHING DANDY (IRE)   10 b.g. Brush Aside (USA) – Hawthorn Dandy (Deep Run) [2002/3 c93, h–: 24g^5 22g^6 20m^4 24g* c23g^3 c20g^4 c26g^2 c24d^4 c24s* 17m^2 Apr 16] lengthy, angular gelding: modest chaser: won handicaps at Kempton (novice) and Taunton in November: novice hurdler: won handicap at Worcester in July: off 5 months, appeared to show considerable improvement when 4 lengths second of 10 to Indien Royal at Cheltenham: effective around 2m and stays 3¼m: acts on firm and soft going. *J. A. B. Old*   **c93 +**
h111

SOMETHING HAPPENED (NZ)   10 b.g. Cache of Gold (USA) – Iseki (NZ) (Brazen Bay (AUS)) [2002/3 h83: 20g^{pu} Mar 17] close-coupled gelding: successful on Flat in New Zealand: very lightly raced over hurdles in Britain, best effort in novices at Wetherby when third in May 2001: appeared to go amiss on return. *O. Brennan*   **h–**

SOMETHING SPECIAL   5 b.g. Petong – My Dear Watson (Chilibang) [2002/3 16s^{pu} Jun 9] compact gelding: no form on Flat or on hurdling debut. *H. E. Haynes*   **h–**

SOME TOOL   6 b.g. Jupiter Island – Melodys Daughter (Sizzling Melody) [2002/3 17g 16m Jul 14] showed nothing in maiden on Flat: well beaten both starts over hurdles. *John A. Harris*   **h–**

SOMOSIERRA (IRE)   8 b.g. Paris House – Island Heather (IRE) (Salmon Leap (USA)) [2002/3 h–: 16d^{pu} May 4] no form over hurdles (tried blinkered): sold £900 Ascot June Sales: second on completed start in points. *V. Thompson*   **h–**

SONEVAFUSHI (FR)   5 b.g. Ganges (USA) – For Kicks (FR) (Top Ville) [2002/3 h117: 20m* 18d^2 17v^2 16d 20v^4 16d^6 20d Apr 4] leggy, useful-looking gelding: fairly useful hurdler: won intermediate at Southwell in May: stays easy 2½m: acts on heavy and good to firm going: blinkered (raced too freely) final start: jumps none too fluently: weak finisher. *Miss Venetia Williams*   **h119 §**

SONIC GIRL (IRE)   8 ch.m. Boyne Valley – So Ladylike (Malinowski (USA)) [2002/3 h–: 16v^6 16s c16s^{pu} c25s^{pu} Mar 7] of little account nowadays: blinkered once. *N. M. Babbage*   **c–**
h–

SONNY JIM   5 b.g. Timeless Times (USA) – Allesca (Alleging (USA)) [2002/3 h90: 16d^5 21d^3 16s^2 16d^3 19d^2 18s^3 21v 19v^4 16m^6 Mar 31] compact gelding: modest hurdler: left J. O'Neill after reappearance: barely stays 21f: acts on any going: blinkered last 2 starts in 2001/2, looked ungenuine when visored on reappearance. *M. D. I. Usher*   **h85**

SON OF A GUN   9 b.g. Gunner B – Sola Mia (Tolomeo) [2002/3 h103: 16g^3 17s^6 25s 24v^{pu} 19g^4 16g* 20g 16m Apr 21] smallish, sturdy gelding: only poor over hurdles in 2002/3, won selling handicap at Fakenham in March: should stay 2½m: raced mainly on good going or softer over hurdles (bumper form on firm): has found little *M. J. Polglase*   **h84**

SON OF ANSHAN   10 b.g. Anshan – Anhaar (Ela-Mana-Mou) [2002/3 c116, h–: c23d^3 c27s* c27d* c21g^F Apr 3] rangy, workmanlike gelding: fairly useful hunter chaser: excelled himself when third in Fox Hunters' at Aintree in 2002 (behind when fell twelfth in latest renewal), won point 3 days later): good efforts on balance of form first 3 starts in 2003, twice winning in good style at Sedgefield in March: stays 27f: acts on heavy and good to firm going: tried blinkered: tongue tied. *G. Tuer*   **c103 +**
h–

SON OF LIGHT (IRE)   8 br.g. Hollow Hand – Leaney Kamscort (Kambalda) [2002/3 c81, h100d: c24m^5 c22g^2 c22m^3 c26m* c26m* c26g^2 Apr 21] useful-looking gelding: winning hurdler: fair chaser: won novices at Uttoxeter in July and Southwell in August: left A. Streeter and off 8 months, creditable second to Our Jolly Swagman in handicap at   **c105**
h–

Newton Abbot: stays 3¼m: acts on soft and firm going: visored once: has looked none too keen. *Miss Venetia Williams*

SON OF ROSS   9 b.g. Minster Son – Nancy Ardross (Ardross) [2002/3 h73?: 22g^{ur} 24m⁵ 27g⁶ 24d Jun 4] tall, angular gelding: won weak novice early in 2001/2, little other form over hurdles. *R. W. Thomson*   **h–**

SON OF SNURGE (FR)   7 b.g. Snurge – Swift Spring (FR) (Bluebird (USA)) [2002/3 22m^F 20g⁴ 22g⁶ 16s⁶ 20v² 20s⁴ 20d 20d 24v^{pu} 24v⁵ 24v⁵ 20v⁴ 24g 22d 27s 21g³ 20g³ 20g⁵ Apr 14] well-made gelding: poor maiden hurdler, sold out of T. Tate's stable 900 gns Doncaster August Sales before reappearance: stays 2½m: tried blinkered, wears cheekpieces nowadays. *W. G. Young*   **h78 ?**

SOON OR LATE   5 ch.g. Kris – Silky Heights (IRE) (Head For Heights) [2002/3 19d Oct 19] leggy gelding: half-brother to winning 2½m hurdler Winged Angel (by Prince Sabo): poor maiden on Flat (stays 2m): ninth of 10 finishers in maiden at Market Rasen on hurdling debut: sold 2,200 gns Doncaster November Sales. *Miss J. A. Camacho*   **h–**

SORBIEDIDITMYWAY (IRE)   4 b.g. Sorbie Tower (IRE) – Wamdha (IRE) (Thatching) [2002/3 F18d Feb 17] IR 1,500Y: first foal: dam, winning hurdler, half-sister to useful 1½m performer Altaweelah: 40/1 and blinkered, pulled very hard when tailed off in bumper on debut. *B. G. Powell*   **F–**

SORELY MISSED (IRE)   8 br.g. Yashgan – Well Honey (Al Sirat (USA)) [2002/3 c–, h79: c19g⁴ c20d^{pu} 16s^{pu} 24m^{pu} Mar 18] well-made gelding: no form over fences: poor handicap hurdler, has lost his way: stays 25f: acts on soft and good to firm going: visored second start, wore cheekpieces final one. *R. Dickin*   **c–** **h–**

SORRENTO KING   6 ch.g. First Trump – Star Face (African Sky) [2002/3 h96: c16m³ c16g³ c16g⁴ c21g* c21m* c25m^F Apr 21] smallish gelding: modest hurdler: successful in novice chases at Sedgefield in September and October: stays 21f: acts on firm and soft going: blinkered (ran poorly) once. *Mrs M. Reveley*   **c93** **h–**

SOSSUS VLEI   7 b.g. Inchinor – Sassalya (Sassafras (FR)) [2002/3 h126: 16d² 16v 16s² 16s² 16d⁵ Mar 6] medium-sized gelding: smart on Flat at best: novice hurdler, fair on balance of form: raced around 2m on good ground or softer (ran poorly on heavy): tends to carry head high, and not an easy ride. *P. Winkworth*   **h102**

SO TEMPTED   4 br.f. So Factual (USA) – Bystrouska (Gorytus (USA)) [2002/3 F17v^{su} F16m^F Mar 18] angular filly: sixth foal: half-sister to fairly useful 6f/7f winner Charlie Sillett (by Handsome Sailor) and winner in Belgium by Green Ruby: dam once-raced half-sister to fairly useful hurdler/chaser Brambleberry, stays 21f: would have finished third but for slipping up in final 1f in mares bumper at Sedgefield on debut: well beaten when fell next time. *N. Wilson*   **F66**

SOUND OF CHEERS   6 br.g. Zilzal (USA) – Martha Stevens (USA) (Super Concorde (USA)) [2002/3 h102: c20v⁴ c21v⁴ c19g^{pu} c20v⁵ c19d⁴ c21s² c16d⁶ c16g² 16g Apr 14] good-topped gelding: modest novice chaser: winning hurdler: ran as if amiss final start: stays 21f: acts on heavy going: tongue tied last 5 starts. *F. Kirby*   **c94** **h–**

SOUNDS COOL   7 b.g. Savahra Sound – Lucky Candy (Lucky Wednesday) [2002/3 h69: 17m⁴ 17m⁴ 19m^{pu} Sep 11] leggy gelding: poor hurdler: raced mainly around 2m: acts on soft and good to firm going: tried visored: joined Mrs S. Smith. *A. Streeter*   **h75**

SOUNDS PROMISING   8 b.g. Profilic – Blakeney Sound (Blakeney) [2002/3 23g^{pu} May 8] 2,600 4-y-o: half-brother to useful chaser up to 3m Sounds Like Fun and useful staying hurdler Master Rastus (both by Neltino): dam unraced: no promise on hurdling debut: won maiden point in March. *R. Wilman*   **c–** **h–**

SOUNDS STRONG (IRE)   14 br.g. Strong Gale – Jazz Bavard (Le Bavard (FR)) [2002/3 c26d⁶ Jun 5] sturdy, lengthy gelding: fair hunter chaser in 2000: always behind at Cartmel in June: stays 3¼m: acts on firm and soft going: often let down by jumping. *Miss A. Armitage*   **c62 x**

SOUNDTRACK (IRE)   10 b.g. Orchestra – Misty Boosh (Tarboosh (USA)) [2002/3 c–, h–: c24m⁶ Apr 22] rangy gelding: fairly useful novice hurdler in 2000/1: disappointing in handicaps since, off 14 months before reappearance: best at 3m+: acts on any going: front runner. *Miss Venetia Williams*   **c–** **h–**

SOUNDZ OF MUZIC (IRE)   8 b.m. Supreme Leader – Southern Princess (Black Minstrel) [2002/3 F20v⁵ 16s⁵ 16s³ 16v⁴ 16v^{bd} 16v 16s* 16g³ 16g⁴ Apr 23] first reported foal: dam winning Irish pointer: twice-raced in bumpers: modest handicap hurdler: won at Thurles in March: good third of 27 to Windmill Flyer in 27-runner event at Cork later in month, finding little: should stay beyond 2m: acts on soft going. *A. J. Martin, Ireland*   **h89** **F68**

SOUTHDOWN HOUSE   7 b.m. Husyan (USA) – Inger-Lea (Record Run) [2002/3   h93
F17s⁴ 20v² 20v⁴ 20g³ Mar 16] third foal: half-sister to winning pointers by Phardante   F63
and Mazaad: dam winning selling hurdler, stayed 2¾m: fourth of 12 in mares bumper at
Folkestone on debut: easily best effort in mares novice hurdles when staying-on second
to Lynrick Lady at Chepstow: will be suited by further than 2½m. *R. Rowe*

SOUTHERN-BE-GEORGE   8 b.g. Be My Chief (USA) – Southern Sky (Comedy   c–
Star (USA)) [2002/3 h94: 24m 27gᵖᵘ c20dᵖᵘ c20m⁴ Jun 3] winning hurdler: well-held   h–
fourth of 5 finishers on completed start in novice chases (hung badly right on debut):
stays 2¾m: acts on firm and soft going: usually makes running. *W. G. M. Turner*

SOUTHERNCROSSPATCH   12 ch.g. Ra Nova – Southern Bird (Shiny Tenth)   c–
[2002/3 c–, h95: 24dᵖᵘ 24s⁶ 26s 23dᵖᵘ 24m⁴ 21m² Apr 21] strong, compact gelding: h87
modest handicap hurdler: stays 27f: acts on good going. *Mrs Barbara Waring*

SOUTHERNDOWN (IRE)   10 ch.g. Montelimar (USA) – Country Melody (IRE)   c92
(Orchestra) [2002/3 c65, h69: c25d² c24dᶠ c25g⁵ c23m² c26m⁴ c26m* c24m* c26g*   h77
c24m⁴ 24d⁴ c24s Jan 3] sparely-made gelding: poor hurdler: modest chaser: improved in
first half of season, winning at Southwell (novice) in August, Bangor (novice handicap)
in September and Southwell again (odds on in 3-runner handicap) in October: stays 27f:
has form on soft/heavy going, best efforts under less testing conditions: tried blinkered/
visored, not in 2002/3. *R. Lee*

SOUTHERN DUNES   7 b.g. Ardkinglass – Leprechaun Lady (Royal Blend) [2002/3   h–
h–: 16mᵖᵘ 17g 21d⁶ Nov 14] of no account: often blinkered. *G. Fierro*

SOUTHERN RIDGE   12 b.g. Indian Ridge – Southern Sky (Comedy Star (USA))   c–
[2002/3 c–, h63: 17g 17m³ Jun 14] sparely-made gelding: well beaten only run over   h62
fences: poor handicap hurdler: best around 2m: acts on good to firm and soft going.
A. S. T. Holdsworth

SOUTHERN STAR (IRE)   8 ch.g. Montelimar (USA) – Flying Pegus (Beau Chap-   c140
eau) [2002/3 c142, h–: c27d² c26g c26s² c28d c24g c36d Apr 5] big, lengthy gelding: h–
useful handicap chaser: ran well when second to Stormez and Historg at Cheltenham,
well held in valuable events 4 other starts (including in Grand National) in 2002/3: should
stay beyond 27f: acts on soft and good to firm going. *Miss H. C. Knight*

SOUTH WEST EXPRESS (IRE)   11 ch.g. Executive Perk – Bohemian Girl   c– x
(Pardao) [2002/3 c66x, h–: 22m c19d³ c26vᵖᵘ c19m Apr 22] shallow-girthed gelding: h–
winning hurdler/chaser, retains little ability: blinkered once: often let down by jumping
over fences. *Mrs D. Thomas*

SOUTH WEST WON   5 b.g. Bedford (USA) – Wood Heath (Heres) [2002/3 F18f⁶   F–
Apr 24] £4,700 4-y-o: half-brother to smart hurdler/chaser Trying Again (by Northern
Game), stays 3m: dam, twice-raced in points, out of half-sister to dam of Irish National
winner Vanton: well beaten in bumper at Fontwell on debut, looking very green. *Miss
S. West*

SOVEREIGN   9 b.m. Interrex (CAN) – Shiny Penny (Glint of Gold) [2002/3 h–: 20g⁴   h90
19m* 22g 22m 22g³ 19m² 19g⁴ 24g⁶ 24f⁶ 22f³ 20m² Apr 21] small mare: modest handicap hurdler: won mares event at Hereford in June: stays 23f: has form on soft going,
races on good or firmer nowadays (acts on firm). *J. F. Panvert*

SOVEREIGN GOLD   6 b.g. Rakaposhi King – Page of Gold (Goldhill) [2002/3 F76:   h–
21d Jan 18] signs of ability in bumper on debut: well held in novice hurdle 14 months
later. *D. R. Gandolfo*

SOVEREIGN GRIT (IRE)   13 ch.g. Sheer Grit – Gorryelm (Arctic Slave) [2002/3   c–
c–, h–: 27mᵖᵘ May 7] sturdy gelding: of little account. *Mrs L. C. Jewell*   h–

SOVEREIGN'S GIFT   7 ch.m. Elegant Monarch – Cadeau d'Aragon (Aragon)   h86
[2002/3 h66: 17g⁴ 17m² 22f⁵ 22d² 24fᵖᵘ 22m² Mar 20] workmanlike mare: modest
maiden hurdler: should stay 3m: acts on firm and good to soft going. *Mrs S. D. Williams*

SOVEREIGN STATE (IRE)   6 b.g. Soviet Lad (USA) – Portree (Slip Anchor)   h78 x
[2002/3 16s⁴ 16vᵖᵘ 16d 19d⁶ 16m³ Apr 21] modest on Flat, remained in 2002: poor
maiden hurdler, sold out of Miss S. Hall's stable 1,200 gns Doncaster November Sales
after debut: best effort in visor final outing: unlikely to stay much beyond 2m: acts on
good to firm going, probably on soft: sloppy jumper. *J. A. Moore*

SPAGHETTI JUNCTION   5 ch.m. Sir Harry Lewis (USA) – Up The Junction (IRE)   h100
(Treasure Kay) [2002/3 16s* 17sᵖᵘ 19v³ 21m⁴ 21m Apr 17] sturdy mare: second foal:
dam, fair hurdler around 2m, half-sister to smart hurdler/useful chaser up to 3m Kates
Charm: won mares novice hurdle at Haydock on debut in November: easily best effort

after when fourth of 16 to Ar Muin Na Muice in valuable mares novice handicap at Newbury: stays 21f: acts on soft and good to firm going. *R. H. Alner*

SPAINKRIS 4 b.g. Kris – Pennycairn (Last Tycoon) [2002/3 16v*dis 16d5 16dur 17g* **h98** 16f6 Mar 29] close-coupled gelding: useful form up to 1m at 2 yrs, probably not so good in 2002 but placed up to 15f, sold out of X. Nakkachdji's stable €38,000 Goffs November Sale: fair juvenile hurdler: won at Ayr (maiden, disqualified on technical grounds) in January and Market Rasen: not fluent, beat Ela Re 1¼ lengths) in March: raced around 2m: acts on heavy going, below form on firm (refused to settle). *A. Crook*

SPANDAU (NZ) 9 br.g. Fiesta Star (AUS) – Koru (NZ) (Diplomatic Agent (USA)) **h73** [2002/3 h–: 17dpu 17d 16s5 17v3 20m Apr 12] well-made gelding: poor handicap hurdler: best efforts around 2m: acts on heavy going. *J. C. Tuck*

SPANISH ARCHER (IRE) 8 b.g. Spanish Place (USA) – Bow Gello (Bargello) **c68** [2002/3 c–, h–: c25dpu c21d* c21g3 c23gpu c23m5 c26m c22m4 20g3 22f4 17m 17s3 16vpu 19d 24v5 Dec 28] tall, angular gelding: poor maiden hurdler/handicap chaser: fortunate to win at Uttoxeter in June: sold out of P. Hobbs's stable 3,000 gns Doncaster September Sales after eighth start, little subsequent form: stays 23f: best efforts on good going or firmer (acts on firm): tried blinkered/visored/tongue tied. *L. Waring*

SPANISH MAIN (IRE) 9 b.g. Spanish Place (USA) – Willow Grouse (Giolla Mear) **c104** [2002/3 c124d, h–: c27d3 c26v4 c30s* c31g5 Apr 24] tall gelding: fair handicap chaser: **h–** came from long way back to win at Exeter in March: thorough stayer: acts on good to firm and heavy going: tried blinkered/visored: has had tongue tied. *N. A. Twiston-Davies*

SPARKEY SMITH (IRE) 11 b.g. Mister Majestic – Jim Says (Jaazeiro (USA)) **c114** [2002/3 c117, h–: 20s c20m2 c17d c22m c20m6 c24g4 Feb 12] one-time fairly useful **h–** hurdler/chaser: left C. Swan after fifth start, well beaten in hunter: third in point after: stays 2½m: acts on soft and good to firm going. *Major General C. A. Ramsay*

SPARKLING CASCADE (IRE) 11 b.m. Royal Fountain – Yukon Law (Goldhill) **c81** [2002/3 c77: c24d2 c26gpu c26m5 c26m2 Aug 26] lengthy mare: poor pointer/novice chaser: stays 3m: acts on good to firm and good to soft going. *A. G. Newcombe*

SPARKLING EMBERS 8 b.g. Regal Embers (IRE) – Lady Pia (Pia Fort) [2002/3 **h–** h–: 17gpu 19dpu May 14] of no account. *C. J. Price*

SPARKLING GOLD (IRE) 9 ch.g. Andretti – Aliceion (Tanfirion) [2002/3 c120, **c116** h116: 20g2 c17mur c24f4 Sep 25] lengthy, angular gelding: fairly useful hurdler/chaser: **h117** creditable efforts both completed starts in 2002/3: stays 3m: acts on any going: not a fluent jumper of fences. *J. E. Kiely, Ireland*

SPARKLING JESS 4 b.f. Alderbrook – Tasmin Gayle (IRE) (Strong Gale) [2002/3 **F–** F17s F16g Mar 2] angular filly: fourth foal: dam, lightly-raced hurdler, half-sister to useful staying hurdler Bawnrock and fairly useful staying chaser Dont Tell The Wife: well held in bumpers. *M. J. Roberts*

SPARKLING LASS 9 gr.m. Nicholas Bill – Sparkling Time (USA) (Olden Times) **c–** [2002/3 c–, h–: 19s 22g 27g Apr 19] angular mare: no longer of any account. *N. G. Ayliffe* **h–**

SPARKLING SWORD 8 gr.m. Broadsword (USA) – Sparkling Time (USA) (Olden **h–** Times) [2002/3 F89: 24g May 24] useful-looking mare: useful form in bumpers in 2000: very lightly raced since, well beaten when favourite in novice on hurdling debut: should be suited by 2½m+. *Miss Venetia Williams*

SPARK OF LIFE 6 b.m. Rainbows For Life (CAN) – Sparkly Girl (IRE) (Danehill **h84** (USA)) [2002/3 h84: 17m5 Jul 15] modest and unreliable on Flat (stays 13f): poor form in 2 novice hurdles. *T. D. McCarthy*

SPARKY GAYLE (IRE) 13 b.g. Strong Gale – Baybush (Boreen (FR)) [2002/3 **c108** c116, h–: c27m3 Apr 11] rangy gelding: has had wind operation: smart chaser at best: won **h–** hunter at Kelso in 2001/2: remote third to Earthmover in similar event at Ayr on return year later: stays 25f: acts on good to firm and heavy going: tongue tied: has broken blood vessel: usually a fine jumper. *A. Parker*

SPECIAL AGENDA (IRE) 9 b.g. Torus – Easter Blade (IRE) (Fine Blade (USA)) **c115 x** [2002/3 c115, h–: c16g* c17d4 c17dur c16dpu c17g5 c17d6 Mar 3] useful-looking gelding: **h–** fair handicap chaser: won at Newton Abbot in May, coming from off strong pace: below form after, often let down by jumping: best around 2m: acts on heavy going. *C. J. Mann*

SPECIAL CONQUEST 5 b.g. El Conquistador – Kellys Special (Netherkelly) **F97** [2002/3 F17g* Apr 19] third foal: brother to fairly useful chaser Kellys Conquest, stays

25f: dam maiden pointer: won maiden bumper at Newton Abbot on debut, keeping on strongly to beat Eljay's Boy 6 lengths: will stay 2½m+. *J. W. Mullins*

SPECIAL CONSTABLE   5 b. or br.g. Derrylin – Lavenham's Last (Rymer) [2002/3 F14d 21s^{pu} Jan 27] 4,000 3-y-o, 10,000 4-y-o: medium-sized gelding: fifth foal: half-brother to 17f hurdle winner Gohh (by Alflora): dam unraced half-sister to high-class staying chaser Cybrandian: no promise in bumper or novice hurdle. *B. I. Case*   h– F–

SPECIALISM   5 ch.g. Spectrum (IRE) – Waft (USA) (Topsider (USA)) [2002/3 16v Dec 4] little form on Flat: failed to settle when well held on hurdling debut. *M. J. Gingell*   h–

SPECIALIZE   11 b.g. Faustus (USA) – Scholastika (GER) (Alpenkonig (GER)) [2002/3 c106, h–: c24g^5 c24g^{pu} c20m c24m^{pu} c20m^4 c21g^4 c21g c26d^2 c21m^{pu} c21g^6 Sep 12] good-bodied gelding: fair handicap chaser, generally below form in 2002/3: barely stays 3¼m: acts on firm and soft going: usually blinkered/visored: difficult ride. *K. R. Burke*   c101 h–

SPECIAL PRESENT   5 ch.g. Presenting – Pitts Special (Pitpan) [2002/3 F95: F16d^2 16m* 18g* Oct 6] useful-looking gelding: fairly useful form when runner-up on 3 of 4 starts in bumpers: unbeaten in 2 outings over hurdles, in novices at Stratford in September and Fontwell (broke down badly run-in) in October: dead. *L. Wells*   h104 F95

SPECTROMETER   6 ch.g. Rainbow Quest (USA) – Selection Board (Welsh Pageant) [2002/3 h109: 16s^2 17d^5 18g^2 19m^2 20d^2 17d* 21g^3 24g^5 Apr 3] leggy gelding: useful handicap hurdler: won competitive 16-runner contest at Cheltenham in December by ½ length from Telimar Prince: generally ran well otherwise, 4½ lengths third of 27 to Xenophon in Coral Cup at same course: finished tired when fifth of 22 to Carlovent at Aintree: barely stays 3m: acts on firm and soft going: takes good hold and is held up: sometimes drifts left: consistent. *P. J. Hobbs*   h143

SPECTROSCOPE (IRE)   4 b.g. Spectrum (IRE) – Paloma Bay (IRE) (Alzao (USA)) [2002/3 16d* 16d^{bd} 16d^4 16d* 17g^4 16g^2 Apr 3]   h137

No horse has yet completed what, if it didn't include a race in Ireland, the British Horseracing Board might grandly call the Juvenile Triple Crown. The Triumph Hurdle at Cheltenham, the Anniversary Hurdle at Aintree and the Champion Four Year Old Hurdle at Punchestown, run over a period of around six weeks in the spring, are without question the most significant events for juvenile hurdlers. All are run at around two miles, though seventeen furlongs over the New Course at Cheltenham is generally much more of a test of stamina than a bare two miles round the sharp Mildmay course at Aintree. After tackling those two contrasting tests successfully, any 'triple crown' contender then requires durability and consistency to be at the same peak of form at Punchestown. Little wonder the feat has proved elusive. The Cheltenham/Punchestown double has been completed

JCB Triumph Hurdle, Cheltenham—
Spectroscope (right) battles gamely to deprive long-time leader Well Chief

Mrs G. Smith's "Spectroscope"

only by Shawiya and Katarino, while the Cheltenham/Aintree double hasn't been achieved since Pollardstown first did it in 1979. Quazar, in 2002, became the first to land the Aintree and Punchestown races and, a year on, his stable-companion Spectroscope came closer than any yet to completing the hat-trick, though he ended up with one victory and two second places, winning the JCB Triumph before an unlucky defeat at Aintree and a clear-cut one at Punchestown.

Spectroscope's campaign had begun with a ready success in an eighteen-runner event at Kempton in October. He was brought down when just behind the leaders at the second last at Cheltenham in November and reportedly came home rather sore and was not seen out again until mid-January, when nearly eight lengths fourth to Bal de Nuit at Kempton. There was nothing in Spectroscope's form to suggest he might play a part in any championship events, and he started at 20/1 for the Triumph after getting back on the winning trail in a ten-runner race at Kempton again in early-February, taking the eye before leading at the last and beating Navale by two and a half lengths after being fifteen lengths adrift three out. Bal de Nuit, Do L'Enfant d'Eau, Far Pavilions and Sporazene—not yet in the form he showed later—were absentees for the Triumph, but the twenty-seven-runner field contained all the other top juveniles headed by the favourite Golden Cross, successful in two Grade 3 races at Fairyhouse and one of six Irish challengers in a season boasting fewer good young hurdlers there than usual. Red Wine, an eight-length scorer at Newbury, and Well Chief, a six-length winner of the Grade 2 Adonis Hurdle at Kempton, came next in the betting followed by Mutineer, successful from Golden Cross in a Grade 2 at Leopardstown. Spectroscope raced close to the pace set by Well Chief and avoided the trouble three flights out where Old California, sharing the lead, fell fatally, bringing down Don Fernando and German raider Moneytrain and badly impeding Dashing Home and Starzaan. Coming under strong pressure from the second last, Spectroscope inched his way up to the leader, who showed no signs of stopping, and got his head in front near the line to win by a head. The staying-on Golden Cross was five lengths away third followed by French-trained Lilium de Cotte. Spectroscope's form was not up to that usually required to land a Triumph Hurdle and he improved on it in the Anniversary Hurdle at Aintree, in which Well Chief, the 2/1 favourite, was widely expected to gain his revenge on Spectroscope, who started at 8/1. Giving 4 lb to most of his opponents, Spectroscope was in touch throughout but landed flat-footed and lost the lead at the last, where he was also crossed, and went down by a head to Triumph sixth Le Duc, with Well Chief two and half lengths behind him. With better luck Spectroscope would probably have won but the same cannot be said of his defeat in the Champion Four Year Old Hurdle at Punchestown in May, after the end of the British season. Sporazene took command early in the straight and Spectroscope was unable to get to him, staying on under pressure to go down by two lengths, four clear of third-placed Golden Cross.

Spectroscope (IRE) (b.g. 1999)	Spectrum (IRE) (b 1992)	Rainbow Quest (b 1981)	Blushing Groom
			I Will Follow
		River Dancer (b 1983)	Irish River
			Dancing Shadow
	Paloma Bay (IRE) (b 1993)	Alzao (br 1980)	Lyphard
			Lady Rebecca
		Adventurine (ch 1984)	Thatching
			Forever Amber

Spectroscope cost 36,000 guineas as a foal and 310,000 guineas as a yearling at the Newmarket October Sales but did not live up to expectations on the Flat, despite winning two middle-distance handicaps at Goodwood. The dam Paloma Bay, who has since produced foals by Danehill, Anabaa and Rainbow Quest, won over six furlongs at two when also placed in the listed Chesham Stakes. She stayed a mile but was out of a sprinting sister to Rustic Amber, successful in the Greenlands Stakes over the minimum trip, with Irish Oaks winner Ambergris as her third dam. Although this is not a family with an abundance of stamina, the sire Spectrum is, like his own sire Rainbow Quest, beginning to look an influence for stamina, and if Spectroscope is to improve significantly it may be when stepped up in trip. Spectroscope has raced only on good ground or softer. *Jonjo O'Neill*

SPECULAR (AUS) 7 b.g. Danehill (USA) – Spyglass (NZ) (Sir Sian (NZ)) [2002/3 15v* 14s² 14g* 15d* 16g* 15g* 16s* Apr 12] half-brother to Australian Group 1 winner at 1m Iron Horse (by Zephyr Zip): dam won 2m Auckland Cup: raced over 40 times on Flat, won over 1½m in Australia: leading hurdler in Australia, successful on 8 of 10 starts, including Lachal Hurdle at Flemington after end of British season: bidding to become first horse in over 60 years to carry more than 70kg to victory in race when unlucky-in-running short-head second to Alobar in Aus \$177,000 Grand National Hurdle there in late-June: stays 2½m: raced on good going or softer: sold reportedly for Aus \$750,000, to join Jonjo O'Neill. *T. Rosolini, Australia*   **h?**

SPEED BOARD (IRE) 11 b.g. Waajib – Pitty Pal (USA) (Caracolero (USA)) [2002/3 c20d c24s³ c25s³ c24s³ c25dur Feb 10] sturdy gelding: one-time fair hurdler/chaser: only poor nowadays, unseated sixth in hunter at Hereford on first outing since leaving F. Flood: third in point following month: stays 25f: unraced on firm going, acts on any other: blinkered. *Dennis Pugh*   **c79 h–**

SPEED VENTURE 6 b.g. Owington – Jade Venture (Never So Bold) [2002/3 h93: 19d 16d 16d 17s⁵ 16d⁴ 19s* 22g Mar 15] sparely-made gelding: modest handicap hurdler: back to best when winning 6-runner event at Hereford in March: stays 19f: raced on good going or softer (acts on heavy): visored last 4 starts, found little on first occasion: tongue tied. *J. Mackie*   **h92**

SPENDID (IRE) 11 b.g. Tidaro (USA) – Spendapromise (Goldhill) [2002/3 c–, h149: 25d³ 25d c26s* c33m³ c29m Apr 26] sturdy gelding: smart hurdler: respectable third to Brother Joe in Grade 2 at Wetherby on reappearance: useful chaser: first start over fences for 2 years, won 8-runner handicap at Doncaster in December by 6 lengths from Random Harvest: not discredited in very valuable events at Ayr (third to Ryalux in Scottish Grand National) and Sandown last 2 starts: best at 3m+: acts on soft and firm going: blinkered once (pulled up): usually races up with pace: usually less than fluent over fences: genuine and consistent. *A. King*   **c138 h145**

SPERIAMO (IRE) 7 b.g. Mandalus – Mares Eat Oats (Ovac (ITY)) [2002/3 F–: **h–**
16m⁶ 22d Oct 22] lengthy, dipped-backed gelding: tailed off in bumper and 2 novice
hurdles (blinkered): sold £450 Ascot February Sales. *G. Brown*

SPIDER BOY 6 b.g. Jupiter Island – Great Dilemma (Vaigly Great) [2002/3 F–: **F76 ?**
F16d F16g³ Mar 23] workmanlike gelding: first form in bumpers when 3 lengths third
of 7 to Romany Dream at Warwick, dictating pace after whipping round at start. *Miss
Z. C. Davison*

SPIDER MUSIC 7 ch.g. Orchestra – Muffet's Spider (Rymer) [2002/3 F91: 20s³ **h91**
20d^{ro} 20g³ 25g⁶ Mar 17] sturdy gelding: fair form in bumpers: easily best effort in novice
hurdles (ran out time before) when 14 lengths third of 17 to Sh Boom at Huntingdon:
should stay beyond 2½m. *Ferdy Murphy*

SPILAW (FR) 7 b.g. Sky Lawyer (FR) – Spinage (FR) (Village Star (FR)) [2002/3 **c71**
c77, h62: c16v⁵ c17s⁴ c21d³ c20v² c21s⁶ c26s⁴ c26s⁴ c24g⁶ Mar 12] angular gelding: **h–**
poor hurdler/chaser: stays 3¼m: acts on heavy going: blinkered once (less than keen).
John Allen

SPINAROUND 5 br.g. Terimon – Re-Spin (Gildoran) [2002/3 F16s 18g Mar 17] first **h–**
live foal: dam unraced half-sister to 1992 Grand National winner Party Politics: needed **F77**
race when well held in bumper at Sandown on debut: jumped poorly on hurdling bow.
N. A. Gaselee

SPINNING SILVER 8 b.g. Nearly A Hand – Paid Elation (Pia Fort) [2002/3 c–, F–: **c–**
17s 20m^{pu} 22m^F 20g⁶ Sep 14] tall, angular gelding: of little account. *D. J. Minty* **h–**

SPINOFSKI 8 b.g. Petoski – Spin Again (Royalty) [2002/3 c112+, h–: c24d² c22g² **c127**
c26s^{ur} c25d² c24s² c24g c24m⁵ Mar 22] angular gelding: fairly useful handicap chaser: **h–**
good efforts when runner-up 4 times in 2002/3, behind Ibis Rochelais at Sandown on last
occasion: stays 3¼m: acts on good to firm and heavy going: usually sound jumper: has
twice refused (when exhausted on second occasion). *P. R. Webber*

SPINONTHERIVER (IRE) 10 b.g. Over The River (FR) – Spindle Tree (Laurence **c–**
O) [2002/3 c24d^{pu} Jan 13] no form in 3 steeplechases in Britain, off 3 years before
reappearance. *Lady Susan Watson*

SPINOSA 5 br.m. Afzal – Rose Water (Waterfall) [2002/3 F16m⁵ Apr 21] 4,600 4-y-o: **F–**
fourth foal: dam unraced: well held in mares maiden bumper at Fakenham. *Mrs P. Sly*

SPIRIT LEADER (IRE) 7 b. or br.m. Supreme Leader – That's The Spirit (Mand- **h143**
alus) [2002/3 h122, F110: 16s² 16v³ 16s* 16s⁵ 16g* 17g*] Mar 13]

Seconditis: an unfortunate condition that can lead to punters catching a
cold. One sufferer with a particularly virulent form of the disease was identified in
the autumn by consultants of the form book. She (yes, it was a she) was so often the
bridesmaid and never the bride. In her failure to make it to the altar Spirit Leader
resembled no-one so much as Adelaide in *Guys And Dolls* as she found herself led
into the runner-up's berth for the eighth time in nine appearances when favourite on
her reappearance. But just as Adelaide manages to get her gambling man in the end,
so those punters who stayed true to Spirit Leader were more than amply rewarded
by the time spring had sprung.

After her reappearance defeat, to Mise Rafturai at Gowran, Spirit Leader
contested five of the hottest handicap hurdles of the season and won three, the
William Hill Handicap at Sandown, the Tote Gold Trophy at Newbury and the
Vincent O'Brien County Hurdle at Cheltenham. To win two major handicap hurdles in one season is a rare occurrence, to win three at any time is even rarer, in one
season almost without precedent. A clean sweep of this particular trio of races had,
however, never previously been realised. Make A Stand, in 1996/7, had won two of
the three, the William Hill and the Tote Gold Trophy, as well as the Lanzarote on
his way to Champion Hurdle success. Prideaux Boy won three major handicaps
over hurdles, the Mecca Bookmakers (as the William Hill was known) in 1984/5
and the Lanzarote and the Swinton in 1985/6, as well as finishing second in an
Imperial Cup and fourth in a County Hurdle. Floyd, in the spring of 1985, won the
Imperial Cup, the County Hurdle and the Queen's Prize on the Flat, which is a
notable treble of a slightly different kind, as is Willie Wumpkins' three successive
victories in the Coral Golden Hurdle Final. No horse has come particularly close to
winning the three races Spirit Leader did. Neblin is the only other to have won the
Tote Gold Trophy (or its predecessor, the Schweppes) and the County Hurdle, in
1987, and Copeland the only other, along with Make A Stand, to have won both the

William Hill (in 1999/00) and the Tote Gold Trophy (in 2001/2). Copeland was also second in the 2000 Tote Gold Trophy but two attempts at the County Hurdle resulted in no better than fifteenth place each time. Ekbalco won both the Mecca Bookmakers and the Imperial Cup in 1980/1 and finished a close second in the following season's Schweppes.

The William Hill was the weakest of the three races that Spirit Leader won. She started a well supported second favourite after another honourable defeat, finishing third on this particular occasion, behind Emotional Moment, in a race at Down Royal which was proving solid form. Making smooth headway from three out at Sandown, Spirit Leader led and made a mistake at the last but galloped on well up the stiff climb to the line and won by four lengths from Moving On Up.

The Tote Gold Trophy was named as a target afterwards but, with a sizeable rise in her handicap mark in the offing (her BHB mark went up 9 lb), there seemed sure to be stronger candidates come the day. A defeat in the Pierse Hurdle in January, in which Spirit Leader did not jump so fluently as usual but seemed beaten on merit when fifth to Xenophon, seemed to confirm that view. However, the Pierse turned out to be just about the strongest handicap hurdle of the season; they had bet 10/1 the field and, by the time Spirit Leader lined up at Newbury, the Leopardstown form had started to work out really well. It was to Spirit Leader's advantage that Xenophon had not been entered for the race (and would probably have been balloted out had he been anyway). Two other serious contenders weren't there either: Emotional Moment, the ante-post favourite, was eliminated at the final declaration stage and the very well handicapped Flame Creek was quixotically reserved for the Champion Hurdle. A maximum twenty-seven lined up for Europe's richest handicap hurdle in which Spirit Leader's main rival turned out to be the Lanzarote Hurdle winner Non So. The attempts of the Jockey Club's senior starter to dispatch the big field were hampered by some runners getting too close to the starting tape. Anyone in the vicinity and Channel 4 viewers heard the increasingly frustrated starter tell the jockeys to 'Get off the tape!' and to 'Do what you are told!' With the jockeys appearing to take very little notice, the Tote Gold Trophy start descended into a shambles. The runners eventually got off when with very little warning—and just after telling the jockeys 'Now keep off the gates'—the starter pressed the lever and gave a call of 'Come on'. Once under way, the race went

William Hill Handicap Hurdle, Sandown—Spirit Leader (noseband) holds off outsider Moving On Up to become only the second Irish-trained winner in the race's history

Tote Gold Trophy (Handicap), Newbury—riderless Calladine leads Spirit Leader over the last; Non So (right), Tikram (left) and long-time leader Benbyas are in close attendance

much as the one at Sandown: Spirit Leader travelled smoothly under a patient ride, improved her position stealthily in the straight and, after challenging approaching the last, overcame being crossed by a loose horse to lead on the run-in and win by a length and a half from Non So. The view put forward by *Timeform Perspective* that 'she owes her connections nothing and the handicapper is surely likely to take her measure now', again seemed a perfectly rational one at the time.

On to the County Hurdle. There were twenty-eight runners this time. There might have been twenty-nine but Xenophon was withdrawn after connections decided against bidding to follow up his success in the previous day's Coral Cup. Non So was in the line-up as was Mise Rafturai, Spirit Leader's conqueror at Gowran back at the start of the season. Mise Rafturai was the gamble of the race, backed at all rates down to 5/1 favourite, but, as inspired plots went, this was more *Crossroads* than *The Usual Suspects*. While the handicapper had done his best to try to take her measure by raising her a further 9 lb, it was in Spirit Leader's favour that the County Hurdle is invariably run to suit a horse that, like her, is produced to lead as late as possible. While Thierry Doumen sent the well-treated Never for home two out, much too soon, and was predictably swallowed up going to the last, Barry Geraghty (taking over from Norman Williamson, who had been on board at

Vincent O'Brien County Handicap Hurdle, Cheltenham— a third valuable handicap for Spirit Leader caps a memorable meeting for Barry Geraghty; runner-up Balapour is second left, the blundering Through The Rye finishes third

Sandown and Newbury) produced Spirit Leader at just about the right moment. He began to celebrate prematurely, however, and Spirit Leader had to work hard close home to hold the late surge of Balapour by a neck with Through The Rye a short head away third and Non So fourth. Geraghty was winning his fifth race of the Festival and snatched the top rider's prize from Richard Johnson. Spirit Leader was a second winner of the meeting for trainer Jessica Harrington, following Moscow Flyer in the Queen Mother Champion Chase. It was intended to run Spirit Leader in the Grade 1 Emo Oil Champion Hurdle at the Punchestown Festival shortly after the end of the British season but she failed to meet the engagement, reportedly not pleasing in her work after a long season. As it turned out, she wouldn't have had to improve much on her County Hurdle form to get in the shake-up against Quazar and Back In Front. In general, though, she has a fair way to go if she is to emulate Make A Stand and progress from a leading performer in big handicaps to a serious contender at championship level.

		Bustino	Busted
Spirit Leader (IRE) (b. or br.m. 1996)	Supreme Leader (b 1982)	(b 1971)	Ship Yard
		Princess Zena	Habitat
		(b 1975)	Guiding Light
	That's The Spirit (b 1984)	Mandalus	Mandamus
		(b 1974)	Laminate
		Flynn's Field	The Parson
		(b 1980)	Russian Queen

Spirit Leader was bought for IR 7,800 guineas at the Fairyhouse August Sale as a three-year-old in 1999. Her main selling points on pedigree were her sire Supreme Leader and her half-brother That's My Man (by Remainder Man), who won all five of his starts over hurdles, including the Royal Bond, before being fatally injured while being prepared for Cheltenham. Beyond that there was next to

Mr D. Thompson's "Spirit Leader"

nothing to recommend Spirit Leader. None of the three dams at the bottom of her pedigree raced. Her grandam Flynn's Field produced a winning pointer and her third dam Russian Queen did little better, with a minor hurdles winner and a winning pointer to her name. The catalogue page at Fairyhouse detailing Spirit Leader's family does actually feature another Tote Gold Trophy winner in King Credo but, as his fourth dam Hal's Maiden, is Spirit Leader's fifth dam the connection is remote to say the least. Spirit Leader has form at two and a half miles, though she raced only at around two in 2002/3. She is waited with and is well served by a true gallop. She has raced on good going or softer and acts on heavy. Spirit Leader is a sturdy mare in appearance and gives the impression she will make a chaser, so a switch to fences may be the best plan with her in 2003/4. Though, as has been said already, she owes her connections nothing. *Mrs J. Harrington, Ireland*

SPIRIT OF DESTINY   6 ch.m. Riverwise (USA) – Tearful Sarah (Rugantino) **h–**
[2002/3 F–: 22g^{pu} Nov 9] small mare: no sign of ability. *C. W. Mitchell*

SPIRIT OF LOVE (USA)   8 ch.g. Trempolino (USA) – Dream Mary (USA) (Marfa **h99**
(USA)) [2002/3 h80: 23d^4 22d^4 24g^F Jun 12] good-topped gelding: smart at one time on Flat (best at 2m+): modest form over hurdles: won novice handicap at Cartmel in June: would have been suited by 3m+: not a fluent jumper: dead. *E. W. Tuer*

SPIRIT OF TENBY (IRE)   6 b.g. Tenby – Asturiana (Julio Mariner) [2002/3 h91: **h84 d**
16g^{pu} 17g^6 20m 16g 22g^6 17m^{pu} 21d 24d Nov 25] small gelding: won novice hurdle at Perth in early-2001/2: disappointing in handicaps since, sold out of C. Mann's stable 5,800 gns Doncaster August Sales after third start: unproven beyond 2m: tried in cheekpieces/visor: sold 1,800 gns Doncaster May Sales. *A. G. Hobbs*

SPIRIT OF THE GREEN (IRE)   5 b.g. Detroit Sam (FR) – Golden Hearted (Cor- **F82 ?**
varo (USA)) [2002/3 F17g^5 Mar 16] 5,000 4-y-o: fourth foal: half-brother to winning 2¾m hurdler Kilcourt Lad (by Valville) and winning pointer by Roi Guillaume: dam, maiden, from family of smart staying hurdler Goldspun: fifth of 11 in maiden bumper at Folkestone on debut, never a threat. *L. Wells*

SPLASH AND DASH (IRE)   8 ch.g. Arcane (USA) – Quilty Rose (Buckskin (FR)) **c103**
[2002/3 c24s* Mar 10] fifth foal: half-brother to winning 2½m chaser Take The Lot (by Commanche Run): dam bumper/1¾m winner on Flat: bought 12,000 gns Doncaster May (2001) Sales: useful pointer, successful 3 times in Britain, including in February: landed odds in novice hunter chase at Stratford, not always fluent but pulling away when left clear 3 out. *Mrs S. J. Hickman*

SPLENDOUR (IRE)   8 b.g. Broken Hearted – Black Trix (Peacock (FR)) [2002/3 **c112**
h110: 20g^4 24s^2 24s^4 16d^4 16v c18d^3 c21v^2 Mar 2] leggy gelding: fairly useful handicap **h115**
hurdler: won at Roscommon in August: fair form when placed both starts over fences: effective at 2m to 3m: acts on any going. *J. R. Cox, Ireland*

SPLODGE   12 b.g. Oedipus Complex – Gardella (Garnered) [2002/3 c–: c25d^{pu} c24d^{pu} **c–**
May 26] close-coupled, workmanlike gelding: winning pointer: well held only completed start in steeplechases: blinkered in 2002/3. *N. A. Callaghan*

SPOOF (IRE)   8 b.g. Good Thyne (USA) – Wraparound Sue (Touch Paper) [2002/3 **h94**
h98: 24d^5 27v^2 20d^5 24v^6 Jan 2] compact gelding: modest handicap hurdler: stays 27f: acts on heavy going. *L. Lungo*

SPORAZENE (IRE)   4 gr.g. Cozzene (USA) – Sporades (USA) (Vaguely Noble) **h138 p**
[2002/3 16d^3 16s^3 16m* Apr 12]
    The juvenile hurdlers of 2002/3 were not a vintage bunch. The French-trained and -raced Nickname is the highest rated four-year-old in this Annual, some way ahead of the best of those raced in Britain and Ireland. Spectroscope is one of those with strongest claims to being the best of that group, having won the Triumph and failed narrowly to concede weight to Le Duc in the Anniversary Hurdle at Aintree, but he was beaten fairly and squarely by Sporazene, who didn't run at either Cheltenham or Aintree, in the Champion Four Year Old Hurdle at Punchestown and, as a result, Sporazene is rated the best in Britain and Ireland. Sporazene's rating is as low as any leading juvenile hurdler since *Chasers & Hurdlers* began, on a par with Grimes in 1996/7 and Sybillin in 1989/90. Such lowly ratings didn't stop Sybillin showing himself a very smart hurdler and high-class chaser subsequently, while Grimes developed into a top-class two-mile hurdler, one of the best of recent years. Rated just behind Grimes in his year were Commanche Court and Bellator

IAWS Champion Four Year Old Hurdle, Punchestown—
Sporazene stakes his claim as the leading juvenile in Britain and Ireland

and they didn't fare so badly subsequently: Commanche Court showed very smart form over hurdles before finishing second in the 2002 Cheltenham Gold Cup, and Bellator was a smart hurdler and high-class chaser. It is far from a hopeless cause for Sporazene to achieve a similar level of form.

Sporazene's emergence as a leading juvenile came late in the day, although he made his debut in theoretically the first significant juvenile hurdle of the season, the Wensleydale at Wetherby in November, formerly a Grade 2 race but now reclassified as listed. He started a well-supported, short-priced favourite, with his home reputation preceding him. However, he looked far from the finished article beforehand and his jumping lacked confidence, and he managed only third behind Newtown Dancer and Tunstall. The game winner wasn't seen again and the second ran below form next time before meeting an untimely end, but the form looks nothing out of the ordinary. Sporazene was returned to Wetherby later in the month and started odds on to gain compensation. He failed to progress as expected, Mistanoora, who developed into a useful juvenile, winning by a wide margin, while Sporazene, again making mistakes, could not even hold second. Sporazene appeared a weak-looking colt who needed time and he was given plenty of it after Wetherby. He also got a visit from the vet and when he returned at Ayr in April it was as a gelding. Some of the fields at the Scottish National meeting were on the thin side, including that for the Purvis Marquees Juvenile Novices' Hurdle in which just four went to post. Despite not coming up to expectations in the autumn, Sporazene started odds on and made short work of his rivals. There were clear indications that he might yet make the sort of impact his early reputation suggested he could, perhaps the most telling that his jumping was altogether more assured.

That said, it was still a very big step up in class to tackle the pick of the four-year-old hurdlers in the Grade 1 at Punchestown. All eleven of his rivals, even the maiden 40/1-chance Laoch Na Mara, had shown better bare form than Sporazene, some of them by some margin, and the form of all the best juvenile races was set to be tested: Spectroscope was joined by the first four Irish-trained runners to chase

854

him home at Cheltenham—Golden Cross (third), Newlands Gold (seventh), Mutineer (eighth) and Dashing Home (tenth)—as well as Nas Na Riogh who unseated rider there, and by Starzaan, impeded when down the field in the Triumph before coming fourth at Aintree. Mutineer and Golden Cross had fought out the best Irish trial for Cheltenham, Dashing Home had won at the National meeting at Fairyhouse and Nas Na Riogh had won the Finale Hurdle at Chepstow. Throw in the Denny winner Party Airs and there could hardly have been a more representative line-up. Sporazene beat the lot of them in some style. Held up in the middle of the field, he again jumped well and travelled with ease, made his move up the hill and led at the flight before the straight, two out, quickening once turned for home and ridden out after the final flight with the race already his. He beat Spectroscope by two lengths, with Golden Cross a further four away in third, Starzaan fourth, Mutineer fifth and Dashing Home sixth. Most of the principals had proved consistent through the season and there is little reason to think they did not give their running.

After the race, trainer Paul Nicholls said Sporazene could be the first serious Champion Hurdle horse he has trained. He has certainly made his name as a trainer of chasers, with a stable consisting largely of graduates from the pointing field or young French-bred horses that are sent over fences sooner rather than later. Although Sporazene has the physique to make a chaser when he fills out, he has a Flat pedigree and his speed and much improved jumping suggest he has some prospect of making the grade as a good two-mile hurdler. At the time of writing, he is generally quoted as fourth favourite for the 2004 Champion Hurdle, behind Rooster Booster, Back In Front and Rhinestone Cowboy. His form does not entitle him to such a position but there aren't that many plausible contenders around. A

Ged Mason & David Jackson's "Sporazene"

race like the Christmas Hurdle at Kempton could provide a further idea of how far Sporazene might go as a hurdler.

Sporazene (IRE) (gr.g. 1999)	Cozzene (USA) (gr 1980)	Caro (gr 1967)	Fortino II
			Chambord
		Ride The Trails (b 1971)	Prince John
			Wildwook
	Sporades (USA) (ro 1989)	Vaguely Noble (b 1965)	Vienna
			Noble Lassie
		Stresa (gr 1975)	Mill Reef
			Ileana

Sproazene ran three times on the Flat in France for Andre Fabre before being sold to join Nicholls' yard. He won an eleven-furlong newcomers race at Chantilly and finished a neck second in a minor event over slightly further, showing fairly useful form. Fabre has quite a connection with Sporazene's family. He trained the dam Sporades, a smart filly who won the mile-and-a-quarter Prix de Flore, and two of her notable half-brothers, Mill Native, who won the Arlington Million, and the high-class miler French Stress, who finished second in the Poulains and the Jacques le Marois. The grandam Stresa bred ten winners in all, among the others the smart two-year-old American Stress and the listed-placed pair Tremplin and Private Talk. Sporazene is Sporades' fifth foal and fourth winner. Best of the others is the smart miler Leave Us Leap (by Summer Squall). Of the remainder, Sojourner (by Gone West) won over seven and a half furlongs while Shalako (by King-mambo) won four times up to a mile and a half in Germany and was a fair hurdler for Philip Hobbs in 2002/3. Since Sporazene, the dam has produced the filly Ile Rousse (by Danehill), who was second on her Flat debut in France in 2002 and Noble Desert (by Green Desert), a 38,000-guinea yearling who is in training with Rae Guest. The third dam Ileana was another smart miler (though out of a good stayer in Romantica). She bred nine winners, notably the Gran Premio di Milano winner Terreno and the high-class two-year-old Antrona, the dam of the good miler Spoleto and grandam of the high-class mile to mile-and-a-quarter colt First Island. This isn't a family where stamina gets much of a look in and Sporazene seems likely to prove best at around two miles for the time being. His best run came on good ground, but it would be unwise to judge his effectiveness or otherwise on soft on what he achieved at Wetherby. *P. F. Nicholls*

SPORTING CHANCE 11 ch.g. Ikdam – Tumbling Ego (Abednego) [2002/3 c–, h–: c19f³ c25g c23m c21m⁴ Jul 14] sturdy gelding: poor pointer/novice chaser: barely stays 25f: acts on firm going. *A. G. Hobbs*   **c76 h–**

SPORTING GESTURE 6 ch.g. Safawan – Polly Packer (Reform) [2002/3 16d Nov 2] half-brother to useful 3m hurdler Upton Park (by High Top) and fair 2m hurdler Regal Reform (by Prince Tenderfoot): fair on Flat (stays 1½m), successful in April: patiently ridden and not given unduly hard time when around 26 lengths eighth of 24 to Jaboune in well-contested novice at Wetherby on hurdling debut: should improve. *M. W. Easterby*   **h82 p**

SPORTSMAN (IRE) 4 b.g. Sri Pekan (USA) – Ardent Range (IRE) (Archway (IRE)) [2002/3 17g⁶ 16m² 16m² 16d⁵ 16d³ Nov 30] leggy gelding: poor maiden on Flat: modest form in juvenile hurdles: will stay beyond 2m: blinkered last 3 starts (didn't look easy ride middle one). *M. W. Easterby*   **h90**

SPOT THEDIFFERENCE (IRE) 10 b.g. Lafontaine (USA) – Spotted Choice (IRE) (Callernish) [2002/3 c129, h–: c26g⁶ c21gᵘʳ c29g Apr 21] tall, useful-looking gelding: fairly useful chaser at best: won point in March: below form in Foxhunter at Cheltenham (bad mistake fifteenth) and Irish Grand National at Fairyhouse (wore cheekpieces): unseated in Fox Hunters' at Aintree (well behind when hampered thirteenth) in between and in cross-country event at Punchestown (6 out when in third) in early-May: best form at up to 25f: raced mainly on good going or softer (acts on heavy): ran well only outing in blinkers. *E. Bolger, Ireland*   **c116 h–**

SPOT THE NATIVE (IRE) 7 ch.g. Be My Native (USA) – Shannon Foam (Le Bavard (FR)) [2002/3 h–: 17d³ 20d³ 20d c16g c27v² c24gᵘʳ c25dᵖᵘ c25gᵘʳ c25g⁴ Mar 17] sturdy gelding: modest maiden hurdler/chaser: stays 27f: acts on heavy going: inconsistent. *Mrs S. J. Smith*   **c88 h87**

SPREAD THE DREAM 5 ch.g. Alflora (IRE) – Cauchemar (Hot Brandy) [2002/3 F16m² Mar 20] fifth foal: dam winning hurdler/chaser, stayed 25f: second to Forever Dream in bumper at Wincanton on debut, looking green. *N. J. Henderson*   **F93**

SPREAD THE WORD   11 b.m. Deploy – Apply (Kings Lake (USA)) [2002/3 c25dpu Feb 6] sparely-made mare: fair pointer, successful in January: no show on hunter chase debut: tried visored. *Mrs O. Bush*

c–
h–

SPREE VISION   7 b.g. Suave Dancer (USA) – Regent's Folly (IRE) (Touching Wood (USA)) [2002/3 h80: 16s² 20d² 16d* 16d⁶ 16v³ 20vpu 16d 17d⁵ 16d Mar 7] smallish gelding: modest hurdler: won maiden at Newcastle in November (subsequently tested positive for morphine): below form last 4 starts: stays easy 2½m: acts on heavy and good to firm going: has had tongue tied: occasionally finds little. *P. Monteith*

h95

SPRIGHTLEY PIP (IRE)   12 gr.g. Roselier (FR) – Owen's Rose (Master Owen) [2002/3 c99, h–: c33gpu c25fpu May 15] good-topped gelding: lightly raced over hurdles: winning pointer: fairly useful modest chaser at best: stayed 3m: acted on firm going: dead. *P. Williams*

c–
h–

SPRINGBOK ATTITUDE   6 b.g. Pharly (FR) – Tugra (FR) (Baby Turk) [2002/3 h82?, F–: 16gpu 17dpu 16spu 16m 16m 20m 17f² 16f³ Oct 10] smallish gelding: poor maiden hurdler: form only around 2m on firm/good to firm going: tried visored/blinkered: has had tongue tied. *B. Llewellyn*

h62

SPRING DAWN   8 gr.g. Arzanni – Another Spring (Town Crier) [2002/3 16d³ 17s² 17s³ 16g Mar 14] workmanlike gelding: fair novice hurdler, placed first 3 starts: likely to prove suited by 2½m: acts on soft going. *N. J. Henderson*

h105

SPRING DOUBLE (IRE)   12 br.g. Seclude (USA) – Solar Jet (Mandalus) [2002/3 c–, h99d: 24g⁶ May 8] leggy, close-coupled gelding: fair handicap hurdler/chaser: below form since winning on reappearance in 2001/2 (lame final start of season): best at 3m+: acts on good to firm and heavy going: effective visored/blinkered or not: often jumps none too fluently, and has run in snatches. *N. A. Twiston-Davies*

c–
h–

SPRINGER THE LAD   6 ch.g. Carlton (GER) – Also Kirsty (Twilight Alley) [2002/3 h79, F77: 17s³ 16d⁴ c21v⁴ c24spu Mar 7] strong gelding: poor form in novice hurdles: no show in 2 novice chases. *D. M. Grissell*

c–
h76

SPRINGFIELD GILDA (IRE)   5 b.m. Gildoran – Ledee (Le Bavard (FR)) [2002/3 F82: F17d² 16dpu Nov 12] modest form in bumpers, runner-up twice: no show in mares maiden at Southwell on hurdling debut. *S. Gollings*

h–
F82

SPRINGFIELD REX   12 ch.g. Oedipus Complex – Scarlet Coon (Tycoon II) [2002/3 c97: c20mpu May 8] medium-sized gelding: winning hunter chaser, little sign of retaining ability: acts on firm going. *D. E. Ingle*

c–

SPRINGFIELD SCALLY   10 ch.g. Scallywag – Ledee (Le Bavard (FR)) [2002/3 h–: 24s* 25d⁴ 22s 21d³ 23s⁵ 24d* 25g 24g Apr 3] quite good-topped gelding: useful handicap hurdler: won at Chepstow in November and Doncaster in March, beating Muck Savage by 5 lengths on latter course: stays 3¼m: acts on good to firm and heavy going: forces pace: tough, genuine and reliable. *S. Gollings*

h132

*Pertemps Handicap Hurdle (Qualifier), Chepstow—
bold front runner Springfield Scally returns to form after a disappointing 2001/2 campaign*

SPRINGFORD (IRE) 11 b.g. King's Ride – Tickenor Wood (Le Bavard (FR)) [2002/3 c90, h–: c25f⁶ May 15] workmanlike gelding: winning chaser: thrice-raced maiden hurdler: won point in January: stays 25f: best form on good going: sometimes finishes weakly. *Mrs Caroline Keevil*
  c–
  h–

SPRING GALE (IRE) 12 b.g. Strong Gale – Orospring (Tesoro Mio) [2002/3 c101, h–: c24gʳᵗʳ c25m³ May 22] rather leggy gelding: fair hunter chaser: refused to race at Fakenham in May: ruined chance by starting very slowly next time: won points in March and April: stays 3½m: acts on soft and good to firm going: has worn blinkers: needs treating with caution. *J. M. Turner*
  c74 §
  h–

SPRING GROVE (IRE) 8 b.g. Mandalus – Lucy Lorraine (IRE) (Buckskin (FR)) [2002/3 c128, h–: c21gᵖᵘ 20d⁴ 19m⁶ Apr 15] workmanlike gelding: fairly useful hurdler/chaser at best: largely disappointing since 2000/1, often shaping as if having problem: should be effective around 2½m: acts on heavy and good to firm going. *R. H. Alner*
  c–
  h–

SPRING PURSUIT 7 b.g. Rudimentary (USA) – Pursuit of Truth (USA) (Irish River (FR)) [2002/3 17s⁵ 16s⁶ 16d Dec 14] brother to fair 2m hurdler First Truth: modest on Flat (best around 1½m) nowadays: poor form in novice company over hurdles, jumping less than fluently. *R. J. Price*
  h81

SPRING ROCK 6 b.g. Rock Hopper – Shaft of Sunlight (Sparkler) [2002/3 F16f F17d Oct 26] half-brother to several winners on Flat up to 2¼m: dam, maiden who stayed 1½m, half-sister to fairly useful 2m hurdler Nocatchim: little show in bumpers/points. *R. M. Whitaker*
  F–

SPRINGWELL ALBERT (IRE) 7 ch.g. Alphabatim (USA) – Red Bit (IRE) (Henbit (USA)) [2002/3 h–, F77: 20gᵖᵘ 17gᵖᵘ Apr 21] quite good-topped gelding: no form over hurdles: reportedly broke blood vessel final outing. *C. Grant*
  h–

SPRINGWELL BOB 7 b.g. Alflora (IRE) – Gokatiego (Huntercombe) [2002/3 16v 20gᵖᵘ Apr 21] tenth foal: brother to bumper winner Alf Lauren and half-brother to fair 2m chaser Strong Views (by Remainder Man) and poor hurdler/chaser Come On Penny (by Rakaposhi King), stays 2½m: dam unraced: no sign of ability in 2 novice hurdles. *C. Grant*
  h–

SPRINGWOOD WHITE 9 gr.g. Sharkskin Suit (USA) – Kale Brig (New Brig) [2002/3 c–: c20mᵘʳ c20m c16g c25g³ Apr 14] modest pointer (dead-heated in January)/hunter chaser: stays 25f: wore cheekpieces final outing. *J. L. Gledson*
  c78

SPUDDLER'S DREAM 6 ch.g. Michelozzo (USA) – Keep On Dreaming (Sunyboy) [2002/3 F17d May 14] first foal: dam winning pointer: won 2½m maiden point on debut, placed next 2 starts: ninth of 16 in bumper at Hereford: fourth in point in January. *P. F. Nicholls*
  F68

SPUD ONE 6 b.g. Lord Americo – Red Dusk (Deep Run) [2002/3 F17d* F17d² 16d⁵ 16g* 18g⁵ 16dᵖᵘ 16f² Apr 21] 25,000 4-y-o: lengthy, good-topped gelding: fifth foal: dam, poor novice hurdler who stayed 2½m, sister to high-class 2m to 2½m chaser Deep Sensation: fairly useful form in bumpers: showed little in November: good second to Cloudy Grey at Hereford next time, though hung and carried head awkwardly: modest novice hurdler: won at Huntingdon in February: raced around 2m: acts on firm and good to soft going: headstrong: blundered last sixth start. *O. Sherwood*
  h98
  F96

SPUMANTE PRINCE 6 b.g. Tromeros – Asti Spumante (FR) (Fireside Chat (USA)) [2002/3 F16m F16g 16gᵖᵘ Feb 27] fifth reported foal: dam, lightly-raced maiden, from family of champion US Flat mare Old Hat: no sign of ability: tried visored. *G. Barnett*
  h–
  F–

SPY BOY (IRE) 7 b.g. Balla Cove – Spy Girl (Tanfirion) [2002/3 h80, F74: 21gᵘʳ 20gᵖᵘ 16m 19g 16m 20mᵘʳ c23m⁶ c24s³ c23g⁴ c17gᵖᵘ c19d c20d⁴ 16v 19s 24v c26sᵖᵘ c17vᵖᵘ Mar 5] leggy gelding: winning hurdler/maiden chaser: tried visored (including for win)/blinkered: sold £600 Ascot April Sales. *S. T. Lewis*
  c–
  h–

SQUANDAMANIA 10 b.g. Ela-Mana-Mou – Garden Pink (FR) (Bellypha) [2002/3 h–: 16vᴿ 20s⁵ 21v⁵ 24v 20s⁵ 27s⁵ Mar 11] tall gelding: handicap hurdler, capable of no more than bad form nowadays: acts on soft going: tried blinkered/visored/in cheekpieces: all 4 wins at Sedgefield. *J. R. Norton*
  h53

SQUARE ONE (IRE) 9 b.m. Mandalus – Deep Dollar (Deep Run) [2002/3 c–: c25dᵖᵘ May 6] lengthy mare: winning pointer (including in February)/hunter chaser: ran poorly in blinkers in May. *C. C. Bealby*
  c–

SQUEEZE BOX (IRE) 4 b.f. Accordion – Spread Your Wings (IRE) (Decent Fellow) [2002/3 F16g² F17g F16g⁶ Apr 14] €26,000 3-y-o: fourth foal: dam modest 2m
  F84

hurdler: easily best effort in bumpers when second in mares event at Musselburgh on debut, carrying head shade awkwardly. *J. Howard Johnson*

SQUEEZE (IRE) 5 b.g. Old Vic – Petaluma Pet (Callernish) [2002/3 F16m⁶ Apr 21] **F77**
seventh foal: half-brother to winning Irish pointer Coolafinka (by Strong Statement): dam placed twice in 2m hurdles in Ireland: signs of just a little ability when sixth of 8 in maiden bumper at Huntingdon on debut. *B. N. Pollock*

SQUIBNOCKET (IRE) 4 b.g. Charnwood Forest (IRE) – Serenad Dancer (FR) **h–**
(Antheus (USA)) [2002/3 16d^F Nov 2] half-brother to fair 2m hurdler Brief Dance (by Brief Truce): modest maiden on Flat: probably stayed 8.5f: fell fatally on hurdling debut. *T. D. Easterby*

STACK THE PACK (IRE) 6 ch.g. Good Thyne (USA) – Game Trix (Buckskin **h90**
(FR)) [2002/3 F98: 19d 24d² Mar 1] rather unfurnished gelding: bumper winner: much better effort in novice hurdles when 21 lengths second to Fern Lord at Newbury: will prove better at 3m than shorter. *T. R. George*

STACKY LIGHT (FR) 10 b.g. Conquistacky (USA) – Lumineuse (BEL) (Lisaro) **c–**
[2002/3 c–, h–: c25g^pu May 4] tall, angular gelding: fair pointer: winner on hunter chase **h–**
debut in 1998/9, no form since: stays 25f: acts on good to soft going: blinkered/visored. *D. Pipe*

STACUMNY BRIDGE (IRE) 5 b.g. Flying Spur (AUS) – Karoi (IRE) (Kafu) **h125**
[2002/3 F16m² F16s* 16v* 16d⁴ 16d³ Mar 22] good sort: will make a chaser: fourth foal: **F99**
half-brother to several winners on Flat: dam 9.5f winner on Flat: fairly useful form in 2 bumpers, winning at Fairyhouse in December: won 4-y-o novice hurdle: won 4-y-o maiden at Leopardstown later in month, beating Arch Stanton a length: ran well when fourth to Sacundai in Grade 2 at Gowran in February and to Back In Front in Grade 1 at Punchestown in April: raced at 2m: acts on heavy going. *M. Halford, Ireland*

STAFFORD KING (IRE) 6 b.h. Nicolotte – Opening Day (Day Is Done) [2002/3 **h86**
17s² 16s³ 20m² 20m² 20g² 20m³ 22g² 25m Oct 29] workmanlike horse: modest maiden on Flat (stays 2¾m): modest novice hurdler: effective around 2m and seems to stay 25f: acts on soft and good to firm going: reliable. *J. G. M. O'Shea*

STAGE AFFAIR (USA) 9 b. or br.g. Theatrical – Wooing (USA) (Stage Door Johnny) **c127**
[2002/3 16v² 16d³ c16d³ c16d² c16g⁵ Mar 11] tall gelding: useful hurdler nowadays: placed in **h144**
Grade 1 events at Leopardstown in December (second to Liss A Paoraigh) and January (third to Like-A-Butterfly): third to Schwartzhalle in Grade 2 novice at Navan on chasing debut: stiff task, well-held sixth to Azertyuiop in Arkle at Cheltenham (blinkered and edgy): raced at 2m: acts on good to firm and heavy going: has had tongue tied. *D. K. Weld, Ireland*

STAGE DIRECTION (USA) 6 b.g. Theatrical – Carya (USA) (Northern Dancer) **h84**
[2002/3 h77: 17g 16m* Jun 19] leggy gelding: modest on Flat (stays 2m), successful in July: poor hurdler: won novice claimer at Worcester in June: raced around 2m, should stay further: acts on good to firm going. *B. J. Llewellyn*

STAKEHOLDER (IRE) 5 ch.g. Priolo (USA) – Island Goddess (Godswalk (USA)) **h–**
[2002/3 F88: 17v 16d 16d Nov 24] angular gelding: fair form in bumpers in 2001/2: well held in 3 novice hurdles. *M. Sheppard*

STALKY 4 ch.f. Bahamian Bounty – La Noisette (Rock Hopper) [2002/3 17m^pu Aug **h–**
17] modest and unreliable on Flat (best form at 5f): no prospect of staying 2m. *G. F. Bridgwater*

STALKY DOVE 6 b.m. Homo Sapien – Sally's Dove (Celtic Cone) [2002/3 F16g⁴ **F74**
F16m⁶ F16f Mar 29] 3,100 4-y-o: third known foal: half-sister to winning hurdler Dove From Above (by Henbit), stays 3¼m: dam, winning 2m hurdler, from family of 1994 Champion Hurdle winner Flakey Dove: poor form in mares bumpers. *W. M. Brisbourne*

STALLONE 6 ch.g. Brief Truce (USA) – Bering Honneur (USA) (Bering) [2002/3 **h81**
16g⁶ 17s³ 16g⁵ 16d^F 16g⁵ Apr 1] modest on Flat (stays 1¼m) nowadays: poor novice hurdler: raced around 2m: acts on soft ground: has had tongue tied: hung left off bridle fourth outing. *N. Wilson*

STAMPARLAND HILL 8 b.g. Gildoran – Woodland Flower (Furry Glen) [2002/3 **c–**
c129, h106: 20d 19d⁴ 16d^pu Apr 9] lengthy gelding: successful on chasing debut, let down **h107**
by jumping other 2 starts: fair handicap hurdler: ran well when fourth at Doncaster in January but well below form both runs either side: bred to stay much further than 19f: probably acts on heavy going: formerly headstrong. *J. M. Jefferson*

STAND ASIDE 7 b.g. In The Wings – Honourable Sheba (USA) (Roberto (USA)) **h104**
[2002/3 20v² 22s³ 24v⁵ Jan 17] sturdy gelding: fair maiden hurdler: good placed efforts
first 2 starts in 2002/3, tailed off final one: should stay 3m: raced on going softer than
good (acts on heavy): has high head carriage. *J. T. Gifford*

STAND EASY (IRE) 10 b.g. Buckskin (FR) – Geeaway (Gala Performance (USA)) **c101 §**
[2002/3 c101, h–: c26v^F c23d^{pu} 24v 22s⁴ 26s³ c25m³ Apr 17] tall gelding: poor maiden **h83 §**
hurdler: fair maiden chaser: first start since sold out of J. Portman's stable 3,000 gns
Doncaster March Sales and looking very well, easily best effort in 2002/3 when third to
Keltic Heritage in novice chase at Cheltenham final start: suited by 3m+: acts on soft and
good to firm going: has worn cheekpieces, better without: often none too fluent over
fences: not to be trusted. *J. R. Cornwall*

STANDIFORD GIRL (IRE) 6 b.m. Standiford (USA) – Pennine Girl (IRE) (Pennine **h–**
Walk) [2002/3 h–: 16s^{pu} 21d 16s Mar 10] small, plain mare: little show over hurdles.
L. A. Dace

STANDING APPLAUSE (USA) 5 b. or br.g. Theatrical – Pent (USA) (Mr Pros- **h70**
pector (USA)) [2002/3 20g^{pu} 20d 20m⁵ Jun 19] ex-Irish gelding: fairly useful on Flat
(stays 1¾m), sold out of D. Weld's stable 20,000 gns Newmarket Autumn (2001) Sales:
first form over hurdles when fifth in maiden at Worcester in June: tongue tied. *Mrs
A. J. Hamilton-Fairley*

STANDING BLOOM 7 ch.m. Presidium – Rosie Cone (Celtic Cone) [2002/3 h77?: **h92**
16g 17s³ 20d² 21s* 20v⁴ 21m Mar 22] medium-sized mare: modest hurdler: won minor
event at Warwick in January: likely to stay beyond 21f: acts on heavy going, bumper form
on good to firm. *Mrs P. Sly*

STANLEY ISLAND 6 b.g. Stani (USA) – Teminny (Grey Love) [2002/3 16m^{pu} 19g^{pu} **h–**
Oct 18] tall, leggy gelding: seventh live foal: dam won 2-runner novice hurdle: no show
in 2 selling hurdles. *M. Sheppard*

STANLEY PARK 5 ch.g. Bold Arrangement – Queen Buzzard (Buzzards Bay) **h–**
[2002/3 F16d 16g 20m^{pu} Apr 21] workmanlike gelding: first foal: dam poor hurdler who **F–**
stayed 2¾m: no sign of ability. *J. R. Weymes*

STANMORE (IRE) 11 b.g. Aristocracy – Lady Go Marching (USA) (Go Marching **c103**
(USA)) [2002/3 c93, h–: c22g^{pu} c20d⁴ c21m³ c21m² c21m* c24m* c20m⁴ c21g³ c24d* **h–**
c24d⁴ c24d⁴ Nov 24] lengthy gelding: fair handicap chaser: won at Southwell in August,
Stratford in September and Fakenham in October: stays 3m: has won on soft going, raced
on firmer nowadays (acts on firm): blinkered twice: usually races prominently: sound
jumper. *Mrs J. A. Saunders*

STANTONBURY PARK 6 gr.g. Neltino – True Divine (True Song) [2002/3 F16m **F–**
Oct 30] workmanlike gelding: has scope: seventh foal: half-brother to fairly useful
hurdler Mullover (by Ra Nova), stays 2½m, and to poor pointer by Broadsword: dam
pulled up in 2 points: well held in bumper at Cheltenham on debut, probably in need of
experience. *S. J. Gilmore*

STANTONS CHURCH 6 b.g. Homo Sapien – Valkyrie Reef (Miramar Reef) [2002/3 **h80**
16d⁵ 16g⁴ 17s³ 20m^{pu} Mar 23] first foal: dam, poor maiden on Flat, won 17f hurdle: poor
form over hurdles: not an easy ride. *H. D. Daly*

STAPLE SOUND 6 b.g. Alflora (IRE) – Loch Scavaig (IRE) (The Parson) [2002/3 **h–**
F–: F17d 20v 16d 20g^{pu} Apr 1] leggy gelding: well held in bumpers and over hurdles: left **F–**
W. McKeown before final start. *James Moffatt*

STAR ANGLER (IRE) 5 b.g. Supreme Leader – So Pink (IRE) (Deep Run) [2002/3 **F94**
F16d² Mar 10] €18,000 4-y-o: third foal: dam 2m hurdle winner: promising second to
Tighten Your Belt in maiden bumper at Stratford on debut. *H. D. Daly*

STAR BLAKENEY 10 b.g. Blakeney – Trikkala Star (Tachypous) [2002/3 c–, h–: **c–**
c20d^{pu} 22m* 21g 20g⁶ 22m³ Sep 7] rangy gelding: poor hurdler/maiden chaser: won **h68**
conditional jockeys selling handicap hurdle at Uttoxeter in June: stays 2¾m: acts on good
to firm and heavy going: tongue tied. *B. D. Leavy*

STAR CATCHER (IRE) 7 b.g. Toulon – Paper Merchant (Hays) [2002/3 h–, F–: **h–**
24v^{pu} 20d Jan 15] no sign of ability: has had tongue tied. *B. G. Powell*

STAR CLIPPER 6 b.g. Kris – Anne Bonny (Ajdal (USA)) [2002/3 h122, F93: 18s² **c122**
16d³ 16s c18v* c20s³ Mar 15] good sort: fairly useful hurdler, below best in 2002/3: good **h113**
start to chasing career when winning maiden at Fairyhouse in March: ran well, though
looked reluctant under pressure, when fourth of 5 to Le Roi Miguel in Grade 1 novice at

Punchestown in May: raced mainly around 2m on good going or softer (acts well on heavy): looked less than keen in blinkers third outing. *N. Meade, Ireland*

STAR CONTROL (IRE)   9 gr.m. Phardante (FR) – Greystar (General Ironside) [2002/3 c–, h69: 20g 22g 26m⁵ Jul 19] workmanlike mare: bad maiden hurdler/chaser: probably stays 3¼m: acts on firm going. *H. J. Evans*   c– h57

STAR COUNCEL (IRE)   7 b.m. Leading Counsel (USA) – Black Avenue (IRE) (Strong Gale) [2002/3 c21g⁵ c20vᶜᵒ c22d c16vᵖᵘ 27s⁵ 21v² 19d⁴ 24g² 22d 24m* Mar 18] angular ex-Irish mare: second foal: dam, poor maiden in bumpers, half-sister to useful 2½m hurdler Frickley: modest handicap hurdler: trained by D. Hughes prior to 2002/3: won over hurdles at Southwell in March: probably stays 27f: acts on any ground: tried blinkered/in cheekpieces: has had tongue tied. *B. S. Rothwell*   c– h86

STARCROSS SADIE   5 b.m. Saddlers' Hall (IRE) – Starr Danias (USA) (Sensitive Prince (USA)) [2002/3 F16g Dec 12] half-sister to 4 winners, including fairly useful 5f/ 7f winner Yaa Wale (by Persian Bold) and 6f (at 2 yrs)/1½m winner Potsclose (by Miswaki): dam lightly raced in USA: well held in mares bumper on debut. *R. A. Fahey*   F–

STAR DYNASTY (IRE)   6 b.g. Bering – Siwaayib (Green Desert (USA)) [2002/3 h85: 16g² 17gᵖᵘ May 3] modest maiden hurdler: lame at Bangor in May, not seen out again: will stay beyond 17f. *D. McCain*   h85

STAR JACK (FR)   8 b.g. Epervier Bleu – Little Point (FR) (Le Nain Jaune (FR)) [2002/3 c114, h–: c22gᵖᵘ c16g c16d² c20d² c24d³ c16d* c16s* 16sᵖᵘ c33mᵖᵘ Apr 12] lengthy, medium-sized gelding: winning hurdler: reportedly had breathing problem when disappointing only start over hurdles in 2002/3: fairly useful handicap chaser: won at Ayr and Wetherby in November: effective at 2m (given test) to 2½m: yet to race on firm going, acts on any other: usually wears cheekpieces: tongue tied: bold jumper. *T. J. Fitzgerald*   c124 h–

STAR OF RAVEN   6 b.m. Sea Raven (IRE) – Lucy At The Minute (Silly Prices) [2002/3 c25gᵘʳ Apr 14] ex-Irish mare: first foal: dam lightly-raced maiden pointer/poor hunter chaser: poor form on second of 3 starts in bumpers: won points in February/March: looked likely winner much of way in maiden hunter at Hexham on chasing debut, though held in second when unseating last. *Joss Saville*   c78

STAR OF WONDER   5 b.m. Celtic Swing – Meant To Be (Morston (FR)) [2002/3 h97: 18m⁴ 22f³ 20m⁵ Jun 19] leggy, sparely-made mare: modest handicap hurdler: effective at 2m, unlikely to stay beyond 2¾m: raced on good going or firmer (acts on firm): usually jumps fluently: consistent. *Lady Herries*   h99

STAR OF WONDER (FR)   8 ch.m. The Wonder (FR) – Teardrops Fall (FR) (Law Society (USA)) [2002/3 c–, h69: 17m c17gᵖᵘ c16sᵖᵘ 16d 16s 16d³ 16d³ 16g⁶ 16vᵖᵘ 19g 21g Mar 12] leggy mare: pulled up all 3 starts over fences: poor hurdler: probably stays 21f: acts on good to soft going: visored/blinkered sixth to ninth starts, also tried in cheekpieces. *John Allen*   c– h61

STAR PERFORMANCE (IRE)   8 ch.g. Insan (USA) – Leallen (Le Bavard (FR)) [2002/3 c25s c20s² c16s⁴ c25s³ c21vᵖᵘ c22g² Apr 20] IR 30,000 4-y-o: workmanlike gelding: fifth foal: half-brother to winning hurdler/top-class staying chaser Lord Noelie (by Lord Americo) and a poor pointer by Roselier: dam, in frame in Irish points, half-sister to smart chaser up to 3m Master Aristocrat VI: winning pointer: fair novice chaser: effective at 2m to 2¾m: acts on soft going: blinkered fifth start. *Oliver McKiernan, Ireland*   c111

STAR PROTECTOR (FR)   4 b.c. Hector Protector (USA) – Frustration (Salse (USA)) [2002/3 16d³ 16s* 16d⁴ Nov 16] sturdy colt: fairly useful on Flat (stays 1½m), claimed from J. Hills £20,000 in August: fair form in juvenile hurdles, winning at Ascot in November: claimed. *R. M. Stronge*   h100

STARRY MARY   5 b.m. Deploy – Darling Splodge (Elegant Air) [2002/3 16s 21d Jan 16] modest on Flat (barely stays 15f): left with plenty to do and shaped with some promise both starts over hurdles, seventh, never a factor, in mares maiden at Ludlow on second occasion: remains likely to do better. *E. L. James*   h73 p

STARS DELIGHT (IRE)   6 ch.g. Fourstars Allstar (USA) – Celtic Cygnet (Celtic Cone) [2002/3 F77: F17m⁴ 16s 16s³ 20v* 19f* Mar 24] workmanlike gelding: modest form at best in bumpers: tailed off on Flat debut in June, then left Mrs L. Jewell: fair hurdler: won maiden at Fontwell and novice at Taunton (easily) in March: will stay beyond 2½m: acts on any going: lame third start. *G. L. Moore*   h104 F71

STAR SEVENTEEN 5 ch.m. Rock City – Westminster Waltz (Dance In Time (CAN)) h–
[2002/3 16g⁶ 16s 16d 17d 19sᵖᵘ Mar 7] half-sister to fair but unreliable hurdler Calldat
Seventeen (by Komaite): fair on Flat (stays 1½m): no form over hurdles (reluctant to start
fourth outing), sold out of P. d'Arcy's stable 13,500 gns Newmarket Autumn Sales after
debut: has pulled hard. *T. H. Caldwell*

STARS OUT TONIGHT (IRE) 6 b.g. Insan (USA) – Go And Tell (Kemal (FR)) c123
[2002/3 h129+, F99: c17g* c16d³ c25d* c24gᵖᵘ Mar 12] rangy, good sort: fairly useful h–
hurdler: similar standard in novice chases, winning at Exeter in October and Wincanton
in February: pulled up in Grade 1 at Cheltenham final start: bred to be better suited by
2½m+ than shorter: yet to race on extremes of going. *Miss H. C. Knight*

STAR TIME (IRE) 4 b.g. Fourstars Allstar (USA) – Punctual (Lead On Time (USA)) h–
[2002/3 F12d 16sᵖᵘ Dec 5] 4,000 3-y-o: first foal: dam unraced: no show in bumper or F–
juvenile hurdle (jumped poorly). *A. G. Hobbs*

STARTING AGAIN 9 b.g. Petoski – Lynemore (Nearly A Hand) [2002/3 c116, h–: c–
c19d⁵ Oct 23] lengthy gelding: fairly useful chaser: shaped as if outing was needed when h–
fifth of 8 to impressive Halexy in handicap at Chepstow only start in 2002/3: effective
around 2m and stays 2¾m: acts on any going. *H. D. Daly*

STAR TROOPER (IRE) 7 b. or br.g. Brief Truce (USA) – Star Cream (Star Appeal) h93
[2002/3 16m 16f⁴ 17s* 18v² 17v* 16d 18d 21d 17g² Apr 21] ex-Irish gelding: half-
brother to useful 2m hurdler Tropical Lake (by Lomond) and fairly useful hurdler I
Remember It Well (by Don't Forget Me), stays 2½m: 1¼m winner on Flat at 3 yrs:
modest handicap hurdler: sold out of E. McNamara's stable 2,200 gns Doncaster October
Sales after second start: won at Sedgefield in November (seller) and December: best
around 2m: acts on heavy going: effective blinkered or not. *Miss S. E. Forster*

STARZAAN (IRE) 4 b.g. Darshaan – Stellina (IRE) (Caerleon (USA)) [2002/3 16g⁴ h129 +
17s* 17g 16g⁴ Apr 3] tall, angular gelding: has scope: useful on Flat (stays 1¾m),
successful twice in 2002 for P. Cole: odds on, confirmed promise of hurdling debut when
winning juvenile maiden at Folkestone in February by 18 lengths from Researcher:
hampered 3 out when held in Triumph Hurdle at Cheltenham next time: improved
form when fourth to Le Duc in Grade 2 at Aintree in April and to Sporazene in Grade 1 at
Punchestown early following month: will be suited by further than 17f: type to make a
useful handicapper. *H. Morrison*

STASHEDAWAY (IRE) 6 b.m. Treasure Hunter – Mugs Away (Mugatpura) [2002/3 c82 p
20g⁵ 17d² 16d³ 20sᵘʳ 20s* 18v⁶ c20s c18sᵇᵈ 16d² 16g* 20g² Apr 20] lengthy mare: half- h118
sister to several winners, notably Irish National winner Glebe Lad (by Le Bavard): dam
lightly raced: poor form on completed outing over fences (capable of better): fairly useful
hurdler: won maiden at Gowran in December and competitive handicap at Cork (beat
King's Opera 6 lengths) in April: ran well at Fairyhouse and Punchestown (in late-April)
subsequently: stays 2½m: acts on soft going. *M. J. P. O'Brien, Ireland*

STASH THE CASH (IRE) 12 b.g. Persian Bold – Noble Girl (Be Friendly) [2002/3 c–
c26dᵖᵘ Jun 5] leggy gelding: has had soft palate operation: one-time fairly useful hurdler: h–
winning chaser: retains little ability: tongue tied. *Miss A. Armitage*

STATE AFFAIRS (IRE) 7 ch.g. Political Merger (USA) – Bridewell Belle (Saulingo) h–
[2002/3 20sᵖᵘ 19sᶠ 19mᵖᵘ Apr 5] short-backed gelding: little sign of ability.
R. Hollinshead

STATE CASINO 6 b.m. State Diplomacy (USA) – Nod And A Wink (Casino Boy) h–
[2002/3 F–: F16dᵖᵘ F17m 16dᵖᵘ 21vᵖᵘ 24sᵖᵘ Feb 24] leggy mare: of no account. *Miss* F–
L. C. Siddall

STATELEY LORD (IRE) 7 br. or b.g. Good Thyne (USA) – Sixfoursix (Balinger) c–
[2002/3 h–: c16sᵖᵘ Jan 14] workmanlike gelding: little sign of ability, including on h–
chasing debut: tongue tied. *G. L. Moore*

STATE OF BALANCE 5 ch.m. Mizoram (USA) – Equilibrium (Statoblest) [2002/3 F–
F17d⁶ F18m Mar 31] second foal: dam, 2-y-o 6f winner, half-sister to winning jumper
Getting Plenty: weak in bumpers. *K. Bell*

STATIM 4 b.f. Marju (IRE) – Rapid Repeat (IRE) (Exactly Sharp (USA)) [2002/3 16s² h111 §
16s² 16s² 16v² 16g Apr 3] leggy filly: fairly useful on Flat (stays 1½m), sold out of
L. Cumani's stable 19,000 gns Newmarket Autumn Sales: fair juvenile hurdler, runner-up
first 4 starts: probably best in blinkers: irresolute. *M. J. P. O'Brien, Ireland*

STATION ISLAND (IRE) 6 ch.g. Roselier (FR) – Sweet Tulip (Beau Chapeau) F79
[2002/3 F16g⁵ Mar 12] IR £7,500 4-y-o: sixth foal: half-brother to several winners,

notably high-class staying chaser Truckers Tavern (by Phardante): dam winning pointer: won second of 2 starts in maiden Irish points in 2002: bought 20,000 gns Doncaster May Sales: fifth of 16 to Eric's Charm in bumper at Huntingdon. *J. Mackie*

STAY LUCKY (NZ) 14 b.g. Sir Sydney (NZ) – Against The Odds (NZ) (Harbor Prince (USA)) [2002/3 c24m^{pu} May 11] rangy gelding: winning chaser: on the downgrade: tried blinkered. *Simon Bloss*
c–
h–

ST BEE 8 br.g. St Ninian – Regal Bee (Royal Fountain) [2002/3 c22v^{ur} c20m c24g^6 c24g^F c20s^{pu} c32v^{pu} c25g^F c25g^4 c25g^5 Apr 14] of little account: sketchy jumper. *W. G. Reed*
c– x
h–

STEADY EDDY 11 ch.g. Scorpio (FR) – Moaning Jenny (Privy Seal) [2002/3 c77, h–: c24m^{pu} c25g^6 Jun 12] poor chaser: won point in April: stays 3¼m: acts on good to firm and good to soft going, possibly not on soft: poor jumper. *N. A. Twiston-Davies*
c80 x
h–

STEEL BELLS (IRE) 14 br.g. Mandalus – Lucy's Pal (Random Shot) [2002/3 c34g^{pu} May 22] lengthy, good-bodied gelding: winning pointer: little sign of ability otherwise: tried blinkered. *A. W. Froggatt*
c–
h–

STEEL EDGE (IRE) 9 ch.g. Torus – Lasting Impression (Proverb) [2002/3 c25d^{ur} c24g^F Mar 2] workmanlike gelding: bumper winner: modest novice chaser in 2000/1: close up going well when unseating eleventh in novice handicap at Hereford on belated return: fell heavily next time: stays 3m: acts on any going. *Miss Venetia Williams*
c–
h–

STEEL MILL (IRE) 8 gr.g. Roselier (FR) – Chatmando (IRE) (Mandalus) [2002/3 c–, h72: 25g^{pu} 25m^3 22d^2 c25g^5 Nov 18] sturdy gelding: won second of 2 starts in Irish points in 2000: modest maiden hurdler: poor maiden chaser: stays 25f: acts on good to firm and good to soft going. *D. J. Caro*
c–
h87

STEEL RIGG (IRE) 11 ch.g. Lancastrian – Cute Play (Salluceva) [2002/3 24d^4 Jun 4] modest maiden chaser: winning hurdler/pointer: tongue tied, poor form when fourth in handicap hurdle in June: seems to stay 3m: raced only on good going or softer (acts on heavy). *Mrs A. Hamilton*
c–
h72 ?

STENNIKOV (IRE) 7 b.g. Good Thyne (USA) – Belle Bavard (Le Bavard (FR)) [2002/3 h103, F99: 19d^2 20v^4 24v Jan 17] rangy gelding: fair maiden hurdler: likely to prove best around 2½m: acts on good to soft going (won bumper on soft): often carries head awkwardly. *P. F. Nicholls*
h110

STEPASTRAY 6 gr.g. Alhijaz – Wandering Stranger (Petong) [2002/3 16s^{pu} Dec 16] modest maiden on Flat (effective at 1¼m, barely at 1¾m): no show in novice on hurdling debut. *R. E. Barr*
h–

STEP IN LINE (IRE) 11 gr.g. Step Together (USA) – Ballycahan Girl (Bargello) [2002/3 c–, h65: c21g May 1] sparely-made gelding: winning chaser: well beaten in hunter at Cheltenham in May: stays 3¼m: acts on firm and soft going: held up. *Mrs Ruth Hayter*
c–
h–

STEP IN SILVER (IRE) 7 gr.g. Step Together (USA) – Seagate (IRE) (Decent Fellow) [2002/3 h85, F–: 20s^{pu} 22d^{pu} c24m^{pu} Apr 10] lengthy, rather leggy gelding: modest maiden hurdler: no form in 2002/3, including on chasing debut: stays 2½m: acts on good to firm going: tried tongue tied. *Jonjo O'Neill*
c–
h–

STEP ON EYRE (IRE) 13 b.g. Step Together (USA) – Jane Eyre (Master Buck) [2002/3 c118§, h–: c22d^4 c25d^{pu} c24m^4 Apr 12] big gelding: one-time useful handicap chaser: won point in March: just fair form in hunters: stays 33f: acts on good to firm and heavy going: tried blinkered: usually jumps soundly: unreliable. *S. Wynne*
c92 §
h–

STEPPES 8 b.g. Jendali (USA) – Asoness (Laxton) [2002/3 c21m 21m 24g* 26g^{pu} 20d^{pu} 24g^{pu} Apr 21] no sign of ability in points: bought 3,000 gns Doncaster May Sales: well held on chasing debut: form over hurdles only when winning weak maiden at Worcester in September: stays 3m. *M. J. Gingell*
c–
h68

STEPPES OF GOLD (IRE) 6 b.g. Moscow Society (USA) – Trysting Place (He Loves Me) [2002/3 F16g* Apr 1] 20,000 4-y-o: sixth foal: half-brother to poor 2m hurdler Grondola (by Indian King) and winner in Germany by Cyrano de Bergerac: dam unraced, from family of high-class middle-distance performer Madam Gay: won bumper at Newcastle on debut by 1¾ lengths from Oodachee, smooth progress from rear to lead over 2f out and keeping on well despite drifting left: sure to improve. *N. G. Richards*
F104 p

STEP QUICK (IRE) 9 ch.g. All Haste (USA) – Little Steps (Step Together (USA)) [2002/3 c24s^2 c24m^2 c19m^2 Apr 21] tall, angular gelding: fair pointer, successful in
c94

April: runner-up all 3 starts in hunter chases: stays 3m: acts on soft and good to firm going. *W. Bryan*

STERLING DOT COM (IRE)   7 b.g. Roselier (FR) – Daddy's Folly (Le Moss) [2002/3 h108: c24s^F c24g^5 c24v^4 c24d c25d^{pu} Jan 27] tall gelding: failed to progress over hurdles after winning maiden in 2001/2: still in front when falling fourteenth on chasing debut, disappointing all 4 subsequent starts: should stay at least 3m: raced on good going or softer (acts on soft): blinkered final outing. *P. J. Hobbs*   **c88** **h–**

STERLING STEWART (IRE)   8 b.g. Insan (USA) – Kyle Eile (IRE) (Callernish) [2002/3 c108, h103: c17g^2 c21f^3 c20m^2 Oct 16] lengthy gelding: fair hurdler: fairly useful chaser: good second to Chergan in handicap at Wetherby final start: should stay beyond 2½m: acts on any going: failed to settle only run in blinkers: reportedly lame second outing. *M. Pitman*   **c119** **h–**

STERO HEIGHTS (IRE)   8 b.g. Shirley Heights – Trystero (Shareef Dancer (USA)) [2002/3 18d^5 24s 20g* 18d^4 20m^2 21g* 20g* 20g^2 Oct 13] maiden on Flat: modest hurdler: won handicaps at Ballinrobe in July, Sedgefield (conditional jockeys) in September and Roscommon in October: stays 21f: best efforts on good/good to firm ground: tried blinkered: tongue tied. *D. Broad, Ireland*   **h97**

STEVE FORD   14 gr.g. Another Realm – Sky Miss (Skymaster) [2002/3 c–, h–: c21g^F May 1] leggy gelding: winning hurdler/chaser, retains little ability: runner-up in point in April. *Mrs S. S. Harbour*   **c–** **h–**

STEVE THE FISH (IRE)   7 ch.g. Dry Dock – Country Clothing (Salluceva) [2002/3 h86: 24d^{pu} c20s^5 c22s^{ur} Dec 28] medium-sized gelding: modest maiden hurdler: well held on completed start over fences: should stay 3m: acts on soft going. *J. A. B. Old*   **c–** **h–**

STEWART'S LAD   6 b.g. Well Beloved – Moneyacre (Veloski) [2002/3 h84, F–: 16m Nov 4] workmanlike gelding: poor maiden hurdler: well held only start in 2002/3: raced mainly around 2m: acts on soft going. *B. D. Leavy*   **h–**

STILA (IRE)   4 b.f. Desert Style (IRE) – Noorajo (IRE) (Ahonoora) [2002/3 18s^{pu} Mar 2] half-sister to modest hurdler Traditional (by Erins Isle), stays 2¾m: poor maiden on Flat: no show on hurdling debut. *B. W. Duke*   **h–**

STILL SPEEDY (IRE)   6 b.g. Toulon – Gorge (Mount Hagen (FR)) [2002/3 F16g F16d F16m^4 Apr 22] IR £14,500 4-y-o: seventh foal: half-brother to fairly useful chaser De Jordaan (by Callernish), stayed 21f: dam maiden: modest form in bumpers, pulling hard. *Noel T. Chance*   **F83**

STING LIKE A BEE (IRE)   4 b.c. Ali-Royal (IRE) – Hidden Agenda (FR) (Machiavellian (USA)) [2002/3 16d 16d 16v^5 16g^3 16d^5 16g^6 Apr 7] small colt: fair maiden around 1m at best on Flat, trained mostly by H. Cecil: poor juvenile hurdler: will prove best around 2m: has reportedly had breathing problem more than once, tongue tied last 3 starts. *J. S. Goldie*   **h73**

STITCH-B (IRE)   10 ch.g. Naheez (USA) – Sea View (Quayside) [2002/3 c–, h–: c20g^{pu} Jun 12] poor hurdler: modest form on first of 2 starts over fences: will prove best at 3m+: best efforts on good going or firmer (acts on firm): only win in blinkers. *P. Beaumont*   **c–** **h–**

ST KILDA   6 b.m. Past Glories – Oiseval (National Trust) [2002/3 F16g F17s^3 F18v^6 F16g^6 21s^3 Mar 10] first reported foal: dam unraced: poor form in bumpers: similar form when well-beaten third in novice at Plumpton on hurdling debut. *Mrs H. M. Bridges*   **h70** **F70**

ST MATTHEW (USA)   5 b.g. Lear Fan (USA) – Social Crown (USA) (Chief's Crown (USA)) [2002/3 19d* 20v^2 21v* 24s^4 Mar 8] sturdy gelding: fair on Flat (barely stays 1¾m), sold out of J. Hills's stable 7,000 gns Newmarket Autumn Sales: fair novice hurdler: won at Doncaster in January and Sedgefield (all out to hold Ragu ½ length) in February: stays 21f (beaten after stamina became an issue when tailed off over 3m): acts on heavy going. *G. M. Moore*   **h109**

ST MELLION PAR (IRE)   9 ch.g. Glacial Storm (USA) – Tenerife Sunset (Boreen (FR)) [2002/3 c–, h–: c25g^6 May 4] well-made gelding: winning hurdler/chaser: ran badly in 2001/2, long way below best at Hereford in May: stays 3m: raced on good going or softer (acts on heavy). *P. J. Hobbs*   **c–** **h–**

STOCKERS PRIDE   8 b.g. Sula Bula – Fille de Soleil (Sunyboy) [2002/3 h99, F75: 22d^{pu} c26v^F c26v^{pu} Feb 10] modest hurdler: no form in 2002/3, last 2 starts over fences: suited by 3m+: acts on heavy going. *S. Woodman*   **c–** **h–**

STOCKS 'N SHARES 7 b.m. Jupiter Island – Norstock (Norwick (USA)) [2002/3 **h78** F17d 17g⁵ 21d 17d* Dec 3] good-topped mare: failed to complete in 2 points in 2001: **F73** poor form in bumpers: not unduly knocked about in mares novices first 2 starts over hurdles: tongue tied, won seller at Hereford in December (subsequently tested positive for morphine): bred to stay at least 2½m: yet to race on extremes of going. *J. White*

STONE COLD 6 ch.g. Inchinor – Vaula (Henbit (USA)) [2002/3 c92, h90: c16m⁶ **c97** c20d⁴ c16d³ c16s⁴ c16g⁶ c20g² c20g² c20d² c23g² Mar 23] angular gelding: modest **h–** handicap chaser: generally in good form in 2002/3, runner-up last 4 starts: stays 23f but effective at much shorter: acts on soft going: usually blinkered: has failed to impress with attitude. *T. D. Easterby*

STONEHENGE (IRE) 6 b.g. Caerleon (USA) – Sharata (IRE) (Darshaan) [2002/3 **c–** c–, h86: c17g c20g⁶ c20dᵖᵘ 19dᵖᵘ 17s Nov 21] angular gelding: little worthwhile form **h–** over fences: left J. W. Mullins after third start: winning hurdler, no show last 2 outings (sold out of A. King's stable £1,100 Ascot November Sales in between): stays 2¾m: acts on firm going: tried visored. *D. Burchell*

STONEHILL PROSPECT 9 b.m. Lightning Dealer – Ditchling Beacon (High **h–** Line) [2002/3 h–: 17s⁵ May 28] of little account. *C. J. Gray*

STONE MOUNTAIN (IRE) 11 gr.g. Mandalus – Dora Frost (Stradavinsky) [2002/3 **c–** c23gᵖᵘ c19gᵖᵘ 17s Dec 26] rangy gelding: second in point: no form in steeplechases or **h–** over hurdles. *C. J. Down*

STONERAVINMAD 5 ch.g. Never So Bold – Premier Princess (Hard Fought) **h–** [2002/3 20d 27sᵘʳ 21s 20g Mar 29] third foal: half-brother to 9.4f winner Rosie Jaques (by Doyoun): dam won at 2m+ on Flat and up to 3½m over hurdles: no form in novice hurdles. *Mrs E. Slack*

STONESBY (IRE) 11 b.g. The Bart (USA) – Maid In The Mist (Pry) [2002/3 c20dᵖᵘ **c–** Mar 4] sparely-made gelding: winning hurdler/chaser, retains little ability. *Geoffrey* **h–** *Deacon*

STONEY PATH 8 b.m. Petoski – Lampstone (Ragstone) [2002/3 h87: 20g* May 22] **h90** lengthy mare: modest hurdler: won novice handicap at Worcester in May, not seen out again: should stay beyond 2½m: acts on good to firm going. *A. King*

STONEY RIVER (IRE) 9 b.g. Riverhead (USA) – Another Space (Brave Invader **c–** (USA)) [2002/3 c85: c25mᵖᵘ May 8] fair pointer: modest form at best in steeplechases: has had tongue tied. *Ms Alison Christmas*

STOP THE MUSIC (IRE) 7 b.g. Lord Americo – Brace Yourself (Castle Keep) **h–** [2002/3 F71: 20d Oct 23] workmanlike gelding: modest form both starts in bumpers in 2001/2: well held in novice at hurdling debut. *S. E. H. Sherwood*

STOPWATCH (IRE) 8 b.g. Lead On Time (USA) – Rose Bonbon (FR) (High Top) **c84** [2002/3 h75: 21m³ 17mᶠ 19m c20d² c20s² c19dᵘʳ c19dᶠ c16gᶠ 16g Mar 12] lengthy **h73** gelding: poor handicap hurdler: runner-up in novice handicap chases at Fontwell and Ludlow: stays easy 21f: acts on soft and good to firm going (possibly not heavy): tried blinkered (raced too freely)/in cheekpieces: inconsistent. *Mrs L. C. Jewell*

STORM A BREWING 7 ch.g. Glacial Storm (USA) – Southern Squaw (Buckskin **h68** (FR)) [2002/3 F83: 22s 26d 25g⁴ Mar 23] angular gelding: poor form over hurdles. *R. M. Stronge*

STORM AHEAD (IRE) 9 b.g. Glacial Storm (USA) – Little Slip (Super Slip) [2002/3 **c–** c–, h79: 22d 16m⁶ c16gᵖᵘ 20g 20dᵖᵘ Apr 25] poor maiden hurdler, left N. Richards after **h–** third start: pulled up both starts in novice chases: probably stays 2½m: act on heavy going: often tongue tied: often finds little. *A. Parker*

STORM BOXER (IRE) 5 b. or br.g. Glacial Storm (USA) – Sarakin (IRE) (Buck- **F100** skin (FR)) [2002/3 F16d* F16g Mar 12] sturdy gelding: second foal: dam, lightly raced in bumpers/over hurdles, half-sister to smart staying hurdler/chaser Unsinkable Boxer: won bumper at Leopardstown on debut by 2½ lengths from Kahuna, running green in front: mid-field in Grade 1 events at Cheltenham and Punchestown subsequently. *Patrick Mullins, Ireland*

STORM CASTLE (IRE) 11 b.g. Carlingford Castle – Strong Rum (Strong Gale) **c91** [2002/3 c99, h–: c25f* c26m² c28m⁶ c26gᵘʳ Mar 13] sturdy gelding: fair hunter chaser: **h–** runner-up at Exeter (later awarded race on technical grounds) in May: won point in February: stays 3¼m: acts on soft and firm going. *Miss J. Wickens*

STORM DAMAGE (IRE) 11 b.g. Waajib – Connaught Lace (Connaught) [2002/3 c126§, h–: c24d² c24s² c31d³ c27d⁵ c24s* Feb 13] angular gelding: fairly useful chaser: won Royal Artillery Gold Cup at Sandown in February, asserting after last when beating Lord Kilpatrick 8 lengths: stays 31f: acts on good to firm and heavy going: tried blinkered, including last 3 starts: often soon off bridle and not one to trust. *P. F. Nicholls*

c126 §
h–

STORMDANCER (IRE) 6 ch.g. Bluebird (USA) – Unspoiled (Tina's Pet) [2002/3 16d^pu 20v^pu 21g^pu Mar 25] workmanlike gelding: half-brother to winning pointer by Jareer: little form on Flat: no form in novice hurdles: has worn cheekpieces. *Mrs Lucinda Featherstone*

h–

STORMEZ (FR) 6 b.g. Ezzoud (IRE) – Stormy Scene (USA) (Storm Bird (CAN)) [2002/3 h143: c23m* c23g* c21g² c32m* c27d* c26g c24g* c24g* c24m* c32g² c33m² c29m² Apr 26]

c151
h–

How many races do you need under your belt in the current season to win at the Cheltenham Festival? If the latest season was anything to go by, the answer is just three, as that was the average number of outings the Cheltenham Festival winners had had before the Festival, the twenty winners having had sixty races between them. Royal Predica and Young Spartacus turned up without a prior run at all, while only three of the winners had had more than four outings: Sudden Shock and Spirit Leader had had five, and La Landiere seven. The fact that the average Festival winner has such a light campaign will be seen by many as evidence of the extent to which Cheltenham overshadows the rest of the season. But one who came close to bucking the trend in no uncertain terms was the Pipe stable's reported 'banker' of the meeting Stormez, who just failed to hold on in the dying strides of the four-mile National Hunt Chase. That was the tenth race of Stormez's season, one which had begun the previous May (less than a month after the end of his previous campaign), and comprised wins in valuable handicaps in both the summer and autumn before continuing successfully through the winter. What's more, his best performances were still to come after Cheltenham. Stormez would therefore have been a most untypical Festival winner, but there are plenty more contradic-

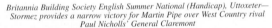

Britannia Building Society English Summer National (Handicap), Uttoxeter—
Stormez provides a narrow victory for Martin Pipe over West Country rival
Paul Nicholls' General Claremont

Intervet Trophy Handicap Chase, Cheltenham—
the third last and Tony McCoy looks to have chosen correctly as Shooting Light (visor) heads Stormez,
but there are four places between the stable companions at the line

tions where Stormez is concerned. For a start, he's no chaser on looks, being a smallish gelding. As shall be seen, he's not bred to be a jumper of any sort, still less a staying chaser, and he was bought with the Champion Hurdle in mind. On top of that, his jumping is less than fluent and he is no easy ride. Yet his bare record for the season tells a story of toughness and considerable improvement: seven wins and four seconds from twelve starts.

Cheltenham looked a long way off, not just on the calendar, when Stormez began his chasing career. He landed the odds in a couple of novice chases at Worcester in May, but the opposition was poor and defeat in a similar event at Newton Abbot later in the month raised questions about whether chasing would really prove his game. The Newton Abbot race was over twenty-one furlongs however, the shortest trip Stormez was to tackle all season, and when upped markedly in distance for the Britannia Building Society English Summer National on his handicap debut over fences at Uttoxeter in June, Stormez made it plain that his future was as a staying chaser. His jumping was still a bit deliberate in the valuable four-mile event but he showed no lack of resolution once headed and got back up near the line to beat General Claremont a neck. When he came back in the autumn, Stormez had been raised a harsh-looking 9 lb for his narrow win and Tony McCoy chose to ride stable-companion Shooting Light instead in the Intervet Trophy Handicap at Cheltenham. But Stormez, under Barry Geraghty, coped surprisingly well with the demands of Cheltenham, jumping fluently in the main, seeing off his stable companion by the last and responding well to beat Southern Star by three quarters of a length. The Hennessy, for which Stormez had now picked up a 6-lb penalty, proved a different matter though, and Stormez trailed in last of nineteen finishers at Newbury, never threatening in what proved the season's most competitive handicap chase.

With his limitations seemingly exposed in top handicap company, Stormez's preparation for the Festival took place in the calmer waters of novice chases again and, after the turn of the year, he completed a hat-trick in small fields at Kempton (twice) and at Newbury in between. He made rather heavy weather of landing the odds in the first of those races at Kempton, racing lazily, but did not need to exert himself unduly for his seventh win of the campaign when beating Sudden Shock in a match there in February. When the pair met on the same terms in the four-mile National Hunt Chase for amateurs at Cheltenham next time, Stormez was the clear form pick, starting at 7/4 in the twenty-four-runner field, but he was unable to hold Sudden Shock's late swoop and was beaten a length after taking up the running two out. That Stormez got to the front at all owed much to the efforts of his promising rider Jamie Moore (who subsequently turned professional), as he was off the bridle a long way from home after some far from fluent jumping.

Martin Pipe has run horses with lesser credentials than Stormez in the Grand National but Stormez skipped Aintree, lining up instead for the Scottish Grand National at Ayr where he started joint-second favourite with Sudden Shock. Stormez found further improvement, going down by a neck to Ryalux. Jumping better than at Cheltenham, Stormez responded well when challenged by the winner in the straight, getting away from the last the quicker before being collared close home. The fact that he managed to repeat that form on his twelfth and final start of the season when favourite for the attheraces Gold Cup at Sandown says much for Stormez's durability, but the bare result—a nine-length defeat by Ad Hoc—hardly tells the whole story. Stormez gave every indication of having had enough for the season but Tony McCoy, typically, was in no mood to take it easy on the final day. Stormez was off the bridle as early as the first fence and was never going well or jumping fluently thereafter. Still well behind jumping the last of the railway fences (four out), he seemed in a hopeless position but began to stay on well from thereon, passing a few stragglers to jump the Pond fence in ninth place and staying on past more beaten rivals after the last. McCoy deserved a medal.

			Last Tycoon (b 1983)	Try My Best
Stormez (FR) (b.g. 1997)	Ezzoud (IRE) (b 1989)			Mill Princess
			Royal Sister II (b 1977)	Claude
				Ribasha
			Storm Bird (b 1978)	Northern Dancer
	Stormy Scene (USA) (ch 1983)			South Ocean
			Drama (ch 1978)	Sir Ivor
				Drury Nell

If his pedigree gives little clue as to the source of his stamina, Stormez's temperament is very much reminiscent of his sire Ezzoud, who died in 1998. He too could be an awkward ride (he lost his rider soon after the start of the King George VI & Queen Elizabeth Diamond Stakes on one occasion) but was just as capable of giving his all in a finish, notably when gaining his second successive win in the Juddmonte International Stakes. It's not just a lack of stamina which makes Stormez's pedigree unusual for one who clearly stays so well, but a predominance of speed. Both his dam and grandam won over six furlongs in Ireland in Robert Sangster's colours, Stormy Scene winning at Leopardstown for John Oxx and Drama winning the Greenlands Stakes at the Curragh for Vincent O'Brien. Great-grandam Drury Nell was a half-sister to the high-class sprinting two-year-old of 1960 Typhoon. Stormy Scene, who died while Stormez was being weaned, produced four other winners, all successful in ordinary company on the Flat in France (none at beyond a mile and a half), Shockadelica (by Machiavellian) also winning there over hurdles and fences. Maintaining the family's sprinting theme, Stormy Scene's unraced daughter Shavya is the dam of the smart French horse Swedish Shave who completed a hat-trick in good company at around five furlongs in the spring—at around the same time his dam's half-brother was performing so well at four miles.

Stormez's 2002/3 campaign came hot on the heels of a busy previous season when he joined Martin Pipe midway through from Christophe Aubert in France. Hopes that he would make into a Champion Hurdle horse were fuelled by his final outing in France when he had beaten Bilboa (who went on to finish third in the Champion) in the Grande Course de Haies d'Enghien. Stormez has proved best at three miles or more though, and he is also proven on any going bar firm which he has yet to encounter. He wears a tongue strap, but could also benefit from the reapplication of a visor which he wore on his final start in 2001/2, as the way he went at Sandown suggests he could become an increasingly difficult ride. Stormez is a tough sort who has already achieved more than most six-year-olds over fences, but he'll be doing very well to enjoy so much success again in 2003/4. *M. C. Pipe*

STORMHILL STAG 11 b.g. Buckley – Sweet Sirenia (Al Sirat (USA)) [2002/3 c112, h–: 22s⁵ c19vᵖᵘ c20v⁴ c19s² c19g² Mar 18] leggy gelding: winning hurdler: fair handicap chaser: creditable second last 2 starts: stays 3m, effective at much shorter: acts on good to firm and heavy going: blinkered twice: has made mistakes and looked difficult ride. *R. Lee*   **c110 h95**

STORM KITTEN (IRE) 5 br.m. Catrail (USA) – Mbunda (Mtoto) [2002/3 F–: 16d Nov 14] little sign of ability. *Miss K. M. George*   **h–**

STORM MAN (IRE) 11 br.g. Glacial Storm (USA) – Devon Royale (Le Prince) [2002/3 c20f May 11] fair form in points but tailed off in 2 hunter chases. *Miss Charlotte Williams*   **c–**

STORM OF GOLD (IRE) 10 b.g. Glacial Storm (USA) – Tipperary Tartan (Rarity) [2002/3 c103, h–: c25d² c31m⁶ c25dᵖᵘ c25s⁴ c26dᵖᵘ c24s⁶ c28g⁶ Mar 17] useful-looking gelding: winning hurdler/chaser: left Miss C. Elliott after second start, badly out of sorts subsequently: stays 31f: acts on soft going: tried in headgear: not an easy ride. *D. L. Williams*   **c103 d h–**

STORM PRINCE (IRE) 6 ch.g. Prince of Birds (USA) – Petersford Girl (IRE) (Taufan (USA)) [2002/3 16d 16d⁵ 16s 21d⁶ Mar 8] smallish gelding: fair juvenile hurdler in 2000/1, winning twice: modest form at best in handicaps on return: best around 2m: acts on soft going: usually forces pace: raced too freely on reappearance: sound jumper. *J. L. Spearing*   **h94**

STORM TIGER (IRE) 12 b.g. Strong Gale – Happy Party (Invited (USA)) [2002/3 c98§, h87§: c16mᵖᵘ 17m³ 17g c16mᶠ Oct 3] good-bodied gelding: winning hurdler: fairly useful chaser at best: form in 2002/3 only when third in handicap hurdle at Market Rasen in June: stays 2½m: acts on good to firm and heavy going: effective visored or not: sketchy jumper of fences: moody and tends to find little. *C. G. Cox*   **c– § h91 §**

STORM VALLEY (IRE) 11 b.g. Strong Gale – Windy Run (Deep Run) [2002/3 c87, h–: c21gᶠ c22s⁵ c24mᵘʳ Mar 18] leggy gelding: winning chaser, has lost his form: has had tongue tied: poor jumper: sold 700 gns Doncaster May Sales. *J. R. Cornwall*   **c– x h–**

STORM WIZARD (IRE) 6 b.g. Catrail (USA) – Society Ball (Law Society (USA)) [2002/3 h74: 17s Mar 7] fair maiden at best on Flat at 3 yrs: poor form on first of 2 outings over hurdles nearly 2 years apart, making mistakes. *D. G. Bridgwater*   **h–**

STORMY BEECH 7 b.g. Glacial Storm (USA) – Cheeny's Brig (New Brig) [2002/3 h–, F–: 22dᵖᵘ 17g 24d 20v⁵ 17s² 16s⁶ 16g* 16v³ 17v* 16d 17s² Mar 11] angular gelding: poor hurdler: sold out of B. Mactaggart's stable 700 gns Doncaster August Sales after reappearance: won handicaps at Catterick (seller) and Sedgefield (novice) in February: best around 2m: acts on heavy going: tried in cheekpieces, blinkered nowadays: has hung left: races freely. *R. Johnson*   **h82**

STORMYFAIRWEATHER (IRE) 11 b.g. Strong Gale – Game Sunset (Menelek) [2002/3 c24mᵖᵘ Mar 22] small, angular gelding: very smart chaser on his day, twice won Cathcart Chase at Cheltenham: no encouragement in handicaps at Newbury and Punchestown (in early-May) after nearly 3 years off with leg injury: stays 25f: has won on soft going, much better form on good/good to firm. *N. J. Henderson*   **c– h–**

STORMY LORD (IRE) 7 br.g. Lord Americo – Decent Shower (Decent Fellow) [2002/3 h99: 16g² 17g* 16g⁵ 16s* 16d³ 20g* Mar 23] fairly useful hurdler: won novice at Carlisle (odds on) in October and handicaps at Ayr in December and Wetherby (beat Exstoto 1¼ lengths, soon clear but tiring over longer trip late on) in March: best effort when just over 2 lengths third to Rhinestone Cowboy in Grade 2 novice at same course: successful at 2½m, probably best around 2m: acts on soft going: has tended to hang/jump left: free-going front runner: type to do well in novice chases in 2003/4. *J. Wade*   **h120**

STORMY PASS 6 b.g. Dolphin Street (FR) – Noble Choice (Dahar (USA)) [2002/3 h–, F–: 20d Oct 23] lengthy, workmanlike gelding: no form in bumpers or over hurdles: won 3-finisher maiden point in March: tried visored/tongue tied. *P. R. Webber*   **h–**

STORMY SKYE (IRE) 7 b.g. Bluebird (USA) – Canna (Caerleon (USA)) [2002/3 h109§: c21g² c20v³ c22s⁴ c20dᶠ c20d³ c20d³ c25gᶠ c26m³ Mar 31] useful-looking gelding: fair handicap hurdler, regressive form in 2001/2: modest novice chaser: would   **c98 § h– §**

have won maiden at Folkestone seventh start but for falling 2 out: stays 25f: acts on good to firm and soft going, probably on heavy: usually blinkered nowadays: often tongue tied prior to 2002/3: hard ride (runs in snatches). *G. L. Moore*

ST PALAIS   4 b.f. Timeless Times (USA) – Crambella (IRE) (Red Sunset) [2002/3 16m 16d² 16d⁶ 16vʳᵒ 22vʳᵒ 17d 26g⁴ 21s 19g 22g⁶ Apr 12] no form on Flat for J. Balding: bad maiden hurdler: seems to stay 3¼m: sometimes wears cheekpieces/visor. *D. L. Williams*   **h68**

STRAIGHT ON (IRE)   12 b.g. Tremblant – Maybird (Royalty) [2002/3 c70, h–: c24g² c25m⁴ May 22] close-coupled gelding: winning hurdler/chaser: best effort in hunters on return from lengthy absence when second to Corston Joker at Fakenham: stays 3m: acts on any going: often blinkered over hurdles. *Mrs S. A. Hodge*   **c94**
h–

STRAIT TALKING (FR)   5 b.g. Bering – Servia (Le Marmot (FR)) [2002/3 h84: 16g 16v⁶ 16d³ 16s 16g² c16dᶠ 16g 16d² 16m* Apr 21] leggy gelding: poor hurdler: won selling handicap at Fakenham in April: fell heavily on chasing debut: likely to prove best around 2m: acts on soft and good to firm going: has worn cheekpieces. *Jedd O'Keeffe*   **c–**
h87

STRATCO (IRE)   9 b. or br.g. Satco (FR) – No Slow (King's Ride) [2002/3 h103: c23f* c21m⁶ Jun 30] sturdy gelding: fair hurdler: created good impression when winning novice at Exeter on chasing debut: reportedly finished lame following month: will stay beyond 23f: acts on good to firm going. *W. W. Dennis*   **c112**
h–

STRATEGIC COURSE (USA)   7 b.g. Alleged (USA) – Danlu (USA) (Danzig (USA)) [2002/3 F17m F16f Sep 15] 1,700 4-y-o: sixth reported foal: brother to very smart middle-distance stayer Strategic Choice and half-brother to 4 winners, including fair hurdler/modest chaser up to 25f Swing West (by Gone West) and smart 1m/1¼m winner Sure Dancer (by Affirmed): dam, probably stayed 1¼m, sister to smart 6f/7f performer Nicholas: looked most temperamental when tailed off in 2 bumpers: visored/blinkered. *C. J. Teague*   **F– §**

STRATH FILLAN   5 b.m. Dolphin Street (FR) – Adarama (IRE) (Persian Bold) [2002/3 h73: 16g⁶ 16m⁶ 16g 20m Mar 23] poor on Flat and over hurdles (well held in 2002/3): sold out of W. Musson's stable 5,000 gns Newmarket Autumn Sales after second start. *H. J. Collingridge*   **h–**

STRAWBERRY HILL (IRE)   9 b.g. Lancastrian – Tudor Lady (Green Shoon) [2002/3 h–: 21m⁵ 21sᵖᵘ 16g⁵ 17d² 20d⁶ Apr 25] poor novice hurdler: should stay beyond 17f. *Miss V. Scott*   **h80**

STRAWMAN   6 b.g. Ela-Mana-Mou – Oatfield (Great Nephew) [2002/3 c–, h78: c21g⁴ c21gᶠ c22mᵖᵘ c26m⁶ c20gᵘʳ c17m³ c18m* c21g² c26mᵖᵘ Sep 24] angular gelding: maiden hurdler: poor novice chaser, left J. Given after third start: won 3-runner event at Fontwell in August: pulled up lame there final outing: stays 21f: acts on good to firm and heavy going: tried visored (has hinted at temperament): often makes mistakes. *C. N. Kellett*   **c78**
h–

STREAMSFORTH LAD (IRE)   6 b.g. Be My Native (USA) – Protrial (Proverb) [2002/3 F72: F16f² F16m⁶ 16d³ 16dᵖᵘ 16v⁵ 21g 21gᵖᵘ 21m⁴ 26m⁴ Apr 5] good-topped gelding: fair form in bumpers: disappointing maiden hurdler: looked temperamental in blinkers last 2 starts: stays 21f: acts on good to soft and good to firm going (bumper form on firm): one to treat with caution. *S. A. Brookshaw*   **h87 §**
F88

STREAMSTOWN (IRE)   9 b. or br.g. Rashar (USA) – Lady Torsil (Torus) [2002/3 c139, h–: c20g Nov 30] useful-looking gelding: useful handicap chaser: inadequate test of stamina only outing in 2002/3: should stay beyond 3½m: raced mainly on good going or softer (acts on heavy): tends to make odd mistake: patiently ridden. *Ferdy Murphy*   **c–**
h–

STREET FIGHTER (FR)   8 b.g. Subotica (FR) – American Order (USA) (Slew O'Gold (USA)) [2002/3 h–: 17dᵖᵘ Oct 19] small gelding: very lightly raced over hurdles, form only on debut in 1998/9: tongue tied and blinkered only start in 2002/3. *Jonjo O'Neill*   **h–**

STREET MAGIC (IRE)   6 br.m. Jolly Jake (NZ) – Corrie's Duchess (IRE) (Burslem) [2002/3 h72p, F72: 20m² 22g³ Nov 9] leggy mare: poor form when placed in mares novice hurdles: stays 2¾m: acts on good to firm going. *N. A. Twiston-Davies*   **h79**

STREET SMART (IRE)   7 gr.g. Roselier (FR) – College Street (IRE) (Strong Gale) [2002/3 24s 22s 24sᵖᵘ 24dᵖᵘ Feb 23] IR 25,000 4-y-o: workmanlike ex-Irish gelding: third foal: dam unraced, out of half-sister to Grand National winner Royal Athlete: little sign of ability in visored events. *C. J. Mann*   **c–**
h–

STREET WALKER (IRE)   7 b.m. Dolphin Street (FR) – Foolish Dame (USA) **h–**
(Foolish Pleasure (USA)) [2002/3 h56: 17d 17s Nov 26] small, angular mare: maiden on
Flat: bad novice hurdler: stays 19f: acts on soft going: tried in headgear. *W. Storey*

STREETWISE KID (IRE)   4 b.g. Dolphin Street (FR) – Perfect Answer (Keen) **h–**
[2002/3 F12d F16s 16gᵖᵘ 16mᵘʳ Apr 2] first foal: dam once-raced half-sister to useful **F–**
hurdler Cotteir Chief, stayed 21f: seems of no account. *C. Roberts*

STRETCHING (IRE)   10 br.g. Contract Law (USA) – Mrs Mutton (Dancer's Image **c70**
(USA)) [2002/3 c24m⁵ Jun 1] close-coupled gelding: selling hurdler/novice chaser: fair **h–**
pointer in 2002, successful twice: stays 21f: acts on good to firm and good to soft going:
effective visored or not. *Miss Joanne Priest*

STREWTH   9 b.g. Cruise Missile – Storm Foot (Import) [2002/3 c20dᵖᵘ c24m⁶ Apr **c79 §**
12] fair pointer: successful 3 times in 2003 prior to sixth of 9 in hunter chase at Bangor. **h–**
Mrs L. Pomfret

STRICTLY SPEAKING (IRE)   6 b.g. Sri Pekan (USA) – Gaijin (Caerleon (USA)) **h92**
[2002/3 h92: 19d⁶ 21vᵖᵘ Dec 4] medium-sized gelding: modest on Flat (stays 14.8f):
modest form over hurdles: likely to prove best up to 2½m: raced on good going or softer.
P. F. I. Cole

STROMIAN HOUSE (IRE)   7 br.g. Rock Hopper – Strike Home (Be My Guest **h62**
(USA)) [2002/3 h–, F–: 22g⁴ 21dᵖᵘ 22sᵖᵘ Dec 6] sturdy gelding: signs of only a little
ability over hurdles. *A. D. Smith*

STROMNESS (USA)   6 ch.g. Trempolino (USA) – Caithness (USA) (Roberto **h139**
(USA)) [2002/3 h142: 25d⁶ 24s* 23s³ 20d⁶ 24m³ 24g³ Apr 2] compact gelding: has had
soft palate operation: useful hurdler: won minor event at Cheltenham in December by 7
lengths from Rum Pointer: tongue tied, best effort when third of 7 to Deano's Beeno
in Grade 2 at Ascot final start: best at 3m+: acts on heavy going, possibly not on good to
firm: has worn crossed noseband. *A. King*

STRONG ARROW (IRE)   10 b.g. Strong Gale – Caesonia (Buckskin (FR)) [2002/3 **c–**
c–, h81: 23g² 23d 24g² 24g⁵ 20s³ 20m⁶ 20g* c20d⁶ 20m⁴ Mar 19] tall gelding: shows **h86**
traces of stringhalt: winning chaser, never dangerous in handicap on final outing for
F. Murphy: modest novice hurdler: won handicap at Fakenham in October: barely stays
3m: acts on heavy going, probably on good to firm: visored twice in 2000/1: inconsistent.
J. A. Supple

STRONG DECISION (IRE)   6 br.g. Mandalus – Francois's Crumpet (IRE) (Strong **h82**
Gale) [2002/3 F88: 21m² Apr 21] rather leggy gelding: trained by W. Jarvis, best effort in
bumpers in 2001/2 when seventh of 25 at Newbury, hanging right: off 15 months and
tongue tied, 5 lengths second of 5 finishers to Barrow in maiden at Huntingdon on
hurdling debut: bred to be suited by greater test of stamina. *M. C. Banks*

STRONG FINISH   8 ch.g. Montelimar (USA) – Atlantic View (Crash Course) [2002/3 **c67 ?**
h67: 22gᵖᵘ 22g⁴ 22d⁵ 24m⁴ c22m⁵ c21m⁵ 21m⁴ c24m² c24m³ Oct 11] lengthy, angular **h72**
gelding: poor maiden jumper: has had tongue tied: sold £2,100 Ascot October Sales.
P. W. Hiatt

STRONG FLOW (IRE)   6 br.g. Over The River (FR) – Stormy Skies (Strong Gale) **h125 p**
[2002/3 24s² 24s* Feb 27] second foal: half-brother to winning pointer Ballyconnell
(by Insan): dam, maiden jumper, half-sister to useful staying chaser Plenty Crack: won
maiden Irish point in 2002: shaped well on hurdling debut, then won 9-runner novice at
Taunton by 17 lengths from Gumption, jumping fluently and always travelling strongly:
exciting prospect. *P. F. Nicholls*

STRONG KING (IRE)   9 b. or br.g. Strong Gale – Mrs Simpson (Kinglet) [2002/3 **c–**
h–: c23dᵖᵘ Jun 3] poor maiden pointer: little show over hurdles or in maiden chase: tried **h–**
visored. *R. Ford*

STRONG MAGIC (IRE)   11 br.g. Strong Gale – Baybush (Boreen (FR)) [2002/3 c94, **c96**
h–: c20s⁵ c24g c24s⁴ c21m² c20d² c24d² c24s⁴ c23g⁴ c22g c24d⁵ Apr 9] workmanlike **h–**
gelding: modest handicap chaser: stays 25f: acts on soft and good to firm going: often
makes running: usually jumps well. *J. R. Cornwall*

STRONG PALADIN (IRE)   12 b.g. Strong Gale – Kalanshoe (Random Shot) [2002/3 **c109**
c121, h–: c22g³ c24d³ c25d⁶ c26m* c26m⁴ Apr 16] rangy, useful-looking gelding: fair **h–**
handicap chaser: won at Fontwell in March: stays 3¼m: acts on firm and soft going: has
run creditably when sweating: sound jumper: consistent. *N. A. Gaselee*

STRONG PROJECT (IRE) 7 ch.g. Project Manager – Hurricane Girl (IRE) **c95**
(Strong Gale) [2002/3 20s^F 24s^3 24s^3 20m* c20s^F 22d^2 22g c22s^F c21m c20d^6 Oct 24] **h116**
fairly useful hurdler: didn't have to be at best to win minor event at Wexford in July: not
fluent and modest form at best over fences: stays 3m: acts on soft and good to firm going.
C. F. Swan, Ireland

STRONG RESOLVE (IRE) 7 gr.g. Roselier (FR) – Farmerette (Teofane) [2002/3 **h87**
h85, F77: 24g^{pu} 16g^3 22s^3 20s^3 20s^5 20d^4 16s^5 24v^{pu} 16d^5 20d^4 16d* 20d^{pu} Mar 15] leggy
gelding: modest hurdler: won maiden at Ayr in March: effective at 2m to 2¾m: acts on
soft going: has shaped as if amiss more than once. *J. Barclay*

STRONG TARTAN (IRE) 9 br.g. Strong Gale – Kemchee (Kemal (FR)) [2002/3 **c89**
c94, h–: 22m^3 c25g^3 c22s^F 24g^{pu} Apr 23] well-made gelding: maiden hurdler: modest **h75**
handicap chaser: stays 25f: acts on good to firm going. *A. Parker*

STRONGTROOPER (IRE) 8 b.g. Doubletour (USA) – Moss Gale (Strong Gale) **c–**
[2002/3 c96, h–: c21g^6 Apr 21] big, angular gelding: twice-raced winning hurdler: mod- **h–**
est chaser: well held in handicap on return from year's absence: stays 3m: acts on good to
firm and good to soft going: often let down by jumping: has been led in. *O. Sherwood*

STRONG VISION (IRE) 12 b.g. Strong Gale – Deep Vision (Deep Run) [2002/3 **c81**
c–: c22d^3 c23m^2 c26g^{pu} c26g^{pu} c26m^{pu} Jul 19] sturdy, lengthy gelding: long-standing
maiden chaser: stays 25f: acts on good to firm and heavy going: blinkered last 4 starts
(ran poorly all bar first occasion). *K. C. Bailey*

ST STEVEN (NZ) 9 b.g. Hula Town (NZ) – Gabby (NZ) (In The Purple (FR)) **c?**
[2002/3 c166, h–: c16d^3 c18s* c18s* c18s^5 c16m^2 Apr 21] leading Australian chaser:
gained second successive win in A. V. Hiskins Steeplechase (premier conditions chase in
Australia) at Moonee Valley in July: won 2002 Nakayama Grand Jump, beaten 5 lengths
by locally-trained Big Taste when third in latest renewal in April: effective at 2m to 25f:
acts on any going. *J. Wheeler, New Zealand*

STUDIO THIRTY 11 gr.g. Rock City – Chepstow Vale (USA) (Key To The Mint **c–**
(USA)) [2002/3 c–, h83: 19d 16g 17m^{pu} Apr 5] leggy gelding: novice chaser: handicap **h–**
hurdler, no sign of retaining ability after lengthy absence in 2002/3: stays 2½m: acts on
soft and good to firm going. *R. J. Price*

STURM UND DRANG 9 ch.g. Selkirk (USA) – Historiette (Chief's Crown (USA)) **c80**
[2002/3 h86: c17g^6 c16g^5 16m^2 Apr 22] modest maiden hurdler, lightly raced: left J. Frost **h88**
and off 10 months, best effort when 9 lengths second of 16 to Knocktopher Abbey at
Chepstow: well held in 2 early-season novice chases: best form around 2m. *C. J. Down*

STYLINO (USA) 6 ch.g. Trempolino (USA) – Smartly Styled (USA) (Cox's Ridge **c–**
(USA)) [2002/3 c20m^4 c21s^{pu} c17m^{pu} Jun 22] ex-French gelding: lightly raced on Flat: **h–**
fair maiden jumper: sold out of M. Rolland's stable 330,000 francs Goffs July (2001)
Sale: no form in Britain: best form around 2m: acts on heavy going: tried blinkered/
tongue tied. *C. C. Bealby*

STYLISH FELLA (USA) 5 b.g. Irish River (FR) – Dariela (USA) (Manila (USA)) **h– §**
[2002/3 h–: 19g^5 24g^{pu} 20g^{pu} 16s Aug 1] little sign of ability over hurdles (has looked
temperamental): tried blinkered. *D. G. Bridgwater*

SUAVE FRANKIE 7 ch.g. Suave Dancer (USA) – Francia (Legend of France (USA)) **h–**
[2002/3 h64: 20d^5 24g^{pu} May 11] poor maiden hurdler: stays 21f. *I. W. McInnes*

SUBA LIN 14 b.m. Sula Bula – Tula Lin (Tula Rocket) [2002/3 c21f^{pu} May 10] poor **c–**
pointer: always behind in hunter chase. *Mrs C. Atyeo*

SUBIACO (GER) 6 b.h. Monsun (GER) – So Sedulous (USA) (The Minstrel (CAN)) **h92**
[2002/3 16d^5 16s^F Feb 14] useful-looking horse: useful on Flat (effective at 10.5f to 2m)
for A. Schutz in Germany, successful 6 times: hung left off bridle when fifth of 16 to
Demi Beau in novice at Doncaster on hurdling debut: weakening in fourth when fell last
in similar event at Sandown next time (looked lame). *B. J. Curley*

SUCH PHUN 5 b.m. Karinga Bay – Bugsy's Sister (Aragon) [2002/3 F–: F16g^5 F17m **h–**
17s^3 17d 19g^6 21g^6 Dec 12] plain mare: signs of only a little ability in bumpers and over **F63**
hurdles. *J. Hetherton*

SUCK YOUR THUMB 9 b.m. Teenoso (USA) – Onaway (Commanche Run) [2002/3 **h– §**
h–§: 16d^{pu} Nov 14] lengthy mare: has shown more temperament than ability over hurdles.
N. A. Twiston-Davies

SUD BLEU (FR)   5 b.g. Pistolet Bleu (IRE) – Sudaka (FR) (Garde Royale) [2002/3   **h120 §**
h117§: 17d* 16d³ 16g² 16s 17v⁴ 17s³ 22d⁵ 18d⁵ Mar 1] tall, useful-looking gelding: fairly
useful hurdler, simple task in novice at Exeter in October: creditable efforts when in
frame after, well below form final outing: raced mainly around 2m on good going or
softer (failed to stay 2¾m): weak finisher. *P. F. Nicholls*

SUDDEN SHOCK (GER)   8 b.g. Motley (USA) – Santalina (Relko) [2002/3   **c129**
h143: c25mᶠ c20dᶠ 21s³ c25d⁴ c24m² c32g* c33m Apr 12]   **h129**
      'The widely-held notion that the day when cavalry can usefully be
employed in war is over because it has been superseded by aeroplanes is based on a
misconception of the powers and limitations of aircraft. Much mischief may result
if the truth is not made known. Those engaged in the breeding of light horses from
which the cavalry obtains its drafts have quite enough inevitable discouragements
to contend against and may well be spared those which spring from ignorance. It is
very essential that the public should know that cavalry is still a necessity and not
merely an ornamental luxury in order that the government may not feel hampered in
any steps they may think it necessary to take to ensure the provision of home-bred
remounts in adequate numbers and quality, both for immediate and prospective
needs.' Not, as might first be thought, a letter sent to the *Racing Post* by a retired
trainer from Berkshire but the opening to a piece that appeared under the heading
'Cavalry Not Obsolete~The Limitations of Aeroplanes' in the *Bloodstock Breeders
Review* of 1920. Resisting change is a perilous business for anyone worried about
being made to look silly eighty years down the line. Well, not so much resisting
change as failing to see what, not just in hindsight, is blindingly obvious. The
Bloodstock Breeders Review between the wars (Great and Second World) wasn't
much concerned with National Hunt racing, contests other than the Grand National
and the Grand Steeple-Chase de Paris meriting barely a mention. Had it extended
its coverage beyond those two races, one of the first to be featured would have been
the National Hunt Chase, then the centrepiece of the National Hunt meeting, as the
Cheltenham Festival is still formally known, and a race of much longer standing
than the Gold Cup and Champion Hurdle. Today, however, the National Hunt
Chase seems a metaphorical cavalry horse among the top flight contests at the
Cheltenham Fesitval. It could be argued that a four-mile novice chase for amateur
riders has no business in a programme of championship races and ultra-competitive

National Hunt Chase Challenge Cup (Amateur Riders'), Cheltenham—
Sudden Shock (left) reverses Kempton placings from his previous start with hot favourite Stormez

Mr Darren C. Mercer's "Sudden Shock"

handicaps that make up the rest of the programme (though it won't look so out of place when a proposed cross-country race is added in 2005). However, just as the banks races at Punchestown and the Queen Alexandra Stakes at Royal Ascot are signature contests that embody the tradition of the fixture, so the National Hunt Chase is important as a fixed point in the ever-revolving universe. Just as the Queen Alexandra is seen by some as a good excuse to get away before the last, so there are those that see the National Hunt Chase as a chance to spend a bit longer in the Guinness tent. Good for them. But those who think the race encapsulates the very spirit of the sport don't want to see a finish fought out by the fourth- or fifth-string novices of two top stables, which is likely to be a regular occurrence after a change in the race conditions in 2002. Horses that had won over hurdles before the start of the current season were formerly excluded, making the race more restrictive than a novice chase. It was the restrictions that gave the race its unique character, whereas now it is just for those not good enough, or too slow, to run in the SunAlliance. It might be won by a better standard of novice but has lost something in the process. Either change it back or scrap it.

The 2003 renewal, the second under the new conditions, was fought out by a smart hurdler and a useful hurdler who had had contrasting seasons as they made the transition to chasing. The favourite Stormez had had a productive time in novices and handicaps over fences, and certainly had form good enough to justify a place in the SunAlliance, but his connections had another leading candidate for that race in It Takes Time. On the other hand, the 25/1-chance Sudden Shock found getting the hang of fences a problem; he fell on his first two starts, then, after a rather disappointing return to hurdling in the Cleeve Hurdle at Cheltenham, was well held at Wincanton and easily outpointed in a match at Kempton, by none other than Stormez. It therefore came as a major surprise that Sudden Shock was able to reverse placings, coming through to pinch the race after travelling strongly in rear to the third last. A blunder at the next hardly halted his progress, and Sudden Shock continued gaining on Stormez after the last, getting up close home and winning by a length. Sudden Shock and Stormez met for a third time in the Scottish Grand National at Ayr the following month, both sent off 6/1 joint-second favourite despite neither looking well handicapped, Stormez, much improved, again missing out narrowly on victory, but Sudden Shock underlining his unpredictability in finishing well held in seventh behind Ryalux. The fourth, sixth and seventh at Cheltenham were all pulled up next time but Hedgehunter, who was possibly unlucky in the race as he was going well when all but falling two out, came a creditable second in the big novice handicap at Punchestown next time. In general, those that ran afterwards underlined the limitations of the form at Cheltenham.

		Best Turn		Turn-To
	Motley (USA)	(b or br 1966)		Sweet Clementine
	(b 1984)	Tipping Time		Commanding II
Sudden Shock (GER)		(b 1966)		Tipping
(b.g. 1995)		Relko		Tanerko
	Santalina	(b 1960)		Relance
	(ch 1974)	Sursum Corda		Le Haar
		(gr 1968)		Ad Altiora

Sudden Shock was raced in Europe before joining Jonjo O'Neill in 2001, winning four times over hurdles in Germany, three in Italy, including in the Corsa Siepi di Merano, and finishing second in the Prix Juigne at Auteuil. His only win over hurdles in Britain came in a listed handicap at Aintree in 2001/2, for which he started 33/1. He is one of eight winners from eleven foals out of his dam, the French middle-distance winner Santalina. Two of the others were useful, the nine-furlong and mile-and-a-quarter winner Salilia (by Nishapour) and the Irish hurdler Sanndila (by Lashkari). Two of the others won over hurdles in France and Germany, including Sudden Shock's brother Sears Tower. Santalina is a half-sister to two above-average Flat performers, Sumayr, who won the Grand Prix de Paris when it was run over fifteen furlongs, and Samata, who stayed a mile and a half and is the dam of the smart French chaser Sprong. The third dam Ad Altiora produced a smart performer both on the Flat and over fences, in the Pouliches winner Altissima and the Prix Ferdinand Dufaure winner Incantando. The useful-looking Sudden Shock was effective at around two and a half miles and on heavy going when trained in Germany, but his best efforts in Britain have been at three miles or more and on good or good to firm going. That though may just be a result of his inconsistency. *Jonjo O'Neill*

SUEZ TORNADO (IRE) 10 ch.g. Mujtahid (USA) – So Stylish (Great Nephew) **c–**
[2002/3 c78, h–: c26g² c26m⁵ c26m⁵ c20fᵖᵘ c26sᵖᵘ Mar 10] sturdy gelding: poor maiden **h–**
jumper, left B. Johnson after fourth start: stays 23f: form only on good ground or firmer: usually blinkered nowadays: has looked reluctant. *K. Tork*

SUHAIL (IRE) 7 b.g. Wolfhound (USA) – Sharayif (IRE) (Green Desert (USA)) **h–**
[2002/3 17g Nov 7] no longer of any account on Flat: tongue tied, well held in seller on hurdling debut. *Jane Southcombe*

SULABAN 7 b.m. Sula Bula – Mariban (Mummy's Pet) [2002/3 F–: c19dᵖᵘ 22mᵖᵘ Apr **c–**
8] no form in varied events: lame final outing. *B. J. M. Ryall* **h–**

SULLANE STORM (IRE) 8 b.g. Glacial Storm (USA) – Heather Point (Pollerton) **c90**
[2002/3 c25dᵖᵘ c24dᵖᵘ c26sᵘʳ c30s c24v* c24m* Apr 22] ex-Irish gelding: fourth foal: dam, winning pointer, half-sister to La Touche Cup winner Howyanow: fair chaser in 2001/2 for E. O'Sullivan: found some form again towards end of 2002/3, won 4-finisher minor event at Taunton in March and 6-runner handicap at Chepstow in April: stays 3m: acts on good to firm and heavy ground: reportedly bled fourth start: sometimes jumps none too fluently. *M. C. Pipe*

SULLYS HOPE 6 b.g. Rock Hopper – Super Sally (Superlative) [2002/3 h109: 16g **h108**
19mᵖᵘ 16m⁴ 16d³ 17d⁴ Dec 13] good-topped gelding: fair handicap hurdler: best around

2m: acts on firm and soft going: tried visored: flashed tail under pressure third outing. *Nick Williams*

SULPHUR SPRINGS (IRE)   11 ch.g. Don't Forget Me – Short Wave (FR) (Trepan (FR)) [2002/3 c133, h–: c24g³ c28m c20m^pu Sep 29] leggy gelding: useful chaser, successful 6 times in 2001/2: creditable effort on reappearance, but very disappointing both starts after: effective at 2½m to 3¼m: acts on soft and firm going: tongue tied nowadays: races prominently. *M. C. Pipe*   **c130** **h–**

SUMBOY (IRE)   9 br.g. Aristocracy – Sign O' The Season (Strong Gale) [2002/3 c–, h–: c25d^pu May 6] no sign of ability: sold 2,000 gns Ascot July Sales. *J. F. Panvert*   **c–** **h–**

SUM LEADER (IRE)   7 b.g. Leading Counsel (USA) – Greenodd (Green Shoon) [2002/3 h116: 24s* 20s² 24s* 16d 22g⁵ 22g⁴ Apr 21] lengthy gelding: fairly useful handicap hurdler: won at Navan in May and June: off 8 months, creditable efforts at Fairyhouse in April and Punchestown 8 days later: stays 3m: acts on good to firm and heavy going: consistent. *G. Keane, Ireland*   **h124**

SUMMER BOUNTY   7 b.g. Lugana Beach – Tender Moment (IRE) (Caerleon (USA)) [2002/3 h–: 16d⁴ 16d 20d^F Nov 24] close-coupled gelding: fair on turf, modest on all-weather Flat (stays 1½m, has virtually refused to race): poor novice handicap hurdler: best around 2m: acts on good to firm and good to soft going. *F. Jordan*   **h84**

SUMMER BREAK (IRE)   6 ch.m. Foxhound (USA) – Out In The Sun (USA) (It's Freezing (USA)) [2002/3 h105d: 16g^pu 20s⁴ Dec 5] angular mare: modest on Flat nowadays: one-time fair hurdler, disappointing since first outing in 2001/2: left I. Williams after reappearance: best efforts at 2m: acts on good to firm and heavy ground: rejoined A. Mullins. *W. J. Musson*   **h–**

SUMMER CHERRY (USA)   6 b.g. Summer Squall (USA) – Cherryrob (USA) (Roberto (USA)) [2002/3 h68: 16d Nov 2] close-coupled gelding: modest on Flat (stays 1½m, sometimes looks none too keen), successful twice in 2002: tongue tied, poor form in 3 starts over hurdles. *Jamie Poulton*   **h–**

SUMMER VILLA   11 b.m. Nomination – Maravilla (Mandrake Major) [2002/3 c–, h–: 16d 16m Jul 18] workmanlike mare: poor 2m hurdler/novice chaser, little sign of retaining ability: usually blinkered: tried tongue tied. *K. G. Wingrove*   **c–** **h–**

SUMUT   4 b.g. Hamas (IRE) – Simaat (USA) (Mr Prospector (USA)) [2002/3 F16d Feb 23] 3,800 3-y-o: fifth foal: closely related to useful 7f winner Al Ihsan and fairly useful 1988 2-y-o 7.5f winner Samut (both by Danehill) and half-brother to winner in Spain by Last Tycoon: dam, 1m winner, out of sister to US Grade 1 6f (at 2 yrs) to 9f winner Rockhill Native: around 18 lengths eighth of 18 in bumper at Ayr on debut: well held in maidens on Flat. *G. A. Swinbank*   **F77**

SUN BIRD (IRE)   5 ch.g. Prince of Birds (USA) – Summer Fashion (Moorestyle) [2002/3 16v² Nov 13] fairly useful on Flat (stays 13f), successful twice in 2002: promising hurdling debut when neck second of 13 to Zamat in novice at Kelso, not always fluent but putting in sustained challenge run-in: open to improvement. *R. Allan*   **h101 p**

SUNCZECH (IRE)   13 b.m. Sunyboy – Miss Prague (Mon Capitaine) [2002/3 c24g⁶ c20d⁵ c20g⁴ Mar 17] successful in points in March and April: poor form in hunter chases. *Mrs S. S. Harbour*   **c72**

SUNDANCE SID (IRE)   7 b.g. Phardante (FR) – The Kid's Sister (Black Minstrel) [2002/3 h–: 16m May 11] little sign of ability: tried visored. *Miss E. C. Lavelle*   **h–**

SUNDAWN LADY   5 b.m. Faustus (USA) – Game Domino (Derring Rose) [2002/3 F16s F17s 20g² 22g² 21m⁵ Apr 21] medium-sized mare: third foal: dam little sign of ability: well beaten in 2 bumpers: poor form over hurdles: stays 2¾m. *C. P. Morlock*   **h78** **F66**

SUNDAY HABITS (IRE)   9 ch.g. Montelimar (USA) – Robertina (USA) (Roberto (USA)) [2002/3 c26m* c26m^ur Apr 21] winning Irish pointer: off nearly 2 years, best effort in steeplechases when winning 5-runner novice handicap (11 lb out of weights) at Plumpton in April, making all: stays 3¼m: acts on good to firm going: tried in tongue strap. *D. P. Keane*   **c77**

SUNDAY RAIN (USA)   6 b.g. Summer Squall (USA) – Oxava (FR) (Antheus (USA)) [2002/3 h94§: 16g* 20s³ 16d³ 16m* 16m² 16m³ 16m 20d³ 19d 16g⁵ Apr 14] well-made gelding: modest hurdler: won intermediate in April and novice in June, both at Hexham: ran at least respectably most other starts: stays 2½m: acts on soft and good to firm going: blinkered (ran poorly) final start in 2001/2: formerly ungenuine. *Miss Lucinda V. Russell*   **h100**

SUNGATES (IRE)   7 ch.g. Glacial Storm (USA) – Live It Up (Le Coq d'Or) [2002/3   **h77**
F90: 24s⁶ 24v⁵ Nov 22] lengthy gelding: third (promoted) in bumper on debut in
early-2001/2: off 18 months, poor form over hurdles: bred to stay well. *A. J. Lidderdale*

SUNGIO   5 b.g. Halling (USA) – Time Or Never (FR) (Dowsing (USA)) [2002/3 h81:   **h97 §**
17gᵖᵘ 16g⁴ 20g* 19dᵖᵘ 21dᵖᵘ 18d⁴ 21vᵖᵘ Dec 4] rangy, unfurnished gelding: fair on Flat
(stays 1½m): modest hurdler: improved form upped in trip when winning novice claimer
at Fontwell in October: stays 2½m: acts on good to soft going: has worn cheekpieces: not
an easy ride and none too reliable. *B. G. Powell*

SUN KING   6 ch.g. Zilzal (USA) – Opus One (Slip Anchor) [2002/3 h97+, F89: 16m*   **h96**
16g* 17m² 20m³ 17d² 19dᵖᵘ 16d Apr 9] leggy gelding: modest hurdler: favourite, won
novices at Wetherby (conditional jockeys) and Towcester (awarded race) in May: stays
2½m: best efforts on good/good to firm going: sometimes races freely/jumps right. *Mrs
M. Reveley*

SUNLIT BOY   11 ch.g. Ardross – Sunlit River (Roi Soleil) [2002/3 c20s c26sᵖᵘ Mar   **c–**
10] rangy gelding: little form over hurdles and fences: tried tongue tied. *J. J. Bridger*   **h–**

SUNNE LORD (IRE)   6 b.g. Mister Lord (USA) – Happy Party (Invited (USA))   **h–**
[2002/3 F16s F17s 19m Apr 5] IR 11,000 3-y-o: seventh foal: half-brother to fairly useful   **F76**
jumper around 2m Storm Tiger (by Strong Gale): dam unraced: never on terms in
bumpers or maiden hurdle. *A. King*

SUNNYARJUN   5 ch.g. Afzal – Hush Tina (Tina's Pet) [2002/3 F16s 16g 19g Apr 19]   **h–**
workmanlike gelding: first foal: dam modest maiden up to 1½m on Flat/over hurdles: **F–**
well held in bumper and 2 starts over hurdles (has pulled hard). *J. C. Tuck*

SUNNY FLIGHT (FR)   9 ch.g. Saint Cyrien (FR) – Sunday Flight (FR) (Johnny   **c150 ?**
O'Day (USA)) [2002/3 c123+, h152: c18v⁵ 18s⁵ c21s¹ꟳ 19s c18s* c27v* c22v⁶ Dec 1]   **h132**
raced exclusively at Auteuil in 2002/3: smart hurdler, just useful form both outings in
2002/3: smart chaser: apparently back to very best when winning Group 3 Prix Ingre in
May by 8 lengths from Ty Benjam, possibly flattered after leaders went too fast: ran badly
in Grand Steeple-Chase de Paris next time, refused fifth in Group 2 in June: earlier
successful twice in autumn, in minor event and Group 1 Prix La Haye Jousselin (rallied
well in very testing conditions to beat Cerilly 5 lengths): stays 27f: raced mainly on soft/
heavy going. *A. Chaille-Chaille, France*

SUNNYSIDE ROYALE (IRE)   4 b.g. Ali-Royal (IRE) – Kuwah (IRE) (Be My   **h65**
Guest (USA)) [2002/3 16d 16s Nov 27] leggy, close-coupled gelding: modest maiden on
Flat (should stay 1¾m): never a factor in juvenile hurdles. *M. W. Easterby*

SUNNY SOMBRERO   6 b.m. Contract Law (USA) – Vitry (Vitiges (FR)) [2002/3   **F–**
F16m F16g Jul 10] 1,700 3-y-o: half-sister to temperamental winning 2m hurdler Script
(by Squill): dam, poor maiden stayed 1½m, half-sister to useful 2m hurdler Hill's Pageant
and useful hurdler/chaser up to 3m Homeson: well held in bumpers at Worcester.
Dr P. Pritchard

SUNRIDGE FAIRY (IRE)   4 b.f. Definite Article – Foxy Fairy (IRE) (Fairy King   **h94**
(USA)) [2002/3 17g* 17d* 17m* 16m⁴ 16s* 16g* 17v⁴ 16d 17d⁵ Mar 18] modest on
all-weather, poor on turf on Flat (should stay beyond 1m): modest juvenile hurdler: won
at Sedgefield and Cartmel in August, Hereford (seller, sold from P. Haslam 7,000 gns) in
September and Leicester (seller) and Catterick (claimer, claimed from Miss K. Marks
£6,000) in November: not at best in handicaps last 3 starts: likely to prove best around
2m: acts on soft and good to firm going. *Ronald Thompson*

SUNRIDGE ROSE   5 b.m. Piccolo – Floral Spark (Forzando) [2002/3 h–: 17m 16mᵖᵘ   **h– §**
16gᵖᵘ May 17] modest on Flat (stays 7f), has refused to race: has also shown more
temperament than ability over hurdles: visored final start. *Andrew Reid*

SUNRISE SPECIAL (IRE)   10 b.g. Peterius – Break of Day (On Your Mark) [2002/3   **c–**
c24sᵖᵘ Nov 9] workmanlike gelding: fair handicap chaser in 2000/1: behind when pulled   **h–**
up and dismounted only subsequent outing: stays 3m: raced mainly on going softer than
good (acts on heavy): has shown temperament under pressure. *P. R. Rodford*

SUNSHAN   7 b.g. Anshan – Kyrenia Sunset (CYP) (Lucky Look (CYP)) [2002/3 c20g⁶   **c75**
c19f⁵ c19g⁶ c19m⁵ Apr 21] workmanlike gelding: winning pointer: little impact in hunter
chases: has red tongue tied. *T. Long*

SUNSHINE BOY   7 b.g. Cadeaux Genereux – Sahara Baladee (USA) (Shadeed   **h84**
(USA)) [2002/3 h94: 22dᵖᵘ 18g³ 22gᵖᵘ Apr 21] workmanlike gelding: modest hurdler: off
17 months and left G. McCourt, form in handicaps in 2002/3 only when third to Guru at

Fontwell, flashing tail under pressure: stays 27f: best on good going or firmer (acts on firm): blinkered once. *Miss E. C. Lavelle*

SUNSHINE HEIGHTS   6 b.m. Golden Heights – Turners Keep (Just A Monarch)   **F68 ?**
[2002/3 F16g⁶ F17m⁶ Sep 11] second foal: dam of little account: signs of only a little ability in bumpers at Worcester and Hereford. *P. R. Hedger*

SUNSHINE LEADER (IRE)   8 b.m. Supreme Leader – Cherry Run (Deep Run)   **c94**
[2002/3 h95: c16v² c25d³ c24v⁶ Dec 28] leggy, lengthy mare: modest hurdler: similar   **h–**
form on steeplechasing debut, let down by jumping both subsequent starts: effective at 2m, should stay 3m: raced on good going or softer (acts on heavy): below form in blinkers final outing in 2001/2. *E. L. James*

SUNTAS (IRE)   8 b.m. Riberetto – Shuil (IRE) (Meneval (USA)) [2002/3 c110, h90:   **c108**
c30d* c32d⁴ c26s c29dᵖᵘ c29gᵖᵘ Mar 14] good-topped mare: maiden handicap chaser: **h–**
won 3-finisher event at Huntingdon in November: ran poorly last 3 starts: stays 3¾m: raced on good going or softer (acts on heavy). *T. R. George*

SUNUVUGUN   11 b.g. Gunner B – Final Melody (Final Straw) [2002/3 c–, h–: c25dᵖᵘ   **c–**
c25m⁵ c20d⁴ c22mᵖᵘ Jul 7] well-made gelding: winning 25f chaser: blinkered final   **h–**
outing: dead. *Mrs D. Thomson*

SUPERB LEADER (IRE)   9 b.g. Supreme Leader – Emmagreen (Green Shoon)   **c102**
[2002/3 17s⁴ c20s³ c17v² c20d⁴ c17g* Mar 22] useful-looking gelding: modest form over   **h84**
hurdles, off 20 months before reappearance: best effort over fences when winning 7-runner maiden at Bangor: stays 21f: acts on heavy going: finished tamely fourth start. *Miss Venetia Williams*

SUPER BLUE (IRE)   6 b.m. Supreme Leader – Tip Marie (IRE) (Celio Rufo) [2002/3   **h–**
F17d F17v⁶ 24vᵖᵘ Jan 17] IR 34,000 3-y-o: useful-looking mare: third foal: half-sister to   **F–**
Irish bumper winner Quick Pick (by Alphabatim): dam unraced, from family of smart chaser up to 25f Tipping Tim: signs of only a little ability in 2 bumpers: no show on hurdling debut. *P. F. Nicholls*

SUPER DOLLAR (IRE)   7 ch.g. Great Commotion (USA) – L'Americaine (USA)   **c97**
(Verbatim (USA)) [2002/3 h96: c17g³ c16s⁶ Jun 9] sturdy gelding: modest handicap   **h–**
hurdler: off 10 months, similar form when under 5 lengths third of 5 finishers in novice at Stratford on chasing debut: fell seventh following month: best up to 19f: acts on soft and firm going. *K. C. Bailey*

SUPER DOLPHIN   4 ch.g. Dolphin Street (FR) – Supergreen (Superlative) [2002/3   **h–**
16d 16s 16d 16d⁶ 16m⁶ Apr 21] modest maiden on Flat (stays 7f, refused to race on reappearance in 2003): form over hurdles only when sixth of 21 in novice at Catterick fourth start: likely to need sharp 2m. *T. P. Tate*

SUPER FELLOW (IRE)   9 b.g. Shy Groom (USA) – Killough (Lord Gayle (USA))   **c132 ?**
[2002/3 c17s⁵ c20s³ c20s c26m* c23f² c24d* c24v⁵ c25d⁴ Apr 4] angular gelding: **h–**
one-time useful handicap hurdler: successful twice in points in 2002: novice chaser: won at Newton Abbot in August and Cheltenham (fortunate) in November: apparently much improved when 18 lengths fourth of 9 to Irish Hussar in Grade 2 at Aintree, probably flattered in steadily-run race: stays 3¼m: acts on any going: blinkered last 3 starts: usually tongue tied: none too consistent. *D. P. Murphy, Ireland*

SUPER GRAN (IRE)   5 b.m. Grand Plaisir (IRE) – Caledon Mist (IRE) (Le Moss)   **F–**
[2002/3 F16fᵖᵘ Sep 15] second foal: dam unraced: showed nothing in bumper: dead. *R. Johnson*

SUPERIOR WEAPON (IRE)   9 b.g. Riverhead (USA) – Ballytrustan Maid (IRE)   **c87**
(Orchestra) [2002/3 c92: c24m² c25mᵖᵘ c22dᵖᵘ Nov 17] modest chaser: poor efforts last 2 starts, 5½ months in between: seems to stay easy 3m: acts on soft and good to firm going: tongue tied. *F. P. Murtagh*

SUPER NOMAD   8 b.g. Nomadic Way (USA) – Super Sue (Lochnager) [2002/3 c108,   **c118**
h–: c16g⁵ c16dᶠ c19gᵖᵘ c19d² 16d⁴ c16g² c17m² Apr 21] strong gelding: winning hurdler: **h110**
fairly useful handicap chaser: good second to Arctic Fancy at Doncaster fourth start: stays 2½m: acts on heavy and good to firm going: has had tongue tied: sound jumper in main. *M. W. Easterby*

SUPER RAPIER (IRE)   11 b.g. Strong Gale – Misty Venture (Foggy Bell) [2002/3   **c–**
c–, h71: 27m⁵ 23d³ 24d⁴ 26m⁵ Aug 12] well-made gelding: one-time fair chaser: poor   **h76**
hurdler nowadays: won conditional jockeys selling handicap at Fontwell in May: best at 3m+ nowadays: acts on soft and good to firm going: visored/blinkered in 2002/3. *Ferdy Murphy*

SUPER ROAD TRAIN   4 b.g. Petoski – Foehn Gale (IRE) (Strong Gale) [2002/3   **F91**
F18m* Mar 31] first foal: dam unraced: won bumper at Plumpton on debut by 1½ lengths
from Gebora. *L. Wells*

SUPER SAMMY   7 br.m. Mesleh – Super Sue (Lochnager) [2002/3 h84, F97: 16m   **h92**
16s² 19g² 19s³ 16v* 21v⁶ 16g 20d² 20g⁶ Mar 29] lengthy mare: modest hurdler: won
mares maiden in January: hinted at temperament final outing: stays 2½m:
raced mainly on good going or softer (acts on heavy). *M. W. Easterby*

SUPER SATCO (IRE)   5 b.g. Satco (FR) – Brae (IRE) (Runnett) [2002/3 F16f⁵ F16d   **F82**
Nov 17] IR £20,000 3-y-o: unfurnished gelding: second foal: dam won 2m hurdle: around
5 lengths fifth of 12 in bumper at Hexham on debut: tailed off in listed event at Cheltenham 2 months later. *Edward Butler, Ireland*

SUPERSHOT (IRE)   5 b.g. Son of Sharp Shot (IRE) – One To Two (IRE) (Astronef)   **F—**
[2002/3 F16g Dec 13] first foal: dam ran once: in rear in bumper at Doncaster on debut.
O. Brennan

SUPERSTAR EXPRESS (IRE)   6 br.g. Jurado (USA) – Easter Bee (IRE) (Phardante   **h—**
(FR)) [2002/3 F—: F16s 16g⁶ 16g 17m Apr 19] lengthy gelding: little worthwhile form: **F—**
has had tongue tied. *J. I. A. Charlton*

SUPRALUNA   4 ch.f. Classic Cliche (IRE) – Spring Flyer (IRE) (Waajib) [2002/3   **F—**
F14d F16f Mar 29] sturdy filly: fourth foal: half-sister to fairly useful hurdlers up to 3m
Miss Tango (by Batshoof) and Roveretto (by Robellino), latter winning 2m chaser: dam,
fair 7f to 9f winner, half-sister to smart sprinter A Prayer For Wings: well held in bumpers
at Newcastle and Haydock. *Mrs M. Reveley*

SUPREME ATTRACTION   6 b.m. Supreme Leader – Tourist Attraction   **h81 p**
(IRE) (Pollerton) [2002/3 F87: 20d³ Dec 12] won mares bumper in 2001/2: 5½ lengths
third of 13 in mares novice at Huntingdon on hurdling debut 10 months later, travelling
strongly but mistakes closing stages: should improve. *Noel T. Chance*

SUPREME BEING (IRE)   6 b.g. Supreme Leader – Parsonetta (The Parson)   **h104**
[2002/3 h111, F92: 22v 20s⁵ 20v³ 20s⁶ 20v⁶ 20s Feb 22] unfurnished gelding: fair
handicap hurdler: below form after third start: should be suited by further than 2½m: acts
on heavy going: effective blinkered or not: has looked less than keen: none too consistent.
Michael Cunningham, Ireland

SUPREME BREEZE (IRE)   8 b.g. Supreme Leader – Merry Breeze (Strong Gale)   **c90 §**
[2002/3 c82, h—: c25dᵘʳ c25g⁴ c24v⁵ c24g⁶ c25d² c25g³ c31g³ Apr 24] winning hurdler: **h—**
maiden chaser, poor on balance early: stays 21f: raced on good going or softer (acts on
soft): effective blinkered or not: prone to mistakes: ungenuine. *Ferdy Murphy*

SUPREME BUCCANEER (IRE)   9 b.g. Supreme Leader – Night Blade (Fine   **c— x**
Blade (USA)) [2002/3 h—, F—: c20d⁵ c19sᵖᵘ c16gⁿᵘ Nov 30] strong gelding: no form: poor   **h—**
jumper of fences. *Mrs S. M. Johnson*

SUPREME CATCH (IRE)   6 b.g. Supreme Leader – Lucky Trout (Beau Charmeur   **c119**
(FR)) [2002/3 h112: c19g⁵ c20d* c21d² Dec 14] workmanlike gelding: won maiden on   **h—**
hurdling bow in 2001/2: better for steeplechasing debut, won novice at Huntingdon in
November, left clear last to beat Another Raleagh 25 lengths: below that form when
length second to Paxford Jack in valuable novice at Cheltenham: likely to be suited by
3m: raced on good going or softer (acts on heavy). *Miss H. C. Knight*

SUPREME CHARM (IRE)   11 b.g. Sovereign Water (FR) – Welsh Charmer (Welsh   **c—**
Captain) [2002/3 c128, h—: c24d⁵ Nov 2] good-topped gelding: fairly useful handicap   **h—**
chaser: lacklustre effort only outing in 2002/3: stays 31f: acts on any going: blinkered
once: often held up: sometimes looks none too keen, though consistent in main.
K. C. Bailey

SUPREME CLASS   6 ch.g. Arrasas (USA) – Gabitats Dominion (Gabitat) [2002/3   **h—**
F17g F16m 16mᵖᵘ Jul 14] first foal: dam unraced: no form in 2 bumpers and novice   **F—**
selling hurdle. *G. N. Alford*

SUPREME CRAFT (IRE)   7 b.m. Warcraft (USA) – Phantom Thistle (Deep Run)   **h—**
[2002/3 F16m⁶ F16m 24m Jul 17] 4,000 4-y-o: half-sister to fairly useful 2¾m hurdler   **F—**
Chilled (by Mandalus) and prolific winning pointer/useful hunter chaser Copper Thistle
(by Ovac): dam, maiden pointer, out of useful staying chaser Tarthistle: signs of ability
only on first start in bumpers, sold afterwards out of Ms A. Embiricos' stable £5,000
Ascot June Sales. *Mrs S. M. Johnson*

SUPREME DAWN (IRE) 6 b.g. Supreme Leader – Tudor Dawn (Deep Run) **F85**
[2002/3 F85: F17d⁴ F16v³ Dec 21] medium-sized, useful-looking gelding: fair form in
frame all 3 starts in bumpers: will stay 2½m. *A. J. Lidderdale*

SUPREME DEVELOPER (IRE) 6 b.g. Supreme Leader – Bettys The Boss (IRE) **h110 +**
(Deep Run) [2002/3 F117: 20s² 16s³ 16s² 18d* 16g Mar 11] well-made gelding: will
make a chaser: smart in bumpers in 2001/2: rather disappointing over hurdles, only
success in 25-runner maiden at Navan in February, beating Tandys Bridge 1½ lengths:
soundly beaten in Grade 1 novices at Cheltenham in March and Punchestown in late-
April: should be suited by 2½m+: acts on soft going: jumps none too fluently. *Anthony
Mullins, Ireland*

SUPREME FORTUNE (IRE) 9 b.g. Supreme Leader – Lucylet (Kinglet) [2002/3 **c97 §**
h119§: 18d 20d³ 16g⁶ 20d² 21d² c21v² c19g² c16d⁴ c16g* Apr 1] close-coupled gelding: **h110 §**
fair hurdler: modest form over fences: jumped soundly when easily winning weak novice
at Newcastle: stays 21f: acts on heavy going, possibly not on good to firm: held up, and
suited by well-run race: finds little. *Mrs M. Reveley*

SUPREME GLORY (IRE) 10 b.g. Supreme Leader – Pentlows (Sheer Grit) [2002/3 **c134**
c140+: c26s⁴ c29vᵖᵘ c24g⁵ c28d c36d² Apr 5] well-made gelding: useful handicap chaser:
suffered leg injury and missed Grand National in 2002: ran creditably in latest renewal,
keeping on strongly from off the pace, when 12 lengths second of 40 to Monty's Pass:
apparently best previous effort (well held otherwise) when last of 5 finishers in Grade 2 at
Newbury: stays 4½m: acts on heavy and good to firm going: sound jumper. *P. G. Murphy*

SUPREME HILL (IRE) 6 br.g. Supreme Leader – Regents Prancer (Prince Regent **h111**
(FR)) [2002/3 F105: 20v³ 20v² 19d⁴ Jan 24] workmanlike gelding: useful bumper
winner: fair form when in frame in novice hurdles: will stay beyond 2½m: raced on going
softer than good (acts on heavy): jumps none too fluently. *C. J. Mann*

SUPREME IRONY (IRE) 10 b.g. Supreme Leader – Florenanti (Floriferous) **c84**
[2002/3 c86, h91: c24g³ c20d³ c24mᵘʳ c21m Jul 4] good-topped gelding: novice hurdler: **h–**
poor on balance of form over fences: won point in March: stays 3m: acts on soft going:
jumped poorly when blinkered first and third starts. *M. J. Roberts*

SUPREME LAD (IRE) 9 b.g. Supreme Leader – April Shade (Harwell) [2002/3 **c108**
c104p, h–: c22dᶠ c25dᵖᵘ Nov 24] big, rangy gelding: fairly useful hurdler in 1999/00: **h–**
very lightly raced over fences since, also second when fell 2 out in novice handicap at
Market Rasen: several mistakes at Aintree following month: should stay 3m: raced on
good going or softer (acts on soft). *M. W. Easterby*

SUPREME LASS (IRE) 7 b.m. Supreme Leader – Falas Lass (Belfalas) [2002/3 **h–**
F88: 19g 16dᵖᵘ 16d Feb 26] won mares bumper in 2001/2: no form over hurdles: bred to
be suited by 2½m+. *G. M. Moore*

SUPREMELY BRIGHT 6 b.m. Supreme Leader – Oh So Bright (Celtic Cone) **F–**
[2002/3 F16g F16d Mar 8] 5,800 4-y-o: second foal: dam, fair hurdler who stayed 2¾m,
from family of Hennessy Gold Cup winner Ever Blessed: tailed off in 2 bumpers, hung
left on debut. *M. J. Ryan*

SUPREMELY RED (IRE) 6 b.g. Supreme Leader – Her Name Was Lola (Pitskelly) **h82**
[2002/3 F80: 22f³ 22gᵖᵘ 22m* 22d 22d 20mᵖᵘ Mar 23] medium-sized gelding: poor
hurdler: won maiden at Newton Abbot in June despite jumping right, markedly so on
several occasions: left M. Pipe, no form in handicaps subsequently: likely to stay 3m: acts
on firm going: visored last 4 starts: not an easy ride. *D. A. Rees*

SUPREME NATIVE (IRE) 7 b.g. Be My Native (USA) – Ballough Bui (IRE) **h103**
(Supreme Leader) [2002/3 h108, F89: 16m³ 17f² 22mᵖᵘ Oct 27] useful-looking gelding:
has been pin-fired: fair novice hurdler: reportedly lame final outing: should stay beyond
19f: raced on good going or firmer (acts on firm): has cocked jaw and probably not an
easy ride. *P. F. Nicholls*

SUPREME OPTIMIST (IRE) 6 b.g. Supreme Leader – Armagale (IRE) (Strong **h95**
Gale) [2002/3 h–p, F85: 17d 16v³ 16s³ Dec 26] fair form when placed over hurdles: bred
to stay 2½m: raced on good going or softer (acts on heavy). *N. G. Richards*

SUPREME PIPER (IRE) 5 b.g. Supreme Leader – Whistling Doe (Whistling Deer) **h104**
[2002/3 F16d³ 17d⁴ 19d² 22d² 20v⁶ Mar 8] useful-looking gelding: chasing type: sixth **F89**
foal: half-brother to winning 2m hurdler Just Bayard (by Kambalda) and 3m chase winner
Lord Graney (by Lord Americo): dam winning hunter chaser: third in bumper at Haydock
on debut (hung left): fair form when runner-up in novice hurdles, beaten 7 lengths by Our
Vic at Taunton and 8 lengths by Grey Brother at Exeter: well held on heavy ground final
start: will stay 3m: acts on good to soft going: takes good hold. *P. J. Hobbs*

SUPREME PRINCE (IRE) 6 b.g. Supreme Leader – Strong Serenade (IRE) **h143**
(Strong Gale) [2002/3 F109: 20d* 20s* 22d* 21g 24d³ Apr 4]

Just over half an hour after Supreme Prince had maintained his unbeaten record by winning the Persian War Novices' Hurdle at Chepstow, his stable-companion One Knight, successful in that event twelve months earlier, took the Rising Stars Novices' Chase on the same card. One Knight was an appropriate winner of his race, given that he went on to win the Royal & SunAlliance Chase at the Cheltenham Festival, and Supreme Prince will do very well to match his exploits when he is sent chasing in the next season. Yet, from what has been seen of Supreme Prince so far, it's not beyond the bounds of possibility. Supreme Prince, like One Knight, is a tall gelding, very much the type to make a chaser; and his form over hurdles is superior to that shown by One Knight in the latter's only season over hurdles. The winner of a bumper at Exeter on his sole start prior to the latest campaign, Supreme Prince created a most favourable impression when justifying favouritism in a novice hurdle at Chepstow in October on his reappearance, and also when doing the same in the Royal British Legion Poppy Appeal Persian War Novices' Hurdle just over two weeks later. Supreme Prince continued his winning run in quite a valuable novice event at Wincanton three months later, although, after a bad mistake three out, he had to work harder than expected to land the odds. His run came to an end when he was upped significantly in class on his next start, in the Royal & SunAlliance Hurdle at Cheltenham. Supreme Prince, a 16/1-shot this time, was a little outpaced, but he did keep on steadily to finish eighth of nineteen to Hardy Eustace, showing useful form in the process. Stepped up to three miles in the Martell Cognac Sefton at Aintree, Supreme Prince showed further improvement in finishing twenty lengths third to Iris's Gift. He had a hard race that day, flat out to go second before the third last and outstayed by Royal Emperor in the battle for the minor placings. A bid of IR 100,000 guineas was required to secure Supreme Prince when he was auctioned as an unraced three-year-old. He probably looked the part even at that early stage, and would also have made plenty of appeal on pedigree, by Supreme Leader out of a mare who won a bumper and a two-mile maiden event over hurdles. Strong Serenade, the dam, is also responsible for That's The Story (by

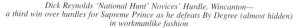

Dick Reynolds 'National Hunt' Novices' Hurdle, Wincanton—
a third win over hurdles for Supreme Prince as he defeats By Degree (almost hidden)
in workmanlike fashion

Montelimar) who was successful in a bumper in 2001 and in a three-mile handicap hurdle at Galway in the latest season. Supreme Prince has been raced only on good ground or softer, and he acts on soft. *P. J. Hobbs*

SUPREME PRIORITY (IRE) 5 b.g. Supreme Leader – Kakemona (Kambalda) [2002/3 F16s F16s³ 22v³ 24d 19d Feb 28] lengthy, useful-looking gelding: fourth foal: half-brother to fairly useful hurdler/chaser around 2m Fiery Ring (by Torus): dam bumper winner: better effort in bumpers (very green on debut) when staying-on third to impressive Sixo at Newbury: poor form over hurdles, trip too short and not knocked about after hampered 2 out final start: may still do better over hurdles at 2½m+. *Jonjo O'Neill* — h74 + F90

SUPREME QUEST (IRE) 7 b.g. Supreme Leader – Hazy River (Over The River (FR)) [2002/3 h102, F79: 24g² 27g* 24gᵖᵘ Sep 12] strong gelding: winning Irish pointer: fair handicap hurdler: visored, won at Stratford in May: weakened quickly before 2 out and pulled up lame at Uttoxeter 4 months later: stays 27f: best efforts on good/good to soft going. *Jonjo O'Neill* — h111

SUPREME SILENCE (IRE) 6 b.g. Bluebird (USA) – Why So Silent (Mill Reef (USA)) [2002/3 h87: 21g c24m³ c25mᵖᵘ Oct 4] angular gelding: poor on Flat (stays 2m), won in July: won novice hurdle early in 2001/2: no form since, including over fences: should stay 3m: tried blinkered/tongue tied: ungenuine. *Jedd O'Keeffe* — c– § h– §

SUPREME SOVIET 13 ch.g. Presidium – Sylvan Song (Song) [2002/3 c88§, h–: c24m* c24d³ c23gᵖᵘ c25m² c25g⁴ c25dᵖᵘ c27d³ c25gᵖᵘ Mar 29] leggy gelding: modest handicap chaser: won at Perth in May: stays 27f: acts on any going: ran out once: unreliable. *A. C. Whillans* — c88 § h–

SUPREME STORM (IRE)   8 b.g. Supreme Leader – Angolass (Al Sirat (USA))   **c96**
[2002/3 h78, F78: c19d⁴ c20g* c20dᵖᵘ Jun 8] strong gelding: poor form in novice hurdles: **h–**
much improved on second start over fences when winning novice handicap at Huntingdon in May: reportedly lame following month: should stay 3m: raced on good going or
softer. *B. G. Powell*

SUPREME TOSS (IRE)   7 b.g. Supreme Leader – Sleemana (Prince Hansel) [2002/3   **h131 p**
F95: 21s* 20s* 24v* Feb 1] rangy, good sort: bumper winner: made excellent start to
hurdling career, winning maiden at Warwick (impressively) and novice at Leicester (not
extended to beat Zilarator 3 lengths) in December and novice at Uttoxeter (upped in trip,
stayed on really well to beat Ar Muin Na Muice 14 lengths) in February: better suited by
3m than shorter: raced on going softer than good (acts on heavy): missed rest of season
due to leg injury but remains very promising chasing prospect. *R. T. Phillips*

SURABAYA (FR)   8 ch.m. Galetto (FR) – Silver Sea (FR) (Gay Mecene (USA))   **c– §**
[2002/3 c61§, h–§: 20d c21mᵖᵘ 22m⁶ 22m 26m³ c24gᵖᵘ 24f⁶ Oct 24] sparely-made mare: **h– §**
bad hurdler/novice chaser: stays 25f: acts on good to firm going: tried blinkered: ungenuine. *F. Jordan*

SUREFAST   8 ch.g. Nearly A Hand – Meldon Lady (Ballymoss) [2002/3 c–, h–: 20g³   **c72**
20g 21s 17d⁶ c24s³ c24f⁶ Mar 24] stocky gelding: poor maiden hurdler/chaser: left   **h75**
P. Rodford after third start: stays 3m: acts on soft ground (possibly unsuited by firm):
sometimes makes mistakes over fences. *S. C. Burrough*

SURE FUTURE   7 b.g. Kylian (USA) – Lady Ever-So-Sure (Malicious) [2002/3 h88:   **h108 +**
25v⁴ 19s³ 22s* 20v² 24s* Dec 27] close-coupled gelding: fair handicap hurdler:
improved in 2002/3, won at Folkestone and Kempton (beat His Song by 8 lengths) in
December: probably better at 2¾m/3m than shorter: acts on soft and good to firm going:
tried blinkered: tongue tied second start: patiently ridden. *R. M. Stronge*

SURE TOUCH   6 ch.g. Sure Blade (USA) – Welsh Lustre (IRE) (Mandalus) [2002/3   **h–**
F81: 20dᶠ 21vᵖᵘ 22d⁵ Nov 21] smallish gelding: modest form in 2 bumpers in 2001/2:
some promise prior to falling 4 out on hurdling debut, never a factor both subsequent
starts: wears cheekpieces. *Jonjo O'Neill*

SURPRISING   8 b.g. Primitive Rising (USA) – Ascot Lass (Touching Wood (USA))   **c108**
[2002/3 h130: 23f* 25d c25d³ c24d⁴ c24d² 22v 22d 25g 24m⁵ Apr 17] lengthy gelding: **h132 d**
useful hurdler: better than ever when winning handicap at Haydock in May: largely
disappointing subsequently, including in novice chases: stays 25f: acts on any going:
usually blinkered: held up: not an easy ride/has found little. *P. J. Hobbs*

SURSUM CORDA   12 b.g. Idiot's Delight – Childhay (Roi Soleil) [2002/3 c102, h–:   **c96 d**
c16d³ c21m⁵ c20d³ c20m⁴ c24g³ Apr 12] sturdy gelding: fair hunter chaser: barely stays   **h–**
3m: acts on any going: tongue tied: has broken blood vessel. *John Wall*

SUSAN'S BOY   7 b.g. Minster Son – Nancy Ardross (Ardross) [2002/3 h62, F62: 19g   **h–**
Dec 13] lengthy gelding: signs of a little ability in bumper and novice hurdle in 2001/2:
tailed off on reappearance: should have been suited by further than 17f: dead. *R. Dickin*

SUSAN WINTOUR (IRE)   6 gr.m. Roselier (FR) – Fine Artist (Fine Blade (USA))   **h–**
[2002/3 F–: 20sᵖᵘ Oct 28] well held both starts in bumpers: fatally injured on hurdling
debut. *H. D. Daly*

SUSEJEBHA (IRE)   7 ch.m. Magical Wonder (USA) – Tribute To Viqueen (Furry   **c70**
Glen) [2002/3 22g³ 16m⁴ c20g⁶ 22f³ 16g³ Apr 21] sparely-made mare: fair pointer: poor   **h71**
form on first of 2 starts in steeplechases (didn't look keen on second occasion): poor
maiden hurdler: stays 2¾m: acts on soft going, probably on firm. *M. C. Pipe*

SUSIE SINATRA   7 ch.m. Jupiter Island – Noire Small (USA) (Elocutionist (USA))   **h–**
[2002/3 h–, F66: 22d⁶ May 4] tall, leggy, useful-looking mare: modest form at best in
bumpers: poor form on second of 2 starts in novice hurdles: sold 1,000 gns Doncaster
May Sales, subsequently unseated in 2 points. *Ian Williams*

SUSPENDID (IRE)   10 b.g. Yashgan – Spendapromise (Goldhill) [2002/3 c111, h–:   **c109**
c32mᵖᵘ c20m² c20m* c20m* Apr 10] sturdy gelding: fair handicap chaser,   **h–**
left C. Egerton after reappearance: back to form at Ludlow last 3 starts, winning twice in
April: stays 21f: acts on good to firm and good to soft going: has had tongue tied: has
broken blood vessels: often races freely. *R. Lee*

SWANEYS HILL (IRE)   7 b.g. Shernazar – Why Me Linda (IRE) (Nashamaa)   **h–**
[2002/3 F–: F16d F17s 17sᵖᵘ Feb 7] no sign of ability: trained by W. Clay on reappear-   **F–**
ance. *F. Lloyd*

SWAN KNIGHT (USA) 7 b. or br.g. Sadler's Wells (USA) – Shannkara (IRE) **h113**
(Akarad (FR)) [2002/3 h113: 17s 16d⁵ 16d² 16m⁶ Mar 22] compact gelding: fairly useful
on Flat (stays easy 1¼m), sold out of R. White's stable 17,000 gns Newmarket July Sales:
fair handicap hurdler: best effort in 2002/3 when sixth to Gin Palace at Newbury final
start: raced around 2m: acts on good to firm and good to soft going. *R. A. Fahey*

SWANSEA BAY 7 b.g. Jurado (USA) – Slave's Bangle (Prince Rheingold) [2002/3 **c126**
h79: c25g c24d⁴ c26g² c23m* c24d* c23g* c23g* c24m⁶ c25m* c25g* c24s⁶ c25dᵖᵘ **h–**
Jan 18] lengthy gelding: winning hurdler: had fine first season over fences, winning
handicaps at Worcester in July, Bangor and Worcester in August, Worcester in September
and Wincanton in October and November: best effort when beating Gola Cher 2½ lengths
in Badger Brewery Chase for last-named success: tailed off in Grade 1 novice at Kempton
next time, reportedly had breathing problem final start: will prove best at 3m+: acts on
heavy and good to firm going: wears cheekpieces: sometimes idles. *P. Bowen*

SWANSEA GOLD (IRE) 12 ch.m. Torus – Show M How (Ashmore (FR)) [2002/3 **c–**
c24fᵖᵘ Mar 24] smallish mare: winning chaser: no sign of retaining ability. *Miss Hilary* **h–**
Handel

SWAZI PRINCE 4 b.g. Rakaposhi King – Swazi Princess (IRE) (Brush Aside (USA)) **F–**
[2002/3 F16g Mar 14] first foal: dam unraced, out of half-sister to useful 2½m chaser
Man of Leisure: not given hard time when well held in bumper on debut. *N. A. Gaselee*

SWEEPING STORM (IRE) 6 ch.g. Glacial Storm (USA) – Sweeping Gold (Quay- **h–**
side) [2002/3 17g³ Oct 11] fifth foal: dam, Irish point/2½m bumper winner, half-sister to
useful staying chaser Tartan Trademark: signs of only a little ability when third of 7 in
novice hurdle at Carlisle on debut: showed some temperament in points subsequently,
best effort when runner-up in March. *J. Wade*

SWEET AUBURN (IRE) 7 b. or br.g. Tidaro (USA) – Sweet View (King's Ride) **h–**
[2002/3 F16v⁵ 20sᵖᵘ 21s Dec 10] IR 2,500 4-y-o: half-brother to 19f chaser winner Wellie **F79**
(by Aristocracy): dam unraced: won maiden Irish point on debut in 2002: bought 17,000
gns Doncaster May Sales: fifth of 14 in bumper at Wetherby, but no promise in 2 novice
hurdles. *Mrs B. K. Thomson*

SWEET BIRD (FR) 6 ch.g. Epervier Bleu – Sweet Virginia (FR) (Tapioca II) **h89**
[2002/3 h94: 21s⁵ 20v⁶ Feb 13] sturdy, lengthy gelding: modest maiden hurdler: will stay
3m: acts on heavy going. *A. M. Hales*

SWEET DIVERSION (IRE) 4 b.g. Carroll House – Serocco Wind (Roi Guillaume **F90**
(FR)) [2002/3 F17s² F17f² Mar 24] €13,500 3-y-o: sixth foal: half-brother to winning
chaser up to 3m Francoskid (by Kambalda): dam once-raced half-sister to fairly useful
staying chaser Captain Brandy: runner-up in 2 bumpers, though possibly unsuited by firm
ground at Taunton on second occasion, wandering under pressure. *P. F. Nicholls*

SWEET LORD (IRE) 12 ch.g. Aristocracy – Sweet And Fleet (Whistling Deer) **c–**
[2002/3 24m⁴ Jul 17] good-topped gelding: useful chaser at best: very lightly raced since **h–**
1998/9, shaping as if race was needed when fourth in novice hurdle at Worcester only
outing in 2002/3: stays 25f: has form on soft going, best efforts on good/good to firm: has
jumped left, and may prove best on left-handed course. *J. A. B. Old*

SWEET MILLY 8 b.m. Milieu – Another Joyful (Rubor) [2002/3 h–: 16g⁴ 16g⁶ 16d³ **h74**
16g 16vᵖᵘ 16g⁴ 16s⁴ 16v³ 17g⁴ Apr 21] poor maiden hurdler: raced mainly around 2m:
acts on heavy going. *J. E. Dixon*

SWEET MINUET 6 b.m. Minshaanshu Amad (USA) – Sweet N' Twenty (High Top) **h85**
[2002/3 h77: 19v⁴ 20g⁴ 18f* Apr 24] lengthy mare: modest hurdler: won mares maiden at
Fontwell by head from Mulhacen, holding on determinedly: stays 2¾m: acts on any
going: blinkered once. *M. Madgwick*

SWEET SENORITA 8 b.m. Young Senor (USA) – Sweet N' Twenty (High Top) **c–**
[2002/3 c126, h–: 22mᵖᵘ 17m⁴ 16g 16mᵘʳ 16g³ Oct 21] sparely-made mare: successful **h77**
both starts over fences: one-time useful hurdler: very disappointing in claimers in 2002/3:
raced mainly around 2m: has won on soft going, better under less testing conditions (acts
on good to firm): headstrong front runner. *M. C. Pipe*

SWEET SENSATION 8 ch.m. Carlingford Castle – Pink Sensation (Sagaro) [2002/3 **h–**
F84: 20m 22sᵖᵘ 19g 17mᵘʳ Apr 26] lengthy, rather sparely-made mare: no encouragement
over hurdles, failing to impress with jumping and attitude. *C. Grant*

SWEET SERENATA 8 gr.m. Keen – Serenata (Larrinaga) [2002/3 h56: 20dᵖᵘ May **h–**
23] lengthy mare: bad maiden hurdler: stays 21f, seemingly not 3m: acts on firm and soft
going: visored once: sold 2,100 gns Doncaster May Sales. *M. E. Sowersby*

Badger Brewery Handicap Chase, Wincanton—a sixth win in seven starts for Swansea Bay (cheekpieces) as he sees off Gola Cher (centre) and Itsonlyme

SWIFT PEARL (IRE) 10 b.g. Persian Mews – Laurestown Rose (Derring Rose) [2002/3 F16s² F16g 20v⁵ F19s⁵ 20s* Aug 4] third foal: dam unraced half-sister to useful chaser up to 25f Greenwood Lad: modest form in bumpers: modest hurdler: best effort when winning maiden at Perth by 11 lengths from Mount Gay: stays 2½m: acts on soft going. *T. M. Walsh, Ireland* **h92 F84**

SWIFT ROSE (IRE) 6 b.m. Roselier (FR) – Clonarctic Slave (Sir Mordred) [2002/3 F16g 20s 16s 18s Mar 5] fifth foal: sister to winning 3m hurdler Swift Pick: dam unraced half-sister to fairly useful jumper Yeoman Broker, stayed 3m: no sign of ability. *Paul Nolan, Ireland* **h– F–**

SWIFT SWALLOW 5 ch.g. Missed Flight – Alhargah (Be My Guest (USA)) [2002/3 F16m³ Apr 21] half-brother to several winners, including 2m winner/winning hurdler Guest Alliance (by Zaffaran) and fairly useful 1990 2-y-o 6f winner Moy River (by Dominion): dam no form: third to Lord Perseus in maiden bumper at Huntingdon on debut. *O. Brennan* **F88**

SWINCOMBE (IRE) 8 b.g. Good Thyne (USA) – Gladtogetit (Green Shoon) [2002/3 c21g c24g* c26g² c25d* c27dᵖᵘ Jan 16] fair chaser: won hunter at Chepstow in May and (having left Miss E. Kelly and been off 7 months) handicap at Wincanton in December: laboured effort final start: stays 3¼m. *R. H. Alner* **c112**

SWINGING THE BLUES (IRE) 9 b.g. Bluebird (USA) – Winsong Melody (Music Maestro) [2002/3 h63: 16g May 26] poor maiden hurdler: likely to prove best at sharp 2m: tried visored: has pulled hard. *C. A. Dwyer* **h–**

SWING WEST (USA) 9 b.h. Gone West (USA) – Danlu (USA) (Danzig (USA)) [2002/3 c20m³ 24g c16s c20sᵖᵘ c24s c20gᵖᵘ Apr 2] leggy horse: winning hurdler/chaser, has lost his way: usually blinkered. *N. F. Glynn, Ireland* **c– h–**

SWORD LADY 5 b.m. Broadsword (USA) – Speckyfoureyes (Blue Cashmere) [2002/3 F17g⁶ Apr 19] 3,600 4-y-o: half-sister to fair hurdler Lorgnette (by Emperor Fountain), stays 3m, and to winning pointer Stearsby: dam, winning hurdler who stayed 2½m, from family of high-class staying chaser Stearsby: never-nearer sixth of 14 in maiden bumper at Newton Abbot on debut. *Mrs S. D. Williams* **F68**

SWORDPLAY 5 ch.g. Kris – Throw Away Line (Cragador) [2002/3 16s² 16m* 16m² 16f* 16d³ 16m* Apr 22] leggy gelding: fairly useful on Flat up to 13f, sold out of **h122**

G. Butler's stable 50,000 gns Newmarket Autumn (2001) Sales: fairly useful hurdler: won maiden at Tramore in August and minor events at Listowel in September and Fairy-house in April: enterprisingly ridden when putting up improved effort to beat Central House 2 lengths at last-named course: held up when below form in Grade 1 novice at Punchestown in late-April: will prove best around 2m: acts on firm and good to soft going: has had tongue tied. *M. J. P. O'Brien, Ireland*

SYLCAN EXPRESS 10 br.g. Sylvan Express – Dercanny (Derek H) [2002/3 c–, h69: 20d 21g⁴ May 30] workmanlike gelding: poor hurdler: stays 21f: acts on soft going: tried visored. *C. N. Kellett* **c– һ66**

SYLV 5 b.m. Ridgewood Ben – High Commotion (IRE) (Taufan (USA)) [2002/3 16m 18m⁶ Aug 23] poor maiden on Flat (probably stays 15.4f): well held both starts over hurdles, not fluent on second occasion. *J. G. Portman* **h–**

SYLVA BOUNTY 4 br.g. Bahamian Bounty – Spriolo (Priolo (USA)) [2002/3 16dᵖᵘ 17gᵖᵘ Mar 17] sturdy gelding: little sign of ability on Flat, sold out of C. Brittain's stable 600 gns Doncaster September Sales: showed nothing in 2 juvenile hurdles. *B. P. J. Baugh* **h–**

SYLVA LEGEND (USA) 7 b.g. Lear Fan (USA) – Likeashot (CAN) (Gun Shot) [2002/3 h97: 16g* 17f⁴ 17g³ 22g* 22f³ c21g⁴ Nov 18] modest hurdler: won handicap at Chepstow in May and novice at Newton Abbot in June: last of 4 finishers in novice at Folkestone (reportedly lame) on chasing debut: stays 2¾m: acts on soft and firm going: often races up with pace. *R. J. Baker* **c– һ97**

SYLVAN TWISTER 4 br.c. First Trump – Storm Party (IRE) (Bluebird (USA)) [2002/3 16sᶠ 17g Mar 16] no form on Flat: well held on completed start over hurdles. *P. Mitchell* **h–**

SYLVIAJAZZ 4 b.f. Alhijaz – Dispol Princess (IRE) (Cyrano de Bergerac) [2002/3 16v Jan 22] tailed off in 1½m maiden at 3 yrs, and in juvenile on hurdling debut. *Miss J. Feilden* **h–**

SYLVIESBUCK (IRE) 6 b.g. Kasmayo – Sylvies Missiles (IRE) (Buckskin (FR)) [2002/3 F16v² 22v⁵ 16s 19d Feb 25] strong gelding: third foal: dam maiden: won only completed start in maiden Irish points in 2002: shaped well when second to Sh Boom in bumper at Wetherby but only modest form at best in 3 novice hurdles. *G. M. Moore* **h86 F95**

T

TAAKID (USA) 8 b.g. Diesis – Tanwi (Vision (USA)) [2002/3 c84, h–: c16d* c16m² c17d⁵ c16g⁵ c20d³ c16m² c17d⁵ c21g³ c21m* c20g³ Oct 12] leggy, angular gelding: modest handicap chaser: won at Hexham (easily) in May and Sedgefield in October: stays 21f: acts on good to soft and good to firm ground: effective tongue tied or not. *Mrs S. J. Smith* **c91 h–**

TABLE MOUNTAIN 7 ch.g. Rock Hopper – Comtec Princess (Gulf Pearl) [2002/3 h–: 16d* Oct 23] medium-sized gelding: useful form in bumpers in 2000/1: much better effort over hurdles when winning novice at Chepstow only start in 2002/3, though wouldn't have won if Taskmaster had not fallen last: should stay at least 2½m: raced on going softer than good. *C. Weedon* **h103**

TABOO TEE 7 br.m. Teenoso (USA) – Temporary Affair (Mandalus) [2002/3 h85, F–: 20gᵖᵘ c21gᵖᵘ c20m⁶ c23g Oct 22] lengthy, rather sparely-made mare: modest maiden hurdler in 2001/2: poor form over fences: should stay beyond 21f: acts on good to firm and good to soft going. *O. Sherwood* **c– h–**

TACIN (IRE) 6 b.g. Supreme Leader – Nicat (Wolver Hollow) [2002/3 21s³ 24dᶠ Mar 1] IR £55,000 4-y-o: well-made gelding: will make a chaser: sixth foal: brother to modest hurdler up to 25f Sister Superior and bumper winners Mrs Avery and Von Carty: dam, maiden, out of useful 2m hurdler The Very Thing: second in Irish point in 2002: better effort over hurdles (held when fell 2 out second start) when third to Fork Lightning in novice at Kempton: should stay 3m. *B. G. Powell* **h112**

TACITA 8 ch.m. Gunner B – Taco (High Season) [2002/3 h68: 24g 20s⁴ 22g Mar 17] lengthy mare: little worthwhile form over hurdles. *M. D. McMillan* **h–**

TACOLINO (FR) 9 ch.g. Royal Charter (FR) – Tamilda (FR) (Rose Laurel) [2002/3 c16g c16g c16fᶠ c20g⁵ c17m* Apr 21] workmanlike ex-Irish gelding: poor maiden hurdler: fair handicap chaser: sold out of A. Moore's stable 9,800 gns Doncaster November Sales after third start: won at Market Rasen in April by 1½ lengths from Super Nomad: **c102 h–**

best form around 2m: acts on good to firm and good to soft ground, probably firm: blinkered once: effective tongue tied or not. *O. Brennan*

TACTFUL REMARK (USA)   7 ch.g. Lord At War (ARG) – Right Word (USA)   **h124**
(Verbatim (USA)) [2002/3 16s* 17g* 17v³ 17gᵖᵘ 16d³ Apr 9] angular gelding: useful at one time on Flat (stays 10.4f), no encouragement in 2 starts in 2002, leaving J. Osborne after second: won novices at Worcester (by distance from Per Amore) and Newton Abbot (made all, on bridle) in June on first 2 outings over hurdles: off 8 months, not quite so good after: raced around 2m on good going or softer (probably unsuited by heavy): free-going sort. *M. C. Pipe*

TADZIO   4 bl.g. Mtoto – Fresher (Fabulous Dancer (USA)) [2002/3 F16g Mar 12] third   **F–**
reported foal: half-brother to useful Flat performer Zuleika Dobson (by Cadeaux Genereux), stays 9f: dam, French 2-y-o 1m winner later successful in USA, half-sister to very smart French 1½m performer Songlines: no show in bumper on debut. *P. R. Webber*

TAFFS WELL   10 b.g. Dowsing (USA) – Zahiah (So Blessed) [2002/3 h89: 16d 17m²   **h93 +**
17g* Aug 9] modest form over hurdles, won novice at Sedgefield very easily in August: will prove best at sharp 2m. *B. Ellison*

TAGAR (FR)   6 b.g. Fijar Tango (FR) – Fight For Arfact (Salmon Leap (USA)) [2002/3   **h103**
h118: 19d³ 16d⁴ 16v Feb 15] close-coupled gelding: fairly useful maiden hurdler at best: below that form in 2002/3: best efforts at 2m: acts on heavy going. *N. J. Henderson*

TAGULA SUN (IRE)   5 b.g. Tagula (IRE) – Dee-Lady (Deploy) [2002/3 F74: F16m⁴   **F84**
Jun 3] compact gelding: well backed, best effort in bumpers when fourth to Reseda at Huntingdon only run in 2002/3: tongue tied after debut. *Jean-Rene Auvray*

TAHRIMA   4 b.f. Slip Anchor – Khandjar (Kris) [2002/3 F16g Feb 22] sister to fairly   **F67 +**
useful hurdler Valedictory, stays 2½m, and fair hurdler around 2m Zamat and half-sister to fairly useful Irish 1½m winner Irdal (by Rainbow Quest): dam, 9f winner, sister to high-class miler Shavian and half-sister to Gold Cup winner Paean: bought unraced out of W. Jarvis's stable 6,500 gns Newmarket February Sales: took good hold and faded straight when seventh of 20 in mares bumper at Huntingdon on debut. *C. A. Dwyer*

TAIL GUNNER   4 gr.g. Vague Shot – Plum Blossom (USA) (Gallant Romeo (USA))   **h–**
[2002/3 17gᵘʳ Sep 28] brother to fair 2m hurdle winner Isitoff and half-brother to modest hurdler at 2½m+ Julietski (by Niniski): modest maiden on Flat (stays 2m) for S. Williams: none too keen and behind when unseating fourth in juvenile seller on hurdling debut. *K. A. Morgan*

TAILLEFER (FR)   7 b.g. Cyborg (FR) – Tourka (FR) (Rose Laurel) [2002/3 c–, h–:   **c–**
c21gᵖᵘ c20dᵇᵈ c22dᵖᵘ 24vᵖᵘ 22d⁶ 22y² 20s* 20s³ Mar 15] tall, leggy gelding: has report-   **h100**
edly had wind operation: fairly useful chaser in 2000/1: refound some form over hurdles towards end of 2002/3, winning handicap at Sandown in February: stays 2¾m: raced on good ground or softer (acts on heavy): tried blinkered. *M. E. D. Francis*

TAILORED (IRE)   9 b.g. King's Ride – Hook's Close (Kemal (FR)) [2002/3 c21gᶠ   **c–**
Nov 9] modest maiden hurdler: fair form when winning novice handicap at Kempton in   **h–**
2000/1 on chasing debut: fell fifth on return: would have stayed 3m: acted on soft and good to firm going: dead. *R. H. Alner*

TAILS I WIN   4 b.g. Petoski – Spinayab (King of Spain) [2002/3 F16v Mar 8] lengthy,   **F–**
plain, sparely-made gelding: second foal: dam no worthwhile form on Flat: showed nothing in bumper on debut. *J. W. Mullins*

TAKAGI (IRE)   8 b.g. Husyan (USA) – Ballyclough Gale (Strong Gale) [2002/3   **c138**
c138, h126: c24s* c26gᵖᵘ c24s² c28sᵖᵘ c25s² 24d³ c29g Apr 21] lengthy, useful-looking   **h122**
gelding: fairly useful hurdler: creditable third in handicap at Navan in March: useful chaser: won Troytown Handicap Chase there in November: good efforts when second to Be My Belle in valuable handicap at Gowran in January and to Rince Ri in Grade 2 at Fairyhouse in February: should stay beyond 25f: probably ideally suited by going softer than good (acts on heavy). *E. J. O'Grady, Ireland*

TAKE A DROP (IRE)   8 b.g. Farhaan – Misquested (Lord Ha Ha) [2002/3 16m 20g   **h104**
F16g* 20m* 16s⁶ 21dᵖᵘ 21d⁵ 24vᵛ⁴ 24s 24m Apr 13] medium-sized gelding: half-brother   **F93**
to fair staying hurdler Fort Deely (by Seamanship): dam unraced, out of half-sister to very smart 2m hurdler Mwanadike: twice-raced on Flat: won bumper at Cork in August: fair hurdler: won maiden at Tramore 4 days later: generally below form subsequently: stays 21f: acts on firm and good to soft going. *S. O'Farrell, Ireland*

TAKE A RAIN CHECK (IRE)   6 b.m. Rainbows For Life (CAN) – Just A Second   **h–**
(Jimsun) [2002/3 h–: 18vᵖᵘ 20vᵖᵘ 22g Apr 12] workmanlike mare: no sign of ability. *C. J. Drewe*

887

TAKE CONTROL (IRE) 9 b.g. Roselier (FR) – Frosty Fairy (Paddy's Stream) [2002/3 c145x, h–: c26g c24d⁴ c29vᶠ c28d c34sᵖᵘ c33m⁶ Apr 12] workmanlike gelding: smart chaser in 2001/2, generally disappointing on return: stays 33f: acts on good to firm and heavy going: tried visored: often let down by jumping. *M. C. Pipe* **c130 x h–**

TAKE FLITE 6 b.g. Cadeaux Genereux – Green Seed (IRE) (Lead On Time (USA)) [2002/3 h114: 16d 16m³ 17g³ 16g² 16m⁴ 16d* 16s 16v² 16gᶠ 16m Apr 22] compact gelding: fairly useful on Flat (stays 1½m), successful in May and March: fairly useful hurdler: didn't have to be at best to win minor event at Cork in October: at least respectable efforts last 3 starts, likely to be in frame when falling last in listed handicap at Aintree: likely to prove best at sharp 2m: acts on good to firm and heavy going: held up. *Anthony Mullins, Ireland* **h119**

TAKE HEED 7 b.g. Warning – Tunaria (USA) (Lyphard (USA)) [2002/3 h–: 16m 17s⁵ 16g* 16d² 16d² 16g⁶ 16d 17g⁶ Mar 16] sturdy gelding: poor hurdler: won conditional jockeys novice handicap at Kempton in November: will prove best around 2m: acts on good to firm and good to soft going: usually tongue tied: tends to finish weakly. *K. A. Morgan* **h78**

TAKE MY SIDE (IRE) 11 b.g. Be My Native (USA) – Fight For It (Strong Gale) [2002/3 c–, h–: c21ˢᵘʳ c20d⁴ c26sᶠ Mar 10] rangy gelding: winning maiden/maiden chaser: no sign of retaining ability: tried blinkered/tongue tied. *Mrs P. Townsley* **c– h–**

TAKE THE BRUSH (IRE) 9 b.m. Brush Aside (USA) – Ballywilliam Girl (Royal Match) [2002/3 c–, h–: c18mᶠ c20gᵖᵘ May 17] winning pointer, little form otherwise: sold £1,150 Ascot June Sales. *J. White* **c– h–**

TAKE THE STAND (IRE) 7 b.g. Witness Box (USA) – Denys Daughter (IRE) (Crash Course) [2002/3 h87: c24dᵖᵘ c23g² c24g* c26m* Mar 31] poor hurdler: fairly useful form in novice chases, successful at Fakenham and Plumpton in March: stays 3¼m: acts on good to firm going: sold to join P. Bowen 20,000 gns Doncaster May Sales. *Ian Williams* **c116 h–**

TAKEYOURTIME 8 b.m. Hatim (USA) – Wand of Youth (Mandamus) [2002/3 h79+: 20d⁴ 20d³ 24d³ 20d² 20g² 16v 24vᵖᵘ 20v⁵ Jan 29] lengthy mare: modest maiden hurdler: best efforts at 2½m: acts on good to firm and heavy going. *A. Scott* **h89**

TAKING (FR) 7 gr.g. Take Risks (FR) – Sonning (FR) (Moulin) [2002/3 c86, h–: c16d⁵ c16m c16g³ c19g⁶ c20d² c21m* c21mᵖᵘ c21m³ c20mᵖᵘ Nov 18] leggy gelding: poor handicap chaser: won at Southwell in July: stays 21f: acts on good to firm and heavy going: blinkered last 5 starts: has had tongue tied: often let down by jumping. *C. N. Kellett* **c81 x h–**

TAKSINA 4 b.f. Wace (USA) – Quago (New Member) [2002/3 F18v F17s 18s⁵ 17g⁶ Apr 19] second foal: dam lightly raced and little worthwhile form over jumps: little sign of ability. *R. H. Buckler* **h– F–**

TALARIA (IRE) 7 ch.m. Petardia – Million At Dawn (IRE) (Fayruz) [2002/3 17dᵖᵘ 17g 17gᵖᵘ 16fᵖᵘ Sep 15] lost her form on Flat and showed nothing over hurdles: has had tongue tied. *C. J. Teague* **h–**

TALARIVE (USA) 7 ch.g. Riverman (USA) – Estala (Be My Guest (USA)) [2002/3 16s² 16s* 16v* 16d² 20s³ 16d² 18d² 16vᵖᵘ Mar 8] smallish, sturdy ex-Irish gelding: first foal: dam, French 2-y-o 9f winner, half-sister to smart French stayer Erudite: maiden on Flat: fairly useful hurdler: trained by J. Berry prior to 2002/3, by J. O'Neill on reappearance: easily won handicaps at Leicester in December and Ayr in January: better form when placed next 4 starts, head second to Covent Garden, pair clear, in Grade 2 novice at Kelso on final occasion: probably stays 2½m: acts on heavy ground: has edged left under pressure. *P. D. Niven* **h125**

TALATHATH (FR) 11 b.g. Soviet Star (USA) – Mashmoon (USA) (Habitat) [2002/3 c72, h–: c22gᵖᵘ c26fᵘʳ Aug 13] workmanlike gelding: winning hurdler: poor maiden chaser: stays 21f: acts on firm and soft going: tried blinkered, not for long time: has had tongue tied. *M. J. Wilkinson* **c69 h–**

TALBOT LAD 7 b.g. Weld – Greenacres Girl (Tycoon II) [2002/3 h86, F95: 17d³ 20g⁵ 20mᵖᵘ 16s c19d⁴ c17v² c16g³ c17g⁵ 20m² 20g⁶ Apr 21] leggy gelding: poor maiden hurdler/chaser: stays 2½m: acts on good to firm and heavy going: tongue tied. *S. A. Brookshaw* **c83 h83**

TALE BRIDGE (IRE) 10 b.g. Tale Quale – Loobagh Bridge (River Beauty) [2002/3 c26gᵖᵘ c25d³ c25gᵖᵘ Apr 5] modest pointer/hunter chaser: won point in February: stays 25f. *Mrs O. Bush* **c82 h–**

TALENT STAR 6 b.g. Mizoram (USA) – Bells of Longwick (Myjinski (USA)) **h–**
[2002/3 16m^pu Oct 19] poor maiden on Flat: no show in maiden on hurdling debut.
A. W. Carroll

TALES OF BOUNTY (IRE) 8 b.g. Ela-Mana-Mou – Tales of Wisdom (Rousillon **c124**
(USA)) [2002/3 h110: 24d* 25d c24s* c24s⁴ Feb 27] lengthy, useful-looking gelding: fair **h114**
handicap hurdler: won at Exeter on return from 18-month absence in November: created
good impression when winning novice at Taunton on chasing debut, jumping well and
beating Another General 5 lengths: most disappointing in similar event there over 2
months later: stays 3m: acts on soft and good to firm going. *P. F. Nicholls*

TALKING TACTICS (IRE) 5 b.g. Bigstone (IRE) – Soviet Pretender (USA) (Ya **h119**
Zaman (USA)) [2002/3 16s 18s 16s 16d* 16v* 16s² Mar 16] first foal: dam unraced
daughter of useful 7f performer Russian Royal: fairly useful novice hurdler: won maiden
at Gowran in February and minor event at Leopardstown in March: raced around 2m: acts
on heavy going. *C. Roche, Ireland*

TALK ON CORNERS (IRE) 8 b.m. Alphabatim (USA) – Shannon Lass (Callernish) **h–**
[2002/3 F16v 16s 18s^pu 22f^pu Apr 21] ex-Irish mare: of no account: left J. Brassil before **F–**
final start. *N. R. Mitchell*

TALLENOE 4 b.f. Rudimentary (USA) – Tino-Ella (Bustino) [2002/3 F17s Jan 14] **F–**
600F, 5,700Y: ninth foal: half-sister to 3 winners, including fairly useful 1997 2-y-o 7f
winner Absolutely Sparklin (by Midyan) and 1¾m winner Doddington Flyer (by Distant
Relative): dam, 1¼m winner, half-sister to dam of Imperial Cup winner Carlito Brigante
and smart 7f/1m performer Sugarfoot: tailed off in mares maiden bumper on debut.
P. R. Webber

TALLISON 5 ch.g. First Trump – Clare Celeste (Coquelin (USA)) [2002/3 F71: F17g **F–**
Jun 17] poor form on first of 2 starts in bumpers (reportedly choked on reappearance):
unseated in point in March. *P. F. Nicholls*

TALLOW BAY (IRE) 8 b.g. Glacial Storm (USA) – Minimum Choice (IRE) (Miner's **c99**
Lamp) [2002/3 c102, h–: c25g⁶ c21s* c21v* c24d⁶ c26d^pu c20s⁵ Mar 10] sturdy gelding: **h–**
modest chaser: twice made all at Folkestone (first a handicap) in January, idling markedly
in novice on second occasion: stays 3¼m: acts on heavy going, pulled up on firm: tried
blinkered. *Mrs S. Wall*

TALL TALE (IRE) 11 b.g. Tale Quale – Prudent Rose (IRE) (Strong Gale) [2002/3 **c65 §**
c77§: c25g³ c25g⁵ c26d³ c27g⁵ c25v⁴ c24d^ur c27s⁴ c25g c27v^pu c27v⁶ c25d⁴ c32v^pu c25g*
Mar 29] tall gelding: poor chaser: won very weak amateur selling handicap at Hexham in
March: probably stays 3½m: acts on good to firm and heavy going: tried in headgear: has
had tongue tied: ungenuine. *R. Johnson*

TAMANGO (FR) 6 gr.g. Klimt (FR) – Tipmosa (FR) (Tip Moss (FR)) [2002/3 h99, **c110**
F97: 19d² 16m² c17d² c20v³ c16v^F 19m³ Apr 15] leggy, lengthy gelding: fair hurdler: **h112**
showed similar ability over fences but didn't impress with jumping: possibly best up to
19f: acts on good to firm and heavy going. *P. J. Hobbs*

TAMBO (IRE) 8 b.g. Shardari – Carmen Lady (Torus) [2002/3 c85, h–: c21v^pu c20m² **c85**
Mar 31] workmanlike gelding: winning hurdler: modest novice chaser: stays 21f: acts on **h–**
good to soft and good to firm going: takes good hold. *M. Bradstock*

TAMING (IRE) 7 ch.g. Lycius (USA) – Black Fighter (USA) (Secretariat (USA)) **h125**
[2002/3 h93: 17g² 16d5 16s* 16d* 20g* 17d 16m³ 20m* 21m* 21d* 20v³ 20v^F 21g Mar
12] compact gelding: fairly useful hurdler: won maiden at Uttoxeter in June and novices
at Wolverhampton and Worcester in July, Huntingdon and Cheltenham in October and
Cheltenham (beat Wouldn't You Agree 4 lengths) in November: long way below form
last 3 starts: stays 21f: acts on soft and good to firm going: has had tongue tied. *Miss
Venetia Williams*

TANA RIVER (IRE) 7 b.g. Over The River (FR) – Home In The Glen (Furry **h129**
Glen) [2002/3 20d² 20v² 20v² 19d* 20v* 20v* Mar 8]
    Tana River landed the valuable European Breeders Fund 'National Hunt'
Novices' Handicap Hurdle Final in March, run for possibly the second last time at
Sandown, the race set to be switched to Cheltenham when the Festival is extended
to four days. The race is set for a boost in prize money and will prove at least as
competitive if and when it does move. Given how well Cheltenham drains these
days, it is unlikely, however, that it will often be run under the sort of very testing
conditions that prevailed at Sandown in 2003. Twelve lined up, after three intended
runners were withdrawn because of the state of the ground, and few of them coped,
particularly with a good pace from an early stage ensuring stamina was at a pre-

The Frisky Fillies' "Tana River"

mium. Tana River, who has an old-fashioned jumping pedigree, proved well served by the test of endurance and put up an improved effort. He looked a most unlikely winner early in the home straight, flat out in a moderate eighth, but gradually made up ground, as those in front faltered, and went right away after taking the lead on the flat, winning by nine lengths from Nonantais. Winners are prone to be flattered under such unusually testing conditions, and that may be the case with Tana River. With three miles likely to show him to even better advantage, however, he may still be able to find the improvement to stay ahead of the BHB handicapper. In any event, his future is more likely to be over fences. Tana River ran four times over hurdles before Sandown after coming from Ireland, where he won his only start in points. He landed the odds with something to spare in novices at Exeter and Leicester but his earlier defeats were of more interest: he came second in novices at Chepstow, beaten by Supreme Prince and Coolnagorna respectively but shaping with abundant promise.

The sturdy Tana River was presumably something of a slow developer. He was sold for just IR 2,000 guineas as a four-year-old and did not make the course until he was six. He is decidedly bred for stamina, being by Over The River out of a Furry Glen mare. His dam Home In The Glen was a winning pointer and has bred one other winner, Forever Friend (by Jurado), successful in a bumper in Ireland. This isn't a distinguished family and Tana River's exploits haven't just benefited his connections—a three-year-old Carroll House half-brother was sold for 36,000 guineas at the Doncaster May Sales. *Miss E. C. Lavelle*

TANDYS BRIDGE (IRE) 7 b.g. Mister Lord (USA) – Danny's Charm (IRE) (Deep Run) [2002/3 F16s* 18v⁵ 22s⁴ 18d² 20v* 22d³ Mar 22] IR 11,000 3-y-o: second living foal: half-brother to fairly useful hurdler/useful chaser The Bunny Boiler (by Tremblant), stays 4¼m: dam unraced: fairly useful form when winning bumper at Navan on debut: **h109 F98**

fair novice hurdler: won maiden at Leopardstown in March: stays 2¾m: acts on heavy going. *N. Meade, Ireland*

TANGO ROYAL (FR) 7 gr.g. Royal Charter (FR) – Nazia (FR) (Zino) [2002/3 c128, h–: c16d^F c17g^F 16s 17d^6 19d^6 19v^3 17g^5 Mar 18] leggy gelding: fairly useful handicap chaser, fell first 2 starts: fair handicap hurdler: stays 2½m: probably acts on any going: tongue tied last 5 outings. *M. C. Pipe*

**c–
h110**

TANIKOS (FR) 4 b.g. Nikos – Tamana (USA) (Northern Baby (CAN)) [2002/3 17v* 16d^3 17g Mar 13] big, workmanlike ex-French gelding: second foal: half-brother to fair maiden hurdler/winning chaser around 2m Tanaiis (by Round Sovereign): dam 1¼m and 13f winner: maiden on Flat: trained by G. Blasco, won juvenile at Lyon Parilly in November on hurdling debut: third to Middlethorpe in novice at Wetherby on British debut: tailed off in Triumph Hurdle at Cheltenham in March, well held in 4-y-o minor event at Punchestown in late-April: will stay 2½m. *N. J. Henderson*

h100 +

TANNERS COURT 6 b.g. Framlington Court – True Nell (Neltino) [2002/3 F17d F16v F16s^3 F17g Mar 16] good-topped gelding: first foal: dam unraced, out of half-sister to top-class staying chaser Spartan Missile: easily best effort in bumpers when third to Back To Ben Alder at Kempton in January: pulled too hard final outing. *Miss C. Dyson*

F88

TANNERS FRIEND 6 b.m. Environment Friend – Glenn's Slipper (Furry Glen) [2002/3 F17s F17d F16s F16g 20g^pu Mar 16] leggy mare: eighth foal: half-sister to poor hurdler Miss Souter (by Sulaafah), stayed 3¼m: dam 2-y-o 7f winner: little sign of ability. *Miss C. Dyson*

**h–
F–**

TANTABANK 5 b.g. Primitive Rising (USA) – Rua Ros (IRE) (Roselier (FR)) [2002/3 F16v Nov 16] big, lengthy gelding: first foal: dam poor hurdler, stayed 25f: shaped as if race was needed when ninth of 14 in bumper at Wetherby on debut. *Mrs S. J. Smith*

F72

TAP DANCE 5 ch.g. Dancing Spree (USA) – Trachelium (Formidable (USA)) [2002/3 h84: 16d 21m^2 21g^2 20f 23d 21v^6 25d^pu 27g^pu 17m Apr 21] angular gelding: poor maiden hurdler: sold out of Miss S. Hall's stable 3,000 gns Doncaster November Sales after fifth start: stays 21f: acts on good to firm going: tried visored/blinkered: has had tongue tied: sometimes takes little interest, and best treated with caution. *M. E. Sowersby*

h79 §

TAP DANCER (IRE) 5 b.g. Sadler's Wells (USA) – Watch Out (USA) (Mr Prospector (USA)) [2002/3 h–: 16m^5 16s^pu Aug 10] leggy gelding: modest on Flat (stays 1¼m): little show over hurdles: needs to settle better. *B. G. Powell*

h–

TAP THE STONE (IRE) 4 b.g. Bigstone (IRE) – Wadeyaa (Green Desert (USA)) [2002/3 16m 16d^pu 16d Nov 24] sturdy gelding: poor maiden on Flat (probably stays 9f): little show in 3 juvenile hurdles: has worn cheekpieces/visor. *J. S. Wainwright*

h–

TARASCO (FR) 7 b.g. Deploy – Moucha (FR) (Fabulous Dancer (USA)) [2002/3 h120: c20s^F c19d^5 c16g* c17g* c17m* Apr 12] close-coupled gelding: fairly useful hurdler: similar form in novice company over fences, winning at Huntingdon (mistakes) and Market Rasen in March and Bangor (beat Kock de La Vesvre 6 lengths) in April: stays 2½m: has won on good to firm ground but goes particularly well on soft/heavy: visored last 2 starts. *P. R. Webber*

**c120
h–**

TARASHANI (IRE) 5 ch.g. Primo Dominie – Tarakana (USA) (Shahrastani (USA)) [2002/3 h67: 18s^4 16v^4 17s^4 Dec 10] poor maiden hurdler: raced around 2m: on good going or softer (acts on heavy): tried visored. *B. Ellison*

h73

TARBOLTON MOSS 8 b.m. Le Moss – Priceless Peril (Silly Prices) [2002/3 h96: c20s^4 c25v^2 c26v^pu c25s^* c32g^3 Mar 21] modest handicap hurdler: fair novice chaser: won maiden at Ayr in February: best effort when third to A Piece of Cake in valuable handicap at Kelso month later: best at 3m+: raced on good going or softer (acts on heavy): sound jumper. *M. Todhunter*

**c107
h–**

TARBOUSH 6 b.g. Polish Precedent (USA) – Barboukh (Night Shift (USA)) [2002/3 16d^6 16g 16g^3 17f^2 Apr 3] sturdy gelding: fairly useful up to 1¼m on Flat, successful twice in 2002 for N. Callaghan: modest form over hurdles: best effort when third to Unleash in maiden at Ludlow in March, travelling comfortably in rear and running on well when shaken up after 2 out (horse and jockey banned, trainer fined under non-triers rule): will need sharp 2m: headstrong. *B. G. Powell*

h96 +

TARDAR (NZ) 7 br.g. Prince Ferdinand – La Magnifique (NZ) (Kampala) [2002/3 16d^3 16s^* 16v^* 21g Mar 12] angular gelding: half-brother to French middle-distance winner La Bijou (by Caerwent): successful 7 times from 1m to around 1½m from 17 starts on Flat in New Zealand: fairly useful novice hurdler: won at Chepstow in December

h121 +

(maiden) and February, idling on second occasion: should stay beyond 2m: has had tongue tied. *Jonjo O'Neill*

TARDISSIMA 5 ch.m. River Falls – Chilibang Bang (Chilibang) [2002/3 F16m F16g Jun 15] first foal: dam 5f to 7f winner: tailed off both starts in bumpers: headstrong. *Mrs H. O. Graham* — **F—**

TARONGO (FR) 5 b.g. Tel Quel (FR) – Rainbow Rainbow (Vision (USA)) [2002/3 h–: 19g^{pu} c19f^F c17g^2 Apr 19] no form: tried visored and tongue tied: keen sort. *Mrs L. C. Taylor* — **c— h—**

TARONGOSHY (IRE) 6 ch.m. Over The River (FR) – October Lady (Lucifer (USA)) [2002/3 h–, F87: 17v 24m^5 21m^{pu} Apr 21] sturdy mare: form over hurdles only when fifth in handicap at Sandown in March, finding little: blinkered last 2 starts: reportedly lame final outing. *M. Pitman* — **h71**

TARSKI 9 ch.g. Polish Precedent (USA) – Illusory (Kings Lake (USA)) [2002/3 h76: 16m* 16s 17m* 16g 19f^2 21f^{pu} Oct 24] smallish gelding: modest hurdler: won maiden at Worcester in July and claimer at Newton Abbot in August: stays 19f: acts on firm going, below form both starts on softer than good: effective visored or not. *W. S. Kittow* — **h87**

TARXIEN 9 b.g. Kendor (FR) – Tanz (IRE) (Sadler's Wells (USA)) [2002/3 h139: c20d* c19v* c21v^2 c20s* c21g^F c20m^2 Apr 12] — **c150 h—**

Tarxien has been a revelation since being bought out of Merrita Jones's stable for 35,000 guineas at the Doncaster Sales in May 2001. Still without a win over jumps at that stage of his career, Tarxien won six of his seven completed starts, developing into a useful hurdler, for his present trainer during 2001/2; and he showed himself a smart novice chaser in his latest campaign, gaining one of his

Scilly Isles Novices' Chase, Sandown—
testing ground, and Tarxien sees out the trip better than Farmer Jack (noseband)

Mr B. A. Kilpatrick's "Tarxien"

three wins in a Grade 1 event at Sandown. Tarxien did well to achieve as much as he did over fences in the latest season because his jumping often left something to be desired. He will need to improve in that department if he's to prove so successful when he graduates to open company in 2003/4.

Tarxien should have been completing a four-timer at Sandown, a mistake two out when beaten a short head by Joss Naylor at Cheltenham on his previous outing probably costing him that race. Tarxien made a successful chasing debut at Cheltenham, trouncing Iverain and seven others; and he followed up with an even better performance in a Grade 2 novice at Ascot, beating Scots Grey by fifteen lengths with Palarshan a further six lengths back in third. Tarxien had only three rivals in the Scilly Isles Novices' Chase at Sandown in February, but they included smart hurdler Telemoss, who had won all three of his starts easily over fences, and Farmer Jack, who had shown useful form when completing a hat-trick on his previous start, at Kempton. The other runner, Irish challenger Ground Ball, cut out the running before steadying the pace after the fourth which resulted in there being very little between the quartet four out. Telemoss was the first to drop away—it transpired that he had broken a blood vessel—and Ground Ball had no more to give after two out, which left Tarxien and Farmer Jack to fight it out. There was nothing between the pair starting up the run-in, but Tarxien was the stouter stayer in the testing ground and forged clear to win by three lengths. Tarxien's jumping let him down on both his starts after Sandown, several mistakes preceding his fall at the sixth in the Cathcart at Cheltenham. Although his jumping was sound enough for much of the way in a Grade 2 novice event at Ayr, it became ragged once he was headed by Vol Solitaire three out; Tarxien was some way below his best in second.

		Kendor (FR) (gr 1986)	Kenmare (gr 1975)	Kalamoun
Tarxien (b.g. 1994)				Belle of Ireland
			Belle Mecene (b 1982)	Gay Mecene
				Djaka Belle
		Tanz (IRE) (b 1988)	Sadler's Wells (b 1981)	Northern Dancer
				Fairy Bridge
			Gull Nook (b 1983)	Mill Reef
				Bempton

Tarxien is bred on Flat-racing lines and ran only on the Flat until he was five, showing fairly useful form and winning five times at a mile and a half to a mile and three quarters for Karl Burke. By the Poule d'Essai des Poulains winner Kendor, Tarxien is the second foal of Tanz, who comes from an excellent middle-distance family. A sister to the smart mile-and-three-quarter-winner Spring and closely related to the King George VI and Queen Elizabeth Stakes winner Pentire, Tanz showed fair form at a mile and a half when trained by Henry Cecil, winning a three-runner maiden at Catterick. She has bred three other winners, the best of whom is the useful filly Tanzilla (by Warning), who stayed eleven furlongs. Tarxien's grandam Gull Nook, out of a half-sister to Shirley Heights, won the Ribblesdale Stakes. There are plenty of other decent Flat winners in the family but it is hard to find any other winners over jumps. Perhaps Tarxien's nearest relative with a success over jumps to its name is Monument, a selling hurdle winner out of a half-sister to the third dam Bempton. The sturdy Tarxien has shown his form on going ranging from good to firm to heavy, but probably needs testing conditions to bring out the best in him when racing at around two and a half miles. Tarxien has raced only at that sort of distance over fences, and might benefit from a return to further. He put up his best performances over hurdles at three miles, including when second to Stromness in a Grade 1 novice event at Aintree. Tarxien, who is thoroughly genuine and consistent, has been fitted with a tongue strap on all his appearances for his present yard. *M. C. Pipe*

TASBOK (IRE) 8 b.g. Posen (USA) – Go Honey Go (General Assembly (USA)) [2002/3 h84: 21g³ 22f⁵ 20sᵖᵘ c21dᶠ Dec 2] medium-sized gelding: poor maiden hurdler: well beaten when falling last in novice handicap on chasing debut: probably stayed 2¾m: acted on firm and good to soft going: tried tongue tied: dead. *R. Rowe* — c– h84

TASKMASTER 6 b.g. Alflora (IRE) – Travail Girl (Forties Field (FR)) [2002/3 F74: 16dᶠ Oct 23] rangy gelding: badly in need of experience in bumper on debut in 2001/2: would have made winning debut over hurdles in novice won by Table Mountain at Chepstow on reappearance but for falling last, not seen out again: will prove suited by further than 2m. *P. J. Hobbs* — h105

TA TA FOR NOW 6 b.g. Ezzoud (IRE) – Exit Laughing (Shaab) [2002/3 h–, F77: 20g⁶ 24m⁴ 22s⁴ 20s³ 24g c21s c25d³ Mar 5] lengthy gelding: modest novice hurdler: won weak race at Hexham in April: jumped sketchily both starts over fences: stays 3m: acts on soft and good to firm going. *P. Beaumont* — c83 h89

TATHMIN 10 b.g. Weldnaas (USA) – Alcassa (FR) (Satingo) [2002/3 h96: c23d* c23d² c23m² c26d³ 26m³ 24d⁵ 24g³ 22d⁵ 26m⁵ Mar 23] sturdy gelding: placed all 4 starts over fences (awarded novice at Wetherby in May), though didn't impress at all with attitude on last 2: modest handicap hurdler: stays 3¼m: acts on good to soft and good to firm going: usually blinkered/visored, tried in cheekpieces final outing (downed tools): not one to trust. *A. King* — c99 § h90 §

TAXBUSTER 11 b.g. Welsh Captain – Indian Cash (Indian Ruler) [2002/3 h–: c17gᶠ May 1] leggy gelding: poor maiden hurdler: had already lost place when falling seventh on chasing debut, not seen out again: may prove best around 2m: acts on good to soft going (best effort in bumpers on firm): races freely. *N. B. Thomson* — c– h–

TEAATRAL 9 b.g. Saddlers' Hall (IRE) – La Cabrilla (Carwhite) [2002/3 c–, h145?: 24s⁵ Dec 31] leggy, good-topped gelding: high-class hurdler at best: bit backward, tailed off in minor event at Cheltenham only start in 2002/3: effective at 2m (given test) to easy 3m: raced on good going or softer (acts on heavy): blinkered: best efforts on right-handed courses: races prominently: unenthusiastic nowadays. *C. R. Egerton* — c– h–

TEA BOX (IRE) 12 b.g. Meneval (USA) – Elteetee (Paddy's Stream) [2002/3 c97, h–: c24g³ May 8] fair hunter chaser: charged tape and unseated before start prior to running below best at Fakenham in May: stays 3m: acts on good to soft going. *M. A. Kemp* — c82 h–

TE AKAU DAN (NZ) 9 b.g. Dance Floor (USA) – Bellandaan (NZ) (Standaan (FR))   c–
[2002/3 c–, h–: 19g^pu Jul 27] sturdy gelding: winning pointer, little worthwhile form   h–
otherwise: tried blinkered/tongue tied. *S. G. Griffiths*

TEAL BAY 11 b.m. Scallywag – Centaura (Centaurus) [2002/3 c24s^5 May 18] rather   c78
leggy, close-coupled mare: modest pointer: none too fluent and never dangerous in hunter   h–
chase at Bangor in May. *P. A. Jones*

TEALBY 6 b.m. Efisio – Al Raja (Kings Lake (USA)) [2002/3 h101p, F105: 16s* 17d^2   h110
16d^2 Dec 26] good-topped mare: fair form over hurdles: easily won mares novice at
Southwell in December: mistakes when neck second to Rhinestone Cowboy in falsely-
run novice at Cheltenham week later, reportedly in season when well below best final
start: has plenty of speed and will prove best around 2m. *Mrs L. Wadham*

TEAM CAPTAIN 9 ch.g. Teamster – Silly Sausage (Silly Answer) [2002/3 c106:   c99
c21f^2 c28g^ur c27g^4 c25m^6 Mar 20] angular gelding: modest chaser: probably stays 3½m:
acts on firm and good to soft going, pulled up on soft: bled from nose final start.
C. J. Down

TEA TIME (IRE) 8 b.g. Glacial Storm (USA) – Blaze of Hope (IRE) (Le Moss)   h–
[2002/3 h–: 22g^pu May 1] no form over hurdles or in points. *R. T. Phillips*

TEDDY MAC (IRE) 6 b.g. Commanche Run – Fraudulento (Orchestra) [2002/3   h–
24g^pu 18s^F Mar 2] 7,800 4-y-o: third foal: dam in frame twice up to 19f over hurdles: fell
fatally on second start over hurdles. *C. Weedon*

TEDO (IRE) 5 ch.g. Beveled (USA) – Gunner Girl (Gunner B) [2002/3 h–: 16m^pu   h–
May 6] no sign of ability. *J. Neville*

TEDSTONE FOX 11 b.g. Bold Fox – Royal Wren (Blast) [2002/3 c76x: c16g c19f^pu   c–
May 15] signs of only a little ability in points and hunter chases: sold £1,300 Ascot
December Sales. *Miss R. S. Reynolds*

TEE-JAY (IRE) 7 ch.g. Un Desperado (FR) – N T Nad (Welsh Pageant) [2002/3   c88
h101, F79: c20s^5 c20d^pu c16g 19d^3 24g 24g^3 20g^2 Mar 29] workmanlike gelding: modest   h99
handicap hurdler: similar form on first of 3 starts over fences: should stay beyond 2½m:
acts on soft going: inconsistent. *M. D. Hammond*

TEELIN 6 b.g. Neltino – Slieve League (IRE) (Roselier (FR)) [2002/3 F16d^3 Mar 19]   F96
first foal: dam, little sign of ability in novice hurdles, sister to useful staying chaser Ebony
Jane: fairly useful form when 1½ lengths third of 10 to Mount Karinga in bumper at
Chepstow on debut. *P. R. Webber*

TEELIN BAY (IRE) 11 b.g. Be My Native (USA) – Fahy Quay (Quayside) [2002/3   c86
c117+, h–: c25g^4 May 8] rather leggy gelding: fairly useful hunter chaser: very disap-   h–
pointing favourite at Kelso (breathing problem) in May: stays 27f: has won on heavy
going, clearly goes well on good to firm: tongue tied. *Miss Pauline Robson*

TEES COMPONENTS (IRE) 8 b.g. Risk Me (FR) – Lady Warninglid (Ela-Mana-Mou)   h141 +
[2002/3 F118+: 24d* 16s^2 24d* 23d^3 Mar 1]
  There was more than three years between Tees Components' racecourse
debut in a bumper and his hurdling debut, which finally came in November, little
more than a month before he turned eight. Part of the reason for the belated switch
to hurdling was that Tees Components missed the whole of the 2000/1 season after
sustaining a hairline fracture to a knee. Connections also made the most of Tees
Components' bumper career, giving him five runs. They had good reason because
Tees Components excelled in that sphere. Narrowly beaten on that debut at Huntingdon (Grand National winner Bindaree made his British debut in third in the
same race), Tees Components won his four remaining starts in bumpers, three at
Wetherby either side of his injury and then a Grade 2 at Chepstow in December
2001. Rated only behind the Cheltenham Champion Bumper first three—Pizarro,
Rhinestone Cowboy and Back In Front—among bumper horses in 2001/2, Tees
Components looked an excellent prospect for novice hurdles, but first he was to
prove himself a useful performer on the Flat. His 2002 campaign began with a
winning debut in a maiden on the all-weather at Lingfield and included a nine-
length win in a handicap at Newmarket in the autumn in between starting a
disappointing favourite for both the Cesarewitch and the November Handicap.
Tees Components' hurdling career got off to the expected good start at
Newcastle where he did not come off the bridle to land the odds from his only
serious rival Royal Emperor, the pair finishing a distance clear. That effort reads

skybet.com River Don Novices' Hurdle, Doncaster—a scintillating performance by Tees Components

even better now, given that Tees Components was one of only three horses all season to defeat Royal Emperor who wound up rated the better horse by 11 lb. Royal Emperor was Tees Components' most notable scalp over hurdles but his more important win—and best effort yet—came when defeating seven other winners in impressive style in the skybet.com River Don Novices' Hurdle at Doncaster in January. Ridden more positively, Tees Components showed himself a class apart, drawing further and further clear in the straight on the bridle and eased virtually to a walk to win by twenty-two lengths from the outsider Tribal Venture. Second favourite Maybe The Business collapsed and died after passing the post a remote fourth and third favourite Coolsan was tailed off when pulled up, but nonetheless, it was hard not to be impressed by Tees Components. In addition, Tribal Venture's subsequent efforts hardly let the form down.

Those races at Newcastle and Doncaster were over three miles, and the drop to two proved Tees Components' undoing at Newcastle in between. He looked sure to land the odds at the last but hung left (as he has on the Flat and in bumpers) when asked for his effort and went down by half a length to Our Armageddon. There were also valid excuses for Tees Components' other defeat, in the Prestige Novices' Hurdle at Haydock after his win at Doncaster. In hindsight, at least, there was no disgrace in being beaten by Iris's Gift in what looked essentially a match, but Tees Components managed only a well-held third after looking a danger before three out and it was probably significant that his stable was under a cloud at the time, resulting in the yard's normally steady stream of winners drying up completely for more than a month. Tees Components still didn't seem himself when well beaten back on the Flat at Doncaster on Lincoln day but he showed he was back in form shortly after the end of the latest jumps season in early-May when slamming some moderate rivals by twenty-five lengths and more in an intermediate hurdle at Kelso.

Tees Components was sold for just 2,000 guineas as a foal and made IR 8,500 guineas as a yearling. He can hardly be said to be a typical product of his sire

Risk Me who has had no shortage of runners but very few of note, the best of them the One Thousand Guineas runner-up Niche and smart and tough six- and seven-furlong performer Branston Abby. Tees Components' dam Lady Warninglid never ran but is a half-sister to this family's other jumper of note, the useful Roberty Lea. Also trained for much of his career by Mary Reveley, Roberty Lea won on the Flat and over fences but was at his best at around two and a half miles over hurdles. Grandam Rosy Lee won at up to a mile and a quarter in France and was a half-sister to the Musidora winner Rimosa's Pet. The latter figures in the pedigree of several good Flat winners, including her son the very smart and consistent six-furlong to one-mile performer Rock City, and daughter Kerrera who was runner-up in the One Thousand Guineas. Tees Components is his dam's only winner so far over jumps but she has also bred the fair stayer La Brief (by Law Society), the mile-and-a-half-winner The Karaoke King (by Sayf El Arab), winners in Germany (by the afore-mentioned Rock City) and Spain (by Pharly), and a full brother to Tees Components named Witz who has won in Italy. Tees Components' five-year-old sister White-house Beauty has shown a little ability in bumpers and maidens in Ireland. Lady Warninglid's yearling by Danzig Connection made 5,500 guineas at Newmarket on the eve of Tees Components' win there in the autumn and it will not come as a surprise to learn that Mary Reveley was the purchaser. However, it is likely that by the time he reaches the racecourse it will be her son Keith who holds the licence at Groundhill Farm, as the trainer announced in the spring her intention to retire by the end of 2004.

		Sharpo	Sharpen Up
	Risk Me (FR)	(ch 1977)	Moiety Bird
	(ch 1984)	Run The Risk	Run The Gantlet
Tees Components		(b 1976)	Siliciana
(b.g. 1995)		Ela-Mana-Mou	Pitcairn
	Lady Warninglid	(b 1976)	Rose Bertin
	(b 1983)	Rosy Lee	Le Haar
		(ch 1969)	Rimosa

Before then, Tees Components has the potential to be a final big-race winner for his trainer. With just five races over hurdles—three impressive wins and two excusable defeats—we may not have seen the best of him yet. A strong gelding, Tees Components stays three miles and acts on good to firm and soft going. He has a tendency to edge left under pressure. *Mrs M. Reveley*

TEETON PRICELESS 8 b.m. Broadsword (USA) – Teeton Frolic (Sunley Builds) [2002/3 c23d^{ur} c24s^F Mar 10] modest pointer, successful in January and February: failed to complete both starts in hunter chases. *Mrs Joan Tice* c–

TEFI 5 ch.g. Efisio – Masuri Kabisa (USA) (Ascot Knight (CAN)) [2002/3 17m^{pu} Jun 1] modest on Flat (stays 1m), successful in February: pulled up early due to slipped saddle on hurdling debut. *S. R. Bowring* h–

TEGUISE 7 ch.m. Tigani – The Ranee (Royal Palace) [2002/3 16g 17d 19g c20m c26d^3 Aug 26] compact mare: no worthwhile form: tried tongue tied. *B. Ellison* c– h–

TEJANO GOLD (USA) 13 ch.g. Tejano (USA) – Nelli Forli (USA) (Broadway Forli (USA)) [2002/3 c20v^{pu} c20d^{pu} Mar 4] narrow gelding: fairly useful hurdler/fair chaser at best: no form in 2 hunters and a point on return from long absence: dead. *F. L. Matthews* c– h–

TEJAQUE 8 b.m. Lord of Arabia – Devil's Gold (Goldfella) [2002/3 22m^{pu} Jul 14] first foal: dam, poor staying novice hurdler, from family of smart staying chaser Tracys Special: signs of a little ability in points: showed nothing on hurdling debut. *Mrs N. S. Sharpe* h–

TELEMOSS (IRE) 9 b.g. Montelimar (USA) – Shan's Moss (Le Moss) [2002/3 h151: c20s* c22v* c16v* c20s⁴ Feb 1] useful-looking gelding: smart hurdler: easily won novice chases at Ayr, Kelso and Newcastle first 3 starts, jumping soundly in main: broke blood vessel when tailed off in Grade 1 novice at Sandown final outing: reported later in month to have suffered knee injury: likely to prove best up to 3m: acts on good to firm and heavy going: worth another chance to confirm promise over fences. *N. G. Richards* c125 p h–

TELIMAR PRINCE (IRE) 7 b.g. Montelimar (USA) – Blakica (Sexton Blake) [2002/3 h109p: 19d* 17d² 16v³ 20d² Feb 17] lengthy, angular gelding: useful hurdler: won handicap at Newbury in November: good placed efforts subsequently, 1½ lengths h139 second of 7 to Classified in Grade 2 at Fontwell final outing: stays 2½m: acts on heavy going. *J. T. Gifford*

TELL ME SEE (IRE)   7 b.m. Glacial Storm (USA) – Bavards Girl (IRE) (Le Bavard (FR)) [2002/3 F16d* 19v^{ur} F18s^{su} 24v* Mar 9] first foal: dam unraced: winning pointer: comfortably won bumper at Thurles in December: best effort over hurdles when winning maiden at Naas in March: stays 3m: acts on heavy going. *John Michael Burke, Ireland*   **h111 F91**

TELL ME WHY (IRE)   7 b.g. Roselier (FR) – Clonarctic Slave (Sir Mordred) [2002/3 h87p: c24d² Dec 21] quite good-topped gelding: fifth of 13 in novice hurdle on debut in 2001/2: off over 10 months, 2½ lengths second to Cool Investment in novice chase at Warwick: will prove best at 3m+: clearly difficult to train. *P. R. Webber*   **c110 h–**

TELMAR FLYER   6 b.m. Neltino – Flying Mistress (Lear Jet) [2002/3 F–: F16d F16m^{su} F16m 20d^{pu} 16v^{pu} Feb 10] lengthy mare: little sign of ability. *J. Cullinan*   **h– F–**

TEME VALLEY   9 br.g. Polish Precedent (USA) – Sudeley (Dancing Brave (USA)) [2002/3 h100§: 16m⁴ 16m 22s 17s* 16g 16d 17d* Apr 8] leggy gelding: modest handicap hurdler: has won 7 times at Sedgefield, including in November and April: stays 19f: acts on soft and good to firm going, possibly not on heavy: effective tongue tied or not: has shown reluctance at start: unreliable. *J. Howard Johnson*   **h99 §**

TEMONY (IRE)   8 ch.g. Tremblant – Lindabell (Over The River (FR)) [2002/3 c16d³ c17s* c20m* c22d^{ur} c22v c24f^F Sep 25] winning hurdler: fair chaser: won maiden at Ballinrobe in June and handicap at Tipperary in July: fell fatally at Listowel: stayed 2½m: acted on good to firm and heavy going. *Anthony Mullins, Ireland*   **c113 h–**

TEMPER LAD (USA)   8 b.g. Riverman (USA) – Dokki (USA) (Northern Dancer) [2002/3 h90: 22m² May 6] neat gelding: has had wind operation: winning hurdler, poor nowadays: stays 2¾m: acts on soft going, probably on firm: effective blinkered or not: tongue tied. *J. Joseph*   **h82**

TEMPLE DOG (IRE)   7 ch.g. Un Desperado (FR) – Shower (Kings Lake (USA)) [2002/3 F108: 16d* 16v* 16d* Mar 15] workmanlike gelding: successful all 3 starts in novice hurdles, at Ayr and Haydock in December and Newcastle in March: stayed on to lead last when beating Tribal Dispute 3½ lengths at last-named course: will be suited by at least 2½m: raced on going softer than good (acts on heavy): open to further improvement granted more of a test. *T. P. Tate*   **h122 p**

TEMPLES TIME (IRE)   5 b.m. Distinctly North (USA) – Midnight Patrol (Ashmore (FR)) [2002/3 h–: 16m⁴ 16g⁴ 20d^{pu} Jun 8] half-sister to 3 winners over jumps, including fairly useful hurdler Viceroy Jester (by Jester), stayed 2½m: modest on Flat (stays 1½m): poor form over hurdles: dismounted final start: should stay beyond 2m. *R. Brotherton*   **h76**

TEMPO (IRE)   11 b.g. Satco (FR) – Arabian Sands (Pollerton) [2002/3 c76, h–: c21g^{ur} May 26] workmanlike gelding: winning hurdler/chaser, retains little ability: stays 2½m: acts on heavy and good to firm going: visored once. *Ian Williams*   **c– h–**

TENACIOUS STAR (IRE)   5 b.g. Fourstars Allstar (USA) – Saltee Sound (IRE) (Buckskin (FR)) [2002/3 F16d 22v^{pu} 17d^{pu} Mar 2] IR £14,000 3-y-o: second foal: dam, lightly raced in points, half-sister to useful 2½m chase winner Man of Leisure: no form in bumper or 2 novice hurdles: dead. *Ferdy Murphy*   **h– F–**

TENDER COVE (IRE)   5 b.g. Balla Cove – Fair Tender (Tender King) [2002/3 h120: 16f Sep 24] close-coupled gelding: useful on Flat (stays 1m): won juvenile maiden in 2001/2 on hurdling debut: best effort since when seventh in 4-y-o handicap at Listowel in September: will prove best at sharp 2m. *Patrick Mullins, Ireland*   **h112**

TENDER TANGLE   8 ch.g. Crested Lark – Red Tango (Legal Tender) [2002/3 h–: 16d^{pu} 16g 16s^F 16m^{ur} Jun 30] little sign of ability, including in point. *F. Jordan*   **h–**

TENDER TOUCH (IRE)   8 gr.m. Weldnaas (USA) – Moments Peace (Adonijah) [2002/3 h71: 16m⁵ 19g⁵ 20m⁵ 20v³ 16s c16g³ Mar 25] leggy mare: poor handicap hurdler: similar level on chasing debut: stays 19f: acts on heavy and good to firm going. *Miss Kate Milligan*   **c63 h67**

TENERIFE FLYER   5 ch.m. Rock City – Nobleata (Dunbeath (USA)) [2002/3 h–: 19g 16g Dec 13] sparely-made mare: of no account. *J. R. Norton*   **h–**

TEN FOURTEEN (IRE)   8 ch.g. Ore – Yonder Bay (IRE) (Trimmingham) [2002/3 21d^{pu} 22f^{pu} May 15] ex-Irish gelding: second foal: brother to fair hurdler/chaser up to 19f Sir Storm: dam unraced: of little account. *Miss Z. C. Davison*   **h–**

TENNESSEE TWIST (IRE)   13 b.g. Buckskin (FR) – Darjoy (Darantus) [2002/3 c–, h–: c33g c34g³ c26d⁴ c24v^{pu} Mar 5] good-topped, attractive gelding: one-time useful   **c84 h–**

staying chaser: best effort in hunters in 2002/3 when third at Uttoxeter: blinkered once. *M. Williamson*

TEN POUNDSWORTH (IRE)   10 ch.g. Orchestra – Rush For Gold (Mugatpura) **c127** [2002/3 c112: c21v* c21s^F Feb 9] lengthy, angular gelding: former hunter chaser: fairly useful form when winning 12-runner Grade 3 novice at Leopardstown in January by 2 lengths from Ground Ball: fell 4 out in Grade 1 novice there (subsequently collapsed and died) following month: stayed 25f: acted on heavy going. *George Stewart, Ireland*

TENSHOOKMEN (IRE)   9 ch.g. Cardinal Flower – April Rise (Prominer) [2002/3 **c100** c20d c19f^{pu} c18d* c18s* c20d c20v⁴ c21s⁶ c20m⁵ c25g^{pu} Apr 20] strong gelding: half-brother to winning pointer Mr Goodbye (by Tremblant): dam ran once: fair handicap chaser: won at Thurles in October and Punchestown in November: best form up to 2½m: acts on soft and good to firm going. *W. F. Codd, Ireland*

TENSILE (IRE)   8 b.g. Tenby – Bonnie Isle (Pitcairn) [2002/3 h131: 23f⁴ c21g* **c119** c21m^F c24m* c26m³ 20g³ 20m* 20s³ 22s⁵ 22f⁵ Mar 29] compact gelding: not fluent in **h128** novice chases, despite winning at Newton Abbot and Stratford early in season: fairly useful handicap hurdler: back to form when winning 4-runner event at Uttoxeter in October: below best after break last 2 outings: stays 3m: acts on any going: has had tongue tied: held up. *P. J. Hobbs*

TENTSMUIR   7 b.m. Arctic Lord – Deep Pier (Deep Run) [2002/3 F77: 20g^{pu} 20v **h72** 24g⁴ Apr 23] sparely-made mare: won weak bumper on debut in 2001/2: poor form in novice hurdles. *D. W. Whillans*

TEORBAN (POL)   4 b.c. Don Corleone – Tabaka (POL) (Pyjama Hunt) [2002/3 **h80** 16m⁶ Mar 23] successful at 6f (at 2 yrs) and 1m on Flat in Poland for B. Chrzanowski, won over 2m at Wolverhampton in April: 12½ lengths sixth of 17 in maiden at Hunting-don on hurdling debut: may do better. *M. Pitman*

TERDAD (USA)   10 ch.g. Lomond (USA) – Istiska (FR) (Irish River (FR)) [2002/3 **c– §** c–, h108§: 19d⁵ 17m 19m^F 17m 16g c22g⁴ c20m^{pu} 21d 19s⁶ 16d³ 16m⁴ 17m Apr 21] big, **h82 §** rangy gelding: one-time fair hurdler, on the downgrade: lightly raced over fences, no show both starts in 2002/3: effective at 2m to 3m: acts on firm and soft going: best in blinkers/visor: ungenuine. *M. C. Chapman*

TEREK (GER)   7 ch.g. Irish River (FR) – Turbaine (USA) (Trempolino (USA)) **h100** [2002/3 h95: 16d⁴ 16g² 16d⁴ Jan 18] tall, leggy, close-coupled gelding: smart on Flat (stays 1¼m) for P. Schiergen in Germany: fair form over hurdles: ½-length second of 17 to Search And Destroy in conditional jockeys novice handicap at Doncaster, hanging left late on: will prove best at sharp 2m: raced on good going or softer: pulls hard. *R. T. Phillips*

TERIDOVE   6 b.g. Terimon – Flakey Dove (Oats) [2002/3 F16d F17s Dec 26] second **F–** foal: dam top-class hurdler up to 21f, won 1994 Champion Hurdle: behind in bumpers at Ludlow and Hereford. *C. J. Price*

TERIMON'S DREAM   6 gr.g. Terimon – I Have A Dream (SWE) (Mango Express) **h–** [2002/3 16d Nov 26] leggy, lengthy gelding: little form on Flat: well held in novice on hurdling debut: sold £1,700 Ascot April Sales. *A. W. Carroll*

TERINO   7 b.g. Terimon – Ashmo (Ashmore (FR)) [2002/3 F87?: 16g⁵ 16m 22d 19s **h–** 16m 16m⁴ Apr 21] signs of only a little ability. *A. E. Jessop*

TERMONFECKIN   5 b.g. Runnett – Crimson Sol (Crimson Beau) [2002/3 F17m³ **h–** F16m³ 20m⁶ Aug 17] sixth foal: dam poor maiden hurdler: third in bumpers at Market **F80** Rasen and Stratford: showed nothing in maiden on hurdling debut. *P. W. Hiatt*

TERTULLIAN (IRE)   4 b.g. Petorius – Fiddes (IRE) (Alzao (USA)) [2002/3 16g **h79** Dec 18] sturdy gelding: fairly useful on Flat (stayed 1¼m), sold out of R. Hannon's stable 45,000 gns Newmarket Autumn Sales: twelfth of 20 in juvenile at Newbury on hurdling debut: dead. *S. Dow*

TESORA MIA   7 ch.m. Mon Tresor – Rocky Affair (Clear Run) [2002/3 F16d 19d^{pu} **h–** Feb 10] eighth foal: dam winning pointer: no show in bumper or mares novice hurdle. **F–** *M. Wellings*

TESTIFY (IRE)   10 b.g. Montelimar (USA) – Test Drive (Crash Course) [2002/3 **h117** h117: 20g⁵ 24s 22g² 22d 22g³ 22g⁶ 24m⁴ 24f⁴ 24s 24d 24d Mar 22] fairly useful handicap hurdler: won at Listowel in September: stays 3m: has won on soft going, best efforts on good or firmer (acts on firm): tongue tied. *M. J. O'Connor, Ireland*

TEST OF LOYALTY   9 b.g. Niniski (USA) – River Chimes (Forlorn River) [2002/3 **c83** c78, h–: c16d⁴ 16d* c17g* c16g⁶ c16g⁵ c17g⁴ c20g⁴ Apr 25] workmanlike gelding: **h–**

maiden hurdler: poor chaser: won handicaps in small fields at Perth in June and Southwell in September: ideally suited by around 2m: acts on soft going. *J. N. R. Billinge*

TEXAS RANGER   5 b.g. Mtoto – Favorable Exchange (USA) (Exceller (USA))   **h125**
[2002/3 h111p: 18m* 16m* 20g* 20m* 22d 21s⁵ 21s⁴ 20v³ 21m 21g Mar 12] compact gelding: fairly useful hurdler: won 4-y-o events at Fontwell (maiden) and Worcester (novice), novice at Fakenham and handicap at Worcester by end of June: well below form most starts after, probably flattered when in mid-division in Grade 1 novice at Cheltenham final one: should stay beyond 2½m: acts on good to firm going: sold 15,000 gns Doncaster May Sales. *C. J. Mann*

THAIX (FR)   6 b.g. Roi de Rome (USA) – Action de Balle (FR) (Cricket Ball (USA))   **h114**
[2002/3 F101p: 18v* Dec 26] well-made gelding: shaped quite well when eighth of 17 in Grade 1 bumper at Punchestown on debut (trained by E. Hales) in 2001/2: won maiden hurdle at Leopardstown 8 months later by 6 lengths from Poachin Again, making running and finding extra when pressed: not seen out again after fracturing cannon bone: will stay 2½m. *M. J. P. O'Brien, Ireland*

THALYS (GER)   5 bl.g. Gold And Ivory (USA) – Tachira (Faraway Times (USA))   **h96**
[2002/3 h82p: 16m² 17s³ 17m² 19m* 20m² Jul 18] good-topped gelding: modest novice hurdler: won weak event at Market Rasen in July: stays 19f: acts on good to firm going: tongue tied last 3 starts. *Mrs H. Dalton*

THAMES (IRE)   5 b.g. Over The River (FR) – Aon Dochas (IRE) (Strong Gale)   **F96**
[2002/3 F16d³ F17g⁴ Apr 5] lengthy, angular gelding: first foal: dam, won 2m chase, half-sister to smart chaser up to 21f Native Charm and useful 2½m chaser Sir Dante: better effort in bumpers when 20 lengths fourth of 21 to Classic Native in Grade 2 at Aintree, staying on having been off bridle long way out: will be suited by 2½m+. *N. J. Henderson*

THANX DIRECTORY (IRE)   4 ch.f. Mukaddamah (USA) – Scanno's Choice (IRE)   **F87**
(Pennine Walk) [2002/3 F14d³ F16d³ F16m* Mar 23] IR 6,000F, 34,000Y: lengthy filly: fifth foal: sister to 3 winners, notably smart British/Hong Kong 1m to 1½m performer Sobriety: dam Irish maiden: progressive form in bumpers, won mares maiden at Huntingdon by ¾ length from Miss Honeypenny: sold 18,000 gns Doncaster May Sales. *T. J. Etherington*

THARI (USA)   6 b. or br.g. Silver Hawk(USA) – Magic Slipper (Habitat) [2002/3   **c122**
h136: c22s* c21m⁴ c20d² c20s^F c20v⁴ 21g 24g c20m* Apr 22] good-topped gelding: **h–**
useful hurdler in 2001/2, well held when returned to smaller obstacles in valuable handicaps at Cheltenham and Aintree: fairly useful novice chaser: won maiden at Galway in September and weakly-contested 3-runner Grade 1 Powers Gold Cup at Fairyhouse in April: fortunate when beating One Night Out 3 lengths at latter, held when left disputing

Powers Gold Cup, Fairyhouse—Thari runs out a very fortunate winner

Mr D. P. Sharkey's "Thari"

lead and hampered 2 out: well beaten in valuable handicap at Punchestown 8 days later: stays 2¾m: acts on heavy ground, probably on good to firm: sometimes tongue tied. *N. Meade, Ireland*

THATCHAM ISLAND 10 ch.m. Jupiter Island – Floreal (Formidable (USA)) [2002/3 24g^pu 22d^pu 17s 16m^pu Mar 31] lengthy, workmanlike mare: winning hurdler, no show in 2002/3: twice-raced novice chaser: fell in point in 2002: stays 2½m: acts on soft and good to firm going: tried visored/blinkered. *Mrs L. P. Baker* **c– h–**

THATCHER ROCK 7 b.g. High Estate – Bellifontaine (FR) (Bellypha) [2002/3 h83, F85: 17s^pu Nov 29] lightly-raced gelding: fair form at best in bumpers: twice-raced in novice hurdles, pulled up only start in 2002/3. *Jonjo O'Neill* **h–**

THATCHERS LONGSHOT 6 ch.g. Gunner B – Formidable Lady (Formidable (USA)) [2002/3 F16s^6 Jun 9] sixth foal: half-brother to winning pointer by Jupiter Island: dam winning 2m hurdler: needed experience when well held in bumper on debut: won maiden point in April. *S. A. Brookshaw* **F–**

THATS ALL FOLKS 6 b.g. Alhijaz – So It Goes (Free State) [2002/3 c104, h98: 19d^6 c21s^2 c17d^3 c16g* c17m^F c21m^2 c21g^2 Aug 9] compact gelding: winning hurdler, claimed from P. Nicholls on reappearance: fair chaser: won handicap at Hexham in June: stays 21f: acts on heavy and good to firm going: sometimes let down by jumping. *M. Todhunter* **c110 h–**

THAT'S FINE 8 ch.g. Good Thyne (USA) – Wing On (Quayside) [2002/3 h90, F91: 22s 24s^2 24d^5 Feb 23] angular gelding: bumper winner: best effort over hurdles when second to Glen Warrior in handicap at Taunton: stays 3m: raced on good to soft/soft going. *R. T. Phillips* **h104**

THATSFOREEL 10 b.g. Scottish Reel – That Space (Space King) [2002/3 c88d: c24d* Apr 9] modest form at best over fences: fit from points (runner-up all 3 starts in **c88**

2003), won hunter chase at Uttoxeter by 8 lengths from Watchyourback: stays 25f: raced on good going or softer: tried blinkered: has looked ungenuine. *Miss Joanne Tremain*

THATS THE CRACK (IRE) 9 b.g. King's Ride – Mighty Crack (Deep Run) [2002/3 c– c83: c25gⁿ Apr 7] tall, lengthy gelding: lightly-raced winning chaser: failed to complete in point and hunter chase in 2003: stays 3m: acts on firm going. *Alan J. Brown*

THE ALLEYCAT (IRE) 12 b.g. Tidaro (USA) – Allitess (Mugatpura) [2002/3 c87: **c83** c17m c16m 17d⁵ c17m* Apr 21] poor chaser: sold out of J. Haldane's stable 1,450 gns **h71** Doncaster October Sales after second start: back to form to win selling handicap at Plumpton: probably best around 2m: raced mainly on good going or firmer (acts on firm): fluent jumper in main. *R. Ford*

THEATRE CALL (IRE) 5 b.g. Old Vic – Jennycomequick (Furry Glen) [2002/3 **F85** F16s⁴ Jan 27] IR £25,000 3-y-o: rather unfurnished gelding: fourth foal: half-brother to useful hurdler Leinster (by Supreme Leader), stays 2½m: dam useful hurdler up to 2¾m and winning chaser in Ireland: shaped like a stayer when 16¾ lengths fourth of 20 to Back To Ben Alder in bumper at Kempton on debut, nearest finish. *J. A. B. Old*

THEATRE LADY (IRE) 5 b.m. King's Theatre (IRE) – Littlepace (Indian King **h–** (USA)) [2002/3 17d 16v Dec 21] workmanlike mare: poor maiden on Flat (stays 9f): well held after taking strong hold both starts over hurdles. *P. D. Evans*

THEATRELAND (USA) 6 b.g. Dynaformer (USA) – Mime (Cure The Blues (USA)) **c– §** [2002/3 h108§: 24m 27g c23dⁿᵘ Jun 8] workmanlike gelding: fair handicap hurdler, **h– §** below form both starts early in 2002/3: dropping away when unseating eleventh in novice at Worcester on chasing debut: stays 3m: acts on good to firm going: has worn blinkers, including when successful: temperamental, and one to leave alone. *S. E. H. Sherwood*

THEATRE OF LIFE (IRE) 4 b.g. King's Theatre (IRE) – Miss Ironwood (Junius **h–** (USA)) [2002/3 17s 17s Nov 28] poor maiden on Flat: well held in 2 juvenile hurdles, blinkered second time. *G. L. Moore*

THE BAJAN BANDIT (IRE) 8 b.g. Commanche Run – Sunrise Highway VII (Dam- **c129** sire Unregistered) [2002/3 h128p: c20v* c21s* c22d² c25dⁿ c24gⁿᵘ Mar 12] medium- **h–** sized gelding: successful on 10 of first 11 starts, including 4 times over hurdles and in novice chases at Carlisle (unimpressive) in November and Ayr in December: flattered by proximity to easy winner It Takes Time when 9 lengths second of 4 at Haydock: ran poorly in Grade 2 at Wetherby (found to have nasal discharge) and Grade 1 at Chelten- ham: should stay 3m: raced mainly on going softer than good (has won on good to firm): sketchy jumper. *L. Lungo*

THE BANDIT (IRE) 6 b.g. Un Desperado (FR) – Sweet Friendship (Alleging **h88 +** (USA)) [2002/3 F91: 17g 19dᶠ 19d⁶ 20m² Mar 23] useful-looking gelding: best effort over hurdles when 8 lengths second of 18 to Bravo in novice handicap at Huntingdon, though wandered and found little under pressure: will stay beyond 2½m: may prove best with exaggerated waiting tactics. *Miss E. C. Lavelle*

THE BARGE (IRE) 10 b.g. Un Desperado (FR) – Marble Owen (Master Owen) **c64** [2002/3 c82, h–: c20s² c17m⁶ Apr 21] winning hurdler: poor form at best over fences: **h–** stays 3¼m: acts on heavy going, probably good to firm: sometimes blinkered. *J. White*

THE BEYTON BEAR (IRE) 7 b.g. Dromod Hill – Reffian (IRE) (Henbit (USA)) **h–** [2002/3 F66: 16dⁿᵘ Mar 7] signs of only a little ability in bumper in 2001/2 and maiden hurdle: dead. *J. N. R. Billinge*

THE BIG'UN 9 b.g. Green-Fingered – Lismore (Relkino) [2002/3 c–: c21sⁿᵘ c20g⁶ **c84** c24g³ Mar 12] good-bodied gelding: novice chaser, poor form in handicaps in 2002/3: stays 3m: blinkered last 2 starts: often makes mistakes/looks less than keen. *G. L. Moore*

THE BIKER (IRE) 6 br.g. Arctic Lord – Glenravel (Lucifer (USA)) [2002/3 F114: **h123 p** 16s* 17v* Nov 19] tall ex-Irish gelding: has scope: useful bumper winner: odds on, made all in novice hurdles at Uttoxeter (impressive) and Newton Abbot in November: looked just to have Mister Wellard's measure when left clear 2 out at latter (hung left off bridle): will stay beyond 17f: looked useful prospect, but not seen out again. *M. C. Pipe*

THE BISCUIT 9 ch.m. Nomadic Way (USA) – Not To Worry (USA) (Stevward) **h–** [2002/3 h–: 24g² Sep 25] well beaten in bumper and over hurdles: tongue tied last 3 starts. *B. Mactaggart*

THE BOILER WHITE (IRE) 15 ch.g. Deep Run – Cill Dara (Lord Gayle (USA)) **c§§** [2002/3 c§§, h–§: c34gⁿᵘ May 22] lengthy gelding: one-time fair hurdler/chaser, but **h– §** thoroughly ungenuine and no form in hunters: tried in blinkers/visor. *E. W. Froggatt*

THE BOLD ABBOT   13 b.g. Derring Rose – Canford Abbas (Hasty Word) [2002/3 **c88**
c73, h–: c25g³ May 1] fair hunter chaser: stays 25f: acts on good to soft going. *Miss* **h–**
S. West

THE BONGO MAN (IRE)   10 b.g. Be My Native (USA) – Fight For It (Strong Gale) **c–**
[2002/3 c–, h123d: 17s^pu 16m⁶ 21m³ 24f* 24d 22v^pu 17g Mar 29] lengthy gelding: **h95**
winning chaser: one-time fairly useful handicap hurdler, only modest nowadays: won at
Taunton in October: stays 3m: acts on any going: has had tongue tied, including at
Taunton: best with waiting tactics. *D. J. Wintle*

THE BOOZING BRIEF (USA)   10 b.g. Turkoman (USA) – Evening Silk (USA) **h–**
(Damascus (USA)) [2002/3 20d^pu 20g⁶ 19g^pu Apr 19] workmanlike gelding: maiden
hurdler, off 3 years before reappearance: tried blinkered: tongue tied. *Miss C. Dyson*

THE BOSUN   6 b.g. Charmer – Sailors Joy (Handsome Sailor) [2002/3 F16d F16m   **F76**
Apr 21] first foal: dam never ran: little impact in bumpers at Fakenham and Huntingdon.
A. E. Jessop

THE BOYS IN GREEN (IRE)   6 b.g. Shernazar – Mursuma (Rarity) [2002/3 16s²   **h113 p**
Mar 16] half-brother to 6 winners, including top-class chaser up to 2½m Direct Route
(by Executive Perk) and smart hurdlers Joe Mac (by Topanoora), raced mainly at 2m, and
Penny A Day (by Supreme Leader), stayed 2½m: dam 1m winner: highly promising
debut when ½-length second to Kniaz in novice hurdle at Punchestown: will improve.
C. Roche, Ireland

THE BREWER   11 ch.g. Dunbeath (USA) – Bell Cord (Beldale Flutter (USA)) **c–**
[2002/3 c–, h65: 16m⁶ 22d* Nov 5] lengthy gelding: maiden chaser: poor hurdler: won **h68**
selling handicap at Folkestone: stays 3m: acts on good to firm and heavy going: tried
blinkered/visored. *J. C. Tuck*

THE BROKEN MAN   10 b.g. Rakaposhi King – School Run (Deep Run) [2002/3 **c80**
c25d⁶ c25g Apr 7] modest pointer: well held in hunter chases: wears blinkers/cheek-
pieces. *Mrs R. L. Elliot*

THE BUNNY BOILER (IRE)   9 b.g. Tremblant – Danny's Charm (IRE) (Arapahos **c– x**
(FR)) [2002/3 c138x, h110+: 24s² 24s* c29v^pu c24s c24g c36d^ur c29m Apr 26] tall, **h129**
useful-looking gelding: fairly useful hurdler, won handicap at Navan in December by
head from Rostropovich: useful handicap chaser, won Midlands Grand National at
Uttoxeter and Irish Grand National at Fairyhouse in 2001/2: failed to make an impact in
valuable events over fences in 2002/3: stays 4¼m: best on going softer than good (acts on
heavy): often let down by jumping. *N. Meade, Ireland*

THEBWLBOY   10 ch.g. Interrex (CAN) – Super Melody (Song) [2002/3 h–: c16g⁵   **c66**
c16m⁴ c16g^pu Jun 22] sturdy gelding: poor hurdler/novice chaser, left D. Gibbs after first **h–**
outing: best around 2m: acts on good to firm going: sold £650 Ascot October Sales.
J. W. Tudor

THE BYEDEIN (IRE)   6 b.m. Alflora (IRE) – Southern Squaw (Buckskin (FR)) **h72**
[2002/3 F62: F16m⁵ 22s 16v⁵ 16d² 20m⁵ 24g⁵ Apr 23] poor form in bumpers and over **F72**
hurdles: seems to stay 3m. *A. H. Mactaggart*

THE CAR CHASER (IRE)   5 ch.g. Great Marquess – Bright Diamond (Never So **h–**
Bold) [2002/3 F16m F16d 18d Nov 11] compact gelding: first foal: dam modest maiden, **F–**
stayed 7f: mid-division at best in bumpers/claiming hurdle. *A. M. Hales*

THE CARDIFF BAY   9 b.g. St Ninian – Comarch (Ancient Monro) [2002/3 h–: **c–**
c21f⁶ May 10] no form over jumps: headstrong: sold 1,000 gns Ascot July Sales. *Mrs* **h–**
Merrita Jones

THE COTTONWOOL KID   11 b.g. Blakeney – Relatively Smart (Great Nephew) **h–**
[2002/3 h72: 22f 22g 22f^pu Aug 13] leggy gelding: has had wind operation: handicap
hurdler, no form in 2002/3: stays 3m: visored/blinkered. *Mrs Merrita Jones*

THE COUNT (FR)   4 b.g. Sillery (USA) – Dear Countess (FR) (Fabulous Dancer **h–**
(USA)) [2002/3 16v³ 16g 17d 16g^pu Mar 29] modest maiden on Flat (barely stays 1¼m):
no form over hurdles: headstrong. *F. P. Murtagh*

THE CROOKED OAK   11 ch.g. Fearless Action (USA) – Life Goes On (Pharly (FR)) **c–**
[2002/3 c82d, h77d: c25d^F May 4] tall gelding: poor chaser/novice hurdler, little form **h–**
since early-2001/2: stays 25f: acts on good to firm going, probably on soft. *K. S. Thomas*

THE CROPPY BOY   11 b.g. Arctic Lord – Deep Cut (Deep Run) [2002/3 c–, h–: **c– x**
c23g^pu 24g⁴ 26g³ 25m Oct 29] angular gelding: of little account nowadays. *Mrs* **h–**
N. S. Sharpe

THE CULDEE (IRE)   7 ch.g. Phardante (FR) – Deep Inagh (Deep Run) [2002/3   **h121**
h121: 22v² 24v³ 24s 16d 25g 22g Apr 21] stocky gelding: fairly useful handicap hurdler,
below form after reappearance: should stay 3m: raced mainly on going softer than good
(acts on heavy). *F. Flood, Ireland*

THE DANGLER (IRE)   10 b.g. Feelings (FR) – Royal Typhoon (Royal Fountain)   **c81**
[2002/3 c78, h–: 22f⁵ c16m³ c21g* c16mᵖᵘ c24s c21g Apr 3] angular gelding: poor   **h73**
chaser: won handicap at Newton Abbot in June: left J. Frost, very stiff tasks last 2 starts:
effective at 2m given a test, and stays 3¼m: acts on firm and soft going: well beaten only
start in blinkers. *Mrs Laura J. Young*

THE DARK FLASHER (IRE)   6 b.g. Lucky Guest – Perpignan (Rousillon (USA))   **h118**
[2002/3 h112: 16s 16s⁶ 16s³ 18s² 16s 16s 16d 16dᶠ 16g² 16m³ Apr 22] leggy gelding:
fairly useful hurdler: good efforts when in frame in handicaps last 2 starts, third of 18 to
High Prospect in valuable event at Fairyhouse: likely to prove best around 2m: acts on
good to firm and heavy going: consistent but often finds little. *C. F. Swan, Ireland*

THE DARK LORD (IRE)   6 b.g. Lord Americo – Khalkeys Shoon (Green Shoon)   **h88**
[2002/3 16g⁴ 16v² Mar 8] IR 12,500 4-y-o: lengthy, rather unfurnished gelding: fourth
foal: dam unraced sister to dam of one-time useful chaser up to 2½m Mulkev Prince: just
over 7 lengths fourth of 13 finishers to Spud One in steadily-run race at Huntingdon,
better effort in novice hurdles: bred to stay beyond 2m. *Mrs L. Wadham*

THE DELL (IRE)   10 b.g. Denel (FR) – Rocks Rose (Little Buskins) [2002/3 c116,   **c125**
h–: c24m² c24g² c29g Apr 21] well-made gelding: fairly useful handicap chaser: good   **h–**
second at Down Royal in May and Cork in March, beaten ¾ length by Native Jack at
latter course: mistakes at vital stages at Fairyhouse (Irish Grand National) and Punchestown (would have been second but for unseating 2 out) subsequently: stays 25f: acts on
good to firm and heavy going: consistent. *Miss F. M. Crowley, Ireland*

THE DUCKPOND (IRE)   6 ch.g. Bob's Return (IRE) – Miss Gosling (Prince Bee)   **h100 +**
[2002/3 F100: F16v⁴ 19gᶠ Dec 18] tall gelding: fairly useful form when in frame in   **F92**
bumpers: would probably have been placed but for falling 2 out in novice won by Calling
Brave at Newbury on hurdling debut: open to improvement. *J. A. B. Old*

THE EENS   11 b.g. Rakaposhi King – Snippet (Ragstone) [2002/3 c86, h–: c24mᵖᵘ   **c–**
c22m⁴ c25v⁴ c28s⁴ c24s⁶ c24f⁵ Mar 29] rather leggy, close-coupled gelding: winning   **h–**
hurdler: modest handicap chaser, below best in 2002/3: stays 27f: acts on good to firm
and heavy going: tried blinkered/in cheekpieces. *D. McCain*

THE EQUALISER   6 b.g. Alflora (IRE) – My Charade (Cawston's Clown) [2002/3   **h–**
F18m⁶ 20sᵇᵈ Dec 2] ninth foal: half-brother to poor staying hurdler Tommy Cooper and   **F77**
modest stayer Smilingatstrangers (both by Macmillion): dam, fair 1¾m winner, half-
sister to smart 6f/7f performer Step Ahead: sixth of 10 in slowly-run bumper on debut:
off bridle when brought down seventh in novice hurdle at Folkestone 7 months later.
M. J. Roberts

THE FAIRY FLAG (IRE)   5 ch.m. Inchinor – Good Reference (IRE) (Reference   **h–**
Point) [2002/3 h96: 20sᵖᵘ 16gᵖᵘ 17m⁵ Apr 26] neat mare: won first 2 starts over hurdles
within 3 days in 2001/2: no form since, off 15 months before reappearance: not sure to
stay much beyond 2m: blinkered final outing. *A. Bailey*

THE FENMAN   5 b.g. Mazaad – Dalgorian (IRE) (Lancastrian) [2002/3 F–: 16mᵖᵘ   **h77**
17s² 16s 16d 19s² 19d³ 25d 21g 22g 16d Apr 9] leggy gelding: poor maiden hurdler:
should stay beyond 19f: acts on soft going: well beaten when blinkered last 3 starts: none
too consistent. *C. N. Kellett*

THE FLYER (IRE)   6 b.g. Blues Traveller (IRE) – National Ballet (Shareef Dancer   **h109**
(USA)) [2002/3 h96: 20d² 19g* 22v⁴ 21d² Dec 21] leggy gelding: fair handicap hurdler:
won at Hereford (unbeaten in 3 starts there) in November by length from Meadows Boy:
stays 2¾m: acts on heavy going: consistent, but not an easy ride. *Miss S. J. Wilton*

THE FRENCH FURZE (IRE)   9 ch.g. Be My Guest (USA) – Exciting (Mill Reef   **c106**
(USA)) [2002/3 h148: 16f 16d² 17d⁶ 16s⁵ c21s* c16gᶠ Mar 25] leggy, close-coupled   **h139**
gelding: useful hurdler: runner-up in Fighting Fifth Hurdle at Newcastle for third year in
succession: tended to jump left in two 4-runner novice chases at Sedgefield in March,
easily landed odds first time and about to win again when falling heavily last second
occasion: stays 21f: acts on heavy and good to firm going: tried blinkered (not since
1999): often front runner but is effective ridden more patiently. *N. G. Richards*

THE FULL NELSON (IRE)   8 b. or br.g. Supreme Leader – Quivering Melody   **h78 ?**
(Lord Ha Ha) [2002/3 22vᵖᵘ 20v⁶ 22d 22s 22d 24s⁴ 22v⁶ 25s Mar 10] workmanlike geld-

ing: poor maiden hurdler: stays 2¾m: raced on going softer than good (acts on heavy): visored/blinkered last 4 starts. *Mrs Jane Galpin*

THE FUNKY MONKEY (IRE) 7 b.g. Roselier (FR) – Rumups Debut (IRE) (Good Thyne (USA)) [2002/3 F–: F17g² F17d 20sᵖᵘ Mar 6] easily best effort in bumpers when length second to Jackson's Bay at Carlisle: jumped poorly on hurdling debut. *A. Parker* — **h–** **F86**

THE GAMBLING LADY 7 b. or br.m. General Gambul – Coach Rd Express (Pony Express) [2002/3 h–: 24vᵖᵘ 21vᶠ Jan 23] leggy, lengthy mare: no form over hurdles: tried tongue tied. *C. Tizzard* — **h–**

THE GATHERER (IRE) 9 b.g. Be My Native (USA) – Reapers Run (Deep Run) [2002/3 h137: 16gᶠ c17sᶠ c16s³ c16dᶠ 17g Mar 13] good-topped gelding: useful hurdler, found nothing off bridle when well held in valuable event at Cheltenham final start: fell 3 times earlier in season, including twice over fences, when in lead and travelling well when coming down 3 out in strongly-contested maiden won by One Night Out at Fairyhouse on chasing debut: should stay 2½m: acts on soft and good to firm going: usually held up. *A. L. T. Moore, Ireland* — **c127** **h–**

THE GENE GENIE 8 b.g. Syrtos – Sally Maxwell (Roscoe Blake) [2002/3 h96: c17d⁵ c19s⁵ 16d³ 17v² Dec 28] workmanlike gelding: modest handicap hurdler: not fluent both starts over fences: effective at 2m, barely stays 2¾m: raced mainly on good going or softer (acts on heavy): tried visored. *R. J. Hodges* — **c85** **h94**

THE GOPHER (IRE) 14 ch.g. General View – Egg Shells (Miami Springs) [2002/3 c96, h–: c23m⁵ c23m⁴ c26m* c26m* c26gᵖᵘ Oct 21] sturdy gelding: fair handicap chaser: won at Southwell in August and Plumpton in September: stays 4m: has won on soft going, much better form on good or firmer (acts on firm): best in blinkers: lazy. *D. J. Wintle* — **c103** **h–**

THE GRANBY (IRE) 9 b.g. Insan (USA) – Elteetee (Paddy's Stream) [2002/3 c119+, h–: 24m⁶ 23s⁴ 24g 24d³ Mar 1] leggy gelding: fairly useful hurdler/chaser: stays 3m: acts on soft and good to firm going. *Mrs M. Reveley* — **c–** **h119**

THE GRANDSON (IRE) 8 b.g. Husyan (USA) – Tarary (Boreen (FR)) [2002/3 h–: 19sᵖᵘ 24gᵖᵘ Aug 24] no sign of ability. *S. T. Lewis* — **h–**

THE GREENKEEPER (IRE) 10 b.g. Beau Sher – Hurricane Hattie (Strong Gale) [2002/3 c–, h–: c26gᶠ Apr 29] lightly raced and no form. *C. Tizzard* — **c–** **h–**

THE GREY BARON 6 gr.g. Baron Blakeney – Topsy Bee (Be Friendly) [2002/3 c24dᵖᵘ c23sᵖᵘ Jan 29] fifth foal: half-brother to fair hurdler/chaser Gottabe (by Gunner B), stays 25f, and fair chaser up to 25f Oscar Wilde (by Arctic Lord): dam, no worthwhile form, half-sister to dam of smart chaser Young Spartacus: tongue tied, showed nothing in 2 outings over fences. *A. Ennis* — **c–**

THE GREY BUTLER (IRE) 6 gr.g. Roselier (FR) – Georgic (Tumble Gold) [2002/3 F16v³ F16g⁴ Apr 2] workmanlike gelding: first known foal: dam temperamental winning hurdler/chaser, best at 2m: fair form when in frame in 2 bumpers at Ascot. *B. De Haan* — **F89**

THE GREY DYER (IRE) 9 gr.g. Roselier (FR) – Tawny Kate (IRE) (Crash Course) [2002/3 c102, h105: c20s² c24dᶠ c25d* c33vᵖᵘ c20vᵖᵘ c25g² Apr 14] lengthy, angular gelding: fair hurdler: best effort over fences when winning handicap at Ayr in December by 3 lengths from Historg: had very tough race next time, found less than seemed likely final outing: stays 25f: raced mainly on going softer than good (acts on heavy). *L. Lungo* — **c116** **h–**

THE GUINEA STAMP 4 b.g. Overbury (IRE) – Gagajulu (Al Hareb (USA)) [2002/3 F16s F16s 17sᵖᵘ 17gᵖᵘ Mar 17] second foal: dam 2-y-o 5f winner: no sign of ability: sold 900 gns Doncaster March Sales. *S. A. Brookshaw* — **h–** **F–**

THE GUY (IRE) 5 b.g. Old Vic – Burn Again (Adonijah) [2002/3 F16f⁴ F16s* F16s³ 16v* 16s⁵ Jan 11] first foal: dam behind in bumper: progressive form in bumpers, winning at Cork in November: fair form both starts over hurdles, winning maiden at Punchestown in December: raced at 2m: acts on heavy going. *M. J. P. O'Brien, Ireland* — **h105** **F100**

THE HEARTY JOKER (IRE) 8 b.g. Broken Hearted – Furryway (Furry Glen) [2002/3 c65, h–: c20d² c21f⁴ c20f³ c21m² c20d³ c21d² c20d³ c19d⁶ Jan 16] lengthy gelding: poor maiden chaser: stays 21f: acts on firm and good to soft going (pulled up only start on softer): front runner. *B. G. Powell* — **c72** **h–**

THE HONEY GUIDE 7 gr.g. Homo Sapien – The Whirlie Weevil (Scallywag) [2002/3 F17d 20gᵖᵘ Apr 23] first foal: dam, modest novice hurdler who stayed 2¾m, half-sister to fairly useful chasers Earlymorning Light, best around 2½m, and Real Tonic, stayed 25f: no show in bumper and maiden hurdle 6 months apart. *Mrs L. B. Normile* — **h–** **F–**

905

THEICECREAMMAN (IRE) 6 ch.g. Glacial Storm (USA) – Miss Cornetto (IRE) **h93**
(Parliament) [2002/3 F19s⁶ F16s³ 16s⁵ F18s⁶ 20s³ 19v 20v* 19m³ Apr 21] ex-Irish **F89**
gelding: first foal: dam unraced half-sister to useful jumper up to 2½m Buckminster and
one-time useful hurdler Vanilla Man, stays 3m: fair form at best in bumpers: modest
hurdler: won 20-runner maiden at Clonmel in February, final outing for L. Young: will
stay beyond 2½m: raced mainly on soft/heavy going. *G. Prodromou*

THE JOKER (IRE) 5 ch.g. Montelimar (USA) – How Doudo (Oats) [2002/3 F18m⁵ **F101**
F18s* F16v* F16v⁴ Feb 8] third foal: dam won 2½m claiming hurdle, half-sister to fairly
useful staying hurdler Mynah Key: never placed to challenge in bumper on debut (trainer
fined, jockey and horse banned): won similar events at Downpatrick in December and
Ayr (fairly useful form, beat Great Chaos 2½ lengths) in January: raced freely final
outing: will be suited by 2½m+. *J. K. Magee, Ireland*

THE KERRY REBEL (IRE) 10 b.g. Gallant Knight – Symphony Orchestra (Orch- **c66**
estra) [2002/3 c–, h–: 24gpu 24d 24g c21g⁴ c26f³ c24m² Sep 14] lengthy, sparely-made **h–**
gelding: poor maiden jumper, left R. Curtis after second start: stayed 3¼m: acted on firm
ground: tried blinkered: dead. *Miss G. Browne*

THE KEW TOUR (IRE) 7 ch.g. Un Desperado (FR) – Drivers Bureau (Proverb) **h107**
[2002/3 25d* 20g* 24g² Apr 24] ex-Irish gelding: fourth foal: half-brother to winning
pointer by Town And Country: dam placed in bumper: winning pointer: bought out of
D. Wachman's stable 11,000 gns Doncaster May Sales: much improved over hurdles,
won conditional jockeys handicap and novice at Wetherby in March: best effort when
second of 5 to Brooklyn Breeze in novice at Perth: stays 25f: front runner. *Mrs S. J. Smith*

THE LAIRD'S ENTRY (IRE) 8 b.g. King's Ride – Balancing Act (Balinger) **h–**
[2002/3 h111, F90: 22g⁶ May 8] big gelding: chasing type: fair form when winning
novice hurdle in 2001/2: left impression all not well final start that season and on
reappearance: should stay beyond 19f: acts on soft going. *L. Lungo*

THE LAMBTON WORM 9 b.g. Superpower – Springwell (Miami Springs) [2002/3 **c–**
h75: 17m⁶ c21gpu Jun 29] poor 2m novice hurdler: showed nothing on chasing debut: acts **h68**
on soft and good to firm going. *G. F. Edwards*

THE LAND AGENT 12 b.g. Town And Country – Notinhand (Nearly A Hand) **c104**
[2002/3 c114, h–: c25f⁴ c21g³ c20m* c21g c20d³ c27spu c18g⁶ c21d⁴ c20s³ c19m* Apr **h–**
21] rangy gelding: fair handicap chaser nowadays: won at Stratford in June and Hereford
in April: barely stays 25f: acts on heavy and good to firm going: has worn cheekpieces.
J. W. Mullins

THE LAST CAST 4 ch.g. Prince of Birds (USA) – Atan's Gem (USA) (Sharpen Up) **h116**
[2002/3 16d⁵ 16s³ 17s* 17s* 17v¹ Jan 1] workmanlike gelding: fair maiden on Flat (stays
1¼m): generally progressive form in juvenile hurdles: made virtually all when winning
at Bangor in November, Market Rasen in December and Cheltenham in January: fairly
useful effort when beating Serotonin 17 lengths at last-named, responding gamely when
left clear soon after last: raced around 2m on going softer than good (acts on heavy).
C. R. Egerton

THE LAST MOHICAN 4 b.g. Common Grounds – Arndilly (Robellino (USA)) **h87**
[2002/3 16d⁴ 16v³ 16d⁵ 19g² 17g² 16d 21m⁴ Apr 21] poor maiden on Flat (stays 1½m):
modest juvenile hurdler: stays 21f. *P. Howling*

THE LAST SHOUT (IRE) 10 b.g. Yashgan – Apia Sunshine (Simbir) [2002/3 c21gpu **c–**
May 1] ex-Irish gelding: well beaten only outing over hurdles: poor pointer, won maiden **h–**
in 2002: always well behind in maiden hunter chase. *Mrs Mair Hughes*

THE LEADER 10 b.g. Ardross – Leading Line (Leading Man) [2002/3 c93, h–: c16g **c92**
c26v² c24v c16v* c18s c16spu Mar 7] rangy gelding: modest and inconsistent handicap **h–**
chaser: won 5-runner race at Folkestone (for third consecutive year) in January: effective
around 2m to 3¼m: raced on good going or softer (acts on heavy): often weak finisher.
P. R. Chamings

THE LEAZES 4 b.g. Shaamit (IRE) – Air of Elegance (Elegant Air) [2002/3 F16gpu **F–**
F17gpu Apr 21] first foal: dam, maiden, from family of top-class staying chaser Kildimo,
Grand National winner Rubstic and very smart staying hurdler Baydon Star: pulled up in
2 bumpers, hung badly right on debut. *A. Dickman*

THE LYME VOLUNTEER (IRE) 6 b.m. Zaffaran (USA) – Dooley O'Brien (The **h105 +**
Parson) [2002/3 F73: F18m 18m⁵ 19f³ 25m³ 24s² 24d* 24v² 24d⁵ 26m* Apr 21] useful- **F–**
looking mare: twice-raced in bumpers: progressed into fair hurdler, won 15-runner
handicap at Ludlow in November and 6-runner novice at Hereford (by 1¼ lengths from
Lodestar) in April: suited by 3m+: acts on heavy and good to firm going. *O. Sherwood*

THE MAJOR (NZ) 10 ch.g. Try To Stop Me – Equation (NZ) (Palatable (USA)) [2002/3 c126: c21g^{pu} c20m^3 c20d^5 c27d^F Nov 24] tall gelding: fairly useful handicap chaser in 2001/2 for Mrs M. Reveley: not so good in 2002/3, best effort when third of 4 finishers at Cheltenham: stays 3m: best efforts on going softer than good (acts on heavy): idles, and held up: makes mistakes. *J. R. Cornwall* **c114 x**

THEMANFROMCARLISLE 7 br.g. Jupiter Island – Country Mistress (Town And Country) [2002/3 F78: c16s^{pu} 16g 19d 20m* 21m^4 Apr 10] tall gelding: won point in 2002: pulled up on steeplechasing debut: best effort over hurdles when making all in 5-runner novice at Fontwell in March: stays 21f: acts on good to firm going: has taken good hold: possibly best on left-handed tracks. *M. Pitman* **c–**
h90

THE MANSE BRAE (IRE) 7 b.g. Roselier (FR) – Decent Preacher (Decent Fellow) [2002/3 h111+: c20m* 24d^5 c21d^6 c24g* c25d* Feb 25] good-bodied gelding: fair hurdler: similar form over fences, successful on 3 of 4 starts, in novices at Bangor in September, Musselburgh in January (tended to jump left) and Catterick in February: will prove best at 3m+: acts on good to firm and good to soft going: has worn cheekpieces: a hard ride. *J. M. Jefferson* **c114**
h103

THE MASARETI KID (IRE) 6 b.g. Commanche Run – Little Crack (IRE) (Lancastrian) [2002/3 F93: F16f* 22m^5 Oct 6] successful twice in bumpers at Hexham, beating Rosidavis by head on reappearance in September: odds on, only fifth of 10 in novice at Kelso on hurdling debut (reportedly hung left): should stay 2¾m. *G. A. Swinbank* **h–**
F93

THE MERRIEMEADE 7 b.m. Mahrajan – Salmon Spirit (Big Deal) [2002/3 21d^F Jan 16] half-sister to winning chaser around 2m Bert House (by Brianston Zipper): dam unraced: disputing lead when falling 5 out in mares maiden hurdle at Ludlow on debut: dead. *C. J. Down* **h–**

THE MERRY MASON (IRE) 7 b.g. Roselier (FR) – Busters Lodge (Antwerp City) [2002/3 h65: 24g* 25m* Oct 16] leggy, good-topped gelding: poor form when winning handicaps at Market Rasen (conditional jockeys) and Wetherby (novice, stayed on dourly having been off bridle long way) in October: likely to prove best given thorough test of stamina: acts on good to firm going: lazy. *J. M. Jefferson* **h85**

THE MIGHTY FLYNN 4 ch.g. Botanic (USA) – Owdbetts (IRE) (High Estate) [2002/3 F16d Apr 25] 12,000 3-y-o: second foal: half-brother to French 6f and 1m winner Ratio (by Pivotal): dam 7f and 1¼m winner: tailed off after taking strong hold in bumper on debut. *P. Monteith* **F–**

THE MINER 5 ch.g. Hatim (USA) – Glen Morvern (Carlingford Castle) [2002/3 F16g^3 F17g^5 Apr 21] second foal: dam 2¼m hurdle winner: fair form in bumpers at Perth and Carlisle 7 months apart. *Miss S. E. Forster* **F83**

THE MINISTER (IRE) 14 br.g. Black Minstrel – Miss Hi-Land (Tyrant (USA)) [2002/3 c25m^6 Jun 1] big, good-topped gelding: winning chaser: fair pointer: jumped poorly back in handicap at Hexham in June: probably stays 27f: acts on firm going. *Miss T. Jackson* **c–**
h–

THE MOG 4 b.g. Atraf – Safe Secret (Seclude (USA)) [2002/3 17d 20m^2 17g^{pu} Mar 29] modest on all-weather, poor on turf on Flat (stays 7f, ungenuine): form over hurdles only when 10 lengths second to easy winner Jacopo in weakly-contested maiden at Southwell, pulling hard: tongue tied. *S. R. Bowring* **h64**

THE MOYNE MACHINE (IRE) 7 b.m. Elbio – Victoria Hall (Hallgate) [2002/3 c16s c16d^6 c20v^3 c16s^3 c20s^5 c16v^2 c18s* c21s^4 Mar 15] leggy, lengthy mare: one-time fair maiden on Flat: winning hurdler: modest over fences, won mares maiden at Thurles in March: not fluent when tailed off in valuable mares novice handicap at Uttoxeter 9 days later: stays 2½m: acts on heavy going: tried tongue tied. *T. Doyle, Ireland* **c97**
h–

THE NAMES BOND 5 b.g. Tragic Role (USA) – Artistic Licence (High Top) [2002/3 16d^5 17s^3 16g^4 16d^2 20v^F Feb 13] close-coupled gelding: modest maiden hurdler: raced mainly around 2m (tired when fell last over testing 2½m): acts on soft and good to firm going: races prominently. *Andrew Turnell* **h89**

THE NEGOTIATOR 9 ch.g. Nebos (GER) – Baie Des Anges (Pas de Seul) [2002/3 c108, h87: c16m^5 c16m^2 c20d* c16m^2 c20d^{pu} c16s^{pu} c20v^F c17g^3 c20g^4 Apr 23] workmanlike gelding: fair chaser: won 4-runner intermediate at Wetherby in May: largely out of sorts afterwards: stays 2¾m, at least as effective at shorter: has form on soft/heavy going, raced mainly on firmer nowadays (acts on firm): has had tongue tied: usually races prominently. *M. A. Barnes* **c114**
h–

THE NELSON TOUCH 6 b.g. Past Glories – Kellys Special (Netherkelly) [2002/3 **h– x** h–, F–: 21s^{pu} 20s 20s^{pu} Dec 27] rather unfurnished gelding: little form in novice hurdles: poor jumper. *J. W. Mullins*

THE NEWSMAN (IRE) 11 b.g. Homo Sapien – Miller Fall's (Stubbs Gazette) **c106** [2002/3 c84, h–: c21g^2 c20m^3 c17m* c17d^6 c20d* c18s* c19g^3 c18f* Apr 24] tall, useful- **h–** looking gelding: fair chaser: had good season, winning handicaps (first 3 novices) at Plumpton (first run after leaving Miss S. Edwards) in October and Fontwell in December, March and April: stays 21f: probably acts on any going: tried blinkered. *G. Wareham*

THE NOBLE MOOR (IRE) 7 br.g. Euphemism – Who Says (IRE) (Amazing Bust) **h–** [2002/3 F75: 16m 21s^{pu} Jan 3] tall gelding: little sign of ability: reportedly distressed final start. *T. R. George*

THE NOMAD 7 b.g. Nomadic Way (USA) – Bubbling (Tremblant) [2002/3 h96, F90: **h108** 20g^2 17d* 17s* 20v* 23d^{pu} 20g* Apr 1] workmanlike gelding: fair novice hurdler: won at Sedgefield in October, Market Rasen (amateurs, fortunate) in November, Wetherby in December and Newcastle (handicap) in April: should stay beyond 2½m: acts on heavy and good to firm going: front runner: genuine. *M. W. Easterby*

THE NORWICH FLY (IRE) 6 b.m. Norwich – The Race Fly (Pollerton) [2002/3 **F95** F16d* F16v^4 F16m^2 Mar 22] leggy ex-Irish mare: half-sister to fair hurdler/one-time fairly useful chaser Champagne Native (by Be My Native), stays 21f, and fair 2½m hurdler Fly Rosey (by Roselier): dam never ran: in frame all 3 starts in bumpers, won at Thurles on debut in October: off 4½ months and left P. Doyle, improved form when ¾-length second of 18 to Yardbird at Newbury: will stay beyond 2m. *Miss E. C. Lavelle*

THE OCTOBER MAN 6 ch.g. Afzal – Florence May (Grange Melody) [2002/3 16d **h71** 16s 16g Nov 20] 15,000 4-y-o: compact gelding: sixth foal: half-brother to fairly useful hurdler/fair chaser Homme de Fer (by Arctic Lord), stays 25f, and winning chaser Flash Gordon (by Gildoran), probably stays 3m: dam, winning pointer/steeplechaser, suited by test of stamina: signs of only a little ability in 3 novice hurdles: bred to be suited by much stiffer test of stamina. *Jonjo O'Neill*

THE ONLY OPTION (IRE) 8 b.m. Phardante (FR) – Sirrah Madam (Tug of War) **h–** [2002/3 h62: 24d^5 23d^{pu} May 23] strong mare: won maiden point in 2002: little form over hurdles: sold 1,200 gns Doncaster May Sales. *R. Tate*

THE OTHER MAN (IRE) 13 b.g. Remainder Man – Amelioras Gran (Northern **c–** Guest (USA)) [2002/3 c25d^{pu} c25d c25g^6 May 24] sturdy gelding: of little account. **h–** *Miss L. C. Siddall*

THE PARSONS DINGLE 8 ch.g. Le Moss – Not Enough (Balinger) [2002/3 h86: **c100** c16g c16d^4 c17v* c17v^4 c18m^{pu} Mar 22] workmanlike gelding: modest form over **h–** hurdles: best effort over fences when winning novice handicap at Bangor in February: ran poorly both subsequent starts: should stay 2½m: acts on heavy going (won bumper on good to firm). *P. R. Webber*

THE PENNYS DROPPED (IRE) 6 ch.g. Bob's Return (IRE) – Shuil Alainn **h100** (Levanter) [2002/3 F79: F16d F18d^2 19g 17s^F 17d^2 Mar 2] sturdy gelding: best effort in **F95** bumpers when runner-up to Novi Sad in maiden at Plumpton: kept on well after mistake 2 out when 1¾ lengths second of 17 to Our Armageddon in novice hurdle at Carlisle: will stay 2½m: raced on good going or softer. *Jonjo O'Neill*

THE PHAIR CRIER (IRE) 8 ch.g. Phardante (FR) – Maul-More (Deep Run) **h–** [2002/3 h123: 20s 24d^{pu} Mar 15] good-topped gelding: fairly useful form when winning novice hurdle at Newcastle in 2001/2: very disappointing all 4 starts since: should stay beyond 3m: raced on good going or softer (acts on soft): reportedly suffers breathing problems. *L. Lungo*

THEPOINTABOUTITIS (IRE) 6 ch.g. Case Law – Boston View (IRE) (Simply **h105** Great (FR)) [2002/3 17m^4 16f* 16g^5 17d^4 16d^6 Nov 15] compact gelding: fairly useful on Flat (stays 1½m) at 4 yrs: fair novice hurdler: won at Clonmel (maiden) in September and Gowran (by 1½ lengths from Stashedaway in 20-runner event) in October: creditable effort in face of stiff task when sixth of 12 to Mutakarrim in Grade 2 at Cheltenham: raced around 2m: acts on firm and soft going, yet to race on heavy. *John F. Gleeson, Ireland*

THE PREACHER MAN (IRE) 8 b.g. Be My Native (USA) – Frankford Run (Deep **c–** Run) [2002/3 c25d^{ur} Mar 1] IR 44,000 4-y-o: ex-Irish gelding: seventh foal: half-brother **h–** to 3 winners, notably top-class chaser Sound Man (by Kemal), stayed 2½m: dam placed in Irish bumper and over hurdles: some promise in novice hurdle and bumper first 2 starts, failed to progress: sold out of C. Roche's stable 5,000 gns Doncaster October (2001)

Sales: won maiden point in February: prominent when unseating fifteenth in novice at Kelso on hunter chase debut. *V. Thompson*

THE PREMIER CAT (IRE) 7 b.g. Glacial Storm (USA) – Carraigaloe (Little Buskins) [2002/3 h124, F–: c20s⁶ c17s* c20s³ c24v² c20v* c24d* c24v² Mar 8] fairly useful hurdler: useful novice chaser: won maiden at Clonmel in November and minor event there (fourth course success) and Grade 3 novice at Navan (beat Intelligent by 4½ lengths) in February: distant second to Native Sessions in novice handicap at latter course final start: will prove best at 2½m+: raced on going softer than good (acts on heavy): sound-jumping front runner. *T. Cahill, Ireland* **c138 h–**

THE PROJECT 7 b.g. Prince of Darkness (IRE) – Kerry Calluna (Celtic Cone) [2002/3 F–: F16d 17s 16gᵖᵘ 22dᵖᵘ Feb 6] tall, lengthy, angular gelding: little sign of ability. *J. C. Fox* **h– F–**

THE PROOF 6 b.g. Rudimentary (USA) – Indubitable (Sharpo) [2002/3 h–: 19g⁵ 17f May 15] lengthy, sparely-made gelding: little form on Flat or in 3 starts over hurdles. *G. B. Balding* **h69 ?**

THE QUADS 11 b.g. Tinoco – Queen's Royale (Tobrouk (FR)) [2002/3 c117, h117: c26sᵖᵘ c31d² c31d* c29vᵖᵘ c26v⁵ c32gᵘʳ Mar 21] leggy gelding: winning hurdler: fairly useful chaser: form in 2002/3 only in cross-country races at Cheltenham second and third starts, winning 10-runner handicap in December by 10 lengths from Eoins Pride: stays 31f: acts on good to firm and heavy going: blinkered last 4 outings: usually tongue tied. *Ferdy Murphy* **c128 ? h–**

THEREALBANDIT (IRE) 6 b.g. Torus – Sunrise Highway VII (Damsire Unregistered) [2002/3 19d 17s⁶ 20d³ 22g* Apr 21] 18,000 4-y-o: half-brother to useful hurdler/chaser The Bajan Bandit (by Commanche Run) and winning hurdler/chaser up to 3m Hennessy Feeds (by Mazaad): dam, 2m winner on Flat/bumper winner, from family of Belmont King and Andy Pandy: progressive hurdler, easily landed odds in handicap at Newton Abbot in April: will stay 3m. *M. C. Pipe* **h107 +**

THE REBEL LADY (IRE) 6 br.m. Mister Lord (USA) – Arborfield Brook (Over The River (FR)) [2002/3 18s⁶ 21d 22d³ 21m 24m³ Apr 10] tall, rather unfurnished mare: third foal: half-sister to winning pointer by Phardante: dam unraced: fourth on first of 2 starts in maiden Irish points in 2002: modest form when placed twice in novice hurdles: stays 3m. *Miss H. C. Knight* **h87 +**

THE RELIC (NZ) 8 b.g. Rua Rukuna (NZ) – Fine Sky (NZ) (Mussorgsky) [2002/3 17vᵖᵘ Nov 6] unplaced in 3 maidens up to 1m on Flat in New Zealand at 4/5 yrs, subsequently winning eventer: weakened quickly having led until fifth in novice at Newton Abbot on hurdling debut. *Miss H. C. Knight* **h–**

THE RENDERER 7 b.g. Homo Sapien – Kingsley (Kings Lake (USA)) [2002/3 F16m Jul 24] second foal: dam won from 1½m to 2m on Flat: showed little in bumper on debut. *Miss S. J. Wilton* **F–**

THE RIGHT CUE (IRE) 9 b.g. Torus – Bo Reynella (IRE) (Le Bavard (FR)) [2002/3 h61: 20g 19mᵖᵘ Jun 4] little form: tried blinkered. *P. R. Rodford* **h–**

THE RILE (IRE) 9 ch.g. Alphabatim (USA) – Donna Chimene (Royal Gunner (USA)) [2002/3 h101?: 20d⁵ 18s⁵ 20s* c21v* c20v² c20d* Mar 7] strong, lengthy gelding: fair handicap hurdler: wide-margin winner of conditional jockeys event at Wetherby in November: successful in novices on 2 of 3 starts over fences at Ayr, comfortably beating Falchion both times: will be suited by 3m: raced mainly on going softer than good (acts on heavy): has won 3 times at Carlisle: jumps fences soundly and probably capable of better still. *L. Lungo* **c116 + h101**

THE RIVER JOKER (IRE) 7 ch.g. Over The River (FR) – Augustaeliza (IRE) (Callernish) [2002/3 h67: 26s* 20s² 24v⁶ 24vᵖᵘ 25d Feb 25] lengthy, angular gelding: will make a chaser: poor handicap hurdler: improved form when winning at Huntingdon in November: poor efforts last 3 starts: stays 3¼m well: acts on soft going. *John R. Upson* **h80**

THE ROAN RUNNER 5 gr.g. Nalchik (USA) – Grey Runner (Crofthall) [2002/3 16m 20gᵖᵘ 20dᵖᵘ Oct 12] lengthy gelding: no form on Flat or in novice hurdles: tried visored. *B. P. J. Baugh* **h–**

THE ROUNDSILLS 9 ch.g. Handsome Sailor – Eye Sight (Roscoe Blake) [2002/3 c73, h–: 16sᵖᵘ c16dᵖᵘ Dec 26] lengthy, sparely-made gelding: winning 2m chaser, lightly raced and little form since 1999/00. *M. Mullineaux* **c– h–**

THE SAWDUST KID 9 ch.g. River God (USA) – Susie's Money (Seymour Hicks (FR)) [2002/3 h96d: c25f⁵ c26gᵖᵘ c21m² c23g⁵ c26m* c26m* c26m* c22g² c24m⁵ **c93 h–**

c24v^{pu} c20d⁴ c26s^{pu} c26f⁶ Apr 24] good-bodied gelding: winning hurdler: modest chaser: won weak handicaps at Fontwell (novice) in August and Southwell and Fontwell (novice) in September: stays 3¼m: acts on firm going, possibly not on softer than good: blinkered fourth outing. *R. H. Buckler*

THE SECRETARY (IRE) 6 b.m. Shernazar – Exemplary Fashion (Master Owen) **h75**
[2002/3 F16g³ 20s³ 21s^{pu} 16s⁶ 24s 24g^{pu} Apr 21] IR 1,000 3-y-o: half-sister to winning **F81**
pointers by Roselier and Over The River: dam, maiden pointer, half-sister to dam of top-class 2½m chaser Dublin Flyer: better effort in bumpers (trained on debut by J. Burns) when third at Worcester on reappearance: form over hurdles only when third of 6 finishers in mares novice at Bangor. *Mrs H. Dalton*

THESEUS (IRE) 7 b.g. Danehill (USA) – Graecia Magna (USA) (Private Account **c107**
(USA)) [2002/3 h124: c17d c17s³ c16m⁴ c20m² c17d c17m³ c16g* c17m* c16f³ c16s **h–**
c17d³ Oct 19] useful-looking gelding: fairly useful hurdler: fair chaser: won maiden at Tralee in August and handicap at Killarney in September: below form last 2 starts: stays easy 2½m: acts on firm and soft going. *P. Hughes, Ireland*

THESIS (IRE) 5 ch.g. Definite Article – Chouette (Try My Best (USA)) [2002/3 17s² **h110**
17s² 16s³ 16d⁶ Apr 4] leggy gelding: fairly useful on Flat (stays 1¼m), sold out of J. Osborne's stable 27,000 gns Newmarket Autumn Sales: fair novice hurdler: runner-up first 2 starts, beaten ¾ length by Desert Air at Taunton on debut: stiff task and made mistakes in Grade 2 at Aintree final outing: likely to prove best around 2m: raced mainly on soft going (may prove suited by less testing conditions). *Miss Venetia Williams*

THE SISTER 6 b.m. Alflora (IRE) – Donna Farina (Little Buskins) [2002/3 20d⁵ 20d⁴ **h79**
Mar 6] half-sister to fairly useful chaser Mountain Path, stayed 3¼m, and winning pointer Don Royal (both by Rakaposhi King): dam, winning hurdler/chaser who stayed 2½m, half-sister to smart staying chaser Realt Na Nona and useful 2m to 2½m hurdler The Hacienderos: some promise when fifth of 13 to Madge Carroll in mares novice hurdle at Huntingdon on debut: disappointing favourite (not fluent) in similar event at Wetherby 12 weeks later: likely to stay beyond 2½m. *Jonjo O'Neill*

THE SKY IS BLUE 7 ch.g. Alflora (IRE) – Mistress Boreen (Boreen (FR)) [2002/3 **c–**
c–, h–: c16d⁴ c21v^{pu} c24g^{pu} Apr 12] sturdy gelding: no form over jumps: reportedly **h–**
distressed final outing: tried tongue tied. *Mrs P. Townsley*

THE SLEEPER 7 b.g. Perpendicular – Distant Cherry (General Ironside) [2002/3 F–: **h–**
F17d 16d 21v 16d Mar 5] first sign of ability when seventh of 21 in novice hurdle at **F–**
Catterick final start, mistake and left behind after 3 out. *H. P. Hogarth*

THE STAFFORD MARE (IRE) 6 b.m. Leading Counsel (USA) – Royal Desire **F–**
(Royal Match) [2002/3 F16s F17s F16d Mar 19] sturdy mare: half-sister to several winners, including fairly useful hurdlers/winning chasers by Nordance, Noels Dancer, stays 3m, and Nordic Prince, stays 3¼m: dam unraced: well held in 3 bumpers. *J. G. M. O'Shea*

THE STAGGERY BOY (IRE) 7 b.g. Shalford (IRE) – Murroe Star (Glenstal **c92**
(USA)) [2002/3 h89: c17g² c16m² c16g⁵ c19v^{pu} c16g⁴ c20m⁴ Mar 31] sturdy gelding: **h–**
modest hurdler/maiden chaser: raced mainly around 2m (quickly beaten after 3 out over 2½m final start): acts on good to firm and good to soft going: often tongue tied. *M. R. Hoad*

THE TALLET 5 ch.g. Alflora (IRE) – Bustle'em (IRE) (Burslem) [2002/3 17s⁵ Feb **h–**
7] second foal: dam, 1m winner, out of half-sister to smart staying hurdler Sandalay: no show in novice hurdle on debut. *D. McCain*

THE TALL GUY (IRE) 7 b. or br.g. Zaffaran (USA) – Mullangale (Strong Gale) **c–**
[2002/3 h–, F91: 25m⁵ c19s^{pu} c25d^F Feb 23] tall gelding: bumper winner: form in novice **h91**
hurdles only on reappearance: failed to complete both starts over fences: stays 25f: acts on good to firm going: tongue tied. *N. A. Twiston-Davies*

THE TEUCHTER 4 b.g. First Trump – Barefoot Landing (USA) (Cozzene (USA)) **h–**
[2002/3 16v 16d 17g⁶ Mar 16] medium-sized gelding: modest middle-distance maiden on Flat, sold out of M. Johnston's stable 4,000 gns Newmarket Autumn Sales: little show in 3 juvenile hurdles. *N. A. Dunger*

THE TILE BARON (IRE) 6 b.g. Little Bighorn – Elegant Miss (Prince Tenderfoot **h–**
(USA)) [2002/3 F70: 16v 16s 17v Jan 21] medium-sized gelding: poor form in bumper: well held all 3 outings over hurdles. *L. Lungo*

THE TIMBERMAN 11 gr.g. Grey Desire – Heldigvis (Hot Grove) [2002/3 c–, h–: **c–**
c21g^F May 3] workmanlike gelding: no form over hurdles: modest pointer, successful in **h–**
2-runner race in April: held when falling in 2 hunter chases: often tongue tied. *Tim Butt*

THE TINKER 8 b.g. Nomadic Way (USA) – Miss Tino (Relkino) [2002/3 c–, h–: c16dᶠ c22vᵘʳ c24gᶠ c16g³ c16g² c17dᶠ c16g⁴ Mar 29] maiden hurdler: fair novice chaser: should stay beyond 2½m: acts on good to soft going: often let down by jumping (would have won on reappearance but for falling last). *Mrs S. C. Bradburne* — c98 x h–

THE TOFF 4 b.f. Overbury (IRE) – Fenian Court (IRE) (John French) [2002/3 F14d F16s⁶ 19d Feb 10] small, stocky filly: first foal: dam, poor 2m hurdler, half-sister to fairly useful 2m hurdlers Kenobico and Penny Native: well held in bumpers and maiden claiming hurdle (visored). *P. D. Evans* — h– F64

THE TUBE (IRE) 5 b.m. Royal Abjar (USA) – Grandeur And Grace (USA) (Septieme Ciel (USA)) [2002/3 h–: 19g 16m 17g⁴ Jul 31] little form on Flat or over hurdles. *P. Bowen* — h–

THE VANLINERS (HOL) 4 b.g. Kadeed (IRE) – For Eve (Forzando) [2002/3 16m Oct 6] second foal: dam never ran: behind in juvenile hurdle on debut. *Mrs H. O. Graham* — h–

THE VILLAGER (IRE) 7 br.g. Zaffaran (USA) – Kitty Wren (Warpath) [2002/3 h123, F105: 20d* c24v* c25d³ c20v² c19d* c25dᵖᵘ Apr 4] workmanlike gelding: bumper winner: fairly useful hurdler, landed odds in handicap at Chepstow in October: at least as good over fences, won novices at Bangor in November and Exeter (beat Bonus Bridge ½ length in 15-runner event) in January: ran much better than pulled up suggests in handicap at Aintree, taking good hold, left in front 4 out but strongly pressed when misjudging next (jumped well otherwise): probably finds 19f a minimum, and will stay beyond 25f: acts on good to firm and heavy going: may yet progress further. *D. J. Caro* — c127 + h117 +

THE WARRIOR (IRE) 7 gr.g. Willie Joe (IRE) – Fast And Straight (IRE) (Shirley Heights) [2002/3 h–, F–: 20mˢᵘ 16g May 24] tall gelding: no form. *T. P. McGovern* — h–

THE WELDER 9 b.g. Buckley – Crystal Run VII (Damsire Unregistered) [2002/3 c–, h–: c21gᵖᵘ Apr 19] workmanlike gelding: no form over hurdles: second in maiden point in 2002, let down by jumping both starts in hunter chases: has had tongue tied. *V. Y. Gethin* — c– h–

THE WHOLE HOG (IRE) 14 b.g. Cataldi – Beeston (Our Babu) [2002/3 c–, h–: c25g⁶ May 8] close-coupled gelding: veteran staying chaser: second in a point in 2002: acts on firm and good to soft going. *K. Robson* — c– h–

THE WILEY KALMUCK (IRE) 9 b.g. Be My Native (USA) – Beecom Silk (English Prince) [2002/3 c93§, h–: c21m⁴ Apr 21] good-topped gelding: modest handicap hurdler/maiden chaser at best: successful 3 times (including walk-over) in points in 2003 prior to well held in novice hunter at Fakenham: stays 25f: acts on good to firm and heavy going: usually blinkered/visored: unreliable. *J. M. Turner* — c– § h–

THE WINKSTER (IRE) 9 b. or br.g. Black Minstrel – Oremus (Marisco) [2002/3 c–, h–: c21mᵖᵘ May 22] once-raced over hurdles: won maiden point in 2002: dropped right away after mistakes in novice at Folkestone on hunter chase debut: has had tongue tied. *Mrs D. M. Grissell* — c– h–

THEYDON STAR (NZ) 6 b.g. Classic Fame (USA) – Hilarity (NZ) (St Hilarion (USA)) [2002/3 h–, F72: 20m⁶ May 7] leggy gelding: sixth in bumper on debut: no form in novice hurdles: sold 3,000 gns Ascot July Sales. *Mrs N. Smith* — h–

THIEVES'GLEN 5 b.g. Teenoso (USA) – Hollow Creek (Tarqogan) [2002/3 F92: F13s⁵ F17s³ F16d⁴ Mar 10] fairly useful form in bumpers, raced freely when around 7 lengths fourth of 9 in maiden at Stratford: bred to be suited by 2½m+. *H. Morrison* — F97

THINK AGAIN (IRE) 9 b.g. Long Pond – Either Or (Boreen (FR)) [2002/3 h–: 17g⁵ 17d 20d⁵ 17s⁵ Nov 26] leggy gelding: bad maiden hurdler: probably stays 2½m: has found little. *R. Craggs* — h60

THISTHATANDTOTHER (IRE) 7 b.g. Bob Back (USA) – Baden (IRE) (Furry Glen) [2002/3 F106: 16m* 16g* 20s² 16d* 16d² 16g⁵ 16m² Apr 12] — h145

For the third successive season, the loss of Sandown's January fixture, due to waterlogging this time around, resulted in the rescheduling of the Tote Tolworth Hurdle. Ascot and Warwick had stepped in to stage this Grade 1 event in 2001 and 2002 respectively, and the latter was set to do so again until its fixture succumbed to frost. Perseverance did pay off, however, and the race eventually took place two weeks after it was originally due to be run, at Wincanton. The venue was very familiar to one of the race's seven contestants Thisthatandtother. He had already made three appearances there and been successful twice, in a bumper in his first season and in novice hurdles on his first two starts in the latest one. Thisthatandtother was sent off second favourite to make it four out of four at the course in the

Tolworth, five-time winner Puntal going off at odds on in what looked a fair renewal of the top mid-season race for two-mile novice hurdlers. The pair dominated
the race as well as the betting, Puntal as usual forcing the pace, tracked by Thisthatandtother who took a good hold. Thisthatandtother was clearly travelling the
better as they began to pull away on the long run to two out. Ridden to challenge at
the last, Thisthatandtother gained the upper hand on the run-in and went on to win
by two and a half lengths. There was a further gap of fourteen lengths back to
third-placed Self Defense, who went on to finish fourth in the Champion Hurdle.
Thisthatandtother himself finished runner-up to subsequent Champion Hurdle third
Rhinestone Cowboy on his next appearance, yet another one at Wincanton. The
race was the Kingwell Hurdle and Thisthatandtother was beaten less than two
lengths, though he was flattered, barely able to get the winner off the bridle. It was
still a smart performance by Thisthatandtother, one which confirmed him as a
leading contender for the Supreme Novices' Hurdle at Cheltenham, where he
started second favourite behind Back In Front. Thisthatandtother finished fifth
behind the impressive Back In Front though he was below form, failing to do
himself justice for the only time in his first season over hurdles. A return to open
company in the Scottish Champion Hurdle, a limited handicap run at Ayr, saw
Thisthatandtother back to form. Receiving 1 lb from the Champion Hurdle sixth In
Contrast, Thisthatandtother finished two and a half lengths second to him, hanging
left under pressure. When Thisthatandtother is seen next, it will be over fences. His
stable has a fine record with its two-mile novice chasers, and the useful-looking
Thisthatandtother has the potential to be up there with the best of them.

Thisthatandtother has been tried once over a distance beyond two miles,
when five lengths second to Coolnagorna in a Grade 2 novice run over an extended
two and a half miles at Sandown in December. He ran close to his best that day, but
was outstayed by Coolnagorna after looking to be travelling much the better before
two out. It would be no surprise if Thisthatandtother were to prove fully effective at
a bare two and a half miles when the emphasis is on speed, soft ground at Sandown

Tote Tolworth Hurdle, Wincanton—Thisthatandtother (noseband) gets the better of odds-on shot Puntal

Mr C. G. Roach's "Thisthatandtother"

Thisthatandtother (IRE) (b.g. 1996)	Bob Back (USA) (br 1981)	Roberto (b 1969)	Hail To Reason
			Bramalea
		Toter Back (ch 1967)	Carry Back
			Romantic Miss
	Baden (IRE) (b 1988)	Furry Glen (b 1971)	Wolver Hollow
			Cleftess
		St Moritz (b 1974)	Linacre
			Machete

having placed it very much on stamina. There's no reason why Thisthatandtother shouldn't stay beyond two miles judged on his pedigree. His sire Bob Back is an influence for stamina, while his dam Baden, a fairly useful Irish hurdler, stayed nineteen furlongs. Baden won three races over hurdles, including a Grade 2 handicap at Fairyhouse, and is a sister to the fairly useful two-mile hurdler/chaser Seon. Their dam St Moritz won both on the Flat and over hurdles in Ireland, and, appropriately, was also successful over jumps in Switzerland. Thisthatandtother is Baden's first foal. Her second, Polar Scout (by Arctic Lord), has shown just modest form at up to two and a half miles over hurdles in Ireland, and is still a maiden. Her then three-year-old filly by Jolly Jake fetched €32,000 at the 2002 Derby Sale. Thisthatandtother has shown his form on ground ranging from good to firm to soft. *P. F. Nicholls*

THIS THYNE   7 b.m. Good Thyne (USA) – Dalkey Sound (Crash Course) [2002/3 **h98** h–, F79: 16d⁶ 23d 22d 26m⁶ 24d* 25m² 23d² 20d² 20sᶠ Dec 7] lengthy mare: fair hurdler: won weak novice handicap at Perth in August: better form when runner-up next 3 starts:

suited by 2½m+: acts on good to firm and good to soft going: tongue tied second start. *Mrs M. Reveley*

THISTLE DO 5 b.g. College Chapel – Fishki (Niniski (USA)) [2002/3 F–: F17d⁶ **h87 d** 27sᵖᵘ 20d⁵ 16v 24gᵖᵘ 19dᵖᵘ 20d Apr 25] lengthy gelding: sixth of 18 on second start in **F79** bumpers: form over hurdles only when fifth in novice at Ayr, left L. Lungo after next outing. *M. D. Hammond*

THISTLEKICKER (IRE) 11 b.g. Mandalus – Miss Ranova (Giacometti) [2002/3 **c–** c–, h76: 16g 16m* 16g 16d³ 16m⁴ 17m³ 17mᶠ 16s 24d⁵ 16g Apr 24] leggy gelding: well **h74** beaten only start over fences: poor hurdler: won conditional jockeys selling handicap at Perth in May: needs sharp 2m on good going or firmer. *Mrs J. C. McGregor*

THOMAS THE DOUBTER 8 ro.g. Roviris – Doubting Donna (Tom Noddy) **c–** [2002/3 c21mᶠ c24mᵖᵘ Apr 22] maiden pointer, runner-up in March and April: failed to complete both starts in hunters, in cheekpieces second time. *S. A. Hughes*

THORN IN OUR SIDE (IRE) 6 b. or br.m. Detroit Sam (FR) – Aintree Rose **h–** (Avocat) [2002/3 F20dᵖᵘ 17g⁶ 16v 16g 16mᵖᵘ Oct 4] third foal: dam of little account: no **F–** sign of ability. *C. S. McKeever, Ireland*

THORPENESS (IRE) 4 b.g. Barathea (IRE) – Brisighella (IRE) (Al Hareb (USA)) **h84** [2002/3 16m 17s³ Nov 21] modest maiden on Flat (best efforts around 1½m) for C. Wall: better effort in juvenile hurdles when 6 lengths third of 16 to Do L'Enfant d'Eau at Hereford. *J. White*

THOSEWERETHEDAYS 10 b.g. Past Glories – Charlotte's Festival (Gala Perform- **c127 +** ance (USA)) [2002/3 c128, h94p: c21d* c24d³ Mar 15] sturdy gelding: useful chaser: left **h–** F. Murphy, won 5-runner hunter at Ayr impressively in March: 11/4 on, very disappointing in similar race at Newcastle 8 days later: stays 21f: raced on good going or softer (acts on soft): reportedly bled from nose final start in 2001/2: bold-jumping front runner. *Miss Pauline Robson*

THOUTMOSIS (USA) 4 ch.g. Woodman (USA) – Toujours Elle (USA) (Lyphard **h98** (USA)) [2002/3 18g* 16g³ Mar 29] ex-French gelding: half-brother to 2m hurdle winner Al Towd (by Kingmambo): maiden on Flat, raced mainly around 1m, sold out of F. Head's stable €6,000 Goffs July Sale: 33/1, won 8-runner juvenile at Kelso in March on hurdling debut by 7 lengths from Thunder Canyon: favourite, failed to improve when third of 8 to Bushido at Hexham 8 days later. *L. Lungo*

THREAD OF HONOUR (IRE) 6 gr.g. Roselier (FR) – Sharkezan (IRE) (Double **F93** Schwartz) [2002/3 F16g F16s³ F16g Mar 2] good-topped gelding: second foal: dam unraced: best effort in bumpers when third of 13 to Music To My Ears at Southwell: will stay beyond 2m. *N. J. Henderson*

THREE CLOUDS 6 b.g. Rainbow Quest (USA) – Three Tails (Blakeney) [2002/3 **h–** h–: 23vᵖᵘ Jan 22] leggy gelding: modest on Flat (stays 2m): no promise in 3 outings over hurdles, sold out of G. L. Moore's stable £800 Ascot December Sales. *C. N. Kellett*

THREE DAYS REIGN (IRE) 9 br.g. Camden Town – Little Treat (Miner's Lamp) **c75** [2002/3 h84: c18m³ Mar 22] robust gelding: modest novice hurdler, lightly raced: not **h–** given hard time when third in novice handicap at Newbury on chasing debut: stays 21f: best efforts on good to firm going: blinkered both starts in 2001/2. *P. D. Cundell*

THREE EAGLES (USA) 6 ch.g. Eagle Eyed (USA) – Tertiary (USA) (Vaguely **h92** Noble) [2002/3 h95: 21f* 19m³ 20mᶠ 20mᶠ Sep 14] small gelding: modest handicap hurdler: made all in 3-runner race at Warwick in May: in lead when falling last 2 starts: effective at 2m to 3m: acts on any going: usually forces pace: game. *A. Bailey*

THREE LIONS 6 ch.g. Jupiter Island – Super Sol (Rolfe (USA)) [2002/3 h107: 22sᵖᵘ **h90** 21dᵖᵘ 16s 17d⁵ Feb 10] leggy gelding: modest hurdler: first form in 2002/3 when making all in 15-runner handicap at Hereford: stays 2½m: acts on soft going: wore cheekpieces second start: has gone in snatches. *R. S. Brookhouse*

THREE SAINTS (IRE) 14 b.g. Rising – Oh Dora (Even Money) [2002/3 c–, h–: **c88** c24s³ May 18] lengthy gelding: winning 2½m chaser: fair hunter, finished alone in 2- **h–** runner race in March: much better effort in hunters at Bangor when third to Lord Harry: blinkered in 1998/9. *W. G. Dutton*

THREE WEEKS 10 ch.g. Formidable (USA) – Zilda (FR) (Zino) [2002/3 h94: 19mᵖᵘ **h–** Jun 1] rather dipped-backed gelding: modest handicap hurdler, no show after 6-month absence on reappearance: stays 19f: acts on soft going: sold 900 gns Doncaster September Sales. *M. J. Wilkinson*

THREEZEDZZ 5 ch.g. Emarati (USA) – Exotic Forest (Dominion) [2002/3 16m⁵ **h98 ?** 16m² 17f⁵ Oct 17] half-brother to winning 17f hurdler Misbehaviour (by Tragic Role):

one-time useful sprinter on Flat, only fair in 2002: best effort in novice hurdles when 4 lengths second to Grave Doubts at Plumpton: will need sharp 2m: pulls hard. *Mrs P. N. Dutfield*

THRILL A MINUTE (IRE)   9 b.g. Be My Native (USA) – Fairy Run (Deep Run)   **c88** [2002/3 c96, h63: c28s² c33vᵖᵘ c25dᵖᵘ c30vᵖᵘ Feb 7] angular gelding: modest handicap   **h–** chaser, out of sorts after reappearance: stays 3½m: raced on good going or softer (acts on heavy): tongue tied 4 of last 5 starts. *Jonjo O'Neill*

THROUGH THE RYE   7 ch.g. Sabrehill (USA) – Baharlilys (Green Dancer (USA))   **h131** [2002/3 h128: 16s⁶ 16v² 16d 16d³ 17g³ 18gᵖᵘ Mar 21] strong gelding: useful handicap hurdler: 66/1 and looking extremely well, close third of 28 to Spirit Leader in County Hurdle at Cheltenham in March, holding narrow advantage when fluffing last: ran poorly at Kelso 8 days later: raced mainly around 2m: acts on heavy going: tongue tied once: usually front runner/races prominently. *E. W. Tuer*

THROWALINE   7 b.g. Thowra (FR) – Stockline (Capricorn Line) [2002/3 F99: 18s²   **h106** 19s* 20m² 22f* Apr 24] smallish gelding: bumper winner: landed odds in novices at Hereford in March and Fontwell in April: better form over hurdles when second in similar events, though no match for Brooklyn Breeze at Ayr third start: will prove as effective at 2¾m as shorter. *P. J. Hobbs*

THROWER   12 b.g. Thowra (FR) – Atlantic Line (Capricorn Line) [2002/3 h91: 20v²   **h102** 19dᵘʳ Jan 25] neat gelding: one-time useful handicap hurdler: stayed 2½m: acted on good to firm and heavy going: tried visored: dead. *W. M. Brisbourne*

THROW THE DEUCE (IRE)   6 b.g. Desert Style (IRE) – Baileys Bride (IRE) (Shy   **c–** Groom (USA)) [2002/3 c–, h93: 19sᵖᵘ Dec 12] fair but temperamental maiden on Flat: **h–** won 2m maiden hurdle in early-2001/2, little other form over jumps: tried blinkered: sold £320 Ascot February Sales. *G. F. Edwards*

THUMPER (IRE)   5 b.g. Grand Lodge (USA) – Parkeen Princess (He Loves Me)   **h98** [2002/3 16g² Mar 12] fair on Flat (stays 1¼m), successful twice in 2002, sold out of R. Hannon's stable 16,000 gns Newmarket Autumn Sales: 5 lengths second of 18 to Crimson Pirate in maiden at Huntingdon on hurdling debut: may do better. *J. Mackie*

THUNDER CANYON (USA)   4 b. or br.g. Gulch (USA) – Naazeq (Nashwan (USA))   **h92** [2002/3 16g⁵ 16s² 18g² 20m³ Apr 21] fairly useful on Flat (stays 1¾m), won 3 times in 2002, sold out of M. Johnston's stable 22,000 gns Newmarket Autumn Sales: modest juvenile hurdler: stays 2½m: acts on soft and good to firm going. *N. G. Richards*

THUNDERED (USA)   5 gr.g. Thunder Gulch (USA) – Lady Lianga (USA) (Secre-   **h–** tariat (USA)) [2002/3 h–: 17gᵖᵘ Aug 9] modest on Flat (stays 1m): showed nothing in 2 starts over hurdles, tailed off first occasion. *G. A. Swinbank*

THUNDERING JAY-SEA   5 ch.m. First Trump – Thunder Bug (USA) (Secreto   **h–** (USA)) [2002/3 17d Nov 5] no form on Flat or on hurdling debut. *J. R. Jenkins*

THUNDERPOINT (IRE)   11 b.g. Glacial Storm (USA) – Urdite (FR) (Concertino   **c75 §** (FR)) [2002/3 c70§, h–§: c19m² c17d⁴ c16g⁵ c24s² c21m⁶ c20m⁵ c19m⁶ Apr 22] smal-   **h– §** lish, lengthy gelding: poor handicap chaser: probably stays 21f (beaten before stamina became issue over 3m): acts on any going: tried visored, blinkered nowadays: temperamental. *R. J. Price*

THURSDAY-FOURBALL (IRE)   9 b.g. Phardante (FR) – Ashville Lady (IRE) (Le   **c– x** Bavard (FR)) [2002/3 c–x, h88: c25dᵘʳ 22f May 15] lengthy, angular gelding: maiden   **h–** hurdler/chaser: sold £500 Ascot November Sales. *R. Curtis*

THWAITES STAR (IRE)   4 b.f. Petardia – Monterana (Sallust) [2002/3 17gᵖᵘ 17d   **h–** 16gᶠ 17gᵖᵘ Sep 28] half-sister to fair but temperamental hurdler Henry Island, stays 21f, and winning 17f hurdler Occam (both by Sharp Victor): disappointing maiden on Flat for A. Berry: no form over hurdles. *R. Johnson*

THYME OF HOPE   5 b.m. Timeless Times (USA) – Wych Willow (Hard Fought)   **F–** [2002/3 F16d Mar 5] fifth foal: dam unraced half-sister to useful 1½m performer Future Perfect: tailed off in bumper on debut. *Mrs M. Reveley*

THYNE WILL TELL (IRE)   8 ch.g. Good Thyne (USA) – Deep Khaletta (Deep   **c137** Run) [2002/3 c115, h119: c21f* c21g* c21dF c20m⁴ Apr 11] lengthy gelding: has report-   **h–** edly suffered knee problems: fairly useful hurdler: useful handicap chaser: improved in 2002/3, won at Newton Abbot in August and Stratford (idled markedly when beating Navarone a length) in October: looked likely to be involved in finish when falling 4 out in race won by Poliantas at Wincanton, ran as if all wasn't well 4 months later: will stay 3m: acts on firm and good to soft going (won bumper on heavy): has broken blood vessels. *P. J. Hobbs*

TIANYI (IRE) 7 b.g. Mujadil (USA) – Skinity (Rarity) [2002/3 h–: 17m 16d 16g[5] 20d **h77** 16m 16f* 16g[2] 17m* 16d 16d[4] Dec 26] angular gelding: poor hurdler: left F. Jordan and off 4 months after fifth start: improved subsequently, won handicaps at Wincanton (novice) and Taunton (made all and idled) in October: raced mainly around 2m: acts on firm and good to soft going: effective with/without headgear: not a fluent jumper or an easy ride. *D. J. Caro*

TIBBIE LUGS 7 ch.g. Turbo Speed – Tina's Song (Tina's Pet) [2002/3 F–: 20s[pu] Nov **h–** 17] no show in bumpers or novice hurdle. *F. P. Murtagh*

TICKTON FLYER 5 b.g. Sovereign Water (FR) – Contradictory (Reprimand) [2002/3 **h98** F91: F16s[2] F17m* F17g* 16g[2] 20v[5] 19d[3] Dec 4] fairly useful in bumpers, won at Market **F100** Rasen in June and September: only modest form in novice hurdles: should stay 2½m+: not a straightforward ride. *M. W. Easterby*

TIDAL REEF (IRE) 11 br.g. Tidaro (USA) – Windsor Reef (Take A Reef) [2002/3 **c–** c–, h–: 22f[pu] 23d[pu] 26m 24g[pu] c24f[pu] Apr 3] winning hunter chaser, no longer of much **h–** account (won 2-runner point in March): tried blinkered. *R. Fielder*

TIED FOR TIME (IRE) 11 b.g. Montelimar (USA) – Cornamucla (Lucky Guy) **c92** [2002/3 c94, h–: c22m[4] Jun 1] tall, useful-looking gelding: fair pointer/hunter chaser: **h–** stays 25f. *A. J. Walker*

TIERNA'S RESPECT 11 b.g. Respect – Tierna's Pet (Laurence O) [2002/3 c–, h–: **c–** c19f[6] Mar 27] tall gelding: of little account. *G. Chambers* **h–**

TIER WORKER 7 b.g. Tenby – On The Tide (Slip Anchor) [2002/3 16d[pu] 16s Feb 8] **h–** sturdy gelding: useful on Flat (stays 1½m) at 3 yrs: not seen again until tailed off in 2 novice hurdles. *T. D. Easterby*

TIFASI (IRE) 13 b.g. Shardari – Tikrara (USA) (Assert) [2002/3 h63: 16d[pu] 16m **h–** Jul 18] leggy gelding: has stringhalt: winning selling hurdler, no show in 2002/3: tried blinkered. *K. G. Wingrove*

TIGERBURNINGBRIGHT (IRE) 9 b.g. Strong Gale – Ring Road (Giolla Mear) **c–** [2002/3 c20d[pu] 22v[pu] 20s[pu] Nov 27] strong gelding: very lightly-raced maiden hurdler: **h–** no sign of retaining ability, including on chasing debut: lame final start. *J. R. Adam*

The MerseyClyde Partnership's "Tighten Your Belt"

TIGER FROG (USA) 4 b.g. French Deputy (USA) – Woodyoubelieveit (USA) **h86**
(Woodman (USA)) [2002/3 16d⁶ 16d 16d 17d Feb 23] lengthy gelding: fair maiden on
Flat (should stay beyond 1¼m), sold out of J. Gosden's stable 18,000 gns Newmarket
Autumn Sales: better effort over hurdles when sixth of 19 in juvenile at Haydock on
debut. *R. C. Guest*

TIGER GRASS (IRE) 7 gr.g. Ezzoud (IRE) – Rustic Lawn (Rusticaro (FR)) [2002/3 **c–**
h91§: c23gᵖᵘ 21s* 22d* 26m* 24g* 24f² 25g² 22v³ Nov 6] lengthy, rather sparely-made **h114 §**
gelding: fair hurdler: left W. Muir after chasing debut (soon tailed off) on reappearance:
right back to best subsequently, winning sellers at Market Rasen (handicap) and Newton
Abbot and handicaps at Hereford and Perth before end of September: stays 3¼m: acts on
any going: usually blinkered/visored: usually looks far from keen, and takes plenty of
driving. *M. C. Pipe*

TIGER GROOM 6 b.h. Arazi (USA) – Rifada (Ela-Mana-Mou) [2002/3 c?, h152: **c119 p**
21s 25d⁶ 24v² 20v³ 19vᶠ c17s² 17g c21g Apr 19] lengthy, angular horse: placed in 1½m **h148**
listed race on Flat in September: smart hurdler, placed at Auteuil in November in Grand
Prix d'Automne (length second to Laveron, pair clear) and Prix Leon Olry-Roederer
(beaten 9 lengths by Katiki): fairly useful maiden over fences, second in minor event at
Enghien in March: well held in Grade 1 events over hurdles and fences at Nakayama last
2 starts: unlikely to stay much beyond 2½m: acts on heavy and good to firm going: held
up. *R. Collet, France*

TIGER ROUGE 8 ch.g. Kinglet – Lake View Lady (Little Buskins) [2002/3 h–, F–: **h–**
20mᵖᵘ May 9] medium-sized gelding: no form. *M. Pitman*

TIGER TALK 7 ch.g. Sabrehill (USA) – Tebre (USA) (Sir Ivor) [2002/3 h88: 17g* **c74**
16d³ 16d5 17m* 17mᵖᵘ 21mᵖᵘ c16g c17s⁵ c17v² c16gᵖᵘ 19g 20g⁶ 17d⁴ 16m⁵ Apr 21] **h86**
angular gelding: modest handicap hurdler: won at Sedgefield in May and Market Rasen
(novices) in June: below best after, and just poor form over fences: unproven beyond 17f:
acts on heavy and good to firm going: effective blinkered or not: has worn cheekpieces.
M. E. Sowersby

TIGER TYPHOON (IRE) 7 b.g. Cataldi – Churchtown Breeze (Tarqogan) [2002/3 **c–**
F74: 16m 17s³ c16dᵖᵘ c16sᵘʳ c20m³ Apr 21] strong gelding: signs of only a little ability: **h76**
should prove suited by 2½m+. *R. J. Hodges*

TIG HILL 7 b.g. Tigani – Grange Hill Girl (Workboy) [2002/3 F16v Nov 16] 5,000 **F73**
6-y-o: fourth foal: half-brother to fairly useful staying chaser Scotton Green (by Ardross):
dam, fair chaser up to 21f, half-sister to useful hurdler up to 2¾m Nineofus: eighth of 14
in bumper at Wetherby: dead. *P. Beaumont*

TIGHTEN YOUR BELT (IRE) 6 b.g. Phardante (FR) – Hi' Upham (Deep Run) **F106**
[2002/3 F16d* F17g³ Apr 5] IR £18,000 4-y-o: useful-looking gelding: fifth foal: half-
brother to top-class chaser Native Upmanship (by Be My Native), stays easy 25f: dam,
poor maiden hurdler/chaser, half-sister to smart hurdler Glassilaun: won completed start
in maiden Irish points in 2002: favourite, impressive when winning maiden bumper at
Stratford in March: looked out-and-out stayer when around 20 lengths third of 21 to
Classic Native in Grade 2 at Aintree, flat out at halfway and staying on dourly. *Miss
Venetia Williams*

TIK-A-TAI (IRE) 8 b.g. Alphabatim (USA) – Carrig Ross (Lord Ha Ha) [2002/3 **c118**
c122, h–: c22g⁵ c21g³ 22d* 22s³ 21dᵖᵘ Jan 18] strong gelding: fairly useful chaser: took **h116**
advantage of lower handicap mark back over hurdles when winning at Fontwell in
November: ran poorly final outing: stays 3m: acts on soft going: has broken blood vessel:
prone to mistakes over fences. *O. Sherwood*

TIKI TAPU 5 b.m. Karinga Bay – Hy Wilma (Jalmood (USA)) [2002/3 F17f³ Oct 17] **F82**
fourth foal: half-sister to 1m winner Leonie Samual (by Safawan): dam, 2-y-o 6f winner,
out of Galtres Stakes winner Hymettus: 3¼ lengths third of 6 to very easy winner Mister
Wellard in steadily-run bumper at Taunton on debut. *R. J. Hodges*

TIKRAM 6 ch.g. Lycius (USA) – Black Fighter (USA) (Secretariat (USA)) [2002/3 **h133**
h126: 16f⁴ 16g² 16sᵖᵘ 16g⁴ 16v 18d* 16v⁴ 16g³ 16v⁶ 20d Apr 4] tall gelding: useful
handicap hurdler: won at Fontwell in December, despite going bit in snatches: in frame
in very competitive events at Ascot and Newbury (best effort, wandered under pressure
when third to Spirit Leader) next 2 starts: should stay 2½m: acts on any going: tried
visored/blinkered (pulled hard): not an easy ride. *G. L. Moore*

TILANJANI (IRE) 6 ch.g. Indian Ridge – Tijara (IRE) (Darshaan) [2002/3 h–, F86: **h–**
16mᵖᵘ May 15] leggy gelding: runner-up final start in bumpers: no form over hurdles,
mainly in sellers: tried visored. *K. A. Morgan*

TIMBERA (IRE) 9 b. or br.g. Commanche Run – Morry's Lady (The Parson) **c135**
[2002/3 c137p, h–: c28s^{pu} c21v^{2} c24g^{4} c29g* Apr 21]   **h–**

With three successes in five years, the Irish, after a long barren spell, seem
to have got the hang of winning the Grand National again and they could well have
a major contender in 2004 with Timbera. Like Bobbyjo and Papillon, his Aintree
credentials have been advertised by his exploits in the Irish Grand National at
Fairyhouse, the latter pair having fought out a close finish to the 1998 Irish National
before winning in successive years at Aintree, in 1999 and 2000. Papillon took part
in three runnings of the Irish National before his Aintree success, while Timbera
was succeeding at the second attempt when winning the Powers Gold Label-
sponsored event in April. Twelve months previously, as a novice, Timbera had been
bang in contention when falling two out, looking likely to finish third at worst
behind The Bunny Boiler had he completed. With the Cheltenham Gold Cup
second Commanche Court in the field that day, Timbera had to race from 10 lb out
of the handicap but a year on he was off his proper mark. As he had not progressed
in three outings in the meantime, Timbera was actually off a lower mark at Fairyhouse than he had been in 2002. He had looked the type to make an impact in his
second season over fences but hadn't run any sort of race on his reappearance in
November and then missed the main part of the season, not being seen out again
until the beginning of March. After a promising second to the progressive novice
Jenniferjo in a handicap over an inadequate twenty-one furlongs at Leopardstown,
Timbera was a little disappointing (or so it seemed at the time) when fourth to
another novice Native Jack over three miles at Cork. As it turned out, this was the
key race so far as the Irish National was concerned. The first four were all in the
line-up at Fairyhouse with Timbera meeting the winner, runner-up The Dell and
third Torduff Boy on terms between 2 lb and 7 lb better. The latest Irish National
looked particularly open, with the betting 8/1 the field. Several of the leading
contenders looked doubtful stayers beforehand, with the favourite Eskimo Jack,
third to Youlneverwalkalone in the Leopardstown Chase and still relatively unexposed, among them. Even less sure to stay, at least on his record rather than
pedigree, was Winning Dream, an impressive two-mile winner last time out and the
gamble of the race with Tony McCoy booked to ride. Ross Moff was another
unproven beyond twenty-five furlongs, unlike his stable-companion Davids Lad,
controversially excluded from the Grand National itself, who had won the race in
2001. Another with a chance and likely to stay was the novice I'vehadit. A notable

Powers Gold Label Irish Grand National Chase (Handicap), Fairyhouse—
an exciting finish is in store as Timbera (left) is led over the last by novice Knock Knock,
Winning Dream (right) and Torduff Boy are next

late absentee was 2002 winner The Bunny Boiler, taken out on account of the ground which was considered on the firm side of good. The Irish Grand National is not often a race for sluggards and certainly wasn't under the prevailing conditions. Timbera was always in a handy position and travelled smoothly for much of the way, coming under pressure after three out and, in a close and exciting finish, getting in front near the post, to beat the outsider Knock Knock by a head with Winning Dream, Davids Lad and Torduff Boy all at spaces of two lengths next across the line. Jumping certainly made the difference for Timbera whose fluent round was in marked contrast to that of Knock Knock who all but lost his rider early on the final circuit. The third and fifth had every chance though probably wouldn't be so close again under conditions which place much more emphasis on stamina. Eskimo Jack faded quickly in the straight and appeared not to stay. The fences told on many of the other leading contenders: Native Jack and Ross Moff fell independently at the sixth, The Dell blundered away his chance five out when bang in contention, I'vehadit jumped badly. Of the first five, only Torduff Boy ran at Punchestown, winning the valuable two-and-a-half-mile handicap for the second year running.

Timbera (IRE) (b. or br.g. 1994)	Commanche Run (b 1981)	Run The Gantlet (b 1968)	Tom Rolfe
			First Feather
		Volley (b 1965)	Ratification
			Mitrailleuse
	Morry's Lady (b 1980)	The Parson (b 1968)	Aureole
			Bracey Bridge
		Mary Escart (b 1965)	Escart III
			Mary's Last

Mrs J. M. Breen's "Timbera"

Timbera comes from an ordinary jumping background. He is the fifth foal and second winner out of the twice-raced Morry's Lady, the other winner La Princesse (by Le Bavard) who was a fair hurdler at up to two and three quarter miles. Neither the grandam Mary Escart nor the third dam Mary's Last raced. The best of Mary Escart's four winners was the fair staying chaser Naughty Nicky. Mary's Last produced eight winners and three of those were above average, the useful staying chaser Vital Moment, the fairly useful hurdler/chaser at up to three miles Turmo-Tang and the fairly useful hurdler Maxwell House. The lengthy Timbera seems sure to stay the Grand National distance if he makes it to Aintree, and he will have plenty going for him. He has raced mainly on going softer than good (acts on heavy) but would be unlikely to face conditions much firmer than at Fairyhouse in the National itself. *D. T. Hughes, Ireland*

TIMBER KING (IRE) 7 b.g. Brief Truce (USA) – Shanntabariya (IRE) (Shernazar) **h137**
[2002/3 h136: 16g* 16d⁶ 16mᵖᵘ Oct 6] lengthy, rather leggy gelding: useful hurdler: won minor event at Tipperary in July: creditable sixth of 24 to Say Again in Galway Hurdle (Handicap) following month: fatally injured in Grade 2 at Tipperary: would have stayed 2½m: acted on soft and good to firm going. *C. Roche, Ireland*

TIMBER STREET (IRE) 6 b. or br.g. Montelimar (USA) – Ware Star (IRE) (Torus) **h–**
[2002/3 F17m² 22dᵖᵘ Oct 31] IR £28,000 4-y-o: first foal: dam unraced sister to high- **F74** class hurdler/top-class chaser up to 3m Bradbury Star: poor form when second to Phar From Fair in bumper at Hereford on debut: favourite, reportedly choked in maiden hurdle at Stratford. *M. Pitman*

TIMBOURINE 5 ch.m. Hatim (USA) – Persian Symphony (IRE) (Persian Heights) **h–**
[2002/3 F16g F17m 20sᵖᵘ Aug 4] first foal: dam 9f and 1½m winner on Flat: showed **F–** nothing in bumpers or maiden hurdle. *C. R. Wilson*

TIME AFTER THYNE 10 b.g. Good Thyne (USA) – Lady Solstice (Vital Season) **c– x**
[2002/3 c–x, h–: 22vᵖᵘ Dec 2] useful-looking gelding: lightly-raced novice hurdler/chaser **h–** (let down by jumping). *Ferdy Murphy*

TIME CAN TELL 9 ch.g. Sylvan Express – Stellaris (Star Appeal) [2002/3 h91: **h–** 27m⁶ 19m Jun 4] well-made gelding: lightly-raced novice hurdler, modest form at best. *A. G. Juckes*

TIMELESS CHICK 6 ch.m. Timeless Times (USA) – Be My Bird (Be My Chief **h69** (USA)) [2002/3 h72: 17m⁵ 17d³ 17g² 21s⁶ Nov 21] angular mare: poor on Flat (stays 8.5f): poor maiden hurdler: best at 2m: acts on good to soft going (no show both starts on soft): blinkered final outing in 2001/2. *J. L. Spearing*

TIME MARCHES ON 5 b.g. Timeless Times (USA) – Tees Gazette Girl (Kalaglow) **h82** [2002/3 17g⁶ 16s* 16g Dec 13] leggy gelding: poor on Flat (stays 1½m): easily best effort over hurdles when winning novice seller at Kelso in November. *Mrs M. Reveley*

TIME N TIDE (IRE) 7 b.g. Namaqualand (USA) – Now Then (Sandford Lad) [2002/3 **h115 §** h98: 17s* 20v 19d² 23sᵖᵘ 20g Apr 2] lengthy gelding: fair handicap hurdler: off 15 months, won at Bangor in November and Doncaster (by 2 lengths from Totally Scottish) in January: disappointing otherwise in 2002/3: should stay beyond 2½m: acts on soft and good to firm going: difficult ride (often soon off bridle). *Jonjo O'Neill*

TIME OF FLIGHT (IRE) 10 ch.g. Over The River (FR) – Icy Lou (Bluerullah) **c102 §** [2002/3 c117, h–: 16d c20d⁴ c16g⁴ Mar 17] compact gelding: fairly useful handicap **h–** chaser/winning hurdler: well held in 2002/3, looking unwilling (not for first time) final start: should stay beyond 2½m: acts on good to firm and heavy going: often tongue tied prior to 2001/2. *Mrs M. Reveley*

TIMES PAST (IRE) 8 b.g. Commanche Run – Orient Moonbeam (Deep Run) **c89** [2002/3 c24g⁴ May 3] IR 5,800 3-y-o: ex-Irish gelding: fourth foal: half-brother to useful **h–** pointer River Swilley (by Over The River): dam lightly-raced hurdler: won bumper and fourth in minor hurdle for W. Flavin: fair pointer, successful twice in 2002: favourite, only fourth of 6 finishers in novice hunter at Bangor. *Mrs Edward Crow*

TIME TEMPTRESS 7 b.m. Timeless Times (USA) – Tangalooma (Hotfoot) [2002/3 **h–** h58: 21gᵖᵘ May 30] small, sparely-made mare: bad maiden hurdler: seems to stay 23f: acts on soft and good to firm going: blinkered only outing in 2002/3. *I. W. McInnes*

TIME TO PARLEZ 12 b.g. Amboise – Image of War (Warpath) [2002/3 c80§, h–: **c73 §** c26m⁶ c26dᵖᵘ c32d c26vᵖᵘ c26s* c26s³ c24s⁶ c26s c28g² c26f⁴ Apr 24] strong gelding: **h–**

poor handicap chaser: won at Plumpton in January: stays 3½m: acts well on soft/heavy going: blinkered once: moody, and not to be trusted. *C. J. Drewe*

TIME TO TELL   7 b.m. Keen – Meet Again (Lomond (USA)) [2002/3 F16d F16d⁴ 18s 22mᵖᵘ 20g⁵ Mar 25] third foal: half-sister to 3 winners, including miler Cool Vibes (by Rock City) and 1¼m seller winner Today Tonite (by Adbass): dam ran 3 times: better effort in maiden bumpers when fourth at Fakenham (had run of things): no show in 3 novice hurdles, running out of Mrs L. Pearce's stable 800 gns Newmarket February Sales after debut. *B. G. Powell*   **h–
F77**

TIMIDJAR (IRE)   10 b.g. Doyoun – Timissara (USA) (Shahrastani (USA)) [2002/3 h67: 16g 16v 19s 17m³ 16m³ Apr 21] neat gelding: poor hurdler nowadays: best around 2m: acts on firm and good to soft going: tried blinkered. *Mrs D. Thomas*   **h70**

TIMPANI (IRE)   7 b.g. Broken Hearted – Queen Kam (IRE) (Kambalda) [2002/3 h–: 18m⁴ 24g³ 22mᵖᵘ 19f Oct 9] won 2 points for D. Pipe in 2002: poor maiden hurdler: probably better at 3m than shorter: visored after reappearance. *M. C. Pipe*   **h79**

TIM'S THE MAN (IRE)   7 gr.g. Roselier (FR) – Pindas (Bargello) [2002/3 16s* 19g 19d⁴ 21g² Mar 3] IR 20,000 3-y-o: good-topped gelding: fourth foal: half-brother to fairly useful hurdler/chaser Spankers Hill (by Monksfield), stayed 25f: dam bumper winner/winning 21f hurdler: fair form at best in bumpers for A. Mullins in 2001/2: easily best effort over hurdles when winning novice at Leicester in November: should stay beyond 2m: raced on good going or softer. *C. J. Mann*   **h96**

TINA COOKE   7 gr.m. Tina's Pet – Up Cooke (Deep Run) [2002/3 F79?: 16mᵖᵘ 17d 22v⁴ 16s 20m⁴ 22gᵖᵘ Mar 29] lengthy mare: signs of only a little ability. *Miss Kate Milligan*   **h–**

TINA'S INDIAN (IRE)   5 b.m. Indian Ridge – Tina's Charm (IRE) (Hatim (USA)) [2002/3 16mᶠ 18gᵘʳ 18d Nov 11] second foal: dam, won around 2m over hurdles, also 9f winner: modest on Flat (should stay 1½m), successful in May: well held in claimer on completed outing over hurdles. *B. G. Powell*   **h–**

TINA'S SCALLYWAG   6 br.m. Baron Blakeney – Southend Scallywag (Tina's Pet) [2002/3 F17g 20v 19g 16d 25d⁶ 25dᵖᵘ Mar 6] leggy mare: fourth foal: half-sister to fair hurdler Red Imp (by Alflora), stayed 2½m: dam modest hurdler stayed 2½m: little form in bumper or over hurdles, tried in cheekpieces final start: sold 2,400 gns Doncaster May Sales. *R. C. Guest*   **h59
F66**

TINA THYNE (IRE)   9 b.m. Good Thyne (USA) – Tiny Tina (Deep Run) [2002/3 h86: 21g⁵ 16v⁵ 16v² 19d⁴ 19v* 16v⁴ 24f⁶ Apr 3] smallish, angular mare: modest hurdler: sold out of T. Tate's stable 8,000 gns Doncaster May Sales after reappearance: won maiden at Taunton in March: reportedly broke blood vessel final outing: ideally needs further than 2m and stays 27f: raced mainly on good going or softer (acts on heavy): effective blinkered/visored or not. *J. G. M. O'Shea*   **h86**

TINDLES BIBLE   11 b.g. Le Coq d'Or – Wedderburn (Royalty) [2002/3 c74, h–: 23dᵖᵘ 23v⁴ 27s⁴ c27s⁶ Dec 10] novice hurdler, fair at best: little show in steeplechases: tried in visor/cheekpieces. *J. S. Wainwright*   **c–
h78 ?**

TINO (IRE)   7 ch.g. Torus – Delphic Thunder (Viking (USA)) [2002/3 c68, h68: c21fᵖᵘ c21m* c25g c19d c24f³ c24m² Apr 10] sturdy gelding: maiden hurdler: poor chaser: won handicap at Folkestone in November: stays 3m: raced mainly on good going or firmer (acts on firm): ran well in blinkers final outing. *J. S. King*   **c73
h–**

TINOVERITAS (FR)   5 b.g. Saint Estephe (FR) – Tinorosa (FR) (Concertino (FR)) [2002/3 F13s² F16v Dec 27] big, rangy gelding: half-brother to 6 winners in France, including 2m hurdler Tinopasa (by No Pass No Sale) and fairly useful 2m chaser Tinozakia (by General Holme): dam won on Flat in France: wouldn't go past when beaten neck by Enitsag in bumper at Exeter on debut: well held in Grade 1 at Chepstow. *P. F. Nicholls*   **F100**

TIN SYMPHONY   5 ch.m. Opera Ghost – Bronze Age (Celtic Cone) [2002/3 F18sᵘʳ F18d F16m⁵ Mar 22] fourth foal: half-sister to 17f hurdle winner Bronzesmith (by Greensmith): dam poor form in bumpers: best effort in bumpers (hung left second start) when fifth of 18 to Yardbird at Newbury. *B. J. M. Ryall*   **F81**

TIOBRAID ARANN   6 b.g. Au Bon – Babs Reflection VII (Damsire Unregistered) [2002/3 F16g F16m Jun 29] non-thoroughbred gelding: dam unraced: tailed off in 2 bumpers at Worcester. *A. W. Carroll*   **F–**

TIP KASH (FR)   6 ch.g. Kashtan (FR) – Tipas (FR) (Tip Moss (FR)) [2002/3 F88: 19s* 20s⁴ 17s⁴ 22g³ 20gᵖᵘ Apr 2] angular gelding: fair hurdler: easily won novice at Market Rasen in November: carried head awkwardly under pressure when third (beaten 2 necks)   **h106**

to Benefit in handicap at same course: stays 2¾m: raced on good going or softer (acts on soft): reportedly lost action second start. *A. M. Hales*

TIPP TOP LORD (IRE) 6 gr.g. Mister Lord (USA) – Dark Fluff (Mandalus) [2002/3 24d⁶ Oct 26] IR £4,000 4-y-o: eighth foal: dam, placed over hurdles, half-sister to fairly useful 2m hurdler Granville Hotel: failed to complete in 3 maiden Irish points in 2002, ran out on third occasion: well beaten in novice on hurdling debut. *N. A. Twiston-Davies* — h–

TIPSY MOUSE (IRE) 7 ch.g. Roselier (FR) – Darjoy (Darantus) [2002/3 c24s^pu 16d 20s 24s⁴ 24s² 25g⁴ Mar 17] workmanlike ex-Irish gelding: brother to 1995 Grand National winner Royal Athlete and to bumper winner, and half-brother to several winners, including one-time useful staying chaser Tennessee Twist (by Buckskin): dam unraced, from family of 1986 Grand National winner West Tip: won maiden Irish point in 2002: pulled up in hunter chase for D. M. O'Brien: modest novice hurdler, easily best effort on fifth outing: will prove best at 3m+: acts on soft ground. *Mrs S. J. Smith* — c– h97

TIP THE SCALES 5 b.g. Dancing Spree (USA) – Keen Melody (USA) (Sharpen Up) [2002/3 h77: 16d 20m Mar 23] medium-sized gelding: poor form in juvenile hurdles in 2001/2, no encouragement in 2 novice handicaps. *Mrs T. J. McInnes Skinner* — h–

TI PUNCH 5 b.g. Jupiter Island – Caipirinha (IRE) (Strong Gale) [2002/3 F17s F18v 19d^pu Jan 24] rather unfurnished gelding: second foal: dam 3m hurdle winner: no show in bumpers or novice hurdle. *A. King* — h– F–

TIRALDO (FR) 10 b.g. Royal Charter (FR) – Tamilda (FR) (Rose Laurel) [2002/3 c70, h–: c26m⁵ c25g c24d* c26m³ c25g^pu Mar 29] compact gelding: one-time fairly useful handicap chaser, only poor nowadays: won weak 4-runner event at Stratford in August: ran moody race after 7-month absence final outing: stays 25f: raced mainly on good going or softer (acts on heavy): blinkered last 4 starts. *A. G. Juckes* — c70 h–

TIRARI (IRE) 4 b.f. Charnwood Forest (IRE) – Desert Victory (Green Desert (USA)) [2002/3 17g^ur 16m⁶ 16s^pu 16g 17g Mar 15] leggy filly: half-sister to winning 2m hurdler Milkat (by Machiavellian): poor on Flat (stays 1½m): little form over hurdles: became worked up beforehand and failed to settle fourth start: visored next time. *C. R. Dore* — h–

TIRIKUMBA 7 ch.m. Le Moss – Ntombi (Trasi's Son) [2002/3 F16g* F16v⁶ F17m⁶ Apr 17] lengthy mare: second foal: dam, won 2½m hurdle, half-sister to fairly useful 2½m to 3m hurdler Grenach: 40/1, won 11-runner mares bumper at Ludlow on debut in December by 9 lengths from Direction: highly tried after, ran well when 8½ lengths sixth of 17 to Amorello in listed mares event at Cheltenham final start: will stay 3m. *S. G. Griffiths* — F95

TIRLEY GALE 11 b.g. Strong Gale – Mascara VII (Damsire Unregistered) [2002/3 c–§, h–: c24m³ May 6] big, rangy gelding: maiden hurdler/winning chaser: best effort in hunters when distant third of 7 to Noyan at Ludlow: won point in January: seems to stay 3m: acts on soft and good to firm going: has shown signs of temperament (refused to race once). *Miss N. Brookes* — c74 § h–

TIRLEY STORM 8 b.g. Tirley Gale – Random Select (Random Shot) [2002/3 c71?, h–: c24m^pu c19m^pu c20d⁴ c19s⁶ c20d c23d^pu c23v c20s Jan 23] rangy gelding: little form. *J. S. Smith* — c– h–

TIS GROMIT 9 b.m. Bedford (USA) – Lac Royale (Lochnager) [2002/3 h69: 24d^pu 23d⁶ 22d⁴ c22v c25s² Feb 11] poor maiden hurdler: easily better effort over fences when neck second to Our Jolly Swagman in 16-runner handicap at Folkestone, soon taking little interest and veering under pressure (rider lost irons): stays 25f: acts on soft going: tried blinkered, wore cheekpieces last 2 starts: ungenuine. *Miss S. West* — c70 § h– §

TISHO 7 ch.m. Sir Harry Lewis (USA) – Sister-In-Law (Legal Tender) [2002/3 F17s* F18s³ F16g⁴ 17g^F Mar 17] rangy mare: fourth foal: dam, novice hurdler stayed 2¾m, from family of high-class 2½m chaser Townley Stone and 1991 Grand National third Auntie Dot: fair form in mares bumpers, successful at Bangor on debut in May: favourite, would probably have made winning debut over hurdles but for falling heavily last in mares maiden at Hereford, length up on Poppet having made running and jumped well. *P. R. Webber* — h94 F93

TISSIFER 7 b.g. Polish Precedent (USA) – Ingozi (Warning) [2002/3 h117: 16d⁵ 16d 16d² 16d⁵ 17g⁵ 16g^F Apr 19] fair handicap hurdler: raced mainly around 2m: acted on soft going: tried visored/in cheekpieces: difficult ride: dead. *Mrs M. Reveley* — h108

TITUS BRAMBLE 6 b.g. Puissance – Norska (Northfields (USA)) [2002/3 c79§, h–§: c26m⁴ May 6] leggy gelding: winning hurdler/novice chaser: placed in points in — c– § h– §

February and April: probably stays 2¾m: acts on good to firm and heavy going: usually blinkered/visored: has had tongue tied: none too keen. *P. C. Ritchens*

TIUTCHEV   10 b.g. Soviet Star (USA) – Cut Ahead (Kalaglow) [2002/3 c164, h–: c16s² c19s* c16gᶠ c21g Apr 19]   **c164 h–**

The Grand Jump. Perhaps it's the name. It probably sounds fine in Japanese. It is the world's richest race over jumps but has yet to engender much more than passing interest in the British racing Press (at least compared to coverage of the Japan Cup or the lengthy build-up accorded the Melbourne Cup) or among British racegoers. Attempts by British-trained runners to land some of the massive prize fund seem to be meeting with less success as the years go by. The Outback Way was third in the inaugural international running in 2000 but, in the two most recent renewals open to European runners (none being allowed in 2001 due to foot and mouth), Cenkos fared best of three British challengers in 2002 in fifth and Armaturk and Tiutchev in the latest renewal managed thirteenth and fourteenth in a field of sixteen. It isn't just the British that are finding it tough. After taking second with Boca Boca in 2000, the French have made little impact, though it was perhaps optimistic to expect Escort Boy, who had shown easily his best form when winning over three and a quarter miles on barely raceable ground, to perform as well at twenty-one furlongs under much firmer conditions, though the other French-trained runner Tiger Groom fared no better. The trouble with the Grand Jump may well be that the nature of the race, with starting stalls, a strong pace, sharp turns, steep gradients on a tight track, is alien to the European-raced horses. The home

Ritz Club Ascot Chase—Tiutchev wins this race for the second time in three years

runners, with one notable exception, have dominated the last two runnings. The New Zealand-trained St Steven, representing Australia, won at Nakayama in 2002 and finished a close third behind Big Taste and Gilded Age in 2003. Tiutchev never got into the race, his jockey Rodi Greene reporting the pace to be 'very, very quick'.

The Grand Jump had been the target for Tiutchev all season. A switch from Nicky Henderson's stable at the start of the campaign was said to have been made specifically because Martin Pipe had handled a previous runner in the Grand Jump (Exit Swinger, last in 2002). Tiutchev was to be prepared for the race with a couple of runs in Britain before contesting the valuable trial race, the Pegasus Jump. The two British runs went fine, though Tony McCoy wouldn't agree with that verdict about the first of them. Reappearing in the Elmbridge Handicap Chase at Sandown in February, a race he had won effectively first time out the year before, Tiutchev looked set for a winning return when two lengths up between the last two fences but he began to tire and was collared by Eskleybrook, a 50/1 shot, out of the handicap and ridden by a veteran amateur at overweight. Tiutchev looked about as good as ever, though, and a second victory in the Ritz Club Ascot Chase two weeks later confirmed the view. As ever, this was not the strongest Grade 1 of the season but, in beating former stable-companion Geos impressively by twelve lengths, Tiutchev recorded a performance that looked as if it would make him a leading contender for the Champion Chase if connections were to have a change of plan. They did. After being available at 12/1 for the Champion Chase immediately after Ascot, Tiutchev was backed down to 5/1 second favourite on the day but failed to settle before falling at the fifth. The Pegasus Jump, a race designed to give the foreign runners experience of the Nakayama circuit, went by without him, Gilded Age winning, with Big Taste third and St Steven fourth.

Tiutchev (b.g. 1993)	Soviet Star (USA) (b 1984)	Nureyev (b 1977)	Northern Dancer
			Special
		Veruschka (b 1967)	Venture VII
			Marie d'Anjou
	Cut Ahead (b 1986)	Kalaglow (gr 1978)	Kalamoun
			Rossiter
		Cut Loose (b 1979)	High Top
			Cutle

Although his season ended in anti-climax, Tiutchev showed on his first two starts that he is still a high-class chaser. With a campaign aimed at purely domestic targets, he could well add further successes in 2003/4. Tiutchev is effective at two miles to two and a half miles and acts on soft and good to firm going (he unseated at the first on his only start on heavy). He has shown a susceptibility to colic over the years which has limited his appearances and made his form a little inconsistent. To provide early warning of any recurrence of the illness, Tiutchev now has closed-circuit television in his box. There is nothing to add to the pedigree details of the rangy Tiutchev which have featured extensively in previous Annuals. *M. C. Pipe*

TOAD HALL 9 b.g. Henbit (USA) – Candlebright (Lighter) [2002/3 20m^{pu} c16g^4 Apr 24] lightly-raced 2½m winning hurdler: last of 4 in novice on chasing debut. *Mrs L. B. Normile* — **c–** **h–**

TOBERLONE 10 b.g. K-Battery – Elisetta (Monsanto (FR)) [2002/3 21g^{pu} May 3] of no account. *J. S. Haldane* — **h–**

TOBESURE (IRE) 9 b.g. Asir – Princess Citrus (IRE) (Auction Ring (USA)) [2002/3 c91, h88: 22d^5 24g 22m* 22g^2 22s^3 25g^6 24g 23d^3 22d^2 22g 24g Apr 23] novice chaser: modest handicap hurdler: won at Kelso in October: stays 25f: acts on soft and good to firm going (bumper form on heavy): tongue tied final outing in 2001/2. *J. I. A. Charlton* — **c–** **h93**

TO BE THE BEST 13 ch.g. Superlative – Early Call (Kind of Hush) [2002/3 c–, h–: 17m c16m Jul 25] tall, good-topped gelding: maiden hurdler/winning chaser: has looked none too keen. *D. A. Lamb* — **c–** **h–**

TOBY 10 b.g. Jendali (USA) – Au Revoir Sailor (Julio Mariner) [2002/3 20d^4 20m^{pu} 22g^{pu} Oct 19] compact gelding: winning hurdler/chaser, though unconvincing over fences: finished lame final start in 2000/1, poor form over hurdles on return (shaped as if amiss final start): seems to stay 3¼m: acts on good to firm and heavy going. *N. G. Richards* — **c–** **h84**

TOBY BROWN 10 b.g. Arzanni – Forest Nymph (NZ) (Oak Ridge (FR)) [2002/3   **c95** h111: c22d² c26g^pu May 22] close-coupled gelding: one-time useful hurdler: modest form   **h–** when runner-up on chasing debut, broke down next time: stayed 3m: acted on soft going: dead. *A. King*

TODAYS MAN 6 b.g. Bigstone (IRE) – Snowgirl (IRE) (Mazaad) [2002/3 h–: 17g^pu   **h–** 17d^pu Aug 26] sturdy gelding: no show in maiden on Flat or over hurdles. *Mrs Dianne Sayer*

TODDEANO 7 b.g. Perpendicular – Phisus (Henbit (USA)) [2002/3 F–: F16g 16d^pu   **h–** Nov 14] no show in bumpers or novice hurdle. *G. Fierro*   **F–**

TOEJAM 10 ch.g. Move Off – Cheeky Pigeon (Brave Invader (USA)) [2002/3 21g⁴   **h68** 17m⁵ Apr 26] poor on Flat (best form at 1m): well held in 2 novice hurdles at Sedgefield: will prove best around 2m. *R. E. Barr*

TOFT HALL (IRE) 8 br.g. Erdelistan (FR) – Countess Christy (Mon Capitaine)   **c–** [2002/3 c20d^F c27s⁵ c24g^pu c25g^pu c25g^ur c25g Apr 14] seventh foal: half-brother to modest chaser If You Believe, stayed 3m, and fair hurdler up to 2¾m Mountmead (both by Jamesmead): dam unraced: won maiden from 5 starts in points in 2002: no form in steeplechases, blinkered last 3 starts. *Mrs A. Hamilton*

TOI EXPRESS (IRE) 7 ch.g. Phardante (FR) – Toi Figures (Deep Run) [2002/3 h93:   **c105** c19m^F c16g² c17m³ c16d* c16g⁹ Sep 14] workmanlike gelding: modest maiden hurdler: **h–** fair form when placed in novice chases at Hereford and Stratford: unimpressive when winning similar events at Newton Abbot (idled) and Worcester (jumped markedly right on occasions and hard ridden to beat only other finisher): stays 19f: acts on good to firm going, probably on good to soft: not an easy ride. *P. J. Hobbs*

TOLCEA (IRE) 4 ch.g. Barathea (IRE) – Mosaique Bleue (Shirley Heights) [2002/3   **h–** 16d^pu Mar 1] well-made gelding: modest maiden on Flat (should stay 1¾m+), sold out of E. Dunlop's stable 4,500 gns Newmarket July Sales: never figured in juvenile on hurdling debut. *W. Storey*

TOLLBRAE (IRE) 6 gr.g. Supreme Leader – Miss Henrietta (IRE) (Step Together   **h98** (USA)) [2002/3 F104: 20s³ 16g² 20v⁴ Mar 7] sturdy gelding: bumper winner: modest form in novice hurdles: stays 2½m. *N. J. Henderson*

TOMBAZAAN (IRE) 7 b.m. Good Thyne (USA) – Master Nidee (Master Owen)   **h81** [2002/3 h82p: 19s⁶ 22s⁵ 16s Dec 26] bumper winner: only poor on balance of form over hurdles, well held in novice handicap final start (tongue tied/reportedly bled): should stay at least 2½m. *G. J. McKeever, Ireland*

TOMCAPPAGH (IRE) 12 br.g. Riberetto – Shuil Suas (Menelek) [2002/3 c79:   **c86 ?** c25d^pu c25m^pu c26v^pu c24d⁶ c24m⁴ c24g^pu c26f^pu Apr 24] lengthy gelding: poor handicap chaser: well out of weights and probably flattered only 2 completed starts in 2002/3: stays 3¼m: acts on heavy and good to firm going. *Mrs S. Wall*

TOM COSTALOT (IRE) 8 gr.g. Black Minstrel – Hop Picker (USA) (Plugged   **c123** Nickle (USA)) [2002/3 c113, h77: c20d³ c20d* c21d* c24d⁶ c24g c21d Apr 4] good-   **h–** topped gelding: maiden hurdler: fairly useful handicap chaser: won at Warwick in November and Cheltenham (beat Merry Minstrel 7 lengths in conditional jockeys event) in December: ridden less prominently than usual when well held in Topham Chase at Aintree final start: seems best around 2½m: acts on soft and good to firm going: jumps soundly: genuine and reliable. *Mrs Susan Nock*

TOM DE SAVOIE (IRE) 10 br.g. War Hero – Black Pilot (Linacre) [2002/3 c105:   **c78 §** c23d⁵ c24m² Apr 21] deep-girthed gelding: fairly useful pointer/hunter chaser on his day: below form in hunters at Leicester (ran in snatches) and Fakenham in 2003: will stay beyond 2m: acts on good to firm and good to soft going: needs treating with some caution. *Mrs Caroline Bailey*

TOMENOSO 5 b.g. Teenoso (USA) – Guarded Expression (Siberian Express (USA))   **h97** [2002/3 h92: 17s³ 16g 16d* 21d* 20m* Apr 19] lengthy gelding: modest handicap hurdler: won at Wetherby and Sedgefield in March and Carlisle in April, putting up best effort when holding Plutocrat by 3½ lengths in 5-runner event at last-named: stays 21f: acts on soft and good to firm going: front runner: genuine. *Mrs S. J. Smith*

TOMFOOLARY (IRE) 6 ch.g. Erins Isle – Liberty Bird (USA) (Danzatore (CAN))   **h–** [2002/3 h72p, F76: 16d Nov 19] lengthy gelding: modest form in bumpers: well beaten in 2 outings over hurdles. *J. A. B. Old*

TOM FRUIT 6 b.g. Supreme Leader – Forever Mine (IRE) (Phardante (FR)) [2002/3   **F103** F16g³ F16s² F16v² F16d* Mar 1] 14,000 4-y-o: tall, quite good-topped gelding: first foal:

dam, won 2½m hurdle in Ireland, out of sister to Stayers' Hurdle winner Rose Ravine: fairly useful in bumpers, impressive when winning at Doncaster by 9 lengths from Music To My Ears: will be suited by 2½m+. *T. D. Easterby*

TOMICH (IRE) 8 b. or br.g. Lord Americo – Gilt Course (Crash Course) [2002/3 c104?, h82: 26g² Oct 12] sturdy gelding: 40/1, won novice at Wincanton on chasing debut in 2001/2: jumped poorly next 2 starts: poor maiden hurdler: stays 2¾m: acts on good to soft going. *Miss A. M. Newton-Smith* **c– h82**

TOMMIE SWIFT 7 b.g. Karinga Bay – Marie Swift (Main Reef) [2002/3 h–, F–: 26gᵖᵘ May 4] no sign of ability. *B. J. Llewellyn* **h– F–**

TOMMY CARSON 8 b.g. Last Tycoon – Ivory Palm (USA) (Sir Ivor) [2002/3 c88, h–: c20g Apr 29] compact gelding: modest handicap chaser in 2001/2: tailed off at Plumpton in late-April: effective at 2½m to 3m: acts on good to firm and heavy going: tried visored/blinkered, not since 1999/00. *Jamie Poulton* **c– h–**

TOMMY TROOPER 8 ch.g. Infantry – Steady Saunter VII (Damsire Unregistered) [2002/3 h105: c16d c16sᶠ 24s 18s⁶ 16s² Feb 12] medium-sized gelding: let down by jumping both starts over fences: modest hurdler: claimed 8,000 gns final outing: should stay 2½m: acts on heavy going, bumper form on good to firm: tongue tied fourth start. *P. F. Nicholls* **c– h96**

TOMMY WOLF 7 ch.g. Little Wolf – Oneninefive (Sayyaf) [2002/3 F17d F17g F16m 22fᵖᵘ Aug 13] second foal: dam won 21f selling hurdle: no sign of ability. *Mrs E. B. Scott* **h– F–**

TOM PINCH (IRE) 14 b.g. Mandalus – Spanish Royale (Royal Buck) [2002/3 c68, h–: c21g³ c21g⁴ c22g⁴ c24mᵘʳ c23gᵖᵘ Jul 10] sturdy gelding: poor handicap chaser: won 2-runner point in March: stays 3m: acts on good to firm and heavy going: has had tongue tied. *J. R. Cornwall* **c68 h–**

TOM'S LAD 10 gr.g. Scallywag – Menquilla (Menelek) [2002/3 20dᵖᵘ Oct 23] workmanlike gelding: lightly raced and no sign of ability: poor jumper. *Lady Connell* **h–**

TOM'S PRIZE 8 ch.g. Gunner B – Pandora's Prize (Royal Vulcan) [2002/3 c112, h88: c24dᶠ c23v² c24v² c24sᶠ c23s* c24d* c25d Apr 4] plain gelding: maiden hurdler: fairly useful handicap chaser: successful at Leicester (improved form) in February and Doncaster (fortunate in 4-finisher quite valuable event, got back up run-in after clear leader unseated last) in March: ran good deal better than placing indicates when seventh of 14 to Master Tern at Aintree final start, still close up when blundering 2 out: stays 3m: acts on good to firm and heavy going: races prominently. *J. L. Spearing* **c125 h–**

TOM'S RIVER (IRE) 11 ch.g. Over The River (FR) – Nesford (Walshford) [2002/3 c100x, h–: 24d⁵ c30d³ c24m⁶ c24d⁴ c24vᵖᵘ c24sᵖᵘ c24sᵖᵘ c21m⁴ c21g³ Apr 19] lengthy gelding: maiden hurdler: modest chaser: sold out of Mrs M. Reveley's stable 12,000 gns Doncaster August Sales after third start (blinkered): well below best for present stable: stays 3¾m: acts on soft going: held up: often let down by jumping. *R. J. Hodges* **c99 x h–**

TOM THE BOMB 7 b.g. Faustus (USA) – Llanon (Owen Dudley) [2002/3 c20mᵖᵘ c26mᵖᵘ 21dᵖᵘ 19dᵖᵘ 22sᵖᵘ Feb 3] half-brother to winning 21f chaser Cader Idris (by St Columbus): dam well beaten on Flat at 2 yrs: runner-up on completed start in maiden points, only sign of ability: raced freely in blinkers final start. *D. R. Wellicome* **c– h–**

TOM TYGRYS 4 b.g. Danzig Connection (USA) – Strath Kitten (Scottish Reel) [2002/3 17s⁶ 16g⁵ 17m⁴ Aug 17] well held on Flat and in juvenile hurdles: visored final outing. *P. S. McEntee* **h–**

TOMWONTPAYALOT 4 gr.g. Overbury (IRE) – Alice Smith (Alias Smith (USA)) [2002/3 F14g² F16g² Apr 2] 15,000 3-y-o: first foal: dam modest hurdler/chaser, stayed 3m: runner-up both starts in bumpers, beaten 2 lengths by Very Optimistic in 19-runner event at Ascot second time: will stay beyond 2m. *B. J. Eckley* **F96**

TONGITA 5 b.m. Petong – Bonita Bee (King of Spain) [2002/3 F66: F17m⁶ F16s 19dᵖᵘ Jan 27] poor form in bumpers, left J. McConnochie after reappearance: showed little on hurdling debut. *B. R. Millman* **h– F64**

TONIOSO 8 b.g. Teenoso (USA) – Sweet Ryme (Rymer) [2002/3 17m⁵ 17d⁶ 17m⁶ Sep 13] 6,500 4-y-o: sturdy gelding: fourth foal: dam unraced, from family of top-class staying chaser Brown Chamberlin: best effort in novice company over hurdles when fifth of 12 to eased Welsh Border at Southwell: will be well suited by further than 17f. *Mrs S. J. Smith* **h72**

TONKA 11 b.g. Mazilier (USA) – Royal Meeting (Dara Monarch) [2002/3 h101: 19g 21d 24d⁶ Jan 16] smallish gelding: fair handicap hurdler, well below form since first **h–**

half of 2001/2: effective at 21f to 3m: acts on heavy going: races prominently: has worn cheekpieces. *D. R. Gandolfo*

TONOCO 10 b.g. Teenoso (USA) – Lady Shoco (Montekin) [2002/3 c–, h–: c20d^F c16d² c24v* c24d³ c24d² c21s^{pu} c21d c25m* Apr 21] tall, lengthy gelding: tubed: fairly useful handicap chaser: won at Haydock in December and Wetherby in April: ridden with more restraint than on previous 2 starts when beating Eau de Cologne a neck in 6-runner race at latter: stays 25f: acts on good to firm and heavy going: tried in tongue strap: sound jumper. *Mrs S. J. Smith*   **c118 h–**

TONY THE PILER (IRE) 7 br.g. Tidaro (USA) – Adabiya (IRE) (Akarad (FR)) [2002/3 h76+: 24g³ 20v² 24v⁵ 20g⁴ Mar 28] small gelding: poor handicap hurdler: stays 3m: raced on good going or softer (acts on heavy): has worn cheekpieces: reluctant to race second start. *N. G. Richards*   **h80**

TONY TIE 7 b.g. Ardkinglass – Queen of The Quorn (Governor General) [2002/3 16s Nov 16] fairly useful on Flat (stays easy 1¼m): well held in maiden on hurdling debut. *J. S. Goldie*   **h–**

TOO FAR TO BRIDGE 6 b.g. Jupiter Island – Catherine Bridge (Pitpan) [2002/3 20v^{pu} Nov 27] tall gelding: sixth foal: half-brother to fair hurdler/chaser around 2m Bungee Jumper (by Idiot's Delight) and bumper winner Finally Fantazia (by True Song): dam, winning hurdler, stayed 2½m: broke blood vessel in novice hurdle at Chepstow on debut. *H. D. Daly*   **h–**

TOO FORWARD (IRE) 7 ch.g. Toulon – One Back (IRE) (Meneval (USA)) [2002/3 h130: 24g^{bd} 24m Apr 17] tall, leggy gelding: useful novice hurdler in 2001/2: chipped a bone in hock in summer, and long way below form on completed outing in handicaps: stays 3m: acts on good to firm and heavy going: carries head awkwardly under pressure, and probably best held up: not always fluent. *M. Pitman*   **h–**

TOO MUCH 5 b.m. Lugana Beach – Dancing May (Tina's Pet) [2002/3 F16m⁶ F16m 16g^{pu} 19m^{pu} Sep 11] third reported foal: dam plater: no form in bumpers or over hurdles: blinkered final start (not fluent). *J. L. Spearing*   **h– F–**

TOORAK (USA) 6 b.g. Irish River (FR) – Just Juliet (USA) (What A Pleasure (USA)) [2002/3 h87: 16g Apr 12] workmanlike gelding: disappointing maiden on Flat/over hurdles. *Mrs T. J. McInnes Skinner*   **h–**

TOO TECHNICAL (IRE) 8 b.g. Archway (IRE) – Another Side (Bold Lad (IRE)) [2002/3 16m 16g 16d⁵ Feb 8] bumper winner: off over 2 years, poor form at best over hurdles. *J. M. Jefferson*   **h78**

TOP AR AGHAIDH (IRE) 5 b.m. Topanoora – Shuil Ar Aghaidh (The Parson) [2002/3 F17m* May 3] fourth foal: half-sister to 2m hurdle winner Rith Ar Aghaidh (by Phardante): dam, very smart staying hurdler, half-sister to useful staying jumper Rawhide, from family of very smart hurdler Liss A Paoraigh and Scottish National winner Baronet: won bumper at Folkestone on debut, reeling in stable-companion Applepie Lady on line having looked held for much of straight: will be suited by further than 17f. *A. J. Lidderdale*   **F84**

TOP BUCK (IRE) 9 b.g. Top of The World – Orlita (Master Buck) [2002/3 h110: c19s* c20d^F Feb 17] tall, useful-looking gelding: fair hurdler: chaser on looks and unbeaten in 2 starts over fences, winning maiden at Ascot (beat High Cotton 5 lengths despite idling) in November and novice at Fontwell (all out after mistake last) in February: effective at 2m to 2¾m: raced on good going or softer (acts on soft): consistent: remains open to improvement over fences. *K. C. Bailey*   **c119 p h–**

TOP LIGHT 7 b.g. Miner's Lamp – Myrtilla (Beldale Flutter (USA)) [2002/3 h–, F74: 21g^{pu} c24m⁴ c24s^F c24d^F 22d c20m^F Apr 19] lengthy gelding: no form over hurdles or fences. *R. H. Buckler*   **c– h–**

TOP NOLANS (IRE) 5 ch.g. Topanoora – Lauretta Blue (IRE) (Bluebird (USA)) [2002/3 16m³ 16m Oct 19] fair on Flat (stays 8.5f), claimed from M. Tompkins £7,000 in July: poor form when third in novice at Uttoxeter on hurdling debut, jinking right at several flights: well held in seller 2 months later. *Miss K. Marks*   **h63**

TOP NOTCH 5 br.m. Alderbrook – Gaygo Lady (Gay Fandango (USA)) [2002/3 F17s⁶ F17s Nov 21] useful-looking mare: half-sister to 21f chase winner in Switzerland by Glenstal and to fair 6f/7f winner Baligay (by Balidar): dam smart 1m winner: well held in bumpers 6 months apart. *K. C. Bailey*   **F–**

TOP OF THE CLASS (IRE) 6 b.m. Rudimentary (USA) – School Mum (Reprimand) [2002/3 h63: 18m Sep 24] lengthy, sparely-made mare: modest on Flat (stays

1¼m), successful twice in 2002: poor maiden hurdler: probably needs easy 2m: raced mainly on good going or softer (probably struggles to stay on heavy): twice visored. *P. D. Evans*

TOP OF THE DEE 6 ch.m. Rakaposhi King – Lavenham's Last (Rymer) [2002/3 **h65** h–, F–: 17s⁶ 16s⁵ 16m 20m³ 17d³ 20m⁴ 17m² 22m³ 17d⁶ Oct 12] rangy, rather unfurnished mare: poor maiden hurdler: probably stays 2½m: tongue tied last 3 outings. *Mrs L. Williamson*

TOP OF THE LEFT 8 b. or br.g. Nomination – Diva Madonna (Chief Singer) [2002/3 **h98 p** 19d Jan 27] good-topped gelding: modest form both starts in novice hurdles in 2000/1: caught the eye when seventh of 18 in similar event at Exeter on return: presumably difficult to train, but remains open to improvement. *Jonjo O'Neill*

TOP OF THE STACK 5 b.g. Syrtos – Just Hannah (Macmillion) [2002/3 F16s 20vᵖᵘ **h–** Jan 29] fourth foal: half-brother to winning hurdler/fair chaser Banjo Hill (by Arctic **F–** Lord), stays 2¾m: dam poor maiden on Flat: no show in bumper or novice hurdle. *B. N. Doran*

TOPOL (IRE) 5 br.g. Topanoora – Kislev (IRE) (Be My Guest (USA)) [2002/3 F74: **h78** 17s 16d 19d Feb 23] useful-looking gelding: poor form in novice hurdles: free-going sort. *Miss H. C. Knight*

TOPPING LASS (IRE) 8 b.m. Topanoora – Grassed (Busted) [2002/3 16g⁵ 20gᵖᵘ **h– §** 22dʳᵗʳ 17s 19d 16v 16dᵖᵘ Feb 25] second foal: sister to bumper winner Hillcrest Manor: dam, won 17f hurdle, placed up to 2m on Flat: third in bumper on debut but little form since, sold out of C. Roche's stable 600 gns Doncaster September Sales after reappearance: usually tongue tied: headstrong and temperamental. *A. W. Carroll*

TOP SAINT (IRE) 9 gr.g. Topanoora – God's Kiss (Godswalk (USA)) [2002/3 h79: **h64** 21d² 24g May 22] sturdy gelding: poor maiden hurdler: stays 23f: acts on good to firm and heavy going: sold 1,100 gns Doncaster October Sales. *Mrs M. Reveley*

TOP STOPPA 5 gr.g. Environment Friend – Orchid Valley (IRE) (Cyrano de Bergerac) **F–** [2002/3 F16f Sep 15] first foal: dam ran twice: raced freely in front when well beaten in bumper at Hexham on debut. *A. Scott*

TOP TEAM 7 b.m. Teamster – Highly Inflammable (USA) (Wind And Wuthering **c–** (USA)) [2002/3 h–, F–: c20m³ c20dᵖᵘ c20dᵖᵘ Jun 8] no sign of ability: tried visored. **h–** *Dr P. Pritchard*

TOP TREES 5 b.g. Charnwood Forest (IRE) – Low Line (High Line) [2002/3 17s⁴ **h75** 17s Nov 28] fair but temperamental maiden on Flat (barely stays 1½m): well held in maiden hurdles at Taunton. *W. S. Kittow*

TORCHE (IRE) 5 b.g. Taos (IRE) – Orchette (IRE) (Orchestra) [2002/3 F17g⁴ Mar **F85** 22] first foal: dam unraced, from family of smart staying chaser Zeta's Lad: outpaced before running on when close fourth of 8 in bumper at Bangor on debut: will be suited by greater test of stamina. *D. J. Caro*

TORDUFF BOY (IRE) 10 b.g. Yashgan – Couleurs Volants (Peacock (FR)) [2002/3 **c131** c123: c22s² c22d 20m² 20f⁴ c24fᵘʳ c17v⁴ c24g³ c29g⁵ Apr 21] workmanlike gelding: **h95** twice-raced over hurdles: useful handicap chaser: creditable efforts in quite valuable event at Cork (third to Native Jack) and Irish Grand National at Fairyhouse (fifth to Timbera): won quite valuable race at Punchestown in early-May for second successive year, beating Michael Mor ¾ length: stays 29f: acts on soft and good to firm going: has had tongue tied, including at Punchestown *Paul Nolan, Ireland*

TORDUFF EXPRESS (IRE) 12 b.g. Kambalda – Marhabtain (Touching Wood **c118** (USA)) [2002/3 c130, h–: c22d² c26d* c36dᵘʳ c31d⁴ Apr 25] rather leggy gelding: smart **h–** hunter chaser, won 2002 Fox Hunters' Chase at Aintree: won 6-runner event at Fontwell (for second year running) in February: prominent long way though held in sixth when unseating 4 out (saddle slipped) in Grand National at Aintree: lacklustre effort later in month: stays 4m: acts on good to firm and heavy going: effective blinkered or not: has flashed tail under pressure, but is reliable. *P. F. Nicholls*

TOREO (FR) 9 ch.g. Bakharoff (USA) – Becerrada (FR) (Tip Moss (FR)) [2002/3 **h–** 20sᵖᵘ 16dᶠ Mar 7] sturdy, lengthy gelding: poor maiden hurdler, failed to complete both starts after near 3-year absence. *J. R. Adam*

TORMENTOSO 6 b.g. Catral (USA) – Chita Rivera (Chief Singer) [2002/3 h74§: **h– §** 16m 20g 16m⁶ 16m Jun 19] small gelding: poor and unreliable maiden hurdler: best around 2m: acted on firm and soft ground: tried visored/tongue tied: dead. *A. G. Hobbs*

TORN SILK 9 b.g. Top Ville – Cut Velvet (USA) (Northern Dancer) [2002/3 c115, h–: c23s* c20d⁴ c25g⁶ c24dᵖᵘ Apr 9] workmanlike gelding: fairly useful handicap chaser: won at Worcester in June: left P. Nicholls and off 9 months, no impact in hunters in spring: stays 3m: acts on any going: visored, usually blinkered: has reportedly broken blood vessels: carries head high: unreliable. *P. England* **c116 d h–**

TOROSAY (IRE) 5 b.g. Presenting – Mazuma (IRE) (Mazaad) [2002/3 F17d⁵ Mar 2] second foal: dam, won 2m hurdle, half-sister to useful juvenile hurdler Lir: under 3 lengths fifth of 15 to Riothamus in bumper at Carlisle on debut. *N. G. Richards* **F98**

TORTUGA DREAM (IRE) 4 b.g. Turtle Island (IRE) – Tycoon's Catch (IRE) (Thatching) [2002/3 16g 16v⁶ 20v 17m Apr 16] lengthy gelding: no show on Flat or over hurdles. *A. Charlton* **h–**

TORTUGAS (FR) 6 b.g. Subotica (FR) – Northern Whisper (FR) (Vacarme (USA)) [2002/3 h73§: 17d c17m⁴ c19m⁴ c24gᶠ c19dᶠ c17mᶠ Apr 21] angular gelding: winning hurdler: little form since 2000/1 (badly let down by jumping over fences): should stay 2½m: tried visored: temperamental. *Mrs H. Dalton* **c54 § h– §**

TORUS STAR (IRE) 14 b.g. Torus – Vulstar (Vulgan) [2002/3 c25dᵖᵘ May 14] ex-Irish gelding: fair pointer, successful 3 times in 2002: no form over hurdles or in steeplechases. *Mrs J. Mathias* **c– h–**

TORY BOY 8 b.g. Deploy – Mukhayyalah (Dancing Brave (USA)) [2002/3 c–, h77+: 17m* 16s³ 21m² 21g⁴ Sep 8] close-coupled gelding: modest on Flat (stays 2m): jumped poorly only outing over fences: modest handicap hurdler: successful at Southwell in July and Stratford in August: stays 3m, effective at much shorter: acts on firm and soft going: tried blinkered/visored. *M. G. Quinlan* **c– h93**

TOSAWI (IRE) 7 b.g. Commanche Run – Deep Satisfaction (Deep Run) [2002/3 h102: 16m⁶ 21d 19s⁴ 24s 22d 16s³ 19v² Mar 4] good-bodied gelding: fair handicap hurdler: stays 21f: acts on heavy and good to firm going: takes good hold. *R. J. Hodges* **h100**

TOSCANINI (GER) 7 b.g. Goofalik (USA) – Tosca Stella (GER) (Surumu (GER)) [2002/3 h82: 16s⁵ 21sᵖᵘ 19v* Mar 4] useful-looking gelding: modest hurdler: won steadily-run 4-runner handicap at Exeter in March: should stay beyond 19f: acts on heavy going: has looked difficult ride. *D. R. Gandolfo* **h89**

TOSHEROON (IRE) 7 b.g. Good Thyne (USA) – Rare Currency (Rarity) [2002/3 21g* 20s³ Nov 2] IR 16,000 3-y-o: useful-looking gelding: fourth foal: half-brother to fairly useful chaser up to 2¾m Shekels (by Orchestra): dam unraced, from family of high-class chaser Fifty Dollars More: fell in maiden Irish point on debut in 2001: promising start over hurdles, won novice at Plumpton in October and third to King Bee in novice handicap at Ascot (drifted under pressure and jumped right last 2): remains open to improvement. *A. M. Hales* **h104 p**

TOSHIBA TIMES 7 b.g. Persian Bold – Kirkby Belle (Bay Express) [2002/3 h92: c16g⁵ c16g⁶ Oct 15] modest hurdler: much better effort over fences (left B. Ellison after reappearance) when fourth of 6 to Jokers Charm in handicap at Sedgefield: raced around 2m: acts on firm and good to soft going: has found little/looked none too keen. *M. Todhunter* **c89 h–**

TOSTI (FR) 7 b.g. Beyssac (FR) – Madame Flibuste (FR) (Rahotep (FR)) [2002/3 c–, h–: c26s⁵ c25dᵖᵘ Dec 17] ex-French gelding, very lightly raced: winning hurdler: poor form only completed start in novice chases in Britain. *C. R. Egerton* **c84 h–**

TOTAL ECLIPSE (IRE) 8 b.g. Be My Native (USA) – Everdancing (Dance In Time (CAN)) [2002/3 17g Sep 6] poor novice hurdler in 2000/1 (tongue tied last 4 starts) for M. Pipe: well beaten only subsequent outing. *A. J. Lockwood* **h–**

TOTALLY SCOTTISH 7 b.g. Mtoto – Glenfinlass (Lomond (USA)) [2002/3 h94: 16mᵘʳ 17d² 17s* 19d² 20s⁵ 18g² Mar 21] rather sparely-made gelding: maiden on Flat: fairly useful handicap hurdler: won at Carlisle (has good record there) in November: improved further when head second to Celtic Vision at Kelso final start: stays 2½m: acts on soft and good to firm going: blinkered/tongue tied on debut: held up, and has looked less than keen under pressure. *Mrs M. Reveley* **h117**

TOTEM DANCER 10 b.m. Mtoto – Ballad Opera (Sadler's Wells (USA)) [2002/3 h–: 21mᵖᵘ Sep 13] successful up to 15f on Flat: lightly raced and little form over hurdles: tongue tied last 2 outings. *B. G. Powell* **h–**

TO THE FUTURE (IRE) 7 ch.g. Bob Back (USA) – Lady Graduate (IRE) (Le Bavard (FR)) [2002/3 c95p, h–: c25dᵖᵘ c25s² c25v* c25sᵖᵘ Feb 23] tall gelding: maiden hurdler: modest chaser: won novice handicap at Ayr in January: reportedly distressed **c96 h–**

final outing: will stay beyond 3¼m: raced on going softer than good (acts on heavy). *A. Parker*

TOTLAND BAY (IRE) 7 br.g. Phardante (FR) – Seanaphobal Lady (Kambalda)   **h100**
[2002/3 h78, F78: 20m⁴ 23d 22g* 22f² 22d³ 22m² 22g² 22m³ 21m² Apr 19] fair hurdler:
won 6-runner maiden at Newton Abbot in July: placed all starts after, off 6 months before
beaten short head by Paynestown Lad in novice at Plumpton final one: stays 2¾m: acts
on firm going, seemingly not on softer than good: reportedly made a noise second start.
J. W. Mullins

TOTO TALECA 6 b.m. Mtoto – Miss Taleca (Pharly (FR)) [2002/3 F–: F16d 19g 19d   **h–**
21vᵖᵘ 16d 17s 17mᵘʳ 17gᵖᵘ Apr 26] leggy mare: of little account. *M. E. Sowersby*   **F–**

TOUCH CLOSER 6 b.g. Inchinor – Ryewater Dream (Touching Wood (USA))   **h67**
[2002/3 F110: 16d 21vᵖᵘ 16d 20gᵖᵘ Mar 29] angular gelding: useful bumper form in
2001/2: also fairly useful form on Flat in 2002, but very disappointing over hurdles.
G. A. Swinbank

TOUCH OF EBONY (IRE) 4 b.c. Darshaan – Cormorant Wood (Home Guard   **h–**
(USA)) [2002/3 17s 17d 16d Feb 28] leggy colt: fair maiden on Flat (stays 1¾m): well
held in juvenile hurdles, raced freely in cheekpieces on debut. *J. Neville*

TOUCH OF LOVE 7 b.h. Pursuit of Love – Nitouche (Scottish Reel) [2002/3 16d⁶   **h117**
16d⁴ 16d* 16d⁴ 17g 16f² 16m⁵ Oct 6] fair on Flat (stays 1¾m): fairly useful handicap
hurdler: won at Naas in July: raced around 2m: acts on soft and firm going: blinkered
once: consistent. *E. J. O'Grady, Ireland*

TOUGH TERMS (IRE) 11 b.g. Welsh Term – Glenardina (Furry Glen) [2002/3   **c98**
c21m* May 22] workmanlike gelding: lightly raced: won 2 points in 2002: first form in   **h–**
steeplechases when winning novice hunter at Folkestone, though still far from foot
perfect (tended to go left). *Miss V. Park*

TOULON CREST (IRE) 6 b.g. Toulon – Another Contact (Martin John) [2002/3   **c88 ?**
F17s F16d F16g c24gᵖᵘ c17m³ Apr 21] rather unfurnished gelding: second live foal: dam   **F–**
winning 2m hurdler: fell in maiden Irish point on debut in 2002: well beaten in bumpers:
better effort in small-field novice chases when third of 4 to Indian Venture at Market
Rasen, possibly flattered: tried tongue tied. *G. Prodromou*

TOULON D'OR (IRE) 6 b.g. Toulon – Rare Currency (Rarity) [2002/3 F–: F17d⁵   **c–**
18m 16m 16g⁶ c20d⁴ c20dᵖᵘ Dec 10] tall gelding: signs of only a little ability in novice   **h–**
events over hurdles and fences. *M. Pitman*   **F–**

TOULON ROUGE (IRE) 6 b.m. Toulon – Master Nidee (Master Owen) [2002/3   **h93**
F88: 20m⁶ 21dᵖᵘ 21s⁶ 21v³ 21s* 21d⁶ 24g* Apr 23] tall, lengthy mare: bumper winner:
modest hurdler: won mares novices at Sedgefield in March and Perth in April: has shown
signs of temperament: stays 3m: acts on heavy going. *Ferdy Murphy*

TOULOUSE (IRE) 6 b.g. Toulon – Neasham (Nishapour (FR)) [2002/3 F16g³ 17s*   **h109**
16d⁵ 22d 19d Feb 23] rangy gelding: will make a chaser: brother to winning 19f hurdler   **F87**
The Matrix and half-brother to fair hurdler/novice chaser Jodesi (by Sandalay), stayed
2½m: dam maiden suited by 1¼m+: third in bumper at Wincanton: created good impression when winning novice at Taunton in December on hurdling debut: better form when
fifth of 18 to Mind How You Go in similar event at Wincanton: very disappointing both
subsequent starts: should stay beyond 17f. *R. H. Alner*

TOULOUSE-LAUTREC (IRE) 7 ch.g. Toulon – Bucks Slave (Buckskin (FR))   **c112 p**
[2002/3 h75, F68: c20s* c21d³ c24v* Dec 20] tall gelding: poor form in novice hurdles: **h–**
already much better over fences: won novice handicaps at Uttoxeter in November and
December, leading 4 out and soon clear when beating Cresswell Quay 14 lengths in latter:
likely to prove better suited to 3m than shorter: raced on going softer than good (acts on
heavy): open to further improvement. *T. R. George*

TOURING-TURTLE (IRE) 11 ro.g. Roselier (FR) – Rossian (Silent Spring) [2002/3   **c– x**
c84x, h–: c18f⁵ c23m Jul 17] leggy gelding: poor chaser: effective around 2½m to 3¼m: **h–**
acts on any going: blinkered final start: has been let down by jumping, including on
reappearance: inconsistent. *C. Tizzard*

TOURNIQUET (IRE) 8 b.g. Torus – Treidlia (Mandalus) [2002/3 25m² 24v³ 22d   **h98**
Feb 6] strong gelding: first foal: half-brother to very smart hurdler Classified (by Roselier), stays 3m: dam unplaced in bumpers: won second of 2 starts in maiden Irish points in
2002: bought 15,500 gns Doncaster August Sales: regressed after 3½ lengths second to
Balinahinch Castle in 5-finisher novice at Warwick on hurdling debut. *D. J. Caro*

TOWN CRIER (IRE)   8 br.g. Beau Sher – Ballymacarett (Menelek) [2002/3 20s^F Jan 30] tall gelding: very lightly raced: well held when fell last in novice hurdle at Southwell after over 2-year absence. *Mrs S. J. Smith*   **h–**

TOWNIE (IRE)   9 ch.g. Camden Town – Pafelto (Ragapan) [2002/3 24g^6 24s 26g Feb 22] workmanlike gelding: fair handicap hurdler in 2000/1: well held after 2-year lay-off, found nothing final start: stays 3m: acts on good to soft and good to firm going: blinkered once: wears tongue strap. *C. P. Morlock*   **h–**

TOWNS ENDER (IRE)   5 b.g. Zaffaran (USA) – Delway (Fidel) [2002/3 F16s F16d 17g^5 Mar 22] IR £44,000 3-y-o: strong, lengthy gelding: fifth foal: brother to fair 2¼m hurdle winner Munster: dam twice-raced sister to very smart 2m hurdler Fidway: well held in 2 bumpers and novice hurdle. *D. J. Caro*   **h–**
F–

TOY BOY (IRE)   5 b.g. Un Desperado (FR) – Too Sharp (True Song) [2002/3 F16d Dec 12] first foal: dam modest hurdler/chaser, stayed 2½m: weakened quickly having led going well 4f out in bumper at Huntingdon on debut. *Miss H. C. Knight*   **F–**

TRABOLGAN (IRE)   5 b.g. King's Ride – Derrella (Derrylin) [2002/3 F16v^2 F16m^2 F16g^2 Mar 12]   **F118**

Trabolgan is rated behind only Liberman (and Rhinestone Cowboy, who had been sent hurdling before Christmas) among the British-trained bumper horses in 2002/3 but, unfortunately for his connections, his best effort came when chasing home Liberman in the Weatherbys Champion Bumper at Cheltenham, his third successive second place in three starts. Trabolgan started favourite when runner-up to Plastic Paddy in the mud at Uttoxeter in December and when beaten a neck by newcomer Chelsea Bridge in a steadily-run event on much less testing ground at Kempton in February. The Kempton effort was useful but not one that made Trabolgan an obvious candidate for Cheltenham, where he was sent off a 50/1-

Mr Trevor Hemmings' "Trabolgan"

chance, stable jockey Mick Fitzgerald choosing to partner Back To Ben Alder, who finished last. A more truly-run race served Trabolgan well and he showed marked improvement, always handy, challenging into the straight and keeping on despite edging right until held close home. He was half a length down at the line, giving his owner and trainer their second runner-up in the race after the ill-fated Inca in 2000. The valuable bumper at Cheltenham's Open meeting in November could be an ideal starting point for 2003/4 before Trabolgan is sent over jumps, in which sphere he is likely to stay two and a half miles. He isn't the only noteworthy member of his family with a touch of seconditis, as his unraced dam Derrella is a sister to the high-class two-mile hurdler Kesslin. His most significant efforts came when finding one too good, as in the Bula Hurdle, the Supreme Novices' and the Breeders' Cup Chase, and even when he was first past the post in a big race, in the Wessel Cable Irish Champion Hurdle, he was demoted by the stewards. Derrella is also a half-sister to Rathconrath, a smart hurdler as a four-year-old and later a useful chaser. Her foals prior to Trabolgan haven't set the world alight but his none-too-younger half-sister Time For An Audit (by Supreme Leader) finished third on her debut in the extremely valuable mares and fillies bumper at the Punchestown Festival shortly after the end of the British season. Trabolgan was rather unfurnished in appearance in his first season but can be expected to fill out and he makes plenty of appeal as a prospective novice hurdler. *N. J. Henderson*

TRACK O' PROFIT (IRE) 11 ch.g. Kambalda – Teazle (Quayside) [2002/3 c95, h–: c24s* c26m³ Apr 17] medium-sized gelding: fairly useful hunter chaser: as good as ever when winning at Taunton in February: not take eye, remote third of 6 finishers to Earthmover at Cheltenham: effective around 2½m to 3¼m: acts on firm and soft going. *Miss S. Young*   **c99 h–**

TRADE DISPUTE (IRE) 11 ch.g. Ela-Mana-Mou – Safety Feature (Be My Guest (USA)) [2002/3 c114, h–: c25dᵖᵘ c25g* c27d* Apr 8] leggy gelding: useful hunter chaser: off nearly a year (reportedly with back problem), shaped as if amiss on reappearance but bounced back to land odds in point and hunters at Kelso in March and Sedgefield (not extended to beat Royal Snoopy 6 lengths) in April: stays 3½m: acts on soft and good to firm going: blinkered once: jumps soundly in main: genuine and consistent. *G. Tuer*   **c116 h–**

TRADING TROUBLE 6 b.g. Petoski – Marielou (FR) (Carwhite) [2002/3 h110: c16v³ c19gꟳ c20s³ Mar 2] medium-sized gelding: fair hurdler: similar form over fences, would have won novice at Catterick but for falling 3 out: stays 2½m: raced on good going or softer (acts on heavy). *J. M. Jefferson*   **c112 h–**

TRADITIONAL (IRE) 7 ch.g. Erins Isle – Noorajo (IRE) (Ahonoora) [2002/3 16s 16v 16g⁵ 18d 16m 24m² 20g* 22m* 22d 24s⁶ 24g⁵ 22d⁴ 22g 22g⁶ Apr 21] close-coupled gelding: won up to 2m on Flat: modest novice hurdler: won at Downpatrick in September (maiden) and October: sold out of P. Rothwell's stable 9,200 gns Doncaster November Sales: best effort in handicaps after when fourth to Wartorn at Wincanton: stays easy 3m: acts on good to soft and good to firm going: blinkered (stiff task) fourth start. *N. J. Hawke*   **h89**

TRAGIC OHIO 4 b.g. Tragic Role (USA) – Kiniohio (FR) (Script Ohio (USA)) [2002/3 F17d* F16d⁴ Mar 19] first foal: dam won 2¼m juvenile hurdle: 50/1, won bumper at Exeter in February on debut by 8 lengths from Gentle Beau: favourite, similar form when fourth of 10 to Mount Karinga at Chepstow, looking in need of greater test of stamina. *M. C. Pipe*   **F102**

TRAINED BYTHE BEST 5 b.m. Alderbrook – Princess Moodyshoe (Jalmood (USA)) [2002/3 h103: 18m 20d³ 20vᵖᵘ Dec 21] leggy mare: fairly useful on Flat (stays 2¼m): fair hurdler: hasn't progressed, and didn't impress with attitude or jumping in handicaps last 2 starts: stays 2½m: acts on good to soft going: tongue tied: one to be wary of. *M. C. Pipe*   **h103 §**

TRAJECTUS 6 b.m. Homo Sapien – Dublin Ferry (Celtic Cone) [2002/3 F16mᵖᵘ F17s Nov 21] fifth foal: half-sister to 3 winners, including winning hurdler/useful chaser Europa (by Jupiter Island), stays 2½m: dam unraced half-sister to top-class 2½m chaser Dublin Flyer: no promise in 2 bumpers. *Mrs H. Dalton*   **F–**

TRAMANTANO 4 b.g. Muhtarram (USA) – Hatta Breeze (Night Shift (USA)) [2002/3 16d³ 17d⁴ 16d⁴ 16d⁴ 16g Mar 11] good-topped gelding: second foal: dam, useful hurdler, half-sister to high-class hurdler/smart chaser Land Afar, effective at 2m to sharp 3m: fairly useful 1¼m winner on Flat for H. Candy: created very good impression when winning juvenile at Newbury in November on hurdling debut, beating Nas Na Riogh 1½   **h121**

lengths: failed to progress as well as expected, generally not fluent: raced around 2m, mainly on good to soft going: reportedly had breathing problem third start, tongue tied afterwards. *N. A. Twiston-Davies*

TRANSATLANTIC (USA) 5 gr.g. Dumaani (USA) – Viendra (USA) (Raise A   h77
Native) [2002/3 16g 16g 16m 19m^pu Apr 21] useful on Flat (stays 9f), below form after winning on reappearance in 2002, sold out of F. J. Houghton's stable 23,000 gns Newmarket Autumn Sales: little encouragement over hurdles, made mistakes and hung right second start: headstrong. *H. D. Daly*

TRANSIT 4 b.c. Lion Cavern (USA) – Black Fighter (USA) (Secretariat (USA))   h87 +
[2002/3 16d^5 16d^5 16g^2 Mar 29] leggy colt: half-brother to fairly useful hurdler around 2½m Taming and useful hurdler around 2m Tikram (both by Lycius): fairly useful maiden on Flat (seems to stay 1½m), sold out of H. Cecil's stable 15,000 gns Newmarket Autumn Sales: modest form over hurdles, 5 lengths second to Bushido in juvenile at Hexham: best effort but didn't look easy ride when seventh of 20 in 4-y-o novice at Punchestown (wore cheekpieces) month later. *B. Ellison*

TRANSLUCID (USA) 5 b.h. Woodman (USA) – Gossamer (USA) (Seattle Slew   h114
(USA)) [2002/3 17g^2 16d^2 16d* 17s^6 Jan 25] angular horse: successful 4 times up to 1½m on Flat, including at Dusseldorf in June: fair form over hurdles, made most to win 22-runner novice at Warwick in November by 3 lengths from Kali des Obeaux: favourite, found little after taking good hold up with pace when sixth of 23 to Keltic Bard in novice handicap at Cheltenham: free-going sort, likely to prove best at 2m. *C. Von Der Recke, Germany*

TRAVELLERS HEIR (IRE) 5 ch.g. Montelimar (USA) – Allaracket (IRE) (The   h90
Parson) [2002/3 F91: F16d^4 16g 21m^2 Mar 19] stocky gelding: fair form in frame both   F87
starts in bumpers: upped in trip, better effort over hurdles when 1¾ lengths second of 6 to Rainbow River in novice at Ludlow, keeping on despite wandering under pressure: may improve again over further still. *H. D. Daly*

TRAVELLING JACK 8 ch.g. Lyphento (USA) – Lady Magenta (Rolfe (USA))   c–
[2002/3 c–: c25d^5 Mar 6] fair pointer, successful twice in 2002: no show in 2 hunter chases, jumped badly first time. *Mrs Laura J. Young*

TREASURE CHEST (IRE) 8 b.g. Last Tycoon – Sought Out (IRE) (Rainbow Quest   h73 §
(USA)) [2002/3 h89§: 22g^6 19s 21v^6 Jan 23] leggy gelding: modest handicap hurdler, out of form around 2m to 3m: acts on good to firm and heavy going: effective blinkered/visored or not: has had tongue tied: temperamental. *M. C. Pipe*

TREASURED COIN 5 b.g. Overbury (IRE) – Slip A Coin (Slip Anchor) [2002/3 h–:   h71
20m^2 24g^pu Sep 15] leggy gelding: well held in maiden on Flat: form over hurdles only when second in novice handicap at Fontwell. *P. Bowen*

TREASURED GUEST 5 b.g. Rainbow Quest (USA) – Free Guest (Be My Guest   h106
(USA)) [2002/3 17m^2 16s* 16d^2 16g^3 16f 20s* 16d Nov 16] good-topped gelding: modest on Flat (stays 13f): fair novice hurdler: won at Kilbeggan (maiden) in July and Wexford in October: stays 2½m: acts on firm and soft going, yet to race on heavy: reliable. *M. Halford, Ireland*

TREASURE DOME (IRE) 9 b.g. Treasure Kay – Royal Saint (USA) (Crimson   c– §
Satan) [2002/3 c–, h–: c21m^pu Apr 21] good-topped gelding: one-time fair 2m hurdler: h–
unreliable pointer nowadays, successful in March: pulled up most other starts in 2003, including in novice hunter. *John Whyte*

TREBLE TROUBLE 7 b.g. Minster Son – Ferneyhill Lady (Menelek) [2002/3 c–:   c–
c20m^pu 24g^pu 25m^F 24s^pu c21v^3 c16s^pu c17g^5 Mar 15] good-topped gelding: winning   h–
pointer: little form otherwise: tongue tied final start. *C. C. Bealby*

TREMALLT (IRE) 12 b.g. Henbit (USA) – Secret Romance (Gala Performance   c110 +
(USA)) [2002/3 c136, h100+: 24s c24s c21s^3 c36d Apr 5] close-coupled gelding: h94 +
winning hurdler: one-time useful handicap chaser, not the force of old: best around 3m nowadays (failed to stay in Grand National): acts on heavy going, probably on good to firm: visored once: front runner: bold jumper, prone to the odd error. *T. R. George*

TRENANCE 5 b.g. Alflora (IRE) – Carmel's Joy (IRE) (Carlingford Castle) [2002/3   F–
F16g Apr 2] sturdy gelding: first foal: dam winning hurdler/chaser, stayed 33f: thirteenth of 19 in bumper at Ascot on debut. *T. R. George*

TRENCROM HILL 6 b.g. Homo Sapien – Sweet On Willie (USA) (Master Willie)   F–
[2002/3 F–: F17d Oct 22] workmanlike gelding: tailed off in 2 bumpers. *R. J. Hodges*

Glenmore Investments Novices' Hurdle, Ascot—Tribal Venture gets off the mark over hurdles

TRESOR DE MAI (FR) 9 ch.g. Grand Tresor (FR) – Lady Night (FR) (Pompon Rouge) [2002/3 c148x, h–: c20d⁴ c19s³ c20g Mar 12] sparely-made gelding: smart chaser: won Grade 1 event at Ascot in 2001/2: creditable third of 7 to Tiutchev in same race in February: well beaten other 2 starts in 2002/3: effective around 2½m to 3m: acts on heavy going: blinkered prior to 2001/2: sketchy jumper. *M. C. Pipe*   **c150 x** **h–**

TRESOR PREZINIERE (FR) 5 b. or br.g. Grand Tresor (FR) – Rose de Martine (FR) (The Quiet Man (FR)) [2002/3 17gᵖᵘ c18g c18g⁵ c17gᶠ c20gᵘʳ c18g* c20g³ c19g³ c19d* c19v c18s³ c16m⁴ c16gᶠ Apr 24] leggy ex-French gelding: fifth foal: half-brother to winning hurdler/chaser up to 19f J'Adore Martine (by Bojador): dam lightly raced and little sign of ability: ran once on Flat: maiden hurdler: won 4-y-o chases at Josselin in August and Angers (left T. Poche after next outing) in October: last of 4 to Tysou in novice at Wincanton, again jumping left, and fell second next time: stays 19f: acts on good to soft going: sometimes blinkered in France. *P. J. Hobbs*   **c?** **h?**

TRES TOUCHE (USA) 6 b. or br.g. Poles Apart (USA) – Princess Smoggy (USA) (Smoggy) [2002/3 h127: 18f² 17f² 19s⁵ 19s* 21s² 20d* 22d² 19f² 20g³ Apr 19] leading American hurdler: won valuable events at Shawan Downs in September and Montpelier in November: second 3 tries in Grade 1 contests, to Flat Top in Breeders Cup at Far Hills and Colonial Cup at Camden, and to Al Skywalker in Carolina Cup at last-named course: stays 21f: acts on firm and soft going: has had tongue tied. *R. Hendriks, USA*   **h?**

TRIBAL COUNTY (IRE) 8 b.g. Erdelistan (FR) – Kismet Dancer (IRE) (Lancastrian) [2002/3 20g 20g 19d 24vᵖᵘ 20g³ 20s* Mar 6] 3,000 4-y-o: workmanlike ex-Irish gelding: first foal: dam ran once: bumper winner: modest hurdler: sold out of M. Morris' stable 8,800 gns Doncaster May Sales after second start: best effort when winning novice at Carlisle by 7 lengths from Chabrimal Minster: should stay beyond 2½m: acts on soft going: usually tongue tied in Ireland: sold 10,000 gns Doncaster May Sales. *Ferdy Murphy*   **h98**

TRIBAL DANCER (IRE) 9 ch.g. Commanche Run – Cute Play (Salluceva) [2002/3   **c116** h112: 24d² c24s⁴ c24s* c26s⁵ c24m² Apr 12] leggy, close-coupled gelding: fair handicap   **h112** hurdler: similar form over fences, won novice at Taunton (idled) in February: would have been at least third but for falling 2 out in valuable novice handicap at Punchestown in late-April: likely to stay beyond 3m: acts on soft and good to good going: not an easy ride (has hung very badly/wandered under pressure). *Miss Venetia Williams*

TRIBAL DISPUTE 6 b.g. Primitive Rising (USA) – Coral Princess (Imperial Fling   **h110** (USA)) [2002/3 F81: F17d 17d⁴ 20d 20g² 16v* 16d² 16d² 16g* 20d Apr 25] big,   **F–** useful-looking gelding: will make a chaser: modest form on first of 2 starts in bumpers: fair novice hurdler: won at Newcastle (handicap) in January and Kelso (beat Gastornis a short head, pair clear) in April: went too freely final outing: should prove as effective at 2½m as 2m: acts on heavy going: had breathing problem third start. *T. D. Easterby*

TRIBAL KING (IRE) 8 b. or br.g. Be My Native (USA) – Island Bridge (Mandalus)   **c111** [2002/3 c105, h–: c20g* c20d* c22d⁶ c25d^pu c24s⁶ Jan 27] lengthy, good sort: winning   **h–** hurdler: fair novice chaser: won at Aintree in May and Wetherby (handicap) in November: went as if amiss last 2 outings: stays 2¾m: raced mainly on good going or softer (won bumper on soft): takes good hold. *Miss H. C. Knight*

TRIBAL RUN (IRE) 8 ch.g. Be My Native (USA) – Queen's Run (IRE) (Deep Run)   **c102** [2002/3 c25v* c25v² c24v² c30d² Feb 8] fourth foal: half-brother to winning hurdler   **h–** Banreme (by Supreme Leader), stays 3m: dam unraced: novice hurdler: won 3 Irish points in 2002: won maiden chase at Hexham in November: better form when runner-up all 3 starts after, beaten 3 lengths by Native Buck in handicap at Catterick final one: stays 3¾m: acts on heavy going: tongue tied. *N. G. Richards*

TRIBAL TRACT (IRE) 9 b.g. Alphabatim (USA) – Wiji Damar (Laurence O)   **c–** [2002/3 c100d: c25d^pu May 6] workmanlike gelding: fair novice chaser at best, disappointing since reappearance in 2001/2: won point in April: should prove best at 3m+: acts on soft going: tried blinkered/tongue tied. *Jonjo O'Neill*

TRIBAL VENTURE (FR) 5 gr.g. Dom Alco (FR) – Babacha (FR) (Latnahc (USA))   **h133** [2002/3 F92: 22s⁶ 24v* 20s⁵ 24d² 23s⁶ 25g³ 24m* Apr 17] rather leggy gelding: novice hurdler: won at Ascot in December and Cheltenham (handicap) in April: useful form when beating Rosco 11 lengths in 11-runner event at latter: third to Inching Closer in Pertemps Final (Handicap) there start before: best at 3m+: acts on good to firm and heavy going: has jumped none too fluently. *Ferdy Murphy*

TRIBAL WARRIOR (IRE) 8 b.m. Muharib (USA) – War Saint (Tug of War)   **c–** [2002/3 c71, h76, F72: c24m⁴ Sep 14] sparely-made mare: poor hurdler: similar form on   **h–** first of 2 starts in steeplechases: stays 23f: acts on good to firm ground (bumper form on firm and good to soft): effective tongue tied or not. *N. B. Mason*

TRICKY TREVOR (IRE) 10 b. or br.g. Arctic Lord – Chancer's Last (Foggy Bell)   **c–** [2002/3 c23d^pu Mar 4] rangy gelding: novice hurdler/chaser: fairly useful pointer   **h–** nowadays, won 5 times in 2002: didn't impress with attitude on hunter debut, seeming to down tools after mistake 7 out: stays 2½m: tried blinkered. *Mrs H. J. Cobb*

TRILLIONAIRE 5 ch.g. Dilum (USA) – Madam Trilby (Grundy) [2002/3 h–: 18m^F   **h74** 16g⁴ 17g⁶ 19m³ 22m⁵ 19d 19d 21d 24v^pu 24m³ 22g 26m⁵ 22g* Apr 26] smallish gelding: poor handicap hurdler: 25/1, won at Market Rasen in April: stays easy 3m: acts on good to firm going: pulls hard. *Miss C. J. E. Caroe*

TRIMSTONE 6 br.g. Bandmaster (USA) – Klairover (Smackover) [2002/3 16d^pu   **h–** 17v⁴ Nov 6] poor maiden on Flat (stays 8.5f): little show in 2 sellers over hurdles. *R. J. Hodges*

TRINITRO 12 ch.g. Northern State (USA) – Mrs Waddilove (Bustino) [2002/3 c21g*   **c123 ?** c21s² c22g² c31d³ c31d^F Dec 13] leggy, lengthy gelding: useful chaser, winner of Norsk Grand National at Ovrevoll in 1999 and 2001: won Svensk Grand National at Stromsholm in June: made most and stuck to task well when 2¾ lengths third of 16 to Famfoni in valuable cross-country event at Cheltenham: fell after briefly taking wrong course there next time: stays 31f: acts on heavy going: blinkered both starts at Cheltenham. *R. Haugen, Norway*

TRINITY BELLE (FR) 5 b.m. Tel Quel (FR) – Razzamatazz (FR) (Always Fair   **h98** (USA)) [2002/3 17g* 18d⁶ 18g* 16s⁴ 17s^pu Apr 16] angular mare: second foal: half-sister to useful 4-y-o chaser Vesuve (by Villez) and winning hurdler/chaser up to 2¾m Gee Whizz (by Turgeon): dam 3-y-o winner/chaser: 9.5f winner on Flat at 3 yrs: won over hurdles at Dieppe in August and Bordeaux (mares event) in November: every chance when fourth in novice at Plumpton: raced around 2m. *G. Macaire, France*

TRINKET (IRE) 5 b.g. Definite Article – Alamiya (IRE) (Doyoun) [2002/3 F89p: **h100 +**
F16m* 16s² 17s³ Nov 29] well-made gelding: confirmed debut promise when winning **F102**
bumper at Worcester in May: fair form when placed both starts in novice hurdles: will
stay beyond 17f. *H. D. Daly*

TRINK HILL 5 ch.m. Good Times (ITY) – Sweet On Willie (USA) (Master Willie) **h–**
[2002/3 F–: F17f⁵ 17vᵖᵘ 16d⁴ 17d 24sᵖᵘ Feb 13] lengthy, rather unfurnished mare: little **F–**
sign of ability. *R. J. Hodges*

TRINLEY MOSS (IRE) 5 b.m. Executive Perk – Rosmere (IRE) (Roselier (FR)) **h–**
[2002/3 16dᵖᵘ Feb 23] first foal: dam unraced: soon tailed off in novice hurdle on debut.
J. S. Haldane

TRIO 7 b.g. Cyrano de Bergerac – May Light (Midyan (USA)) [2002/3 16gᴿ Aug 26] **h– §**
fairly useful at one time on Flat for N. Hamilton, modest on return from lay-off in 2001
and went wrong way temperamentally (refused to race once): very reluctant to race and
refused first on hurdling debut. *J. R. Boyle*

TRIOS VENTURE 8 ch.g. Bedford (USA) – Hunting Cottage (Pyjama Hunt) [2002/3 **c–**
c75, h–: 21gᵖᵘ May 30] workmanlike gelding: maiden hurdler: poor form only completed **h–**
start over fences: best form around 2m: acts on soft going. *Miss E. C. Lavelle*

TRIPLE CROWN (IRE) 10 b. or br.g. Tidaro (USA) – Noreen Beag (Thatching) **c–**
[2002/3 c–, h–: c24m⁵ May 6] little form, including in points. *R. M. Bluck* **h–**

TRIPLE GLORY (IRE) 4 b.f. Goldmark (USA) – Trebles (IRE) (Kenmare (FR)) **h74**
[2002/3 16g² 18m⁴ 17gᵘʳ 17sᵖᵘ Nov 18] angular filly: modest maiden on Flat, well held in
2002: poor form in juvenile hurdles: may prove best over 2m. *Mrs P. N. Dutfield*

TRIPLE RUM (IRE) 6 b.g. Be My Native (USA) – Pegus Gold (Strong Gale) [2002/3 **F103**
F16s* F16g Mar 12] good-topped gelding: third foal: dam placed in bumpers: well held
in point in 2002: bought €3,800 Fairyhouse August Sale: 50/1-winner of 18-runner
bumper at Naas in February: well beaten in Grade 1 events at Cheltenham and
Punchestown. *James Leavy, Ireland*

TRISTAN LUDLOW (IRE) 7 gr.g. Roselier (FR) – Surely Madam (Torenaga) **h111**
[2002/3 h103, F–: 22s² 21d² Jan 15] good-topped gelding: won maiden point in Ireland in
2001: fair maiden hurdler: runner-up both starts in 2002/3: likely to be suited by 3m: acts
on soft going: has looked none too easy ride. *Jonjo O'Neill*

TRIUMPH OF HOPE 7 b.g. Nomadic Way (USA) – Welton Stratagem VII (Damsire **h–**
Unregistered) [2002/3 20s⁶ 20g Apr 1] second foal: dam unraced: well held in 2 novice
hurdles. *C. Grant*

TRIVIAL (IRE) 11 b.m. Rakaposhi King – Miss Rubbish (Rubor) [2002/3 c–, h85: **c–**
20m* 20m³ 17s c21sᴿ 20g⁵ 20g³ Apr 14] quite good-topped mare: modest hurdler: won **h85**
maiden at Perth in May: winning pointer, has failed to complete in 2 steeplechases: stays
3m: acts on good to firm and good to soft going, possibly not on soft. *J. E. Brockbank*

TROCHILIDAE (IRE) 7 b.m. Alphabatim (USA) – Quincy Bay (Buckskin (FR)) **h–**
[2002/3 F–: 19sᵖᵘ Nov 28] smallish mare: no sign of ability. *A. J. Wilson*

TROEDRHIWDALAR 6 b.m. Gunner B – Delladear (Sonnen Gold) [2002/3 F16d **h–**
F17f 17m 24m³ 24sᵖᵘ Feb 27] first living foal: dam unraced: little sign of ability. *Mrs* **F–**
D. A. Hamer

TROOPER 9 b.g. Rock Hopper – Silica (USA) (Mr Prospector (USA)) [2002/3 c73§, **c85 §**
h–§: 16d³ c20m⁵ 20d⁶ c25m² c25gᵖᵘ c27g² c27d* c27v² c24d⁵ c28sᵖᵘ c27v³ 27vᵖᵘ c24s³ **h87 §**
c25gᵖᵘ c28g³ c27m* Apr 26] lengthy gelding: modest hurdler/chaser: won at Sedgefield
in October (handicap) and April (novice): stays 27f: acts on any going: visored/blinkered:
ungenuine. *A. Crook*

TROOPER COLLINS (IRE) 5 b.g. Dolphin Street (FR) – Born To Fly (IRE) (Last **h86**
Tycoon) [2002/3 h95: 20s 26m⁴ 24g³ Aug 24] workmanlike gelding: modest maiden
hurdler: won points in March and April: stays 3m: best form on good going: tried
blinkered, including last 2 outings: has had tongue tied. *Jonjo O'Neill*

TROUBLE AHEAD (IRE) 12 b.g. Cataldi – Why 'o' Why (Giolla Mear) [2002/3 **c118 x**
c125, h–: c25d⁵ c20d³ c24m⁵ c20g³ Apr 23] good-topped gelding: fairly useful handicap **h–**
chaser: best effort in 2002/3 when third to Hunters Tweed at Perth final start: should stay
beyond 3m: acts on good to firm and heavy going: seems best on right-handed tracks:
prone to mistakes. *Miss Venetia Williams*

TROUBLE NEXT DOOR (IRE) 5 b.g. Persian Bold – Adjacent (IRE) (Doulab **c94 p**
(USA)) [2002/3 h94: c16m² Mar 20] made all in 2 juvenile hurdles in 2001/2: similar **h–**

form when second of 4 to Tysou in novice chase at Wincanton on return: will probably prove best around 2m: acts on firm going: free-going sort: should improve over fences. *N. P. Littmoden*

TROUBLE'N'STRIFE   6 b.m. Endoli (USA) – Midsummer Breeze (Tumble Wind   h–
(USA)) [2002/3 F–: 16d⁶ 17g⁵ Jun 22] no sign of ability: tried blinkered. *Mrs S. D. Williams*

TROUBLESHOOTER   5 b.g. Ezzoud (IRE) – Oublier L'Ennui (FR) (Bellman (FR))   h66
[2002/3 17g 20f³ Sep 15] modest maiden at 2 yrs, well held on Flat since: never near to challenge when seventh in novice on hurdling debut, though not given hard time: pulled too hard when tailed off next time: sold 1,800 gns Doncaster October Sales, won point in March. *G. A. Swinbank*

TROYSGREEN (IRE)   5 b.g. Warcraft (USA) – Moylena (Bustomi) [2002/3 F16g   h– §
23sᶠ 20dᵖᵘ 16dᵖᵘ 24dᵖᵘ Feb 7] IR 10,000 3-y-o: has scope: second foal: dam, winning   F–
pointer, half-sister to useful 2m hurdlers Eddie Wee and Helynsar: won 2½m maiden 4-y-o Irish point on debut in 2002: bought 32,000 gns Doncaster May (2002) Sales: well held in bumper: has shown more temperament than ability over hurdles (tried blinkered): joined P. Niven. *Jonjo O'Neill*

TRUCKERS TAVERN (IRE)   8 ch.g. Phardante (FR) – Sweet Tulip (Beau   c166
Chapeau) [2002/3 c143, h–: c25v³ c24vᶠ c24d* c24g³ c26g² Mar 13]   h–
His stable's faith in Truckers Tavern as a potential Gold Cup horse ultimately turned out to be well placed. But there were plenty of doubters along the way, Timeform among them, until Truckers Tavern handsomely justified his home reputation when finishing a remarkable second in the Cheltenham Gold Cup in March, running way above any form he had previously shown. Trainer Ferdy Murphy campaigned Truckers Tavern mostly at around two miles as a novice when he won three times at the minimum trip and came fourth to Moscow Flyer in the Arkle Trophy at the Cheltenham Festival, after being beaten by Harbour Pilot in the Dr P. J. Moriarty Novices' Chase over twenty-one furlongs, the longest trip he had encountered outside points before the latest season. Murphy, however, never had any doubt that Truckers Tavern was essentially a stayer. 'We knew last season he was a three-mile horse but I didn't want to go down the SunAlliance route which is why he went for the Arkle,' he said in a pre-season interview which left readers in no doubt that Truckers Tavern was 'the star of our show' at Wynbury Stables. Incidentally, Alverton (who won both) and Desert Orchid are the only Gold Cup winners since *Chasers & Hurdlers* began to have contested the Arkle in their novice campaign. However, Best Mate would have done so had the 2001 Festival not been cancelled due to the foot and mouth outbreak, while the 2002 Gold Cup runner-up Commanche Court ran in the 2000 Arkle.

Truckers Tavern's reappearance was delayed by an autumn dry spell. He had been due to start off his campaign at Wetherby in early-November and, after being declared for the abandoned First National Gold Cup at Ascot in November, he eventually reappeared under top weight in a fairly valuable handicap over twenty-five furlongs at Kelso in early-December. It was a race he might have been expected to win if he was really going to make it to the top in his second season over fences. Starting favourite, he went down by three quarters of a length and a length to Hugo de Grez and Ryalux, staying on dourly and giving the impression he would have gone close to winning but for losing ground after hitting the second last. A trip to Ascot for the Silver Cup later in the month ended in ignominy: heavily-backed Truckers Tavern, who was clearly expected to come on considerably for his reappearance, fell at the first.

Truckers Tavern did confirm next time, however, that he was a young chaser still on the upgrade when gaining his most important victory to date in the Bet Direct Peter Marsh Chase at Haydock in January. He pulled clear from the second last with another Gold Cup-bound northern chaser Hussard Collonges and stayed on really well to get on top on the flat, winning by two and a half lengths. Truckers Tavern received 15 lb from Hussard Collonges at Haydock and, on form, still had plenty to find to make any impression in the Gold Cup. If he'd been ours, he would probably, at this stage, have been aimed at the Red Square Vodka Gold Cup, back at Haydock in early-March, rather than the Cheltenham Gold Cup. The view that Truckers Tavern hadn't done enough to earn his place in the Gold Cup field seemed

Bet Direct Peter Marsh Chase (Limited Handicap), Haydock—Truckers Tavern (left) makes the most of a 15 lb weight pull with fellow northern Gold Cup hopeful Hussard Collonges

to be confirmed when he was beaten by two other Gold Cup entries Valley Henry and Chives in the AON Chase at Newbury in February, pushed along from soon after halfway and making no impression on the leaders when none too fluent at the second last, one of a number of mistakes he made in the race. Truckers Tavern belied his odds of 33/1 at Cheltenham, finishing ahead of Valley Henry and Chives, and everything else in the field except Best Mate. The Gold Cup, even on the prevailing good ground, still represented the stiffest test of stamina Truckers Tavern has faced in his career. Though off the pace and seemingly struggling to keep up at times, he stayed on down the final hill, after a mistake three out, and kept on well to take second on the run-in, finishing ten lengths behind Best Mate and two and a half lengths off third-placed Harbour Pilot who also stayed on dourly to be nearest at the finish. Neither Truckers Tavern nor Harbour Pilot ever threatened, both seemingly flattered as the race was run. It remains to be seen whether either proves capable of reproducing the form in a less well-run race, or at a shorter distance. If Truckers Tavern is returned to Cheltenham for the 2004 Gold Cup, his chances of going one better would be enhanced by softer going, placing more emphasis on stamina.

		Pharly (ch 1974)	Lyphard
	Phardante (FR) (b 1982)		Comely
Truckers Tavern (IRE) (ch.g. 1995)		Pallante (b 1970)	Taj Dewan
			Cavadonga
	Sweet Tulip (b 1979)	Beau Chapeau (ch 1963)	High Hat
			Beau Co Co
		Belle Mackay (b 1969)	Even Money
			Tarpine

The big, well-made Truckers Tavern was a 50,000-guinea purchase at the Doncaster May Sales in 2000. He had been successful three times in Irish points but made only one appearance for his new stable in the 2000/1 season—recording a very impressive victory in a novice hurdle at Wetherby—before being sidelined with heat in a leg. Then came the flying start to his chasing career in 2001/2 in which, for the most part, front-running tactics were employed over the shorter distances at which he was campaigned. As Truckers Tavern showed in the latest season, he is just as effective held up. Sweet Tulip, the dam of Truckers Tavern, was a point-to-point winner in Ireland where she was also placed over hurdles and in a hunter chase. She is also the dam of the fair hurdler Sophronia (by Strong Gale), a winner at up to two and a half miles, and of the modest three-mile chaser Lovable Outlaw (by Henbit). Sweet Tulip was also represented on the racecourse in the latest season by the six-year-old Station Island (by Roselier) who showed a little ability in a bumper at Huntingdon on his only start. Truckers Tavern, who was tongue tied on his racecourse debut and also on his four most recent starts, has been raced only on good going or softer, and acts on heavy. *Ferdy Murphy*

TRUE BLUE VICTORY (IRE) 7 b.g. Catrail (USA) – Russian Ribbon (USA) (Nijinsky (CAN)) [2002/3 h127p: 20s 16v⁵ 16s 16d* 16v Mar 8] useful-looking gelding: fairly useful hurdler: easily best effort in 2002/3 when winning handicap at Naas in February by 1½ lengths from Cailin's Perk: best at 2m: acted on going softer than good (possibly not at best on heavy): tongue tied prior to 2002/3. *T. M. Walsh, Ireland* **h127**

TRUE DESTINY 6 b.m. Afzal – Wenrisc (Boreen (FR)) [2002/3 F17g* F17m Apr 17] workmanlike mare: first foal: dam poor novice hurdler, stayed 21f: won mares bumper at Market Rasen on debut by neck from Hello Dee: tailed off in listed event at Cheltenham following month: likely to be suited by at least 2½m. *Miss Venetia Williams* **F83**

TRUE LIES 6 ch.m. King's Signet (USA) – Lysithea (Imperial Fling (USA)) [2002/3 h–, F72: 17v 21v 17s Feb 13] small, angular mare: poor form in bumpers, none over hurdles. *C. Tizzard* **h–**

TRUE NORTH (IRE) 8 b.g. Black Monday – Slip A Loop (The Parson) [2002/3 h89: 24dᵖᵘ 22s 20d³ 22v* 24v* 24v* 24v² Mar 13] fair hurdler: won handicaps at Kelso in December and Ayr and Newcastle (conditional jockeys) in January, last 2 within 5 days: suited by 2¾m+: raced only on good going or softer (acts well on heavy). *L. Lungo* **h114**

TRUE ROSE (IRE) 7 ch.m. Roselier (FR) – Naar Chamali (Salmon Leap (USA)) [2002/3 16s⁵ 21d 16d* 16d⁵ 16v³ c16g³ Mar 29] workmanlike mare: third foal: dam, lightly-raced maiden, half-sister to dam of useful hurdler up to 3m Out Ranking: won maiden Irish point in 2002: bought 15,000 gns Doncaster May Sales: poor novice hurdler: won weak mares event at Catterick in February: should stay beyond 2m: raced on good going or softer (acts on heavy). *J. R. Turner* **c78 h84**

TRULY GOLD (IRE) 4 ch.g. Goldmark (USA) – Truly Flattering (Hard Fought) [2002/3 16v⁴ 16s 16m* Apr 19] fair on Flat (stays 1½m), successful in blinkers in October: fair form in juvenile hurdles, winning maiden at Cork by 4 lengths from Laoch Na Mara. *M. Halford, Ireland* **h109**

TRUMP CARD 6 b.g. Distant Relative – Tell No Lies (High Line) [2002/3 F16s F16s F16s⁴ 20s^F 20g³ 16g F19m* Apr 19] leggy gelding: third foal: half-brother to fairly useful winner up to 9f Honest Borderer (by Selkirk): dam useful winner up to 1½m: poor form over hurdles: easily best effort in bumpers when winning at Cork by ½ length from Our Handyman: stays easy 2½m: acts on soft and good to firm going: blinkered third and fourth starts. *C. F. Swan, Ireland* **h79 F98**

TRUMPER 7 b.g. First Trump – Sayida-Shahira (Record Run) [2002/3 h82§: 21g c21m⁵ c25g³ c22dᵖᵘ c26sᵖᵘ c21s⁴ c25s⁵ c24g Mar 11] rather unfurnished gelding: poor maiden hurdler/chaser: stays 25f well: best form on good going or softer (acts on heavy): wore cheekpieces last 4 starts, blinkered previous 2: has reportedly had breathing problems: unreliable. *J. T. Gifford* **c75 § h– §**

TRUMPINGTON 5 ch.m. First Trump – Brockton Flame (Emarati (USA)) [2002/3 h87: 21m⁶ 22m³ 25d² 24m² 22d⁴ Aug 10] modest maiden hurdler: stays 3m: acts on soft and good to firm going: has hung/looked none too keen under pressure. *D. G. Bridgwater* **h85**

TRUSTING PADDY (IRE) 6 b.g. Synefos (USA) – Homefield Girl (IRE) (Rahotep (FR)) [2002/3 F82: F16d F16s⁶ 17v⁴ 19d⁴ 16v³ Mar 8] lengthy gelding: modest form in bumpers: poor form over hurdles: stays 19f. *L. A. Dace* **h82 F82**

TRUSTING TOM 8 b.g. Teamster – Florista (Oats) [2002/3 c94: c22d* c20d² c25d⁴ c24sᵘʳ c21d² c24d⁵ c20d³ Mar 4] sturdy gelding: fair handicap chaser: won novice at Market Rasen in October: continued in good form, third at Punchestown in late-April: **c104**

stays 25f: raced on good going or softer: effective blinkered or not: reportedly distressed final start: consistent. *C. C. Bealby*

TRUSTYOURINSTINCTS (IRE)   5 ch.g. Brief Truce (USA) – Mitsubishi Diamond (Tender King) [2002/3 16d^{pu} Nov 15] angular gelding: half-brother to 2 winning hurdlers, including Perugino Diamond (by Perugino), useful around 2m: little form on Flat: no show in Grade 2 novice on hurdling debut. *S. O'Farrell, Ireland*   h–

TRY ME AND SEE   9 ch.g. Rock City – Al Raja (Kings Lake (USA)) [2002/3 h–: 17s 23s^5 16s Dec 16] good-topped gelding: fairly useful form in bumpers in 1997/8: off 4 years, no form in 4 starts over hurdles since: has had tongue tied. *A. M. Crow*   h–

TRYSULL DREAM (IRE)   4 b.f. Mujadil (USA) – Emma's Whisper (Kind of Hush) [2002/3 16m^5 Sep 29] poor maiden on Flat: fifth of 9 finishers in poor juvenile on hurdling debut. *C. A. Dwyer*   h–

TSANGA   11 b.g. Rakaposhi King – Audrina (Young Generation) [2002/3 c–, h–: 24m^6 c22m^4 c20m^5 c27m^3 c26m^{pu} Aug 12] leggy gelding: one-time fair hurdler: poor form in novice chases: stays 27f: acts on firm and good to soft going: effective blinkered or not: tongue tied. *C. Grant*   c67 h–

TSUNAMI   7 b.m. Beveled (USA) – Alvecote Lady (Touching Wood (USA)) [2002/3 c70, h82: c19g 16g 17d^6 21g^6 20g^6 c20g^{ur} Apr 14] sparely-made mare: poor handicap hurdler/maiden chaser: stays 21f: probably acts on any going: tried visored. *B. D. Leavy*   c– h79

TUBBER ROADS (IRE)   10 b.g. Un Desperado (FR) – Node (Deep Run) [2002/3 c113: c25g^{pu} May 1] good-topped gelding: developed into useful hunter chaser in 2002: pulled up at Cheltenham (lame) in May and in point in February: stays 3m: acts on soft and good to firm going: often races up with pace: genuine. *M. G. Hazell*   c–

TUCACAS (FR)   6 gr.m. Highest Honor (FR) – Three Well (FR) (Sicyos (USA)) [2002/3 h135p: 16f^6 21d^2 22d^{pu} 25g 20d^{pu} Apr 4] leggy mare: useful hurdler: best effort when winning intermediate handicap at Cheltenham in November by ¾ length from Samasakhan: efforts probably best ignored on account of trip next 2 starts, ran moody race in first-time visor final outing: stays 21f, likely to prove as effective at 2m: acts on any going. *M. C. Pipe*   h137

TUCKER FENCE   4 br.g. So Factual (USA) – Daisy Topper (Top Ville) [2002/3 16g Feb 12] modest on Flat (stays 1m), sold out of J. Balding's stable 1,600 gns Doncaster November Sales: tailed off in juvenile on hurdling debut. *Ian Emmerson*   h–

TUDOR GALE (IRE)   10 b.m. Strong Gale – Orra Beg (Dear Gazelle) [2002/3 c–§, h–§: c19g^F May 4] lengthy, sparely-made mare: no worthwhile form since 1998/9: refused to race only appearance in blinkers: has had tongue tied: one to leave alone. *A. G. Juckes*   c– § h– §

TUDOR KING (IRE)   9 br.g. Orchestra – Jane Bond (Good Bond) [2002/3 c82, h66: 20m^6 c23m c21m* c24m^{ur} c21g^{ur} 22m 21f^3 c24d^{pu} 20m c20m* Apr 19] rather sparely-made gelding: maiden hurdler: poor handicap chaser: won at Southwell in August and Plumpton in April: barely stays 25f: acts on soft and firm going: races prominently: often let down by jumping: inconsistent. *J. S. King*   c82 x h65 §

TUDOR NATIVE   7 b.m. Distinct Native – Tudorfield Girl (Tudorville) [2002/3 24g^{pu} Apr 23] second foal: dam winning pointer: showed nothing in mares novice hurdle on debut. *A. Parker*   h–

TUDOR NICKOLA   11 ch.m. Nicholas Bill – Cottage Melody (Super Song) [2002/3 h–: 18m^{ur} 22m^{pu} Mar 20] lengthy, angular mare: of no account: has had tongue tied. *P. D. Purdy*   h–

TUESDAY (IRE)   8 b.g. Satco (FR) – Beech Glen (Furry Glen) [2002/3 c105, h119: c17s^4 c22s^3 Feb 12] workmanlike gelding: fairly useful hurdler: fair maiden chaser: effective at 2m to 2¾m: acts on any going. *W. P. Mullins, Ireland*   c109 h–

TUFF JOINT (IRE)   5 b. or br.g. Good Thyne (USA) – The Furnituremaker (Mandalus) [2002/3 F17d F16d Apr 25] sixth known foal: brother to modest hurdler/chaser Dene View, stays 21f, and half-brother to 2 winners by Strong Gale, including one-time fairly useful chaser Strong Chairman, stays 27f: dam, poor maiden jumper, half-sister to useful staying chaser Mr Gossip: well beaten in 2 bumpers: sold 6,500 gns Doncaster May Sales. *C. Grant*   F–

TUFTEX KING   6 b.g. Syrtos – More Laughter (Oats) [2002/3 F17d 16d 16d 16s 17d 16d 16g 17f^{ro} 16m Apr 21] medium-sized gelding: second foal: dam bad novice hurdler: h80 d F–

soundly beaten in bumper and over hurdles: tried blinkered: pulls hard: ran out eighth start: sold 1,000 gns Doncaster May Sales. *Ian Williams*

TUFTY HOPPER   6 b.g. Rock Hopper – Melancolia (Legend of France (USA))   **h107**
[2002/3 16d⁵ 27s* 27v* 25d³ 24dᶠ 26m* Mar 23] sturdy gelding: modest on Flat (stays easy 2m) for P. Howling: fair novice hurdler: won at Sedgefield in November and December and Huntingdon (handicap) in March: stays 27f: acts on heavy and good to firm going: carries head high. *Ferdy Murphy*

TULACH ARD (IRE)   8 b.g. Erdelistan (FR) – Noon Hunting (Green Shoon)   **c–**
[2002/3 h95: 20d⁶ 24v⁴ c20vᶠ c21sᵘʳ 20d* Mar 2] quite good-topped gelding: failed to   **h101**
complete in 2 novice chases: fair hurdler: improved effort when winning novice handicap at Carlisle despite wandering under pressure: stays 2½m (seemingly not 3m): raced on good going or softer (acts on soft): possibly not an easy ride. *A. Parker*

TULLIMOSS (IRE)   8 b.m. Husyan (USA) – Ballynattin Moss (Le Moss) [2002/3   **h70**
h–, F73: 20m³ 20g⁴ 22g⁶ 22v² 20dᶠ 24g⁶ 22d 22dᵖᵘ 22g Apr 7] poor maiden hurdler: should stay 3m: acts on good to firm and heavy going: has had tongue tied. *J. N. R. Billinge*

TULLONS LANE   8 b.g. Riverwise (USA) – Pallanda (Pablond) [2002/3 c–, h–:   **c88**
c21mᵖᵘ c18d* c20d⁶ c20s⁶ c16s⁴ c17v² c18s² c20dᵖᵘ c18s c21mᵖᵘ c18fᵖᵘ Apr 24] lengthy,   **h–**
angular gelding: modest chaser: 11 lb out of handicap, won weak amateur event at Fontwell in November: let down by jumping 3 of last 4 starts: best efforts around 2m on going softer than good (acts on heavy). *N. R. Mitchell*

TULSA (IRE)   9 b.g. Priolo (USA) – Lagrion (USA) (Diesis) [2002/3 h–: 16g May 26]   **h–**
compact gelding: maiden hurdler: no form since 2000/1: blinkered once. *L. Montague Hall*

TUMBLEWEED GLEN (IRE)   7 ch.g. Mukaddamah (USA) – Mistic Glen (IRE)   **c82**
(Mister Majestic) [2002/3 c69, h–x: c16g⁶ c19m⁴ c19m² Apr 21] angular gelding: poor   **h– x**
maiden hurdler/chaser: stays 2½m: acts on soft and good to firm going: effective blinkered or not. *P. Kelsall*

TUNSTALL (USA)   4 b.g. Bahri (USA) – Princess West (GER) (Gone West (USA))   **h111**
[2002/3 16m* 16d² 16s⁵ 16dᶠ Jan 25] good-topped gelding: fair maiden on Flat (stayed 1¼m): won juvenile at Wetherby on hurdling debut in October: best form when second in listed juvenile there following month: dead. *T. D. Easterby*

TURAATH (IRE)   7 b.g. Sadler's Wells (USA) – Diamond Field (USA) (Mr Prospector   **h99**
(USA)) [2002/3 h87: 21m² 20dᵖᵘ 20m⁹ 19d* 20s 22dᶠ Mar 6] stocky gelding: modest handicap hurdler: left G. McCourt and off 6 months, won conditional jockeys event at Taunton in January, despite hanging left and carrying head high: stays 2¾m: acts on good to firm and good to soft going, possibly unsuited by soft: running creditably when falling when blinkered final outing: tried tongue tied: none too reliable. *P. J. Hobbs*

TURBO (IRE)   4 b.g. Piccolo – By Arrangement (IRE) (Bold Arrangement) [2002/3   **h114**
17d⁶ 16d³ 17g 16gᵖᵘ Apr 3] close-coupled gelding: useful on Flat (stays 1¼m) for G. Balding: fair form in juvenile hurdles, tending to wander when third to Red Wine at Newbury second start: showed nothing in Triumph Hurdle at Cheltenham and Grade 2 at Aintree (reportedly had breating problem) last 2 runs: will prove best with emphasis on speed at 2m: blinkered final outing. *Miss Venetia Williams*

TURBO MOWER   5 b.g. Turbo Speed – Fruids Park (Royal Fountain) [2002/3 F–:   **h–**
24dᵖᵘ Oct 26] medium-sized gelding: no show in bumper or novice hurdle. *W. G. Young*

TURGEONEV (FR)   8 gr.g. Turgeon (USA) – County Kerry (FR) (Comrade In Arms)   **c144**
[2002/3 c152, h–: c20d³ c20d c16s² c16gᵘʳ c16d⁶ c16m² c16g c16g Apr 3] tall gelding: **h–**
smart chaser in 2001/2: not so good in 2002/3, best efforts when placed in handicaps at Wetherby first and third starts: best around 2m: acts on any going: usually held up nowadays: usually sound jumper. *T. D. Easterby*

TURN BACK   4 b.f. Pivotal – Trachelium (Formidable (USA)) [2002/3 17s⁶ 16g Mar   **h–**
23] half-sister to fairly useful 2m hurdler Uniform (by Unfuwain) and fair 2m hurdler Innes (by Inchinor): fair at best on Flat: signs of ability when well held in 2 juvenile hurdles. *Miss S. E. Hall*

TURNED OUT NICE   5 b.m. Ezzoud (IRE) – Green Seed (IRE) (Lead On Time   **h89**
(USA)) [2002/3 16d⁴ 16d 16g³ Apr 24] half-sister to fairly useful hurdler around 2m Take Flite (by Cadeaux Generaux): never dangerous in 1¼m maiden on Flat debut at 4 yrs for J. Bethell: best effort in novice hurdles when third to Laouen at Perth final start: likely to prove best around 2m. *P. Beaumont*

941

TURN OF PHRASE (IRE) 4 b.g. Cadeaux Genereux – Token Gesture (IRE) (Alzao **h100**
(USA)) [2002/3 16s⁵ 16d 16g* 16f² 16g⁵ Apr 19] lengthy gelding: fair on Flat (stays
1¼m): fair juvenile hurdler: won maiden at Wetherby in March: likely to prove best with
emphasis on speed around 2m: acts on firm going: went bit in snatches when running
creditably fourth start. *R. A. Fahey*

TURN THE TIDE 6 b.m. Derrylin – Mermaid Bay (Jupiter Island) [2002/3 h–, F–: **h74**
20m⁵ 22f² 21spu Jan 23] poor maiden hurdler: stays 2¾m: best efforts on firm/good to
firm going. *A. King*

TURN TO BLUE 4 b.g. Bluegrass Prince (IRE) – Alvecote Lady (Touching Wood **h–**
(USA)) [2002/3 16mpu 16m 16d Nov 13] sparely-made gelding: half-brother to winning
hurdler up to 2½m Tsunami (by Beveled): modest maiden on Flat (stays 1¼m): little
show in 3 juvenile hurdles: has worn cheekpieces. *J. C. Fox*

TURN TWO (IRE) 6 ch.g. Montelimar (USA) – Rock And Rye (The Parson) [2002/3 **c119**
c22s³ c20sur c16s* c20dF c24vR Mar 8] well-made gelding: sixth foal: half-brother to
winning 2¼m hurdler Gimme Gimme (by Shardari): dam, bumper winner, out of half-
sister to very smart chaser Rainbow Warrior: fairly useful form over fences, best efforts
when winning maiden at Naas in February and when third to Rule Supreme in valuable
novice handicap at Punchestown (tongue tied) in April: effective at 2m to 25f: acts on soft
going. *N. Meade, Ireland*

TURSAL (IRE) 14 b.g. Fine Blade (USA) – Turlough Pet (Retieme) [2002/3 c26d Jun **c–**
8] workmanlike gelding: fair pointer, successful twice in April: well beaten in maiden **h– §**
hunter in June: ran out once over hurdles. *A. R. Campbell*

TURTLEBACK (IRE) 5 b.g. Turtle Island (IRE) – Mimicry (Thatch (USA)) [2002/3 **h129**
h129: 16v² 18s* 16v³ 16d5 17g Mar 13] strong, well-made gelding: fairly useful hurdler:
won minor event at Fairyhouse in November: ran well when seventh of 28 to Spirit
Leader in valuable handicap at Cheltenham final start: will prove best around 2m: raced
on good going or softer (acts on heavy). *E. J. O'Grady, Ireland*

TURTLE DANCER (IRE) 5 b.g. Turtle Island (IRE) – Love Me Please (IRE) **h100**
(Darshaan) [2002/3 h113: 17g* 17g⁶ Sep 6] third start over hurdles when winning novice
at Sedgefield in August by 2½ lengths from Yorkshire (who conceded 36 lb): ran poorly
there following month, not seen out again: tried blinkered. *B. Ellison*

TURTLE LOVE (IRE) 4 b.f. Turtle Island (IRE) – A Little Loving (He Loves Me) **h67**
[2002/3 17gpu 16d⁶ 16d 17d⁶ 16g 17g² Apr 26] modest on Flat (stays 9.4f): poor form
over hurdles: best at sharp 2m: blinkered, tried to refuse on hurdling debut (trained by
B. Ellison). *K. A. Morgan*

TUSCAN TEMPO 4 ch.g. Perugino (USA) – Fact of Time (Known Fact (USA)) **h–**
[2002/3 17f⁶ 16d 17s⁶ 17dF 16spu 17gpu Mar 18] workmanlike gelding: poor maiden on
Flat (stays 1m), sold out of R. Hannon's stable £1,500 Ascot August Sales: no worthwhile
form over hurdles. *G. F. Edwards*

TUSCARORA (IRE) 4 b.f. Revoque (IRE) – Fresh Look (IRE) (Alzao (USA)) **h73**
[2002/3 16g⁵ Nov 23] fair on Flat (best at 6f/7f), successful in January and April (for
A. Carroll): raced freely and weakened between last 2 when fifth of 21 in juvenile claimer
at Catterick on hurdling debut. *P. C. Haslam*

TUSKA RIDGE (IRE) 10 b.g. Zaffaran (USA) – McBrides Reject (Avocat) [2002/3 **c90 §**
c–, h87: 16mur c24s* c25sR c17spu 22g 21m² 27g⁴ c21d² c20f⁴ c24fur c24sR 22s 20s c16dR **h87 §**
24d Mar 22] medium-sized gelding: modest handicap hurdler/chaser: won over fences at
Navan in May: stays 27f: acts on firm and soft going: has refused several times and not
one to trust. *J. J. Lambe, Ireland*

TUXEDO JUNCTION (NZ) 8 br.g. Little Brown Jug (NZ) – Just Kay (NZ) (St **c93 +**
Puckle) [2002/3 17g³ 20g⁴ c20d⁴ Jun 8] rather leggy gelding: poor maiden hurdler: made **h82**
virtually all in novice handicap at Worcester on chasing debut, jumping soundly: stays
2½m: acts on soft and good to firm going: looked open to improvement over fences but
not seen out again. *P. J. Hobbs*

TWEED 6 ch.g. Barathea (IRE) – In Perpetuity (Great Nephew) [2002/3 h82§: 21d⁵ **h– §**
Nov 4] sturdy gelding: fairly useful at best on all-weather Flat (stays 2m), not so good on
turf: maiden hurdler: blinkered, jumped poorly and weakened tamely only start in 2002/3:
should stay well beyond 2m: less than keen. *J. R. Best*

TWELI 6 b.g. Deploy – Flying Fantasy (Habitat) [2002/3 F17m³ F16m² F17d F17d **h88**
16mⁿ Mar 23] lengthy gelding: half-brother to fairly useful hurdler/fair chaser Round **F84**
Robin (by Royal Academy), stays 3m, and to poor hurdler Famille (by Top Ville): dam

lightly-raced sister to 1000 Guineas winner Flying Water: modest form when placed in bumpers first 2 starts: fourth of 17 to Pirandello in maiden at Huntingdon on hurdling debut: will stay 2½m. *I. A. Wood*

TWICE AS GOOD (IRE) 9 b.g. Good Thyne (USA) – Twice As Fluffy (Pollerton) [2002/3 h87: c19g⁶ c23g⁴ c24sᵖᵘ c24gᵖᵘ Apr 19] quite good-topped gelding: bumper winner: modest maiden hurdler/chaser: ran as if amiss last 2 starts: likely to prove best around 3m: raced on good going or softer (acts on heavy). *K. C. Bailey* **c87** **h–**

TWIN-CYLINDER (IRE) 10 br.g. Mandalus – Gemini Stone (Le Bavard (FR)) [2002/3 c19dᵖᵘ c19m³ Jun 4] maiden pointer: has shown little in 2 steeplechases. *R. Lee* **c–**

TWISCOMBE 8 br.m. Arctic Lord – Flying Cherub (Osiris) [2002/3 F–: 17gᵖᵘ May 1] sturdy mare: no sign of ability. *Mrs J. G. Retter* **h–**

TWISTED LOGIC (IRE) 10 b.g. Tremblant – Logical View (Mandalus) [2002/3 c124, h–: c23g² c25d⁵ c24m³ c24m³ c24d c25d* c23v³ c25dᵖᵘ c26m² c23f* c24m⁵ Apr 12] smallish, sturdy gelding: fairly useful handicap chaser: won at Exeter in December and March: stays 3¼m: acts on firm and soft going: blinkered once: prone to mistakes. *R. H. Alner* **c124** **h–**

TWO FOR JOY (IRE) 8 br.m. Mandalus – Misty Joy (General Ironside) [2002/3 h113: c24gꟳ c23d³ May 23] sturdy mare: fair hurdler: modest form on completed start in novice chases: will probably stay beyond 3m: raced on good going or softer. *C. R. Egerton* **c85** **h–**

TWOFORTEN 8 b.g. Robellino (USA) – Grown At Rowan (Gabitat) [2002/3 h–: 17m 18m Sep 24] no worthwhile form over hurdles: blinkered once: sometimes looks none too keen. *P. Butler* **h–**

TWO HUGE 5 gr.g. Norton Challenger – Rainy Miss (IRE) (Cheval) [2002/3 F16g² Apr 2] workmanlike gelding: first foal: dam winning pointer: never a factor in bumper at Ascot on debut. *N. A. Twiston-Davies* **F–**

TWO LORDS 11 b.g. Arctic Lord – Doddycross (Deep Run) [2002/3 c–, h–: 22g 24m 24s³ 20g⁵ 24mᵖᵘ Jul 24] workmanlike gelding: winning hurdler: retains little ability: tried blinkered: tongue tied: has broken blood vessels: reportedly lame final start. *Mrs A. C. Tate* **c–** **h–**

TWO TEARS 9 gr.g. Silver Owl – Vomero (NZ) (Church Parade) [2002/3 c–, h–: 22d⁵ c19s* c20s* c24v* c19dᵖᵘ c19s⁴ c19sᵖᵘ Feb 26] leggy gelding: poor maiden hurdler: fair chaser: won handicaps at Taunton, Bangor and Taunton again in December: well below form next 2 starts and lame final outing: stays 3m: acts on heavy going. *N. J. Hawke* **c101** **h–**

TWOTENSFORAFIVE 10 b.g. Arctic Lord – Sister of Gold (The Parson) [2002/3 c79, h–: c23mᵖᵘ c23m⁴ c22mꟳ c21m³ c19d* c19s⁶ c23d⁵ c19v⁵ Dec 28] angular gelding: poor chaser: won selling handicap at Chepstow in October, out of sorts otherwise in 2002/3: stays 3m: acts on good to firm and heavy going: tried blinkered. *P. R. Rodford* **c79** **h–**

TWOTIMING GENT (IRE) 10 b.g. Broken Hearted – Dual Express (Giolla Mear) [2002/3 16s 16s 24d 22g³ 27gᵖᵘ Mar 25] fifth foal: dam won around 2m over hurdles: form over hurdles only when third in handicap at Killarney in July: stays 2¾m: won bumper on heavy going: blinkered last 2 starts. *Niall. J. Donohoe, Ireland* **h76**

TY BENJAM (FR) 7 b.g. Cyborg (FR) – Pampa Maid (FR) (Pampabird) [2002/3 c149?, h139: c21sꟳ c25g³ c25s² c22v c22s Apr 13] useful hurdler: useful chaser on balance of form, won Group 2 Prix des Drags at Auteuil (found more than rivals when beating Cerilly 2½ lengths) in June: earlier creditable placed efforts in Gran Premio di Merano (length third to Present Bleu) in September, Grand Steeple-Chase d'Enghien (length behind Astonville) in November and Group 3 at Auteuil in May: stays 25f: acts on heavy going, apparently on good to firm. *G. Le Paysan, France* **c140** **h–**

TYNDARIUS (IRE) 12 b.g. Mandalus – Lady Rerico (Pamroy) [2002/3 c117, h–: c22s³ c25vᵖᵘ c24dᵖᵘ c21sᵖᵘ Mar 11] strong gelding: fairly useful handicap chaser at best, out of sorts in 2002/3: effective around 2m and stays 25f when conditions aren't very testing: acts on heavy going: blinkered final outing: joined J. Hetherton. *I. W. McInnes* **c–** **h–**

TYRRELLSPASS (IRE) 6 b.g. Alzao (USA) – Alpine Chime (IRE) (Tirol) [2002/3 h–: 16vᵖᵘ 16s 16g Sep 14] 1¼m winner on Flat in Spain at 3 yrs, no form in 2002: no form over hurdles: left S. Donohoe, twelfth of 24 in selling handicap at Worcester final start: raced at 2m. *J. D. Frost* **h–**

Gala Casinos Novices' Chase, Ayr—Tysou is the sole finisher

TYSOU (FR)   6 b.g. Ajdayt (USA) – Pretty Point (Crystal Glitters (USA)) [2002/3   **c132 +**
c118p, h141: c16d* c16s³ c16g³ c16m* c16gᶠ c16m* Apr 11] angular gelding: useful   **h–**
handicap hurdler: useful novice chaser: won in small fields at Sandown in November,
Wincanton in March and Ayr (finished alone) in April: will prove best around 2m: acts on
good to firm and good to soft going, possibly not on softer: races freely. *N. J. Henderson*

U

UGIE GIRL   4 gr.f. Passing Point (IRE) – Nawtinookey (Uncle Pokey) [2002/3 F16g   **F–**
Mar 23] first foal: dam, bad novice hurdler/chaser, stayed 2½m: tailed off in bumper on
debut. *A. C. Whillans*

ULTIMATE GOLD (IRE)   9 b.g. Good Thyne (USA) – Golden Mela (Golden Love)   **c81**
[2002/3 h91: c16dᵖᵘ c20m³ Nov 18] sturdy gelding: modest maiden hurdler: better effort   **h–**
over fences when third of 5 finishers in handicap at Leicester on return from 6-month
absence: should stay 3m. *K. C. Bailey*

ULUSABA   7 b.g. Alflora (IRE) – Mighty Fly (Comedy Star (USA)) [2002/3 c–, h98:   **c94**
c16d³ c17g⁴ c17s⁴ c17m⁵ 16s⁶ c17m* c17d² c20m⁴ c16g c16g 17g* c16v⁴ c16v⁶ c19m*   **h98**
Feb 28] neat gelding: modest hurdler/chaser: won handicaps over fences at Southwell
(novice) in August and Doncaster in February and over hurdles at Market Rasen in
October: stays 2½m: acts on good to firm and good to soft going (no form on heavy):
usually visored/blinkered: tongue tied: not always fluent over fences. *R. C. Guest*

944

ULVICK STAR (IRE) 11 b.g. Lord Americo – She's Approaching (Ragapan) c–
[2002/3 c–: 20g⁴ 20m⁶ 25dᵖᵘ 24d³ 26gᵖᵘ c23gᵘʳ 26m⁴ 25mᵖᵘ Oct 16] compact gelding: h–
winning pointer: little worthwhile form over hurdles or in steeplechases: stays 3m: acts
on good to firm and good to soft going: tried visored. *M. J. Gingell*

UMBOPA (USA) 5 b.g. Gilded Time (USA) – How Fortunate (CAN) (What Luck h–
(USA)) [2002/3 16dᵖᵘ 17v⁵ Nov 6] good-topped gelding: fair on Flat (should stay 1¾m)
for K. Burke, often shaped as if amiss in 2002: showed nothing in 2 starts over hurdles, in
cheekpieces on first occasion and blinkers (looked less than keen) on second. *P. Bowen*

UMBRELLA MAN (IRE) 7 ch.g. Insan (USA) – Askasilla (IRE) (Lucky Mick- c114
mooch) [2002/3 h101: c20d⁵ c16g³ c20d* c20s⁴ c21dᶠ c20m² Apr 2] tall, rangy gelding: h–
fair maiden hurdler: similar form over fences, won handicap at Ludlow in January: stays
2½m: acts on soft and good to firm going: takes good hold: wandered under pressure
when running well final start. *Miss H. C. Knight*

UNCLE ARTHUR (IRE) 9 b.g. Satco (FR) – Lady-Easton (Oats) [2002/3 25g⁴ c–
24g* 24d³ 22g 24m² 24f⁵ 24m Apr 13] lengthy gelding: winning pointer: bumper winner: h116
well beaten only completed start in hunter chases: fairly useful handicap hurdler: won at
Bellewstown in July: stays 25f: acts on firm and good to soft going. *M. Halford, Ireland*

UNCLE BERT (IRE) 13 b.g. Ovac (ITY) – Sweet Gum (USA) (Gummo) [2002/3 c85
c20gᵖᵘ c20m³ c16g³ c16g² c20d⁵ c20v⁵ c21d² c21m² Apr 26] rangy gelding: modest h–
handicap chaser: stays 21f: acts on any going: often races prominently. *Miss Lucinda
V. Russell*

UNCLE CLOCKWISE 6 gr.g. Absalom – Summer Flower (Nomination) [2002/3 h–
16dᵖᵘ 17fᵖᵘ May 15] second foal: dam modest hurdler around 2m: little sign of ability.
Miss Z. C. Davison

UNCLE MICK (IRE) 8 b.g. Ikdam – Kandy Kate (Pry) [2002/3 c93, h107: c19gᶠ c93
22v⁴ 24v² 24d 24s⁴ 21s⁶ 25s c25g² c26g* Apr 21] medium-sized gelding: fair handicap h113
hurdler: modest form on 2 completed outings over fences, won maiden at Newton Abbot
in April: best at 2¾m+: acts on heavy going: visored all starts over hurdles in 2002/3:
sometimes let down by jumping. *C. Tizzard*

UNCLE TEDDY (IRE) 10 b.g. Arctic Cider (USA) – Ishtar (Dike (USA)) [2002/3 c93
c95, h–: c19g³ c20g⁵ c25g* c23g² c25m⁵ Sep 11] rather sparely-made gelding: winning h–
hurdler: modest chaser: won selling handicap at Hereford in June: stays 25f: acts on firm
going: blinkered/visored over hurdles. *Miss E. C. Lavelle*

UNCLE TOM 12 b.g. Scallywag – Reebok (Scottish Rifle) [2002/3 c25d⁵ May 14] c–
modest pointer: tailed off on hunter chase debut. *Mrs M. Marfell*

UNCLE WALLACE 7 b.g. Neltino – Auntie Dot (Hallodri (ATA)) [2002/3 h113p, c112
F93: c16m⁴ c18s³ c21d³ c20d⁴ Feb 7] lengthy, useful-looking gelding: fair novice h–
hurdler: similar form last 2 starts in novice chases: stays 21f, likely to be at least as
effective back at shorter: acts on soft going (bumper form on good to firm). *P. R. Webber*

UNDER CONSTRUCTION (IRE) 5 b.g. Pennekamp (USA) – Madame Nureyev h87
(USA) (Nureyev (USA)) [2002/3 17v³ 17s Nov 28] half-brother to 2 poor hurdlers: fair
on Flat (stays 1½m): much better effort over hurdles when third in novice at Newton
Abbot. *G. A. Ham*

UNDERLEY PARK (IRE) 9 ch.g. Aristocracy – Even Bunny VII (Damsire Unreg- c–
istered) [2002/3 c–, h–: 26dᶠ Jun 5] poor maiden hurdler in 1998/9: very lightly raced and h–
no form over hurdles or in steeplechases since: won maiden point in March. *R. Ford*

UNDER THE SAND (IRE) 6 b.g. Turtle Island (IRE) – Occupation (Homing) h126
[2002/3 h121: 16d⁶ 16v² 16v 17s³ 20vᶠ 21m 16v Mar 8] sturdy gelding: fairly useful
handicap hurdler: easily best efforts in 2002/3 when placed: not certain to stay 2½m: acts
on heavy going (possibly not on good to firm). *P. J. Hobbs*

UNDERTHESCOREBOARD (IRE) 7 b.g. Executive Perk – Down The Garden h–
(IRE) (Good Thyne (USA)) [2002/3 25dᵖᵘ May 30] 30,000 4-y-o: second foal: dam
unraced half-sister to useful staying chaser Darkorjon: no sign of ability in intermediate
hurdle at Wetherby on debut. *Jonjo O'Neill*

UNDER THE THUMB 9 b.g. Sunley Builds – Solhoon (Tycoon II) [2002/3 c78, c–
h76: 20g c20d c24s⁵ c19sᵖᵘ 16d Dec 26] maiden hurdler/winning chaser: out of sorts in h–
2002/3: sold £450 Ascot February Sales. *C. P. Morlock*

UNDER WRAPS (IRE) 9 b.g. In The Wings – Wrapping (Kris) [2002/3 c–, h–: c–
c24dᵖᵘ c29sᵖᵘ c30sᵖᵘ c30dᵖᵘ 24d Mar 2] good-topped gelding: fairly useful hurdler/chaser h–

in 2000/1, badly out of sorts since: left J. O'Neill after third start: usually blinkered, also tried in cheekpieces: ungenuine. *J. Howard Johnson*

UNGARETTI (GER) 6 b.g. Law Society (USA) – Urena (GER) (Dschingis Khan) **h96**
[2002/3 h100: 23m⁴ 25v 25s⁴ 26g^F 24g⁴ 26g 24m Apr 12] rangy gelding: modest handicap hurdler: won at Ludlow in February: may prove best up to 3m: acts on heavy going, possibly not on good to firm: has had tongue tied. *Ian Williams*

UN JOUR A VASSY (FR) 8 b.g. Video Rock (FR) – Bayalika (FR) (Kashtan (FR)) **c116**
[2002/3 c116, h100: c24m² c20d^F c20d⁶ c24m² c24f² Apr 3] leggy gelding: fairly useful **h–**
handicap chaser: runner-up 3 times in 2002/3: stays 25f when emphasis is on speed: acts on firm and good to soft going. *P. F. Nicholls*

UNLEASH (USA) 4 ch.g. Benny The Dip (USA) – Lemhi Go (USA) (Lemhi Gold **h126 p**
(USA)) [2002/3 16v³ 17d³ 16g* 16g* Apr 19] leggy gelding: useful on Flat (stays 2m), sold out of Sir Mark Prescott's stable 44,000 gns Newmarket Autumn Sales: progressive juvenile hurdler: favourite, won at Ludlow (maiden, easily) in March and Stratford (handicap, not extended to beat Crownfield 3½ lengths) in April: will stay beyond 2m: capable of better still. *P. J. Hobbs*

UNLIMITED FREE (IRE) 9 ch.g. Ile de Chypre – Merry Madness (Raise You Ten) **c96**
[2002/3 c100, h78: c25f⁴ c24s⁶ c22m⁵ Mar 21] useful-looking gelding: maiden hurdler: **h–**
modest chaser: sold out of O. Sherwood's stable Doncaster August Sales after reappearance: below best in hunters last 2 starts: stays 25f: acts on soft and firm going: has jumped right. *Mrs S. Alner*

UNSIGNED (USA) 5 b. or br.g. Cozzene (USA) – Striata (USA) (Gone West (USA)) **h–**
[2002/3 16f May 10] fairly useful on Flat (probably stays 2m): pulled hard when well held in novice on hurdling debut. *R. H. Buckler*

UNTIDY DAUGHTER 4 b.f. Sabrehill (USA) – Branitska (Mummy's Pet) [2002/3 **h83**
16d 16d 16d² 17v⁵ 16d 17d⁵ 17m* 16d 17m⁷ Apr 16] half-sister to winning hurdler/useful handicap chaser Ei Ei (by North Briton), stays 2½m: fair maiden on Flat (best around 1m), sold out of R. Hannon's stable 9,500 gns Newmarket July Sales: poor hurdler: went with more zest tried in cheekpieces when winning mares handicap at Sedgefield, despite several mistakes: will prove best around 2m: acts on good to firm and good to soft going. *B. Ellison*

UNTOLD STORY (USA) 8 b.g. Theatrical – Committed Miss (USA) (Key To Con- **h–**
tent (USA)) [2002/3 19d^pu May 14] good-topped gelding: no show over hurdles. *G. A. Ham*

UPESI 7 b.m. Regal Embers (IRE) – Dawn Melody (Lighter) [2002/3 F17g F17d Oct **F–**
12] sturdy mare: first foal: dam well beaten in 2 bumpers: of no account in bumpers. *J. L. Spearing*

UPGRADE 9 b.g. Be My Guest (USA) – Cantanta (Top Ville) [2002/3 c154, h–§: **c150 §**
c21m² c21d^F c20d⁵ 21g^pu c21m³ Apr 16] lengthy gelding: one-time smart hurdler: smart **h– §**
chaser: temperamental displays most starts in 2002/3: best around 2½m: acts on soft and firm going: blinkered last 2 starts: often front runner: tends to idle: best avoided. *M. C. Pipe*

UP IN FLAMES (IRE) 12 br.g. Nashamaa – Bella Lucia (Camden Town) [2002/3 **h59**
16g 17d³ 20g⁶ Apr 1] rather sparely-made gelding: bad maiden hurdler: best around 2m: acts on good to soft going: tongue tied. *Mrs G. S. Rees*

UPON A THYNE (IRE) 6 br.m. Good Thyne (USA) – Brown Willows (IRE) **h–**
(Kemal (FR)) [2002/3 F16m⁴ F17s 16d^pu Dec 26] 3,500 4-y-o: first foal: dam, placed in **F–**
points, from family of high-class staying chaser Cahervillahow: signs of only a little ability: dead. *P. G. Murphy*

UPRIGHT IMA 4 b.f. Perpendicular – Ima Delight (Idiot's Delight) [2002/3 F16m³ **F80**
Mar 23] first live foal: dam fair hurdler: stayed 2¾m: staying-on third of 11 in mares maiden bumper at Huntingdon on debut. *Mrs P. Sly*

UPRIVER RUN 4 ch.g. Alderbrook – Uplift (Bustino) [2002/3 F12g F17s F16m Mar **F72 ?**
20] small, leggy gelding: first live foal: dam 2m winner on Flat: signs of only a little ability in 3 bumpers. *R. Rowe*

UPSWING 6 b.g. Perpendicular – Moorfield Lady (Vicomte) [2002/3 17d 16d 20g^pu **h–**
Apr 1] fourth foal: dam, modest 2m hurdler/chaser, half-sister to useful 2-y-o 5f performer Indiana Pencil: no sign of ability in 3 novice hurdles. *R. Johnson*

UP THE CLARETS (IRE)   8 b.g. Petardia – Madeira Lady (On Your Mark) [2002/3   h72
h78: 17m³ Jul 25] tall, leggy gelding: poor handicap hurdler nowadays: none too fluent
when third at Sedgefield, only start in 2002/3: stays 2½m: acts on good to firm and heavy
going: tried blinkered: inconsistent. *D. McCain*

UP THE GLEN (IRE)   9 b.g. Tale Quale – Etrenne (Happy New Year) [2002/3 h–:   h92
20v* 27s² 20s³ 19s⁵ Feb 27] angular gelding: modest hurdler: made all in weak selling
handicap at Hexham in November: barely stays 27f: raced on going softer than good (acts
on heavy). *R. T. Phillips*

UP THE KYBER   6 b.g. Missed Flight – Najariya (Northfields (USA)) [2002/3 h–:   h–
17s 16dᵖᵘ Dec 4] maiden on Flat, poor form in 2002: signs of only a little ability over
hurdles. *M. D. Hammond*

UPTOWN LAD (IRE)   4 b.g. Definite Article – Shoka (FR) (Kaldoun (FR)) [2002/3   h81
16d 16d⁶ 17v 17v² Feb 11] poor maiden on Flat (stays 1¼m), sold out of Mrs
A. Duffield's stable 1,700 gns Doncaster October Sales: similar form over hurdles: will
prove best around 2m. *R. Johnson*

UP YOUR STREET   8 b.m. Petoski – Air Streak (Air Trooper) [2002/3 h81: 24d³   h76
May 6] sparely-made mare: maiden pointer: poor novice hurdler: stays 3¼m well: acts on
good to soft going. *J. Neville*

URBAN HYMN (IRE)   7 ch.g. College Chapel – Soltura (IRE) (Sadler's Wells (USA))   c87
[2002/3 h101: 16s⁶ 17v³ c16g⁴ c16g⁶ c16d⁴ Mar 18] close-coupled gelding: modest   h99
handicap hurdler: below that level in 3 novice chases: stays easy 21f: acts on heavy and
good to firm going: blinkered once. *Ferdy Murphy*

URGA (FR)   12 ch.g. Baby Turk – Pampa Girl (FR) (Pampabird) [2002/3 c156, h118:   c152
c22s³ c29s³ 18s* c22s³ c22v³ c22s⁴ Apr 13] leggy gelding: veteran chaser: hasn't   h118 +
won over fences since 1998/9, but regularly in frame in top company at Auteuil, including
in last 2 runnings of Grand Steeple-Chase de Paris, best effort in a year when third to Line
Marine in May: fairly useful form over hurdles, won minor event at Auteuil in September:
stays 29f: raced mainly on soft/heavy ground. *G. Chaignon, France*

US FOUR (IRE)   13 b.g. Mandalus – Rock Plant (Ovac (ITY)) [2002/3 c16d c19mᵖᵘ   c–
Apr 21] sturdy gelding: fair hunter chaser in 2000: well beaten on return (trained first start   h–
by S. Magnier): stays 2½m: acts on good to firm and good to soft going: usually
blinkered. *Miss S. A. Loggin*

USK VALLEY (IRE)   8 b.g. Tenby – Penultimate (USA) (Roberto (USA)) [2002/3   c–
h70: c19d⁴ c25gᶠ Mar 16] poor maiden hurdler: never a factor on completed start over   h–
fences: should stay beyond 2½m: raced on good going or softer (acts on heavy).
P. R. Chamings

V

VAGUE IDEA   10 gr.g. Tout Ensemble – Roodle Doodle (Rugantino) [2002/3 c85, h–:   c94
c25g* c25d³ c21s⁵ c24mᵘʳ c20d⁶ c26m⁶ c27m⁵ Apr 11] fair hunter chaser: fortunate to   h–
win at Hereford in May: well held all starts in handicaps: stays 25f: acts on soft going.
O. J. Carter

VAIGLY NORTH   5 b.m. Minshaanshu Amad (USA) – Straight Gold (Vaigly Great)   h–
[2002/3 F16d⁵ F16s F16m³ F17m⁶ 20gᵖᵘ Apr 14] third known foal: dam fair hurdler up to   F74
2½m/modest up to 2m on Flat: poor form in bumpers: sold out of A. Newcombe's stable
3,200 gns (privately) Doncaster January Sales: no show on hurdling debut. *J. A. Moore*

VALERIO   7 b.g. Be My Native (USA) – Laurello (Bargello) [2002/3 h121p: 16d*   h124
16vᵖᵘ 22v⁵ 24gᵖᵘ Apr 3] tall gelding: impresses in appearance: will make a chaser: fairly
useful handicap hurdler: won at Newbury in November by 2½ lengths from Haditovski:
stays 2¾m: acts on heavy going. *N. J. Henderson*

VALEUREUX   5 ch.g. Cadeaux Genereux – La Strada (Niniski (USA)) [2002/3 h104:   h99
17sᶠ 16d³ 16d³ 16d³ Feb 23] tall gelding: modest maiden hurdler: likely to prove best
around 2m: raced only on good to soft/soft going: may not have ideal temperament.
J. Hetherton

VALFONIC   5 b.g. Zafonic (USA) – Valbra (Dancing Brave (USA)) [2002/3 h89p: h106 d
16m* 16g* 17g⁵ 17m⁴ 16m³ 16d⁶ 17v⁵ 17d 19sᵖᵘ Feb 13] fair handicap hurdler: won at
Southwell and Worcester in May, attempting to run out last when completing hat-trick at

latter course: badly out of sorts last 6 starts, visored first 5 of those: not sure to stay much beyond 2m: acts on good to firm going: usually tongue tied. *M. C. Pipe*

VALHALLA GOLD 9 ch.g. Golden Lahab (USA) – Key Harvest (Deep Diver) **h–**
[2002/3 17g^{pu} Sep 6] half-brother to 2 winners by Sonnen Gold, including winning 2m hurdler Golden Vest: dam unraced: no show only start on Flat or on hurdling debut. *B. Ellison*

VALHALLA (IRE) 10 b.g. Brush Aside (USA) – Eimers Pet (Paddy's Stream) [2002/3 **c–**
c–, h77: 20s^6 20d^2 22s^5 17d^{pu} 20g^{ur} Jun 15] good-topped gelding: poor maiden hurdler/ **h75**
chaser: looked to sustain serious injury final start: stays 2¾m: acts on soft and good to firm going: has had tongue tied: none too consistent. *R. F. Fisher*

VALIGAN (IRE) 10 gr.g. Roselier (FR) – Wonderful Lilly (Prince Hansel) [2002/3 **c–**
c121, h–: c28d^4 Feb 8] sparely-made gelding: fairly useful handicap chaser in 2001/2: **h–**
well held last 3 starts that season and in hunter at Catterick on reappearance: finished alone in point in March: suited by 3m+: acts on heavy going: tried visored/in cheekpieces. *T. P. Tate*

VALIGNANI (IRE) 11 b.g. Law Society (USA) – When Lit (Northfields (USA)) **c§§**
[2002/3 c§§, h§§: 18m^5 20v^{pu} 25g^{pu} Jul 15] small, close-coupled gelding: winning **h§§**
hurdler/maiden chaser: hopelessly ungenuine nowadays: tried blinkered/visored, also wore eyecover last 2 starts: one to leave severely alone. *M. C. Pipe*

VALJEAN (IRE) 7 b.g. Alzao (USA) – Escape Path (Wolver Hollow) [2002/3 h–: **c59**
16g^{pu} c16m^4 Apr 5] medium-sized gelding: no form over hurdles: left W. M. Brisbourne, **h–**
won maiden point in March: well held on hunter chase debut. *Ms Myfanwy Miles*

VALLEY ERNE (IRE) 12 b.g. King's Ride – Erne Gold VII (Damsire Unregistered) **c108 x**
[2002/3 c106x, h121: c24m^6 24s^6 16g^5 20d c22d^2 22d^{pu} c21v c17d^6 Mar 22] **h115**
lengthy gelding: veteran handicap hurdler/chaser at best: form in 2002/3 only over hurdles third start and over fences at Punchestown in early-May: effective at 2m, barely stays 25f: acts on heavy and good to firm going: usually races prominently: often let down by jumping over fences. *Michael Cunningham, Ireland*

VALLEY HENRY (IRE) 8 b.g. Step Together (USA) – Pineway VII (General **c172**
Ironside) [2002/3 c146p, h–: c21m* c24s* c25s^4 c24g* c26g^4 c25g^4 Apr 3] **h–**
    Valley Henry's fluctuating reputation ended on a flat note in the latest season when he was a well-beaten favourite, only fourth of six finishers behind First Gold, in the Martell Cognac Cup Chase at Aintree. The performance illustrated Valley Henry's continuing fallibility in a chasing career which, so far, has been distinguished neither by consistency nor reliability. Valley Henry's jumping provided the main cause for concern in his first season over fences when he failed to complete the course in three of his eight races, including in the Feltham Chase and the Royal & SunAlliance. He ended that season on a high note, however, jumping fluently and winning the Future Champion Novices' Chase at Ayr in fine style, looking a very good prospect. Barry Geraghty rode him for the first time at Ayr and has partnered him in all his races since, except for the Fieldspring Desert Orchid Chase, a limited handicap in which he ran off a BHB mark of 151 at Wincanton on his reappearance in October. Ridden by Mick Fitzgerald on what was his first run outside novice company, Valley Henry survived a first-fence blunder to land the odds from the smart but temperamental Upgrade, the pair having the race between them up the home straight and Valley Henry regaining the initiative with a good jump at the last before going on to a seven-length victory.
    Valley Henry's jumping looked assured when he landed the odds with ease in a four-runner intermediate chase at Sandown in December, though his technique wasn't really tested in a steadily-run affair. The Ericsson Chase at Leopardstown, rather than the King George at Kempton, was earmarked as Valley Henry's Christmas target. But the race went by without him and the focus was on his Gold Cup credentials by the time he was next seen out in the Pillar Property Chase at Cheltenham at the end of January. Starting second favourite to the ill-fated Bacchanal in an event that looked likely to prove an informative Gold Cup trial, Valley Henry ran a stinker, dropping away tamely early on the final circuit and trailing in last of four finishers. Some poor jumping, particularly early on, could not excuse his effort which was simply too bad to be true.

AON Chase, Newbury—Valley Henry (noseband) re-enters the Gold Cup picture with victory over Chives

Whatever ailed Valley Henry at Cheltenham—'he never went in the ground, even going to the start', Geraghty reported—certainly did not affect him a fortnight later in the AON Chase at Newbury. Valley Henry's connections had planned to send him straight to the Gold Cup if things had gone well in the Pillar, but that race raised questions that needed to be answered before a final decision was taken about Valley Henry's participation at the Festival. His trainer's faith in Valley Henry's championship potential was restored with the best performance of the horse's career up to that time in the AON Chase, which carried a £100,000 bonus linked to Gold Cup success. Gold Cup sponsors the Tote slashed Valley Henry's Cheltenham odds from 40/1 to 10/1 immediately after he came home two and a half lengths and seven lengths ahead of Chives and Truckers Tavern. Jumping fluently, leading six out and always going best in the home straight, Valley Henry looked a completely different horse to the one who had flopped in the Pillar, the only slight blemish on his performance coming when he wandered on the run-in after appearing to idle in front. There was much to admire about Valley Henry at Newbury, though he still had something to find on the form-book—the way we read it anyway—to play a leading role in the Gold Cup. Much continued to be made by connections of the difference in the state of the going in the Pillar (soft) and the AON (good) and the stable announced that Valley Henry would not run in the Gold Cup unless the going was good or firmer. Valley Henry has won several times on soft going—it was soft when he won at Sandown—but there is probably something in the theory that less testing ground is to his advantage because fewer flaws are exposed in his jumping.

Starting at 14/1, Valley Henry ran a tremendous race on good going in the Gold Cup, one which in our view merited his being rated the second-best horse in the field. Valley Henry didn't see out the trip in a truly-run race so well as the placed horses Best Mate, Truckers Tavern and Harbour Pilot, but his trainer was spot-on when he said afterwards: 'If we'd ridden him to finish second to Best Mate, he probably would have finished second, but we took him on from the top of the hill and just ran out of petrol from the last.' Valley Henry, jumping well in the main, was held up about fourth or fifth, always moving smoothly. He and Best Mate were clearly travelling better than their rivals at the top of the hill and Valley Henry was looking the only real danger to Best Mate when making a mistake at the fourth last. Shaken up and still holding every chance three out, Valley Henry was unable to quicken and faded into fourth in the closing stages, beaten ten lengths, two and a half lengths and a neck. Judged on his Gold Cup performance, Valley Henry certainly has the potential to win a major race in the next season. If everything were to fall into place for him on the day, for example, he could run very well in the King George at Kempton on Boxing Day.

949

Valley Henry (IRE) (b.g. 1995)	Step Together (USA) (gr 1976)	Big Spruce (b or br 1969)	Herbager
			Silver Sari
		Feet First (ro 1968)	Native Dancer
			Next Move
	Pineway VII (ch 1981)	General Ironside (gr 1973)	Sea Hawk II
			Come Dancing
		Balyerne (b or br 1972)	Shackleton
			Straight News

The rangy Valley Henry is, by some way, the best performer sired by the Power Gold Cup Chase winner Step Together. Valley Henry is a non-thoroughbred, the fourth known foal of Pineway VII, a winning Irish pointer. Pineway VII has also produced the winning hurdler/fair Irish two-mile chaser Templevalley (by King's Ride) and her fifth known foal, Ask Henry (by Jolly Jake), was also in training with Nicholls in the latest season when he showed fairly useful form in novice chases and was successful at Chepstow in January. *P. F. Nicholls*

VALLEYMORE (IRE) 7 br.g. Jolly Jake (NZ) – Glamorous Brush (IRE) (Brush Aside (USA)) [2002/3 F16d 17s⁴ 20d² 20v³ 20s* 22s* 22fᵖᵘ Mar 29] lengthy gelding: type to make a chaser: first foal: dam unraced: won second of 2 starts in Irish points in 2001: bought 20,000 gns Doncaster May (2001) Sales: poor form in bumper: much improved over hurdles when winning handicaps at Haydock (valuable novice, beat Simply Supreme 11 lengths) in February and Uttoxeter (easily beat Dungarvans Choice 8 lengths) in March: favourite, seemed unsuited by much firmer ground at Haydock (jumped right) final outing: stays 2¾m: acts on soft going: remains open to improvement. *S. A. Brookshaw*

h117 p
F74

VALPARISA (FR) 5 br.m. Priolo (USA) – Valuable (FR) (Top Ville) [2002/3 F17d^{pu} **F—**
Oct 12] compact mare: fifth foal: half-sister to 3 middle-distance winners on Flat in
France: dam 1¼m winner in France at 3 yrs: broke down in mares bumper on debut.
J. Neville

VALUABLE (IRE) 6 b.m. Jurado (USA) – Can't Afford It (IRE) (Glow (USA)) **F—**
[2002/3 F16s F16m Dec 17] strong, well-made mare: first foal: half-sister to fairly useful
bumper winner Mitchelstown (by Topanoora): dam, ran twice at 2 yrs, half-sister to
useful sprinter Clever Caption: well beaten in 2 bumpers and seller on Flat: sold 1,700
gns Doncaster May Sales. *Mrs A. Duffield*

VANDAS CHOICE (IRE) 5 b.g. Sadler's Wells (USA) – Morning Devotion (USA) **h102**
(Affirmed (USA)) [2002/3 F14d⁴ F16v³ F16d⁵ 16g⁵ 16g* Apr 25] brother to useful 1m **F86**
and 9f winner First Night and closely related to several above-average Flat winners,
notably Oaks and Irish Derby winner Balanchine and Derby third Romanov: dam, 2-y-o
6f winner, stayed 1½m: fair form in bumpers: stepped up debut effort over hurdles
previous day to win maiden at Perth by 1¾ lengths from Kymani Prince: will stay beyond
2m. *Mrs L. B. Normile*

VAN DE VELDE 4 ch.g. Alhijaz – Lucky Flinders (Free State) [2002/3 16d 23v 16s **h—**
Feb 12] disappointing maiden on Flat: has failed to make a splash over hurdles. *R. Wilman*

VANORMIX (FR) 4 gr.g. Linamix (FR) – Vadsa Honor (FR) (Highest Honor (FR)) **h120**
[2002/3 16g² 17v^{ur} 16d 19d* 19d* 16m⁴ Mar 22] sturdy gelding: second foal: brother to
very smart 1m/9f winner Vahorimix and useful 3-y-o Vadalix: dam, won twice around
1½m in France, half-sister to dam of Breeders Cup Mile winner Val Royal: fair maiden
up to 1¼m on Flat, sold out of A. Fabre's stable €60,000 Goffs July Sale: fairly useful
juvenile hurdler: favourite, won novices at Exeter in January and February (easily beat
Howrwenow 6 lengths): also might have won but for unseating after last (rider lost iron)
at Cheltenham second start: stays 19f: acts on heavy ground (not discredited on good to
firm). *M. C. Pipe*

Red Square Vodka 'Fixed Brush' Novices' Hurdle Final Bonus Race (Handicap), Haydock—
much improved form by 33/1-shot Valleymore

VA PENSIERO (GER)   4 b.c. Java Gold (USA) – Velvet Blue (Exactly Sharp (USA))   h–
[2002/3 16v⁶ Dec 20] maiden on Flat: favourite, well held in juvenile seller at Uttoxeter on hurdling debut. *C. Von Der Recke, Germany*

VARYKINOV (IRE)   14 b. or br.g. Roselier (FR) – Royal Handful (Some Hand)   c–
[2002/3 c84, h–: 24s⁵ Feb 26] sturdy gelding: fair hunter chaser in 2002: well held in   h–
amateur novice hurdle on return: stays 3¼m: acts on heavy going: effective blinkered or not. *M. G. Rimell*

VATIRISK (FR)   6 gr.g. Take Risks (FR) – Vatipan (FR) (Trepan (FR)) [2002/3 h115:   h120
16s⁴ 17g² 22d* 20f⁵ 16s⁶ 16v Mar 2] lengthy gelding: fairly useful handicap hurdler: won at Galway in August: below form following break final 2 starts: stays 2¾m: acts on soft and firm going: has worn blinkers/tongue strap. *E. J. O'Grady, Ireland*

VEGAS VIC (IRE)   5 b.m. Old Vic – Princess Breda (IRE) (Long Pond) [2002/3   F–
F14d Nov 26] unfurnished mare: first foal: dam, winning Irish pointer, half-sister to use-ful chaser Ask The Butler, stayed 2¾m: showed nothing in bumper on debut. *G. Brown*

VEILED DANCER (IRE)   10 b.m. Shareef Dancer (USA) – Fatal Distraction   c71
(Formidable (USA)) [2002/3 22g 22f⁶ 21m⁶ c25d⁶ c24g⁶ c28g⁴ Mar 17] compact mare: h62
winning pointer: poor maiden hurdler: better effort on completed starts in steeplechases (jumped poorly in between) when fourth of 7 from 12 lb out of handicap at Fontwell: stays easy 3½m: acts on firm and good to soft going. *A. S. T. Holdsworth*

VELMEZ   10 ch.g. Belmez (USA) – Current Raiser (Filiberto (USA)) [2002/3 h71:   c–
c16m 22g 22m c19dᶠ Oct 23] sturdy gelding: winning hurdler: virtually no form since   h–
early-2000/1, including over fences: stays 3m: acts on firm going, probably on soft: visored/blinkered. *B. J. Llewellyn*

VELVET SWORD   8 b.m. Broadsword (USA) – Marney Barle (Julio Mariner)   h73
[2002/3 20m 20m⁵ 22m²ⁿ Jul 14] leggy mare: poor maiden hurdler/pointer, lightly raced. *R. Hollinshead*

VENEGUERA (IRE)   10 b.g. Satco (FR) – Orlita (Master Buck) [2002/3 c99§, h101:   c– §
24gᵖᵘ 21m⁴ 22m⁶ 24f* 26s 26sᵖᵘ 21d⁶ Jan 15] lengthy gelding: maiden chaser: modest   h90 §
handicap hurdler: off 4 months, won at Ludlow in October: out of form otherwise in 2002/3: stays 3¼m: acts on any going: sometimes blinkered earlier in career: lazy sort, often needs plenty of driving. *K. C. Bailey*

VENN OTTERY   8 b.g. Access Ski – Tom's Comedy (Comedy Star (USA)) [2002/3   c–
c–, h–: 19gᵖᵘ c20g⁴ c16sᵖᵘ 19m c16g⁴ c16mᶠ c22m c25mᶠ Apr 12] rangy gelding: of little   h–
account: headstrong. *O. J. Carter*

VENTUREMORE   7 br.g. Green Adventure (USA) – Admire-A-More (Le Coq d'Or)   h83
[2002/3 F–: 18g 16m⁶ 16g⁶ 16m³ 16s³ 16g 16g⁴ Apr 7] tall gelding: poor novice hurdler: raced around 2m: acts on soft and good to firm going: takes strong hold. *P. Monteith*

VENTURE TO FLY (IRE)   9 ch.g. Roselier (FR) – Fly Run (Deep Run) [2002/3   c107
c–p, h–: c20v⁴ c21dᵖᵘ Dec 9] sturdy gelding: fair hurdler: off a year, similar form only   h–
completed start over fences: should prove best at 3m+: raced on going softer than good (acts on heavy). *N. G. Richards*

VERDE LUNA   11 b.g. Green Desert (USA) – Mamaluna (USA) (Roberto (USA))   c68
[2002/3 20m 21s 16s c26m* 26m⁵ c19d c24m⁶ c23m⁶ Nov 18] sparely-made gelding: h–
form outside points since 1998/9 only when winning weak handicap chase at Fontwell in August: stays 3¼m: acts on good to firm going: blinkered/visored: has had tongue tied. *A. G. Hobbs*

VERIDIAN   10 b.g. Green Desert (USA) – Alik (FR) (Targowice (USA)) [2002/3   c81
h111: 17g⁴ 17s³ c16g⁴ c17gᵖᵘ 20sᵖᵘ 16d⁵ 16d⁵ Nov 25] compact gelding: fair handicap   h116 d
hurdler: let down by jumping both starts over fences: badly out of sorts returned to hurdles, left B. Llewellyn after fifth outing: stays 2½m: acts on soft and good to firm going, probably on heavy: below form only run in blinkers: held up. *G. F. Bridgwater*

VERNEY BIRD (IRE)   6 b.m. Prince of Birds (USA) – Verney Run (Deep Run)   h123
[2002/3 h122, F90: 20s² Dec 8] compact mare: fairly useful hurdler: good second to Aimess Mark in handicap at Punchestown only start in 2002/3: stays 2½m: acts on soft going. *M. Halford, Ireland*

VERO BEACH   7 ch.g. Nicholas Bill – My Moody Girl (IRE) (Alzao (USA)) [2002/3   h?
27g⁵ Apr 19] workmanlike gelding: well beaten in bumpers in 2000/1: fifth of 9 in claimer at Newton Abbot on hurdling debut, not fluent and probably flattered in steadily-run race. *Mrs S. D. Williams*

VERSAILLES 4 b.g. Bluegrass Prince (IRE) – Fabulous Pet (Somethingfabulous **h–**
(USA)) [2002/3 17s^{pu} 16d^{pu} Jan 18] half-brother to winning juvenile hurdler Baisse
d'Argent (by Common Grounds) and modest hurdler/chaser Broadgate Flyer (by Silver
Kite), stays 3m: modest maiden on Flat (bred to be suited by 1¼m+), sold out of Mrs
J. Ramsden's stable 3,000 gns Newmarket Autumn Sales: no show in 2 juvenile hurdles.
D. Burchell

VERSICIUM (FR) 9 ch.g. Mister Sicy (FR) – Verdurine (FR) (General Holme (USA)) **c106**
[2002/3 c102, h95: c17m* c17g³ c16m^{pu} c16m² Oct 3] winning hurdler: fair handicap **h–**
chaser: off 9½ months, won at Southwell in July: best around 2m: acts on firm and soft
going: visored: front runner: has been let down by jumping, but largely consistent.
M. C. Pipe

VERT ESPERE 10 ch.g. Green Adventure (USA) – Celtic Dream (Celtic Cone) **h99**
[2002/3 h80: 20m² 24m⁵ 19m* 21g² 20g² 20m^{pu} Apr 21] big, workmanlike gelding:
modest handicap hurdler: won at Market Rasen in August: ran well next 2 starts, then left
A. Streeter: stays 3m: acts on firm and good to soft going. *Mrs J. Candlish*

VERY DARING 13 b.g. Derring Rose – La Verite (Vitiges (FR)) [2002/3 c–, h–: **c–**
c21g^{pu} May 1] workmanlike gelding: virtually no form outside points: tried visored/ **h–**
blinkered. *Miss N. L. Elliott*

VERY OPTIMISTIC (IRE) 5 b.g. Un Desperado (FR) – Bright Future (IRE) (Satco **F102 p**
(FR)) [2002/3 F16g* Apr 2] €64,000 4-y-o: rather unfurnished gelding: first foal: dam
unraced half-sister to fairly useful chaser Pennybridge, stays 3m: favourite, won
19-runner bumper at Ascot on debut by 2 lengths from Tomwontpayalot, smooth
headway 5f out but green off bridle and taking time to get on top: open to improvement.
Jonjo O'Neill

VERY TASTY (IRE) 6 ch.g. Be My Native (USA) – Jasmine Melody (Jasmine Star) **h–**
[2002/3 h–, F–: 20m^{pu} Jun 1] no sign of ability in bumper or over hurdles. *M. Todhunter*

VESUVE (FR) 4 b.g. Villez (USA) – Razzamatazz (FR) (Always Fair (USA)) [2002/3 **c133**
15v^F 16d* 15d³ 17s* 18s⁶ 18s⁵ c17v² c17s² c17s² c20s³ c20v² Apr 26] third foal: half- **h111**
brother to winning hurdler/chaser up to 2¾m Gee Whizz (by Turgeon) and winning
hurdler around 2m Trinity Belle (by Tel Quel): dam useful 3-y-o hurdler/chaser: fair
hurdler, won 3-y-o minor event at Auteuil in July: much better over fences, second on 4
of 5 completed starts, best effort when beaten ½ length by Gorfou de Maspie in Group 2
in April: will stay beyond 2½m: raced mainly on soft/heavy going: usually blinkered.
G. Macaire, France

VETRANIO (IRE) 6 ch.g. Hubbly Bubbly (USA) – Cool Charm (Beau Charmeur **h66**
(FR)) [2002/3 F16d⁶ F18v⁶ 19d Feb 28] 15,000 4-y-o: second foal: half-brother to **F79**
winning pointer by Lanfranco: dam, winning pointer, from family of Pizarro: shaped like
a stayer both starts in bumpers: well-beaten ninth of 18 in novice at Newbury on hurdling
debut: will be suited by greater test of stamina. *N. M. Babbage*

VIADUCT (IRE) 7 b.g. Archway (IRE) – Decent Essence (Decent Fellow) [2002/3 **c92**
c28g² c24s³ c24v³ c25s⁴ c26g c24s* Apr 9] strong gelding: fair hunter chaser: won **h–**
at Wexford in March: out of depth in Foxhunter at Cheltenham 4 days earlier: stays 3½m:
acts on heavy going: tried blinkered: tongue tied. *I. Kingston, Ireland*

VICARS DESTINY (IRE) 5 b.m. Sir Harry Lewis (USA) – Church Leap (Pollerton) **h93**
[2002/3 F72: F17d F16d² F16v² 20d³ 20d* 24v* 20g^{pu} Apr 2] leggy mare: fair form in **F92**
bumpers: confirmed promise of hurdling debut when winning mares novice at Wetherby
in March: unruly at start there and didn't impress with attitude when pulled up at Ascot
final start: should stay 3m: raced on good going or softer (runner-up in bumper on heavy).
Mrs S. Lamyman

VICAR'S LAD 7 b.g. Terimon – Proverbial Rose (Proverb) [2002/3 F17s⁴ F17d 26d⁵ **h68**
Feb 23] 15,000 3-y-o: third foal: brother to 17f hurdle winner Flinders Chase and **F85**
half-brother to 2½m hurdle winner Bansha House (by Ardross): dam, winning pointer, in
frame up to 27f in steeplechases: better effort in bumpers at Hereford when fourth of 17
to Miller's Boy, outpaced after mistake eighth when fifth of 11 finishers in novice there
on hurdling debut: will prove suited by good test of stamina. *N. A. Twiston-Davies*

VICENTIO 4 br.g. Vettori (IRE) – Smah (Mtoto) [2002/3 F16d F16d F16g⁶ F17g Apr **F81**
26] 8,500Y: smallish, workmanlike gelding: third living foal: dam unraced, out of
half-sister to US Grade 1 winners Upper Nile and De La Rose: signs of only a little ability
in bumpers. *T. J. Fitzgerald*

VIC PLUM (IRE) 5 b. or br.m. Lord Americo – Naujella (Malinowski (USA)) **F–**
[2002/3 F16v F14d F16g Feb 12] 600 4-y-o: seventh foal: half-sister to fair hurdler/

winning chaser Plumbob (by Bob Back), stays 3¼m: dam maiden on Flat: tailed off in bumpers. *W. G. Young*

VICTORIA RYAN (IRE) 5 b.m. Good Thyne (USA) – No Not (Ovac (ITY)) [2002/3 F16g F16g Apr 14] €1,700 4-y-o: eighth foal: sister to winning pointer and half-sister to fair hurdler Elmside (by Brush Aside), stays 2¾m: dam once-raced, from family of smart chasers up to 3m Bells Life: well held in 2 bumpers. *J. R. Norton*   **F–**

VICTORIA'S BOY (IRE) 10 b.g. Denel (FR) – Cloghroe Lady (Hardboy) [2002/3 c83, h–: c24d⁴ c22m c21mᵖᵘ Jul 19] strong gelding: poor handicap chaser: stays 25f: acts on soft and good to firm ground: tried blinkered: sold 3,600 gns Doncaster August Sales: won 3-runner point in April. *T. D. Walford*   **c75 h–**

VICTORIA STONE 6 b.m. Old Vic – Lampstone (Ragstone) [2002/3 F16sᵖᵘ Jan 3] ninth foal: half-sister to several winners, notably smart 2m chaser Martin's Lamp (by Martinmas) and useful chaser Hurricane Lamp (by Derrylin), stayed 3m: dam, novice hurdler/chaser, half-sister to useful 2m hurdler Red Power: pulled up lame in bumper on debut. *A. King*   **F–**

VICTOR LASZLO 11 b.g. Ilium – Report 'em (USA) (Staff Writer (USA)) [2002/3 c80§, h–: c17d⁴ c22m c20m⁵ c22m c20d³ c16g⁴ c21g⁴ c20g⁵ Sep 26] smallish gelding: poor maiden chaser: effective at 2m to easy 25f: acts on firm and good to soft going: tried visored: usually tongue tied: unreliable. *R. Allan*   **c74 § h–**

VICTORY GUNNER (IRE) 5 ch.g. Old Vic – Gunner B Sharp (Gunner B) [2002/3 F16s F16s⁵ F17g² F17g Apr 5] medium-sized gelding: first foal: dam unraced sister to useful juvenile hurdler Son of A Gunner: best effort in bumpers (fairly useful form) when ½-length second to Samby in maiden at Folkestone: out of depth final start. *C. Roberts*   **F99**

VICTORY ROLL 7 b.g. In The Wings – Persian Victory (IRE) (Persian Bold) [2002/3 h103: 16v 16d Mar 10] close-coupled gelding: fair handicap hurdler, off 12 months before reappearance: raced mainly around 2m on going softer than good (acts on heavy): visored once. *Miss E. C. Lavelle*   **h96**

VIC TOTO (FR) 6 b.g. Kaid Pous – Koberta (FR) (Don Roberto (USA)) [2002/3 h155: 21s² 25d² 19s* 20s* 24v⁴ 18v⁴ 20s⁴ Apr 21] angular gelding: very smart hurdler: raced exclusively at Auteuil: won 2 Group 3 events in autumn, Prix de Compiegne (impressively, beat Rougenoir 8 lengths) and Prix Carmarthen (beat Galant Moss 2 lengths), making all each time: not at best subsequently: effective at 2¼m and stays 25f: raced on going softer than good: forces pace: genuine. *Mlle F. Forneron, France*   **h156**

VIDI CAESAR (NZ) 8 b.g. Racing Is Fun (USA) – Vidi Vici (NZ) (Marauding Roman Empire) [2002/3 16d 16d³ Mar 5] sturdy gelding: maiden on Flat, in frame up to 1¼m: poor form in novice hurdles won by Middlethorpe at Wetherby and Catterick. *R. C. Guest*   **h77**

VIGOUREUX (FR) 4 b.g. Villez (USA) – Rouge Folie (FR) (Agent Bleu (FR)) [2002/3 16v² 17v* 16s⁵ 16m³ Apr 12] first foal: dam once-raced: twice-raced in juvenile hurdles at Enghien in November for M. Rolland, winning on second occasion: better subsequent effort when 21 lengths third of 4 to easy winner Sporazene at Ayr. *S. Gollings*   **h94**

VIKING BUOY (IRE) 11 ch.g. Pimpernels Tune – Clare's Crystal (Tekoah) [2002/3 17s c16v³ c18s c24s 21m⁵ 21m³ Apr 21] tall gelding: half-brother to smart staying hurdler/chaser Earthmover (by Mister Lord): one-time fair hurdler/chaser for D. Kiely, only poor nowadays: stays 25f: acts on any going: tried blinkered. *Mrs P. Townsley*   **c– h68**

VILLA 7 b.g. Jupiter Island – Spoonhill Wood (Celtic Cone) [2002/3 F96: F16v* Nov 27] good-topped gelding: progressive in bumpers, useful form when beating Earl's Kitchen 3½ lengths in 15-runner event at Chepstow in November: will be suited by 2½m+. *M. C. Pipe*   **F110**

VILLAGE COPPER 11 b.g. Town And Country – Culm Valley (Port Corsair) [2002/3 c–: c24m⁴ c21m⁴ May 22] non-thoroughbred gelding: modest hunter chaser: successful in point in March: stays 3m: acts on good to firm going. *Mrs Ruth Hayter*   **c81**

VILLAGE KING (IRE) 10 b.g. Roi Danzig (USA) – Honorine (USA) (Blushing Groom (FR)) [2002/3 c133§, h–: c24m² c27d⁴ Nov 24] good-bodied gelding: useful handicap chaser: much better effort in autumn when clear second to Run For Paddy at Chepstow: probably stays 3½m: acts on heavy and good to firm going: blinkered once (ran creditably): sometimes takes little interest, including over National fences at Aintree in November (had fallen twice over them previously). *P. J. Hobbs*   **c137 § h–**

VILLAGE QUEEN (IRE) 6 ch.m. Good Thyne (USA) – Lady Henbit (IRE) (Henbit (USA)) [2002/3 19s 16d Dec 26] IR 2,200 3-y-o: second foal: dam unraced, top-class   **h–**

staying chaser from family of top-class staying chaser The Dikler: well beaten in mares novice hurdles. *P. J. Hobbs*

VILLAIR (IRE) 8 b.g. Valville (FR) – Brackenair (Fairbairn) [2002/3 c–, h76: c20d^F 16d* c20s² c20s⁴ c20s⁵ c17v^F c20g² c20s* Mar 10] long-backed gelding: poor hurdler: won novice seller at Towcester in May, sold out of D. Stoddart's stable 5,800 gns at Doncaster later in month: modest chaser: improved last 2 starts, won 6-runner handicap at Plumpton by ¾ length from Burwood Breeze: stays 2½m: raced on good going or softer (acts on soft): tried blinkered, usually when successful: has run in snatches and looked none too keen (carried head high at Plumpton). *C. J. Mann* **c92 h74**

VILPRANO 12 b.g. Ra Nova – Village Princess (Rolfe (USA)) [2002/3 h107: 22d⁴ 24m⁵ 26s³ 24g⁵ 22s 24s⁴ 25g⁵ 23v⁶ 27v³ 24s³ 24v³ 24m 27g Apr 25] smallish, leggy gelding: fair handicap hurdler, on the downgrade in 2002/3: best at 3m+: acts on any going: has won with/without visor and has worn cheekpieces: often soon off bridle. *James Moffatt* **h107 d**

VINCENT VAN GOGH (IRE) 8 b.g. Executive Perk – Rare Picture (Pollerton) [2002/3 c94, h–: c24f* c24s² c25d⁶ c24s c21d² c21d⁵ Feb 15] tall gelding: modest chaser: won handicap at Taunton (third course success) in October: generally below form after next outing, probably flattered fifth one: stays 3m: acts on firm and soft going: has broken blood vessel: no form on left-handed courses: often none too fluent: has failed to impress with attitude. *R. J. Hodges* **c98 h–**

VINO TINTO (IRE) 9 b.g. Glacial Storm (USA) – Pure Spec (Fine Blade (USA)) [2002/3 c91, h–: c25g³ Mar 15] tall gelding: maiden hurdler: fair pointer/hunter chaser, tended to carry head high when close third to Westerton at Market Rasen: stays 25f: raced on good going or softer (acts on heavy): tried blinkered/tongue tied. *Mrs C. M. Mulhall* **c91 h–**

VIOLENT 5 b.m. Deploy – Gentle Irony (Mazilier (USA)) [2002/3 h–: 16m Jun 19] modest at best on Flat (barely stays 1½m), no form since April 2002: showed little in 2 runs over hurdles. *Jamie Poulton* **h–**

VIRAC BOY (IRE) 10 b.g. Tremblant – Supreme Cherry (Buckskin (FR)) [2002/3 16d 24g^{pu} 25v⁶ 22v⁵ 25s⁶ Mar 10] winning pointer: little form over hurdles. *Miss G. Browne* **c– h–**

VIRGIN SOLDIER (IRE) 7 ch.g. Waajib – Never Been Chaste (Posse (USA)) [2002/3 h113p: 16m* 17m* 16m³ 16m² Oct 16] angular gelding: fairly useful on Flat (stays 2¼m): fairly useful handicap hurdler: won at Stratford and Bangor in September: very good 2½ lengths second to Welsh Main at Wetherby: stays 2½m: acts on good to firm and good to soft going. *G. A. Swinbank* **h126**

VIRTUOSO 9 b.g. Suave Dancer – Creake (Derring-Do) [2002/3 c106, h–: 19m⁶ c16s⁶ c19d⁶ c21s⁴ c16d⁶ Feb 10] leggy, sparely-made gelding: winning hurdler: fair handicap chaser in 2001/2 for C. Mann: has lost his form: raced mainly around 2m: acts on heavy going, below form once than good: blinkered once. *B. G. Powell* **c– h–**

VISCOUNT BANKES 5 ch.g. Clantime – Bee Dee Dancer (Ballacashtal (CAN)) [2002/3 h–: 17s^{pu} Mar 7] no form over hurdles: in frame in 2 maiden points. *W. G. M. Turner* **h–**

VISIBILITY (FR) 4 gr.g. Linamix (FR) – Visor (USA) (Mr Prospector (USA)) [2002/3 16d³ 17d² 16s* 16d⁴ 16g⁵ Mar 14] tall, leggy, angular gelding: fairly useful on Flat (stays 10.5f), sold out of A. Fabre's stable €45,000 Goffs Arc Sale: fairly useful juvenile hurdler: won at Leicester in February by 7 lengths from Lewis Island: failed to impress with attitude and jumping final start: raced around 2m on good going or softer (acts on soft). *M. C. Pipe* **h117**

VITAL ISSUE (IRE) 11 b. or br.g. Electric – Dreamello (Bargello) [2002/3 c25g^{pu} c34g* c28m Jun 1] strong gelding: fairly useful hunter chaser on his day: won at Uttoxeter in May: stays 4¼m: acts on heavy going. *M. J. Brown* **c109 h–**

VITELUCY 4 b.f. Vettori (IRE) – Classic Line (Last Tycoon) [2002/3 17s⁴ 16m² Mar 18] modest on Flat (should stay beyond 13f), claimed from A. Balding £8,000 after winning in February: better effort over hurdles when second in weakly-contested mares novice at Southwell. *Miss S. J. Wilton* **h80**

VIVA BINGO (IRE) 7 ch.g. Phardante (FR) – Kitty Frisk (Prince Tenderfoot (USA)) [2002/3 F16s² F16g³ F16g⁵ F16d 16s 23v^{pu} 17v^{pu} 20m 16m Apr 21] angular gelding: brother to smart 2m hurdler Kimanicky: dam maiden: modest in bumpers: sold out of D. P. Kelly's stable 4,000 gns Doncaster November Sales: no form over hurdles. *M. J. Gingell* **h– F83**

VIVALDI ROSE (IRE) 8 b.m. Cataldi – Peaceful Rose (Roselier (FR)) [2002/3 h–, F77: 16d^{pu} 23d 21v³ c21g^{pu} c20g⁴ Apr 21] little sign of ability. *L. Lungo*   **c– h62**

VODKA BLEU (FR) 4 b.g. Pistolet Bleu (IRE) – Viva Vodka (FR) (Crystal Glitters (USA)) [2002/3 F16s* F16d* F17g^{ur} Apr 5] leggy, unfurnished ex-Irish gelding: fifth foal: brother to 2 winners, including fairly useful French hurdler Rosmadec, and half-brother to 2 others, including useful miler Macchiato (by Starborough): dam, French 7f to 1m winner, out of smart 1974 2-y-o Oak Hill: won first 2 starts in bumpers, 9-runner events at Leopardstown in January (trained by E. Hales) and Haydock (7/2 on, had to be firmly ridden to beat Provocative a head, pair clear) in March: unseated before halfway in Grade 2 at Aintree. *M. C. Pipe*   **F103**

VODKA INFERNO (IRE) 6 ch.g. Moscow Society (USA) – Corrie Lough (IRE) (The Parson) [2002/3 F91: F16d³ F16d 25g^{pu} Jan 18] medium-sized gelding: fair form in bumpers: far from fluent in novice at Catterick on hurdling debut: should stay at least 2½m. *C. R. Egerton*   **h– F87**

VOLANO (FR) 5 b.g. Pistolet Bleu (IRE) – Vouivre (FR) (Matahawk) [2002/3 h121: 16g⁵ 16v 17s⁴ 16d^F Mar 10] small, well-made gelding: fairly useful hurdler: respectable efforts in handicaps at Newbury (fifth to Never) and Cheltenham (fourth to Native New Yorker) in 2002/3: running at least as well when falling 2 out at Stratford: likely to prove best at 2m: raced on good going or softer. *N. J. Henderson*   **h119**

VOL SOLITAIRE (FR) 5 b.g. Loup Solitaire (USA) – Vol Sauvage (FR) (Always Fair (USA)) [2002/3 h141: c17s* c16g^F c16d* c16d² c16s* c17d* c16g⁴ c16g² c20m* Apr 12] good-topped gelding: leading British-trained juvenile hurdler of 2001/2: again among the best novice chasers of 2002/3: successful in small fields at Bangor in October, Warwick (4-y-o event, by 3½ lengths from Palarshan) in November, Cheltenham in   **c151 h–**

Ashleybank Investments Future Champion Novices' Chase, Ayr—
a final win for the ill-fated Vol Solitaire

December, Kelso in March and Ayr (Grade 2, by 19 lengths from Tarxien) in April: also ran well seventh and eighth starts, fourth of 21 to Palarshan in valuable handicap at Cheltenham and second to stable-companion Le Roi Miguel in Grade 1 at Aintree: stayed 2½m: acted on good to firm and heavy going: often front runner: sound jumper: dead. *P. F. Nicholls*

VRUBEL (IRE) 4 ch.g. Entrepreneur – Renzola (Dragonara Palace (USA)) [2002/3 **h–** 16s^pu 16g Mar 14] fair at best on Flat (stays 9f), successful in June, sold out of N. Callaghan's stable 11,000 gns Newmarket Autumn Sales: no show in 2 starts over hurdles. *H. J. Collingridge*

VULCAN LANE (NZ) 6 ch.g. Star Way – Smudged (NZ) (Nassipour (USA)) [2002/3 **h73** 16s 16g 17v⁴ Jan 21] compact gelding: won at 9f on Flat in New Zealand: poor form in novice hurdles. *N. B. Mason*

W

WADERS (IRE) 9 b.g. Good Thyne (USA) – Lochda (Crash Course) [2002/3 c–, h–: **c–** c24m⁶ Apr 22] rangy gelding: winning chaser: won points in March and April before well **h–** beaten in hunter at Chepstow: stays 3¼m: acts on soft going: refused to race once. *Miss Gayle Evans*

WADSWORTH (NZ) 10 br.g. Kirmann – Guard The Gold (NZ) (Imperial Guard) **c–** [2002/3 c–, h89: 16m³ 18d⁶ Aug 2] leggy gelding: let down by jumping over fences: mod- **h89** est hurdler: raced mainly around 2m: acts on firm and good to soft going. *B. P. J. Baugh*

WAFFLES OF AMIN 6 b.g. Owington – Alzianah (Alzao (USA)) [2002/3 16g 17s **h–** Feb 13] small gelding: poor on Flat (seems to stay easy 2m): well held in 2 maiden hurdles. *S. Kirk*

WAGGY (IRE) 7 b.g. Cataldi – Energance (IRE) (Salmon Leap (USA)) [2002/3 F16g **h–** F16m⁵ 26d^pu Feb 23] second foal: dam, 2m hurdle winner, half-sister to fairly useful 2m **F82** jumper Nordic Thorn: better effort in bumpers (hung badly right on debut) when fifth of 10 at Huntingdon: weakened quickly 4 out in 3¼m novice at Hereford on hurdling debut 9 months later. *S. E. H. Sherwood*

WAGNER (IRE) 6 b. or br.g. Lure (USA) – Tapaculo (Tap On Wood) [2002/3 16g **h102** 17g 20s* 21d² 20v 24g* 24d⁴ 27g³ Apr 25] fair handicap hurdler, off nearly 20 months before reappearance: won at Bangor in October and Market Rasen in March: good efforts last 2 starts: best at 3m+: acts on heavy going: effective tongue tied or not. *Jonjo O'Neill*

WAHIBA SANDS 10 b.g. Pharly (FR) – Lovely Noor (USA) (Fappiano (USA)) **c147** [2002/3 c157, h–: c16s³ c24s⁶ c16g⁶ c19s⁴ c16m³ c20d⁵ c21m⁵ c16m³ Apr 26] tall, **h–** useful-looking gelding: very smart chaser at best: not so good in 2002/3, one of better efforts third of 5 to Seebald in very valuable minor event at Sandown final start, not finding much off bridle: stays 21f: acts on heavy and good to firm going: can race lazily (wore cheekpieces/visor last 2 outings). *M. C. Pipe*

WAIMEA BAY 4 b.f. Karinga Bay – Smart In Sable (Roscoe Blake) [2002/3 F17g² **F?** Apr 21] second foal: dam modest 2m hurdler: well-beaten second in 5-runner mares bumper at Newton Abbot on debut. *P. R. Hedger*

WAINAK (USA) 5 b.g. Silver Hawk (USA) – Cask (Be My Chief (USA)) [2002/3 **h88** h77: 16s² 17d² 16g³ 16m⁴ 20s² 20d⁴ 20g³ 20g³ Apr 23] close-coupled gelding: modest novice hurdler: stays 2½m: acts on soft and good to firm going: tried in headgear: consistent, but is hard ride. *Miss Lucinda V. Russell*

WAIN MOUNTAIN 7 b.g. Unfuwain (USA) – Mountain Memory (High Top) [2002/3 **c130** c122, h–: c19v² c19v⁴ Dec 20] good-topped gelding: fairly useful chaser: better effort in **h–** handicaps in 2002/3 when 4 lengths second of 4 to Asador at Chepstow: stays 3¼m: raced on going softer than good (acts on heavy): tends to flash tail under pressure. *J. A. B. Old*

WAIT FOR THE WILL (USA) 7 ch.g. Seeking The Gold (USA) – You'd Be **h118** Surprised (USA) (Blushing Groom (FR)) [2002/3 h73+: 17m² May 3] tall gelding: useful on Flat (stays 1¾m), won 4 times in 2002: placed all 3 starts over hurdles, fairly useful form when 1¼ lengths second to Foreman in steadily-run maiden at Folkestone in May: blinkered since debut. *G. L. Moore*

WAIT FOR THIS (IRE) 8 b.g. Torus – Bar You Try (Bargello) [2002/3 c97, h103: **c84** c24g⁴ c28m^pu c25m^pu 22m 24f Oct 17] winning hurdler/chaser: little form in 2002/3, **h–**

looked none too keen in blinkers final start: better at 3m than shorter: acts on firm and good to soft going: usually tongue tied. *C. J. Down*

WAKEUP SMILING (IRE) 5 b.g. Norwich – Blackmiller Lady (Bonne Noel) [2002/3 F16s F16g3 F18m3 Mar 31] unfurnished gelding: fifth foal: dam Irish maiden: well-backed favourite, best effort in bumpers when third of 19 to Flower of Pitcur at Huntingdon: flashed tail final start. *Miss E. C. Lavelle* **F92**

WALCOT LAD (IRE) 7 b.g. Jurado (USA) – Butty Miss (Menelek) [2002/3 h–, F–: 22m3 19g 16s5 20m5 16m3 Sep 7] poor maiden hurdler: stays 2¾m: acts on good to firm and good to soft going: blinkered/visored. *B. A. Pearce* **h70 ?**

WALK ON BY 9 gr.g. Terimon – Try G'S (Hotfoot) [2002/3 c77, h–: c16m3 c16s2 c16g6 c21mF 20s c22m* c20mpu c19d4 c26mur c24spu Nov 14] workmanlike gelding: maiden hurdler: poor handicap chaser: won at Fontwell in August: stays 2¾m: acts on firm and soft going: often blinkered. *J. S. King* **c81 h–**

WALK ON SEAS (IRE) 8 b.g. Shardari – Over The Seas (North Summit) [2002/3 19s 19s 18v4 21d4 18v 19s2 20v2 Apr 26] leggy, close-coupled gelding: fourth foal: half-brother to 2 winning hurdlers by Project Manager: dam fairly useful 2m hurdler: fairly useful hurdler: last of 4 in slowly-run 21f minor event at Cheltenham: creditable second in handicaps at Auteuil last 2 starts, behind Malone in very valuable 19-runner event on second occasion: acts on heavy going. *F. Doumen, France* **h123**

WALTER PLINGE 7 b.g. Theatrical Charmer – Carousel Zingira (Reesh) [2002/3 h68: c21g3 c21gF5 20gpu 24gpu 17spu 21g 20g* Apr 21] compact gelding: poor hurdler: back to form when winning selling handicap at Uttoxeter: similar form on first of 2 starts over fences: stays 21f: acts on good to firm and good to soft going: tongue tied last 2 outings. *A. G. Juckes* **c68 h68**

WALTER'S DESTINY 11 ch.g. White Prince (USA) – Tearful Sarah (Rugantino) [2002/3 c108§, h–: c25gpu c25d4 c25d4 c25d3 c24spu c25m3 c26gpu Apr 19] lengthy gelding: fair handicap chaser on his day: acts on good to firm and heavy going: has looked hard ride (may benefit from headgear): unreliable. *C. W. Mitchell* **c103 § h–**

WALTZING ALONG (IRE) 5 b.g. Presenting – Clyduffe Fairy (Belfalas) [2002/3 F16d3 F16g4 Apr 14] IR £20,000 3-y-o: fourth foal: dam unraced: in frame in bumpers at Catterick and Hexham. *L. Lungo* **F88**

WANNA SHOUT 5 b.m. Missed Flight – Lulu (Polar Falcon (USA)) [2002/3 h–: 16mpu 16g 16d6 19d Nov 26] rather leggy mare: modest on Flat (stays 1¼m): no form over hurdles: tried in blinkers/cheekpieces. *R. Dickin* **h–**

WARD SEVENTEEN 6 b.g. Supreme Leader – Kerris Melody (Furry Glen) [2002/3 F17s Nov 21] fifth foal: half-brother to bumper winner Star Diva (by Toulon) and winning pointer by Derrylin: dam of little account: eighth of 17 in bumper at Hereford on debut. *R. S. Brookhouse* **F–**

WAREYTH (USA) 4 b. or br.g. Shuailaan (USA) – Bahr Alsalaam (USA) (Riverman (USA)) [2002/3 16spu 17d 16dpu 17f 16mur Apr 21] tall gelding: signs of ability on Flat, sold out of M. Channon's stable 15,500 gns Newmarket July Sales: no form in juvenile hurdles (trained by Jane Southcombe on debut). *R. H. Buckler* **h–**

WARJAN (FR) 6 b.g. Beaudelaire (USA) – Twilight Mood (USA) (Devil's Bag (USA)) [2002/3 h–: 16s* 16d 16g 17g Mar 13] lengthy gelding: has had wind operation: fairly useful handicap hurdler: improved in 2002/3, won at Sandown in November, quickening smartly in falsely-run race to beat Hawadeth a neck: good ninth to Spirit Leader in Tote Gold Trophy at Newbury third start, mid-field behind same horse in County Hurdle at Cheltenham: raced around 2m on good going or softer (acts on heavy). *R. T. Phillips* **h124**

WARM FRONT 6 b.m. Bustino – Princess Hotpot (IRE) (King's Ride) [2002/3 F17s May 18] modest form on first of 2 completed starts in bumpers, trained in 2000/1 by M. Easterby. *Miss H. C. Knight* **F–**

WARMINGHAMSHARPISH 6 b.m. Nalchik (USA) – Tilstock Maid (Rolfe (USA)) [2002/3 F17s F16g5 F16m2 F16f* Oct 10] unfurnished mare: second foal: dam unraced: fair form in bumpers, won at Ludlow by 3½ lengths from Streamsforth Lad. *W. M. Brisbourne* **F87**

WARNER FOR PLAYERS (IRE) 12 br.g. Good Thyne (USA) – Bramble Hatch (Pry) [2002/3 c94, h–: c20v2 Feb 7] leggy gelding: modest chaser: second of 3 finishers to Wise Prince in hunter at Bangor: won 3-runner point in April: should stay beyond 25f: goes well on soft/heavy going: front runner. *S. Wynne* **c96 h–**

WAR PAINT (IRE) 11 gr.g. Zaffaran (USA) – Rosy Posy (IRE) (Roselier (FR)) [2002/3 c83, h–: 19d Nov 26] strong, rangy gelding: won maiden point in 2002, let down by jumping on steeplechasing debut: fair form on second of 3 outings over hurdles, no show in handicap in November. *M. Sheppard*   c– h–

WARRBOW 12 gr.g. Fast Frigate – Dam Unregistered (Damsire Unknown) [2002/3 c21mᵖᵘ May 22] maiden pointer. *S. Garrott*   c–

WARREN BOY 13 b.g. Hotfoot – Artaius Rose (FR) (Artaius (USA)) [2002/3 c16gᶠ May 1] sturdy gelding: winning hunter chaser: well held when fell heavily 3 out at Cheltenham in May. *T. L. Jones*   c– h–

WARRLIN 9 b.g. Warrshan (USA) – Lahin (Rainbow Quest (USA)) [2002/3 c99, h–: c25d² c16fᶠ c22g* Sep 28] sparely-made gelding: winning hurdler: modest novice chaser: made hard work of simple task in 4-runner event at Market Rasen, and not seen out again: barely stays 25f: acts on any going. *C. W. Fairhurst*   c97 h–

WARTON CRAG 7 b.g. Tina's Pet – Majestic Form (IRE) (Double Schwartz) [2002/3 F–: 17dᵖᵘ Jun 5] showed nothing in bumper or on hurdling debut. *D. Moffatt*   h–

WARTORN (IRE) 8 b.g. Warcraft (USA) – Alice Minkthorn (Party Mink) [2002/3 h91?: 19d⁵ 21d 17d 19v² 19d² 21s 21s³ 22d* Mar 6] workmanlike gelding: modest hurdler: won 21-runner handicap at Wincanton: should stay 3m: raced on going softer than good (acts on heavy). *J. S. King*   h95

WAR TUNE 7 b.g. Warrshan (USA) – Keen Melody (USA) (Sharpen Up) [2002/3 h88: c21g⁵ 20d² 20m* Jun 19] workmanlike gelding: modest hurdler, claimed from G. Edwards £6,000 second start: won 17-runner maiden at Worcester in June: stays 2½m: acts on soft and good to firm going: swishes tail under pressure: none too consistent. *B. D. Leavy*   c– h88

WAS A DRIVE (IRE) 9 b.g. Yashgan – Alan's Rosalinda (Prefairy) [2002/3 c81: c20dᵖᵘ c20v³ c21sᶠ c20g Apr 14] poor handicap chaser, little form in 2002/3: should stay beyond 2½m: acts on heavy going. *Miss Kate Milligan*   c–

WASHINGTON PINK (IRE) 4 b.g. Tagula (IRE) – Little Red Rose (Precocious) [2002/3 17s³ 17g² 17d² 16g* 16g³ 16m⁴ 16m Oct 16] compact gelding: fair on Flat (likely to prove best up to 1½m): modest juvenile hurdler: made all in maiden at Uttoxeter in September: raced around 2m: acts on soft and good to firm going. *C. Grant*   h90

WASSL STREET (IRE) 11 b.g. Dancing Brave (USA) – One Way Street (Habitat) [2002/3 c23sᵖᵘ Feb 12] angular gelding: winning hurdler/chaser up to 23f: always behind only outing (suffered overreach) since 2000: successful only start in visor. *R. Lee*   c– h–

WATCH IT 5 b.g. Sea Raven (IRE) – Magic Penny (Sharrood (USA)) [2002/3 F80: F16d F16g⁴ Apr 1] modest form in bumpers, found little both starts in 2002/3: free-going sort. *M. Todhunter*   F78

WATCH THE DOVE 6 b.g. Afzal – Spot The Dove (Riberetto) [2002/3 F93: 16g³ 20v⁶ 17v² 17s² 17d⁴ 21m⁶ Mar 21] angular gelding: modest novice hurdler: stays 21f: acts on good to firm and heavy going: consistent. *C. Tizzard*   h90

WATCHYOURBACK (NZ) 9 ch.g. Watchman (NZ) – English Lass (NZ) (English Harbour) [2002/3 c24d² c21mᶠ Apr 21] winning hurdler: fair pointer: similar form when second to Thatsforeel at Uttoxeter on hunter chase debut: fell fifth in novice event at Fakenham: stays 3¼m: acts on good to firm and good to soft going: visored/tongue tied in 2002/3. *M. Trott*   c82 h–

WATERBERG (IRE) 8 b.g. Sadler's Wells (USA) – Pretoria (Habitat) [2002/3 c123+, h103+: c22s² c24dᵖᵘ 22v⁴ 22d c24s⁴ c20g⁴ Mar 28] smallish, workmanlike gelding: winning hurdler: fairly useful novice chaser in 2001/2: disappointing in handicaps, reportedly bled from nose final outing: stays 3m: raced on good going or softer (acts on heavy): blinkered last 2 starts. *H. D. Daly*   c98 h–

WATER FONT (IRE) 11 b.g. Lafontaine (USA) – Belle Savenay (Coquelin (USA)) [2002/3 c104, h–: c28gᵖᵘ c32mᵖᵘ c28dᵖᵘ Feb 8] angular gelding: has been hobdayed: fair handicap chaser in early-2001/2: pulled up all 3 starts in steeplechases in 2002/3 (left J. O'Neill after second one), later placed in small-field points: stays 27f: acts on firm and soft going, well held only run on heavy: tried blinkered: has been let down by jumping. *Mrs J. Williamson*   c– h–

WATERHALL 10 b.g. River God (USA) – Tuneful Queen (Queen's Hussar) [2002/3 20g 22d⁵ 22sᵖᵘ 26g² 26g⁶ Mar 12] workmanlike gelding: poor maiden hurdler: stays 3¼m: acts on soft and good to firm going. *J. M. P. Eustace*   c– h69

WATER KING (USA) 4 b.c. Irish River (FR) – Brookshield Baby (IRE) (Sadler's Wells (USA)) [2002/3 16g 17s 16s[4] 16g[3] 16m[5] Apr 19] fairly useful maiden on Flat (stays 1¼m), sold out of E. Dunlop's stable 11,000 gns Newmarket Autumn Sales: poor form when in frame over hurdles: raced around 2m: acts on soft going. *G. Brown* **h84**

WATERLILY (IRE) 4 b.f. Revoque (IRE) – Cochineal (USA) (Vaguely Noble) [2002/3 F16m* Apr 21] sixth foal: half-sister to 2 winners, including useful 1995 2-y-o 1m winner Ski Academy (by Royal Academy): dam maiden, stayed at least 11.7f: won 13-runner mares maiden bumper at Fakenham on debut by 6 lengths from Maryland: open to improvement. *M. J. Wallace* **F92 p**

WATERLOO PARK (IRE) 7 b.m. Alphabatim (USA) – Waterloo Sunset (Deep Run) [2002/3 F94: F16m[2] 16d[pu] Aug 4] leggy, lengthy mare: fair form in bumpers: won on debut in 2001/2 (very reluctant to race next time): sold out of N. Chance's stable 16,000 gns Doncaster May Sales after reappearance: again reluctant to set off on hurdling debut: has been early to post: temperamental. *P. M. J. Doyle, Ireland* **h– §** **F94**

WATERSHIP DOWN (IRE) 6 b.g. Dolphin Street (FR) – Persian Myth (Persian Bold) [2002/3 c80, h61: c23m[5] c21f[2] c23g[2] c24d c24v[pu] Nov 22] leggy gelding: well held over hurdles: modest chaser: stays 23f: acts on firm and good to soft going, possibly not on heavy: has looked none too keen. *B. G. Powell* **c86** **h–**

WATER SPORTS (IRE) 5 b.m. Marju (IRE) – Water Splash (USA) (Little Current (USA)) [2002/3 16g 16v 21d[pu] 20s[3] Mar 2] lengthy mare: half-sister to smart chaser up to 21f Stately Home (by Fools Holme) and winning hurdler around 2½m Teller of Tales (by Arazi), and to Derby runner-up Blue Judge (by Rainbow Quest): dam, fairly useful 1½m winner, half-sister to fairly useful hurdlers Court Circular, a stayer, and Moat Garden, best at 2m: fair on Flat, 11f winner in France at 3 yrs for Mme C. Head-Mareek: first form over hurdles (trained by P. Webber first 3 starts) when third in novice handicap at Fontwell, jumping poorly: stays 2½m: blinkered last 2 outings. *N. A. Twiston-Davies* **h69**

WATERSPRAY (AUS) 5 ch.g. Lake Coniston (IRE) – Forain (NZ) (Nassipour (USA)) [2002/3 16d 16s[3] 19d[5] 17f[w] Apr 3] small, angular gelding: maiden on Flat, runner-up 3 times over 1m from 5 starts in Australia: modest form over hurdles: won weak handicap at Taunton by 3 lengths from Never Can Tell: seems to stay 19f: acts on firm and soft going. *J. L. Spearing* **h93**

WATSON LAKE (IRE) 5 b.g. Be My Native (USA) – Magneeto (IRE) (Brush Aside (USA)) [2002/3 F16s[2] F16v* F16g Mar 12] IR £70,000 3-y-o: tall, good sort: third foal: dam unraced half-sister to fairly useful hurdler up to 3m Truth Be Told, from family of smart 3m chaser Garamycin: progressive form in bumpers first 3 starts, won at Down Royal in November by 8 lengths from Laurel View, pair well clear: left E. Hales, always rear in Grade 1 at Cheltenham: will stay at least 2½m. *N. Meade, Ireland* **F110**

WAVERBECK (IRE) 6 ch.m. Accordion – Belle Dame (IRE) (Executive Perk) [2002/3 F16v[5] F16g Dec 28] first foal: dam unraced half-sister to smart hurdler Spirit Leader and useful 2m hurdler Thats My Man: soundly beaten in 2 bumpers. *F. S. Storey* **F–**

WAVE ROCK 8 br.g. Tragic Role (USA) – Moonscape (Ribero) [2002/3 c134, h–: 19d* 20g[2] c21m[5] c20d[3] c21d c20g[pu] c16s[4] c16g[f] c16g[pu] c20m[ur] Apr 26] neat gelding: fairly useful handicap hurdler, won at Hereford in May: useful handicap chaser: creditable third to Cyfor Malta in Thomas Pink at Cheltenham in November: below form after until again unseating 2 out in quite valuable event at Sandown (looked very well) final start, 3 lengths clear and looking likely winner: stays 2½m: acts on heavy and good to firm going: blinkered: has hung left. *P. J. Hobbs* **c134** **h120**

WAYNESWORLD (IRE) 5 b.g. Petoski – Mariners Mirror (Julio Mariner) [2002/3 F16g F16s 20d[pu] Apr 9] 14,000 4-y-o: smallish gelding: first foal: dam fair hurdler/fairly useful chaser, stayed 3¼m: better effort in bumpers when mid-division at Doncaster on debut: pulled up in novice hurdle. *D. J. Caro* **h–** **F78**

WAYWARD BUTTONS 9 b.g. Nomadic Way (USA) – Lady Buttons (New Brig) [2002/3 c100, h–: c25g[4] c21d[5] Apr 8] modest chaser: trained by C. Dennis, close fourth of 7 in hunter at Market Rasen: stays 25f: acts on good to soft going: tongue tied final start: has found little. *M. Todhunter* **c98 §** **h–**

WAYWARD COVE 6 b.m. Karinga Bay – Wayward Pam (Pamroy) [2002/3 F–: F17m 16m[f] 19f[5] Oct 9] rather unfurnished mare: well held in bumpers and on completed start over hurdles. *J. A. Hodges* **h–** **F–**

WAZARO (IRE) 6 b.h. Alzao (USA) – Wildbahn (Be My Guest (USA)) [2002/3 17s[2] 18g[6] 19d[5] Mar 10] useful on Flat (stays 9f), successful 4 times, including on sand at **h–**

Dortmund and Neuss in February: well beaten over hurdles, including in seller. *C. Von Der Recke, Germany*

WEARERICH 6 ch.m. Alflora (IRE) – Weareagrandmother (Prince Tenderfoot (USA)) [2002/3 F17s F17s^{pu} Jan 28] workmanlike mare: fourth reported foal: sister to 21f hurdle winner Alfy Rich and half-sister to fair hurdler Granny Rich (by Ardross), stays 2½m: dam winning hurdler/1m and 12.5f winner on Flat: well beaten in bumper on debut: broke blood vessel next time. *P. M. Rich*   F–

WEAVER GEORGE (IRE) 13 b.g. Flash of Steel – Nephrite (Godswalk (USA)) [2002/3 c121, h–: c25d^3 c25d^{pu} 26s^4 c30d^2 c24d^6 c21g^5 c26d^3 c25g* c26s^{pu} c25v c25v^5 c25s^{pu} c24d^5 c24g^{pu} Apr 1] leggy gelding: winning hurdler: fair handicap chaser: fourth course success at Kelso in October: out of form subsequently: best at 3m+: acts on any going: tried visored/blinkered, wears cheekpieces nowadays: has won 6 times at Sedgefield: usually comes from off pace. *W. Storey*   c113 h–

WEAVER SAM 8 ch.g. Ron's Victory (USA) – Grove Star (Upper Case (USA)) [2002/3 h–: 20s^{pu} Dec 6] leggy gelding: bumper winner: no form over hurdles: tried blinkered. *K. R. Burke*   h–

WEAVERS CHOICE 10 ch.g. Sunley Builds – Wedding Song (True Song) [2002/3 c83: c22d^{pu} c20d^6 Mar 4] fair pointer, won in January: largely below that form in hunter chases. *Mrs Joan Tice*   c–

WEB MASTER (FR) 5 b.g. Arctic Tern (USA) – Inesperada (Cariellor (FR)) [2002/3 F16d^3 F16g Mar 17] leggy gelding: second foal: dam, 1¼m to 15f winner in France, half-sister to useful hurdlers Fataliste and Miss Fara: easily better effort in bumpers when third of 18 to Monet's Garden at Ayr. *C. Grant*   F93 ?

WEE DANNY (IRE) 6 b.g. Mandalus – Bonne Bouche (Bonne Noel) [2002/3 17m 22m^6 27g^4 22m^5 Aug 23] ex-Irish gelding: brother to smart hurdler/high-class chaser up to 25f Boca Boca and half-brother to fair staying chaser Baile Na Gcloch (by Pollerton) and fairly useful 2m chaser The Brewmaster (by Torus): dam placed twice on Flat at 3 yrs: poor novice hurdler: stays 27f. *L. A. Dace*   h70

WEEJUMPAWUD 13 b.m. Jumbo Hirt (USA) – Weewumpawud (King Log) [2002/3 c80, h–: c20g^3 Apr 30] leggy mare: one-time fairly useful hunter chaser: none too fluent in intermediate chase at Hexham in April: stays 25f: acts on good to firm going, probably on heavy. *Miss S. E. Forster*   c– h–

WEE JUNIOR 7 gr.g. Alflora (IRE) – Sheer Gold (Yankee Gold) [2002/3 c24m^{pu} Apr 22] sixth foal: half-brother to useful pointer Perfect Light (by Salmon Leap): dam very smart staying hurdler: twice-raced in points, won maiden in March: pulled up lame on steeplechase debut. *O. A. Little*   c–

WEET AND SEE 9 b.g. Lochnager – Simply Style (Bairn (USA)) [2002/3 c–, h88: c17g^5 16m^F 16m^4 16d* 16m 17m 16s c16f^6 16s 16d Nov 14] leggy gelding: let down by jumping over fences: poor hurdler: won seller at Wolverhampton in July: badly out of sorts last 5 starts: stays 2½m: acts on good to firm and heavy going: tried in cheekpieces. *T. Wall*   c71 h74

WEE WILLOW 9 b.m. Minster Son – Peak Princess (Charlottown) [2002/3 h–: 26d^3 22v^4 24v^4 27g^3 Mar 25] smallish mare: poor novice hurdler: stays 27f. *D. W. Whillans*   h60

WELBURN BOY 11 b.g. Kalaglow – Teevano (Blakeney) [2002/3 c67, h–: c25s^{pu} c26v^{pu} c20s^6 c25s 21g^6 20g^{pu} Apr 21] lightly-made gelding: poor staying hurdler/chaser, little form since 2000/1: blinkered/tongue tied. *M. Sheppard*   c– h–

WELCOME EXCHANGE 4 b.f. Most Welcome – Santarem (USA) (El Gran Senor (USA)) [2002/3 16s^{pu} Nov 9] no form on Flat or on hurdling debut. *J. J. Bridger*   h–

WELCOME NEWS 5 ch.m. Bob Back (USA) – Rosie O'Keeffe (IRE) (Royal Fountain) [2002/3 F16d Mar 8] third foal: half-sister to winning pointer by Alflora: dam unraced half-sister to useful chaser up to 3m Highfrith, out of half-sister to high-class 2m chaser I'm A Driver: well held in mares maiden bumper at Warwick on debut. *Mrs H. Dalton*   F–

WELCOME TO UNOS 6 ch.g. Exit To Nowhere (USA) – Royal Loft (Homing) [2002/3 16v^3 16g^2 16d^2 16d^3 19d^3 17m^2 Apr 26] sturdy gelding: modest novice hurdler: barely stays 19f: acts on good to firm and heavy going: usually waited with. *Mrs M. Reveley*   h99

WELDUNFRANK 10 b.g. Weld – Damsong (Petong) [2002/3 h54: 16m^2 Jun 3] tall gelding: poor 2m maiden hurdler: acts on soft and good to firm going. *W. M. Brisbourne*   h68

Singapore Airlines Adonis Juvenile Novices' Hurdle, Kempton—
a muddling race but Well Chief still impresses

WELL CHIEF (GER)   4 ch.g. Night Shift (USA) – Wellesiena (GER) (Scenic)   **h134**
[2002/3 17s* 16m* 17g² 16g³ Apr 3]

Tony McCoy's latest season, one in which he rode two hundred and fifty-seven winners, became champion for a record-equalling eighth time and became the most successful jump jockey ever in terms of number of winners, was described by the man himself as a 'disaster'. He may have since taken a more positive view of the 2002/3 season, given that he sustained a broken arm barely two months into the next campaign, but part of the reason for his dissatisfaction with the latest season was that he fell short of notching up three hundred winners, his principal target at the start of the campaign. When quantity of winners is as much of a motivation as quality, as it clearly is to McCoy, a Taunton maiden hurdle carries the same weight as a Cheltenham Gold Cup. Missing out on the Martin Pipe-trained hurdling new-comer Well Chief in just such a maiden hurdle in February will be seen by McCoy as one of the ones that got away in his pursuit of the triple century.

McCoy was on the Venetia Williams-trained odds-on favourite Thesis at Taunton instead, a sure sign seemingly of there being little confidence in the Pipe camp in Well Chief's chances but, Thesis having led over the last, it was Well Chief, a weak 12/1 chance, who gained the upper hand on the run-in under Tom Scuda-more to win by five lengths. Even with McCoy in the saddle on his next outing, Well Chief was still not accorded the sort of respect normally afforded a horse representing the trainer/owner, Martin Pipe/David Johnson combination. He started 7/1 third favourite for the Singapore Airlines Adonis Juvenile Novices' Hurdle at Kempton, a recognised trial for the Triumph. In contrast to the unheralded Well Chief, his two main rivals Saintsaire (10/11) and East Tycoon (9/4) had both been well touted. Saintsaire's reputation was such that he headed some ante-post lists for the Triumph even before he made an impressive hurdling debut at Newbury in Dec-ember, while East Tycoon had been well backed when also impressing on his debut at Doncaster in January. The slowly-run Adonis turned out to be a poor rehearsal for the hurly-burly of the Triumph. Nobody wanted to jump off in front and it took the field nearly thirty seconds to reach the first flight. But despite failing to settle, it was Well Chief who coped best with the way the race was run, jumping fluently, leading after three out and having the race sewn up when jinking slightly left going to the last. Unconsidered Mughas and Duke of Earl were separated by a neck, six lengths behind, while East Tycoon and Saintsaire could finish only fourth and fifth respectively of the seven runners, neither having things go their way in a muddling race.

For all the weaknesses of the Adonis as a Triumph Hurdle trial, Well Chief (McCoy's choice among four Pipe-trained runners) started third favourite at Cheltenham and improved again from Kempton. Pulling his way to the front early on, he remained there until Spectroscope overhauled him near the line to win by a head. Now proven as one of the best juvenile hurdlers around, Well Chief was strongly supported to turn the tables on Spectroscope on Aintree's flatter track in the Anniversary Hurdle. However, Well Chief could only match the form he'd shown at Cheltenham, finishing behind Spectroscope again, the pair of them finding the Triumph sixth Le Duc too strong.

Well Chief (GER) (ch.g. 1999)	Night Shift (USA) (b 1980)	Northern Dancer (b 1961)	Nearctic
			Natalma
		Ciboulette (b 1961)	Chop Chop
			Windy Answer
	Wellesiena (GER) (b 1994)	Scenic (b 1986)	Sadler's Wells
			Idyllic
		Weltkrone (ch 1982)	Lord Udo
			Weltdame

Well Chief's level of form on the Flat in Germany for Ralf Suerland made it all the more surprising that he'd been unfancied for his hurdling debut in such a modest contest. However, Martin Pipe revealed later that Well Chief had been gelded after his arrival from Germany 'but he had a rough time of it and at one stage I didn't think we'd get him on a racecourse this season.' Well Chief won twice at

Mr D. A. Johnson's "Well Chief"

around a mile and a quarter in Germany, including a listed race at Dortmund, and later acquitted himself well in Group 3 company. That's better form than anything shown by his closest relatives. Well Chief is the first foal of his dam Wellesiena who failed to win in five starts but was placed in a listed trial for the Preis der Diana. Grandam Weltkrone was unraced, while great grandam Weltdame was a minor winner in Germany out of a mare named Weltwunder who was second in the Preis der Diana, the German classic for middle-distance fillies. Weltwunder has a number of good descendants in Germany but the name that will mean most to British racegoers is that of her great granddaughter Zahrat Dubai, who won the Musidora and Nassau Stakes. The angular Well Chief is rather lacking physical scope. However he fares from now on, he's likely to prove best at around two miles. He acts on soft and good to firm ground, and is an exuberant sort who wears a crossed noseband. *M. C. Pipe*

WELLFRANKO (IRE)   8 b.g. Camden Town – Electana (Electrify) [2002/3 h92: 16d 16m Mar 31] small, angular gelding: form over hurdles only when winning 2m conditional jockeys novice handicap at Uttoxeter in 2001/2: left F. Murphy after reappearance. *Miss Z. C. Davison*   h–

WELLIE (IRE)   10 b.g. Aristocracy – Sweet View (King's Ride) [2002/3 c81x, h–: c20s^{pu} c16g^{pu} c19f⁵ c19m² c19m* Apr 22] tall gelding: poor chaser: made all in selling handicap at Chepstow: stays 19f: acts on good to firm and good to soft ground: tends to pull hard/made mistakes. *S. J. Gilmore*   c85 x h–

WELLINGTON HALL (GER)   5 b.g. Halling (USA) – Wells Whisper (FR) (Sadler's Wells (USA)) [2002/3 17s^F 16g 16v^{pu} 16v Feb 15] ex-German gelding: seemingly useful on Flat for P. Schiergen, successful twice around 11f: would probably have finished close second but for falling last in maiden at Taunton on hurdling debut: not fluent and failed by long way to repeat that form, blinkered final outing. *A. Charlton*   h99 d

WE'LL MAKE IT (IRE)   5 b.g. Spectrum (IRE) – Walliser (Niniski (USA)) [2002/3 h92§: 16d 16s² 17s 20v 17g* 16g² 21m³ Apr 19] angular gelding: fair hurdler: won novice handicap at Folkestone in March: best form at 2m: acts on soft going: usually blinkered: irresolute. *G. L. Moore*   h101 §

WELLOW (IRE)   7 b.g. Unblest – Alpine Sunset (Auction Ring (USA)) [2002/3 c–, h–: 19m^{pu} 16v⁶ Feb 1] workmanlike gelding: little form and has hinted at temperament. *Miss C. J. E. Caroe*   c– h–

WELL THEN NOW THEN (IRE)   8 b.m. Supreme Leader – Northern Dandy (The Parson) [2002/3 h93: 24s* 24s* 24d⁵ 26d^{pu} Feb 23] angular mare: fair hurdler: improved efforts when winning at Uttoxeter (mares handicap) in November and Southwell (novice) in December: reportedly broke down final start: seems best at 3m+: raced on good going or softer (acts on heavy). *H. D. Daly*   h112

WELSH BORDER   5 ch.g. Zafonic (USA) – Welsh Daylight (Welsh Pageant) [2002/3 h121p: 17g⁴ 17d* 17m* 20g^{rtr} 18m⁶ Sep 24] fairly useful hurdler: successful in novices at Market Rasen and Southwell in August: refused to race fourth start, virtually refused to do so on final one: will stay 2½m: one to leave alone. *G. Prodromou*   h110 §

WELSH DREAM   6 b.g. Mtoto – Morgannwg (IRE) (Simply Great (FR)) [2002/3 h98: 16d² May 1] useful-looking gelding: half-brother to fair 2m hurdler Penybont (by Unfuwain): modest on Flat (stays 2m), successful 3 times in 2002, sold out of P. Haslam's stable 2,500 gns Doncaster September Sales: modest form when placed in 2 maiden hurdles, second at Kelso in May. *P. C. Haslam*   h88 +

WELSH MAIN   6 br.g. Zafonic (USA) – Welsh Daylight (Welsh Pageant) [2002/3 h98p: 16m³ 16s³ 16g^F 16m² 16m* Oct 16] sturdy gelding: fairly useful handicap hurdler: won at Wetherby by 2½ lengths from Virgin Soldier: raced at 2m: acts on good to firm and good to soft going: consistent. *S. J. Magnier*   h116

WELSH MARCH (IRE)   11 b.g. Over The River (FR) – Welsh Tan (Welsh Saint) [2002/3 c107: c17s⁶ c16d^F c16d c24v⁵ c20s^{pu} Feb 24] strong gelding: fairly useful chaser at best: badly out of sorts since reappearance in 2001/2, including only outing over hurdles. *G. M. Moore*   c– h–

WELSH MISTRESS   4 ch.f. Master Willie – Llanfihangel Lass (Gildoran) [2002/3 F16s 19d^{ur} Feb 10] first foal: dam unraced, out of half-sister to useful hurdler Winston Run, probably stayed 3m: tailed off in bumper: jumped badly right and unseated fourth in maiden claimer on hurdling debut. *P. D. Evans*   h– F–

WELSH PARK (IRE) 10 ch.g. Balinger – Welsh Escort (Welsh Captain) [2002/3 c–, h54: 25g^{pu} Jul 15] compact gelding: yet to complete in points/steeplechases: bad hurdler: best efforts on good going or firmer: blinkered. *A. P. James*   **c–**   **h–**

WEMYSS QUEST 8 b.g. Rainbow Quest (USA) – Wemyss Bight (Dancing Brave (USA)) [2002/3 h108: c20g* Jun 12] quite good-topped gelding: fair hurdler: won novice at Market Rasen on chasing debut by 10 lengths from Lord Fleet, looking second best when left in front last: stays 25f: acts on firm and good to soft going (below form on soft/heavy): effective tongue tied or not: should improve over fences: joined Miss V. Williams. *Ferdy Murphy*   **c89 p**   **h–**

WEND'S DAY (IRE) 8 br.g. Brief Truce (USA) – Iswara (USA) (Alleged (USA)) [2002/3 16g* 16d^2 20v^6 Dec 20] strong, lengthy gelding: modest hurdler: won claimer at Plumpton in October: stays 19f: acts on soft ground: tongue tied: sold 2,500 gns Doncaster May Sales. *A. M. Hales*   **h98**

WENRIC PET 7 br.m. Petoski – Jervandha (Strong Gale) [2002/3 F17m F17d Oct 12] compact mare: third foal: dam, no form over hurdles, half-sister to fairly useful chaser up to 2½m Buckland Lad: well held in 2 bumpers. *J. C. Tuck*   **F–**

WENSLEY BLUE (IRE) 4 b.g. Blues Traveller (IRE) – Almasa (Faustus (USA)) [2002/3 17g^5 16s^6 Nov 27] big, good-topped gelding: poor maiden on Flat (stays 11f): poor form in 2 juvenile hurdles. *P. C. Haslam*   **h77**

WENSUM DANCER 6 b.m. Shareef Dancer (USA) – Burning Ambition (Troy) [2002/3 16d^3 16s* 16d^6 16g^6 16f^6 16f^{pu} 16d 16g Mar 30] half-sister to smart staying hurdler Her Honour (by Teenoso) and winning pointer by Lidhame: fair on Flat (stays 2m), successful twice in August: fair handicap hurdler: won at Limerick in July: raced mainly around 2m: acts on firm and soft going: tongue tied. *T. Hogan, Ireland*   **h107**

WERE IN TOUCH (IRE) 5 b.g. Old Vic – Winterland Gale (IRE) (Strong Gale) [2002/3 F18v* Feb 10] first foal: dam never ran: odds on, won maiden bumper at Plumpton on debut by length from Bramlynn Brook, despite tending to edge left: open to improvement. *P. F. Nicholls*   **F98 p**

WERE NOT STOPPIN 8 b.g. Mystiko (USA) – Power Take Off (Aragon) [2002/3 h62: 16m^5 16g^3 16m* 19g^3 22d^5 17m^6 16d^{pu} 20g^{pu} Mar 23] good-topped gelding: poor hurdler: awarded novice handicap at Uttoxeter in June: stays 19f: acts on firm ground, possibly not on softer than good. *R. Bastiman*   **h80**

WESLEY'S LAD (IRE) 9 b. or br.g. Classic Secret (USA) – Galouga (FR) (Lou Piguet (FR)) [2002/3 h–: 16g^6 19s 19s^6 Dec 12] tall gelding: handicap hurdler, modest nowadays: stays 2½m: acts on soft and good to firm going. *D. Burchell*   **h94**

WEST ASIDE (IRE) 9 b.g. Brush Aside (USA) – Chancy Belle (Le Bavard (FR)) [2002/3 h–: c26s^{ur} Feb 26] winning Irish pointer: little show otherwise. *T. P. McGovern*   **c–**   **h–**

WEST COASTER (IRE) 5 gr.g. Be My Native (USA) – Donegal Grey (IRE) (Roselier (FR)) [2002/3 F84: 16g^F 16d 16d^3 19s^6 20m Mar 23] lengthy, good-topped gelding: best effort over hurdles when third to River City in novice at Doncaster in January: should stay at least 2½m. *Miss H. C. Knight*   **h89**

WESTCOUNTRY LAD 13 b.g. General Surprise – Charmezzo (Remezzo) [2002/3 c–: c26s^5 May 28] angular gelding: fair pointer: yet to translate that form to hunter chases. *Mrs P. Bond*   **c72**

WEST END DANCER (USA) 6 b.m. West By West (USA) – Chateau Dancer (USA) (Giacometti) [2002/3 20d^{pu} 19s^{pu} Dec 5] angular mare: poor hurdler in 2000/1: little sign of retaining ability: tried visored/blinkered. *P. S. McEntee*   **h–**

WESTENDER (FR) 7 b.g. In The Wings – Trude (GER) (Windwurf (GER)) [2002/3 h143: 17v^3 16g^2 16m^3 Apr 12]   **h159**

    In well-run championship races the cream ought to come to the top. In the Champion Hurdle, by and large, it does. In the last twenty runnings, only 50/1-shot Beech Road in 1989 has won at odds of 20/1 or more. But outsiders knock on the door with surprising regularity. In the same twenty-year period, the Champion Hurdle runner-up has started at odds of 20/1 or longer on no fewer than ten occasions. Cima (1984) and Robin Wonder (1985) were second starting at 66/1, while 50/1-chances Boreen Prince (1983) and Royal Derbi (1993) also found only one too good. The latest outsider to take second in the Champion was 33/1-chance Westender, who finished eleven lengths behind Rooster Booster. As those odds suggest, Westender put up a career-best effort at Cheltenham (where he was the paddock pick, incidentally), but to describe his performance simply does not tell half the story. Following what was generally a rather shambolic start to the race, Westender was reluctant to jump off and was off the bridle throughout, needing a crack behind the saddle as early as after the first flight. Rodi Greene's persistence began to pay off as Westender made headway after the fifth and, after narrowly avoiding being brought down when stable-companion Copeland fell in front of him three out, Westender challenged for second entering the straight and held that position to the line despite continuing to look less than willing. Tony McCoy had received all the plaudits for surviving a last-flight blunder on Westender in a valuable handicap at the track the previous season, but Greene, riding Westender for the first time, deserves as much credit for the way he handled the horse in the Champion.

Westender was finishing second at the Festival for the second year running. Twelve months earlier, he had run Like-A-Butterfly (only tenth in the Champion Hurdle) to a neck in the Supreme Novices' Hurdle. Westender had actually been as low as 10/1 for the Champion Hurdle in his novice season after winning his first five completed starts over hurdles, but defeat in the Ladbroke Handicap at Ascot led to Westender's connections taking the novice option at that year's Festival. Westender's starting price for the latest Champion Hurdle implied that he was not the same horse in his second season over hurdles, though the truth was that there was little evidence to go on as his second season amounted to just one race prior to

Mr Matt Archer & Miss Jean Broadhurst's "Westender"

the Festival. In a handicap at Cheltenham on New Year's Day he finished third under top weight to the up-and-coming Flame Creek, himself considered worth his place in the Champion Hurdle. Raced only on good or good to firm going previously over hurdles, Westender made an encouraging reappearance under vastly different conditions, only done with when tiring in the heavy ground from the last. Westender shared top weight with Flame Creek in the Scottish Champion Hurdle at Ayr on his only start after the Festival but couldn't repeat his Cheltenham effort. Making the running this time, when none of the others went on, Westender was soon beaten after being headed three out and finished third of the four finishers behind the Champion Hurdle sixth In Contrast.

			Sadler's Wells	Northern Dancer
Westender (FR) (b.g. 1996)	In The Wings (b 1986)		(b 1981)	Fairy Bridge
			High Hawk	Shirley Heights
			(b 1980)	Sunbittern
	Trude (GER) (b 1981)		Windwurf	Kaiseradler
			(b 1972)	Wiesenweime
			Tamina	Spy Well
			(b 1972)	Tania

The tall, close-coupled Westender's pedigree was covered in last year's Annual, the only update being that his dam has since had another winner in Germany where Tempi Passati (by Marju) was successful in 2002. Raced only at around two miles, Westender has yet to race on firm ground but acts on any other. Blinkered nowadays, he is a lazy type, and the Champion Hurdle was not the first time he had shown signs of reluctance—on his hurdling debut he had had to be pulled up after attempting to run out. *M. C. Pipe*

WESTERN BLUEBIRD (IRE) 5 b.g. Bluebird (USA) – Arrastra (Bustino) [2002/3 **h–** h67: 16s 16d 25d^{pu} 20g^{pu} Apr 1] leggy gelding: fair on Flat (probably best around 1½m), sold out of H. Morrison's stable 9,000 gns Newmarket July Sales: no worthwhile form over hurdles: tried in cheekpieces. *Miss Kate Milligan*

WESTERN CHIEF (IRE) 9 b.h. Caerleon (USA) – Go Honey Go (General Assem- **c90** bly (USA)) [2002/3 c94, h–: c26m² Aug 23] angular horse: well held all 3 runs on Flat in **h–** 2002: modest handicap chaser: creditable second at Fontwell only start in 2002/3: stays 3¼m: acts on firm and good to soft going: tried visored: tongue tied. *D. L. Williams*

WESTERNMOST 5 b.g. Most Welcome – Dakota Girl (Northern State (USA)) **h103** [2002/3 h99: 17s² 17d* 16m² 17d² 21m² Oct 1] workmanlike gelding: modest maiden on Flat (stays 1¾m): fair hurdler: won novice at Cartmel in June: stays 21f: acts on heavy and good to firm going. *M. Todhunter*

WESTERN RIDGE (FR) 6 b.g. Darshaan – Helvellyn (USA) (Gone West (USA)) **h72 p** [2002/3 h–: 17s 16v 17m² Apr 8] close-coupled gelding: fair on Flat (stays 15f): first form over hurdles when second of 6 in conditional jockeys handicap at Exeter final start: should do better. *B. J. Llewellyn*

WESTERN SUN 13 b.g. Sunyboy – Running Valley (Buckskin (FR)) [2002/3 c–, h–: **c–** c25g^{pu} May 4] strong gelding: of little account. *J. L. Needham* **h–**

WESTERTON (IRE) 10 b.g. Glacial Storm (USA) – Killiney Rose (Buckskin (FR)) **c92** [2002/3 c24s³ c25g* Mar 15] workmanlike gelding: one-time fair hurdler: off 2 years, **h–** fair form in 2 hunter chases on return, won at Market Rasen by ½ length from Mullensgrove: stays 25f: acts on heavy going: has room for improvement in his jumping. *F. A. Hutsby*

WESTFIELD JOHN 8 ch.g. Little Wolf – Moonbreaker (Twilight Alley) [2002/3 **c–** h–, F73: 20g⁴ c20m³ Jun 1] big, workmanlike gelding: no form over hurdles or in novice **h–** chase: won points in February, March and April (dead-heat). *Ferdy Murphy*

WESTGATE RUN 6 b.m. Emperor Jones (USA) – Glowing Reference (Reference **h87** Point) [2002/3 17m⁴ 17g³ 21m³ 16g* 16d 16g² Dec 12] leggy mare: modest on Flat (stays 1½m): similar form over hurdles: won mares novice at Hexham in October: stays 21f: acts on good to firm going: sometimes jumps poorly. *R. A. Fahey*

WEST GLORY (IRE) 9 b.g. Phardante (FR) – The Kid's Sister (Black Minstrel) **h–** [2002/3 20g^{pu} Mar 17] workmanlike ex-Irish gelding: fourth foal: dam unraced: pulled up both outings over hurdles 3½ years apart. *I. W. McInnes*

WEST HILL ROSE (IRE) 8 gr.m. Roselier (FR) – Clonmeen Official (Official) **c96** [2002/3 h107: 24v⁵ c23d² c26v⁶ c30sᵖᵘ Mar 4] leggy mare: fair hurdler: shaped well when **h100** second to One Knight in novice at Exeter on chasing debut: very disappointing both subsequent starts, going with little zest: thorough stayer: raced on good going or softer (acts on heavy). *V. R. A. Dartnall*

WESTMEATH LAD 6 ch.g. Primo Dominie – Re-Release (Baptism) [2002/3 F70: **h75** F16g² 16g 17d Aug 26] rather leggy gelding: best effort in bumpers when second at **F86** Hexham on reappearance: signs of some ability in 2 outings over hurdles: needs to become more tractable. *M. Todhunter*

WESTMINSTER CITY (USA) 7 b.g. Alleged (USA) – Promenade Fan (USA) **h–** (Timeless Moment) (USA)) [2002/3 h81?: 16mᵖᵘ 19gᵖᵘ Jul 27] signs of only a little ability over hurdles: left G. Brown after reappearance. *Jean-Rene Auvray*

WESTMORLAND (IRE) 7 b.g. Phardante (FR) – Ticking Over (IRE) (Decent **h98 +** Fellow) [2002/3 h93: 24g* May 11] fair hurdler: won handicap at Hexham in May, not seen out again: will prove best at 3m+: acts on heavy going. *L. Lungo*

WESTON COURT 9 b.g. Scottish Reel – Lady Westown (Town And Country) [2002/3 **h–** 19s Feb 27] third foal: dam winning hurdler, stayed 3m: tailed off in novice hurdle on debut. *P. G. Murphy*

WESTON MARAUDER 6 b.g. Unfuwain (USA) – Rushing River (USA) (Irish River **h–** (FR)) [2002/3 F17g 16mᵖᵘ Mar 23] 2,600 6-y-o: second foal: dam unraced, from family **F–** of high-class American horse Cryptoclearance: no form in bumper or maiden hurdle. *M. J. Gingell*

WESTON ROCK 4 b.g. Double Eclipse (IRE) – Mossberry Fair (Mossberry) [2002/3 **F74** F16g⁶ Jan 17] eighth foal: half-brother to winning hurdler/fair chaser around 2m Pegasus Bay (by Tina's Pet) and winning pointer by Infantry: dam winning hurdler: never-nearer sixth of 15 in bumper at Musselburgh. *T. D. Walford*

WESTORM (IRE) 12 br.g. Strong Gale – Little Peach (Ragapan) [2002/3 16m⁵ **h–** 16mᵖᵘ Jun 3] no longer of much account. *P. W. Hiatt*

WEST PACES (IRE) 9 br.g. Lord Americo – Spanish Royale (Royal Buck) [2002/3 **c94** 19d c24sᵖᵘ c21dᶠ c20g³ c24m² Apr 10] sixth foal: half-brother to poor 3m chaser Tom **h–** Pinch (by Mandalus) and to 2 winning pointers: dam, won 2m chase in Ireland, sister to dam of useful 2½m to 3m chaser Headwind: won Irish point in 1999: no show on hurdling debut: modest form when placed in novice chases: will stay beyond 3m. *G. B. Balding*

WESTWINDS 11 b.g. Vital Season – April's Crook (Crozier) [2002/3 c77: c21gᵖᵘ **c–** c25d⁶ c25g Jun 12] big gelding: poor chaser: showed little in 2002/3: blinkered on reappearance. *M. J. Coombe*

WHALEEF 5 b.g. Darshaan – Wilayif (USA) (Danzig (USA)) [2002/3 17s⁶ 16d Jan **h–** 15] half-brother to poor 2m hurdler Royal Allegiance (by Kris): fairly useful on Flat (stays 1½m) nowadays: well held in 2 novice hurdles. *P. R. Webber*

WHASS URRP (IRE) 4 b.g. Desert King (IRE) – Blue Burgee (USA) (Lyphard's **h–** Wish (FR)) [2002/3 19dᵖᵘ Feb 25] poor maiden on Flat (should stay 1m), sold out of J. M. Bradley's stable £750 Ascot October Sales: tongue tied, no show in novice over hurdling debut. *M. E. Sowersby*

WHATACHARLIE 9 b.g. Nicholas Bill – Zulu Dancer (Sula Bula) [2002/3 c19g **c–** c26m³ Apr 21] sturdy gelding: has reportedly been tubed: winning pointer, no form in steeplechases: tongue tied. *D. P. Keane*

WHATAFELLOW (IRE) 13 ch.g. Arapahos (FR) – Dara's March (March Parade) **c87** [2002/3 c–: c34g⁴ c24d³ Apr 9] workmanlike gelding: prolific winning pointer/winning hunter chaser, fair nowadays: stays 3¼m: acts on good to firm going: blinkered. *Mrs Edward Crow*

WHAT A FIDDLER (IRE) 10 ch.g. Orchestra – Crowenstown Miss (Over The River **c91** (FR)) [2002/3 c111, h–: c26d* c32v⁶ Mar 13] fairly useful hunter chaser: didn't need to **h–** be at best to win at Cartmel in June: well beaten in handicap 9 months later: stays 3¼m: acts on good going. *J. S. Haldane*

WHAT A MAN (IRE) 6 b.g. Beau Sher – Cactus Wren (IRE) (Remainder Man) **h99 p** [2002/3 F16s⁴ 21d⁵ Jan 18] IR 4,000 3-y-o: has scope: first foal: dam unraced: won 2 of 3 **F94** starts in Irish points: shaped as if in need of stiffer test of stamina in bumper at Ludlow and novice hurdle at Kempton (fifth of 9 to Lord Sam): will be suited by 3m: open to improvement. *T. R. George*

WHAT A MONDAY   5 b.g. Beveled (USA) – Raise Memories (Skyliner) [2002/3 **F92** F16s* F16g F16g³ Mar 12] lengthy, angular gelding: second known foal: dam, maiden on Flat and over hurdles, out of half-sister to smart 2-y-o Varingo: fair form in bumpers: won at Worcester in June: creditable third at Huntingdon final start: stiff task in Grade 2 at Newbury in between. *K. Bell*

WHATAREYOUHAVING   7 b.g. Derrylin – Simple Mind (Decent Fellow) [2002/3 **c–** h116: 22g 24d⁴ c22sᵖᵘ Nov 10] leggy gelding: fair handicap hurdler: no show on chasing **h113** debut: stays 3m: raced on good going or softer (acts on heavy). *Henry De Bromhead, Ireland*

WHATASHOCK   8 b.g. Never So Bold – Lady Electric (Electric) [2002/3 c23dᵖᵘ Dec **c–** 19] medium-sized gelding: won all 4 completed starts in points in 2002: shaped better than being pulled up suggests in novice chase at Exeter, close up until lack of a recent outing told. *A. King*

WHATAWIZARD (IRE)   6 br.g. Hubbly Bubbly (USA) – Justine's Way (USA) **h–** (Buffalo Lark (USA)) [2002/3 F16s 20v 17s⁶ 24d⁶ 26m Apr 5] IR £10,000 4-y-o: tall **F–** gelding: seventh foal: half-brother to 21f hurdle winner Michaels Dawn (by Woodman): dam 11f winner: no sign of ability. *R. Dickin*

WHAT A WONDER (IRE)   8 gr.g. Roselier (FR) – Lady Abednego VII (Damsire **c83 §** Unregistered) [2002/3 c96§, h113: 22v⁵ 24m⁵ c25d⁴ c26s⁵ c25g⁴ 27g Apr 25] lengthy **h102 §** gelding: fair handicap hurdler, below form in 2002/3: poor maiden chaser, usually let down by jumping: should stay beyond 25f: acts on heavy and good to firm going: blinkered after reappearance: temperamental. *Ferdy Murphy*

WHATEVER FOR   5 b.m. Daar Alzamaan (IRE) – Manx Monarch (Dara Monarch) **F–** [2002/3 F16m Dec 17] second foal: dam, maiden who stayed 1m, out of half-sister to smart miler Soprano: looked in need of experience (hung badly right home turn) when last of 11 in bumper on debut. *F. P. Murtagh*

WHAT ODDS (IRE)   7 b.g. Torus – Merrywell (Mugatpura) [2002/3 c24vᵖᵘ c25s* **c112 p** Feb 22] strong gelding: brother to winning pointer Verywell and half-brother to a winning pointer by Garryowen: dam winning pointer: winning pointer, including in November (twice) and January: successful twice from 3 starts in hunter chases, including at Fairy-house in February and Punchestown (by 10 lengths from Sheltering) in April: will stay beyond 25f: acts on heavy going: front runner: open to further improvement. *T. K. Geraghty, Ireland*

WHAT'S THE BUZZ   12 ch.g. Ardross – Cherry Opal (Saint Denys) [2002/3 c25d **c–** Mar 5] sturdy, lengthy gelding: maiden hurdler/chaser: placed twice in points in 2003: **h–** showed nothing in novice hunter in between. *Joss Saville*

WHAT'S THE COUNT   7 gr.g. Theatrical Charmer – Yankee Silver (Yankee Gold) **h98** [2002/3 h–: 16g⁵ 20d³ 22s⁴ 17v² 21v² 22v 21m Mar 31] lengthy gelding: modest maiden hurdler: stays 2¾m: acts on heavy ground: usually tongue tied: free-going sort. *B. R. Johnson*

WHAT'S THE SCORE (IRE)   9 ch.g. Orchestra – Silent Twirl (Piaffer (USA)) **c109** [2002/3 c20d² c20s⁵ c18sᵖᵘ c22s c24s³ c21sᵖᵘ c20s³ c21v⁴ c17d² Mar 22] tall gelding: fair **h–** handicap chaser: won at Punchestown in January and April: effective around 2m to 25f: acts on heavy going: races prominently: tongue tied after fifth start. *D. T. Hughes, Ireland*

WHAT'S UP BOYS (IRE)   9 gr.g. Supreme Leader – Maryville Bick (Malacate **c–** (USA)) [2002/3 c161, h–: c25dF Nov 2] leggy, lengthy gelding: high-class chaser: fell **h–** sixth in Grade 2 at Wetherby on reappearance, reportedly sustaining injuries which kept him out for rest of season: stays 4½m: acts on good to firm and heavy going: effective blinkered or not: has gone in snatches and not looked easiest of rides. *P. J. Hobbs*

WHAT YOU KNOW (IRE)   9 b.g. Be My Guest (USA) – Flamme d'Amour (Gift **h76 §** Card (FR)) [2002/3 20g 16g* 19f* 16s 22d 19d Jan 16] angular gelding: poor hurdler: off 3 years before reappearance: won conditional jockeys selling handicaps at Worcester in September and Exeter in October: poor efforts on softer ground last 3 starts: stays 19f: acts on firm going: tried blinkered/visored/tongue tied: has been reluctant to race: not one to trust. *Mrs D. A. Hamer*

WHAT YOU MEAN   8 ch.g. Kasakov – Lonely Lass (Headin' Up) [2002/3 h76: 20s⁵ **h–** 21s 16vᵖᵘ 19dᵖᵘ Feb 25] angular gelding: maiden hurdler: no form in 2002/3: visored third start. *J. R. Norton*

WHEREAREYOUNOW (IRE)   6 ch.g. Mister Lord (USA) – Angie's Delight   **c132**
(London Gazette) [2002/3 22d⁴ 21d⁵ c25d⁵ c21v³ c21s⁴ c24s² c24g Mar 11] IR £14,500   **h107**
4-y-o: rather unfurnished gelding: seventh foal: brother to winning pointer Spring
Cabbage: dam winning pointer: won second of 2 starts in maiden Irish points in 2002:
much better effort in novice hurdles when fifth at Cheltenham in November: useful form
over fences: good fourth to La Landiere in novice handicap there in January: stays 21f:
raced only on good going or softer (acts on heavy). *N. A. Twiston-Davies*

WHERE EAGLES DARE (USA)   6 b.g. Eagle Eyed (USA) – Velveteen (USA)   **h–**
(Pirateer (USA)) [2002/3 20dᵖᵘ May 30] modest maiden on Flat (stays 1¾m): completed
once from 4 starts in points in 2002: tongue tied, showed nothing on hurdling debut.
M. E. Sowersby

WHETHER THE STORM (IRE)   7 b.g. Glacial Storm (USA) – Minimum Choice   **c93**
(IRE) (Miner's Lamp) [2002/3 h–: c20d⁴ c21v⁴ c24dᵖᵘ Jan 13] strong gelding: lightly   **h–**
raced: winning hurdler: best effort in novice chases when fourth to Scots Grey at Huntingdon in November: stays 2½m: raced on good going or softer. *Miss H. C. Knight*

WHISPERING HOLLY   4 b.g. Holly Buoy – Stuart's Gem (Meldrum) [2002/3   **F–**
F17g Apr 26] seventh foal: brother to winning hurdler Gem of Holly, stays 21f: dam
unraced: no show in bumper on debut. *R. S. Wood*

WHISPERING JOHN (IRE)   7 b.g. Grand Plaisir (IRE) – London Anne (London   **c–**
Bells (CAN)) [2002/3 19d² 21d 16d c20dᶠ Feb 17] IR 35,000 4-y-o: rangy gelding: **h104**
fourth foal: half-brother to 2 winners, including fairly useful staying chaser/winning
hurdler Iffeee (by Forties Field): dam 2m hurdle winner: runner-up both starts in Irish
points in 2002: best effort in novice hurdles when second to Robber Baron at Exeter in
November: sixth when falling 4 out in novice chase final start: should stay beyond 19f.
P. F. Nicholls

WHISTFUL SUZIE (IRE)   6 ch.m. Eurobus – Ah Suzie (IRE) (King's Ride)   **h73**
[2002/3 h–, F–: 20mᵇᵈ 20g⁶ 16g⁵ Oct 19] first form when fifth in novice hurdle at Kelso
in October. *Mrs S. C. Bradburne*

WHISTLING DIXIE (IRE)   7 ch.g. Forest Wind (USA) – Camden's Gift (Camden   **h130**
Town) [2002/3 h130: 16f³ 17d⁴ 16v 16s⁶ 16vᶠ 16s 22v³ Feb 1] angular gelding: useful
handicap hurdler: looked back to best in valuable event won by Chauvinist at Ascot fifth
start, still travelling strongly when falling 2 out: disappointing at Leopardstown next
time: creditable efforts at Sandown (third to Chopneyev) in February and Punchestown
(fourth to Blue Away) in late-April: effective at 2m to 2¾m: acts on any going: patiently
ridden. *Mrs M. Reveley*

WHISTLING SONG   8 ch.m. True Song – Sancal (Whistlefield) [2002/3 c–: c17gᶠ   **c–**
Apr 26] little sign of ability. *R. Dickin*

WHITASIDE (IRE)   9 b. or br.g. Brush Aside (USA) – Flying Silver (Master Buck)   **h97**
[2002/3 21m² 20g* 19s² Nov 21] IR 20,000 4-y-o: fifth foal: half-brother to winning
2½m hurdler French Buck (by Phardante) and to prolific winning pointer Rip Van Winkle
(by Le Bavard): dam, winning 2m hurdler/chaser, half-sister to dam of useful staying
chaser Keep Talking: modest form in novice hurdles: won weak event at Hexham in
October: likely to stay beyond 21f. *Mrs S. J. Smith*

WHITEBONNET (IRE)   13 b.g. Rainbow Quest (USA) – Dawn Is Breaking (Import)   **h– §**
[2002/3 h–§: 27sᵖᵘ May 28] lengthy gelding: winning hurdler: no form since 2000/1:
blinkered/visored. *C. F. C. Jackson*

WHITE DOVE (FR)   5 b.m. Beaudelaire (USA) – Hermine And Pearls (FR) (Shirley   **h65**
Heights) [2002/3 16mᵘʳ 17d⁶ 19s³ 17m⁴ Aug 17] poor maiden on Flat and over hurdles:
likely to prove best at 2m: headstrong. *R. Dickin*

WHITE IN FRONT   12 ch.g. Tina's Pet – Lyaaric (Privy Seal) [2002/3 c90, h–:   **c84**
c16m³ c17d³ c16g⁴ c19gᶠ c19s⁶ c20d Jan 16] lengthy gelding: poor chaser: best around   **h–**
2m: acts on firm and soft going: effective blinkered or not. *Mrs A. Price*

WHITENZO (FR)   8 b.g. Lesotho (USA) – Whitengy (FR) (Olantengy (FR)) [2002/3   **c142**
c140, h138: c25d⁵ c26g⁴ c24d c24dᵖᵘ c25d⁵ c29m Apr 26] tall gelding: useful hurdler/   **h–**
chaser: ruined chance with bad mistake 4 out over fences first 2 starts, rallying well when
fourth to Be My Royal in Hennessy Cognac Gold Cup (Handicap) at Newbury: subsequent form only when respectable fifth to Master Tern in handicap at Aintree: stays 3¼m:
unraced on firm going, acts on any other. *P. F. Nicholls*

WHITE ROCK LADY   5 b.m. Rock Hopper – Don't Tell Jean (Petong) [2002/3 **h–** F16m F16m 20m 20m Oct 24] sturdy mare: third foal: dam poor and temperamental **F–** maiden on Flat, stayed 7f: well held in bumpers and novice hurdles. *R. D. E. Woodhouse*

WHITFIELD WARRIOR   5 ch.g. Husyan (USA) – Valentines Day (Doctor **F92** Pangloss) [2002/3 F16d⁴ Feb 1] workmanlike gelding: fourth foal: dam unraced: better for race, fourth of 16 to Crossbow Creek in bumper at Wetherby on debut. *J. R. Turner*

WHITLEY GRANGE BOY   10 b.g. Hubbly Bubbly (USA) – Choir (High Top) **c72 ?** [2002/3 h–: c16d⁶ c25d^F c21g^ur c21d⁶ c27m³ Apr 26] tall gelding: winning hurdler: signs **h–** of only a little ability over fences. *A. J. Lockwood*

WHO CARES WINS   7 ch.g. Kris – Anne Bonny (Ajdal (USA)) [2002/3 h100: 20s^pu **h94** 22s² 22g Mar 15] sparely-made gelding: modest hurdler: stays 2¾m: acts on soft and good to firm going. *J. R. Jenkins*

WHO DARES WINS   10 b.g. Kala Shikari – Sarah's Venture (Averof) [2002/3 c93, **c88 d** h96: c26v³ c26v³ c24v 24v⁴ c26s⁶ c32v⁵ Mar 13] tall gelding: maiden hurdler: modest **h–** handicap chaser: creditable effort in 2002/3 only on reappearance: dour stayer: best on soft/heavy going: tried blinkered/in cheekpieces. *C. Grant*

WHO IS EQUINAME (IRE)   13 b.g. Bob Back (USA) – Instanter (Morston (FR)) **c–** [2002/3 c–, h–: c21g c16d^pu May 13] close-coupled gelding: modest pointer nowadays, **h–** successful in April: well beaten in 3 hunters: acts on good to firm and heavy going: blinkered: sometimes sweats and is edgy. *W. J. Warner*

WHOSE LINE IS IT   5 gr.g. Sharp Deal – Madame Ruby (FR) (Homing) [2002/3 **F88** F16s⁶ F16m² F17g³ Apr 19] angular gelding: half-brother to fair hurdler Got News For You (by Positive Statement), stays 21f: dam, fair 17f hurdle winner, half-sister to fairly useful 2m hurdler Might Move: placed 2 out of 3 starts in bumpers, though dictated pace and possibly flattered when third in maiden at Newton Abbot final start. *N. J. Hawke*

WHO'S THE MAN   9 gr.g. Arzanni – Tommys Dream (Le Bavard (FR)) [2002/3 c–, **c–** h–: c24g⁴ c24g c17g^pu Apr 7] lengthy gelding: lightly raced and little worthwhile form. **h–** *N. M. L. Ewart*

WHO'S TO SAY   17 b.g. Saher – Whisht (Raise You Ten) [2002/3 c–, h–: 20s 22g **c–** 22g Jun 29] lengthy gelding: veteran chaser/hurdler, retains little ability: tried blinkered/ **h–** visored. *Dr P. Pritchard*

WIDEMOUTH BAY (IRE)   5 br.g. Be My Native (USA) – Lisaleen River (Over **F117** The River (FR)) [2002/3 F16g* F16s* F16g³ Mar 12]

Here's a mystery to puzzle Arthur C. Clarke: How was Widemouth Bay possibly allowed to start at 33/1 for the Champion Bumper at the Cheltenham Festival? Here was a horse with a good pedigree, a top trainer/jockey combination and some of the best form going into the race (only Cornish Rebel and, marginally, Liberman looked to have better), yet he was out among the rags. Turning for home, anyone betting in running would have had Widemouth Bay just about favourite as he was poised behind the leader, going best of all. Though he couldn't quicken well enough when ridden, and then had to be switched, he went down only by half a length and a length to Liberman and an even bigger outsider in Trabolgan. Widemouth Bay had won both his starts before Cheltenham, showing a good turn of foot at Wincanton on his debut in November to gain an impressive success in a race which worked out well, then doing really well to get up and dead heat with the front-running Ashley Brook, whom he had allowed plenty of rope, at Ludlow in January. That was undoubtedly a smart effort, one good enough, if repeated, to reach the frame at Cheltenham. Perhaps the expected Irish domination of the race swayed the market, plus the fact that the scene of Widemouth Bay's latest performance had been, after all, only Ludlow.

Widemouth Bay is a lengthy gelding who still looked rather unfurnished at Cheltenham. He was bought for IR £70,000 at the 2001 Derby Sale. By Be My Native, Widemouth Bay is the third foal out of Lisaleen River, a fair hurdler at up to three miles for Michael Hourigan. The first two include a winning pointer by Royal Fountain. Lisaleen River is a half-sister to five winners, chief among them the useful hurdler at up to three miles Abbot of Furness and the fairly useful chaser Plastic Spaceage, who was effective from two miles to three and a quarter miles.

Mrs J. F. Deithrick's "Widemouth Bay"

Widemouth Bay is bred to stay at least two and a half miles, though his efforts in bumpers suggest he won't necessarily need a test of stamina. He is one of the brightest prospects for novice hurdles in 2003/4 and it will be both a surprise and a disappointment if he turns up priced at anything near a true 33/1-chance in either the Supreme Novices' or the SunAlliance Hurdle. *P. J. Hobbs*

WILD ABOUT HARRY   6 ch.g. Romany Rye – Shylyn (Hay Chas) [2002/3 F16s⁴   **F91**
F16s F16g Apr 14] workmanlike gelding: sixth foal: half-brother to 2 bumper winners by Push On: dam unraced half-sister to Foxhunter winner Elmboy: fourth to Classic Native in bumper at Warwick on debut: failed badly to repeat that form in 2 similar events, sold out of L. G. Cottrell's stable 11,000 gns Doncaster January Sales before final start. *A. R. Dicken*

WILD BAVARD (IRE)   11 b.g. Le Bavard (FR) – Wild Deer (Royal Buck) [2002/3   **c88 ?**
c26g³ May 25] strong gelding: best effort in steeplechases when third to Jabiru in hunter at Newton Abbot in May. *A. W. Congdon*

WILD BLADE (IRE)   10 ch.g. Meneval (USA) – Tuney Blade (Fine Blade (USA))   **c–**
[2002/3 c–, h–: c25dᵖᵘ May 6] tall gelding: winning hurdler: no form in 2 handicap   **h–**
chases: tried visored: has looked none too keen under pressure: sold 1,200 gns Doncaster September Sales, placed twice in points subsequently. *Noel T. Chance*

WILD DREAM   8 b.m. Derrylin – Vedra (IRE) (Carlingford Castle) [2002/3 F114:   **h93 p**
17g³ 21d* Nov 26] sturdy, lengthy mare: useful in bumpers: better effort in mares novice hurdles when easy winner at Warwick in November: will stay beyond 21f: has run out (in points)/hung badly left: made mistakes both starts over hurdles: likely to prove best on left-handed track: no easy ride but open to further improvement. *S. Pike*

972

WILDFIELD RUFO (IRE)   8 b.g. Celio Rufo – Jersey Girl (Hardboy) [2002/3 c99: c24d^F c25d^F 22v^2 24v^2 24v* 24s Feb 24] rangy gelding: winning hunter chaser: fair form switched to hurdles, easily won novice at Ayr in February: stays 25f: acts on heavy and good to firm going: consistent. *Mrs K. Walton*   **c–**
h103

WILD HADEER   9 ch.g. Hadeer – Wild Moon (USA) (Arctic Tern (USA)) [2002/3 h87: 20g May 8] sturdy gelding: modest handicap hurdler: well below form in seller at Chepstow in May, not seen out again: stays 21f: acts on soft going: blinkered. *John R. Upson*   **h–**

WILD KNIGHT (IRE)   6 b.g. Jurado (USA) – Knight's Maid (Giolla Mear) [2002/3 F17f^2 F16m* 22d^F 20s^4 22d^pu 16m^2 16g^3 Apr 25] IR £25,000 4-y-o: medium-sized gelding: second foal: half-brother to winning pointer by Orchestra: dam won 2¼m chase in Ireland: fair form in bumpers, won weakly-contested event at Chepstow in October: fair novice hurdler: likely to prove best around 2m: acts on firm going: takes strong hold: not an easy ride. *P. F. Nicholls*   **h105**
F94

WILD ROMANCE (IRE)   8 b.g. Accordion – Mandy's Last (Krayyan) [2002/3 h123: 16d^F 16d^2 16v^5 16g^5 Mar 23] smallish gelding: fairly useful hurdler in 2001/2: best effort in handicaps in 2002/3 when second at Wincanton in December: raced mainly around 2m, only on good going or softer over hurdles (acts on heavy). *D. J. Wintle*   **h110**

WILD SPICE (IRE)   8 b.g. Mandalus – Curry Lunch (Pry) [2002/3 h–: 22g* 20g^ur 27g* 20d^6 c20d c24d^5 c26v^2 c24d^F c25d^2 c24g^5 Apr 2] smallish gelding: fair handicap hurdler, won at Exeter and Stratford in May: fair novice chaser, though often let down by jumping: stays 27f: acts on heavy going. *Miss Venetia Williams*   **c107**
h112

WILFIE WILD   7 b.g. Nomadic Way (USA) – Wild Child (Grey Ghost) [2002/3 c25d^pu May 4] second foal: brother to winning pointer: dam modest hunter chaser, stayed 25f: won maiden point in 2002: not fluent and showed little on chasing debut. *Mrs Lynne Ward*   **c–**

WILFRAM   6 b.g. Fraam – Ming Blue (Primo Dominie) [2002/3 16d 16g 19f^2 19m^6 22g^4 22g Apr 19] modest and inconsistent on Flat (seems best up to easy 1¼m): poor novice hurdler: stays 2¾m: acts on firm going: often wears cheekpieces: didn't impress with attitude final start. *J. M. Bradley*   **h77**

WILFUL LORD (IRE)   6 b.g. Lord Americo – Dotties Girl (IRE) (Remainder Man) [2002/3 21v 19g 25g Mar 17] 3,500 4-y-o: tall, rather unfurnished gelding: second foal: dam ran once in points: well held in 3 novice hurdles. *J. Wade*   **h–**

WILLA THYNE (IRE)   9 br.m. Good Thyne (USA) – Florella (Royal Fountain) [2002/3 h–: 20d^pu 16m^5 Jun 1] of little account nowadays: tried visored/tongue tied. *R. Allan*   **h–**

WILLIAM GEORGE (IRE)   4 b.g. Turtle Island (IRE) – Lady's Dream (Mazilier (USA)) [2002/3 16s 18m^6 16m 16d^pu 16s^ur 17d 16d^5 16m^pu Mar 31] sturdy gelding: fair maiden on Flat (stays 1m), sold out of K. Ryan's stable 3,200 gns Newmarket Autumn Sales: showed little over hurdles: will need bare 2m: tried in blinkers/cheekpieces. *J. Joseph*   **h–**

WILLIAM LIONHEART   9 b.g. Henbit (USA) – Come To Tea (IRE) (Be My Guest (USA)) [2002/3 c24s c23d^ur c22v^5 c23d^4 Jan 27] sturdy gelding: winning pointer, signs of only a little ability otherwise. *Mrs Jane Galpin*   **c65**
h–

WILLIAM O'DEE (NZ)   14 br.g. Exceptionnel – Fiducia O'Dee (NZ) (Sir Godfrey (FR)) [2002/3 c94, h–: c21s^4 May 28] smallish gelding: fair hunter chaser: ran poorly at Newton Abbot in May: will prove best up to 21f: acts on good to firm and heavy going: free-going front runner. *G. Chambers*   **c–**
h–

WILLIE JOHN DALY (IRE)   6 b.g. Mister Lord (USA) – Murphy's Lady (IRE) (Over The River (FR)) [2002/3 F16s^4 F16s^2 F19v* F16s^6 Feb 8] IR £9,500 4-y-o: first foal: dam winning pointer: fairly useful form in bumpers, successful at Naas in January: stays 19f. *D. Coffey, Ireland*   **F100**

WILLIE MAKEIT (IRE)   13 b.g. Coquelin (USA) – Turbina (Tudor Melody) [2002/3 c21f^4 c24m c19g^pu Apr 2] rather sparsely-made gelding: veteran hunter chaser, on the downgrade: tried blinkered. *Mrs A. L. Tory*   **c–**
h–

WILLOUGHBY FLYER   5 b.g. Homo Sapien – Jane's Daughter (Pitpan) [2002/3 25m^5 21d 24s^pu 25g^pu Mar 23] IR £2,300 3-y-o: eighth foal: half-brother to one-time fairly useful chaser River Don (by Over The River), stays 25f, and to fair chaser Mister Muddypaws (by Celtic Cone), stays 4m: dam, unplaced in bumpers/points in Ireland,   **h–**

half-sister to useful hurdler up to 3m Trust The King: not fluent and no form in novice hurdles. *John R. Upson*

WILLOUGHBY'S BOY (IRE)   6 b.g. Night Shift (USA) – Andbell (Trojan Fen) **h–**
[2002/3 16d Nov 12] smallish gelding: fair up to 1¼m on Flat: failed to settle and shaped like non-stayer in novice on hurdling debut. *B. Hanbury*

WILLOW RUN (NZ)   9 b.g. Conquistarose (USA) – Crazy Lady (NZ) (One Pound **h73 §** Sterling) [2002/3 h80: 16m 17s 16s 16g 16d Feb 8] medium-sized gelding: poor hurdler: raced mainly around 2m: acts on soft and good to firm going: tried blinkered/in cheekpieces: sometimes tongue tied: unreliable. *B. Ellison*

WILLOW WONDER   4 ch.f. Greensmith – Walnut Way (Gambling Debt) [2002/3 **h–** 17sᵖᵘ Nov 18] sixth foal: dam, fairly useful chaser, stayed 2¾m: no sign of ability on Flat or on hurdling debut. *M. R. Hoad*

WILL SHE   5 b.m. Bollin William – She's A Madam (Kabour) [2002/3 F17m F16g **F–** F17m Jul 25] first foal: dam of little account: well held in 3 bumpers: tongue tied. *M. E. Sowersby*

WILL'SILLYSHANKERS   8 b.g. Silly Prices – Hannah's Song (Saintly Song) **h–** [2002/3 h–: 19d 24dᵖᵘ Jun 8] quite good-topped gelding: little sign of ability: tried visored. *G. A. Ham*

WILLS PERK (IRE)   8 ch.m. Executive Perk – Brandy Hill Girl (Green Shoon) **c– x** [2002/3 c63x: c25g May 11] signs of only a little abilty in steeplechases: won point in April: should stay beyond 21f: acts on soft going: has had tongue tied: usually makes mistakes. *N. B. Mason*

WILL TELL   5 b.g. Rainbow Quest (USA) – Guillem (USA) (Nijinsky (CAN)) [2002/3 **F93** F17d F16d⁴ Apr 25] 25,000 3-y-o: tall gelding: fifth foal: half-brother to useful 2m hurdler Goss (by Linamix) and fair chaser Guilder (by Groom Dancer), stays 2½m: dam, third over 11.5f on only start, closely related to smart winner up to 1½m Lydian and half-sister to Ribblesdale winner Ballinderry, herself dam of Prix du Jockey Club winner Sanglamore: much better effort in bumpers (trained on debut by T. Etherington) when fourth of 17 to Flight Command at Perth, wandering as he tired. *Mrs S. J. Smith*

WILLY WILLY   10 ch.g. Master Willie – Monsoon (Royal Palace) [2002/3 c–, h90: **c–** 16m² 16d⁵ 19m⁵ c22dᵖᵘ Dec 10] tall, angular gelding: winning hurdler/chaser, poor **h80** nowadays: stays easy 21f: acts on firm going: free-going front runner. *G. Brown*

WILTON BRIDGE (IRE)   9 b.g. Clearly Bust – Pai-Collect (Paico) [2002/3 c16s⁴ **c96** c21v⁴ c21sᵘʳ c20gᵘʳ Apr 23] winning hurdler: modest handicap chaser: effective at 2m to **h–** 3m: unraced on firm going, acts on any other. *A. J. Martin, Ireland*

WIN ALOT   5 b.g. Aragon – Having Fun (Hard Fought) [2002/3 h73: 17m² 24mᵖᵘ **h76** 17g⁶ 22g⁵ Apr 26] sturdy gelding: modest maiden on Flat (barely stays 1¾m): poor handicap hurdler: probably stays 3m, effective at much shorter: acts on good to firm going: has hinted at temperament. *S. R. Bowring*

WINCHESTER   8 ch.g. Gunner B – Tracy Jack (David Jack) [2002/3 c22v³ c19g* **c115** c25d² c23g³ c20g⁶ Apr 3] good-topped gelding: winning hurdler: fairly useful novice **h–** chaser, off 20 months before reappearance: won at Catterick in January by 15 lengths from Supreme Fortune: improved form when 3½ lengths third to Random Harvest in handicap at Wetherby fourth start: stays 25f: raced on good going or softer (acts on heavy): tends to jump left. *K. A. Ryan*

WINDFOLA   4 b.f. Sovereign Water (FR) – Sainte Martine (Martinmas) [2002/3 **F68** F16g⁵ Feb 12] third foal: dam winning chaser up to 23f: fifth of 15 in mares bumper at Musselburgh on debut. *R. D. E. Woodhouse*

WINDLE BROOK   11 b.g. Gildoran – Minigale (Strong Gale) [2002/3 c92, h–: c19g **c93 §** c26d³ c23m² c24gᵖᵘ c24dᵖᵘ c23gᵖᵘ Oct 22] workmanlike gelding: modest handicap **h–** chaser: form in 2002/3 only when second at Worcester in June: showed plenty of temperament otherwise: stays 3m: acts on firm and good to soft going (possibly not on soft): has been tongue tied: unreliable. *K. C. Bailey*

WINDROSS   11 b.g. Ardross – Dans Le Vent (Pollerton) [2002/3 c132, h–: c24sᵖᵘ **c–** c25d² Apr 4] rangy gelding: useful handicap chaser: off 13 months (reportedly due to **h–** suspensory trouble), showed nothing on reappearance: fell third next time: stays 25f: acts on soft and good to firm going: usually waited with/has found little. *A. King*

WINDY VALLEY (IRE)   10 gr.g. Roi Guillaume (FR) – My Bonny Girl (Bonne **c–** Noel) [2002/3 c86, h87: c21fᵖᵘ c20mᶠ 22mᶠ 20g² 18m⁴ 24gᵖᵘ Sep 15] leggy gelding: **h87**

modest handicap hurdler/maiden chaser: stayed 3m: acted on soft and firm going: was blinkered and tongue tied: dead. *Mrs A. J. Hamilton-Fairley*

WINGED ANGEL   6 ch.g. Prince Sabo – Silky Heights (IRE) (Head For Heights) [2002/3 h–: 20g⁵ 16g² 20d* 20g* Jun 15] modest novice hurdler: won 2 handicaps at Hexham in June, finishing lame in second: likely to prove better suited by 2½m than shorter: raced only on good/good to soft going: held up. *L. Lungo*   **h95**

WINGED HUSSAR   10 b.g. In The Wings – Akila (FR) (Top Ville) [2002/3 h100§: 17s⁴ 16s² 17s 19d⁵ c17g² Mar 22] lengthy gelding: fair maiden hurdler: runner-up in maiden at Bangor on chasing debut: should stay beyond 2m: raced on good going or softer (acts on soft): ungenuine. *D. R. Gandolfo*   **c94 §** **h101 §**

WINGED LADY (GER)   4 b.f. Winged Love (IRE) – Wonderful Lady (GER) (Surumu (GER)) [2002/3 16d Mar 10] ex-German filly: successful once over 9f from 3 starts on Flat at 3 yrs for M. Hofer: well held in juvenile on hurdling debut. *A. G. Juckes*   **h–**

WINGS OF HOPE (IRE)   7 b.g. Treasure Hunter – She's Got Wings (Bulldozer) [2002/3 h90§: 22mᶠ 19gʳᵒ 20g6 20m² 20s⁵ 20g³ 24g⁵ 21f* 21f* 21g 19mᵖᵘ Apr 21] close-coupled, quite good-topped gelding: modest hurdler: won minor event and novice handicap at Ludlow in October: showed little after 5-month absence last 2 starts: stays 25f: acts on any ground: tried blinkered: irresolute. *C. J. Hemsley*   **h87 §**

WINNIE   8 br.m. Presidium – Sindur (Rolfe (USA)) [2002/3 h65: 25g⁵ 22fᵖᵘ 22s⁴ 17v c20gᶠ Mar 12] rather sparely-made mare: poor maiden hurdler: fell seventh on chasing debut: tried blinkered, has worn cheekpieces: has had tongue tied: sold £800 Ascot April Sales. *Miss A. M. Newton-Smith*   **c–** **h–**

WINNIE THE POOH   9 br.g. Landyap (USA) – Moorland Nell (Neltino) [2002/3 c–, h72: 17g 22fᵖᵘ 22m² 17dᵖᵘ c16gᵖᵘ Apr 21] poor maiden hurdler on balance: no show either start over fences: stays 2¾m. *J. D. Frost*   **c–** **h78**

WINNING DREAM (IRE)   9 b.g. Hollow Hand – Lottosprite (IRE) (Sandalay) [2002/3 c16s⁶ c17d* c29g³ Apr 21] strong gelding: fairly useful handicap chaser: much improved last 2 starts, easily beating What's The Score 12 lengths at Navan in March and third to Timbera in Irish Grand National at Fairyhouse: effective around 2m and clearly stays easy 29f: acts on soft going. *Oliver McKiernan, Ireland*   **c126**

WINN'S PRIDE (IRE)   12 b.g. Indian Ridge – Blue Bell Girl (Blakeney) [2002/3 c103, h–: c20s³ c16v² c19g c20m⁵ c24m Jul 18] leggy gelding: modest handicap chaser: probably best around 2½m: acts on any going: visored once. *R. Hollinshead*   **c94** **h–**

WINTER BROOK   5 b.m. Alderbrook – Oats For Notes (Oats) [2002/3 F12g 17g Mar 17] 5,000 3-y-o: leggy mare: first foal: dam, poor form in bumpers/points, from family of Sun Alliance Hurdle winner Rebel Song: well held in bumper and mares maiden hurdle. *G. B. Balding*   **h–** **F–**

WINTER GALE (IRE)   11 b. or br.g. Strong Gale – Winter Fox (Martinmas) [2002/3 c93, h–: c16m c24dᵖᵘ c20d⁶ Jun 4] lengthy gelding: poor handicap chaser: placed first 3 starts in points in 2003: stays 25f: acts on good to firm and good to soft going: blinkered once in bumpers. *M. W. Easterby*   **c73** **h–**

WINTER GARDEN   9 ch.g. Old Vic – Winter Queen (Welsh Pageant) [2002/3 16s⁶ 16v⁵ 16g Feb 12] useful-looking gelding: bought out of A. Moore's stable 8,500 gns Doncaster May Sales: one-time useful handicap hurdler, very much on downgrade: no encouragement over fences (refused to race once): stays 21f: acts on heavy and good to firm going: tried blinkered/tongue tied. *Miss Lucinda V. Russell*   **c–** **h93**

WINTERTIDE   7 b.g. Mtoto – Winter Queen (Welsh Pageant) [2002/3 21d⁴ 22d² Feb 17] has scope: useful bumper winner: fairly useful maiden on Flat (stays 2½m), sold out of R. Fahey's stable 18,000 gns Newmarket Autumn Sales: fair form in novice hurdles at Kempton and Fontwell: likely to stay 3m: won a race. *M. Pitman*   **h110**

WINTER WHISPER (IRE)   8 b.g. Jurado (USA) – Princess Annabelle (English Prince) [2002/3 c20sᵖᵘ 19f⁴ c21gᶠ c19m Apr 21] IR 6,400 3-y-o: medium-sized gelding: tenth foal: half-brother to 2 winning hurdlers, including 2½m winner Bold Tipperary (by Orchestra): dam 1½m winner: winning hurdler/chaser, left E. O'Grady prior to reappearance: headstrong and just modest in hunter chases in Britain: stays 2½m: acts on good to firm and heavy ground: often tongue tied. *Mrs Susan E. Busby*   **c84** **h–**

WIN THE TOSS   11 b.g. Idiot's Delight – Mayfield (USA) (Alleged (USA)) [2002/3 c–, h–: c26m c16d⁶ c21gᵘʳ c19gᵖᵘ Apr 2] leggy, angular gelding: winning hurdler: poor on balance of form in points (successful twice in April) and hunter chases: not certain to stay much beyond 2½m: acts on any going: tried blinkered/tongue tied. *P. York*   **c69** **h–**

WISE ADVICE (IRE) 13 b.g. Duky – Down The Aisle (Godswalk (USA)) [2002/3   **c82**
c70, h–: c24m³ c19g^pu Apr 2] lengthy gelding: veteran chaser: third in hunter at   **h–**
Huntingdon in May: dead-heated in point in April: acts on firm and good to soft going:
tried visored/blinkered. *M. A. Kemp*

WISE KING 13 b.g. Rakaposhi King – Sunwise (Roi Soleil) [2002/3 c120, h–: c20d^F   **c115**
c20g⁴ c21d* c19g⁵ c21g³ Apr 21] lengthy gelding: fairly useful handicap chaser: first win   **h–**
in nearly 4 years when beating Fluff 'N' Puff 4 lengths at Wincanton in February: stays
3m: acts on soft and good to firm going. *J. A. B. Old*

WISE MAN (IRE) 8 ch.g. Mister Lord (USA) – Ballinlonig Star (Black Minstrel)   **c–**
[2002/3 c22d 20m 16d³ 22g² Mar 21] IR 8,400 4-y-o: sixth foal: brother to winning   **h100**
hurdler Lords Best, stays 2¾m, and half-brother to fair hurdler/chaser Ballinagreen (by
Henbit), stays 3m: dam unraced: fair maiden hurdler/chaser: off 7 months and left
A. Moore, creditable efforts over hurdles last 2 starts: stays 2½m: yet to race on firm
going, acts on any other: often tongue tied (not in Britain). *N. W. Alexander*

WISE PRINCE (IRE) 11 b.g. Denel (FR) – Kissowen (Pitpan) [2002/3 c95: c25g³   **c95 §**
c22d³ c28g⁴ c20v* c24v⁴ Mar 5] fair hunter chaser: won at Bangor in February: stays
3½m: acts on good to firm and heavy going: threw away winning chance by going
violently left on reappearance: remains one to treat with caution. *Mrs Edward Crow*

WISE TALE 4 b.g. Nashwan (USA) – Wilayif (USA) (Danzig (USA)) [2002/3 16d   **h74**
16d^F 16v Jan 2] half-brother to poor 2m hurdler Royal Allegiance: fair maiden up to 1¾m
on Flat (possibly unsuited by ground softer than good): poor form in juvenile hurdles, all
on ground softer than good: visored second start. *P. D. Niven*

WISHBONE ALLEY (IRE) 8 b.g. Common Grounds – Dul Dul (USA) (Shadeed   **h–**
(USA)) [2002/3 h–: 17s^pu Nov 21] no form over hurdles: most unlikely to stay 2m: tried
in cheekpieces. *K. G. Wingrove*

WISHFUL VALENTINE 7 ch.g. Riverwise (USA) – Wishful Dream (Crawter)   **h–**
[2002/3 h–: 22d^pu 24v^pu 22g Apr 19] sturdy, plain gelding: no form over hurdles.
C. W. Mitchell

WISLEY WARRIOR 12 b.g. Derring Rose – Miss Topem (Mossberry) [2002/3 c–x,   **c– x**
h–: c33g^pu May 1] workmanlike gelding: winning chaser: no show in hunter: poor jump-   **h–**
er. *C. R. Willes*

WITCH'S BREW 6 b.m. Simply Great (FR) – New Broom (IRE) (Brush Aside   **h94**
(USA)) [2002/3 17v⁶ 16v³ 16v² 16g² 16d* 21s⁴ 20g² 19g³ Apr 26] lengthy mare: modest
maiden on Flat (stays 1½m): similar form over hurdles, won mares novice handicap at
Catterick in February: stays 2½m: acts on heavy going. *T. D. Easterby*

WITH A DASH 5 ch.g. Afzal – Oh So Ripe (Deep Run) [2002/3 F16m Feb 22] 2,800   **F–**
4-y-o: workmanlike gelding: sixth foal: dam poor 2m novice hurdler: well held in bumper
on debut. *N. A. Twiston-Davies*

WITH A TWIST (GER) 5 ch.g. Alwuhush (USA) – Walkona (IRE) (Local Suitor   **h–**
(USA)) [2002/3 h118: 17v 16d^F Jan 25] smallish, good-bodied gelding: fairly useful form
over hurdles: tailed off in handicap on reappearance, fell fatally next time. *C. J. Mann*

WITHCOTE JEM 8 gr.g. Norton Challenger – Jem Jen (Great Nephew) [2002/3   **h–**
16g^F 22s^ro Nov 2] half-brother to fair 2m hurdler Crystal Beam (by Crystal Glitters),
later successful over fences in Germany and winning pointer by Glint of Gold: dam fairly
useful 1¼m winner: no promise in 2 novice hurdles. *A. Scott*

WITHCOTE WELCOME 8 gr.g. Norton Challenger – Welcoming Arms (Free   **h–**
State) [2002/3 23v^pu Nov 16] no sign of ability in maiden on Flat (trained by B. Ellison)
or selling hurdle. *A. Scott*

WITHCOTE WIZARD 7 gr.g. Norton Challenger – Roses To Rachel (Artaius   **h–**
(USA)) [2002/3 17g^pu 20f⁴ Sep 15] sixth foal: brother to winner 1m winner in Slovakia: dam,
placed twice in USA, half-sister to 2000 Guineas third Huntingdale: showed nothing in 2
novice hurdles. *A. Scott*

WITHOUT A DOUBT 4 b.g. Singspiel (IRE) – El Rabab (USA) (Roberto (USA))   **F89**
[2002/3 F16d³ F16m Mar 22] leggy gelding: fifth foal: half-brother to 3 winners, including useful 6f/7f winner Filfilah (by Cadeaux Genereaux) and Canadian Grade 2 11f
winner Muntej (by Muhtarram): dam, 2-y-o 1m winner, out of Breeders' Cup Juvenile
Fillies winner Brave Raj: bought unraced out of J. Hammond's stable 14,000 gns
Newmarket Autumn Sales: much better effort in bumpers at Newbury when third to
Bourbon Manhattan. *M. Pitman*

WITHOUT PRETENSE (USA)   5 b.g. St Jovite (USA) – Spark of Success (USA)   **h63**
(Topsider (USA)) [2002/3 16m 19d 17d^pu 16d 17f^4 Mar 27] ex-Irish gelding: half-brother
to fairly useful 2m hurdler Fearsome Factor (by Alleged) and winner over jumps in Czech
Republic by Lear Fan: lightly-raced maiden on Flat, best effort at 7f: poor maiden hurdler,
sold out of D. Weld's stable 6,000 gns Doncaster September Sales after reappearance:
will prove best around 2m. *N. G. Ayliffe*

WITNESS TIME (IRE)   7 b.g. Witness Box (USA) – Lisnacoilla (Beau Chapeau)   **h93**
[2002/3 F80: 20v 20s^5 20v^5 26d* Feb 23] strong, workmanlike gelding: improved form
over hurdles when winning novice at Hereford by 5 lengths from Joe Deane, making most
and running on strongly despite wandering under pressure: clearly suited by 3m+: raced
on good going or softer (acts on heavy). *B. J. Eckley*

WITNEY (IRE)   9 b.m. Strong Gale – Euroblend (IRE) (The Parson) [2002/3 h–:   **h–**
22d 20g^4 20m 24m^pu 21m^5 Sep 13] sturdy mare: no worthwhile form over hurdles.
P. T. Dalton

WITNEY O'GRADY (IRE)   10 ch.g. Ring of Ford – C B M Girl (Diamonds Are   **h–**
Trump (USA)) [2002/3 h71?: 17s^pu 24g^pu Apr 21] strong, lengthy gelding: winning
pointer: no worthwhile form over hurdles. *Miss L. V. Davis*

WIZADORA   8 gr.m. Safawan – Shrood Biddy (Sharrood (USA)) [2002/3 c–§, h–:   **c§§**
c16d^rtr May 13] lengthy mare: little form and temperamental to boot: tried blinkered/   **h§§**
tongue tied. *Mrs S. Davies*

WIZARD O' WASS   5 ch.g. Imp Society (USA) – Sabeel (Local Suitor (USA))   **F–**
[2002/3 F17v^5 F16d^5 F16g Mar 29] first foal: dam, poor novice hurdler, half-sister to
one-time fairly useful hurdler Shu Gaa: pulled hard and showed little in bumpers.
J. R. Turner

WIZARDTREE   4 ch.g. Presidium – Snow Tree (Welsh Pageant) [2002/3 F16d Feb   **F–**
15] plain gelding: eleventh foal: brother to bumper winner Presidentree and half-brother
to fair hurdler up to 2½m Bodentree (by Rambo Dancer): dam, middle-distance winner,
out of half-sister to smart stayer Celtic Cone: little show in bumper on debut. *R. S. Brookhouse*

WOLF SPIDER   6 gr.m. Norton Challenger – Milly Green (No Loiterer) [2002/3   **h–**
19d^pu 24s^pu 22g Mar 21] lengthy mare: fourth foal: dam, twice-raced on Flat, half-sister
to top-class staying chaser Burrough Hill Lad: no sign of ability. *A. Scott*

WOMAN   5 b.m. Homo Sapien – La Princesse (Le Bavard (FR)) [2002/3 F16f F16m   **F–**
F16d^ur Nov 17] 1,200 4-y-o: leggy mare: second foal: dam, fair hurdler who stayed 2¾m,
half-sister to Irish Grand National winner Timbera: no sign of ability. *H. J. Manners*

WONDERFUL MAN   7 ch.g. Magical Wonder (USA) – Gleeful (Sayf El Arab (USA))   **h80**
[2002/3 h–: 17g^F 16m^2 16d^2 16d^3 16m^5 Apr 11] good-topped gelding: poor novice hurdler: raced around 2m: acts on good to firm and good to soft going. *R. D. E. Woodhouse*

WONDERFUL REMARK   7 b.m. Golden Heights – Queen of Dreams (Ti King   **h– §**
(FR)) [2002/3 h–, F–: 17m 16m^pu Jun 19] no worthwhile form over hurdles: tried   **F–**
blinkered: has looked ungenuine. *G. J. Smith*

WONDER WEASEL (IRE)   10 b.g. Lancastrian – The She Weasel (Gulf Pearl)   **c136**
[2002/3 c128, h112p: c27d^4 c25s* c33v^3 c28d^4 c36d^F Apr 5] sturdy gelding: once-raced   **h–**
over hurdles: useful handicap chaser: in good form in 2002/3, won at Wetherby in
December by length from Heidi III: good fourth to Shotgun Willy in valuable event at
Haydock fourth start: fell third in Grand National at Aintree final outing: stays 3½m: acts
soft and good to firm going, probably heavy: blinkered (reportedly choked) once, wore
cheekpieces after reappearance. *K. C. Bailey*

WONDER WINGS   6 ch.g. Lir – Ginger Wings (Ginger Boy) [2002/3 F18f^4 Apr 24]   **F74**
first foal: dam poor novice hurdler/chaser who stayed 2½m: fourth of 9 to Cockatoo
Ridge in bumper at Fontwell on debut. *G. L. Moore*

WONTCOSTALOTBUT   9 b.m. Nicholas Bill – Brave Maiden (Three Legs) [2002/3   **c101**
c90, h111d: c26m^3 22v^2 c26d* c24s 24g c26d^3 c26s^4 c25m* Apr 21] smallish mare: fair   **h109**
hurdler/chaser, trained until after reappearance by M. Wilkinson: won novice chases at
Fontwell in December and Hereford (mares, wore cheekpieces) in April: will stay beyond
3¼m: acts on good to firm and heavy going: twice visored. *B. De Haan*

WOODFIELD GALE (IRE)   10 b.g. Strong Gale – Excitable Lady (Buckskin (FR))   **c96 §**
[2002/3 c107d, h–: c22g^pu c20d^4 c19g^3 c25d^2 c24g^6 c25g^2 c25d^2 Mar 6] useful-looking   **h–**
gelding: modest handicap chaser: left F. Murphy after second start: in frame 5 of 7 outings

in 2002/3, throwing away winning chance by idling on final occasion: stays 25f: acts on any going: tried blinkered: often none too fluent: not one to trust. *T. D. Easterby*

WOODLAND KING (IRE)   11 b.g. King's Ride – Bilma (IRE) (Glenstal (USA)) [2002/3 c26g^{pu} c21f^3 c26d^5 c23g^{pu} Oct 22] useful-looking gelding: thrice-raced hurdler: maiden chaser: sold out of A. Moore's stable 3,200 gns Ascot February (2000) Sales: runner-up in point in 2002: little worthwhile form back in steeplechases: stays 2¾m: acts on soft and firm going. *D. C. Turner*   c88 ?
h–

WOODLAND PARK (USA)   5 b.g. Woodman (USA) – Yemanja (USA) (Alleged (USA)) [2002/3 h–: 23g^3 26g* May 30] good-topped gelding: modest hurdler: won weak novice handicap at Huntingdon in May: stays 3¼m. *Mrs D. Haine*   h93

WOODLANDS BEAU (IRE)   11 b.g. Beau Sher – Never Intended (Sayyaf) [2002/3 c101x: c26m^4 c25g^2 May 24] workmanlike gelding: modest handicap chaser: won points in March (2) and April: stays 3¼m: acts on any going: usually blinkered/visored: sketchy jumper. *R. H. Alner*   c85 x

WOODLANDS HIPOWER   8 b.m. Risk Me (FR) – Hallowed (Wolver Hollow) [2002/3 16g^{ur} May 17] well held in bumpers in 1999/00: unseated first on hurdling debut. *P. A. Pritchard*   h–

WOODLANDS POWERGEN   10 br.g. Rich Charlie – Hallowed (Wolver Hollow) [2002/3 20s^{pu} Dec 5] no sign of ability. *P. A. Pritchard*   h–

WOODWIND DOWN   6 b.m. Piccolo – Bint El Oumara (Al Nasr (FR)) [2002/3 h76: 16m^3 17d^3 16g^3 16m^2 c16m* c16g^2 c16g^2 c17s^{pu} 20f* Sep 15] modest form in novice chases, won at Sedgefield in July: poor hurdler: won handicap at Hexham (reportedly finished lame) in September: stays 2½m: acts on firm and good to soft going: tried blinkered/visored: held up: not an easy ride. *M. Todhunter*   c87
h82

WOODYS DEEP OCEAN (IRE)   7 b.g. Be My Native (USA) – Von Carty (IRE) (Supreme Leader) [2002/3 h114, F103: 19g 18d^2 16s^3 16s* 16s* 16s^3 16d 16g^4 Apr 21] lengthy gelding: fair hurdler: won maiden at Fairyhouse in November and novice at Gowran in December: raced mainly at 2m: acts on soft going. *N. Meade, Ireland*   h113

WOODY'S DELIGHT   5 b.m. Hatim (USA) – Woodram Delight (Idiot's Delight) [2002/3 F17g Mar 28] seventh foal: half-sister to fairly useful staying chaser Bank Avenue (by Homo Sapien): dam unraced half-sister to dual Scottish National winner Androma and useful staying chaser Bigsun: last of 10 in bumper on debut. *M. A. Barnes*   F–

WOODYS WIDGET   8 b.m. Rislan (USA) – Woodland Firefly (Mins Baby) [2002/3 22f^{pu} Aug 13] first foal: dam modest pointer: completed once from 7 starts in maiden points: showed nothing on hurdling debut. *W. W. Dennis*   h–

WOOLLEY   9 b.g. Welsh Captain – Singing Hills (Crash Course) [2002/3 c–, h–: 22g^4 May 17] workmanlike gelding: poor maiden hurdler: stays 2¾m: acts on heavy going: has had tongue tied: sold 3,500 gns Doncaster August Sales, runner-up 3 times in points subsequently. *John Allen*   c–
h80

WOOLLY WINSOME   7 br.g. Lugana Beach – Gay Ming (Gay Meadow) [2002/3 h–: 17m May 3] sturdy gelding: no form over hurdles: jumped sketchily in blinkers only start in 2002/3. *G. Brown*   h–

WOR BOBBY (IRE)   5 br.g. Warcraft (USA) – Pil Eagle (FR) (Piling (USA)) [2002/3 F16g F16v^{pu} Jan 29] fifth foal: half-brother to fair hurdler/chaser up to 3m Mitchleldean (by Be My Native) and winning 2½m hurdler Brave Eagle (by Roselier): dam once-raced half-sister to fairly useful staying hurdler Quini Eagle: modest form on first of 2 starts in bumpers: dead. *B. Ellison*   F78

WORKAWAY   7 b.g. Alflora (IRE) – Annicombe Run (Deep Run) [2002/3 h–, F89: 20m^3 16g* 17d^5 16s^2 16d^6 17g^5 Apr 21] modest handicap hurdler: made all at Kelso in October: stays 2½m: acts on good to firm and heavy going: has broken blood vessel: free-going sort. *A. Parker*   h86

WORKING GIRL   6 b.m. Morpeth – Workamiracle (Teamwork) [2002/3 F17d 16s 18s 16d^3 Mar 10] second foal: dam once-raced daughter of useful staying chaser Armagnac Princess: well held in bumper on debut: signs of only a little ability over hurdles. *J. D. Frost*   h60
F–

WORLD VISION (IRE)   6 ch.g. Denel (FR) – Dusty Lane (IRE) (Electric) [2002/3 F16m^4 F17g^3 F20f F16m 16s 20d Feb 23] IR £20,000 4-y-o: leggy ex-Irish gelding: first foal: dam unraced, from family of top-class hurdler Aonoch: fell fifth in maiden Irish   h–
F90

point on debut in 2002: fair form at best in bumpers, sold out of C. Swan's stable 20,000 gns Doncaster August Sales after third start: well held in 2 novice hurdles. *Ferdy Murphy*

WORLD WIDE WEB (IRE) 7 b.g. Be My Native (USA) – Meldrum Lass (Buckskin (FR)) [2002/3 h112: c24d⁴ c22d 19s 16d⁵ 16s* 16s* c16g Mar 16] tall, good sort: fairly useful hurdler: improved form fifth and sixth starts, winning handicaps at Sandown (conditional jockeys) and Chepstow, in latter having more in hand than margin suggests when beating Canada 1½ lengths: caught eye on chasing debut but finished last both subsequent outings over fences, jumping with no confidence in handicap final one (odds on): effective at 2m given test and stays 3m: raced only on good going or softer (acts on soft): ran well only try in blinkers. *Jonjo O'Neill*
c99
h123 +

WORTHY MAN 6 b.g. Homo Sapien – Marnworth (Funny Man) [2002/3 F–: F17dᵖᵘ Feb 23] rangy gelding: has scope: no form in 2 bumpers. *T. R. George*
F–

WOT ABOUT ME (IRE) 8 b.g. Jolly Jake (NZ) – Time Please (Welsh Saint) [2002/3 c–, h–: c21gᵖᵘ c16dᵖᵘ Mar 4] little sign of ability outside points. *Mrs P. J. Ikin*
c–
h–

WOTAN (IRE) 5 ch.g. Wolfhound (USA) – Triple Tricks (IRE) (Royal Academy (USA)) [2002/3 h–: 20v Mar 7] leggy gelding: modest maiden on Flat (stays 13f): little show over hurdles. *R. Curtis*
h–

WOT NO CASH 11 gr.g. Ballacashtal (CAN) – Madame Non (My Swanee) [2002/3 c77, h–: c18f³ c16g⁵ c17mᵖᵘ c17m⁵ Apr 21] poor handicap chaser: best around 2m: acts on soft and firm going. *R. C. Harper*
c65
h–

WOTSITOOYA (IRE) 11 b.g. Rashar (USA) – Droppey Loops (Over The River (FR)) [2002/3 c112+, h94: 16d⁵ 20m c22d² 24s⁴ c24f 24m* c28sᶠ 24d² c24g c29g⁶ Apr 21] lengthy gelding: fair form over hurdles, won novice at Limerick in October: fair handicap chaser: good efforts when second in Galway Plate in July and valuable event at Punchestown in early-May, also ran well in Irish National at Fairyhouse in April: stays 29f: acts on good to firm and heavy going. *M. J. P. O'Brien, Ireland*
c113
h106

WOULDN'T YOU AGREE (IRE) 7 ch.g. Toulon – Mention of Money (Le Bavard (FR)) [2002/3 F106p: F16s* 16d² 20m* 16m* 21d² Nov 17] tall gelding: won at Galway in July on second of 2 starts in bumpers: fairly useful novice hurdler: won at Galway (maiden) and Tipperary in August and at Tipperary again in October: off 5½ months, well below form in Grade 1 at Punchestown in early-May: clearly effective at 2m, bred to stay beyond 21f: tongue tied fourth outing. *C. Roche, Ireland*
h122
F106

WOULD YOU BELIEVE 7 gr.g. Derrylin – Ramelton (Precipice Wood) [2002/3 c23gᶠ c24d³ Dec 21] ex-Irish gelding: sixth foal: dam unraced half-sister to fairly useful chaser up to 3m Roscoe Harvey: well beaten in bumper in 2001/2 for W. Durkan: unbeaten in 3 Irish points in 2002: in narrow lead when falling 3 out in maiden at Leicester on steeplechasing debut: third to Cool Investment in novice at Warwick next time. *K. C. Bailey*
c109

WRAGS TO RICHES (IRE) 6 b.g. Tremblant – Clonea Lady (IRE) (Lord Ha Ha) [2002/3 F18d F16d⁵ F17s² Dec 26] 9,000 4-y-o: second foal: dam unraced half-sister to useful hurdler up to 3m Glazeaway, out of half-sister to smart 2½m hurdler/chaser Danny Harrold: easily best effort in bumpers when neck second to Mickey Croke at Hereford final start. *K. C. Bailey*
F101

WRANGEL (FR) 9 ch.g. Tropular – Swedish Princess (Manado) [2002/3 c–, h92: 17d⁵ 16s 16dᵖᵘ 17s 17s⁶ 17d³ 16g³ 16m⁶ Apr 21] good-topped gelding: poor handicap hurdler: raced mainly around 2m: acts on soft and good to firm going. *B. J. Llewellyn*
c–
h83

WREKENGALE (IRE) 13 br.g. Strong Gale – Wrekenogan (Tarqogan) [2002/3 c95, h–: c30m³ c31mᵖᵘ May 22] tall gelding: fair hunter chaser: stays 31f: acts on any going: tried blinkered: often tongue tied: inconsistent. *Neil King*
c89
h–

WRENS ISLAND (IRE) 9 br.g. Yashgan – Tipiton (Balboa) [2002/3 c96: c19gᵖᵘ c23m* c24m* c23gᵖᵘ c24m c20g⁵ c27g⁵ Dec 12] well-made gelding: fair handicap chaser: won at Worcester in July and Uttoxeter in August: stays 3m: best efforts on good to firm going: often a front runner. *R. Dickin*
c102

WUN CHAI (IRE) 4 b.g. King's Theatre (IRE) – Flower From Heaven (Baptism) [2002/3 17mᵖᵘ 19s⁵ 17g* 16g Apr 12] modest maiden up to 1¼m on Flat: 50/1, best effort over hurdles when making all in juvenile at Hereford in March: likely to prove best around 2m. *F. Jordan*
h84

WUNDERWOOD (USA) 4 b.g. Faltaat (USA) – Jasoorah (IRE) (Sadler's Wells (USA)) [2002/3 F12g⁶ Dec 18] unfurnished gelding: half-brother to useful German 9f to 1¾m winner Aljaarif and UAE 7.5f/1m winner Iljasoor (both by Rainbow Quest): dam,
F74

1m (at 2 yrs) and 1½m winner, granddaughter of Irish 1000 Guineas/St Leger winner Pidget: sold unraced out of A. Stewart's stable 12,000 gns Newmarket Autumn Sales: showed some ability when sixth to Royal Rosa in bumper at Newbury on debut: successful in 1¼m maiden on Flat debut in January. *Lady Herries*

WUXI VENTURE 8 b.g. Wolfhound (USA) – Push A Button (Bold Lad (IRE)) [2002/3 16s³ 16v⁶ 16d⁵ 17s* 16d⁶ 18g² Mar 17] small, sturdy gelding: fair handicap hurdler, missed 2001/2: won steadily-run race at Bangor in February: will prove best around 2m: acts on soft going, yet to race on firmer than good over hurdles: patiently ridden. *Miss Venetia Williams* **h110**

WYCHNOR KING (IRE) 9 b. or br.g. Torus – Eva's Fancy (Distinctly (USA)) [2002/3 h–: c20d^pu May 26] big gelding: no worthwhile form. *M. Mullineaux* **c–**
h–

WYCHNOR PRINCESS (IRE) 8 ch.m. Montelimar (USA) – Forty One (IRE) (Over The River (FR)) [2002/3 h–, F–: c17m^pu 21g^pu Aug 1] leggy mare: more temperament than ability. *L. R. James* **c– §**
h– §

WYNBURY FLYER 8 ch.g. Risk Me (FR) – Woolcana (Some Hand) [2002/3 c–, h–: c19d c20v⁶ c16s^pu Jan 30] workmanlike gelding: winning hurdler/chaser: showed little in 2002/3. *R. Lee* **c–**
h–

WYNYARD DANCER 9 b.m. Minster Son – The White Lion (Flying Tyke) [2002/3 c20m* Jun 1] poor maiden hurdler: won hunter chase at Hexham in June: stays 3m: acts on good to firm going. *Mrs G. Sunter* **c80**
h–

X

XAIPETE (IRE) 11 b.g. Jolly Jake (NZ) – Rolfete (USA) (Tom Rolfe) [2002/3 c118, h112: 16d³ 19m 17m⁶ 16g⁴ c17g 16g³ c16g³ 16d³ c16g² c16d³ c16d² c17g⁶ c16s⁴ c16v* 16d⁶ c16g³ 16g³ c20g* c20g^F Apr 12] useful-looking gelding: modest handicap hurdler: fairly useful handicap chaser: won at Ayr (first win in 2½ years) in January and Carlisle in March: stays 2½m: acts on any going: held up: has pulled hard. *R. C. Guest* **c116**
h94

XELAROC 5 ch.m. Karinga Bay – Valkyrie Reef (Miramar Reef) [2002/3 F16g Feb 27] second foal: dam won 17f hurdle: never a factor in mares bumper at Ludlow: withdrawn after proving troublesome in preliminaries on intended debut in December. *S. Gollings* **F68**

XELLANCE (IRE) 6 b.g. Be My Guest (USA) – Excellent Alibi (USA) (Exceller (USA)) [2002/3 16m⁵ 16d 16d 20s 21m³ 17m³ 19m* Apr 21] angular gelding: half-brother to several winners over jumps, including fairly useful hurdler Arabian Moon (by Barathea), stays 3m: fairly useful on Flat (stays 2½m) for M. Johnston: modest hurdler: trained first 4 starts by B. Leavy: best effort when winning novice handicap at Hereford by ¾ length from Gielgud: stays 21f: acts on good to firm going. *P. J. Hobbs* **h88**

XENOPHON (IRE) 7 b.g. Toulon – Fureen (Furry Glen) [2002/3 h116p: 16s² 16s* 21g* Mar 12] **h145 p**

'With a horse like this there is no point in going for Mickey Mouse races—one big one like this makes up for ten little ones.' There are few shrewder trainers around than Tony Martin and he provided another fine example of how to place a horse to maximum advantage when, from just three starts in 2002/3, Xenophon won two of the most valuable handicaps of the season, the Pierse at Leopardstown and the Coral Cup at the Cheltenham Festival. Or as Mark Costello rather neatly put it in *The Irish Field* after the first of those victories: 'When the Greek historian and general Xenophon wrote about the art of horsemanship in 360BC he neglected to include a chapter on "how to get them handicapped". Perhaps . . . Tony Martin will publish his thoughts on the subject sometime. They would make fascinating reading.'

Xenophon was past his fifth birthday when he made his debut in May 2001 on the first of three starts in maiden hurdles. He was a 25/1 chance when down the field that day and again when second in an ordinary contest at Punchestown eight months later. He then won over nineteen furlongs at Naas at the end of January 2002, driven out and showing form not much better than the time before. That was it for another nine months. Xenophon reappeared in a competitive but not especially valuable handicap at Punchestown at the start of November and ran a promising race, coming from well off the pace two out to take second to Cloone River, beaten a length and a half. That earned Xenophon a rise of 3 lb from the Turf Club handicapper, which was more than fair as the form worked out well. In addition, further improvement looked sure to be forthcoming. The original plan with Xenophon was to run in the valuable two-mile handicap at the Open meeting at Cheltenham later in the month (a race Rooster Booster won) but a minor setback meant he had to wait for the Pierse. This is often the strongest handicap hurdle of the whole year in Ireland and the latest renewal looked especially open, with the market leaders in a field of twenty-eight sent off at 10/1, Xenophon a 12/1-chance. As was only to be expected, any number were in contention two out but once Xenophon made his move, coming to lead on the bridle at the last, the outcome wasn't in doubt and he just needed shaking up to hold Colourful Life by two lengths.

Xenophon wasn't entered for the Tote Gold Trophy—and probably wouldn't have got a run had he been—so the Coral Cup and a step up in trip was next. He was raised 10 lb for the win at Leopardstown (his trainer among those kicking up a fuss about discrepancies between British and Irish marks) but that began to seem far from punitive as those in his wake came out and franked the form: the third Camden Tanner ran a good second in the valuable Sandown Handicap and the fifth Spirit Leader won the Tote Gold Trophy. In all, by the Cheltenham Festival ten of the next twelve home in the Pierse had run again over jumps and all but three of them had run well next time. There was no 10/1 the field this time. Available at 8/1 in the morning, Xenophon was heavily backed and went off favourite at half those odds. Despite another big field and an otherwise open contest, Xenophon won in very similar style and every bit as impressively, produced to lead at the last then staying on strongly up the hill, scoring by three and a half lengths from Samon.

Pierse Hurdle (Handicap), Leopardstown—Xenophon (noseband) makes light of his inexperience to beat British raider Colourful Life (spots) and Camden Tanner

Xenophon was left in the County Hurdle at the overnight stage but wasn't asked to bid for a second win in two days. He wasn't seen out again after Cheltenham, and, although he is likely to go up at least another 10 lb, plenty more improvement looks on the cards and it will be no surprise if he proves able to defy the handicapper. The valuable three-mile handicap at Cheltenham's Open meeting in the autumn might be a good starting point. Longer term, a switch to chasing has been mooted and the lengthy Xenophon certainly has the physique to make an impact over fences as well.

Xenophon (IRE) (b.g. 1996)	Toulon (b 1988)	Top Ville (b 1976)	High Top / Sega Ville
		Green Rock (ch 1981)	Mill Reef / Infra Green
	Fureen (b or br 1985)	Furry Glen (b 1971)	Wolver Hollow / Cleftess
		Sneem (br 1974)	Rum / Magical Music

Xenophon comes from the first crop of the St Leger winner Toulon, whose death in 1998 is beginning to look a significant loss to NH breeding, given that he is also responsible for Kingscliff, Rockstown Boy and Solerina. There certainly isn't much to get excited about in the lower half of Xenophon's pedigree. His dam Fureen and grandam Sneem were both winners on the Flat, Fureen twice at a mile as a four-year-old. She has bred one winner apart from Xenophon, Magua (by Be My Native), a fair two-mile hurdler for Martin's stable. Sneem produced two other winners, a pointer and the fairly useful hurdler at up to two and a half miles Lottie's Fury. Xenophon will probably prove best at two and a half miles or more in due course. He made his debut on firm going and has raced on good or softer since. *A. J. Martin, Ireland*

XERXES (FR) 5 gr.g. Sir Brink (FR) – Sirta (FR) (Le Pontet (FR)) [2002/3 F16g Mar 2] leggy gelding: fourth foal: half-brother to 2 winners, including French chaser around 2½m Harielle II (by Un Numide): dam useful chaser up to 23f in France: well beaten in bumper on debut. *Jonjo O'Neill* **F–**

XIBALBA 6 b.g. Zafonic (USA) – Satanic Dance (FR) (Shareef Dancer (USA)) [2002/3 16gpu Apr 1] half-brother to winning French hurdler by Subotica: fair at best on Flat (stays 1¼m) for C. Brittain: no encouragement in novice claimer on hurdling debut: sold 600 gns Doncaster May Sales. *Mrs M. Reveley* **h–**

XTRA 5 b.g. Sadler's Wells (USA) – Oriental Mystique (Kris) [2002/3 17s3 Jan 28] angular gelding: smart on Flat (will stay at least 1¾m), successful once from 3 starts in **h89**

2002, sold out of L. Cumani's stable 120,000 gns Newmarket Autumn Sales, and gelded: favourite, jumped fluently in main when third to Kalca Mome in novice at Taunton on hurdling debut. *J. A. B. Old*

Y

YAHESKA (IRE) 6 b.m. Prince of Birds (USA) – How Ya Been (IRE) (Last Tycoon) **h–** [2002/3 h68: 16g Sep 14] poor maiden on Flat: form over hurdles only when winning seller at Hereford in 2001/2: sold £1,200 Ascot October Sales. *J. M. Bradley*

YAKAREEM (IRE) 7 b.g. Rainbows For Life (CAN) – Brandywell (Skyliner) **c85** [2002/3 h88: c16g³ c17dᵘʳ c17m⁴ c18m² c17m⁴ c25m² c24f² c24f* c24mᶠ c18d² c24dᵖᵘ **h–** Nov 25] compact gelding: winning hurdler: modest novice chaser: won weak 4-runner amateur handicap at Ludlow in October: effective at 2m to easy 3m: acts on firm and good to soft going: has had tongue tied, not in 2002/3: has been reluctant at start. *D. G. Bridgwater*

YANKEE CROSSING (IRE) 5 b.g. Lord Americo – Ath Leathan (Royal Vulcan) **F–** [2002/3 F16s F16d Mar 1] close-coupled, useful-looking gelding: first foal: dam unraced half-sister to fairly useful jumper up to 3m Aughrim Hill, out of half-sister to smart staying hurdler Hill of Slave: well beaten in 2 bumpers. *Jonjo O'Neill*

YANKEE JAMIE (IRE) 9 b.g. Strong Gale – Sparkling Opera (Orchestra) [2002/3 **c114 p** h90p: c20dᵖᵘ c22sᵖᵘ c25g² c21d* c25s* c24gᶠ Jan 28] lengthy, angular gelding: progressive **h101 +** chaser: won 2 handicaps at Ayr in December (first a novice): fair handicap hurdler: completed hat-trick at Musselburgh in January: stays 25f: acts on soft going: reportedly suffers breathing problems. *L. Lungo*

YANKIE LORD (IRE) 11 b.g. Lord Americo – Coolstuff (Over The River (FR)) **c91 x** [2002/3 c93?: c24gᶠ c16g² c17sᵖᵘ c24m⁵ c24g⁵ c20gᵖᵘ c20g⁵ c20g³ c20g⁵ c20g⁶ Apr 23] rangy gelding: modest handicap chaser nowadays: effective at 2m to 3m: acts on good to firm and heavy going: often races up with pace: error prone. *Mrs J. C. McGregor*

YANN'S (FR) 7 b.g. Hellios (USA) – Listen Gyp (USA) (Advocator) [2002/3 h113: **c124** 16d⁴ c20d² c20d² c24s* c25s² Feb 23] lengthy, angular gelding: fair handicap hurdler: **h102** fairly useful novice chaser: won at Taunton in February: stays 25f: acts on heavy going: tends to swish tail: sound jumper. *R. T. Phillips*

YANUS 5 b.g. Inchinor – Birsay (Bustino) [2002/3 h98: 20m² 16g⁵ 16m⁶ Oct 6] small **h90** gelding: modest maiden hurdler: probably stays 2½m: acts on soft and good to firm going: has worn cheekpieces. *J. S. Goldie*

YARDBIRD (IRE) 4 b.g. Moonax (IRE) – Princess Lizzie (IRE) (Homo Sapien) **F93** [2002/3 F16m* F16m Apr 22] €22,000 3-y-o: medium-sized gelding: second foal: dam unraced half-sister to useful staying chaser Hoh Warrior: won bumper at Newbury on debut in March by ¾ length from The Norwich Fly: tended to hang right much of way when 10½ lengths seventh to Newmill in Land Rover Bumper at Fairyhouse next time. *Noel T. Chance*

YASPLEEZDO (IRE) 9 ch.g. Yashgan – By All Means (Pitpan) [2002/3 c–: c26m **c–** c21dᵇᵈ Jun 3] little sign of ability. *G. Brown*

YAYO (IRE) 7 b.g. Petit Loup (USA) – Cuixmala (FR) (Highest Honor (FR)) [2002/3 **c–** 16s³ 24d² 20g³ c22s c16s c20s c17s c18s Nov 28] fairly useful hurdler: no form over **h118** fences: effective at 2m to 3m: acts on soft going: usually tongue tied. *C. Roche, Ireland*

YDOWEDOIT 5 ch.g. Bollin William – Scalby Clipper (Sir Mago) [2002/3 F18m **F–** Mar 31] 3,000 4-y-o: third foal: dam lightly-raced daughter of useful hunter chaser Lady Annapurna: always behind in bumper on debut. *K. F. Clutterbuck*

YDRAVLIS 5 ch.m. Alflora (IRE) – Levantine Rose (Levanter) [2002/3 22dᵖᵘ 17sᵖᵘ **h–** Jan 28] fifth foal: sister to hurdle winner up to 2½m Fragrant Rose and half-sister to fair hunter chaser Derryrose (by Derrylin), stays 27f: dam winning hurdler, stayed 25f: no sign of ability. *D. J. S. ffrench Davis*

Y-DUG (IRE) 8 b.g. Wakashan – Jerpoint Sparkle (Roselier (FR)) [2002/3 h–, F–: **h–** 19mᵖᵘ Jun 4] seems of little account. *P. Bowen*

YELLOW SKY 5 b.m. Gildoran – Summer Sky (Skyliner) [2002/3 F16d F17m 16d **h–** Dec 26] half-sister to 4 winners, including fair sprinters by Emarati and Whittingham and **F–** modest 2m hurdler/fair 6f to 9f winner Whispering Dawn (by Then Again): dam, fair

2-y-o 5f winner, half-sister to smart 7f to 10.5f winner Lucky Scott: well beaten in bumpers and mares novice hurdle. *P. F. Nicholls*

YEOMAN'S POINT (IRE)   7 b.g. Sadler's Wells (USA) – Truly Bound (USA) (In Reality) [2002/3 h133: 20s* 25d² 21g 24g Apr 3] good-topped gelding: useful handicap hurdler: won Tote Silver Trophy at Chepstow in November by 5 lengths from Chicago Bulls: good second to Native Emperor in valuable event at Cheltenham next time: off 4 months, well held in valuable races at Cheltenham (blinkered) and Aintree last 2 starts: stays 25f: acts on soft going. *C. Roche, Ireland*   **h133**

YER 'UMBLE (IRE)   12 b.g. Lafontaine (USA) – Miners Girl (Miner's Lamp) [2002/3 24dᵖᵘ c24mᵖᵘ c24d c26g³ Apr 21] stocky gelding: winning hurdler/chaser, off 2 years before reappearance: probably retains little ability: tried blinkered/visored. *J. K. Cresswell*   **c–** **h–**

YESYES (IRE)   8 b.g. Supreme Leader – Barton Bay (IRE) (Kambalda) [2002/3 c26gᵖᵘ 19d 16s* 19sᵖᵘ Dec 26] 19,000 4-y-o: useful-looking gelding: first foal: dam unraced, out of half-sister to top-class staying chaser Barton Bank: showed little in hunter chase on debut for G. Deacon: form over hurdles only when 33/1-winner of novice at Plumpton in November: should stay beyond 2m: breathing problem final start. *Miss E. C. Lavelle*   **c–** **h96**

YEWCROFT BOY   12 ch.g. Meadowbrook – Another Joyful (Rubor) [2002/3 20g⁴ Sep 26] poor and very lightly-raced maiden hurdler: won maiden point in February. *A. Parker*   **h–**

YOB (IRE)   4 b.c. Common Grounds – First Veil (Primo Dominie) [2002/3 17dᵖᵘ Aug 2] poor maiden on Flat (stays 6f): tongue tied, showed little in juvenile on hurdling debut. *P. D. Evans*   **h–**

YOGI (IRE)   7 ch.g. Glacial Storm (USA) – Good Performance VII (Damsire Unregistered) [2002/3 20g 16s 18s 16g⁴ 16mᵖᵘ 20s 16s 16d 16v² 20s⁴ 16s* 20s⁵ 16s* 16v* 20s 16g⁵ Apr 21] leggy gelding: second foal: dam unraced half-sister to top-class chaser Very Promising: dual bumper winner: fair handicap hurdler: won at Thurles in January, Clonmel in February and Thurles (novice) and Naas in March, last 2 within 4 days: stays 2½m: acts on heavy going: below form all starts in blinkers. *Thomas Foley, Ireland*   **h114**

YORKIE MORGANS   7 b.g. Manhal – Placid Fury (Sovereign King) [2002/3 F17s 22dᵖᵘ 16dᶠ 16m Apr 22] second reported foal: dam unraced: no sign of ability: headstrong. *Mrs D. A. Hamer*   **h–** **F–**

YORK RITE (AUS)   7 ch.g. Grand Lodge (USA) – Amazaan (NZ) (Zamazaan (FR)) [2002/3 h–: 17g⁵ 20d* Nov 24] strong gelding: poor hurdler: better effort in 2002/3 when winning selling handicap at Fakenham: stays 2½m. *N. B. Mason*   **h66**

YORKSHIRE EDITION (IRE)   10 br.g. Strong Gale – Rent A Card (Raise You Ten) [2002/3 c95, h–: c25f* c25mᵖᵘ c32m⁶ Jun 30] strong, good sort: modest chaser nowadays: best effort in 2002/3 when winning handicap at Wincanton (fifth course success) in May despite idling: stays 3½m: acts on good to soft going, best efforts on firmer (acts on firm): takes good hold. *P. F. Nicholls*   **c95** **h–**

YORKSHIRE (IRE)   9 ch.g. Generous (IRE) – Ausherra (USA) (Diesis) [2002/3 20g* 17s* 16g* 19m* 19m* c20s³ 17g² 20s⁴ 16s⁶ 21s⁶ 24dᵖᵘ 16v⁶ Feb 1] workmanlike gelding: smart on Flat (stays 2¾m), sold out of P. Cole's stable 24,000 gns Doncaster March (2002) Sales: fairly useful novice hurdler: landed odds in facile style at Chepstow, Bangor, Huntingdon, Stratford and Market Rasen between May and July: well below form last 5 starts (tried to run out eleventh one): also tried to run out in novice at Market Rasen only start over fences (not fluent): should stay 3m: best form on good/good to firm going (acts on soft/heavy on Flat): blinkered final outing: free-going sort. *D. L. Williams*   **c–** **h124 §**

YOU CAN CALL ME AL   6 b.g. Almoojid – Coraletta (Buckley) [2002/3 F16s⁵ F16m Jun 29] 500 3-y-o: rather leggy gelding: first foal: dam unraced, out of useful hurdler up to 21f Coral Delight: little sign of ability in bumpers or points. *O. O'Neill*   **F–**

YOULNEVERWALKALONE (IRE)   9 b.g. Montelimar (USA) – In My Time (Levmoss) [2002/3 c137, h161: c24s* c21d³ c24v* c24g* c36dᵖᵘ Apr 5]   **c151** **h–**

     Youlneverwalkalone had acquired the reputation among layers of being something of a bookies' friend at Cheltenham but, after several unsuccessful visits to Prestbury Park over the years, he finally came good at the latest Festival. Youlneverwalkalone finished only third as 5/4 favourite for the Supreme Novices' Hurdle in 2000, failed to complete in both the Bula Hurdle and Cleeve Hurdle when well supported for both races the following season, and finished last in the Arkle Trophy in 2002. He was beaten for a fifth time at Cheltenham when sent off the 7/2 second favourite for the Tripleprint Gold Cup in December, finishing a creditable third nonetheless behind Fondmort in a race that probably wasn't run to suit him.

Youlneverwalkalone's record at home in Ireland was in marked contrast to what he had been able to show at Cheltenham. By the time of the latest Festival, he had had fifteen races in Ireland, winning nine of them and being placed in the six others. He won both his starts in Ireland in the latest season, a minor chase at Thurles nine days before the Tripleprint and, ridden for the first time by Barry Geraghty, the valuable Pierse Leopardstown Handicap Chase in January. As a novice, Youlneverwalkalone gave the impression that he barely stayed two and a half miles but his wins at Thurles and Leopardstown came over three miles. The Thurles race was against inferior opposition, being restricted to horses who had won no more than one chase. Although placed in better company, Youlnever-walkalone's only win as a novice had come in a beginners chase at Navan. The Leopardstown Handicap was an altogether stronger affair, though the presence of the high-class pair Foxchapel King and Rince Ri meant that second favourite Youlneverwalkalone and favourite Eskimo Jack were the only other members of the eleven-runner field able to run off their allotted marks. The race was delayed for an unusual reason when smoke from a fire at a construction site next to the track started blowing across the course, causing the second fence after the winning post to be omitted. Ridden more prominently than in the Tripleprint the time before, Youlneverwalkalone moved up to the leaders three out, led on the bridle at the last, and was ridden out to beat Foxchapel King (who gave him 23 lb) a length. Youlneverwalkalone saw his race out more satisfactorily than on some previous occasions.

Despite his unconvincing record at Cheltenham, Youlneverwalkalone was one of the leading contenders for the eighteen-runner William Hill National Hunt Handicap Chase, although nothing like so heavily backed as on some of his previous visits. With Geraghty again in the saddle, he started at 7/1 behind the 5/1 joint-favourites Joss Naylor, unbeaten in three novice chases, and leading Grand

Pierse Leopardstown Handicap Chase—Barry Geraghty makes a winning start on Youlneverwalkalone (No.3); Foxchapel King is upsides at the last

William Hill National Hunt Handicap Chase, Cheltenham—Youlneverwalkalone confirms himself a tougher battler than previously with a narrow win over Haut Cercy (white face)

National hope Ad Hoc, who was having his first run of the season over fences. Youlneverwalkalone broke his Cheltenham duck with a much improved effort, travelling with his customary fluency, making smooth headway to reach the heels of Haut Cercy two out and finally getting the better of that rival close home to win by three quarters of a length, showing plenty of resolution to do so. Ad Hoc put himself spot-on for the National by finishing nine lengths back in third, but now Youlneverwalkalone also entered calculations for Aintree, looking one of the better-treated entries in the light of an improved effort at Cheltenham.

Youlneverwalkalone was available at 50/1 for the Grand National when the weights came out and a best-priced 20/1 following his Cheltenham win. The subject of continued support up to the off at Aintree led to his starting the 8/1 joint-second favourite. A Ladbrokes spokesman predicted 'All the signs suggest Youlneverwalkalone will be the best-backed horse in Grand National history', presumably an attempt at generating a self-fulfilling prophecy, with the name striking a chord, in particular, with many football fans on Merseyside. There was no denying Youlneverwalkalone's status as a popular choice for the National on the day, despite the fact that, with conditions threatening to be on the firm side at Aintree, Youlneverwalkalone's participation had hung in the balance in the build-up to the race. On the only outing of his career on ground firmer than good he had tended to hang and most of his wins had come in the mud. The *Racing Post*'s headline on April 1st— 'Youlneverwalkalone unlikely to run, Roche warns public'—was no April Fool, though it might just as well have been: with connections satisfied that conditions were suitable, Youlneverwalkalone's participation in the National was confirmed four days later. In hindsight, it must have been a decision connections regretted. Youlneverwalkalone broke down going to the twelfth fence, though it was only after jumping it that his rider was able to pull him up. His injury, a broken off-fore cannon bone, needed nine weeks' treatment at the University of Liverpool and his racing future must be in doubt, the fracture reportedly requiring ten screws.

Youlneverwalkalone (IRE) (b.g. 1994)	Montelimar (USA) (b 1981)	Alleged (b 1974)	Hoist The Flag
			Princess Pout
		L'Extravagante (br 1973)	Le Fabuleux
			Fanfreluche
	In My Time (b 1974)	Levmoss (b 1965)	Le Levanstell
			Feemoss
		Time To Leave (b 1967)	Khalkis
			Dawn Chorus

It was only in the latest season that Youlneverwalkalone finally matured into the horse both his physique and pedigree promised. A tall, good sort, he had always looked a chaser in the making though, until the latest Festival, his form over fences had always been overshadowed by his earlier high-class hurdling form.

Youlneverwalkalone's breeding suggested he'd stay at least three miles, though that too was something which was proved only rather belatedly. Youlneverwalkalone's pedigree has been covered in previous Annuals though, stressing the stamina elements, suffice to say here that his dam had already produced a Cheltenham Festival winner in the dual Stayers' Hurdle winner Galmoy, while Youlneverwalkalone shares his sire, Montelimar, with the Grand National winner Monty's Pass. Another respect in which Youlneverwalkalone developed in the latest season was that his tendency to finish tamely on occasions was replaced by a more resolute attitude. That factor was as instrumental as any in gaining him that elusive win at Cheltenham. *C. Roche, Ireland*

YOU NEVER LEARN 9 b.g. Aydimour – Briglen (Swing Easy (USA)) [2002/3 c–, h–: c16d^{pu} Apr 29] sturdy gelding: lightly raced and little worthwhile form. *Mrs L. Wadham* **c–**
h–

YOUNG AMERICAN (IRE) 7 br.g. Hamas (IRE) – Banana Peel (Green Dancer (USA)) [2002/3 h115: 20d^2 20s^8 22s* 25v^{pu} 22d^{pu} 24d^6 20g^{pu} Mar 23] useful-looking gelding: fairly useful hurdler: won handicap at Haydock in November by length from Roveretto: well below form subsequently, reportedly lame final start: stays 3m, at least when conditions aren't testing: acts on good to firm and heavy going: tried blinkered: races prominently. *Jonjo O'Neill* **h117**

YOUNG BOUNDER (FR) 4 b. or br.g. Septieme Ciel (USA) – Far But Near (USA) (Far North (CAN)) [2002/3 F16d Mar 1] unfurnished gelding: sixth foal: half-brother to French 3-y-o 6.5f (at 2 yrs) to 1m winner Bon Eleve (by Mujtahid) and fair hurdler/fairly useful chaser up to 25f Corniche (by Marju), latter also fairly useful up to 2m on Flat: dam, 2-y-o 6f winner on only start, out of Coronation Stakes winner Kesar Queen: failed to settle when last of 13 in bumper on debut. *N. A. Twiston-Davies* **F–**

YOUNG BUCK (IRE) 9 ch.g. Glacial Storm (USA) – Lady Buck (Pollerton) [2002/3 c–, h119: c21g^4 20d^5 19m^2 17g^3 16s^2 21m^4 19g^6 Nov 7] medium-sized gelding: no form in 3 starts over fences: fair hurdler: stays 2¾m: acts on soft and good to firm going: often blinkered/visored: usually tongue tied. *Ferdy Murphy* **c–**
h106

YOUNG BUTT 10 ch.g. Bold Owl – Cymbal (Ribero) [2002/3 21s^{pu} 16s^6 17g 16m^5 Mar 31] sparely-made gelding: poor maiden hurdler: raced mainly around 2m: acts on good to soft going: tried blinkered. *L. A. Dace* **h65**

YOUNG CHEVALIER 6 b.g. Alflora (IRE) – Mrs Teasdale (Idiot's Delight) [2002/3 h60, F–: c20d^F 20s 24g Jan 17] rangy, unfurnished gelding: little sign of ability: headstrong. *J. R. Adam* **c–**
h–

YOUNG CLAUDE 6 b.g. Le Moss – Deirdres Dream (The Parson) [2002/3 20d 23s^3 25g^3 25d^{pu} Feb 8] tall, unfurnished gelding: chasing type: second foal: half-brother to very smart staying chaser Young Kenny (by Ardross): dam lightly-raced half-sister to useful chaser Aughavogue: poor form over hurdles: likely to need 3m+. *P. Beaumont* **h81**

YOUNG DALESMAN 10 br.g. Teenoso (USA) – Fabulous Molly (Whitstead) [2002/3 h114: 24d^{pu} 24g^4 Sep 28] workmanlike gelding: fair handicap hurdler: stays 3m: acts on good to firm and heavy going: joined Mrs J. Candlish. *A. Streeter* **h107**

YOUNG DANCER (IRE) 5 b.g. Eurobus – Misquested (Lord Ha Ha) [2002/3 F16s Feb 14] good-topped gelding: seventh foal: half-brother to fair staying hurdler Fort Deely (by Seamanship) and fair hurdler Take A Drop (by Farhaan), stays 21f: dam unraced, from family of very smart 2m hurdler Mwanadike: not knocked about unduly when seventh of 15 in bumper at Sandown on debut. *V. R. A. Dartnall* **F91**

YOUNG DEVEREAUX (IRE) 10 b. or br.g. Lord Americo – Miss Iverk (Torus) [2002/3 c128, h–: c16v* c16g* c19s^{pu} Feb 15] **c154**
h–

Another lengthy lay-off, or perhaps even retirement, beckoned for the injury-plagued Young Devereaux when he was pulled up after two out, looking ill at ease, in the Ascot Chase in February. Although reported to be sound the next day and still a possible for the Champion Chase the week before Cheltenham, the fact that Young Devereaux missed the remainder of the season doesn't augur well for his prospects of adding significantly to the number of appearances he has made in a career spanning six seasons. Young Devereaux had run in a couple of bumpers in Ireland before being bought by present connections for 26,000 guineas at the Doncaster May Sales in 1998, and he has contested just nine races since. That he

cantorindex.co.uk Handicap Chase, Ascot—
Young Devereaux survives a mistake at the last to hold off Seebald

has won five of them and also developed into a smart chaser, despite being so difficult to train, reflects great credit on those involved with him.

Young Devereaux's leg troubles surfaced early on in his career, and he was fired after easily landing the odds in a maiden hurdle at Chepstow on his second start for Paul Nicholls. A faller on his chasing debut the following season, Young Devereaux then created a good impression when winning novice chases at Uttoxeter and Folkestone, but further problems kept him off the course for all of the 2000/1 season, and restricted him to just one outing in 2001/2, when second to Cyfor Malta in a quite valuable handicap at Newbury. So Young Devereaux was still very short of experience when he returned after twelve months off to contest the seven-runner cantorindex.co.uk Handicap at Ascot in December. According to his trainer Paul Nicholls, Young Devereaux had only been schooled once in between the two races, and that had been on the previous morning! Young Devereaux's lack of practice showed and he did well to survive a bad mistake at the first and made further errors four out and at the final fence. Yet he still managed to travel strongly for a long way and he came again after the last of those errors had handed the advantage to Seebald, going on to win by a length. There was a sad postscript to the race, the eleven-year-old Get Real, a high-class chaser at his best, having to

Tote Exacta Chase (Limited Handicap), Kempton—
Ascot placings are confirmed despite a 10 lb turnaround in the weights

be put down after suffering injuries as a result of a fall two out. Remarkably, the number of races that Get Real ran in at Ascot alone is two more than Young Devereaux's total number of appearances to date. Young Devereaux and Seebald were in opposition again a month later, the pair among nine entries for the Tote Exacta Chase, a Grade 2 limited handicap instituted as a replacement for Ascot's Victor Chandler Chase which was a victim of the weather. In a repeat of Ascot, Young Devereaux and Seebald, the latter 10 lb better off, finished first and second separated by a length. They had the race to themselves after Fondmort took a crashing fall three out, a close third but under pressure at the time. Young Devereaux, 5 lb out of the handicap, was still on the bridle when taking the lead off Seebald at the tenth, and he would have won more convincingly but for being none too fluent at the last two fences.

Young Devereaux (IRE) (b. or br.g. 1993)	Lord Americo (b 1984)	Lord Gayle (b 1965)	Sir Gaylord / Sticky Case
		Hynictus (b 1968)	Val de Loir / Hypavia
	Miss Iverk (b 1986)	Torus (b 1976)	Ribero / Lighted Lamp
		Marsha's Daughter (b 1979)	Merrymount / Marsha

Young Devereaux is a half-brother to Oscar Performance (by Roselier), a winner over hurdles and placed over fences for Bob Buckler in the current season. Their dam Miss Iverk was placed in a bumper in Ireland but the next two mares on the bottom line of the pedigree were both unraced. The grandam Marsha's Daughter is a sister to the very smart staying chaser Ivan King. Young Devereaux, a rangy, good-looking gelding, is effective at two miles to two and a half miles. He has raced only on good going or softer and acts on heavy. *P. F. Nicholls*

Paul K. Barber, Mick Coburn, Colin Lewis 2's "Young Devereaux"

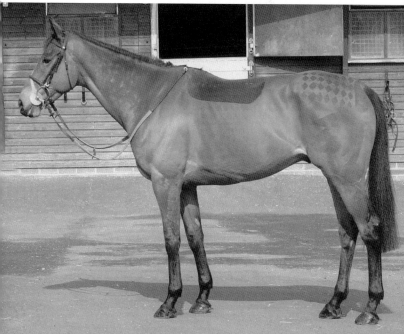

YOUNG JOKER (IRE) 7 b.g. Jolly Jake (NZ) – Ara View (Rontino) [2002/3 c123, h68: 19m³ c17gᵖᵘ Nov 30] close-coupled gelding: twice-raced over hurdles, modest form when third in novice at Hereford on reappearance: much improved chaser in late-2001/2: let down by jumping in handicap at Newbury (reportedly lame) in November: stays 19f: acts on soft and good to firm going: races prominently. *N. A. Twiston-Davies* **c–** **h87 +**

YOUNG LIRRUP 5 ch.g. Lir – Blue-Bird Express (Pony Express) [2002/3 F–: F17s⁶ F17s Jan 28] compact gelding: poor form in bumpers: has hinted at temperament (tried to run out on debut). *W. S. Kittow* **F68**

YOUNG OTTOMAN (IRE) 7 b.g. Mandalus – Lone Run (Kemal (FR)) [2002/3 h120: c22d³ c25d⁴ c24g² c26v* c32g³ Mar 12] well-made, lengthy gelding: fairly useful hurdler: fairly useful novice chaser: won at Plumpton in February: good third to Sudden Shock in National Hunt Chase at Cheltenham final start: stayed 4m: raced only on good going or softer (acted on heavy): dead. *V. R. A. Dartnall* **c123** **h–**

YOUNG OWEN 5 b.g. Balnibarbi – Polly Potter (Pollerton) [2002/3 F–: 16s⁵ 17sᵖᵘ 16dᵖᵘ Mar 7] rather leggy gelding: signs of a little ability in 2 bumpers: poor form on hurdling debut (not knocked about), disappointing both subsequent starts. *R. A. Fahey* **h71**

YOUNG SPARTACUS 10 b.g. Teenoso (USA) – Celtic Slave (Celtic Cone) [2002/3 c132, h–: c20g* Mar 12] **c154** **h–**

'He should be odds on,' Martin Pipe stated of his Thomas Pink Gold Cup favourite Chicuelo. 'A million to one,' was how a spokesperson from Henry Daly's stable reportedly summed up the chances of their runner Young Spartacus in the Mildmay of Flete. Inside information isn't always what it's cracked up to be. As he has had more National Hunt winners than any other trainer in history, Pipe needs no defending, and, as a pupil of the late Tim Forster, a touch of pessimism is not too surprising in Henry Daly. The Ludlow trainer, whose first Festival success was registered by Relaxation in the 2000 National Hunt Chase, went close on the first day of the 2003 Festival when Haut Cercy lost out in a battle up the hill with Youlneverwalkalone in the National Hunt Handicap. 'I know you are meant to be gracious in defeat—but damn,' said Daly. After that reverse, a refusal to talk up Young Spartacus's chance on the day was understandable. The trainer later reported that the prime reason for his running was that there were no alternative engagements for a horse with his BHB mark.

The most obvious reason for passing over Young Spartacus in the Mildmay of Flete was that he had not raced for four hundred and twenty-four days. Successful on three of his four completed starts in 2000/1, including the Racing Post Chase, Young Spartacus was below form on all three outings during 2001/2 and ended that campaign in February with a leg injury. In January of the latest season it was reported that Young Spartacus had completed his first piece of serious work without

Mildmay of Flete Challenge Cup Handicap Chase, Cheltenham—Young Spartacus (centre) makes light of a fourteen-month absence to beat the Henderson-trained duo Fondmort and Scots Grey (grey)

repercussions and that it would take six to eight weeks to get him back to full fitness. The Mildmay of Flete was just under nine weeks away. The bookmakers' assessment of Young Spartacus's chance on the day was not quite so bleak as that of the stable, but he was as long as 33/1 with the major firms on the morning of the race, before eventually going off at 16/1. Presumably not because of stable money. Backed down to favouritism in a nineteen-runner field was J. P. McManus's 2000 Tripleprint Gold Cup winner Go Roger Go. Young Spartacus also had a previous course-and-distance win to his name, from January 2001, but victory in the Mildmay of Flete surpassed that and all his other previous achievements. Go Roger Go unseated his rider at the fourth and Goguenard unseated his spectacularly at the second last—when about two lengths up, travelling strongly but pecking on landing—after which it was Young Spartacus, ridden by Richard Johnson, who emerged in front. He took a narrow advantage and stayed on well to register a four-length success over the 2002 Tripleprint winner Fondmort. Johnson picked up a five-day ban from the stewards for marking the horse with his whip. Daly went on to take the following day's Grand Annual Chase with Palarshan.

		Teenoso (USA) (b 1980)	Youth (b 1973)	Ack Ack
Young Spartacus (b.g. 1993)				Gazala
			Furioso (b 1971)	Ballymoss
				Violetta III
		Celtic Slave (ch 1977)	Celtic Cone (ch 1967)	Celtic Ash
				Fircone
			Branded Slave (b 1970)	Arctic Slave
				Brand X

In addition to Young Spartacus, three other offspring of the broodmare Celtic Slave ran during the latest season: the fair novice hurdler Alpine Slave (by

Mr B. G. Hellyer's "Young Spartacus"

Alflora) won a race for Josh Gifford in March and youngster Rakalakey (by Rakaposhi King) showed promise in two bumpers for Daly, while the modest mare Cream Gorse (by Alflora) struggled to complete in novice chases. Young Spartacus, his dam and grandam were all bred by his owner's father, Young Spartacus's dam Celtic Slave being a fair hurdler and usefully useful chaser who stayed well. Young Spartacus does not have quite the same stamina resources, for while he won the Racing Post Chase over three miles at Kempton and was a creditable fourth over a furlong further in the Punchestown Gold Cup seven weeks after the latest Mildmay of Flete, his performance at Punchestown reinforced the impression that three miles is the limit of his stamina as he travelled well to four out but tired after the second last, eventually finishing nineteen lengths behind the winner First Gold. A strong gelding, Young Spartacus has form close to his best on heavy going, but his very best efforts have been on good. He jumps to his right but that has not prevented his recording two of his most important victories at left-handed Cheltenham. *H. D. Daly*

YOUNG STEVEN   12 b.g. Singing Steven – Adoration (FR) (Dancer's Image (USA)) [2002/3 c–, h–: c25d³ c24g⁵ Feb 12] leggy gelding: winning chaser: little form after 2000/1: stayed 27f: acted on any going: tried blinkered/visored: dead. *Mrs J. M. Hollands*   **c67**
h–

YOUNG TERN   5 b.g. Young Ern – Turnaway (Runnett) [2002/3 17vᵖᵘ Mar 10] modest on Flat (seems to stay 1¼m): no show in seller on hurdling debut. *B. J. Llewellyn*   **h–**

YOUNG THRUSTER (IRE)   10 b.g. Over The River (FR) – Bit of Fashion (Master Owen) [2002/3 c101, h–: c25d³ c26s⁶ c24dᵘʳ c26d² Nov 26] lengthy, good sort: fair handicap chaser: stays 3¾m: acts on heavy and good to firm going: races prominently. *N. A. Twiston-Davies*   **c101**
h–

YOUNG TOMO (IRE)   11 b.g. Lafontaine (USA) – Siege Queen (Tarqogan) [2002/3 c96, h–: c27gᵖᵘ c25m³ c27g⁴ Oct 15] sturdy gelding: modest handicap chaser in 2001/2: well below form in 2002/3: blinkered: front runner: sold 6,000 gns Doncaster November Sales, fifth in point in February. *J. Howard Johnson*   **c–**
h–

Modern City Living Handicap Chase, Ascot—
Tony McCoy and You're Agoodun win the race for the second year running

YOUNG WHACK (IRE)   9 br.g. Phardante (FR) – Flash Parade (Boreen (FR))   **c116**
[2002/3 c116, h–: c22m* 20m³ c23s c17dᵖᵘ c20m* Apr 12] good sort: winning hurdler: **h111**
fairly useful chaser: won novice at Downpatrick in May and handicap at Listowel in
September: effective at 2m to 3m: acts on soft and firm going: has had tongue tied: sold
to join J. H. Johnson 26,000 gns Doncaster May Sales. *N. Meade, Ireland*

YOUNG WILL   4 b.g. Keen – Barkston Singer (Runnett) [2002/3 F12d Nov 13] third   **F—**
foal: dam, 1m winner at 2 yrs, became temperamental: well held in bumper on debut. *Mrs*
Lucinda Featherstone

YOUNICO   8 b.g. Nordico (USA) – Young Wilkie (Callernish) [2002/3 c74§, h–§:   **c– §**
c21fᵖᵘ May 10] winning pointer: poor maiden chaser: tried blinkered: not one to trust.   **h– §**
Paul O. J. Hosgood

YOUPEEVEECEE (IRE)   7 b.g. Little Bighorn – Godlike (Godswalk (USA))   **h87**
[2002/3 F90: 24vᵖᵘ 19d⁴ 19s³ 21m⁶ 20mᵘʳ Apr 12] modest novice hurdler: stays 19f: acts
on soft going: has looked difficult ride. *Mrs J. Candlish*

YOUR A GASSMAN (IRE)   5 b.g. King's Ride – Nish Bar (Callernish) [2002/3   **F100**
F16d³ Apr 25] sixth foal: half-brother to Irish bumper winner Brenny's Pearl (by Good
Thyne): dam unraced sister to very smart chaser at 2½m+ Addington Boy: favourite,
encouraging third to Flight Command in bumper at Perth on debut. *Ferdy Murphy*

YOU'RE A DIAMOND   5 ch.m. Superlative – Diamond Tip (Homing) [2002/3   **F—**
F16dᵖᵘ F16gᵖᵘ Sep 15] fifth foal: dam maiden: stayed 1m: pulled up in 2 bumpers.
T. P. Walshe

YOU'RE AGOODUN   11 ch.g. Derrylin – Jennie Pat (Rymer) [2002/3 c141x, h–:   **c144 x**
c24d* c24sᵖᵘ c28d² c26g c36dᵘʳ Apr 5] medium-sized gelding: useful handicap chaser: **h—**
won at Ascot in November for second year running: excellent ¾-length second to
Shotgun Willy in valuable event at Haydock in March: stays 3½m: acts on heavy and
good to firm going: visored/blinkered: often let down by jumping (unseated nineteenth in
Grand National final start). *M. C. Pipe*

YOU'RE SPECIAL (USA)   6 b.g. Northern Flagship (USA) – Pillow Mint (USA)   **c101**
(Stage Door Johnny) [2002/3 h110: c20d² Mar 15] workmanlike gelding: fair hurdler: **h—**
similar form when second to Diceman in novice at Newcastle on chasing debut: barely
stays 3m: acts on soft and good to firm going: has tongue tied: consistent. *P. C. Haslam*

YOUR MY ANGEL (IRE)   7 b.m. Commanche Run – Marshtown Fair (IRE) (Cam-   **h67**
den Town) [2002/3 17m⁴ Apr 26] IR 3,000 4-y-o: first foal: dam, lightly raced in points,
from family of useful Irish 2½m chaser The Lady's Master: won mares maiden Irish point
in 2001: bought 8,000 gns Doncaster November (2001) Sales: shaped as if retaining
ability when remote fourth of 7 finishers in conditional jockeys novice at Sedgefield on
hurdling debut, not given unduly hard time. *Ferdy Murphy*

YOURS SO COOL   6 ch.g. Karinga Bay – Laurel Diver (Celtic Cone) [2002/3 F–: 20v³   **h101**
Feb 11] sturdy gelding: well held in bumper on debut in 2001/2: blinkered, fair form when
third to Palua in maiden at Folkestone on hurdling debut. *M. C. Pipe*

YOUR TURN ROSIE   8 b.m. Relief Pitcher – Bremhill Rosie (Celtic Cone) [2002/3   **h—**
F–: 19g May 4] no sign of ability in mares bumper or novice hurdle. *I. R. Brown*

YVANOVITCH (FR)   5 b.g. Kaldounevees (FR) – County Kerry (FR) (Comrade In   **h92 +**
Arms) [2002/3 16g 16g⁵ 16g⁵ 16d Mar 1] big, strong ex-French gelding: chasing type:
half-brother to fair hurdler/smart chaser around 2m Turgeonev (by Turgeon): well held in
2 races on Flat at 3 yrs, sold out of J. Barbe's stable 8,000 gns Doncaster May (2001)
Sales: signs of ability in 4 races over hurdles at Newbury: best efforts when fifth: showed
up long way in handicap final start: likely to prove best at bare 2m. *Mrs L. C. Taylor*

Z

ZAAJER (USA)   7 ch.g. Silver Hawk (USA) – Crown Quest (USA) (Chief's Crown   **h—**
(USA)) [2002/3 h86: 17d⁶ Dec 3] sturdy gelding: modest form at best over hurdles: ran as
though something amiss in seller only run in 2002/3: should stay beyond 2m. *J. A. B. Old*

ZABADI (IRE)   11 b.g. Shahrastani (USA) – Zerzaya (Beldale Flutter (USA)) [2002/3   **c—**
c108, h–: c20g⁶ 16g⁵ c20g⁶ c20s⁴ c18s⁶ c16s⁵ Mar 7] rangy gelding: handicap chaser: **h—**
out of form in 2002/3: tried blinkered: often a weak finisher. *Miss Venetia Williams*

ZABRISKIE POINT 4 b.f. Overbury (IRE) – Brownhill Lass (Sunyboy) [2002/3 **F–**
F16v F16g Feb 12] third foal: dam modest chaser, stayed 3m: well held in 2 mares
bumpers. *Mrs J. C. McGregor*

ZACOPANI (IRE) 11 b.g. Lafontaine (USA) – Take A Dare (Pragmatic) [2002/3 c–, **c–**
h88: c24g c25g^{pu} c25g^{ur} Mar 29] lengthy gelding: winning hurdler/chaser: largely out of **h–**
form since 2000/1: blinkered/visored. *R. Ford*

ZAFARABAD (IRE) 9 gr.g. Shernazar – Zarafa (Blushing Groom (FR)) [2002/3 **c138 §**
c134, h125: c24f* c24v³ c24m c24g⁴ Apr 25] sturdy gelding: winning hurdler: useful **h–**
handicap chaser: won valuable event at Kempton in October by 1½ lengths from Audacter: well held all 3 subsequent starts: stays 3m: acts on firm and soft going: usually
blinkered: races mostly right-handed: usually races up with pace: not one to trust.
P. J. Hobbs

ZAFARELLI 9 gr.g. Nishapour (FR) – Voltigeuse (USA) (Filiberto (USA)) [2002/3 **c–**
c–, h78: 24m^{pu} 21s Jul 20] tall, leggy gelding: poor handicap hurdler: no show in 2002/3: **h–**
stays 27f: acts on good to firm and heavy going: effective blinkered/visored or not: has
looked none too keen. *J. R. Jenkins*

ZAFFAMORE (IRE) 7 ch.g. Zaffaran (USA) – Furmore (Furry Glen) [2002/3 h91: **c123**
c20d⁴ c24s⁵ c20d* c20d c24m^{pu} c24m² Apr 2] strong gelding: twice-raced hurdler: fairly **h–**
useful novice chaser: won at Ludlow in November and January: below form last 3 starts:
should stay 3m: acts on good to soft going. *Miss H. C. Knight*

ZAFFARAN IN EDEN (IRE) 6 ch.m. Zaffaran (USA) – Edenapa (Peacock (FR)) **h91**
[2002/3 22d² 17g⁴ F20v Aug 7] eighth foal: half-sister to winning pointer by Homo **F–**
Sapien: dam unraced: won twice in Irish points in 2002: much better effort over hurdles
when second in maiden at Downpatrick in June: ninth of 16 in mares bumper at Sligo
final start. *C. S. McKeever, Ireland*

ZAFFARANNI (IRE) 7 ch.m. Zaffaran (USA) – Nimbi (Orchestra) [2002/3 h96: **c103**
c24d⁴ c25s⁴ c20d* c25s^{pu} c21s^{ur} c25m^{pu} Apr 21] big, good sort: winning hurdler: fair **h–**
novice chaser: won handicap at Newbury in November and mares event at Huntingdon
(unimpressive) in December: generally let down by jumping otherwise: should stay
beyond 3m: acts on soft going, held when pulled up lame on good to firm final start.
D. J. Caro

ZAFFARAN WINDS (IRE) 8 b.m. Zaffaran (USA) – Sharpwinds (Tumble Wind **c65**
(USA)) [2002/3 c–, h–: c20g² May 17] workmanlike mare: winning pointer: poor maiden **h–**
steeplechaser: often tongue tied. *Mrs Marilyn Scudamore*

ZAFFRE D'OR (IRE) 6 b.g. Zaffaran (USA) – Massinetta (Bold Lad (IRE)) [2002/3 **F–**
F16d Mar 1] 20,000 4-y-o: has scope: brother to fair hurdler Zaffre Noir, stays 3m, and to
winner in USA: dam modest maiden on Flat: better for race, well-beaten seventh of 13 in
bumper at Newbury on debut, leading and disputing until 4f out. *M. Pitman*

ZAFFRE NOIR (IRE) 7 b.g. Zaffaran (USA) – Massinetta (Bold Lad (IRE)) [2002/3 **h–**
h112: 20d^{pu} May 4] tall, lengthy gelding: fair hurdler: well below form in handicap in
May, not seen out again: probably stays 3m: acts on any going: races prominently.
M. Pitman

ZAGGY LANE 11 b.g. Prince of Peace – Meldon Lady (Ballymoss) [2002/3 c106, **c115 d**
h–: c24d² c26s² c29s⁴ c30s⁴ c27d² c28v⁵ c25d⁴ c24s⁴ c24m³ Apr 22] workmanlike **h–**
gelding: handicap chaser: fairly useful form when second at Uttoxeter on reappearance,
below that level subsequently: best at 3m+: acts on good to firm and heavy going:
blinkered once. *S. C. Burrough*

ZAHAALIE (USA) 11 ch.g. Zilzal (USA) – Bambee T T (USA) (Better Bee) [2002/3 **c–**
21g⁴ Mar 14] small gelding: poor hurdler: off 2 years, signs of retaining ability when **h–**
fourth in claimer at Warwick on return: effective at 2m to 3m: acts on good to firm and
heavy going: blinkered once. *J. A. Pickering*

ZAIDAAN 7 b.g. Ezzoud (IRE) – River Maiden (USA) (Riverman (USA)) [2002/3 h–: **h84**
16m* 16m 16g³ 20g³ Oct 9] poor hurdler: well backed, returned from lengthy absence to
win selling handicap at Worcester in June: reportedly lame next time (final outing for
G. McCourt): probably best around 2m, though beaten too far out to blame lack of
stamina over further final start: acts on good to firm going. *D. J. Wintle*

ZALEEM (IRE) 6 b.g. Kahyasi – Zallaka (IRE) (Shardari) [2002/3 F87: 16d^{pu} Apr **h–**
9] fair form at best in bumpers in 2001/2: showed nothing in novice hurdle on belated
reappearance: tried visored. *Mrs J. Candlish*

ZAMAT   7 b.g. Slip Anchor – Khandjar (Kris) [2002/3 h80: 16g* 18s* 16v* 17d 16s⁵   **h113**
16d* 20s⁵ 18g⁶ Mar 21] lengthy gelding: fair hurdler: much improved in 2002/3, winning
novice handicap in May and conditional jockeys handicap and novice in November, all at
Kelso, and handicap at Ayr in February: raced mainly around 2m: acts on heavy going.
P. Monteith

ZAMHAREER (USA)   12 b.g. Lear Fan (USA) – Awenita (Rarity) [2002/3 c73, h–:   **c–**
c30d⁵ Jun 8] smallish gelding: veteran chaser: stiff task on reappearance: in frame several   **h–**
times in points subsequently: stays 29f: acts on good to firm and heavy going: tried
visored: has had tongue tied. *R. Ford*

ZAMIR   4 ch.g. Zamindar (USA) – Fairy Flax (IRE) (Dancing Brave (USA)) [2002/3   **h–**
16d Nov 30] little form on Flat: showed nothing on hurdling debut. *A. Crook*

ZAMORIN   4 b.g. Zafonic (USA) – Armeria (USA) (Northern Dancer) [2002/3 16m   **h–**
16s Dec 27] angular gelding: modest on Flat (stays 1½m), sold out of R. Charlton's stable
5,000 gns Doncaster August Sales and gelded, successful in November: well held in 2
juvenile hurdles: sold £2,600 Ascot April Sales. *P. S. McEntee*

ZANTANA BOY (IRE)   5 ch.g. Zaffaran (USA) – Ardtana (IRE) (Cidrax (FR))   **F–**
[2002/3 F16s Feb 14] 19,000 4-y-o: leggy gelding: third foal: dam unraced: tailed off in
bumper on debut. *D. J. Caro*

ZAPATA HIGHWAY   6 ch.g. Bold Arrangement – Trailing Rose (Undulate (USA))   **h–**
[2002/3 F–: 16m 16gᵖᵘ 16d Nov 29] good-topped gelding: no sign of ability.
D. R. C. Elsworth

ZARBARI (IRE)   4 b.g. Kahyasi – Zarlana (IRE) (Darshaan) [2002/3 F17g Apr 21]   **F–**
first foal: dam, 1m winner, half-sister to smart 7f/1m filly Zarannda, from family of one-
time smart 2m hurdler Zabadi: tongue tied, well beaten in bumper on debut. *D. McCain*

ZARZA BAY (IRE)   4 b.g. Hamas (IRE) – Frill (Henbit (USA)) [2002/3 16d Dec 14]   **h73**
half-brother to fair hurdler Sudest (by Taufan), stays 3m: modest but temperamental on
Flat (stays 1¾m): none too fluent when seventh of 14 in juvenile at Fakenham on hurdling
debut. *K. R. Burke*

ZAYTA (FR)   8 b.m. Zayyani – La Toscanella (FR) (Riverton (FR)) [2002/3 c129x,   **c– x**
h110: 24d c17vᵖᵘ Dec 1] leggy mare: fairly useful hurdler: mid-field in handicap at   **h117**
Gowran (tongue tied) in October: fairly useful chaser, ran poorly final start: should stay
beyond 2½m: acts on soft going. *Mrs J. Harrington, Ireland*

ZELENSKY (IRE)   4 b.g. Danehill Dancer (IRE) – Malt Leaf (IRE) (Nearly A Nose   **h–**
(USA)) [2002/3 16vᵖᵘ Jan 17] disappointing maiden on Flat: pulled up after failing to
settle in juvenile claimer on hurdling debut. *Jean-Rene Auvray*

ZELOSO   5 b.g. Alzao (USA) – Silk Petal (Petorius) [2002/3 17s⁴ 17g⁴ 16m 16dᵖᵘ   **h92 §**
16gᵖᵘ 16g⁴ 19m* 19g³ 20m⁵ 19m 21mᵖᵘ Apr 10] half-brother to winning hurdler/chaser
Head Gardener (by Be My Chief), stays 3¾m: one-time fairly useful on Flat (stays 1¼m),
no form in 2002: modest hurdler: won conditional jockeys handicap at Hereford in
September: stays 19f: acts on soft and good to firm going: blinkered/visored after
hurdling debut: moody last 2 starts and not one to trust. *M. F. Harris*

ZETAGALOPON   5 b.m. Petong – Azola (IRE) (Alzao (USA)) [2002/3 h–: 17dᵖᵘ 16d   **h–**
Dec 26] no show over hurdles: tried blinkered (reluctant to race)/in cheekpieces: sold
£700 Ascot February Sales. *C. L. Popham*

ZIGGY'S WAY   8 b.g. Teenoso (USA) – Onaway (Commanche Run) [2002/3 h84:   **c–**
c24sᵖᵘ Feb 26] sturdy, lengthy gelding: poor maiden hurdler: no show on chasing debut.   **h–**
Mrs A. Barclay

ZILARATOR (USA)   7 b.g. Zilzal (USA) – Allegedly (USA) (Sir Ivor) [2002/3   **h107 §**
h112p: 20s² 16v⁴ 16s² 21s⁵ 22gʳᵗʳ Apr 19] good-topped gelding: fair maiden hurdler:
increasingly let down by jumping and temperament in 2002/3: stays 2½m: acts on soft
going: not to be trusted. *P. J. Hobbs*

ZOFFANY (IRE)   6 b.g. Synefos (USA) – Shining Green (Green Shoon) [2002/3   **h101**
16d* 16d Jan 13] fifth known foal: half-brother to Irish 17f winner Wadablast (by Milk of
The Barley): dam unraced half-sister to top-class hurdler Mighty Mogul: won novice
hurdle at Haydock on debut, held when left clear last by fall of Always Rainbows:
disappointing in similar event at Doncaster next time. *M. Todhunter*

ZOLTANO (GER)   5 b.g. In The Wings – Zarella (GER) (Anatas) [2002/3 16d⁴ 16s²   **h110**
16vᶠ 16v² Jan 14] workmanlike gelding: dam won on Flat/over hurdles (17f) in Germany:
won twice around 1¼m on Flat, including at Hoppegarten in March: left P. Rau in May:

shaped well when fourth in well-contested novice at Wetherby on hurdling debut: well below that form when runner-up (promoted on second occasion) in 2 maidens at Ayr subsequently, leading when falling 2 out in another novice at Wetherby in between. *M. Todhunter*

ZSARABAK 6 br.g. Soviet Lad (USA) – Moorefield Girl (IRE) (Gorytus (USA)) [2002/3 h102: 17g* 16g⁴ 16d c20g³ Jun 12] close-coupled gelding: fair handicap hurdler: won on return from 8-month absence at Bangor in May: poor form when third in novice at Market Rasen on chasing debut (reportedly distressed): barely stays 2½m: best efforts on good/good to firm going: effective visored or not: tried tongue tied: joined P. Niven. *Jonjo O'Neill*   **c77** **h106**

ZURS (IRE) 10 b.g. Tirol – Needy (High Top) [2002/3 h109: 17m³ c16gᶠ 17m² 20d⁶ 18d² 16s⁴ 16d⁴ 16gᵖᵘ Apr 19] leggy gelding: fell fifth on chasing debut: fair hurdler: several creditable efforts in 2002/3, though ran poorly final start (first outing after leaving J. O'Neill): best around 2m: acts on good to firm going, probably on soft. *H. J. Collingridge*   **c–** **h107**

ZYGOMATIC 5 ch.g. Risk Me (FR) – Give Me A Day (Lucky Wednesday) [2002/3 F17m³ F16g³ F17d 16sᵖᵘ 17s 16d 16d 20d Mar 15] sturdy gelding: seventh foal: brother to 3 winners, including modest Colin's Choice, stayed 11.7f, and half-brother to another: dam little form: fair form when third in bumpers first 2 starts: little worthwhile form over hurdles. *R. F. Fisher*   **h62** **F85**

ZYGO (USA) 11 b.g. Diesis – La Papagena (Habitat) [2002/3 16g Dec 18] disappointing maiden on Flat (barely stays 1¼m): no form in 2 starts over hurdles nearly 5 years apart. *M. Pitman*   **h–**

ERRATA & ADDENDA

'Chasers & Hurdlers 2000/01'

Idiome (FR)   dam unplaced on Flat and over jumps, not unraced

'Chasers & Hurdlers 2001/02'

Classified (IRE)   P210 line 19: third dam was not unraced
Court Dreaming   did not race in 2001/2
Seebald (GER)   P827 line 3: placed three times, not ran three times

PROMISING HORSES

Selected British-trained horses in *Chasers & Hurdlers* thought capable of noteworthy improvement are listed under the trainers for whom they last ran.

R. ALLAN
Sun Bird (IRE) 5 ch.g h101p

R. H. ALNER
Cracking Dawn (IRE) 8 b.g h— c125p
Gotham (IRE) 6 gr.g h101p
Millcroft Seaspray (IRE) 7 br.g h116 c115p
No Visibility (IRE) 8 b.g h— c130p
Sir Rembrandt (IRE) 7 b.g h— c138p

MRS S. ALNER
Kingscliff (IRE) 6 b.g c137P

K. C. BAILEY
First Flight 7 br.g h— c—p
Longshanks 6 b.g h97 c93p
Top Buck (IRE) 9 b.g h— c119p

C. C. BEALBY
Silken Thyne 7 b.g h123p

P. BEAUMONT
Flight Command 5 ch.g F103p
Jodante (IRE) 6 ch.g h83p F83

S. A. BROOKSHAW
Valleymore (IRE) 7 br.g h117p F74

NOEL T. CHANCE
Beyond The Pale (IRE) 5 b.g h114p F103
Chief Witness (IRE) 7 b.g h116p
Murphy's Cardinal (IRE) 7 b.g h128p F97
Sea Ferry (IRE) 7 b.g h105 c—p
Supreme Attraction (IRE) 6 b.m h81p

H. D. DALY
Clever Thyne (IRE) 6 b.g h98 c—p
Coursing Run (IRE) 7 ch.g h— c109p
Hand Inn Hand 7 b.g h— c141p
Jivaros (IRE) 5 b.g h— c104p
Maconnor (IRE) 6 b.g h106p
Majority Verdict 7 b.g h100p
Make Haste Slowly 6 b.g h102p
Palarshan (FR) 5 b.g h— c140p

M. W. EASTERBY
Gastornis 5 ch.g h113p F97
Sporting Gesture 6 ch.g h82p

C. R. EGERTON
Cock of The North (IRE) 6 b.g h98p
Dragon Hunter (IRE) 8 b.g h— c—p

D. R. C. ELSWORTH
Pawn Broker 6 ch.g h88p

FRANCIS ENNIS, IRELAND
Askthejudge (IRE) 4 b.g h111p

P. D. EVANS
Diamond Max (IRE) 5 b.g h94p

R. A. FAHEY
Beseiged (USA) 6 ch.g h105p F96

J. D. FROST
Fire Ranger 7 ch.m h—p F82
Grey Brother 5 gr.g h111p F90

D. R. GANDOLFO
Red Socialite (IRE) 6 ch.g h107p

T. R. GEORGE
Toulouse-Lautrec (IRE) 7 ch.g h— c112p
What A Man (IRE) 6 b.g h99p F94

T. K. GERAGHTY, IRELAND
What Odds (IRE) 7 b.g c112p

C. GRANT
Beckley (IRE) 7 b.g h104p

B. DE HAAN
Crimson Pirate (IRE) 6 b.g h103p

A. M. HALES
Hello Stranger (IRE) 7 gr.g h92p
Tosheroon (IRE) 7 b.g h104p

N. J. HENDERSON
Bareme (FR) 4 b.g h119p
Daprika (FR) 5 b.m h102 c91p
Irish Hussar (IRE) 7 b.g h— c152p
King Player (IRE) 6 b.g F101p
Oyster Shell (IRE) 6 b.g h72p
Placid Man (IRE) 9 br.g h— c113p

P. J. HOBBS
Amplifi (IRE) 6 b.g h100p
Moscow Whisper (IRE) 6 b.g h105p F85
Mr Fluffy 6 br.g h113p
One Knight (IRE) 7 ch.g h— c150p
Unleash (USA) 4 ch.g h126p

J. R. JENKINS
Amir Zaman 5 b.g h104p

J. HOWARD JOHNSON
Chevet Girl (IRE) 8 ch.m h106 c97p
Covent Garden 5 b.g h128p
Lord Transcend (IRE) 6 gr.g h148p

S. KIRK
Halland Park Lad (IRE) 4 ch.g h96p

MISS H. C. KNIGHT
Alvino 6 b.g h112p
Caribbean Cove (IRE) 5 gr.g h99p F73
Chase The Sunset (IRE) 5 ch.g h83p F—
Chelsea Bridge (IRE) 5 b.g F105p

MISS E. C. LAVELLE
Gig Harbor 4 b.c h—p
Immola (FR) 7 b.g h106p F76

N. P. LITTMODEN
Trouble Next Door (IRE) 5 b.g h— c94p

L. LUNGO
Ashleybank House (IRE) 6 b.g h85p F89
Brooklyn Breeze (IRE) 6 b.g h127p F99
Captain's Leap (IRE) 7 ch.g h80p
Cook O'Hawick (IRE) 6 b.g h65p F69
Kidithou (FR) 5 b.g h98p F95
Laouen (FR) 5 br.g h124p F109

Monolith 5 b.g h71p
Mr Woodentop (IRE) 7 b.g h120 c104p
Only Once 8 b.g c117p
Silvertown 8 b.g h125p
Yankee Jamie (IRE) 9 b.g h101+ c114p

C. J. MANN
Showpiece 5 b.g h107p

H. MORRISON
Kylkenny 8 b.g h89p

FERDY MURPHY
Kagram (IRE) 8 ch.g h—p
Wemyss Quest 8 b.g h— c89p

P. F. NICHOLLS
Azertyuiop (FR) 6 b.g h— c159p
Dusky Light 5 b.m h81p F77
Joly Bey (FR) 6 ch.g h100p c137
Le Roi Miguel (FR) 5 b.g h— c156p
Onwardsandupwards (IRE) 4 b.g F89p
Sporazene (IRE) 4 gr.g h136p
Strong Flow (IRE) 6 br.g h125p
Were In Touch (IRE) 5 b.g F98p

JONJO O'NEILL
Ballylusky (IRE) 6 b.g h119 c96p
Blood Sub (IRE) 6 b.g h106P F95
Cambrian Dawn 9 b.g h— c115p
Campaign Trail (IRE) 5 b.g h127p
East Tycoon (IRE) 4 ch.g h121p
Feel The Pride (IRE) 5 b.m h96p
Fern Lord (IRE) 6 ch.h h115p
Hasty Prince 5 ch.g h125p
Hey Ref (IRE) 6 b.g h114p F101
Keen Leader (IRE) 7 b.g h— c151p
Longterm (IRE) 6 b.g h110p F112
Multeen River (IRE) 7 b.g h118p
Over Anxious (IRE) 7 ch.g h118p
Rhinestone Cowboy (IRE) 7 b.g h156p F123
Saratov (GER) 4 b.g h112p
Top of The Left 8 b.g h98p
Very Optimistic (IRE) 5 b.g F102p

A. PARKER
Em's Royalty 6 b.g h100p
For Your Ears Only (IRE) 7 b.g h—p F91

R. T. PHILLIPS
Supreme Toss (IRE) 7 b.g h131p

S. PIKE
Wild Dream 8 b.m h93p

D. PIPE
Lord Atterbury (IRE) 7 ch.g c126p

M. C. PIPE
Fortune Island (IRE) 4 b.g h111p
Gone Far (USA) 6 b.g h120p
Isard III (FR) 7 gr.g h127p c—p
Jurancon II (FR) 6 b.g h125 c118p
Maragun (GER) 7 b.g h119 c—p
Our Vic (IRE) 5 b.g h140p
Penny Pictures (IRE) 4 b.c h115p
Rakaposhi Lass 7 b.m h97p F116+
The Biker (IRE) 6 br.g h123p

B. G. POWELL
Colonel Frank 6 b.g h113p F90
Glanamana (IRE) 7 b.g h— c99p

MRS M. REVELEY
Bewleys Hotels (IRE) 7 ch.g h96p c88p
Diamond Sal 5 b.m F100p
Florida Rain (IRE) 7 b.g h111p
Icy River (IRE) 6 ch.g h73p F80

N. G. RICHARDS
Bob The Piler 7 b.g h78p
Broken Knights (IRE) 6 ch.g h117p F107
Byron Lamb 6 b.g h— c126p
Monet's Garden (IRE) 5 gr.g F98p
Paperprophet 5 b.g h114p F91
Steppes of Gold (IRE) 6 b.g F104p
Telemoss (IRE) 9 b.g h— c125p

K. A. RYAN
Gralmano (IRE) 8 b.g h135 c126p

S. E. H. SHERWOOD
Ballybrophy (IRE) 8 gr.g h— c111p

J. S. SMITH
Glen Warrior 7 b.g h98p

T. P. TATE
Hot Weld 4 b.g F99p
Temple Dog (IRE) 7 ch.g h122p

MRS A. M. THORPE
Madam Mosso 7 b.m h97 c97p

N. A. TWISTON-DAVIES
Lord Maizey (IRE) 6 b.g c108p F100

N. WAGGOTT
Fred's In The Know 8 ch.g h113 c112p

M. J. WALLACE
Waterlily (IRE) 4 b.f F92p

MRS S. D. WILLIAMS
Master Billyboy (IRE) 5 b.g h109p

MISS VENETIA WILLIAMS
Alpha Noble (GER) 6 b.g h90p
Effectual 10 b.g h124 c105p
Grand Finale (IRE) 6 b.h h91p

P. WINKWORTH
Instant Appeal 6 gr.g h101p F—

P. YORK
Jackie Jarvis (IRE) 6 b.m c103p

998

SELECTED BIG RACES 2002/03

Prize money for racing abroad has been converted to £ sterling at the exchange rate current at the time of the race. The figures are correct to the nearest £.

1 **Swinton Hcap Hdle (Gr 3) (A) (148) (4yo+) £31,900**   2m (8)

INTERSKY FALCON *JonjoO'Neill* 5-11-10[148] (b) LCooper 11/2   1
GRALMANO (IRE) *KARyan* 7-10-0[124] GLee .... 6/1   ½ 2
WHISTLING DIXIE (IRE) *MrsMReveley* 6-10-5[129] ADempsey 12/1   3 3
Tikram *GLMoore* 5-9-10[125] MFoley[5] .... 10/1   ¾ 4
Monkerhostin (FR) *OSherwood* 5-10-0[129] RFlavin[5] 10/1   1¾ 5
Tucacas (FR) *MCPipe* 5-10-11[135] APMcCoy 3/1f   8 6
Happicat (IRE) *PRWebber* 7-9-7[124] MrATinkler[7] 33/1   4 7
Milligan (IRE) *MissVenetiaWilliams* 7-11-4[142] ADobbin 5/1   16 8
Fait Le Jojo (FR) *PJHobbs* 5-10-10[134] RJohnson 7/1   5 9
Belle d'Anjou (FR) *MCPipe* 5-10-6[130] TScudamore 14/1   6 10
The French Furze (IRE) *NGRichards* 8-11-0[143] PRobson[5] 33/1   6 11

Interskyracing.com & Mrs Jonjo O'Neill 11ran 3m32.40

2 **Britannia Building Society English Summer National**   4m110y (24)
       (Hcap Chase) (B) 0-140(133) (5yo+) £32,500

STORMEZ (FR) *MCPipe* 5-11-8[133] (t) APMcCoy 11/2   1
GENERAL CLAREMONT (IRE) *PFNicholls* 9-10-9[114] RWalsh .... 9/2f   nk 2
ARDENT SCOUT *MrsSJSmith* 10-10-6[111] SDurack 20/1   1½ 3
Ashgar (USA) *PJHobbs* 6-10-9[114] (b) PFlynn 12/1   21 4
Mister One *CTizzard* 11-12-0[133] RJohnson 9/1   22 5
Yorkshire Edition (IRE) *PFNicholls* 9-9-11[105] RPMcNally[3] 25/1   8 6
Dear Deal *CTizzard* 9-10-10[115] (b) AThornton .... 16/1   dist 7
No More Hassle (IRE) *JAkehurst* 9-10-10[115] ARoss 16/1   4 8
Emperor Scras (IRE) *NGRichards* 7-11-3[122] (t) BHarding .... 6/1   f
Dancetillyoudrop (IRE) *PFNicholls* 11-10-8[120] MrChristianWilliams[7] ..... 10/1   ur
Cherokee Boy *BJMRyall* 10-10-6[111] RGreene .... 33/1   pu
Lisdante (IRE) *MrsSJSmith* 9-10-6[111] WMarston .... 13/2   pu
Suspendid (IRE) *CREgerton* 9-10-4[109] JAMcCarthy .... 12/1   pu
Water Font (IRE) *JonjoO'Neill* 10-10-0[105] (b) LCooper .... 25/1   pu

Mr D. A. Johnson 14ran 8m08.28

3 **Summer Hdle (Hcap) (B) 0-140(134) (4yo+) £23,200**   2m1f110y (8)

PUNTAL (FR) *MCPipe* 6-11-10[134] APMcCoy 6/1   1
LOOP THE LOUP *MrsMReveley* 6-10-6[121] (b) PAspell[5] 14/1   4 2
COTOPAXI (IRE) *MissVenetiaWilliams* 6-10-2[112] BJCrowley.................. 14/1   4 3
1 WHISTLING DIXIE (IRE) *MrsMReveley* 6-11-7[131] ADempsey 11/1   3 4
Spectrometer *PJHobbs* 5-10-8[118] RJohnson .... 6/1   nk 5
Romero *MissECLavelle* 6-10-0[110] (v) TJMurphy 25/1   3½ 6
Inducement *RMStronge* 6-10-2[112] BFenton .... 25/1   hd 7
Patriot Games (IRE) *CFSwan,Ireland* 8-11-1[125] CFSwan 4/1f   1 8
Borani *SGollings* 7-10-1[111] TScudamore 33/1   7 9
Rigmarole *PFNicholls* 4-10-6[118] (t) BJGeraghty 14/1   3½ 10
Court of Appeal *BEllison* 5-10-0[110] RWakley 40/1   20 11
Taming (IRE) *MissVenetiaWilliams* 6-10-9[119] MAFitzgerald.................. 10/1   1¼ 12
Magic Combination (IRE) *LLungo* 9-10-8[118] ADobbin .... 7/1   ½ 13
1 Gralmano (IRE) *KARyan* 7-11-5[129] GLee .... 7/1   pu
Jaboune (FR) *AKing* 5-11-2[126] (t) WMarston .... 10/1   pu
Let's Fly (FR) *MrsMReveley* 7-10-0[110] SDurack .... 16/1   pu

Mr Terry Neill 16ran 4m09.71

4 **Summer Plate (Hcap) (Chase) (B) 0-140(136) (5yo+) £37,700**   2½m (15)

CHICUELO (FR) *MCPipe* 6-10-4[116] (v) APMcCoy 15/8f   1
STAR JACK (FR) *JGFitzGerald* 7-10-0[117] (t) PRobson[5] 20/1   5 2
LOGICIAN (NZ) *IABalding* 11-11-10[136] MBradburne 14/1   2½ 3
Phar From A Fiddle (IRE) *PFNicholls* 6-10-7[119] BJGeraghty 6/1   3 4
Joint Account *RTate* 12-10-13[130] MrsFNeedham[5] 20/1   9 5
Ei Ei *MCChapman* 7-10-8[120] WMWorthington 33/1   6 6
Billy Nomaite *MrsSJSmith* 8-10-1[113] WMarston .... 16/1   ur
Demasta (NZ) *NJHenderson* 11-11-9[135] MAFitzgerald .... 8/1   pu
Korakor (FR) *IanWilliams* 8-11-9[135] ADobbin .... 20/1   pu

Lord York (IRE) *MTodhunter* 10-11-4[130] (v+t) SDurack .... 40/1   pu
Bleu Superbe (FR) *MissVenetiaWilliams* 7-11-2[128] BJCrowley .... 6/1   pu
Monitor *GMLyons,Ireland* 8-10-10[122] (t) CO'Dwyer.................................... 10/1   pu
Donadino (IRE) *CFSwan,Ireland* 9-10-6[118] DJCasey .... 12/1   pu
The Negotiator *MABarnes* 8-10-4[116] CMcCormack...................................... 50/1   pu
Saragann (IRE) *PJHobbs* 7-10-3[115] RJohnson .... 9/1   pu

Mrs Belinda Harvey 15ran 4m57.84

GALWAY Wednesday, Jul 31   GOOD to SOFT

5   **Galway Plate (Gr B Hcap Chase) (135) (4yo+) £58,022**   2¾m (14)

ROCKHOLM BOY (IRE) *MichaelHourigan* 9-10-5[117] KHadnett[5]............. 20/1   1
WOTSITOOYA (IRE) *MJPO'Brien* 10-10-1[113] DJHoward[5] 14/1   3½ 2
RIDGEWOOD WATER (IRE) *NMeade* 10-9-10[103] PMoloney 25/1   3 3
RISK ACCESSOR (IRE) *CRoche* 7-11-5[126] (t) RWalsh .... 15/2   ½ 4
Prince of Pleasure (IRE) *DBroad* 8-10-6[113] BMCash .... 12/1   ½ 5
Monty's Pass (IRE) *JamesJosephMangan* 9-11-10[131] BJGeraghty.............. 16/1   6
Keeponthesunnyside (IRE) *TimothyDoyle* 10-9-9[105] JJMansell[3] 14/1   7
Torduff Boy (IRE) *PaulNolan* 9-11-2[123] MAFitzgerald 9/1   8
Fier Goumier (FR) *ALTMoore* 7-10-1[108] DJCasey 16/1   9
Royal Jake (IRE) *NMeade* 8-11-2[123] PCarberry 7/1f   10
Hill Society (IRE) *NMeade* 10-11-7[128] (b) JLCullen 33/1   11
Ghadames (FR) *WMBrisbourne,GB* 8-10-6[113] TPTreacy 20/1   12
Nuzum Road Makers (IRE) *MichaelCunningham* 11-10-5[112] (b) JRBarry ... 20/1   13
Danaeve (IRE) *GKeane* 7-10-12[119] KPGaule 16/1   14
Super Franky (IRE) *CByrnes* 9-11-11[135] PPO'Brien[3] 25/1   15
Vanilla Man (IRE) *PatrickMullins* 9-10-9[116] SDurack .... 14/1   f
Bregogue (IRE) *PO'Keeffe* 8-10-6[113] MrDNRussell.................................. 20/1   f
Colm's Rock (IRE) *MissFMCrowley* 11-10-8[120] SGMcDermott[5]................. 33/1   ur
Temony (IRE) *AnthonyMullins* 7-10-3[113] RGeraghty[3] .... 12/1   ur
4 Monitor *GMLyons* 8-10-12[119] (t) CO'Dwyer .... 25/1   pu
Rash Decision (IRE) *AnthonyMullins* 7-10-2[109] KAKelly .... 33/1   pu
Brilliant Star (NZ) *SABrookshaw,GB* 10-9-11[107] MPMadden[3] .... 33/1   pu

M. G. H. Syndicate 22ran 5m39.50

GALWAY Thursday, Aug 1   GOOD to SOFT

6   **Guinness Galway Hdle (Hcap) (Gr B) (147) (4yo+) £57,706**   2m (9)

SAY AGAIN (IRE) *PaulNolan* 6-10-7[126] JLCullen 16/1   1
MUTAKARRIM *DKWeld* 5-10-3[122] (b) BJGeraghty 12/1   2 2
JUST OUR JOB (IRE) *DTHughes* 7-12-0[147] KAKelly .... 25/1   sh 3
TOUCH OF LOVE *EJO'Grady* 6-9-11[116] JECasey.................................... 12/1   2½ 4
Bob What (IRE) *PatrickMullins* 8-9-12[124] (t) RMPower[7] 20/1   2 5
Timber King (IRE) *CRoche* 6-11-8[141] PMoloney 11/1   6
Moratorium (USA) *NMeade* 7-10-8[127] PCarberry 9/1   7
Galway Breeze (IRE) *ALTMoore* 7-9-11[116] DJCasey 16/1   8
Sharpaten (IRE) *PHughes* 7-10-9[133] GTHutchinson[5] 25/1   9
Garvivonnian (IRE) *EdwardPMitchell* 7-9-8[118] LAHurley[5] 33/1   10
Take Flite *AnthonyMullins* 5-9-10[118] RGeraghty[3] 25/1   11
Czar of Peace (IRE) *WPMullins* 4-9-11[117] JRBarry 33/1   12
Patsy Veale (IRE) *JQueally* 7-10-10[129] RWalsh 10/1   13
Flint Knapper *PatrickOBrady* 8-10-1[127] RCColgan[7] 25/1   14
Balapour (IRE) *PatrickOBrady* 4-10-6[129] JPElliott[3] 12/1   15
Sum Leader (IRE) *GKeane* 6-10-12[131] MAFitzgerald 9/1   16
Anxious Moments (IRE) *CFSwan* 7-10-10[129] CFSwan 11/2f   17
Aleemdar (IRE) *MJPO'Brien* 5-9-11[121] DJHoward[5].............................. 20/1   18
Experimental (IRE) *PJRothwell* 8-10-3[125] (b) NMulholland[3] 16/1   19
Pillar Rock (USA) *NMeade* 6-9-10[115] KPGaule.................................... 33/1   20
Clever Consul (IRE) *AJMartin* 7-9-7[112] PFlynn 20/1   21
Emperors Guest *PatrickMullins* 4-10-2[122] ADobbin 25/1   22
Well Fella (USA) *CMcCarthy* 4-9-9[120] SACurtis[5] 33/1   23
John James (IRE) *JHScott* 6-9-7[112] PACunningham 50/1   24

Mr Sean Duggan 24ran 3m56.10

LISTOWEL Wednesday, Sep 25   FIRM

7   **Guinness Kerry National Hcap Chase (Gr A) (135) (4yo+) £53,386**   3m (15)

5 MONTY'S PASS (IRE) *JamesJosephMangan* 9-11-9[130] BJGeraghty............. 9/1   1
PUTSOMETNBY (IRE) *KFO'Brien* 6-9-10[103] GCotter............................ 20/1   2 2
NATIVE PERFORMANCE (IRE) *MichaelHourigan* 7-9-6[104]
   GTHutchinson[5] .... 10/1   nk 3
SPARKLING GOLD (IRE) *JEKiely* 8-10-4[116] PJCrowley[5]..................... 16/1   4 4
Glacial Sygnet (IRE) *JamesJosephMangan* 9-9-7[100] (b+t) JRBarry.............. 14/1   ½ 5
2 General Claremont (IRE) *PFNicholls,GB* 9-11-2[123] RWalsh 8/1   6

Fnan *NMeade* 6-10-10[117] PCarberry 5/1f   7
5   Wotsitooya (IRE) *MJPO'Brien* 10-10-6[118] DJHoward[5] 7/1   8
  Chevalier Errant (IRE) *JRAdam,GB* 9-11-2[126] MIFoley[3] 16/1   9
  Eoins Pride (IRE) *EBolger* 7-9-0[100] (t) SCurling[7] 25/1   10
  Gladiateur IV (FR) *PJHobbs,GB* 8-12-0[135] NWilliamson .... 14/1   f
5   Colm's Rock (IRE) *MissFMCrowley* 11-10-6[118] SGMcDermott[5] .... 33/1   f
5   Temony (IRE) *AnthonyMullins* 7-10-3[113] RGeraghty[3] .... 14/1   f
  Ballinarrid (IRE) *PaulARoche* 9-9-2[100] LAHurley[5] .... 20/1   f
5   Rockholm Boy (IRE) *MichaelHourigan* 9-11-9[130] JCulloty .... 12/1   bd
5   Torduff Boy (IRE) *PaulNolan* 9-11-2[123] MAFitzgerald .... 7/1   ur
  Tuska Ridge (IRE) *JJLambe* 9-9-2[100] MDGrant[5] .... 66/1   ur
  Andretti Castle (IRE) *MichaelJMcDonagh* 7-9-10[103] (b) PMoloney .... 14/1   pu

Dee Racing Syndicate 18ran 5m44.70

TIPPERARY Sunday, Oct 6   GOOD to FIRM

8   **John James McManus Memorial Hdle (Gr 2) (4yo+)** £32,704   2m (9)

1   INTERSKY FALCON *JonjoO'Neill,GB* 5-11-12 (b) LCooper 3/1   1
6   BOB WHAT (IRE) *PatrickMullins* 8-11-5 (t) RWalsh 14/1   1½ 2
  IN CONTRAST (IRE) *PJHobbs,GB* 6-11-12 PCarberry 7/4f   10 3
  Rostropovich (IRE) *MFMorris* 5-11-12 DJCasey 20/1   4 4
  Scottish Memories (IRE) *NMeade* 6-11-12 PCarberry 4/1   2 5
3   Patriot Games (IRE) *CFSwan* 8-11-5 CFSwan 16/1   6
6   Just Our Job (IRE) *DTHughes* 7-11-5 KAKelly .... 7/1   bd
  Ballyhampshire Boy (IRE) *SeanAherne* 6-11-9 BJGeraghty .... 8/1   su
6   Timber King (IRE) *CRoche* 6-11-12 PMoloney .... 9/1   pu

Intersky Racing/Mrs JJ O'Neill 9ran 3m45.20

LIMERICK Sunday, Oct 13   GOOD

9   **Munster National Hcap Chase (Gr C) (137) (4yo+)** £24,375   3m (16)

  MORE THAN A STROLL (IRE) *ALTMoore* 10-10-0[133] (t) CO'Dwyer 6/1   1
  ARCTIC COPPER (IRE) *NMeade* 8-10-1[134] (b) PCarberry 5/2   1 2
7   MONTY'S PASS (IRE) *JamesJosephMangan* 9-10-4[137] BJGeraghty 7/4f   2½ 3
7   Rockholm Boy (IRE) *MichaelHourigan* 9-9-9[133] GTHutchinson[5] 7/2   2 4
7   Ballinarrid (IRE) *PaulARoche* 9-10-0[133] DJCasey 25/1   20 5
5   Prince of Pleasure (IRE) *DBroad* 8-9-7[133] RCColgan[7] .... 10/1   f

Mrs D. Grehan 6ran 6m03.20

KEMPTON Saturday, Oct 26   GOOD to SOFT

10   **Platinum Security Hdle (B) (4yo+)** £8,151   2m (8)

  ROOSTER BOOSTER *PJHobbs* 8-11-8 NWilliamson 15/8   1
  MR COOL *MCPipe* 8-11-8 APMcCoy 4/6f   7 2
  MANDOOB *BRJohnson* 5-11-0 (t) GSupple .... 50/1   dist 3
  Ben Ewar *KOCunningham-Brown* 8-11-8 BFenton .... 14/1   dist 4
  Look Sharp (FR) *TWall* 5-11-0 RGreene .... 33/1   pu

Mr Terry Warner 5ran 3m52.16

WINCANTON Sunday, Oct 27   GOOD to FIRM

11   **Desert Orchid Chase (Ltd Hcap) (Gr 2) (A) (154) (5yo+)** £23,200   2m5f (17)

  VALLEY HENRY (IRE) *PFNicholls* 7-11-7[151] MAFitzgerald 4/5f   1
  UPGRADE *MCPipe* 8-11-10[154] APMcCoy 7/2   7 2
  CELIBATE (IRE) *CJMann* 11-10-4[134] NFehily 11/1   6 3
  Peccadillo (IRE) *RHAlner* 8-10-4[134] AThornton 6/1   19 4
  Wave Rock *PJHobbs* 7-10-6[136] (b) PFlynn 7/1   2 5
  Good Lord Murphy (IRE) *DrPPritchard* 10-9-13[134] DrPPritchard[5] .... 100/1   f

Mr Paul K. Barber 6ran 5m00.89

WETHERBY Saturday, Nov 2   GOOD to SOFT

12   **Peterhouse Group Charlie Hall Chase (Gr 2) (A) (5yo+)** £29,000   3m1f (18)

  MARLBOROUGH (IRE) *NJHenderson* 10-11-0 MAFitzgerald 7/2   1
  HUSSARD COLLONGES (FR) *PBeaumont* 7-11-5 RGarritty 9/1   2 2
  GINGEMBRE (FR) *MrsLCTaylor* 8-11-0 AThornton .... 14/1   nk 3
  Grey Abbey (IRE) *FPMurtagh* 8-11-4 (t) BHarding 11/1   8 4
  Whitenzo (FR) *PFNicholls* 6-11-0 RThornton 14/1   16 5
  What's Up Boys (IRE) *PJHobbs* 8-11-6 (b) PFlynn .... 5/2f   f
  Lord Noelie (IRE) *MissHCKnight* 9-11-0 JCulloty .... 3/1   ur
  Moscow Express (IRE) *MissFMCrowley,Ireland* 10-11-10 JRBarry .... 14/1   pu

Sir Robert Ogden 8ran 6m22.70

13   **John Smith's West Yorkshire Hdle (Gr 2) (A) (4yo+)** £17,400   3m1f (12)

  BROTHER JOE (NZ) *PJHobbs* 8-11-0 JCulloty 5/1   1
  BOSS DOYLE (IRE) *MFMorris,Ireland* 10-11-8 (b) DJCasey 5/2f   15 2

SPENDID (IRE) *AKing* 10-11-8 WMarston 8/1   6 3
Frosty Canyon *PRWebber* 9-11-0 RGarritty 11/1 1¼ 4
Ad Hoc (IRE) *PFNicholls* 8-11-0 MAFitzgerald... 9/2   ½ 5
Stromness (USA) *AKing* 5-11-4 RThornton 7/2   9 6
Bindaree (IRE) *NATwiston-Davies* 8-11-0 CLlewellyn 12/1 21 7

Sir Robert Ogden 7ran 6m10.37

NAVAN Sunday, Nov 3   SOFT

14   **Philips Electronics Lismullen Hdle (Gr 2) (4yo+) £20,440**   2½m (11)

    LIMESTONE LAD (IRE) *JBowe* 10-11-13 PCarberry 4/5f   1
    LISS A PAORAIGH (IRE) *JEKiely* 7-11-8 BJGeraghty............................... 11/4   2 2
    KADOUN (IRE) *MJPO'Brien* 5-11-7 (b) CFSwan.................................... 10/1 25 3
    Sacundai (IRE) *EJO'Grady* 5-11-7 NWilliamson 11/2   7 4
    Hat Or Halo (IRE) *NiallJDonohoe* 10-11-4 PMoloney .... 14/1 dist 5
    Catch Ball *WPMullins* 6-10-13 SCurling 16/1   6
  6 Balapour (IRE) *PatrickOBrady* 4-10-13 (t) JPElliott .... 14/1   ur

Mr James Bowe 7ran 4m50.90

AUTEUIL Sunday, Nov 3   HEAVY

15   **Grand Prix d'Automne (Hdle) (Gr 1) (5yo+) £69,340**   3m (16)

    LAVERON *FDoumen,France* 7-10-8 TDoumen 6/10   1
    TIGER GROOM *RCollet,France* 5-10-3 CPieux 1 2
    EL FUEGO (FR) *BBarbier,France* 10-10-8 CGombeau 10 3
    Vic Toto (FR) *MlleFForneron,France* 5-10-3 LDeLaRosa....................................   8 4
    Turnium (FR) *AChaille-Chaille,France* 7-10-8 PSourzac......................   5 5
    Killerine (FR) *J-PDelaporte,France* 7-10-8 JMarion............................   2 6
    Rougenoir (FR) *RELecomte,France* 9-10-8 (b) FBenech............................   6 7
    San Sebastian *MRolland,France* 8-10-8 (b) PChevalier........................   2 8

Dirk G. Grauert 8ran 6m45.00

EXETER Tuesday, Nov 5   GOOD

16   **William Hill Haldon Gold Cup Chase (Limited Hcap) (Gr 2) (A)**   2m1f110y (12)
    (165) (5yo+) £24,360

    EDREDON BLEU (FR) *MissHCKnight* 10-11-10[165] (t) JCulloty 10/1   1
    SEEBALD (GER) *MCPipe* 7-10-13[154] APMcCoy............................... 1/1f 10 2
    ARMATURK (FR) *PFNicholls* 5-10-12[153] RWalsh 5/2 21 3
    Castle Prince (IRE) *RJHodges* 8-10-4[145] RGreene............................ 100/1   2 4
    Latalomne (USA) *BEllison* 8-10-12[153] MAFitzgerald 7/2 19 5
    Ichi Beau (IRE) *FerdyMurphy* 8-10-4[145] (t) TJMurphy 33/1 27 6

Mr Jim Lewis 6ran 4m10.72

CHEPSTOW Saturday, Nov 9   SOFT

17   **Tote Exacta Rising Stars Nov Chase (Gr 2) (A) (4yo+) £17,980**   2m3f110y (16)

    ONE KNIGHT (IRE) *PJHobbs* 6-11-4 PFlynn 11/4   1
    LE ROI MIGUEL (FR) *PFNicholls* 4-10-5 APMcCoy 8/11f   5 2
    HAND INN HAND *HDDaly* 6-11-4 WMarston.................................. 6/1   4 3
    Gentle Rivage (FR) *NATwiston-Davies* 8-11-4 CLlewellyn.......................... 12/1 28 4
    Kittenkat *NRMitchell* 8-10-13 SCurran.................................... 50/1 18 5
    Twotensforafive *PRRodford* 9-11-4 SBurrough............................. 100/1 dist 6
    Monte Cristo (FR) *MrsLCTaylor* 4-10-5 NFehily .... 25/1   ur

Mr R. Gibbs 7ran 5m02.20

WINCANTON Saturday, Nov 9   GOOD

18   **Elite Hdle (Ltd Hcap) (Gr 2) (A) (137) (4yo+) £20,300**   2m (8)

    SANTENAY (FR) *PFNicholls* 4-11-7[134] TJMurphy 15/8f   1
    CASTLESHANE (IRE) *SGollings* 5-10-9[122] JCulloty .... 6/1   ½ 2
    QUAZAR (IRE) *JonjoO'Neill* 4-11-10[137] (t) ADobbin 10/3 1¼ 3
  1 Tikram *GLMoore* 5-10-3[123] MrJEMoore[7].. 4/1   7 4
    Running Man (FR) *PRWebber* 8-10-11[124] TDoyle .... 5/1 sh 5
    Pietro Bembo (IRE) *MissECLavelle* 8-10-12[125] AThornton........................ 16/1 dist 6

The Hon Mrs Townshend 6ran 3m39.75

DOWN ROYAL Saturday, Nov 9   SOFT

19   **Killultagh Properties Ltd Chase (Gr 3) (5yo+) £20,701**   2¼m (12)

    MOSCOW FLYER (IRE) *MrsJHarrington* 8-12-0 BJGeraghty 4/11f   1
    KADARANN (IRE) *PFNicholls,GB* 5-11-6 RWalsh............................... 5/2 20 2
    FIERY RING (IRE) *JRHFowler* 7-11-2 RGeraghty... 8/1 dist 3

Mr Brian Kearney 3ran 4m45.90

20   **James Nicholson Championship Chase (Gr 1) (5yo+) £53,503**   3m (15)

  9 MORE THAN A STROLL (IRE) *ALTMoore* 10-11-10 (t) CO'Dwyer......... 20/1   1

SEE MORE BUSINESS (IRE) *PFNicholls,GB* 12-11-10 (b) RWalsh 2/1f 5 2
GIVE OVER (IRE) *EUHales* 9-11-10 MrDNRussell 8/1 9 3
Florida Pearl (IRE) *WPMullins* 10-11-10 BJGeraghty 9/4 15 4
Cregg House (IRE) *PatrickMullins* 7-11-10 PCarberry.............................. 25/1 dist 5
9 Rockholm Boy (IRE) *MichaelHourigan* 9-11-10 KHadnett .... 25/1 ur
Foxchapel King (IRE) *MFMorris* 9-11-10 DJCasey .... 11/4 pu

Mrs D. Grehan 7ran 6m29.10

AUTEUIL Sunday, Nov 10   HEAVY

21   Prix La Haye Jousselin (Chase) (Gr 1) (5yo+) £78,821   3m3f110y (22)
SUNNY FLIGHT (FR) *AChaille-Chaille,France* 8-10-8 PSourzac 6/1 1
CERILLY (FR) *JBertrandeBalanda,France* 5-10-4 LMetais.................................. 5 2
INNOX (FR) *FDoumen,France* 6-10-8 TDoumen 8 3
Batman Senora (FR) *PRago,France* 6-10-8 CGombeau 10 4
Fustrien du Paon (FR) *AChaille-Chaille,France* 6-10-8 GRiviere 3 5
Champion Veronais (FR) *FDanloux,France* 12-10-8 SBeaumard .... dist 6
El Paso III (FR) *BSecly,France* 10-10-8 CPieux .... pu

Mr P. Boiteau 7ran 7m29.00

22   Grande Course de Haies Des 4 Ans (Gr 1) (4yo) £60,191   2½m110y (12)
KARLY FLIGHT (FR) *AChaille-Chaille,France* 4-10-1 PSourzac............. 11/10 1
FOREMAN (GER) *FDoumen,France* 4-10-5 TDoumen 5 2
KOTKITA (FR) *BSecly,France* 4-10-1 CPieux 1½ 3
Saint Des Saints (FR) *GMacaire,France* 4-10-5 BGicquel.............................. 4 4
Abyce (FR) *J-PGallorini,France* 4-10-5 TMajorcryk.................................... 15 5
Ticket To Ride (FR) *TTrapenard,France* 4-10-5 BChameraud.......................... 3 6
Dorado (FR) *YPorzier,France* 4-10-5 BDelo 10 7

Mr P. Boiteau 7ran 5m18.00

CHELTENHAM Saturday, Nov 16   GOOD to SOFT (Old Course)

23   Tote Bookmakers Hcap Hdle (L) (A) (155) (4yo+) £31,175   3m1f110y (13)
NATIVE EMPEROR *JonjoO'Neill* 6-10-4[133] LCooper 13/2 1
YEOMAN'S POINT (IRE) *CRoche,Ireland* 6-10-3[132] CFSwan................. 10/3f 1¼ 2
IT TAKES TIME (IRE) *MCPipe* 8-11-12[155] APMcCoy .... 4/1 ½ 3
Springfield Scally *SGollings* 9-10-6[135] GLee 14/1 8 4
Guard Duty *MCPipe* 5-9-7[129] (t) MrJEMoore[7] .... 33/1 nk 5
Roveretto *MrsMReveley* 7-9-10[130] PAspell[5] 14/1 15 6
Surprising *PJHobbs* 7-9-7[136] (b) MAFitzgerald .... 4/1 ¾ 7
Tales of Bounty (IRE) *PFNicholls* 7-9-7[129] NCarter[7] 20/1 1½ 8
Do It On Dani *MrsAMThorpe* 7-9-9[129] WHutchinson[5] 33/1 3 9
Carlovent (FR) *MCPipe* 7-11-2[145] TScudamore 33/1 3½ 10
13 Spendid (IRE) *AKing* 10-11-8[151] RThornton 10/1 15 11

R. & E. H. Investments Ltd 11ran 6m24.20

24   Intervet Trophy Hcap Chase (L) (A) (161) (5yo+) £34,800   3m3f110y (21)
2 STORMEZ (FR) *MCPipe* 5-10-6[142] (t) BJGeraghty 5/1 1
SOUTHERN STAR (FR) *MissHCKnight* 7-10-2[137] JCulloty........................ 4/1 ¾ 2
GOOD SHUIL (IRE) *TJTaaffe,Ireland* 7-9-9[135] PAspell[5] 12/1 4 3
Wonder Weasel (IRE) *KCBailey* 9-10-0[135] NWilliamson 12/1 7 4
Shooting Light (IRE) *MCPipe* 9-11-12[161] (v) APMcCoy 3/1f 9 5
Murt's Man (IRE) *PFNicholls* 8-10-2[137] RWalsh................................... 10/1 1 6
Noble Lord *RTPhillips* 9-10-0[135] MBradburne...................................... 10/1 dist 7
Jocks Cross (IRE) *MissVenetiaWilliams* 11-10-5[140] BJCrowley .... 9/1 pu
Somemanforoneman (IRE) *CJMann* 8-10-0[135] (b) NFehily...................... 20/1 pu
Maidstone Monument (IRE) *MrsAMThorpe* 7-10-0[135] SDurack .... 100/1 pu

Mr D. A. Johnson 10ran 7m12.39

25   Thomas Pink Gold Cup Chase (Hcap) (Gr 3) (A) (157) (5yo+)   2½m110y (15)
£58,000
CYFOR MALTA (FR) *MCPipe* 9-11-9[154] BJGeraghty................................. 16/1 1
POLIANTAS (FR) *PFNicholls* 5-10-9[140] TJMurphy.................................. 25/1 7 2
11 WAVE ROCK *PJHobbs* 7-10-2[133] (b) RWakley................................... 16/1 5 3
Foly Pleasant (FR) *MissHCKnight* 8-11-5[157] (t) RBiddlecombe[7] 14/1 1 4
Killultagh Storm (IRE) *WPMullins,Ireland* 8-10-6[137] DJCasey.................... 33/1 ½ 5
Mr Baxter Basics *MissVenetiaWilliams* 11-10-0[131] BJCrowley 14/1 4 6
4 Korakor (FR) *IanWilliams* 8-10-2[133] DRDennis.................................... 20/1 8 7
Turgeonev (FR) *TDEasterby* 7-11-3[148] RGarritty.................................. 33/1 10 8
5 Risk Accessor (IRE) *CRoche,Ireland* 7-10-0[131] LCooper 14/1 13 9
Red Ark *NBMason* 9-10-4[135] (t) KJohnson... 16/1 28 10
Its Time For A Win (IRE) *WPMullins,Ireland* 10-10-9[140] RWalsh .... 8/1 f
Perfect Fellow *MissHCKnight* 8-10-0[131] JCulloty................................. 5/1 f
Exit Swinger (FR) *MCPipe* 7-11-5[150] RGreene...................................... 12/1 ur

1003

| | 4 | Chicuelo (FR) *MCPipe* 6-10-1[132] (v) APMcCoy | 2/1f | pu |
| | | Batswing *BEllison* 7-10-0[131] NWilliamson | 33/1 | pu |

Mr D. A. Johnson 15ran 5m11.53

CHELTENHAM Sunday, Nov 17   GOOD to SOFT (Old Course)

26 **November Nov Chase (Gr 2) (A) (4yo+) £17,400**   2m (12)

		AZERTYUIOP (FR) *PFNicholls* 5-11-9 RWalsh	5/4f	1
		GOLDEN ALPHA (IRE) *MCPipe* 8-11-7 APMcCoy	3/1	16 2
		STARS OUT TONIGHT (IRE) *MissHCKnight* 5-11-7 JCulloty	4/1	8 3
	1	Fait Le Jojo (FR) *PJHobbs* 5-11-7 PFlynn	13/2	4 4
		Mumaris (USA) *MarkCampion* 8-11-3 VTKeane	33/1	dist 5
		Lord Fleet (IRE) *JRCornwall* 8-11-3 JAMcCarthy	100/1	26 6

Mr J. Hales 6ran 3m59.34

27 **Rehabilitation of Racehorses Hdle (Hcap) (L) (A) (155) (4yo+) £29,000**   2m110y (8)

	10	ROOSTER BOOSTER *PJHobbs* 8-11-12[155] SDurack	7/1	1
	18	QUAZAR (IRE) *JonjoO'Neill* 4-10-8[137] (t) LCooper	6/1	9 2
		DARK'N SHARP (GER) *RTPhillips* 7-10-0[129] JMogford	13/2	1½ 3
		Benbyas *DCarroll* 5-10-0[129] TJMurphy	25/1	3 4
	16	Latalomne (USA) *BEllison* 8-9-13[131] VTKeane[3]	20/1	9 5
		Dream With Me (FR) *MCPipe* 5-10-5[134] (v) APMcCoy	7/2f	12 6
		Docklands Limo *GFBridgwater* 9-10-6[135] EHusband	50/1	12 7
	8	In Contrast (IRE) *PJHobbs* 6-11-3[146] RWalsh	5/1	f
		Eternal Spring (IRE) *JRFanshawe* 5-10-13[142] MAFitzgerald	4/1	f
		Wild Romance (IRE) *DJWintle* 7-10-0[129] JCulloty	100/1	f
	3	Loop The Loup *MrsMReveley* 6-9-9[129] (b) PAspell[5]	16/1	bd

Mr Terry Warner 11ran 3m57.49

28 **Open Bumper (Standard Open NHF) (L) (4, 5 and 6yo) £10,570**   2m110y

		RHINESTONE COWBOY (IRE) *JonjoO'Neill* 6-10-11 MrJPMagnier[7]	9/4f	1
		LIBERMAN (IRE) *MCPipe* 4-11-7 APMcCoy	9/2	1 2
		INCA TRAIL (IRE) *MissHCKnight* 6-11-4 JCulloty	4/1	5 3
		Bold Bishop (IRE) *JIACharlton* 5-11-1 BGibson[3]	16/1	2 4
		Beyond The Pale (IRE) *NoelTChance* 4-10-13 DCrosse[5]	14/1	1½ 5
		Nil Desperandum (IRE) *MissFMCrowley,Ireland* 5-11-4 RWalsh	12/1	1¾ 6
		Captain Flinders (IRE) *CJMann* 5-11-0 NFehily	33/1	3½ 7
		Limerick Leader (IRE) *PJHobbs* 4-11-0 RJohnson	10/1	3½ 8
		Mohawk Brave (IRE) *KCBailey* 4-10-9 DFlavin[5]	33/1	3½ 9
		Riders Revenge (IRE) *PMJDoyle,Ireland* 4-11-0 TJMurphy	25/1	¾ 10
		Vodka Inferno (IRE) *CREgerton* 5-10-11 MFoley[3]	50/1	1 11
		Autumn Stroll (IRE) *CFSwan,Ireland* 4-11-0 CFSwan	33/1	hd 12
		Pimlico (IRE) *JTGifford* 4-11-0 PHide	33/1	½ 13
		Phar From Fair (IRE) *LWells* 5-11-7 MAFitzgerald	20/1	sh 14
		Champagne Harry *NATwiston-Davies* 4-11-0 CLlewellyn	50/1	2 15
		Kingscote Thunder (IRE) *NoelTChance* 5-11-0 TDoyle	33/1	18 16
		Fiery Creek *DJWintle* 5-10-2 PGriffiths[7]	66/1	3½ 17
		Sento (IRE) *AKing* 4-11-4 RThornton	20/1	9 18
		Trusting Paddy (IRE) *LADace* 5-10-9 CBolger[5]	50/1	5 19
		Ardan Glas (IRE) *PMJDoyle,Ireland* 5-11-0 PaulMoloney	33/1	6 20
		Looks Like Value (IRE) *KCBailey* 6-10-7 CHonour[7]	33/1	1½ 21
		Marshal Murat (IRE) *CREgerton* 4-11-0 JAMcCarthy	20/1	1½ 22
		Super Satco (IRE) *EdwardButler,Ireland* 4-11-0 NMulholland	50/1	13 23
		Woman *HJManners* 4-10-2 MrTGreenway[7]	100/1	ur

Mrs John Magnier 24ran 4m06.66

HAYDOCK Sunday, Nov 17   GOOD to SOFT

29 **Edward Hanmer Memorial Chase (Ltd Hcap) (Gr 2) (A) (157) (5yo+) £30,000**   3m (17)

		KINGSMARK (IRE) *MTodhunter* 9-11-10[157] DRDennis	10/3	1
		CHIVES (IRE) *MissHCKnight* 7-10-10[143] RichardGuest	3/1f	1½ 2
		BOBBY GRANT *PBeaumont* 11-10-12[145] RGarritty	16/1	19 3
		Exit To Wave (FR) *PFNicholls* 6-10-7[140] (t) AThornton	13/2	16 4
	12	Grey Abbey (IRE) *FPMurtagh* 8-11-2[149] (t) BHarding	4/1	2½ 5
	2	Lisdante (IRE) *MrsSJSmith* 9-10-1[137] DElsworth[3]	25/1	dist 6
		Kadou Nonantais (FR) *OSherwood* 10-10-1[139] (b) RFlavin[5]	33/1	f
		Jimmy Tennis (FR) *MissVenetiaWilliams* 5-10-4[138] BJCrowley	14/1	ur
		Ever Blessed (IRE) *PJHobbs* 10-10-4[137] TScudamore	8/1	ur

Sir Robert Ogden 9ran 6m06.92

NAVAN Sunday, Nov 17   SOFT

30 **Morgiana Hdle (Gr 2) (4yo+) £18,631**   2m (10)

| | 14 | LIMESTONE LAD (IRE) *JBowe* 10-12-0 PCarberry | 8/11f | 1 |

1004

	14	LISS A PAORAIGH (IRE) *JEKiely* 7-11-9 BJGeraghty	2/1	11	2
		KNIFE EDGE (USA) *MJPO'Brien* 7-11-11 DJCasey	9/1	10	3
	8	Ballyhampshire Boy (IRE) *SeanAherne* 6-11-1 NWilliamson	7/1		f

Mr James Bowe 4ran 3m55.30

31   **Tote Exacta 'Monksfield' Nov Hdle (Gr 3) (4yo+) £14,904**   2½m (12)

PIZARRO (IRE) *EJO'Grady* 5-11-3 NWilliamson	4/1	1
SOLERINA (IRE) *JBowe* 5-10-12 DJCasey	7/1	2 2
NONCHALANT (IRE) *MissFMCrowley* 4-10-10 (b) SGMcDermott[5]	10/1	20 3
Montayral (FR) *PHughes* 5-11-3 BJGeraghty	5/4f	1½ 4
Native Design (IRE) *MJO'Connor* 5-10-12 CO'Dwyer	12/1	20 5
I Can Imagine (IRE) *RobertTyner* 7-10-7 (t) PJCrowley[5]	20/1	6
Colca Canyon (IRE) *MrsJHarrington* 5-11-3 KAKelly	33/1	7
Compostello (IRE) *NMeade* 7-11-6 PCarberry	8/1	8
Jolly Moonbeam (IRE) *MichaelHourigan* 5-11-1 PGHourigan	7/1	f

Mr Edward Wallace 9ran 5m00.20

ASCOT Friday, Nov 22   HEAVY

32   **PricewaterhouseCoopers Ascot Hdle (Gr 2) (A) (4yo+) £18,600**   2½m (11)

	BARACOUDA (FR) *FDoumen,France* 7-11-8 TDoumen	2/5f	1
10	MR COOL *MCPipe* 8-11-0 APMcCoy	11/1	nk 2
23	CARLOVENT (FR) *MCPipe* 7-11-0 RGreene	22/1	30 3
	Landing Light (IRE) *NJHenderson* 7-11-8 MAFitzgerald	4/1	dist 4

Mr J. P. McManus 4ran 5m52.95

HUNTINGDON Saturday, Nov 23   GOOD to SOFT

33   **Peterborough Chase (Gr 2) (A) (5yo+) £32,725**   2½m110y (16)

	BEST MATE (IRE) *MissHCKnight* 7-11-10 JCulloty	8/15f	1
	DOUZE DOUZE (FR) *GMacaire,France* 6-11-0 JaquesRicou	7/2	8 2
	GEOS (FR) *NJHenderson* 7-11-0 MAFitzgerald	8/1	2½ 3
	Tresor de Mai (FR) *MCPipe* 8-11-10 APMcCoy	14/1	dist 4
16	Castle Prince (IRE) *RJHodges* 8-11-0 LTibbatts	150/1	dist 5

Mr Jim Lewis 5ran 5m06.54

AINTREE Sunday, Nov 24   GOOD to SOFT

34   **Tote Becher Chase (Hcap) (B) (147) (5yo+) £37,700**   3m3f (Nat.) (22)

2	ARDENT SCOUT *MrsSJSmith* 10-9-11[123] DEIsworth[3]	14/1	1
	AMBERLEIGH HOUSE (IRE) *DMcCain* 10-10-5[128] ADobbin	9/2f	24 2
	BLOWING WIND (FR) *MCPipe* 9-11-8[145] APMcCoy	5/1	17 3
	Village King (IRE) *PJHobbs* 9-10-12[135] RJohnson	11/2	2½ 4
	Smarty (IRE) *MPitman* 9-10-8[131] (b) TJMurphy	12/1	6 5
	Skillwise *TDEasterby* 10-10-0[123] RMcGrath	40/1	8 6
	Heidi III (FR) *MrsLWilliamson* 7-10-0[123] BHarding	25/1	10 7
	Scotton Green *TDEasterby* 11-9-11[123] DO'Meara[3]	33/1	4 8
	Impertio *PBeaumont* 8-10-0[123] BStorey	40/1	5 9
13	Bindaree (IRE) *NATwiston-Davies* 8-11-10[147] CLlewellyn	11/1	f
	Browjoshy (IRE) *KCBailey* 9-10-7[130] (b) AThornton	25/1	f
	Moor Lane *IABalding* 10-10-5[128] (v) MBradburne	7/1	f
	The Major (NZ) *JRCornwall* 9-10-0[123] ARoss	66/1	f
	Goguenard (FR) *MrsSJSmith* 8-10-6[129] WMarston	10/1	ur
	Shannon Gale (IRE) *CRoche,Ireland* 10-10-0[123] PaulMoloney	12/1	pu

Mrs Alicia Skene & W. S. Skene 15ran 7m13.10

CLONMEL Sunday, Nov 24   HEAVY

35   **Morris Oil Chase (Gr 2) (5yo+) £22,771**   2½m (14)

	BEEF OR SALMON (IRE) *MichaelHourigan* 6-10-13 PCarberry	7/2	1
	SACKVILLE (IRE) *MissFMCrowley* 9-11-12 DJCasey	4/1	3½ 2
20	CREGG HOUSE (IRE) *PatrickMullins* 7-11-3 DNRussell	11/2	6 3
12	Moscow Express (IRE) *MissFMCrowley* 10-11-12 RWalsh	7/2	25 4
	Alcapone (IRE) *MFMorris* 8-11-12 BJGeraghty	2/1f	ur

Mr B. J. Craig 5ran 5m32.60

AUTEUIL Sunday, Nov 24   HEAVY

36   **Prix Leon Olry-Roederer (Hdle) (Gr 2) (5yo+) £50,159**   2½m110y (12)

	KATIKI (FR) *J-PGallorini,France* 5-9-13 CPieux	47/10	1
15	LAVERON *FDoumen,France* 7-11-1 TDoumen		4 2
15	TIGER GROOM *RCollet,France* 5-10-6 LMetais		5 3
15	El Fuego (FR) *BBarbier,France* 10-10-8 (b) CGombeau		3 4
	Galant Moss (FR) *MCPipe,GB* 8-10-8 AKondrat		1 5
	Metchnikoff (FR) *PChatelain,France* 6-10-3 J-LCarracillo		8 6
21	Batman Senora (FR) *PRago,France* 6-10-3 (b) OAuge		¾ 7

1005

Brazil (FR) *MRolland,France* 7-10-6 (b) PChevalier.. nk 8
Arielle (FR) *EPilet,France* 6-9-13 BDelo 8 9

Mme A. Poisot-Gantes 9ran 5m15.00

NEWBURY Friday, Nov 29 GOOD TO SOFT

37 **Worcester Nov Chase (Gr 2) (A) (5yo+) £17,400**   3m (18)

	LUCKY BAY (IRE) *MissHCKnight* 6-11-2 JCulloty.....................................	14/1	1
	JOLY BEY (FR) *PFNicholls* 5-11-8 RWalsh	7/2	5 2
17	ONE KNIGHT (IRE) *PJHobbs* 6-11-9 RJohnson	11/8f	12 3
	High Cotton (IRE) *DRCElsworth* 7-11-2 BFenton	14/1	2½ 4
	Moss Harvey *JMJefferson* 7-11-9 GLee	9/4	1 5
	Keltic Heritage (IRE) *LADace* 8-11-2 (t) CBolger	50/1	6 6

Executive Racing 6ran 6m06.69

NEWBURY Saturday, Nov 30 GOOD

38 **Cantor Sport Long Distance Hdle (Gr 2) (A) (4yo+) £17,400**   3m110y (12)

	BACCHANAL (IRE) *NJHenderson* 8-11-0 MAFitzgerald............................	7/2	1
23	NATIVE EMPEROR *JonjoO'Neill* 6-11-4 ADobbin	9/2	5 2
	DEANO'S BEENO *MCPipe* 10-11-0 APMcCoy..	9/4f	3 3
13	Boss Doyle (IRE) *MFMorris,Ireland* 10-11-0 (b) DJCasey.......................	16/1	9 4
8	Rostropovich (IRE) *MFMorris,Ireland* 5-11-0 (t) NWilliamson	20/1	1½ 5
13	Brother Joe (NZ) *PJHobbs* 8-11-8 PCarberry	11/4	2 6
	Garruth (IRE) *PFNicholls* 8-11-0 (b) TJMurphy......................................	50/1	24 7
14	Catch Ball *WPMullins,Ireland* 6-10-9 RWalsh	40/1	¾ 8

Lady Lloyd Webber 8ran 5m51.95

39 **Hennessy Cognac Gold Cup Chase (Hcap) (Gr 3) (A) (162) (5yo+)**   3¼m110y (21)
       £60,900

	BE MY ROYAL (IRE) *WPMullins,Ireland* 8-10-0[136] DJCasey....................	33/1	1
12	GINGEMBRE (FR) *MrsLCTaylor* 8-10-13[149] AThornton	16/1	½ 2
	HARBOUR PILOT (IRE) *NMeade,Ireland* 7-10-3[139] PCarberry	11/1	1½ 3
12	WHITENZO (FR) *PFNicholls* 6-10-2[138] RWalsh......................................	25/1	2½ 4
12	Hussard Collonges (FR) *PBeaumont* 7-11-4[154] RGarrity	9/1	1 5
	Carbury Cross (IRE) *JonjoO'Neill* 8-10-9[145] (b) SDurack	33/1	1 6
	Gunther McBride (IRE) *PJHobbs* 7-10-2[138] RJohnson.............................	12/1	2½ 7
13	Frosty Canyon *PRWebber* 9-10-6[142] (v) TDoyle	14/1	7 8
12	Marlborough (IRE) *NJHenderson* 10-11-9[159] MAFitzgerald	12/1	2½ 9
20	Give Over (IRE) *EUHales,Ireland* 9-10-1[137] DNRussell.........................	20/1	1¼ 10
12	Lord Noelie (IRE) *MissHCKnight* 9-11-12[162] JCulloty.........................	33/1	5 11
	Take Control (IRE) *MCPipe* 8-10-11[147] TScudamore	20/1	6 12
24	Southern Star (IRE) *MissHCKnight* 7-10-1[137] TJMurphy	20/1	1¾ 13
29	Ever Blessed (IRE) *PJHobbs* 10-10-0[136] PFlynn	50/1	7 14
	Infrasonique (FR) *MrsLCTaylor* 6-9-9[136] PJBrennan[5].........................	50/1	5 15
	Bounce Back (USA) *MCPipe* 6-10-11[147] APMcCoy.................................	13/2f	½ 16
	Moral Support (IRE) *JSMoore* 10-10-0[136] BFenton	66/1	5 17
	Red Striker *NBMason* 8-10-7[143] (t) RichardGuest	25/1	15 18
24	Stormez (FR) *MCPipe* 5-10-11[148] (t) PaulMoloney	16/1	7 19
34	Bindaree (IRE) *NATwiston-Davies* 8-10-11[147] CLlewellyn....................	50/1	ur
	Crocadee *MissVenetiaWilliams* 9-10-0[136] BJCrowley............................	50/1	f
	Gola Cher (IRE) *AKing* 8-10-0[136] (b) RThornton..................................	12/1	f
	Iznogoud (FR) *MCPipe* 6-10-11[147] RGreene..	20/1	pu
	Takagi (IRE) *EJO'Grady,Ireland* 7-10-5[141] NWilliamson	14/1	pu
	Direct Access (IRE) *LLungo* 7-10-0[136] ADobbin..................................	11/1	pu

Mrs V. O'Leary 25ran 6m35.81

NEWCASTLE Saturday, Nov 30 GOOD to SOFT

40 **Pertemps 'Fighting Fifth' Hdle (Gr 2) (A) (4yo+) £29,000**   2m (9)

8	INTERSKY FALCON *JonjoO'Neill* 5-11-8 (b) LCooper...........................	11/10f	1
1	THE FRENCH FURZE (IRE) *NGRichards* 8-11-0 BHarding.......................	9/1	6 2
	MARBLE ARCH *HMorrison* 6-11-0 MBradburne	13/8	8 3
	October Mist (IRE) *MrsMReveley* 8-11-0 ADempsey..............................	9/1	7 4
18	Castleshane (IRE) *SGollings* 5-11-0 GLee	16/1	9 5
	Didifon *NPMcCormack* 7-11-0 BStorey	200/1	7 6

Interskyracing.com & Mrs Jonjo O'Neill 6ran 3m55.00

FAIRYHOUSE Saturday, Nov 30 SOFT

41 **betfair.com Juv 3-Y-O Hdle (Gr 3) (3yo) £14,399**   2m (10)

	GOLDEN CROSS (IRE) *MHalford* 3-10-9 CFSwan	2/1	1
	MIRPOUR (IRE) *EGriffin* 3-10-9 (b) BJGeraghty	7/2	4 2
	DASHING HOME (IRE) *NMeade* 3-10-4 JUPower[5]	7/4f	6 3
	Dyrick Daybreak (IRE) *DavidAKiely* 3-9-13 (t) KHadnett[5]	7/1	1 4

Achates (IRE) *WMRoper* 3-9-13 SGMcDermott[5] 12/1   8 5
Chief Mosconomo *TMWalsh* 3-10-4 GTHutchinson[5] 16/1   6
South West Nine (IRE) *JTGorman* 3-10-4 GCotter 16/1   7
Blackagino (IRE) *TO'Neill* 3-10-1 JPElliott[3] .... 66/1   pu

Mrs H. Johnson 8ran 4m06.50

FAIRYHOUSE Sunday, Dec 1   HEAVY

42   **Boylesports Royal Bond Nov Hdle (Gr 1) (4yo+) £28,797**   2m (10)

HARDY EUSTACE (IRE) *DTHughes* 5-11-12 KAKelly 5/1   1
BACK IN FRONT (IRE) *EJO'Grady* 5-11-12 NWilliamson 4/1   1½ 2
MACS VALLEY (IRE) *WPMullins* 5-11-12 RWalsh............................... 8/1   9 3
6   Mutakarrim *DKWeld* 5-11-12 (b) BJGeraghty .... 11/4   ½ 4
Rosaker (USA) *NMeade* 5-11-12 PCarberry 14/1   2 5
Friend's Amigo (IRE) *PMJDoyle* 5-11-12 CFSwan............................. 2/1f   6
Whithworth Ben (IRE) *PatrickMorris* 5-11-12 CO'Dwyer..................... 16/1   7
Rupununi (IRE) *FrancisEnnis* 5-11-12 GCotter 20/1   8
Native Sparkle (IRE) *THogan* 5-11-7 KHadnett 10/1   9
Social Order (IRE) *MJPO'Brien* 4-11-7 (b) DJCasey........................... 25/1   10

Mr Laurence Byrne 10ran 4m04.67

43   **Pierse Group Drinmore Nov Chase (Gr 1) (5yo+) £30,854**   2½m (16)

LE COUDRAY (FR) *CRoche* 8-11-12 BJGeraghty 1/1f   1
BARROW DRIVE *AnthonyMullins* 6-11-12 (t) JCulloty 3/1   6 2
19   FIERY RING (IRE) *JRHFowler* 7-11-12 RGeraghty.............................. 14/1   dist 3
Thari (USA) *NMeade* 5-11-10 (t) PCarberry .... 8/1   dist 4
Boneyarrow (IRE) *WPMullins* 6-11-12 RWalsh.................................. 8/1   f
Native Scout (IRE) *DHassett* 6-11-12 (t) NWilliamson .... 8/1   pu
Native Sessions (IRE) *NMeade* 7-11-12 DJCasey.............................. 10/1   pu
Cyborsun (FR) *ALTMoore* 5-11-10 CO'Dwyer .... 12/1   pu
Come In Moscow (IRE) *JohnJosephMurphy* 6-11-7 KHadnett .... 33/1   pu

Mr John P. McManus 9ran 5m25.69

44   **Ballymore Properties Hatton's Grace Hdle (Gr 1) (4yo+) £30,854**   2½m (11)

30   LIMESTONE LAD (IRE) *JBowe* 10-11-12 BJGeraghty 8/15f   1
8   SCOTTISH MEMORIES (IRE) *NMeade* 6-11-12 PCarberry...................... 7/2   8 2
NED KELLY (IRE) *EJO'Grady* 6-11-12 NWilliamson .... 6/1   dist 3
Colonel Braxton (IRE) *DTHughes* 7-11-12 KAKelly 9/1   20 4
14   Balapour (IRE) *PatrickOBrady* 4-11-7 (t) JPElliott .... 40/1   dist 5

Mr James Bowe 5ran 5m09.37

WINCANTON Thursday, Dec 5   GOOD to SOFT

45   **Tote Exacta Levy Board Int Chase (Ltd Hcap) (B) (154) (5yo+) £17,922**   2m5f (17)

25   POLIANTAS (FR) *PFNicholls* 5-10-13[143] TJMurphy 9/2   1
GOLDEN GOAL (GER) *MissVenetiaWilliams* 6-10-8[138] AThornton............ 10/1   1½ 2
FONDMORT (FR) *NJHenderson* 6-10-13[143] MAFitzgerald 5/2   1¼ 3
Royal Auclair (FR) *MCPipe* 5-11-10[154] APMcCoy 9/4f   28 4
Thyne Will Tell (IRE) *PJHobbs* 7-10-4[134] RJohnson .... 5/1   f
Juralan (IRE) *MissHCKnight* 7-10-5[135] JCulloty... 14/1   pu

Mr Mark Tincknell 6ran 5m19.78

SANDOWN Friday, Dec 6   SOFT

46   **GQ Winter Nov Hdle (Gr 2) (A) (4yo+) £14,500**   2½m110y (9)

COOLNAGORNA (IRE) *JonjoO'Neill* 5-11-4 ADobbin 6/4f   1
THISTHATANDTOTHER (IRE) *PFNicholls* 6-11-4 BJGeraghty................. 11/4   5 2
SELF DEFENSE *MissECLavelle* 5-11-0 FKeniry... 8/1   26 3
Lady Laureate *GCBravery* 4-10-9 WMarston 25/1   10 4
Domenico (IRE) *JRJenkins* 4-11-0 JCulloty.. 16/1   dist 5
Master George *PJHobbs* 5-11-4 RJohnson.. 7/1   f
Calling Brave (IRE) *NJHenderson* 6-11-4 MAFitzgerald .... 6/1   ur

Mrs G. Smith 7ran 5m11.39

47   **GQ Future Stars Chase (Int) (B) (5yo+) £10,972**   3m110y (22)

11   VALLEY HENRY (IRE) *PFNicholls* 7-11-10 BJGeraghty.......................... 8/13f   1
INTELLIGENT (IRE) *MrsJHarrington,Ireland* 6-10-12 MAFitzgerald 8/1   4 2
HAUT CERCY (FR) *HDDaly* 7-10-8 RJohnson... 9/2   5 3
Maximize (IRE) *MissHCKnight* 8-11-10 JCulloty 5/1   5 4

Mr Paul K. Barber 4ran 6m30.18

CHEPSTOW Saturday, Dec 7   SOFT

48   **John Hughes Rehearsal Chase (Ltd Hcap) (L) (A) (162) (5yo+)**   3¼m110y (22)
    £23,200

20   SEE MORE BUSINESS (IRE) *PFNicholls* 12-11-10[162] (b) AThornton 2/1jf   1

39   BINDAREE (IRE) *NATwiston-Davies* 8-10-4[142] CLlewellyn.......................... 8/1   7 2
RUGGED RIVER (IRE) *RHAlner* 7-9-13[142] RWalford[5]................................. 7/2   2 3
Supreme Glory (IRE) *PGMurphy* 9-10-4[142] LAspell................................ 2/1jf 22 4
29 Jimmy Tennis (FR) *MissVenetiaWilliams* 5-10-4[142] BJCrowley .... 11/1 dist 5

Mr Paul K. Barber & Sir Robert Ogden 5ran 7m12.33

SANDOWN Saturday, Dec 7   SOFT

49   **Henry VIII Nov Chase (Gr 2) (A) (4yo+) £20,100**   2m (13)

    IMPEK (FR) *MissHCKnight* 6-11-2 JCulloty.. 5/4f   1
17 LE ROI MIGUEL (FR) *PFNicholls* 4-10-5 RWalsh... 6/4 1½ 2
    TYSOU (FR) *NJHenderson* 5-11-6 MAFitzgerald... 3/1 dist 3

Mr Jim Lewis 3ran 3m57.79

50   **Mitsubishi Shogun Tingle Creek Trophy Chase (Gr 1) (A) (5yo+)**   2m (13)
    £58,000

    CENKOS (FR) *PFNicholls* 8-11-7 RWalsh.. 6/1   1
16 EDREDON BLEU (FR) *MissHCKnight* 10-11-7 (t) JCulloty 13/2 14 2
    WAHIBA SANDS *MCPipe* 9-11-7 APMcCoy.. 10/1 15 3
    Flagship Uberalles (IRE) *PJHobbs* 8-11-7 RJohnson 15/8f   9 4
    Get Real (IRE) *NJHenderson* 11-11-7 MAFitzgerald 66/1 3½ 5
19 Moscow Flyer (IRE) *MrsJHarrington,Ireland* 8-11-7 BJGeraghty.................. 2/1   ur

Mrs J. Stewart 6ran 3m59.31

51   **William Hill Heap Hdle (L) (A) 0-150(148) (4yo+) £40,600**   2m110y (8)

    SPIRIT LEADER (IRE) *MrsJHarrington,Ireland* 6-10-0[122] NWilliamson 9/2   1
    MOVING ON UP *CJMann* 8-10-0[122] (b) NFehily 20/1   4 2
    HAWADETH *VRADartnall* 7-10-0[122] JCulloty 16/1   4 3
    Deep Sunset (IRE) *NJHenderson* 6-9-7[127] MrATinkler[7] 7/1 1½ 4
32 Mr Cool *MCPipe* 8-11-5[148] MrJEMoore[7] 12/1   8 5
 3 Whistling Dixie (IRE) *MrsMReveley* 9-8-8[130] MAFitzgerald .... 14/1 nk 6
    Samon (GER) *MCPipe* 5-10-13[135] APMcCoy... 4/1f ½ 7
    Idaho d'Ox (FR) *MCPipe* 6-10-6[128] (v) TScudamore 20/1   1 8
27 Quazar (IRE) *JonjoO'Neill* 4-11-2[138] (t) BJGeraghty 5/1   6 9
    Sud Bleu (FR) *PFNicholls* 4-10-1[123] RWalsh... 7/1   7 10
 3 Jaboune (FR) *AKing* 5-10-5[127] RJohnson.. 10/1 dist 11
18 Pietro Bembo (IRE) *PCRitchens* 8-10-0[122] FKeniry .... 66/1 ½ 12

Mr D. Thompson 12ran 4m06.63

PUNCHESTOWN Sunday, Dec 8

52   **John Durkan Memorial Punchestown Chase (Gr 1) (5yo+) £37,500**   2½m (14)

    NATIVE UPMANSHIP (IRE) *ALTMoore* 9-11-12 CO'Dwyer 5/4f   1
    RINCE RI (IRE) *TMWalsh* 9-11-12 RWalsh.. 5/1   3 2
    FIRST GOLD (FR) *FDoumen,France* 9-11-12 TDoumen 5/2 1½ 3
20 More Than A Stroll (IRE) *ALTMoore* 10-11-12 (t) BMCash 6/1 15 4
35 Alcapone (IRE) *MFMorris* 8-11-12 BJGeraghty.. 14/1 15 5

Mrs John Magnier 5ran 5m24.50

CHELTENHAM Friday, Dec 13   GOOD to SOFT (New Course)

53   **Ian Williams' Owners Nov Chase (Gr 2) (A) (5yo+) £14,500**   3m1f110y (21)

    SIR REMBRANDT (IRE) *RHAlner* 6-11-4 AThornton 7/2   1
23 IT TAKES TIME (IRE) *MCPipe* 8-11-0 APMcCoy .... 1/1f ½ 2
    THE VILLAGER (IRE) *DJCaro* 6-11-4 TScudamore 5/1 22 3
    Iverain (FR) *PFNicholls* 6-11-4 RWalsh... 7/1 ¾ 4
    Whereareyounow (IRE) *NATwiston-Davies* 6-11-4 CLlewellyn.................... 50/1 21 5
    Rushing Again *DrPPritchard* 7-11-0 MissPGundry................................. 100/1   ur
    Tribal King (IRE) *MissHCKnight* 7-11-4 TJMurphy .... 20/1 pu

A & D Enterprises (Poole) Ltd 7ran 6m35.13

CHELTENHAM Saturday, Dec 14   GOOD to SOFT (New Course)

54   **40th Anniversary Heap Chase (B) 0-145(144) (5yo+) £14,102**   2m110y (14)

19 KADARANN (IRE) *PFNicholls* 5-11-12[144] RWalsh 7/1   1
    RED BLAZER *MissHCKnight* 11-11-3[135] JCulloty.. 6/1 15 2
    GLENELLY GALE (IRE) *ALTMoore,Ireland* 8-10-6[124] CO'Dwyer............ 5/1   8 3
    Master Tern (USA) *JonjoO'Neill* 7-10-7[125] DJCasey 13/2   9 4
    Barren Lands *KBishop* 7-10-0[118] RGreene.. 16/1 dist 5
26 Golden Alpha (IRE) *MCPipe* 8-10-12[130] APMcCoy .... 5/2f ur
 4 Demasta (NZ) *NJHenderson* 11-11-3[135] MAFitzgerald .... 7/1 pu
    Ritual *MissJacquelineSDoyle* 7-9-9[118] DCrosse[5]................................... 25/1 pu

Notalotterry 8ran 4m05.60

55   **Tripleprint Juv Nov Hdle (Gr 2) (A) (3yo) £11,600**   2m1f (8)

    DON FERNANDO *MCPipe* 3-11-7 APMcCoy 10/11f   1

LILIUM DE COTTE (FR) *GMacaire,France* 3-11-4 JaquesRicou .... 20/1   ¾ 2
NAS NA RIOGH (IRE) *NJHenderson* 3-10-13 MAFitzgerald .... 7/1   dh 2
Tramantano *NATwiston-Davies* 3-11-7 CLlewellyn 4/1   11 4
Duke of Earl (IRE) *SKirk* 3-11-7 SDurack .... 12/1   ½ 5
Turbo (IRE) *MissVenetiaWilliams* 3-11-0 NWilliamson 10/1   8 6
Silver Charmer *HSHowe* 3-10-9 RGreene 50/1   21 7

Lucayan Stud 7ran 4m12.16

56   **Tripleprint Gold Cup (Hcap Chase) (Gr 3) (A) (164) (5yo+)** £58,000   2m5f (17)

45   FONDMORT (FR) *NJHenderson* 6-10-5[143] MAFitzgerald 5/1   1
25   FOLY PLEASANT (FR) *MissHCKnight* 8-11-3[155] (t) JCulloty 7/1   6 2
     YOULNEVERWALKALONE (IRE) *CRoche,Ireland* 8-10-1[139] CO'Dwyer .. 7/2   6 3
25   Cyfor Malta (FR) *MCPipe* 9-11-12[164] APMcCoy 10/3f   6 4
     Fadalko (FR) *PFNicholls* 9-11-10[162] RWalsh 12/1   4 5
45   Golden Goal (GER) *MissVenetiaWilliams* 6-10-0[138] NWilliamson 8/1   8 6
25   Wave Rock *PJHobbs* 7-10-0[138] (b) RJohnson 25/1   7 7
25   Killultagh Storm (IRE) *WPMullins,Ireland* 8-10-0[138] DJCasey 14/1   9 8
25   Exit Swinger (FR) *MCPipe* 7-10-12[150] RGreene 14/1   2 9

Mr W. J. Brown 9ran 5m26.15

57   **Victor Chandler Bula Hdle (Gr 2) (A) (4yo+)** £43,500   2m1f (8)

27   ROOSTER BOOSTER *PJHobbs* 8-11-4 RJohnson 11/8f   1
32   LANDING LIGHT (IRE) *NJHenderson* 7-11-8 (b) MAFitzgerald 6/1   2½ 2
33   GEOS (FR) *NJHenderson* 7-11-0 NWilliamson .... 7/1   hd 3
40   Marble Arch *HMorrison* 6-11-0 APMcCoy 6/1   2½ 4
     Never (FR) *FDoumen,France* 5-11-4 TDoumen 12/1   3 5
40   The French Furze (IRE) *NGRichards* 6-11-0 BHarding........................... 25/1   2½ 6
     Fifth Generation (IRE) *DrPPritchard* 12-11-0 RGreene .... 300/1   dist 7
     Hors La Loi III (FR) *JRFanshawe* 7-11-8 (t) RWalsh .... 13/2   f
     Al Skywalker (USA) *JenniferMajette,USA* 9-11-8 TJFoley .... 33/1   pu

Mr Terry Warner 9ran 4m03.19

58   **Tripleprint Bristol Nov Hdle (Gr 2) (A) (4yo+)** £14,500   3m (12)

     IRIS'S GIFT *JonjoO'Neill* 5-11-7 APMcCoy 13/8f   1
13   AD HOC (IRE) *PFNicholls* 8-11-4 RWalsh .... 7/4   nk 2
     PRIESTS BRIDGE (IRE) *NATwiston-Davies* 6-10-9 CLlewellyn .... 5/1   dist 3
     Lords Best (IRE) *AKing* 6-11-7 RJohnson 7/1   9 4
     Chanticlier *KCBailey* 5-11-0 NWilliamson 25/1   2 5
     Blazing Batman *DrPPritchard* 9-11-0 RGreene .... 200/1   dist 6
     Battle Warning *PBowen* 7-11-0 SDurack .... 25/1   pu

Mr Robert Lester 7ran 5m58.52

HAYDOCK Saturday, Dec 14   GOOD to SOFT

59   **Tommy Whittle Chase (Gr 2) (A) (5yo+)** £31,000   3m (18)

35   SACKVILLE (IRE) *MissFMCrowley,Ireland* 10-11-8 TJMurphy 3/1   1
29   BOBBY GRANT *PBeaumont* 11-10-12 RGarritty 11/2   1½ 2
29   KINGSMARK (IRE) *MTodhunter* 9-11-4 DRDennis 8/11f   1½ 3
39   Take Control (IRE) *MCPipe* 8-11-4 TScudamore 8/1   10 4

Mr Seamus O'Farrell 4ran 6m22.84

CORK Sunday, Dec 15   SOFT

60   **O'Connell Transport Hilly Way Chase (Gr 3) (5yo+)** £16,666   2m (11)

35   BEEF OR SALMON (IRE) *MichaelHourigan* 6-11-12 TJMurphy 2/1   1
     RIVER CLODAGH (IRE) *HenryDeBromhead* 8-11-6 (b) JRBarry 20/1   4½ 2
     FADOUDAL DU COCHET (FR) *ALTMoore* 9-11-2 CO'Dwyer 15/8f   6 3
     Copernicus *PHughes* 7-11-9 MAFitzgerald .... 4/1   nk 4
     Noble Buck (IRE) *JQueally* 6-10-11 IJPower[5] 20/1   2½ 5
     Donna's Princess (IRE) *GDucey* 7-10-11 DNRussell 33/1   6
     Rathbawn Prince (IRE) *DTHughes* 10-11-6 KAKelly................................ 8/1   f
     Penny Rich (IRE) *THogan* 8-10-13 (t) KHadnett[3] .... 14/1   f

Mr B. J. Craig 8ran 4m11.30

NAVAN Sunday, Dec 15   SOFT

61   **Giltspur Scientific Hdle (4yo+)** £8,333   2½m (12)

44   LIMESTONE LAD (IRE) *JBowe* 10-11-12 PCarberry 1/2f   1
30   LISS A PAORAIGH (IRE) *JEKiely* 7-10-11 BJGeraghty.......................... 7/4   6 2
44   BALAPOUR (IRE) *PatrickOBrady* 4-10-8 (t) JPElliott[5] 16/1   25 3
     Tommy Dee (IRE) *WRock* 8-10-12 RWalsh 150/1   7 4
     Yangtze (IRE) *RichardJButler* 8-10-5 RCColgan[7] .... 200/1   dist 5

Mr James Bowe 5ran 4m56.40

62   **Barry & Sandra Kelly Memorial Nov Hdle (Gr 3) (4yo+)** £20,833   2½m (12)

31   SOLERINA (IRE) *JBowe* 5-11-2 PCarberry 13/8   1

1009

              KICKING KING (IRE) *TJTaaffe* 4-10-10 BJGeraghty 6/1   8 2
31   PIZARRO (IRE) *EJO'Grady* 5-11-7 NWilliamson 8/13f   25 3
     Rose Perk (IRE) *ESheehy* 6-10-10 CFSwan 33/1   6 4
     Mistletoeandwine (IRE) *SJTreacy* 4-10-5 RWalsh 16/1   20 5

     Mr John P. Bowe 5ran 4m58.60

     ASCOT Friday, Dec 20   HEAVY

63   Cantor Sport Long Walk Hdle (Gr 1) (A) (4yo+) £40,200   3m1f110y (14)
38   DEANO'S BEENO *MCPipe* 10-11-7 APMcCoy 14/1   1
32   BARACOUDA (FR) *FDoumen,France* 7-11-7 TDoumen 4/11f   1 2
38   NATIVE EMPEROR *JonjoO'Neill* 6-11-7 LCooper .... 5/1   dist 3
38   Brother Joe (NZ) *PJHobbs* 8-11-7 MAFitzgerald .... 12/1   pu
     Young American (IRE) *JonjoO'Neill* 6-11-7 CFSwan .... 50/1   pu

     Axom 5ran 6m42.30

64   Kennel Gate Nov Hdle (Gr 2) (A) (4yo+) £14,500   2m110y (9)
     KOPECK (IRE) *JTGifford* 4-11-0 LAspell 33/1   1
 3   PUNTAL (FR) *MCPipe* 6-11-7 APMcCoy 8/13f   2 2
22   FOREMAN (GER) *TDoumen,France* 4-11-7 TDoumen 7/2   20 3
     Shalako (USA) *PJHobbs* 4-11-4 RJohnson 12/1   19 4
     Dumaran (IRE) *IABalding* 4-11-4 TJMurphy 10/1   14 5
     Adjawar (IRE) *HMorrison* 4-11-0 MAFitzgerald .... 33/1   pu
     Atum Re (IRE) *PRWebber* 5-11-0 BFenton .... 33/1   pu
     Grand Finale (IRE) *MissVenetiaWilliams* 5-11-0 BJCrowley.................... 14/1   pu

     Mr P. H. Betts 8ran 4m22.58

     ASCOT Saturday, Dec 21   HEAVY

65   cantorindex.co.uk Hcap Chase (B) (154) (5yo+) £31,000   2m (12)
     YOUNG DEVEREAUX (IRE) *PFNicholls* 9-10-1[129] RWalsh 3/1   1
16   SEEBALD (GER) *MCPipe* 7-11-12[154] APMcCoy 11/2   1 2
     SHAMAWAN (IRE) *JonjoO'Neill* 7-10-4[132] LCooper 11/4f   2½ 3
     Davoski *MissVenetiaWilliams* 8-11-8[150] TJMurphy 7/1   13 4
27   Dark'n Sharp (GER) *RTPhillips* 7-11-6[148] RJohnson .... 4/1   f
50   Get Real (IRE) *NJHenderson* 11-10-12[140] MAFitzgerald .... 14/1   f
25   Batswing *BEllison* 7-10-2[130] NFehily .... 16/1   ro

     Paul K.Barber,Mick Coburn,Colin Lewis 2 7ran 4m15.84

66   Silver Cup (Hcap Chase) (L) (A) (158) (5yo+) £31,000   3m110y (20)
     BEHRAJAN (IRE) *HDDaly* 7-11-12[158] RJohnson 7/1   1
29   EXIT TO WAVE (FR) *PFNicholls* 6-10-6[138] (t) RWalsh .... 6/1   nk 2
     ZAFARABAD (IRE) *PJHobbs* 8-10-9[141] (b) APMcCoy .... 15/2   dist 3
21   Innox (FR) *FDoumen,France* 6-10-10[142] TDoumen .... 15/2   ½ 4
     Truckers Tavern (IRE) *FerdyMurphy* 7-10-8[140] (t) DNRussell.............. 2/1f   f
39   Carbury Cross (IRE) *JonjoO'Neill* 8-10-13[145] (b) LCooper .... 15/2   pu
     Ikrenel Royal (IRE) *NJHenderson* 6-10-7[139] MAFitzgerald .... 6/1   pu

     The Behrajan Partnership 7ran 6m42.40

67   Ladbroke Hdle (Hcap) (L) (A) 0-150(148) (4yo+) £58,000   2m110y (9)
     CHAUVINIST (IRE) *NJHenderson* 7-10-0[122] NWilliamson 15/2   1
51   IDAHO D'OX (FR) *MCPipe* 6-10-3[125] (v) GSupple 50/1   15 2
27   BENBYAS *DCarroll* 5-10-5[132] PJBrennan[5] .... 20/1   ½ 3
18   TIKRAM *GLMoore* 5-10-2[124] TJMurphy 12/1   1 4
 1   Monkerhostin (FR) *OSherwood* 5-10-8[130] (s) SStronge 40/1   9 5
51   Mr Cool *MCPipe* 8-11-2[145] MrJEMoore[7] 33/1   10 6
     Bernardan (GER) *MCPipe* 6-10-9[131] APMcCoy 14/1   2½ 7
     Keltic Bard *CJMann* 5-10-0[122] NFehily 25/1   15 8
     Holy Orders (IRE) *WPMullins,Ireland* 5-10-8[130] (b) RWalsh 4/1f   11 9
     Milkat (IRE) *WPMullins,Ireland* 4-9-7[122] MrNPMadden[7].................. 12/1   6 10
     Under The Sand (IRE) *PJHobbs* 5-10-5[127] RJohnson 14/1   3 11
     Volano (FR) *NJHenderson* 4-10-3[125] JRKavanagh............................... 16/1   27 12
 6   Anxious Moments (IRE) *CFSwan,Ireland* 7-10-4[126] CFSwan 8/1   14 13
     Majlis (IRE) *TRGeorge* 5-10-9[131] (b) DNRussell.............................. 50/1   dist 14
51   Whistling Dixie (IRE) *MrsMReveley* 5-10-5[127] ADempsey................. 16/1   f
     Polar Red *MCPipe* 5-11-12[148] (v) BFenton .... 25/1   pu
     Valerio *NJHenderson* 6-10-12[134] MAFitzgerald................................. 8/1   pu
     Giocomo (IRE) *JonjoO'Neill* 4-10-11[133] LCooper .... 16/1   pu
51   Moving On Up *CJMann* 8-10-4[126] (b) JAMcCarthy.......................... 25/1   pu
 6   Czar of Peace (IRE) *WPMullins,Ireland* 4-10-1[122] NMulholland[3]........ 33/1   pu

     Mrs E. Roberts & Nick Roberts 20ran 4m24.50

68   cantorsport.co.uk Noel Nov Chase (Gr 2) (A) (4yo+) £18,000   2m3f110y (16)
     TARXIEN *MCPipe* 8-11-8 (t) APMcCoy 1/1f   1

                                         1010

SCOTS GREY *NJHenderson* 7-11-6 MAFitzgerald 7/2   15 2
PALARSHAN (FR) *HDDaly* 4-10-5 RJohnson.. 5/2   6 3
Mercato (FR) *JRBest* 6-11-2 (t) BHitchcott.................................... 50/1   dist 4
Placid Man (IRE) *NJHenderson* 8-11-2 JRKavanagh .... 20/1   pu
The Staggery Boy (IRE) *MRHoad* 6-11-2 (t) SStronge .... 100/1   pu

Mr B. A. Kilpatrick 6ran 5m20.63

KEMPTON Thursday, Dec 26

69   **Feltham Nov Chase (Gr 1) (A) (5yo+) £29,000**   3m (19)

       JAIR DU COCHET (FR) *GMacaire,France* 5-11-7 JaquesRicou 5/2   1
       LE SAUVIGNON (FR) *PFNicholls* 8-11-7 RWalsh 2/1f   6 2
       BOLD INVESTOR *JonjoO'Neill* 5-11-7 APMcCoy 7/2   5 3
       One Night Out (IRE) *WPMullins,Ireland* 6-11-7 RJohnson...................... 11/1   23 4
   37 Lucky Bay (IRE) *MissHCKnight* 6-11-7 TJMurphy 12/1   4 5
       Swansea Bay *PBowen* 6-11-7 (s) TScudamore.. 10/1   dist 6
       Go White Lightning (IRE) *MBradstock* 7-11-7 JPMcNamara .... 66/1   pu

Mrs F. Montauban 7ran 6m19.02

70   **Pertemps Christmas Hdle (Gr 1) (A) (4yo+) £43,500**   2m (8)

   40 INTERSKY FALCON *JonjoO'Neill* 5-11-7 (b) CFSwan 1/1f   1
   18 SANTENAY (FR) *PFNicholls* 4-11-7 TJMurphy 20/1   3 2
       DAVENPORT MILENIUM (IRE) *WPMullins,Ireland* 6-11-7 RWalsh 11/2   6 3
   57 Hors La Loi III (FR) *JRFanshawe* 7-11-7 (t) CO'Dwyer 11/4   13 4
   57 Marble Arch *HMorrison* 6-11-7 MAFitzgerald................................. 7/1   1¼ 5
       Yorkshire (IRE) *DLWilliams* 8-11-7 RJohnson............................... 66/1   24 6

Interskyracing.com & Mrs Jonjo O'Neill 6ran 3m57.83

71   **Pertemps King George VI Chase (Gr 1) (A) (5yo+) £87,000**   3m (19)

   33 BEST MATE (IRE) *MissHCKnight* 7-11-10 APMcCoy 11/8f   1
   39 MARLBOROUGH (IRE) *NJHenderson* 10-11-10 TJMurphy 14/1   1½ 2
   38 BACCHANAL (IRE) *NJHenderson* 8-11-10 MAFitzgerald........................ 10/3   4 3
   20 Florida Pearl (IRE) *WPMullins,Ireland* 10-11-10 RWalsh 8/1   12 4
   52 Native Upmanship (IRE) *ALTMoore,Ireland* 9-11-10 CO'Dwyer 7/1   13 5
   50 Wahiba Sands *MCPipe* 9-11-10 TScudamore 66/1   18 6
   33 Douze Douze (FR) *GMacaire,France* 6-11-10 CGombeau.................... 12/1   pu
   50 Flagship Uberalles (IRE) *PJHobbs* 8-11-10 RJohnson .... 10/1   pu
   39 Lord Noelie (IRE) *MissHCKnight* 9-11-10 JPMcNamara............................ 40/1   pu
   24 Shooting Light (IRE) *MCPipe* 9-11-10 (v) RGreene .... 25/1   pu

Mr Jim Lewis 10ran 6m18.06

LEOPARDSTOWN Thursday, Dec 26   HEAVY

72   **Denny Gold Medal Nov Chase (Gr 1) (4yo+) £41,667**   2m1f (11)

   43 LE COUDRAY (FR) *CRoche* 8-11-12 BJGeraghty 8/13f   1
       BUST OUT *MrsJHarrington* 6-11-12 PCarberry .... 5/2   ½ 2
       RICARDO *BrianNolan* 8-11-12 GCotter 10/1   20 3
    6 Say Again (IRE) *PaulNolan* 6-11-12 JLCullen .... 8/1   ¾ 4
       Quadco (IRE) *PAFahy* 8-11-12 KAKelly .... 14/1   dist 5

Mr John P. McManus 5ran 4m35.10

LIMERICK Thursday, Dec 26   SOFT

73   **Guinness Greenmount Park Nov Chase (Gr 2) (5yo+) £18,750**   2½m (14)

   47 INTELLIGENT (IRE) *MrsJHarrington* 6-11-5 RMPower 9/2   1
   43 BARROW DRIVE *AnthonyMullins* 6-11-8 MrJJCodd 5/4f   5 2
       THE PREMIER CAT (IRE) *TCahill* 6-11-5 JRBarry 6/1   12 3
       Be My Belle (IRE) *SJTreacy* 6-11-0 TPTreacy 5/2   7 4
       Just In Debt (IRE) *PMJDoyle* 6-11-5 MrJTMcNamara .... 6/1   ¾ 5

Mr Norman Moore 5ran 5m14.90

CHEPSTOW Friday, Dec 27   HEAVY

74   **Western Daily Press Finale Juv Hdle (Gr 1) (A) (3yo) £20,880**   2m110y (7)

   55 NAS NA RIOGH (IRE) *NJHenderson* 3-10-9 MFoley 5/1   1
       LEWIS ISLAND (IRE) *NATwiston-Davies* 3-11-0 CLlewellyn 10/3   11 2
       LOUGAROO (FR) *GMacaire,France* 3-11-0 CGombeau 9/2   19 3
   55 Lilium de Cotte (FR) *GMacaire,France* 3-11-0 JaquesRicou .... 10/3   dist 4
       He's The Biz (FR) *NickWilliams* 3-11-0 DRDennis.............................. 100/1   dist 5
       Le Duc (FR) *PFNicholls* 3-11-0 (b) PJBrennan .... 14/1   f
       Fast Mix (FR) *MCPipe* 3-11-0 APMcCoy... 3/1f   pu
       Flaming Spirt *JSMoore* 3-10-9 DCrosse .... 100/1   pu

Brian Twojohns Partnership 8ran 4m20.74

75   **Coral Welsh National (Heap Chase) (Gr 3) (A) (147) (5yo+) £43,500**   3m5f110y (22)

       MINI SENSATION (IRE) *JonjoO'Neill* 9-10-4[125] ADobbin........................... 8/1   1

29	CHIVES (IRE) *MissHCKnight* 7-11-12[147] RichardGuest	10/1	7 2
	GUNNER WELBURN *IABalding* 10-10-6[127] BFenton	5/2f	13 3
39	FROSTY CANYON *PRWebber* 9-11-7[142] (v) TDoyle	20/1	1¾ 4
24	Murt's Man (IRE) *PFNicholls* 8-10-9[135] MrChristianWilliams[5]	50/1	9 5
	Frantic Tan (IRE) *DJCaro* 10-10-10[131] CLlewellyn	16/1	8 6
	Royal Tommy (IRE) *RHBuckler* 10-10-7[128] MBradburne	33/1	dist 7
59	Take Control (IRE) *MCPipe* 8-11-12[147] APMcCoy	16/1	f
	It's Himself *AJMartin,Ireland* 10-10-5[126] (t) TJMurphy	7/1	f
39	Bounce Back (USA) *MCPipe* 6-11-12[147] RGreene	25/1	pu
	The Bunny Boiler (IRE) *NMeade,Ireland* 8-11-3[143] IJPower[5]	5/1	pu
48	Supreme Glory (IRE) *PGMurphy* 9-11-7[142] LAspell	20/1	pu
48	Rugged River (IRE) *RHAlner* 7-10-7[131] RWalford[3]	8/1	pu
	Ackzo *DMcCain* 9-10-7[128] (b) GLee	40/1	pu
	Native Buck (IRE) *TRGeorge* 9-9-9[121] DCrosse[5]	14/1	pu
	The Quads *FerdyMurphy* 10-10-0[121] (b+t) JRKavanagh	33/1	pu

Mr J. P. McManus 16ran 8m15.44

NEWBURY Saturday, Dec 28 SOFT

76 **Stan James Challow Nov Hdle (Gr 1) (A) (4yo+) £20,300** 2m5f (10)

46	COOLNAGORNA (IRE) *JonjoO'Neill* 5-11-7 APMcCoy	4/6f	1
46	CALLING BRAVE (IRE) *NJHenderson* 6-11-7 MAFitzgerald	5/1	29 2
46	LADY LAUREATE *GCBravery* 4-11-2 BFenton	40/1	13 3
	Maybe The Business *PFNicholls* 6-11-7 RThornton	4/1	8 4
	Texas Ranger *CJMann* 4-11-7 NFehily	25/1	6 5
70	Yorkshire (IRE) *DLWilliams* 8-11-7 JAMcCarthy	20/1	1½ 6
	No Collusion (IRE) *NoelTChance* 6-11-7 SDurack	10/1	pu

Mrs G. Smith 7ran 5m16.80

LEOPARDSTOWN Saturday, Dec 28 Chase course: HEAVY, Hurdles course: SOFT

77 **2003 Special Olympics Nov Hdle (4yo+) £12,500** 2½m (10)

42	HARDY EUSTACE (IRE) *DTHughes* 5-11-8 KAKelly	9/10f	1
28	NIL DESPERANDUM (IRE) *MissFMCrowley* 5-11-5 RWalsh	8/1	¾ 2
	FOTA ISLAND (IRE) *MFMorris* 6-11-11 DJCasey	12/1	5 3
	Satco Express (IRE) *ESheehy* 6-11-11 CFSwan	5/1	4 4
	Mystic Lord (IRE) *NMeade* 5-11-5 PCarberry	12/1	dist 5
	Plenty of Ice (IRE) *CRoche* 5-11-5 PMoloney	9/2	f

Mr Laurence Byrne 6ran 4m56.89

78 **woodiesdiy.com Christmas Hdle (Gr 2) (4yo+) £20,833** 3m (12)

61	LIMESTONE LAD (IRE) *JBowe* 10-11-11 PCarberry	4/6f	1
38	BOSS DOYLE (IRE) *MFMorris* 10-11-9 (b) DJCasey	14/1	9 2
	BANNOW BAY (IRE) *CRoche* 7-11-11 CFSwan	6/4	2½ 3
	Coolaness (IRE) *MsMFlynn* 9-11-4 JRBarry	100/1	dist 4
38	Catch Ball *WPMullins* 6-11-2 RWalsh	25/1	4½ 5
	Oa Baldixe (FR) *NMeade* 8-11-7 BJGeraghty	33/1	6

Mr James Breen 6ran 6m09.82

79 **Ericsson Chase (Gr 1) (5yo+) £62,500** 3m (17)

60	BEEF OR SALMON (IRE) *MichaelHourigan* 6-11-9 TJMurphy	5/1	1
44	COLONEL BRAXTON (IRE) *DTHughes* 7-12-0 NWilliamson	20/1	6 2
39	HARBOUR PILOT (IRE) *NMeade* 7-12-0 PCarberry	6/1	sh 3
20	Foxchapel King (IRE) *MFMorris* 9-12-0 DJCasey	8/1	6 4
59	Sackville (IRE) *MissFMCrowley* 9-12-0 BJGeraghty	7/1	4 5
52	Rince Ri (IRE) *TMWalsh* 9-12-0 RWalsh	3/1	6
52	First Gold (FR) *FDoumen,France* 9-12-0 TDoumen	11/4f	7

Mr B. J. Craig 7ran 6m40.82

LEOPARDSTOWN Sunday, Dec 29 HEAVY

80 **Paddy Power Dial-A-Bet Chase (Gr 2) (5yo+) £18,750** 2m1f (9)

50	MOSCOW FLYER (IRE) *MrsJHarrington* 8-11-12 BJGeraghty	4/9f	1
30	KNIFE EDGE (USA) *MJPO'Brien* 7-11-12 RWalsh	8/1	5 2
	GO ROGER GO (IRE) *EJO'Grady* 10-11-10 NWilliamson	20/1	5 3
60	Copernicus *PHughes* 7-11-7 JLCullen	12/1	2½ 4
9	Arctic Copper (IRE) *NMeade* 8-11-7 (b) PCarberry	10/1	dist 5
52	Alcapone (IRE) *MFMorris* 8-11-12 DJCasey	8/1	pu

Mr Brian Kearney 6ran 4m41.54

81 **Paddy Power Hcap Chase 0-140(131) (4yo+) £62,308** 3m (14)

	COQ HARDI DIAMOND (IRE) *NMeade* 8-9-11[103] GTHutchinson[3]	14/1	1
	SATCOSLAM (IRE) *LWhitmore* 7-10-8[111] GCotter	25/1	7 2
	CLONMEL'S MINELLA (IRE) *MichaelHourigan* 11-9-7[99] RPMcNally[3]	14/1	14 3
	BENNIE'S PRIDE (IRE) *EJO'Grady* 6-10-6[109] NWilliamson	16/1	14 4

Billy The Snake (IRE) *PHughes* 9-10-9[112] JLCullen 9/1   3 5
Delgany Royal (IRE) *DTHughes* 10-11-4[121] KAKelly 16/1   6
31   I Can Imagine (IRE) *RobertTyner* 7-10-3[109] (t) KHadnett[3] 7/1   7
Orthez (IRE) *EGriffin* 8-9-6[102] (b) MFBates[7] 33/1   8
Woodenbridge Natif (IRE) *NMeade* 7-10-5[108] PCarberry 8/1   9
31   Montayral (FR) *PHughes* 5-11-3[125] RMPower[5] .... 20/1   f
Precious Music (IRE) *GerardFarrell* 9-10-11[114] BJGeraghty .... 13/2   f
Supreme Arrow (IRE) *DWachman* 7-9-10[102] MDGrant[3] .... 33/1   f
Golden Storm (IRE) *MissFMCrowley* 5-10-12[120] SGMcDermott[5] .... 16/1   ref
Kirmar (IRE) *PAFahy* 8-10-5[108] KPGaule .... 25/1   ref
Good Vintage (IRE) *NMeade* 7-9-10[104] (b) MFMooney[5] .... 12/1   ref
35   Cregg House (IRE) *PatrickMullins* 7-12-0[131] RWalsh .... 20/1   pu
39   Moral Support (IRE) *JSMoore,GB* 10-10-6[126] DJHoward[3] .... 50/1   pu
Kings Valley (IRE) *NMeade* 8-11-5[122] CO'Dwyer .... 20/1   pu
Jaguar Claw (IRE) *MissFMCrowley* 7-10-4[107] JRBarry .... 16/1   pu
43   Come In Moscow (IRE) *JohnJosephMurphy* 6-9-12[104] JPElliott[3] .... 33/1   pu
Finians Ivy (IRE) *AJMartin* 7-9-11[100] DJCasey .... 11/2f   pu

Mrs Catherine Howard 21ran 6m55.97

CHELTENHAM Wednesday, Jan 1   HEAVY (New Course)

82   **George Stevens Hcap Hdle (B) 0-150(145) (4yo+) £15,300**   2m1f (8)

FLAME CREEK (IRE) *NoelTChance* 7-10-11[130] SDurack 10/3   1
SONEVAFUSHI (FR) *MissVenetiaWilliams* 5-10-0[119] NWilliamson 3/1f   6 2
WESTENDER (FR) *MCPipe* 7-11-12[145] (b) APMcCoy 11/2   3½ 3
51   Sud Bleu (FR) *PFNicholls* 5-10-1[120] RWalsh 13/2   2½ 4
General *MrsNSmith* 6-10-3[122] LAspell 7/1   10 5
67   Majlis (IRE) *TRGeorge* 6-10-9[128] (b) DNRussell...................................... 50/1   18 6
Per Amore (IRE) *PJHobbs* 5-10-1[120] (b) RJohnson.................................... 50/1   27 7
Diamond Joshua (IRE) *MESowersby* 5-10-11[130] BHarding 50/1   7 8
With A Twist (GER) *CJMann* 5-10-12[131] NFehily .... 16/1   dist 9

Martin Wesson Partners 9ran 4m26.00

CORK Saturday, Jan 4   SOFT

83   **McCarthy Insurance Group Pension & Investment Advisors INH**   2m
     Flat (5yo+) £5,601

MASTEROFFOXHOUNDS (IRE) *DWachman* 8-11-11 MrJPMagnier[7] 7/4   1
POKER PAL (IRE) *DTHughes* 6-11-11 (t) MrRLoughran[7] 6/1   5 2
ROCKSTOWN BOY (IRE) *CByrnes* 5-11-7 MrMJFerris[7] 11/10f   1 3
Polly's Dream (IRE) *PatrickCarey* 7-11-6 MrROHarding[7].......................... 12/1   15 4
Shake It Easy (IRE) *RobertTyner* 5-11-0 MrDerekO'Connor[7] 25/1   2 5
Dunbrody Millar (IRE) *MichaelCullen* 5-11-0 MrNPMadden[7] 14/1   6
Back To Gales (IRE) *PatrickMullins* 6-10-13 MrKJMercer[7]........................ 10/1   7
Supreme Shadow (IRE) *TGO'Leary* 5-11-2 MrPFenton 12/1   8
Coolgarrane (IRE) *TimothyDoyle* 8-11-4 MrAJMcNamara[7] 12/1   9
Owensher (IRE) *TAShirley* 7-11-6 MrSOO'Brien[5] 20/1   10

Mrs John Magnier 10ran 4m02.30

LEOPARDSTOWN Sunday, Jan 12   Chase course: HEAVY, Hurdles course: SOFT

84   **Pierse Leopardstown Hcap Chase (159) (5yo+) £42,208**   3m (16)

56   YOULNEVERWALKALONE (IRE) *CRoche* 9-10-5[136] BJGeraghty............. 7/2   1
79   FOXCHAPEL KING (IRE) *MFMorris* 10-12-0[159] DJCasey...................... 13/2   1 2
ESKIMO JACK (IRE) *ALTMoore* 7-10-2[133] CO'Dwyer 5/2f   3½ 3
81   Delgany Royal (IRE) *DTHughes* 11-9-11[131] GTHutchinson[3] 33/1   10 4
Michael Mor (IRE) *NMeade* 9-10-0[131] PCarberry 14/1   4 5
79   Rince Ri (IRE) *TMWalsh* 10-11-13[158] RWalsh 13/2   6
Pikachu Blue (IRE) *MrsSABramall* 7-10-0[131] GCotter 25/1   7
5   Royal Jake (IRE) *NMeade* 9-10-0[131] (b) NWilliamson 16/1   8
81   Precious Music (IRE) *GerardFarrell* 10-10-0[131] TJMurphy....................... 14/1   9
Dark Magic (IRE) *PaddyFennelly* 12-10-1[132] JCulloty................................ 25/1   f
Macs Gildoran *WPMullins* 9-10-0[131] JRBarry .... 13/2   pu

Mr John P. McManus 11ran 6m35.10

85   **Pierse Hdle (Extended Hcap) 0-140(133) (4yo+) £51,071**   2m (8)

XENOPHON (IRE) *AJMartin* 7-10-11[120] MAFitzgerald 12/1   1
COLOURFUL LIFE (IRE) *MrsMReveley,GB* 7-10-6[115] ADobbin 25/1   2 2
CAMDEN TANNER (IRE) *RobertTyner* 7-10-12[121] DNRussell.................. 16/1   ¾ 3
EMOTIONAL MOMENT (IRE) *TJTaaffe* 6-11-2[125] NWilliamson............... 11/1   ¾ 4
51   Spirit Leader (IRE) *MrsJHarrington* 7-11-4[132] RMPower[5] 14/1   2 5
Cailin's Perk (IRE) *JamesMorrissey* 9-10-11[125] APLane[5] 33/1   6
The Dark Flasher (IRE) *CFSwan* 6-10-7[116] DJCasey................................ 20/1   7
Janidou (FR) *ALTMoore* 7-10-9[118] CO'Dwyer... 12/1   8

	Junior Fontaine (FR) *ALTMoore* 6-10-5[117] DJHoward[3]	16/1	9
67	Milkat (IRE) *WPMullins* 5-10-8[117] RWalsh	16/1	10
	Evening Scent *MrsJHarrington* 7-10-10[119] BJGeraghty	10/1jf	11
	Some Buzz (IRE) *TMWalsh* 8-9-11[109] GTHutchinson[3]	10/1jf	12
	True Blue Victory (IRE) *TMWalsh* 7-11-5[128] GCotter	25/1	13
67	Anxious Moments (IRE) *CFSwan* 8-11-6[129] CFSwan	16/1	14
67	Holy Orders (IRE) *WPMullins* 6-11-3[133] (b) SCurling[7]	25/1	15
	King Carew (IRE) *MichaelHourigan* 5-9-12[114] (b) SJCraine[7]	33/1	16
67	Whistling Dixie (IRE) *MrsMReveley,GB* 7-11-9[132] AJDempsey	14/1	17
	Sharp Act (USA) *PHughes* 5-9-10[105] PFlynn	25/1	18
	Eastern Tribute (USA) *ACWhillans,GB* 7-10-6[118] IJardine[3]	100/1	19
	Mr Sneaky Boo (IRE) *MichaelHourigan* 7-11-2[125] APMcCoy	14/1	20
	Lisaan (IRE) *WDurkan* 6-10-7[123] (b) MrNPMadden[7]	33/1	21
	Fairwood Heart (IRE) *PJRothwell* 6-9-12[112] DO'Leary[5]	66/1	22
	Greywell (IRE) *MissElizabethDoyle* 6-9-10[105] TPTreacy	12/1	23
	Star Clipper *NMeade* 6-11-6[129] (b) PCarberry	25/1	24
	Newhall (IRE) *FFlood* 5-11-5[128] FJFlood	20/1	f
6	Emperors Guest *PatrickMullins* 5-10-7[121] IJPower[5]	50/1	f
	Rare Ouzel (IRE) *AJMartin* 7-9-13[108] TJMurphy	16/1	f
61	Balapour (IRE) *PatrickOBrady* 5-11-2[128] (t) JPElliott[3]	33/1	ur

Lane Syndicate 28ran 3m56.98

HAYDOCK Saturday, Jan 18   Chase course: GOOD to SOFT, Hurdles course: SOFT

86	**Premier Stayers' Hdle (Gr 2) (A) (5yo+)** £23,200		2m7f110y (12)
	LORD TRANSCEND (IRE) *JHowardJohnson* 6-11-0 ADobbin	8/1	1
63	DEANO'S BEENO *MCPipe* 11-11-8 APMcCoy	5/6f	nk 2
13	STROMNESS (USA) *AKing* 6-11-4 RThornton	2/1	20 3
	The Granby (IRE) *MrsMReveley* 9-11-0 ADempsey	50/1	10 4
23	Springfield Scally *SGollings* 10-11-0 SDurack	20/1	½ 5
	Rum Pointer (IRE) *RHBuckler* 7-11-0 CLlewellyn	14/1	dist 6

Transcend (Hair and Beauty) Limited 6ran 6m10.31

87	**Peter Marsh Chase (Ltd Hcap) (Gr 2) (A) (155) (5yo+)** £34,800		3m (18)
66	TRUCKERS TAVERN (IRE) *FerdyMurphy* 8-10-9[140] (t) DNRussell	9/2	1
39	HUSSARD COLLONGES (FR) *PBeaumont* 8-11-10[155] RGarritty	3/1f	2½ 2
34	GOGUENARD (FR) *MrsSJSmith* 9-10-4[135] WMarston	20/1	10 3
48	Bindaree (IRE) *NATwiston-Davies* 9-10-11[142] CLlewellyn	16/1	6 4
39	Iznogoud (FR) *MCPipe* 7-11-2[147] APMcCoy	8/1	2½ 5
	Royale de Vassy (FR) *MissVenetiaWilliams* 9-9-13[135] FWindsorClive[5]	20/1	4 6
39	Whitenzo (FR) *PFNicholls* 7-10-10[141] JTizzard	4/1	11 7
	Barton *TDEasterby* 10-11-8[153] ADobbin	7/2	26 8
	Scotmail Boy (IRE) *JHowardJohnson* 10-10-4[135] SDurack	100/1	dist 9

Mrs M. B. Scholey 9ran 6m27.45

88	**Red Square Vodka Champion Hdle Trial (Gr 2) (A) (4yo+)** £23,200		2m (8)
82	FLAME CREEK (IRE) *NoelTChance* 7-11-6 SDurack	9/4	1
40	OCTOBER MIST (IRE) *MrsMReveley* 9-11-2 ADempsey	14/1	13 2
	ILNAMAR (FR) *MCPipe* 7-11-10 APMcCoy	11/10f	nk 3
	Mister McGoldrick *MrsSJSmith* 6-11-2 DElsworth	14/1	6 4
57	The French Furze (IRE) *NGRichards* 9-11-2 ADobbin	6/1	22 5
	Epitre (FR) *MFHarris* 6-11-2 OMcPhail	16/1	5 6
57	Fifth Generation (IRE) *DrPPritchard* 13-11-2 JTizzard	100/1	18 7

Martin Wesson Partners 7ran 3m37.25

KEMPTON Saturday, Jan 18   Chase course: GOOD, Hurdles course: GOOD to SOFT

89	**Tote Exacta Chase (Ltd Hcap) (Gr 2) (A) (161) (5yo+)** £46,400		2m (13)
65	YOUNG DEVEREAUX (IRE) *PFNicholls* 10-10-4[141] RWalsh	9/2	1
65	SEEBALD (GER) *MCPipe* 8-11-5[156] RJohnson	11/2	1 2
65	DARK'N SHARP (GER) *RTPhillips* 8-10-11[148] RJohnson	10/3jf	9 3
54	Demasta (NZ) *NJHenderson* 12-10-1[141] MFoley[3]	50/1	9 4
	Redemption *PRWebber* 8-10-4[141] (b) AThornton	11/1	hd 5
71	Wahiba Sands *MCPipe* 10-11-10[161] TScudamore	25/1	17 6
60	Fadoudal du Cochet (FR) *ALTMoore,Ireland* 10-10-4[141] CO'Dwyer	12/1	21 7
56	Fondmort (FR) *NJHenderson* 7-11-1[152] NWilliamson	10/3jf	f
25	Turgeonev (FR) *TDEasterby* 8-10-9[146] RMcGrath	7/1	ur

Paul K.Barber,Mick Coburn,Colin Lewis 9ran 3m52.53

90	**HBLB Middlesex Nov Hdle (B) (5yo+)** £12,458		2m5f (10)
	LORD SAM (IRE) *VRADartnall* 7-11-8 JCulloty	11/10f	1
	SH BOOM *JonjoO'Neill* 5-11-4 LCooper	7/2	1¾ 2
67	CHAUVINIST (IRE) *NJHenderson* 8-11-8 MFoley	2/1	4 3
	Wintertide *CJMann* 7-10-12 NFehily	33/1	20 4

1014

	What A Man (IRE) *TRGeorge* 6-10-12 RWalsh	20/1	2½	5
	Cherry Brandy *MissHCKnight* 7-10-12 JPMcNamara	100/1	14	6
	Sovereign Gold *DRGandolfo* 6-10-12 LStephens	100/1	22	7
	Distant Sky (USA) *PMitchell* 6-10-12 PHide	100/1	3	8
	Harry's Dream *JWMullins* 6-10-12 AThornton	66/1		pu

Plain Peeps 9ran 5m14.32

WINCANTON Saturday, Jan 18   GOOD to SOFT

91 Tote Tolworth Hdle (Gr 1) (A) (4yo+) £23,800 2m (8)

46	THISTHATANDTOTHER (IRE) *PFNicholls* 7-11-7 TJMurphy	11/4		1
64	PUNTAL (FR) *MCPipe* 7-11-7 BJGeraghty	4/6f	2½	2
46	SELF DEFENSE *MissECLavelle* 6-11-7 FKeniry	25/1	14	3
	Dispol Rock (IRE) *DrPPritchard* 7-11-7 DrPPritchard	250/1	dist	4
64	Kopeck (IRE) *JTGifford* 5-11-7 LAspell	11/2	dist	5
	Limited Edition (IRE) *MPitman* 5-11-7 MBradburne	40/1		f
	Fair Question (IRE) *MissVenetiaWilliams* 5-11-7 BJCrowley	16/1		pu

Mr C. G. Roach 7ran 3m51.10

PAU Sunday, Jan 19   HEAVY

92 Grand Prix de Pau (Chase) (Gr 3) (5yo+) £32,353 3¼m110y

	ESCORT BOY (USA) *JOrtet,France* 5-11-1 FBarrao	6/4		1
	LINE MARINE (FR) *CAubert,France* 6-10-3 LMetais	20	2
	IDOLE DES FONTAINES (FR) *CDiard,France* 7-10-8 SZuliani	10	3
	Chant Royal (FR) *MdeMontfort,France* 11-10-6 (b) TBerthelot	20	4
75	The Quads *FerdyMurphy,GB* 11-10-9 (b) MrDNRussell	1	5
	Coraya (FR) *PChevillard,France* 7-9-13 (b) SRSimon	10	6
	Paladin (FR) *JOrtet,France* 8-11-1 (b) AKondrat	10	7
	Kho Tao (FR) *JOrtet,France* 7-11-1 CPieux		ur
	Bingo Bell (FR) *PBoisgontier,France* 6-10-8 CCheminaud		f
	Haut de Gamme (FR) *J-PTotain,France* 8-10-8 DLesot		f
	Argent Vif (FR) *J-PTotain,France* 8-10-6 BThelier		f
	Iclan de Molieres (FR) *ELeenders,France* 7-10-12 CDubourg		pu
	Iryntzau d'Airy (FR) *JOrtet,France* 7-10-6 (b) TBarcellini		pu

Mme G. Brami 13ran 6m56.00

CHELTENHAM Saturday, Jan 25   SOFT

93 Timeform Nov Hcap Chase (B) (135) (5yo+) £12,818 2m5f (17)

	LA LANDIERE (FR) *RTPhillips* 8-11-12[135] RJohnson	9/2		1
	IBIS ROCHELAIS (FR) *AEnnis* 7-10-7[116] JAMcCarthy	14/1	6	2
	SEA DRIFTING *FerdyMurphy* 6-10-2[111] (s) DNRussell	8/1	sh	3
53	Whereareyounow (IRE) *NATwiston-Davies* 6-11-0[123] CLlewellyn	14/1	hd	4
	Ask The Natives (IRE) *PFNicholls* 9-11-5[128] RWalsh	11/2	dist	5
	Pendle Hill *PBeaumont* 8-9-12[110] DO'Meara[3]	16/1	3½	6
	Irish Hussar (IRE) *NJHenderson* 7-11-7[130] BJGeraghty	5/2f		f
	Pharpost (IRE) *MissVenetiaWilliams* 8-10-1[110] BJCrowley	7/1		f
	Ideal du Bois Beury (FR) *MCPipe* 7-10-11[120] APMcCoy	12/1		pu
	Princesse Grec (FR) *DrPPritchard* 5-10-0[118] VSlattery	100/1		pu

Mrs R. J. Skan 10ran 5m35.62

94 Byrne Bros Cleeve Hdle (Gr 1) (A) (4yo+) £44,625 2m5f110y (10)

	CLASSIFIED (IRE) *MCPipe* 7-11-8 APMcCoy	8/11f		1
67	MR COOL *MCPipe* 9-11-8 TScudamore	11/1	1	2
	SUDDEN SHOCK (GER) *JonjoO'Neill* 8-11-8 BJGeraghty	9/1	16	3
76	Texas Ranger *CJMann* 5-11-8 NFehily	33/1	22	4
	Comex Flyer (IRE) *PFNicholls* 6-11-8 (t) RWalsh	9/1	sh	5
27	Eternal Spring (IRE) *JRFanshawe* 6-11-8 JCulloty	10/3		f

Mr D. A. Johnson 6ran 5m31.01

95 Pillar Property Chase (Gr 2) (A) (6yo+) £49,600 3m1f110y (20)

66	BEHRAJAN (FR) *HDDaly* 8-11-6 RJohnson	9/2		1
56	FOLY PLEASANT (FR) *MissHCKnight* 9-11-6 (t) JCulloty	7/1	14	2
39	GINGEMBRE (FR) *MrsLCTaylor* 9-11-0 AThornton	11/2	dist	3
47	Valley Henry (IRE) *PFNicholls* 8-11-6 BJGeraghty	10/3	26	4
71	Bacchanal (IRE) *NJHenderson* 9-11-10 (b) RWalsh	3/1f		f
56	Cyfor Malta (FR) *MCPipe* 10-11-6 APMcCoy	6/1		ur

The Behrajan Partnership 6ran 6m54.89

96 Ladbroke Trophy Chase (Hcap) (L) (A) (157) (5yo+) £23,200 2m5f (17)

	LADY CRICKET (FR) *MCPipe* 9-11-12[157] (b) APMcCoy	9/2f		1
65	SHAMAWAN (IRE) *JonjoO'Neill* 8-10-4[135] NFehily	11/1	nk	2
	HERMES III (FR) *NJHenderson* 8-10-5[136] RJohnson	13/2	3½	3
	Ballinclay King (IRE) *FerdyMurphy* 9-11-0[145] DNRussell	9/1	2	4

Katarino (FR) *NJHenderson* 8-10-9[143] MFoley[3] 7/1   11 5
45   Poliantas (FR) *PFNicholls* 6-11-2[147] RWalsh .... 8/1   ½ 6
Horus (IRE) *MCPipe* 8-10-11[142] BJGeraghty 6/1   3½ 7
Halexy (FR) *MissVenetiaWilliams* 8-10-0[131] BJCrowley 9/1   13 8
Just Jasmine *KBishop* 11-10-6[137] FKeniry 16/1   3½ 9
Akarus (FR) *MCPipe* 8-9-8[132] MrJEMoore[7] 66/1   1¾ 10
34   Blowing Wind (FR) *MCPipe* 10-10-10[141] TScudamore 25/1   3 11
Be My Manager (IRE) *MissHCKnight* 8-10-0[131] JCulloty .... 20/1   nk 12
Arlequin de Sou (FR) *PJHobbs* 9-10-0[131] (b) PFlynn 33/1   3½ 13
Run For Paddy *MrsHDalton* 7-10-9[140] PGHourigan .... 12/1   pu
Banner Gale (IRE) *DrPPritchard* 14-10-0[131] VSlattery .... 100/1   pu

Mr D. A. Johnson 15ran 5m35.41

97   **Wragge & Co Finesse Juv Nov Hdle (Gr 2) (A) (4yo) £17,400**   2m1f (8)

MONEYTRAIN (GER) *CVonDerRecke,Germany* 4-11-0 RThornton 25/1   1
55   DON FERNANDO *MCPipe* 4-11-8 APMcCoy 7/4   1½ 2
SAINTSAIRE (FR) *NJHenderson* 4-11-4 RJohnson 6/4f   2 3
74   Le Duc (FR) *PFNicholls* 4-11-0 (b) RWalsh 8/1   2½ 4
Ken's Dream *MsAEEmbiricos* 4-11-0 SFox 33/1   4 5
Kadara (IRE) *RHAlner* 4-11-3 AThornton 13/2   12 6
Correct And Right (IRE) *JWMullins* 4-10-9 FKeniry 66/1   4 7
Quarter Masters (IRE) *GMMoore* 4-11-0 JCulloty 66/1   10 8
Sculptor *CJMann* 4-11-0 NFehily 66/1   13 9
74   Lougaroo (FR) *GMacaire,France* 4-11-8 BGicquel 25/1   1¼ 10
Gainful *GFHCharles-Jones* 4-10-9 GRichards .... 100/1   dist 11

Mrs T. Hamann 11ran 4m27.66

DONCASTER Saturday, Jan 25   GOOD to SOFT

98   **skybet.com River Don Nov Hdle (Gr 2) (A) (4yo+) £17,400**   3m110y (11)

TEES COMPONENTS *MrsMReveley* 4-11-8 ADempsey 4/5f   1
TRIBAL VENTURE (FR) *FerdyMurphy* 5-11-11 JMMaguire 33/1   22 2
COWBOYBOOTS (IRE) *LWells* 5-11-4 BFenton 10/1   8 3
76   Maybe The Business *PFNicholls* 7-11-4 JTizzard 5/1   5 4
Well Then Now Then (IRE) *HDDaly* 8-11-3 RForristal 11/1   11 5
Silver Knight *TDEasterby* 5-11-4 (b) RGarritty 10/1   7 6
76   Yorkshire (IRE) *DLWilliams* 9-11-8 FHouston .... 20/1   pu
Coolsan (IRE) *RHAlner* 8-11-4 TJMurphy .... 8/1   pu

Tees Components Ltd 8ran 6m16.45

99   **Great Yorkshire Chase (Hcap) (L) (A) 0-145(140) (5yo+) £32,567**   3m (18)

BARRYSCOURT LAD (IRE) *MCPipe* 9-10-1[115] RGreene 9/2   1
RYALUX (IRE) *ACrook* 10-11-4[132] RMcGrath .... 14/1   hd 2
TONOCO *MrsSJSmith* 10-9-11[114] DElsworth[3] 9/1   9 3
DONNYBROOK (IRE) *RDEWoodhouse* 10-9-11[114] PWhelan[3] 66/1   3 4
Shardam (IRE) *NATwiston-Davies* 6-10-8[122] JGoldstein 12/1   1 5
Tom Costalot (IRE) *MrsSusanNock* 10-9-8[125] AntonyEvans[3] 14/1   2½ 6
Carryonharry (IRE) *MCPipe* 9-11-4[132] GSupple 16/1   11 7
Quality First (IRE) *MrsHDalton* 10-10-11[125] JMogford .... 33/1   hd 8
84   Precious Music (IRE) *GerardFarrell,Ireland* 10-10-3[117] TJMurphy .... 20/1   ¾ 9
75   Gunner Welburn *AMBalding* 11-11-7[135] BFenton .... 11/2   nk 10
Robbo *MrsMReveley* 9-11-7[135] (s) ADempsey 16/1   4 11
7   Chevalier Errant (IRE) *JRAdam* 10-10-9[123] WMarston 50/1   2½ 12
Paris Pike (IRE) *FerdyMurphy* 12-12[140] RichardGaunt .... 40/1   f
84   Delgany Royal (IRE) *DTHughes,Ireland* 11-10-9[123] KAKelly .... 25/1   ur
69   Bold Investor *JonjoO'Neill* 6-11-10[138] LCooper .... 3/1f   pu
Gun'n Roses II (FR) *TDEasterby* 9-11-10[138] RGarritty .... 33/1   pu
Ballybough Rasher (IRE) *JHowardJohnson* 8-11-2[130] GLee .... 20/1   pu
Random Harvest (IRE) *MrsMReveley* 14-10-6[120] JTizzard .... 50/1   pu

Roseberry Racing 18ran 6m13.13

LEOPARDSTOWN Sunday, Jan 26   Chase course: SOFT, Hurdles: GOOD to SOFT

100   **Baileys Arkle Challenge Cup Nov Chase (Gr 1) (5yo+) £32,072**   2m1f (11)

72   BUST OUT *MrsJHarrington* 7-11-12 BJGeraghty 11/10f   1
43   NATIVE SCOUT (IRE) *DHassett* 7-11-12 (t) KHadnett 12/1   1 2
RATHGAR BEAU (IRE) *ESheehy* 7-11-12 TJMurphy 16/1   2 3
72   Ricardo *BrianNolan* 9-11-12 GCotter 25/1   1½ 4
Jurado Express (IRE) *ALTMoore* 7-11-12 CO'Dwyer 7/1   12 5
69   One Night Out (IRE) *WPMullins* 7-11-12 JRBarry 14/1   6
Alexander Milenium (IRE) *WPMullins* 7-11-12 RWalsh .... 7/1   f
Soltero (IRE) *MrsJHarrington* 7-11-12 PCarberry .... 5/1   f

B. B. Horse Racing Club 8ran 4m33.99

101 AIG Europe Champion Hdle (Gr 1) (4yo+) £57,237   2m (8)

	LIKE-A-BUTTERFLY (IRE) *CRoche* 9-11-5 CFSwan	6/4f	1
78	LIMESTONE LAD (IRE) *JamesBowe* 11-11-10 BJGeraghty	15/8	hd 2
	STAGE AFFAIR (USA) *DKWeld* 9-11-10 DJCasey	10/1	13 3
44	Scottish Memories (IRE) *NMeade* 7-11-10 PCarberry	3/1	9 4
	Turtleback (IRE) *EJO'Grady* 5-11-6 NWilliamson	66/1	25 5

Mr John P. McManus 5ran 4m01.74

THURLES Thursday, Jan 30   SOFT

102 Kinloch Brae Chase (Gr 2) (6yo+) £21,523   2½m (14)

71	NATIVE UPMANSHIP (IRE) *ALTMoore* 10-11-12 CO'Dwyer	1/4f	1
80	ARCTIC COPPER (IRE) *NMeade* 9-11-8 (b) PCarberry	6/1	3½ 2
35	MOSCOW EXPRESS (IRE) *MissFMCrowley* 11-11-12 RWalsh	6/1	½ 3
	Ollar Rose *JamesDevereux* 8-11-0 JLCullen	66/1	20 4
	Asabache (IRE) *PO'Keeffe* 8-11-5 KHadnett	500/1	pu

Mrs John Magnier 5ran 5m30.60

SANDOWN Saturday, Feb 1   Chase course: SOFT, Hurdles course: HEAVY

103 Elmbridge Hcap Chase (B) (164) (5yo+) £12,483   2m (13)

	ESKLEYBROOK *VYGethin* 10-10-3[148] MrDMansell[7]	50/1	1
	TIUTCHEV *MCPipe* 10-11-12[164] APMcCoy	7/4f	2 2
	DEVON VIEW (IRE) *PFNicholls* 9-10-0[138] JTizzard	11/2	2 3
56	Wave Rock *PJHobbs* 8-10-0[138] (b) RJohnson	14/1	6 4
	Extra Jack (FR) *PFNicholls* 11-10-0[138] (b) SDurack	11/1	13 5
89	Redemption *PRWebber* 8-9-11[138] MFoley[3]	4/1	f
4	Bleu Superbe (IRE) *MissVenetiaWilliams* 8-10-0[138] BJCrowley	4/1	pu

Mr V. Y. Gethin 7ran 4m10.44

104 Agfa Hdle (B) (5yo+) £12,180   2m110y (8)

57	ROOSTER BOOSTER *PJHobbs* 9-11-8 RJohnson	2/7f	1
91	SELF DEFENSE *MissECLavelle* 6-11-0 FKeniry	14/1	½ 2
	TELIMAR PRINCE (IRE) *JTGifford* 7-11-0 LAspell	8/1	13 3
	Over The First (IRE) *CFSwan,Ireland* 8-11-4 DJCasey	10/1	24 4
	Misconduct *JGPortman* 9-10-9 DRDennis	50/1	15 5
98	Yorkshire (IRE) *DLWilliams* 9-11-0 (b) SDurack	33/1	dist 6
	Royal Racer (FR) *JRBest* 5-11-0 BHitchcott	100/1	pu

Mr Terry Warner 7ran 4m19.30

105 Scilly Isles Nov Chase (Gr 1) (A) (5yo+) £34,100   2½m110y (17)

68	TARXIEN *MCPipe* 9-11-6 (t) APMcCoy	15/8f	1
	FARMER JACK *JWMullins* 7-11-6 AThornton	2/1	3 2
	GROUND BALL (IRE) *CFSwan,Ireland* 6-11-6 DJCasey	10/1	15 3
	Telemoss (IRE) *NGRichards* 9-11-6 RichardGuest	2/1	dist 4

Mr B. A. Kilpatrick 4ran 5m33.71

106 Tote Scoop6 Sandown Hcap Hdle (Gr 3) (A) (137) (4yo+) £34,800   2¾m (11)

	CHOPNEYEV (FR) *RTPhillips* 5-10-5[116] RJohnson	15/8f	1
85	CAMDEN TANNER (IRE) *RobertTyner,Ireland* 7-10-12[123] JCulloty	11/2	¾ 2
85	WHISTLING DIXIE (IRE) *MrsMReveley* 7-11-2[127] ADempsey	11/1	6 3
	Ballylusky (IRE) *JonjoO'Neill* 6-10-9[120] DJCasey	9/1	1¾ 4
67	Valerio *NJHenderson* 7-11-6[134] MFoley[3]	14/1	10 5
	Lorenzino (IRE) *JonjoO'Neill* 6-11-5[130] SDurack	33/1	7 6
86	Rum Pointer (IRE) *RHBuckler* 7-11-0[125] CLlewellyn	12/1	5 7
93	Ideal du Bois Beury (FR) *MCPipe* 7-10-13[131] (v) DHoward[7]	33/1	7 8
	Chicago Bulls (IRE) *AKing* 5-11-0[125] RThornton	14/1	¾ 9
	Jollie Bollie (IRE) *MissVenetiaWilliams* 8-11-5[135] FWindsorClive[5]	12/1	10 10
	Mane Frame *HMorrison* 8-10-0[111] LAspell	16/1	11 11
23	Surprising *PJHobbs* 8-11-8[133] (b) SStronge	16/1	dist 12
32	Carlovent (FR) *MCPipe* 8-11-12[137] APMcCoy	12/1	pu

Mrs Claire Smith 13ran 5m58.71

107 Agfa Diamond Hcap Chase (B) 0-145(143) (5yo+) £29,000   3m110y (20)

	IRIS BLEU (FR) *MCPipe* 7-11-2[133] TScudamore	12/1	1
75	FROSTY CANYON *PRWebber* 10-11-8[139] (v) TDoyle	15/2	23 2
	LORD JACK (IRE) *NGRichards* 7-10-10[130] PRobson[3]	11/2	¾ 3
	Ifni du Luc (FR) *NJHenderson* 7-10-10[130] MFoley[3]	13/2	nk 4
39	Gunther McBride (IRE) *PJHobbs* 8-10-8[137] RJohnson	9/2f	6 5
	Indian Chance *DrJRJNaylor* 9-9-11[117] RWalford[3]	25/1	10 6
	Bramblehill Duke (IRE) *MissVenetiaWilliams* 11-11-1[132] BJCrowley	20/1	2½ 7
	Mothers Help *DLWilliams* 8-10-0[117] SDurack	66/1	14 8
	Prancing Blade *NATwiston-Davies* 10-10-0[117] CLlewellyn	66/1	8 9
	Lancastrian Jet (IRE) *HDDaly* 12-10-3[120] JTizzard	12/1	3½ 10

You're Agoodun *MCPipe* 11-11-12[143] (v) APMcCoy .... 9/1   pu
75 Rugged River (IRE) *RHAlner* 8-11-1[132] AThornton .... 14/1   pu
    Windross *AKing* 11-11-0[131] RThornton .... 10/1   pu
    Handyman (IRE) *PJHobbs* 9-10-9[126] JCulloty .... 16/1   pu

Mr D. A. Johnson 14ran 6m42.35

UTTOXETER Saturday, Feb 1   HEAVY

108   Singer & Friedlander National Trial (Hcap Chase) (L) (A) (145)   3½m (21)
    (6yo+) £47,600

75 MINI SENSATION (IRE) *JonjoO'Neill* 10-11-3[136] BJGeraghty 5/2   1
34 ARDENT SCOUT *MrsSJSmith* 11-10-13[132] WMarston 7/1   12 2
    HISTORG (FR) *FerdyMurphy* 8-10-10[129] DNRussell 2/1f 14 3
59 Bobby Grant *PBeaumont* 12-11-12[145] RGarritty 10/1   5 4
    Zaggy Lane *SCBurrough* 11-10-0[119] LCummins .... 20/1 hd 5
    Kemal's Council (IRE) *JonjoO'Neill* 7-10-4[123] TJMurphy .... 4/1   f
    Echo's of Dawn (IRE) *JohnRUpson* 11-10-0[119] PFlynn .... 14/1   pu

Mr J. P. McManus 7ran 8m32.13

WETHERBY Saturday, Feb 1   GOOD to SOFT

109   Weatherbys Towton Nov Chase (Gr 2) (A) (5yo+) £20,825   3m1f (18)

    KEEN LEADER (IRE) *JonjoO'Neill* 7-11-6 LCooper 8/11f   1
    JUNGLE JINKS (IRE) *GMMoore* 8-11-6 RMcGrath 10/1 24 2
47 HAUT CERCY (FR) *HDDaly* 8-11-6 NWilliamson 9/1 14 3
37 High Cotton (IRE) *DRCElsworth* 8-11-2 (b) BFenton 25/1 1¾ 4
    Gottabe *MrsSJSmith* 10-11-2 PGHourigan 50/1 17 5
    The Bajan Bandit (IRE) *LLungo* 8-11-2 ADobbin .... 3/1   pu

Mrs Stewart Catherwood 6ran 6m43.68

110   Rossington Main Nov Hdle (Gr 2) (A) (4yo+) £17,400   2m (9)

28 RHINESTONE COWBOY (IRE) *JonjoO'Neill* 7-11-8 NWilliamson 1/3f   1
    ALWAYS RAINBOWS (IRE) *BSRothwell* 5-11-5 (v) ARoss 14/1 1¾ 2
    STORMY LORD (IRE) *JWade* 7-11-8 BHarding .... 66/1   ½ 3
    Dancing Bay *NJHenderson* 6-11-5 JPMcNamara 6/1   6 4
    Spainkris *ACrook* 4-10-5 JCrowley 9/1 19 5
    Argento *GMMoore* 6-11-1 RMcGrath 40/1   4 6
    Tier Worker *TDEasterby* 7-11-1 DO'Meara .... 66/1   pu

Mrs John Magnier 7ran 4m05.57

PUNCHESTOWN Sunday, Feb 2   SOFT

111   Byrne Group Plc Nov Hdle (Gr 2) (5yo+) £21,523   2m (9)

62 KICKING KING (IRE) *TJTaaffe* 5-10-13 BJGeraghty 5/2f   1
    CENTRAL HOUSE *DTHughes* 6-11-2 (t) KAKelly 6/1   4 2
    WOODYS DEEP OCEAN (IRE) *NMeade* 7-11-2 PCarberry 8/1   4 3
    Georges Girl (IRE) *FFlood* 5-10-8 FJFlood 6/1   8 4
    Florida Coast (IRE) *JamesBowe* 8-11-2 DJCasey .... 13/2   ¾ 5
42 Macs Valley (IRE) *WPMullins* 6-11-5 RWalsh 9/1   6
    Commanche Course (IRE) *TGO'Leary* 7-11-2 TJMurphy 20/1   7
    Lease *TJTaaffe* 5-10-13 MrTGFreyne 100/1   8
    Curraghmore Thyne (IRE) *AJMartin* 6-10-11 KHClarke 200/1   9
83 Masteroffoxhounds (IRE) *DWachman* 8-11-2 NWilliamson .... 7/2   pu

Mr Conor Clarkson 10ran 4m05.80

112   Byrne Group Plc Tied Cottage Chase (Gr 3) (5yo+) £17,219   2m (11)

80 MOSCOW FLYER (IRE) *MrsJHarrington* 9-12-0 BJGeraghty 2/7f   1
80 COPERNICUS *PHughes* 8-11-10 PCarberry 12/1   9 2
    COMMANCHE COURT (IRE) *TMWalsh* 10-12-0 RWalsh 7/1   4 3
56 Killultagh Storm (IRE) *WPMullins* 9-11-7 DJCasey 8/1 3½ 4
43 Fiery Ring (IRE) *JRHFowler* 8-11-4 RGeraghty[3] 25/1 13 5

Mr Brian Kearney 5ran 4m35.20

WINCANTON Thursday, Feb 6   GOOD to SOFT

113   Annual Members Hcap Hdle (D) 0-125(122) (4yo+) £5,073   2m (8)

    OUR VIC (IRE) *MCPipe* 5-11-10[120] APMcCoy 4/6f   1
    GREEN IDEAL *NJHenderson* 5-11-4[117] MFoley[3] 20/1   1 2
    REVIEWER (IRE) *HMorrison* 5-11-12[122] MBradburne 16/1 17 3
    Brooklyn's Gold (USA) *IanWilliams* 8-11-7[117] DRDennis 8/1 12 4
    World Wide Web (IRE) *JonjoO'Neill* 7-10-12[108] LCooper .... 33/1 hd 5
    Firestone (GER) *AWCarroll* 6-10-9[97] (t) JCulloty 8/1   5 6
3 Rigmarole *PFNicholls* 5-11-3[120] (t) NCarter[7] 14/1   8 7
    Clarendon (IRE) *PJHobbs* 7-11-9[119] RJohnson 11/1 16 8
    Hot Shots (FR) *MPitman* 8-11-2[112] TJMurphy .... 14/1   ur

Lord Native (IRE) *NJHenderson* 8-10-7[110] MrATinkler[7] .... 25/1   pu

Mr D. A. Johnson 10ran 3m53.63

NEWBURY Saturday, Feb 8   GOOD

114   **Sodexho Prestige Game Spirit Chase (Gr 2) (A) (5yo+) £31,000**   2m1f (13)

54	KADARANN (IRE) *PFNicholls* 6-11-4 JTizzard	5/1	1
50	CENKOS (IRE) *PFNicholls* 9-11-10 RWalsh	5/6f	8 2
96	LADY CRICKET (FR) *MCPipe* 9-11-5 (b) APMcCoy	2/1	4 3
33	Castle Prince (IRE) *RJHodges* 9-11-0 LAspell	150/1	dist 4
96	Just Jasmine *KBishop* 11-10-13 RGreene	20/1	ur

Notalotterry 5ran 4m04.27

115   **Tote Gold Trophy Hdle (Hcap) (Gr 3) (A) (157) (4yo+) £69,600**   2m110y (8)

85	SPIRIT LEADER (IRE) *MrsJHarrington,Ireland* 7-10-0[131] NWilliamson ...	14/1	1
	NON SO (FR) *NJHenderson* 5-9-11[131] MFoley[3]	9/2f	1½ 2
67	TIKRAM *GLMoore* 6-10-0[131] LAspell	25/1	3½ 3
27	IN CONTRAST (IRE) *PJHobbs* 7-10-13[144] RJohnson	6/1	1 4
67	Benbyas *DCarroll* 6-9-12[134] PJBrennan[5]	16/1	1½ 5
67	Monkerhostin (FR) *OSherwood* 5-10-0[131] JCulloty	33/1	sh 6
51	Quazar (IRE) *JonjoO'Neill* 5-10-10[141] (t) ADobbin	11/1	1½ 7
67	Bernardon (GER) *MCPipe* 7-10-0[131] (v) GSupple	66/1	4 8
	Warjan (FR) *RTPhillips* 6-9-11[131] AntonyEvans[3]	66/1	sh 9
67	Polar Red *MCPipe* 6-10-0[148] (v) MrJEMoore[7]	50/1	½ 10
90	Chauvinist (IRE) *NJHenderson* 8-10-7[138] BJGeraghty	14/1	1 11
3	Gralmano (IRE) *KARyan* 8-10-0[131] BFenton	9/1	½ 12
	Atlantic Rhapsody (FR) *TMWalsh,Ireland* 6-10-1[132] RWalsh	25/1	2½ 13
67	Moving On Up *CJMann* 9-10-0[131] (b) NFehily	50/1	1¼ 14
	Copeland *MCPipe* 8-11-12[157] (v) RGreene	20/1	¾ 15
	Regal Exit (FR) *NJHenderson* 7-10-2[133] TJMurphy	25/1	sh 16
	Haditovski *JMackie* 7-9-11[131] (v) CRafter[3]	66/1	3 17
88	October Mist (IRE) *MrsMReveley* 9-10-6[137] ADempsey	33/1	2½ 18
65	Davoski *MissVenetiaWilliams* 9-10-4[135] DNRussell	50/1	½ 19
91	Puntal (IRE) *MCPipe* 7-11-2[147] APMcCoy	10/1	1¼ 20
	Joe Cullen (IRE) *IanWilliams* 8-9-9[131] WHutchinson[5]	40/1	3½ 21
94	Mr Cool *MCPipe* 9-10-11[142] TScudamore	25/1	5 22
85	Holy Orders (IRE) *WPMullins,Ireland* 6-10-0[131] (b) JRBarry	20/1	16 23
	Scolardy (IRE) *WPMullins,Ireland* 5-10-7[143] RMPower[5]	25/1	8 24
82	Majlis (IRE) *TRGeorge* 6-10-0[131] (b) RThornton	66/1	nk 25
67	Giocomo (IRE) *JonjoO'Neill* 5-10-6[137] SDurack	40/1	12 26
	Calladine (IRE) *CRoche,Ireland* 7-10-3[134] PaulMoloney	25/1	ur

Mr D. Thompson 27ran 3m50.17

116   **AON Chase (Gr 2) (A) (6yo+) £41,650**   3m (18)

95	VALLEY HENRY (IRE) *PFNicholls* 8-11-6 BJGeraghty...............................	4/1	1
75	CHIVES (IRE) *MissHCKnight* 8-11-6 RichardGuest...................................	3/1	2½ 2
87	TRUCKERS TAVERN (IRE) *FerdyMurphy* 8-11-6 (t) DNRussell	5/1	7 3
45	Royal Auclair (FR) *MCPipe* 6-11-10 APMcCoy.......................................	12/1	6 4
75	Supreme Glory (IRE) *PGMurphy* 10-11-6 LAspell.....................................	66/1	15 5
71	Marlborough (IRE) *NJHenderson* 11-11-10 TJMurphy	6/4f	f

Mr Paul K. Barber 6ran 5m54.34

117   **AON Standard Open NHF (Gr 2) (A) (4, 5 and 6yo) £11,600**   2m110y

	CORNISH REBEL (IRE) *PFNicholls* 6-11-2 RWalsh	12/1	1
	CLOUDY GREY (IRE) *MissECLavelle* 6-11-9 BFenton	9/2	11 2
	SIXO (IRE) *MCPipe* 6-11-9 RGreene	6/1	1 3
	Be Fair *DECantillon* 5-11-9 JCulloty	16/1	1¾ 4
	Control Man (IRE) *MCPipe* 5-11-9 APMcCoy	4/1	3½ 5
	He's The Boss (IRE) *RHBuckler* 6-11-6 FMBerry	8/1	¾ 6
	Patriarch Express *GAHarker* 6-11-6 NHannity[3]	16/1	¾ 7
28	Bold Bishop (IRE) *JonjoO'Neill* 6-11-6 FMBerry	5/2f	4 8
28	Limerick Leader (IRE) *PJHobbs* 5-11-2 RJohnson	10/1	7 9
	Earl's Kitchen *CTizzard* 6-11-6 JTizzard	66/1	3 10
	What A Monday *KBell* 6-11-6 SCurran..	66/1	1¼ 11
	Rakassa *HJManners* 5-10-4 MrJamesDavies[7]	100/1	18 12
	Passenger Omar (IRE) *NoelTChance* 5-11-2 (t) SDurack	66/1	6 13
	Jonanaud *HJManners* 4-9-13 MrJEMoore[7]	100/1	3 14
	Kausse de Thaix (FR) *AMHales* 5-11-2 NWilliamson	66/1	3 15
	Paphian Bay *FerdyMurphy* 5-11-2 DNRussell	50/1	10 16
	Bruern (IRE) *MrsMaryHambro* 5-11-2 VSlattery	100/1	2 17
	Gazump (IRE) *NATwiston-Davies* 5-10-13 AntonyEvans[3]	100/1	1½ 18
	Black Kite (IRE) *HJManners* 4-9-13 LStephens[7]	100/1	12 19
	Money Mountain *JABOld* 6-11-2 LAspell..	66/1	10 20

1019

Hurricane Dipper (IRE) *MissAMNewton-Smith* 5-11-2 HOliver.................. 100/1 nk 21
Camden Dolphin (IRE) *BAPearce* 6-10-8 CRafter[3] 150/1 1½ 22
Mantel Mini *BAPearce* 4-9-8 RLucey-Butler[7] .... 100/1 dist 23

Mr C. G. Roach 23ran 3m51.53

LEOPARDSTOWN Sunday, Feb 9   SOFT

118   Cashmans Bookmakers Spring Juv Hdle (Gr 2) (4yo) £21,242   2m (8)

     MUTINEER (IRE) *DTHughes* 4-11-3 (b+t) KAKelly 6/1   1
41   GOLDEN CROSS (IRE) *MHalford* 4-11-3 CFSwan .... 7/2   hd 2
     KENILWORTH (USA) *PatrickOBrady* 4-11-0 JLCullen 4/1   8 3
     Party Airs (USA) *DKWeld* 4-11-6 BJGeraghty.. 10/3f   9 4
     Lost In The Rain (IRE) *NMeade* 4-11-0 (t) PCarberry 14/1   3½ 5
     Newlands Gold (IRE) *MJPO'Brien* 4-11-0 (b) RWalsh 5/1   6
41   Dyrick Daybreak (IRE) *DavidAKiely* 4-10-9 (t) DJCasey 14/1   7
     American Isle (IRE) *JSBolger* 4-11-0 CO'Dwyer .... 33/1   pu

Seven To Eleven Syndicate 8ran 4m11.87

119   Deloitte And Touche Nov Hdle (Gr 1) (5yo+) £31,863   2¼m (9)

62   SOLERINA (IRE) *JamesBowe* 6-11-5 PCarberry 11/10f   1
77   HARDY EUSTACE (IRE) *DTHughes* 6-11-10 KAKelly 9/4   2 2
77   NIL DESPERANDUM (IRE) *MissFMCrowley* 6-11-10 RWalsh 13/2   14 3
     Hi Cloy (IRE) *MichaelHourigan* 6-11-10 TJMurphy.................................. 7/1   hd 4
     Kadiskar (IRE) *CRoche* 5-11-7 (t) PMoloney 7/1   2 5
42   Native Sparkle (IRE) *THogan* 6-11-5 KHadnett 40/1   6

Mr John P. Bowe 6ran 4m42.95

120   Dr P J Moriarty Nov Chase (Gr 1) (5yo+) £44,608   2m5f (14)

73   BARROW DRIVE *AnthonyMullins* 7-11-12 (t) JCulloty 6/1   1
     NOMADIC *NMeade* 9-11-12 PCarberry .... 16/1   dist 2
     BALLYAMBER (IRE) *WPMullins* 8-11-12 RWalsh .... 14/1   nk 3
84   Eskimo Jack (IRE) *ALTMoore* 7-11-12 CO'Dwyer 5/1   3 4
72   Le Coudray (FR) *CRoche* 9-11-12 BJGeraghty .... 8/15f   f
     Minella Leisure (IRE) *MichaelHourigan* 9-11-12 TJMurphy .... 33/1   f
     Ten Poundsworth (IRE) *GeorgeStewart* 10-11-12 DNRussell .... 12/1   f

Mrs B. Lenihan 7ran 5m50.87

121   Hennessy Cognac Gold Cup (Gr 1) (5yo+) £66,078   3m (17)

79   BEEF OR SALMON (IRE) *MichaelHourigan* 7-12-0 TJMurphy 1/1f   1
79   COLONEL BRAXTON (IRE) *DTHughes* 8-12-0 NWilliamson 7/2   4 2
79   HARBOUR PILOT (IRE) *NMeade* 8-12-0 (b) PCarberry .... 6/1   nk 3
84   Rince Ri *TMWalsh* 10-12-0 (b) RWalsh 9/1   1 4
71   Florida Pearl (IRE) *WPMullins* 11-12-0 BJGeraghty .... 11/2   pu

Mr B. J. Craig 5ran 6m37.76

122   Raymond Smith Memorial Hunters Chase (5yo+) £7,667   3m (17)

     SHELTERING (IRE) *EJO'Grady* 11-11-11 MrGElliott[3] 7/4jf   1
     DORANS PRIDE (IRE) *MichaelHourigan* 14-11-7 MrROHarding[7] 11/4   10 2
     JOE BLAKE (IRE) *IRFerguson* 8-12-0 MrJTMcNamara............................. 7/4jf   12 3
     Bellaney Lady (IRE) *GeorgeStewart* 9-11-2 MrLJGracey[7]........................... 10/1   dist 4
     Cortynan (IRE) *PatrickJFGillespie* 11-11-7 MrTMPeoples[7] .... 66/1   f
     Taurean Son (IRE) *MrsDFoster* 10-11-7 MrPBuchanan[7] .... 50/1   f
     Executive Games (IRE) *PaulJohnGilligan* 6-11-2 MrMDarcy[7].................... 50/1   f

Mrs Stewart Catherwood 7ran 6m44.09

ASCOT Saturday, Feb 15   Chase course: SOFT, Hurdles course: HEAVY

123   Amlin Reynoldstown Nov Chase (Gr 2) (A) (5yo+) £27,300   3m110y (20)

109   KEEN LEADER (IRE) *JonjoO'Neill* 7-11-10 LCooper 11/10   1
93   WHEREAREYOUNOW (IRE) *NATwiston-Davies* 6-11-3 CLlewellyn .... 33/1   dist 2
     Indian Scout (IRE) *BDeHaan* 8-11-10 LCummins .... 14/1   f
69   Jair du Cochet (FR) *GMacaire,France* 6-11-10 JaquesRicou.................... 1/1f   ur

Mrs Stewart Catherwood 4ran 6m46.01

124   William Hill Hcap Hdle (B) 0-140(132) (4yo+) £29,000   2½m (11)

     KORELO (FR) *MCPipe* 5-10-8[115] APMcCoy...................................... 4/1   1
106   CHOPNEYEV (FR) *RTPhillips* 5-11-6[127] RJohnson.............................. 5/2f   1¼ 2
     FORMAL BID (USA) *CCBealby* 6-10-8[115] JCulloty 16/1   12 3
82   Sonevafushi (FR) *MissVenetiaWilliams* 5-11-2[123] BJCrowley 16/1   23 4
106   Carlovent (FR) *MCPipe* 8-11-4[132] MrJEMoore[7] 33/1   1½ 5
85   Colourful Life (FR) *MrsMReveley* 7-10-9[116] AThornton..................... 9/2   12 6
     Half The Pot (IRE) *RRowe* 8-10-1[108] BFenton...................................... 33/1   ½ 7
68   Mercato (FR) *JRBest* 7-10-10[117] TJMurphy....................................... 7/1   9 8
     Prokofiev (USA) *JonjoO'Neill* 7-11-1[122] (b) LCooper............................ 16/1   ½ 9

67	Under The Sand (IRE) *PJHobbs* 6-11-3[124] MAFitzgerald	10/1	f
	Eluna *IanWilliams* 5-11-6[127] DRDennis	33/1	pu
	Exstoto *RAFahey* 6-10-3[113] PWhelan[3]	16/1	pu
	Mr D. A. Johnson 12ran 5m22.82		

125 Ritz Club Ascot Chase (Gr 1) (A) (5yo+) £59,500   2m3f110y (16)

103	TIUTCHEV *MCPipe* 10-11-7 APMcCoy	15/8f	1
57	GEOS (FR) *NJHenderson* 8-11-7 MAFitzgerald	11/2	12 2
33	TRESOR DE MAI (FR) *MCPipe* 9-11-7 RGreene	12/1	1¼ 3
89	Wahiba Sands *MCPipe* 10-11-7 TScudamore	16/1	3½ 4
56	Fadalko (FR) *PFNicholls* 10-11-7 TJMurphy	10/1	dist 5
71	Douze Douze (FR) *GMacaire,France* 7-11-7 (t) BGicquel	5/1	ur
89	Young Devereaux (IRE) *PFNicholls* 10-11-7 JTizzard	4/1	pu
	The Liars Poker Partnership 7ran 5m12.84		

WINCANTON Saturday, Feb 15   GOOD to SOFT

126 Country Gentlemen's Association Chase (L) (A) (5yo+) £23,800   3m1f110y (21)

48	SEE MORE BUSINESS (IRE) *PFNicholls* 13-11-12 (b) RWalsh	7/4	1
107	IRIS BLEU (FR) *MCPipe* 7-11-12 TScudamore	13/8f	9 2
79	FIRST GOLD (FR) *FDoumen,France* 10-11-12 TDoumen	9/4	1 3
108	Zaggy Lane *SCBurrough* 11-11-2 JPMcNamara	50/1	dist 4
96	Banner Gale (IRE) *DrPPritchard* 14-11-2 DrPPritchard	200/1	dist 5
	Mr Paul K. Barber & Sir Robert Ogden 5ran 6m31.72		

127 Axminster Kingwell Hdle (Gr 2) (A) (4yo+) £29,750   2m (8)

110	RHINESTONE COWBOY (IRE) *JonjoO'Neill* 7-11-6 NWilliamson	8/11f	1
91	THISTHATANDTOTHER (IRE) *PFNicholls* 7-11-6 RWalsh	7/2	1¾ 2
70	HORS LA LOI III (FR) *JRFanshawe* 8-11-10 (t) ADobbin	10/3	14 3
88	Fifth Generation (IRE) *DrPPritchard* 13-11-2 DrPPritchard	300/1	30 4
	San Suru (GER) *MHofer,Germany* 9-11-2 (b) PGehm	100/1	21 5
94	Eternal Spring (IRE) *JRFanshawe* 6-11-6 (t) TDoyle	16/1	f
	Mrs John Magnier 6ran 3m45.25		

GOWRAN PARK Saturday, Feb 15   GOOD to SOFT

128 The Red Mills Trial Hdle (Gr 2) (4yo+) £23,675   2m (9)

14	SACUNDAI (IRE) *EJO'Grady* 6-11-9 CFSwan	7/4	1
61	LISS A PAORAIGH (IRE) *JEKiely* 8-11-6 BJGeraghty	4/6f	1½ 2
115	CALLADINE (IRE) *CRoche* 7-11-9 MrAPCrowe	14/1	13 3
	Stacumny Bridge (IRE) *MHalford* 5-11-0 PCarberry	12/1	1 4
85	Cailin's Perk (IRE) *JamesMorrissey* 9-10-12 DJCasey	14/1	1½ 5
	Saywhat (IRE) *PatrickAKinsella* 5-11-0 DJHoward	500/1	6
	Malm Syndicate 6ran 4m04.80		

FONTWELL Monday, Feb 17   GOOD to SOFT

129 Collins Stewart National Spirit Hdle (Gr 2) (A) (4yo+) £23,200   2½m (10)

94	CLASSIFIED (IRE) *MCPipe* 7-11-10 APMcCoy	8/13f	1
104	TELIMAR PRINCE (IRE) *JTGifford* 7-11-2 LAspell	7/1	1½ 2
94	COMEX FLYER (IRE) *PFNicholls* 6-11-2 (t) RWalsh	10/1	2 3
1	Milligan (IRE) *MissVenetiaWilliams* 8-11-9 RJohnson	20/1	12 4
	Marcus William (IRE) *BGPowell* 6-11-2 BFenton	50/1	1 5
86	Stromness (USA) *AKing* 6-11-2 RThornton	4/1	¾ 6
	Alka International *MrsPTownsley* 6-11-2 (b) TJMurphy	100/1	3 7
	Mr D. A. Johnson 7ran 5m03.53		

KEMPTON Friday, Feb 21   GOOD to FIRM

130 Dovecote Nov Hdle (Gr 2) (A) (4yo+) £17,400   2m (8)

115	PUNTAL (FR) *MCPipe* 7-11-8 APMcCoy	4/5f	1
51	JABOUNE (FR) *AKing* 6-11-8 RJohnson	6/1	11 2
	CARACCIOLA (GER) *NJHenderson* 6-11-8 MAFitzgerald	7/1	17 3
	Demi Beau *CJMann* 5-11-1 NFehily	3/1	11 4
	Amir Zaman *JRJenkins* 5-11-1 AThornton	33/1	13 5
	Rolex Free (ARG) *MrsLCTaylor* 5-11-1 AThornton	66/1	24 6
	Mr Terry Neill 6ran 3m48.76		

131 betfair.com Rendlesham Hdle (Gr 2) (A) (4yo+) £23,800   3m110y (12)

86	DEANO'S BEENO *MCPipe* 11-11-10 APMcCoy	1/1f	1
	PALUA *MissECLavelle* 6-11-2 BFenton	4/1	12 2
129	STROMNESS (USA) *AKing* 6-11-2 RThornton	10/3	8 3
115	October Mist (IRE) *MrsMReveley* 9-11-2 ADempsey	8/1	2½ 4
115	Moving On Up *CJMann* 9-11-2 (b) NFehily	12/1	dist 5
	Axom 5ran 6m01.75		

132 betfair.com Nov Chase (C) (5yo+) £12,753   3m (19)

39	STORMEZ (FR) *MCPipe* 6-11-10 (t) APMcCoy	2/9f	1
94	SUDDEN SHOCK (GER) *JonjoO'Neill* 8-11-3 JRKavanagh	10/3	11 2

Mr D. A. Johnson 2ran 6m25.88

133 Pendil Nov Chase (Gr 2) (A) (5yo+) £20,300   2½m110y (17)

17	HAND INN HAND *HDDaly* 7-11-7 RJohnson	3/1	1
	DRUID'S GLEN (IRE) *JonjoO'Neill* 7-11-3 BJGeraghty	16/1	5 2
68	SCOTS GREY *NJHenderson* 8-11-3 MAFitzgerald	9/4jf	½ 3
23	Roveretto *MrsMReveley* 8-11-3 ADobbin	12/1	21 4
	Epervier d'Or (FR) *PFNicholls* 5-11-3 (t) RWalsh	9/4jf	9 5
17	Monte Cristo (FR) *MrsLCTaylor* 5-10-10 AThornton	33/1	16 6
	Colonial Sunset (IRE) *DrPPritchard* 9-11-3 MrJEMoore	100/1	1½ 7
	Jaybejay (NZ) *MCPipe* 8-11-3 APMcCoy	12/1	pu

Patrick Burling Developments Ltd 8ran 5m03.98

134 Singapore Airlines Adonis Juv Nov Hdle (Gr 2) (A) (4yo) £17,400   2m (8)

	WELL CHIEF (GER) *MCPipe* 4-11-2 APMcCoy	7/1	1
	MUGHAS (IRE) *AKing* 4-10-12 RThornton	12/1	6 2
55	DUKE OF EARL (IRE) *SKirk* 4-11-5 SDurack	14/1	nk 3
	East Tycoon (IRE) *JonjoO'Neill* 4-11-5 BJGeraghty	9/4	3 4
97	Saintsaire (IRE) *NJHenderson* 4-11-2 MAFitzgerald	10/11f	nk 5
	Master Papa (IRE) *NATwiston-Davies* 4-11-2 CLlewellyn	33/1	½ 6
	Miss Koen (IRE) *DLWilliams* 4-10-7 GusBrown	200/1	19 7

Mr D. A. Johnson 7ran 4m06.29

135 Racing Post Chase (Hcap) (Gr 3) (A) (152) (5yo+) £58,000   3m (19)

93	LA LANDIERE (FR) *RTPhillips* 8-11-7[147] WMarston	5/1jf	1
107	GUNTHER MCBRIDE (IRE) *PJHobbs* 8-10-8[134] RJohnson	5/1jf	3 2
99	RYALUX (IRE) *ACrook* 10-11-0[140] RMcGrath	14/1	1 3
99	Carryonharry (IRE) *MCPipe* 9-10-5[131] (v) GSupple	33/1	10 4
	Montreal (FR) *MCPipe* 6-10-4[130] APMcCoy	7/1	1¼ 5
108	Historg (FR) *FerdyMurphy* 8-10-2[128] DNRussell	25/1	2½ 6
89	Fondmort (FR) *NJHenderson* 7-11-12[152] MAFitzgerald	8/1	1 7
66	Exit To Wave (FR) *PFNicholls* 7-11-2[142] (t) RWalsh	9/1	1¾ 8
47	Maximize (IRE) *MissHCKnight* 9-10-10[136] JCulloty	9/1	4 9
25	Red Ark *RCGuest* 10-9-13[132] (t) MrLMcGrath[3]	25/1	1¼ 10
66	Zafarabad (IRE) *PJHobbs* 9-11-0[140] (b) TJMurphy	16/1	25 11
99	Bold Investor *JonjoO'Neill* 6-10-12[138] BJGeraghty	10/1	3½ 12
66	Carbury Cross (IRE) *JonjoO'Neill* 9-11-4[144] (b) SDurack	14/1	21 13
25	Chicuelo (FR) *MCPipe* 7-11-2[142] (v) TScudamore	14/1	pu

Mrs R. J. Skan 14ran 5m53.99

136 Red Square Vodka Prestige Nov Hdle (Gr 2) (A) (4yo+) £17,850   2m7f110y (12)

58	IRIS'S GIFT *JonjoO'Neill* 6-11-9 BJGeraghty	8/13f	1
58	PRIESTS BRIDGE (IRE) *NATwiston-Davies* 7-11-1 CLlewellyn	33/1	17 2
98	TEES COMPONENTS *MrsMReveley* 8-11-9 ADempsey	7/4	19 3
	Simply Supreme (IRE) *MrsSJSmith* 6-11-6 WMarston	10/1	29 4
	Happy Hussar (IRE) *DrPPritchard* 10-11-2 DrPPritchard	200/1	sh 5

Mr Robert Lester 5ran 5m53.45

137 Red Square Vodka Gold Cup Chase (Hcap) (Gr 3) (A) (155) (5yo+) £63,800   3½m110y (22)

	SHOTGUN WILLY (IRE) *PFNicholls* 9-11-12[155] RWalsh	10/1	1
107	YOU'RE AGOODUN *MCPipe* 11-10-12[141] (v) RThornton	40/1	¾ 2
126	IRIS BLEU (FR) *MCPipe* 7-11-6[149] TScudamore	13/2f	sh 3
24	WONDER WEASEL (IRE) *KCBailey* 10-10-0[134] (s) DFlavin[5]	10/1	5 4
24	Jocks Cross (IRE) *MissVenetiaWilliams* 12-10-6[135] BJCrowley	66/1	6 5
107	Frosty Canyon *PRWebber* 10-10-10[139] (v) TDoyle	7/1	nk 6
116	Supreme Glory (IRE) *PGMurphy* 10-10-5[134] LAspell	20/1	5 7
87	Bindaree (IRE) *NATwiston-Davies* 9-10-11[140] CLlewellyn	14/1	4 8
	Hugo de Grez (FR) *AParker* 8-10-5[137] PRobson[3]	12/1	5 9
39	Southern Star (IRE) *MissHCKnight* 8-10-11[140] JCulloty	8/1	8 10
135	Carbury Cross (IRE) *JonjoO'Neill* 9-10-12[144] TSiddall[3]	33/1	2½ 11
75	Take Control (IRE) *MCPipe* 9-11-0[143] RGreene	25/1	3 12
108	Bobby Grant *PBeaumont* 12-10-11[140] RGarritty	20/1	10 13
108	Ardent Scout *MrsSJSmith* 11-10-0[132] DElsworth[3]	11/1	6 14
34	Amberleigh House (IRE) *DMcCain* 11-10-0[129] WMarston	40/1	8 15
108	Mini Sensation (IRE) *JonjoO'Neill* 10-11-5[148] BJGeraghty	8/1	pu

Kit Smartie (IRE) *DMForster* 11-10-0[129] (s+t) JRKavanagh......................... 33/1   pu

Mr C. G. Roach 17ran 7m25.40

SANDOWN Saturday, Mar 8   HEAVY

138   EBF NH Nov Hcap Hdle Final (Gr 3) (A) (120) (4 to 7yo) £29,000   2½m110y (9)

	TANA RIVER (IRE) *MissECLavelle* 7-11-12[120] BFenton............................. 7/1		1
	NONANTAIS (FR) *MBradstock* 6-11-10[118] MBatchelor.............................. 12/1	9	2
	BENBECULA (IRE) *PRWebber* 6-11-6[114] (v) JAMcCarthy 11/1	1½	3
	Handy Money *MJRyan* 6-10-12[106] MAFitzgerald 16/1	9	4
	Be My Destiny (IRE) *MPitman* 6-11-4[112] RJohnson 10/1	7	5
	Supreme Piper (IRE) *PJHobbs* 5-10-12[106] PFlynn..................................... 8/1	6	6
	Celtic Vision (IRE) *JonjoO'Neill* 7-11-7[115] (t) LCooper........................... 7/2f		pu
	Jupiter de Bussy (FR) *LLungo* 6-11-4[112] ADobbin.................................. 10/1		pu
	His Nibs (IRE) *MissVenetiaWilliams* 6-11-2[110] BJCrowley...................... 10/1		pu
	Master Trix (IRE) *MPitman* 6-10-11[108] CRafter[3].................................... 8/1		pu
	Russian Gigolo (IRE) *NATwiston-Davies* 6-10-6[100] CLlewellyn 25/1		pu
	Lord Nellsson *JSKing* 7-10-0[94] RGreene.. 20/1		pu

The Frisky Fillies 12ran 5m32.69

139   Sunderlands Imperial Cup Hdle (Hcap) (B) 0-150(134) (4yo+)   2m110y (8)
£29,000

124	KORELO (FR) *MCPipe* 5-11-6[128] APMcCoy.. 9/4f		1
85	NEWHALL (IRE) *FFlood,Ireland* 5-11-2[124] FJFlood 16/1	6	2
	LAWZ (IRE) *CJMann* 9-10-13[121] NFehily.. 33/1	2½	3
	CANADA *MCPipe* 5-10-11[119] RGreene.. 14/1	1½	4
124	Mercato (FR) *JRBest* 7-10-7[115] LCummins.. 33/1	2	5
115	Tikram *GLMoore* 6-11-5[134] MrJEMoore[7].. 33/1	2½	6
88	Mister McGoldrick *MrsSJSmith* 6-11-8[133] DElsworth[3]...................... 16/1	¾	7
51	Hawadeth *VRADartnall* 8-11-3[125] JCulloty... 8/1	6	8
	Bound *MLWadham* 5-10-3[114] (t) CRafter[3].. 50/1	nk	9
67	Idaho d'Ox (FR) *MCPipe* 7-11-4[126] (v) TScudamore 25/1	nk	10
85	Janidou (FR) *ALTMoore,Ireland* 7-10-8[116] DJCasey............................. 12/1	25	11
110	Dancing Bay *NJHenderson* 6-11-0[122] MAFitzgerald 10/1	2½	12
	Serenus (USA) *DRCEllsworth* 10-10-0[115] MrONelmes[7]........................ 50/1	sh	13
85	True Blue Victory (IRE) *TMWalsh,Ireland* 7-11-9[131] RWalsh 12/1	½	14
124	Under The Sand (IRE) *PJHobbs* 6-11-0[122] RJohnson.......................... 14/1	5	15
115	Bernardon (GER) *MCPipe* 7-11-4[126] (v) GSupple 50/1	20	16
	Talarive (USA) *PDNiven* 7-10-7[115] ADobbin... 13/2		pu

Mr D. A. Johnson 17ran 4m22.83

CHELTENHAM Tuesday, Mar 11   GOOD (Old Course)

140   Gerrard Wealth Management Supreme Nov Hdle (Gr 1) (A) (4yo+)   2m110y (8)
£58,000

42	BACK IN FRONT (IRE) *EJO'Grady,Ireland* 6-11-8 NWilliamson.............. 3/1f		1
111	KICKING KING (IRE) *TJTaaffe,Ireland* 5-11-8 BJGeraghty 13/2	10	2
115	CHAUVINIST (IRE) *NJHenderson* 8-11-8 MAFitzgerald 20/1	4	3
67	Keltic Bard *CJMann* 6-11-8 NFehily... 50/1	3	4
127	Thisthatandtother (IRE) *PFNicholls* 7-11-8 RWalsh 9/2	nk	5
	Limerick Boy (GER) *MissVenetiaWilliams* 5-11-8 ADobbin.................... 33/1	2½	6
130	Jaboune *AKing* 6-11-8 RJohnson... 50/1	1¾	7
28	Inca Trail (IRE) *MissHCKnight* 7-11-8 JCulloty..................................... 14/1	1¼	8
42	Mutakarrim *DKWeld,Ireland* 6-11-8 (b) TJMurphy............................... 14/1	nk	9
42	Rosaker (USA) *NMeade,Ireland* 6-11-8 PCarberry 11/1	2½	10
	Lirfox (FR) *MCPipe* 6-11-3 APMcCoy... 12/1	½	11
55	Tramantano *NATwiston-Davies* 4-11-0 (t) CLlewellyn............................ 100/1	1¼	12
	Dangerously Good *RCGuest* 5-11-8 (v) RichardGuest........................... 66/1	6	13
	Joueur d'Estruval (FR) *WPMullins,Ireland* 6-11-8 CFSwan................... 14/1	4	14
	Detonator (FR) *IanWilliams* 5-11-8 DRDennis....................................... 100/1	11	15
	Supreme Developer (IRE) *AnthonyMullins,Ireland* 6-11-8 CO'Dwyer...... 20/1	5	16
	North Point (IRE) *RCurtis* 5-11-8 JGoldstein... 50/1	dist	17
	Prince Dimitri *MCPipe* 4-11-0 TScudamore 66/1	22	18
	Arch Stanton (IRE) *WPMullins,Ireland* 5-11-8 DJCasey 25/1		su

D. Cox 19ran 3m56.62

141   Irish Independent Arkle Challenge Trophy Chase (Gr 1) (A) (5yo+)   2m (12)
£81,200

26	AZERTYUIOP (FR) *PFNicholls* 6-11-8 RWalsh 5/4f		1
49	IMPEK (FR) *MissHCKnight* 7-11-8 JCulloty... 6/1	11	2
	ISIO (FR) *NJHenderson* 7-11-8 MAFitzgerald 10/1	1	3
105	Farmer Jack *JWMullins* 7-11-8 AThornton.. 7/1	3	4
133	Hand Inn Hand *HDDaly* 7-11-8 RJohnson 10/1	5	5
101	Stage Affair (USA) *DKWeld,Ireland* 9-11-8 (b) BJGeraghty.................... 20/1	15	6

1023

100	Ricardo *BrianNolan,Ireland* 9-11-8 GCotter	100/1	18 7

100 Ricardo *BrianNolan,Ireland* 9-11-8 GCotter 100/1   18 7
      Adamant Approach (IRE) *WPMullins,Ireland* 9-11-8 PCarberry .... 7/1   f
49 Le Roi Miguel (FR) *PFNicholls* 5-11-3 APMcCoy .... 11/1   f
      Mr J. Hales 9ran 3m56.67

142   Smurfit Champion Hdle Challenge Trophy (Gr 1) (A) (4yo+)   2m110y (8)
     £174,000

104 ROOSTER BOOSTER *PJHobbs* 9-12-0 RJohnson 9/2   1
82 WESTENDER (FR) *MCPipe* 7-12-0 (b) RGreene 33/1   11 2
127 RHINESTONE COWBOY (IRE) *JonjoO'Neill* 7-12-0 NWilliamson 5/2f   3 3
104 Self Defense *MissECLavelle* 6-12-0 FKeniry .... 100/1   ¾ 4
70 Intersky Falcon *JonjoO'Neill* 6-12-0 (b) LCooper 5/1   2½ 5
115 In Contrast (IRE) *PJHobbs* 7-12-0 BJGeraghty 25/1   4 6
57 Landing Light (IRE) *NJHenderson* 8-12-0 (b) MAFitzgerald 14/1   2 7
115 Holy Orders (IRE) *WPMullins,Ireland* 6-12-0 (b) JRBarry 100/1   2 8
70 Santenay (FR) *PFNicholls* 5-12-0 RWalsh 33/1   5 9
101 Like-A-Butterfly (IRE) *CRoche,Ireland* 9-11-9 CFSwan .... 13/2   hd 10
101 Scottish Memories (IRE) *NMeade,Ireland* 7-12-0 PCarberry 25/1   4 11
70 Marble Arch *HMorrison* 7-12-0 TJMurphy 25/1   1 12
88 Flame Creek (IRE) *NoelTChance* 7-12-0 SDurack 14/1   16 13
115 Scolardy (IRE) *WPMullins,Ireland* 5-12-0 DJCasey 66/1   3½ 14
115 Copeland *MCPipe* 8-12-0 (v) APMcCoy .... 25/1   f
      Iberus (GER) *MCPipe* 5-12-0 (v) TScudamore .... 100/1   f
127 Hors La Loi III (FR) *JRFanshawe* 8-12-0 (t) ADobbin .... 14/1   rtr
      Mr Terry Warner 17ran 3m54.55

143   William Hill NH Hcap Chase (Gr 3) (A) (161) (5yo+) £46,400   3m110y (19)

84 YOULNEVERWALKALONE (IRE) *CRoche,Ireland* 9-10-11[142] BJGeraghty 7/1   1
109 HAUT CERCY (FR) *HDDaly* 8-10-0[131] RJohnson .... 10/1   ¾ 2
58 AD HOC (IRE) *PFNicholls* 9-11-0[145] RWalsh 5/1jf   9 3
135 MAXIMIZE (IRE) *MissHCKnight* 9-10-1[132] TJMurphy 20/1   1¼ 4
      Djeddah (FR) *FDoumen,France* 12-10-2[133] (b) TDoumen 50/1   4 5
135 Historg (FR) *FerdyMurphy* 8-10-0[131] DNRussell .... 14/1   ½ 6
107 Bramblehill Duke (IRE) *MissVenetiaWilliams* 11-10-0[131] PFlynn 33/1   3 7
137 Southern Star (IRE) *MissHCKnight* 8-10-6[140] DElsworth[3] 14/1   1 8
116 Royal Auclair (FR) *MCPipe* 6-11-7[152] RGreene 20/1   8 9
75 The Bunny Boiler (IRE) *NMeade,Ireland* 9-10-11[142] PCarberry 25/1   9 10
      Joss Naylor (IRE) *JonjoO'Neill* 8-10-9[140] LCooper 5/1jf   1¼ 11
      Satchmo (IRE) *EJO'Grady,Ireland* 11-10-1[132] NWilliamson 16/1   18 12
95 Foly Pleasant (FR) *MissHCKnight* 9-11-13[158] (t) JCulloty 16/1   17 13
      Fatehalkhair (IRE) *BEllison* 11-10-0[134] VTKeane[3] 40/1   6 14
84 Foxchapel King (IRE) *MFMorris,Ireland* 10-12-2[161] DJCasey .... 20/1   ur
87 Iznogoud (FR) *MCPipe* 7-10-12[143] (v) TScudamore .... 9/1   ur
137 Carbury Cross (IRE) *JonjoO'Neill* 9-10-10[141] SDurack .... 20/1   pu
      Go Ballistic *RTPhillips* 14-10-9[140] WMarston .... 33/1   pu
      Mr J. P. McManus 18ran 6m16.99

144   Fulke Walwyn Kim Muir Challenge Cup Hcap Chase (Amat) (B)   3m110y (19)
     0-140(140) (5yo+) £29,000

      ROYAL PREDICA (FR) *MCPipe* 9-10-13[134] (t) MrSSMcHugh[7] 33/1   1
93 IBIS ROCHELAIS (FR) *AEnnis* 7-10-5[122] MrLMcGrath[3] 4/1f   10 2
60 RATHBAWN PRINCE (IRE) *DTHughes,Ireland* 11-11-8[139] MrRLoughran[3] 40/1   ¾ 3
135 MONTREAL (FR) *MCPipe* 6-10-12[129] MrJEMoore[3] .... 12/1   ½ 4
96 Katarino (FR) *NJHenderson* 8-11-5[140] MrSWaley-Cohen[3] 25/1   2½ 5
135 Carryonharry (IRE) *MCPipe* 9-11-2[130] (v) MrGordonElliott .... 20/1   ½ 6
      Samuel Wilderspin *RLee* 11-11-4[132] (t) MrGCarenza .... 16/1   ¾ 7
107 Ifni du Luc (FR) *NJHenderson* 7-10-12[129] MrATinkler[3] 14/1   6 8
99 Tom Costalot (IRE) *MrsSusanNock* 8-10-11[125] MrJMPritchard 25/1   2½ 9
      Spinofski *PRWebber* 8-10-1[120] MrMBaldock[5] 9/1   5 10
96 Be My Manager (IRE) *MissHCKnight* 9-8-12[125] MrSMorris[3] 33/1   2½ 11
123 Whereareyounow (IRE) *NATwiston-Davies* 6-10-2[123] MrTGreenway[7] 25/1   13 12
      Lanmire Tower (IRE) *SGollings* 9-10-10[124] (b) MrAFitzgerald 33/1   1¾ 13
107 Lord Jack (IRE) *NGRichards* 7-10-11[130] (t) MrROHarding[5] 14/1   10 14
      Silver Steel *CRoche,Ireland* 8-10-13[127] MrAPCrowe 6/1   1½ 15
      Dorans Gold *PFNicholls* 9-11-1[129] MrChristianWilliams 25/1   2½ 16
87 Royale de Vassy (FR) *MissVenetiaWilliams* 9-11-0[128] AO'Keeffe .... 20/1   ½ 17
      Skippers Cleuch (IRE) *LLungo* 9-11-0[128] MrBRHamilton .... 20/1   dist 18
34 Moor Lane *AMBalding* 11-10-13[130] MrPJColville[3] .... 14/1   ur
25 Mr Baxter Basics *MissVenetiaWilliams* 12-10-6[121] MrsThomas[7] ...... 33/1   ur
      Burlu (FR) *MCPipe* 9-11-1[132] MrHNaggar[3] .... 20/1   pu
      Rith Dubh (IRE) *JonjoO'Neill* 11-10-13[127] (b) MrJTMcNamara .... 14/1   pu
      Northern Sound (IRE) *PaulARoche,Ireland* 10-10-6[125] MrDRoche[5] ... 40/1   pu
      Mr P. A. Deal, J. S. Dale & A. Stennett 23ran 6m23.22

145   Pertemps Final (Hcap Hdle) (L) (A) (140) (5yo+) £34,800   3m1f110y (13)

	INCHING CLOSER *JonjoO'Neill* 6-11-2[130] BJGeraghty	6/1f	1
	ROYAL EMPEROR (IRE) *MrsSJSmith* 7-11-6[137] DElsworth[3]	14/1	sh 2
98	TRIBAL VENTURE (FR) *FerdyMurphy* 5-10-6[120] DNRussell	33/1	12 3
	RAVENSWOOD (IRE) *MCPipe* 6-11-3[131] (t) TScudamore	7/1	1¾ 4
23	Guard Duty *MCPipe* 6-10-8[122] (t) GSupple	33/1	2 5
	Creon *JonjoO'Neill* 8-10-8[122] CFSwan	14/1	2 6
	Dubai Seven Stars *MCPipe* 5-10-7[121] PCarberry	25/1	3½ 7
124	Carlovent (FR) *MCPipe* 8-11-3[131] (v) NWilliamson	33/1	¾ 8
38	Rostropovich (IRE) *MFMorris,Ireland* 6-11-3[131] (t) DJCasey	14/1	¾ 9
	Ballysicyos (FR) *MCPipe* 8-11-3[131] TJMurphy	33/1	2½ 10
	Proper Squire (USA) *CJMann* 6-10-8[122] (b) NFehily	20/1	nk 11
	Kerrigand (FR) *MCPipe* 6-10-9[123] (v) RGreene	25/1	nk 12
106	Surprising *PJHobbs* 8-10-8[122] (b) MAFitzgerald	33/1	1½ 13
106	Ballylusky (IRE) *JonjoO'Neill* 6-10-6[120] LCooper	14/1	hd 14
	The Culdee (IRE) *FFlood,Ireland* 7-10-5[119] FFlood	33/1	11 15
86	Springfield Scally *SGollings* 10-11-6[134] SDurack	25/1	4 16
	Farinel *ALTMoore,Ireland* 7-10-8[122] CO'Dwyer	7/1	4 17
	No Discount (IRE) *TMWalsh,Ireland* 9-10-7[121] RWalsh	20/1	6 18
1	Tucacas (FR) *MCPipe* 6-11-9[140] MrGElliott[3]	40/1	8 19
	Miss Fara (FR) *MCPipe* 8-10-2[123] MrJEMoore[7]	33/1	28 20
	Mirjan (IRE) *LLungo* 7-10-10[124] ADobbin	16/1	1¼ 21
124	Chopneyev (FR) *RTPhillips* 5-11-7[135] RJohnson	13/2	20 22
106	Rum Pointer (IRE) *RHBuckler* 7-10-6[120] RThornton	33/1	f
37	Moss Harvey *JMJefferson* 8-11-8[136] GLee	33/1	pu

Mrs N. L. Spence 24ran 6m20.97

CHELTENHAM Wednesday, Mar 12   GOOD (Old Course)

146   Royal & SunAlliance Nov Hdle (Gr 1) (A) (4yo+) £58,000   2m5f (10)

Order as they passed the post

119	HARDY EUSTACE (IRE) *DTHughes,Ireland* 6-11-7 KAKelly	6/1	1
76	COOLNAGORNA (IRE) *JonjoO'Neill* 6-11-7 ADobbin	4/1	1¼ 2
62	PIZARRO (IRE) *EJO'Grady,Ireland* 6-11-7 NWilliamson	2/1f	1 3
90	Lord Sam (IRE) *VRADartnall* 7-11-7 WMarston	10/1	3½ 4
64	Foreman (GER) *TDoumen,France* 5-11-7 TDoumen	11/1	¾ 5
9	Sh Boom *JonjoO'Neill* 5-11-7 LCooper	14/1	sh 6
119	Nil Desperandum (IRE) *MissFMCrowley,Ireland* 6-11-7 RWalsh	25/1	2 7
	Supreme Prince (IRE) *PJHobbs* 5-11-7 PFlynn	16/1	2½ 8
	Little Sport (IRE) *AScott* 6-11-7 GHills	100/1	4 9
94	Texas Ranger *CJMann* 5-11-7 NFehily	150/1	10 10
	Double Honour (FR) *PJHobbs* 5-11-7 RJohnson	25/1	2½ 11
	Saitensohn (GER) *JonjoO'Neill* 5-11-7 GusBrown	33/1	½ 12
119	Native Sparkle (IRE) *THogan,Ireland* 6-11-2 KHadnett	150/1	3 13
	Rosslea (IRE) *MissHCKnight* 5-11-7 JCulloty	66/1	nk 14
	Mossy Green (IRE) *WPMullins,Ireland* 9-11-7 CFSwan	33/1	2 15
130	Puntal (FR) *MCPipe* 7-11-7 APMcCoy	14/1	3 16
	Moore's Law (USA) *MJGrassick,Ireland* 5-11-7 PCarberry	100/1	6 17
76	Calling Brave (IRE) *NJHenderson* 7-11-7 MAFitzgerald	33/1	27 18
119	Hi Cloy (IRE) *MichaelHourigan,Ireland* 6-11-7 TJMurphy	50/1	f

Mr Laurence Byrne 19ran 5m05.89

147   Royal & SunAlliance Chase (Gr 1) (A) (5yo+) £81,200   3m110y (19)

37	ONE KNIGHT (IRE) *PJHobbs* 7-11-4 RJohnson	15/2	1
123	JAIR DU COCHET (FR) *GMacaire,France* 6-11-4 JaquesRicou	4/1	1¾ 2
120	BARROW DRIVE *AnthonyMullins,Ireland* 7-11-4 (t) BJGeraghty	9/1	10 3
93	Sea Drifting *KAMorgan* 6-11-4 NFehily	100/1	16 4
123	Keen Leader (IRE) *JonjoO'Neill* 7-11-4 LCooper	9/4f	12 5
53	It Takes Time (IRE) *MCPipe* 9-11-4 APMcCoy	3/1	5 6
	Iris Royal (FR) *NJHenderson* 7-11-4 MAFitzgerald	16/1	pu
26	Stars Out Tonight (IRE) *MissHCKnight* 6-11-4 JCulloty	14/1	pu
109	The Bajan Bandit (IRE) *LLungo* 8-11-4 ADobbin	33/1	pu

Mr R. Gibbs 9ran 6m14.71

148   Queen Mother Champion Chase (Gr 1) (A) (5yo+) £145,000   2m (12)

112	MOSCOW FLYER (IRE) *MrsJHarrington,Ireland* 9-12-0 BJGeraghty	7/4f	1
102	NATIVE UPMANSHIP (IRE) *ALTMoore,Ireland* 10-12-0 CO'Dwyer	12/1	7 2
114	CENKOS (FR) *PFNicholls* 9-12-0 RWalsh	7/1	3 3
125	Geos (FR) *NJHenderson* 8-12-0 MAFitzgerald	25/1	5 4
71	Flagship Uberalles (IRE) *PJHobbs* 9-12-0 (b) RJohnson	12/1	5 5
50	Edredon Bleu (FR) *MissHCKnight* 11-12-0 (t) JCulloty	12/1	2½ 6
114	Kadarann (IRE) *PFNicholls* 6-12-0 JTizzard	9/1	1¼ 7

1025

	121	Florida Pearl (IRE) *WPMullins,Ireland* 11-12-0 PCarberry	12/1	10	8
	27	Latalomne (USA) *BEllison* 9-12-0 VTKeane	25/1		f
	89	Seebald (GER) *MCPipe* 8-12-0 NWilliamson	14/1		f
	125	Tiutchev *MCPipe* 10-12-0 APMcCoy	5/1		f

Mr Brian Kearney 11ran 3m53.78

149 **Coral Cup (Hcap Hdle) (Gr 3) (A) (148) (5yo+) £43,500** 2m5f (10)

	85	XENOPHON (IRE) *AJMartin,Ireland* 7-11-0[130] MAFitzgerald	4/1f	1
	51	SAMON (GER) *MCPipe* 6-11-3[133] DJCasey	25/1	3½ 2
	3	SPECTROMETER *PJHobbs* 6-11-8[138] RJohnson	10/1	1 3
	85	EMOTIONAL MOMENT (IRE) *TJTaaffe,Ireland* 6-11-4[134] BJGeraghty	7/1	3 4
	139	Korelo (FR) *MCPipe* 5-11-5[135] APMcCoy	8/1	½ 5
	131	Moving On Up *CJMann* 9-10-8[124] (b) NFehily	50/1	4 6
		Bow Strada *PJHobbs* 6-11-4[134] SDurack	40/1	1 7
		Persian Waters (IRE) *JRFanshawe* 7-10-11[127] AThornton	20/1	sh 8
		Aimees Mark (IRE) *FFlood,Ireland* 7-10-7[123] FJFlood	33/1	nk 9
		Anatar (IRE) *MCPipe* 5-10-8[124] TScudamore	50/1	2 10
		Majestic (IRE) *IanWilliams* 8-10-12[135] (b+t) WAWorthington[7]	40/1	1¼ 11
	106	Camden Tanner (IRE) *RobertTyner,Ireland* 7-11-11[131] NWilliamson	14/1	½ 12
	115	Quazar (IRE) *JonjoO'Neill* 5-12-1[148] (t) RFlavin[3]	25/1	4 13
		Tardar (NZ) *JonjoO'Neill* 7-10-7[123] (t) LCooper	12/1	½ 14
		See You Sometime *JWMullins* 8-11-7[137] JTizzard	25/1	2 15
	106	Chicago Bulls (IRE) *AKing* 5-10-5[121] RThornton	33/1	5 16
	43	Thari (USA) *NMeade,Ireland* 6-11-5[135] (t) PCarberry	20/1	1 17
	115	Benbyas *DCarroll* 6-11-0[135] PJBrennan[5]	33/1	3½ 18
	115	Mr Cool *MCPipe* 9-11-4[141] MrJEMoore[7]	33/1	2 19
	106	Ideal du Bois Beury (FR) *MCPipe* 7-10-9[125] GSupple	33/1	3½ 20
	36	Galant Moss (FR) *MCPipe* 9-11-5[135] (v) TJMurphy	66/1	9 21
	135	Chicuelo (IRE) *MissVenetiaWilliams* 7-10-13[132] (v) DJHoward[3]	33/1	2½ 22
	3	Taming (IRE) *MissVenetiaWilliams* 7-10-9[125] DNRussell	33/1	sh 23
		Arabian Moon (IRE) *SDow* 7-11-3[133] PFlynn	33/1	18 24
	23	Yeoman's Point (IRE) *CRoche,Ireland* 7-11-5[135] (b) CFSwan	8/1	19 25
	11	Upgrade *MCPipe* 9-11-12[142] (b) RGreene	50/1	pu
	27	Dream With Me (IRE) *MCPipe* 6-11-4[134] (t) RWalsh	33/1	pu

Lane Syndicate 27ran 5m03.84

150 **NH Chase Challenge Cup (Amat) (Nov) (B) (5yo+) £26,100** 4m (24)

	132	SUDDEN SHOCK (GER) *JonjoO'Neill* 8-11-7 MrDWCullen	25/1	1
	132	STORMEZ (FR) *MCPipe* 6-12-0 (t) MrJEMoore	7/4f	1 2
		YOUNG OTTOMAN (IRE) *VRADartnall* 7-11-11 MrJMPritchard	10/1	13 3
	109	High Cotton (IRE) *DRCElsworth* 8-11-7 MrLMcGrath	25/1	hd 4
		Moorlands Again *CTizzard* 8-11-11 MrNHarris	33/1	10 5
	69	Lucky Bay (IRE) *MissHCKnight* 7-11-11 MrRBurton	10/1	hd 6
		Ask Henry (IRE) *PFNicholls* 7-11-11 MrChristianWilliams	8/1	4 7
		Majed (IRE) *PFNicholls* 7-11-7 (v) MrGordonElliott	20/1	6 8
	133	Druid's Glen (IRE) *JonjoO'Neill* 7-12-0 MrJJTMcNamara	8/1	1¾ 9
	81	Clonmel's Minella (IRE) *MichaelHourigan,Ireland* 12-12-0 MrROHarding	33/1	7 10
	17	Kittenkat *NRMitchell* 9-11-2 MrJSnowden	100/1	½ 11
		Hedgehunter (IRE) *WPMullins,Ireland* 7-11-11 MrJJCodd	10/1	13 12
		Christy's Pride (IRE) *CWeedon* 11-11-2 AO'Keeffe	100/1	9 13
		Paxford Jack *MFHarris* 7-12-0 MissPGundry	25/1	12 14
		Mackinus (IRE) *PAFahy,Ireland* 7-11-11 MrJTCarroll	100/1	3½ 15
		Over The Storm (IRE) *MissHCKnight* 6-11-11 MrAGCostello	8/1	23 16
		Dunowen (IRE) *THyde,Ireland* 8-11-11 (b) MrTPHyde	66/1	f
		Dealer Del *CJDown* 9-11-11 MrLJefford	100/1	ur
	93	Princesse Grec (FR) *DrPPritchard* 5-10-7 MrESelter	200/1	ur
		Dionn Righ (IRE) *JHowardJohnson* 8-12-0 MrAFitzgerald	33/1	pu
		Dark Room (IRE) *JonjoO'Neill* 6-11-11 MrAPCrowe	25/1	pu
		Lanmire Glen (IRE) *EBolger,Ireland* 6-11-11 MrAFleming	50/1	pu
		Bonny Boy (IRE) *DARees* 8-11-7 (v) MrEWilliams	100/1	pu
		Even More (IRE) *RHAlner* 8-11-7 MrRYoung	50/1	pu

Mr Darren C. Mercer 24ran 8m21.96

151 **Mildmay of Flete Challenge Cup Hcap Chase (L) (A) (164) (5yo+) £43,500** 2½m110y (15)

		YOUNG SPARTACUS *HDDaly* 10-10-9[147] RJohnson	16/1	1
	135	FONDMORT (FR) *NJHenderson* 7-10-13[151] MAFitzgerald	11/2	4 2
	133	SCOTS GREY *NJHenderson* 8-9-7[138] MrATinkler[7]	16/1	4 3
	81	CREGG HOUSE (IRE) *PatrickMullins,Ireland* 8-9-9[138] (b) RMPower[5]	25/1	3 4
	114	Lady Cricket (FR) *MCPipe* 9-11-12[164] (b) APMcCoy	8/1	5 5
	96	Horus (IRE) *MCPipe* 8-10-3[141] RGreene	14/1	7 6
	125	Fadalko (FR) *PFNicholls* 10-11-3[155] BJGeraghty	20/1	3½ 7
	16	Armaturk (FR) *PFNicholls* 6-10-11[149] JTizzard	12/1	3½ 8

1026

	96	Blowing Wind (FR) *MCPipe* 10-10-1[139] TScudamore	20/1	2½ 9
	102	Arctic Copper (IRE) *NMeade,Ireland* 9-10-5[143] PCarberry	16/1	20 10
	125	Tresor de Mai (FR) *MCPipe* 9-11-0[152] DJCasey	25/1	3½ 11
		Chergan (IRE) *MrsSCBradburne* 10-10-0[138] MBradburne	100/1	22 12
		Arctic Fancy (USA) *MissHCKnight* 10-10-0[138] TJMurphy	50/1	10 13
		Europa *TPTate* 7-10-1[139] JMMaguire	8/1	f
	80	Go Roger Go (IRE) *EJO'Grady,Ireland* 11-10-2[140] NWilliamson	5/1f	ur
	87	Goguenard (FR) *MrsSJSmith* 9-10-2[140] WMarston	11/1	ur
		Silence Reigns *PFNicholls* 9-10-0[138] RWalsh	14/1	ur
	96	Hermes III (FR) *NJHenderson* 8-10-0[138] JRKavanagh	9/1	pu
	45	Juralan (IRE) *MissHCKnight* 8-10-0[138] JCulloty	66/1	pu

Mr B. G. Hellyer 19ran 5m04.78

152		**Weatherbys Champion Bumper (Standard Open NHF) (Gr 1) (A)**		**2m110y**
		(4, 5 and 6yo) £23,200		
	28	LIBERMAN (IRE) *MCPipe* 5-11-6 APMcCoy	2/1f	1
		TRABOLGAN (IRE) *NJHenderson* 5-11-6 SDurack	50/1	½ 2
		WIDEMOUTH BAY (IRE) *PJHobbs* 5-11-6 RJohnson	33/1	1 3
	117	Bold Bishop (IRE) *JonjoO'Neill* 6-11-6 (b) FMBerry	50/1	½ 4
		Miller's Bay *MissHCKnight* 5-11-6 JCulloty	50/1	5 5
		Bourbon Manhattan *AKing* 5-11-6 OMcPhail	14/1	¾ 6
		Govamix *DKWeld,Ireland* 5-11-6 PJSmullen	10/1	1½ 7
		Kim Fontaine (FR) *WPMullins,Ireland* 5-11-6 MrJJCodd[5]	40/1	1¾ 8
	117	He's The Boss (IRE) *RHBuckler* 6-11-6 CLlewellyn	100/1	3½ 9
		Royal Alphabet (IRE) *WPMullins,Ireland* 5-11-6 RWalsh	11/1	1½ 10
		Classic Native (IRE) *JonjoO'Neill* 5-11-6 LCooper	66/1	sh 11
	117	Cornish Rebel (IRE) *PFNicholls* 6-11-6 BJGeraghty	9/2	2½ 12
	117	Patriarch Express *GAHarker* 6-11-3 NHannity[3]	33/1	sh 13
		Storm Boxer (IRE) *PatrickMullins,Ireland* 5-11-6 RHughes	25/1	¾ 14
		McGruders Cross (IRE) *AnthonyMullins,Ireland* 5-10-13 MrJPMagnier[7]	14/1	¾ 15
		Mr Babbage (IRE) *WPMullins,Ireland* 5-11-6 DJCasey	33/1	2½ 16
		Crossbow Creek *MGRimell* 5-11-3 MrMRimell[1]	66/1	3 17
		Dizzy's Dream (IRE) *NMeade,Ireland* 5-11-6 PCarberry	14/1	1¾ 18
		Kahuna (IRE) *ESheehy,Ireland* 6-11-6 CFSwan	33/1	5 19
		Triple Rum (IRE) *JamesLeavy,Ireland* 5-11-6 PaulMoloney	50/1	2½ 20
	117	Be Fair *DECantillon* 5-11-6 MHills	20/1	2½ 21
		Watson Lake (IRE) *NMeade,Ireland* 5-11-6 NWilliamson	20/1	12 22
		Davenport Democrat (IRE) *WPMullins,Ireland* 5-11-6 MrJANash	33/1	4 23
		Back To Ben Alder (IRE) *NJHenderson* 6-11-6 MAFitzgerald	8/1	4 24
		Dempsey (IRE) *MPitman* 5-11-6 TJMurphy	33/1	pu

Mr D. A. Johnson 25ran 3m52.31

CHELTENHAM Thursday, Mar 13   GOOD (New Course)

153		**JCB Triumph Hdle (Gr 1) (A) (4yo)** £58,000		**2m1f (8)**
		SPECTROSCOPE (IRE) *JonjoO'Neill* 4-11-0 BJGeraghty	20/1	1
	134	WELL CHIEF (GER) *MCPipe* 4-11-0 APMcCoy	7/1	hd 2
	118	GOLDEN CROSS (IRE) *MHalford,Ireland* 4-11-0 CFSwan	11/2f	5 3
	74	Lilium de Cotte (FR) *GMacaire,France* 4-11-0 BGicquel	25/1	1¼ 4
	134	Mughas (IRE) *AKing* 4-11-0 RThornton	20/1	4 5
	97	Le Duc (FR) *PFNicholls* 4-11-0 RWalsh	40/1	3½ 6
	118	Newlands Gold (IRE) *MJPO'Brien,Ireland* 4-11-0 DJCasey	33/1	sh 7
	118	Mutineer (IRE) *DTHughes,Ireland* 4-11-0 (b+t) KAKelly	10/1	nk 8
		Red Wine *JAOsborne* 4-11-0 JAMcCarthy	13/2	nk 9
	41	Dashing Home (IRE) *NMeade,Ireland* 4-11-0 PCarberry	25/1	1½ 10
		King Solomon (FR) *MissVenetiaWilliams* 4-11-0 PFlynn	50/1	4 11
		Fortune Island (IRE) *MCPipe* 4-11-0 ADobbin	33/1	3 12
		Starzaan (IRE) *HMorrison* 4-11-0 MBradburne	16/1	¾ 13
		Little Rort (IRE) *MJGrassick,Ireland* 4-11-0 (t) JECasey	66/1	2 14
	134	Saintsaire (FR) *NJHenderson* 4-11-0 MAFitzgerald	14/1	1½ 15
		Overstrand (IRE) *MrsMReveley* 4-11-0 ADempsey	66/1	¾ 16
		Its Wallace Jnr *MissSWest* 4-11-0 JGoldstein	100/1	¾ 17
	55	Turbo (IRE) *MissVenetiaWilliams* 4-11-0 GLee	66/1	9 18
	134	Duke of Earl (IRE) *SKirk* 4-11-0 SDurack	50/1	3½ 19
		Tanikos (FR) *NJHenderson* 4-11-0 JRKavanagh	50/1	12 20
	97	Ken's Dream *MsAEEmbiricos* 4-11-0 SFox	66/1	1¾ 21
		Andy Gin (FR) *PJHobbs* 4-11-0 RJohnson	20/1	1 22
	118	Kenilworth (USA) *PatrickOBrady,Ireland* 4-11-0 JCullen	33/1	dist 23
		Old California (IRE) *MCPipe* 4-11-0 RGreene	16/1	f
	97	Don Fernando *MCPipe* 4-11-0 TScudamore	12/1	bd
	97	Moneytrain (GER) *CVonDerRecke,Germany* 4-11-0 NWilliamson	14/1	bd
	74	Nas Na Riogh (IRE) *NJHenderson* 4-10-9 MFoley	16/1	ur

Mrs G. Smith 27ran 4m00.28

154	**Bonusprint Stayers' Hdle (Gr 1) (A) (4yo+) £85,260**		3m (12)
63	BARACOUDA (FR) *FDoumen,France* 8-11-10 TDoumen	9/4jf	1
136	IRIS'S GIFT *JonjoO'Neill* 6-11-10 BJGeraghty	7/1	¾ 2
101	LIMESTONE LAD (IRE) *JamesBowe,Ireland* 11-11-10 PCarberry	9/4jf	5 3
129	Classified (IRE) *MCPipe* 7-11-10 APMcCoy	8/1	13 4
128	Liss A Paoraigh (IRE) *JEKiely,Ireland* 8-11-5 CFSwan	20/1	17 5
131	Deano's Beeno *MCPipe* 11-11-10 RGreene	25/1	5 6
	Galileo (POL) *TRGeorge* 7-11-10 JMMaguire	11/1	14 7
63	Brother Joe (NZ) *PJHobbs* 9-11-10 (b) RWalsh	14/1	1¾ 8
131	Palua *MissECLavelle* 6-11-10 TJMurphy	66/1	dist 9
	Crazy Horse (IRE) *LLungo* 10-11-10 ADobbin	80/1	pu
63	Native Emperor *JonjoO'Neill* 7-11-10 LCooper	20/1	pu
	Mr J. P. McManus 11ran 5m41.31		

155	**Tote Cheltenham Gold Cup Chase (Gr 1) (A) (5yo+) £203,000**		3¼m110y (22)
71	BEST MATE (IRE) *MissHCKnight* 8-12-0 JCulloty	13/8f	1
116	TRUCKERS TAVERN (IRE) *FerdyMurphy* 8-12-0 (t) DNRussell	33/1	10 2
121	HARBOUR PILOT (IRE) *NMeade,Ireland* 8-12-0 (b) PCarberry	40/1	2½ 3
116	Valley Henry (IRE) *PFNicholls* 8-12-0 BJGeraghty	14/1	nk 4
95	Behrajan (IRE) *HDDaly* 8-12-0 RJohnson	14/1	1½ 5
112	Commanche Court (IRE) *TMWalsh,Ireland* 10-12-0 RWalsh	8/1	1½ 6
116	Chives (IRE) *MissHCKnight* 8-12-0 RichardGuest	25/1	4 7
126	See More Business (IRE) *PFNicholls* 13-12-0 (b) JTizzard	16/1	17 8
137	You're Agoodun *MCPipe* 11-12-0 (v) APMcCoy	50/1	¾ 9
121	Colonel Braxton (IRE) *DTHughes,Ireland* 8-12-0 KAKelly	33/1	12 10
116	Marlborough (IRE) *NJHenderson* 11-12-0 MAFitzgerald	20/1	10 11
	Modulor (FR) *MCPipe* 11-12-0 (v) RGreene	200/1	10 12
121	Beef Or Salmon (IRE) *MichaelHourigan,Ireland* 7-12-0 TJMurphy	5/1	f
126	First Gold (FR) *FDoumen,France* 10-12-0 TDoumen	33/1	pu
87	Hussard Collonges (FR) *PBeaumont* 8-12-0 RGarritty	8/1	pu
	Mr Jim Lewis 15ran 6m38.98		

156	**Christie's Foxhunter Chase Challenge Cup (B) (5yo+) £23,200**		3¼m110y (22)
	KINGSCLIFF (IRE) *MrsSAlner* 6-12-0 MrRYoung	11/4f	1
	BRIGHT APPROACH (IRE) *MrsOBush* 10-12-0 MissPGundry	20/1	2½ 2
	LAST OPTION *RTate* 11-12-0 MrsFNeedham	16/1	½ 3
	Earthmover (IRE) *PFNicholls* 12-12-0 MrChristianWilliams	5/1	¾ 4
	County Derry *JScott* 10-12-0 MrNHarris	14/1	5 5
	Spot Thedifference (IRE) *EBolger,Ireland* 10-12-0 MrJTMcNamara	14/1	15 6
	Araminta *MrsLPomfret* 9-11-9 MrMMackley	50/1	3 7
122	Sheltering (IRE) *EJO'Grady,Ireland* 11-12-0 MrGordonElliott	13/2	3½ 8
	Jabiru (IRE) *MrsKMSanderson* 10-12-0 MrRWoollacott	33/1	22 9
	Polaris Flame (IRE) *MrsDFoster,Ireland* 10-11-9 MrPBuchanan	33/1	3½ 10
	Our Boy *JGCromwell,Ireland* 8-12-0 (t) MrBRHamilton	66/1	6 11
	Mr Dow Jones (IRE) *KGoldsworthy* 11-12-0 MrRBarber	33/1	8 12
	Quetal (IRE) *MrsLauraJYoung* 10-12-0 MrJamesYoung	13/2	11 13
	Viaduct (IRE) *JKingston,Ireland* 7-12-0 (t) MrPCashman	50/1	½ 14
	Nahthen Lad (IRE) *JADanahar* 14-12-0 (v) MassVSturgis	100/1	5 15
122	Dorans Pride (IRE) *MichaelHourigan,Ireland* 14-12-0 MrROHarding	16/1	f
	False Tail (IRE) *JJLambe,Ireland* 11-12-0 MrDWCullen	33/1	f
	Family Business (IRE) *DPipe* 7-12-0 (v) MrLJefford	33/1	bd
	Storm Castle (IRE) *MissJWickens* 11-12-0 MissJWickens	100/1	ur
	Backsheesh (IRE) *GTuer* 8-12-0 (t) MrGTuer	50/1	pu
	Fair Wind (IRE) *MrsHBartlett* 11-12-0 (b) MrMGMiller	66/1	pu
	Galway (IRE) *MrsMarilynScudamore* 10-12-0 MrRBurton	50/1	pu
	Garolo (FR) *MrsFBrowne* 13-12-0 (b) MissSSamworth	66/1	pu
	Mr Smudge *MrsFJMarriott* 11-12-0 MrAndrewMartin	100/1	pu
	Mr A. J. Sendell 24ran 6m49.75		

157	**Cheltenham Grand Annual Chase Challenge Cup (Hcap) (L) (A)** **(153) (5yo+) £43,500**		2m110y (14)
68	PALARSHAN (FR) *HDDaly* 5-10-0[134] MBradburne	8/1	1
25	RISK ACCESSOR (IRE) *CRoche,Ireland* 8-10-1[130] SDurack	20/1	3 2
89	DARK'N SHARP (GER) *RTPhillips* 8-11-2[145] RJohnson	13/2	¾ 3
	VOL SOLITAIRE (FR) *PFNicholls* 5-10-8[142] RWalsh	7/1	¾ 4
	Ross Moff (IRE) *AJMartin,Ireland* 10-10-0[129] (t) TJMurphy	6/1f	½ 5
135	Red Ark *RCGuest* 10-9-9[129] (s+t) MrLMcGrath[5]	20/1	½ 6
100	Native Scout (IRE) *DHassett,Ireland* 7-10-8[137] (t) BJGeraghty	7/1	3½ 7
56	Exit Swinger (FR) *MCPipe* 8-11-0[143] RGreene	14/1	nk 8
25	Korakor (FR) *IanWilliams* 9-10-0[129] DRDennis	33/1	1¼ 9
84	Royal Jake (IRE) *NMeade,Ireland* 9-10-0[129] (b) PCarberry	25/1	7 10
	Harvis (FR) *MissVenetiaWilliams* 8-10-0[129] GLee	25/1	½ 11
	Lord Grey (IRE) *DPKelly,Ireland* 10-10-0[129] JCulloty	33/1	3½ 12

1028

89	Turgeonev (FR) *TDEasterby* 8-11-1[144] RGarritty		16/1	1	13
	Got One Too (FR) *NJHenderson* 6-10-11[140] MAFitzgerald		16/1	dh	13
114	Castle Prince (IRE) *RJHodges* 9-9-9[129] AHoneyball[5]		150/1	25	15
54	Golden Alpha (IRE) *MCPipe* 9-10-6[135] APMcCoy		10/1		f
103	Wave Rock *PJHobbs* 8-10-2[131] (b) ADobbin		25/1		f
103	Eskleybrook *VYGethin* 10-11-3[153] MrDMansell[7]		16/1		pu
103	Bleu Superbe (FR) *MissVenetiaWilliams* 8-10-4[138] AO'Keeffe[5]		20/1		pu
89	Fadoudal du Cochet (FR) *ALTMoore,Ireland* 10-10-8[137] DJCasey		9/1		pu
	Passereau (FR) *CNKellett* 7-10-0[129] TDoyle		100/1		pu

Mrs A. L. Wood 21ran 3m58.74

---

158   **Cathcart Challenge Cup Chase (Gr 2) (A) (5yo+) £46,400**   2m5f (17)

135	LA LANDIERE (FR) *RTPhillips* 8-10-12 RJohnson	5/4f	1
93	IRISH HUSSAR (IRE) *NJHenderson* 7-11-0 MAFitzgerald	14/1	1½ 2
84	MACS GILDORAN *WPMullins,Ireland* 9-11-3 RWalsh	25/1	5 3
120	Le Coudray (FR) *CRoche,Ireland* 9-11-3 (t) BJGeraghty	5/1	7 4
96	Poliantas (FR) *PFNicholls* 6-11-7 TJMurphy	12/1	4 5
87	Barton *TDEasterby* 10-11-12 RGarritty	20/1	7 6
115	Regal Exit (FR) *NJHenderson* 7-11-0 RichardGuest	20/1	¾ 7
143	Iznogoud (FR) *MCPipe* 7-11-7 PCarberry	16/1	dist 8
105	Tarxien *MCPipe* 9-11-3 (t) RGreene	10/3	f

Mrs R. J. Skan 9ran 5m12.63

---

159   **Vincent O'Brien County Hcap Hdle (Gr 3) (A) (145) (5yo+) £37,700**   2m1f (8)

115	SPIRIT LEADER (IRE) *MrsJHarrington,Ireland* 7-11-7[140] BJGeraghty	10/1	1
85	BALAPOUR (IRE) *PatrickOBrady,Ireland* 5-10-0[124] (t) MFMooney[5]	25/1	nk 2
	THROUGH THE RYE *EWTuer* 7-10-9[128] GLee	66/1	sh 3
115	NON SO (FR) *NJHenderson* 5-11-5[138] MAFitzgerald	10/1	5 4
140	Jaboune (FR) *AKing* 6-10-8[127] RJohnson	25/1	sh 5
	Direct Bearing (IRE) *DKWeld,Ireland* 6-10-5[124] (b) PCarberry	7/1	¾ 6
101	Turtleback (IRE) *EJO'Grady,Ireland* 5-10-11[130] DNRussell	20/1	sh 7
115	Polar Red *MCPipe* 6-11-12[145] (v) RGarritty	25/1	2½ 8
139	Idaho d'Ox (FR) *MCPipe* 7-10-7[126] (v) TScudamore	66/1	¾ 9
57	Never (FR) *FDoumen,France* 6-11-1[142] TDoumen	9/1	hd 10
	Full Irish (IRE) *LLungo* 7-11-1[134] MBradburne	25/1	2½ 11
115	Monkerhostin (FR) *OSherwood* 5-10-12[131] TJMurphy	10/1	7 12
	Miss Cool *MCPipe* 7-9-12[124] (v) MrJEMoore[7]	33/1	½ 13
115	Warjan (FR) *RTPhillips* 6-10-7[126] WMarston	33/1	½ 14
115	Joe Cullen (IRE) *IanWilliams* 8-10-0[122] WHutchinson[3]	33/1	4 15
	Image de Marque II (FR) *MCPipe* 7-11-1[134] (t) DJCasey	33/1	¾ 16
	The Gatherer (IRE) *ALTMoore,Ireland* 9-11-5[138] CO'Dwyer	33/1	1¾ 17
1	Belle d'Anjou (FR) *PJHobbs* 6-10-5[124] SDurack	50/1	11 18
40	Castleshane (IRE) *SGollings* 6-10-5[124] RThornton	25/1	14 19
	Phardante Flyer (IRE) *PJHobbs* 9-10-11[130] PFlynn	16/1	16 20
72	Say Again (IRE) *PaulNolan,Ireland* 7-11-2[135] JCullen	25/1	dist 21
129	Comex Flyer (IRE) *PFNicholls* 6-11-2[135] (t) RWalsh	25/1	f
	Mixsterthetrixster (USA) *MissTMIde* 7-10-4[128] MrGBarfoot-Saunt[5]	40/1	f
139	Hawadeth *VRADartnall* 8-10-6[125] JCulloty	25/1	bd
	Maragun (GER) *MCPipe* 7-10-4[123] GSupple	50/1	bd
	Native New Yorker (IRE) *RRowe* 8-10-11[130] LAspell	10/1	pu
	Tactful Remark (USA) *MCPipe* 7-10-5[124] RGreene	20/1	pu
	Mise Rafturai (IRE) *PaulNolan,Ireland* 5-10-2[121] CFSwan	5/1f	pu

Mr D. Thompson 28ran 3m58.36

UTTOXETER Saturday, Mar 15   SOFT

160   **Midlands Grand National Chase (Hcap) (L) (148) (6yo+) £58,000**   4¼m (24)

73	INTELLIGENT (IRE) *MrsJHarrington,Ireland* 7-10-5[132] RMPower[5]	6/1	1
96	AKARUS (FR) *MCPipe* 8-9-11[106] MrJEMoore[7]	33/1	1½ 2
	JURANCON II (FR) *MCPipe* 6-10-1[123] RJohnson	8/1	28 3
	RIVER BUG (IRE) *JamiePoulton* 9-10-0[122] (b) LCummins	25/1	18 4
144	Silver Steel *CRoche,Ireland* 10-10-5[127] BJGeraghty	8/1	27 5
75	Native Buck (IRE) *TRGeorge* 10-10-3[125] JMMaguire	12/1	dist 6
	Mini Sensation (IRE) *JonjoO'Neill* 10-11-12[148] ADobbin	20/1	pu
137	Take Control (IRE) *MCPipe* 9-11-5[141] RGreene	20/1	pu
135	Exit To Wave (FR) *PFNicholls* 7-11-3[139] (t) RWalsh	20/1	pu
	Polar Champ *MCPipe* 10-11-0[136] (v) TScudamore	16/1	pu
	Galapiat du Mesnil (FR) *PFNicholls* 9-10-13[135] JTizzard	50/1	pu
99	Robbo *MrsMReveley* 9-10-9[131] RThornton	33/1	pu
	Coole Spirit (IRE) *MissECLavelle* 10-10-6[128] NWilliamson	4/1f	pu
	Just Maybe (IRE) *MissVenetiaWilliams* 9-9-12[125] (b) AO'Keeffe[5]	9/1	pu
108	Kemal's Council (IRE) *JonjoO'Neill* 7-10-1[123] LCooper	9/1	pu
	Sad Mad Bad (USA) *MrsMReveley* 9-10-0[122] (v) ADempsey	40/1	pu

Kildorragh (IRE) *LWells* 9-9-11[122] PWhelan[3].. 25/1   pu

Norman Moore 17ran 9m26.57

NEWBURY Saturday, Mar 22   GOOD to FIRM

161 **European Breeders Fund Crandon Park Stud Mares' NH Nov Hdle**   2m5f (11)
Final (Ltd Hcap) (L) (A) (121) (4yo+ f+m) £29,000

AR MUIN NA MUICE (IRE) *JonjoO'Neill* 7-11-10[121] BJGeraghty 11/8f		1
GLENMOSS TARA (IRE) *NGRichards* 5-11-0[111] BHarding........................ 11/2	2½	2
BLUE RIDE (IRE) *PFNicholls* 6-10-8[110] PJBrennan[5]............................... 4/1	4	3
SPAGHETTI JUNCTION *RHAlner* 5-10-5[102] AThornton 33/1	10	4
Angel Delight *MissVenetiaWilliams* 7-9-13[101] AO'Keeffe[5] 40/1	5	5
Fragrant Rose *MissHCKnight* 7-10-7[109] RBiddlecombe[5]...................... 12/1	3½	6
Ask Me What (IRE) *MissVenetiaWilliams* 6-10-1[101] PRobson[3]............... 33/1	2½	7
The Rebel Lady (IRE) *MissHCKnight* 6-10-4[101] JCulloty......................... 40/1	5	8
Mini Mandy *RHBuckler* 7-10-4[101] (b) LAspell 25/1	2	9
Scottish Dance *NJHenderson* 6-10-4[101] (t) MAFitzgerald 14/1	1	10
Lynrick Lady (IRE) *JGPortman* 7-10-4[101] TJMurphy 33/1	4	11
Standing Bloom *MrsPSly* 7-10-4[101] WMarston.. 33/1	7	12
Native Approach (IRE) *NJHenderson* 6-10-4[101] JRKavanagh................. 25/1	dist	13
Ragu *FerdyMurphy* 5-10-4[101] SDurack 50/1	3½	14
Long Shot *NJHenderson* 6-9-11[101] MrATinkler[7] 40/1		f
Macnance (IRE) *RLee* 7-10-4[106] TJPhelan[5].. 10/1		ur

Mrs G. Smith 16ran 4m59.59

NAVAN Saturday, Mar 22   GOOD to SOFT

162 **Slane INH Flat (4yo+)** £5,163   2m

BRAVE INCA (IRE) *CAMurphy* 5-11-11 MrPJColville[5]........................... 3/1f		1
DOORS TO MANUAL (FR) *CharlesO'Brien* 5-11-13 MrAPCrowe[3] 5/1	7	2
PEDINA (IRE) *GMLyons* 5-11-2 MissNCarberry[7]................................... 10/1	sh	3
Away Home (IRE) *MJPO'Brien* 5-11-11 (t) MrDWCullen[5]....................... 9/1	2	4
Mitchelstown (IRE) *CRoche* 5-11-9 (t) MrJPMagnier[7]............................ 6/1	1½	5
Rugged Jacket (IRE) *DTHughes* 6-11-13 MrRLoughran[5]...................... 13/2		6
Izntitgreat (IRE) *JAO'Connell* 5-10-11 MrAELynch[7]........................... 20/1		7
31 Native Design (IRE) *MJO'Connor* 6-11-6 (t) MrDerekO'Connor[7] 13/2		8
Ballon Rose (IRE) *PDelaney* 5-10-13 MrPGMurphy[5]............................ 33/1		9
Sanamour (IRE) *SJTreacy* 5-11-2 MrMDarcy[7]....................................... 16/1		10
Street Colour *NMeade* 5-11-2 MrNPMadden[7].. 8/1		11
Grandello (IRE) *MichaelCullen* 5-11-4 MrJJCodd[5] 25/1		12
Go Johnny Go Go (IRE) *DBroad* 4-10-10 MrCJSwords[5]........................ 20/1		13
Soaring Peak (IRE) *NMeade* 5-11-2 MrDMacAuley[7].............................. 14/1		14
That's Magic (IRE) *DMFogarty* 6-11-10 MrPFahey[3] 12/1		15
Not Today Sir (IRE) *DBroad* 5-11-2 MrDFO'Regan[7]............................. 16/1		16
Camels Cross (IRE) *MichaelKiernan* 5-11-2 MrRLCully[7] 25/1		17
Right Jack (IRE) *PAFahy* 4-10-8 MrJTCarroll[7]...................................... 33/1		18
Matthew Anthony (IRE) *JFTormey* 7-11-11 MrPFenton.......................... 20/1		19
Tsessebe (IRE) *JRHFowler* 6-10-13 MrRO'Sullivan[7].............................. 14/1		20
Johnson (IRE) *JeremiahJohnO'Neill* 6-11-4 MrJMBarcoe[7].................... 25/1		21
Wing Back (IRE) *MFMorris* 5-11-9 (t) MrKRO'Ryan ....* 10/1		22
Drumdowney Lad (IRE) *MartinKinane* 4-10-10 MrPCashman[5] 33/1		23
Cedar Dale (IRE) *CPDonoghue* 5-11-9 MrJPDempsey 14/1		pu

Novices Syndicate 24ran 3m58.00

AINTREE Thursday, Apr 3   GOOD

163 **Martell Cognac Nisa Today's Hcap Hdle (L) (A) (144) (5yo+)**   3m110y (12)
£23,200

145	CARLOVENT (FR) *MCPipe* 8-10-11[129] (v) APMcCoy 16/1		1
145	ROSTROPOVICH (IRE) *MFMorris,Ireland* 6-10-12[130] (t) NWilliamson 16/1	1½	2
	KEEPATEM (IRE) *MFMorris,Ireland* 7-10-2[120] DJCasey 8/1	½	3
85	FAIRWOOD HEART (IRE) *PJRothwell,Ireland* 6-9-9[118] RMPower[5] 12/1	1½	4
149	Spectrometer *PJHobbs* 6-11-12[144] RJohnson.. 7/1	4	5
23	Do It On Dani *MrsAMThorpe* 8-10-0[118] SDurack...................................... 66/1	3½	6
98	Silver Knight *TDEasterby* 5-10-0[118] DO'Meara..................................... 25/1	1¼	7
146	Little Sport (IRE) *AScott* 6-10-9[127] TJMurphy 8/1	5	8
146	Calling Brave (IRE) *NJHenderson* 7-10-7[125] RWalsh............................. 20/1	9	9
145	Guard Duty *MCPipe* 6-10-3[121] (t) RGreene 20/1	1½	10
149	Yeoman's Point (IRE) *CRoche,Ireland* 7-11-2[134] CFSwan 12/1	4	11
145	Miss Fara (FR) *MCPipe* 8-9-9[118] MrJEMoore[5]...................................... 40/1	8	12
145	Inching Closer *JonjoO'Neill* 6-11-10[142] BJGeraghty 13/2f	15	13
145	Springfield Scally *SGollings* 10-10-13[131] GLee.................................... 33/1	2½	14
145	Ballysicyos (FR) *MCPipe* 8-10-10[128] TScudamore 25/1	1	15
145	Old Rouvel (USA) *AKing* 12-10-8[126] RThornton.................................. 33/1	dist	16

1030

145	Proper Squire (USA) *CJMann* 6-9-13[120] (b) DCrosse[3]	25/1	dist 17
149	Thari (USA) *NMeade,Ireland* 6-11-1[133] PCarberry	33/1	12 18
149	Majestic (IRE) *IanWilliams* 8-10-9[134] (b+t) WAWorthington[7]	20/1	f
	Too Forward (IRE) *MPitman* 7-11-1[133] JCulloty	50/1	bd
136	Priests Bridge (IRE) *NATwiston-Davies* 7-10-2[120] CLlewellyn	16/1	bd
106	Valerio *NJHenderson* 7-10-13[131] MAFitzgerald	16/1	pu

C. M., B. J. & R. F. Batterham 22ran 6m09.84

164 **Martell Cognac Cup Chase (Gr 2) (A) (5yo+)** £87,000   3m1f (19)

155	FIRST GOLD (FR) *FDoumen,France* 10-11-2 (b) TDoumen	14/1	1
151	LADY CRICKET (FR) *MCPipe* 9-11-7 (b) APMcCoy	6/1	14 2
155	COMMANCHE COURT (IRE) *TMWalsh,Ireland* 10-11-6 RWalsh	10/3	¾ 3
155	Valley Henry (IRE) *PFNicholls* 8-11-12 BJGeraghty	11/8f	14 4
155	Marlborough (IRE) *NJHenderson* 11-11-12 (s) MAFitzgerald	9/1	7 5
158	Barton *TDEasterby* 10-11-7 ADobbin	12/1	20 6
52	More Than A Stroll (IRE) *ALTMoore,Ireland* 11-11-12 (t) CO'Dwyer	20/1	pu

Mr J. P. McManus 7ran 6m22.44

165 **Red Rum Chase (Hcap) (L) (A) (146) (5yo+)** £40,600   2m (12)

157	GOLDEN ALPHA (IRE) *MCPipe* 9-11-3[135] APMcCoy	7/1	1
157	DARK'N SHARP (GER) *RTPhillips* 8-11-10[146] RJohnson	4/1f	10 2
157	RISK ACCESSOR (IRE) *CRoche,Ireland* 8-10-11[133] SDurack	7/1	1¼ 3
	LOG ON INTERSKY (IRE) *JHowardJohnson* 7-10-2[124] GLee	10/1	6 4
65	Batswing *BEllison* 8-10-0[122] TJMurphy	25/1	½ 5
157	Harvis (IRE) *MissVenetiaWilliams* 8-10-3[125] NWilliamson	25/1	15 6
4	Lord York (IRE) *IanWilliams* 11-10-8[130] (b) DRDennis	12/1	1 7
157	Lord Grey (IRE) *DPKelly,Ireland* 10-10-2[124] PCarberry	16/1	11 8
157	Turgeonev (FR) *TDEasterby* 8-11-4[140] RGarritty	10/1	5 9
54	Glenelly Gale (IRE) *ALTMoore,Ireland* 9-10-6[128] CO'Dwyer	12/1	8 10
	Abalvino (FR) *PRWebber* 9-10-7[129] (t) TDoyle	14/1	11 11
	Heavenly Stride *DMcCain* 7-10-0[122] BHarding	66/1	f
157	Bleu Superbe (FR) *MissVenetiaWilliams* 8-10-2[138] BJCrowley	33/1	pu
16	Ichi Beau (IRE) *FerdyMurphy* 9-10-11[133] (t) DNRussell	33/1	pu
157	Wave Rock *PJHobbs* 8-10-9[131] JCulloty	20/1	pu
158	Regal Exit (FR) *NJHenderson* 7-10-5[127] MAFitzgerald	10/1	pu

Mr D. A. Johnson 16ran 3m56.22

166 **Martell Cognac Fox Hunters' Chase (B) (6yo+)** £24,375   2m5f110y (Nat.) (18)

	DIVET HILL *MrsAHamilton* 9-12-0 MrDJewett	11/2	1
	GENERAL WOLFE *TWDennis* 14-12-0 MrTDennis	16/1	11 2
	I'M THE MAN *MrsSHShirley-Beavan* 12-12-0 MrJCookson	66/1	nk 3
	Irbee *PFNicholls* 11-12-0 (b) MissCTizzard	14/1	2 4
	Epsilo de La Ronce (FR) *SFlook* 11-12-0 MrDMansell	25/1	½ 5
	Gallant Glen (IRE) *PerryHarding-Jones* 10-12-0 MrSMorris	16/1	13 6
	Private Pete *LadyConnell* 10-12-0 MrRCope	33/1	6 7
	Folly Road (IRE) *DLWilliams* 13-12-0 MissLHorner	50/1	6 8
	Down (FR) *RWaley-Cohen* 12-12-0 MrSWaley-Cohen	66/1	2 9
	Esprit de Cotte (FR) *RGurney* 11-12-0 MrPYork	50/1	dist 10
	The Dangler (IRE) *MrsLauraJYoung* 10-12-0 MrAMichael	100/1	dist 11
	Dam The Breeze *EvanWilliams* 10-12-0 MrEWilliams	50/1	f
156	Sheltering (IRE) *EJO'Grady,Ireland* 11-12-0 MrGordonElliott	9/2f	f
	Son of Anshan *GTuer* 10-12-0 (t) MrPYork	8/1	f
	Winter Whisper (IRE) *MrsSusanEBusby* 8-12-0 (t) MrFHutsby	100/1	f
	Bitofamixup (IRE) *MJRoberts* 12-12-0 (t) MrsJGordon	100/1	ur
156	Family Business (IRE) *DPipe* 7-12-0 (b) MrRHFowler	16/1	ur
	Master Wood *CGrant* 12-12-0 MrTGreenall	13/2	ur
	Mullensgrove *DLowe* 9-12-0 MissSPhizacklea	50/1	ur
156	Spot Thedifference (IRE) *EBolger,Ireland* 10-12-0 MrJTMcNamara	5/1	ur
	Laganside (IRE) *JFWMuir* 10-12-0 MrJMuir	66/1	pu

Mr Ian Hamilton 21ran 5m42.66

167 **Ember Inns Anniversary 4-Y-O Nov Hdle (Gr 2) (A) (4yo)** £63,800   2m110y (9)

153	LE DUC (FR) *PFNicholls* 4-11-0 RWalsh	33/1	1
153	SPECTROSCOPE (IRE) *JonjoO'Neill* 4-11-4 BJGeraghty	8/1	hd 2
153	WELL CHIEF (GER) *MCPipe* 4-11-4 APMcCoy	2/1f	2½ 3
153	Starzaan (IRE) *HMorrison* 4-11-0 MBradburne	9/1	1¼ 4
	Harchibald (FR) *NMeade,Ireland* 4-11-0 (t) PCarberry	20/1	5 5
153	Mughas (IRE) *AKing* 4-11-0 RThornton	14/1	8 6
153	Moneytrain (GER) *CVonDerRecke,Germany* 4-11-4 NWilliamson	10/1	3 7
	Allude (IRE) *CJMann* 4-11-0 TJMurphy	100/1	sh 8
153	King Solomon (FR) *MissVenetiaWilliams* 4-11-0 BJCrowley	33/1	1¼ 9
	Mistanoora *NATwiston-Davies* 4-11-0 (b) RBiddlecombe	66/1	18 10
	Do L'Enfant d'Eau (FR) *PJHobbs* 4-11-0 RJohnson	5/1	3 11

	74	Lewis Island (IRE) *NATwiston-Davies* 4-11-0 CLlewellyn	25/1	3 12
		Statim *MJPO'Brien,Ireland* 4-10-9 (b) DJCasey	25/1	14 13
	153	Ken's Dream *MsAEEmbiricos* 4-11-0 SFox	66/1	dist 14
		Brigadier du Bois (FR) *MrsLWadham* 4-11-0 LAspell	150/1	6 15
		Far Pavilions *GASwinbank* 4-11-0 MAFitzgerald	7/1	pu
		Gabor *GLMoore* 4-11-0 PHide	50/1	pu
		Ryders Storm (USA) *TRGeorge* 4-11-0 JMMaguire	100/1	pu
	153	Turbo (IRE) *MissVenetiaWilliams* 4-11-0 (b) ADobbin	66/1	pu

Mrs J. Stewart 19ran 4m04.21

168   Martell Cognac Nov Hcap Chase (B) (135) (5yo+) £24,895   2½m (15)

		MIDLAND FLAME (IRE) *MissHCKnight* 8-10-9[118] JCulloty	14/1	1
	135	BOLD INVESTOR *JonjoO'Neill* 6-11-12[135] BJGeraghty	12/1	2½ 2
		INDALO (IRE) *MissVenetiaWilliams* 8-10-13[122] BJCrowley	20/1	8 3
	144	MONTREAL (FR) *MCPipe* 6-11-11[134] APMcCoy	7/2f	8 4
		Royal Beluga (USA) *TRGeorge* 6-10-0[109] JAMcCarthy	25/1	¾ 5
		Winchester *KARyan* 8-10-9[118] GLee	16/1	hd 6
		Cape Stormer (IRE) *PFNicholls* 8-10-11[120] RWalsh	7/1	14 7
		Lauderdale *MissLucindaVRussell* 7-9-11[109] PRobson[3]	50/1	2½ 8
	133	Jaybejay (NZ) *MCPipe* 8-11-6[129] TScudamore	33/1	4 9
	26	Fait Le Jojo (FR) *PJHobbs* 6-11-7[130] PFlynn	7/1	f
		Kock de La Vesvre (FR) *MissVenetiaWilliams* 5-10-12[125] RJohnson	25/1	f
		Night Fighter (GER) *RCGuest* 8-9-9[109] (s+t) MrLMcGrath[5]	33/1	f
		Avalanche (FR) *JRBest* 6-11-0[123] MBradburne	7/1	ur
		Hunters Tweed *PBeaumont* 7-10-12[121] RGarritty	8/1	ur
	147	Iris Royal (FR) *NJHenderson* 7-11-5[128] MAFitzgerald	12/1	pu
		Fireball Macnamara (IRE) *MPitman* 7-10-10[119] TJMurphy	20/1	pu

Mr Trevor Hemmings 16ran 5m05.96

169   St Austell Brewery Mersey Nov Hdle (Gr 2) (A) (4yo+) £29,000   2½m (11)

		LEINSTER (IRE) *DTHughes,Ireland* 6-11-0 KAKelly	12/1	1
		CRYSTAL D'AINAY (FR) *AKing* 4-10-7 RThornton	14/1	7 2
		AINE DUBH (IRE) *KevinFO'Donnell,Ireland* 6-10-9 CFSwan	66/1	17 3
		Skibb (IRE) *MFMorris,Ireland* 6-11-3 DJCasey	100/1	25 4
		Negresko (FR) *MCPipe* 4-10-10 (v) RGreene	100/1	8 5
	42	Friend's Amigo (IRE) *PMJDoyle,Ireland* 6-11-3 RWalsh	11/2	2½ 6
		Euro Bleu (FR) *MrsLWadham* 5-11-3 LAspell	100/1	12 7
	162	Native Design (IRE) *MJO'Connor,Ireland* 6-10-9 (t) CO'Dwyer	100/1	12 8
	146	Coolnagorna (IRE) *JonjoO'Neill* 6-11-8 BJGeraghty	11/10f	f
	55	Silver Charmer *HSHowe* 4-10-2 RFarrant	100/1	f
	146	Puntal (FR) *MCPipe* 7-11-8 RJohnson	20/1	pu
	149	Korelo (FR) *MCPipe* 5-11-5 APMcCoy	9/2	pu
	140	Inca Trail (IRE) *MissHCKnight* 7-11-0 JCulloty	16/1	pu
		Julies Boy (IRE) *TRGeorge* 6-11-0 JMMaguire	100/1	pu
	146	Sh Boom *JonjoO'Neill* 5-11-0 GLee	7/1	pu

Mr Cathal M. Ryan 15ran 5m01.25

AINTREE Friday, Apr 4   GOOD to SOFT

170   Martell Cognac VS Thresher Hcap Chase (B) (140) (5yo+) £26,000   3m1f (19)

	54	MASTER TERN (USA) *JonjoO'Neill* 8-11-1[129] ADobbin	5/1	1
	99	SHARDAM (IRE) *NATwiston-Davies* 6-10-8[122] CLlewellyn	11/1	1¼ 2
	157	ROSS MOFF (IRE) *AJMartin,Ireland* 10-11-1[129] (t) MAFitzgerald	9/2f	7 3
	143	Fatehalkhair (IRE) *BEllison* 11-10-9[126] VTKeane[3]	50/1	4 4
	87	Whitenzo (FR) *PFNicholls* 7-11-10[138] RWalsh	14/1	1 5
	80	Alcapone (IRE) *MFMorris,Ireland* 9-11-12[140] BJGeraghty	33/1	3½ 6
		Tom's Prize *JLSpearing* 8-11-0[128] JCulloty	14/1	5 7
	107	Windross *AKing* 11-10-13[127] RThornton	25/1	f
	96	Run For Paddy *MrsHDalton* 7-11-10[138] TJMurphy	14/1	pu
	144	Rathbawn Prince (IRE) *DTHughes,Ireland* 11-11-10[138] KAKelly	12/1	pu
	151	Horus (IRE) *MCPipe* 8-11-9[137] APMcCoy	6/1	pu
	53	The Villager *DJCaro* 7-11-1[129] TScudamore	8/1	pu
	99	Ballybough Rasher (IRE) *JHowardJohnson* 8-10-12[126] GLee	16/1	pu
		Berlin Blue *RMStronge* 10-10-10[124] SStronge	20/1	pu

Mr J. P. McManus 14ran 6m33.61

171   Laurel Pub Company Top Nov Hdle (Gr 2) (A) (4yo+) £29,000   2m110y (9)

	140	LIMERICK BOY (GER) *MissVenetiaWilliams* 5-11-0 ADobbin	5/1	1
		MAN O'MYSTERY (USA) *PRWebber* 6-11-0 TDoyle	11/2	4 2
	140	LIRFOX (FR) *MCPipe* 6-11-0 RGreene	12/1	12 3
		Ontos (IRE) *AScott* 7-11-0 TJMurphy	50/1	nk 4
		Glenhaven Nugget (IRE) *EJO'Grady,Ireland* 7-11-3 NWilliamson	7/2	5 5
		Thesis (IRE) *MissVenetiaWilliams* 5-11-0 BJCrowley	33/1	13 6

153	Don Fernando *MCPipe* 4-11-2 APMcCoy	3/1f	18	7
91	Limited Edition (IRE) *MPitman* 5-11-0 JCulloty	66/1	6	8
	Pro Dancer (USA) *PMJDoyle,Ireland* 5-11-0 RWalsh	40/1	10	9
159	Jaboune (FR) *AKing* 6-11-3 RJohnson	6/1	25	10
130	Caracciola (GER) *NJHenderson* 6-11-3 MAFitzgerald	20/1		pu
	Spud One *OSherwood* 6-11-0 RFlavin	100/1		pu

Favourites Racing 12ran 4m10.21

172 **Martell Cognac Melling Chase (Gr 1) (A) (5yo+)** £87,000   2½m (16)

148	NATIVE UPMANSHIP (IRE) *ALTMoore,Ireland* 10-11-10 CO'Dwyer	5/4f		1
148	SEEBALD (GER) *MCPipe* 8-11-10 APMcCoy	4/1	1	2
148	KADARANN (IRE) *PFNicholls* 6-11-10 JTizzard	12/1	18	3
148	Cenkos (FR) *PFNicholls* 9-11-10 RWalsh	11/2	5	4
125	Wahiba Sands *MCPipe* 10-11-10 NWilliamson	16/1	20	5
148	Edredon Bleu (FR) *MissHCKnight* 11-11-10 (t) JCulloty	5/1	dist	6

Mrs John Magnier 6ran 5m08.63

173 **Martell Cognac Sainsbury's Topham Chase (Hcap)**   2m5f110y (Nat.) (18)
     (B) 0-150(140) (5yo+) £40,600

	CLAN ROYAL (FR) *JonjoO'Neill* 8-10-2[116] LCooper	12/1		1
158	MACS GILDORAN *WPMullins,Ireland* 9-11-8[136] RWalsh	5/1f	2½	2
157	EXIT SWINGER (IRE) *MCPipe* 8-11-12[140] APMcCoy	12/1	3½	3
	MR BOSSMAN (IRE) *RCGuest* 10-10-8[122] (s) HOliver	12/1	2½	4
	Falcon du Coteau (FR) *AJMartin,Ireland* 10-10-0[114] TJMurphy	25/1	2	5
99	Quality First (IRE) *MrsHDalton* 10-11-0[128] DNRussell	20/1	sh	6
103	Extra Jack (FR) *PFNicholls* 11-10-11[125] (b) ADobbin	33/1	2	7
	Jeremy Spider *CTizzard* 10-10-6[120] JTizzard	25/1	9	8
157	Royal Jake (IRE) *NMeade,Ireland* 9-10-10[124] PCarberry	20/1	6	9
144	Be My Manager (IRE) *MissHCKnight* 8-10-7[121] JCulloty	25/1	nk	10
	Native Beat (IRE) *JRHFowler,Ireland* 8-9-7[114] MissDDuggan[7]	66/1	4	11
99	Tonoco *MrsSJSmith* 10-9-12[115] DElsworth[3]	12/1	5	12
34	Shannon Gale (IRE) *CRoche,Ireland* 11-10-2[116] PaulMoloney	25/1	8	13
	Indian Gunner *DrJRJNaylor* 10-10-3[117] RThornton	10/1	2½	14
	Cassia Heights *SABrookshaw* 8-9-7[114] (t) JamesDavies[7]	66/1	5	15
	Nosam *RCGuest* 13-10-2[116] (t) KJohnson	25/1	15	16
144	Tom Costalot (IRE) *MrsSusanNock* 8-10-6[123] AntonyEvans[3]	14/1	1¼	17
151	Chergan (IRE) *MrsSCBradburne* 10-10-1[115] MBradburne	25/1	6	18
	Mulkev Prince (IRE) *DPearson* 12-10-2[116] PHide	33/1	16	19
144	Mr Baxter Basics *MissVenetiaWilliams* 12-10-13[127] BJCrowley	20/1		f
155	Modulor (FR) *MCPipe* 11-10-9[123] (v) RGreene	25/1		f
81	Come In Moscow (IRE) *JohnJosephMurphy,Ireland* 7-9-11[114] KHadnett[3]	50/1		f
160	Exit To Wave (FR) *PFNicholls* 7-11-9[137] (t) AThornton	25/1		ur
144	Ifni du Luc (FR) *NJHenderson* 7-10-12[126] JRKavanagh	20/1		ur
	Canadiane (FR) *MCPipe* 8-9-12[117] MrJEMoore[5]	16/1		ur
11	Good Lord Murphy (IRE) *DrPPritchard* 11-10-6[125] DrPPritchard[5]	100/1		pu
	Ceanannas Mor (IRE) *NJHenderson* 9-10-5[119] MAFitzgerald	25/1		pu
150	Paxford Jack *MFHarris* 7-10-0[114] OMcPhail	20/1		pu
	Lambrini Gold *DMcCain* 9-10-0[114] (t) BHarding	100/1		pu

Mr J. P. McManus 29ran 5m39.04

174 **Martell Cognac Sefton Nov Hdle (Gr 1) (A) (4yo+)** £46,400   3m110y (13)

154	IRIS'S GIFT *JonjoO'Neill* 6-11-4 BJGeraghty	10/11f		1
145	ROYAL EMPEROR (IRE) *MrsSJSmith* 7-11-4 DElsworth	12/1	8	2
146	SUPREME PRINCE (IRE) *PJHobbs* 6-11-4 PFlynn	12/1	12	3
136	Simply Supreme (IRE) *MrsSJSmith* 6-11-4 WMarston	66/1	22	4
146	Hardy Eustace (IRE) *DTHughes,Ireland* 6-11-4 KAKelly	4/1	dist	5
	Balladeer (IRE) *MissHCKnight* 5-11-4 ADobbin	100/1	dist	6
146	Pizarro (IRE) *EJO'Grady,Ireland* 6-11-4 NWilliamson	5/1		f
138	Master Trix (IRE) *MPitman* 6-11-4 TJMurphy	100/1		ur
	Balinahinch Castle (IRE) *MrsLBNormile* 6-11-4 MBradburne	100/1		pu

Mr Robert Lester 9ran 6m22.66

175 **Happy Shopper Mildmay Nov Chase (Gr 2) (A) (5yo+)** £43,500   3m1f (19)

158	IRISH HUSSAR (IRE) *NJHenderson* 7-11-2 MAFitzgerald	3/1		1
147	IT TAKES TIME (IRE) *MCPipe* 9-11-7 APMcCoy	15/8f	5	2
37	JOLY BEY (FR) *PFNicholls* 6-11-7 RWalsh	6/1	7	3
	Super Fellow (IRE) *DPMurphy,Ireland* 9-11-7 (b+t) JCullen	50/1	6	4
147	Sea Drifting *KAMorgan* 6-11-2 NFehily	20/1	29	5
150	Lucky Bay (IRE) *MissHCKnight* 7-11-9 JCulloty	12/1		pu
144	Ibis Rochelais (FR) *AEnnis* 7-11-7 ADobbin	7/1		pu
	Far Dawn (USA) *JGallagher* 10-11-2 JMogford	100/1		pu
	Jakari (FR) *HDDaly* 6-11-2 RJohnson	7/1		pu

Major Christopher Hanbury 9ran 6m35.00

1033

176 Clark's Brewery Hcap Hdle (L) (A) (140) (4yo+) £23,200   2½m (11)

8	PATRIOT GAMES (IRE) *CFSwan,Ireland* 9-10-4[126] CFSwan	16/1		1
115	GRALMANO (IRE) *KARyan* 8-10-6[128] GLee	10/1	1½	2
139	CANADA *MCPipe* 5-10-0[122] RGreene	16/1	5	3
149	EMOTIONAL MOMENT (IRE) *TJTaaffe,Ireland* 6-11-1[137] BJGeraghty	3/1f	6	4
149	Samon (GER) *MCPipe* 6-11-4[140] APMcCoy	5/1	hd	5
124	Colourful Life (IRE) *MrsMReveley* 7-10-0[122] ADempsey	12/1	1	6
159	Monkerhostin (FR) *OSherwood* 6-10-6[128] JCulloty	12/1	8	7
7	Fnan *NMeade,Ireland* 7-10-8[130] PCarberry	14/1	5	8
	Murray River (FR) *MCPipe* 7-9-11[124] (v+t) MrJEMoore[5]	9/1	12	9
139	Tikram *GLMoore* 6-10-1[132] LAspell	9/1	14	10
	Exalted (IRE) *TAKCuthbert* 10-10-0[122] BHarding	100/1	4	11
145	Dubai Seven Stars *MCPipe* 5-9-11[122] DJHoward[3]	12/1	16	12
145	Farinel *ALTMoore,Ireland* 7-10-0[122] (b) DJCasey	14/1	13	13
124	Sonevafushi (FR) *MissVenetiaWilliams* 5-9-7[122] (b) JamesDavies[7]	25/1	6	14
145	Tucacas (FR) *MCPipe* 6-11-1[137] (v) TScudamore	33/1		pu
	Achilles Wings (USA) *MissKMGeorge* 7-10-0[122] SDurack	100/1		pu

Mr J. P. McManus 16ran 5m06.31

AINTREE Saturday, Apr 5
Mildmay Course: GOOD, Grand National Course: GOOD to SOFT

177 Cordon Bleu Hcap Hdle (L) (A) (142) (5yo+) £23,200   2m110y (9)

	RISKY REEF *AndrewLee,Ireland* 6-10-7[123] RWalsh	20/1		1
	ALTAY *RAFahey* 6-9-13[118] PWhelan[3]	7/1	1¾	2
113	BROOKLYN'S GOLD (USA) *IanWilliams* 8-10-0[123] JamesDavies[7]	16/1	3	3
	EDMO HEIGHTS *TDEasterby* 7-10-0[116] DO'Meara	40/1	1	4
159	Idaho d'Ox (FR) *MCPipe* 7-10-7[123] (v) TScudamore	25/1	nk	5
139	Newhall (IRE) *FFlood,Ireland* 5-10-11[127] FJFlood	9/1	2	6
159	Hawadeth *VRADartnall* 8-10-7[123] JCulloty	25/1	3	7
159	Never (FR) *FDoumen,France* 6-11-12[142] TDoumen	6/1	4	8
149	Dream With Me (FR) *MCPipe* 6-11-0[130] (t) RGreene	50/1	3	9
159	Non So (FR) *NJHenderson* 5-11-9[139] MAFitzgerald	12/1	6	10
159	Polar Red *MCPipe* 6-11-12[142] (v) APMcCoy	10/1	2½	11
159	Full Irish (IRE) *LLungo* 7-11-1[131] ADobbin	14/1	16	12
	Chevet Girl (IRE) *JHowardJohnson* 8-11-1[116] PAspell[3]	66/1	11	13
159	Maragun (GER) *MCPipe* 7-10-4[120] GSupple	50/1	1¼	14
139	Mister McGoldrick *MrsSJSmith* 6-10-12[131] DElsworth[3]	33/1	7	15
82	Per Amore (IRE) *PJHobbs* 5-10-2[118] (b) RJohnson	25/1	¾	16
	Mythical King (IRE) *RLee* 6-10-1[122] AO'Keeffe[5]	16/1	17	17
6	Take Flite *AnthonyMullins,Ireland* 6-10-1[117] CFSwan	11/2f		f
	Grave Doubts *KBishop* 7-10-7[123] (t) BFenton	14/1		pu

Ergon Syndicate 19ran 3m56.71

178 Martell Maghull Nov Chase (Gr 1) (A) (5yo+) £67,000   2m (12)

141	LE ROI MIGUEL (FR) *PFNicholls* 5-11-1 RWalsh	9/4		1
157	VOL SOLITAIRE (FR) *PFNicholls* 5-11-1 JTizzard	10/3	11	2
141	IMPEK (FR) *MissHCKnight* 7-11-4 JCulloty	6/4f	hd	3
100	Rathgar Beau (IRE) *ESheehy,Ireland* 7-11-4 BJGeraghty	8/1		f
49	Tysou (FR) *NJHenderson* 6-11-4 MAFitzgerald	16/1		f

Mrs J. Stewart 5ran 3m52.06

179 Martell Cognac Aintree Hdle (Gr 1) (A) (4yo+) £87,000   2½m (11)

128	SACUNDAI (IRE) *EJO'Grady,Ireland* 6-11-7 RWalsh	9/1		1
142	ROOSTER BOOSTER *PJHobbs* 9-11-7 RJohnson	5/4f	hd	2
142	LIKE-A-BUTTERFLY (IRE) *CRoche,Ireland* 9-11-2 CFSwan	11/2	7	3
149	Quazar (IRE) *JonjoO'Neill* 5-11-7 (t) BJGeraghty	25/1	1	4
86	Lord Transcend (IRE) *JHowardJohnson* 6-11-7 GLee	11/1	6	5
142	Copeland *MCPipe* 8-11-7 (v) APMcCoy	7/1	5	6
148	Geos (FR) *NJHenderson* 8-11-7 MAFitzgerald	20/1	25	7
149	Mr Cool *MCPipe* 9-11-7 TScudamore	66/1	1	8
142	Hors La Loi III (FR) *JRFanshawe* 8-11-7 (t) ADobbin	16/1	¾	9
159	Balapour (IRE) *PatrickOBrady,Ireland* 5-11-7 (t) JCullen	33/1	dist	10
142	Self Defense *MissECLavelle* 6-11-7 FKeniry	20/1		pu

Malm Syndicate 11ran 4m51.80

180 Martell Cognac Grand National Chase (Hcap) (Gr 3) (A) 0-110(158) (6yo+) £348,000   4½m (30)

9	MONTY'S PASS (IRE) *JamesJosephMangan,Ireland* 10-10-7[139] BJGeraghty	16/1		1
137	SUPREME GLORY (IRE) *PGMurphy* 10-10-2[134] LAspell	40/1	12	2
137	AMBERLEIGH HOUSE (IRE) *DMcCain* 11-10-4[136] GLee	33/1	2	3
99	GUNNER WELBURN *AMBalding* 11-10-2[134] BFenton	16/1	14	4

	Montifault (FR) *PFNicholls* 8-10-4[136] JTizzard	33/1	11 5
137	Bindaree (IRE) *NATwiston-Davies* 9-10-11[143] CLlewellyn	25/1	1 6
143	Carbury Cross (IRE) *JonjoO'Neill* 9-10-12[144] LCooper	25/1	18 7
151	Blowing Wind (FR) *MCPipe* 10-10-9[141] TScudamore	20/1	6 8
	Tremallt (IRE) *TRGeorge* 12-10-2[134] JMMaguire	200/1	7 9
155	Behrajan (IRE) *HDDaly* 8-11-12[158] RJohnson	22/1	7 10
143	Djeddah (FR) *FDoumen,France* 12-10-1[133] (b) TDoumen	66/1	9 11
150	Majed (FR) *MCPipe* 7-10-5[137] (v) RGreene	200/1	8 12
144	Royal Predica (FR) *MCPipe* 9-10-2[134] (t) MrJEMoore	33/1	dist 13
143	Southern Star (IRE) *MissHCKnight* 8-10-8[140] DElsworth	66/1	26 14
143	Bramblehill Duke (IRE) *MissVenetiaWilliams* 11-10-0[132] BJCrowley	200/1	f
143	Maximize (IRE) *MissHCKnight* 9-10-4[136] JCulloty	16/1	f
137	Wonder Weasel (IRE) *KCBailey* 10-10-5[137] (s) JPMcNamara	50/1	f
144	Burlu (FR) *MCPipe* 9-10-0[132] (b) GSupple	200/1	f
	Killusty (IRE) *CREgerton* 9-10-4[136] ADobbin	12/1	f
155	You're Agoodun *MCPipe* 11-10-9[141] VThornton	50/1	ur
151	Goguenard (FR) *MrsSJSmith* 9-10-2[134] WMarston	28/1	ur
151	Fadalko (FR) *PFNicholls* 10-11-7[153] SDurack	100/1	ur
143	Ad Hoc (IRE) *PFNicholls* 9-11-1[147] PCarberry	9/1	ur
143	The Bunny Boiler (IRE) *NMeade,Ireland* 9-10-10[142] JCullen	50/1	ur
144	Katarino (FR) *NJHenderson* 8-10-8[140] MAFitzgerald	50/1	ur
39	Red Striker *RCGuest* 9-10-8[140] (t) MrLMcGrath	50/1	ur
160	Polar Champ *MCPipe* 10-10-4[136] (v) DJHoward	200/1	ur
	Mantles Prince *AGJuckes* 9-10-3[135] OMcPhail	200/1	ur
	Torduff Express (IRE) *PFNicholls* 12-10-3[135] (b) TJMurphy	33/1	ur
160	Robbo *MrsMReveley* 9-10-0[132] (s) ADempsey	100/1	ur
95	Gingembre (FR) *MrsLCTaylor* 9-11-9[155] AThornton	14/1	pu
137	Shotgun Willy (IRE) *PFNicholls* 9-11-9[155] RWalsh	7/1f	pu
155	Chives (IRE) *MissHCKnight* 8-11-5[151] RichardGuest	10/1	pu
137	Iris Bleu (FR) *MCPipe* 7-11-3[149] APMcCoy	8/1	pu
96	Ballinclay King (IRE) *FerdyMurphy* 9-10-12[144] DNRussell	50/1	pu
143	Youlneverwalkalone (IRE) *CRoche,Ireland* 9-10-11[143] CO'Dwyer	8/1	pu
24	Good Shuil (IRE) *CJManson* 8-10-3[135] NFehily	200/1	pu
157	Red Ark *RCGuest* 10-10-0[132] (s+t) KJohnson	100/1	pu
	Empereur River (FR) *JOrtet,France* 11-10-0[132] MrPPailhes	250/1	pu
151	Cregg House (IRE) *PatrickMullins,Ireland* 8-10-3[135] DJCasey	50/1	ref

Dee Racing Syndicate 40ran 9m21.24

181 Martell Reserve Nov Hunt Chase (B) (5yo+) £12,025   3m1f (19)

	LORD ATTERBURY (IRE) *DPipe* 7-12-0 MrRHFowler	7/4f	1
	ARCTIC TIMES (IRE) *EugeneMO'Sullivan,Ireland* 7-12-0 MrWMO'Sullivan	9/2	dist 2
	EDGAR GINK (IRE) *LCorcoran* 9-12-0 MrRMcCarthy	10/1	3½ 3
	Hazel Reilly (IRE) *MrsSarahLDent* 12-11-9 MrLBates	14/1	3½ 4
	Paddies Boy (IRE) *JJLambe,Ireland* 8-12-0 MrDWCullen	20/1	5 5
	Good Good (IRE) *FJBrennan* 9-11-9 (t) MrJAJenkins	50/1	dist 6
	Blyth Brook *WTReed* 11-12-0 MrRMorgan	25/1	pu
	Border Light *HJManners* 10-12-0 MrACharles-Jones	40/1	pu
	Don Royal *JScott* 9-12-0 MrDEdwards	50/1	pu
	Paddy For Paddy (IRE) *GLLandau* 9-12-0 MrRBurton	7/2	pu
	Porlock Hill *JScott* 9-12-0 MrNHarris	50/1	pu
	Tale Bridge (IRE) *MrsOBush* 10-12-0 MrJMPritchard	66/1	pu

Mr P. J. Finn 12ran 6m17.80

182 Martell Champion Standard NHF (Gr 2) (A) (4, 5 and 6yo) £17,400   2m1f

152	CLASSIC NATIVE (IRE) *JonjoO'Neill* 5-11-1 RFlavin[3]	25/1	1
152	BE FAIR *DECantillon* 5-11-1 DCrosse[3]	20/1	2½ 2
	TIGHTEN YOUR BELT (IRE) *MissVenetiaWilliams* 6-10-13 AO'Keeffe[5]	10/1	17 3
	Thames (IRE) *NJHenderson* 5-10-11 MrATinkler[7]	25/1	½ 4
	Eric's Charm (FR) *OSherwood* 5-10-11 OKozak[7]	15/2	3½ 5
	Dark Character *GASwinbank* 4-10-5 JamesDavies[7]	33/1	2½ 6
	Ashley Brook (IRE) *KBishop* 5-11-1 RPMcNally[3]	33/1	6 7
	Salhood *SGollings* 4-10-9 PRobson[3]	50/1	3 8
	El Vaquero (IRE) *MissHCKnight* 5-10-13 RBiddlecombe[5]	16/1	2 9
117	Rakassa *HJManners* 5-10-6 MrJAJenkins[7]	100/1	nk 10
	Armaguedon (FR) *LLungo* 5-10-13 GBerridge[5]	4/1	9 11
	Red Knight (IRE) *CRoche,Ireland* 5-11-4 MrAPCrowe[3]	14/1	9 12
	Baron Monty (IRE) *CGrant* 5-11-1 DElsworth[3]	100/1	2½ 13
	John Oliver (IRE) *EJO'Grady,Ireland* 5-11-4 MrPFenton	3/1f	14 14
	Patricksnineteenth (IRE) *PRWebber* 6-11-4 KRenwick	25/1	nk 15
	Victory Gunner (IRE) *CRoberts* 5-11-1 RForristal[3]	100/1	1¾ 16
	Behzad (IRE) *DMcCain* 4-10-9 VTKeane[3]	100/1	24 17
152	Dempsey (IRE) *MPitman* 5-11-1 CRafter[3]	33/1	dist 18

Fathom *MrsLBNormile* 5-11-1 KHadnett[3] .... 150/1 dist 19
Vodka Bleu (FR) *MCPipe* 4-10-7 MrJEMoore[5] .... 11/2 ur
Flower of Pitcur *TRGeorge* 6-11-1 PJBrennan[3] .... 50/1 pu

Ray & Sue Dodd Partnership 21ran 4m06.13

AYR Saturday, Apr 12   GOOD to FIRM

183   **Future Champion Nov Chase (Gr 2) (A) (5yo+)** £21,700   2½m (17)

178 VOL SOLITAIRE (FR) *PFNicholls* 5-11-6 RWalsh 3/1 1
158 TARXIEN *MCPipe* 9-11-10 (t) APMcCoy 9/4 19 2
141 FARMER JACK *JWMullins* 7-11-10 AThornton 15/8f 7 3
149 Bow Strada *PJHobbs* 6-11-3 RJohnson .... 5/1 dist 4
    Early Edition *OJCarter* 7-11-3 MrDHDunsdon .... 200/1 f

Mr B. C. Marshall 5ran 4m52.11

184   **Scottish Champion Hdle (Ltd Hcap) (Gr 2) (157) (4yo+)** £24,800   2m (9)

142 IN CONTRAST (IRE) *PJHobbs* 7-10-13[146] RJohnson 2/1 1
140 THISTHATANDTOTHER (IRE) *PFNicholls* 7-10-12[145] RWalsh 6/1 2½ 2
142 WESTENDER (FR) *MCPipe* 7-11-10[157] (b) APMcCoy 11/8f 6 3
    Hitman *MPitman* 8-10-4[137] BFenton 25/1 25 4
142 Flame Creek (IRE) *NoelTChance* 7-11-10[157] SDurack .... 5/1 pu

Mr Tony Staple 5ran 3m38.31

185   **Gala Casinos Daily Record Scottish Grand National Chase (Hcap)**   4m1f (26)
    (Gr 3) (A) (161) (5yo+) £63,800

135 RYALUX (IRE) *ACrook* 10-10-5[140] RMcGrath 15/2 1
150 STORMEZ (FR) *MCPipe* 6-10-10[145] (t) APMcCoy .... 6/1 nk 2
 23 SPENDID (IRE) *AKing* 11-10-5[140] RThornton 12/1 20 3
    KERRY LADS (IRE) *MissLucindaVRussell* 8-10-0[135] KRenwick .... 40/1 ¾ 4
180 Shotgun Willy (IRE) *PFNicholls* 9-11-12[161] (b) RWalsh 8/1 3 5
160 Take Control (IRE) *MCPipe* 9-10-2[137] (v) RGreene 18/1 6 6
150 Sudden Shock (GER) *JonjoO'Neill* 8-10-3[138] BJGeraghty 6/1 6 7
137 Kit Smartie (IRE) *DMForster* 11-10-0[135] (b) DO'Meara 50/1 4 8
151 Scots Grey *NJHenderson* 8-10-4[139] MAFitzgerald .... 16/1 f
170 Berlin Blue *RMStronge* 10-10-0[135] BFenton .... 25/1 f
135 Gunther McBride (IRE) *PJHobbs* 8-10-1[136] RJohnson .... 7/2f ur
    Sir Frosty *BJMRyall* 10-10-0[135] (t) MBradburne .... 20/1 ur
173 Exit To Wave (FR) *PFNicholls* 7-10-2[137] (b+t) JTizzard .... 33/1 pu
    Enrique (GER) *PJHobbs* 8-10-0[135] ADobbin .... 20/1 pu
144 Carryonharry (IRE) *MCPipe* 9-9-9[135] (v) MrJEMoore[5] .... 16/1 pu
170 Fatehalkhair (IRE) *BEllison* 11-10-0[138] VKeane[3] .... 50/1 pu
  4 Star Jack (FR) *TJFitzgerald* 8-9-11[135] (s+t) PRobson[3] .... 50/1 pu
156 Last Option *RTate* 11-9-9[135] MrsFNeedham[5] .... 25/1 pu
160 Sad Mad Bad (USA) *MrsMReveley* 9-10-0[135] (v) ADempsey .... 100/1 pu

Mr William Lomas 19ran 8m12.33

CHELTENHAM Wednesday, Apr 16   GOOD to FIRM (New Course)

186   **Silver Trophy Chase (Ltd Hcap) (Gr 2) (152) (5yo+)** £29,000   2m5f (17)

158 POLIANTAS (FR) *PFNicholls* 6-11-1[143] RWalsh 6/1 1
151 FONDMORT (FR) *NJHenderson* 7-11-10[152] MAFitzgerald 9/4jf 10 2
149 UPGRADE *MCPipe* 9-11-8[150] (b) TJMurphy 25/1 9 3
103 Redemption *NATwiston-Davies* 8-10-7[135] CLlewellyn 11/2 9 4
172 Wahiba Sands *MCPipe* 10-11-6[148] (s) APMcCoy 12/1 2 5
180 Fadalko (FR) *PFNicholls* 10-11-8[150] (b) BJGeraghty 8/1 5 6
165 Dark'n Sharp (GER) *RTPhillips* 8-11-3[145] RJohnson .... 9/4jf ur

Mr Mark Tincknell 7ran 5m08.66

NAKAYAMA Saturday, Apr 19   GOOD

187   **Nakayama Grand Jump (Chase) (4yo+)** £422,654   2m5f55y

    BIG TASTE (JPN) *TNakao,Japan* 5-10-0 KTsuneishi 112/10 1
    GILDED AGE (JPN) *SMatsumoto,Japan* 6-10-0 RochelleLockett 9/10f 1½ 2
    ST STEVEN (NZ) *JWheeler,NewZealand* 9-10-0 BScott 37/10 3½ 3
    Kanetoshi Governor (JPN) *ANomura,Japan* 8-10-0 TKosaka .... 11/2 nk 4
    Mejiro Raiden (JPN) *MOkubo,Japan* 7-10-0 YImamura 42/1 2 5
    Daiwa Dur (JPN) *IShimada,Japan* 7-10-0 TTanaka 115/10 7 6
    Meisho Wakashio (JPN) *KIkezoe,Japan* 9-10-0 NKado 55/1 2½ 7
    Yu Fuyoho (JPN) *SMatsumoto,Japan* 6-10-0 KIdetsu 55/1 1¾ 8
    Cheers New Power (JPN) *SMasuzawa,Japan* 8-10-0 KMiura 173/1 6 9
 92 Escort Boy (USA) *JOrtet,France* 5-10-0 FBarrao .... 23/1 dist 10
    Hizen Hokusho (JPN) *MIto,Japan* 7-10-0 TOehara 48/1 5 11
    Just Bandit (JPN) *SKobiyama,Japan* 7-10-0 YYokoyama 150/1 3½ 12
151 Armaturk (FR) *PFNicholls,GB* 6-10-0 JTizzard 42/1 1 13

```
148  Tiutchev MCPipe,GB 10-10-0 RGreene ......................................... 21/1  dist 14
 36  Tiger Groom RCollet,France 6-10-0 TMajorcryk ........................... 45/1  1¼ 15
     Silver Archer (NZ) CAmrein,NewZealand 12-10-0 FLeahy................. 97/1  dist 16

Mr U. Big 16ran 4m48.90
```

188 Dan Moore Memorial Hcap Chase (141) (4yo+) £26,712   2m1f (13)

```
112  KILLULTAGH STORM (IRE) WPMullins 9-10-12¹³⁴ RWalsh...................... 5/2f  1
170  ALCAPONE (IRE) MFMorris 9-11-3¹³⁹ BJGeraghty ............................. 5/1  hd 2
151  ARCTIC COPPER (IRE) NMeade 9-11-5¹⁴¹ PCarberry............................. 3/1  3 3
165  Glenelly Gale (IRE) ALTMoore 9-10-11¹³³ CO'Dwyer ....................... 7/1  7 4
112  Fiery Ring (IRE) JRHFowler 8-10-8¹³³ RGeraghty³........................... 7/1  13 5
100  Jurado Express (IRE) ALTMoore 7-10-11¹³³ DJCasey .......................... 6/1  pu
```

Mrs Rose Boyd 6ran 4m09.46

189 Irish Grand National Chase (Hcap) (146) (5yo+) £73,000   3m5f (24)

```
     TIMBERA (IRE) DTHughes 9-10-12¹³⁰ (t) JCulloty......................... 11/1  1
     KNOCK KNOCK (IRE) DWachman 6-9-13¹²⁰ MDGrant³......................... 20/1  hd 2
     WINNING DREAM (IRE) OliverMcKiernan 9-10-5¹²³ APMcCoy ............. 9/1  2 3
     DAVIDS LAD (IRE) AJMartin 9-12-0¹⁴⁶ (t) TJMurphy........................ 10/1  2 4
  7  Torduff Boy (IRE) PaulNolan 10-10-4¹²⁵ (t) GTHutchinson³ .............. 14/1  2 5
  7  Wotsitooya (IRE) MJPO'Brien 11-10-0¹¹⁸ PMoloney ........................ 14/1  6
120  Eskimo Jack (IRE) ALTMoore 7-11-1¹³³ CO'Dwyer ......................... 8/1f  7
 81  Kirmar (IRE) PAFahy 9-10-0¹¹⁸ KPGaule ...................................... 33/1  8
 81  Good Vintage (IRE) NMeade 8-10-0¹¹⁸ PCarberry ........................... 20/1  9
166  Spot Thedifference (IRE) EBolger 10-10-10¹²⁸ (s) DJCasey.............. 28/1  10
 39  Takagi (IRE) EJO'Grady 8-11-13¹⁴⁵ NWilliamson .......................... 20/1  11
     Princess Symphony (IRE) ESheehy 7-9-7¹¹⁸ AJDonoghue⁷.............. 25/1  12
     Beausheram (IRE) JamesMKiernan 9-9-11¹¹⁸ RGeraghty³................. 33/1  13
170  Rathbawn Prince (IRE) DTHughes 11-11-5¹³⁷ KAKelly ................... 14/1  14
     The Dell (IRE) MissFMCrowley 10-10-7¹²⁵ RGeraghty..................... 12/1  15
     I'vehadit (IRE) DTHughes 9-10-5¹²⁸ MrRLoughran⁵........................ 12/1  16
173  Falcon du Coteau (FR) AJMartin 9-10-0¹¹⁸ JRBarry ...................... 20/1  17
     Native Jack (IRE) ALTMoore 9-10-9¹³⁰ DJHoward³......................... 14/1  f
170  Ross Moff (IRE) AJMartin 10-10-11¹²⁹ (t) MAFitzgerald................... 9/1  f
100  One Night Out (IRE) WPMullins 7-10-6¹²⁴ RWalsh .......................... 14/1  f
 81  Satcoslam (IRE) LWhitmore 8-10-0¹¹⁸ GCotter................................. 25/1  pu
```

Mrs J. M. Breen 21ran 7m44.37

190 Prix Leon Rambaud (Hdle) (Gr 2) (5yo+) £34,138   2½m110y (12)

```
 22  KARLY FLIGHT (FR) AChaille-Chaille,France 5-10-1 PSourzac............... 11/1  1
     GREAT LOVE (FR) PBoisgontier,France 5-10-10 CCheminaud ................. 3/1  15 2
     SOLARIUS (FR) JBertrandeBalanda,France 6-10-3 LMetais.................... 14/1  1 3
 15  Vic Toto (FR) MlleFForneron,France 6-10-10 LDeLaRosa.......................... 5 4
     Ibardine (FR) BdeMontzey,France 6-10-3 NDesoutter ............................ 6 5
     Royal Atalza BBarbier,France 6-10-3 (b) CGombeau .......................... sn 6
 36  Katiki (FR) J-PGallorini,France 6-10-6 CPieux................................. rtr
```

Mr P. Boiteau 7ran 5m02.00

191 Powers Gold Label Hcap Hdle Series Final (130) (4yo+) £40,345   2m (9)

```
     HIGH PROSPECT (IRE) PaulNolan 5-10-0¹⁰² NWilliamson ...................... 5/1f  1
 85  JUNIOR FONTAINE (FR) ALTMoore 6-10-10¹¹⁵ DJHoward³ .............. 14/1  ½ 2
 85  THE DARK FLASHER (IRE) CFSwan 6-10-13¹¹⁵ DJCasey ................. 16/1  ¾ 3
     HEALY'S PUB (IRE) OliverMcKiernan 7-10-10¹¹⁹ RCColgan⁷ .............. 8/1  2 4
     Classic Note (IRE) AJMartin 8-9-8⁹⁶ GCotter .................................. 8/1  ½ 5
     Right Job (IRE) PJFlynn 8-11-2¹²¹ IJPower³ .................................... 12/1  6
 85  Some Buzz (IRE) TMWalsh 8-10-6¹⁰⁸ RWalsh ............................... 10/1  7
177  Take Flite AnthonyMullins 6-11-3¹¹⁹ BJGeraghty ........................... 7/1  8
177  Newhall (IRE) FFlood 5-11-5¹²⁶ APLane⁵ ..................................... 12/1  9
  6  Pillar Rock (USA) CFSwan 7-10-8¹¹⁰ KAKelly .............................. 25/1  10
139  Janidou (IRE) ALTMoore 7-10-12¹¹⁴ CO'Dwyer ............................. 11/1  11
159  Mise Rafturai (IRE) PaulNolan 5-11-2¹²¹ GTHutchinson³ .................. 12/1  12
 85  Emperors Guest PatrickMullins 5-10-11¹¹³ (s) TJMurphy .................. 20/1  13
  8  Bob What (IRE) PatrickMullins 9-11-9¹³⁰ (t) RMPower⁵ ................... 9/1  14
     An Modh Direach (IRE) TMWalsh 9-11-9¹³⁰ (b) MrNPMadden⁷.................. 25/1  15
179  Balapour (IRE) PatrickOBrady 5-11-9¹³⁰ MFMooney⁵ ...................... 16/1  f
     Blue (IRE) NMeade 7-10-13¹¹⁵ PCarberry ...................................... 20/1  f
```

Estival Park (IRE) *DonalKinsella* 6-9-7[95] PACarberry .... 33/1   ur

Mr Alec Scallan 18ran 3m40.52

SANDOWN Friday, Apr 25   FIRM

192 **Concept Hdle (B) (4yo+) £34,800**   2m110y (8)

142	SANTENAY (FR) *PFNicholls* 5-11-6 RWalsh	7/4	1
179	COPELAND *MCPipe* 8-11-6 (v) APMcCoy	8/15f	7 2
10	BEN EWAR *KOCunningham-Brown* 9-11-6 AThornton	50/1	14 3
	Scented Air *JDCzerpak* 6-11-1 LAspell	100/1	5 4
	Jalons Star (IRE) *MQuinn* 5-11-6 SCurran	200/1	24 5
180	Mantles Prince *AGJuckes* 9-11-6 OMcPhail	25/1	dist 6

The Hon Mrs Townshend 6ran 3m43.18

SANDOWN Saturday, Apr 26   GOOD to FIRM

193 **'Press The Red Button To Bet attheraces' Hdle (B) (4yo+) £29,000**   3m (12)

163	ROSTROPOVICH (IRE) *MFMorris,Ireland* 6-11-5 (s+t) NWilliamson	4/1	1
154	DEANO'S BEENO *MCPipe* 11-11-9 APMcCoy	8/13f	sh 2
163	CARLOVENT (FR) *MCPipe* 8-11-5 (v) TScudamore	8/1	dist 3
	Glacial Sunset (IRE) *AJLidderdale* 8-11-5 TDoyle	10/1	5 4
	Ennel Boy (IRE) *NMBabbage* 10-11-5 TJMurphy	50/1	5 5
	Darina's Boy *LWells* 7-11-5 RJohnson	33/1	dist 6

Mr M. A. Kilduff 6ran 5m39.41

194 **Queen Elizabeth The Queen Mother Celebration Chase (B) (5yo+)**   2m (13)
£59,500

172	SEEBALD (GER) *MCPipe* 8-11-6 APMcCoy	11/8	1
172	CENKOS (FR) *PFNicholls* 9-11-10 RWalsh	5/4f	1¼ 2
186	WAHIBA SANDS *MCPipe* 10-11-6 (v) NWilliamson	33/1	9 3
188	Alcapone (IRE) *MFMorris,Ireland* 9-11-6 BJGeraghty	16/1	4 4
179	Geos (FR) *NJHenderson* 8-11-6 MAFitzgerald	7/1	dist 5

The Macca & Growler Partnership 5ran 3m49.94

195 **attheraces Gold Cup Chase (Hcap) (Gr 3) (A) (161) (5yo+) £87,000**   3m5f110y (24)

180	AD HOC (IRE) *PFNicholls* 9-10-10[145] RWalsh	7/1	1
185	STORMEZ (FR) *MCPipe* 6-10-12[147] (t) APMcCoy	9/2f	9 2
185	GUNTHER MCBRIDE (IRE) *PJHobbs* 8-10-1[136] RJohnson	7/1	1¼ 3
137	FROSTY CANYON *PRWebber* 10-10-2[137] (v) TDoyle	9/1	½ 4
158	Iznogoud (FR) *MCPipe* 7-10-8[143] BFenton	25/1	hd 5
75	Bounce Back (USA) *MCPipe* 7-10-8[143] TScudamore	12/1	4 6
143	Foxchapel King (IRE) *MFMorris,Ireland* 10-11-12[161] DJCasey	33/1	1 7
185	Spendid (IRE) *AKing* 11-10-5[140] RThornton	16/1	8 8
180	The Bunny Boiler (IRE) *NMeade,Ireland* 9-10-7[142] MAFitzgerald	25/1	dist 9
170	Whitenzo (FR) *PFNicholls* 7-10-3[138] BJGeraghty	14/1	7 10
180	Killusty (IRE) *CREgerton* 9-10-7[142] NWilliamson	5/1	pu
180	Montifault (FR) *PFNicholls* 8-10-1[136] JTizzard	8/1	pu
180	Royal Predica (FR) *MCPipe* 9-10-0[135] (t) RGreene	14/1	pu
180	Burlu (FR) *MCPipe* 9-9-11[135] (b) DJHoward³	66/1	pu
	Moving Earth (IRE) *AWCarroll* 10-10-0[135] NFehily	66/1	pu
37	Keltic Heritage (IRE) *LADace* 9-10-0[135] (t) TJMurphy	20/1	pu

Sir Robert Ogden 16ran 7m20.87

AUTEUIL Saturday, Apr 26   HEAVY

196 **Prix Amadou (Hdle) (Gr 2) (4yo) £43,448**   2m3f110y (12)

	NICKNAME (FR) *J-PGallorini,France* 4-10-10 TMajorcryk	21/10	1
	BULOUGUN (FR) *MRolland,France* 4-9-11 PChevalier		1 2
	KAPGARDE (FR) *GMacaire,France* 4-10-6 BGicquel		8 3
	Malcom (FR) *BSecly,France* 4-10-3 CCheminaud		1 4
	L'Interprete (FR) *TTrapenard,France* 4-10-3 AKondrat		6 5
	Fidelety (FR) *BSecly,France* 4-9-11 JaquesRicou		¾ 6
	Cheler (FR) *BSecly,France* 4-10-3 BChameraud		8 7
	Homme du Bourg (FR) *PHDemercastel,France* 4-10-1 FBenech		8 8
	Katoune (FR) *MmeSylvieAudon,France* 4-10-3 PSourzac		f
	Royaleety (FR) *TCivel,France* 4-10-10 CPieux		pu
	Empereur du Monde (FR) *J-PGallorini,France* 4-10-3 LGerard		pu
	Goffriler (FR) *J-LLaval,France* 4-10-1 LMetais		pu

Mrs Daniel Wildenstein 12ran 5m08.91

PUNCHESTOWN Tuesday, Apr 29   GOOD

197 **BMW Chase (Gr 1) (5yo+) £51,847**   2m (11)

| 148 | FLAGSHIP UBERALLES (IRE) *PJHobbs,GB* 9-12-0 RJohnson | 8/1 | 1 |
| 188 | ARCTIC COPPER (IRE) *NMeade* 9-12-0 (s) NWilliamson | 25/1 | 6 2 |

188	KILLULTAGH STORM (IRE) *WPMullins* 9-12-0 (b) DJCasey	14/1	4½ 3
148	Latalomne (USA) *BEllison,GB* 9-12-0 ADobbin	13/2	2 4
151	Tresor de Mai (FR) *MCPipe,GB* 9-12-0 RGreene	16/1	9 5
80	Knife Edge (USA) *MJPO'Brien* 8-12-0 MAFitzgerald	10/1	6
148	Moscow Flyer (IRE) *MrsJHarrington* 9-12-0 BJGeraghty	4/11f	ur

Mr J. P. McManus 7ran 4m08.13

198   Evening Herald Champion Nov Hdle (Gr 1) (5yo+) £36,806   2m (9)

140	BACK IN FRONT (IRE) *EJO'Grady* 6-11-12 NWilliamson	4/11f	1
171	LIMERICK BOY (GER) *MissVenetiaWilliams,GB* 5-11-11 ADobbin	7/1	2½ 2
77	FOTA ISLAND (IRE) *MFMorris* 7-11-12 DJCasey	8/1	7 3
128	Stacumny Bridge (IRE) *MHalford* 5-11-11 TJMurphy	20/1	1½ 4
	Swordplay *MJPO'Brien* 5-11-11 DNRussell	12/1	13 5
111	Central House *DTHughes* 6-11-12 KAKelly	16/1	6
169	Aine Dubh (IRE) *KevinFO'Donnell* 6-11-7 PMoloney	33/1	7
	Khetaam (IRE) *NMeade* 5-11-11 (b) BJGeraghty	16/1	8
111	Woodys Deep Ocean (IRE) *NMeade* 5-11-12 RJohnson	25/1	pu

Mr D. Cox 9ran 3m49.07

PUNCHESTOWN Wednesday, Apr 30   GOOD

199   Punchestown Heineken Gold Cup (Gr 1) (5yo+) £66,667   3m1f (17)

164	FIRST GOLD (FR) *FDoumen,France* 10-12-0 (b) TDoumen	7/4f	1
121	RINCE RI (IRE) *TMWalsh* 10-12-0 MAFitzgerald	12/1	6 2
172	NATIVE UPMANSHIP (IRE) *ALTMoore* 10-12-0 CO'Dwyer	11/4	7 3
151	Young Spartacus *HDDaly,GB* 10-12-0 RJohnson	10/1	6 4
148	Florida Pearl (IRE) *WPMullins* 11-12-0 BJGeraghty	9/1	3½ 5
195	Foxchapel King (IRE) *MFMorris* 10-12-0 DJCasey	12/1	6
155	Hussard Collonges (FR) *PBeaumont,GB* 8-12-0 RGarritty	9/2	f

Mr J. P. McManus 7ran 6m15.30

200   Colm McEvoy Auctioneers Nov Hcap Chase (133) (5yo+) £38,750   3m1f (17)

	RULE SUPREME (IRE) *WPMullins* 7-11-7[128] DJCasey	12/1	1
150	HEDGEHUNTER (IRE) *WPMullins* 7-11-4[125] BJGeraghty	11/4f	3½ 2
	TURN TWO (IRE) *NMeade* 6-10-9[116] (t) JCulloty	16/1	1 3
150	CLONMEL'S MINELLA (IRE) *MichaelHourigan* 12-10-7[114] TJMurphy	16/1	2½ 4
77	Mystic Lord (IRE) *NMeade* 6-10-7[119] (t) RMPower[5]	20/1	5 5
	Killultagh Thunder (IRE) *WPMullins* 7-10-2[114] MrJJCodd[5]	20/1	6
189	Good Vintage (IRE) *NMeade* 8-10-4[114] (s) KHadnett[3]	14/1	7
73	Just In Debt (IRE) *PMJDoyle* 7-11-9[130] NWilliamson	10/1	8
189	Princess Symphony (IRE) *ESheehy* 7-10-9[116] JLCullen	14/1	9
81	Bennie's Pride (IRE) *EJO'Grady* 7-10-7[114] KWhelan	20/1	10
163	Thari (IRE) *NMeade* 6-11-3[124] MAFitzgerald	14/1	11
	Star Performance (IRE) *OliverMcKiernan* 8-10-9[116] CO'Dwyer	16/1	12
14	Kadoun (IRE) *MJPO'Brien* 6-11-9[133] DJHoward[3]	8/1	f
	Tribal Dancer (IRE) *MissVenetiaWilliams,GB* 9-10-8[115] BJCrowley	16/1	f
	Diceman (IRE) *MrsSJSmith,GB* 8-10-7[114] DSElsworth	12/1	f
109	Jungle Jinks (IRE) *GMMoore,GB* 8-11-11[132] RGarritty	12/1	bd
170	Shardam (IRE) *NATwiston-Davies,GB* 6-11-7[128] CLlewellyn	6/1	ur
43	Native Sessions (IRE) *NMeade* 8-11-5[129] (t) IJPower[3]	14/1	pu

Mr John P. Lynch 18ran 6m17.88

201   Paddy Power Champion INH Flat (Gr 1) (4yo+ m) £13,542   2m

	ROYAL ROSA (FR) *NJHenderson,GB* 4-11-6 MrAFitzgerald	14/1	1
152	ROYAL ALPHABET (IRE) *WPMullins* 5-11-8 MrJJCodd[5]	4/1	3½ 2
	KILDARE (IRE) *DTHughes* 6-11-9 MrRLoughran[5]	20/1	1½ 3
	Lady Toulon (IRE) *DMFogarty* 5-11-5 MrPFahey[3]	33/1	1½ 4
	Flexible Action (IRE) *JEKiely* 5-11-10 MrAPCrowe[3]	9/2	¾ 5
83	Rockstown Boy (IRE) *CByrnes* 5-11-6 MrDerekO'Connor[7]	16/1	6
	Kickham (IRE) *EJO'Grady* 7-12-0 MrPFenton	6/4f	7
	Arctic Force (IRE) *PaulARoche* 6-11-7 MrDRoche[7]	33/1	8
	Buffalo Bill (IRE) *DWachman* 7-11-7 MrJPMagnier[7]	11/1	9
152	Storm Boxer (IRE) *PatrickMullins* 5-11-6 MrKJMercer[7]	20/1	10
	Penny Fiction (IRE) *DMLeigh* 6-11-2 MrTGFreyne[7]	33/1	11
	Fairwood Present (IRE) *PJRothwell* 5-11-6 MrDGPorter[7]	25/1	12
	Zum See (IRE) *NMeade* 4-10-13 MrNPMadden[7]	10/1	13
	The Galway Man (IRE) *AnthonyMullins* 6-11-7 MrSKRyder[7]	16/1	14
	Kilrossanty (IRE) *HenryDeBromhead* 4-11-3 MrTPHyde[3]	16/1	15
	King of The Arctic (IRE) *DKWeld* 5-11-13 MrKRO'Ryan[7]	20/1	16
100	Alexander Milenium (IRE) *WPMullins* 7-12-0 MrJANash	12/1	17
152	Triple Rum (IRE) *JamesLeavy* 6-12-0 MrJTMcNamara	33/1	18
	It's Official (IRE) *JohnJosephMurphy* 4-10-13 MrAJMcNamara[7]	33/1	19

Million In Mind P'ship 12 19ran 3m42.74

202 **Champion Stayers' Hdle (Gr 1) (4yo+)** £43,056   3m (14)

142	HOLY ORDERS (IRE) *WPMullins* 6-11-12 (b) JRBarry	6/1	1
179	SACUNDAI (IRE) *EJO'Grady* 6-11-12 NWilliamson	9/10f	½ 2
193	ROSTROPOVICH (IRE) *MFMorris* 6-11-12 (s+t) MAFitzgerald	9/2	13 3
176	Fnan *NMeade* 7-11-12 TJMurphy	16/1	2 4
164	Commanche Court (IRE) *TMWalsh* 10-11-12 RWalsh	6/1	2½ 5
	Colonel Monroe (IRE) *EJO'Grady* 6-11-12 BJGeraghty	33/1	6

Mr Allan McLuckie 6ran 5m55.10

203 **IAWS Champion Four Year Old Hdle (Gr 1) (4yo)** £47,361   2m (9)

	SPORAZENE (IRE) *PFNicholls,GB* 4-11-0 RWalsh	7/1	1
167	SPECTROSCOPE (IRE) *JonjoO'Neill,GB* 4-11-0 BJGeraghty	4/1	2 2
153	GOLDEN CROSS (IRE) *MHalford* 4-11-0 TJMurphy	7/2f	4 3
167	Starzaan (IRE) *HMorrison,GB* 4-11-0 JCulloty	10/1	¾ 4
153	Mutineer (IRE) *DTHughes* 4-11-0 KAKelly	8/1	2 5
153	Dashing Home (IRE) *NMeade* 4-11-0 NWilliamson	5/1	6
118	Party Airs (USA) *DKWeld* 4-11-0 DTEvans	16/1	7
41	Mirpour (IRE) *EGriffin* 4-11-0 (s) ADobbin	20/1	8
153	Newlands Gold (IRE) *MJPO'Brien* 4-11-0 DJCasey	14/1	9
203	Laoch Na Mara (USA) *TGMcCourt* 4-11-0 MrPJCasey	40/1	10
153	Nas Na Riogh (IRE) *NJHenderson,GB* 4-10-9 MAFitzgerald	10/1	11
153	Kenilworth (USA) *PatrickOBrady* 4-11-0 JLCullen	14/1	12

Ged Mason &. David Jackson 12ran 3m48.43

204 **Swordlestown Cup Nov Chase (Gr 1) (5yo+)** £36,597   2m (11)

178	LE ROI MIGUEL (FR) *PFNicholls,GB* 5-11-5 RWalsh	8/11f	1
178	IMPEK (FR) *MissHCKnight,GB* 7-11-12 JCulloty	9/4	6 2
178	RATHGAR BEAU (IRE) *ESheehy* 7-11-12 BJGeraghty	7/1	2 3
85	Star Clipper *NMeade* 6-11-12 NWilliamson	25/1	20 4
188	Jurado Express (IRE) *ALTMoore* 7-11-12 CO'Dwyer	14/1	5 5

Mrs J. Stewart 5ran 4m10.13

205 **Emo Oil Champion Hdle (Gr 1) (5yo+)** £56,250   2m (9)

179	QUAZAR (IRE) *JonjoO'Neill,GB* 5-11-13 (t) ADobbin	7/2	1
198	BACK IN FRONT (IRE) *EJO'Grady* 6-12-0 NWilliamson	8/11f	1 2
	IN THE FORGE *MHalford* 6-12-0 (t) BJGeraghty	14/1	8 3
177	Risky Reef *AndrewLee* 6-12-0 RWalsh	9/1	25 4
171	Glenhaven Nugget (IRE) *EJO'Grady* 7-12-0 TJMurphy	12/1	1½ 5
128	Cailin's Perk (IRE) *JamesMorrissey* 9-11-9 DJCasey	20/1	6

Mr C. D. Carr 6ran 3m52.75

206 **Menolly Homes Champion Nov Hdle (Gr 1) (4yo+)** £38,750   2½m (12)

	NOBODY TOLD ME (IRE) *WPMullins* 5-11-6 RWalsh	9/1	1
	JACK HIGH (IRE) *WRock* 8-11-12 DNRussell	12/1	5 2
	PAY IT FORWARD *MrsJHarrington* 5-11-11 BJGeraghty	12/1	3 3
174	Pizarro (IRE) *EJO'Grady* 6-11-12 NWilliamson	11/8f	2½ 4
146	Hi Cloy (IRE) *MichaelHourigan* 6-11-12 TJMurphy	16/1	2½ 5
	Jim (FR) *JTRDreaper* 6-11-12 JCulloty	14/1	6
169	Leinster (IRE) *DTHughes* 6-11-12 KAKelly	8/1	7
146	Double Honour (FR) *PJHobbs,GB* 5-11-11 CO'Dwyer	12/1	8
140	Joueur d'Estruval (FR) *WPMullins* 6-11-12 JRBarry	14/1	9
140	Rosaker (USA) *NMeade* 6-11-12 ADobbin	8/1	10
	Wouldn't You Agree (IRE) *CRoche* 7-11-12 PMoloney	10/1	11
	Kings Orchard (IRE) *NMeade* 6-11-12 IJPower	16/1	12
	Atlantic Crossing (IRE) *PBeaumont,GB* 6-11-12 RGarritty	33/1	pu

Amber Syndicate 13ran 4m54.52

207 **Prix La Barka (Hdle) (Gr 2) (5yo+)** £44,681   2m5f110y (14)

190	KARLY FLIGHT (FR) *AChaille-Chaille,France* 5-10-1 PSourzac	4/10f	1
190	GREAT LOVE (FR) *PBoisgontier,France* 5-10-10 CCheminaud		10 2
190	KATIKI (FR) *J-PGallorini,France* 6-10-6 CPieux		5 3
206	Nobody Told Me (IRE) *WPMullins* 5-9-13 DJCasey		2½ 4
	Samson (FR) *LAudon,France* 6-10-3 AKondrat		2 5
190	Solarius (FR) *JBertrandeBalanda,France* 6-10-3 LMetais		2 6
149	Galant Moss (FR) *MCPipe,GB* 9-10-6 PChevalier		2½ 7
190	Royal Atalza *BBarbier,France* 6-10-3 ELequesne		15 8
202	Holy Orders (IRE) *WPMullins,Ireland* 6-10-6 (b) JRBarry		dist 9
	Mary Terse (FR) *JMesnil,France* 5-9-9 (b) FBarrao		pu

Mr P. Boiteau 10ran 5m26.84

208   **Grand Steeple-Chase de Paris (Gr 1) (5yo+)** £153,191   3m5f (23)

92	LINE MARINE (FR) *CAubert,France* 6-10-3 CPieux	17/10 1
36	BATMAN SENORA (FR) *IanWilliams,GB* 7-10-8 (b) CGombeau	10 2
	URGA (FR) *GChaignon,France* 12-10-8 PBrechet	sh 3
15	Rougenoir (FR) *RELecomte,France* 10-10-8 (b) HServeau	¾ 4
	Ilare (FR) *EChevalierduFau,France* 7-10-8 TDoumen	8 5
21	Cerilly (FR) *JBertrandeBalanda,France* 6-10-8 PChevalier	15 6
	Princelou (FR) *NMadamet,France* 6-10-8 JaquesRicou	5 7
21	Sunny Flight (FR) *AChaille-Chaille,France* 9-10-8 PSourzac	pu
	Jerico Vallis (FR) *JBertrandeBalanda,France* 6-10-8 LMetais	pu
21	El Paso III (FR) *BSecly,France* 11-10-8 BGicquel	pu
92	Idole Des Fontaines (FR) *CDiard,France* 7-10-8 (b) SZuliani	pu

Mme G. Vuillard 11ran 7m37.38

AUTEUIL Saturday, Jun 14   GOOD to SOFT

209   **Prix Alain du Breil (Gr 1) (4yo)** £55,458   2m3f110y (12)

196	NICKNAME (FR) *J-PGallorini,France* 4-10-6 TMajorcryk	18/10 1
196	BULOUGUN (FR) *MRolland,France* 4-10-1 PChevalier	1/1f 6 2
196	KATOUNE (FR) *MmeSylvieAudon,France* 4-10-1 CPieux	8/1 2½ 3
196	Cheler (FR) *BSecly,France* 4-10-6 CCheminaud	10 4
196	Homme du Bourg (FR) *PHDemercastel,France* 4-10-6 FBenech	2 5
196	L'Interprete (FR) *TTrapenard,France* 4-10-6 (b) AKondrat	2½ 6
	Klakos (FR) *JLesbordes,France* 4-10-6 JMarion	3 7
	Grabels (FR) *JBertrandeBalanda,France* 4-10-6 LMetais	ur
	Kiss And Cry (FR) *BdeMontzey,France* 4-10-1 NDesoutter	pu

Mrs Daniel Wildenstein 9ran 4m40.67

210   **Grande Course de Haies d'Auteuil (Gr 1) (5yo+)** £87,148   3m1f110y (16)

207	NOBODY TOLD ME (IRE) *WPMullins,Ireland* 5-9-13 DJCasey	31/1 1
207	KARLY FLIGHT (FR) *AChaille-Chaille,France* 5-9-13 PSourzac	1/5f 2 2
207	KATIKI (FR) *J-PGallorini,France* 6-10-8 CPieux	8/1 2 3
	Trespass (FR) *MRolland,France* 5-10-3 PChevalier	6 4
207	Samson (FR) *MmeSylvieAudon,France* 6-10-8 AKondrat	20 5
	Malone (FR) *JBertrandeBalanda,France* 5-10-3 LMetais	15 6
195	Iznogoud (FR) *MCPipe,GB* 7-10-8 TDoumen	10 7
179	Mr Cool *MCPipe,GB* 9-10-8 RGreene	dist 8

Amber Syndicate 8ran 6m27.01

INDEX TO SELECTED BIG RACES

Abalvino (FR) c165
Abyce (FR) 22[5]
Achates (IRE) 41[5]
Achilles Wings (USA) 176[pu]
Ackzo c75[pu]
Adamant Approach (IRE)
  c141[F]
Ad Hoc (IRE) 13[5], 58[2], c143[3],
  c180[ur], c195*
Adjawar (IRE) 64[pu]
Aimees Mark (IRE) 149
Aine Dubh (IRE) 169[3], 198
Akarus (FR) c96, c160[2]
Alcapone (IRE) c35[ur], c52[5],
  c80[pu], c170[6], c188[2], c194[4]
Aleemdar (IRE) 6
Alexander Milenium (IRE)
  c100[F], F201
Alka International 129
Allude (IRE) 167
Al Skywalker (USA) 57[pu]
Altay 177[2]
Always Rainbows (IRE) 110[2]
Amberleigh House (IRE) c34[2],
  c137, c180[3]
American Isle (IRE) 118[pu]
Amir Zaman 130[5]
Anatar (IRE) 149
Andretti Castle (IRE) c7[pu]
Andy Gin (FR) 153
Angel Delight 161[5]

An Modh Direach (IRE) 191
Anxious Moments (IRE) 6, 67,
  85
Arabian Moon (IRE) 149
Araminta c156
Arch Stanton (IRE) 140[su]
Arctic Copper (IRE) c92[5], c805,
  c102[2], c151, c188[3], c197[2]
Arctic Fancy (USA) c151
Arctic Force (IRE) F201
Arctic Times (IRE) c181[2]
Ardan Glas (IRE) F28
Ardent Scout c23[3], c34*, c108[2],
  c137
Argento 110[6]
Argent Vif (FR) c92[F]
Arielle (FR) 36
Arlequin de Sou (FR) c96
Armaguedon (FR) F182
Armaturk (FR) c16[3], c151,
  c187
Ar Muin Na Muice (IRE) 161*
Asabache (IRE) c102[pu]
Ashgar (USA) c24
Ashley Brook (IRE) F182
Ask Henry (IRE) c150
Ask Me What (IRE) 161
Ask The Natives (IRE) c93[5]
Atlantic Crossing (IRE) 206[pu]
Atlantic Rhapsody (FR) 115
Atum Re (IRE) 64[pu]

Autumn Stroll (IRE) F28
Avalanche (FR) c168[ur]
Away Home (IRE) F162[4]
Azertyuiop (FR) c26*, c141*

Bacchanal (IRE) 38*, c71[3],
  c95[F]
Back In Front (IRE) 42[2], 140*,
  198*, 205[2]
Backsheesh (IRE) c156[pu]
Back To Ben Alder (IRE) F152
Back To Gales (IRE) F83
Balapour (IRE) 6, 14[ur], 44[5],
  61[3], 85[ur], 159[2], 179, 191[F]
Balinahinch Castle (IRE) 174[pu]
Balladeer (IRE) 174[6]
Ballinarrid (IRE) c7[F], c9[5]
Ballinclay King (IRE) c96[4],
  c180[pu]
Ballon Rose (IRE) F162
Ballyamber (IRE) c120[3]
Ballybough Rasher (IRE)
  c99[pu], c170[pu]
Ballyhampshire Boy (IRE) 8[su],
  30[F]
Ballylusky (IRE) 106[4], 145
Ballysicyos (FR) 145, 163
Banner Gale (IRE) c96[pu],
  c126[5]
Bannow Bay (IRE) 78[3]

Baracouda (FR) 32^*, 63^2, 154^*
Baron Monty (IRE) F182
Barren Lands $c54^5$
Barrow Drive $c43^2$, $c73^2$, $c120^*$, $c147^3$
Barryscourt Lad (IRE) $c99^*$
Barton c87, $c158^6$, $c164^6$
Batman Senora (FR) $c21^4$, 36, $c208^2$
Batswing $c25^{pu}$, $c65^{ro}$, $c165^5$
Battle Warning 58^{pu}
Beausheram (IRE) c189
Beef Or Salmon (IRE) $c35^*$, $c60^*$, $c79^*$, $c121^*$, $c155^F$
Be Fair $F117^4$, F152, $F182^2$
Behrajan (IRE) $c66^*$, $c95^*$, $c155^5$, c180
Behzad (IRE) F182
Bellaney Lady (IRE) $c122^4$
Belle d'Anjou (FR) 1, 159
Be My Belle $c73^4$
Be My Destiny (IRE) 138^5
Be My Manager (IRE) c96, c144, c173
Be My Royal (IRE) $c39^*$
Benbecula (IRE) 138^3
Benbyas 27^4, 67^3, 115^5, 149
Ben Ewar 10^4, 192^3
Bennie's Pride (IRE) $c81^4$, c200
Berlin Blue $c170^{pu}$, $c185^F$
Bernardon (GER) 67, 115, 139
Best Mate (IRE) $c33^*$, $c71^*$, $c155^*$
Beyond The Pale (IRE) F285
Big Taste (JPN) $c187^*$
Billy Nomaite $c4^{ur}$
Billy The Snake (IRE) $c81^5$
Bindaree (IRE) 13, $c34^F$, $c39^{ur}$, $c48^2$, $c87^4$, c137, $c180^6$
Bingo Bell (FR) $c92^F$
Bitofamixup (IRE) $c166^{ur}$
Blackagino (IRE) 41^{pu}
Black Kite (IRE) F117
Blazing Batman 58^6
Bleu Superbe (FR) $c4^{pu}$, $c103^{pu}$, $c157^{pu}$, $c165^{pu}$
Blowing Wind (FR) $c34^3$, c96, c151, c180
Blue (IRE) 191^F
Blue Ride (IRE) 161^3
Blyth Brook $c181^{pu}$
Bobby Grant $c29^3$, $c59^2$, $c108^4$, c137
Bob What (IRE) 6^5, 8^2, 191
Bold Bishop (IRE) $F28^4$, F117, $F152^4$
Bold Investor $c69^3$, $c99^{pu}$, c135, $c168^2$
Boneyarnon (IRE) $c43^F$
Bonny Boy (IRE) $c150^{pu}$
Borani 3
Border Light $c181^{pu}$
Boss Doyle (IRE) 13^2, 38^4, 78^2
Bounce Back (USA) c39, $c75^{pu}$, $c195^6$
Bound 139
Bourbon Manhattan $F152^6$
Bow Strada 149, $c183^4$

Bramblehill Duke (IRE) c107, c143, $c180^F$
Brave Inca (IRE) $F162^*$
Brazil (FR) 36
Bregogue (IRE) $c5^F$
Brigadier du Bois (FR) 167
Bright Approach (IRE) $c156^2$
Brilliant Star (NZ) $c5^{pu}$
Brooklyn's Gold (USA) 113^4, 177^3
Brother Joe (NZ) 13^*, 38^6, 63^{pu}, 154
Browjoshy (IRE) $c34^F$
Bruern (IRE) F117
Buffalo Bill (IRE) F201
Bulougun (IRE) 196^2, 209^2
Burlu (FR) $c144^{pu}$, $c180^F$, $c195^{pu}$
Bust Out $c72^2$, $c100^*$
Cailin's Perk (IRE) 85^6, 128^5, 205^6
Calladine (IRE) 115^{ur}, 128^3
Calling Brave (IRE) 46^{ur}, 76^2, 146, 163
Camden Dolphin (IRE) F117
Camden Tanner (IRE) 85^3, 106^2, 149
Camels Cross (IRE) F162
Canada 139^4, 176^3
Canadiane (IRE) $c173^{ur}$
Cape Stormer (IRE) c168
Captain Flinders (IRE) F28
Caracciola (GER) 130^3, 171^{pu}
Carbury Cross (IRE) $c39^6$, $c66^{pu}$, c135, c137, $c143^{pu}$, c180
Carlovent (FR) 23, 32^3, 106^{pu}, 124^5, 145, 163^*, 193^3
Carryonharry (IRE) c99, $c135^4$, $c144^6$, $c185^{pu}$
Cassia Heights c173
Castle Prince (IRE) $c16^4$, $c335$, $c114^4$, c157
Castleshane (IRE) 18^2, 40^5, 159
Catch Ball 14^6, 38, 78^5
Ceanannas Mor (IRE) $c173^{ur}$
Cedar Dale (IRE) $F162^{pu}$
Celibate (IRE) $c11^3$
Celtic Vision (IRE) 138^{pu}
Cenkos (FR) $c50^*$, $c114^2$, $c148^3$, $c172^4$, $c194^2$
Central House 111^2, 198^6
Cerilly (FR) $c21^2$, $c208^6$
Champagne Harry F28
Champion Veronais (FR) $c21^6$
Chanticlier 58^5
Chant Royal (FR) $c92^4$
Chauvinist (IRE) 67^*, 90^3, 115, 140^3
Cheers New Power (JPN) c187
Cheler (FR) 196, 209^4
Chergan (IRE) c151, c173
Cherokee Boy $c2^{pu}$
Cherry Brandy 90^6
Chevalier Errant (IRE) c7, c99
Chevet Girl (IRE) 177
Chicago Bulls (IRE) 106, 149
Chicuelo (FR) $c4^*$, $c25^{pu}$, $c135^{pu}$, 149
Chief Mosconomo 41^6

Chives (IRE) $c29^2$, $c75^2$, $c116^2$, c155, $c180^{pu}$
Chopneyev (FR) 106^*, 124^2, 145
Christy's Pride (IRE) c150
Clan Royal (FR) $c173^*$
Clarendon (IRE) 113
Classic Native (IRE) F152, $F182^*$
Classic Note (IRE) 191^5
Classified (IRE) 94^*, 129^*, 154^4
Clever Consul (IRE) 6
Clonmel's Minella (IRE) $c81^3$, c150, $c200^4$
Cloudy Grey (IRE) $F117^2$
Colca Canyon (IRE) 31
Colm's Rock (IRE) $c5^{ur}$, $c7^F$
Colonel Braxton (IRE) 44^4, $c79^2$, $c121^2$, c155
Colonel Monroe (IRE) 202^6
Colonial Sunset (IRE) c133
Colourful Life (IRE) 85^2, 124^6, 176^6
Come In Moscow (IRE) $c43^{pu}$, $c81^{pu}$, $c173^F$
Comex Flyer (IRE) 94^5, 129^3, 159^F
Commanche Course (IRE) 111
Commanche Court (IRE) $c112^3$, $c155^6$, $c164^3$, 202^5
Compostello (IRE) 31
Control Man (IRE) $F117^5$
Coolaness (IRE) 78^4
Coole Spirit (IRE) $c160^{pu}$
Coolgarrane (IRE) F83
Coolnagorna (IRE) 46^*, 76^*, 146^{2d}, 169^F
Coolsan (IRE) 98^{pu}
Copeland 115, 142^F, 179^6, 192^2
Copernicus (IRE) $c60^4$, $c80^4$, $c112^2$
Coq Hardi Diamond (IRE) $c81^*$
Coraya (FR) $c92^6$
Cornish Rebel (IRE) $F117^*$, F152
Correct And Right (IRE) 97
Cortynan (FR) $c122^F$
Cotopaxi (IRE) 3^3
County Derry $c165^5$
Court of Appeal 3
Cowboyboots (IRE) 98^3
Crazy Horse 154^{pu}
Cregg House (IRE) $c205$, $c35^3$, $c81^{pu}$, $c151^4$, $c180^R$
Creon 145^6
Crocadee $c39^F$
Crossbow Creek F152
Crystal d'Ainay (FR) 169^2
Curraghmore Thyne (IRE) 111
Cyborsun (FR) $c43^{pu}$
Cyfor Malta (IRE) $c25^*$, $c56^4$, $c95^{ur}$
Czar of Peace (IRE) 6, 67^{pu}
Daiwa Dur (JPN) $c187^6$
Dam The Breeze $c166^F$
Danaeve (IRE) c5
Dancetillyoudrop (IRE) $c2^{ur}$
Dancing Bay 110^4, 139
Dangerously Good 140

Darina's Boy 193[6]
Dark Character F182[6]
Dark Magic (IRE) c84[F]
Dark'n Sharp (GER) 27[3], c65[F], c89[3], c157[3], c165[2], c186[ur]
Dark Room (IRE) c150[pu]
Dashing Home (IRE) 41[3], 153, 203[6]
Davenport Democrat (IRE) F152
Davenport Milenium (IRE) 70[3]
Davids Lad (IRE) c189[4]
Davoski c65[4], 115
Dealer Del c150[ur]
Deano's Beeno 38[3], 63*, 86[2], 131*, 154[6], 193[2]
Dear Deal c2
Deep Sunset (IRE) 51[4]
Delgany Royal (IRE) c81[6], c84[4], c99[ur]
Demasta (NZ) c4[pu], c54[pu], c89[4]
Demi Beau 130[4]
Dempsey (IRE) F152[pu], F182
Detonateur (FR) 140
Devon View (IRE) c103[3]
Diamond Joshua (IRE) 82
Diceman (IRE) c200[F]
Didifon 40[6]
Dionn Righ (IRE) c150[pu]
Direct Access (IRE) c39[pu]
Direct Bearing (IRE) 159[6]
Dispol Rock (IRE) 91[4]
Distant Sky (USA) 90
Divet Hill c166*
Dizzy's Dream (IRE) F152
Djeddah (FR) c143[5], c180
Docklands Limo 27
Do It On Dani 23, 163[6]
Do L'Enfant d'Eau (FR) 167
Domenico (IRE) 46[5]
Donadino (IRE) c4[pu]
Don Fernando 55*, 97[2], 153[bd], 171
Donna's Princess (IRE) c60[6]
Donnybrook (IRE) c99[4]
Don Royal c181[pu]
Doors To Manual (FR) F162[2]
Dorado (FR) 22
Dorans Gold c144
Dorans Pride (IRE) c122[2], c156[F]
Double Honour (FR) 146, 206
Douze Douze (FR) c33[2], c71[pu], c125[ur]
Down (FR) c166
Dream With Me (FR) 27[6], 149[pu], 177
Druid's Glen (IRE) c133[2], c150
Drumdowney Lad (IRE) F162
Dubai Seven Stars 145, 176
Duke of Earl (FR) 55[5], 134[3], 153
Dumaran (IRE) 64[5]
Dunbrody Millar (IRE) F83[6]
Dunowen (IRE) c150[F]
Dyrick Daybreak (IRE) 41[4], 118

Earl's Kitchen F117
Early Edition c183[F]

Earthmover (IRE) c156[4]
Eastern Tribute (USA) 85
East Tycoon (IRE) 134[4]
Echo's of Dawn (IRE) c108[pu]
Edgar Gink (IRE) c181[3]
Edmo Heights 177[4]
Edredon Bleu (IRE) c16*, c50[2], c148[6], c172[6]
Ei Ei c46
El Fuego (FR) 15[3], 36[4]
El Paso III (FR) c21[pu], c208[pu]
Eluna 124[pu]
El Vaquero (FR) F182
Emotional Moment (IRE) 85[4], 149[4], 176[4]
Empereur du Monde (FR) 196[pu]
Empereur River (FR) c180[pu]
Emperor Ross (IRE) c2[F]
Emperors Guest 6, 85[F], 191
Ennel Boy (IRE) 193[5]
Enrique (GER) c185[pu]
Eoins Pride (IRE) c7
Epervier d'Or (FR) c133[5]
Epitre (FR) 88[6]
Epsilo de La Ronce (FR) c165[5]
Eric's Charm (FR) F182[5]
Escort Boy (USA) c92*, c187
Eskimo Jack (IRE) c84[3], c120[4], c189
Eskleybrook c103*, c157[pu]
Esprit de Cotte (FR) c166
Estival Park (IRE) 191[ur]
Eternal Spring (IRE) 27[F], 94[F], 127[F]
Euro Bleu (FR) 169
Europa c151[F]
Evening Scent 85
Even More (IRE) c150[pu]
Ever Blessed (IRE) c29[ur], c39
Exalted (IRE) 176
Executive Games (IRE) c122[F]
Exit Swinger (FR) c25[ur], c56, c157, c173[3]
Exit To Wave (FR) c29[4], c66[2], c135, c160[pu], c173[ur], c185[pu]
Experimental (IRE) 6
Exstoto 124[pu]
Extra Jack (FR) c103[5], c173

Fadalko (FR) c56[5], c125[5], c151, c180[ur], c186[6]
Fadoudal du Cochet (FR) c60[3], c89, c157[pu]
Fair Question (IRE) 91[pu]
Fair Wind (IRE) c156[pu]
Fairwood Heart (IRE) 85, 163[4]
Fairwood Present (IRE) F201
Fait Le Jojo (FR) 1, c26[4], c168[F]
Falcon du Coteau (FR) c173[5], c189
False Tail (IRE) c156[F]
Family Business (IRE) c156[bd], c166[ur]
Far Dawn (USA) c175[pu]
Farinel 145, 176
Farmer Jack c105[2], c141[4], c183[3]
Far Pavilions 167[pu]
Fast Mix (FR) 74[pu]

Fatehalkhair (IRE) c143, c170[4], c185[pu]
Fathom F182
Fidelety (FR) 196[6]
Fier Goumier (FR) c5
Fiery Creek F28
Fiery Ring (IRE) c19[3], c43[3], c112[5], c185[5]
Fifth Generation (IRE) 57, 88, 127[4]
Finians Ivy (IRE) c81[pu]
Fireball Macnamara (IRE) c168[pu]
Firestone (GER) 113[6]
First Gold (FR) c52[3], c79, c126[3], c155[pu], c164*, c199*
Flagship Uberalles (IRE) c50[4], c71[pu], c148[5], c197*
Flame Creek (IRE) 82*, 88*, 142, 184[pu]
Flaming Spirt 74[pu]
Flexible Action (IRE) F201[5]
Flint Knapper 6
Florida Coast (IRE) 111[5]
Florida Pearl (IRE) c20[4], c71[4], c121[pu], c148, c199[5]
Flower of Pitcur F182[pu]
Fnan c7, 176, 202[4]
Folly Road (IRE) c166
Foly Pleasant (FR) c25[4], c56[2], c95[2], c143
Fondmort (FR) c45[3], c56*, c89[F], c135, c151[2], c186[2]
Foreman (GER) 22[2], 64[3], 146[4]
Formal Bid (USA) 124[3]
Fortune Island (IRE) 153
Fota Island (IRE) 77[3], 198[3]
Foxchapel King (IRE) c20[pu], c79[4], c84[2], c143[ur], c195, c199[6]
Fragrant Rose 161[6]
Frantic Tan (IRE) c75[6]
Friend's Amigo (IRE) 42[6], 169[6]
Frosty Canyon 13[4], c39, c75[4], c107[2], c137[6], c195[4]
Full Irish (IRE) 159, 177
Fustrien du Paon (FR) c21[5]

Gabor 167[pu]
Gainful 97
Galant Moss (FR) 36[5], 149, 207
Galapiat du Mesnil (FR) c160[pu]
Galileo (POL) 154
Gallant Glen (IRE) c166[6]
Galway Breeze (IRE) 6
Galway (IRE) c156[pu]
Garolo (FR) c156[pu]
Garruth (IRE) 38
Garvivonnian (IRE) 6
Gazump (FR) F117
General 82[5]
General Claremont (IRE) c2[2], c7[6]
General Wolfe c166[2]
Gentle Rivage (FR) c17[4]
Georges Girl (IRE) 111[4]
Geos (FR) c33[3], 57[3], c125[2], c148[4], 179, c194[5]
Get Real (IRE) c50[5], c65[F]
Ghadames (FR) c5

Gilded Age (JPN) c187[2]
Gingembre (FR) c12[3], c39[2], c95[3], c180[pu]
Giocomo (IRE) 67[pu], 115
Give Over (IRE) c20[3], c39
Glacial Sunset (IRE) 193[4]
Glacial Sygnet (IRE) c7[5]
Gladiateur IV (FR) c7[F]
Glenelly Gale (IRE) c54[3], c165, c188[4]
Glenhaven Nugget (IRE) 171[5], 205[5]
Glenmoss Tara (IRE) 161[2]
Go Ballistic c143[pu]
Goffriler (FR) 196[pu]
Goguenard (FR) c34[ur], c87[3], c151[ur], c180[ur]
Go Johnny Go Go (IRE) F162
Gola Cher (IRE) c39[F]
Golden Alpha (IRE) c26[2], c54[ur], c157[F], c165*
Golden Cross (IRE) 41*, 118[2], 153[3], 203[3]
Golden Goal (GER) c45[2], c56[6]
Golden Storm (IRE) c81[R]
Good Good (IRE) c181[6]
Good Lord Murphy (IRE) c11[F], c173[pu]
Good Shuil (IRE) c24[3], c180[pu]
Good Vintage (IRE) c81[R], c189, c200
Go Roger Go (IRE) c80[3], c151[ur]
Got One Too (FR) c157
Gottabe c109[5]
Govamix F152
Go White Lightning (IRE) c69[pu]
Grabels (FR) 209[ur]
Gralmano (IRE) 1[2], 3[pu], 115, 176[2]
Grandello (IRE) F162
Grand Finale (IRE) 64[pu]
Grave Doubts 177[pu]
Great Love (FR) 190[2], 207[2]
Green Ideal 113[2]
Grey Abbey (IRE) c124, c29[5]
Greywell (IRE) 85
Ground Ball (IRE) c105[3]
Guard Duty 23[5], 145[5], 163
Gunner Welburn c75[3], c99, c180[4]
Gun'n Roses II (FR) c99[pu]
Gunther McBride (IRE) c39, c107[5], c135[2], c185[ur], c195[3]

Haditovski 115
Halexy (FR) c96
Half The Pot (IRE) 124
Hand Inn Hand c17[3], c133*, c141[5]
Handyman (IRE) c107[pu]
Handy Money 138[4]
Happicat (IRE) 1
Happy Hussar (IRE) 136[5]
Harbour Pilot (IRE) c39[3], c79[3], c121[3], c155[3]
Harchibald (FR) 167[5]
Hardy Eustace (IRE) 42*, 77*, 119[2], 146*, 174[5]
Harry's Dream 90[pu]
Harvis (FR) c157, c165[6]

Hat Or Halo (IRE) 14[5]
Haut Cercy (FR) c47[3], c109[3], c143[2]
Haut de Gamme (FR) c92[F]
Hawadeth 51[3], 139, 159[bd], 177
Hazel Reilly (IRE) c181[4]
Healy's Pub (IRE) 191[4]
Heavenly Stride c165[F]
Hedgehunter (IRE) c150, c200[2]
Heidi III (FR) c34
Hermes III (FR) c96[3], c151[pu]
He's The Biz (FR) 74[5]
He's The Boss (IRE) F117[6], F152
Hi Cloy (IRE) 119[4], 146[F], 206[5]
High Cotton (FR) c37[4], c109[4], c150[4]
High Prospect (IRE) 191*
Hill Society (IRE) c5
His Nibs (IRE) 138[pu]
Historg (FR) c108[3], c135[6], c143[6]
Hitman (IRE) 184[4]
Hizen Hokusho (JPN) c187
Holy Orders (IRE) 67, 85, 115, 142, 202*, 207
Homme du Bourg (FR) 196, 209[5]
Hors La Loi III (FR) 57[F], 70[4], 127[3], 142[rr], 179
Horus (IRE) c96, c151[6], c170[pu]
Hot Shots (FR) 113[ur]
Hugo de Grez (FR) c137
Hunters Tweed c168[ur]
Hurricane Dipper (IRE) F117
Hussard Collonges (FR) c12[2], c39[5], c87[2], c155[pu], c199[F]

Ibardine (FR) 190[5]
Iberus (GER) 142[F]
Ibis Rochelais (FR) c93[2], c144[2], c175[pu]
I Can Imagine (IRE) 31[6], c81
Ichi Beau (IRE) c16[6], c165[pu]
Iclan de Molieres (FR) c92[pu]
Idaho d'Ox (FR) 51, 67[2], 139, 159, 177[5]
Ideal du Bois Beury (FR) c93[pu], 106, 149
Idole Des Fontaines (FR) c92[3], c208[pu]
Ifni du Luc (FR) c107[4], c144, c173[ur]
Ikrenel Royal (FR) c66[pu]
Ilare (FR) c208[5]
Ilnamar (FR) 88[3]
Image de Marque II (FR) 159
Impek (FR) c49*, c141[2], c178[3], c204[2]
Impertio c34
I'm The Man c166[3]
Inca Trail (IRE) F28[3], 140, 169[pu]
Inching Closer 145*, 163
In Contrast (IRE) 8[3], 27[F], 115[4], 142[6], 184*
Indalo (IRE) c168[3]
Indian Chance c107[6]
Indian Gunner c173

Indian Scout (IRE) c123[F]
Inducement 3
Infrasonique (FR) c39
Innox (FR) c21[3], c66[4]
Intelligent (IRE) c47[2], c73*, c160*
Intersky Falcon 1*, 8*, 40*, 70*, 142[5]
In The Forge 205[3]
Irbee c166[4]
Iris Bleu (FR) c107*, c126[2], c137[3], c180[pu]
Irish Hussar (IRE) c93[F], c158[2], c175*
Iris Royal (FR) c147[pu], c168[pu]
Iris's Gift 58*, 136*, 154[2], 174*
Iryntzau d'Airy (FR) c92[pu]
Isio (FR) c141[3]
It's Himself c75[F]
It's Official (IRE) F201
Its Time For A Win (IRE) c25[F]
Its Wallace Jnr 153
It Takes Time (IRE) 23[3], c53[2], c147[6], c175[2]
I'vehadit (IRE) c189
Iverain (FR) c53[4]
Iznogoud (FR) c39[pu], c87[5], c143[ur], c158, c195[5], 210
Izntitgreat (IRE) F162

Jabiru (IRE) c156
Jaboune (FR) 3[pu], 51, 130[2], 140, 159[5], 171
Jack High (IRE) 206[2]
Jaguar Claw (IRE) c81[pu]
Jair du Cochet (FR) c69*, c123[ur], c147[2]
Jakari (FR) c175[pu]
Jalons Star (IRE) 192[5]
Janidou (FR) 85, 139, 191
Jaybejay (NZ) c133[pu], c168
Jeremy Spider c173
Jerico Vallis (FR) c208[pu]
Jim (FR) 206[6]
Jimmy Tennis (FR) c29[ur], c48[5]
Jocks Cross (IRE) c24[pu], c137[5]
Joe Blake (FR) c122[3]
Joe Cullen (IRE) 115, 159
John James (IRE) 6
John Oliver (IRE) F182
Johnson (IRE) F162
Joint Account c4[5]
Jollie Bollie (IRE) 106
Jolly Moonbeam (IRE) 31[F]
Joly Bey (FR) c37[2], c175[3]
Jonanaud F117
Joss Naylor (IRE) c143
Joueur d'Estruval (FR) 140, 206
Julies Boy (IRE) 169[pu]
Jungle Jinks (IRE) c109[2], c200[bd]
Junior Fontaine (FR) 85, 191[2]
Jupiter de Bussy (FR) 138[pu]
Jurado Express (IRE) c100[5], c188[pu], c204[5]
Juralan (IRE) c45[pu], c151[pu]
Jurancon II (FR) c160[3]
Just Bandit (JPN) c187
Just In Debt (IRE) c73[5], c200
Just Jasmine c96, c114[ur]

Just Maybe (IRE) c160pu
Just Our Job (IRE) 6³, 8bd

Kadara (IRE) 97⁶
Kadarann (IRE) c19², c54*, c114*, c148, c172³
Kadiskar (IRE) 119⁵
Kadoun (IRE) 14³, c200F
Kadou Nonantais (FR) c29F
Kahuna (IRE) F152
Kanetoshi Governor (JPN) c187⁴
Kapgarde (FR) 196³
Karly Flight (FR) 22*, 190*, 207*, 210²
Katarino (FR) c96⁵, c144⁵, c180ur
Katiki (FR) 36*, 190rr, 207³, 210³
Katoune (FR) 196F, 209³
Kausse de Thaix (FR) F117
Keen Leader (IRE) c109*, c123*, c147⁵
Keepatem (IRE) 163³
Keeponthesunnyside (IRE) c5
Keltic Bard 67, 140⁴
Keltic Heritage (IRE) c37⁶, c195pu
Kemal's Council (IRE) c108F, c160pu
Kenilworth (USA) 118³, 153, 203
Ken's Dream 97⁵, 153, 167
Kerrigand (FR) 145
Kerry Lads (IRE) c185⁴
Khetaam (IRE) 198
Kho Tao (FR) c92pu
Kickham (IRE) F201
Kicking King (IRE) 62², 111*, 140²
Kildare (IRE) F201³
Kildorragh (IRE) c160pu
Killerine (FR) 15⁶
Killultagh Storm (IRE) c25⁵, c56, c112⁴, c188*, c197³
Killultagh Thunder (IRE) c200⁶
Killusty (IRE) c180F, c195pu
Kilrossanty (IRE) F201
Kim Fontaine (FR) F152
King Carew (IRE) 85
King of The Arctic (IRE) F201
Kingscliff (IRE) c156*
Kingscote Thunder (IRE) F28
Kingsmark (IRE) c29*, c59³
King Solomon (FR) 153, 167
Kings Orchard (IRE) 206
Kings Valley (IRE) c81pu
Kirmar (IRE) c81R, c189
Kiss And Cry (FR) c209pu
Kit Smartie (IRE) c137pu, c185
Kittenkat c175⁵, c150
Klakos (IRE) 209
Knife Edge (USA) 30³, c80², c197⁶
Knock Knock (IRE) c189²
Kock de La Vesvre (FR) c168F
Kopeck (IRE) 64*, 91⁵
Korakor (FR) c4pu, c25, c157
Korelo (FR) 124*, 139*, 149⁵, 169pu

Kotkita (FR) 22³

Lady Cricket (FR) c96*, c114³, c151⁵, c164²
Lady Laureate 46⁴, 76³
Lady Toulon (FR) F201⁴
Laganside (IRE) c166pu
La Landiere (FR) c93*, c135*, c158*
Lambrini Gold c173pu
Lancastrian Jet (IRE) c107
Landing Light (IRE) 32⁴, 57², 142
Lanmire Glen (IRE) c150pu
Lanmire Tower (IRE) c144
Laoch Na Mara (USA) 203
Last Option c156³, c185pu
Latalomne (USA) c16⁵, 27⁵, c148F, c197⁴
Lauderdale c168
Laveron 15*, 36²
Lawz (FR) 139³
Lease 111
Le Coudray (FR) c43*, c72*, c120F, c158⁴
Le Duc (FR) 74F, 97⁴, 153⁶, 167*
Leinster (IRE) 169*, 206
Le Roi Miguel (FR) c17², c49², c141F, c178*, c204*
Le Sauvignon (FR) c69²
Let's Fly (FR) 3pu
Lewis Island (IRE) 74², 167
Liberman (IRE) F28², F152*
Like-A-Butterfly (IRE) 101*, 142, 179³
Lilium de Cotte (FR) 55², 74⁴, 153⁴
Limerick Boy (GER) 140⁶, 171*, 198²
Limerick Leader (IRE) F28, F117
Limestone Lad (IRE) 14*, 30*, 44*, 61*, 78*, 101², 154³
Limited Edition (IRE) 91F, 171
Line Marine (FR) c92², c208*
L'Interprete (FR) 196⁵, 209⁶
Lirfox (FR) 140, 171³
Lisaan (IRE) 85
Lisdante (IRE) c2pu, c296
Liss A Paoraigh (IRE) 14², 30², 61², 128², 154⁵
Little Rort (IRE) 153
Little Sport (IRE) 146, 163
Logician (NZ) c4³
Log On Intersky (IRE) c165⁴
Long Shot 161F
Look Sharp (FR) 10pu
Looks Like Value (IRE) F28
Loop The Loup 3², 27bd
Lord Atterbury (IRE) c181*
Lord Fleet (IRE) c26⁶
Lord Grey (IRE) c157, c165
Lord Jack (IRE) c107³, c144
Lord Native (IRE) 113pu
Lord Nellsson 138pu
Lord Noelie (IRE) c12ur, c39, c71pu
Lord Sam (IRE) 90*, 146³
Lords Best (IRE) 58⁴

Lord Transcend (IRE) 86*, 179⁵
Lord York (IRE) c4pu, c165
Lorenzino (IRE) 106⁶
Lost In The Rain (IRE) 118⁵
Lougaroo (FR) 74³, 97
Lucky Bay (FR) c37*, c69⁵, c150⁶, c175pu
Lynrick Lady (IRE) 161

Mackinus (IRE) c150
Macnance (IRE) 161ur
Macs Gildoran c84pu, c158³, c173²
Macs Valley (IRE) 42³, 116⁶
Magic Combination (IRE) 3
Maidstone Monument (IRE) c24pu
Majed (IRE) c150, c180
Majestic (IRE) 149, 163F
Majlis (IRE) 67, 82⁶, 115
Malcom (FR) 196⁴
Malone (FR) 210⁶
Mandoob 10³
Mane Frame 106
Man O'Mystery (USA) 171²
Mantel Mini F117
Mantles Prince c180ur, 192⁶
Maragun (GER) 159bd, 177
Marble Arch 40³, 57⁴, 70⁵, 142
Marcus William (IRE) 129⁵
Marlborough (IRE) c12*, c39, c71², c116F, c155, c164⁵
Marshal Murat (IRE) F28
Mary Terse (FR) 207pu
Master George 46F
Masteroffoxhounds (IRE) F83*, 111pu
Master Papa (IRE) 134⁶
Master Tern (USA) c54⁴, c170*
Master Trix (FR) 138pu, 174ur
Master Wood c166ur
Matthew Anthony (IRE) F162
Maximize (IRE) c47⁴, c135, c143⁴, c180F
Maybe The Business 76⁴, 98⁴
McGruders Cross (IRE) F152
Meisho Wakashio (JPN) c187
Mejiro Raiden (JPN) c187⁵
Mercato (FR) c68⁴, 124, 139⁵
Metchnikoff (FR) 36⁶
Michael Mor (IRE) c84⁵
Midland Flame (IRE) c168*
Milkat (FR) 67, 85
Miller's Bay F152⁵
Milligan (FR) 1, 129⁴
Minella Leisure (IRE) c120F
Mini Mandy 161
Mini Sensation (FR) c75*, c108*, c137pu, c160pu
Mirjan (IRE) 145
Mirpour (IRE) 41², 203
Misconduct 104⁵
Mise Rafturai (IRE) 159pu, 191
Miss Cool 159
Miss Fara (FR) 145, 163
Miss Koen (IRE) 134
Mistanoora 167
Mister McGoldrick 88⁴, 139, 177

Mister One c2[5]
Mistletoeandwine (IRE) 62[5]
Mitchelstown (IRE) F162[5]
Mixsterthetrixster (USA) 159[F]
Modulor (FR) c155, c173[F]
Mohawk Brave (IRE) F28
Money Mountain F117
Moneytrain (GER) 97*, 153[bd], 167
Monitor c4[pu], c5[pu]
Monkerhostin (FR) 1[5], 67[5], 115[6], 159, 176
Montayral (FR) 31[4], c81[F]
Monte Cristo (FR) c17[ur], c133[6]
Montifault (FR) c180[5], c195[pu]
Montreal (FR) c135[5], c144[4], c168[4]
Monty's Pass (IRE) c5[6], c7*, c9[3], c180*
Moore's Law (USA) 146
Moorlands Again c150[5]
Moor Lane c34[F], c144[ur]
Moral Support (IRE) c39, c81[pu]
Moratorium (USA) 6
More Than A Stroll (IRE) c9*, c20*, c52[4], c164[pu]
Moscow Express (IRE) c12[pu], c35[4], c102[3]
Moscow Flyer (IRE) c19*, c50[ur], c80*, c112*, c148*, c197[ur]
Moss Harvey c37[5], 145[pu]
Mossy Green (IRE) 146
Mothers Help c107
Moving Earth (IRE) c195[pu]
Moving On Up 51[2], 67[pu], 115, 131[5], 149[6]
Mr Babbage (IRE) F152
Mr Baxter Basics c256[6], c144[ur], c173[F]
Mr Bossman (IRE) c173[4]
Mr Cool 10[2], 32[2], 51[5], 67[6], 94[2], 115, 149, 179, 210
Mr Dow Jones (IRE) c156
Mr Smudge c156[pu]
Mr Sneaky Boo (IRE) 85
Mughas (IRE) 134[2], 153[5], 167[6]
Mulkev Prince (IRE) c173
Mullensgrove c166[ur]
Mumaris (USA) c26[5]
Murray River (FR) 176
Murt's Man (IRE) c24[6], c75[5]
Mutakarrim 6[2], 42[4], 140
Mutineer (IRE) 118*, 153, 203[5]
Mystic Lord (IRE) 77[5], c200[5]
Mythical King (IRE) 177

Nahthen Lad (IRE) c156
Nas Na Riogh (IRE) 55[2], 74*, 153[ur], 203
Native Approach (IRE) 161
Native Beat (IRE) c173
Native Buck (IRE) c75[pu], c160[6]
Native Design (IRE) 31[5], F162, 169
Native Emperor 23*, 38[2], 63[3], 154[pu]
Native Jack (IRE) c189[F]

Native New Yorker (IRE) 159[pu]
Native Performance (IRE) c7[3]
Native Scout (IRE) c43[pu], c100[2], c157
Native Sessions (IRE) c43[pu], c200[pu]
Native Sparkle (IRE) 42, 119[6], 146
Native Upmanship (IRE) c52*, c71[5], c102*, c148[2], c172*, c199[3]
Ned Kelly (IRE) 44[3]
Negresko (FR) 169[5]
Never (FR) 57[5], 159, 177
Newhall (IRE) 85[F], 139[2], 177[6], 191
Newlands Gold (IRE) 118[6], 153, 203
Nickname (FR) 196*, 209*
Night Fighter (GER) c168[F]
Nil Desperandum (IRE) F28[6], 77[2], 119[3], 146[6]
Noble Buck (IRE) c60[5]
Noble Lord c24
Nobody Told Me (IRE) 206*, 207[4], 210*
No Collusion (IRE) 76[pu]
No Discount (IRE) 145
Nomadic c120[2]
No More Hassle (IRE) c2
Nonantais (FR) 138[2]
Nonchalant (IRE) 31[3]
Non So (FR) 115[2], 159[4], 177
Northern Sound (IRE) c144[pu]
North Point (IRE) 140
Nosam c173
Not Today Sir (IRE) F162
Nuzum Road Makers (IRE) c5

Oa Baldixe (FR) 78[6]
October Mist (IRE) 40[4], 88[2], 115, 131[4]
Old California (IRE) 153[F]
Old Rouvel (USA) 163
Ollar Rose c102[4]
One Knight (IRE) c17*, c37[3], c147*
One Night Out (IRE) c69[4], c100[6], c189[F]
Ontos (GER) 171[4]
Orthez (IRE) c81
Our Boy (IRE) c156
Our Vic (IRE) 113*
Overstrand (IRE) 153
Over The First (IRE) 104[4]
Over The Storm (IRE) c150
Owensher (IRE) F83

Paddies Boy (IRE) c181[5]
Paddy For Paddy (IRE) c181[pu]
Paladin (FR) c92
Palarshan (FR) c68[3], c157*
Palua 131[2], 154
Paphian Bay F117
Paris Pike (IRE) c99[F]
Party Airs (USA) 118[4], 203
Passenger Omar (IRE) F117
Passereau (FR) c157[pu]
Patriarch Express F117, F152
Patricksnineteenth (IRE) F182

Patriot Games (IRE) 3, 8[6], 176*
Patsy Veale (IRE) 6
Paxford Jack c150, c173[pu]
Pay It Forward 206[3]
Peccadillo (IRE) c11[4]
Pedina (IRE) F162[3]
Pendle Hill c93[6]
Penny Fiction (IRE) F201
Penny Rich (IRE) c60[F]
Per Amore (IRE) 82, 177
Perfect Fellow c25[F]
Persian Waters (IRE) 149
Phardante Flyer (IRE) 159
Phar From A Fiddle (IRE) c4[4]
Phar From Fair (IRE) F28
Pharpost (IRE) c93[F]
Pietro Bembo (IRE) 18[6], 51
Pikachu Blue (IRE) c84
Pillar Rock (USA) 6, 191
Pimlico (IRE) F28
Pizarro (IRE) 31*, 62[3], 146[2], 174[F], 206[4]
Placid Man (IRE) c68[pu]
Plenty of Ice (IRE) 77[F]
Poker Pal (IRE) F83[2]
Polar Champ c160[pu], c180[ur]
Polaris Flame (IRE) c156
Polar Red 67[pu], 115, 159, 177
Poliantas (FR) c25[2], c45*, c96[6], c158[5], c186*
Polly's Dream (IRE) F83[4]
Porlock Hill c181[pu]
Prancing Blade c107
Precious Music (IRE) c81[F], c84, c99
Priests Bridge (IRE) 58[3], 136[2], 163[bd]
Prince Dimitri 140
Princelou (FR) c208
Prince of Pleasure (IRE) c55*, c9[F]
Princesse Grec (FR) c93[pu], c150[ur]
Princess Symphony (IRE) c189, c200
Private Pete c166
Pro Dancer (USA) 171
Prokofiev (USA) 124
Proper Squire (USA) 145, 163
Puntal (FR) 3*, 64[2], 91[2], 115, 130*, 146, 169[pu]
Putsometnby (IRE) c7[2]

Quadco (IRE) c72[5]
Quality First (IRE) c99, c173[6]
Quarter Masters (IRE) 97
Quazar (IRE) 18[3], 27[2], 51, 115, 149, 179[4], 205*
Quetal (IRE) c156

Ragu 161
Rakassa F117, F182
Random Harvest (IRE) c99[pu]
Rare Ouzel (IRE) 85[F]
Rash Decision (IRE) c5[pu]
Rathbawn Prince (IRE) c60[F], c144[3], c170[pu], c189
Rathgar Beau (IRE) c100[3], c178[F], c204[3]
Ravenswood (IRE) 145[4]

Red Ark c25, c135, c157[6], c180[pu]
Red Blazer c54[2]
Redemption c89[5], c103[F], c186[4]
Red Knight (IRE) F182
Red Striker c39, c180[ur]
Red Wine 153
Regal Exit (FR) 115, c158, c165[pu]
Reviewer (IRE) 113[3]
Rhinestone Cowboy (IRE) F28*, 110*, 127*, 142[3]
Ricardo c72[3], c100[4], c141
Riders Revenge (IRE) F28
Ridgewood Water (IRE) c5[3]
Right Jack (IRE) F162
Right Job (IRE) 191[6]
Rigmarole 3, 113
Rince Ri (IRE) c52[2], c79[6], c84[6], c121[4], c199[2]
Risk Accessor (IRE) c5[4], c25, c157[2], c165[3]
Risky Reef 177*, 205[4]
Rith Dubh (IRE) c144[pu]
Ritual c54[pu]
River Bug (IRE) c160[4]
River Clodagh (IRE) c60[2]
Robbo c99, c160[pu], c180[ur]
Rockholm Boy (IRE) c5*, c7[bd], c9[4], c20[ur]
Rockstown Boy (IRE) F83[3], F201[6]
Rolex Free (ARG) 130[6]
Romero 3[6]
Rooster Booster 10*, 27*, 57*, 104*, 142*, 179[2]
Rosaker (USA) 42[5], 140, 206
Rose Perk (IRE) 62[4]
Rosslea (IRE) 146
Ross Moff (IRE) c157[5], c170[3], c189[F]
Rostropovich (IRE) 8[4], 38[5], 145, 163[2], 193*, 202[3]
Rougenoir (FR) 15, c208[4]
Roveretto 23[6], c133[4]
Royal Alphabet (IRE) F152, F201[2]
Royal Atalza 190[6], 207
Royal Auclair (FR) c45[4], c116[4], c143
Royal Beluga (USA) c168[5]
Royale de Vassy (FR) c87[6], c144
Royaleety (FR) 196[pu]
Royal Emperor (IRE) 145[2], 174[2]
Royal Jake (IRE) c5, c84, c157, c173
Royal Predica (FR) c144*, c180, c195[pu]
Royal Racer (FR) 104[pu]
Royal Rosa (FR) F201*
Royal Tommy (IRE) c75
Rugged Jacket (IRE) F162[6]
Rugged River (IRE) c48[3], c75[pu], c107[pu]
Rule Supreme (IRE) c200*
Rum Pointer (IRE) 86[6], 106, 145[F]
Run For Paddy c96[pu], c170[pu]
Running Man (FR) 18[5]
Rupununi (IRE) 42

Rushing Again c53[ur]
Russian Gigolo (IRE) 138[pu]
Ryalux (IRE) c99[2], c135[3], c185*
Ryders Storm (USA) 167[pu]

Sackville (IRE) c35[2], c59*, c79[5]
Sacundai (IRE) 14[4], 128*, 179*, 202[2]
Sad Mad Bad (USA) c160[pu], c185[pu]
Saint Des Saints (FR) 22[4]
Saintsaire (FR) 97[3], 134[5], 153
Saitensohn (GER) 146
Salhood F182
Samon (GER) 51, 149[2], 176[5]
Samson (FR) 207[5], 210[5]
Samuel Wilderspin c144
Sanamour (IRE) F162
San Sebastian 15
San Suru (GER) 127[5]
Santenay (FR) 18*, 70[2], 142, 192*
Saragann (IRE) c4[pu]
Satchmo (IRE) c143
Satco Express (IRE) 77[4]
Satcoslam (IRE) c81[2], c189[pu]
Say Again (IRE) 6*, c72[4], 159
Saywhat (IRE) 128[6]
Scented Air 192[4]
Scolardy (IRE) 115, 142
Scotmail Boy (IRE) c87
Scots Grey c68[2], c133[3], c151[3], c185[F]
Scottish Dance 161
Scottish Memories (IRE) 8[5], 44[2], 101[4], 142
Scotton Green c34
Sculptor 97
Sea Drifting c93[3], c147[4], c175[5]
Seebald (GER) c16[2], c65[2], c89[2], c148[F], c172[2], c194*
See More Business (IRE) c20[2], c48*, c126*, c155
See You Sometime 149
Self Defense 46[3], 91[3], 104[2], 142[4], 179[pu]
Sento (IRE) F28
Serenus (USA) 139
Shake It Easy (IRE) F83[5]
Shalako (USA) 64[4]
Shamawan (IRE) c65[3], c96[2]
Shannon Gale (IRE) c34[pu], c173
Shardam (IRE) c99[5], c170[2], c200[ur]
Sharp Act (USA) 85
Sharpaten (IRE) 6
Sh Boom 90[2], 146[5], 169[pu]
Sheltering (IRE) c122*, c156, c166[F]
Shooting Light (IRE) c24[5], c71[pu]
Shotgun Willy (IRE) c137*, c180[pu], c185[5]
Silence Reigns c151[ur]
Silver Archer (NZ) c187
Silver Charmer 55, 169[F]
Silver Knight 98[6], 163
Silver Steel c144, c160[5]

Simply Supreme (IRE) 136[4], 174[4]
Sir Frosty c185[ur]
Sir Rembrandt (IRE) c53*
Sixo (IRE) F117[3]
Skibb (IRE) 169[4]
Skillwise c34[6]
Skippers Cleuch (IRE) c144
Smarty (IRE) c34[5]
Soaring Peak (IRE) F162
Social Order (IRE) 42
Solarius (FR) 190[3], 207[6]
Solerina (IRE) 31[2], 62*, 119*
Soltero (IRE) c100[F]
Some Buzz (IRE) 85, 191
Somemanforoneman (IRE) c24[pu]
Sonevafushi (FR) 82[2], 124[4], 176
Son of Anshan c166[F]
Southern Star (IRE) c24[2], c39, c137, c143, c180
South West Nine (IRE) 41
Sovereign Gold 90
Spaghetti Junction 161[4]
Spainkris 110[5]
Sparkling Gold (IRE) c7[4]
Spectrometer 3[5], 149[3], 163[5]
Spectroscope (IRE) 153*, 167[2], 203[2]
Spendid (IRE) 13[3], 23, c185[3], c195
Spinofski c144
Spirit Leader (IRE) 51*, 85[5], 115*, 159*
Sporazene (IRE) 203*
Spot Thedifference (IRE) c156[6], c166[ur], c189
Springfield Scally 23[4], 86[5], 145, 163
Spud One 171[pu]
Stacumny Bridge (IRE) 128[4], 198[4]
Stage Affair (USA) 101[3], c141[6]
Standing Bloom 161
Star Clipper 85, c204[4]
Star Jack (FR) c42[5], c185[pu]
Star Performance (IRE) c200
Stars Out Tonight (IRE) c26[3], c147[no]
Starzaan (IRE) 153, 167[4], 203[4]
Statim 167
Storm Boxer (IRE) F152, F201
Storm Castle (IRE) c156[ur]
Stormez (FR) c2*, c24*, c39, c132*, c150[2], c185[2], c195[2]
Stormy Lord (IRE) 110[3]
Street Colour F162
Stromness (USA) 136[3], 86[3], 129[6], 131[3]
St Steven (NZ) c187[3]
Sud Bleu (FR) 51, 82[4]
Sudden Shock (GER) 94[3], c132[2], c150*, c185
Sum Leader (IRE) 6
Sunny Flight (FR) c21*, c208[pu]
Super Fellow (IRE) c175[4]
Super Franky (IRE) c5
Super Satco (IRE) F28

Supreme Arrow (IRE) c81[F]
Supreme Developer (IRE) 140
Supreme Glory (IRE) c48[4], c75[pu], c116[5], c137, c180[2]
Supreme Piper (IRE) 138[6]
Supreme Prince (IRE) 146, 174[3]
Supreme Shadow (IRE) F83
Surprising 23, 106, 145
Suspendid (IRE) c2[pu]
Swansea Bay c69[6]
Swordplay 198[5]

Tactful Remark (USA) 159[pu]
Takagi (IRE) c39[pu], c189
Take Control (IRE) c39, c59[4], c75[F], c137, c160[pu], c185[6]
Take Flite 6, 177[F], 191
Talarive (USA) 139[pu]
Tale Bridge (IRE) c181[pu]
Tales of Bounty (IRE) 23
Taming (IRE) 3, 149
Tana River (IRE) 138*
Tanikos (FR) 153
Tardar (NZ) 149
Tarxien c68*, c105*, c158[F], c183[3]
Taurean Son (IRE) c122[F]
Tees Components 98*, 136[3]
Telemoss (IRE) c105[4]
Telimar Prince (IRE) 104[3], 129[2]
Temony (IRE) c5[ur], c7[F]
Ten Poundsworth (IRE) c120[F]
Texas Ranger 76[5], 94[4], 146
Thames (IRE) F182[4]
Thari (USA) c43[4], 149, 163, c200
That's Magic (IRE) F162
The Bajan Bandit (IRE) c109[pu], c147[pu]
The Bunny Boiler (IRE) c75[pu], c143, c180[ur], c195
The Culdee (IRE) 145
The Dangler (IRE) c166
The Dark Flasher (IRE) 85, 191[3]
The Dell (IRE) c189
The French Furze (IRE) 1, 40[2], 57[6], 88[5]
The Galway Man (IRE) F201
The Gatherer (IRE) 159
The Granby (IRE) 86[4]
The Major (NZ) c34[F]
The Negotiator c4[pu]
The Premier Cat (IRE) c73[3]
The Quads c75[pu], c92[5]
The Rebel Lady (IRE) 161
Thesis (IRE) 171[6]
The Staggery Boy (IRE) c68[pu]
The Villager (IRE) c53[5], c170[pu]
Thisthatandtother (IRE) 46[2], 91*, 127[2], 140[5], 184[2]
Through The Rye 159[3]
Thyne Will Tell (IRE) c45[F]
Ticket To Ride (FR) 22[6]
Tier Worker 110[pu]
Tiger Groom 15[2], 36[3], c187
Tighten Your Belt (IRE) F182[3]
Tikram 1[4], 18[4], 67[4], 115[3], 139[6], 176

Timbera (IRE) c189*
Timber King (IRE) 6[6], 8[pu]
Tiutchev c103[2], c125*, c148[F], c187
Tom Costalot (IRE) c99[6], c144, c173
Tommy Dee (IRE) 61[4]
Tom's Prize c170
Tonoco c99[3], c173
Too Forward (IRE) 163[bd]
Torduff Boy (IRE) c5, c7[ur], c189[5]
Torduff Express (IRE) c180[ur]
Touch of Love 6[4]
Trabolgan (IRE) F152[2]
Tramantano 55[4], 140
Tremallt (IRE) c180
Tresor de Mai (FR) c33[4], c125[3], c151, c197[5]
Trespass (FR) 210[4]
Tribal Dancer (IRE) c200[F]
Tribal King (IRE) c53[pu]
Tribal Venture (FR) 98[2], 145[3]
Triple Rum (IRE) F152, F201
Truckers Tavern (IRE) c66[F], c87*, c116[3], c155[2]
True Blue Victory (IRE) 85, 139
Trusting Paddy (IRE) F28
Tsessebe (IRE) F162
Tucacas (FR) 1[6], 145, 176[pu]
Turbo (IRE) 55[6], 153, 167[pu]
Turgeonev (FR) c25, c89[ur], c157, c165
Turnium (FR) 15[5]
Turn Two (IRE) c200[3]
Turtleback (IRE) 101[5], 159
Tuska Ridge (IRE) c7[ur]
Twotensforafive c176
Tysou (FR) c49[3], c178[F]

Under The Sand (IRE) 67, 124[F], 139
Upgrade c11[2], 149[pu], c186[3]
Urga (FR) c208[3]

Valerio 67[pu], 106[5], 163[pu]
Valley Henry (IRE) c11*, c47*, c95[4], c116*, c155[4], c164[4]
Vanilla Man (IRE) c5[F]
Viaduct (IRE) c156
Victory Gunner (IRE) F182
Vic Toto (FR) 15[4], 190[4]
Village King (IRE) c34[4]
Vodka Bleu (FR) F182[ur]
Vodka Inferno (IRE) F28
Volano (FR) 67
Vol Solitaire (FR) c157[4], c178[2], c183*

Wahiba Sands c50[3], c71[6], c89[6], c125[4], c172[5], c186[5], c194[3]
Warjan (IRE) 115, 159
Water Font (IRE) c2[pu]
Watson Lake (IRE) F152
Wave Rock c11[5], c25[3], c56, c103[4], c157[F], c165[pu]
Well Chief (GER) 134*, 153[2], 167[3]
Well Fella (USA) 6

Well Then Now Then (IRE) 98[5]
Westender (FR) 82[3], 142[2], 184[3]
What A Man (IRE) 90[5]
What A Monday F117
What's Up Boys c12[F]
Whereareyounow (IRE) c53[5], c93[4], c123[2], c144
Whistling Dixie (IRE) 1[3], 3[4], 51[6], 67[F], 85, 106[3]
Whitenzo (FR) c125, c39[4], c87, c170[5], c195
Whithworth Ben (IRE) 42
Widemouth Bay (IRE) F152[3]
Wild Romance (IRE) 27[F]
Winchester c168[6]
Windross c107[pu], c170[F]
Wing Back (IRE) F162
Winning Dream (IRE) c189[3]
Wintertide 90[4]
Winter Whisper (IRE) c166[F]
With A Twist (GER) 82
Woman F28[ur]
Wonder Weasel (IRE) c24[4], c137[4], c180[F]
Woodenbridge Natif (IRE) c81
Woodys Deep Ocean (IRE) 111[3], 198[pu]
World Wide Web (IRE) 113[5]
Wotsitooya (IRE) c5[2], c7, c189[6]
Wouldn't You Agree (IRE) 206

Xenophon (IRE) 85*, 149*

Yangtze (IRE) 61[5]
Yeoman's Point (IRE) 23[2], 149, 163
Yorkshire Edition (IRE) c2[6]
Yorkshire (IRE) 70[6], 76[6], 98[pu], 104[6]
Youlneverwalkalone (IRE) c56[3], c84*, c143*, c180[pu]
Young American (IRE) 63[pu]
Young Devereaux (IRE) c65*, c89*, c125[pu]
Young Ottoman (IRE) c150[3]
Young Spartacus c151*, c199[4]
You're Agoodun c107[pu], c137[2], c155, c180[ur]
Yu Fuyoho (JPN) c187

Zafarabad (IRE) c66[3], c135
Zaggy Lane (IRE) c108[5], c126[4]
Zum See (IRE) F201

INDEX TO PHOTOGRAPHS

PORTRAITS & SNAPSHOTS

Horse	Age & Breeding	Copyright	Page
Adamant Approach ..	9 b.g Mandalus – Crash Approach	*Caroline Norris*	30
Ad Hoc	9 b.g Strong Gale – Knockarctic	*Bill Selwyn*	32
Amorello	5 b.m Be My Native – Soundsgoodtome	*Dinah Nicholson*	46
Ar Muin Na Muice	7 ch.m Executive Perk – Raashideah	*Bill Selwyn*	59
Azertyuiop	6 b.g Baby Turk – Temara	*Bill Selwyn*	70
Back In Front	6 br.g Bob Back – Storm Front	*Caroline Norris*	76
Baracouda	8 b.g Alesso – Peche Aubar	*John Crofts*	88
Beef Or Salmon	7 ch.g Cajetano – Farinella	*Caroline Norris*	101
Be Fair	5 br.g Blushing Flame – Tokyo	*Claire Williams*	103
Behrajan	8 b.g Arazi – Behera	*Dinah Nicholson*	105
Best Mate	8 b.g Un Desperado – Katday	*Dinah Nicholson*	118
Bold Bishop	6 b.g Religiously – Ladybojangles	*Bill Selwyn*	131
Brave Inca	5 b.g Good Thyne – Wigwam Mam	*Peter Mooney*	139
Cenkos	9 ch.g Nikos – Vincenza	*Bill Selwyn*	169
Chauvinist	8 b.g Roselier – Sacajawea	*Dinah Nicholson*	176
Chelsea Bridge	5 b.g Over The River – Anguillita	*Dinah Nicholson*	177
Chives	8 b.g Good Thyne – Chatty Actress	*Dinah Nicholson*	182
Chopneyev	5 b.g Goldneyev – Pierre de Soleil	*Dinah Nicholson*	184
Cloudy Grey	6 gr.g Roselier – Dear Limousin	*Clare Williams*	193
Colonel Braxton	8 b.g Buckskin – Light The Lamp	*Peter Mooney*	196
Coolnagorna	6 b.g Warcraft – Mandalaw	*Bill Selwyn*	204
Copeland	8 b.g Generous – Whitehaven	*Bill Selwyn*	205
Cyfor Malta	10 b.g Cyborg – Force Nine	*Bill Selwyn*	219
Dashing Home	4 b.g Lahib – Dashing Rose	*Peter Mooney*	227
Deano's Beeno	11 b.g Far North – Sans Dot	*Bill Selwyn*	232
Do L'Enfant d'Eau	4 ch.g Minds Music – L'Eau Sauvage	*Bill Selwyn*	245
Don Fernando	4 b.c Zilzal – Teulada	*Bill Selwyn*	247
Emotional Moment ..	6 b.g Religiously – Rosceen Bui	*Caroline Norris*	267
Farmer Jack	7 b.g Alflora – Cheryls Pet	*Clare Williams*	281
First Gold	10 b.g Shafoun – Nuit d'Or II	*John Crofts*	291
Flagship Uberalles	9 br.g Accordion – Fourth Degree	*Bill Selwyn*	294
Flame Creek	7 b.g Shardari – Sheila's Pet	*Clare Williams*	297
Florida Pearl	11 b.g Florida Son – Ice Pearl	*Caroline Norris*	301
Foly Pleasant	9 ch.g Vaguely Pleasant – Jeffologie	*Dinah Nicholson*	304
Fondmort	7 b.g Cyborg – Hansie	*Dinah Nicholson*	306
Geos	8 b.g Pistolet Bleu – Kaprika	*Dinah Nicholson*	324
Gingembre	9 ch.g Le Nain Jaune – Teuphaine	*Clare Williams*	327
Golden Alpha	9 b.g Alphabatim – Gina's Love	*Bill Selwyn*	336
Golden Cross	4 b.g Goldmark – Fordes Cross	*Peter Mooney*	337
Hand Inn Hand	7 b.g Alflora – Deep Line	*Dinah Nicholson*	354
Harbour Pilot	8 b.g Be My Native – Las-Cancellas	*Peter Mooney*	356
Hardy Eustace	6 b.g Archway – Sterna Star	*Peter Mooney*	360
Haut Cercy	8 b.g Roi de Rome – Mamoussia	*Dinah Nicholson*	364
Holy Orders	6 b.g Unblest – Shadowglow	*Caroline Norris*	377
Hussard Collonges	8 b.g Video Rock – Ariane Collonges	*Alec Russell*	384
Impek	7 b.g Lute Antique – Attualita	*Dinah Nicholson*	392
Inching Closer	6 b.g Inchinor – Maiyaasah	*Bill Selwyn*	395
In Contrast	7 b.g Be My Native – Ballinamona Lady	*Bill Selwyn*	397
Intelligent	7 b.g Religiously – Culkeern	*Caroline Norris*	402
Intersky Falcon	6 ch.g Polar Falcon – I'll Try	*Bill Selwyn*	406
Irish Hussar	7 b.g Supreme Leader – Shuil Ard	*Dinah Nicholson*	412
Iris's Gift	6 gr.g Gunner B – Shirley's Gift	*Bill Selwyn*	416
Isio	7 b.g Silver Rainbow – Swifty	*Dinah Nicholson*	420
Joly Bey	6 ch.g Beyssac – Rivolie	*Bill Selwyn*	438
Joss Naylor	8 b.g Be My Native – Sister Ida	*Bill Selwyn*	440
Kadarann	6 b.g Bigstone – Kadassa	*Bill Selwyn*	448
Keen Leader	7 b.g Supreme Leader – Keen Gale	*Bill Selwyn*	459
Keltic Bard	6 b.g Emperor Jones – Broughton Singer	*Clare Williams*	461
Kicking King	5 b.g Old Vic – Fairy Blaze	*Caroline Norris*	466
Kingscliff	6 b.g Toulon – Pixies Glen	*Bill Selwyn*	474

Korelo	5 b.g Cadoudal – Lora du Charmil	*Bill Selwyn*	485
Lady Cricket	9 ch.m Cricket Ball – Lady Mariza	*Bill Selwyn*	490
La Landiere	8 b.m Synefos – As You Are	*Dinah Nicholson*	496
Le Coudray	9 b.g Phantom Breeze – Mos Lie	*Caroline Norris*	505
Leinster	6 br.g Supreme Leader – Jennycomequick	*Peter Mooney*	510
Le Roi Miguel	5 b.g Point of No Return – Loumir	*Bill Selwyn*	513
Liberman	5 b.g Standiford – Hail To You	*Bill Selwyn*	516
Limerick Boy	5 b.h Alwuhush – Limoges	*Clare Williams*	522
Limestone Lad	11 b.g Aristocracy – Limestone Miss	*Peter Mooney*	526
Lord Atterbury	7 ch.g Mister End – Tammyiris	*Bill Selwyn*	537
Lord Sam	7 b.g Supreme Leader – Russian Gale	*Bill Selwyn*	543
Macs Gildoran	9 b.g Gildoran – Shamrock Bridge	*Caroline Norris*	553
Marlborough	11 br.g Strong Gale – Wrekenogan	*Dinah Nicholson*	566
Mini Sensation	10 b.g Be My Native – Minorettes Girl	*Bill Selwyn*	585
Monty's Pass	10 b.g Montelimar – Friars Pass	*Peter Mooney*	607
More Than A Stroll	11 ch.g Pennine Walk – Jenny's Child	*Caroline Norris*	612
Moscow Flyer	9 b.g Moscow Society – Meelick Lady	*Caroline Norris*	617
Mutineer	4 gr.g Highest Honor – Miss Amy R	*Peter Mooney*	630
Nas Na Riogh	4 b.f King's Theatre – Abstraite	*Dinah Nicholson*	635
Native Upmanship	10 ch.g Be My Native – Hi'upham	*Caroline Norris*	641
Never	6 b.g Vettori – Neraida	*John Crofts*	646
Nobody Told Me	5 b.m King's Theatre – Thats Luck	*Caroline Norris*	655
One Knight	7 ch.g Roselier – Midnights Daughter	*Bill Selwyn*	670
Our Vic	5 b.g Old Vic – Shabra Princess	*Bill Selwyn*	677
Palarshan	5 b.g Darshaan – Palavera	*Dinah Nicholson*	683
Palua	6 b.g Sri Pekan – Reticent Bride	*Clare Williams*	684
Pizarro	6 ch.g Broken Hearted – Our Swan Lady	*Caroline Norris*	701
Poliantas	6 b.g Rasi Brasak – Popie d'Ecorcei	*Bill Selwyn*	706
Puntal	7 b.g Bering – Saveur	*Bill Selwyn*	718
Quazar	5 b.g Inzar – Evictress	*Bill Selwyn*	722
Rhinestone Cowboy	7 b.g Be My Native – Monumental Gesture	*Bill Selwyn*	744
Rince Ri	10 ch.g Orchestra – Mildred's Ball	*Peter Mooney*	747
Risky Reef	6 ch.g Risk Me – Pas de Reef	*Peter Mooney*	749
Rooster Booster	9 gr.g Riverwise – Came Cottage	*Bill Selwyn*	762
Rosaker	6 b.g Pleasant Tap – Rose Crescent	*Peter Mooney*	764
Royal Alphabet	5 b.g King's Theatre – A-To-Z	*Caroline Norris*	768
Royal Predica	9 ch.g Tip Moss – Girl Vamp	*Bill Selwyn*	773
Royal Rosa	4 ch.g Garde Royale – Crystalza	*Dinah Nicholson*	775
Rule Supreme	7 b.g Supreme Leader – Book of Rules	*Caroline Norris*	779
Ryalux	10 b.g Riverhead – Kings de Lema	*Alec Russell*	784
Sacundai	6 b.g Hernando – Shahdiza	*Caroline Norris*	788
Santenay	5 b.g Mister Mat – Guigone	*Bill Selwyn*	795
Say Again	7 gr.g Celio Rufo – Tricia's Pet	*Peter Mooney*	799
Seebald	8 b.g Mulberry – Spartina	*Bill Selwyn*	806
See More Business	13 b.g Seymour Hicks – Miss Redlands	*Bill Selwyn*	808
Self Defense	6 b.h Warning – Dansara	*Clare Williams*	810
Sh Boom	5 b.g Alderbrook – Muznah	*Bill Selwyn*	817
Shotgun Willy	9 ch.g Be My Native – Minorettes Girl	*Bill Selwyn*	822
Solerina	6 b.m Toulon – Deep Peace	*Peter Mooney*	840
Spectroscope	4 b.g Spectrum – Paloma Bay	*Bill Selwyn*	847
Spirit Leader	7 b.m Supreme Leader – That's The Spirit	*Caroline Norris*	852
Sporazene	4 gr.g Cozzene – Sporades	*Bill Selwyn*	855
Sudden Shock	8 b.g Motley – Santalina	*Bill Selwyn*	874
Supreme Prince	6 b.g Supreme Leader – Strong Serenade	*Bill Selwyn*	882
Tana River	7 b.g Over The River – Home In The Glen	*Clare Williams*	890
Tarxien	9 b.g Kendor – Tanz	*Bill Selwyn*	893
Thari	6 b.g Silver Hawk – Magic Slipper	*Peter Mooney*	901
Thisthatandtother	7 b.g Bob Back – Baden	*Bill Selwyn*	913
Tighten Your Belt	6 b.g Phardante – Hi' Upham	*Clare Williams*	916
Timbera	9 b.g Commanche Run – Morry's Lady	*Peter Mooney*	919
Trabolgan	5 b.g King's Ride – Derrella	*Peter Mooney*	931
Valley Henry	8 b.g Step Together – Pineway VII	*Bill Selwyn*	950
Well Chief	4 ch.g Night Shift – Wellesiena	*Bill Selwyn*	963
Westender	7 b.g In The Wings – Trude	*Bill Selwyn*	966
Widemouth Bay	5 br.g Be My Native – Lisaleen River	*Bill Selwyn*	972
Young Devereaux	10 b.g Lord Americo – Miss Iverk	*Bill Selwyn*	989
Young Spartacus	10 b.g Teenoso – Celtic Slave	*Dinah Nicholson*	991

RACE PHOTOGRAPHS

Race and Meeting	Copyright	Page
Agfa Diamond Handicap Chase (Sandown)	*George Selwyn*	409
Agfa Hurdle (Sandown)	*Bill Selwyn*	760
AIG Europe Champion Hurdle (Leopardstown)	*Peter Mooney*	519
Amlin Reynoldstown Novices' Chase (Ascot)	*Ed Byrne*	458
AON Chase (Newbury)	*Ed Byrne*	949
AON Standard Open National Hunt Flat Race (Newbury)	*George Selwyn*	207
Ascot United Football Club Novices' Hurdle (Ascot)	*Ed Byrne*	627
Ashleybank Investments Future Champion Novices' Chase (Ayr)	*Alec Russell*	956
Ashleybank Investments Scottish Borders National (Kelso)	*John Grossick*	51
attheraces.co.uk Handicap Chase (Sandown)	*George Selwyn*	832
attheraces Gold Cup Chase (Handicap) (Sandown)	*John Crofts*	31
Auckley Handicap Chase (Doncaster)	*Alec Russell*	273
Axminster Kingwell Hurdle (Wincanton)	*Bill Selwyn*	743
Badger Brewery Handicap Chase (Wincanton)	*George Selwyn*	885
Baileys Arkle Perpetual Challenge Cup Novices' Chase (Leopardstown)	*Peter Mooney*	151
Ballymore Properties Champion Stayers' Hurdle (Punchestown)	*Peter Mooney*	376
Ballymore Properties Hatton's Grace Hurdle (Fairyhouse)	*Caroline Norris*	524
Bet attheraces 0800 083 83 83 Novices' Hcap Chase (Sandown)	*Bill Selwyn*	389
Bet Direct Peter Marsh Chase (Limited Handicap) (Haydock)	*Bill Selwyn*	938
betfair.com Rendlesham Hurdle (Kempton)	*George Selwyn*	230
Betfair Open Bumper (Cheltenham)	*Ed Byrne*	741
Bewley Hotels & EBF National Hunt Fillies Championship Bumper (Punchestown)	*Caroline Norris*	738
BMW Chase (Punchestown)	*Ed Byrne*	293
Bonusprint Stayers' Hurdle (Cheltenham)	*Ed Byrne*	86
Britannia Building Society English Summer National (Uttoxeter)	*Alan Wright*	866
Byrne Bros Cleeve Hurdle (Cheltenham)	*Ed Byrne*	190
Byrne Group plc Novices' Hurdle (Punchestown)	*Peter Mooney*	465
Byrne Group plc Tied Cottage Chase (Punchestown)	*Caroline Norris*	615
cantorindex.co.uk Handicap Chase (Ascot)	*Ed Byrne*	988
cantorsport.co.uk Silver Cup (Handicap Chase) (Ascot)	*George Selwyn*	104
Cantor Sport Long Distance Hurdle (Newbury)	*George Selwyn*	72
Cantor Sport Long Walk Hurdle (Ascot)	*Ed Byrne*	229
Cashmans Bookmakers Spring Juvenile Hurdle (Leopardstown)	*Peter Mooney*	629
Cathcart Challenge Cup Chase (Cheltenham)	*Ed Byrne*	495
Cheltenham Grand Annual Chase Challenge Cup (Handicap)	*Ed Byrne*	682
Christie's Foxhunter Chase Challenge Cup (Cheltenham)	*Alec Russell*	473
Clark's Brewery Handicap Hurdle (Aintree)	*Ed Byrne*	688
Claydon Horse Exercisers Maiden Hurdle (Stratford)	*George Selwyn*	723
Colm McEvoy Auctioneers Novices' Handicap Chase (Punchestown)	*Peter Mooney*	778
Concept Hurdle (Sandown)	*George Selwyn*	794
Concord Juvenile Filing Products Juvenile Hurdle (Cheltenham)	*Alec Russell*	78
Connaught plc John Bull Chase (Wincanton)	*Ed Byrne*	261
Coral Cup (Handicap) (Cheltenham)	*John Crofts*	982
Coral Welsh National (Handicap Chase) (Chepstow)	*Ed Byrne*	584
Cordon Bleu Handicap Hurdle (Aintree)	*Peter Mooney*	748
Country Gentlemen's Association Chase (Wincanton)	*Bill Selwyn*	807
Dan Moore Memorial Handicap Chase (Fairyhouse)	*Caroline Norris*	468
Deloitte And Touche Novices' Hurdle (Leopardstown)	*Peter Mooney*	839
Denny Gold Medal Novices' Chase (Leopardstown)	*Caroline Norris*	504
Dick Reynolds 'National Hunt' Novices' Hurdle (Wincanton)	*Bill Selwyn*	881
Doncaster Bloodstock Sales Future Champions Novices' Chase (Cheltenham)	*Ed Byrne*	689
Doncaster Racecourse Sponsorship Club Novices' Chase	*Alec Russell*	419
Dr P. J. Moriarty Novices' Chase (Leopardstown)	*Bill Selwyn*	91
Duggan Brothers Porterstown Handicap Chase (Fairyhouse)	*Caroline Norris*	311
easyodds.com The Price Is Right Handicap Chase (Sandown)	*W. Everitt*	469
Edward Hanmer Memorial Chase (Limited Handicap) (Haydock)	*Alec Russell*	477
Elmbridge Handicap Chase (Sandown)	*Bill Selwyn*	271
Ember Inns Anniversary 4-Y-O Novices' Hurdle (Aintree)	*Alec Russell*	507
Emo Oil Champion Hurdle (Punchestown)	*Bill Selwyn*	721
Ericsson Chase (Leopardstown)	*Caroline Norris*	99

European Breeders Fund Crandon Park Stud Mares 'National Hunt' Novices' Hurdle Final (Limited Handicap) (Newbury)	Ed Byrne	58
European Breeders Fund Novices' Chase (Kempton)	Ed Byrne	132
Evening Herald Champion Novices' Hurdle (Punchestown)	Ed Byrne	75
Evening Herald December Festival Hurdle (Leopardstown)	Peter Mooney	530
Extraman Henry VIII Trophy Novices' Chase (Sandown)	W. Everitt	391
Faucets For Mira Showers Silver Trophy Chase (Limited Handicap) (Cheltenham)	Alec Russell	705
Favourites Racing Handicap Chase (Haydock)	Ed Byrne	333
Frenk Pengelly Novices' Hurdle (Kempton)	Ed Byrne	307
Fulke Walwyn Kim Muir Challenge Cup Handicap Chase (Cheltenham)	John Crofts	772
Gala Casinos Daily Record Scottish Grand National Chase (Ayr)	Alec Russell	783
Gala Casinos Novices' Chase (Ayr)	Alec Russell	944
Gerrard Wealth Management Rossington Main Novices' Hurdle (Wetherby)	Ed Byrne	742
Gerrard Wealth Management Kennel Gate Novices' Hurdle (Ascot)	Ed Byrne	482
Gerrard Wealth Management Dovecote Novices' Hurdle (Kempton)	Bill Selwyn	717
Gerrard Wealth Management Supreme Novices' Hurdle (Cheltenham)	George Selwyn	74
Glenmore Investments Novices' Hurdle (Ascot)	Ed Byrne	934
Golden Miller Handicap Chase (Cheltenham)	Alec Russell	578
Gouldings Richland Galmoy Hurdle (Gowran)	Peter Mooney	796
GQ Winter Novices' Hurdle (Sandown)	George Selwyn	203
Grande Course de Haies d'Auteuil	Ed Byrne	654
Grande Course de Haies d'Auteuil	Bertrand	654
Grand Prix d'Automne (Auteuil)	Ed Byrne	502
Gras Savoye Grand Steeple-Chase de Paris (Auteuil)	Ed Byrne	528
Green Hammerton Novices' Chase (Wetherby)	Alec Russell	442
Guinness Galway Hurdle (Handicap)	Caroline Norris	798
Guinness Kerry National Handicap Chase (Listowel)	Caroline Norris	598
Happy Shopper Mildmay Novices' Chase (Aintree)	George Selwyn	411
HBLB Middlesex Novices' Hurdle (Kempton)	George Selwyn	542
HBLB Twickenham Novices' Chase (Kempton)	W. Everitt	280
Heathorns Handicap Chase (Sandown)	George Selwyn	262
Hennessy Cognac Gold Cup (Leopardstown)	Caroline Norris	100
Hennessy Cognac Gold Cup Chase (Handicap) (Newbury)	Bill Selwyn	326
Hennessy Cognac Gold Cup lead-in (Newbury)	George Selwyn	109
Hipcover Gras Savoye-Prix La Barka (Auteuil)	Ed Byrne	453
Ian Williams' Owners Novices' Chase (Cheltenham)	Ed Byrne	830
IAWS Champion Four Year Old Hurdle (Punchestown)	Caroline Norris	854
IAWS Thyestes Handicap Chase (Gowran)	Peter Mooney	108
Independent Newspaper November Novices' Chase (Cheltenham)	Bill Selwyn	68
INH Stallion Owners EBF Novices' Hurdle (Punchestown)	Peter Mooney	838
Intervet Trophy Handicap Chase (Cheltenham)	Ed Byrne	867
Irish Independent Arkle Challenge Trophy Chase (Cheltenham)	George Selwyn	69
Isle of Skye Blended Whisky-Kelso Novices' Chase (Haydock)	Alec Russell	423
James Nicholson Wine Merchant Championship Chase (Down Royal)	Peter Mooney	611
JCB Triumph Hurdle (Cheltenham)	Alec Russell	846
John Durkan Memorial Punchestown Chase	Caroline Norris	639
John James McManus Memorial Hurdle (Tipperary)	Caroline Norris	404
John Smith's Midlands Grand National Chase (Uttoxeter)	Alec Russell	401
John Smith's West Yorkshire Hurdle (Wetherby)	Alec Russell	145
Kilcock Novices' Chase (Naas)	Caroline Norris	729
Ladbroke Hurdle (Handicap) (Ascot)	Ed Byrne	175
Ladbroke Racing Handicap Hurdle (Fairyhouse)	Caroline Norris	678
ladbrokes.com Handicap Chase (Newbury)	Ed Byrne	380
Ladbroke Trophy Chase (Handicap) (Cheltenham)	Ed Byrne	489
Laurel Pub Company Top Novices' Hurdle (Aintree)	Alec Russell	521
Light Infantry Plate (Novices' Hurdle) (Doncaster)	Alec Russell	363
Martell Champion Standard National Hunt Flat Race (Aintree)	Ed Byrne	188
Martell Cognac Aintree Hurdle	Peter Mooney	787
Martell Cognac Cup Chase (Aintree)	Ed Byrne	289
Martell Cognac Golden Cross Inn Fox Hunters' Chase (Aintree)	Peter Mooney	242

1052

Martell Cognac Grand National Chase (Handicap) (Aintree)	*George Selwyn*	599
Martell Cognac Grand National Chase (Handicap) (Aintree)	*Liverpool Daily Post & Echo*	600
Martell Cognac Grand National Chase (Handicap) (Aintree)	*George Selwyn*	601
Martell Cognac Grand National Chase (Handicap) (Aintree)	*Peter Mooney*	601
Martell Cognac Grand National Chase (Handicap) (Aintree)	*George Selwyn*	602
Martell Cognac Grand National Chase (Handicap) (Aintree)	*Bill Selwyn*	603
Martell Cognac Grand National Chase (Handicap) (Aintree)	*Liverpool Daily Post & Echo*	603
Martell Cognac Grand National Chase (Handicap) (Aintree)	*Alec Russell*	604
Martell Cognac Grand National Chase (Handicap) (Aintree)	*Alec Russell*	605
Martell Cognac Grand National Chase (Handicap) (Aintree)	*Peter Mooney*	606
Martell Cognac Melling Chase (Aintree)	*George Selwyn*	640
Martell Cognac Nisa Today's Handicap Hurdle (Aintree)	*Ed Byrne*	162
Martell Cognac Novices' Handicap Chase (Aintree)	*George Selwyn*	577
Martell Cognac Safeway Red Rum Chase (Handicap) (Aintree)	*Peter Mooney*	335
Martell Cognac Sainsbury's Topham Chase (Handicap) (Aintree)	*George Selwyn*	187
Martell Cognac Sefton Novices' Hurdle (Aintree)	*Peter Mooney*	415
Martell Cognac V.S. Thresher Handicap Chase (Aintree)	*Alec Russell*	570
Martell Maghull Novices' Chase (Aintree)	*Ed Byrne*	511
McCabe Builders Ltd Boyne Hurdle (Navan)	*Caroline Norris*	266
McCallum Corporate Consulting Peterborough Chase (Huntingdon)	*Ed Byrne*	113
Menolly Homes Champion Novices' Hurdle (Punchestown)	*Peter Mooney*	653
Menolly Homes Novices' Hurdle (Fairyhouse)	*Caroline Norris*	331
Mildmay of Flete Challenge Cup Handicap Chase (Cheltenham)	*Bill Selwyn*	990
Mitsubishi Shogun Tingle Creek Trophy Chase (Sandown)	*Ed Byrne*	168
Modern City Living Handicap Chase (Ascot)	*George Selwyn*	992
Morgiana Hurdle (Navan)	*Healy Racing Photography*	523
National Hunt Chase Challenge Cup (Amateur Riders') (Cheltenham)	*John Crofts*	873
Paddy & Helen Cox Memorial Newlands Chase (Naas)	*Caroline Norris*	54
Paddy Power Champion INH Flat (Punchestown)	*Bill Selwyn*	774
Paddy Power Dial-A-Bet Chase (Leopardstown)	*Caroline Norris*	614
Pertemps Aviation Resources Feltham Novices' Chase (Kempton)	*Ed Byrne*	428
Pertemps Christmas Hurdle (Kempton)	*George Selwyn*	405
Pertemps Final (Handicap Hurdle) (Cheltenham)	*John Crofts*	394
Pertemps Handicap Hurdle (Qualifier) (Haydock)	*Alec Russell*	770
Pertemps Handicap Hurdle (Qualifier) (Chepstow)	*Bill Selwyn*	857
Pertemps King George VI Chase (Kempton)	*George Selwyn*	115
Peterhouse Group Charlie Hall Chase (Wetherby)	*Alec Russell*	565
Pierse Hurdle (Handicap) (Leopardstown)	*Caroline Norris*	981
Pierse Leopardstown Handicap Chase	*Peter Mooney*	985
Pillar Property Chase (Cheltenham)	*Ed Byrne*	104
Powers Gold Cup (Fairyhouse)	*Caroline Norris*	900
Powers Gold Label Irish Grand National Chase (Fairyhouse)	*Caroline Norris*	918
Premier Stayers' Hurdle (Haydock)	*Alec Russell*	544
Press & Journal Handicap Chase (Perth)	*John Grossick*	643
'Press The Red Button To Bet attheraces' Hurdle (Sandown)	*John Crofts*	766
Pricewaterhousecoopers Ascot Hurdle	*George Selwyn*	84
Prix Alain du Breil-Course de Haies d'Ete des Quatre Ans (Auteuil)	*Ed Byrne*	650
Punchestown Heineken Gold Cup	*Ed Byrne*	290
Queen Elizabeth The Queen Mother Celebration Chase (Sandown)	*John Crofts*	805
Queen Mother Champion Chase (Cheltenham)	*Ed Byrne*	500
Queen Mother Champion Chase (Cheltenham)	*Bill Selwyn*	616
Quinns of Baltinglass Chase For The La Touche Cup (Punchestown)	*Ed Byrne*	147
Racing Post Chase (Handicap) (Kempton)	*Bill Selwyn*	494
Read The Racing Post Before You Bet Pendil Novices' Chase (Kempton)	*Ed Byrne*	353
Red Mills Trial Hurdle (Gowran)	*Caroline Norris*	786
Red Square Vodka Champion Hurdle Trial (Haydock)	*Alec Russell*	296
Red Square Vodka 'Fixed Brush' Novices' Hurdle Final Bonus Race (Handicap) (Haydock)	*Alec Russell*	951

Red Square Vodka Gold Cup Chase (Handicap) (Haydock)	*George Selwyn*	821
Red Square Vodka Prestige Novices' Hurdle (Haydock)	*Ed Byrne*	414
Rehabilitation of Racehorses Hurdle (Handicap) (Cheltenham)	*Ed Byrne*	758
Ritz Club Ascot Chase	*Bill Selwyn*	923
Rosling King 'National Hunt' Novices' Hurdle (Ascot)	*Ed Byrne*	418
Royal & SunAlliance Chase (Cheltenham)	*John Crofts*	669
Royal & SunAlliance Novices' Hurdle (Cheltenham)	*Peter Mooney*	359
Royal Bank of Scotland 'National Hunt' Novices' Hurdle (Ayr)	*Alec Russell*	144
Samsung Electronics Scottish Champion Hurdle (Limited Handicap) (Ayr)	*Alec Russell*	396
Scilly Isles Novices' Chase (Sandown)	*George Selwyn*	892
Singapore Airlines Adonis Juvenile Novices' Hurdle (Kempton)	*Ed Byrne*	962
Singer & Friedlander National Trial (Handicap Chase) (Uttoxeter)	*Bill Selwyn*	584
skybet.com Castleford Chase (Wetherby)	*Alec Russell*	323
skybet.com Great Yorkshire Chase (Handicap) (Doncaster)	*Alec Russell*	93
skybet.com River Don Novices' Hurdle (Doncaster)	*Alec Russell*	896
Smurfit Champion Hurdle Challenge Trophy (Cheltenham)	*George Selwyn*	761
Sodexho Prestige Game Spirit Chase (Newbury)	*Ed Byrne*	447
sportingoptions.co.uk Long Distance Hurdle (Ascot)	*George Selwyn*	231
Sporting Index Chase (Cross Country) (Cheltenham)	*Bill Selwyn*	278
Stan James Handicap Chase (Newbury)	*Ed Byrne*	259
St Austell Brewery Mersey Novices' Hurdle (Aintree)	*Ed Byrne*	509
Stone Street Novices' Chase (Folkestone)	*Ed Byrne*	514
Sunderlands Bookmakers Novices' Chase (Sandown)	*George Selwyn*	385
Sunderlands Imperial Cup Hurdle (Handicap) (Sandown)	*W. Everitt*	484
Swordlestown Cup Novices' Chase (Punchestown)	*Ed Byrne*	512
Systems By Design Worcester Novices' Chase (Newbury)	*Ed Byrne*	548
Tattersalls (Ireland) European Breeders Fund Mares' Novices' Chase (Uttoxeter)	*Alec Russell*	737
Telectronics Systems 'National Hunt' Auction Novices' Hurdle (Cheltenham)	*Alec Russell*	148
Thomas Pink Gold Cup Chase (Handicap) (Cheltenham)	*Bill Selwyn*	218
Timeform Novices' Handicap Chase (Cheltenham)	*Ed Byrne*	493
Tommy Whittle Chase (Haydock)	*Alec Russell*	785
Tote Becher Chase (Handicap) (Aintree)	*Alec Russell*	56
Tote Cheltenham Gold Cup Chase (Cheltenham)	*Bill Selwyn*	116
Tote Cheltenham Gold Cup Chase (Cheltenham)	*Ed Byrne*	117
Tote Exacta Chase (Limited Handicap) (Kempton)	*W. Everitt*	988
Tote Exacta Handicap Chase (Wetherby)	*Ed Byrne*	388
Tote Exacta 'Monksfield' Novices' Hurdle (Navan)	*Healy Racing Photography*	700
Tote Gold Trophy (Handicap) (Newbury)	*Ed Byrne*	851
Tote Scoop6 Handicap Hurdle (Wetherby)	*Bill Selwyn*	82
Tote Scoop6 Lanzarote Hurdle (Handicap) (Kempton)	*George Selwyn*	658
Tote Scoop6 Sandown Handicap Hurdle (Sandown)	*George Selwyn*	183
Tote Scoop6 Summer Plate (Handicap Chase) (Market Rasen)	*Alec Russell*	179
Tote Tolworth Hurdle (Wincanton)	*Bill Selwyn*	912
Tripleprint Gold Cup (Handicap Chase) (Cheltenham)	*Bill Selwyn*	305
Tripleprint Juvenile Novices' Hurdle (Cheltenham)	*Ed Byrne*	246
Unicoin New Homes Chase (Handicap) (Cheltenham)	*Ed Byrne*	80
United House PFI Handicap Hurdle (Ascot)	*George Selwyn*	252
Victor Chandler Bula Hurdle (Cheltenham)	*Ed Byrne*	759
Victor Ludorum Juvenile Novices' Hurdle (Haydock)	*Ed Byrne*	282
Vincent O'Brien County Handicap Hurdle (Cheltenham)	*George Selwyn*	851
Weatherbys Champion Bumper (Standard Open National Hunt Flat Race) (Cheltenham)	*Bill Selwyn*	515
Weatherbys Towton Novices' Chase (Wetherby)	*Ed Byrne*	457
Weatherbys Travel 'National Hunt' Novices' Hurdle (Uttoxeter)	*Ed Byrne*	216
Western Daily Press Finale Juvenile Hurdle (Chepstow)	*Ed Byrne*	634
William Hill Haldon Gold Cup (Limited Handicap) (Exeter)	*Bill Selwyn*	260
William Hill Handicap Hurdle (Ascot)	*Ed Byrne*	483
William Hill Handicap Hurdle (Sandown)	*Ed Byrne*	850
William Hill National Hunt Handicap Chase (Cheltenham)	*John Crofts*	986
Wilmot-Smith Memorial Cup (Hunters' Chase) (Wetherby)	*Ed Byrne*	258
woodiesdiy.com Christmas Hurdle (Leopardstown)	*Caroline Norris*	525
Wragge & Co Finesse Juvenile Novices' Hurdle (Cheltenham)	*Ed Byrne*	594

CHAMPIONS FROM THE 'CHASERS & HURDLERS' SERIES

Best Two-Mile Chaser

75/76	Lough Inagh	**167**	89/90	Desert Orchid	**187**
76/77	Skymas	**156**	90/91	Desert Orchid	**178**
77/78	Tingle Creek	**154**	91/92	Remittance Man	**173**
78/79	Siberian Sun	**151**	92/93	Katabatic	**161 ?**
79/80	I'm A Driver	**163**	93/94	Viking Flagship	**166**
80/81	Anaglogs Daughter	**171**	94/95	Viking Flagship	**169**
81/82	Rathgorman	**170**	95/96	Klairon Davis	**177**
82/83	Badsworth Boy	**179**	96/97	Martha's Son	**177**
83/84	Badsworth Boy	**177**	97/98	One Man	**176**
84/85	Bobsline	**164 +**	98/99	Direct Route	**166**
85/86	Dawn Run	**167**	99/00	Flagship Uberalles	**176**
86/87	Pearlyman	**171**	00/01	Flagship Uberalles	**175**
87/88	Pearlyman	**174**	01/02	Flagship Uberalles	**170**
88/89	Desert Orchid	**182**	02/03	Moscow Flyer	**170 p**

Best Staying Chaser

75/76	Captain Christy	**182**	89/90	Desert Orchid	**187**
76/77	Bannow Rambler	**163**	90/91	Desert Orchid	**178**
77/78	Midnight Court	**164**	91/92	Carvill's Hill	**182**
78/79	Gay Spartan	**166**	92/93	Jodami	**174 p**
79/80	Silver Buck	**171**	93/94	The Fellow	**171**
80/81	Little Owl	**176**	94/95	Master Oats	**183**
81/82	Silver Buck	**175**	95/96	One Man	**179**
82/83	Bregawn	**177**	96/97	One Man	**176**
83/84	Burrough Hill Lad	**175**	97/98	Cool Dawn	**173**
	Wayward Lad	**175**	98/99	Suny Bay	**176**
84/85	Burrough Hill Lad	**184**	99/00	See More Business	**182**
85/86	Burrough Hill Lad	**183**	00/01	First Gold	**180**
86/87	Desert Orchid	**177**	01/02	Best Mate	**173**
87/88	Desert Orchid	**177**		Florida Pearl	**173**
88/89	Desert Orchid	**182**	02/03	Best Mate	**182**

Best Novice Chaser

75/76	Bannow Rambler	**152 p**	90/91	Remittance Man	**153 p**
76/77	Tree Tangle	**159 §**	91/92	Miinnehoma	**152 p**
77/78	The Dealer	**145**	92/93	Sybillin	**156**
78/79	Silver Buck	**151**	93/94	Monsieur Le Cure	**156 p**
79/80	Anaglogs Daughter	**156**	94/95	Brief Gale	**159**
80/81	Clayside	**145**	95/96	Mr Mulligan	**154**
81/82	Brown Chamberlin	**147 p**	96/97	Strong Promise	**171 +**
82/83	Righthand Man	**150**	97/98	Escartefigue	**171 p**
83/84	Bobsline	**161 p**	98/99	Nick Dundee	**164 +**
84/85	Drumadowney	**159**	99/00	Gloria Victis	**172**
85/86	Pearlyman	**150**	00/01	Bacchanal	**161 p**
86/87	Kildimo	**151 p**		Shotgun Willy	**161**
87/88	Danish Flight	**156 p**	01/02	Moscow Flyer	**159 p**
88/89	Carvill's Hill	**169 p**	02/03	Beef Or Salmon	**165 p**
89/90	Celtic Shot	**152 p**			

Best Two-Mile Hurdler

75/76	Night Nurse	**178**	89/90	Kribensis	**169**
76/77	Night Nurse	**182**	90/91	Morley Street	**174**
77/78	Monksfield	**177**	91/92	Granville Again	**165 p**
78/79	Monksfield	**180**	92/93	Mighty Mogul	**170**
79/80	Sea Pigeon	**175**	93/94	Danoli	**172 p**
80/81	Sea Pigeon	**175**	94/95	Alderbrook	**174 p**
81/82	For Auction	**174**	95/96	Alderbrook	**174**
82/83	Gaye Brief	**175**	96/97	Make A Stand	**165**
83/84	Dawn Run	**173**	97/98	Istabraq	**172 +**
84/85	Browne's Gazette	**172**	98/99	Istabraq	**177 +**
85/86	See You Then	**173**	99/00	Istabraq	**180**
86/87	See You Then	**173**	00/01	Istabraq	**180**
87/88	Celtic Shot	**170**	01/02	Limestone Lad	**167**
88/89	Beech Road	**172**	02/03	Rooster Booster	**170**

Best Staying Hurdler

75/76	Comedy of Errors	**170**	77/78	Monksfield	**177**
76/77	Night Nurse	**182**	78/79	Monksfield	**180**

79/80	Pollardstown	167	92/93	Sweet Duke	161
80/81	Daring Run	171 +	93/94	Sweet Glow	162
81/82	Daring Run	171	94/95	Dorans Pride	167
82/83	Gaye Brief	175	95/96	Pleasure Shared	163 p
83/84	Dawn Run	173	96/97	Paddy's Return	164
84/85	Bajan Sunshine	162	97/98	Paddy's Return	168
85/86	Gaye Brief	167	98/99	Deano's Beeno	165
86/87	Galmoy	165		Princeful	165
87/88	Galmoy	160	99/00	Limestone Lad	177
88/89	Rustle	169	00/01	Le Sauvignon	178
89/90	Trapper John	159	01/02	Baracouda	169 +
90/91	King's Curate	164	02/03	Baracouda	175
91/92	Nomadic Way	162			

Best Novice Hurdler

75/76	Grand Canyon	159	89/90	Regal Ambition	151
76/77	Outpoint	154	90/91	Ruling	167
77/78	Golden Cygnet	176	91/92	Royal Gait	164 p
78/79	Venture To Cognac	162	92/93	Montelado	150 P
79/80	Slaney Idol	143	93/94	Danoli	172 p
80/81	Dunaree	159	94/95	Alderbrook	174 p
81/82	Angelo Salvini	149	95/96	Pleasure Shared	163 p
82/83	Dawn Run	168	96/97	Make A Stand	165
83/84	Desert Orchid	158	97/98	French Holly	151 P
84/85	Asir	148 p	98/99	Barton	153 p
85/86	River Ceiriog	158 p	99/00	Monsignor	158 p
86/87	The West Awake	153 p	00/01	Baracouda	172
87/88	Carvill's Hill	157 p	01/02	Intersky Falcon	152 p
88/89	Sondrio	152 p	02/03	Iris's Gift	172
	Wishlon	152 +			

Best Juvenile Hurdler

75/76	Valmony	157	89/90	Sybillin	138
76/77	Meladon	149	90/91	Oh So Risky	149 p
77/78	Major Thompson	144	91/92	Staunch Friend	151 p
78/79	Pollardstown	141	92/93	Shawiya	141 p
79/80	Hill of Slane	144	93/94	Mysilv	144 p
80/81	Broadsword	144	94/95	Kissair	143 p
81/82	Shiny Copper	141	95/96	Escartefigue	159
82/83	Sabin du Loir	147 p	96/97	Grimes	138 p
83/84	Northern Game	142	97/98	Deep Water	149 p
84/85	Out of The Gloom	151	98/99	Hors La Loi III	162 p
85/86	Dark Raven	153 p	99/00	Grand Seigneur	148 p
86/87	Aldino	154	00/01	Jair du Cochet	163
87/88	Kribensis	143 p	01/02	Scolardy	147
88/89	Royal Derbi	144	02/03	Nickname	142

Best National Hunt Flat Race Performer

93/94	Aries Girl	123	99/00	Quadco	129
94/95	Dato Star	120	00/01	The Bajan Bandit	128
95/96	Wither Or Which	122	01/02	Pizarro	123
96/97	Florida Pearl	124		Rhinestone Cowboy	123
97/98	Alexander Banquet	126	02/03	Rhinestone Cowboy	123
98/99	Monsignor	122			

Best Hunter Chaser

75/76	Otter Way	143	90/91	Mystic Music	143 ?
76/77	Under Way	124	91/92	Rushing Wild	127 p
77/78	Spartan Missile	133	92/93	Double Silk	122 p
78/79	Spartan Missile	133 +	93/94	Double Silk	130 p
79/80	Rolls Rambler	132		Elegant Lord	130 p
80/81	Spartan Missile	169	94/95	Fantus	139 p
81/82	Compton Lad	142	95/96	Elegant Lord	138 p
82/83	Eliogarty	147	96/97	Celtic Abbey	136 p
83/84	Venture To Cognac	149		Fantus	136
84/85	Further Thought	141	97/98	Earthmover	140 p
85/86	Ah Whisht	148	98/99	Castle Mane	148 p
86/87	Observe	146	99/00	Cavalero	142
87/88	Certain Light	147	00/01	Sheltering	136
88/89	Call Collect	142 p	01/02	Torduff Express	130
89/90	Mystic Music	143	02/03	Kingscliff	137 P

REVOLUTIONISE YOUR RACING @
timeform.com

Timeform Race Cards for every meeting available for immediate download for £5.50 per meeting!

Timeform Daily Form Guide, exclusive to our internet site, provides ratings and commentaries for any individual race for only £1.50!

Horse Enquiry facility lets you see the up-to-date commentary, rating and Perspective history for any horse on the Timeform database for 50p!

Bonus Credits when you deposit £50 or more!

Before you bet know what we know!

19 Timeform, Timeform House, Halifax, West Yorkshire HX1 1XF